THE OXFORD COMPANION TO
CLASSICAL CIVILIZATION

THE OXFORD COMPANION TO CLASSICAL CIVILIZATION

EDITED BY
SIMON HORNBLOWER
AND
ANTONY SPAWFORTH

Oxford   New York
OXFORD UNIVERSITY PRESS
2004

OXFORD

UNIVERSITY PRESS

Great Clarendon Street, Oxford OX2 6DP

Oxford University Press is a department of the University of Oxford.
If furthers the University's objective of excellence in research, scholarship,
and education by publishing worldwide in

Oxford New York

Auckland Bangkok Buenos Aires Cape Town Chennai
Dar es Salaam Delhi Hong Kong Istanbul Karachi Kolkata
Kuala Lumpur Madrid Melbourne Mexico City Mumbai Nairobi
São Paolo Shanghai Singapore Taipei Tokyo Toronto

Oxford is a registered trade mark of Oxford University Press
in the UK and in certain other countries

Published in the United States
by Oxford University Press Inc., New York

British Library Cataloguing in Publication Data
Data available

Library of Congress Cataloging in Publication Data
Data available
ISBN 0–19–860958–2 (paperback)
ISBN 0–19–861034–3 (hardback)

1 3 5 7 9 10 8 6 4 2

Typeset by Selwood Systems
Midsomer Norton
Printed in Great Britain by
Butler & Tanner Ltd.
Frome, Somerset

Contents

Preface

This new *Oxford Companion to Classical Civilization* is an up-to-date and authoritative, but handily sized, encyclopaedia about the civilizations of Greece and Rome and their more or less immediate neighbours. The contributors number just over 300 of the world's most distinguished classical scholars. The aim of the *Companion* is to make available to an even wider readership the essential material from the very successful third (1996) edition of the *Oxford Classical Dictionary (OCD³)*, but in a cheaper and less weighty format. We have achieved the shorter length by omitting entries which we thought too technical or recondite for the readership we envisage, and by removing the specialist bibliographies attached to particular entries, adding instead a select general bibliography at the back of the book. We have *not* however shortened individual entries in any other way (except that we have retained only the general, introductory section of the long *OCD³* entry on 'music'; the *Companion* entry thus becomes 'music in Greek and Roman life'). Readers can therefore be assured that all the expert material from *OCD³* included in this *Companion* is undiluted and unabridged. Naturally, however, it has been edited so as to achieve internal consistency: the copious cross-references which were such a feature of *OCD³* have either been adapted so that they refer to material elsewhere in the *Companion* or replaced by explanations, where the cross-reference was to a technical term which no longer has its own entry.

A notable feature of the *Companion* is its many illustrations, which we hope succeed in adding a further dimension which will interest and stimulate readers to a fuller understanding of life in the ancient world. Here we are indebted to Professor Brian Sparkes, who made the initial selection of pictures and provided a great deal of further help to the picture researcher. Our policy on illustration has been not just to cover archaeological entries (sites, places, and so on) but as far as possible to reflect all the different scholarly areas represented in the book, underlining the great breadth of the *Companion* text and of its parent volume.

At the Press we pay tribute to the enthusiasm and support of the commissioning editor, Michael Cox. We were enormously fortunate in that Pam Coote, in-house editor for *OCD³*, performed the same job for this volume with her usual diligence, sympathy, and wisdom. We are also grateful for the expertise of, respectively, Tom Chandler (copy-editor), Sandra Assersohn (picture-research), Kim Richardson (maps and chronology), and Leofranc Holford-Strevens (for assistance with the thematic listing of entries).

SIMON HORNBLOWER
ANTONY SPAWFORTH
1998

List of maps

Index to Initials of Contributors

Contributors

R.A.K.   Robert A. Kaster
S.J.K.   Simon J. Keay
A.W.L.   Andrew William Lintott
B.M.L.   Barbara M. Levick
D.G.L.   D. G. Lateiner
G.E.R.L.   Geoffrey Lloyd
J.A.O.L.   Jakob Aall Ottesen Larsen
J.F.La.   John F. Lazenby
K.L.   H. Kathryn Lomas
L.B.L.   Lillian B. Lawler
R.J.L.   Roger J. Ling
R.O.A.M.L.   R. O. A. M. Lyne
W.L.   W. Liebeschuetz
W.A.L.   William Allison Laidlaw

A.M.   Arnaldo Momigliano
A.Mot.   André Motte
B.C.McG.   Brian C. McGing
C.A.M.   Catherine A. Morgan
C.A.Ma.   Charles Anthony Martindale
C.B.M.   Christopher B. Mee
D.J.Ma.   David J. Mattingly
D.M.M.   Douglas Maurice MacDowell
F.G.B.M.   Fergus Graham Burtholme Millar
G.W.M.   Glenn W. Most
H.Ma.   Herwig Maehler
I.Mo.   Ian Morris
J.F.Ma.   John F. Matthews
J.L.Mo.   John L. Moles
J.R.M.   Jennifer R. March
J.R.Mo.   John R. Morgan
J.V.M.   J. V. Muir
K.M.   Klaus Meister
M.J.M.   Martin J. Millett
O.Ma.   Olivier Masson
O.Mu.   Oswyn Murray
P.C.M.   Paul C. Millett
R.M.   Russell Meiggs
R.H.M.   Ronald Haithwaite Martin
S.M.   Stephen Mitchell
V.A.M.   Valerie A. Maxfield
W.M.M.   William M. Murray

A.N.   Alexander Nehamas
B.N.   Barry Nicholas
D.P.N.   Damien P. Nelis
J.A.N.   J. A. North
L.F.N.   Lucia F. Nixon
M.C.N.   Martha C. Nussbaum

D.O.   Dirk Obbink
J.M.O'B.   John Maxwell O'Brien
R.G.O.   Robin G. Osborne

A.J.P.   A. J. Parker
C.B.R.P.   C. B. R. Pelling
D.S.P.   David S. Potter
F.N.P.   Frederick Norman Pryce
H.N.P.   Holt N. Parker
J.G.F.P.   Jonathan G. F. Powell
J.J.P.   Jeremy James Paterson

J.J.Po.   J. J. Pollitt
J.R.P.   John Robert Patterson
J.R.T.P.   John Richard Thornhill Pollard
N.P.   Nicholas Purcell
P.J.P.   P. J. Parsons
R.C.T.P.   Robert Christopher Towneley Parker
S.G.P.   Simon Geoffrey Pembroke
S.R.F.P.   Simon R. F. Price
T.W.P.   T. W. Potter
V.P.-D.   Vinciane Pirenne-Delforge

B.L.R.   Barney L. Rickenbacker
C.R.   Charlotte Roueché
C.C.R.   Christopher C. Rowland
C.J.R.   Christopher J. Rowe
D.A.R.   Donald Andrew Frank Moore Russell
D.H.R.   Deborah H. Roberts
D.W.R.   Dominic W. Rathbone
D.W.R.R.   David William Robertson Ridgway
E.E.R.   Ellen E. Rice
G.W.R.   Geoffrey Walter Richardson
H.J.R.   Herbert Jennings Rose
I.A.R.   Ian Archibald Richmond
J.B.R.   James Boykin Rives
J.M.R.   Joyce Maire Reynolds
J.S.R.   Jeffrey Stuart Rusten
J.S.Ri.   John Stuart Richardson
J.W.R.   John William Rich
K.R.   Kurt Raaflaub
L.D.R.   Leighton Durham Reynolds
N.J.R.   Nicholas J. Richardson
N.K.R.   N. K. Rutter
O.R.   Oliver Rackham
P.R.   Philip Rousseau
P.J.R.   P. J. Rhodes
R.B.R.   R. B. Rutherford
T.R.   Tessa Rajak

A.Sch.   Albert Schachter
A.F.S.   Andrew F. Stewart
A.H.S.   Alan Herbert Sommerstein
A.J.S.S.   Antony J. S. Spawforth
A.M.S.   Anthony M. Snodgrass
A.N.S.-W.   A. N. Sherwin-White
C.G.S.   Chester G. Starr
C.S.-I.   Christiane Sourvinou-Inwood
D.E.S.   Donald Emrys Strong
D.G.J.S.   D. Graham J. Shipley
D.N.S.   David N. Sedley
E.M.S.   Edith Mary Smallwood
E.T.S.   Edward Togo Salmon
G.S.   Gisela Striker
H.S.   Henri Seyrig
H.S.-W.   Heleen Sancisi-Weerdenburg

H.P.S.   Hans Peter Syndikus
J.Sca.   John Scarborough
J.Sch.   John Scheid
J.B.S.   John B. Salmon
J.-F.S.   Jean-François Salles
J.H.S.   John Hedley Simon
J.R.S.   J. Robert Sallares
K.S.S.   Kenneth S. Sacks
M.S.S.   Martin Stirling Smith
M.S.Sp.   M. Stephen Spurr
R.A.S.S.   Richard A. S. Seaford
R.B.E.S.   Rowland B. E. Smith
R.J.S.   Robin J. Seager
R.R.K.S.   Richard R. K. Sorabji
S.S.-W.   Susan Mary Sherwin-White

C.C.W.T.   Christopher C. W. Taylor
C.J.T.   Christopher J. Tuplin
D.J.T.   Dorothy J. Thompson
G.J.T.   G. J. Toomer
J.D.T.   J. David Thomas
J.M.C.T.   Jocelyn M. C. Toynbee
R.T.   Rosalind Thomas
R.Th.   Romila Thapar
R.A.T.   Richard Allan Tomlinson
R.S.O.T.   R. S. O. Tomlin
S.C.T.   Stephen C. Todd
S.M.T.   Susan M. Treggiari

H.S.V.   H. S. Versnel
J.T.V.   J. T. Vallance
M.V.   Michael Vickers

A.G.W.   Arthur Geoffrey Woodhead
A.J.W.   A. J. Woodman
B.H.W.   Brian Herbert Warmington
D.W.   David Whitehead
E.H.W.   Eric Herbert Warmington
F.R.W.   Francis Redding Walton
H.D.W.   Henry Dickinson Westlake
H.T.W.-G.   Henry Theodore Wade-Gery
J.Wi.   Josef Wiesehöfer
L.C.W.   Lindsay Cameron Watson
M.W.   Michael Winterbottom
M.Wil.   Margaret Williamson
M.L.W.   Martin Litchfield West
M.M.W.   M. M. Willcock
N.G.W.   Nigel Guy Wilson
R.B.B.W.   Robert B. B. Wardy
R.J.A.W.   Roger J. A. Wilson
S.E.C.W.   Susan E. C. Walker
T.E.J.W.   Thomas E. J. Wiedemann

B.Z.   Bernhard Zimmermann

Thematic Listing of Entries

All entries in the book are listed here according to broad subject areas. Many entries relate to more than one subject and accordingly appear under more than one heading.

HISTORY

Greek prehistory, history, & politics
agrarian laws and policy
Alexandria
armies, Greek and Hellenistic
Asia Minor
Athens (history)
banks
booty
bribery, Greek
brigandage
Carthage
citizenship, Greek
class struggle
colonization, Greek
colonization, Hellenistic
Crete, Greek and Roman
Cyprus
Delian League
democracy, Athenian
economy, Greek
economy, Hellenistic
federal states
finance, Greek and Hellenistic
freedmen, freedwomen
freedom in the ancient world
Greece (prehistory and history)
Hellenism, Hellenization
imperialism
Ionian Revolt
Macedonia
magistracy, Greek
mercenaries
metics
Minoan civilization
Mycenaean civilization
nomads
oligarchy
polis
politics
population, Greek
propaganda
Sicily
Spain
Sparta
status, legal and social
sycophants
tyranny

Roman history & politics
Actium
Africa, Roman

agrarian laws and policy
Alexandria
armies, Roman
Asia, Roman province
banks
booty
bribery, Roman
brigandage
Britain, Roman
Carthage
citizenship, Roman
class struggle
colonization, Roman
consul
dictator
economy, Roman
equites
Etruscans
finance, Roman
freedom in the ancient world
Gaul (Cisalpine)
Gaul (Transalpine)
imperialism
limes
magistracy, Roman
mercenaries
nomads
Notitia Dignitatum
patricians
patronage (non-literary)
plebs
politics
population, Roman
procurator
propaganda
proscription
provincia/province
publicani
Romanization
Rome (history)
senate
Sicily
Spain

Historical individuals
Aeschines
Agrippa
Agrippina
Alcibiades
Alexander the Great
Antigonus Gonatas
Antigonus the One-eyed
Antiochus III
Antoninus Pius
Antony, Mark

Atticus
Augustus
Aurelius, Marcus
Brutus
Caesar, Julius
Caracalla
Catiline
Cato the Elder
Cato the Younger
Cincinnatus
Claudius
Cleisthenes
Cleopatra VII
Clodia
Clodius Pulcher, Publius
Commodus, Lucius Aurelius
Constantine I
Coriolanus
Crassus
Demosthenes
Diocletian
Dionysius I
Domitian
Elagabalus
Epaminondas
Eucratides I
Fabius Maximus Verrucosus, Quintus
Flamininus
Gaius (Caligula)
Germanicus
Gordian III
Gracchus, Gaius
Gracchus, Tiberius
Hadrian
Hannibal
Julia
Julian
Lepidus
Livia
Lycurgus
Lysander
Lysimachus
Maecenas, Gaius
Marius, Gaius
Messallina
Mithradates VI
Nero
Nerva, Marcus Cocceius
Nicias
Paul, St
Pericles
Philip II
Pisistratus
Pompey

Ptolemy I
Ptolemy II
Pyrrhus
Scipio Aemilianus
Scipio Africanus
Sejanus
Septimius Severus, Lucius
Sertorius, Quintus
Severus Alexander
Silius Italicus
Solon
Sulla
Tarquinius Superbus, Lucius
Themistocles
Tiberius
Titus
Trajan
Tullius, Servius
Vespasian

Near Eastern Studies
Ai Khanoum
Babylonia
Bactria
Cleopatra VII
Cyrus the Great
Darius I
Egypt
Icaros
India
Nemrut Dag
Orientalism
Palmyra
Parthia
Persepolis
Persia
Phoenicians
Ptolemy I
Ptolemy II
Seleucids
Seleucus I
Syria
Xerxes I

Historiography
Ammianus Marcellinus
Appian
Arrian
Cassius Dio
Diodorus
Ephorus
Eusebius
genealogy
Herodotus
Hieronymus of Cardia

Thematic Listing of Entries

Abbreviations

Frontin.	Frontinus	IG	Inscriptiones Graecae (1873–)
Str.	Strategemata	ILabraunda	J. Crampa (ed.), Labraunda Swedish
G&R	Greece and Rome, NS (1954/5–)		Excavations and Researches 3 (1
Gai. Inst.	Gaius, Institutiones		and 2): The Greek Inscriptions
Gell.	Aulus Gellius		(1969 and 1972)
NA	Noctes Atticae	Il.	Iliad
Gow–Page, GP	A. S. F. Gow and D. L. Page, The	ILLRP	Inscriptiones Latinae Liberae Rei
	Greek Anthology: Garland of Philip		Republicae, ed. A. Degrassi, vol.
	and some Contemporary Epigrams,		1² (1965), 2 (1963)
	2 vols. (1968)	ILS	see Dessau
Gow–Page, HE	A. S. F. Gow and D. L. Page, The	IMagn.	O. Kern (ed.), Die Inschriften von
	Greek Anthology: Hellenistic		Magnesia am Maeander (1900)
	Epigrams, 2 vols. (1965)	IMylasa	W. Blümel, Die Inschriften von Mylasa
Gow–Scholfield	A. S. F. Gow and A. F. Scholfield,		(2 vols., 1987–8)
	Nicander: the Poems and Poetical	ISestos	J. Krauss, Die Inschriften von Sestos
	Fragments (1953)		und der Thrakischen Chersones
GVI	W. Peek, Griechische Vers-Inschriften 1:		(1980)
	Grab-Epigramme (1955)	Isid.	Isidorus
Harp.	Harpocration	Etym.	Etymologiae
Harv. Stud.	Harvard Studies in Classical Philology	Isoc.	Isocrates
HCT	A. W. Gomme, A. Andrewes, and	Bus.	Busiris
	K. J. Dover, A Historical	Antid.	Antidosis
	Commentary on Thucydides, 5 vols.	Paneg.	Panegyricus
	(1945–81)	IVO	Inschriften von Olympia, ed. W.
Hdt.	Herodotus		Dittenberger and K. Purgold
Hell. Oxy.	Hellenica Oxyrhynchia		(1896)
Hermog.	Hermogenes	JACT	Joint Association of Classical
Prog.	Progymnasmata		Teachers
Hes.	Hesiod	JCS	Journal of Classical Studies
Op.	Opera et Dies	Jeffery, LSAG	L. Jeffery, Local Scripts of Archaic
Theog.	Theogonia		Greece, 2nd edn., rev. A. Johnston
Hippoc.	Hippocrates		(1990)
Aer.	De aera, aquis, locis	Jer.	Jerome
Mul.	De mulierum affectibus	Ab Abr.	Ab Abraham, the chronological
Nat. mul.	De natura muliebri		reckoning from the first year of
Virg.	De virginibus morbis		Abraham followed in Jerome's
VM	De vetere medicina		translation and enlargement of
Hippol.	Hippolytus		Eusebius' Chronicle
Haer.	Refutatio omnium haeresium	De vir. ill.	De viris illustribus
Hist.	Historia	JHS	Journal of Hellenic Studies
Hom.	Homer	Joseph.	Josephus
Il.	Iliad	AJ	Antiquitates Judaicae
Od.	Odyssey	Ap.	Contra Apionem
Hom. Hymn Dem.	Homeric Hymn to Demeter	BJ	Bellum Judaicum
Hor.	Horace	JRA	Journal of Roman Archaeology
Ars P.	Ars poetica	JRS	Journal of Roman Studies
Carm.	Carmina or Odes	Julian.	Julianus imperator
Carm. saec.	Carmen saeculare	Or.	Orationes
Epist.	Epistulae	Just. Epit.	Justinus, Epitome (of Trogus)
Epod.	Epodi	Juv.	Juvenal
Sat.	Satirae or Sermones	KA	see Kassel–Austin
HR	History of Religions	Kassel–Austin, PCG	R. Kassel and C. Austin, Poetae
HRRel.	see under Peter		Comici Graeci, vol. 1 (1983), 2
Hsch.	Hesychius		(1991)
Hyg.	Hyginus	Keil, Gramm. Lat.	H. Keil, Grammatici Latini, 8 vols.
Fab.	Fabulae		(1855–1923; repr. 1961)
Hymn. Hom. Ap.	Hymnus Homericus ad Apollinem	Kern	O. Kern
Hymn. Hom. Cer.	Hymnus Homericus ad Cererem	Orph. frag.	Orphica Fragmenta (1922)
Hymn. Hom. Merc.	Hymnus Homericus ad Mercurium	Kirk–Raven–Schofield,	G. S. Kirk, J. E. Raven, and M.
Hyp.	Hyperides	The Presocratic	Schofield, The Presocratic
Lyc.	For Lycophron	Philosophers	Philosophers, 2nd edn. (1983)
Iambl.	Iamblichus	LGPN 1	P. M. Fraser and E. Matthews (eds.),
VP	Vita Pythagorae		A Lexicon of Greek Personal Names
IE	Indo-European		1 (1987)

Thematic Listing of Entries

Abbreviations

A. GENERAL

abr.	abridged/abridgement	Gk.	Greek	Ol.	Olympiad
adesp.	adespota	ha.	hectare/s	OP	Old Persian
app.	appendix	Hebr.	Hebrew	orig.	original (e.g. Ger./Fr.
app. crit.	apparatus criticus	hyp.	hypothesis		orig. [edn.])
b.	born	*i.a.*	*inter alia*	OT	Old Testament
bibliog.	bibliography	ibid.	ibidem, in the same work	oz.	ounce/s
bk.	book	IE	Indo-European	plur.	plural
c.	*circa*	in.	inch/es	pref.	preface
cent.	century	introd.	introduction	*Proc.*	*Proceedings*
cm.	centimetre/s	Ion.	Ionic	ps.-	pseudo-
comm.	commentary	kg.	kilogram/s	pt.	part
d.	died	km.	kilometre/s	pub.	published
Dor.	Doric	lb.	pound/s	ref.	reference
end	at/nr. end	lit.	literally	repr.	reprint, reprinted
ed.	editor, edited by	L.	Linnaeus	rev.	revised/by
edn.	edition	Lat.	Latin	schol.	scholiast or scholia
Eng.	English	m.	metre/s	ser.	series
esp.	especially	mi.	mile/s	Skt.	Sanskrit
f., ff.	and following	ml.	millilitre/s	Suppl.	Supplement
fl.	floruit	mod.	modern	T	*testimonium* (i.e. piece of
Fr.	French	Mt.	Mount		ancient evidence about an
fr.	fragment	n., nn.	note, notes		author)
ft.	foot/feet	n.d.	no date	trans.	translation, translated by
g.	gram/s	no.	number	yd.	yard
Ger.	German	NT	New Testament		

B. AUTHORS AND BOOKS

Note [--] names of authors or works in square brackets indicate false or doubtful attributions
A small number above the line indicates the number of an edition

AAA	*Athens Annals of Archaeology*	*ANRW*	*Aufstieg und Niedergang der römischen*
AE	*L'Année Épigraphique*, published in		*Welt* (1972–)
	Revue Archéologique and separately	*Ant. Class.*	*L'Antiquité classique*
	(1888–)	Apollod.	Apollodorus mythographus
Ael.	Aelianus	*Bibl.*	*Bibliotheca*
VH	*Varia Historia*	*Epit.*	*Epitome*
Aen.	*Aeneid*	App.	Appian
Aen. Tact.	Aeneas Tacticus	*B Civ.*	*Bella civilia*
Aesch.	Aeschylus	*Pun.*	*Libykē*
Ag.	*Agamemnon*	*Syr.*	*Saunitikē*
Cho.	*Choephoroe*	Apul.	Apuleius
Eum.	*Eumenides*	*Apol.*	*Apologia*
Pers.	*Persae*	*Met.*	*Metamorphoses*
PV	*Prometheus Vinctus*	Ap. Rhod.	Apollonius Rhodius
Sept.	*Septem Contra Thebas*	*Argon.*	*Argonautica*
Supp.	*Supplices*	Ar.	Aristophanes
Aeschin.	Aeschines	*Ach.*	*Acharnenses*
In Ctes.	*Against Ctesiphon*	*Av.*	*Aves*
In Tim.	*Against Timarchus*	*Eccl.*	*Ecclesiazusae*
AJAH	*American Journal of Ancient History*	*Eq.*	*Equites*
AJPhil.	*American Journal of Philology*	*Lys.*	*Lysistrata*
AK	*Antike Kunst*	*Nub.*	*Nubes*
Alcm.	Alcman	*Plut.*	*Plutus*
Andoc.	Andocides	*Ran.*	*Ranae*

Thesm.	Thesmophoriazusae
Vesp.	Vespae
Arch. Anz.	Archäologischer Anzeiger in Jahrbuch des [kaiserlichen] deutschen archäologischen Instituts (JDAI)
Arist.	Aristotle
[Ath. Pol.]	Athēnaiōn politeia
Cael.	De Caelo
De an.	De anima
Eth. Eud.	Ethica Eudemia
Eth. Nic.	Ethica Nicomachea
Gen. an.	De generatione animalium
Gen. corr.	De generatione et corruptione
Hist. an.	Historia animalium
[Lin. ins.]	De lineis insecabilibus
Metaph.	Metaphysica
Mete.	Meteorologica
[Oec.]	Oeconomica
Part. an.	De partibus animalium
Ph.	Physica
Poet.	Poetica
Pol.	Politica
[Pr.]	Problemata
Rh.	Rhetorica
Top.	Topica
Aristid. Or.	Aristides, Orationes
Aristox.	Aristoxenus
Fr. hist.	Fragmenta historica
Arr.	Arrian
Anab.	Anabasis
ARV²	J. D. Beazley, Attic Red-Figure Vase-Painters, 2nd edn. (1963)
ASAA	Annuario della Scuola archeologica di Atene e delle Missioni italiane in Oriente
Asc.	Asconius
Mil.	Commentary on Cicero, Pro Milone
Ath.	Athenaeus
Athenaeum	Athenaeum (Pavia), NS (1923–)
Ath. pol.	Athēnaiōn politeia (Aristotelian); see also Xen. for 'Old Oligarch' i.e. Ps.-Xen. Ath. Pol.
ATL	B. D. Meritt, H. T. Wade-Gery, and M. F. McGregor, The Athenian Tribute Lists 1–4 (1939–53)
August.	Augustine
De civ. D.	De civitate Dei
Ep.	Epistulae
Austin	M. M. Austin, The Hellenistic World from Alexander to the Roman Conquest (1981)
Bagnall and Derow	R. S. Bagnall and P. Derow, Greek Historical Documents: The Hellenistic Period (1981)
BCH	Bulletin de Correspondance Hellénique
BÉ	Bulletin épigraphique, pub. in Revue des études grecques
Beazley, ABV	J. D. Beazley, Attic Black-figure Vase Painters (1956)
ARV²	Attic Red-figure Vase Painters, 2nd edn. (1963)
BGU	Berliner Griechische Urkunden (Ägyptische Urkunden aus den Kgl. Museen zu Berlin)

BHisp.	Bellum Hispaniense
BICS	Bulletin of the Institute of Classical Studies, London
Broughton, MRR	T. R. S. Broughton, The Magistrates of the Roman Republic (1951–2); Suppl. (1986: supersedes Suppl. 1960)
BSA	Annual of the British School at Athens (1895–)
Budé	Collection des Univ. de France, publiée sous le patronage de l'Assoc. Guillaume Budé
Burkert, GR	W. Burkert, trans. J. Raffan, Greek Religion (1985)
Burkert, HN	W. Burkert, trans. P. Bing, Homo Necans (1983)
Caes.	Caesar
B Civ.	Bellum Civile
B Gall.	Bellum Gallicum
CAH	Cambridge Ancient History, 2nd edn. (1961– ; 1st edn. 1923–39)
Callim.	Callimachus
Aet.	Aetia
Epigr.	Epigrammata
Hymn 3	Hymn to Artemis
Hymn 4	Hymn to Delos
Hymn 5	Hymn to Athena
Cato, Agr.	Cato, De agricultura or De re rustica
Orig.	Origines
Catull.	Catullus
CCAG	Catalogus Codicum Astrologorum Graecorum, ed. F. Cumont and others 9 vols.
CEG	P. A. Hansen, Carmina Epigraphica Graeca, 2 vols. (1983–9)
Celsus, Med.	Celsus, De medicina
Charisius, Gramm.	Charisius, Ars grammatica
Chiron	Chiron: Mitteilungen de Kommission für alte Geschichte und Epigraphik des deutschen archäologischen Instituts
Chron. Pasch.	Chronicon Paschale
CIA	Corpus Inscriptionum Atticarum (1825–)
Cic.	Cicero (Marcus Tullius)
Acad. post.	Academica posteriora
Att.	Epistulae ad Atticum
Balb.	Pro Balbo
Brut.	Brutus or De Claris Oratoribus
Cael.	Pro Caelio
Deiot.	Pro rege Deiotaro
De or.	De oratore
Div.	De divinatione
Dom.	De domo sua
Fam.	Epistulae ad familiares
Fin.	De finibus
Flac.	Pro Flacco
Font.	Pro Fonteio
Har. resp.	De Haruspicum responso
Leg.	De legibus
Leg. agr.	De lege agraria
Mur.	Pro Murena
Nat. D.	De natura deorum
Off.	De officiis

Orat.	*Orator ad M. Brutum*
Planc.	*Pro Plancio*
Q Fr.	*Epistulae ad Quintum fratrem*
Rosc. Am.	*Pro Sexto Roscio Amerino*
Scaur.	*Pro Scauro*
Sest.	*Pro Sestio*
Sull.	*Pro Sulla*
Top.	*Topica*
Tusc.	*Tusculanae disputationes*
Verr.	*In Verrem*
CIJ	*Corpus Inscriptionum Iudaicarum,* ed. J.-B. Frey (1936–52)
CIL	*Corpus Inscriptionum Latinarum* (1863–)
CJ	*Classical Journal*
Clem. Al.	Clemens Alexandrinus
Protr.	*Protrepticus*
Strom.	*Stromateis*
Cod. Iust.	*Codex Iustinianus*
Cod. Theod.	*Codex Theodosianus*
Collingwood–Wright, *RIB*	R. G. Collingwood, R. P. Wright, and others, *The Roman Inscriptions of Britain* (1965–)
Columella, *Rust.*	Columella, *De re rustica*
Cook, *Zeus*	A. B. Cook, *Zeus: A Study in Ancient Religion,* vol. 1 (1914), 2 (1925), 3 (1940)
CPhil.	*Classical Philology*
Courtney, *FLP*	E. Courtney, *The Fragmentary Latin Poets* (1993)
CQ	*Classical Quarterly*
CR	*Classical Review*
CR Acad. Inscr.	*Comptes rendus de l'Académie des Inscriptions et Belles-lettres*
Cron. Erc.	*Bolletino del Centro internazionale per lo studio dei papyri ercolanesi*
Curt.	Q. Curtius Rufus
Davies, *APF*	J. K. Davies, *Athenian Propertied Families 600–300 BC* (1971)
Davies, *EGF*	M. Davies, *Epicorum Graecorum Fragmenta* (1988)
PMGF	*Poetarum Melicorum Graecorum Fragmenta* (1991)
DB	Inscription of Darius I at Bisutun
Def. tab. Wünsch	R. Wünsch, *Defixionum Tabellae* (= *IG* 3/3) (1897)
Dem.	Demosthenes
De cor.	*De corona*
Epit.	*Epitaphius*
Meid.	*Against Meidias*
Dessau, *ILS*	H. Dessau, *Inscriptiones Latinae Selectae* (1892–1916)
*DFA*³	A. W. Pickard-Cambridge, rev. J. Gould and D. M. Lewis, *Dramatic Festivals of Athens,* 3rd edn. (1988)
Dig.	*Digesta*
Dio Cass.	Dio Cassius
Dio Chrys.	Dio Chrysostomus
Or.	*Orationes*
Diod. Sic.	Diodorus Siculus
Diog. Laert.	Diogenes Laertius
Dion. Hal.	Dionysius Halicarnassius
Ant. Rom.	*Antiquitates Romanae*
Comp.	*De compositione verborum*
Lys.	*De Lysia*
Pomp.	*Epistula ad Pompeium*
Rhet.	*Ars rhetorica*
DK	H. Diels and W. Kranz, *Fragmente der Vorsokratiker,* 6th edn. (1952)
Donat.	Aelius Donatus
Vit. Verg.	*Vita Vergilii*
Dumézil, *ARR*	G. Dumézil, *Archaic Roman Religion* (1987; Fr. orig. 1974)
EJ	V. Ehrenberg and A. H. M. Jones, *Documents Illustrating the Reigns of Augustus and Tiberius,* 2nd edn. (1976)
Enn. Ann.	Ennius, *Annales*
Epicurus	Epicurus
Ep.	*Epistulae*
Ep. Hdt.	*Epistula ad Herodotum*
Ep. Men.	*Epistula ad Menoeceum*
Ep. Pyth.	*Epistula ad Pythoclem*
Sent. Vat.	*Vatican Sayings,* = *Gnomologium Vaticanum*
RS	*Ratae sententiae*
Eratosth.	Eratosthenes
Etym. Magn.	*Etymologicum Magnum*
Eur.	Euripides
Alc.	*Alcestis*
Andr.	*Andromache*
Bacch.	*Bacchae*
Cyc.	*Cyclops*
El.	*Electra*
Hec.	*Hecuba*
HF	*Hercules furens*
Hipp.	*Hippolytus*
IA	*Iphigenia Aulidensis*
IT	*Iphigenia Taurica*
Med.	*Medea*
Or.	*Orestes*
Rhes.	*Rhesus*
Supp.	*Supplices*
Euseb.	Eusebius
Chron.	*Chronica*
Hist. eccl.	*Historia ecclesiastica*
Praep. evang.	*Praeparatio evangelica*
Vit. Const.	*Vita Constantini*
Eust.	Eustathius
Prooem. ad Pind.	*Eustathii prooemium commentariorum Pindaricorum,* ed. F. W. Schneidewin (1837)
Eutocius, *In Arch. circ. dim.*	Eutocius, *In Archimedis circuli dimensionem*
Farnell, *Hero-Cults*	L. R. Farnell, *Greek Hero-Cults and Ideas of Immortality* (1921)
Festus, *Gloss. Lat.*	W. M. Lindsay's second edn. of Festus in his *Glossaria Latina,* vol. 4
FGrH	F. Jacoby, *Fragmente der griechischen Historiker* (1923–)
FIRA	see Riccobono, *FIRA*
Firm. Mat.	Firmicus Maternus
Err. prof. rel.	*De errore profanarum religionum*
FPG	F. W. A. Mullach, *Fragmenta Philosophorum Graecorum* (1860–81)

Frontin.	Frontinus	*IG*	*Inscriptiones Graecae* (1873–)
Str.	*Strategemata*	*ILabraunda*	J. Crampa (ed.), *Labraunda Swedish*
G&R	*Greece and Rome*, NS (1954/5–)		*Excavations and Researches* 3 (1
Gai. *Inst.*	Gaius, *Institutiones*		and 2): *The Greek Inscriptions*
Gell.	Aulus Gellius		(1969 and 1972)
NA	*Noctes Atticae*	*Il.*	*Iliad*
Gow–Page, *GP*	A. S. F. Gow and D. L. Page, *The*	*ILLRP*	*Inscriptiones Latinae Liberae Rei*
	Greek Anthology: Garland of Philip		*Republicae*, ed. A. Degrassi, vol.
	and some Contemporary Epigrams,		1² (1965), 2 (1963)
	2 vols. (1968)	*ILS*	see Dessau
Gow–Page, *HE*	A. S. F. Gow and D. L. Page, *The*	*IMagn.*	O. Kern (ed.), *Die Inschriften von*
	Greek Anthology: Hellenistic		*Magnesia am Maeander* (1900)
	Epigrams, 2 vols. (1965)	*IMylasa*	W. Blümel, *Die Inschriften von Mylasa*
Gow–Scholfield	A. S. F. Gow and A. F. Scholfield,		(2 vols., 1987–8)
	Nicander: the Poems and Poetical	*ISestos*	J. Krauss, *Die Inschriften von Sestos*
	Fragments (1953)		*und der Thrakischen Chersones*
GVI	W. Peek, *Griechische Vers Inschriften* 1:		(1980)
	Grab-Epigramme (1955)	Isid.	Isidorus
Harp.	Harpocration	*Etym.*	*Etymologiae*
Harv. Stud.	*Harvard Studies in Classical Philology*	Isoc.	Isocrates
HCT	A. W. Gomme, A. Andrewes, and	*Bus.*	*Busiris*
	K. J. Dover, *A Historical*	*Antid.*	*Antidosis*
	Commentary on Thucydides, 5 vols.	*Paneg.*	*Panegyricus*
	(1945–81)	*IVO*	*Inschriften von Olympia*, ed. W.
Hdt.	Herodotus		Dittenberger and K. Purgold
Hell. Oxy.	*Hellenica Oxyrhynchia*		(1896)
Hermog.	Hermogenes	JACT	Joint Association of Classical
Prog.	*Progymnasmata*		Teachers
Hes.	Hesiod	*JCS*	*Journal of Classical Studies*
Op.	*Opera et Dies*	Jeffery, *LSAG*	L. Jeffery, *Local Scripts of Archaic*
Theog.	*Theogonia*		*Greece*, 2nd edn., rev. A. Johnston
Hippoc.	Hippocrates		(1990)
Aer.	*De aera, aquis, locis*	Jer.	Jerome
Mul.	*De mulierum affectibus*	*Ab Abr.*	*Ab Abraham*, the chronological
Nat. mul.	*De natura muliebri*		reckoning from the first year of
Virg.	*De virginibus morbis*		Abraham followed in Jerome's
VM	*De vetere medicina*		translation and enlargement of
Hippol.	Hippolytus		Eusebius' Chronicle
Haer.	*Refutatio omnium haeresium*	*De vir. ill.*	*De viris illustribus*
Hist.	*Historia*	*JHS*	*Journal of Hellenic Studies*
Hom.	Homer	Joseph.	Josephus
Il.	*Iliad*	*AJ*	*Antiquitates Judaicae*
Od.	*Odyssey*	*Ap.*	*Contra Apionem*
Hom. Hymn Dem.	*Homeric Hymn to Demeter*	*BJ*	*Bellum Judaicum*
Hor.	Horace	*JRA*	*Journal of Roman Archaeology*
Ars P.	*Ars poetica*	*JRS*	*Journal of Roman Studies*
Carm.	*Carmina* or *Odes*	Julian.	Julianus imperator
Carm. saec.	*Carmen saeculare*	*Or.*	*Orationes*
Epist.	*Epistulae*	Just. *Epit.*	Justinus, *Epitome* (of Trogus)
Epod.	*Epodi*	Juv.	Juvenal
Sat.	*Satirae* or *Sermones*	KA	see Kassel–Austin
HR	*History of Religions*	Kassel–Austin, *PCG*	R. Kassel and C. Austin, *Poetae*
HRRel.	see under Peter		*Comici Graeci*, vol. 1 (1983), 2
Hsch.	Hesychius		(1991)
Hyg.	Hyginus	Keil, *Gramm. Lat.*	H. Keil, *Grammatici Latini*, 8 vols.
Fab.	*Fabulae*		(1855–1923; repr. 1961)
Hymn. Hom. Ap.	*Hymnus Homericus ad Apollinem*	Kern	O. Kern
Hymn. Hom. Cer.	*Hymnus Homericus ad Cererem*	*Orph. frag.*	*Orphica Fragmenta* (1922)
Hymn. Hom. Merc.	*Hymnus Homericus ad Mercurium*	Kirk–Raven–Schofield,	G. S. Kirk, J. E. Raven, and M.
Hyp.	Hyperides	*The Presocratic*	Schofield, *The Presocratic*
Lyc.	*For Lycophron*	*Philosophers*	*Philosophers*, 2nd edn. (1983)
Iambl.	Iamblichus	*LGPN* 1	P. M. Fraser and E. Matthews (eds.),
VP	*Vita Pythagorae*		*A Lexicon of Greek Personal Names*
IE	Indo-European		1 (1987)

LGPN 2	M. Osborne and S. Byrne (eds.), *A Lexicon of Greek Personal Names* 2 (1994)	Nic.	Nicander
		Alex.	*Alexipharmaca*
LIMC	*Lexicon Iconographicum Mythologiae Classicae* (1981–)	Non.	Nonius
		OGI	*Orientis Graeci Inscriptiones Selectae*
Lindsay, *Gloss. Lat.*	W. M. Lindsay, *Glossaria Latina* (1930)	*ORF* and *ORF*⁴	see Malcovati, *ORF*
		Orph.	Orphica
Livy, *Epit.*	Livy, *Epitomae*	frs.	see Kern
Per.	*Periochae*	Ov.	Ovid
Loeb	Loeb Classical Library	*Am.*	*Amores*
[Longinus], *Subl.*	[Longinus], *On the Sublime*	*Ars am.*	*Ars amatoria*
LP	E. Lobel and D. L. Page, *Poetarum Lesbiorum Fragmenta* (1955)	*Fast.*	*Fasti*
		Her.	*Heroides*
LSAG	see Jeffery, *LSAG*	*Ib.*	*Ibis*
LSAM	F. Sokolowski, *Lois sacrées de l'Asie Mineure* (1955)	*Medic.*	*Medicamina faciei*
		Met.	*Metamorphoses*
LSCG	F. Sokolowski, *Lois sacrées des cités grecques* (1969)	*Pont.*	*Epistulae ex Ponto*
		Rem. am.	*Remedia amoris*
LSS	F. Sokolowski, *Lois sacrées des cités grecques: Supplément* (1962)	*Tr.*	*Tristia*
		Page, *FGE*	D. L. Page, *Further Greek Epigrams* (1981)
Luc.	Lucan	*GLP*	*Greek Literary Papyri* (Loeb, 1942)
Lucian		*PMG*	*Poetae Melici Graeci* (1962)
Alex.	*Alexander*	*P. Antinoop.*	*Antinoopolis Papyri* (1950–67)
Catapl.	*Cataplus*	Paus.	Pausanias
Dial. meret.	*Dialogi meretricii*	*P Berol.*	*Berlin Papyri*
Hermot.	*Hermotimus*	*PCG*	see Kassel–Austin
Hist. conscr.	*Quomodo historia conscribenda sit*	*PColon.*	*Kölner Papyri* (1976–)
Ind.	*Adversus indoctum*	*PCPS*	*Proceedings of the Cambridge Philological Society*
Macr.	*Macrobii*		
Lucil.	Lucilius	*PEleph.*	*Elephantine Papyri* (1907)
Lucr.	Lucretius	*Peripl. M. Rubr.*	*Periplus Maris Rubri*
LXX	Septuagint	Peter, *HRRel.*	H. Peter, *Historicorum Romanorum Reliquiae*, vol. 1² (1914), 2 (1906)
Macrob.	Macrobius		
Sat.	*Saturnalia*	Petron.	Petronius
Malcovati, *ORF*	H. Malcovati, *Oratorum Romanorum Fragmenta* (2nd edn. 1955; 4th edn. 1967)	*Sat.*	*Satyrica*
		Pf.	R. Pfeiffer
		PG	see Migne
Marcellin.	Marcellinus	*PGM*	K. Preisendanz and others (eds.), *Papyri Graecae Magicae: Die griechischen Zauberpapyri*, 2 vols., 2nd edn. (1973–4)
Marm. Par.	*Marmor Parium* (*IG* 12 (5), 444)		
Mart.	Martial		
Spect.	*Spectacula*		
Marx	F. Marx, *C. Lucilii Carminum Reliquiae* (1904–5)	Pherec.	Pherecydes
		Philo	Philo Judaeus
M. Aur. *Med.*	Marcus Aurelius, *Meditations*	*CW*	Edition of Philo Judaeus by L. Cohn and P. Wendland (1896–1916)
MDAI	*Mitteilungen des deutschen archäologischen Instituts*		
		Leg.	*Legatio ad Gaium*
Men.	Menander	*Philol.*	*Philologus*
Dys.	*Dyskolos*	Philostr.	Philostratus
MH	*Museum Helveticum*	*VA*	*Vita Apollonii*
Migne, *PG*	Migne, *Patrologiae Cursus*, series Graeca	*VS*	*Vitae sophistarum*
		Phot.	Photius
PL	*Patrologiae Cursus*, series Latina	*Bibl.*	*Bibliotheca*
ML	R. Meiggs and D. Lewis, *A Selection of Greek Historical Inscriptions to the End of the Fifth Century BC*, rev. edn. (1988)	Pind.	Pindar (ed. B. Snell and H. Maehler, 1987–8)
		Isthm.	*Isthmian Odes*
Mon. Anc.	*Monumentum Ancyranum*	*Nem.*	*Nemean Odes*
Muson.	Musonius Rufus	*Ol.*	*Olympian Odes*
M–W	R. Merkelbach and M. L. West, *Fragmenta Hesiodea* (1967)	*Pyth.*	*Pythian Odes*
		PL	see Migne
Nauck	see *TGF*	Pl.	Plato
Nauck/Snell	see *TGF*	*Alc.*	*Alcibiades*
Nep.	Nepos	*Ap.*	*Apologia*
Att.	*Atticus*	*Chrm.*	*Charmides*

Abbreviations

Cra.	Cratylus	PMGF	see Davies, PMGF
Grg.	Gorgias	PMich.	Michigan Papyri (1931–)
[Hipparch.]	Hipparchus	PMur	Discoveries in the Judaean Desert of
Hp. mai.	Hippias maior		Jordan, 1–6 (1955–77)
Leg.	Leges	Poll.	Pollux
Phd.	Phaedo	Onom.	Onomasticon
Phdr.	Phaedrus	Polyaenus, Strat.	Polyaenus, Strategemata
Plt.	Politicus	Polyb.	Polybius
Prt.	Protagoras	Porph.	Porphyry
Resp.	Respublica	Abst.	De abstinentia
Symp.	Symposium	De antr. nymph.	De antro nympharum
Soph.	Sophista	Plot.	Vita Plotini
Tht.	Theaetetus	Powell, Coll. Alex.	U. Powell, Collectanea Alexandrina
Ti.	Timaeus		(1925)
Plaut.	Plautus	POxy.	Oxyrhynchus Papyri (1898–)
Amph.	Amphitruo	Prisc. Inst.	Priscian, Institutio de arte grammatica
Mil.	Miles gloriosus	Proc. Brit. Acad.	Proceedings of the British Academy
Plin.	Pliny (the Elder)		(1903–)
HN	Naturalis historia	Procop.	Procopius
Plin.	Pliny (the Younger)	Goth.	De bello Gothico
Ep.	Epistulae	Prudent.	Prudentius
Pan.	Panegyricus	C. Symm.	Contra Symmachum
PLM Vollmer/Morel	Poetae Latini Minores ed. Vollmer, 1	Perist.	Peristephanon
	(1909) emendavit Morel³ (1935)	PSI	Papiri Greci e Latini, Pubblicazioni
PLRE	Prosopography of the Later Roman		della Società italiana per la ricerca
	Empire 1, ed. A. H. M. Jones and		dei papiri greci e latini in Egitto
	others (1970); 2 and 3, ed. J. R.		(1912–)
	Martindale (1980–92)	PTeb.	Tebtunis Papyri (1902–76)
Plut.	Plutarch	Ptol.	Ptolemaeus mathematicus
Mor.	Moralia	Geog.	Geographia
Amat.	Amatorius	Tetr.	Tetrabiblos
De Alex. fort.	De fortuna Alexandri	PVindob.	Papyrus Vindobonensis
De exil.	De exilio	PVS	Proceedings of the Vergil Society
[De mus.]	De musica	Quint.	Quintilian
De Pyth. or.	De Pythiae oraculis	Inst.	Institutio oratoria
Prae. coniug.	Praecepta coniugalia	Radke, Götter	G. Radke, Die Götter Altitaliens (1960;
Prae. ger. reip.	Praecepta gerendae reipublicae		2nd edn. 1979)
Vit.	Vitae Parallelae	Radt	see TrGF
Alex.	Alexander	RE	A. Pauly, G. Wissowa, and W. Kroll,
Ant.	Antonius		Real-Encyclopädie d. klassischen
Arat.	Aratus		Altertumswissenschaft (1893–)
Arist.	Aristides	Rev. Arch.	Revue archéologique
Cat. Mai., Min.	Cato Maior, Minor	RG	see Mon. Anc.
Cic.	Cicero	Rh. Mus.	Rheinisches Museum für Philologie
Cim.	Cimon		(1827–), NS (1942–)
Cleom.	Cleomenes	RIB	see Collingwood–Wright
Crass.	Crassus	Riccobono, FIRA	S. Riccobono, Fontes Iuris Romani
Eum.	Eumenes		Antelustiniani (1941)
Lyc.	Lycurgus	Richardson, Topog. Dict.	L. Richardson, A New
Mar.	Marius	Ancient Rome	Topographical Dictionary of
Nic.	Nicias		Ancient Rome (1992)
Num.	Numa	RK	see Wissowa
Pel.	Pelopidas	RRC	M. H. Crawford, Roman Republican
Per.	Pericles		Coinage (1974)
Phil.	Philopoemen	RSC	Rivista di Studi Classici, Turin
Pomp.	Pompeius	Sall.	Sallust
Rom.	Romulus	Cat.	Bellum Catilinae or De Catilinae
Sol.	Solon		coniuratione
Sull.	Sulla	Hist.	Historiae
Them.	Themistocles	Iug.	Bellum Iugurthinum
Thes.	Theseus	schol.	scholiast or scholia
Tim.	Timoleon	Schol. Bern.	Scholia Bernensia ad Vergilii bucolica et
X orat.	Vitae decem oratorum		georgica, ed. Hagen (1867)
PMG	see Page, PMG	Schol. Flor. Callim.	Scholia Florentina in Callimachum

SEG	*Supplementum epigraphicum Graecum* (1923–)	*Aug.*	*Divus Augustus*
		Calig.	*Gaius Caligula*
Semon.	Semonides	*Claud.*	*Divus Claudius*
Sen.	Seneca (the Elder)	*Dom.*	*Domitianus*
Controv.	*Controversiae*	*Galb.*	*Galba*
Suas.	*Suasoriae*	*Gram.*	*De grammaticis*
Sen.	Seneca (the Younger)	*Illustr.*	*De viris illustribus*
Clem.	*De clementia*	*Iul.*	*Divus Iulius*
Ep.	*Epistulae*	*Ner.*	*Nero*
Q. Nat.	*Quaestiones naturales*	*Poet.*	*De Poetis*
Serv.	Servius	*Rel. Reiff.*	*Reliquiae,* ed. Reifferscheid
Praef.	*Praefatio*	*Rhet.*	*De rhetoribus*
Sext. Emp.	Sextus Empiricus	*Tib.*	*Tiberius*
Math.	*Adversus Mathematicos*	*Tit.*	*Divus Titus*
Pyr.	*Outlines of Pyrrhonism*	*Vesp.*	*Divus Vespasianus*
SHA	Scriptores Historiae Augustae	*Vit.*	*Vitellius*
Alex. Sev.	*Alexander Severus*	*Vita Hor.*	*Vita Horatii*
Ant. Pius	*Antoninus Pius*	*Suppl. Hell.*	H. Lloyd-Jones and P. Parsons
Hadr.	*Hadrian*		(eds.), *Supplementum*
Heliogab.	*Heliogabalus*		*Hellenisticum,* Texte und
M. Ant.	*Marcus Aurelius Antoninus (Caracalla)*		Kommentare no. 11 (1983)
		Suppl. Mag.	R.W. Daniel and F. Maltomini
Marc.	*Marcus*		(eds.), *Supplementum Magicum,*
Prob.	*Probus*		Papyrologica Coloniensia
Sherk, *Augustus*	R. E. Sherk, *Rome and the Greek East*		16/1–2, 2 vols. (1989–91)
	to the Death of Augustus,	*SVF*	H. von Arnim, *Stoicorum Veterum*
	Translated Documents of		*Fragmenta* (1903–)
	Greece and Rome 4 (1984)	*Syll.*3	W. Dittenberger, *Sylloge*
Sherk, *Hadrian*	*The Roman Empire: Augustus to*		*Inscriptionum Graecarum,* 3rd edn.
	Hadrian, Translated Documents		(1915–24)
	of Greece and Rome 6 (1988)	Syme	R. Syme
Simon.	Simonides	*RP*	*Roman Papers,* 7 vols. (1979–91)
Simpl.	Simplicius	Tac.	Tacitus
in Phys.	*in Aristotelis de Physica Commentarii*	*Agr.*	*Agricola*
		Ann.	*Annales*
Smallwood, *Docs*	E. M. Smallwood, *Documents*	*Dial.*	*Dialogus de oratoribus*
. . . . Nerva	*illustrating the Principates of*	*Germ.*	*Germania*
	Nerva, Trajan and Hadrian (1966)	*Hist.*	*Historiae*
Docs. . . . Gaius	*Documents illustrating the Principates*	TAPA	*Transactions of the American*
	of Gaius, Claudius and Nero (1967)		*Philological Association*
Snell–Maehler	see Pind.	Ter.	Terence
Soph.	Sophocles	*Ad.*	*Adelphoe*
Aj.	*Ajax*	*An.*	*Andria*
Ant.	*Antigone*	*Eun.*	*Eunuchus*
El.	*Electra*	*Haut.*	*H(e)autontimorumenos*
OC	*Oedipus Coloneus*	*Hec.*	*Hecyra*
OT	*Oedipus Tyrannus*	*Phorm.*	*Phormio*
Phil.	*Philoctetes*	Tert.	Tertullian
Trach.	*Trachiniae*	*De spect.*	*De spectaculis*
Sor. *Gyn.*	Soranus, *Gynaeceia*	*TGF*	A. Nauck, *Tragicorum Graecorum*
Spengel–Hammer	C. Hammer, *Rhetores Graeci ex*		*Fragmenta,* 2nd edn. (1889);
	recognitione Leonardi Spengel		Suppl. by B. Snell (1964)
	(1894): 2nd edn. of vol. 1/2 of	*Them. Or.*	Themistius, *Orationes*
	Spengel, *Rhet.*	Theoc.	Theocritus
Stat.	Statius	*Id.*	*Idylls*
Achil.	*Achilleis*	Theophr.	Theophrastus
Silv.	*Silvae*	*Caus. pl.*	*De causis plantarum*
Theb.	*Thebais*	*Char.*	*Characteres*
Steph. Byz.	Stephanus Byzantius or Byzantinus	*Hist. pl.*	*Historia plantarum*
Stob.	Stobaeus	Theopomp.	Theopompus Historicus
Flor.	*Anthologion*	Thgn.	Theognis
Suda	Greek lexicon formerly known as	Thuc.	Thucydides
	Suidas	Tib.	Tibullus
Suet.	Suetonius	*TrGF*	B. Snell, R. Kannicht, S. Radt (eds.),

	Tragicorum Graecorum Fragmenta, 4 vols. (1971–85), vol. 1² (1986)	Wissowa, *RK*	G. Wissowa, *Religion und Kultus d. Römer,* 2nd edn. (1912)
Val. Max.	Valerius Maximus	Xen.	Xenophon
Varro, *Ling.*	Varro, *De lingua Latina*	*An.*	*Anabasis*
Rust.	*De re rustica*	*Cyn.*	*Cynegeticus*
Vell. Pat.	Velleius Paterculus	*Cyr.*	*Cyropaedia*
Verg.	Virgil	*Hell.*	*Hellenica*
Aen.	*Aeneid*	*Hier.*	*Hiero*
Catal.	*Catalepton*	*Lac.*	*Respublica Lacedaemoniorum*
Ecl.	*Eclogues*	*Mem.*	*Memorabilia*
G.	*Georgics*	*Oec.*	*Oeconomicus*
Vit. Ar.	*Vita Aristophanis,* ed. F. Dübner, *Scholia Graeca in Aristophanem* (1846), *Prolegomena* II	*Symp.*	*Symposium*
		Vect.	*De vectigalibus*
		XPf	Inscription of Xerxes I at Persepolis (so-called 'Harem Inscription')
Vitr.	Vitruvius		
De arch.	*De architectura*	XPh	Inscription of Xerxes I at Persepolis (so-called 'Daiva Inscription')
W	see West, *GLP* and *IE²*		
Walbank, *HCP*	F. W. Walbank, *A Historical Commentary on Polybius,* 3 vols. (1957–79)	*YClS*	*Yale Classical Studies*
		ZPE	*Zeitschrift für Papyrologie und Epigraphik*
West, *GLP*	M. L. West, *Greek Lyric Poetry* (1993)		
IE²	*Iambi et Elegi,* 2nd edn. (1989)		

How to use this Book

This book is designed for easy use but the following notes may be helpful to the reader.

Chronological span The period covered is from the middle of the second millennium BC to the 6th century AD, with the main concentration of coverage focused on 800 BC to AD 300. For a brief outline, see the Chronology on pp. 789–93.

Alphabetical arrangement Entries are arranged in letter-by-letter alphabetical order of their headwords, which are shown in bold type.

Names In all cases the forms of names used are those that are the most familiar. Thus, Roman individuals of the Republican and imperial periods (up to about AD 275) are listed under their surname (*cognomen*) rather than the family name (*nomen*). For example, Cicero is listed under C rather than under his family name of Tullius, and the great general Publius Cornelius Scipio Aemilianus Africanus is listed under the familiar form 'Scipio Africanus', rather than under his family name of Cornelius. Similarly, Roman emperors, who often had long names, are listed under their usual short form, such as Nero, and the full name follows in parentheses.

In antiquity, the Latin alphabet did not contain the letter J and only in medieval times were many Roman names, such as Iulius, written with a J. In this book, we have retained the 'I' spellings except for those names which occur as headwords, which the reader would naturally look for under J.

Note that the Roman forename (*praenomen*) Gaius is conventionally abbreviated C. (not G.) and similarly Gnaeus is abbreviated Cn. not Gn.

Greek names are normally spelt in their more familiar Latinized or Anglicized forms (that is, 'Pericles' not 'Perikles').

Transliteration of Greek Except where its use was thought essential to the subject-matter or context of the entry, Greek has been transliterated, with long vowels indicated by macrons (ō, ē).

Cross references An asterisk (*) in front of a word in the text signals a cross-reference to a related entry which may be interesting to look up. Similarly, 'see' or 'see also' followed by a headword in SMALL CAPITALS is used to cross-refer when the precise form of headword to which the reader is being pointed does not occur naturally in the text.

Thematic listing of entries The list of entries under major topics at the front of the book (see pp. xi–xiv) offers another means of access to the material, in that it allows the reader to see at a glance all the entries relating to a particular subject—such as women's studies or Greek mythology—without needing to know the precise entries to look up.

References to classical texts and commentaries are given in abbreviated form in the entries, for the benefit of classics students and others who may wish to follow them up. Details of these sources are given in full at the front of the book (pp. xv–xxii).

Contributors' initials are given at the end of each entry, and a key to these initials is provided on pp. ix–x.

abortion was controversial in antiquity. Doctors taking the Hippocratic Oath (see MEDICINE, § 1.5) swore not to administer abortifacients, but other Hippocratic texts suggest that prostitutes (see PROSTITUTION, SECULAR) often employed abortion. A *Lysias fragment suggests that abortion was a crime in Athens against the husband, if his wife was pregnant when he died, since his unborn child could have claimed the estate. Greek temple inscriptions show that abortion made a woman impure for 40 days (see POLLUTION).

The Stoics (see STOICISM) believed that the foetus resembled a plant and only became an animal at birth when it started breathing. This attitude made abortion acceptable. Roman jurisprudence maintained that the foetus was not autonomous from the mother's body. There is no evidence for laws against abortion during the Roman republic. It was common during the early Roman empire (e.g. Ov. *Am.* 2. 14), and was practised for many reasons, e.g. for family limitation, in case of *adultery, or because of a desire to maintain physical beauty. Soranus (*Gynaecology* 1. 59–65, Eng. trans. 1956) distinguished deliberate from spontaneous abortion, and abortion from *contraception. He accepted abortion if the woman's life was in danger. Galen and Dioscorides mention many plant products used, either orally or by vaginal suppository, to provoke abortions. Some plants, e.g. aristolochia and squirting cucumber, can indeed have such effects. Mechanical methods were also used.

The emperors *Severus and *Caracalla towards AD 211 introduced the first definite ban on abortion in Rome as a crime against the rights of parents, and punished it with temporary exile. The spread of *Christianity changed attitudes. The *Teachings of the Apostles*, the first Christian document to mention abortion, condemned it, as did the *Letter of Barnabas*, Tertullian, and many later writers. Christians regarded abortion, once the foetus was fully formed (40 days after conception), as murder of a living being.

J. R. S.

Academy, public *gymnasium at Athens, sacred to the hero Academus, north-west of the Dipylon gate. It gave its name to the school founded there by *Plato in the early 4th cent. and maintained by an unbroken line of successors until the 1st cent. BC. The school's private property was never there, but, at least during the 4th cent., at Plato's nearby house.

The Early Academy is the phase of doctrinal Platonism under Plato himself (d. 347) and his successors Speusippus, Xenocrates, Polemon, and Crates.

The 'New Academy' is the phase, from c.269 to the early or mid-1st cent. BC (its further subdivision, Sext. Emp. *Pyr.* 1. 220, is a later imposition), in which the school, initially under Arcesilaus, interpreted true Platonism as scepticism. Dialectical criticism of doctrines, usually Stoic, was orchestrated to demonstrate *akatalēpsia*, the impossibility of knowledge, resulting in *epochē*, suspension of judgement. Carneades, its most influential head (mid-2nd cent.), was a systematic critic of all doctrines. His successors disagreed about his true intentions: Clitomachus (scholarch c.128–c.110) regarded his arguments as still promoting *epochē*, but Metrodorus of Stratonicea and Philon of Larissa (possibly the last scholarch, c.110–c.79) considered their intent doctrinal, albeit fallibilist, with the 'convincing' (*pithanon*) an adequate basis for both action and philosophical judgement. *Cicero's main philosophical works reflect his allegiance to the Philonian Academy.

In 87 BC, when the Academics were refugees from Athens, Philon was openly challenged by his disciple Antiochus of Ascalon, whose 'Old Academy' claimed to return to the doctrines of the 'ancients', meaning especially Plato and *Aristotle. Thereafter the Academy as an institution disintegrated (whether Antiochus ever became scholarch is uncertain), although the title 'Academic' lived on (cf. *Plutarch).

D. N. S.

Achilles, son of Peleus and Thetis; greatest of the Greek heroes in the Trojan War; central character of *Homer's *Iliad*.

His name may be of Mycenaean Greek origin, meaning 'a grief to the army'. If so, the destructive Wrath of Achilles, which forms the subject of the *Iliad*, must have

been central to his mythical existence from the first. He was the recipient of hero-cults in various places, but these no doubt result from his prominence in the epic, and do nothing to explain his origins.

In Homer he is king of Phthia, or 'Hellas and Phthia', in southern *Thessaly, and his people are the Myrmidons. As described at *Il.* 2. 681–5 the size of his kingdom, and of his contingent in the Trojan expedition (50 ships), is not outstanding. But in terms of martial prowess, which is the measure of excellence for a Homeric hero, Achilles' status as 'best of the Achaeans' is unquestioned. We are reminded of his absolute supremacy throughout the poem, even during those long stretches for which he is absent from the battlefield.

His character is complex. In many ways he carries the savage ethical code of the Homeric hero to its ultimate and terrifying conclusion. When *Agamemnon steals his concubine Briseis in *Il.* 1, his anger at the insult to his personal honour is natural and approved by gods and men; but he carries this anger beyond any normal limit when he refuses an offer of immense compensation in *Il.* 9. Again, when he finally re-enters the war (*Il.* 19) after the death of his friend Patroclus, his ruthless massacre of Trojans, culminating in the killing of *Hector (*Il.* 22), expresses a 'heroic' desire for revenge; but this too is taken beyond normal bounds by his contemptuous maltreatment of Hector's dead body (*Il.* 22. 395–404, 24. 14–22).

But what makes Achilles remarkable is the way in which his extreme expression of the 'heroic code' is combined with a unique degree of insight and self-knowledge. Unlike Hector, for instance, Achilles knows well that he is soon to die. In his great speech at *Il.* 9. 308–429 he calls the entire code into question, saying that he would rather live quietly at home than pursue glory in the Trojan War; but it is his 'heroic' rage against Agamemnon that has brought him to this point. In his encounter with Lycaon at *Il.* 21. 34–135, his sense of common mortality (the fact that Patroclus has died and Achilles himself will die) is a reason, not for sparing his suppliant, but for killing him in cold blood. Finally at *Il.* 24, when Priam begs him to release Hector's body, it is human feeling, as well as the gods' command, that makes him yield (507–70); but even then he accepts a ransom, and his anger still threatens to break out afresh (568–70, 584–6).

Later writers seldom treated the subject-matter of the *Iliad* (though *Aeschylus did so, portraying Achilles and Patroclus as lovers: fr. 134a). But they did provide many further details of Achilles' career, often derived from other epics such as the *Cypria* and *Aethiopis*. As a boy he was brought up by the wise *Centaur Chiron on Mt. Pelion. Later his mother Thetis, knowing that he would be killed if he joined the expedition to Troy, hid him at the court of King Lycomedes on Scyros, disguised as a girl (this episode is treated in the unfinished *Achilleis* of *Statius). There he fell in love with the king's daughter Deidamia, who bore him a son, Neoptolemus. *Odysseus discovered his identity by trickery and he joined the Greek army at Aulis,

where he was involved in the story of Iphigenia (see *Euripides' *Iphigenia at Aulis*). On the way to Troy he wounded Telephus. His exploits at Troy included the ambush and killing of Priam's son Troilus, a story linked with that of his love for Priam's daughter Polyxena. After the events of the *Iliad* he killed two allies of the Trojans: the *Amazon queen Penthesilea, with whom he is also said to have fallen in love, and the Ethiopian king Memnon. Finally he was himself killed by Paris and *Apollo (as predicted at *Il.* 22. 358–60). The fight over his body, and his funeral, are described in a dubious passage of the *Odyssey* (24. 36–94). His famous arms (described at *Il.* 18. 478–613) were then given to Odysseus (see *Sophocles' *Ajax*). After the fall of Troy his ghost demanded the sacrifice of Polyxena (see Euripides' *Hecuba*). A curious story, going back to Ibycus (fr. 10 Page), is that in Elysium he married *Medea (see also Paus. 3. 19. 13 for Achilles and Helen on the White Island). Several of these episodes, including the ambush of Troilus and the killing of Penthesilea, were popular with vase painters.

A late addition is the familiar motif of Achilles' heel: Thetis sought to make the infant Achilles invulnerable by dipping him in the Styx, but omitted to dip the heel by which she held him, and it was there that he received his death-wound. This is alluded to by Hyginus (107) and Statius (*Achil.* 1. 134, 269), but we have no full account until Servius and 'Lactantius Placidus'. A. L. B.

Actium (see ◀ Map 1, Ab ▶), a flat sandy promontory at the entrance to the Ambracian Gulf, forming part of the territory of Anactorium, as well as the NW extremity of Acarnania. A cult of *Apollo was located here as early as the 6th cent. BC to judge from the torsos of two archaic *kouroi* found on the cape in 1867. At this time, or soon thereafter, a temple stood on a low hill near the tip of the promontory where games were celebrated in honour of the god as late as the end of the 3rd cent. BC. In 31 BC the cape was the site of Mark *Antony's camp, and gave its name to the naval battle, fought just outside the gulf, in which he was defeated by Octavian, the future *Augustus (2 September). A few years later, when Octavian founded *Nicopolis on the opposite (northern) side of the strait, he took care to enlarge Apollo's sanctuary at Actium by rebuilding the old temple and adding a monumental naval trophy. In ship-sheds constructed in the sacred grove at the base of the hill, he dedicated a set of ten captured warships, one from each of the ten classes that had fought in the battle (Strabo 7. 7. 6). He also revitalized the old Actian Games by transferring them to a new venue outside Nicopolis. The quinquennial games, called Actia, were modelled on the Olympian festival, and were later imitated by several other Greek cities (see GAMES). An Actian 'era' was established, whose initial date is variously placed between 30 and 28 BC. W. M. M.

Acts of the Apostles The second of two volumes which continues the story of the rise and spread of

Achilles An Athenian clay water jar (late 6th cent. BC) depicts the vengeful Achilles about to drag Hector's body behind his chariot—an example of the excessive behaviour which distinguishes his portrayal in *Homer.

*Christianity begun in the gospel of Luke. Its textual history poses peculiar interpretative problems as it is extant in two versions, the longer in Codex Bezae. Its narrative starts with Jesus' ascension in Jerusalem and ends with *Paul preaching in Rome, where he had been taken after his appeal to Caesar (i.e. the emperor). The focus of the material on the earliest Jerusalem church around Peter and, later in the book, on the Christian career of Paul shows the concern of the author to relate the Jewish and Gentile missions and to demonstrate their basic unity. Only occasional glimpses are offered of the conflict in early Christianity which is evident in the Pauline corpus (e.g. Acts 6: 1 and 15). Acts has for a long time been a cause of great controversy between those who maintain the substantial authenticity of its historical account (while allowing for its apologetic interests) and those who see the document as a work of skilful narrative propaganda whose historical value is negligible. Knowledge of contemporary Graeco-Roman institutions should not mask the difficulties in accepting the historicity of Acts, a particular problem being the reconciliation of the accounts of Paul's career in Acts, Gal. 1–2, and the Corinthian correspondence. The references to Paul's theology indicate a markedly different set of ideas from what we find in the letters to the Romans and Galatians. For this and other reasons Acts has proved to be disappointing to the historian of Christian origins as a source for early Christian history. The history of the Jerusalem church after the start of the Pauline mission is only touched on in so far as it helps the author explain Paul's career as apostle to the Gentiles. Whereas Luke's gospel portrays Jesus as a Palestinian prophet with a controversial, indeed subversive, message for Jewish society, there is little in Acts (apart from the idealized accounts of the common life of the Jerusalem church) of that radicalism. The antagonism to *Jews and the sympathetic account of Roman officials evident in the gospel of Luke is continued in Acts, and a conciliatory attitude towards Rome has been suggested. Jews in Acts are regarded as responsible for the harassment of nascent Christianity, though there are occasional glimpses of more openness to Judaism elsewhere in the book than the concluding verses would indicate.

Various suggestions have been made with regard to its (and the related gospel of Luke's) purpose. These have included an apologia for Christianity to the Roman state, an explanation for the delay of the Parousia (Second Coming) by stressing the role of the Church in the divine purpose, an essay in anti-Jewish polemic, and a defence of Paul when his case was heard in Rome. Like his contemporary *Josephus the author of Acts seeks to demonstrate that divine providence is at work, though for the latter there is nothing in the emergence of a strange Jewish messianic movement to contradict the Jewish tradition, since it is rather the inevitable continuation of it.   C. C. R.

adoption

Greek Greeks counted on their heirs for support in old *age, and for continuation of their *oikoi* (families) and care of their tombs after death. But high mortality ensured that many had no surviving children. Adoption was a common recourse, probably encouraged by the great variation in fertility characteristic of populations with unreliable means of *contraception. The fullest accounts can be provided for Gortyn (on Crete) and Athens in the Classical period.

The law code of Gortyn apparently modifies prior practice. It permits an adult male to adopt anyone he chooses, including someone without full membership in the community, even if he already has legitimate children; however, the inheritance of those adopted in such circumstances is less than it would be if they were themselves natural children. Adoptive fathers are to announce the adoption to a citizen assembly and make a stipulated payment to their *hetaireia* (in this context, a kind of kinship group); they may also publicly disavow the adoption, and compensate those adopted with a set sum. Neither women nor minors may adopt.

At Athens, we hear of three forms of adoption, differing chiefly in the manner in which those adopted entered into their inheritance. These involved living parties (*inter vivos*), a will (testamentary adoption, said to have been introduced by *Solon), or the provision of an heir for a man already deceased. (Such posthumous adoptions did not require the prior agreement of the adoptive father.) As at Gortyn, only adult male citizens could adopt. However, Athenians' freedom of action was more limited: they could adopt only in the absence of legitimate sons, and then no one other than citizens. Magistrates could not adopt or be adopted until their accounts had been rendered; those who were *atimoi* (subject to civic disability) could not be adopted. Adopted sons could not themselves adopt in some or all cases. But fathers with daughters only could adopt; they might also marry their daughters to their adopted sons. In practice, adopters tended to choose adults, as these were more likely to survive and (according to the orators) had already given good evidence of their character, and sons were preferred to daughters. Those adopted would often have inherited anyway by the laws governing intestacy; adoptions of others were likely to be challenged by closer kin. Their claims might be furthered by the belief, apparent in other contexts as well, that adoption did not generally forge links of loyalty and intimacy equal to those of blood (e.g. Pl. *Leg.* 9. 878a; Dem. *Epit.* 4). Adoptions by will could also be attacked on the legal grounds that the adopter had acted when mad or senile, under the influence of drugs, illness, or a woman, or under coercion. Adopted children severed their connections with their natural fathers, though not their mothers. They could return to their *oikos* of birth if they left a natural son as heir to their adoptive *oikos*.

Adoption at Athens has often been viewed in the context of the community's concern for the survival of individual *oikoi*, a concern thought to be reflected in the responsibilities of the eponymous archon (a magistrate). Other Greek *poleis* (see POLIS) provide parallels: the role of the kings in adoptions at *Sparta (Hdt. 6. 57), the tradition that Philolaus, the lawgiver of Thebes, used adoption to maintain the number of *klēroi*, 'inheritable estates' (Arist. *Pol.* 2. 1274ᵇ5). However, recent scholarship tends towards contrary conclusions: the *polis* was not concerned to maintain separate *oikoi* through adoption, though individuals certainly were; adoption was essentially a private matter, regulated by the phratries and demes (sub-groups of the citizen body) into which adopted children were introduced, in which the archon took no initiative; heirs had no legal obligation to continue an *oikos* through posthumous adoption. Furthermore, arguments (based on the disappearance of testamentary adoption) that continuation of the *oikos* ceased to be a goal of adoption after the 4th cent. probably read too much into the silence of our literary sources.

Almost all our evidence for adoption in the Hellenistic and Roman periods comes from numerous inscriptions from throughout the Greek world, especially Rhodes. These reveal a bewildering inconsistency in terminology, even within the same community, perhaps attesting to differences in formal procedures and consequences now unclear. They also indicate that Greeks might change their names on adoption. 　　　　　　　　　　M. G.

Roman *Adoptio* is a legal act by which a Roman citizen enters another family and comes under the *patria potestas* (paternal authority) of its chief. Since only a *paterfamilias* (usually father or grandfather) could adopt, women could not (except in later law by imperial grant). When the adopted person, male or female, was previously in the paternal power of another, the act was *adoptio*; when a male who was not in paternal power but himself the head of a family, it was *adrogatio*. Women could not be adrogated. Both acts involved a *deminutio capitis minima*, a reduction of legal status.

Adrogatio fused two families, for with the adoptee (*adrogatus*) all under his power (*potestas, manus*) and his property pass into the family of the adopter (*adrogator*). In early times *adrogatio* was publicly validated by a vote of the curiate assembly, preceded (since it extinguished a family and its cult) by an investigation by the pontiffs; by the time of Cicero, 30 lictors represented the *curiae*. Since the assembly met only in Rome, *adrogatio* could take place only there, until (by *Diocletian's time at latest) imperial rescript replaced the vote.

Adoptio of a person in power (of any age) was a more private act performed before a praetor or governor. Its form was the same as that of emancipation (*emancipatio*, the release of a child from power), except that after the third sale the buyer did not free the child but collusively claimed that he/she was in his power. Under Justinian (see JUSTINIAN'S CODIFICATION), these formalities were replaced by a declaration before a magistrate.

The effect of both *adoptio* and *adrogatio* was to place the adopted person for all legal purposes in the same position as if he/she had been a natural child in the power of the adopter. The adoptee took the adopter's name and rank and acquired rights of succession in his new family, losing those held in the old family. 'Adoption imitates nature' (*Inst. Iust.* 1. 11. 4), so an adoptive relationship barred marriage and the adopter had to be older than the adoptee (a rule allegedly flouted by the adoption of P. *Clodius Pulcher). Bachelors and men physically incapable of reproduction (except if they had been castrated) could adopt. Adoption could be reversed by emancipation.

Adoption (of both kinds), since it created paternal power and continued the agnatic family, was originally the prerogative of men only. Adoption by women, 'to console them for the loss of children', was allowed by later emperors, as was adrogation of women: this shows a new conception. Safeguards grew up, especially for young children and their property.

Since adoption destroyed the adoptee's succession rights in the old family and a subsequent emancipation would destroy rights in the new family, Justinian drastically changed *adoptio* to allow the adoptee to retain rights in the old family, except where the adopter was a close relative, e.g. maternal grandfather.

The testamentary adoptions recorded in non-legal sources in the late republic and Principate apparently created only an obligation (from which the praetor could give dispensation) to take the testator's name. So T. Pomponius *Atticus inherited from his mother's brother Caecilius and became formally Q. Caecilius Q. f. Pomponianus Atticus (Cic. *Att.* 3. 20); the future emperor Galba for some time bore a name taken from the family of his stepmother, Livia Ocellina: L. Livius Ocella (Suet. *Galb.* 3–4). Caesar's adoption of his great-nephew C. Octavius (see AUGUSTUS) was ratified by a posthumous *adrogatio*.

Adoption of adult men was a convenient recourse for childless aristocrats and for emperors in need of successors. 　　　　　　　　A. B.; B. N.; S. M. T.

adultery

Greek At Athens, a law (attributed to Draco or *Solon) allowed a man who killed another he found in the sexual act with his wife, mother, sister, daughter, or concubine held for the purpose of bearing free children, to plead justifiable homicide; such adulterers might also be held for ransom. It is probable that there was also a *graphē* (legal suit) against adulterers, possible that those caught in the act were delivered to the 'Eleven' for summary execution or trial. Adulterous wives had to be divorced, and were excluded from public sacrifices. As for unmarried women, Solon supposedly permitted a *kurios* ('controller', male representative at law) to sell a daughter or sister into slavery if he discovered she was not a virgin. No instances are known, however, and indeed some husbands too probably preferred to respond (or not) to adultery without recourse to the law, so avoiding public dishonour. Many states are said to have allowed adulterers to be killed with impunity

(Xen. *Hiero* 3. 3). But the law code of Gortyn (on Crete) envisages adulterers paying ransoms, varying with the status of the parties and the setting of the acts, and pecuniary penalties are stipulated in some marriage contracts from Hellenistic Egypt. Punishments in other (mostly later) communities stress public humiliation. Laws at both Athens and Gortyn provided protection against entrapment and false accusations. There was allegedly no Lycurgan (see LYCURGUS) law against adultery at *Sparta, a tradition informed by the custom by which Spartans could share their wives with fellow citizens for procreative purposes. (See MARRIAGE LAW (*Greek*).)   M. G.

Roman Roman tradition ascribed to fathers and husbands great severity in punishing illicit sexual behaviour by daughters or wives. Such misconduct was *stuprum* in married or unmarried women, an offence against chastity (*pudicitia*); *adulterium* described sexual intercourse between a married woman and a man other than her husband. Until the legislation of *Augustus, regulation was chiefly in the hands of the family: adultery probably always justified divorce; a family council might advise the *paterfamilias* (husband or father in whose power the woman was) on this and other sanctions, possibly including execution. The immediate killing of adulterers/adulteresses taken in the act was defensible (morally and in court) but probably not legally prescribed. Other physical violence against the adulterer is a literary commonplace. Adultery in the late republic, like the seduction or rape of an unmarried woman, entitled the father or husband to sue the man for damages (for *iniuria*, insult) and not only to divorce the wife but to retain part of her dowry. Magistrates occasionally proceeded against adulterers/adulteresses.

Augustus, in the Julian law on repression of adulteries (*lex Iulia de adulteriis coercendis vel sim.*, *Dig.* 48. 5), passed apparently shortly after the marriage law of 18 BC, made illicit sexual intercourse (extramarital intercourse by and with a respectable free woman) a crime, to be tried by a special court under a praetor (in practice, often the senate). The law detailed restricted circumstances in which homicide by father or husband was justifiable. The normal judicial penalty for adulterers was *relegatio* (banishment) to different islands, and partial confiscation of property and dowry (one half). The husband with clear evidence had to divorce or be liable to a charge of procuring (*lenocinium*; penalties similar). On divorce, husband or father might bring an accusation within 60 days, or anyone within the next four months. A woman might not be accused while married.

Penalties were increased by Christian emperors. *Constantine I introduced the death penalty (which Justinian confirmed (see JUSTINIAN'S CODIFICATION)), but allowed only the husband or the wife's relatives to prosecute.

Adultery by the husband was not *adulterium* (unless his partner was a married woman), but his intercourse with a respectable unmarried woman (or male) constituted *stuprum* and in the 5th cent. AD (*Cod. Iust.* 5. 17. 8) his adul-

tery in the matrimonial home or with a married woman entitled his wife to divorce him without incurring the penalties then imposed for unjustified divorce. (See MARRIAGE LAW (*Roman*).)   A. B.; B. N.; S. M. T.

Aegae (Vergina) in northern Pieria (see ◀Map 1, Ba▶), overlooking the coastal plain of *Macedonia. Founded by the first of the Temenid kings and thereafter the site of their tombs, it has been made famous by Manolis Andronikos, who excavated a pre-Temenid cemetery of tumuli and then, in 1977, three royal tombs of the 4th cent. BC. Two were intact. The frescos, the offerings in gold, silver, ivory, and bronze, and the weapons were of the highest artistic quality. Tomb II was almost certainly that of *Philip II (for an alternative view, that his son, Philip III Arrhidaeus, was buried here, see E. Borza, *In the Shadow of Olympus* (1990), 256 ff.). Earlier and later burials have also been found. Theatre, palace, and acropolis stand above the cemetery area. Excavations continue.   N. G. L. H.

Aeneas, character in literature and mythology, son of Anchises and the goddess *Aphrodite. In *Homer's *Iliad* he is a prominent Trojan leader (see TROY), belonging to the younger branch of the royal house (13. 460–1, 20. 179–83, 230–41), and has important duels with Diomedes (5. 239 ff.) and *Achilles (20. 153 ff.), from both of which he is rescued by divine intervention. His piety towards the gods is stressed (20. 298–9, 347–8), and *Poseidon prophesies that he and his children will rule over the Trojans (20. 307–8).

This future beyond the *Iliad* is reflected in the version in the lost epic *Iliu Persis* ('Fall of Troy') that Aeneas and his family left Troy before its fall to retreat to Mt. Ida, which led later to accusations of his treachery (e.g. *Origo gentis Romanae* 9. 2–3). The departure of Aeneas from Troy is widely recorded, and the image of Aeneas' pious carrying of his father Anchises on his shoulders in the retreat is common in Greek vases of the 6th cent. BC found in Etruria (see ETRUSCANS), and occurs in 5th- and 4th-cent. Attic literature (Soph. fr. 373 Radt, Xen. *Cyn.* 1. 15). The further story of Aeneas' voyage to Italy may have existed as early as the 6th or 5th cent. BC (Stesichorus fr. 205 Davies; Hellanicus, *FGrH* 4 F 84), but seems well established by the 3rd cent. (Timaeus, *FGrH* 566 F 59). Following recent excavations at Lavinium, claims have been made for hero-cult of Aeneas there as early as the 4th cent. BC, but these must remain unproven; it is not easy to link this with other attestations of cult for Aeneas as Jupiter Indiges (e.g. Dion. Hal. *Ant. Rom.* 1. 64. 5; Livy 1. 2. 6).

The list of Aeneas' westward wanderings towards Italy is already long and contradictory by the 1st cent. BC (cf. Dion. Hal. 1. 44–64), including cities and cults supposedly named after him in Thrace, Chalcidice, Epirus, and *Sicily, and visits to *Delos and *Crete. A visit to *Carthage, possibly involving a meeting with Dido, is certainly part of the itinerary by the time of *Naevius' *Bellum Punicum* (3rd cent. BC), where it is seen as an ancestral cause of the enmity between Rome and Carthage. As Rome confronted a Greek-speaking Mediterranean world in the 3rd cent. BC, it found it politically and culturally useful to claim as its founder Aeneas, famous through his appearance in Homer but also an enemy of the Greeks; a particular stimulus was the invasion of Italy by *Pyrrhus of Epirus (280 BC), who claimed descent from Achilles and saw Rome as a second Troy (Paus. 1. 12. 2). In consequence, Roman poets (e.g. *Ennius), historians (e.g. Cato the Elder), and antiquarians (e.g. Varro) stressed the Trojan origins of Rome; considerations of chronology eventually led to the view that Aeneas founded not Rome but a preceding city, Lavinium, and that Rome's eponymous founder *Romulus was his distant descendant.

*Virgil's version of the Aeneas-legend in the *Aeneid* aims at literary coherence rather than antiquarian accuracy. Aeneas' wanderings, apart from the stay at Carthage, are compressed into a single book (*Aeneid* 3); his war in Latium is the subject of the second half of the poem, and he appears there and at other times to have some typological link with *Augustus (cf. *Aen.* 8. 680 and 10. 261), who claimed him as ancestor (1. 286–8). The Virgilian Aeneas' central traits of *pietas* (dutiful respect) and martial courage continue his Homeric character, but he is also a projection of the ideal patriotic Roman, subordinating personal goals to national interest. And yet he never renounces his human vulnerability; he is in despair in his first appearance in the poem (1. 92 ff.), he is deeply affected by love for Dido (4. 395, 6. 455), and the poem ends not with his triumphant apotheosis, anticipated earlier (1. 259–60, 12. 794–5), but with his emotional killing of Turnus in a moment of passion.

The success of the *Aeneid* meant that few innovations were made in the Aeneas-legend by later writers; subsequent Aeneas-narratives are clearly crafted from existing materials, principally Virgil (e.g. Ov. *Met.* 13. 623–14. 608, *Origo gentis Romanae* 9. 2–15. 4).   S. J. Ha.

Aeneas Tacticus, probably the Stymphalian general of the Arcadian League in 367 BC (Xen. *Hell.* 7. 3. 1); anyway the earliest (-surviving) and most historically interesting of the ancient military writers (*tactici*). Of several treatises only his *Siegecraft* (*Poliorcetica*) is extant, internally datable to the mid-4th cent. via the clustering of contemporary illustrations of its precepts (and linguistically important for its embryo form of the *koinē*, i.e. standard Greek). Concerned more with defence against than prosecution of siege-warfare, it offers unique insights into the stresses of life in small communities with warfare and revolution constantly threatening.   D. W.

Aeschines (*c.*397–*c.*322 BC), Athenian orator whose exchanges with *Demosthenes in the courts in 343 and 330 provide a large part of the evidence for the relations of Athens and Macedon in the 340s and the 330s. His origins were sufficiently obscure to allow Demosthenes' invention full play. He probably did not receive the usual formal training in rhetoric, but after military service of some distinction in the 360s and early 350s, and a period as an actor, he embarked on a public career as a supporter first briefly of Aristophon and then of Eubulus, during whose supervision of the city's finances Aeschines' brother, Aphobetus, was a theoric commissioner (responsible for distribution of grants for attendance at festivals). In 347/6 both Aeschines and Demosthenes were members of the Council of 500 and their disagreements led to sixteen years of enmity. Early in 346 (though many have dated the affair to 348/7) when alarming news reached Athens of the extension of Macedonian influence to Arcadia, Eubulus supported by Aeschines took the lead in urging Athens to protest to Arcadia and to seek to organize a Common Peace, which would provide for common action against aggressors and so make it unnecessary for any state to seek Macedonian help. Aeschines was sent on an embassy to Megalopolis where he sought to dissuade the assembly of the Arcadians from dealings with *Philip II. Whether through the indifference of the Greek states or through the new threat to Greece caused by the refusal of the Phocian tyrant, Phalaecus, to permit access to Thermopylae, the key-point for the defence of Greece, the initiative of Eubulus and Aeschines proved abortive. An embassy of ten, including Aeschines and Demosthenes, was hastily sent to negotiate peace terms with Philip. Their return to the city was closely followed by a Macedonian embassy, and on the 18th and 19th of the month Elaphebolion, when the peace was debated and voted, Aeschines played a notable if ineffectual part. Demosthenes, realizing that peace was essential and that the only form of peace which Philip would accept was a plain alliance with Athens and her allies of the Second Athenian Confederacy, made himself responsible for getting the decree of Philocrates passed: Aeschines strove without success for a Common Peace open to all the Greeks. The ten ambassadors then set off again to secure Philip's oath to the treaty which he did not render until his forces were in position to attack Phocis. When the ambassadors returned with this alarming news, it was decided in the Council to recommend an expedition to save Phocis, but by the 16th of the month Skirophorion, when the people met, it was known that Philip had occupied Thermopylae; Demosthenes' proposal was not even read out and he was himself shouted down. Aeschines then made a speech, which Demosthenes chose to regard as proof that Aeschines had been won over by Macedonian bribery. The truth was probably far different; since Phocis could not be saved, Aeschines sought to reconcile the Athenians to the fact by reporting vague suggestions of Macedonian proposals for central Greece which were very much what Athens was seeking.

From that day Demosthenes was implacably opposed to Aeschines as well as determined to destroy the Peace, while Aeschines was gradually won over to support it and seek its extension into a Common Peace. In 346/5 Demosthenes with the support of Timarchus began a prosecution of Aeschines for his part in the peace negotiations; Aeschines replied by charging Timarchus with breach of the law forbidding those whose misconduct was notorious from addressing the assembly; the *Against Timarchus* was successful and Demosthenes was forced to recognize that the time was not ripe to attack Aeschines. By mid-343 the mood of Athens had clearly begun to change; early in the year Philocrates had been successfully prosecuted by *Hyperides and in the *De falsa legatione* Demosthenes attacked Aeschines, the advocate of merely amending a discredited peace, as if he had been the orator really responsible in 346 for Athens' accepting the Peace. Aeschines replied in a speech of the same title and, supported by Eubulus and Phocion, was narrowly acquitted. Aeschines continued to have some influence in the assembly, and in 340/39 was sent as one of Athens' representatives to the Amphictionic Council (see DELPHI), on which occasion he appears to have displayed a serious lack of judgement in relation to the affairs of central Greece: at a time when the war against Philip had recommenced and there was a clear need to avoid exacerbating the divisions of Greece, Aeschines replied to Locrian charges against Athens with such a vigorous attack on the conduct of the Amphissans that hostilities began and Philip was the more easily able to intervene.

Aeschines was a member of the embassy sent to negotiate with Philip after the battle of Chaeronea (338), but from then on he withdrew from politics only to re-emerge on two occasions when circumstances seemed favourable for an attack on Demosthenes. The first was in early 336 when Ctesiphon proposed that Demosthenes should be crowned in the theatre at the festival of the Dionysia for the excellence of his services to the city: earlier Demosthenes had been similarly honoured without protest but, at a time when Demosthenes' gloomy predictions after Chaeronea seemed mocked by the opening of the Macedonian invasion of Persia, Aeschines indicted the decree under the *graphē paranomōn* (law against unconstitutional proposals). However, the murder of Philip made the future too uncertain for Aeschines to be confident of success, and he decided not to proceed with the indictment for the moment. In 330 after the defeat of Persia at Gaugamela (331) and the failure of the revolt of King Agis III of Sparta, which Demosthenes had chosen not to support, Athens was in almost complete isolation with no prospect of liberation from Macedon, and Aeschines thought the moment suitable for him to proceed with his prosecution of Ctesiphon. In the *Against Ctesiphon*, after adducing minor, if perhaps valid, legalistic considerations concerning the details of the original decree, he reviewed the career of Demosthenes, somewhat selectively, and sought to show that Demosthenes was unworthy of the crown. In the *De corona* Demosthenes replied with all the devastating effect that his great rhetorical gifts could command, and Aeschines failed to secure the necessary fifth of the jury's votes to save him from a fine and the limitation of the right to prosecute. He chose to retire from Athens to Rhodes, where he taught rhetoric.

The supremacy of Demosthenes as an orator has to a large extent beguiled posterity into the opinion that he alone fully appreciated the menace of Macedon and correctly diagnosed the causes of Philip's success, and Aeschines has been represented as an opportunist with little judgement and less principle. In fact, there was no obvious way of saving Athens and Greece, and it is probable that Aeschines no less than Demosthenes sought to maintain his city's power and independence.

Speeches The only genuine speeches of Aeschines known to the critics of the Roman period were the three that we have: a fourth, concerning *Delos, was rejected by Caecilius. Aeschines was a man of dignified presence and fine voice, who deprecated the use of extravagant gestures by an orator, preferring a statuesque pose. Proud of his education, he displays it by frequent quotation of poetry. In the use of historical argument he cannot compare with Demosthenes, but in a battle of wits he more than holds his own. His vocabulary is simple but effective, though occasional obscurities may be found in his sentences. Ancient critics ranked him lower than he deserves; the fact is that he was not aiming at literary perfection; his object was to produce a powerful effect on his audiences, and he was justified by the result.   G. L. C.

Aeschylus (*see facing page*)

Africa (*Libya), exploration Africa was distinguished from Asia as the third continent by *c.*500 BC, with the Nile, later usually the Red Sea, as divider; but its interior and, even at the most extended period of knowledge, its coasts south of Cape Delgado on the east and Cape Yubi on the west, remained substantially unknown, locations of marvels and geographical features uncertainly identifiable (Ptol. *Geog.* 4). Some believed it circumnavigable (Hdt. 4. 42) and triangular in shape (Strabo 17. 3. 1), but no circumnavigation is satisfactorily attested, and there are modern scholars who think it impracticable for ancient ships; pure theorizing could account for the traditions. An inconsistent belief in a land bridge from Africa to Asia in fact prevailed (Ptol. 7. 3. 6).

In Egypt, and to some extent in Cyrenaica, Greeks could supplement autopsy with local information, cf. Herodotus on the Nile valley (2. 29–31), the inland route therefrom, via oases, possibly to the Atlas (4. 181–3), and a Libyan foray perhaps reaching the Niger, more probably Chad (not the Nile as he supposed; 2. 32–3). Extended knowledge of the Red Sea and NE coasts came from *Alexander the Great's Indian expedition, more under Ptolemaic rule in Egypt and still more in Roman times as a result of increasing trade with India (see especially, *Peripl. M. Rubr.*; Ptol. *Geog.* 4). Penetration up the Nile valley was furthered under Augustus by the campaign of Gaius Petronius against the Ethiopians (Strabo 17. 1. 54) and an investigative mission which probably reached southern Nubia in Nero's reign (Sen. *QNat.* 5. 8. 3–5); but it was checked by swamps; the geographer Ptolemy, however, recorded lakes sighted by a

[*continued on p. 12*]

Aeschylus

Aeschylus, Athenian tragic dramatist *Life* (?525/4–456/5 BC) Aeschylus was probably born at *Eleusis in 525/4 BC (*Marm. Par.*). He fought in two great battles in which the Greeks defeated the invading Persians: the battle of Marathon in 490 (*Marm. Par.*; *Vita* 4, 11) and probably at Salamis (Ion of Chios, *FGrH* 392 F 7). His first tragic production was in 499 (*Suda* ai 357 with π 2230), his first victory in 484 (*Marm. Par.*); thereafter he may have been almost invariably victorious, especially after the death of Phrynichus *c.*473 (he gained thirteen victories altogether, *Vita* 13). Of his surviving plays, *Persians* was produced in 472 (his *chorēgos* or financial backer being the young *Pericles) and *Seven against Thebes* in 467. *Suppliants*, part of a production which won first prize over *Sophocles (*POxy.* 2256. 3), must be later than *Seven* (despite the predominant role of the chorus and other features once thought to prove it very early); its exact date is uncertain. The *Oresteia* (comprising *Agamemnon*, *Choephori* ('Women Bearing Drink-offerings') and *Eumenides*, with the lost satyr-play *Proteus*) was Aeschylus' last production in Athens, in 458. He had already visited *Sicily once, possibly twice, at the invitation of Hieron of Syracuse, composing *Women of Aetna* in honour of Hieron's newly founded city of Aetna (*Vita* 9) and producing *Persians* at Syracuse (ibid. 18; Eratosth. in schol. Ar. *Frogs* 1028); after the production of the *Oresteia* he went there again, dying at Gela in 456/5. *Prometheus Bound*, if by Aeschylus (see below), may have been composed in Sicily and produced posthumously. His epitaph (*Vita* 11) makes no reference to his art, only to his prowess displayed at Marathon; this estimate of what was most important in Aeschylus' life—to have been a loyal and courageous citizen of a free Athens—can hardly be that of the Geloans and will reflect his own death-bed wishes (cf. Paus. 1. 14. 5) or those of his family.

Two sons of Aeschylus themselves became dramatists, Euphorion (who also restaged many of his father's plays) and Euaeon. A nephew, Philocles, was the founder of a dynasty of tragedians that lasted over a century.

Works (° denotes a known satyr-play). Aeschylus' total output is variously stated at between 70 and 90 plays. Seven plays have survived via medieval manuscripts, of which *Prometheus Bound* is of disputed authenticity (it was possibly composed by Euphorion and produced by him as Aeschylus' work). In addition there survive substantial papyrus fragments of °*Netfishers* (*Diktyoulkoi*) and °*Spectators at the Isthmian Games* (*Theōroi* or *Isthmiastai*).

Many of Aeschylus' productions were connected 'tetralogies', comprising three tragedies presenting successive episodes of a single story (a 'trilogy') followed by a satyr-play based on part of the same or a related myth. This seems to have been common practice in his day, though the production of 472 (*Phineus*, *Persians*, *Glaucus of Potniae*, and °*Prometheus the Fire-kindler*) is an exception. Four tetralogies are securely attested: (1) the *Oresteia* (see above); (2) *Laius*, *Oedipus*, *Seven against Thebes*, °*Sphinx*; (3) *Suppliants*, *Egyptians*, *Danaids*, °*Amymone*; (4) a *Lycurgeia* comprising *Edonians*, *Bassarids*, *Young Men* (*Neaniskoi*), and °*Lycurgus*. At least seven other tetralogies can be reconstructed with a fair degree of probability: (5) *Myrmidons*, *Nereids*, *Phrygians* (satyr-play unknown), based on *Iliad* 16–24; (6) *Ghost-raisers* (*Psychagōgoi*), *Penelope*, *Bone-gatherers* (*Ostologoi*), °*Circe*, based on the *Odyssey* but apparently with an innovative ending; (7) *Memnon*, *The Weighing of Souls* (*Psychostasia*), *Phrygian Women* (satyr-play unknown), based on the cyclic *Aethiopis*, ending with the funeral of Achilles; (8) *The Award of the Arms* (*Hoplon Krisis*), *Thracian Women*, *Women of Salamis* (satyr-play unknown), centring on the death of Ajax; (9) *Semele*, *Wool-carders* (*Xantriai*), *Pentheus*, and perhaps °*The Nurses of Dionysus*, on the birth of Dionysus and his conflict with Pentheus (cf. *Euripides' *Bacchae*); (10) *Eleusinians*, *Women* (?) *of Argos*, *Epigoni*, and perhaps °*Nemea*, on the recovery of the bodies of the Seven against Thebes and their sons' war of revenge; (11) *Lemnian Women*, *Argo*, *Hypsipyle*, °*Cabiri*, on the story of Hypsipyle and Jason. In some cases two tragedies seem to be connected but no third related one can be identified: (12)

Prometheus Bound and *Prometheus Unbound* (if, as is likely, the title *Prometheus the Fire-bearer* (*Pyrphoros*) is no more than a variant form of °*Prometheus the Fire-kindler* (*Pyrkaeus*)); (13) *Phorcides* and *Polydectes* (with °*Netfishers*), with Perseus as hero; (14) *Mysians* and *Telephus*.

Aeschylean plays not mentioned above include *Archer-nymphs* (*Toxotides*), on the death of Actaeon; *Athamas*; *Atalanta*; *Callisto*; *Carians* or *Europa*; °*Cercyon*; *Chamber-makers* (*Thalamopoioi*); *Children of Heracles*; *Cretan Women* (on the story of Polyidus); *Daughters of the Sun* (*Heliades*); *The Escort* (*Propompoi*); *Glaucus the Sea-god*; °*Heralds* (*Kerykes*); *Iphigenia*; *Ixion*; °*The Lion*; *Niobe*; °*Oreithyia*; *Palamedes*; *Perrhaebian Women* (whose central character was Ixion); *Philoctetes* (see Dio Chrys. *Or.* 52); *Priestesses* (*Hiereiai*); °*Sisyphus the Runaway* and *Sisyphus the Stone-roller* (if these two are different plays).

Technique Aeschylus was the most innovative and imaginative of Greek dramatists. His extant plays, though covering a period of only fifteen years, show a great and evolving variety in structure and presentation.

The three earlier plays (*Persians*, *Seven*, and *Suppliants*) are designed for a theatre without a *skēnē* (see THEATRES (GREEK AND ROMAN), STRUCTURE) but containing a mound or elevation (tomb of Darius, Theban acropolis, Argive sanctuary, the two latter with cult-images on them). There are two actors only; the main interactions are less between character and character than between character and chorus (often expressed in 'epirrhematic' form, i.e. dialogue between singing chorus and speaking actor), and in two cases the chorus open the play in marching anapaests. There is a wide variety of structural patterns, some of them (like *Sept.* 375–676, with its seven pairs of speeches punctuated by short choral stanzas) probably unique experiments, but all built round the basic framework of a series of episodes framed by entries and exits and separated by choral songs. The pace of the action is usually rather slow.

By 458 the dramatist had available to him a *skēnē* and probably an *ekkyklēma* (wheeled platform) and *mēchanē* (crane) also, as well as a third actor. Aeschylus makes imaginative, and once again very varied, use of the new opportunities. After composing the first half of *Agamemnon* entirely in his old style (with no actor–actor dialogue whatever), he centres the play on a verbal trial of strength between *Agamemnon and Clytemnestra, meanwhile keeping Cassandra long silent and then making her narrate Agamemnon's death prophetically before it happens. The house and its entrance are firmly controlled throughout by the 'watchdog' Clytemnestra. In the second half of *Choephori* the action increasingly accelerates as the climax approaches, and then abruptly slows as Clytemnestra for a time staves off her doom with brilliant verbal fencing. In *Eumenides* a series of short scenes, full of surprises and changes of location, and including a trial-scene with some virtuoso four-sided dialogue, leads to a conclusion mainly in the old epirrhematic mode for one actor and chorus (with a second chorus at the very end).

Aeschylus' plots tend to be characterized, not by abrupt changes of direction (*peripeteiai*), but by a build-up of tension and expectation towards a climax anticipated by the audience if not by the dramatis personae. He was quite capable of contriving *peripeteiai* when he wished, as witness *Seven against Thebes* where the whole action pivots on Eteocles' discovery that he has unwittingly brought about a combat between himself and his brother and thus fulfilled his father's curse; the trilogy form, however, encourages sharp changes of direction and mood between plays rather than within them.

In general the central interest in Aeschylean drama is in situation and event rather than in character. Even quite major figures in a play (like Pelasgus or Agamemnon's son Orestes) can be almost without distinctive character traits: if their situation gives them effectively no choice how to act, their personal qualities are irrelevant and are ignored. On the other hand, characters who make (or have previously made) decisions vitally affecting the action, when alternative choices were possible, are portrayed as far as is necessary for illuminating these decisions: Eteocles is usually calm and rational but can be carried away by strong emotions, Agamemnon is one who values prestige above all other considerations. The character most fully drawn is Clytemnestra, because the plot requires her to be a unique individual, 'a woman with a man's mind'. In the *Oresteia* several minor characters are drawn with marked vividness, less perhaps for their own sake than to focus special attention on what they have to say.

For similar reasons, Aeschylean choruses usually have a strong and distinctive personality. Their words are often of utmost importance in drawing attention to the deeper principles underlying events (even when they do not themselves fully understand these principles or their implications) and, together with their music and dance, in establishing the mood and theme of a whole play. The women of *Seven*, dominated almost throughout by fear, contrast sharply with the Danaids, utterly determined in their rejection of marriage and coercing Pelasgus by a cool threat of suicide; the Argive elders of *Agamemnon*, enunciators of profound moral principles yet unable to understand how these principles doom Agamemnon to death, share a trilogy with the Erinyes (i.e. the Eumenides or Furies), hellish bloodsuckers yet also divine embodiments of these same principles. Aeschylus' choruses often have a substantial influence on the action; the Danaids and the Erinyes are virtually the protagonists of their plays, the women's panic in *Seven* causes Eteocles' promise to fight in person, while in *Choephori* it is the chorus who ensure that Aegisthus is delivered unguarded into Orestes' hands. Sometimes a chorus will surprise the audience near the end of a play (as when the Argive elders defy Aegisthus); it is a distinctly Aeschylean touch in *Prometheus Bound* when the hitherto submissive Oceanids resolve to stay with Prometheus despite Hermes' warning of apocalyptic destruction impending.

Aeschylus' lyric style is smooth and flexible, and generally easier of immediate comprehension than that of *Pindar or Sophocles, provided the listener was attuned to a vocabulary that tended towards the archaic and the Homeric. In iambic dialogue, where he had fewer models to follow, he sometimes seems stiff compared with Sophocles or Euripides, though he can also create an impression of everyday speech through informal grammar and phraseology. He excels at devising patterns of language and imagery, elaborating them down to minute detail, and sustaining them all through a play or a trilogy.

Patterns of metre (and presumably of music) are likewise designed on a trilogic scale; in the *Oresteia* ode after ode ponders the workings of justice in syncopated iambics and lecythia, with variations and deviations to suit particular contexts (epic-like dactyls for the departure of the expedition to Troy, ionics for Helen's voyage and her welcome by the Trojans). Aeschylus' lyrics are mostly simple and perspicuous in structure, here too resembling *Alcman or *Stesichorus more than Pindar or Sophocles. He makes extensive use of marching anapaests as preludes to (and occasionally substitutes for) choral odes, and also in quasi-epirrhematic alternation with lyrics. The regular speech-verse is the iambic trimeter, but the trochaic tetrameter (characteristic of early tragedy according to Arist. *Poet.* 1449ᵃ22) appears in *Persians* and *Agamemnon*.

Aeschylus is consistently bold and imaginative in exploiting the visual aspects of drama. The contrast between the sumptuous dress of Atossa at her first, carriage-borne entry and the return of Xerxes alone and in rags; the chaotic entry of the chorus in *Seven*; the African-looking, exotically dressed Danaids and their confrontation with brutal Egyptian soldiers; the purple cloth over which Agamemnon walks to his death, and the display of his corpse in the bath-tub with Cassandra beside him and Clytemnestra 'standing where I struck' (a scene virtually repeated in *Choephori* with a different killer and different victims); the Erinyes presented anthropomorphically on stage (probably for the first time), yet tracking Orestes like hounds by the scent of blood; the procession that ends the *Oresteia*, modelled on that at the Great Panathenaea—these are far from exhausting the memorable visual images in only six or seven plays, quite apart from numerous careful touches of detail (e.g. at the end of *Agamemnon* where Aegisthus, that 'woman' of a man, alone of those on stage has neither weapon nor staff in his right hand).

Thought Aeschylus, like all truly tragic writers, is well aware of, and vividly presents, the terrible suffering, often hard to justify in human terms, of which life is full; nevertheless he also believes strongly in the ultimate justice of the gods. In his surviving work (leaving aside *Prometheus*), all human suffering is clearly traceable, directly or indirectly, to an origin in some evil or foolish action—Xerxes' ill-advised decision to attempt the conquest of Greece; Laius' defiance of an oracular warning to remain childless; the attempt by the sons of Aegyptus to force the Danaids to be their wives; the adultery of Thyestes with Atreus' wife; the abduction of Helen by Paris. The consequences of these actions, however, while always bringing disaster to the actors, never end with them, but spread to involve their descendants and ultimately a whole community; some of these indirect victims have incurred more or less guilt on their own account, but many are completely innocent. In some of Aeschylus' dramas, like *Persians* or the Theban trilogy, the action descends steadily towards a nadir of misery at the end. In the *Oresteia*, however, presumably also in the Odyssean trilogy, and not improbably in the Danaid trilogy, it proves to be possible to draw a line under the record of suffering and reach a settlement that promises a better future; each time a key element in the final stages is the substitution of persuasion for violence, as when in the *Oresteia* a chain of retaliatory murders is ended by the judicial trial of Orestes, and the spirits of violent revenge, the Erinyes, are persuaded to accept an honoured dwelling in Athens.

In dramas of the darker type described above, the gods are stern and implacable, and mortals often find themselves helpless prisoners of their own or others' past decisions; though they may still have considerable freedom to choose how to face their fate (compare the clear-sighted courage of Pelasgus or Cassandra with Xerxes or Agamemnon). Elsewhere, especially perhaps in Aeschylus' latest work, a different concept of divinity may appear. In the *Oresteia* ethical advance on earth, as the virtuous Electra and an Orestes with no base motive succeed the myopic Agamemnon and the monstrous Clytemnestra, is presently answered by ethical advance on Olympus as the amoral gods of *Agamemnon* and *Choephori* turn in *Eumenides* into responsible and even loving (*Eum.* 911, 999) protectors of deserving mortals. Something similar may well have happened in the Prometheus plays.

Aeschylus is intensely interested in the community life of the *polis*, and all his surviving genuine works have strong political aspects. He seems to be a strong supporter of democracy (a word whose elements first appear together in the phrase *dēmou kratousa cheir*, 'the sovereign hand of the people', *Supp.* 604) and of Athens' wars of the early 450s, while recognizing the overriding importance of avoiding civil conflict by conciliating rival interests (*Eum.* 858–66, 976–87). To later generations, who from time to time continued to see his plays (cf. Ar. *Ach.* 10), Aeschylus, who may have come of age in the year of *Cleisthenes' reforms and whose death coincided with the peak of Athenian power, was (as in Aristophanes' *Frogs*) the poet of Athens' greatness, of the generation of Marathon where he had lived what to him was the supreme day of his life. See also TRAGEDY, GREEK.   A. H. S.

sailor driven off course near Zanzibar, which he took to be the source of the Nile (*Geog.* 1. 9; presumably Victoria and Albert Nyanza), and had also heard of the Mountain of the Moon whose snows fed them (*Geog.* 4. 8. 2; perhaps Mt. Kilimanjaro).

In the north-west, local knowledge, both of the coastal hinterland and of the west coast, may have been less readily available before the fall of Carthage. What became known then was soon supplemented by Roman exploration, often undertaken for military purposes. Already in 146 BC *Scipio Aemilianus had dispatched *Polybius with a fleet down the west coast (Plin. *HN* 5. 9, 10). Later landmarks were the Jugurthine War (but Sallust's account is disappointing); campaigns by Lucius Cornelius Balbus under Augustus and Valerius Festus under Vespasian against the Garamantes in the Fezzan (Plin. *HN* 5. 36–8), and by Suetonius Paulinus under Claudius in the Atlas mountains (ibid. 5. 14–15); investigative missions, probably

under Domitian, attributed to Iulius Maternus and Septimius Flaccus (perhaps identical events), from Tripolitania via the Garamantes, possibly to Chad (Ptol. *Geog.* 1. 8. 4).

Archaeological evidence, constantly accruing, is not always easy to interpret since artefacts might penetrate further than travellers in the packs of native traders and raiders; but a scatter of recently reported inscriptions may suggest Mediterranean contacts further south than expected, e.g. in the Fezzan, the Hoggar mountains of Algeria, and the Canaries, while the announcement of Roman pottery found on Zanzibar accords with the literary record.

See GEOGRAPHY; MAPS.   J. M. R.

Africa, Roman (see ◀ Map 4, Ad ▶) The Punic Wars made Rome heir to the Carthaginian empire (see CARTHAGE). In 146 BC she left most territory in the hands of the Numidian king Masinissa's descendants, but formed a new province (Africa) in the most fertile part. This covered about 13,000 sq. km. (5,000 sq. mi.) of north and central Tunisia, northeast of a boundary line (the *fossa regia*, 'the royal ditch') from Thabraca to Hadrumetum; it was governed by a praetor from Utica. Except for Utica and six other towns of Phoenician origin which had supported Rome rather than Carthage in the Punic Wars, most of the land became *ager publicus* (see AGRARIAN LAWS AND POLICY). Although the attempt by Gaius *Gracchus to found a Roman colony at Carthage failed, Roman and Italian traders and farmers settled in the province in large numbers, and many of *Marius' veterans settled west of the *fossa regia*. After the battle of Thapsus in 46 BC *Caesar added to the existing province (thenceforth called Africa Vetus, 'Old Africa') the Numidian territory of Juba I (Africa Nova, 'New Africa'). Caesar's colonial foundations in Africa included Clupea, Curubis, and Neapolis, and his intention to colonize Carthage afresh was carried out by Octavian, the future *Augustus. A substantial territory in Numidia based on Cirta was given to Caesar's supporter Publius Sittius.

Under Augustus, after various boundary changes, the united province, now called Africa Proconsularis, extended from Arae Philaenorum, on the western edge of Cyrenaica, to the river Ampsagas (Rhummel) in eastern Algeria. At least eleven colonies were founded in Proconsularis, in addition to the thirteen colonies settled on the coast of Mauretania (the rest of which was ruled by the client king Juba II). Africa Proconsularis was governed from Carthage by a proconsul, who (unusually for the governor of a province not controlled by the emperor) also commanded the Legio III Augusta, then stationed at Ammaedara. Under Gaius command of the legion was handed over to an imperial legate who became responsible for the government of Numidia and the frontier districts. The provincialization of North Africa was completed by *Claudius with the creation of two provinces in Mauretania. Resistance to Roman rule on the fringes of the Sahara and in the mountainous regions such as the Kabylie and Aurès was no more than sporadic, and for over three centuries the whole area from Cyrenaica to the Atlantic was protected by only a single legion and auxiliaries. The southern frontier ran approximately from Arae Philaenorum through Cydamus (Gadhamès), Nefta, Vescera (Biskra), and Auzia (Aumale) to the Atlantic south of Volubilis.

Urban life in North Africa was of pre-Roman origin, both Punic and (under Punic influence) Numidian. In spite of the destruction of Carthage, a number of towns of Phoenician or Carthaginian origin survived on the coast, such as Hadrumetum and Lepcis Magna; further west, Icosium (Algiers), Iol (Caesarea), Tingis, and Lixus appear to have been pre-Roman settlements of some size. In a few places Carthaginian language and institutions survived into the 2nd cent. AD, as inscriptions demonstrate; spoken Punic lasted much longer and was still being used, at least in rural areas, in *Augustine's day (*Ep.* 66. 108. 14, 209. 3).

Over large areas of the interior the influence of Carthaginian civilization on the indigenous tribes was profound, especially in central Tunisia and in the region of Cirta where Numidian kings had encouraged it. Under Roman control, however, urbanization occurred on a vastly increased scale, and refounded Carthage became the largest city in the western empire after Rome (see URBANISM (*Roman*)). Over 600 communities ranked as separate *civitates* (citizen communities), of which a large number in due course obtained the rank of *municipium* or *colonia*. The area of densest urbanization was around Carthage and the Bagradas valley, where some of the towns were only a dozen miles apart. Some, like Ammaedara and Theveste, were established on the sites of early legionary fortresses; Lambaesis grew out of the settlement outside the final fortress chosen for Legio III Augusta; others, like Timgad and Diana Veteranorum, were settled as colonies for retired legionaries. Roman *equites* of African origin are known from the mid-1st cent. AD, soon followed by senators. During the 2nd cent. African senators (the best-known being the orator Fronto) formed the largest western provincial group. The influence of Africans reached its height under *Septimius Severus, who was born at Lepcis Magna.

The wealth of Africa was proverbial throughout the Roman period, and consisted largely of agricultural products. Of these corn was certainly the most important and with Egypt Africa replaced Sicily as Italy's major supplier during the empire (see FOOD SUPPLY (*Roman*)). The Bagradas valley and the region around Cirta and Sitifis were productive corn-growing districts, but polyculture throughout North Africa was common. Especially from the 2nd cent. *olive-growing and the production of oil for export became an increasingly important part of the African economy, especially in the drier regions of Proconsularis, around Cillium and Sufetula in central Tunisia, and near Thysdrus and Sullecthum in eastern Tunisia, as well as further west in Numidia and Mauretania. *Wine was also exported from Tripolitania, Proconsularis, and Mauretania, although on a much smaller scale. The maintenance of irrigation systems, some clearly of pre-Roman origin, and the efficient collection and conservation of what little rain-water there was, were essential to successful cultivation. Africa was famed as a place where large estates in the hands of a few men were commonplace, the largest landowner being the emperor, but there were plenty of medium-sized estates as well, the majority of them owned not by Italians but by prosperous members of the Romano-African urban élite, whose wealth was so conspicuously displayed in the showy public monuments they paid for in their home towns. Our knowledge of the administration of imperial estates, and the relationship between tenants (*coloni*) and lessees (*conductores*), is best known from a series of 2nd-and early 3rd-cent. inscriptions from the Bagradas valley. Other exports from Africa included fish-sauce (*garum*), especially from Proconsularis (see FISHING); marble, especially the prized yellow *marmor Numidicum* from Simitthus; wood, especially the citrus-wood for furniture-making from Mauretania (see TIMBER); dyes, for which the island of Mogador off western Morocco was famous; an orange-red pottery ('African red slip-ware'), which despite its simplicity gained a Mediterranean-wide export market at the zenith of its production in the 4th and 5th cents. (see POTTERY, ROMAN); and wild animals destined for *amphitheatres in Italy and elsewhere, including lions, leopards, and *elephants, the capture of which is featured on a number of African *mosaics (e.g. from Hippo Regius and Carthage). The arts flourished, with several vigorous local schools of sculptors working in both limestone and marble, while mosaic workshops (*officinae*), in response to the demand for elaborate polychrome figured mosaics in both private houses and public buildings such as baths, adopted from the second quarter of the 2nd cent. onwards an original and creative approach to mosaic design which by the 4th cent. had left its influence on mosaic floors in Italy and several other provinces as well.

During the 3rd cent. the African provinces continued to prosper, and suffered less from imperial usurpations than most provinces of the Roman west; the failure of the emperor Gordian I had, however, serious repercussions. *Christianity established itself more firmly than in any other western province, first in the cities, but making rapid strides in Numidia after *c*.200. The works of Tertullian and Cyprian were of considerable importance in the development of Latin Christianity.

In the emperor *Diocletian's administrative changes, the provinces of Tripolitania, Byzacena, Numidia, Mauretania Sitifensis, and Mauretania Caesariensis formed the diocese of Africa, Africa Proconsularis being strictly outside the diocesan system, and Mauretania Tingitana forming part of the diocese of Spain. The military forces of the area were put under a 'count of Africa' (*comes Africae*), and the frontier was divided into districts each under a *praepositus limitis* (frontier commander), a system unique in the empire (see LIMES).

Throughout the 4th and early 5th cent., North Africa was affected by serious divisions among Christians; the Donatists, condemned as schismatics by imperial legislation from Constantine onwards, were particularly strong in rural areas of Numidia and Mauretania, where social discontent was growing and where central government's authority was increasingly in decline. Nevertheless the area remained prosperous in comparison with the devastated provinces of northern Europe, and the collapse of Africa to the Vandals (Carthage was captured in 439) was a grievous blow, not least for the corn supply. The invaders found Africa easy prey, since the defensive system was designed for policing work and the suppression of sporadic tribal revolts rather than full-scale invasion.

W. N. W.; B. H. W.; R. J. A. W.

after-life See ART (FUNERARY); DEATH, ATTITUDES TO; DEAD, DISPOSAL OF; HADES

Agamemnon, in mythology son of Atreus (or, occasionally, of Atreus' son Pleisthenes), brother of Menelaus, and husband of Clytemnestra; king of Mycenae, or Argos, and, in *Homer, commander-in-chief of the Greek expedition against *Troy, taking with him 100 ships, the largest single contingent (*Il.* 2. 569–80). He had a son, Orestes, and three daughters, Chrysothemis, Laodice, Iphianassa (*Il.* 9.145); Iphigenia, whom Homer does not mention, seems to be a later substitution for Iphianassa, as does *Electra for Laodice (Xanthus, fr. 700 *PMG*).

Homer depicts Agamemnon as a man of personal valour, but lacking resolution and easily discouraged. His quarrel with *Achilles, who withdrew in anger and hurt pride from battle when Agamemnon took away his concubine Briseis, supplies the mainspring of the *Iliad*'s action, with Achilles' refusal to fight leading to tragedy. The *Odyssey* (1. 35 ff., 4. 512 ff., 11. 405 ff., 24. 96 f.) tells how, on Agamemnon's return home, Aegisthus, Clytemnestra's lover, treacherously set on him and his men at a banquet and killed them all, Clytemnestra also killing his Trojan captive Cassandra, daughter of King Priam. Eight years later Orestes came from Athens and avenged his father's murder (1. 304 ff.). This whole story became a favourite one among later authors, who retold it with various elaborations and changes. *Aeschylus, for instance, makes Clytemnestra a powerful and awe-inspiring female who, quite alone, kills Agamemnon after she has pinioned him in a robe while he is unarmed in his bath (*Ag.* 1379–98).

The epic *Cypria* is the earliest evidence of the sacrifice of Agamemnon's daughter Iphigenia. Agamemnon caught a stag, then boasted that he was a better huntsman than *Artemis, whereupon the offended goddess held the Greek fleet wind-bound at Aulis. The seer Calchas told them to appease her by sacrificing Iphigenia, whom they sent for on the pretext of marriage to Achilles. Here the guilt for the killing seems to be laid on the Greeks in general; moreover Iphigenia was snatched away and made immortal by Artemis, who left a deer on the altar in her place (as in *Euripides' *Iphigenia in Tauris*). But again matters are very different in Aeschylus, where Iphigenia is simply a child, dead, and Agamemnon himself her killer, for which Clytemnestra never forgave him.

In historic times Agamemnon had a cult in Laconia and at Tarentum, Clazomenae, and Chaeronea: see Farnell, *Hero-Cults* 321 and n. 55; also Mycenae. Agamemnon appears occasionally in art from the 7th cent. BC in a variety of scenes, mostly relating to the war at Troy: see O. Touchefeu and I. Krauskopf, *LIMC* 1/1. 256–77; also A. J. N. W. Prag, *The Oresteia: Iconographic and Narrative Tradition* (1985). Agamemnon in Homer: O. Taplin in C. Pelling (ed.), *Characterization and Individuality in Greek Literature* (1990). H. J. R.; J. R. M.

age The division of life into age-groups was prominently adhered to in antiquity, though there was considerable disagreement as to their precise identification. The Pythagorean philosophers (see PYTHAGORAS) identified four

(Diod. Sic. 10. 9. 5), whereas Hippocratic writers (see MEDI-CINE § 4) acknowledged seven ages of man, each seven years in length (Poll. 2. 4). Since adult society was primarily organized on a two-generational principle, a threefold division probably served most practical purposes, viz. *pais*, *neos*, and *gerōn* in Greek, *puer*, *iuvenis*, and *senex* in Latin. Mental ability was judged to be strictly a function of ageing, as indicated by the fact that there were minimum age qualifications for administrative and executive posts. So an Athenian councillor had to be 30 years old, as, probably, did an ephor at *Sparta (see also AGE CLASSES). Similarly the Roman *cursus honorum* or ladder of office prescribed minimum ages for all magistracies. Belief in the magical power inherent in certain numbers, notably seven and three, meant that certain ages were believed fraught with danger. *Augustus is said to have expressed considerable relief 'at having survived my climacteric, the sixty-third year' (Gell. *NA* 15. 7. 3). Censorinus' *De die natali* (*On Birthdays*) provides an invaluable compilation of information about age terminology, etc.

There is little evidence with which to estimate the age structure of the population of ancient Rome, and even less that of ancient Greece because Greek funerary monuments, unlike Roman ones, rarely record age at death except in the case of extreme youth and extreme longevity. What follows must therefore be treated with extreme caution, as must any such model. It is estimated that in Rome 'more than a quarter of all live-born Roman babies died within their first year of life' (K. Hopkins, *Population Studies* (1966), 246-64). About one-third of the children who survived infancy were dead by the age of 10. Upper-class females in their early teens tended to marry males who were at least ten years older. In Rome, however, the legal age for marriage was 12 and 14 for males and females respectively (see MARRIAGE LAW). Sepulchral inscriptions, no doubt biased in favour of the upper classes, suggest that in the Roman world the median age of death was 34 years for wives and 46.5 for husbands. The study of skeletal remains from Classical Athens has produced comparable results, viz. 35 for women and 44 for men. Life expectancy was appreciably lower for *women at all social levels, largely because of the debilitating and often lethal effects of *childbirth. Probably less than one per cent of the population attained the age of 80 and anyone who did so was judged remarkable, as [*Lucian's] catalogue of octogenarians in *Macrobii* suggests. Notwithstanding the brevity of human life, threescore years and ten still constituted the proper quota of years (cf. Solon 27. 17f. West, *IE²*). Maximum life-span, viz. about 100 years, appears to have been the same in antiquity as it is today. Old age is commonly described as hateful and detestable in classical literature and many lives would have been characterized by increasing incapacitation and loss of mobility from the beginning of the third decade onwards. (The study of skeletal remains at the Romano-British cemetery at Cirencester indicates that 80 per cent of the population suffered from osteoarthrosis). Particularly disadvantaged and scorned were spinsters and widows. Certain races had a reputation for extreme longevity, notably the long-lived Ethiopians, whose life-span was put at 120 years. Many Greeks and Romans would only have had an approximate notion of their exact age in years, as the expression *P(lus) M(inus)* 'more or less', which is frequently found on Roman tombstones, indicates. See POPULATION.

R. S. J. G.

age classes A method of social and political organization in *Sparta and *Crete in the Classical period. Traces of analogous institutions in other Greek states permit the hypothesis that age-class systems played an important role in the development of the *polis* throughout the Greek world in earlier periods. In the Spartan *agōgē* (educational system) boys were removed from their parents at the age of 7 and allocated in annual age classes (*bouai*, 'herds') to tutors who were responsible for their upbringing. At 12 the boys entered paederastic relationships with young adults (e.g. King Agesilaus II and Lysander, the future general). The *krypteia*, a head-hunting ritual with a police function, occurred at initiation into adulthood, after which all members of each age class married simultaneously. Age-class control of marriage, along with segregation of the sexes until the age of 30, probably had important demographic consequences linked to Sparta's manpower problems. Completion of the various stages of the system, which also provided the basis for military organization, conferred political rights and duties. In old age some individuals obtained considerable political power through membership of the *gerousia* (council of elders).   J. R. S.

agōnes See GAMES.

agora, Greek term for an area where people gather together, most particularly for the political functions of the *polis*, normally sited centrally in cities (as at Priene), or at least central to the street lines where the actual centre may be occupied by other features (such as the Acropolis at Athens); the area was sacred, and could be treated like a temenos or sacred precinct. In unplanned cities its shape depends on the nature of the available site, irregular at Athens, on low-lying ground bordered by rising land to west (the Kolonos Agoraios) and south (the slopes of the Acropolis). In planned cities the required number of blocks in the regular grid plan are allocated, giving a strictly rectangular shape. (See URBANISM (*Greek and Hellenistic*).)

Architecturally, the agora need be no more than the space defined by marker stones rather than buildings, as, originally, at Athens. When spectacular buildings develop for the various functions of the agora, they are placed along the boundary, which they help to define, rather than in the agora space. These include lawcourts, offices, and meeting-places for officials (and the formal feasting which was part of their office). These may be integrated with extended porticoes—stoas—and it is these that come to dominate the architecture of the agora, often with long

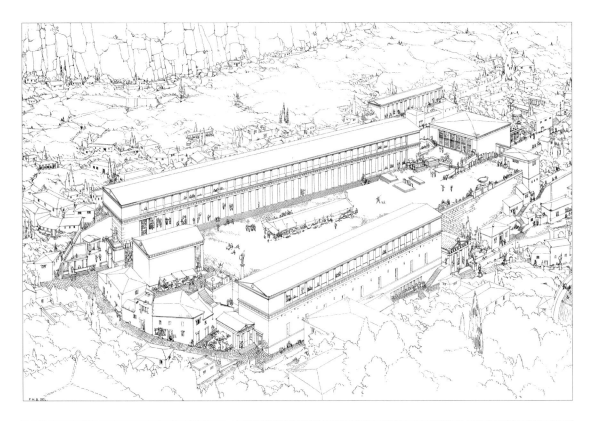

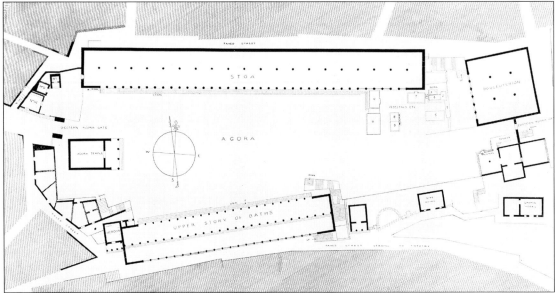

agora Restored view and plan of the agora (2nd cent. BC) at Assos, a Greek city in NW *Asia Minor. The combination of religious and political buildings with a market and public amenities was typical of the Greek agora.

lines of rooms behind them, though not infrequently as colonnades pure and simple. Such colonnades, extended along the boundaries, define the agora more obviously than marker stones and are normal in the developed (and particularly the planned) agoras of the 4th cent. BC and the Hellenistic period.

In unplanned agoras, streets normally run through the open area; thus the 'Panathenaic Way' enters the Athenian agora at its north-west corner, and leaves at the south-east. As the buildings on the borders develop, the agora tends more and more to be closed off, streets being diverted to pass outside the surrounding stoas, with perhaps one main street being allowed through (though by Roman times this may have to pass through formal, and closable, gateways).

The central area of the agora was the locality for special monuments and dedications, statue groups such as the Tyrannicides (the killers of Hipparchus son of *Pisistratus) at Athens, the line of exedrae at Priene. So long as the space was needed for crowds (all those voting in an *ostracism at Athens, as an extreme example) it had to remain open; it was only with the restricted political life of Greek cities in the Roman period that it might include large buildings such as the odeum (small theatre or concert-hall) of Agrippa at Athens. See ATHENS (TOPOGRAPHY).   R. A. T.

agrarian laws and policy Allocation of land by the community is attested in the Greek world at the times of new city foundations (colonies; see COLONIZATION, GREEK), and when land was annexed (so-called cleruchies). There is also some evidence for legislation restricting the disposal of allotments by sale or inheritance, in order to maintain the original land-units which sustained the households. On the other hand, there developed strong resistance to the notion of redividing the city's territory so as to change the proportions of private landholdings: a promise not to propose anything of the kind was included in the oath of the Athenian jurymen. See also SPARTA.

At Rome agrarian legislation played a large part in the history of the republic and the struggles between the aristocracy and the *plebs. It is hard to know how far we should trust the evidence about the early republic, since often the details of the narratives in *Livy and *Dionysius of Halicarnassus seem to have been elaborated in the light of late-republican experience. However, we can be confident that there were laws about land and it is highly probable that they were connected, as Roman tradition maintained, with plebeian discontent. Legislation arose originally from annexation of land after Roman military expansion. It thus concerned land which was the public territory of the Roman people (ager publicus), not land belonging to private individuals (private land remained free from interference by the community except where it could be shown that a public right existed over it, such as access to a water supply). One type of law established new cities (colonies) with their associated land, a second assigned new allotments in a wide tract of territory, such

as those in the Sabina and the ager Gallicus in Picenum, a third (de modo agrorum) did not positively assign land to anyone but restricted the exploitation at will of unassigned public land by reference to area occupied or number of beasts grazed. The first known law of the last type, the lex Licinia of 367 BC, was probably a response to the opportunities created by the acquisition of all the land of Veii. During the middle republic, when Italy and Cisalpine Gaul were gradually subjected to Roman power, land demands were satisfied by new allocations. However, in the late 2nd cent. BC, with a rising number of landless and a shortage of new land available for distribution in the peninsula, the *Gracchi passed laws which sought to recover what was still technically public land from wealthy men who were exploiting it illegally to excess, and to redistribute it to the poor. This was regarded by wealthy landholders as a radical and subversive move. Nevertheless the Gracchan programme was largely completed and such redistribution seems to have remained part of agrarian policy until the death of Marcus Livius Drusus (*tribune of the plebs 91 BC), though settlements were also made in territory acquired by conquest abroad (we know of land-assignment in Africa, the Balearics, Corsica, Greece, and Gaul, both Cisalpine and Transalpine). The Social and Civil Wars followed by *Sulla's proscriptions led de facto to great changes in landholding in Italy, which favoured the greater landholders against the peasants. Some attempt was made to return to Gracchan policies in the late republic (Publius Servilius Rullus' bill of 63 BC, *Caesar's legislation of 59 BC), but the chief means of public acquisition of land in Italy now had to be purchase from private individuals. The proscriptions by the triumvirs (see AUGUSTUS) after Caesar's murder made land available for distribution to their soldiers, but Augustus returned to purchase in order to secure land for his veterans after *Actium.   A. W. L.

agricultural implements
Greek The *technology of Greek *agriculture was simple, and apparently underwent little development. Breaking up the ground, which was fundamental to sowing, weed-control, and preservation of moisture, was achieved by simple symmetrical ploughs, which did not turn the soil, or by mattock and hoe. Ploughs and mattocks occasionally appear on vases and the (all wood) plough is described at length in Hesiod (Op. 427 ff.). Cereals were reaped with a curved sickle, and vines and olives pruned with an implement which is scarcely distinguishable.

The processing of crops required more sophisticated equipment. Threshing cereals required a stone floor on which the grain was threshed by animal hoofs or perhaps animal-drawn sledges, the runners of which may have been toughened by the addition of obsidian flakes; winnowing was by basket and shovel. Pressing grapes could be done by human feet in a basket, vat, or stone press-bed, but olives had to be crushed (see OLIVE). The earliest (archaeological) evidence for an olive mill is late 5th-cent. BC; it is

agricultural implements Iron tools (sickles, pruning knife, hoe, spade-sheath, and plough coulter) from Roman Britain. The widespread availability of such tools to ordinary farmers was one of the achievements of Roman *trade and *technology.

not clear how olives were crushed before that time. An Archaic Attic vase shows an olive press which exploits leverage and counterweights, and vessels specially constructed to facilitate the separation of oil and water survive from the late bronze age. Screw presses seem to be a Hellenistic innovation.   R. G. O.

Roman Roman agricultural implements comprised slaves (see SLAVERY), animals, and tools (Varro, *Rust.* 1. 17. 1). Only the third category is reviewed here. The essential similarity between the inventories in *Cato the Elder (*Agr.* 10, 11) and Palladius (1. 42) some 600 years later indicates technological stability or stagnation, depending on one's point of view. (This very stability has enabled researchers working in Mediterranean areas little affected by mechanized agriculture to interpret with some security the growing archaeological evidence, the ancient representations in art, and the Roman agricultural writers.) Yet while innovations such as the Gallic reaping machine (Plin. *HN* 18. 296; Palladius, 7. 2. 2–4) were rare, improvements in design were common. Examples include: in arable cultivation, the plough (e.g. Plin. *HN* 18. 171–2) and threshing sledge (Varro, *Rust.* 1. 52. 2); and, in arboriculture, the vine-dresser's knife, trench-measuring devices (Columella, *Rust.* 4. 2. 5, 3. 13. 11), and wine- and oil-presses (Plin. *HN* 18. 317). Different vari-

eties of basic tools existed (e.g. twelve types of *falx*) due to regional custom (cf. Varro, *Rust.* 1. 50. 1–3), agricultural conservatism despite the introduction of new designs, and the needs of diverse soils and crops. While a *villa estate might keep different varieties of each basic implement for specialized uses (e.g. Varro, *Rust.* 1. 22. 5), the subsistence cultivator would fully exploit one multi-purpose implement. Such was the *rastrum*, thought to characterize peasant agriculture (Verg. *Aen.* 9. 607–8), which was used for clearing rough land, for turnip cultivation, and for breaking up clods of earth left after ploughing (Columella, *Rust.* 3. 11. 3, 2. 10. 23; Plin. *HN* 18. 180). While some improved designs resulted from the desire for elevated production, implements like the reaping machine, the long-handled scythe, and, perhaps, the harrow, developed as a result of labour shortage (Plin. *HN* 18. 296, 261, 180). Wooden equipment might be home-made, but metal and stone implements were purchased, thus stimulating the local economy (Cato, *Agr.* 22. 3–4, 135; Varro, *Rust.* 1. 22). See AGRICULTURE, ROMAN; TECHNOLOGY.   M. S. Sp.

agricultural writers Agricultural manuals, written by practising landowners, flourished at Rome from *Cato the Elder (*c.*160 BC) to Palladius (*c.* mid-5th cent. AD), enjoying higher status than other technical literature. Greece had produced notable works (*Varro knew more than 50, *Rust.* 1. 1. 8–11), but written mostly from a philosophical or scientific viewpoint; and an influential (non-extant) Punic work by Mago had been translated into both Greek and Latin (Varro ibid.; Columella, *Rust.* 1. 1. 13). Agriculture, as gradually defined and systematized (earlier Greek, Punic, and Roman writers had wandered off the topic: Varro, *Rust.* 1. 2. 13), embraced, in Varro's work (*c.*37 BC), arable cultivation, livestock, arboriculture, market gardens, luxury foods, slave management, and villa construction. A century later, Columella doubted whether one man could know it all (*Rust.* 1. *praef.* 21; 5. 1. 1), and, from the early empire onwards, specialized works appeared, such as Iulius Atticus' monograph on vines (Columella, *Rust.* 1. 1. 15). While Varro criticized the Greek writer Theophrastus for excessive theory (*Rust.* 1. 5. 2), modern scholars in their turn have doubted the practicality of the Roman writers. Recent rural archaeology has given grounds for greater confidence. The excavated *villa at Settefinestre in Etruria has substantiated in remarkable detail the recommendations of Varro and Columella, as has the discovery of a large vineyard at *Pompeii. But the agricultural writers describe not just one ideal type of estate. Crop by crop they discuss a variety of methods of cultivation, according to species, soil, topography, and custom—a regional diversity confirmed by archaeological survey. See also AGRICULTURE, ROMAN.   M. S. Sp.

agriculture, Greek The agriculture of Greece in the historical periods shared the basic cultigens and techniques of most of the other contemporary civilizations of the Mediterranean. Life was sustained by barley and wheat, sown mostly in the autumn as field crops dependent on rainfall between autumn and spring. Hulled barley (two- and six-row) and hulled wheat (emmer and einkorn), introduced to the Aegean from the near east in the neolithic period, remained important crops. Naked wheats, especially tetraploid, durum wheat, evolved in the first millennium BC, but hexaploid bread wheat, better in colder climates, was imported from the north shores of the Black Sea. Cultivation with a simple wooden plough (ard), sometimes tipped with iron, to break up the surface of the soil for receiving seeds in autumn, is treated as normal by ancient sources but recently doubts have arisen as to whether smallholders could produce enough to feed a pair of plough-oxen in addition to their own households. For them hand cultivation by spade and hoe must have been common (see AGRICULTURAL IMPLEMENTS).

The practice of leaving half the land in uncultivated fallow is also regarded as normal by our sources while repeated ploughing of the fallow was desirable. But again, smallholders may have been forced to risk long-term depletion of the soil by resting much less than half their land each year. Some leguminous field crops (broad beans and various lentils (pulses)) were known in Mycenaean times and in *Homer. By the 4th cent. BC they were recommended as partial alternatives to fallow (either as crops in

their own right or as green manure to be ploughed under); it is not clear how early or how widely they were employed in rotation with wheat and barley. The moisture and soil requirements of wheat made it an often unreliable crop in the Greek *climate. Barley, somewhat less nutritious and much less esteemed, was probably grown more widely. Frequent local crop failures required supplementation through trade with less affected neighbours or over longer distances. While it is unlikely that overseas settlements of the 8th and 7th cents. BC had as a prime goal assistance to the grain supply of the mother cities, once established in Magna Graecia (roughly, south Italy) and *Sicily or, later, on the northern Black (Euxine) Sea coast and its approaches, the existence of surpluses in the new settlements at times of shortages in the old lessened the chances of famine and set in motion rhythms of trade with far-reaching consequences. How early the larger Greek towns came to depend on imported grain is disputed. Some have seen Athenian colonies on the Hellespont in the later 6th cent. as established on the route of the city's grain supply, but for Athens explicit evidence comes only in the late 5th cent. Meanwhile by *c.*470 BC the Ionian city of Teos included interference with the city's grain supply among the targets of public curses (ML 30; Fornara, no. 63).

Other crops, chiefly olives, grapes, and the vegetables and fruits grown in irrigated gardens (*kēpoi*), supplemented the largely cereal diet. *Olive oil and *wine also permitted *trade, not least for the acquisition of grain in times of shortage. Greek settlement was rarely at elevations or latitudes too cold for the olive. Since the trees matured slowly (in 10–15 years), they were planted for long-term benefits and not in large numbers everywhere. Olive cultivation was not demanding once young trees had been established and no longer needed irrigation, but harvesting and, with only primitive *technology (though improved in the 4th cent. BC and again in Roman times), oil production required much labour. By contrast, vines grew fast and demanded much hard work from the start.

For the Greeks improvement of agricultural property meant, after the creation of suitable plots of land, investment in trees and vines together with the necessary equipment, including store-rooms and containers for storing and shipping oil and wine. However, interplanting of cereals, pulses, vines, and trees in a single plot, or polyculture using separate plots, were probably always more common than specialization in a single crop.

Animal husbandry on a small scale (plough-oxen and mules, donkeys as pack animals, some sheep, goats, and pigs) probably had a place on all but the smallest properties. Larger herds were moved to mountain pastures in the summer (so-called transhumance; see PASTORALISM). The value of manuring was appreciated and organic wastes were collected conscientiously from settlements and applied especially to trees and vines. But the amount available in the absence of lush pastures and large numbers of cattle close to the farms limited its effect.

Nowhere in old Greece did the geography and the

nature of the agriculture favour large, unitary estates farmed by a large labour-force, though properties increased in size in Hellenistic and especially Roman times. The wealthy usually owned several parcels of land whose environmental diversity may have been advantageous. Poorer farmers were more limited. The particular agricultural regimes in use varied with local social and economic conditions as well as with geography. *Thessaly's extensive good grain land was long controlled by a small upper class and farmed by a large population of serfs, as were Laconia and Messenia, less suited to grains but probably slow to develop crops for trading. The islands of Chios and Corcyra had rich estates concentrating on vines and olives and cultivated by unusually large numbers of slaves (see SLAVERY).

Attica (the territory of *Athens) up to the Peloponnesian War (431–404 BC) was also known for its fine country houses, a measure of rural prosperity (Thuc. 2. 65. 2). Its relatively large landless (or inadequately landed) population were not primarily farm labourers, and significant use of slave labour by the top three property classes is indicated. But for all except the rich, hired or slave labour only supplemented that of the landowner and his family.

The range of possibilities open to the Greek farmer for increasing production were restricted and most required additional labour. Intensity and efficiency of agricultural production were neither uniform nor static, nor independent of social and economic factors, even if the ideal of self-sufficiency (autarkeia) was prevalent and other relevant concepts were largely unexamined. The agricultural information in *Xenophon's Oeconomicus, informative for us, was no doubt banal. But beginning in the 4th cent. BC an extensive technical literature developed (cf. references in Theophrastus' botanical writings) which was used by Roman writers (see AGRICULTURAL WRITERS) but is almost entirely lost to us.   M. H. J.

agriculture, Roman By modern standards Roman agriculture was technically simple, average yields were low, transport was difficult and costly, and storage was inefficient. This limited urbanization (and hence 'industrialization') and obliged the bulk of the population to live and work on the land. Nevertheless, in the late republic and earlier Principate agriculture and urbanization (see URBANISM (Roman)) developed together to levels probably not again matched until the late 18th cent. Roman agriculture broadly fits the ahistoric pattern which is commonly seen as characteristic of the Mediterranean region: based on the triad of cereals, vines (see WINE), and *olives, at the mercy of a semi-arid *climate with low and unreliable rainfall, and dominated by small farms practising a polyculture aimed principally at self-sufficiency and safety. But two factors—the geophysical diversity of Italy (let alone of Rome's provinces), and the effects of political and social developments—led to historically important variations between areas and across time in the organization and practice of agriculture. The last 40 years have seen an enormous growth in archaeological research—surface survey of rural areas, excavations of farmsteads, study of the ancient environment (through pollen, seeds, bones)—which is taking our knowledge and understanding of Roman agriculture far beyond what could be discovered from the evidence of the literary sources.

In archaic Rome the land seems to have been controlled by the élite, and the majority of Romans were dependent labourers (nexi). The concept of private ownership of land (ager privatus) had probably developed by the late 6th cent. BC, and by the later 4th cent. Rome had become a state of citizen-smallholders. The political aim behind this development was the creation of a large conscript army of smallholders who could afford to arm themselves (the assidui); as this army defeated Rome's Italian neighbours the Roman state annexed tracts of their territories which were often distributed in small plots to create more assidui, although some was left as nominally 'public' land (ager publicus) and appears to have been dominated by the élite who now used enslaved enemies as their main agricultural workforce. This cycle of conquest, annexation, and settlement continued, almost without interruption, into the early 2nd cent. BC, and settlement schemes, albeit thereafter using confiscated land, continued into the early Principate. The face of Italy was changed: forests were cleared and drainage schemes undertaken, as in south Etruria and in the Po valley; the territories of the ubiquitous Roman colonies were divided into small farms of similar size by rectangular grids of ditches, banks, and roads (*centuriation) which are often still traceable today; these examples and the obligation on most of Rome's Italian allies to supply infantry on the Roman model encouraged the wider diffusion of this pattern of peasant smallholding.

Rome's massive overseas expansion in the 2nd and 1st cents. BC boosted agricultural developments which had already begun in the 3rd cent. The large and long-serving armies of conquest required huge supplies of grain, wine, wool, and leather, the Celtic aristocracy under and beyond Roman rule enthusiastically adopted wine-drinking as a mark of status, and the city of Rome swelled as the capital of an empire and the centre for conspicuous consumption and display by its increasingly wealthy leaders. The boom in demand for agricultural produce, and the continuous supply of cheap slave labour, encouraged the élite to expand their landholdings and to invest in market-oriented production. A significant differentiation between larger and smaller farms emerges in the archaeological record, and also regional patterns of types of agriculture. While in southern Italy relatively extensive forms of agriculture, that is, cereal cultivation using chain-gangs of slaves and large-scale stockbreeding with seasonal movement between upland summer pastures and winter stations in the coastal plains (transhumance), were probably predominant, central western Italy (the semicircle around Rome and her main ports) was dominated by the so-called '*villa system', that is intensive production on medium-sized estates (around 25 to 75 ha.; 60 to 180 acres) of wine, olive oil, and other cash crops, including wheat, vegetables, fruit (see FOOD AND DRINK), and also small game and poultry, with a permanent nucleus of skilled slave labour topped up at seasonal peaks with casual labour hired from the free rural poor. These forms of agriculture flourished into the 2nd cent. AD with some reorientation: consumption by the frontier-based armies of the Principate and the Celtic aristocracy was increasingly met by the development of local Roman-influenced agricultural production, but the growth of Rome and general urbanization of Italy in the Augustan period greatly increased domestic demand in Italy. Roman estate owners showed considerable interest in technical and technological improvements, such as experimentation with and selection of particular plant varieties and breeds of animal, the development of more efficient presses and of viticultural techniques in general, concern with the productive deployment and control of labour, and, arguably, a generally 'economically rational' attitude to exploitation of their landholdings (see TECHNOLOGY). A technical literature of estate management emerged, drawing on Carthaginian and Hellenistic predecessors, which is represented to us principally by the manuals of Cato the Elder, *Varro, and Columella (see AGRICULTURAL WRITERS).

The development of this estate agriculture put pressure on the peasant smallholders, although military needs led to some dramatic and bitterly opposed attempts to revive an independent peasantry in central Italy, notably the Gracchan programme (see GRACCHUS, TIBERIUS and GAIUS) of the later 2nd cent. and the settlement schemes for veterans in the 1st cent. BC. The decline of the peasantry should not be exaggerated: excavated small farms show that some peasants too produced for and profited from the same markets as the large estates, and in hillier areas and the Po (Padus) valley the peasantry remained strong. But as the Roman army became mercenary and then, under Augustus, professional and more cosmopolitan, the political will to maintain an independent peasantry in Italy gradually evaporated, and it seems that peasants increasingly became tenants rather than owners of small farms. The problems of the 3rd cent. AD reduced the inflow of imperial revenues to Rome and Italy, and as the level of urbanization and demand for agricultural produce declined, so did intensive farming. Large estates were becoming more concentrated in the hands of fewer noble families (and the Church), and the legal standing of the poor declined further. The result was a tendency, not general but widespread, to move to more extensive agriculture based on the labour of tied tenants (coloni), although paradoxically this was the period in which Roman-influenced estate agriculture flourished most in some of the less troubled provinces, notably Britain and Egypt. See AGRICULTURAL IMPLEMENTS; PASTORALISM.   D. W. R.

Agrippa (Marcus Vipsanius Agrippa), the lifelong friend and supporter of *Augustus, was born in 64, 63, or even 62 BC of obscure but probably well-to-do family (he neglected his undistinguished family name). He accompanied Octavius (the future Octavian and Augustus) to Rome from Apollonia after *Caesar's murder, helped him to raise a private army, prosecuted Cassius in the court set up by Quintus Pedius in 43, and was prominent in the war against Mark *Antony's brother Lucius Antonius (Pietas). After being *tribune of the plebs in 43 or a little later, and so entering the *senate, he was urban praetor in 40. As governor of Gaul in 38 he suppressed a rebellion in Aquitania, led a punitive expedition across the Rhine, and either now or in 20 settled the Ubii on the left bank. As *consul (37) he fitted out and trained a new fleet for Octavian's war against *Pompey's son Sextus Pompeius, converting the *lacus Avernus* near Cumae into a harbour (portus Iulius) for the purpose, and in 36 won two decisive naval engagements at Mylae and Naulochus, where his improved grapnel was highly effective. In 35–34 he took part in the Illyrian War. Although an ex-consul he held the aedileship in 33, contributing greatly to Octavian's popularity. In 31 his vigorous naval operations were the primary cause of Mark Antony's defeat; at *Actium he commanded the left wing. He next (31–29), with *Maecenas, managed affairs in Italy in Octavian's absence. On Octavian's return he helped carry out a purge of the senate and a census (29–28) and he held second and third consulships in the crucial years 28 and 27. In 23 Augustus, ill and embroiled in political controversy, handed him his signet-ring, conferring an unofficial status (most importantly in the eyes of the armies) that would have meant his supremacy if Augustus had died. He was entrusted with a mission in the eastern half of the empire, probably with proconsular power, which he carried out from Mytilene on *Lesbos. The claim that rivalry with Augustus' nephew Marcus Claudius Marcellus had sent him into virtual exile cannot be substantiated. More likely it was a constitutional crisis, with Agrippa put in easy reach of the armies of the Balkans and Syria if Augustus' position were undermined or his life threatened. He was recalled in 21 to represent Augustus in Rome; in 20 he proceeded to Gaul and in 19 to Spain where he quelled the Cantabri. In 18 he was given tribunician power (see TRIBUNE OF THE PLEBS, end of entry) for five years, a power held otherwise only by Augustus, and his *imperium* was renewed for the same period. In 13 his tribunician power was renewed for five more years, and his *imperium* apparently made superior to that of all other holders, like that of Augustus (the extent and development of Agrippa's powers, outlined in the fragmentary papyrus (*Kölner Pap.* 1 (1976), 10 = EJ 366) that contains part of Augustus' funerary elogium on him, remains controversial). As a *quindecimvir sacris faciundis* or member of a college whose job it was to look after certain ritual texts (from before 37) he assisted in the celebration of the Secular Games in 17. His second mission to the east (17/16–13) is notable for the establishment of Polemon of Pontus in the Bosporan kingdom, the settlement of veterans at Berytus and Heliopolis, and his friendship with Herod and benevolent treatment of the *Jews. Early in 12 he went to Pannonia where there was a danger of revolt, but fell ill on his return and died about the end of March. After a public funeral he was buried in the mausoleum of Augustus.

Agrippa's wealth was spent freely in the service of the Roman people and the empire, winning him lasting popularity. He restored the sewers of Rome and reorganized the water supply, constructing two new *aqueducts (Iulia, 33 BC, and Virgo, 19 BC), and a network of distribution installations. Virgo fed Rome's first public *baths, close to his Pantheon, and the expanded Saepta Iulia (26 BC), all in a huge recreational area. He also built a granary (horrea Agrippiana) behind the Forum (*forum Romanum) and a new bridge over the Tiber. Constructions in the provinces included buildings at Nemausus (mod. Nîmes) and a road system radiating from Lugdunum (mod. Lyon). By his will Augustus received the greater part of his property, including the Thracian Chersonese (Gallipoli); he also made generous bequests to the people of Rome.

He wrote an autobiography (now lost) and a geographical commentary (also lost, but used by *Strabo and *Pliny the Elder) from which a map of the empire was constructed, to be displayed after his death on the porticus Vipsaniae (see MAPS).

Agrippa was married three times: in 37 to Caecilia Attica, in 28 to Augustus' niece the elder Marcella, whom he divorced in 21 to marry Augustus' daughter *Julia. The first two wives produced daughters, Attica's including Vipsania Agrippina (the 'Elder Agrippina'), the first wife of the later emperor *Tiberius, Marcella's the Vipsania who married Publius Quinctilius Varus. Iulia had three sons, Gaius and Lucius Caesar, who were adopted by Augustus in 17, and Agrippa Postumus; and two daughters, Julia the Younger and the Younger *Agrippina; through her he was grandfather and great-grandfather respectively of the emperors *Gaius and *Nero.

Agrippa, portrayed as upright, simple, and modest, a man who subordinated his ambitions to those of Augustus, was by 12 BC a partner nearly equal in power. Refusing three *triumphs (19 BC onwards) and failing even to report his Spanish successes inhibited private men from applying and contributed to the end of such triumphs. Like his advocacy of public display of works of art (he was a noted collector), it went against the interests of the ruling class, who boycotted his funeral games. To Augustus he may sometimes have been an embarrassment.

G. W. R.; T. J. C.; B. M. L.

Agrippina, Iulia Agrippina, 'the Younger Agrippina' (AD 15–59), eldest daughter of *Germanicus and Vipsania Agrippina ('the Elder Agrippina'), was born on 6 November AD 15 at Ara Ubiorum. In 28 she was betrothed to Cn. Domitius Ahenobarbus, to whom she bore one son, the later emperor *Nero, in 37. During the principate of her brother *Gaius (37–41) her name, like those of her sisters, was coupled with the emperor's in vows and oaths; but when she was discovered at Mogontiacum (mod. Mainz) late in 39 to be involved in the conspiracy of

Gnaeus Cornelius Lentulus Gaetulicus, she was sent into banishment. She was recalled by her uncle *Claudius, who married her in 49. Aided by Marcus Antonius Pallas, the younger *Claudius, who married her in 49. Aided by Marcus Antonius Pallas, the younger *Seneca, and Sextus Afranius Burrus, she quickly achieved her ambitious purpose. Receiving for herself the title Augusta, she persuaded Claudius to adopt Nero as guardian of his own son Britannicus. She was generally believed to have poisoned Claudius, to make room for Nero (54). In the years of Nero's rule she was almost co-regent with him but, after Pallas had fallen in 55 and Burrus and Seneca turned against her, she lost her power. In March 59 she was murdered at Baiae by a *freedman, Anicetus, acting on Nero's instructions. She wrote an autobiography.

J. P. B.; A. J. S. S.

Ai Khanoum (see ◀Map 2a, Cb▶), Greek Hellenistic city excavated (1965–78) by the French archaeological delegation in Afghanistan, is situated in the eastern part of *Bactria, at the junction of the river Oxus (mod. Amu Darya) and a tributary of the left bank, the Kokcha river, at the frontier between Afghanistan and the former Soviet Union. The Greek name of the city is uncertain. It seems to have been built as a fortified frontier town, to guard against the nomadic tribes to the north and the mountain peoples to the east (the Badakhshan range). It was founded, commanding a fertile plain, by the end of the 4th cent. or in the early 3rd cent. BC, in an area where there had been earlier settlement, as indicated by an irrigation system and an Achaemenid fortress. Ai Khanoum passed from Seleucid control to that of the so-called Indo-Bactrian kings, certainly by the reign of *Eucratides (c.172–155 BC) of Bactria. In c. the mid-2nd cent. BC it was destroyed by invasions from the Saca tribes. The buildings discovered include administrative quarters, a temenos (sacred precinct), a *gymnasium, a theatre, several rich private dwellings, a citadel where a garrison was installed, a palace built on the Persian style, and two temples built to Mesopotamian plan and decorated in Mesopotamian style. The site was surrounded by vast, impressive fortifications.   S. S.-W.

Aias (Lat. *Ajax*). (1) Son of Telamon, king of Salamis, hence Aias Telamonius. He brought twelve ships from Salamis to Troy (*Il.* 2. 557). In the *Iliad* he is of enormous (pelōrios) size, head and shoulders above the rest (3. 226–9), and the greatest of the Greek warriors after *Achilles (2. 768–9). His stock epithet is 'bulwark (herkos) of the Achaeans', and his characteristic weapon a huge shield of seven-fold ox-hide. He clearly has the better of *Hector in a duel (7. 181–305) after which the heroes exchange gifts, Aias giving Hector a sword-belt in return for a sword; and he is at his memorable best when with unshakeable courage he defends the Greek wall and then the ships (see esp. 15. 676–88, 727–46, 16. 101–11). He is also a member of the Embassy to Achilles, when he gives a brief but effective appeal to Achilles on friendship's grounds (9. 624–42). At

Ai-Khanoum Exedra (recess with benches) in the *gymnasium at Ai-Khanoum—a witness to the *Hellenism of this outpost of Hellenistic *colonization in modern Afghanistan.

Patroclus' funeral games he draws a wrestling match with *Odysseus, strength against cunning (23. 708–39).

The lost epic *Aethiopis* told how after Achilles' death Aias carried his body off the field of battle while Odysseus kept back the Trojans (cf. *Od.* 5. 309 f.). Another such epic, the *Little Iliad*, told how the arms of Achilles were then adjudged to Odysseus instead of Aias, who went mad with anger, killed the herds of the Greeks, believing them to be the Greek leaders, and then committed suicide. *Sophocles dramatizes these later events in his *Ajax*, but at the end of the play Aias is taken to an honourable burial, in marked contrast to his treatment in the *Little Iliad* (fr. 3 Davies) where he is denied the customary burial honours (see J. R. March, *BICS* 1991–2, 1–36). In the *Odyssey*, when Odysseus is in Hades, he meets the shade of Aias who, in anger at his loss of Achilles' arms, refuses to speak and stalks away in magnificent silence (11. 543–64).

In the Hesiodic *Great Ehoiai* (fr. 250 M–W) and thence in Pindar (*Isthm.* 6. 35 ff.) *Heracles visits Telamon and, standing on the lion-skin, prays that his new-born son may be as stout (*arrēktos*) as the skin; *Zeus, in answer, sends an eagle, *aietos*, and hence the baby is named Aias. From this develops the story (Lycoph. 455 ff.; cf. Aesch. *Thracian Women*, fr. 83 Radt) that Aias was invulnerable save at one point, where the skin had not touched him when (in this version) he was wrapped in it. It was later said that when he killed himself his blood flowed on the ground and there sprang up the iris (*hyakinthos*) which also commemorates the death of Hyacinthus; hence the markings on its petals recall the hero's name (*Aias—aiai*, see Ov. *Met.* 13. 394 ff.). Aias had a cult in Salamis, Attica, Megara (?), the Troad, and Byzantium: see Farnell, *Hero Cults*, 305 ff. and n. 58.

Scenes from Aias' life popular in art, some from the 7th cent. BC, are combats with Hector and others, dicing with Achilles, lifting Achilles' body, the argument and voting about Achilles' arms, and (an especial favourite) his suicide: see O. Touchefeu, *LIMC* 1/1. 312–36.

(2) Son of Oïleus or Ileus, the Locrian chieftain. In Homer Aias leads the Locrian contingent to Troy with 40 ships (*Il.* 2. 527 ff.). He is 'much lesser' than Telamonian Aias (hence often called the Lesser Aias), quick-footed, and often paired with his great namesake as a brave fighter. He can, however, be an unpleasant character, on occasion grossly rude (23. 473 ff.), hated by *Athena (*Od.* 4. 502), and finally drowned by *Poseidon for blasphemy against the gods while scrambling ashore after shipwreck (*Od.* 4. 499–511).

In the *Iliu Persis* he dragged Cassandra away from the statue of Athena to rape her, and in so doing loosened the statue from its plinth. This is a favourite scene in archaic and classical art: see O. Touchefeu, *LIMC* I/1. 339–49. In historic times the Locrians sent two virgins annually to serve in the temple of Athena at Ilium (*Troy) in expiation of this crime, the Locrians maintaining that this penalty was imposed for 1,000 years.   H. J. R.; J. R. M.

Ajax See AIAS.

Alcaeus, *lyric poet, of Mytilene on *Lesbos. Probably born c.625–620 BC, since he was old enough to participate in the struggle against Athens for Sigeum near Troy in the last decade of the century in which Pittacus distinguished himself (fr. 428; Hdt. 5. 95; Diog. Laert. 1. 74; Strabo 13. 1. 38). Lesbian politics at this period were violent and confused. The ruling dynasty, the Penthilidae, who traced their descent from Orestes, were weakened and finally overthrown by two successive coups (Arist. *Pol.* 1311^{b}26, 29). Power passed to a tyrant named Melanchrus, who was overthrown by a faction headed by Pittacus and Alcaeus' brothers c.612–609 (*Suda*, entry under *Pittakos*; Diog. Laert. 1. 74); Alcaeus (perhaps too young—fr. 75) was not involved (Diog. Laert. 1. 74). A new tyrant, Myrsilus, emerged, who was opposed unsuccessfully by a faction of exiles including Pittacus and Alcaeus (frs. 129, 114); Pittacus subsequently allied himself with Myrsilus, while his former comrades continued the struggle in exile (frs. 129, 70). After Myrsilus' death the people elected Pittacus *aisymnētēs* (dictator) to ward off Alcaeus' faction (frs. 70, 348; Arist. *Pol.* 1285^{a}35 ff.). Internal divisions within the faction contributed to its failure to oust Pittacus (fr. 70). Pittacus' marriage alliance with the Penthilidae probably belongs to this period (fr. 70), as may Alcaeus' journey to Egypt and his brother Antimenidas' service abroad (frs. 432, 350). An ancient critic (*POxy.* 2506. 98) indicates at least three periods of exile. Alcaeus' poetry is full of attacks on and abuse of Pittacus, for perjury and faithlessness, low birth (probably false), drunkenness, unbridled ambition, and physical defects (frs. 72, 129, 348; Diog. Laert. 1. 81). Popular opinion was with Pittacus, as in general is that of posterity. The tradition that Pittacus subsequently pardoned Alcaeus (Diog. Laert. 1. 76) is suspect.

Alcaeus' poetry was divided by the Alexandrians into at least ten books. It was monodic, and was composed in a variety of lyric metres in two- or four-line stanzas, including the alcaic stanza, named after him. The dialect is predominantly Lesbian vernacular, but epicisms are admitted. His range is rivalled only by *Archilochus in the Archaic period. He dealt with politics, war, wine, love, hymns to the gods, moralizing, and myth (though possibly both moralizing and myth were always subordinated to specific contexts). There is considerable variety in the treatment of each theme. Politics may be dealt with through personal abuse or the grandeur of myth and ritual or both (frs. 72, 129, 298; Diog. Laert. 1. 81); the invitation to drink may be supported by myth (fr. 38A) or the imperatives of the weather (frs. 338, 347). He is open to a range of influences. In his use of lyric for abuse he blurs the difference between lyric and iambus. His hymns are influenced by the rhapsodic tradition. Fr. 347 recasts a passage of *Hesiod in lyric form. He has a vivid descriptive power and an impressive vigour, particularly in his arresting openings; his control of form and mood (the developed contrasts of frs. 42 and 338, the changes of mood and register in fr. 129, the extended metaphor of storm for civil strife in fr. 326, the accelerating tempo of the list in fr. 140) is often underrated. He was popular at Attic *symposia and a favourite with *Horace (*Carm.* 1. 32. 5 ff., 2. 13. 26 ff.).   C. C.

Alcibiades (451/0–404/3 BC), son of Cleinias, Athenian general and politician. Brought up in the household of his guardian *Pericles, he became the pupil and intimate friend of *Socrates. A flamboyant aristocrat, he competed in politics with the new-style demagogues, and his ambitious imperialism drew Athens into a coalition with Argos and other enemies of *Sparta. This policy, half-heartedly supported by the Athenians, was largely discredited by the Spartan victory at Mantinea (418). Though Alcibiades temporarily allied with *Nicias to avoid *ostracism, the two were normally adversaries and rivals, and when Alcibiades sponsored the plan for a major Sicilian expedition, Nicias unsuccessfully opposed it. Both were appointed, together with Lamachus, to command this expedition (415). After the mutilation of the herms (see HERMES), Alcibiades had been accused of involvement in other religious scandals, and soon after the fleet reached Sicily he was recalled for trial. He escaped, however, to Sparta, where he encouraged the Spartans to send a general to Syracuse, and to establish a permanent Spartan post at Decelea in Attica (which was eventually done in 413).

In 412 he was involved in Sparta's decision to concentrate on the Aegean rather than the Hellespont, but he soon lost the confidence of the Spartans and fled to the Persian satrap Tissaphernes. He tried to secure his return to Athens by obtaining the support of Persia and bringing about an oligarchic revolution, but the negotiations with Persia were unsuccessful. The Athenian fleet at *Samos appointed him general, and for several years he skilfully directed operations in the Hellespont, winning a brilliant victory at Cyzicus in 410. On returning to Athens in 407 he was cleared of the religious charges hanging over him and was appointed to an extraordinary command; but when a subordinate was defeated by *Lysander at Notium (406) he withdrew to Thrace, and his approach to the Athenians before Aegospotami was rebuffed (405). After he had taken refuge with the Persian Pharnabazus, he was murdered in Phrygia through the influence of the Thirty Tyrants (see ATHENS (HISTORY) and LYSANDER).

Alcibiades was a competent military leader and a master of intrigue, but his personal ambition and the excesses of his private life aroused the distrust of the Athenians, and he was not given the chance to show whether his ambitious policies, carried out under his leadership, could bring about success.   H. D. W.; P. J. R.

Alcman, *lyric poet, active in the mid- to late 7th cent. BC in *Sparta. His birthplace was disputed. Some believed him a Laconian, i.e. Spartan, while a number of ancient authors made him a Lydian (*Anth. Pal.* 7. 18, 19, 709; Ael. *VH* 12. 50; *Suda*, entry under *Alkman*, *POxy.* 2389, 2506, 3542; Vell. Pat. 1. 18. 2); the latter version (derived from fr. 16) was further emboidered to make him a freed slave (Heraclid Pont. *Excerp. Polit.* 9). The *Suda* credits him with six books of lyric songs (*melē*); a group called 'Diving women'/ 'Swimming women' (*kolymbōsai*), of which no certain trace survives, may have made up one of these or a seventh book. The lyric songs, mostly choral, included maiden-songs (*partheneia*), which were probably arranged into two books by Alexandrian scholars (Steph. Byz. entry under *Erusichē*). We also hear of hymns and wedding-songs (*hymenaioi*). The *Suda* credits him with love-poetry, and fragments with erotic content survive (58, 59a).

The most important surviving works are fragments of two maiden-songs found on papyri. The first (fr. 1) shows many features of the developed choral lyric: a myth (1–35), gnomic moralizing (36 ff.), and (probable but not certain, since the opening is lost) framing reference to the present occasion. An account of the death of the sons of Hippocoon is followed by a gnomic transition (36 ff.) on divine punishment and mortal limitation. The rest of the fragment is devoted to praise of two females who play a major role in the ritual (Hagesichora and Agido) and description (with humorous self-deprecation) of the chorus. The song was performed at dawn (41 f., 60 ff.). The identity of the goddess honoured (87, *Aotis*, lit. 'the goddess at the dawn') is unclear (conjectures include Helen, *Artemis Orthia, Phoebe daughter of Leucippus), likewise the nature of the festival, though many scholars detect a reference to a rival choir (60 ff.); there is uncertainty about the details of the myth and its relevance to the occasion. The second (fr. 3), more fragmentary, poem also concentrates on the actions of the leading figure (Astymeloisa). Both poems share a richness of sensuous imagery and a pronounced homoerotic tenor. There is an evident taste for puns, and a proliferation of proper names, many of significance only to the original audience. Alongside this parochiality we find a taste for the distant and exotic (1. 59, 100; cf. frs. 90, 148 ff.). Together the two songs show a gaiety and humour not usually associated with Sparta. Some other fragments come from maiden-songs (16, 26, 29, 38, 59b, 60), but many defy classification. Alcman's descriptive power is shown in an account of the sleep of nature (fr. 89, context unknown). Mythic narrative is attested by a number of fragments (e.g. fr. 69 Niobe; fr. 77 addressed to Paris; fr. 69 the stone of Tantalus; fr. 80 *Odysseus and Circe). The songs are composed in the Laconian vernacular, with intermittent epic and aeolic forms. The poetry had achieved classic status by the late 5th cent. (Ar. *Lys.* 1247 ff.). C. C.

alcoholism

Greece The ancient Greeks were unfamiliar with modern concepts of alcoholism, but they were well aware of self-destructive drinking and the effects of habitual drunkenness. In the *Odyssey*, *Homer makes a speaker note that wine is a bane to those who drink it excessively, and identifies overindulgence as the cause of the *Centaur Eurytion's vile behaviour (21. 293–8). In *Hades, Homer's Elpenor admits that heavy drinking was a key factor in his fatal plunge from Circe's roof (*Od.* 11. 61). *Pythagoras is credited with the dictum that drinking to achieve drunkenness is a training-ground for madness, and he advises drunkards to take an unflinching look at their inebriate behaviour if they wish to alter it (Stob. *Flor.* 3. 18. 23, 33). In the *Republic*, *Plato writes about men who welcome any excuse to drink whatever wine is available (475a). *Aristotle's treatise *On Drunkenness* has been lost, but his extant works confirm an abiding interest in wine's pernicious effects. *Plutarch's *Moralia* deplores the vicious cycle exhibited by habitual drunkards who seek wine in the morning to remedy their hangovers, noting that wine not only reveals the character but can alter it as well (127f, 799b–c). The value of abstention was recognized by the ancient Greeks, and Athenaeus devotes considerable attention to water-drinkers in *The Deipnosophists* (2. 44b–f); abstainers, however, were rare in Greek antiquity. Athenaeus and Aelian discuss those groups—the Macedonians, for example—who drank with heroic intensity. Cleomenes I (see SPARTA), *Alcibiades, *Philip II of Macedon, *Alexander the Great, Dionysius II of Syracuse, and Demetrius Poliorcetes ('the Besieger') can be counted among the most renowned topers of the ancient Greek world. In classical antiquity, however, allegations of intemperance often serve as vehicles for character assassination; thus, each case must be considered on its own merits.

Rome The ancient Romans were as interested in the harmful effects of excessive drinking and chronic intoxication as their Greek counterparts. In *On the Nature of Things*, *Lucretius writes that wine's fury disturbs the soul, debilitates the body, and provokes quarrels (3. 476–83). The younger *Seneca warns that habitual drunkenness so weakens the mind that its consequences are felt long after the drinking has stopped (*Ep.* 83. 26). He notes that some men become so tolerant of wine that even though they are inebriated they appear to be sober (*Ep.* 83. 11). Seneca also suggests that drunkenness tends to disclose and magnify character defects (*Ep.* 83. 19–20). In his *Natural History*, *Pliny the Elder finds irony in the fact that men spend hard-earned money on something that can damage the mind and cause madness (14. 137). Like the Greeks, Pliny comments on truth in wine ('*in vino veritas*'), but emphasizes that the truths therein revealed are often better left unspoken (*HN* 14. 141). Seneca's and Pliny's descriptions of the psychological and physical effects of chronic intoxication presage modern observations: memory loss, identity confusion, narcissistic self-indulgence, antisocial behaviour, impaired speech and vision, distended stomach, halitosis, quivering, vertigo, insomnia, and early death (Sen.

Ep. 83. 21, 95. 16; Plin. *HN* 14. 142). *Sulla, *Cato the Younger, Marcus Tullius Cicero (son of the famous orator), Mark *Antony, *Julia (daughter of Augustus), and the emperors *Tiberius, *Claudius, Vitellius, and *Commodus are among the prominent Romans accused of notorious tippling.

The alcoholic beverage of choice for both the ancient Greeks and Romans was *wine, customarily diluted with water, except perhaps in the case of the Macedonians who were reputed to drink their wine *akratos*, or unmixed. Distilled spirits, such as brandy and whisky, had not yet been invented, and beer was looked upon as a swinish potation better left to barbarians.   J. M. O'B., B. L. R.

Alexander the Great (*see facing page*)

Alexandria (see ◀Map 2, Bb▶) was founded by *Alexander the Great in 331 BC when he took *Egypt from the Persians. It was developed principally by the first two Ptolemies, who made it the capital of their kingdom and the main Mediterranean port of Egypt (see PTOLEMY I and II). It was founded as a theoretically autonomous city (*polis*) of the traditional Greek type, modelled in several respects on Athens: it had an exclusive hereditary citizenship organized by demes (local districts; see DEMOCRACY, ATHENIAN), prob-ably with an assembly (*ekklēsia*), council (*boulē*), and annu-ally elected magistrates, it had its own territory, restricted to citizen-owners and exempt from direct royal taxation, its own coinage, and its own laws. Its founding citizens were recruited from all over the Greek world; there were also numerous non-citizen residents of Egyptian and other ethnic origin, including a large Jewish community which acquired special privileges though not full citizenship. Alexandria soon became one of the largest and grandest cities of the Mediterranean world, famed for the monu-mental magnificence of its two main intersecting streets, its palace-quarter with the tomb of Alexander and the Museum and Library, its Serapeum (see EGYPTIAN DEITIES), *gymnasium, and pharos, the lighthouse at the entrance to its two capacious artificial harbours. As a royal capital Alexandria could not be a normal *polis*: its coinage and, probably, its laws were used throughout Egypt; in the course of the dynastic struggles of the later Ptolemies, in which its citizens naturally took a prominent part, Alexandria was, it seems, punished with the loss of its *ekklēsia* and *boulē*, and its magistrates became more like royal officials. These struggles also ignited the notorious antagonism between the 'Greek' citizen-body and the Jewish community, which continued to flare up in the Roman period (see JEWS).   [*continued on p. 30*]

Alexandria A late-antique school at Alexandria. The lecturer's seat is visible at the centre of the U-shaped lecture-hall. Alexandria retained its eminence as an intellectual centre throughout Roman times.

Alexander the Great

Alexander the Great (Alexander III of Macedon), 356–323 BC, son of *Philip II and Olympias.

1. As crown prince he was educated by *Aristotle (from 342); he was his father's deputy in Macedon (340) and fought with distinction at the battle of Chaeronea (338). Philip's last marriage created a serious rift, but a formal reconciliation had been effected by the time of his death (autumn 336), and Alexander was proclaimed king against a background of dynastic intrigue, in which his rivals (notably Amyntas, son of Perdiccas, and the faction of Attalus) were eliminated. A show of force in southern Greece saw him acknowledged Philip's successor as *hēgemōn* of the League of Corinth; and in 335, when the Thebans took advantage of his absence campaigning on the Danube and rebelled, he destroyed the city and enslaved the survivors. The exemplary punishment enabled him to leave the Greek world under the supervision of Antipater with little fear of revolt, while he turned to the war of revenge against Persia.

2. In early 334 Alexander led his grand army across the Hellespont. In all some 43,000 foot and 5,500 horse (including the expeditionary force under Parmenion), it was the most formidable array ever to leave Greek soil. The Macedonians were its indispensable nucleus. The infantry phalanx, *c*.15,000 strong and armed with the fearsome 6-metre (19½-foot) pike (*sarisa*), comprised a guard corps (hypaspists) and six regionally levied battalions (*taxeis*); and the cavalry, originally 1,800 strong, was also divided into regional squadrons (*ilai*). In pitched battle the phalanx, in massed formation, was practically unbreakable on level ground, and Alexander was able to generate a cavalry charge from the flank which had decisive momentum. The men of the hypaspists, usually supplemented by Agrianian javelin-men and the corps of archers, were deployed in rapid-moving columns along with the cavalry,

Alexander the Great This Roman copy (the 'Azara' herm, 2nd cent. AD) of a lost Greek original probably reflects the god-like image of Alexander created by his favourite sculptor, Lysippus.

and were an irresistible combination in mountain warfare. These units were far superior to any they encountered (except arguably the armoured cavalry of *Bactria), and, supplemented by a large reserve of secondary troops (Thracians, Illyrians, and the hoplites of the Corinthian League), they gave Alexander an overwhelming military advantage.

3. Alexander's superiority was immediately asserted at the river Granicus (334), where a composite satrapal army was outmanœuvred and its large mercenary phalanx exterminated. That allowed him to march directly to occupy Sardis, *Ephesus, and Miletus. The most serious threat came from a superior Persian fleet, which sustained the stubborn defence of Halicarnassus, and Alexander took the gamble of demobilizing his own fleet and abandoning the coast. He moved east via Lycia, Pamphylia, and Phrygia (where he 'cut' the Gordian knot, fulfilling a presage of empire), and largely ignored a major Persian counter-offensive in the Aegean, which—fortunately for him—the Great King (Darius III) crippled by withdrawing a large segment of the fleet to swell his royal army (summer 333). Alexander made Cilicia his base for the critical campaign and lured the vast Persian army into the narrow coastal plain south of Issus, where its numbers were ineffective. He disrupted the front line with his standard cavalry charge from the right and gradually forced the entire Persian army into panic retreat. This overwhelming victory (c. November 333) gave him control of the near east as far as the Euphrates. There was some resistance, notably at Tyre and Gaza, which he crushed in exemplary fashion, preferring protracted and costly sieges (seven months at Tyre) to diplomacy and negotiation. All challenges were met directly, whatever the human cost.

4. After a winter (332/1) in Egypt, which was surrendered peacefully, he invaded Mesopotamia and won his crowning victory at Gaugamela (1 October 331). Darius' forces were outmanœuvred again, on chosen ground and unrestricted plain; Alexander sacrificed his left wing, leaving it to be enveloped while he extended the enemy line to the right, created a gap and drove inwards at the head of his cavalry. Again a general rout ensued, and Mesopotamia in turn lay open to him. Babylon and Susa fell without resistance, and he forced the Persian Gates against determined opposition to occupy the heartland of Persis (winter 331/0). At Persepolis he acquired the accumulated financial reserves of the Persian empire and incinerated its great palace during (it would seem) an orgiastic *symposium, subsequently representing it as the final act of the war of revenge. That in effect came during the summer of 330 when Darius fled from his last refuge at Ecbatana, to be murdered by his closest entourage (led by Bessus, satrap of Bactria). Alexander honoured his rival's body and closed the war by discharging his Hellenic troops *en masse.*

5. A new challenge arose when Bessus, who had withdrawn to his satrapy, proclaimed himself King of Kings under the regnal name Artaxerxes V. He appointed counter-satraps in central Asia and fomented revolt. Alexander left his satraps to cope with the insurgency, while he moved in a great swathe through Areia, Drangiana, and Arachosia (east Iran and west Afghanistan) and crossed the Hindu Kush to invade Bactria (spring 329). Bessus was soon gone, arrested in his turn by his nobles and surrendered to Alexander for exemplary punishment. Shortly afterwards, when Alexander reached the NE limit of the empire (the Syr-Darya), a new uprising began in Sogdiana (Uzbekistan), rapidly spreading south to Bactria. One of Alexander's (non-Macedonian) columns was ambushed by the insurgents' nomad auxiliaries west of Marakanda (Samarkand), a military and moral reverse which impressed the need for slow, systematic pacification. The conquest of the area fortress by fortress witnessed deliberate massacre, enslavement, and transplantation of recalcitrant populations, and, when the revolt ended (spring 327), the north-eastern satrapies were left exhausted under a large garrison of mercenaries and a network of new city foundations, in which a Hellenic military élite was supported by a native agrarian workforce—the invariable model for the dozens of Alexandrias he founded in the eastern empire.

6. From Bactria Alexander moved into *India at the invitation of the local dynasts of the Kabul valley and Punjab. He was nothing loath to reaffirm the traditional Achaemenid claims to the Indus lands. Resistance was treated as rebellion, and his progress through Bajaur and Swat was marked by

massacre and destruction, as in Sogdiana. Even the remote rock-fortress of Aornus (Pir-sar) was reduced by siege at the cost of prodigious hardship, to demonstrate that there was no escape from his dominion. The spring of 326 saw him at Taxila, east of the Indus, poised for a campaign against Porus, who held the Jhelum (Hydaspes) against him. After a series of diversionary manœuvres he crossed the river under cover of a spring thunderstorm and defeated Porus, whose war *elephants could not compensate for his cavalry inferiority. The victory was commemorated in two city foundations (Bucephala and Nicaea), and a remarkable issue of silver decadrachms depicts Alexander (crowned by victory) in combat with Porus and his elephant. Alexander continued eastwards, crossing the rivers of the Punjab in the face of an increasing monsoonal deluge, until his troops' patience was exhausted. They refused to cross the Hyphasis (Beas) and invade the Ganges river system, and Alexander reluctantly acceded. A river fleet (commissioned in the summer) was ready at the Hydaspes by November 325, and the army proceeded by land and water to the southern Ocean. The journey was marked by a singularly vicious campaign against the Malli, unprovoked except by their failure to offer submission, and Alexander's impetuousness cost him a debilitating chest wound. Further south the kingdoms of Sambus and Musicanus were visited with fire and slaughter when their allegiance wavered, and, as he approached his base in the Indus delta (Patalene), the natives fled in terror (July 325).

7. Alexander now returned to the west, deputing Nearchus to take his fleet across the southern coastline while he led the main army through the Gedrosian desert (Makran), in emulation—so Nearchus claimed—of *Cyrus the Great and Semiramis. The horrors of heat and famine which ensued were considerable, but perhaps exaggerated in the sources, which attest no great loss of life among the Macedonian army. Reunited with the fleet in Carmania (c. December 325), he returned to Persepolis and Susa (March 324), where some 80 of his staff joined him in taking wives from the Persian nobility. For the next year there was a lull in campaigning (except for a punitive expedition against the Cossaeans of the Zagros), but there were grandiose preparations in the Levant, where he commissioned a war fleet allegedly 1,000 strong, some of which was conveyed to Babylon in summer of 323. The first stage of conquest was certainly the Persian Gulf and Arabian littoral, which Alexander intended to conquer and colonize, but the sources, in particular the memoranda (*hypomnēmata*) reported by *Diodorus Siculus, refer to projects of conquest in the western Mediterranean aimed at Carthage and southern Italy—and plans are even alleged of a circumnavigation of Africa. The reality is perhaps beyond verification, but it is likely enough that Alexander conceived no practical limit to his empire.

8. Alexander's monarchy was absolute. From the outset he regarded Asia Minor as liberated territory only in so far as he displaced the Persians, and he announced the fact of possession by imposing his own satraps upon the erstwhile Persian provinces. By 332 he regarded himself as the proper ruler of the Persian empire, and after Gaugamela he was acclaimed king of Asia. From 330 his status was displayed in his court dress, which combined the traditional Macedonian hat (*kausia*) and cloak with the Persian diadem, tunic, and girdle. He used Persian court ceremonial and promoted Persian nobles, but there is no evidence of a formal 'policy of fusion' with Persians and Macedonians assimilated into a single ruling class. Except for a brief moment at Opis the Macedonians were entrenched in a position of superiority. The Susa marriages would indeed give rise to a mixed offspring (as would the liaisons of his soldiers with native women), but in both cases the ultimate aim was probably to counter the regional and family loyalties which had been the curse of both Persian and Macedonian monarchs. At another level he had cut across the traditional regional basis of his army and introduced Iranians even to the élite Companion cavalry. There was to be a single loyalty—to the crown.

9. Alexander naturally experienced opposition in various forms. His Macedonian troops proved increasingly reluctant to be enticed into further conquest. He gave way once, at the Hyphasis, but at Opis (324) he confronted their contumacious demands for repatriation with summary executions and a devastating threat to man his army exclusively from Persians. He had deliberately made his Macedonians dispensable and demonstrated the fact. The same ruthlessness marked his reaction to

opposition at court. He isolated and struck down Parmenion because of his resistance to imperial expansion, and the adolescent pages, who seriously threatened his life for reasons which are obscure (but probably based on antipathy to the new absolutism), were tortured and stoned to death. Insubordination was as intolerable as conspiracy. Alexander's return to the west in 325/4 witnessed a spate of executions of satraps who had exceeded their authority or arrogated power (e.g. Astaspes in Carmania, Orxines in Persis). Misgovernment as such was a secondary consideration, as is shown by his remarkable offer of pardon to Cleomenes, financial administrator in Egypt. Relations with the Greek world became increasingly strained. At first the machinery of the Corinthian League was effective; and the challenge by Agis III of Sparta had limited support and was quickly crushed (? spring 330). But Alexander undermined the provisions of the league by his Exiles' Decree (324), which threatened Athens' possession of *Samos and gave almost every city the problem of repatriating long-term exiles. The last year of his reign was punctuated by tense and heated diplomacy, and his death was the catalyst for general war in southern Greece.

10. Given Alexander's uncompromising claims to sovereignty it can be readily understood how he came to conceive himself divine. A Heraclid by lineage, he believed himself the descendant of *Heracles, Perseus, and (ultimately) *Zeus, and by 331 he had begun to represent himself as the direct son of Zeus, with dual paternity comparable to that of Heracles. He was reinforced in his belief by his pilgrimage (in 331) to the oracle of Ammon (recognized as a manifestation of Zeus at Siwa), and thereafter styled himself son of Zeus Ammon. But divine sonship was not divinity, and by 327, after conquest had followed conquest, Alexander was encouraged (particularly in the liberated atmosphere of the symposium) to believe that his achievements deserved apotheosis at least as much as Heracles'. *Proskynēsis*, the hierarchical prostration of inferior to superior, was *de rigueur* at the Persian court, but Alexander attempted to extend it to Macedonians and Greeks, for whom the gesture was an act of worship. The experiment failed, thanks to the resistance of Callisthenes, but the concept remained, and there is an anecdotal (but probable) tradition that he wrote to the cities of Greece in 324, suggesting that it would be appropriate for divine honours to be voted him along with a hero-cult for his deceased favourite, Hephaestion. Cults were certainly established, predominantly in Asia Minor, and persisted long after his death, eclipsing the largely ephemeral worship of his successors.

11. Portraits of Alexander tend to follow the model created by his favourite sculptor, Lysippus, who perpetuated the leftward inclination of his neck and the famous *anastolē* (hair thrown back from a central parting). His profile, first illustrated on the 'Alexander sarcophagus' (311), appears repeatedly on coins, most strikingly on the commemorative tetradrachms of *Lysimachus. His personality is far more elusive, thanks to the tendency in antiquity to adduce him as a moral example of good or evil and the propensity of moderns to endue him with the qualities they would admire in themselves. His reputation for invincibility, which he studiously fostered, has been a source of fascination (notably for *Pompey, *Trajan, and Napoleon), mostly for ill. The process began when he died (10 June 323) after a ten-day illness (which contemporaries ascribed to poison), and the marshals who sought to emulate him rapidly dismembered his empire.   A. B. B.

When Egypt came under Roman rule the citizens of Alexandria retained most of their surviving privileges; they were also used extensively in the new administration of the province, and only they, in Egypt, could acquire Roman *citizenship. Despite several appeals to the Julio-Claudian emperors, Alexandria only regained a *boulē* (council) in AD 200/1 when *Septimius Severus granted councils to all the cities of Egypt; this development, and the universal grant of Roman citizenship in AD 212, undermined Alexandria's political primacy in Egypt, but not her Mediterranean-wide economic and cultural importance. With over 500,000 inhabitants, Alexandria was the second city of the Roman empire; it was also the main port of the eastern Mediterranean for state and private shipping, straddling the luxury trade between India and Rome. Fine public and private buildings continued to be erected, and the arts and crafts and intellectual pursuits flourished: notable were glassware manufacture and *medicine. In the 3rd cent. AD the reputed see of St Mark the evangelist became one of the main centres of the Christian Church, revitalizing Alexandria's claims to intellectual, artistic, political, and economic prominence within and beyond Egypt.   D. W. R.

Amazons Athenian ceramic bowl showing a trousered Amazon rider attacking a fallen Greek, *c*.470 BC. The theme was popular in Greek art, especially after the Persian Wars, when Amazons were compared with Persians, another 'womanly' foe from the east.

Amazons, mythical race of female warriors. The name was popularly understood as 'breastless' (*maza*, 'breast') and the story told that they 'pinched out' or 'cauterized' the right breast so as not to impede their javelin-throwing (Apollod. 2. 5. 8, Strabo 11. 5. 1). No real etymology is known.

Epic Amazons exist in order to be fought, and ultimately defeated, by men in an Amazonomachy ('Amazon-battle'). Already in the *Iliad* we hear of Bellerophon killing them in Lycia (6. 186), their defeat at the river Sangarios (near Pessinus, 3. 189), and a tomb of Myrrhine outside Troy (2. 814, cf. Strab. 12. 8. 6). In Arctinus' *Aethiopis* their Thracian queen, Penthesilea 'daughter of *Ares', arrives to help the Trojans, but *Achilles kills her (and Thersites for alleging Achilles loved her). *Heracles' ninth labour was to fetch the girdle of the Amazon queen, Hippolyte, resulting in another Amazonomachy (Apollod. 4. 16). *Theseus joined Heracles and as a result had to defeat an Amazon invasion

of Attica, a story told in a late 6th-cent. BC *Theseid* (story in Plut. *Thes.* 26).

Cult/commemoration Amazon tombs are frequent in central Greece, presumably because of local Amazonomachy myths. They are found at Megara (Paus. 1. 41. 7), *Athens (Paus. 1. 2. 1), Chaeronea, and Chalcis—as well as in *Thessaly at Scotussa and Cynoscephalae (Plut. *Thes.* 27). There was an Amazoneum (shrine of Amazons, implying tombs and cult) at Chalcis and Athens. At Athens there were annual sacrifices to the Amazons on the day before the Thesea. Many Asia Minor settlements were founded by Amazons: Amastris, Sinope, Cyme, Pitana, Priene, Mytilene (*Lesbos), *Ephesus, Smyrna, Myrina (Diod. Sic. 3. 55. 6, Strab. 11. 5. 4). At Ephesus Hippolyte and her Amazons set up a *bretas* (old wooden statue) of Artemis and established an annual circular dance with weapons and shields (Callim. *Hymn* 3. 110; Pind. fr. 174 Snell–Maehler), as performed in historical times by maidens.

Ethnography Amazons, appropriately for a group inverting normal Greek rules, live at the edge of the world. Their usual homeland is next to a river Thermodon in the city of Themiscyra in remote Pontic *Asia Minor (Aesch. *PV* 723–5, Pherec. *FGrH* 3 F 15). Real Amazons would need men for procreation. *Diodorus Siculus' Amazons at the Thermodon cripple their male children (2. 45), but his second set, in Libya (3. 53–4), have house-husbands to whom they return (like Greek males) after their period of military service. In Pseudo-Callisthenes, *Alexander Romance* (2. 25), they keep men across a river. It is part of the mythologizing of *Alexander the Great that stories were quick to surface that he had met Amazons and threatened (Arr. *Anab.* 7. 13; Plut. *Alex.* 46) or pleasured (Diod. Sic. 17. 77) their queen.

Matriarchy and Message Especially since J. J. Bachofen's *Mutterrecht* (1859), Amazons have been used as evidence for an actual matriarchy in prehistoric times. This has seemed an attractive counter to modern male prejudices, but mistakes the nature of myth. Women warriors and hunters are quite frequent in myth and folk-tale (Stith Thompson F 565) and inversely reflect the actual distribution of roles between the sexes. It may be that such inversion in Greece goes back to rituals of the initiation of maidens (cf. Ephesus) and youths (cf. the Thesea), where the definition of gender roles is at issue.

Art Amazonomachies and genre studies of Amazons are represented copiously in art from the late 7th cent. on, propelled by their special importance at Athens. *LIMC* catalogues 819 items.   K. D.

Ammianus Marcellinus (c. AD 330–95), the last great Latin historian of the Roman empire, was born at Syrian *Antioch. His early entry, c.350, into the élite corps of *protectores domestici* may indicate family connections with the imperial service at Antioch, in which case an early acquaintance with the Latin language could be inferred, as well as the Greek which formed the base of his literary education. Assigned by Constantius II to the personal staff of the general Ursicinus, Ammianus saw service in north Italy, Gaul, Germany (the early campaigns of *Julian), Illyricum, and Mesopotamia. It was here, in the siege and capture by the Persians of Amida (mod. Diarbekir) in 359, that the first phase of Ammianus' military career came to an end. He escaped from the city, but Ursicinus was dismissed from office in the aftermath of its fall. Ammianus seems to have returned to Antioch, but subsequently participated in the disastrous Persian campaign of Julian (363). In later years he travelled—to the Black Sea and Egypt, southern Greece, possibly to a Thracian battlefield from the Gothic invasions of 376–8—before he came to Rome in the mid-380s. It was here that he completed his history. The work is composed in 31 books, of which the first thirteen, covering the period from Nerva to 353, seem from the nature of a reference to them by the grammarian Priscian already to have been lost by the early 6th cent. The earlier of the lost books were

apparently not very full or original, but the scale of the narrative enlarged as Ammianus approached his own day. The surviving books describe in great detail the events and personalities of Ammianus' active lifetime through a period of just 25 years, covering the reigns of Constantius II and Julian (353–63), the brief tenure of Jovian (363–4), the joint reigns of Valentinian I (364–75) and Valens (364–78), and the usurpation of Procopius (366). The culmination of the work is the Gothic invasions of 376–8 and the battle of Hadrianople (9 August 378) at which Valens was killed. The period from 378 to the time of publication is alluded to only in passing references which are, however, of value in judging the date of composition of the work; the latest datable events referred to are of 390 and 391, and the history was probably completed very soon after this.

In the earlier books, narrating his service under Ursicinus, Ammianus' own experiences form a major element, and events are largely seen through the often biased eyes of his patron; with their vivid narrative of sometimes very detailed events and the subjectivity of their judgements, these books have seemed to readers to resemble personal memoir rather than formal history. Despite his own participation—which was at a less privileged level than his experiences with Ursicinus—his narrative of the Persian campaign of Julian is less personally involved, relying sometimes on written sources, and the books on Valentinian and Valens are less detailed, and despite moments of intense involvement, not focused on the author's own experiences. The centrepiece of the history was the government, first in Gaul as Caesar and then in the east as sole Augustus, of Julian the Apostate. Ammianus deeply admired Julian, particularly for his military and administrative abilities. He was openly critical of other aspects of Julian's regime, not least his religious policies.

Himself a pagan of a more traditional cast, Ammianus disliked Julian's intolerance, and was hostile to the emperor's devotion to excessive sacrifice, and of his submission to the influence of philosophers who, in the end with disastrous results, indulged Julian's interest in Neoplatonic techniques of divination. The extent to which Ammianus was himself a polemical writer is debated. He did not adopt the openly ideological stance against *Christianity taken by his younger contemporary Eunapius (whose work he seems to have used from time to time). He is however scathing, in satirical fashion, about the ostentation of the bishops of Rome, criticizes those of *Alexandria for their ambition, and ironically refers to the failure of Christianity to live up to its 'pure and simple' professions.

Ammianus' elaborate, individual, and often very intense style is notable for its strong pictorial sense and for its ability to portray character, in which it displays the influence of physiognomical writing and exploits often very vivid comparisons of human character with that of wild beasts. It contains many passages, especially of military narrative, in which individuals are shown at close quarters and in situations of personal stress and great danger. It is influenced too by the language of *satire, as when Ammianus denounces the behaviour of the nobility and common people of Rome, or the behaviour of lawyers. The subject-matter is wide, and the history contains many geographical and ethnographical digressions (describing the non-Roman as well as the Roman worlds), as well as scientific and antiquarian excursuses, in which the author's Greek culture is acknowledged, sometimes with quotations of Greek words in which Ammianus refers to Greek as his 'own' first language. The sources for the lost books are not known, except that Ammianus' back-references do not indicate the large-scale use of Greek sources that would have been possible for him, and there are occasional traces of the lost Latin history known as 'Enmann's *Kaisergeschichte*' which can be seen in other Latin writers of the period such as Aurelius Victor and Eutropius. For the contemporary period, Ammianus' narrative was based on personal knowledge and the accounts of eyewitnesses— those 'versati in medio' referred to in the preface of book 15; some of these, such as the eunuch Eutherius and the senator Praetextatus, can be convincingly identified. Ammianus does not mention the orator Symmachus, and was certainly not the anonymous historian addressed by Symmachus in *Epistolae* 9. 110. In general, his affinities with Roman 'senatorial' circles have been much exaggerated by historians.

Ammianus' work, justly admired by Gibbon, is a classic of Latin historiography, though whether the influence of *Tacitus is more than formal (it would explain the starting-point at the reign of Nerva) is debated. The influence of *Sallust is indicated from time to time, but the most persuasive literary influence is clearly that of *Cicero, whose writings are constantly referred to and alluded to. Greek authors, like *Herodotus, *Thucydides, and *Polybius, are acknowledged at suitable moments but do not seem otherwise to have exercised any real influence upon Ammianus' manner. *Homer and *Virgil are effectively used to give epic scale and colour to the narrative. Affinities with contemporary Latin prose writers are not obvious or extensive; the most obvious, both as to style and content, is perhaps the imperial legislation collected in the Theodosian Code—a comparison by which Ammianus, a lover of settled government and respect for institutions, might not have been offended. See HISTORI-OGRAPHY, ROMAN. J. F. Ma.

amphitheatres The earliest surviving permanent amphitheatres are found in Campania, the well-preserved example at *Pompeii, called *spectacula* by its builders (*CIL* 10. 852), being the only closely datable example (*c*.80 BC). At Rome, although gladiatorial games were held in the *forum Romanum from an early date with spectators accommodated in temporary wooden stands, the first permanent building was erected by Titus Statilius Taurus in the Campus Martius only in 29 BC. Nero built a much larger wooden structure there, destroyed by the fire of AD 64. Rome finally gained a permanent, monumental amphitheatre with the *Colosseum. Amphitheatres are common in the western provinces from the late republic but are rarer in the east, where from the 2nd cent. AD onwards many *theatres were instead adapted for this purpose. The use of gladiatorial techniques for training the Roman army led to small amphitheatres also becoming a normal adjunct of military *camps, the earliest surviving examples being Augustan. These and many of the minor amphitheatres in the provinces were cut into the natural rock or formed from simple earth mounds; wooden structures also continued to be built (Tac. *Ann.* 4. 62). The earliest masonry arenas such as Pompeii and Merida (8 BC) had retaining walls to support earth mounds; self-contained monumental masonry structures (e.g. Arles (Arelate; see next page), El Djem), combining radial and annular vaulted passages to solve problems of access and circulation for large numbers of spectators, mainly appear under the inspiration of the Colosseum. The amphitheatre should be distinguished from the *ludus* or gladiators' training-school, generally having much less seating and a proportionately larger arena. See GLADIATORS. I. A. R.; J. D.

Anacreon, *lyric poet, native of Teos. Little is known of his life. Born perhaps *c*.575–570 (Eusebius gives his floruit as 536/5), he probably joined in the foundation of Abdera in Thrace by the Teans fleeing before the threat of the Persian general Harpagus in 545 (Strabo 14. 1. 30; Aristox. fr. 12 Wehrli, Hdt. 1. 168). He joined the court of Polycrates, tyrant of Samos (Hdt. 3. 121), the most illustrious Greek of the day; *Strabo claims that his 'whole poetry is full of mention of Polycrates' (14. 1. 16), though there is no reference in surviving fragments. Tradition made Anacreon and Polycrates rivals for the love of a Thracian boy, Smerdies, whose hair Polycrates cut off in a fit of jealousy (Stob. 4. 21. 24; Ath. 12. 540e; Ael. *VH* 9. 4); this may be false inference from Anacreon's poetry. After the murder of Polycrates by the Persian satrap Oroetes he joined the Pisistratid court at Athens (see PISISTRATUS); allegedly Pisistratus' son Hipparchus sent a warship to fetch him ([Pl.] *Hipparch.* 228c). According to Plato (*Chrm.* 157e) he praised the family of Critias (grandfather of the oligarch Critias, whose lover he was (schol. Aesch. *PV* 128)). After Hipparchus' murder he may have gone to Thessaly (*Anth. Pal.* 6. 136, 142, if correctly attributed). The fragments suggest that he lived to old age, though the figure of 85 years ([Lucian] *Macr.* 26) cannot be verified. The tradition that he died by choking on a grape (Val. Max. 9. 12) displays the mythopoeia typical of ancient *biography.

He composed in elegiac distichs, iambic and trochaic rhythms, lyric stanzas consisting of glyconics with pherecratean clausula, and ionics (including a form with anaclasis named Anacreontic after him). The dialect is Ionic vernacular with some epicisms. The range of what survives is narrow. Wine and love (both homosexual and heterosexual) figure prominently. His control of form produces an appearance of effortlessness. Many poems

amphitheatres The amphitheatre and (background) theatre at Arelate (Arles), in S. Gaul (late 1st cent. AD). In the Roman west the amphitheatre was the usual setting for *gladiatorial and wild-beast shows; in the east *theatres were adapted instead.

have an epigrammatic quality. Words are positioned with great effect, as in the fr. 357, a prayer to *Dionysus, with the play on the beloved's name and closing revelation that this is a love poem; 358 with the contrast between the fluent first and staccato second half reflecting the move from enchantment to rejection; 395 with its closing wordplay; and 360 with the closing image of the beloved boy as charioteer of the poet's soul. Striking images for love abound (396, 398, 413). Delicacy, wit, paradox, irony, and self-mockery are prominent, as in 417, addressed to a coy girl, represented as a reluctant filly, 347 which laments the loss of a boy's hair in mock-epic terms, the bathos of 359, the idea of riotous decorum in 356a. He also produced biting abuse in the iambic tradition (346, 372, 388). Later sources ascribe maiden-songs to him (Ath. 13. 600d); a possible fragment survives (501). His work was edited by the Alexandrians into at least six books. His wit inspired a corpus of frivolous imitations in and after the Hellenistic period, the *Anacreontea*, which until the 19th cent. were believed to be his work.   C. C.

anatomy and physiology

I The examination of the parts of the body, their forms, location, nature, function, and interrelations (to adapt the list provided by Aulus Cornelius Celsus in the proem to book 1 of the *De medicina*)—whether through dissection (*anatomia*, the title of several ancient medical works, and of a lost work by *Aristotle) or as part of more abstract speculation about natural causes (*physiologia*)—was a concern not only for doctors. Physiology did not have the restricted range it has today; in antiquity it covered all kinds of speculative investigation into nature—in areas ranging from the search for the *soul and its physical location in the body to the explanation of organic processes in animals and plants. This means that ancient medical writers often paid close attention to the work of those whom we might regard today as having quite different concerns. Much early Greek cosmology, for example, was concerned (directly or indirectly) with problems surrounding the nature and origins of life, and the relations between the macroscopic structures of the universe and the microscopic structures of the body. Several Presocratic philosophers of nature advanced speculative models to explain physiological and pathological processes in terms of the transformation and balanced arrangement of one or more types of principal matter which they believed to constitute the universe as a whole. (Ideas of balance and imbalance, democracy and tyranny, symmetry and asymmetry can be seen shaping many different areas of Greek thought, cosmological, political, and physiological.) The influence, both positive and negative, of early cosmological models on Hippocratic physiological theories was often profound—so much so that the author of the Hippocratic treatise *On Ancient Medicine* directed a strong attack on those doctors who borrowed unverifiable hypotheses from the philosophers. See MEDICINE §4.

Modern critics of Greek medicine—particularly those with scientific or medical backgrounds themselves—are often struck by the lack of agreement (even amongst ancient specialists) over the description of the human body's internal structures. And it is true that even in the Hippocratic corpus there is no single, dominant anatomical or physiological treatise. In fact there is little unambiguous, early evidence for dissection as an investigative tool either in the study of anatomy or in the development of physiological theories. It does seem surprising to find Aristotle noting towards the end of the 4th cent. (after the bulk of the Hippocratic treatises were written) that 'the internal parts of the body, especially those of man, are unknown. We must as a result refer to the parts of other creatures with a nature similar to that of humans' (*Hist. an.* 494[b]). Even Galen several hundred years later was still relying on dissections of the Barbary ape for his knowledge of some aspects of human anatomy—yet Galen himself was struck by the lack of interest in anatomy amongst the earliest Greek doctors.

The reasons for this state of affairs (which seemed as surprising to many later Greek medical authorities as it does to some of us today) are extremely complex and this article aims merely at summary and general description. Galen's explanation was simple: The earliest doctors treated medicine as a craft, and medical knowledge was handed down from father to son. There seemed little point in writing down information which could more readily be obtained by direct inquiry. In contrast, conventional modern explanations of the situation have tended to focus on the widespread ancient taboos against dissection—especially human dissection—which persisted throughout antiquity. Such taboos there certainly were, however surprising this may seem in societies which otherwise tolerated the murder of men and women in the name of public entertainment. In spite of evidence that the dissection of animals played an increasingly important role in the study of human medicine after Aristotle, it is not at all easy to assess the status of the early, pre-Aristotelian evidence.

While it is widely believed that early in the 5th cent. BC Alcmaeon of Croton pursued anatomical studies of animals, there is little agreement (modern or ancient) as to just how far he went. Later ancient witnesses attribute to him pioneering work on the anatomy of the eye and its communication with the brain, the ear, the nasal passages, and the embryo, and more controversially the blood-vascular system (DK 24 A 5–18). As none of his own work survives intact, we are hardly in a position to judge just how far his research was based on autopsy, let alone its general motivations. The judgement of the early evidence is further complicated by the problem of the lack of technical anatomical vocabulary. Much apparently technical information may have been more or less common knowledge. At Aristophanes' *Frogs* 134 for instance, the comic Dionysus fears that by jumping off a tall building he will 'destroy two rissole wrappers of his brain'; should this metaphor have occurred in a medical treatise, we might immediately assume that it displayed more or less specialized autoptic experience of the brain. In fact it is not until Hellenistic times that a detailed anatomical vocabulary develops in earnest, and even then it grows by naming parts of the body through analogy with familar external objects. This is the procedure which had already been advocated by the author of the Hippocratic treatise *On Ancient Medicine* (22) to aid the comprehension of the functions of internal parts, of which he had only the vaguest idea: 'It is necessary to learn about [internal structures] from external ones which are evident to us,' he notes. The problem of anatomical nomenclature, its poverty and the lack of standardization was still so serious in the 2nd cent. AD that Rufus of Ephesus and Galen himself devoted several treatises specifically to this subject.

Acute observations of physiological processes such as respiration, sensation, digestion, and excretion, were often incorporated into highly speculative theories without these observations themselves being the subject of practical verification. It seems that traditional anatomical models could also take on authoritative status in some quarters. Scenes of wounding in the Homeric epics point to the existence of traditional models to describe the internal structure of the body which became part of the furniture for some medical writers. For instance, *Il.* 13. 545–9: 'Antilochus watched Thoon as he turned around, and then rushed at him, thrusting. He severed the whole vein (*phleps*) which runs right up the back to the neck—he severed the whole of it. Thoon fell back and lay in the dust, stretching out both his hands to his friends.' In some cases it was a long time before this kind of literary tradition was displaced by the results of autopsy. A much later ancient commentator on this Homeric passage noted that 'here the poet is an anatomist. He refers to the so-called "hollow vein" [*koilē phleps*, the Greek term for the *vena cava*] which runs from the right of the spine, from the liver, passes over the diaphragm to the heart and from there to the neck.' Homer is a special case, of course, and the non-medical writers often preserve important observations which were never taken up at all. The phenomenon of contagion, for example, described by *Thucydides in his account of the great plague at Athens in 430 BC (2. 47), and hinted at in the first choral ode of Sophocles' *Oedipus*, was not examined in detail by the very doctors whom Thucydides tells us were the first to suffer.

II Much early work on the structure of the body focused on the skeleton and the vascular system. One of the earliest surviving accounts of the way in which parts communicate with each other is preserved by Aristotle; it is striking for the few signs it shows of close acquaintance with the physical appearance of the structures it describes. Aristotle reports (*Hist. an.* 512^{a}4 ff.) that Diogenes of Apollonia in the 5th cent. had posited a blood-vascular system of ducts (*phlebes*) distributed throughout the body, divided into two independent networks each serving one side of the body. The network on the right originated in the liver, and was probably called *hēpatitis*, while that on

the left, *splēnitis*, came from the spleen. It is likely that surface anatomy (especially in connection with parts like the neck where internal structures stand out) played a part in the establishment of models such as this one; perhaps experience derived from the practice of therapeutic measures such as venesection was also relevant. Most significant, perhaps, is the underlying assumption here that the bilateral symmetry exhibited by the body externally should in some way be reflected internally.

Vessels, pores, and ducts, visible and theoretical, figure prominently in many ancient physiological theories. It is not clear from Aristotle's account of Diogenes exactly what the vessels carried, nor what function his model played in his physiological theory. One late doxographical source (Aëtius, DK 64 A 29) reports that they carried air. (Air was known to be necessary to life and vital for the functioning of the senses; it was not known until much later, of course, exactly what happened to inspired air. A large group of ancient theorists, many of them still active in Galen's day, believed that inspired air (*pneuma*) passes from the lungs via the heart into the arteries). Diogenes' 'ducts' probably carried a variety of fluids around the body, including air. Diogenes may or may not have been a doctor himself; certainly he was a cosmologist, and it seems likely that his physiological and anatomical work was related to his cosmology, and in particular to his idea that air has some kind of elemental status, and is to be associated with the cognitive faculties in animals.

Aristotle mentions two other similar early models of internal anatomical structures; one he attributes to the otherwise unknown Syennesis of Cyprus, and the other to Polybus, supposed by many to have been the son-in-law of Hippocrates. An account similar to that of Polybus appears in the Hippocratic treatise *On the Nature of Man* (ch. 11); it might be noted that the surviving Hippocratic accounts of vascular anatomy are not as a rule as detailed as these three cited by Aristotle. (Although, as exceptions, one should note the little-known Hippocratic treatises *On the Nature of Bones*, *On Anatomy*, *On Fleshes*, and the later (4th-cent.) work *On the Heart*.)

Along with early work on the anatomy of the vascular system comes speculation about the seat of cognition, and the ways in which the senses communicate with each other and the so-called 'command centre' of the body. Some early authorities, including in all probability Alcmaeon of Croton, Diogenes of Apollonia, and by implication the author of the Hippocratic *Sacred Disease*, argued for the brain's primary role here, but *Plato moved the command centre to the heart (*Ti.* 70a ff.), followed by Aristotle and Diocles of Carystus. The debate continued until Galen reasserted the very early primacy of the liver in the 2nd cent. AD.

In the Hippocratic writings, then, pathological commentary and physiological theory tend to be more detailed than empirical knowledge of internal anatomy. The author of *Sacred Disease*, famous for the argument that epilepsy has a natural cause, offers a convenient example of the priority of theory, even in cases where autopsy is brought to the fore. He insists that epilepsy has its origin in the brain; assuming that the human brain is fundamentally the same as the brain in all other animals, he describes the examination of the brain of a similarly afflicted goat. 'On opening the head', he claims, 'the brain will be found to be wet, full of fluid, and foul-smelling—persuasive proof that the disease and not a deity is causing the harm.' Adherents of humoral theories similarly tended to locate the source of the humours in specific organs which seemed a priori to be appropriate. Typically for many Hippocratic authors, bile comes from the liver and phlegm from the head. External examination of the state of the most prominent vessels which allowed the communication of these fluids through the body could be an important part of a general assessment of the state of the body.

III With *Aristotle, there is much stronger evidence that physiological theory can be related to empirical investigation. (Some modern scholars hold that Aristotle may even have dissected a human embryo, but the evidence (*Hist. an.* 583^{b}14) is inconclusive. It seems unlikely, on balance, that Aristotle dissected human subjects.) In the first book of the treatise *On the Parts of Animals*, Aristotle stresses the importance of autopsy as a preliminary to theory, however disagreeable this may be. In the *History of Animals*, he went on to provide detailed, observationally based accounts of the vascular system and the internal geography of the body, and a whole range of physiological theories explaining digestion, respiration, etc. in the treatises which make up the so-called *Parva naturalia*. See ANIMALS, KNOWLEDGE ABOUT § II.

IV After Aristotle, it seems that more and more doctors began to employ animal dissection—including vivisection—but human dissection probably remained the exception and not the rule. Diocles of Carystus (credited by Galen with having composed the first anatomical handbook (fr. 23 Wellmann)) made important observations about the anatomy of the womb (fr. 27 Wellmann). Praxagoras of Cos is traditionally credited with drawing the distinction between veins and arteries, and doing important work on neural anatomy. As the teacher of Herophilus of Chalcedon, Praxagoras stands at the beginning of one of the most fruitful periods of anatomical investigation in the history of medicine. Herophilus' and Erasistratus' work in dissection—notably human dissection—led to a dramatic development of anatomical knowledge. Celsus reports that they were given condemned criminals and performed vivisections on them; although the evidence for this has been questioned in some quarters, most modern scholars seem to accept its plausibility, and, at the very least, it seems likely that Herophilus was one of the first physicians to make systematic use of human dissection. He made important discoveries about the anatomy of the eye, the male and female reproductive systems, and the blood-vascular system. Most famous, perhaps, was his work on the nerves; it seems likely that he

was the first to discern them, and perhaps the first to make the distinction between motor and sensory nerves.

In Hellenistic physiological theory we find the marriage of physics and anatomy developing in many ways. Erasistratus, credited by Galen with new anatomical work on the structure of the heart and the blood-vascular system, developed a theory which explained the origins of the body in terms of agglomerations of an elemental complex of vein, artery, and nerve. Asclepiades of Bithynia seems to have taken this type of idea further, reducing the body's component parts to elementary corpuscles and pores whose constant motion accounted for the change and unpredictability of physiological and pathological phenomena. The Asclepiadean theory, with its insistence that health and disease—indeed all physiological processes—can be understood in terms of the proper movement of these corpuscles in the pores, had the effect of dampening commitment to anatomical investigation amongst his many intellectual progeny. But not all; although the Methodists argued that the study of anatomy was rather beside the point, given their insistence that all the doctor needed to know about disease could be learned from the phenomenal presentation of two or three morbid states in the body, Soranus of Ephesus made a considerable contribution to female anatomy in his *Gynaecology*. At the beginning of this work, Soranus notes that 'since we are now about to pass to the section on gynaecological hygiene, it will first be necessary to explain the nature of the female parts. Some of this can be learned directly, some from dissection. And since dissection, although useless, is nevertheless studied for the sake of profound learning, we shall also teach what has been discovered by it' (I. 2. 5, trans. O. Temkin). There follows a remarkably detailed account of the anatomy of the female reproductive system. (See GYNAECOLOGY.)

Not all doctors placed anatomy at the service of physiology. Another group, active from the 2nd cent. BC onwards, associated themselves more or less directly with a current in Pyrrhonian scepticism, and marshalled powerful arguments against the value of physiological speculation in the practice of medicine. Pointing to the kinds of disagreements amongst dogmatic exponents of medical theories which had so frustrated even the Hippocratic author of *On Ancient Medicine*, it was argued that experience was the only true teacher in medicine. Medical empiricism placed restrictions on the amount of research it was sensible for a doctor to pursue given the futility of theory-building, although anatomical investigation of accident victims remained—as it always had been—a valid way of gathering knowledge.

V Galen's very importance as anatomist and physiologist makes any detailed treatment here quite impossible, and any summary treatment would be misleading. Best simply to quote Galen's own advice to the intending student of his anatomical and physiological theories, adapted from his work *On the Order of his Own Books*. '... *On Bones, for*

Beginners. This is the first part of the course of anatomy; … then … approach the *Anatomical Administrations*. This work teaches the parts revealed in anatomy, their size, position shaping, interrelations, appearance, and similarities with each other. The man who is experienced in the observation of these things through anatomy will then go on to learn about their activities—their natural activities, written about in three books of comment entitled *On the Natural Faculties*. The faculties of the soul, as they are called, are dealt with in several other works, of which *On the Anatomy of the Dead* [lost] comes first, and then two books *On the Anatomy of the Living* [lost], and besides these, two more *On Anatomical Disagreements* [lost]. Next after these come three books *On the Motion of the Abdomen and the Lungs* [lost], two *On the Causes of Respiration*, and four books *On the Voice*. In the same category comes the work *On the Movement of the Muscles*. I have set out my investigations into the "ruling part", and all the other inquiries into physical and psychical activities in a number of books which I wrote *On the Doctrines of Hippocrates and Plato*. Next comes the specialized work *On the Seed*, and then *On the Anatomy of Hippocrates*. The treatise *On the Usefulness of the Parts* follows on all these.

'The material origins of the generation of all things in existence lie in the four elements, which are naturally mixed completely with one another, and which act on one another. This is proved in the first book of *On [Medical] Names*, and in *On the Elements according to Hippocrates*. I do not cover everything relating to the proof of the elements in this little book, but only those features of it which were used by Hippocrates. For the most complete account of the science of the elements of the body the reader is referred to what I said in book 13 of *On Demonstration* [lost], and in books 5 and 6 of *On the Doctrines of Asclepiades* [lost]. … Three books of comments *On Mixtures* follow the work *On the Elements according to Hippocrates*, and after these the treatise *On the Faculties of Simple Drugs*, followed by the treatise *On Compound Drugs*. In the first books the mixtures present in animals are discussed along with the special features of each, and in the third book the discussion is about the mixture of drugs. If you like, whether after two or after three books, you may read about the *Best Constitution of the Body* [lost], *On the Good State of Being*, and *On Anomalous Bad Temperament*, in that order …'

Galen's own work, and his summary of his predecessors' work, played the dominant role in preserving ancient anatomical and physiological knowledge for the Middle Ages and Renaissance. On this and the individual medical writers mentioned above, see MEDICINE.   J. T. V.

Andocides (*c*.440–*c*.390 BC), a member of a distinguished aristocratic family, whose grandfather had been one of the ten Athenian envoys who negotiated the Thirty Years Peace of 446. In 415, shortly before the great expedition to Sicily was due to depart, the Athenians were greatly dismayed one morning to discover that in the night the statues of *Hermes around the city had been mutilated:

Hermes being the god of travellers, this act was presumably intended to affect the progress of the expedition, but it was also taken, curiously, as a sign that the democracy itself was in danger. In the subsequent accusations the young Andocides and his associates in a club (*hetaireia*), which was probably suspected of oligarchic tendencies, were named as having shared both in the mutilations and in profane parodies of the Eleusinian mysteries (see DEMETER; ELEUSIS), and were arrested. Andocides, to secure immunity and, as he claimed, to save his father, confessed to a share in the mutilations and gave an account of the whole affair which, though it may have been far from the truth, was readily accepted by the Athenians. This secured his release, but shortly afterwards, when the decree of Isotimides, aimed at him especially, forbade those who had confessed to an act of impiety to enter temples or the *Agora, Andocides preferred to leave the city and began to trade as a merchant, in which role he developed connections all over the Aegean and in Sicily and Italy. In 411, seeking to restore himself to favour at Athens, he provided oars at cost price to the fleet in Samos, and shortly afterwards returned to Athens to plead for the removal of the limitation on his rights. Unfortunately for him, the revolution of the Four Hundred (see ATHENS (HISTORY)) had just installed in power the very class of citizens whom his confession had affected, and he was put into prison and maltreated. Released, perhaps at the fall of the Four Hundred, he returned to his trading, in the course of which he was for a while imprisoned by Evagoras, the king of Cyprus. At some time after the re-establishment of the democracy in 410, he returned to the city to renew his plea (the speech *De reditu* belongs to this occasion) but he was again unsuccessful. Returning finally under the amnesty of 403, he resumed full participation in public life, and in 400 (or 399) successfully defended himself in the *De mysteriis* against an attempt to have him treated as still subject to the decree of Isotimides: the sixth speech of the Lysian corpus (see LYSIAS), *Against Andocides*, was delivered by one of his accusers. In 392/391 he was one of the Athenian envoys sent to Sparta to discuss the making of peace, and on his return in the debate in the assembly he delivered the *De pace* urging acceptance of the proffered terms, which were in fact very similar to those of the King's Peace of 387/386. The Athenians, however, rejected the peace, and Andocides and the other envoys were prosecuted by the young Callistratus. Andocides anticipated condemnation by retiring into exile, and we hear no more of him.

Speeches In addition to the three speeches mentioned above, there is a fourth speech, *Against Alcibiades*, preserved under his name, which purports to be concerned with an *ostracism in 415; most scholars regard this as a forgery. Fragments of four other speeches are preserved.

Greek and Roman critics discovered in Andocides faults which, according to their canons, were serious; and admittedly the faults are there. He sometimes carries the use of parenthesis to absurd extremes; he cannot keep to one point at a time; his style is so loose that the argument is hard to follow. On the other hand, this inconsequential method of expression is at times effective, giving the impression of an eagerness which outruns premeditated art. He possessed a natural gift of expression, a fine flow of words, and a good narrative style. He was not a professional rhetorician, and if he neglected scholastic rules, it can at least be claimed for him that he was successful on his own unconventional lines.   G. L. C.

animals, attitudes to This was the subject of a huge debate among the philosophers. Already in the 6th and 5th cents. BC *Pythagoras and Empedocles had attacked the killing or maltreatment of animals, partly on the grounds that transmigration made us literally akin to them. But vegetarianism was made difficult by the mutual interconnections between religious sacrifice and meat-eating. Justice was treated as a gift of God to benefit humans, not animals, both by *Hesiod and in the myth ascribed to Protagoras in *Plato's *Protagoras*. Little was conceded by Democritus' extending considerations of criminal justice to dangerous animals.

The decisive step, however, was taken not by the Presocratics, but by *Aristotle, who denied reason and belief to animals. Compensatingly, he allowed them a rich perceptual life, which he carefully disentangled from reliance on reason or belief. In ethics, he surprisingly combined the view that animals can be praised and blamed for their voluntary acts with the view that we owe them no justice, because we have nothing in common, and can conduct a just war against them. Aristotle's successor Theophrastus disagreed. We are, in an extended sense, akin (*oikeioi*) even in reasonings, and killing non-dangerous animals is unjust.

The Epicureans and Stoics (see EPICURUS; STOICISM) sided with Aristotle in denying reason to animals, and hence justice. Only *Plutarch was to ask 'why not kindness, if not justice?' The Epicurean rationale, clearest in Hermarchus, is that justice is owed only where there is a contract, hence only among rational agents, *pace* Democritus. The Stoics denied that animals, as non-rational, could be treated as belonging (*oikeiōsis*: lit. a welcoming into the household)— and that despite the prevalence of animal pets. Hence justice could not be extended to them. Unlike Aristotle, they denied animals memory, emotion, foresight, intention, and voluntary acts.

From then on, the philosophical debate turned on animal rationality. Animal pain and terror were seldom cited before Porphyry. Pythagoras and Apuleius exploited them only in the case of humans transformed into animals. Outside philosophy, attitudes were sometimes broader. The Athenians punished a man for flaying a ram alive. When *Pompey staged a slaughter of *elephants, the public was more concerned for the terrified elephants, the Stoic *Seneca for the loss of human life. The philosophers' praise of animals is sometimes only to downgrade humans (the *Cynics) or glorify the Creator (*Augustine),

while vegetarianism was often based merely on ascetic or medical grounds.

The chief defenders of animals, in response to the Stoics, were the Neopythagoreans and certain Platonists. Defences are recorded in Philon *De animalibus* and Origen *Against Celsus*. Plutarch's *Moralia* contains three treatises in defence. But by far the most important work is Porphyry's *On Abstinence from Animal Food*. Of its four books, the first records the case against animals, but forbids meat on ascetic grounds; the second rejects animal sacrifice; the third claims rationality and justice for animals; the fourth is an anthropology of vegetarian nations. But Porphyry's probable pupil Iamblichus felt it necessary to reinstate sacrifice. To defend this, he reinterpreted Pythagoras' and Plato's belief in transmigration of human souls into animals, the first as excluding sacrificial animals, the second as metaphorical. He denied a rational soul to animals, and his pupil Theodore insisted that human souls could act on animals only by remote control, not by genuine transmigration.

The western Christian tradition was fatefully influenced by Augustine who ignored the pro-animal side of this debate and backed the Stoic ground for killing animals, thus departing from such predecessors as Arnobius and Lactantius, who had allowed animals rationality.

Given the extensive use of animals in antiquity, it would have been as hard to give up killing them as to give up slaves, and one of the justifications offered was that civilization would break down.

See also ANIMALS, KNOWLEDGE ABOUT; SACRIFICE, GREEK and ROMAN.   R. R. K. S.

animals, knowledge about

I Animals are the mirror of nature, claimed *Epicurus (quoted in Cic. *Fin.* 2. 32), echoing a view widely held in different ways throughout antiquity. But others added that animals mirror culture as well; Greek and Roman writing and thinking about animals was as often ethical as what we might call scientific in character. Hardly surprisingly, the archaeological record provides ample evidence that animals were closely observed by artists, and further evidence for the ancient study of animals comes from early medical observations about the role of animals and animal products in human regimen. Yet the term *zōologia* seems not to occur in any surviving classical work, and the earliest English uses of 'zoology' refer more often than not to the study of the medicinal uses of animal products.

In the Homeric epics, animals exemplify many types of human qualities. Lions are brave, deer are prone to flight, bees swarm like crowds of people, dogs tread the treacherous path between loyalty and servility. (The story of Odysseus' dog, who died of joy on recognizing the scent of his long-lost master, was regarded by the later medical Empiricists as a miracle of diagnosis.) A great many similar examples can be found in the early Greek lyric poets. In the late 7th cent. BC, Semonides of Amorgos wrote a poem comparing animals with different types of women; the only good woman is like a bee, the best of a terrible collection. Specific qualities retain their associations with specific animals. *Herodotus' story of Arion's rescue from pirates by a dolphin stands at the head of a long line of similar tales about these intelligent and compassionate creatures. Much later, *Plutarch marvelled at the society of ants in their anthills, and in a series of treatises (including the *De sollertia animalium*, *De esu carnium*, and *Bruta animalia ratione uti*) considered the problems of whether animals have souls and the capacity for reason, and feeling. (The debate about the minds of animals, the morality of killing them for sport and food, or even using them as beasts of burden, was a lively one.) If Plutarch allowed animals some degree of intellect, the opposing view that animals possessed vitality (*anima*) without rationality (*animus*) was perhaps dominant; thus man and animals were kept apart. The ethical, metaphorical, use of animals to explain the organization of human society reaches its fullest expression in the anecdotal zoology of Aelian, which was composed in the time of Hadrian, in the Aesopic collection of Fables, and ultimately in the medieval bestiaries.

Animals were also organized physically. The Romans in particular collected animals from all over the world in zoos and menageries, often preserving monstrous creatures from unnatural births as aids to divination.

Early philosophers of nature were not innocent of these ethical concerns. There was a considerable amount of cross-fertilization between what we might call ethical (or psychological) and 'scientific' zoology; *Aristotle for instance makes frequent observations about the social behaviour of animals in the *Historia animalium*, and throughout the zoological works he cites poets, dramatists, and historians as well as less 'high' literary sources. Yet the question of the physiological origins of animal life was, of course, a central concern for many Presocratic cosmologists, and fragments survive of a number of biological theories. Amongst the earliest surviving accounts is that of Anaximander, who is reported to have claimed that living creatures were generated in moisture, perhaps slime, protected by thorny bark, and that they grew drier and more self-supporting with age. Animals are soon able to sustain themselves, he claimed, but man alone, born initially inside some kind of fish, lacks self-sufficiency and needs prolonged nursing. Anaximander's account is notable for the importance it accords the animal's environment in its development. In Empedocles' theory on the other hand, blood, bones, and flesh arose out of combinations of the elements. They then formed solitary limbs which wandered the earth in search of other parts with which to combine. The evidence for Empedocles refers to monstrous creatures, men with the faces of oxen, and oxen with the faces of men, which lived during the early stages of the development of man. (See ANATOMY AND PHYSIOLOGY; ANTHROPOLOGY.)

Early evidence for the systematic study of animal physiology is sparse, and signs of attempts at zoological taxon-

omy still more so. In one well-known early case, the author of the Hippocratic treatise *On Regimen* 2 organizes the (mainly edible) animals which concern him into land, sea, and air creatures (2. 46–8), with further subdivisions on the basis of whether they are wild or domestic. (See MEDICINE §4) Medical writers continued to preserve and amplify observations about the dietary and pharmaceutical properties of animals and animal products including hair, urine, and excrement.

Non-medical authors had their own interests. *Plato is particularly associated with the use of a method (variously applied) which involved the progressive division of objects into typical pairs. Setting up patterns based on pairs of opposed *differentiae*, he might divide animals into 'walking' or 'aquatic', and aquatic in turn into 'winged' and 'water dwelling', and so on. It is not at all clear how far Plato developed this way of thinking in the direction of animal taxonomy, and the main Platonic texts (*Soph.* 220a–b, *Plt.* 264d, *Leg.* 823b) offer far from consistent examples of the uses to which division might be put. On the other hand, Aristotle seems to have Plato's method of division in mind at several points where he is himself apparently dealing with the problems of animal classification (e.g. in *Top.* 6). Plato's successor as head of the *Academy, Speusippus, is credited in a few fragments with having written a work *On Similarities*, in which animals with similar appearances may have been grouped together (see Ath. 105b). Speusippus is also credited with some new coinages in which some scholars see signs of taxonomical concerns—the word *malakostraka*, for instance, to describe soft-shelled creatures is particularly associated with him. On balance, however, very little is known about Speusippus, and the motivations behind Plato's method of division are certainly not linked primarily to zoological taxonomy.

II The earliest surviving systematic studies of the physical nature of animals are those of Aristotle—many would insist that no one in antiquity after Aristotle rivalled the breadth and depth of his interests. The biological treatises account for well over 20 per cent of the surviving Aristotelian corpus, and lists of Aristotle's works preserved by Diogenes Laertius and Hesychius suggest that there is much more that has not survived. In spite of the amount of material, there is little agreement today even about the aims of Aristotle's zoological investigations. It is probably fair to say—though some are reluctant to go even this far—that he was the first to devise a detailed zoological taxonomy and that this formed an important part of his general study of the *physics of the sublunary sphere. (His pupil Theophrastus carried this work further, applying Aristotelian methods to botany.)

In his famous exhortation to the study of animals (*De partibus animalium* I. 5), Aristotle speaks of the low status enjoyed by the enterprise—some philosophers, he says, considered the subject matter trivial or even disagreeable—but he maintains that the study of even the meanest of creatures is worth while if only because the means to discover their beauty, form, and purpose are close at hand. Modern disagreement about the nature of Aristotle's zoological enterprise is due in part to the difficulty of arranging the relevant treatises in a clear chronological sequence. (In particular, it is very difficult to decide exactly when most of Aristotle's empirical research was done. Some scholars feel that much must have been done during his stay on the island of Lesbos, in his middle years; others argue that the practical investigation was done late in life, after he had laid the theoretical foundations of his philosophy.) Aristotle himself would have us approach his work on animals as an example of his scientific method in action and in this briefest of summaries it is convenient to follow, albeit cautiously, Aristotle's own plan.

In the treatises which make up the so-called *Organon* (in particular, the *Posterior Analytics*), Aristotle set out the goals of scientific inquiry. He stressed the importance of firm, logically tested scientific knowledge, and elaborated the deductive apparatus for its achievement. In practice, Aristotle's method meant that he could begin an investigation into animals, for example, by collecting the relevant material—observations, information from others, along with the results of a preliminary assessment of these data, all of which go to make up what he calls the 'phenomena', together with the opinions of earlier authorities. Not all the phenomena are the result of autopsy—Aristotle himself acknowledges debts to all kinds of people, and the elder *Pliny noted that with the help of *Alexander the Great, Aristotle was able to order thousands of fowlers, fishermen, beekeepers, hunters, and herdsmen to inform him about every creature they encountered (*HN* 8. 44). None the less, Aristotle's commitment to personal, autoptic research, often through dissection, must not be forgotten.

The results of the first step in Aristotle's zoological investigation are set out in the *Historia animalium* ('Researches into Animals'). The range covered is extraordinary—the lives, breeding habits, and structure of some 540 different genera. Modern students of the Life Sciences tend to highlight certain areas of practical research in which Aristotle was ultimately deemed by modern standards to have been particularly successful. The following (traditional) list is far from complete. (*a*) Investigations of the developing chick, the classical embryological subject ever since. (*b*) Detailed descriptions of the habits and development of octopuses and squids. (*c*) Anatomical accounts of the four-chambered stomach of ruminants, of the complex relations of the ducts, vessels, and organs in the mammalian generative system, and of the mammalian character of porpoises, dolphins, and whales, all unsurpassed until the 17th cent. (*d*) Accounts of exceptional modes of development of fish, among them a dog-fish (*Mustelus laevis*), the young of which is linked to the womb by a navel cord and placenta much as in a mammal. The accuracy of Aristotle's observations was confirmed only a century ago.

Such a huge amount of raw material needed to be organized in some provisional way; listing the 'differences'

between animals, Aristotle arranged his evidence in the *Historia animalium* under preliminary headings. He drew a broad distinction, for example, between bloodless and blooded creatures. Bloodless animals (of which he enumerates around 120 altogether) are of four main types, usually rendered in the following way: cephalopods (*malakia*), crustacea (*malakostraka*), testacea (*ostrakoderma*), and insects (*entoma*). Blooded animals include man, viviparous quadrupeds and cetacea, oviparous quadrupeds and animals without feet, birds, and fish. This is seen in itself as an exercise in taxonomy by many modern scholars, but while taxonomy is certainly implicit throughout the work, Aristotle himself seems quite clear about his own goals. At *Hist. an.* 1. 1–6, he offers a list of very broad genera into which animals can be placed, but does not explain the list, remarking at 1. 6 that his talk of animal genera at this stage in the inquiry is a 'kind of sample of the range of subjects and attributes which we will need to think about. We will go into these problems in detail later on.'

In the *De partibus animalium* ('On the Parts of Animals') problems of division are addressed in detail, as are other theoretical questions about the relative importance of the various causal factors which all need to be understood if an animal's existence is to be properly explained. In general, Aristotle advocates investigating the attributes common to a group of animals, then explaining their existence ultimately in terms of their purpose (the Final Cause). He also includes accounts of the matter from which they come (the Material Cause), the process which led to their generation (the Efficient Cause), and their shape (the Formal Cause). The parts of animals are divided into those whose division yields a part which can be called by the same name as the whole—flesh, hair, bone, blood, marrow, milk, cartilage, etc.—sometimes called *homoiomeria* or 'uniform' parts (dealt with especially at *Hist. an.* 3. 2–17, and *Part. an.* 2. 1–9), and those whose division yields something with a different name—hands for instance, whose parts cannot be called 'hands', faces, skeletal structures, the internal organs, and so on. These are the *anhomoiomeria* or 'non-uniform' parts, and they are chiefly described and their functions discussed at *Hist. an.* 1. 7–14, 2. 8–12, 3. 1–11, and *Part. an.* 2–4. Concentrating attention exclusively on these characteristics as a prelude to explanation is not enough, and Aristotle criticizes certain of his predecessors for privileging the matter of an animal, and the material aspects of its generation, over its *raison d'être*. Empedocles, for example, is criticized for explaining the articulation of the spine in man by arguing that the foetus is twisted in the womb. Aristotle on the other hand argued that the vertebrae exist because they existed in the father, because they allow movement, and because without them the offspring could not become a man. Aristotelian explanation in zoology is dominated by questions of purpose and function.

Aristotle's licence to study the biological world was bought partially by insisting that the kind of reality which Plato would only allow his perfect Forms exists in the forms of things around us. While the Creator of Plato's physical world strives to copy the Forms with varying degrees of success, Aristotle argued that the good of a particular animal, or part of an animal, is explicable in terms of that animal's contribution to its own survival, or the survival of its species. This does not lead to inflexibility; some things may be necessarily so without any obvious purpose—the colour of one's eyes, the existence of breasts in men, and so on—but Aristotelian teleological explanation can deal even with them as instances of natural necessity. (The discussion of so-called 'inessential characteristics' occupies much of *De generatione animalium* 5.)

At the beginning of book two of the *Parts of Animals*, then, Aristotle is able to say, 'I have set forth the parts out of which each of the animals is composed, and their number, in the *History of Animals*. Now I must examine the causes by which each animal has the nature it does, leaving aside what was said in the *History*.' In the following three books, Aristotle proceeds to develop his classification, and in particular his ideas about how different groups and subgroups can be practically distinguished. The language Aristotle uses to describe these different groups and types varies somewhat. Terms like *genos* ('kind') and *eidos* (often translated 'species') are to some extent context-relative, even if the Aristotelian species are themselves fixed and unchanging.

Problems related to the origins and means of animal locomotion are investigated in the *De motu animalium* ('On the Movement of Animals') and the *De incessu animalium* ('On the Progression of Animals'). But how does the soul move the body? What is the ultimate source of movement? Aristotle elaborates his ideas about the 'unmoved mover' in many different contexts, but the specific problems raised here lead into the detailed investigation presented in the *De anima* ('On the Soul'). Physiological and psychological problems—the nature of respiration, life and death, dreams, perception, etc.—are investigated in the nine short treatises which make up the *Parva naturalia*.

The temptation to portray Aristotle as a proto-Linnaeus, held back only by his speculative understanding of physiological processes, has proved a very strong one. Others are so keen to resist this temptation that they seek quite different motivations behind the zoology. They argue that Aristotle's central concern in gathering all the biological data is to test practically the theoretical and logical devices he developed in the *Organon*. It seems more reasonable to tread a middle path, which allows a proper appreciation of the striking amount of highly detailed, empirical research of great quality which is preserved in the Aristotelian zoological treatises, whilst also keeping in mind the role of Aristotle's conception of science and scientific method in guiding his eyes.

III Zoological research of the type pursued by Aristotle seems subsequently to have been pursued with little commitment, although there is evidence to suggest that Diocles of Carystus performed animal dissections. Where

botanical research (see BOTANY) often yielded important benefits in areas such as pharmacy, the pure study of animals attracted remarkably few students, and later, non-ethical, work on animals tends either to be practical—for example, in the form of anatomical studies for doctors who were fundamentally concerned with humans but unable to dissect them freely—or related to sport. There survive a number of prose and verse works on hunting, shooting, and fishing in the style of *Xenophon's Cynegetica*, or the hexameter poetry of Oppian. There also survives a considerable corpus of veterinary writings in both Greek and Latin.

Pliny's *Natural History* contains the most extensive collection of zoological and botanical material after Aristotle and Theophrastus. In fact, much of it comes ultimately from Aristotle and Theophrastus, although the material is not organized according to the same kinds of principles. Pliny begins his (often anecdotal) account of animals with those that live on land (book 8). First comes the elephant, a creature which possesses a variety of human characteristics, or qualities that closely resemble them, including language, memory, sense of honour, and piety. Pliny evinces a romantic sympathy for many creatures; he relates the story of a literate elephant who was able to trace in Greek on the sand 'I, the elephant, wrote this' (8. 6). Creatures in the sea form the subject of book 9; birds and insects are dealt with in book 11, which ends with an enumeration of creatures notable for their small size. Animals, for Pliny, have their own worlds, their own societies, their own discoveries, which they make by accident, lacking the *ratio*—power of reasoning—necessary to solve their problems by deliberation. It might reasonably be said that this was the animal world which antiquity handed on to the Middle Ages.

J. T. V.

anthropology It is probably misleading, though not entirely inappropriate, to use this word to describe the ancient study of man and society. Misleading, because anthropology did not really exist as the kind of discrete discipline it is today. What follows here is a very brief summary of some central anthropological themes from antiquity, gathered from a variety of sources and contexts, ethical, scientific, and literary.

The Greeks and Romans developed a range of ideas about their own identity and the identity of others; about the nature of human societies, their history, and organization. It is well known that many Greeks designated non-Greek speakers '*barbarian'—after the Greek verb for 'babble'—and language of course remained an important index of racial and cultural difference. (*Herodotus's *History* introduced many Greeks to foreigners and their customs for the first time: Hdt. 4. 183 notes that the Egyptian Trogodytae 'squeak like bats'; elsewhere, e.g. Aesch. *Ag.* 1050, Hdt. 2. 57, Theoc. *Id.* 15. 87 ff., etc., strange tongues are likened to the language of birds.) Language served equally to differentiate Greek-speaking groups—the various Greek dialects had their own distinctive written as well as spoken forms. But thought was also given by poets, philosophers, doctors, and others to defining what it is to be human (an *anthrōpos*), what separates mankind from animals and gods, men from women, men and women from children, and so on. Amongst many possible examples, one might mention the use of animal similes and metaphors in the Homeric epics (see HOMER) as aids to understanding human behaviour, Semonides' misogynistic poem attributing various animal characteristics to different kinds of women (see ANIMALS, KNOWLEDGE ABOUT), the Hesiodic *Works and Days* (see HESIOD) where man is distinguished from brute beasts through his possession of justice, and medical works concerned with issues such as the physiological difference between male and female, and the validity of using the study of animal physiology and anatomy to illuminate the human body (see ANATOMY AND PHYSIOLOGY; MEDICINE). To develop only the last point, many medical theories were formulated against a background of the assumed inferiority of the female sex. The natural world of *Aristotle—to take just one example— has man as opposed both to woman and mankind firmly placed in the centre; several hundred years later, the Methodist physician Soranus in his *Gynaecology* was still investigating the implications for the study of pathology of his belief that there are diseases specific to *women (see GYNAECOLOGY).

Moreover, there was widespread and sustained interest throughout Graeco-Roman antiquity in explaining the progress and evolution of human—not just Greek—civilization, language, culture, and behaviour. Modern scholars have tended to condense the variety of ancient models of human history into two broad lines of argument. One line is represented most clearly by the Homeric and Hesiodic poems, and argues nostalgically that human society declined from an ancient 'golden age' through other ages of increasing metallic baseness to the present. The 'golden age' type of model is especially common in poetry (both Latin and Greek) from *Pindar to *Juvenal and beyond. The other type of argument has it that civilization gradually progressed through the discovery of technological, political, and linguistic benefits. A fragment of the Presocratic philosopher Xenophanes offers a convenient illustration of this type of position: 'The Gods did not show everything to mortals from the beginning, but through investigation mortals have discovered over time what is better' (DK 21 B 18). On this view, man has some control over his progress.

Two distinct threads have in turn been discerned in this developmental model of human society. One, which has something in common with an influential strain of ancient empiricism, is represented ultimately by *Lucretius (especially book 5 of *On the Nature of the Universe*), *Diodorus Siculus, *Vitruvius, and parts of *Pliny the Elder, *Natural History* 7, and its origins are thought by many to lie with Democritus of Abdera. This group tends to the view that accidental discoveries like that of fire, the use of metals, links between diet and health, and so on provided the

impetus for most major changes in society. On the second thread, the teleological view is taken that mankind's weakness in the face of a hostile world led to the development of essential means of protection. This 'challenge and response' model is associated with Protagoras (in Plato's dialogue of that name), with *Plato himself (who mapped out the ideal way forward in the *Republic*), Aristotle, and to some extent the Stoic Posidonius of Apamea.

Behind this apparently straightforward dichotomous summary there lies much that is not at all straightforward. For a start, there was no single, orthodox 'Myth of the Golden Age' in which life for mankind becomes progressively worse with time. (Note, for example, the highly elaborate myth of ages set before the young Socrates at Pl. *Plt.* 269c–d.) Baser metallic ages, even in Hesiod, still have their good points, and Hesiod's golden age is apparently devoid of normal humans altogether—only godlike creatures remote and free from toil and grief (*Op.* 110–20). And the Roman encyclopaedist Aulus Cornelius Celsus held (*On Medicine* 1, proem 1) that in the distant past medicine was only necessary for the treatment of wounds and other injuries because men lived virtuous and moderate lives. Yet the development of medicine, he suggests, has gone a long way towards counteracting the effects of the decline in moral standards.

Generalization, then, is difficult. Certain philosophical models which allow that human society is capable of improvement often insist that this improvement is dependent on men embracing the appropriate philosophical way of life. (This is as true of Epicureans (see EPICURUS) like Lucretius as it is of Plato.) Moreover, it should be added that even those who saw social institutions and the arts constantly progressing had no place for progress on the part of nature herself—say, by suggesting that animal species too might be in a state of constant development. On the contrary, philosophers and natural scientists from Anaximander to Aristotle and beyond seem to have held that the successful adaptation of animals to their environment was simply the result of one-off changes in their form. See RACE.   J. T. V.

Antigonus Gonatas (*c*.320–239 BC), king of Macedonia (*c*.277/6–239 BC), son of Demetrius Poliorcetes ('the Besieger') and Phila. (The meaning of his nickname 'Gonatas' is unknown.) He served under his father in Greece in 292, commanded his possessions there from 287, and took the royal title on Demetrius' death in 282, though he failed to gain Macedonia until 277/6. Before then his military ability won widespread recognition, not only in Macedonia, through a major victory near Lysimacheia in 277 over Celts who had overrun Macedonia and Thrace. Cassandreia still resisted him for ten months but his dynastic alliance with Antiochus I, whose sister Phila he married, ended Seleucid competition. *Pyrrhus occupied western Macedonia and Thessaly in 274 but his death in 272 removed this threat. In Greece Demetrius' old naval bases—Piraeus, Chalcis, Corinth, and Demetrias—guaranteed Antigonus' influence, and although an alliance led by Athens and Sparta and supported by *Ptolemy II Philadelphus tried to eject the Macedonians (in the 'Chremonidean War' of c.267–261), Athens finally had to capitulate. Subsequently Antigonus, in alliance with Antiochus II, took the offensive in Ptolemy's preserve, the SE Aegean—a naval victory near Cos (perhaps 254) caused a modest spread of Macedonian influence which was reinforced by Antigonus' son Demetrius' marrying Antiochus II's sister Stratonice. In Greece Antigonus became notorious for controlling cities by supporting tyrants, a practice which saved garrison troops but provoked serious local opposition, especially in the Peloponnese, where the Achaean Confederacy exploited dissatisfaction to extend its influence, even taking Corinth in 243. Nevertheless Demetrias, Chalcis, and the Piraeus remained Macedonian. In Macedonia Antigonus seems to have aimed at restoring the court tradition of *Philip II. In particular his own intellectual interests, fostered in his youth in southern Greece, led to frequent visits to Pella by historians, poets, and philosophers. The larger cities of the kingdom—at least Amphipolis, Pella, Cassandreia, and Thessalonica—encouraged by the stable conditions, acquired some limited rights of self-government, which were widely recognized before Antigonus' death. Antigonus also helped establish his dynasty by regulating the succession. His son Demetrius played a major part, from the 260s onwards, both in military and civil capacities; some historians even think he used the royal title in Antigonus' last years. Antigonus' long period of rule—37 years—and cautious policies provided a desperately needed consolidation for Macedonia. Characteristic for his later reputation is his reported comment, even if not authentic, that kingship is honourable servitude.

R. M. E.

Antigonus the One-eyed (Monophthalmos) (c.382–301 BC), Macedonian noble, was prominent under *Philip II and governed Greater Phrygia for *Alexander the Great (334–323). Victorious in three battles over Persian refugees from Issus (332), he remained unchallenged in his satrapy until he fell foul of the regent Perdiccas whom he denounced to Antipater in Macedon (322), unleashing the First Coalition War. For his services he was given command of the campaign against Eumenes of Cardia and the remnants of the Perdiccan factions. In 319 he defeated both groups spectacularly, and Antipater's death, on the heels of his victories, encouraged him in his supremacist ambitions. He supported Cassander against the regent Polyperchon, and took the war against Eumenes (Polyperchon's appointee as royal general) into central Asia. The victory at Gabiene (316) gave him control of territory from the Hindu Kush to the Aegean, but his success brought immediate war with his erstwhile allies: Cassander, *Lysimachus, and *Ptolemy (I) (315). The 'Peace of the Dynasts' (summer 311) briefly ratified the status quo, but it was a dead letter from the first. *Seleucus

I invaded Babylon in 311 with Ptolemy's support, provoking full-scale war, and Ptolemy resumed hostilities in 310. Antigonus directed his attention to the Greek world, broadcasting his predilection for freedom and autonomy, and ultimately reactivated the Corinthian League of Philip II as a weapon against Cassander (303/2). Athens welcomed him and his son, Demetrius Poliorcetes 'the Besieger' with open arms and exaggerated honours (307), and in the following year the two had themselves proclaimed kings (basileis). But the achievements belied the propaganda. The invasion of Egypt (306) was abortive, as was Demetrius' year-long siege of *Rhodes (305/4). Finally the coalition of 315 was reforged. At Ipsus (in Phrygia) the combined Antigonid forces were defeated decisively and Antigonus died in battle. His ambitions had been too patent, his resources inadequate to contain the reaction they provoked.

A. B. B.

Antioch (see ◀Map 2, Cc▶), in *Syria, one of the Seleucid royal capitals, on the left bank of the river Orontes, some 24 km. (15 mi.) from the sea, was founded in 300 BC by *Seleucus I, in a favourable position between his Anatolian and eastern possessions, on the edge of a large and fertile plain. Seleuceia, at the mouth of the Orontes, became its harbour. The king transferred thither the 5,300 Athenian and Macedonian settlers whom *Antigonus the One-eyed had planted at Antigoneia nearby in 307, and his successors enlarged the city and adorned it with splendid buildings. Little of Seleucid Antioch has survived, but it is known to have been laid out on a grid plan (see URBANISM). It contained a large Aramaic-speaking and also a Jewish community, whose privileges were said to go back to Seleucus I. The Antiochenes played a large part in the dynastic struggles of the later Seleucid era. After an interlude of Armenian rule (83–66 BC) it was annexed by *Pompey (64 BC) and became the capital of the province of Syria; it was made an autonomous city by Caesar (47 BC). Having sided with Pescennius Niger it was in AD 194 degraded by *Septimius Severus, but in 201 restored to its former rank, to which *Caracalla added the title of colony. Antioch administered an extensive territory. With a population of around 250,000, it was the third city of the east, after *Alexandria and Seleuceia on the Tigris, and later Constantinople (see BYZANTIUM). Its wealth was derived above all from its being a centre of civil, military, and later ecclesiastical administration of much of the near east, but also from its position on the commercial road from Asia to the Mediterranean, and the production of wine and olive oil. Rivalry of the patriarchates of Antioch and of Alexandria and the conflicting theologies of the two sees contributed to the Christological controversies, which after the councils of Ephesus (431) and Chalcedon (451) resulted in the establishment of separate Nestorian and Monophysite churches, and greatly reduced the influence of the patriarchs of Antioch. In the 6th cent. Antioch was weakened by earthquakes and plague. It was sacked by the Persians (540), and occupied by them 611–28. Deprived of its administrative role after being captured by the Arabs (641), Antioch survived, a smaller but still major city. For Antioch's personification in art see *LIMC* 1/1 (1981), 840–51.

A. H. M. J.; H. S.; W. L.; S. S.-W.

Antiochus III ('the Great') (*c*.242–187 BC), second son of Seleucus II, succeeded to the *Seleucid throne as a young man, after the assassination of his elder brother, Seleucus III. He faced many problems within the empire: in the east, a rebellion in Media led by the satrap Molon (222), with the support of the satrap of Persis, Alexander (brother of Molon); Molon invaded Babylonia, seized the royal capital, Seleuceia on Tigris, and took the title 'king'. In the west, Achaeus, viceroy of Seleucid Asia Minor, was in revolt and in control of the royal capital of Sardis. The Ptolemies still retained control of Seleuceia-Pieria in north *Syria.

Within the next 25 years, Antiochus, 'restitutor orbis', overcame the revolt of Molon (Polyb. 5. 51–4), regained Seleuceia-Pieria (219), re-established control over Sardis (213), and in 212 began his *anabasis* (march up-country) to the 'Upper Satrapies', bringing Commagene and Armenia under direct Seleucid rule; he restored Seleucid suzerainty over *Parthia and *Bactria (210–206), renewed links with the *India of the Mauryas (Polyb. 11. 39. 11–12) and, on his return, mounted a naval expedition to the Persian Gulf, where the Seleucids controlled the island of *Icaros, and waged a campaign against Gerrha, but in the end agreed a treaty that allowed the former status of the Gerrhaeans as independent to continue (Polyb. 13. 9. 4–5). It was as a result of these campaigns that Antiochus was given the epithet *megas* (Great), the *terminus ante quem* of which is 202 BC. In campaigns (202–198) Antiochus finally established lasting Seleucid control over southern Syria, Phoenicia, and Judaea after initial invasions (221, 219, 217, when he was defeated by Ptolemy IV at the battle of Raphia). Then (198) Antiochus launched an onslaught against Ptolemaic possessions in Lycia and Caria, which he took over (new inscriptions attest to the disruption and turmoil that this caused to the local populations). He moved thence to Thrace (197/6), where he refounded Lysimachea (Livy, 33. 38; App. *Syr.* 1). The campaign into Thrace, always (since Seleucus I) claimed as Seleucid, brought Antiochus up against the imperialistic Roman republic. In the protracted diplomatic exchange of 196–193, he and the senate were at cross purposes, and finally he invaded Greece. He was defeated by the Romans in two land battles, at Thermopylae in Greece and at Magnesia in Asia Minor (190). He also lost a naval campaign to them.

By the peace of Apamea (188), Antiochus ceded Seleucid satrapies in Anatolia, north of the Taurus (e.g. Lydia, Phrygia, Mysia, Caria), retaining in southern Anatolia Pamphylia and Rough and Smooth Cilicia. He still ruled a huge realm, from southern Turkey, through Syria and Palestine to Babylonia, Iran, and central Asia. After his defeat by Rome, Antiochus was again on campaign to the 'Upper Satrapies', where, disastrously, he pillaged the temple of Bel/Zeus in Elymais, and died from his injuries.

Antiochus stands out as one of the most dynamic and successful of the Seleucid kings. The centrality of Babylon (and so of *Babylonia) and of his eastern empire is mirrored in a newly published Babylonian astronomical diary (188/7), which shows Antiochus participating in rituals in the temple of Esagila (Babylon), before he embarked on his ill-fated, second *anabasis*.

Antiochus was married (221) to Laodice, daughter of Mithradates of Pontus, who gave Antiochus four sons, of whom Seleucus IV and Antiochus IV ruled as kings.

His reign was marked by continuous military campaigns to reconsolidate the Seleucid empire. He was also the first Seleucid to have organized, on a satrapal basis, a state *ruler-cult for the king, the *progonoi* (his ancestors), and, by 193, his queen, Laodice.

G. T. G.; S. S.-W.

Antiphon, of the deme (local district; see DEMOCRACY, ATHENIAN) of Rhamnus (*c*.480–411 BC), the first Attic orator whose works were preserved. From a prominent family, he participated in the intellectual movement inspired by the *sophists, taking a particular interest in law and rhetoric; he reportedly taught *Thucydides, among others. Many (though not all) scholars are now inclined to identify him with Antiphon 'the Sophist' (Xen. *Mem.* 1. 6), fragments of whose work *Truth* are concerned with the nature of justice and the relationship between *nomos* ('law, convention') and *physis* ('nature').

Thucydides (8. 68) praises Antiphon highly for ability (*aretē*), intelligence, and power of expression, adding that he stayed in the background himself but made his reputation giving advice to others. He credits Antiphon with planning the oligarchic coup that overturned the democratic constitution of Athens for a few months in 411 BC (for this, the regime of the 'Four Hundred', see ATHENS, (HISTORY)). When democracy was restored, most leaders of the coup fled, but Antiphon and Archeptolemus remained to stand trial for treason; both were convicted and executed. Antiphon's speech in his own defence, a small papyrus fragment of which survives, was the finest speech Thucydides knew. When congratulated by Agathon on its brilliance, Antiphon replied that he would rather have satisfied one man of good taste than any number of common people (Arist. *Eth. Eud.* 1232[b] 7).

Antiphon was apparently the first to compose speeches for other litigants and thus the first to write them down. His clients included well-known political figures and foreign allies of Athens. We have six complete works: three courtroom speeches and three *Tetralogies*. All concern homicide cases, though the fragmentary speeches treat many other issues. The courtroom speeches and the datable fragments come from the last two decades of Antiphon's life (430–411). In *Against the Stepmother* (1) a young man accuses his stepmother of having employed a servant-woman to poison his father. He may have brought the case from a sense of duty, for he offers little evidence. In *The Murder of Herodes* (5) a Mytilenean is accused of murdering Herodes during a sea voyage: Herodes went ashore one stormy night and never returned. He defends his innocence by appeal both to facts and to probabilities (*eikota*), and accuses his opponent of trumping up the charge for political reasons and personal gain. In *On the Chorus Boy* (6) a *chorēgos* ('chorus-leader', i.e. a man who trained and paid for a festival chorus; see TRAGEDY, GREEK §1.4) is accused of the accidental death of a boy who was given a drug to improve his voice. The *chorēgos* argues that he was not even present at the time and that the prosecution is politically motivated.

The *Tetralogies* are Antiphon's earliest works. Their authenticity is disputed, but their arguments concerning probability, causation, and similar issues fit the period and Antiphon's interests. Using the sophistic method of contrasting arguments (Protagoras' *Antilogiae*) and displaying a self-conscious virtuosity, the *Tetralogies* illustrate methods of argument that could be applied to a wide variety of cases. Each consists of four speeches for hypothetical cases, two on each side. In the *First Tetralogy* (2) a man is murdered and circumstantial evidence points to the accused, who argues that others are more likely (*eikos*) to be the killers. In the *Second Tetralogy* (3) a boy is accidentally killed by a javelin; the defence argues that the boy himself, not the thrower, is guilty of unintentional homicide because he was the cause of his own death. In the *Third Tetralogy* (4) a man dies after a fight and the accused argues that the victim is to blame because he started it.

Antiphon stands at the beginning of the tradition of literary Attic prose. He is an innovator and experimenter; he is fond of antithesis (in both word and thought), poetic vocabulary, the use of participles, and occasionally extreme asyndeton. In comparison to successors like *Lysias, Antiphon lacks grace of expression, clarity of organization, and the vivid presentation of character, but the force and variety of his arguments may account for his success.   M. Ga.

anti-Semitism (pagan). The anti-Jewish movements of Graeco-Roman antiquity have led to scholarly debate over (*a*) their causes and (*b*) their relationship to 'anti-Semitism'—i.e. the modern (and mainly western) phenomenon of ideologically driven prejudice against *Jews and the Jewish religion (see RELIGION, JEWISH). The episodes most discussed are the measures of *Seleucid King Antiochus IV and his successors in Judaea, the *stasis* (civil unrest) between *metic Jews and 'Greek' citizens in the eastern Roman provinces (above all *Syria and *Alexandria), and the series of expulsions of Jews from Rome. As to (*a*), scholarly argument focuses on how far, if at all, ancient anti-Jewishness in essence was a response to the religious and cultural alterity (see BARBARIAN) of Jews, described with varied reactions (sympathy included) by classical writers from Hecataeus on (the 'substantialist' model); or whether (the 'functionalist' model) it was grounded in concrete, localized conflicts (at Alexandria, Jewish aspirations to Greek citizenship; Greek resentment of Roman protection of the Jews). As to (*b*), many scholars

see 'anti-Semitism' as a modern concept unsuited for retrojection to antiquity; others claim to recognize a unique type of ancient antipathy directed at the Jews alone, prefiguring the (in some ways related) phenomenon of Roman hostility to and persecution of early *Christianity.
                                                                    A. J. S. S.

Antoninus Pius, Roman emperor AD 138–61, born at Lanuvium in Latium in 86, was the son of Titus Aurelius Fulvus (consul 89) and grandson of another Aurelius Fulvus (consul 70 and 85), from Nîmes (Nemausus). His mother Arria Fadilla was daughter of Arrius Antoninus (consul 69 and 97), whose names he bore as well as Boionius from his maternal grandmother: Titus Aurelius Fulvus Boionius Arrius Antoninus. He married Annia Galeria Faustina, and became consul in 120. Apart from the traditional magistracies, his only posts were those of imperial legate in Italy (an innovation of *Hadrian), in his case in Etruria and Umbria, where he owned land, and proconsul of Asia (135–6).

His links with the Annii Veri, combined with his wealth,

Antoninus Pius A slab from a monumental altar at *Ephesus (shortly after AD 169) shows members of the imperial family—Marcus *Aurelius, Antoninus Pius, the boy Lucius Verus, and *Hadrian—at the *adoption of Verus in AD 138. Adoption ensured unprecedented stability in the imperial succession for much of the 2nd cent. AD.

popularity, and character, led Hadrian to choose him as adoptive son and successor on the death of Lucius Aelius Caesar. Given *imperium* and the *tribunicia potestas* (powers of a *tribune of the *plebs*) on 25 February 138, he became Imperator Titus Aelius Aurelius Antoninus Caesar and at Hadrian's wish adopted both the young son of L. Aelius (the future Lucius Verus) and his nephew by marriage Marcus Annius Verus (Marcus *Aurelius). His accession at Hadrian's death, 10 July 138, was warmly welcomed by the senate, which overcame its reluctance to deify Hadrian at Antoninus' insistence and named him Pius in acknowledgement of his loyalty. His wife Faustina was named Augusta and his only surviving child, also Annia Galeria Faustina, was betrothed to Marcus Aurelius Caesar, his nephew and elder adoptive son. Pius became consul for a second term and *Pater Patriae* ('father of the fatherland') in 139, consul for a third term in 140 with Marcus Aurelius as colleague, and held one further consulship, in 145, again with Marcus Aurelius, whose marriage to the younger Faustina took place the same year. On the birth of a child to this couple in late 147, M. Aurelius received *tribunicia potestas* and Faustina (whose mother had died in 140) became Augusta. The dynastic succession thus clearly established—but, despite Hadrian's intention, the younger adoptive son received neither any powers nor the name Caesar—Antoninus' longevity and steady hand made 'Antonine' a byword for peace and prosperity. This impression is largely influenced by Publius Aelius Aristides' *To Rome*, delivered in 143 or 144, by the portrayal of the tranquil life of the imperial family, entirely confined to Italy, in Fronto's *Letters*, by the impressive tribute to Antoninus in M. Aurelius' *Meditations*, and by the uniformly favourable attitude of the scanty historical sources.

Hadrian's policies were rapidly changed in some areas: the consular legates for Italy, unpopular with the senate, were abolished, and southern Scotland reconquered by the governor Quintus Lollius Urbicus, Hadrian's *Wall being replaced by the 'wall of Antoninus' between Forth and Clyde. This campaign, for which Antoninus took the acclamation 'Imperator' for the second time in late 142, was the only major war, but Moorish incursions in North Africa were dealt with by sending reinforcements to Mauretania in the 140s, minor campaigns kept the peace in Dacia, a show of force at the beginning of the reign deterred a Parthian invasion, and in the late 150s a minor extension of territory in Upper Germany was marked by the construction of a new 'outer' *limes* (frontier). Direction of military policy (and much else) was doubtless left to the guard prefect Marcus Gavius Maximus, who held office for almost the entire reign. The statement in the SHA (*Ant.* 5. 3) that he kept 'good governors in office for seven or even nine years' seems to be mistaken; the senatorial *cursus honorum* (career path) —and other parts of the imperial system—settled down in a stable pattern, contributing to the emperor's popularity with the upper order. Two conspiracies against him are mentioned in the SHA (*Ant.* 7. 3–4), the second, that of Cornelius Priscianus, 'who dis-

turbed the peace of the province of Spain' being thus referred to in the *fasti Ostienses* for 145, but no further details are known. A highlight of the reign was the celebration of Rome's 900th anniversary in 148, when Antoninus' otherwise thrifty financial policy was relaxed (by a temporary debasement of the silver coinage). He cut down on excess expenditure, although relieving cities affected by natural disasters, and left a surplus of 675 million denarii at his death. In spite of his conservatism and sceptical attitude towards Greek culture, Greeks advanced to the highest positions in his reign (Tiberius Claudius Atticus Herodes, consul 143, being the best-known case); other provincials also rose, not least from Africa, helped by the prominence of Fronto, a native of Cirta. The long, peaceful reign allowed the empire a breathing-space after Trajan's wars and Hadrian's restless travels. Antoninus' last watchword for the guard, 'equanimity', sums up his policy well; but he was angry with 'foreign kings' in his last hours and clouds were looming. He died at Lorium near Rome on 7 March 161 and was deified 'by universal consent'.   A. R. Bi.

Antony, Mark (Marcus Antonius), Roman statesman and general. 1. The truth of his career and personality has been heavily overlaid by legend, as first hostile propaganda presented him as a villain, then romantic biography turned him into a figure of tragic self-destruction.

2. Eldest son of Marcus Antonius (Creticus), he was born in 83 (or, less likely, 86) BC. His youth was allegedly dissipated. He distinguished himself as cavalry commander under Aulus Gabinius in Palestine and Egypt (57–4), then joined *Caesar in Gaul, where, apart from an interval in Rome (53–2), he remained till the end of 50; in 51 he was quaestor. As tribune in 49 he defended Caesar's interests in the senate, fled to his camp when the 'last' (i.e. emergency) 'decree' was passed (*senatus consultum ultimum*), took part in the fighting in Italy, and was left in charge of Italy during Caesar's Spanish campaign. In 48 he served in Greece and commanded Caesar's left wing at Pharsalus. Caesar then sent him to impose order on Italy as his 'master of the horse' (*magister equitum*) (till late in 47), but he was only partly successful, and he held no further post till 44 when he was Caesar's consular colleague. On 15 February 44 he played a prominent role in the incident of the Lupercalia, offering a diadem which Caesar refused.

3. After the Ides of March he at first played a delicate game, combining conciliation of the Liberators with intermittent displays of his popular and military support. He acquired and exercised a strong personal dominance, but this was soon threatened by the emergence of Octavian (the future *Augustus), and the two locked in competition for the Caesarian leadership. Octavian deftly acquired support and allies, and by early 43 Antony faced an armed coalition consisting of Decimus Iunius Brutus Albinus, whom he was blockading in Mutina, the consuls Aulus Hirtius and Gaius Vibius Pansa Caetronianus, both moderate Caesarians, and Octavian, backed by the senate's

authority and Cicero's eloquence. In April he was compelled by reverses at Forum Gallorum and Mutina to retreat into Gallia Narbonensis. He was however joined there by the governors of the western provinces, Marcus Aemilius *Lepidus, Gaius Asinius Pollio, and Lucius Munatius Plancus, and subsequently reconciled with Octavian.

4. By the *lex Titia* (November 43) Antony, Lepidus, and Octavian were appointed 'triumvirs for the restoration of the state' for five years. The *proscription of their enemies (especially the wealthy) was followed in 42 by the defeat of Cassius and *Brutus at Philippi, which firmly established Antony's reputation as a general. By agreement with Octavian he now undertook the reorganization of the eastern half of the empire; he also received Gaul, strategically vital if there were to be any renewal of fighting in the west. In 41 he met *Cleopatra at Tarsus and spent the following winter with her in Egypt. Their twins Alexander Helios and Cleopatra Selene were born in 40. The defeat of his brother Lucius Antonius (Pietas) in the Perusine War compelled him to return to Italy early in 40, despite the Parthian invasion of *Syria; but a new agreement was reached at Brundisium whereby Antony surrendered Gaul, which Octavian had already occupied, and married Octavian's sister Octavia. The division of the empire into east and west was becoming more clear-cut. At Misenum in 39 the triumvirs extended their agreement to Sextus Pompeius, after which Antony returned with Octavia to the east. By 38 his lieutenant Publius Ventidius had expelled the Parthians from Syria. In 37, new differences between Antony and Octavian were settled at Tarentum, and the Triumvirate was renewed for another five years; but this time he left Octavia behind when he left for the east, and renewed his association with Cleopatra on a firmer basis. Their third child Ptolemy Philadelphus was born in 36.

5. This liaison had political attractions. Egypt was one of several important kingdoms which Antony strengthened and expanded; nor did he grant all that Cleopatra wished, for he refused to take territory from Herod of Judaea, another able and valued supporter. The allegiance of the east was courted by religious *propaganda. By 39 he had already presented himself as *Dionysus in Athens, and he and Cleopatra could now be presented as Osiris and Isis (or *Aphrodite; for Osiris and Isis see EGYPTIAN DEITIES), linked in a sacred marriage for the prosperity of Asia (cf. Plut. *Ant.* 26). But in 36 Antony's Parthian expedition ended in a disastrous reverse, while the defeat of Sextus Pompeius and the elimination of Lepidus correspondingly strengthened Octavian. It still seems to have been some time before Antony accepted that a decisive clash with Octavian was inevitable. At first he continued to concentrate on the east, planning a further invasion of Parthia and annexing Armenia in 34: this was marked in *Alexandria by a ceremony (hostile sources regarded it as a sacrilegious version of a Roman triumph after which Cleopatra and her children—including Caesarion, whom Antony provocatively declared to be Caesar's acknowledged son—were paraded

in national and regal costumes of various countries, just as if they might inherit them dynastically. The propaganda exchanges with Octavian intensified in 33, then early in 32 Octavian intimidated many of Antony's supporters, including the consuls Gnaeus Domitius Ahenobarbus and Gaius Sosius, into leaving Rome. Antony divorced Octavia; then Octavian outrageously seized and published Antony's will, in which he allegedly left bequests to his children by Cleopatra and requested burial in Alexandria. Octavian proceeded to extract the annulment of Antony's remaining powers and a declaration of war against Cleopatra: Antony would now seem a traitor if he sided with the national enemy.

6. The spring and summer of 31 saw protracted military engagements in western Greece. Antony's initial numerical superiority was whittled away by *Agrippa's skilful naval attacks, then during the summer Antony was deserted by most of his most influential Roman supporters, including Plancus, Marcus Titius, and Domitius Ahenobarbus: they had allegedly been alienated by Cleopatra's presence. In September 31 Cleopatra and Antony managed to break the blockade at *Actium and escape southwards, but the campaign was decisively lost, and their supporters defected to Octavian in the following months. Antony committed suicide as Octavian entered Alexandria (August 30).

7. For all its romanticism, much of Plutarch's portrayal of Antony carries some conviction—the great general, with unusual powers of leadership and personal charm, destroyed by his own weaknesses. But it is easy to underestimate his political judgement. True, Octavian won the war of propaganda in Italy, but till a late stage Antony continued to have strong support from the east and from influential Romans (many old republicans preferred him to Octavian). He looked the likely winner until the Actium campaign itself, and it is arguable that military rather than political considerations sealed his downfall. His administrative arrangements in the east were clear-sighted, and most were continued by Augustus.

8. His only literary publication was a pamphlet of *c.*33, 'On his own Drunkenness', evidently a reply to Octavian's aspersions rather than a tippler's memoir. Specimens of his epistolary style can be seen in *Cicero's correspondence, the thirteenth *Philippic*, and *Suetonius' *Augustus*.

9. Antony was married ?(1) to Fadia, though this is more likely to have been a careless affair; (2) to his cousin Antonia, daughter of Gaius Antonius 'Hybrida', whom he divorced in 47; (3) in 47 or 46, to Fulvia; (4) in 40, to Octavia. By Antonia he had a daughter, also called Antonia; by Fulvia two sons, Marcus Antonius Antyllus and Iullus Antonius; by Octavia two daughters, Antonia the Elder and Antonia the Younger, through whom he was the ancestor of the emperors *Gaius, *Claudius, and *Nero. His 'marriage' to Cleopatra would not have been seen as such by an Italian audience.   C. B. R. P.

Aphrodisias (see ◀Map 2, Bb▶) (mod. Geyre in south-western Turkey), was a Carian city, probably established in the 2nd cent. BC as the political centre of 'the Plarasans and Aphrodisians' (Plarasans dropped from the description under *Augustus); site of vigorous prehistoric and Archaic communities honouring a mother-goddess, called *Aphrodite perhaps from the 3rd cent. BC and later identified with Roman Venus. That identification encouraged a special relationship with Rome and with the family of *Caesar; so Aphrodisias resisted *Mithradates VI in 88 BC and the Liberators after Caesar's death, earning privileges which Rome conferred in 39 BC and confirmed up to the late 3rd cent. AD. The wall-circuit, *c*.3.5 km. (2.2 mi.) long and containing many inscribed blocks reused, a stadium, and columns have always been visible; excavation has now uncovered civic buildings and much sculpture, which is sometimes distinguished and often technically interesting. Intellectual pursuits were prized too—famous Aphrodisians included the novelist Chariton, the philosophers Adrastus and the philosophical commentator Alexander, and, in the late 5th cent. AD, Asclepiodotus. Numerous inscriptions, including an 'archive' of official communications from Rome inscribed on a wall in the theatre, throw important light on Roman history, late antiquity, ancient entertainments, and the Jewish Diaspora.

It was associated with the province of Asia to the mid-3rd cent. AD, then became part, perhaps capital, of Phrygia-Caria, and, under *Diocletian, capital of Caria, from which it derived its modern name. J. M. R.

Aphrodite Born from the severed genitals of Uranus according to *Hesiod (*Theog.* 188–206), or in the Homeric version (see HOMER) daughter of *Zeus and Dione (*Il.* 5. 370–417), Aphrodite is the representative among the gods of an ambivalent female nature combining seductive charm, the need to procreate, and a capacity for deception, elements all found in the person of the first woman, Pandora (Hes. *Op.* 60–8). There is no agreement on her historical origins; the Greeks themselves thought of her as coming from the east (Hdt. 1. 105, Paus. 1. 14. 7), and in literature she is frequently given the name Cypris, 'the Cyprian'. (See CYPRUS.) The double tradition of her birth shows how the Greeks felt Aphrodite to be at the same time Greek and foreign, but also, on the level of mythology, that they perceived her as a powerful goddess whom it would be prudent to place under the authority of Zeus.

Aphrodite's cults extend very widely over the Greek world, though her temples and festivals cannot compete with those of the other great figures of the pantheon. Cyprus is the home of her most famous cults, for instance at Paphos and Amathus. There, probably in the Archaic period, the name Aphrodite became attached to an indigenous goddess who was also subject to numerous oriental influences. In Greece itself, one or more cults of Aphrodite are known in every region. She was worshipped above all as presiding over sexuality and reproduction—necessary for the continuity of the community. Thus in many cities girls about to be married sacrificed to Aphrodite so that their first sexual experience might be propitious (e.g. Paus. 2. 32. 7, 34. 12). This is the particular sphere of Aphrodite, compared with other goddesses involved in marriage like *Hera and *Demeter, a function especially emphasized in the Argolid by the mythological connections between cults of Aphrodite and the story of the Danaids. The close bond which the Greeks felt to exist between human fertility and the fruitfulness of the land lies behind Aphrodite's connections with vegetation and the earth in general: as Melainis at Corinth (Paus. 2. 2. 4) and Mantinea (Paus. 8. 6. 5) the 'black' Aphrodite shows her power over the 'black earth' as well as her links with the powers of the night. In Athens, Aphrodite en kēpois, 'in gardens', was worshipped together with Athena at the Arrephoria, a rite concerned with fertility and with the sexuality of the arrhephoroi as future wives of citizens (Paus. 1. 27. 3). This Aphrodite was also worshipped by prostitutes. Epithets such as Hetaira ('courtesan') and Porne ('prostitute') show her as protectress of this profession, whose essential stock-in-trade was seduction. Corinth was particularly well known for the beauty and luxurious living of its prostitutes, who certainly revered the local Aphrodite. All the same, it is unlikely that her sanctuary on Acrocorinth was the location of an institutionalized form of what is usually called 'sacred prostitution'. The only source for such a remarkable practice in a Greek context, *Strabo (8. 6. 21 (378–9 C)), places it in a vague past time, and is surely influenced by the eastern practices with which he was familiar. Herodotus also mentions a similar practice in several parts of the Mediterranean area, and his silence in regard to Corinth should invite caution. See PROSTITUTION, SACRED and SECULAR.

If Aphrodite was worshipped primarily by women, men also took part in her cult, notably in connection with her role as patron of seafaring (Aphrodite Euploia, Pontia, Limenia: e.g. *IG* 2². 2872, Paus. 2. 34. 11). Aphrodite is also concerned with magistrates in their official capacity, being the deity of concord and civic harmony. The title Pandemos, which is hers conspicuously in Athens (*IG* 2². 659), indicates her protection of the whole citizen body, but she can also be linked with a particular civic office (e.g. as Stratagis in Acarnania (*IG* 9². 1. 2. 256), and as Epistasie on Thasos (J. Pouilloux, *Thasos* 1, no. 24)). In this context, she is frequently associated with *Hermes, Peitho (Persuasion), and the Charites (Graces). Thus *Plato's interpretation of the epithets Urania and Pandemos as indicating respectively exalted and common love (*Symp.* 180d–181) is completely unfounded. The title Urania, 'heavenly', occurs frequently in cult and refers to the power of the goddess who presides over every type of union. It is with this epithet that the name Aphrodite is used as the Greek designation of foreign goddesses, a process found already in *Herodotus and which accelerates with the syncretisms of the Hellenistic period. The title also expresses one of Aphrodite's ambiguities, making her simultaneously 'daughter of Uranus' and 'the goddess who has come from elsewhere'. According to Pausanias, there were several statues showing an armed Aphrodite, particularly at Sparta (3. 15. 10; 3. 23. 1). Considering the special characteristics of the upbringing of Spartiate girls, it is not too surprising that the goddess of femaleness should be given male attire, but the actual examples of the type scarcely permit us to see in her a war-goddess, except in connection with a protecting role such as she has at Corinth. Her association with *Ares, prominent in the literary tradition, has more to do with a wish to bring opposites together than with any similarity of function.

From *Sappho to *Lucretius, literature celebrates the power of love and the dominion of Aphrodite. Ares, Adonis, Hermes, and *Dionysus are all at various times given as her lovers, as is the mortal Anchises, but apart from a few isolated examples these associations do not appear in cult.   V. P.-D., A. Mot.

Apollo, Greek god, son of *Zeus and Leto, brother of *Artemis, for many 'the most Greek of Greek gods' (W. F.

Otto). Among his numerous and diverse functions, healing and purification, prophecy, care for young citizens, for poetry, and music are prominent (see Pl. *Cra.* 404d–405e). In iconography, he is always young, beardless, and of harmonious beauty, the ideal ephebe (see GYMNASIUM) and young athlete; his weapon is the bow, and his plant the laurel.

His name is absent from Linear B (while Paean, his later epiclesis and hymn, appears as *Paiawon* in the pantheon of Mycenaean Cnossus). In *Homer and *Hesiod, his myth and cult are fully developed, and his main centres, *Delos and *Delphi, are well known (Delian altar of Apollo, *Od.* 6. 162; Delphic shrine, *Il.* 9. 405 and *Od.* 8. 80; stone of Cronus, *Theog.* 499) though none goes back to the bronze age: Apollo's cult must have been introduced and brought to Panhellenic importance during the Dark Ages. Epic poetry, where Apollo is prominent, had its decisive share in this development. The key document is the *Homeric Hymn to Apollo*; it consists of two aetiological parts, a Delian part which tells the story of Apollo's birth and a perhaps earlier

Apollo This Athenian 'white-ground' cup (c.470 BC) depicts Apollo as a handsome youth. The lyre, his favoured instrument, denotes his association with *music, poetry, and, more generally, *education.

Delphic part about the foundation of the oracular shrine in Delphi; opinions about structure and date vary, though a date in the 7th cent. BC for the Delian, and one slightly later for the Delphic part are plausible.

The origins of Apollo are debated; after earlier theories explaining the god from the sun (following an identification as old as the 5th cent., and adding the linguistic argument that the epiclesis *Lykeios* would derive from the stem *luc-*, as in latin *lux*), partisans of an Anatolian, esp. Lycian, origin relied upon the same epiclesis and upon his mother's name being Lycian and connected with *lada*, 'earth'; the French excavations in Lycian Xanthus proved both assumptions wrong. More promising is the connection with Dor. *apella*, 'assembly', i.e. annual reunion of the adult tribesmen which also introduces the young men into the community (W. Burkert, *Rh. Mus.* 1975, 1–21). This explains his widespread role as the divinity responsible for the introduction of young initiated adults into society: he receives the first cut hair at the end of *initiation (Hes. *Theog.* 347, mentioning Apollo together with *kourai*, 'girls', i.e. nymphs, and rivers), and his cult has to do with military and athletic training (for Apollo Lycius at Athens, M. Jameson, *Archaiognosia* 1980, 213–35; the 'Wolf-Apollo' has to do with Archaic wolf-warriors) and with the citizen-right of the sons (for Apollo Delphinius, F. Graf, *MH* 1979, 2–22). His cult on the lonely island of Delos, where Leto gave birth after long search, became the religious focus of Archaic Ionia (*Hymn. Hom. Ap.* 147) at least from the late 8th cent. onwards; before this date, archaeology shows a more regional, Cycladic influence. While a Delian temple of Artemis was present already in the 8th cent. (bronze age origin and continuity are contested), a temple of Apollo was built only in the mid-6th cent.; his cult centred around the famous altar of horns (parallels from Archaic Drerus on Crete, from *Ephesus, and from Boeotian Hyampolis, are now archaeologically attested).

Apollo's interest in music and poetry could derive from the same source, music and poetry having an educational role in Greece (see EDUCATION, GREEK). Apollo's instrument is the lyre whose well-ordered music is opposed to the ecstatic rhythms of flute and drums which belong to *Dionysus and Cybele; according to the *Homeric Hymn to Hermes*, he received it from Hermes, its inventor. He is, together with the *Muses, protector of epic singers and cithara-players (Hes. *Theog.* 94); later, he is Musagetes, 'Leader of the Muses', in Pindar (fr. 91c Snell–Maehler) and on Archaic images. When philosophy takes over a similar educational function, he is associated with philosophy, and an anecdote makes him the real father of *Plato.

His own song, the paean (*paian*; see L. Käppel, *Paian*, 1993), is sung and danced by the young Achaeans after the sacrifice to Apollo when bringing back Chryseis to her father (*Il.* 1. 473): even if not necessarily a healing-song in this passage, it was understood as such later and was accordingly transferred to Asclepius as well. In the *Iliad*, Paieon could still be understood as an independent healing god (5. 401); later, it is an epiclesis of Apollo the Healer.

The Ionian Apollo *iatros* ('Healer') had cult in most Black Sea cities, and as *Medicus* Apollo was taken over by the Romans during a plague in the 5th cent. (Livy 4. 25. 3, see below). Only the rise of *Asclepius in the 5th and 4th cents. eclipsed this function, though in Epidaurus, where Apollo took over a bronze age hill-sanctuary of Maleatas, Apollo Maleatas preceded Asclepius in official nomenclature until the imperial period. In *Iliad* 1 he is responsible both for sending and for averting the plague. The image of a god sending plague by shooting arrows points to the ancient near east where Reshep 'of the arrow' is the plague-god in bronze age Ugarit/Ras Shamra and on Cyprus; details of iconography point to a transfer from Cyprus to Spartan Amyclae—and in the Archaic Dorian world of Crete and Sparta, the paean is first attested as an individual poetical genre (Plut. [*De mus.*] 9. (1134c)); both in *Il.* 1. 473 and in the cultic reality of the Spartan Apollo, paean and *kouroi* ('young men') are closely connected.

Disease is the consequence of impurity, healing is purification—in myth, this theme later crystallized around Orestes whom Delphic Apollo cleansed of the murder of his mother, and of the concomitant madness. Oracular Apollo (see ORACLES) is often connected with purification and plague; he decreed the Cyrenean purification laws (6th cent., R. Parker, *Miasma* (1983), 332–51) and the setting up of his statue to avert the Athenian plague of 430 BC (Paus. 1. 3. 4, 10. 11. 5). But this is only a small part of the much wider oracular function which Apollo had not only in his shrines at Delphi and the Ptoion (a Boiotian oracular sanctuary) on the Greek mainland, and at Branchidae, Claros, and Gryneum in Asia Minor, but also in his relationship with the Sibyl(s) and other seers like Bacis or Cassandra; while the Sibyls are usually priestesses of Apollo (e.g. Erythrae, *PL* 8. 450, or Cumae, Verg. *Aen.* 6. 77), Cassandra refused Apollo as a lover. Apolline prophecy was usually ecstatic: the Delphic Python was possessed by the god (in NT Greek, *pūthōn* is 'ventriloquist'), as were the Sibyls (see Verg. *Aen.* 6. 77–80), Cassandra, young Branchus (Callim. fr. 229 Pf.), and Bacis; and the priest of Claros attained ecstasy through drinking water (Tac. *Ann.* 2. 54). Apollo's supreme wisdom is beyond human rationality.

In Archaic and Classical Greece, Delphi was the central oracular shrine (see the quest of Croesus, Hdt. 1. 46). Though his cult had grown out of purely local worship in the 8th cent., myth saw its foundation as a primordial event, expressing it in the theme of dragon-slaying (*Hymn. Hom. Ap.* 287–374; see J. Trumpf, *Hermes* 1958, 129–57, and J. Fontenrose, *Python* (1959)); alternative myths gave an even longer prehistory to Apollo's taking over and his temple-building (C. Sourvinou-Inwood, *'Reading' Greek Culture* (1991), 192–216, 217–43). Like isolated Delos, marginal Delphi achieved international political importance in Archaic Greece simply for being marginal. But from his role as a political adviser, Apollo acquired no further political functions—and only a marginally moralistic character.

In Italy, Apollo's arrival in Rome during a plague in 433 BC was due to a recommendation of the Sibylline Books

(Livy 4. 25. 3): to avert the plague, a temple of Apollo Medicus was vowed and built just outside the *pomerium*, where there had already been an *Apollinar*, presumably an open cult-place of the god (Livy 3. 63. 7, for the year 449). In Etruria (see ETRUSCANS), no cult of Apollo is attested, though his name, in the form *Aplu*, is read in mythological representations (with a Greek iconography): the form shows that the name was taken over from Latin *Apollo*, not directly from the Greek (A. Pffifig, *Religio Etrusca* (1975), 251). Until the time of Augustus, the temple of Apollo Medicus was the only Roman temple of the god, and healing his main function; the Vestals addressed him as 'Apollo Medice, Apollo Paean' (Macrob. *Sat.* I. 17. 15). Mainly in response to Mark *Antony's adoption of Dionysus, and perhaps already stimulated by the victory of Philippi which Caesar's heirs had won in the name of Apollo, *Augustus made Apollo his special god (P. Zanker, *The Power of Images in the Age of Augustus* (1988), 48–53). In 31 BC, Augustus vowed a second temple to Apollo in Rome after the battle of Actium, where, from his nearby sanctuary, the god was said to have helped against Mark Antony and Cleopatra; the temple was built and dedicated in 28, close to the house of Augustus on the Palatine, with a magnificent adjoining library. See ORACLES.   F. G.

Apollonius of Rhodes (Apollonius Rhodius), a major literary figure of 3rd-cent. BC *Alexandria, and poet of the *Argonautica*, the only extant Greek hexameter *epic written between *Homer and the Roman imperial period.

Life Our main sources are: *POxy.* 1241, a 2nd-cent. AD list of the librarians of the Royal Library at *Alexandria; two *Lives* transmitted with the manuscripts of *Argon.* which probably contain material deriving from the late 1st cent. BC; an entry in the Byzantine dictionary known as the *Suda*. (I) All four state that Apollonius was from Alexandria itself, though two 2nd-cent. AD notices point rather to Naucratis. The most likely explanation for the title 'Rhodian' is thus that Apollonius spent a period of his life there, which would accord well with what we know of his works (cf. below), though it remains possible that he or his family came from *Rhodes. (2) Apollonius served as librarian and royal tutor before *Eratosthenes (*POxy.* 1241), and probably in succession to Zenodotus, thus *c.*270–245 BC. It is to this period that the *Argonautica* should be dated. (3) All four sources make him a pupil of *Callimachus, which probably reflects beliefs about the indebtedness of his poetry to Callimachus (cf. below). (4) The *Lives* give confused and contradictory accounts of withdrawal to Rhodes after a poor reception for his poetry in Alexandria. Nothing of value can be retrieved from these stories, which may well be fictions based on the existence of a text of at least *Argon.* I which differed significantly from the vulgate (the *proekdosis*, cited six times by the scholia to *Argon.* I). (5) Very flimsy ancient evidence has been used by some scholars to construct a 'quarrel' between Apollonius and Callimachus concerning poetic questions, particularly the value and style of epic. The many striking parallels between the works of Callimachus and the *Argonautica*, however, argue against, rather than for, any serious dispute; moreover, Apollonius does not appear in the list (*PSI* 1219) which seeks to identify Callimachus' opponents, the Telchines, and Roman poets clearly align Apollonius with, rather than against, Callimachus. Two episodes in the *Argonautica* handle the same material as two poems of *Theocritus (Hylas, cf. *Id.* 13; Amycus and Polydeuces, cf. *Id.* 22), and this offers no reason to doubt the dating derived from other sources.

Lost works (I) Poems (cf. Powell, *Coll. Alex.* 4–8). *Canobus*: choliambic poem on Egyptian legends. *Foundation Poems* in hexameters on Caunus, Alexandria, Naucratis, Rhodes, and Cnidus; poems of this type reflect the deep Alexandrian interest in local history and cult. Many other lost poems may also be assumed, including probably epigrams (cf. Ant. Lib. *Met.* 23); an extant epigram attacking Callimachus (*Anth. Pal.* 11. 275) is very doubtfully ascribed to Apollonius. (2) Prose Works. Apollonius' scholarly interests were reflected in many works (cf. R. Pfeiffer, *History of Classical Scholarship* I (1968), 144–8), including a monograph on Homer (*Against Zenodotus*). *Archilochus and *Hesiod were also among the poets discussed by Apollonius; he defended the authenticity of the *Shield of Heracles* (hypothesis (introduction) A to the poem) and probably rejected Hesiodic authorship of the *Ornithomanteia* which was transmitted after *Works and Days* (corrupt scholium to *Op.* 828).

Argonautica Hexameter epic on the Argonautic legend in four long books totalling 5,835 preserved verses. Fifty-two manuscripts are known, and a large body of papyri attests to the popularity of the poem in later antiquity. It was very important at Rome, where it was translated by the neoteric Publius Terentius Varro Atacinus, is a major influence on *Catullus 64 and *Virgil's *Aeneid*, and, with the *Aeneid*, forms the basis of *Valerius Flaccus' *Argonautica*.

Books 1–2 deal with the outward voyage, to recover the golden fleece, from Iolcus in *Thessaly to the Colchian city of Aia at the extreme eastern edge of the Black (Euxine) Sea (in modern Georgia), which is ruled over by Aeëtes, the cruel son of *Helios. The major events of this voyage are a stay at Lemnos where the local women, who have murdered the entire male population, seize the chance for procreation, and Jason sleeps with Queen Hypsipyle (I. 609–910); the loss of *Heracles from the expedition (I. 1153–1357); a boxing-match between Amycus, king of the Bebrycians, and Polydeuces (2. 1–163); meeting with the blind prophet Phineus whom the Argonauts save from the depredations of the Harpies and who, in return, tells them of the voyage ahead (2. 168–530); passage through the Clashing Rocks (*Symplēgades*) which guard the entrance to the Black Sea (2. 531–647); meeting on the island of Ares with the sons of Phrixus, who fled Greece on the golden ram (2. 1030–1230). In Book 3 Jason asks Aeëtes to grant him the fleece; this the king agrees to do on the condition that Jason ploughs an enormous field with fire-breathing bulls, sows it with dragon's teeth, and slays the armed warriors who rise up from the ground. Jason succeeds in this, because, at the instigation of Jason's protector Hera, the king's daughter, *Medea, falls in love with the hero and supplies him with a magic salve to protect him and give him superhuman strength. In Book 4 Medea flees to join the Argonauts and secures the fleece for them from the grove where it is guarded by a sleepless dragon. The Argonauts flee via a great river (the Danube) which is pictured as flowing from the Black Sea to the Adriatic; at the Adriatic mouth, Jason and Medea lure her brother, Apsyrtus, who commands the pursuing Colchians, to his death, a crime for which Zeus decides that they must be purified by Medea's aunt Circe who lives on the west coast of Italy. They reach Circe via rivers (the Po (Padus) and the Rhône) imagined to link NE Italy with the western Mediterranean. From there they sail to Drepane (Corfu), Homer's Scheria, where Jason and Medea are married, and are then driven to the wastes of Libya where they are again saved by divine intervention. They finally return home by way of Crete, where Medea uses her magic powers to destroy the bronze giant Talos who guards the island.

The central poetic technique of Apollonius is the creative reworking of *Homer. While the Hellenistic poet takes pains to avoid the repetitiveness characteristic of Archaic epic, Homer is the main determinative influence on every aspect of the poem, from the details of language to large-scale narrative patterns, material culture, and technology (e.g. sailing) which is broadly 'Homeric' (but note 'Hellenistic' architectural features at 3. 215 ff.). This is most obvious in set scenes such as the Catalogue of Argonauts (1. 23–233), corresponding to Homer's Catalogue of Ships, the description of the cloak Jason wears to meet Hypsipyle (1. 721–67), corresponding to the Shield of *Achilles, the meeting of *Hera, *Athena, and *Aphrodite on Olympus at the start of book 3 which finds many forerunners in Homer, the scenes in the palace of Aeëtes, corresponding to the scenes of the *Odyssey* on Scheria, and the voyage in the western Mediterranean, corresponding to *Odysseus' adventures on his way home. These scenes function by contrast: the Homeric 'model' is the base-text by which what is importantly different in the later poem is highlighted. Individual characters too owe much to Homeric predecessors, while also being markedly different from them: e.g. Jason/Odysseus, Medea/Nausicaa and Circe. After Homer, the two most important literary influences are Pindar's account of the Argonauts (*Pyth.* 4) and Euripides' *Medea*; the events of the tragedy are foreshadowed in a number of places in the epic—perhaps most strikingly in the murder of Apsyrtus who goes to his death 'like a tender child' (4. 460)—and in one sense the epic shows us that the events of the tragedy were 'inevitable', given the earlier history of Jason and Medea.

A fundamental principle of composition for Apollonius is discontinuity, a feature shared with the poetics of Callimachus. The *Argonautica* is constantly experimental. This shows itself, for example, in the organization of the narrative both within books (e.g. book 2 where scenes of action—Amycus, the Harpies—stand in sharp contrast to long passages of ethnography and geography, and book 4 where different Argonauts and Medea take turns to play leading roles) and between books (thus book 3 stands apart as a tightly-knit drama of its own). Apollonius' principles of characterization have also frequently been misunderstood; the two main sides of Medea's character—impressionable virgin and dangerous sorceress—are only confusing if viewed from the perspective of that 'consistency' which *Aristotle prescribed for dramatic character. Apollonius is rather interested in the similarities and differences between the power of love, the power of persuasion, and the power of drugs, and this interest is explored through the presentation of Medea, whose character is thus a function of the narrative. Jason's character, on the other hand, brings persuasion and stratagem to the fore (cf. esp. his testing (*peira*) of the crew after the passing of the Clashing Rocks (2. 607–49), and the praise of *muthos* and *mētis* at 3. 182–93). His story is of the familiar type of rite of passage (cf. Orestes, *Theseus, etc.) in which a young man must accomplish a dangerous set of tasks before assuming his rightful position (in this case a kingship which had been usurped by Pelias); that Jason seems often overwhelmed (*amēchanos*) by the enormity of what he must do and only finally accomplishes it through Medea's help finds many parallels in related stories, but also marks the difference between his exotic story and that of the Homeric heroes. With the partial exception of some of Odysseus' adventures, magic and fantasy have little role in Homer, whereas they had always had a prominent position in the Argonautic myth and are very important in the *Argonautica*. Discontinuity is also seen in the divine element of the epic where different Olympian gods—Athena, *Apollo, and Jason's main protector, *Hera—and other minor divinities are all prominent at one time or another.

In common with other Alexandrian poetry, the aetiology of cult and ritual is very important in the *Argonautica*. Apollonius' scholarly learning, visible also in his detailed manipulation of earlier texts, here emphasizes how the Argonautic voyage is in part a voyage of acculturation establishing Greek tradition. The repeatedly positive evaluation of Greek culture (including cult and ritual) should be connected with the Ptolemaic context of the work; the Ptolemies promoted themselves as the true heirs and champions of Classical Greek culture, and this strain should not be overlooked in the epic. It is even possible that the characters of King Alcinous and Queen Arete owe not a little to *Ptolemy II Philadelphus and his sister/wife. Just as Ptolemaic ideas are thus inscribed into prehistory, Apollonius also mixes the temporal levels of his poem in other ways too. One is by emotional authorial 'intrusions' (e.g. 1. 616–19, 2. 542–5, 4. 445–9) which strongly differentiate the *Argonautica* from the 'impersonal' Homeric poems; these are one manifestation of the strong literary self-consciousness of an epic which is much concerned with displaying the problems of *how* one writes epic poetry. Another is by reflections of Hellenistic science within the mythical material of the poem; Aphrodite bribes her son with a ball which is also a cosmic globe of a kind familiar in Apollonius' time (3. 131–41), Medea's suffering reflects contemporary physiological theories (3. 762–3), and Mopsus' death from snakebite (4. 1502–36) is a very typical mixture of Alexandrian medicine and myth.

The language of Apollonius is based on that of Homer, constantly extended and varied by analogy and new formation, but Apollonius also draws upon the vocabulary of the whole high poetic tradition. Metrically, his hexameter shows similar developments to Callimachus' and Theocritus', and dactylic rhythm is more predominant than in Homer. Complex, enjambed sentences and syntactically sophisticated indirect speech reveal the possibilities open to the poet of written, rather than oral, epic.

The *Argonautica* is a brilliant and disturbing achievement, a poem shot through with intelligence and deep ironies. Its reception at Rome is in stark contrast to its reception by modern critics who have tended to see it as a failed attempt to write like Homer; more recently, however, it has become the subject of serious literary study, and is thus coming into its own.   R. L. Hu.

Apollonius of Tyana, a Neopythagorean holy man, whose true history and persona it is scarcely possible to grasp. According to the only full account, the highly untrustworthy 'biography' of Philostratus, he was born at Tyana in Cappadocia at the beginning of the 1st cent. AD and survived into the reign of *Nerva. He led the life of an ascetic wandering teacher, visited distant lands (including India), advised cities (e.g. Sparta), had life-threatening encounters with *Nero and *Domitian, whose death he simultaneously prophesied (Philostr. 8. 25–6; cf. Cass. Dio 67. 18), and on his own death underwent heavenly assumption. He was the object of posthumous cult attracting the patronage of the Severan emperors; pagan apologists compared him favourably to Jesus. An epigram from Cilicia (*SEG* 28. 1251; 31. 1320, not before the 3rd cent. AD) describes him as 'extinguishing the faults of men'. Of his writings there survive some doubtfully authentic letters and a fragment of his treatise *On Sacrifices*.

H. J. R.; A. J. S. S.

Appian of Alexandria, Greek historian. Born in *Alexandria at the end of the 1st cent. AD, he experienced the Jewish rising of AD 116/17, became a Roman citizen, moved to Rome as an advocate and eventually gained, through the influence of his friend Marcus Cornelius Fronto, the *dignitas* of a *procurator under *Antoninus Pius, which enabled him to devote his time to writing a Roman History. After the preface and book 1 on early Rome in the period of the kings, this work is arranged ethnographically, dealing with the individual peoples as Rome conquered them: book 2, Italians; 3, Samnites; 4, Celts; 5, Sicilians; 6, Iberians; 7, *Hannibal; 8,

Carthaginians (Libyans and Nomads), 9, Macedonians and Illyrians; 10, Greeks and Ionians; 11, Syrians (Seleucids) and Parthians; and 12, *Mithradates VI; 13–17 treat the Civil Wars; 18–21, the wars in Egypt; 22, the century up to *Trajan; 23, Trajan's campaigns against Dacians, Jews, and Pontic peoples; and 24, Arabians. A survey of Rome's military and financial system was apparently not yet written when Appian died in the 160s. The preface, books 6–9, and 11–17 survive complete, apart from 8b on the Nomads and 9a on the Macedonians (of which only fragments exist) as well as 11b on the Parthians (11b was perhaps unfinished at Appian's death; the textual tradition preserves a Byzantine fake instead); 1–5 are fragmentary, 10 and 18–24 lost.

In order to accommodate a millennium of Roman history in a single work, Appian greatly, but not always successfully, reduced the material he chose from a variety of Greek and Latin authors, among them *Hieronymus of Cardia, *Polybius, and Roman annalists like Gaius Asinius Pollio, *Caesar, and *Augustus. Since some of his valuable sources, especially on the Civil Wars, are otherwise lost, his work gains historical importance for us, even though it does not simply reproduce these sources. Recent research has stressed Appian's own conscious contribution not only in choosing, reducing, and organizing the material, but also in the independent composition of speeches, in the introduction of episodes from the rhetorical repertoire, and in detailed interference with the sources in view of his avowed aims: a proud citizen of Alexandria, Appian makes events in Egypt the climax of his work; a convinced monarchist, he explains, not always correctly, Roman republican institutions to his Greek audience (papyri show that his work was read in Dura Europus); a stout conservative, he regards a lack of popular concord, as witnessed in the Civil Wars, as cataclysmic; unusually interested in administration and finance, he preserves more social and economic information than most historiographers; above all, an ardent admirer of Rome, Appian explains her success through reference to the Romans' good counsel, endurance, patience, moderation, and, especially, overall virtue.   K. B.

aqueducts In a Mediterranean climate, correcting the accidents of rainfall distribution through the management of water-sources transforms *agriculture by extending the growing-season through the dry summer by means of irrigation, allows agglomerations of population beyond the resources of local springs or wells, eases waterlogging through drainage in the wetter zones, and protects against floods caused by violent winter rainfall. The societies of the semi-arid peripheries had long depended on water-strategies such as irrigation drawn from perennial rivers, or the *qanat* (a tunnel for tapping ground-water resources).

Hydraulic engineering was therefore both useful and prestigious. It was quickly adopted by the nascent cities of the Greek world and their leaders: ground-level aqueducts bringing water from extra-mural springs into Greek cities were at least as old as the 6th cent. BC: notable late-Archaic examples are at Athens, using clay piping (see ATHENS

aqueducts The Pont du Gard, one of the best-preserved Roman aqueducts, guaranteed the water supply of Nemausus (mod. Nîmes), but also served as a costly statement of civic pride.

(TOPOGRAPHY), and on *Samos, where the water was channelled by a rock-hewn tunnel through the acropolis—a remarkable engineering feat on which Herodotus (3. 60) comments. In the Classical period, an aqueduct system is attested for the refounded city of Priene, presumably when it was moved to its new site in the 4th cent. BC. Water from springs at a distance of 2 km. (1¼ mi.), and above the level of the city, was fed through a terracotta pipe 25 cm. (10 in.) in diameter set in a trench covered with marble slabs and leading to a distribution tank within the city walls.

A more elaborate system was constructed in the 2nd cent. BC by Eumenes II at *Pergamum. A copious spring 25 km. (15½ mi.) (in a direct line) north of the city was brought through an extended pipeline, following the contours. This was constructed in various materials. It led to a basin from which it flowed under pressure through iron pipes (supported by stone blocks at intervals) up to the top of the citadel. The basin is at a height of 386 m. (1,266 ft.) above sea-level: at its lowest point, the pipe crossed a valley at only 175 m. (574 ft.) before rising to the citadel at c.330 m. (1,083 ft.). (*Vitruvius (8. 6. 5) says the Greeks call this system a *koilia*.) This system may have helped inspire the first important aqueduct at Rome, the aqua Marcia of 144 BC.

The city was, however, already served by two waterleats, for the most part in underground tunnels, called aqua Appia (312 BC) and aqua Anio Vetus (272); both were prestige works like the first generation of public roads, with which they had associations, and in the case of the Anio Vetus drawing to Rome the water of the river Anio from its upper course a considerable distance away. The ease of tunnelling in the volcanic tufa of Rome's neighbourhood had combined with the problems of water management on a relatively wet west-facing coast to create an indigenous tradition of hydraulic engineering in Etruria, where extensive networks of land drains (*cuniculi*) were developed.

A supply of copious clean water was needed for a steadily increasing population. Most aqueducts, moreover (more or less legally), provided some water for irrigation in the market-garden belts in and around city walls, while some were used to turn water-mills (notably at Barbégal near Arles). But the growing popularity of water-intensive services such as *baths and fountains also promoted the development of the aqueduct system, while there was considerable kudos to be gained by such spectacular reworkings of the dispositions of nature. By the imperial period, aqueducts became a widespread status symbol, and the great bridges (like the Pont du Gard on the aqueduct at Nîmes (Nemausus) or that at Segovia in Spain) which are so famous today owe something to the need for visibility and show.

Imperial benefaction created the most ambitious projects. As a sign of Rome's status as world-capital and to supply their elaborate waterworks Agrippa and Augustus added three aqueducts to its supply (the first after the aqua Tepula of 125 BC), and established an administrative infrastructure for maintaining the system. Aquae Iuliae or Augustae became standard in the repertoire of what favoured cities in Italy might receive: the longest of all was that which conveyed the water of the Serino spring to the cities of Campania. The Claudian aqueducts at Rome, aqua Claudia and Anio Novus, were also on the most ambitious scale, with very long sections on arches to maintain the head of water necessary for access all across the city of Rome. Further additions to the network were made under Trajan and Caracalla (for his baths): we know less about the period after the work of Sextus Iulius Frontinus, our outstandingly detailed description of Rome's aqueducts in about AD 100. Dues were payable for private use of water, but no attempt was made in any city to cover the cost of the system, which always remained a public benefaction.   R. A. T.; N. P.

Ara Pacis, a monumental altar erected at Rome in the northern Campus Martius near the via Lata (Corso), considered one of the major products of Augustan public art. It was voted in 13 BC by the senate, as *Augustus records in his Testament (see RES GESTAE), to commemorate his safe return from Gaul and Spain; and finished in 9 BC. The altar proper was surrounded by a walled precinct (11.6 × 10.6 m.; 38 × 34¾ ft.) with entrances to east and west, and decorated with sculptured reliefs on two tiers. Internally there were festoons slung from ox-heads above and fluting below; externally the lower frieze was filled with complex acanthus scrolls, above which on the east and west were mythological panels, on the north and south a religious procession showing the imperial family, lictors, priests, magistrates, and representations of the Roman people. Smaller reliefs on the inner altar showing Vestals (see VESTA AND VESTALS), priests, sacrificial animals, etc., continue the procession on the outer walls. The event represented by this procession has been much disputed, a *supplicatio* (formal period of public rejoicing) of 13 BC being recently proposed rather than the consecration of the altar itself.

Several of the sculptured slabs were brought to light about 1568, others in 1859 and 1903. In 1937–8 the site was thoroughly explored and the monument reconstructed, with most of its surviving sculptures, between the Mausoleum of Augustus and the Tiber. See SCULPTURE, ROMAN.   J. D.

archaeology, classical (*see facing page*)

archaeology, underwater The potential richness of the sea for salvage or accidental finding of sunken valuables was recognized from earliest times, but the possibility of defining meaningful groups of wrecked material or of interpreting submerged sites scarcely predates the widespread adoption of underwater breathing-apparatus in the 20th cent. Standard apparatus, supplied with compressed air from the surface, as used by sponge divers, enabled the discovery and partial excavation of rich 1st-cent. BC cargoes at Antikythera (1900–1) and Mahdia (1908–13), but the unwieldy equipment, reliance on untrained working

[*continued on p. 59*]

classical archaeology

classical archaeology, properly the study of the whole material culture of ancient Greece and Rome, is often understood in a somewhat narrower sense. Epigraphy, the study of inscriptions on permanent materials, is today more widely seen as a branch of historical rather than of archaeological enquiry; while numismatics, the study of coins, has become a largely independent discipline. The chronological limits are also open to debate. In the case of the Greek world, it has become common to distinguish 'ancient' from 'prehistoric', and to treat the archaeology of early Greece—at any rate down to the late bronze age—as lying outside the scope of classical archaeology. For Italy, the same is true down to a later date, after the beginning of the iron age. There is wider agreement in treating the collapse of pagan civilization as the terminus at the lower end.

No less important than these explicit divisions are the unwritten, yet widely accepted constraints on the range of material culture accepted as appropriate for study. These constraints, which have helped to maintain an intellectual distance between classical and other archaeologies, have privileged the study of works of representational art and monumental architecture as the core, sometimes almost the entirety, of the subject. A second prominent attitude, one which indeed inspired the study of the material remains of antiquity in the first place, has been attention to the surviving ancient texts, with the aim of matching them with material discoveries. These assumptions can be traced back to the earliest stages of the history of the discipline; topographical exploration, which also began very early, understandably shared the same deference to the texts. The collection of works of art, a prerogative of wealth rather than of learning, helped to confer on the subject in its early years a social prestige at least

archaeology, classical The first 'excavations' (1811/12) at the Apollo-temple, Bassae (Arcadia), rediscovered and removed its sculptures. The recovery of fine architecture and artworks for long remained the chief concern of classical archaeology in Greece.

as prominent as its intellectual. From Renaissance times in Italy and France, from the early 17th cent. in England, and from somewhat later in other parts of northern Europe and North America, these forces propelled the subject forward. Such excavation as took place before the mid-19th cent. was usually explicitly directed towards the recovery of works of art, with the textual evidence serving as a guide or, where it was not directly applicable, as a kind of arbiter. Once the volume of available finds reached a certain critical mass, a further motive came into play: that of providing models for the better training of artists and architects.

Textual evidence, collectors' preference, and the frequency of recovery combined to make *sculpture pre-eminent among the visual arts. It has retained this place even when the reaction against classicism has deprived it of virtually any bearing on contemporary artistic practice. From 1500 on, the finds from Rome and other Italian sites furnished an increasingly rich body of material. To J. J. Winckelmann (1717–68) belongs the credit for first attempting a systematic organization of this evidence, the limitations of whose range were hardly yet suspected. Only in the opening years of the 19th cent., with the transport of the Parthenon, Bassae, and Aegina sculptures to London and to Munich, did even the learned world begin to glimpse the true range of classical sculpture. From then on, leadership in this field passed to Germany: art history played a prominent part in university education there, and a German Institute in Rome was established as early as 1829. Over the next hundred years, the rate of new discoveries was on its own enough to maintain the vitality of this branch of study, with Adolf Furtwängler (1853–1907) as its most distinguished exponent. A period of consolidation then kept it alive until a series of new finds, some of them from underwater exploration, brought about a further revival of interest in the late 20th cent. (See ARCHAEOLOGY, UNDERWATER.)

With classical *painting, the natural starting-point was the rich series of murals excavated at *Herculaneum, *Pompeii, and other sites from the Vesuvian destruction of AD 79, in the years from 1739 on. Some reflection of lost Greek masterpieces was recognized in these, but in this case there was no salvation to come from the later recovery of the originals. Instead, attention was diverted to Greek painted vases which (though not yet recognized as Greek) had begun to appear in numbers in Italian graves in the 1720s (see POTTERY, GREEK). Then, later in the same century, the foundations were laid for a branch of classical archaeology which, for the first time, owed almost nothing to the surviving textual evidence. Interest was at first directed to the interpretation of the figured scenes on the vases. Late in the 19th cent., there was a shift to the increasingly detailed study of classification, chronology, and, above all, attribution of the works to individual artists. This phase, with which the name of Sir John Beazley (1885–1970) is inseparably associated, lasted for three generations and absorbed the energies of some of the most distinguished figures in the history of the discipline. With Beazley's death, the unique authority of his attributions was no longer available and there was a marked reversion to the study of the content of the scenes (see IMAGERY). Two other strong directions in recent ceramic studies have been laboratory work on the composition of the clay and the closer investigation of the contexts in which the vessels were made, used, and exchanged. Meanwhile Roman wall-painting and *mosaic came to be increasingly treated as manifestations of Roman culture in its own right, rather than as reflections of lost Greek work. The interaction of such art with its architectural setting has become a particular object of research. The study of classical *architecture itself, a central pillar of the discipline during its formative, 'instructional' period, has become a progressively more specialized field, with a largely separate group of practitioners.

The modern history of fieldwork in the Greek world—that is, its redirection towards the goal of recovery of the entire range of the preserved material culture—began with the adoption of a more systematic strategy in the excavation of Pompeii from 1860 on, and received its greatest single stimulus from the discoveries of Schliemann at *Troy, Mycenae, and Tiryns in the 1870s and 1880s. The revelation that the soil could still hold secrets on the scale of whole civilizations—those of the bronze age Aegean—whose existence had not previously been suspected, acted as a spur to many other large-scale projects. In Greece, these have primarily been directed at the great sanctuaries, with the German expedition to *Olympia (1875–) giving a notable lead, followed by the Greek excavations on the Athenian Acropolis (1882– ; see ATHENS (TOPOGRAPHY)), the French missions to *Delphi (1892–) and *Delos (1904–), and a number of others. Large areas of major settlement-sites have also been excavated, notably by the Americans at Corinth (1896–), Olynthus (1928–38), and the *Agora of Athens (1931–). Many of these projects are still in progress, adding vastly to knowledge and providing a training-ground for future practitioners. In Italy, the work has had a broader focus throughout, inspired perhaps by the continuing success of work at the Vesuvian sites. The greatest single focus of interest has naturally been Rome itself, where the discoveries cover almost every aspect of ancient urban life and span a chronological range of many centuries. By far the most extensive field of activity, however, involving intensive work in at least thirty modern countries, has been the archaeology of the Roman empire. While continental Europeans integrated this work into the study of classical antiquity of the historical period, English-speaking archaeologists were quick to turn to the possibilities opened up in the field of Aegean prehistory, in the Cyclades and, after Evans's sensational discoveries at Cnossus, in Crete (see MINOAN CIVILIZATION). Thus, within the space of a couple of generations, classical archaeology came to adopt an entirely new role as an instrument of general historical enquiry.

The most prominent recent innovation in fieldwork has been the introduction of intensive surface survey, first in central and southern Italy, then in the Aegean area and certain provinces of the Roman empire. This technique involves the systematic searching of a tract of landscape, without discrimination in favour of 'likely' locations, to find traces of the pattern of past settlement and activity, sometimes of a specific period but more often of all periods. In contrast with excavation, it is directed at the acquisition of regional knowledge, especially for the rural sector. In all these activities, the use of scientific techniques—for determining the provenance of manufactured objects, for the fuller classification of organic matter, for detection of buried features, and especially for dating—has become increasingly common. In the last-named field, the most striking progress has been made by dendrochronology which, by building up a sequence from a series of trees extending backwards in time, makes it possible to offer absolute dates for tree-rings in structural timbers and other large wooden objects.

Classical archaeology is probably the fastest-changing branch of Classical Studies. One symptom of this is that it is no longer possible to secure universal assent to any definition of its role, either within the study of the Classics or within world archaeology. But pluralism, at least in this case, is a sign of vitality.

A. M. S.

divers, and exclusion of archaeological direction from involvement under water remained serious limitations on progress. Self-contained breathing-apparatus (the aqualung) came into widespread use after 1945, and resulted in the growth of diving for sport and pleasure; many ancient wrecks were discovered, especially in southern France, and the importance of this resource was recognized by F. Benoit. However, he did not direct operations under water, and his main underwater project, the excavation at the islet of Le Grand Congloué (1952–7), has subsequently been shown to have confused two superimposed Roman wrecks. *In situ* recording and interpretation were developed especially by P. Tailliez at the Roman wreck of Le Titan, southern France (1957), but the combination of these techniques with archaeological project-design and report-preparation did not mature until the establishment of a French national underwater archaeological service in 1967, which, beginning with A. Tchernia (1967–70), has

developed both field techniques and also regular publications. In Italy, N. Lamboglia recognized the value of wreck sites in the 1940s, and established an underwater archaeological institute which carried out important excavations, e.g. at Albenga, though until recent years there remained a gap between the archaeological director (who dived only in an observation bell) and the excavation team of technicians. Meanwhile, British and American field-archaeology traditions resulted in the impact of H. Frost and P. Throckmorton on underwater sites, especially in the emphasis on methodical observation and recording before any excavation; this found expression in the successful Cape Gelidonya project (Lycia) led by G. F. Bass, which finally established underwater archaeology as a respectable, worthwhile branch of the discipline. Subsequently, work on shipwrecks has developed successfully not only under the aegis of foreign expeditions, notably those of the Institute of Nautical Archaeology, but

archaeology, underwater Excavation of a bronze-age merchantman wrecked off the S. coast of Turkey (Ulu Burun) c.1350 BC. A floating treasury of metals, minerals and exotic products, it is one of over 1,000 shipwreck sites known from the Mediterranean, and is the earliest ship to be found in the open sea.

also through the growth of national and university institutes in Israel, Greece, Italy, France, Spain, and Croatia. Important developments have included the integration of excavation, post-excavation, conservation, and reconstruction of wrecks (notably at Kyrenia, Cyprus), and the development of remote sensing and of remotely operated or piloted submersibles for survey below the effective free-diving limit (50–70 m.; 160–230 ft.). Meanwhile, the study of sea-level change and submerged settlement-sites, notably by N. C. Flemming, has emphasized the significant information which can be recovered from underwater sites (e.g. the plan of the bronze-age settlement on the isle of Elaphonisos, off SE Peloponnese), and the importance of underwater investigation for understanding ancient harbours, not least Caesarea (by A. Raban). See RIACE WARRIORS. A. J. P.

Archilochus, Greek iambic and elegiac poet, from Paros. He mentioned Gyges, who died *c*.652 BC (fr. 19), and a total solar eclipse which was almost certainly that of 6 April 648 (fr. 122); a memorial to his friend Glaucus, son of Leptines (fr. 131), in late 7th-cent. lettering, has been found on Thasos, where Archilochus spent part of his life (*SEG* 14. 565). His poetry was concerned with his personal affairs and with contemporary public events—politics, shipwrecks, war, etc. Its tone varied widely, from grave to gay, from pleasantly bantering to bitter. Archilochus was famous throughout antiquity for the stinging wit with which he lashed his enemies and sometimes his friends, and for what appeared to be carefree admissions of outrageous conduct such as fleeing from battle and abandoning his shield (fr. 5), or compromising young ladies. He repeatedly attacked one Lycambes, who had (or so the ancients understood) betrothed his daughter Neobule to Archilochus but later revoked the agreement. The vengeful poet then produced a series of poems in which he recounted in the most explicit detail the sexual experiences that he and others had enjoyed with both Neobule and her sister. This (so the legend goes) induced Lycambes and his daughters to hang themselves for shame. We have several fragments from sexual narratives (e.g. frs. 30–48). However, in the 'Cologne Epode' discovered in 1974 (fr. 196a) Neobule is represented as available for Archilochus but he dismisses her as overblown and promiscuous, while gently seducing the younger sister. The whole business has to be considered against the background of the Ionian *iambos* and its conventions of bawdy narrative and abuse of individuals.

The ancients arranged Archilochus' work in four sections: Elegiacs, (iambic) Trimeters, (trochaic) Tetrameters, and Epodes, with a couple of inauthentic pieces (frs. 322–4) tagged on at the end. Most celebrated were the Epodes, songs in simple strophes usually made up of a hexameter or iambic trimeter plus one or two shorter cola. Most famous of all was the first Epode, in which Archilochus remonstrated with Lycambes using the fable of the fox and the eagle (frs. 172–81). He used an animal fable in at least one other Epode (frs. 185–7). The lubricious material is con-

centrated in the Trimeters, though they also contained some serious pieces. The Tetrameters and Elegiacs were also of mixed character, but Archilochus clearly favoured tetrameters for elevated subjects such as accounts of battles (e.g. frs. 94, 98) and warnings of political dangers (frs. 105–6). Several of the elegiac fragments (8–13) lament men drowned at sea. M. L. W.

architecture (*see following page*)

archives

Greek (*ta dēmosia grammata* and variations; *archeion* is mainly Hellenistic). In Archaic Greece, documentation was minimal, laws being the most important public documents; lists of officials and agonistic victors (see GAMES) were evidently recorded (and later published), but the public inscriptions themselves were probably the 'stone archives' (see RECORDS AND RECORD-KEEPING). Temples were safe deposits from early on (e.g. Heraclitus deposited in a temple a copy of his own book), and might contain public inscriptions: hence they often came to house the archives of the city: e.g. the Athenian Metroon, also a shrine; archives of 2nd-cent BC Paros. Documents were also kept separately by the officials concerned, or in their offices (on wooden tablets (*pinakes*), or whitened boards (*leukōmata*), or papyri), e.g. the Athenian cavalry archive, the records of the *pōlētai* (Athenian officials who sold or leased state property) (*Ath. pol.* 47–8), and there was little centralization. Athens acquired a central archive, the Metroon, in the late 5th cent. BC; manned by slaves, this housed official documents of the Council and assembly, i.e. mainly decrees, some foreign letters, and treaties with other cities (previously kept in the Council chamber or *bouleutērion*, or else on stone); the laws were probably not kept there until the late 4th cent., nor were private documents like *Epicurus'* will. Even after the creation of the Metroon, public inscriptions are regarded as authoritative texts. There is a general increase in documentation and hence of archive use from the 4th cent., though the extent and sophistication of archives in Egypt must be exceptional (cf. the piecemeal organization in 2nd-cent. Paros, *Chiron* 1983, 283 ff.). Public archives are increasingly used, and sometimes compulsory (Arist. *Pol.* 1321b), for private documents (contracts etc.) in the Hellenistic period. The registration of property and documentation of other transactions is particularly elaborate in Ptolemaic and Roman *Egypt.

Roman (*tabularia*, from *tabulae* as 'records'). Rome's early records were rudimentary: lists of magistrates (*fasti*), copies of treaties, and priestly records, which were not systematically organized till the late 4th cent. The main archive was the *aerarium*, in the temple of Saturn, established in the early republic and supervised by urban quaestors. It contained copies of laws and decrees of the senate (*senatus consulta*), which were not valid until properly deposited (Suet. *Aug.* 94; Plut. *Cat. Min.* 16–18); also *acta senatus* (later), public contracts, records of official

[*continued on p. 65*]

architecture

Greek The forms of Greek architecture evolved essentially in the 7th and 6th cent. BC. After the collapse of *Mycenaean civilization, construction methods relapsed into the simplest forms of mud-brick and timber, mostly in small hut structures, the main exception being the great 10th-cent. apsidal building at *Lefkandi, over 30 m. (100 ft.) in length and flanked by wooden posts, supporting a thatched roof, a form echoed also in early structures at Thermum in Aetolia.

The development of the Archaic period centred on temples, which in terms of size and expense always constituted the most important building type in the Greek world. Some of the earliest examples such as the little temple of *c.*750 BC at Perachora retained the apsidal form, while one at Eretria (the early temple of *Apollo Daphnephoros) was curvilinear. This soon gives way to the rectangular cella, in major buildings entered by a porch at one end, balanced by a similar but false porch at the back (west Greek temples omit this in favour of an adytum, an internal room at the back of the cella) and surrounded by a colonnade. Such temples of the first part of the 7th cent. BC as that to Poseidon at Isthmia, and to *Hera at the Argive and Samian Heraia were, like Lefkandi, 'hundred-footers' (*hekatompeda*), with steps and wall-footings of cut stone (at Isthmia the walls imitated timber-reinforced mud-brick but were constructed entirely in limestone), but with wooden columns. It is assumed these were already anticipating the forms of the Classical orders of architecture though there is no material proof of this.

Construction in stone, employing the Doric or Ionic orders, developed in the late 7th cent. BC, when the Greeks began to have direct experience of Egypt, learning the methods of quarrying and working stone. The architectural form of temples built early in the 6th cent. BC, the temples of *Artemis at Corcyra (Doric), and the *oikos* of the Naxians, *Delos—probably a temple of Apollo—(Ionic), shows that the arrangements and details of the orders were established by then, and in the case of Doric, these clearly imitate forms evolved from the earlier wooden structures. Thereafter architecture as applied to temples is a matter of refinement and improvement, rather than radical development and change. Ionic architects (especially in the Cyclades) were already using marble in the early 6th cent. Limestone remained the normal material in the Peloponnese, even for major temples such as that of *Zeus at *Olympia (*c.*470 BC), and in the temples of Sicily and Italy, but the opening of the quarries of Pentelicon in the late 6th cent. led to the splendid series of Athenian marble temples of the 5th cent.

Refinement concentrated on detail: the balance of proportions in all parts of the structure, in the precise form of column, capital, entablature, and above all the decorative mouldings. Colour was also used, now generally lost from temples and other normal buildings but well preserved on the façades and interiors of the built Macedonian vaulted tombs of the 4th cent. and later (such as the royal tombs at Vergina; see AEGAE). Here the façades, which imitate temple and related architectural forms, have their painted decoration perfectly preserved because they were buried immediately after the decoration was added. In Doric, clearly, this also evolved with the wooden buildings, whose structural divisions it emphasizes. The colours are harsh, positive blues and reds, with some patterning in contrasting yellow and gold. Refinement of architectural form involves the use of subtle curves rather than straight lines for the profiles of the columns: these evolve from the cruder curvature of early Doric, perhaps itself derived from the naturalistic curvature of Egyptian plant-form columns, and curvature of the temple base or crepis carried up to the entablature may be intended to correct optical illusion, as also the slight inward inclination of columns. Ionic buildings always used slender columns; Doric, very massive at first, becomes more slender—though the continued refinement into the Hellenistic period suggests that the 5th-cent. marble forms of Periclean Athens were not recognized as ideal and Ictinus' interest in the mathematical relationship of various parts, particularly the ratio $2^2:3^2$, demonstrated in the Parthenon, is not generally imitated.

The procedures of design employed by architects are uncertain. Scale plans are known in Egypt, but their use in Greece was probably restricted by lack of drawing material and the limitations of the Greek numerical system, particularly for fractions. Procedures were more likely based on experience and tradition, details of layout being worked out *in situ*. 'Examples' (*paradeigmata*), probably full-scale, of detailed elements would be supplied to the quarries and craftsmen as necessary. Structural systems were simple, based on the principle of post and beam, and dimensions were restricted by the size of available timber beams, generally not more than 12 m. (39 ft.); more complex woodworking systems may have been used in Macedon, where the palace at Vergina has rooms with a free span of more than 16 m. (52¼ ft.). Macedon also developed the vault in the 4th cent. BC but this was not utilized generally in Greek architecture except for the Macedonian tombs and, in Hellenistic times, for gateways in fortifications. In temple architecture there is no complexity of plan, apart from the totally exceptional Erechtheum at Athens.

Other building forms evolve more slowly, and are always influenced by concepts employed in temples. Usually they are less lavish, and economy in construction is an important factor. Colonnades, which had developed largely as a decorative or prestige factor, could be employed extensively in more utilitarian structures, either as free-standing buildings (stoas) or extended round courtyards, both providing scope for adding rooms behind the resulting portico, which could be put to a variety of purposes. As a result, a new principle of architectural design emerges. Temples were essentially free-standing buildings, viewed from the surrounding space. Buildings based on the courtyard principle, which by the 6th cent. had been adapted as the normal arrangement for Greek *houses, were intended to be seen from within, from the space they surrounded. These developments are seen in more progressive places, such as Athens in the 5th cent. BC, particularly in the buildings surrounding the *Agora. *Theatre structures were still relatively undeveloped, and the theatre at Athens did not attain architectural form until the construction of the stone-seated auditorium in the second half of the 4th cent. Buildings might now be more complex in plan, though simple rectangles, or rectangular courtyards, were still preferred, with single roof levels. Curvilinear forms are rare, restricted to a few circular buildings (such as the tholos, and the curvilinear auditorium of theatres). Some complex plans exist, such as the Propylaea to the Athenian Acropolis (436–432 BC), or the near contemporary Erechtheum, but even here it can be seen that the architect is constrained to think in terms of the juxtaposition of rectangular blocks, though using different roof levels, rather than a fully integrated overall design.

It is the Hellenistic age which sees the widest application of Greek architectural forms, with developed arrangements, based on courtyard principles, for exercise grounds and planned agoras. Much structure remained in mud-brick and timber, but there was now more application of stone construction, with columns, to buildings other than temples. Here the simpler Doric order was generally preferred to Ionic. There are some distinctive regional or local developments such as the tall tenement houses of *Alexandria, of which some footings, in regular ashlar blocks, have been discovered. In *Pergamum idiosyncratic architectural forms evolve, employing the local stone, trachyte, not generally used in Greek architecture; but more significant here are the variations in traditional styles, such as the introduction of a palm-leaf capital, and walls formed from inner and outer skins of squared stone with rubble packing, as well as variations in the details of the conventional orders. In the Hellenistic period generally there is some impact of non-Greek architectural form; and although in Ptolemaic Egypt there is a distinctive separation between the Greek form and the continuation of an Egyptian tradition, the development of the more ornate Corinthian order, in the Seleucid kingdom particularly, may well reflect the influence of a local taste derived from earlier architectural usage.

The establishment of Roman authority over the former Hellenistic kingdoms did not lead to any abrupt change in forms of architecture. The troubled years of the early 1st cent. BC must have imposed something of a moratorium on building; but with the establishment of the Augustan Principate conditions favourable to construction returned. (There was something of a false dawn under *Caesar.) Buildings in Athens are either developed from Hellenistic prototypes (the Odeum of Agrippa) or conceived as Classical derivatives (the temple of Rome and Augustus on the Acropolis, based on the details of the Erechtheum). In Asia Minor the distinctive pulvinated masonry style of the 2nd cent. BC continues into the 1st cent. AD. Many of the public buildings of Ephesus were reconstructed in the 1st cent. AD in Hellenistic form. Temples in the Greek areas were normally built with a stepped crepis (though they may well employ the Corinthian order); only 'official' Roman buildings such as the temple of Trajan at Pergamum are based on podia with steps only at the front. In the 2nd cent. this gives way to a more universal Roman style, ornately decorated, habitually using column shafts of smooth, coloured marbles and other stones. Even so, the construction did not employ Roman concrete techniques, though mortared work, and brickwork, occur more regularly. See ATHENS (TOPOGRAPHY); URBANISM.

R. A. T.

Roman Roman architecture represents the fusion of traditional Greek elements, notably the trabeated orders, with an innovative approach to structural problems resulting in the extensive exploitation of the arch and vault, the evolution of a new building material, concrete, and, probably, the development of the roof truss. While the orders remained synonymous with the Greek-inspired architecture of temples and porticoes, it was the structural experiments which facilitated the creation of new building types in response to the different political, social, and economic conditions of Rome's expanding empire.

The importance of the orders reflects the early pre-eminence of temple architecture in central Italy, where the Tuscan order evolved probably under the inspiration of Archaic Greek Doric. By the 2nd cent. BC distinctive Italian forms of Ionic and Corinthian were also in widespread use beside more purely Hellenistic Greek forms. The fully Roman form of Corinthian, distinguished by the scroll-shaped modillions of the cornice, probably of Alexandrian origin, emerged as a concomitant to the growing use of marble in public building during the Augustan age. Among the numerous variants on the Corinthian capital, the most successful was the Composite, combining the acanthus-clad bell of the Corinthian with the diagonal volutes of the Italic Ionic. A purely decorative use of the orders, incorporating many features later to be associated with the Italian 'baroque', was particularly common in the 2nd and 3rd cents. AD, gaining impetus from the increasing availability of various precious marbles. Monumental columnar façades, two to three storeys high, decorated theatre stages throughout the empire, and the device was also employed in the eastern empire and at Rome for public fountains, *libraries, and large bath-buildings (see BATHS). Colonnaded streets also became popular.

New building types evolved in the 3rd and 2nd cents. BC, some, such as the *amphitheatre, purely Roman, while *baths and *theatres, for example, showed more influence from Hellenistic Sicily and Magna Graecia. Sophisticated timberwork allowed for the roofing of large spans in the basilica, covered theatre (*odeum*), and atrium house (see HOUSES, ITALIAN), while the adoption of barrel-vaulting for terracing structures such as villa platforms and monumental sanctuaries (e.g. sanctuary of Fortuna at Praeneste) provided the basic structural system later used in utilitarian buildings such as the Porticus Aemilia and in free-standing theatres and amphitheatres. The high status of the orders in Roman architectural thought led to them being applied as decorous adjuncts to arcuated façades already by the late republic (e.g. the Forum façade of the Tabularium), a motif which found full expression in buildings such as the theatre of Marcellus and the Colosseum and which was to have a strong influence on Renaissance and later architecture.

The decisive developments in Roman concrete architecture in the early imperial period also took place in the context of domestic or non-traditional building types, such as *Nero's *Domus Aurea* (Golden House), *Domitian's palace on the Palatine, and Hadrian's villa at Tibur as well as the great imperial baths, which in turn influenced the later Basilica of Maxentius; the Pantheon, as a temple, is exceptional. The flexibility and structural properties of the new material were used to create an architecture in which the dominant factor was not the solid masonry but the space which it enclosed. Instead of the structural rationality and sculptural quality of Classical Greek architecture, this was an architecture of illusion and suggestion, inspired by the ephemeral pavilions of Hellenistic palaces, in which subtly curvilinear forms based on complex geometries in plan and elevation, splendidly lit and clothed in light-reflecting material such as marble veneer and coloured-glass mosaic, contrived to negate the solidity of the structures themselves. Here too the columnar orders often formed an integral part of the visual effect, e.g. in the *frigidaria* of the imperial bath-buildings, although their structural role was generally negligible. Treatment of exteriors remained simple and traditional, often decorated in either veneer or stucco imitation of ashlar, although in the later empire the curves of the vaults were often allowed free expression outside as well as inside (e.g. the Hunting Baths at Lepcis Magna). It was this exploitation of interior space which found its logical conclusion in the architecture of Byzantium and remains the most important Roman contribution to all subsequent architectural thought.

J. D.

oaths, lists of public debtors, and Marcus *Aurelius' new register of Roman births. It is unclear how strictly the archives were separated from the *aerarium*'s financial functions; the closely associated monumental complex nearby on the slopes of the Capitol certainly contained a *tabularium* (CIL 1². 737), though its conventional identification as a Public Record Office is incorrect (it may in fact be the Atrium Libertatis). Romans continue to speak of records going into the *aerarium* (e.g. Tac. *Ann*. 3. 51). Access was not always straightforward (SEE RECORDS AND RECORD-KEEPING). Another archive was used by the *plebs* in the temple of Ceres (holding *plebiscita* and *senatus consulta*); censors' records went into the temple of the Nymphs and Atrium Libertatis; and private archives, e.g. of ex-officials, were also commonly kept (cf. Cic. *Sull*. 42). Inscriptions, like the bronze tablets of laws visible on the Capitol, formed a public source of reference. Under the empire, the focus is increasingly on the emperor's archival records, often called the *tabularium principis*: the emperor's *commentarii* (memoranda) included imperial edicts and letters (cf. Plin. *Ep*. 10. 65, 66); *commentarii* recording grants of Roman *citizenship (recorded in the *tabula Banasitana*) were established by *Augustus (*JRS* 1973, 86 ff.). R. T.

Ares, the Greek war-god as embodiment of the ambivalent (destructive but often useful) forces of war, in contrast to Athena who represents the intelligent and orderly use of war to defend the *polis*.

The name is perhaps attested on Linear B tablets from Cnossus (SEE MINOAN CIVILIZATION) and, in a theophoric name, from Thebes. In *Homer's *Iliad*, his image is mostly negative: he is brazen, ferocious, 'unsatiable with war', his cry sounds like that of 'nine or ten thousand men', Zeus hates him (*Il*. 5. 890 f.), he fights on the Trojan side, his attendants are Deimos 'Fear' and Phobos 'Panic', and he is often opposed to *Athena (see esp. *Il*. 15. 110–42). On the other hand, a brave warrior is 'a shoot from Ares', and the Danai are his followers. In epic formulae, his name is used as a noun ('the frenzy of fighting'); this must be

metonymy, although the god's name could have originated as a personification of the warrior's ecstasy (Ger. *wuot*). As with the ecstatic *Dionysus, the myth (*Il*. 13. 301) of his origin in Thrace (roughly mod. Bulgaria) illustrates this position outside the ordered, 'Greek' world of the *polis and has no historical value.

Mythology makes Ares the son of *Zeus and *Hera (Hes. *Theog*. 922, together with their daughters Hebe and Eileithyia), thus inscribing him in Zeus' world-order, and the lover of *Aphrodite (*Od*. 8. 267–366) whose eroticism is at least as liable to subvert the *polis* order (as her birth-legend and some rites suggest). Offspring of Ares and Aphrodite are Deimos and Phobos (Hes. *Theog*. 934), *Eros (Simonides, 575 *PMG*; it underlines the subversive aspect of Eros), the artificial Anteros (Cic. *Nat. D*. 3. 60), and Theban Harmonia. Among other children of Ares, unruly and disruptive figures abound (Diomedes the Thracian, Cycnus the brigand, Phlegyas the eponym of the ferocious Phlegyans).

Cults of Ares are rare, and details for ritual lacking; what we know confirms the god's functions, and his marginality. Temples are known chiefly from Crete (Cnossus, Lato, Biannos, perhaps Olus) and the Peloponnese (Argos, Troezen, Megalopolis, Therapne, Geronthrae, Tegea), but also from Athens and Erythrae. Cretan towns offer sacrifices to Ares and Aphrodite (ML 42), who appear in interstatal and ephebic oaths; their combination seems to be typical for Archaic bands of warriors (see Plut. *Pel*. 19 who associates them with the homosexual bond among young warriors). See HOMOSEXUALITY. The Tegean women sacrifice to Ares *gunaikothoinas*, 'Who feasts the women' (Paus. 8. 48. 4), in a ritual of reversal which fits the nature of Ares. In Athens, he has a temple in the rural town of Acharnae and a priest together with Athena Areia, and the two figure in the ephebic oath as the warlike protectors of the city's young soldiers, together with the pair Enyo and Enyalius.

In Thebes, mythology makes him the ancestor of the town (Aesch. *Sept*. 105): Cadmus slays the dragon whom some authors declare to be the offspring of Ares (schol.

Soph. *Ant.* 126) and marries Harmonia, the daughter of Ares and Aphrodite. Actual Theban cult, however, is extremely reticent about Ares: again, he as well as Harmonia seem to belong to the Archaic heritage of warfare (see above); given his nature, it would be impossible to make him the central deity of a town.

In literature from Homer onwards, Ares is identified with Enyalius (e.g. *Il.* 13. 519 and 521, 17. 211, but see *Il.* 2. 651, etc.) whose name Homeric formulae also use as a noun and who is attested in Mycenaean Cnossus. In cult, the two are functionally similar but distinct war-gods, sometimes with cults in the same town; Enyalius is especially common in NE Peloponnese, but receives a marginal dog-sacrifice in Sparta (Paus. 3. 14. 9) where his cult statue was fettered (Paus. 3. 15. 7).

In Rome, Ares was identified with *Mars; the Augustan temple of Ares on the Athenian Agora (perhaps the transferred 4th-cent. temple of Acharnae) meant Mars as the ancestor of Rome; Greek Ares would have been unthinkable on an agora.

In early art, Ares appears exclusively in mythological scenes, together with the other gods (divine assemblies, as for the wedding of Peleus and Thetis or on the Parthenon frieze). First a bearded warrior, he is later shown naked and young (Parthenon frieze), as a warlike ephebe (see GYMNASIUM) with whom not only the Athenians connected him.

F. G.

Aristophanes, the greatest poet of the Old Attic Comedy (see COMEDY (GREEK), OLD), was the son of Philippus and the father of Araros. It has been inferred (wrongly, perhaps) from *Ach.* 652 ff. that he lived, or owned property, on Aegina. Since he considered himself too young in 427 BC (Ar. *Nub.* 530 f. with schol.) to produce a play himself, he is unlikely to have been born earlier than 460 and may have been born as late as 450. He died in or shortly before 386. Eleven of his plays survive; we have in addition 32 titles (some of them alternative titles, and some certainly attributed to other authors) and nearly a thousand fragments and citations. The surviving plays, and the datable lost plays (°) are:

427: °*Banqueters*, produced by Callistratus. It contained (frs. 198 and 222 and *Nub.* 529 with schol.) an argument between a profligate son and his father and also between the profligate and a virtuous young man.

426 (City Dionysia festival): °*Babylonians*, produced by Callistratus. Dionysus was a character in the play (fr. 70), and by its 'attacks on the magistrates' it provoked a prosecution—apparently unsuccessful—by the politician Cleon (schol. Ar. *Ach.* 378).

425 (Lenaea festival, first prize): *Acharnians* ('*Ach.*'), produced by Callistratus; the 'hero' makes, and enjoys to the full, a private peace-treaty.

424 (Lenaea, first prize): *Knights* ('*Eq.*'), produced by Aristophanes himself; Cleon is savagely handled and worsted in the guise of a favourite slave of Demos, and a sausage-seller replaces him as favourite.

423 (City Dionysia, bottom prize): *Clouds* ('*Nub.*'), ridiculing *Socrates as a corrupt teacher of rhetoric. We have only the revised version of the play, dating from the period 418–416; the revision was not completed and was never performed (schol. *Nub.* 552).

422 (Lenaea, second prize): *Wasps* ('*Vesp.*'), produced by Philonides, ridiculing the enthusiasm of old men for jury-service.

421 (City Dionysia, second prize): *Peace* ('*Pax*'), celebrating the conclusion of peace with Sparta.

414 (Lenaea): °*Amphiaraus*, produced by Philonides (hyp. 2 Ar. *Av.*).

414 (City Dionysia, second prize): *Birds* ('*Av.*'), produced by Callistratus, a fantasy in which an ingenious Athenian persuades the birds to build a city in the clouds and compels the gods to accept humiliating terms.

411: *Lysistrata* ('*Lys.*'), produced by Callistratus, in which the citizens' wives in all the Greek states compel their menfolk, by a 'sex strike', to make peace; and *Thesmophoriazusae* ('*Thesm.*')—datable in relation to *Euripides' *Helena* and *Andromeda*, and by political references—in which the women at the Thesmophoria (see DEMETER) plan to obliterate Euripides, and an elderly kinsman of his takes part in their debate, disguised as a woman.

408: the first °*Plutus* (schol. Ar. *Plut.* 173).

405 (Lenaea, first prize): *Frogs* ('*Ran.*'), in which *Dionysus goes to Hades to bring back Euripides, finds that he has to be the judge in a contest between *Aeschylus and Euripides, for the throne of poetry in *Hades, and ends by bringing back Aeschylus.

392: *Ecclesiazusae* ('*Eccl.*'); the date depends on a partially corrupt scholium or ancient textual note (on *Eccl.* 193) and on historical references, and a case can be made for 391. In this play the women take over the running of the city and introduce community of property.

388: the second *Plutus* ('*Plu.*'), in which the god of wealth is cured of his blindness, and the remarkable social consequences of his new discrimination are exemplified.

After 388: °*Aiolosikon* and °*Cocalus*, both produced by Aristophanes' son Araros (hyp. 4 Ar. *Plu.*). *Cocalus* anticipated some of the characteristics of Menander (see COMEDY (GREEK), NEW), according to the ancient *Life* of Aristophanes 1 pp. 1, 3.

In the first period, down to 421, Aristophanes followed a constant procedure in the structure of his plays, particularly in the relation of the parodos (entry of the chorus) and the parabasis (address by the chorus to the audience) to the rest of the play. From *Av.* onwards we see significant changes in this procedure, culminating, in *Eccl.* and *Plu.*, in the introduction of choral songs irrelevant to the action of the play (indicated in our texts by the word *chorou*), and in *Plu.* the chorus seems, for the first time, something of an impediment to the unfolding of the plot (see COMEDY (GREEK), MIDDLE). At the same time *Eccl.* and *Plu.* show a great reduction (though not a disappearance) of strictly topical reference. The evidence suggests that Aristophanes was a leader, not a follower, in the changes undergone by comedy in the early 4th cent. BC. Aristophanes' language is colourful and imaginative, and he composes lyric poetry in every vein, humorous, solemn, or delicate. He has a keen eye and ear for the absurd and the pompous; his favoured weapons are parody, satire, and exaggeration to the point of fantasy, and his favourite targets are men prominent in politics, contemporary poets, musicians, scientists, and philosophers, and—as is virtually inevitable in a comedian writing for a wide public—manifestations of cultural change in general. His sympathetic characters commonly express the feelings of men who want to be left alone to enjoy traditional pleasures in traditional ways, but they are also ingenious, violent, and tenaciously self-seeking in getting what they want. Having been born into a radical democracy which had been created and strengthened by his father's and grandfather's generations, Aristophanes nowhere advocates oligarchic reaction, least of all in 411, when this reaction was an imminent reality. His venomous attack on Cleon in *Eq.* is adequately explained by Cleon's earlier attack on him (see above), and his treatment of other politicians does not differ significantly from the way in which 'we' satirize 'them' nowadays. No class, age-group, or profession is wholly exempt from Aristophanes' satire, nor is the citizen-body as a whole, and if we interpret his plays as moral or social lessons we never find the lesson free of qualifications and complications. In *Eq.* Cleon is worsted not by an upright and dignified man but by an illiterate and brazen cynic who beats him at his own game. In *Nub.* Socrates' 'victim' is foolish and dishonest, and in the contest between Right and Wrong, Right, who is characterized by bad temper, sexual obsession, and vacuous nostalgia, ends by 'deserting' to the side of Wrong. In *Thesm.* Euripides, sharply parodied in much of the play, triumphs in the end. In *Ran.* the end of the contest between Aeschylus and Euripides finds Dionysus in a state of complete irresolution. Modern sentiment admires the heroine of *Lys.*, but possibly Aristophanes and his audience found preposterous much in her which seems to us moving and sensible. Aristophanes' didactic influence (as distinct from his influence in raising the intellectual and artistic standards of comedy) does not seem to have been significant. Plato (*Ap.* 18bc, 19d) blames him for helping to create mistrust of Socrates. On the other hand, *Ach.* and *Lys.* do not seem to have disposed the Athenians to negotiate for peace (*Pax* did not mould public opinion, but fell into line with it), and Cleon was elected to a generalship shortly after the first prize had been awarded to *Eq.* The fact that Aristophanes survived not only Cleon's attacks but also (with other comic poets) two oligarchic revolutions (see DEMOCRACY, ATHENIAN) and two democratic restorations should not be forgotten.

Aristophanes was intensively studied throughout antiquity, and the plays which are now lost, as well as those which have survived, were the subject of commentaries (cf. schol. Ar. *Plu.* 210).

See also COMEDY (GREEK), OLD and MIDDLE; LITERARY CRITICISM IN ANTIQUITY, paras. 2, 3. K. J. D.

Aristotle (*see following page*)

armies, Greek and Hellenistic Apart from what little archaeology can tell us, our earliest evidence comes from *Homer, but it is uncertain how far the poems can be taken as depicting real warfare. To some extent, what happens on Homeric battlefields is dictated by the nature of the poetry. However, with the possible exception of those from Locris (*Il.* 13. 714 ff.), all troops are implied to be of the same type, and there is no cavalry, even the chariots not being organized as a separate force and only rarely being used for a massed charge (e.g. 15. 352 ff.), despite Nestor's advice (4. 303 ff.). Nestor also recommends subdivision into *phylai* ('tribes') and phratries (kinship groups) (2. 362 f.), and other passages suggest organization into lines and files (e.g. 3. 77, 4. 90), but the constant use of the throwing-spear implies a loose formation except in particular circumstances (e.g. 16. 211 ff.).

By Tyrtaeus' time (mid-7th cent. BC), the fundamental distinction between 'heavy' infantry fighting hand-to-hand and 'light', missile-armed infantry, has appeared, at any rate in *Sparta, but the chariot has disappeared, and there is still no cavalry. What organization there is, is based on the three Dorian *phylai*. Archaeological evidence confirms that by the mid-7th cent. BC hoplites (heavy infantrymen) had appeared, and thereafter, for some three centuries, they dominated the battlefield, though some states (e.g. *Macedonia and *Thessaly) relied more on cavalry and the Boeotians also had fine cavalry in addition to hoplites. Some of the less urbanized areas (e.g. Aetolia) also still tended to make more use of light, missile-armed troops, and all states probably had them. Most armies seem to have been recruited on a local basis. For instance, after the reforms of *Cleisthenes, Athenian hoplites were divided into ten units (*taxeis*) based on the ten *phylai*, and the cavalry was similarly divided into two groups of five units.

Most Greek troops were essentially militia. Cavalry and hoplites were drawn from the more well-to-do since they mostly provided their own equipment. Possibly for this reason, there appears to have been little or no training at least until the 4th cent., and very little organization. The smallest unit in the Athenian army, for example, seems to have been a *lochos*, probably consisting of several hundred men, and the same may have been true of the Argive and Theban armies).

The exception was Sparta. Not only were Spartan soldiers trained from boyhood and liable for service from 20 to 60, but their army was highly organized, giving it an ability to manœuvre that other armies lacked, At the beginning of the 5th cent. it may have consisted of five *lochoi*, but these were possibly already subdivided into *enōmotiai* (cf. Hdt. 1. 65. 5), and by 418 BC at the latest, when there were at least six *lochoi*, possibly twelve, each was subdivided into four *pentēkostyes* and sixteen *enōmotiai*, with a proper chain of command (Thuc. 5. 66. 3, 68. 3).

By *Xenophon's time the largest unit was the *mora*, of which there were again six, but it is not certain how many

[*continued on p. 74*]

Aristotle

Aristotle (384–322 BC) was born in Stagira in Chalcidice. 1. His father Nicomachus, a member of the medical guild of the Asclepiadae (see ASCLEPIUS), was court physician to Amyntas II of Macedonia, and Aristotle may have spent part of his childhood at the court in Pella. Although his interest in biology may have developed early because of his father's career, there is no evidence that he began systematic study. Asclepiad doctors taught their sons dissection, but Aristotle probably did not receive this training, since both of his parents died when he was extremely young.

2. At the age of 17 he travelled to Athens and entered *Plato's *Academy, remaining until Plato's death in 348/7 BC. Plato's philosophical influence is evident in all of Aristotle's work. Even when he is critical (a great part of the time) he expresses deep respect for Plato's genius. Some scholars imagine that no dissent was tolerated in the Academy; they therefore conclude that all works in which Aristotle criticizes Plato must have been written after Plato's death. This is implausible. Plato's own work reveals a capacity for searching self-criticism. Frequently these criticisms resemble extant Aristotelian criticisms. An attractive possibility is that the arguments of his brilliant pupil were among the stimuli that led Plato to rethink his cherished positions.

3. At Plato's death Aristotle left Athens, probably because of political difficulties connected with his Macedonian ties. (He may also have disapproved of the choice of Speusippus as Plato's successor.) Accepting an invitation from Hermias, ruler of Assos and Atarneus in the Troad and a former fellow student in the Academy, he went to Assos, where he stayed until Hermeias' fall and death in 345, marrying his adopted daughter Pythias. While at Assos, and afterwards at Mytilene on *Lesbos, he did the biological research on which his later scientific writings are based. (The treatises refer frequently to place-names and local species of that area.) His observations, especially in marine biology, were unprecedented in their detail and accuracy. (His work remained without peer until the time of Harvey (1578–1657), and was still much admired by Darwin.)

4. Invited by *Philip II of Macedon to Pella in 342 BC, he became tutor to Philip's son *Alexander the Great. His instruction focused on standard literary texts, but probably also included political theory and history. Aristotle's opinion of his pupil's philosophical ability is unknown, but in later years their relationship was distant. In the *Politics* Aristotle writes that rule by a single absolute monarch would be justified only if the person were as far superior to existing humans, in intellect and character, as humans are to beasts. He conspicuously fails to mention any case in which these conditions have been fulfilled.

5. In 335, after a brief stay in Stagira, Aristotle returned to Athens. As a resident alien (*metic) he could not own property, so he rented buildings outside the city, probably between Mt. Lycabettus and the Ilissus. Here, in what was called the Lyceum, he established his own school. (The school later took its name from its colonnade or *peripatos*.) He delivered some popular lectures, but most of his time was spent in writing or lecturing to a smaller group of serious students, including some, such as Theophrastus and Eudemus, who achieved distinction. He amassed a considerable library, and encouraged his students to undertake research projects, especially in natural science and political history (where he projected a collection of historical and comparative descriptions of 158 regimes).

6. Pythias died early in this period; they had one daughter. For the rest of his life Aristotle lived with a slave-woman named Herpyllis, by whom he had a son, Nicomachus. Although in his will Aristotle praises Herpyllis' loyalty and kindness, he freed her from legal slavery only then. On the death of Alexander in 323 BC, an outbreak of anti-Macedonian feeling forced Aristotle to leave Athens once again. Alluding to the death of *Socrates, he said that he was leaving to prevent the Athenians from

'sin[ning] twice against philosophy'. He retired to Chalcis, where he died in 322 of a digestive illness.

7. Aristotle left his papers to Theophrastus, his successor as head of the Lyceum. *Strabo reports that Theophrastus left them to Neleus of Scepsis (in Asia Minor), whose heirs hid them in a cellar, where they remained unused until a rich collector, Apellicon, purchased them and brought them to Athens early in the first century BC. This is seriously misleading. There is copious evidence that some of Aristotle's major works were used by his successors in the Lyceum, as well as by *Epicurus and numerous Alexandrian intellectuals (see ALEXANDRIA). At this stage the works were not edited in anything like the form in which we know them. A list of Aristotle's works, probably dating from the 3rd cent. BC, appears to cover most of the major extant texts under some description, as well as a number of works now lost. Among the lost works are dialogues, some of which were still well known in *Cicero's Rome. Apparently their style was different from that of the extant works: Cicero describes it as 'a golden river'. We can reconstruct portions of several lost works through reports and citations.

8. When *Sulla captured Athens (86 BC), Apellicon's collection was brought to Rome, where it was edited around 30 BC, by Andronicus of Rhodes, whose edition is the basis for all subsequent editions. Andronicus grouped books into works, arranged them in a logical sequence, and left copious notes about his views on authenticity. We possess most of the works he considered genuine and important, in manuscripts produced between the 9th and 16th cents. The transmission during the intervening period is represented by several papyrus fragments, plus the extensive papyri from which the (dubious) *Athenaion politeia* (*Constitution of the Athenians*) has been edited. Several of the Greek commentaries produced between the 3rd and 6th cents. AD show evidence of access to now lost elements of the manuscript tradition, and can prove useful in establishing the text.

9. The extant works may be classified as follows:

(a) Logic and Metaphysics: *Categories, De interpretatione, Prior Analytics, Posterior Analytics, Topics, Sophistici elenchi* (= *Top.* 9), *Metaphysics*.

(b) Nature, Life, and Mind: *Physics, De caelo, De generatione et corruptione, Meteorologica* (bk. 4 of dubious authenticity), *Historia animalium, De partibus animalium, De motu animalium, De incessu animalium, De generatione animalium, De anima, Parva naturalia* (including *De sensu, De memoria, De somno, De somniis, De divinatione per somnum, De longitudine et brevitate vitae, De iuventute, De respiratione*).

(c) Ethics, Politics, Art: *Eudemian Ethics, Nicomachean Ethics, Politics; Magna moralia* (probably not written up by Aristotle, but closely based on Aristotelian lectures); *Athenaion politeia* (authorship disputed); *Rhetoric; Poetics*.

Of the works surviving only in fragments, the most important and substantial is *Peri ideōn* (*On the Forms*), a critical discussion of Plato's theories; also significant are the dialogues *On Philosophy* and *On the Good*, and the *Protrepticus*.

Clearly spurious works transmitted along with the corpus include *De mundo, De spiritu, De coloribus, De audibilibus, Physiognomonica, De plantis, De mirabilibus auscultationibus, Mechanica, Problemata* (a compilation of materials from the school), *De lineis insecabilibus, Ventorum situs, De Melisso, Xenophane, Gorgia, De virtutibus et vitiis, Oeconomica, Rhetorica ad Alexandrum*.

10. Many questions have been raised about the status of the 'Aristotelian corpus'. The most plausible view is that the extant treatises are written lectures. The exact wording of most of the material is Aristotle's. We cannot rely on the order of books within a treatise as Aristotelian, or even the grouping of distinct books into a single treatise. All titles and many introductory and concluding sentences are likely to be the work of later editors. Cross-references may be genuine if well integrated with their context. Throughout we are faced with textual problems, some of which require the transposition of substantial passages for their solution. Some sections, furthermore, may have been left poorly organized by Aristotle himself, and are best regarded as assorted notes that were never worked into a finished discussion (for example, *De anima* 3. 6–7). The most serious philosophical problems raised by the state of the corpus come from its duplications: (a) multiple discussions of a single problem, and (b)

a single discussion repeated in more than one context. There are many cases of the first type; here we must ask whether differences amount to incompatibility or are best explained by a difference of perspective or starting-point. Doublets of the second type may be very brief, or they may be several books long; sometimes repetition is verbatim, sometimes with changes. *Metaphysics* 1 and 13 have many chapters in common, with small but significant changes. *Metaphysics* 11 compiles material from other books of the *Metaphysics* and the *Physics*. Books 5–7 of the *Nicomachean Ethics* also appear as books 4–6 of the *Eudemian Ethics*. In each case, we must ask how likely it is that Aristotle himself would have put the repeated portion in both contexts himself. If such a hypothesis creates problems with the overall argument of the work, we should ask whether it is clear that Aristotle himself must have noticed those problems.

11. The medieval tradition led us to view Aristotle's work as a closed, consistent system without internal chronological development. This view of the corpus was overthrown early in the 20th cent. by Werner Jaeger's important work, which convincingly presented evidence of development and stressed the flexible undogmatic character of Aristotle's philosophizing (whether or not one agrees with Jaeger's particular chronological story). Thereafter, however, scholars sometimes went to an opposite extreme, hastily assuming incompatibility and making irresponsible use of developmental explanations. In general, it is crucial to recognize the extent to which Aristotle's problems and questions in a particular work dictate his approach to an issue.

12. Aristotle was the first Greek philosopher to attempt a general account of validity in inference. The *Prior Analytics* is thus a towering achievement; though displaced in the Hellenistic period by Stoic propositional logic, it became the dominant account of formal logic from the early Middle Ages until the early 20th cent. The *Topics* and the *Sophistici elenchi* show Aristotle's keen interest in methods of dialectical argumentation and in the analysis of common fallacies and paradoxes; they give us a vivid picture of the philosophical culture of Aristotle's time.

13. In the *Posterior Analytics* Aristotle sets out the conditions under which scientific demonstration will convey genuine understanding (*epistēmē*). Conclusions must be deducible, ultimately, from first principles that are true, basic, necessary, and explanatory of the other conclusions of the science. The scientist has understanding when he is able to show how the more basic principles of his science explain the less basic. (In this sense, understanding must always be of the universal, since particulars cannot become part of a deductive explanatory structure of this sort; this does not mean, however, that Aristotle thinks our grasp of particulars shaky or prone to sceptical doubt.) *Posterior Analytics* 2. 19 argues that understanding is based on the experience of many particulars, and requires the achievement of *nous* concerning the first principles. Although *nous* has often been taken to be a special faculty of mind that grasps first principles a priori, it is probably best understood to be mental insight into the explanatory role of principles that the thinker knows and uses already on the basis of experience. Thus Aristotelian science does not require an a priori foundation.

14. In *Metaphysics* 4, Aristotle undertakes the defence of two especially basic logical principles: the Principle of Non-Contradiction and the Principle of the Excluded Middle. Non-Contradiction, which is called 'the most basic starting-point of all', is established not by a proof from other principles, but by an 'elenctic demonstration', i.e. one that establishes that the opponent who challenged this law actually must rely on it if he is to think and speak at all. For to say anything definite he must rule something out—at the least, the contradictory of what he sets forth.

15. Throughout his work Aristotle is intensely concerned with experience, including the record of experience contained in what people say. It is common for an inquiry, in science as well as in ethics, to begin by 'setting down the *phainomena*', the 'appearances', which usually include perceptual observation and the record of reputable belief, frequently as embodied in language. Aristotle clearly believes that scientific inquiry involves examining common conceptions as well as looking at the world;

indeed the two frequently interpenetrate, as in the inquiries into time and place in the *Physics*. Aristotle is also very careful to survey the views of the reputable thinkers who have approached a problem. As he states at the start of his inquiry into number in *Metaphysics* 13, he can hope in this way to avoid making the same mistakes, and can perhaps hope to progress a little beyond what the tradition has already accomplished. Although we may find fault with his treatment of one or another previous thinker, he was the first Greek thinker to make engagement with the books of others a central part of his method.

16. 'Metaphysics' is not an Aristotelian term (it refers to the placement of that work 'after the *Physics*' in ancient editions), but Aristotle's study of the most general characteristics of things gives subsequent metaphysics its agenda. Aristotle holds that the central question about that which is (*to on*), for both his predecessors and himself, has been a question about *ousia*, usually translated 'substance'. Since *ousia* is a verbal noun formed from the participle *on*, this is not a perspicuous statement. But from Aristotle's procedures we can get a better idea of his problem. Two questions appear to drive the search for substance: a question about *change*, and a question about *identity*. Since a central part of our experience of nature is that of change—the cycle of the seasons, changes in living bodies—an account of nature needs to find a coherent way to speak about process. Following Plato's *Theaetetus*, Aristotle holds that this, in turn, requires the ability to single out some entities as (relatively) stable 'subjects' or 'substrates' (*hypokeimena*) of change, things to which the change happens. At the same time, discourse about the world also requires asking and answering the question 'What is it?' about items in our experience. This means being able to say what it is about an individual that makes it the very thing it is, and to separate that aspect from more superficial attributes that might cease to be present while the individual remained the same. This question, Aristotle holds, leads us to search for (what we now call) the thing's 'essence' (here we borrow a Ciceronian rendering of Aristotle's odd yet homely term, *to ti ēn einai*, 'the what it is to be'). The two questions might seem to point in opposite directions: the first in the direction of matter as the basic substance, since that persists while animals and people are born and die; the second in the direction of the universal, since 'human being' or 'tree' seem promising accounts of the 'what is it' of particulars. But it is Aristotle's view that in reality the two must be held closely together and will ultimately converge on a single account of the basic substances. For any adequate theory of change must single out as its substrates items that are not only relatively enduring, but also definite and distinct; and any account of the essence of a particular should enable us to say what changes it can undergo while still remaining one and the same. Aristotle pursues the two prongs of his question through several treatises, with results that appear to undergo development and are always difficult to interpret.

17. In the early *Categories*, Aristotle argues that the 'primary substances' and substrates of change are physical individuals, such as 'this human being' and 'this horse' (as contrasted both with individual qualities, quantities, relations, etc., and also with universals of all types). On the other hand, we can only individuate and identify them via 'secondary substances', species universals such as 'human being' and 'horse'. Unlike Platonic forms, secondary substances have no existence apart from physical individuals, but they are fundamental to our grasp of them. In *Physics*, and *Gen. corr.*, Aristotle brings matter into the picture and asks about its relation to form or organization. Although he ultimately rejects the notion that a thing's matter is substance, and more basic than its organization, he is apparently driven to grant that some cases of change—the comings-to-be and passings-away of substances—have to be explained with reference to material substrates.

18. Aristotle's culminating inquiry into substance, in *Metaph.* 7–8, is the subject of endless interpretative controversy. On one plausible reading, Aristotle concludes that the most basic substrates are also the essences of things, and that both of these are identical with the *form* (*eidos*) of a thing as a member of a certain species, for example, the humanness (characteristic human organization) of Socrates. This form is a particular in the sense that Socrates is a distinct human being from Coriscus;

on the other hand, the account of Socrates' essence or form mentions only those features he shares with other species members. In other words, what Socrates really is, and what must remain the same about him while other attributes change, is his characteristic species organization.

19. Other major topics in Aristotle's metaphysical work include *potentiality* and *actuality* (concepts linked to substance and invoked in explaining the forms of living things); *number* (Aristotle attacks the Platonist separation of numbers from things); *unity* (organic living beings have more than artefacts); and the nature of the *study of being* itself (it may become a general study with substance as its focal point). In *Metaphysics* 12, Aristotle articulates his idea of god as an eternally active and unaffected substance, whose activity is thinking and who inspires movement in the heavenly spheres by becoming an object of their love.

20. The *Metaphysics* describes the development of philosophy as a search for explanations of natural events that inspire wonder. In the *Physics* Aristotle describes the types of explanation a natural philosopher should be prepared to give. He begins from the question 'Why?' (*dia ti*)—asked either about a thing or a complex state of affairs; he suggests that there are four basic ways in which we can answer such a 'why' question. First, we may cite the materials of which a thing is composed. This answer is inadequate on its own, since we need to be able to pick out the thing as a structure of a certain sort before we can enumerate its constituents. Second, we may mention a thing's form or characteristic organization. Third, we may mention some agent or event that made the event or thing come about—this sort of answer is called by Aristotle 'the origin of change', and by the tradition 'the efficient cause'. Finally, we may mention 'the end' or 'that for the sake of which' a thing is. Aristotle insists frequently that we should explain processes or subsystems of creatures by showing how they contribute to the overall functioning of the creature. The characteristic organization of a species is in that sense an 'end' towards which processes should be seen as contributing. Whether Aristotle invokes teleological explanations to relate one species to another species is highly uncertain, as is the question whether such explanations apply to the non-living. The *Physics* also contains valuable discussions of place, time, and the nature of change.

21. Aristotle's work on *psychē* (*De anima*) is a general study of life and the living. After criticizing materialist and Platonist accounts of *psychē*, he defends the view that *psychē* is the substance of a living thing; he argues that this substance will be not its material constituents but its species-form. His working definition is that *psychē* is the 'first entelechy of a natural organic body'. 'First entelechy' takes the place of 'form' in order to stress the fact that it is not actual functioning (e.g. seeing or thinking) that is the *psychē*, but the organization-to-function. 'Organic' seems to mean 'equipped with materials that are suitable for performing these functions'. Aristotle goes on to give more concrete accounts of self-nutrition, reproduction, perceiving, imagining, and thinking; these inquiries are further developed in the *Parva naturalia* and, in some cases, the biological writings.

22. Aristotle's ethical treatises search for an adequate account of *eudaimonia*, a term usually translated 'happiness', but which might more perspicuously be understood as 'human flourishing'. There is general agreement that *eudaimonia* is the 'target' of human choice, and that it involves being active. Reflection, Aristotle holds, will show common candidates such as pleasure and honour to be inadequate accounts of what *eudaimonia* is; it must be understood as 'activity of soul in accordance with complete excellence'. This complex end has many constituent elements; Aristotle investigates a long list of excellences of character (such as courage, moderation, generosity, justice), which are, in general, stable dispositions to choose activities and to have responses that are neither excessive nor deficient in each area of choice; this 'mean' standard is given by looking to the choices of the 'person of practical wisdom', i.e. to paradigms of human excellence. Excellence of character requires and is required by practical wisdom, an excellence of the intellect.

23. Aristotle stresses the fact that practical wisdom requires a grasp of many particulars, which must be derived through experience. Like medicine and navigation, good judgement (in law as well as in ethics) requires a grasp of rules laid down in advance, but also the ability to adjust one's thinking to the complex requirements of the situation that is at hand. His account of 'equity' (*epieikeia*) in public judgement is continuous with reflections on that theme in the Greek orators; it has had enormous influence in the history of western law. Closely connected to Aristotle's accounts of practical wisdom are his reflections on voluntary action and excusing factors, and on choice (*prohairesis*), which is involved, it seems, in the specification of *eudaimonia* into its constituent parts as well as in more concrete operations.

24. Friendship (*philia*), Aristotle holds, is one of the most important elements in a good human life. Even if one were free of need and doing well in all other respects, one would still view life as not worth living without friends. Aristotle seems to hold that any genuine friendship requires mutual awareness and mutual activity seeking to benefit the other for the other's own sake. Friendships, however, come in different types, according to the characteristics of the parties that are the ground or basis for the friendship. There are friendships of pleasure, of utility, and of character, the last being both the most stable and the richest.

25. In two separate discussions Aristotle argues that pleasure is not equivalent to the good. (His accounts of pleasure differ, and may not be compatible.) In the final book of the *Eth. Nic.* he then goes on to praise the life that is devoted to contemplating the eternal. He appears to praise this activity not just as one among the other constituents of *eudaimonia*, but as something of supreme value, to which maximal attention should be given where possible. Scholars have long disagreed about whether these chapters are consistent with the more inclusive picture of *eudaimonia* that appears to emerge from the rest of the work; incompatibilist interpretations have much force. But however we resolve these questions, the chapters give evidence of Aristotle's high evaluation of the contemplative life, and complicate the task of describing the relationship between Aristotle's ethical thought and Plato's.

26. The investigation of human flourishing is a part of the science of politics, since legislators need to know about human ends in order to design schemes that promote these ends. But *political theory requires, in addition, a critical and empirical study of different regimes, and an attempt, on that basis, to consider what the best form of government would be. In the process, Aristotle makes Greek philosophy's most distinguished contribution to *economic theory.

27. Aristotle's great rhetorical treatise argues, against Platonic strictures, that rhetoric can be a systematic science. Defining rhetoric as 'the capability of recognizing in each case the possible means of persuasion', he argues for its autonomy and offers a comprehensive discussion of persuasion through speech. The work includes many discussions of broader interest, including a survey of ordinary beliefs about many ethical topics, and an analysis of the major emotions (see RHETORIC, GREEK).

28. Aristotle's *Poetics* should be read in close connection with his ethical writings, which insist, against Plato, that good people can sometimes fall short of *eudaimonia* through disasters not of their own making. Tragic action, Aristotle holds, inspires two emotions in its audience: *pity* (a painful emotion felt at the undeserved and serious suffering of another person), and *fear* (a painful emotion felt at the thought of serious disasters impending). We pity the tragic hero as someone undeserving of his misfortune, and fear for him, seeing him as someone similar to ourselves. (Plato's *Republic* had argued that both of these emotions are pernicious: literature that inspires them should be removed.) In this way, poetry proves more philosophical than historical narration, since it presents universals, things 'such as might happen' in a human life. Like other forms of representation (*mimēsis*), it gives rise to the pleasure of learning and recognition. The tragic hero's reversal inspires pity if it is due not to wickedness of character but rather to some *hamartia*, by which Aristotle seems to mean some error in

action, sometimes blameworthy and sometimes not. Scholars will never agree on the proper interpretation of the *katharsis* through pity and fear that is the result of watching tragic action. But it should be observed that 'purgation' is only one possibility, and a problematic one; another possibility, perhaps more in keeping with the rest of Aristotle's argument, is that the emotional experience, by removing obstacles to our recognition of the mutability of human life, 'cleans up' or 'clears up' our muddled view of human fortunes. The central concepts of this work remain disputed and in need of close scholarly argument.

29. Aristotle's achievements have been fundamental to a great deal of the subsequent history of western philosophy. His undisputed greatness has produced at times an attitude of deference that he probably would have deplored. On the other hand, few if any philosophers have so productively stimulated the inquiries of other distinguished philosophers; few philosophers of the remote past, if any, are so conspicuously alive in the range of questions they provoke and in the resourcefulness of the arguments they offer.

See ANATOMY AND PHYSIOLOGY; ANIMALS, KNOWLEDGE ABOUT; BOTANY; EXPERIMENT; PHYSICS.   M. C. N.

armies, Greek and Hellenistic A fragment from a public monument (early 4th cent. BC) showing a display of the Athenian cavalry. In Greek warfare the cavalry was never a battle-winner before the rise of *Macedonia, when it came into its own.

sub-units each contained. Xenophon (*Respublica Lacedaemoniorum* II. 4) appears to imply 4 *lochoi*, 8 *pentēkostyes*, and 16 *enōmotiai*, but it is possible that there were really 2, 8, and 32. It is thus also not possible to determine the strength of a *mora*, for which the sources give totals varying from 500 to 1,000: if each contained sixteen *enōmotiai*, its total strength was 640, if thirty-two, 1,280. By Xenophon's time the cavalry was also organized into *morai*, of unknown size, with the rich providing the horses, but not as in other states actually serving.

The Spartan ideal was clearly an army of citizen-hoplites (*homoioi*, lit. 'equals', see SPARTA § 2), but by 425 it appears that they only made up *c*.40 per cent, and there were fewer still by the time of the battle of Leuctra (371). It is usually assumed that the numbers were made up by *perioikoi*, but it is possible that Spartans who had lost their full citizenship (*hypomeiones*) continued to serve in the army, and that the *perioikoi* (subject neighbours) were always separately brigaded.

The defeat of the Spartan army at Leuctra ushered in a short period of Theban dominance, and saw the beginnings of a new form of warfare, in which the traditional hoplite phalanx (close-packed formation) was combined with cavalry and other arms. These changes culminated in the army of *Alexander the Great, but it is possible that the chief innovator was his father, *Philip II. Macedonia had long had good cavalry, known as 'hetairoi' (i.e. 'companions' of the king), but it was possibly Philip who first raised and organized the 'pezetairoi' or 'foot companions', who, with the 'hypaspistai' (lit. 'shield-bearers'), possibly derived from the old royal guard, constituted the heavy infantry. By Alexander's time the *pezetairoi* were divided into *taxeis* of 1,500 men, subdivided down to files of sixteen men, though still called 'decads'; the hypaspists into *chiliarchai* of 1,000 men, then possibly subdivided in a similar way to the *pezetairoi*.

But what marked Alexander's army out from its predecessors was the number of different types of unit all interacting with each other—*pezetairoi* and hypaspists, light infantry armed with missiles, heavy and light cavalry. Alexander's conquests owed as much to his soldiers' ability to cope with any situation, as to his own strategic and tactical skills.

Under his successors there was a tendency for the cavalry to decline, with a corresponding increase in the importance of the phalanx. The latter's unwieldiness was sometimes compensated for by interspersing more mobile infantry units among the heavy infantry, notably by *Pyrrhus in his Italian campaigns, and the vulnerability of the phalanx to flank attacks was also sometimes offset by drawing up a second line. But, in the end, the Macedonian-type army proved no match for the Roman legions, and manpower problems, particularly in Macedonia itself, meant that its kings could not afford to lose even a single battle, whereas the Romans could survive even the most appalling defeats. See ARMIES, ROMAN.

J. F. La.

armies, Roman

Monarchy–3rd cent. AD Traditionally, King Servius *Tullius (*c*.580–530 BC), made the first attempt to channel the resources of the Roman state into military organization by dividing the citizens into wealth groups, so that the weapons they could afford determined their military role, with the richest serving as cavalry. Below these groups were the *capite censi* ('assessed by a head-count'), men with no property, who were excluded from the army. Military service, therefore, although integral to the duties of citizenship, was also a privilege. This organization of the citizens probably emerged gradually and not through the act of an individual, but there is little clear evidence for the early army until *Polybius in the 2nd cent. BC. By *c*.400 BC a small allowance had been introduced for each soldier to help pay his expenses on active service. The body of infantry was called the *legio* ('levying', legion) and by 311 had been divided into four legions; these were supported by contingents of Rome's Italian allies and subjects, grouped in formations comparable in size to the legions and commanded by Roman officers. Archers and other specialist fighters were supplied by *mercenaries.

The Punic Wars (see ROME (HISTORY) § 1.4) stretched Roman manpower resources to the limit. The system of recruitment had been designed for a small city-state fighting short annual campaigns in Italy. Rome now waged long wars, sometimes overseas, and after the defeat of *Carthage in 201 BC, began to acquire provinces that needed a permanent military presence. Consequently, there was a reduction in the property qualification for military service. The annual levy selected citizens of military age (17–46), who were expected to serve for up to six consecutive campaigns but be available for enlistment for up to sixteen years, or ten years in the case of a cavalryman. The army was commanded by the chief magistrates, the consuls.

Throughout the 2nd cent. there was increasing discontent with the levy as Rome faced a series of foreign wars, and the property qualification was further reduced. Then in 107 BC the consul *Marius extended this practice by accepting volunteers from the propertyless and had them equipped at the state's expense for the war in Africa. Undoubtedly conscription along the normal lines still continued, but many volunteers probably chose to serve for sixteen years, and this contributed to the development of a professional, long-term army. The consequences of the Social War (91–87 BC) were also far-reaching, since Rome's defeated Italian allies were absorbed into the citizen body, significantly increasing the reservoir of manpower. Non-Italians now provided auxiliary forces of cavalry (*auxilia*). But the state had no policy of granting appropriate discharge payments to its troops. Generals, often holding long-term commands, used their reputation, and promises of generous benefits, to recruit men with whom they then built up a personal rapport. Increasingly soldiers owed their allegiance to their commander rather than to the Roman state, and became instruments of violent political change. The precedent set by *Sulla in 88 BC of seizing power by military might was not to be expunged, and the republic succumbed to the rival mercenary armies of military dynasts.

*Augustus united these fragmented legions in loyalty to his person and created a fully professional, standing army. This was not revolutionary in itself, but his detailed provision for the troops' service conditions and emoluments, the incorporation of the non-citizen *auxilia* into the formal military structure, the establishment of a personal bodyguard (praetorians), the permanent policing of Rome, and the apportionment of legions and *auxilia* as permanent garrisons of individual provinces, shaped Roman military thinking until the 3rd cent. AD and made military organization an integral part of imperial policy. The most striking development in the command of the Roman army was that from the end of the 1st cent. AD onwards, the emperor, who in his nomenclature and public portrayal bore the attributes of a Roman general, took personal charge of all major campaigns. J. B. C.

Late empire The army of the late empire is brilliantly described by *Ammianus Marcellinus, and its order of battle (c. AD 395) survives in the *Notitia Dignitatum, but its evolution is obscure. As pressure upon the frontiers grew, *Septimius Severus increased the number of legions and, by recruiting the praetorian guard from them, protected himself from other usurpers and formed a strategic reserve. This was supplemented on campaign by the usual frontier detachments. Emperors assumed personal command and, if they proved incompetent like *Severus Alexander, the army replaced them. Promotion of professional soldiers culminated in Gallienus' exclusion of senators from military service, and the premium on mobility in his creation of a separate cavalry force.

This 'élite', as the emperor Aurelian's army is called, was used by Diocletian (285–305) to reinforce frontier armies now increasingly commanded by professional *duces* (generals). But despite his emphasis on fixed defences, Diocletian retained a small mobile army of new units like the *comites* cavalry and the *Ioviani* and *Herculiani* legions. Units though numerous were comparatively small, and were conscripted from German prisoners and volunteers, as well as from soldiers' sons and peasants. Soldiers still received a cash payment (*stipendium*), but it was supplemented by free rations and regular donatives in gold and silver. *Constantine I, however, was the true innovator who greatly enlarged the mobile army with new units like the Germanic auxiliaries and by reducing the frontier armies. He disbanded the praetorian guard, and replaced its prefects as his lieutenants-general with a master of infantry (*magister militum*) and a master of cavalry (*magister equitum*). He created the distinctive strategy of the 4th cent.—frontiers garrisoned by *limitanei* (frontier units), *comitatenses* (mobile army-units) held in reserve—which was crippled by the Goths' defeat of the emperor Valens at Adrianople (378). So many *comitatenses* were lost here that

the western empire was ultimately unable to preserve the logistic base its army required. R. S. O. T.

arms and armour

Greek Most Homeric references to arms and armour are best interpreted in connection with *Minoan and Mycenaean armaments, known from such representations as those on the shaft-grave daggers (see MYCENAEAN CIVILIZATION). The characteristic armour here is a figure-of-eight-shaped shield made from a single ox-hide and swung from the neck by a strap. The only other protection was a helmet. The chief weapon was a long rapier-like sword. Towards the end of the bronze age this style was displaced by the use of a much smaller round shield carried on the arm; a change which involved the addition of a breastplate and greaves, while the sword became shorter and was used for cut as well as thrust. In the Homeric poems the champions begin by throwing spears at each other, and when these are gone they proceed to close combat with swords.

The standing type of the Archaic and Classical soldier was the hoplite (heavy infantryman), ultimately derived from the soldier of the transition to the iron age. The trend now was towards heavier armour and fighting based on weight of manpower. Shields were made of bronze and leather, and spears and swords of iron. In addition hoplites wore breastplates, greaves, and helmets as defensive armour. The spear as used by hoplites and cavalry had become a pike for thrusting, not throwing, and was usually some 2 m. (c.7 ft.) in length. Only light-armed troops and some light cavalry used instead the throwing-spear (*akontion*). Along with the use of the spear as a pike, the sword (at least of the Athenian hoplite) had developed a short, straight-edged blade; it could only be used for very close fighting.

The 4th cent. saw the evolution of a more flexible type of equipment than the hoplite's. Experiments were first made with the peltast (light infantryman), but the final change was the establishment of the Macedonian type as employed in the phalanx (close-packed infantry formation). The spear (*sarisa*) was increased still more in length to a maximum of just over 5 m. (17 ft.), and the shield reduced to a small target carried on the arm. The different ranks of the phalanx used different lengths of spear. The equipment for light-armed infantry and light- and heavy-armed cavalry was also specialized at this period. At all periods, soldiers competed over the excellence of their armour (e.g. Thuc. 6. 31. 3), some of which might be highly decorated. H. W. P.; M. V.

Roman Artistic representations, military treatises, other literary and subliterary references, and archaeological artefacts are the main sources of information. Pre-imperial artefacts are sparse and come mainly from siege sites. Imperial finds are most plentiful, associated mainly with ordered dismantlement-deposits in frontier installations. Late Roman equipment is again sparse, final site-abandonments being less ordered. Roman military equipment represented a constantly evolving and adapting *mélange* of cultural traits.

In the regal and early republican periods the Roman infantry was equipped on the Greek hoplite (heavy infantryman) model. A long thrusting-spear (*hasta*) was the chief offensive weapon, and the defensive armour varied with individual wealth, the richest men having cuirasses (*loricae*), round shields, greaves, and helmets of Greek or Italic form.

By the mid-2nd cent. BC, however, the heavy javelin (*pilum*) replaced the *hasta* in the first two lines (*hastati* and *principes*) of the legion (see ARMIES, ROMAN). A short sword was used for close fighting, a Spanish form of which became dominant. Men of all three lines carried a long, curving, oval shield of Italic origin with a Celtic boss and central spine. Helmets were of the Celtic 'Montefortino' type. A bronze plate (*pectorale*) was worn by the poorer soldiers, and a coat of mail (*lorica hamata*) by the richest. The legionary light infantry (*velites*) had a small round shield, light javelins, sword, and helmet. The legionary cavalry wore a helmet and cuirass, and carried a round shield and spear. The allies (*socii*) were probably armed in corresponding fashion. During the last century of the republic (if not before) the *pilum* became universal for legionary infantry, a change associated perhaps with organization into cohorts (tactical units), relaxing property qualifications, and increased state equipment supply.

In the first two centuries AD new forms of helmets developed from Celtic models. The legionary shield continued to be large and curving, but oval, sub-oval, and rectangular variants were in contemporary use. Scale, mail, and articulated-plate cuirasses were current. The latter (modern usage: '*lorica segmentata*') consisted of steel plates articulated on leather strips, and developed from the first half of the 1st cent. AD into the 3rd. Additional arm- and leg-armour was also sometimes worn. Spears and light javelins were carried by some legionaries instead of *pila*, and all continued with the short sword. Auxiliary infantry and cavalry were also armoured in mail or scale (not plate), but large flat shields of varying shapes were carried. Infantry used short swords, cavalry the long Celtic *spatha*. The majority carried spears and/or javelins, while specialist units carried composite bows or lances (cavalry). Horsemen used Celtic saddlery, wore special helmet types, and had sports armour for training and displays.

The 3rd cent. saw distinctions between legionary and auxiliary and infantry and cavalry equipment disappear— all now carried slightly dished, oval shields (not curved), and wore mail or scale (the '*lorica segmentata*' eventually going out of use). Cavalry helmet forms were adopted by infantry. The legionary *pilum* was generally replaced by a variety of spears and light javelins. Short swords continued in use but *spathae* took over as the main bladed weapon.

Increased emphasis on cavalry involved the use of heavily armoured mounted troops (*catafractarii*, *clibanarii*) on the Parthian/Sasanid model. Into the late Roman period infantry continued to be armoured; some troops

arms and armour, Greek Bronze panoply from a 7th-cent. BC grave at Argos. The bell-shaped corslet, later of leather or linen, was a standard item in the equipment of the Greek heavy infantryman (hoplite).

carried flat, round Germanic shields; but a major change came with the introduction of simple, mass-produced infantry and cavalry 'Ridge' helmets *c.* AD 300.

In all periods the *mercenaries, allies, native levies, etc., valued for their specialized fighting skills, used their own ethnic military equipment.

Military status, especially during the imperial period, was defined by the right to carry arms and especially by military waist-belts. Fittings on the latter constantly evolved but were usually decorative and noisy.

Equipment was manufactured in cities and was largely a matter of individual acquisition and ownership before the 1st cent. BC. Thereafter, the state organized production, manufacture, and supply (individual ownership continued in the Principate), based principally on legionary work-shops and craftsmen. Army expansion necessitated the establishment of additional, city-based, state arms factories from *c.* AD 300 onwards. J. C. N. C.

Arrian (Lucius Flavius Arrianus), *c.* AD 86–160, the histo-rian. Born in Nicomedia in Bithynia, he held local office and pursued studies with the Stoic philosopher Epictetus, whose lectures he later published (allegedly verbatim) as the *Discourses* and summarized in the *Encheiridion* ('Manual'). In Greece between 108 and 112 he attracted the friendship of *Hadrian, who later adlected him to senato-rial rank and after his consulate (?129) employed him for six years (131–7) as legate of Cappadocia. Subsequently he retired to Athens, where he held the archonship (145/6), and perhaps survived into the reign of Marcus *Aurelius.

One of the most distinguished writers of his day, Arrian represented himself as a second *Xenophon and adopted a style which fused elements of Xenophon into a composite, artificial (yet outstandingly lucid) diction based on the great masters, *Herodotus and *Thucydides. The *Cynegeticus* is an explicit revision of Xenophon's mono-graph in the light of the revolution in hunting brought by the Celtic greyhound; and Xenophon's influence is demon-strable in the short essays he wrote in Cappadocia: the *Periplus* (*c.*131), the *Essay on Tactics* (136/7), and, most remarkable, the *Order of Battle against the Alans*, which expounds his tactics to repel the incursion of the Alans (135) in the style of Xenophon's *Cyropaedia*.

Celebrated as a philosopher in his lifetime, Arrian is today principally known as a historian. Works now lost include the eight-book *Bithyniaca*, the history of his native province from mythical times to its annexation by Rome, and the seventeen-book *Parthica* with its detailed narrative of *Trajan's campaigns (probably the source for *Cassius Dio). His most famous work deals with the age of *Alexander the Great. The period after Alexander's death (323–319 BC) was covered expansively in the ten books of *Affairs after Alexander* (significant fragments of which survive on palimpsest and papyrus). The only extant history is the so-called 'Anabasis of Alexander', a history of Alexander the Great in seven books from his accession to his death. A short companion piece, the *Indike*, provides a

digest of Indian memorabilia, based explicitly upon Megasthenes, *Eratosthenes, and Nearchus (see INDIA), and recounts Nearchus' voyage from south India to Susa. Arrian's work is conceived as a literary tribute to Alexander's achievements, to do for him what *Homer had done for *Achilles, and the tone is eulogistic, mitigating standard criticisms and culminating in a panegyric of extraordinary intensity. The sources Arrian selected were *Ptolemy I and Aristobulus, contemporaries and actors in the events and appropriately favourable to Alexander; and the narrative is in the main worked up from material they provided, supplemented by *logoi* ('stories'), mostly from late rhetorical sources and chosen for their colour. Arrian's priority was excellence of style, not factual accuracy. Consequently his account is rich in detail and eminently readable, but is marred by demonstrable errors and mis-understandings. A. B. B.

art, ancient attitudes to
Artists and their work The Greeks regularly equated art with craft, *technē*, which *Aristotle defined as the 'trained ability (*hexis*) of making something under the guidance of rational thought' (*Eth. Nic.* 1140^{a}9–10). Until the late Hellenistic period, there is no evidence that sculpture and painting were viewed as fundamentally different from shoemaking or any other profession which produced a product. Although a number of writers betray an instinc-tive recognition of a qualitative difference between the visual arts on the one hand and utilitarian crafts on the other, no formal distinction was ever made between the 'fine arts' and other arts in Greek thought.

From an aristocratic point of view artists were regarded as social inferiors because they were obliged to do physical work for others, and this type of life was held to have a degrading effect on their bodies and minds (Xen. *Oec.* 4. 2–3; Arist. *Pol.* 1281^b 1–3; Lucian, *Somnium* 6–9). Although this aristocratic prejudice is documented throughout an-tiquity, there is also evidence that not everyone adhered to it. Artists like Phidias, Polyclitus, Parrhasius, and Zeuxis were clearly respected in their own time, and the quality and value of their work was recognized (Xen. *Mem.* 1. 4. 3; Isoc. *Antidosis* 2). Respect for the art of painting in particu-lar seems to have grown during the Classical period, and in the late 4th cent. BC, under the influence of the prestigious painter Pamphilus, painting was added to the normal cur-riculum of Greek education (Plin. *HN* 35. 77).

The modest position of artists in most Greek social and philosophical thought did not prevent some of them from attaining considerable prestige and even wealth. Phidias was part of *Pericles' inner circle; the painter Polygnotus, whom Plutarch describes as 'not just one of the common workmen' (*Cim.* 4. 6), served as Cimon's artistic impre-sario; the family of the sculptor *Praxiteles belonged to the upper level of Athenian society in the 4th cent., and one of Praxiteles' sons, the sculptor Cephisodotus the Younger, undertook costly liturgies (self-funded work for the state); and in the Hellenistic period a number of sculptors are recorded to have held magistracies and been the recipients of honours in various Greek cities. The reputation and influence of artists was further enhanced by the *patronage of Hellenistic monarchs. *Alexander the Great gave special status to Lysippus and Apelles, for example; Demetrius Poliorcetes ('the Besieger') treated the painter Protogenes with special favour; and the early Ptolemies (see PTOLEMY I and II) invited prominent artists to their court.

In the late Hellenistic period a new theory of artistic creativity was developed in which certain artists, especially Phidias, were recognized as inspired visionaries whose insight (*phantasia*) and creative ability surpassed that of ordinary people and made them sages of a sort. This '*phantasia* theory', which grew out of an amalgam of *Stoicism and Platonic idealism (see PLATO), left its mark on a variety of Roman and late Greek writers (e.g. *Cicero, Dio Cocceianus or Chrysostom, and Plotinus) but was never part of the mainstream of Greek thought about art.

Evolving uses of art, Greek   There was a significant distinction in the Greek world between public and private art. The major arts of sculpture and painting fall primarily, if not exclusively, into the category of public art, which had two subdivisions: works with a religious purpose, such as cult images, temple sculptures, and votive offerings; and works with a political or cultural commemorative function, such as portraits of civic leaders, personifications of political ideas, paintings of famous battles, and victory monuments connected with public competitions (see GAMES). Funerary sculpture, although usually privately commissioned, was essentially public in function and also belongs to the commemorative category. Although public monuments usually had a decorative aspect, there seems to have been hardly any public art that was designed to be purely decorative. Even stage paintings in the theatre were created for public religious festivals.

Small-scale works of art which had a primarily decorative purpose, such as paintings on Greek *pottery, engravings on *gems, and jewellery, belong to the category of private art. Some terracotta statuettes may fall into this class, although the majority of these were probably votive. In the 4th cent. BC figural *mosaic pavements became an increasingly common decorative element in private houses, and Plutarch's story of *Alcibiades' efforts to compel the painter Agatharchus to decorate his house (*Alc.* 16) suggests that mural paintings could also be part of domestic decoration, at least in aristocratic circles.

Over time there were two major shifts of emphasis within these categories. First, beginning in the 5th cent. BC, the line between religious and commemorative–political art became blurred as traditional subjects were adapted to convey political meanings (e.g. the Amazonomachy, the Gigantomachy; see AMAZONS; GIANTS). The sculptures of the Parthenon at Athens and the great altar and other Attalid dedications at *Pergamum are notable examples of this trend. Second, as the idea of acquiring works of art for

private delectation developed among Hellenistic monarchs, the major arts of sculpture and painting gradually also became part of the world of private art.

Evolving uses of art, Roman   Art in Rome had the same functions that it had in Greece, but private patronage of artists played a much wider role in the Roman world, and the commemorative aspect of public art tended to have a different emphasis.

The formation of private art collections was a distinctive phenomenon of the later Roman republic and was apparently first stimulated by the vast quantities of Greek art taken as *booty by the Romans in the 3rd and 2nd cent. BC. Captured sculptures and paintings were first used to adorn triumphal processions and subsequently to decorate villas and houses of the triumphators. In time, possessing an art collection became a badge of cultural sophistication, and the drive to acquire collections spread beyond the world of victorious generals. When the supply of looted works of art dried up, the demand created by collectors was met by Greek artists who migrated to Rome, and some of them, like the sculptor Arcesilaus, were able to command huge prices for their work (Plin. *HN* 35. 155–6). By the 1st cent. BC a lively 'art world' had taken shape, populated not only by artists and collectors but also by dealers and even forgers. One significant outcome of this development was the creation of Europe's first public art galleries, in which extensive private collections could be exhibited.

Although historical subjects were occasionally depicted in Greek art, the Romans were much more consistently interested than the Greeks in using the arts to record the details of specific historical events. Public buildings, for example, frequently bore inscriptions celebrating the largess and achievements of the prominent citizens who had built them, and both paintings and relief sculptures documented military campaigns and important public ceremonies. See ARA PACIS.

A fusion of this deep-seated historical self-consciousness with the growing importance of private patronage in late republican Rome resulted in a significant expansion of the scope of ancient *portraiture. The Greeks had produced portraits only of prominent public figures (e.g. military men and civic leaders). By the early empire, however, Roman portraits came to be commissioned not only by rulers and aristocrats but also by citizens of relatively humble status, such as freedmen.

Art criticism   Ancient criticism of the visual arts was of four kinds. (*a*) Professional criticism, that is, criticism current among artists themselves. This focused on various technical achievements and improvements and was often propagated through professional treatises, like the *Canon* of Polyclitus. A number of these were used and cited by *Pliny the Elder and *Vitruvius. The idea for such treatises seems to have originated among architects in the 6th cent. BC and was adopted by sculptors and painters in the Classical period. In the 3rd cent. the principles of professional criticism were incorporated into the first histories of sculpture and painting, which described these arts as pro-gressing through a series of technical improvements towards a state of formal perfection. (*b*) Moralistic aesthetics. In Classical Greek philosophy the visual arts were viewed as forms of imitation, *mimēsis*, and their value was assessed on the basis of the moral and intellectual value of what they imitated (e.g. Plato's criticism of painting for its failure to imitate reality, *Resp.* 10. 596e–597e, and Aristotle's praise of 'moral' painters like Polygnotus in *Poet.* 1450ᵃ23 and 1448ᵃ1). The *phantasia* theory of the late Hellenistic and Roman periods, the essence of which is best preserved in Philostratus (early 3rd cent. AD), *VA* 6. 19, perpetuated this moralistic tradition in criticism but shifted its emphasis from *mimēsis* to the artist's spiritual insight. (*c*) Popular appreciation of *mimēsis*. Throughout antiquity there was a tradition of informal criticism which praised works of art for imitating nature so closely that the viewer was deceived into thinking that the work of art was 'real'. In the Archaic period this may have involved attributing magical qualities to works of art (as in the folk-tales about the works of the legendary craftsman Daedalus preserved in *Diodorus Siculus, 4. 76. 1–6). Later, in the hands of writers like Pliny, the Philostrati, and Callistratus, the marvellous power of illusionism is the dominant theme. (*d*) Stylistic analogy with rhetoric and literature. Cicero, *Brut.* 70, Quintilian, *Inst.* 12. 10. 1–10, and *Dionysius of Halicarnassus in his essays on orators used the developmental histories that grew out of professional criticism as analogies for the stylistic development of rhetoric, prose, and poetry. This type of criticism is of particular interest in art history because it took note of the importance of personal styles in sculpture and painting and approached the idea of style with sympathy and understanding.

See ART, FUNERARY, GREEK and ROMAN; ARTISANS AND CRAFTSMEN; EKPHRASIS; IMAGERY; PAINTING, GREEK and ROMAN; SCULPTURE, GREEK and ROMAN   J. J. Po.

art, funerary, Greek This article covers both architecture and art made specifically to mark and monumentalize the grave; for grave goods (which may be of any sort, and in Greece were rarely, it seems, custom-made for the tomb): see DEAD, DISPOSAL OF.

Bronze age (*c*.3000–*c*.1100 BC). The earliest monumental funerary architecture occurs in the Mesara plain of Crete, where hundreds of circular stone tholos-tombs were erected during the third millennium, each housing multiple burials. Late Minoan rulers were occasionally buried in sumptuous built tombs, like the Royal Tomb at Isopata and the Egyptian-style Temple Tomb at Cnossus (see MINOAN CIVILIZATION). On the mainland, the 16th-cent. shafts of Grave Circle A at Mycenae were surmounted by limestone slabs showing battles and hunts from chariots, and from *c*.1400 the élite were buried in corbelled tholos-tombs, of which several hundred are known from all over Greece; the largest and most famous is the so-called Treasury of Atreus at Mycenae (see MYCENAEAN CIVILIZATION).

Early iron age and geometric period (*c*.1100–*c*.700). Greek monumental tomb-architecture stopped with the destruction of the Mycenaean palaces *c*.1200. Until recently, the subject's history would have resumed in the 8th cent., when large vases became popular in Athens as tomb-markers. In 1981, however, two rich 10th-cent. burials were discovered at *Lefkandi in Euboea, surmounted by an apsidal building 10 m. wide and 50 m. long (11 × 55 yds.): the earliest Greek hero-shrine or heroon. Such heroa were eventually to become a common feature of the Greek landscape. They assumed a wide variety of forms, from the simple triangular enclosure above the graves of seven late 8th-cent. heroes of Eretria to the heroon that Cimon built at Athens shortly after 474 to receive *Theseus' bones, lavishly embellished with frescos by the painter Micon.

Earth mounds topped by undecorated stone slabs were popular as grave-markers in many geometric communities, but at Athens and Argos large vases performed this function after *c*.800. At Athens, massive craters stood on men's graves and amphorae on women's, decorated with multifigured battles and funerals. Despite attempts to identify these scenes as episodes from Homer, they are probably all taken from contemporary life. The Argive vases are no less monumental, though quite different iconographically: their repertoire of birds, horses, fish, water, and men apparently reflects the landscape and inhabitants of the Argive plain. In other communities, most notably on Crete, the bronze-age practice of burial in tholoi persists or is intentionally revived.

Archaic period (*c*.700–*c*.480). The period's chief innovations were the funerary statue and carved gravestone. *Kouroi* (standing, usually nude, youths) marked graves on Thera by *c*.630, and some argue that the type was introduced for this purpose. Funerary *korai* (standing, draped, young women) appear shortly after 600, as do painted and sculptured gravestones. At Athens, these steles soon became extremely lavish, until banned by sumptuary legislation (Cic. *Leg.* 2. 26. 64), apparently *c*.490. Athletes, warriors, hunters, and elders are common subjects; women and children far less so. The less wealthy or less pretentious continued to favour earth mounds, though built tombs of stone or brick appeared around 600. These were sometimes embellished with clay plaques painted with mourning scenes; sets survive signed by Sophilus, Lydus, Execias, and others.

In other areas, funerary art varied widely. *Kouroi* rarely stood over graves in central and southern Greece, but often did so in Miletus and *Samos. These cities' rich traditions of funerary sculpture also included *korai*, seated figures, and lions. Sarcophagi were popular in east Greece: Rhodians favoured plain stone ones, Clazomenians lavishly-painted clay ones. Aeolians and Macedonians liked large tumuli, Thessalians preferred tholos-tombs; and so on.

Classical period (*c*.480–*c*.330). At Athens, the legislation mentioned above decreed that no tomb could be made by

art, funerary, Greek Grave-marker for a young man from Athens (c.340 BC). The idealization of the deceased (handsome, athletic) and the reflective mood are typical of Athenian gravestones in the 4th cent. BC.

869

more than ten men in three days. So whereas high-quality grave-steles with single figures in relief remain in vogue in the Cyclades and Thessaly, until c.430 Attic funerary art is restricted to white-ground lecythi: small, clay oil-flasks usually painted with domestic or mourning scenes in applied colour. Some show scenes at the tomb itself, complete with lecythi standing on the stepped bases of the simple stone slabs that now served as tomb-markers.

Around 430, for reasons perhaps relating either to the outbreak of the Peloponnesian War (431) or the plague (429), grave-steles began to reappear in Athens. At first echoing Cycladic models, they soon developed a standard repertoire of subjects: athlete, warrior, mistress and maid, father and son, married couple, family group, funeral banquet, and so on. Though most are in the form of naiskoi ('miniature shrines') in high relief, low-relief slab-steles furnished a cheap alternative; stone lecythi were also popular, and unmarried women received marble loutrophoroi ('water-jars'). Dead and living are often linked by a handshake, and the mood is usually sombre. During the 4th cent., the steles became larger and more elaborate, until Demetrius of Phalerum banned them in 317; they were often imitated elsewhere in Greece.

In Asia Minor, Greek architects and sculptors built sumptuous tombs for local rulers. In Lycia, the most elaborate is the 'Nereid Monument' from *Xanthus, now in the British Museum. Constructed c.380, it consisted of a square podium embellished with battle-reliefs and surmounted by a small Ionic temple; Nereids stood between the columns, and other friezes, a sculptured pediment, and acroteria decorated its entablature, cella, and roof. The Carian ruler Mausolus used many elements of this design for his *Mausoleum at Halicarnassus. Begun around 365, this most grandiose of all sculptured tombs was widely imitated.

Hellenistic period (c.330–c.30). *Alexander the Great's sumptuous hearse, described by *Diodorus Siculus (18. 26 ff.), set a new standard in funerary magnificence. His own mausoleum at *Alexandria, the so-called Sema, has disappeared, but other royal tombs have survived. In Macedonia, kings and aristocrats were buried in vaulted chambers painted with a wide variety of subjects: hunts, Amazonomachies (see AMAZONS), Centauromachies (see CENTAURS), *Hades and *Persephone, chariot-races, and so on. The most famous of these, tomb II at Vergina (see AEGAE), was probably constructed for King Philip III Arrhidaeus and Eurydice (d. 317/6), not *Philip II (d. 336), as proposed by its excavator. Sculptured monuments range from the 'Alexander Sarcophagus' from Sidon in Phoenicia (probably made for Abdalonymus, Alexander's puppet king), through the mausoleum at Belevi near *Ephesus (perhaps constructed for *Lysimachus, d. 281), to Antiochus I of Commagene's hierothesion at *Nemrut Dağ in eastern Turkey (c.40).

The extinction of the Attic gravestone industry in 317 prompted an exodus of sculptors to Rhodes, Macedonia, and Alexandria, where painted or carved imitations of Attic steles continued into the 3rd cent. Thereafter, Alexandrians interred their dead in underground *necropoleis*, decked out like houses with colonnaded or pilastered façades, and often painted inside. In *Cyrene, faceless female busts set over rock-cut tombs probably represent Persephone. A rich local stele tradition develops in the Asian cities around 200, featuring either funeral banquets or family groups where the dead are overtly heroized. Inscriptions also tell of built heroa with bronze funerary statues of the deceased, but few examples (and no statues) survive. In Tarentum, naiskoi embellished with reliefs of heroic fights, Achilles' last journey, and so on, are popular from c.330 to 250. See IMAGERY.   A. F. S.

art, funerary, Roman Early republican tombs at Rome have none of the decorative features of contemporary Etruscan funerary art (see ETRUSCANS), but by the mid to late republic some aristocratic tombs show a desire for elaboration (e.g. the sarcophagus of Lucius Cornelius Scipio Barbatus and the façade of the tomb of the Scipio family, painted and decorated with statues in niches). From the last years of the republic onwards funerary art ceased to be the prerogative of the rich: even *freedmen and slaves decorated their tombs and bought funerary monuments. Several media were used to decorate the tomb outside and inside, and to provide memorials for the dead. The exterior might have decorations in relief (stone or terracotta) alluding to the deceased's offices or profession (e.g. fasces and curule chair for a magistrate, or a scene of everyday business such as the baking depicted on the tomb of the baker Marcus Vergilius Eurysaces). Portraits of the deceased, represented in the round or in relief, were also popular, especially with freedmen in the late republic and early empire. Inside the tomb there were sculptured free-standing monuments, including the containers for the remains of the deceased—ash-chests in the early empire and, increasingly from c. AD 100 onwards, sarcophagi. There were also commemorative monuments such as grave altars or cippi. The interior of the tomb itself might be decorated with stucco, *painting, and mosaic. Stucco provided architectural and figured decoration for niches in the walls (e.g. the first tomb of the Caetennii and the tomb of the Valerii in the Vatican cemetery, and was also used on the ceilings, which could be subdivided into a complex pattern of smaller fields by stucco mouldings, each containing a painted or stuccoed motif (e.g. tombs 'of the Pancratii' and 'of the Valerii' on the via Latina, Rome). Painting provided colour, but also a variety of motifs placed inside niches, on ceilings, and on walls. In the catacombs painting was the dominant form of decoration, but here biblical stories and Christian symbols replaced the pagan ones in use elsewhere. *Mosaic was used primarily for the floors of tombs, but also appears on ceilings and walls (the most spectacular being the ceiling decoration of the small tomb of the Iulii—tomb M—in the Vatican cemetery, with Christ/Helios in his chariot amid a design of vines on a gold background).

Outside Rome, different areas of the empire developed

their own types and styles of funerary monument and art: tombs of many kinds were decorated with sculpture, both statues and reliefs (e.g. the tomb of the Secundinii at Augusta Treverorum (Trier), with its scenes both of everyday life and of mythology). Tombstones or grave-steles were also used in many areas to mark the grave and commemorate the deceased (e.g. the numerous tombstones of both soldiers and civilians from Roman Britain).

The iconographic repertoire of Roman funerary art is particularly rich. Motifs might refer directly to the deceased: *portraiture, whether full-length or in bust form, was popular throughout the imperial period, and portraits are found both on the façades of tombs and on a variety of monuments such as sarcophagi, where they can appear both in relief on the chest and as a reclining figure on the lid. The deceased might also be represented engaged in an everyday activity, on their death-bed, or in heroized and idealized form, with the attributes of a deity or hero, and women might be represented with the beauty and attributes of *Venus. Battle and hunt scenes, designed to show the deceased's manliness, were widely used on sarcophagi, as were other scenes designed to suggest his virtues. Mythological scenes were extremely popular, and a wide selection of episodes from Greek mythology was used in all contexts, but again especially on sarcophagi. Motifs from the natural world (plants, birds, and animals) abound, possibly reflecting the desire to have one's tomb surrounded by a luscious garden teeming with life. In addition there was a host of other motifs, such as cupids, seasons, sphinxes, and griffins, which could be combined in a number of different ways. Clearly some of these designs had a significance beyond their surface meaning, and alluded allegorically to beliefs in and hopes for an afterlife existence: however, this is an area of much scholarly disagreement, some maintaining that virtually all motifs used in funerary contexts have an eschatolological meaning, others remaining more sceptical (e.g. some think that scenes of Tritons and Nereids swimming through the sea allude to the *soul on its journey to the Islands of the Blest, while others deny the motif any such significance). As the imperial period progressed the mystery religions (see MYSTERIES), with their promise of salvation, gained in popularity, and Bacchic themes (see DIONYSUS) and Heracles (paradigm of a mortal attaining immortality: see HERACLES) appeared more frequently in funerary art.

Much of the private, non-state art of Rome was funerary, and the production of sarcophagi in particular became a major industry, with partially carved chests travelling considerable distances. Although some individual choice of design was possible, and some highly idiosyncratic pieces survive, for most purposes, standardized motifs taken from pattern books were used, personalization being achieved by the addition of an inscription or portrait. Nevertheless, commemoration of the dead, on as lavish a scale as could be afforded, was a major concern for most Romans of the imperial period. See DEAD, DISPOSAL OF; IMAGERY; SCULPTURE, ROMAN.   G. D.

Artemis Daughter of *Zeus and Leto, *Apollo's elder twin sister, a very important Olympian deity, a virgin and a huntress, who presided over crucial aspects of life. She presided over women's transitions, most crucially their transformation from *parthenos* (virgin) to (fully acculturated and fully 'tamed') woman (*gynē*; see INITIATION), and over *childbirth and *kourotrophein* (the rearing of children). She was also concerned with male activities, often (as at Sparta, see below) with their rites of transition to adulthood, also hunting and certain aspects of war. Like all deities, she had different cults in the different parts of the Greek world, but the above-mentioned concerns are part of her Panhellenic persona and recur commonly in local cults; the same is even more strongly the case with her firm association with the wild and her persona as protector of young animals as well as of hunting. It is possible to perceive that the core of her personality is a concern with transitions and transitional marginal places, such as marshes, junctions of land and water and so on, and marginal situations. There is some merit in this, but since such classifications are inevitably culturally determined, we cannot be sure whether this was indeed a core aspect of Artemis or a culturally determined construct created by our own assumptions and preferred conceptual schemata at a time when transitions and things marginal are at the forefront of scholarly discourse—especially since deities were complex beings and did not begin with one function which was then expanded.

In the Classical period Artemis' iconography crystallized into a particular version of the iconographical schema 'young *parthenos*', a version that includes several variants; usually she has a bow and arrow, and she is often associated with a deer. One of Artemis' epithets, it should be noted, is Elaphēbolos (the 'Shooter of Deer'), after which was named the month Elaphebolion. Sometimes, especially in the Archaic period, she was represented through the schema of *Potnia Thērōn*, 'Mistress of the Animals', usually winged, flanked by animals. Very rarely she is shown with wings but not as a Potnia Thērōn, that is, not flanked by animals. Many, but not all, scholars believe that her name appears in the Linear B tablets of Pylos (PY Es 650. 5; Un 219. 5; see MYCENAEAN CIVILIZATION). One of the religious nexuses that contributed to the making of the divine persona that crystallized in the figure of the historical Greek goddess Artemis is the 'Potnia Thērōn' facet of a *Minoan goddess. It is for this reason that Artemis sometimes became associated or identified with another 'later transformation' of that goddess, Britomartis/Dictynna.

In *Homer, Artemis was, like Apollo, on the side of the Trojans. She was a death-bringing deity, for she sent sudden death to women (cf. e.g. *Od.* II. 171–3), as Apollo did to men. Apollo and Artemis together killed the children of Niobe, who had boasted about the large number of children she had in comparison to Leto's two. She or Apollo, or both, killed Tityus who had tried to rape Leto (or, in Euphorion fr. 105 Powell, Artemis herself). Some of the more important myths assigning her the role of punishing deity are that of Actaeon (whom she transformed into a stag and had torn apart by his own hounds), that of her companion Callisto (for having lost her chastity to Zeus), and her demand that Iphigenia (see AGAMEMNON) be sacrificed. According to one version of his myth she killed the hunter Orion for insulting her.

In Attica her most important cults are those of Artemis Brauronia, Munichia, Tauropolos, and Agrotera. As Brauronia and Munichia she was above all concerned with female transitions, especially that from *parthenos* to *gynē*. At her sanctuaries at *Brauron and Munichia little girls between the ages of 5 and 10 served Artemis as *arktoi* (bears), a pre-menarche ritual that turned girl-children into marriageable *parthenoi*. Artemis Brauronia was, in general, a women's goddess, and she included a strong kourotrophic function. Artemis Munichia was also a *kourotrophos*, and in addition she was also concerned with *ephēboi* (youths undergoing paramilitary service); at her festival, the Munichia, ephebes sailed from Zea to the harbour of Munichia in 'the sacred ships', and held races at sea. Then they processed for Artemis and sacrificed, celebrations said to be in commemoration and thanksgiving for the battle of Salamis. The cult of Artemis Phosphoros was also associated with that of Munichia at Munichia, while the torch-bearing Artemis, the iconographical representation of Artemis as Phosphoros, is one of the most frequently encountered types among the votives, especially votive reliefs, found at Brauron (L. Kahil, *AK* 1977, 86–98, and in W. G. Moon (ed.), *Ancient Greek Art and Iconography* (1983), 231–44; L. Palaiokrassa, *To hiero tēs Artemidos Mounichias* (1991), and *MDAI (A)* 1989, 1–40; C. Sourvinou-Inwood, *Studies in Girls' Transitions* (1988); P. Brulé, *La Fille d'Athènes* (1987), 179 ff.). The cult of Artemis Tauropolos at Halae Araphenides (E. Attica) appears to have been associated with a boys' initiation ceremony, reflected in the rite described at Eur. *IT* 1439 ff. as having been ordained by Athena. She ordered Orestes to take Artemis' Tauric statue to Athens, and set it up in a sanctuary that he was to found at Halai. There Artemis was to be worshipped as Tauropolos, and at her festival (as a compensation for the aborted sacrifice of Orestes) the sword was to be held to a man's throat and blood spilled. (F. Graf, *Antike Welt* 1979, 33–41; H. Lloyd-Jones, *JHS* 1983, 87–102.)

Artemis Agrotera had some involvement with war. The Spartans sacrificed a goat to her before battle, while the Athenians, we are told, before the battle of Marathon vowed to sacrifice to Artemis Agrotera as many goats as enemies killed. In the event they could not find enough goats, so they vowed to sacrifice 500 a year, which they did, on her festival on 6 Boedromion, which thus involved a strong element of thanksgiving for Marathon. This festival included a procession to the temple in which the ephebes took part. The sanctuary of Artemis Agrotera was periurban, at Agrae. The overwhelming (though not universal) scholarly opinion is that the temple of Artemis Agrotera is to be identified with the so-called Ilissus temple, built by the architect Callicrates. (On Artemis and war cf. Burkert,

HN, 65–7; J.-P. Vernant, *Mortals and Immortals* (collected essays ed. F. I. Zeitlin) (1991), 244–57, and *Figures, Idoles, Masques* (1990), 162–81; H. W. Parke, *Festivals of the Athenians* (1977); P. Ellinger, *Arch. Anz.* 1987, 88–99 and *Quaderni urbinati di cultura classica* 1978, 7–35.)

In some places, including Athens, Artemis' role as protector of women in childbirth is expressed through her epithet Loch[e]ia (cf. e.g. Eur. *IT* 1097, *Supp.* 958; *IG* 2². 4547; Sokolowski, *LSCG* 154 A 16–17 (Cos)). Elsewhere it is expressed in her identification with Eileithyia (cf. e.g. Artemis Eileithyia in various Boeotian towns: A. Schachter, *Cults of Boeotia* 1 (1981), 94, 98, 101–6); cf. on both epithets Plut. *Mor.* 658 f. It has been suggested that in *IG* 2². 4547 Eileithyia is not a separate deity but belongs with *Artemidi Lochiai* as a second epithet (M. Guarducci, in D. W. Bradeen and M. F. McGregor (eds.), *Phoros* (1974), 60).

At Sparta Artemis had several cults, the most important of which was that of Artemis Orthia, a cult closely associated with the *agōgē* or state training, the long process through which Spartan boys became élite warriors and citizens, though Artemis Orthia also had other functions, not least ones pertaining to female concerns, and there was clearly a close association between Artemis Orthia and Eileithyia since many dedications to Eileithyia were found in this sanctuary. (R. M. Dawkins (ed.), *The Sanctuary of Artemis Orthia* (1929); C. Calame, *Les Chœurs de jeunes filles en Grèce archaïque* (1977), 276–97; J.-P. Vernant, *Mortals and Immortals* (1991), 225–43; R. Parker, in A. Powell (ed.), *Classical Sparta* (1989), 151–2.)

A ritual practice broadly comparable to the Attic *arkteia* (but in much closer proximity to marriage) has been convincingly reconstructed (P. Clement, *Ant. Class.* 1934, 393–409) as having been associated with the Thessalian cults of Artemis Pagasitis at Pagasae-Demetrias and Artemis Throsia at Larissa, the *nebreia*, which consisted of the consecration of girls to Artemis for a certain period during which they were called *nebroi* (fawns). (Cf. also K. Dowden, *Death and the Maiden* (1989), 41–2; P. Brulé, *La Fille d'Athènes* (1987), 191.)

At Patrae the festival Laphria in honour of Artemis Laphria included a procession in which the virgin priestess rode in a chariot drawn by deer and the holocaust sacrifice of many animals; these were thrown alive into the altar enclosure, and included wild animals such as deer and boar, which were not normally sacrificed in Greek religion (cf. Paus. 7. 18. 8–13; G. Piccaluga in *Le Sacrifice dans l'antiquité*, Entretiens Hardt 27 (1981), 243–77).

The cult of Artemis at *Ephesus (on which cf. A. Bammer, *Das Heiligtum der Artemis von Ephesos* (1984)) includes Asiatic elements; but this does not make Artemis an eastern goddess.

Artemis was often identified with other goddesses whose name she sometimes bore as an epithet, for example, besides Artemis Eileithyia referred to above, Artemis Hecate (cf. e.g. Aesch. *Supp.* 675–7).

C. S.-I.

artillery Evidence for Greek and Roman artillery comes from the surviving technical treatises, incidental historical and subliterary references, and, most importantly, finds of both machine-fittings and projectiles. The latter at present date from the 2nd cent. BC to the 4th cent. AD.

In 399 BC artificers of *Dionysius I apparently invented the first artillery piece (Diod. Sic. 14. 42. 1). The *gastraphetēs* shot arrows only, and somewhat resembled an early medieval crossbow. Propulsion force was supplied by a composite bow, which, being too powerful for a man to draw by hand, was bent by means of a slide and stock. Later *gastraphetai*, some of which were stone-throwers, used a winch and had a stand.

Torsion catapults appeared around 340 BC, possibly invented by *Philip II's engineers. Stock, winch, and base remained much the same, but two springs, bundles of rope made from animal sinew, horsehair, or human hair, and held at high tension in a metal-plated wooden frame, now provided propulsive power. Torsion machines improved continuously in efficiency through the Roman period. From *c*.270 BC a technical literature of calibrating formulae and standard dimensions developed. However, torsion catapults did not supersede the large non-torsion types before the later 3rd cent. and small composite machines continued into the late Roman period.

The torsion *katapeltēs oxybelēs* shot bolts only (main calibres: one to four bolt), the *lithobolos* hurled stone-shot (weights of ten *minae* to three talents). Both types had a maximum effective range well in excess of 300 m. (330 yds.). Schramm reached 387 m. (423 ft.) with a full-size reproduction of a two-cubit (approx. 100-cm./40-in.) machine employing horsehair springs. Modifications devised between 200 and 25 BC are reflected in machines described by *Vitruvius, and by fittings from Ephyra, Mahdia, and Ampurias.

Each imperial Roman legion had integral artillery specialists and workshops to design, manufacture, repair, and deploy its *c*.70 *catapultae* and *ballistae* (cf. 1st-cent. AD Cremona finds; also *ILS* 2034). The small but powerful engines illustrated on Trajan's Column and described by Heron of Alexandria (*chiroballistra*), with all-metal frames, were probably developed in the 1st cent. AD. They continued in use into the late Roman period, as evidenced by finds from Lyons, Gornea, and Orsova, and the accounts of Vegetius, Procopius, and Mauricius. By the 4th cent. AD the one-armed, stone-throwing *onager* was also developed.

Artillery figured most prominently in sieges, especially those associated with Rome's eastern wars, and its use spread to the Persian Sasanids through Roman contacts. Whilst the 4th-cent BC Phocian general Onomarchus and *Alexander the Great used artillery in the field, lack of mobility restricted it before the Roman period. Long range made artillery a valuable naval weapon (e.g. Demetrius Poliorcetes ('the Besieger') off Cypriot Salamis and *Agrippa at Naulochus). J. C. N. C.

artisans and craftsmen (see ART, ANCIENT ATTITUDES TO; INDUSTRY; MARKETS AND FAIRS). In Greece the prejudices of the (largely landowning) citizen-élites against the activities of 'mechanics' (*banausoi*), often slaves, *freedmen, or *metics, subjected artisans to formal handicaps in the oligarchic *polis, including limitation of political rights (Ptolemaic *Cyrene: *SEG* 9. 1, para. 8, unfortunately corrupt), restriction of their freedom of movement (Thessalian cities: Arist. *Pol.* 7. 12, 1331ᵃ31–5), and exclusion from the *gymnasium (Beroea in the 2nd cent. BC: P. Gauthier and M. Hatzopoulos, *Meletemata* 1994, 21, line 29), although in the Athenian *democracy their social standing was higher, notwithstanding the condescension of Athenian 'intellectuals'. Craftsmen themselves could be proud of their products, if the 'signatures' on painted *pottery are really those of their makers, as too of their occupations, to judge from the Athenian artisans who stated them in their dedications, including a 'washerwoman' (*pluntria*) (A. Raubitschek, *Dedications from the Athenian Acropolis* (1949), 464–5), the last a reminder of the considerable involvement of women in the humbler crafts, especially *textile production (see *IG* 2². 1553–78 with M. Tod, *Epigraphica* 1950, 3 ff.). Although entrepreneurs could prosper through artisanal activity, craftsmen as a group were largely powerless, since the citizen-group, beyond taxing sales and charging rents for market- and workshop-space, had no interest in promoting industry as such.

The larger scale of the Roman economy gives greater visibility to the entrepreneurial artisan in Roman society, such as the contract-baker Marcus Vergilius Eurysaces, whose grandiose tomb at Rome still stands (Richardson, *Topog. Dict. Ancient Rome*, entry under Sep. Eurysacis), although there is little clear evidence for manufacturing enterprises of more than local significance and—apart from the exceptional case of brick production—the Roman élite cannot easily be linked with manufacture. On the other hand, upper-class disdain for the crafts, as at Cic. *Off.* 1. 42, hardly encouraged the open admission of such links, which certainly accounted for some of the wealth of successful Roman freedmen. Roman craftsmen are widely attested in rural villages as well as cities.

A. J. S. S.

Asclepius (Lat. *Aesculapius*), hero and god of healing.

In *Homer's *Iliad*, he is a hero, the 'blameless physician' (formula in *Il.* 4. 405, 11. 518), taught by the *Centaur Chiron (*Il.* 4. 219); his two sons, the physicians Machaon and Podalirius, lead a contingent from Tricca in Thessaly (*Il.* 2. 729–33). Late Archaic authors fit him into two different genealogies: in a Thessalian version alluded to in a Hesiodic poem (fr. 60 M–W; see HESIOD) and narrated more fully in *Pindar (*Pyth.* 3), he was the son of *Apollo and Coronis, daughter of Phlegyas. Coronis had become Apollo's beloved, but then married the mortal Ischys; when a raven denounced the girl to the god, he (or his sister *Artemis) killed her, but snatched the unborn baby from the pyre, and entrusted him to Chiron. When grown up, Asclepius became a great healer who even raised men from the dead, which provoked *Zeus into killing him with his thunderbolt. Angered, Apollo retaliated by killing the Cyclopes who had made the thunderbolt; in order to punish him, Zeus sent him into servitude with Admetus, king of Pherae in Thessaly. In the Hesiodic *Catalogues*, however, Asclepius is the son of Arsinoë, daughter of Messenian Leucippus (Hesiod fr. 50 M–W), although the story must have followed about the same course as in Pindar, with Asclepius' death by lightning and Apollo's anger and servitude (frs. 51, 52, 54b, c). Thus, already in the 6th cent. BC two local versions of the myth are well attested and show a very early double location of Asclepius; in both, Apollo is already present. A later, Epidaurian version retained 'the daughter of Phlegyas' (Coronis or Aigle) as mother but made Epidaurus his birth-place, where the baby was exposed, nurtured by a goat, and protected by a dog (Paus. 2. 26. 3; hence the sacred dogs and the prohibition of goat sacrifice in Epidaurus).

The two early local myths complicate the question of his local origin. It seems prudent to assume two Archaic foci of a healer-cult of Asclepius, in Tricca in Thessaly and in Messenia. Unlike ordinary heroes, Asclepius must have been very early emancipated from the attachment to a local grave; this allowed him to develop a god-like stature, though in most places he stayed attached to his father Apollo. Tricca had 'the oldest and most famous sanctuary' of Asclepius (Strabo 9. 5. 17, p. 437) which is still archaeologically unknown, while the Asclepieum of Messene has revealed an important Hellenistic complex of inner-city sanctuaries briefly described by Pausanias (4. 31. 10), whose pre-Hellenistic roots are still unknown.

Expansion of Asclepius must have begun in late Archaic times; both Cos and Epidaurus became famous during the 5th cent. The E. Aegean island of Cos was the home of a school of physicians which was organized in a pseudo-gentilicial way (i.e. as if it was a *genos* or kinship-group): following the lead of the Homeric *Asclēpiadai*, they all called themselves the descendants of Asclepius or Asclepiadae (Pl. *Phdr.* 270c). Local tradition insisted on a Triccan origin (Herod. 2. 97). The site of an early sanctuary is uncertain; when, in 366/5 BC, the city of Cos was rebuilt, Asclepius received a sanctuary in a grove of Apollo Cyparissius (*LSAM* 150 A, dated 325–300 BC); the famous oath, sworn to Apollo, Asclepius, (his daughters) Hygieia and Panacea, 'and all gods and goddesses', belongs to the same period. At Epidaurus, Asclepius must have arrived in about 500 BC when his first sanctuary was built below the hill-sanctuary of Apollo Maleatas where cult went back to the bronze age (first *ex-voto*: Jeffery, *LSAG* 180). Epidaurus became the centre for later expansion. Already in the 5th cent., Asclepius had come to Sicyon (NE Peloponnese), brought on a mule cart and in the form of his snake (Paus. 2. 10. 3). Similarly, the god sent his snake to Athens where he arrived in 420/19, coming by sea to his sanctuary in the port of Piraeus (see the account in the Telemachus monument, reconstructed by L. Beschi, *ASAA* 1967/8, 381–436 and *AAA*

1983, 31–43); not long after, he was transferred by cart, together with Hygieia, to his main city sanctuary on the west slope of the Acropolis, well above the theatre of Dionysus. Perhaps already in the 4th cent. BC, a certain Archias who had found healing in Epidaurus, brought the cult to *Pergamum (Paus. 2. 26. 8f.). To cure a plague in 293 BC, the Sibylline books caused the Romans to fetch the god's snake by ship from Epidaurus to Rome, where the snake chose the Tiber island as its home (Livy 10. 47. 7), but a 5th-cent. dedication from Tuscany points to much earlier acquaintance with the cult elsewhere in peninsular Italy, and the architectural layout of the Hellenistic Asclepieum at Fregellae shows Coan influence (F. Coarelli, *Fregellae* 2 (1986)). Epidaurian foundations might in their turn become foci for further Asclepiea, like the one in Cyrenean Balagrae from which derives the sanctuary on Crete at Lebena, or Pergamum mother of the Smyrnaean sanctuary (Paus. 2. 26. 9). The origins of many other Asclepiea are less well documented, but not necessarily late—the Olympian dedication of Micythus of Rhegium who lived in Tegea (central Peloponnese) after 467 BC dates Asclepius' Tegean cult not much later than the Coan or Epidaurian one (Paus. 5. 26. 2); this sanctuary, as many others in the Peloponnese, might derive from Messenia, not from Epidaurus—though later combinations obscure the picture, like the cult of Machaon in Messenian Gerenia (Paus. 3. 26. 9).

The success of Asclepius was due to his appeal to individuals in a world where their concerns became more and more removed from *polis* religion and even from the healer Apollo whose appeal still was discernible in his expansion to Rome in 433 BC and in his popularity in the Black (Euxine) Sea towns: with the one exception of Asclepius' transfer to Rome, it was individuals who were responsible for the expansion. The hero, 'best of the physicians', son of Apollo but still enough of a human to try to cancel death, the fundamental borderline between man and god in Greek thinking, was more easily accessible than Apollo who could proclaim lofty indifference towards man and his destiny (*Il.* 21. 462–6); even as a god, Asclepius was never so distant (see the very personal attachment of Aelius Aristides (see SECOND SOPHISTIC) in the 2nd cent. AD to Pergamene Asclepius).

Most Asclepiea share common features. The children of Asclepius, his sons Machaon and Podalirius and his daughter Hygieia, have cult in most, as has Apollo whom official inscriptions from Epidaurus always name before Asclepius. Most sanctuaries contain a sacred snake, some—like Epidaurus—also sacred dogs. A central feature of the cult is incubation, the receiving of dreams in which the god prescribes the healing; such dreams are preserved in the long 'Sacred Stories' of Aelius Aristides and in the accounts of more or less miraculous healings inscribed in Epidaurus, Pergamum, Lebena, and Rome (M. Guarducci, *Epigrafia greca* 4 (1978), 143–66; H. Müller, *Chiron* 1987, 193–233). Often, actual medical therapy followed the dream: Asclepiea developed into sacred hospital and nursing-homes, but, owing to their wide appeal, also constituted meeting-places for local intellectuals and places of philosophical instruction (as in Cilician Aegae, Philostr. *VA* I. 7). Besides the healing rites, other rituals are possible (initiatory dedications of ephebic hair in Cycladic Paros (*IG* 12. 2. 173); burnt sacrifices in Titane (Paus. 2. 12. 7) with archaic cult images). Most Asclepiea were situated outside the town, sometimes on the seashore or in a lone valley, or at least in a marginal position in town. They share such sites with oracular shrines; both constituted places where man could meet the divine directly (in his sanctuary, Asclepius 'reveals himself in person to man', Philostr. *VA* I. 7).

In iconography, Asclepius generally appears as a mature, bearded man, similar to Zeus, but with a milder expression; a beardless Asclepius, as portrayed by the sculptors Calamis and Scopas, is the exception. His most constant attributes are the staff (see ritual 'putting up the staff' at Cos, [Hippoc.] *Ep.* II. 778 Kühn) and the snake, often coiled about the staff. Generally, the god is standing; in the famous chryselephantine statue from Epidaurus (Paus. 2. 27. 2, see coins), the god is seated, the staff in his left hand, his right extended above the head of a serpent, and beside the throne lies a dog. F. G.

Asia, Roman province (see ◀Map 4, Dc▶) Attalus III of *Pergamum bequeathed his kingdom to the Romans. After his death in 133 BC it was constituted as *provincia Asia* by Manius Aquillius. Originally it consisted of Mysia, the Troad, Aeolis, Lydia, Ionia, the islands along the coast, much of Caria, and at least a land corridor through Pisidia to Pamphylia. Part of Phrygia was given to Mithradates V Euergetes of Pontus and was not made part of the province until 116 BC. Lycaonia was added before 100 and the area around Cibyra in 82 BC. After 80 BC, the SE portion was removed and joined to the new province of Cilicia, as were the Phrygian assize-districts of Laodicea, Apamea, and Synnada between 56 and 50 BC. Under the empire Asia included all the territory from Amorium and Philomelium in the east to the sea; it was bounded in the north by Bithynia, in the south by Lycia, and on the east by Galatia.

The province of Asia was rich in natural resources and in the products of agriculture and industry. Woollen fabrics were a speciality of the interior. Long-established trade routes ran from the interior along the valleys of the Hermus and the Maeander rivers to the harbours of the Aegean. Roman republican governors and capitalists exploited the new province with predatory rapacity and aroused widespread hatred, which was exploited by *Mithradates VI when he stirred up much of Asia to revolt between 88 and 85 BC. Allegedly 80,000 Italians were murdered in a single day at his instigation. After defeating Mithradates *Sulla reorganized the province in 85/4 BC and revised the administrative pattern into eleven assize-districts. This occasion marked the beginning of a new era for many cities, especially in the interior regions of Lydia and Phrygia. Methods of taxation were taken over from the Attalids, but Roman innovations included new customs

arrangements introduced by a law of 75 BC, which, with several revisions, was still in force in AD 62. Asia continued to suffer from heavy taxation and arbitrary exactions through the civil wars of the late republic. The province had the misfortune to pick the losing side in the wars between Mithradates and Rome, between *Pompey and *Caesar, between the tyrannicides (Caesar's murderers *Brutus and Cassius) and Mark *Antony, and between Antony and Octavian, the future *Augustus. Neither victors nor losers in these wars hesitated to milk its rich resources. The principate of Augustus brought relief and was welcomed with genuine hope and enthusiasm, which is reflected above all in the organization of *ruler-cult, both at provincial and civic level, throughout the province.

Asia was now governed by a proconsul (a promagistrate, in this case an ex-*consul; see PROVINCE) who normally served for one year, assisted by three legates (*legati*) and a quaestor. He traditionally landed at *Ephesus, the headquarters of the republican *publicani* (tax-collectors) and later of the imperial *procurators, but spent much of his time visiting the assize centres (*conventus*) of the province according to a fixed rotation, where he heard cases and conducted other judicial business. The structure of the assize-districts is illustrated by an inscription of the Flavian period from Ephesus, which lists the assize centres and the smaller cities which were subordinate to them. Ephesus eclipsed the old Attalid capital of *Pergamum, although these cities and Smyrna remained locked in rivalry for the rank of leading provincial city. The other assize centres included Adramyttium, Cyzicus, Synnada, Apamea, Miletus, Halicarnassus (*JRS* 1975, 64–91).

Under the Principate new cities were created in the interior regions of Mysia, Lydia, and Phrygia; the province thus comprised a conglomeration of self-governing cities on which the Roman system of provincial government depended. The cities were responsible for local administration, for their own finances and building (sometimes under the supervision of a *curator*, an official of the central government), for law and order on their territories, and for tax collection. The province was represented as a unity by the council (*koinon*) of Asia, a general assembly of representatives from all the cities and other communities, which met annually in one of the five provincial cities (Ephesus, Smyrna, Pergamum, Sardis, and Cyzicus) and organized the provincial imperial cult. The high priests (*archiereis*) of Asia are probably to be distinguished from other provincial officials called Asiarchs, but the relationship of the two posts remains controversial. Progress towards provincial unity, however, was always hampered by inter-city rivalry, particularly among the communities of the west coast and the Maeander valley.

Asia was supposedly one of the ungarrisoned provinces of the empire. No full legions were stationed there, but legionary detachments were present at various periods at the Phrygian cities of Apamea and Amorium, there was an auxiliary cohort stationed at Phrygian Eumeneia, and smaller contingents of soldiers were regularly used to patrol routes through mountainous areas. During the 3rd cent. AD soldiers were increasingly present in hitherto peaceful rural areas, leading to conflict and bitter complaints from the rural civilian population.

In the first two centuries AD the cities of Asia enjoyed great prosperity, attested by splendid ruins and handsome monuments, and reflected, for instance, in the panegyric speeches of Aelius Aristides (see SECOND SOPHISTIC). The wealth of inscriptions, locally minted coins, and material remains makes Asia one of the best documented of all Roman provinces. The cities had changed from autonomous city-states into administrative centres, but countless inscriptions attest the eagerness of members of the city aristocracies for public service, their generosity in providing civic amenities (doubtless at the expense of the rural populations which they exploited), and the entry of many families into the senatorial and equestrian orders. The glittering and extravagant society of the coastal cities, with their wealthy rhetors and sophists, contrasts with the traditional, rural-based society of the Anatolian interior. Urbanization brought Graeco-Roman culture up-country, but the basic Anatolian character of the population of regions such as Lydia and Phrygia was of enduring importance and was particularly conspicuous in their religious cults. The strict, self-disciplined morality of Anatolian pagan belief in the hinterland of the province of Asia provided fertile ground where Jewish and early Christian groups flourished. Much of the interior had apparently converted to Christianity before the beginning of the 4th cent.

In the 3rd cent. AD the province suffered not only from the indiscipline of the soldiery and a general decline in voluntary civic generosity, but also from a collapse in security prompted by Gothic invasions of the 250s and 260s, which led many cities to pull down their public buildings to provide material for hastily improvised fortifications. As the political and strategic emphasis shifted away from the Aegean to the Anatolian plateau and to the overland routes between the Balkans and the eastern frontier, Asia lost some of its former prominence and was divided into seven smaller provinces by Diocletian (285–305). In the political order of the 4th cent. the leading cities which served as new provincial capitals—such as Ephesus, Sardis, and *Aphrodisias—retained much of their former glory, but most of the cities of the interior declined until they were barely distinguishable from villages.

W. M. C.; E. W. G.; S. M.

Asia Minor (see ◀ Map 2 ▶)

Pre-Classical Palaeolithic and mesolithic occupation was in caves and rock-shelters and has left simple paintings. The neolithic (*c*.8000–6500 BC) brought settlement in plains and valleys, growth of villages, and the domestication of plants and animals. Vigorous wall-paintings at Çatal Hüyük and clay statuary at Hacılar emphasize hunting, virility, fertility, and childbirth. Painted pottery first appears in the chalcolithic (*c*.6500–3400 BC). An economic upsurge in the early bronze age (*c*.3400–2000 BC) was made possible by developments in metallurgy, attested in metalwork from Troy and from royal burials at Alaca Hüyük, and was perhaps stimulated by Mesopotamian demand for native Anatolian metals. Greater wealth led to universal fortification of settlements and the rise of citadels (e.g. *Troy) and of palaces (e.g. Norşun Tepe). By the middle bronze age (*c*.2000–1700 BC) Assyrians had trading-stations in central Anatolia on which indigenous rulers at (e.g.) Kültepe, Alişar, and Acemhöyük imposed levies. Cuneiform (wedge-shaped) writing was introduced. In the late bronze age (*c*.1700–1200 BC) the Hittites dominated central Anatolia from Hattuša (mod. Boğazköy). Extreme western and northern regions remained largely independent, but a north Syrian province was administered from Carchemish. Famine and Sea-Peoples are thought to have been responsible for extinguishing the state *c*.1200 BC, but the royal line continued at Carchemish and in other north Syrian kingdoms, where Hittite culture survived into the iron age (*c*.1200–700 BC). Central Anatolia was dominated by the Phrygians (capital at Gordium) and eastern Anatolia by the kingdom of Urartu.

D. F. E.

Classical The geographical term Asia Minor is used to denote the westernmost part of the Asian continent, equivalent to modern Turkey between the Aegean and the Euphrates. The western and southern coastal fringes were part of the Mediterranean world; the heartland of Asia Minor lay in the interior of Anatolia, comprising the hilly but fertile uplands of Phrygia, the steppic central plateau, and the rugged and harsh country of Cappadocia. These areas were framed by the Pontic ranges which rise steeply from the Black Sea in the north, and the long range of the Taurus which snakes through southern Anatolia from Lycia to the Euphrates and separates Asia Minor from Syria. In the Graeco-Roman period the region's history is illuminated by an almost limitless flood of historical information, which makes it possible to identify the separate languages, cultures, and religious traditions of its various regions—Bithynia, Mysia, Lydia, Caria, Lycia, Pisidia, Cilicia, Cappadocia, Galatia, Paphlagonia, and Pontus—and also to document the influence of external powers and cultures, above all of Persia, Greece, and Rome. Asia Minor was one of the economic powerhouses of the Persian empire. Much of the population of eastern Anatolia had strong Iranian connections, and Persian settlements were also widespread in the west after the mid-6th cent. BC. Many endured until late antiquity. Greek influence—*Hellenism—was naturally strongest in the coastal areas, where Greeks had established settlements between *c*.1100 and 600 BC. The cultural process, however, was not one-way, and the Greeks of Caria and Pamphylia were also much influenced by pre-existing Anatolian cultures. During the 4th cent. BC Hellenization spread to the indigenous inhabitants of Pisidia and Lycia in the southwest; most of the interior, however, was barely touched before the 1st cent. BC. Roman rule made the strongest impact. In the time of Hadrian Asia Minor was divided into six provinces: Asia, Pontus and Bithynia, Galatia, Lycia and Pamphylia, Cilicia, and Cappadocia, although provincial boundaries and administrative arrangements were more flexible in Anatolia than in almost any other part of the empire. The creation of an all-embracing road network, the universal *ruler-cult, the founding of cities to act as administrative centres, a permanent military presence, and the creation of far-reaching systems of taxation (see FINANCE, ROMAN) forged a new society in Asia Minor, which was as much Roman as it was Anatolian.

The indigenous regional cultures of Asia Minor, however, survived until the end of antiquity, preserving their native languages and their religious practices, above all in the rural parts of the interior and in the mountains. These were only finally erased by the spread of Christianity, which became strongly rooted as early as the 3rd cent. and extended, except for obstinate, usually urban, pockets of paganism, across the whole of the peninsula by the end of the 4th cent. Neither Christianity nor the introduction of Islam by the Turks between the 11th and 14th cents. obliterated the basic patterns of Anatolian life, which were rooted in a traditional rural economy. There was a continuity of population and settlement pattern which can be observed even in contemporary Turkey, where the modern peasant is manifestly the descendant of his Hittite or, indeed, neolithic forebears.   S. M.

astrology, the art of converting astronomical data (i.e. the positions of the celestial bodies) into predictions of outcomes in human affairs. Astrology developed in the Hellenistic age, essentially as an import from Babylon, which equally furnished many of its astronomical parameters. *Alexandria was its major centre. By the 1st cent. BC, it had emerged as a sophisticated technical art, commanding widespread credence and respect. So it remained until the late empire, when its incompatibility with *Christianity led to its formal suppression (though not extinction).

There are several branches of astrology, of which the most important is genethlialogy, the art of foretelling an individual's life from the positions of the stars (i.e. sun, moon, planets, and fixed stars) at birth or conception. The basic astronomical data for calculating a 'nativity' (i.e. a horoscope) are (*a*) the positions of the seven known planets (including sun and moon) relative to one another (their 'aspects') and to the twelve signs of the zodiac, and (*b*) the position of the circle of the zodiac (and thus of the planets moving round it) relative to a second circle of twelve 'places' (mod. 'houses') whose cardinal points ('centres') are the rising- and setting-points on the horizon and the zenith and nadir. The whole may be likened to a complex clock whose seven hands (the planets) turn counter-clockwise at various mean speeds (from the moon's month to Saturn's almost 30 years) against a dial whose twelve hours are the signs of the zodiac; simultaneously, the dial and its hands together rotate clockwise (in a

24-hour period corresponding to the apparent daily revolution of the heavens) against a second, fixed dial which is the local frame of reference for the nativity, itself divided into twelve sectors (the 'places') with the rising and setting points at 9 and 3 o'clock and the zenith and nadir at about 12 and 6. The astrologer reads this clock at the time of birth and then assigns meanings, in terms of the 'native's' destiny, character, and occupation, to the various positions and relationships in the 'nativity'. In antiquity, as now, astronomical tables rather than direct observation were used.

Actual horoscopes survive from antiquity, both simple (as in papyrus fragments) and complex (as in professional treatises, e.g. the *Anthologies* of Vettius Valens, mid-2nd cent. AD). Astrology was popular with all classes; similarly, astrologers spanned a wide social and intellectual range. At the pinnacle were men such as Thrasyllus and his son Balbillus who were theoreticians and practitioners of the art, confidants and functionaries of emperors from *Tiberius to *Vespasian, and connected by marriage both to powerful Romans (*Sejanus and, also under Tiberius, Macro) and to the Greek client-kings of Commagene (SE *Asia Minor). Because it was so widely believed, astrology was potentially subversive of public order. Accordingly, astrologers were periodically expelled from Rome, and Augustus forbade both consultations in private and those concerning deaths (AD 11).

From a modern perspective it is the postulated link, causal or semiotic, between celestial and terrestrial events that renders astrology suspect. Most ancients took that link for granted, under a belief in a 'universal sympathy' which connects all parts of the cosmos in a harmoniously functioning whole. *Stoicism legitimized divination of all sorts, and the worship of the stars, especially the sun (see HELIOS), added further authority to astrology, as did the common belief in the *soul's celestial origin and destiny. Many intellectuals accordingly accepted and justified the art, including such astronomers as Ptolemy who makes a well-reasoned case (*Tetrabiblos* 1. 1–3) that astrology is but the application of *astronomy, in a necessarily fallible way, to the sublunary environment. There were, however, sceptics and critics, among the most cogent being Sextus Empiricus (*Math.* bk. 5), late 2nd cent. AD, and Favorinus of Arles (reproduced in summary by Gell. *NA* 14. 1), early 2nd cent. AD; and low-grade practitioners preying on the superstitious attracted inevitable scorn.   R. L. B.

astronomy 1. The use of the heliacal rising and setting of prominent stars or star-groups to mark points in the year is found in the earliest literature of the Greeks (*Homer and *Hesiod, e.g. *Op.* 619 ff.), and no doubt goes back to prehistoric times. This 'traditional' Greek astronomy continued (with some refinements borrowed from 'scientific' astronomy) to the end of antiquity. It was embodied in the 'astronomical calendars' (or *parapēgmata*, so called from the practice of sticking a peg to mark the current day in holes along the sides) which began with Meton and

astronomy The high level of craftsmanship attained by Greek astronomical instruments is shown by this device, recovered from a 1st-cent. BC shipwreck off the SE coast of Greece. The bronze fragment belongs to a complex mechanism representing the relative motions of sun and moon.

Euctemon in the 5th cent. BC and of which several examples are preserved in manuscript and on stone. These mark important points of the year (including solstices and equinoxes), and use the risings and settings of stars as a basis for weather predictions (the latter already in Hesiod).

2. Scientific astronomy in Greece hardly predates the 5th cent. BC. The cosmological speculations of the earlier Presocratics are irrelevant, and the scientific feats attributed to some of them (e.g. Thales' prediction of an eclipse) by later writers are unworthy of belief. However, some of the basic concepts necessary to later astronomy were enunciated in the course of the 5th cent. Parmenides (A 44 DK) mentioned the sphericity of the earth and stated that the moon receives its light from the sun (B 15). Empedocles went beyond this to infer the cause of solar eclipses (B 42), as did Anaxagoras. Yet how unfamiliar this was even to an educated man of the late 5th cent. is shown by the remark of *Thucydides (2. 28) that solar eclipses *seem* to occur only at new moon. There seems to have been general ignorance about the planets: Democritus (later 5th cent. BC), according to *Seneca (*QNat* 7. 3. 2), said that he *suspected* that there were several (*plures*) planets but gave neither number nor names. Significant for the future development of Greek astronomy is the transmission of elements from *Babylonia (which had a tradition of observational astronomy going back to the 8th cent. BC): the twelve signs of the zodiac appear in Greece perhaps as early as the late 6th cent. (if the lines quoted from Cleostratus of Tenedos (DK 6) are genuine); certainly the nineteen-year luni-solar cycle of Meton was derived from Babylon; but this, like Meton's solstice observations, is still directed towards the goals of 'traditional' astronomy.

3. The 4th cent. saw the introduction of the most characteristic Greek contribution to astronomical theory, the idea that the apparently irregular motions of the heavenly bodies should be explained by geometrical models based on uniform circular motion. Later sources attribute this to *Plato (Simplicius on Arist. *Cael.* 219^{a}23), but although it is not inconsistent, in a general sense, with views expressed in his dialogues, the only certainty is that the first system embodying this idea was constructed by Plato's contemporary Eudoxus. It is significant that Eudoxus was also the first to establish axiomatic rigour in geometry: we may conjecture that it was this success which led to the notion of extending the explanatory power of geometry to other fields, including the heavens. Eudoxus' system of 'homocentric spheres', centred on the fixed, spherical earth, and rotating with uniform motions about different poles, combined simplicity with mathematical ingenuity, and was able, in principle, to account for the retrogradations of the planets and the latitudinal deviations of all bodies, including the moon. The observational elements involved were few, namely crude synodic and sidereal periods for the planets and the moon. Yet even these represent a considerable advance over the ignorance prevalent 50 years earlier: Eudoxus is the first Greek who is *known* to have recognized all five planets (the passages in Plato, *Resp.* 616d–617b and *Ti.* 38c ff., where the five planets are hinted at, may well have been written later than Eudoxus' book). Here again we may suspect Babylonian influence in the observational data, particularly since there are Mesopotamian elements also in the description of the constellations which Eudoxus published. For all its mathematical elegance, Eudoxus' system exhibited serious discrepancies from easily observable facts. In particular no homocentric system could account for the obvious variations in size and brightness of e.g. the moon and Venus. Nevertheless Callippus modified Eudoxus' model to eliminate some of the grosser discrepancies, and this revised model has come down to us because *Aristotle accepted it (*Cael.*, *Metaph.* 1073^{a}14–1074^{b}14), transforming what had probably been for Eudoxus a purely geometrical scheme into a physical mechanism with contiguous solid spheres. Scientific astronomy in the 4th cent. remained at this purely theoretical level: practical astronomy was concerned with traditional topics, the calendar (Eudoxus' *Octaeteris* and Callippus' 76-year cycle), and the risings and settings of stars. The earliest extant astronomical works, those of Autolycus and Euclid, are little more than a treatment of the latter in terms of elementary geometry.

4. At an unknown date, probably not long after Callippus, the epicyclic and eccentric hypotheses for planetary motion were proposed. These provided a remedy for the most glaring defect of the homocentric system, by producing variation in the distance of a heavenly body, while at the same time giving a simple representation of the 'anomalies' (variations in speed and direction) of the bodies; they became the standard models used in Greek theoretical astronomy. No doubt the complete geometric

equivalence of epicyclic and eccentric forms (under suitable conditions), which was assumed in the planetary theory of Apollonius (Ptolemy, *Almagest* 12. 1), was discovered soon after these models were proposed. One might conjecture that it was in examining the transformation of one to the other that Aristarchus of Samos (*c.*280 BC) came to the realization that one can transpose the geocentric universe to a heliocentric one, and so put forward his famous hypothesis. This, like the earlier suggestion of Heraclides Ponticus that the earth rotates on its axis, appears never to have been taken seriously by practising astronomers, although the grounds for rejecting it were 'physical' rather than astronomical. The 3rd cent. probably saw much astronomical activity, but our knowledge of it, derived mostly from incidental remarks in the *Almagest*, is slight. There was more observation, of solstices by Aristarchus and Archimedes, of the declinations of fixed stars (presumably for delineating a star-globe) by Aristyllus and Timocharis, and of the moon (including eclipses) by Timocharis. But theoretical astronomy remained at the stage of explaining the phenomena by means of geometrical models and deriving the mathematical consequences. This is evident in Apollonius' use of the epicyclic/eccentric hypothesis to determine stationary points on planets' orbits, and also in the single astronomical work surviving from this time, Aristarchus' treatise on the distances of the sun and moon: this is a mathematical exercise showing how the limits for those distances can be derived from certain numerical assumptions (about the inaccuracy of which the author appears unconcerned, although it must have been obvious). The topic of the distances of the heavenly bodies was much discussed, by Archimedes and Apollonius amongst others, but no one before Hipparchus devised a reliable method of computing even the moon's distance.

5. Astronomy was transformed by Hipparchus between *c.*145 and 125 BC. His great innovation was the idea of using the geometrical models, which his predecessors had developed to *explain* the phenomena, in order to *predict* or calculate them for a given time. He did not himself fully succeed in this (we are specifically informed that he renounced any attempt at constructing a theory of the planets), but he contributed several essential elements, including the development of trigonometry, ingenious methods for the application of observational data to geometrical models, and the compilation of observations, not only of his own and other Greeks, but especially from the massive Babylonian archives (to which he seems to have had privileged access). Although sporadic Mesopotamian influences appear in Greek astronomy from at least the time of Meton, it is apparently Hipparchus who was the main conduit to the Greek world of Babylonian astronomy, including not only observations, but also astronomical constants (e.g. very accurate lunar periods), the sexagesimal place-value notation for expressing fractions, and methods of calculation. The latter were sophisticated arithmetical procedures for predicting celestial phenom-

ena, and now that the original cuneiform documents have been analysed, it seems likely that it was the Babylonian success in applying mathematical methods to astronomical prediction which inspired Hipparchus to attempt the same within the Greek theoretical framework. He got as far as constructing a viable epicyclic model for the moon, and made many other individual advances, including the discovery of the precession of the equinoxes, to which he was perhaps led by noticing the discrepancy between the year-length which he had derived from observations of equinoxes (the tropical year) and that used by the Babylonians (which was in fact a sidereal year). He also recorded a large number of star positions to be marked on his star-globe.

6. The history of astronomy in the 300 years between Hipparchus and Ptolemy is very obscure, because the unchallenged position of the *Almagest* in later antiquity resulted in the loss of all earlier works on similar topics. However, the evidence from Indian astronomy (the *siddhāntas* based on lost Greek treatises from late Hellenistic times) and from Greek papyri shows that the process begun by Hipparchus was continued by his successors, who produced predictive mathematical models for all the heavenly bodies. This undoubtedly contributed to the enormous growth in genethlialogical *astrology (which requires calculating the celestial positions for a given time) in the period following Hipparchus. But theoretical astronomy was characterized by a bewildering profusion of Babylonian arithmetical methods (which Hipparchus himself had not hesitated to use, even in his lunar theory), combined with geometrical planetary models which, although producing numerical results, lacked logic and consistency. This situation satisfied the professional needs of astrologers such as Ptolemy's contemporary Vettius Valens, but was repugnant to the scientific purism of Ptolemy himself. In his magisterial *Almagest* (*c.* AD 150) he ignores (apart from an occasional contemptuous aside) the work of his immediate predecessors, singling out Hipparchus as the sole peer worthy of his imitation and criticism. Starting from first principles, and rigidly excluding arithmetical methods, he constructed an edifice of models for sun, moon, planets, and fixed stars based on a combination of epicycles and eccentrics employing uniform circular motions, the numerical parameters of which he determined by rigorous geometrical methods from carefully selected observations. These were supplemented by tables allowing the computation of all celestial positions and phenomena pertinent to ancient astronomy, to a suitable accuracy (Ptolemy regarded agreement with observation within 10′ of arc as acceptable). The result is a work of remarkable power and consistency, which dominated astronomy for 1,300 years.

7. Ptolemy himself regarded his work as provisional, but it was treated as definitive by his ancient successors, who produced nothing of significance in astronomy, confining themselves to explicating the *Almagest* (and other treatises by him), despite the fact that there were serious defects in

it even by ancient standards, notably in the solar theory, producing errors which increased with the lapse of time. That these were completely unnoticed in later antiquity is an indication both of the lack of independent observation and of the state of the science after Ptolemy. However, important corrections to the solar theory and other individual details of Ptolemaic astronomy were made after it experienced a revival through its transmission to the Islamic world (the *Almagest* was translated into Arabic *c*. AD 800), but even there the edifice as a whole remained undisturbed, and criticisms of Ptolemy were concerned mainly with his alleged violation of the principle of uniform circular motion in introducing the equant. Ancient astronomy did not begin to become obsolete until Copernicus, and the process was not completed until Kepler.

8. The astronomy of the Greeks covered only a part of what is now comprised in the term. It can be considered the most successful of the ancient applied sciences, if one accepts the ancient view that its task is confined to describing and predicting observed motions by means of a consistent mathematical model. Physical astronomy, however, remained at a very low level (like physics in general). But it is not entirely ignored even in the *Almagest*, and in his *Planetary Hypotheses* Ptolemy attempted to fit the kinematical models of the *Almagest* into a unified physical system. This was based on Aristotelian notions, including the crucial thesis that nature is not wasteful. In it Ptolemy describes a universe in which each planetary 'shell' is contiguous with that of the bodies immediately above and below it. This system enabled him to compute the absolute dimensions and distances of all parts of the universe out to the sphere of the fixed stars, which he found to be less than 20,000 earth-radii from the central earth (less than the distance from the earth to the sun by modern computation). This vision of a small and completely determined universe, although not universally accepted even in late antiquity, became the canonical view in the Middle Ages, in both east and west, and is enshrined in biblical exposition and learned poetry as well as in the works of professional astronomers. It was a strong argument against consideration of the heliocentric hypothesis, which entailed a vastly larger universe in which the fixed stars were at enormous distances.   G. J. T.

Athena In *Iliad* 5. 733–7, *Homer describes how Athena took off the finely-wrought robe 'which she herself had made and worked at with her own hands' and 'armed herself for grievous war'. This incident encapsulates the paradoxical nature of a goddess who is as skilled in the preparation of clothes as she is fearless in battle; who thus unites in her person the characteristic excellences of both sexes. At the greater Panathenaea festival in Athens, she was presented with a robe, the work of maidens' hands, which traditionally portrayed that battle of the gods and giants in which she was the outstanding warrior on the side of the gods.

Her patronage of crafts is expressed in cults such as that of Athena Erganē, Athena the Craftswoman or Maker; it extends beyond the 'works' of women to carpentry, metalworking, and technology of every kind, so that at Athens she shared a temple and a festival with *Hephaestus and can, for instance, be seen on vases seated (in full armour!) in a pottery. Her love of battle is seen, as we saw, in myth, and also in such cults as that of Athena Victory (*Nike); she is regularly portrayed fully armed, one leg purposefully advanced, wearing her terror-inducing aegis (a large all-round bib with scales, fringed with snakes' heads and decorated with the head of the female monster Gorgo).

She is also closely associated with the masculine world in her mythological role as a helper of male heroes, most memorably seen in her presence beside Heracles on several of the metopes of the temple of *Zeus at *Olympia. Indeed her intervention in battle often takes the form of 'standing beside' a favourite (e.g. *Il*. 10. 278–94). (She has accordingly been seen as every man's ideal elder sister, in contrast to the tomboy Artemis and sexy Aphrodite (P. Friedrich, *The Meaning of Aphrodite* (1978)); but these modern western categories scarcely fit the Greek family.) Her virginity is a bridge between the two sides of her nature. Weaving is a characteristic activity of ordinary young girls, but a perpetual virgin, who is not subject to the distinctively feminine experience of *childbirth, is a masculine woman, a potential warrior.

The warlike Athena is scarcely separable from Athena Polias, the goddess of the Acropolis (see ATHENS (TOPOGRAPHY)) and protectress of cities. 'City-protecting' was most commonly performed by goddesses rather than gods; and the other great protectress was the other great warrior-goddess of the *Iliad*, Athena's close associate *Hera. Athena exercised this function in many cities besides Athens, including Sparta and (in the *Iliad*) Troy. Athens was unique only in the degree of prominence that it assigned her in this role.

A few cult titles and festivals of Athena seem to indicate interests other than those discussed so far; and it has often been suggested that her familiar classical functions have been pared down from a much broader original competence. But this is too much to deduce from stray allusions to cults the details of which are usually very little known. The 'Athena Mother' of Elis (Paus. 5. 3. 2) is a puzzle; and Athena's limited intrusions upon the preserves of other gods at Athens—the cult of Athena of Health (Hygieia) for instance—may simply reflect a tendency of city-protecting gods to have a finger in every pie.

Athena is unique among Greek gods in bearing a connection with a city imprinted in her very name. The precise linguistic relation between place and goddess is teasingly difficult to define: the form of her name in early Attic inscriptions is the adjectival *Athēnaia*, which suggests that she may in origin be 'the Athenian' something, the Athenian Pallas for instance (*Pallas Athēnaiē* being a regular Homeric formula). But this account still leaves the shorter name-form Athena unexplained. Athenians themselves, of course, stressed the goddess's association with their city enthusiastically. She was foster-mother of the early king of Athens Erechtheus/Erichthonius, and had competed, successfully, with Poseidon for possession of Attica. In Panhellenic mythology, however, she shows no special interest in Athens or in Athenian heroes. The association with Athens does not appear to affect her fundamental character.

Her most important myth is that of her birth from the head of Zeus. It stresses her unique closeness to Zeus, a vital quality in a city-protecting goddess, and at the same time the gap that divides her, a child without a mother, from the maternal side of femininity. In the oldest version (Hes. *Theog.* 886–90) Zeus became pregnant with Athena after swallowing Metis; she was thus also a kind of reincarnation of *mētis*, 'cunning intelligence'.

It has in fact been suggested that Athena's characteristic mode of action, a mode that unifies her apparently diverse functions while differentiating them from those of other gods with which they might appear to overlap, is the application of *mētis*. Her *mētis* appears obviously in her association with crafts and in her love (Hom. *Od.* passim) for wily *Odysseus; more obliquely, it is argued, it is for instance to be seen in her title Hippia, 'of horses', which she acquires via a product of *mētis*, the bridle, whereas *Poseidon Hippius embodies the animal's brute strength. In warfare she would express rational force, *vis temperata*, in contrast to the mindless violence of Ares. One may doubt, however, how fundamental the opposition to Ares and the role of *mētis* in fact are in defining her military function.

Precursors of Athena have been identified in Mycenaean military or palace-protecting goddesses; the only solid evidence is a tantalizing reference in a Linear B tablet from Cnossus to A-ta-na po-ti-ni-ja.   R. C. T. P.

Athens (history) (*see following page*)

Athens (topography) (see ◀Map 1, Cc▶)

Acropolis, the central fortress and principal sanctuary of *Athena, patron goddess of the city. In the later 13th cent. BC the steep hill was enclosed by a massive wall. Within, there are Mycenaean terraces, perhaps once supporting traces of 'the strong house of Erechtheus' (Hom. *Od.* 7. 81), the mythical Athenian king. The first monumental temples and sculptural dedications date to the 6th cent. BC. Two large Doric temples of limestone with marble trim were built, along with a half-dozen small temples or treasuries. Later quarrying has obliterated the foundations of all but one of the peripteral temples (*c.*510 BC) which stood on the north side of the hill, just south of the later Erechtheum. A marble temple, the Older Parthenon, was under construction on the south half of the hill in 480 BC when the Persians took and sacked the city. The debris from this devastation was buried on the Acropolis and no major construction took place for about a generation. In the 450s a monumental bronze statue of Athena Promachus was set up to celebrate victory over the Persians and in the second half of the 5th cent. four major

buildings were constructed at the instigation of *Pericles, with the artist Phidias as general overseer. First came the Parthenon (447–432); the Propylaea (437–432), gateway to the Acropolis, occupied the western approaches to the citadel. Soon after, an old shrine of Athena Nike (Victory) was refurbished and a small temple of the Ionic order, tetrastyle amphiprostyle in plan, was built just outside the Propylaea. Finally, the Erechtheum was constructed during the last quarter of the 5th cent. Only a few buildings were added to the Acropolis in later times: a sanctuary of Brawhen bronzes were stored. A tall pier built just outside the Propylaea in the 2nd cent. BC first carried statues of Eumenes II and Attalus II, kings of *Pergamum and benefactors of Athens, later replaced by one of *Agrippa. The Roman presence in Greece is reflected on the Acropolis by the construction after 27 BC of a small round temple dedicated to Roma and Augustus and built in an Ionic order closely copying the Erechtheum.

Environs of the Acropolis Numerous sanctuaries clustered around the base of the Acropolis rock. The sanctuaries of 'the nymph' (7th cent. BC), *Asclepius (420 BC), and *Dionysus (*c.*500 BC) were on the south slope. The theatre of Dionysus was built of limestone and marble in the 330s BC and renovated several times in the Roman period. To the west was a stoa built by King Eumenes II of Pergamum (197–159 BC) and beyond that the local millionaire Herodes Atticus built a huge odeum (concert-hall) in memory of his wife Regilla (*c.* AD 160). The ground east of the theatre was taken up by the odeum of Pericles (*c.*443 BC), a replica of the tent of Xerxes, captured by the Greeks at the battle of Plataea (479 BC). A broad street lined with tripods set up by victorious *chorēgoi* (producers) in the choral lyric contests led from the theatre around the east end and north side of the Acropolis. The small Corinthian Lysicrates monument (335 BC) is the best-preserved surviving tripod base. In this eastern area were to be found several other cults (Aglaurus, Dioscuri, *Theseus), as well as the *Prytaneion*, hearth of the city (all unexcavated). The north side of the Acropolis sheltered cults of *Aphrodite and *Eros, *Pan, *Apollo, and *Demeter and *Persephone (Eleusinium). The Areopagus, a low hill north-west of the Acropolis, was the seat in early times of a council and lawcourt as well as a shrine of the Eumenides (Furies). St *Paul addressed the court of the Areopagus, though by the 1st cent. AD the council almost certainly met in the lower city and not on the hill.

Agora, the civic centre of Athens was located north-west of the Acropolis on ground sloping down to the Eridanus river. Traversed by the Panathenaic Way, the Agora was a large open square reserved for a wide variety of public functions, lined on all four sides by the principal administrative buildings of the city. First laid out in the 6th cent. BC, it remained a focal point for Athenian commerce, politics, and culture for centuries, surviving the Persian sack of 480 BC and the Sullan siege of 86 BC (see SULLA). Here in the

[*continued on p. 96*]

history of Athens

Prehistory The more substantial remains of later periods have largely effaced prehistoric settlement evidence, apart from subterranean features like tombs and wells, whose distribution suggests that the characteristic settlement pattern from early times was a nucleus around the Acropolis and a wider spread of hamlets and farms. The settlement's earlier history is obscure, but it clearly became one of the more significant Mycenaean centres (see MYCENAEAN CIVILIZATION), as indicated by wealthy 14th-cent. BC tombs and the later 13th cent. BC fortification and water-supply system on the Acropolis. Twelfth-cent. remains are scanty, but cemetery evidence indicates a wide spread of communities, mostly small, by the Submycenaean phase; overall, the evidence offers no support for the theory that Athens attracted large 'refugee' groups.

History Tradition held that *Theseus was responsible for the *synoecism, in the political rather than physical sense, of the Athenian (Attic) state. More prosaically put, this would imply a unified kingdom, centred on Athens, in the late bronze age. But if there was any such kingdom it did not survive the collapse of Mycenaean civilization and the synoecism is now generally put *c*.900 BC after a tumultuous period in which refugees from Attica settled in Ionia (W. *Asia Minor) from *c*.1050 BC onwards. Athenian imperial *propaganda later exaggerated the organized character of this process, turning it into a movement of *colonization which would justify the metropolis (mother-city) making hegemonical demands of the 'daughter-cities'. Another later propaganda item was the myth of 'autochthony' (Attica had 'always had the same inhabitants'). This was false, but useful for scoring off the Dorian Greek 'newcomers'.

The Attic countryside was settled from the centre in the 8th cent. by 'internal colonization': Athens was not among the first genuinely colonizing states. The early Attic state was aristocratic and politically hardly distinctive. There was nothing even embryonically democratic about the annual *archontes* who began in 684/3 BC and were the chief officers of state: Thuc. 1. 126, correcting Hdt. 5. 70 which says an obscure group ran Athens, the '*prytaneis* of the naukraries', a title which implies ships (*nau-*). But early Athenian naval activity is plausible, because Attica's long coastline is one of the features which did make it exceptional. Others were an imposing city acropolis, with its own water-supply; a mountain-system which formed a first line of defence for Athens itself; and valuable resources in the silver-bearing Laurium region of east Attica.

In 632 'the Athenians', a collective noun now first used as a political agent, resisted Cylon's attempt at a *tyranny; there is no reason to link this rejection of constitutional upheaval with Draco's law-code in the 620s. Athens' first overseas settlement at Sigeum (NW Asia Minor) in *c*.610 may be an indicator of economic restlessness of the kind which produced *Solon. His economic and political reforms in the 590s created an Attica of smallholders; enhanced Athenians' sense that they were a political élite; and widened eligibility for political office. But proper democracy was still in the future and Solon could not save Athens from the tyranny, later in the 6th cent., of *Pisistratus and his sons. The tyranny was not oppressive until shortly before the end (510), and did more for Athens' later military and naval prominence than 5th-cent. historians allowed.

It was *Cleisthenes in 508 who, after a short phase of aristocratic struggle, established the democracy which provoked Persia by helping the Ionian Revolt, and then defeated Persia at Marathon (490) and ten years later at Salamis (480) and Plataea (479). The Cleisthenic state was however aristocratic in many ways and full democracy did not arrive until the 460s and the reforms associated with Ephialtes and *Pericles. But meanwhile Athens had in 478/7 become an imperial city: see DELIAN LEAGUE. Against a background of increasing tension with Sparta, the displaced leader of Greece, the Athenians now capitalized on their Persian War achievement. Military successes against Persia culminated in the battle of the Eurymedon in the early 460s, and more subject-allies were brought under Athenian control; art and architecture, poetry and rhetoric continued to insist on the Persian Wars theme in a way hardly guessable from the history of *Thucydides. The Athenian empire survived the First Peloponnesian War of *c.*461–446, though the Thirty Years Peace of 446 ended Athens' ten-year control of Boeotia (central Greece). But increasing Athenian expansionism in the early 430s alarmed Sparta and the outbreak in 431 of the 27-year Peloponnesian War ended the *Pentekontaetia* or 50-year period from the Persian Wars; this was the period of maximum Athenian cultural achievement.

In the Archidamian War (431–421), the Spartans failed in their programme of 'liberating' Greece from the tyrant city, Athens. Nor did Athens' catastrophic Sicilian Expedition of 415–413 or the oligarchic regime of the Four Hundred (411), or even the definite commitment of wealthy Persia to the Spartan side (407) end the war, which included Athenian successes like Cynossema (411), Cyzicus (410), and Arginusae (406) before the final defeat at Aegospotami in 405. Athens became a subject-ally of Sparta and a second, Spartan-sponsored oligarchy took power in 404, the Thirty Tyrants.

But by a recovery even more remarkable than that of 413, Athens climbed back to independent and even semi-imperial status in the early 4th cent. Fifth-century Athens had been an imperial, Hellenistic Athens was a university, city; 4th-cent. Athens was something in between. Democracy was restored in 403 and the constitution was mildly reformed, though not in a way which can be associated with any named reformer. From now on the democracy was more efficient but noticeably less radical (see DEMOCRACY, ATHENIAN). In foreign affairs, Athens soon dared to confront the Spartans as one of the coalition which fought the Corinthian War of 395–386 and, remarkably, included Sparta's recent backer Persia. The battle of Cnidus of 394 was a naval victory over Sparta, won by a Persian-sponsored fleet but with an Athenian commander, Conon. The King's Peace of 386 (see GREECE, HISTORY) ended this first phase of Athenian recovery. But Spartan aggressions and unpopularity enabled Athens to launch a Second Athenian Confederacy in 378.

Initially the confederacy was successful and welcome: its members included Thebes, now a rising power. Athens defeated Sparta at Naxos and Alyzia in the mid-370s. But Thebes' defeat of Sparta at Leuctra in 371 led to a *rapprochement* between Athens and Sparta in the 360s. Meanwhile Athenian attempts to turn their empire into something more like its 5th-cent. predecessor, especially attempts to recover Amphipolis and the cleruchy put in on *Samos in 366, were unpopular. Major island allies rebelled in the Social War of 357–355. Because of distractions like this and the Third Sacred War (356–345), not to mention sheer short-sightedness, it was not until 351 that Athens and *Demosthenes realized the threat posed by *Philip II of Macedon. A brief war (early 340s) ended with the Peace of Philocrates (346); Athens now acknowledged the loss of Amphipolis. The end, militarily, to Athenian great-power status came in 338 at Chaeronea, though modern historians rightly insist that this did not signal either the death of the *polis* generally or of Athens in particular.

The Athens of the politicians Eubulus and Lycurgus pursued, in the 330s and 320s, ostensibly backward-looking policies of retrenchment which actually anticipate Athens' Hellenistic role as cultural centre. Athens did not openly resist *Alexander the Great, but when at the end of his life he restored Samos to the Samians, Athens embarked on and was defeated in the Lamian War of 323–322 (naval battles of Abydos and Amorgos, land battle of Crannon), after which democracy was suppressed. There were however later democratic restorations and reactions, the first as early as 318 (democracy installed by the Macedonian general Polyperchon).

Under Cassander (ruler of Macedonia), Athens was ruled tyrannically by Demetrius of Phalerum (318–307), a period of peace but imposed cultural austerity. He was expelled by the rapturously welcomed Antigonid Macedonian Demetrius Poliorcetes ('the Besieger'). Another Cassander-supported tyrant Lachares seized power in 300; the hoplite general Charias resisted him unsuccessfully in 296 in the name of democracy. Lachares fell in 294 and Athens submitted to the Antigonids for much of the century until the 220s; the exceptions were a precarious period of freedom in the 280s/early 270s (a period associated with the name of the patriot commander Olympiodorus) and the Chremonidean

War of the 260s, which ended with Athens' surrender in 262 (see ANTIGONUS GONATAS). In the 220s, under the regime of Euryclides and Miccion, Athens managed to stay on good terms with the Ptolemies as well as with Macedon, as Rome's shadow lengthened over Greece.　　　　　S. H.

Roman (see GREECE, ROMAN). Friendly with Rome from 229 BC (Polyb. 2. 12. 8), Athens was rewarded for her support against King Perseus of Macedonia with the gift of *Delos (166 BC), its possession fuelling an economic boom, peaking by 100 BC (S. Tracy, *Harv. Stud.* 1979, 213 ff.) and linked with (if not prompting) a copious ('New Style') silver coinage. In 88 BC, under the tyrant Aristion, Athens enthusiastically supported *Mithradates VI; the city was sacked as a result by *Sulla (86 BC), and a timocratic constitution imposed, but it retained 'free' status (Strabo 9. 1. 20). From the 50s BC on *philhellenism prompted Roman nobles, then emperors, to become benefactors of the city. *Hadrian transformed it with a lavish building programme and made it the seat of the Panhellenion (an inter-provincial organization of Greek cities). Thereafter it flourished culturally as a centre of Greek rhetoric (see SECOND SOPHISTIC), and it remained a bastion of philosophy, above all (from *c.* AD 400) Neoplatonism, until *c.*530. Damaged by the Herulian Goths (267) and besieged by the Visigothic leader Alaric (396; see ROME, HISTORY), the city acquired major new buildings in the 5th cent., notably the vast 'Palace of the Giants'. *Christianity was slow to make inroads; the Parthenon may not have become a church before the 6th cent.　　　　　A. J. S. S.

Classical period were to be found the *bouleutērion* (council-house), the Tholos (public dining-hall), the Metroon (archives), mint, lawcourts, and magistrates' offices (Royal Stoa, and South Stoa I), along with sanctuaries (Hephaisteion, Altar of the Twelve Gods, Stoa of Zeus Eleutherius, Apollo Patrous), fountain-houses, and stoas (Stoa Poecile, Stoa of the Herms). More large stoas (Attalus II, Middle Stoa, South Stoa II) were added in the 2nd cent. BC. To the 2nd cent. perhaps should be dated (controversial) the elaborate octagonal marble water-clock known today as the Tower of the Winds, built some 200 m. (220 yds.) east of the Agora. This eastern area was later occupied by the market of Caesar and Augustus, which supplanted many of the commercial functions of the old Agora. In the 2nd cent. AD a huge peristyle court with library was built by Hadrian just to the north of the Roman market. Roman additions to the Agora also reflect Athenian prominence in cultural and educational affairs: an odeum given by *Agrippa (*c.*15 BC) and a library dedicated by Pantaenus (*c.* AD 100). Badly damaged and partially abandoned as the result of the sack by the Herulian Goths in AD 267, the Agora was finally destroyed by Alaric and the Visigoths in AD 395.

Pnyx, the meeting-place of the Athenian assembly (*ekklēsia*), was built on a low ridge west of the Acropolis. Originally laid out in either *c.*500 or 462/1 BC, and remodelled in 403 under the Thirty Tyrants (Plut. *Them.* 19; see ATHENS)), the final phase was built in *c.*340 BC. This third phase consists of a rock-cut speaker's platform (*bēma*) and a massive curved retaining wall for the auditorium. Stoas were laid out on the ridge above but never finished. By the Hellenistic period most meetings took place in the theatre of Dionysus, and a small open-air sanctuary of Zeus

Hypsistus was established just south-east of the *bēma* in the Roman period. North of the Pnyx the ridge was given over to the worship of the Nymphs, while the south end of the ridge (the Museum) was the site first of a Macedonian garrison fort in Hellenistic times and then the marble tomb of Philopappus, member of the deposed royal house of Commagene in SE Asia Minor (d. AD 114/16).

South-east Athens In this quarter of town were to be found the oldest cults of the city: Dionysus in 'the Marshes', Olympian Zeus, Gē (Earth), and Pythian Apollo (Thuc. 2. 15). Best preserved is the colossal Olympieum. The centre of *Hadrian's worship in the Greek world, it was approached through an arch bearing inscriptions delineating the old town of Theseus from the new Athens built by Hadrian (*IG* 2². 5185). Nearby, to the north, a gymnasium with a sanctuary of Apollo Lyceus gave its name to *Aristotle's school, the Lyceum. Other shrines and the old Enneakrounos fountain-house lay further out, along the banks of the Ilissus river. Across the river lay the Panathenaic stadium, built by the statesman Lycurgus (338–326 BC), rebuilt in marble by Herodes Atticus (AD 139–44), and restored in 1896.

Fortifications An Archaic city wall was replaced in 479 BC, immediately after the Persian sack, by a new expanded circuit, hastily constructed at the behest of Themistocles (Thuc. 1. 90). Its length of 6¼ km. (4 mi.) was pierced by at least fifteen gates, the principal one being the Dipylon, to the north-west. Moats and outer walls were added in the 4th cent. in response to threats from Macedonia, and a large extension was added to the east in Roman times. Destroyed in AD 267, the walls were replaced in part by a new, much more constricted, circuit, though the outer wall was eventually refurbished as well. Communication between Athens and the harbours of Piraeus was assured by means of three Long Walls.

Cemeteries Burials were made outside the city walls, all around the circuit. The principal cemetery, known as the Ceramicus, lay along the two major roads leading northwest from the city. It was used as a burial ground from *c*.1100 BC until the 6th cent. AD, and excavations have recovered hundreds of graves, along with sculptured and inscribed grave-markers. In this same vicinity lay the *dēmosion sēma*, the state burial ground for the war-dead as well as other notables. Further on lay the *Academy.

J. McK. C.

athletics

Greek At the core of Greek athletics was an individual's hard physical struggle in order to gain victory over an opponent; hence, it included not only (as 'athletics' implies nowadays) track and field events but also boxing, wrestling, and equestrian events, and excluded team competitions, fun-running, and performances aimed at setting records (cf. the derivation of 'athletics' (from the root *athl*-

denoting struggle, competition for a prize, and misery). Athletics was a popular activity; valuable contemporary evidence for it is provided by vase-paintings and the victory odes of *Pindar and *Bacchylides.

The first substantial description of Greek practice comes from *Homer's account of the funeral games for Patroclus (*Il.* 23. 262–897; cf. *Od.* 8. 120–30). Eight events are mentioned there (*chariot-racing, boxing, wrestling, running, javelin,* an event similar to fencing, throwing the weight, and archery); the five in italics regularly formed the central part of all later games.

From the middle of the 5th cent. the four major venues for athletics competitions were the Olympian (see OLYMPIA), Pythian (see DELPHI), Nemean (at Nemea, NE *Peloponnese), and Isthmian (at Corinth) Games. The running-races were the *stadion* (a length of the stadium, 192 m. (210 yds.) at Olympia), *diaulos* (there and back), and *dolichos* (twelve laps at Olympia). There was no marathon or event of similar length, although according to Herodotus (6. 105) Phidippides, who ran from Athens to Sparta (490), trained as an ultra-distance runner for the purpose of delivering messages. A race in armour, derived

athletics Athenian ceramic oil-jar of *c.*525 BC, given as a prize in the Panathenaic *games, showing a jumper, discus-thrower, and two javelin throwers. Male nudity was a feature of Greek athletics.

from military training, was introduced into athletics programmes at the end of the 6th cent., and there was a pentathlon consisting of long-jump, *stadion*, discus, javelin, and wrestling. At the Olympian and Pythian Games there were separate events for men and boys, while at the Nemean and Isthmian Games there was also an intermediate category for youths (*ageneioi*, lit. 'beardless').

Training took place in the *gymnasium, or *xystos* (covered colonnade); for the running events, especially the *dolichos*, long training-runs must have been done outside the confines of these buildings. The need for athletes to have a suitable diet was widely recognized (Hippoc. *VM* 4; Arist. *Eth. Nic.* 2. 6. 7; Pl. *Resp.* 410b; Paus. 6. 7. 10). Sometimes an athlete's father would act as his coach (Pind. *Isthm.* 6. 72–3); often, past victors became coaches (Melesias of Athens, Pind. *Ol.* 8. 54–64; Iccus of Tarentum, Paus. 6. 10. 5). Before the Olympia, the wise precaution was taken of making competitors swear by Zeus that for the previous ten months they had trained properly (Paus. 5. 24. 9). When training or competing, athletes covered their bodies with olive oil to keep off the dust and were generally naked, though there is some disputed evidence pointing to the use of loincloths (e.g. Thuc. 1. 6. 5 and the Perizoma group of vases, Beazley, *ABV* 343–6; see M. McDonnell, *JHS* 1991, 182–93). Male sexual interest in young athletes, admired for their physique, was commonplace (e.g. Xen. *Symp.* 1. 2–10; Aeschin. *In Tim.* 156–7; see HOMOSEXUALITY).

Women competed at Olympia in separate games, the Heraea in honour of *Hera; there was just one event, a shortened *stadion*-race (Paus. 5. 16. 2–3). During the men's athletics, married women were forbidden to watch, but virgin girls were permitted (Paus. 6. 20. 9), a custom perhaps derived from a conception of the games as an occasion for girls to meet future husbands.

It is hard to evaluate athletics performances, because running-races were not timed, and distances in field events not measured; one indication that standards may have been low is the fact that Pausanias records many examples of men who had been able to win in several different types of event (cf. Paus. 6. 3. 7, 6. 13. 3, 6. 15. 8–9).

Roman At Rome colourful *circus spectacles (especially chariot-racing) and ball games were the most popular sporting activities. But *Augustus promoted traditional athletics, staging athletics competitions in the Campus Martius and exhibition-running in the Circus (Suet. *Aug.* 43. 1–2); he himself was keen on watching boxing (45. 2). Ultra-distance running was also practised: 'Some men can do 160 [Roman] miles in the Circus' (Plin. *HN.* 7. 84). Interest in athletics was maintained by the establishing of Greek-style games at Rome and elsewhere. In (?)4 BC *Tiberius won the chariot-race at the Olympian Games; from then on, Romans (mostly either eastern provincials with Roman citizenship, or those with sufficient authority to bend the rules, as Nero did in 67 BC) won at Olympia with increasing regularity. See GAMES.   S. J. I.

atomism Ancient philosophers developed a rich variety of atomistic theories. The best way to approach this tradition is by recognizing that *atomon* means 'indivisible', and then considering what 'indivisibility' might mean and why some thinker might advocate it.

Thus, Leucippus and Democritus (both 2nd half of the 5th cent. BC) were particularly concerned to counter arguments from the Eleatic philosophical school (founded at Italian Elea, late 6th cent. BC denying the possibility of plurality and change (Arist. *Gen. corr.* A 8)). Zeno of Elea (early 5th cent. BC) had argued that since what is, is all alike (a thesis the atomists accept), it contains no differentiations permitting a merely finite division. But the alternative, divisibility anywhere, was supposedly equivalent to divisibility everywhere, and this was taken to yield the absurdity that being divides into nothing. Thus what is, is indivisible. The atomists responded by insisting, paradoxically, that what is not, is: divisibility everywhere is still absurd, but what is, is divided up to a point, with portions of nothing or void differentiating the structure of reality and separating off individual atoms which are internally indivisible because solid or homogeneous. 'What is not is' sounds like a blatant contradiction; how might the atomists have defended it? Perhaps void was not empty space itself, but rather 'the empty', a negative occupant of space. Qua nothing, void is not; but qua occupier of a place—wherever there are no atoms—it is. The existence of not-being also accounts for change, albeit in a limited sense. The Eleatic Melissus (mid-5th cent. BC) had identified not-being with void and contended that it is a necessary but unfulfillable condition for the occurrence of change: the atomists' place-occupying nothing fulfils it.

A third Eleatic argument, again from Melissus, may well have radically constrained the atomists' conceptions of these elements and their possible relations. Elaborating his denial that change occurs, Melissus argued that 'the arrangement which was earlier does not perish, nor does an arrangement which is not come into being' (DK 30 fr. 7). As a result, no group subject to rearrangement of its constituent members can exist, because such rearrangement would involve impossible change. Thus, the familiar objects of the apparent macroscopic world cannot truly exist, since such objects suffer rearrangement. Contrary to traditional interpretations, however, it is arguable that the atomists could not have identified macroscopic objects with microscopic collections of atoms and void. Such groupings would be equally vulnerable to Melissus' attack, for *ex hypothesi* arrangements of atoms and void can alter no more than collections of anything else. The microscopic world comprises individual atoms, not groups of them; change permitted by the introduction of void is only relative change in position, not in any intrinsic feature of the atoms. Numerous reports in fact have Leucippus and Democritus asserting that atoms and the void alone are real, and that no authentic unity can emerge from plurality. The striking pessimism about what can be known which marks the first phase of Greek atomism, usually described as a sceptical evaluation of the reliability of the senses, is the proper reaction to a stark world where every appearance of real change or aggregation is a delusion.

Democritus may have had a mathematical argument for atomism too (Plut. *Mor.* 1079e). When a cone is cut parallel to the base, if the surfaces produced are equal, the 'cone' will be a cylinder; if unequal, a ziggurat. Possibly Democritus, choosing the second horn of the dilemma, maintained that these mathematical steps would be atomic magnitudes. Less conjectural evidence of finitist mathematics is to be found in the Platonic tradition. The report that *Plato identified indivisible lines as the source of the line (Arist. *Metaph.* 992ᵃ 19–22) does not determine whether they are physical or ideal. But later Platonists, perhaps Xenocrates (late 4th cent. BC), deployed arguments whose ontological commitments are precise, e.g. that the Forms of Line, Surface, and Body are indivisible, as otherwise their parts would be prior to them ([Arist.] *Lin. ins.* 968ᵃ9–13).

The brilliant dialectician Diodorus Cronus (around 300 BC) transformed philosophical conceptions of indivisibility and profoundly influenced the future course of atomic theory. Perhaps under the influence of Aristotle (*Ph.* 6. 1–4, 10), Diodorus argued that although it is never true that anything is moving, things have moved (Sext. Emp. *Math.* 10. 119–20). If something moves, it is moving now, at the present instant, and thus in the present time. Since any division in the present would divide it without remainder into past and future, it must be partless and so atomic. Movement must thus take a certain whole number of time-atoms. Now a thing can occupy only a single place in a partless time; so, a finite number of places equinumerous with the time-atoms will have been traversed, provided no intervals between the starting- and stopping-points were skipped. Hence, movement in partless time entails traversal of partless places. Finally, these spatial atoms require atoms of matter: were some matter smaller than its atomic space, that space would be part empty, and so not partless. A material atom gets into different places when it occupies successive spatial atoms for the duration of successive temporal atoms. Partless matter fills partless space throughout partless segments of time; accordingly, it never moves, but nevertheless has moved. Significantly, Diodorus insisted on 'very small and partless body' rather than 'atom' as the technical designation for bits of matter (frs. 116–17 Giannantoni), and his material 'atoms' are a consequence of very different arguments from those which provoked Leucippus and Democritus. True, his partless bodies are indivisible, because division would be into the parts they lack; but partlessness rather than indivisibility is their defining characteristic.

It was on grounds of explanatory economy that *Epicurus contended that the totality of things is body and void; everything else which might seem to be in its own right, such as qualities, events, and time, cannot exist apart from body, but is one or another attribute of it (Lucr. 1. 449–82). Void, again the precondition for motion, is the exception, being identified as place, which when empty exists independently of body. Thus if it is correct to attribute the conception of void as a place-occupying nothing to the earlier atomists, Epicurus may rank as the first Greek thinker explicitly to articulate the idea of space as extension pure and simple.

Only at this juncture does Epicurus introduce atomism. The ultimate constituents of compound bodies must be atomic and unalterable, since otherwise everything would be pulverized into nothing (*Ep. Hdt.* 40–1). The indivisible atoms themselves consist of minimal parts reminiscent of and perhaps prompted by Diodorus' 'small and partless bodies' (*Ep. Hdt.* 57). Two major considerations lead to the postulation of minimal parts. First, in a Zenonian spirit, an infinite division of a finite body would yield an infinity of particles each possessing magnitude and together constituting a body of infinite size—thus contradicting the premise that it is finite. The limit of division is parts themselves indivisible, because partless. Second, a conceptual argument: were the mind to scan an infinite collection of parts, it would reach infinity, which is impossible. In obedience to the linkage between varieties of atomism pioneered by Aristotle and Diodorus, Epicurus also advocated temporal atoms (Sext. Emp. *Math.* 10. 142–54).

As *Lucretius amply demonstrates, atomic features and events are intended to explain causally a great many macroscopic phenomena. Much modern scholarship thus supposes that Epicureanism was a reductive theory which identifies without remainder familiar objects and occurrences with what happens on the atomic level. Yet Epicureans believe that free volition, an attribute of the macroscopic mind, directly influences atomic matter (Lucr. 2. 251–83). Although Epicurus is a thoroughgoing materialist—there is nothing but body and void—he does not believe there is nothing but atoms and void, and we have strong evidence that the bodies which are our minds exert a causal influence downwards which is not subject to the laws of atomistic motion, but rather interrupts them.

Even this partial and skeletal survey suffices to prove that the rubric 'Greek atomism' covers a bewilderingly rich range of alternative theories; ironically, the only stimulus not to be found is the first to occur to a modern reader, the evidence of empirical experiment. Leucippus and Democritus inaugurated atomism in reaction to Eleatic arguments against plurality and change; 'atomicity', that is, 'indivisibility', is truly the focal point of their system. In sharp contrast, Diodorus argued for temporal, spatial, and material partlessness; his scheme does indeed yield indivisibility, but only as a by-product of his argument against ongoing movement. Again, Epicurus' case for both atomicity and partlessness is sensitive to yet other considerations, and his philosophy as a whole is better regarded as 'materialistic' rather than 'atomistic', to avoid the danger of mistaking his theory for a reductive one. The debate over finitist mathematics is sensitive to a further, distinct set of arguments.

This diversity has been often obscured by a tendency to

assimilate all these thinkers to a standard list of atomistic commitments, which usually includes a desire to provide comprehensive reductive explanations, especially in psychology. If Leucippus and Democritus denied reality to all arrangements, they were not in the position to explain them, reductively or not. Diodorus did not engage in any project of scientific explanation taking him beyond his argument for partlessness. Epicurus did entertain explanatory ambitions, but they were antireductionist. Many of the most celebrated doctrines associated with these philosophers are not atomistic *per se*. Democritus argued against the reliability of the senses by adducing their conflict, rejecting relativism, and thus denying that we have perceptual access to truth; while this epistemology neatly complements his atomism by leaving rational rather than empirical investigation of microscopic reality unassailed, there is no logical connection with his metaphysics. Likewise, no convincing case has been made for any link between Epicurus' atomism and his theological and ethical views. What is crucial for his brief against immortality and divine intervention in human affairs is that the *soul is a temporary physical compound and that there is a naturalistic mechanism to account for 'supernatural' visions. That the soul is made of atoms and that *dreams are explained in atomistic terms are both incidental to his fundamental materialism. Since divisibility arguments and the possibility that materialism carries reductive implications continue to provoke deep philosophical disputes, the legacy of ancient atomism retains perennial interest.   R. B. B. W.

Atticus (Titus Pomponius Atticus), b. 110 BC as the son of a cultured *eques* (see EQUITES) of a family claiming descent from Pompilius Numa, legendary second king of Rome, was later adopted (see ADOPTION) by a rich uncle (Quintus Caecilius), whose wealth he inherited. He was a friend of *Cicero from boyhood (Cicero's brother Quintus married Atticus' sister), and Cicero's *Letters to Atticus*, probably published in the reign of *Nero (though parts were known to some before), are the best source for his character, supplemented by an encomiastic biographical sketch by his friend Cornelius Nepos. In 85 Atticus left Italy after selling his assets there, in order to escape the civil disturbances he foresaw. He lived in Athens until the mid-60s (hence his *cognomen* 'Atticus', i.e. 'Athenian'), among other things studying Epicurean philosophy (see EPICURUS), to which however he never wholly committed himself. Henceforth he combined a life of cultured ease (*otium*) with immense success in various business activities and an infallible instinct for survival. He privately urged Cicero to determined action on behalf of the *optimates* ('best men'), with whom he sympathized, but himself refused to take sides in politics and personally assisted many prominent politicians from *Marius to Octavian (see AUGUSTUS), without regard for their differences and conflicts. He was Cicero's literary adviser and had his works copied and distributed. He himself wrote a *Liber Annalis* (a chronological table of world, and especially Roman, history), which became a standard work, eulogistic histories of some noble families, and minor works. (All are lost.) He lived to become a friend of *Agrippa, who married his daughter. In 32 he committed suicide when incurably ill.   E. B.

Augustine, St (Aurelius Augustinus) (AD 354–430), was born at Thagaste (mod. Souk Ahras, Algeria), son of Patricius, a modest town councillor of pagan beliefs, and a dominant Catholic mother, Monica. Educated at Thagaste, Madauros, and *Carthage, he taught rhetoric at Thagaste, Carthage, and Rome and (384–6) as public orator at Milan, then the capital of the emperor Valentinian II. Patronized at Rome by Symmachus, the pagan orator, he hoped, by an advantageous marriage (to which he sacrificed his concubine, the mother of a son, Adeodatus—d. *c.*390) to join the 'aristocracy of letters' typical of his age. At 19, however, he had read the *Hortensius* of *Cicero. This early 'conversion to philosophy' was the prototype of successive conversions: to Manicheism, a Gnostic sect promising Wisdom, and, in 386, to a Christianized Neoplatonism patronized by Ambrose, bishop of Milan. Catholicism, for Augustine, was the 'Divine Philosophy', a Wisdom guaranteed by authority but explored by reason: 'Seek and ye shall find', the only scriptural citation in his first work, characterizes his life as a thinker.

Though the only Latin philosopher to fail to master Greek, Augustine transformed Latin *Christianity by his Neoplatonism: his last recorded words echo the Neoplatonist philosopher Plotinus. Stimulated by abrupt changes—he was forcibly ordained priest of Hippo (Bone, Algeria) in 391, becoming bishop in 395—and by frequent controversies, Augustine developed his ideas with an independence that disquieted even his admirers. He has left his distinctive mark on most aspects of western Christianity.

Augustine's major works are landmarks in the abandonment of Classical ideals. His early optimism was soon overshadowed by a radical doctrine of grace. This change was canonized in an autobiographical masterpiece, the *Confessions* (*c.*397–400), a vivid if highly selective source for his life to 388 and, equally, a mirror of his changed outlook. *De doctrina Christiana* (begun 396/7) sketched a literary culture subordinated to the Bible. *De Trinitate* (399–419) provided a more radically philosophical statement of the doctrine of the Trinity than any Greek Father. *De civitate Dei* (413 to 426) presented a definitive juxtaposition of Christianity with literary paganism and Neoplatonism, notably with Porphyry. After 412, he combated in Pelagianism views which, 'like the philosophers of the pagans', had promised men fulfilment by their unaided efforts. In his *Retractationes* (427) Augustine criticized his superabundant output of 93 works in the light of a Catholic orthodoxy to which he believed he had progressively conformed—less consistently, perhaps, than he realized.

Letters and verbatim sermons richly document Augustine's complex life as a bishop; the centre of a group of sophisticated ascetics, the 'slave' of a simple congregation, he was, above all, a man dedicated to the authority of the Catholic Church. This authority had enabled his restless intellect to work creatively: he would uphold it, in Africa, by every means, from writing a popular song to elaborating the only explicit justification in the early Church of a policy of religious persecution. J. F. Ma.

Augustus (*see following page*)

Aurelius, Marcus, emperor AD 161–80, was born in 121 and named Marcus Annius Verus. His homonymous grandfather, Marcus Annius Verus, from Ucubi (Espejo) in Baetica, consul for the third time (as *ordinarius*) in 126 and city prefect, a relative of *Hadrian and an influential figure, brought him up after his father's early death. His mother Domitia Lucilla inherited the fortune created by Gnaeus Domitius Afer. From early childhood Marcus was a favourite of Hadrian, who nicknamed him *Verissimus*. At the age of 15 he was betrothed at Hadrian's wish to Ceionia Fabia, daughter of the man Hadrian adopted as Lucius Aelius Caesar. In 138 Hadrian ordered his second heir *Antoninus Pius, whose wife was Marcus' aunt Annia Galeria Faustina, to adopt Marcus along with Aelius' son Lucius: he now became Marcus (Aelius) Aurelius Verus Caesar. When Hadrian died, Marcus was betrothed to Antoninus' daughter, his own cousin Annia Galeria Faustina (the younger), instead of Ceionia. Quaestor in 139, first elected consul in 140 and again in 145, he married in the latter year; his first child was born on 30 November 147; the next day he received *tribunicia potestas* (see TRIBUNE OF THE PLEBS) and *imperium* and Faustina became Augusta (*fasti Ostienses*). Marcus was educated by a host of famous teachers, one being the orator Fronto; many of their letters survive. His leaning to philosophy, already manifest when he was 12, became the central feature of his life. He was much influenced by Quintus Iunius Rusticus (elected to a second consulship in 162), son or grandson of the Stoic 'martyr' (see STOICISM) of AD 93, and by the teaching of Epictetus. Although Marcus is called a Stoic, his *Meditations* (see below) are eclectic, with elements of Platonism and Epicureanism as well. Further, he was much indebted to Antoninus, who receives a lengthier tribute than anyone else in the *Meditations* (1. 16; another version, 6. 30). His tranquil family life is vividly portrayed in his correspondence and recalled with affection in the *Meditations*. Faustina bore him further children; several died in infancy, but the couple had four daughters when Marcus succeeded Antoninus on 7 March 161; and Faustina was again pregnant.

Marcus at once requested the senate to confer the rank of co-emperor on his adoptive brother Lucius, as Hadrian had intended. Lucius took Marcus' name Verus, while Marcus assumed that of Antoninus. There were thus two Augusti for the first time, equal rulers, except that only Marcus was Pontifex Maximus (head of the *pontifices*: see PRIESTS) and he had greater *auctoritas*. The coinage proclaimed the *concordia Augustorum* (concord of the emper-

ors), L. Verus was betrothed to Marcus' eldest daughter Lucilla, and the *felicitas temporum* (happiness of the times) was further enhanced when Faustina gave birth to twin sons on 31 August, their names honouring Antoninus (T. Aurelius Fulvus Antoninus) and Lucius (L. Aurelius Commodus). But Antoninus' death had unleashed trouble on the frontiers: in Britain, dealt with by Sextus Calpurnius Agricola; Upper Germany, to which Marcus' close friend Aufidius Victorinus, Fronto's son-in-law, was sent; along the Danube; and, most seriously, in the east. The Parthians seized Armenia and defeated the governor of Cappadocia, who took his own life, and invaded Syria. It was decided that an expeditionary force was needed, to be led by L. Verus, with an experienced staff. Verus left Italy in 162 and was based at Antioch until 166 (with a visit to Ephesus in 164 to marry Lucilla), but was merely a figurehead. After the expulsion of the Parthians from Armenia by Statius Priscus (163), he took the title Armeniacus (accepted by Marcus in 164), crowning a new king, Sohaemus. Other generals, notably Avidius Cassius, defeated the Parthians in Mesopotamia: Ctesiphon was captured and Seleuceia on the Tigris sacked at the end of 165. Verus became Parthicus Maximus, Marcus following suit after a short delay. In 166 further success led to the title Medicus. But plague had broken out in the eastern army; the threat in the north was becoming acute—the dispatch of three legions to the east had weakened the Rhine–Danube *limes. Verus was obliged to make peace, celebrating a joint triumph with Marcus (12 October 166). Each became Pater Patriae ('Father of the Fatherland') and Marcus' surviving sons, *Commodus (whose twin had died) and Annius Verus (b. 162), became Caesar.

Marcus planned a new campaign to relieve the Danube frontier. New legions, II and III Italicae, were raised in 165; V Macedonica, formerly in Lower Moesia, was moved to Dacia on its return from the east. But the *plague, reaching Rome in 166, delayed the expedition until spring 168; meanwhile Pannonia and Dacia were both invaded. The emperors went to the Danube in 168 and reinforced the frontier, stationing the new legions in western Pannonia under Quintus Antistius Adventus (*ILS* 8977). They wintered at Aquileia, where the plague broke out; the praetorian prefect Furius Victorinus was a victim and Galen, the imperial physician, refused to stay. At Verus' insistence, he and Marcus also left in January 169, but Verus had a stroke on the journey and died a few days later. Marcus deified him and obliged the widowed Lucilla to marry the Syrian *novus homo* (first of his family to reach the senate) Tiberius Claudius Pompeianus, who had distinguished himself in Pannonia. In spite of further bereavement—his younger son Verus died—he pressed on with preparations, auctioning imperial treasures to raise funds, and returned north, to Sirmium, in autumn 169.

Apparently planning to annex territory beyond the Danube, he launched an offensive in spring 170, but incurred a severe defeat. The Marcomanni and Quadi of Bohemia and Slovakia invaded, outflanked Marcus, and

[*continued on p. 107*]

Augustus

Augustus (63 BC–AD 14), the first emperor at Rome, who presided over the inception of much of the institutional and ideological framework of the imperial system of the first three centuries AD. The long survival of his system, and its association with a literary milieu that came to be regarded as the golden age of Latin literature, make him a uniquely important figure in Roman history, but no narrative history of his lifetime survives except for the account of *Cassius Dio (incomplete 6 BC–AD 14), and the rest of the evidence is very deeply imbued with partisan spirit of various kinds. An estimation of his personal contribution is hard to achieve.

Son of a *novus homo* or first man of his family to reach the senate (Gaius Octavius, praetor 61, d. 59, from Velitrae in the Alban Hills), the younger Gaius Octavius was typical enough of the milieu of junior senators in the third quarter of the 1st cent., perceiving that the way to success lay through the support of the great dynasts for their agents and followers. In this he had a head start: his mother Atia (of a family from Aricia, next door to Velitrae) was the daughter of *Caesar's sister, which made Octavius one of the closest young male relatives of the dictator, a connection emphasized when in 51 BC he gave the funeral oration for his maternal grandmother. In 47 he was made pontifex (see PRIESTS); with Caesar in Spain in 45, he was enrolled as a patrician, and when the dictator drew up his will (13 September 45) he adopted the 17-year-old Octavius and made him his heir. The young man spent the winter in study at Apollonia in Dalmatia, but reacted with decision and alacrity when Caesar was murdered and the will read. Over the next months he consolidated his position as the leader of the friends of Caesar, commemorating his adoptive father, and wooing his veterans; a course of action which brought him into conflict with Mark *Antony, and support of the cause against him which was victorious at Mutina (April 43), after which he seized the consulship by force. At Bononia the differences between him, Antony, and *Lepidus were resolved and the Triumvirate (board of three men assuming supreme authority in the state) established. The next years were marked by the crushing of Antony's brother Lucius Antonius (Pietas) and wife Fulvia at Perusia, with singular violence, the settling of veterans, on confiscated land, and the *proscriptions, in which he was as ruthless as the others. He married Scribonia as a gesture to Sex. Pompeius (*Pompey's son), and she bore his only child *Julia (in 39 he divorced her to marry *Livia); to seal the political dispositions made at Brundisium in October 40 Antony married his sister Octavia. All the politicians of the time made use of *imperium*, one of the only surviving constitutional principles of any potency, and Caesar's heir now took the first name Imperator.

Over the 30s, events combined with astute responses enabled Imperator Caesar to represent himself as defender of an Italian order. His principal local rival for this position, Sex. Pompeius (finally defeated at Naulochus in 36), he represented as a pirate-leader. He took advantage of his control of the ancient centre of *imperium* and (especially through the singular post-consular aedilate of *Agrippa in 33) maintained the favour of the disaffected and volatile *populus* (people) who still in theory granted it. After a half-hearted attempt to attain some military reputation against a foreign enemy (the Illyrians) he turned to representing Antony in *Alexandria as alien, immoral, and treacherous. In 32 a formal oath expressed the mass loyalty of Italy to his cause. The advantages of this policy were not wholly symbolic. Italy offered material resources, manpower, and the land with which to reward its loyalty. Imp. Caesar and his close supporters of these years and afterwards (especially Agrippa, Titus Statilius Taurus, and *Maecenas) were victorious against Antony, whose pro-Egyptian policy and failure in Armenia had lost him much of his eastern support. The battle of *Actium (31 BC) was the turning-point; the capture of Alexandria in the next year ended the war and led to the incorporation of Egypt in the empire. Victory in the east, the vindication of his political promises in Italy, and the booty of the Ptolemies gave him an unassailable position, soon expressed in terms of divinity.

Augustus This trophy, set up in 6 BC at La Turbie (above Monaco), commemorated Augustus' victory over 44 Alpine tribes, resulting in the province of Alpes Maritimae, constituted in 14 BC. Military operations under Augustus doubled the size of the empire and helped to maintain the prestige of his regime.

From his consulship of 31 (he held it every year down to 23) there began a down-playing of the irregularity of the triumviral system, which culminated in a formal restoration of the *res publica* (constitutional organs of state), a restoration in the sense of repair or revival rather than a return to a different constitution. He returned to Rome in mid-29, triumphed, beautified the city by the dedication of important temples, and signalled an end to war by the closing of the temple of *Janus. Agrippa was his colleague in the consulship for 28 and 27: at the beginning of 27 he made the formal gesture of reinstating the magistrates, senate (reduced in numbers through a purge of undesirable elements), and people in their old constitutional role. In return he received a major grant of proconsular *imperium*, and many honours, including the name Augustus, and departed to carry out the military duties of his new command.

Before 7 BC Augustus spent a great deal of time in the provinces (only in 23, 18, 17, and 12 did he spend the whole year in Rome, and he was absent for the whole of 26/25, 21/20, and 15/14). The Civil Wars had shown that power at Rome was to be won in the provinces, and with ever greater numbers of Roman citizens outside Italy, Augustus had to form an empire-wide system. The creation of a huge proconsular *provincia on the model of the commands of Pompey and the triumvirs, which gave Augustus *imperium* over most of the *milites* (troops) of the *res publica*, was the core of this, and the most important part of the 'settlement' of 27. Delegation was essential in so unwieldy an entity, and, like his predecessors, Augustus appointed senatorial legates and equestrian prefects to serve his *imperium*. If these men ran units which were analogous to the *provinciae* of the proconsuls who continued to be sent to the parts of the Roman dominion that lay outside Augustus' command, that is not to say that the settlement envisaged two types of province. Such an innovation would have been far less subtle than the skill with which the legal flexibility of the assignment of proconsular commands and the convenient precedents of the previous generation were adapted to Augustus' purpose.

There were difficulties, since holders of *imperium* had been accustomed to a greater independence than Augustus could afford to allow them. Already in 30 the claim of Marcus Licinius Crassus (grandson of *Crassus) to the *spolia opima* (spoils offered by a Roman general who had slain an enemy leader in single combat) had tested the limits of self-determination; this bid for an antique honour was, characteristically, thwarted by a display of greater erudition from Augustus. Egypt's temptations proved too much for even the equestrian prefect Gaius Cornelius Gallus (26). Marcus Primus came to grief because his informal instructions were inconsistent (c.24). In 23, again following the precedent of Pompey, the proconsular *imperium* was clearly labelled *maius* (superior), which also clarified the position of the other holders under Augustus of wide-ranging commands, such as Agrippa and Gaius Caesar.

The maintenance of the loyalty of the soldiers finally depended on Augustus' capacity to pay them. That in turn depended on the organization of revenues so that they would regularly accrue to him directly. A simple fiscal logic thus operated which transformed the empire: previously, the maintaining of cash flows to the centre, where they might be squandered by one's enemies, was of little interest to provincial governors. Now, the efficiency of the exaction system was the only guarantee of the survival of the new order. The whole world was enrolled, and noticed it (Luke 2: 1, even if the process was not so sudden as the experience of the province of Judaea implied). Taxation was reformed and new provinces made so that their tribute might swell Augustus' takings. The enthusiastic imposition of such burdens caused rebellion and disaster, especially in Germany. A military treasury on the Capitol announced the theoretical centrality of the fiscal arrangements to the whole *imperium* from AD 6.

The incorporations of this period doubled the size of the provincial empire: NW Spain and the provinces of the Alps and the Alpine foreland, Raetia, Noricum, and Pannonia, with Germania and Moesia beyond them, saw most of the military aggression, the provincialization of Galatia (central *Asia Minor) and Judaea (see JEWS) being relatively peaceful. A reasonably high level of military activity was a sensible ingredient in Augustan political strategy, and provided the glory which fuelled the *auctoritas* (prestige) of the ruling cadre. Some of this took the form of expeditions which bore no fruit in terms of the all-important taxation, either directly (or in some cases ever): like Augustus' own trip to the Danube (35–33 BC), Aelius Gallus' Arabian campaign (25–24), and the wars in southern Egypt of Cornelius Gallus (29) and Gaius Petronius (25). The main point of such trips was the glamour of the geography and ethnography, celebrated in poetry and on Agrippa's *map, which propagated the belief that Augustus' Rome ruled the whole inhabited world. This impression was reinforced by Augustus' generally successful use (continued in the east from Antony's careful practice) of the traditional diplomatic relations with local magnates, kings, or communities, in places outside the direct *imperium* of a Roman governor. Ritual courtesies on both sides could suggest that the empire included *India or *Britain, and had a practical role in settling outstanding issues with Parthia in 20 in a negotiation which Augustus made a great deal of. When a serious military threat appeared, in the shape of the Pannonian Revolt, 'the worst war since those against Carthage', or the German war that followed the massacre of Quinctilius Varus and his three legions, the system all but collapsed.

For all his absences, Rome itself was at the heart of Augustus' vision. City-foundations in the provinces, and benefactions to existing *coloniae* (colonies) and *municipia* (municipalities), encouraged the imitation of the metropolis and the recognition of that constituency of Italians spread across the Mediterranean world that had played such a vital part in the Civil Wars. He could not avoid a real concern for the urban populace of Rome itself, who caused major disturbances of the traditional kind at intervals throughout his ascendancy. In 23, the choice of *tribunicia potestas* (see TRIBUNE OF THE PLEBS) as the 'indication of the highest station', and the way in which Augustus counted the years of his 'reign' thereafter, signalled also his descent from the *populares* (popular politicians) of the late republic, many of whose policies he continued (albeit sometimes with a show of reluctance): he made provision against famine, fire, and flood, and reorganized the districts of the city (spreading his own cult in the process). The popular assembly duly ratified his legislation, and was represented *en masse* in displays of loyalty at important moments.

*Varro had taught the Romans to be at home in their own city, and Augustus was an eager interpreter of the process. The ancient messages of cult and civic ritual offered many opportunities, which he was making use of already in the 30s. After Actium the serious development of the cult of Palatine Apollo as a parallel for Capitoline Jupiter, and the restoration of dozens of Rome's ancient sanctuaries; after 12 (when he finally became Pontifex Maximus or head of the college of *pontifices* (see PRIESTS) on the death of Lepidus) the formation of the House of the Pater Patriae, in 2 BC the inauguration of a replacement forum (the forum Augustum: see ROME (TOPOGRAPHY)), to which many state ceremonies were removed; throughout the creation of a 'suburb more beautiful than the city' on the Campus Martius, for the amenity of the populace: the reduplication of Rome's glories cleverly allowed him to be a new founder without damaging the old system, and to surpass all past builders and benefactors without the solecism of departing from or belittling their precedent. He thus underlined his relationship with the previous centuries of Roman history in a Roman Whig history that culminated in his ascendancy.

His management of *lex* (statute) was equally historic: giving his name to far more *leges* than any legislator before him, and announcing his control of the legislative assembly in the process, he became the city-founding lawgiver of the new Rome. The control of religion, that mirror of the *res publica*, was the interpretative vehicle of much of this, and learning, interpretation, and doctrine, of law or ritual precedent, history or geography, were the indispensable servants of all these projects. Hence the cultural and literary acme that later generations of Romans perceived at this epoch. These processes came together in the pivotal years 19–17 BC, when he had made the last modifications to his position in the *res publica*, settled the eastern and western provinces, and acquired his first grandson (Gaius Caesar, the child of Julia and Agrippa). Now came the ethical and social laws, and in 17 the great celebration of the divine diuturnity that the Fates had given to Rome by making her populace virtuous and therefore fecund, in the *ludi saeculares* (Secular Games).

His concern for the institutions of state allowed him to insert himself into the annals of Roman history as a continuator or reformer rather than as an intruder or revolutionary, while the inherent flexibility of the institutions gave him a wonderful repertoire of gambits both for shaping opportunities for political success for his supporters and for social promotion, of which the most important form of all was the identification of a successor to his office. The very happy accident of his long life allowed readjustment of many of his innovations in a process of trial and error, a refining process which explains the success and long survival of many of them: the city prefect, the public *postal service, the *vigiles* (fire brigade), and so on.

The arrangement of a successor proved the most difficult task of all. The calculation of *auctoritas* in which he excelled, and which his very name evoked, entailed that no merely dynastic principle could be guaranteed; it would belittle his own carefully constructed practical reputation for real ability to have a successor who owed everything, as he had done, to a name. At the same time he had been unable (and had perhaps not wanted) to avoid accumulating honours for his family, and using for that very consolidation of *auctoritas* the image of a Father and the model of the state as a super-household, one conducted like his own and under his benign but omnicompetent tutelage. There was in the end a dissonance between the role of those who had to be permitted to acquire the necessary *auctoritas* to maintain the image of effective governance, especially through largely factitious military escapades, and the need to rely on his own blood-line to keep alive the charisma of his own divine associations. Agrippa was a compliant assistant in the public sphere, and Livia happy and expert at propagating the necessary pictures in the private; but *Tiberius and Drusus, Livia's children by her first marriage, were not good at being second fiddle, and *Julia, his daughter and only child, on whom the whole dynastic construction relied, nearly wrecked the whole thing by probably calculated sexual misbehaviour. This called into question the credentials of the model family, the legitimacy of her offspring, and the feasibility of using ethics as a constitutional strategy, while potentially irradiating her partners (who included Antony's son Iullus Antonius) with her share of the ancestral charisma.

The dynastic policy was not overtly monarchic either, however, and what saved Augustus was the fact that he had (since he did not have the option of destroying them wholesale) re-created the Roman aristocracy and given them a new role in his social system. As an antidote to the Civil War social mobility was to be curbed; *freedmen were discouraged from promotion, the *plebs* was indulged but controlled; the two upper classes were encouraged to procreate, and each had its precise place in the religious system, at the theatre, and in government. As an ornament to the whole thing, and to camouflage the prerogatives that he ascribed to his own family, survivors of the great lines of the historic Roman past were encouraged to live up to their ancestors' images, and given an honorific but circumscribed part to play in a system whose regulation, through his censorial function, it was Augustus' job to manage. Hence—and the power derived also from his fatherly pretensions—the ethical content of much of his legislation, which did the nobility the credit of thinking them worthy of the past while giving their arbiter a useful way of coercing them if they failed to live up to it. The seeds of the disastrous use of the laws on *adultery and *maiestas* (treason broadly defined) over the next generations were therefore sowed by Augustus, who was not himself faced by any very coherent opposition.

Later authors dated the establishment of the imperial monarchy to 31 or 27 BC. In many ways, as Augustus probably saw, and *Tacitus appreciated, the new arrangements, many times modified, and threatened by diverse instability, could not be regarded as established until someone had succeeded to them, and then shown himself willing to continue their essentials. Although the *optimus status* ('best state of affairs') was in most respects in place by the climax of the legislative phase and the announcement of the *saeculum* in 17, and the pinnacle of *auctoritas* was commemorated in 2 BC, the

Augustan empire could have been dissolved in AD 14. The achievement of Augustus lay in the flexibility with which he and his advisers responded to a period of striking social change in the Mediterranean world, the legacy of the Roman/Italian diaspora of the previous century. But in controlling a dynamic process there is more continuity and less revolution than is usual in the foundation of a monarchy, and that may well help to account for the stability of the system that Augustus' successors developed out of his innovations. See also ROME (HISTORY) § 2.1.   N. P.

swept over the Julian Alps, sacking Opitergium (Oderzo) and besieging Aquileia. It was the worst such crisis since the German invasions at the end of the 2nd cent. BC. Desperate measures, led by Pompeianus and Publius Helvius Pertinax, cleared Italy, Noricum, and Pannonia. The Marcomanni were defeated as they tried to recross the Danube with their booty. But the Balkans and Greece were invaded by the Costoboci, requiring further emergency measures, and Spain was ravaged by the Moors, dealt with by Marcus' friend Victorinus. Marcus, based at Carnuntum, first used diplomacy to detach some tribes from the 'barbarian conspiracy'; some peoples were settled within the empire. The offensive, resumed in 172, is depicted at the start of the Aurelian column in Rome. In spite of the death of the praetorian prefect Vindex, the Marcomanni were defeated: victory was claimed, with the

Aurelius, Marcus Aerial view of Carnuntum, a legionary fortress on the Danube, where Marcus was based during the Marcomannic wars and wrote part of his *Meditations*. The civil settlement, made a municipality under *Hadrian, is in the left foreground.

title Germanicus. In a battle against the Quadi Roman troops were saved by a 'rain miracle', shown on the column, later claimed to have been achieved by the prayers of Christian legionaries; Marcus gave the credit to the Egyptian Hermes 'Aerius'. In 173 he pacified the Quadi, moving to Sirmium in 174 to take on the Sarmatian Jazyges of the Hungarian plain. After some successes, he was obliged to make an armistice when Avidius Cassius, who had had special powers in the east, was proclaimed emperor. The revolt collapsed after three months, but Marcus, now Sarmaticus, toured the east, taking Faustina, who died in late 175 and was deified, and Commodus. He went through Asia and Syria to Egypt, returning via Athens to Rome. Here he held a triumph (23 December 176) and raised Commodus to Augustus. In summer 178, renewed warfare in the north took him northwards again. He remained, evidently planning to annex Marcomannia and Sarmatia, until his death (17 March 180).

Marcus has been universally admired, as a philosopher-ruler, to the present day, criticized only for leaving his unworthy son as successor. This no doubt seemed the best way to ensure stability, and he left Commodus experienced advisers, including his numerous sons-in-law. Despite Marcus' lack of military experience he took personal command against the first wave of the great *Völkerwanderung* that ultimately destroyed the empire, setting an example that inspired his contemporaries in the view of *Ammianus (31. 5. 14).   A. R. Bi.

Meditations Marcus is most famous for a work his subjects never saw, the intimate notebook in which he recorded (in Greek) his own reflections on human life and the ways of the gods, perhaps before retiring at night. The title *Meditations* is purely modern: *ta eis heauton* ('to himself'), found in our MSS, may not go back to the author, but is surely accurate. Internal evidence suggests that he was past his prime when he wrote (2. 2, and other references to his age or imminent death), and that at least parts were composed during his lengthy campaigns against the German tribes. It seems to have survived almost by accident; it was unknown to the writers of his time and for long afterwards, but seems to have surfaced in the 4th cent. (Them. *Or.* 6. 81c, not a certain allusion). In general the closest analogies for the thought are with the Stoic philosopher Epictetus (mid-1st–2nd cent. AD), but Marcus is interested less in sustained exposition. The style, often eloquent and poetic, can also be compressed, obscure, and grammatically awkward. All of this is understandable if he was writing memoranda for his eyes alone.

Although divided by moderns into twelve 'books', the work seems not to have a clear structure. Brief epigrams are juxtaposed with quotations (usually of moral tags, occasionally of longer passages: esp. 7. 38–42, 11. 30–9) and with more developed arguments on divine providence, the brevity of human life, the necessity for moral effort, and tolerance of his fellow human beings. Frustratingly, these *pensées* are almost invariably generalized: we do not learn Marcus' secret thoughts about his family, members of the court, or military policy. We do, however, get some idea of his personality and preoccupations.

The first book of the *Meditations* is a different matter, being more coherent than the others; it may have been composed independently. Here Marcus goes through a list of his closer relatives and several teachers, recording what he owes to each—in some cases a specific lesson, but more often a general moral example. This list culminates in two long passages on what he owes to his predecessor *Antoninus Pius, and to the gods (1. 16 and 17). Though often allusive and obscure, these give us unique access to the mind of an ancient ruler, and the whole book is a precious personal document.

In the rest of the work, though technical discussion of Stoic doctrine is avoided, certain recurrent themes stand out: the need to avoid distractions and concentrate on making the correct moral choice; the obligation of individuals to work for the common good (e.g. 6. 54: 'What does not benefit the hive does not benefit the bee'); the unity of mankind in a world-city (4. 4; cf. G. R. Stanton, *Phronesis* 1968, 183 ff.); insistence on the providence of the gods, often combined with rejection of the Epicurean alternative that all is random movement of atoms (e.g. 6. 17, 8. 39). Duty and social responsibility are strongly emphasized; Marcus was keenly aware of the temptations of power (e.g. 5. 16, 6. 30 'do not be Caesarified'). Thoughts of providence lead him to contemplate the vastness of time and space, and the guiding pattern that according to the Stoics gives order to the universe (e.g. 10. 5). There is also a more melancholy note, of resignation and pessimism. Though determined to persevere in his moral efforts, the author is often resigned to their futility (8. 4; 9. 29 'who will change men's convictions?'). Hymns to the grandeur and order of the universe (4. 23, 5. 4) can give way to revulsion and disgust (8. 24). Above all, Marcus is fascinated by life's transience and the way in which all great men, even philosophers and emperors, pass on and are forgotten (4. 32, 33, 48, 50, etc.). His most lasting achievement is a work which has inspired readers as different as Sir Thomas Browne, Matthew Arnold, and Cecil Rhodes.

R. B. R.

Babylonia (see ◀Map 2, Dd▶), country in south Iraq, stretching from modern Baghdad to the Arab-Persian Gulf, drained by the Euphrates and Tigris rivers. Settlement (dependent on irrigation) is first attested in the sixth millennium BC. The population was mixed; non-Semitic Sumerian dominates the literary record in the third millennium, gradually replaced by Semitic Akkadian in the second millennium, which in turn was displaced by Aramaic in the later first millennium.

Babylonia's political pattern until the 15th cent. BC was one of contending city-states, some of which succeeded in imposing control on their rivals (e.g. Agade: 2340–2200; Third Dynasty of Ur: 2100–2000; Babylon: 1760–1595). From then on, Babylonia formed a territorial state with Babylon as its capital. Babylonia was subject to Assyria from the late 8th cent. until the Babylonian general, Nabopolassar, fought back the Assyrians and, with Median help, destroyed Assyria's empire (626–609). Nabopolassar founded the Neo-Babylonian empire, stretching from Palestine to the Iranian frontier, ruled from Babylon. The most famous Neo-Babylonian king was his son, Nebuchadnezzar II (604–562), who rebuilt Babylonia's cities extensively and sacked Jerusalem (587). The last Neo-Babylonian ruler, Nabonidus (555–539), was defeated in battle at Opis by *Cyrus the Great of Persia (559–530), who turned Babylonia's imperial territory into a single satrapy of the Achaemenid empire (see PERSIA). It was divided early in *Xerxes I's reign (486–465) into two provinces: the satrapy of Babylonia stretched from the Persian Gulf to Assyria and north-west to the east bank of the Euphrates. *Alexander the Great conquered Babylonia in 331, detaching its northern region (Mesopotamia); he planned to turn Babylonia into one of his chief bases. *Seleucus I and *Antigonus the One-eyed disputed, and fought for, control of Babylonia (316–309) and it became a core-region of the Seleucid empire. After lengthy struggles (141–127), Babylonia came under Parthian control in 126, and henceforward formed part of the empires of the Arsacids (see Parthia), then the Sasanids. Babylonia's strategic location on north–south and east–west routes and its legendary fer-

tility (Hdt. 1. 193; Strabo 16. 1. 14) meant that it continued to play an important role in the Persian, Seleucid, Parthian, and Sasanian periods. Important royal centres were founded by Seleucus I at Seleuceia on Tigris and by the Parthians at Ctesiphon.

Babylonian learning, writing, cultic, and literary traditions proved tenacious, and survived alongside the increased use of new languages (such as Aramaic, Persian, and Greek). The latest cuneiform text dates to AD 78. Classical writers frequently confused Babylonia with Assyria, to which the Babylonian scholar Berosus (fl. 290 BC) objected with little effect. Babylonia was perceived by Greeks and Romans as the source of astronomical and astrological lore. They associated this activity with 'Chaldaeans'—the name of a number of tribal groups in Babylonia. There is no evidence that Babylonians ever linked any particular learning with these tribes. *Astronomy and *mathematics were an important and highly developed part of Babylonian scholarship; most of the latest preserved cuneiform texts are of this scientific nature. To what degree Babylonian astronomy and mathematics influenced Greek science is debated. See ASTROLOGY.
A. T. L. K.

Bacchanalia can be used to mean either 'Bacchic festival' or 'Bacchic places of worship', but usually translates the Greek *mysteries (*orgia*), with special reference to the worship suppressed by the Roman authorities in 186 BC. We have an account of the suppression in Livy (39. 8–18) and an inscribed version of the senatorial decree (*ILLRP* 511) against the cult, in the form in which it was circulated to the allied states of Italy. These sources can be supplemented by references in *Plautus' plays and now by archaeological evidence to show that the Bacchic cult, perhaps of south-Italian Greek origin, was widespread in Italy, central and south, decades before the senate chose to act against it. The form of the Italian cult seems to differ from other Hellenistic examples in admitting men as well as women to the mysteries and in increasing the frequency of meetings. It is a matter of debate how far the cult's followers were forming a movement of protest against the Roman authorities.

The surviving decree concentrates on the structure of Bacchic cells—their oaths of loyalty, their organization and funding, their membership, their property. This suggests that it was the power of cell-leaders over worshippers, cutting across traditional patterns of family and authority, that disturbed the senate, rather than alleged criminal actions or orgiastic rites; but any allegation would have helped in the discrediting of a powerful and well-embedded cult; Livy's vivid account has valuable elements, and in substance shows knowledge of the decree itself; but its highly literary elaboration shows the influence of the senate's propaganda against the cult.

The senate's persecution succeeded at least in removing the cult from prominence, though artistic evidence shows its long-sustained influence. Later Italian evidence, especially the great Bacchic inscription of Agripinilla (2nd cent. AD), show a domesticated, family version of the cult, well subordinated to élite authority.

See DIONYSUS.   J. A. N.

Bacchylides (c.520–450 BC), lyric poet, of Iulis in Ceos (mod. Kea), son of Midon (or Midylus, *Etym. Magn.* 582, 20), nephew of *Simonides (Strabo 486, *Suda*, entry under 'Bakchulidēs'). His floruit was given as 480 by *Chron. Pasch.* 162b (304. 6), as 467 and 451 by *Eusebius–Jerome (the entry in Eusebius, *Chron.* Ol. 87.2 = 431 BC, refers to a flute-player Bacchylides mentioned by the comic poet Plato in his *Sophistai*, fr. 149 KA, *PCG* 7. 494, see G. Fatouros, *Philol.* 1961, 147). The assumption that he was younger than *Pindar (Eust. *Prooem. ad Pind.* 25 = schol. Pind. 3, p. 297. 13 Dr.) is unfounded and unlikely in view of the early date of his poem in praise of the young prince Alexander, son of Amyntas (fr. 20b Snell–Maehler), who succeeded his father as King Alexander I of Macedonia in c.494. Although Bacchylides was one of the canonical nine lyric poets (*Anth. Pal.* 9. 184 and 571; schol. Pind. 1, p. 11. 20 Dr.), and although he was well known in Hellenistic and Roman times (imitated by Horace, *Carm.* 1. 15, quoted by Strabo, Plutarch, [Longinus], *Subl.*, and by the emperor *Julian who 'enjoyed reading him', as Amm. Marc. 25. 4. 3 says), only a handful of lines had survived in quotations when a papyrus containing his book of victory odes almost complete and the first half of his book of *dithyrambs was found at Meīr, near Al-Kussīah, south of Hermopolis, in 1896 and published by F. G. Kenyon in 1897. Since then, remains of fifteen more papyri have been attributed to him, and two papyri contain scholia on his epinician odes and dithyrambs. The known dates of his epinician odes are: 476 (5, for the tyrant Hieron of *Syracuse's horse-race victory at Olympia, also celebrated by Pindar, *Ol.* 1), 470 (4, for Hieron's chariot victory at Delphi, for which Pindar sent *Pyth.* 1), 468 (3, for Hieron's chariot victory at Olympia), and 452 (6, for Lachon's sprint victory as a boy at Olympia); likely dates are: c.485 (13) and 454 or 452 (1 and 2); the Third Dithyramb (17, 'The Youths' or 'Theseus') seems

to date from the early 490s; it is really a paean sung by a Cean choir at *Delos. Bacchylides spent some time in exile in the Peloponnese (Plut. *De exil.* 14). Like Simonides and Pindar, he may have stayed at Syracuse as Hieron's guest (Ael. *VH* 4. 15), but the alleged rivalry between him and Pindar seems to be a figment of some ancient biographers.

His patrons, apart from Hieron of Syracuse, included athletes from Ceos, Aegina, Phlius, Metapontum, and *Thessaly; a poem in honour of a magistrate of Larissa seems to have been added at the end of the book (14b, cf. Pindar's *Nem.* 11). Several of his dithyrambs were composed for competitions at Athens (15?, 18, 19, 23?), one for Sparta (20). The Alexandrian editors gave them titles and arranged them in alphabetical order. Stylistically, his dithyrambs are like ballads, using lively narrative, often allusive and selective, as well as direct speech. They exploit the pathetic potential of the myths, as do those epinician odes which contain a mythical narrative as their centrepiece. *Dith.* 2 (16, 'Heracles' or 'Deianira'?) appears to assume familiarity with *Sophocles's *Trachiniai*; *Dith.* 4 (18, 'Theseus') is unique in being a dialogue between the chorus as people of Athens and the chorus leader, their king, Aegeus; this may have been influenced by Attic drama (plays like Aesch. *Supp.* or *Pers.*), rather than being an archaic form of dithyramb. Bacchylides also wrote hymns (frs. 1–3), paeans, of which fr. 4 + 22 contains a fine eulogy of peace, processional songs (frs. 11–13), maidensongs (Plut. *De mus.* 17), dancing-songs (hyporchemata, frs. 14–16), songs about love (erotica, frs. 17–19), and songs of praise (encomia?, frs. 20–20f). Didymus wrote a commentary on the epinician odes and probably also on other books. The textual transmission must have broken off sometime in the Roman period; later authors like Athenaeus and Clement of Alexandria seem to quote from anthologies.   H. Ma.

Bactria (see ◀Map 2a, Cb▶), enormous region lying (roughly) between the Oxus river (Amu-Darya) to the north and the Hindu Kush to the south; the term occasionally also includes Sogdiana to the north (Tadjikistan/ Uzbekistan). The Achaemenid *Persian satrapy (Bāxtriš) is cited several times in the *Persepolis tablets. Because of the silence of the classical sources, Bactrian history only becomes more fully recoverable with *Alexander the Great, who had to fight tough battles here. Recent excavations have profoundly enhanced our knowledge, especially excavation of the site of *Ai Khanoum, a Hellenistic city, (possibly) founded by Alexander himself, on the upper Oxus (Alexandria Oxiana?). Surveys in eastern Bactria, on both banks of the Oxus, have revealed that the agricultural prosperity, for which the country was famed, goes back to the bronze age. From this time on, networks of irrigation canals were constructed, which were maintained and extended throughout the Achaemenid and Hellenistic periods. Under the early *Seleucids, Bactria was extensively colonized, and Bactra (mod. Balkh) served as a temporary residence for Antiochus (the future Antiochus I), son of *Seleucus I. Inscriptions found on several Bactrian sites have provided new insights into Iranian and Greek settlement and into the process of acculturation. A Graeco-Bactrian kingdom was created by Seleucid breakaway satraps. This secession is generally thought to have been achieved by Diodotus c.230 BC, linked to the invasion by the Parni (see PARTHIA) of the Iranian plateau, but this chronology is debated. In 206, following a campaign by *Antiochus III, the Graeco-Bactrian king Euthydemus I accepted Seleucid supremacy. In the reign of Eucratides I, people from beyond the Oxus invaded Bactria and destroyed the city of Ai Khanoum c.145 BC. At the end of Heliocles' reign (c.130 BC), another invasion virtually obliterated the Greek presence in Bactria.   P. B.

banks in antiquity supplied a selection of the services familiar from their modern counterparts. None the less, the essential banking function, receipt of deposits which might then be lent at interest to a different set of customers, appears only fleetingly in ancient texts (Dem. 36. 11). Many temples, both Greek and Roman (e.g. *Apollo on *Delos, Castor and Pollux at Rome) took deposits and even lent money; but deposits remained untouched and cash was lent from the temple's own funds. Similarly, moneylenders who lent from their own resources, even on a regular basis, were not bankers; nor were usurers, specializing in short-term, high-interest loans of small sums—the common Greek term is *obolostatēs* ('a lender of obols'). Banking in the Greek world appears to have evolved out of professional money-changing: a response to the multiplicity of state coinages (*trapezitēs* or 'banker' refers to the *trapeza* or changer's table). Changers, and presumably bankers, existed all over the Classical and Hellenistic Greek worlds, but our knowledge is concentrated in Athens, where, from the 4th cent. BC, the names are known of some twenty bankers. Money-changing remained important; otherwise, the emphasis and impact of the services provided by Athenian bankers is disputed. Modernizing approaches treat banks as central not only to fringe economic activity, but to the whole *polis*: primarily through the linked taking of deposits and extension of credit. Alternative readings, stressing differences between ancient and modern economies, see bankers (often themselves non-Athenians) as more marginal to the citizen structure of the *polis*, providing a peripheral range of credit and other services (including acting as witnesses and guarantors). The majority of their clients would then be persons themselves not fully integrated into the *koinōnia* (community) of the *polis*: traders, other visitors to Athens, and a minority of citizens who urgently needed money or the support of specialist banking skills. Not disputed is the wealth of the most successful Athenian bankers. Pasion, beginning as a bankers' slave, gained his freedom, took over control of his former masters' bank, and eventually became a citizen. Remarkably, his own banking slave, Phormion, followed an almost identical path from rags to riches (Isoc. 17; Dem. 36, 45, [46], [49], [52]). Bankers from

the Greek world seem to have operated in isolation; there is no clear evidence for any integrated banking system. A letter of credit is introduced to an Athenian jury as something needing explanation (Isoc. 17. 35 ff.). This is in contrast to Ptolemaic *Egypt, where surviving papyri reveal a complex system of giro payments and bills of exchange. There was a range of banking institutions, changing through time: a network of royal or state banks (based on *Alexandria with branches in local capitals, banks operated on license, private banks, and *logeutēria* (royal treasuries). By the 2nd cent. BC, and into the Roman period, the scene was dominated by state and private banks.

For the Roman west, literary evidence for banking operations is unsystematic. The basic problem is distinguishing between wealthy men of affairs who might offer financial services, including credit (e.g. *Atticus) and professional dealers in money. Whereas the former might be wealthy through ownership of land, the latter were generally of lower status, made most of their living through financial transactions, and might be organized into *collegia* (private clubs). Three identifiable groups had banking interests: *argentarii*, *coactores argentarii*, and *nummularii*. The earliest testimony from Rome and Italy (down to c.100 BC) mentions only *argentarii*, who resembled Greek *trapezitai* in offering a range of functions: changing, deposit, and credit. Specialization is evident from the 1st cent. BC, with *argentarii* continuing to take deposits and lend, but money-changing becoming the province of the *nummularii*. There also emerge from c.50 BC the *coactores argentarii*, who offered credit facilities to those purchasing goods at auction. This marks a possible partial break with the tendency for credit in antiquity to be economically non-productive. Against this (as for the Greek world), there is no hard evidence for Roman bankers lending in maritime loans. Though possibly prosperous, none of these financiers came from the upper end of society: Mark *Antony could insult Octavian (the future *Augustus) by claiming his grandfather was an *argentarius* (Suet. *Aug*. 2. 6; cf. 4. 2 for *nummularius*). Nor did they number among their clients the Roman élite, who generally had their own safe deposits and sources of credit. As in Athens, Italian bankers regularly crop up in connection with the affairs of merchants (as indicated by the affairs of Caecilius Iucundus, auctioneer at *Pompeii). This tripartite system of finance was restricted to the western empire, and possibly only to Italy. Even there, from AD 200, distinctions begin to disappear, with a return to the idea of the all-embracing *argentarius*. A final (if problematic) perspective on Roman banking from the 6th cent. AD is provided by the *Digest*.   P. C. M.

barbarian Social groups frequently assert their cohesiveness by emphasizing the differences between themselves and 'outsiders'. Individuals belong to a range of groups, and which they choose to emphasize will depend on particular historical situations. While we associate Classical culture primarily with emphasis on *citizenship (member-

barbarian Gaulish prisoners on a Roman triumphal arch at Carpentras (France). Rome took over from Greek thought the idea of the barbarian. Classification of conquered peoples (like Gauls) as (inferior) barbarians offered a justification of Roman *imperialism.

ship of a *polis*), Classical Greek literature also assigns considerable importance to defining a common Greek identity and creating the figure of the 'barbarian' in contrast.

That contrast was not important in Archaic literature. The factors that brought it to the fore were (*a*) the imposition of Persian control over western *Asia Minor from the mid-6th cent. BC and the successful armed resistance to Persia by many Greek states in 480/79 BC (see GREECE (HISTORY)); (*b*) justification of Athenian hegemony over the *Delian League on the grounds that Greeks should unite to continue resistance against Persia; and (*c*) the appearance of considerable numbers of non-Greek slaves at Athens (where the economic exploitation of the indigenous poor had been curtailed by *Solon's *seisachtheia* (alleviation of *debt)).

With *Aeschylus' *Persians* (performed 472 BC), a consistent image of the barbarian appears in Athenian literature and art. Apart from a lack of competence in Greek (e.g. Ar. *Thesm*.), the barbarian's defining feature is an absence of the moral responsibility required to exercise political freedom: the two are connected, since both imply a lack of *logos*, the ability to reason and speak (sc. Greek) characteristic of the adult male citizen. Barbarians are marked by a lack of control regarding sex, food, and cruelty. In *Homer, the breaking of such taboos had been associated with super-human heroes; in Classical thought, they were 'barbarous' (the myth of Tereus, thought originally to have been a Greek (Megarian) hero, includes rape, tearing out a tongue, a mother's murder of her own child, and cannibalism: consequently Tereus had to be reclassified as a 'barbarian' (Thracian) king). Absence of political freedom entails rule by tyrants, and frequently women, and the use of underhand weaponry like bows and poison; the absence of moral self-control entails the wearing of wasteful and 'effeminate' clothing, drinking wine neat, and enjoying emotional ('Lydian' or 'Ionian') music. Somatic differences might be used by writers (or vase-painters) to reinforce the image of the barbarian, but it did not matter whether the typology was black African or Thracian. See RACE.

The Greek/barbarian polarity continued to be a major element in Greek literature throughout antiquity; it compensated for the military and political powerlessness of Greek cities in the Hellenistic and Roman periods. Along with other elements of Greek culture, it became part of the ideological baggage of Latin literature. Its importance in practical terms is less clear: 'barbarians' were excluded from the *games at *Olympia and other religious ceremonies, e.g. at *Eleusis, and a 4th-cent. BC lawcourt speech could make capital out of an opponent's alleged 'barbarian' descent (Dem. *Meid*. 149 f.). Roman rhetoric, too, could represent opponents, both non-Roman and Roman, as either 'barbarians' or 'barbarous' (Cic. *Font*., etc.; representations of *Cleopatra (VII) or Boudicca (see BRITAIN)), though such language masked much more real distinctions (principally that between the Roman citizen and the non-citizen), and Roman moral discourse symbolized disapproval in different terms (e.g. Etruscan luxury). While

some Greek intellectuals stretched the polarity to its limits (Isoc. *Paneg*. and *Philippus*; Arist. *Pol*. 1. 2–7 and 3. 14 on barbarians being slaves 'by nature'), others questioned the usefulness of the concept (Pl. *Resp*. 262de). The polarity might be associated with a more universal distinction between 'us' at the centre of the world and 'them' at the periphery: the barbarians who inhabited the 'edge' of the world might be savages without laws, settled homes, or agriculture (see NOMADS), but alternatively they might have created an earthly paradise (the Hyperboreans (legendary Apollo-worshippers in the far north), the 'Kingdom of the Sun' in the Indian Ocean). Like kings, women, children, old people, or slaves, some barbarians might be closer to the divine world than the adult male citizen (Celtic Druids, Persian magi, Indian gymnosophists; cf. the Christian Salvian of Marseille's positive judgement of 5th-cent. AD Germanic invaders).

In the Hellenistic period, the distinction between Greek and barbarian came to be seen as insignificant even by some of those imbued by the literary culture (*Stoicism); its irrelevance was explicitly expressed by Christians (Colossians 3: 11; 1 Corinthians 7: 21; cf. Acts 8: 27). Nevertheless the prejudice against 'barbarians' remained latent in the literary tradition, to be exploited by late-antique Christians like Prudentius (*C. Symm*. 2. 807–19) as well as non-Christians such as *Ammianus Marcellinus when they wished to parade their scholarship. With the rediscovery of *Aristotle in the 12th cent., it became one of the roots of western self-definition first against Muslims and the 'orient', and later against subject populations around the globe. See ORIENTALISM.   T. E. J. W.

baths one of the most characteristic and widely distributed types of Roman buildings, had their origins in the Greek world where public baths were common from at least the 4th cent. BC. Surviving 3rd-cent. Greek baths centre on a series of hip-baths arranged around the walls of one or more rooms, often circular (*tholoi*), with niches above the tubs, and were furnished with hot water which was poured over the seated bather. Baths of this type are found in southern Italy (e.g. Stabian baths, *Pompeii, first phase) and *Sicily, where, together with local traditions of therapeutic baths at volcanic springs and fumaroles, they were instrumental in the development of the purely Roman type. These replaced the individual tubs with communal pools, and often incorporated the dry sweating-rooms (*laconica*) and exercise grounds (*palaestrae*) of the Greek *gymnasium in the same establishment (Stabian baths, later phases; Republican baths at Regio VIII, 5, Pompeii). The basic features of these early Roman baths were a changing-room (*apodyterium*), an unheated *frigidarium* with a cold-water basin, an indirectly heated warm room (*tepidarium*) sometimes containing a tepid pool, and a strongly heated room (*caldarium*) containing a hot plunge pool and a separate water-basin on a stand (*labrum*). The evolution of the hypocaust (under-floor) and wall-heating systems after c.100 BC, replacing the less efficient braziers,

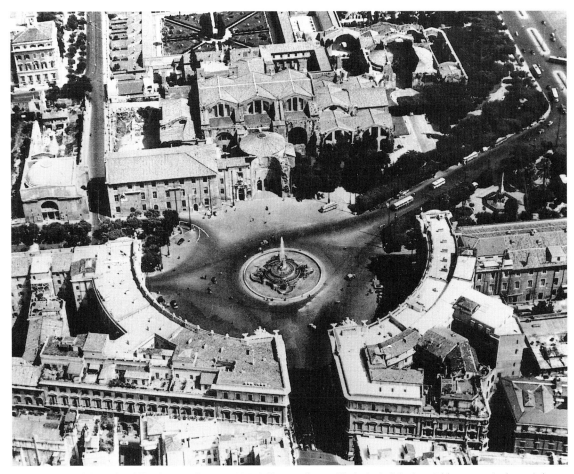

baths Air view of the baths of *Diocletian at Rome, AD 305–6. The grandiose public baths built by imperial *patronage in the capital spawned numerous paler imitations in the provinces.

and the introduction of window-glass in the 1st cent. AD permitted the development of an elaborately graded system (Sen. *Ep*. 90. 25; Celsus, *Med*. 1. 4, 2. 17) often with the incorporation of several wet and dry sweating-rooms (*sudatoria*). With increasingly assured water supply to towns (see AQUEDUCTS), large cold and even heated swimming-pools (*piscina*, *natatio*) also became common adjuncts.

Public baths, often located near the forum (civic centre), were a normal part of Roman towns in Italy by the 1st cent. BC, and seem to have existed at Rome even earlier. The baths in the Campus Martius donated to the Roman people by *Agrippa *c.*20 BC set new standards of luxury and architectural elaboration, and heralded a new civic role for the baths in the towns of the empire. At Rome they were followed by the baths of *Nero, *Titus, and *Trajan, the latter being the first of the truly monumental complexes set in a vast enclosure containing *gardens, lecture-halls, *libraries, and other cultural facilities, reflecting the influence of the Hellenistic gymnasium. The symmetrical plan

of the bathing-block, perhaps originating with the baths of Nero, centred on a triple cross-vaulted *frigidarium*, and incorporating a large *natatio* and twin colonnaded *palaestrae*, sometimes interpreted as basilical halls, was highly influential both at Rome (baths of *Caracalla and *Diocletian) and in the provinces with such buildings as the Antonine baths at *Carthage, the Barbara baths at Augusta Treverorum (Trier), and the Hadrianic baths at Lepcis Magna in *Africa. Even when the architectural form was not imitated so closely, the influence of the 'imperial' type can be seen in the increased size and elaboration of many baths in the provinces from the late 1st cent. onwards, along with an increase in the amount of space devoted to non-bathing functions. Regional variations developed, central Italy and North Africa producing many buildings of highly complex curvilinear plan (e.g. at Hadrian's villa near Tivoli and Thenae in Tunisia). Roman-style baths were widely adopted in the eastern provinces, forming a distinctive type in Asia Minor (e.g. at *Ephesus and Miletus) where they were assimilated to the Hellenistic gymnasium.

Bathing occupied a central position in the social life of the day; by the 2nd cent., any community of any substance, civil and military, had at least one set of public baths, while private baths are common in country *villas and in wealthier town houses. Larger towns often had one or more substantial buildings (*thermae*) which were showpieces for the community as well as a number of smaller, privately owned *balnea* to serve everyday needs. See HOUSES, ITALIAN; WATER. J. D.

bilingualism Widespread bilingualism at some level was characteristic of the ancient world, whether we look for (*a*) bilingual *communities*, in which two languages are in use (e.g. official and popular languages, written and nonwritten, formal and informal), or (*b*) bilingual individuals who know two languages at some level. Perfect capacity in two languages, a modern ideal, was probably both rare and unnecessary, and, despite Hdt. 8. 144 on Greek (see GREEK LANGUAGE), the close modern identity of language and nation seems to have been relatively unimportant. But bilingualism implies language choice: according to context, the associations of each language, or social ambition. Latin and especially Greek were the languages of culture and education (in the Roman empire, Latin was the language of law and army), as well as power, so that while many other languages coexisted alongside Latin and Greek, neither Greeks nor Romans ever had to impose their language on others. Greek and Roman writers tended to be uninterested in other languages, or they were never written down, so our evidence (written) is slight and misleading (e.g. we learn about Getic in Tomis (on the Black Sea) from *Ovid's complaints (e.g. *Pont.* 4. 13, 17 ff.), not from inscriptions).

Greek unwillingness to learn other languages, linked to their assurance of cultural superiority, is well known (Momigliano). *Herodotus learned no other languages (and suffered at interpreters' hands: e.g. 2. 125), Greek thinkers say little about foreign languages or revealingly categorize languages simply as Greek or *barbarian (e.g. *Plato, *Cratylus*). Yet this monolingualism may be more characteristic of the literary élite and of high culture. Other Greeks must have acquired other languages: e.g. the Ionian and Carian *mercenaries in Egypt in the Archaic period, the Greeks in Persian service, e.g. the doctor Democedes (see D. M. Lewis, *Sparta and Persia* (1977), 12–15), traders and colonizers—Massalia (in Transalpine *Gaul) was still trilingual in the 1st cent. BC—and often married non-Greek women (cf. for the reverse, the unfortunate Scylas, Hdt. 4. 78 ff., with Scythian father and Greek mother). The orientalizing period (8th–7th cent. BC) of Greek culture is hard to envisage with merely monolingual Greeks. Late 5th-cent. Athens has a mixture of customs and languages 'from all the Greeks and barbarians' (*Ath. pol.* 2. 8). However, by the Classical period, the bilinguals in a Greek city would be mainly foreigners, traders,

and slaves, i.e. outsiders (e.g. Scythian archers, Ar. *Eccl.* 1001–225).

The picture becomes more complex with *Alexander the Great's conquests of large non-Greek-speaking areas. The idea that Greek was always imposed as the language of administration in the Hellenistic kingdoms is increasingly doubtful. In the Seleucid empire, there is a mixture of Greek and Aramaic in the administration and, at least east of Asia Minor, evidence for bilingual Greeks. In Ptolemaic Egypt, Greek did become the language of administration; the extent to which Egyptians learnt Greek and became bilingual, however, or Greeks integrated at all into Egyptian society, is extremely difficult to gauge, and some recent work stresses bilingualism and at least limited interaction. There is evidence for individuals with double names, one Egyptian, one Greek, and for scribes fluent in both demotic and Greek. So the weight of administrative documents in Greek may hide greater Egyptian participation. Individual bilingualism, especially among prominent and ambitious Egyptian officials, must have been widespread.

The Roman empire was bilingual at the official, and multilingual at the individual and non-official, level. With the increasing Hellenization of Rome itself (see HELLENISM), educated Romans were expected to be bilingual in Latin and Greek, especially from the 1st cent. BC, at least for cultural purposes (there were tensions: *Juvenal complains about women who irritate their husbands by speaking Greek, *Sat.* 6. 184 ff.). The orator Quintilian advised that children start learning Greek before Latin (*Inst.* 1. 1. 12–14). Greek was widely used in diplomatic activity from the republic: P. Licinius Crassus, proconsul of Asia in 131 BC who spoke five Greek dialects (Val. Max. 8. 7. 6), was exceptional, but by Cicero's time, interpreters were not always needed for Greek in the senate (Cic. *Fin.* 5. 89, with *Div.* 2. 131). *Tiberius tried, too late, to discourage Greek in the senate, a rare case of Latin chauvinism (Suet. *Tib.* 71: this failed). Most Roman emperors were fluent in Greek: Marcus *Aurelius, despairing of Latin, wrote his private *Meditations* in Greek; while *Septimius Severus may have been trilingual (Lat., Gk., Punic), *Severus Alexander perhaps better at Greek than Latin (SHA *Alex. Sev.* 3. 4).

The Romans made remarkably little attempt to impose Latin on the empire. The language of administration in the west was certainly Latin, and ambitious provincials simply had to acquire it themselves (P. Brunt, *Imperial Themes* (1990), 267 ff.). In the Greek-speaking east, administration was mostly conducted in Greek, mainly from pragmatism, and edicts, imperial constitutions, and letters sent by Rome to Greek cities were usually translated into Greek first (and inscribed in Greek). Greek speakers were markedly unenthusiastic about learning Latin, and Roman colonies in the east were linguistically quickly absorbed. However the extent of bilingual inscriptions implies there was no strict single language policy (see J. Kaimio, *The Romans and the Greek Language* (1979)). Decisions of the Roman courts were probably always given in Latin, and Latin was necessary in law for certain documents for Roman citizens. With the widening of Roman *citizenship (AD 212), Severus Alexander (222–35) allowed Greek in the wills of Roman citizens. From the 4th cent., Latin was increasingly used in government and court when the government transferred to the east; this was deplored by educated Greeks. Greek became less widely known even in educated circles in the west from the 4th cent. (cf. Symmachus, *Epistolae* 4. 20).

The many other languages in the Roman empire tend to be submerged in our evidence because they were unwritten, or non-literary, and many gain prominence with Christian preoccupations, but must always have been there: e.g. Gallic, Getic, neo-Phrygian, Aramaic, Coptic, and Syriac which develop as literary languages after AD 200, Iberian, Thracian, Punic (noted by St *Augustine), not to mention Hebrew. Romanized provincials presumably knew the 'vernacular' as well as Latin, and the languages each had their own milieu. The Roman army in particular brought together a multilingual force where the lingua franca was Latin (cf. Tac. *Hist.* 2. 37, 3. 33, for problems of polyglot armies). This substratum is indicated by the later adaptation of Roman law to the extension of Roman citizenship: Ulpian allowed 'even Punic, Gallic, Syriac, and other languages' for certain transactions (trusts) under Roman law (*Dig.* 32. 11 pref.). See also TRANSLATION.

R. T.

biography, Greek 1. Biography in antiquity was not a rigidly defined genre. *Bios*, 'life', or *bioi*, 'lives', could span a range of types of writing, from *Plutarch's cradle-to-grave accounts of statesmen to Chamaeleon (*c.*350–after 281 BC)'s extravagant stories about literary figures, and even to Dicaearchus (fl. *c.*320–300 BC)'s ambitious *Life of Greece*. Consequently the boundaries with neighbouring genres—the encomium, the biographical novel on the model of *Xenophon's *Cyropaedia*, the historical monograph on the deeds of a great man like *Alexander the Great—are blurred and sometimes artificial. One should not think of a single 'biographical genre' with acknowledged conventions, but rather of a complicated picture of overlapping traditions, embracing works of varying form, style, length, and truthfulness.

2. The impulse to celebrate the individual finds early expression in the dirge (song of lamentation) and the funeral oration; organization of a literary work around an individual's experiences is as old as the *Odyssey* (see HOMER), and various *Heracleids* and *Theseids* seem to have treated their subjects' deeds more comprehensively. In the 5th cent. biographical interest was pursued in various ways. Ion of Chios gossiped about contemporary figures in his 'Visits' (*Epidemiai*, a book of reminiscences), while Stesimbrotus wrote colourfully on the Athenian politicians Themistocles, Thucydides son of Melesias, and *Pericles. The historian *Thucydides included selective sketches of several figures, notably the regent Pausanias (see SPARTA) and Themistocles. In the 4th cent. appeared two influential encomia, *Isocrates' *Evagoras*, enumerating its subject's

qualities in a loosely chronological framework, and Xenophon's *Agesilaus*, giving first a focused narrative of achievements, then a catalogue of virtues. Xenophon's *Cyropaedia* also set the model for the idealizing and largely fictional biographical novel, while his 'Socratic Memoirs' (*Memorabilia*), along with the Platonic corpus, developed the personality of Socrates in different literary forms.

3. *Aristotle gave biography a new impetus. Under his influence interest in ethical and cultural history encouraged the writing of more generalized *bioi*. Dicaearchus and Clearchus of Soli treated different lifestyles; Theophrastus' *Characters* are clearly related; while Dicaearchus' three-volume *Life of Greece* traced the origins of contemporary Greek culture. Aristoxenus of Tarentum wrote Lives of philosophers, in which an interest in lifestyle combined with malicious stories about *Socrates' irascibility and *Plato's plagiarism. This anecdotal style heralds a distinctive style of biography of cultural figures. Chamaeleon's Lives of various poets were notable for their wild inferences of biographical data from an author's work, and his model was followed by Hermippus of Smyrna (3rd cent. BC), Satyrus (who adopted dialogue form), and Sotion (early 2nd cent. BC?), who presented in thirteen books a *diadochē*, 'succession', of great philosophers. This tendency to collect Lives in series became a standard mode of presenting intellectual history, and the 'succession' of teachers and pupils was a helpful idiom for explaining influences. Little can be said of the literary form of these works, except that it varied.

4. Biography of political figures is more problematic. Dicaearchus presented philosophers as men of action as well as intellectuals, and the active life was prominent in discussion of lifestyles; several monographs also approximated to biographies or to series of biographical sketches, such as *Theopompus' *Philippica*, Phaenias' *On the Sicilian Tyrants*, and Idomeneus' *On the (Athenian) Demagogues*. Both Phaenias and Idomeneus also wrote on the Socratics, and other works similarly spanned politicians and intellectuals: Hermippus of Smyrna included (often mythical) lawgivers in his series, and Satyrus treated *Philip II. But political history had an adequate alternative mode of presentation in the various forms of *historiography, which themselves increasingly stressed human personality.

5. Rather than clear-cut political *bioi*, we thus have works with biographical affinities. The impact of *Alexander the Great was here important. Such early monographs as those of Cleitarchus, Ptolemy I (see PTOLEMY I and II) and Aristobulus centred on the king's person; the fragmentation of the Hellenistic world into dynasties encouraged monographs on other kings, such as Duris' four-volume *History of Agathocles* (see SYRACUSE), and perhaps the works on Agathocles and *Pyrrhus which formed a four-volume supplement to *Timaeus' *History*. The biographical novel on the model of *Cyropaedia* also revived, with its typical emphasis on a king's upbringing. Onesicritus' *How Alexander Was Brought Up* belongs here, and so later does Nicolaus of Damascus' *On Augustus' Life and Education*. This genre

overlapped with encomium, which also flourished: *Polybius 10. 21 mentions his earlier three-volume work on the Achaean statesman Philopoemen (2nd cent. BC), and distinguished the 'inflation' appropriate to that work from the truthfulness required of continuous history. The monographs may not have been full on childhood, and ranged beyond their subject's personal achievements; the novels (see NOVEL, GREEK) were largely idealized and partly fictional. But the biographical interest of these works is still strong, and the dividing line from biography is not clear.

6. About 240 BC Antigonus of Carystus displayed a new accuracy in describing contemporary philosophers; and in the scholarly atmosphere of *Alexandria there developed a different style of biography, revaluing the findings of the Peripatetics (Aristotle's school) and re-establishing their chronological data. Commentaries and epitomes called for biographical introductions, which generally avoided chronological narrative: between the particulars of birth and death short notes elucidated the mode of life, friends, students, works, etc. Typical of this school is Posidonius' pupil Jason of Nysa; later Didymus' *On Demosthenes* collects many learned items in conjunction with a commentary on the *Philippics* of *Demosthenes. The artistic pretensions of this tradition are not great.

7. A type of autobiography goes back to early lyric poetry, to Xenophon's *Anabasis*, and to such self-defences as Isocrates' *Antidosis*, Demosthenes' *On the Crown*, and Plato's *Seventh Letter*. By the 3rd cent. men of action were elaborating the memoir: the Achaean statesman Aratus was here most influential. With Nicolaus of Damascus' *Autobiography* the technique extends to an intellectual figure; he finds a follower in *Josephus.

8. The Christian Gospels have points of contact with the Greek tradition, with their charismatic hero and their anecdotal narrative texture. A different moral earnestness is found in Plutarch's *Parallel Lives*, which mark a considerable new achievement. Their scale, ambition, and historical sobriety are hard to parallel in the antecedent traditions; so is the depth of characterization. Important here is the technique of comparison of a Greek and Roman hero, drawing attention to nuances of personality. The moralizing is sometimes subtle; the psychological interest is uneven, but can be penetrating.

9. Philostratus' *Life of Apollonius* (see APOLLONIUS OF TYANA) veers towards hagiography: readers would probably not have taken it as literal truth. Eunapius (4th cent. AD) broke up the Alexandrian form. More learned were the Neoplatonist biographies of Porphyry and Marinus. The first book of Marcus *Aurelius provides a more exploratory form of intellectual autobiography. The doctor Galen is similar but less perceptive, while *Lucian's *Dream* is more playful; Libanius (4th cent. AD) goes back to the model of Isocrates' *Antidosis*. Diogenes Laertius exemplifies the abridging and synthesizing of the materials of literary biography.

Much of Greek biography is lost; the range and richness of its remains are still striking.   C. B. R. P.

biography, Roman I. Roman biography did not wholly derive from its Greek equivalent: their own political and family customs led Romans to value the recording of the deeds of their great men. We hear of songs at banquets praising the famous, of dirges (*neniae*) at funerals, and of a native tradition of funeral laudations (*laudationes funebres*). Such laudations were preserved and kept among the family records, together with the likenesses (*imagines*) of distinguished ancestors: Cicero (*Brut.* 62) complains about the inaccuracies of these laudations. Sepulchral inscriptions were important too, and became very elaborate, often giving details of private as well as public matters (cf. the 'laudations' of Murdia and Turia, *CIL* 6. 2. 10230 and 1527, 31670). The flavour of such formal memorials is as recurrent in Roman biography as that of encomium in the Greek counterpart; it is, for instance, one of the elements detectable in *Tacitus' *Agricola*.

2. The competitive quest for glory also stimulated writers to self-justification and self-defence. The award of a triumph might depend on the bulletins sent home by generals; such writing naturally goes back to an early period. More elaborate apologetic or propagandist autobiography found a natural home in Rome: examples were the three books of Marcus Aemilius Scaurus, the five or more of Publius Rutilius Rufus, and Quintus Lutatius Catulus' single book *On his Consulship and his Achievements*. The twenty-two books of *Sulla's memoirs owed something to the Greek precedent of Aratus of Sicyon (3rd cent. BC). *Caesar's *Commentaries* presented a particularly nuanced form of self-projection; *Cicero too wrote about his own career and achievement both in Latin and in Greek. Under the Principate, it was especially members of the imperial family who wrote political memoirs: *Augustus, *Tiberius, *Agrippina, *Hadrian, *Septimius Severus.

3. Justification was not limited to autobiography. Gaius *Gracchus' two books *To Pomponius* presented a picture of his brother Tiberius *Gracchus which similarly contributed to contemporary debate. Equal generosity, even when the political point was less immediate, was surely to be found in the memoirs written by clients or freedmen of the great, Marcus Tullius Tiro on Cicero and Plotus on the Pompeii (Suet. *Rhet.* 6, cf. Peter, *HRRel.* I. cclxxxiii–cclxxxiv). Such works can be hard to distinguish from the historical monograph: in his letter to Lucius Lucceius (*Fam.* 5. 12) Cicero seems to assume that such a monograph will naturally centre on a single person and his achievements, and playfully pleads for a liberal attitude to the truth. *Sallust's extant monographs notably avoid such a sharp focus on Jugurtha or *Catiline, but Gaius Oppius' work on Caesar may belong here.

4. The political heat of the late republic produced further writings designed to praise and defend, or sometimes attack, not only political actions but private character or philosophy. The influence of forensic rhetoric, so often describing the life of client or opponent, is here strong. The death of *Cato the Younger inspired works by

Cicero and *Brutus, which were answered first by Aulus Hirtius, then by Caesar's own counterblast the *Anticato*; this in its turn was countered by Munatius Rufus. Lucius Calpurnius Bibulus wrote on the other philosopher-statesman, Brutus. These works represent the beginnings of a considerable literature, a blend of martyrology and ideological propaganda, which came to cluster around the Stoic opponents of the 1st-cent. Principate (see STOICISM). *Deaths of Famous Men*, such as Gaius Fannius' three books on *Nero's victims, dwelt especially on the theatrical martyrdoms: Quintus Iunius Arulenus Rusticus' *Life* of Thrasea Paetus and Herennius Senecio's of Helvidius Priscus are mentioned by Tacitus in the preface to his *Agricola*, and this must have been a further influence on that work. *Agricola* too explores political life under a tyrant, though it praises restrained collaboration rather than ostentatious martyrdom; its use of an individual's life to sketch a political ambience is most deft.

5. Jerome named *Varro, Cornelius Nepos, Hyginus, Santra, and *Suetonius in a canon of biographers (*De vir. ill.* 2. 821 Vull.). The contributions of Hyginus and Santra are obscure, but the list still brings out the range of literary form which the genre could accommodate. Varro may be named for his *On Poets* or for his *Imagines* ('Likenesses', a work which added some sort of brief description to a series of 700 portraits), or even for his *Life* (*Vita*) *of the Roman People*, a Roman imitation of Dicaearchus. Besides longer works on *Cato the Elder and on Cicero, Nepos wrote sixteen or eighteen books containing some 400 short *Lives*: the series *On Foreign Generals* survives, together with *Cato* (an abbreviation of the longer version) and the more elaborate and eulogistic *Atticus*, both it seems from the series *On Roman Historians*. His enterprise owed something to Greek writing 'On Famous Men', and Nepos was perhaps trying to make the great men of history accessible to a wider Roman audience. Suetonius' *Caesars* pointedly reduce the element of historical narrative, instead providing a learned survey of an emperor's character and behaviour under a series of headings. There is some generic similarity with his lives of grammarians and rhetors, but the scale and ambition is much greater. The style of the *Caesars* proved congenial as spectators increasingly saw Roman history in terms of the ruling personality, and biography supplanted historiography as the dominant mode of record: Marius Maximus and then the *Historia Augusta* continued Suetonius and followed his model.

6. There is little intimacy in Roman biography. Much Latin poetry is self-revealing and self-analytical, but the most ambitious formal autobiography and biography centred on public figures, and exploration of spiritual life is felt as inappropriate. Cicero (*Brut.* 313 ff.) does tell us something of his education and development, analysing his debt to various teachers; but there are no Latin pieces of self-exploration comparable with Marcus *Aurelius' *Eis Heauton* ('To himself') until we reach St *Augustine.

C. B. R. P.

biology See ANATOMY AND PHYSIOLOGY; ANIMALS, KNOWLEDGE ABOUT; BOTANY; GYNAECOLOGY.

body The history of the body is a discipline which emerged in the 1980s; it questions the extent to which the body is 'natural', and asks whether all societies have experienced the body in the same way. The combined classical and Christian heritage of western civilization has assigned the body a subordinate place in its value systems, but dichotomies such as mind/body and soul/body are by no means universal. The subject is associated in particular with the work of Foucault, although his studies of the classical world have been criticized for relying unduly on élite philosophical texts, neglecting Rome, and ignoring female sexuality.

It is in medical texts that the differences between ancient and modern experiences of the body are perhaps most obvious. For many centuries, Graeco-Roman *medicine included the belief that the womb could move around the body, and debate existed on such issues as the seat of consciousness (the liver, the heart, and the brain were suggested) and the origin of male seed (from the brain, the blood, or the whole body). The female body was seen as unstable; strong affinities existed between the top and bottom, so that defloration deepened the voice, while menstrual blood could come out of the nose (see GYNAECOLOGY).

Another clear distinction between our own society and the ancient world concerns nakedness. Clothing was one of the features believed to set humanity apart from the animals. In *Homer, nakedness is associated with vulnerability and shame; Odysseus covers himself before Nausicaa (*Od.* 6. 126–9). For the Greeks of the Classical period, however, nudity becomes the costume of the citizen; because male nudity is seen as normal, only *barbarians are represented as feeling shame when a man is seen naked (Hdt. 1. 10. 3 on the Lydians). Female nudity, meanwhile, continues to be associated with vulnerability and shame; the girls of Miletus (W. Asia Minor) are persuaded to end a mass suicide epidemic by the threat of exposure after death (Plut. *Mor.* 249bd). Nudity is also associated with *initiation (e.g. *Brauron) and fertility. In Athenian vase-paintings, men are represented naked in outdoor scenes, never in private domestic space. Women are generally shown naked only in private scenes when nudity is to be expected—for example, when washing—or when they are about to be killed or raped. In Etruscan art, in contrast, men wear shorts or loincloths in situations when Greek men would be shown naked—for instance when exercising (see ATHLETICS). In Roman art, nudity continues to be the costume of the male hero.

From childhood, the body needed to be controlled. Roman child-nurses were advised on how to mould the shape of the body, by swaddling and massage (Sor. *Gynaeceia* 2. 15, 32). For men, correct control of the body was a further part of the costume of a good citizen. The orator, in particular, was advised on every aspect of presentation of self (e.g. Cic. *Off.*; Quint. *Inst.* 11. 3) (see RHETORIC, LATIN). The state too had a role in controlling the body, by instilling obedience through *education and, above all, through military training. Physiognomy used the body to reveal character, but recognized that individuals could learn to conceal their faults by changing their outward appearance. From Pandora's adornment by the gods onwards, women were represented as deceptive and frivolous, their elaborate clothing, wigs, and make-up concealing the vices underneath. Both Greek and Roman sources praise the unadorned woman (e.g. Xen. *Oec.* 10. 2–13; Seneca, *De consolatione* 16), while Roman sumptuary legislation tried to set limits on the expense of women's clothing (see DRESS).

*Augustine (e.g. *De civ. D.* 19. 13) draws a parallel between the ordered arrangement of the parts of the body and the ordered arrangement of the appetites of the soul. Peace and health consist of both. Within the order of nature, the soul must control the body and reason the appetites, just as master controls slave and man controls woman. Some Christians positively valued neglect of the body—seen in abstinence from food and sex, or lack of interest in one's appearance—as evidence of a proper rejection of this world, whereas Graeco-Roman philosophy urged the care of the body as evidence of the virtue of *enkrateia* or self-control.

The body is also a central metaphor for political and social order. In Livy, Menenius Agrippa (*consul 503 BC) uses the body as an analogy for the body politic; the rest of the body revolts against the stomach (i.e. senate), perceived as idle, but soon weakens and has to recognize its dependence (2. 32). Disease in the body politic was a way of expressing social disorder. H. K.

Boeotian confederacy See FEDERAL STATES.

books, Greek and Roman (*see following page*)

booty 'It is a law established for all time among all men that when a city is taken in war, the persons and the property of its inhabitants belong to the captors' (Xen. *Cyr.* 7. 5. 73). This universal ancient conception is reflected in the wide range of meanings of the ancient terminology for 'booty' (notably *leia*, *laphura*, and *ōpheleia* in Greek, *praeda* and *spolia* in Latin). It referred not just to movable and inanimate objects (e.g. precious metals), but could also include animals and livestock, human beings, and even whole cities and territory. War, for instance, was one of the major suppliers of the slave trade (see SLAVERY). It was rare after *Homer for wars to be fought solely and openly for acquisitive purposes. But it was always assumed that success in war would lead to appropriation by the victor of the property and persons of the vanquished, and sometimes of territory as well. Hence the largest sudden transfers of wealth in the ancient world were the result of successful warfare: for example *Sparta's conquest of Messenia (see PELOPONNESE) and the Messenians in the late

8th cent. BC, the Persian Wars (see GREECE, (HISTORY)) and their sequels, *Alexander the Great's conquest of the Persian empire and the wars of the Successors, who all regarded their conquests as 'spear-won territory', and the numerous wars of the expanding Roman republic. On a smaller scale raiding between neighbouring states was endemic, as were *piracy at sea and *brigandage on land, except when a stronger power was able to impose peace in its sphere of influence (Athens in the 5th cent., Rhodes in the Hellenistic period, Rome under the empire). Throughout antiquity, it was also assumed that armies would sustain themselves from the territory in which they operated. M. M. A.

botany From earliest times, Greeks and Romans had expert familiarity with plants and their growth cycles; agriculture dominates, alongside acute command of medicinal herbs, including production of oils and perfumes. Exact nomenclatures were quite irrelevant; everyone 'knew' plants and flowers carpeting fields and mountain valleys in season; flower metaphors became common in *Homer

[*continued on p. 124*]

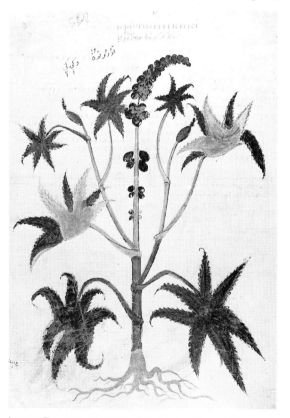

botany The castor oil plant as illustrated in a 6th-cent. AD copy of the herbal of Pedanius Dioscorides (1st cent. AD). His work, 'Materials of Medicine', lists around 700 plants and is an important source of knowledge about earlier Greek botany.

Greek and Roman books

Greek and Roman books Books existed in Egypt long before they came into use in Greece. Systems of writing had been invented and developed for administrative purposes in both Egypt and Mesopotamia by *c*.3000 BC. While the Sumerians and Babylonians (see BABYLONIA) used clay tablets for their cuneiform (wedge-shaped) scripts, the Egyptians used papyrus (made from the marsh plant *Cyperus papyrus*). A blank sheet of papyrus was found in the tomb of the vizier Hemaka in Saqqara of *c*.3000 BC. The oldest surviving inscribed papyrus texts are the temple accounts of Abusir of *c*.2450 BC. A number of fine statues of seated scribes of the same period suggests that this profession was already well established and that writing had been practised for centuries, long enough for the 'hieratic' script to develop through the adaptation of hieroglyphs to the use of reed-brush and papyrus. The hieroglyph for 'book-roll' is first attested in the first dynasty (*c*.3000–2800 BC), and Egyptian literature was supposed to have begun with the writings of Imhotep, the architect of the first pyramid under King Djoser in the third dynasty (*c*.2600 BC). Religious books were kept in temples; although temple 'libraries', i.e. chambers designated for the storage of books, have survived only in Ptolemaic temples (Edfu, Philae, ed-Tod), literary references to books and libraries suggest their existence in the Middle Kingdom (thirteenth dynasty, *c*.1700 BC), and *Diodorus Siculus (1. 47, using the account of Hecataeus) describes the library in the Ramesseum at Egyptian Thebes.

The papyrus plant grew mainly in the swamplands of lower Egypt and especially the Nile delta. It was used for many purposes: to make ropes, sandals, baskets, boats, and—most importantly—writing material. The Greeks called it *byblos* or *biblos* (see below), later *papyros* (first attested in Theophr. *Hist. pl.* 4. 8. 2), believed to be derived from Egyptian *pꜣ-n-pr-ꜥꜣ* 'that of Pharaoh', which suggests that its manufacture and marketing were a royal monopoly. The *locus classicus* describing its manufacture is Plin. *NH* 13. 74–82 (translation and discussion in N. Lewis, *Papyrus in Classical Antiquity* (1974), 34–69). The triangular-sectioned stem is cut into segments *c*.30–40 cm. (12–16 in.) long, from which the outer hull is then removed; the white pith is sliced lengthwise into thin strips, which are placed vertically parallel to each other on a plane surface; over these, a second layer of strips is placed horizontally, and the ends squared off. They are then pressed in presses (*prelis*); the plant's natural juice glues the layers firmly together. After drying, the sheet is smoothed with a stone or a sea-shell. According to *Pliny the Elder, twenty sheets (*kollēmata, plagulae*) were then glued together to form a roll (*chartēs, charta*), on average 6–8 m. (20–26 ft.) long (in Pharaonic times, too, papyrus rolls of twenty sheets had been standard). If a longer roll was required, it had to be manufactured specially. The narrow edge (*kollēsis*, 'gluing') of a sheet which, in Greek books, overlaps that of the sheet to its right is usually 20–25 mm. (¾–1 in.) wide. In rolls of Egyptian texts, however, the right-hand sheet overlaps the one to its left, so that the scribe, writing from right to left, had his reed brush travelling 'downhill' over the joins. If this was the way in which rolls were originally manufactured, Greek scribes turned them upside down, so that they, too, could write 'downhill' over the joins. The sheets on the inside of the roll show horizontal fibres; in this way the joins are better protected from being pulled apart. Only the first sheet of the roll has its vertical fibres on the inside, at right angles to those of the following sheets; this is the 'protocol' (*prōtokollon*) which protected the outside of the book when it was rolled up; it was sometimes a parchment sheet (cf. [Tib.] 3. 1. 9), or reinforced with parchment. Whether the ends of rolls were similarly reinforced is not clear; the surviving ends of book-rolls show no sign of an *eschatocollion* (Mart. 2. 6. 3). Rollers (*umbilici*, Hor. *Epist.* 14. 8; Mart. 4. 89) with decorative knobs (*cornua*, Mart. 11. 107) attached to the last sheet survive in some rolls from *Herculaneum but none have been found in Egypt.

As the pen runs more smoothly along the fibres than across, the scribes normally used the inside of the roll first where the glued join (*kollēsis*) runs at right angles to the fibres; this is conventionally called 'recto', its back 'verso', but these terms should only be used with regard to codices ('recto' = right-hand page), whereas for rolls the terms 'front'/'back', or 'inside'/'outside' are preferable. In some rolls, however, the writing runs across the fibres on the inside, parallel to the joins, in long lines from edge to edge. Such rolls (*rotuli*) were employed only for Greek and Latin documents, never for literary texts which were designed for continuous reading. Documents, on the other hand, were often glued together to form rolls, the blank backs of which could then be used for literary texts (for private use, not for sale). As the inside of the roll was nearly always used first, a dated document may provide a *terminus post quem* for the literary text; the reverse case (document on the back of a book roll, cf. Mart. 8. 62) is relatively rare. Papyrus rolls were dressed with cedar-oil (*kedria*, *cedrium*) to protect them against worms (Vitr. *De arch.* 2. 9. 13).

A papyrus roll would take a book of *Thucydides, or a play of *c.*1500 lines, or two to three books of *Homer. The length of the books of *Apollonius Rhodius' *Argonautica*, or the books of *Polybius, *Strabo, or *Diodorus Siculus, may have been determined by this standard format. The text is arranged in columns (*selides*, *paginae*); the number of lines per column, usually between 25 and 45, varies with the height of the column and the size of the writing. The length of the lines also varied; in hexameter and trimeter poetry it was determined by the verse, but lyric poetry and prose were (at any rate, from the 2nd cent. BC onwards) written in shorter lines of between 5 and 10 cm. (2–4 in.), with an average of between 18 and 25 letters per line. Some book-rolls have wide upper and lower margins as well as generous spaces between columns. Sometimes a line accidentally omitted from the text is added in the upper or lower margin, usually with a reference mark.

Apart from papyrus, leather was also used in Egypt to produce rolls for literary texts. The *Annals* of Thutmosis III were written on leather rolls and deposited in the temple of Amūn at Karnak. The inscription in the library of the Edfu temple also lists leather rolls. In the ancient near east, leather was widely used as a writing material. Ctesias, writing late 5th cent. BC, describes (in Diod. Sic. 2. 32. 4) the 'royal hides' (*basilikai diphtherai*) which the Persians used for their chronicles; from Persia, leather rolls may have come into use in Ionia and then in other parts of Greece. In Italy, too, animal hides were used at an early stage (Dion. Hal. 4. 58). While leather had to be tanned, vellum or parchment was manufactured by placing the hide in slaked lime for some days; then flesh and hairs were scraped off and the hide was rubbed with calcium oxide, stretched in a frame, and finally smoothed with pumice. The name 'parchment' (*pergamēnē*, *pergamena*) is derived from *Pergamum, which became a centre of production and export in the 2nd cent. BC when papyrus from Egypt was in short supply. The earliest extant Greek documents on vellum (parchment), however, prove that the manufacturing process had been known earlier.

In the production of books parchment played only a minor role compared with papyrus, which remained the dominant writing material throughout Greek and Roman antiquity. In *Crete, papyrus may have been used as early as the second millennium BC, as strands of papyrus have been found baked into Minoan clay sealings. Egyptian papyrus was also exported to Phoenicia (see PHOENICIANS) and beyond; the story of Wen-Amūn (11th cent. BC) mentions 500 rolls of finished papyrus sent to Byblos in return for timber. The fact that in Greek (Aesch. *Supp.* 947, Hdt. 2. 100, etc.) *byblos* means 'papyrus roll' suggests that originally it may have been imported from Byblos (mod. Jubayl, Lebanon), Phoenician Gubla. So it is at least possible that papyrus as a writing material was known in the Greek world in Mycenaean times, but there is as yet no firm evidence for its use as a vehicle for Greek literature before *c.*500 BC when book-rolls of papyrus first appear on Attic vases. Herodotus' remark (5. 58) that the Ionian Greeks had used leather rolls at a time when papyrus was scarce, and hence kept the word *diphthera* ('hide') for 'book' (*byblos*), does not rule out early acquaintance with papyrus. In the 8th cent. BC, papyrus is mentioned in cuneiform texts in Assyrian accounts as 'reeds from Egypt', and an 8th-cent. palimpsest papyrus written in Hebrew has come to light near Murabba'at on the Dead Sea (*PMur.* 17 = *Discoveries in the Judaean Desert* (1960), 2, pp. 93–100).

Although writing may have been employed early on in the composition of Greek poetry (and the complex structure of both *Iliad* and *Odyssey* is hardly conceivable without it), the performance of poetry continued to be oral throughout the Archaic and Classical periods. When the poet Archilochus (7th cent. BC) describes himself as a 'woeful messenger-stick' (*achnymenē skytalē*, fr. 185 W), he does not necessarily imply that his epode was transmitted on a piece of papyrus or leather, wrapped round a stick. On the other hand, much of early epic poetry is reflected in both lyric poetry and black-figure vase-painting, Corinthian and Attic (see POTTERY, GREEK), and it seems doubtful whether this can be accounted for by oral transmission (by itinerant rhapsodes (professional poetry-reciters) and choirs) alone. It is therefore reasonable to assume that book-rolls played a part in the transmission of Greek poetry in the 7th and 6th cent., if only as *aides-mémoire* to the performers. In the 6th cent., the tyrants Polycrates of Samos and *Pisistratus of Athens are said to have been admired for their collections of books (Athen. 1. 3a). Pisistratus is credited with a revision of the texts of Homer which until then had been 'confused' (Cic. *De or*. 3. 137); he is also said to have inserted lines about Salamis and *Theseus into the texts (*Il*. 2. 558, *Od*. 11. 631). On the other hand, [Pl.] *Hipparch*. 228b says that Pisistratus' son Hipparchus brought the poems of Homer to Attica and forced the singers at the Panathenaea festival to perform them—in preference, perhaps, to other early epics. In any case, there clearly was, in the later 6th cent., an authoritative text of Homer which served as a basis for rhapsodic recitals at the Panathenaea.

From *c*.500 onwards, book-rolls (evidently of papyrus) appear on Attic vases; as far as the writing can be identified, they all contain poetry. The Duris cup in Berlin of *c*.485 BC (Beazley, *ARV*² 431. 48) illustrates the use of book-rolls in schools, and Ar. *Nub*. 961–72 describes the 'ancient education' (*archaia paideia*), i.e. in the schools of *c*.500 BC, where the children were made to memorize epic poetry and to sing it in the traditional mode. Reading books for pleasure is mentioned in Eur. *Erechtheus* (fr. 369 N, of 422 BC?), and in Ar. *Ran*. 52 f. (405 BC) *Dionysus says he read *Euripides' *Andromeda* on board ship. The earliest references to booksellers are in the playwright Eupolis, late 5th cent. BC (fr. 327 KA, *PCG* 5. 485), and in *Plato (*Ap*. 26d), where *Socrates says that a copy of the philosopher Anaxagoras could be bought 'from the orchestra' (in the Agora of Athens?) for one drachma 'at most'. The term 'bookseller' (*bibliopōlēs*) is first attested in Theopompus the comic poet, active *c*410–370 BC (fr. 77 Kock). *Xenophon (*An*. 7. 5. 12–14) refers to 'many written books' being exported on ships from Athens to the Black Sea, and in *Mem*. 4. 2. 10 *Socrates asks Euthydemus whether he wants to become a rhapsode, having bought the complete works of Homer.

The intellectual revolution of the *sophists and the interest in dithyrambs and tragedy boosted demand for books in Athens, where book production and the book trade flourished in the 4th cent. BC. It made the vast collecting activities of *Aristotle and his pupils possible and led to the formation of *libraries, notably that of Aristotle himself (Strabo 13. 608).

The oldest surviving specimens of literary papyrus rolls date from the second half of the 4th cent. The Timotheus papyrus (*PBerol*. 9875, *Persians*), found at Abusir north of Memphis, written in long lines in large, clumsy letters, may antedate *Alexander the Great's conquest of Egypt. The carbonized papyrus roll found at Derveni in *Macedonia, a commentary on an Orphic cosmogony, is written in small letters (*c*.2 mm. (⁄₁₀ in.) high) in a careful, skilled hand which makes the columns look almost like *stoichēdon* inscriptions (i.e. exactly aligned vertically). Given the regularity and elegance of Attic writing on vases and also of private letters on lead tablets, such as the letter of Mnesiergus in Berlin (*Syll*.³ 1259), the Derveni papyrus has a far stronger claim to being a typical representative of a 4th-cent. book. From the beginning of the Ptolemaic period through to the 8th cent. AD, an uninterrupted series of book-rolls and, later, codices chiefly from Egypt illustrates the development of Greek (and, to a lesser extent, Latin) books and their scripts.

The Museum and the Library at *Alexandria, founded by *Ptolemy I, became the most important centre of scholarship, and literary criticism in particular, for centuries to come. The work of the Alexandrian scholars led to a standardization in the formats of Greek books and in the layout of the texts. While in early 3rd-cent. BC texts of poetry, verse (other than hexameters and trimeters) is not written metrically, books from the 2nd cent. BC onwards show lyric passages arranged in short metrical units or *kōla*; their colometry is preserved in the medieval manuscripts of *Pindar's *epinikia* and the choruses of Attic drama (see TRAGEDY; COMEDY). Prose texts are usually set out in fairly narrow columns in lines of equal length. Aids to the reader, such as spaces between sentences, punctuation, or horizontal dashes (*paragraphoi*) in the left-hand margin or between line-beginnings, very rare at first, become more frequent in the 2nd and 1st cents. BC and increasingly common during the Roman period, as do accents and breathings. The librarian Aristarchus (*c*.216–144 BC) devised a system of critical reference signs to alert the reader to textual problems and their discussions in commentaries; most of these appear in book-rolls, though not always with the functions assigned them by Aristarchus. Commentaries (*Hypomnēmata*) were written in rolls separate from the texts on which they comment, but the rolls carrying texts often have notes or excerpts from commentaries in the margins, although they are rarely as copious as in the Louvre papyrus of *Alcman's *Partheneion*.

Greek book-rolls continued the Egyptian tradition of book illumination; the surviving illustrated papyri are mostly scientific or mathematical books, or magical papyri; fragments of illustrated papyrus rolls of Homer or drama are very rare. Book illumination becomes more common only in the later Roman period, with the victory of the codex (see below). Titles, too, were added, either in the left-hand margin against the opening line, or at the end of a book under its last line. Title-tags (*sillyboi*) were sometimes appended to book-rolls. Book titles first came into use with Attic drama, because the titles of plays had to be entered for the competition. While the older lyric poems are usually referred to by their opening lines, Aristophanes (*Nub.* 553 f.) quotes Eupolis' *Marikas* by title and then his own play, the *Knights* (*tous hēmeteras Hippeas*). *Dithyrambs, too, may have been entered for competitions by their titles, perhaps as early as the 6th cent., if Herodotus' statement that the cithara-player Arion (around 600 BC) 'gave his dithyrambs names' (*onomosanta*, 1. 23) is to be trusted. Prose works in the 5th and 4th cents. BC generally do not seem to have had titles, even though Plato (*Politicus* 284b) refers to his dialogue *Sophist* by this title (*en tōi Sophistēi*). Normally, prose works, too, are referred to by quoting their opening words, a practice which may have been promoted by *Callimachus's catalogue of the Alexandrian library, the *Pinakes* ('Panels'). The division of longer works into books must be attributed to the Alexandrian scholars who edited them.

Rolls were kept on shelves, or in boxes or buckets (*teuchos, capsa, scrinium*). Sometimes rolls were kept in a vellum cover (*diphthera, paenula*) with a coloured label. The vellum label with *Pindaros holos* ('The Complete Pindar', *PAntinoop.* 1. 21) may have been attached to a box or bookcase containing the seventeen books of the Alexandrian edition. While private libraries had boxes or movable cases, as did the library of King Eumenes II (197–158 BC) of Pergamum, the great public libraries of early imperial Rome had bookcases inserted in niches (*thyris, fenestra*) in the walls. This is a feature of both Egyptian temples (Edfu, Philae, ed-Tod: see above) and Coptic monasteries; it seems probable that *Caesar saw them in Alexandria (in the Serapeum library?) and hence planned to introduce them in Rome's first public library, a plan which the historian Asinius Pollio carried out after Caesar's death in the Atrium Libertatis, thus creating the model for *Augustus' library on the Palatine.

The most important innovation in the shape of the book was Roman in origin. The codex was created when the wooden panels of writing-tablets fastened together with thongs were replaced by parchment (*membrana*). At first used as notebooks (Hor. *Sat.* 2. 3. 2; Quint. *Inst.* 10. 3. 31), parchment codices had come into use for classical literature by the 1st cent. AD (Mart. 14. 184–92 advertises them as cheap pocket editions), while the normal form of the book was, in the Latin west as in the Greek east, the papyrus roll. What eventually established the codex was its adoption by the Christians; the vast majority of biblical and NT texts from the early 2nd cent. onwards are in codex form. Pagan classical authors appear in parchment and papyrus codices from the 2nd cent. AD and more frequently in the 3rd; by the 4th cent., three out of four literary texts were in codex form.

Codices were assembled from quires consisting of wide sheets folded vertically in the middle and then stitched together along the fold. Quires of four or five sheets (*quaterniones, quiniones* = 8 or 10 leaves) are common, thinner or thicker quires are exceptional and may be early experiments. Sheets of papyrus were often placed so that on facing pages the direction of the fibres was the same (recto pages with horizontal and vertical fibres alternating), but the alternative arrangement (i.e. vertical facing horizontal fibres, and vice versa) is not uncommon. Vellum sheets were usually arranged with hair sides facing and flesh sides facing. While papyrus sheets in Greek book-rolls, and in codices of the 2nd and 3rd cents., rarely exceed 35 cm. (13¾ in.) in height and 23 cm. (9 in.) in width, wider sheets (30–35 cm.: 12–13¾ in.) were often used in Greek and Coptic codices of the 4th, 5th, and 6th cents., when large parchment codices were also common. Small formats (even miniature codices like the Cologne parchment codex of the life of Mani with pages of 38 × 45 mm. (1½ × 1¾ in.)) are also found in this period.

The text was written before the sheets were stitched together, usually in one column per page, prose texts sometimes in two narrow columns like those in rolls (more frequently in parchment than in papyrus codices). Pagination is frequent; sometimes quires are also numbered on their first pages. Codices were bound between wooden panels covered in leather. Papyrus codices remained common in Egypt until the late 6th cent.; elsewhere, parchment codices begin to prevail from the later 3rd cent. onwards. For codices, the advantages of parchment over papyrus are obvious: less fragile folds, greater durability, greater capacity, and they are easier to use. *Constantine I ordered 50 parchment copies of the Scriptures for the churches in Constantinople, and Jerome records that the papyrus manuscripts in the library of Caesarea in Palestine, having become worn by use, were replaced by parchment codices.

Little is known about the book trade in the Greek world, probably because the private copy always remained the commonest form of book production. In the 4th cent. there seem to have been itinerant booksellers who 'carried around' bundles of *Isocrates' speeches (Dion. Hal. *Isoc.* 18). More information is available on the book trade in Rome from the 1st cent. BC onwards, and some publishers like *Cicero's friend *Atticus, or the Sosii, Horace's publishers, or *Martial's and the orator Quintilian's publisher, Tryphon, are well attested; *Pliny the Younger (*Ep.* 11. 11. 2) was surprised to learn that booksellers in Lyons (Lugdunum) were selling his books. The evidence for book prices is scanty and contradictory; on the whole, it seems that in Rome books were not expensive: Martial quotes 5 denarii as the price of a luxury edition of his poems (1. 117), while a cheap one would cost 6 to 10 sesterces (1. 66). Palimpsests, i.e. texts written on reused papyrus or parchment after the original writing had been rubbed or washed off, were cheaper still (Catull. 22).   H. Ma.

and the lyric poets. There is nothing esoteric about early botanical lore; locals understood their plants—from various wheats and vegetables to the widespread poisons (hemlocks, mandrake, the opium poppy, etc.)—and they spoke of parts (roots, seeds, flowers, stems, leaves) *as* plants providing particulars: food, medicines, poisons, oils, beverages (wine, beer).

Botany figures in Mycenaean Greek texts, suggesting a sophisticated perfume and perfumed oil industry at Pylos, Cnossus, and elsewhere (see MYCENAEAN CIVILIZATION). Few species are imported exotics, and Homer's flowers are likewise local, e.g. the saffron crocus (*Il.* 14. 348: *Crocus sativus* L.), galingale (*Il.* 21. 351; *Od.* 4. 603: *Cyperus longus* L.), lotus (*Il.* 14. 348: *Lotus corniculatus* L.), the bluebell (*Il.* 14. 348: *Cyclamen graecus* Link), the asphodel (*Od.* 11. 359, 24. 13: *Asphodelus ramosus* L.), the laurel or bay (*Od.* 9. 183: *Laurus nobilis* L.), and others. Homer mentions the opium poppy and its sleep-inducing latex (*Il.* 8. 306–7; *Od.* 4. 220–30: *Papaver somniferum* L.), but the poet credits it to Egypt, an anomaly since *P. somniferum* is native to Asia Minor.

Influence also came from herbalists of Assyrian origin; *Aristotle's *dēmiourgos* (*Pol.* 1282ᵃ3) mirrors a hoary tradition of skilled rootcutters (the *rhizotomoi*) who gained their craft and plied their trade in the countryside. Interwoven with medical botany is religion and myth, and typical is Homer's 'gift' of the unknown *moly* to Odysseus (*Od.* 10. 305) to ward away *Circe's evil drug (*Od.* 10. 394), a gift from *Hermes, long celebrated as the deity who gave herbs to man: 'O Hermes, benefactor, discoverer of drugs' (*PGM* 8. 27 f.). Moderns need not untangle this medley of beliefs about botany: the ancient mind did not wall *magic away from pure philosophy, any more than there were strict divisions between botany and herbal lore. Deep traditions speak through the poetry of *Sappho and Theognis (mid-6th cent. BC), using flowers and herbs in metaphor with telling effect; Sappho speaks of cassia (Supp. 20C2: *Cinnamomum cassia* Blume), roses blooming, the tender chervil, and flowery melilot (all no. 96. 11. 13–14 (Loeb 1, p. 120)), along with edible chickpeas (no. 143 (Loeb, 1, p. 156)). Locals knew what plants were like nettles, and Theognis

(537) knows the nasty effects of squill (*Urginea maritima* (L.) Baker), long storied in tales of what a community *pharmakos* endured. Not coincidental is *pharmakos* = 'scapegoat' and the neuter *pharmakon* usually = 'drug' or 'magical spell'.

Debate began early about the nature of plants in relationship to other forms of life. Aristotle, *De an.* 410^{b}22, in noting faulty Orphic notions on how plants breathe, indicates how old was this discussion; speculation on *Medea's *pharmakon* (lulling to sleep the golden fleece's guardian reptile) also was quite early: the singer Musaeus, semi-legendary and pre-Homeric, stated that Medea used a drug with *arkeuthos*, the prickly juniper, *Juniperus oxycedrus* L. (schol. on Ap. Rhod. 4. 156), faithfully reproduced by *Apollonius Rhodius in his *Argonautica* many centuries later. Musaeus wrote poems on healing plants: Theophrastus (*Hist. pl.* 9. 19. 2) cites Musaeus and *Hesiod on the properties of *tripolion*, the sea starwort (*Aster tripolium* L.), encapsulating folk tradition with accuracy in citation and current use: 'It is useful for every good treatment, and they dig it up at night, pitching a tent there.' *Pindar (*Pyth.* 3. 51–3) says that traditional medical treatments of *Asclepius were incantations, surgery, soothing potions, and amuletic drugs, reflecting *medicine's dual therapies, herbal drugs and surgery. Athenian playwrights record well-known herbs and plants with some frequency; e.g. *Sophocles' lost *Rhizotomoi* ('Rootcutters' = Macrob. *Sat.* 5. 19. 9–10) noted the professional status of rootcutters and herbal experts, even as Medea uses *thapsia*, the deadly carrot (*Thapsia garganica* L.), to induce frenzy; *Aristophanes' *Peace* (712) and *Lysistrata* (89) show the commonplace use of pennyroyal (*Mentha pulegium* L.) as a female contraceptive; these examples could be severally multiplied.

Striking is the *mélange* of herbal lore and specific plants indicated for women's ailments (see GYNAECOLOGY) in the Hippocratic *Diseases of Women* and similar tracts (see MEDICINE §4.2); there are over 300 identifiable species, collected expertise of midwives (also recorded by the gifted Soranus of Ephesus in his *Gynaecology* (*c.* AD 117)). Analogy was crucial: the Hippocratic *Nature of the Child* and the shorter *Seed* liberally employ agricultural terms; the author (probably mid- or late 4th cent. BC) is well acquainted with growth patterns in plants, from seed through germination into seedling, a 'youth', followed by maturity and senescence. Aristotle incorporated plants into his scheme of living things, endowing them with three faculties of the *soul: nutrition, growth, reproduction, but not motion or perception. Pseudo-Aristotle, *Plants*, summarizes ideas on botany at the Lyceum, but it is Theophrastus (*c.*370–288/5 BC) who provides the best Greek account of botany in *Inquiry into Plants* (*Hist. pl.*) and *Causes of Plants* (*Caus. pl.*); as Aristotle's foremost student, Theophrastus certainly echoed his mentor's paradigms of nature.

An acute observer of plants, Theophrastus distinguished long before modern botany between dicotyledons and monocotyledons, based on precise morphology; he is not ignorant of plant sexes (viz. *Hist. pl.* 2. 8. 1 on fertilization in figs; 2. 8. 4 on fertilization in date palms; cf. Hdt. 1. 193 on similar understanding about Assyrian figs and palmtrees), but chooses to tabulate by forms, flower to fruit, defining flowers as epigynous, perigynous, and hypogynous, showing that he understood the essential relation of flowering to fruiting; anticipating Dioscorides, Theophrastus notes geography to account for differences in shapes and properties of plants when used as medicines—and very good are his descriptions of plants and their parts (root, stem, leaves, flowers, seeds or fruits, and so on), their cultivation as crops or as pot-herbs—and he often quotes from the ubiquitous *rhizotomoi*, the special uses of plants, from medicines to quasi-magical potions and aphrodisiacs; book 9 of *Hist. pl.* is a priceless document in its own right, the first herbal manual in Greek to survive.

Hellenistic botany extended its scope, resulting in part from the far-flung expeditions of *Alexander the Great into India; many spices trickled into Greek cooking and pharmacy owing to voyages to *India, fairly common by 200 BC. Much Hellenistic botany and pharmacology is lost excepting citations, especially by Dioscorides of Anazarbus (fl. *c.* AD 65), *Pliny the Elder's marvellous pot-pourri, the *Natural History* of AD 77, the doctor Galen of Pergamum (AD 129–after 210), and a few others. The *Preface* of Dioscorides' *Materia medica* demonstrates use of earlier Greek texts, and through Dioscorides, Pliny, Galen, etc. we know of Iollas of Bithynia (? 250–200 BC), Heraclides of Tarentum (fl. *c.*100 BC), Crateuas (fl. *c.*100 BC), Asclepiades of Bithynia (d. 92 BC.), Andreas (d. 217 BC), as well as Dioscorides' near-contemporaries Sextius Niger, Julius Bassus, Niceratus, Petronius, Diodotus, and several more. Pliny's botany is good when he remains in Italy, but his polymathic curiosity led him to copy all non-Italian sources as being of equal merit; Pliny's plants compared with corollary passages in Dioscorides (both independently used Sextius Niger's lost works) display reasonable accuracy, and species and genera are often keyed with some assurance. Crateuas produced an illustrated herbal, but it is not ancestral to most later illuminated herbals (e.g. the Vienna Dioscorides of AD 512). Together, Pliny and Dioscorides provide details of about 600 species; Pliny gives much on various wheats and vines, vegetables, apples, olives (following in the steps of *Cato the Elder, and *Varro), and several cultivars, while Dioscorides provides precise accounts—though not much morphology—of medically useful plants, arranged according to a drug affinity system (what the drug did when given to a patient for a particular ailment). Botanical drugs likewise figure heavily in the works of Galen of Pergamum, who quotes voluminously from earlier authorities, attempting (unsuccessfully) to organize his materials.

Among writers in Latin, Celsus' *De medicina* (*c.* AD 37) has a good account of medical plants, derived partially from Hellenistic sources, and Scribonius Largus' *Compositiones* (AD 43 or later) details 242 botanicals (from *abrotanum* (*Artemisia abrontanum* L., a wormwood) to *zea*

(*Triticum spelta* L., spelt)), 36 minerals, 27 animal products (beeswax, honey, eggs, beaver testicle, etc.); Scribonius carefully considers certain poisonous drugs (e.g. aconite, hyoscyamus, hemlock (*Conium maculatum* L.), various mushrooms, the opium poppy), crucial at the Roman imperial court (Scribonius was physician to *Claudius, who succumbed to mushroom poisoning in AD 54). *Compositiones* in turn became a source for several later Latin texts in medical botany, including the *De medicamentis* by Marcellus Empiricus (*c.* AD 400), a trove of Gallicisms creeping into Latin.

Characteristic of botanical and pharmacological texts is continuous adaptation of written documents to local conditions; numerous 'substitution lists' in Greek and Latin were circulating by AD 200, clearly seen in the Galenic tract by that title. By AD 400, the major lines of Graeco-Roman medical botany—as well as pure botany, best discerned in the works of Theophrastus—are well defined; certain flowering-plant families are well represented in folklore, agriculture, and botany: prominent among the dicotyledons are Labiatae, Umbelliferae, Boraginaceae, Ranunculaceae, Convulvulaceae, Compositae, Salicineae, Rosaceae, Cruciferae, Leguminosae, Solanaceae, and Coniferae; and frequently included among the monocotyledons are Liliaceae, Gramineae, and Orchideae; there is detailed expertise on trees and woods, as well as fungi, lichens, and algae. See AGRICULTURAL WRITERS; CONTRACEPTION; OLIVE; TIMBER; WINE.   J. Sca.

boulē, council of 500 at Athens. See DEMOCRACY, ATHENIAN, §§2 and 3.

Brauron (see ◖Map 1, Cc◗), site of a sanctuary of *Artemis on the east coast of Attica (the rural territory of *Athens) at the mouth of the river Eridanos. It is included in the Athenian local historian Philochorus' (4th cent. BC) list of twelve townships united by *Theseus (*FGrH* 328 F 94). Archaeological evidence indicates human presence in the area of the sanctuary and the acropolis above it from neolithic times onwards, and there is an important late Helladic cemetery nearby. In the sanctuary itself there is a continuous tradition from protogeometric on, with a temple built in the 6th cent. (Phot. *Lexicon*, entry under *Braurōnia*) and an architecturally innovative *pi*-shaped stoa with dining-rooms built in the later part of the 5th cent. Flooding in the early 3rd cent. BC led to the abandonment of the site. Some traditions associate the Pisistratids (see PISISTRATUS) with Brauron (Photius, as above), or with the local residential centre called Philaidai which lay a short distance inland from the sanctuary (Pl. [*Hipparch*.] 228b).

Cult activity at Brauron was particularly associated with the *arkteia*, a ritual, known also at the sanctuary of Artemis Munichia in the Piraeus, the port of Athens, in which young girls between the ages of 5 and 10 'became' bears. The aetiological myth for the *arkteia* related that this service was required of all Athenian girls before marriage because of an incident in which a bear belonging to the

sanctuary had been killed after becoming savage with a young girl (schol. Ar. *Lys.* 645). Modern scholars suggest that the ritual was a rite of passage (see RITUAL; INITIATION) which marked the physical maturation of pubescent girls and prepared them for taming by marriage by stressing their wildness. Some pottery vessels of a shape particularly used for dedications to Artemis (*krateriskoi*) excavated at Brauron show naked girls running and part of a bear, and scholars have suggested that these illustrate the ritual. The sanctuary included a cave sacred to Iphigenia, daughter of *Agamemon, and dedications were also made in celebration of successful *childbirth. The Brauronia was a quadrennial festival organized by *hieropoioi* appointed by the city by lot, and involved a procession from Athens out to Brauron. We also hear of a sacred hunt.   R. G. O.

breast-feeding was a proof of maternal devotion and, according to some philosophers, a good woman's duty (there is a detailed discussion in Gell. *NA* 12. 1). It was acknowledged to be tiring, but it increased the mother's affection for the child, and the baby was thought to be morally, as well as physically, influenced by the milk it drank and the milk's provider: breast-milk was explained as a further transformation of the blood which had gone to form the embryo. Mothers who were unwilling to breast-feed might be blamed for laziness, indifference, or vanity about their breasts. But wet-nursing was a standard practice. The Greek and Latin words for 'nurse' (*titthē, trophos*; *nutrix*) have the primary meaning of someone who feeds the child; the bond between nurse and nursling was acknowledged to be strong and is often commemorated in inscriptions. There has been extensive recent discussion on the psychological effects of shared child-rearing.

Soranus (*Gynaecology* 2. 11. 18, *c.* AD 117) prefers that the mother should breast-feed, but advises the use of a wet-nurse if the mother is ill or may become exhausted. He recommends giving boiled honey (the equivalent of glucose) with or without goat's milk (which is closest in composition to human milk) for the first two days of a newborn's life, then, if possible, using a wet-nurse until the mother's body has stabilized after *childbirth and her milk is less heavy. (The manuscripts have the figure twenty for the number of days this takes; some editors correct to three.) Soranus notes that some doctors think breast-feeding should start at once. He devotes several chapters (2. 12. 19–15. 29) to the choice of a wet-nurse, explaining how to test her milk and to ensure that she leads a healthy life: in particular, she should not drink *wine, which affects the milk as well as making her incapable. He envisages a wet-nurse who lives in the household, and recommends employing several so that the child is not dependent on one. At 2. 17. 36–40 Soranus gives detailed instructions on how and when to feed the child: he does not approve of feeding on demand, but does not specify the number of feeds per day; 2. 21. 46–8, on weaning, suggests that the child will not be ready for solid food before the sixth month, or for complete weaning until the third or fourth half-year when the teeth can deal with food; the majority of wet-nursing contracts from Egypt (see below) also envisage breast-feeding for two years. In the section on childbirth, 2. 5. 7–8 offers treatments for engorged breasts and for suppressing lactation in women who do not intend to breast-feed. Plutarch (*Mor.* 609e) praises his wife for undergoing surgery to her nipple so that she could continue nursing. Some folk remedies for breast problems are included in *Pliny the Elder's *Natural History* (28. 77. 250; 30. 45. 131).

Because breast-milk was explained as a transformation of surplus blood, which would otherwise be shed in menstruation or used in the growth of an embryo, nursing women were advised (Soranus, 2. 12. 19) to abstain from sexual activity: even if they did not become pregnant, intercourse might stimulate menstruation, and would in any case cause disturbance to the milk and the nursling. The contraceptive effect of lactation was thus reinforced. One motive for not breast-feeding may have been the mother's wish for more children.

Contracts with wet-nurses, which survive from Egypt, set out the rules of life which the wet-nurse must follow to safeguard her milk supply. Wages were low in comparison with those of a trained weaver, but the total cost of hiring a wet-nurse, for instance to rear a foundling child, was a large investment. Contracts include provision for the return of wages, and further penalty clauses, if the child dies or the nurse becomes unable to feed. The wet-nurse in these contracts may be free-born and living outside the household (if so, she must make regular visits for the child to be inspected), or may be a slave hired from another owner. Within households, slave mothers may have been obliged to hand over children to a wet-nurse so that they could return to work.

Several Greek deities have a title Kourotrophos, meaning 'concerned with child-rearing', but no Greek or Roman goddess is specifically concerned with lactation and there are few examples in art of the 'nursing goddess'.

E. G. C.

bribery, Greek Much of the Greek vocabulary for bribery is noticeably neutral ('persuade by gifts / money', 'receiving gifts'), although pejorative terms like 'gift-swallowing' are found as early as *Hesiod (*Op.* 37 ff.). In Attic tragedy, we hear of accusations of bribery against e.g. seers like Tiresias (Soph. *OT* 380 ff.); Thucydides' *Pericles (2. 60. 5, cf. 65. 8) finds it necessary to say that he has *not* taken bribes; clearly the normal expectation was that politicians did. Accusations of bribery are frequent in the 4th-cent. orators, partly because it was necessary to prove bribery in order to make a treason accusation (*eisangelia*) stick: Hyp. 4. 29 f. Hyp. 5. 24 f. implies an Athenian distinction between bribes taken for and against the interests of the state; the latter type have been called 'catapolitical' (D. Harvey, *CRUX* (1985), 76 ff.). See also CORRUPTION. S. H.

bribery, Roman, Latin *ambitus*, a 'going round', is related to *ambitio*, the pursuit of public office, but always,

unlike *ambitio*, denotes reprehensible activity which has been declared illegal.

Specifically it refers to obtaining electoral support (see ELECTIONS AND VOTING (*Roman*)) through gifts, favours, or the promise of these. According to *Polybius, the Romans had made the manifest use of money to buy votes a capital offence, but we have no other evidence for this in the last two centuries of the republic (the early books of Livy refer to laws in 432, 358, and 314 BC, the last two of which at least may have some historical substance). In 181 BC a *lex Cornelia Baebia* instituted a system of non-capital trials, which was developed in the late republic by further laws about *ambitus* and related matters—the use of bribery agents, associations, and expenditure on public dinners. These laws seem to have been a response to greater competition for office. However, Roman tradition did not discourage the cultivation of voters through material benefits (see especially the *Commentariolum Petitionis* and Cicero, *Pro Murena*). What established politicians disliked was, first, the stealing of votes by 'new men' (a *novus homo* was, roughly, the first man of his family to reach the senate or consulship) who outbid former patrons and, second, the damage this caused to traditional claims of *patronage. In the late republic the distortion of politics by massive expenditure became scandalous in spite of the new legislation. Under the Principate, in so far as genuine competition for office persisted, *ambitus* remained an issue both in Rome and, perhaps more importantly, in the municipalities throughout the empire. The fact that penalties do not seem to have been very severe (Suet. *Aug.* 40. 1) suggests toleration of traditional behaviour. See also CORRUPTION.

A. W. L.

brigandage (Gk. *lēsteia*, Lat. *latrocinium*), the unlawful use of personal violence to maraud by land, was not condemned wholesale by the Classical Greeks. A carry-over from pre-state times, it remained a respectable occupation among some communities (Thuc. 1. 5). In the 3rd cent. BC central Greece was dominated by the Aetolians, whose confederacy (see FEDERAL STATES) protected, indeed quasi-institutionalized, their traditional way of life as bandits and pirates. As with Aetolia, brigandage was particularly prevalent in geographically more marginal zones, especially uplands, over which even the ancient empires exercised only nominal control (in the heart of the Persian empire note the Uxii, Arr. *Anab.* 3. 17. 1; Isauria, in SE Asia Minor, is the classic Roman case), and where pastoral mobility (see NOMADS) facilitated illegal behaviour. With the Roman state's claim to the monopoly of force, *latrocinium* acquired a wider semantic range than modern 'brigandage' (it included e.g. 'feuding' and 'raiding'). The urban populations saw brigandage as such as an all-pervasive threat beyond the city gates (this was true even in Italy at the height of empire). In its attempts to control bandits (never permanently successful, not least because they often had the support of élite landowners), the Roman state relied on the army, including the occasional all-out campaign (as by

*Augustus in the Alps: Strabo 4. 6. 6), more usually on the uncoordinated efforts of local *police and vigilantes (western cities had their *viatores*, 'road patrols', eastern ones their *diogmitai* commanded by irenarchs, lit. 'peace-keepers'), backed up by the most brutal forms of exemplary punishment of culprits. Whether antiquity knew the phenomenon of the 'social bandit' (E. Hobsbawm, *Bandits*, 2nd edn. (1985)) is debated, although the admiring tales attached to a few 'super-brigands' (Iulius Maternus; Bulla Felix) suggest the ideological appeal of such a type. See PIRACY.   A. J. S. S.

Britain, Roman (*see facing page*)

Brutus (Marcus Iunius Brutus), son of another Marcus Iunius Brutus and of Servilia, born (probably) 85 BC, was adopted by his uncle (?) Quintus Servilius Caepio by 59 and was henceforth called Q. Caepio Brutus. Brought up by *Cato the Younger, he was educated in oratory and philosophy and long retained a fierce hatred for his father's murderer *Pompey. In 58 he accompanied Cato to *Cyprus and in 56 lent a large sum to Cypriot Salamis at 48 per cent interest p.a., contrary to the *lex Gabinia*, procuring a senate decree to validate the loan. As moneyer (perhaps 55) he issued coins showing *Libertas* (*freedom) and portraits of his ancestors Lucius Iunius Brutus (who overthrew *Tarquinius Superbus) and Gaius Servilius Ahala, the tyrannicide (*RRC* 433). As quaestor in 53 he went to Cilicia with Appius Claudius Pulcher, whose daughter he had married, and there lent King Ariobarzanes I of Cappadocia a large sum, probably to enable him to pay interest on his huge debt to Pompey. When *Cicero succeeded Appius, he found that an agent of Brutus had been made prefect of cavalry to extort money from Salamis and that five Salaminian senators had been killed. He cancelled the appointment, but to avoid offence to Brutus gave a similar post to Brutus' agent in Cappadocia and recognized the validity of the loan to Salamis (Cic. *Att.* 5. 21–6. 1). In 52 Brutus defended Titus Annius Milo and in a pamphlet attacked Pompey's wish for a dictatorship, but in 50 they both defended Appius against Publius Cornelius Dolabella, and in 49 he joined the republican cause and was formally reconciled with Pompey. After the battle of Pharsalus (48 BC) he successfully begged Caesar for pardon and, no doubt through Servilia's influence, became one of his protégés. He was made a pontifex (see PRIESTS) and in 47 sent to govern Cisalpine Gaul, while Caesar went to Africa to fight Cato and the republicans. During this time he developed relations with Cicero, who dedicated various philosophical and rhetorical works to him and, at his request, wrote a eulogy of Cato after Cato's death. (Finding it unsatisfactory, Brutus wrote one himself.) Although he now divorced Claudia and married Cato's daughter Porcia, widow of Marcus Calpurnius Bibulus, he remained on good terms with Caesar, met him on his return from Munda, assured Cicero of Caesar's laudable optimate intentions, and was made *praetor urbanus* (urban praetor)

for 44 and designated consul for 41. But when Caesar became *dictator perpetuus* ('perpetual *dictator': February 44), Brutus, reminded of his heritage, joined, and *ex officio* took the lead in, the widespread conspiracy that led to Caesar's assassination before his departure for his Parthian War. Outmanœuvred by Mark *Antony, whose life he had spared on the Ides of March, he and Cassius (Gaius Cassius Longinus) had to leave Rome and, failing to win popular approval, left Italy for Greece (August 44). With Antony now openly against them, Brutus collected close to 400 million sesterces from the treasuries of Asia and Syria and confiscated the supplies Caesar had prepared for his campaign. He and Cassius gradually seized all the eastern provinces, building up large armies, partly of veterans. When Cicero, in his *Philippics*, swung the senate behind them, they received *imperium maius* in the east. Brutus captured, and later executed, Antony's brother Gaius Antonius; after P. Cornelius Dolabella's death he acquired Asia and completed its conquest, and during 43 and 42 squeezed it dry for his armies. The money was turned into a large coinage (*RRC* 500–8) and Brutus, alone among the republicans, put his own head on one of the gold coins. He also won the title of *imperator* in Thrace. In 42 he and Cassius, with about 80,000 legionaries plus auxiliaries, twice met Antony and Octavian (the future *Augustus) at the battle of Philippi (42 BC). In the first battle Cassius, defeated by Antony, committed suicide, while Brutus impressively defeated Octavian. In a second battle, forced on Brutus, he was defeated, deserted by his soldiers, and also committed suicide. His body was honourably treated by Antony.

Arrogant, rapacious, calculatingly ambitious, Brutus yet professed a deep attachment to philosophy. Cicero admired but never liked him, and ignored his warnings not to trust Octavian. A renowned orator, with an austere and dignified style, he despised Cicero's as 'effeminate and spineless' (Tac. *Dial.* 18. 5). His literary works (philosophy, historical epitomes, poetry) are lost, as are his letters, except for a few surviving among Cicero's. With Cassius, he was officially condemned under the empire, but revered by many as the last defender of Roman freedom.   E. B.

Byzantium (see ◀Map 1, Ea▶), a famous city on the European side of the south end of the Bosporus, between the Golden Horn and the Propontis (mod. sea of Marmara). The Greek city occupied only the eastern tip of the promontory, in the area now covered by the Byzantine and Ottoman palaces of Constantinople / Istanbul. The evidence of cults and institutions confirms the claim of the city of Megara (between Athens and Corinth) to be the main founder, but groups from the Peloponnese and central Greece probably also participated in the original colony, which is to be dated 668 (Hdt. 4. 144) or 659 BC (Euseb. *Chron.*). Little material earlier than the late 7th cent. BC has yet emerged from excavations. Except during the Ionian Revolt (see GREECE, HISTORY) the city was under Persian control from *Darius I's Scythian expedition until

[*continued on p. 131*]

Roman Britain

Roman Britain (see ◀Map 5, Ba▶), the province of Britannia. The oldest name of the island known to us is Albion; the earliest form of the present name, *Prettania*, was used by the Greeks. The Latin *Britannia* was in use by the 1st cent. BC. It has no direct Celtic origin and is probably a Latin abstraction from an earlier form.

The iron-age communities of Britain showed a variety of social organization, although all were agrarian peoples organized into tribal territories dominated by a range of enclosed settlement sites. Many were agriculturally sophisticated and had developed an impressive Celtic art style. The peoples of the south-east had a long history of shared culture with northern Gaul. The islands were known to the Mediterranean world from at least the 3rd cent. BC. After 120 BC, as trading contacts between Transalpine Gaul and areas to the north intensified, Britain began to receive goods such as wine amphorae, and Gallo-Belgic coinage was introduced. Close political contacts with northern Gaul provided the pretext for *Caesar's expeditions in 55 and 54 BC and the context for the migration of the Belgae from Gaul to Britain which he mentions (*BGall*. 5. 12). His campaigns did not result in conquest, although he imposed tribute on King Cassivellaunus (supreme commander of the south-east Britons) before withdrawing. Contacts with the continent intensified with the *Romanization of Gaul from *Augustus onwards, and Rome maintained an interest in British affairs. Several burials of this period include luxury Roman goods probably sent as diplomatic gifts. Enhanced external contact stimulated internal political change culminating in the expansion of the Catuvellauni (the most powerful southern British tribe) who, under their king Cunobelinus, obtained territorial dominance in the south-east.

Annexation had apparently been contemplated by Augustus and *Gaius but was only achieved by *Claudius in AD 43. The army of four legions, with *auxilia*, quickly overran the territory of the Catuvellauni, with a set-piece battle at Camulodunum (Colchester). The army then moved west and north so that by the time of the revolt of Boudicca, queen of the Iceni in East Anglia (AD 60/1), the lowlands south of the Trent and much of Wales were held. Romanization was under way and towns were well established at *Londinium, Verulamium (St Albans), and Colchester. The revolt was crushed

Britain, Roman This collection of church silver from Water Newton (probably *c.* AD 300) may well be the earliest of its kind. The inscriptions on some pieces reveal the patronage of wealthy women donors. The extent of *Christianity's acceptance in 4th-cent. Britain, however, is disputed.

but territorial expansion slowed for perhaps a decade. A succession of able Flavian governors enlarged the province by completing the conquest of Wales and pushing into Scotland. The last of these, Gnaeus Iulius Agricola (c. AD 77/8–83/4), advanced far into Scotland and defeated the Caledonians in a great battle at mons Graupius. Its location is unknown but camps associated with his campaigns have been identified as far north as the Moray Firth. After his withdrawal the rest of Scotland remained unconquered and there began a gradual retreat, eventually to the Tyne–Solway line (by the period of Trajan). The Stanegate road which marked this line became a *de facto* frontier until the construction of the *wall of Hadrian from c. AD 122. Although Scotland was again occupied first in the period c.139–64, when the wall of Antoninus (between the Forth and the Clyde) was the frontier, and then during *Septimius Severus' campaigns of 208–11, it was never successfully incorporated, and Hadrian's Wall remained the effective permanent frontier of the province.

Britain was an imperial province which contained a very substantial military garrison throughout the Principate. In the 2nd cent. AD the army comprised three legions—II Augusta at Isca (Caerleon), XX Valeria Victrix at Deva (Chester), and VI Victrix at Eburacum (York)—and perhaps 75 auxiliary units. These were predominantly based in the north and Wales and brought considerable wealth to these regions, which nevertheless remained less Romanized than areas to the south and east.

Local government was based on the Gallic cantonal system, with the following sixteen *civitates* (civic communities) known: the Brigantes (capital at Aldborough), Parisi (Brough-on-Humber), Silures (Caerwent), Iceni (Caistor-by-Norwich), Cantiaci (Canterbury), Carvetii, Durotriges (Dorchester, Dorset, and also later Ilchester), Dumnonii (Exeter), Corieltauvi (not Coritani) (Leicester), Catuvellauni (Verulamium/St Albans), Atrebates (Silchester), Belgae (Winchester), and Cornovii (Wroxeter). In addition there were four *coloniae* (Roman colonies) at Colchester (founded AD 49), Lindum (Lincoln, 90–6), Glevum (Gloucester, 96–8), and York (early 3rd cent.), together with Londinium which, although the provincial capital, is of uncertain status. The *civitates* were large and as many as seventy lesser urban centres served the countryside away from the principal towns. Although relatively large, none of the towns was well provided with public buildings. Most of those known are of later 1st- and 2nd-cent. date. During the 2nd and 3rd cents. most towns (including the lesser centres) were provided with defences, although there is debate over why these were built. In the 4th cent. the principal towns continued to be occupied but they became characteristically residential rather than productive centres. Although important as defended locations, none of them survived with urban characteristics for long into the 5th cent.

The single province of the Principate, governed from London, was divided in the early third century into Upper (with its capital at London) and Lower (capital York). A further subdivision into four provinces (Maxima Caesariensis, capital London; Flavia Caesariensis, capital Lincoln; Britannia Prima, capital Cirencester; and Secunda, capital York) took place under Diocletian. Valentia, known in northern Britain in the 4th cent., was probably the result of a further division of Secunda, although its location remains obscure.

The countryside was already extensively farmed before the conquest and agriculture remained the mainstay of the province with perhaps 90 per cent of the late Roman population of about 3.6 million living rurally. Most of these people continued to inhabit traditional farmsteads with only about one in a hundred sites becoming a *villa. Villa-building began soon after the conquest and continued steadily through the 2nd and 3rd cents. with a peak in both numbers and opulence during the 4th cent. The villas were generally modest by Mediterranean standards and most developed piecemeal through the aggrandizement of existing houses. *Mosaics were common by the 4th cent. and there is abundant evidence for the existence of a wealthy, rurally based aristocracy in southern Britain.

Other economic activities known from archaeology show growth to a peak of prosperity during the 4th cent. Metal extraction (for gold, silver, and lead) began very soon after the conquest but did not become dominant. Local craft-based production was widespread, its success attested by the very abundant collections of objects found on most settlements. In the early empire there was great dependence on other provinces for the supply of consumer goods, imported initially through the military supply networks. Later local production grew to sustain the bulk of the province's needs and very substantial manufactures for items like pottery developed, especially in rural locations in the south and east (see POTTERY, ROMAN). None of these, however, became major exporters to other provinces.

Art and culture in Britain developed as a hybrid of Celtic and classical features. The religions of the Mediterranean spread to Britain with the army and administrators, but the Celtic gods were worshipped across most of the province. However, they took on new forms, with the increased use of Romano-Celtic styles of temple architecture (first found at the end of the iron age) and the adoption of Latin epigraphy on altars and dedications. Particular gods are associated with certain regions and *civitates*. Many soldiers also adopted Celtic gods whom they identified with gods of the Roman pantheon. Christianity is found throughout the province in the 4th cent., although the extent of its acceptance is disputed. In art new materials (especially stone sculpture and mosaic) supplanted the metalwork used in the iron age La Tène styles. Not all the results are aesthetically pleasing today but some mosaics show an innovatory blend of ideas. Latin was widely adopted, although a study of the graffiti illustrates that writing was most used on military and urban sites (see VINDOLANDA TABLETS).

During the later empire Britain enjoyed relative peace compared with other provinces. A series of usurpers emerged from the province, Albinus (193–6), Carausius (286–93), Allectus (293–7), Magnus Maximus (383–8), and Constantine III (407). Problems with raiders from across the North Sea may have led to the piecemeal construction of the Saxon Shore forts from the middle of the 3rd cent. onwards. These and other coastal installations in the north and in Wales hint at increasing military threats, although the continued use of the traditional style of garrisons on Hadrian's Wall, combined with the general absence of the late Roman field army, implies that there were few serious military problems. In 367 there were concerted barbarian attacks from the north, which necessitated a military campaign, although the account by *Ammianus Marcellinus probably exaggerated these events. There is little else to suggest any serious military threats until early in the 5th cent. By then the depleted British garrison could not cope and the more pressing threats to Rome herself prevented aid from being sent. Britain, left to defend herself, gradually fell to the Saxons.

M. J. M.

478. In the Athenian empire (see DELIAN LEAGUE) it paid fifteen talents' tribute or more, deriving its wealth from tuna fishing and from tolls levied on passing ships. The city also had an extensive territory not only in European Thrace (roughly mod. Bulgaria) but also in Bithynia and Mysia in NW Asia Minor. It revolted from Athens in 440–439 and 411–408. Although under Spartan control after the battle of Aegospotami (405) alliance coins show that it joined the anti-Spartan sea league formed after the battle of Cnidus in 394. It became a formal ally of Athens from c.378 to 357 and also when resisting *Philip II of Macedon in the siege of 340–339. The goddess Hecate is supposed to have helped the besieged on this occasion and her symbols, the crescent and star (later adopted as the emblem of the Turkish state), appear on the city coinage. It suffered from the attacks and exactions of the Galatians in the 270s but picked the winning side in Rome's Macedonian wars in the 2nd cent. BC. Byzantium's strategic position enabled it to enjoy privileged status under the Roman empire, which did not, however, protect the city from the depredations of passing armies and rapacious officials. All privileges were lost when it supported Pescennius Niger against *Septimius Severus, and fell after a two-year siege (AD 193–5; *Cassius Dio, 75. 12. 1, gives a brilliant although exaggerated account). Severus reduced Byzantium to village-status and caused much destruction, but rebuilding soon followed and traces of the subsequent Severan restoration have been archaeologically identified. *Constantine I refounded Byzantium as New Rome, Constantinople, on 11 May 330, extending its bounds to new city walls and adorning it with magnificent new buildings.

A. J. G.; S. M.

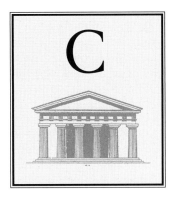

Caesar, Julius (*see page 134*)

cakes (flour-based sweetmeats or fancy breads) were given many names in Greek and Latin, of which the most general were *pemmata*, *popana* in Greek, *liba* (sacrificial cakes) and *placentae* (from the Greek *plakountes*) in Latin. The Greeks especially had a vast number of different kinds, and several monographs were written on the subject (on these see Ath. 3. 109b–116a, 14. 643e–648c; Poll. 6. 72 ff.). Most were regarded as a luxurious delicacy, to be eaten with fruit after the main course at a special meal. Cakes were also very commonly used in *sacrifice, either as a peripheral accompaniment to the animal victim or as a bloodless sacrifice. Sacrificial cakes very often had a special form characteristic of the relevant divinity or rite; among the more spectacular examples are the Attic *amphiphōn*, stuck with lights and offered to *Artemis on the full-moon day, or the Sicilian *mullos*, shaped like female genitals and offered to the Two Goddesses, *Demeter and *Persephone. Many votive cakes, modelled in terracotta, have been found at Demeter's sanctuary in Corinth.   E. Ke.

Caligula, Roman emperor. See GAIUS.

Callimachus, of *Cyrene, Greek poet and scholar, 'Battiades' (*Epigr.* 35), i.e. son (or descendant?) of Battus; his grandfather was a general (*Epigr.* 21). He flourished under *Ptolemy II (285–246 BC and continued into the reign of Ptolemy III (246–221 BC: *Suda*); he mentions the Celtic invasion of 279 (*Hymn* 4. 171 ff.; fr. 379); the marriage (*c*.275) and apotheosis (270? 268?) of Arsinoë II Philadelphus, sister-wife of Ptolemy II (frs. 392, 228); and the Laodicean War of 246/5 (fr. 110). Other work for Berenice II, wife of Ptolemy III (*Epigr.* 51?, frs. 387–8, *Suppl. Hell.* 254 ff.), and perhaps the *Victory of Sosibius* (fr. 384), belong to the same late period. Callimachus stood close to the *Alexandrian court; it may be accident that we have no works datable between Arsinoë's death and the accession of Berenice (herself a princess of Cyrene).

Callimachus was credited with more than 800 books

(*Suda*). Michael Choniates, *c*. AD 1200, may still have possessed copies of *Aetia* and *Hecale*. But, apart from the six hymns and some sixty epigrams, and a selection from the prose *Paradoxa* (fr. 407), only fragments now survive. The Milan *Diegeseis*, a papyrus of *c*. AD 100, contains summaries of the poems, in the order *Aetia*, *Iambi*, *Lyrica*, *Hecale*, *Hymns*.

Works 1. *Aetia*, in four books (some 4,000 lines in all?): a miscellany of elegiac pieces, from extended epigrams (fr. 64, on the tomb of *Simonides; fr. 114, on the Delian statue of *Apollo) to narratives of 100–200 lines (frs. 67–75, Acontius and Cydippe; *Suppl. Hell.* 254–69, *Victory of Berenice*). The common subject is 'origins': the origins in myth or history of Greek cults, festivals, cities, and the like. Episodes are chosen and rehearsed with antiquarian relish. In the 'prologue' (fr. 1) the poet answers the critics who complain that he does not compose a 'continuous poem' on the deeds of kings or heroes: poetry should be judged by art, not quantity; Apollo recommended the slender Muse, the untrodden paths; better be the cicada than the braying mule. Like *Hesiod, he had met the *Muses, in a dream, and they related the *Aetia* to him (fr. 2). Books 1 and 2 were structured, at least in part, by a dialogue between the poet-researcher and the Muses; books 3 and 4 are framed by the substantial court-poems *Victory of Berenice* and *Lock of Berenice*. Within books, poems may be grouped thematically. The 'epilogue' (fr. 112) recalls Hesiod's meeting with the Muses; and leads over to the 'pedestrian field of the Muses', i.e. (probably) to the *Iambi*. It is generally (but controversially) argued that the *Aetia* went through two editions: the poet in old age added 'prologue' and 'epilogue', and perhaps books 3–4 entire.

2. *Iambi*: thirteen poems, written in scazons or other iambic metres. In the first, the Archaic poet Hipponax speaks, returned from the dead; in the last, the poet names Hipponax as the exemplar of the genre. Personal invective (1–5), and the fable (2, 4), play their part, as in the traditional *iambus* (jesting and ribaldries in certain festivals). But these poems range much wider: 6 (the statue of *Zeus at

cakes Ceramic cakes in *likna* (winnowing baskets), left as offerings in the sanctuary of *Demeter and Kore at Corinth. They imitate the real-life cakes accompanying Greek *sacrifice. (The right-hand object was stolen from the Corinth Museum in 1990 and is as yet unrecovered.)

*Olympia) reads as an epodic epigram, 8 as an iambic epinician; 7–11 record various *aitia*; 12 celebrates a birth. The framing poems continue literary polemic: in 1 against quarrelling scholars, in 13 against those who think that an author should confine himself to a single genre.

3. Miscellaneous poems include the lyric *Apotheosis of Arsinoë* (fr. 228), and the elegiac epinician for Sosibius (fr. 384).

4. *Hecale*, a hexameter narrative of something over 1,000 lines. *Theseus leaves Athens secretly to face the bull of Marathon; a storm breaks; he takes shelter in the cottage of the aged Hecale; he leaves at dawn and subdues the bull; he returns to Hecale, finds her dead, and founds the deme (country district) of Hecale and the sanctuary of Zeus Hekaleios in her memory. This heroic (but not Homeric) material was deviously elaborated, with Hecale rather than Theseus at the centre. The scene of rustic hospitality became famous; talking birds diversify the narrative; the action ends in another *aition*, perhaps drawn from the *Atthis* (local histories of Athens).

5. The *Hymns* reanimate the traditional (Homeric) form, but with no view to performance. The hymns to Zeus, *Artemis, and *Delos (nos. 1, 3, 4) elaborate the god's birth and virtues with quizzical learning and virtuoso invention. Those to Apollo (no. 2), *Athena (no. 5), and *Demeter (no. 6) are framed as dramas, in which the narrator-celebrant draws the hearer into an imagined ritual; 6 (Doric hexameters) and still more 5 (Doric elegiacs) deliberately cross generic boundaries (see genre).

6. The *Epigrams* (a selection preserved in Meleager's anthology) cover the full range of literary, erotic, dedica-

tory, and sepulchral themes; scattered fragments (frs. 393–402) hint at more.

7. Callimachus wrote prose works on nymphs; on athletic contests (see GAMES); on the foundation of islands and cities; on winds, on rivers, on 'marvels', and on birds; on 'barbarian customs' and on local names of fish and of months. He was among the founders of lexicography and paradoxography (descriptions of marvels). The *Pinakes* ('Tables of Those who have Distinguished themselves in Every Form of Culture and of What they Wrote') presented, in 120 books, a bibliography of Greek literature and a catalogue of the Library of *Alexandria, organized by subject ('rhetoric', 'laws', 'miscellaneous prose'); they included some biographical notes, and cited the first line of each work, and the number of lines. Callimachus also 'arranged' the poems of *Pindar and *Bacchylides (fr. 450, *Suppl. Hell.* 293).

Callimachus often states his preferences in poetry and among poets. He defends shorter (and discontinuous) poems (fr. 1), the small drop from the pure spring (*Hymn* 2. 107 ff.), diversity of genre (*polueidia*) (fr. 203); 'a big book equals a big evil' (fr. 465), 'slim' poetry (fr. 1. 24) is better than 'thick' (fr. 398). This 'new' aesthetic (which might seem less novel if we had the poetry of the 4th cent.) quotes the example of past poets. Callimachus invokes Hesiod (frs. 2, 112; *Epigr.* 27), and condemns the Epic Cycle or collection of early Greek epics (*Epigr.* 28); Homer is all-present, but formal emulation and verbal pastiche are rigorously avoided. From Pindar he borrows the critical images of the 'fine flower' (*Hymn* 2. 112, *Isthm.* 7. 18) and the 'carriage road' (fr. 1. 25–8, *Pae.* 7b. 11). Mimnermus (late

[*continued on p. 137*]

Julius Caesar

Julius Caesar (Gaius Iulius Caesar), born 100 BC (Suet. *Iul.* 88. 1), of a *patrician family without social equals, as descendants of *Venus and *Aeneas, but with little recent political success. His father's sister Iulia married Gaius *Marius, and her cousins Lucius Iulius Caesar and Gaius Iulius Caesar Strabo Vopiscus profited by his unforeseen success, but Caesar's father never became consul. Lucius Cornelius Cinna, while in power, gave Caesar his daughter Cornelia in marriage and made him *flamen Dialis* as successor to Lucius Cornelius Merula—a post of supreme honour but normally precluding a consulship (no doubt thought unattainable). *Sulla, after his victory, annulled his enemies' measures, including this appointment, but as a fellow patrician spared Caesar's life, even though he refused to divorce Cornelia and voluntarily resign his priesthood.

Most of the next decade Caesar spent in Asia, studying and winning military distinction, including a victory over an advance force of *Mithradates VI and a *corona civica* (the Roman Victoria Cross); but two prosecutions of ex-Sullani (Gnaeus Cornelius Dolabella and Gaius Antonius), although unsuccessful, established his fame as an orator. In 73 he was co-opted a pontifex (see PRIESTS), largely through family connections, and returned to Rome. Elected military tribune, he supported amnesty for the associates of Marcus Aemilius Lepidus. As quaestor 69, before going to his province of Further Spain, he lost both his aunt Iulia and his wife. He conducted their funerals in the grand aristocratic manner, stressing his aunt's (and thus partly his own) descent from kings and gods (Suet. *Iul.* 6. 1) and, for the first time since Sulla, displaying Marius' *imago* (wax funerary mask) and distinctions in public. (He no doubt similarly displayed Cinna's at Cornelia's funeral.) On his return from Spain he found the Latin colonies beyond the Po (Padus) vigorously demanding Roman citizenship and supported their agitation, but did nothing to further their cause in Rome. He supported the laws of Aulus Gabinius and Gaius Manilius, conferring extraordinary commands on *Pompey (clearly a most useful patron), and he married Pompeia, a granddaughter of Sulla. With Pompey overseas, he courted another powerful ex-Sullan, *Crassus, Pompey's enemy, joining him in various political schemes in return for financial support, which enabled Caesar to spend large sums as curator of the Appian Way and as aedile (65). In 64, in charge of the murder court, he resumed his vendetta against Sulla by offering to receive prosecutions of men who had killed citizens in Sulla's proscription.

In 63 Quintus Caecilius Metellus Pius' death left the chief pontificate vacant, a post normally held by eminent ex-consuls. Although two (Publius Servilius Isauricus, to whom Caesar was bound in loyalty as to his old commander in Cilicia, and Quintus Lutatius Catulus) sought the office, Caesar announced his candidacy and through lavish bribery won the election. This and his election to a praetorship for 62 established him as a man of power and importance. He supported *Catiline, who advocated a welcome cancellation of debts, but covered his tracks when Catiline turned to conspiracy. The consul *Cicero, who to the end of his days was convinced of Caesar's involvement, had to proclaim his innocence. In his prosecution of Gaius Rabirius he left the legality of the so-called *senatus consultum ultimum* ('ultimate' i.e. emergency decree of the senate) in doubt, and when Cicero wanted the death penalty under that decree for the conspirators betrayed by the Allobrogan envoys (the Allobroges were a Gallic tribe), Caesar persuaded most senators to vote against it, until a speech by *Cato the Younger changed their minds.

As praetor he joined the tribune Quintus Caecilius Metellus Nepos in agitating for the recall of Pompey against Catiline's forces. Suspended from office, he demonstratively submitted, and the senate, eager to avoid alienating him, reinstated and thanked him. In December, when Pompeia was *ex officio* in charge of the rites of the Bona Dea, from which men were strictly excluded, Publius *Clodius Pulcher gained access disguised as a woman—it was said, in order to approach Pompeia in her husband's absence—and was ejected. Caesar, while asserting the innocence of Clodius (a man congenial to him and worth cultivating) and of Pompeia, divorced her, proclaiming that his household must be free even from suspicion. With his consulship approaching, he could now seek a more advantageous marriage.

But first he had to go to his province of Further Spain. His creditors applied for an injunction to stop him from leaving, and he was saved from this unprecedented indignity by Crassus' standing surety for part of his debts: his provincial spoils would cover the rest. He now 'had to make a bigger profit in one year than Verres had in three' (W. Will, *Julius Caesar: Eine Bilanz* (1992)) and, largely neglecting his routine duties, he concentrated on attacking independent tribes. The booty enabled him to clear his debts and pay large sums into the treasury, all without incurring a risk of prosecution. About mid-60 he returned to Rome, was voted a *triumph by a co-operative senate, and prepared to claim his consulship. There was a technical obstacle: to announce his candidacy for the consulship he had to enter Rome long before the triumph could be arranged, but that would forfeit his *imperium* and right to triumph. The senate was ready to give him a dispensation, but his enemy Cato, although only an ex-tribune, arranged to be asked to speak and talked the proposal out. Caesar decided to put power before glory and entered the city.

He now could not afford to lose, so he needed allies and a massive infusion of money. A brilliant stroke secured both. In his absence Pompey and Crassus had failed—partly because each had opposed the other—to obtain what they respectively wanted from the senate: ratification of Pompey's eastern settlement and land for his veterans, and a remission of part of the price offered for the tithe of Asia by the *publicani*. Caesar, on good terms with both, persuaded them to support his candidacy: he promised to give each what he wanted without harm to the other, provided they refrained from mutual opposition. Pompey now persuaded his wealthy friend Lucius Lucceius to join Caesar in his canvass: in return for paying the expenses for bribery (no doubt with Crassus' help), he could expect to succeed through Caesar's popularity. But Caesar's enemies, led by the upright Cato, collected a huge bribery fund for Cato's son-in-law Marcus Calpurnius Bibulus, who secured second place after Caesar.

As consul Caesar appealed to the senate for co-operation in formulating the laws to satisfy his allies. Frustrated by his enemies, he passed them in the assembly by open violence, aided by friendly tribunes. Bibulus withdrew to his house, announcing that he was stopping all future meetings of the assemblies by watching the sky for omens. This unprecedented step, of doubtful legality, was ignored by Caesar, who satisfied Pompey and Crassus and went on to pass further legislation, *i.a.* on *repetundae* (extortion) and on the publication of senate debates. Pompey and Crassus, satisfied (especially) with his assuming the onus for his methods, now joined him in an open alliance (sometimes erroneously called the 'First Triumvirate'). Pompey married Iulia and Caesar married Calpurnia, whose father, Lucius Calpurnius Piso Caesoninus, was made consul 58, with Pompey's aide Gabinius as colleague. For further insurance, Clodius was allowed to become a plebeian and tribune 58. Caesar's reward was a law of Vatinius, giving him Illyricum and Cisalpine Gaul for five years. The senate obligingly added Transalpine Gaul. Early in 58 attempts to prosecute Caesar were averted, and moderates in the senate attempted conciliation by offering to have his legislation re-enacted in proper form. But Caesar refused, since this would admit guilt and impair his *dignitas* (personal honour). The breach between him and the senate majority thus became irreparable.

A movement by the Helvetii (a Celtic people who in about 100 BC had migrated to an area in modern Switzerland) gave him an unforeseen chance of starting a major war, which after nearly a decade and many vicissitudes led to the conquest of the whole of Gaul. It was in Gaul that he acquired the taste and the resources for monarchy and trained the legions that could 'storm the heavens' (*BHisp.* 42. 7). Young Roman aristocrats flocked to him to make their fortunes, vast sums (sometimes made palatable as loans) flowed into the pockets of upper-class Romans and, as gifts, to cities and princes, to support Caesar's ambitions. The depleted treasury received none of the profits and was forced to pay for his legions. In his triumphs of 46 (see below) he displayed 63,000 talents of silver and spent about 20,000 of his own money (together enough to create the fortunes of 5,000 *equites*), much of it booty from

Gaul. Plutarch, on the basis of Caesar's figures, reports that a million Gauls were killed and another million enslaved. Requisitions of food and punitive devastations completed human, economic, and ecological disaster probably unequalled until the conquest of the Americas.

In Rome Caesar's position remained secure until 56, when his bitter enemy Lucius Domitius Ahenobarbus, confident of becoming consul 55, promised to recall and prosecute him, and Cicero, back from exile, hoped to detach Pompey from him. Crassus informed him of what was going on, and they summoned Pompey to Luca, where he was persuaded to renew the compact. Pompey and Crassus became consuls 55, receiving Spain and Syria respectively for five years, while Caesar's command was renewed for five years in Gaul; Pompey was to stay near Rome to look after their interests, governing Spain through legates. But the alliance soon disintegrated. Iulia died (54) and Crassus, attacking Parthia, was killed at Carrhae (53). In 52 Pompey married a daughter of Caesar's enemy Quintus Caecilius Metellus Pius Scipio and made him his colleague as consul. Caesar now secured legal authorization to stand for a consulship in absence in 49; but the legality of this became doubtful, and his claim that it included the right to retain *imperium* (hence immunity from prosecution) was denied by his enemies. (The legal position is obscured by partisan distortion.) Pompey was gradually (perhaps reluctantly) forced to co-operate with them, to avoid a consulship by Caesar in 48, which would have left him irreversibly at Caesar's mercy. In 49 Caesar invaded Italy and started a civil war, nominally to defend the rights of tribunes who had been forced to flee to him for protection, but in fact, as he later admitted (Suet. *Iul.* 30. 4), to escape conviction and exile.

He rapidly overran Italy, where there were no reliable veteran legions to oppose him. As he moved down the peninsula, he kept making specious peace offers, retailed with considerable distortion in book 1 of his *Civil War*. Ahenobarbus was forced to surrender at Corfinium, and Pompey, knowing that Italy was untenable, to the chagrin of his aristocratic supporters crossed to Greece, hoping to strangle Italy by encirclement. Caesar broke it by defeating Pompey's *legati* in a brilliant campaign in Spain and then taking Massalia (Marseille). In 48 he crossed to Greece, though Pompey controlled the seas, and besieged him at Dyrrhachium. A tactical defeat there turned into *de facto* strategic victory when Pompey withdrew to Thessaly, where both sides received reinforcements. Persuaded, against his better judgement, to offer battle at Pharsalus, Pompey was decisively defeated, escaped to Egypt, and was killed. Caesar, arriving there in pursuit, intervened in a domestic conflict over the kingship and was cut off for months in Alexandria, until extricated by troops from Asia Minor and a Jewish force under Antipater. He spent three more months in Egypt, chiefly with *Cleopatra, whom he established on the throne and who after his departure bore a son whom she named Ptolemy Caesar. Then, moving rapidly through Syria and Asia Minor, he reorganized the eastern provinces, easily defeated Pharnaces II at Zela, and in September 47 returned to Italy. There he had to settle an army mutiny and serious social unrest, fanned during his absence by Marcus Caelius Rufus and Titus Annius Milo and after their death by Publius Cornelius Dolabella.

Meanwhile the republican forces had had time to entrench themselves in Africa, where Metellus Scipio assumed command, aided by Juba I. Caesar landed in December. After an inauspicious beginning he gained the support of Bocchus II and Publius Sittius and, deliberately inviting blockade at Thapsus, won a decisive victory that led to the death of most of the republican leaders (including Scipio and Cato). On his return he was voted unprecedented honours and celebrated four splendid triumphs (20 September—1 October 46), nominally over foreign enemies, to mark the end of the wars and the beginning of reconstruction. But Gnaeus Pompeius Magnus (Pompey's son), soon joined by his brother Sextus Pompeius and Titus Labienus, consul for the second time, raised thirteen legions in Spain and secured much native support. In November Caesar hurriedly left Rome to meet the threat. The Pompeians were forced to offer battle at Munda (near Urso) and were annihilated with the loss of 30,000 men in Caesar's hardest-fought battle. After reorganizing Spain, with massive *colonization, he returned to Rome and celebrated a triumph over 'Spain'.

Caesar had been *dictator (briefly), nominally for holding elections, in 49, consul for the second time

48, and dictator for the second time after Pharsalus; he was consul for the third time and *curator morum* ('supervisor of public morals') in 46 and dictator for the third time (designated for ten years ahead, we are told: Cass. Dio 43. 14. 3) after Thapsus; he held his fourth, sole, consulship for nine months and his fourth dictatorship in 45, and was consul for the fifth time and (from about February) *dictator perpetuo* (see *RRC* 480/6 ff.) in 44. The specification of his dictatorships after the first is lost in the *fasti* (official calendars and records of magistracies), but at least the third and fourth were probably, like Sulla's, *rei publicae constituendae* ('for settling the republic'). Apart from epigraphic evidence (see Broughton, *MRR* 3. 108), this is suggested by Cicero's references and by the fact that the work of reform began after Thapsus. The specification (if any) of the perpetual dictatorship is beyond conjecture. In addition to introducing the Julian calendar, his most lasting achievement, he considerably increased the numbers of senators, priests, and magistrates, for the first time since *c.*500 created new patrician families, founded numerous colonies, especially for veterans and the city *plebs*, and passed various administrative reforms. His great-nephew Octavian (the future *Augustus), adopted by Caesar in his testament in 45, was made a pontifex (see PRIESTS) aged about 16 and, although he had no military experience, was designated *magister equitum* ('master of the horse') in 44, aged 18. Caesar, although he adopted the dress and ornaments of the old Roman kings, refused the invidious title of *rex* (king), but, thinking gods superior to kings (Suet. *Iul.* 6. 1), aimed at deification (see RULER-CULT), which after gradual approaches he finally achieved shortly before his death (Cic. *Phil.* 2. 110: Mark *Antony was designated his *flamen*; see PRIESTS). It was the culmination of increasingly unprecedented honours voted by the senate (Cass. Dio lists them at various points), perhaps in part to see how far he would go, and he accepted most of them.

He had no plans for basic social, economic, or constitutional reforms, except to graft his divine and hereditary rule onto the republic. The abyss this opened between him and his fellow *nobiles* made him uncomfortable, and he planned to escape from Rome to wage a major Parthian war. As all remembered the disruption caused by his temporary absences during the Civil Wars, the prospect of being ruled by an absent divine monarch for years ahead proved intolerable even to his friends. He was assassinated in the Curia (senate-house), in a widespread conspiracy hastily stitched together to anticipate his departure, on 15 March 44.

Caesar was a distinguished orator in the 'Attic' manner, believing in 'analogy' (on which he wrote a treatise, *De analogia*) and in the use of ordinary words (Gell. *NA* 1. 10. 4). His speeches, at least some of which were published, and his pamphlet attacking Cato's memory, are lost. Seven books on the Gallic War (an eighth was added by Aulus Hirtius) and three on the Civil War survive, written to provide raw material for history and ensure that his point of view would prevail with posterity. Distortion at various points in the *Civil War* is demonstrated by evidence surviving in Cicero's correspondence. For praise of Caesar's style, see Cic. *Brut.* 262 (strongly tinged by flattery).   E. B.

6th cent. BC) and Philitas (late 4th cent. BC) exemplify the short poem, Ion of Chios (5th cent. BC) *polueidia*. Antimachus (fl. 400 BC), *Plato, and Praxiphanes (end of 4th–mid-3rd cent. BC) are variously dispraised (frs. 398, 589, 460). Of contemporaries, Callimachus commends Aratus (*Epigr.* 27, fr. 460); the story of his quarrel with *Apollonius Rhodius (and of the *Ibis*, frs. 381–2) is now generally discounted.

Callimachus says little about Egypt (though some have tried to find Pharaonic ideology in *Hymn* 4). From Alexandria he looks to Greece, and the Greek past; he has a scholar's systematic knowledge of the Greek literary inheritance, an exile's feeling for the old country and its links (through *aitia*) with the contemporary world. His work often reaches out to the archaic world, crossing the centuries of drama and prose—to Hesiod, Hipponax, Pindar. But this past is transmuted. Verbal borrowing is rare; genres are shifted or mixed, myth transformed by mannerism, words and motifs juxtaposed in post-modern incongruities. *Victoria Berenices* may serve as an example. This epinician is also an *aition* (the foundation of the Nemean Games (see ATHLETICS). It borrows words from Pindar, and story from Bacchylides, in the wrong dialect (Ionic) and the wrong metre (elegiac). The narrative dwells not on *Heracles but on the rustic hospitality of the peasant Molorcus; Molorcus' war with the mice parallels

Heracles' fight with the lion. Callimachus' poems are (by epic standards) short; various in style, metre, and genre; experimental in form, recondite in diction, polished in versification, devious, elaborate, allusive, and sometimes obscure (the earliest surviving papyrus, within a generation of Callimachus' death, includes an explanatory paraphrase). To Roman poets he became the exemplar of sophistication, *princeps elegiae* ('master of elegy': Quint. *Inst.* 10. 1. 58): *Catullus translated him (66), *Propertius invokes him (3. 1. 1). The *Aetia* in particular stands behind *Ovid's *Fasti* and Propertius 4; *Georgic* 3 begins with an allusion to it. But classicizing snobbery took him to represent technique without genius (Ov. *Am.* 1. 15. 14).

Callimachus commands an extraordinary variety of tone: tongue-in-cheek epic (*Hecale* fr. 74 Hollis), versified statistics (*Iambus* 6), classic pathos (*Epigr.* 19), Catullan elegance (fr. 401). The scholarship is integral to the poetry, which even quotes its own sources (frs. 75. 54, 92. 3, *Schol. Flor. Callim.* 35?). But irony and invention dominate.

P. J. P.

camps When *Polybius (6. 27–32) described the construction of a military camp (*castra*) c.143 BC, he was referring to a well-established practice. *Livy, writing of 294 BC, assumes the existence of a fixed layout, without explaining it (10. 32. 9). The invention of castrametation by the Romans was probably connected with orientation, town planning, and land division, which themselves were associated with augural practices. Land division, with its careful delineation of areas and use of boundary lines intersecting at right angles, was well suited to military planning. Roman camp-building techniques emphasize the professionalism of their military establishment.

Archaeological and aerial surveys have revealed about 400 marching-camps in *Britain, generally square or oblong in shape, protected by a ditch and rampart of turves surmounted by a palisade, and with at least four gates, often guarded by a ditch or curving extension of the rampart (*clavicula*). Some were construction, or practice camps (to teach soldiers building techniques); others were large enough to accommodate an army (e.g. a group in SE Scotland of 67 ha. (165 acres), perhaps associated with the campaigns of *Septimius Severus in AD 208). At *Masada in Judaea several siege camps with their internal stone walls have survived.

However, archaeological evidence rarely illuminates the internal layout of temporary camps. According to Polybius, when a consular army of two legions and an equal number of allies encamped, the general's tent (*praetorium*) was located in a central position, with an open space (*forum*) on one side, and the quaestor's tent (*quaestorium*) on the other. In front of these were the tribunes' tents. The main street (*via principalis*—about 30 m. (33 yds.) wide), ran parallel to the *praetorium*, being intersected at right angles by other streets along which were encamped the legions and allies. The most important of these streets was the *via praetoria* (about 15 m. (16¼ yds.) wide), which

formed a T-junction opposite the *praetorium*. The legionary cavalry was positioned in troops on either side of the *via praetoria*; then the legionary infantry (grouped respectively as *triarii*, *principes*, and *hastati*) in maniples, with the *triarii* back to back to the cavalry. In front of the *triarii* ran other roads parallel to the *via praetoria*, beyond which were positioned the *principes* back to back to the *hastati*. Beyond the *hastati* the allied cavalry and infantry were similarly encamped. The *via quintana*, running parallel to the *via principalis*, divided the first to fifth maniples from the sixth to tenth. Behind the *praetorium* were the élite allied infantry and cavalry, and local auxiliary troops. The camp was square, surrounded by a ditch, rampart, and palisade, with a space (*intervallum*) of about 60 m. (66 yds.) from the tents. Each of the two main roads of the camp led to fortified gates. Polybius perhaps refers to half of a four-legion camp, when both consular armies were camping together. In the complete layout they would be positioned back to back, in a camp of oblong shape, with the legions and allies at either end. However, when a two-legion army encamped alone, the layout was perhaps changed to accommodate the *praetorium* between the two legions, as apparently confirmed by a camp excavated in Spain, associated with Roman attempts to capture Numantia in the 150s BC.

The *De munitionibus castrorum* ('On Camp Fortifications'), an anonymous treatise (probably 2nd cent. AD), is a theoretical work, presumably for the guidance of military surveyors, and differs significantly from Polybius' version. The tripartite rectangular layout contained a combined *praetorium* and *principia* (headquarters), in front of which ran the *via principalis*, intersected at right angles by the *via praetoria*; here in the *praetentura* (one-third of the layout), auxiliaries were encamped in centuries, and also behind the *praetorium* along the *via quintana* in the *retentura* (the remaining two-thirds), where the *quaestorium* was now situated; praetorians were encamped next to the *praetorium*, and legionaries next to the *intervallum* along the *via sagularis*, encircling the entire camp.   J. B. C.

capitalism is a term freighted with heavy ideological baggage. For economists and historians working within a Marxist tradition (see MARXISM AND CLASSICAL ANTIQUITY) it has a specific reference to an advanced socio-economic formation in which value, profit, and rationality are determined according to the productive modalities and mentalities of large-scale competitive businesses and price-fixing markets. On this view, the economies of Greece and Rome would be classed as pre- or non-capitalist. For non-Marxists of various stripes, capitalism in the sense of the productive deployment, especially investment, of fixed or variable capital assets may occur within a wider range of political, social, and economic contexts, including the societies of Greece and Rome.

The disagreement is not only ideological. To define Greece and Rome as pre-capitalist may imply also, for instance, the view that 'the economy' as a separately instituted sphere did not exist in classical antiquity and that the ancients therefore did not, because they could not, practise economic analysis properly so called (see ECONOMY, GREEK); or that ancient economic institutions with apparent modern equivalents in fact functioned quite differently from their modern counterparts or namesakes—ancient *banks, for example, being seen as merely glorified money-changers and usurers rather than lenders of risk or venture capital for productive economic investment. Those who, in contrast, regard the economy of the ancient world or local sectors thereof as in some useful sense capitalist detect differences of scale and sophistication rather than of fundamental nature.

Such ideological and pragmatic disagreements have a century-long pedigree within Ancient History, going back to the creative controversy between Karl Bücher and Eduard Meyer over the proper periodization of world history in economic perspective. They received a further injection of fuel in the second quarter of the 20th cent. from the anthropologically influenced theorist Karl Polanyi, whose outlook owed more to Max Weber than to Karl Marx. But his 'substantivist' views engendered an equal and opposite reaction from those who, without necessarily accepting the pejorative labels of 'formalists' or 'modernizers' that Polanyi and his followers had foisted upon them, nevertheless argued that the ancients were motivated by a recognizably capitalist rationality and to that end instituted processes of wealth-creation susceptible of analysis in the formal terms of neoclassical micro-economic theory, including such mathematical tools as Leontief-style input–output tables.

The dispute shows no sign of proximate resolution, and indeed cannot formally be resolved in the absence of the requisite quantities of the right types of evidence, above all data amenable to statistical or quasi-statistical analysis. But whereas for exponents of the 'capitalist' hypothesis that absence is merely an accident of non-survival, for the Marxist or Weberian 'primitivists' it is itself further evidence in support of their classificatory hypothesis.

P. A. C.

Caracalla, nickname (from his Celtic dress) of Marcus Aurelius Antoninus (AD 188–217), emperor AD 198–217. Elder son of *Septimius Severus, originally called Septimius Bassianus; renamed after Marcus *Aurelius and made Caesar in 195. Augustus in 198, he was consul for the first time with his father in 202 and for the second time with his brother Publius Septimius Geta in 205, when he had his hated father-in-law Gaius Fulvius Plautianus killed. Consul for the third time in 208, again with Geta, whom he also hated, he accompanied his father to *Britain, sharing command against the Caledonians. When Severus died, he and Geta abandoned Scotland, making the *wall of Hadrian the frontier again, and returned to Rome. After having Geta killed (26 December 211), a drastic purge followed. To conciliate the soldiers, he raised their pay, creating financial problems. One solution was the 'Antonine

constitution' (see CITIZENSHIP, ROMAN); he simultaneously doubled the inheritance tax paid only by citizens, which funded the *aerarium militare* (military treasury). In 215 a new coin was struck, the so-called *antoninianus*, evidently tariffed at two denarii, but weighing only 1.5: this was to lead to inflation.

In 213 he fought the Germanic Alamanni (the first time they are mentioned), evidently gave the Raetian *limes* a stone wall, and became Germanicus Maximus. In 214 he attacked the Danubian Carpi and reorganized Pannonia, each province now having two legions (Britain was split into two provinces at this time; Hither Spain was also subdivided). Obsessed by *Alexander the Great, he raised a Macedonian phalanx and went east in his footsteps, through Asia and Syria to *Alexandria, where large numbers who had mocked him were killed. When his offer to marry a Parthian princess was rejected, he attacked Media. While preparing a further campaign he was murdered near Carrhae (8 April 217). His successor Macrinus deified him as Divus Antoninus Magnus.

A. R. Bi.

careers

Greek In virtually all the Greek-speaking areas, pressures to evolve clear career structures in public life were countered by social or political considerations, thereby preventing the emergence of recognizable *cursus honorum* (career paths) on the Roman republican model. Though, for example, *Thucydides (5. 66. 3–4) credited the Spartan army with a clear hierarchical command structure, promotions and careers within it were by appointment and co-optation rather than by election. Hence they were as much a matter of belonging to a notable lineage, or of influence with kings or ephors, as of merit. At Athens a simple hierarchy of military command in both infantry and cavalry is attested, while re-election to the post of general (*stratēgos*) was common and helped to provide a clear career path for professional soldiers, often interspersed with spells of mercenary command abroad. In contrast, careers in civilian office-holding in Classical Athens were effectively precluded by the short-term tenure and non-repeatability of office, by collegiality, and above all by selection by lot. A young politician had to use the assembly (see DEMOCRACY, ATHENIAN) rather than office-holding, and tended to begin by lawcourt advocacy or by serving a senior politician as his 'friend' or 'flatterer' (e.g. [Dem.] 59. 43) before establishing his own position and his own clique of followers. Public career structures in other Greek states are barely traceable for lack of detailed evidence.

The Hellenistic courts developed more of a career structure, alike for their ministers, envoys, and army commanders, ostensibly formalized by the growth of graded titles such as 'friend', 'first friend', 'companion', and 'relative' (of the king). (See FRIENDSHIP, RITUALIZED.) However, here too patronage could easily override merit, status was precarious, and recruitment as much a matter of family succession as of individual promise.

Outside public life, some professions such as doctors or

performing artists formed guilds with their own procedures and officers, but little in the way of formalized career structures is perceptible.

    J. K. D.

Roman Ancient society was not so organized as to provide a course of professional employment which affords opportunity for advancement. The Latin phrase normally translated as 'career' is the Ciceronian *cursus honorum*, which refers to the series of elective magistracies open to senators: those of quaestor, held at 30 from *Sulla's legislation onwards, but five years younger under the Principate; of aedile; of praetor, held at 39 under the late republic, but by some at 30 under the Principate; and of *consul, held at 42 after Sulla (cf. the career of *Cicero), by patricians at 33 under the Principate, and by 'new men' (*novi homines*, i.e. the first of a family to reach the consulship) at 38 or later. Successful election to these posts depended on birth and achievement (cf. Tac. *Ann.* 4. 4: high birth, military distinction, and outstanding gifts in civil life, i.e. forensic or political oratory, knowledge of the law: note the order). Success might be achieved not only in the magistracy that preceded but in preliminary offices civil and military (as one of the *vigintisexviri* (six boards of minor magistrates) or *tribuni militum* (six legionary tribunes)), and in positions held at Rome, in Italy, or the provinces, under the republic often involving command of troops, that normally followed the praetorship and consulship (propraetorships and proconsulships, allocated by seniority and by lot); or that were devised under the Principate to get previously neglected work done (e.g. curatorships of roads in Italy). After AD 14 elections were effectively conducted in the senate and a man's success depended on the verdict of his peers or on his ability to strike bargains with his rivals' supporters; but *Augustus' *lex Iulia de maritandis ordinibus* (see MARRIAGE LAW, ROMAN) provided speedier advancement for men married with children, while the opinion of the emperor, known or surmised, was of great and increasing weight (cf. *ILS* 244. 4; Pliny, *Pan.* 66), hence too the favour of his advisers. Some posts, notably legionary commands and governorships of regions that were part of his 'province' (e.g. *Syria, *Gaul (Transalpine) outside Narbonensis), were in his direct gift, though the senate ratified such appointments (both types of officer were 'legates (*legati*) of Augustus'). The influence exercised by the emperor has given rise to the view that there was a special type of career 'in the Emperor's service' regularly involving particularly speedy advancement (especially between praetorship and consulship) enjoyed by 'military men' (*viri militares*). A more cautious hypothesis is that men advanced themselves using what gifts they had; those who took to army life necessarily were the appointees of the emperor. Each appointment was ad hoc and might depend on a number of factors, e.g. current needs, a man's availability, experience, record, current effectiveness of his supporters, but precedent was also relevant.

    The word 'career' is often applied to the posts offered by the emperor to men of equestrian and lower status, whether in official positions (e.g. *praefectus praetorio* = prefect of the praetorian guard, or *procuratores Augusti* in his provinces, supervising tax collecting) or as his private agents (also *procuratores*) managing his private estates (see PROCURATOR). But although such posts mostly had their distinctive standing, and were normally preceded by up to three military posts, and although (because of this) recognizable patterns of advancement developed (cf. the two Trajanic 'careers' *ILS* 1350 and 1352), appointments were again ad hoc, *ad hominem* (cf. *AE* 1962, 183), intermittent, and accepted on a basis of mutual goodwill, with character rather than professionalism the overt criterion. Imperial freedmen and even slaves who held subordinate positions in the organizations enjoyed lower standing, but their continuous service over long periods of time justifies the application of the term 'career' to their activities (see FREEDMEN; SLAVERY).

    In the army below the rank of tribune it is legitimate to speak of a career, since the minimum period of service outside the praetorian guard was 20 years. Men frequently record their advance through minor posts of privilege (e.g. *tesserarius*, 'Officer Commanding the Watchword') to (e.g.) one of the 60 centurionates of a legion, or upwards through legionary centurionates (e.g. *ILS* 2653).

    Elsewhere the word is inappropriate; outside the limited state apparatus the ancient world lacked the great organizations that now provide methodical advancement in business and industry.

    B. M. L.

Carthage (*see facing page*)

Cassius Dio (*c.* AD 164–after 229), Greek senator and author of an 80-book history of Rome from the foundation of the city to AD 229. His full name was perhaps Lucius Cassius Dio, as on M. M. Roxan, *Roman Military Diplomas* 2 (1985), no. 133 ('Cl.' on *AE* 1971, 430, could attest the further name 'Claudius', but is probably a stone-cutter's error; 'Cocceianus' may have been added in Byzantine times through confusion with Dio of Prusa). Dio came from a prominent family of Nicaea in Bithynia (mod. Iznik). His father, Cassius Apronianus, entered the senate, attaining a consulship and several governorships. Dio's senatorial career was even more distinguished. He was praetor in 194 and suffect consul probably *c.*204. From 218 to 228 he was successively *curator* (state finance official) of *Pergamum and Smyrna, proconsul of *Africa, and legate first of Dalmatia and then of Upper Pannonia. In 229 he held the ordinary consulship with *Severus Alexander as colleague and then retired to Bithynia. Dio lived through turbulent times: he and his fellow senators quailed before tyrannical emperors and lamented the rise of men they regarded as upstarts, and in Pannonia he grappled with the problem of military indiscipline. These experiences are vividly evoked in his account of his own epoch and helped to shape his view of earlier periods.

    Dio tells us (72. 23) that, after a short work on the

[*continued on p. 144*]

Carthage

Carthage (*Qrtḥdšt* (= 'New Town'); Gk. *Karchēdōn*; Lat. *Carthago*) (see ◀Map 4, Ac▶), a *Phoenician colony and later a major Roman city on the coast of NE Tunisia.

History According to tradition (*Timaeus, *FGrH* 566 fr. 60) Carthage was founded from Phoenician Tyre in 814/13 BC, but no archaeological evidence has yet been found earlier than the second half of the 8th cent. BC. The site provided anchorage and supplies for ships trading in the western Mediterranean for gold, silver, and tin, and soon outstripped other Phoenician colonies because of its position, its fertile hinterland, and its better harbour.

Trade was more important to Carthage throughout its history than perhaps to any other ancient state. Initially most of it was conducted by barter with tribes in Africa and Spain, where metals were obtained in return for wine, cloth, and pottery; but early contact with the Greek world is shown by the presence of Athenian amphorae (transport jars) in the earliest levels at Carthage. Voyages of exploration were undertaken along the Atlantic coast of North Africa and Spain. Carthage controlled much of the trade in the western Mediterranean, settling its own trading-posts in addition to those founded by the Phoenicians, so that Carthaginian influence extended from Tripolitania to Morocco, as well as to western Sicily, Sardinia, and southern Spain. From the 4th cent. Carthage also exported agricultural produce and was integrated into the wider Hellenistic *economy of the Mediterranean world. Pottery from levels of the last Punic phase (first half of the 2nd cent. BC) shows significant quantities of imports from Greece, Italy, and the Iberian peninsula.

Carthage was ruled at first by a governor (*skn*), responsible to the king of Tyre; whether by the 7th cent. she had her own kings (*mlk*) is far from clear. At any rate by the 6th cent. the constitution had become oligarchic, headed by at first one, later two 'judges' (*špṭm*), called *suffetes* in Latin; they were elected annually on a basis of birth and wealth. Military commands were held by separately elected generals. There was a powerful 'senate' of several hundred life-members. The powers of the citizens were limited. A body of 104 judges scrutinized the actions of generals and other officials. Largely through this body the ruling class was successful in preventing the rise of *tyranny either through generals manipulating the mercenary armies or officials encouraging popular discontent. Military service was not obligatory on Carthaginians, whose population was too small to control a large citizen army; instead mercenaries were hired from various western Mediterranean peoples.

In the 5th cent., owing to setbacks in Sicily, Carthage occupied much of the hinterland of north and central Tunisia, and settled agriculture flourished. The native Numidian population in the areas to the west of Carthage adopted settled urbanism and other elements of Punic culture and religion from the late 3rd cent. onwards, and especially under enlightened rulers such as Masinissa (238–148), so that considerable parts of North Africa outside formal Carthaginian control were already to a greater or lesser extent Punicized before the arrival of Rome.

The chief external policy of Carthage was control of the sea routes to the west. From c.600 BC it was clear that rival claims must lead to war between *Etruscans, Carthaginians, and Greeks. The westward thrust of Phocaea (western Asia Minor) and her colony Massalia (mod. Marseille) was crushed off Alalia in Corsica by the Etruscan and Carthaginian fleets (c.535). This led to the consolidation of Carthaginian control of southern and western Sardinia and parts of southern Spain. Earlier the general Malchus (fl. 580–550 BC?) had won successes in *Sicily, where the western end of the island remained in Carthaginian hands down to the 3rd cent. BC. For three centuries Carthaginians and Greeks fought intermittently for Sicilian territory and the allegiance of Sicans, Sicels, and Elymians. In 480 BC a great Carthaginian army under Hamilcar was defeated at Himera by the tyrants Gelon and Theron. His grandson Hannibal avenged the defeat by destroying Himera (409) and a succession of Greek cities on

Carthage In the 2nd cent. BC Punic Carthage reached its greatest extent, including these houses on the Byrsa hill, built over an archaic cemetery. When Carthage was refounded by *Augustus as a Roman colony, the hill lay at the centre of the Roman street grid.

the south coast; but the ensuing wars with *Dionysius I of Syracuse ended with Carthaginian power confined to the far west of the island, and with the destruction of one of their three cities, Motya (to be replaced by the new Carthaginian stronghold of Lilybaeum, mod. Marsala). The tyrant Agathocles of Syracuse (d. 289/8) later carried the war into Africa, but was defeated near Tunis (307).

With Rome Carthage concluded treaties in 508 and 348, in which she jealously guarded her monopoly of maritime trade while refraining from interference in Italy. When *Pyrrhus attacked (280), her fleet helped Rome to victory. But sixteen years later Sicilian politics brought the two states into open conflict. Carthaginian intervention on the side of the Mamertines at Messina in 264 precipitated the first of the Punic Wars (see ROME (HISTORY) §4), which ended in the destruction of Carthage (146 BC). Rome decreed that neither house nor crop should rise again. But Carthaginian blood survived, and the awesome pantheon still persisted: worship of Baal-Hammon, Tanit, Eshmoun, and Melqart was too deep-rooted in many parts of North Africa to die with the destruction of Carthage, and it was to continue, under a thinly Romanizing veneer, until the rise of *Christianity.

Carthage never developed a distinctive art of her own, but was content to copy and adapt styles imported from Egypt and Greece. She manufactured and exported carpets, rugs, purple dyes, jewellery, pottery, lamps, tapestry, timber, and hides. Her agricultural skill, which made excellent use of the fertile Tunisian plains, profited her Roman conquerors: Mago's 32 books on scientific farming were translated into Latin; see AGRICULTURAL WRITERS.

The site of Carthage was too attractive to remain unoccupied for long. The attempt of Gaius *Gracchus to establish the colony of Junonia on suburban land failed, but the city was colonized by Augustus in fulfilment of Caesar's intentions, and became the capital of Africa Proconsularis (see AFRICA, ROMAN). By the 2nd cent. AD Carthage had become the second city only to Rome in the western Mediterranean. A few urban troops and a cohort of the Third Augustan legion sufficed to keep order. But through his control of the vital African corn-trade, the proconsul was a potential danger to the emperor, as shown by the rebellions of Clodius Macer (68) and Gordian I (238).

Carthage became an outstanding educational centre, especially famous for orators and lawyers. In the 3rd cent. the genius of the apologist Tertullian and the devotion of Cyprian (bishop of Carthage) made her a focus of Latin Christianity. Her bishop held himself the equal of the bishop of Rome, and Carthage played a great part in establishing western Christianity on lines very different from the speculation of the Greek churches. As a great Catholic stronghold she fought against the Donatist heresy. When the Vandals overran Africa, she became the capital of the Vandal king Gaiseric (428–77) and his successors, who embraced the Arian version of *Christianity. After the Roman general Belisarius' victory over the Vandals (533–4) Catholicism was restored on stricter lines. Carthage remained loyal to the eastern Roman empire and beat off the earlier Muslim invasions, until captured in 697.

Topography Carthage was founded on part of a large peninsula which stretched eastwards from lagoons into the gulf of Tunis; the isthmus linking it to the mainland further west is *c*.5 km. (3 mi.) wide at its narrowest point. Scanty remains of houses of the last quarter of the 8th cent. BC have been found, at one point up to 350 m. (380 yds.) from the shore, suggesting that the settlement then was already of considerable size; but the original nucleus, if there really was a colony here a century earlier to correspond with the traditional foundation date, has yet to be found. Little is known of the archaic urban layout, but surface evidence and cemeteries to the north and west suggest that it covered at least 55 ha. (136 acres). Pottery kilns and metal-working quarters have been identified on its fringes, and the *tophet*, where child sacrifice to Baal and Tanit took place, has been located on the south; this was in continuous use from the later 8th cent. down to 146 BC. Substitution of animal for child was practised from the start: one in three archaic sacrifices in the sector excavated in the 1970s were of animals, declining to one in ten in the 5th/3rd cent. BC.

In the late 5th cent. massive fortifications, 5.20 m. (17 ft.) wide, were erected with projecting towers and gates; Livy (*Epit.* 51) says they were 32 km. (20 mi.) long. Substantial houses, some with peristyles and simple *terrazzo* or tessellated floors, are known from the Hellenistic period, when the city reached its greatest extent: a new area of housing was laid out on the slopes of the Byrsa hill soon after 200 BC, covering an archaic necropolis. Also to the last Punic phase belong the two artificial harbours to the south near the *tophet*, one rectangular (later adapted into an elongated hexagon), the other circular around a central island. The first was the commercial harbour, and the latter housed the warships of the Carthaginian navy: *Appian reports a ship-shed capacity of 220 vessels here. Little is known of the disposition of the harbour(s) at an earlier date.

Roman Carthage has suffered greatly from stone-robbing, but the regular Augustan street grid centred on the Byrsa hill is known in detail, as well as the position of the principal public buildings, including the *amphitheatre on the western outskirts, the circus on the south-west, the theatre, and the odeum. The 2nd cent. AD saw the apogee of the city's prosperity: a massive forum and basilica, the biggest known outside Rome, was erected on the Byrsa in Antonine times, and also Antonine is the huge and lavish bath-house down by the sea, designed on a symmetrical layout like the great imperial *baths of Rome. It was probably to supply it that Carthage's 132-km. (82-mi.) *aqueduct was constructed, the longest anywhere in the Roman world. The forum on the Byrsa is unlikely to have been the only one: recent work (since 1990) near the coast midway between the Antonine baths and the harbours, alongside the *cardo maximus* (a main thoroughfare), has revealed part of what is probably the forum of the Augustan city; a Punic temple, perhaps that of *Apollo mentioned by Appian as bordering the Punic agora, has been located below. The 4th cent. and later saw a rash of extramural church-building, and *c.*425 a massive new defensive circuit was erected on the landward side against the Vandal threat; despite it the city fell easily to the Vandals in 439. Several houses of the 5th and 6th cents. are known, when Carthage continued to prosper: survey work in the Carthaginian hinterland shows rural settlement at its densest in the 5th and 6th cents., matching and even outstripping that of the 2nd and 3rd cents.

W. N. W.; B. H. W.; R. J. A. W.

dreams and portents presaging the accession of *Septimius Severus, he went on to write first a history of the wars following the death of *Commodus and then the *Roman History*, and that for this work he spent ten years collecting material for events up to the death of Severus (211) and a further twelve years writing them up. Nothing survives of the early works or of other historical writings attributed to Dio by the Suda (a 10th-cent. AD Byzantine lexicon). The dates of composition of the *Roman History* are disputed, but the most natural interpretation of Dio's words is that he began work *c.*202. His plan was to continue recording events after Severus' death as long as possible, but absence from Italy prevented him giving more than a cursory account of the reign of Severus Alexander and he ended the history with his own retirement (80. 1–5).

The *Roman History* is only partially extant. The portion dealing with the period 69 BC to AD 46 (36. 1. 1–60. 28. 3) survives in various MSS, with substantial lacunae after 6 BC. For the rest we depend on excerpts and the Byzantine epitomes of the 12th-cent. historian Zonaras (down to 146 and 44 BC to AD 96) and the 11th-cent. monk Xiphilinus (from 69 BC to the end).

Like its author, the work is an amalgam of Greek and Roman elements. It is written in Attic Greek, with much studiedly antithetical rhetoric and frequent verbal borrowings from the classical authors, above all *Thucydides. The debt to Thucydides is more than merely stylistic: like him, Dio is constantly alert to discrepancies between appearances and reality. In its structure, however, the history revives the Roman tradition of an annalistic record of civil and military affairs arranged by the consular year. Dio shows flexibility in his handling of the annalistic framework: there are many digressions, usually brief; external events of several years are sometimes combined in a single narrative cluster; introductory and concluding sections frame the annalistic narratives of emperors' reigns.

For his own times Dio could draw on his own experience or oral evidence, but for earlier periods he was almost entirely dependent on literary sources, chiefly earlier histories. Attempts to identify individual sources are usually futile. Dio must have read widely in the first ten years, and in the ensuing twelve years of writing up he probably worked mainly from his notes without going back to the originals. Such a method of composition may account for

some of the history's distinctive character. It is often thin and slapdash; errors and distortions are quite common, and there are some surprising omissions (notably the conference of Luca (see CAESAR)). However, Dio does show considerable independence, both in shaping his material and in interpretation: he freely makes causal links between events and attributes motivations to his characters, and many of these explanations must be his own contribution rather than drawn from a source.

One notable feature of the work is the prominence of the supernatural: Dio believed that divine direction played an important part in his own and others' lives and he devoted much space to portents. Another is the speeches, which are free inventions and sometimes on a very ample scale. Many of them are commonly dismissed as mere rhetorical set-pieces, but they generally have a dramatic function, often heavily ironic. In *Maecenas' speech of advice to *Augustus (52. 14–40) Dio combines an analysis of the problems facing Augustus and of the imperial system as it evolved under the emperors with a sketch of how he himself would have liked to see the empire governed.

The *Roman History* is dominated by the change from the republic to the monarchy of the emperors, repeatedly endorsed by Dio on the grounds that only monarchy could provide Rome with stable government. The late republic and the triumviral years are accorded much more space than other periods. Dio anachronistically treats the conflicts of the late republic as struggles between rival contenders for supreme power. His account of the settlement of 27 BC perceptively explores the ways in which it shaped the imperial system under which he still lived (53. 2. 6–21. 7). Dio's treatment of individual emperors' reigns reflects the values and interests of the senator: his overriding concern is with the respects in which emperors measured up to or fell short of senators' expectations.　　J. W. R.

Catiline (Lucius Sergius Catilina), of *patrician, but not recently distinguished, family, served with *Pompey and *Cicero under Gnaeus Pompeius Strabo in the Social War (91-89 BC: see ROME (HISTORY) §1.5). He next appears as a lieutenant of *Sulla both in the *bellum Sullanum* after Sulla's invasion of Italy and in the *proscriptions when, incited by Quintus Lutatius Catulus, he killed his brother-in-law Marcus Marius Gratidianus. There is no further record of him until his praetorship (68 BC), after which he governed Africa for two years. Prosecuted *repetundarum* (i.e. on a charge of provincial extortion) on his return, he was prevented from standing for the consulship for 65 and 64, but was finally acquitted with the help of his prosecutor P. *Clodius Pulcher. In 66/5 he was said to be involved in a plot with Publius Autronius and Sulla's kinsman Publius Sulla; the details are obscured by gossip and propaganda, and his involvement is doubtful. Frustrated ambition now became his driving force. In the elections for 63 he made a compact with Gaius Antonius 'Hybrida' and gained the support of *Caesar and *Crassus, but was defeated by Cicero. He then began to champion the cause of the poor and dispossessed: dissolute aristocrats, bankrupt Sullan veterans, and those whom they had driven from their lands. Again defeated for 62, he organized a widespread conspiracy with ramifications throughout Italy. Cicero, kept informed by his spies, could not take decisive action owing to lack of sufficient support, for Catiline—an old Sullan, a patrician, and now a demagogue—was both popular and well connected. In November Cicero succeeded in frightening Catiline into leaving Rome to join a force of destitute veterans in Etruria. Soon afterwards, some Allobrogan envoys, carelessly given letters by conspirators in Rome, provided Cicero with the written evidence he needed. The leaders of the conspiracy in Rome were arrested and, after a long debate and a vote in the senate, executed. The consul Antonius marched out against Catiline, who was caught between two armies and was defeated and killed by Marcus Petreius near Pistoria (early January 62). Cicero was hailed as saviour of Rome, but was open to the charge of having executed citizens without trial.   E. B.

Cato the Elder (Marcus Porcius Cato) or 'Cato the Censor' (234–149 BC) was a dominant figure in both the political and the cultural life of Rome in the first half of the 2nd cent. BC. A *novus homo* (roughly, the first man of his family to become a senator and/or consul), he was born at Tusculum, but spent much of his childhood in the Sabine country, where his family owned land. He served in the Hannibalic War, winning particular praise for his contribution at the battle of the Metaurus in 207. He embarked on a political career under the *patronage of the patrician Lucius Valerius Flaccus, who was his colleague in both consulship and censorship. As quaestor 204 he served under *Scipio Africanus in Sicily and Africa; a constant champion of traditional Roman virtues, he looked with disfavour on Scipio's adoption of Greek customs and relaxed military discipline in Sicily, but the story that he came back to Rome to express his criticisms must be rejected. He is said to have returned from Africa via Sardinia, bringing thence the poet *Ennius to Rome. He was plebeian aedile 199 and praetor 198, when he may have carried the *lex Porcia* which extended the right of *provocatio* (appeal to the people against the action of a magistrate) to cases of scourging. He governed Sardinia, expelling usurers and restricting the

demands made on the Sardinians for the upkeep of himself and his staff. He reached the consulship in 195: after unsuccessfully opposing the repeal of the *lex Oppia*, he went to Spain, where, in a campaign which may have extended into 194, he suppressed a major rebellion, extended the area under Roman control, and arranged for the exploitation of the gold and silver mines; he returned to Rome to celebrate a triumph. In 191, as military tribune, he played an important part in the defeat of *Antiochus III at Thermopylae, and was sent to Rome by Manius Acilius Glabrio to report the victory.

Cato was constantly engaged in court cases, both as prosecutor or prosecution witness and as defendant. He was an instigator of the attacks on the Scipios (Africanus and his brother Lucius Cornelius Scipio Asiagenes), and two of his other targets, Quintus Minucius Thermus and Glabrio, can be seen as allies of the Scipios. The attack on Glabrio was connected with the censorial elections of 189, when Cato and Flaccus stood unsuccessfully. Five years later they were elected, having stood on a joint programme of reversing the decline of traditional morality. They were severe in their review of the rolls of the senate and the *equites*, removing Lucius Flamininus from the senate and depriving Scipio Asiagenes of his public horse. High levels of taxation were imposed on what the censors regarded as luxuries, and the public contracts were let on terms most advantageous for the state and least so for the contractors. They undertook extensive public works, including major repairs and extensions to the sewage system. The controversies caused by his censorship affected Cato for the rest of his life. But he courted conflict and spoke his mind to the point of rudeness. He rigidly applied to himself the standards he demanded of others and made a parade of his own parsimony: when in Spain he had made a point of sharing the rigours of his soldiers.

Though he held no further public offices Cato continued to play an active role in politics. He was probably an augur. He opposed the modification of the *lex Baebia* of 181 which had provided for the election of only four praetors in alternate years, and of the *lex Orchia*, a sumptuary law. Soon after 179 he attacked Marcus Fulvius Nobilior, and in 171 was one of the patrons chosen by the peoples of Spain to present their complaints against Roman governors. A critical remark about King Eumenes II of *Pergamum in 172 and speeches in 167 against declaring war on *Rhodes and in favour of leaving Macedonia free are probably part of a general reluctance to see Rome too directly involved in eastern affairs. It was also in 167 that he opposed the attempt by Servius Sulpicius Galba to block the *triumph of Lucius Aemilius Paullus; Cato's son later married a daughter of Paullus, and it thus seems that the old enmity between Cato and the family of the Scipios was at an end. In the last years of his life, after serving on an embassy to *Carthage in 153, Cato convinced himself that the existence of Carthage constituted a serious danger to Rome; he ended each speech in the senate by saying that Carthage must be destroyed. Despite the opposition of Publius Cornelius Scipio Nasica Corculum war was eventually declared in 149. Shortly afterwards came the last speech of Cato's life, against Galba.

Cato has rightly been called the 'virtual founder of Latin prose literature'. Among works that were known to later generations—though not necessarily intended for publication by Cato himself—but of which we know little, are the *Ad filium* ('to his son'), perhaps no more than a brief collection of exhortations, a letter to his son, the *De re militari* ('on military matters'), a work dealing with civil law, the *Carmen de moribus*, probably a prose work on behaviour, and a collection of sayings.

Cato was the foremost orator of his age, and made many speeches. Over 150 were known to *Cicero, and we possess fragments of eighty. There can be little doubt that he intended his speeches to survive, though it is an open question whether he revised them for publication and conceived of himself as creating Latin oratory as a literary genre.

Previous Roman historians, starting with Fabius Pictor, had written in Greek; Cato's *Origines*, begun in 168 and still in progress at the time of his death, was the first historical work in Latin. It consisted of seven books. The first dealt with the foundation of Rome and the regal period; Cato had little or nothing to say about the early republic. The second and third covered the origins and customs of the towns of Italy (the title of the work is appropriate only for these three books). His approach was probably influenced by Greek *ktisis* (foundation) literature and/or *Timaeus. The remaining books described Rome's wars from the First Punic War onwards. Cato is said to have written in a summary fashion, though some episodes were given detailed treatment, and he devoted more space to the events of the period during which he was writing; the last two books cover less than twenty years. He chose to omit the names of generals and included at least two of his own speeches (those on behalf of the Rhodians and against Galba).

The only work of Cato which survives intact is the *De agri cultura* ('on agriculture'). It is concerned not with agriculture as a whole, but principally with giving advice to the owner of a middle-sized estate, based on slave labour, in Latium or Campania, whose primary aim was the production of wine and olive oil for sale. It also includes recipes, religious formulae, prescriptions, and sample contracts. The work is disordered and some have wondered whether Cato himself is responsible for the shape of the text as we have it. See further appendix, below.

Cato sometimes expressed great hostility to all things Greek: in the *Ad filium* he called the Greeks a vile and unteachable race; in 155, worried by the effect their lectures were having on Roman youth, he was anxious that an embassy of Athenian philosophers should leave Rome rapidly. But he knew Greek well and had a good knowledge of Greek literature. His objections were to an excessive *philhellenism and he probably thought that contemporary Greeks were very different from the great figures of the past.

Cato was married twice, to Licinia and to Salonia (daughter of one of his clients), and had a son by each wife; the first died as praetor-designate in 152; the second, born when his father was 80, was the grandfather of Cato the Younger; see next article.   J. Br.

Appendix: Cato the Elder, De agri cultura 'Cato first taught agriculture to speak Latin' (Columella *Rust.* 1. 1. 12). The work (*c*.160 BC) was both innovative and part of an established Greek genre. Indications of acquaintance with Greek technical literature are clear, while the largely shapeless structure of the treatise reflects the infancy of Roman prose writing. Later authors (Varro, *Rust.* 1. 2. 12–28) defined and systematized *agriculture, discarding Cato's recipes and encomium of cabbage. Cato wrote for the young man who expected to make money and to enhance his public reputation by successful agriculture (3. 2). Thus the *villa should be sited near good access routes (1. 1. 3), and wine and oil stored until prices are high (3. 2). The treatise's essential subject is the slave-staffed villa in Latium and Campania practising mixed farming with an emphasis on vines and *olives. The archaeological record documents a gradual spread of villa sites in these regions from the beginning of the 2nd cent. BC and a remarkable diffusion of Italian *wine-amphorae (transport jars) in the western Mediterranean from the mid-2nd cent. BC.   M. S. S.

Cato the Younger (Marcus Porcius Cato), 'of Utica' ('Uticensis') (95–46 BC), great-grandson of Cato the Elder (see preceding entry), nephew of Marcus Livius Drusus, and brought up in the Livian household with the children of his mother's marriage to Gnaeus Servilius Caepio. Quaestor probably in 64, in 63 he became tribune-designate in order to check Quintus Caecilius Metellus Nepos, supported Lucius Licinius Murena's prosecution, and intervened powerfully in the senate to secure the execution of the Catilinarians (see CATILINE). As tribune he conciliated the mob by increasing the numbers eligible to receive cheap corn, but in all else remained uncompromising; *Cicero (*Att.* 1. 18. 7; 2. 1. 8) deplores his lack of realism which prevented revision of the Asian tax-contracts (61)—thus alienating the *equites—and which frustrated every overture of *Pompey until the coalition between Pompey, *Caesar, and *Crassus was formed. In 59 he opposed Caesar obstinately and was temporarily imprisoned, but next year P. *Clodius Pulcher removed him by appointing him to undertake the annexation of *Cyprus. Though King Ptolemy of Cyprus (an illegitimate son of Ptolemy IX of Egypt and brother of Ptolemy XII Auletes) killed himself and Cato's accounts were lost on the voyage home, his reputation for fairness remained unimpaired. After Luca (see POMPEY) he persuaded his brother-in-law Lucius Domitius Ahenobarbus not to give up hope of being elected consul for 55, but Domitius' candidature collapsed because of physical intimidation by the supporters of Pompey and Crassus. Publius Vatinius defeated Cato for the praetorship by bribery, but Cato was eventually praetor in 54. In 52, abandoning his constitutional principles, he supported Pompey's election as sole consul; he himself stood for 51 but failed. In the war he tried to avoid citizen bloodshed but resolutely followed Pompey: he served in Sicily, but was expelled from there by Gaius Scribonius Curio. Then he served in Asia, and held Dyrrhachium during the campaign of Pharsalus (48). After Pompey's defeat, Cato joined the quarrelling Pompeians in Africa and reconciled them; he had Quintus Caecilius Metellus Pius Scipio made general. During the war he governed Utica with great moderation, and was honoured by the city's inhabitants when after Thapsus in April 46 he committed *suicide rather than accept pardon from Caesar, an act which earned him the undying glory of a martyr.

Cato's constitutionalism, a mixture of *Stoicism and old Roman principles, was genuine. After death he was more dangerous than ever to Caesar, who in his *Anticato*, a reply to Cicero's pamphlet *Cato*, pitched the hostile case too high, and allowed the fame of Cato's life and death to give respectability to the losing side, and to inspire later political martyrs: 'the victors had their cause approved by the gods, the vanquished by Cato' (Lucan 1. 128).

G. E. F. C.; M. T. G.

Catullus (Gaius Valerius Catullus), the Roman poet, came from a distinguished propertied family of Verona but spent most of his life in Rome. The dates of his life are incorrectly transmitted in the *Chronicle* of Jerome but can be approximately reconstructed. He was probably born in 84 BC or a little earlier, and probably died in 54 BC: at any rate, there is no trace in his work of events subsequent to 55 BC. Since he was sent to Rome as a young man, his family were probably thinking of a political career, but he seems to have had no great ambitions in this area. His only public activity, so far as we know, was service on the staff of the propraetor Gaius Memmius, who was governor of Bithynia in 57–56 BC. In general, the political events of the turbulent decade he passed in Rome are little mentioned in his work. On one occasion his politically active friend Gaius Licinius Calvus involved him in a literary campaign against the triumvirs, especially *Caesar (with his minion, Mamurra), but this outburst of ill-humour did not last and when Caesar magnanimously offered him his hand in reconciliation, he did not refuse it (Suet. *Iul.* 73).

If Catullus was only marginally involved in politics, he was at the centre of the radical social change that marked the end of the republic. He lived in the circles of the *jeunesse dorée* (the *delicata iuventus* as Cicero called them) who had turned away from the ideals of early Rome and embraced Hellenistic Greek culture. This environment affected not only Catullus' outlook and views but also his language, which acquired a facility previously unknown in Roman literature. In a literary sense also Catullus was surrounded by like-minded individuals. A whole group of young poets, the so-called 'neoterics', shared the same rejection of traditional norms and the same search for new

forms and content, and, as in their lifestyle, Hellenistic culture provided the most important model. In these same aristocratic circles Catullus met the married woman whom he called 'Lesbia'. He depicts her as self-assured, beautiful, and cultured, and regards her becoming his lover as the peak of felicity. But when he realizes that she has been false to him with a succession of partners, his happiness turns to despair. The ups and downs of this affair provide Catullus with the central theme of his poetry. His love poetry is completely different from the light-hearted frivolity of Hellenistic literature, as presented in the epigrams of the *Greek Anthology*; he sought in love not sexual transport but a deep human union which would last a whole lifetime. Apuleius (*Apol.* 10) tells us that behind the name Lesbia was a Clodia, and this seems to offer a secure historical context, since we know of a *Clodia with similar characteristics living in Rome at this time, the sister of *Clodius Pulcher and wife to the consul of 60 BC, Quintus Caecilius Metellus Celer. Cicero gives a picture of her in his *Pro Caelio* which for all its bias must have had some basis in life. The identity of Lesbia and Clodia was for a long time thought secure, but has often been questioned in the 20th cent. Nevertheless, even if the identification cannot be proved, Cicero's picture of the historical Clodia is instructive for the social background to Catullus' poetry.

Catullus died young, and left behind only a slim corpus of work amounting to 114 poems of extremely varied length and form. The book is primarily ordered on metrical grounds. Sixty short poems in lyric or iambic metres are followed by poems 61–8, which are long poems in a variety of metres: the remainder of the book consists of epigrams. Another structural principle groups the elegies and epigrams together—that is, all the poems in elegiacs (65–116). Within these major sections, the ordering is again not random. In the short poems, as far as possible, a succession of poems in the same metre is avoided: the only exceptions are the many poems in phalaecean hendecasyllables, which often of necessity must be placed together, and the two short closural poems, 59 and 60. In the long poems, the first and last are metrically related to the neighbouring shorter poems: poem 61 is in lyric metre, 65–8 in elegiacs. A series of cycles may also be noticed in the content; the most important of these is the Lesbia cycle at the beginning of the book (2, 3, 5, 7, 8, 11), telling the story of Catullus' love affair from their first courtship through the height of passion to estrangement and the final breakup of the affair. It is then up to the reader to place the rest of the Lesbia poems, which are not ordered chronologically, within this framework. There is another Lesbia cycle in the epigrams (70–87), though it is more loosely constructed and not completely chronological. Further cycles of related poems include those dealing with the dubious pair of friends Furius and Aurelius (15–26) and with Gellius (74–91, and then 116). Other motifs, such as the trip to Bithynia, the Iuventius poems, and the invectives against Caesar, are distributed throughout the book. This apparently careless arrangement has led some to believe that

Catullus did not order the book himself, but that it is the result of posthumous publication. The principles of ordering mentioned above, however, seem more likely to go back to the poet himself, and a similar variety may be discerned in various reconstructions of Hellenistic books, such as the *Garland* of Meleager.

The three major groupings of poems within the corpus differ considerably in their approach. The short poems (1–60) contain much that one might term 'social poetry' from a thematic point of view, though they also include expressions of stronger emotions. These poems are certainly not, as has sometimes been thought, artless productions of a moment's reflection: Catullus models himself in them on the elegance and facility of the shorter Hellenistic forms. The group of longer poems in more elevated style begins with two wedding poems (61–2): poem 63 describes the fate of a young man who has become a devotee of *Cybele, the 'epyllion' (miniature epic) 64 contrasts happy and unhappy love in the stories of Peleus and Ariadne, and 65–8 are a series of elegiac poems on various themes. Poem 66 (with the introductory poem 65) contains a translation of the *Lock of Berenice* which concludes *Callimachus' *Aetia*; 68 (possibly two connected poems), is often seen as a precursor of the love elegies of *Propertius and *Tibullus. The epigrams (69–116) differ radically from the other poems. Even when they deal with the painful circumstances of the poet's own life, they are never simply representations of a momentary emotion, but rather reflective analyses of a situation or the poet's own experience.   H. P. S.

censorship See INTOLERANCE, INTELLECTUAL AND RELIGIOUS.

Centaurs (Greek *Kentauroi*), a tribe of 'beasts' (*Il.* 1. 268, 2. 743), human above and horse below; the wild and dangerous counterpart of the more skittish *satyrs, who are constructed of the same components but conceived of as amusing rather than threatening creatures. In both cases it is the very closeness of the horse to humanity that points up the need to remember that a firm line between nature and culture must be drawn. Pirithous the king of the Lapiths, a Thessalian clan, paid for his failure to absorb this lesson when he invited the Centaurs to his wedding-feast; the party broke up in violence once the guests had tasted *wine, that quintessential product of human culture (Pindar fr. 166 Snell–Maehler), and made a drunken assault on the bride (see the west pediment of the temple of Zeus at *Olympia). 'Ever since then', says Antinous in the *Odyssey* (21. 303), 'there has been conflict between Centaurs and men.' Their uncontrolled lust, violence, and greed for alcohol (see ALCOHOLISM) challenge the hard-won and ever fragile rules of civilization, which are symbolically reasserted by the victories of *Heracles (whose wife Deianira the Centaur Nessus tried to rape) and *Theseus (who sometimes fights alongside his friend Pirithous in the wedding-fight) over the savage horde. Centaurs belong to the forested

Centaurs Terracotta figurine of a Centaur, *c*.950–900 BC, from *Lefkandi.

mountains of Arcadia (see PELOPONNESUS) and northern Greece, the fringes of human society, so it is natural that in the 'Centauromachies' (battle-scenes between Lapiths and Centaurs) so popular in Archaic art (e.g. the François vase) they fight with uprooted trees and boulders against armed and disciplined Greek heroes; it is with fir-trunks that they pound the invulnerable Lapith Caeneus into the ground.

Their double-natured ambivalence is further emphasized in traditions which single out two of their number, Chiron and Pholus, as wise and civilized exceptions to the general rule. Pholus, it is true, eats his steak raw like an animal when entertaining Heracles in his Arcadian cave (Apollod. 2. 5. 4), but his self-control is shown by the fact that he is capable of holding his liquor—a specially aged vintage donated by Dionysus—until the other members of his tribe scent the bouquet of the wine, go berserk, and have to be shot down by Heracles. Chiron is a more complex character, blurring the human–animal boundary still further: vase-painters often make the point by giving him human rather than equine front legs and draping him in decorous robes. His bestial side is demonstrated by the way he feeds the baby *Achilles, deserted by his mother Thetis, on the still-warm blood of the hares which in art he

centuriation Aerial photography has been instrumental in revealing traces of ancient centuriation, as here in Italy's Po valley, where the system originated with the great wave of Roman *colonization in (Cisalpine) *Gaul in the 2nd cent. BC.

habitually carries over his shoulder as a portable game-larder (hence, in turn, the savagery of the hero); but he is also a source of wisdom on natural medicine (*Il.* 4. 219, 11. 831), and is recorded as an educator of the Argonaut Jason and *Asclepius as well as Achilles.

By the 5th cent. BC, Centaurs (like *Amazons) come to symbolize all those forces which opposed Greek male cultural and political dominance; at Athens, on the Parthenon metopes, with their heroically nude boxers and wrestlers, the triumph over Persia is a clear subtext. Of later literary treatments, *Ovid's magnificently gory, over-the-top account of the Lapith wedding (*Met.* 12. 210 ff.) is not to be missed.

A. H. G.

centuriation, a system of marking out the land in squares or rectangles, by means of *limites*, boundaries, normally prior to distribution in a colonial foundation. (The units above and below the *centuria* are explained by *Varro, *Rust.* 1. 10.) The practice appears with the second phase of Latin colonization (see COLONIZATION, ROMAN) beginning after 338 BC, perhaps at much the same time as apparently similar approaches in such cities of Magna Graecia (Greek S. Italy) as Heraclea and Metapontum. (There is no good evidence that in the Roman world the earliest stage involved marking out only in strips, rather than in squares or rectangles.) Centuriation was widespread in Italy between the 4th cent. BC and the early empire, spreading to the provinces with the projected colony of *Carthage-Junonia in 122 BC. In so far as a single plot of land in a single location was distributed, the practice was not rational in the normal conditions of Mediterranean agriculture: peasant strategies probably depended then as now on farming scattered plots with different soils, altitudes, and aspects, and therefore minimizing the risk of total crop failure; and marriage and inheritance probably rapidly fragmented originally unitary holdings. Those centuriation systems which remain visible today are on the whole those in relatively homogeneous terrain, especially where the *limites* between lots were also ditches which served for drainage, as in the Po valley. *Limites* might otherwise be anything from a drystone wall to a row of markers. The *limites* which run east–west are usually known as *decumani*, those which run north–south as *cardines* or *kardines*. There is an abundant, if often desperately obscure, literature on centuriation and similar matters in the writings of the *gromatici* or *agrimensores*, land surveyors, dating from the 2nd cent. AD to the late empire and beyond. The identification, never mind dating, of centuriation systems known only from aerial photographs is often uncertain in the extreme.

M. H. C.

chariots See TRANSPORT, WHEELED.

chastity

Before Christianity Chastity was not recommended in classical Greek *medicine before the physician Soranus (early 2nd cent. AD). In pagan religion, certain goddesses chose to remain virgins (e.g. Hestia/*Vesta, *Artemis/*Diana) and some priestesses—not necessarily those serving virgin goddesses—remained life virgins (e.g. Artemis Hymnia in Arcadia, Paus. 8. 13. 1) while others could only hold the position until the age of marriage (e.g. *Poseidon at Calauria, Paus. 2. 33. 3). They did not support their other human followers who emulated this behaviour (e.g. *Euripides' Hippolytus).

In contrast to the Hippocratics (see MEDICINE § 4) who believed a girl must be 'opened up' for the sake of her health, Soranus recommended perpetual virginity as positively healthful for both men and women (*Gynaeceia* 1. 30–2). These chapters were omitted in the Latin versions of his work compiled in late antiquity. He argued that desire harms the body, and loss of seed is damaging to health, while pregnancy and *childbirth exhaust the body. However, Soranus ends the section by conceding that intercourse is necessary for the continuance of the human race.

In contrast to Christian writers of the early Roman empire (see below), Soranus recommends virginity neither for spiritual health nor as part of rejecting the world, but to make the present life easier.

H. K.

Christian Celibacy and asceticism are endemic to *Christianity and are typical of the distinctive outlook on life which runs throughout much of early Christian literature. The lifestyle of John the Baptist and the canonical gospels' portrayal of the celibacy of Jesus and his eschatological message set the pattern for subsequent Christian practice. While the influence of Graeco-Hellenistic ideas cannot be ruled out, particularly Platonism (see PLATO), the background to this form of religious observance is to be found in the ascetical practices of certain forms of sectarian Judaism. The level of purity demanded by the Qumran sect (see DEAD SEA SCROLLS) reflects the regulations with regard to sexual activity in Leviticus and the requirements laid upon men involved in a holy war in Deuteronomy (probably explaining the reference to virginity in Rev. 14: 4). Elsewhere there is evidence that asceticism was a central part of the mystical and apocalyptic tradition of Judaism (e.g. Dan. 10). The centrality of eschatological beliefs for Christianity meant that from the earliest period there was a marked component of Christian practice which demanded a significant distance from the values and culture of the present age. The hope for the coming of a new age of perfection in which members of the Church could already participate placed rigorous demands on those who would join. Some evidence suggests that baptized men and women thought that they had to live like angels (cf. Luke 20: 35), putting aside all those constraints of present bodily existence which were incompatible with their eschatological state. *Paul's approach in 1 Cor. 7 in dealing with the rigorist lifestyle of the Corinthian ascetics is typical of the compromise that evolved, in which there is a grudging acceptance of marriage and an exaltation of celibacy. The emerging monastic movement, therefore, drew on a long history of ascetical practice which was taken to extremes in some Encratite circles.

C. R.

chemistry See PHYSICS.

childbirth

childbirth was generally the concern of women, either family and neighbours or experienced midwives who were sometimes ranked as doctors, but male doctors expected to be called in for difficult cases. Several treatises in the Hippocratic corpus (see MEDICINE §4) include some discussion of childbirth. *On the Nature of the Child* ascribes the onset of labour to the movement of the foetus, which breaks the membranes. *Diseases of Women* says that prolonged and unsuccessful labour usually means a difficult presentation, stillbirth, or multiple birth. Suggestions include vigorous shaking to stimulate delivery, and drugs to speed labour (*ōkytokia*); if all else fails, the doctor may resort to embryotomy, the extraction by instruments of a foetus which is stillborn or impossible to deliver alive. The uterus is envisaged as a container rather than as a powerful muscle, and labour is described as pains not contractions. *Aristotle (*Hist. an.* 586^b) notes that pains can occur in the thighs and the lower back as well as the lower abdomen, and that women can help delivery by effort and correct breathing. Dissection by Herophilus, in the 3rd cent. BC, revealed that the uterus is muscular, and in the 2nd cent. AD Galen (*Nat. Fac.* 3. 3) argues that it has the power to retain or expel the foetus.

The most detailed account of labour and delivery is in the 1st-cent. AD handbook written by Soranus (early 2nd cent. AD) for midwives, the *Gynaecology*. Soranus envisages delivery on a birthing-chair, or on a hard bed if the mother is weak. He does not discuss contractions or distinguish stages of labour, but does describe dilation of the cervix and the breathing-technique to be used in delivery. Pain relief is provided by warm cloths on the abdomen and sharp-scented things to smell, and Soranus emphasizes that the midwife and helpers must reassure the mother and be careful not to embarrass her. At the birth, the midwife signals whether the baby is male or female, then lays the baby on the ground and assesses whether it is 'worth rearing'. She judges when to cut and tie the umbilical cord, cleans and swaddles the baby, and puts it to bed.

Soranus invokes psychological and physical factors in the mother, as well as big babies, multiple births, and abnormal presentations, to explain difficult labour. He offers techniques for relieving a narrow or obstructed cervix (these do not include episiotomy) and for turning a foetus, but makes no mention of obstetric forceps or of Caesarean section as an alternative to embryotomy: a mother could not have survived the trauma of a Caesarean. He has no confidence in drugs, induced sneezing, and shaking to stimulate delivery of the baby or the placenta, and disapproves of cold baths, tight swaddling, and hard beds for newborns. He notes the belief that delivery is impeded if the woman's hair or belt is tied, and the reluctance of some midwives to cut the cord with iron.

Maternal mortality, like neonatal and infant mortality, is often assumed to have been high, but estimates of the maternal death rate range from 5 in 20,000 to 25 in 1,000. Women may have died from exhaustion and haemorrhage in a difficult delivery (especially if they had poor health or were very young) or from eclampsia, a kind of epilepsy which can now be detected early; puerperal fever occurred, but infection is relatively unlikely in home delivery.

In Greek tradition, childbirth ritually polluted those present because blood was shed, and delivery on sacred ground was therefore forbidden (see POLLUTION). Olympian goddesses are not represented as giving birth. The deities most often invoked in labour were *Artemis Eileithyia (sometimes regarded as separate deities) or *Hera in Greece, *Juno Lucina in Rome. Roman childbirth rituals are briefly described by *Augustine (*De civ. D.* 6. 9), but his source is the antiquarian *Varro rather than common practice. There are also allusions to rituals in which the father lifts the child from the earth (*tollere liberum*) or carries the child round the hearth (*amphidromia*), but these would not always be practicable—for instance, in a house with no central hearth or when the baby was born on the upper floor of a tenement—and it was the name-day celebration, approximately ten days after the birth, which publicly acknowledged the child as a family member.   E. G. C.

chorégos, 'chorus-leader', i.e. the man who trained and paid for a festival chorus. See TRAGEDY, GREEK §1.4.

Christianity (*see page 153*)

Chrysostom, Dio See DIO OF PRUSA.

Cicero (*see page 159*)

Cincinnatus (Lucius Quincius Cincinnatus), a *patrician listed in the *fasti* as suffect consul (see CONSUL) in 460 BC. In 458, according to tradition, when a Roman army under the consul L. Minucius Esquilinus Augurinus was besieged by the Aequi on Mt Algidus, Cincinnatus was called from the plough and appointed *dictator. Within fifteen days he assembled an army, defeated the Aequi, triumphed, laid down his office, and returned to his ploughing. The story was frequently cited as a moral example, illustrating the austere modesty of early Rome and its leaders. An area on the right bank of the Tiber called the 'Quinctian Meadows' (*prata Quinctia*) was regarded as the site of Cincinnatus' four-*iugera* farm (Liv. 3. 26. 8). He is said to have been appointed dictator a second time in 439 BC during the Spurius Maelius crisis (this man was a wealthy plebeian— see PLEBS—who made an attempt at a *tyranny in 439 BC but was killed by Gaius Servilius Ahala); Cicero says that it was on this occasion that he was called from the plough (*De sen.* 56). It was this detail that was firmly fixed in the Roman tradition; the historical context was less certain. The campaign of 458 recalls the rescue of C. Minucius in 217, and Cincinnatus' supposedly crushing victory is suspect, since the Aequi returned to the attack again in 457 and 455.   T. J. Co.

circus, the Roman arena for chariot-racing. The most important at Rome was the Circus Maximus (*c*.650 × 125 m.: *c*.711 × 137 yds.), in the Murcia valley between the Palatine and Aventine, traditionally founded in the regal period and progressively adorned during the republic. The distinctive form with parallel sides and one semi-circular end fitted with tiered seating, and with twelve starting gates (*carceres*) at the open end, was created under *Caesar and preserved in the monumental rebuilding by *Trajan. The area was divided into two tracks by a long central barrier (*euripus* or *spina*), marked at the ends with conical turning-posts (*metae*) and decorated with Augustus' obelisk and other monuments, including the movable eggs and dolphins which marked the ends of the seven laps in each race. Four, six, eight, or twelve teams of horses competed under different colours, red and white at first (Tert. *De spect.* 5, 9), then also green (Suet. *Calig.* 55) and blue (Suet. *Vit.* 7), *Domitian's purple and gold (Suet. *Dom.* 7) being temporary. Other circuses at Rome included the Circus Flaminius in the Campus Martius, formalized *c*.220 BC but without permanent seating, and the Vatican Circus of *Gaius and *Nero (Plin. *HN* 36. 74; 16. 201), the site of Christian martyrdoms, close to the later St Peter's basilica. Best preserved is the Circus of Maxentius outside the city on the via Appia, dedicated in AD 309 (*ILS* 673).

Circuses are found elsewhere in Italy and in many parts

of the empire. In the east those of *Antioch and *Alexandria were famous, while Spain provides notable examples such as Merida (Emerita Augusta) and Urso, the latter famous for its racing-stables (Plin. *HN* 8. 166). In the late empire circuses became increasingly associated with the emperor and were built in connection with imperial residences as at Constantinople (see BYZANTIUM) and Milan (Mediolanum).

J. D.

Cisalpine Gaul See GAUL (CISALPINE).

cities See POLIS; URBANISM.

citizenship, Greek Greek citizenship stemmed from the fusion of two distinct but related elements, (*a*) the notion of the individual state as a 'thing' with boundaries, an ongoing existence, and a power of decision, and (*b*) the notion of its inhabitants participating in its life as joint proprietors. The first element was a product of the various processes of state formation which eroded personal chieftainship by centralizing power and exercising it through a growing number of offices or magistracies with limited length of tenure: at first denoted by an extended use of the word *polis*, it later engendered the more abstract term *politeia*, 'polity', 'constitution', or 'commonwealth'. The second element developed from the informal but ineradicable roles which *Homer already portrays as being played in communal life by the *dēmos* (the territory or settlement and its inhabitants) and the *laos* (the people in terms of roles—especially military—and relationships): reflected in various ways in early texts such as ML 2 (Dreros on *Crete), ML 8 (Chios), or the Great Rhetra of *Sparta (Plut. *Lyc.* 6), it was formalized in the word *politēs* (citizen) and in the assembly (*ekklēsia*, *apellai*, etc.) as an institution. The fusion of the two elements was expressed in the fundamental phrase 'to have a share in the polity' (*metechein tēs politeias*), which is widespread in Greek texts. It implied that all citizens shared in public responsibilities (deciding, fighting, judging, administering, etc.) and in public privileges (access to land, distributions, or power) as if they were shareholders in a company.

Political pressures and political theory (cf. especially Arist. *Pol.* 3) crystallized round the questions 'Should shares be equal?' and 'Who should be a citizen?'. Aspirations towards equality, opposed by oligarchs, were expressed by terms such as *homoioi* ('peers', full Spartiates), *isēgoria* ('freedom to speak in assembly'), and *isonomia* ('equity of power between rulers and ruled'), by the diffusion of power among the citizenry, and by the notion of 'ruling and being ruled by turn' which shaped *Aristotle's functional definition of citizenship (*Pol.* 1277ᵃ27). In consequence, the boundary between citizen and non-citizen needed explicit definition. Some formulations admitted all free residents, as *Cleisthenes' reform in Athens probably did. Others required descent from a real or imagined founder or group, and therefore emphasized legitimacy of birth. Others envisaged 'those best able to help (the city)

with their property and persons' (Thuc. 8. 65. 3), or (as in Sparta) disfranchised those unable to contribute fully to the common table. Such formulations tended to equate citizenship with the four abilities—to fight, to vote, to hold office, to own land—and thereby to make citizen bodies into closed, privileged, all-male corporations, outside which lay various inferior or adjunct statuses such as *perioikoi* ('dwellers-round'), *metoikoi* (*metics) or *paroikoi* ('resident free aliens'), and *apeleutheroi* ('freedmen'). However, need and advantage forced states to make individual exceptional enfranchisements, e.g. for men with particular resources or talents (cf. the seer Teisamenus, Hdt. 9. 33). Collective grants (e.g. ML 94) or amalgamations of citizenship also remained rare except as a product of *synoecisms such as *Rhodes or Megalopolis (Arcadia).

Such exclusivity gradually broke down in the Hellenistic period, as citizenship became more an honour and a status than a function. The purchase of citizenship became a common practice, as did plural citizenship or the mutual permeability of citizenship represented by treaties of *isopoliteia* ('equal citizenship'). By the Roman period active citizenship in the Greek states required previous service in the upper-class *ephēbeia* (see GYMNASIUM).

J. K. D.

citizenship, Roman In both the Greek and the Roman world in the Archaic period, it seems that communities were open to the arrival of people from elsewhere, at all social levels, whether one thinks of *Hesiod's father, Demaratus of Corinth (mid-7th cent.) in Tarquinii (see ETRUSCANS), the Tarquins (see TARQUINIUS SUPERBUS), or Attus Clusus and his followers in Rome. Detailed rules for citizenship were of course developed in both civilizations, as the city evolved, in the 7th to 5th or 6th to 5th cents. BC. In the case of Rome, though the details are obscure, Roman citizenship clearly developed in dialogue with the citizenships of other Latin communities. It involved the observance of the Roman civil law; and the struggles of the plebeians gradually brought protection for citizens from magisterial *imperium*.

At all events, Roman citizenship came to possess two features which distinguished it from *polis citizenship and which later surprised Greek observers: the automatic incorporation of freed slaves of Romans into the Roman citizen body; and the ease with which whole communities of outsiders could be admitted as citizens. By the time Rome faced the invasion of *Hannibal in 218 BC, she had a long history of giving citizenship to Italian communities, either with the vote (*optimo iure*) or without the vote (*sine suffragio*). (The latter communities, as with Arpinum, the place of origin of *Marius and *Cicero, were usually later granted the vote.) Apart from Roman communities of these two types and allies, *socii*, Italy also contained numerous Latin communities, whose members shared a number of rights with Romans and whose citizenships were interchangeable with that of Rome, and vice versa, if the person concerned changed domicile. One of the rights shared with Romans was *conubium* (right of marriage). A

[*continued on p. 158*]

Christianity

Christianity Classicists have traditionally found interesting both the Christian cult itself and Christian attitudes to Greek and Roman culture and the imperial state. Recent research encourages equal attention to the *Jews. Christianity began as a Jewish sect and changed its relationship with the Jewish community at a time when both groups were affected by later Hellenism. Christians laid claim to an antiquity rooted in the history of ancient Israel, while at the same time they sought the tolerance, interest, and loyalty of the pagans around them.

The first followers of Jesus inhabited a political system, the Roman empire, that regarded Jews as singular. Strategic prudence had recognized in Herod the Great (confirmed as king of Judaea in 40 BC) a useful ally against opponents of Roman expansion and against rivals for power in Rome itself. The Jews, monotheists who identified closely their religion and their ethnicity, survived thus in the Roman context only because exceptions were made: suspending in this instance a characteristic readiness to absorb the religion of an alien people, Rome allowed them a controlled political independence in several territories (although Judaea itself, after Herod's death, passed under direct administration).

Many Jews lived willingly with resulting contradictions. Yet such compromise had long caused division among them. Following the conquests of *Alexander the Great, intercourse with Hellenistic culture (see HELLENISM) had seemed advantageous to some; but the resolution of the 'devout' and the revolt of the Maccabees against the Seleucid Antiochus IV (168/7 BC) had shown that traditional values were far from dead. Now the encroachment of Rome gave new edge to revulsion from the Gentile world, and the frequent brutality of the conquerors strengthened the hand of those more dubious about the benefits of alliance.

Jesus lived, therefore, in a divided Palestine. The rule of Rome and the fortunes of her Jewish allies seemed secure; but the cruelty of Herod had kept alive strong forces of resistance and revolt. One cannot avoid asking where Jesus stood on issues of religious and political loyalty, although his native Galilee was subject to a tetrarch rather than a Roman governor during his lifetime.

It is likely that Jesus reflected several tendencies in the Judaism of his day. Followers saw him variously as a forerunner of the rabbis, holy man, wonder-worker, rebel, and prophet. Attempts to decide how he saw himself have proved difficult. When we set side by side the NT (New Testament) reports and our knowledge of Galilee at the time, the wonder-working holy man appears his most likely guise. He emphasized the imminent ending of the visible world and the judgement of God upon it. He promoted also a sense of liberty, to be enjoyed by those willing to repudiate family, career, and a sense of 'sin'. That, and the number of his followers in the volatile atmosphere of Jerusalem at pilgrimage time, was enough to set him at odds with the Jewish high-priestly establishment, wedded to the social order required by Rome.

Those who had not known Jesus well, if at all, were less simple and less dramatic in their interpretations. The NT reveals how they broadened the religious context within which he was seen as significant, in pagan as well as Jewish terms. They also postponed the consummation he had seemed to herald. Partly as a consequence, they felt it proper to debate the value and authority of the Roman dispensation and the contrasting force of Jewish tradition. They also passed judgement on Temple and synagogue. Those characteristic centres of Jewish cult did not differ entirely from other religious traditions. In spite of strident voices defending the unique and separate quality of their life, some elements of the religious practice of the Jews invited comparison with paganism. Blood *sacrifice, priesthood, ritual purity, dietary law, the preservation and study of sacred texts, speculation about the nature and purposes of God and about human virtue—all took a Jewish form but also identified Judaism as a religion among others: for those categories of thought and practice were familiar to many in the ancient world. Thus Christian criticism, operating within the Jewish tradition, highlighted a potential for realignment, inviting the attachment of additional or alternative meanings to the religious practice of the Jews themselves.

At a time, therefore, when Jews were divided over the nature of their privilege and separation, one group among them began actively to seek recruits among the Gentiles. Distance from other Jews was not achieved simply. The destruction of the Temple in AD 70, occurring in the midst of the earliest Christian readjustment, was built into the Church's founding documents. The Jewish revolts of 115–17 and 132–5, however, attracted little Christian comment. The Church's distinctiveness, by then, was more obvious. Christian texts with a strong Jewish flavour, like *1 Clement* (*c*.96) and Hermas' *Shepherd* (early to mid-2nd cent.), gave way to more deliberate competition for both respectability and a claim on the past. The 'apologist' Justin Martyr (d. *c*.165), while defending his new religion against the Roman élite, asserted also against Jews, in his *Dialogue with Trypho*, Gentile claims to the heritage of Israel and a natural alliance between the OT (Old Testament) and classical cosmology.

The Christian writer Origen of Alexandria (*c*.185–254) established in the next generation (especially after his move to Palestinian Caesarea in 230) a new style of dialogue with Jews, all in pursuit of his own biblical research. The Jews in Palestine had by that time acquired new confidence, after the disasters of 66–73 and 132–5. Their rabbinic leaders had completed the publication of the Mishnah (a collection of legal opinions); and, under the leadership of a Patriarch, a disciplined community had been set in place, contrasting markedly with enduring elements of Hellenistic Jewry elsewhere. Origen became the architect of a mature Christian biblical exegesis. His purpose was to demonstrate in Christianity the fulfilment of OT prophecy. He focused, as had Justin, more on the significance of Jesus than on the inadequacy of the Law. A 'spiritual' understanding was required to detect fulfilment, assisted to a limited extent by the allegory beloved of the Jewish writer Philo (early 1st cent. AD). Yet Origen remained dependent on the Jewish exegesis he hoped to undermine. His most notable attack on paganism, the *Against Celsus*, required extensive defence of Jewish thought. His more homiletic works addressed an enduring ambiguity in Christian life, affected by converts from Judaism only slightly less exaggerated or precise in their mixed loyalty than the Ebionites and Nazarenes of the age.

Origen's African contemporary, the 'apologist' Tertullian (*c*.160–225), is noted chiefly for rigorist theology (reflecting in part an admiration for the martyrs) and for attacks on Gnosticism. Tertullian probably had little to do with real Jews. His work *Against the Jews* was chiefly directed against pagans. It was, rather, the gnosticizing Marcion (d. *c*.160) who led Tertullian to develop his views on the justice and providence of the OT God and the status of Jesus as Messiah. (Marcion, for his part, had appeared to reject the OT dispensation completely.) Displaying in the process some debt to bishops Melito of Sardis (d. *c*. AD 190) and Irenaeus of Lyons (d. *c*. AD 200), as well as to Justin, Tertullian thus transmitted a specifically western approach to OT exegesis that influenced his fellow Africans bishop Cyprian of Carthage (d. 258) and *Augustine (354–430) and all Latin theology.

The real sense, however, of a seamless inclusion of the OT within the Christian tradition came with *Eusebius of Caesarea (*c*.260–*c*.340). He had been reared in the tradition of Origen. Famous for his *History of the Church*, which contributed much to a sense of continuity between the orthodox Christians of Constantine's reign and the faith and practice of the Apostolic age, his *Preparation of the Gospel* and *Demonstration of the Gospel* are no less significant for their Christian appropriation of the Hebrew past.

The toleration of Christianity by the Roman state made it less necessary to compete with Judaism for the favour of the state and heralded a sharp decline in Jewish–Christian relations. Yet the arrogant vitriol of bishop John Chrysostom of Constantinople (*c*.347–407) shows that a challenge from Jewish ideas was still perceived by Christians, at least at *Antioch, centuries after the death of Jesus. Unflagging antagonism remained a major engine of the Church's development, compelling it to adopt yet more distinguishing forms and attitudes of its own. The differences between Christianity and Judaism apparent or desirable in 4th-cent. eyes were, naturally, not those that had struck Hermas or Justin. Even Jerome (d. 420), Scripture scholar though he was, found himself in circumstances very different from those of Origen. Yet the shifting quality of the debate implied a lasting insecurity of definition. Faced from within by new divisions and critics of its administration and discipline, the 4th-cent. Church was still not ready to label itself finally. Moreover, the confidence of the Theodosian Code (the collection of imperial laws published 429–38) that heresy was a thing of the past proved laughable in the light of Monophysite secession and the persistent Arianism among the barbarians of the west.

In that long process of Christian self-definition in relation to Judaism, crucial in determining the character of Christianity itself, three sensitivities stand out, concerning sacrifice, text, and morality.

The interpretation of sacrifice separated Christians at an early stage. Jews retained an attachment to priest and victim, but in the context of the desert Tabernacle rather than the Temple (almost certainly by that time destroyed). From then on, Christians saw themselves as competing for the heritage of priesthood as well as of the synagogue tradition. The Church continued to emphasize the symbolic priesthood of the heavenly Jesus and developed its own priestly caste, which presided over a eucharistic cult with strong sacrificial elements. The word 'bishop' quickly acquired an official meaning (1 Tim. 3: 1); but clear priestly association with the Eucharist (absent in the *Didache*, where the bishop is seen as teacher and prophet, 15. 1, and vague in *1 Clement*, in spite of an asserted need for succession, 44) does not occur until Ignatius of Antioch (d. *c*.107), *Letter to the Philadelphians* 4 (which links 'bishop' with 'Eucharist' and 'altar'). Subsequent development was inexorable; but not every Christian assembly demanded the presence and action of a bishop or priest until the 3rd cent.

Priesthood and sacrifice implied atonement: for sacrifice had to have a purpose. *Paul had presented the execution of Jesus as an expiation for sin (Col. 1: 20, Rom. 3: 25)—the sin of Adam and the sin of individual men and women. Christianity thus adopted on its own terms the historical perspective of restoration to God's favour enshrined in the Jewish Scriptures, paying less attention to political or tribal triumph in a Messianic age and more to cosmic and psychological divisions between creatures and creator, the defeat of sin, and the heavenly destiny of redeemed humanity.

Christians argued against the Jewish interpretation of the texts that they shared. Christian appropriation demanded a new sense of what drove the ancient writers. God's words and actions and the inspired utterances of prophets were now focused on Jesus. The evident meaning of older texts had often to be wrenched so far in a new direction that 'exegesis', methodical interpretation, took centuries to achieve a Christian maturity and depended in part on the literary skills of the pagan élite. Once again, Origen illustrates the process. The allegorical tradition, filtered to some extent through Philo, allowed him access to the 'spiritual' meaning of the Bible; but other traditional skills of criticism and analysis were required, which the rabbis were equally aware of, and which Origen just as keenly applied. Moreover, since Jesus was an historical figure, the prophecies typical of Scripture were, after the time of Jesus himself, robbed of further purpose. 'Prophecy' suddenly attracted suspicion in place of reverence. The most famous victims of that prejudice were the adherents of Montanism (a prophetic movement in Asia Minor) of the late 2nd and early 3rd cents. Their combination of ecstatic prophecy, apocalyptic expectation, and ascetic rigour (which successfully attracted Tertullian) can be found thereafter in varying proportions among many movements both critical and schismatic. Opponents favoured a closed 'canon' of Scripture (finally achieved only in the 4th cent.): no documents later than a certain date were regarded as 'inspired'. Interpretation was no longer expected to yield surprise but simply reinforced a significance already totally achieved.

The attitudes that established a textual canon were also influential in defining authority: for one had to know who was entitled to expound the significance of Scripture. Agreement on that issue kept pace with the developing style of Christian priesthood: in the end, the bishop and his assistants claimed exclusive rights to exegesis, just as they claimed the right to preside over the sacrificial cult of the Church.

Finally, Christians developed a new moral theory not based on the OT; and that, too, served to separate them from Jewish contemporaries. Their emphasis was on love, as opposed to law—such were the terms in which they explained themselves, though with little justice to the Jews. They tapped other ethical traditions also: later *Stoicism especially. Increasing sophistication can be traced through the *Shepherd*, the 2nd-cent. *Sentences of Sextus*, and the *Pedagogue* of Clement of Alexandria (*c*.150–*c*.215). The Greek ascetic tradition made its appeal to the more committed. Surprise at a failure in love would be naïve: more significant was the enduring Christian attachment to law (which made anti-Jewish polemic a tortured enterprise). With the tolerance of *Constantine I, the Church was ready to take advantage of the law of the state. For some time, however, it had been developing its own legal system, represented by the decrees of Church councils, of which the archetype is described in Acts 15. Other early councils, of the 2nd cent., were mustered against perceived errors such as those of Montanism (Euseb. *Hist. Eccl.* 5. 16) or in relation to the date of Easter—a sensitive issue *vis-à-vis* the Jews (Euseb. *Hist. Eccl.* 5. 24). Evidence of gathering momentum is provided by African practice in the 3rd cent. (beginning with allusions in Cyprian, *Ep.* 71. 4, 73. 3). Council decisions continued to focus mainly on ecclesiastical order; but moral prescriptions were frequently implied or stated and spilled inevitably into the lives of ordinary men and women.

The Christian cult acquired, under the same influence, an increasingly formal character. The development of a calendar (exemplified by the Chronographer of AD 354), particularly relating to the ceremonies of initiation during Lent and Easter, augmented by the celebration of Epiphany and, later, Christmas and by commemorations of the martyrs, enfolded Christians in a detailed regime. A series of strictures and public ceremonies impinged upon the wayward, involving a modicum of public shame and defining the steps whereby they might be reconciled to both God and their fellows. (An early model is presented in *1 Clement* 57. 1. Vague evidence accumulates in Clem. Al. *Strom.* 2. 13. Details emerge only with Tert. *De paenitentia* 8. 9. 4 and Cyprian *De lapsis* 29; *Ep.* 55. 29.) All Christians, to a greater or lesser degree, were exhorted to undertake a life of self-discipline, marked by traditionally habitual patterns of prayer, fasting, and generosity.

While thus strengthening its self-definition against Judaism, Christianity faced the task of relating to other cults. It presented itself from an early stage as a universal religion. It did not merely invite adherence but demanded it: all men and women were thought able to achieve their destiny only within its embrace. One possible response to so aggressive an invitation was resentment; and here we touch upon the so-called 'persecution' of Christianity by the Roman state. Legal proceedings against the Church were intermittent and often moderate; violent demonstrations outside the law were unusual. The heroism revered in the *Acts of the Martyrs* seems to have been invited as often as it was imposed. Nevertheless, we find occasional confrontation. The famous attack by *Nero on Christians in Rome in 64 had no lasting impact or significance. The traditionally accepted oppression by *Domitian in the 90s has gained its notoriety mostly from the misleading obscurity of Melito (Euseb. *Hist. Eccl.* 4. 26. 9 f.). More generally significant in political terms may have been the situation described in *Pliny the Younger's *Ep.* 10. 96 f. of 112; but *Trajan's insistence on the observance of legal procedure and the avoidance of harassment says as much as his governor's distaste. Christians in that period may have attracted suspicion partly through a presumed association with rebellious Jews. As the political hopes of the Jews began to fade and the self-effacing preoccupations of rabbinic society gathered strength, Christians were exposed as possible enemies of the state in their own right. It was then that famous martyrs made their names—Polycarp of Smyrna and Justin Martyr in 165 and those condemned at Lyons in 177. Yet the pleas of Melito and the 'apologist' Athenagoras (mid-2nd cent. AD) cannot disguise the local quality of such reversals. Outbursts under the emperors *Septimius Severus and Maximinus Thrax (235–8) were similarly limited. It was not until the middle of the 3rd cent. that forceful opposition was sanctioned by central authority. Severe threats to the stability of the state had by that time fostered new anxieties about loyalty; but the growing strength of the Church made it less susceptible to intolerance. The short-lived brutality of Decius (249–51) and the dissipated attacks of Valerian (253–60) were foiled by that resilience—proved as much by the Church's readmission of the weak as by its admiration for the strong. The new confidence was even more evident under the

Diocletianic persecution from 303 until the emperor Galerius' deathbed surrender in 311 (see DIOCLETIAN).

Throughout the prior period, several paradoxes had been laid bare, connected with the universal vision of the Church, the analogous breadth of Rome's claims to government, and its desire to tolerate nevertheless a variety of religious beliefs and practices. State and Church faced similar problems: how should one balance universalist demands and individual variety? The state's solution was to demand, in the interest of unity, a minimum but inescapable conformity in religious practice and to display, when it came to controlling belief, a prudent reticence. The devotee of an alien cult should not oppose, at least, the gods of Rome. The difference between loyalty to the empire and enthusiasm for local deities was more easily made clear with the growth of the imperial (*ruler-) cult (which called for the simplest obeisance) and the extension of Roman *citizenship in 212. Christians resolutely branded that policy a subterfuge, demanding particular rights for what they thought of in their case as absolute values, undermining at once the freedom of the individual and the authority of the state.

They pursued the same embarrassing tactics in their broader dialogue with the classical world. As they acquired the vocabulary and adopted the habits of Greek philosophy, so they began to make their own points on the issues that philosophy had traditionally addressed: the nature of the divine and the visible world, the significance of texts, the canons of moral education and behaviour, the uses of ritual, the shape of history, and the character of its major figures. Such usurpation made them eventually impossible to ignore. The stages of encroachment are represented by the very writers who composed polemic against the Jews—1 Clement, the apologists, the *Alexandrians, and the Africans—and culminate in the added reflection that came with more assured success in the 4th-cent. Cappadocians and the writings of Bishop Ambrose of Milan (d. 397) and *Augustine. Method counted for as much as ideas: for with genre—letter, dialogue, homily, or life—Christians absorbed models as well as techniques, which affected their notions of community and conviction as much as of virtue or divinity. Thus they invaded the classrooms, libraries, temples, and debating-chambers of their adversaries long before they gained positions of public authority and power. Infuriatingly, they began to impose peculiar meanings on what the majority of their fellows had long been accustomed to say: so, while they could appear reassuringly familiar and traditional as a Mediterranean cult among others, they were constantly found to be undermining that to which they appeared to subscribe.

Christian engagement with Jewish tradition and classical culture made a distinctive contribution to the religious life of the Mediterranean world. The Christian view of God was subtle. It combined attachment to transcendence and monotheism with a sense of personal dynamism in the godhead— potent, purposeful, and affectionate. Correspondingly, the relation of the individual to that divinity engaged every level of human experience, bodily and spiritual, from hunger, fear, and desire to insight and self-sacrifice. Such beliefs were made formal in the doctrines of the Trinity and the Incarnation, both in their way indebted to pagan and Jewish antecedents. There was also in Christianity a clear system of authority and leadership: the bishop was its own brilliant, proper, and lasting creation. Heir to Jewish priesthood and biblical learning, he provided both the focus and the generative impulse, through baptism and mission, for a stable community. The sacramental liturgy, reinforced by singing, processions, and the veneration of dead heroes and exemplars, enabled the Church to act out its beliefs through symbol and recollection. The past was especially valuable to the Christian, once correctly understood. The canon of sacred texts, the succession of priests, the interpretations of Scripture, and the customs of discipline and worship all conspired to produce a vision of where time was leading the Church and rescued it from the disoriented ambiguities of Gnosticism. Finally, Christians developed their own morality, founded on the conviction that each person was created by God and destined for his lasting company; a morality that valued, therefore, the whole human being, refined by continence, expanded by selfless generosity, and rewarded by bodily resurrection.

Such, at least, was the 'orthodox' view; but it was never taken for granted. 'Orthodoxy' was established only slowly and was constantly challenged by men and women who claimed the title

'Christian'. The nature of their dissent or variety sprang in part from the fact that they had found other ways of relating to Jewish and pagan tradition. A more anthropomorphic view of God, indifference to sacramental worship, suspicion of the clergy and preference for charismatic leadership and personal inspiration, a love of myths and symbols in the place of literal history, mistrust of the *body and a corresponding desire for 'spiritual' experience and fulfilment—all such emphases diffracted the pattern of Christian development, yet seemed no less Christian for that. It is neither possible nor just to isolate groups that represented those tendencies precisely: that was the ploy of their enemies. What seemed clear choices in the cause of self-definition, especially when they attempted to exclude either pagans or Jews, were normally made in circumstances of confusion, which they by no means brought to an end. The tidy writings of Irenaeus and Epiphanius of Cypriot Salamis (d. 403) teem with supposedly undesirable eccentrics; but those 'heretics' may have seemed to others at the time no more than ordinary Christians. The image of the Gnostic or the Montanist, of the Encratite or rigorist ascetic, often the product of prejudice and horror, can disguise a more complicated variety that represented nevertheless the Christian norm.

We cannot content ourselves, therefore, with a straightforward account of Christian triumph over pagan and Jew. It was simply that certain answers to fundamental questions began to seem more acceptable to some Mediterranean people—answers in a debate pursued by some in all parties about the nature of creation, the destiny of the cosmos and the individual, the status of sacred texts, the substantiality of the visible world, the use of ritual and law, and the proper styles of religious authority. The new answers were thought to deserve the label 'Christian'; but what had happened was that the controlling element in a whole society had changed its mind about the meaning of history and experience.

Can we be sure about the scale of that development? It is impossible to judge the size of the Christian population at any one time. Surviving reports are marred by hyperbole, ignorance, and convention. Archaeology and inscriptions are statistically haphazard and impervious to individual sentiment. Suffice it to say that within certain urban communities, particularly in the east, Christians formed a sizeable minority and occasionally even a majority in the late 3rd cent. The difficult question is why. Breeding and friendship must have played a large part in the expansion of Christianity—perhaps always larger than that of convincing oratory. What remains textually of Christian address was not necessarily disseminated broadly. We know little more about the *reception of the Christian message than we do about that of any ancient document. With the advent of toleration, it is likely that expediency, laziness, and fear played as much a part then as they do now. Talk of 'superstition' is misleading. Features of religious life supposedly attractive to a superstitious mind had always been available in traditional cult. The change of allegiance demands more subtle explanations. See RELIGION, JEWISH.

P. R.

child born to two Romans was a Roman; but so was a child born to a Roman father and a mother from a people possessing conubium.

All citizens, after the abolition of the ban on conubium between patricians and plebeians, had conubium; they were also liable to *tributum and military service. If they had the vote, they were also eligible to stand for magistracies. (Individuals were occasionally deprived of the vote as a punishment, becoming aerarii, 'payers'.) It is not certain whether communities without the vote were bound by the Roman civil law or not.

In the course of the 2nd cent. BC, grants of citizenship dried up, except for a few communities sine suffragio granted the vote; and Rome sought also to restrict the access of Latins to Roman citizenship. Attempts were made to respond to the desire of Latins and Italians alike for citizenship, by Marcus Fulvius Flaccus in 125 BC, by Gaius *Gracchus in 122 BC, and by Marcus Livius Drusus in 91 BC. The failure of Flaccus provoked the revolt of Fregellae (near mod. Leprano); and when the last attempt failed, most of the allies went to war with Rome to achieve their end, the so-called Social War; and in order to ensure the loyalty of the rest, as also of the Latins, who had for the most part remained loyal, Rome granted them citizenship by the lex Iulia of 90 BC. Although the details of the process are obscure, citizenship was in fact also extended to former rebels. By the time of *Sulla, Italy south of the Po (Padus) and former Latin colonies north of the Po were Roman, with the possible exception of the

[continued on p. 167]

Cicero

Cicero, Marcus Tullius Cicero, the famous orator.

Life The first of two sons of a rich and well-connected *eques* (see EQUITES, *origins and republic*) of Arpinum, he was born on 3 January 106 BC, the year following the first consulship of *Marius, with whose family (also from Arpinum) his grandmother Gratidia had marriage connections. His intelligent and ambitious father (who was to die in the year of Cicero's canvass for the consulship), advised perhaps by Lucius Licinius Crassus, gave his two sons an excellent education in philosophy and rhetoric in Rome and later in Greece, with their two first-cousins as their fellow students. Cicero did military service in 90/89 under *Pompey's father, Gnaeus Pompeius Strabo, and attended legal consultations of the two great Scaevolae (both called Quintus Mucius Scaevola). He conducted his first case in 81 (*Pro Quinctio*) and made an immediate reputation through his successful defence of Sextus Roscius of Ameria on a charge of parricide in 80, a case which reflected discreditably on the contemporary administration of the dictator *Sulla. Cicero was then from 79 to 77 a student of philosophy and oratory both in Athens and in *Rhodes, where he heard Posidonius; he visited Publius Rutilius Rufus at Smyrna.

He returned to Rome, his health greatly improved, to pursue a public career, and was elected quaestor for 75, when he served for a year in western Sicily, and praetor for 66, in each case at the earliest age at which he could legally become a candidate. By securing the condemnation of Gaius Verres for extortion in Sicily in 70 he scored a resounding success against Quintus Hortensius Hortalus, eight years his senior, whom he was to replace as the leading figure at the Roman bar. In a cleverly disarming speech delivered during his praetorship (*De imperio Cn. Pompei*) he supported, against strong opposition from the so-called 'optimates' ('best men', i.e. the office-holding upper class), the tribune Gaius Manilius' proposal to transfer the command in the war against *Mithradates to Pompey; this was the first public expression of his admiration for Pompey who was, with occasional short interruptions, henceforward to be the focus of his political allegiance. He was elected consul for 63—the first *novus homo* (first man from his family to reach the consulship) with no political background whatever since 94—because, in a poor field (including *Catiline, who had tried for the office twice before), his reputation as an orator and his cultivation of aristocrats, *equites*, and prominent Italians paid off. Hampered by a weak and indeed suspect colleague, Gaius Antonius 'Hybrida', Cicero did very well to secure evidence which convinced the senate of the seriousness of Catiline's conspiracy. After the 'last [i.e. emergency] decree' (*senatus consultum ultimum*) was passed, and Catiline left Rome for his army in Etruria, five conspirators prominent in Roman society and politics, including a praetor, Publius Cornelius Lentulus Sura, were arrested and executed on 5 December (the Nones). Although, after debate, the senate, influenced by *Cato the Younger, had recommended their execution, the act itself, a violation of the citizen's right to a trial, could be justified only by the passing of the last decree and was Cicero's personal responsibility. Though approved in the first moment of panic by all classes of society in Rome, its legality was strictly questionable, and Cicero was unwise to boast as loudly of it as he did (even in a long and indiscreet letter to Pompey in the east, *Sull.* 67, *Planc.* 85, cf. *Fam.* 5. 7). He published his speeches of 63, including those against Catiline, in 60, wrote of his action in prose and verse, in Greek and Latin, and invited others, including Posidonius, to do the same; and to the end of his life he never wavered in his belief that he had acted rightly and had saved Rome from catastrophe.

Though it was unlikely that he would escape prosecution, Cicero refused overtures from *Caesar, which might have saved him at the price of his political independence. In 58 Publius *Clodius Pulcher, whom he had antagonized in 61 when Clodius was charged with incest, moved a bill as *tribune re-enacting the law that anyone who had executed a citizen without trial should be banished. Without awaiting prosecution Cicero fled the country, to Macedonia, and Clodius passed a second bill, which Cicero regarded as unconstitutional, declaring him an exile. His house on the Palatine was destroyed by Clodius' gangsters, part of its site to be made a shrine of Liberty, and his villa at Tusculum was also badly damaged. With Pompey's belated support and with the support of the tribune Titus Annius Milo, who employed violence as irresponsibly as Clodius had done in the previous year, Cicero was recalled by a law of the people on 4 August 57 and was warmly welcomed on his return both in Italy and in Rome, which he reached on 4 September.

He returned to a busy winter, fighting to secure adequate public compensation for the damage to his property and, in the senate and in the courts, supporting those chiefly responsible for his recall. Hopes of dissociating Pompey from his close political connection with Caesar, attempts which Clodius was employed by Caesar to interrupt, were at an end when Caesar, Pompey, and *Crassus revived their political union at Luca in April 56, and Cicero was sharply brought to heel (*Att.* 4. 5, on his 'palinode' or recantation; cf. *Fam.* 1. 9 for his later account of his conversion). He at once spoke warmly in the senate (e.g. in *De provinciis consularibus*) and on the public platform in favour of Caesar, as of a long-standing political friend. He claimed that it was the act of a realist, a *sapiens*, to accept the indisputable predominance of the Three ('temporibus adsentiendum', *Fam.* 1. 9. 21) and only revealed in conversation and in letters to such close friends as T. Pomponius *Atticus the deep wound which his pride—his *dignitas*—had suffered. He took no more part in the collapsing world of republican politics, devoting himself to writing, which he never regarded as anything but a poor substitute for active political life (the *De oratore* was published in 55, and the *De republica* finished in 51); and he was humiliated by briefs which, under pressure from Pompey and Caesar, he was forced to accept. He defended Publius Vatinius successfully and Aulus Gabinius unsuccessfully in 54. He was humiliated too by his failure, in a court packed with troops, to defend Milo adequately when, with the case already prejudiced, Milo was impeached for the murder of Clodius early in 52. The period brought him one consolation, when he was elected augur in 53 or 52 in the place of his earlier protégé, young Publius Licinius Crassus, who had been killed at Carrhae (53 BC, the battle against *Parthia in which his father Crassus as commander was killed).

Cicero was out of Rome during the eighteen months preceding the outbreak of the Civil War, being selected under regulations following Pompey's *lex de provinciis* of 52 to govern Cilicia as proconsul from summer 51 to summer 50. He was a just, if not a strong, governor, but he regarded his appointment with horror as a second relegation from Rome. However, his dispatches recording the successful encounter of his troops with brigands on mons Amanus earned a *supplicatio* (ritual thanksgiving) at Rome and he returned, the *fasces* of his lictors wreathed in fading laurels, hoping that he might celebrate a triumph. Instead he was swept into the vortex of the Civil War.

Appointed district commissioner at Capua by the government, he did not at first follow Pompey and the consuls overseas. Caesar saw him at Formiae on 28 March 49, and invited him to join the rump of the senate in Rome on terms which with great resolution Cicero refused to accept (*Att.* 9. 11a, to Caesar; 9. 18). His long indecision up to this point, which was anything but discreditable, was now at an end, and he joined the republicans in Greece, irritating their leaders by his caustic criticism, himself dismayed by the absence of any idealistic loyalty on their part to the cause of republicanism. After the battle of Pharsalus (48 BC), in which he took no part, he refused Cato's invitation to assume command of the surviving republican forces and, pardoned by Caesar, he returned to Italy. But political life was at an end, and he was utterly out of sympathy with Caesar's domination. All that he could do was to return to his writing, his only important speech being that delivered in the senate in 46 (the year in which the *Brutus* was written) in praise of Caesar's pardon of Marcus Claudius Marcellus (consul 51), who had done so much to precipitate the outbreak of the Civil War.

That Cicero was not invited to participate in the conspiracy to kill Caesar in 44 is not insignificant. He hailed the news of the murder on 15 March with intemperate delight (e.g. *Fam.* 6. 15). Political life began again, and Cicero had all the prestige (*auctoritas*) of a senior consular. Within three months he was saying openly that Mark *Antony should have been killed too (*Att.* 15. 11. 2). He accepted the overtures of the young Caesar (Octavian; see AUGUSTUS), uncritical of the lawlessness of many of his acts, misled by his youth into a mistaken underassessment of his political acumen, and he closed his eyes to the fact that Octavian could never be reconciled to *Brutus and Cassius. He struggled in speech after speech (the *Philippics*, the first delivered on 2 September 44, the last on 21 April 43) to induce the senate to declare Antony a public enemy. After Antony's defeat in Cisalpine Gaul in April 43, Octavian fooled Cicero for a time, perhaps with the suggestion that they might both be consuls together. But Octavian's intentions were different. After his march on Rome to secure the consulship for himself and his uncle Quintus Pedius, and the formation of the Triumvirate, he did not oppose Antony's nomination of Cicero as a victim of the *proscriptions which were the inauguration of the new regime (for this phase see ROME (HISTORY) §1.5). The soldiers caught Cicero in a not very resolute attempt to escape by sea. His slaves did not desert him, and he died with courage on 7 December 43.

In politics he hated Clodius, with good reason, and he hated Marcus Crassus and, at the end of his life, Antony. For the character of Cato, eleven years his junior, he had unqualified respect, and he published a panegyric of Cato in 45, after his death; but in politics, especially in the years following Pompey's return from the east in 62, he thought Cato's uncompromising rigidity (his *constantia*) impolitic, and Cato never concealed his distaste for Cicero's policy of temporizing expediency, both at this period and when he capitulated to the Three in 56. With Pompey Cicero never established the intimacy to which, particularly after Pompey's return in 62, he aspired, suggesting that he might play a second Laelius to Pompey's Scipio. Few of his contemporaries, perhaps, held him in higher esteem than did his constant opponent Caesar who, though often with an imperiousness which Cicero could not tolerate, was always friendly in his approach. Cicero was not a discriminating judge of the political intentions of others, being far too susceptible to, and uncritical of, flattery; and he was inevitably condemned to a certain political isolation. Loyally and not very critically devoted to the existing republican constitution, and fascinated by the mirage of a political consensus ('concordia ordinum'), he was never a liberal reformer (*popularis*); yet he was never completely acceptable to the established *optimates*, the worst of whom despised his social origin, while the rest mistrusted his personality as much as he mistrusted theirs. And, not having the *clientela* of the noble or of the successful general, he lacked *auctoritas*. It was this political isolation which (cf. *Att.* 1. 17; 1. 18. 1, of 61/60 BC) enhanced the importance for him of his close association with the knight Titus Pomponius Atticus, a man of the highest culture in both Greek and Latin, his banker, financial adviser, publisher, and most generous and tolerant friend.

His marriage to Terentia had issue: a daughter Tullia, to whom he was devoted, whose death in 45 was the hardest of the blows which afflicted his private life, and a son called (like himself) Marcus Tullius Cicero. His marriage survived the storms and stress of thirty years, until he grew irritated with Terentia and divorced her in winter 47/6, to marry the young Publilia, from whom in turn he was almost immediately divorced. Cicero was a good master to his slaves and, with the rest of his family, was devoted to Tiro, to whom twenty-one of his letters in *Fam.* 16 are addressed. He gave him his freedom in 53, 'to be our friend instead of our slave', as his younger brother Quintus Tullius Cicero wrote (*Fam.* 16. 16. 1).

Cicero, who was never a really rich man, had eight country residences, in Campania, at Arpinum, at Formiae, and, his suburban villa, at Tusculum; in Rome he was extremely proud of his house on the Palatine, which he bought in 62 for 3½ million sesterces (*Fam.* 5. 6. 2).

Apart from the surviving histories of the late republic and, in particular, Plutarch's Lives of Cicero and of his outstanding contemporaries, the bulk of our knowledge of him derives from his own writings, in particular from his letters, only a minority of which were written with any thought of publication. His reputation has therefore suffered from the fact that we have intimate knowledge of the most private part of his personal life; in this respect he has been his own worst enemy, and his critics have given undue prominence to his extremes of exaltation and depression and to the frequent expression of his evident vanity. (See J. P. V. D. Balsdon, 'Cicero the Man', in T. A. Dorey (ed.), *Cicero* (1965).)

J. P. B.; M. T. G.

Works Speeches

Fifty-eight speeches of Cicero survive in whole or part; numerous others were unpublished or lost (88 are recorded by Crawford).

Cicero's normal practice, if he decided to publish a speech, was to 'write up' (*conficere*) a version after the event. In one case we know that he delivered a speech from a script (*Post reditum in senatu*); otherwise it seems that only a few important passages, chiefly the exordium and peroration, were written out *in extenso* beforehand. The published versions of court speeches in many instances certainly represent a shortened version of the actual proceedings, as shown by Humbert; the examination of witnesses is largely omitted, and some sections of argumentation are represented only by headings. The extent to which Cicero changed the content or emphasis of his speeches when preparing them for publication is disputed. It has been thought that the speeches were regularly altered to suit the political circumstances of the time of publication, rather than the time of delivery. On the other hand, it has been pointed out that Cicero's overt reason for publication was to provide examples of successful oratory for posterity to imitate and admire, and this would naturally place limits on the degree of alteration that could reasonably be made, as would the presence among his readership of a substantial number of those who had been present at the delivery of the speech.

In certain cases there is firm evidence that our text does not represent a speech that was actually delivered. The five speeches of the *Actio secunda in Verrem* were prepared for use in court but were never actually delivered, since Verres withdrew into exile after the *Actio prima*. The second *Philippic* was not delivered as a speech, but circulated as a pamphlet, although it observes the conventions of a senatorial speech. But these are exceptions. The *Pro Milone* is an exception in another way, being a rare example of an unsuccessful speech that was nevertheless published; our sources claim or imply that they had access to a transcript (complete with interruptions) of the actual speech, which differed from Cicero's published version, although it is not proved that the difference in content was much greater than in the case of most of Cicero's other speeches (J. N. Settle, *TAPA* 1963, 268–80).

Cicero's reputation as an orator depended on consistent practical success, although his detractors in antiquity made as much capital out of his relatively rare failures as their modern equivalents have done. In these successes a large part must have been played by his manner of delivery, of which virtually no impression can be given by a written speech; yet it is possible to see in the published versions something of the powers of advocacy that made Cicero the leading courtroom orator of his time (this has been brought out particularly clearly by Stroh). The political speeches are perhaps more difficult for a modern reader to appreciate: Cicero's self-glorifications and his unbridled invectives tend to repel those brought up in a modern western society, while adverse judgement of his political position can hinder appreciation of his oratory. It is easy to be cynical about what *Juvenal called the 'divine Philippic' (the Second) without coming to terms with the historical circumstances that produced this and other speeches, and the oratorical qualities that made them into objects of near-universal admiration.

The style of Cicero's speeches did not remain entirely uniform. As he himself observed, in his youth he had a tendency to exuberance (so-called Asianism), best exemplified in the *Pro Roscio Amerino* (cf. F. Solmsen, *TAPA* 1938, 542–56); this was later tempered by increasing maturity and by a change in oratorical fashion. The style also depended to some extent on the occasion; there are variations in manner between Cicero's addresses to senate and people, to a full jury, and to a single arbitrator, and Cicero himself talks of the different styles appropriate for the different sections of a speech (plain for narration, grand for the final appeal to the emotions, etc.). However, Cicero's speeches throughout his life are consistent in their rhythmical regularity, their smooth and balanced sentence-construction, and their careful choice of vocabulary and idiom (on the style of the speeches, see Laurand). Cicero's style was criticized by some of his contemporaries for lacking vigour (Tac. *Dial.* 18) and by later rhetoricians for longwindedness and lack of quotability (ibid. 22).

Cicero made good use of the theories of rhetoric current in his time, and, still more, of the great classical models of Athenian oratory. Most of the ancient structural conventions, figures of speech, and standard modes of argument can be exemplified from his writings, and some of the speeches were consistently taken as copy-book examples by later rhetoricians such as Quintilian; but Cicero never merely followed the rules for their own sake, and examples can be found of highly effective departures from the recommended practice of the rhetoricians.

Of the extant speeches, three belong to the period before Cicero's Sicilian quaestorship (*Pro Roscio Amerino*, from Cicero's first major public trial in 80 BC, together with *Pro Quinctio* and *Pro Roscio Comoedo*). Then follows the series of speeches from the trial of Verres in 70: *Divinatio in Caecilium*, the *Actio prima in Verrem*, and the five speeches of the *Actio secunda* generally referred to as the Verrines. The *Pro Tullio*, *Pro Fonteio*, and *Pro Caecina* date from 69. Two of the extant speeches belong to Cicero's praetorship, the *Pro lege Manilia* (alias *De imperio Cn. Pompei*) and the *Pro Cluentio*. Of the 'consular' orations which Cicero himself published (a collection of twelve according to *Att.* 2. 1. 3; but see W. C. McDermott, *Philologus* 1972, 277–84), we have the three speeches *De lege agraria contra Rullum*, the *Pro Rabirio perduellionis reo*, and the four Catilinarians; the *Pro Murena* also dates from this year. From the years succeeding the consulship the *Pro Sulla*, *Pro Archia* (both 62), and *Pro Flacco* (59) survive. Another group is formed by the speeches made on returning from exile in 57 and in the following year: *Post reditum in senatu*, *Post reditum ad Quirites*, *De domo sua*, *De haruspicum responsis*, *Pro Sestio*, *In Vatinium interrogatio*. To the year 56 also belong the senatorial speech *De provinciis consularibus* and the defences of Caelius Rufus and Lucius Cornelius Balbus; the invective *In Pisonem* was published in 55. From 54 we have the *Pro Plancio* and the *Pro Rabirio Postumo*. In 52, Cicero defended Titus Annius Milo without success, publishing a version of the speech before departing to govern Cilicia. In 46–45, Cicero addressed the victorious Caesar on behalf of Marcus Claudius Marcellus, Ligarius, and King Deiotarus of Galatia. Otherwise Caesar's dictatorship offered no opportunity for Cicero to exercise his forensic gifts, and he devoted himself to the writing of treatises on rhetoric and philosophy. During his brief return to public life in 44–43, Cicero delivered the series of speeches known (at his own joking suggestion: *Ad Brut.* 2. 3. 4) as the *Philippics*, which directly or indirectly expressed his opposition to Mark *Antony; cf. DEMOSTHENES. Fourteen of these survive; at least three more have been lost.

Works on Rhetoric

(a) *De inventione*, written in Cicero's youth, is a treatise on some techniques of rhetorical argument, which has a close resemblance to parts of the anonymous *Rhetorica ad Herennium* (once falsely attributed to Cicero).

(b) *De oratore* (55 BC), *Brutus*, and *Orator* (46) represent Cicero's major contribution to the theory of (Latin) *rhetoric, and he himself grouped them with his philosophical works. They present an idealized picture of the orator as a liberally educated master of his art, a picture in which the technical aspects of Greek rhetorical theory still have their place, but are supplemented by knowledge of literature, philosophy, and general culture, and by the qualities of character required of the ideal Roman aristocrat. This was endorsed by later Roman authors such as *Quintilian, and it was one of the formative influences on Renaissance ideals of character and education. The *De oratore* was closely linked with the more ambitious *De republica* which followed it, and the ideal orator depicted in the former is little different from the ideal statesman in the latter. The *Brutus* is devoted largely to a history of Roman oratory, while the *Orator* deals with more technical points of style. These last two works were written against a background of controversy regarding the desirable style or styles in oratory, in the course of which Cicero had been criticized for persisting (as it seemed) in the 'Asian' fashions of his younger days, and a plain 'Attic' style had been held up as an ideal. Cicero reacts to this by attempting to demonstrate that different styles are effective for different purposes, that there was more variety in actual Athenian oratory than the 'Atticists' allowed, and that the ideal orator should be master of several styles, including (where appropriate) the Ciceronian grand manner itself, for which *Demosthenes, rather than the Asian rhetoricians, is claimed as a precedent. Although this controversy was in some senses an ephemeral one, these works contain much of interest concerning the way Roman orators regarded their art, and the *Brutus* is a mine of prosopographical information (see PROSOPOGRAPHY) as well as of Roman rhetorical criticism.

(*c*) Cicero's minor works on the subject comprise: *Partitiones oratoriae*, a dialogue in which Cicero instructs his son in the elements of the art (the date is uncertain, but it must belong to a time at which Cicero's son was approaching maturity); *Topica*, written in 44 BC and dedicated to Gaius Trebatius Testa, an exposition of the content of *Aristotle's work of the same title; and *De optimo genere oratorum*, of disputed authenticity, an introduction to translations (which may or may not have existed) of *Aeschines' *In Ctesiphontem* and Demosthenes' *De corona*.

Poems

Cicero early acquired a reputation as a bad poet on the basis of two lines from his autobiographical compositions, 'o fortunatam natam me consule Romam' ('O happy Rome, born in my consulship') and 'cedant arma togae, concedat laurea laudi' ('yield arms to the toga, the bay to achievement') (the variant *linguae* 'to the tongue', was probably satirical). The only obvious faults of these lines are a naïve self-esteem and a somewhat old-fashioned taste for assonance; in general, Cicero was a competent enough versifier, and despite his admiration for the older poets, his verse technique is more modern than that of his contemporary *Lucretius. He appears at times to have had serious poetic ambitions and to have regarded verse-writing as more than an amateur's accomplishment. It is perhaps less surprising in an ancient than it would be in a modern context that he chose to make verse a vehicle for personal propaganda, in the *Consulatus suus* (of which a substantial passage is quoted by Cicero himself in *Div.* 1. 17) and *De temporibus suis*. Apart from these, Cicero composed an original (probably fairly short) epic poem on his fellow Arpinate *Marius; this must have been in circulation in the 50s BC (he refers to it at the beginning of the *De legibus*). The only part of his poetry to survive in a manuscript tradition is the so-called *Aratea*, 469 lines from a verse translation of Aratus' *Phaenomena*; this is of interest as part of the tradition of adapting Hellenistic didactic poetry and as a precursor of *Virgil's *Georgics*. There are some other scattered fragments of lost poems, and Cicero translated a number of passages of Greek poetry ad hoc for quotation in his philosophical works (in preference to the original Greek).

Letters

Cicero's surviving correspondence is an invaluable collection of evidence for his biography, for the history of the time, and for Roman social life. The sixteen books *Ad familiares* were published after Cicero's death by his freedman Tiro. Cicero's letters to *Atticus were preserved (without the replies) by the latter and seen by Cornelius Nepos (Nep. *Att.* 16. 2–4, referring to a collection in 11 books). They were in circulation in the reign of Nero and later, but the silence of Asconius suggests that they were not available to him. Our present collection *Ad Atticum* consists of sixteen books, probably an augmented version of the collection known to Nepos. We also have the smaller collections *Ad Quintum fratrem* (including the *Commentariolum petitionis*) and *Ad Brutum*. Further collections of Cicero's letters apparently existed in antiquity. The *Ad familiares* collection contains, in addition to Cicero's own, letters from a variety of correspondents to him.

The letters were not in any sense written for publication; as far as is known, it was not until 44 BC that Cicero thought of publishing a selection of them (*Att.* 16. 5. 5; cf. *Fam.* 16. 17. 1), and it is not clear that this idea was ever put into practice in that form. They vary greatly in their level of formality. At the one extreme they include official dispatches and letters of a semi-public nature on matters of political importance, whose style is similar to that of the public speeches; at the other may be found casual notes to members of the family and informal exchanges with Atticus, often highly allusive and colloquial.   J. G. F. P.

Philosophica

Apart from the treatises on rhetoric, an important part of the Hellenistic philosophical curriculum (though see below), these fall into two parts: (*a*) the writings on political philosophy and statecraft of the years immediately preceding Cicero's governorship of Cilicia, and (*b*) the works on epistemology, ethics, and theology (standing in the place of physics) which were produced in the incredibly short period between February 45 and November 44. Cicero gives a list and account of his own philosophical writings at *Div.* 2. 1.

In the *De republica*, a dialogue between *Scipio Aemilianus, Gaius Laelius, and others, of which we have only parts of the six books (including the *Somnium Scipionis*, preserved as a whole by Macrobius), Cicero discusses the ideal state, always with an eye on the history of the Roman republic, and favours a constitution combining elements of all three main forms, monarchy, oligarchy, and democracy. His discussion reflects the political conditions of the time and looks to a wise counsellor (for which part Cicero may at one time have cast *Pompey) as a remedy for Rome's political sickness. But its chief attraction for posterity lay in its assertion of human rights and of man's participation in humanity and the cosmos, a notion which eclectic developments in *Stoicism and Cicero's own predilections helped to foster. Cicero probably worked on the *De legibus* immediately after the *De republica* (cf. *Leg.* 1. 15), but did not publish it. (It does not appear in the list in *Div.* 2. 1 ff., and is not specifically mentioned in the letters.) In the three extant books (Macrobius quotes from a fifth book, and the reference to *iudicia* in 3. 47 has generally been taken to point to the subject of the fourth book) Cicero expounds the Stoic conception of divinely sanctioned Law, based on reason, and discusses legal enactments connected with religion and magistracies, drawing heavily on the 2nd-cent. BC Stoic Diogenes of Babylon.

Politically inactive under Caesar's dictatorship, the death of his daughter Tullia finally led Cicero to seek consolation in writing about philosophical subjects which had always interested him, from the early days of his studies under the Epicureans Phaedrus and Zeno of Sidon (cf. EPICURUS), the Academics Philo of Larissa, Antiochus of Ascalon, at Athens and on *Rhodes the Stoic Posidonius, through the years of his association with Diodotus the Stoic (who lived and died in his own home), to the time immediately after the Civil War, when Gaius Matius urged him to write on philosophy in troubled times (*Fam.* 11. 27. 5). What had formerly been for Cicero a useful exercise (cf. *Tusc.* 2. 9, and his claim at *Orat.* 12 to be a product of the *Academy rather than of the rhetoricians' workshops) and a source of oratorical material (cf. *De or.* 1. 5 and *Orat.* 113 ff.; the *Paradoxa Stoicorum*, published, it seems, as late as the beginning of 46, may be an exercise in the preparation of such material) became now a haven of refuge (*Fam.* 7. 30. 2), a *doloris medicina* (*Acad. post.* 1. 11). Cicero needed to reassure himself, and hoped as well to make a name for himself as a philosophical writer (at *Off.* 1. 2 ff. he admits his inferior philosophical knowledge, but contraposes his virtues as a stylist). But Cicero was well prepared for the task, having learnt Stoic dialectic from Diodotus, rhetoric and arguing both sides of a question from the Peripatetics, while the Academics had taught him to refute any argument. In addition Cicero had heard, and listened carefully, to the most charismatic philosophers of his time, the showmen of the day. He had a profound admiration and respect for *Plato (*deus ille noster*—'our divine Plato': *Att.* 4. 16. 3) and *Aristotle. His claim to look to *Socrates (*Acad.* 1. 3) belies his sceptical method of inquiry and emphasis on ethics. He aimed above all at giving the Romans a philosophical literature and terminology, which would take the place of the Greek philosophers, on whom the Romans had been hitherto intellectually dependent. The surviving work of the Hellenistic philosophers suggests that Cicero would not be alone in following his Greek sources closely in order to engage them polemically. But some scholars have understood Cicero's words: '*apographa* sunt, minore labore fiunt; verba tantum adfero quibus abundo' ('They are copies. They're no trouble. I just bring the words, and I've plenty of them': *Att.* 12. 52. 3) too seriously (i.e. without a hint of false modesty), and Shackleton Bailey has suggested that they do not even pertain to the *philosophica*. More trustworthy are Cicero's claims (*Off.* 1. 6) to follow the Stoics (in that work) not as a mere translator but drawing from Stoic sources as he thinks fit, and (*Fin.* 1. 6) to add his own criticism (*iudicium*) and arrangement (*scribendi ordo*) to the chosen authority.

Several lost works probably came first: a *De gloria* (a eulogy of *Cato the Younger); the *Consolatio*, an attempt to console himself for the loss of his daughter Tullia (and unique in being addressed to himself); and the *Hortensius*, a plea for the study of philosophy, which profoundly affected St *Augustine (it turned him to God: *Conf.* 3. 4. 7). The list in *Div.* 2. 1 shows that Cicero swiftly proceeded with the construction of what is by his own description an encyclopaedia of Hellenistic philosophy: the protreptic *Hortensius* is followed by the *Academica*, on epistemology or theory of knowledge (especially concerned with the criterion of truth), originally in two books, entitled *Catulus* and *Lucullus*, of which only the second survives, but later recast in four books, of which we possess part of the first (*Academica posteriora*). It treats of the views of the New Academy after Arcesilaus, and in particular of Carneades on the impossibility of attaining certain knowledge, but conceding some *realia* as more compelling or probable than others. The recommendation (*Div.* 2. 150) to give unprejudiced consideration to different theories before approving *simillima veri* appealed to Cicero, who sometimes portrayed himself as belonging to this philosophical school (*Tusc.* 2. 5, 4. 47). In fact Cicero remained generally true to Philon's early teaching, rejecting the possibility of certain knowledge, but retaining and asserting the right to adopt whatever position seemed most compelling on each occasion.

Thus in questions of ethics Cicero often inclined towards Stoic doctrine as he recoiled from the Epicurean, as is evident in the *De finibus bonorum et malorum*, where he compiles and answers in turn the theories on the *summum bonum* ('highest good') propounded by the Epicureans and Stoics, before giving the views of Antiochus' so-called 'Old Academy' in book 5. From this encyclopaedic survey of the various schools' positions on ethics, Cicero turned in the *Tusculan Disputations* to the problems of the psychology of the happy life: death, grief, pain, fear, passion, and other mental disorders, and of what is essential for happiness, including (according to the Stoics) virtue. Concerned largely to allay his own doubts, and impressed by Stoic teaching on these subjects, he writes here with a passionate intensity and lyrical beauty.

As in the case of the contemporary Epicurean Philodemus, theological speculation stands for Cicero in the place of a full account of natural philosophy and physical causes (such as is found, for example, in *Lucretius, Epicurus, or Chrysippus, though *Tusc.* 1 also treats materialism in its concern for the material composition of the soul and a rational chain of causation). Thus Cicero next composes *De natura deorum* in three books, each devoted to the view of a different school (Epicurean, Stoic, Academic) on the nature of the gods and the existence of the divine, its role in human culture and the state. Having allowed Cotta to present the sceptical Academic view in book 3, after Velleius' presentation of the Epicurean in book 1, and Balbus' of the Stoic in book 2, Cicero rounds off the debate with a typically Academic expression of his own opinion: that the Stoic's argument is more likely to be right (*ad veritatis similitudinem ... propensior* 3. 95). In a later work, Stoic beliefs concerning Fate and the possibility of prediction are examined, with more use of anecdote and quotation perhaps indicative of a popular exposition, in the two books of the *De divinatione*, published just after Caesar's murder (*Div.* 2. 4). In this case Cicero displays no sympathy with the views of the Stoics, whose commitment to the validity of divination was based on complex principles of logic and cosmic sympathy. Cicero's pious reaffirmation (2. 148) of his belief in the existence of a divine being, maintaining that it is prudent to keep traditional rites and ceremonies, belies his concerns in matters of theology and religion for the state above all else. Finally, the fragmentary *De fato* discusses the more specialized problem of volition and decides against Stoic determinism.

Equally specialized are the two genial and polished essays *Cato Maior de senectute* (written probably just before Caesar's murder and included in *Div.* list) and the *Laelius de amicitia*, which show once again Cicero's anxiety to reassure or occupy himself in times of stress and danger, and his last work on moral philosophy, *De officiis* (finished November 44), aims at giving advice, based on Stoic precepts and in particular (for books 1 and 2) on the teachings of Panaetius, on a variety of problems of conduct (ostensibly to Cicero's son).

These three works, along with the *Tusc.* and the *Somnium Scipionis*, were the most popular among readers in the Middle Ages, when the work of Cicero the politician and orator was almost forgotten, to be rediscovered in the Renaissance. Cicero's influence on European thought and literature ensured that what he found interesting and important in Greek philosophy became the philosophical curriculum of the Renaissance and Enlightenment. His achievement stands out as the creator of philosophical vocabulary in Latin, and as a philosophical stylist.

J. H. S.; D. O.

Ligurians; actual registration in the Roman census, however, remained very incomplete.

The last generation of the Roman republic and the civil wars which followed witnessed demands for citizenship in those areas of Italy which still did not have it—demands which were satisfied by *Caesar—and the increasing spread of citizenship overseas as a reward for service of one kind or another, in the Greek world as well as in the west. In the established imperial system, Roman citizens enjoyed in theory and often in practice protection against the *imperium* of a provincial governor, and a relatively favourable tax status.

Roman citizenship continued to spread, for three principal reasons. (1) Communities were granted Latin status and their magistrates automatically acquired Roman citizenship, a right which was probably created after the Social War for new Latin communities north of the Po and perhaps in Liguria. (2) Citizenship was granted to auxiliaries and their families on discharge. (3) Legionaries were supposed to be recruited among citizens only, but were clearly also recruited among provincials and deemed to be citizens. Their families on their discharge—between *Augustus and *Septimius Severus serving soldiers could not marry—if their wives were of citizen status, helped to spread Roman citizenship. (4) In the East, from *Pompey on, citizenship was conferred on individuals, typically members of the provincial city-élites.

Citizenship was finally granted to virtually all the free population of the empire by *Caracalla, in the so-called Antonine constitution. But by this time, the right to vote had long disappeared; provincial Romans had lost their exemption from taxation; and many of the most important personal privileges of citizenship had been restricted to the élite, the *honestiores*, as opposed to the *humiliores*. And thereafter the essential distinction was between slave and free—which also in due course became less important with the depression of the status of the free tenant—and, within those who were still free men, between *honestiores* and *humiliores*.

M. H. C.

Civil Wars, Roman See ROME (HISTORY).

citizenship, Roman Grants of Roman citizenship were the most important of the privileges conferred on veteran auxiliaries in the Roman imperial army. This Latin 'diploma' (two inscribed bronze tablets wired together) records a grant to one Gemellus on 17 July AD 122.

Claros (see ◀Map 1, Ec▶), *oracle and grove of *Apollo belonging to the city of Colophon (western Asia Minor). The oracle appears to have been founded by the 8th cent. BC, as stories about its foundation appear in the *Epigoni* (attributing the foundation to Manto), *Hesiod mentions the site in connection with a contest between the seers Calchas and Mopsus, and it is mentioned as a residence of Apollo in the Homeric *Hymn to Apollo*. The sanctuary was discovered 1907, and an excavation, begun under the direction of Louis Robert in the 1950s, turned up the oracular chamber under the temple and numerous inscriptions relating to its operation. On the basis of these inscriptions and literary texts, we know that there were 'sacred nights' upon which the consultations would take place, when there would be a procession of consultants to the temple of Apollo with sacrifices and singing of hymns. Consultants would then hand over questions to the priests who would descend into the adytum (innermost sanctuary), through the blue marble-faced corridors underneath the temple, to a place outside the room in which the divine spring flowed. Within this room the *thespiōdos*, a man, would drink from the spring and utter his responses to the questions of each consultant. These would then be written down in verse by the *prophētēs* and delivered to the consultants. An inscription of Hellenistic date confirms *Tacitus' statement that the Colophonians imported people of Ionian Greek descent to act as prophets (*thespiōdoi*), though he confuses the issue by mentioning only one official instead of two.

Inscriptions are now revealing the nature of Claros' clientele among the cities of Asia Minor and further afield in greater detail. These inscriptions, along with various discussions in the literature of the empire, reveal that Claros was one of the most important oracular sites in Asia Minor from roughly the 3rd cent. BC to the mid-3rd cent. AD. A number of responses are preserved on inscriptions and in the *Tübingen Theosophy*.   D. S. P.

class struggle, as a concept and phrase, is indelibly associated with the Marxist tradition of socio-historical analysis and practical political endeavour. 'The history of all hitherto existing society is the history of class struggles', is the opening sentence of the first main section of *The Communist Manifesto* (1848). Karl Marx, moreover, did not only apply the phrase to the societies of Greece and Rome (among others) but also acknowledged his debt to the 'giant thinker' *Aristotle for demonstrating, as he saw it, the general utility of the concept for historical analysis and explanation. See MARXISM AND CLASSICAL ANTIQUITY. Marx, however, nowhere in his voluminous writings gave an extended and coherent definition of 'class', which remains one of the most essentially contested terms in all socio-historical theory. His omission has been variously repaired by historians sympathetic to Marxist theory. Conversely, the very applicability and utility of any definition of class for the understanding of Greece and Rome have been equally passionately denied.

Economic class is an objective actuality, a relationship subsisting among persons similarly placed in an economic system. But when used as a dynamic term of historical analysis, or a fortiori as a political slogan, it may comport also a psychological ingredient of self-consciousness, so that membership of a certain economic class may crucially determine the members' conscious behaviour towards each other and towards members of another class or classes. Economic classes, moreover, in order properly to constitute classes, are usually thought of as being in some relation of hierarchy and antagonism towards each other. Definition of class-membership is difficult enough for any society, but it is often held that the societies of Greece and Rome raise peculiarly recalcitrant obstacles.

Suppose that people are classed according to their relationship to the means and labour of economic production: between those who do and do not own such means, between those who do or do not have to work for a living and/or for others. Are the richest Roman senator (see SENATE) and the non-working owner of a relatively modest pottery manufactory therefore to be placed in the same class? Or consider ownership of land, always the most basic and coveted means of production. In most Greek cities at most periods non-citizens were normally debarred from legal ownership of land, even if they happened to possess the economic means to work it (see CITIZENSHIP, GREEK). That legal obstacle could be circumvented by leasing land from others, but would that place the lessee in the same class as the citizen lessor?

If class definition is problematic for the ancient world, so too is the identification of class struggle. In so far as chattel slaves were legally rightless and limitlessly exploitable productive labourers, they stood in a relationship of class to their masters and mistresses, but in what sense could they be said to have conducted a 'class struggle' against them? Outright slave revolts (see SLAVERY) were rare, and there is little or no sense of a shared consciousness of identity and purpose among them. On the other hand, the masters and mistresses may justly be held to have waged a constant class struggle against their slaves, with the aid of those free non-slaveowners who identified their interests with the maintenance of the institution of slavery (as practically all ancient free people almost always did).

By contrast, in political struggles within the citizen estates of the Greek world (*stasis*), as in the city of Rome under the late republic, there is no doubting the high degree of self-conscious solidarity between the two great antagonistic groups of the 'rich' and the 'poor' (otherwise known as 'the few' and 'the many', and a host of other binary terms). Since the root of their antagonism lay in differential ownership of the means of production, and the aim of their struggle was often the control of the organs of government, this looks very much like class struggle—except that the classes are defined not purely by economic but by a mixture of economic and legal criteria, and the solidarity of 'the poor' was less organic and more soluble than that of 'the rich'.

P. A. C.

Claudius (Tiberius Claudius Nero Germanicus), 10 BC–AD 54, the emperor Claudius I, born at Lugdunum, Lyons (1 August), the youngest child of Nero Claudius Drusus (the younger brother of *Tiberius) and of Antonia (Mark *Antony's younger daughter). Hampered by a limp, trembling, and a speech defect, all perhaps due to cerebral palsy, and by continual illnesses, he received no public distinction from *Augustus beyond the augurate, and was twice refused a magistracy by Tiberius. Enactments of AD 20, the *tabula Siarensis* (ZPE 55 (1984), 58 f., fr. 1, II. 6f.; 19–21) and the *senatus consultum de Cn. Pisone patre* (ed. W. Eck and others, forthcoming) I. 148, like Tac. *Ann.* 3. 18. 4, illustrate his low position in the imperial family. Claudius retained the status of a knight until on 1 July 37 he became suffect consul with his young nephew, the emperor *Gaius; for the rest of the reign he received little but insults. What role, if any, he played in planning the assassination of Gaius in 41 is disputed. After the murder he was discovered in the palace by a soldier, taken to the praetorian barracks, and saluted emperor while the *senate was still discussing the possibility of restoring the republic. Senators did not easily forgive him for the way he came to power, but he had the support of the army: the revolt of Lucius Arruntius Camillus Scribonianus in Dalmatia (42) was short-lived. Claudius stressed his bond with guard and legions and, making up for previous inexperience, briefly took a personal part in the invasion of *Britain (43). The capture of Camulodunum occasioned an impressive pageant, and Claudius made a leisurely progress back to Rome for his *triumph (44). By the end of his principate he had received 27 salutations as *imperator*, more than any other emperor until *Constantine I. He was also consul four more times (42, 43, 47, and 51), and revived the office of censor, which he held with his favourite Lucius Vitellius in 47–8.

Although he reverted from the pretentious absolutism of Gaius (whose acts, however, were not annulled wholesale), and stressed civility to the senate, the precariousness of his position made him liable to take sudden and violent action against threats real, imagined by himself, or thought up by advisers; offenders who were given a trial were often heard by few advisers in private. His early career and mistrust of the senate led him to rely on the advice of freedmen, especially Narcissus and Pallas, whose influence and wealth were hated; but his dependence on his third and fourth wives Valeria *Messal(l)ina and Iulia *Agrippina was due as much to their political importance as to uxoriousness. Messallina was the mother of his only surviving son Britannicus, born 41 (Claudius' earlier wives, Plautia Urgulanilla and Aelia Paetina, left him only with a daughter, Antonia). She was hard to dislodge for that reason, but fell in 48, in what looks like a struggle between freedmen on the one hand and senators and knights on the other. Agrippina, daughter of Claudius' popular brother *Germanicus, was a figure in her own right, and particularly desirable after the loss of face entailed by Messallina's fall. Nero, the son she brought with her, was more than

three years older than Britannicus, and in 50 he was adopted by Claudius as a partner for his own son to assure their joint accession to power; in 53 Nero married Claudius' daughter Claudia Octavia. But while Nero's career was accelerated, with a grant of proconsular power outside Rome coming in 51, Britannicus was pushed aside. Claudius' death on 13 October 54 conveniently made it impossible for him to give his natural son the toga of manhood, but the story that he was poisoned by Agrippina has been questioned.

In youth Claudius wrote works on Etruscan and Carthaginian history (see ETRUSCANS; CARTHAGE). From *Livy he acquired a knowledge of Roman history, and he was steeped in religion and tradition, but his celebration of the Secular (hundred-year) Games (47), extension of the *pomerium* (Rome's religious boundary), and taking of the *augurium salutis* ('augury of security', 49) had the political purpose of reassuring the Roman people about the stability and success of his regime.

Claudius paid particular attention to the welfare of the populace. Building the harbour at *Ostia and draining the Fucine Lake (central Italy) were intended to secure or increase the grain supply, as was his offer of privileges to those who invested in the construction of grain ships.

Claudius' interest in government, from which he had been excluded, inclined him to intervene whenever he found anything amiss, and he berated senators who failed to take an active part in debate. He was particularly interested in jurisdiction, and was indefatigable, if emotional and inconsistent, in dispensing justice. Legislation had clear aims: to discourage sedition; to protect inheritance within the clan and the rights of individual property owners; more 'liberal' measures increased the rights of slaves, women, and minors. Arguments for his legislation invoked traditional *mores* and the upholding of status, but in his senatorial speech advocating the admission of Gauls to the senate, Claudius' preoccupation with the place of innovation in Roman life shows him coming to terms with changes in economy and society.

Claudius was noted for generosity with the citizenship, though his advisers also sold it without his knowledge. (See CITIZENSHIP, ROMAN.) A few widespread grants of Latin rights, along with his favourable response to the request of long-enfranchised Gallic chieftains for permission to stand for senatorial office (resented by existing senators), made him seem more generous than he was: proved merit was his own criterion for grants. Administrative changes have also been given undue weight, as also the influence of the *freedmen, who were emerging in previous reigns and have wrongly been claimed to have become the equivalent of modern 'ministers' as part of a policy of 'centralization'. Claudius' grant of additional jurisdiction to provincial *procurators, and the introduction of that title for equestrian governors of provinces, previously called 'prefects', simply relieved him of the job of hearing appeals and stressed the dependence of the governors upon their emperor.

Claudius added other provinces to the empire besides

Claudius Sardonyx cameo (see GEMS) portraying Claudius in the guise of *Jupiter (mid.-1st cent. AD). Since cameos circulated in private, they offered a medium for more overt imperial self-advertisement than was usually thought suitable for public monuments.

Cleopatra VII

171

Britain, although that left few resources for an active policy against the Germans: the two Mauretanias (whose last king, Ptolemy, had been executed by Gaius), Lycia (43), and Thrace (46); and he resumed overseas colonization. His dealings with Judaea and the Parthians, however, were inept. In Judaea (see JEWS) the procurators who replaced the deceased King Agrippa I in 44 proved unsatisfactory, and by 54 Claudius' eastern governors had allowed the Parthians to gain control of Greater Armenia, a serious blow to Roman prestige.

Claudius was deified on death, enhancing his adoptive son's prestige, but in Nero's early years the failings of the regime (influence of women and freedmen, corruption, trials held in private, the bypassing of the senate, favour to provincials), were excoriated: *Seneca's *Apocolocyntosis* reveals the tone. Under *Vespasian a more balanced view prevailed and Claudius' temple was completed, but *Tacitus, though he exploits Claudius' speeches, is merciless. Modern writers have overreacted, exaggerating his purposefulness in encouraging the development of the provinces; his accession and survival, preserving the imperial peace, and his recognition of social changes were his main domestic achievements.   J. P. B.; B. M. L.

Cleisthenes, Athenian politician, of the Alcmaeonid family, son of Megacles and Agariste, daughter of Cleisthenes tyrant of Sicyon. He was archon (magistrate) under the Pisistratid tyrant Hippias in 525/4 BC, but later in Hippias' reign the Alcmaeonids went into exile and put pressure on Sparta through the *Delphic oracle to intervene in Athens and overthrow the tyranny. In the power vacuum which followed, Cleisthenes and Isagoras were rivals for supremacy; Isagoras obtained the archonship (the supreme magistracy) for 508/7; but Cleisthenes appealed for popular support with a programme of reform. Isagoras appealed to King Cleomenes I of *Sparta, who came to Athens with a small force, invoked the hereditary curse of the Alcmaeonids, and forced Cleisthenes and others to withdraw; but he met with strong popular resistance and was forced to withdraw in turn, taking Isagoras with him. Cleisthenes returned, and his reforms were enacted and put into effect.

Cleisthenes' main achievement was a new organization of the citizen body. The four Ionian tribes (*phylai*) and other older units were left in existence but deprived of political significance. For the future each citizen was to be a member of one of 139 local units called 'demes' (*demoi*), and the demes were grouped to form 30 new *trittyes* ('thirds') and 10 new *phylai*; citizenship and the political and military organization of Attica were to be based on these units (e.g. *Solon's council, *boulē*, of 400 became a council of 500, with 50 members from each tribe and individual demes acting as constituencies). The main purpose of the reform was probably to undermine the old channels of influence (and perhaps to give the Alcmaeonids an advantageous position in the new system); its main appeal to the ordinary citizens was perhaps the provision of political

machinery at local level; and working this machinery educated the citizens towards democracy. (See DEMOCRACY, ATHENIAN.) The institution of *ostracism is almost certainly to be attributed to Cleisthenes.

In the 5th cent. Cleisthenes came to be regarded as the founder of the democracy, but in the political disputes at the end of the century the democrats looked further back, to Solon or even to *Theseus.   T. J. C.; P. J. R.

Cleopatra VII (69–30 BC), the final and best known of the Ptolemies (see EGYPT (Ptolemaic)), was daughter of Ptolemy XII (Auletes). On the latter's death in 51 she became queen, alone at first and subsequently with her younger brothers, first Ptolemy XIII (who opposed Caesar) and then (47–45) with Ptolemy XIV. A joint reign with Ptolemy XV Caesar (Caesarion, reputedly Caesar's son) is recorded from 45 BC. Her later children by Mark Antony were the twins Alexander and Cleopatra (b. 40 BC after Antony's winter in *Alexandria), and Ptolemy Philadelphus (b. 36). In 37/6 she marked Antony's gift to her of Chalcis in Syria by instituting a double numeration of her regnal years (year 16 = 1). She died at her own hand (and the bite of a royal asp) soon after Octavian (see AUGUSTUS) took Alexandria on 3 August 30.

Best known for her successful relations first with *Caesar who besieged and captured Alexandria in 48–47, and later with Mark *Antony, following a colourful encounter at Tarsus (SE *Asia Minor) in 41, she managed to increase her kingdom territorially in return for financial support. Caesar restored *Cyprus to Egypt and in 34, in a magnificent ceremony at Alexandria, Cleopatra appeared as Isis (see EGYPTIAN DEITIES) to mark the division of the earlier kingdom of *Alexander the Great between the royal couple and their children. Cleopatra ruled Egypt and and Caesarion Cyprus as Queen of Kings and King of Kings; Antony's children Alexander Helios (the Sun) and Ptolemy Philadelphus were named kings east and west of the Euphrates respectively, with Cleopatra Selene (the Moon) queen of *Cyrene. The symbolism of the ceremony was more important than any reality.

Internally Cleopatra was strong, using her position as pharaoh to gain backing from all the people. To her title of Philopator ('father-loving') was added Philopatris ('loving her country') (*BGU* 14. 2377. 1) and her support for the traditional Egyptian bull-cults is recorded at both Memphis and Armant. In the final struggle against Octavian, however, she confiscated temple lands. In Greek she was known also as Thea Neotera, 'the younger goddess'. An expert linguist, she was reportedly the first Ptolemy to have known Egyptian, and *Plutarch reports it was her conversation rather than her looks which formed the secret of her success.

The legend of Cleopatra has proved even more powerful than her historical record. Thanks to her successful liaisons with men of power she was named as the author of treatises on hairdressing and cosmetics. Her exploitation of Egyptian royal symbolism with its eastern tradition

Cleopatra VII Silver coin inscribed 'Queen Cleopatra, the younger goddess', minted c.34 BC. In *Plutarch's view her success lay in her conversation, not her looks.

of luxury was used against her by her antagonists; for Roman poets she was 'monster' and 'wicked woman'. Her visit to Rome in 46–44 achieved little but embarrassment for Caesar. Following his murder, her attempts to aid the Caesarians in 42 were thwarted by Cassius (one of Caesar's murderers), and by contrary winds. The summons to Tarsus by Antony followed. Her liaison with Antony formed the focus of Octavian's propaganda, based on fear of Egyptian wealth. Yet the skilful manipulation of power by this queen preserved Egypt from the direct rule of Rome longer than might otherwise have been the case. See ACTIUM. D. J. T.

climate The ancient climate was very similar to the modern climate. The Mediterranean climate is character-ized by cool, wet winters and hot, dry summers. There is a very high degree of interannual climatic variability, which makes farming (see AGRICULTURE) risky and sometimes causes *famines. The ordinary run of interannual climatic variability is taken for granted by literary sources. Only exceptional years stood a chance of being recorded. The rain, predominantly in winter, is usually adequate for dry-farming of cereals, and for evergreen trees resistant to the summer drought. However, it is not sufficient for dense coniferous or deciduous forests. Westerly winds bring most of the rain, so that areas in the rain shadow on the eastern side of Greece, e.g. Attica (the rural territory of

Athens), are much drier than regions in western Greece. Rainfall often takes the form of short, intense showers. It runs off the land and does not help plants. There are sta-tistical correlations between cereal yields, total annual pre-cipitation, and the monthly distribution of rainfall during the year. The winters generally remain warm enough for plants like the olive-tree, with a low degree of frost toler-ance, while the summers are hot enough to support sub-tropical vegetation. The Mediterranean climate and much of the flora associated with it is quite young in terms of geological time. For ancient views on the weather see *Aristotle's *Meteorologica*, and Theophrastus, *On Weather Signs*.

Various methods are used to investigate the ancient climate. Palynology (pollen studies) enables us to make inferences about climate by examining the geographical distribution in antiquity of plants with known climatic requirements. Theophrastus' botanical works also indicate that the mean temperature c.300 BC was within a degree of modern values. In the future the most important source of information will probably be tree-ring studies. We can con-struct tree-ring chronologies (dendrochronology) reaching as far back as several thousand years ago, and then make inferences about climate in each year from the thickness of the ring. This technique has already been employed on subalpine conifers to show that the year 218 BC, when *Hannibal crossed the Alps, was a mild year, helping to explain the success of Hannibal's audacious enterprise. Information derived from tree-ring studies should eventually resolve a number of controversies among modern historians about the possibility that there were secular climatic variations in antiquity. J. R. S.

Clodia, second of the three sisters of Publius *Clodius Pulcher, born *c.*95 BC, had married her first cousin Quintus Caecilius Metellus Celer by 62 (Cic. *Fam.* 5. 2. 6). Her bitter enemy *Cicero (but gossip said she had once offered him marriage, Plut. *Cic.* 29) paints a vivid picture of her in his *Letters* from 60 BC onwards, and above all in the *Pro Caelio* of April 56. Her affair with *Catullus—the identification with Lesbia is widely admitted—began before the death of Metellus in 59, which Clodia was said to have caused by poison: by the end of that year Marcus Caelius Rufus was her lover. After the Caelius case her political importance ceases, but she may have been still alive in 45 BC (Cic. *Att.* 12. 38, etc.). G. E. F. C.; R. J. S.

Clodius Pulcher, Publius, youngest of six children of Appius Claudius Pulcher (consul 79). He was born *c.*92 BC (since quaestor in 61). In 68 he incited the troops of his brother-in-law Lucius Licinius Lucullus to mutiny in Armenia. When prosecuting *Catiline in 65 he was, according to Cicero, in co-operation with the defence. On his return to Rome he had been apparently friendly with *Cicero (Plut. *Cic.* 29), but in May 61 Cicero gave damaging evidence against him when he was on trial for trespassing on the Bona Dea festival disguised as a woman the previous December. However Clodius was narrowly acquitted by a jury said to have been heavily bribed. Next year, on returning from his quaestorian province of *Sicily, he sought transference into a plebeian *gens* (see PLEBS): this was at first resisted, but in March 59 *Caesar as pontifex maximus (senior member of the *pontifices*: see PRIESTS) presided over the *comitia curiata* (assembly of citizens voting in units called *curiae*) at which the adoption was ratified. There were suggestions of subsequent disagreements with Caesar and *Pompey and of his departure from Rome, but in the event he was elected tribune for 58. His measures included free corn for the *plebs*, restoration of *collegia* (private clubs), repeal or modification of the *leges Aelia et Fufia*, grant of new provinces to the consuls Aulus Gabinius and Lucius Calpurnius Piso Caesoninus, a bill exiling those who had condemned Roman citizens to death without popular sanction, a bill confirming the exile of Cicero (who departed in late March), the dispatch of *Cato the Younger to *Cyprus, and the grant of title of king and control of Pessinus (central *Asia Minor) to Brogitarus ruler of the Galatian tribe of the Trocmi. Clodius then turned against Pompey, allowing the escape of the Armenian prince Tigranes, threatening Pompey's life, and (Cic. *Dom.* 40; *Har. resp.* 48) suggesting that Caesar's acts of 59 were invalid because of Marcus Calpurnius Bibulus' religious obstruction. These attacks on Pompey were continued in 57, especially over the question of Cicero's recall, and in the early part of Clodius'

aedileship in 56; but after the conference at Luca (see CAESAR) his attitude changed and by agitation and violence he helped to bring about the joint consulship of Pompey and *Crassus in 55. He still continued to control large sections of the urban *plebs* (*plebs urbana*). He stood for the praetorship of 52 but owing to rioting the elections had not been held when he was murdered by Titus Annius Milo on 18 January of that year. His clients among the *plebs* burned the senate-house as his pyre.

Clodius, who like two of his sisters used the 'popular' spelling of his name, probably saw the tribunate as a vital step in his political career: revenge on Cicero need not have been his main aim in seeking transfer to the *plebs*, nor (despite Cic. *Dom.* 41; *Sest.* 16) Caesar's aim in granting it. Moreover, the view that Caesar was at any time his patron seems misconceived. In 58–56 he may have been allied with Crassus; but he was surely both opportunist and independent, for before as well as after Luca he was friendly with various *optimates* (Cic. *Fam.* 1. 9. 10, 19), and in 53 he was supporting the candidates of Pompey for the consulship (Asconius, 26, 42). The one consistent motif is his courting of the urban *plebs* and the promotion of its interests. The daughter of his marriage to Fulvia was briefly married to Octavian (later *Augustus) in 42. G. E. F. C.; A. W. L.

closure, the sense of finality or conclusiveness at the end of a work or some part of it. In addition to the basic fulfilment of expectations raised by particular texts, some ancient genres show marked closural conventions; examples include the choral coda of Euripidean tragedy, the *plaudite* of Roman comedy (see COMEDY, LATIN), and the rhetorical peroration. We also find a variety of closural modes across genres: authorial self-reference, generalization, prophecy, prayer, motifs such as death, marriage, ritual, and departure. Our understanding of ancient closure is limited by what we have; some endings have been lost, some works were never finished, and some extant endings may be interpolations. Our uncertainties about ancient closural convention in turn lead us to disagree about whether in fact we do possess the actual endings of works such as *Herodotus' *Histories*, *Euripides' *Iphigenia at Aulis*, *Lucretius' *De Rerum Natura*, and *Catullus 51. Even when we have the ending we may have difficulties in assessing closure. Closure may be unexpected or false, undercut or ironized; it is often hard to interpret the effect on closure of the audience's knowledge of later events in the continuing myths from which so many ancient narratives are taken. *Aristotle tells us in the *Poetics* that a plot must have an ending, which follows from something but from which nothing follows (ch. 7), and that different endings suit different genres (ch. 13); further discussion of closure may be found in the rhetorical tradition and in remarks on particular endings. But the most telling ancient comment on the interpretative significance of endings as the opportunity for what B. H. Smith calls 'retrospective patterning' is to be found in *Solon's advice at Herodotus 1. 32: that we call no one happy until death. D. H. R.

Cocceius Nerva, Marcus, Roman emperor. See NERVA.

coinage, Greek

Definitions Coinage to the Greeks was one of the forms of money available to measure value, store wealth, or facilitate exchange. Coins were made from precious metal such as gold or silver, or from a copper alloy; they were of regulated weight and had a design (type) stamped on one or both sides. Lumps of bullion too could be weighed to a standard and stamped with a design, but the stamp on a coin indicated that the issuing authority, normally a state or its representative(s), would accept it as the legal equivalent of some value previously expressed in terms of other objects, including metal by weight. Merchants and others therefore were expected to accept it in payment. A coin of precious metal might weigh the same as the equivalent value of bullion, but would normally weigh less, to cover minting costs and, in varying degrees, to make a profit for the mint: in other words, coins were overvalued relative to bullion.

The scope of Greek coinage is wide, both geographically and chronologically. In the Archaic and Classical periods many of the Greek communities established around the Mediterranean and Black Seas produced coins, and they often influenced their neighbours to do the same: Persians (see PERSIA) in western *Asia Minor, Carthaginians (see CARTHAGE) in North Africa and Sicily, *Etruscans in Italy, Celts in western Europe. The coins of these peoples, although they usually bear images and inscriptions appropriate to their traditions, were in general inspired by Greek models, and they tend to be catalogued as part of Greek coinage. After 334 the conquest of the Persian empire by *Alexander the Great inaugurated a massive extension of the area covered by coinage, in particular in the successor kingdoms, Syria, Egypt, and so on. In effect the term Greek coinage includes most of the non-Roman coinage of the ancient world issued between the Straits of Gibraltar and NW India.

Beginnings Literary and archaeological evidence combine to show that coinage began in western Anatolia, at the point of contact between Greek cities on the Aegean coast and the Lydian kingdom in the interior. The first coins were of electrum, an alloy of gold and silver occurring naturally in the river Pactolus, which flowed into the Hermus to the west of Sardis, the Lydian capital. A date of *c*.600 BC or a little later for their introduction fits their appearance in a miscellaneous deposit of jewellery and figurines discovered in the foundations of the temple of Artemis at *Ephesus, and also the subsequent development of coinage in Asia Minor and the wider Aegean world. The first coins of electrum were followed in Lydia by coins of pure gold and silver, with the type of confronting foreparts of a lion and of a bull. Such coins have traditionally been attributed to the Lydian king Croesus (*c*.561–547), but hoard evidence suggests that most, if not all, are later than his reign and were part of the coinage issued in the area by the Persians.

Purpose In the modern world the role of coinage in everyday buying and selling is clear, but this does not mean that similar commercial reasons prompted its introduction. Coins were not necessarily advantageous in large transactions, and their usefulness in exchanges between cities was inhibited by various factors, including the diversity of weight-standards in the Greek world. For example, the weight of the drachma differed in cities as close together as Aegina, Corinth, and Athens. As for small transactions, few early coinages included the necessary range of small denominations. It is true that one of these was the electrum coinage produced in the 6th cent. in Ionia, but even the lowest known denomination (‰) represented a large sum. Given the nature of the earliest coins—in particular their standardized weights and the lion's head that features on many of them—it is a plausible hypothesis that they were issued to make a large number of uniform and high-value payments in an easily portable and durable form, and that the authority or person making the payment, perhaps to *mercenaries, was the king of Lydia. For the original recipients coins were simply another form of movable wealth, but many pieces might thereafter be exchanged for goods or services and so pass into general circulation as money. But the progress towards a monetary economy was by no means straightforward or immediate. The fact that many of the early electrum coins are covered in small punch-marks suggests that it was some time before such coins were universally acceptable.

Minting Technique: Implications for Study The first task of the Greek moneyer was to create from metal of the required quality the blanks, or flans, of suitable shape and correct weight. Blanks were normally made by casting, that is, pouring the molten metal into moulds. (In the Greek world coins themselves were rarely made by casting.) To convert the blank into a coin it was struck with dies made from either toughened bronze or iron, and hand-engraved in negative (*intaglio*). One die, which was to produce the obverse, was set in an anvil. The blank was placed on top of it and the metal forced into the die beneath by a short stout bar (*charaktēr*), its butt resting on the blank while its top was struck with a hammer. On the earliest coins the butt simply reproduced its own rough surface on the reverse; at a later stage, in many places by the end of the 6th cent., the practice arose of engraving the butt also with a device, thus creating a coin with types on both sides.

Minting was thus a relatively simple process, but at each stage there are implications for the modern study of its products. At the preparatory stage great care was generally taken to ensure both the purity of the metal and the accurate weight of the blanks: modern methods of non-destructive metal analysis can detect any significant differences in the composition of a metal alloy and thus help to classify the coins or to signal a change of monetary policy. Sometimes it was not—for whatever reason—con-

(a)

(b)

(c)

coinage, Greek Greek cities used their coinage to project a local identity in a variety of ways. (*a*) An issue of Sicilian Naxos (*c*.530–510 BC) used a grape-cluster and a portrait of *Dionysus to celebrate Naxian wine. (*b*) An issue of *Pergamum (AD 180–92) adroitly couples the suckling of its mythical founder Telephus, son of *Heracles, with a portrait of *Commodus, the new Hercules (Roman Heracles). (*c*) Kings used coins to present the royal image. Here *Eucratides I of *Bactria appears as a warleader and claims the title Great King (*Megas Basileus*).

venient to prepare fresh blanks, and new types were over-struck on old coins. In cases where the undertypes were not totally obliterated by the restriking process, such 'over-strikes' can provide valuable evidence for relative dating and for the circulation of coins. When the blanks were being struck, the alignment of the two dies might be fixed or it might be variable: similarities or differences in the patterns of alignment may again help to classify or date some coins. Studies of the dies employed are of fundamental importance in modern numismatics. A single coin in isolation can provide a certain amount of information, but the significance of the information is immeasurably enhanced when two or more coins can be shown to have been struck from the same die(s). Coins sharing dies in this way must normally have been struck at the same place and at approximately the same time. Furthermore, since in practice the punch dies were more exposed to wear and/or damage than anvil dies and tended to be discarded more frequently, it is often possible to build up a sequence of issues sharing either an obverse or a reverse die. Finally, die-studies form the basis of attempts to estimate the size of a coinage. Using a variety of statistical methods, it may be possible to work out from a sample of dies the total number of dies used to produce a given coinage. To estimate the amount of bullion required, that total must be multiplied by the number of coins that were struck from each die. But in any individual case, that figure is elusive. There is no means of telling when a particular die was under-used, though conversely there is frequently evidence for the use of dies in an advanced stage of deterioration, and dies were sometimes recut, to repair them or to update them. The size of an issue of coins depended on many factors, not least the availability of bullion.

Coin Types The type of a Greek coin is a mark of its origin, whether a community or an individual. The earliest coins, found in the temple of Artemis at Ephesus, had types only on the obverse and their variety makes it difficult to assign them to a specific minting authority. The commonest type, a lion's head, has been attributed to the kingdom of Lydia; others, such as a seal's head or a recumbent lion, may belong to Phocaea and Miletus (western *Asia Minor) respectively. The significance of the earliest types was not usually reinforced by any letter or inscription. On one coin from the Ephesian Artemisium with the type of two lions' heads the inscription WALWEL has been read. This cannot refer to king Alyattes of Lydia (c.610–560) since another name, KALIL, has been identified on a similar issue. The identity of these persons remains unknown. Rather more revealing are the inscriptions on two early coins showing a stag. One has a simple name in the uncontracted genitive, *Phaneos*, 'of Phanes', the other reads *Phanos emi sēma* 'I am the badge of Phanes'. The identity of the Phanes referred to is not known (a mercenary captain of that name from Halicarnassus (SW Asia Minor) employed in Egypt in the 530s is too late for the coin), but with a different name and device the formula occurs on an archaic seal-stone probably from Aegina (J. Boardman, *Archaic Greek Gems* (1968), no. 176). The analogy makes clear the origin of a coin type in the personal seal or badge of the authority responsible for its issue. Apart from these examples coin legends are rare in the 6th cent. By its end the initial letter or letters of an ethnic might be introduced (as a *koppa* on coins of Corinth or *Athe* on those of Athens), and in course of time the tendency was to lengthen the inscription. When written out in full it was frequently in the genitive case, signifying [a coin] of whoever the issuing authority was.

After an initial period of variation the types of individual cities settled down and changed little: familiarity encouraged acceptability. Most coin types are connected with religion in the widest sense. Sometimes a divinity is represented directly, in other cases indirectly, through an animal or an attribute. Even some of the types illustrating a local product belong in this category: for example an ear of barley can symbolize *Demeter, goddess of crops. Many types refer to local myths or religious traditions, for example those connected with the foundation of a city. Only rarely do types refer to historical events, at least in the Archaic and Classical periods. In this respect they share the preference of Greek art in general for the allusive and symbolic, rather than for direct and literal references to political matters.

The Spread of Coinage (*Archaic and Classical*) Electrum, with its variable content of gold and silver, did not last long as the primary metal for coining, and in the second half of the 6th cent., with a few exceptions such as Cyzicus, Phocaea, and Mytilene, the coin-producing cities of Asia Minor turned exclusively to silver. Coinage in gold became a rarity both there and elsewhere, although from the early 5th cent. the Persians issued gold darics with the same type as their silver sigloi, a crowned figure representing the king of Persia. ('Darics' were so named by the Greeks after the Persian king Darius I (522–486); 'siglos' is a Greek form of the Semitic 'shekel'.) These coins were issued for use in those parts of the Persian empire in closest contact with the Greeks, and the institution of coinage did not initially travel far to the east of its birthplace in western Asia Minor.

To the west and north the story was different. By c.550 coinage had crossed the Aegean to communities close to the isthmus of Corinth—Aegina, Corinth, and Athens—and not much later had taken root among the Greek cities and the tribes of the Thraco-Macedonian area (see MACEDONIA). The rich metal resources of the latter gave rise to coinage in a remarkable range of denominations, including the heaviest of all Greek silver coins, the double octadrachm. Such coins travelled far, especially to the east, and may have been made for export. The first Athenian coins, the so-called *Wappenmünzen* ('heraldic coins'), share some of the characteristics of the early coins of Asia Minor, notably their changing types, their lack of any indication of origin, and the use of electrum as well as silver for some issues. In the later part of the 6th cent., perhaps under the tyrant Hippias (527–510), these issues were replaced by the famous 'owls', with obverse helmeted head of *Athena, reverse owl, and the abbreviated name of the city. These coins too travelled a long way, another example of the export in the form of coin of silver mined in the territory of the issuing state.

From the Aegean area the medium of coinage spread rapidly to the western Greeks settled around the coasts of southern Italy and Sicily, France, and Spain. Early Corinthian coinage in particular influenced some of the first coinages in the west both in production technique and because imported Corinthian coins were often used as flans for overstriking. There was also a notable willingness to experiment: the first Italian coins were made using the sophisticated 'incuse' method, unique in the Greek world, in which the obverse type appears normally in relief, while on the reverse a closely similar version of the same type is struck in negative, the two types exactly aligned. To the western cities also belong the first bronze coins, at Thurii (S. Italy) from c.440, at Acragas (Sicily) from c.430, and thus the development of the idea of fiduciary coinage in which the worth of a coin was not related to the intrinsic value of its metal content. The coins of the western Greeks attained the highest standards of artistic excellence and especially in the late 5th and early 4th cents. the careers of many of the artists can be traced from their signatures on dies.

Hellenistic

In the 4th cent. the Greek world of independent city-states began to give way in the eastern and western Mediterranean to the ambitions of individuals and the growing power of Rome. In the east the exploitation by *Philip II of Macedon of the mines of Pangaeus after 356 left a rich legacy of coinage in gold and silver which was adapted and expanded by his son *Alexander the Great to cover the whole near east. He adopted the Attic weight-standard for both his gold and silver coinage, and struck coins with the same designs at more than one mint. After Alexander's death in 323, the currency system he had put in place remained remarkably stable. In the world of territorial states and kingdoms that emerged in the 3rd cent. only *Ptolemy I in Egypt introduced major innovations in the types and weights of his coins, to produce an autonomous system of coinage. The change to larger political units, kingdoms, states, and leagues was reflected in the coinage. Many individual cities coined from time to time, but mostly in bronze; only Athens and Rhodes coined continuously in silver down to the 1st cent. BC. Coins with Alexander's types played an important role as international currency, especially in Asia Minor, where 'posthumous Alexanders' were produced in quantity until 175 BC and even later.

The types of Hellenistic coins, like those of earlier periods, are for the most part religious in content; and although they display a strong historical consciousness in line with the culture of the time, they rarely refer directly to historical events. The major innovation was the introduction of the portrait of a ruler. Few portraits of living persons have been recognized on Greek coins before Ptolemy I shortly after 305/4. A reverse of Abdera (north Aegean coast) in the last quarter of the 5th cent. realistically depicts a male head which might be the portrait of an individual (Pythagores) named on the coin. In the 4th cent. fine portraits occur on the coins of Persian satraps or Lycian dynasts in Asia Minor (e.g. Pericles of Limyra). From the Hellenistic period we have a whole gallery of portraits of rulers in which idealized images of royal power are often combined with realism and insight into character. On the far eastern fringes of the Hellenistic world the kings of *Bactria are known to us largely through their brilliant coin-portraits. See PORTRAITURE.

In the last two centuries BC, as Roman power spread inexorably eastwards, Hellenistic coinage evolved new forms. League coinages had already played a leading role, for example those of the Arcadian and Achaean Confederacies (see FEDERAL STATES) in Greece. At Athens 'New Style' coinage began around 170, and *Pergamum at about the same time began to issue cistophoroi, so called from the adoption as their obverse type of a *cista mystica*, a basket used in the celebration of the rites of *Dionysus. After the battle of *Actium (31 BC) Rome's control over the eastern Mediterranean was complete and Greek coinage had virtually ceased. The subsequent plethora of city coinages with Greek legends and local types which were issued in the eastern provinces of the Roman empire (the so-called 'Greek imperials') until well into the later 3rd cent. AD are more Roman in appearance and conception; see COINAGE, ROMAN.   N. K. R.

coinage, Roman There are two related stories about Roman coinage, the one of its internal evolution, the other of its progressive domination of the Mediterranean world, its use throughout the Roman empire, and finally its fragmentation into the coinages of the successor kingdoms in the west and the Byzantine empire in the east.

Rome under the kings and in the early republic managed without a coinage, like the other communities of central Italy, with the episodic exception of some Etruscan cities; bronze by weight, *aes rude*, with a pound of about 324 g. (11¼ oz.) as the unit, served as a measure of value, no doubt primarily in the assessment of fines imposed by a community in the process of substituting public law for private retribution; this stage of Roman monetary history is reflected in the *Twelve Tables. The progressive extension of Roman hegemony over central Italy brought booty in the form of gold, silver, and bronze; the means to create a coinage on the Greek model were at hand. The stimulus was probably provided by Roman involvement with the Greek cities of Campania (west central Italy), with the building of the via Appia in the late 4th cent. BC; Rome had struck a diminutive coinage of bronze at Neapolis after 326 BC, with the legend *PΩMAIΩN*, 'of the Romans'; she now struck a coinage of silver pieces worth two (probably)

drachmas, with the legend ROMANO, otherwise indistinguishable from the Greek coinages of the south. But the
continuing irrelevance of coinage to Rome emerges from
the fact that there was nearly a generation before the next
issue, probably contemporary with the Pyrrhic War. (See
PYRRHUS.) From this point, there is a virtually unbroken
sequence of Roman coinage to the end of the Roman
empire in the west.

To the basis of silver didrachms was added a token
coinage in bronze; the curious decision was also taken to
produce a cast bronze coinage, the unit (or *as*) of which
weighed a pound; this coinage is now known as *aes graue*,
though the Latin writers who spoke of the bronze coinage
of early Rome as *aes graue* probably had little idea of what
was involved. Bronze currency bars were also cast for a
short time, in the period of the Pyrrhic and First Punic
Wars (see ROME (HISTORY) §1.4), now very misleadingly
known as *aes signatum* (to a Roman, this phrase simply
meant 'coined bronze'). It is striking that even now the
coinage of Rome remained on a relatively small scale,
compared with those of Carthage and the Greek cities of
Italy.

The silver coinage with its token coinage in bronze
(changing the ethnic in due course from ROMANO to
ROMA) and the heavy cast bronze coinage went on side by
side down to the outbreak of the Second Punic War in 218
BC. It is probably in this period that Roman coinage penetrated the territories of the peoples of the central
Apennines for the first time; and it is likely that, just as military needs may explain much of the production of Roman
coinage in this period, so it was returning soldiers who
carried it to Samnite and other communities.

The enormous strain of the war against *Hannibal led
to a reduction in the metal content of the heavy cast
bronze coinage, an emergency issue of gold and finally the
debasement of the silver coinage. The first coinage system
of Rome collapsed and in or about 211 BC a new system was
introduced; it included a new silver coin, the denarius,
which remained the main Roman silver coin until the 3rd
cent. AD. The issue was financed initially by unprecedented
state levies on private property, thereafter by booty as the
war went better for Rome. The unit (or *as*) of the bronze
coinage by this stage weighed only about two ounces (54
g.: 2 oz.), the denarius (or 'tenner') was worth ten of these;
there were subsidiary denominations in both silver—
including a piece known as the victoriatus, without a mark
of value, weighing three-quarters of the denarius, but with
a low and erratic silver content—and bronze and a short-
lived issue of gold. The end of the war saw the virtual cessation of minting by other Italian communities; and
coinage other than Roman on the whole disappeared
rapidly from circulation in Italy. When the Italians produced a rebel coinage in 90–88 BC, it was modelled on the
denarius, apart from a single issue of gold, in which they
anticipated *Sulla (see below).

Despite the creation of the denarius, bronze remained
the most important element in the Roman monetary

system for some years; a belief similar to those held by
*Cato the Elder even led to the virtual suppression for a
decade of the silver coinage, a symbol of increasing wealth
and of declining public morality. But the consequences of
Rome's conquest of the world could not be suppressed for
ever; the *booty in silver *inter alia* which flowed into Rome
from 194 BC onwards and the mines in *Macedonia which
Rome controlled from 167 BC found expression in a vastly
increased issue of silver coinage from 157 BC. It became
normal for Rome to coin in a year as much as a Greek city
might coin in a century; and it was only with Sulla that the
mint abandoned the practice of producing a large part of
what was needed each year as new coin; the mint then
went over to what remained standard practice, to top up
revenues already in the form of Roman coin with issues
largely from newly mined metal. In the years after 157 BC,
the coinage came accurately to reflect the position of
Rome as ruler of the world by omitting the ethnic: no
identification was needed.

The relative unimportance of the bronze coinage after
157 BC led to the cessation of production of the as and to
the production of its fractions on a very reduced weight
standard; and in about 141 BC the bronze coinage was effectively devalued when the denarius was retariffed as the
equivalent of 16, not 10, asses; its name, however, remained
unchanged. By the end of the 2nd cent. BC, victoriati in circulation weighed only about half a denarius; and halves of
the denarius, or quinarii, were henceforth intermittently
struck, often for the Po valley or Provence (see below).

The period after the Second Punic War saw the beginning of the process whereby Roman coinage came to be
the coinage of the whole Mediterranean world. The denarius rapidly became the silver coin of Sicily, flanked both by
Roman bronze and by bronze city issues. In Spain, the
Romans permitted or encouraged the creation of silver
and bronze coinages modelled on the denarius coinage,
probably in the 150s BC. In the Po valley and in Provence,
the Romans accepted for their own purposes the local
monetary unit, equivalent to half-a-denarius, and indeed
on a number of occasions struck such a unit for those
areas. By way of contrast, the Greek east remained largely
uninfluenced by Roman monetary structures until the 1st
cent. BC. But as more and more of the Mediterranean
world came under direct Roman rule and became involved
in the civil wars that brought the republic to an end, so
the use of Roman monetary units and Roman coins
spread, to Africa, Greece and the east, and Gaul. Only
Egypt, incorporated in 30 BC, remained monetarily isolated
from the rest of the Roman world.

The military insurrection of Sulla in 84 BC had seen the
production of a gold as well as a silver coinage, the availability of the metal combining with an urgent need for
coinage to pay his soldiers; the precedent of Sulla was followed by *Caesar in this if in no other respect: the vast
quantities of gold derived as booty from Gaul and Britain
were converted in 46 BC by Aulus Hirtius (consul 43) into
the largest gold issue produced by Rome before the reign

of *Nero; by 44 BC the distribution of gold coins, or aurei, to the troops was a normal occurrence. Caesar's rival *Pompey had become from the exploitation of the provinces of the east the wealthiest man of his time; in attempting successfully to outdo him in wealth as well as in prestige, Caesar in effect superseded the state as a minting authority.

The civil wars which followed the death of Caesar saw the production of coinage in a variety of metals—including bronze on more than one standard—by most of the rival contenders; unity of minting authority and uniformity of product returned when the last survivor of the civil wars finally suppressed the institutions of the free state and established an autocracy. The coinage of Caesar Octavianus (see AUGUSTUS) became the coinage of Rome.

Meanwhile, the types displayed by the Roman republican coinage had also come to mirror accurately the escalating internal conflict of the nobility. By 211 BC, the production of coinage was in the hands of men called moneyers, young men at the beginning of a political career. The possibilities offered by the coinage for self-advertisement gradually became apparent during the 2nd cent. BC and by the last third of the century the issue produced by a moneyer was as far as its types were concerned effectively a private concern; a moneyer might recall his town of origin, the deeds of his ancestors, eventually the contemporary achievements of a powerful patron; with Caesar, the coinage began to display his portrait, an overtly monarchical symbol; even *Brutus, the self-styled Liberator, portrayed on his last issue two of the daggers which had murdered Caesar on one side and his own portrait on the other side. In striking contrast to Mark *Antony, the future Augustus gradually suppressed on his coinage any reference to his lieutenants; and the coinage with which he paid the troops who defeated Antony and *Cleopatra VII at the battle of *Actium was already a coinage which displayed only the portrait and attributes of a single leader.

One important change in the structure of this coinage took place under Augustus: the silver fractions of the denarius, which had filled the gap between the denarius and the as, were largely replaced by orichalcum multiples of the as, the sestertii, and dupondii which are among the most familiar components of the Roman imperial coinage. At the same time, the as and the smallest denomination now struck, the quadrans, or quarter, were produced in pure copper. The most probable view is that the letters SC on the new base metal coinage of Augustus reflect the fact that the new structure was endorsed by a decree of the senate (s(enatus) c(onsultum)); the reform perhaps involved the revaluation of surviving republican asses, heavier than Augustan asses, as dupondii.

The mainstream coinage of the Roman empire, then, consisted of aurei and denarii, at a ratio of 1 : 25, and base metal fractions. Although at all periods much, even most, was struck at Rome, this was not necessarily so: it is likely that between Augustus and the changes under *Nero most of the precious metal coinage was struck in Gaul. In addi-

tion, the empire continued in the east to produce coinages modelled on the earlier coinages of a number of areas, for instance cistophori in Asia till the 2nd cent. AD, tetradrachms in *Syria till the early 3rd cent. AD, tetradrachms in Egypt till *Diocletian (285–305). But the shift of minting from Gaul to Rome began a process of concentration of minting which lasted till the Severans (see ROME (HISTORY)). Thereafter, the evolution of the empire saw an inexorable tendency for more and more of the mainstream coinage to be produced in the provinces, though there were ebbs and flows in the pattern. And the base metal coinage of the east consisted for a long time not of the familiar sestertii, dupondii, asses, and quadrantes of the mint of Rome, but of a range of provincial bronze coinages. The kaleidoscopic variety of the coinage of the empire was completed by hundreds of city coinages, in the west till *Claudius, in the east (the so-called 'Greek imperials') till the 3rd cent. AD. All these coinages, however, were probably based on, or compatible with, Roman monetary units. It is less clear how far the empire formed a single circulation area: the most probable view is that even mainstream coinage, once it had reached an area, tended to stay there, even in the 1st and 2nd cents. AD; but there is no doubt that the compartmentalization of circulation became even more marked with the shift from a monetary to a natural economy in the third century AD (see below).

The monetary system of the Roman empire always operated on very narrow margins. It is possible to calculate that in normal times perhaps 80 per cent of the imperial budget was covered by tax revenues, the rest by the topping up of what came in with coins minted from newly mined metal. Prudent emperors managed; the less prudent did not.

In AD 64 Nero reduced the weight of the aureus and the weight and fineness of the denarius; and despite attempts under the Flavians (*Vespasian, *Titus, *Domitian) to reverse the trend, the next century and a half saw a slow decline in the silver content of the denarius, paralleled by a similar or worse decline in that of the provincial 'silver' coinages. *Commodus further reduced the weight of the denarius and *Septimius Severus drastically reduced its fineness; while *Caracalla chose to issue a coin, known to modern scholars as the antoninianus, with the weight of about one and a half denarii, but (probably) the face value of two. Since the imperial portrait bore a radiate crown, not the laurel wreath of the denarius, the coin may have been known as a 'radiate'. The tax-paying population of the Roman empire was not to be deceived and the state found its revenues increasingly arriving in the form of recent issues of poor quality, while older issues of better quality were hoarded or melted down. The combination of this process with the increasing demands on the empire as barbarian pressure increased led from AD 238 onwards to the complete collapse of the silver coinage: the denarius ceased to be produced and by AD 270 the antoninianus had ceased to contain more than a trifling percentage of silver. The weight even of the gold unit fluctuated, presumably as emperors divided what was in the kitty by the number of aurei it was necessary to pay out. In a sense, all that happened was that what had always been the underlying reality was revealed: an agricultural surplus supported an army and a bureaucracy. For on the whole taxes and payments were slow to catch up with the declining value of the coinage; and as the monetary circle—levies of taxes, payments to soldiers and others, payments to cultivators for grain for soldiers and others, providing the source for yet further levies of taxes—became increasingly meaningless, so it became ever more apparent that the 'real' wage of a soldier, for instance, was his ration of corn. And the institutional structures of the empire slowly changed to accommodate this fact.

At the same time, the sheer bulk of coinage produced and its appalling quality facilitated the production of imitations: the *nummularii*, whose profession it had been to test for forgeries, could not cope. A large part of the hoards of the late 3rd cent. AD, particularly in the west, is made up of coins known to modern scholars as 'barbarous radiates'.

By a series of reforms, the details of which remain obscure, Aurelian and the immediately subsequent emperors attempted to reform and stabilize the coinage. Aurelian (270–5) produced coins marked *XXI* or *KA* (in Greek), to indicate 5 per cent silver content; and there followed coins marked *XI* or *IA* (in Greek), to indicate 10 per cent silver content. The next major reform is that of Diocletian, who stabilized the gold coinage at 60 aurei to the Roman pound, restored a pure silver coinage at 96 units to the pound, and produced in addition a large bronze denomination with some silver content, known at the time as the nummus, and also small bronze pieces, doubles with a radiate head and no silver content, the ultimate descendants of Caracalla's double denarius, and singles with a laureate head. The gold unit was henceforth known as the solidus. Further adjustment was necessary in AD 301, the year of the Prices Edict, when Diocletian issued a revaluation edict, attested by the coins and by one of the two texts on a fragmentary inscription from *Aphrodisias. Diocletian also consolidated the distribution of production in twelve to fifteen mints distributed through most of the Roman empire; their products on the whole circulated in the areas where they were struck.

*Constantine I reduced the weight of the solidus to 72 to the Roman pound, but managed not to wreck the system completely; his gold coin remained standard for many centuries. A pure silver piece, however, never again played a major part in production or circulation, except to a certain extent between about AD 350 and 400. Nor did the Diocletianic nummus really survive, though some of the bronze issues of his successors approach it in diameter. Rather the coinage of the late Roman empire consists essentially of solidi and vast quantities of small bronze denominations of changing face value. There is a long series of reforms and revaluations, until some sort of stability is finally achieved in the 5th cent. AD, with the emergence of very small bronze nummi, followed by the substantial 'reforms' associated with the names of Anastasius and Justinian (527–65). It is this pattern which is initially replicated by the coinages of the successor kingdoms of the west, before they develop the silver coinages characteristic of the Middle Ages. In the east, the coinages of the Arab successors to much of the territory of the Byzantine empire are likewise of silver. See FINANCE, ROMAN.

M. H. C.

colonization, Greek 'Colonization', in the language of a former imperial power, is a somewhat misleading definition of the process of major Greek expansion that took place between *c.*734 and 580 BC. In fact, the process itself was not so much 'Greek' as directed in different ways and for different reasons by a number of independent city-states (see POLIS). This at least emerges with relative clarity from both the historical and the archaeological evidence. For the rest, the mass of general and particular information that has accumulated under these two headings is only rarely susceptible to a single uncontroversial interpretation. Although the position has greatly improved since the 1930s, it is still only too true that archaeologists and ancient historians do not always appreciate each other's aims and methods—a problem that is exacerbated by the fact that on the subject of colonization ancient no less than modern authors are more than usually influenced by their own political agenda and accordingly more than usually liable to project the priorities, practices, and terminology of their own times onto the much earlier events they purport to describe.

The actual course of early Greek expansion is reasonably clear, in terms both of the areas colonized and of the identity of the chief colonizing cities: Chalcis, Eretria, Corinth, Megara, Miletus, and Phocaea. Of these, the Euboean cities (Chalcis, Eretria) must rank as pioneers. Eretrian Corcyra (on mod. Corfu) was the first Greek colony in the Adriatic, which suggests that it was intended mainly as a way-station on the route to the west; and the primarily Chalcidian foundation of Cumae on the bay of Naples is the most northerly as well as the earliest (before 725) Greek colony on the mainland of southern Italy—known to later historians as Magna Graecia. Cumae was a logical extension of the pre-colonial Euboean venture at the *emporion* (trading place) of Pithecusae (mod. Ischia), itself a result of earlier commercial experience—not least in a Levant that had been aware of western resources (Sardinia) since the bronze age. Chalcidians extended their reach to eastern Sicily with the foundation of Naxos in 734, soon followed by Leontini and Catana; on the straits of Messina, they were joined by Cumaeans at Zancle, whence Mylae provided much-needed land, and control of the vital passage was completed at Rhegium *c.*720. Nearer home, the Chalcidice peninsula takes its name from the early and extensive Euboean presence on the northern shores of the Aegean, notably at Torone (Chalcis; this is controversial) and at Mende, founded by Eretria, as was Methone (for refugees from Corcyra) on the gulf of

Salonica. The Euboean domination of this area, motivated by land hunger rather than commerce, was not broken until c.600, when Corinth established Potidaea to trade with *Macedonia. By then, Corinthians (and Corinthian pottery) had long enjoyed a substantial western presence, built on precolonial experience that had extended to expatriate ceramic production at Euboean Pithecusae. In 733, Corinth evicted the Eretrians from their port of call at Corcyra and founded *Syracuse, which had the best harbour in eastern Sicily and for long conditioned the history of nearby Megara I Iyblaea, founded by Corinth's near neighbour at home, Megara—which elsewhere gained control by c.660 of the approaches to the Black (Euxine) Sea with Chalcedon and the superior site of *Byzantium.

Early Euboean and Corinthian achievements in the west concentrated the attention of others, both on the west itself and on other areas as yet unopened. Of the former, the Achaeans were responsible from c.720 for Sybaris, Croton, Caulonia (founded from Croton), Metapontum, and Poseidonia (i.e. Paestum, probably founded from Sybaris)—the latter, on the Tyrrhenian coast, was situated at the end of an overland route from the south that provided a serious challenge to the well-established trade (ultimately with Etruria) through the straits. In the last decades of the 8th cent., *Sparta founded its only colony by taking

possession of the finest port in south Italy, Tarentum; Rhodians and Cretans (see RHODES; CRETE) combined to establish Gela on the south coast of Sicily in 688; Locri Epizephyrii is said to have been founded by settlers from Locris in central Greece in 673, Siris from Colophon in Ionia (western *Asia Minor) before 650. By now, daughter-foundations were a standard feature of the western scene: two of them, Selinus and Acragas, representing extensions into western Sicily by Megara Hyblaea and Gela respectively, boast temples that are no less magnificent than those of Greece itself.

At the other end of the Greek world, the literary evidence is less reliable than it is for the west, and excavation has been less extensive: but it is claimed that Miletus founded a great number of cities along the Turkish coast to Trapezus, north from the Bosporus to the Danube, and in the Crimea. In a completely different direction, Thera founded *Cyrene in North Africa c.630. And from c.600, Phocaeans safeguarded their far western trade by founding colonies on the Mediterranean coast on either side of the Rhône delta: Massalia (mod. Marseille), Nicaea (mod. Nice), and Antipolis (Antibes) in what is now southern France, and the aptly named Emporion in northern Spain.

It is no exaggeration to say that by 580 all the most obvious areas in the then available world had been occupied to at least some extent by Greeks. The factors that influenced any given colonizing city, or indeed the foundation of any given colony, were inevitably many and various: it is not possible to compile a generally applicable assessment of the interlocking claims of overpopulation and land hunger at home, opportunities for commercial or social advancement abroad, 'internal' (Greek vs. Greek) rivalry and reaction to external pressure. No less various were the relations between colony and mother city, and the effects of Greek colonization on the indigenous inhabitants of the regions colonized. Many different natural resources were doubtless targeted for exploitation, and markets were accordingly made: but the cultural 'Hellenization of the *barbarians' (see HELLENISM) was at no time consciously planned, nor did all the 'barbarians' share the unswerving predilection for the Greek point of view displayed by all ancient and most modern commentators on colonial matters. It remains true that the history of the Greeks abroad is an indispensable element of the history of the Greeks at home.   D. W. W. R.

colonization, Hellenistic *Plutarch, in the eulogy of his hero *Alexander the Great (*De Alex. fort.*), made the foundation of cities the linchpin of the achievement of Alexander, who wished to spread Greek civilization throughout his realm. Although we must be mindful of the predictable ideology which has structured Plutarch's argument, as well as distrustful of the number of cities attributed to the conqueror (70!), it is nevertheless true that Alexander's conquest opened the countries of the middle east to Greek immigration. The Greeks, however, could only imagine life in cities with Greek-style houses, streets, public buildings, civic institutions, and a rural territory where the colonists could hold plots of land (*klēroi*). Begun by Alexander, usually as military colonies rather than cities proper (*Alexandria in Egypt is an exception), this policy was followed by his successors and developed further by the *Seleucids. Every region of their empire was included, but it is possible to distinguish four arenas in particular: *Babylonia (including Susiana and the Persian Gulf), where Seleuceia on Tigris filled the role of royal residence (Akk. *āl šarrūti*), and the military colonists of the islet of *Icaros (mod. Failaka) held land-grants; north *Syria, the 'new Macedon', sown with dynastic foundations (*Antioch, Apamea, Seleuceia in Pieria, Laodicea-on-the-Sea); *Asia Minor, where new cities were planted on older sites (e.g. Celaenae/Apamea, Laodicea-Lycus, etc.); and, last but not least, central Asia, where the best-documented example is *Ai Khanoum (perhaps originally an Alexandria). All the foundations received a Greek and/or Macedonian population, as the onomastic evidence shows; the Seleucids wanted, in effect, 'to create *Greek* colonies and to instal citizens of Greek cities in Phrygia, in Pisidia, and even in the Persian Gulf region' (Louis Robert). When Antiochus I (281–261) wanted to strengthen the city of Antioch-Persis, he asked Magnesia ad Maeandrum (western Asia Minor) to send a contingent of new colonists. Even the most distant foundations remained in direct contact with their Aegean

counterparts: we know, for example, that the philosopher Clearchus of Soli, a pupil of Aristotle, stayed at Ai Khanoum, leaving as evidence a copy of the Delphic maxims; the family of the Graeco-Bactrian king Euthydemus I (last quarter of the 3rd cent. BC) came from Magnesia ad Maeandrum, and influences from the Maeander valley are also detectable in a statuette found in the Bactrian sanctuary of Takht-i Sangin; the Greek inscriptions found in Arachosia use a language and syntax which imply regular links with the Aegean cities. However, the Graeco-Macedonian dominance in the new cities implies neither an enforced Hellenization of the local peoples nor their marginalization. (See HELLENISM.) In Babylonia, what is striking is the continuity and survival of traditional social, political, and religious institutions. Anu-uballit, governor of Uruk in the reign of Seleucus II (240–225), is a specially interesting case: he had received permission from the Seleucid king to add to his Babylonian name the Greek 'Nikarchos'; at the same time he continued to watch over and care for the Babylonian sanctuaries of the city.   P. B.

colonization, Roman The earliest colonies of Roman citizens were small groups of 300 families at *Ostia, Antium (mod. Anzio, 338 BC), and Tarracina (mod. Terracina, 329 BC). Others were added as the Roman territory expanded, through reluctance to maintain a permanent fleet. In 218 there were 12 such '*coloniae maritimae*'. The older view that such small communities were to serve as garrisons guarding the coasts of Italy, and even their title, have been disputed and a more political 'Romanizing' or 'urbanizing' purpose envisaged. (See ROMANIZATION; URBANISM.) *Coloni* retained Roman citizenship because the early colonies were within Roman territory, and were too small to form an independent *res publica*; some colonies, such as those at Antium and Minturnae (295 BC), seem to be part of a double community, rapidly assimilated, even if the relations between the two populations is obscure. Later 'double communities', though often doubted, are attested, as at Interamnia Praetuttiorum (*ILLRP* 617 f.). Citizen colonies are distinct from Latin, which, though largely manned by Romans, were autonomous states established outside Roman territory and with acknowledged strategic aims, clear for the 6,000 sent to Alba Fucens in 303 BC; the two-*iugera* plots ascribed to Tarracina (however supplemented by access to undistributed land) were smaller than those allotted to Latin colonists (15 at Vibo Valentia, mod. Monteleone, in 192 BC). '*Coloniae maritimae*' seem to have been normally exempt from legionary service, though the exemption was revocable, and *coloni* were bound not to absent themselves by night from their colonies in time of war. (Arguments brought against this *vacatio militiae* are not wholly convincing.)

About 177 BC the system of citizen colonies was reorganized. They were assimilated to Latin colonies, and the use of the latter to all appearances abandoned. Henceforth citizen colonies were large—2,000–5,000 men—and were employed for the same purpose as Latin colonies formerly.

It should not be assumed, however, that all the original Roman colonies remained small and static. Puteoli (194 BC), mod. Pozzuoli, though exceptional because of its position, was showing administrative complexity and magisterial jurisdiction in a public building contract of 105 BC (*ILLRP* 518). It is worth noting too that the first deployment of large Roman colonies is in Cisalpina (2,000 at Parma and Mutina, 183 BC), where the strategic and cultural situation was different from that of 4th-cent. Latium. Generous allotments of land were given to the new colonies and their internal organization was changed also. They remained citizen colonies but received extensive powers of local government for their annual magistrates—*duoviri, praetores*, or *duoviri praetores*—and council (*consilium*). Not many of the new-style colonies were founded till the time of Tiberius and Gaius *Gracchus, when a further change took place in their employment. Henceforth they were founded for social and political as much as for strategic reasons, either as emigration schemes for the landless or to provide for veteran soldiers. They could, as with the Sullan settlements in Etruria and *Pompeii (see SULLA), cause friction with the original inhabitants and give rise to unrest, notably the revolts of 78 and 63 BC.

The first foundation outside Italy was the Gracchan Junonia at *Carthage (122 BC). Its charter was revoked, but the *coloni* retained their allotments. In 118 BC Narbo Martius in Provence was successful despite senatorial objections. In 103 and 100 BC, Lucius Appuleius Saturninus (*tribune of the plebs 103) and *Marius proposed large-scale colonization in certain provinces, and effected a few settlements in Africa, Corsica, and Provence. But extensive colonization outside Italy became regular only under *Caesar and Octavian (the future *Augustus), when, reflecting the change in the locus of political power, colonies began to adopt the names of their founders and benefactors as titles of honour (so *Colonia Claudia Ara Agrippinensium*, Cologne, AD 50). Some colonists were still being drawn from the civilian population, notably at the refounding of Carthage and Corinth and at Urso in Spain (all about 44 BC). Such exceptional colonies were known as *coloniae civicae*. Augustus, discharging his veterans and avoiding Italy after 27 BC, established numerous colonies not only in Narbonensis (see GAUL (TRANSALPINE)), the Spanish provinces, *Africa, and Mauretania, but also in the east. There had already been Caesarian foundations in *Asia Minor (e.g. Apamea Myrlea). After the battle of Philippi (42), Octavian gave veterans Italian land (Cass. Dio 49. 14 records the allocation to Campanian Capua of Cretan territory in compensation), but the Perusine war (42) showed that if not sent home (*RG* 16) they would have to be settled elsewhere, and the numbers of Antonian troops to be discharged indicated the east. (See MARK ANTONY.) Augustan colonies were thickly scattered, mainly on the seaboard of Greece and NW Asia Minor. In Pisidia (25 BC), surrounding the mountains that sheltered the rebellious Homanadenses, and at Berytus (c.14 BC), mod. Beirut, they provided a military presence when legions could not

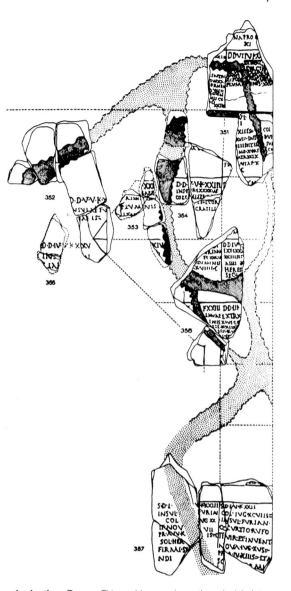

colonization, Roman This marble map shows the colonial plots of land created by *centuriation of islands formed by the river Rhône in the territory of Arausio (Orange), a veteran-colony. As was usually the case with Rome's overseas colonies, Arausio was founded on land taken from subject peoples.

be afforded. In the east an existing *polis* could survive colonization: at Iconium in Phrygia and at Ninica in Cilicia, both in Asia Minor, native communities continued; colonization may be seen as part of a movement in populations that included the individual settlement of Italian businessmen, soldiers, and others, as well as the creation of hybrids like *Nicopolis in Epirus: colonization was sometimes unofficial in both east and west. In the later republic, casual immigrants established the *pagus* and *conventus civium romanorum*, 'community of Roman citizens', in native settlements, thus forming the basis of future *municipia*, municipalities.

Eastern colonies used the standard constitution of *duoviri* and *ordo* (see below); where there was a genuine settlement the use of Latin for official purposes was persistent, and the eastern colonies were a fruitful source of senators and *equites, for their size, but the overall picture, in language, constitution, religion, and architecture, is of a rich mix. To possess a Capitolium (temple of *Jupiter) was important, and some colonies, Ariminum (268 BC and Augustan), Puteoli, Pisidian Antioch (25 BC), were miniature Romes (Gell. *na* 16. 13. 8 f.), even organized into seven districts (*vici*). if colonies sent to places where native communities already existed provided the latter with the model of how Romans and Italians lived, and brought some means of following it, that was incidental (see ROMANIZATION). None the less, the original communities would often eventually receive citizenship and coalesce with the colony.

Eastern colonization continued under *Claudius and *Vespasian (Ptolemais, AD 51, mod. Acco; Caesarea in Palestine, *c.* AD 70) but increasingly became a means of enhancing the status of existing cities (even though the concomitant privileges did not include exemption from tribute) rather than of finding homes for veterans or of constructing military outposts. *Colonia Aelia Capitolina* (Jerusalem, AD 135) was a special punitive case (see JEWS). Claudius also began the regular colonization of the Balkan provinces and the northern frontier, which continued till *Hadrian. Thenceforth no new colonies were founded. Instead, the title colony with *ius coloniae* became a privilege increasingly sought out by *municipia* as the highest grade of civic dignity. The process began when Claudius conferred the title on the capital cities of certain Gallic communities, but only became considerable in the 2nd cent.

The arrangements for local government in Caesarian and imperial colonies were a more complex development of the earlier system. Colonial magistracies were always more standardized than municipal and eventually came to resemble a small-scale replica of the Roman constitution; so the 300 families of early Roman colonies echoed threefold divisions of the Romulan state. (Hence the later popularity of the *ius coloniae*, 'colonial status'.) However, the evolution of constitutions in Italy was very gradual. *Duoviri iure dicundo* ('two magistrates for interpreting the law') appear under the republic only at Pompeii and Ostia. While there is evidence for standardization in Cic. *Leg. agr.* 2. 92 f., and Caesar was responsible for developments in connection with his agrarian legislation, the *lex Mamilia Roscia Peducaea Alliena Fabia* (FIRA 12, 138 no. 12), archaic elements persisted ('*manus iniectio*' occurs in the Caesarian law for Urso, 177 no. 21 (= Dessau, *ILS* 6087), 61). Aediles and sometimes quaestors are also attested, the former before republic passed into empire: at Venusia the colony began electing quaestors in 34 BC (*fasti Venusini*, CIL 9. 422). The census was taken by *duoviri quinquennales* ('quinquennial magistrates'), replaced

in some Italian colonies by *censores*. Even under the empire individuality was not wiped out: Abellinum had *censores*, *praetores duoviri*, and *aediles duoviri*, the last apparently unique, and some colonies in Narbonensis may have had *quattuorviri* (A. Degrassi, *Scritti vari* 1 (1962), 127–43; aediles 179–83). Ex-magistrates passed into the council of decuriones, sometimes called *conscripti*. See CENTURIATION; MAGISTRACY, ROMAN. A. N. S.-W.; B. M. L.; E. H. B.

Colosseum, the medieval name of the Amphitheatrum Flavium, near the colossus of *Nero on the site of the lake of Nero's palace, the Domus Aurea (Golden House). Begun by *Vespasian, it was continued by *Titus, and dedicated in June AD 80. *Domitian was probably responsible only for the complex substructures of the arena. The building measures 188 × 156 m. (205 × 170 yds.) along the axes, and is 52 m. (170 ft.) high. The travertine façade has three storeys of superimposed arcades framed by half columns of the Doric, Ionic, and Corinthian orders, surmounted by a masonry attic decorated with Corinthian pilasters on a low podium; there are windows in the podium and in the spaces between the pilasters, alternating with bronze shields. There were also mast-corbels for the awning, worked by sailors. The seating, supported by concrete vaults, was in three tiers, with standing room above it. The arena was cut off by a fence and a high platform carrying marble chairs for guilds and officials, including boxes for the emperor and magistrates on the short axis. The arena was floored in timber, covering cages for beasts, mechanical elevators, and drains. Audiences, estimated at 50,000, were marshalled outside the building in an area bordered by bollards, and held tickets corresponding to the 76 numbered arcades, whence an elaborate system of staircases serviced all parts of the auditorium.

The amphitheatre was restored by *Nerva and *Trajan (CIL 6. 32254–5), *Antoninus Pius (SHA *Ant. Pius* 8), after the fires of 217 (Cass. Dio 78. 25; SHA *Heliogab.* 17; *Alex. Sev.* 24; *Maximus et Balbinus* 1. 14) and of 250 (Jer. *Ab Abr.* 2268), after 442 (CIL 6. 32094), and in 523 (Cassiod. *Var.* 5. 42). I. A. R.; D. E. S.; J. D.

comedy (Greek), Old (*see facing page*)

comedy (Greek), Middle (*see page 186*)

comedy (Greek), New (*see page 189*)

comedy, Latin This term has come to be synonymous with *fabula palliata* ('drama in a Greek cloak'), since the *palliatae* of *Plautus and *Terence are the only complete Latin comedies to have survived from antiquity. But there were other types of comedy in Latin (*Atellana*, a masked drama named from the town Atella in Campania; *togata*, '(drama) in a toga'; mime; and others), and there was clearly some overlap of subject-matter, titles, and style between the various types. *Varro praised Titinius (?first half of 2nd cent. BC), Terence, and Quinctius Atta for their

[*continued on p. 190*]

Greek comedy

Old Comedy 1. For practical purposes, 'Old Comedy' is best defined as the comedies produced at Athens during the 5th cent. BC. An early form of comedy was composed in *Sicily, the connection of which with Attic comedy is hypothetical. At Athens itself no transition from Old to Middle Comedy occurred precisely in 400 BC, but the two extant plays of *Aristophanes which belong to the 4th cent. differ in character from his earlier work, above all in the role of the chorus (see para. 2 below). The provision of comedies at the City Dionysia festival each year was made the responsibility of the relevant magistrate in 488/7 or 487/6 BC ('eight years before the Persian Wars' of 480–479 BC), *Suda*, entry under *Chiōnidēs*; cf. *IG* 2². 2325); *Aristotle's statement (*Poet.* 1449ᵇ2) that before then comic performances were given by 'volunteers' (*ethelontai*) is probably a guess, but a good one. Comedies were first included in the Lenaea festival shortly before 440 BC. Before and after the Peloponnesian War (431–404) five comedies were performed at each festival; there is evidence that the number was reduced to three during the war, but this question is controversial. In the 4th cent. comedies were performed also at the Rural Dionysia (cf. Aeschin. 1. 157), festivals of Dionysus held in the local districts of Athens, and it is likely, given the existence of early theatres in several of these districts (demes: see DEMOCRACY, ATHENIAN), that such performances were widespread before the end of the 5th cent. No complete plays of any poet of the Old Comedy except Aristophanes survive, and he belongs to the last stage of the genre, but we have a great many citations from the work of his elders (notably Cratinus, 2nd half of the 5th cent.) and contemporaries (notably Eupolis). Some of these support generalizations about Old Comedy based on Aristophanes, but where support is absent or doubtful it is important to remember Aristophanes' date and not to assume that the structural features common to his earliest plays constitute, as a whole, a formula of great antiquity.

2. The chorus, which had 24 members (cf. Ar. *Av.* 297 ff., with scholia (ancient commentaries) and on *Ach.* 211), was of primary importance in Old Comedy, and very many plays (e.g. *Babylonians*, *Banqueters*, *Acharnians*) take their names from their choruses. In Aristophanes (the practice may have been different in Cratinus) the chorus addresses the audience in the parabasis, which has a central position in the play, and again at a later stage. In parts of the parabasis the chorus maintains its dramatic role (as Acharnians, knights, clouds, jurymen, etc.), while in others it speaks directly for the poet; in the former case dramatic illusion is partly broken, in the latter case wholly. The entry of the chorus is sometimes a moment of violence and excitement; it may be (as in *Acharnians* and *Wasps*) hostile to the 'hero' of the play, and it has to be won over; thereafter it is on his side, applauding and reinforcing what he says and does. It is possible that the sequence hostility–contest–reconciliation between chorus and hero was a common formula.

3. The plots of Old Comedy are usually fantastic. In their indifference to the passage of time, the ease with which a change of scene may be assumed without any complete break in the action (places which in reality would be far apart can be treated as adjacent), and the frequency of their references to the audience, the theatre, and the occasion of performance, they resemble a complex of related charades or variety 'turns' rather than comedy as we generally understand the term. The context of the plot is the contemporary situation. In this situation, a character takes some action which may violate the laws of nature (e.g. in Aristophanes' *Peace* Trygaeus flies to the home of the gods on a giant beetle in order to release the goddess Peace from imprisonment and bring her back to earth) or may show a complete disregard for practical objections (e.g. in Aristophanes' *Acharnians* Dicaeopolis makes a private peace treaty with his country's enemies and enjoys the benefits of peace). Events in Old Comedy are sometimes a translation of metaphorical or symbolic language into dramatic terms, sometimes the realization of common fantasies; they involve supernatural beings of all kinds and the talking animals familiar in folklore. The comic possibilities of the hero's realization of his fantasy are

often exploited by showing, in a succession of short episodes, the consequences of this realization for various professions and types. The end of the play is festive in character (Aristophanes' *Clouds* is a striking exception), a kind of formal recognition of the hero's triumph, but the logical relation between the ending and the preceding events may be (as in Aristophanes' *Wasps*) very loose, as if to drown the question 'But what happened *then*?' in the noise of song and dance and to remind us that we are gathered together in the theatre to amuse ourselves and Dionysus by a cheerful show.

4. Men prominent in contemporary society are vilified, ridiculed, and parodied in Old Comedy. Sometimes they are major characters, either under their own names (e.g. '*Socrates' in *Clouds* and '*Euripides' in *Thesmophoriazusae*) or under a very thin disguise (e.g. the 'Paphlagonian slave' in *Knights*, who is the politician Cleon (d. 422)). Many plays, e.g. *Hyperbolus* and *Cleophon*, actually bore real men's names as their titles. The spirit in which this treatment was taken by its victims and by the audience raises (and is likely always to raise) the most difficult question in the study of Old Comedy. A man would hardly become a comic poet unless he had the sense of humour and the natural scepticism which combine to make a satirist, and prominent politicians are always fair game for satire. Equally, artistic or intellectual change is a more obvious and rewarding target for ridicule than traditional practices and beliefs. There is nothing in the comic poets' work to suggest that as a class they positively encouraged an oligarchic revolution, and their own art was characterized by elaborate and continuous innovation. There is some evidence (schol. Ar. *Ach.* 67, cf. schol. Ar. *Av.* 1297) for attempts to restrict the ridiculing of individuals by legislation; the evidence for their scope and effect is scanty.

5. Mythology and theology are treated with extreme irreverence in Old Comedy; some plays were burlesque versions of myths, and gods (especially *Dionysus) were made to appear (e.g. in Aristophanes' *Frogs* and Cratinus' *Dionysalexandros*) foolish, cowardly, and dishonest. Yet the reality of the gods' power and the validity of the community's worship of them are consistently assumed and on occasion affirmed, while words and actions of ill-omen for the community are avoided. It is probable that comic irreverence is the elevation to a high artistic level (the bard Demodocus' tale of *Ares and *Aphrodite in *Od.* 8 may be compared) of a type of irreverence which permeates the folklore of polytheistic cultures. The essential spirit of Old Comedy is the ordinary man's protest—using his inalienable weapons, humour and fantasy—against all who are in some way stronger or better than he: gods, politicians, generals, artists, and intellectuals.

6. The actors wore grotesque masks, and their costume included artificial exaggeration (e.g. of belly and phallus or erect penis) for comic effect; the phallus may have been invariable for male roles until the 4th cent. No limit seems to have been set, in speech or action, to the humorous exploitation of sex (normal and unorthodox) and excretion, and the vocabulary used in these types of humour eschews the euphemism characteristic of prose literature.

7. Most of the extant comedies of Aristophanes require for their performance four actors and, on occasion, supernumeraries, whose responsibilities can be precisely defined. Performance by three actors plus supernumeraries is possible only if we give the latter a degree of responsibility which blurs the distinction between actor and supernumerary.

See also: ARISTOPHANES.   K. J. D.

Middle Comedy The term 'Middle Comedy' was coined by a Hellenistic scholar (?Aristophanes of Byzantium) as a convenient label for plays produced in the years between Old and New Comedy (*c*.404–*c*.321 BC). This was a time of experiment and transition; different types of comedy seem to have predominated at different periods; probably no single kind of play deserves to be styled 'Middle Comedy' to the exclusion of all others.

The defeat of Athens in 404 BC vitally affected the comic stage; the loss of imperial power and political energy was reflected in comedy by a choice of material less intrinsically Athenian and more cosmopolitan. In form at least the changes began early. *Aristophanes' *Ecclesiazusae* ('Assemblywomen':

Old Comedy S. Italian pottery bowl (krater), 400–380 BC, showing a comedy performed on a raised stage by actors wearing comic masks, padding, and phalluses.

New Comedy Roman *mosaic from Mytilene (*Lesbos) with scene from the play 'Girl from Samos' (*Samia*, inscribed top left) by Menander, a title savouring of the love-interest which the plots of New Comedy favoured.

probably 393 BC) and *Plutus* ('Wealth': 388), now generally acknowledged to be early examples of Middle Comedy, reveal the atrophy of the comic chorus. The parabasis has disappeared; instead of lyrics specially composed for the chorus, interpolated pieces (*embolima*) were used at points marked in the MSS by the word *chorou*, '(song) of the chorus'. Already in the *Plutus* the lines expressly written for the chorus are virtually reduced to an entrance dialogue and duet. This decline of the chorus was probably gradual but not rectilinear. Throughout the period plays that took their titles from the chorus (e.g. Eubulus' *Stephanopolides* ('Garland-sellers'), cf. Heniochus fr. 5) continued to be written, and examples can be found of choruses that still conversed with the actors (Aeschin. 1. 157, 345 BC; cf. Alexis fr. 239 KA = 237 K) or sang specially composed lyrics (Eubulus frs. 102, 103 KA = 104, 105 K). Yet the typical New-Comedy chorus, which took no part in the plot, must have become the norm by the end of the period, together with the five-act structure that its four unscripted interludes made possible.

The dangling phallus and grotesque padding of Old-Comedy costume were probably given up during the period, but it is uncertain whether this was the result of legislation (the politician Lycurgus' theatrical reforms 338–*c*.325/4) or a change in popular taste.

Yet the specific flavour of Middle Comedy remains elusive. The pronouncements of ancient scholarship (e.g. Platonius 10–11 Kaibel = 50ff. Perusino, emphasizing the lack of political criticism and the popularity of mythological burlesque; *Aristotle, *Eth. Nic.* 4. 6, 1128ª22 ff., claiming that contemporary comedy had replaced the foul language of Old Comedy with innuendo) seem reasonably accurate, provided they are not interpreted too rigidly. In the absence of any complete play (after the *Plutus*) judgements about Middle Comedy almost entirely depend on the interpretation of a large number of fragments, often quoted along with their play-titles, but it cannot be stressed too greatly that the bias of the main preserver of these fragments, Athenaeus, may give a distorted impression of the part that descriptions of food and drink played in Middle Comedy.

Even so titles and fragments, when carefully examined, can be very informative. The variety of subject, especially in contrast with New Comedy, is striking. Plays with political themes were still produced, mainly but not exclusively in the early part of the period (notable titles are Eubulus' *Dionysius*, Mnesimachus' *Philip*), and politicians such as *Demosthenes and Callimedon were frequently ridiculed, if rarely criticized outright. As in Old Comedy, philosophers were pilloried and their views comically misrepresented; *Plato and the Pythagorean sects (see PYTHAGORAS) seem to have been the commonest victims. In the earlier part of the period mythological burlesque played a prominent role, doubtless continuing Old-Comedy traditions. There may have been two main types of such burlesque: straight travesty of a myth, with or without political innuendo, and parody of tragic (especially *Euripidean) versions. The aim was often to reinterpret a myth in contemporary terms; thus *Heracles is asked to select a book from the musician Linus' library of classical authors (Alexis fr. 140 KA = 135 K), and Pelops (see OLYMPIA §1) complains about the meagre meals of Greece by contrast with the Persian king's roast camel (Antiphanes fr. 172 KA = 170 K). Popular also were riddles, long descriptions of food and feasting (often in extravagantly poetic language or anapaestic dimeters), and the comedy of mistaken identity (Middle-Comedy originals have been suggested for *Plautus' *Menaechmi* ('The Brothers Menaechmus') and *Amphitruo*).

Numerous fragments and titles show that the presentation of contemporary types, manners, and pursuits (e.g. *kitharōidos*/lyre-player, *mempsimoiros*/fault-finder, *skyteus*/cobbler, *philothēbaios*/the 'I love Thebes' man) was a characteristic of Middle Comedy. This interest in the details of ordinary life may well have been associated with the development of one particular type of play, which dealt with a series of more or less plausible everyday experiences such as love affairs and confidence tricks, and featured a group of stock characters ultimately (though with the distortions of caricature) drawn from life. This was the type of play that later prevailed in New Comedy. Virtually all its stock figures (e.g. cooks, parasites, pimps, soldiers, courtesans, angry or avaricious old men, young men in love) can be identified in the fragments and titles of Middle Comedy. Although several of these characters can be traced back, at least embryonically, to Old Comedy (thus the braggart soldier has a prototype in the

Lamachus of Aristophanes' *Acharnians*; Eupolis named one play *Kolakes*, 'Parasites', after its chorus; courtesans were title-figures in several of Pherecrates' comedies), it is clear that the middle of the 4th cent. had the greatest influence on their typology. That was the time when, for instance, the cook began to receive his typical attributes of braggadocio and garrulousness, and the parasite or sponger to be called regularly by this name (*parasitos*) in place of the older term *kolax*.

Plots of the standard New-Comedy pattern can already be detected in the surviving fragments of Middle Comedy; Alexis' *Agonis* (datable to *c*.340–330 BC) featured a courtesan named Agonis, a young man in love, and probably too a confidence trick and recognition. Some of the typical plot elements (e.g. low trickery, the clever slave) go back to Old Comedy and probably beyond that to popular farce; others (e.g. recognition scenes) owe much to tragedy, especially Euripides. Although several of the sources are disputed, the part played by Middle Comedy in the complicated story of the development of the typical New-Comedy plot must not be underestimated. Aristophanes is said to have introduced rape and recognition into comedy, but only in a mythological burlesque, the *Cocalus*, a late play written in the Middle-Comedy period. Rapes and recognitions are likely to have been themes of other Middle-Comedy burlesques such as Eubulus' *Auge* and *Ion* and Anaxandrides' *Helen*, all perhaps incorporating parodies of Euripidean tragedies which were famous for their rapes and recognitions. Consequently, when the *Suda* (α 1982) claims that it was Anaxandrides who invented 'love affairs and the rapes of maidens', this probably means that this comic poet was the first to use them as incidents of contemporary life in a non-mythological framework.

To 57 poets Athenaeus attributes more than 800 plays. We know the names of about 50 poets, many of them non-Athenian but writing for the Attic stage. The most important are Alexis (who continued writing well into the New-Comedy period), Anaxandrides, Antiphanes, Eubulus, and Timocles.

The fragments of all the Middle-Comedy poets are superbly edited by Kassel and Austin, *PCG* 2, 3/2, 4, 5, 7; this supersedes the older editions by Meineke, Kock, and Edmonds, although Kock's numbering of the fragments was standard previous to Kassel and Austin, and Edmonds's edition (Middle Comedy in vol. 2, 1959) adds a lively but inaccurate English translation. Eubulus is edited also by R. L. Hunter (1983), Alexis by W. G. Arnott (1996).   W. G. A.

New Comedy, comedy written from the last quarter of the 4th cent. BC onwards, but generally regarded as ending its creative heyday in the mid-3rd cent., composed mainly but not exclusively for first performance at Athens. At some stage the author of an anonymous treatise on comedy reckoned to know that there were 64 playwrights of New Comedy, of whom the most distinguished were Philemon, Menander, Diphilus, Philippides, Posidippus, and Apollodorus (*Prolegomena de comoedia*, ed. W. J. W. Koster (1975), 10); the first three are commonly seen as the leading playwrights of the period, and above all Menander, who, though not the most successful in his own lifetime, was soon recognized as the outstanding practitioner of this type of drama. The volumes of Kassel and Austin, *Poetae Comici Graeci* include nearly 80 playwrights dated with some probability as active between 325 and 200, and over 50 of later date; but many are simply names (or even fragments of names) found on inscriptions. A large number of fragmentary papyrus texts are believed to be from New Comedy (because of their similarity to identifiable texts), but they remain anonymous.

Texts of Menander (and perhaps others) circulated widely until the 7th cent. AD but were then completely lost; only with the discovery of papyri from Egypt in the 20th cent. did it again become possible to form a picture of some plays at first hand. In the mean time, knowledge of the genre was based very largely on the Latin adaptations by *Plautus and *Terence, though there are also echoes in later Greek authors such as Alciphron (2nd or 3rd cent. AD) and *Lucian. Even now we have perhaps 8 per cent of Menander's total output and otherwise very little in Greek except scrappy fragments and short quotations. But there is enough in common between the surviving Greek remains and the Latin adaptations for us to feel confident about picking out certain features as characteristic of the genre as a whole (see pp. 186–9 on Middle Comedy).

Athens continued (at least at first) to be the magnet that attracted playwrights like Diphilus and Philemon from far away. But the plays themselves were quickly exported all over the Greek-speaking world, as is shown by the large number of terracotta masks and other artistic representations that have been discovered and by the evidence for travelling companies of 'artists of Dionysus'. Although Athenian citizenship and marriage-laws are integral to many of the plays, the presentation of characters, situations, and relationships is true to such universal elements of human experience that the plays could be enjoyed then as now by audiences far removed from Athens. Political references are rare and subordinate to the portrayal of the private and family life of fictional individuals; there are social tensions (between rich and poor, town and country, citizens and non-citizens, free and slave, men and women, parents and children), but they are not specific to one time or place. Love or infatuation (always heterosexual) plays a part and is regularly shown triumphing over obstacles in a variety of contexts. But this is not the only ingredient; Menander excelled at the sympathetic portrayal of many kinds of personal relationship and of the problems that arise from ignorance, misunderstanding, and prejudice. These generate scenes that the audience can perceive as comic because of their own superior knowledge, enjoying the irony of the situation; but Menander often plays games with his audience's expectations as well. Menander may have been exceptional, both in the skill with which he handled all these elements and altogether in the elegance and economy of his plot-construction; but this is the type of play that is accepted as typical of New Comedy.

The playwrights' skill lay partly in their ability to give fresh treatment to familiar material. In some ways comedy had become simpler and tamer by the end of the 4th cent.: there was little metrical variety (and the chorus was reduced to performing interludes that marked the act-breaks in a standard five-act structure) and very little obscenity (the costume of male characters no longer included a phallus), and the exuberant fantasies of Old Comedy were not found. But there were boastful stock characters (such as cooks, parasites or spongers, and soldiers), stock situations (such as the rediscovery of long-lost children), and familiar comic routines (such as the door-knocking scene which is central to the presentation of the main character in the third act of Menander's *Dyscolus* and can be traced back to Aristophanes' *Acharnians*). The terracottas show that there was also a standard repertoire of masks; some correspond closely with the descriptions in the list of 44 'masks of New Comedy' by the scholar Pollux of Naucratis (*Onom.* 4. 143–54, 2nd cent. AD), but the status of that list is unclear since the repertoire must have evolved flexibly. It has been suggested that particular masks were attached to particular names and that in some sense the same character was seen to appear in play after play with the same name and mask; on the whole the evidence of the plays tells against this.   P. G. M. B.

character-drawing, combining authors of *palliata* and *togata* in the same list, and both types were influenced by Menander (see above p. 189). The creative heyday of the *palliata* is thought to have been from Livius Andronicus (2nd half of the 3rd cent. BC) to Turpilius (?d. 103 BC), that of the *togata* from Titinius to Atta; most productions cannot be dated, but the two types probably flourished side by side in the mid-2nd cent. BC. This may reflect a development within the *palliata*; at first happy to allow the inclusion of Roman elements in its Greek setting (as seen most clearly in the plays of Plautus), it came to favour greater consistency and thereby perhaps encouraged the development of a separate type of comedy with an Italian setting.

Plautus and Terence continued to be performed, and new *palliatae* to be written, at least until the time of *Horace, and *togatae* too were occasionally revived; but the comic stage came to be dominated by the coarser *Atellana*

(still performed in *Juvenal's day) and above all (for several centuries) the mime. The comedies of Pomponius Bassulus (?early 2nd cent. AD) and his ?contemporary Vergilius Romanus were doubtless written for recitation, like the *togatae* mentioned by Juvenal at about the same time.

*Livy's account of the evolution of drama at Rome (7. 2; cf. Hor. *Epist.* 2. 1. 139 ff.) does not explicitly distinguish comedy from tragedy, and its value is questionable. But it does include an informal tradition of 'jests in improvised verse' as a relevant factor in the period before Livius Andronicus introduced plays with coherent plots. The Romans were doubtless also familiar with native Italian traditions such as the *Atellana* before they began to enjoy the *palliata*, and there are clear signs of the influence of the former on the latter, at least in our texts of Plautus; in turn, when the *Atellana* became scripted in the time of Sulla, it was influenced by the *palliata*. Furthermore, knowledge of

Greek drama was widespread in southern Italy well before Livius Andronicus, and many Romans must have seen or heard of performances in Greek by travelling 'artists of Dionysus' (though perhaps not normally in Rome itself); such performances may themselves have influenced the native Italian traditions.

It is generally assumed that all actors were male, except in mimes. They certainly wore masks in *Atellana*, almost certainly in *palliata*, and perhaps also in *togata*, but not in mimes.

For an attempt to show that satyr-plays were written and performed at Rome, see T. P. Wiseman, *JRS* 1988.

See also ENNIUS; NAEVIUS.   P. G. M. B.

commerce See TRADE.

Commodus, Lucius Aurelius, sole emperor AD 180–92, one of twin sons born to M. *Aurelius and Faustina in August 161, the first emperor 'born in the purple'. Given the title Caesar in 166, he was summoned to his father's side after the usurpation of Avidius Cassius, the governor of Syria, in 175, received *imperium* and *tribunicia potestas* (SEE TRIBUNE OF THE PLEBS) at the end of 176, and was consul in 177, now Augustus and co-ruler. He was married in 178 to Bruttia Crispina and left Rome with Marcus for the second Marcomannic War. On his father's death on 17 March 180 he became sole emperor, taking the names Marcus Aurelius Commodus Antoninus, rapidly made peace, and abandoned the newly annexed territories, holding a triumph in October 180.

Major wars were avoided during the reign, the exception being in Britain, where, following a breach of the northern frontier, victories were won by Ulpius Marcellus, for which Commodus assumed the title Britannicus in AD 184. There were minor disturbances on the Danube frontier and in Mauretania (NW Africa), and serious problems with *brigandage and deserters, as well as mutinies in the British army. Commodus at first retained his father's ministers, e.g. the guard prefect Taruttienus Paternus, but after an assassination attempt in 182, in which the emperor's sister Annia Aurelia Galeria Lucilla was implicated, Paternus was dismissed and soon killed along with many others. The guard prefect Tigidius Perennis effectively ran the government from 182 to 185, when he was lynched by mutinous troops. Marcus Aurelius Cleander, the freedman chamberlain, was the next favourite to hold power, even becoming guard prefect. After his fall in 190, following riots at Rome, power was shared by the emperor's favourite concubine Marcia, the chamberlain Eclectus, and (from 191) the guard prefect Quintus Aemilius Laetus. Commodus, by now obsessively devoted to performing as a *gladiator, appeared to be dangerously deranged. Proclaiming a new golden age, he shook off his allegiance to his father's memory, calling himself Lucius Aelius Aurelius Commodus, as well as eight other names, including Hercules Romanus: each month was given one of these names; Rome itself became the *Colonia Commodiana*. Numerous senators had

been executed; others feared the same fate, and Laetus, probably with the connivance of Publius Helvius Pertinax (consul 175) and others, had Commodus strangled in the night of 31 December 192. His memory was at once condemned, but was restored by *Septimius Severus in 195.

A. R. Bi.

confederacies See FEDERAL STATES.

Constantine I (*see following page*)

Constantinople See BYZANTIUM; CONSTANTINE.

consul, the title of the chief annual civil and military magistrates of Rome during the republic. Two consuls were elected annually for most, if not all, of the republic by the *comitia centuriata* (wealth-based citizen-assembly voting in centuries) at a meeting called for the purpose, normally by a consul, exceptionally by a *dictator, *interrex* (a *patrician senator chosen to supervise consular elections when both consuls died in office), or military tribune with consular power. Before 153 BC their year of office began on 15 March (possibly earlier in the years before *c.*220), thereafter on 1 January.

According to tradition the dual annual magistracy succeeded immediately to the kingship. Most of the powers of the king (including military command and the right to summon the senate and the people, but excluding certain religious functions, reserved for the *pontifices* (see PRIESTS) and the *rex sacrorum*, 'king for sacred rites', a patrician priest) fell to a pair of annual magistrates, called originally praetors (Livy 3. 55. 12; Festus 249 Lindsay) and subsequently consuls, the powers now tempered by the principle of collegiality and limited tenure of office. Against this it has been held that the dual collegiate system must have been some time in developing, and scholars have pointed to the fact that for most of the years from 448 to 368 there were more than two chief magistrates (the military tribunes) and to Livy 7. 3. 5, where an 'ancient law' (*lex vetusta*) is referred to that mentions a *praetor maximus*, taken to refer to a sole (or pre-eminent) chief magistrate. The title praetor (from *prae-ire*, to go before; the etymology of 'consul' is not clear) suggests military leadership, and many have seen in the *praetor maximus* the supreme magistrate of the early republic, with the fully collegiate magistracy appearing in its final dual form only much later, perhaps as late as 367. The traditional view that republic and dual magistracy were coeval is supported by the *fasti* (inscribed records of consuls), which show a succession of two annual consuls in the years before 451, and was apparently in place by the time *Polybius wrote (see 3. 22. 1–2). The testimony of the *fasti* has yet to be successfully impugned, and modern supporters of the traditional view have seen in Livy's *praetor maximus* a descriptive reference to the senior (but not more powerful) of the two collegial magistrates or an indication of the superiority of their office. The Greek translations (*stratēgos* for praetor

[*continued on p. 195*]

Constantine I

Constantine I, 'the Great' (Flavius Valerius Constantinus) (*c.* AD 272/3–337), born at Naissus, was son of Constantius I and Helena. When his father was appointed Caesar (293) Constantine remained as a tribune at the court of Diocletian (ruled 285–305). He fought alongside the emperor Galerius against Persia (298) and the Sarmatians (299), and was at Nicomedia (Bithynia) in 303 and again in 305 when Diocletian abdicated. Constantius was now senior Augustus; his eastern partner Galerius reluctantly released Constantine for service with his father. Constantine, fearing interception by the western Caesar, Flavius Valerius Severus, hastened to *Britain to aid his father against the Picts.

When Constantius died at York (306), his troops proclaimed Constantine Augustus; Galerius gave this rank to Severus, but grudgingly conceded Constantine the title Caesar. Based mainly at Trier, Constantine ruled his father's territories of Spain, Gaul, and Britain. At Rome Maxentius usurped power; Severus and then Galerius failed to dislodge him. For Constantine an alliance with Maxentius was welcome. The usurper's father, the former emperor Maximian, returned to power, visited Constantine in Gaul (307), and gave him the title Augustus and his daughter Fausta in marriage. Constantine sheltered Maximian when driven from Rome after failing to depose his son (308). At the conference of Carnuntum on the Danube Galerius gave the title Augustus to Licinius; like Maximinus in the east, Constantine spurned the style *filius Augustorum* (son of the Augusti) and retained that of Augustus, which Galerius recognized (309/10). Meanwhile he defended the Rhine, warring against the Franks (306–7), raiding the territory of the Bructeri, and bridging the river at Cologne (Colonia Agrippinensis, 308). He was campaigning against the Franks (310) when Maximian tried to regain power. Constantine forced him to surrender and commit suicide. As the connection with the Herculian dynasty was now discredited, a hereditary claim to the throne was invented for Constantine: it was alleged that his father had been related to Claudius II (268–70). On the death of Galerius (311), Maximinus and Licinius narrowly avoided war when partitioning his territories, and as Maximinus looked for support to Maxentius, Constantine looked to Licinius. In 312 Constantine invaded Italy. Victorious over Maxentius' northern forces near Turin and Verona, he marched on Rome. Maxentius gave battle at Saxa Rubra, was defeated, and was drowned near the Mulvian Bridge across the Tiber. The senate welcomed Constantine as liberator and made him, not Maximinus, senior Augustus. He took over the rule of Italy and Africa, and disbanded the praetorian guard which had supported Maxentius.

Two years earlier it had been given out that Constantine had seen a vision of his tutelary deity the sun-god *Apollo accompanied by Victory (see NIKE) and the figure XXX to symbolize the years of rule due to him. By the end of his life Constantine claimed to have seen a (single) cross above the sun, with words 'Be victorious in this'. At Saxa Rubra, Constantine as the result of a dream sent his soldiers into battle with crosses (and no doubt other symbols) on their shields; heavily outnumbered, he defeated Maxentius. No more, yet no less, superstitious than his contemporaries, he saw the hand of the Christian God in this, and the need to maintain such support for himself and the empire. (See CHRISTIANITY.) From that moment he not merely restored Christian property but gave privileges to the clergy, showered benefactions on the Church, and undertook a massive programme of church-building. At Rome a basilica was provided for the Pope where the barracks of the mounted branch of the praetorians had stood, and other churches, most notably St Peter's, followed. His religious outlook may have undergone later transformations, and was affected by his encounters with problems in the Church. In Africa he confronted the Donatist schism: the Donatists (members of a puritanical church of the martyrs) objected to the largess for their opponents and appealed to him. To the *vicarius* (supreme governor) of Africa, a 'fellow worshipper of the most high God', he wrote (314) of his fear that failure to achieve Christian unity would cause God to replace him with another emperor. Sincerity is not determinable by historical method; it is, in any case, not incompatible with a belief that consequential action may have political advantage. He had been present at Nicomedia when persecution began in 303; he knew that the problem with Christianity was that its exclusiveness stood in the way of imperial unity. If he threw in his lot with the Christians, there could be no advantage if they were themselves not united. Following a papal council in 313, his own council at Arles (Arelate) in 314, and his investigation into the dispute, he saw the refusal of the Donatists to conform as obtuse. From 317 he tried coercion; there were exiles and some executions. Totally failing to achieve his object, he left the Donatists to God's judgement (321). Weakness in the face of a movement widespread in Africa was seen when the Donatists seized the basilica Constantine built for the Catholics at Cirta; he left them in possession and built the Catholics another one.

At Milan (Mediolanum, 313) he met Licinius, and gave him his half-sister Constantia in marriage. Back at Nicomedia, Licinius published regulations agreed with Constantine on religious freedom and the restoration of Christian property (the so-called Edict of Milan). Licinius struck down Maximinus, and the two emperors were left to rule in harmony. In 313 the Rhine frontier engaged Constantine's attention; in 314 after attending the council of Arles he campaigned against the Germans; in 315 he spent two months in Rome.

The concord with Licinius was unstable. A first war was decided in Constantine's favour by victories at Cibalae (316) and Campus Ardiensis. Licinius ceded all his European territories except for the diocese of Thrace. In 317 Crispus and Constantine II, sons of Constantine, and Licinius II, son of Licinius, were made Caesars. Constantine spent 317–23 in the Balkans. Licinius became increasingly distrustful of him and suspicious of his own Christian subjects, whom he began to persecute. Constantine defeated a Gothic invasion (323) but was accused by Licinius of usurping his function; war followed. Constantine was victorious at Adrianople, in the Hellespont, and at Chrysopolis, and forced the abdication of Licinius at Nicomedia (324). Though his life was spared after his wife intervened with her brother, Licinius was later accused of plotting and executed, with his Caesar Martinianus (325); the Caesar Licinius II was executed in 326. Implication in the supposed plot may have been the excuse also for Constantine to remove one of the consuls of 325, Proculus. In a mysterious scandal, he even ordered the deaths of his son Crispus and his wife Fausta (326). Only one usurpation is recorded in the rest of his reign: Calocaerus in Cyprus (334), who was burnt alive by the emperor's half-brother Dalmatius.

On 8 November 324 Constantine made his third son Constantius II Caesar and founded Constantinople on the site of *Byzantium. The need for an imperial headquarters near the eastern and Danubian frontiers had been seen by Diocletian, who preferred Nicomedia, mod. Izmit, NW Turkey; Constantine will have recognized the strategic importance of Byzantium in his war with Licinius. The city's dedication with both pagan rites and Christian ceremonies took place on 11 May 330. From the beginning it was 'New Rome', though lower in rank. Pagan temples and cults were absent, but other features of Rome were in time reproduced (Constantius II (337–61) upgraded the city council to equality with the Roman senate). To speak of the foundation of a capital is misleading; yet a permanent imperial residence in the east did in the end emphasize division between the empire's Greek and Latin parts.

In a reunited empire Constantine was able to complete *Diocletian's reforms and introduce innovations. The separation of civil and military commands was completed. A substantial field army was created under new commanders, *magister equitum* (master of the horse) and *magister peditum* (in charge of the infantry), responsible directly to the emperor: its soldiers (*comitatenses*) had higher pay and privileges than the frontier troops (*limitanei*). The number of Germans seems to have increased, especially in the higher ranks. Praetorian prefects and *vicarii* (overall governors in charge of the dioceses or groupings of provinces) now had purely civilian functions. In a reorganization of the government, the *magister officiorum* (master of the offices) controlled the imperial bureaus (*scrinia*), a new corps of guards (*scholae*) which replaced the praetorians, and a corps of couriers and agents (*agentes in rebus*); the *quaestor sacri palatii* (quaestor of the sacred palace) was chief legal adviser; the

Constantine I Portrait of Constantine I from Rome. The soldier-emperors of the later 3rd cent. were shown in Roman *portraiture as tough and ill-shaven. With the imperial recovery, Constantine revived the clean-shaven look.

comes sacrarum largitionum (count of the sacred largesses) and the *comes rei privatae* (in charge of the imperial domains) handled those revenues and expenditures not controlled by the praetorian prefects. The emperor's council (*consistorium*) had the above as permanent members, as well as *comites* (counts). These at first were men who served at court or as special commissioners, but the title 'count' was soon given freely as an honour. He also resuscitated the title of patrician. He tried vainly to stop *corruption in the steadily growing bureaucracy. He gave senatorial rank freely, and reopened many civilian posts to senators who began to recover some of their lost political influence. From his reign survive the first laws to prevent tenant farmers and other productive workers, not to mention town councillors, from leaving their homes and work. His open-handedness harmed the economy: taxation (mostly in kind) rose inexorably despite the confiscation of the vast temple treasures. He established a gold coinage of 72 solidi to the pound, but the other coinage continued to depreciate (see COINAGE, ROMAN).

Resident now in the more Christianized east, his promotion of the new religion became more emphatic. He openly rejected paganism, though without persecuting pagans, favoured Christians as officials, and welcomed bishops at court, but his actions in Church matters were his own. He now confronted another dispute which was rending Christianity, the theological questions about the nature of Christ raised by the Alexandrian priest Arius. To secure unity Constantine summoned the council which met at Nicaea (mod. Iznik) in 325 (later ranked as the First Ecumenical Council), and proposed the formula which all must accept. Dissidents were bludgeoned into agreement; but bishop Athanasius of Alexandria's view that his opponents had put an unorthodox interpretation on the formula was seen by Constantine as vexatious interference with attempts to secure unity. Even if his success in this aspect was superficial, he nevertheless brought Christianity from a persecuted minority sect to near-supremacy in the religious life of the empire.

He spent the generally peaceful last dozen years of his reign in the east or on the Danube, though he visited Italy and Rome (326), and campaigned on the Rhine (328/9). Victory over the Goths (332) was followed (334) by a campaign against the Sarmatians, many thousands of whom were then admitted within the empire as potential recruits. In 336 he fought north of the Danube, even recovering part of the lost province of Dacia. The empire's prestige seemed fully restored; a Persian war loomed but did not break out until after his death.

His youngest son Constans gained (333) the title Caesar already held by Constantine II and Constantius II. A believer in hereditary succession, Constantine groomed these to succeed along with his nephews Dalmatius (Caesar 335) and Hannibalianus, hoping they would rule amicably after his death. Baptized when death approached (such postponement was common at the time), he died near Nicomedia (22 May 337).   R. P. D.

and *stratēgos hypatos*, or *stratēgos* or *hypatos* alone, for consul) may be indicative, but they are not attested before the early 2nd cent. BC and seem more likely to reflect contemporary Greek perceptions than Roman antiquities.

As the highest office of state the consulship figured in the 'struggle of the orders' between patricians and plebeians (see PLEBS). Analysis of the *fasti*, however, suggests that the tradition may have been wrong in regarding the consulship as an office from which plebeians were at one time excluded by law. Plebeian consuls were, nevertheless, few in the 5th cent., and it was not until 367 BC that a Licinian plebiscite required the election of at least one plebeian consul and not until 342 that this became regular in fact. The first entirely plebeian college held office in 172.

The consul's power, or *imperium, was effectively that of

the king, limited by the period of office and the presence of a colleague with the same *imperium*. The importance of the principle of collegiality here is reflected in the fact that if a consul died or resigned, his colleague was bound to hold an election to fill his place for the remainder of the year (as suffect consul). Over time, some functions were removed from the consuls. The conduct of the census was taken over by the censors from 443, and civil jurisdiction passed effectively to the praetor from 366. In the city consuls could exercise *coercitio*, a general power of enforcing order and exacting obedience to their commands, but the extent of their power within the city (*imperium domi*) was subject from the earliest times to *provocatio* (appeal made to the Roman people against the action of a magistrate). The power of the consul in the field (*imperium *militiae*) was virtually unrestricted, as symbolized by the addition of the axe to the fasces (bundles of rods—emblems of magisterial authority) when the consul left the city on campaign. It was probably not until a law of *Cato the Elder in the 190s that the citizen's right of *provocatio* was extended beyond the precincts of the city. The consuls could and usually did act together, for example in calling the senate or an assembly, and use of the veto (*intercessio*) against one another was rare. When division of labour in the city was indicated, this might be arranged by agreement or by lot, or by use of the custom whereby each assumed duties (and the fasces) for a month at a time. When both consuls were on campaign together, the normal practice was for each to assume overall command for a day at a time.

Under the empire consuls continued, but in an appropriately attenuated way. With *Augustus consular *imperium* came to be part of the emperor's arsenal and to be held by the emperor independently of the office of consul itself. With the suppression of the centuriate assembly and popular election, the emperors either recommended the candidates or held the office themselves. The position continued to confer honour, as is indicated by the increasing use of pairs of suffect consuls during the same year after the initial brief tenure of the *consules ordinarii* ('ordinary consuls'), who gave their name to the year as the republican consuls had done. The republican age limits (fixed initially by the *lex Villia annalis* of 180 BC and later by a law of *Sulla's dictatorship; in the late republic no one under 42 could be elected) were often disregarded as imperial relatives and protégés were signalled by the bestowal upon them of the consulship. In these circumstances children might become consuls, and the future emperor Honorius was made consul at his birth in AD 384. The consulship continued in the western empire for 150 years after that.

P. S. D.

contraception played a minor role in Hippocratic medicine, where the emphasis was rather on helping women to conceive. (See MEDICINE §4.) The exception is a substance called 'misy', possibly copper ore, recommended as having the power to prevent conception for a year (e.g. Hippoc. *Mul.* 1. 76 and *Nat. mul.* 98). It was erroneously believed that the most fertile time of the month was just before or just after a menstrual period, when the womb was open to receive semen. Any attempt to use this information in reverse, in order to avoid conception, would thus in fact have led to intercourse at the most fertile days of the month.

However, it has been argued that many of the remedies given as general gynaecological cures (see GYNAECOLOGY) in the ancient medical tradition did in fact contain substances, mostly of plant origin, effective both as contraceptives and as early-stage abortifacients. Some substances were used as barriers; for example, sponges soaked in vinegar or oil, or cedar resin applied to the mouth of the womb. These could have acted as spermicides. Others could either be

taken orally or used as pessaries, and included pomegranate skin, pennyroyal, willow, and the squirting cucumber, which forcefully ejects its seeds. The degree to which these would have been effective is, however, very difficult to assess. The widespread practice of polypharmacy, by which a combination of several different remedies were used at once, together with the use of amulets, other magical techniques, and non-fertile sexual positions would have made it difficult to judge which method was responsible in the event of a long period without pregnancy ensuing. There is considerable debate also over the use of coitus interruptus, which is not discussed in the sources (see, however, 'landing in the grassy meadows' in *Archilochus, *PColon.* 7511 = SLG 478²) but which is nevertheless assumed by some modern commentators to have been widespread. The physician Soranus (early 2nd cent. AD) recommends a form of withdrawal by the female partner, in order to prevent the ejection of semen deep into the womb, as well as sneezing after intercourse, washing the vagina, and drinking cold water (*Gynaeceia* 1. 20).

An additional problem is that, although some distinction between *abortion and contraception was made in the ancient world—at least by Soranus (*Gynaeceia* 1. 20)—conception was often seen as a process, and any intervention in early pregnancy could thus be seen as 'contraceptive'. This confusion is heightened by the fact that the substances used as contraceptives or abortives would perhaps also work as emmenagogues. What was envisaged as action to bring on a delayed period could thus have been an early abortion—or, indeed, vice versa. See BOTANY.

H. K.

conversion The term implies rejection of one way of life for another, generally better, after brief and intense insight into the shortcomings of self or the demands of circumstance. Ancient religious cult did not require such radical or sudden shifts. Devotees could embrace one allegiance without renouncing others. Observance was intensified by addition rather than by exchange, even in the case of initiation to a mystery. A. D. Nock (*Conversion* (1933)) made much of the account of Lucius in Apuleius (*Conversion* 138–55—the allusions are to Isis). Lucius' metamorphosis owed more to miracle, however, than to will-power, although the conversion of others may have been invited (Apul. *Met.* 11. 15).

It is common to suggest that only *Christianity, and to a lesser extent Judaism (see JEWS), could muster a sharp sense of exclusive loyalty, so that adherence to either cult demanded rejection of some other practice. Two considerations undermine that view.

First, the characteristic word for conversion in the NT, *metanoia*, was used also by classical philosophers. Its chief meaning was to come to one's senses in a new and different way. While Marcus *Aurelius, for example (M. Aur. *Med.* 8. 10), and *Plutarch (e.g. *Tim.* 6. 2; *Mar.* 10. 4) generally retained the narrow sense of inconstancy or regret, other texts are more dramatic—e.g. *Poimandres* 28 (*Corpus Hermeticum*, ed. Nock and Festugière 1. 16 f.) and the *Tabula* of Cebes, ed. K. Praechter 1893 (§§ 9–11). In the words used by Hierocles, 'conversion is the beginning of philosophy' (*FPG* 1. 451 f.). Such writers could take their cue, in any case, from the classic insights of *Plato (*Resp.* 7. 4).

Latin was strikingly weak in its corresponding word-power. *Conversio* remained resolutely wedded to its physical origins and even in a moral sense had more to do with association than with psychological attitude. Commonly quoted passages such as Cic. *Nat. D.* 1. 27 and Plin. *Ep.* 9. 13. 18 are ambiguous or narrow. There was among the Romans a contrasting admiration for *constantia*, in the sense of steadfastness, whereby those deserving moral approbation were as likely to maintain the gifts and inclinations of their breeding as to renounce their past in favour of novel commitments.

Second, the literature of Christian conversion frequently describes a change of heart based on existing association with the Church. The classic example of *Augustine (*Confessions* 8. 6–8, 12) echoes the experience of many men and women in the century before him (and *Seneca's 'sudden change' is a striking anticipation, *Ep.* 6. 1 f.). Antony and Basil of Caesarea (d. 379) were already sprung from pious Christian families. Bishop Ambrose of Milan (d. 397), by contrast, although similarly placed, was embarrassed to find himself on the verge of baptism and episcopacy with no respectable conversion to his name.

The perceived meanings of conversion, therefore, prompt us to attach equal importance to breeding or intimate friendship in the growth of the Christian community. Baptism, even when postponed because of its demands, was not identified with conversion. The term should be reserved for the experience of a narrower body of men and women, who felt a need to carry religious commitment to new heights not far removed from the ambitions of pagan philosophers. Mass attachment to the Church after Constantine, on the other hand, was more circumspect than passionate. The sermons addressed by bishops to their expanding flocks are telling in their exhortations. The level of intensity they recommended was clearly greater than their cautious hearers had achieved.   P. R.

cookery The religious importance of *sacrifice gave cooking a powerfully expressive role in ancient society: the order of the exposing of meat to different sources of heat, especially boiling and roasting, mattered ritually. The public meat-cook (*mageiros*) was a man; other food preparation was among the private, household tasks of an adult woman (see HOUSEWORK). Food could be prepared at the hearth of the city and consumed as a public activity, like the meals of the Athenian *prytaneion* (state dining facility); it was more normally regarded as a household matter. But the staples of domestic diet (see MEALS), especially grains (of which there was a considerable variety), could also be cooked in special forms as offerings (a wide range of sacred breads and *cakes is known).

Cereals could be boiled (like pulses, which were also important) or made into coarse or fine flours, which could also be boiled; the heat necessary for bread-making makes provision of communal ovens desirable outside very large households. The spread of bakeries is a part of a gradual, partial, controversial, and never very advanced displacement of cookery from the household, reaching its acme in the Roman tavern, with its cheap wine and cooked food a sign of the advantages available to urban populations. Even in urban settings much cooking was still done in the household on a brazier, using techniques like the sealed broiling of the *clibanus* or roasting-pot; samovar-like water-heaters, often highly ornamented, were also used. Casual finds and the kitchens of *Pompeii and *Herculaneum have provided copious information on practical technique, not for all that yet exhaustively studied (see illustration on following page).

The standard pattern of meals remained the combination of nutritious staples with tasty condiments. Quality in food reflected the excellence of these, and became—by 5th-cent. BC. Athens if no earlier—an ingredient in social stratification. Raw materials were carefully calibrated: their places of origin acquired precise reputations. The preparation of speciality vegetables or meats through careful tending was part of the process. The combination of condiments, often exotic—for instance as sauces based on fish products (see FISHING), *wine and its derivatives, *olive oil, or the cooking juices of fish or meat—was also a matter for considerable ingenuity and skill, and this (rather than the precise execution of the cooking and serving of the food) was the base of the claim of the ancient connoisseur to knowledge of an *ars*.

Ancient *cuisine* did therefore become *haute*, and resembled the high style in the cooking of other élites in being to some extent regional (the specialities of the various homes of *truphē*, 'luxury', such as south Italy, are an example). There was therefore a considerable literature, much of it comic or semi-serious; but although Athenaeus provides a huge store of culinary anecdote and quotation from earlier sources, and the moral indignation of the Roman writers spices it with tales of culinary excess, reinforced by occasional description like Trimalchio's parody meal in *Petronius Arbiter's *Satyricon*, the reconstruction of *system* and *style*, as opposed to the understanding of individual recipes, in ancient cooking still rather eludes us, and the only surviving text on cookery, [Apicius] *De re coquinaria*, with its odd combination of the bizarre and the everyday, helps surprisingly little.   N. P.

Coriolanus, Gnaeus Marcius Coriolanus (Gaius in Dion. Hal. and Plutarch), a Roman aristocrat who supposedly received his surname from his part in the Roman capture of Corioli from the Volsci (493 BC). According to the story he went into exile when charged with tyrannical conduct and opposing the distribution of grain to the starving *plebs*. Welcomed by the Volscians of Antium, he became their leader in a war against Rome. In two devastating

campaigns he captured a series of Latin towns and led his forces to the gates of Rome, where he was persuaded to turn back by his mother Veturia and his wife Volumnia (in Plutarch they are named as Volumnia and Vergilia respectively). He was then killed by the Volscians (although Quintus Fabius Pictor, fr. 17 Peter, believed that he lived into old age). It is uncertain how much, if any, of this famous story is based on fact. Coriolanus does not appear in the *fasti*, and although *Livy makes him a *patrician (as indeed the plot of the story requires), in historical times the Marcii were a plebeian clan (see PLEBS). The setting of the story recalls a time when the Volscians overran southern Latium and threatened the very existence of Rome; this conforms to what is otherwise known (partly from archaeological evidence) of the situation around 490 BC. Finally, the tale of a Roman becoming leader of the Volsci is an example of 'horizontal social mobility', a phenomenon that occurs in other stories of this period (e.g. Tarquinius Priscus, Appius Claudius Crassus Inregillensis Sabinus, Mastarna) and may be a genuine feature of the society of central Italy in the archaic period.   T. J. Co.

corn supply See FOOD SUPPLY.

corruption is a difficult term; its use largely a matter of perspective. Indeed, from a modern, western point of view, many practices widely accepted in antiquity seem both immoral and detrimental to good government. But beyond underlining the difference between classical societies and our own, the imposition of expectations or prescriptions derived from contemporary ideals does little to advance our understanding of the past.

Charges of corruption (fraud, *bribery, double-dealing, peculation, or the sale of offices) must always be viewed against the norms of the society in which the accusation is made. It should also be recognized that the majority of the surviving classical evidence comes from works whose primary purpose is denigration. Accusations of corruption—along with other vices and depravities—were part of a complex moralizing rhetoric of execration intended to damn an opponent in as many memorable ways as possible. These claims should be accorded the same degree of credibility as invective concerning dubious ancestry, sexual perversion, or physical deformity.

It is within this framework that texts on corruption should be read. The insults traded between the 4th-cent. BC Athenian orators *Demosthenes and *Aeschines were an accepted part of their rivalry and their advocacy of competing political programmes (Dem. *De cor.* 126 ff.; Aeschin. *In Ctes.* 102 ff.). Such abuse was unexceptional. In his speech against Verres (governor of Sicily, 73–71 BC) *Cicero included accusations of extortion, bribery, and taxation fraud (Cic. *Verr.* esp. 2. 3). These were aspects of a long, lurid, and highly rhetorical description of Verres' vices—indispensable elements in any properly constructed character assassination. More broadly, before accepting Cicero's version, it should be noted that provincial governorships were widely regarded as a legitimate source of income (Cicero himself did well while governor of Cilicia) and that very few cases of maladministration were ever successfully prosecuted in the Roman courts.

Of course, in the ancient world there were those who acted illegally or immorally. Sometimes they were caught and punished. In AD 38, the citizens of *Alexandria secured the conviction of Avillius Flaccus, a former prefect of Egypt, on charges of extortion. He was exiled and later—in a display of imperial probity—executed on the orders of the emperor *Gaius (Philo, *In Flacc.* esp. 125 ff.). In the early 3rd cent. AD, the emperor *Severus Alexander discovered an official receiving money for his (apparently illusory) influence at court; a practice known colloquially as *fumum vendere*—selling smoke. In one of the blunter examples of imperial wit, Severus ordered a fire of wet logs to be made. The offender was suffocated to death (SHA *Alex. Sev.* 36). But, again, these incidents must be seen in context. On the whole, they represent isolated reactions. They are attempts to police particularly blatant or excessive abuses or to eliminate rivals, rather than evidence of any widespread condemnation of these practices themselves. No doubt the majority played safe, following the maxim of the emperors Septimius Severus and *Caracalla that governors should be careful to take 'neither everything, nor every time, nor from everyone' (*Dig.* 1. 16. 6. 3).

The continued acceptance of activities which we would regard as corrupt has been seen by some commentators as a sign of an unchecked moral and administrative malaise. These conclusions should be handled with care. It is not clear that officials who profited from their offices were any less reprehensible, or any less effective, than early modern tax farmers. For officials—otherwise unsalaried—the charging of fees for their services was a convenient way both of securing an income and of regulating the many demands on their time. Equally, in societies where access to power and position was dominated by networks of influential connections (see PATRONAGE (NON-LITERARY)), it may be that the payment of money offered an important, alternative channel of advancement. In turn, for peasants, the payment of fees—albeit irksome—offered a simple and affordable means of mollifying a hostile and ever-threatening officialdom.

These are possibilities. But when dealing with highly emotive or unashamedly moralizing terms, they indicate the importance of viewing the classical world in its own context. Sweeping condemnations of the persistence or toleration of 'corruption' should be resisted. If we insist on judging the ancient world against contemporary standards, we will not achieve much—other than a misplaced smugness as to our own superiority.   C. M. K.

Crassus (Marcus Licinius Crassus), son of Publius Licinius Crassus (consul 97 BC), escaped from Lucius Cornelius Cinna's occupation of Rome (87) to Spain, joined *Sulla after Cinna's death, played a prominent part in regaining Italy for him, and made a fortune in Sulla's *proscriptions.

cookery Bronze cooking pots in the cramped kitchen servicing the House of the Vettii at *Pompeii, a relatively lavish Italian *house equipped with two or three dining areas.

After his praetorship he defeated Spartacus, leader of a slave revolt (72–71 BC), but *Pompey, after crucifying many fugitives, claimed credit for the victory, deeply offending Crassus. Formally reconciled, they were made *consuls 70 and presided over the abolition of Sulla's political settlement, though his administrative reforms were retained. During the next few years Crassus further increased his fortune and, relying on his connections, financial power, and astuteness, gained considerable influence. After 67, overshadowed by Pompey's commands (which he had opposed), he is associated by our sources with various schemes to expand his power and perhaps gain a military command. As censor 65, he tried to enrol the Transpadanes (see GAUL (CISALPINE)) as citizens and to have *Egypt annexed; he was foiled by his colleague Quintus Lutatius Catulus and their quarrel forced both to abdicate. Always ready to help eminent or promising men in need of aid, he shielded the suspects in the 'first conspiracy' of *Catiline and supported Catiline until the latter turned to revolution and a programme of cancelling debts. He may have supported the agrarian law of Publius Servilius Rullus (63). A patron of *Caesar (without, however, detaching him from Pompey), he enabled him to leave for his province in 62 by standing surety for part of his debts. On Caesar's return, he was persuaded by him to give up his opposition to Pompey, which during 62–60 had prevented both of them from gaining their political objectives, and to join Pompey in supporting Caesar's candidacy for the consulship. As consul (59), Caesar satisfied him by passing legislation to secure remission of one-third of the sum owed by the *publicani of Asia for their contract (Crassus presumably had an interest in their companies), and he now joined Pompey and Caesar in an open political alliance. After Caesar's departure for Gaul he supported *Clodius Pulcher, who soon proved to be too ambitious to make a reliable ally and tried to embroil him with Pompey and Cicero. He welcomed Cicero on his return from exile, but in 56 alerted Caesar to the attempts by Cicero and others to recall him and attach Pompey to the *optimates* (lit. 'the best men'). Caesar and Crassus met at Ravenna and Pompey was persuaded to meet them at Luca (mod. Lucca) and renew their alliance. The dynasts' plans were kept secret, but it soon became clear that Pompey and Crassus were to become consuls for a second time by whatever means proved necessary and to have special commands in Spain and Syria respectively assigned to them for five years, while they renewed Caesar's command for five years.

Late in 55, ignoring the solemn curses of the tribune Gaius Ateius Capito, Crassus left for Syria, determined on a war of conquest against *Parthia. He won some early successes in 54 and completed financial preparations by extorting huge sums in his province. In 53 he crossed the Euphrates, relying on his long-neglected military skills and the recent ones of his son Publius Crassus. Although deserted by King Artavasdes II of Armenia and the king of Osroëne, he continued his advance into unfamiliar territory. After Publius died in a rash action, he himself was caught in a trap by the Surenas (the Parthian king's hereditary commander) near Carrhae (Mesopotamia) and, trying to extricate himself, died fighting.

After playing the game of politics according to the old rules, in which he was a master, he in the end found that unarmed power no longer counted for much in the changed conditions of the late republic, and he died while trying to apply the lesson. His death helped to bring Caesar and Pompey into the confrontation that led to the Civil War.
E. B.

Crete, Greek and Roman (see ◀Map 4, Cc▶) (for prehistoric Crete see MINOAN CIVILIZATION). Evidence for the history of the island comes both from literary sources, inscriptions, and coins and from excavation and (increasingly) field survey. The transition from bronze to iron age is still not fully understood, but some sites go back into the Dark Ages (Dictaean cave; the Idaean cave—finds start in the 8th cent.; refuge sites, e.g. Karphi and Vrokastro), but in historical times the island was predominantly Dorian Greek (Eteocretan, a non-Greek language, was used in places in the Archaic period, and traces survived into the 2nd cent. BC). Cretans prided themselves that *Zeus was born on Crete, they developed a peculiar temple form, and also eschewed the hero-cults found on the Greek mainland. Of *Homer's 'Crete of the hundred cities' over 100 names survive, but there seem to have been in the Classical and Hellenistic periods only about 40 city-states: Archaic Dreros, Prinias, and Axos, and 5th–2nd-cent. Lato, are well known archaeologically; Cnossus, Gortyn, and Lyttus were initially the most important, along with Cydonia and Hierapytna. The island's position on the sea-routes to and from *Cyprus, the Levant, and *Egypt secured it an important place in the development of Archaic Greek art: important innovations were attributed to the mythical Cretan Daedalus. It had a reputation as the home of mercenary slingers and archers, and of lawgivers (see LAW IN GREECE). Aristocratic society persisted in the island, and the constitutions (though without kings) resembled that of *Sparta, which was said to have been derived from Crete, and impressed *Plato and *Aristotle. In the Classical period the island lay outside the mainstream of Greek history. From the mid-3rd cent. her foreign relations centred on the new and unstable Cretan League, the Attalid dynasty (see PERGAMUM), and the intrigues of Macedon. In 216 BC the cities accepted King Philip V of Macedon as protector, but strife soon returned, both against Rhodes and still more between the cities, especially Cnossus and Gortyn. By this time Crete was reputed as a home of pirates second only to Cilicia (see PIRACY). Their activities were encouraged by Philip, who realized his hope of thereby injuring Rhodes. The pirates supported *Mithradates VI of Pontus against Rome, and when Marcus Antonius (Creticus) intervened to punish them, he was beaten off Cydonia (71), but Quintus Caecilius Metellus (Creticus) crushed the islanders (69–67). Crete

curses A Latin curse tablet on lead from the Sacred Spring at Aquae Sulis (Bath) in Roman *Britain. Springs and wells, since they gave access to the underworld, were popular sites for depositing curses.

became a Roman province, united with *Cyrene, under a senator of praetorian rank, and the old league became the provincial council; from the 4th to 7th cent. AD Crete formed a province on its own in the diocese of Macedonia. *Jews are known on Crete from the 1st cent. BC to the 5th cent. AD, and Christians from the earliest times (St Paul's Epistle to Titus). The prosperity of the island under Roman rule was disrupted by major *earthquakes in the 4th cent., though between c.450 and 550 numerous Christian basilicas were built. From the early 7th cent. Crete was increasingly vulnerable to raids by Slavs and then Arabs, to whom it fell in AD 827–8.

W. A. L.; L. F. N.; S. R. F. P.

curses A curse is a wish that evil may befall a person or persons. Within this broad definition several different types can be distinguished, according to setting, motive, and condition. The most direct curses are maledictions inspired by feelings of hatred and lacking any explicit religious, moral, or legal legitimation. This category is exemplarily represented by the so-called curse tablets (Gk. *katadesmos*, Lat. *defixio*), thin lead sheets inscribed with maledictions intended to influence the actions or welfare of persons (or animals). If a motive is mentioned it is generally inspired by feelings of envy and competition, especially in the fields of sports and the (amphi)theatre, litigation, love, and commerce. Almost without exception these texts are anonymous and lack argumentation or references to deserved punishment of the cursed person(s). If gods are invoked they belong to the sphere of death, the Underworld, and witchcraft (*Demeter, *Persephone,

*Hermes). In later times the magical names of exotic demons and gods abound. Spirits of the dead are also invoked, since the tablets were often buried in graves of the untimely dead as well as in sanctuaries and wells of chthonian deities (gods of the earth). The tablets might be rolled up and transfixed with a needle and sometimes 'voodoo dolls' were added. These tablets first appear in the 6th cent. BC with often simple formulas ('I bind the names of …') and develop into elaborate texts in the imperial age. More than 1,500 have been recovered.

Also included in the well-known collections of *defixiones*, yet a distinct genre, are prayers for justice or 'vindictive prayers'. Often inscribed on lead tablets, but also in other media, they differ from the binding curses in that the name of the author is often mentioned, the action is justified by a reference to some injustice wrought by the cursed person (theft, slander), the gods invoked belong to the great gods (including for instance *Helios), and they are supplicated in a submissive way to punish the culprit and rectify the injustice. This variant becomes popular only in the Hellenistic and Roman periods and is found all over the Roman empire, but especially in *Britain.

Both these types of curse are concerned with past and present occurrences. Another type refers to future events. Conditional curses (imprecations) damn the unknown persons who dare to trespass against certain stipulated sacred or secular laws, prescriptions, treaties (e.g. the famous curses from Teos in W. *Asia Minor, *Syll.*[3] 37–8). They are prevalent in the public domain and are expressed by the community through its representatives (magistrates, priests). The characteristic combination of curse and prayer, a feature they share with judicial prayer, is already perceptible in the Homeric term *ara*. The culprit thus found himself in the position of a man guilty of sacrilege and so the legal powers could enforce their rights even in cases where only the gods could help. A special subdivision in this category is the conditional self-curse as contained in oath formulae. Here, too, the person who offends against the oath invokes the curse he has expressed himself and the wrath of the gods. Similar imprecations, both public and private, are very common in funerary inscriptions against those who violate graves, especially in Asia Minor. All these curses may be accompanied with ritual actions, and most of them have left traces in literature, especially in 'curse poetry'. H. S. V.

cursus honorum, 'career-path' at Rome. See CAREERS, ROMAN.

Cybele (Gk. *Kybelē*; Lydian form *Kybēbē*, Hdt. 5. 102), the great mother-goddess of Anatolia, associated in myth, and later at least in cult, with her youthful lover Attis. Pessinus in Phrygia (in central *Asia Minor) was her chief sanctuary, and the cult appears at an early date in Lydia. The queen or mistress of her people, Cybele was responsible for their well-being in all respects; primarily she is a goddess of fertility, but also cures (and sends) disease, gives oracles, and, as her mural crown indicates, protects her people in war. The goddess of mountains (so *Mētēr oreia*; Meter Dindymene), she is also mistress of wild nature, symbolized by her attendant lions. Ecstatic states inducing prophetic rapture and insensibility to pain were characteristic of her worship (cf. especially Catull. 63).

By the 5th century BC Cybele was known in Greece, was early associated with *Demeter (H. Thompson, *Hesp.* 1937, 206) and perhaps with a native 'Mother of the Gods', but except possibly for such places as Dyme and Patrae in the NW *Peloponnese (Paus. 7. 17. 9; 20. 3), and private cult associations at Piraeus, the port of *Athens where Attis also was honoured, it is likely that the cult was thoroughly Hellenized. (See HELLENISM.) Cybele was officially brought to Rome from Asia Minor 205–204 (for the conflicting legends see H. Graillot, *Le Culte de Cybèle* (1912), ch. 1), but under the republic, save for the public games, the Megalesia, which were celebrated by the aediles and the old *patrician families, and processions of the priests of Cybele with the participation of one of the colleges of Roman *priests, the *quindecimviri sacris faciundis* (Lucr. 2. 624 f.; Luc. 1. 599 f.), she was limited to her Palatine temple and served only by oriental priests (Dion. Hal. *Ant. Rom.* 2. 19. 3 ff.). The consultation of the Sibylline books (see ORACLES) and the cult of Cybele were under the control of the *quindecimviri sacris faciundis*. The cycle of the spring festival, mentioned in public documents from *Claudius' reign, while not fully attested till AD 354, began to take form then. The rites began on 15 March with a procession of the Reed-bearers (*cannophori*), and a sacrifice for the crops. After a week of fastings and purifications, the festival proper opened on the 22nd with the bringing of the pine-tree, symbol of Attis, to the temple. The 24th was the Day of Blood, commemorating the castration and probably the death of Attis. The 25th was a day of joy and banqueting, the Hilaria, and after a day's rest the festival closed with the ritual bath (*Lavatio*) of Cybele's image in the Almo. The rubric for the 28th (*Initium Caiani*) is apparently unrelated. The relation of this spring festival to the Hellenistic mysteries of Cybele is uncertain. Of the later mysteries, in which Attis figured prominently, we again know little. The formulae preserved (Firm. Mat. *Err. prof. rel.* 18; Clem. Al. *Protr.* 2. 15) mention a ritual meal; the carrying of the *kernos*, a vessel used in the *taurobolium* ('bull-sacrifice') to receive the genitals of the bull; and a descent into the *pastos*, probably an underground chamber where certain rites were enacted; but one can also think in terms of a metaphor for *initiation.

The ritual of the *taurobolium* originated in Asia Minor, and first appears in the west in the cult of Venus Caelesta (i.e. -is) at Puteoli (mod. Pozzuoli) in AD 134 (*ILS* 4271, but cf. 4099 of AD 108). From the Antonine period, numerous dedications to Cybele and Attis record its performance in this cult 'ex vaticinatione archigalli' (i.e. with official sanction), on behalf of the emperor and the empire. From Rome the rite spread throughout the west, notably in *Gaul (Transalpine). It was performed also on behalf of individuals, and was especially popular during the pagan revival, AD 370–90. In the rite, the recipient descended into a ditch and was bathed in the blood of a bull, or ram (*criobolium*), which was slain above him (Prudent. *Perist.* 10. 1011–50). It was sometimes repeated after twenty years; one late text (*ILS* 4152) has 'taurobolio criobolioq. in aeternum renatus', 'reborn into eternity through the *taurobolium,* and *criobolium*' (a concept possibly borrowed from *Christianity), but in general the act was considered rather a 'thing done' for its own value than as a source of individual benefits. There has been much speculation, ancient (e.g. *Julian, *Or.* 5. 9. 168d f.) and modern, about Cybele and her cult, but these theories are either late allegorizations or, in the latter case, inspired by the modern 'myth' of the Great Mother.

A belief in immortality was perhaps part of the cult from early times, and the after-life may at first have been thought of as a reunion with Mother Earth. Later, Attis became a solar god, and he and Cybele were regarded as astral and cosmic powers; there is some evidence that the *soul was then thought to return after death to its celestial source.

Thanks to its official status and early naturalization at Rome and in *Ostia, the cult spread rapidly through the provinces, especially in Gaul and *Africa, and was readily accepted as a municipal cult. Its agrarian character made it more popular with the fixed populations than with the soldiery, and it was especially favoured by women.

Cybele is generally represented enthroned in a *naiskos* ('shrine'), wearing either the mural crown or the *calathos* ('basket'), carrying a libation-bowl and drum, and either flanked by lions or bearing one in her lap.

F. R. W.; J. Sch.

Cynics ('the dog-like'), term used of the philosopher Diogenes (*c.*412/3–*c.*324/1 BC) 'the dog' (so called for his shamelessness) and his followers. The genesis, status, significance, and influence of Cynicism were anciently controversial and remain so. Interpretative problems arise from Cynic behaviour and sayings, from the loss of nearly all Cynic writings (though this matters less in the case of Cynicism than of other philosophies), and from diverse distortions in the ancient traditions (invention of sayings and anecdotes; artificial integration of Cynicism into a formal philosophical succession from *Socrates to the Stoics (see STOICISM)).

Cynicism was never a formal philosophical school but rather a way of life grounded in an extreme primitivist interpretation of the principle 'live according to nature'. Diogenes having discovered the true way of life, there was relatively little diversity or development within Cynicism, though 'hard' Cynics (rigorous exponents of the original prescription, found at all periods) can be distinguished from 'soft' Cynics (who compromised varyingly with existing social and political institutions), practical Cynicism from literary Cynicism (Cynicism as written or written about), and Cynics (in some sense) from those influenced by Cynicism.

'Hard' Cynicism was best expounded by Diogenes and (to some extent) Crates of Thebes (d. *c*.288/285 BC). From 320 to 220 BC 'soft' Cynicism was diversely represented by Onesicritus, whose *History* portrayed *Alexander the Great as a Cynic philosopher-king; the eclectics Bion of Borysthenes, court philosopher of *Antigonus Gonatas, and Teles, schoolteacher; and Cercidas, politician, lawgiver, and social reformer. Practical Cynicism declined in the 2nd and 1st cents. BC but revived in the early empire. Greek cities swarmed with Cynics. Cynicism produced remarkable individuals (Demetrius, friend of *Seneca; *Dio of Prusa; in the 2nd cent. AD Demonax, Peregrinus, and Oenomaus). The Roman authorities inevitably clashed with 'hard' Cynics (*qua* anarchists). Later, Cynic and Christian ascetics were sometimes confused, sometimes distinguished. (Some scholars even claim Jesus as a Cynic.) Cynics are mentioned until the 6th cent. Continental European philosophy has shown some interest in Cynicism.

Cynicism greatly influenced Greek and Roman philosophy, rulership ideology, literature, and (later) religion. Crates' follower Zeno founded *Stoicism, a development of Cynicism with a proper theoretical grounding: Stoic ethics are essentially Cynic ethics, Stoic cosmopolitanism a development of Cynic; Diogenes' *Republic* influenced Zeno's and Chrysippus'. The legitimacy of Cynicism was debated within Stoicism, reactions ranging from nearly total acceptance (Ariston of Chios) to partial acceptance (Zeno, Chrysippus), to rejection (Panaetius of Rhodes), to bowdlerizing and idealizing redefinition (Epictetus). More broadly, the very extremeness of Cynic positions on material possessions, individual ethics, and politics catalysed the definition of other philosophies' positions: apart from the Stoics, the Epicureans (see EPICURUS), though greatly influenced by Cynic ethics, polemicized against Cynicism. Diogenes and Crates are generally celebrated in popular philosophy. While the Cynic king is a moral concept wholly antithetical to the worldly king, Onesicritus (following Antisthenes, the associate of Socrates, and *Xenophon) facilitated appropriation and redefinition of that concept by rulership ideology (as later in Dio of Prusa's Kingship Orations); see KINGSHIP. Cynic ethics influenced Christian asceticism.

To maximize their audience the Cynics (despite avowed rejection of literature) wrote more voluminously and variously than any ancient philosophical school: relatively formal philosophical treatises, dialogues, tragedies, historiography, letters, diatribes, various kinds of poetry and of literary parody, prose–poetry hybrids. The Cynic diatribe, anecdotal tradition, satiric spirit, and serio-comic discourse had enormous and varied philosophical and literary influence (e.g. on the diatribes of Seneca and *Plutarch; philosophical biography and the gospels; Roman *satire; the epistles of *Horace, St *Paul, and Seneca; *Lucian).

J. L. Mo.

Cyprus (see ◀Map 2, Cc▶), third largest Mediterranean island (9,282 sq. km.: 3,584 sq. mi.), was of strategic and economic importance to the *Mediterranean and near

eastern powers, and significant both to their relations with western Asia and with one another. It is vulnerable to the power politics of its neighbours, by one or other of whom it has often been occupied or governed, and whose mutual conflicts have sometimes been fought out on its soil or its seas. Though mountainous (the highest points on its Troödos and Kyrenia ranges are 1,951 and 1,023 m. (6,403 and 3,357 ft.) respectively), its central plain (Mesaoria) is fertile, while its extensive piedmont and river-valley systems are suited to crop and animal husbandry. The island suffers intermittently from serious seismic disturbance. Rainfall is uncertain, drought endemic, and fertility dramatically responsive to irrigation capacity. Copper ore, chiefly located in the Troödos foothills at the junction of igneous and sedimentary deposits, has been exploited since prehistory. *Timber resources played a major role in the region's naval history.

The character of the first human traces, found with extinct pleistocene animal species at the Akrotiri (*Aetokremnos* rock-shelter, with a carbon-14 date of *c*.8000 BC) is uncertain, as is their relationship with the *c*.6000 BC pre-ceramic neolithic phase, best seen at the type-site, Khirokitia, but distributed at numerous other locations, coastal and inland. Successive phases of neolithic and chalcolithic settlement embrace a 3,500-year period; excavation has established the general character of several sites spanning this period, yet origins and interrelationships between its successive episodes are alike uncertain. The gradual introduction of metal technology during the third millennium greatly accelerated social and material development; the main stimulus may have been the disruption and dispersal of more advanced societies in adjacent Anatolia (see ASIA MINOR). The 1,500 years of the Cypriot bronze age (early, middle, and late) were marked by a progression from isolated rural communities linked by shared traits in material civilization (typifying the late third millennium) to what by the 13th cent. had become an urbanized hierarchical society, enriched by the international exchange systems in which raw copper played a major role (symbolized by the cargoes of the wrecked Ulu Burun and Cape Gelidonya ships off SW Turkey). This change saw a shift from the north and south piedmont of the Kyrenia mountains to the south and east coasts, to new towns founded at the end of middle Cypriot (17th cent.) at river mouths (Enkomi, Maroni, Palaepaphos) or on natural harbours (Citium, Hala Sultan Tekke). While Egypt and the cities of the Levant (notably the kingdom of Ugarit, SE Turkey) enjoyed regular exchanges with Cyprus, Minoan Crete played a part and, from *c*.1400 Mycenaean Greece was prominent, even dominant (see MINOAN and MYCENAEAN CIVILIZATION). The island was literate during late Cypriot, using the Cypro-Minoan script. Objective proof of the identification of Cyprus with the 'Alasya' of Hittite, Egyptian, Ugaritic, and other documents remains elusive, for all its appeal. The final bronze-age years (1200–1050) knew turbulence, violence—and remarkable prosperity, in which there was a fruitful coalescence of the native

Cypriot with migrant Aegean and Levantine elements that produced a distinguished but short-lived material civilization whose ceramic design, metalwork, *ivory carving, and glyptic were pre-eminent; perhaps iron technology was disseminated westward at this time. By 1050 virtually all the old settlements had been abandoned, in some cases to be replaced nearby by communities under the strongest Greek influence yet seen, including Mycenaean types of tomb and, very probably, the Arcadian dialect. This process may dimly be reflected in the legends, where figures from the *Nostoi* (returns of various Greek heroes after Troy) are credited with the foundation of the later cities—Teucer at Salamis, Agapenor at Paphos, etc. Classical Cypriot script, adapted from Cypro-Minoan, lasted for some purposes almost to 200 BC (and was the vehicle too for the undeciphered Eteo-Cyprian of Amathus, east of mod. Limassol).

The iron-age settlement-pattern was based on a nexus of city-kingdoms (sometimes seen as a Mycenaean legacy)— Salamis, Citium, Amathus, Paphos, Curium, Soli, Marion, Tamassus, Idalium, Chytri—which largely lasted throughout antiquity. Citium was for long a *Phoenician city (Phoenician influence was very strong elsewhere in the island), Amathus was 'Eteocypriot'. The kings ruled as autocrats; only at Idalium may power have been shared with a '*dēmos*' ('people'). The 8th- and 7th-cent. 'royal' tombs at Salamis suggest both the wealth and foreign connections of these rulers. From the late 8th cent., if no earlier, Cyprus was sucked into east Mediterranean politics; its kings acknowledged at least the nominal suzerainty of a succession of great powers. The Sargon II stela said to have been found at Citium (Larnaka) reports the submission of the kings to Assyria in 709; the information is repeated on other Assyrian documents. While the 7th cent. seems to have been largely a period of independence, the island was dominated by Egypt in the earlier 6th cent. In 545 came voluntary submission to *Persia; there was Cypriot help for the Persians in the Carian War, the conquest of *Babylonia and, in 525, their attack on Egypt. Sufficient independence remained for the kings to issue their own coinage, starting c.538 with Euelthon of Salamis (the same Euelthon to whom Pheretime of *Cyrene vainly appealed for help against her son Arcesilas III—further symptom of independence). When *Darius I reorganized the empire, Cyprus found itself in the fifth satrapy with *Phoenicia and Syria-Palestine; tribute was imposed, but the amount is unknown. The cities (except Amathus) joined the *Ionian Revolt, egged on, it seems, by dissidents who gained control in Salamis, where crucial land and sea battles were fought. Though the Ionian fleet was victorious, ashore the Cypriots were defeated, and their leader, Onesilus, killed. The cities were reduced by the Persians, Soli holding out the longest. The Cypriots had an uncomfortable time in the subsequent long struggle between Greece and Persia; their ships fought poorly on the Persian side in the Persian Wars of 480–479 (see GREECE (HISTORY)). The island was constantly campaigned over during Athenian efforts under the statesman Cimon to deny it to the Persians, but Cimon's death during the 449/8 campaign raised the siege and, temporarily, pro-Persian rulers became everywhere dominant; but the Teucrid king of Salamis, Evagoras I (c.411–374) was conspicuously pro-Greek, in fact as well as theory. Later, the kings intervened decisively on behalf of *Alexander the Great at the siege of Tyre in 331, where their ships were badly mauled. Alexander's Successors (Diadochi), usually violently, abolished the city-kings, and with them any pretence of an independent Cyprus. The island became part of the Ptolemaic share of Alexander's legacy (see PTOLEMY I) and thereby lost most of what remained of its idiosyncratic material civilization. In the 1st cent. BC the island passed to and fro between Roman and Ptolemaic rule until its final annexation after *Actium by Octavian, the future *Augustus. In 22 BC it was ceded as a minor public province. Its Roman history was (apart from serious *earthquakes and the Jewish revolt of 115/16 (see JEWS)) relatively tranquil and—to judge from surviving monuments at Salamis, Curium, and Nea Paphos— prosperous.

H. W. C.

Cyrene (mod. Shahat) (see ◖Map 2, Ac◗), the major Greek colony in Africa (see COLONIZATION, GREEK), was founded from Thera (mod. Santorini) c.630 BC, and reinforced by later groups of colonists, who were, before the Hellenistic period, predominantly Dorian Greeks. It gave its name to the surrounding territory (mod. Cyrenaica), apparently claiming authority (sometimes resisted) as *mētropolis* (mother-city) of all Greek settlements there; it is not always clear whether ancient references to Cyrene are to the city or to this territory. Information about it has been significantly increased by 20th-cent. excavation; there is now material evidence from at least the 7th cent. BC to at least the 7th cent. AD, but its interpretation is often debatable.

For the foundation, the account in Herodotus (4. 150–8) is supplemented by an inscription purporting to give the substance of the Theraean decree which organized the colonial expedition (SEG 9. 3, 20. 714); after two initial failures, a site was found, with indigenous Libyan help, on the northern edge of the Gebel Akhdar, 621 m. (2,037 ft.) above and c.12 km. (7½ mi.) from the sea, in a fertile area with a freshwater spring and normally good rainfall, but shading into pre-desert southwards; other Greek settlements followed swiftly, for example a dependent port near by, the city of Taucheira further off. Communications with these and exploitation of the country required Libyan co-operation, which was withdrawn on arrival of a new wave of colonists in the 6th cent. Libyan/Egyptian opposition was defeated c.570 and Greek expansion continued, with more dependent settlements and the cities of Barca and Euhesperides. Evidence for the Libyan relationship is unsatisfactory. Within city territories they presumably provided dependent labour; outside them they were free, although in the adjacent pre-desert perhaps tributary, and, apparently, peaceable; Herodotus notes their Hellenization (see HELLENISM), as well as their cultural influence on Greeks (4. 170–1, 186, 189); there was intermarriage and, by the Hellenistic period, marked racial mixture. Hostile raiding, sometimes serious, may have been initiated by more distant tribes (Diod. Sic. 3. 49). Cyrene's own territory became unusually large for a *polis, with organized villages reminiscent of Attic demes (i.e. constitutional sub-districts as well as rural districts); its cereals, vines, olives, and grazing were notable, and the grazing extended into the pre-desert, which was also the source of the silphium plant, Cyrene's characteristic export and emblem; like silphium-collection, animal husbandry must often have been in the hands of Libyans. The horses were particularly famous, horse-drawn chariots became a feature of Cyrene's armies, and chariot-racing, with teams victorious in Greek *games (Pind. *Pyth.* 4, 5), a predilection of the rich. The resultant wealth financed buildings, sculptures, painting, and a tradition of learning and literature; if the great names (e.g. the philosophers Aristippus and Carneades, *Callimachus, and *Eratosthenes) cluster in the Classical and Hellenistic periods, Roman Cyrene made some contribution to the Hadrianic Panhellenion (an Athens-based organization of Greek cities) and in late antiquity produced the Christian Neoplatonist Synesius (c. AD 370–413).

The founder (Aristoteles Battus) and his heirs ruled as kings. The dynasty survived civic unrest and revolution as well as family infighting, submitted to *Persia in 525, but recovered independence in the 5th cent.; it was finally overthrown c.440. The subsequent republican regime is obscure; 4th-cent. monuments suggest a prosperous élite and further expansion, perhaps including an extension of influence, to Great Catabathmus (Sollum) in Marmarica, and Arae Philaenorum (Ras el Aali) in Syrtica; this, it has been suggested, would open access to trans-Saharan trade-goods. All Cyrenaica offered allegiance to *Alexander the Great. After his death, and an attempted coup by the adventurer Thibron, it became a dependency of the Ptolemaic kingdom of *Egypt. *Ptolemy I gave Cyrene a moderately oligarchic constitution under which his own authority was ensured by his permanent office as *stratēgos*, 'general' (SEG 9. 1). A date in 322–321 is now generally accepted for this, but almost all dates and many details after that are disputed. He and his successors aroused some local opposition, and their representatives tended to assert independence (Ophellas, Magas); briefly, in the middle of the 3rd cent., there was, apparently, a free interlude when Demophanes and Ecdelus established a federation of the cities; but it ended when Magas' daughter Berenice married Ptolemy III. Cyrene seems to have been the royal capital but must have lost prestige through Ptolemaic patronage of the other cities (Berenice/Euhesperides, Arsinoë/Taucheira, Ptolemais/Barca), especially if it was a Ptolemy who raised her port to city-status as Apollonia (but the earliest evidence for this is of 67 BC); all cities presumably lost cohesion by the introduction of new colonists beholden to the Ptolemies (certainly Jews and probably ex-soldiers of the Ptolemaic army); while in the 2nd cent.

Ptolemy Physcon (later Ptolemy VIII of Egypt) enlisted diplomatic support from Rome and reinforced it by bequeathing Cyrenaica to Rome should he leave no heir (SEG 9. 7). At his death in 116 there were in fact heirs, two of whom, as is now known, succeeded him in turn, Ptolemy IX of Egypt and Ptolemy Apion; but when Apion died in 96 the kingdom did pass to Rome, who accepted the royal property but gave the cities freedom.

Internal factions and external pressures (piratical assaults, perhaps coinciding with Libyan raiding) caused a breakdown of order; the senate authorized annexation in 75/4, but the organization of the new province is uncertain. *Pompey's defeat of the pirates (see PIRACY) in 67 relieved one pressure but the Roman Civil Wars brought others, especially severe when Mark *Antony garrisoned Cyrene and restored Cyrenaica to the Egyptian crown. After *Actium, Cyrenaica was combined with *Crete in a public *province governed by an annual praetorian proconsul, whose main seat in Cyrenaica was at Cyrene, where the provincial council also met. The imperial-period monuments suggest modest prosperity, evoking standard signs of élite loyalty to Rome; but it was sharply interrupted c.2 BC–AD 2 by a Marmaric War, after which a small Roman garrison was introduced to guard the Syrtican approaches to Cyrenaica, again in 115–17 by a Jewish Revolt (see JEWS), after which legionary veteran colonists were sent to compensate for the casualties, and under Claudius II Gothicus (AD 268–70) when there was another Marmaric War (SEG 9. 9), from whose effects Cyrene may have been slower to recover; that perhaps explains why *Diocletian (ruled 285–305) preferred Ptolemais as metropolis of his new province of Upper Libya. This was a loss of status to Cyrene which altered her civic character, but the life and works of Synesius seem to show that intellectual pursuits continued there; and, despite severe earthquake damage in the late 4th cent. and further Libyan raiding in the 5th, her Christian monuments are not negligible. Some life survived on the site after the Arab invasions in the 7th cent.

J. M. R.

Cyrus the Great (OP *Kuruš*), son of Cambyses I, who became c.557 BC king of the small kingdom of Anshan in *Persia, at that time subject to the Median king. Beginning in 550 he fought extensive campaigns in which he conquered, respectively, Media (550/49), Sardis and Lydia (W. *Asia Minor) (546), *Babylonia, and the neo-Babylonian empire (539). At some point (before or after 539?) he conquered central Asia. He was thus the first Persian king to bring together territories into an imperial framework, to whose organization he contributed substantially. In general, the Greek (especially the *Cyropaedia* of *Xenophon), Babylonian ('Cyrus cylinder'), and Judaean sources (Ezra) present him as a conqueror welcomed by the local inhabitants. This apologetic tendency reflects both the expectations nourished by certain groups (e.g. the *Jews, who received permission to return to Jerusalem) and a policy continued by his successors: i.e. forging collaborative links with the local élites. This willingness to accommodate local conditions went hand-in-hand with tight control, as shown by the fact that land was confiscated to benefit the crown and Persian nobility. The royal administration also maintained a close watch over the fiscal obligations of the Babylonian sanctuaries. His achievement as founder of the empire was symbolized by the building of a royal residence in Persia, Pasargadae, where his tomb was also constructed. He was buried here by his son, Cambyses II, after his death in 530 following a campaign in central Asia.

P. B.

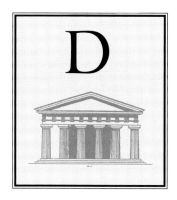

dancing From earliest times, the dance played an important role in the lives of the Greeks, and was sometimes regarded by them as the invention of the gods. It was generally associated with music and song or poetry in the art called *mousikē*, and frequently made use of a body of conventionalized gestures (*cheironomia*). The dance had a place in religious festivals, in the secret rites of *mysteries, in artistic competitions, in the education of the young, and even in military training, especially in *Sparta. People danced at weddings, at funerals, at the 'naming-days' of infants, at harvests, at victory celebrations, in after-dinner merrymaking, in joyous dance processions (*kōmos*) through the streets, in animal mummery, and even in incantations. Performances by professional dancers were enjoyed, especially at the *symposium; such dancers were almost all slaves and *hetairai* (lit. 'companions', a type of female prostitute: see PROSTITUTION, SECULAR).

Among particularly famous dances of the Greeks were the *geranos* (a nocturnal serpentine dance the name of which is probably derived from the root †*ger-*, 'to wind', and not from the word for 'crane'); the pyrrhic and related dances by men and boys in armour; the *partheneion*, a song-dance performance by maidens; the *hyporchēma*, a lively combination of instrumental music, song, dance, and pantomime; the skilful 'ball-playing' dance; and the uproarious *askōliasmos*, performed on greased wineskins. In the worship of *Dionysus the wild *oreibasia*, or 'mountain-dancing' of frenzied women, by classical times was toned down into a prepared performance by a *thiasos*, or group of trained devotees.

In the Athenian theatre, the *tyrbasia* of the cyclic choruses, the lewd *kordax* of comedy, the stately *emmellia* of tragedy, and the rollicking *sikinnis* of the satyr-play were distinctive. The actors in the *phlyakes*–plays of Magna Graecia (S. Italy) apparently at times burlesqued the dignified dances of the religious festivals.

The Romans were much more restrained than the Greeks in their use of the dance. Some of them, including *Cicero (*Mur.* 6. 13), openly expressed contempt for dancers. There are records of a few ancient dances used in religious ceremonies—e.g. the leaping and 'three-foot' dances (*tripudia*) of the armed Salii and the Arval Brothers (both ritual sodalities honouring respectively *Mars and the Dea Dia), and the 'rope dance' of maidens in honour of *Juno (Livy 27. 37. 12–15). *Etruscan and Greek dancers, from the 4th cent. BC on, exerted some influence, and the introduction of various oriental cults brought noisy and ecstatic dances to Rome. Dancing by professionals, usually slaves, often furnished entertainment at dinner-parties. With the coming of the pantomime (a form of mime set to music), popular interest in the dance became great. See MUSIC.   L. B. L.; A. J. S. S.

Darius I (OP *Darāyavauš*); son of Hystaspes, a Persian of noble lineage already known in the reigns of *Cyrus the Great and Cambyses II. He seized power after a bloody struggle against an individual said by him to have been the magus Gaumata. It is quite possible that the person he in fact assassinated was Bardiya (Gk. Smerdis), the brother of Cambyses (522 BC). He then had to quell numerous revolts by subject peoples and deal with the insubordinate Oroites, satrap of Sardis (W. *Asia Minor). His achievements were commemorated for posterity, in text and picture, on the rock of Bisitun in Media (SW of the Caspian Sea). To mark what he presented as a refoundation of the empire, he created two new royal residences: Susa in Elam (SW Iran) and *Persepolis in *Persia. He also extended the empire in the east (Indus valley) and west (Thrace). Soon after his brutal crushing of the *Ionian Revolt (*c.*500–493), he put Datis in command of an army which conquered the Aegean islands, before meeting a setback at the battle of Marathon (490; see GREECE (HISTORY)). Until his death in 486, Darius worked to perfect the administration and tributary structure of the empire, as shown by a famous passage in *Herodotus (3. 89–97). It is illustrated even better by the thousands of Elamite tablets found in the treasury and fortifications of Persepolis.   P. B.

dead, disposal of Correct disposal of the dead was always a crucial element in easing the *soul of the deceased into the next world. However, the forms of burial varied enormously. Great significance was attached to the choice of inhumation, cremation, or some other rite (e.g. Hdt. 3. 38; Lucr. 3. 888–93), but there is rarely any reason to see a direct correlation between specific methods and specific racial, class, or religious groups.

Greece In prehistory there was enormous variation. An inhumation burial is known from mesolithic times in the Franchthi cave (Argolid), while in *Thessaly cremation cemeteries go back to early neolithic. In the early bronze age rich grave goods were sometimes used, particularly in the multiple inhumation tombs of the Cyclades and *Crete. In the late bronze age, there was for the first time considerable uniformity on the mainland, with multiple inhumations in rock-cut chamber-tombs being the norm. In early *Mycenaean times a few people were buried in spectacular tholos-(beehive) tombs. Very large cemeteries of chamber-tombs have been found at Mycenae and other sites. This pattern extended as far north as Thessaly, but in *Macedonia and Epirus (NW Greece) individual inhumation in stone-lined cist-graves, grouped together under mounds of earth, was normal. After the destruction of the Mycenaean world c.1200 BC, regional variations returned in the 'Dark Age'. Inhumations in cists with the body contracted were normal at Argos; cremation on a pyre with just a handful of the ashes scattered in the grave at *Lefkandi; on Crete, chamber-tombs with multiple inhumations until about 1000, and then multiple cremations with the ashes placed in urns. At Athens, adult rites changed frequently—inhumations in cists in the 11th cent.; cremations with the ashes in urns, c.1000–750; inhumations in earth-cut pit-graves, c.750–700; cremations in the grave itself, c.700–550; and then inhumations in pit-graves, tile-covered graves, or sarcophagi from about 550 onwards. Early archaeologists associated both cist burial and cremation with the 'Dorian invasion' (mythical Greek migration into the *Peloponnese after *Troy's fall) at various times, but these correlations are not convincing.

There were, however, a few generally observed rules. Cremation with the ashes placed in a metal urn (usually bronze), in the Homeric style, tended to be associated with warrior burials throughout antiquity. Children were rarely cremated, and in most places infants were buried inside amphoras or storage pots. Starting in the 6th cent. there was a general trend towards simpler burials, which may have been accompanied by sumptuary laws. Inhumation in pit-graves or tile graves was adopted for adults in most parts of Greece by the 6th or 5th cent. The main exception was western Greece, where adults were inhumed in giant storage pots from the Dark Age to Hellenistic times.

Rich grave goods and elaborate tomb markers went out of style everywhere for most of the 5th cent., but returned around 425. There was a great flowering of funerary sculpture at Athens in the 4th cent. Funerary spending escalated still further after 300, and in the 3rd–1st cents. BC the massive 'Macedonian'-style vaulted tombs, often with painted interiors, are found all over Greece. The most spectacular of these are the late 4th-cent. royal tombs, possibly of *Philip II and his court, at Vergina in Macedonia (see AEGAE). Athens was an exception to this general pattern. *Cicero (*Leg.* 2. 66) says that the Macedonian governor Demetrius of Phalerum banned lavish tombs, probably in 317, and indeed no monumental burials are known from Attica between then and the 1st cent. BC. *Lucian (*On Mourning* 21) called cremation a 'Greek custom', but he was probably thinking in purely literary terms, drawing on classical passages such as Hdt. 3. 38. In Roman times inhumation was the strict rule throughout the whole Greek east, although the precise forms varied—from tile graves at Athens to chamber-tombs at Cnossus on *Crete, built tombs at Dura Europus (*Syria), and spectacular rock-cut tombs at Petra (Arabia). Greek settlers in the near east, from *Egypt to *Bactria, generally adopted rites very similar to the local population's practices.

Rome Burial customs in prehistoric *Italy were as varied as those in Greece. The earliest graves found at Rome date to the 10th cent. BC, and include both urn cremations and inhumations. There is, however, no reason to see these as belonging to different racial groups. Roman burials were until about 100 BC generally rather simple, in marked contrast to their neighbours the *Etruscans, who built complex chamber-tombs which often housed cremations in unusual urns, accompanied by rich grave goods. From the 8th cent. on the customs of southern Italy were heavily influenced by Greek settlers, and inhumation generally replaced cremation. Impressive local traditions of tomb-painting developed, particularly in Campania.

At Rome itself, few burials are known from republican times, suggesting that rites were so simple as to leave few archaeological traces. Across most of Europe in the 5th–3rd cents. the bulk of the population was disposed of relatively informally, often by exposing the body on platforms. In Italy there is some evidence for mass burial of the poor in huge open pits. The use of these *puticuli* at Rome in the late republic is mentioned by *Varro (*Ling.* 5. 25; cf. Hor. *Sat.* 1. 8; Festus, entry under 'puticuli'), and a few were excavated in the 1880s. By the 3rd cent. BC some of the rich were being cremated with their ashes placed in urns and buried in communal tombs. By the 1st cent., cremation was the norm, and according to Cicero (*Leg.* 2. 57) and *Pliny the Elder (*HN* 7. 187) even the ultra-conservative Cornelii (see SCIPIO) gave up inhumation in 78 BC. At about the same time, Roman nobles began building very elaborate tombs modelled on those of the Greek east, with monumental sculptures and elaborate stone architecture.

The spiralling cost of élite tombs ended abruptly under *Augustus, who built himself a vast mausoleum. Other nobles were careful to avoid being seen as trying to rival the splendour of the imperial household. Simpler tombs, organized around modest altars, came into fashion for the very rich, while the not-quite-so-rich and the growing number of funerary clubs (*collegia*) adopted the *columbarium* (a word meaning 'dovecot', coined by modern scholars). The earliest example dates to *c*.50 BC, but they became common after *c*. AD 40. They were barrel-vaulted brick and masonry tombs with niches for urns, usually holding 50–100, although one example found at Rome in 1726 held 3,000 urns.

Urn cremation was adopted all over the western empire in the 1st and 2nd cent. AD, although there were always significant local variations. By about AD 150, the empire can be divided into a cremating, Latin-using west and an inhuming, Greek-using east. But during the 2nd cent. members of the Roman élite adopted inhumation, probably as a conscious emulation of Hellenistic practices, and in the 3rd cent. this rite gradually swept across the whole west. The change has no obvious links to *Christianity or any other religious movement. However, it was certainly convenient for the spread of Christianity, which generally opposed cremation, which destroyed the body and posed difficulties for some visions of the day of resurrection. By the late 4th cent., certain practices found widely in western cemeteries—an east–west orientation, the use of lime on the walls of the grave, and the decline of grave goods—might indicate the presence of Christians. At Rome itself, there was a general shift around 300 away from traditional cemeteries in favour of catacombs and burial within basilical churches.

See further ART, FUNERARY, GREEK and ROMAN; DEATH, ATTITUDES TO.   I. Mo.

Dead Sea Scrolls, documents made of leather and papyrus, and, in one case, of copper, found between 1947 and 1956 in caves near Qumran by the Dead Sea. The scrolls, written by Jews, are mostly in Hebrew and Aramaic, but a small number are in Greek. Many are fragments of biblical texts from the Old Testament and from Jewish religious compositions otherwise only preserved through Christian manuscript traditions. The scrolls were written in the last centuries BC and 1st cent. AD.

Of particular significance in the study of Judaism in this period are the texts composed by sectarians, who are probably to be identified with *Jews who used the nearby site at Qumran as a religious centre. These texts include community rules, hymns, liturgical texts, calendars, and works of bible interpretation. Among this last group is found the *pesher* type of interpretation, characteristic of this sect and rarely found elsewhere in Jewish literature, in which the real meaning of scriptural passages is alleged to lie in hidden allusions to more recent events.

The Community Rule (1QS, also called the Manual of Discipline), a composite work found in various manuscripts in different caves, laid down the rules for initiation into the community and for living within it. The Rule of the Congregation or Messianic Rule (1QSa) gives regulations for the eschatological integration of the 'congregation of Israel' into the sectarian community. The

Damascus Rule (CD) is also attested in a medieval manuscript (the Zadokite Fragments) discovered in Cairo in 1896. The War Rule (1QM) is a rather different text which regulates the behaviour of the 'sons of light' in the eschatological war against the 'sons of darkness'. The Temple Scroll (11QT) contains a systematic statement of the regulations pertaining to the Temple cult, derived from the Pentateuch but with frequent non-biblical additions which are presented as the direct words of God. Numerous fragments of the scrolls are still unedited and it is certain that more sectarian material will be recognized in the remaining material.

How many of those documents were originally composed by adherents of one particular sect is debated. If the scrolls were deposited in the caves for safe keeping, they may have been placed there by more than one group, perhaps after the destruction of the Jerusalem Temple in AD 70. The contents of the Copper Scroll (3Q15), a prosaic list of the hiding-places of an immensely valuable treasure, might support this hypothesis, but finds of multiple copies of some sectarian texts in different caves may suggest that only one sect was responsible for placing them there. In that case doctrinal differences between texts must be accounted for by supposing either variant branches of the sect or a gradual development of the sect's ideas over time.

Many attempts have been made to connect the scrolls to the Jewish groups of this period known from other sources. Most such attempts assume that the scrolls were deposited by the inhabitants of the site at Qumran, where excavation revealed a small community, isolated in the desert, with a deep concern for ritual purity. The most plausible of such identifications is with the Essenes, who are known primarily from descriptions by Philo of Alexandria, *Josephus, and *Pliny the Elder. However, the classical evidence is equivocal and contradictory, and some aspects of the Essene society depicted there do not fit the evidence from the scrolls, so that those who hold this hypothesis have to consider the scrolls community as Essenes of a peculiar type. It may be better to take the sectarian material in the scrolls as evidence of a type of Judaism otherwise unknown. See RELIGION, JEWISH.

M. D. G.

death, attitudes to

Greek The Greek attitude towards *Hades is best summed up by *Achilles, 'I'd rather be a day-labourer on earth working for a man of little property than lord of all the hosts of the dead' (*Od*. 11. 489–91). The Homeric dead are pathetic in their helplessness, inhabiting draughty, echoing halls, deprived of their wits (*phrenes*), and flitting purposelessly about uttering batlike noises (*Od*. 24. 5 ff.). Athenian lawcourt speeches urge the jury to render assistance to the dead as if they were unable to look after their own interests (e.g. Lys. 12. 99). The precise relationship between the living body and the *psychē* (spirit of the dead) is unclear, since the latter is only referred to in connection with the dead. The necessity of conducting burial rites (e.g. *Il.* 23. 71) and the insult to human dignity if they are omitted (cf. Soph. *Ant. passim*) are frequently mentioned in literature. Except in philosophy and Orphism (cf. Pind. *Ol.* 63–88; Pl. *Resp* 2. 363c–e, *Phd.* 113d–114c; see ORPHISM), belief in a dualistic after-life is largely absent from Greek eschatology. In *Homer the Underworld judge Minos merely settles lawsuits between the litigious dead (*Od.* 11. 568–70). Only gross sinners (e.g. Tantalus, Tityus, and Sisyphus) receive retributive punishment, while the favoured few end up in the Elysian Fields (4. 561 ff.). Fear of the after-life was therefore largely absent (but cf. Pl. *Resp.* 1. 330d). Though powerless in themselves the dead had access to the infernal powers, notably Pluto (Aedoneus) and Persephone, for which reason folded lead plaques (*katadesmoi*) inscribed with *curses bearing the name of the person to be 'bound down' were occasionally placed in graves.

The deceased's journey to the next world was effected by elaborate ritual conducted by the relatives of the deceased, primarily women. The funeral, from which priests were debarred for fear of incurring *pollution, was a three-act drama which comprised laying out the body (*prothesis*), the funeral cortège (*ekphora*), and the interment. We only rarely hear of undertakers (*nekrothoptoi, nekrophoroi*) and other 'professionals'. We know of no burial 'service' as such. Cremation and inhumation were often practised concurrently in the same community, with no apparent distinction in belief. From *c*.500 BC intramural burial was forbidden in Athens (cf. Plut. *Lyc.* 27 for Sparta). No tomb-cult was practised in early times, but in Classical Athens women paid regular visits to the grave. Offerings included *cakes and *choai*, i.e. libations mainly of pure *water. The attention that the dead received from the living in this period was judged to be so important that it constituted a reason for adopting an heir (Isae. 2. 36, 7. 30). In the Archaic period a funeral provided a perfect showcase for the conspicuous display of aristocratic wealth, power, and prestige, and many communities passed legislation designed to limit its scope and magnificence (e.g. [Dem.] 43. 62 and Plut. *Sol.* for *Solonian legislation; *Syll.*³ 1218 for Iulis on Keos).

Funerary ritual was substantially modified for those who died in their prime, the unburied dead, victims of murder, *suicides, heroes, etc. Special sympathy was felt towards those who died at a marriageable age but unmarried. To underline their pathos, a stone marker in the form of a *loutrophoros* (i.e. vase used in the nuptial bath) was placed over the grave. Victims of murder were vengeful and malignant, as indicated by the grisly practice of cutting off their extremities. Most powerful were the heroic dead, who even in *Plutarch's day still received blood *sacrifice (Plut. *Aristides* 21).

Geometric vases depict only the *prothesis* and *ekphora*, whereas Athenian white-ground *lēkythoi* (oil flasks) frequently depict tomb-cult (see POTTERY, GREEK). Hades is rarely represented in Greek art (but cf. Paus. 10. 28–31 for Polygnotus' lost painting at Delphi, the *Nekyia*) or in literature (*Od.* 11 and Ar. *Frogs* are notable exceptions; cf. too

'Orphic' gold leaves). Though the belief in Hades as the home of the undifferentiated dead predominated and never lost its hold over the popular imagination (cf. its persistence as a theme in epitaphs), other concepts include the transformation of the dead into stars (e.g. Castor and Pollux), their absorption into the upper atmosphere or aether (e.g. *IG* 1³. 1179), the Pythagorean (e.g. DK 14, 8a) and Platonic (e.g. *Phd.* 107d) belief in transmigration, and the indistinct 'blessedness' promised to initiates in the *mysteries of *Eleusis. See PLATO; PYTHAGORAS.

Roman In the Roman tradition death is conceived of essentially as a blemish striking the family of the deceased, with the risk of affecting all with whom it had contact: neighbours, magistrates, priests, and sacred places. For this reason ritual established a strict separation between the space of the deceased and that of the living. Cypress branches announced the blemished house, and on days of sacrifices for the dead sanctuaries were closed.

The time of death spanned above all the period when the deceased's corpse was exposed in his or her home, its transport to the cemetery, and its burial. These operations were usually completed after eight days. The transformation of the corpse was achieved in the course of 40 days. The deceased did not, in the course of the funerary ritual, arrive at life eternal, but joined, as it were, a new category: those members of the community, the *di manes*, who lived outside towns on land set aside for this purpose and managed by the *pontifices* (see PRIESTS). The legal status of these tombs was that of the *religiosum*. The *di manes* were thought of as an undifferentiated mass or (rather) a collective divinity (Romans spoke of the *di manes* of such-and-such a person), and received regular cult during the Parentalia festival of 13–21 February and at other times. The immortality which they enjoyed was conditional on the existence of descendants, or at least of a human presence (a proprietor of the land on which the tomb was located, or a funerary *collegium* or club), since it was the celebration of funerary cult, in the form of sacrifices, which ensured the deceased's survival.

The unburied dead were called *lemures* and thought of as haunting inhabited areas and disturbing the living. Usually anonymous (being no longer integrated into any social context) they none the less received cult at the Lemuria festival in May, supposedly to appease them.

Along with these forms of survival, conceived generally as menacing and undesirable, there existed a third belief about life after death—deification. Combining Roman tradition with Hellenistic practices and ideas deriving from Hellenistic philosophy, the deification of exceptional individuals was instituted at Rome after *Caesar's assassination. Thereafter elevation to the status of a god (*divus*) by a senatorial decree (*senatus consultum*) became the rule for emperors and some members of their families (see RULER-CULT).

To these traditions was added, from the last centuries of the republic on, a series of Hellenistic concepts, ranging from speculation about the immortality of the soul to images of hell. Verse epitaphs prove that these ideas were rarely exclusive and coherent. We are dealing with speculations rather than beliefs capable of shaping a person's whole existence.

See DEAD, DISPOSAL OF.   R. S. J. G., J. Sch.

debt, the creation of obligations in cash or kind, existed at all levels of society throughout the ancient world: from loans of seed and implements between peasants (Hes. *Op.* 396 ff., 453 ff.) to lending of small sums and household objects between city-dwellers (Theophr. *Char. passim*), from borrowing to cope with unforeseen crises (Dem. 53. 4 ff.) to substantial cash loans between the wealthy to support an élite lifestyle (Ar. *Nub.*; Plut. *Mor* 827 ff.). More generally, the partly random testimony of papyri from Ptolemaic and Roman *Egypt hints at the likely frequency of loan transactions in other times and places, largely concealed by the perspective of surviving sources. The part played by debt in funding *trade and commerce is disputed; but always to the fore were the socio-political implications of widespread indebtedness, plausibly linked with the so-called 'Solonic Crisis' (see SOLON) in Archaic Athens and the 'Struggle of the Orders' in early *Rome. In time of siege or revolution, the indebted could be a force to be reckoned with (Aen. Tact. 5. 2, 14. 1; Thuc. 3. 81.). Athens after Solon was exceptional in its successful prohibition of loans secured on the person (*Ath. pol.* 6. 1); debt-bondage and other forms of debt-dependence were common throughout the remainder of the Greek and Roman worlds. Frequent laws intended to regulate debt were rarely enforceable and generally had only limited or temporary effect. Forms of debt-bondage continued in Rome long after the *lex Poetelia de nexis* (326 BC), which reputedly prohibited imprisonment for debt. Wider implications of indebtedness were also apparent at the upper end of society. Wealthy Athenians risked their status by raising loans on the security of property to fulfil *eisphora* (tax) and prestigious liturgy (public works) obligations. In the late Roman republic, indebtedness was intertwined with élite politics: the massive debts incurred by politicians in the pursuit of power could result in credit crises (49 BC, on the eve of the Civil War) and, in extreme cases, point the way to revolution (the conspiracy of *Catiline). A possible alternative was exploitation of the provincials: *Cicero, while governor in Cilicia (S. Asia Minor), records with more dismay than surprise loans at usurious rates of interest by *Brutus to the nearby city of Salamis on *Cyprus, and by *Pompey to Ariobarzanes III, king of neighbouring Cappadocia (*Att* 5. 21; 6. 1).   P. C. M.

Delian League, modern name for the alliance formed 478/7 BC against the Persians. ('Athenian empire' might be a better title for this article, but not all students of *imperialism admit that Athens had an empire in the full sense). In 478 the Greeks, led by the Spartan Pausanias, campaigned in *Cyprus and secured *Byzantium; but Pausanias abused his power and was recalled to Sparta. At the request of the allies, who pleaded Pausanias' behaviour and 'Ionian (Greek) kinship' (Thuc. 1. 95. 1), Athens accepted leadership. The Peloponnesians acquiesced (some evidence suggests reluctance), and a new alliance was formed with its headquarters on the sacred island of *Delos—a traditional Ionian festival centre but with an appeal to Dorian islanders also. Athens provided the commander of the allied forces and settled which cities were to provide ships and which money; the treasurers also, ten *hellēnotamiae*, were Athenians, and the Athenian politician Aristides made the first assessment. But at the outset policy was determined at meetings on Delos at which every member, including Athens, had just one equal vote. The nucleus of the alliance was formed by the Ionian cities of the west coast of *Asia Minor, the Hellespont (Dardanelles), and the Propontis (mod. sea of Marmara), and most of the Aegean islands. Chios, *Samos, *Lesbos, and some other states with a naval tradition provided ships; the remainder brought annual tribute to the treasury at Delos. Members took permanently binding oaths of loyalty.

At first the anti-Persian objectives were vigorously pursued. Persian garrisons were driven out of Thrace (except at Doriscus on the Hebrus) and Chersonesus; Greek control was extended along the west and south coast of Asia Minor; new members joined until there were nearly 200. The climax was the Athenian general Cimon's victory at the river Eurymedon, SW Asia Minor (466). Meanwhile Carystus in Euboea was forced to join (*c*.472), Cycladic Naxos tried to secede and was forced back in (*c*.467), and in 465 wealthy Thasos (N. Aegean) revolted because of Athenian encroachment on Thasian mainland holdings. Thasos surrendered 462 and stiff terms were imposed, but nearby on the Strymon a large colony of Athenian allies was wiped out by the local inhabitants. If Cimon made a first peace of Callias with Persia, after Eurymedon it ended with his *ostracism and fighting against Persia resumed in 460, when a strong Athenian force sailed to Cyprus to support Inarus, a Libyan prince in revolt from Persia. The Egyptian expedition ended in disaster for Athens in 454, and in that year the treasury was moved from Delos to Athens (?for security in this moment of peril; but the date of the move is not absolutely certain). But Athenian power spread in Greece and the Aegean: the Dorian island of Aegina was coerced in 458, and the First Peloponnesian War gave Athens control over Boeotia 457–446: it now seems that the Boeotian towns Orchomenus and Acraephnium were actually tributary members of the league, which should therefore not be regarded as purely maritime. At sea Cimon, back from ostracism, led a force to Cyprus but this phase of resumed expansion ended with his death at the end of the 450s. Meanwhile Athens exploited the *propaganda potential of *Apollo's sanctuaries at Delos and Delphi; a struggle took place throughout the century between Athens and the Peloponnesians at this level as well as the military (see DELPHI).

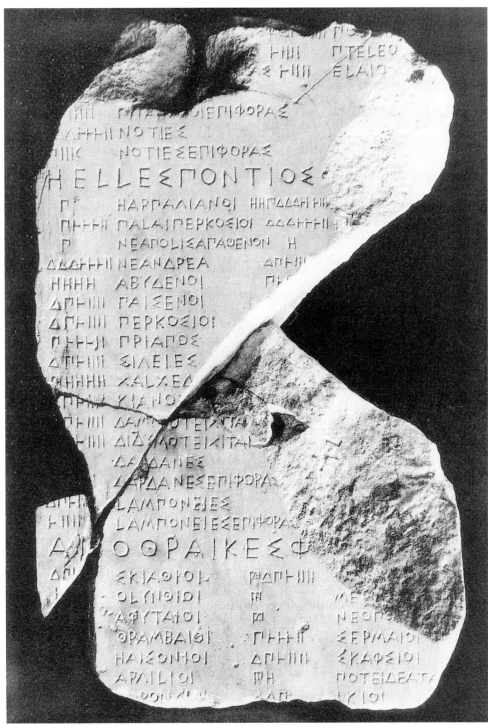

Delian League Fragment from one of the inscribed lists set up on the Athenian Acropolis as a record of the quotas set aside for *Athena from the annual payments of the allies. The lists give a valuable indication of which states paid tribute, and how much they paid, from one year to another.

The main Callias Peace of 450, if historical, restricted Persian movement west of Phaselis (SW Asia Minor) and outside the Black Sea, and Persia made other concessions. The removal of the original justification of the league led to restlessness among Athens' allies, but this was checked and tribute-levying (perhaps discontinued for a year) was resumed. Cleruchies (a type of Athenian citizen colony) and other repressive institutions were now imposed, though the greater bulk of epigraphic evidence after mid-century creates a risk of confusing first occurrence with first attestation. The first known cleruchy was at Andros 450, also perhaps Naxos and Euboea (Carystus); Chersonesus was settled by *Pericles in 447. By now only Chios, Samos, and Lesbos contributed ships, the rest paid tribute and had no effective means of resisting. Epigraphic evidence suggests a shift to harsher terminology, 'the allies' being replaced by 'the cities which the Athenians rule'; and the greater proliferation of visually and symbolically formidable imperial inscriptions in allied states may itself have functioned increasingly as a repressive device in the years after 460. This sombre league-into-empire picture of gradually increasing oppression (ATL, R. Meiggs, *The Athenian Empire* (1972)) has been challenged (M. Finley, *Economy and Society in Ancient Greece* (1981), ch. 3), less by the offering of a more cheerful one than by the insistence that Athenian behaviour had never been anything but harsh (e.g. Cimon's coercion of Scyros in the 470s). In favour of the 'gradual deterioration' view is Thuc. I. 99, an important chapter. Equally serious is the questioning of traditional criteria for dating of Attic inscriptions; techniques of laser enhancement have been used to down-date ML 37 (Athenian alliance with Sicilian Segesta) from 458/7 to 418, see SEG 39. I. If this dating wins general acceptance, not only does important evidence for early Athenian ambitions in the west disappear, not to mention possible damage done to the credit of *Thucydides, but some fundamental epigraphically-based assumptions about the development of Athenian imperial policy may have to go. But at time of writing the issue is open. The new technique needs to be more generally tested, not just applied to one fragmentary and desperately disputed text.

Boeotia revolted in 447 or 446, Athens was defeated at Boeotian Coronea, and this deepened the crisis—revolts by Megara and Euboea, and a Spartan invasion—which was settled by the Thirty Years Peace (446). In 440 Samos defied Athens, was besieged and subdued and forced to pay a large indemnity. Whether or not a technical democracy was now installed or an *oligarchy tolerated is uncertain; it was perhaps more important to Athens, here and elsewhere, that the governing group should be pro-Athenian. Back at Athens, the people's courts or *dikastēria* (see LAW AND PROCEDURE, ATHENIAN) played a major part in the control of empire.

When the Peloponnesian War began (431), this Athenian control was firm; Spartan hopes for large-scale revolt from Athens were disappointed, nor did the Spartans make best use of their opportunities, e.g. on Lesbos, which Athens

crushed. In 425 the Athenians increased the tribute assessment to nearly 1,500 talents (the original assessment is said to have been 460 talents). In 416 when Cycladic Melos refused to join the alliance, Athens reduced the island and enslaved the women and children, a small-scale atrocity but one long remembered against Athens. After the Sicilian disaster of 415–413 Chios, Miletus, Thasos, Euboea, and other key places revolted, but even this wave of revolt was contained, partly because of Persian behaviour and Spartan limpness, partly because Athens had learned to avoid counter-productive reprisals.

The Athenian empire brought benefits to the poorer cities: *piracy was suppressed to the great advantage of *trade, and the Athenian navy offered well-paid service, particularly attractive to the population of the islands. Pride in Athenian imperial success and cultural achievement may not have been confined to Athens' own citizens, though these are not aspects on which our main source Thucydides dwells. He does not even bring out the extent to which the upper classes at Athens benefited (as inscriptions like *Hesperia* 1953, 225 ff. attest) from overseas territorial possessions in the empire, acquired in defiance of local rules. But such possessions help to explain why there was so little principled objection to the empire, and the democracy which ran it, on the part of the Athenian social and intellectual élite. They also show that the literary picture of solidarity between the Athenian dēmos (common people) and the dēmos in the allied states is too simple. Thucydides or rather one of his speakers hints that the allies would prefer independence from either Athens or Sparta. Nevertheless, and in Athens' favour, the same chapter (8. 48) is surely right to acknowledge that at worst, arbitrary judicial process and violent killings could be expected from the oligarchies which Sparta had to offer instead.

The allies did not in fact make much contribution to the defeat of Athens, and when Sparta took Athens' place the cities soon had reason to regret the change. In less than 30 years they again united under Athenian leadership in the Second Athenian Confederacy. But it is a significant indicator of the reasons for Athenian unpopularity in 431 (Thuc. 2. 8) that in 377 Athens repudiated cleruchies, garrisons, and overseas possessions. R. M.; S. H.

Delos (see ◀Map 1, C c▶), a small Aegean island (3 sq. km.: 1.2 sq. mi.) between Myconos and Rheneia, regarded in antiquity as the centre of the Cyclades. Composed of gneiss and granite, it is barren and almost waterless and was incapable of supporting its inhabitants.

Delos, the only place to offer shelter to Leto, was the birthplace of her children *Apollo and *Artemis, as recounted in the Archaic *Homeric Hymn to Apollo*. This was the basis of its historical importance. It was also the burial-place of the Hyperboreans (legendary race of Apollo-worshippers in the far north). Anius was its heroic founder, son and priest of Apollo, later associated with the Trojan cycle.

Early bronze age occupation on Mt. Cynthus was succeeded by a *Mycenaean settlement on the low ground later occupied by the sanctuary. Two Mycenaean graves were later identified as the tombs of the Hyperborean maidens (the Theke and the Sema). Continuity of cult into historic times is unlikely.

Delos was colonized by Ionian Greeks c.950 BC but the sanctuary's prominence originates in the 8th cent. It became the principal cult centre of the Ionians of the Cyclades, *Asia Minor, Attica, and Euboea, and was perhaps the centre of an Ionian amphictiony (cultic league of neighbours). Naxos and Paros were its most conspicuous patrons in the early Archaic period. In the later 6th cent. first *Pisistratus and then the tyrant Polycrates of *Samos asserted their authority. The Athenians purified the island by removing burials within view of the sanctuary and perhaps built a temple of Apollo (the pōrinos naos). Polycrates dedicated Rheneia to Apollo, providing the basis for the sanctuary's subsequent wealth. Delos emerged unscathed from the Persian Wars (490–479 BC) and subsequently became the meeting-place and treasury of the *Delian League. After their removal to Athens in 454 BC the Athenians assumed administration of the sanctuary but did not impose tribute. In 426 BC Athens carried out a second purification, clearing all burials and depositing their contents in the Purification Trench on Rheneia. Henceforth women about to give birth and the dying had to be removed to Rheneia. They also reorganized their quadrennial festival (the Delia), celebrated with particular splendour by *Nicias in 417 BC, perhaps to inaugurate the new temple of Apollo. In 422 BC the Delians were expelled by Athens on a charge of impurity but were soon recalled. Its independence following liberation in 405 BC was short-lived, administration of the sanctuary reverting to Athens from 394 BC.

Athenian domination lasted until *Antigonus the One-eyed's foundation of the League of Islanders in 314 BC, championed by the Ptolemies in the early 3rd cent. but redundant after the Chremonidean War (260s). For a century and a half Delos was independent and functioned as a normal city-state, with an archon as its chief magistrate and the sanctuary's administration entrusted to a board of hieropoioi (religious officials). This was a period of extensive new public building, some provided by foreign patrons (e.g. the stoas of *Antigonus Gonatas and Philip V of Macedon). These and the festivals instituted by successive Hellenistic kings were more a display of religious patronage than an assertion of political domination. Although Delos' population remained relatively small (c.3,000–4,000) it began to develop as a commercial centre, attracting foreign bankers and traders, Italians prominent among them.

Independence ended in 166 BC when Rome handed control of Delos to Athens. Its inhabitants were expelled and replaced by Athenian cleruchs (citizen-colonists). Delos was made a free port to the detriment of Rhodian commerce (see RHODES). In conjunction with its commercial growth in the later 2nd and early 1st cent. its population expanded enormously and it became increasingly cosmopolitan, merchants and bankers from Italy and the Hellenized East forming distinct communities. Delos became the most important market for the slave trade (see SLAVERY). Although Athenians filled the civic posts (chief magistrate, the epimelētēs), guilds and associations of the foreign communities and trading groups administered their own affairs. Sacked in 88 BC by Archelaus, *Mithradates VI's general, and again in 69 BC by pirates (see PIRACY), Delos never recovered its former greatness. By the end of the 1st cent. BC its importance as a sanctuary as well as a commercial centre were lost. Its decline, which became a *topos in Roman literature, owed as much to shifts in trading-patterns as the destructions. A small community survived into late antiquity.

The cults of Apollo, Artemis, and Leto were naturally the most prominent and among the most ancient, though none need be earlier than the 8th cent. Apollo was the focus of the annual Ionian festival (the panēgyris) celebrated with games, singing, and dancing. Individual cities sent delegations to the major festivals and some, such as Andros, Ceos (mod. Kea), and Carystus (Euboea), had their own oikoi (buildings) within the sanctuary. It was administered by boards of officials responsible for managing the property of Apollo and guarding the temple treasures, as well as maintaining the buildings of the officially recognized cults. However, as in any normal *polis, the gods charged with other communal concerns were given due attention, each having its own cult and annual festival. From the late 3rd cent. and especially after 166 BC foreign cults multiplied, reflecting the cosmopolitan character of the city. Most were of oriental origin, such as Sarapis, Isis (see EGYPTIAN DEITIES), and the Syrian gods Hadad and Atargatis, but Italian divinities, such as the Lares compitales, also occur and, from the early 1st cent. BC, a *synagogue served the Jewish community. Many were the concern of private groups and not officially recognized.

Among the more curious cult rituals were the sacred offerings sent to Delos by the Hyperboreans, passed from city to city along a fixed route, apparently modified under Athenian influence to pass through Attica. The 'crane' dance (geranos; see DANCING; PYGMIES), initiated by *Theseus and the Athenian youths returning from *Crete, was performed at the Altar of Horns. *Callimachus alludes to self-flagellation around the altar and gnawing the trunk of the sacred olive.

The archaeological exploration of Delos, conducted by the French school since 1873, has unearthed the sanctuary and large parts of the ancient city. Its public buildings, commercial installations, and residential quarters, combined with a mass of epigraphic documentation from the 4th cent. BC, give a detailed picture of its political, religious, social, and economic history. Nevertheless, the identification of many of the monuments is disputed.

Most of the ancient cults lay in the low ground on the sheltered west side of the island. Here were the temples of Apollo, the Artemision, and, to the north, the Letoon, as well as the Dodekatheon (sanctuary of the twelve gods) and others not securely identified. In the same area are the *oikoi* of various cities, dining-rooms, and the altars; the site of the Altar of Horns (the *keratinos bōmos*), reputedly built by Apollo himself, is debated. The Heraion, one of the earliest temples, stood apart at the foot of Mt. Cynthus, whose peak was crowned by a sanctuary of *Zeus and *Athena. The cult of Anius was housed in the *archēgesion* (founder's shrine) in the north-east. Originally the sanctuary was approached from the north, passing the Lion Terrace, but subsequently it was entered from the south. The later cults, especially those of oriental origin, were for practical and religious reasons concentrated below Mt. Cynthus and around its peak. The synagogue, on the NE coast, was isolated from the other sacred areas. Many of the associations named after a particular divinity (e.g. the Poseidoniasts of Berytus, mod. Beirut, and the Hermaists) combined cult with commercial and social functions.

The sanctuary of Apollo was also the focus for the city's political institutions, housing the *prytaneion* (*hôtel de ville*), the *bouleutērion* (council-chamber), and *ekklēsiastērion* (assembly hall). Associated with the social and religious life of the city were the hippodrome, *stadium, and *gymnasium on the low ridge north-east of the sanctuary. North of the Sacred Lake were two palaestras and on the lower slopes of Cynthus, in the old town, was the theatre. Around the sanctuary and encroaching on the sacred precincts were many of the commercial establishments, such as the markets of the Delians and the Italians.

Warehouses fringed the shore south of the port. Residential areas surrounded the sanctuary on the north, east, and south. No trace of the early city remains. The old town of the 3rd cent., with its unsystematic plan of winding streets and irregular houses, lay to the south at the base of Mt. Cynthus. The expansion of habitation in the later 2nd and early 1st cent. matched the increase in population after 166 BC. Houses of this period are larger, more regular, and organized on a rectilinear street grid. Their affluence testifies to the wealth of the city. Many contain *mosaics and traces of wall-paintings and the largest have colonnaded courts. Some 15,000 clay sealings found in one house are all that remains of a private *archive. Delos remained unwalled until 69 BC when, following the pirate sack, the Roman commander Triarius constructed a wall encompassing the main sanctuary and the residential areas to its north and south. The city's vast necropolis covered the SE shore of Rheneia.   R. W. V. C.

Delphi (see ◖Map 1, Bc◗) (See also DELPHIC ORACLE). Delphi, one of the four great panhellenic *sanctuaries (the others are Isthmia, *Olympia, Nemea), is on the lower southern slopes of Mt. Parnassus, *c.*610 m. (2,000 ft.) above the gulf of Corinth.

Before 300 BC There was an extensive *Mycenaean village in the *Apollo sanctuary at the end of the bronze age; the area was resettled probably during the 10th cent., and the

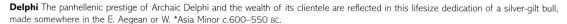

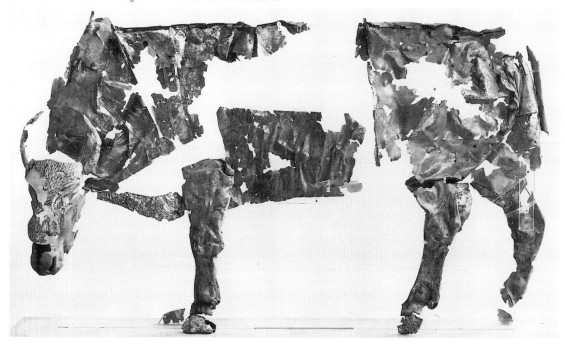

Delphi The panhellenic prestige of Archaic Delphi and the wealth of its clientele are reflected in this lifesize dedication of a silver-gilt bull, made somewhere in the E. Aegean or W. *Asia Minor c.600–550 BC.

first dedications (tripods and figurines) appear *c.*800. The settlement was probably relocated after the first temple was built (late 7th cent.). The first archaeological links are with Corinth and Thessaly. The 6th-cent. *Homeric Hymn to Apollo* says Apollo chose Cretans for his Delphic priests, and early Cretan metal dedications have been found, but Cretan material could have come via Corinth, and Cretan priests may have been invented because *Crete was distant i.e. this is a way of stressing the end of local domination. The first Pythian Games were held in either 591/0 or 586/5.

The sanctuary, for which our main literary evidence is *Pausanias 10, consisted of a temenos (sacred precinct) enclosed by a wall. Inside it were the monuments dedicated by the states of Greece to commemorate victories and public events, together with about twenty 'treasuries' (the oldest are those of Cypselid Corinth; Sicyon (northern *Peloponnese), *c.*560; Cnidus (SW Asia Minor), *c.*550; and Cycladic Siphnos, *c.*525), a small theatre, and the main temple of Apollo to which the Sacred Way wound up from the road below. The Persian Wars (490–479) were architecturally celebrated with special panache, and heroes like the Athenian general Miltiades were commemorated more assertively here (Paus. 10. 10) than was possible back at democratic Athens. The first temple was destroyed by fire in 548 BC; debris, including many votives (notably gold-and-ivory statuary), was buried under the Sacred Way. This destruction led to an architectural reorganization of the temenos. The great new temple was constructed in the late 6th cent. with help from the noble Athenian Alcmaeonid clan, and was itself destroyed by *earthquake in 373. A new temple was built by subscription. The physical organization of the Delphic oracle is controversial.

Delphi was attacked by the Persians in 480 and by the Gauls in 279 BC, but suffered little damage. Excavations were begun by French archaeologists in 1880, when the village of Kastri was moved from Delphi to its present site some way away. Apart from the revelation of the main buildings of the enclosure and the remains of numerous buildings (such as the base of the Serpent Column and the Spartan general *Lysander's victory-monument for the battle of Aegospotami), there have been notable finds of sculpture: the metopes of the Sicyonian building and the metopes of the Athenian treasury, the frieze of the Siphnian treasury, pedimental sculptures of the 'Alcmaeonid' temple, the bronze Charioteer, and the remnants of? the 4th-cent. sculptor Lysippus' memorial for a Thessalian dynast (the 'Daochos monument'). Below the modern road and the Castalian Spring are public buildings (palaestra, etc.), the mid-7th-cent. temple of Athena Pronaia, the 4th-cent. tholos, and the treasury of Massalia (Marseille, *c.*530), in the area called the Marmaria, where there are also boulders which have fallen from the rocks above (the Phaedriades).

The affairs of the sanctuary were administered by an ancient or ostensibly ancient international organization, the Delphic Amphictiony (cultic league of 'dwellers-around'). Influence at Delphi could be exercised in various ways and (mostly) via this amphictiony: by imposing fines for religious offences, by declaring and leading sacred wars, and by participation in prestigious building projects. Thus from the age of Archaic *tyranny to the Roman period, Delphi (like other pan-Hellenic sanctuaries but more so, because of its centrality and fame) was a focus for interstate competition as well as for contests between individuals. The four sacred wars are therefore only the moments when such competition flared up into overt military clashes. But even 'conventional' wars like the Peloponnesian Wars had a religious aspect: Sparta's foundation of Heraclea Trachinia (in central Greece) during the Archidamian War (431–421) was arguably an attempt to increase *Sparta's influence in the amphictiony. And at all times in Greek history, control of *Thessaly was desirable because Thessaly had a built-in preponderance of amphictionic votes. In the 3rd cent. BC the power of Aetolia (see FEDERAL STATES) was linked to its possession of Delphi, and significantly Rome's first alliance with a Greek state (212 or 211) was with Aetolia.

Delphi was also a *polis, which issued decrees that survive on stone. But one decree (*CID* i, no. 9) suggests abnormality in that the phratry (kinship group) of the Labyadae is found handling some of the business (e.g. rules about conduct of funerals) which would elsewhere have been the concern of the *polis* proper rather of a kinship group.

Finally, Delphi had military importance as a place of muster in central Greece (e.g. Thuc. 3. 101).

After 300 BC New Hellenistic powers used patronage of Delphi to gain legitimacy; the Aetolian Confederacy certainly (see FEDERAL STATES), and perhaps Attalus I of *Pergamum, made dedications promoting their victories against the Gauls as pan-Hellenic services. The appropriation (168 BC) by the victorious Lucius Aemilius Paullus of a monument destined for the defeated King Perseus of Macedonia announced *de facto* Roman domination of the sanctuary. Although *Augustus reformed the amphictiony (mainly to serve the interests of *Nicopolis) and *Domitian repaired the temple (AD 84), the only emperor to take a real interest in Delphi was *Hadrian, who held the city's archonship twice, toyed with enlargement of the amphictiony (ending up instead founding the Panhellenion, an Athens-based organization of Greek cities), and sponsored building (*Syll.*³ 830); whether the orchestrator (*kathēgemōn*) of Roman Delphi's beautification in a debated passage of *Plutarch (*De Pyth. or.* 409c) is Hadrian or the author himself, a Trajanic priest of Apollo, is debated. A regional Greek interest in the cult endured into the 3rd cent. AD, but international attention was now confined largely to *tourism and the Pythian Games. Delphi was still a 'sacred city' (*hiera polis*) under Constans (AD 337–350) (*Syll.*³ 903d); the steps in the installation of *Christianity remain obscure.   C. A. M., S. H., A. J. S. S.

Delphic oracle *Oracle of *Apollo. Its origins are dated to the very end of the 9th cent. BC and eventually it developed into the most important Greek oracle. It was consulted by *poleis* (see POLIS) as well as individuals, and played an important guiding role in the formation of the Greek *poleis* and in *colonization; it gave guidance on *pollution, 'release from evils', (rarely) laws, and, above all, cult. The story that Apollo was not the original owner of the oracle, but replaced an earlier deity (different versions naming different deities, but all including Gaia or Themis, or both) does not reflect cult history; it is a myth, expressing the perception that at Delphi the chthonian (lit. 'of the earth'), dangerous, and disorderly aspects of the cosmos have been defeated by, and subordinated to, the celestial guide and lawgiver. Apollo's oracle has tamed the darker side of the cosmos—both at the theological (Gaia's defeat) and at the human level: it therefore gives men divine guidance through which they can cope with this side of the cosmos.

The earliest temple for which there is evidence belongs to the second half of the 7th cent. The temple whose remains are visible was built in the 4th cent. Its predecessor was built in the last quarter of the 6th cent. after the earlier temple had been burnt down in 548/7. The oracular consultation took place in the adytum (innermost sanctuary), in which stood the omphalos (navel), a stone marking the centre of the world as determined by *Zeus, who released two eagles, one from the east and one from the west, which met at Delphi (cf. Pind. fr. 54). Another story makes the omphalos the mythical Python's (see APOLLO) or *Dionysus' tomb. Also in the adytum grew a laurel-tree, but the chasm with the vapours is a Hellenistic invention. The enquirer had to pay a consultation tax called *pelanos* (which had begun as a bloodless offering and kept the name when it became a monetary contribution). At the altar outside the temple was offered the preliminary sacrifice before the consultation, the *prothysis*, which on regular consultation days was offered by the Delphic *polis* on behalf of all enquirers. On other days it was offered by the enquirer—to be more precise, on behalf of the enquirer by the *proxenos* (local representative) of his city: non-Delphians were treated at the Delphic oracle as *xenoi*, foreigners, worshipping at the sanctuary of another *polis*. If the preliminary ritual was successful, i.e. if the animal had reacted as it should when sprinkled with *water (cf. Plut. *Mor.* 437a, 438a–b), it was sacrificed, and the enquirer entered the temple, where he offered a second *sacrifice, depositing either a whole victim or parts of one on a *trapeza*, offering-table, at the entrance of the adytum. He then probably went with the *prophētai* (interpreters) and other cult personnel to a space from which he could not see the Pythia (see below) in the adytum. The Pythia, who had prepared herself by purification at the Castalian Spring, burnt laurel leaves and barley meal on the altar called *hestia* inside the temple (which came to be seen as the common hearth of Greece); crowned with laurel, she sat on the tripod, became possessed by the god, and, shaking a laurel, prophesied under divine inspiration—a state which may correspond to what in non-religious explanatory models would be considered a self-induced trance. Her pronouncements were then somehow shaped by the *prophētai*. Exactly what form the Pythia's pronouncements took and what the *prophētai* did are matters of controversy. One possibility is that she felt that she received partial signs transmitting fragmentary visions— *not* gibberish—and that the *prophētai* interpreted these, shaping them into coherent, if ambiguous, responses; this was not an attempt to hedge their bets, but a result of the ambiguity inherent in the god's signs and the Greek perception that ambiguity is the idiom of prophecy, that there are limits to man's access to knowledge about the future: the god speaks ambiguously, and human fallibility intervenes and may misinterpret the messages.

The most important of the oracle's religious personnel (consisting of Delphians) were: the Pythia, an ordinary woman who served for life and remained chaste throughout her service; the *prophētai*; the *hosioi*, who participated in the ritual of the consultation and shared tasks with the *prophētai*, and the priests of Apollo. The Pythia is not mentioned in the oldest 'document' informing us about the Delphic cult and oracle, the *Homeric Hymn to Apollo*, where the god gives oracular responses 'from the laurel-tree' (393–6), an expression that corresponds closely to that ('from the oak-tree') used in the *Odyssey* (14. 327–8; 19. 296–7) for the prophecies at Dodona (NW Greece), where the oak-tree spoke the will of *Zeus, which was interpreted by priests. A similar practice involving the laurel may perhaps have been practised at Delphi at an early period. Whether divination by lot was practised at Delphi as a separate rite is a matter of controversy. Control of the oracle was in the hands of the Delphic Amphictiony (cultic league of 'dwellers-around'), run by the amphictionic council, whose duties included the conduct of the pan-Hellenic Pythian Games, the care of the finances of the sanctuary, and the upkeep of the temple. The amphictiony, we are told, fought a war against nearby Crisa and defeated it; this is the First Sacred War, the historicity of which has been doubted, but the traditional date for its end (*c*.590 BC) coincides with the beginning of a period of transformation, a serious upgrading of the sanctuary, not the least of its manifestations being the building of several treasuries. The first Pythian Games were held to celebrate the amphictiony's victory. Other Sacred Wars took place subsequently, of which the fourth ended in 338 with the victory of *Philip II of Macedon at the battle of Chaeronea. It is not true that the oracle's influence had diminished as a result of its suspect position in the Persian Wars (490–479). Its influence continued, only its 'political' role inevitably diminished in the radically changed circumstances of the Hellenistic and Graeco-Roman world.   C. S.-I.

deme, local district/village. At Athens, see CLEISTHENES.

Demeter, the Greek goddess of corn, identified in Italy with Ceres. The second part of her name means 'mother', and *dē* (or *da*) was thought to mean 'earth' in antiquity, but the Greeks had a separate goddess of the Earth, and Demeter came later in the pantheon, as granddaughter of Ge (Gaia) and sister of *Zeus. An alternative modern theory connects *dē* with *dēai*, the Cretan word for 'barley' (cf. *xeia*, 'spelt'), but this is linguistically doubtful. She is, however, certainly the goddess who controls all crops and vegetation, and so the sustainer of life for men and animals. In early epic corn is called 'Demeter's grain' (*dēmēteros aktē*), and in a Homeric simile 'blonde Demeter' herself winnows grain from chaff (*Il.* 5. 500 f.). Her daughter by Zeus, *Persephone (Attic Pherrephatta), was called simply *Korē*, 'the Girl', and the two were so closely linked that they were known as 'the Two Goddesses' (*tō Theō*) or even sometimes as 'the Demeters' (*Dēmēteres*). Because the life of plants between autumn and spring is one of hidden growth underground, Persephone was said to have been carried off by her uncle *Hades, lord of the Underworld, and compelled to spend the winter months with him as his wife, returning to the upper world with the flowers of spring. Thus as Kore she was a deity of youth and joy, the leader of the Nymphs (young women divinities), with whom she looked after the growth of the young, but as Hades' wife she was also queen of the dead, governing the fate of *souls, and thus an awesome and dread goddess.

As deities of *agriculture and growth, associated with a settled rhythm of life, Demeter and Kore were regarded as important influences in the development of civilization. Their title Thesmophoros was traditionally interpreted as due to their role as givers of law and morality. The Greek religious calendar was closely linked to the farmer's year, and many of their festivals coincided with the seasonal activities of ploughing, sowing, reaping, threshing, and storing the harvest. One of the most important and widespread, the Thesmophoria, normally took place in autumn (11–13th of the month Pyanopsion in Athens), near to sowing-time, and included ceremonies intended to promote fertility. Like many festivals of Demeter, it was secret and restricted to women. Their secrecy seems to have been due primarily to the sense of awe and fear generated by contemplation of the powers of the earth and Underworld.

The most important festivals of Demeter and Kore were the ceremonies of *initiation known as '*mysteries', the most famous of which were those of *Eleusis. By guaranteeing to initiates the favour of the goddesses, they offered above all the promise of a better fate after death, but they also promised prosperity in life, personified by Plutus (Wealth), who was the child of Demeter, born from her union with the Cretan hero Iasion 'in a thrice-ploughed field' (Hom. *Od.* 5. 125–8; cf. Hes. *Theog.* 969–74, *Hymn. Hom. Cer.* 486–9).

Many legends told how, when Demeter was searching for her daughter after Hades had carried her off, she received information or hospitality from the local inhabitants of different places in Greece, and in gratitude taught them how to practise agriculture and to celebrate her rituals. The chief claimants for this honour were Eleusis and *Sicily, her most important cult centres. The oldest and best-known version of the myth is the *Homeric Hymn to Demeter*, an *epic poem probably of the Archaic period. This tells how, after Kore was carried off, Demeter wandered the earth in search of her, disguised as an old woman, until she came to Eleusis where she was welcomed by the family of King Celeus. She became the nurse of his baby son Demophon, and tried to immortalize him by anointing him with ambrosia and holding him in the fire at night to burn away his mortality. She was interrupted by Metanira, Celeus' wife, and so prevented from making him immortal. Instead, she revealed her true identity, promised Demophon heroic honours after death, and ordered the Eleusinians to build her a temple and altar. She then withdrew to her new temple and caused a universal *famine, until Zeus was forced to order Hades to release her daughter. Hades, however, gave Persephone a pomegranate seed to eat, and because she had tasted food in the Underworld she was compelled to spend a third part of every year there, returning to earth in spring. Demeter then restored the fertility of the fields and taught the princes of Eleusis how to perform her mysteries, whose absolute secrecy is stressed. The poem closes with the promise of divine favour to the initiates both in life and after death.

The Great Mysteries at Eleusis were celebrated in early autumn (in the Athenian month Boedromion), and were preceded by the Lesser Mysteries at Agrae, just outside Athens, in spring (in the month Anthesterion). Some modern scholars have rejected the predominant ancient view which connected Persephone's absence with winter, arguing that her descent should coincide with the storing of seed-corn in underground granaries after harvest, during the period of summer dryness, to be taken out in autumn for sowing. This fits some near eastern myths of a similar type about a disappearing deity, but the story was never understood in this way by the Greeks, and the traditional explanation agrees much better with the agricultural condition of Greece itself.

The famine, in the *Homeric Hymn*, reflects another form of the belief that the death of vegetation has a divine cause. Persephone's absence and Demeter's anger and grief both combine to create sterility. The hymn assumes the existence of agriculture already before the Rape, but the Athenians in the Classical period claimed that Demeter had given to Triptolemus, one of the princes of Eleusis, the gifts of corn and the arts of agriculture, and that he then travelled over the world teaching these to other nations.

Sicily was always regarded as especially consecrated to the Two Goddesses, and in the Hellenistic and Roman periods versions of the myth of Kore which placed her Rape and Return here became popular. She was said to have been carried off from a meadow near Enna in the centre of the island, and to have disappeared underground at the site of the spring Cyane near *Syracuse, where an annual festival was held. Other major festivals took place at the times of harvest and sowing.

In Arcadia (central *Peloponnese) Demeter was worshipped with *Poseidon. The Black Demeter of Phigaleia and Demeter Erinys of Thelpusa were both said to have taken the form of a mare and to have been mated with by Poseidon in horse-shape, and at Phigaleia she was shown as horse-headed. Their offspring were Despoina ('the Mistress') and (at Thelpusa) the horse Arion. At Phigaleia she was also said to have caused a universal famine because of her anger both with Poseidon and over the loss of her daughter (Paus. 8. 25 and 42).

These motifs of Demeter's anger and a consequent famine recur in the story of Erysichthon, who incurred her wrath by trying to cut down a grove sacred to her, although warned by the goddess in disguise not to do so. She punished him with an insatiable hunger which ruined all his household (Callim. 6).

A unique genealogy of Demeter makes her the mother of *Artemis (Aesch. fr. 333 Radt): Herodotus says that this was due to syncretism (mingling) with Egyptian mythology (2. 156. 5–6).

In art Demeter is shown both on her own and with Persephone, with related figures of cult such as Hades and Triptolemus, and in groups with the other Olympian deities. Particularly popular scenes are those of the Rape and Return of Persephone, and the Mission of Triptolemus. She carries a sceptre, ears of corn and a poppy, or torches, and she and her daughter are often portrayed as closely linked and similar in iconography.

N. J. R.

democracy, Athenian (see following page)

Demosthenes (see page 225)

Diana (root †*dyw*-'the bright one' (cf. *Jupiter), originally a moon goddess, *contra* Altheim, *Griechische Götter im alten Rom* (1930), 93 ff.), an Italian goddess anciently identified with *Artemis, from whom she took over the patronage of margins and savageness. But the modalities of this evolution remain puzzling (moonlight as the contrary of daylight, and so of civilized life?). Her cult was widespread; see Birt in Roscher, *Lex.* 1. 1003–4 for details. One of her most famous shrines was on Mt. Tifata near Capua (Vell. Pat. 2. 25. 4 and elsewhere in literature, supported by much inscriptional evidence); the name Tifata means 'holm-oak grove' (Festus 503. 14 Lindsay), which suits Diana's character as a goddess of the wilderness. Most famous of all was her ancient cult near Aricia (on the shore of the volcanic lake known as the Mirror of Diana, *Speculum Dianae*, below the modern Nemi, i.e. *nemus*, 'grove'). Her temple stood in a grove, which was recorded as dedicated to her by Egerius Baebius (?) of Tusculum, *dictator Latinus* (Cato, *Orig.* 2, fr. 21 Jordan). It was therefore an old religious centre of the Latin League and it is probable, though direct proof is lacking, that the foundation of her temple (probably preceded by an altar) on Rome's Aventine hill, traditionally by Servius *Tullius (Livy 1. 45. 2 ff.), was an

attempt to transfer the headquarters of this cult to Rome, along with, what Livy mentions (ibid. 3), the headship of the league. See further, for the Massiliote and Ephesian connections of the Aventine temple, ARTEMIS.

That she was later largely a goddess of women is shown by the processions of women bearing torches (symbols of her name and original function) in her honour at Aricia (Prop. 2. 32. 9–10; Ov. *Fast.* 3. 268–9), also by the character of many of the votive offerings there, which have clear reference to children and *childbirth (Wissowa, *RK* 248). Her links with women, along with slaves (Festus 460. 33 ff. Lindsay) and asylum (Dion. Hal. *Ant. Rom.* 4. 26. 3), seem to inscribe her within the frame of her real field of action—namely, margins.

At Aricia she was associated with the nymph Egeria, and Virbius, an obscure male deity (Ov. *Met.* 15. 544; Servius on *Aen.* 7. 84 and 761). Identifications with foreign deities are common all over the west.

H. J. R.; J. Sch.

dictator, an extraordinary supreme magistracy at Rome, used first in military, later in domestic crises.

In Latin cities we find the name 'dictator' given to a regular magistracy, but there is no evidence that this was ever Roman practice. As an emergency magistracy the dictatorship is found frequently in the annals of the Roman republic down to the end of the 3rd cent. BC; it was not used during the 2nd cent. but reappeared in a more powerful form, when granted to *Sulla and then *Caesar. Possible parallels are the Oscan (see ITALY) *meddix tuticus* and the *Etruscan *zilath* or *purth*, but there is no reason to derive the Roman office from them. Although *Fabius Maximus Verrucosus is said to have been elected dictator in the centuriate assembly (*comitia centuriata*, Livy 22. 8), normally dictators were simply nominated in public by a magistrate with *imperium (*consul, praetor, or *interrex*) after authorization by the senate—for Sulla and Caesar the authorization was provided by a law. The dictator's function was either to command the army or to perform a specific task, such as holding elections or dealing with a sedition. His 24 lictors (attendants) indicated not so much a revival of the kingship, as *Appian *BCiv.* 1. 98–9 suggests, as a concentration of the powers of the consuls. The dictator (who was also known as *magister populi*, master of the infantry, and had to get permission to mount a horse while in office) immediately appointed a cavalry commander (*magister equitum*) as his subordinate. Existing magistrates remained in office but were generally subordinate to him. Originally dictators resigned as soon as their task was completed, being permitted at most to remain in office for six months. They were therefore not appropriate for emergency overseas commands, and specially chosen proconsuls were used instead. Contrary to the antiquarian tradition about the origin of the dictatorship, in the middle and later republic the dictator's actions were in theory exempt neither from veto by the *tribunes of the *plebs* (Livy 27. 6. 5) nor from *provocatio* (appeal to the Roman People) (Livy 8. 33. 8). Nor was he himself free from

[*continued on p. 224*]

Athenian democracy

Athenian democracy from 508/7 to 322/1 BC is the best known example in history of a 'direct' democracy as opposed to a 'representative' or 'parliamentary' form of democracy.

1. Ideology Today democracy is invariably a positive concept, almost a buzz-word, whereas *dēmokratia* in ancient Greece was a hotly debated form of constitution, often criticized by oligarchs and philosophers (see PHILOSOPHERS AND POLITICS) alike. The Athenian democrats themselves, however, connected *dēmokratia* with the rule of law (Aeschin. 1. 4–5) and, like modern democrats, they believed that democracy was inseparably bound up with the ideals of liberty and equality (Thuc. 2. 37). Democracy was even deified, and in the 4th cent. BC offerings were made to the goddess Demokratia (IG 2². 1496. 131–41).

Dēmokratia was what the word means: the rule (*kratos*) of the people (*dēmos*), and decisions of the assembly were introduced with the formula *edoxe tō dēmō*, 'it seemed good to the people' (IG 2². 28). When an Athenian democrat said *dēmos* he meant the whole body of citizens, irrespective of the fact that only a minority turned up to meetings of the assembly (Aeschin. 3. 224; Thuc. 8. 72). Critics of democracy, on the other hand, especially the philosophers, tended to regard the *dēmos* as a class, i.e. the 'ordinary people' (Arist. *Pol.* 1291ᵇ17–29; *Ath. pol.* 41. 2) or the 'city poor' who by their majority could outvote the minority of countrymen and major property-owners (Pl. *Resp.* 565a).

The fundamental democratic ideal was liberty (*eleutheria*, see FREEDOM), which had two aspects: political liberty to participate in the democratic institutions, and private liberty to live as one pleased (*zēn hōs bouletai tis*) (Arist. *Pol.* 1317ᵃ40–ᵇ17; Thuc. 7. 69. 2). The most important aspect of liberty was freedom of speech (*parrhēsia*) which in the public sphere was every citizen's right to address his fellow citizens in the political assemblies, and in the private sphere was every person's right to speak his mind (Dem. 9. 3). The critics of democracy, especially the philosophers, took democratic *eleutheria* to be a mistaken ideal that led to a deplorable pluralism and prevented people from understanding the true purpose in life (Pl. *Resp.* 557b–558c).

The democrats' concept of equality was not based on the view that all are equal (although the philosophers wanted to impute this view to the democrats, Arist. *Pol.* 1301ᵃ28–35). The equality advocated by the democrats was that all should have an equal opportunity to participate in politics (*isonomia*, Hdt. 3. 80. 6; Eur. *Supp.* 353, 408, 441), especially an equal opportunity to speak in the political assemblies (*isēgoria*, Hdt. 5. 78; Dem. 15. 18) and that all must be equal before the law (*kata tous nomous pasi to ison*, Thuc. 2. 37. 2). The concept of equality was purely political and did not spread to the social and economic sphere of society.

2. Institutions A description of the political system must focus on the 4th cent. BC, especially on the age of *Demosthenes (355–322) where the sources are plentiful enough to allow a reconstruction of the democratic organs of government.

Political rights were restricted to adult male Athenians. Women, foreigners, and slaves were excluded (Dem. 9. 3). An Athenian came of age at 18 when he became a member of his father's deme (constitutional sub-unit) and was enrolled in the deme's roster (the *lēxiarchikon grammateion*, Aeschin. 1. 103); but, as *ephēboi* (see GYMNASIUM), most young Athenians were liable for military service for two years (*Ath. pol.* 42) before, at the age of 20, they could be enrolled in the roster of citizens who had access to the assembly or *ekklēsia* (the *pinax ekklēsiastikos*, Dem. 44. 35). And full political rights were only obtained at the age of 30 when a citizen was allowed to present himself as a candidate at the annual sortition of magistrates (Xen. *Mem.* 1. 2. 35) and jurors (*Ath. pol.* 63. 3) (who served as both legislators and judges).

The citizen population totalled some 30,000 adult males over 18, of whom some 20,000 were over 30 and thus in possession of full political rights. The population of Attica—citizens, foreigners, and slaves of both sexes and all ages—may have amounted to some 300,000 persons. (See POPULATION, GREEK.)

Any citizen over 20 had the right to speak and vote in the people's assembly (*ekklēsia*) (Xen. *Mem.* 3. 6. 1). The people met 40 times a year (*Ath. pol.* 43. 3), mostly on the Pnyx hill (Aeschin. 3. 34); a meeting was normally attended by at least 6,000 citizens, the quorum required for (among other things) ratification of citizenship decrees (Dem. 59. 89), and a session lasted a couple of hours only (Aeschin. 1. 112). The assembly was summoned by the 50 *prytaneis* (see below) and chaired by the nine *proedroi*, 'chairmen' (*Ath. pol.* 44. 2–3). The debate consisted of a number of speeches made by the politically active citizens, and all votes were taken by a show of hands (*cheirotonia*), assessed by the *proedroi* without any exact count of the hands (ibid. 44. 3) (see ELECTIONS AND VOTING). The Athenians distinguished between laws (general and permanent rules, called *nomoi*) and decrees (temporary and/or individual rules, called *psēphismata*, Andoc. 1. 87); see LAW AND PROCEDURE, ATHENIAN. The assembly was not allowed to pass *nomoi* but did, by decree, make decisions on foreign policy and on major issues of domestic policy (*Ath. pol.* 43. 6). Furthermore, the people in assembly were empowered (*a*) to elect the military and financial magistrates (ibid. 43. 1, 44. 4); (*b*) to initiate legislation (*nomothesia*) by appointing a panel of legislators (*nomothetai*, Dem. 3. 10–3); and (*c*) to initiate a political trial (*eisangelia eis ton dēmon*) by appointing a panel of judges (a *dikastērion*, *Ath. pol.* 43. 4).

Citizens over 30 were eligible to participate in the annual sortition of a panel of 6,000 jurors (*hoi omomōkotes*, Ar. *Vesp.* 662) who for one year served both as legislators (Dem. 24. 21) and as judges (ibid. 148–51). When a *nomos* was to be enacted, the assembly decreed the appointment, for one day only, of a board of e.g. 1,000 legislators (*nomothetai*) selected by lot from the 6,000 jurors (Dem. 24. 20–38; Aeschin. 3. 38–40). Having listened to a debate the *nomothetai* decided by a show of hands all amendments to '*Solon's laws', i.e. the Solonian law code of 594/3 as revised and codified in 403/2 (Andoc. 1. 82–5). Boards of *nomothetai* were appointed only infrequently, and to legislate once in a month was considered excessive (Dem. 24. 142).

Jurisdiction was much more time-consuming. The popular courts (*dikastēria*) met on roughly 200 days in a year. On a court day members of the panel of 6,000 jurors showed up in the morning in the Agora (see ATHENS (TOPOGRAPHY)), and a number of courts were appointed by sortition from among those who presented themselves. These courts consisted of 201 or 401 judges each in private actions and 501 or more in public actions. Each court was presided over by a magistrate and in a session of some eight hours the judges had to hear and decide either one public action or a number of private actions (*Ath. pol.* 63–9). The two most important types of political trial were (i) the public action against unconstitutional proposals (*graphē paranomōn*), brought against proposers of decrees (Aeschin. 3. 3–8), and (ii) denunciation to the people in assembly (*eisangelia eis ton dēmon*, Hyp. 3. 7–8), used most frequently against generals charged with treason and *corruption (Dem. 13. 5).

In addition to the decision-making organs of government (*ekklēsia*, *nomothetai*, *dikastēria*) Athens had about 1,200 magistrates (*archai*), elected from among citizens over 30 who presented themselves as candidates (Lys. 6. 4). About 100 were elected by the *ekklēsia* (Aeschin. 3. 14) whereas the other 1,100 were chosen by lot (Dem. 39. 10), viz. 500 councillors and *c*.600 other magistrates, often organized in boards of ten with one representative from each tribe (IG 2². 1388. 1–12). The period of office was restricted to one year and a magistrate selected by lot could only hold the same office once whereas elected magistrates could be re-elected (*Ath. pol.* 62. 3). Before entering office magistrates had to undergo an examination (*dokimasia*) before a *dikastērion* (ibid. 55. 2–5) and, on the expiration of their term of office, to render accounts (*euthynai*) before another *dikastērion* (ibid. 54. 2; 48. 4–5).

The magistrates' principal tasks were to summon and preside over the decision-making bodies, and to see to the execution of the decisions made (Arist. *Pol.* 1322^{b}12–17). Apart from routine matters, the magistrates could not decide anything but only prepare the decisions (ibid. 1298^{a}28–32). The council of five hundred prepared business for the *ekklēsia* (*Ath. pol.* 45. 4) and the *nomothetai* (Dem. 24. 48), the other magistrates for the *dikastēria* (Aeschin. 3. 29).

democracy, Athenian This inscribed law against *tyranny (337/6 BC), passed at Athens in the tense period following *Philip II's victory at Chaeronea, stresses the democratic context with a relief of Demokratia (democracy) crowning Demos (the people).

By far the most important board of magistrates was the council of five hundred (*hē boulē hoi pentakosioi*). It was composed of 50 persons from each of the ten tribes who for a tenth of the year (a prytany of 36 or 35 days) served as *prytaneis*, i.e. as executive committee of the council, which again served as executive committee of the assembly. The council met every day except holidays in the *bouleutērion* on the Agora to run the financial administration of Athens and to consider in advance every matter to be put before the people (*Ath. pol.* 43. 2–49. 5).

Of the other boards of magistrates the most important were the ten generals (*stratēgoi*) who commanded the Athenian army and navy (ibid. 61. 1–2), the board for the Theoric Fund (*hoi epi to theōrikon*) who in the 350s under the politician Eubulus supervised the Athenian financial administration (Aeschin. 3. 24–5), and the nine archons, who in most public and private actions had to summon and preside over the popular courts and supervised the major festivals, e.g. the Panathenaea and the Dionysia (*Ath. pol.* 55–9).

In all matters the initiative was left to the individual citizen, in this capacity called *tōn Athenaiōn ho boulomenos hois exestin* (SEG 26. 72. 34). At any time about 1,000 citizens must have been active as speakers and proposers of *nomoi* and *psēphismata* or as prosecutors and *synēgoroi* before the people's court. But it was always a small group of about twenty citizens who more or less professionally initiated Athenian policy. They were called *rhētores* (Hyp. 3. 4, 8) or *politeuomenoi* (Dem. 3. 29–31), whereas the ordinary politically active citizen is referred to as an *idiōtēs* (Dem. *prooem.* 13). There were no political parties and the people did not just vote according to the crack of their leaders' whip. But by persuasion and charisma major political leaders sometimes succeeded in dominating the political assemblies for a longer period, as did *Pericles from 443 until his death in 429 (Thuc. 2. 65. 10), and *Demosthenes in the period 341–338 (Dem. 18. 320).

The ordinary citizens were reimbursed for their political activity as *ekklēsiastai*, or *nomothetai* or *dikastai* or *bouleutai* (*Ath. pol.* 62. 2; Dem. 24. 21). Very few of the magistrates were paid on a regular basis, but many obtained perquisites instead (Isoc. 7. 24–7). Speakers and proposers in the political assemblies were unpaid, and those who attempted to make a profit out of politics were regarded as *sycophants and liable to punishment (Dem. 59. 43).

The council of the Areopagus was a survival of the Archaic period and in the period 461–404 mainly a court for cases of homicide (Philochorus, *FGrH* 328 F 64). In the 4th cent., however, the activity of the Areopagus was again progressively enlarged in connection with the attempts to revive the 'ancestral' or 'Solonian' democracy (Din. 1. 62–3; Lycurg. 1. 52).

3. History In 510 BC the Pisistratid tyrants (see PISISTRATUS) were expelled from Athens, but the revolution ended in a power struggle between the returning aristocrats led by *Cleisthenes and those who had stayed behind led by Isagoras. With the help of the ordinary people (the *dēmos*) Cleisthenes successfully opposed Isagoras (Hdt. 5. 66–73) and, reforming the Solonian institutions of 594 BC, he introduced a new form of popular government which was in fact arising in several Greek city-states at the time. The term *dēmokratia* can be traced back to c.470 (*SEG* 34. 199; Aesch. *Supp.* 604) and may go back to Cleisthenes' reforms of 508/7 (Hdt. 6. 131. 1). Cleisthenes' major reforms were to divide Attica into 139 municipalities (demes or *dēmoi*) which, in turn, were distributed among ten tribes (*phylai*). Citizen rights were linked to membership of a deme, and a council of 500 (*boulē*) was introduced, with 50 representatives from each of the ten tribes, and a fixed number of seats assigned to each of the demes (*Ath. pol.* 21. 2–6). Finally, to avoid a repeat of the power struggle of 510–507 Cleisthenes introduced *ostracism (ibid. 22. 1, 3–4).

During the next century the new democracy was buttressed by other reforms: in 501 command of the army and navy was transferred from the polemarch to a board of ten popularly elected generals (*stratēgoi*) (*Ath. pol.* 22. 2). In 487/6 the method of selection of the nine archons was changed from election to selection by lot from an elected short list (ibid. 22. 5). The politician Ephialtes' reforms of 462 deprived the council of the Areopagus of its political powers which were divided between the assembly, the council of five hundred, and the popular courts (ibid. 25. 2). Shortly afterwards, on the initiative of Pericles, political pay was introduced for the popular courts (Arist. *Pol.* 1274ᵃ8–9) and the council or *boulē* (*IG* 1³. 82. 20), so that even poor citizens could exercise their political rights. Athenian citizenship became a much-coveted privilege, and in 451 Pericles had a law passed confining *citizenship to the legitimate sons of an Athenian mother as well as father (*Ath. pol.* 26. 4).

The defeats in the Peloponnesian War (431–404) resulted in a growing opposition to democracy and twice the antidemocratic factions succeeded for some months in establishing an *oligarchy, in 411 a moderate oligarchy led by the council of Four Hundred (Thuc. 8. 47–98, *Ath. pol.* 29–33) and in 404–3 a radical oligarchy under a junta which fully earned the name 'the Thirty Tyrants' (Xen. *Hell.* 2. 2–4; *Ath. pol.* 35–8; Diod. Sic. 14. 3. 7). In 403/2 democracy was restored in a modified form. Legislation (in 403) and all jurisdiction in political trials (in *c.*355) were transferred from the people in assembly to the panel of 6,000 jurors acting both as legislators (*nomothetai*) and judges (*dikastai*). In the 330s a kind of minister of finance was introduced (*ho epi tē dioikēsei*) (*SEG* 19. 119). He was elected for a four-year period and could be re-elected, and for twelve consecutive years the administration of Athens was entrusted to the politician Lycurgus (Hyp. fr. 139 Sauppe). These and other reforms were allegedly a return to the 'ancestral' or 'Solonian' democracy (Andoc. 1. 83; Aeschin. 3. 257), but the gradual and moderate transformation of the democratic institutions came to an abrupt end in 322/1 when the Macedonians after their victory in the Lamian War (323–322 BC) abolished the democracy and had it replaced by a 'Solonian' oligarchy (Diod. Sic. 18. 18. 4–5). During the Hellenistic age democracy in some form was restored several times i.e. in 318/17, 307–298(?), 287–103, and 88–85.

4. *Tradition* Between 322 BC and *c.* AD 1850 Athenian democracy was almost forgotten, and, if mentioned, the focus was on the mythical 'Solonian democracy' known from *Plutarch's *Life of Solon* and *Aristotle's *Politics* (1273ᵇ35–1274ᵃ21). It was not until *c.*1800, when history began to emerge as a scholarly discipline, that the Athenian democratic institutions were studied seriously and reconstructed, e.g. by August Böckh, from sources such as *Thucydides, Demosthenes, and inscriptions. And it was only from *c.*1850 that the new understanding of Classical Athenian democracy was connected, principally by George Grote, with a budding interest in democracy as a form of government, though now in the form of a 'representative' or 'parliamentary' democracy and no longer as an 'assembly' democracy in which power was exercised directly by the people.   M. H. H.

prosecution after leaving office (*CIL* 1². 583. 8–9). Although after 202 BC no short-term dictators were appointed, it appears that this was contemplated in 54/3 BC, and in 52, on the senate's advice, *Pompey was created sole consul instead (senators apparently feared he might abuse dictatorial power). Both Sulla and Caesar, when they were appointed to this office in order to lend constitutional form to their *de facto* supremacy, were given the task of restoring the constitution. Cicero portrays *Scipio Aemilianus dreaming that he would be appointed to a dictatorship with this function (*Rep.* 6. 12), and the anachronistic fiction suggests that in the 50s BC such a wide-ranging office was now acceptable to many of Cicero's readers. However, when Caesar was eventually appointed *dictator perpetuus*, 'dictator for life', this completely subverted the original notion of the dictatorship as an emergency office: it became a quasi-monarchy.   A. N. S.-W.; A. W. L.

Dio (Cassius), historian. See CASSIUS DIO.

Dio of Prusa, (Dio Cocceianus), later called Chrysostom, 'golden-mouthed') (*c.*AD 40/50–after 110), Greek orator and popular philosopher. Born of wealthy family in Prusa (mod. Bursa, NW Turkey) in Bithynia, Dio began a career as a rhetorician at Rome, but soon fell under the spell of the Stoic philosopher Musonius Rufus (see STOICISM). Involved in a political intrigue early in the reign of *Domitian, he was banished (*relegatus*) both from Rome and from his native province, and spent many years travelling through Greece, the Balkans, and Asia Minor as a wandering preacher of Stoic-*Cynic philosophy. Rehabilitated by *Nerva, he became a friend of *Trajan, but continued to travel widely as an epideictic orator. He later retired to his family estates in Bithynia and became a notable in the province (he figures in the *Letters* of *Pliny the Younger as the defendant in a prosecution arising out of a public building contract).

Of the 80 speeches attributed to him, two are actually the work of his pupil Favorinus of Arles. Many are display-

[*continued on p. 229*]

Demosthenes

Demosthenes (384–322 BC), the greatest Athenian orator. When Demosthenes was 7 years old his father died, leaving the management of his estate to his brothers, Aphobus and Demophon, and a friend, Therippides. The trustees mismanaged the business, and Demosthenes at the age of 18 found himself almost without resources. He claimed his patrimony from his guardians, who spent three years in attempts to compromise. In the mean time, he was studying rhetoric and legal procedure under *Isaeus and at 21 he brought a successful action against his guardians, but two more years elapsed before he received the remnants of the property. By now he was engaged in the profession of *logographos* (speech-writer) and the reputation gained in private cases led to his being employed as an assistant to prosecutors in public trials.

From 355/4 onwards he came more and more to devote himself to public business. It is not clear how far Demosthenes' sympathies were engaged in his first public trials, the prosecutions of the politicians Androtion and Leptines in 355 and of Androtion's associate, Timocrates, in 353: *Against Androtion* and *Against Timocrates* he wrote for a Diodorus, and in any case the political tendency of the trials is unsure; *Against Leptines* Demosthenes did deliver himself, and, since Leptines' law was defended by the politician Aristophon, it is possible that all three trials centred on his policy and that Demosthenes was one of his opponents. This would be consistent with the policy he supported in *On the Symmories* in 354/3: a rumour came that the king of Persia was preparing to attack Greece, as he had threatened to do in 356/5, and Demosthenes, arguing that the city was not properly prepared, opposed the advocates of war, certainly not the Eubulus group, possibly that of Aristophon. In 353/2 he turned on the politician Eubulus: *On the Syntaxis* seems directed partly against the allocation of surpluses to the *theōrika* (state grants to Athenian citizens to attend major festivals at the Theatre)—at § 30 he sneers about the public works of Eubulus—and partly against the policy of abstaining from all but essential military enterprises.

For the next few years Demosthenes was regularly on the losing side and of minor importance. Early in 352 in *For the Megalopolitans* he argued in favour of promising to support Arcadia, if Sparta carried out her plan of exploiting Thebes' preoccupation with the Third Sacred War: since Athens based her policy on concord with Phocis and *Sparta, the decision to do no more than give a guarantee to Messenia was probably right. A few months later Demosthenes wrote *Against Aristocrates* for use in the attack on a proposal to honour Charidemus in gratitude for his offices in the cession of the Chersonesus by the Thracian ruler Cersobleptes: the speech is notable both as a source of information about the law of homicide and also for the manner in which it regards Cersobleptes, not *Philip II of *Macedonia, as the real enemy in the north. Demosthenes did not yet see what was plain to those he opposed. In late 352 Philip's attack on Cersobleptes carried him very near the Chersonesus, and Demosthenes' eyes were opened. In 351 he delivered the *First Philippic* which pleaded for more vigorous prosecution of the war for Amphipolis: his proposals were not accepted; deeper involvement in the long fruitless struggle may have seemed to endanger the power to defend the vital areas of Thermopylae and Chersonesus. Late in 351 in *On the Liberty of the Rhodians* he urged support of the Rhodian *dēmos* against the oligarchs supported by the Carian dynasty (see RHODES): but the Persian attack on Egypt prompted caution, and Demosthenes' arguments were far from strong. In mid-349 Olynthus (Chalcidice), which had by then lapsed from Philip's alliance, was attacked by Philip and appealed to Athens for help: in the three *Olynthiacs*, delivered in quick succession, Demosthenes demanded the fullest support and, in the last, an end to the law assigning surpluses to the *theōrika*; again he scathingly alluded to the works of Eubulus. There is, however, no reason to suppose that the three expeditions voted were not supported by Eubulus or indeed that they satisfied Demosthenes, and the implementation of his proposals might have brought even greater disaster than the loss of

Olynthus. Early in 348 the party of Eubulus involved the city in a costly and inconclusive intervention in Euboea to prevent the island falling into the control of those hostile to Athens: Demosthenes later claimed to have been alone in opposing the expedition; either he was not truthful or he had taken a curious view of Athens' interests. One consequence of his opposition to Eubulus was that he became embroiled in an absurd wrangle with Midias, a prominent supporter of Eubulus, who had slapped his face at the Dionysia festival of 348: the case was settled out of court and the speech *Against Midias* was never delivered.

In mid-348, before the fall of Olynthus, Demosthenes successfully defended Philocrates when he was indicted under the *graphē paranomōn* (public action against unconstitutional proposals) for his proposal to open negotiations with Philip, and in 347/6, when Demosthenes like *Aeschines was a member of the council of five hundred, the partnership continued and Demosthenes played a leading part in securing acceptance of the Peace of Philocrates. On the two embassies to Macedon he cut a poor figure before Philip and got on badly with his fellow ambassadors, but the decisive moment came after the second embassy's return when in the assembly on 16 Scirophorion, it was known that Philip had occupied the Gates of Thermopylae and that Phocis could not be saved. Demosthenes was shouted down and Aeschines made the speech to which Demosthenes constantly recurred. What Demosthenes wanted that day is not clear: if he did want the city to denounce the new Peace, to march out to support Phocis attacked by the Macedonians and *Thessalians from the north and the Thebans from the south, his judgement was seriously awry. From that day Demosthenes determined to undo the Peace. Shortly after, however, in *On the Peace* he counselled caution, and for the moment contented himself with the attack on Aeschines from which he was forced to desist by the successful countercharge against his own associate, Timarchus.

The year 344 brought Demosthenes his opportunity to attack the Peace. Rumours reached Athens that Philip was preparing to intervene in the Peloponnese in support of Argos and Messene, and Demosthenes went on an embassy to those cities to warn them of the dangers of consorting with Philip: Philip protested, and shortly after Demosthenes' return the embassy of Python and all Philip's allies protested against his misrepresentations, and offered to turn the Peace into a Common Peace (i.e. applicable to all cities); first reactions were favourable, but in the assembly Hegesippus succeeded in having the status of Amphipolis referred to Philip—an oblique way of sabotaging the whole affair—while Demosthenes' contribution was the *Second Philippic* in which he denounced Philip as not worth an attempt at negotiation. (The alternative reconstruction would deny this conjunction and put Python's embassy in early 343.) In mid-343, after the success of the orator Hyperides' prosecution of Philocrates, Demosthenes judged the moment suitable to resume his attack on Aeschines; *On the False Embassy* sought to exploit the support of Eubulus' party for continuing the Peace and to suggest that Aeschines was really responsible for Philip's use of the peace negotiations to intervene in Phocis in 346. With the support of Eubulus and Phocion, Aeschines was acquitted by a narrow margin.

With the final collapse in early 342 of proposals to amend the Peace, Philip either began to intervene directly in Greece or was represented by Demosthenes as so doing, and amidst mounting hostility to Macedon Demosthenes went on an embassy to the Peloponnese to set about the organization of an Hellenic alliance for the war he was determined to have. For the moment his efforts came to little, but in 341 in *On the Chersonese* and shortly after, in the *Third Philippic*, he defended the aggressive actions of Diopeithes against Cardia in the NE Aegean by arguing that, since Philip's actions already amounted to war, it was absurd to heed the letter of the Peace. Not long after, he delivered the *Fourth Philippic* (of which the authenticity was long doubted but is now widely accepted); in it Demosthenes appears so confident of his control that he dismissed the notion of harm being done by the theoric distributions in words inconceivable in 349, and he successfully demanded an appeal to Persia to join in attacking Philip. In 341/0 he also formed an alliance with *Byzantium, and by autumn 340, when Philip finally declared war and seized the Athenian cornfleet, Demosthenes was in full charge of the war he had sought, though he was unable to restrain Aeschines from his unwise intrusion at Delphi into the rivalries of central Greece (see AESCHINES). In mid-339 he moved the suspension of the allocation of surpluses to the *theōrika*, and with Thebes unlikely to side with Philip after having expelled the Macedonian garrison from the Gates, Demosthenes could expect not to have to face Philip in Greece. The sudden seizure of Elatea in Phocis threw Athens into horrified perplexity, but Demosthenes proposed and effected alliance with Thebes, which he later pretended always to have wanted, and Athens and Thebes fought side by side at Chaeronea in autumn 338.

Demosthenes was present at the battle, and returned so quickly to organize the city's defences that Aeschines could accuse him of running away. He provided corn, repaired the walls, and was so much the man of the hour that he was chosen to deliver the Funeral Oration for 338. With Philip in Greece, the people looked to Demosthenes and he successfully met the frequent attacks on him in the courts. In 337/6 he was theoric commissioner, and Ctesiphon proposed that he be crowned at the Dionysia for his constant service to the city's best interests: perhaps encouraged by the opening of the Macedonian attack on Persia, Aeschines indicted Ctesiphon, but with the changing events of the next few months he preferred for the moment to let the case lapse. Demosthenes, hoping that the death of Philip was the end of Macedonian domination in Greece, sought to foment troubles for his successor, but *Alexander the Great quickly marched south and Demosthenes had to accept the new monarch. In 335 Demosthenes actively aided the Thebans in their revolt and narrowly escaped being surrendered to Alexander. From then on he seems to have looked to Persia to accomplish the liberation of Greece: such at any rate seems to be the meaning of the many charges of receiving money from the Persians. Demosthenes gave no support to the revolt of the Spartan king Agis III at any stage and, when Persia was crushed at Gaugamela (331) and the revolt collapsed, Athens was left in disastrous isolation. Aeschines seized the opportunity to renew his attack on Demosthenes through Ctesiphon. The case was heard in mid-330, and Demosthenes defended his acts in *On the Crown*, which is his masterpiece. He declined to fall into the trap of discussing recent events and with supreme art interspersed his discussion of events long past with lofty assertions of principle. Fewer than one-fifth of the jury voted for Aeschines, and he retired to Rhodes. Demosthenes was left in triumph, and the city settled down to acceptance of Macedonian rule, until in 324 word reached Greece that at the coming Olympian Games Alexander's emissary Nicanor was to make public a rescript ordering the restoration of exiles. Since this would affect the Athenian cleruchy (citizen colony) on *Samos, an agitation began which was to end in the Lamian War (323–322 BC). Demosthenes led a deputation as *architheōros* to protest. Subsequently he engaged in the discussion at Athens about divine honours (see RULER-CULT) for Alexander, having also taken the lead in dealing with the sudden appearance of Alexander's fugitive treasurer Harpalus by proposing first that Harpalus be kept prisoner and his money stored on the Acropolis, and later that the Areopagus investigate the losses. It is difficult to assess Demosthenes' policy in this year: he may have foreseen the new uprising under Leosthenes leading to the Lamian War and planned to involve Athens, but, since the especial ally of Leosthenes was Hyperides, who led the attack on Demosthenes in the prosecution of early 323, Demosthenes appears to have been at odds with the war-party. Equally unsure is his guilt in the Harpalus trial: the Areopagus declared him guilty of appropriating 20 talents, and he was found guilty and fined 50 talents, but, even if he did take the money, he may have intended to use it in service of the state; the whole affair is most obscure. He retired into exile, and lent his support to Hyperides in the creation of the alliance for the Lamian War. He was then recalled to Athens, but after the Macedonian victory at Crannon in 322 he left the city again, and was condemned to death by the decree of Demades. Pursued by the agents of Antipater, ruler of Macedon, he committed suicide in Calauria (mod. Poros) (322).

Modern opinions of Demosthenes' political importance have varied greatly, often in discernible relation to contemporary events. He has been lauded as a solitary champion of liberty and censured as the absurd opponent of progress. With the latter view English scholars have, happily, had little sympathy, but the high esteem in which the works of Demosthenes have been rightly held as works of art has tended to obscure the possibility that, while his devotion to liberty is one of the supreme monuments of liberty, his methods and his policies were not the best suited to attain their end, and that those of his opponents, which we must largely infer from his attacks, were no less directed to maintaining the city's power and independence, and perhaps more apt.

Demosthenes has much to say about Philip's success being due to *bribery and was convinced that his own opponents had been corrupted, but in his obsession with this dubitable view he seems blind to the real problem of his day, which was how Greece could be united to counter effectively the military power of the new national state so far greater than the power of any single city-state. There was much to be said against Demosthenes' determination to involve the full military resources of Athens in a war in the north, in particular that in such a war Athens stood to gain most and the other Greeks would not unite for that result. For the defence of Greece itself against invasion there was a real hope of uniting the cities in a Common Peace, and this appears to have been the policy of Demosthenes' opponents. There was perhaps more enthusiasm than judgement in his military assessments, and since the defeat of Chaeronea appears to have produced a Greece that could never wholeheartedly unite in a war of liberation, it is possible that, if such a decisive battle was inevitable, his opponents might have united Greece for it more effectively. But the situation of Greece was tragic, and Demosthenes was certainly of heroic stature.

Private lawcourt speeches (*dikai*). The series of private speeches begins with those against Aphobus and Onetor (363–362), in which Demosthenes claimed recovery of his property from his guardians, and continues throughout his life (*Against Dionysodorus*, 323–322). Several private speeches attributed (perhaps wrongly) to Demosthenes were delivered on behalf of the Apollodorus who was his opponent in the *For Phormion*. The speech *For Phormion* (350) and the first *Against Stephanus* (349; the second *Stephanus* is undoubtedly spurious) raise a question of professional morality. Pasion, the banker, appointed his chief clerk Phormion trustee for his sons; the elder son, Apollodorus, subsequently claimed a sum of money allegedly due to him, but Phormion proved that the claim had been settled some years previously. Apollodorus then prosecuted Stephanus, one of Phormion's witnesses, for perjury. If, as *Plutarch states, Demosthenes wrote *Stephanus A* as well as *For Phormion*, he was guilty of a serious breach of faith, for while the earlier speech extols Phormion's character, the later one contains insinuations against him. The evidence for the authenticity of *Stephanus A* is, however, inconclusive (cf. L. Pearson, *Antichthon* 1969, 18–26). Aeschines asserts that Demosthenes showed to Apollodorus a speech composed for Phormion, but this may be a misrepresentation of some attempt by Demosthenes to act as mediator.

The subjects of the private speeches include guardianship, inheritance, claims for payment, maritime loans, mining rights, forgery, trespass, assault, etc. In the *Callicles* (which has flashes of humour, seldom found in Demosthenes) the plaintiff alleges that the defendant has flooded his land by blocking a watercourse; in the *Conon*, a brilliant piece of writing, combining Lysianic grace (see LYSIAS) and Demosthenic force, some dissolute young rowdies and their father are summoned for assault.

Demosthenes had many rivals in his lifetime; but later critics considered him the greatest of the orators. His claim to greatness rests on his singleness of purpose, his sincerity, and his lucid and convincing exposition of his argument. In many instances he produces a great effect by the use of a few ordinary words. In his most solemn moments his style is at its plainest and his language most moderate. A master of metaphor, he uses it sparingly, and hardly at all in his most impressive passages. His style varies infinitely according to circumstances; sometimes as simple as *Lysias, now polished like *Isocrates, again almost as involved as *Thucydides, he follows no scholastic rule; long and short periods follow each other, or are mingled with passages in the running style not according to any regular system. Thus his carefully prepared utterances give an impression of spontaneity. Such was his control of language that he was generally able to avoid hiatus without any dislocation of the order of words. He had an instinctive aversion to a succession of short syllables, and even tribrachs are of comparatively rare occurrence.

G. L. C.

speeches, but others, e.g. those delivered before the assembly and council at Prusa, deal with real situations. His themes are varied: mythology, the Stoic-Cynic ideal monarch, literary criticism, popular morality, funeral orations, rhetorical descriptions, addresses to cities, etc. He sees himself as a teacher of his fellow men, and his stock ideas are the Stoic concepts of *physis* ('nature'), *aretē* ('virtue'), and *philanthrōpia* ('philanthropy'). His language and style are Atticist, though he avoids the extreme archaism of some representatives of the *Second Sophistic, and often aims at an easy, almost conversational style, suggestive of improvisation. *Plato and *Xenophon are his main models. Dio idealizes the Hellenic past, and feels himself the heir to a long classical tradition, which he seeks to revive and preserve. His Stoic-Cynic philosophy has lost its erstwhile revolutionary *élan*, and become essentially conservative, though he still insists on the philosopher's right to free speech and criticism. His Greek patriotism is in no way anti-Roman. Like his contemporary *Plutarch, he reflects the attitudes and culture of the upper classes of the eastern half of the empire, who were beginning to reach out to a share in political power. He gives a vivid and detailed picture of the life of his times.

R. B.; N. G. W.

Diocletian (Gaius Aurelius Valerius Diocletianus), originally named Diocles. Of obscure origins, born in Dalmatia perhaps in the early 240s AD, he rose to command the *domestici* (bodyguard) of the emperor Numerianus on the Persian campaign of 283–4. When Numerianus was killed by his praetorian prefect Aper, the army proclaimed Diocles Augustus at Nicomedia (20 November 284); he killed Aper. He campaigned (285) against Numerianus' brother Carinus, who was killed at Margus. A usurper Iulianus was also removed, and Diocletian was sole emperor. Visiting Italy, he proclaimed his comrade-in-arms Maximian as Caesar and sent him to suppress the Bacaudae (insurgent peasants in Gaul and northern Spain). Maximian was made Augustus (286) and spent the next years defending Gaul. Diocletian spent most of his reign on the Danube or in the east. In 287 he installed Tiridates III as king of Armenia and reorganized the Syrian frontier. He campaigned on the Raetian frontier (288); he fought the Sarmatians (285 or 289), and the Saracens (290).

But the problems of the empire remained serious. On 1 March 293 he established the 'tetrarchy'. To the two Augusti, now known as Iovius and Herculius respectively to emphasize their quasi-divine authority, were added Caesars, Constantius and Galerius; these were adopted into the Jovian or Herculian houses by the marriage of Galerius to Diocletian's daughter Valeria and of Constantius to Maximian's (?step-)daughter Theodora. The arrangement would provide an imperial presence in different areas; it might deter usurpers; and the Caesars might become acceptable to the armies and live to succeed as Augusti (but it is most unlikely that the Augusti had yet planned to abdicate). To raise the dignity of the imperial office Diocletian adopted an oriental court ceremonial (*adoratio*) and seclusion. Each tetrarch had his own staff (*comitatus*), and was often on the move in his territory, though Nicomedia, Trier (Augusta Treverorum), and Sirmium (on the Sava river in Pannonia (Inferior)) often provided an imperial residence; Rome was of lesser importance. In practice the empire was divided into two; Maximian and Constantius ruled the west, Diocletian and Galerius the east. Diocletian employed Galerius in Oriens until 299, thereafter on the Danube. Diocletian defeated the Sarmatians (294) and campaigned against the Carpi (296); many Bastarnae (a German tribe) and Carpi were settled on Roman soil. In Egypt a revolt broke out (297) under Domitianus and Aurelius Achilleus; present in person, Diocletian suppressed this after a long siege of *Alexandria, reorganized the administration of *Egypt, and negotiated with the Nobatae on the extreme southern frontier (298). Meanwhile he had sent Galerius to deal with the situation on the Syrian frontier: the Persian king Narses had expelled Tiridates from Armenia. Though defeated in his first campaign, Galerius won a total victory (298) and added significant territories to the empire. Campaigning by Constantius continued on the Rhine, but from 298 there was a general lull in rebellions and wars; tetrarchic authority was secure.

Diocletian pursued systematically a long-established policy of dividing provinces into smaller units; by 314 there were about 100, twice the number of a century earlier (see PROVINCIA). The purpose was to ensure closer supervision, particularly over law and finance, by governors and their numerous staffs; critics saw it as leading to never-ending condemnations and confiscations. All provinces were governed by equestrian *praesides* except Asia and Africa (by senatorial proconsuls) and the divisions of Italy (by senatorial officials called *correctores*). To oversee the *praesides*, Diocletian grouped the provinces into twelve new 'dioceses', each under a new equestrian official, the *vicarius* or 'deputy' of the praetorian prefects. In the later part of his reign, Diocletian began an important reform, separating military from civil power in frontier provinces; groups of provincial armies were put under the command of *duces* ('dukes'), so that *praesides* were left with civilian duties only. Senators remained excluded from military commands. His conception of defence was conservative; he made little or no effort to increase the size of the élite field army (*comitatus*), which had been formed in the late 3rd cent. But a huge programme of building and reconstruction of defensive works was undertaken on all frontiers, and these were to be held by sheer force of numbers; the size of the Roman army was perhaps nearly doubled.

The army and the increase of administrative personnel were a heavy financial burden. Diocletian reformed the system of taxation to take inflation into account and to regularize exactions in kind. Taxation was now based on the *iugum*, a new concept, a unit of land calculated from its productivity as much as by its area, and on the *caput*, the unit of human resource. Most revenue and expenditure was now in kind; every year an assessment of all levies payable on each fiscal unit was declared (*indictio*) by the praetorian prefects. By the Currency Edict (301) Diocletian attempted to create a unified currency, doubling the value of at least some coins and decreeing that the retariffed currency be used both for paying debts to the *fiscus* (central imperial treasury) and in private contracts. But he could not establish confidence in this revaluation. Late in 301 he tried to halt inflation by the Price Edict. In great detail this fixed maximum prices and wages; despite savage penalties it became a dead letter, as goods disappeared from the market.

Many legal decisions show Diocletian's concern to maintain or resuscitate Roman law in the provinces. He was an enthusiast for what he understood of Roman tradition and discipline, to reinforce imperial unity: hence he decreed the suppression of the theosophical sect known as the Manichees. This policy forms the backdrop to the persecution of Christians, undertaken possibly on the insistence of Galerius. (See CHRISTIANITY.) Earlier attempts had been made to purge the court and the army, but the first persecuting edict, issued at Nicomedia (23 February 303), was designed to prevent the Church from functioning, by requiring the burning of Scriptures and the demolition of churches, and the banning of meetings for worship; recusants were deprived of any rank, and thus made liable to torture and summary execution and prevented from taking action in court; imperial freedmen were re-enslaved. In Gaul and Britain Constantius contented himself with demolishing churches, and the later edicts were not promulgated outside the areas controlled by Diocletian and Galerius. The second edict imprisoned all clergy; the third released them, but they were to sacrifice first. The fourth edict ordered a universal sacrifice, but implementation was patchy, most severe it seems in Palestine and Egypt.

Late in 303 Diocletian visited Rome for the only time, to celebrate with Maximian his *vicennalia* (the 20th anniversary of his accession). A collapse in health caused him to return to Nicomedia, where on 1 May 305 he abdicated (Maximian reluctantly did the same at Milan), leaving Constantius and Galerius as Augusti, with Flavius Valerius Severus and Gaius Galerius Valerius Maximinus as Caesars. He attended Galerius' conference at Carnuntum (308) but refused to reassume the purple and spent his last years at Salonae (mod. Split); remains of the palace he built survive. He died about 312. His wife Prisca and only child Valeria were exiled by Maximinus and beheaded by the emperor Valerius Licinianus Licinius (Augustus from 308 to 325). Diocletian's genius was as an organizer; his measures did much to preserve the empire in the 4th cent., and many lasted much longer in the east. The tetrarchy as such broke down when Diocletian's personality was removed, but for most of the 4th cent. more than one emperor was the rule. His reforms were completed by *Constantine I, who introduced further innovations, most notably in the army and in religion.   R. P. D.

Diodorus of Agyrium, Sicily (hence Diodorus Siculus) is the author of the *Bibliothēkē* ('Library'), a universal history from mythological times to 60 BC. Only 15 of the original 40 books survive fully (bks. 1–5; 11–20); the others are preserved in fragments. Despite his claim to cover all of known history, Diodorus concentrates on Greece and his homeland of Sicily, until the First Punic War (264–241 BC), when his sources for Rome become fuller. But even in its fragmentary state, the *Bibliothēkē* is the most extensively preserved history by a Greek author from antiquity. For the period from the accession of *Philip II of Macedon to the battle of Ipsus (301 BC), when the text becomes fragmentary, it is fundamental; and it is the essential source for classical Sicilian history and the Sicilian slave rebellions of the 2nd cent. BC. For many individual events throughout Graeco-Roman history, the *Bibliothēkē* also sheds important light.

Diodorus probably visited *Egypt *c*.60–56 BC, where he began researching his history. By 56, he may have settled in Rome, completing the *Bibliothēkē* there around 30. He read Latin and had access to written materials in Rome, but, despite his admiration for *Caesar, there is no evidence that he personally knew Romans of prominence. Diodorus originally intended to cover events to 46; perhaps the dangers of writing contemporary history of a turbulent period influenced his decision to conclude with the year 60.

Books 1–6 include the geography and ethnography of the *oikoumenē* ('inhabited world') and its mythology and paradoxology (description of marvels) prior to the Trojan War; bks. 1–3 cover the east, bks. 4–6 the west. Of special significance are the description of Egypt in bk. 1, drawn from Hecataeus of Abdera; the discussion of India in bk. 2, drawn from Megasthenes (see INDIA); passages from the works of Agatharchides in bk. 3; and the highly fragmentary material in bk. 6, derived from Euhemerus of Messene.

The fully preserved historical books cover 480–302 and are organized annalistically, with Olympian, Athenian archon, and Roman consular years synchronized—often erroneously. The fragmentary final books, which draw on Posidonius, are probably organized episodically. Occasionally including the same incidents from different authorities or failing to understand the organizational habits of an individual author, Diodorus created numerous, sometimes serious doublets.

The main source for most of the narrative of the Greek mainland is *Ephorus; *Hieronymus of Cardia is the prime authority for the outstanding narrative of the Diadochi (*Alexander the Great's successors). Sicily receives important independent attention, in which Diodorus employs *Timaeus extensively. For much of the later Roman period, Diodorus follows *Polybius closely, as the preserved Polybian text shows; he employs Posidonius for many events after 146. But the 19th-cent. belief that all of Diodorus' sources could be identified proved over-confident and attempts to make such identifications continue to provoke great controversy. Further, because few of his sources survive outside his own work, precisely what Diodorus has taken verbatim, what he has confused and entered in error, and what he has consciously interpolated are matters of great dispute. It appears at least that certain themes recur throughout the *Bibliothēkē* independently of Diodorus' current source. Character assessments, with a strong insistence on personal and collective morality, and an emphasis on the civilizing power of individual benefactors suggest late Hellenistic influence and therefore Diodorus' own philosophy.   K. S. S.

diolkos, stone trackway across the isthmus of Corinth, for transporting ships and/or cargoes between the Saronic and the Corinthian gulfs. Archaeology suggests a date under the tyrant Periander (*c*.627–587 BC; there is literary evidence that he considered a canal. Wheeled wagons ran in carved grooves *c*.1.5 m. (5 ft.) apart; traffic probably moved in one direction at a time. *Triremes used it during the Peloponnesian War (431–404 BC), perhaps after modifications; but it was probably constructed for merchant vessels. It may quickly have become incapable of transporting most vessels fully laden, so that cargoes alone were carried. It was used by a fleet as late as AD 883.   J. B. S.

Dionysius I, born *c*.430 BC, son of Hermocritus, a well-to-do *Syracusan; wounded (408) in Hermocrates' attempted coup; secretary to the generals (406), he distinguished himself in the Acragas (mod. Agrigento) campaign. By unscrupulous demagogy he secured the dismissal of the generals and his own election as general plenipotentiary (a title he may have used until 392), obtained a bodyguard, occupied and fortified the citadel (Ortygia), and assumed control of the state. With a large allied army, he failed to raise the siege of Gela (405), but crushed a revolt of the aristocracy (confiscating their properties), and concluded the Peace of Himilco, which stripped Syracuse of her possessions. Besieged in Ortygia by the rebellious Syracusans (404–3), he came to terms with them (less the exiled aristocracy), giving them, although disarmed, a measure of autonomy. After subjugating eastern Sicily (south of Messana (mod. Messina)) with a mercenary army (402–399), he prepared for war with *Carthage, fortifying Epipolae, amassing war-material, building a huge fleet, rearming the Syracusans, hiring mercenaries, and forming matrimonial alliances with Syracuse (Andromache, sister of Dionysius' father-in-law Dion) and Locri Epizephyrii (Doris). He invaded the Carthaginian province (397) and stormed Motya (Mozia), but (396) retired before Himilco to Syracuse; here, following the defeat of his navy off Catana (Catania), he was besieged until 395, when, with some Corinthian and Spartan aid, he overthrew Himilco's plague-stricken forces. He restored his east Sicilian empire (incorporating Messana), attacked Rhegium (Reggio) and countered a new Carthaginian threat (395–2); but when the Syracusan army mutinied, he concluded a peace with Carthage (392) that recognized his suzerainty of eastern Sicily. He again attacked Rhegium (390) and starved it into

diolkos View of the *diolkos*, the stone haulway across the isthmus of Corinth probably built *c*.600 BC. Its chief aim was probably to levy dues on *trade, especially the long-distance seaborne commerce between the Aegean and Italy and the west.

surrender (387), allied himself with the Lucanians (mod. Basilicata), crushed the forces of the Italiot League on the Eleporus (Galliparo) (389), and incorporated Iapygia (southern Calabria) in his empire. The year 388 witnessed the fiasco of Dionysius' *Delphic embassy. In 387 he helped Sparta to impose the King's Peace on Greece; and in 386 a palace conspiracy (probably) led to the banishment of some of his courtiers, including his brother Leptines (later recalled) and the historian Philistus. To improve his supply of silver, timber, horses, and mercenaries, he extended his power into the Adriatic, founding colonies and establishing friendly relations with the Senones. He raided Pyrgi (384), the port of Caere (mod. Cerveteri). The chronology and details of his greatest war (383–probably 375), against the Italiots and allied Carthage, are unclear, owing to a failure in the transmission of *Diodorus' text (15. 15–17, 24). Attacking Thurii, he lost his fleet in a storm, but he gained Croton. In Sicily he routed the Carthaginians at Cabala but was totally defeated at Cronium (Leptines was killed), and made a peace that established the Halycus (Platani) as the common frontier. He sent expeditions to Greece (369, 368), to assist Sparta against the Boeotians; and Athens, hitherto hostile, voted him a crown and (368) conferred her citizenship on him and his sons. He again invaded western Sicily

(368) and besieged Lilybaeum (Marsala), but his fleet was captured at Drepana (Trapani) and he concluded an armistice. At the Lenaea festival at Athens in 367 his play, *The Ransom of Hector*, won the prize, and a mutual defence treaty was negotiated, whose ratification was perhaps prevented by his death.

Dionysius, who probably styled himself *archōn* (ruler) of Sicily, was a born leader of men, in peace and war; orator and diplomat, planner and administrator, patron of religion, of his native city, of literature and the arts, a dramatist perhaps no worse than the generality in an age of decline—above all, the greatest soldier that, apart from the Macedonians, ancient Greece produced. He applied mind to warfare, introducing *artillery, Phoenician siege-technique, and the quinquereme (warship rowed by oarsmen grouped in fives). He could handle large *mercenary armies and small light-infantry detachments; he appreciated the importance of reconnaissance. If his subordinates had not constantly let him down, he might well have achieved his life's ambition, to drive the Carthaginians from Sicily. Dionysius represents the irruption onto the historical scene of the new individualism of his age. Portrayed by the anecdotal tradition, above all by the *Academy, as the archetypal tyrant—paranoid, oppressive, obsessed with power—he looms through the historical tradition (*Diodorus (and Polyaenus), going back through *Ephorus and *Timaeus to Philistus) rather as the first of the Romantic 'great men'; the precursor of *Alexander the Great, *Hannibal, and Napoleon: obsessed not with power but with glory.
B. M. C.

Dionysius of Halicarnassus, Greek critic and historian, lived and taught *rhetoric at Rome, arriving 'at the time *Augustus put an end to the civil war', and publishing the first part of his *Roman Antiquities* (*Rhōmaikē archaiologia*) 22 years later (*Ant. Rom.* 1. 7). This great work was in twenty books, going down to the outbreak of the First Punic War; we have the first eleven (to 441 BC), with excerpts from the others. Dionysius used the legends of Rome's origins to demonstrate that it was really a Greek city, and his whole history is an erudite panegyric of Roman virtues. It is also very rhetorical, abounding in long speeches. He doubtless thought of it as exemplifying his literary teaching, which was directed towards restoring Classical prose after what he saw as the aberrations of the Hellenistic period. The treatises in which he developed this programme seem mostly to have been written before the *Antiquities*, though their chronology is much disputed. These are: (1) *On imitation* (*Peri mimēseōs*), in three books, of which only fragments survive; the judgements on individual authors coincide largely with those in Quintilian *Inst.* 10. 1; (2) a series of discussions of individual orators (*Lysias, *Isocrates, *Isaeus, *Demosthenes), prefaced by a programmatic statement of distaste for 'Asianic' rhetoric, hope for an 'Attic' revival, and the writer's consciousness that this happy change is due to the good taste of the Roman governing class; (3) a group of occasional works:

*On Dinarchus, On *Thucydides* (important), two letters to Ammaeus (one on Demosthenes' alleged indebtedness to Aristotle, the other on *Thucydides), and a letter to Cn. Pompeius on *Plato, of whose 'dithyrambic' style Dionysius was very critical; (4) *On Arrangement of Words* (*De compositione verborum, Peri suntheseōs onomatōn*), the only surviving ancient treatise on this subject, full of interesting observations on euphony and onomatopoeic effects (note especially ch. 20, on *Odyssey* 11. 593–6); this was a fairly late work, but the second part of *Demosthenes* (35 ff.) presupposes it.

For all the traditional terminology and character of Dionysius' criticism—he frequently gives the impression of 'awarding marks' for good qualities narrowly and unimaginatively defined—he is an acute and sensitive stylistic critic, whose insights deserve attention; and he understood the importance of linking historical study (e.g. on questions of authenticity) with the purely rhetorical and aesthetic.
D. A. R.

Dionysus (Linear B *Diwonusos*) is the twice-born son of *Zeus and Semele. His birth alone sets him apart. Snatched prematurely from the womb of his dying mother and carried to term by his father, he was born from the thigh of Zeus. Perceived as both man and animal, male and effeminate, young and old, he is the most versatile and elusive of all Greek gods. His myths and cults are often violent and bizarre, a challenge to the established social order. He represents an enchanted world and an extraordinary experience. Always on the move, he is the most epiphanic god, riding felines, sailing the sea, and even wearing wings. His most common cult name was *Bakch(e)ios* or *Bakchos*, after which his ecstatic followers were called *bakchoi* and *bakchai*. Adopted by the Romans as *Bacchus*, he was identified with the Italian Liber Pater. Most importantly, while modern scholars regard Dionysus inevitably as a construct of the Greek imagination, in the eyes of his ancient worshippers he was a god—immortal, powerful, and self-revelatory.

Throughout antiquity, he was first and foremost the god of *wine and intoxication. His other provinces include ritual madness or *ecstasy (*mania*); the mask, impersonation, and the fictional world of the theatre; and, almost antonymically, the mysterious realm of the dead and the expectation of an after-life blessed with the joys of Dionysus. If these four provinces share anything in common that illuminates the nature of this god, it is his capacity to transcend existential boundaries. Exceptionally among Greek gods, Dionysus often merges with the various functions he stands for and thus serves as a role model for his human worshippers. In the Greek imagination, the god whose myths and rituals subvert the normal identities of his followers himself adopts a fluid persona based on illusion, transformation, and the simultaneous presence of opposite traits. Both 'most terrible and most sweet to mortals' in Attic tragedy (Eur. *Bacch.* 861), he was called 'Eater of Raw Flesh' (*Omēstēs*, on *Lesbos, Alcaeus fr. 129. 9 L–P, *POxy*. 53. 3711) as well as 'Mild' (*Meilichios*, on Naxos, *FGrH* 499 F 4) in actual cult.

The name Dionysus appears for the first time on three fragmentary Linear B tablets from *Mycenaean Pylos (Western Peloponnese and Khania (Crete) dated to *c*.1250 BC. The tablets confirm his status as a divinity, but beyond that they reveal little about his identity and function in Mycenaean religion. One of the Pylos tablets may point to a tenuous connection between Dionysus and wine; on the Khania tablet, Zeus and Dionysus are mentioned in consecutive lines as joint recipients of libations of honey. But, thus far no physical remains of his cult have been identified with absolute certainty. A Dionysiac connection has been claimed for several archaeological discoveries; none convinces. The most spectacular is the discovery in the early 1960s of a large number of terracotta statues in a late Cycladic shrine at Ayia Irini on Ceos 9 (mod. Kea). Tentatively dated to 1500–1300 BC, these fragmentary, nearly life-sized figures represent mature women who stand or, perhaps, dance. A much later deposit of Attic drinking-vessels was found in the same room; among them is a scyphus of *c*.500 BC inscribed with a dedication to Dionysus by Anthippus of Iulis (*SEG* 25. 960). According to the excavators, the temple was in continuous use from the 15th to the 4th cent. BC. This remarkable find does not prove, however, that Dionysus was worshipped on the site before the Archaic period, let alone continuously from the bronze age to the Classical period. Given the prominence of women in *Minoan (i.e. bronze-age Cretan) religion generally, it is equally far-fetched to identify these figures as Dionysus' female attendants, whether nymphs (young female divinities), nurses, or *maenads. Yet typical features of Dionysus and his religion—including wine and ivy; divine epiphanies and ecstatic forms of worship; women dancing, handling snakes, or holding flowers; the divine child and nurturing females; and bulls with and without anthropomorphic features—are all prominent in Aegean, especially Cretan religion and art. The earliest Dionysus may indeed be sought in the culture of Minoan Crete.

If we had more information on the bronze age Dionysus, he would probably turn out to be a complex figure with a substantial non-Greek or Mediterranean component. Absolute 'Greekness' is a quality that few, if any, Greek gods can claim. This is especially true of their names. If Dionysus signifies '†nysos (son?) of Zeus', as some linguists believe, the god's name would be half Greek and half non-Greek (not Thracian, however, as its occurrence in Linear B demonstrates). But such etymological neatness is just as improbable as a divine name derived from the god's genealogy. Hardly more plausible is the derivation from *nysai*, the dubious designation for three nymph-like figures on a vase fragment by Sophilus (Beazley, *ABV* 39. 15). Attempts to derive the name Semele from Phrygian, *bakchos* from Lydian or *Phoenician, and *thyrsos*—the leafy branch or wand carried by the god and his followers—from Hittite (see ASIA MINOR), though highly speculative, reflect the wide spectrum of potential cross-

cultural contacts that may have influenced the early formation of Dionysus and his cult.

In Archaic epic, Dionysus is referred to as a 'joy for mortals' (*Il*. 14. 325) and 'he of many delights' (Hes. *Theog*. 941). The source of all this pleasure is wine, the god's ambivalent 'gift' (Hes. *Op*. 614) which brings both 'joy and burden' (Hes. fr. 239. 1). Dionysus 'invented' wine, just as *Demeter discovered *agriculture (Eur. *Bacch*. 274–83). By a common metonymy, the wine-god is also synonymous with his drink and is himself 'poured out' to the other gods as a ritual liquid (*Bacch*. 284). Libations (liquid offerings) of mixed or, occasionally, unmixed wine accompanied every animal *sacrifice; wineless libations were the exception. In vase-painting, Dionysus is never far from the wine. Surrounded by cavorting *satyrs and silens, nymphs, or maenads he presides over the vintage and the successive stages of wine-making on numerous black-figure vases. Holding in one hand a grapevine and in the other one of his favourite drinking-vessels, either a cantharus or a rhyton, he is often depicted receiving wine from a male or female cupbearer such as Oenopion, his son by Ariadne, or pouring it on an altar as a libation, or lying on a couch in typical symposiast posture (see SYMPOSIUM). Yet he is never shown in the act of consuming his own gift. His female followers, too, keep their distance from the wine, at least in maenadic iconography. While maenads may carry drinking-vessels, ladle wine, or pour it, they are never shown drinking it.

Longus' Dionysiac love story of Daphnis and Chloe (see NOVEL, GREEK) culminates in the celebration of the vintage on the Lesbian estate of Dionysophanes, whose name evokes the divine epiphanies (appearances) of Dionysus. Wine festivals were celebrated in many regions of the Greek world; in Elis (western *Peloponnese) as well as on the Aegean islands of Andros, Chios, and Naxos, they were accompanied by wine miracles. The oldest festival of Dionysus, the Ionian-Attic Anthesteria, was held each spring. In Athens, the highlight consisted of the broaching of the new wine followed by a drinking-contest. On this occasion, as on others, citizen women were excluded from the ceremonial drinking of wine. The admixture of wine and water was allegorized as the nurturing of Dionysus by his mythical nurses (*FGrH* 325 F 12, 328 F 5), or more ominously, as the 'mixing of the blood of *Bakchios* with fresh-flowing tears of the nymphs' (Timotheus, *PMG* fr. 780). In Attica, myths were told which connected the arrival of Dionysus and the invention of the wine with the murder of Icarius (schol. D *Il*. 22. 29; *LIMC* Dionysos/Bacchus no. 257). Here and elsewhere, Dionysiac myths emphasize the darker aspects of the god, and the perversion of his gifts.

Of Dionysus' four provinces, wine is the most dominant; it often spills over into the other three. Drunkenness can cause violence and dementia (Pl. *Leg*. 2. 672d, 6. 773d, *mainomenos oinos*). Yet the ritual madness associated with Dionysus in myth and cult had nothing to do with alcohol or drugs. Seized by the god, initiates into Bacchic rites acted much like participants in other possession cults.

Their wild dancing and ecstatic behaviour were interpreted as 'madness' only by the uninitiated. As numerous cultic inscriptions show, the actual worshippers did not employ the vocabulary of madness (*mania*, *mainesthai*, *mainades*) to describe their ritual ecstasy; rather, they used the technical but neutral language of *bakcheia* and *bakcheuein*. The practitioners of *bakcheia* were usually women; the exception is Scyles, the 'mad' Scythian king who danced through the streets of Olbia—an early centre of the Dionysus cult—as a *bakchos* (Hdt. 4. 79). While men, too, could 'go mad' for Dionysus, they could not join the bands (*thiasoi*) of maenadic women who went 'to the mountain' (*eis oros*) every other year in many Greek cities to celebrate their rites. Their notional leader was always the god himself (Eur. *Bacch.* 115 f., 135 ff.; Diod. Sic. 4. 3. 2–3), who appears already in the Homeric version of the Lycurgus myth—the earliest reference to maenadic ritual—as Dionysus *mainomenos*, 'the maddened god' (*Il.* 6. 132). Known mainly from post-classical inscriptions and prose authors like *Plutarch and *Pausanias, ritual maenadism was never practised within the borders of Attica. Athenian maenads went to *Delphi to join the Delphic Thyiads on the slopes of Mt. Parnassus (Soph. *Ant.* 1126–52; Plut. *De mul. vir.* 13. 249e–f; Paus. 10. 4. 3). Halfway between Athens and Delphi lies Thebes, the home town of Dionysus and 'mother city (*mētropolis*) of the Bacchants' (Soph. *Ant.* 1122), from where professional maenads were imported by other cities (*I. Magn.* 215). Erwin Rohde and E. R. Dodds were the first scholars to take a comparative approach to the psychological and anthropological aspects of maenadic ritual and behaviour, but they ignored the fundamental distinction between *mythology and *ritual.

In poetry and vase-painting, Dionysus and his mythical maenads tear apart live animals with their bare hands (*sparagmos*) and eat them raw (*ōmophagia*). But the divinely inflicted madness of myth was not a blueprint for actual rites, and the notion that maenadism 'swept over Greece like wildfire' (Rohde, Nilsson, Dodds) is a Romantic construct that has to be abandoned along with the suggestion that the maenads sacramentally consumed Dionysus in the shape of his sacred animal. The 'delight of eating raw flesh' (Eur. *Bacch.* 139) appears in maenadic myth, where it can escalate into cannibalism. In the entire cultic record, however, omophagy is mentioned only once. In a maenadic inscription from Miletus (SW *Asia Minor), the following directive occurs: 'Whenever the priestess performs the rites of sacrifice on behalf of the [entire] city, no one is permitted to "throw in" (deposit?) the *ōmophagion* before the priestess has done so on behalf of the city' (*LSAM* 48, 276/5 BC). Although the ritual details escape us, a piece of raw meat was apparently deposited somewhere for divine or human consumption. The mere reference to eating raw flesh is significant, given that sacrificial meat was normally roasted or cooked. In this instance, the perverted sacrifice, a mainstay of Dionysiac myth, has left its mark also on Dionysiac cult.

Dionysiac festivals were ubiquitous throughout the Greek world; in Athens alone there were seven such festivals in any given year, five of which were dedicated chiefly to Dionysus—Oschophoria, Rural Dionysia, Lenaea, Anthesteria, and City Dionysia. The name Oschophoria commemorates the ritual carrying of vine branches hung with bunches of grapes. The Lenaea and both Dionysia featured performances of *tragedy and *comedy. Apart from the new wine, the Anthesteria celebrated the spring time arrival of Dionysus from across the sea. Less is known about two other Dionysiac festivals at Athens, the *Theoinia* and the *Iobakcheia* ([Dem.] 59. 78). Festivals of Dionysus were often characterized by ritual licence and revelry, including reversal of social roles, cross-dressing by boys and men, drunken comasts in the streets, as well as widespread boisterousness and obscenity. In Athens as throughout Ionian territory, monumental phalli (erect penises) stood on public display, and phallophoric processions paraded through the streets (Semos of Delos, *FGrH* 396 F 24). But, unlike *Pan or the *Hermes of the herms (pillars surmounted with a bust and, when male, given genitalia), Dionysus himself is never depicted with an erection. The god's dark side emerged in rituals and aetiological myths concerned with murder and bloodshed, madness and violence, flight and persecution, and gender hostility (as during the Agrionia). Throughout the Athenian Anthesteria festival, merrymaking predominated, but it was punctuated by ritual reminders of a temporary suspension of the normal structures of daily life—the invasion of the city by spirits of evil, or by the dead, or by strangers called 'Carians'; the silent drinking at separate tables, explained by the myth of the matricide Orestes' arrival in Athens and the fear of pollution it provoked; the 'sacred marriage' (*hieros gamos*) of the wife of the *basileus* (an Athenian magistrate) to Dionysus; and the cereal meal prepared on the festival's last day for the dead or for Hermes Chthonios and the survivors of the Great Flood.

Tragedy and comedy incorporate transgressive aspects of Dionysus, but they do so in opposite ways. While comedy re-enacts the periods of ritual licence associated with many Dionysiac festivals, tragedy dramatizes the negative, destructive traits of the god and his myths. *Aristotle connected the origins of tragedy and comedy with two types of Dionysiac performance—the *dithyramb and the phallic song respectively. Yet, in his own analysis of the tragic genre, he ignored not only Dionysus but also the central role of the gods in the drama. In addition to the mask worn by the actors in character, including the disguised god himself in both *Bacchae* and *Frogs* (see ARISTOPHANES), the choral dance is the most palpable link between Attic drama and Dionysiac ritual. Tragic and comic choruses who refer to their own dancing invariably associate their choral performance with Dionysus, *Pan, or the maenads. Despite Aristotle's silence, tragedy in particular has a lot to do with Dionysus. The tragedians set individual characters, entire plays, and indeed the tragic genre as a whole in a distinct Dionysiac ambience (see COMEDY (GREEK); TRAGEDY, GREEK).

The god so closely associated with exuberant life is also connected with death, a nexus expressed as 'life–death–life' in one of the Dionysiac-Orphic (see ORPHEUS) bone inscriptions from Olbia. '*Hades and Dionysus are the same' according to the philosopher Heraclitus (fr. 15 DK). On an Apulian funerary crater (4th cent BC) by the Darius painter, Dionysus and Hades are shown in the Underworld each grasping the other's right hand while figures from Dionysiac myth surround them (Toledo 1994.19). A sacred tale ascribed to Orpheus and modelled on the Osiris myth describes the dismemberment of Dionysus Zagreus by the Titans and his restoration to new life; his tomb was shown at Delphi (Orph. fr. 35 Kern; Callim. fr. 643 Pf.). According to another myth, Dionysus descends to the Underworld to rescue Semele from Hades (Iophon, *TrGF* 22 F 3); Aristophanes' comic parody of the god's catabasis (descent) has Dionysus retrieve *Aeschylus (Ar. *Frogs*). In a related ritual, the Argives summoned Dionysus ceremonially 'from the water' with the call of a trumpet hidden in thyrsi 'after throwing a lamb into the abyss for the gatekeeper', i.e. for Hades (Plut. *De Is. et Os.* 35. 364 f). Dionysus loomed large in the funerary *art and after-life beliefs of Greeks and Romans alike. In many regions of the ancient world, tombs were decorated with Dionysiac figures and emblems like the maenad, the cantharus, and the ivy, or bore inscriptions with a Dionysiac message. The tombstone of Alcmeionis, chief maenad in Miletus around 200 BC, announces that 'she knows her share of the blessings'— a veiled reference to her eschatological hopes (*GVI* 1344). Found in tombs from southern Italy to *Thessaly, the so-called Orphic gold tablets contain ritual instructions and Underworld descriptions for the benefit of the deceased. Two ivy-shaped specimens refer to a ritual rebirth under the aegis of Dionysus, and to wine-drinking in the after-life; a third identifies the dead person as a Bacchic initiate (*mystēs*) (see DEATH, ATTITUDES TO).

No other deity is more frequently represented in ancient art than Dionysus. Until about 430 BC, Dionysus is almost invariably shown as a mature, bearded, and ivy-wreathed adult wearing a long chiton often draped with the skin of fawn or feline, and occasionally presenting a frontal face like his satyrs; later he usually appears youthful and beardless, effeminate, and partially or entirely nude. From his earliest depictions on Attic vases signed by Sophilus and Clitias (c.580–570 BC) to the proliferating images of the god and his entourage in Hellenistic and Roman imperial times, Dionysiac iconography becomes more varied while remaining remarkably consistent in its use of certain themes and motifs. Major mythical subjects comprise the Return of *Hephaestus and the Gigantomachy (see GIANTS); Dionysus' birth and childhood; his punishments of Lycurgus, Pentheus, and the impious sailors whom he turns into dolphins; and his union with Ariadne (as on the Derveni crater of c.350 BC from Macedonia). Cult scenes in vase-painting include those on the so-called Lenaea vases, which show a makeshift image of Dionysus—fashioned from a mask attached to a pillar—surrounded by women carrying or ladling wine. It is unclear whether these settings refer to a single festival or represent an artistic montage of authentic ritual elements. The Hellenistic friezes of his temples at Teos and Cnidus displayed the thiasos (group of worshippers) of satyrs, maenads, and *Centaurs; in the theatre at Perge (S. Asia Minor), we find scenes from the god's mythical life. Most conspicuously, sarcophagi of the imperial period abound with scenes from Dionysiac mythology such as the god's birth and his Indian triumph—the theme of the 5th cent. AD Nonnus of Panopolis' monumental epic.

The very existence of Dionysus in the Mycenaean pantheon came as a complete surprise when it was first revealed by Michael Ventris in 1953. Already in antiquity Dionysus was considered a foreign god whose original home was Thrace or Phrygia and who did not arrive on the Greek scene until the 8th cent. BC. The Thracian origin of Dionysus achieved the status of scholarly dogma with the second volume of Rohde's *Psyche* (1894). In Rohde's view, the Thracian Dionysus invaded Greece, where his wild nature was ultimately civilized and sublimated with the help of the Delphic *Apollo, a process commemorated in the myth of Dionysus' exile abroad, the resistance with which his cult was met upon its arrival in Greece, and his ultimate triumph over his opponents. Rohde's Dionysus—*barbarian but happily Hellenized, occasionally wild but mostly mild—appealed to successive generations of scholars from Jane Harrison to Dodds. Wilamowitz derived Dionysus from Phrygia and Lydia rather than Thrace, while Nilsson adopted a theory of multiple foreign origins. As early as 1933, however, Walter F. Otto (*Dionysus: Myth and Cult*, 1965, Eng. trans.) dissented, emphasizing instead the Greek nature of Dionysus as the epiphanic god who comes and disappears. According to Otto, the myths of Dionysus' arrival—with their dual emphasis on resistance to his otherness as well as on acceptance of his gifts—articulate the essential aspects of the god's divinity rather than the historical vicissitudes of the propagation of his cult. Otto's version of a polar and paradoxical Dionysus categorizes the diversity of Dionysiac phenomena, thus making them more intelligible. It has been argued, after Otto, that the 'foreign' Dionysus is a psychological rather than a historical entity which has more to do with Greek self-definition and the 'Dionysus in us' than with the god's actual arrival from abroad. More recently, Dionysus has emerged as the archetypal 'Other'—in a culturally normative sense—whose alterity is an inherent function of his selfhood as a Greek divinity. However, if such abstractions are pushed too far, Dionysus ceases to be the god he was to the Greeks—present in his concrete manifestations, and in the perplexing diversity of his myths, cults, and images—and becomes a modern concept.   A. H.

disease, the main cause of death in antiquity, is a topic for which there are more sources than for most aspects of life in the ancient world, thanks principally to the Hippocratic corpus (see MEDICINE, §4), Aretaeus of

Cappadocia, and the numerous works of his contemporary, Galen of Pergamum (2nd cent. AD). Additional information may be obtained from palaeopathology, the study of diseases found in human skeletal remains. Ancient medical literature concentrates on chronic and endemic diseases, rather than the major epidemic diseases. In fact the Greek word *epidēmios*, in a medical context, means 'endemic' rather than 'epidemic'.

Malaria and tuberculosis are the most prominent diseases in ancient literature. Malaria occurred in antiquity in three forms, vivax, the commonest, falciparum, the most dangerous, and quartan. All three produce fevers recurring every two or three days which were noticed easily, if not understood, by ancient doctors. The epidemiology of malaria in antiquity resembled that of recent times. In the highly seasonal Mediterranean climate malaria occurs mainly in the summer and autumn and affects adults at least as much as children, helping to explain its importance for ancient doctors. It depends for its transmission on certain species of mosquitoes, and was probably absent from some regions where these vectors did not occur. It is not necessarily associated with marshy environments. The chronology of the spread of malaria in the Mediterranean is disputed. All three types existed in Greece in the 4th cent. BC, but it is uncertain how long before that falciparum malaria had been present. The disease which struck the Athenian forces outside *Syracuse during the Peloponnesian War (see ATHENS (HISTORY)) may have been falciparum malaria, which was not yet present in Attica, but this interpretation is controversial. W. H. S. Jones argued that the spread of malaria caused the decline of ancient Greek civilization, but this hypothesis is an exaggeration. Similar theories have been advanced to explain the decline of the *Etruscans, and it has also been argued that malaria did not exist in Sardinia before *Phoenician and Roman colonization.

Tuberculosis mostly affected young adults. One Hippocratic text describes it as invariably fatal, probably an exaggeration, but Aretaeus (above) gives the best ancient description of tuberculosis. Both human pulmonary and bovine tuberculosis were present in antiquity. It was probably common in crowded urban centres.

Ancient authors say hardly anything about childhood diseases, but enteric diseases such as infantile viral diarrhoea and amoebic dysentery probably accounted for most of the high infant mortality observed in cemeteries. Chickenpox, diphtheria, mumps, and whooping cough are all described in connection with attacks on adults, but there is no definite evidence for measles or rubella in antiquity. Cholera was absent. The presence of influenza is uncertain, but the common cold certainly existed. Leprosy was probably endemic in the near east in the bronze age and spread slowly westwards in the Hellenistic period. It probably only occurred sporadically. There is no conclusive evidence for gonorrhoea or syphilis, but some sexually transmitted diseases certainly existed, such as genital herpes and trachoma. The latter was also the main infectious cause of blindness.

disease Disease was one of the chief reasons for the prevalence of congenital deformity in antiquity. This Hellenistic ivory statuette depicts a hunchback with Pott's disease.

Heart disease is not prominent in ancient literature, but palaeopathology suggests that underlying conditions such as atherosclerosis were common. Some cancers were well known. Galen states that breast cancer was common.

Some chronic malnutrition diseases were quite common, especially in childhood, e.g. iron-deficiency anaemia, rickets, bladder-stone disease, and night blindness. The Greeks and Romans also took an interest in diseases of plants and animals because of their importance in agriculture. See PLAGUE.   J. R. S.

dissection See ANATOMY AND PHYSIOLOGY §4; ANIMALS, KNOWLEDGE ABOUT; VIVISECTION.

dithyramb, choral song in honour of *Dionysus; the origins of dithyramb, and the meaning of the word itself, have been the subject of speculation since antiquity. There are three phases in the history of the genre: (1) pre-literary dithyramb; (2) the institutionalization of dithyramb in the 6th cent. BC; and (3) the latest phase, which began in the mid-5th cent.

Already in phase (1) dithyramb was a cult song with Dionysiac content. It was sung by a group of singers under the leadership of an *exarchōn*, as shown by the oldest piece of literary evidence, *Archilochus fr. 120 West. Phase (2) has its roots in the cultural and religious policies of the tyrants (see TYRANNY; PISISTRATUS) and the young Athenian democracy (see DEMOCRACY, ATHENIAN; TRAGEDY, GREEK). *Herodotus (1. 23) says that the musician Arion in late 7th-cent. Corinth was the first to compose a choral song, rehearse it with a choir, and produce it in performance, and that he finally gave the name 'dithyramb' to this new kind of choral song. (Some scholars take *ōnomasanta* to mean 'he gave it a title', but titles are not associated with dithyrambs before the 5th cent.). Lasus of Hermione (6th cent. BC) is connected with dithyramb at Athens: he organized a dithyrambic contest in the first years of the democracy. Each of the ten Athenian tribes entered the competition with one chorus of men and one of boys, each consisting of 50 singers. The financing of the enterprise (payment for the poet, the trainer of the chorus (*chorodidaskalos*), and the pipe-player; and the cost of equipping the chorus) was the responsibility of the *chorēgos* (financial backer). The winning *chorēgos* could put up a tripod with a dedicatory inscription in the Street of the Tripods. The dithyrambic contest was a competition between the tribes, not the poets, who are never mentioned on the victory inscriptions. Dithyrambs were performed at the following Athenian festivals: the City or Great Dionysia, the Thargelia, the (Lesser) Panathenaea, the Prometheia, the Hephaestia; cf. Lys. 21. 1–4; ps.-Xen. *Constitution of the Athenians* 3. 4; Antiphon 6. 11. The first victor at the Dionysia at Athens was the otherwise unknown Hypodicus of Chalcis (509/8 BC). In the first part of the 5th cent. *Simonides (with 56 victories), *Pindar, and *Bacchylides were the dominant dithyrambic poets. Pindar's dithyrambs (frs. 70–88 Maehler) are recognizable as such by their Dionysiac character. The standard content of a Pindaric dithyramb included some mention of the occasion which had given rise to the song, and of the commissioning *polis*; praise of the poet; narration of a myth; and some treatment of Dionysiac theology. By contrast, Bacchylides' dithyrambs, with the exception of *Io*, lacked these topical allusions. Hence the difficulties of classification which have been felt since Alexandrian times (see ALEXANDRIA): there was a discussion between Aristarchus and *Callimachus over whether the *Cassandra* of Bacchylides (fr. 23 Snell–Maehler) was a dithyramb or a

paean: *POxy*. 2368. From the mid-5th cent. (phase 3), dithyramb became the playground of the musical avant-garde, as we see from the criticisms of Pherecrates (fr. 155 K–A) and the reaction of Pratinas (fr. 708 Page). Melanippides, Cinesias, Timotheus, and Philoxenus are the best-known exponents of phase (3): they introduced astrophic form (i.e. their poems were not arranged according to strophe and antistrophe), instrumental and vocal solos, and 'mimetic' music. In the course of the 4th cent., a recognizably dithyrambic manner and idiom developed, and penetrated other lyric genres also. Songs with dithyrambic content were composed, like Philoxenus' *Banquet*; and in Middle Comedy (see COMEDY, GREEK (MIDDLE)) we find fairly long passages in dithyrambic style. In the Hellenistic period dithyrambs were performed at the festivals of the Delia and Apollonia on *Delos; and at the City Dionysia in Athens until the 2nd cent. AD. But post-Classical fragments (citations) allow no confident judgement about these compositions.

Our knowledge of dithyrambic poetry, esp. Pindar and Bacchylides, is based chiefly on papyrus finds. For phase (3) we are chiefly dependent on citations by *Athenaeus and on the criticisms of the comic poets and *Plato.   B. Z.

divorce See MARRIAGE LAW.

Domitian (Titus Flavius Domitianus), son of the emperor *Vespasian, was born on 24 October AD 51, and remained in Rome during his father's campaign against Aulus Vitellius. Surrounded on the Capitol with his uncle, Flavius Sabinus, he managed to escape and on Vitellius' death was saluted as Caesar by the Flavian army, though the real power lay in the hands of Gaius Licinius Mucianus until Vespasian's arrival. In 71 he participated in the triumph of Vespasian and Titus, and between 70 and 80 held seven consulships, being twice ordinary consul (73 and 80; see CONSUL). Although Domitian exercised no formal power, he was clearly part of the dynastic plan, and there is no convincing evidence that he was kept in the background or consumed by jealousy of his brother, whom he succeeded smoothly in 81.

The literary sources, especially *Tacitus and *Pliny the Younger, represent a senatorial tradition hostile to Domitian. But this is a legitimate and important viewpoint, illustrating the tension between aristocratic officials and autocrat. *Suetonius' account, though basically hostile, is more balanced and suggests that a more favourable view did exist, apart from the flattery of poets like *Statius and *Martial.

Domitian was conscientious in the performance of his duties, adopting a stance of moral rectitude, maintaining public decency at shows, and showing respect for religious ritual; three Vestal virgins (see VESTA) suffered capital punishment for breaking their vows of chastity; later, Cornelia, the chief Vestal, was buried alive. He promoted festivals and religious celebrations, showing particular devotion to *Jupiter and *Minerva, and performed the Secular Games; many public buildings were erected, completed, or restored, including the Capitol, the Colosseum, and a great palace on the Palatine. For the people there were frequent spectacles and banquets, though his cash grants were restrained. He raised military pay by a third, and bestowed by edict additional privileges on veterans and their families; he remained popular with the army and praetorians.

Domitian administered legal affairs diligently and tried to suppress corruption. Suetonius' contention that he achieved equitable provincial administration through careful supervision of officials and governors (*Dom.* 8. 2) has been challenged, but other evidence indicates that Domitian, although authoritarian in his attitude to the provinces (e.g. his abortive order to cut down at least half the provincial vineyards), tried to impress probity and fairness on his appointees; he sensibly granted rights of ownership to those who had appropriated tracts of unused land (*subseciva*); Pliny the Younger's letters to *Trajan show that Domitian's administrative decisions were generally endorsed. The role and influence of equestrians in the administration increased in his reign, but as part of a continuing trend rather than deliberate policy. The effectiveness of his management of imperial finances is disputed, but he probably left a surplus in the treasury; his confiscation of the property of his opponents was for political rather than financial reasons.

Domitian was the first reigning emperor since *Claudius in 43 to campaign in person, visiting the Rhine once, and the Danube three times. Frontinus in his *Strategemata* reports favourably on Domitian's personal control of strategy and tactics. In 82/3 he fought a successful war against the Chatti on the middle Rhine, brought the Taunus area under Roman control, and accepted a triumph and the name 'Germanicus'. But the military balance was shifting towards the Danube, and in 85 the Dacians, under king Decebalus, invaded Moesia killing its governor, Oppius Sabinus. Domitian came in person in 85 and 86; and after the defeat and death of Cornelius Fuscus (praetorian prefect), Tettius Iulianus, governor of Upper Moesia, won a victory at Tapae in 88. Since Domitian was facing trouble from the Marcomanni and Quadi in Pannonia, he made peace with Decebalus before launching a campaign against them (spring 89); at the end of 89 he celebrated another triumph. Then early in 92 a legion was destroyed in Pannonia by an incursion of the Sarmatian Iazyges and the Suebi, which was eventually contained under Domitian's personal direction. There was also considerable military activity in Britain, where Gnaeus Iulius Agricola continued the invasion of northern Scotland; his recall in 84 after an unusually long governorship of seven years, probably reflects military needs elsewhere rather than imperial jealousy.

Domitian failed to find a working relationship with the *senate. He was sometimes tactless and did not conceal the reality of his autocracy, holding ten consulships as emperor, wearing triumphal dress in the senate, having 24 lictors, and becoming *censor perpetuus* in 85, symbolically in charge of the senate; his manner was arrogant, and he allegedly began an official letter: 'Our lord god orders that this be done'. There was a conspiracy in 87, and a rebellion in 89 by Lucius Antonius Saturninus, governor of Upper Germany. He apparently had little support among his troops and was easily crushed, but Domitian thereafter forbade two legions to be quartered in one camp. He became more ruthless against presumed opponents, and factions in the aristocracy produced many senators willing to act as accusers. The executions of at least twelve ex-consuls are recorded in the reign, mainly for dissent or alleged conspiracy, and not because they were Stoics (see STOICISM), although Domitian did expel philosophers. The emperor himself observed: 'no one believes in a conspiracy against an emperor until it has succeeded'. The execution in 95 of Flavius Clemens, his cousin, whose sons he had adopted as heirs, was a mistake since it seemed that no one now was safe. A plot was formed by intimates of his entourage possibly including his wife, Domitia, and he was murdered on 18 September 96; his memory was condemned by the senate. J. B. C.

drama See TRAGEDY, GREEK and LATIN; COMEDY (GREEK), OLD, MIDDLE, and NEW; COMEDY, LATIN.

dreams fascinated the ancients as much as they do us, though it is illegitimate to employ Freudian categories in interpreting ancient dreams: their categories must not be subverted by our own culturally relative theories. Most ancients accepted that there were both significant and non-significant dreams (e.g. Hom. *Od.* 19. 562–7: true dreams come from gates of horn, delusory dreams from gates of ivory; cf. Verg. *Aen.* 6. 893–6). This basic division might itself be subdivided, most elaborately into a fivefold classification: non-predictive dreams, subdivided into *enhypnia* caused by the day's residues and *phantasmata* or distorted visions that come between sleeping and waking states; predictive dreams subdivided into: *oneiroi* that need symbolic interpretation, *horamata* or prophetic visions, and *chrēmatismata* or advice from a god (e.g. Macrob. *in Somn.* I. 3). The last category is well attested epigraphically by votives put up by people as the result of successful advice or instructions from a god received in a dream, and in the remarkable diary kept by Aelius Aristides which included numerous visions of *Asclepius and other gods. Dreams were indeed an important aspect of diagnosis in sanctuaries of Asclepius.

The idea that dreams could be significant, but might need professional interpreters, is found from Homer onwards (*Il.* 1. 62–7, 5. 148–51; Hdt. 5. 55–6; Theophr. *Char.* 16. 11). Dream-books were written from the 5th cent. BC onwards; the only surviving example from antiquity is that by Artemidorus.

Philosophers and others discussed whether dreams had a divine origin. The Hippocratic author of the treatise *On the Sacred Disease* urged that dreams were caused merely by disturbances in the brain, and the author of *On Regimen* 4 explained how to use dreams for medical diagnosis. *Plato argued that some dreams came from the gods and were reliable sources of knowledge, *Aristotle that physiological explanations applied, while *Epicurus and *Lucretius located dreams in a theory about the nature of sense perceptions. For *Cicero the possibility of prophetic dreams was an example of divination that worked in practice, but which was impossible to justify theoretically (*Div.* I. 39–65, 2. II9–48, with Pease's comm.). Cicero also used a dream narrative (the Dream of Scipio) as part of his *Republic*, the part to which Macrobius devoted his commentary.

Christian texts also developed the importance of dream visions, in a variety of styles: the Book of Revelation or the *Shepherd* of Hermas both stand as reports of visions; the *Martyrdom of St Perpetua* includes a vivid firsthand report of a dream vision she had of her martyrdom; Synesius, *On Dreams* (AD 405–6) offered an allegorical interpretation of dreams. Eight handbooks of dream interpretation survive from the Byzantine period.   S. R. F. P.

dress In classical antiquity, items of clothing and jewellery were major personal possessions. The prominence of drapery, i.e. clothing, in Greek and Roman art reflects the importance of dress in daily life.

Most garments were made of wool, though linen was used for some tunics and underclothing and silk was worn by richer women; most frequently, the fibre was left undyed, though women's clothes were more colourful than men's; the clothing of both sexes commonly had areas of decoration in wool dyed either with 'real purple' from sea snails or in imitation of purple; such decoration was generally very simple, consisting of woven bands and geometric motifs; figurative decoration, where it occurred, was usually tapestry-woven and only rarely embroidered. Clothes were made of large pieces of cloth with simple outlines which had been woven to shape on traditional looms; though certain garments were characteristic of the Greeks and others of the Romans there was no real difference between Greek and Roman clothes in techniques or materials; most classical garments belonged either to the category of mantles and cloaks that were 'thrown around' and for which the general terms were *periblēma* and *amictus*, or to those items, including tunics, that were 'entered into', *endyma* and *indumentum*; the former often served at night as blankets; all clothes were cleaned by washing and were stored folded-up in chests.

Draped mantles were the characteristic garment of freeborn citizens. The mantle worn by Greek men, and eventually by men and women throughout the eastern Mediterranean and by Roman women, was the *himation*, in Latin *pallium* or *palla*. This was a rectangle, measuring approximately 2.8 × 1.75 m. (9 × 6 ft.), which could be draped in various ways but which was usually supported on the left arm, leaving the right arm free. The mantle worn by Roman men, the Etruscans, and, originally, Roman women too was the *toga, a semicircular piece of cloth which over time became extremely large.

Cloaks were worn by men, either pinned on the right shoulder or joined at the front of the body. Pinned cloaks, used especially by horsemen, could be rectangular or semicircular: two Roman military cloaks, the *paludamentum* and the *sagum* (of Celtic origin), were rectangular; *chlamys*, the old Greek term for a pinned cloak, had by the 1st cent. AD come to mean specifically a semicircular cloak. The closed cloaks, in Latin *birrus* and *paenula*, were also based on semicircles and, being hooded, were suitable for travellers.

The traditional Greek woman's garment, the *peplos*, somewhere between a mantle and a tunic, was an approximately square piece of cloth worn with the top third or so folded over and pinned on both shoulders. By the 4th cent. BC the *peplos* had been largely replaced in the cities by the *himation* but was still worn in the country and by all women during cold weather.

According to tradition, the *peplos*, *himation*, and toga had all at first been worn without a tunic. However, the tunic, *chiton* or *tunica*, had an early history as an independent garment and by the 4th cent. the combination of draped mantle and tunic was the normal form of civilian dress for both men and women. Most tunics were sleeveless, made of two rectangular pieces joined at the sides and on the shoulders or of a single piece folded lengthways or widthways. An alternative to sewing, used to fasten women's tunics on the shoulders, was a series of button-like discs around which fabric from both front and back was wrapped and tied. Sleeved tunics only became common in the late Roman period, when two clearly defined varieties emerged, the narrow-sleeved tunic known in Latin as *strictoria*, and the wide-sleeved *dalmatica*. While the dalmatic was worn ungirt, tunics generally were worn with a belt, *zōnē* or *cingulum*, as had been the *peplos*.

Underclothes, like tunics, were probably worn more widely than ancient art or literature suggests. A tunic of linen was often worn under a tunic of wool and men probably mostly wore a triangular loincloth (*perizōma*, and perhaps also *zōnē*; Lat. *subligar* or *licium*), as did women in menstruation. A number of cloth bands were also used as underclothes, notably the *strophion* or *mamillare*, with which women bound their breasts.

Garments used on the extremities of the bodies illustrate a number of non-woven techniques: the Greek woman's *sakkos* or hairnet was made by a method now known as sprang; stretchy socks, *sokkoi*, employed a looping technique resembling knitting; certain men's hats and some foot-coverings were made of felt, *pilos* or *pilleus*. Leather was the usual material for shoes and sandals but, except in the army, was not employed for clothing. Fur, characteristic of barbarian dress, was not used at all.

The simplicity and conservatism of classical dress was set off, in the case of women, by elaborate coiffures, jewellery and make-up. For both men and women, hairstyles and footwear shapes changed more rapidly than those of clothing and are consequently a better guide when dating works of art. See TEXTILE PRODUCTION.

                                                            H. G.-T.

earthquakes The Mediterranean is a zone of intense earthquake activity because the plates carrying Africa and Europe are slowly moving together, according to the theory of plate tectonics. Notable earthquakes in antiquity include: *Sparta *c*.464 BC, where an age class perished; Helice in Achaea 373 BC, where the city was submerged under the sea; *Rhodes 227/6 BC, when the Colossus statue collapsed; *Pompeii AD 62, which suffered severe damage. Some destructions of Mycenaean and Minoan palaces are also attributed to earthquakes. Earthquakes were associated with *Poseidon in mythology: Poseidon the Homeric 'earth-shaker' (*ennosigaios*) was fervently worshipped also as 'earth-holder' (*gaiaochos*) and 'stabilizer' (*asphalios*), in Sparta and elsewhere. King Agesipolis of Sparta was as distinctly unusual in his pragmatic approach to an earthquake in the Argolis in 388 BC (Xen. *Hell.* 4. 7. 4–5) as Herodotus (7. 129. 4) was in his rationalist, seismological explanation of Thessalian geomorphology (see THESSALY). Ancient philosophers and 'scientists', however, frequently speculated about the causes of earthquakes (Sen. *QNat.* bk. 6). Thales thought that the earth moved upon the primeval waters. Anaximenes reckoned that variations in wetness and aridity caused cracks in the earth. Several philosophers, including Anaxagoras, Democritus, *Aristotle, and Posidonius, produced theories which involved water or air entering the earth and causing explosions.

P. A. C., J. R. S.

ecology (Greek and Roman) A modern concept with numerous antecedents in antiquity, when attitudes towards nature (*physis*) varied greatly. The Presocratic philosopher Empedocles devised the theory of the four elements, leading to the idea of opposites and the theory of the four humours (Hippoc. *Nature of Man* 4–8), in which an imbalance of the humours causes disease. Different climates cause different humours to prevail in different peoples, producing the theory of environmental determinism in Hippocrates (*Aer.*). The observed regularities in nature led to a belief in purpose in nature. *Herodotus (3. 107–9) thought that different types of animal had different rates of reproduction appropriate to their natures, an argument for purposeful creation. Other arguments invoked in favour of purposeful creation included the unity and harmony of the universe; the apparent design of human organs, e.g. the eye (*Socrates in Xen. *Mem.* 1. 4. 4–15); the regularities in astronomical phenomena, which led to *astrology and Ptolemy's theory (*Tetr.*) of cosmic environmentalism in which the stars influence life on earth; and the idea that the creator acted like an artisan, a theory—very important for *Plato (*Ti.* 27–33), *Cicero, and the younger *Seneca—that was adopted by the early Christian Fathers and laid the foundations for natural theology in later ages. *Aristotle (e.g. *Pol.* 1256ᵃ⁻ᵇ) turned the concept of purpose in nature into an all-embracing teleology, but rejected Plato's artisan deity. Possibly Aristotle thought that nature advances unconsciously towards ends. Theophrastus expressed doubts about teleology in biology, invented plant biogeography, and considered climatic change caused by human modification of the environment. The Epicureans (see EPICURUS) rejected design in nature. The Stoics (see STOICISM) fused the aesthetic attitude towards nature, evident in Hellenistic bucolic poetry, with utilitarian attitudes. The earth is beautiful and useful.

J. R. S.

economic theory (Greek) It is a commonplace that the Greek philosophers had no economic theory. Three reasons are advanced for this absence: (1) the merely embryonic existence of the relevant institutions, especially the market; (2) aristocratic disdain for *trade and exchange; (3) the priority assigned to ethical concerns over technical considerations of exchange and accumulation. While each of these claims contains some truth, the third assumes a modern conception of the autonomy of economics against which ancient theory may make a pertinent challenge.

*Plato's discussion of the market is sketchy. The *Republic* describes the creation of a market in the 'first city'; money (see COINAGE, GREEK) will be used for internal exchange, and barter for foreign trade. In the Ideal City the lowest class, ruled by bodily appetites, is also called the money-making class. The ideal city of *Laws* 5 will have no money, and strict lower and upper limits on amount of ownership. The market legislation of bks. 8 and 11 permits money, but most transacting is done by aliens; again, the state fixes strict limits to acquisition and ownership.

Economic analysis proper begins in *Aristotle's *Politics*. Fundamental to the entire discussion is the idea that material goods are tools of human functioning. Their proper use has a limit set by those requirements. Poverty placing one beneath this limit is a problem for public planning; accumulation above this limit is 'unnatural' and morally problematic. Thus Aristotle criticizes the saying of *Solon, 'Of wealth no boundary stands fixed for men'. The accumulation of goods began as a way of ensuring the presence of needed resources. Because some of these had to be imported from a distance, barter arose; barter led, in turn, to the temporary accumulation of surpluses useful for trade. Eventually coin money was introduced to facilitate deferred exchanges. This, however, gave rise to the idea of accumulating a surplus without reference to need or limit, as if wealth were an end in itself.

Aristotle's analysis is pertinent to recent criticisms of welfare and development economics which appeal to notions of human functioning in interpreting economic notions such as 'the standard of living' and 'the quality of life'.

Elsewhere, Aristotle analyses the relationship between level of wealth and political behaviour, arguing that the essential difference between *democracy and *oligarchy lies in whether rule is by the poor or the rich; it happens that in every city the poor are many and the rich are few.

Hellenistic thought about money focuses on limiting the desire for possessions. Stoic teleology (see STOICISM) is the background for Adam Smith's conception of the 'invisible hand', which should not be understood apart from Stoic ideas of providence and justice. See ECONOMY, GREEK and HELLENISTIC; WEALTH, ATTITUDES TO.   M. C. N.

economy, Greek Even if there was 'an economy' in ancient Greece (see CAPITALISM), Greece itself was not a single entity, but a congeries of more than a thousand separate communities. One should therefore speak of Greek economies rather than the Greek economy, and for simplicity's sake it is convenient to divide them into three groups, types, or models. First, there is the 'Archaic' group of which *Sparta can stand as the representative instance. At the opposite extreme is Athens, distinguished both by the exceptional size and number of its economic transactions, and by the exceptional sophistication of its economic institutions. In between fall the vast range of 'normal' Greek cities or communities, differentiated from the latter chiefly in the scale, and from the former principally in the nature, of their economic arrangements.

Consider the last group first. Our 'economy' is derived from the ancient Greek word *oikonomia*, but this meant originally and usually the management of a private household (*oikos*) rather than that of a 'national' economy (see

HOUSEHOLD, GREEK). Ideally, for sound prudential reasons as well as ideological, moral, or political ones, each 'normal' Greek household (comprising a two-generation nuclear family, free and unfree dependants, slaves, animals, land, and other property) aimed to be as self-sufficient as possible, making all due allowance for the basic constants of the changing domestic life-cycle, and the amount and nature of available land and labour. Household economy in Greece was overwhelmingly rural economy, the number of genuine cities or even genuinely urban residential centres being countable on the fingers of a single hand. See URBANISM, GREEK.

Most Greeks living in 'normal' communities were peasants of one description or another, farming a couple of hectares (say, 5 acres) planted to a mix of cereals (mainly barley, some wheat) and xerophytic crops (*olives, grapevines (see WINE), figs above all). Small stock animals, especially sheep and goats (see PASTORALISM, GREEK), constituted a necessary, not a purely optional, complement to agriculture and herbiculture in the absence of artificial fertilizers. In some areas local conditions favoured specialization in one or other crop, or an exceptional amount of stockraising. In coastal settlements there were always some specialist fishermen (see FISHING), but, apart from the Black Sea, Greek waters were not especially favourable to sizeable and predictable shoals of easily catchable fish. Fish remained something of a luxury food by comparison with the staple 'Mediterranean triad' (grain, wine, olive oil) of the Greek peasant diet.

In practice, of course, self-sufficiency remained for most an ideal rather than a lived actuality, so that economic exchange of various kinds was obligatory (see TRADE, GREEK). But such exchanges were typically conducted between individuals—neighbours or at any rate members of the same community—either directly and by barter in kind or through the use of some monetary medium in the local village or town market. The economy of Athens was wholly exceptional in the degree to which the very viability of the civic community depended on the exchange through long-distance trade of a staple commodity, grain (see FOOD SUPPLY). Fortunately, and not incidentally, Athens was exceptionally blessed with a near-unique means of paying for such imports in the shape of the silver (strictly, argentiferous lead) deposits in the Laurium district of SE Attica. The mines were worked almost entirely by chattel-slave labour (see SLAVERY). To ensure that the silver bullion was channelled productively into the grain trade the Athenian community instituted a wide range of preferential measures backed by severe and enforceable legal sanctions against both citizen and non-citizen miscreants. Athens was also fortunate, and unusual, in that much of Attica's soil and climate was peculiarly well suited to olive cultivation; the export of olive oil was officially encouraged from as early as 600 BC.

These factors permitted the development in the course of the 5th cent. BC of a genuinely urban sector of the Athenian citizen population, concentrated in what was almost a second city around the port of Piraeus. But most of those directly and exclusively engaged in Piraeus commerce, as in the other non-agricultural sectors of Athenian economy, were non-Athenian and often non-Greek foreigners, resident (free *metics and slaves) and transient. Both absolutely and as a proportion of the total population (which itself was hypertrophied by 'normal' Greek standards) the foreign element was sensibly greater in Athens than in any other Greek community.

Sparta in its economy as in some other respects represented the opposite pole from Athens. So far from being encouraged as economically desirable or even necessary, foreigners—Greek as well as non-Greek—were periodically expelled from Sparta (xenēlasiai). The Spartans did regularly practise economic exchange, but within rather than outside their territory, and with a politically subordinate free population known as perioikoi, on whom they depended, not least, for supplies of iron. Agriculture and stockraising were left to, or rather forced upon, a subjugated local population of helots, Greek in speech and culture but servile in status. By dint of exploiting the helots, the Spartans themselves contrived to do no economically productive work whatsoever (except in the sense that war, 'the business of Ares', was itself a means of production). Some other Greek communities exploited workforces of a similar collective character and servile status, but none combined that exploitation with the Spartans' peculiar disdain of all non-military forms of economic activity. The Spartans were not unique in refusing to coin silver or bronze for economic or political purposes, but their retention of a non-convertible domestic 'currency' of iron spits nicely symbolizes their economic eccentricity. See COINAGE, GREEK.   P. A. C.

economy, Hellenistic The regions brought under the control of the Hellenistic kingdoms showed little economic unity or uniformity. Land use systems ranged from irrigation regimes in Egypt, Mesopotamia, and parts of Iran (Polyb. 10. 28) through widespread dry farming to the nomad or transhumant *pastoralism of the deserts and the mountains. Land tenure arrangements included, besides private beneficial ownership at all levels of magnitude, land owned by cities, cantons, or temples but rented out to individuals or worked by 'slaves of the shrine' (hierodouloi), and above all land owned by the kings. Such land might be held in direct tenure and worked by serfs, or alienated to large-scale proprietors (e.g. Austin nos. 180 and 185), or bestowed as allotments (klēroi) in various ways on individuals in return for military service, or have its use and revenues assigned to individuals (dōrea). Such lands mostly had arable and arboricultural use in producing the basic Mediterranean triad (cereals, vines (see WINE), *olives) and other supplementary foodstuffs, while other land uses included pasturage, ornamental ground such as the ex-Persian paradeisoi, quarries, mines, and forests.

Most foodstuff production will have been consumed locally, but some established long-distance flows continued, such as corn from Egypt to the Aegean, cattle and slaves (see SLAVERY) from the Black Sea (Polyb. 4. 38), or spices and precious stones from India to the Mediterranean. They may well have grown in importance in the Hellenistic period, thereby assisting the growth and enrichment of entrepôt and trading cities such as *Rhodes, *Alexandria, and Petra. Such cities seem also to have become the main centres of both the production and the consumption of fine decorative goods such as silverware, and jewellery, while the creation and use of more basic artefacts remained local unless used, as amphorae universally were, as containers for transport and storage. The growth in the numbers of coin-hoards and of shipwrecks during the period, together with the development of institutions (e.g. public and private *banks) and installations (harbours, lighthouses, etc.), suggest an increase both in the volume of trade and in the monetization of some transactions: the activities of Cretan and other pirates (see PIRACY) increased accordingly.

Rulers and polities affected all such economic activities by their needs, exactions, and benefactions. Old and new Greek cities levied taxes and rents on transactions, statuses, properties, and commodities, but rarely covered expenses comfortably. They tended instead to elicit loans, donations, or endowments from wealthy and benevolent citizens or outsiders, whose services prompted honorary decrees (e.g. Austin nos. 98 and 113) and shifted power relationships in their favour (see EUERGETISM). On a larger scale kings and rulers did the same, redistributing resources via systematic taxation to pay for armies and wars, courts and bureaucracy, gifts and benefactions, disaster relief and city foundations. For fiscal reasons all royal governments showed some interest in increasing the productive capacity of their territories, e.g. by opening mines, extending the agrarian base or transplanting species, but the older picture of a managed 'royal economy' is not now accepted, even for Egypt. The political act with the biggest impact on the Hellenistic economy was probably Rome's creation of a free port at *Delos in 166 BC, which moved some trade routes and badly damaged Rhodes (Polyb. 30. 31).

J. K. D.

economy, Roman The economic history of Rome from the first, like all ancient Mediterranean economies, involved the interaction of the circumstances of local *agriculture with the available *labour supply in the context of opportunities for interregional redistribution in which the exchange of other commodities was involved. It is now certain that from the 7th cent BC. Rome was privileged among other Tiber valley communities as a centre for the movement of people and materials from peninsular Italy out into the world of Mediterranean contacts. The Romans believed that they had imported cereals from Campania from at least the early 5th cent., and that they had freed their citizens from the risk of debt-bondage (nexum; see DEBT) at the end of the 4th. It was important to their self-image that they considered the area around their city to be of only moderate productivity, and that it had been assigned in lots from an early period to citizens who worked them independently. Historically, this enthusiasm for the lot was of more significance in the concept of public ownership of land, and the practice of dividing and assigning it (*ager publicus*). This was attested in the formation of new *tribus* in the 4th cent. and widely practised in the establishment of *coloniae* in the 3rd and 2nd cents., especially on land which had belonged to defeated opponents of Rome (see COLONIZATION, ROMAN). But the exploitation of allotted land was perhaps never intended to be in theory, and was certainly not in practice, a matter of basic household subsistence. It rapidly became linked with the formation of estate centres (*latifundia*) for the production of cash crops for mass-marketing, the *villas of the late republican landscape, which were also central to the cultural life of the wealthy families which owned them. The cities grew as *markets and centres of processing, administration, and consumption of the products of this agriculture, and as centres for the control and management of a mutable labour force which included, as a result in part of the victories of the 2nd cent. BC, significant numbers of slaves (see SLAVERY), though their large-scale use in agriculture was generally perceived by the Roman tradition as undesirable. From the beginnings of the large-scale export of *wine from Italy in the mid-2nd cent. the network of economic exchanges involved entrepreneurs, Roman military forces in the field, more or less dependent consumers inside and outside Roman territory, and the city of Rome itself in an increasingly complicated web, in which the non-agricultural resources of the growing imperial state, especially metals, were an important ingredient. The development over the next centuries of this state of affairs saw frequent changes in the specifics of the geography of the centres of exchange, and the favoured places of investment in production: *olive oil and wine remained important, though we should recall that they are particularly visible archaeologically, and the production of Baetica, Africa, and Tripolitania transformed these regions, with concomitant gain to their market centres and port outlets. The economy of the empire included significant connections with networks of exchange reaching across northern Europe, central Asia, and the Sahara, but most importantly via the Red Sea with the increasingly complex economy of the Indian Ocean area, to which *Alexandria was central. Rome itself was a consumer on an enormous scale, and therefore exerted a considerable influence on Mediterranean production and exchange, which were also promoted by the need to pay state exactions in cash. But the complexity of the network, the continued local interdependence of the regions of the empire, and the existence of very many smaller centres of consumption, management, and marketing, ensured that the economic life of the Roman world was not wholly oriented on Rome. The social and political forms of economic life were sophisticated and various, though they did not much resemble the practices of early modern Europe: the role of

ex-slaves (see FREEDMEN) and the public contract may be singled out, while the availability of credit and the nature of accounting deserve further investigation. See ARTISANS AND CRAFTSMEN; COINAGE (ROMAN); INDUSTRY; TRADE, ROMAN. N. P.

ecstasy In classical Greek the term *ekstasis* may refer to any situation in which (part of) the mind or body is removed from its normal place or function. It is used for bodily displacements, but also for abnormal conditions of the mind such as madness, unconsciousness, or 'being beside oneself'. In the Hellenistic and later periods the notion is influenced by the Platonic concept of 'divine madness', a state of inspired possession distinct from lower forms of madness and as such providing insights into objective truth. *Ekstasis* now acquires the notion of a state of trance in which the soul, leaving the body, sees visions (Acts 10: 10; 22: 17). In later, especially Neoplatonist theory (Plotinus, Porphyry), *ekstasis* is the central condition for escape from restraints of either a bodily or a rational-intellectual nature and thus becomes the gateway to the union with the god (*unio mystica*); see DIONYSUS. H. S. V.

education, Greek (*see following page*)

education, Roman (*see page 249*)

Egypt (see ◀Map 2, Bd▶)
Ptolemaic In the period from the death of *Alexander the Great in 323 BC until the defeat of *Cleopatra with Antony at Actium in 31 BC the Egyptian throne was held by Macedonians, and from 304 by the one family, the Prolemies (who were descended from Alexander's general *Ptolemy I son of Lagus). Externally the main problem remained the extent of the kingdom, while internally the nature of administrative control and relations with the native Egyptians formed the major concerns of this new resident dynasty of foreign pharaohs. For the modern observer it is the incomplete nature of the historical record which presents problems. Contemporary historical analysis is limited in period (*Polybius, *Diodorus Siculus), much of it concentrating on the scandalous and sensational (Pompeius Trogus, Justin), and while numerous papyri and ostraca, preserved through the dry desert conditions, join with inscriptions to make Egypt better documented than other Hellenistic kingdoms, these illustrate the details of administration and everyday life without its wider context.

Territorially the Nile valley formed a natural unit. Ptolemy I added *Cyrene and *Cyprus to the kingdom, both significant territories in Ptolemaic history. Under *Ptolemy II control was extended over much of the Aegean and the coast of *Asia Minor organized as the Island League; this was later lost. But the territory most fought over with the Seleucid rulers of Syria was Coele ('Hollow') Syria: Palestine and the Gaza strip. This strategic area was Ptolemaic until the battle of Panion in 200,

[*continued on p. 251*]

Greek and Roman education

Greek education *1. Early Period* Greek ideas of education (*paideia*), whether theoretical or practical, encompassed upbringing and cultural training in the widest sense, not merely schooling and formal education. The poets were regarded as the educators of their society, particularly in the Archaic period, but also well into the classical, when *Plato could attack *Homer's status as educator of Greece (e.g. *Resp.* 606e, and generally, bks. 2, 3, 10; cf. Xen. *Symp.* 4. 6 for the conventional view). Much education would have taken place in an aristocratic milieu informally through institutions like the *symposium (as in the poetry of Theognis) or festivals (cf. the children reciting *Solon's poetry at the Apaturia, Pl. *Ti.* 21b), backed up by the old assumption that the aristocracy possessed inherited, not instructed, excellence. Important educational functions were seen by some in the relationship of a boy and an older lover (see HOMOSEXUALITY); or in the very institutions of the city-state (*polis), the city festivals and rituals (e.g. Aeschin. 3. 246; see N. Loraux, *Invention of Athens* (1986; Eng. trans.). Even in the 4th cent. BC, Plato (*Laws*), for instance, saw the laws as performing educational functions, Lycurgus of Athens the democratic processes; cf. DEMOCRACY, ATHENIAN.

There is a tendency in modern work to overformalize Greek education. Before the 5th cent. BC, there must have been some sort of training for any specialized skills (cf. the scribal skills needed by the Mycenaeans), but most of this was probably on an ad hoc and quite individual basis (more like an apprenticeship, as was surely the case with oral epic bards). The evidence for early schooling (i.e. formal group teaching) is remarkably slight: the school laws attributed to Solon (594 BC) by Aeschines (1. 9 ff.) may be later and are in any case primarily about morality; the traditions about Chiron (see CENTAURS) (cf. *Il.* 9. 443) as ideal educators, teaching their charges all the known skills may reflect some form of early aristocratic instruction. The earliest school mentioned is at Chios, in 494 BC (Hdt. 6. 27); we also hear of schools at Astypalaea (an Aegean island between Amorgos and Nisyros) in 496 BC (Paus. 6. 9. 6), at Troezen in 480 (Plut. *Them.* 10), at Mycalessus in Boeotia in 413 (Thuc. 7. 29), and less reliably, among allies of the Mytilenaeans in *c*.600 (Ael. *VH* 7. 15). Fifth-cent. Attic vase-paintings show scenes of schooling (see Beck). But it is likely that at least before the mid-5th cent., education was elementary in our terms, probably confined to the aristocratic strata, and organized simply for individuals (the figure of the later *paidagōgos* may have retained something of an earlier individual tutor; cf. Xen. *Mem.* 2. 2. 6 on home education). That education would also be non-technical, and, as indicated by discussions of the 'old' and the 'new' education in the 5th cent. (cf. Ar. *Clouds*), would be primarily concerned with music and gymnastics. This type of education, or at least its higher levels, was transformed by the *sophists and their successors in to one involving the techniques of prose rhetoric, which then came to form the most typical part of ancient education at the higher level.

2. Sparta Certain Dorian states like *Crete and Classical *Sparta practised a totalitarian and militaristic form of education controlled by the state. By Classical times, Sparta had adapted its educational system entirely for the purposes of maintaining military strength. From the age of 7 the child was entirely under the control of the state, living in barracks away from parents. The aim of education was to produce efficient soldiers, and though their training included *music and how to read and write, physical education received first priority (see Xen. *Lac.*; Plut. *Lyc.*). Girls, too, were also educated in the interests of the state, to be the future mothers of warriors (Xen. *Lac.* 1. 3–4): gymnastics and sport were emphasized, as well as music and *dancing.

3. Classical Athens **Elementary education**
It is unclear how early elementary schooling began in Athens (from which most evidence comes): explicit evidence for schools (see above) is much later than the introduction of the alphabet to Greece in the mid-8th cent. BC, and though it has been thought that the alphabet implies schools to teach it,

instruction at this low level could have been carried out without formal institutions. However, *ostracism at Athens may presuppose widespread basic *literacy in the time of *Cleisthenes, and schooling is definitely attested for early 5th-cent. Greece.

There were three main elements to elementary education, normally taught in different establishments. The *paidotribēs* dealt with gymnastics, games, and general athletic fitness, mainly in the palaestra (e.g. Pl. *Grg.* 452b, *Prt.* 313a). The *kitharistēs* taught music and the works of the lyric poets, the lyre school inheriting the musical education of the Archaic period. The *grammatistēs* taught reading, writing, and arithmetic, as well as literature, which consisted of learning by heart the work of poets, especially Homer, who were regarded as giving moral training (see Protagoras on the moral function of music and poetry, *Prt.* 326a). Thus after learning the alphabet (see Pl. *Resp.* 402a–b; *Plt.* 227e–278b, for the methods of learning to read), pupils would progress to learning the poets by heart (*Prt.* 325e). Gymnastics and music (including poetry), then, were the fundamentals. The 'Old Education' parodied in *Aristophanes's *Clouds* (961–1023) gives most emphasis to physical education and music, saying nothing about letters, either because it was a minor element or too basic to mention. But the predominance of music—which included poetry and dance, and emphasized actual performance—and physical training in the basic Greek education is attested elsewhere (e.g. Pl. *Resp.* 376e); the conservative Plato sees lack of musical training (*achoreutos*) as synonymous with lack of education (*apaideutos*) (*Leg.* 654a–b).

In a single day, the pupil might start with gymnastics, then proceed to the lyre school, and end with letters. But the system was private and fee-paying, far from rigid, and parents might not want their children to participate in all three. Girls as we see from vase-painting, might be educated in all three elements, as well as dancing, though not normally in the same schools as boys or to the same extent. The teacher was normally a free man enjoying the same social status (and remuneration) as a doctor— though in fact often not so highly regarded (cf. *Demosthenes on *Aeschines, *De cor.* 265). Assistants might be slaves or free men. Boys were always accompanied to school by a *paidagōgos*, a slave and highly trusted part of the family (cf. Themistocles', Hdt. 8. 75), who helped to bring up the child and at school must have been a helpful overseer. Discipline at school was strict: the symbol of the *paidotribes'* power to punish was the forked stick, of other teachers the *narthex* (cane). Pupils regularly had to recite what they had learned, and the regular public competitions (all illustrated in vase-scenes), whether literary, musical, or athletic, were an important forum for proving their skill.

The development of group schooling, in which the education previously reserved for the aristocracy is spread to other citizens, may be related, at least in Athens, to the development of the *democracy, but cannot have originated with it. The balance between the physical and intellectual aspects may not have been as harmonious as some modern observers have suggested; it was certainly disputed by Greek thinkers, and the military uses of physical education may have given that side ascendancy (cf. *Prt.* 326 b–c, on gymnastics as useful training for war. Xenophanes (*c.*500) (DK 21 B 2) and *Euripides scoffed at the *athletic (and aristocratic) ideal, while *Pindar, perhaps Aristophanes, and *Xenophon (*Cyn.* 13) supported it. Plato, *Isocrates, and Aristotle (*Pol.* 8) subordinated the physical side to the intellectual.

Higher education

From the late 5th cent. it was possible to pursue further and more specialist education by joining one of the courses offered by the *sophists, or listening to their lectures and disputations. Or there were the specialized schools of *rhetoric or philosophy or of *medicine (possible early 'schools' (e.g. of medicine, Hdt. 3. 129, 131), may have been more like loose semi-religious foundations). The most famous were Isocrates' school of rhetoric, founded about 390 BC, Plato's *Academy with its scientific, mathematical, and philosophical curriculum founded soon after, and Aristotle's Lyceum (see ARISTOTLE, para. 5), founded in 335 BC. Some of these higher schools prescribed propaedeutic courses (e.g. geometry for Plato's Academy), which have been seen as the origin of 'secondary education'.

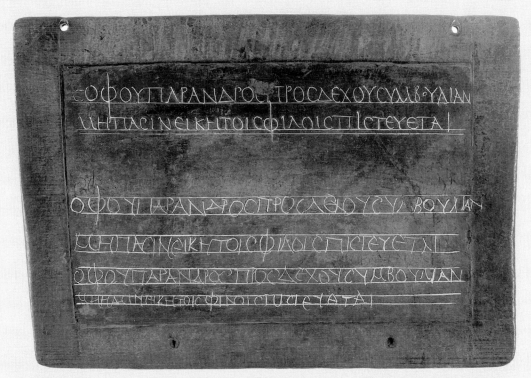

education, Greek Learning to write, along with reading, dominated Greek elementary education. This wooden tablet (2nd cent. AD) shows a Greek maxim in the master's hand (top) and the pupil's two copies. Such maxims were used as school texts.

The great educators and theorists

The sophists were itinerant teachers, who offered education for a fee on a variety of specialized and technical subjects. In general, they claimed to teach political virtue (*aretē*), and most laid great stress on skills useful for political life, especially rhetoric (e.g. *Prt.* 318e–319a). In that sense they rivalled the poets' claim as educators; they offered techniques useful in the Athenian democracy (and open to anyone who could pay), and in charging for their services, aroused much distrust. They were progressive and pragmatic in their views and methods, and belonged to the liberal, democratic tradition of Greek education. They were effectively the first to create a standard teaching system at an advanced level, and the first to include the basic sciences in their schema (note especially the polymath Hippias, *Prt.* 318e). But they were part of the mainstream of Greek cultural heritage, which they accepted, taught, and enhanced, and against which *Socrates and *Plato reacted so violently. Their ideas initiated and propelled the ferment of discussion about education—including the 'nature versus nurture' debate—that continued so intensely in the 4th cent.

Socrates, on the other hand, distrusted the sophists' claim to be able to teach everything, or indeed even to know anything. Socrates sought not to impart a body of knowledge, but to progress, with his followers, in seeking it. In the educational sphere, he seems to have had a rather conservative reliance on innate gifts; his great influence lies in the famous 'Socratic' method of teaching (below), and in his equation of virtue with knowledge. Plato, however, gives us the most extensive theory of education, in the *Republic* and, in a less extreme form, the *Laws*, where he sets forth the ideal state of a totalitarian mould, influenced by Sparta, and a corresponding system of education in which everything, including most forms of literature and art, which does not serve the interests of the state, is rigidly excluded: his elementary education, for all citizens to the age of 17 or 18, was otherwise rather conservative. Plato's

Timaeus provided the Middle Ages with the rationale for their quadrivium: though this in fact derived ultimately from Hippias' insistence (*Prt.* 318e) on the four sciences, namely arithmetic, geometry, astronomy, and music. In his early works he strongly opposed the teaching of rhetoric, but later allowed it to be taught in the Academy alongside the more important scientific, mathematical, and philosophical studies. His concept of an educational establishment with permanent buildings, specialist teachers, and an integrated curriculum, may be seen as a precursor of the secondary school (see *Resp.* 536–41 for the appropriate age-range for each stage in Plato's scheme), his founding of the Academy, an association of scholars, as the first university. It was, however, the Lyceum (see ARISTOTLE, para. 5), which became the greatest research institute of antiquity. In *Isocrates' educational innovations, one sees the further development of the rhetorical side of late 5th-cent. culture, as opposed to the philosophical emphasized by Plato and left by Isocrates as marginal to the ultimate rhetorical focus. He owed much to the sophists in subject-matter and teaching methods; his educational aims were to train (a few) students in morality and political skill, hence rhetoric (e.g. *Panathenaicus* 30–2; *Antidosis* 231; *Contra Sophistas* 21), and ultimately to produce political leaders. Other subjects were subservient to the pursuit of rhetorical skill: among these was knowledge of the past, and he distinguished between useful, or cultural, and purely disciplinary subjects like eristic and mathematics (*Antidosis* 261–9). His teaching methods also laid immense stress on the literary composition of prose, seeking to oust the dominant position of the poets in education. It was this primarily rhetorical basis of further education that became the dominant characteristic of ancient education.

Teaching methods
Private tuition, individual tuition, and teaching in small groups are all attested, even for gymnastics (Pl. *Plt.* 294d–e). Learning by heart, for the purposes of recitation, was standard. Even Plato accepted the usefulness of games in elementary education (arithmetic), though he was generally hostile to any experimentation in scientific teaching. At a higher level, pedagogic techniques were most developed in rhetorical teaching. Students memorized commonplaces, stock situations, and stock phrases, along with sample passages like Gorgias' *Funeral Oration* as material for later improvisation (on which much store was set). Psychology, techniques of persuasion, and the art of arguing both sides of a case were also taught. In addition, the sophists, and in particular, Isocrates, supplemented this with further general knowledge (see RHETORIC, GREEK).

The sophists developed both the dialectical method and the lecture, which might take the form of the display *epideixis* or the full technical lecture, which even Plato frequently used though he preferred dialectic. The dialectic method involves question and answer, in which the respondent makes a real contribution to discussion (as opposed to the Socratic technique). This method was developed by Isocrates into a seminar technique of group discussion and criticism. The Socratic method proceeds by reducing the pupil to a state of *aporia* (or puzzlement) and admission of complete ignorance (not to mention irritation), and then drawing out knowledge by a process of questioning, a process of intellectual 'midwifery' (Pl. *Tht.* 150c). It is well illustrated in the geometry lesson of Plato's *Meno* (see *Meno* 85d–86b for the Socratic explanation given there). *Xenophon advocated the 'activity' method in the *Cyropaedia* where pupils learn justice by practising it in real-life group situations.

4. Hellenistic Education For the Hellenistic period, there is a wealth of inscriptions which illuminate the public side of education, and rich papyrological evidence for school activity (e.g. school exercises). The pattern of education established in Classical Athens was brought in the early years of the Hellenistic era to a definitive form which endured with only slight changes to the end of the ancient world. Greater attention was paid to the education of the ordinary citizen, as reflected in the many separate philosophical treatises on education by thinkers such as Aristippus, Theophrastus, Aristoxenus, Cleanthes, Zeno, Chrysippus, Clearchus, and Cleomenes. There is definitely an extension of elementary education, with generous foundations set up in some cities to fund teachers: at Teos

(*Syll.*³ 578 = Austin no. 120) all free boys were to receive education; *Rhodes, funded by Eumenes II of *Pergamum (Polyb. 31. 31), probably came nearest to universal public education (for boys) in antiquity (cf. also at *Delphi, *Syll.*³ 672 (= Austin no. 206), and Miletus, *Syll.*³ 577 (= Austin no. 119)). Girls also received more education than before (e.g. Teos, Pergamum), but cannot have been educated everywhere as fully as boys. But how far one can really claim universal education among Greek children in the period is controversial, and formal education was surely mostly confined to the cities. Greek *paideia* was now regarded as the essential badge of Greekness, and educational institutions—particularly the *gymnasium—were thought necessary to maintain, or assert, Greek identity.

Organization

Education was still mostly paid for by parents, but generous private benefactions in some cities provided for teachers' salaries (esp. Teos, Miletus, Delphi, Rhodes, above), and the cities seem to have taken more formal interest in education, organizing ephebic institutions (see GYMNASIUM) and regulating private benefactions themselves. Most had one gymnasium, some more. This would be the focus for physical training, which became transformed into an educational centre with schooling for *paides* (12–17) and ephebes: some space was devoted to schooling and lectures, with teachers of literature, philosophy, music (though the evidence suggests that this was not universal: the law from Beroea (*BÉ* 1978, 274 = Austin no. 118) implies the activity was overwhelmingly athletic). Thus it was a centre for Greek culture in the widest sense. The gymnasiarch (*kosmētēs* in Athens), a state official, was elected for a year to run the gymnasium, and to supervise all aspects of the education (public or private) of the *epheboi* or *neoi* (ex-ephebes, i.e. in their twenties). He might be expected to contribute financially, buying oil or providing extra oil for athletic activity (very widely attested), and paying for one or more teachers' salaries. The increasing financial burdens of the office led to its decay in imperial times to a mere liturgy with wealth the only qualification. The *paidonomos* had similar duties for elementary education. Girls also sometimes had special officials (e.g. Smyrna, Pergamum). These officials organized numerous public competitions and awards, sometimes paid for by the gymnasiarch: preserved lists of prizewinners mention (among others) those successful in reading, writing, painting, recitation, verse and song-writing, running, boxing. Class loads tended to be high, as the recorded complaints of teachers indicate, and the social standing of teachers rather low.

Other innovations of this period were the concentration of all educational activity into a single building; examinations; and the formal division of pupils into educational age groups, though these seem to vary from place to place: *paides* (boys), aged 12–17, *epheboi*, aged 18–20 in Athens (younger elsewhere), and *neoi*, ex-ephebes, in their twenties. The ephebate, which began as a predominantly military training organized for young men by the state, and in Athens was reinvigorated in the 330s as a two-year training, spread over the Greek world with enormous vitality, and became a kind of cultural-athletic institution for the leisured classes. This came (in Athens from the late 2nd cent. BC) to include intellectual studies in its make-up, though as sport took first place, it is questionable how intellectual any of this education really was.

Elementary and secondary education

Elementary education was dominated by learning to read and write, and learning by heart, by what seem from the papyri to be unnecessarily tedious methods (sport, of course, was also important). At secondary level, adolescents progressed to an overwhelmingly literary curriculum that still involved learning by rote and recitation, and was dominated by the reading and exposition of texts under the care of the *grammaticus*. The canonization of classical literature progressed rapidly, and anthologies used for teaching crystallized certain authors and passages in the educational curriculum. Physical education and music continued; the ancient idea of the *enkyklios paideia*, or general education, was evolved to include the four main sciences, following Hippias, and looking forward to the Seven Liberal Arts of the Middle Ages (grammar, rhetoric, dialectic, geometry, arithmetic, astronomy, music). But it is unclear how keenly the scientific subjects were really pursued, and literary studies seem to oust the others. The Classics, particularly Homer, were studied in minute detail and according to rigidly formal rules. The study of grammar (in the modern sense) was added later (1st cent. BC), also composition, and preliminary rhetorical material.

Higher education

After secondary level there were several options of varying levels. The *ephēbeia* did include further cultural studies (literature, rhetoric, philosophy) accompanied by lectures and *libraries; similarly with the older *neoi*. But for really serious 'higher education' in the recognizably modern sense, there were the great centres of learning—Athens, Pergamum, and Rhodes for philosophy and rhetoric; Cos, Pergamum, or Ephesus for medicine; *Alexandria for the whole range of higher studies.

The teachers

Teachers were elected by the cities for a year at a time and supervised by the gymnasiarch and *paidonomos*. There were three grades of literary teacher: the *grammatistēs* (elementary level), *grammaticus* (secondary), and rhetor or sophist (higher). The *paidonomos* and ephebes might engage skilled itinerant teachers for short periods. Ordinary teachers received little more pay than a skilled workman, private ones less than those provided with a salary by the city: music teachers received most, then the literary teacher, then the *paidotribēs*. A good teacher would receive gifts, prizes, and sometimes tax-exemption (teachers were exempt from the salt tax in Ptolemaic Egypt).

See also LITERACY; ORALITY.   F. A. G. B.; R. T.

Roman education

1. Early Italy and the republic There is very little reliable evidence bearing upon formal education in the early period. Education was then certainly centred on the family and was probably based upon apprenticeship supervised by the father—in poorer homes an apprenticeship to agriculture or trade, in more aristocratic circles to military service and public life (what later became known as the *tirocinium militiae* and the *tirocinium fori*). The authority of the father, legalized as *patria potestas*, was absolute and could only in theory be questioned by the censors. The Roman mother had a more restricted, domestic role but she too was traditionally expected to take a personal, central responsibility and to set a strong moral example. It is not certain when reading and writing became a serious part of Roman education: the 7th-cent. BC ivory writing-tablet with inscribed alphabet found at Marsiliana d'Albegna and 6th-cent. bucchero (pottery) models of wooden writing-tablets (*tabulae ansatae*) from Etruria may imply that *literacy was then already becoming a part of everyday life. Institutions like the religious calendars, the census, and the codification of the *Twelve Tables point in this direction and by the end of the 4th cent. BC it would certainly have been hard for a Roman senator to do without reading and writing. It is not known how such elementary instruction was given though it was often reckoned to be a parental responsibility; references to schools in the 5th and 4th cents. BC are probably anachronistic.

2. The later republic and the empire As Rome's contacts with the Greek-speaking world grew in the 3rd and 2nd cent. BC, a predominantly Greek pattern of education evolved (see EDUCATION, GREEK), omitting however the *gymnasium and emphasis on competitive physical education. Aristocratic Roman families often employed Greek-speaking tutors for their children (Livius Andronicus and *Ennius were early and conspicuous examples) and these tutors—often slaves or freedmen—commonly taught both Greek and Latin; competence in both languages remained a feature of an upper-class education until the western and eastern empires parted company. This tradition of tutors in wealthy families continued alongside the growth of schools. A freedman, Spurius Carvilius, is credited with opening the first fee-paying school for elementary reading and writing in the second half of the 3rd cent. BC and thereafter the elementary teacher (*ludi magister* or *litterator*) running a small school became a lowly, noisy, and familiar part of Roman life. The Greek custom of a family *paedagogus* who took the children to and from school and supervised their life and habits was also adopted; the custom burgeoned especially after the Third Macedonian War when cheap, well-qualified Greek slaves became easily available. The second stage of education was in the hands of the *grammaticus* who taught language and poetry and who might be either a private tutor with a family or a teacher with his own school. He could be a person of some learning and consequence. Teachers of *rhetoric, the third stage of Greek and Roman education, first appear in the 2nd cent. BC at Rome—Crates of Mallus was said to have been influential—and, in the absence of Latin instructional material, taught Greek theory and practice. Latin materials corresponding to the Greek rhetorical manuals appeared in the 1st cent. BC (e.g. the *Rhetorica ad Herennium*) and Plotius Gallus is said to have opened the first school for teaching rhetoric in Latin about 94 BC. Cicero's works on oratory were a major contribution to teaching rhetoric in Latin and Quintilian's *Institutio Oratoria* published about AD 95 includes a developed and humane picture of Roman rhetorical training at its best. From the middle of the 2nd cent. BC, when three visiting Greek philosophers made a great impression with their lectures in Rome, philosophy could play a significant part in the education of some wealthier young Romans. Teachers were soon available in Italy, though no philosophical schools were founded in Rome until Plotinus and Porphyry attracted pupils in the 3rd cent. AD: the young were glad to travel and to visit one of the four famous schools in *Athens or other centres where philosophers taught. From the 1st cent. AD there were law schools at Rome which founded an important tradition of legal education culminating in the great law school at Berytus (mod. Beirut) in the eastern empire. Augustus attempted with some success to use Roman and Italian traditions to create a Roman counterpart to the Greek *ephebeia* (see GYMNASIUM) in the revival of the *lusus Troiae* at Rome and the *collegia iuvenum* in the Italian cities; in this there was more than a hint of political education. Later emperors, local communities, and benefactors like *Pliny the Younger sometimes subsidized charitable and educational activity from personal interest, generosity, public duty, or political expediency but there was nothing like national or regional provision for education.

3. Levels and subjects of study The three levels of Roman education represented by the *ludi magister*, the *grammaticus*, and the rhetor were probably never rigidly differentiated. Although formal education usually began when children were about 7 years old and transfers to the *grammaticus* and rhetor frequently happened at about the ages of 12 and 15 respectively, progress between the levels was often more a matter of achievement than age group; the roles of teachers sometimes overlapped considerably. All three levels followed a Greek pattern: the elementary teacher, for instance, taught reading by the familiar progression—letters, syllables, words—with much use of the gnomic example sentence (*sententia*). Writing and some basic mathematics were also his province. Echoes of the ancient schoolroom can be heard in the *colloquia* ('discourses') which occur in the bilingual school-books known as the *Hermeneumata*. The *grammaticus* advanced the study of both language and poetry (rarely prose). As Roman grammarians like *Varro and Remmius Palaemon adapted Alexandrian grammatical theory to Latin (especially that of Dionysius Thrax, some systematic morphology was taught; syntax was rather diffusely approached via correctness of speech and the avoidance of solecism. In teaching poetry, attention was paid to expressive reading (*lectio*) followed by the teacher's explanation (*enarratio*) and, where appropriate, analysis (*partitio*). Homer's pre-eminent place in Greek schools was originally taken by poets like Livius Andronicus (who supplied the *Odyssey* in Saturnian verse translation), Naevius, and Ennius. Quintus Caecilius Epirota is credited with the introduction of contemporary poetry to Roman schools in 26 BC and later Virgil supplanted most earlier poets (Terence becoming the Roman counterpart to Menander). The teaching of rhetoric followed the Greek model closely with a series of preliminary exercises (*progymnasmata*—sometimes taught by the *grammaticus*) leading on to the theory and practice of declamation with the two major groupings of *suasoriae* (advice offered in historical or imaginary situations) and *controversiae* (court-room cases). The five traditional parts of rhetoric were the basis of instruction: *inventio*, *dispositio*, *elocutio*, *memoria*, and *actio* (see RHETORIC, LATIN). The teaching of philosophy which young Romans encountered seems to have been based very much upon studying the works of the founder of a philosophical school and the commentaries of his successors.

4. Schools and teachers Elementary teachers usually seem to have worked in suitable spaces in public porticoes or squares, in hired accommodation off the street, or in their own rooms; the idea of the school as a dedicated building is misleading. The *grammaticus* and the rhetor probably commanded better but not institutional accommodation. It is likely that most schools were small and though the monthly fees doubtless varied, such evidence as there is suggests that elementary teachers of some kind were affordable by all but the poor. Towns but not villages under the empire might be expected to have teachers and schools. Boys were almost certainly in a majority but some girls did attend too. The regular equipment for pupils consisted of waxed or whitened wooden writing-tablets, pen, and ink (though exercises were certainly written on papyrus when it could be afforded). In the elementary school lessons began at dawn and discipline was strict and unashamedly physical. There is some evidence for the education of slaves in *paedagogia* or training-schools attached to wealthy houses; the training sometimes included reading and writing as well as the household tasks required of them.

The status of elementary teachers was low; many were ex-slaves and had only a small and hazardous income. The *grammaticus* was better respected and *Suetonius' *De grammaticis* gives sketches of a poor but not ill-regarded profession. The rhetor could charge higher fees and the most famous could become men of some consequence under the empire. The ratio of maximum fees payable to the *ludi magister*, the *grammaticus*, and the rhetor in Diocletian's Price Edict was 1:4:5. The rhetor was at first an object of some suspicion in Rome; in 161 BC rhetors were expelled from the city and Latin rhetoricians suffered the same fate in 92 BC. However, from the time of *Caesar teachers were more favoured; now and then they received various immunities, exemptions, and privileges by imperial edict, though imperial patronage was largely reserved for the highest levels. *Vespasian for instance endowed imperial chairs in Greek and Latin rhetoric at Rome, *Quintilian being the first holder of the Latin chair; Marcus *Aurelius endowed four chairs of philosophy and a chair of rhetoric at Athens. Emperors and politicians looked for visibility and prestige in exchange for their generosity.   J. V. M.

when it passed to Seleucid control. The final episode in the struggles of these two kingdoms came in 168 when Antiochus IV's successful invasion of Egypt was halted at Eleusis (a suburb of *Alexandria) by Roman intervention. To the south the doubtful loyalty of the Thebaid proved an ongoing threat to the traditional unity of Upper and Lower Egypt. The area was in revolt from 206 to 186, under the control of rebel kings Haronnophris and Chaonnophris and again for three years from 88. The destruction of Egyptian Thebes by Ptolemy IX brought relative peace to the south for 75 years. See NATIONALISM (Hellenistic and Roman).

Internally the Ptolemies used local expertise as they set up their royal administration based on the traditional divisions or nomes of Egypt. Self-governing cities were few: Alexandria, which served as capital from 312 BC, the Greek Delta port of Naucratis and Ptolemais (mod. El-Menshā) founded by Ptolemy I as a Greek city in the south. Through a hierarchical bureaucracy, taxation of rich agricultural land and of the population and their livestock was based on a thorough census and land-survey. Greek was gradually introduced as the language of the administration and Greeks were privileged, both socially and in the tax-structure. The categorization however of Greek was now not an ethnic one, but rather one acquired, through employment and education. The wealth of the country (from its irrigation-agriculture and from taxes) was employed both for further development in the countryside (with agricultural initiatives and land-reclamation, especially in the Fayūm) and, in Alexandria, for royal patronage and display. The cultural life of the capital, with the Museum and *Library strongly supported under the early Ptolemies, played an important role in the definition of contemporary Hellenism.

Like other Hellenistic monarchs, the Ptolemies depended for security on their army, and Ptolemaic troops were tied in loyalty to their new homes by land-grants in the countryside. From the reign of Ptolemy VI local *politeumata* were also founded as settlements for both soldiers and attached civilians. As the flow of immigrant recruits grew less, Egyptian troops were increasingly used, a development Polybius noted (5. 107. 3) as dangerous to the country. These troops too might become settlers (cleruchs) in the countryside (with smaller plots), as might the native police and other security forces. Land was further used in gift-estates to reward high-ranking officials; the *dioikētēs* ('finance minister') Apollonius under Ptolemy II was one of these.

In a soft approach to Egyptian ways, the Ptolemies early recognized the importance of native temples, granting privileges, and supporting native cults. For the Ptolemies were both Egyptian pharaohs and Greek monarchs. The new god Sarapis with his human aspect, an extension of the native Osiris-Apis bull, typifies this dual aspect of the period. Royal co-operation—for mutual ends—with the high priests of Memphis, central city of Lower Egypt where from the reign of at least Ptolemy V the king was crowned Egyptian-style, contrasts with the problems posed by the breakaway tendencies of Thebes and Upper Egypt. General tolerance and even financial support for native temples characterize the religious policy of the regime. In the important field of law two separate legal systems continued in use.

The sister-marrying Ptolemaic dynasty is, from the late 3rd cent., consistently represented as in decline. From the mid-2nd cent. the shadow of Rome loomed large, yet Egypt was the last Hellenistic kingdom to fall under Roman sway.   D. J. T.

Roman After two centuries of diplomatic contacts, Egypt was annexed as a province of the Roman people in 30 BC by Octavian (*Augustus) after his defeat of Mark *Antony and *Cleopatra. Although the Romans adapted many individual elements of the centralized bureaucracy of the Ptolemaic kingdom, and although the emperor could be represented as a pharaoh, the institutions of the Ptolemaic monarchy were dismantled, and the administrative and social structure of Egypt underwent fundamental changes. The governor (prefect) and other major officials were Roman *equites appointed, like the administrators of other 'imperial' provinces, by the emperor for a few years. Egypt was garrisoned with three, later two, legions and a number of auxiliary units. For private business pre-existing Egyptian and Greek legal forms and traditions were generally respected, but under the umbrella of the principles and procedures of Roman law. A closed monetary system based on the Alexandrian silver tetradrachm was maintained, but the tetradrachm was made equivalent to the Roman denarius. The Egyptian temples and priesthood were allowed to keep most of their privileges, but in tacit return for the ubiquitous spread of the Roman imperial cult (see RULER-CULT). Local administration, previously entrusted to salaried officials and private contractors, was gradually converted to a liturgic system, in which ownership of property brought an obligation to serve. This was enabled by Augustus' revolutionary conversion of the category of 'cleruchic' land, allotments held in theory at royal discretion in return for military service, into fully private property, of which there had been very little in Ptolemaic Egypt. The Romans also increased the status of the towns and their inhabitants. Alexandria enjoyed the greatest privileges, but the *mētropolis* ('mother-city', i.e. chief town) of each regional administrative unit (nome), was under

Augustus given some self-administration through liturgic magistrates, then encouraged to erect public buildings and to behave like cities elsewhere, until in AD 200/1 *Septimius Severus granted *boulai* (councils) to Alexandria and all the *mētropoleis*. As part of this urbanization the Romans introduced a strict social hierarchy with ethno-cultural overtones: Roman and Alexandrian citizens were legally marked off, mainly by their exemption from the poll-tax, from the other inhabitants, who were called 'Egyptians'. Within the category of 'Egyptians' the metropolites (original residents of the *mētropoleis*) enjoyed some privileges, principally a reduced rate of poll-tax, and within them a theoretically hereditary group of 'Hellenic' descent, defined by membership of the *gymnasium, formed the socio-political élite of each *mētropolis*. Large private estates developed in the 2nd cent. and flourished in the 3rd, so that Egypt, like other eastern provinces, was dominated and run by a local 'Greek', urban-based landowning aristocracy. Despite urbanization, the bulk of the population remained peasants, many of them tenant-farmers of 'public' (previously 'royal') and 'sacred' land for the traditional, variable, but quite high, rents in kind. The imperial government exported some of this tax-wheat to feed Rome, but it was equally if not more interested in the cash revenues of Egypt. Roman tax-rates often followed Ptolemaic precedent, though the annual poll-tax in cash was a striking novelty; the chronic fiscal problems uniquely documented in the papyri were probably typical of much of the ancient world. Whether economic conditions were better or worse than in previous periods is difficult to judge. The single greatest disaster of the Roman period was the Antonine plague of the mid-160s to 170s, but the country seems to have recovered fully by the early 3rd cent. Generally Roman Egypt had a vigorous and increasingly monetized economy. The main cultural division was between the 'Hellenic' life of the metropolites and the village life of the Egyptian-speaking majority, even after the universal grant of Roman citizenship in 212. But most peasants were involved in the money economy, many acquired some literacy in Greek, and the scale of urbanization implies considerable social mobility. The political and fiscal reforms of *Diocletian at the end of the 3rd cent., capping longer-term developments such as the growth of *Christianity—which led to the re-emergence of Egyptian as a literary language (Coptic)—brought about another social, administrative, and cultural revolution which marked the end of 'Roman' Egypt. Egypt remained a province of the Byzantine empire until it came under Arab rule in AD 642. (See RACE; FOOD SUPPLY, ROMAN.)
                                                              D. W. R.

Egyptian deities The Graeco-Roman view of Egyptian religion is sharply fissured. Despite Hdt. 2. 50. 1 (comm. A. B. Lloyd, 1975–88), many writers of all periods, and probably most individuals, found in the Egyptians' worship of animals a polemical contrast to their own norms (though cf. Cic. *Nat. D.* 1. 29. 81 f.), just as, conversely, the Egyptians turned animal-worship into a symbol of national identity (cf. Diod. Sic. 1. 86–90). The first Egyptian divinity to be recognized by the Greek world was the oracular Ammon of the Siwa oasis (Hdt. 2. 54–7); but *oracles have a special status. The only form of Late-period Egyptian religion to be assimilated into the Graeco-Roman world was to a degree untypical, centred on anthropomorphic deities— Isis, Sarapis, and Harpocrates—and grounded in Egyptian vernacular enthusiasm quite as much as in temple ritual. The other gods which became known in the Graeco-Roman world, Osiris, Anubis, Apis, Horus, Bubastis, Agathodaemon, Bes, etc., spread solely in their train. Moreover, especially in the Hellenistic period, a nice balance was maintained between acknowledgement of their strangeness (Isis *Taposirias*, *Memphitis*, *Aigyptia*, etc.) and selection of their universal, 'hearkening', 'aiding', 'saving' roles.

From the late 4th cent. BC, these cults were most commonly introduced into the Greek world, primarily to port- and tourist-towns, by (Hellenized) Egyptians, i.e. immigrant metics: cf. *IG* II. 4. 1299, comm. H. Engelmann (1975²). Sometimes they were introduced by Greeks who had served or lived in Egypt (e.g. *SEG* 38. 1571, 217 BC). There is a growing consensus that they were often indirect beneficiaries of Ptolemaic political suzerainty. Within a generation or two they became sufficiently attractive to Greeks of some social standing to be able to press for recognition as *thiasoi* (group of worshippers of a god): it was when they proselytized among the citizen body that they were regulated by city governments and incorporated as civic deities. Full-time Egyptian priests were then obtained for larger temples, and subordinate *synodoi* (associations) formed, e.g. *melanephoroi* (lit. 'the black-clad'), *pastophoroi* ('shrine-carriers'), analogous to a development widespread in Late-period Egypt. In many smaller communities the Greek model of annual priesthoods was adopted. (See PRIESTS.) In the west, Isis reached Campania from *Delos in the late 2nd cent. BC. At Rome the situation was initially volatile: the private *Isium Metellinum* (75–50 BC) and an illegal shrine on the Capitol were pulled down in 53 BC (Dio Cass. 40. 47. 3, cf. 42. 26. 2). The first public temple was the *Iseum Campense* (43 BC). The cults became attractive to members of the decurial class in the 1st cent. AD, spreading from Italy unevenly into the western empire. Neither slaves nor the poor are anywhere much in evidence.

R. L. G.

ekklesia, democratic assembly at Athens. See DEMOCRACY, ATHENIAN, §§2 and 3.

ekphrasis, an extended and detailed literary description of any object, real or imaginary. 'There are *ekphraseis* of faces and objects and places and ages and many other things' (Hermog. *Prog.* 10; cf. Dion. Hal. *Rhet.* 10. 17, Lucian, *Hist. conscr.* 20, Apthonius, *Progymnasmata* 12). The rhetoricians thus systematized into a rhetorical exercise (*progymnasma*) a poetic technique stretching from the description of the shield of Achilles in the *Iliad* to that of Hagia Sophia by Paulus Silentiarius. Most were of works of art. *Ekphraseis* was a work by Callistratus, and *Eikones* was the title of works by Philostratus, *Lucian, and others.

J. S. R.

Elagabalus (Marcus Aurelius Antoninus), emperor (AD 218–22), was the son of Sextus Varius Marcellus and Julia Soaemias Bassiana, niece of Julia Domna, the wife of *Septimius Severus. Born probably in 203, as Varius Avitus Bassianus, he was holding the priesthood, hereditary in his mother's family, of Elagabalus the presiding deity of Emesa in Syria, in 218, when his mother and grandmother Julia Maesa used him as figurehead of a rebellion against Macrinus. He was proclaimed to be the son of his mother's cousin *Caracalla and renamed M. Aurelius Antoninus after him. After the victory, he took the cult of the god by whose name he is known to Rome, which he reached in July 219. In late 220 his intention to make Elagabalus ('deus Sol invictus', 'the invincible sun-god') supreme god of the empire aroused open hostility at Rome when he divorced his first wife Julia Paula and married the Vestal virgin Aquilia Severa, a 'sacred marriage' to match the union of the god with Juno Caelestis. He was forced to adopt his cousin Alexianus, renamed Alexander (26 June 221), and to divorce Aquilia in favour of a descendant of Marcus *Aurelius, Annia Faustina; but by the end of 221 he took Aquilia back and tried to get rid of Alexander. This provoked renewed outrage, which came to a head with his murder on 11 March 222 and replacement by Alexander. His flouting of conventions in the choice of officials, combined with disgust at the orgiastic ceremonial of the Syrian cult had proved too much for senate, praetorians, and *plebs* alike. See SEVERUS ALEXANDER.

A. R. Bi.

elections and voting

Greek In the Greek states voting was used in councils, assemblies, and lawcourts; appointments were made by election or by allotment or sometimes by a combination of the two. In Athens and elsewhere *psēphisma* (from *psēphos*, 'voting-stone') became the standard word for a decree of the council (*boulē*) or assembly (*ekklēsia*), and *cheirotonia* ('raising hands') was used for elections; but in Athens (see DEMOCRACY, ATHENIAN) voting was normally by show of hands (not precisely counted) in the council and assembly both for decrees and for elections, but by ballot in the lawcourts. Ballots seem first to have been used on occasions when a count was necessary to ensure that a quorum was achieved, but by the end of the 5th cent. BC it had been realized that voting by ballot could be secret voting. In *Sparta voting by acclamation survived to the Classical period for elections and for decrees of the assembly. In the Hellenistic and Roman periods some decrees of some states report numbers of votes cast for and against.

P. J. R.

Roman At Rome adult male citizens had the right to vote to elect the annual magistrates, to make laws, to declare war and peace, and, until the development of the public courts in the late republic, to try citizens on serious charges. But the remarkable feature of the Roman system was that matters were never decided by a simple majority. Votes were always cast in assigned groups, so that a majority of individual votes decided the vote of each group, and a majority of groups decided the vote of the assembly as a whole. The three groupings of the 30 *curiae* (the most ancient divisions), centuries (*centuriae*), and tribes (**tribus*) made up the different types of *comitia* (assembly).

In the two important *comitia* the overall procedures for voting were similar. Cicero (*Flac.* 15) noted that Romans considered matters and voted standing up, whereas the Greeks sat down. The vote was preceded by a *contio*, a public meeting, to present the issues or the candidates involved. The presiding magistrate dissolved this by the command to the citizens to disperse (*discedere*) into the areas roped off for each group. From their enclosures the groups of citizens proceeded, when called, across raised gangways (*pontes*), erected at the site of the assembly. Originally each voter was asked orally for his vote by one of the officials (*rogatores*), who put a mark (*punctum*) against the appropriate name or decision on his official tablet. From 139 to 107 BC a series of four laws introduced the secret ballot. Now the voter was handed a small boxwood tablet covered in wax on which he recorded his vote with a stylus. In most cases a single letter was sufficient: in legislation, V for assent (*uti rogas*) and A for dissent (*antiquo*); in judicial cases I for acquittal (*libero*) and C for condemnation (*condemno*); in elections the voter was expected to write the names for himself (**Cato the Younger is supposed to have rejected many votes clearly written in the same hand, Plut. *Cat. Min.* 46). The completed tablet was then dropped into a tall wickerwork voting-urn (*cista*) under the control of guardians (*custodes*), who forwarded it to the tellers (*diribitores*). The process of casting the vote is illustrated on a coin of Publius Licinius Nerva of the late 2nd cent. BC. In the *comitia centuriata* people voted successively, class by class, and the results were announced as they went along. In the *comitia tributa* successive voting was used in legislative and judicial assemblies, but simultaneous voting probably in elections. This may explain why legislative assemblies regularly took place in a variety of places, some quite restricted, such as the **forum Romanum, Capitol, and Circus Flaminius (see CIRCUS), while the large spaces of the Campus Martius were needed for elections. It was here that Caesar planned a huge building, the Julian Enclosures (Saepta Iulia), to house the electoral process. The project was continued by the triumvir **Lepidus and completed in 26 BC under Augustus by **Agrippa, who was also responsible for beginning a connected building to house the tellers (the Diribitorium).

The lot played a vital role in the electoral process. It was used to pick the tribe (designated as the *principium*) or the century (*centuria praerogativa*) which voted first and provided a lead for the other voters. The lot also determined the order of voting by the tribes or the order in which the votes were announced. This was important, because the first candidates to achieve a simple majority of the groups were declared elected up to the number of posts available, even though they might not have polled the largest number of votes, if all the votes of all the groups had been counted.

The significance for Roman politics of this elaborate and time-consuming voting process has often been played down by historians. However, the great lengths to which members of the élite went to win votes is testimony to the fact that the voting assemblies represent a truly democratic element in republican Rome. In typical Roman fashion the voting procedures, in a modified form, remained under the Principate, even when the substantive decision-making had passed to the emperor and the senate. J. J. P.

Electra, in mythology: (1) daughter of Oceanus and Tethys, wife of Thaumas, mother of Iris and the Harpies (Hes. *Theog.* 265 ff.).

(2) Daughter of Atlas and Pleione, and one of the Pleiades (Apollod. 3. 10. 1); mother by Zeus of Dardanus and Iasion (ibid. 3. 12. 1).

(3) Daughter of **Agamemnon and Clytemnestra, and sister of Orestes. She does not appear in epic, the first certain mention of her being in the *Oresteia* of **Stesichorus (fr. 217 Davies, *PMGF*), although she was said to be Homer's Laodice, renamed because of her long unwedded state (*Il.* 9. 145, cf. Xanthus fr. 700 *PMG* Page). Our major source for her story is Athenian tragedy, where she plays a central role in Orestes' vengeance on Clytemnestra and her lover Aegisthus for the murder of Agamemnon. Her first appearance is in the *Choephori* of **Aeschylus, where she is unalterably hostile to her mother and Aegisthus, welcoming her brother, joining with him in an invocation to Agamemnon's ghost, but not actively involved in the killings. In fact here the focus is still mainly on Orestes, with Electra disappearing from view once the vengeance begins. But her role is very much developed in **Sophocles and **Euripides.

In Sophocles' *Electra*, the main focus of the play is Electra herself, a steadfast, enduring figure, passionately grieving her father's murder and passionately set on revenge. She rescued Orestes, then a young child, from his father's murderers (12, 296–7, 1132–3), and now longs for his return. The move from despair to joy in the scene where she laments over the urn, believing it to hold the ashes of her dead brother, then learns that the man beside her is in fact the living Orestes himself, gives us perhaps the most moving recognition scene in extant tragedy. She is a strong and determined character who, when she believes Orestes dead, is willing to kill Aegisthus entirely unaided (947 ff., 1019 ff.); then, when it comes to the murder of Clytemnestra, she urges Orestes on, shouting out to him at the first death-cry of her mother, 'Strike, if you have the strength, a second blow' (1415).

In Euripides' *Electra* she is even more active in the murder: Orestes is weak and indecisive, and it is Electra who is the dominant figure, driving him to kill Clytemnestra and even grasping the sword with him at the moment of murder (1225), although afterwards she is as full of remorse as before she was full of lust for revenge. In Euripides' *Orestes* she appears as a desperately faithful nurse and helper to her mad brother, abetting him and his comrade Pylades in their attacks on Helen and Hermione. In some accounts she later marries Pylades (Eur. *El.* 1249; *Or.* 1658 f.; Hyg. *Fab.* 122, where she also meets Orestes and Iphigenia at Delphi and nearly murders the latter, who she thinks has murdered him).

There is no certain representation of Electra in art before the beginning of the 5th cent. BC, where she is present at the murder of Aegisthus; later her meeting with Orestes at the tomb of Agamemnon became popular: see I. McPhee, *LIMC* 3/1. 709–19.   H. J. R.; J. R. M.

elegiac poetry, Greek This may be initially defined as poetry in elegiac couplets (hexameter followed by pentameter), one of the most popular metres throughout antiquity. The term *elegeion*, normally meaning 'elegiac couplet', is derived from *elegos*, a sung lament that must have been characteristically in this metre, but the metre was always used for many other purposes. We also find the feminine *elegeia*, 'elegy', i.e. a poem or poetry in elegiacs.

A stricter definition distinguishes between elegiac poetry (elegy) and epigram (which was often but not necessarily in elegiac metre). Elegy, in the early period, was composed for oral delivery in a social setting, as a communication from the poet to others; an epigram was information written on an object (a tombstone, a dedication, etc.). The distinction was not always so clear after the 4th cent. BC, when the epigram came to be cultivated as a literary genre, but on the whole it can be sustained. As Greek *epigram has its own entry in this volume, we shall concentrate here on elegy.

All archaic elegy is in (epic-) Ionic dialect (see GREEK LANGUAGE, §4), whatever the author's provenance, and the form must have evolved among Ionians side by side with hexameter poetry. It is already established on both sides of the Aegean by *c*.650 BC when the first recorded elegists appear: *Archilochus, Callinus, and Tyrtaeus. From then till the end of the 5th cent. BC elegy was a popular medium; some poets used no other. Extant poems vary in length between two lines and 76 (*Solon fr. 13 West); Solon's *Salamis* was of 100 (Plut. *Sol.* 8. 2), while such poems as Mimnermus' *Smyrneis* and *Simonides' *Battle of Plataea* may have been longer still.

Many pieces presuppose the *symposium as the setting in which they were designed to be heard (e.g. Thgn. 467, 503, 825, 837, 1047, 1129; Xenophanes 1; Simon. eleg. 25 W; Dionysius Chalcus 1–5; Ion 26–7). Theognis (239–43) anticipates that (his elegies addressed to) Cyrnus will often be sung by young men at banquets in a fine, clear voice to the accompaniment of *auloi* (flutes, oboes). There are other mentions of an aulete accompanying the singing of elegy in the symposium (Thgn. 533, 825, 941, 943, 1056), and an

early 5th-cent. vase-painting (Munich 2646) shows a reclining symposiast with words of an elegiac verse issuing from his mouth while an aulete plays. Presumably there were conventional melodies that the aulete could repeat or vary for as long as required, without his having to know what verses were to be sung, as he would need to in the case of lyric. Certain elegists (Tyrtaeus, Mimnermus) are said to have been auletes themselves. Other settings are occasionally suggested: carousal through the streets after the party (Thgn. 1045, cf. 1065, 1207, 1351); a military encampment (Archil. 4; Thgn. 887, 1043); a public square in the evening (? Thgn. 263). Elegiac laments may sometimes have been sung at funerals, and these or other elegiac compositions at certain festivals where prizes were awarded for aulody, i.e. singing to *aulos* accompaniment, as happened at the Pythian festival (i.e. held at *Delphi) in 586 BC (Paus. 10. 7. 4–6) and at the Panathenaea (at Athens) from about 566.

A common use of elegy in the 7th cent. was in exhorting the poet's fellow citizens to fight bravely for their country (Callinus 1, Tyrtaeus 10–12 W, as well as Mimnermus 14 W, Solon 1–3 W); Callinus' opening 'How long will you lie there?' may imply the symposium setting. In other poems of Tyrtaeus and Solon the exhortation is political, presumably not delivered before a mob but to a social gathering from which participants might pass the message on to other gatherings. Solon, at least, also wrote elegies of a more personal, convivial character. Mimnermus was famous for elegies celebrating the pleasures of love and youth. He also used the versatile elegiac for his *Smyrneis*, a quasi-epic (for the symposium?), complete with invocation of the Muses, on the Smyrnaeans' heroic repulse of the Lydians around the time of the poet's birth.

The largest surviving body of archaic elegy is the collection of poems and excerpts, some 1,400 lines in all, transmitted under the name of Theognis. He is actually only one among many poets represented, ranging in date from the 7th to the early 5th cent. BC. Here we find a wide cross-section: political and moralizing verse, social comment, personal complaint, convivial pieces, witty banter, love poems to nameless boys. Other items are reflective or philosophic, and develop an argument on some ethical or practical question. This dialectic element was a feature of elegy from the start, but became more prominent later, for example in Xenophanes and Euenus.

With the publication of *POxy*. 3965, Simonides now appears as the major 5th-cent. elegist. He used the medium to celebrate the great battles of 480/79 BC; his grandiose poem on Plataea (eleg. 10–17 W) recalls Mimnermus' *Smyrneis*. His more personal poetry is now also represented by some fine fragments. Lesser 5th-cent. elegists include Euenus, Dionysius Chalcus, Ion of Chios, and Critias. They are all symposium-oriented, and this is still the situation in what looks like an early 4th-cent. piece, Adesp. eleg. 27 W. But the symposium was fast losing its songfulness, and elegy in the classical style was drying up. Isolated poems are quoted from Philiscus of Miletus and *Aristotle, containing posthumous tributes to *Lysias and *Plato respectively.

Meanwhile, Antimachus' use of elegiac metre for a long mythological poem, his *Lyde*, set a new pattern. (The existence of long antiquarian elegiac poems by Semonides, Xenophanes, and Panyassis is doubtful.) Antimachus and (nominally) Mimnermus were the two principal models for Hellenistic elegists such as Philitas, Hermesianax, Phanocles, Alexander Aetolus, *Callimachus (*Aetia*), *Eratosthenes (*Erigone*), who combined romantic subject-matter with mythological learning, sometimes on a large scale. But the metre was now taken up again by many poets for diverse purposes; witness its use for a hymn (Callim. *Hymn.* 5), a bucolic singing-contest (Theoc. *Id.* 8. 33 ff.), medicinal didactic (Nic. frs. 31–2 Gow–Scholfield, Eudemus in *Suppl. Hell.* 412A). This last application continued into the 1st cent. AD (Aglaias, Philon of Tarsus, Andromachus). Otherwise the elegiac metre rather fell out of favour under the empire except for epigrams. Gregory of Nazianzus made some use of it, and it appears in a 4th-cent. encomium of a Beirut professor (*PBerol.* 10558).   M. L. W.

elegiac poetry, Latin *Ennius introduced the elegiac couplet into Latin (Isid. 1. 39. 15); four epigrams, epitaphic in form, survive under his name (*var.* 15–24 Vahlen; 43–6 Courtney). Lucilius (bks. 22–5) used the metre for epitaphs and other short poems descriptive of slaves. An anecdote in Aulus Gellius (19. 9) offers an early glimpse of elegiac epigram on erotic themes, Hellenistic in flavour (Valerius Aedituus, Porcius Licinus, and Quintus Lutatius Catulus, *c.*150–100 BC); a Pompeian wall bears witness to the popular diffusion of such work in the second quarter of the 1st century BC (D. O. Ross Jr., *Style and Tradition in Catullus* (1969), 147–9). The careers of *Catullus and *Ovid bound the elegiac genre's most concentrated and distinctive period of Roman development. In particular, by early Augustan times elegy emerges as the medium for cycles of first-person ('subjective') poems describing the tribulations, mostly erotic, of a male poet who figuratively enslaves himself to a single (pseudonymous) mistress, distances himself from the duties associated with public life, and varies his urban *mise en scène* with escapist appeals to other worlds, mythological (*Propertius, Ovid) or rural (*Tibullus). 'Love-elegy', though the term is widely used by modern critics, was not for the Romans a formal poetic category. However a canonical sequence of Cornelius Gallus (as originator), Tibullus, Propertius, and Ovid is explicitly offered by Ovid (*Tr.* 4. 10. 53–4; cf. *Ars Am.* 3. 536–8); and Quintilian's later adoption of this same canon to represent Latin elegy at large arguably reflects the central role of Augustan 'love-elegy' in defining the genre. Among elegiac works by other hands in the *Corpus Tibullianum* especially noteworthy is the group associated with the female poet Sulpicia.

The question of Greek precedent for the format of Latin 'love-elegy' has long been disputed. Propertius repeatedly pairs *Callimachus and Philitas as literary models. The latter is among a number of late Classical and Hellenistic elegists who wrote extended poems in which (this is controversial) mythological narratives may have been framed or unified by 'subjective' discussion of the poet's own beloved (cf. esp. Antimachus, test. 7 Wyss, *POxy.* 3723); Catullus 68 has been adduced as a possible link to such a tradition. This search for origins remains inconclusive, and is further hampered by a lack of reliable knowledge concerning Gallus; the new fragment published in 1979 only adds to the uncertainty concerning the format and development of Gallan elegy. More accessible are continuities in Augustan 'love-elegy' with the erotic conceits of short Hellenistic epigram, and with the situations and characters of New Comedy. Most immediately important is the influence of Catullus' portrait of Lesbia as developed piecemeal in the elegiac epigrams, in 68, and in the polymetrics.

Even in the heyday of 'love-elegy', the associations of the genre were never exclusively amatory. *Versibus impariter iunctis querimonia primum,* | *post etiam inclusa est voti sententia compos*, 'Verses unequally joined framed lamentation first, then votive epigram': Horace's interest (*Ars P.* 75–6) in defining the genre in terms of its traditional origins finds some reflection in the practice of his own elegiac contemporaries (cf. Ovid's poem of mourning for Tibullus at *Am.* 3. 9. 3–4). With its stress upon separation and loss, and its morbid flights of fancy (especially in Propertius), Roman elegiac love may be implicated from the outset in funereal lament. The association with votive epigram is no less available for reclamation: allusions to fictional inscriptional contexts, funereal or otherwise dedicatory, abound in literary elegy. To some extent, as in Greek, the elegiac couplet is an all-purpose metre, save that its sphere of operation can often be defined negatively as 'not epic'. The paired contrasts between public and private, martial and peaceful, hard and soft, weighty and slight which dominate the aesthetic and moral vocabulary of late republican and early imperial poetry are associated above all with an opposition between *epic and elegy, deriving ultimately from Callimachus' *Aetia* prologue. Epic is constantly immanent within elegy as the term against which it defines itself— even in those long narrative elegies which come near to closing the gap between the two genres. Ovid's career as an elegist, from 'subjective' *Amores* to epistolary *Heroides*, didactic *Ars Amatoria*, aetiological *Fasti*, funereal *Tristia*, and vituperative *Ibis*, is the pre-eminent demonstration of the ability of a classical Roman genre to expand its range without losing its identity.

After Ovid the metre was used chiefly for epigrams and short occasional poems (many examples in *Anthologia Latina*). The use of elegy for epigram reached a peak in the work of *Martial, whose couplets can excel Ovid's in wit and technical virtuosity. The elegiac couplet is favoured by many late antique poets, including Ausonius and Claudian, but generally with no strong sense of linkage between metre and subject-matter.

Metre The elegiac hexameter differs little from the heroic. The special effects appropriate to epic were not often required in elegiac writing, and the general character of the line is smooth and fluent. Of five pentameters by Ennius which survive four end in disyllables, and it may be that this rhythm was the most satisfactory to the Roman ear: certainly, though the epigrammatists mentioned above, para. 1, and Catullus freely admitted words of from three to five syllables to the end of the line, following Greek practice, the disyllabic ending became the rule in Propertius' later poems and in Ovid (however, in *Her.* 16–21, the *Fasti*, and the poems of exile he reverts occasionally to the looser usage). After Catullus elision became both rarer and, when used, less harsh. These developments were undoubtedly dictated by artistic preferences, but Catullus' 'un-Augustan' usages must not be interpreted as evidence of technical incapacity: the occasionally harsh rhythms of e.g. poem 76 are part of the designed effect of the poem (cf. E. Harrison, *CR* 1943, 97 ff.; Ross, 115 ff.). From the very beginning the Latin couplet, unlike the Greek, tended to be self-contained: genuine enjambment between couplets is extremely rare. For modern Latin verse-writing, from the Renaissance onwards, the strict Ovidian form of the couplet has generally been the preferred model. It is above all ideally suited to pointed expression, conveyed through variation and antithesis: half-line responding to half-line, pentameter to hexameter, couplet to couplet.

E. J. K.; S. E. H.

elephants Although ivory was known to the prehistoric Greeks and is mentioned in *Homer, they first encountered war-elephants at the battle of Gaugamela in 331 BC. The ivory probably came originally from Africa, but the first war-elephants were Indian (*Elephas maximus*). Although not used by *Alexander the Great, war-elephants were used by his successors, particularly the *Seleucids and Ptolemies.

When the Seleucids gained control of the Indian sources, the Ptolemies managed to capture and train African 'forest' elephants (*Loxodonta africana cyclotis*), then found in the hinterland of the Red Sea. Smaller than Indian elephants, they are not to be confused with East African 'bush' elephants (*Loxodonta africana*), the latter being larger than the Indian and unknown to the ancients. The 'forest' elephant is now almost extinct, but until comparatively recently was still found in the Gambia. The main difference between the two types was that the Indian was large enough to carry a howdah containing one or more missile-armed soldiers in addition to the mahout, whereas the African carried a single mahout, and although he could carry javelins, the elephant itself was the main weapon. When the two types met at the battle of Raphia 217 BC, the Africans were defeated, but they were heavily outnumbered.

The Romans first encountered elephants when *Pyrrhus used Indians in his invasion of Italy, hence the term 'Lucanian cows'. Both at Heraclea in 280 BC and at A(u)sculum Satrianum in 279, they had considerable success, in the first routing the Roman cavalry—untrained

horses will not face elephants—in the second actually breaching the Roman infantry line after it had been driven back by Pyrrhus' phalanx.

By this time the Carthaginians were also using African elephants, drawn from the forests of the Atlas region. They fought against the Romans in the First Punic War (see ROME (HISTORY), §1.4 in Sicily and in the defeat of Marcus Atilius Regulus in Africa. Their appearance is clearly shown on Carthaginian coins minted in Spain. *Hannibal, famously, took elephants across the Alps in 218 BC. They helped win his first victory at the Trebia, but all save one died during the winter of 218/17. This carried Hannibal through the marshes of the Arno in 217, and may be the one called 'Surus', mentioned by *Cato the Elder (in Plin. *HN* 8. 5. 11). But although Hannibal received more in 215, and used them in an attempt to break the siege of Capua in 211, it was only at the battle of Zama that he used them again in quantity, and there *Scipio Africanus nullified their effectiveness by opening lanes through his ranks.

The Seleucids continued until their downfall to make use of elephants, but although the Romans also sometimes used them in war (e.g. at Cynoscephalae, Numantia, and Thapsus), they were mainly kept for the arena or ceremonial. During the empire there was an imperial herd in Latium. It is strange that they were never used as pack-animals or for road-building, as they were by the British army as late as the Second World War.

J. F. La.

Eleusis (see ◀Map 1, Cc▶), the most famous deme (local district: see DEMOCRACY, ATHENIAN) in Athens after Piraeus, on a land-locked bay with a rich plain, was a strong prehistoric settlement but merged with Athens sometime before the 7th cent. BC. Its hill (called Akris) and sanctuary were enclosed by fortification walls in the late 6th cent., and it became one of the three main fortresses for the defence of western Attica (with Panakton and Phyle). There was an important theatre of *Dionysus there, and the sanctuary of *Demeter and Kore (see PERSEPHONE) was the site of many festivals of local or national importance (Eleusinia, Thesmophoria, Proerosia, Haloa, Kalamaia), but the fame of Eleusis was due primarily to the annual festival of the *Mysteries, which attracted initiates from the entire Greek-speaking world. Within the sanctuary of the Two Goddesses the earliest building that may be identified as a temple is geometric. Its replacement by increasingly larger buildings (two in the Archaic period, two attempted but not completed in the 5th cent.), culminating in the square hall with rock-cut stands built under *Pericles, the largest public building of its time in Greece, bears eloquent witness to the ever increasing popularity of the cult. The unusual shape of this temple reflected its function as hall of initiation (usually called Anaktoron, sometimes Telesterion). Destroyed by the Costobocs in 170 AD, it was rebuilt under Marcus *Aurelius, who also brought to completion the splendid propylaea, a copy of the Propylaea on the Athenian Acropolis. In this he followed the initiative of *Hadrian, who was primarily responsible for the physical

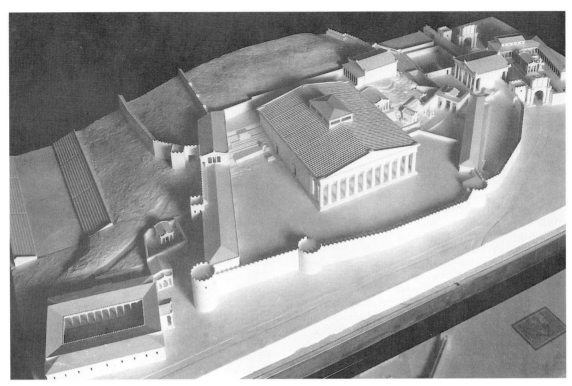

Eleusis Model showing the sanctuary of Eleusis following rebuilding in the later 2nd cent. AD. The hall of initiation dominates the complex. The monumental propylaea (gateway) to the right, rebuilt by Marcus *Aurelius, reflects the intense Roman interest in the cult.

renewal of the sanctuary in the 2nd cent. The sanctuary evidently ceased to exist after AD 395.   K. C.

Ennius, Quintus (239–169 BC), an immigrant of upper-class Messapian origin brought to Rome in 204 by *Cato the Elder (consul 195) and given the *citizenship in 184 by Quintus Fulvius Nobilior (consul 153). Cato found him serving in a Calabrian regiment of the Roman army in Sardinia. At Rome he made himself acceptable to the Cornelii, the Sulpicii, and the Caecilii as well as to the Fulvii. He lived in a modest house on the Aventine and taught Greek and Latin grammar to the young men of the great families. He composed plays for the public festivals down to the year of his death, although never, like Livius Andronicus, acting roles in them. He also composed a large amount of non-dramatic verse and at least one work in prose. Marcus Fulvius Nobilior took him on his staff to Aetolia in 189. Biographers noted a fondness for alcohol and declared him to have died of gout.

Three titles (*Caupunculus, Pancratiastes, Telestis* (?)) have the smell of the (Greek) New Comedy (see COMEDY (GREEK), NEW). To some of the twenty recorded tragic titles (*Achilles, Aiax, Alcmeo, Alexander, Andromacha, Andromeda, Athamas, Cresphontes, Erechtheus, Eumenides, Hectoris Lytra, Hecuba, Iphigenia, Medea, Melanippa, Nemea, Phoenix, Telamo, Telephus, Thyestes*) are attached fragments suffi-

ciently extensive to indicate that Ennius had a particular liking for *Euripides and that he translated his tragedies in the free manner Latin poets had been using for half a century. Compared with Euripides, he seems to us to have written rather grandly. To Cicero's contemporaries, comparing him with Pacuvius and Accius, he seems to have made his personages use the everyday language (*Orat.* 36). He also wrote a play in the tragic style on an incident of early Roman history (*Sabinae*) and another on Nobilior's deeds in Aetolia (*Ambracia*). The character of the *Scipio* is disputed.

A narrative poem in fifteen units on the history of the Roman people from the loss of Troy to the seizure of Ambracia and the triumphal return of the elder Nobilior was intended by Ennius to do better what *Naevius had attempted in his *Carmen belli Poenici*. Its title, the (*libri*) *Annales*, appropriated that of the record which the *pontifices* (see PRIESTS) kept in notoriously simple prose of religiously significant events. Instead of the ancient *Camenae*, Ennius invoked the *Musae* (*Muses), newly imported and given a home by Nobilior in a new temple on the Campus Martius. He represented himself as a reincarnation of Homer and replaced the Saturnian verse with a Latin version of the dactylic hexameter rather closer to the Homeric pattern than, say, the verses of the stage were to those of the Classical Athenian tragedians and comedians. The archaic vocabulary used by Livius and Naevius was pruned but some items survived, and many novelties appropriate to dactylic metrical patterns of an openly Greek origin were introduced. Books 1–3 took Ennius' story down to the expulsion of the last king and the foundation of the republic; 4–6 dealt with the reduction of Etruria and Samnium and the seeing off of the Epirote king *Pyrrhus; 7–9 with the driving of the Carthaginians back to North Africa and the incorporation within the Roman state of the old Greek cities of southern Italy and Sicily; 10–12 with the campaigns of the first decade of the 2nd cent. on the Greek mainland and in Spain; 12–15 with the defeats inflicted on Philip V of Macedon, *Antiochus III, and the Aetolian Confederacy. The poem emphasized the constant expansion of the Roman empire and the eclipse suffered by the Greek states which had sacked Troy and by their descendants. The gods of Olympus were made to support and assist the expansion. There was little on the other hand about the internal politics of the city of Rome. A number of Ennius' themes were foreign to the old Greek epic tradition. e.g. autobiography, literary polemic, grammatical erudition, and philosophical speculation.

Ennius added a further three books to the *Annales* in the last years of his life. These books featured the deeds of junior officers, rather than those of the generals, in the wars of the 180s and 170s against the Istrians, Ligurians, and other minor tribes.

Whereas it had been the custom to write epitaphs for leading men in Saturnian verses and even in senarii, Ennius composed pieces on *Scipio Africanus (d. 184) and on himself in a Latin version of the elegiac couplet. The notion that Scipio's soul may have been assumed into heaven went against conventional Roman doctrine on the after-life, as did the deification of Romulus narrated in the first or second book of the *Annales*.

The *Epicharmus* presented, in trochaic septenarii of the theatrical type, an account of the gods and the physical operations of the universe. The poet dreamed he had been transported after death to some place of heavenly enlightenment.

The *Euhemerus* presented a theological doctrine of a very different type in a kind of mock simple prose modelled on the Greek of the early Hellenistic writer Euhemerus of Messene and earlier theological writers. According to this doctrine the gods of Olympus were not supernatural powers still actively intervening in the affairs of men, but great generals, statesmen, and inventors of olden times commemorated after death in extraordinary ways. The relationship of such a view to what Ennius expounded in the *Annales*, the epigrams, and the *Epicharmus* can only be guessed at.

The *Hedyphagetica* must have seemed to move from yet another philosophical position. It took much of its substance from the gastronomical epic of Archestratus of Gela, a work commonly associated with Epicureanism. A reference to Ambracia suggests Ennius' own mature experience. The eleven extant hexameters have prosodical features avoided in the more serious *Annales*.

The *Sota* employed a metrical form associated with Sotades and probably presented similar themes in a similar tone.

The remains of six books of *Saturae* show a considerable variety of metres. There are signs that Ennius sometimes varied the metre within a single composition. A frequent theme was the social life of Ennius himself and his upper-class Roman friends and their intellectual conversation. Some scholars have detected the influence of *Callimachus' *Iambi*. The character of the *Protrepticus*/*Praecepta* is obscure.

Ennius stands out among Latin writers for the variety of the works he produced. Some of his tragedies were still performed in the theatre during the late republic. The *Annales* was carefully studied by *Cicero, *Lucretius, *Catullus, *Virgil, *Ovid, and *Lucan, and its text was still available in the Flavian period. Recitations were given during the time of *Hadrian. Copies had become rare by the 5th cent., but a reader of Orosius' *Histories* obtained access to one. Commentators on Virgil's *Aeneid* liked to point out borrowings from the older poem. Nonius Marcellus is the only late writer who can be shown to have read any of the tragedies. Apuleius was able to find in a library a copy of the *Hedyphagetica* and Lactantius one of the *Euhemerus*. See TRAGEDY, LATIN.

H. D. J.

Epaminondas (d. 362 BC), Theban general, famous for his victories at the battles of Leuctra and Mantinea. Of his early career little is known. He is said to have been a pupil of Lysis of Tarentum, and to have saved the life of Pelopidas at Mantinea, presumably during the Spartan siege in 385, but played a minor role in the liberation of Thebes in 379, and in the subsequent rebuilding of the Boeotian Confederacy. However, by 371 he was one of the boeotarchs (Boeotian federal officials), and, as such, represented Thebes at the peace conference in Sparta, walking out when the Spartan king Agesilaus refused to allow him to take the oath on behalf of the Boeotians as a whole.

Although all seven boeotarchs were at Leuctra, Epaminondas was clearly regarded as the architect of victory, and was re-elected for 370. Late in the year he went to the aid of the Arcadians, and was largely responsible for the crucial decision to press on with the invasion of the Spartan homeland—the first in historical times—and, above all, to free Messenia. In the summer of 369 he led a second invasion of the Peloponnese, which succeeded in further eroding Spartan influence, without quite matching previous triumphs. But his successes and, possibly, high-handed behaviour, aroused jealousy, and he was not re-elected boeotarch for 368, though legend has it that while serving as an ordinary hoplite (heavy infantryman) he was called upon to rescue the Boeotian army when it got into difficulties in *Thessaly. Re-elected for 367, his third invasion of the Peloponnese finally put an end to Sparta's 300-year-old Peloponnesian League. The removal of the fear of Sparta, however, aroused old antagonisms, and by 362

Thebes found herself fighting many of her erstwhile allies in alliance with Sparta. At the battle of Mantinea, Epaminondas was killed in the moment of victory.

Though an innovative tactician, Epaminondas' strategic and political sense may be questioned. His attempt to challenge Athenian supremacy at sea in 364 had little lasting effect, and some of his dealings in the Peloponnese were questionable. But his traditional nobility of character presumably reflects how he appeared to contemporaries, and he possibly lacked the ruthlessness necessary to impose Thebes' will on her quarrelsome allies, once they ceased to fear Sparta. He may honestly have wanted to create an alliance of independent states in which Thebes would be no more than first among equals.   J. F. La.

Ephesus (see ◀Map 1, Ec▶), city at the mouth of the river Caÿster on the west coast of *Asia Minor, which rivalled and finally displaced Miletus, and owing to the silting up of both harbours since antiquity has itself been displaced by Izmir (Smyrna) as the seaport of the Maeander valley. Ephesus was founded by Ionian colonists led by Androclus son of Codrus. It had little maritime activity before Hellenistic times, was oligarchic in temper, and open to indigenous influences. The city maintained itself against the Cimmerians and also Lydia until its capture by Croesus, who contributed to the construction of the great temple of Artemis. Under *Persia it shared the fortunes of the other coastal cities; it was a member of the *Delian League, but revolted c.412 BC and sided with Sparta. The Archaic Artemisium, burnt down in 356 BC, was rebuilt in the 4th cent. BC, the Ephesians refusing *Alexander the Great's offer to fund the cost (Strabo 14. 1. 22). The city was replanned by *Lysimachus, considered one of their city-founders by later Ephesians, and passed with the kingdom of Attalus III of *Pergamum to Rome in 133 BC. An enthusiastic supporter of *Mithradates VI (88–85 BC), it was deprived by Sulla of its free status. Under the Principate it eclipsed Pergamum as the economic and administrative hub of provincial *Asia. Seat of Roman officialdom and one of the province's *conventus* (assize) centres, it was also its chief centre for the (Roman) *ruler-cult and thrice *neōkoros* (having a temple to the Roman emperor) by the early 3rd cent. AD. Acts of the Apostles ch. 19 gives a vivid picture of the Artemisium's religious and economic importance for the Roman city. As seen today Ephesus is the product of the prosperous centuries of late antiquity, when it was the seat of the governor of Diocletian's reduced province of Asia and a metropolitan archbishopric. Among urban developments was the creation of the Arcadiane, a major colonnaded thoroughfare with street lighting, dominated by statues of the four evangelists. Several important Christian shrines include the tomb of St John, where Justinian built a major basilica, round which the Byzantine town grew after Arab attacks in the 7th cent. Ephesus again became an administrative centre in the 8th cent., and remained important until captured by the Turks in 1304.
                    W. M. C.; J. M. C.; C. R., A. J. S. S.

Ephorus, of Cyme (c.405–330 BC), a historian whose now lost work is of great importance because *Diodorus Siculus followed it extensively. In antiquity, he was thought to have been a student of *Isocrates; there are in fact clear echoes of Isocratean sentiments in the Ephoran parts of Diodorus, and some of the character assessments found in Diodorus are in the Isocratean style. His pro-Athenian bias might also have come from Isocrates.

The 30-book *History* avoided the mythological period—although it included individual myths—beginning with the Return of the Heraclidae and reaching the siege of Perinthus, in 340. His son, Demophilus, completed the work with an account of the Third Sacred War. His work was grand in scope and far longer than 5th-cent. histories. According to *Polybius, he was the first universal historian, combining a focus on Greek history with events in the barbarian east. Ephorus may have been the first historian to divide his work by books, and he provided each with a separate proem. Individual books were apparently devoted exclusively to a particular area (southern and central Greece, Macedonia, Sicily, Persia), but within each book events were sometimes retold episodically, sometimes synchronistically.

Ephorus drew on a diversity of sources, historical and literary, at times using good judgement (he preferred the Oxyrhynchus historian to *Xenophon), at other times making unfortunate choices (he coloured *Thucydides's account with material from 4th-cent. pamphleteers). Of special interest to Ephorus were migrations, the founding of cities, and family histories (see GENEALOGY).

The *History* was widely quoted in antiquity and was generally complimented for its accuracy (except in military descriptions). It was known to Polybius and was extensively used by *Strabo, Nicolaus of Damascus, Polyaenus, *Plutarch, and possibly Pompeius Trogus. But its greatest significance lies in the probability that Diodorus followed it closely for much of Archaic and practically all of Classical Greek history. In paraphrasing Ephorus, Diodorus supplies critical information, especially about 4th-cent. mainland history.

His other works include a history of Cyme, a treatise on style, and two books 'On Discoveries' which aimed at satisfying the demand for popular information on diverse topics characteristic of the period.   K. S. S.

epic The purely metrical ancient definition of epic, or *epos, epē* (lit. 'word', 'words'), as verse in successive hexameters includes such works as Hesiod's didactic poems and the philosophical poems of the Presocratics. In its narrower, and now usual, acceptance 'epic' refers to hexameter narrative poems on the deeds of gods, heroes, and men, a kind of poetry at the summit of the ancient hierarchy of genres. The cultural authority of epic throughout antiquity is inseparable from the name of *Homer, generally held to be the earliest and greatest of Greek poets; the *Iliad* and the *Odyssey* establish norms for the presentation of the heroes and their relation with the gods, and for the omniscience of the inspired epic narrator. According to Herodotus (2. 53), Homer and Hesiod established the names, functions, and forms of the Greek gods; a typical specimen of the biographical and critical idolatry of Homer in later antiquity is found in the pseudo-Plutarchan *On the Life and Poetry of Homer*.

Post-Cyclic Greek epics on mythical or legendary subjects included Panyassis' *Heraclea* (5th cent. BC) and Antimachus' *Thebais* (late 5th cent. BC); Antimachus' scholarly and self-conscious reworking of the epic traditions anticipated the Alexandrian scholar-poets such as *Apollonius Rhodius, the author of the surviving *Argonautica* (mid-3rd cent. BC). Historical epic began with Choerilus of Samos' *Persica* (late 5th cent. BC), and flourished in the panegyrical epics written to heroize the achievements of *Alexander the Great and his successors, as well as in nationalistic epics like Rhianus of Bene's *Messeniaca*; but such works did not enjoy a long life (fragments in *Suppl. Hell.*).

The history of epic in Rome begins with Livius Andronicus' translation in the native Saturnian verse of the *Odyssey* (3rd cent. BC). This was followed by *Naevius' historical epic in Saturnians, the *Bellum Poenicum*. The commemorative and panegyrical functions of epic particularly appealed to the Romans; for a century and a half the classic Roman epic was *Ennius' *Annals*, the hexameter narrative of Roman history (finished before 169 BC). Republican generals and statesmen had themselves commemorated in both Greek and Latin epics; *Cicero gives a portrait of a typical Greek epic panegyrist in his speech in defence of Aulus Licinius Archias, and himself composed autobiographical epics on his own successes. *Virgil revolutionized the genre by combining the legendary and the historical strands of epic in the *Aeneid*, which immediately established itself as the central classic of Roman literature. Later Latin epics, both legendary (*Ovid's *Metamorphoses*, *Statius' *Thebaid*, *Valerius Flaccus' *Argonautica*) and historical (*Lucan's *Bellum civile*, *Silius Italicus' *Punica*), are composed through a continuous dialogue with the *Aeneid*.

In later antiquity panegyrical (Claudian in Latin; for the Greek fragments see E. Heitsch (ed.) *Die griechischen Dichterfragmente der römischen Kaizerzeit: 1. Abh. der Akademie der Wissenschaften in Göttingen, ph.-hist. Kl. 3. Folge no. 49/1961 (²1963); II. no. 58/1964 1)* and mythological (Quintus Smyrnaeus, Nonnus) epic continued in abundance. Virgil and his Latin successors were the main models for the epics of the Latin Middle Ages and the Renaissance.   P. R. H.

Epicurus (b. *Samos, 341 BC; d. Athens, 270 BC), moral and natural philosopher. His father Neocles and mother Chaerestrate, Athenians of the deme (local district: see DEMOCRACY, ATHENIAN) Gargettus, emigrated to the Athenian cleruchy (citizen settlement) in Samos. As a boy he was taught by a Platonist, Pamphilus. He served as an ephebe (see GYMNASIUM) in Athens, when Xenocrates was head of the *Academy and *Aristotle was in Euboean

Chalcis; the playwright Menander was in the same class of the ephebate as Epicurus. He rejoined his family, who had then settled on the Asian mainland at Colophon. At this time or earlier he studied under Nausiphanes, from whom he learnt about the *atomist philosophy of Democritus. At 32 he moved to Mytilene in *Lesbos, then to Lampsacus on the Hellespont; at both places he set up a school and began to acquire pupils and loyal friends.

About 306/7 he bought a house in Athens, with a garden that became the eponymous headquarters of his school of philosophy. Apart from occasional visits to Asia Minor, he remained in Athens until his death in 270, when he bequeathed his garden and school to Hermarchus of Mytilene (his will survives, in Diog. Laert. 10, the main source for his biography).

The Epicurean school (The Garden). He and his followers lived together, secluding themselves from the affairs of the city and maintaining a modest and even austere standard of living, in accordance with the Master's teaching. They included slaves and women. Contemporary Epicureans mentioned in the literature were his most devoted companion, Metrodorus of Lampsacus, who died before Epicurus; Leontius and his wife Themista, also of Lampsacus; Hermarchus, his successor; and a slave called Mys.

The school was much libelled in antiquity and later, perhaps because of its determined privacy, and because of Epicurus' professed hedonism. The qualifications that brought this hedonism close to asceticism were ignored, and members of rival schools accused the Epicureans of many kinds of profligacy. In Christian times, Epicureanism was anathema because it taught that man is mortal, that the cosmos is the result of accident, that there is no providential god, and that the criterion of the good life is pleasure. Hence such caricatures as Sir Epicure Mammon, in Ben Jonson's *Alchemist*, and the modern use of the word 'epicure'.

Writings Diog. Laert. 10. 26 reports that Epicurus wrote more than any of the other philosophers—about 300 rolls. Most of these are now lost. Fragments of his 37 books *On Nature* survive in the volcanic ash at *Herculaneum, and efforts to restore and interpret them, begun around 1800, are now in progress with renewed vigour. The following three letters and two collections of maxims have been preserved intact, the first four all in Diog. Laert. 10: (1) Letter to Herodotus (*Hdt.*): a summary of his philosophy of nature; (2) Letter to Pythocles (*Pyth.*): a summary of astronomy and meteorology; (3) Letter to Menoeceus (*Men.*): a less technical summary of Epicurean morality; (4) *Kyriai doxai* (*KD*), *Ratae sententiae*, or *Principal Doctrines*: 40 moral maxims; (5) *Sent. Vat.* (*VS*): 81 similar short sayings identified in a Vatican manuscript by C. Wotke in 1888.

Present-day knowledge and appreciation of Epicurean philosophy depends very largely on the great Latin epic poem of his later follower, *Lucretius' *De rerum natura*.

Epicurus Part of a massive inscription in which a local philosopher, Diogenes of Oenoanda in SW *Asia Minor, presented basic doctrines of Epicureanism to his fellow-citizens, probably in the 2nd cent. AD. The text is evidence for the continuing appeal of Epicurus into the Christian era.

Doctrines The purpose of philosophy is practical: to secure a happy life. Hence moral philosophy is the most important branch, and physics and epistemology are subsidiary. (For this tripartition, see Sext. Emp. *Math.* 11. 169, and for the comparative evaluation *KD* 11 and Diog. Laert. 10. 30).

1. Epistemology

The main sources are *Hdt.*, Lucr. 4, and critical comments in Sext. Emp. *Math.* Epicurus held that sense perception is the origin of knowledge, and defended its reliability with a physical account of it. Physical objects, being made of atoms, give off from their surface thin films of atoms, called *eidōla*, which retain the shape and some other characteristics of their parent body and implant its appearance on the sense organs of the perceiver. This appearance is somehow transmitted to the soul-atoms which constitute the mind. The appearance itself is never false: falsehood occurs only in the opinion (*doxa*) the mind forms about it. If appearances conflict, a closer look or a sound argument or experience of the context may serve to 'counter-witness' all but one consistent set of opinions: in some cases (especially in astronomy, where no closer look is possible) we must accept that all beliefs not counter-witnessed are somehow true.

Epicurus was apparently not able to articulate an explanation of concept-formation and theorizing by minds made of atoms and void. The extant texts show frequent use of analogical reasoning, from phenomena to theoretical entities.

2. Physics

Epicurus adopted the atomist theories (see ATOMISM) of Democritus, with some changes that can often be seen as attempts to answer Aristotle's criticisms.

The original atomist theory was a response to the Eleatic school of Parmenides, Zeno of Elea, and Melissus. Arguments about Being and Not-being show that there must be permanent elements—atoms of matter. Arguments about divisibility show that there must be indivisibles—construed by Epicurus as inseparable parts of atoms. The observed fact of motion proves that there must be empty space in which atoms can move.

Change is explained as the rearrangement of unchangeable atoms. The universe is infinite, both in the number of atoms and in the extent of space. Our cosmos, bounded by the region of the heavenly bodies, came into being through random collisions of suitable atoms, and it will some day dissolve again into its component atoms. It is one of an indefinite number of cosmoi, past, present, and future.

Atoms move naturally downwards at constant and equal speed because of their weight, unless they collide with others. But they would never collide unless some of them sometimes swerved from the straight downward path. (This postulate, which also accounts for the self-motions of animals (see below), is not mentioned in any surviving text of Epicurus, but is set out at some length by Lucretius, 2. 62–332, mentioned by other classical writers, and generally agreed to have been advanced by Epicurus himself.)

Gods exist, atomic compounds like everything else, but take no thought for this cosmos or any other, living an ideal life of eternal, undisturbed happiness—the Epicurean ideal. It is good for men to respect and admire them, without expecting favours or punishments from them.

Both creation, as in *Plato's *Timaeus*, and the eternity of the cosmic order, as in *Aristotle's world picture, are rejected: natural movements of atoms are enough to explain the origin and growth of everything in the world. A theory of the survival of the fittest explains the apparently purposeful structure of living things.

Epicurus was a thoroughgoing physicalist in his philosophy of mind. The soul is composed of atoms, all extremely small but distinguished by shape into four kinds: fire, air, and breath (but all somehow different from their ordinary namesakes), and a fourth, unnamed kind. At death the component atoms are dispersed.

The swerve of atoms somehow accounts for the possibility of actions performed by choice, by humans and some other animals: without the swerve, apparently, all actions would be as fully determined as the fall of a stone dropped from a height. How this works is a matter of continuing controversy.

3. Moral philosophy

'We say that pleasure is the beginning and end of living happily' (*Men.* 128). It is a datum of experience that pleasure is naturally and congenitally the object of human life. Since it is a fact, however, that some pleasures are temporary and partial, and involve pain as well, it is necessary to distinguish between pleasures, and to take only those which are not outweighed by pains. Pain is caused by unsatisfied desire; so one must recognize that those desires that are natural and necessary are easily satisfied; others are unnecessary. The limit of pleasure is the removal of pain; to seek always for more pleasure is simply to spoil one's present pleasure with the pain of unsatisfied desire. Pleasure is not so much the process of satisfying desires (*kinetic* pleasure) but rather the state of having desires satisfied (*katastematic* pleasure).

Pleasure of the *soul, consisting mainly of contemplation or expectation of bodily pleasure, is more valuable than bodily pleasure. The ideal is *ataraxia*, freedom from disturbance. The study of philosophy is the best way to achieve the ideal. By teaching that the soul, made of atoms as the body is, dies with the body, it persuades us that after death there is no feeling: what happens after our death, like what happened before our birth, is 'nothing to us'. By teaching that the gods do not interfere and that the physical world is explained by natural causes, it frees us from the fear of the supernatural. By teaching that the competitive life is to be avoided, it removes the distress of jealousy and failure; by teaching one how to avoid intense emotional commitments, it frees us from the pain of emotional turmoil. (The main sources are Epicurus *Men.*, *KD*, and *VS*, and Lucretius 3 and 4.)

Epicurean moral philosophy thus finds room for most of the conventional Greek virtues of the soul; its main difficulty is to justify the virtues that are concerned with the well-being of other people—especially justice. Those who are wise will avoid injustice, Epicurus argues, because one can never be certain of remaining undetected. But Epicurean morality was less selfish than such statements made it appear. The Epicurean communities were famous even among their enemies for the friendship which bound members to each other and to the founder.   D. J. F.

epigram, Greek

Archaic An epigram was originally nothing more than an inscription on an object or monument to say whose it is or who made it, who dedicated it to which god, or who is buried beneath it. The earliest known are in hexameters (*CEG* 1. 432 and 454, the Dipylon oenochoe and Pithecusae scyphus, both *c*.720 BC), but by *c*.500 they were predominantly in what was to be the classic metre of epigram, the elegiac couplet. The earliest consist largely of formulae (e.g. τύμβος ὅδ᾽ ἐστί, στῆθι καὶ οἴκτιρον, ... ἐπέθηκε θανόντι, ... μ᾽ ἀνέθηκε 'this is tomb (of so-and-so), stand and take pity ... (so-and-so) set up (this) for the deceased ... (so-and-so) dedicated me') plus the appropriate proper names in stereotyped epicizing phraseology. The material in Peek, *GVI* 1 (limited to epitaphs) is arranged by such formulae.

Classical Epigrams written for monuments are normally anonymous; the earliest signed by the author date from *c*.350 (*CEG* 2. 819, 888. ii). The first poet credited with writing epigrams is *Simonides, though only one of the many ascribed to him (Page, *FGE* 119–23, 186–302) can be accepted, the simple and dignified epitaph on the seer Megistias (Hdt. 7. 228; *FGE* 195–6). Many others are attributed in Hellenistic and later times to famous poets (Page, *FGE*), but even if authentic present generic problems. For example, the couplet πολλὰ πιὼν καὶ πολλὰ φαγὼν καὶ πολλὰ κακ᾽ εἰπών | ἀνθρώπους κεῖμαι Τιμοκρέων Ῥόδιος 'I, Timocreon the Rhodian, lie here after drinking and eating a lot and uttering a lot of abuse' (*FGE* 252) is certainly a 5th-cent. parody of funerary epigram, but at the time it would have been called a scolium and sung at the *symposium. It is hard to believe *Euripides wrote the undistinguished distich that *Plutarch read on a monument to the Athenians who died in Sicily (*FGE* 155–6), but there seems no reason to doubt *Aristotle's authorship of the epigram on a statue of his friend Hermias at Delphi (*FGE* 31–2). On the other hand, the love epigrams attributed to *Plato are 'plainly Alexandrian in tone, contents and style' (Page, *FGE* 125–7). Down to *c*.400 BC study of the epigram is in effect limited to anonyma: P. Friedländer and H. Hoffleit, *Epigrammata* (1948) remains a useful companion to *CEG* 1–2.

Hellenistic With the 3rd cent. we find an enormous expansion of non-inscriptional epigram. Reitzenstein distinguished two schools: the Dorian-Peloponnesian and Ionian-Alexandrian. The first represents a natural development from inscriptional poetry: literary embellishments of epitaphs and dedications. Fictitious dedications were a neat way to treat the lives of humble folk rather than kings and generals, through the different objects vowed by rustics, hunters, and fishermen—or even hetairai. Anyte of Tegea wrote on women and children and pastoral themes, epitaphs on animals rather than humans. Leonidas of Tarentum was the most influential writer of this school, influential too in establishing an ornate style and dithyrambic vocabulary as its medium. Asclepiades and *Callimachus wrote about wine, women, boys, and song, renewing the themes of Classical sympotic elegy and lyric, though they were selective in the motifs they treated, investing them with that combination of allusiveness, conciseness, and wit that were ever after to be the hallmarks of the genre (Giangrande, in *L'Épigramme grecque*, Entretiens Hardt (1968)). The simple exchange between passer-by and tomb we find in Classical epitaphs is expanded into witty dialogue under the influence of mime. The epitaph is developed into poems on those long as well as recently dead, and epigrams on writers are especially common (M. Gabathuler, *Hell. Ep. auf Dichter*, 1937). The dedication also evolved into the *ekphrasis on a work of art, another form with a long future. In addition to more conventional themes, Alcaeus of Messene wrote political lampoons. Poets would vie with each other in treating the same themes.

Early Hellenistic epigrams were often quite long and in metres other than elegiacs. Most of the major poets published books of *epigrammata*. The first known to consist entirely of elegiacs (on the evidence of the Milan roll) is Posidippus. It has sometimes been argued that epigrams were now 'book-poetry', but they continued to be written for their original function as well as for the symposium. Callimachus and Posidippus in particular wrote a number of epigrams for Alexandrian monuments. Hellenistic epigrams on victors in the games became less factual and more literary, characterized by mythological allusion and motifs from Classical epinicion (J. Ebert, *Epp. auf Sieger* (1972), 19–22, 191–2, 205–8). The Milan roll has revealed that Posidippus wrote almost twenty epigrams on equestrian victors.

Graeco-Roman Epigrammatists of the late republic and early empire, most now writing for Roman patrons, represent a striking change of direction, away from the erotic and sympotic (with the exception of Philodemus and Marcus Argentarius) to the ecphrastic (i.e. involving extended and detailed descriptions of real or imagined objects) and epideictic: jokes, paradoxa, witty anecdotes, invitations to dinner, epigrams to accompany presents or congratulate on birthdays or the cutting of a son's first beard. The late 1st cent. AD saw the development of the satiric epigram, best represented by the Neronian Lucillius: attacks on the faults, not of individuals, but of entire classes and professions (doctors, athletes, thin men). There was also a short-lived revival of the erotic with Rufinus (under Nero) and the pederastic with Straton (under Hadrian).

Not the least interesting development of the 3rd and 4th cent. is the re-emergence of the anonymous inscriptional epigram. Honorific inscriptions that in the early empire would have been in prose are increasingly in verse, often verse of some distinction and elegance. There is unfortunately no modern corpus, but many are quoted and discussed in L. Robert's *Épigrammes du Bas-Empire* (1948).

Byzantine Towards the end of the 4th cent. the Alexandrian schoolmaster Palladas wrote satiric epigrams with a difference, powerful, pessimistic tirades against his profession, and rueful laments on the impotence of a declining paganism. At the same time Gregory of Nazianzus (*Anth. Pal.* bk. 8) was writing epigram after epigram on his family (12 on his father, 52 on his mother), conventional in every respect (vocabulary, imagery, variation, point) except their Christianity and their disregard of Classical prosody. The age of Justinian saw a remarkable renaissance of the classicizing epigram. Agathias, Paul the Silentiary, Macedonius the consul, Julian the Egyptian, and many other professional men and civil servants returned to Hellenistic models, writing erotic, sympotic and dedicatory poems in a remarkably homogeneous style, a fusion of the traditional conventions and motifs with the bombast and metrical refinement of Nonnus. Their literary paganism is so thoroughgoing that we are astonished by the occasional use of the same style and vocabulary to describe a Christian icon (R. C. McCail, *Byzantion* 1971, 205–67). This was the end of creative writing in the genre.

A. D. E. C.

equites

Origins and republic The early history of the cavalry at Rome is overlaid with legend and speculation. The kings are said to have enrolled 300 *celeres* or *trossuli* (later doubled) for the legion. They wore loincloths, tunics with the *clavus* (stripe), *trabeae* (short embroidered cloaks), and *mullei* (strapped red shoes); they were armed with lances and their horses were adorned with *phalerae* (silver disks). Their insignia, in various adapted forms, later became the distinctive attire of patricians, magistrates, and senators. Twelve hundred *equites* were allegedly added by Servius *Tullius. These 1,800 had their horses supplied and maintained by the state (hence *equites equo publico*), out of the property taxes paid by widows and orphans. They had to serve ten campaigns. In the centuriate assembly they formed eighteen *centuriae*, later including (it seems) those too old for service. This voting privilege survived in essence as long as the assembly. In the classical republic these *equites* were enrolled by the censors, after financial, physical, and moral scrutiny (*recognitio*). At least since 304 BC, though rarely in the late republic, they paraded to the Capitol in the *transvectio* on 15 July. Men of aristocratic birth always had preference for enrolment.

About 400 BC, men on their own horses (*equites equo privato*) were added to the cavalry. They did not share the voting privilege, but were given at least some of the status marks, of the others. In the 3rd cent. Roman cavalry proved increasingly ineffective in war and by 200 was largely replaced by *auxilia*. But *equites* retained their social eminence and became a corps from which officers and the staffs of governors and commanders were drawn. This new 'equestrian' service was within the reach of any wealthy and well-connected family and the old exclusiveness was undermined. In 129 senators (but not their non-senatorial relatives) were excluded from the equestrian centuries (Cic. *Rep.* 4. 2). Whatever the motive, this marks the beginnings of the later *ordo equester* as a distinct body. Gaius *Gracchus excluded senators from service on the *repetundae* (extortion) court. Although the positive qualifications for service are largely lost, various considerations, especially the need to exclude senators (*FIRA* 7 ll. 13 and 16), make it certain that the jurors were not defined as registered *equites equo publico*, i.e. the qualification must have been by wealth. The law on the Asian taxes is therefore also unlikely to have defined bidders as belonging to that class. Gracchus' prescription was followed in other *quaestiones* (tribunals), permanent or special; as a result, the composition of juries became, for a generation (106–70), an object of bitter contention between the senatorial and the equestrian *ordo*, firmly establishing their distinctness.

Another result was the transformation of the *ordo* itself. Pliny (*HN* 33. 34) derives the later *ordo equester* from the Gracchan jurors, and what evidence we have supports him. The wealthy *publicani* gradually became the dominant element on juries and within the *ordo*: Cicero could rhetorically identify them with it. The 'public horse' and the annual parade are nowhere mentioned in our ample record of the age of Cicero, except for one political demonstration by *Pompey in 70. Between 70 and at least 50, there were no censorships culminating in a *lustrum*, so the list of strictly defined *equites* could not be kept up. By 50 (even), the influx of Italians, to whose leading men the jury courts had been opened since 70, made a return to the old restriction politically impossible. The law of Lucius Roscius Otho allocating special rows of seats to *equites* probably confirmed the definition by wealth: we cannot be certain, but Cicero (quoted by Asc. p. 78 C) links it with the judiciary law of Lucius Aurelius Cotta, which certainly did. The attested objection of the *plebs* was no doubt precisely to that definition: the Roman *plebs* never objected to traditional status distinctions.

The new *ordo* was a disparate body. Round an aristocratic Roman core (men like *Atticus) were grouped leading men from colonies and *municipia*, *publicani*, and even *negotiatores* (businessmen)—many of similar background, but some self-made men. Free birth and a landed interest were prerequisites for social recognition (cf. Cic. *Off.* 1. 51). Senators and *equites* in the late republic, thus formed a plutocracy sharing both landed and business interests, in a continuous range of proportions.

In social standing, *equites* were almost equal to senators, freely intermarrying even with patrician nobles and gaining entry to the senate (though not the consulate) if they wanted it (see Cic. *Sest.* 97). But as a class they preferred the pursuit of money and pleasure to political responsibility, and they thus formed the non-political section of the upper class rather than (as in the empire) an intermediate class. Their history is an important part of that of the late republic, particularly in view of their control of the *quaestiones* during most of that time. Various *populares* tried to mould them into a political force opposed to the senate and the *nobilitas*; but their social and economic interests, especially after the enfranchisement of Italy, were basically too similar to permit this. *Sulla, after decimating them in the proscriptions, followed the example of Marcus Livius Drusus the Younger and

deprived them of leadership by adlecting the most prominent survivors to the senate, and of power by taking the courts from them. But strengthened by the influx of Italians and by increasing financial power, wooed by Pompey, and largely restored to the courts by the law of Cotta, they rose to unprecedented influence in the 60s, when Cicero and the senate—aware of the basic community of interests of the two classes—tried to unite them behind the *principes* in a *concordia ordinum*. Yet, though often united on a single issue (e.g. against threats to financial stability by demagogues or threats to freedom of profiteering by statesmen), sometimes even for a lengthy period, they were too disparate in composition and too non-political to form a stable grouping. Preventing necessary reform (especially in the provinces), they remained a disruptive and irresponsible element with no programme or allegiance, until the Civil War substituted military for economic power. Caesar deprived them of the Asian tithe, but opened a new avenue for them by making prominent *equites* like Gaius Oppius and Lucius Cornelius Balbus—a splendid example of a non-traditional *eques*—his political and financial agents. The support of these men, as well as the precedent, proved important to Augustus.   E. B.

Imperial period Under the emperors the *equites* constituted a second aristocratic order which ranked only below the senatorial order in status. *Equites* in the wider sense (see below) provided the officer corps of the Roman army and held a wide range of posts in the civil administration (see PROCURATOR) as it developed from its limited beginnings under *Augustus.

The precise criteria for membership of the order remain disputed. On a wider definition, which will be accepted here, all Roman citizens of free birth who possessed the minimum census qualification of 400,000 sesterces automatically qualified as members of the order. Thus when *Pliny the Younger (*Ep.* 1. 19) offered a friend from Comum a gift of 300,000 sesterces 'to make up the wealth required of an *eques*', he implies that this gift of itself would be sufficient to make his friend an *eques*. However, it remains possible that these were necessary but not sufficient criteria and that, in addition, some formal act of authorization, perhaps even the grant of the public horse (see below), by the emperor was necessary.

The equestrian order, widely defined, was much more numerous than the senatorial order and socially and politically (in terms of the range of its public roles) more heterogeneous. Although the total number of *equites* at any time cannot be determined, already under Augustus they were relatively numerous. Strabo records that recent censuses had revealed 500 men of equestrian census at both Gades and Patavium (Strabo 169, 213C). During the course of the first two centuries the possession of equestrian rank spread widely through the provinces. This diffusion mirrored the extension of Roman *citizenship. From the beginning of the Principate Baetica and Narbonensis are well represented, in the 1st cent. AD and after Africa and the

Greek east. Far fewer *equites* are attested in the Danubian provinces, Germany, Gaul, and Britain. The vast majority of the order came to be constituted by the landed gentry of the municipalities of Italy and of the cities of the most urbanized provinces. Although these men were eligible to take up the military and civilian posts reserved for *equites*, the majority of them continued rather to play a local political role as senior local magistrates and councillors or as high priests of the imperial cult.

Within the order three specific subsets of unequal importance can be identified, namely the holders of the public horse (*equus publicus*), the jurors at Rome, and the military and civilian office-holders. The re-emergence of the category of *equites equo publico* under Augustus formed part of his traditionalist social policies. He restored the long disused parade (*transvectio*) of July 15, while allowing men handicapped by age or ill health to parade on foot, and those over 35 to have the choice of retaining or giving up the (notional) *equus publicus*; the occasion was also combined with an examination by Augustus of the physical and moral fitness of these *equites*. On one occasion more than 5,000 men are recorded as taking part in this ceremony (Dion. Hal. *Ant. Rom.* 6. 13). This subset of *equites* formed a distinct corporation which might dedicate statues or play a role in the funeral of an emperor. The grant of this status was at the discretion of the emperor who could also withdraw it.

Augustus also established four boards (*decuriae*) of jurors (*iudices*), each of 1,000 men, who were of equestrian rank but, according to *Pliny the Elder (*HN* 33. 30–3), were not as such called *equites* until AD 23. Owing to the pressure for places Gaius added a fifth *decuria*. Like the public horse the status of juror was solely in the gift of the emperor. For example a Q. Voltedius Optatus Aurelianus, from Carthage, was granted the public horse by *Trajan and entry to the *decuriae* by *Hadrian; another local notable from Africa received both statuses from *Antoninus Pius (*ILS* 9406–7). Both statuses, as dignities conferred by the emperors, came to some extent to be honorific privileges which did not necessarily involve the expectation of the exercise of actual duties at Rome. Both statuses cease to be attested after the first part of the 3rd cent.

Within the political system of the Principate the most significant, if a minority, subset of equestrians was constituted by those who served as equestrian officers in the army and as senior civil administrators. Each year there were about 360 posts available for senior officers of equestrian rank: prefectures of cohorts, military tribunates, and prefectures of cavalry units. A minority of these officers were not typical equestrian landed gentry but instead ranking soldiers who had attained the rank of senior centurion (*primipilus*) in a legion and thereby acquired equestrian status. Tenure of these officer-posts was normally the necessary precursor for advancement to the senior civil administrative posts, reserved for *equites*, though from the early 2nd cent. tenure of the post of *advocatus fisci* became an alternative precursor. In the provinces emperors appointed *equites* as procurators who had prime responsibility for fiscal administration; at Rome from the reign of Augustus key posts, such as the praetorian prefecture or the prefecture of the corn supply, were reserved for equestrians. From the late 1st cent. the posts of the palatine officials, for example, control of the imperial correspondence, were transferred from freedmen to equestrians. Senior equestrian administrators formed with senior senators the political élite of the empire. They intermingled socially with senators; they married into senatorial families; like senators they could be summoned to serve on the emperor's *consilium* (emperor's body of advisers). Sons of leading equestrian officials were the prime source of recruitment of new senatorial families. On occasion, especially under *Vespasian and Marcus *Aurelius, senior equestrians might be adlected by the emperor into the senate.

From the latter part of the 2nd cent. equestrian officials began to acquire regular appellations of rank—*vir eminentissimus* ('most renowned') for the praetorian prefects, *vir perfectissimus* ('most accomplished') for the other prefects and higher procurators, *vir egregius* ('excellent') for the rest. In the course of the 3rd-cent. crisis equestrian officers, often men who had risen to equestrian status via the chief centurionate, began to replace senators as army commanders and provincial governors. This process culminated in the reforms of *Diocletian under whom the higher military posts and almost all administrative posts passed into the hands of *equites*. During the first half of the 4th cent. repeated attempts were made to confine equestrian rank to office-holders and to exclude *curiales* (town councillors). In the same period the title *perfectissimus* (*egregius* disappears under *Constantine I) was extended downwards to officials of minor rank, eventually being awarded in three grades. By the end of the century this process had been overtaken by a similar diffusion of senatorial honours among officials, and at this point the equestrian order ceases to be a recognizable element in the Roman state.

F. G. B. M.; G. P. B.

Eratosthenes, of *Cyrene (*c*.285–194 BC), pupil of *Callimachus and Lysanias of Cyrene. After spending several years at Athens, where he came under the influence of Arcesilaus and Ariston of Chios, he accepted the invitation of Ptolemy III Euergetes to become royal tutor and to succeed *Apollonius of Rhodes as head of the Alexandrian Library. He thus became a member of the Cyrenaean intelligentsia in Alexandria, of which the central figure was Callimachus. His versatility was renowned and criticized, and the eventual Alexandrian verdict was to describe him as *bēta*, 'B-class' (that is to say, not 'second rate' but 'next after the best specialist in each subject'), and *pentathlos*, an 'all-rounder'. Others, more kindly, called him 'a second Plato' (see PLATO). In more than one field, however, and particularly in chronology and mathematical and descriptive *geography, of which, thanks to *Strabo, we know most, his work long retained much of its authority.

Works (almost entirely lost in direct quotation).

1. Literary criticism. Eratosthenes evidently attached considerable importance to his researches in this field, for we are told by *Suetonius that he was the first scholar to call himself by the proud title of *philologos*. His most important work seems to have been the treatise *On Ancient Comedy*, in at least twelve books; this dealt with literary, lexical, historical, and antiquarian matters, and problems of the authorship and production of plays.

2. Chronology. His *Chronographiai* represented the first scientific attempt to fix the dates of political and literary history. He also compiled a list of Olympian victors. In this field his most significant achievement (later abandoned) was to replace a partly mythical pre-historic chronology by one based on supposedly assured data (the fall of *Troy).

3. Mathematics. He investigated a wide range of mathematical and geometrical problems and was accepted as an equal by Archimedes, who addressed his *Methodus* to him, after the death of his earlier disciple Conon of *Samos. In his *Platonicus* (perhaps a dialogue) he apparently discussed mathematical definitions and the principles of music. Among his geometrical works were the *On Geometrical Means* and *On the Duplication of the Cube*. The latter included his poem on that well-worn theme, addressed to Ptolemy III. In his *On the Measurement of the Earth* (probably a preliminary work to his *Geographica*) he treated mathematical geography, calculating with a higher degree of accuracy than his predecessors the circumference of the earth. He was the first systematic geographer, and the *Geographica* (three books) dealt with mathematical, physical, and ethnographical geography, being based on a division of continents on a geometrical basis into 'seals' (*sphragīdes*), a term perhaps borrowed from contemporary Ptolemaic terminology of land-measurement. The work opened with a sketch of the history of the subject, with especial reference to the Homeric poems, and this, along with the mathematically more exact work of Hipparchus, formed the main source of Strabo's theoretical geography in books 1–2. For the Asiatic section his work was based to a considerable extent on the data provided by the bematists (surveyors) of *Alexander the Great and the early *Seleucids.

4. Philosophy. His works in this field, the *Platonicus*, mentioned above, and the *Ariston* (named after the Chian philosopher Ariston whom Eratosthenes had heard with some scepticism in Athens) were severely criticized by Strabo for their dilettanteism, but we know virtually nothing of their contents, and Strabo, as a good Stoic, was nettled by Eratosthenes' disenchantment with his Stoic teachers. (See STOICISM.) Archimedes, in sending to Eratosthenes the text of his *Methodus*, called him 'a leader of philosophy' ($\phi\iota\lambda o\sigma o\phi\acute{\iota}\alpha\varsigma$ $\pi\rho o\epsilon\sigma\tau\acute{\omega}\varsigma$), and there is no reason to regard this as polite condescension. It seems likely that these philosophical writings belong to the pre-Alexandrian phase of Eratosthenes' career.

5. Poetry. As a poet Eratosthenes for the most part eludes us, though his 'Alexandrian' characteristics are evident in theme and occasional quotation. His statement that the aim of poetry is to entertain, not to instruct, reflects a coherent *ars poetica*. His short epic *Hermes* described the birth of the god *Hermes, his youthful exploits, and his ascent to the planets. The short epic *Anterinys* or *Hesiod* dealt with the death of *Hesiod and the punishment of his murderers. [Longinus] (*Subl.* 33. 5) praises the elegy *Erigone*, which told the myth of Icarius and his daughter, as 'a faultless little poem' ($\delta\iota\grave{\alpha}$ $\pi\acute{\alpha}\nu\tau\omega\nu$ $\mathring{\alpha}\mu\acute{\omega}\mu\eta\tau o\nu$ $\pi o\iota\eta\mu\acute{\alpha}\tau\iota o\nu$). These, however, have vanished, and the longest surviving fragments of his versatile muse are the delightful poem on the Duplication of the Cube (see above), and the short piece on the youth of Hermes.

Eratosthenes' intellectual calibre is seen both in chance utterances which reveal him as a man of insight and conviction (perhaps also of prejudice) and also in an occasional glimpse of a wide moral and political comprehension, notably in his comment in his *Geographica* (Strab. 66) that Greek and 'barbarian' (the Indians and the Arians, the Romans and the Carthaginians, 'with their wonderful political systems') should be judged by the unique criterion of morality and not of race (see BARBARIAN). His candour and independence of judgement may go some way towards explaining that, although the names of some of his direct pupils are known, he seems to have established no lasting following associated with his name; we hear of no 'Eratostheneioi', as there were 'Callimacheioi', 'Aristarcheioi', and others. See GEOGRAPHY; MAPS.   P. M. F.

Eros, god of love. Eros personified does not occur in Homer, but the Homeric passages in which the word *erōs* is used give a clear idea of the original significance. It is the violent physical desire that drives Paris to Helen, Zeus to Hera, and shakes the limbs of the suitors of Penelope (*Il.* 3. 442, 14. 294; *Od.* 18. 212). A more refined conception of this Eros who affects mind and body appears in the Archaic lyric poets. Because his power brings peril he is cunning, unmanageable, cruel (Alcman 36; Ibycus 6; Sappho 136; Thgn. 1231); in *Anacreon he smites the lovestruck one with an axe or a whip. He comes suddenly like a wind and shakes his victims (Sappho, Ibycus). Eros is playful, but plays with frenzies and confusion. He symbolizes all attractions which provoke love. He is young and beautiful, he walks over flowers, and the roses are 'a plant of Eros' of which he makes his crown (*Anacreonta* 53. 42). He is sweet and warms the heart (Alcman 101).

With Himeros ('Desire') and Pothos ('Longing'), Eros is a constant companion of *Aphrodite, although he can appear with any god, whenever a love story is involved. Hesiod seems to have transformed the Homeric conception of Eros. Although he describes Eros in terms almost identical with Homer as the god who 'loosens the limbs and damages the mind', he also makes him, together with Earth and Tartarus, the oldest of all gods, all-powerful over gods and men. With Eros as a cosmic principle, Parmenides found a place for him, perhaps as the power which leads contrasts together. This philosophic conception contributed to the Epicurean picture of omnipotent Eros (Ath. 13. 561), took abstruse mythological shape in Orphic cosmogonies (Ar. *Av.* 696) (see ORPHEUS), and formed the background for Plato's discussions of Eros in *Symposium* and *Phaedrus*.

Hellenistic poets continue the more playful conception of Anacreon, the tricks Eros plays on mortals, the tribulations of those who try to resist him, and the punishments he receives for his misdeeds. His bow and arrows, first mentioned by Euripides (*IA* 548–9), play a great part in these accounts. Frequently a plurality of Erotes is introduced (*Anacreonta*; *Anth. Pal.*; Ap. Rhod. 3. 452, 687, 765, 937) because both love and the god who symbolized it could multiply.

Eros had some ancient cults and much individual worship. He was always the god of love directed towards male as well as female beauty. Hence his images in the gymnasia, his cult among the Sacred Band in Thebes (Ath. 13. 561f, 602a), and the altar in Athens erected by the tyrant Hippias' lover (Ath. 13. 609d). As a god of fertility Eros is celebrated in the very old cult in Thespiae (Paus. 9. 27. 1–5), and in the joint cult with Aphrodite on the north slope of the Athenian Acropolis. In Thespiae Eros was represented by an aniconic image; in Athens phallic symbols have been found in the sanctuary. In both cults festivals were celebrated; that in Thespiae, called Erotidia, incorporated art, athletics, and equestrianism. Altars to Eros at the *Academy in Athens and the gymnasium at Elis were matched by ones to Anteros (Paus. 1. 30. 1, 6. 23. 3), whom Eros sometimes wrestles. In Philadelphia, worshippers called themselves Erotes; other cult centres include Leuctra, Velia (in south Italy), and Parium in Mysia.

Eros in Archaic art is hard to differentiate from other winged males. An Attic plaque shows him wingless. On vases, he appears alone, carrying lyre or hare, or in myth, especially accompanying Aphrodite, winged, boyish, sometimes with bow and arrows. During the Classical period he increasingly associates with women, in domestic scenes or weddings. He appears in military and athletic scenes, and was painted by Zeuxis and Pausias. The Erotostasia occurs occasionally. Scopas' group of Eros, Pothos, and Himeros at Megara is an early sculpture. In the Hellenistic period, he is a putto, common in terracottas and with Psyche.   G. M. A. H.; J. R. T. P.; K. W. A.

ethnicity (see RACE). In social science usage, a term coined (in 1953) to describe that condition 'wherein certain members of a society in a given social context choose to emphasize as their most meaningful basis of primary extrafamilial identity certain assumed cultural, national or somatic traits' (O. Patterson in N. Glazer and P. Moynihan (eds.), *Ethnicity* (1975) 308); a socio-political strategy of selective advantage enacted within a dominant political organization, which rests on insistence upon the significance of group distinctiveness and identity, and the rights that derive from it. Ethnic identity is not a 'natural' condition, but rather a self-conscious statement using selected cultural traits as diacritical marks. Ethnic groups are thus mutually exclusive, and are more usually constituted with reference to kinship than to territory. Dynamic and strongly contextualized, ethnic expression is characteristic of complex societies.

In the ancient Greek world, ethnicity is of importance in two principal areas. First, in the context of the *ethnos*, a category of state which existed alongside the *polis, but which is only rarely treated by ancient sources. *Ethnē* are diverse, with no single form of constitution. They are characterized by the fact that by contrast with *poleis* (which retained total autonomy), individual communities surrendered some political powers (usually control of warfare and foreign relations) to a common assembly. Their inhabitants were thus required to express a range of local and regional loyalties of varying degrees of complexity and strength. By contrast with *poleis*, the role of urban centres in *ethnē* varied greatly; settlement structures range from a high degree of urbanization and local autonomy (e.g. Boeotia, which was tantamount to a collection of small *poleis*) to scattered small villages with little urban development (e.g. Aetolia). According to *Aristotle (*Pol.* 1326[b]), *ethnē* are characterized by their large populations. Although the *ethnos* is sometimes equated with primitive tribalism, social and political developments from the 8th cent. BC onwards (in religion and *colonization, for example) often bear comparison with evidence from *poleis*, and the *ethnos* was a varied and long-lived phenomenon. Equally, *ethnē* have been seen as the origin or precursors of the federal states created from the 4th cent. onwards (e.g. the Achaean and Aetolian Confederacies). These, however, incorporated many former *poleis*, and relations between citizen groups were thus more formally constituted, often drawing on earlier concepts of *sympoliteia* and *isopoliteia* ('joint / equal citizenship').

In Hellenistic and Roman times, the concept of ethnicity may be applied to a variety of 'outsider' groups (e.g. Jews) who sought or were accorded particular status or rights within a broader imperial context. Hence the status and political role of these groups varied over time, and ancient sources are often imprecise in distinguishing between ethnic groups, the *natio* (or nation, usually the dominant ethnic group in a region), and the tribe (which in the case of the Roman division of state, may originally have been constituted on an ethnic basis). See NATIONALISM; RACE.   C. A. M.

Etruscans (Tyrsenoi, Tyrrheni, Etrusci), historically and artistically the most important of the indigenous peoples of pre-Roman Italy, and according to *Cato the Elder the masters of nearly all of it (Serv. on *Aen.* 11. 567)—a claim confirmed by archaeology for the area between the Tridentine Alps and the gulf of Salerno. Modern research has raised the status of Etruscan civilization to a level that is demonstrably superior to the traditional picture of a poor relation of Greece and a mysterious prelude to Rome.

The conflict in the sources between the Etruscans' alleged eastern (Hdt. 1. 94) and autochthonous (Dion. Hal. *Ant. Rom.* 1. 25–30) origins has been resolved by D. Briquel's convincing demonstration that the famous story of an exodus, led by Tyrrhenus from Lydia to Italy, was a deliberate political fabrication created in the Hellenized milieu of the court at Sardis in the early 6th cent. BC. Herodotus' authority is not diminished by this: his account is indeed prefaced by the words 'The Lydians say …'. Archaeologically, M. Pallottino's hypothesis of ethnic formation in Etruria itself has long provided the best explanation of the facts: the possessors of the indigenous Villanovan culture between the Arno and the Tiber were iron age Etruscans, who gained much in the 9th and 8th cents. from the interest shown by the outside world in their mineral resources, and in the 7th were able to acquire and commission luxury goods and adornments of east Mediterranean ('orientalizing') types for the tombs of their 'princes'. Foremost among the early bearers of outside influences were the Euboean traders who had established themselves at Pithecusae by the mid-8th cent.: their alphabet was modified to accommodate the pre-existing phonetic systems already characteristic of different Etruscan-speaking zones, and there can be little doubt that it is the first western Greeks who are ultimately responsible for the exaggerated perception of ethnic unity ('Tyrsenoi') in an area that had in fact inherited a significant degree of regional individuality from its final bronze age.

The continuity in settlement and in the basic culture of the 8th and 7th cents. at the mainstream Villanovan–Etruscan centres was accompanied by major developments both in society and in artistic production. The *praenomen–nomen* combination, a clear sign of proto-urban organization, is attested epigraphically from the beginning of the 7th cent., as are recognizably local schools of fine painted pottery, soon joined by *bucchero* (the only exclusively Etruscan product), bronze-work, and jewellery—categories in which the contributions of native Etruscan and expatriate Greek and Levantine specialists and entrepreneurs are inextricably linked. Oil and wine were also produced and exported on a large scale by the mid-6th cent. By then, too, the social class represented by the early orientalizing princely tombs had given way to a broader, *polis*-based, category of prosperous merchants and landowners. Their last resting-places take the form of single-family chamber-tombs, ranged along streets in well-planned cemeteries which have yielded a rich harvest of imported vases from all the best Attic black-figure and red-figure workshops. The chambers at Tarquinii and a few other centres have preserved the largest extant complex of pre-Roman painting in the classical world: prior to the 4th cent., its naturalistic and frequently cheerful depiction of banquets, games, and hunting affords a welcome glimpse of the 'real' Etruscan character underneath the veneer of Hellenization (see HELLENISM) constituted by the mass of prestige goods imported (and made locally) not only for deposition in tombs but also—and increasingly—to supply the votive requirements of major sanctuaries like that at Pyrgi.

The expansion of some Etruscan centres beyond the relatively narrow confines of Etruria proper began at an early stage with the foundation of the Tarquin dynasty at Rome by Lucius Tarquinius Priscus (reigned traditionally 616–578). The presence of the Tarquins, who turned Rome into a city, doubtless facilitated control of the land route to Campania, where Volturnus (Capua) became the chief Etruscan city. To the north, Felsina (Bologna) enjoyed a similar status in the Po valley from the late 6th cent., when growing Greek activity on land and at sea to the south made it imperative to cultivate new markets—not least with the mysterious Celtic communities north of the Alps, who had acquired a taste for the contents of the fine bronze flagons made in Vulci when Arruns of Clusium (Chiusi) set off to entice them into Italy for his own purposes at the end of the 5th cent. (Livy 5. 33). In the event, the Celts added their own not inconsiderable weight to the pressure on the Etruscans that was already building up from Rome (whence the Tarquins were expelled in 509), from the Greek south (where the battle of Cumae was lost in 474) and from other quarters as well (the Carthaginians and the Italic peoples). Of these, the inexorable advance of Rome into Etruria and Umbria was by far the most serious threat to the survival of what was still an essentially cantonal phenomenon as distinct from a nation: city-states, loosely organized in a League of Twelve Peoples, capable of meeting in council at the federal sanctuary of Voltumna near Volsinii—and of denying federal assistance to Veii, threatened by Rome since the end of the 5th cent., for primarily religious reasons. Livy's comment (5. 1. 6) on this episode, to the effect that the Etruscans paid more attention than any other people to religious considerations, is one of the relatively few positive statements about the Etruscans in the ancient sources: no Etruscan literature has survived, and Greek and Roman authors were far from objective observers of such matters as commercial rivalry (which they defined as piracy) and social customs (notably those concerning the position of women) that were not those of Greece and Rome.   D. W. R. R.

Eucratides I ('the Great'), Graeco-Bactrian king *c.*170–145 BC. His brilliant but warlike reign marked the climax of Greek rule in *Bactria(-Sogdiana). Just. *Epit.* 61. 6. 1–5 compares him to Mithradates the Great of Parthia, while Apollodorus of Artemita (quoted at Strabo 15. 1. 3) calls him 'ruler of a thousand cities'. His parents Heliocles and Laodice, commemorated on a special series of his coins, are otherwise unknown; however, Laodice is portrayed wearing a diadem and was therefore from a royal family. Some believe her to be a sister of *Antiochus III the Great, but most scholars reject this view and associate her with either the family of Diodotus II or Euthydemus I. Eucratides apparently seized power in Bactria, and then waged wars in Sogdiana, Arachosia, Drangiana, Aria, and finally NW India. His principal adversary was probably

King Demetrius I (son of Euthydemus I), though some argue for Demetrius II. After enduring a long siege, Eucratides overcame Demetrius and claimed the territories of Parapamisadae and Gandhara. It is likely that he also defeated the relatives of Demetrius I, including the ephemeral kings Euthydemus II, Agathocles, and Pantaleon. A campaign against Menander I is also possible.

The career of Eucratides may be traced in his voluminous coinage, which is among the finest and most innovative from antiquity. Besides commemorating his parents, he portrayed himself in heroic pose and added the epithet 'Great' to his royal title. His standard coin-type, the charging Dioscuri, seems to celebrate the famous cavalry of Bactria. South of the Hindu Kush mountains, he issued rectangular and bilingual coins (Greek/Prakrit) on an Indian standard for local commerce. He also struck the largest known gold coin from the ancient world, a numismatic masterpiece weighing 20 staters (169 g.: almost 6 oz.).

Eucratides was brutally assassinated c.145 BC by one of his sons, probably Plato. Another son, Heliocles 'the Just', avenged the crime, but Bactria-Sogdiana soon fell victim to nomadic invaders from the north and Parthian encroachment from the west. F. L. H.

euergetism, neologism of French scholarship (*évergétisme*, from *euergetēs*, 'benefactor') to describe the socio-political phenomenon of voluntary gift-giving to the ancient community. Embracing the beneficence of Hellenistic kings and Roman emperors, whose subjects saw such philanthropy as a cardinal virtue of rulers (see KINGSHIP), it has been studied in recent years above all in relation to the *polis, of which benefaction by wealthy citizens (including women) becomes a defining characteristic from the 3rd cent. BC until late antiquity, as is attested by thousands of honorific inscriptions memorializing donors; it is also a feature of republican Rome, where the liberalities of senators in kind at least (public building, spectacle) resemble that of their humbler Greek contemporaries, and of the (Mediterranean) Roman city in general. In Greece the origins of euergetism go back to the aristocratic ideal of liberality found in Homer and echoed by Aristotle, who included acts of 'magnificence' (*megaloprepeia*) such as feasting the city among the virtues of the well-born man (*Eth. Nic.* 1119^{b}19–1122^{a}17). In Classical Athens beneficence in this tradition, while lingering into the 5th cent., was essentially inimical to the ideal equality of Athenian *democracy, which preferred instead to impose on rich citizens the compulsory duty of the liturgy. Although 4th-cent. Athens conferred the title 'benefactor' on foreigners, only in the 3rd cent. does the type of the 'benefactor politician' emerge clearly in the Greek city, as with one Boulagoras of Samos (c.245 BC), who combined office-holding with gifts from his own purse to his city, in return receiving a crown and inscription (*Syll.*³ 366 = Austin no. 113). *Aristotle saw munificence in office as a cynical device of rich oligarchs (*Pol.* 1321^{a}31–42); P. Veyne (*Bread and*

Circuses (abr. Eng. trans., 1990)) sees Hellenistic 'benefactor politicians' as symptomatic of a weakening of democracy (see DEMOCRACY, NON-ATHENIAN) in favour of increasing dependence on the rich few. Others (following P. Gauthier, *Les cités grecques et leurs bienfaiteurs* (1985)) postpone this 'decline' until the advent of Roman domination, when (largely unaccountable) regimes of gift-giving notables in effect became the system of government in the Greek city; it is to this phase (from c.150 BC) that the extreme forms of honours for local benefactors, including cult, belong (as well as the hailing of the Romans by some Greek cities as 'common benefactors', *koinoi euergetai*). Civic euergetism was a mixture of social display, patriotism, and political self-interest. It was not charity, since its main beneficiary was the citizen-group, although its increasing embrace under Roman rule of the whole city (i.e. slaves and foreigners) prepared the way for the emergence of bishops and wealthy lay Christians as local benefactors, whose protection and material assistance, however, now specifically included the *humiliores* (non-élite persons). Probably at no time was the economic significance of euergetism as great as the vast number of honorific inscriptions might suggest.
A. J. S. S.

Euripides (*see facing page*)

Eusebius, of Caesarea (c. AD 260–339), prolific writer, biblical scholar and apologist, effective founder of the Christian genres of Church history and chronicle, and the most important contemporary source for the reign of *Constantine I. His intellectual formation at Caesarea in Palestine owed much to the influence of Pamphilus (martyred 310), by whom he was apparently adopted, and to their joint use of the library of Origen. From his election as bishop of Caesarea c.313 until his death in 339, Eusebius played a significant role in ecclesiastical politics in the eastern empire. He attended and assented to the decisions of the council of Nicaea in 325, having been readmitted to communion after recanting his earlier views; but though he delivered a speech at the dedication of Constantine's church of the Holy Sepulchre in Jerusalem (335) and encomia for the emperor's *decennalia* (315–16) and *tricennalia* (335–36), he was probably not such a confidant of Constantine as has commonly been supposed. He was present at the council of Tyre in 335 as an opponent of Athanasius, and shortly afterwards at Jerusalem when Arius was readmitted to the church. His *Life of Constantine*, left unfinished at his death, sought to create the impression of a harmonious and consistent imperial religious policy from the accession of Constantine (306) to the reign of his three sons, beginning in September 337.

Eusebius wrote biblical commentaries, in which the profound influence exerted on him by Origen is tempered by his own historical perspective; his *Onomasticon*, 'a biblical gazetteer', is an important source for the historical geography of Palestine. The two editions (? before 303 and 325–6) of his lost *Chronicle*, represented by Jerome's Latin

[*continued on p. 275*]

Euripides

Euripides, Athenian tragic playwright.

Career Euripides was born probably in the 480s. He first took part in the dramatic competitions of the City Dionysia at Athens in 455 BC, the year after the death of *Aeschylus (Life 32: he came third; the plays included *Daughters of Pelias*, his first treatment of the story of *Medea); he died in 407–6, leaving, like *Sophocles later in the same year, plays still unperformed (*Iphigeneia at Aulis*, *Alcmaeon in Corinth*, *Bacchae*: schol. Ar. *Frogs* 67), with which he won a last, posthumous victory (*Suda*, entry under the name). His first victory came only in 441 (*Marm. Par.* 60; plays unknown). He won again in 428 (hypothesis ('preface') to *Hippolytus*), but in his lifetime won only four victories at the Dionysia (*Suda*): he was thus far less successful in the competition than Aeschylus (thirteen victories) or Sophocles (eighteen victories). In 438 he was defeated by Sophocles (hyp. *Alc.*; Euripides' plays were *Cretan Women*, *Alcmaeon in Psophis*, *Telephus*, *Alcestis*); in 431 he was third to Aeschylus' son, Euphorion, and Sophocles (hyp. *Med.*: his plays were *Medea*, *Philoctetes*, *Dictys*, *Theristae*); in 415 second to Xenocles (Ael. *VH* 2. 8; Euripides' plays were *Alexander*, *Palamedes*, *Trojan Women*, *Sisyphus*); in 409 second, perhaps to Sophocles (hyp. *Phoen.*; his plays included *Phoenissae* and perhaps *Oenomaus* and *Chrysippus*). In 408 he probably competed at the Dionysia for the last time with plays that included *Orestes* (schol. *Or.* 371). Soon afterwards he left Athens on a visit to Macedon, as guest of the Hellenizing king Archelaus, and wrote a play there about an eponymous ancestor of the king (much as Aeschylus had written a play about the foundation of the city of Aetna while in Syracuse as guest of the tyrant, Hiero). He never returned to Athens but died in Macedon. There is no good reason to accept the ancient tradition that he had left Athens an embittered man, finally despairing after a series of defeats by almost unknown playwrights (Satyrus, Life of Eur. fr. 39; Philodemus *de vitiis*, col. 13: Satyrus' Life is largely a work of fiction).

Plays Euripides wrote some ninety plays (*Suda*, entry under the name). By chance we have more than twice as many of them as we have plays by either Aeschylus or Sophocles. They fall into two categories: the first, a group of ten plays which have been transmitted to us in our medieval manuscripts complete with the accumulation of ancient notes and comments that we call scholia. They represent the same kind of volume of 'selected plays' as we have for the other two playwrights. They are: *Alcestis*, *Medea*, *Hippolytus*, *Andromache*, *Hecuba*, *Trojan Women*, *Phoenissae*, *Orestes*, *Bacchae*, and *Rhesus*. The last is probably not by Euripides; the plays are in their likely chronological order; *Bacchae* has lost its scholia and the end of the play is partly missing. The other nine plays are: *Helen*, *Electra*, *Heraclidae*, *Heracles*, *Suppliant Women*, *Iphigenia at Aulis*, *Iphigenia among the Taurians*, *Ion*, *Cyclops*. They have been transmitted in only a pair of closely related 14th-cent. manuscripts (known as L and P); they have no scholia and they are in a rough (Greek) alphabetical order. There is little doubt that they represent the chance survival of one volume (perhaps two) of the 'complete plays' of Euripides, which circulated in alphabetical order, as we know from ancient lists of plays and collections of 'hypotheseis' (prefaces) to the plays (see Barrett, ed. *Hippolytos*, 45–61): they therefore represent a random sample of Euripides' work. Nine of the surviving plays are dated: *Alcestis* (438), *Medea* (431), *Hippolytus* (428), *Trojan Women* (415); *Helen* (412); *Phoenissae* (409); *Orestes* (probably 408); *Bacchae* and *Iphigenia at Aulis* (between 408 and 406). The remaining plays can be dated more roughly but with some confidence on the evidence of Euripides' writing of the verse of spoken dialogue in his plays. Statistical studies have shown that the tendency he clearly displays to write an ever freer, looser iambic verse line, by replacing 'long' syllables with pairs of 'short', is steadily progressive and not subject to sudden fluctuations (Dale, ed., *Helen*, with references to earlier work). The likely sequence (with approximate dates) is: *Heraclidae* (430), *Andromache* (426), *Hecuba* (424), *Suppliant Women* (422), *Electra* (416), *Heracles* (414), *Iphigenia among the*

Taurians (413), *Ion* (410). The satyr-play *Cyclops* is late, probably around 408. We also have, mostly from papyrus texts, sizeable fragments of several other plays: *Telephus, Cretans, Cresphontes, Erechtheus, Phaethon, Alexander, Oedipus, Hypsipyle, Archelaus* (in their probable chronological order).

'Realism', fragmentation, formalism   Ever since Aristophanes' portrayal of Euripides, in his play *Frogs*, as an intellectual iconoclast who insisted on confronting the darker and more disturbing aspects of everyday reality (*Frogs* 959), and Aristotle's quotation of an opaque remark attributed to Sophocles, to the effect that he (Sophocles) presented men 'as they ought to be', while Euripides presented them 'as they are' (*Poet.* 1460^{b}33 ff.), Euripides has tended to be read as a 'realist'. Plays such as *Trojan Women* (which sharply focuses on the savage brutality of war, in the middle of war); *Aeolus* (which takes incest as its theme: we know of it only from its 'hypothesis') and *Cretans* (whose action turns on sexual intercourse between a woman and a bull) have been cited in evidence. Moreover it has seemed obvious to many critics (already in antiquity: [Longinus], *Subl.* 15. 4–5) that a naturalistic treatment of human psychology, particularly female psychology, is another hallmark of Euripidean theatre: witness Medea, Phaedra, Hecuba, Electra, Creusa but also Ion, Orestes (in *Orestes*), and Pentheus. It is undoubtedly true that there are strands of 'realism' in Euripides' writing for the theatre: for example, Medea's presentation of herself as mistrusted 'foreigner' and oppressed and exploited 'woman' (*Med.* 214–58) and her subsequent slow, tortured progress to infanticide; Orestes sickened and eventually driven mad by the corrosive effects of guilt (*Or.* 34–45; 208–315, including the only 'mad scene' in extant Greek tragedy); or the voyeurism of Pentheus in *Bacchae*. But these are strands only in an extremely fragmented whole. For it is arguable that a vision of human experience as inherently fragmented and as defined by the co-existence of disparate, even contradictory, strands forms the very heart of Euripidean sensibility.

If we go back to *Medea* and read it attentively, we shall find that the Medea we have encountered in the passage already referred to exists, within the world of the play, alongside other Medeas: before the passage mentioned, she has been heard off-stage, giving incoherent voice only to pain and articulate only in universal cursing and damnation, of herself and her own children as well as of her enemies; immediately after it, she is transformed into a subtle adversary who patently and easily outwits her most powerful enemy. Subsequently she becomes successively brilliant orator, pathetic victim, devious manipulator, exultant (and uncanny) avenger, tormented mother until her final metamorphosis (involving a stunning *coup de théâtre*) into the demonic figure who, in an aerial chariot drawn by snakes, closes the play with prophecies and taunts sent down from beyond his reach upon the husband who deserted and humiliated her.

Hippolytus too introduces us to a similarly fragmented world: the play is framed by the appearance of two human-like divinities, cool, articulate, and frighteningly rational in their revenges; in between it is given over to humans, in three very disparate and distinct 'movements'. The first of these movements comprises the uncanny and disturbing passage across the stage of Hippolytus, who, it is clear, lives apart in a world of his own making and companioned by his own, personal, chorus; as he leaves, we are confronted, first, by a world of women, characterized by an intimacy which is warm and close but also painful, and by a Phaedra, who is successively delirious with hunger and unspoken sexual desire and then, immediately, rational, articulate, and analytical in presenting her decision to take her own life. That world is shattered by its own intimacies, which lead by slow degrees but with a sense of psychologically convincing inevitability first to deadly revelation and then to misguided intervention. The intervention goes terrifyingly astray. Phaedra dies and the world of women in which she has lived is replaced by a world of men, that of her husband and Hippolytus, the stepson with whom she had, by Aphrodite's will, fallen obsessively in love. This male world is characterized no longer by intimacy and warm relationship but by distance and cold rhetoric: in this world there is no communication, only speech-making and the cut-and-thrust of distichomythia (the formal exchange of pairs of lines). The scene ends in Theseus' invocation of a male divinity, his own father, to destroy his son and it is followed at once by the messenger's description of that destruction: the description demonstrates that divinity is not human, but bestial and capable of tearing men literally apart and of bringing about the annihilation of all that they have made.

Moreover, Euripidean 'realism' is conveyed to the reader/spectator through the medium of a marked, if equally fragmented, formalism. It has been a stumbling-block for many critics that Euripidean theatricality is expressed in stiffly formal, often detached, 'set pieces'. Euripides characteristically opens his plays with a markedly non-naturalistic 'prologue', in the form of a monologue, which acts as a kind of separate overture. Almost as characteristically he closes them with a detached tailpiece: the shape of the action is broken and brought to a halt by the intervention, sometimes (as in *Medea*) of a character from that action, now transformed, but more often a divinity (as in *Hippolytus, Andromache, Suppliant Women, Electra, Iphigenia among the Taurians, Ion, Helen, Orestes, Bacchae*). The divinity often apparently makes a highly theatrical apparition off the ground in mid-air, the so-called '*deus ex machina*' (already a problem for Aristotle: *Poet.* 1454^{b}2 ff.). Confrontation between dramatic persons frequently takes the form of an exchange of symmetrical and brilliantly rhetorical speeches, transparently forensic in tone, a special kind of bravura set-piece which modern scholars have called an *agōn*.

Innovation and recurrence In *Frogs* Aristophanes presents Euripides (comically) as a compulsive innovator and subverter of tradition. In his handling of the traditional stories which he (like the other 5th-cent. playwrights) took as the material out of which to make his plays, he clearly innovates: Medea's infanticide; Heracles' killing of his wife and children after, not before, the labours; Electra's marriage to a peasant farmer; the trial of Orestes before the Argive assembly; Thebes, years after Oedipus' discovery of the truth, still inhabited by Iocasta, Oedipus, and Antigone (and by a transient chorus of Phoenician girls!)—all these seem to be Euripidean innovations. There is a kind of restlessness to Euripidean experimentation (*Phoenissae* provides a good example) that many critics have taken to be definitive of his theatrical imagination. But innovation is not in itself a peculiarly Euripidean trait: Aeschylus (especially in *Suppliant Women* and *Oresteia*) and Sophocles (especially in *Philoctetes*) both gave themselves the freedom to reshape traditional stories in order to create new fictional worlds for the tragic theatre.

At least as characteristic of Euripides is the tendency to create theatre, almost obsessively, out of recurring dramatic situations which echo and resonate with each other. Very often these situations have women at their centre, women as victims and/or deadly avengers: examples are *Medea, Hippolytus, Andromache, Hecuba, Electra, Trojan Women, Ion, Helen, Iphigenia at Aulis*. Sometimes structural echoing (as between *Medea* and *Hippolytus*), situational parallels (as between *Electra* and *Orestes* or between *Hecuba* and *Trojan Women*), or emotional resonances (as between *Medea* and *Ion*) almost give the impression that the later play is a reworking of the earlier. Similarly *Bacchae* recurs to the theme of divine revenge through the subjugation and perversion of human will that he had treated in *Hippolytus*. But these are not 'revivals' under another name. Each reworking offers a different vision of the human condition and these disparate visions are enacted in very different structural forms: the ending of *Hecuba*, for example, is quite other than, and carries a very different sense of '*closure' from, that of *Trojan Women*.

Speech and song: the late plays The late plays of Euripides (roughly those of the last decade of his life, the plays that come after *Trojan Women* and *Heracles*) have thrown up major problems of interpretation and have led to strong critical disagreement. In so far as there has been a consensus, plays such as *Iphigenia among the Taurians, Ion*, and *Helen* have been characterized as 'escapist' or as 'tragicomedies', while others such as *Phoenissae, Orestes* and *Iphigenia at Aulis* (*Bacchae*, it is agreed, is somehow 'different') have been called 'epic theatre' or 'melodrama'. The underlying assumption has been that Euripides has turned away from the painful realities of tragic experience to offer his audiences less demanding, more 'entertaining' forms of theatre: the very real sufferings caused by the Peloponnesian War (431–404 BC) between Athens and the Spartan alliance have often been invoked in explanation.

The late plays are also often seen as the moment in Athenian theatre history when the chorus goes into terminal decline: its songs become fewer, more 'irrelevant' to the action and more purely decorative in function. (The charge of 'irrelevance' has indeed been laid against Euripides' use of the chorus even in his earliest surviving plays, for example in the third *stasimon* of *Medea*, ll. 824–65.) The two issues (of the changing nature of late Euripidean theatre and the 'decline of the chorus') need to be taken together.

Sung and spoken text together form the 'script' of the Greek tragic theatre from the earliest surviving play, Aeschylus' *Persians* of 472 BC, to the last, Euripides' *Bacchae* and *Iphigenia at Aulis* and Sophocles' *Oedipus at Colonus*, and in almost all the plays that we have actors and chorus both sing and speak (it is generally assumed that the spoken lines marked 'Chorus' in our manuscripts were in fact spoken only by the chorus-leader). But song is the characteristic mode of choral utterance and speech that of actors. In the late plays of Euripides this distinction becomes very much less clear as actors are increasingly given arias and duets to sing and moments of great emotional intensity in these plays are marked by such songs. Thus, for example, Creusa's anguished and distracted aria of self-revelation at *Ion* 859–922; the recognition duet of Menelaus and Helen at *Helen* 625–97; the murder scene of *Orestes* 1246–1310; and the final encounter and last farewells of Antigone and Oedipus at *Phoenissae* 1539–81, 1710–57. Sung text is also used to convey young innocence at *Ion* 82–183 and *Phoenissae* 103–92. At the same time choral songs are becoming more infrequent, though the stanzas that form them are getting longer.

Moreover, Euripides increasingly uses 'astrophic' song, that is song not composed of the responding, metrically 'rhymed' stanzas that throughout the history of tragedy had characterized the song of both chorus and actors. We have external evidence that connects these changes to new developments in musical composition, developments that were seemingly designed to make possible freer, aurally less predictable vocal lines. The key figure in these developments appears to have been Euripides' younger contemporary, Timotheus, who is plausibly associated with Euripides in a number of ancient anecdotes. Such music and the writing that goes with it, composed of long sentences, free in syntax, that seem to float without ultimate closure (they are brilliantly parodied by Aristophanes in *Frogs*), are clearly the medium for a different perception of human experience than that of the earlier plays. It is not that Euripides' perception is no longer 'tragic' (though a number of the late plays, such as *Ion*, *Iphigenia among the Taurians*, and *Helen*, do end with apparent 'happiness'); rather Euripides now seems to see human beings not just as articulately analytical in confronting suffering but simultaneously as living in a world of shifting, unstable, and often contradictory emotions. It is through song, and the associative juxtaposition of sensations, thoughts, and experiences that have always characterized Greek song, that such fleeting and unstable forms of consciousness are conveyed in the late plays.

Alongside this almost operatic use of song, Euripides also employs in the late plays other new formal devices to create new versions of the tragic. They include vastly extended passages of stichomythia (exchanges of single lines, dialogue at its most tensely formal) and the use of metres taken from much older forms of tragedy, such as the trochaic tetrameter (*Or.* 729–806, which includes 25 successive lines divided between two speakers, shows both formal devices together). The result is a series of plays whose emotional atmosphere is much more difficult to seize and characterize. Their themes still include human isolation and inexplicable suffering, failures of communication, the victimization of women, and the drive to revenge, even the terrors of madness, themes that have marked earlier Euripidean theatre but in a bewildering variety of new dramatic modes.

The last two plays that we have, *Bacchae* and *Iphigenia at Aulis*, point up the paradoxical and disconcerting multiplicity of Euripides' theatrical imagination. *Bacchae* eschews almost all the formal innovations of the other late plays (though not the freer iambic verse nor the extended stichomythia scenes) and offers a vision of human experience that combines a stark and shocking view of the power of divinity with a luxuriant but ambiguous emotionalism which veers from joyful calm to exultant savagery: men and women are crushed and overwhelmed by collision with a divine power which they cannot comprehend. *Iphigenia at Aulis* takes us into another world. It makes much use of actor arias and duets (including an extended passage of sung text given to Agamemnon, as well as long arias for Iphigenia); it deploys greatly extended passages of stichomythia, much of it in trochaic tetrameters and involving free use of broken lines. The choral songs are more numerous than in other late plays and the first of them (the entry-song of the chorus) is very long. Above all it creates an emotionally charged but unstable world marked by botched deception and exciting disclosure, by an anti-hero, Agamemnon, who is tormented by indecision, and by a young Iphigenia, who combines a childlike innocence with heroic self-determination. The worlds of *Iphigenia* and of *Bacchae* barely touch and yet, in the theatre, they were juxtaposed, played one after the other before the same audience. They attest not merely the variety of Euripides' theatrical imagination (to the very end of his life) but also a fact that we should always remember: that his audiences, like those of Aeschylus and Sophocles, were accustomed to the experience of tragedy not in the form of a single play but as a sequence of three disparate tragic fictions, rounded off by anti-tragic burlesque. The disparateness of Euripides' theatrical imagination plays to that expectation.

J. P. A. G.

version and by an Armenian translation, synthesized Old Testament, near eastern, and Graeco-Roman history into a continuous chronological sequence accompanied by chronological tables. The object, as in his *Ecclesiastical History*, was to demonstrate that God's plan for salvation subsumed the whole of history. The same thinking lay behind his *Preparation for the Gospel* and *Proof of the Gospel* (after 313), apologetic works in which pagan philosophy is refuted and the Roman empire seen as the necessary background for the coming of Christ and the establishment of Christianity. The *Preparation* reveals Eusebius' immense debt to the library of Origen, with its many citations from Greek historians, Philo Judaeus, and especially Middle Platonist philosophy. An early work, *Against Hierocles*, attacks the comparison of the pagan Apollonius of Tyana with Christ; in the *Preparation* the main target is Porphyry, whose anti-Christian arguments Eusebius systematically set out to refute. The later *Theophany* (325–6 or later), extant in Syriac translation, and his last works repeat many of the same apologetic themes.

Eusebius' integrity as a historian has often been challenged, and indeed the later part of his ten-book *Ecclesiastical History* (which may have been begun in the 290s but only reached its final form in 324–5) was successively extended and clumsily revised as immediate circumstances changed. The *Life of Constantine*, in four books, has seemed so suspect on the grounds of bias and inconsistencies that Eusebian authorship has been denied. But the authenticity of the many documents cited or mentioned has been vindicated in one major case by the identification of the same text on papyrus, and modern scholarship is more willing than before to recognize the complexity of Eusebius' methods. The citation of documentary evidence marks both works off from secular historiography. However, Eusebius' aim was not so much objectivity as

persuasion: close study of the reworking of parts of the *Ecclesiastical History* in the *Life of Constantine* shows that he deliberately developed and enhanced his own earlier argument in the light of later reflection. Both works reflect the powerful impact of Christian persecution on Eusebius' thought but unlike the *Ecclesiastical History*, which took its main shape before or during the persecution of 303–13, and went on to cover only the part of Constantine's reign up to the defeat of Licinius in 324, the much later *Life of Constantine* reflects Eusebius' mature, if one-sided, understanding of the implications of a Christian imperial system.

A. M. C.

experiment Greek and Roman scientists did not refer directly to the experimental method. However, in a variety of contexts they described testing procedures that were clearly deliberate investigations designed to throw light on problems or to support theories. Examples can be found in the Presocratic philosophers, the Hippocratic writers, *Aristotle, Erasistratus, Ptolemy, and Galen.

We should distinguish first the areas where experimental investigation is possible from those where it is not. Direct experiments in astronomy are out of the question. This was also true, in antiquity, in relation to most problems in meteorology (thunder and lightning) and in geology (*earthquakes). In such cases ancient scientists often conjectured analogies with other more accessible phenomena that were directly investigable. Thus Anaximenes may have tried to support Anaximander's theory of lightning as caused by wind splitting the clouds by suggesting that it is like the flash of an oar in water. Similarly some of the experimental interventions described in the Hippocratic writers (see MEDICINE §4) incorporate an element of analogy. The writer of *Diseases* 4, for instance, describes a system of intercommunicating vessels which can be filled or emptied by filling or emptying one of them. He uses this to explain the movements of the humours between the main sources in the body (stomach, heart, head, spleen, liver). What this shares with an experiment is the careful construction of an artificial set-up. Where it differs from experiment in the strict sense is that its relevance to the physiological problem discussed depends entirely on the strength of the analogy suggested (in this case a mere conjecture).

Sometimes, however, direct interventions are proposed. Examples can be given from *physics, harmonics, optics, physiology, and *anatomy. Thus Aristotle states that he has proved by testing (*pepeiramenoi*) that sea water on evaporation becomes fresh (*Meteor.* 358^b 16 ff.): however he then goes on to claim that the same is true of other flavoured liquids including wine—a typical risky extension of an experimental result. In harmonics, testing procedures were used by pre-Platonic Pythagoreans (see PYTHAGORAS) in their investigations of the numerical relations expressed by the concords of octave, fifth, and fourth, although later writers who report that those relations were discovered by Pythagoras himself are generally untrustworthy. Some such reports claimed, for example, that he made that discovery by weighing hammers that gave certain notes: yet that would not yield the result described.

Optics provides one of our fullest examples of a series of careful experiments, though the results have been adjusted to suit the general theory proposed. In his *Optics* (5. 8 ff.) Ptolemy describes his investigations of refraction between three pairs of media (from air to water, air to glass, and water to glass). He describes the apparatus used and records the results to within a half degree for angles of incidence at 10-degree intervals. However, the results all exactly confirm the general 'law' that takes the form $r = ai \div bi^2$, where r is the angle of refraction, i the angle of incidence, and a and b constants for the media concerned. Elsewhere he provides convincing experimental proof of the elementary laws of reflection (3. 3), to establish, for instance, that the angle of incidence equals the angle of reflection.

Experiments in the strict sense were attempted also in the life sciences. Erasistratus described one in which a bird is kept in a vessel without food for a given period of time, after which he weighed the animal together with the visible excreta and compared this with the original weight. This he took to show that there are invisible effluvia from animals—again an overinterpretation of a correct result. Galen used experimental *vivisections on animals to investigate a variety of problems. He showed the peristalsis of the stomach in one, and produced a detailed account of the courses of the nerves in systematic experiments on the spinal cords of pigs. In the latter case no general theory is at stake: what the experiments reveal is the precise connection between vital functions and particular nerves.

Ancient scientists thus showed considerable ingenuity in devising testing procedures. However what this exemplifies is not so much the idea of a crucial experiment, an ideally neutral means of adjudicating between theories antecedently deemed to be of equal plausibility, as the appeal to tests specifically to support or to falsify a theory. In this way, experiments in antiquity are an extension, though an important one, of the use of evidence.

G. E. R. L.

Fabius Maximus Verrucosus, Quintus, grandson or great-grandson of Quintus Fabius Maximus Rullianus, as consul 233 BC celebrated a *triumph over the Ligurians and unsuccessfully opposed the agrarian bill of Gaius Flaminius. He was censor 230, consul for the second time 228, and *dictator (probably) 221. In 218 he perhaps opposed an immediate declaration of war on *Carthage. Dictator again in 217, after the Roman defeat at Lake Trasimene, he began his famous policy of attrition, believing that Hannibal could not be defeated in a pitched battle; this earned him the name 'Cunctator' (the Delayer). He allowed Hannibal to ravage the Campanian plain, but then blocked his exits; Hannibal, however, escaped by a stratagem. Opposition to Fabius' policy at Rome led to his *magister equitum* (master of the horse), Marcus Minucius Rufus, receiving *imperium* equal to his. When Minucius was enticed into a rash venture, Fabius rescued him. The traditional policy of fighting fixed battles was resumed in 216, but after the disaster at Cannae there was no alternative to Fabius' policy. With the help of his position as the senior member of the college of *augures*—he is said to have been an augur since 265—he became suffect consul for the third time for 215, operating in Campania. He was re-elected for 214, helped to recapture Casilinum and had a number of successes in Samnium. In 213 he perhaps served as legate to his son. Direct control of affairs now passed to other men, but Fabius reached his final consulship in 209, when he recaptured Tarentum and was made *princeps senatus* (acknowledged senior senator). In 205, together with Quintus Fulvius Flaccus, he strongly opposed *Scipio Africanus' plan to invade Africa. He was no doubt alarmed by Scipio's growing prestige, but genuinely believed that taking the war to Africa posed unnecessary dangers. It was Scipio who brought the war to an end, but Fabius' cautious strategy which made victory possible. Fabius died in 203. He had been *pontifex* (see PRIESTS) since 216 as well as augur, a distinction unique until *Sulla and *Caesar.

J. Br.

Failaka (off Kuwait). See ICAROS.

family, Roman English 'family' has connotations which have changed during its long history and vary according to context. Biologically, an individual human being is related to parents, through them to ascendants, aunts, uncles, siblings, and cousins, and may, by sexual intercourse with someone of the opposite sex, in turn become a parent, linked by blood to descendants. Blood relations for Romans were *cognati*, the strongest ties normally being with parents and children and the siblings with whom an individual grew up. Relationship established through the sexual tie of marriage was *adfinitas*; kin by marriage were *adfines* (in strict usage from engagement until dissolution of the marriage). Law initially stressed blood relationship through males: *agnati* (father's other children, father's siblings, father's brothers' children, a man's own children, etc.) inherited on intestacy. By entering *manus* (marital power), a married woman came into the same agnate group as husband and children; if she did not, her legal ties and rights were with her natal family.

The group under the power of a *paterfamilias* (father or grandfather), whether or not they lived under the same roof, was sharply distinguished; there might be other living agnates outside this group. Agnatic forebears were present in family consciousness as recipients of ritual, as *imagines* (portraits) in an aristocratic house, and as links between the living. For the Romans, *familia* could originally mean the patrimony; its more normal usages were to describe (1) those in the power of a *paterfamilias*, kin, or slaves, or (2) all the agnates who had been in such power, or (3) a lineage, like the Julian house, or (4) a group or household of slaves (Ulpian, *Dig.* 50. 16. 195. 1–4) A lineage in the broadest possible sense, a group allegedly descended from a common mythical ancestor, was *gens*; its members shared a middle name (*nomen gentilicium*), e.g. Tullius/a, as members of an agnatic *familia* might share a last name (*cognomen*), e.g. Cicero. (The class of those sharing a *gentilicium* extended to newly enfranchised citizens, slaves, and their descendants.) *Domus*, besides meaning the building in which someone lived (home or residence: see HOUSES, ITALIAN), covers (1) the *household of free, slave, and freed persons and (2) a broader kinship group including cognates (e.g. the imperial 'family' or dynasty, *domus Caesarum*). Increasingly, descent in the female line (*maternum genus*) came to be valued in sentiment, appraisal of status, and inheritance practices.

The nuclear family is described, in relation to its male head, as consisting of wife and children (*uxor liberique*). Similarly a list of those closest to a particular individual would be drawn up to suit various contexts: Cicero for instance in writing to his brother Quintus at an emotional moment might stress his brother, his daughter, his own son, his nephew (his only surviving close kin), his wife (*QFr.* 1. 3. 3). In relation to an individual, the kin or affines who count change with the phases of life and accidents of survival. The evidence of epitaphs illustrates close family ties as they existed at the time of commemoration: the person(s) who pay for a monument may do so out of love, duty as kin, or duty as beneficiary/ies. Where the commemorator is specified we get a glimpse of how the family operated, as we do from juristic sources, e.g. on dowry or succession, or literary sources, which chiefly reflect the expectations and practice of the upper classes. Although ties with remoter relations by blood or marriage are acknowledged when they exist, emphasis is normally on the nuclear family (one's wife/husband and children, or parents and siblings). In the absence of these, as for soldiers debarred from legal marriage or ex-slaves who theoretically had no parents and in practice might have been prevented from forming a family, comrades or fellow freedmen/women (*coniliberti/ae*) might form a substitute family. S. M. T.

famine Catastrophic breakdowns in the production and distribution of essential foodstuffs, resulting in exceptionally high mortality from attendant epidemic *diseases, were rare in the ancient world. The typical natural and man-made causes of famine were omnipresent: crop failure caused by the unreliable Mediterranean rainfall (see CLIMATE) or pests and diseases, destruction in war, state oppression and incompetence, poor arrangements for transport, storage, and distribution, and profiteering by the élite. Specific food-shortages of varying intensity and chronic malnutrition of the poor were common, but most of the population were subsistence farmers whose primary strategy of production was to minimize risk, and the political culture helped town-dwellers to pressure their leaders to resolve food crises before they became critical. The exaggerated references to 'famine' in the ancient sources echo the political rhetoric of an urban society where famine was a frequent threat but a very infrequent experience. Local climatic variation meant that relief supplies were normally available within the region, given the political will to obtain them. The severe food-shortages over extensive areas of the eastern Mediterranean world attested in 328 BC, AD 45-7 (the 'universal famine' of Acts 11: 28), and AD 500 were quite exceptional. Most famines were local, brief, and primarily man-made, such as the three best-attested famines in Athens of 405/4, 295/4, and 87/6

BC, all the result of siege, or the food-shortages at Rome in 67 BC and AD 5-9, the former apparently intensified, if not caused, by Pompey's manipulation of the supply network, the latter by the diversion of supplies to emergency military operations in Dalmatia and Germany. See FOOD SUPPLY. D. W. R.

fantastic literature, or fiction of the unreal, took two forms in antiquity: (*a*) fantasies of travel beyond the known world; (*b*) stories of the supernatural. Both look back to the Phaeacian tales in the *Odyssey*, which became a byword for the unbelievable (cf. [Longinus] *Subl.* 9. 14).

From the Hellenistic period we know of a series of descriptions of imaginary lands, such as those by Euhemerus, Hecataeus of Abdera, and Iambulus. Their primary purpose was social and moral comment, but they often seem to have been authenticated by an adventure story, which provided entertainment but also drew attention to the question of how literally they were to be believed. Antiphanes of Berge's account of the far north was so transparently fictitious that 'Bergaean' became synonymous with 'fantasist'. Although these works were criticized as falsehoods, some recognized that undisguised fiction represented an area of licence for the imagination (e.g. Strabo 2. 3. 5). Fantasies of this kind are parodied in the space-travel of Lucian's *True History*, but, despite his satirical programme, Lucian's invention acquires its own fantastic momentum.

Tales of the supernatural also make doubt and belief their central theme. Lucian's *Philopseudes* tells stories of ghosts and magic, including the Sorcerer's Apprentice, while mocking those who believe them. Fantastic episodes occur in the novels, notably of Iamblichus and Apuleius, whose characters share the reader's hesitation as to the nature of the phenomena (see NOVEL). The fragments of Phlegon of Tralles contain the story of an amorous revenant, while Philostratus (*VA* 4. 25) narrates the detection of a vampire. Photius (*Bibl.* cod. 130) knew the collection of ghost stories of the neoplatonist Damascius (d. *c*. AD 458), but most literature of this kind has been lost. Papyrus fragments include two ghosts (*POxy.* 1368, from the *Phoenicica* of Lollianus; *PMich.* inv. 3378) and a wizard (*PMich.* inv. 5+*PPal. Rib.* 152).

The two strands of fantasy united in the *Wonders beyond Thule* of Antonius Diogenes, which combined travel beyond real geography with witchcraft, Pythagorean philosophy, and self-conscious authentication, all arguably intended to subvert the reality of the perceptible world. J. R. Mo.

federal states are found in the Greek world from the late 6th cent. BC. The term is used of those organizations in which the separate city states (see POLIS) of a geographical and ethnic region were combined to form a single entity at any rate for purposes of foreign policy, while for local purposes retaining their separate identity as city states and their separate citizenship. Thus Boeotia was a federal state in which the individual communities were still regarded as cities, whereas Attica formed the city-state of Athens and the demes (local districts: see DEMOCRACY, ATHENIAN) did not have the degree of autonomy appropriate to cities. Tribal states in the less urbanized parts of Greece were like federal states in that the tribal organization comprised units with a considerable degree of local autonomy. There is no ancient Greek term which precisely denotes a federal state: the words most often used are *koinon* ('commonwealth') and *ethnos* ('nation'; see ETHNICITY). An account follows of some of the more important federations.

The earliest evidence of a federal state is in (probably) 519 BC, when Plataea resisted incorporation in a Boeotian federal state dominated by Thebes and gained the protection of Athens (Hdt. 6. 108); there are references to the boeotarchs, the chief magistrates of the federation, in 480–479 (Paus. 10. 20. 3; Hdt. 9. 15. 1). The federation may have broken up after the Persian Wars, and for a time Boeotia was controlled by Athens, but it was revived after 446 and we have evidence for its basic mechanisms (Thuc. 5. 38. 2; *Hell. Oxy.* 19 Chambers). The individual cities had similar constitutions, with one quarter at a time of the full citizens who satisfied a property qualification acting as a probouleutic council. The federation was based on electoral units, eleven after 427 and perhaps nine before; the largest cities with their dependencies accounted for more than one unit, while the smallest were grouped together to form a unit; each unit provided one boeotarch and 60 members of a council of 660, and within the council one quarter at a time acted as the probouleutic body. In 386 *Sparta regarded the federation as infringing the principle of autonomy enshrined in the Peace of Antalcidas or King's Peace, and insisted on its dissolution. The federation as revived in the 370s again had electoral units and boeotarchs, but its decision-making body was an assembly, and it was dominated to a greater extent by Thebes. Thebes was destroyed after revolting against *Alexander the Great in 335, and was refounded *c.*316; the federation survived in the Hellenistic period, based now not on electoral units but on cities.

*Thessaly was divided regionally into four tetrads, each of which came to be headed by a tetrarch; the tetrads could combine to elect a single leader, the *tagos*, but there seem to have been substantial periods when there was no *tagos*, either because the need for one was not felt or because dissension made the appointment of an agreed leader impossible. The peoples of the surrounding mountains were *perioikoi* ('dwellers around'), whom the Thessalians controlled when they were strong enough to do so. During the 5th cent. cities developed, and became more important than the tetrads. At the end of the century a dynasty of tyrants came to power in Pherae; *c.*375 Jason of Pherae obtained the title of *tagos*; in the 360s the opponents of Pherae, led by the Aleuadae family of Larissa, organized themselves in a *koinon* with an *archōn* ('ruler') and four polemarchs ('war-rulers'); appeals for support to

Macedon and to Thebes culminated in the overthrow of the tyrants by Philip II of Macdeon in 352 and his being made *archōn* of Thessaly. In the course of his later interventions Philip revived the old tetrarchies. Thessaly survived into the Hellenistic period as a federation of cities under the control of the Macedonian king, and a new federation was created by the Romans in 194.

In Arcadia moves towards unity in the 5th cent. seem not to have gone very far, but a federal state was founded after the battle of Leuctra and a new capital was created for it at Megalopolis. There was an assembly of the Ten Thousand, probably all citizens, and also a council; the chief magistrates were 50 *damiorgoi* ('public workers'), representing the cities in proportion to their size, and a single *stratēgos* ('general'). Before long the federation split: one of the two divisions certainly claimed to be the Arcadian *koinon* and the other may have done so. No more is heard of an Arcadian League after the 320s.

The Aetolian Confederacy (like the Achaean, see below) began as a tribal state in the Classical period, and in the Hellenistic period developed into organizations with members from outside their original *ethnos*. The Aetolians in the 5th and 4th cents. had both tribal units and city units, and some kind of federal organization. When the confederacy expanded, in the 3rd cent., neighbouring peoples were designated *telē* and perhaps given a status equivalent to that of one of the three Aetolian tribes, while more distant recruits were given *isopoliteia* ('equality of citizenship') either with an Aetolian city or with the whole confederacy. The confederacy had an assembly which held two regular meetings a year, with voting by individuals, a large representative council, and a smaller executive committee, the *apoklētoi* ('those called away'); the principal magistrates were the *stratēgos* and the hipparch ('cavalry commander').

The Achaean Confederacy already had outside members in the 4th cent. It broke up at the end of the century but was revived in 281/0 and began to acquire outside members in 251/0. There were four regular *synodoi* ('meetings') a year, attended by both a representative council and an assembly, in both of which voting was by cities; later in the 3rd cent. major questions of foreign policy were transferred to extraordinary *synklētoi* ('summoned meetings'), which involved usually both council and assembly but sometimes only the council. The confederacy had two *stratēgoi* until 255, one thereafter. The individual cities of the confederacy continued to have an active political life of their own.　　　　J. A. O. L.; P. J. R.

finance, Greek and Hellenistic The collective deployment of resources by the community inevitably has sociopolitical implications (who pays? who benefits?). But public finance in Greek states rarely had economic aims beyond the broad balancing of incomings and outgoings: demand-management through running a budget deficit or surplus was unknown. *Oikonomia* ('economics') as applied to state finance preserved autarkic attitudes appropriate to its original meaning of 'household management' (Xen. *Mem.* 3. 4).

finance, Greek and Hellenistic An inscribed decree (late 4th cent. BC) records honours awarded by an Athenian deme (village) to two *chorêgoi* (financial backers) of local dramatic performances. In finance, as in other ways, an Athenian deme behaved like a *polis* in miniature.

Recurring expenditure (primarily on administration, cult, ambassadors, defence, maintenance of fortifications, gymnasia, and public buildings) would be met from a variety of revenues (rents and royalties from state property, including mines and quarries, court fees and fines, taxes on non-citizens, sales taxes, excise duties and customs dues). Collection of taxes was regularly farmed out by auction to private individuals (*Ath. pol.* 47. 2 ff). Extraordinary expenditure (typically through warfare or food shortage; occasionally, on public building) was met through ad hoc measures: property and poll taxes, public loans, creation of monopolies, *epidoseis* (contributions), or confiscations ([Arist.] *Oec.* 2). Warfare itself was seen as potentially productive (Arist. *Pol.* 1256ᵇ), and might occasionally prove so. Systems of Greek public finance may be assessed in so far as they conform to or deviate from these norms.

Minoan and Mycenaean communities seem to have been unique in the Greek world in their degree of direct, central control over resources. The testimony of the Linear B tablets, in conjunction with extensive storage facilities within the palaces, suggests a 'redistributive' system of economic exchange, rigidly controlled from the centre (there are parallels in temple-based economies of the near east; see MINOAN and MYCENAEAN CIVILIZATION). All this ended with the onset of the so-called Dark Age (*c.*1100 BC). The well-stocked storerooms of the *Odyssey* (2. 337 ff.) may dimly recall Mycenaean palaces, but redistribution was replaced in the world of Homer by *reciprocity between and within aristocratic *oikoi* (households). Resources were deployed by the giving of gift and counter-gift: in return for their contributions to the élite, the people received protection (*Il.* 12. 310 ff.; *Od.* 13. 13 ff.). Arrangements in Archaic and even Classical *Sparta resembled Homeric organization in the near absence of any centralized system of finance. The mainstay of the regime was the agricultural produce appropriated from the helots (state slaves) by individual Spartiates, who passed on a portion to their *sussition* (public mess). Details are obscure (the *perioikoi* ('dwellers round about'—not full citizens) may have made contributions in cash or kind), but the small scale of resources under central control helps to account for the poor showing of late 5th-cent. Sparta as a city (Thuc. 1. 10). Much the same might be said of the rudimentary systems of finance (e.g. the *naukrariai* and *kōlakretai* in Athens) deployed by the aristocracies dominating early Archaic *poleis*. Archaic tyrants provide a stark contrast: their characteristically heavy expenditure on public buildings and central, civic institutions gave the *polis* a new, urban emphasis. Necessary resources were raised by a combination of personal taxes and other, extraordinary measures: in Athens, a tax on agricultural produce (Thuc. 6. 54). Also characteristic of Archaic tyranny was the effective merging of the tyrant's own resources with those of the state (*Ath. pol.* 16. 1). The ending of *tyranny caused an immediate reaction against the tyrants' financial methods: taxes on the person became a symbol of oppression, restricted to non-citizens and those of low status.

Archaic Athens broadly conformed to this pattern; as late as the 480s, it was proposed that a windfall gain of 100 talents from the silver mines at Laurium be parcelled out among the citizen body (*Ath. pol* 22. 7). Shortly after, Athenian finances were transformed by the acquisition of a tribute-paying empire (see DELIAN LEAGUE). Figures from the eve of the Peloponnesian War give a crude impression of scale: from a total annual revenue (internal and external) of approximately 1,000 talents (Xen. *An.* 7. 1. 27) some 600 talents derived from the empire (Thuc. 2. 13). This made possible the maintenance of a massive navy, an extended programme of public building, provision of public pay, and the accumulation on the Acropolis of a strategic reserve of at least 6,000 talents (Thuc. 2. 13). Against this, expenses of war were heavy: one talent in pay to keep one trireme at sea for one month. As the

Peloponnesian War progressed, there was (in addition to an upward reassessment of the tribute in 425: ML 69) increasing reliance on payments of *eisphora*—an extraordinary property tax falling on the wealthy. By contrast, the Spartan system was poorly placed to generate the resources needed for extended warfare. Appeals for contributions from sympathetic individuals proved inadequate (ML 67), and only massive subventions of Persian gold made possible the eventual Spartan victory. The importance of imperial revenues for Athens' *democracy became apparent in the 4th cent., when the range of public payments was actually extended to include assembly pay and payments from the theoric fund. Collective aspirations may be read into the explicit aim behind the proposals in *Xenophon's *Poroi* ('Revenues'): maintenance of the citizen body at public expense. Attempts to revive the tribute-paying empire failed and heavier burdens therefore fell on the wealthy (Xen. *Oec.* 2. 5 ff.). The degree to which increasing demands disrupted and alienated the Athenian élite is disputed. There emerged in the course of the 4th cent. a group of financial experts (including Eubulus and culminating in Lycurgus), who occupied tailor-made offices and made the most of Athens' internal resources.

Characteristic of finance in Classical Athens was the liturgy system, placing the élite under an obligation to perform public services (notably the *trierarchy and *chorēgia* (financing choruses for festivals)). Liturgies were an integral part of the democratic system: in return for public services, liturgists might (or might not) receive popular consideration in politics and the courts. Significantly, Aristotle (*Pol.* 1321ᵃ) recommends that oligarchies attach expensive duties to high public office, so excluding all but the wealthy. The citizens of 4th-cent. Pharsalus in *Thessaly handed over their acropolis and control of their finances to their wealthiest citizen; in return he used his fortune as a revolving loan-fund, smoothing out imbalances in income and expenditure (Xen. *Hell.* 6. 1. 2) This privileging of wealth ties in with the broadly post-democratic practice of *euergetism, common in Hellenistic cities. The *euergetēs* ('benefactor') earned enhanced status, and possibly material rewards, by making donations in cash or kind to the advantage of the citizen body.

Amongst the Hellenistic monarchies, Ptolemaic *Egypt had a system of public finance of exceptional complexity. Revenues from farmland were assessed in painstaking detail and collected directly; collection of dues from vineyards, orchards, and gardens was farmed out. Additionally, the *apomoira* (a tax on wine, fruit, and vegetables) was assessed by royal officials, but the right to collect was sold to contractors. Customs dues were graduated from 20 to 50 per cent, according to the goods involved (contrast the flat 5 per cent tax from Classical Athens). There were varying rates of tax on sale and gift of property and privileges (e.g. tax concessions) and, apart from sundry minor taxes (including a poll tax), intricately organized *monopolies on an extended range of goods and services. Other Hellenistic kings raised revenue from their subject cities partly by imposing specific taxes, partly by levying contributions (*phoros*), which were creamed off internal revenues, raised in the usual ways.   P. C. M.

finance, Roman 'Taxes are the sinews of the state'. So claimed both Cicero and the great jurist Ulpian. Despite this recognition of the central importance of taxation no systematic ancient treatment of Roman public finance survives. Extended financial documents are also rare (though see now the elaborate schedule of the *portoria* (customs duties) of Asia, *AE* 1989, 681). Therefore many details about (e.g.) the allocation and collection of taxes or about the character of fiscal institutions such as the *fiscus*, *patrimonium*, and the *res privata* remain obscure and disputed. Despite the serious deficiencies in our evidence the broad features of the history and development of Roman public finance through the republic and the Principate to the later empire can be delineated with some confidence.

In the republic there were, traditionally, two major types of revenue namely the regular *vectigalia* (public revenues and rents) and the *tributum*, an extraordinary (in principle) levy on the property of Roman citizens. The total size of this levy was decided by the *senate and varied from year to year. The earliest detailed account of republican public finance survives in the sketch of the Roman constitution in the sixth book of *Polybius, reflecting conditions in the mid-2nd cent. BC. The *aerarium*, the central depository of the state for both cash and documents, was managed by two urban quaestors; but all decisions as to payments from it were made by the senate. On setting out on campaign a *consul could draw funds on his own responsibility. But further payments, for the supplies, clothes, or pay of the army, had again to be authorized by the senate. The senate also made a quinquennial grant to the censors, on the basis of which they let out contracts for building and repairs of public buildings in Rome and the *municipia* and *coloniae* (municipalities; colonies) of Italy and for the exploitation of public properties—rivers, harbours, gardens, *mines, and land. Ultimate control of the contracts, for instance in altering the terms, again lay with the senate.

The most important development, not reflected in Polybius' account of the last two centuries of the republic, was the acquisition of a territorial empire overseas. At first resources were extracted from the conquered via *booty and war indemnities, in the medium term by the imposition of regular taxation (tribute) in cash or kind. Provincial governors (and their quaestors) were responsible for the supervision of the collection of tribute and for expenditure in their province. After 123 BC in Asia certainly (and perhaps elsewhere) the process of collection of tribute was contracted out to *publicani. Two prime consequences ensued from this development. First, the levying of tribute on Roman citizens in Italy was abandoned from 167 BC onwards. Secondly, the revenues of the state were greatly increased. On one speculative estimate (Frank, *Econ. Survey* 1. 141) annual revenues in the early 2nd cent. BC were 12.5 to

15 million denarii. By the late 60s BC they had increased to 50 million; and according to a difficult passage of Plutarch (*Pomp.* 45), Pompey's great conquests in the 60s further increased revenues to either 85 or 135 million. The continuing access of new revenues both meant that Rome's continuous wars were in the long term self-financing and allowed the creation of novel forms of public expenditure such as the distribution of subsidized, later free, corn to Roman citizens. (See FOOD SUPPLY.) Even so, as in many pre-industrial societies, public revenues remained modest in relation to the private wealth of the élite. So the fortune of *Crassus alone amounted to 48 million denarii.

The establishment of imperial rule entailed far-reaching changes in public finance and the creation of an elaborate fiscal state. First, although the senate retained the function of making routine votes of funds, effective control over the state's finances came to lie with the emperor and his agents. Under Augustus we meet for the first time the publication of general accounts (*rationes*) of the public funds. At his death full details of the state's finances were in the hands of his personal slaves and freedmen. The public post of *a rationibus* (first held by imperial freedmen, later by senior equestrians) soon emerged. By the late 1st cent. AD this official was responsible for estimating the revenues and expenditure of the state. Secondly, direct taxation in the provinces, in the form of the poll tax and the land tax, was placed on a new footing through the introduction by *Augustus and *Agrippa of periodic provincial censuses. These mapped out the human and physical resources of the provinces and formed the basis for the assessments of tribute for each city and its territory. Whenever a new province was annexed, a census was taken. Provincial governors and imperial procurators supervised the collection of tribute; the process of collection devolved on the individual civic authorities. Thirdly, Rome's revenues were vastly increased, although no secure figures survive. The annexation of new provinces (that of Egypt in 30 BC was especially important) of itself increased revenues. A new array of indirect taxes were introduced. The most important were, probably, the *vicesima hereditatum* (5 per cent tax on inheritances) of AD 6 (hypothecated to the discharge payment for veterans) and the *quinta et vicesima venalium mancipiorum* (4 per cent tax on the sale of slaves) of AD 7 (hypothecated to the pay of the *vigiles*). The first three centuries AD also saw the steady accretion of landed property (via legacies, gifts, and confiscations) in the hands of the emperor. The importance of revenue from such crown property was considerable, if unquantifiable, and is already manifest in Augustus' own account, in his *Res gestae*, of his expenditure on public needs. By the late 2nd cent. there were two departments of crown property, the *patrimonium* and the *res privata*, though the distinction between them remains obscure. This formidable array of revenues (tribute in cash and kind, indirect taxes, revenues from crown property) enabled the imperial state to carry out, on a *routine* basis, key political functions such as the distribution of the corn-dole at Rome, the upkeep of the

imperial court, the construction and maintenance of an elaborate road network (see ROADS) across the empire, the payment of salaries to senatorial and equestrian officials, and, above all, the funding of the vast standing armed forces of c.350,000 men. This fiscal system was predicated, in its mature form in the 2nd cent., on a basic predictability of expenditure and revenue and on the state's ability to exercise uncontested authority over the territory of the empire. However, potential problems in the form of sudden emergencies or increases in expenditure were already apparent in the later 2nd cent. The great northern wars under Marcus *Aurelius rapidly depleted the reserves of the treasury. In turn the major pay rises for the army of *Septimius Severus and *Caracalla were funded in part by significant debasements of the silver coinage. (See COINAGE, ROMAN.) The generalized political and military crisis, which enveloped the empire from the 230s onwards, was to shatter the fiscal apparatus and its preconditions. The state's ability to raise revenues was undermined by its failure to maintain routine central authority over the empire; the census-system collapsed, invasion and civil war destroyed accumulated capital and crops. To meet its needs the state resorted to irregular and arbitrary requisitions in kind and to runaway debasement of the coinage. By the 260s the precious-metal content of the silver coinage had been reduced to about 5 per cent. Hyper-inflation wrecked the whole monetary system.

A measure of stability was only restored to the public finances with the reassertion of central authority over the empire. *Diocletian, in a striking repetition of the measures of Augustus, re-established censuses throughout the empire. Payments of tax (predominantly in kind) were assessed by units of population (*capitatio*) and of land (*iugatio*), although the principles and workings of this system, which certainly varied from area to area, are still subject to debate. The finances of the empire were now managed through three departments. The *res privata* dealt primarily with imperial property. The *sacrae largitiones* controlled mines, mints, and state factories, collected taxes and levies in cash, and paid donatives (irregular disbursements) to the troops. The office of the praetorian prefects, the most important of the three, was responsible for the rations of soldiers and officials, for the maintenance of the *cursus publicus* (see POSTAL SERVICE) and of most public buildings, and for calculating annually the required rate of the indiction to produce the supplies in kind.   G. P. B.

fishing Fish populations of the *Mediterranean are less abundant than those of the oceans. Gradients of temperature and salinity resulting from the depth and the closure of the ecosystem, however, promote the life cycle of several important species on the continental shelves (but see FOOD AND DRINK). The migratory habits of many important species bring them into contact with many Mediterranean islands and coastlands.

Since the routes of the shoals are far from predictable, places where their movements are topographically constrained (such as straits like Messina, the Bosporus, or Hellespont, or lagoons and their entries) are of obvious importance. Numbers are very variable from year to year: gluts occur, but dearth is so frequent as to make it unwise to make fish protein more than a supplement (if a locally and occasionally important one) to a subsistence diet. The nutritional usefulness is greatly increased by processing to make the resource sustainable in times of general dearth, and movable inland or by sea: drying and salting are the principal techniques, and the evaporite salt of pans on the fringes of lagoons used for fishery anyway constituted an important symbiotic resource. The salt in salt fish (with the minerals in the fish) was probably of as much dietary importance as the protein.

Even in conditions of glut, and assuming very favourable conditions for fishing, total yields cannot have constituted an important aggregate contribution to the protein needs of even small ancient populations, compared with cereal or legume staples. They did, however, play a significant role in diversifying a diet based on those staples, which was important both nutritionally and culturally in the classic Mediterranean pairing of staple and 'relish'—in Greek *opson*. Salted or pickled fish was the *opson par excellence* (the mod. Greek *psari*, 'fish', is derived from *opsarion*), and widely available for use in small quantities.

To the producer, this demand gave the catch the economic status of a cash crop, and enabled the secondary purchase of more protein than could easily have been acquired through consuming the fish. On this base of widely disseminated eating of fish-pickle, the fisherman could rely on a still more lucrative market in fresh fish which could fetch high prices in luxury provision markets. This combination of an urbane—and urban—ready availability of fish *opsa* with the opulent associations of fresh fish prized by the connoisseur underlies the great prominence of fish in the Athenian comic tradition. What had been characteristic of Athens became a feature of most towns in the Hellenistic and Roman periods; study of the amphorae reveals the scale and complexity of the trade in *garum* (as the pickle came to be known), while the competitive consumption of the exquisites of high society provided a continuing stock of anecdote about colossal prices and singular specimens. The fisherman became a type of opportunism and poverty, proverbially wild, but a familiar and parasitical accompaniment to all that was best about stylish living.

Fishing in the open sea was chancy and hazardous, but essential for the most prized fish. Many local markets were supplied from the rocky shores. The fisheries of the formerly extensive wetland lagoons of the Mediterranean coasts were the easiest to develop artificially, because they were sheltered, shallow, and had controllable inlets and outlets, and systematic pisciculture grew from their management. Both archaeological and literary evidence shows the extent to which Roman pisciculture developed, and the elaboration of fishponds for both fresh and salt-water fish. Processing plants for making pickle were also built on a grand scale, from the early Hellenistic period in the Black Sea area, and in the Roman period on the coasts of southern Spain and Mauretania. This economy depended on, and is an interesting indicator of, a developed interdependence of markets in the Mediterranean.   N. P.

Flamininus (Titus Quinctius Flamininus). Born *c*.229 BC, military tribune 208 under Marcus Claudius Marcellus, then quaestor, probably at Tarentum in south Italy, where he held praetorian **imperium* for some years from 205. Decemvir for distributing land to **Scipio Africanus'* veterans 201, he concurrently became triumvir to supplement Venusia (200). In 198, against some opposition but with the support of the veterans he had settled, he was elected **consul* and sent to take over the war against Philip V of Macedon with a new army and a new political approach. After driving Philip from a strong position in the Aous gorge separating Macedonia from Epirus, he moved towards central Greece against stiff resistance, but with his brother's help forced the Achaean Confederacy into alliance and now gained some further allies. Meeting Philip late in 198, he demanded the evacuation of all of Greece (unacceptable to Philip at this point), but apparently hinted to Philip that the **senate might modify the terms. He instructed his friends in Rome to work for peace if he could not be continued in command and for war if he could complete it; he was prorogued, and the senate insisted on his terms. In spring 197, after gaining the alliance of most of Greece, he decisively defeated Philip by superior tactical skill at the battle of Cynoscephalae. He now granted Philip an armistice on the same terms, which the senate confirmed as peace terms. Advancing implausible excuses, he refused to allow his Aetolian allies to annex some cities promised to them. He thus secured a balance of power in the north, but gravely offended the Aetolians, making them eager to welcome **Antiochus III. In a spectacular ceremony (see Polyb. 18. 46) he announced the unrestricted freedom of the Greeks in Europe at the Isthmian games of 196 and persuaded a reluctant senate commission that this pledge had to be carried out if Greek confidence was to be retained against Antiochus, who was about to cross into Europe. He now initiated a diplomatic effort to keep Antiochus out of Europe and deprive him of the Greek cities in Asia Minor. The final settlement of Greece involved a difficult war against the Spartan tyrant Nabis (see SPARTA), nominally as head of an almost Panhellenic alliance. The settlement paralleled that with Philip: Nabis was left to rule Sparta, to secure a balance of power between him and Rome's Achaean allies. In 194 all Roman troops were withdrawn. Henceforth Flamininus was showered with honours (including divine honours) in Greece. He issued a commemorative gold coin with his portrait (*RRC* 548) and left for Rome to celebrate an unparalleled three-day triumph (Livy 34. 52). A bronze statue with a Greek inscription was erected to him in Rome by his Greek clients (Plut. *Titus* 1. 1).

In 193 he was entrusted with secret negotiations with

Antiochus' envoys; when they refused his offer of undisturbed possession of Asia in return for withdrawal from Europe, he proclaimed to the Greek world that Rome would liberate the Greeks of Asia from Antiochus. Sent to Greece to secure the loyalty of the Greeks and of Philip, he was partly successful; but Demetrias, afraid of being surrendered to Philip, became an Aetolian bridgehead for Antiochus. He remained diplomatically active in 191–190, both in the war and in Peloponnesian affairs, handing Messene over to the Achaeans and annexing Zacynthus for Rome. In 189 he was censor. In 183, sent to Asia on an embassy, he unsuccessfully tried to intervene in Peloponnesian affairs on his way, then took it upon himself to demand the extradition of *Hannibal from Prusias I of Bithynia. (Hannibal committed suicide.) With the senate working to substitute Demetrius, Philip's pro-Roman younger son, for Perseus as designated successor, he hatched a plot to substitute Demetrius for Philip as king (see Polyb. 23. 3, cf. 7; Livy 40. 23, denying the charge). The result was Demetrius' execution (181). After this failure he disappears from public affairs until his death (174).

A typical patrician noble, he saw his world in terms of personal ambition, Roman patriotism, family loyalty, and patron–client relationships. He was the first to develop a policy of turning the Greek world—cities, leagues, and kings—into clients of Rome and of himself, nominally free or allied, but subject to interference for Rome's advantage. The Greeks, whom he had liberated, he expected to follow his instructions even without a public mandate. Aware of Greek history and traditions, he attracted many Greeks by charm and tact, but aroused antagonism by unscrupulous trickery. Midway between arrogant imperialists and the genuine philhellenes of a later period, he laid the foundations of the uneasy acceptance of Roman hegemony by the Greek world. See also PHILHELLENISM.   E. B.

food and drink The ancient diet was based on cereals, legumes, oil, and wine. Cereals, especially wheat and barley, were the staple food and the principal source of carbohydrates. They were eaten in many different ways, e.g. as porridge and bread. The rich could afford a more diversified diet and ate less cereal than the poor. Athenaeus describes many types of bread and *cakes. Probably only the rich could afford 'white' bread, but even the best bread available in antiquity was much coarser than modern bread.

Legumes (field beans, peas, chick-peas, lentils, lupins, etc.), a common find in archaeological excavations at *Pompeii, were an important part of the diet. They were incorporated into bread and complemented cereals because they are a rich source of protein.

The Greeks used the generic term *opson* for 'food eaten with bread or other cereal products' (*sitos* and *frumentum*). Fish, which might be fresh, dried, or pickled, occupied a prominent place in *opson*, especially at Athens. It was important as a source of protein and oils. Many species were known. However, fish are scarce in the Mediterranean because of the absence of large stretches of continental shelf off the coast (see FISHING). They probably did not make a major contribution to the diet. Shellfish were also eaten.

*Olive oil was the main source of fats, which are necessary to make a cereal-based diet palatable. Fats, which have a very high calorific value, were also obtained from other sources, e.g. sesame oil. The use of butter was a mark of barbarians; so was the drinking of beer and to some extent that of milk. Milk was generally used for making cheese. The most important beverage was *wine, usually diluted and often artificially flavoured. It was even consumed by young children. Honey was used for sweetening.

Meat was a luxury for most people. In classical Athens it was generally eaten only at feasts accompanying religious festivals. (See SACRIFICE.) Poultry, game, and eggs played a large part in Roman cookery, but there was comparatively little butcher's meat, apart from pork and sometimes veal. Peasants generally kept pigs. Wild birds (partridges, quails, pheasants) were also eaten. The soldiers of the Roman army had a higher standard of living and a more varied diet than the bulk of the population of the Roman empire.

For ordinary people vegetables (e.g. onion, garlic, turnip, radish, lettuce, artichoke, cabbage, leek, celery, cucumber) provided the most important addition to the basic diet. Wild plants were also gathered for eating. Among fruit, figs, grapes, apples, and pears played a leading part. (Potato, tomato, most citrus fruits, and banana were not available in antiquity.) Sauces, such as the Roman fish-sauce *garum* (see FISHING), and condiments and herbs were very popular. The Romans disliked the natural tastes of most cooked foods. This partiality for flavourings is an important thread of continuity from past to present in Mediterranean cookery. See COOKERY.   J. R. S.

food supply

Greek For Greek city-states of the Archaic and Hellenistic periods the ethos of self-sufficiency (*autarkeia*) dominated the ideology of food supply. In reality few Greek cities ever outgrew the food production capacities of their territory and the small number which did responded by intensifying agricultural production. This is well documented in the case of Athens. However, most Greek states operated in politically and environmentally unstable conditions. Weather (see CLIMATE) and warfare posed constant, but unpredictably timed, hazards. Consequently, some degree of shortfall in food supply could be expected perhaps as often as once in five years.

By 'food' (*sitos*) is meant cereals. Though other crops were grown and important in the ancient Greek diet, grain was the preferred staple, especially wheat and barley Hence shortfalls in these crops proved the most problematic at all levels. Grain was at the heart of the political discourses which evolved around the problem of food supply in most city-states.

Grain was grown not by cities but by individual households, on private land. Therefore shortages had to be met with ad hoc measures on the part of government, city-states virtually never having either central grain production or storage facilities. General shortfalls in the cereal harvest enhanced class tensions, since wealthy landowners would not have suffered to the same degree as small-scale cultivators. Shortfalls also provided opportunities for the rich to gain political capital and to manipulate grain supplies. From the 4th cent. BC onwards, benefactions of grain by wealthy individuals are regularly documented in inscriptions, and become part of the political strategies employed in élite competition for power (see EUERGETISM).

City-states were empowered to do little in the likely event of grain shortage. Only one free, state-sponsored, grain distribution is known (Samos: *SEG* 1. 366). Generally states behaved as middlemen, aiming to encourage imports, or donations and subsidized sales by the rich (e.g. *IG* 5. 1. 1379; J. Pouilloux, *Choix d'inscriptions grecques* (1960), no. 34, p. 126; *IDélos* 442A 101; 399A 69–73). Incentives might be offered to private traders, but many were not citizens, and the profits they made were greatly resented (Lys. 22).

It is sometimes difficult to ascertain how 'genuine' food shortages were. It is perhaps significant that with one possible exception, barley, which was considered inferior for food, was not imported. Wheat, the preferred cereal (and most of the time probably the prerogative of the rich) was the usual grain from overseas. It is difficult to know how much of this imported wheat the poor ever ate. However, ensuring the supply of wheat itself became a political issue, as is shown by the careful diplomacy with which the Bosporan kingdom (a major supplier of wheat to Athens) was treated. See AGRICULTURE, GREEK; FAMINE.　L. F.

Roman The growth of Rome to a city of perhaps 250,000 inhabitants in the time of Gaius and Tiberius *Gracchus and of up to one million under *Augustus, far outstripping the productive capacity of her hinterland, created an unprecedented demand for imported foodstuffs. The supplying of Rome was always left mainly to private enterprise, and the main source was always Italy (including Sicily and Sardinia), but the political pressure on the Roman government to deal with actual or feared shortages led to some institutionalized public underpinning of the mechanisms of supply, which were enabled by exploitation of Rome's imperial revenues. In the early and middle republic individual magistrates competed either to win popular favour by securing extra supplies from subject or allied states where they had some personal influence, or to win noble approval by quashing popular complaints. Gaius *Gracchus took the momentous step of establishing a regular public distribution of a set monthly ration of grain (*frumentatio*) at a set price to adult male citizen residents, which Publius *Clodius Pulcher made free in 58 BC. Other legislation alternately cut and increased the number of entitled recipients, called the *plebs frumentaria*, until in 2 BC Augustus stabilized it at or below 200,000. Augustus also reorganized the system of storage and distribution under an imperial appointee of equestrian status called the *prae-fectus annonae*, who also had a more general remit to watch over food supplies. This public supply (*annona*), drawing on the grain paid to the state as rent or tax in Sicily, Africa, and (from 30 BC) Egypt, helped the privileged minority who held tickets of entitlement (*tesserae*), which could be inherited or sold. But the monthly ration did not meet a family's need for grain, and the tickets did not necessarily go to the poor. All residents will still have relied on the private market to some extent (or, if they had them, on produce from their farms), and the majority will have used it for most of their supplies. Shortages could and did occur, especially in the supply of wheat, leading emperors to make ad hoc interventions to hold down prices, or stimulating long-term improvements such as the successive new ports at *Ostia. Wealthy private individuals often gave free meals or tokens for food to their clients, but this generosity was unreliable and also not particularly directed at the poor. At the end of the 2nd cent. AD *Septimius Severus added free *olive oil to the rations received by the *plebs frumentaria*, and in the 270s Aurelian added free pork and cheap *wine, and the monthly wheat ration was replaced with a daily issue of bread. As Rome ceased to be the empire's capital in the 4th cent., the responsibility for maintaining supplies to the decreasing population fell first on the senatorial nobility and then on the Church. See also FAMINE.　D. W. R.

Forma urbis, a plan showing the city of Rome after AD 203 at a scale of roughly 1 : 240, engraved on 151 slabs of marble decorating a wall of the temple of Peace, perhaps in the office of the *praefectus urbi* (urban prefect). About 10 per cent of the total remains, some fragments being known only from Renaissance drawings. A few pieces appear to belong to an earlier version presumably from the Flavian complex. See illustration on following page.　J. D.

forum Romanum, the chief public square of Rome, surrounded by monumental buildings, occupied a swampy trough between the Palatine, Velia, Quirinal, and Capitol. The edges of the marsh were covered with cemeteries of early iron-age settlements on the surrounding hills, until the area was made suitable for building in the late 7th cent. BC by the canalizing of the Cloaca Maxima, and the deposition of considerable quantities of fill. The Regia and temple of *Vesta were traditionally associated with this period, while the earliest dated monuments are the temples of Saturnus (497 BC: Livy 2. 21) and Castor (484 BC: Livy 2. 20, 42). The forum became the centre of Roman religious, ceremonial, and commercial life, as well as the political activities which took place in the adjacent Comitium; balconies (*maeniana*) were in 338 BC built above the shops surrounding the forum, to allow for the viewing of the gladiatorial shows which took place there. Butchers and fishmongers were, however, soon relegated to the *macellum* (see MARKETS AND FAIRS) and *forum piscarium*, as more monumental buildings were constructed around the forum. Basilicas (public halls) were introduced in 184 BC by

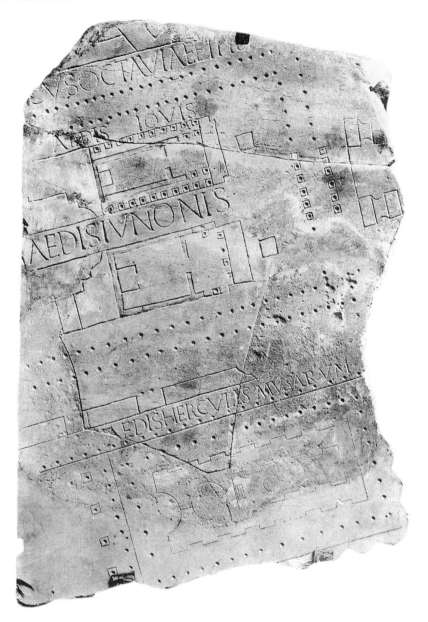

Forma urbis Fragment of the *Forma urbis* or marble plan showing the city of Rome after AD 203. It shows a group of 2nd-cent. BC. *temples: those of Jupiter (Aedes Iovis) and Juno (Aedes Iunonis) were the first temples in Rome faced with marble; the third, for Hercules and the Muses, was funded and adorned with Greek *booty.

*Cato the Elder (Livy 39. 44); his work was soon imitated by the basilica Aemilia et Fulvia (179 BC) on the north side of the square, and basilica Sempronia (170 BC) on the south.

The growing population of Rome and the increasing importance of popular politics were reflected by the transfer from the Comitium to the forum of the *comitia tributa* in 145 BC; in 121 Lucius Opimius restored the temple of Concord, following the death of Gaius *Gracchus and his supporters, and built a new adjacent basilica. In the same year the first triumphal arch, to Quintus Fabius Maximus (Allobrogicus), was set up over the via Sacra beside the

Regia. The temple of Castor was rebuilt in 117 (Cic. *Scaur.* 46).

Much of the present setting, however, is due to *Sulla, *Caesar, and *Augustus. Sulla rebuilt the Curia on a larger scale to accommodate the senate of 600 members, obliterating much of the Comitium in the process; Caesar planned a new basilica Iulia, to replace the old basilica Sempronia, which, like his Curia Iulia, was finished by Augustus. After Caesar's assassination a column was erected to mark the site of his pyre and later (29 BC) replaced by the temple of Divus Iulius; this, and the adja-

forum Romanum The open area of the forum seen through the columns of the temple of *Antoninus Pius and Faustina. Under the empire new additions served chiefly to glorify the Roman emperors, as also with (middle ground) the triumphal arch of *Septimius Severus.

cent Parthian arch of Augustus (19 BC), had the effect of monumentalizing the east end of the forum. New Rostra in front of the temple of Divus Iulius faced the 'old' Rostra, rebuilt by Caesar and then Augustus. Many ancient monuments were restored: the Regia (36 BC), the basilica Aemilia (14 BC), and the temples of Saturnus (42 BC), Castor (AD 6), and Concordia (AD 10).

Comparatively few changes were made to the topography of the forum under the empire; the imperial fora, the Campus Martius, and the Palatine provided more scope for emperors keen to make their mark on the city. New temples were, however, dedicated to deified emperors and empresses (Augustus, *Vespasian, *Antoninus Pius, and Annia Galeria Faustina) while Domitian set up an equestrian statue of himself in AD 91; and the arch of Septimius Severus was built in AD 203. A major fire in AD 283, however, provided an opportunity for a major reconstruction under Diocletian, with a row of monumental columns set up in front of the basilica Iulia, and the Curia rebuilt. Later structures included a statue of Stilicho and the column of Phocas (AD 608). I. A. R.; D. E. S.; J. R. P.

freedmen, freedwomen Emancipated slaves were more prominent in Roman society (little is known of other Italian societies before their enfranchisement) than in Greek city-states or Hellenistic kingdoms (see SLAVERY). In Greek the words *apeleutheros/a* and *exeleutheros/a* are used; in Latin *libertus/a* designates the ex-slave in relation to former owner (*patronus/a*), *libertinus/a* in relation to the rest of society. In Greek communities, freed slaves usually merged with other free non-citizens. In Rome, the slave freed by a citizen was normally admitted to citizenship (see CITIZENSHIP, ROMAN). A slave might be released from the owner's control by a fictitious claim before a magistrate with executive power (*imperium*) that he/she was free (manumission *vindicta*), by being ordered to present himself to the censors for registration as a citizen (manumission *censu*: in these forms public authority attested citizen status and made it impossible for the slave to be a slave), or by will (manumission *testamento*, where implementation of the owner's command was postponed until he/she died and depended on acceptance of the inheritance and public validation). A slave freed informally lacked citizenship and other rights, but was protected by the praetor, until Augustus introduced Latin rights, with the possibility (expanded by later emperors) of promotion to full citizenship. Augustus also, by the Fufio-Caninian law of 2 BC (introducing a sliding scale to limit the number of slaves who could be freed by will) and the Aelio-Sentian law of AD 4 (a comprehensive law, which included minimum ages for slave and manumitter and barred from citizenship slaves deemed criminal), regulated the previously untrammelled right to manumit.

In Greece, the ex-slave might be bound to perform services while the ex-owner lived; in Rome, continuing dependency took the form of part-time services (*operae*; *libertae* married with patron's consent were exempt from paying these to a male patron), possible remunerated work, the obligation of dutifulness, and some inheritance rights for the patron and descendants against the freed slave's heirs other than non-adopted children. Freedmen were usually registered in the four urban voting tribes (*tribus*), excluded from major public offices and military service, but given a role in local elective office and cult. Children born after their mother's manumission were free-born and under no legal disabilities, though servile descent might be remembered (especially by the upper classes) for several generations. Freed slaves document their activity in urban trades and crafts; the most prominent, wealthy, and envied were usually freed by the upper classes: literature emphasizes the exceptions—writers such as *Terence, the fictitious millionaire Trimalchio (see PETRONIUS ARBITER) or the bureau-chiefs of the early emperors such as Narcissus and Marcus Antonius Pallas. M. I. F.; S. M. T.

freedom in the ancient world (*see following page*)

friendship, ritualized (or guest-friendship), a bond of trust, imitating kinship and reinforced by rituals, generat-

[*continued on p. 290*]

freedom in the ancient world

freedom in the ancient world On the individual and social levels, the distinction between free and unfree is as old as slavery, and individual or collective freedom from dues, taxes, and other obligations as old as communities with centralized government. These concepts are attested in Egyptian and Mesopotamian documents and the Hebrew Bible. Nevertheless to these civilizations—as to ancient China—the concepts of free citizens or of political freedom were unknown. Typically, near-eastern societies were characterized by a plurality of statuses 'between slavery and freedom' (Pollux) and ruled by autocratic and divinely sanctioned monarchs or an absolute divine law. Obedience and integration into a given order were the prime virtues; the rise and fall of empires and cities, protection from foreign enemies, or, individually, status change or protection from domestic exploitation were seen as results of divine will. Such conditions were not conducive to recognizing freedom as a political value. Despite their charter myth of liberation from Egyptian slavery, even the Hebrews (see JEWS) began to use freedom politically only under Hellenistic influence. About Phoenician city-states we know too little to judge.

Eleutheros and *liber* probably both derive from IE †*leudh-* (perhaps initially 'grow'), designating the legitimate member of a descent group or community. The distinction free–unfree is attested in the earliest Greek and Roman texts (Linear B, Homer (e.g. *Il.* 6. 455, 463), *Twelve Tables). As 'chattel *slavery' became predominant, earlier status plurality was often replaced by a sharp contrast: slave–free. *Freedmen were enfranchised in Rome but not in Greece (see CITIZENSHIP, GREEK and ROMAN).

Current evidence indicates that freedom was first given *political* value by the Greeks, in a world of small *poleis* (see POLIS) which were not subject to imperial control, where power was not centralized, autocratic, or divinely sanctioned but broadly distributed, and communal well-being depended on many citizens, so that early forms of equality survived and gained importance over time. Loss of freedom was frequent, both for individuals (war, piracy, debt bondage), and communities (tyranny).

Nevertheless, freedom was articulated politically only when Lydian and especially Persian expansion to the Aegean for the first time subjected Greek *poleis* to foreign rule, often supporting local tyrants (see TYRANNY). This danger of double 'enslavement' and the confrontation with the autocratic Persian state made the Greeks aware of the free character of their societies. Earliest allusions to political freedom and the emergence of an abstract noun (*eleutheria*) date to the Persian Wars of 480/79 and their aftermath (e.g. *Aeschylus, *Persae* 403).

Vowing the continued defence of Greek liberty against Persia. Athens assumed leadership in the *Delian League (478) which was soon converted into a naval empire; allies became subjects who could hope only to preserve self-administration (*autonomia*). Freedom quickly deteriorated into a political slogan. In the Peloponnesian War (431–404), *Sparta propagated the liberation of Hellas from Athens as 'tyrant city' (*polis tyrannos*) though primarily protecting its own interests and soon turning oppressor itself.

Domestically, freedom initially meant 'absence of tyranny'. Constitutional development was dominated first by 'order' (*eunomia*—see LYCURGUS), then by equality (*isonomia*), which, in democracy, eventually included all citizens, thus approximating *isonomia* to *demokratia* (Hdt. 3. 80. 6.). *Eleutheria* was claimed by democracy when democracy and *oligarchy were perceived as mutually exclusive, partisan forms of rule, so that the *dēmos* ('people') could be free only by controlling power itself (ps.-Xen. *Ath. pol.* 1. 6, 9). Similarly, a new term for 'freedom of speech' (*parrhēsia*) supplemented 'equality of speech' (*isēgoria*). Rejecting the extension of full rights to all citizens, oligarchs accepted as 'free citizens' only those wealthy enough to engage in liberal arts and occupations (*eleutherios paideia*, *eleutherioi technai*) and communal service. When *eleutherios* was set against *eleutheros* the concept of the 'free citizen' was divided ideologically, as proportional equality was opposed to numerical equality. Aristotle later included liberality (*eleutheriotēs*) in his analysis of virtues (*Eth. Nic.* 4. 1).

In the 4th cent. BC Sparta, Athens, and Thebes claimed to promote the liberty of those subjected by others. The liberty of the Greeks in Asia, sacrificed by Sparta in 412, was definitively yielded in the King's Peace (386). The charter of the Second Athenian Confederacy (379/8) guaranteed the members' *eleutheria* and *autonomia*. The Messenian helots (state slaves of Sparta) were freed by Thebes after the battle of Leuctra (371). To end continuous internecine warfare, *Isocrates called for a pan-Hellenic crusade against Persia to liberate the Hellenes—a programme realized by *Alexander the Great only after Greek liberty was crushed at the battle of Chaeronea (338).

In the Hellenistic period, politics were controlled by the great powers; local autonomy was the best that could be attained. Yet the kings, competing for political and material support, presented themselves as protectors of Hellenic civilization and liberty. Declarations of freedom for the Hellenes were thus an old tradition when, after his victory over Philip V of Macedon, *Flamininus in 196 pronounced that the king's Greek subjects 'shall be free, exempt from tribute, and subject to their own laws' (Livy 33. 32. 5–6).

The use of freedom in philosophy was more complex. Fifth-century *sophists emphasized the strong individual's right to erupt from enslavement by the conventions of *nomos* and rule over the weaker in accordance with nature (*Antiphon, Callicles in *Plato's *Gorgias*). Others contested the validity of traditional social distinctions; Alcidamas declared slavery as contrary to nature. Despite *Aristotle's elaborate refutation (*Politics* 1), this view was echoed by the Stoics (see STOICISM) and discussed thoroughly by Roman jurists. Yet other sophists propagated cosmopolitanism, individualism, and 'freedom from the state' (Aristippus).

One aspect of democratic *eleutheria* was 'to live as you like' (Arist. *Pol.* 1317^b 11). Plato caricatured such 'excessive' freedom in *Republic* 8–9; Isocrates denounced it when advocating *patrios politeia* ('ancestral constitution': *Areopagiticus*. 20). Generally, *Socrates and his pupils avoided *eleutheria*. Originating in popular morality (echoed in *Euripides), the notion of freedom from all kinds of dependencies (especially material goods and passions) induced generations of thinkers (Antisthenes, Diogenes the Cynic, Bion) to stress self-control (*sōphrosynē*, *enkrateia*) as decisive means to achieve inner freedom.

Loss of political freedom and the need for new orientations gave philosophy broad appeal as a means to achieve happiness (*eudaimonia*). Despite fundamental differences, both Epicureans (*Sent. Vat.* 77) and Stoics (Epictetus 4. 1) believed in freedom as the goal and principle of life. (See EPICURUS; STOICISM.)

Lack of contemporary sources allows no certainty about the process by which *libertas* was politicized in Rome. The expulsion of the kings or the struggle for abolition of debt bondage are possible contexts. The late republican élite developed an aristocratic concept of *libertas*, supporting equality and opposing *regnum* ('kingship') and extraordinary power of individuals and factions. By contrast, the *libertas populi* was not egalitarian and did not aim at political participation. It was primarily defensive, focusing on equality before the law and the protection of individual citizens from abuse of power by magistrates. *Libertas* rested on institutions, *ius*, and *lex*; it was embodied by the *tribunes and their rights of *provocatio* (appeal) and *auxilium* ('defence' of the property and persons of members of the *plebs*); these are called the *duae arces libertatis tuendae* ('twin poles of the defence of liberty': Livy 3. 45. 8). In late republican conflicts *libertas* was claimed by *populares* against oppression by *optimates* ('best men'—i.e. the office-holding upper class: thus connected with the secret ballot) or a *factio paucorum* ('party of the few') (Caes. *BCiv.* 1. 22. 5; Augustus, *RG* 1).

During the empire, power was concentrated in one man's hands. Although *libertas* remained a favoured slogan of imperial ideology, nevertheless, according to *Tacitus (*Agr.* 3. 1), *principatus ac libertas* were not reconciled before *Nerva. Even so, liberty was increasingly reduced to the elementary meaning of security and protection under the law.

While freedom lost political significance, *eleutheria*/*libertas* became an important element in Christian teaching, emphasized especially by *Paul. Through God's gift and Christ's sacrifice his followers are liberated from sin, the finality of death, and the old law. Such freedom, however, involves subjection to the will of God: Christ's followers are God's 'slaves'. The freedom promised to Christians

is available to all humans, including the lowly and slaves, but it is not of this world and does not militate against existing social dependencies and political or ethical obligations. Accordingly, Christians did not oppose slavery as an institution, but in accepting slaves into their community they anticipated the universal brotherhood of the free expected in another world.

K. R.

ing affection and obligations between individuals belonging to separate social units. In Greek sources this bond is called *xenia*, *xeiniē*, and *xeineiē*; in Latin, *hospitium*. The individuals joined by the bond (usually men of approximately equal social status) are said to be each other's *xenos* or *hospes*. As the same terms designated guest–host relationships, *xenia* and *hospitium* have sometimes been interpreted in modern research as a form of hospitality. *Xenia*, *hospitium*, and hospitality do overlap to some extent but the former relationships display a series of additional features which assimilate them into the wider category called in social studies ritualized personal relationships, or pseudo-kinship. The analogy with kinship did not escape the notice of the ancients themselves. According to the *Aristotelian *Magna Moralia*, *xenia* was the strongest of all the relationships involving affection (*philia*) (2. 1381^{b}29). Aulus *Gellius wrote that a relationship with a *hospes* should take precedence over kinship and marriage in matters of affection and obligation (*NA* 5. 13. 5).

The lexicographer Hesychius defined *xenos* as 'a friend (*philos*) from abroad', and this definition holds good for the Roman *hospitium*: a ritualized friendship dyad could consist, for example, of an Athenian and a Spartan, a Thessalian and a Persian, a Carthaginian and a Syracusan, or a Roman and an Epirote, but very rarely consisted of two Athenians or two Romans. From its first appearance in *Homer (e.g. *Il.* 6. 224–5) onwards, ritualized friendship has been abundantly attested in both Greek and Latin sources from all periods and areas of classical antiquity. In late antiquity, it disappears from view. There are good reasons to assume, however, that it was gradually annexed by the Christian Church, since it reappears in a new guise in the early medieval variants of godparenthood: Latin *compaternitas*, and Byzantine *synteknia*.

One feature that ritualized friendship shared with kinship was the assumption of perpetuity: once the relationship had been established, the bond was believed to persist in latent form even if the partners did not interact with one another. This assumption had two practical consequences. First, the bond could be renewed or reactivated after years had elapsed, a variety of symbolic objects signalling that it once existed (*symbolon*, *pista*, *tessera hospitalis*). Secondly, the bond did not expire with the death of the partners themselves, but outlived them, passing on in the male line to their descendants.

If ritualized friends belonged to separate social units, how did their paths come to cross? Random encounters were made possible by the extraordinary geographic mobility of the Greeks and Romans, as well as by circumstances such as wars, festivals, and *colonization. Stories of how two eminent people first met and developed a liking for each other, and how they (or their descendants) recognized each other after many years of separation, undoubtedly exercised a special fascination over the ancients (e.g. Hdt. 3. 139 ff.).

The beginning of the relationship had to be marked with a ceremony, as did the reactivation of a relationship after many years. The rites of initiation into *xenia* and *hospitium* consisted of a diversity of symbolic elements enacted in sequence: a solemn declaration ('I make you my *xenos*', and 'I accept you'), an exchange of symbolic gifts, a handshake, and finally feasting (Xen. *Hell.* 4. 1. 39; Curt. 6. 5. 1 ff.; Cic. *Deiot.* 8; Livy 23. 9. 3–4; Aeschin. 3. 224. See SYMPOSIUM). The rites were obviously intended to lend the bond an aura of sacrosanctity, rendering it indissoluble. In practice, the bond could fade away through disuse. Its moral context was, however, such that only exceptionally was it interrupted by means of a formal ceremony (e.g. Hdt. 4. 154. 4, 3. 43. 2).

Ritualized friends were, by virtue of their prescribed duties, veritable co-parents. A *xenos* or *hospes* was supposed to show a measure of protective concern for his partner's son, to help him in any emergency, and to save his life (Hom. *Il.* 21. 42; Dem. 50. 56; Hdt. 9. 76; Lys. 18. 10; Plaut. *Mil.* 133–45). A father's partner in relation to the former's son was designated by a technical term: *patrikos* (or *patroos*) *xenos* in Greek, and *paternus hospes* in Latin. If the natural father was absent, ill, or dead, this paternal friend was expected to act as a substitute father. According to *Euripides' *Electra* and *Orestes*, for instance, Orestes was brought up, following the murder of his father *Agamemnon, in the household of Agamemnon's *xenoi*. Similarly, in real life, the Hellenistic statesman Aratus, following the murder of his father, was brought up in the household of his father's *xenoi* at Argos (Plut. *Arat.* 2–3). Cicero relates that on sensing danger he sent his children to the court of his *hospes* Deiotarus, king of Galatia (*Att.* 5. 17, cf. 18. 4). Neglect of coparental duties was strongly disapproved of, often evoking violent emotions (Eur. *Hec.* 689–714; Aeschin. 3. 225). Betrayal of ritualized friendship in general sometimes appears as a sin against the gods (Diod. Sic. 20. 70. 3–4).

In conformity with the coparental obligations, a father was supposed to name a son after his partner. The custom is more often found in Greek than in Roman sources (Thuc. 8. 6. 3; Diod. Sic. 14. 13. 5; Hdt. 3. 55). No explanation of its rationale survives, but a belief that some of the paternal friend's character traits will be passed on to the child with his name can be inferred from the paternal friend's obligation to take a share in the child's education (Hom. *Il.* 9. 483 ff., with Plut. *Phil.* 1; Livy 9. 36. 3, 42. 19. 3).

Ritualized friendship was an overwhelmingly upper-class institution in both Greece and Rome. The people involved in it belonged to a small minority, renowned for their wealth and identified by lofty titles such as 'hero', 'tyrant', satrap, 'nobleman', 'consul', 'governor', and 'emperor'. Throughout antiquity, such people lent each other powerful support, often at the expense of their inferiors, so frequently that ritualized friendship may justly be regarded as a tool for perpetuating class distinctions. The forms of mutual support practised included the exchange of valuable resources (e.g. money, troops, or grain), usually designated gifts, and the performance of important services (e.g. opportune intervention, saving life, catering for every need) usually designated benefactions (Greek *euergesiai*, Latin *beneficia*: see EUERGETISM). The circulation of these goods and services created what may be described as networks of ritualized friendship. The Greek and Roman worlds differed markedly in how these informal networks were integrated into their wider political systems.

In the world reflected in the Homeric poems, *xenia* and the networks to which it gave rise were of paramount importance to the hero. The hero abroad found in a *xenos* an effective substitute for kinsmen, a protector, representative, and ally, supplying in case of need shelter, protection, men, and arms; the community was not sufficiently organized to interfere with this sort of co-operation. The relationship being largely personal, ritualized friendship was, together with marriage, the Homeric forerunner of political and military alliances. The emergence of the *polis during the 8th and 7th cents. BC was accompanied by significant interactions between its nascent systems and this pre-existing network of personal alliances. Nor did the fully-fledged *polis* lead to the abolition of this network: throughout the Classical age, dense webs of ritualized friendship still stretched beyond its bounds, at times facilitating, at times obstructing the conduct of foreign affairs (e.g. Andoc. 2. 11; Thuc. 2. 13). For the upper classes of the Classical age, these networks offered an alternative means to the civic system of pursuing their own interests. In the Hellenistic age, the circles of 'friends' (*philoi*) came to be recruited from among the personal or paternal *xenoi* of the kings; having turned royal officials, these members of governing élites are often found to be acting as mediators between the kings and their own communities of origin, deriving substantial benefits from both systems. The impact of *xenia* upon the Greek civic system is most evident in the creation by the *polis* of *proxenia*, a bond of trust, clearly modelled upon *xenia*, between a *polis* and a prominent individual outside it.

Under the republic, prominent Romans maintained extensive ties of *hospitium* with prominent non-Romans both elsewhere in Italy and overseas. In the lawcourts, for instance, both *Cicero and *Caesar defended members of the aristocracy from various Italian communities. Pompey had hereditary ties of *hospitium* with the Numidian king Juba (Caes. *BCiv.* 2. 25), while Mark *Antony was an ancestral *xenos* of the Herods of Judaea (Joseph. *AJ* 14. 320). *Livy was probably attributing contemporary customs to an earlier age when he assigned to the Etruscan king *Tarquinius Superbus motives epitomizing the role of ritualized friendship in a country of separate communities: 'the Latin race he strove particularly to make his friends, so that his strength abroad might contribute to his security at home. He contracted with their nobles not only ties of *hospitium* but also matrimonial connections' (Livy 1. 49. 9). The sort of upper-class coalitions reflected in this example could, however, easily be overpowered by the state, and therefore posed less of a threat to the Roman community than such coalitions previously had to any single Greek city-state. Rome followed in Greece's footsteps by devising *hospitium publicum*, a public institution analogous to *proxenia*, modelled on *hospitium*.

Hospitium, like *patronage, was instrumental in the *Romanization of local élites (Livy 9. 36. 3, 42. 19. 3–6), in their upward social mobility, and in their integration into the Roman ruling class (e.g. Cic. *Clu.* 25. 165, with *Vir. ill.* 80. 1). Within the Roman empire, the communities in which ritualized friends lived gradually became part of a larger-scale political system, and this change tended to relax the principle that ritualized friends must belong to separate communities. Fronto saw nothing unusual in characterizing as a *hospes* a friend who originated from the same African city as himself, and a 2nd-cent. AD inscription from Spain sees *hospitium* as compatible with kinship ties (*Ad amicos* 1. 3; *CIL* 2. 2633).

G. He.

Gaius, the emperor, 'Caligula' (Gaius Iulius Caesar Germanicus, AD 12–41), son of *Germanicus and Agrippina the Elder, born at Antium (31 August). In 14–16 he was on the Rhine with his parents and, dressed in miniature uniform, was nicknamed 'Caligula' ('Bootee') by the soldiers. He went with his parents to the east in 17 and, after Germanicus' death in 19, lived in Rome with his mother until her arrest in 29, then successively with Livia and Antonia until he joined *Tiberius on Capreae. The downfall of Tiberius' favourite *Sejanus in 31 was to Gaius' advantage, and it was probably engineered by him and associates such as the prefect of the watch (*vigiles*) Macro, who also benefited. After the death of his brother Drusus Iulius Caesar in 33 Gaius was the only surviving son of Germanicus and, with Tiberius Iulius Caesar Nero 'Gemellus'—*Claudius' claim not being considered—next in succession. He became pontifex (see PRIESTS) in 31 and was quaestor two years later, but received no other training in public life. Tiberius made Gaius and Gemellus joint heirs to his property, but, supported by Macro, now prefect of the praetorian guard (*praefectus praetorio*), Gaius was proclaimed emperor (16 March 37), Tiberius' will being declared invalid by the senate, although his acts as a whole were not invalidated; Gaius made an appropriately perfunctory effort to have him deified.

Gaius' accession was greeted with widespread joy and relief, and his civility promised well. One symbolic gesture was the restoration of electoral choice to the popular assemblies, taken from them in 14 (it failed and Gaius had to revert to Tiberian procedure). Gaius needed to enhance his authority and held the consulship four times, in 37 (suffect, so that the men in office in March were not disturbed), 39, 40 (sole consul), and 41; he became Pater Patriae (father of his country), a title refused by Tiberius, on 21 September, 37. In the early months of his rule he honoured the memory of his mother, father, and brothers and spoke abusively of Tiberius. Antonia, a restraining influence, died on 1 May 37. In October Gaius was seriously ill; Philon Judaeus' view (*Leg.* 14, 22) that this unhinged him has been given too much attention. But the illness may

have brought the succession question into prominence: some time before 24 May 38, Gaius executed both Macro and his rival Gemellus. In 39 Gaius quarrelled with the senate, revised his attitude towards Tiberius' memory, announcing the return of slandering the emperor as a treasonable offence. The same year he married his fourth wife, Milonia Caesonia, who had already borne him a daughter, proving her fertility. The autumn and winter of 39–40 Gaius spent in Gaul and on the Rhine; a conspiracy was revealed whose leader, Gnaeus Cornelius Lentulus Gaetulicus, commander of the Upper Rhine army, was executed. This conspiracy may be connected with the simultaneous disgrace of his brother-in-law (and possible successor) Marcus Aemilius Lepidus and of Gaius' surviving sisters *Agrippina ('Agrippina the Younger') and Iulia Livilla. After his return to Rome (in ovation, on 31 August 40) Gaius was in constant danger of assassination, having no successor to avenge him, displayed increasing brutality, and was murdered in the palace on 22 or 24 January 41. His wife and daughter were also murdered.

The government of Gaius was autocratic and capricious, and he accepted extravagant honours which came close to deification. His reign has been interpreted as a departure from the Augustan Principate to a Hellenistic monarchy. Rather, Gaius seems to have been engaged in discovering the limits of his power ('for me anything is licit', Suet. *Calig.* 29). He was a person of the highest descent (he once banished *Agrippa from his ancestry by postulating incest between Augustus and his daughter *Julia), which helps to account for the unprecedented attention paid to his sisters, Iulia Drusilla, whose death in 38 was followed by a public funeral and consecration, Livilla, and Agrippina; he possessed an exceptional intellect and a cruel and cynical wit; and he demanded exceptional homage and was savage if his superiority was not recognized. A gifted orator, who delivered Livia's funerary oration at the age of 17, he enjoyed writing rebuttals of successful speeches. By insisting on primacy in everything Gaius left even courtiers no role of their own. He had terrified the senators, humiliated officers of the praetorian guard (who carried out the assassination), and only the masses seem to have regretted his passing.

Gaius was a keen builder, interested in the state of Italy's roads and in Rome's water supply (he began the aqua Claudia (see AQUEDUCTS) and Anio Novus). For the sake of the grain supply he began to improve the harbour at Rhegium in south Italy. He also completed the reconstruction of the theatre of Pompey and created a circus in the Vatican; other constructions were for his own pleasure, for instance the bridge of boats from Puteoli to Bauli (39), an ephemeral extravagance to outdo *Xerxes or overawe a Parthian hostage.

Gaius' high expenditures were economically advantageous, ending the sluggishness of Tiberius' regime. His achievements abroad, with the exception of his deployment of client rulers, were negative. He probably raised two new legions (XV and XXII Primigeniae) for an invasion of Germany or *Britain. However, his forays into Germany in the autumn of 39 may have been exercises intended to restore discipline after the fall of Gaetulicus and to commemorate the campaigns of Germanicus in 13–16 (the famous collection of sea shells, 'spoils of Ocean', probably alludes to the North Sea storms that Germanicus had encountered); here the Chauci and Chatti were still causing trouble in 41. The conquest of Britain was only mooted, and was considered achieved when Cunobelinus' (Cymbeline's) son Adminius came to render homage (Gaius could not afford to leave the centres of empire in 39–40). By deposing and executing Ptolemy of Mauretania he provoked a war that was brought to an end only in the next reign. For the Jews under Gaius see below.

J. P. B.; B. M. L.

Gaius and the Jews Soon after his accession, Gaius conferred a kingship in Palestine upon his friend, the Herodian Agrippa I. However, their understanding did not prevent discord between the inconsistent emperor and his Jewish subjects. A savage conflict between Jews and Greeks in *Alexandria stood unresolved when Gaius died. The prefect, Aulus Avillius Flaccus, seemingly abandoning any pretence at even-handedness when Gaius succeeded, had backed the Greek side in the long-standing dispute with the Jews over citizen rights. Agrippa I, visiting *en route* for his kingdom, was mocked by the Greek crowd and a pogrom thereby unleashed. It was on the emperor's birthday that Jews who had survived the assaults on the Jewish quarter were rounded up in the theatre and made to eat pork. While Gaius did have Flaccus arrested and replaced in late 38, he disdainfully ignored the delegations sent to Rome by both groups, leaving his successor to investigate and settle the matter.

Among the Jews of Palestine, Gaius' policy was heading for disaster when he died. A statue of the emperor was to be placed in the Jerusalem Temple and worshipped: this was perhaps Gaius' reaction to the Alexandrian Jewish delegation (Josephus), perhaps a response to the destruction by Jews at Jamnia, of their pagan neighbours' altar to the emperor (Philo). Stalling by Publius Petronius, governor of Syria, apparently sympathetic to Jewish pleas, delayed developments; and the intervention of Agrippa, whose long and perhaps genuine letter to Gaius is quoted by Philo, is alleged to have effected the abandonment of the plan. Philo claims that it was then reinstated by secret orders; but this he could scarcely have known. In general lines, however, the events are well documented: Philo was a participant, heading the Alexandrian Jews' delegation to Gaius, while *Josephus offers two distinct accounts of the events in Palestine. T. R.

games (*see following page*)

gardens Two strands of landscape management coalesce in ancient Mediterranean garden culture: the intensification of agricultural production in fertile places where a high input of *labour can achieve very high yield per unit area; and the local improvement of the amenity of the natural environment for human activities of all kinds, like building a house but relying much more on what nature provides. Both, above all else, depend on use of *water, and are inextricably linked.

Culturally, the main traditions (including the amenity of plants and trees in *Minoan art) all go back to the gardens of the Fertile Crescent. The Persian combination of preserve and pleasure known as *paradeisos* has a special place. Early Greek intensive horticulture created places whose amenity, for abundance of shade or the presence of water, was esteemed (already in Homer, esp. *Od.* 7. 112 f.), and this was the style of the famous Garden of the philosopher *Epicurus. Trees were planted in *sanctuaries for their cultic significance or for shade, and by extension, in public places such as the *agora. But a high aesthetic tradition dates only from the domestication of the *paradeisos* in the 4th cent. BC and especially the Hellenistic and Roman periods.

This garden-art aimed particularly at reshaping place, and gave rise to the Roman name of formal gardening, *ars topiaria* (which went far beyond 'topiary', though this was one of its techniques). Use of slopes, views of different scenery, the deployment of architectural adjuncts and numerous sculptures, and the evocation of specific literary or traditional landscapes or stories were among the themes (as in *Hadrian's villa at Tibur); natural features such as springs, streams, hills, caves, and woods, were improved or created *ex novo*. In all this plants were important, but not central; specimen exotics (*viridia*, whence *viridiarium*) evoked alien worlds (as birds and animals, which might also be ultimately destined for the table, did too) or pleased through scent, foliage contrast, or shade. Flowers were prized, but in Mediterranean conditions and before much improvement of the strain, were very limited in their season (hence the value of twice-blooming roses) and grown more for their use in garlands than for their effect in a bed.

Remembering the days when a *hortus* was the lot of a

[*continued on p. 295*]

games

games (*agōnes*), in the special sense of formal contests, usually in honour of a Greek god or local hero.

Before 300 BC Prior to the 8th cent. BC they seem to have been small-scale events, centring round a shrine or sanctuary. But the *agōn* (agonistic festival) at *Olympia came to acquire a special status: traditionally founded in 776 BC, by the end of the 8th cent. it was, because of the wide range of *athletic contests it offered and its lack of political ties, attracting increasing numbers of foreigners (especially from among the athletic Spartans) and was organized as a Panhellenic *agōn* (i.e. the contests were open to all Greeks). With interstate relationships assuming increased importance during the 7th cent., local *agōnes* were reorganized at other places too. The Pythian Games at *Delphi became Panhellenic in 582 BC; its range of athletics events followed the Olympian model, but it preserved its identity and associations with *Apollo through its emphasis on musical competitions. With the reorganization of the Isthmian (*c*.581) and Nemean Games (*c*.573), a group of four Panhellenic *agōnes* came to form an athletics circuit (*periodos*), as the Olympics, World Championships, European, and Commonwealth Games do for some athletes nowadays. At Athens the festival of the Great Panathenaea (founded 566) was also Panhellenic, but for athletes never achieved the status of the other four. Despite this development, local *agōnes* with athletics contests continued to flourish: *Pindar's victory-odes mention more than 20 local games (cf. *Ol.* 13. 107–13; also Simon. *Epig.* 43 Page), and a 5th-cent. Laconian inscription records 72 victories won by Damonon and his son Enymacratidas at eight *agōnes* in the Peloponnese (*IG* 5. 1. 213, trans. W. Sweet, *Sport and Recreation in Ancient Greece: A Sourcebook with Translations* (1987), 145–6).

Contests were often in athletics, but music, poetry, and equestrian events were also popular. *Hesiod won a poetry-singing competition in Chalcis (*Op.* 657); the Pythian Games included three types of musical contest (singing to the accompaniment of cithara or aulos, and solo aulos) and a painting competition (Pliny *HN* 35. 58). In Athens tragedies, comedies, and dithyrambs (choral songs) were performed in competitions at the City Dionysia, and at the Panathenaea rhapsodes (professional reciters of poetry) competed in Homer-reciting contests. Horse- and chariot-races were mainly entered by wealthy individuals who paid charioteers or jockeys to ride on their behalf, and hoped for political prestige from good performances (cf. Alcibiades' boast, Thuc. 6. 16. 2). The chariot-race was often long (about 14 km. (nearly 9 mi.) at the Olympian Games) and dangerous (Pind. *Pyth.* 5. 49–51: the victor was the only one of 40 starters to finish with chariot intact). Beauty contests, drinking contests, and even a wool-carding contest are also recorded.

At the four major Panhellenic *agōnes*, victors were honoured with a wreath: olive at Olympia, laurel at the Pythian Games, varieties of *selinon* (parsley or celery) at the Isthmus and Nemea (but cf. hyp. c *Nem.*, hyp. b *Isthm.*; Paus. 8. 48. 2). At other venues wreaths were made of date-palms (Paus. 8. 48. 2) or myrtle (Pind. *Isthm.* 4. 88). The victor might also be showered with leaves (*phyllobolia*). On returning home he could receive more substantial rewards: free supplies of food (*sitēsis*), the privilege of a front seat (*prohedria*) when spectating at *agōnes*, and gifts. Athens was especially generous to victors: *Solon passed legislation to award Athenian victors at Olympia 500 drachmae (Plut. *Sol.* 23; monetary prizes are however anachronistic at this early date—see COINAGE, GREEK), and at the Great Panathenaea in the 4th cent. BC money, gold crowns, bulls, and large numbers of amphorae containing olive oil were awarded as prizes (*IG* 2². 2311, trans. S. Miller (ed.), *Arete: Greek Sports from Ancient Sources*, 2nd edn. (1991) 80–3; 100 amphorae, *c*.4,000 l. (880 gal.), for a victor in the men's *stadion* race, a very valuable prize). Local *agōnes* also awarded prizes: silver cups at Sicyon (Pind. *Nem.* 10. 43), a bronze shield at Argos, and a thick cloak at Pellene (Pind. *Ol.* 7. 83, 9. 97–8).

To lose in a contest was shameful, and the incidence of failure-induced depression and mental illness is likely to have been high (cf. Pind. *Ol.* 8. 68–9, *Pyth.* 8. 81–7; Paus. 6. 9. 6).

After 300 BC The spread of 'periodic' contests in the Greek style is a defining feature of post-Classical *Hellenism. In the 3rd and 2nd cents. BC they were sponsored by kings (the Alexandrian Ptolemaea and Pergamene Nicephoria) and leagues (the Soteria of *Delphi, by the Aetolian Confederacy) as well as cities great and small (e.g. the plethora of Boeotian *agōnes* by *c.*50 BC: A. Gossage, *BSA* 1975, 115 ff.). Under the Roman Principate this expansion continued; provincial cities founded new games as late as AD 275–6; by the 3rd cent. they were celebrated from *Carthage to Zeugma in Syria. At Rome they were first introduced under *Nero, followed by *Domitian (the Capetolia of 86), *Gordian III (the *agōn* for Athena Promachos of 242) and Aurelian, whose *agōn* of the Sun (274) was still celebrated under *Julian. Frowned on by Christianity, Greek games (shorn of pagan ritual) none the less survived until at least 521, when Justinian banned the Olympia of *Antioch.

The distinctiveness of 'sacred' games, celebrating a deity (often the city's patron god or, under Rome, the *ruler-cult) and (at first) offering only a symbolic prize (typically a crown, *stephanos*), is fundamental. In the Hellenistic age the recognition of new 'sacred' games required cumbersome interstate diplomacy by the promoter (best attested with the Leucophryena of Magnesia on the Maeander in W. Asia Minor (*I. Magn.* 16–87)). From 30 BC Roman emperors decided 'the gift of a sacred contest', weighing up cost, a city's record of loyalty and, in 3rd-cent. Cilicia (SE Asia Minor), its support for imperial troop-movements. An élite group of 'iselastic' games emerged, often named after one of the famous games of the 'ancient circuit' (*archaia periodos*), and distinctive for the privileges which victors could demand of their home cities, notably a triumphal entry, pension (*opsonion*), and tax-immunity (*ateleia*). Otherwise there were prize-games (*thematitai, themides*), also subject to Roman control.

'Sacred' contests comprised a sacrifice, to which other Greek cities sent representatives (*theōroi* or more often, under Rome, *synthytai*), and a profane festival (*panēgyris*), often incorporating *markets and fairs, as well as the contests proper, supervised by an *agōnothetēs*. Funding of new contests relied heavily on civic *euergetism; infrequently emperors—notably *Hadrian (C. P. Jones, *JRA* 1990, 487)—stepped in.

Whatever the qualitative view taken of post-Classical agonistic culture (for contests in ruler-encomium see A. Hardie, *Statius and the* Silvae (1983)), its power in the shaping of later Hellenism is undeniable, and the limits of its diffusion suggest the limits of Hellenism. See ATHLETICS; COMEDY (GREEK); MUSIC; TRAGEDY, GREEK. S. J. I.; A. J. S. S.

citizen, the whimsical Roman élite labelled its suburban garden-palaces 'vegetable gardens', *horti*, and these often achieved remarkable levels of costly and allusive complexity. On a humbler scale, the features of *ars topiaria* were widely disseminated across the Roman world. For our understanding, the town gardens of *Pompeii are especially important, with the garden-paintings which complemented them (see p. 296), but good examples come also from Fishbourne in Britain and Conimbriga in Portugal, Thuburbo Maius in Africa and several cities of southern France. N. P.

Gaul (Cisalpine) (see ◀Map 5, Cc▶) The prosperous northern region of modern Italy, comprising the Po (Padus) plain and its mountain fringes from the Apennines to the Alps, was known to the Romans as Cisalpine Gaul. In the middle republic it was not even considered part of Italy, which extended only to the foothills of the Apennines along a line roughly from Pisa to Rimini (Ariminum). Beyond the Apennines lay Gaul, a land inhabited by Celtic peoples whom the Romans looked upon with fear and wonder. (See GAUL (TRANSALPINE).)

The background to this situation is difficult to reconstruct in detail. Archaeological evidence broadly confirms literary reports of *Etruscan settlement in Emilia-Romagna during the 6th cent. BC, and of the infiltration of Celtic peoples from beyond the Alps during the 5th and 4th cents. Rich warrior graves of the iron age Golasecca culture in Piedmont and Lombardy point to a warrior aristocracy similar to that of the Halstatt culture of central Europe; and these same Golasecca sites during the 5th and 4th cents. contain increasing amounts of La Tène material. Further south there is evidence of a growing Celtic presence in Emilia-Romagna, where Etruscan and La Tène graves are found side by side in the same cemeteries.

gardens A wall-painting from *Pompeii (*c.* AD 70) evokes Roman garden-art. It shows a statue of Mars, lush planting, and exotic birds.

The most detailed literary account of the Gallic occupation of the Po valley is that of *Livy (5. 34–5), who describes a succession of migrations by different tribes, beginning with the Insubres, who moved into the region around Milan (Mediolanum) in the 6th cent. BC. They were followed, in the course of the next two centuries, by the Cenomani, Libui, Salui, Boii, and Lingones. The last group to arrive were the Senones, who by the start of the 4th cent. had occupied the strip of land along the Adriatic known as the *ager Gallicus*. This account, which can be supplemented by other sources, is compatible with the archaeological evidence, although the latter implies a process of gradual infiltration rather than violent invasions. By the early 4th cent. the Gauls had completely displaced the Etruscans in the Po valley, and had begun to make occasional raids across the Apennines into peninsular Italy (in one of which, in *c.*386 BC, they sacked Rome). Further Gallic invasions occurred sporadically throughout the 4th and 3rd cents. (Polyb. 2. 18–31), culminating in the great invasion of 225 BC, which the Romans and their Italian allies defeated at Telamon.

The Romans responded by invading Cisalpine Gaul, which they overran in a three-year campaign of conquest ending with the capture of Mediolanum (Milan) in 222. Their efforts to consolidate the conquest, which included the foundation of colonies at Placentia (Piacenza) and Cremona, were however interrupted by *Hannibal's invasion, which prompted the Gauls to rebel. After defeating Hannibal, the Romans resumed their plan of conquest, which they completed in 191 with a victory over the Boii, the most powerful of the Cisalpine Gallic tribes. The colonies at Placentia and Cremona were refounded (190 BC), and further colonies were settled at Bononia (= Bologna, 189 BC), Parma, and Mutina (both 183). In 187 the via Aemilia (from which the modern region of Emilia takes its name) was constructed from Ariminum to Placentia. As a result of this great programme of colonization (still evident in aerial photographs which show traces of *centuriation throughout the region), virtually all of the land south of the Po was occupied by settlers from peninsular Italy, while the northern part of the plain remained largely in the hands of its Celtic inhabitants, who were henceforth known to the Romans as Transpadani.

After the Social War of 91–89 BC (see ROME, HISTORY §1.5) Cisalpine Gaul was formally separated from Italy and became a Province, with its southern border at the Rubicon; but all the colonial settlers who were not already Roman Citizens were enfranchised. The rest of the free population, which effectively meant the Transpadani, were given Latin rights, a decision that they greatly resented; the demand for full citizen rights became a hot political issue in the following decades, until the Transpadani were finally enfranchised by Caesar in 49. In 42 Cisalpine Gaul was fully integrated within Italy, and under Augustus was divided into four of the eleven administrative regions of Italy (VIII–XI).

In the centuries after 200 BC Cisalpine Gaul was rapidly and thoroughly Romanized, and few traces of Celtic language and culture remained by the time of the empire. An area of rich agricultural land, much of which was reclaimed by Roman drainage schemes in the lower Po valley, Cisalpine Gaul achieved great prosperity; by the time of *Strabo, who gives an eloquent description of it (5. 1. 12, 218 C), it had become what it still is today, one of the most wealthy and prosperous parts of Europe.   T. J. Co.

Gaul (Transalpine) (see ◀Map 5▶) comprised the area from the Pyrenees and the Mediterranean coast of modern France to the English Channel, and the Atlantic to the Rhine and the western Alps. As a geopolitical entity, it emerged in the 1st cent. BC and lasted into the 5th cent. AD. Augustus divided Gaul into four provinces: Narbonensis, Lugdunensis, Aquitania, and Belgica. The Flavians annexed the Agri Decumates and attached them to Upper Germany—carved, like Lower Germany, out of Belgica. *Diocletian subdivided all six Gallic provinces, making a total of thirteen.

Gaul was predominantly Celtic in culture, but it did not include the Celts of the Danube and northern Italy; and it contained Ligurians and Iberians in the south, and Germanic immigrants in the north-east. The south had also been heavily influenced by Greek *colonization. Hence 'Gaul' was not a natural unit, but a Roman artefact. In order to protect the route to Spain, Rome helped Massalia (Marseille) against bordering tribes. The result was, in 121 BC, the formation of 'the Province' (*Provincia*), from the Mediterranean to Lake Geneva, with its capital at Narbo. In 58–50 BC, Caesar seized the remainder of Gaul, justifying his conquest by playing on Roman memories of savage attacks over the Alps by Celts and Germans. Italy was now to be defended from the Rhine.

Initially, indeed, the Romans treated the Gauls as barbarians. They disparaged Gaul beyond the Province as *Gallia Comata*—'Long-haired Gaul', and generally mismanaged the Province itself. However, Gaul was not far behind Rome. Ligurian communities had long emulated Massilia; and, in the Celtic core, Caesar found nations (*civitates*) establishing urban centres (*oppida*) which, though hardly classical cities, had significant socio-economic functions. Under the more prudent rule of the emperors, the Province, now Narbonensis, was seeded with military colonies, and became a land of city-states, comparable with Italy. In the other 'Three Gauls', colonies were few and the *civitates* were retained, but their leaders vied with each other in acquiring the conquerors' culture.

The *Romanization of northern Gaul is illustrated by the dominance of Latin, and the emergence of the Graeco-Roman city. The *civitates* were too large to be city-states, but they contained towns that could be designated as their administrative centres and developed, under local magnates, in accordance with classical criteria. Most were unwalled. On the land, Romanization took the form of *villas—at this time working farms as much as country residences.

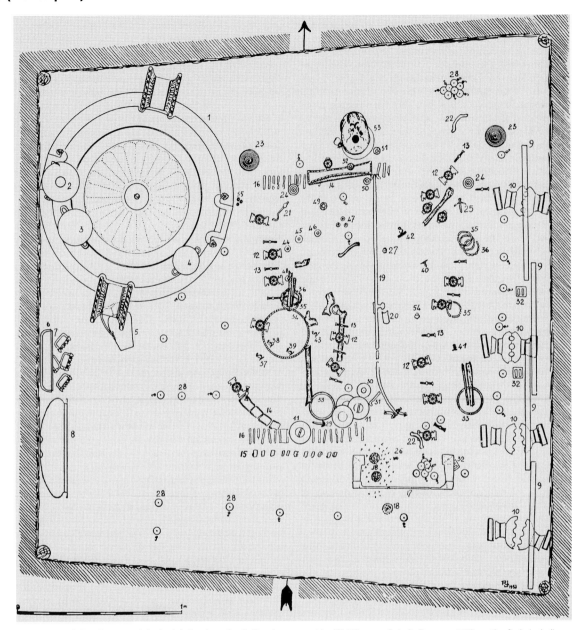

Gaul, Transalpine Drawing of the burial chamber of a Gallic aristocrat at Vix (Châtillon-sur-Seine), France, c.500 BC, the finds including Mediterranean imports of wine-drinking vessels. From the 2nd cent. BC this taste of the Celtic élites was expressed in imports of Italian *wine, until S. Gaul itself became a wine-exporter in the 1st cent. AD.

The population of Gaul was large: c.10,000,000. Agriculture flourished. One of the great engines of its success was the Rhine army, which stimulated trade by purchasing supplies from the interior. Commerce was facilitated by an extensive road- and river-network. The metropolis of high imperial Gaul was Lugdunum (Lyons), at a main junction of these networks. There was little resistance to Roman rule. Localized revolts in AD 21 and 69–70 were easily suppressed; they probably accelerated the demise of the pre-Roman aristocracy. Few Gauls subsequently involved themselves in Roman imperial careers.

Early Roman Gaul came to an end late in the 3rd cent.

External pressures exacerbated internal weaknesses, and neglect of the Rhine frontier resulted in barbarian invasions and civil war. For a while Gaul was governed by a separate line of emperors (beginning with Postumus). Though order was restored, much had changed: the Agri Decumates were abandoned; and cities began to be fortified. However, there had still been no move to gain independence; and, after the restructuring of the empire by Diocletian and Constantine I, Gaul enjoyed stability and enhanced prestige.

For Rome renewed its commitment to defend Italy from the Rhine. A praetorian prefect was based in northern Gaul, usually in Augusta Treverorum (Trier), and rulers frequently sojourned there. Though the frontier was occasionally broken, it was always restored. There was a recovery of economic prosperity, though uneven. Trier was endowed with magnificent buildings, but most cities never recovered their former grandeur. The upper classes now eagerly sought posts in the imperial administration, making much of their rhetorical skills (the 4th cent. saw the blossoming of Gallic education). When not at court, influential Gauls, such as Ausonius, favoured the country life and built themselves palatial villas. Christianity spread; an episcopal hierarchy developed, and monasticism was introduced.

From 395, the division of the empire between eastern and western rulers again caused the neglect of the Rhine frontier, reflected in the transfer of the Gallic prefect to Arelate (Arles). By 418, as the consequence of Germanic invasion and civil war, Franks and Burgundians were established over the Rhine, and the Visigoths in Aquitania. These were kept in check, until the death of Flavius Aetius and the growing debility of the western government created a power-vacuum. The 460s and 470s saw Visigothic encroachment on Roman territory to the east, while the Burgundians expanded westwards from Savoy. In 476, the last imperial possessions in the south were ceded to the Visigoths.

Gaul suffered badly. Refugees fled southwards, only to find high taxation and corruption. Yet, as is evident from the writings of Sidonius Apollinaris, the aristocracy remained remarkably resilient. Down to the mid-5th cent., its members tolerated the Germans while still looking to Rome for status and protection. Thereafter, they increasingly worked for the barbarian kings. Thus, at least in the centre and south of the country, the Gallo-Roman cultural legacy was bequeathed intact to the successor-kingdoms.

Roman Gaul seemed destined to become Visigothic Gaul until, late in the 5th cent., Clovis led the Salian Franks south, and eventually drove the Visigoths into Spain.

J. F. Dr.

Gellius, Aulus, Roman miscellanist, born between AD 125 and 128, author of *Noctes Atticae* ('Attic Nights') in twenty books. Internal evidence suggests publication *c.*180; an apparent echo in Apuleius' *Apology*, sometimes used to support an earlier date, can be otherwise explained. A probable reference in Fronto apart, all knowledge of Gellius comes from his work: reconstruction of his life depends on the assumption, so far unfalsified, that his anecdotes, even if fictitious, are not anachronistic. There are slight but uncertain indications that he came from a Roman colony in Africa: however, most of his life was spent at Rome. He studied with Sulpicius Apollinaris, and knew Fronto; but the deepest impression was made on him by Favorinus. He spent at least a year in Athens completing his education as a pupil of Calvenus Taurus; he visited Tiberius Claudius Atticus Herodes in his summer retreat at Cephisia, attended the Pythian Games of (probably) August 147, and enjoyed the life of a student and a tourist. After his return he was appointed a judge to try private cases (14. 2. 1); but his interest in the law is essentially antiquarian.

The *Noctes Atticae* (of which we lack the start of the preface, the end of bk. 20, and all bk. 8 except the chapter-headings) is a collection of mainly short chapters, based on notes or excerpts he had made in reading, on a great variety of topics in philosophy, history, law, but above all grammar in its ancient sense, including literary and textual criticism. According to his preface, Gellius conceived the notion of giving literary form to his notes during the long winter's nights in Attica (whence the title), but completed the project (some 30 years later) as an instructive entertainment for his children. Variety and charm are imparted by the constant changes of topic, purportedly reproducing the chance order of Gellius' notes (a cliché of such works), and by the use of dialogue and reminiscence as literary forms for conveying information; the dramatizations are generally fictitious, though in settings based on Gellius' own experience. The characters of Gellius' friends and teachers are finely drawn; the fictitious persons are less individual.

Gellius is well read in Latin, less so in Greek (though he shows some knowledge of Homeric scholarship); his judgement is sensible rather than incisive. His style blends the archaic, the self-consciously classical, and the new: he lifts words from early authors but also invents new ones, he construes *plenus* only with the genitive but occasionally admits *quod* clauses instead of accusative and infinitive. He shares the age's preference for Early Latin and Sallust over Augustan and Silver writers, but admires *Virgil and will hear no ill of *Cicero (10. 3; 17. 5); most striking, however, is his liking for Claudius Quadrigarius, of whom he supplies almost half the extant fragments.

In later antiquity Gellius was diligently read by Nonius Marcellus, *Ammianus, and Macrobius; in the Middle Ages he was excerpted in several florilegia. For the Renaissance he was a well-spring of learning and a model for humanistic writing; though displaced from his central position and disparaged along with his age, he has never lacked readers who relish not only the information he conveys, the quotations he preserves, and the reflections he arouses, but also the charm of his style and his infectious love of books.

L. A. H.-S.

(a)

(b)

(c)

(d)

gems A selection of engraved gems used as personal seals, showing a variety of devices, stones, and dates: (a) youth restraining a horse on a chalcedony scarab (Greek, 6th cent. BC); (b) woman-harpist on a rock crystal scarab (Greek, 5th–4th cent. BC); (c) man's ? portrait on a garnet ringstone (Greek, 3rd–1st cent. BC); (d) *Odysseus (right) with Diomedes on a cornelian (Roman).

gems Precious stones were valued in antiquity as possessing magical and medicinal virtues, as ornaments, and as seals when engraved with a device. Such engravings (intaglios) in soft media like steatite or *ivory are found in early Minoan days; the use of hard stones dates from the middle Minoan age. Late Minoan and Mycenaean gems have a rich repertory of human and animal designs; the favoured shapes are the lenticular (round) and amygdaloid (sling-stone) (see MINOAN and MYCENAEAN CIVILIZATION). In sub-Mycenaean and geometric times the art of working hard stones was largely lost. A revival in the 7th cent. BC is usually associated with the island of Melos, and the commencement of Classical gem engraving in the 6th cent. is marked by the introduction of the scarab (beetle) form of seal from Egypt. This was soon abandoned in Greece for the scaraboid, which omits the beetle-back. The late 5th and 4th cents. mark the high point of Greek gem engraving. In Hellenistic times the choice of subjects grows restricted, but excellent work was done in portraiture. In Italy the Etruscans used the scarab until the 3rd cent.; gems of the later Roman republic show a wide range of subjects, combined with clumsiness of execution. With Augustus begins the large series of 'Graeco-Roman' gems. A period of indifferent work in the middle empire is succeeded by a revival under Constantine I.

Several gem-engravers are recorded in literature, e.g.

Pyrgoteles, who worked for *Alexander the Great; others are known from their signatures on extant stones, though many signatures are false. Engravers of gems used the drill and the wheel. These had to be coated with powdered emery (of which Naxos was and is an important source), except for working softer stones such as steatite, which was consequently often used in the earlier periods. The stones most favoured for engraving in view of their durability, moderate hardness, and absence of grain were quartzes, especially those of the crypto-crystalline variety such as agate, plasma, jasper, carnelian, and most popular of all, sard. Red garnet, amethyst, lapis lazuli were much prized in jewellery. Cameos in which design and background were in contrasted colours were made of layered stones such as onyx and sardonyx. Of the hardest stones, emeralds, aquamarines, and sapphires were rarely engraved, while the diamond, probably unknown before the 1st cent. AD, was not even cut. The diamond-point, however, was sometimes used for engraving other stones. Imitations of gems in glass paste were apparently much in demand; in the British Museum collection they even outnumber sards. Glass imitations of rock crystal and red garnet were considered particularly convincing.

F. N. P.; D. E. E.; M. V.

genealogy, the enumeration of descent from an ancestor. Legendary pedigree was particularly important in Greece. Before fighting, *Homeric heroes boast of their ancestry, citing between two and eight generations of ancestors (e.g. *Il.* 6. 145–211, Glaucus). *Hesiod's poetry is preoccupied with legendary ancestry (*Theogony, Catalogue of Women*); even aristocrats in Classical Athens (which put more stress on recent achievements) claimed descent from important local and Homeric heroes, and thence from the gods: cf. the Philaid genealogy (Marcellin. *Life of Thucydides* 3); *Andocides was descended from *Odysseus and therefore *Hermes (Hellanicus, *FGrH* 323a F 24), *Alcibiades from Eurysaces (and *Zeus) (Pl. *Alc.* I. 121a), *Plato from *Solon and Codrus (Plut. *Sol.* I. 2). Other groups, cities, colonies, or tribes (see ETHNICITY), might trace descent from a single legendary figure, and genealogies were sometimes akin to king-lists (e.g. *Sparta), or assimilated with lists of office-holders. Some of the first prose writers recorded (or worked out) genealogies, mostly legendary, as well as their chronological implications: Hecataeus of Miletus (c.500 BC), Acusilaus of Agos, Pherecydes, Hellanicus. Genealogies and their enumeration were evidently popular (Polyb. 9. 1. 4), especially in Sparta, as Hippias found (Pl. *Hp. mai.* 285d), despite Plato's criticisms (*Tht.* 174e ff.). They reflect the enormous significance attributed by the Greeks to origins and the original ancestor in determining the character of future generations. Prestige, status, even moral character, might be derived from the original progenitor, preferably legendary, heroic, or divine. (The Romans, more interested in their recent ancestors (Polyb. 6. 53 f.) only adopted the Greek penchant for legendary ancestry in the course of

Hellenization (see HELLENISM) from the 2nd cent. BC (T. P. Wiseman, *G&R* 1974, 153 ff.).) Political and tribal affiliations might, similarly, be seen in genealogical terms. Given the value of the original ancestor, it is therefore unsurprising that the intervening links were sometimes vague or forgotten, and it may be the professional genealogists who did much to create continuous and coherent stemmata (R. Thomas, *Oral Tradition and Written Record in Classical Athens* (1989)). However, intermediate ancestors would also, obviously, carry prestige or opprobrium, and unsuitable ancestors would drop from view. Such is the moral or political importance of ancestry, that genealogy tends to reflect the current position or claims of a family, and thus it is usually the least reliable of historical traditions. Numerous inconsistencies would arise from the symbolic reflection of current status in past genealogy, and it is these contradictions which the genealogists were in part trying to resolve.

R. T.

genre, a grouping of texts related within the system of literature by their sharing recognizably functionalized features of form and content. Theory of genre as such is quite lacking in antiquity (its place is taken by theories of *imitatio*) and ancient theoretical discussions of specific literary genres are few and for the most part unsatisfactory. They operate according to criteria which are one-sidedly formal (generally metrical), thematic (the characters' moral or social quality, the general subject-matter), or pragmatic (the situation of performance), but scarcely attempt to correlate or justify them; they are more interested in classifying existing works than in understanding the mechanisms of literary production and reception and are directed to the needs of the school and the library, not to the critic's; they bungle some genres (lyric) and ignore others (the novel). Rhetorical handbooks sometimes distinguish among oratorical genres, but the precise relation between their (often pedantic) prescriptions and the literary works remains uncertain.

*Plato (*Resp.* 3. 392d–394c) differentiates a number of existing poetic genres in terms of their constitutive modes of presentation: mimetic (tragedy, comedy), diegetic (dithyramb), or mixed (epic). But among the theoreticians it is only *Aristotle who provides in a nutshell a genuinely complex theory, combining considerations of form, content, the author's and audience's psychology, metre, language, performance, traditionality, and evolution. Yet his surviving *Poetics* focuses mostly upon a single genre and is often elliptical and tentative: it furnishes many of the elements of a useful theory but does not fully work them out. Later theories tend restrictively to prescribe appropriate contents or style (*Horace, *Ars poetica*), to speculate about historical origins (Hellenistic theories of tragedy and pastoral), or to list the multiplicity of transmitted forms (Proclus' *Chrestomathia*).

Modern attempts to found genre theories upon these ancient discussions have usually been sterile. Instead, more progress can be made by concentrating upon the actual practice of ancient poets, which reflects a much more sophisticated and supple sense of how genres really function. In Archaic Greece, poetic genres seem to have been defined not only by immanent characteristics of form and content but also by communally recognized, often ritually sanctioned situations of performance. The gradual emancipation of literature from such performative contexts facilitated the poets' awareness of and artistic experimentation with genres. Even before the Hellenistic period, poets designated genres by the names of their 'inventors' (*Homer for epic, *Archilochus for iambic invective) and *Euripides and *Aristophanes ironically juxtaposed elements from disparate genres. But the Hellenistic philologists' classification of earlier literature into catalogues and canons made it easier for poets definitively to isolate formal and thematic constants as specifiable rules for determining generic identity: already Accius wrote, *nam quam varia sint genera poematorum, Baebi, quamque longe distincta alia ab aliis, nosce* ('Learn, Baebius, how various the genres of poems are and how much they differ from one another': Charisius, *Gramm.* 141. 34 = Accius fr. 8 Funaioli); and a strong interest in genres is obvious among the Augustan poets, manifested for example in *Virgil's exploration of the boundary separating elegy from pastoral (*Ecl.* 10), in Horace's discussion of the 'empty slot' of Augustan tragedy (*Epist.* 2. 1), and in *Ovid's witty experimentation with new and paradoxical genres (*Heroides, Remedia amoris*).

Much confusion has been caused in modern times both by attempts to hypostasize genres, attributing to them an existence independent of the particular literary works, and by the opposed overreaction, denying the very existence of genres. But even without handbooks, genres function within texts as a way of reducing complexity and thereby not only enriching, but even enabling literary communication: for, by guiding *imitatio* and identifying as pertinent the strategic deployment of topoi (see TOPOS) and of conspicuous stylistic and thematic features, they select only certain contexts out of the potentially infinite horizon of possible ones. Hence genre is not only a descriptive grid devised by philological research, but also a system of literary projection inscribed within the texts, serving to communicate certain expectations to readers and to guide their understanding.   G. B. C., G. W. M.

geography The Homeric poems (see HOMER) display a quite complex sense of place, and of the ordering of the world, in which there is already a notable sense of theory. The *Iliad*'s *Catalogue of Ships* systematically evoked the Greek homeland, and its names remained recognizable for the most part (though in some cases perhaps by learned re-creation); the wider world was much less precisely docketed (making later authorities such as *Eratosthenes believe—the theory of *exōkeanismos*—that Homer had deliberately relegated *Odysseus' wanderings to a vague outer darkness), and there was therefore much less onomastic continuity. The listing of such places begins more recognizably in *Hesiod, and some quite elaborate conception of the layout of the *Mediterranean was clearly associated with the complex movements of people and materials in the Archaic periods, and indeed already present in the Phoenician, Euboean, and Corinthian ambits of the 8th cent. BC; the choice of name for the later *apoikiai* (overseas settlements) reflects a geographical sophistication in which the toponyms of the homeland are replicable in an alien world, a habit of thought which remained common in Macedonian and Roman practice (see COLONIZATION, GREEK). From the relatively undocumented practice of the Archaic period the practical literature of coastwise description or *periploi* developed, to be given a *prōtos heuretēs* (discoverer) in Scylax of Caryanda, and first represented for us by the 4th-cent. text known as [Scylax] or pseudo-Scylax. The first notion of geographical description as a discipline is connected conceptually: the *periodos gēs* ('circuit of the earth') that goes back to the Hesiodic corpus.

Geography by the 5th cent. had three distinct strands: this small-scale documentation of the actualities, as of particular sea routes; wider theories about the layout of land and sea on a global scale; and ideas about the place of the *oikoumenē* (inhabited world) in the order of the cosmos. Both of the more theoretical approaches are apparent in Hecataeus of Miletus and *Herodotus (who combined a geographical and ethnographical perspective): it is plausible to suggest an origin in 6th-cent. Ionia, in which new approaches to the physical nature of the universe, inspired in part by contacts with the Fertile Crescent and Egypt, combined with the active seafaring experience of states like Miletus and Samos. The role of *Pythagoras (who postulated a spherical earth) and his followers should also be noted. The invention of the map was attributed to Anaximander.

Learned geography, in tandem with *astronomy, came during the 4th cent. to an advanced understanding of the nature of the earth as a rotating sphere of a realistic size (the role of *Aristotle and Dicaearchus should be noted); and the theory of the latitudinal zones or *klimata* was refined. A mathematical geography emerged (limited in the end by the available instruments), advanced in the work of Eratosthenes of Cyrene and Hipparchus of Nicaea, which culminated in the 2nd cent. AD in the work of Claudius Ptolemy, the most detailed attempt made in antiquity to project the layout of the physical and human world on the surface of the globe. By 300 BC it was known to the informed that the *oikoumenē* of which detailed information was available could only occupy a small portion of the northern hemisphere. It was also at this time, by coincidence or not, that the idea of accumulating information systematically on the edges of received knowledge began, in a way that suggests comparison with the 'voyages of discovery' in the first age of European colonialism. The work of the companions and followers of *Alexander the Great, above all, established a link between formal geography and political dominion which was to be of great importance to the Roman experience. It also offered, through the development of the ethnographic tradition, an analytical content for the genre which went beyond description and cataloguing, though it continued to use these techniques.

Eratosthenes, whose contribution, in late 3rd-cent. *Alexandria, to *geōgraphia* as a separable discipline was enormous, needs separate consideration. He set new standards of verification by rejecting the Homeric tradition and insisting on a clear distinction between fictitious wonder-descriptions and the recording of fact, established a blend of descriptive and mathematical geography as a new genre, made the mapping of the *oikoumenē* its centre, systematized the deployment of a system of co-ordinates of latitude and longitude in order to do so, and applied the benefits of Ptolemaic statecraft: for instance his accurate estimate of the earth's circumference depended on the measurement of *Egypt in the interests of land management, and his theory of the *sphragides*, conceptual units for the subdivision of space, was also indebted to agrimensorial practice.

Geographical ordering became central to the formation of administrative units. Borrowing perhaps from the geographically defined satrapies of the Achaemenid Persian dominion, the Athenians had subdivided their *archē* ('empire') in a practical way into five units. Geographical organization of a sometimes complex kind was also a feature of the states of Alexander and his Successors (*Diadochi*), and the usefulness of correct topographical information for coercion and exaction was established. In this way geographical work in the Hellenistic period, by *Timaeus, Eratosthenes, Artemidorus, *Polybius, Posidonius, and eventually *Strabo, had a practical relationship to history, and came to be a major ingredient in the self-definition of the nascent Roman, Mediterranean-wide state. Roman contributions were of a practical kind: the *commentarii* (memoranda) of commanders and governors; *Caesar has a place of honour here, blending the claim to practical personal observation with Herodotean ethnographical themes; later exemplars, such as Licinius Mucianus, consul AD 70 and 72, were more given to the thaumatological: Strabo was not complimentary about the Roman contribution to geography (3. 4. 19 (166 C)). The Augustan epoch, with its spectacular universal claims to rule in time and space, made very full use of the geographical tradition in its construction of images, while putting it to practical use too. Thereafter geography as such became an ingredient in the encyclopaedic tradition, and the later authors who survive are mainly excerptors or epitomizers of the earlier tradition (like the elder *Pliny's geographical excursus in *Natural History* 2–6). The exceptions are Pomponius Mela, who represents an attempt at a Latin geography, and *Arrian's rather self-conscious *periplous* of the Euxine (Black Sea), deliberately mixing the *genres, as was common at the time.

N. P.

Germanicus, Germanicus Iulius Caesar (before adoption Nero Claudius Drusus Germanicus), elder son of Nero Claudius Drusus and Antonia, was born 24 May 15 or 16 BC and adopted in AD 4 by his uncle *Tiberius. As Tiberius was immediately adopted by *Augustus, Germanicus became a member of the Julian *gens* (family) in the direct line of succession; and his career was accelerated by special dispensations. He served under Tiberius in Pannonia (7–9), and Germany (11). In 12 he was consul, and in 13, as commander-in-chief in Gaul and Germany, he won his first salutation as *imperator* (EJ 368) in a campaign against the Germans, clearing them out of Gaul and re-establishing order there. By now he was a popular figure, held like his father to entertain 'republican' sentiments, and his affability contrasted with Tiberius' dour reserve. But, though by no means incapable, he was over-emotional, and his judgement was unsteady. When, on the death of Augustus, the lower Rhine legions mutinied, his loyalty was proof against the (perhaps malicious) suggestion that he should supplant Tiberius, but his handling of the situation lacked firmness: he resorted to theatrical appeals and committed the emperor to accepting the mutineers' demands. On dynastic matters the two were at one, but their political style was different, and there was soon a marked difference of view as to how Germany should be handled, Tiberius adhering to the precept of the dying Augustus that rejected immediate territorial advance.

In the autumn of 14 Germanicus led the repentant legions briefly against the Marsi. But he was eager to emulate his father and reconquer parts of Germany lost after the defeat of Publius Quinctilius Varus. He campaigned in the spring of 15 against the Chatti, Cherusci, and Marsi, and rescued the pro-Roman Cheruscan Segestes from Arminius. In the summer he attacked the Bructeri, reached the *saltus Teutoburgiensis*, paid the last honours to Varus, and recovered legionary standards: after an indecisive battle with the Cherusci under Arminius, his forces suffered heavy losses on their way back. For the main campaign of 16 a great fleet was prepared and the troops were transported via his father's canal and the lakes of Holland to the Ems, whence they proceeded to the Weser and defeated Arminius in two battles at Idistaviso (near Minden) and somewhat to the north; the fleet suffered considerable damage from a storm on its homeward journey.

Although Germanicus claimed that one more campaign would bring the Germans to their knees, Tiberius judged that results did not justify the drain on Roman resources, and recalled him to a *triumph (26 May 17) and a command to reorder the 'overseas' provinces as proconsul with *maius* ('greater') *imperium* (subordinate to that of Tiberius). Germanicus entered on his second consulship (18) at Nicopolis, crowned Zeno, son of Polemon, king of Armenia (so winning an *ovatio*—a lesser honour than a triumph), and reduced Cappadocia and Commagene to provincial status. In 19 he offended Tiberius by entering Egypt, which Augustus had barred to senators without permission, and by the informal dress he wore there; his reception was tumultuous (EJ 320(b), 379; Smallwood, *Docs. … Gaius* 370, lines 24–7). On his return to Syria the enmity between him and Gnaeus Calpurnius Piso, whom Tiberius had appointed governor as a check on Germanicus, led to his ordering Piso to leave the province. He fell mysteriously ill, and on 10 October died near *Antioch, convinced that Piso had poisoned him. His death—compared by some with that of *Alexander the Great—provoked widespread demonstrations of grief and in Rome suspicion and resentment; many honours were paid to his memory; his ashes were deposited in the mausoleum of Augustus at Rome. His reputation remained as an overwhelming political advantage to his brother and descendants.

Germanicus married Agrippina the Elder (Vipsania Agrippina), the daughter of *Agrippa and *Julia. She bore him nine children, among whom were Nero Iulius Caesar (d. 31), Drusus Iulius Caesar (d. 33), *Gaius (later emperor), *Agrippina the Younger, Iulia Drusilla, and Iulia (sometimes called Livilla). Eloquent and studious, he wrote comedies in Greek (all lost) and Greek and Latin epigrams; he also translated into Latin the *Phaenomena* of Aratus, bringing it up to date and adding further matter on the planets and the weather. A. M.; T. J. C.; B. M. L.

Giants, a mythological race of monstrous appearance and great strength. According to *Hesiod they were sons of Ge (Earth) from the blood of Gaia/Uranus which fell upon earth; he describes them as valiant warriors (*Theog.* 185). *Homer considers them a savage race of men who perished with their king Eurymedon (*Od.* 7. 59). The prevailing legend of the fight of the gods and the Giants was formulated in Archaic epics and was embroidered by many later writers. A substantial account is given by Apollodorus (1. 6. 1.). When the gods were attacked by the Giants they learned that they could win only if they were assisted by a mortal. They called in *Heracles, who killed the giant Alcyoneus and many others with his arrows. *Zeus, who led the gods, smote with his thunderbolt Porphyrion who attempted to ravish *Hera; *Athena killed Pallas or Enceladus; *Poseidon crushed Polybotes under the rock that became the island of Nisyros (Strabo 489); *Apollo shot Ephialtes; *Hermes slew Hippolytus; *Dionysus killed Eurytus and many other Giants besides who were caught in his vine; and Hephaestus aided the gods, throwing red-hot iron as missiles. The Giants were defeated and were believed to be buried under the volcanoes in various parts of Greece and Italy, e.g. Enceladus under Etna. Bones of prehistoric animals were occasionally believed to be bones of giants.

The Gigantomachy was one of the most popular myths in Greece and accordingly the names of participants and the episodes of the battle vary from writer to writer and from representation to representation. Zeus, Heracles, Poseidon, and later Athena, are the usual protagonists. In its early stage the myth seems to represent a variation of the popular motif of the tribe that attempted to dethrone the gods; in a more advanced stage of culture the myth

was interpreted as the fight of civilization against barbarism.

In art the Giants are first shown as warriors or wild men, later as snake-legged monsters. The most famous sculptural renderings are found on the Archaic treasury of the Siphnians at *Delphi and on the Hellenistic altar of *Pergamum. G. M. A. H.

gladiators, combatants at games Gladiatorial combats, held at the funerals of dead warriors in Etruria (see ETRUSCANS), were introduced to Rome (perhaps by way of Samnium and Campania) in 264 BC, when three pairs fought at the funeral games given in honour of Iunius Pera. Down to *Caesar's Games in 46 BC the justification (or pretext) was always the death of a male relative, but these were in part commemorative of Caesar's daughter *Julia, in part not commemorative at all. These contests, like beast-fights, became increasingly important as a route to popular favour for their promoter, forming an important, though normally brief (because highly expensive) item in games held at Rome and in other towns. However, five thousand pairs fought in eight different games given by *Augustus (*RG* 22. 1) and the same number in a single series of games given by *Trajan to celebrate the conclusion of the Dacian War in AD 107. At Rome the original venue was the *forum Romanum. The first stone amphitheatre was built by Statilius Taurus under Augustus, but it was only with the building of the Flavian amphitheatre (*Colosseum) that Rome had a specialized venue larger than those in quite small Italian towns (the fine amphitheatre to be seen at Pompeii goes back to the early years of the Sullan colony). Antiochus IV Epiphanes introduced these games to the Syrian capital, *Antioch, c.170 BC and later they spread to all parts of the Roman empire. Gladiators were of four types: the *murmillo*, with a fish for the crest on his helmet, and the Samnite, both heavily armed with oblong shield, visored helmet, and short sword; the *retiarius*, lightly clad, fighting with net and trident; and the Thracian with round shield and curved scimitar. Prisoners of war and condemned criminals were compelled to fight as gladiators. Those who fought on a professional basis were either slaves, bought for the purpose, or free volunteers who for a fee bound themselves to their owner by an oath (*auctoramentum gladiatorium*) which permitted him to kill or maim them (in practice a gladiator was too valuable an investment to be wasted outside the games and the life of a defeated combatant was often spared by the audience's wish). They were trained in schools under a *lanista* (who was sometimes a retired gladiator) and might be acquired as an investment, to be hired or sold to games-promoters. In the late republic they were frequently used as the core of a gang or armed entourage. It appears that even members of the senatorial and equestrian orders were attracted to a gladiatorial career, which had a macabre glamour deriving from courage, physical strength, and sexual potency. In consequence there was legislation under Augustus and

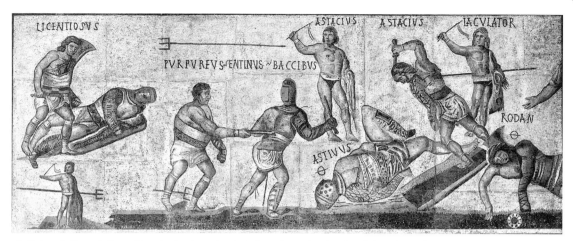

gladiators A 4th-cent. Roman *mosaic showing pairs of gladiators in combat. In spite of the violence depicted, in practice the lives of defeated gladiators were often spared by popular demand.

*Tiberius to prevent members of these orders becoming gladiators (B. M. Levick, *JRS* 1983, 97 ff.), which remained an infamous profession (*Dig.* 28. 2. 3 pref.). After *Domitian gladiatorial games could only be given at Rome by emperors; outside Rome they required official sanction. Restrictions on games in the towns of the empire seem to be related more to the expenditure involved for the promoters than to any distaste. Opposition to the idea of such games centred on their being bloodshed for fun, but for

*Cicero (*Tusc.* 2. 41) and the younger *Pliny (*Pan.* 33. 1) this did not apply if those fighting were condemned criminals. Gladiatorial combats were first prohibited in AD 325, when *Constantine I decided that they were too bloodthirsty a peacetime activity (*Cod. Theod.* 15. 12. 1; *Cod. Iust.* 11. 44).

J. P. B.; A. W. L.

glass (*hyalos* (also 'rock crystal'), Lat. *vitrum*). The art of producing a vitreous surface on stone, powdered quartz

glass A selection of Roman glassware. The invention of glass-blowing (1st cent. BC) allowed the cheap mass-production of what formerly had been a relatively expensive product.

(faience), or clay was known in pre-dynastic Egypt and passed to Crete during the second millennium BC. Glazed objects are common on Greek sites of the Archaic period, some of them Egyptian imports, others probably made locally. In Hellenistic and Roman times Egypt and Asia Minor were centres of fabrication of glazed wares, which often imitated bronze.

Objects composed entirely of glass paste begin to appear in Egypt about 1500 BC, when two allied processes seem to have been in use: modelling molten glass about a core of sand, and pressing it into an open mould. The chief Mycenaean glass is dark blue imitating lapis lazuli, used for beads, inlays, and architectural ornaments. In the 6th cent. small vases made by the sand-core process became known in Greece; they have opaque blue, brown, or white bodies and a marbled effect was produced on their surface by means of a comb or spike. In the Hellenistic period mould-made bowls come into fashion; these were produced mainly in Egypt. Here the tradition of opaque polychrome glass was continued into Roman times with *millefiori* bowls, in which marbled and other polychrome patterns were formed by fusing glass canes of various colours and pressing them into moulds. In the same tradition are the vessels in two layers carved in imitation of hard-stone cameos: the Portland vase in London is the best-known example.

The invention of glass-blowing in the 1st cent. BC (probably in Syria) wrought great changes in the glass industry, which, hitherto limited to relatively expensive surrogates for luxury goods, now became capable of cheap mass-production, but even then the most highly valued glass was 'colourless and transparent, as closely as possible resembling rock crystal' (Plin. *HN* 36. 198). Glass was used in the home and for funerary furniture. Glass-works have been located in many provinces, but in the later western empire, Belgic Gaul and Germany had taken the place of Italy and southern Gaul. Even Britain had some glass-works. The vessels, even when plain, show much variety of form, and there are several styles of decoration—tooling or applying relief ornament to the surface when warm, cutting or engraving or painting when cold. Window glass, made by a primitive process of rolling, was known at *Pompeii, and later became common; in the later empire also begins the use of glass for mirrors. Gemstones were imitated in glass paste at all periods from the 7th cent. BC onwards (see GEMS). Burning-glasses were used, and these may conceivably have been used as magnifying glasses by gem engravers; spectacles were unknown.   F. N. P.; M. V.

Gordian III (Marcus Antonius Gordianus), grandson of Gordian I by a daughter, was forced on Balbinus and Pupienus as their Caesar and, after their murder (mid AD 238), saluted emperor by the praetorians at the age of 13. The conduct of affairs was at first in the hands of his backers but, as fiscal and military difficulties increased, it passed to the praetorian prefect Gaius Furius Sabinius Aquila Timesitheus (241). Timesitheus prepared a major

campaign against Persia which, beginning in 242, achieved substantial success before his death, by illness, in 243. Gordian replaced Timesitheus with one of the latter's protégés, Marcus Iulius Philippus, who continued the war. However, the Roman army suffered defeat near Ctesiphon in Mesopotamia, and shortly afterwards Gordian died of his wounds (early 244). He was succeeded by Philippus.

Though the period of the Gordians shows some of the characteristics of the 3rd-cent. 'crisis', it is best interpreted as a reversion to the Severan monarchy after the aberrance of Maximinus.   J. F. Dr.

Gorgias of Leontini (*c*.485–*c*.380 BC), one of the most influential of the *sophists, important both as a thinker and as a stylist. He is said to have been a pupil of Empedocles; his visit to Athens as an ambassador in 427 is traditionally seen as a landmark in the history of rhetoric, introducing Sicilian techniques into the Athenian tradition of oratory (see RHETORIC, GREEK). However this may be, his stylistic influence was enormous. The extant *Encomium of Helen* and *Defence of Palamedes*, as well as the fragment of his *Epitaphius* (DK 82 B 6), illustrate clearly the seductions of his antithetical manner, with its balancing clauses, rhymes, and assonances: antithesis, homoeoteleuton, and parisosis became known as the 'Gorgianic figures'. There is a wonderful parody of the style in Agathon's speech in *Plato's *Symposium* (194e–197e). At the same time, these speeches also contain serious reflection on the power of words (*logos*) and on moral responsibility. We also possess summaries of a philosophical work (Sext. Emp. *Math.* 7. 65 ff. = DK 82 B 3, and *On Melissus, Xenophanes, and Gorgias* (preserved among the works of *Aristotle, 974^a–980^b Bekker). From these, it is apparent that Gorgias argued that 'nothing is', and even if anything is, it cannot be known, or indicated by one person to another. How serious these sceptical arguments were has been much debated.   D. A. R.

Gracchus, Gaius (Gaius Sempronius Gracchus), younger brother of Tiberius Gracchus (see next entry), served under his cousin and brother-in-law *Scipio Aemilianus at Numantia. A member of his brother's land commission, he supported the plans of Marcus Fulvius Flaccus in 126 BC, then went to Sardinia as quaestor. Returning before his commander in 124, he was accused before the censors but acquitted, and elected tribune for 123 and again for 122, when he was joined by Flaccus, by then *consularis* and *triumphalis* (i.e. having been consul and having celebrated a *triumph). After laws meant to avenge his brother and secure himself against a similar fate, he embarked on a programme of reform, aided by friendly colleagues. The most important measures were: (1) a *lex frumentaria* (corn law) assuring citizens of wheat, normally at a subsidized price; (2) laws providing for the resumption of land distribution and the foundation of colonies, including one on the ritually cursed site of *Carthage, which Gracchus himself, as commissioner, helped to establish; (3) laws regulating army service and providing for public works—all these to gain the support of the *plebs* and relieve poverty and exploitation; (4) a law to have the *decuma* (grain tax) of the new province of Asia sold by the censors in Rome; (5) laws (probably two) regulating *repetundae* (provincial extortion) trials, the second (passed by Manius Acilius Glabrio) introducing elements of criminal procedure and taking juries from the *equites*—these to protect provincials from magistrates' rapacity, to secure the treasury's major revenue against peculation, and to set up members of the non-political class to control politicians; (6) a law to make the senate's designation of consular provinces immune to tribunician veto and to have it before the elections—this to remove the most important administrative decision of the year from personal prejudice. This law shows how far he was from being a 'democrat'.

Finally, in 122, he proposed to offer citizenship to Latins and Latin status to Italian allies, both to protect them from the excesses of Roman magistrates and to make them subject to his brother's agrarian law. The law was opposed by Gaius Fannius, whom he had supported for the consulship, and by Marcus Livius Drusus, who outbid him with an unrealistic colonial programme. It was defeated, and Gracchus was not re-elected. In 121, with his legislation under attack, Gracchus, supported by Flaccus, resorted to armed insurrection. It was suppressed after the first use of the so-called *senatus consultum ultimum* (a declaration of emergency), they and many of their supporters were killed, others executed after arrest.

Gaius Gracchus had more ambitious plans than his brother, whose memory he revered. He saw the need for major administrative reforms. A proud aristocrat, he wanted to leave the Senate in charge of directing policy and the magistrates in charge of its execution, subject to constitutional checks and removed from financial temptation, with the people sharing in the profits of empire without excessive exploitation of the subjects. The ultimate result of his legislation was to set up the *publicani* as a new exploiting class, not restrained by a tradition of service or by accountability at law. But this did not become clear for a generation, and he cannot be blamed for not foreseeing it.   E. B.

Gracchus, Tiberius (Tiberius Sempronius Gracchus), elder brother of the preceding and son of Tiberius Sempronious Gracchus (consul 177) and Cornelia (daughter of *Scipio Africanus), served at Carthage under his cousin *Scipio Aemilianus, who married his sister. As quaestor in Spain (137 BC), he used his father's connections to save the army of Gaius Hostilius Mancinus by a treaty later disowned by the senate on Scipio's motion. Thus attacked in his *fides* (good faith) he joined a group hostile to Scipio: his father-in-law Appius Claudius Pulcher, *princeps senatus* (designated senior senator) and augur; the consul for 133 Publius Mucius Scaevola and his brother Publius Licinius Crassus Dives Mucianus, both eminent lawyers and *pontifices* (see PRIESTS). As tribune 133, in

Scipio's absence, he proposed, with their aid and advice, a law designed to solve Rome's interlocking problems: departure or expulsion of small landowners from their properties, leading to insuperable difficulties in recruiting armies; danger from increasing numbers of slaves; and lack of an assured food supply for the capital. The law reaffirmed the long-ignored limit of 500 *iugera* (c.135 *ha.*) of arable public land per person and instituted a commission (to which he, his brother Gaius (see above) and his father-in-law were ultimately elected) to find and confiscate surplus land and distribute it in small lots to poor citizens. A compromise offering 250 additional *iugera* for each child was withdrawn when it failed to secure his opponents' acceptance of the law. Following good precedent and with his eminent supporters' approval, he submitted the law to the *plebs* without previous discussion in the senate. It was vetoed by Marcus Octavius, taken to the senate for adjudication, and rejected. Gracchus nonetheless resubmitted it, and Octavius persisted in his veto, both contrary to *mos maiorum* (ancestral custom). To end the unprecedented impasse Gracchus had Octavius removed from office—again an unprecedented step, but without objection by the other tribunes, who did not veto it. When Pergamene envoys brought news of Attalus III of *Pergamum's death and will, leaving his estate to Rome, Gracchus (with whom they probably stayed owing to his father's *hospitium* (see FRIENDSHIP, RITUALIZED) with the dynasty) proposed to prejudge the issue of acceptance, ignoring the senate's traditional right to guide foreign affairs, and to distribute Attalus' property to Roman citizens, perhaps as equipment grants for his new allotment-holders.

He next sought re-election, to escape certain conviction on charges of *perduellio* (activity hostile to the state). This last unprecedented step alienated earlier supporters and increased fear of tyranny among opponents. When the consul Scaevola refused to stop him by force, the *pontifex maximus* (see PRIESTS) Publius Cornelius Scipio Nasica Serapio led a mob of senators and their clients 'to save the Republic'. Gracchus and many of his supporters were killed on the Capitol, others were later punished by a commission under Publius Popillius Laenas, consul 132. The land commission, however, continued unimpeded until 129.

His tribunate marks the beginning of 'the Roman Revolution': the introduction of murder into politics and the breakdown of *concordia* (the tradition of not pushing legal powers to extremes) on which the republic was based. See also AGRARIAN LAWS AND POLICY.   E. B.

Greece (geography) (see ◀Map 1▶) Greece with the Aegean basin is part of the great mountain zone running from the Alps to the Himalayas. For 70 million years the land mass of Africa has been burrowing irresistibly under Europe. This mighty force has displaced, shattered, crumpled, and stretched the rocks, creating mountain ranges, ocean trenches, gorges, and upland basins. The Cretan island arc displays one of Europe's most dramatic changes of level, from the Hellenic trench, 4,335 m. (14,222 ft.) deep, immediately to the south, to peaks up to 2,456 m. (8,058 ft.) high on *Crete itself. Northward lies the Cycladic chain of volcanoes, from Nisyros through Santorini (Thera) and Melos to Methana, the volcano within sight of Athens. Mainland mountains range from Taygetus (2,407 m.: 7,897 ft.) in the south through Parnassus (2,457 m.: 8,061 ft.) to Olympus in the north, at 2,917 m. (9,570 ft.) the highest peak in modern Greece. Mountain-building continues, as shown by frequent *earthquakes in ancient and modern Greece.

The geology is very varied. Most of the higher mountains are of hard limestone, but there are also phyllites, gneisses, granites, serpentines, and volcanic rocks. Softer marls, sandstones, and clays, occurring at lower altitudes, were laid down during periods of submergence later in geological history.

Erosion has gone on since the mountains began to form: whole mountain ranges have been carried away and their remains deposited to form new rocks. It was particularly active during the ice ages, 2 million to 12,000 years ago, when there were violent changes of climate (although little development of glaciers). Erosion has created cultivable land in the plains, into which sediments were washed off the hillsides. It continues conspicuously in the Pindus mountains, the northern *Peloponnese, and *Rhodes; elsewhere, as in Crete, most deposits are strongly consolidated and hold together despite very steep slopes. Erosion has been increased by human activity, but by how much is controversial.

Greece is rather poor in minerals. Clay for pottery comes from definite local sources. Sometimes limestone has been turned into a crystalline form under great pressure; hence the marbles of Paros, Naxos, Thasos, and of Pentelicon in Attica. Small deposits of iron ore are frequent, but tin and most of the copper for making bronze had to be imported. The silver-mines of Laurium were essential to the economy of Athens.

Greece has a sharply seasonal Mediterranean *climate. The winter rainy season (typically October–May) is warm, seldom frosty, and the time of activity and growth. The dry season of summer is hot, rainless, relentlessly sunny, and is the dead season. The mountains intercept rain-bearing depressions, producing a disparity between the wet west of Greece (e.g. Ioannina, 1,195 mm. (47 in.) of rain in an average year) and the dry east (Athens, 384 mm.: 15 in.). The west coast of Asia Minor is again well watered in winter (Smyrna, 719 mm.: 28 in.). Summer temperatures sometimes reach 40°C (104°F), especially inland, but are tolerable because of north winds and dry air. Mountain areas, as in Pindus and Arcadia, are difficult to live in all the year, because there are cold winters as well as dry summers: the growing season is very short, and frost-sensitive crops, especially olives, cannot be grown.

The prehistoric climate, as inferred from pollen cores, had been less arid than today's. How far climate differed in Classical times is uncertain. Known fluctuations such as the Little Ice Age (1550–1750 AD) forbid us to assume it as constant. Ancient accounts suggest that it may have been slightly less strongly seasonal than today, with rivers more dependable and snow less rare. The deadly heat of the *kávsoma* (heatwave) in the modern Athenian summer is aggravated by the urban microclimate and air pollution.

Traditional Greek *agriculture, now much in decline, was based on cereals, olives, vines, and herding animals. (New World crops—potato, tomato, tobacco, maize—were unknown in antiquity.) It involved seasonal hard work, ploughing, sowing, picking olives, and tending vines; an unhurried harvest; and long periods of relative leisure.

Inland transport is relatively easy for a mountainous country; it was seldom difficult to make *roads between the fertile basins. Seafaring called for great skill: the coasts are wild and terrible with cliff-bound promontories, razor-edged reefs, and surf-pounded beaches. There were few good harbours, and no tide to help in getting in or out. Sailors feared the sea in winter, and land travel was then difficult because of flooded fords. O. R.

Greece (prehistory and history) *(see facing page)*

Greek language

1. Introduction In the Classical period Greek was spoken in mainland Greece (including the Peloponnese), in the islands of the Aegean (including Crete, Rhodes, and Cyprus), and in the Greek colonies in Asia, Africa, and Italy. It is the European (and Indo-European) language with the longest attested history; the first documents belong to the second half of the second millennium BC and there is no real break between ancient Greek and the modern language of Greece. Most of the evidence from the 8th cent. BC until now is written in the Greek alphabet, but at an early stage two syllabic scripts were also in use: Linear B in the second half of the second millennium rendered the Greek spoken by the exponents of Mycenaean civilization, while a distantly related script, syllabic Cyprian, was used for the local dialect of Cyprus from the end of the second millennium to the 3rd cent. BC. The language changed in time: conventionally we distinguish an ancient period which goes from the first attestation of Mycenaean Greek (in Linear B) to the end of Hellenistic Greek (roughly in AD 300), a Byzantine and medieval period (until c.1650), and a modern period. Here we concentrate on the central period of ancient Greek in the 5th and 4th cents. BC. After a general account of its development we give a very brief discussion of the main features of the language.

2. Origins Greek is related to language groups such as Italic, Germanic, Indo-Iranian, Celtic, Slavic, Anatolian, Armenian, Albanian, etc., all of which descend from an unattested parent language (conventionally called Indo-European or IE), which we partially reconstruct through comparative and historical studies. It is not possible to

[*continued on p. 317*]

prehistory and history of Greece

Stone Age The stone age is divided into the palaeolithic (to *c*.9000 BC), mesolithic (*c*.9000–7000 BC) and neolithic (7th–4th millennia BC); metallurgy began during the neolithic, before the conventional neolithic–bronze age transition.

Classical Greece was an essentially agricultural society and as such can trace its origins back to the first farming communities in Greece in the early neolithic (7th millennium BC). Some at least of the domestic livestock and crop species were introduced from the near east, but Greece had long been occupied by palaeolithic and mesolithic gatherer-hunters (e.g. at Franchthi cave, Argolid). It is unclear whether the first farmers were of indigenous, immigrant or mixed stock. Known early farming settlements (e.g. Argissa) are heavily concentrated in the fertile lowlands of the eastern mainland, particularly in *Thessaly. The southern mainland and smaller Aegean islands, the heartland of both bronze age palatial civilization and the Classical *polis*, were not widely colonized by farmers until the later neolithic and early bronze age (5th–3rd millennia BC). The earliest farmers laid the biological foundations of Classical agriculture, growing a range of cereal and pulse crops and keeping sheep, goats, cattle, and pigs. The vine was a significant resource (possibly cultivated) by *c*.5000 BC, but systematic use of the *olive and the introduction of the horse and donkey are not attested until the bronze age. There is no evidence for the plough in neolithic Greece, and early farming may have resembled the intensive 'horticulture' and small-scale stock-rearing still practised in some hill-villages, rather than the extensive agriculture and specialized *pastoralism which dominate the present landscape and, to some extent, the ancient sources. Neolithic subsistence was probably based on grain crops, with livestock most important as an alternative food source after crop failure. Farmers introduced fallow deer to many islands, making hunting a viable option, but the principal mechanisms for coping with the risk of crop failure in the arid south-east of Greece were social. Field surveys indicate that early farmers lived in small village communities. Excavations at sites such as Sesklo and Nea Nikomedeia have shown that the basic residential and economic unit was a family household, but houses were crowded close together and cooking facilities were located outdoors, ensuring social pressure to share cooked food. In the colonization of agriculturally marginal regions, sharing with close neighbours will have been less effective as a defence against local crop failure. Here a dispersed pattern of 'hamlet' settlements developed, with greater emphasis on distant social ties. Distant social contacts are more difficult to cultivate than close neighbours but are potentially more effective as a source of hospitality in the event of local crop failure. Early neolithic communities were probably egalitarian in the sense that there was no inequality independent of age, gender, and ability. Villages rarely grew to a size demanding institutionalized authority to maintain order. In some late neolithic (6th-millennium BC) villages (e.g. Dimini), however, a central house was segregated within a large courtyard and probably housed some sort of community leader. From the final neolithic (5th millennium BC) onwards, settlements frequently exceeded the organizational limits of egalitarian society. The economic isolation of the family household was now reinforced by moving cooking facilities into an internal 'kitchen' (as at Sitagroi) or walled yard (as at Pevkakia), suggesting that sharing between neighbours had given way to centrally controlled redistribution. By the end of the neolithic, with consolidation of the domestic mode of production and the attendant struggle between household self-sufficiency and indebted dependence on a wider community, the most basic elements of Classical rural society may already have been in place.

P. H.

Bronze age Viewed at its broadest, the history of bronze-age Greece seems a cyclical alternation between periods of expansion, fuelled by increasingly intensive exploitation of the land and

Greece (prehistory and history) The battle of Salamis between the Persian and Greek fleets (480 BC) was fought in the straits between the island of Salamis (foreground) and the Athenian mainland to the east. What actually happened is obscure, but the Persian fleet was defeated and soon afterwards withdrew to Asia Minor.

involvement in overseas exchange, and contraction to a more nearly self-sufficient 'village' level. While warfare and population movement may have been additional contributory factors in periods of decline, they are unlikely to have played a very significant role; in particular, there is no good evidence that a 'coming of the Greeks' (at whatever date this is placed) had a very marked impact. Rather, the most significant development was the establishment of the *Minoan civilization of *Crete, which evidently did not use the Greek language, but had an essential formative influence on the *Mycenaean civilization, which evidently did, at least in its core region, the southern mainland. The effective domination of the Aegean by Mycenaean civilization from the 14th cent. BC onwards marks a step towards the creation of 'Greece'; but the development of many characteristic features of later Greek civilization was a very complex process, much of which took place after the bronze age (cf., for the most typical form of religious *sacrifice, N. Marinatos and B. Bergquist, in R. Hägg, N. Marinatos, and G. Nordquist, *Early Greek Cult Practice* (1988)).

Obviously this is very different from the picture of early Greece that *Thucydides built up (1. 1–20) from analysis of his only available source, the legendary traditions; these gave no suggestion of the length of that past, the long-term stability of the agricultural economy, the importance of exchange, the high level of social organization in the palace societies, or the very existence of 'pre-Greek' civilizations. This is hardly surprising, for to judge from other cultures the primary purpose of such traditions is not the transmission of factual information but the validation of claims to territory and status (see ORALITY), and they can only too readily be tampered with, as in the historical period in Greece. The most vivid elements in the traditional material, the Homeric epics, belong to a genre that cannot be expected to offer a wholly realistic picture of life; but where their setting is realistic, it is becoming increasingly apparent that, while incorporating late bronze-age details, it has much more to do with the Dark Age.

O. T. P. K. D.

Archaic, Classical, Hellenistic
'Dark Ages'
(*c*.1100–776 BC). The period after the Mycenaean collapse and before the 8th-cent. BC renaissance is traditionally regarded and described as the Dark Age of Greece. For several centuries after the disappearance of Linear B, writing ceases to be a category of evidence, and the only other source of information, archaeology, shows that contact even between closely neighbouring communities sank (e.g. in Attica) to low levels. But this picture has been modified by brilliant 10th-cent. finds at *Lefkandi on Euboea, attesting eastern connections and memories of a Mycenaean past. The Dark Age of Greece should not, in fact, be seen entirely negatively, but as an exploratory period in which Greece itself was gradually resettled by pioneers (the prime instance is Attica, see ATHENS, HISTORY), and in which Greeks settled areas like Ionia for the first time. But the word colonization, which implies a central organizing authority, is not yet appropriate for this sort of tentative internal expansion and haphazard overseas movement. And the absence of writing had its positive side, the creation in an originally oral mode of the great epics of *Homer, the *Iliad* and *Odyssey*.

Archaic age
(776–479 BC). The conventional date for the beginning of the historical period of Greece is 776 BC, the date of the first Olympian Games on the reckoning of Hippias of Elis. This is probably not too far out for the event in question; but the early 8th cent. was a turning of the page in several other ways as well. Iron began to be worked with new sophistication; the alphabet was taken over from the east; and colonies began to be sent out in a more organized way (see COLONIZATION, GREEK), above all from Euboea, which between 750 and 730 colonized Cumae and Pithecusae in the west and was involved in Al Mina in the east. The 8th cent. was also the age of *polis* formation and political *synoecism, perhaps themselves a result, in part, of the colonizing movement, but also of the rise of religious leagues or *amphictionies*. (Religious factors have certainly been urged in recent years by students of the emergent *polis*: it has been remarked that *polis* formation was marked by the placing of *sanctuaries, often and for no obvious reason dedicated to *Hera, at the edge of *polis* territory.) Some of all this, not just writing, but perhaps even the idea of the self-determining *polis* community, may actually be Phoenician not Greek in inspiration, and there was a famous and perhaps influential early first-millennium amphictiony of Israel. But whatever the truth about Semitic primacy, early Greek society soon acquired distinctive features and institutions, most of which continued to be important in Classical times and later. Among these were athletics and religiously based athletic events like the Olympian Games, already mentioned (see GAMES); the *gymnasium which provided training for both athletics and its elder brother, warfare; the *symposium, at which aristocratic values were inculcated; and *homosexuality, which was related to all the other phenomena just mentioned. Some other characteristic features of Greek society are more easily paralleled elsewhere, e.g. ritualized *friendship, but institutionalized proxeny which developed out of this, was specifically Greek: this was a system of the diplomatic representation of state *x* in state *y* by nationals of state *y*.

All this contributed to such shared Greek consciousness as there was (see ETHNICITY; NATIONALISM), but the chief way in which early Greek states interacted was through warfare, a paradoxical activity in that in Greece at most periods it was a ritualized, i.e. shared, activity, but at the same time war is, obviously, an assertion of separateness (see WARFARE, ATTITUDES TO). Equally the four great panhellenic ('all-Greek') sanctuaries, *Olympia, *Delphi, Isthmia, Nemea, were a symbol of what Greeks had in common, but they were also a focus for interstate competition exercised in various ways (see DELPHI), and constituting an alternative to war; indeed struggles for influence at sanctuaries sometimes developed into wars proper, so-called Sacred Wars. And sanctuaries were the repositories of tithes or tenth-fractions of the *booty which was a reason for and result of warfare; this booty was often turned into dedications, producing a connection between great art and great suffering which was noticed by Jacob Burckhardt.

The first war which can be called in any sense general was the Lelantine War (late 8th cent.) fought by Chalcis and Eretria for control of the plain between them; each side had allies from further away and links with rival colonial networks have been suspected. But exaggeration on the part of ancient, and anachronism on the part of modern, writers make the truth about this early conflict hard to establish. If there were networks at this time they are less likely to have been firm interstate groupings for purposes of trade or politics than informal systems of aristocratic friendships between entrepreneurial individuals like Sostratus of Aegina, whose prosperous commercial activities in Italy were interestingly illuminated by archaeology and epigraphy in the 1970s.

Commercial and economic prosperity on the one hand, and individual dynamism on the other, combined on *Thucydides' view to produce *tyranny. There is much to be said for this: colonization and trade were connected, and the combination meant that Greece was exposed to luxuries on a new scale. But the chief modern explanation for tyranny is military, in terms of hoplite (heavy-armed infantry) warfare, a partial repudiation of individual aristocratic fighting methods, corresponding to that political repudiation of control by hereditary aristocracies which was the essence of tyranny. A main attraction of this theory is coincidence of time: the first tyrannies, of Pheidon at Argos and Cypselus at Corinth, are best put at mid-7th cent., when hoplites appear.

Two states which did not have tyrannies in this first phase are *Sparta and *Athens, indeed Sparta famously avoided tyranny until Hellenistic times. Sparta was remarkable in other ways also, for instance by not sending out many colonies in the historical period (with the important exception of Tarentum, Greek Taras, in south Italy) but above all in having annexed its next-door neighbour Messenia in the later 8th cent. The inhabitants were turned into state slaves or helots. Other neighbours of Sparta became *perioikoi*, a subordinate status to which some communities of Laconia also belonged. Sparta later became a tight and repressive place, but Archaic Sparta guaranteed political power to the *damos* or people—meaning perhaps only the class of hoplite fighters—at an impressively early date (?7th cent.) when democracy elsewhere was still in the future. But the political momentum at Sparta was lost, partly through the need to hold down Messenia and the helots; this in turn called for the strict *agōgē* (the public upbringing of Spartan boys). Simple infantry strength enabled Sparta to coerce much of the *Peloponnese by the later 6th cent., though propaganda also helped, the deliberate muting of Sparta's unpopular Dorian aspect.

Athens was also unusual among Greek states, above all in the size of its directly controlled territory, Attica, its natural assets (including a supply of silver), and its physical suitability for a naval role (see ATHENS, HISTORY). Athens, like Sparta, avoided tyranny in the 7th cent., but unlike Sparta, Athens did experience an attempt at one at this time, the failed coup of Cylon *c*.630. But a generation later *Solon's reforms (594) both resembled and circumvented—for the moment—tyrannical, anti-aristocratic solutions carried out elsewhere. His creation of a new *boulē* ('council') of 400 members was an important move towards democracy, as was the opening of high political office on criteria of wealth not birth; but even more crucial was abolition of the demeaning if not always economically crippling status of hectemorage (the payment of one sixth of agricultural produce). Indirect but important consequences of this abolition were the development of a self-conscious citizen élite (see CITIZENSHIP, GREEK) and the related rise of chattel-*slavery. Solon also permitted appeal to the *dikastērion* (see DEMOCRACY, ATHENIAN; LAW AND PROCEDURE, ATHENIAN), and legislated in the social sphere; but some of the detailed traditions about his economic reforms are suspect because they imply the existence of *coinage, which in fact begins in the middle of the 6th cent., too late to be relevant to developments at the beginning of it (though accumulation of gold and silver may well be relevant, cf. above on the effects of colonization).

Solon's reforms were critical for the longer-term development of Athens and indeed Greece, but in the short term they were a failure because Athens did after all succumb, for much of the second half of the 6th cent., to a tyranny, that of *Pisistratus and his sons Hippias and Hipparchus. Under these rulers, Athenian naval power was built up, a vigorous foreign policy pursued, splendid buildings erected, and roads built. But the tyrants were driven out in 510 and *Cleisthenes reformed the Athenian constitution in a democratic direction in 508/7.

Meanwhile Achaemenid *Persia had been expanding since *Cyrus the Great overthrew Croesus of Lydia in 546, and the new power had begun to encroach on the freedom of the East Greeks in Ionia and even islands like *Samos. The Athenians, like other mainland Greeks, were insulated from immediate danger by their distance from geographical Ionia, but they were in the racial and religious senses Ionians too, and when in 499 the *Ionian Revolt broke out, itself perhaps the result of restlessness induced by awareness of Cleisthenes' democratic reforms, Athens sent help to the rebels, who, however, were defeated at Lade (494).

How far this help provoked the Persian Wars, by drawing *Darius I's vengeful attention to Athens, and how far they were simply an inevitable consequence of Persian dynamism, is not clear from the account of our main source *Herodotus. A first expedition led by Datis and Mardonius failed at the battle of Marathon, in Attica (490); then at the battles of Thermopylae, Artemisium, Salamis (all 480), and Plataea (479) a far larger Persian invasion by *Xerxes was beaten back. The Greek successes of the Persian Wars were of enormous importance in conditioning Greek attitudes to themselves, to each other, and to the '*barbarian' (as Persians were now more aggressively defined), for centuries to come. The victories were immediately commemorated by state dedications in the great sanctuaries (above all Delphi and Olympia, except that Nemea got no big dedication. Poetry by *Aeschylus and *Simonides, and the prose of Herodotus, signalled the Great Event in literature, as did buildings on the Athenian acropolis; only *Thucydides and his speakers show some impatience with the theme.

The pentekontaetia

(c.50-year period 480–430 BC). In the west (Italy and Sicily), the Greek states shared the culture of their *mētropoleis* ('mother-cities') in Greece itself (see esp. OLYMPIA), but there were differences. Here Greeks (like North African *Cyrene with its Berber neighbours) always had to live alongside non-Greeks, both relatively small-scale but vigorous indigenous groups like Messapians in the hinterland of Taras (Tarentum), and great powers like *Etruscans in central Italy, or *Carthage whose base was in North Africa but which had outposts in Sicily. Herodotus reports a huge massacre of Tarentines by Messapians c.470 and this threat conditioned much of Tarentine history for centuries. And at Himera and Cumae the western Greeks under their tyrants Gelo and Hiero defeated Carthage and the Etruscans in battles which contemporaries compared to the high points of the Persian Wars. But inter-Greek tensions were no less acute: Croton and Locri (Epizephyrii) fought a great Archaic battle at the Sagra river, and when Thurii in the mid-5th cent. replaced Archaic Sybaris, destroyed in 508, it soon found itself at war with neighbouring Taras. But more peaceful developments were possible, as at Elea, where a medical school connected with the cult of *Apollo 'Ouliades' flourished from the 5th cent. BC to Roman times; Parmenides was involved with it. Athenian and Peloponnesian interest in the west was always lively, partly for grain and partly for shipbuilding *timber from south Italy; but partly also because ties of *kinship between colonies and *mētropoleis* were taken seriously.

The great struggle of the 5th cent. was between Athenians and the Peloponnesians led by Sparta. The germs of this are detectable even in the Persian Wars, and when the Athenians took over the leadership of Greece in 487 (see DELIAN LEAGUE), Sparta's response was mixed. But Sparta, despite having crushed for the moment the perennially ambitious rival Argos in 494, had internal problems in the Peloponnese and, for several years from the mid-460s, difficulties with the helots to cope with. So stretched were the Spartans that they invited the Athenians in to help them against the helots, but the Athenian democracy moved on a step in just this period (the reforms of Ephialtes) and the Athenians under Cimon were dismissed from Sparta. Sparta's troubles meant that the Athenian empire was able to expand without check from the Greek side until the end of the 460s and the outbreak of the First Peloponnesian War (460–446), when Sparta did, as often in its history, take some action to protect or further its interests (including religious) in central Greece. So far from curbing Athenian expansion, that war saw Athenian influence rise to its maximum extent: for over ten years after the battle of Tanagra Athens even controlled Boeotia (457–446). It may be that the take-over was possible because

Athens capitalized on *stasis* (civic dissension) inside the cities of Boeotia. (Throughout Classical Greek history there was a risk that *stasis* would open the door to outside interference. But Thucydides may be right to link it particularly with the period introduced by the main Peloponnesian War: in the *pentekontaetia* a degree of stability was guaranteed by the existence of two power blocs: contrast the post-431 period and the 4th cent.) Democratic Athens did not however insist on democracy in Boeotia, allegedly permitting oligarchies instead; nor is it certain that the Boeotian Confederacy ceased to exist in the Athenian period, although Athens' departure in 446 may have led to a federal reorganization.

Despite preoccupations in Greece, Athens in this period continued the struggle against Persia which was the ostensible purpose of the Delian League; but after the Eurymedon victory of 466 a preliminary 'peace of Callias' may have been made. A great Athenian expedition against Persia in Egypt in the 450s failed utterly, and in 450 the main Callias peace was made, though this is controversial. Thereafter, until 413, Athens and Persia were in a state of uneasy peace.

The Peloponnesian War

The First Peloponnesian War ended with the Thirty Years Peace of 446, and this instrument regulated Athenian–Spartan relations until the great Peloponnesian War of 431–404. The Archidamian War, ended by the Peace of *Nicias, failed to achieve the Peloponnesian objective of 'liberating' Greece, i.e. breaking up the Athenian empire. *Propaganda, such as the exploiting of sanctuaries like Delphi and Ionian *Delos, was as much a weapon as open fighting. Athenian exuberance climbed to its highest level in 415, when the Sicilian expedition was launched, to end in catastrophe two years later. Persia re-entered the picture in 413, an important moment because it introduced a long phase of Greek history, ending only with *Alexander the Great, in which Persia's voice would often be decisive. As Athens and Sparta wore each other down, other emergent powers like *Macedonia, itself destined to overthrow Persia eventually, grew in resources and self-confidence, especially under the strong rule of Archelaus; and Thebes, another 4th-cent. giant, profited from the war, notably by annexing Plataea in 427. Small states tried to protect their territorial integrity by aligning with the strongest and closest power of the moment.

The Fourth Century

The end of the war in 404 coincided with another equally momentous event, the establishment in power of *Dionysius I in Sicily, the prototype for many a 4th-cent. and Hellenistic strong man: tyranny, in fact, revives. Even in conservative Sparta there are traces of personality cult, detectable in *Lysander's victory monument at Delphi for the final victory at Aegospotami. And he got cult at *Samos. See RULER-CULT, GREEK.

Lysander's methods were harsh, and Spartan aggression in this period led, startlingly soon after the end of the Peloponnesian War, to the outbreak of the anti-Spartan Corinthian War, ended by the King's Peace (386). This curtailed Sparta's activities in Asia Minor (of which the most famous episode was the *Anabasis* or Persian expedition of Xenophon and the Ten Thousand, in its initial phase a covertly Spartan operation to replace Artaxerxes II by his brother Cyrus the Younger). But the price of eliminating Sparta was surrender of the region to Persia, and a general Greek political retreat east of the Aegean. However over the next 50 years cultural *Hellenism advanced, alongside Persian and indigenous culture, through activity by e.g. the Carian satrap Mausolus.

Much strengthened in Greece by the King's Peace, Sparta proceeded to fresh aggressions in north and central Greece, always a tendency when domestic or other preoccupations permitted. Sparta's coercion of Olynthus aroused no general protest but the occupation of the Cadmea (acropolis) of Thebes in 382 shocked and alarmed Greek opinion, and in 379 Thebes was liberated with Athenian help. Thebes and other places now joined a Second Athenian Confederacy (378). But as Thebes' power itself grew, especially after it defeated Sparta at the battle of Leuctra (371), Athens and Sparta found themselves driven together in the 360s when Thebes tried to usurp Athens' position at sea and (with more success) to weaken Sparta in the Peloponnese by founding Arcadian Megalopolis and reconstituting Messenia after centuries and equipping it with a new physical centre, the city of Messene.

*Philip II of Macedon succeeded to a politically weak but economically strong Macedon in 359, which he rapidly strengthened further at the expense of all his neighbours, Greeks included. The story of Athens' diplomatic relations with him is intricate (see DEMOSTHENES); features of the Peace of Philocrates may indicate that he planned a Persian invasion as early as 346, but he was obliged to defeat the Greeks at the battle of Chaeronea in 338 before the expedition could start. In the event he was assassinated in 336. Alexander, his son, carried the project through (334–323) in a whirlwind campaign which took him to Egypt, Persia, Afghanistan, India, and the Persian Gulf. For the campaigns see ALEXANDER THE GREAT. The city-foundations of Alexander are the most important part of his legacy but hard to estimate in detail: archaeological evidence is spectacular (see AI KHANOUM) but patchy, and the literary record is contaminated by rivalries between Seleucids and Ptolemies (see below).

Hellenistic period

(323–31 BC). After Alexander died aged 32 there was never much chance that the unity of his improvised empire would be perpetuated by any one of his Successors—the name given not to an orderly sequence of post-Alexander rulers (they adopted the title 'king' in a rush in 306) but to a whole clutch of his former marshals (the 'Diadochi'), controlling different areas but at overlapping times. The 'satrapies' were distributed at Babylon in 323 and again at Triparadeisus in 320; another arrangement was reached in 311. The generation after Alexander's death is full of complex military and political history, recorded by *Hieronymus of Cardia, who described the Successors' attempts to acquire as much 'spear-won territory' as possible, while mouthing slogans about the 'freedom of the Greeks' (see FREEDOM IN THE ANCIENT WORLD); the closest any of them got to a dominant position was *Antigonus the One-Eyed (helped by his son *Demetrius Poliorcetes ('the Besieger')), but his desire to reconstruct Alexander's empire is not certain and anyway he was killed at Ipsus in 301. This battle and Corupedion (281), where Seleucus defeated *Lysimachus of Thrace, determined that Asia would be Seleucid, though Lysimachus' defeat also led indirectly to the emergence of an important minor kingdom, that of the Pergamene Attalids. See PERGAMUM.

The first and longest-lasting Successor empire to establish itself was that of the Ptolemies (see PTOLEMY I) in Egypt, partly because its physical base was self-contained and hard to strike at. But Ptolemaic foreign policy was not insular or pacific; the dynasty had overseas possessions such as *Cyprus and *Crete, exercised hegemonical policies in Greece and the Aegean, and fought six Syrian wars in the Hellenistic age against the *Seleucids, the most spectacularly successful of all the Successor rulers.

Seleucid methods owe much to Achaemenid Persia, but were innovative too; but as with Alexander, the difficulty of assessing Seleucid urbanization is particularly tantalizing (the Ptolemies founded only one Greek city in Egypt, Ptolemais Hermiou). Recent writers urge that Mesopotamia as opposed to Anatolia or Syria was the engine-room of Seleucid power, and claim that Babylonian and other non-Greek elements in Seleucid culture played a prime role. Evidence from epigraphy (inscriptions) continues to emerge about these topics; Seleucid history is at the time of writing in a state of exciting flux: new finds, work, and insights can be expected, making confident generalization unusually precarious.

Macedon itself was much fought over and partitioned: at different times it was subject not only to Demetrius Poliorcetes, but to Cassander, Lysimachus, and *Pyrrhus of Epirus. Not until after 276 did Demetrius' son *Antigonus Gonatas consolidate the kingdom properly. Thereafter under the Antigonid rulers (Antigonus Doson; Demetrius II; Philip V) Macedon reverted to something like its historical role as it had been before it ballooned under Alexander, though older conceptions of an essentially Macedonian kingdom, supporting its supporters in Greece, have had to be modified in the light of new evidence from Labraunda in Caria for 3rd-cent. Antigonid activity in the area.

In Greece itself a major development of the age (already adumbrated in the 4th cent.) was the further development of federations or leagues (see FEDERAL STATES), not just the old-established Boeotian Confederacy, but the Arcadian (with its centre at Megalopolis), the Achaean, and the Aetolian, which controlled Delphi for much of the 3rd cent. Sparta's history continues to be distinctive: it stayed out of the Achaean Confederacy until the 190s. Social problems were more acute here than elsewhere, but not different in kind.

Rome made its first decisive eastern intervention in 229, the first Illyrian War; but significant contacts, e.g. with Egypt, antedate this. Philip V's alliance with *Hannibal meant that there would certainly be an eventual Roman reckoning with Macedon, and Philip was defeated in 197 at Cynoscephalae and his son Perseus at Pydna in 168, after which Macedon was divided into four republics. Meanwhile the Seleucid Antiochus IV had been defeated at the battle of Magnesia in Asia Minor in 190, though the resulting Peace of Apamea was an amputation not a death: Seleucid power in the east was unaffected, nor should the rise of new splinter kingdoms and states in *Bactria and Judaea, for example, be straightforwardly taken as indicating terminal Seleucid decline.

The Achaean Confederacy rose against Rome in 146 and was smashingly defeated; Corinth was destroyed.   S. H.

Roman

After 146 BC Rome supervised Greece through the governors of Macedonia; a separate province called Achaia was first created in 46 BC. Parts of Greece supported *Mithradates VI in 88 BC, *Athens with enthusiasm, and suffered accordingly in Sulla's campaigns; the earliest evidence for regular Roman taxation follows. Until Actium Greece remained a theatre for Roman warfare, piratical and civil, imposing heavy demands on her cities, sometimes met with difficulty, as at Gytheum in 71 BC (*Syll.*[3] 748 = Sherk, *Augustus* 74). In the early Principate, with Roman *philhellenism conferring few tangible benefits, the mainland Greeks at first remained—with the notable exception of *Sparta—reluctant subjects; there was unrest at Augustan Athens, and the imperial cult in Greece shows a retarded development, with no supra-city collaboration on record before *Nero. Reconciliation was hardly advanced by the colonial foundations of Caesar at Corinth and Augustus at Patrae and Nicopolis, the last two accompanied by enforced movements of local populations and cults; nor by Rome's proprietary attitude to Greece's heritage, evinced by imperial projects to translate works of art and even a whole cult (*Eleusis) to Rome (Suet. *Calig.* 22; *Claud.* 25). Nero's short-lived restoration of Greece's autonomy in AD 66 (date: T. Barnes, *JRA* 1989, 252–3), in spite of causing local hardship (*IG* 4[2]. 80–1 = Sherk, *Hadrian* 73), won him some Greek approval. Under Trajan the recruitment of Roman senators from Athens and Sparta advanced Greek political integration; writing at the time, *Plutarch (*Praec. ger. reip.*) counselled resigned acceptance of Roman dominion. *Hadrian conferred benefaction throughout the province; his foundation of the Panhellenion (AD 131/2) promoted an influx of easterners to Greece, among them the travel-writer *Pausanias. In the later 2nd and early 3rd cents. AD Greece flourished as a cultural centre (see GAMES; SECOND SOPHISTIC). Levels of prosperity varied regionally; ancient writers stress depopulation in Roman Greece, but the archaeological evidence for an emptied countryside down to 200 (S. Alcock, *Graecia Capta* (1993)), rather than merely confirming this picture, may point as well to greater nucleation (i.e. rural villages and migration to urban centres); certainly some cities now prospered, as could a small place like Aedepsus; *tourism was probably a significant source of wealth. The Heruli (267) damaged Athens, prompting Athenian self-defence. In the 4th cent. gradual Christianization wound down traditional cults, although the Panathenaea were still being celebrated *c.*410 (*IG* 2[2]. 3818 with *PLRE* 2 'Plutarchus' 2). In 396 Alaric sacked Corinth, Argos, and Sparta, prompting a wave of defensive building throughout the province. Recent archaeology shows a previously unsuspected prosperity in the 5th–6th cents., down to the Slav invasions (from 582); many basilical churches were built, and the countryside was densely populated.   A. J. S. S.

establish whether Greek belongs to a specific subgroup of IE; the old theory that it was closely related to Latin or Italic has long since been exploded. It shares a number of features with Armenian and Indo-Iranian, but they are not sufficient to define specific subgroups. The ancient belief that the language was autochthonous cannot be accepted; Indo-European speakers must have reached Greece from elsewhere, though the language may have acquired its main characteristics in Greece itself. Some specific features which distinguish ancient Greek from the Indo-European parent language are listed below.

3. Dialects When we speak of Greek we often mean Attic, i.e. the dialect of Athens. Yet from the Mycenaean period until the late Hellenistic period there was no standard Greek language and all cities or regions had different forms of speech, which they transmitted to their colonies. Even Mycenaean is only one of the varieties of second-millennium Greek. These local 'dialects' had equal or similar status and presumably most of them were mutually intelligible. Until the late 4th cent. BC (and often much later) they were used in normal oral intercourse and for written documents, laws, letters, etc. The contemporary inscriptions provide the best evidence for the differences, which encompass phonology, morphology, syntax, and lexicon (e.g. Lesbian παίσᾱς, 'of all' (fem.), Attic πάσης; Lesbian ἔμμεναι 'to be', Attic εἶναι; Thessalian αἰ μά κε κις, Arcadian εἰ δ' ἄν τις, Ionic-Attic ἐὰν δέ τις 'but if anyone' with a different order of the indefinite pronoun and the potential particle κε/ἄν from e.g. Phocian αἰ δέ τις κα; West Greek λε(ί)ω 'I want', Attic θέλω). On the basis of shared features modern scholars classify the various forms of Greek (partly on the model of the ancient grammarians) into groups: Ionic-Attic, Arcado-Cyprian, Aeolic (which includes Lesbian, Boeotian, and Thessalian), Doric (which includes dialects like Laconian, Argolic, etc.), and North-West Greek.

In spite of the absence of a standard language, from the 5th cent. BC at the latest—but probably much earlier—the Greeks thought of themselves as speaking a common language; for Herodotus (8. 144) τὸ Ἑλληνικόν ('Hellenism') was based on shared blood, language, customs, and religion. See HELLENISM AND HELLENIZATION. Greek was not identified with any of the dialects, but by the early 3rd cent. the Athenians were reproached for behaving as if Greek and Attic were the same thing (Posidippus, fr. 30 KA). In the same period we begin to find that in the local inscriptions the dialect is sometimes replaced by a form of language which is very close to Attic though not identical with it; it is the beginning of the so-called Ionic-Attic *koinē dialektos* (common language), which eventually prevailed and provided Greece with a standard language from which the later dialects developed. By the end of the 2nd cent. BC most local inscriptions were no longer in dialect; in contrast with the many dialects of the earlier colonies, the language brought to Asia and Africa by *Alexander the Great and his Successors was a form of *koinē*. For a brief period

other forms of common language, such as the so-called Doric *koina* of Peloponnese, prevailed in certain areas of mainland Greece, but in the end they were all replaced by the *koinē* (in the inscriptions at least).

4. Literary Greek Literary texts too were composed in different dialects but the dialect was mostly determined by the literary genre and its origin rather than by the author's origin. *Hesiod, who spoke Boeotian (an Aeolic dialect), composed hexameters in the same mixed dialect (based on Ionic) as Homer, while *Pindar, also a Boeotian, wrote choral poetry in a very different mixed dialect which included some Doric features. The iambic trimeters of Attic tragedy are written in a very literary Attic heavily influenced by Homer and by Ionic, but the choruses are written in Doric or rather in a literary form of Attic with superimposed Doric features (μάτηρ for Attic μήτηρ 'mother', etc.). Notice that for the literary dialects we tend to speak, as the grammarians did, of Aeolic, Ionic, and Doric rather than of Thessalian, Euboean, Cretan, and the like (Attic and Lesbian are exceptions), since the dialect used does not normally show features specific of a town or locality: it is more a generic colouring.

The history of literary Greek starts with *Homer, i.e. with a poetic language which, because of the various stages of its formulaic development, is remote from the language of normal conversation and under an Ionic patina includes both late and early features as well as features of different dialects: Mycenaean, Aeolic, Ionic. Because of its cultural importance and its wide diffusion epic poetry provided a common linguistic ground for a linguistically divided culture; in spite of its Ionic colouring the epic language is used for Tyrtaeus' elegiac poetry which exhorted the Doric Spartans to war and for the verses of the oracle at Delphi, a North-West Greek city. The risk was that the prestige and all-pervading influence of the epic language might have led to the fossilization of all literary language. Yet the dialects—and the way in which they were tied to different literary genres—provided a source for linguistic renewal. Elegiac poetry was composed in epic language but some forms of it were in a more or less purified form of Ionic. We have melic poetry in Lesbian (*Sappho and *Alcaeus), Ionic (*Anacreon) and even Boeotian (Corinna, though we are uncertain about the date); in these texts we observe not only the phonology and morphology of the various dialects but presumably also some new lexicon and the characteristics of a simpler style. Iambic and trochaic verses favoured Ionic and we find in Hipponax' poetry, for instance, a rich vocabulary full of colloquialisms and of foreign words; *Archilochus too comes much closer to the language of conversation than Homer. Comedy, which can be in Attic but also in Doric, allows colloquialisms not tolerated in tragedy. Yet the multiplicity of literary dialects also leads to new forms of artificiality. The language of choral poetry is a mixed language which is characterized by a 'Doric' (i.e. non-Attic-Ionic) patina, but in fact exploits elements of all forms of poetry. The result of so much mixture may be magnificent as in Pindar but may also sound baroque: *Aristophanes' parody of Pindar (*Av.* 941 ff.) makes this clear. Literary prose can, though need not, be closer to conversational language. Its first forms came from Ionia; even a Doric doctor like Hippocrates wrote of medicine in Ionic. Attic literary prose, which started in the 5th cent., shows clear signs of Ionic influence but eventually acquires linguistic forms and a style of its own. We have limited evidence for Doric prose.

In Hellenistic times the use of the literary dialects becomes more artificial; *Theocritus wrote his *Idylls* in epic language, in Doric, and in Aeolic (i.e. Lesbian), a *tour de force* which reflects the learned style of Alexandrinian poetry. At a later stage we find deliberate attempts to spurn the *koinē* and to prefer an accurate imitation of Attic. At the same time a prose text like the New Testament shows both Semitic influences and a higher level of colloquial simplicity.

5. Development The presence of dialects effectively prevents us from treating the development of Ancient Greek as a continuous process from Homer (or Mycenaean) to the *koinē*. Yet some changes seem to be widely attested in the Greek-speaking area either because of similar structural forces or because of mutual influences between dialects. In the official or literary language the complexity of sentences increases and the simpler patterns are reserved for the colloquial style or specific rhetorical effects. The article, which is absent from Mycenaean and still vestigial in Homer, is generalized in all dialects and is used to nominalize adjectives, participles, infinitives, and whole sentences. A new abstract and technical vocabulary is created through the use of suffixation (-ικος, -ισμος, -μα, etc.) or of composition. Greek is the one European language in which we can follow the independent creation of an abstract or technical vocabulary; the other languages, Latin included, directly or indirectly exploited Greek as a model or as a source of loan words.

6. Linguistic Features We list here some of the main features of ancient Greek, with special reference to classical Attic.

Phonology
The phonological system of Classical Attic is relatively well known. In the Classical period the vocalic system had five short vowels ([a, e, o, i, y]) written α, ε, o, ι, υ and seven long vowels ([a:, ε:, e:, ɔ:, o:, i:, y:]), written α, η, ει, ω, oυ, ι, υ (the letters in square brackets [ ] are phonetic symbols, with the colon indicating length). Four diphthongs were relatively frequent: [ai, au, eu, oi], written αι, oι, αυ, ευ. The so-called long diphthongs ([a:i, ε:i, ɔ:i]), i.e. αι (or ᾳ), ηι (or ῃ), ωι (or ῳ), were rarer and tended either to merge with the short diphthongs or to lose the second element.

The consonantal system included the dental fricative [s], the glottal fricative [h] (the rough breathing) which had a

very limited distribution, and four sonorants: the two liquids [l, r] and the two nasals [n, m]. The nine stops were organized according to three modes of articulation (voiceless, voiceless aspirate, and voiced) and three places of articulation: labial ([p, pʰ, b]), dental ([t, tʰ, d]), velar ([k, kʰ, g]). Unlike the modern language Ancient Greek had geminate consonants such as [pp, ll, mm] etc.

Some dialects have five long vowels (a:, e:, o:, u:, i:), instead of seven, and in most dialects we find a [u, u:] pronunciation of υ. The distribution of vowels also differs. Attic and Ionic changed the inherited [a:], which is preserved in all other dialects, into [ε:], written η, though in Attic this change was never completed and after [e], [i], [r] the sound reverted to [a:]. Hence Doric and Aeolic μάτηρ vs. Attic-Ionic μήτηρ and Attic χώρᾱ vs. Ionic χώρη. The tendency to monophthongize dipthhongs, which is typical of later Greek, is implemented earlier in dialects like Boeotian.

The consonantal system is relatively stable in all varieties of Greek, but some dialects still preserve [w] (written with Ϝ, the so-called digamma), which was lost in Attic. Other dialects tend to change the aspirated stops into fricatives at an early stage or to lose the (secondary) intervocalic [s] which is found elsewhere. Hence Laconian σιός 'god' for Attic θεός, where σ- may well indicate a dental fricative [θ] (cf. English *th*) and Laconian Μώhα 'Muse' corresponding to Attic Μοῦσα.

The system just described contrasts with that reconstructed for Indo-European. The Indo-European 'laryngeal' consonants were lost; the voiced aspirate stops (†bʰ etc.) yielded voiceless aspirates; the vocalic resonants †r̥, †l̥, †m̥, †n̥ were replaced by vowels or combinations of consonant and vowel, while the consonantal variants [j, w] of *i* and *u* tended to disappear; the inherited labiovelar stops (†kʷ, gʷ, gʷʰ) merged with velars, dentals, or labials, depending on the environment. Indo-European *s* changed to *h* word-initially before a vowel and internally between vowels, where it was eventually lost; all word-final stops were lost and final -*m* changed to -*n*. Not all of these changes are pre-Mycenaean, but those concerning the aspirates, the vocalic resonants, †*s*, probably final †-*m*, and the final stops are. Other changes involved sound clusters and differed in the various dialects; in Mycenaean, Arcado-Cyprian, Ionic-Attic, and Lesbian, but not in Doric and North-West Greek, -*ti* became -*si* (cf. Att. δίδωσι 'gives' and Dor. δίδωτι); in most dialects (including Ionic) *[kj, tj] became [ss], but in Attic and Boeotian we find [tt] (cf. Ion. θάλασσα, Att. θάλαττα).

Morphology and Syntax
Greek is a heavily inflected fusional language where the different grammatical categories are mostly marked by suffixes (nominal and verbal endings) or, far less frequently, by prefixes (e.g. the verbal augment or the reduplication). Infixation in verbs like λαμβ-άνω 'I take' vs. ἔ-λαβ-ον 'I took') is at best marginal. Note that one unsegmentable morpheme fulfils various functions: [o:], written -ου in

πολίτου 'of the citizen' marks genitive, singular, and masculine. Suffixation and composition are the two most productive means of word-formation.

Nouns and adjectives are classified into inflexional classes (declensions) according to their phonological shape (*o*-stems, *a*-stems, consonantal stems). In the Classical period the nominal inflexion distinguished five cases (nominative, vocative, accusative, genitive, dative), three numbers (singular, dual, plural) and three genders (masculine, feminine, and neuter). Later developments led to the loss of the dual (which in some dialects is absent from the earliest attestations) and even later ones to that of the dative. Gender was determined by agreement patterns rather than by semantic factors or the phonological shape of the word (ἵππος, 'horse/mare' can be masculine or feminine without any difference in inflexion). It was normal (though not compulsory) to use masculine and feminine for males and females but words for inanimate objects could be masculine, feminine, or neuter. In progress of time inflexional classes came to be tied to gender as is the case in Modern Greek. At the same time in Hellenistic Greek we witness a drastic simplification of the earlier inflexional variety.

Verbal morphology is highly complicated. A first distinction is between finite and non-finite forms; the former are characterized by personal endings for the singular, dual, and plural (there is not a full complement of dual endings and they too tend to disappear). The latter include participles, verbal adjectives, and infinitives, which are marked by special suffixes and share some of the syntactical, and in some instances morphological, properties of the noun.

In the finite verb the main grammatical categories are aspect, which indicates the way in which action etc. is envisaged (durative or imperfective, punctual or aoristic, stative or perfective), time (present, past, future), mood (indicative, subjunctive, optative, and imperative), voice (active, middle, passive), person (first, second, and third singular, dual or plural). Most verbs have three main stems (distinguished by vocalic alternation or affixation or more rarely by different roots) which indicate different aspects: durative/imperfective (e.g. πειθ- with the present πείθω 'I persuade, am persuading' and the imperfect ἔπειθον 'I was persuading'), or punctual/aoristic (e.g. πεισ- with the aorist ἔ-πεισα 'I persuaded'), or stative/perfective (e.g. πεποιθ- with the perfect πέποιθα 'I am persuaded' and the pluperfect ἐπεπείθειν 'I was persuaded'). Except for the future the so-called tenses (present, imperfect, aorist, perfect, pluperfect, future, future perfect) in the nonindicative moods and the non-finite forms mark primarily contrasts of aspect, while the indicative forms indicate both time and aspect distinctions: Xen. *Cyr.* 5. 5. 22 ἐλθὼν οὖν ἔπειθον αὐτούς, καὶ οὓς ἔπεισα τούτους ἔχων ἐπορευόμην σοῦ ἐπιτρέψαντος, 'I went (part. aorist) and I tried to persuade them (imperfect) and keeping (part. present) with me those whom I persuaded (ind. aorist) I continued in my expedition (imperfect), since you allowed

it (part. aorist).' The perfect is a special case; it starts indicating a state (πέποιθα 'I am convinced') and then develops a resultative use often accompanied by new forms (5th cent.: πέπεικα 'I have persuaded'), which makes it very similar to the aorist. Eventually it is lost and replaced by periphrastic forms. Contrasts of voice and person are marked by the endings. The middle voice emphasizes the participation or the involvement of the subject: active δικάζω 'I sit/am sitting in judgement', middle δικάζομαι 'I go/am going to law (on my own behalf)'. There are a few forms marked by suffixes which are exclusively passive, but otherwise the middle has also passive value, a pattern which will eventually prevail.

Word order is relatively free. The verb may precede or follow the object; similarly the subject may precede or follow the verb. Clitic particles tend in the early stages to occupy the second position in the clause (Xen. *Hell.* 3. 1. 11 ὁ ἀνήρ σοι ὁ ἐμὸς καὶ τἆλλα φίλος ἦν . . . 'my husband was devoted to you in other things too ...'), but they often gravitate towards the word with which they have the closest semantic links. In Homer we still find preverbs separated from verbs in so-called tmesis (ἐπὶ . . . ἔτελλε), but there too and in Classical prose 'preverbs' are either compounded with verbs (cf. ἐπέτελλε 'enjoined') or serve as prepositions which 'govern' an inflected noun. The simple sentence may be limited to a verb without expressed subject (ὕει 'it rains'). In longer sentences grammatical agreement is regular: the verb normally agrees in number with the subject; the adjective agrees in number, gender, and case with the noun to which it refers. Attic, however, preserves the inherited rule by which a subject in the neuter plural can agree with a verb in the singular: τὰ ζῷα τρέχει, 'animals run'. Nominal sentences composed of subject and predicate without any finite verb are frequent: Thuc. 2. 43. 3 ἀνδρῶν γὰρ ἐπιφανῶν πᾶσα γῆ τάφος, 'for of famous men the whole earth [is] a memorial'. Attic prose develops complex forms of subordination; dependent clauses with finite verbs are normally introduced by conjunctions or relative pronouns, while verbs of saying and other verbs may be followed by 'accusative with infinitive' constructions: Xen. *Hell.* 2. 2. 10 ἐνόμιζον δὲ οὐδεμίαν εἶναι σωτηρίαν . . ., 'they believed that there was no escape'.

Dialects show considerable morphological differences, partly determined by their different phonological development, partly by separate analogical processes (cf. e.g. the Aeol. dat. plur. of the type πόδεσσι 'to the feet', with a new ending -εσσι, vs. Att. -σι in ποσί). They do not, however, differ substantially in their morphosyntactic categories. Some syntactic differences are well known (e.g. Arcadian and Cyprian construe prepositions like ἐς (Att. ἐκ) and ἀπύ (Att. ἀπό) with the dative instead of the genitive found in Attic; Elean uses the optative in commands, etc.); others may not have been detected. Even so, there is remarkable similarity in the whole of the Greek-speaking area. If contrasted with IE, Greek has lost some case distinctions: the IE ablative and genitive have merged into the Greek genitive, and similarly the instrumental, locative, and dative into the Greek dative. The extensive use of prepositions is new. The complex arrangement of the verbal system is largely inherited and shows remarkable similarities with that of Indo-Iranian (Vedic and Greek are the only languages to preserve the distinction between optative and subjunctive). Greek has introduced new regularities—the creation of a contrast between middle and active perfect and of a resultative perfect; the pluperfect (to match the imperfect), the future, a separate passive, etc. Later developments show a preference for analytic rather than synthetic forms. It is still disputed how far IE allowed subordination, but the complex patterns found in Greek prose are certainly due to innovation. Perhaps the most important development is the creation of the article. In Homer ὁ, ἡ, τό still largely function as demonstrative or relative pronouns but in Classical prose they are used as articles. The article allows the creation of nominal forms which would be impossible otherwise (e.g. τὸ κακόν, τὸ εὖ, τὸ εἶναι, lit. 'the bad', 'the well', 'the be') and also marks the distinction between attributive and predicative function as in ὁ καλὸς παῖς or ὁ παῖς ὁ καλός 'the handsome boy' as contrasted with καλὸς ὁ παῖς 'the boy (is) handsome'. The development of intellectual language owes more to the article than to any other syntactical feature of Greek.

Lexicon

Though lexical differences between dialects are commonplace, if we allow for phonological differences, most of the basic vocabulary of Greek is shared by all dialects. The bulk of the early Greek lexicon is built on inherited Indo-European roots but numerous words cannot be etymologized and presumably belonged to pre-Greek populations. They include nouns and place names ending in -ινθος and -σσος / -ττος and a number of words for flora, fauna, etc. of Mediterranean origin (σῦκον 'fig', μίνθη 'mint', etc.). In addition even by Mycenaean times we find words of Semitic origin like σήσαμον 'sesame', κύμινον 'cummin', χρυσός 'gold', χιτών 'tunic', etc. In the Classical period it is noticeable that the cultural insularity of the Greeks and their reluctance to learn foreign languages led to very few borrowings from the outside; by contrast the later contacts with the Romans produced a large crop of loanwords or calques. New vocabulary is normally built via suffixation and composition; both processes are productive all through the history of the language. Compounds are characteristic of literary language (where they may be new creations or may be taken from the epitheta of the religious language and the formulae of oral poetry), but also occur in everyday language: the flavour of Pindar's μελησίμβροτος 'which is an object of care to men' or of the comic σαρκασμο-πιτυο-κάμπτης 'sneering pine-bender' (Aristophanes) is different from that of the innumerable -πώλης compounds of Attic inscriptions (κριθοπώλης 'barley seller', ἀρτοπώλης 'bread seller', etc.) which have only practical overtones.   A.M. Da.

gymnasium In Greek cities, the gymnasium originated as a place of exercise for the citizens specifically to fit the *epheboi*, 'ephebes', for the rigours of service as hoplites i.e. heavy-armed infantrymen. (Ephebes were (i) at 4th-cent. Athens, boys aged 18–20 in paramilitary training; (ii) more generally, well-to-do boys passing through a voluntary one-year finishing school.) At first gymnasia were no more than an open space, with a water supply, often sited in conjunction with a sanctuary or shrine; and late as the 5th cent. BC gymnasia seem not to have needed architectural development, shade and shelter being provided rather by groves of trees. Descriptions of the Athenian gymnasia, the Lyceum, Cynosarges, and above all the Academy conform with this (see ATHENS (TOPOGRAPHY)).

Frequented also by older citizens, and particularly from the connection with the 4th-cent. philosophers, they became more intellectual centres. Though the element of exercise was never lost, the concept of education became more important. Some—those at Athens in particular—through the interests of the philosophical schools became in effect universities. More usually in the cities of the Hellenistic age they functioned as secondary schools. More specialized architecture was required, and the gymnasia became enclosed areas, their buildings arranged largely on the courtyard principle. The *Academy at Athens acquired such a courtyard, with shrine-building and fountain-house, but is badly preserved and not fully understood. Better-preserved examples are found in the Asia Minor cities. The lower gymnasium at Priene is adjacent to the stadium which provides *athletic facilities. The gymnasium itself is wholly a school building, comprising a small courtyard with rooms opening off. One, its walls liberally inscribed by the pupils, is the classroom; another provides tubs and running cold water for washing. The gymnasium at *Pergamum is larger and more complex (the details partly obscured by the later intrusion of a Roman bath-building) but included its own running-track. A similar running-track, roofed but with ample ventilation, has been identified next to the so-called forum of Caesar at *Cyrene, indicating that this was originally a colonnaded exercise ground of a Hellenistic gymnasium.

Gymnasia were generally provided by the city. That at *Alexandria was situated at the centre of the city, close to the agora. As a centre of education it became a focus for the maintenance of Greek identity in the face of non-Greek settlement and Roman political control.

In their function as schools gymnasia continued to flourish in the Greek cities during the Roman period. In the west the exercise facilities were more usually developed in the context of the bath-buildings, especially at Rome in the imperial thermae (see BATHS). See EDUCATION, GREEK.   R. A. T.

gynaecology existed in the ancient world as a medical specialism, but its separate identity was not always permitted by wider medical theories. The significant question was this: do women have diseases peculiar to their sex, or are they subject to the same conditions as men, only requiring a separate branch of medicine to the extent that they have different organs to be affected? In other words, is gynaecology necessary?

The majority of the surviving gynaecological treatises come from the Hippocratic corpus (see MEDICINE §4) and probably date to the late 5th and early 4th cents. BC. These treatises include three volumes of *Gynaecia* (*Mul.*), usually translated as 'Diseases of Women', but which can also mean women's sexual organs, menstruation, or therapies for women's diseases. In contrast to the rest of the Hippocratic corpus, these texts include long lists of remedies using plant and animal ingredients. The third volume concerns the treatment of barren women. A separate short treatise discusses the medical problems of unmarried girls at puberty (*Virg.*) while others focus on the process of generation. A large number of the case histories in *Epidemics* trace the progress of disease in women patients.

In keeping with a culture in which women could be seen to constitute a separate 'race', *Mul.* I. 62 criticizes those doctors who make the mistake of treating the diseases of women as if they were men. For the Hippocratics of the *Gynaecia*, women require a separate branch of medicine because they are seen as fundamentally different from men, not merely in their reproductive organs, but in the texture of their flesh, seen as 'wet' and 'spongey', like wool. Because of this texture, women are thought to absorb more fluid from their diet, menstruation being necessary to remove the surplus. There was, however, no uniformity on female difference, other Hippocratic texts applying identical principles—such as the theory of 'critical days', in which certain numbered days were seen as those on which the crisis in a disease occurred—to diseases of both men and women.

The debate on the status of gynaecology continued. Alexandrian anatomy, associated in particular with Herophilus, moved from fluids to organs, and women came to be seen more as reverse males than as a separate race. Whereas men's reproductive organs are outside, women were seen as having the same organs inside. Papyri show that Hippocratic recipes for women's diseases continued to be transmitted. Soranus summarizes the position before his own time; writers such as the early 4th-cent. BC Diocles of Carystus and the Empiricist sect believed there were conditions specific to women, while the 3rd-cent. Erasistratus and Herophilus, together with writers of the Methodist persuasion (see MEDICINE §5.3), believed there were not. Instead, Methodists thought that the same principles governed all diseases, men and women being made of the same materials behaving according to the same rules. Soranus himself claimed that although some conditions, such as pregnancy and lactation, were specific to women, their diseases were not generically different. Galen (*Parts of Medicine* I. 2–3 and 5. 8) lists as legitimate medical specialisms pediatrics and geriatrics, but not gynaecology.

Despite these changes from Hippocratic beliefs, some forms of therapy for women's diseases continued to be used more readily than in the treatment of men with analogous conditions. Foremost among these was the fumigation, in which vapours were passed into the womb through its mouth. These were believed to open the womb, thus permitting retained matter to be expelled and semen to enter. Ancient gynaecological recipes, like purificatory ritual, made use of sulphur, asphalt, squill, and laurel, as well as animal excrement.

Beliefs about the interior of the female body were also remarkably persistent, despite evidence to the contrary. For example, although Herophilus discovered the ovaries and the uterine ligaments, the function of the former was not understood—women continued to be seen as containers for male seed—and the presence of the latter was not widely seen as contradicting the Hippocratic notion that the womb was capable of some degree of movement within the body. Instead, the 'wandering womb' theory was merely rephrased, for example being seen in terms of 'sympathy' between upper and lower parts of the body permitting the latter to cause symptoms in the former. See ANATOMY AND PHYSIOLOGY; BOTANY; CHILDBIRTH.

H. K.

Hades, son of Cronus and Rhea (Hes. *Theog.* 453–56) and husband of *Persephone (*Od.* 10. 491), is 'Lord of the dead' (*Il.* 20. 61) and king of the Underworld, the 'house of Hades' (Hom., Hes.), where he rules supreme and, exceptionally, administers justice (Aesch. *Supp.* 228–31, *Eum.* 273–5). After Homer, Hades is not only the god of the dead, but also the god of death, even death personified (Semon. 1. 14; Pind. *Pyth.* 5. 96, *Nem.* 10. 67, *Isthm.* 6. 15; Soph. *Ant.* 581; Eur. *Alc.* 262; R. Seaford on Eur. *Cyc.* 397). Hades refers normally to the person; in non-Attic literature, the word can also designate the Underworld (*Il.* 23. 244; *Od.* 11. 635; Heraclitus DK 22 B 98; Anac. 50. 9 f. Page, Luke 16. 23). Cold, mouldering, and dingy, Hades is a 'mirthless place' (*Od.* 11. 94; Hes. *Op.* 152–5). The proverbial 'road to Hades' (Lucian *Catapl.* 14) is 'the same for all' (*Anth. Pal.* 7. 477. 3 f., 11. 23. 3). Aeacus, son of *Zeus, 'keeps the keys to Hades' (Apollod. *Bibl.* 3. 12. 6; cf. *GVI* 1906. 4, *PGM* iv 1464 f.); the same is said of Pluton (Paus. 5. 20. 3), Anubis (love charms from Roman Egypt: *PGM* iv 341 f., 1466 f.; *Suppl. Mag.* 2. 299, entry under *kleis*, and Christ (Rev. 1. 18). The 'gates of Hades' (*Il.* 5. 646) are guarded by 'the terrible hound', Cerberus, who wags his tail for the new arrivals, but devours those attempting to leave (Hes. *Theog.* 311 f., 767–73). Hades, too, was sometimes perceived as an eater of corpses (Soph. *El.* 542 f.). Without burial, the dead cannot pass through Hades' gates (*Il.* 23. 71–4; Eur. *Hec.* 28–54). Once inside, they are shrouded in 'the darkness of pernicious Hades' (*SEG* 26. 1139. 9).

Like the Erinyes/Eumenides ('Angry/Kindly Ones') and *Demeter ('Earth-mother', cf. Eur. *Bacch.* 275 f., Derveni papyrus col. 18 (*ZPE* 47 (1982) after p. 300)), Hades lacked a proper name; as in the case of other nameless chthonians ('gods of the earth', as opposed to Olympians, 'of the heavens'), his anonymity was a precaution (Pl. *Cra.* 403a7). He was referred to by descriptive circumlocutions as 'chthonian Zeus' (*Il.* 9. 457; M. L. West on Hes. *Op.* 465), 'the chthonian god' (Hes. *Theog.* 767), 'king of those below' (Aesch. *Pers.* 629), 'Zeus of the departed' and 'the other Zeus' (Aesch. *Supp.* 156 f., 231), 'the god below' (Soph. *Aj.* 571; Eur. *Alc.* 424), or simply 'lord' (Eur. *Alc.* 852). As the

Lord of the Dead, he was dark and sinister, a god to be feared and kept at a distance. Paradoxically, he was also believed to 'send up' good things for mortals from his wealth below (West on Hes. *Theog.* 969; Ar. fr. 504 K–A; Pl. *Cra.* 403a3–5); he is a 'good and prudent god' (Pl. *Phd.* 80d7).

The two opposite but complementary aspects of his divinity are reflected in a host of positive and negative epithets. Of the latter, Hades, 'the invisible one' according to ancient etymology (E. R. Dodds on Pl. *Grg.* 493b4, cf. Soph. *Aj.* 607, but modern linguists are divided on this), recalls the darkness of his realm. The 'wolf's cap of Hades', worn by *Athena in the *Iliad* (5. 844 f.) and by Aita/Hades in Etruscan art (*LIMC* 'Hades/Aita' nos. 5–6, 10–12, 21), makes its wearers invisible (Ar. *Ach.* 390; Pl. *Resp.* 612b). Other negative epithets are 'hateful' (*Il.* 8. 368 *stugeros*, like the Styx, 'implacable and adamant' (*Il.* 9. 158), 'tearless' (Hor. *Carm.* 2. 14. 6) and 'malignant' (*baskanos*, cf. M. W. Dickie, *ZPE* 100 (1994), 111–14). Epithets which euphemistically address his benign and hospitable aspects include Clymenus ('Renowned'), Euboulcus ('Good Counsellor': Nic. *Alex.* 14; *GVI* 2030. 9), Euchaites ('the Beautiful-haired One': Clarian oracle *ISestos* 11. 24, *c.* AD 166), Eukles ('Of Good Repute': Orph. fr. 32 c–e 2 Kern; Hsch. ε 6926), Hagesilaos ('Leader of the People': Aesch. fr. 406 Radt; A. W. Bulloch on Callim. *Hymn* 5. 130; *GVI* 1370. 2), Pasianax ('Lord over All': *Def. tab.* Audollent, nos. 43–4), Polydektes or Polydegmon ('Receiver of Many': *Hymn. Hom. Cer.* 9, 17), Polyxeinos ('Host to Many': Aesch. fr. 228 Radt; Callim. fr. 285 Pf.), and Pluton ('Wealth', *ploutos*, personified; cf. Soph. fr. 273 Radt). Originally a divinity in his own right, during the 5th cent. BC Pluton became Hades' most common name in myth as well as in cult (first attested on a phiale by Douris, *LIMC* 'Hades' no. 28, *c.*490 BC; Soph. *Ant.* 1200, Pl. *Grg.* 523a4, Isoc. 9. 15; *IG* i³. 5. 5, 386. 156, 2². 1363. 21 'priestess of Pluton', 1672. 169, 1933. 2; *Hymn. Orph.* 18).

Hades was not a recipient of cult (Soph. *Ant.* 777–80). Like Thanatos, 'Death', he was indifferent to prayer or offerings (Aesch. fr. 161 Radt; Eur. *Alc.* 424). The abnormal cult of Hades at Elis, with a temple open once a year, then only to the priest (Paus. 6. 25. 2 f.), and his *temenos* at Mt.

Minthe near Pylos (Strabo 8. 344) are the exceptions that prove the rule. But throughout the Greek world—at *Eleusis, *Sparta, *Ephesus, Carian Cnidus, and Mytilene on *Lesbos, among numerous other places—he received cult in his beneficial aspect as Pluton, often alongside his consort *Persephone. The couple were widely worshipped as Pluton and Kore (IG 2². 1672. 182, 4751; CEG 2. 571); at Eleusis, they were also known as Theos and Thea. Pluton is related to the Eleusinian cult figures Plutus and Eubouleus as well as to other friendly chthonians such as Zeus Meilichios and Zeus Eubouleus. In various curse tablets, however, he is invoked along with *Demeter and Kore or, more menacingly, with the Erinyes, Hecate, *Hermes, Moirai, and Persephone (J. G. Gager, *Curse Tablets and Binding Spells from the Ancient World* (1992), nos. 53, 84, 89, 110, 134); *curses in the name of Hades and Persephone are less common (*Def. tab.* R. Wünsch, no. 102b13–16; W. Peek, *Kerameikos* 3 (1941), 98 no. 9. 18). So-called Plutonia marked entrances to the Underworld (Strabo 5. 244).

Apart from the story of Persephone's abduction by him, few myths attach to Hades. By giving her the forbidden food of the dead to eat—the pomegranate—he bound Demeter's daughter to return periodically to his realm (*Hymn. Hom. Cer.* 370 ff.). Their union was without issue; its infertility mirrors that of the nether world (Apollodorus of Athens, *FGrH* 244 F 102a2). When the sons of Cronus divided the universe amongst themselves, Hades was allotted the world of the dead, Zeus obtained the sky, and Poseidon the sea (R. Janko on *Il.* 15. 185–93; Richardson on *Hymn. Hom. Cer.* 86). As ruler of the dead, Hades was always more ready to receive than to let go (Aesch. *Pers.* 688–90). Two kindred gods, Demeter and *Dionysus, as well as heroes like *Heracles, *Theseus, and *Orpheus descended alive to Hades and returned to earth. Ordinary mortals went there to stay; Alcestis, Eurydice, and Protesilaus were among the few allowed to leave (cf. Plat. *Symp.* 179c). Heracles wrestled with Thanatos (Eur. *Alc.* 843–9) and wounded Hades with his arrows (*Il.* 5. 395–7; Paus. 6. 25. 2 f.). Hades' mistress Minthe or Menthe was changed into the mint plant by Persephone (Strabo 8. 344, Ov. *Met.* 10. 728–30; cf. Oppian, *Halieutica* 3. 486 ff.).

Alcestis' death vision of Hades, who comes to get her, is dim but frightening (Eur. *Alc.* 259–62 Diggle: 'Someone is leading me, leading me away—don't you see?—to the hall of the dead. He stares at me from under his dark-eyed brow. He has wings—it's Hades!'). In Greek art, Hades and Pluton—differentiating between the two is not always possible—are wingless human figures lacking any terrifying aspects. Zeus-like and bearded, Hades–Pluton is a majestic, elderly man holding a sceptre, twig, cornucopia, pomegranate, or cantharus. On some vases, Hades is shown averting his gaze from the other gods (*LIMC* nos. 14, 22, 148). Unlike Hades, Thanatos is represented with wings (Eur. *Alc.* 843; often in vase-painting, e.g. Euphronius, calyx-crater, New York, Met. Mus. 1972.11.10; Thanatos Painter, lecythus, London, BM D 58). Conceptually and

iconographically, Dionysus (Heraclitus fr. 15 DK) and Sarapis (H. Heubner on Tac. *Hist.* 4. 83 f.) in their chthonian aspects have affinities to Hades–Pluton.

Hades was the universal destination of the dead until the second half of the 5th cent. BC, when we first hear of the souls of some special dead ascending to the upper air (*aithēr*), while their bodies are said to be received by the earth (Athenian epitaph, c.432 BC, IG 1³. 1179. 6 f. = CEG 1. 10. 6 f.; Eur. *Supp.* 533 f.; CEG 2. 535, 558). Notably, the souls of the heroized daughters of Erechtheus 'do not go to Hades', but reside in heaven (Eur. *Erech.* fr. 65. 71 f. Austin). The various Underworld topographies found in Homer (*Od.* 11) and Virgil (*Aen.* 6), in the esoteric gold leaves containing descriptions of Hades, and in the apocryphal *Apocalypse of Peter* reflect changing constructs of the afterlife. See DEATH, ATTITUDES TO.   A. H.

Hadrian (Publius Aelius Hadrianus), emperor AD 117–38. The Aelii of Italica in southern Spain were among the earliest provincial senators; his mother Domitia Paulina was from Gades (mod. Cádiz). When his father died, Hadrian became the ward of *Trajan, his father's cousin, and of Publius Acilius Attianus (85). Early devotion to Greek studies earned the nickname, *Graeculus* ('little Greek'); a passion for hunting was apparent when he visited Italica (90). After the vigintivirate (a minor magistracy), he was tribune in Legio II Adiutrix (95) and V Macedonica (96). Sent to congratulate Trajan on his adoption in 97, he remained in Upper Germany as tribune of XXII Primigenia, under Lucius Iulius Ursus Servianus, husband of his sister Paulina. In 100 he married Trajan's great-niece Sabina Augusta, a match arranged by Pompeia Plotina, a devoted supporter. As Trajan's quaestor (101) he had to polish his Latin (his 'rustic accent' was mocked). He joined Trajan for the First Dacian War (101–2); was *tribune of the *plebs*; then legate of I Minervia in the Second Dacian War (105–6), perhaps being praetor *in absentia*. He governed Lower Pannonia and was suffect consul (108). When Trajan's closest ally Lucius Licinius Sura died, Hadrian took over as imperial speech-writer. In 112 he was archon at Athens, where he was honoured with a statue; its inscription (ILS 308 = Smallwood 109) confirms the career in the SHA. When the Parthian expedition began (October 113), he joined Trajan's staff, becoming governor of Syria at latest in 117; and was designated to a second consulship for 118. His position was thus very strong when Trajan died at Selinus in Cilicia on 8 August 117. The next day his adoption by Trajan was announced. A single aureus with the reverse HADRIANO TRAIANO CAESARI (*BM Coins, Rom. Emp.* 3. lxxxvi, 124) cannot dispel the rumours that Plotina had staged an adoption after Trajan died. Hadrian was disliked by his peers and had rivals, but the army recognized him; the senate had to follow suit. Plotina and the guard prefect Attianus took Trajan's body to Rome, while Hadrian faced the crisis in the east. He abandoned the new provinces (Armenia, Mesopotamia, and Assyria), dismissed Trajan's favourite Lusius Quietus from his command in Judaea, and

Hadrian View of the Canopus, an ornamental piece of water providing a view for diners, one of the many exotic features of Hadrian's villa at Tibur (Tivoli), the largest ever built. Like all early Roman emperors, Hadrian worked from home, and governance as well as leisure filled his visits to Tibur.

probably wintered at Nicomedia, leaving Catilius Severus as governor of Syria. A rising in Mauretania, no doubt provoked by the dismissal of Quietus, a Moor, was suppressed by Hadrian's friend Quintus Marcius Turbo. Britain was also disturbed; Quintus Pompeius Falco, governor of Lower Moesia, was probably sent to Britain to restore control when Hadrian reached the Danube in spring 118. He negotiated with the Roxolani and evidently evacuated the Transdanubian part of Lower Moesia annexed by Trajan. Gaius Iulius Quadratus Bassus, governor of Dacia, had died campaigning; Hadrian summoned Turbo to govern part of Dacia, with Lower Pannonia. Dacia was divided into three provinces. Turbo, an equestrian, was given the same rank as a prefect of Egypt.

Meanwhile Attianus was active. Four ex-consuls, Gaius Avidius Nigrinus, Cornelius Palma Frontonianus, Publilius Celsus, and Lusius Quietus, were killed for plotting treason. When Hadrian reached Rome (9 July 118), the senate was hostile. He claimed not to have ordered the executions but took steps to win popularity. First came a posthumous triumph for Trajan's Parthian 'victory'. Crown-gold (*aurum coronarium*) was remitted for Italy and reduced for the provinces; a new, more generous, largess was disbursed to the *plebs*; overdue tax was cancelled on a vast scale; children supported by the *alimenta* received a bounty, bankrupt senators a subsidy; lavish gladiatorial games were held.

Hadrian, consul for the second time for 118, took as colleague Pedanius Fuscus, husband of his niece Iulia: Fuscus was a likely heir. In 119 he was consul for the third and last time, and changed guard prefects. One new prefect was Septicius Clarus, to whom the younger Pliny had dedicated his Letters; *Suetonius Tranquillus, protégé of Pliny and Septicius' friend, became *ab epistulis* (in charge of imperial correspondence). The second prefect was Turbo: he was to take charge during Hadrian's absences, together with Marcus Annius Verus, a senator of Spanish origin, linked by kinship to Hadrian. Verus, consul for the second time in 121 and urban prefect, was rewarded by a third consulship in 126. On 21 April 121, the birthday of the city, Hadrian inaugurated a vast temple of *Venus and Roma in the forum Romanum, designed by himself: one of many fields in which he dabbled and claimed expertise. A poet, he boasted of his cithara-playing and singing, was expert in mathematics—and in military science. A favourite occupation was debating with sophists (see SECOND SOPHISTIC). Favorinus yielded: 'who could contradict the Lord of Thirty Legions?' To the legions Hadrian now turned, leaving in 121 for the Rhineland. In Upper Germany and Raetia he erected a continuous palisade, Rome's first artificial *limes*, symbolizing his policy of peace within fixed frontiers. Legions and *auxilia*—with a few exceptions—were to remain in the same bases, local recruiting became prevalent. Hadrian set out to improve discipline and training—*Arrian was to dedicate his *Tactica* to Hadrian, registering the emperor's innovations. In 122 he crossed to Britain, taking his friend Platorius Nepos, promoted from Lower Germany to Britain, and VI Victrix. The empress Sabina, the prefect Septicius, and Suetonius also went. An obscure imbroglio involving these three led to the men's dismissal. The main business was 'the wall to separate Romans and barbarians', as the SHA *vita* tersely puts it. The *wall of Hadrian was far more elaborate than any other *limes*: the bridge at the eastern end of the wall bore his name, Pons Aelius (Newcastle upon Tyne)—perhaps he designed it. From Britain he made for Spain, via southern Gaul, where he commemorated his horse in verse and Plotina with a basilica (she died early in 123). He wintered at Tarragona, calling a meeting of delegates from the peninsula: military service was on the agenda. Italica was not favoured with a visit, although—showing disdain—he granted it the status of *colonia*. Conscious perhaps of the coming 150th anniversary of 27 BC, Hadrian now shortened his names to Hadrianus Augustus: a claim to be a new founder of the empire.

A Moorish uprising was dealt with at this time, perhaps without his personal involvement. News from the east determined his next move. Perhaps visiting Cyrenaica *en route*—he resettled refugees from the Jewish uprising in a new city (Hadrianopolis)—his goal was the Euphrates, to confirm peace with Parthia. After an extensive tour of Asia Minor, he sailed (autumn 124) to Athens. There he was initiated in the Eleusinian *mysteries, visiting many other cities before his return to Rome, via Sicily, in summer 125. He stayed in Italy for three years, touring the Po valley for six months in 127; during this period he created four 'provinces' in Italy, each with a consular governor. The senate was displeased—Antoninus abolished them (see ANTONINUS PIUS). In 128 he accepted the title *pater patriae* ('father of the fatherland'); then began his last tour with a visit to Africa and Mauretania, creating another *limes*; he lectured the troops at Lambaesis, displaying his knowledge of manœuvres (Smallwood 328). Briefly at Rome in late summer, he crossed to Athens, where he wintered again, dedicated the Olympieum and assumed the name Olympius. After participating in the mysteries (spring 129), he went via Ephesus to Syria, wintering at Antioch, visiting Palmyra in spring 130, and going through Arabia and Judaea to Egypt. In Judaea he founded a *colonia* at Jerusalem, Aelia Capitolina; and banned circumcision: measures to Hellenize the Jews—a fatal provocation. Hadrian was accompanied not only by Sabina but by a young Bithynian, Antinous: his passion for the youth, embarrassing to many Romans, was a manifestation of his *Hellenism. After inspections of *Pompey's and *Alexander the Great's tombs, debates in the Museum, and hunting in the desert, a voyage on the Nile ended in tragedy: Antinous was drowned. Hadrian's extreme grief was only assuaged by declaring his beloved a god (duly worshipped all over the empire) and naming a new city on the Nile (perhaps already planned) Antinoöpolis. Hadrian

went from Egypt to Lycia; by the winter of 131–2 he was back at Athens, to inaugurate the Olympieum and found the Panhellenion, the culmination of his philhellenism.

In 132 the Jews rebelled under Bar Kokhba, rapidly gaining control of considerable territory. Hadrian was briefly in Judaea, summoning his foremost general, Sextus Iulius Severus, from Britain to crush the revolt. It lasted until 135; by then Hadrian had been back at Rome for a year, worn out and ill, staying mostly at his Tibur (Tivoli) villa. In 136 he turned his mind to the succession. The aged Servianus and his grandson Fuscus had aspirations; but Hadrian hated both and forced them to suicide. To universal surprise, he adopted one of the consuls of 136, as Lucius Aelius Caesar. It may have been remorse for the killing of Nigrinus, Aelius' stepfather, in 118. But Aelius died suddenly on 1 January 138. Hadrian now chose Aurelius Antoninus (Pius) and ensured the succession far ahead by causing him to adopt in turn his nephew Marcus (= Marcus *Aurelius) and Aelius' young son Lucius Verus). Marcus, a favourite of Hadrian and grandson of Annius Verus, had been betrothed to Aelius' daughter. Hadrian died (10 July 138) with a quizzical verse address to his restless soul. He was buried in his new mausoleum (Castel Sant'Angelo) and deified by a reluctant senate. An intellectual and reformer (the Perpetual Edict, codified by Salvius Iulianus, and the extension of Latin rights (see CITIZENSHIP, ROMAN) were major measures), by his provincial tours, amply commemorated on the coins, by his frontier policy, and promotion of Hellenism, he made a deep impact on the empire.   A. R. Bi.

Hadrian's Wall See WALL OF HADRIAN.

Hannibal (*see following page*)

Hector, in mythology son of Priam and Hecuba, husband of Andromache and father of Astyanax (*Il.* 6. 394 ff.), and the greatest of the Trojan champions. In *Homer's *Iliad* he first appears leading the Trojans out to battle (2. 807 ff.); he reproaches Paris for avoiding Menelaus (3. 38 ff.), and arranges the truce and the single combat between the two (85 ff.). He takes a prominent part in the fighting of books 5 and 6, but in the latter goes back to the city for a while to arrange for offerings to be made to the gods. He thus meets Andromache and Astyanax on the city walls in one of the best-known scenes of the *Iliad*, then returns with Paris to the battle. In book 7 he challenges any Greek hero to single combat, and is met by the greater *Aias, who has rather the better of the encounter; they part with an exchange of gifts. In book 8 he drives the Greeks back to their camp and bivouacs on the plain. In the long battle of books 11–17 he takes a prominent part, leading the main attack on the fortifications of the Greek camp which nearly succeeds in burning the Greek ships. During the battle he is struck down with a stone thrown by Aias (14. 409 ff.), but restored to strength by *Apollo at the command of Zeus (15. 239 ff.). He kills Patroclus (16. 818 ff.),

[*continued on p. 327*]

Hannibal

Hannibal, Carthaginian general. He was born in 247 BC, the eldest son of Hamilcar Barca. After making Hannibal swear an oath never to be a friend of Rome, Hamilcar took him to Spain in 237, where he stayed during the commands of both his father and his brother-in-law Hasdrubal, marrying a Spaniard from Castulo. In 221 he assumed the supreme command in Spain on the death of Hasdrubal (confirmed by the popular assembly at Carthage) and reverted to his father's policy by attacking the Olcades, who lived on the upper Anas (Guadiana). In 220 he advanced beyond the Tagus (Tajo) as far as the Durius (Duero), defeating the Vaccaei and the Carpetani. Regarding Rome's alliance with Saguntum (Sagunto) as a threat to Carthage's position in Spain, he decided to defy her, and put pressure on Saguntum. He rejected a Roman protest, and after consulting Carthage began the siege of Saguntum in spring 219, knowing that war with Rome would result, and took the city eight months later.

Hannibal had decided, without waiting for a Roman declaration of war, to take the initiative by invading Italy; probably less with the object of destroying Rome than of detaching her allies (an expectation warranted by Carthage's experience in her wars with the Greeks) and so weakening her that she would give up Sicily, Sardinia, and Corsica, and undertake not to molest Carthage's North African and Spanish empire. He left his capital, Carthago Nova (mod. Cartagena) in May 218, with a professional army of 90,000 infantry and 12,000 cavalry (Iberians, Libyans, and Numidians) and *elephants, leaving his brother Hasdrubal to hold Spain; and subdued, regardless of cost, the area between the Ebro and the Pyrenees. He remained there until September, presumably in the expectation of meeting and destroying the army of the consul Publius Cornelius Scipio before invading Italy. Then, with 50,000 infantry, 9,000 cavalry, and 37 elephants, he marched to the Rhône, avoided battle with Scipio (belatedly *en route* to Spain), and continued towards the Alps, which he crossed in about fifteen days, with great difficulty and enormous loss of life. The route he took remains a matter for conjecture: he seems to have marched up the valley of the Isère, past Grenoble, and then perhaps took the difficult Col du Clapier pass, having missed the easier Mt. Cenis pass. He arrived in the area of Turin about the end of October, defeated P. Cornelius Scipio (who had returned to Italy) in a cavalry skirmish at the Ticinus (Ticino) near Pavia, and then, having been joined by many Gauls, won the first major battle of the war at the Treb(b)ia, a little to the west of Placentia (Piacenza), against the combined forces of Scipio and Ti. Sempronius Longus (end of December). In May 217 Hannibal crossed the Apennines (losing an eye in the passage of the Arno), ravaged Etruria, and with the help of early-morning fog, trapped the consul Gaius Flaminius in an ambush at Lake Trasimene. Flaminius and 15,000 men were killed and 10,000 captured. Hannibal proceeded to Apulia, and thence to Samnium and Campania, while the dictator Quintus *Fabius Maximus Verrucosus embarked on his strategy of following Hannibal but avoiding a pitched battle. Hannibal returned to Apulia (eluding Fabius) for the winter. In 216 he inflicted a devastating defeat on both consuls, who commanded over-strength armies, at Cannae; only 14,500 Romans and allies escaped death or captivity. After each battle he dismissed the Italian prisoners to their homes while holding the Romans (see e.g. Livy 22. 58).

Cannae led to the defection of southern Italy, including Capua (S. Maria Capua Vetere), the second city in Italy, and part of Samnium; but central Italy and all the Latin colonies remained loyal to Rome, and with Roman commanders avoiding another pitched battle, Hannibal achieved little in the following three years (215–213), although he concluded an alliance with Philip V of Macedon (215), and helped to bring about the revolt of *Syracuse (214). He received no assistance from Spain, where Hasdrubal was on the defensive, and little from Carthage. He failed to gain control of a port, despite attacks on Cumae, Neapolis (Naples), Puteoli (Pozzuoli) and Tarentum (Taranto), and his persistent assaults on Nola were repulsed; several towns were recaptured by Rome, notably Casilinum (Capua) and Arpi (near Foggia). In 212, however, he captured Tarentum by stealth, although the citadel remained in Roman control, and this was followed by the defection of three neighbouring Greek cities. In 211, in an attempt to relieve the siege of Capua (begun the previous year), Hannibal marched on Rome itself but failed to force the Romans to withdraw troops from Capua, and returned to the south; soon afterwards Capua fell, its fall being preceded by that of Syracuse. Hannibal was now being pressed ever further south—from 212–11 onwards, with one possible exception, he spent every winter in the extreme south of Italy—and suffered a further blow in 209 when Fabius recaptured Tarentum. In 208, however, he caught both consuls in an ambush in Lucania; one, Marcus Claudius Marcellus, was killed immediately, his colleague fatally wounded. In Spain, *Scipio Africanus had captured Carthago Nova (209) and defeated Hasdrubal at Baecula (Bailen) (208). Hasdrubal slipped out of Spain, but in 207 his defeat and death on the Metaurus (Metauro) dashed Hannibal's hopes of receiving reinforcements. Hannibal was now confined to Bruttium, where he stayed until 203—in 205 he could not prevent Scipio recapturing Locri Epizephyrii—when he was recalled to Africa to defend Carthage. After abortive peace negotiations with Scipio, he was decisively defeated at Zama (202), and successfully urged his countrymen to make peace on Rome's terms.

Hannibal now involved himself in domestic affairs; as sufete (chief magistrate) in 196 he introduced constitutional reforms to weaken the power of the oligarchs, and reorganized the state's finances so that the war indemnity could be paid to Rome without levying additional taxes. His enemies reacted by alleging to Rome that Hannibal was intriguing with *Antiochus III of Syria. When a Roman commission of enquiry arrived, Hannibal fled, ultimately reaching Antiochus (195). He urged Antiochus to go to war with Rome; he asked for a fleet and an army with which to stir Carthage to revolt, or, failing that, to land in Italy. He accompanied Antiochus to Greece in 192, and advised him to bring Philip V into the war and invade Italy. In 190, bringing a fleet from Syria to the Aegean, he was defeated by the Rhodians off Side. The peace agreed between Rome and Antiochus provided for his surrender; he fled to Crete and then to Prusias I of Bithynia, whom he supported in his war with Eumenes II of Pergamum. In 183 or 182 *Flamininus persuaded Prusias to surrender Hannibal, a fate which he preempted by taking poison.

Hannibal has been widely acknowledged, in both antiquity and modern times, as one of the greatest generals in history. He brought to perfection the art of combining infantry and cavalry, he understood the importance of military intelligence and reconnaissance and he commanded the unflagging loyalty of his troops. But he failed against Rome because all the assumptions upon which his policy and his strategy were based—that huge numbers of Gauls would follow him to Italy, that Carthage would recover the command of the sea and reinforce him from Africa and that Hasdrubal would bring him reinforcements from Spain, and, above all, that Rome's confederation would break up following Rome's defeat in the field—proved fallacious. Roman propaganda accused Hannibal of perfidy and cruelty; as far as the latter charge is concerned, although he could be chivalrous at times, his attitude to those who resisted him was uncompromising. But the record of Rome's treatment of defectors makes far grimmer reading.

B. M. C.

and strips him of his arms despite the efforts of the Greeks. After the appearance of *Achilles at the trench, full of rage at Patroclus' death, Hector again bivouacs on the plain, against the advice of Polydamas (18. 249 ff.). After the Trojan rout on the following day, he alone refuses to enter Troy, but stands his ground and waits for Achilles despite the entreaties of his parents (22. 35 ff.). At Achilles' approach he flees, but after a long chase halts, deceived by Athena into thinking that Deiphobus has come to his aid. In the subsequent fight he is killed, and with his dying words begs Achilles to return his body to Priam, then predicts Achilles' own death (22. 337 ff.). But Achilles, still overcome with rage and hatred, drags Hector's body behind his chariot, though the gods keep it safe from harm. Finally, when Priam comes by night to the Greek camp to beg for the return of his son (24. 189 ff.), Achilles' anger is eased and replaced by pity. The body is ransomed, an eleven-day truce is agreed, and the *Iliad* ends with Hector's funeral. Later poets add nothing of importance to Homer's account.

Hector is depicted in art from the 7th cent. on, setting out for battle, fighting Aias or some other hero, meeting his death at Achilles' hands, and his body being dragged and ransomed: see O. Touchefeu, *LIMC* 4. 1 (1988), 482–98.

H. J. R.; J. R. M.

Helios, the sun. In early Greece Helios was always treated with reverence but received little actual cult. Anaxagoras' announcement that the 'sun was a red-hot mass' caused outrage (DL 2. 12, etc.) and it was not uncommon to salute and even pray to the sun at its rising and setting (Pl. *Symp.* 220d, *Leg.* 887e, cf. Hes. *Op.* 339, and for respect Pl. *Ap.* 26c), but *Aristophanes can treat the practice of sacrificing to sun and moon as one that distinguishes *barbarians from Greeks (*Pax* 406). Hence evidence for actual cults is scarce and usually cannot be shown to be ancient (Farnell, *Cults* 5. 419 f.; but for Athens in the 3rd cent. BC see now *SEG* 33. 115. 12). The exception was *Rhodes, where Helios—subject in fact of the original 'colossus of Rhodes'—was the leading god and had an important festival, the Halieia (Nilsson, *Feste*, 427); the myth explaining this prominence is told in Pindar, *Ol.* 7. 54 ff. In Homer he is invoked and receives an offering as witness to an oath (*Il.* 3. 277), and his all-seeing, all-nurturing power is often stressed in poetry (see Aesch. *Cho.* 984–6 with A. F. Garvie's note).

His most important myth concerned his son Phaethon (too weak to manage the immortal horses, and likely to ignite the world as a result, Phaethon was struck down by Zeus). He is regularly conceived as a charioteer, who drives daily from east to west across the sky (a conception with both Indo-European and near-eastern parallels). His journey back each night in a cup is already attested in Mimnermus fr. 12 West (for many further early poetic references see Ath. 469c ff.).

The identification of the Sun with *Apollo was familiar in the 5th cent. BC but did not become canonical until much later (doubts still in Callim. *Hecale* fr. 103 Hollis): *Aeschylus in *Bassarides* probably associated it with *Orpheus, the religious innovator (M. L. West, *Studies in Aeschylus*, (1990), 38–42), and a passage in *Euripides (*Phaethon* 225 Diggle) where it appears unambiguously for the first time also mentions (whether for this reason or another is unclear) 'those who know the secret names of the gods'. (The identification is also attested for the scientists Parmenides and Empedocles: DK 28 A 20, 31 A 23). The 'visible gods' of heaven acquired new prominence in the astral religion of *Plato, and Cleanthes the Stoic named the sun the 'leading principle' (*hēgemonikon*) of the world (*SVF* 1. 499). Through indirect influence from philosophy, worship of Helios probably became more common in the late Hellenistic period and after. But it was not until the later Roman empire that Helios Sol grew into a figure of central importance in actual cult.

R. C. T. P.

Hellenism, Hellenization, Greek culture and the diffusion of that culture, a process usually seen as active. The relation between the two modern words is controversial: should the longer word be avoided (see ORIENTALISM) because of its suggestion of cultural imperialism? (Cf. G. W. Bowersock, *Hellenism in Late Antiquity* (1990) xi): 'Hellenization is … a modern idea, reflecting modern forms of cultural domination.')

The ancient terminology is interesting but treacherous. The earliest use of the verb 'Hellenize' is in a linguistic context: Thucydides 2. 68 says the Amphilochian Argives were 'Hellenized as to their present language' by the Ambraciots. But the extra words 'as to … language' perhaps (though see *CR* 1984, 246) indicate that the word normally had a wider, cultural sense. Nevertheless, 'Hellenism' in the Classical period is not quite on all fours with 'Medism' (i.e. Persian sympathies), a word which has a political tinge. The asymmetry is interesting because it underlines the absence, in the evidence which has come down to us, of a non-Greek point of view from which political sympathy with Greece could be expressed.

But the most famous use of 'Hellenism' is at 2 Maccabees 4: 13, cf. Acts of the Apostles 6: 1; 9: 29 for 'Hellenists'. Here too it seems that more is meant than just speaking Greek. *How* much more, is disputed.

In modern times the 19th-cent. historian J. G. Droysen, taking his cue above all from the Maccabees and Acts passages, gave 'Hellenismus' (the German is best not translated) a powerful and extended sense, not just 'correct Greek' but 'fusion of Greek and non-Greek'. Droysen associated the word with a particular period, that between *Alexander the Great and the victory of Octavian (later *Augustus) at *Actium. It was in this period, the 'Hellenistic Age', that Greek culture was most intensely diffused; this diffusion was seen as a success story, not least because it made possible the eventual rise and spread of *Christianity.

The post-colonial, late 20th cent. has reacted against such a simple picture. In the Droysenian and post-Droysen view of the ancient world there was arguably (cf. M. Bernal, *Black Athena* (1987-)) some neglect of the non-Greek, especially the Semitic, contribution to Greek achievements. Even in the study of the religion and art of the Archaic period (see GREECE (HISTORY)) the near-eastern element has recently (W. Burkert, *The Orientalizing Revolution* (1992)) been stressed, though this too is a controversial topic (see R. Osborne, *Journal of Mediterranean Archaeology* 1993, 231 ff.).

'Hellenization or Hellenism?' is a question best approached by considering the main alleged agents of the process of Hellenization (alternatively phrased, 'the main vehicles of Hellenism').

Conventionally, Hellenization has in modern times been associated with the post-Alexander period, so that as we have seen the word 'Hellenistic' was (and is) regularly confined to the centuries 336–31 BC. But inscriptional evidence, above all that collected and edited by the great French epigraphist Louis Robert, has shown that in the Persian empire of the Achaemenids (5th and 4th cents. BC), Greek

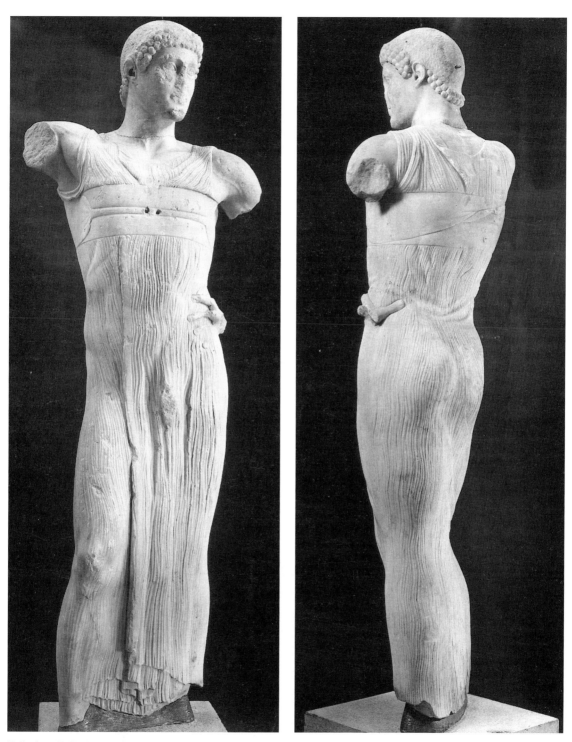

Hellenism, Hellenization This life-size marble statue of a charioteer, carved c.460 BC, was found in 1979 at Motya, one of the great military and commercial strongholds of *Carthage in *Sicily. Undoubtedly carved by a Greek hand, it exemplifies the Hellenic cultural influence to which this Carthaginian enclave was open.

language and even constitutional forms were adopted by dynasts in Lycia like Pericles of Limyra and by Mausolus and his family. Such adoption was perfectly compatible with anti-Greek political behaviour, as the career of Mausolus himself demonstrates. (There is a parallel here with the ambiguities of *philhellenism in the Roman period.) And rulers like Mausolus did strange things with the Greek governmental apparatus they copied: Greek eyebrows would lift at the sight of a decree like that (*ILabraunda* no. 40) by which Mausolus and his sister/wife Artemisia conferred block proxeny (essentially an individual honour, see GREECE (HISTORY)) on the citizens of Cnossus on *Crete, in a decree which opens 'it seemed good to Mausolus and Artemisia', just like a two-person *polis. And Mausolus avoided the great Panhellenic sanctuaries, preferring the local Carian shrines like Sinuri and Labraunda: this is a sort of 'Carianization' alongside the more obvious, *and surely real*, Hellenization. See ASIA MINOR.

Such patriotic retention or reinvention of local culture goes right through the history of post-Classical Asia Minor. It is true that places like Aspendus or Side 'discovered' their Greek origins in the early Hellenistic period when it was convenient to do so (see e.g. *SEG* 34. 282, Argos /Aspendus link); Greeks expressed this sort of thing in terms of '*kinship', *syngeneia*; that is, the relation between *mētropolis* (mother-city) and daughter-city. (The idea is not just Hellenistic, note already Thuc. I. 95. I, the justification for the *Delian League in terms of kinship between Ionians.) Fictitious descents and *genealogies were popular, especially Argive (*Philip II and Alexander the Great themselves claimed Argive descent, cf. Hdt. 5. 22 and Thuc. 5. 80;). But against such assertions of Greekness, real, exaggerated, or imagined, must be set the survival (or artificial resurrection?) of Iranian and other indigenous proper names into the Roman imperial period, and ambiguous cultural behaviour like that of Mausolus, already considered.

Alexander's own aims in this department have not escaped the re-examination to which the rest of his behaviour and career have been exposed in the years since the Second World War. *Plutarch's enthusiastic view of Alexander the Hellenizer was always suspect, and the opposite, modern, view—Hellenization as an instrument of oppression—was never wholly convincing. P. Briant (see his entry COLONIZATION, HELLENISTIC in this book) now offers a subtler conception: the indigenous populations were neither marginalized on the one hand, nor subjected to enforced Hellenization on the other. Whatever Alexander's intentions, exciting new evidence like that from Kandahar in Afghanistan (perhaps Alexandria in Arachosia, see *SEG* 30. 1664) shows that the Greek culture introduced by him flourished thousands of miles from the old Greek centres (see too AI KHANOUM; and note *SEG* 20. 326, a bilingual (Greek and Aramaic) Buddhist text from 3rd-cent. BC Kandahar).

Similar, though worse, problems of understanding arise with the *Seleucids. Their foundation of enduring Greek *poleis* (see POLIS) has long been reckoned as an impressive Hellenizing achievement, and here too (see ICAROS, mod. Failaka) epigraphic evidence speaks eloquently about geographical areas on which the literary sources are silent. But recent work (A. Kuhrt and S. M. Sherwin-White, *Hellenism in the East* (1987) and Sherwin-White and Kuhrt, *From Samarkhand to Sardis* (1993)) has tended to emphasize the continuity between Achaemenid *Persian and Babylonian structures (see SELEUCIDS in this book). Traditionalists will however still wish (see esp. F. Walbank, *LCM* 13 (1988), 108 ff.) to protest that the Seleucids never forgot that they were a Graeco-Macedonian dynasty; and we still await a full re-examination of C. Habicht's striking statistics (*Vierteljahrschr. für Soziologie* 1958, 1 ff.) about the small number of indigenous personnel employed by the Seleucids. At present his case has not been overthrown.

In one troubled area of policy, Seleucid treatment of the *Jews, the modern debate has been specially lively (M. Hengel, *Judaism and Hellenism* (1974); Millar, *Journal of Jewish Studies* 1978, 1 ff.). How far are early 2nd-cent. developments (see *MACCABEES) to be attributed to a 'Hellenizing party' in Judaea itself and how much to Seleucid insistence?

At Rome too, the acceptance or rejection of cultural Hellenism remained an issue (see PHILHELLENISM; CATO THE ELDER) even after the possibility of Greek or Macedonian military or political victories over Rome had evaporated.

The Greek *polis* and its culture not only survived into the Roman period; the introduction of the *polis* was the normal method by which Romans imposed their own authority in the Greek east (though '*polis*' by that time did not quite mean the same as in the days of the Delian League; see further ROMANIZATION (the east), and F. Millar in M. H. Hansen (ed.), *The Ancient Greek City State* (1993)). There is plenty of evidence, especially epigraphic, for élite acceptance of this long-lasting blend of Greek and Roman values. But inscriptions and literary texts are never the whole story; and in Asia Minor, in particular, the attachment to cultural systems other than those of Hellenism continues to be traceable until very late dates. Large allowance must, then, be made both for the tastes of groups other than the élites whom alone our evidence allows us to see, and for the assertive awareness, by the élites themselves, of the non-Greek dimension to their own past. This is particularly true of Asia Minor. Nevertheless it is remarkable that highly traditional Greek forms of discourse should have been used to negotiate a relationship with non-Greek culture in the Hellenistic period proper. It is also remarkable that these same traditional literary forms (including and especially *rhetoric and *epigram), and also that traditional pagan Greek *religion (including and especially *oracles (see R. Lane Fox, *Pagans and Christians* (1986)), should have propelled Hellenism as far into late antiquity as they did. Even in Byzantine antiquity, Christian epigrammatists catch perfectly the idioms of pagan Hellenism. See also GREEK LANGUAGE; JULIAN.

S. H.

Hephaestus, Greek god of fire, of blacksmiths, and of artisans. The name, of uncertain etymology, has no certain attestation in Linear B, though there is the possibility of reading a theophoric name in Minoan Cnossus.

In *Homer, Hephaestus is so closely connected with fire that earlier scholars felt tempted to derive the god from the element: he owns the fire (e.g. *Il.* 9. 468) and helps fight Scamandrus with it (*Il.* 21. 328–82); in a formula, his name is metonymically used for fire (*Il.* 2. 426 etc.). On the other hand, he is the divine master-artisan who fabricates *Achilles' shield and miraculous automata, self-moving tripods (*Il.* 18. 373–9), golden servant maidens (ibid. 417–21), or watchdogs for king Alcinous (*Od.* 7. 91–4, after oriental models). In the divine society of Homer, he is an outsider: he works, even sweats (*Il.* 18. 372); he is laughed at when he tries to replace Ganymedes (*Il.* 1. 571–600); he is married to *Aphrodite but cuckolded (*Od.* 8. 267–366); his feet are crippled (in Archaic iconography they are turned backwards): the outsider even lacks divine bodily perfection. His mother *Hera had conceived him without a male partner (Hes. *Theog.* 927; *Zeus as father *Il.* 1. 578, 14. 338; *Od.* 8. 312), as Gaia had done with some monsters; seeing the crippled offspring, she cast him out of Olympus, and he grew up with the sea goddesses Eurynome and Thetis (*Il.* 18. 395–405); or Zeus had thrown him out because he had sided with Hera, and he had landed on Lemnos where the indigenous Sinties tended him (*Il.* 1. 590–4). But he is not to be underestimated: his works evoke wonder; when serving the gods he intentionally provokes laughter; and he takes his cunning revenge on *Ares and Aphrodite and on Hera, and is brought back into Olympus (Alc. 349 LP). Thus, the Homeric picture preserves among an aristocratic society the physiognomy of a cunning blacksmith whose professional skills are highly admired and secretly feared, and whose social skills should not be underrated. It is very much the position blacksmiths have in Archaic societies. With the exception of Athens (see below), later mythology continues without fundamentally new concepts. His workshop was located beneath active volcanoes, especially Etna, and the Cyclopes were assigned to him as his workmen; he was also connected with natural fires, like the one on Lycian Olympus (Sen. *Ep.* 79. 3). That he had created mankind (Lucian, *Hermot.* 20) is but a witty extrapolation from his role in the creation of Pandora (Hes. *Op.* 70 f.).

Foremost among his cult places is the island of Lemnos where he landed when thrown out from Olympus. One of its two towns is called Hephaestia, with a sanctuary whose priest was eponymous. He is connected with the mysteries of the Cabiri whose father he was (Hdt. 3. 37; Samothracian mythology according to Strabo 10. 3. 20 f., 472 C) and whose ritual structure may derive from secret societies of blacksmiths. The Homeric Sinties were regarded as pre-Greek Thracians (Stephanus of Byzantium entry under *Lēmnos*) or *Etruscans (*Tyrsēnoi,* schol. Ap. Rhod. 1. 608), and the cult in the Lemnian sanctuary of the Cabiri begins before the Greek settlement; thus, non-Greek elements play a role in this cult, reinforcing the marginality of Hephaestus.

Better known is the Athenian cult where he is connected with Athena, the goddess of cunning intelligence. In his sanctuary above the Agora ('Theseion'), which was built after 450 BC, there stood a group of Hephaestus and Athena Hephaestia, set up in 421/0 by Alcamenes (Cic. *Nat. D.* 1. 83). At the same time, the festival Hephaestia in honour of Hephaestus and Athena was reorganized as a *pentetēris* (festival celebrated every fifth year) with a splendid torch-race and lavish sacrifices (*LSCG* 13): the splendour of the festival reflects the position of artisans in the Athenian state. The same holds true for the Chalkeia on the last day of Pyanopsion, a festival dedicated to Athena and Hephaestus when the artisans went in procession through the town (Soph. fr. 844 Radt). The god was also important in the Apaturia when the participants in their best robes and with torch in hand offered a hymn and a sacrifice to the god (Harp. entry under *lampas*). Here and in the Hephaestia, the torch alludes to the theme of new fire (which is also present in the Lemnian cult). Athenian mythology tells of Hephaestus' abortive attempt to rape *Athena; from his spilled semen grew Erichthonius, the ancestor of the autochthonous Athenians—the myth explains Hephaestus' role in the Apaturia and the theme of (new) beginnings.

He was very early identified with Roman Volcanus (F. Coarelli, *Il foro romano: periodo arcaico* (1983), 177) and with Etruscan Sethlans.

In Archaic iconography, Hephaestus appears especially in the scene of his return to Olympus under the guidance of *Dionysus. He is also shown helping Zeus to give birth to Athena (east pediment of the Parthenon) and in the assembly of the gods. The statue of a standing Hephaestus by Alcamenes with a discreet indication of his limp was famous (Cic. *Nat. D.* 1. 83).   F. G.

Hera This major figure in the pantheon, daughter of Cronus and wife of *Zeus, is already attested by name on two Mycenaean tablets, one from Thebes (TH Of 28), the other from Pylos (PY Tn 316), where she appears together with Zeus. Boeotia and especially the *Peloponnese are precisely the two regions of Greece where the cult of Hera is most prevalent. According to Homer (*Il.* 4. 51–2), Hera's favourite cities were Argos, *Sparta, and Mycenae; several cults are actually attested at Sparta, and her most famous sanctuary was on the hill dominating the Argive plain, where there was a temple perhaps from the 8th cent. BC. Sanctuaries with buildings at least as ancient are known at Perachora, Tiryns (on the site of the megaron of the Mycenaean palace), and *Olympia. Of island sites, the best known is the sanctuary on *Samos, where the main building, rebuilt in the 6th cent. BC, was mentioned by Herodotus, who comments on its magnificence (3. 60). Thus, as Burkert observes (*GR* 131), the most ancient and important temples were those of Hera. Her cults also spread at an early date to the colonies of the west, where later she became identified with the Roman *Juno. Her sanctuaries on the Lacinian promontory (near Croton) and at the mouth of the Sele (near Paestum) were much frequented.

In the Classical period, Hera's distinguishing feature compared with other goddesses is her double connection with royalty and marriage. In this way she is closely associated with Zeus, who made her 'last of all, his flourishing wife' (Hes. *Theog.* 921). Her queenliness and noble beauty are abundantly stressed in her epithets and in artistic representations. The ancient formula *potnia Herē* is succeeded by that of *basileia*, 'queen'. She is described as 'golden-throned', and is often thus represented, sometimes seeming to surpass her husband in importance: at Olympia, an Archaic statue showed Zeus standing beside Hera enthroned, while in the Argive Heraion the famous chryselephantine statue by Polyclitus represented the god in the form of a cuckoo perched on the sceptre held by the goddess—in her other hand she held a pomegranate; and on her head-dress were figures of the Charites and the Horae (Paus. 2. 17. 3–4). One of Plato's myths (*Phdr.* 253b) clearly underlines her royal qualities: according to this the followers of Hera are those who seek in love a 'kingly nature'.

Marriage is stressed constantly in Hera's myths and cults. It is attested by epithets such as Gamelia, Gamostolos, Syzygia, Zeuxidia, and especially Teleia, sometimes in connection with Zeus Teleios. Rituals in her honour connected with a sacred marriage are recorded in various places, notably in Athens, where this marriage served as a social and institutional paradigm: at the festival of Theogamia, celebrated in Gamelion, the divine couple were given the title of *prytaneis tōn gamōn* 'magistrates of marriages' (schol. on Ar. *Thesm.* 973–6). In Crete, the marriage was re-enacted annually by the river Theren 'in imitation of weddings' (Diod. Sic. 5. 72. 4). But Hera was not only the patron of marriages; she was often given the title of *Parthenos*, 'girl', and associated with prenuptial rites, including sometimes the lying together of the two sexes (Callim. fr. 75 Pf.; cf. Homer, *Il.* 14. 295 with scholia). Marital separation, suggested by Hera's mythology, is also evoked in cult, particularly at Plataea (Paus. 9. 3. 3; Euseb. *Praep. evang.* 3. 1. 6) and at Stymphalus, where Hera was called simultaneously *Pais* 'child', *Teleia* 'wife', and *Chēra* 'widow' or 'separated', thus covering the whole life of women, with its turning-points. An Argive ritual, whereby every year the statue of Hera was bathed in a spring at Nauplia to restore the goddess's virginity (Paus. 2. 38. 2) indicates the recurrent nature of these separations.

Motherhood, though part of Hera's personality, is little stressed, particularly in cult. Her children are *Ares, Hebe, and Eileithyia, goddess of childbirth, whose name she bears at Argos; in her sanctuary at Paestum, she is sometimes shown as a *kourotrophos* ('child-nurturer'). She suckled *Heracles, a scene often shown on Etruscan mirrors, but her relationship with the hero, whose name could be taken to mean 'glory of Hera', is ambivalent. She acted as nurse to monsters born to Earth, the Lernaean Hydra and the Nemean lion; in addition she was the sole parent of the monster Typhon and also, according to

Hesiod (*Theog.* 927–8), Hephaestus, whom she produced in anger, to defy her husband. But these episodes by their exceptional nature in fact illustrate Hera's close links with the marriage bond, which she herself protects and guarantees.

The marriage of Zeus and Hera is part of a complex symbolism including the natural world of plants and animals. This is shown by Hera's oldest sanctuaries, which are often situated in fertile plains away from urban settlements. The statue of Polyclitus mentioned above is relevant here. The sacred marriage described by Homer (*Il.* 14. 346–51), despite the alterations due to epic, still bears traces of this natural symbolism, and we also find mentioned the flourishing garden at the edge of the Ocean, which served as marriage-bed for the two deities (e.g. Eur. *Hipp.* 748–51). We can see a relationship between the goddess called Boōpis ('ox-eyed') and herds of cows, and also with horses, especially in connection with a sacred marriage. Io, changed into a heifer by Zeus in bull form, was the priestess of Hera at Argos, where Hera's rule extended over the animal herds of the plain. At *Olympia, where Hera Hippia ('of horses') was worshipped alongside *Poseidon Hippios, contests among girls had been established in honour of the goddess by Hippodamia in thanks for her marriage to Pelops. These facts may be linked with two other chthonian features, isolated as they are: the oracles of Hera, at Perachora and Cumae, and the funerary cult given to *Medea's children in one of Hera's sanctuaries at Corinth.

Hera was also worshipped as protector of cities and other social groups, especially at Argos and on Samos; Alcaeus calls her *pantōn genethla*, 'mother of all' (fr. 129 LP), in a hymn of invocation where she appears between Zeus and Dionysus. It is in this context that she is sometimes shown armed. At Argos the prize at the games held during the Heraia festival was a shield. Despite this protecting function, it is noteworthy that literary presentations, from the *Iliad* onwards, tend to stress the destructive and capricious side of Hera's nature.

As with most of the Greek pantheon, Hera's origins are unclear. There is no certain etymology for her name; if the modern consensus sees Linear B *Era* as the feminine of *hērōs*, this itself has given rise to differing interpretations. The supporters of an Indo-European origin from the root †*yer* explain the name variously as meaning 'heifer', 'the goddess of the year', or 'a girl of marriageable age'. Others incline towards a pre-Greek origin for both Mycenaean words. But a solution to the problem of the name would not explain the whole issue of Hera's origin. Associated as she is with Zeus from the Mycenaean period onwards, it is clear that Hera preserves certain characteristics of an Indo-European divine couple; but in her sovereign power, tending towards the universal, it is difficult not to see traces of an Aegean great goddess.   A. Mot., V. P.-D.

Heracles, the greatest of Greek heroes. His name is that of a mortal (compare Diocles), and has been interpreted as 'Glorious through *Hera'. In this case, the bearer is taken

Heracles An Athenian vase (c.490 BC) shows the conventional image of Heracles in Greek art as a bearded, athletic male in his prime, carrying his club and lion-skin cape. Here he defends his seizure of the Delphic tripod.

as being—or so his parents would hope—within the protection of the goddess. This is at odds with the predominant tradition (see below), wherein Heracles was harassed rather than protected by the goddess: perhaps the hostility was against worshippers of Heracles who rejected allegiance to the worshippers of Hera on whom the hero depended. This could have happened when Argos had established control over the Heraion (a temple to Hera, some distance from Argos itself) and Tiryns (possibly reflected in an apparent falling-off of settlement at Tiryns late in the 9th cent. BC: A. Foley, *The Argolid 800–600 BC* (1988), 40–2). Some of the inhabitants of Tiryns might have emigrated to Thebes, taking their hero with them. Traditionally Heracles' mother and her husband (Alcmene and Amphitryon) were obliged to move from Tiryns to Thebes, where Heracles was conceived and born (*LIMC* 1/1. 735). However, there is no agreement over the etymology of the name, an alternative version deriving its first element from 'Hero'.

Heracles shared the characteristics of, on the one hand, a hero (both cultic and epic), on the other, a god. As a hero, he was mortal, and like many other heroes, born to a human mother and a god (Alcmene and *Zeus; Amphitryon was father of Iphicles, Heracles' twin: the bare bones of the story already in Homer, *Il.* 14. 323–4). Legends arose early of his epic feats, and they were added to constantly throughout antiquity. These stories may have played a part in the transformation of Heracles from hero (i.e. a deity of mortal origin, who, after death, exercised power over a limited geographical area, his influence residing in his mortal remains) to god (a deity, immortal, whose power is not limited geographically).

Outside the cycle of the Labours (see below), the chief events of Heracles' life were as follows: Hera pursued him with implacable enmity from before his birth, which she managed to delay until after that of Eurystheus. She then sent serpents to Thebes to attack Heracles in his cradle, but the infant strangled them. Later, she drove him mad and caused him to murder his Theban wife, Megara, and their children (there are different versions). In his youth, Heracles led the Thebans in their successful revolt against Minyan Orchomenus. He also took part in an expedition against Troy and sacked Oechalia (*LIMC* 5/1. 111–13), accompanied the Argonauts (113–14), founded the *games at *Olympia, and ultimately died by burning on Mt. Oeta (128–9: death came as a relief against the poison given him inadvertently by his wife Deianira, who had hoped to regain his love thereby: the dying *Centaur Nessus, from whom Heracles rescued his wife, had given her the poison as a love potion. She used it when Heracles took up with Iole).

The Labours themselves (twelve is the canonical number, but there is little agreement on the full complement) support, by their geographical distribution, the contention that, however popular Heracles became in other parts of the ancient world, his origins were in the *Peloponnese, and more specifically in the Argolid. He was sent to perform them by Eurystheus of Argos, to whom he was bound in vassalage. Six belong to the northern part of the Peloponnese, and might be taken to represent either a gradual spread of Argive ambitions in that region, or, with equal likelihood, the growing popularity of Heracles over a steadily widening area. These tasks were to deal with (1) the Nemean lion (northern border of the Argolid); (2) the Lernaean Hydra (SW Argolid); (3) the Erymanthian boar (NW Arcadia); (4) the hind of Ceryneia (Achaea); (5) the Stymphalian birds (NE Arcadia); (6) the stables of Augeas (Elis). The other Labours are situated at the ends of the habitable world or beyond: the Cretan bull to the south, the horses of the Thracian Diomedes to the north, the quest for the belt of the *Amazon queen to the east, the search for the cattle of Geryon to the west, the apples of the Hesperides at the edge of the world, and Cerberus in the world of the dead. Many but not all of the Labours are already depicted in Greek art of the geometric and early Archaic periods (*LIMC* 5/1. 5–111 and 187). Also early to appear are two feats outside the canon, a fight against Centaurs (187), and a struggle with *Apollo for the Delphic tripod (133–43 and 187). The encounters with Centaurs take place in Arcadia and Thessaly; the fight with Apollo might reflect a struggle for political control over *Delphi between its inhabitants and those of Malis (Trachis and Mt. Oeta). A good survey of Heracles' Labours (*Praxeis*) and *Parerga* (incidental labours) in art is given by T. H. Carpenter, *Art and Myth in Classical Greece* (1991), 117–34.

The iconography of Heracles was firmly established by the Archaic period, but even before then it is possible to identify him from the subject-matter. The major identifying symbols were the lion-skin cape and hood (flayed from the Nemean lion), his club, and his bow and arrows (*LIMC* 5/1. 183–6).

Throughout his life and many adventures, Heracles was guided closely by *Athena (*LIMC* 5/1. 143–54), by whom he was introduced to Olympus after his death (122–8). The apotheosis of Heracles was represented in literature and art by giving him—after his death—a wife in the person of Hebe, i.e. 'youth', or rather the embodiment of the prime of life, for it is the permanent possession of this boon which most distinguishes gods from men. The story is attested definitely by the 6th cent. BC (121–2 and 160–5). In popular cult, Heracles was recognized and invoked as a god from at least late in the 6th cent. (for example, the inscription *CEG* 1. 309 = *IG* 1². 825 from Phaleron). *Herodotus (2. 44. 5) writes approvingly of those Hellenes who worshipped Heracles both as an immortal Olympian and as a hero. The practice must have been common, if not widespread (cf. Pind. *Nem.* 3. 22: Heracles a 'hero god').

As in the case of Apollo, his divine rival for the Delphic tripod, the cult of Heracles spread at least partly through the absorption of local cult figures—in Heracles' case, mostly heroic—of similar nature. Individuals adopted Heracles as a more or less personal patron; at the communal level, he presided over ephebes (young men in military training) as their ideal in warfare and their patron in military training, whence his patronage of the *gymnasium (a role often shared with *Hermes), and over the young in general. He was primarily associated with the activities of men rather than women, which may explain the regulations barring women from his rites or even his sanctuaries, e.g. *LSS* 63 (Thasos), *LSAM* 42 (Miletus). Occasionally, however, the character of the local hero whom Heracles had deposed might override the general practice, as in the case of the western Boeotian Charops Heracles, who was served by a priestess.

The geographical distribution of his cults is, as one might expect, as wide as that of his legends. Interestingly, evidence from Tiryns and Argos, although early in the former, is sparse (Tiryns: *SEG* 30. 380. 15a, first half of the 6th cent.; Argos: his name scratched on two fragments of an Attic crater of the fourth quarter of the 5th cent., *BCH* 1989, 721). That he was established at Thebes by the Homeric period cannot be doubted, although the earliest contemporary evidence for cult occurs in the 5th cent. He was worshipped fairly widely throughout Boeotia, and neighbouring Attica.

One of the earliest places to produce archaeological evidence for a cult of Heracles is the sanctuary on Mt. Oeta, site of his immolation. Another important early site is at Thasos, where evidence extends from soon after the foundation of the colony. The Thasian cult exemplifies several features of the worship of Heracles: first, his treatment as a god; second, his function as *promachos*, champion or protector, of the community (particularly its urban centre); third, the tendency to syncretize Heracles with other deities, local or otherwise, in the case of Thasos, the other being Melqart of Tyre.

The sanctuary at Thasos, which may be typical, included not only a sacrificial area, but also a temple and extensive dining-facilities (the last often illustrated in vase-painting and so probably typical); descriptions of other Herakleia (e.g. at Thebes: Paus. 9. 11. 4–7) would lead us to expect the existence of extensive athletic facilities as part of the complex. All of this public devotion to bodily well-being would have helped to produce the impression of Heracles as a boisterous glutton.

As noted above, Heracles was adopted by individuals or states as a symbol or protecting deity, to which numerous towns named after him bear eloquent testimony. Boeotian Thebes used Heracles as its symbol from at least the second half of the 5th cent. BC, if not earlier. In the preceding century *Pisistratus of Athens made Heracles his personal divine protector and legitimator of his actions (but see IMAGERY; PROPAGANDA). The Macedonian royal family ('Argeads') claimed lineal descent from Heracles for similar motives (see HELLENISM; KINSHIP). Most notoriously, however, the Dorian rulers of the *Peloponnese sought to legitimate their claims to sovereignty by tracing their descent to Heracles through his sons, the Heraclidae, who, as the tale was told, 'returned' to the Peloponnese from the north to claim their inheritance.   A. Sch.

Herculaneum (see ◀Map 3, Bc▶) Roman *municipium* (municipality) on a spur of Vesuvius commanding the coast-road, 8 km. (5 mi.) south-east of Naples (Strabo 5. 4. 8). An independent member of the Samnite league centred on Nuceria in the 4th cent. BC and subsequently allied to Rome, it joined the allied cause in the Social War of 91–89 BC (see ROME (HISTORY), §1.5): Oscan civic institutions were replaced by Roman ones in 89 BC. Its origins are still obscure, though the regular street-plan and the name suggest that it may have been a dependency of the Greek *apoikia* (colonial settlement) at Naples (perhaps of the 6th or 5th cent.).

Recent discoveries have made its municipal life seem comparably vigorous with its neighbours', but restricted hinterland, limited communications, and a small harbour denied it much economic opportunity. On present evidence, the streets (whose plan is more regular than that of *Pompeii) show little sign of heavy traffic (nor are there stepping-stones for pedestrians); shops and workshops are unobtrusive. As the centre of a resort-coast, however, renowned for its beauty and salubrious climate, and close enough to Naples to be a kind of luxury suburb, the town benefited from the wealth of local proprietors (including Roman senators). The grandest property (known from its rifling in 1750–61), the Villa of the Papyri, north-west of the town, on terraces overlooking the sea, was embellished with gardens, waterworks, and statues and inspired the mod. Getty Museum, Malibu (USA). The name derives from the 1785 papyrus scrolls found there. Though carbonized, these can be painstakingly unrolled: Epicurean in taste (see EPICURUS), they include many of the works of Philodemus of Gadara. Many of the town houses were also expensively equipped. See HOUSES, ITALIAN.

The town was damaged by the *earthquake of AD 63 and obliterated by the eruption of AD 79. Deeply buried by ash which solidified to form a tufaceous rock, the remains (especially organic material such as wood or papyrus) are better preserved, but much more difficult to excavate, than those of Pompeii. The first explorations, using tunnels, date from the early 18th cent.; some 5 ha. (12 acres) have since been completely uncovered (representing only about a quarter of the urban core and inner suburbs). The houses appear less atrium-centred and generally more varied in plan than those of Pompeii; they preserve considerable evidence of the upper storeys (e.g. the Casa a Graticcio, built of rubble in a timber frame). Public buildings, mostly dating from the Julio-Claudian period, are much less well attested (a theatre and basilica were recorded by the first excavators: a modest forum, essentially the widening of the Decumanus Maximus, and a large palaestra lie on the edge of the existing site). On the ancient coast are important baths (the 'Terme Suburbane'), and recent work has uncovered the skeletal remains of many dozens of the inhabitants killed at the harbour while attempting to escape the eruption.

N. P.

Hermes Already attested among the Mycenaean pantheon (tablets from Cnossus in *Crete, Pylos, and Thebes), the god has no original connection with the *herma* or cairn of stones, as was once thought. Myths about Hermes are mostly concerned with his childhood, told in the *Homeric Hymn to Hermes* (last third of the 6th cent. BC). He was the son of *Zeus and the nymph Maia, born on Mt. Cyllene in Arcadia. On the day of his birth, he left his cradle, found a tortoise which he made into a lyre, then went to Pieria where he stole 50 cows belonging to *Apollo, which he led backwards to a cave where he sacrificed two and hid the others, before returning to Cyllene; finally he made up the quarrel with Apollo. Later, he invented the syrinx (pipe) and was taught divination by Apollo. Apart from these stories of his childhood, Hermes plays only a secondary part in other myths. He has no recognized wife, but two sons, Eudorus and *Pan, are attributed to him. He is characterized by a great variety of functions. Above all, he is a messenger god, who carries out the orders of Zeus with due respect. In this capacity, he appears as a subordinate deity, giving the ultimatum of Zeus to Prometheus, for instance, or acting as his go-between when he is enamoured of Ganymedes. He is generally well-disposed, and negotiates the ransom of *Hector with pleasantness and good humour. His titles stress his speed and beneficence. He is also the god who guides: he shows transhumant shepherds the way and leads teams of animals; he guides people, especially travellers, for whom he marks out the route in the form of a pillar or herm (see below). He takes divine children to safety (thus he gives *Dionysus to the Nymphs of Nysa, as depicted in the famous statue by Praxiteles, and Arcas to Maia, and is generally a patron of children (*Heracles, *Achilles); he also helps heroes such as Perseus, for whom he obtains the bronze sickle used by the hero to decapitate Medusa, and Heracles. He leads *Hera, *Aphrodite, and *Athena to Paris, the judge in their beauty contest. As god of movement, he is leader of the Nymphs and the Charites. Finally as *psychopompos* (one who escorts *souls), he leads the dead to *Hades, summoning them to the journey beyond, taking them by the hand and accompanying them on to Charon's boat.

Another aspect of Hermes is that of a god of abundance, fertility, and prosperity (*Hymn. Hom. Merc.* 529). He is the patron of herdsmen and of the fruitfulness of herds and flocks; he is himself a cowherd and shepherd (ibid. 491–4). This form of Hermes is called Nomios, 'pastoral' and Epimelios, 'presiding over sheep', and is often shown in art as Hermes *kriophoros* ('ram-bearing'), especially in Arcadia and Boeotia. He is also sometimes a 'lord of animals', of horses in particular. More generally, he is the god of every kind of prosperity. The herm, a quadrangular pillar topped with a head, with tenons on its sides and a phallus on the front, was very popular from the end of the 6th cent. onwards, and not only recalls Hermes' powers of fertility but, as an apotropaic talisman, also guarantees the success of all sorts of undertakings. It is found in towns both at the threshold of houses and inside them, and

Hermes Four-cornered pillars called 'herms', featuring a bust of Hermes and an erect phallus (symbolizing masculine strength), were set up in public and at private doorways as protectors of houses and cities. This 6th-cent. BC example comes from the Aegean island of Siphnos.

became a sort of mascot bringing luck both to cities and to individuals (the mutilation of the herms at Athens was perceived as a bad omen on the eve of the Sicilian expedition: Thuc. 6. 27. 3). In the same context, Hermes is also the god of trade (on Delian seals of the Hellenistic age he appears holding a purse).

Hermes is an ingenious god, expert in both technology and magic. From his birth onwards, he was skilled in trickery and deception, and in the *Homeric Hymn* (292) he is 'prince of thieves'. Even in cult, he is attested as trickster and thief (Hermes Dolios at Pellene in Achaea and Hermes Kleptes in Chios). But most often he uses his power in mischief, illusion, and mystery. He creates a lyre out of the shell of a tortoise, he puts on his feet sandals which erase footprints. He is an expert in knots and chains. Like a magician he knows how to put the enemy camp to sleep (*Iliad* 24) and to call up the dead. As a corollary, this god of *mētis* (prudence, cunning) and of mediation (see L. Kahn, *Hermès passe ou les ambiguités de communication* (1978)), has no part in violence. He is the least warlike of the gods; he is dragged into the battle with the *Giants, and linked with murder only in the story of the monster Argos. He prefers persuasion to weapons, and appears frequently as patron of orators. He can also be a musician: he is the inventor of the syrinx, and accompanies the dances of the Nymphs and the Charites. Only in a late period, as Hermes Trismegistus ('thrice-greatest'), does he come to preside over mystical revelations, as the successor to the Egyptian god Thoth and god of the 'hermetic'. A final function of Hermes, attested above all from the 4th cent. BC, is that of god of athletes—one linked, no doubt, to the youthful appearance and charm which the god assumed for seduction (*Il.* 24. 376–7, 433). See ATHLETICS. In this role he is frequently associated, particularly in the *gymnasium, with *Heracles. He even became, at a late date, the god of the school and of *education.

Hermes' main aspects are shown in his physical appearance and iconography. His attributes are the caduceus (*kērukeion*), the herald's sign which he almost always carries, the traveller's hat (*petasos* or *pilos*), with or without wings, and the winged sandals which evoke his quality of speed. He is generally bearded in the earlier period, but an unbearded type develops from the 4th cent. onwards. He is clothed in a *chlamys* or a *chlaina*, with sometimes a furry leopard-skin. Side by side with this very frequent representation of the god of herds and flocks, the god of music, the messenger and guide, or the chthonian god (e.g. as subterranean guide), we find the herm (see above), whose identity as Hermes is sometimes stressed by a caduceus painted on the shaft. This form, attested in sculpture as well as on vases, was very popular and could symbolize most of the functions of the god. In some cases, especially to indicate Hermes as god of the gymnasium, the pillar wears a cloak.

The cult of Hermes is particularly widely diffused in the Peloponnese, where Pausanias mentions numerous myths, rituals, cults, and herms. Passing over the more ordinary examples (Pellene, Pheneos, and Mt. Cyllene, Megalopolis,

Tegea, Corinth, Argos), we may point out the oracular ritual in front of a pillar of Hermes at Pharae in Achaea (Paus. 7. 22. 2). In Athens, Hermes had a very ancient cult (cf. the *xoanon* or ancient statue dedicated on the Acropolis by Cecrops), and in the form of the herm he was present everywhere in the city. The Hermaia, a young boys' festival, were celebrated in his honour. His cult is also attested in Boeotia (Tanagra) and in the Cyclades: at *Delos he is the god of the gymnasium. At Cydonia in Crete, the Hermaia were a popular festival where slaves took the part of their masters. Hermes was not a major divinity, but because he was essentially kindly, he was one of the most familiar gods in the daily lives of the Greeks.   M. J.

Herodotus (*see following page*)

Hesiod, one of the oldest known Greek poets, often coupled or contrasted with *Homer as the other main representative of early epic. Which was the older of the two was much disputed from the 5th cent. BC on (Xenophanes in Gell. *NA* 3. 11. 2; Hdt. 2. 53; *Ephorus, *FGrH* 70 F 101, etc.): Homer's priority was carefully argued by Aristarchus, and generally accepted in later antiquity. Hesiod's absolute date is now agreed to fall not far before or after 700 BC. Of his life he tells us something himself: that his father had given up a life of unprofitable sea-trading and moved from Aeolian Cyme to Ascra in Boeotia (*Op.* 633–40); that he, as he tended sheep on Mt. Helicon, had heard the *Muses calling him to sing of the gods (*Theog.* 22–35, a celebrated passage); and that he once won a tripod for a song at a funeral contest at Chalcis (*Op.* 650–60). For his dispute with Perses see below (2). He is said to have died in Hesperian Locris (Thuc. 3. 96, etc.), but his tomb was shown at Orchomenus (Arist. fr. 565 Rose, *Certamen* 14, Paus. 9. 38. 3). For the story of his meeting and contest with Homer see *Certamen Homeri et Hesiodi* (A. Rzach, Teubner ed. *Hesiod*[3] (1913), 237 ff.). The poems anciently attributed to him are as follows (only the first three have survived complete, and only the first two have a good claim to be authentic):

1. The *Theogony*. The main part of the poem, which is prefaced by a hymn to the Muses (1–104; cf. the *Homeric Hymns*), deals with the origin and genealogies of the gods (including the divine world-masses Earth, Sea, Sky, etc.), and the events that led to the kingship of *Zeus: the castration of Uranus by Cronus, and the overthrow of Cronus and the Titans, the 'former gods' (424), by the Olympians. This 'Succession Myth' has striking parallels in Akkadian and Hittite texts, and seems originally to have come from the near east. Hesiod's version shows some stylistic awkwardness and inconcinnity, but is not without power. Interlaced with it are the genealogies, which run smoother. The first powers born are Chaos, Earth, and (significantly) *Eros (116–22). From Chaos and Earth, in two separate lines, some 300 gods descend; they include personified abstracts, whose family relationships are clearly meaningful. There is an interesting passage in praise of the un-Homeric goddess Hecate (411–52), further myths, notably

[*continued on p. 341*]

Herodotus

Herodotus of Halicarnassus (now Bodrum on the Aegean coast of Turkey), historian. 1. 'Herodotus of Halicarnassus' are (in Greek) the first two words of a long historical narrative, the earliest we possess. It looks back to the fall of the Lydian kingdom in western Turkey in 545 BC and forwards to events in the early 420s, during the great war between Athens and Sparta, but it has as its focus and *raison d'être* (1. 1) the 'war between Greeks and non-Greeks', which we call the Persian Wars. We do not know exactly when it was written but it was already familiar in Athens in 425 BC, when *Aristophanes parodied its opening chapters in one of his plays (*Ach.* 515 ff.). We know very little about the life of its author: he nowhere claims to have been an eyewitness or participant in any of the major events or battles that he describes (unlike *Aeschylus), but records conversations with those who were (8. 65, 9. 16) and with the grandsons of those involved in events of the late 6th cent. (3. 54; cf. 3. 160, 4. 43 where Herodotus' informant may well be the exiled grandson of the Persian Zopyrus, referred to in 3. 160). This fits with the dating of his birth traditional in antiquity ('a little before the Persian Wars', Dion. Hal. *Thuc.* 5; '484 BC', Gell. *NA* 15. 23). But the latter date is suspicious: it is 40 years before the foundation of the Athenian colony at Thurii in southern Italy in which Herodotus is said to have taken part and where he is said to have spent the rest of his life and died (Steph. Byz., entry under *Thourioi*: his grave was shown there; Aristotle, *Rh.* 3. 9, already refers to him as 'Herodotus of Thurii'); 40 years is an ancient biographer's formula for his subject's age at a turning-point in his life and the whole chronology may be imaginary. His birthplace, Halicarnassus in Caria, was a Greek city, founded some 500 years earlier, but by Herodotus' time it was subject to *Persian control; it lay on the extreme western edge of the great empire that had its administrative centre three months' journey (5. 50) to the east, in Iran. Intermarriage with the neighbouring non-Greek population, who were Carians, was widespread (ML 32) and Herodotus was a cousin of the Halicarnassian epic poet Panyassis, who had a Carian name. He seems to have taken part in political struggles against the Persian-nominated tyrant Lygdamis, grandson of the Artemisia who figures prominently in his narrative (7. 99; 8. 68–9, 87–8, 93, 101–3); these struggles ended in Panyassis' death and Herodotus' exile. Most of what Herodotus tells us about himself concerns his travels and enquiries (see (3) below). He is likely to have died where his allusions to later events themselves end, in the 420s; he may well have been less than 60 when he died.

2. Herodotus' narrative is built from smaller narratives and from summaries of events that are peripheral to his main concern. These smaller narratives, often told in rich detail and equipped with verbatim reports of many conversations, are sometimes told in Herodotus' own person; sometimes in the special syntax which ancient Greek reserves for things reported on another's authority. They are generally linked by chronological succession (particularly, at the beginning, the succession of eastern kings), and as cause and effect; but sometimes they go temporarily backwards (effect is followed by its explanatory cause in another story) or move sideways, to take in events elsewhere which throw light on something in the main line of the story. Their starting-point is in answer to the question with which Herodotus ends his first sentence: 'What caused Greeks and non-Greeks to go to war?'. After surveying traditions (Persian and Phoenician, according to Herodotus) which traced the origin of the conflict to the reciprocal abduction of legendary princesses (Io, Europa, *Medea, Helen: 1. 1–5), Herodotus declares his own view that the story cannot reliably be taken back beyond the reign of the Lydian king Croesus (1. 5), who began the process of absorbing the Greek communities of the Aegean coast into his kingdom and whose fall brought the power of Persia into contact with these communities, which were promptly forced into submission. The first book explains how these events occurred, deals with the Persian conquest of the Median kingdom which embroiled Lydia and led to its annexation by Persia, and continues the expansionist reign of the Persian king *Cyrus the Great to his death in battle in 530 BC. Book 2 takes the form of a massive excursus on the geography, customs, and history of

*Egypt, which was the next target of Persian expansionism, under Cyrus' son and successor, Cambyses. Book 3 continues the reign of Cambyses down to his death in 522 BC, after a failed attempt to invade Ethiopia; it goes on to describe the turmoil that followed and the eventual emergence of *Darius I as the new king of Persia, and deals with his administrative settlement of the empire (3. 88–97). Book 4 covers Darius' abortive attempt to subdue the nomadic Scythian tribes who lived to the north and east of the Danube and across southern Russia, and deals also with Persian expansion along the North African coast. Book 5 traces further Persian expansion, into northern Greece and the southern Balkans, and narrates the unsuccessful attempt of the Aegean Greek communities to free themselves from Persian control (the so-called Ionian Revolt: 5. 28–38, 98–6. 42): Herodotus signals, ominously, the fatal support that Athens gave to that revolt (5. 97). Book 6 begins the story that runs continuously to the end of Herodotus' narrative in book 9: the Persian determination to have revenge for Athenian interference in the affairs of its empire and the first seaborne attack on mainland Greece, an attack which was defeated at Marathon in 490 BC. Books 7–9 embrace the huge expedition mounted in 480–479 by Darius' son and successor, *Xerxes, and the Greek response to that threat; the opening engagements, at sea off Artemisium and on land at Thermopylae; the climactic battles of Salamis and Plataea, which forced the Persian army and navy to withdraw to the north; and the carrying of the war back across the Aegean, ending in the battle of Mycale, on the Turkish coast opposite *Samos. At various points, episodes in the history of Greek communities not at first directly in contact with Persian power, such as *Sparta, *Athens, Corinth, and Samos, are interleaved, often at length, with the main narrative of Persian expansion as they explain how these communities became involved or failed for a time to be involved, until all are seamlessly joined together in books 7–9.

3. The stories from which Herodotus' narrative is built derive sometimes (as we have seen) from distinguished individuals, sometimes from 'collective' informants ('the Corinthians say …'; 'we Spartans have a story …'; 'I heard the story in Proconessus and Cyzicus …'). Occasionally his source may have been a document (for example, his description of the satrapy system set up by Darius to administer the Persian empire). But the overwhelming mass of his material must derive from oral tradition and that tradition will always have been local, even familial. Thus the overall conception of a narrative that would draw on these local traditions but would connect them so as to span more than 70 years and take in much of the known world was Herodotus' own, and it is his most brilliant and original achievement. Herodotus did not speak any language other than Greek but he writes of interpreters in Egypt (2. 154) and at the Persian court (3. 38, 140), where also there were Greek officials in high places. He writes repeatedly of what was told to him in an astonishing range of places: where he could, he preferred to trust what he could see for himself (2. 99; cf. 2. 147, 4. 81, 5. 59) and could enquire into (Herodotus' word for 'enquiry' is historiē, which brought the word 'history' into the languages of Europe). Where he could not, he listened (see ORALITY). He writes of enquiries made in the northern Aegean, in southern Italy, round the shores of the Black Sea (Euxine), in Egypt (where he travelled as far up the Nile as Elephantine: 2. 29), at Dodona in NW Greece, and at *Cyrene in Libya; of things seen on the Dnieper in southern Russia; in *Babylon on the Euphrates; at Tyre in Lebanon; of talking to Carthaginians (see CARTHAGE) and to the inhabitants of *Delphi. He is familiar with the geography of Samos, of Attica, and of the Nile delta, which he compares to the mouth of the Acheloüs river in NW Greece, as well as to the coast of Turkey from Troy south to the Maeander. He takes for granted a detailed knowledge of the topography of *Delos, of the Athenian Acropolis, and of Delphi. Everywhere he writes of what was said to him by 'the locals'. It is of the essence of Herodotus' method of historiē that he builds the process of enquiry into his narrative: he writes not only of his sources, their agreements and disagreements, but also of his own belief and disbelief at what he is told (he is, he writes, under an obligation to report what was said to him, but under no obligation to believe it: 7. 152. 3); sometimes too he records his inability to decide, or the impossibility of arriving at an answer to some question he is enquiring into (sometimes because it is beyond the reach of human memory; sometimes because it lies too far away, too far beyond the limits of his travels). Unlike *Thucydides, he

does not present his account of the past as smoothly authoritative, the result of work not to be done again (Thuc. 1. 23) but as one man's struggle, not always successful, to discover and record what heroic men, non-Greek as well as Greek, have achieved, before those achievements are obliterated by time (1. 1).

4. It is not merely Herodotus' travels that cover an astonishing range but also his understanding of the variety of human experience. He does not disguise the fact that the Greek-speaking world was the cultural as well as the geographical centre of his perceptions. But he writes, almost always open-mindedly, of the differences that distinguish Persians from Scythians, Babylonians, Indians, and Egyptians, as well as from Greeks. For Egypt, he has a model to help him understand the way their world works: it is simply the world of other men upside down; the Egyptians do the opposite of what is universal elsewhere, just as the Nile behaves in a way that inverts the behaviour of all other rivers by flooding in high summer (2. 35). He is less sure of what makes Persian culture cohere but describes what seem to him its distinctive features (the features, that is, that make the Persians un-Greek: 1. 131–40). He is relatively unsuccessful too in grasping the 'ideologies' that made one religion different from another. That is hardly surprising: he records religious practice everywhere with precision, but he has nothing to teach him the 'meaning' of *ritual, as he has for Greek religion in the epic poems of *Homer and *Hesiod (2. 53). He is sure that for all men, however much they know of other cultures, their own culture is superior (3. 38). But when he is faced with something totally alien to his experience and to Greek experience generally, such as the culture of the Scythian nomads, who have no aspect of permanence to their lives (no statues, altars, or temples, except to *Ares, the god of war; no agriculture, no buildings, no walls or settlements even), though he can admire their ability to escape Persian domination by never staying to confront the enemy ('for the rest', he writes, 'I do not like them': 4. 46). They offer him no point of resemblance and they do not fit. None the less, he describes their culture also dispassionately. For Herodotus it is important that things should fit: he is at home with symmetries. He is persuaded of the truth of a story of young Nasamonian tribesmen wandering across the Sahara and finding a great river flowing west–east, because the river they found must have been the Nile. Its identity is guaranteed by the symmetry of its course with that of the Danube, which flows west–east from the Pyrenees and then turns south, as the Nile turns north, to flow out 'opposite the Nile' (2. 32–3)! But such a priori geography exists alongside acute empirical observation of the world around him, as in his defence of the proposition that the land of Lower Egypt is the product of the Nile's silting over ten or twenty thousand years (2. 11–12).

5. Herodotus' vast narrative coheres because it is strung on two lines of connection which pass through time. The first is kinship; the second *reciprocity. Reciprocity is the demand that all men respond to what is done to them with like for like ('equals for equals', in Herodotus' own phrase: 1. 2): with good for good and with hurt for hurt. The demands of reciprocity are absolute, admit of no exceptions and, Herodotus believes, are common to all men. They also outlive time, since they are inherited. The principle of reciprocity is essential to Herodotus' writing: to answer the question 'why did this happen?' it is necessary to ask the further question: 'to what previous act was this act a response?' The chain of reciprocity may reach far back and encompass many people. Thus the search for a 'beginning' is common to all narrative and it is no surprise that, faced with the question 'why did non-Greeks and Greeks go to war [in the 5th cent. BC]?', Herodotus finds an answer in events far distant in space and more than three generations in the past, with Croesus of Lydia and his 'beginning of wrongful acts against Greeks' (1. 5). It is the logic of reciprocity that explains not only the two Persian invasions of Greece but also, for example, the bitter hostility between Athens and Aegina, which lasted from the mid-6th cent. until the Athenians expelled the Aeginetans from their island in 431 BC (5. 82–7: Herodotus describes it as 'owed from before') and the complex of obligations which tied Persia, Sparta, Corinth, and Corcyra together in their several relationships with Samos over more than a generation (3. 44–53, 139–40). For the most part, the question 'why?' is not a problem for Herodotus. Events that are too uncanny, shocking, or momentous for merely human explanation call into play the actions of

divinity which are assumed also to be determined by the logic of reciprocity (1. 90–1, 6. 75, 82, 7. 133–7). He seems too to be at ease with the question of the 'meaning' of events. Both in his own person and also in the person of various 'warners' who appear in his narrative (men such as *Solon; the Egyptian pharaoh Amasis; Xerxes' uncle, the Persian Artabanus, and Croesus, after his downfall), the thread of events seems to be illuminated by general statements: 'human success stays nowhere in the same place', Herodotus (1. 5); 'divinity is jealous and disruptive', 'man is the creature of chance', and 'in everything one must look to the end', 'Solon' (1. 32); 'there is a cycle of human experience: as it revolves, it does not allow the same men always to succeed', 'Croesus' (1. 207). These look to add up to what D. Lateiner (*The Historical Method of Herodotus* (1989)) has called Herodotus' 'historical philosophy'. But they do not in reality fit together; rather they are what ancient Greeks called *gnōmai* (maxims or aphorisms) and their function is closer to that of the proverb than to any 'law' of historical process: they are not discountenanced by contradiction. Nor do references to 'what was going to be', to motions of a man's 'portion', or 'what is assigned' make Herodotus a historical determinist. Rather they represent the storyteller's sense of the shape of his story. Closer perhaps to the heart of Herodotus' sense of things are 'wonder' (a very Herodotean word) at human achievement, the 'great and wonderful deeds of men' (1. 1) and the emotional undercurrent to events that so often gives his narrative a tragic colour: two compelling and haunting examples are the story of the deadly quarrel between Periander, the tyrant of Corinth, and his own son (3. 49–53: characteristically, the story is introduced to explain another event, Corinthian and Corcyrean involvement in the affairs of Samos), and the astonishing moment at Abydos when Xerxes, in the act of mounting his great invasion of Greece and engaged in reviewing his vast invasion force, bursts into tears on reflecting that in a hundred years not one of these splendid warriors would be living (7. 45–7: his uncle, Darius' brother Artabanus, replies that more painful still is the fact that in so short a life there was not one who would not, again and again, wish himself dead to escape the distress of living).

6. The singularity of Herodotus' methods and achievement has always meant that he was problematic to his readers. He has been read with most enthusiasm and greatest understanding in periods of the rapid expansion of men's horizons, such as the Hellenistic period of *Alexander the Great's eastern conquests and in the Age of Discovery. But two adverse responses constantly recur: the first that he is a mere storyteller, charming perhaps but not a serious historian (that view, without the acknowledgement of charm, goes back to Thucydides (1. 21–2; cf. Aristotle, *Gen. an.* 3. 5)); the other view is that he is a liar. This view also has ancient supporters (especially *Plutarch in his bizarre essay, *On the Malice of Herodotus:* Plutarch's beloved Thebes does not emerge very well from Herodotus' account of events). But it was revived at the end of the last century by Sayce and is currently championed by Fehling and Armayor: D. Fehling's view (*Herodotus and his 'Sources'* (Eng. trans. 1989)) would make the untravelled Herodotus the inventor of plausible-sounding encounters with 'those who should know' about the fantastic events he wishes to pass off as veracious. There are problems, certainly, about believing everything that Herodotus says he saw or was told but they are not so great as the problem of recognizing Fehling's Herodotus in the text that we have. J. P. A. G.

the aetiological tale of Prometheus (521–616), and a detailed description of Tartarus (720–819). The poem ends with the marriages of Zeus and the other Olympians, and a list of goddesses who lay with mortal men. This last section, which refers to Latinus (1013) and led on to the *Catalogue* (below, 4), is agreed to be post-Hesiodic, though opinions vary as to where the authentic part ends.

2. The *Works and Days*, abbr. '*Op.*' This poem, apparently composed after the *Theogony* (cf. 11–24 with *Theog.* 225), would be more aptly entitled 'the Wisdom of Hesiod'. It gives advice for living a life of honest work. Hesiod

inveighs against dishonesty and idleness by turns, using myths (Prometheus again, with the famous story of Pandora, 42–105; the five World Ages, 106–201), parable (202–12), allegory (286–92), proverbial maxims, direct exhortation, and threats of divine anger. The sermon is ostensibly directed at a brother Perses, who has bribed the 'kings' and taken more than his share of his inheritance (37–9); but Perses' failings seem to change with the context (cf. 28 ff., 275, 396), and it is impossible to reconstruct a single basic situation. Besides moral advice, Hesiod gives much practical instruction, especially on agriculture

(381–617, the year's 'Works'), seafaring (618–94), and social and religious conduct (336–80, 695–764). There is a fine descriptive passage on the rigours of winter (504–35). The final section, sometimes regarded as a later addition, is the 'Days' (765–828), an almanac of days in the month that are favourable or unfavourable for different operations. Some ancient copies continued with an *Ornithomanteia*, a section on bird omens. The poem as a whole is a unique source for social conditions in early Archaic Greece. It has closer parallels in near eastern literatures than in Greek, and seems to represent an old traditional type. (*Virgil's *Georgics*, though much influenced by Hesiod, are shaped by the Hellenistic tradition of systematic treatment of a single theme.)

It has always been the most read of Hesiodic poems. There was even a 'tradition' that it was Hesiod's only genuine work (Paus. 9. 31. 4); but he names himself in *Theog.* 22, and links of style and thought between the two poems confirm identity of authorship. Both bear the marks of a distinct personality: a surly, conservative countryman, given to reflection, no lover of women or of life, who felt the gods' presence heavy about him.

3. The *Shield* (*Aspis*), abbr. '*Sc.*', is a short narrative poem on Heracles' fight with Cycnus, prefaced by an excerpt from the fourth book of the *Catalogue* giving the story of Heracles' birth (1–56). It takes its title from the disproportionately long description of Heracles' shield (139–320), which is based partly on the shield of Achilles (*Il.* 18. 478–609), partly on the art of the period *c.*580–570 (R. M. Cook, *CQ* 1937, 204 ff.; this proves that Aristophanes of Byzantium was right in denying the poem to Hesiod). Disproportion is characteristic of the work; the Homeric apparatus of arming, divine machination, brave speeches, and long similes is lavished on an encounter in which two blows are struck in all. Parts of the description of the shield betray a taste for the macabre.

4. The *Catalogue of Women* or *Ehoiai* was a continuation of the *Theogony* in five books, containing comprehensive heroic *genealogies with many narrative annotations. Numerous citations and extensive papyrus fragments survive. The poem was accepted as Hesiod's in antiquity, but various indications point to the period 580–520 BC.

5. Other lost poems. (*a*) Narrative: *Greater Ehoiai* (genealogical); *Melampodia* (at least three books; stories of famous seers); *Wedding of Ceyx*; *Idaean Dactyls*; *Aegimius* (at least two books; alternatively ascribed to Cercops of Miletus or Clinias of Carystus). (*b*) Didactic: *Precepts of Chiron* (addressed to *Achilles; see CENTAURS); *Astronomy* (risings and settings—and myths?—of principal stars); *Greater Works*. A few fragments of most of these poems survive.   M. L. W.

heterosexuality and *homosexuality are not strictly applicable to the Graeco-Roman world (this remains controversial). Discussions of sex could focus on either pleasure or procreation. Pleasures were categorized and valued on the distinction between active (penetrating an orifice with a penis) and passive. Heterosexual acts (not people) were distinguished from homosexual not as radically differing pleasures but primarily on the basis of social consequence: only the former produce children.

What was most important in heterosexual acts was the status of the woman and the man's degree of responsibility towards her and her offspring: wife, concubine, hetaira, prostitute, slave ([Dem.] 59. 112, 122). The purpose of wives was to produce legitimate children (Xen. *Mem.* 2. 2. 4; Men. *Dys.* 842; *FIRA* 3. 17). Marriage was primarily a nexus of social and economic exchange (see MARRIAGE LAW). Love between husband and wife was neither necessary nor expected (Lucr. 4. 1278–87; but contrast Cimon and Isodice, Sulla and Valeria). However, mutual respect, affection, and love could and did arise (*IG* 2². 12067, Dem. 40. 27, Plin. *Ep.* 7. 5). Expressions of wives' love for husbands are common, seldom the reverse (*ILS* 7472). Wives were expected to be modest even during sex (Plaut. *Amph.* 839–42; Lucr. 4. 1268–77; Plut. *Praec. coniug.* 16–18). Later marriage contracts specify sexual responsibilities for both partners (*PEleph.* 1; cf. Plut. *Sol.* 20). A strict double standard was enforced. Men had recourse to hetairai (courtesans) for love affairs and sophisticated entertainment, or to prostitutes for quick relief (see PROSTITUTION, SECULAR). Slaves, male or female, could be routinely used for sex (Muson. 12). Concubinage offered a stable, legal (sometimes contractual) status to those for whom marriage was impossible or undesirable.

Control of wives' sexuality (virginity, *adultery) was important to assure the legitimacy of the children (Lys. 1. 33–5; [Dem.] 59. 112–13) and so social stability. Athenian fathers could sell their corrupted unmarried daughters into slavery (Hyp. *Lyc.* 1. 12–13; Plut. *Sol.* 23: no known cases). Tests (if ever applied) for virginity were mostly magical: the hymen was not fully recognized even by anatomists.

Adultery meant intercourse with a married woman; she was the object of adulteration. The offence was against her husband and a matter of 'self-help' justice until the *lex Iulia*. A man caught in the act (seduction or rape) with another's wife, mother, sister, daughter, or concubine, could be killed, sexually abused, or fined. Cuckoldry, however, was less of an obsession than in later 'Mediterranean' societies. Adulterous wives must be divorced ([Dem.] 59. 85–8; *Dig.* 48. 5. 2. 2) and were barred from public ceremonies. Roman law permitted fathers to kill adulterous daughters (*Dig.* 48. 5. 23–4). Rape of a free male or female was subject to monetary fine; half for a slave (Lys. 1. 32; Plut. *Sol.* 23).

Female orgasm is acknowledged (Hippoc. *De genitura* 4; Ar. *Lys.* 163–6; Lucr. 4. 1192–1207; Ov. *Ars am.* 2. 682–4) but largely ignored by the (male) sources. At the same time women were thought to be sexually voracious ([Hes.] fr. 275M–W). Roman (and to a lesser extent Greek) sources illustrate a marked scale of pleasure for the actor and humiliation for the object: vagina, anus, mouth. Anal intercourse, considered a Spartan proclivity (Ath. 13. 602a; Ar. *Lys.* 1148–74), was also practised as a form of birth control

(Hdt. 1. 61) and perhaps as a substitute for defloration early in marriage (for Rome, *Priapea* ed. A. Baehrens, *PLM* 3. 7–8; Sen. *Controv.* 1. 2. 22; Mart. 11. 78). Receiving fellatio was especially prized. Cunnilingus was most vile and degrading to the giver (Ar. *Eq.* 1280–9, *Vesp.* 1280–3; Gal. 12. 249 Kühn; Mart. 11. 61).

Reproduction was controlled through infant exposure, contraception, and *abortion. Most forms of *contraception were useless but some barriers (wool and wax pessaries) or mild spermatocides (e.g. cedar oil) may have been intermittently successful. Coitus interruptus is almost never attested (Archil. 196a West ?). Surgical abortion was dangerous and avoided by the doctors (Sor. *Gyn.* 1. 65; Ov. *Am.* 2. 13–14); oral or vaginal drugs were largely ineffective.

Vase-painting (*c.*575–450 BC) and other artistic (e.g. mirrors) and literary sources illustrate a wide variety of postures for intercourse. Black-figure favours standing rear-entry; red-figure shows greater use of couches. Intercrural sex with women seems unknown. Though the man is always the dominant partner, the positions seem to have few symbolic overtones. Sexual violence, group-sex, as well as occasional scenes of tenderness (kisses, caresses, eye-contact) are shown. Sex reappears in Hellenistic and Roman decorative arts, depicting primarily heterosexual intercourse of individual couples in domestic rather than symposiastic settings (see SYMPOSIUM).

Love as a theme in literature shows a marked periodicity. The personal celebrations of the lyric poets largely disappeared in the Classical age. Love re-emerged in New Comedy (see COMEDY (GREEK), NEW) and the *novel (adumbrated in *Aristophanes' *Lysistrata*) in a predominantly social, domestic, and hence heterosexual form. Hellenistic poetry focused on forbidden and pathological love (Ap. Rhod. 3; Theoc. 2). *Epigram worked conceits on pleasure and pain with both women and boys. Roman comedy transmitted some of this to Latin poetry. *Catullus made romantic love in our sense central to his life and poetry. The theme of erotic passion was continued by the elegists, parodied by *Ovid, and largely disappeared from the western tradition until its rediscovery in Courtly Love. See EROS; PORNOGRAPHY. H. N. P.

Hieronymus of Cardia historian and statesman, was in the entourage of his fellow Cardian (and relative?) Eumenes, acting as his emissary at the siege of Nora (319/18 BC) and passing to the court of *Antigonus the One-eyed after Eumenes' death at the battle of Gabiene (316). He served with Antigonus in Syria (312/1) and at the battle of Ipsus (301), and under Demetrius Poliorcetes ('the Besieger') governed Thebes after its revolt in 293. He ended his days with *Antigonus Gonatas. His great history spanned the period from *Alexander the Great's death (323) to at least the death of *Pyrrhus (272). It was *Diodorus Siculus' authority for Greek affairs in bks. 18–20, and was used extensively by *Plutarch, *Arrian, and Justin. The extant fragments only hint at its dimensions and content.

The main evidence is Diodorus' digest of his work, which in bks. 18–20 abruptly rises to a quality not found elsewhere in the *Bibliothēkē*. Excellently informed (see, for instance, the description of the battle lines at Paraetacene and Gabiene, which Hieronymus witnessed), he supplied documentation such as the texts of Alexander's Exiles' Decree and Polyperchon's *diagramma* (edict) of 319/18, and carefully explained the motives of the various protagonists (particularly Eumenes and Antigonus Monophthalmus). The lively and lucid narrative was varied by pertinent digressions like the descriptions of Alexander's funeral car and the Indian practice of suttee. He was not without bias, understandably favourable to Eumenes and Antigonus Gonatas, and markedly unsympathetic to Athenian democracy, but there is nothing to equal the sustained prejudice of Polybius, his only Hellenistic rival in 'pragmatic history'. (For this term see POLYBIUS.) A. B. B.

Hippocrates, Hippocratic corpus See MEDICINE §4.

historiography, Greek That Greeks invented history-writing is not certain: the Jewish 'Succession Narrative' in the books of Samuel and Kings antedates every Greek claimant to be the first historian. But direct Jewish influence on Greece is unlikely, and much biblical narration is a tram not a bus—driven by divine not humanly contingent causal forces.

*Homer is not historiography and is slippery ground for the historian. But his characters show awareness of the past and are impelled by an urge to leave glory to posterity; thus *Achilles sings of the famous deeds of men and Helen weaves into a web the story of the sufferings she has herself brought about. The poet himself speaks of 'men who exist nowadays' by contrast with inhabitants of the world he describes. *Genealogies, of the sort that feature in Homeric battle-challenges, are essential to a historical perspective on human events, and they form the link between Homer and Hecataeus of Miletus, the first true Greek historian: he wrote a prose work on genealogy, as well as a description of the world known to him, and a work on mythology. His younger critic and improver was *Herodotus: the urge to correct and improve on a predecessor is one of the main dynamics of Greek historiography. But the prose of Hecataeus was not Herodotus' only stimulus: Herodotus' nine-book work may owe at least as much to poets who (unlike Homer) did treat historical events in verse: it is now known that *Simonides handled the Persian War in detail and compared it explicitly to the Trojan War (*POxy.* 3965). The implications of this for the understanding of the beginnings of Greek historiography have yet to be properly drawn.

Herodotus' repudiation of myth was less explicit and famous than that of *Thucydides, but equally or (because earlier) more important: Herodotus restricts himself to historical time and to information he can check. How far he did check that information has been controversial since antiquity, but the sceptical case has not been made out. On the contrary Herodotus' work shows many authentic traces of the oral tradition (see ORALITY) on which its author drew.

Thucydides knew and reacted against Herodotus' work and there are obvious differences, above all a more linear narrative which concerned itself more narrowly with male activities like war and politics. But there are similarities too; thus Homeric influence is detectable in detail not just on Herodotus but on Thucydides also, who has a rhetoric of his own and should not be crudely opposed to Herodotus as *literacy is opposed to orality: Thucydides' famous preface declares his work to be *not so much* a prize composition (a word which hints at the displays of the *sophists) as a possession for ever. This formulation does not exclude recitation of sections in high finish, or even performance of debates and dialogue. By including (i.e. inventing) speeches at all, both historians were copying Homer, and Thucydides' very difficult speeches resemble Homer's in that their style is different from the narrative.

Western Greece, i.e. Italy and Sicily, developed its own historiography, which however borrowed from and interacted with that of old Greece. Thus Antiochus of Syracuse may have written his account to supplement Herodotus' gappy treatment of the west; but Antiochus was in his turn drawn on by Thucydides; who was then a close model for Philistus, who straddles the 5th and 4th cents.

Antiochus and Philistus were in effect local historians, though Sicily is a big place and they were hardly parochial figures. Similarly local historians studied the great states of old Greece, producing above all the *Atthides* or histories of Athens. The first Atthidographer was, however, not an Athenian at all, Hellanicus of Mytilene on Lesbos. But the great 4th- and 3rd-cent. Atthidographers, Androtion and Philochorus, were Athenians who used their literary works to express definite political viewpoints; theirs was not directionless antiquarianism.

The main stream of historiography after Thucydides was, however, navigated, as so often in the ancient world, by more cosmopolitan and restless writers, like the exiled Athenian *Xenophon. His preoccupation in the *Hellenica* with the Peloponnese is marked but his perspective is just too wide for this work to be called local history. He takes his chronological starting-point and some other obvious external features from Thucydides, but his religious values and his use of the illuminating digression are more reminiscent of Herodotus. His *Anabasis* is a snapshot of Persian Anatolia which reveals his gifts as a social historian and is a prime source for modern students of religion and warfare.

Thucydides never ceased to have influence even in the 4th cent. when to find him cited by name is rare, though another and more hard-headed continuator of Thucydides than Xenophon, the Oxyrhynchus historian, does mention him. *Aeneas Tacticus, not an intellectual, shows knowledge both of Thucydides' narrative and his speeches, and Thucydides' remarks on speeches were discussed by Callisthenes, whose *Hellenica* (used by *Ephorus later in the 4th cent. and thus at one remove by *Diodorus Siculus)

faintly transmits an important alternative tradition to that of Xenophon. 'Faintly', because Callisthenes resembles other big names of 4th-cent. Greek historiography in that he survives only in 'fragments' or quotations. The same is true of Ephorus, whose universal history, enormously popular in antiquity, drew on Thucydides for the 5th cent., then on the Oxyrhynchus historian (late 5th and early 4th), then on Callisthenes (? from the King's Peace of 386 BC onwards). But Ephorus also comes down to us mediated by Diodorus. The sources of Diodorus' Persian material for the 4th cent. (Ctesias? Dinon) are disputed, even more so his Sicilian material. Ephorus was one 'Sicilian' source but it is hard to know how much to attribute to *Timaeus, a major figure in Greek understanding of the west.

Another Thucydidean continuator and partial imitator (he echoes the Thucydidean Funeral Speech) was *Theopompus, who wrote about *Philip II of Macedon in a way which may owe something to Thucydides' fascination with the individual *Alcibiades. But the great individual of the age was *Alexander the Great, whose 'Deeds' were reported by Callisthenes, by Dinon's son Cleitarchus (the source of Diodorus book 17 and of the vulgate tradition about Alexander generally), and by Arrian's sources *Ptolemy I and Aristobulus. Alexander, the new *Achilles as his historians presented him or as he presented himself, and his glorious Deeds take us back to Homer where this survey began.   S. H.

historiography, Hellenistic In an age that witnessed the conquests by *Alexander the Great and his Successors and then the Roman succession to virtually all that had been theirs, Greeks substantially expanded history-writing to include new themes, styles, and genres. In the 1st cent. BC *Dionysius of Halicarnassus claimed that the day was not long enough for him to recite the names of all the historians (*Comp.* 4. 30). The increase in history-writing was due to the necessity to explain new events, lands, and peoples. It was nurtured by the patronage of Hellenistic monarchs and Roman aristocrats and by the growth of *libraries and centres of scholarship, most notably in *Alexandria and Pergamum, and finally in Rome.

Most of that rich and diverse writing is lost. Substantial parts of *Polybius, *Diodorus Siculus, and Dionysius of Halicarnassus survive, as do some of the works of *Appian, *Arrian, *Cassius Dio, Herodian, and *Plutarch from the Roman period. Fragments from the lost works of nearly a thousand historians, preserved by later authors as quotations or paraphrases, are collected in F. Jacoby's *Die Fragmente der griechischen Historiker* (*FGrH*). Although still incomplete, it is a treasure trove of information and, arranged by genre, presents an organizational scheme which helps make sense of the complex subject. Work on it has now (1994) been resumed by an international team.

Spanning centuries and continents, Hellenistic historiography, however, defies categorization. The ancients themselves did not submit history to the same rigours or canons as they did philosophy, rhetoric, and science; nor was history part of the educational curriculum. Rhetoricians, apparently far more often than historians themselves, commented on the principles of history writing, usually by evaluating historical narrative for style. Hellenistic history never developed acknowledged classics. Egyptian papyri, as well as literary references, suggest that *Herodotus, *Thucydides, and *Xenophon (followed by *Theopompus and *Ephorus) continued throughout antiquity to be the best-known historians. Polybius, the most renowned Hellenistic historian, was not read closely a century after he wrote (so Dionysius of Halicarnassus). The Attic revival made these Classical writers better objects of rhetorical imitation.

Rhetoric played an important role in the development of narrative. Historians had, since Thucydides, added speeches for variety, colour, and dramatic tension. *Isocrates, a practitioner of the epideictic style of oratory, influenced Theopompus and Ephorus to include also character assessments in passing moral and practical judgements on their subjects. Perhaps related is the development of so-called tragic history. The invocation of highly emotive scenes lent drama to the narrative and entertained the reader. Although Polybius, in choosing a more utilitarian approach, inveighed against the use of tragic history as counterfactual (he attacked especially Phylarchus), a few episodes in his surviving narrative also bear its influence.

Local chronicles—important in the development of Classical historiography—continued to be produced in abundance in the Hellenistic period. But other genres emerged. Biography developed fully, with its Hellenistic emphasis on individual characterization and character type. Satyrus and Cornelius Nepos were precursors of *Plutarch, *Suetonius, Philostratus, Eunapius, and other pagan and Christian hagiographers. Ethnographies became important for explaining the new lands under Greek and then Roman control, and even traditional narratives contained much ethnographic material, leading to amalgams such as the works of *Strabo and *Pausanias. Indeed, the novel emerged from the same spirit of discovery, with many of the romances situated in exotic lands and the main characters 'historical' figures, such as Alexander the Great, Ninus, and Semiramis. Despite their interest in ethnography, Hellenistic historians rarely learned local languages and frequently forced their interpretations of foreign cultures into categories familiar to Greek audiences. Megasthenes idealized the social structure of India in Greek philosophical constructions, as did Hecataeus of Abdera in his analysis of Egypt; Polybius, who spent two decades in Italy, presented a description of Roman political institutions (book 6) based on an Aristotelian model of government (see ARISTOTLE) and marred by an inability to understand Romans on their own terms.

The most significant historical genre that developed in the Hellenistic period was universal history. The Roman conquest made the study of the *oikoumenē* ('inhabited world') a compelling topic, a subject initially treated by Polybius (although *Timaeus had been the first to cover Rome at length). The growth of universalistic philosophies, especially *Stoicism, brought another unifying theme: the power of the common good. Diodorus Siculus used the theme of individual benefactors and civilizing agents haphazardly, but Posidonius could suggest, with some ambivalence, that Roman might represented a unifying force for the common benefit of all. This notion, reinterpreted, became influential with Christian writers such as St *Augustine. But few practitioners of universal history were broadly inclusive of other ethnic groups except as they came into contact with Graeco-Roman civilization. Universalistic historiography became truly ecumenical only when it abandoned time-bound narrative in the form of Judaeo-Christian apocalyptic and prophecy.

Just as Thucydides implicitly acknowledged and followed Herodotus, a series of later historians built their narratives on previous ones. This succession of historical works helped develop the notion of historical tradition, with historians increasingly quoting from and drawing on past works (no more evident than in the case of Plutarch). It also spawned the belief that historical narrative could be created without primary research: Diodorus Siculus and Arrian (to choose extremes in quality) compiled narratives based on accepted earlier traditions. New interpretations of past events were generally derived from rationalizing or from new perspectives, rarely from new research. The very diversity and abundance of Hellenistic history-writing assured a widespread acceptance of the principle that the past, as well as the present, needed to be recalled and reinterpreted—if not also reinvestigated. It encouraged the invocation of history for justification of present policy or for *propaganda, such as occurred in the generally anti-Roman Sibylline oracles. In the Greek revival of the 2nd cent. AD (see SECOND SOPHISTIC), Arrian consciously modelled his works after Xenophon's, as if an echo of Classical form and style would bestow legitimacy.

Greek historiography profoundly influenced its Roman counterpart (beginning with Quintus Fabius Pictor who wrote in Greek) and created the paradigms of historical investigation in other Mediterranean lands. *Maccabees II, an epitome of Jason of Cyrene's larger work in Greek, contains episodes in the style of tragic history, and *Josephus' *Jewish Antiquities* reflects the work of Dionysius of Halicarnassus. Manetho's study of Egypt and Berossus' history of Babylonia are based on Hellenistic examples of history-writing. Although early Christian historiography departs conceptually by identifying a pre-existing spirit that was to outlast all history, some books of the New Testament, especially Luke and *Acts of the Apostles, bear the influence of Hellenistic historiography and rhetorical devices. Christian hagiography develops from the Greek biographical tradition, and *Eusebius, who initiated ecclesiastical history, drew heavily on documents in a manner similar to his Greek predecessors.

See the articles on individual historical writers. K. S. S.

historiography, Roman Presentation of the Roman past was firmly rooted in the Roman present. Historians proclaimed a desire to help and inspire contemporary readers in their public life (e.g. Sall. *Iug.* 4; Livy, pref. 10; Tac. *Ann.* 4. 32–3), and the past was often moulded to provide antecedents for contemporary events or rephrased in contemporary terms, sometimes for tendentious reasons, sometimes just to make the story more excitingly familiar. Roman writers were also more often public men than their Greek counterparts (e.g. *Cato the Elder, *Sallust, Gaius Asinius Pollio, *Tacitus), and their contemporary narrative told of events in which they had played a part: the result was an emphasis on this recent history, which usually comprised the bulk even of those works which covered Rome's history from its foundation (*ab urbe condita*).

Still, historiography was not simply a masked version of the memoir. It aspired to tell the story of the Roman state, not just of an individual's experiences. At first this usually involved an outline of Rome's history from its beginnings, with special emphasis on the inspiring foundation stories. The result was an hourglass structure, with most space given to the beginnings and the present, and a sketchier account of the period in between: that is already visible in Quintus Fabius Pictor, traditionally the earliest Roman historian, and survives in most of his *ab urbe condita* successors (including *Ennius, who did much to shape the Roman view of history). Another aspect, as Cicero (*De or.* 2. 51–3) ruefully observed, was the evocation of traditional Roman *annales*. Writers may only rarely have consulted the *annales maximi* themselves, but the texture of such material—bare lists of omens, magistrates, triumphs, etc.—was still familiar; Cato fr. 77 and Sempronius Asellio frs. 1–2 (both ed. Peter) protested at the historical inadequacy of such catalogues, but versions of these lists figured even in the developed genre, usually conferring an aura of tradition and antiquity. The annalistic structure, organizing material in a year-by-year fashion, also became regular.

Rome took her past seriously; it became part of that seriousness to insist that its history was told with suitable literary and rhetorical art (cf. Cic. *Leg.* 1. 5, *De or.* 2. 36). For Fabius Pictor and his early successors—Lucius Cincius Alimentus, Aulus Postumius Albinus, Gaius Acilius—this meant writing in Greek, thus fitting Roman history into the mainstream of Hellenistic historical literature, which greatly influenced its Roman equivalent; the use of Greek also promoted the presentation of Rome to a cultured Greek audience as Rome advanced eastwards. The Latin prose genre was pioneered by Cato, whose *Origines* extended the focus to the Italian cities, and Lusius Cassius Hemina; but the change of languages did not end the influence of Greece, nor reduce the literary pretensions. From an early stage history drew a great deal from rhetoric, including many clear boons: an eye for evidence, a nose for bias, an alertness to arguments from probability, the capacity to impose structure on recalcitrant material. But rhetorical virtuosity also promoted the imaginative expansion of the past. Second- and first-cent. BC writers filled out the bare annalistic record with circumstantial narrative, sometimes creatively reconstructing what 'must have' happened, sometimes glorifying a family or providing a precedent, sometimes simply for artistic effect. The voluminous works of Gnaeus Gellius in the 2nd cent. and Valerius Antias in the 1st seem to have been particularly rich in such elaboration.

This should not obscure the commitment to discovering the truth, however much it might then be embellished and strengthened with supporting detail. Writers do discuss the reliability of questionable material, with varying critical acumen (e.g. Livy 2. 21, 6. 1, 38. 56–7; Tac. *Ann.* 4. 10–11, 13. 20); *Livy's predecessors aspired to find out new facts as well as provide a new artistic veneer (pref. 2). There was no clear distinction between antiquarianism and historiography at least in the 2nd cent. BC, and even later writers show some respect for documentary sources, e.g. Gaius Licinius Macer and Quintus Aelius Tubero with the 'linen books', and perhaps Tacitus with the senatorial *acta* (official record of proceedings). Still, Roman writers doubtless underestimated the sheer difficulty of discovering distant truth. Cicero (*De or.* 2. 62–3) insists on truthfulness as the first law of history, but gives most emphasis and thought to the rhetorical 'superstructure' (*exaedificatio*) built on this acknowledged 'foundation' (*fundamentum*); when *Pliny the Elder, *Ep.* 5. 8, considered writing ancient history, he considered it 'easy to find out about, but burdensome to bring together'. Writers might identify their sources' political bias; they rarely asked more searching questions about the texture and origin of their material.

Partisan bias was intensified by the struggles of the Gracchan age (see TIBERIUS and GAIUS GRACCHUS), and these accentuated the concentration on the present. One aspect was a stepping up of the reinterpretation of the past in contemporary terms: this seems to have typified the work of Lucius Calpurnius Piso Frugi, then in the 1st cent. Gaius Licinius Macer. The more straightforward development was the tendency to omit earlier history altogether. Asellio combined this with a Polybian determination (see POLYBIUS) to emphasize important interpretative strands; he apparently began in 146 BC, perhaps deliberately beginning where Polybius stopped. A number of writers carried on this practice of continuation, self-consciously producing a serial canon of Roman history: thus, it seems, Sisenna continued Asellio, and Sallust's *Histories* continued Sisenna. A middle position, less exclusively contemporary but still eschewing the distant past, was occupied by Quintus Claudius Quadrigarius, who apparently began with the Gallic sack (387 BC), and earlier by Lucius Coelius Antipater, whose work on the Second Punic War introduced the historical monograph to Rome. Cicero (*Leg.* 1. 6–7) stresses the stylistic advances made by Coelius and Sisenna, but he felt that Rome was still waiting for her great national historian. Cicero never wrote the work himself.

*Sallust's *Bellum Catilinae* and *Bellum Iugurthinum* abandoned annalistic form and developed the monograph, using these two episodes to illustrate themes of wider significance, especially that of moral decline. The analysis is schematic, but is carried through with concentration and structural deftness; and Sallust moulded an appropriate style, concise, epigrammatic, rugged, and abrupt. Meanwhile *Caesar had written a different sort of monograph in his commentaries; their form leaves them outside the mainstream, but he still adapted techniques from historiographic rhetoric to fit his insidiously persuasive plainness of manner. Asinius Pollio wrote of the Civil War (between Caesar and *Pompey) and its antecedents, beginning with 60 BC. His incisive and independent analysis influenced the later Greek versions of *Appian and *Plutarch.

Pollio was less influential in Rome itself, largely because *Livy's 142-book *ab urbe condita* came to dominate the field. The great Roman history had been written at last. Livy offered something new, with a more even treatment of past and present: the great bulk of his history was pre-contemporary, partly, as he explains in the preface, because decline was relatively recent, and the best ethical examples were to be found in the earlier centuries. His moralizing is, however, more than Roman bias; it is also a form of explanation, isolating the strengths which carried Rome to its success, and might yet prove her salvation. The preface suggests that his contemporary books may have projected a less rosy view of Rome's morality, with degeneration explaining the less happy developments of the last century.

As in other genres, an Augustan classic had a stifling effect, and Livy's bulky eminence deterred rivals. History too changed, and the early Principate shows writers balancing traditional forms with a new world where the achievements of the Roman people, with the annual rhythm of changing magistracies, no longer captured the central themes of imperial reality. Velleius Paterculus controlled his recent narrative around leading individuals, Caesar, *Augustus, and *Tiberius, and treated his material with rhetorical exuberance. His enthusiasm for the new world contrasted with Aulus Cremutius Cordus' nostalgia for the old, and Cremutius paid with his life; the elder Seneca dealt more safely with the transition from republic to Principate. Trogus had earlier set Roman history in its universal context; Hyginus and Valerius Maximus collected *exempla*; at some point Quintus Curtius Rufus turned to Greece, and wrote in Roman style about *Alexander the Great's heroics. A more traditional style was followed by Aufidius Bassus and his continuator *Pliny the Elder, though their general histories were complemented by detailed studies of particular wars. Marcus Servilius Nonianus, Cluvius Rufus, and Fabius Rusticus also wrote substantial works.

*Tacitus' achievement is accentuated by this background. In many ways he was highly traditional. He kept the annalistic form; he chose relatively recent events; he wrote of senate and generals, not just emperors and courts. Yet the old forms are at odds with their content, so often pointing the contrast with the republic. The annual rhythms are overridden by the impact of emperors and their changing characters; further themes cut across the years and reigns—the power of advisers and the great ladies of the court, the regrettable necessity of one-man rule in a world unfit to rule itself, the inert senators who exchange hypocrisies with their prince. Brilliant rhetorical sharpness and devastating analysis serve each other well. Livy, at least in his surviving books, was the historian of a romanticized past; Tacitus exposed dispiriting reality.

Tacitus defied imitation as much as did Livy. Imperial historiography was always in danger of collapsing into imperial biography; that had been clear since Velleius, and from the 2nd cent. AD biography dominated the field (see BIOGRAPHY, ROMAN). The classical historians stimulated epitomes (Ampelius, Justin, Eutropius, Festus, Obsequens) or at most rhetorical reformulation (Florus, Granius Licinianus, Exsuperantius); they were not imitated until the last flowering of the genre with *Ammianus Marcellinus, who finally addressed a great theme, and was adequate to the task.   C. B. R. P.

history of classical scholarship See SCHOLARSHIP, ANCIENT and SCHOLARSHIP, HISTORY OF CLASSICAL.

Homer (*see following page*)

homosexuality No Greek or Latin word corresponds to the modern term *homosexuality*, and ancient Mediterranean societies did not in practice treat homosexuality as a socially operative category of personal or public life. Sexual relations between persons of the same sex certainly did occur (they are widely attested in ancient sources), but they were not systematically distinguished or conceptualized as such, much less were they thought to represent a single, homogeneous phenomenon in contradistinction to sexual relations between persons of different sexes. That is because the ancients did not classify kinds of sexual desire or behaviour according to the sameness or difference of the sexes of the persons who engaged in a sexual act; rather, they evaluated sexual acts according to the degree to which such acts either violated or conformed to norms of conduct deemed appropriate to individual sexual actors by reason of their gender, age, and social status. It is therefore impossible to speak in general terms about ancient attitudes to 'homosexuality', or about the degree of its acceptance or toleration by particular communities, because any such statement would, in effect, lump together various behaviours which the ancients themselves kept rigorously distinct and to which they attached radically divergent meanings and values. (Exactly the same things could be said, of course, and with equal justification, about *heterosexuality.)

It is not illegitimate to employ modern sexual terms and concepts when interrogating the ancient record, but particular caution must be exercised in order not to import modern, western sexual categories and ideologies into the

[*continued on p. 351*]

Homer

Homer 1. The ancient world attributed the two epics, the *Iliad* and the *Odyssey*, the earliest and greatest works of Greek literature, to the poet Homer. Against this general consensus a few scholars at *Alexandria argued for different authorship of the two poems; and modern critics, in the 150 years after Wolf (1795), went further and questioned the unity of authorship of each poem. However, the difficulties on which these 'analysts' based their discussions have been resolved through a greater understanding of oral poetry, and now most scholars see each as the work of one author. Whether he was the same for both remains uncertain. They have a great deal of common phraseology, but the *Odyssey* is less archaic in language and more repetitive in content, it views the gods rather differently, and for a few common things it uses different words. Such changes might occur in the lifetime of one person. As nothing reliable is known about Homer, perhaps the question is not important.

There is some agreement to date the poems in the second half of the 8th cent. BC, with the *Iliad* the earlier, about 750, the *Odyssey* about 725. This was the age of colonization in the Greek world (see COLONIZATION, GREEK), and it may be no accident that the *Iliad* shows an interest in the north-east, towards the Black (Euxine) Sea, while much of the *Odyssey* looks towards the west. In *Od.* 6. 7–10 many have seen an echo of the founding of a Greek colony. As to Homer himself, the *Iliad* at least suggests a home on the east side of the Aegean Sea, for storm winds in a simile blow over the sea from Thrace, from the north and west (9. 5), and the poet seems familiar with the area near Miletus (2. 461) as well as that round *Troy (12. 10–33). Moreover, the predominantly Ionic flavour of the mixed dialect of the poems suits the cities of the Ionian migration on the other side of the Aegean. Chios and Smyrna have the strongest claims to have been his birthplace.

2. The *Iliad* is the longer of the two by a third, consisting of over 15,600 lines, divided into 24 books. The book division seems to have been later than the original composition, although the books do in many cases represent distinct episodes in the plot (e.g. books 1, 9, 12, 16, 22, 24). There is now broad agreement that we have the poem virtually as it was composed, with the exception of book 10, where the evidence for later addition is strong. For the rest, an individual intelligence is shown by the theme of the anger of *Achilles, begun in the quarrel with *Agamemnon in 1, kept before us in the Embassy of 9, transferred from Agamemnon to *Hector in 18, and resolved in the consolation of Priam, Hector's father, in 24; also by the tight time-scale of the epic, for, in place of a historical treatment of the Trojan War (see TROY), the *Iliad*, from book 2 to 22, records merely four days of fighting from the tenth year, separated by two days of truce. Even the beginning and end add only a few weeks to the total.

Thus the action is concentrated, but the composition subtly expands to include the whole war, with echoes from the beginning in books 2 to 4, and the final books repeatedly looking forward to the death of Achilles and the fall of Troy. The centre is occupied by a single day of battle between 11 and 18, with the Trojans temporarily superior, Greek leaders wounded, their strongest and most mobile fighter (Achilles) disaffected, only Ajax (see AIAS (1)) and some warriors of the second rank holding the defence. The turning-point is in 16, when Patroclus, acting on a suggestion from Nestor in 11, persuades Achilles to let him go to the rescue of their comrades, and thus starts the sequence that leads to his own death (16), Achilles' return (18), Hector's death (22), and the conclusion of the epic (24).

3. High among the qualities of the *Iliad* is a vast humanity, which justifies comparison with Shakespeare. The poet understands human behaviour and reactions. There are numerous well-differentiated portraits of leading figures, introduced on the Greek side in the first four books, whose successes in action reinforce their heroic status, and whose personal feelings and relationships are expressed in the very frequent speeches. Figures of the second rank (e.g. Meriones, Antilochus) support the leaders; and a large number of minor characters, who appear only to be killed, add a sense of the pathos and waste of war, through background details, particularly reference to families at home.

The Trojans have their leaders too, but their efforts are essentially defensive, and the desperate situation of their city, and the threat to the women and children, contrast with the more straightforward heroics of the Greeks. Three women of Troy, Hecuba, Andromache, and Helen, appear at key moments in books 6 and 24, the first two also in 22.

There is also what Pope called 'invention', a constant brilliance of imagination infusing the reports of action, speeches of the characters, and descriptions of the natural world. The language has a kind of perfection, due to a combination of phrases worn smooth by traditional use and the taste and judgement of the poet; and features which had been technical aids to the oral bard seem to have assumed the form of art in the *Iliad*—the use of formulae and repeated story patterns, ring-composition in the construction of speeches, the pictorial effects of extended similes.

4. The *Odyssey*, about 12,000 lines long, was probably composed in its present form in imitation of the already existing *Iliad*. Its 24 books show exact construction. Four books set the scene in Ithaca ten years after the end of the war, and send Odysseus' son Telemachus to two of the most distinguished survivors, Nestor at Pylos and Menelaus at *Sparta, in search of news of his father. The next four show Odysseus himself released from the island of Calypso and arriving at the land of the Phaeacians (Scheria), a half-way house between the fairy-tale world of his adventures and the real world of Ithaca which awaits him. There, in 9 to 12, he recounts his adventures to the Phaeacians. That completes the first half; the second is devoted to Odysseus' return home, the dangers he faces, and his eventual slaughter of the suitors of his wife Penelope. In book 15, the two strands of the first half are brought together, when Telemachus returns from Sparta and joins his father.

For reasons difficult to guess, the quality of composition fades at the end, from 23. 296, which the Alexandrian scholars Aristophanes of Byzantium and Aristarchus confusingly describe as the 'end' of the *Odyssey*. However, at least two parts of the 'continuation' (i.e. what follows 23. 296) are indispensable for the completion of the story—the recognition of Odysseus by his old father Laertes, and the avoidance of a blood feud with the relatives of the dead suitors.

5. The *Odyssey* is a romance, enjoyable at a more superficial level than the heroic/tragic *Iliad*. We can take sides, for the good people are on one side, the bad on the other. Even the massacre of the suitors and the vengeance on the servants who had supported them are acceptable in a story of this kind. The epic depends very much more than the *Iliad* on a single character; and Odysseus has become a seminal figure in European literature, with eternal human qualities of resolution, intellectual curiosity, and love of home. Apart from books 9 to 12, the settings are domestic, Ithaca, Pylos, Sparta, and Scheria (the land of the Phaeacians). The effect of this is that the gentler qualities of politeness, sensitivity, and tact come into play, as in the delicate interchanges between Odysseus and Nausicaa (the princess on Scheria) and her parents. On the other hand, the boorish behaviour of the suitors shows a break-down of the social order.

For many readers the adventures are the high point. The Lotus-eaters, Cyclops, king of the winds, cannibal giants, witch Circe, Sirens, Scylla, and Charybdis are part of the folk-tale element in western consciousness. They are prefaced by a piratical attack on a people in Thrace, near Troy, and concluded on the island of the Sun, an episode which results in the elimination of Odysseus' surviving companions, leaving him alone to face the return home. In the middle, in book 11, comes the visit to the Underworld, where he sees figures from the past and receives a prophecy of the future.

The combination of precision of observation and descriptive imagination is on a par with the *Iliad*; examples are Odysseus in the Cyclops' cave, Odysseus in his own house among the suitors of his wife, the recognition by his old dog Argos. One gets the impression, however, more strongly with the *Odyssey* than the *Iliad*, that the tale has been told many times before, and some superficial inconsistencies may be the effect of variant versions (e.g. the abortive plans for the removal of the arms in 16. 281–98).

6. The dactylic hexameter has a complex structure, with from twelve to seventeen syllables in the lines, and some precise metrical requirements. Milman Parry demonstrated that features of

composition, notably pervasive repetition in the phraseology, derive from the practice of illiterate oral bards, who would learn the traditional phrases (formulae) in their years of apprenticeship; see ORALITY. This explains many aspects that worried analytical critics since the days of the Alexandrian critics; for repetition of a half-line, line, or sequence of lines had been taken by readers used to the practice of later poets as evidence for corruption in the text, and an adjective used inappropriately had seemed to be a fault, instead of the inevitable consequence of the use of formulae.

Of equal significance to the repetition of formulaic phrases in the composition of oral poetry is the repetitive, though flexible, use of what are called typical scenes, patterns in the story, sometimes described as 'themes'. These range from the four arming-scenes in the *Iliad* (in books 3, 11, 16, 19), scenes of arrival and departure, performance of sacrifices, descriptions of fighting, to the repeated abuse directed at Odysseus in the second half of the Odyssey. Such 'themes' performed a parallel function to the formulae, giving the experienced bard material for the construction of his songs in front of an audience.

Virtually all scholars now accept that oral poetry theory has added to our understanding. Difference remains about whether Homer himself was an illiterate bard, or whether his position at the end of a long tradition shows a bard using the possibilities of literacy while still retaining the oral techniques. The ultimate problem of the survival of the two epics is inextricably bound up with this question. Three possibilities divide the field. Either the poet composed with the help of writing, the Greek alphabet having become available at just the right time; or the poems were recorded by scribes, the poet himself being illiterate; or they were memorized by a guild of public reciters ('rhapsodes') for anything up to 200 years (there being evidence for a written text in Athens in the 6th cent.).

7. The language in which the poems are composed contains a mixture of forms found in different areas of the Greek world. The overall flavour is Ionic, the dialect spoken on Euboea, other islands of the eastern Aegean such as Chios, and on the mainland of Asia Minor opposite them. Attic Greek was a subdivision of Ionic, but Atticisms in the epic dialect are rare and superficial. Second in importance to Ionic in the amalgam is Aeolic, the dialect of north Greece (Boeotia and *Thessaly) and the northern islands such as *Lesbos. Where Aeolic had a different form from Ionic, the Aeolic form mostly appears as an alternative to the Ionic in the epic language when it has a different metrical value. More deeply embedded are certain words and forms which belonged to the dialect of southern Greece in the Mycenaean age, sometimes described as Arcado-Cypriot, because it survived into historical times in those two widely separated areas of the Greek world. See GREEK LANGUAGE.

The historical implications of all this are obscure. The geographical location during the Mycenaean age of the speakers of what later became Ionic and Aeolic was necessarily different from that in historical times; and the dialects themselves obviously developed differently in different areas. What is clear, however, is that the linguistic picture is consistent with that presented by oral theory. Some features are very ancient (often preserved in the formulaic phrases), some quite recent. An important conclusion is that late linguistic forms are not to be seen as post-Homeric interpolations, but more probably come from the language of the poet himself, while earlier ones had reached him through the tradition. It is noted that the similes in the *Iliad* contain a high proportion of 'late' forms.

8. The assumed date of the Trojan war falls in the 13th cent. BC, towards the end of the Mycenaean age; for the Mycenaean palaces on the mainland were destroyed from about 1200. There is thus a gap of some four and a half centuries between the date of composition of the *Iliad* (about 750) and the legendary past which is its setting. The 8th cent. is essentially more important for the epics than the 13th; but the history of the Mycenaean age and of the shadowy times that lay between is naturally of the greatest interest. Here archaeologist and historian combine. We have the extraordinary discoveries of Schliemann at Mycenae, and the excavations at Troy itself by Schliemann (1870–90), Blegen (1932–8), and Korfmann (1981–   ). Historical evidence from the 13th cent. has come to the surface. It is, however, unsafe to assume too close a connection with Homer. For the passage of time, and a retrospective view of a heroic age, have moved the picture nearer to fiction than reality. Only fossilized memories of the

Mycenaean age survive in his work (see MYCENAEAN CIVILIZATION).

After the destruction of the palaces a long Dark Age intervened, lightened to some extent recently by the discovery at *Lefkandi in Euboea of a city with important trade connections in the 10th and 9th cents. It must have been during the Dark Age that heroic poetry developed and spread, even if (as seems probable) it originated in the Mycenaean age. Historians see in the epics reflections of the society and political aspirations of this period, even of the 8th cent. See GREECE (PREHISTORY AND HISTORY).

9. Hexameter poetry continued after Homer, with Hesiod and the *Homeric Hymns*, and the (largely lost) poems of the so-called Epic Cycle, which described the two legendary wars of the heroic age, those against Thebes and Troy. The Theban epics are lost, but for the Trojan we have summaries of the contents of six poems (*Cypria, Aethiopis, Little Iliad, Sack of Troy (Iliu Persis), Returns (Nostoi), Telegony (Telegonia)*, which had been fitted round the *Iliad* and *Odyssey* to create a complete sequence from the marriage of Peleus and Thetis to the death of Odysseus. The summaries, attributed to 'Proclus' (perhaps a grammarian of the 2nd cent. AD), are found in some manuscripts of the *Iliad*. These cyclic epics were obviously later than the Homeric poems, and from a time when oral composition had ceased and public performance was by rhapsodes, not traditional bards. Their significance for us is that they represent the subject-matter of heroic poetry as it was before Homer; for the *Iliad* itself, being the individual creation of a poet of genius, was not typical. Thus, by a time reversal, the partially known later material can make some claim to priority over the earlier. A school of 'neoanalysts' argues that episodes in books 8 (rescue of Nestor), 17 (recovery of the body of Patroclus), 18 (mourning of Thetis), and 23 (funeral games) echo situations connected with Achilles in the repertoire of the oral bards, which later appeared in the cyclic *Aethiopis*. The importance of this is that it seems to give us an insight into the creativity of the *Iliad* poet. See EPIC.   M. M. W.

interpretation of the ancient evidence. Hence, students of classical antiquity need to be clear about when they intend the term 'homosexual' descriptively—i.e. to denote nothing more than same-sex sexual relations—and when they intend it substantively or normatively—i.e. to denominate a discrete kind of sexual psychology or behaviour, a positive species of sexual being, or a basic component of 'human sexuality'. The application of 'homosexuality' (and 'heterosexuality') in a substantive or normative sense to sexual expression in classical antiquity is not advised.

Greek and Roman men (whose sexual subjectivity receives vastly greater attention in the extant sources than does women's) generally understood sex to be defined in terms of sexual penetration and phallic pleasure, whether the sexual partners were two males, two females, or one male and one female. The physical act of sex itself required, in their eyes, a polarization of the sexual partners into the categories of penetrator and penetrated as well as a corresponding polarization of sexual roles into 'active' and 'passive'. Those roles in turn were correlated with superordinate and subordinate social status, with masculine and feminine gender styles, and (in the case of males, at least) with adulthood and adolescence. Phallic insertion functioned as a marker of male precedence; it also expressed social domination and seniority. The isomorphism of sexual, social, gender, and age roles made the distinction between 'activity' and 'passivity' paramount for categorizing sexual acts and actors of either gender; the

distinction between homosexual and heterosexual contacts could still be invoked for certain purposes (e.g. Ov. *Ars am.* 2. 682–4; Achilles Tatius 2. 33–8), but it remained of comparatively minor taxonomic and ethical significance.

Any sexual relation that involved the penetration of a social inferior (whether inferior in age, gender, or status) qualified as sexually normal for a male, irrespective of the penetrated person's anatomical sex, whereas to *be* sexually penetrated was always potentially shaming, especially for a free male of citizen status (e.g. Tac. *Ann.* II. 36). Roman custom accordingly placed the sons of Roman citizens off limits to men. In Classical Athens, by contrast, free boys could be openly courted, but a series of elaborate protocols served to shield them from the shame associated with bodily penetration, thereby enabling them to gratify their male suitors without compromising their future status as adult men.

Pederasty Paiderastia is the word that the Greeks themselves employed to refer to the sexual pursuit of 'boys' (*paides* or *paidika*; Lat. *pueri*) by 'men' (*andres; viri*). The conventional use of the term 'boy' to designate a male in his capacity as an object of male desire is somewhat misleading, because males were customarily supposed to be sexually desirable to other males mostly in the period of life that extended from around the time of puberty (which probably began quite late in the ancient Mediterranean) to the arrival of the full beard (see AGE); the first appearance of down on a boy's cheeks represented to some the peak of his sexual attractiveness, whereas the presence of more fully developed hair on the male face, buttocks, and thighs typically aroused in men intense sexual distaste. By 'boy', then, the ancients designated what we would call an adolescent rather than a child. Moreover, 'man' and 'boy' can refer in both Greek and Latin to the senior and junior partners in a pederastic relationship, or to those who play the respective sexual roles appropriate to each, regardless of their actual ages. A boy on the threshold of manhood might assume the sexual role of a boy in relation to a man as well as the sexual role of a man in relation to another boy (e.g. Xen. *Symp.* 8. 2), but he might not play both roles in relation to the same person. Although some Athenian men may have entertained high-minded intentions towards the boys they courted, it would be hazardous to infer from their occasional efforts at self-promotion (Pl. *Symp.* 184c–185b; Aeschin. *In Tim.* 132–40) that Greek pederasty aimed chiefly at the education and moral improvement of boys instead of at adult sexual pleasure.

Sexual relationships between women are occasionally described by male authors in the vocabulary used to articulate distinctions of age and sexual role in pederasty (e.g. Iut. *Lyc.* 18. 4, *Amat.* 763a), but solid evidence for a comparable polarization of sexual roles in female same-sex sexual relations is lacking.

Periodization The most remarkable feature of ancient same-sex sexual relations is the longevity of the age-structured, role-specific, hierarchical pattern that governed all respectable and virtually all recorded sexual relationships between males in classical antiquity. There is evidence for the existence of such a pattern as early as Minoan times and as late as the end of the Roman empire in the west. *Homer, to be sure, did not portray *Achilles and Patroclus as lovers (although some Classical Athenians thought he implied as much (Aesch. frs. 135, 136 Radt; Pl. *Symp.* 179e–180b; Aeschin. *In Tim.* 133, 141–50)), but he also did little to rule out such an interpretation, and he was perhaps less ignorant of pederasty than is sometimes alleged: he remarks that Ganymedes was carried off to be. the gods' cupbearer because of his beauty (*Il.* 20. 232–5) and he singles out for special mention the man who was—with the exception of Achilles—the most beautiful man in the Greek host (*Il.* 2. 673–4). (Male beauty contests are well documented in the Greek world from Hellenistic times; they may have been institutionalized earlier.)

Sexual relations between males at Rome conformed closely to the age-differentiated, role-specific pattern documented for Greece. The traditional belief that Roman men regarded 'homosexuality' with repugnance and that its presence at Rome was the result of Greek influence is mistaken. To be sure, sexually receptive or effeminate males were harshly ridiculed, and the public courtship of free boys (which the Romans thought of as 'Greek love') was discountenanced as severely as was the seduction of free girls; however, the sexual penetration of male prostitutes or slaves by conventionally masculine élite men, who might purchase slaves expressly for that purpose, was not considered morally problematic. We do hear a good deal more from Roman sources about adult pathics (Sen. *QNat.* 1. 16. 1–3; Petron. *Sat.* 92. 7–9, 105. 9; Juv. *Sat.* 9) and about the sexual pursuit by adult males of male beloveds who had passed beyond the stage of boyhood (Suet. *Galb.* 22). None the less, as in Greece so in Rome did masculinity consist not in the refusal of all sexual contact with males but in the retention of an insertive sexual role and in the preservation of bodily (particularly anal) inviolability.

'Greek Love' The fullest testimony for Greek pederastic norms and practices derives from Classical Athens, but surviving evidence from elsewhere in the Greek world largely accords with the Athenian model. Greek custom carefully differentiated the sexual roles assigned to men and to boys in their erotic relations with one another. Good-looking boys supposedly exerted a powerful sexual appeal that men, even when good-looking, did not. Accordingly, men were assumed to be motivated in their pursuit of boys by a passionate sexual desire (*erōs*) which the boys who were the targets of that desire did not conventionally share, whence the Greek habit of referring to the senior partner in a pederastic relationship as a *subject* of desire, or 'lover' (*erastēs*), and the junior partner as an *object* of desire, or 'beloved' (*erōmenos*). A boy who chose to 'gratify' (*charizesthai*) the passion of his lover might be actuated by a variety of motives, including (on the baser end of the scale) material gain or social climbing and (on the higher end) affection, esteem, respect, and non-passionate love (*philia*), but—although a man might stimulate a boy sexually—neither sexual desire nor sexual pleasure represented an acceptable motive for a boy's compliance with the sexual demands of his lover. Even pederastic relationships characterized by mutual love and tenderness retained an irreducible element of emotional and erotic asymmetry, as is indicated by the consistent distinction which the Greeks drew in such contexts between the lover's *erōs* and the beloved's *philia*. By contrast, women were believed capable of returning their male lovers' sexual passion, and so could be spoken of as exhibiting *anterōs* ('counter-desire')—a term never applied in an erotic sense in the Classical period to boys, except by *Plato in a highly tendentious philosophical context (*Phdr.* 255c–e).

The asymmetries structuring pederastic relationships reflected the underlying division of sexual labour. Whereas a boy, lacking his lover's erotic motivation, was not expected to play what the Greeks considered an 'active' sexual role—he was not expected, that is, to seek a sexual climax by inserting his penis into an orifice in his lover's body—a man was expected to do just that, either by thrusting his penis between the boy's thighs (which was considered the most respectful method, because it did not violate the boy's bodily integrity) or by inserting it into his rectum. Respectable erotic relations between men and boys preserved the social fiction, to which some honourable lovers may even have adhered in actual practice, that sexual penetration of the boy took place only between the legs (the so-called intercrural position), never in the anus or—what was even worse—in the mouth. It was not a question of what people actually did in bed (the boy was conventionally assumed to be anally receptive to his older lover) so much as how they behaved and talked when they were out of bed. Hence the story about Periander, the 6th-cent. BC tyrant of Ambracia, who asked his boy, 'Aren't you pregnant yet?': the boy, who had apparently raised no objection to being anally penetrated on repeated occasions, was sufficiently outraged by this question when it was put to him aloud—and doubtless in the presence of others—that he responded by killing the tyrant in order to recover his masculine honour (Plut. *Amat.* 768f).

The Greek insistence on drawing a clear distinction between the beloved's *philia* and the lover's *erōs* reveals its purpose in this context. Whatever a boy might do in bed, it was crucial that he not seem to be motivated by passionate sexual desire for his lover, because sexual desire for an adult man signified the desire to be penetrated, to be subordinate—to be like a woman, whose pleasure in sexual submissiveness disqualified her from assuming a position of social and political mastery. A boy who indicated that he derived any enjoyment from being anally receptive risked identifying himself as a *kinaidos*, a pathic, a catamite: no modern English word can convey the full force of the ancient stigma attached to this now-defunct identity. Similarly, a man who retained as his beloved a boy on the threshold of manhood thereby cast doubt on his own masculinity, for if the grown boy was not himself a *kinaidos*, then the man who continued to love him must be. And since both Greek men and Greek women (if we credit the desires imputed to the latter by male authors) liked males who looked young, any man who either did look or who tried to look younger than his years exposed himself to the suspicion of harbouring pathic desires or adulterous intentions.

Origins and Causes Scholars have speculated about the factors responsible for the visibility and cultural prestige accorded to pederasty in Greek culture. Among the explanations commonly advanced are: (1) Greek males were driven to seek romance and sexual gratification with other males, *faute de mieux*, by the seclusion and enforced intellectual impoverishment of *women; (2) pederasty was a vestige of earlier male *initiation rituals which featured sexual contact between men and boys. Against the first explanation it may be objected that the seclusion of women was less an actual social practice than an occasional social ideal, that the plentiful availability of both male and female prostitutes (see PROSTITUTION, SECULAR) argues for the existence in some men of specifically pederastic preferences, and that many societies rigorously separate male and female social spheres without also promoting pederasty. In assessing the limited explanatory value of the initiatory model, it is important to notice, first

of all, that pederastic rites of passage are more fully (though still scantily) attested in Crete and the Peloponnese than in Attica; next, that Classical Athenian pederasty proceeded by means of elective pair-bonding, not by the compulsory induction of entire *age classes (individual boys had to be courted, unless they were prostitutes, and they could always withhold their consent); and, finally, that pederastic sex was not a prerequisite for admission to any rank or group membership in Athenian society, and it could in fact lead to the forfeiture of certain privileges, if a boy conducted himself disreputably. Moreover, recent comparative work in ethnography has shifted the burden of explanation by establishing that age-structured and role-specific patterns of same-sex sexual contact are relatively common in pre-industrial cultures, whereas the homosexual/heterosexual pattern is rare, and tends to be limited to the modern, western, industrialized world.

Lesbianism Evidence for sexual relations among women in antiquity is sparse, although ancient writers did on occasion represent women as erotically attracted to one another (e.g. Pl. *Symp.* 191e; Ov. *Met.* 9. 666–797). In an irony all too typical of the state of preservation of ancient sources, the earliest attestation of female homoerotic desire occurs in the work of a male author—namely, in the *partheneia* of the late-7th-cent. Spartan poet *Alcman, who wrote choral odes to be performed by a cohort of unmarried girls in which individual maidens extol the beauty and allure of named favourites among their leaders and age-mates (frs. 1, 3 Page, *PMG*). Further expressions of homoerotic desire can be found a few decades later in the fragmentary poetry of *Sappho, who came from Mytilene on the island of *Lesbos, whence the 19th cent. derived its euphemism for female homosexuality, 'lesbianism'. In antiquity, by contrast, at least from the 5th cent. BC, 'Lesbian' sex referred to fellatio and Sappho figured as a prostitute; the earliest association of Lesbos with female homoeroticism dates to the 2nd cent. AD (Lucian, *Dial. meret.* 5. 2; cf., however, Anac. fr. 358 Page, *PMG*). The interpretation of Sappho's poems is complicated by the fact that no writer of the Classical period found their homoeroticism sufficiently remarkable to warrant mention (although a red-figure Attic hydria, attributed to the Polygnotus group, from about 440 BC portrays Sappho in what may be a female homoerotic setting (Beazley, *ARV²* 1060, no. 145)); the earliest to touch on it were the Augustan poets of the late 1st cent. BC (Hor. *Carm.* 2. 13. 24–5; Ov. *Her.* 15. 15–19, *Tr.* 2. 365). So either Sappho's earlier readers and auditors saw nothing homoerotic in her poems or they saw nothing remarkable in Sappho's homoeroticism. The Sapphic tradition may have been revived by the Hellenistic poet Nossis of Locri.

Perhaps the cultural predominance of the penetration model of sex obscured non-penetrative eroticism among conventionally feminine women, for which in any case there seems to have been no established terminology. The female same-sex sexual practice that imperial Greek and

Roman writers alike singled out for comment was 'trib-adism', the sexual penetration of women (and men) by other women, by means of either a dildo or a fantastically large clitoris. Although the word *tribas* is attested for the first time in Greek in the 2nd cent. AD, an equivalent Latin loan word crops up in the previous century (Phaedrus 4. 15(16). 1; Sen. *Controv.* 1. 2. 23) and the figure of the hyper-masculine phallic woman may be considerably older. The tribade makes memorable appearances, though not always under that name, in imperial literature (Sen. *Ep.* 95. 21; Mart. 1. 90, 7. 67, 7. 70; Lucian *Dial. meret.* 5): she is repre-sented as a shaven-headed butch, adept at wrestling, able to subjugate men and to satisfy women.

Deviance and Toleration Ancient sources are informed by the routine presumption that most free adult males, what-ever their particular tastes, are at least capable of being sexually attracted by both good-looking boys and good-looking women; such attraction was deemed normal and natural. No specifically sexual stigma attached to the act of sexual penetration of a woman, boy, foreigner, or slave by a man, although certain kinds of sexual licence incurred disfavour (the expenditure of extravagant sums of money on prostitutes of either sex, the corruption of free boys, and the adulterous pursuit of citizen women were regarded as signs of bad character in a man and even as actionable offences at Athens; the seduction of free youth of either sex was criminalized as *stuprum* at Rome). Thus, it would not have been unexpected to ask of a man who confessed to being in love whether his object was a boy or a woman, and at least one surviving marriage-contract from Hellenistic *Egypt (*PTeb.* 1. 104) commits the prospec-tive husband not to maintain either a female concubine or a male beloved. The most glamorous and boastworthy same-sex liaison in Greece was that between a free man and a free boy of good family, unaffected by considerations of material gain and untainted by suggestions of sexual degra-dation; a respectable citizen could brag about such a rela-tionship in the lawcourts. And the song of Harmodius and Aristogiton, which celebrated the pederastic couple who supposedly killed one of the Pisistratids and thereby freed Athens from tyranny, functioned in the democratic period as something like the Athenian national anthem.

Not all expressions of same-sex eroticism were approved by the ancients. They did not have a concept of sexual per-version, but they did stigmatize forms of sexual behaviour which they considered shameful, unconventional, or unnatural. Plato is exceptional in treating pederasty (along with female homosexuality) as unnatural in the *Laws* (636b–c, 838–41), although some later moralizing writers did so treat it (along with other civilized luxuries such as warm baths and potted plants: Sen. *Ep.* 122. 7–8). Women who prefer women over men incur male disapproval from Hellenistic times (Asclepiades 7 (Gow–Page, *HE* 1. 46, no. 7)). But what principally seemed deviant to the ancients was sexual behaviour at odds with a person's gender identity and social status—that is, sexual receptivity in men and

sexual insertivity in women, both interpreted as signs of gender inversion. Ancient writers occasionally speculated about the causes of inversion: their explanations range from ingenious physiological hypotheses (Arist. [*Pr.*] 4. 26; Phaedrus 4. 15(16)) to observations about the tyranny of pleasure (Pl. *Grg.* 494c–e) and imputations of pathology (Arist. *Eth. Nic.* 7. 5. 3–4 = 1148^{b}26–35); Caelius Aurelianus, *On chronic diseases* (ed. I. Drabkin), 4. 9). D. M. H.

Horace (*see facing page*)

household

Greek The household (*oikos*) was the fundamental social, political and economic unit of ancient Greece (Arist. *Pol.* 1. 2), though its precise links into larger political and eco-nomic structures changed regionally and over time. At one level was a co-resident group, many (though not all) of whose members were kin or affines (related by marriage). Patrilateral kinship was probably more common than matrilateral in household settings, since marriage was patrilocal, i.e. women tended to move into their husband's house and household on marriage. Though a nuclear family (parents and children) might form the household's core, there is considerable evidence for the regular appear-ance of stem families (nuclear family plus a grandparent) and various kinds of extended families, especially incorpo-rating unmarried female relatives (aunts, sisters, nieces, cousins, etc.). The senior man in the household usually took charge of 'official' relations with the outside world and acted as the head of household (*kyrios*). None the less, women never relinquished membership of the household into which they were born and might move back into it if the marriage were dissolved. Women, then, usually lived out their lives in two households, men in only one.

Households also included many non-kin members, of lower, non-citizen status. Most notable were slaves, who belonged to most of the well-off households mentioned in the sources; see SLAVERY. But other dependants such as freedmen or women might also be present (the household in Demosthenes 47 included an old, ex-slave nurse who must have been of metic status; see METICS). Lodgers (*Antiphon) might also have been considered household members during their sojourn. Households, especially wealthy ones, must often have been quite large. Given the relatively small size of even rich Greek *houses (e.g. at 4th-cent. BC Olynthus the size-range of houses was 150–300 m.²: 1600–3200 ft.²), living conditions must have been crowded by modern standards. See HOUSES, GREEK.

The concept of the household rose above its physical reality and covered not only people but property, land, and animals as well. At this level the households of the élite fre-quently expanded in scope beyond the co-resident unit to include other estates, farms, and businesses. The house-hold formed the most significant structure of economic management in ancient Greece. (See ECONOMY, GREEK.) Transmission of property to the succeeding households of the next generation was via partible inheritance. Because

[*continued on p. 359*]

Horace

Horace (Quintus Horatius Flaccus) was born on 8 December 65 BC in Venusia in Apulia (mod. Venosa) and died on 27 November 8 BC (*Epist.* 1. 20. 26–7; Life). Thanks to the almost complete preservation of *Suetonius' Life (*Vita Hor.*) and numerous biographical allusions in the poetry, we are relatively well informed about his life. His father was a *freedman (*Sat.* 1. 6. 6, 45–6), though this need not mean, as some have supposed, that he had come as a slave from the east. Even an Italian could have been enslaved as a result of the Social War of 91–89 BC (see ROME (HISTORY), §1.5), in which Venusia was captured by Rome. Horace presents himself as brought up in the old Italian style (cf. *Sat.* 1. 4. 105–29 with Ter. *Ad.* 414–19) and his father may well have come from Italy itself. The father had a fairly small landholding in Venusia (*Sat.* 1. 6. 71) but in his role as *coactor* (public auctioneer) obtained what was clearly not an inconsiderable amount of money (*Sat.* 1. 6. 86, Life); otherwise he could not have afforded to send his son to Rome and then Athens for an education that was the equal of that of a typical upper-class Roman of the time (*Sat.* 1. 6. 76–80, *Epist.* 2. 1. 70 f.; Life). This ambitious education was clearly intended to help Horace to rise in society, and at first this plan met with success. While in Athens, Horace joined the army of *Brutus as a *tribunus militum* or military tribune (*Sat.* 1. 6. 47 f.; Life), a post usually held by *equites*. But all these high hopes were brought to nothing by the fall of Brutus and the loss of the family's property (*Epist.* 2. 2. 46–51). Horace counted himself lucky to be able to return to Italy, unlike many of his comrades-in-arms, and to obtain the reasonably respectable position of *scriba quaestorius* (*Sat.* 2. 6. 36 f.; Life). It was in this period that he wrote his first poems (*Epist.* 2. 2. 51 f.), which brought him into contact with *Virgil and Varius Rufus. They recommended him to *Maecenas, then gathering around him a circle of writers; and when Maecenas accepted him into this circle in 38 BC (*Sat.* 1. 6. 52–62, 2. 6. 40–2), and later gave him the famous Sabine farm, his financial position was secure. His property put him in the higher reaches of the *equites* census (cf. *Sat.* 2. 7. 53) and he now possessed the leisure to devote himself to poetry. He was acquainted with many leading Romans, and on friendly terms with a considerable number of them, most notably his patron Maecenas. In his later years *Augustus also sought to be on close terms, as several letters written in a warm and candid tone attest (Life). But Horace knew well how to preserve his personal freedom. Augustus offered him an influential post on his personal staff (*officium epistularum*) but Horace turned this down (Life) and as *Epistle* 1. 7 demonstrates he showed a similar independence towards Maecenas.

Works
Epodes

The *Epodes* or *Iambi* (cf. *Epod.* 14. 7; *Epist.* 1. 19. 23) form a slender book of 17 poems. They include some of Horace's earliest poems, written before the encounter with Maecenas, but work on them continued throughout the 30s BC and poems 1 and 9 allude to the battle of *Actium: the collection as a whole seems to have been published around 30 BC. Horace's formal model was *Archilochus, the founder of *iambus*, to whom he joins Hipponax (*Epod.* 6. 13 f.; *Epist.* 1. 19. 23–5). He thus introduced for the first time into Rome not only the metrical form of early Greek iambus, but also some of the matter (cf. *Epod.* 10, which is closely related to the disputed papyrus fragment Archilochus 79a Diels = Hipponax 115 West). Horace's adoption of this early form may be compared with the incorporation of classical and pre-classical motifs in the visual art of the day, but it did not represent a rejection of the Callimachean principle (see CALLIMACHUS) that every detail of a poem should be artistically controlled and contribute to the overall effect. Even the 'archaic' epodes are written in a style of painstaking elegance. The central theme of iambic poetry was traditionally invective, that is personal attack, mockery, and satire (*Epist.* 1. 19. 25, 30 f.; cf. Arist. *Poet.* 1448^{b}26 ff.), and Horace may have taken up the genre in his affliction after the battle of Philippi (42 BC) as a way of preserving his self-respect in hard times. But only some of the *Epodes* are invectives (4, 5, 6, 8, 10, 12, 17), and even in these the targets are either anonymous or figures about whom we know next to nothing. Horace clearly avoids the sort of personal attacks on important contemporary figures that we find in *Catullus. A different aspect of early Greek poetry is taken up in *Epodes* 7 and 16. Just as the early Greek poets (including Archilochus: cf. fr. 109 West with *Epod.* 16. 17 ff.) on occasions addressed themselves to the general public, so in these poems Horace represents himself as warning and exhorting the Roman people. There are no iambic elements in the poems to Maecenas: *Epod.* 3 is a joke, *Epod.* 14 an excuse, and in *Epod.* 1 and 9 one friend talks to another in the context of the decisive struggles of 31 BC. Other epodes take up motifs from other contemporary genres (elegy in 11 and 15, pastoral in 2) but with significant alterations of tone: Horace ironically breaks the high emotional level of the models with a detached and distant *closure. Epode 13 anticipates a theme of the *Odes* (cf. *Carm.* 1. 7).

Satires

Contemporaneously with the *Epodes*, Horace composed his two books of *satires (*Satira*: 2. 1. 1, 2. 6. 17). He also calls them *Sermones*, 'conversations' (2. 3. 4, *Epist.* 1. 4. 1, 2. 1. 250, 2. 2. 60), which suits their loose colloquial tone that seems to slide from one subject to another almost at random. The first book contains ten satires, the second eight. The earliest datable reference is to the 'journey to Brundisium' undertaken with Maecenas and his circle in 38 or 37 BC and described at length in *Sat.* 1. 5, the latest is to the settlement of veterans after the civil war in 30 BC (*Sat.* 2. 6. 55 f.). Some of the poems may have been written before 38, but there is no evidence that any are later than 30. Horace's model is Lucilius, but he represents himself as determined to write with greater care and attention to form (*Sat.* 1. 4, 1. 10, 2. 1), and thus, again, as a follower of Callimachus (cf. especially *Sat.* 1. 10. 9–15, 67–74). Another difference from Lucilius is that Horace's satires are less aggressive. While the pugnacious poet of the 2nd cent. took sides in the political struggles of his time, Horace chooses a purely private set of themes. In *Sat.* 1. 4 and 2. 1 he represents personal abuse as a typical element in satire, but declares that he himself does not attack any contemporary public figures. When he names people as possessed of particular vices, as in the *Epodes* they are either unknown or no longer alive, and it is clear that the names represent types rather than individual targets. The criticism of vice occurs less for its own sake than to show the way to a correct way of life through an apprehension of error. In these passages Horace comes close to the doctrines and argument-forms of popular philosophy (so-called diatribe), even if he rejects the sometimes fanciful tone of the Cynic-Stoic wandering preachers; see CYNICS; STOICISM. His style is rather to tell the truth through laughter (*ridentem dicere verum*), and not only to show others the way but also to work at improving himself and making himself more acceptable to his fellow human beings (*Sat.* 1. 4. 133–8). The autobiographical aspect of many satires is another Lucilian element. Just like Lucilius, he makes his own life a subject for his poetry, and his personal situation is a central theme of poems like *Sat.* 1. 4, 1. 6, 1. 9, and 2. 6, and a partial concern in many others. Both books are arranged according to theme. In the first book, related poems are grouped together in three groups of three: 1–3 are diatribes, 4–6 are autobiographical, and 7–9 relate anecdotes, while in the last poem of the book Horace offers a retrospective look at the individuality of his satiric production. In contrast to the first book, the poems of the second book are mostly dialogues. They are arranged so that poems from the second half of the book parallel poems of the first in motif: in the dialogues of *Sat.* 1 and 5 an expert is asked for advice, the theme of 2 and 6 is the value of a simple life on the land, in 3 and 7 Horace faces some decidedly dubious representatives of popular philosophy who inflict long sermons on him, and the theme of 4 and 9 is the luxuriousness of contemporary Roman banqueting.

Odes (Carmina)

After the publication of the *Epodes* and *Satires* around 30 BC, Horace turned to lyric poetry. The earliest datable reference is in *Odes* 1. 37, which celebrates Augustus' defeat of *Cleopatra at Actium in 31 BC, though it is not impossible that some odes were written earlier than this: 1. 14, for instance, on the 'ship of state', whose situation fits best the time before Actium (though the poem is open to different interpretations, and it has even been doubted whether it is in fact a political allegory at all). At any rate, the first three books of the *Odes*, 88 poems in all, seem to have been published as a collection in 23 BC. The concluding poem, 3. 30, looks back on the work as a completed unit, and does not envisage a sequel. After the composition, at Augustus' bidding, of the *Carmen saeculare* in 17, however, a fourth book of 15 poems was added, which also seems to have been inspired by Augustus (Life).

Horace declares that his main literary model in the *Odes* was the early Greek *lyric poetry from *Lesbos, especially that of *Alcaeus (*Carm.* 1. 1. 33 f., 1. 32, 3. 30. 13 f.; *Epist.* 1. 19. 32 f.). He is indebted to this model for the metrical form of the *Odes* but he also begins a series of poems with an almost literal translation of lines by Alcaeus (the so-called 'mottoes'), which serve as a springboard for his own developments (e.g. 1. 9, 1. 18, 1. 37, 3. 12). He also takes over motifs from other early lyric poets, such as *Sappho (1. 13), *Anacreon (1. 23), and *Pindar (1. 12, 3. 4, and some of the higher-style poems in book 4). His view of this early poetry, however, is that of a poet trained in the modern contemporary Hellenistic style: the *Odes* are not written in the simple language of the archaic models but are full of the dense and sophisticated allusivity that was the inevitable result of the complex literary world of Augustan Rome. He also takes over a number of themes from Hellenistic poetry, especially from Greek *epigram (cf. 1. 5, 1. 28, 1. 30, 3. 22, 3. 26).

Although the major themes of the *Odes* are the usual ones of ancient poetry, Horace's treatment of them is, as far as we can tell, markedly different. The hymns to the gods, for instance, are not meant for cult performance but encounter the world of Greek divinity more with aesthetic pleasure than in an act of pious worship. His love poetry takes a different line from that of his contemporaries. While Catullus and the elegists (see ELEGIAC POETRY, LATIN) had tended to make a single beloved the focus of their life and poetry, Horace's poems are concerned with a variety of women (and boys; see HOMOSEXUALITY). Although passionate obsession is not entirely alien to the *Odes*, typically Horace tries to free himself from extreme emotion and move himself and his beloved towards a calm and cheerful enjoyment of the moment. The sympotic poetry (see SYMPOSIUM) diverges distinctively from that of Alcaeus. Horace does not set out to drown his sorrows, but to give himself and his friends at the drinking-party a brief moment of freedom from care, in poems which, as earlier in the *Satires*, lead often to reflection on the right way to live one's life. Friendship is an important theme throughout the *Odes*: they are hardly ever soliloquies, but poems addressed to a friend offering help and advice. The political themes begun in the *Epodes* are taken further. Although Horace declines to celebrate Augustus or Agrippa in the traditional Roman form of panegyric epic (1. 6, 1. 12), from the time of the poem celebrating the defeat of Cleopatra (1. 37) on he offers explicit praise of the new ruler as one who had brought peace and through his policies maintained it. He also declares his support for the attempt by Augustus to restore 'ancient Roman' customs and morality (3. 1–6 and 3. 24). In the later *Ode* 3. 14, in the *Carmen saeculare*, and in the poems of book 4 the panegyric of the Augustan epoch comes even more to the fore, and it is celebrated as an epoch of peace, a second golden age.

Horace's *Odes* differ in one essential respect from the norms of modern, especially post-Romantic, lyric poetry. Modern lyric strives as far as possible for a unity of atmosphere within one poem, but this is found in Horace only in his shortest poems. More commonly, as F. Klingner *Studien zur römischen und griechischen Literatur* (1964) noted, within a single poem there are significant movements and changes in content, expression, and stylistic level. Poems written in high style with important content often conclude with a personal and apparently insignificant final turn. In other odes, the whole poem moves considerably from the content or atmosphere of the opening, most often from a distressed or agitated emotional level to a dissipation of tension. In other odes again, a concrete situation gives rise to thoughts which move far away from it, with the result that the meaning of the poem seems to rest on these general reflections rather than in the poem's situation. And a fourth possibility is a form of ring-composition: an opening section is followed by a second part very different in content and tone, and the final section then returns to the mood of the opening. A harmonious balance is also aimed at in the order of poems within the books. Poems of important content and accordingly a high stylistic register tend to be placed at the beginning and end of books, with lighter poems placed next to them for contrast (cf. 1. 4, 1. 5, 2. 4, 2. 5, 3. 7–3. 10 towards the beginning of books, 3. 26, 3. 28, 4. 12 towards the end). In contrast, the first book ends with the light, cheerful short sympotic poem 1. 38, preceded by the weighty victory poem 1. 37.

Epistles *book 1*

After the publication of the *Odes*, Horace returned to hexameter poetry and the conversational style of his earlier *Sermones*, but this time in the form of letters addressed to a variety of recipients. Although Lucilius had written satires in the form of letters, the notion of a complete book of verse epistles was comparatively novel. The poems are naturally not real letters actually sent to their addressees, but the choice of the letter-form was a literary device which gave Horace a concrete starting-point and a unified speech-situation. The dating of the collection is uncertain: the last line of *Epistles* 1. 20 refers to the consuls of 21 BC, and many would place the publication in that year, but 1. 12. 26 seems to refer to the defeat of the Spanish Cantabri in 19 BC (Cass. Dio 54. 11). In the programmatic *Epistle* 1. 1 Horace grounds his choice of the new form in his advancing old age: philosophical reflection and a concentration on questions of how to lead one's life now suit him better than the usual themes of lyric. The philosophical meditation that this declaration places at the centre of his work is an essential theme of the book, but not its only concern. Horace writes also more generally of the circumstances of his own life, and offers his friends various forms of counsel. Many elements recall the *Satires*, but the choice of the letter-form brings a more unified tone to the varied content. The last epistle (1. 20) is an address to the book itself, portrayed as a young slave eager to be free of its master.

Epistles *book 2*, Ars poetica

From *Satires* 1. 4 and 1. 10 on, poetry itself had been a constant concern of Horace's poetry, and this becomes the central theme of the two long poems of *Epistles* book 2 (2. 1. to Florus and 2. 2 to Augustus) and the *Ars poetica*. These poems are again hard to date: but *Epist*. 2. 2. 141 ff. contrasts a philosophical concern for the right way of life with the themes of lyric in similar terms to *Epist*. 1. 1 and the two poems are unlikely to be far apart chronologically. *Epist*. 2. 2 is thus probably written before Horace's resumption of lyric poetry in book 4 of the *Odes* (17 BC). On the other hand *Epist*. 2. 1. 132–7 probably alludes to the *Carmen saeculare*, and 2. 1. 252 seems to recall *Odes* 4. 14. 11 f. from the year 15. Thus the letter to Augustus (2. 1) seems to be later than the letter to Florus (2. 2). The dating of the *Ars poetica* is particularly controversial: in 301–9 Horace says that he is not currently writing (lyric) poetry, but this ironic remark can be situated either before or after *Odes* book 4. The interpretation of all three letters is difficult, because their logical articulation is deliberately obscured by the colloquial tone of a *sermo* or conversation and their various themes are interwoven without clearly marked transitions between them. The great commentary of C. O. Brink has however made many points clearer. In the letter to Augustus (2. 1), Horace complains that the taste of the contemporary public turns more to the cheap theatrical effects of earlier Latin writers than the authors of his own generation. He sees this as unfair, and accuses the older writers of being careless and deficient in taste. The letter to Florus (2. 2.) is more personal. In it, Horace explains to his friend why he no longer writes poetry but has turned to philosophy, and offers a candid picture of the restrictions and difficulties of a poet's life at Rome. The *Ars poetica* begins with the proposition that every poem must be a unified whole (1–41), and after a few verses on the necessary ordering of material (42–4) turns to poetic language and the correspondingly appropriate style (45–118). Lines 119–52 then move via a sliding transition to the choice of material and its treatment, with examples taken both from epic and from drama. Lines 153–294 concentrate on the various genres of dramatic poetry, and in the final section (295–476), after another sliding transition, the reader is offered general rules for the poet's craft. This varied subject-matter is given unity by the recurring insistence on values such as appropriateness, clarity, and artistic composition. Horace's teaching lies in the tradition of *Aristotle's school, the Peripatetic, though the *Ars* does not draw directly on the extant *Poetics* and *Rhetoric* but on later versions of the school's doctrine, particularly (according to the ancient commentator Pomponius Porphyrio) the early Hellenistic philosopher Neoptolemus of Parium. There are striking parallels between the *Ars* and the meagre fragments we possess of Neoptolemus, but it is not impossible that other works also lie behind the *Ars*. At any rate, Horace's own contribution lies less in offering a new view of the existing tradition than in his poetic transformation of it through images and vignettes.   H. P. S.

the household conceptually constituted the limits of trust and loyalty, businesses and long-term financial arrangements rarely expanded beyond it. Even on the death of the head of household, male heirs (normally brothers) did not necessarily divide all the economic resources and construct two new households (Lys. 32).   L. F.

Roman 'Household' is the usual English translation of Latin *familia*, a term to which the jurist Ulpian (*Dig.* 50. 16. 195. 1–5), understanding its application to both property and persons, assigned several meanings: the physical household; the persons comprising a household (e.g. patron and freedman); a body of persons united by a common legal tie such as all kin subject to a living *paterfamilias* (male with paternal authority in law), or a body more loosely connected such as all agnatically related kin; a body of slaves, or slaves and sons; and all blood descendants of an original family founder. (To some degree *familia* overlapped with the term *domus*.) Accordingly, study of the Roman household can range from archaeological investigation of the physical structures in which Romans lived (see HOUSES, ITALIAN) to the exclusive history of *slavery. But it is now primarily associated with the field of family history, the principal constituents of which are the composition, organization and evolution of the family through its life-course. Understood ideally to comprise a married couple, their children, the house in which they lived, and their common property (which could include human property), the household in *Cicero's view (*Off.* 1. 54) was the very foundation of society. The special case of Roman *Egypt apart, it is about the household at the social level Cicero represents that most is known.

The orientation of the household was strictly patriarchal, with its head (*paterfamilias*) wielding enormous power (*patria potestas*) over his dependants, including the power of life and death over his children and slaves. In reality the implicit harshness of the regime towards adult children who, unless emancipated, could not become legally independent and own property until their fathers died, was probably tempered by demographic factors that released many from its constricting effects as they reached their early and mature adult years. The role of the *materfamilias*, stereotypically conceived, was subordinate and, beyond reproduction in marriage, largely confined to matters of domestic management in a context where ideas

of economic self-sufficiency were all-important. It does not follow, however, that Roman wives and mothers were devoid of all social and economic power, as the example of Cicero's wife Terentia indicates. The ideal was propagated that marriage (see MARRIAGE LAW) was a union for life, but because of early spousal death and divorce both men and women might anticipate a succession of marriages through their adult lives. This frequently produced family and household reconstitution, with principals commonly finding themselves aligned in complex familial arrangements, involving both kin and non-kin members. Accordingly the composition of the Roman household was far from simple, its membership constantly in flux, and, especially because of the presence of servants (to whom the day-to-day care of children was often entrusted), not at all confined to immediate nuclear attachments.   K. R. B.

houses, Greek Private houses of the Classical and Hellenistic periods were basically the same throughout the Greek world. Most rooms opened onto one or more sides of a small, rectangular courtyard, as did a doorway to the street, often preceded by a short passage. Windows were few and small and living areas were not visible from the street. An upper storey, reached by a ladder or, more rarely, a built stairway, was common but is often hard to detect. Construction was in mud-brick or rubble on stone socles. Interior walls were plastered and often painted simply, mostly in red and white. Floors were of beaten earth. In most houses, on the ground floor, one or two rooms with heavier floors and provisions for bathing, heating water, and cooking can be identified, but cooking could take place on simple hearths or portable braziers in any room or in the courtyard. The concept of the hearth and its goddess, Hestia, symbolized the identity and cohesion of the *household (*oikos*) but formal, fixed hearths were not common, nor were *altars for domestic ritual.

A larger room, facing south for winter sunshine, and shaded by a shallow porch, may often have served as the principal living-room in the type of house that has been termed *prostas* (it is especially clear at Priene). A type with a long porch or room fronting more than one other room has been called the *pastas* type (favoured at Olynthus, Thasos, and Eretria). Roofs were either pitched and covered with brush and terracotta tiles (or only by brush) or flat, depending on regional climate and traditions.

Frequently a more elaborately decorated room with a distinctive floor-plan served to receive guests, predominantly men (it was usually called the *andrōn*, 'men's room'). The floor, in cement, was raised slightly around all four sides for the placement of dining-couches, usually five, seven, or eleven in number, which resulted in the room's doorway being off-centre (see SYMPOSIUM). The lower rectangle in the middle of the room was sometimes decorated with pebble *mosaics. The *andrōn* has been found in modest as well as large houses, in country as well as town, all over Greece, but is lacking at Thasos.

Women's quarters are mentioned in literary sources but cannot be securely identified in the surviving architecture and are not simply to be equated with the second storey. Rather, certain rooms or areas of the house, depending on the composition and needs of the inhabitants, were assigned primarily to women. The house as a whole may have been regarded as women's domain (see WOMEN), apart from the *andrōn* and wherever unmarried men, slave or free, slept. No distinct quarters for slaves are distinguishable architecturally, although female slaves might be separated by a locked door from the male.

The household was an economic as well as social unit. Much of the processing and storage of the products of the family's land took place in the house. Stone parts of oil-presses have been found in the houses of towns inhabited mostly by farmers. Wells, cisterns for rainwater, and pits for collecting waste for manure are found in courtyards; see WATER. If a craft was practised that too took place in the house; distinctive workshops are rare. One room, opening onto the street, was sometimes separated to serve as a shop, not necessarily occupied by the residents of the house. Houses could be home to several persons or families, especially in cities like Athens with large transient, foreign, and slave populations (see METICS; SLAVERY).

The same general concept and design of the private house was used in city, village, and countryside. In the last the courtyard might be larger to accommodate animals and equipment and commonly a tower of two or three storeys, round or square, and more heavily built than the rest, was entered from the courtyard. Such towers, often the only conspicuous remains of houses in the countryside, have been identified in towns as well. They appear to have been used primarily for the safe keeping of goods and persons, slave and free, especially, but not only, in more isolated locations.

The development of the Greek house is inseparable from that of the settlement. Houses were contiguous, sharing party-walls. The privacy of each adjacent unit and the concomitant independence of each *oikos* were vital. When new settlements were established, streets were laid out orthogonally (see URBANISM); initially house plots were probably of uniform size, though in the course of time changes occurred. The modesty of the Classical houses of all classes is striking. Large houses with two courtyards are first found in Eretria in the 4th cent. BC and in towns of the Hellenistic period. Courtyards may have a peristyle on four sides. Only in the Hellenistic and Roman periods do some Greek houses approximate to the descriptions of the Roman author *Vitruvius (*De arch.* 6. 7). The palaces of monarchs and tyrants (see TYRANNY) took the form of elaborations of the larger private houses.   M. H. J.

houses, Italian The social structures which underlay the Greek house, a *household unit (in Greek, *oikos*), which was capable of representing both a citizen lot in the space of the town, and the symbolic abode of the head of a lineage, were shared by Italy in the period of its first *urbanism. Where there was an idea of equality among a limited group of ruling families the two ideas coalesced comfortably. *Etruscan urbanism shows signs of both ends of this spectrum; fine aristocratic houses are known, which tally with the power and pretensions of what we know of some of the city élites, while the urban texture of places like Marzabotto resembles the topography of wider citizen franchise as seen at Olynthus or Priene. The discoveries of the 1980s on the slopes of the Palatine hill at Rome showed how already in the 6th cent. BC the Roman élite was living along the Sacred Way (via Sacra), beside the Forum, in a series of roughly equal *oikopeda* (house-plots) of considerable size which formed the base of the topography of the area until the great fire of AD 64. The Roman aristocracy thus identified itself with a historic home in the city centre as much as any early modern or modern aristocrat with a feudal estate in the countryside. Something similar may be guessed for other Italian aristocracies of tenacious traditions like that of Tarquinii.

This is the background to the first really copious evidence, the 3rd–2nd-cent. BC houses of *Pompeii, which show a regular plan and a systematic division of urban space, but a very considerable variety of size and levels of wealth, the House of the Faun being absolutely outstanding by the standards of anywhere in the Mediterranean world. In these houses it is relatively easy to identify the features which *Vitruvius, our principal literary source, regarded as canonical, but their evolution in different parts of Italy should not be taken for granted. The traditional houses of the centre of Rome seem also to have adhered to the basic pattern of atrium with rooms round it; where more space was available, this traditional arrangement could be combined with peristyles and gardens, offering scope for planned suites of rooms, interesting light effects, and amenities such as ornamental plantings or fountains, and providing more flexible spaces for living, entertaining, politics, and the cultural activities which were integral to upper-class life. The politicians of the late republic were credited with various changes to the use of houses; and luxury in domestic appointments was thought to have taken off dramatically in the 1st cent. BC; but the setting for both processes seems to have been the traditional 'Pompeian/Vitruvian' house.

The salient feature of this traditional plan was the atrium—a rectangular space open to the sky at the centre,

houses, Italian The Italian house was a religious unit under the protection of household gods. This wall-painting from a house at
*Pompeii depicts (centre) the *genius* (guardian) of the male head of the house or *paterfamilias,* flanked by two Lares, gods of the home.

columned in the more elaborate forms, with wide covered spaces on each of the four sides, one of which gave onto the outside world through a vestibule. Originally the site of the family hearth, whose smoke caused the blackening (*ater*) which gave the place its name, this was also the abode of the household deities, and housed the copies of the funerary masks which were the sign of the family's continuity and identity. The adjacent rooms, including a *tablinum* and *cubicula*, were in fact flexible in their use, and this flexibility is the key to the understanding of all Roman domestic space, even in very much more elaborate dwellings. A *triclinium* for convivial dining was an early and frequent adjunct, but meals could be taken in a variety of different rooms, if they were available, according to season and weather.

*Augustus' house on the Palatine, reached by passing along the street of venerable aristocratic addresses (the houses had been rebuilt many times) from the Forum, consisted of an amalgamation of several *domus* of the traditional sort, so that he could enjoy the advantages of considerable space while claiming moderation in his domestic circumstances. The building of very large complexes nearby under *Gaius (for example, the platform of the 'Domus Tiberiana', which supported a country villa in the heart of Rome) and *Nero, whose Golden House (Domus Aurea) spread over a large section of the city centre and took playful manipulation of Roman domestic tradition to the limit, took a different line, but *Domitian's enormous palace, overpowering and monarchic in its axiality though it was, is recognizably an ancient *domus* on a hugely inflated scale.

For most inhabitants of the Roman city, however, this spacious life was impossible; it was normal to live in someone else's property, and in much less space. The wealthy had long accommodated slaves, dependants, and visitors around the principal spaces of their houses—on the street frontages, from which the principal rooms were averted, on upper floors, or even under the floors of the main premises, in warrens of small rooms. Parts of the *domus* accessible from outside could be let profitably for accommodation or for a variety of economic activities. Purpose-built rental accommodation, in the form of whole blocks in the city or its environs given over to the sort of unit that fringed a normal *domus*, goes back at least to the middle republic. The demand for such premises grew so fast that those who could afford to build them saw a valuable source of rental income, and a style of architecture developed which had this type of dwelling-space in mind. By the imperial period, multi-storey tenement blocks, which are usually known as *insulae*, housed all but a tiny fraction of the population of Rome and other big cities. Not all this accommodation was of low quality; some was sited in attractive areas, some *cenacula* (apartments) were sufficiently large, those on the lower floors were not inconvenient (the 'Garden Houses' at *Ostia for instance), and many people of quite high status could afford no better. The introduction of kiln-fired brick almost certainly made these developments safer and more salubrious than had been the case in the republic. Estimates of the living conditions in the *insulae* we know best, those of Ostia—where we cannot tell if we are looking at privileged or marginal housing—illustrate a more general difficulty in the study of the Roman house, that of understanding the density of occupation and the pattern of human interaction represented by the layout of rooms. Scholarship has concentrated on typology rather than function, and has been given to making facile assumptions about standards of comfort, convenience, and cleanliness based on modern cultural stereotypes. Despite the enormous quantity of archaeological explanation, ancient domestic society still needs investigation.

The atrium proved remarkably tenacious. But by late antiquity the houses of even the topmost élite had adopted in preference the looser arrangements of porticoes and reception rooms which had been developed in suburban villas (*horti*, see GARDENS) and the country *villa.   N. P.

housework, a specifically female task, was evidently not of interest to male authors, and there are no surviving household accounts or instructions. 'Women's work' meant weaving and the other tasks required in fabric-making: cleaning and carding wool, spinning and dyeing thread. *Xenophon, in the *Oeconomicus*, envisages a young wife whose only domestic training is in fabric-making: he suggests that she can train slaves to make fabric, supervise household supplies, equipment, and labour, and, for exercise, fold clothes and bedding and knead dough. Columella (*Rust.* 12. 1–3) says that the bailiff's wife on a Roman estate should supervise wool-working and preparation of meals, and should ensure that the kitchens, the shelters for animals, and especially the sickroom are clean. But there is silence on the details of ordinary daily tasks: providing meals and washing up; washing and drying clothes and household textiles; cleaning the house and its equipment, including fireplaces, braziers, and lamps; and, in many households, tending plants, poultry, and domestic animals. There are inscriptions recording the jobs of slaves in great Roman households, but they specify the more prestigious tasks of the dining-room staff and personal attendants.

The most informative sources on everyday housework are Christian texts on virginity, which (if addressed to women) emphasize the burdens of the harassed housewife or (if addressed to men) minimize the tasks for which a man might want a female partner: washing clothes, making beds, lighting fires, and cooking (see COOKERY). Some household equipment has survived relatively well, especially pottery, metal furniture and tableware, and stone tables and benches, but there are few examples of wooden furniture or textiles. See HOUSEHOLD; HOUSES, GREEK and ITALIAN; TEXTILE PRODUCTION.   E. G. C.

hubris, intentionally dishonouring behaviour, was a powerful term of moral condemnation in ancient Greece; and in Athens, and perhaps elsewhere, it was also treated as a serious crime. The common use of *hubris* in English to suggest pride, over-confidence, or any behaviour which may offend divine powers, rests, it is now generally held, on misunderstanding of ancient texts, and concomitant and over-simplified views of Greek attitudes to the gods have lent support to many doubtful, and often over-Christianizing, interpretations, above all of Greek tragedy.

The best ancient discussion of *hubris* is found in *Aristotle's *Rhetoric*: his definition is that *hubris* is 'doing and saying things at which the victim incurs shame, not in order that one may achieve anything other than what is done, but simply to get pleasure from it. For those who act in return for something do not commit *hubris*, they avenge themselves. The cause of the pleasure for those committing *hubris* is that by harming people, they think themselves superior; that is why the young and the rich are hubristic, as they think they are superior when they commit *hubris*' (*Rh.* 1378^{b}23–30). This account, locating *hubris* within a framework of ideas concerned with the honour and shame of the individual, which took a central place in the value-systems of the ancient Greeks, fits very well the vast majority of texts exploiting the notion, from *Homer till well after Aristotle's own time (with the notable exception of some philosophically significant developments in some of *Plato's later works). While it primarily denotes gratuitous dishonouring by those who are, or think they are, powerful and superior, it can also at times denote the insolence of accepted 'inferiors', such as women, children, or slaves, who disobey or claim independence; or it may be used to emphasize the degree of humiliation actually inflicted on a victim, regardless of the agent's intention; some cases, especially applied to verbal insults, may be humorously exaggerated; and revenge taken to excessive or brutal lengths can be condemned as constituting fresh *hubris*.

Hubris is most often the insulting infliction of physical force or violence: classic cases are Meidias' punch on *Demosthenes' face in the theatre (see Demosthenes 21), and the assaults by Conon and sons on the speaker of Demosthenes 54, when the middle-aged Conon allegedly gloated over the body of their battered victim in the manner of a triumphant fighting-cock. Further common forms of hubristic acts are sexual assaults (rape, seduction, or deviant practices), where emphasis is thereby placed on the dishonour inflicted on the victims or on the male householders responsible for them. Since states too seek to protect their honour, *hubris* is commonly applied to invasions, imperialist 'enslavement', or military savagery, often, but not exclusively, when committed by '*barbarian' powers. In consequence, Greek cities took *hubris* very seriously as a political danger, both to their collective freedom and status, and as communities functioning internally through respect for law and the well-being of their members. Unchecked *hubris* was held to be characteristic of *tyrannies, or of *oligarchies or democracies serving their own class (depending on one's viewpoint), and to be a major cause of *stasis* or civil wars. In Athens, probably from *Solon's laws of the early 6th cent. BC, a legal action for *hubris* existed, and its public significance was signalled by the possibility of the heaviest penalties, and by the fact that the action was (as a *graphē*; see LAW AND PROCEDURE, ATHENIAN , §3) open to any Athenian with full citizen rights, not restricted to the victim of the dishonour. While our limited evidence suggests that the action was infrequently used, its ideological importance as a safeguard for poorer citizens in the democracy was none the less considerable.

Hubris is not essentially a religious term; yet the gods naturally were often supposed to punish instances of it, either because they may feel themselves directly dishonoured, or, more frequently, because they were held to uphold general Greek moral and social values. Nor is it helpful to see Greek tragedy centrally concerned to display the divine punishment of hubristic heroes; tragedy focuses rather on unjust or problematic suffering, whereas full-scale acts of *Hubris* by the powerful tend to deprive them of the human sympathy necessary for tragic victims.

N. R. E. F.

Hyperides (389–322 BC), prominent Athenian statesman, rated by the ancients second only to *Demosthenes amongst the canonical Ten Orators. He studied rhetoric under *Isocrates and began his career by writing speeches for others (i.e. he was a *logographos*). His political career opened with an attack on Aristophon in 363/2. There were other, perhaps numerous, such prosecutions of leading figures, the most notable being his successful prosecution of Philocrates in 343 which heralded his future bitter opposition to Macedon (see PHILIP II), and after the battle of Chaeronea (338 BC) he assumed a leading role. Immediately after the action in which 1,000 Athenians had died and 2,000 were captured, he sought to provide replacements by making *metics citizens and freeing slaves; he was himself duly indicted for this unconstitutional measure but it showed his determination to resist, as did indeed his prosecution of Demades and other collaborationists and his vigorous plea to the Athenians not to accede to *Alexander the Great's demand in 335 for Demosthenes and others (amongst whom Hyperides was counted by *Arrian, but *Plutarch *Dem.* 23 makes it clear enough that he was not one). In 324/3 he led the attack on Demosthenes and others who were accused of appropriating the money deposited by Harpalus. Presumably he wanted it for the coming revolt against Macedon. Indeed Hyperides was the chief supporter of Leosthenes and of Athenian action in the Lamian War of 323–322 BC. Fittingly he was chosen to deliver the Funeral Oration of late 323, a speech of which much survives. With the collapse of the Greek resistance, Hyperides had to flee. He was captured and put to death, Antipater, in one version, first ordering the cutting out of the tongue which had so bitterly assailed him and Macedon, a not ignoble end for one of the heroes of Greek liberty.

Works Although in antiquity of the 77 speeches preserved under the name of Hyperides over 50 were regarded as genuine, except for a few fragments his work was unknown to moderns until 1847. Between that year and 1892 papyri were discovered containing several of his speeches, in whole or in part, most notably the all too fragmentary attack on Demosthenes of 324/3.

In general tone he is akin to *Lysias. He borrowed words and phrases from comedy, thus bringing his language into touch with the speech of everyday life. 'Longinus' *On the Sublime* draws attention to his wit, his suavity and persuasiveness, his tact and good taste. He can be sarcastic and severe without becoming offensive; his reproof often takes the form of humorous banter. He speaks with respect of his adversaries and avoids scurrilous abuse.

G. L. C.

Icaros (mod. Failaka), an island off Kuwait, at the mouth of an ancient course of the Euphrates river. It was settled from the third millennium BC, and visited by an expedition sent by *Alexander the Great to the Persian Gulf (Strabo 16. 3. 2): *Ikaros* might be the Hellenization (i.e. Greek version) of a local name. The *Seleucids built a fortress on Failaka, in use from the early 3rd to the mid-2nd cent. BC: it is 60 m. (200 ft.) square, and two temples were excavated inside the walls; two other sanctuaries were found outside. Greek material and inscriptions attest a Macedonian settlement which probably served as a military—and naval—outpost on the maritime route to *India. After the fall of the Seleucid empire, the island temporarily came under Characenian domination in the 1st cent. AD. A Christian church of the 6th cent. has recently been excavated.

J.-F. S.

imagery The identification of scenes in sculpture, painting, and the minor arts has long been a major activity of classical *archaeology, although it has traditionally been accorded less emphasis than the identification of artists' hands. In all the figurative arts conventional schemes were developed, sometimes under the influence of near-eastern iconography, for portraying particular mythological figures and episodes, and the use and development of these schemes can now conveniently be studied through the *Lexicon Iconographicum Mythologi ae Classicae* (=LIMC, 1981–). Individual artists exploited conventional imagery not simply by replicating it, but by playing variations on a theme or by echoing the conventional scheme for one episode when portraying a different one. An extreme form of this is iconographic parody.

The origins of particular iconographic schemes, and the reasons why the popularity of scenes changes over time, are rarely clear. Ceramic vessels may owe some of their imagery to lost gold or silver plate, and some vases can reasonably be held to take over the imagery of lost wall-paintings or of famous sculptures, such as the Tyrannicides group, although it is also possible in some cases that vase-painting influenced subsequent sculptural imagery.

Influence from drama (see TRAGEDY, GREEK and COMEDY, GREEK) has also frequently been alleged: few images in Attic vase-painting represent scenes from tragedies on stage in any straightforward way, but direct representation of scenes from comic drama is popular in 4th-cent. BC south Italian pottery. In the Greek world, public sculpture often carried broadly political meaning, using the otherness of more or less fantastic figures, *Centaurs or *Amazons, to define the behaviour of the good citizen. Whether particular mythical images on pottery also carry political significance, and the popularity of particular scenes at particular times is a result of their value as political *propaganda, is more hotly debated. At Rome, sculptural style as well as imagery were used to convey political points, particularly during the empire, and the Classical and Hellenistic Greek and republican Roman heritage was manipulated to political ends.

Recently, much work has been devoted to the non-mythological imagery on painted pottery, and has exploited this to excavate the ideology of the Greek city, stressing the way in which imagery can create ways of seeing as well as reflect them. Changes in the popularity of particular scenes or types of scene over time, at least when those changes extend over the work of several different painters, may indicate changing social agendas. There is no doubt that the imagery on pots has a close relationship with the use to which those pots are put, and this can be seen particularly clearly with both vessels deposited in graves and vessels used at the *symposium, many of which are, in one way or another, self-referential. One of the most valuable sources of information here lies in the way in which painters restrict scenes of certain types of activity to imaginary characters, such as *satyrs. But it is obviously problematic to assume that the attitudes displayed at the symposium were shared by society as a whole. The chance preservation of extensive areas of private housing at *Pompeii and *Herculaneum, enables us to see programmes of imagery with which some rich individuals surrounded themselves, and the care and originality with which they constructed visual narratives out of linked imagery.

Icaros View of the 3rd–2nd-cent. BC Greek *temple inside the *Seleucid fortress on Icaros, an island off Kuwait (mod. Failaka). Seleucid interest in the Persian gulf was a legacy from *Alexander the Great, whose unrealized plans to conquer and colonize eastern Arabia reflect the region's importance in the lucrative ancient *trade in incense and spices.

Images were an extremely important part of religious cult. Cult statues sometimes incorporated whole programmes of mythical imagery, as in the Athena Parthenos. In the Roman world religious imagery became increasingly complex, and more or less arcane symbolic programmes are associated with mystery cults. Christianity, with its use of types and antitypes drawn from pagan mythology as well as from both Old and New Testaments, further enriched the interpretative range of familiar imagery. See ART, ANCIENT ATTITUDES TO; ART, FUNERARY; MYTHOLOGY; PAINTING; PISISTRATUS; POTTERY; PROPAGANDA; SCULPTURE.

R. G. O.

imperialism

Carthaginian See CARTHAGE.

Greek and Hellenistic One Greek definition of *freedom included the ability of a state to exercise rule over others (cf. Hdt. 1. 210; Thuc. 8. 68. 4; Arist. *Pol.* 1333^b38–1334^a2; Polyb. 5. 106. 4–5). The 5th-cent. BC Athenians justified their rule over other Greeks by appealing to the motives of fear, honour, and interest: 'it has always been the law that the weaker should be subject to the stronger' (Thuc. 1. 76. 2). *Thucydides himself interpreted the early history of Greece as the gradual emergence of greater powers with the ability to control superior resources (1. 1–19). It was common for the major states to seek to dominate weaker ones, as *Syracuse in Sicily, especially under the tyrants (see TYRANNY), and Sparta and Athens on the mainland of Greece and in the Aegean (see DELIAN LEAGUE). Smaller states did the same: for example Elis in the NW Peloponnese claimed to hold neighbouring cities through the right of conquest (Xen. *Hell.* 3. 2. 23), and Sinope extracted tribute from her colonies on the Black (Euxine) Sea (Xen. *An.* 5. 5. 7–10). But the fragmentation of the Greek world into hundreds of states, the consequent dispersion of resources, and the strong Greek attachment to independence and its symbols, all militated against the emergence of lasting empires in the Greek world, and even inhibited the formation of durable alliance systems except in special circumstances. The territorial empires of the near east, based on deliberate military conquest and the imposition of regular tribute on subjects, were long familiar to the Greeks (cf. Hdt. 1. 6 on the Lydians, 1. 95–6 and 130 on the succession of empires from the Assyrians to the Persians, 3. 89–97 on the tribute of the Persian empire; see PERSIA. But this eastern model did not transfer easily to Greek conditions. Athens' exceptional success in the 5th cent. encouraged emulation by others, but also stimulated the resistance of smaller states to encroachments on their independence and the imposition of regular tribute (cf. the manifesto of the Second Athenian Confederacy in 377, Tod no. 123). Hence the numerous failures of Greek interstate relations in the 4th cent.: the Greeks never successfully bridged the gap between alliance or league (see FEDERAL STATES) on the one hand, and empire on the other. The future lay rather with military monarchies that could command greater resources and work on a scale that would eventually transcend the Greek world itself. *Dionysius I of Syracuse, Jason of Pherae, and Mausolus of Caria may variously be seen as precursors to *Philip II of Macedon. His transformation of Macedonian power provided the basis for *Alexander the Great's conquest of the Persian empire and the subsequent emergence of the kingdoms of the Successors ('Diadochi'). The new Macedonian monarchies in Asia, culturally part of the Greek world, became heirs to the former eastern empires and their methods. But the Antigonid rulers of Macedon (e.g. *Antigonus the One-eyed; Demetrius Poliorcetes ('the Besieger'); *Antigonus Gonatas; later Antigonid rulers including Philip V and Perseus) never succeeded in devising a formula that would permanently reconcile the Greek mainland to their domination. This failure facilitated Roman intervention, hence eventually the absorption of much of the Hellenistic world into the Roman empire.

M. M. A.

Persian See PERSIA.

Roman Although 'imperialism' was first used to describe the growth of the colonial empires of the European powers in the late 19th and early 20th cents., it is now frequently used in the context of the expansion of Roman power in Italy and particularly of the creation of its Mediterranean and European empire from the 3rd cent. BC to the 1st cent. AD.

Rome in the early and middle republican periods (5th to 2nd cents. BC) was a profoundly military society, as can be seen for instance from the military nature of the political power of the city's magistrates (*imperium*), the need of any aspiring magistrate to have performed ten years of military service (Polyb. 6. 19. 4), and the religious and political importance attached to the triumph. By the end of the war with *Pyrrhus in 272 BC, Rome controlled the greater part of Italy south of the river Po by a network of relationships which had grown out of the fighting against the Aequi, Volsci, and *Etruscans in the 5th and early 4th cents., the Latins and the Campanians in the mid-4th cent. (leading to the dissolution of the Latin federation in 338), and the Samnites and other south Italians, of which the final stage was the Pyrrhic wars (see PYRRHUS). Some communities (mostly former Latin and Campanian allies) were incorporated into the Roman people (though geographically distinct from it, and often without full political rights), and the remainder were classified as allies (*socii*), either as part of a reconstituted 'Latin' alliance or with a separate treaty of their own. Of these, only the Roman communities were properly speaking part of the expanded city of Rome, while the allies were under an obligation to provide military assistance and (especially in the case of the Latins) held certain rights from the Romans.

In the period of the two great wars against the Carthaginians (264–241 and 218–202 BC; see ROME (HISTORY) §1.4), the Romans, backed by this military alliance, became involved in wars in *Sicily, Sardinia, Corsica, *Spain, *Greece, and North Africa (see AFRICA, ROMAN). From this grew the beginnings of the Roman empire outside Italy. Roman commanders were assigned commands by the senate by the allocation of a *provincia or area of responsibility. Such *provinciae were not essentially territorial, nor were they permanent; but in areas in which the Romans wished to exercise a long-term military control through the presence of armed forces it became necessary to allocate a *provincia on a regular basis. Sometimes this seems to have occurred considerably later than the conflict that initially brought Roman soldiers to the area. The Carthaginians were defeated in Sicily by 241 and Sardinia was seized in 238, but Roman praetors were sent to these islands on a regular basis only from 227 BC (Livy, *Per.* 20; Pomponius, *Dig.* 1. 2. 2. 32). Similarly in Spain, although it was a *provincia from the beginning of the Second Punic War in 218, praetors were only sent on a regular basis from 196 (Livy 32. 27–8). Within this essentially military pattern, other elements of imperial control developed, particularly taxation of the local communities and jurisdiction exercised by Roman commanders over non-Romans.

In the first half of the 2nd cent. BC, and especially in the context of the wars with the Hellenistic powers of the eastern Mediterranean, Roman imperialism took a different form. Roman armies were sent to Greece during the Macedonian wars and to Asia Minor to fight against the Seleucid king, *Antiochus III. Here long-term *provinciae* were not established when the fighting ended, and control of the regions was exercised in a more remote fashion, through treaties and diplomacy. For *Polybius however, writing in the second half of the century, this represented an extension of Roman control as real as that exercised directly in the western Mediterranean (Polyb. 1. 1); and although Macedonia became a long-term province after the failure of Andriscus' attempt to seize the throne there (149/8 BC), Polybius seems to regard this as no more than a different and more direct form of the domination which the Romans already held.

Further large-scale additions were made as a result of the organization of the east by *Pompey, following the defeat of *Mithradates VI of Pontus (66–62 BC), and of the campaigns of *Caesar in Gaul (58–49 BC). The largest expansion, however, came under *Augustus, who not only completed the conquest of the Iberian peninsula but also added the new provinces of Raetia, Noricum, Pannonia, and Moesia along the line of the river Danube. It appears that he was only prevented from a further expansion into that part of Germany between the Rhine and the Elbe by the disastrous defeat of Publius Quinctilius Varus in AD 9, which led to the loss of three legions. Thereafter, apart from *Claudius' conquest of southern Britain in 42, *Trajan alone (97–117) made further large-scale additions, of which only Dacia and Arabia survived the retrenchment of his successor, *Hadrian.

Although the mechanisms of Roman imperialism are fairly clear, the motivation of the Romans has been the subject of much debate. It was long believed, following Mommsen, that their intentions were essentially defensive, and only incidentally expansionist. Modern scholars have rejected this view, and have suggested alternative motives, including economic benefits (which undoubtedly resulted from the growth of the empire) and a desire for territorial annexation. Whatever else was the case, it is clear that throughout the period of expansion, the political classes at Rome were determined that other states should do what Rome required of them, and, although it is dangerous to attempt to provide a single explanation of so complex a phenomenon as Roman imperialism, it would appear that it was changes in the Roman understanding of what were the most effective means of achieving this control that shaped the way the empire grew. J. S. Ri.

imperium was the supreme power, involving command in war and the interpretation and execution of law (including the infliction of the death penalty), which belonged at Rome to the kings and, after their expulsion, to *consuls,

military tribunes with consular power (from 445 to 367 BC), praetors, *dictators, and masters of the horse (*magistri equitum*). Viewed generally, *imperium* represents the supreme authority of the community in its dealings with the individual, and the magistrate in whom *imperium* is vested represents the community in all its dealings. In practical terms, *imperium* may be seen as the power to give orders and to exact obedience to them (cf. *imperare*, to command). It was symbolized by the *fasces* (rods of office) borne by the lictors, of which the dictator had 24, the consul 12, and the praetor 6, to which was added the axe when the magistrate left the precincts of the city. Later in the republic *imperium* was held also by proconsuls and propraetors, who were either ex-magistrates or private individuals upon whom a special command had been conferred (*privati cum imperio*), and by members of certain commissions (e.g. boards for the distribution of land, Cic. *Leg. agr.* 2. 28). Its application was increasingly restricted: first, when two consuls (originally two 'praetors') replaced the king, by the principle of collegiality and tenure of office limited to one year; the dictator, who had no colleague, held office for a maximum of six months. Secondly, by the *leges Valeriae* (traditionally of 509, 449, and 300 BC) and the *leges Porciae* (probably of the early 2nd cent. BC), magistrates were not allowed to execute citizens at Rome without trial owing to the citizen's right of *provocatio* (appeal) to the people. This right of appeal was extended, whether by a *lex Porcia* or, possibly, by convention, to citizens abroad. Thirdly, the *imperium* of promagistrates was generally restricted to the bounds of their *provinciae*. *Imperium* needed ratification by a *lex curiata*, a convention which persisted at least to the end of the republic (Cic. *Leg. Agr.* 2. 26; *Fam.* 1. 9. 25). To a promagistrate (whether ex-magistrate or *privatus cum imperio*), *imperium* was granted for a year at a time, or until his commission was achieved. Grants of *imperium* for a specified term of several years occur only towards the end of the republic, the earliest being the grant of *imperium* to *Pompey for three years by the *lex Gabinia* of 67 BC; this *imperium* was further distinguished by being *infinitum*, i.e. not subject to the usual territorial limits of a *provincia*.

Under the republic, in case of conflict, the *imperium* of a consul, with twelve fasces, could probably override that of a praetor, who held six. As between consuls and proconsuls, each with twelve fasces, the consul could override the proconsul by virtue of the *auctoritas* (prestige) of his office. Conflict in the same area between proconsuls arose first in 67 between Pompey (pursuing pirates with proconsular *imperium*; see PIRACY) and Quintus Caecilius Metellus (Creticus), proconsul of *Crete. So, in 57, the question of allowing Pompey, in virtue of his corn commission, *imperium* greater than that of other proconsuls was mooted, and *Brutus and Cassius were granted *imperium maius* in the east by the senate in 43.

Octavian (the future *Augustus) held *imperium*, first *pro praetore* and later as consul, in 43, as triumvir (member of board of three with Mark *Antony and M. Aemilius

*Lepidus) from 42 to 33, and as consul in 31–23 (and, from 27, as proconsul of a large number of provinces). When in 23 he resigned the consulship, his proconsular *imperium* was made *maius*, and it was provided that it could be exercised from within the city. By this same enactment (or by another in 19 BC according to Cass. Dio 54. 10. 5) Italy was included within the field of his *imperium*. *Imperium* was granted to him for ten-year periods in 27 and 8 BC and AD 3 and 13, and for five-year periods in 18 and 13 BC. It was voted to succeeding emperors at their accession by the senate (cf. *ILS* 229, with Tac. *Ann.* 12. 69, referring to *Nero's accession), though ratification of the senate's decree by a *lex curiata* probably remained a formal requirement (Gai. *Inst.* 1. 5, and cf. *FIRA* I². 15, the *lex 'de imperio Vespasiani'*, where the *imperium* is defined; see VESPASIAN).

Imperium maius was sometimes granted to others besides the emperor for the creation of a single military command, as to *Germanicus in the east in AD 17 (Tac. *Ann.* 2. 43) and to Corbulo in AD 63 (Tac. *Ann.* 15. 25). It might also be conferred as a way of associating an individual with the *imperium* of the emperor and thereby signalling him as a suitable successor, as with *Tiberius (Tac. *Ann.* 1. 3; Vell. Pat. 2. 121).

As Rome's dominion came to extend overseas in the 3rd and 2nd cents. BC (see IMPERIALISM, ROMAN), it was conceived of in terms of the power to issue orders and to exact obedience to them (so Polyb. 3. 4. 2–3 and elsewhere), in terms, that is, of *imperium* (cf. Cato (Censorius) fr. 164 Malcovati). The first official expression of this is found in Greek. The treaty between Rome and Thracian Maronea from the 160s BC (*SEG* 35. 823) refers to 'the Roman people and those under them', and this standard phrase appears in Latin in Rome's treaty with Callatis on the Black Sea (*ILLRP* 516, from the early 1st cent. BC) as 'the Roman people and those under their *imperium*' ([… *poplo Rom*]ano quei[ve] sub inperio [eius erunt …]). It was with reference to the principle and nature of supreme authority within the state that the authority of Rome itself over others was perceived and defined, and so it was to the *imperium Romanum* of the republic that the Roman empire succeeded.

P. S. D.

incest, sexual intercourse or marriage with close kin, was restricted throughout classical antiquity. However, terminology and the particular relations prohibited varied with place and time. Though *mētrokoitēs*, 'mother's bedmate', occurs in Hipponax, most of the Greek words referring to specific close-kin unions are much later in date and no general word for incest is found before the Byzantine period. *Incestum*, attested as a Latin technical term from the late republic, carries connotations of impurity absent from the Greek vocabulary. Sexual relations involving parent and child were forbidden everywhere we have evidence; their occurrence in Greek myth generally evokes horror, yet the participants are sometimes marked as numinous by their transgression of the usual limits of human conduct. Siblings of the same father could marry at

*Athens, of the same mother at *Sparta. Even marriages between full siblings were recognized among the Greeks of Hellenistic and Roman *Egypt, an unusual practice perhaps intended to preserve the ethnic identity of a small and isolated settler élite and the privileges to which it provided access. Siblings by adoption might marry under Roman law if one of them was first emancipated from *patria potestas* (the legal authority of a *paterfamilias*, usually a father or grandfather). But marriages between nieces and paternal uncles—encouraged in the Athenian epiclerate, (when the niece was an 'heiress' who had no son)—were made legal only in the time (and the marital interests) of *Claudius, and were outlawed again by Constantius II and Constans (*Cod. Theod.* 3. 12. 1). Marriages between men and their sisters' daughters, granddaughters, and great-granddaughters, or between men and their aunts, were forbidden throughout. Despite a tradition that marriages between first cousins were once unknown, they are attested for the 3rd cent. BC and unremarkable until banned by Theodosius I in about AD 384 or 385. (The ban was lifted in 409, *Cod. Theod.* 3. 10. 1.) Allegations of incest were aimed at political opponents at both Athens (Cimon, *Alcibiades) and Rome (Publius *Clodius Pulcher). Public legal sanctions at Athens, if any, are unknown. In republican Rome, offenders are said to have been thrown from the Tarpeian Rock, though the penalty in classical law was deportation, and that only in the cases of closest kin. Women involved in incestuous marriages with collateral kin might escape punishment entirely, though extramarital incest risked the usual penalties for adultery. But the Christian emperors imposed harsher provisions.

M. G.

India (see ◀Map 2a▶) This country had early trade connections with the Persian Gulf, but it remained unknown to Mediterranean peoples until the extension of the Persian empire to the Indus and the voyage of Darius' admiral Scylax down the Kabul and Indus rivers and perhaps round Arabia to Suez (Hecataeus, *FGrH* 264 F 244–9; Hdt. 3. 98 ff., 4. 44). Even so, India remained a land of fable and wonders (as in the *Indica* of Ctesias, *c.*400 BC); it was believed to lie in the farthest east, yet Indians were confused with Ethiopians, and in popular belief India and Ethiopia formed one country. The conquests of *Alexander the Great (327–325) brought more accurate knowledge of NW India as far as the river Hyphasis (Beas) and vague information about the Ganges valley and Sri Lanka; and the voyage of Nearchus reopened a sea connection with the Persian Gulf. *Seleucus I controlled the north-west but *c.*302 conceded the control to the Mauryan king Chandragupta. He kept a resident named Megasthenes at Chandragupta's court at Pataliputra (Palibothra), who published much detail about India (see ARRIAN; DIODORUS SICULUS; STRABO); and King Ashoka in the 3rd cent. sent embassies to the Hellenistic kings. In the 2nd cent. NW India was occupied by the Graeco-Bactrian rulers (see BACTRIA); but the rise of the Parthian empire (see PARTHIA) separated India from the Greek lands, and

India Marble Roman sarcophagus (c. AD 180), showing the Indian triumph of Bacchus, the Roman *Dionysus. His fabled wars in India, a familiar subject in later classical literature and art, were modelled after the eastern campaigns of *Alexander the Great, with whom a more accurate western knowledge of India begins.

invaders from central Asia (c.80–30 BC) obliterated the Greek principalities in the Indus valley. In the 1st cent. AD Chinese silk reached the Roman dominions through India, but land communications with India remained irregular. The chief routes to India were (1) via Meshed and the Bolan and Mula passes, (2) via Merv, Balkh, Kabul, and Peshawar. Roman connections with this area, although not direct, are evident from the excavations at sites such as Sirkap (Taxila) and Begram.

Sea communications between India and the Persian Gulf were maintained by the *Seleucids, but were interrupted under Parthian rule. Direct travel from Egypt to India was impeded for long by the Arabs of Yemen, whose monopoly of trade was not seriously challenged by the Ptolemies of *Egypt, and the voyages of Eudoxus to India were not too successful. The Arab obstruction was removed by the great appetite of Rome for eastern luxuries in the prosperous days of *Augustus, and by the discovery of open-sea routes from Aden to India. In the 1st cent. BC, or soon after, observation of the monsoon encouraged mid-ocean routes leading to various points on the western coast where settlements were subsequently established (Plin. *HN* 6. 96–100). Augustus received Indian envoys (Cass. Dio 54. 9), and Greek and Levantine merchants organized a regular trade from Egypt. In Augustus' day 120 ships sailed to India every year, and under his early successors the drain on Roman money to pay for Indian imports caused occasional anxiety (Plin. *HN* 6. 101, 12. 84). But recent studies suggest that this drain was illusory. The main goals of visitors from the Roman world were western India and the Chera, Chola, and Pandya kingdoms of south India. The principal

imports to Rome were perfumes, spices (especially pepper), *gems, *ivory, pearls, Indian textiles, and Chinese silk. The Romans exported linen, coral, *glass, base metals, 'Arretine' tableware (see POTTERY, ROMAN), *wine in amphorae, etc., and also sent quantities of gold and silver (and later copper) coins, of which large hoards have been found in south India and the eastern Deccan as well as some clay *bullae* ('amulets') of Roman coins. Roman artefacts occur in western India, the Deccan, and southern India at sites such as Nasik, Nevasa, Kolhapur, Akota, and Karvan; at Ter, Bhokardan, Brahmagiri, Chandravalli, Maski, Kondapur; and at Amaravati and Sisupalagarh.

The chief markets on the west coast were Barbaricon and Barygaza (mod. Broach) and the southern towns of Muziris (? Cranganore) and Nelcynda (? Kottayam). Beyond Cape Comorin the Greeks visited Colchoi (Kolkai), Camara (perhaps Kaveripattinam), a trading-station now called Arikamedu near Pondicherry (? Poduce), and Sopatma (? Madras); a few reached the Ganges mouth and brought news of Burma, Malaya, and the Thinae or Sinae (in south China). Greek traders figure in Tamil literature as residents in ports and some inland centres (AD 70–140). The Maldives and Laccadives came into this circuit, Sri Lanka (Taprobane) was circumnavigated; and one Alexander, taking advantage of the bay of Bengal monsoon, is said to have sailed past Burma and Malaya to Vietnam and even to China proper (Ptol. *Geog.* 7. 1–2). A few Roman artefacts of the 2nd cent. AD were found at Oc-eo in Cambodia and on the Mekong river. These could have come in the course of the Roman trade with India being extended eastwards by Indian traders.

Nevertheless, Greek geographers always underrated the extent of India's southward projection and exaggerated the size of Sri Lanka. From *c.* AD 200 direct Graeco-Roman trade declined, communications with India passed into the hands of intermediaries (Arabians, Axumites, Sasanid Persians), and India again became a land of fable to the Mediterranean world. The founders of Christian settlements in India came largely from Persia.

E. H. W.; R. Th.

industry (Greek and Roman). Industry in the sense of hard labour (Gk. *ponos*; Lat. *labor*) the Greeks and Romans knew all too much about; total freedom from productive labour (*scholē*, *otium*) remained a governing ideal from one end of pagan antiquity to the other. But industry in the modern sense of large-scale manufacturing businesses they knew hardly at all, let alone as the characteristic form of manufacturing unit. That role was always filled by the individual workshop (*ergastērion*), and it is no accident that the largest Greek or Roman industrial labour force on record barely tipped over into three figures. Nor did élite Greeks and Romans value labourers any more highly than *labour as such; this was partly because manual labour, even when not actually conducted by slaves (see SLAVERY), was nevertheless always apt to attract the opprobrium of slavishness. As Herodotus (2. 167) put it, the Corinthians despised manual craftsmen (*cheirotechnai*) the least, the *Spartans the most—but all élite Greeks despised them. On the other hand, they always felt boundless admiration for skill (*technē*, *ars*), and some forms of ancient pre-industrial craftsmanship demanded that quality in the highest degree. See ART, ANCIENT ATTITUDES TO; ARTISANS AND CRAFTSMEN.

Craftsmanship in stone, wood, bone, earth, and leather, as well as the use of colour for painting and of fire for cooking, were palaeolithic inventions; textiles, fired

industry Imaginative reconstruction of a large-scale fishery excavated at Cosa, central Italy, with a fish farm, saltery, and kilns for making transport jars (amphorae). Dating from the 2nd–1st cent. BC, the complex illustrates the relatively large scale of Roman industry in certain exceptional areas.

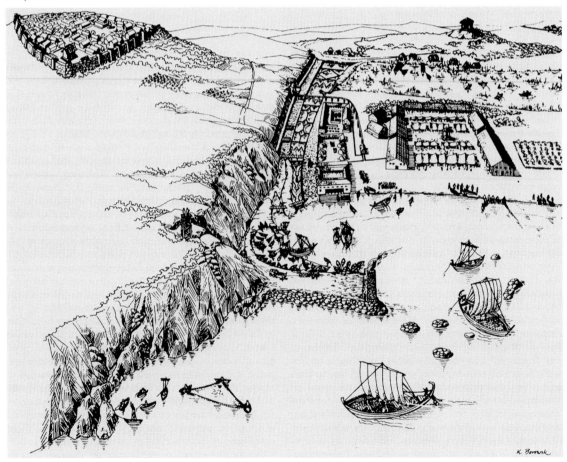

K. Borork

pottery, architecture, and shipbuilding were neolithic discoveries. Metalwork and glass-making began with the bronze age, as did the oversight of craftsmanship by written prescription and the imposition of exact measures and weights in the Minoan and Mycenaean palace-economies. Besides smiths and glaziers the Linear B tablets present an array of specialist craftsmen including potters, brewers, jewellers, leather-workers, and perfumiers. See MINOAN and MYCENAEAN CIVILIZATION.

*Homer and *Hesiod mention a considerable variety of craftsmen, some of the more expert and specialized being non-Greek. But only the metalworkers had their own workshops, and this is in accord with the florescence of bronze-working associated with the great Panhellenic sanctuaries of *Olympia (from the 10th cent. BC), *Delphi (9th), and *Delos (8th) in particular. Their standards were eventually matched by the potters and (if they were separate) vase-painters, above all those of *Athens, Argos, and Corinth; the latter too could boast at least one shipbuilder of distinction by 700 BC (Thuc. 1. 13. 3). In the course of the 7th and 6th cents. workshops and studios proliferated, no longer tied principally to sanctuaries. Depictions of potters, leather-workers, and smiths occur on Attic black- and red-figure vases, themselves often products of the highest craft and finish. As is revealed both by the workers' names (Lydus = 'the Lydian', Amasis (Egyptian), Epictetus = 'the purchased') and by an isolated painted text (Lydus 'the slave'), many of the craftsmen were not only not Athenian citizens but non-Greek slaves.

The concomitant development of the Athenian empire and the Piraeus in the 5th cent. BC provided a further stimulus to Greek craftsmanship, both quantitative and qualitative. No one, according to *Plutarch, would wish actually to be Phidias, but the products of Phidias' extraordinary craft skill were universally admired. The anonymous labours of an army of stone-carvers have left us a legacy of accomplished dressed masonry and decorative sculptural detail carved in the hardest material (marble). Gem-cutters like Dexamenes of Chios and die-engravers (see COINAGE, GREEK) like those who produced the decadrachms of *Syracuse were hardly less accomplished. At Athens craftsmanship interacted with high culture and politics in interesting ways. Plato's *Socrates was fond of analogies from craftsmanship, and the real Socrates was reputedly the son of a stonemason. The fathers of Cleon, *Isocrates, and *Demosthenes made their piles through employing skilled slave craftsmen—tanners, flute-makers, and cutlers respectively. But the biggest 'industrialists' on record in Classical Athens were the metic brothers (see METICS) Polemarchus and *Lysias (the latter a noted speech-writer), even if it is not absolutely certain that their 120 slaves all worked full time in the family shield-making business (exceptionally lucrative, thanks to the Peloponnesian War of 431–404 BC). A more usual size of workshop was the one staffed by ten slaves owned by *Aeschines' opponent Timarchus. Some such skilled slaves were privileged to be set up in business on their own account by their masters. The craftsmen of Athens were sedentary—indeed, in the case of the mine-slaves who extracted and processed the argentiferous lead ores of Laurium, possibly shackled. But itinerant Greek craftsmen operated as far afield as south Russia (within the Scythian sphere) and the Alps, working on the spot under commission from local potentates. There may also have been a few wandering craftsmen in rural districts of Greece during the Classical period.

The Hellenistic age produced a growth of the Greek *ergastērion* system but also to some degree marked a return to the Mycenaean pattern of palace-centred industries. Textile and food production were affected. Several glass-producers of the 1st cent. BC and a potter, Aristion, of c.200 BC seem to have had workshops in more than one town. Glass-blowing was invented in the second half of the 1st cent. BC. The Ptolemies (see EGYPT (Ptolemaic)) 'nationalized' several Egyptian crafts: the production of papyrus scrolls, oil, perfumes, textiles (other than woollen), and beer became government monopolies. Craftsmen in these trades became government employees, who were controlled by tax-farmers and government officials, received salaries, and, in the production of oil, a share of the profits. A government production-schedule was issued annually, and the workers received their tools and raw materials from central stores. Large enterprises for fish-curing, metalworking, and brick-making were also properties of the Ptolemies.

In Rome of the kings (c.750–500 BC), according to tradition, specialized crafts of metal- and leather-workers, potters, dyers, musicians, and *fabri* (all-purpose handymen) were organized in societies known as *collegia*. In later republican times (coeval with the Hellenistic age) Roman craftsmanship developed on Greek lines. This was a period of enormous expansion of the Roman empire and intense specialization of all kinds of economic activity (see ECONOMY, ROMAN), and among the many imports to Rome and Italy from the Greek east were not only staple foodstuffs and luxury finished goods but skilled Greek craftsmen, not a few of whom had been reduced to servitude by their slave-hungry imperial masters. These worked generally on a larger scale, though not usually according to radically different legal or economic conditions, than their free and slave counterparts in the old country. As in old Greece, an attempt was made to erect social barriers between the political élite and the sordid business of production and commerce, but even the Roman senate was not entirely devoid of manufacturing entrepreneurs; the big names of Gaius Rabirius Postumus with his large *terra sigillata* workshops, C. Sestius and his stamped wine-amphorae, and Lucius Domitius Ahenobarbus and his stamped bricks are examples. The large and assured demand provided by Roman armies outside Italy was often a vital factor stimulating the production and distribution of consumable commodities. The politicization of the *collegia* at Rome was another late republican phenomenon, prompting official measures to dissolve or curb them.

Under the Principate craftsmanship of the Greek and

Roman workshop type spread throughout the provinces of the empire. Remnants of administered economy persisted, especially in mining districts, temples, and public domains; but even the Ptolemaic monopolies were broken up or changed into monopolistic concessions for small districts farmed out to independent craftsmen. The local markets of provincial districts were furnished with bricks, coarse pottery, cheap leather goods and metalwork, *terra sigillata*, cheap textiles, and so on by craftsmen working from public and private estates. There were, however, local exceptions to the general pattern both in scale and in management; an apparently huge private-enterprise development of olive-growing and *olive oil distribution in Cyrenaica (see CYRENE), traceable physically through the surviving containers (*amphorae*), and an imperially inspired development of stone quarries in the mons Claudianus area of Egypt, are just two conspicuous instances.

During what appears to have been the general crisis of the 3rd cent. AD control of industry and craftsmanship began to revert to centralized, imperial direction. Diocletian's reforms aimed at rendering the compulsory organization of labour final. The number of independent workshops decreased everywhere, and the state provided for its own requirements by establishing manufactories in all provinces and by regulating the more important *collegia* of craftsmen throughout the empire. Sons had to follow their father's trade, and large taxes were levied on the corporations collectively. Gradually, and especially during the reign of Justinian I (6th cent. AD), they received privileges that enabled them to influence prices, to buy raw materials cheaply for all members, to regulate production and sale, workshop capacity, and size of membership. See also TECHNOLOGY; TRADE.

P. A. C.

initiation is the set of rituals which transforms girls and boys into adults. In Greece, these rituals were the combined product of the Indo-European heritage and indigenous traditions, as the Minoan frescos show (see MINOAN CIVILIZATION). In historical times full rituals can be found only in Sparta and Crete, but scattered notices from other cities and the mythological tradition about the 'career' of heroes, such as *Achilles and *Theseus, suggest that puberty rites once existed all over Greece. *Apollo and *Artemis were the most important gods connected with these rites.

The Greeks had no term for initiation, but various cities used the term *agōgē*, literally 'the leading of a horse by one's hand', and related words. This view reflects itself not only in archaic poetry, where boys and girls are often addressed as foals and fillies, but also in mythological onomastics: youths connected with initiation regularly have names with the element *hippos* ('horse'): Leucippus, Leucippides, Melanippe, etc. Clearly, youths were seen as wild animals, who had to be domesticated before entering adult society.

Regarding girls, our best information comes from Sparta, where their 'education' prepared them for motherhood through physical exercises and dancing in choruses. aristocratic girls had to pass through a lesbian relationship (see HOMOSEXUALITY) to mark the contrast with their final destination, marriage; a similar custom existed on Lesbos where *Sappho instructed aristocratic girls. Special stress was laid on the enhancing of the girls' physical beauty: not unusually, a beauty contest concluded the girls' initiation. See BRAURON.

Male puberty rites survived into the 4th cent. BC on *Crete, where at the age of 17, after an informal training, sons of aristocrats together with boys of lower classes were gathered into bands, *agelai* or 'herds of horses', which were supervised by their fathers. Here they received a training in dancing, singing, hunting, fighting, and letters. The rites were concluded with a brief stay in the countryside, where the aristocratic youth passed through a homosexual affair (see HOMOSEXUALITY). The festivals in which the new adults showed off to the community belong to the most important ones of Crete.

Similar rites existed in Sparta, but their character changed after the Messenian Wars. The *agōgē* was extended by the introduction of *age classes and training became increasingly harsher when Sparta's position started to depend on a decreasing number of citizens. In Athens the original initiatory structures had disintegrated in the course of the Archaic age, but its 'military service', the *ephēbeia* (see GYMNASIUM), still displays various initiatory features.

In Rome, boys' initiation did not survive into the republic, but the traditions about *Romulus and Remus with their band of youths and run-away criminals strongly suggest its one-time existence, as does the myth of Caeculus of Praeneste.

J. N. B.

interest, rates of As in modern industrial society, the ancient world had a complex of rates of interest, varying across time and space. There, however, the similarity ends: ancient interest rates are more social than economic indicators and cannot be read to reveal trends over time. Underlying rates of interest were fixed by custom and stayed stable over long periods: from the 5th to the 2nd cent. BC the temple of *Apollo on *Delos lent money at 10% p.a. (akin to a tithe?). In 4th-cent. Athens, the 'prevailing' rate of interest seems to have been 12% p.a. (literally, 'one drachma interest on each mina lent per month'). The major distinction in loan transactions lay between charging interest and lending interest-free: a pre-existing personal relationship between lender and borrower was thought to preclude the taking of interest. A rate of 1% per month was apparently seen in Athens as reasonable for an 'impersonal' loan transaction (Dem. 27. 17; *Ath. pol.* 52). Particular circumstances could result in higher rates: high risk of default (3% per month: Lys. fr. 38 Gernet–Bizos), unsecured, short-term lending of small sums (25% per day: Theophr. *Char.* 6. 9). As the great majority of loans was raised to cover unforeseen, often emergency expenditure, the charging of interest could be seen as exploitation of the borrower's misfortune (Dem. 45. 69); hence a part of the opposition to lending at interest from *Plato (*Leg.* 742c) and [*Aristotle] (*Pr.* 950ª28 ff.). Compound interest (*anatokismos*) was seen as particularly exploitative (Ar. *Nub.* 1155 f.; Pl. *Leg.* 842d). The major exception was maritime loans, from which the borrower could hope to make a profit, justifying the charging of anything between 12¼ and 30% (possibly more) on the sum lent for the duration of the voyage. From the Roman world, Tacitus (*Ann.* 6. 16) singled out lending at interest as a long-standing social problem. The *fenus unciarium* of the *Twelve Tables may well refer to an annual interest maximum of 100%. Throughout Roman history, attempts were made to fix maximum rates of interest: the *lex Genucia* of 342 BC apparently banned all lending at interest. This and less extreme measures were undermined by the practical needs of borrowers (App. *BCiv.* 1. 54) and the power of creditors. *Brutus avoided the official interest maximum of 12% in the province of Cilicia (and possibly the whole empire) by virtue of a special decree from the senate (Cic. *Att.* 6. 1, 2). Justinian I (6th cent. AD; see JUSTINIAN'S CODIFICATION) attempted to match annual interest maxima to specific circumstances: *c*.5% for cash loans, 12½% for loans in kind, and 4% for loans made by senators. With greater realism, Athenian law forbade any restriction on the charging of interest (Lys. 10. 18).

P. C. M.

intolerance, intellectual and religious For most Greek states our evidence is too poor and patchy for us to be able to say much. We know a little about 5th-cent. BC Athens. Sir K. Popper famously praised it as an 'open society' but the tolerance of that society had limits. There is some evidence for literary censorship, though of a haphazard and perhaps ineffective sort. Phrynichus got into trouble near the beginning of the century for putting on a *tragedy dealing with a sensitive political topic (Hdt. 6.21). Between 440 and 437 BC there were formal restrictions on ridicule in theatrical comedy (Fornara no. III with the important discussion of 'political censorship' at *DFA*³ 364; cf. COMEDY (GREEK), OLD, §4). On the other hand there were no 'witch-hunts' against intellectuals, though Anaxagoras and other associates of *Pericles were prosecuted in the courts. Anaxagoras' ostensible offence was impiety, and the decree of Diopeithes (Plut. *Per.* 32), if historical, would provide hard evidence for public control of religious teaching. *Alcibiades and others were punished severely for parodying the Eleusinian *mysteries (see ANDOCIDES), but Dover is right that the offending action was not necessarily 'the product of earnest intellectual inquiry'. The reasons for *Socrates' execution in 399 are still disputed by scholars, but political considerations were surely at least as relevant as religious: Socrates was critical of the *democracy and its institutions, and had taught prominent oligarchs (see OLIGARCHY). *Aeschines (1.173) in the mid-4th cent. explicitly makes the latter point, which could not be made openly in 399 because of the amnesty granted to oligarchs compromised by involvement with the Thirty Tyrants (see GREECE, HISTORY).

In the Hellenistic period the poet Sotades incurred severe, perhaps capital, punishment for his outspokenness, but he went quite far in his criticism of the *incest of *Ptolemy II. The historian Philochorus was put to death by *Antigonus Gonatas for being too partial to the same Ptolemy. The most notable (actually unique) instance of Hellenistic religious persecution was the *Seleucid Antiochus IV's treatment of the *Jews. In Rome, censors, despite their name, were not responsible for literary or artistic censorship in the modern meaning of the word. Book-burning is however attested in authoritarian periods of Roman history (see e.g. Cassius Dio 56. 27. 1). Roman attitudes to foreign religions were generally cosmopolitan; see RELIGION, ROMAN. The suppression of the *Bacchanalia in 186 BC was exceptional. For Roman treatment of Jews see JEWS and GAIUS: *Gaius and the Jews*; for persecution of Christians see CHRISTIANITY. See also PHILOSOPHERS AND POLITICS; ANTI-SEMITISM.

S. H.

Ionian Revolt The eastern Greeks, prosperous and compliant subjects of *Persia from *c*.546/5 BC, remained uniquely quiet at *Darius I's irregular accession. Further Persian expansion in *Egypt, the Black Sea, and Thrace, however, increased imperial tax-exactions and reduced Hellenic market-share and attractive mercenary opportunities. Resenting *barbarian overlords, autocratic regimes (see TYRANNY), and conscript service for Persian power, most Ionian cities (on the modern west coast of Turkey) followed the Milesian Aristagoras in deposing local tyrants (499; Hdt. 5. 37). Significant Athenian and Eretrian assistance arrived to raze Sardis, a satrapal capital. Ethnic religious assembly (the federal sanctuary known as the 'Panionium'), political organization, and intercity operations proved eastern Greek capacities for unified action. Hellespontines, Carians, and many Cypriots consequently joined the rebels. Samian and Lesbian interests (see LESBOS; SAMOS), however, diverged from Milesian and Carian. Inadequate revenues and budgetary mechanisms and disputed military hierarchies further crippled determination.

Persia mobilized and defeated Hellenes and allies at *Ephesus, *Cyprus, and Carian Labraunda, then reconquered Anatolian territories by amphibious, triple-pronged, city-by-city advances. Both commands welcomed a decisive naval battle near crucial Miletus (at Lade, 494; Hdt. 6. 6–17). Approximately 70,000 allied Greeks in 353 ships, capable Dionysius of Phocaea commanding, faced 600 largely Phoenician vessels. Co-operation among the predominantly Chian, Samian, Milesian, and Lesbian contingents—rivals to begin with—collapsed when battle commenced. Persian 'politics' and bribery succeeded where sheer force had not. Many fought bravely, but most Samians had agreed to defect. Miletus was sacked, the inhabitants killed, enslaved, or expatriated. The coastal and island mop-up was easy and ruthless (6. 18–20, 31–3).

*Herodotus' account, based on surviving losers' biased reconstructions, replays and exasperatedly explains the defeat. Like the westerners' later edifying victory, the eastern Greeks' edifying defeat demanded heroes and villains. Short-sighted tyrants, Ionian disorganization, and military disinclination are blamed throughout. Ionian achievements are trivialized or negated, as each *polis* castigated the others' motives (6. 14). Herodotus condemned the liberation as doomed from birth (5. 28, 97, 6. 3, 27), but his facts allow alternative reconstructions. Initial successes and co-ordination suggest that liberation was possible.

Revolt produced four positive results. The Persian general Mardonius replaced the unpopular Hellenic tyrants on Persia's western borders with more democratic regimes. Another prominent Persian, Artaphernes, renegotiated tribute collections (6. 42–3). Persian westward expansion was delayed. The autonomous Balkan Greeks, observing the risks of capitulation and resistance to Persia, realized that independence could be preserved.   D. G. L.

Isaeus, Athenian speech-writer (c.420–340s BC)

Life The skimpy ancient biographical tradition ([Plut.] *Mor.* 839e–f, *Dionysius of Halicarnassus' critical essay *Isaeus*, and a Life preceding the speeches in the main MSS) preserves his father's name, Diagoras, but was uncertain whether he was Athenian or from Chalcis in Euboea. *Isocrates reportedly taught him, but he plainly also studied *Lysias' speeches and was himself a teacher of *Demosthenes and author of a *technē*, a speech-writer's manual. His working life extended from c.389 to the 350s, perhaps to 344/3 if a lengthy quotation by Dionysius traditionally printed as speech 12 was by him and is correctly dated. The ancient tradition had his activity extend down to the reign of *Philip II of Macedon.

Works As a professional speech-writer (*logographos*) in Athens, he specialized in inheritance cases. Some 64 speech-titles were known in antiquity, 50 of which were reckoned genuine. Eleven survive complete, of which four can be internally dated (speech 5 in 390 or 389, 6 in 364 or 363, 7 in 355 or 354, and 2 in the 350s), while stylometric criteria have been plausibly used by R. F. Wevers (*Isaeus: Chronology, Prosopography, and Serial History* (1969)) to date the remainder. The subject-matter of his speeches is fundamental for Athenian social history, lying as it does where the study of Athenian legal practice converges with those of oratorical professionalism, property acquisition strategies, and private familial behaviour.

Style Dionysius chose him, with Lysias and Isocrates, to illustrate the older style of Attic oratory, and devoted a shrewd and sympathetic essay to him, comparing his style to that of Lysias. As he rightly said, though each speech is superficially lucid, he so 'uses insinuations and preliminary expositions and contrived divisions of material . . . and embroiders his speeches by alternating argument with emotional appeal' that he gained 'a reputation for wizardry and deceit' (*Isaeus* 3 and 4). The accuracy of Dionysius' judgement can be confirmed by following the analyses in Wyse's classic edition, a masterpiece of sceptical deconstruction.   J. K. D.

Isocrates (436–338 BC), Athenian orator of central importance. Although he lacked the voice and the confidence ever to address a large audience and so played no direct part in the affairs of the state, his written speeches, which presumably were of some influence on public opinion, provide us with a most valuable commentary on the great political issues of the 4th cent. His system of education in rhetoric exercised a profound effect on both the written and the spoken word: his many pupils included the historians *Ephorus and *Theopompus, the atthidographer Androtion, and the orators *Hyperides and *Isaeus. Judgements of his importance have variously treated him as the prophet of the Hellenistic world, and as the specious adulator of personal rulers, but, admired or despised, he cannot be neglected in the study of his age.

Life As son of a rich man, he studied under Prodicus, *Gorgias in Thessaly, Tisias, and the moderate oligarch, Theramenes. He was also a follower of *Socrates. Thus, while the Peloponnesian War (431–404 BC) was destroying both his father's fortune and his city's, he was receiving his education from teachers who included the critics of democracy and empire, and the effect was lasting.

In the 390s he turned his theoretical training to account and wrote speeches for others to use in the courts. Orations 16–21 belong to this early phase. Soon discontented with the profession of *logographos* (speech-writer), he began to train others in rhetoric. In *Against the Sophists* he advertised his principles, and of the early writings the *Helen* and *Busiris* displayed his skill on themes already treated by others. It was perhaps in this period before the King's Peace of 386 BC that he opened a school on Chios. The *Panegyricus*, published in 380 after ten years of composition, was his version of a conventional subject celebrated by Gorgias and Lysias; its demand that the Greeks unite under the shared hegemony of Athens and Sparta was familiar, and the long period of composition suggests that it was intended to be an enduring masterpiece of its kind, not, as some have supposed, a topical plea for the establishment of the Second Athenian Confederacy. One of Isocrates' most distinguished pupils was the Athenian general Timotheus whom at some stage Isocrates had accompanied on campaign and served by writing his dispatches to the Athenian people, and as a result of Timotheus' successes Athens was able in 375 to make the peace which embodied the principle of the shared hegemony. Despite the fact that Persia's position in the peace was unchanged, Isocrates lauded it, perhaps partly on personal grounds, and began to address pleas, very similar in form to the *Philippus* of 346, to eminent individuals begging them to assume the lead against Persia, first Agesilaus, then *Dionysius I, then Alexander of Pherae in *Thessaly (cf. Speusippus' *Letter to Philip* 13) and later perhaps Archidamus III of Sparta (cf. *Epistle* 9, of doubtful authenticity). Their reaction is not recorded, nor that of other Greeks, but the ambitious proposals of Jason of Pherae suggest that Isocrates' pleas were to some not wholly impractical.

In 373 when Thebes seized Plataea, he composed the *Plataïcus* purporting to be a speech to the Athenian assembly urging reprisals, and this may have been a sincere manifestation of antipathy to Thebes as a disruptive rival to Athens and Sparta. Likewise the *Archidamus* (366), the imagined speech of the future Spartan king about the Peace of 366/5, may reflect Isocrates' own inclinations. But other writings in this period can hardly be much more than rhetorical exercises, viz. the orations *To Nicocles* (*c*.372), *Nicocles* (*c*.368), and *Evagoras* (*c*.365).

The failure of Athens in the Social War of 357–355 (see ATHENS, HISTORY) and the perilous financial position of the state in 355 stirred Isocrates to denounce in the *De pace* the war policy of the imperialists as the way to bankruptcy, and to demand, in place of the limited peace being made with the allies, a Common Peace and the solution of economic difficulties by the foundation of colonies in Thrace: on the question of a Panhellenic crusade the speech is strikingly silent; the Persian ultimatum of 355 had ruled it out for the moment. The speech is a companion piece to the *Poroi* of *Xenophon; both writings illuminate the financial and foreign policy of Eubulus. Shortly after, in the *Areopagiticus*, Isocrates advocated return to a sober constitution under which the Areopagus would exercise its ancient general supervision of all aspects of life: although some would ascribe the speech to the period before the Social War, it probably belongs to 354 when the supporters of Chares were beginning to raise their heads again, and in view of the impending prosecution of Timotheus Isocrates may have been in a gloomy mood about the future of Athens under its existing constitution. The treatise must have made a curious impression on his countrymen. Certainly by 353 Isocrates was very much on the defensive. By then he had amassed wealth unprecedented for his profession, and by the law of Periander (? 357) he had become liable to frequent *trierarchies; challenged in 354/3 to an *antidosis* (a kind of legal challenge which might result in an exchange of properties), Isocrates had emerged from the court unsuccessful and, imagining himself as a second Socrates, felt moved to write his apologia in the *Antidosis* of 353, in which he criticized his rivals and gave some account of what he himself professed. This is the chief source of our knowledge of his system of education.

In 346 he published his most important treatise, the *Philippus*. Written between the voting of the Peace of Philocrates and *Philip II of Macedon's intervention in Phocis, it expounded afresh the programme of the *Panegyricus* and called on Philip 'to take the lead of both the concord (*homonoia*) of the Hellenes [Greeks] and the campaign against the *barbarians' (§16) and to relieve the misery of Greece by planting colonies in the western satrapies of the Persian empire (§120). In the following year, when Philip instead of beginning the crusade had got himself wounded in war against northern barbarians, Isocrates sent a further letter (*Epistle* 2) urging Philip to begin the campaign against Persia and so acquit himself of slanderous accusations about his real intentions; there is no suggestion here that Isocrates thought of a League of Corinth (see PHILIP II) as the necessary instrument for Philip's leadership of 'the concord of the Hellenes'. We do not know how Isocrates reacted to Philip's proposal to extend the peace brought in 344 by his old pupil Python, but shortly after the collapse of this diplomatic initiative in early 342, he began the last of his great treatises, the *Panathenaicus*, the completion of which was delayed by illness until 339. It was in part personal apologia, in part a comprehensive comparison of Athens and Sparta greatly to the glory of the former. Nowhere did he manifest any further interest in the great theme of the *Panegyricus* and the *Philippus*. Events had disappointed him and the epistles *To Alexander* (? 342) and *To Antipater* (? 340) were purely personal. One last effort remained. After discussion with Antipater, when after the battle of Chaeronea (338 BC) he came to negotiate, Isocrates wrote an appeal to Philip (*Epistle* 3) to set about the programme of the *Philippus*. The Peace of Demades was the answer, and at the time of the annual burial of the dead in autumn 338 Isocrates starved himself to death.

Significance In the realm of political ideas large claims have been made for Isocrates as the man who inspired Philip with the idea of attacking Persia, who envisaged not only the form of Hellenic league that established concord and defined the relation of Greece and the Macedonian kings but also the flowering of Greek culture in the Hellenistic world. These claims cannot be substantiated. The various writings addressed to Philip probably helped Philip to form a clearer idea of the nature and strength of the Panhellenist movement the support of which he needed, but that they did more is a conjecture against which Isocrates' own words in *Epistle* 3 (§3) contend. His ideas about the partnership of Philip and the Greeks appear from the treatises to have been very imprecise, and the fact that he was said to have sent substantially the same epistle to Philip as to Agesilaus suggests that he sought little more than a good general for the campaign. As to the role of the new colonies, he appears not to have thought of a dispersion of Greeks beyond Asia Minor, and far from the leavening of barbary he spoke as if Greek cities would form separate free entities surrounded by barbarians, ruled as barbarians had to be ruled. For the colonies were to effect merely the removal from Greece of the impoverished, and he had no vision of the prosperity that could and did flow from the creation of new trading areas. On the other hand, Isocrates did provide answers to the two great problems of his age, viz. the discord (*stasis*) within cities due to poverty, and the discord between cities due to petty ambitions and rivalries, and one has only to compare the views of *Plato and *Aristotle to see that, naïve as Isocrates seems, he was by far the most practical; neither of the philosophers explained how cities were to be kept from destroying each other, and their plans for ensuring concord within the city by controlling the growth of population contrast unfavourably with Isocrates' proposals to settle in prosperity those whose poverty was the source of revolutionary violence.

Much has been made of the somewhat imprecise proposals for curing the ills of *democracy in the *Areopagiticus*. It is to be noted that these proposals are part of a long tradition deriving from his early master, Theramenes, and found fulfilment in the arrangements of Demetrius of Phalerum: Isocrates was not alone. In his other writings the tone is very different, and this outburst may have been occasioned largely by the serious condition of Athens after the Social War.

In the history of education Isocrates has an important place. See EDUCATION, GREEK. The details of his system remain somewhat obscure, but it would seem that his pupils received under his personal supervision a course of instruction which was neither purely speculative nor a mere training in rhetoric. He disdained the business of the lawcourts as well as 'astrology, geometry, and the like' which at best, he held, did no harm but were of no use 'either in personal matters or in public affairs', and he eschewed the logic-chopping of dialectic, 'the so-called eristic dialogues'. For him the true concern of higher education was 'discussion of general and practical matters', the training of men for discussion and action in the sphere of the practical. What exactly such 'great affairs' were he did not specify, but it would seem that the sort of matters discussed in his own speeches provided the themes for his pupils' speeches which were to be well, that is persuasively argued.

In all this he was in contrast to *Plato whose teaching was at once highly theoretical and essentially dogmatic. Plato aimed to teach men what to think, Isocrates how to argue. There was, not surprisingly, tension between the two and (though many have denied it) with delicate irony Plato in the *Phaedrus* (279a) sneered at Isocrates, who defended himself and his system in the *Antidosis*.

Writings Of the 60 orations extant under his name in Roman times, 25 were considered genuine by *Dionysius of Halicarnassus, and 28 by Caecilius. Twenty-one survive today; six are court speeches. Of the nine letters extant the authenticity of 1, 3, 4, and 9 has been questioned but never disproved.

The works of Isocrates represent Attic prose in its most elaborate form. Dionysius (*Comp.* 23) compared it to 'closely woven material', or 'a picture in which the lights melt imperceptibly into shadows'. He seems, in fact, to have paid more attention to mere expression than any other Greek writer. He was so careful to avoid hiatus that Dionysius could find no single instance in the whole of the *Areopagiticus*; he was very sparing even in the elision of short vowels, and crasis, except of *kai* and *an*, occurs rarely. Dissonance of consonants, due to the repetition of similar syllables in successive words, and the combination of letters which are hard to pronounce together, is similarly avoided. These objects are attained without any perceptible dislocation of the natural order of words. Another

characteristic of the style is the author's attention to rhythm; though avoiding poetical metres, he considered that prose should have rhythms of its own, and approved of certain combinations of trochee and iambus. His periods are artistic and elaborate; the structure of some of the longer sentences is so complex that he overreaches himself; he sacrifices lucidity to form, and becomes monotonous. His vocabulary is almost as pure as that of *Lysias, but while the simplicity of Lysias appears natural, the smoothness of Isocrates is studied.   G. L. C.

Italy (see ◀Map 3▶) The name *Italia*, probably a Graecized form of Italic *Vitelia* (= 'calf-land'), was originally restricted to the southern half of the 'toe' but was gradually extended. By 450 BC it meant the region subsequently inhabited by the Bruttii (Theophr. *Hist. pl.* 5. 8); by 400 it embraced Lucania as well (Thuc. 6. 4, 7. 33); Campania was included after 325, and by *Pyrrhus' day (early 3rd cent. BC) Italia as a geographical expression meant everything south of Liguria and Cisalpine Gaul (Zonar. 8. 17; see GAUL (CISALPINE)); this area, however, only acquired political unity after the Social War of 91–89 BC (see ROME (HISTORY), §1.5). Cisalpine Gaul was not officially incorporated until *Augustus' time when, accordingly, Italy reached its natural Alpine frontiers. Unofficially, however, whatever the administrative divisions, the whole country south of the Alps had been called Italy from *Polybius' time onwards. The Augustan poets also call Italy *Hesperia* (= 'the western land'), *Saturnia* (= strictly Latium), *Oenotria* (= strictly SW Italy), *Ausonia* (= 'the land of the Ausones', *Opica* to the Greeks; strictly Campania).

Italy's greatest length is roughly 1,100 km. (680 mi.); the greatest breadth of the peninsula proper is some 240 km. (150 miles). Its long coastline possesses comparatively few, mostly indifferent ports, Genoa (Genua), Spezia, Naples (Neapolis), Tarentum, Brundisium, Ancona, and Pola being noteworthy exceptions. In compensation, however, Italy could exploit its central position to build a Mediterranean empire. Mountains, valleys, and plains in juxtaposition feature the Italian landscape. On the north are the Alps, a natural but not impossible frontier: the Carnic Alps pass is not formidable and the Brenner from time immemorial has been used by invaders attracted by Italy's pleasant climate, fertility, and beauty; the Alps actually are steeper on the Italian side. Between Alps and Apennines lies the indefensible north Italian plain watered by the Po (Padus). The Apennines traverse peninsular Italy, impeding but not actually preventing communications; the ancients' belief that they abounded in minerals was erroneous, since Italy only possessed some alluvial gold, copper (Etruria), iron (Elba), and marble (Liguria).

Despite fertile upland valleys the mountain districts usually permitted only a relatively frugal existence. The plains, however, were amazingly productive, being enriched partly by volcanic activity (Euganean district in the north, Alban hills in Latium, mons Vultur in Apulia, the still-active Vesuvius in Campania), partly by fertilizing silt carried down by numerous rivers which in winter contained adequate amounts of water. (Northern Italy also possessed important lakes, but not central and southern Italy apart from Trasimene, Fucinus, and water-filled craters like Albanus and Avernus.) Italy's natural products were consequently abundant and varied: *olives, various fruits, cereals, *timber, etc., even though some typically Italian products of today e.g. oranges and tomatoes, were unknown in antiquity. The variety is explained chiefly by the varied climate, which is temperate if not cold in the mountains and northern Italy and warm if not hot in southern Italy. Possibly the ancient climate was slightly more equable; malaria (see DISEASE) was certainly less prevalent. Italy contains excellent pasturage; in many districts ranching supplanted agriculture. Also its seas abound in fish (see FISHING).

Italy was thus well adapted to support human life, and did so from palaeolithic times. Agriculturally based neolithic settlements first appear in some parts of the peninsula around 5000 BC, and metal technology in the third millennium BC. During the bronze age (the so-called Apennine culture of the second millennium BC), the first settlements in naturally-defended positions are found, especially in western central Italy. There was some trade with, and perhaps colonization by, the Mycenaeans in SW coastal areas from about 1400. In the flatlands of Emilia, around Modena (Mutina), Parma, and Piacenza (Placentia), there emerged in the middle to late bronze age the *terramara* culture, with low-lying villages built on piles; a mould for casting a *terramara*-type axe has been found at Mycenae. From the late second millennium BC, there began to develop the 'proto-Villanovan' and then the Villanovan cultures. Iron came into limited use, and during the 8th cent. BC, contact was established between Etruria, Latium, and the early Greek colonies in southern Italy (see COLONIZATION, GREEK). This was a stimulus to, and a profound influence upon, the emergence of the *Etruscan cities, which grew out of Villanovan settlements in Etruria. The cities of Latium, including Rome, likewise expanded. Elsewhere in Italy an immensely diverse mosaic of peoples began to achieve cultural and political identities. Down the east coast were Veneti, Picenes, Daunians, Peucetians, and Messapians. In the mountainous backbone of Italy were Ligurians, Umbrians, Sabines, Samnites, Volsci, Lucanians, and the Bruttii of Calabria; the Samnites in particular expanded out of their homelands in the 5th cent. BC. The coastal fringes of SW and southern Italy, together with *Sicily, comprised Magna Graecia. In the north, Gauls settled from c.400 or before. In the west, apart from the Etruscans, there were the Latins of Latium, the related Faliscans and Hernici, Aurunci-Ausones, and Oenotri (= Sicels?). Some 40 languages were spoken altogether, and the peoples varied greatly in culture and level of civilization. Italy's mountainous topography accentuated and perpetuated such divergences.

Ultimately, the peoples of Italy were for the first time united under the hegemony of Rome. This was a protracted task, occupying the half-millennium between the 5th cent. BC and the reign of Augustus. *Romanization was slow and uneven, but was aided by the gradual creation of a new road network; by the founding of citizen, Latin and, later, veteran, colonies; and by the diffusion of the Latin language, mass-produced Roman goods, new concepts of town planning, and the spread of Romanized villas and farms. It was also fuelled by the profits brought in through the wars of conquest, which encouraged public and private patronage, as a means of social and political advantage.

With Italy finally unified, Augustus divided it into eleven administrative districts (*regiones*):

I. Latium, Campania, Picentini district
II. Apulia, Calabria, Hirpini district
III. Lucania, *ager Bruttius*
IV. Region inhabited by Samnites, Frentani, Marrucini, Marsi, Paeligni, Aequiculi, Vestini, Sabini
V. Picenum, Praetuttii district
VI. Umbria, *ager Gallicus*
VII. Etruria
VIII. Gallia Cispadana
IX. Liguria
X. Venetia, Istria, Cenomani district
XI. Gallia Transpadana

From the late 1st cent. AD, Italy's political and commercial pre-eminence began to wane. The process accelerated under the African and Syrian Severan dynasty (193–235), and, under Diocletian, the imperial court moved to Mediolanum (Milan), 300. Diocletian also initiated administrative changes, so that by *Constantine I's time, Italy was divided into sixteen provinces which now included Sicily, Sardinia, Corsica, and Raetia. *Christianity made relatively gradual progress in Italy after the edict of Milan (313) until the later 4th cent., a major period of church building in Rome, Milan, and elsewhere. In 404 the imperial court moved to the well-protected town of Ravenna, and when the Ostrogoths under Odoacer deposed the last western Roman emperor, Romulus Augustulus, in 476, Ravenna was retained as a capital, and further embellished. The Byzantine reconquest (535–54) was soon checked by the Lombard invasions of 568.   E. T. S.; T. W. P.

ivory (GK. *elephas*, Lat. *ebur*), a material derived from the tusk of the Asiatic or African *elephant or the tooth of the hippopotamus. Capable of being carved in the round, or in relief, used as inlay, as a veneer, turned on a lathe, or even moulded, ivory was a multi-purpose commodity that was imported into the Mediterranean from North Africa and the Levant. The Old Persian for the Nile delta meant 'The Tusks'. There were flourishing schools of ivory-working in bronze age Crete (see MINOAN CIVILIZATION), but many 'Minoan' statuettes in museums outside Greece are suspected forgeries. Rich finds of ivory inlays at Nimrud, Arslan Tash, and other near-eastern sites have echoes in ivory objects found at *Ephesus, *Samos, *Delphi, and in

ivory Ivory plaque showing *Dionysus, satyr, and maenad, from the 'Prince's Tomb', *Aegae (late 4th cent. BC). Such plaques, sometimes with added gilding, commonly decorated Greek luxury furniture.

Laconia. At all periods, furniture was decorated with ivory plaques. Ivory was used for the flesh parts of cult statues (e.g. Phidias' chryselephantine Athena Parthenos and his *Zeus at *Olympia), and for temple doors.   J. B.; M. V.

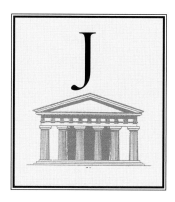

Janus, god of door and gate (*ianua*) at Rome. Like a door, he looked both ways, and is therefore depicted as a double-headed and bearded man (the image chosen for many early Roman coins). More generally he controlled beginnings, most notably as the eponym of the month January (he was named first in prayer, e.g. Livy 8. 9. 6, the *devotio* (ritual self-sacrifice) of Publius Decius Mus), and was linked with the symbolism of the gate at the beginning and end of military campaigns (the bad omen of the departure of the Fabii from Rome before their destruction at the battle of the Cremera involved going through the right-hand *ianus* or arch of the city-gate instead of the left, Livy 2. 49. 8). This was most famously expressed in the ritual of the closing of the temple of Janus Geminus in the Forum in times of complete peace: under Numa, in 235 BC, three times under *Augustus, and more frequently in the imperial period. *Domitian transferred the cult to a new shrine in the forum 'Transitorium'.

This shrine (as depicted on coins) was little more than a gateway itself. It was probably *geminus*—'twin'—in being a four-way arch, like the 'arch of Janus' which survives in the forum Boarium (the porta Triumphalis through which victorious generals crossed the *pomerium* (religious boundary) into the city probably had this shape). There are serious topographical problems about the nature and relationship of the other ancient shrines of Janus along the Sacred Way, which may have been related to crossings of the early watercourses in the area. A sanctuary in the forum Holitorium was Gaius Duilius' monument for his victory at Mylae (260 BC).

Janus was a god of considerable importance (*divom deus*, god of gods, in the *Hymn of the Salii*, Varro, *Ling.* 7. 27; for cosmic significance, Ov. *Fast.* 1. 101 f.). The *rex sacrorum* sacrificed to him in the Regia (see ROME (TOPOGRAPHY)) on the *Dies Agonalis* of 9 January.   N. P.

Jews (*see following page*)

Josephus (Flavius Iosephus) (b. AD 37/8) was a Greek historian but also a Jewish priest (see JEWS) of aristocratic descent and largely Pharisaic education, and a political leader in pre-70 Jerusalem. Though a zealous defender of Jewish religion and culture, his writing is largely hostile to the various revolutionary groups, whom he regarded as responsible for the fall of the Temple: his theology centres on the idea that God was currently on the Romans' side. Participation in a delegation to Rome (*c.*64) impressed on him the impracticality of resistance. When the Jerusalem leaders put him in charge of Galilee, he played an ambiguous role. He was besieged at Jotapata, but when captured, evaded a suicide pact and, he claims, was freed when his prophecy of *Vespasian's accession came true. He remained close to *Titus until the fall of Jerusalem, making several attempts to persuade the besieged city to surrender. He was given Roman citizenship, and, after the war, an imperial house to live in in Rome, a pension, and land in Judaea.

He first wrote an account of the war, now lost, in Aramaic for the Jews of Mesopotamia. Most, if not all, of the seven books of the Greek *Jewish War* appeared between 75 and 79. The first book and a half sketch Jewish history from the Maccabean revolt (see MACCABEES) to AD 66. Much of the rest is based on Josephus' own experience, together with eyewitness reports from others and, probably, the diaries (*commentarii*) of Vespasian and Titus. The triumph at Rome over *Judaea capta* is described in detail. The *Jewish Antiquities*, in twenty books, published in 93/4, is a history of the Jews from the Creation to just before the outbreak of revolt, ostensibly for Greek readers. The biblical history of the first ten books depends not only on the Hebrew and Greek Bibles, but also on current Jewish oral interpretation. For the post-biblical period, works of Jewish-Hellenistic literature such as the Letter of Aristeas, 2 Esdras, and 1 Maccabees (see MACCABEES) are adapted. In the later part, there is a substantial dependence on the histories of Nicolaus of Damascus. The famous *testimonium* to Jesus is partly or even wholly an interpolation. Appended to the *Antiquities* was the *Life*—not a full autobiography, but a defence of Josephus' conduct in Galilee, responding to his critics, especially Iustus of Tiberias. The *Against Apion* was an apologia for Judaism in two books,

[*continued on p. 383*]

Jews

Jews (in Greek and Roman times). The Jews at the beginning of the period were an ethnic group with distinctive religious practices. In the course of the period, the religious definition acquired new emphasis, and significant numbers of Jews became Jews by conversion rather than birth.

Palestine A demographically mixed region, this was understood to be the homeland of the Jews throughout the period, though in fact housing a minority of them. More precisely, the Jews belonged to the small area around Jerusalem known in Greek as *Ioudaia*, whence the name *Ioudaioi*. However, the two revolts against Roman rule brought about the physical exclusion of the Jews from their centre.

From 538 to 332 BC the Jews of Palestine were a part of the Persian empire (see PERSIA). Coins reveal that their territory was called Yehud and the Persian governor *pekah*. The high priest seems to have been the highest Jewish official. A century of Ptolemaic rule (see EGYPT (PTOLEMAIC)) followed *Alexander the Great's death. The Zeno papyri illuminate in general the administration and economic life of the area, and reveal the high-level dealings of Tobias, a Jewish landowner east of the Jordan, with the Ptolemaic governor Apollonius.

In 200 Palestine passed into *Seleucid hands, and the pressure of Hellenism was manifested, first in dissension within the high-priestly families, and then in Antiochus IV's installation of a pagan cult in the Temple (168/7 BC), which was resisted by the *Maccabees. Only in 142 BC was the Seleucid garrison expelled from Jerusalem. For the next 80 years, the Jews were ruled by the hereditary Hasmonean high priests, attaining complete autonomy after the death of Antiochus VII in 134 BC. The expansion of Jewish territory involved a phenomenon new to Judaism, the conversion of the neighbouring peoples, Idumaeans and Ituraeans, at least partly by force.

*Pompey's intervention in 63 BC, occasioned by a quarrel between the two sons of the defunct queen, Alexandra Salome, led to the installation of one of them, Hyrcanus, and to the reduction of the kingdom, with the freeing of the conquered Greek cities. Aulus Gabinius organized the ethnarchy in 57 into five self-governing communities, with Hyrcanus remaining as ethnarch until his removal by the Parthians and the appointment of the Idumaean convert Herod as ruler.

In AD 6 Judaea was annexed, together with Samaria and Idumaea, to form the Roman province of Judaea, administered by equestrian officials (prefects, later procurators). A census in that year crystallized opposition and generated an ideology of resistance. Called by *Josephus the 'fourth philosophy', this tendency was evidently the source of the subsequent, more famous rebel groupings, *sicarii* and zealots. A pattern of procuratorial misgovernment enlisted the sympathies of the Jewish crowd in Jerusalem and of the poor in Galilee to the anti-Roman cause. The high-priestly and landowning élites criticized Rome only under extreme provocation, as when the emperor *Gaius attempted to have his statue placed in the Temple (39/40). The installation of Marcus Iulius Agrippa I (41–4) by Claudius was to prove merely a brief interlude in the regime of the procurators. Famines, banditry, and the breakdown of the working relationship between the Jewish ruling class and Rome marked the years before the outbreak of the First Jewish Revolt in AD 66. The Temple sacrifices for the emperor's welfare were terminated, and a provisional government in Jerusalem appointed regional leaders (including the historian *Josephus), chose a demotic high priest by lot, abolished debt, and issued its own freedom coinage. But the Jews were deeply divided politically. In Galilee the conflict between pro- and anti-war elements made resistance ineffectual. In besieged Jerusalem, three rebel factions conducted a civil war until the last stages of the siege.

In 70 the Judaean victory of *Vespasian and *Titus, confirmed by the burning of Jerusalem and the (perhaps accidental) destruction of the Temple, was crucial in consolidating the Flavian seizure of power. Much was made of 'Judaea capta' in Flavian *propaganda, culminating in the *triumph over the Jews. Jewish-owned land in Judaea was expropriated.

From 70 the province of Judaea was governed by legates and a legion (X Fretensis) was stationed in Jerusalem. Jewish religious and cultural life centred for a generation on Jamnia (Jabneh), an enclave on the Judaean coast, where a new definition of Judaism without a Temple was evolved by the first rabbis.

The revolt in the Diaspora under Trajan, in 115–18, produced disturbances in Palestine, suppressed by Lusius Quietus. Of greater significance was the second great revolt in Palestine, led by Bar Kokhba. Its long-term causes are ill-documented, but the immediate triggers were *Hadrian's prohibition of circumcision, and his plan to turn Jerusalem into the Roman colonia of Aelia Capitolina. After the costly suppression of this revolt, in 135, the name of the province became *Syria Palaestina, another legion (VI Ferrata) was stationed in Galilee, and, according to Christian sources, Jews were altogether excluded from Jerusalem.

A further revolt occurred under *Antoninus Pius, in spite of his exemption of the Jews from Hadrian's ban on circumcision. Later, the Jews are said to have supported Avidius Cassius; and a rebellion in the time of *Septimius Severus is probably associated with the rising of Pescennius Niger.

During the 3rd cent. Jewish life flourished in Galilee: *synagogues began to proliferate, in villages as well as towns; rabbinic influence on daily life grew; and Jews played their part in some of the newly refurbished cities, notably Caesarea. The patriarch, located successively in several Galilean towns, operated as the representative of the Jews of Palestine and was closely associated with the rabbis. Greek was widely used by the educated élite, though the first great rabbinic compilation, the Mishnah, was written in Hebrew, c.200. Prosperous Jews from the Syrian and Phoenician Diaspora were buried, alongside rabbis, in heavily figurative sarcophagi, in the spacious vaults and catacombs of Beth Shearim.

This vigorous community life, and the building of synagogues, continued into the era of Christianization (see CHRISTIANITY) in the Holy Land which followed the conversion of *Constantine I, when sites associated with biblical events became focuses of *pilgrimage. But from then on there were spiritual claims to Jerusalem, Judaea, and Galilee which rivalled those of the Jews.

A destructive Jewish revolt in Palestine, allegedly centred on a supposed Messiah, is ascribed by one source to the reign of Gallus Caesar (350/1). This may have been a protest against Christian anti-Jewish legislation. But it was left to a pagan emperor, *Julian the Apostate, to plan for the rebuilding of the Jewish Temple and the restoration there of the blood sacrifices. An earthquake, a fire, and various supernatural manifestations put a stop to the construction; and a year later (363) Julian was dead.

The Diaspora The dispersion of the Jews began in 586 BC, when Nebuchadnezzar took the inhabitants of Jerusalem into captivity. Many of them did not return when permitted by *Cyrus the Great of *Persia in 538, but remained voluntarily in *Babylonia, where flourishing communities existed for centuries, producing in late antiquity the greatest monument of rabbinic learning, the Babylonian Talmud. During the Hellenistic period, many Jews migrated from Palestine and also from Babylonia, settling around the eastern Mediterranean, especially in Syria, Asia Minor, and Egypt. Jewish military colonists had lived at Elephantine for centuries, and now they were joined by new military and civilian settlers in both countryside and town. The community at *Alexandria became the most important in the Diaspora, the splendour of its synagogue a byword, its mixed Jewish-Greek culture highly creative. Numbers alone made the Jews prominent inhabitants of the city. But by the 1st cent. AD there were sizeable communities in most of the cities of the eastern Mediterranean. The *Acts of the Apostles is important testimony to the local prominence of synagogues.

Expansion to Italy and the west began later, but the community in Rome was established by the mid-2nd cent. BC. Jews taken as slaves after the various wars in Palestine swelled the numbers of the Diaspora, as in due course did the voluntary attachment of pagans to the Jewish synagogues of Rome. Inscriptions from the Jewish catacombs of Rome reveal the existence of eleven synagogues in the 2nd to 4th cents. AD, whose names suggest an earlier, in some cases an Augustan, foundation.

Diaspora Jews retained their identity and the basic religious practices of Judaism—male circumcision, observance of the sabbath, and other festivals (notably Tabernacles) and the avoidance of non-kosher meat. Until AD 70, their allegiance to the Temple and to Jerusalem as their mother city was signalled by the payment of the Temple tax and by the practice of pilgrimage at the major agricultural festivals.

At the same time, inscriptions concerning Jewish benefactions and commemorations from many cities in the eastern Roman empire make it clear that the Jews adapted to their varied environments. Greek was their native language. In Cyrenaica, at Berenice, there were Jewish town-councillors and Jewish ephebes (see GYMNASIUM) as early as the 1st cent. AD. In the 3rd cent. the phenomenon is quite common. Non-Jews expressed attachment to the Jewish synagogue by becoming benefactors, 'God-fearers' (or sympathizers), and proselytes. The great Jewish inscription from *Aphrodisias shows an association of Jews and proselytes subscribing to a memorial together with a separate group of 'God-fearers', including councillors.

The advocacy of Hyrcanus and the Herodians, together with their own diplomacy, gained for Jewish communities in the Roman provinces the patronage successively of *Caesar, of Mark *Antony, and of *Augustus. In their disputes with their neighbours, they were assisted by Roman decrees which upheld their right to observe their customary practices; and these decrees were adopted empire-wide as precedents. Synagogues, though classed as *collegia* (associations), were exempted by Caesar from his general ban. The right to raise, deposit, and transmit the Temple tax was upheld. Sometimes, special food markets were permitted, sometimes exemption granted from court appearances on the sabbath or from military service which rendered sabbath observance impossible. Christian authors were later to describe Judaism as a *religio licita* ('legitimate religion') in the Roman empire on the basis of these arrangements; see RELIGION, ROMAN. Furthermore, after the destruction of the Temple, the two-drachma (half-shekel) tax paid by all adult Jewish males to the Temple was extended to women and children, diverted to *Jupiter Capitolinus, and deposited in the new *fiscus iudaicus* (Jewish fisc or treasury). *Domitian's exactions were notoriously harsh, but *Nerva issued coins announcing his removal of the abuses. Implicit in the taxation was an official acknowledgement of the existence of Jewish communities, and this also contributed to the Christians' sense that the Jews had been 'legalized'.

Periodic expulsions of the Jews from the city of Rome were short-lived and did not undermine their standing elsewhere. Three expulsions of the Jews are recorded: in 139 BC; by *Tiberius in AD 19; and by *Claudius. The authorities' fear of disturbance and of un-Roman practices, rather than overt proselytizing, was the immediate cause of anti-Jewish measures, as of those against other alien cults and practices. The Jews do not appear to have been actively seeking converts during this period. It was not until the reign of *Septimius Severus that conversion to Judaism was forbidden; even then, there was no Jewish 'mission'.

In spite of—or because of—Jewish acculturation, friction between Jews and their neighbours was not uncommon. In Alexandria, anti-Semitic literature was produced in the Hellenistic period; but it was the Roman annexation of Egypt which shook a centuries-long political equilibrium by redefining the privileges accorded to Alexandrian citizens, and excluding the Jews from them. In AD 38, a visit of Marcus Iulius Agrippa I to Alexandria sparked the first pogrom in Jewish history, when synagogues were burnt, shops looted, and the Jews herded into a ghetto. Trouble returned in 66, at a time when the outbreak of revolt in Palestine also provoked Greek—Jewish violence in a number of Syrian cities. The failure of the revolt saw further attacks on urban Jews.

In 115 the Jews of Cyrenaica rose against their pagan neighbours and against the Roman authorities, inflicting considerable damage and targeting pagan temples. The uprising, which suggests considerable frustration, spread to Alexandria and other parts of Egypt; and to *Cyprus, where it was furthered by a charismatic leader. The rebellion in 116 in *Trajan's new Mesopotamian province, coinciding with these events, brought in the Jews of Babylonia. The revolts were suppressed by Quintus Marcius Turbo with considerable effort. An era of more peaceful coexistence for the Jewish Diaspora ensued, and the increasingly high profile of Jewish communities in some cities is attested by excavated remains of synagogues. The case of Sardis is particularly noteworthy, where a massive synagogue adjoined the city's main baths-complex, and was refurbished several times, well into the Christian era. The legal restrictions placed on Jews by the Christian emperors of the 4th and 5th cents. did not in the first instance crush the activities of the synagogues. See ANTI-SEMITISM.   T. R.

demonstrating its antiquity in comparison with Greek culture, and attacking anti-Semitic writers, from the 3rd cent. BC to Apion. Josephus' writings were preserved by the early Church.   E. M. S.; T. R.

judges, foreign, modern coinage to describe a judge or panel of judges (*xenikon dikastērion*) sent by one Greek city to hear lawsuits in another, often on the basis of a shared tie of *kinship (*syngeneia*). Attested mainly from honorific decrees on stone, these judges—commonly between one and five with a secretary—are known from the 4th cent. BC until the Antonines, but above all in Hellenistic times (see HELLENISM), when their dispatch could be orchestrated by kings or royal officials, as well as the Greek leagues (*koina*). They are found hearing both public and private suits, including disputes over written contracts (*sumbolaia*); long backlogs in local courts are a frequently cited reason for their presence. References to foreign judges who restored concord (*homonoia*) among citizens link this demand for impartial jurisdiction with the internal unrest (*stasis*), often based on the indebtedness of the poor to the rich, which marked many Greek cities in Hellenistic times.
                    A. J. S. S.

Julia, only daughter of *Augustus (by Scribonia), was born in 39 BC and betrothed in 37 to Marcus Antonius Antyllus. She was brought up strictly by her father and stepmother *Livia. In 25 she married her cousin Marcus Claudius Marcellus and in 21 *Agrippa, to whom she bore Gaius and Lucius Caesar, the younger Julia, Agrippina the Elder (Vipsania Agrippina), and Agrippa Postumus. Her third marriage, to *Tiberius (in 11), is said to have been happy at first, but estrangement followed, and her behaviour may have contributed to Tiberius' decision to retire from Rome in 6. In 2 BC Augustus learned of her alleged adulteries (e.g. with Iullus Antonius) and banished her to Pandateria; in AD 4 she was allowed to move to Rhegium. Scribonia voluntarily shared her exile. Augustus forbade her burial in his mausoleum, and Tiberius kept her closely confined and stopped her allowance, so that she died of malnutrition before the end of AD 14. Macrobius (*Sat.* 2. 5) speaks of her gentle disposition and learning, and gives anecdotes attesting her wit.   T. J. C.; R. J. S.

Julian 'the Apostate' (Flavius Claudius Iulianus), emperor AD 361–3, was born at Constantinople in 331, the son of a half-brother of *Constantine I, Julius Constantius. After his father's murder in dynastic intrigues of 337, Julian was placed by Constantius II in the care of an Arian bishop and from 342 was confined for six years on an imperial estate in Cappadocia. He impressed his Christian tutors there as a gifted and pious pupil (see CHRISTIANITY), but his reading of the Greek classics was inclining him in private to other gods. In 351, as a student of philosophy, he encountered pagan Neoplatonists and was initiated as a theurgist by Maximus of Ephesus. For the next ten years Julian's pagan 'conversion' remained a prudently kept secret. He continued his studies in Asia and later at Athens until summoned to Milan by Constantius to be married to the emperor's sister Helena and proclaimed Caesar with charge over Gaul and Britain (6 November 355). Successful Rhineland campaigns against the Alamanni and Franks between 356 and 359 proved Julian a talented general and won him great popularity with his army. When Constantius ordered the transfer of choice detachments to the east the army mutinied and in February 361, probably with tacit prompting, proclaimed Julian Augustus. Constantius' death late that year averted civil war and Julian, now publicly declaring his paganism, entered Constantinople unopposed in December. A purge of the imperial court quickly followed, drastically reducing its officials and staff. In his brief reign Julian showed remarkable energy in pursuit of highly ambitious aims. An immediate declaration of general religious toleration foreshadowed a vigorous programme of pagan activism in the interest of '*Hellenism': the temples and finances of the ancestral cults were to be restored and a hierarchy of provincial and civic pagan priesthoods appointed, while the Christian churches and clergy lost the financial subsidies and privileges gained under Constantine and his successors. Though expressly opposed to violent persecution of Christians, Julian overtly discriminated in favour of pagan individuals and communities in his appointments and judgements: measures such as his ban on the teaching of classical literature and philosophy by Christian professors and his encouragement of charitable expenditure by pagan priests mark a determination to marginalize Christianity as a social force. His attempts to revive the role of the cities in local administration by restoring their revenues and councils and his remarkable plan to rebuild the Jewish Temple at Jerusalem are best appraised in the light of this fundamental aim.

Julian's military ambitions centred on an invasion of *Persia intended to settle Rome's long-running war with Sapor II. To prepare his expedition he moved in June 362 to

*Antioch, where his relations with the mainly Christian population deteriorated markedly during his stay. The expedition set out in March 363 but despite some early successes it was already in serious difficulties when Julian was fatally wounded in a mêlée in June 363. He left no heir (Helena died childless in 360, and Julian did not remarry), and after his death the reforms he had initiated quickly came to nothing.

Julian's personal piety and intellectual and cultural interests are reflected in his surviving writings, which show considerable learning and some literary talent. They include panegyrics, polemics, theological and satirical works, and a collection of letters, public and private. Of his anti-Christian critique, *Against the Galileans*, only fragments remain. His own philosophic ideology was rooted in Iamblichan Neoplatonism and theurgy. How forcefully it impinged on his public religious reforms is controversial: on one view, they were directed more to the founding of a Neoplatonist 'pagan Church' than to a restoration of traditional Graeco-Roman polytheism, and their potential appeal to the mass of contemporary pagans was correspondingly limited.

R. B. E. S.

Julius Caesar see CAESAR, JULIUS.

Juno, an old and important Italian goddess and one of the chief deities of Rome. Her name derives from the same root as *iuventas* (youth), but her original nature remains obscure. G. Wissowa's argument (*Religion und Kultus d. Römer*, 2nd. edn. (1912)) that she developed from the *iuno* attributed to individual women is probably mistaken, since that concept apparently arose during the republic on the analogy of the *genius*. On the other hand, her roles as a goddess of women and as a civic deity were both ancient and widespread, and it is difficult to give priority to either. Juno was widely worshipped under a number of epithets throughout central Italy. Some of her important civic cults in Rome were in fact imported from this region. Thus in the 5th cent. BC Juno Regina was brought from the *Etruscan town of Veii and received a temple on the Aventine. Also apparently Etruscan in origin was the Capitoline Triad of *Jupiter, Juno, and *Minerva; the Capitoline Juno was by the late republic also identified as Regina ('Queen'), and regularly carried that epithet in the imperial period. Another imported cult was that of Juno Sospita, the chief deity of Lanuvium (mod. Lanuvio), which from 338 BC onwards was administered jointly with Rome. The distinctive iconography of this goddess, who wears a goatskin and carries a spear and shield, indicates a martial character; Dumézil believed that her full epithet, Sospita Mater Regina, confirmed his thesis that Juno was originally trivalent, with influence over military prowess, fertility, and political organization. The cult of Juno Lucina, the goddess of childbirth, appears both in Rome and in other parts of Latium. The foundation-day of her temple on the Esquiline, 1 March, was traditionally celebrated as the Matronalia, when husbands gave presents to their wives.

Peculiar to Rome is Juno Moneta, whose cult dates to the 4th cent. BC. The ancient association of her epithet with *monere* (to warn) is usually accepted, but its origins are unknown. The first mint in Rome was later located in or near her temple on the *arx*, hence the derivation of 'money' from Moneta. Other epithets, such as Pronuba, belong more to poetry than cult. The Roman conception of Juno's character was deeply affected by her identification with similar goddesses of other cultures. The most important was the Greek *Hera: her mythology and characteristics were largely adopted for Juno, who was thus firmly established by the time of *Plautus as the wife of Jupiter and the goddess of marriage. The great goddess of *Carthage, Tanit, was also identified at a relatively early date with Juno, but had much less influence on her character. Apart from her part in the Capitoline Triad, Juno played a relatively minor role in the provinces. The exceptions are northern Italy, where the mother goddesses were sometimes called *iunones*, and Africa, where Juno Caelestis was heir to the cult of Tanit.

J. B. R.

Jupiter (*Iuppiter*), sovereign god of the Romans, bears a name referring to the 'luminous sky' (†*Dyew-pater*), the first member of which is etymologically identical with that of *Zeus. He was known to all Italic peoples.

Even if associated with the sky, storms, and lightning, Jupiter was not just a god of natural phenomena. These expressed and articulated, in fact, his function as sovereign divinity. Jupiter was sovereign by virtue of his supreme rank and by the patronage derived from exercise of the supreme power. His supreme rank was signified by the fact that the god or his priest was always mentioned at the head of lists of gods or priests, and that the climactic point of the month, before the waning of the moon, was sacred to him in particular (Macrob. *Sat.* 1. 15. 14). In addition, the Roman symbol of power, the sceptre (*sceptrum*), belonged to him and functioned as his symbol (Festus 81 Lindsay). This privilege was described by the traditional epithets of *optimus maximus*, 'the best and the greatest', or by the title *rex* given him by the poets (cf. G. Radke, *Entwicklung der Gottesvorstellung und der Gottesehrung in Rom* (1987), 241 ff.). His patronage of the exercise of sovereign power expressed itself in the fact that no political action could be accomplished without his favourable and prior judgement, expressed through the auspices and in the celebration of the *triumph, representing the fullest exercise of Roman supremacy. Between these two poles the figure of Roman Jupiter must be constructed.

In rituals as well as in mythical narratives (see G. Dumézil, *Les Dieux souverains des Indo-Européens* (1977)), the exercise of sovereignty by Jupiter, which made him into a deity with a political function, is presented under two aspects. On the one hand Jupiter was patron of the violent aspect of supremacy. As well as falling lightning, the Roman triumph, ending at his temple, represented the inexorable side of this power. From this point of view it is understandable that the grape and its product, *wine, were placed under his patronage. But Jupiter was also a political god, who agreed to exercise power within the limits imposed by law and good faith. It was he who took part in the institution of *templa*, those inner spaces in which the important activities of the Roman people took place, and patronized the *nundinae*, traditional days of popular assembly (Macrob. *Sat.* 1. 16. 30). It was he too who, by means of the auspices, conferred legitimacy on the choices and decisions of the Roman people. Finally, he was the patron of oaths and treaties, and punished perjurers in the terrible manner appropriate.

From the end of the regal period, the most brilliant of Jupiter's seats was his temple on the Capitol, which he shared with *Juno Regina (in the cella or chamber to the left) and *Minerva (in the right-hand cella). This triad constituted the group of patron deities of the city of Rome, whose well-being was the subject of an annual vow (Livy 41. 14. 7 ff.); under the empire, vows for the health of the ruler and his family were celebrated on 3 January. The first political action of the new consuls was the acquittal of these vows, formulated the previous year, and their utterance afresh. The anniversary of the Capitoline temple was celebrated during the Ludi Romani (4–19 September) on the Ides of September (13 September). On the Ides of November, during the Ludi Plebei or Plebeian Games (4–17 November; see PLEBS), a great banquet was celebrated on the Capitol (*Iovis epulum*), reuniting the Roman élite around the supreme god, along with Juno and Minerva. It was to the Capitol as well, and specifically to the *arx*, that the procession concluding the 'rites of the Ides', *sacra idulia*, ascended (Festus 372 Lindsay, entry under 'sacram viam'). Finally, the Ludi Capitolini, celebrated in honour of Jupiter Feretrius (15 October, Plut. *Rom.* 25; *Schol. Bern.* on Verg. *G.* 2. 384), their date of foundation uncertain, point to a third ancient sanctuary of Jupiter on the Capitol. Jupiter Feretrius, whom it is difficult to separate from Jupiter Lapis or 'Stone' (see Gell. *NA* 1. 21. 4; Livy 1. 24. 8, 30. 43. 9; Festus 102. 11 Lindsay), was invoked in treaties; the famous flint used in the most solemn oaths was kept there, as well as the *sceptrum* by which oaths were taken (Festus 81. 16 Lindsay). A tradition reactivated by *Augustus attributed to Jupiter the 'first' *spolia opima*, i.e. spoils offered by a Roman general who had slain an enemy leader in single combat (Festus 204. 8 Lindsay; cf. J. Rüpke, *Domi militiae* (1990), 217 ff.).

Jupiter was frequently associated with other deities. From a very early period an association thought by many to reflect Indo-European ideas linked him with *Mars and Quirinus. On the Capitol he shared his temple with Juno and Minerva. Near this temple were found deities who fell in some sense within his orbit: Fides and the problematic Dius Fidius, patrons of good faith and oaths.

The special priests of Jupiter were the *flamen Dialis* and his wife and, where the auspices were concerned, the *augures* (*interpretes Iovis optimi maximi*, 'interpreters of Jupiter Best and Greatest', Cic. *Leg.* 2. 20). J. Sch.

Justinian's codification is a term loosely used to describe the three volumes (*Codex, Digesta* or *Pandectae, Institutiones*) in which Justinian (AD 527–65) tried to restate the whole of Roman law in a manageable and consistent form, though this restatement, which runs to over a million words, is too bulky and ill-arranged to count as a codification in the modern sense.

Ninety years after the Theodosian Code of 438 a new codex (collection of laws) was needed to collect the laws enacted in the intervening period. Justinian, with a keen sense of his predecessors' neglect and his own superior dedication, seized the opportunity to carry out part of the programme envisaged by Theodosius II in 429. This involved including all imperial laws in one volume and ensuring that the laws in it were consistent with one another (C. *Haec* pref.). Within a few months of becoming emperor in 527, he ordered a commission of ten, mostly present or recent holders of public office, to prepare a comprehensive collection of imperial laws including those in the three existing codices (*Gregorianus, Hermogenianus*, and *Theodosianus*), so far as they were still in force, together with more recent laws (*novellae*). The laws were to be edited in a short and clear form, with no repetition or conflict, but attributed to the emperors and dates at which they had originally been issued. The commission contained some lawyers but its head was the politically powerful non-lawyer, John of Cappadocia. Within fourteen months the *Codex Iustinianus* in twelve books (*libri*) was finished and on 7 April 529 was promulgated as the exclusive source of imperial laws, the earlier codes being repealed (C. *Summa*). Its practical aim was to curtail lawsuits; and its compilation was widely regarded as a major achievement. It fitted a vision in which Justinian saw himself as rapidly restoring and extending the empire, in which process military and legal achievements would reinforce one another (C. *Summa* pref.). This 529 *Codex* does not survive, but the second edition of 534 does.

Besides the laws in the *Codex*, C. *Summa* allowed the writings of the old lawyers of authority to be cited in court. Their views not infrequently conflicted, the conflicts being settled by counting heads according to the Law of Citations of 426. In 429 Theodosius II had looked forward to a time when this voluminous material could be arranged under subject-headings and harmonized. Probably, though the matter is controversial, Justinian from the start intended to undertake the further project of collecting, condensing, and amending the rest of Roman law, provided someone could organize it: the incentive to outdo Theodosius still applied. At any rate, Justinian first arranged for the 50 most prominent conflicts between the old writers to be settled (*Quinquaginta decisiones*), then in December 530 (C. *Deo auctore*) ordered that these old works, which ran to over 1,500 books (*libri*), be condensed in 50 books and given the title *Digesta* ('Ordered Abstracts') or *Pandectae* ('Encyclopaedia'). For that purpose he set up a second commission consisting of élite lawyers under the quaestor Tribonianus, who had shown his mettle as a member of the earlier commission, along with another official, four law professors, and eleven advocates. They were to read the works of authority, none of them written later than about AD 300, and excerpt what was currently valid. As for the *Codex*, the commissioners were to edit the texts in a clear form with no repetition or contradiction. Thirty-nine writers were used for the compilation. The commission was not to count heads but to choose the best view, no matter who held it. In the upshot Ulpian, who provided two-fifths of the *Digesta*, was their main source; Paulus provided one-sixth.

The commission worked rapidly and the *Digesta* or *Pandectae* was promulgated on 16 December 533 (C. *Tanta/Dedōken*). The speed of the operation has led some scholars to suppose that the commissioners, instead of reading the original sources, worked from previous collections of material. But nothing on the required scale has been traced, and Tribonianus would have dismissed reliance on secondary sources as disreputable, even supposing it escaped detection. Time was saved in another way. As F. Bluhme discovered in 1820, the works to be read were divided into three groups, extracts from which are generally kept together in the finished *Digesta*. The inference is that three subcommittees were appointed to read the three groups of works; and the operation was perhaps further subdivided within the committees. Justinian, in whose palace the commission was working, could be relied on to see that the timetable was kept to, as he did with the construction of Hagia Sophia.

The compilers had authority not merely to eliminate obsolete or superfluous texts but to alter those they kept. The extent to which they made use of this power is controversial. In any event, if the new version of a text differed from the old, the new prevailed, on the theory that Justinian was entitled to amend the previous law as he wished. But the amended texts were 'out of respect for antiquity' attributed to the original authors and books. This was a compromise, unsatisfactory from a scholarly point of view, which enabled Justinian to claim that everything in the *Digesta* was his, while in fact often reverting to the law as it was before 300.

The practical aims of the *Digesta* were to shorten lawsuits and provide a revised law syllabus to be used in the schools of Berytus (mod. Beirut) and Constantinople (C. *Omnem*). To complete the reform of law-teaching Justinian ordered Tribonianus and two of the professors to prepare an up-to-date edition of the famous 2nd-cent. AD law teacher Gaius' lectures, the *Institutiones*, making use also of other elementary teaching books by writers of authority. The professors perhaps each drafted two books, while Tribonianus brought the whole up to date by adding an account of recent legislation, especially Justinian's. The *Institutiones*, like the *Digesta*, was promulgated in December 533. It has survived and was for many centuries a successful students' first-year book. Then in 534 a second edition of the *Codex* of 529 was produced, which included the reforming laws of the intervening five years. This also

has survived. The codification was now at an end. To avoid conflicting interpretations, commentaries on it were forbidden. Justinian, however, continued to legislate without pause, mainly in Greek, and private collections of his later laws (*novellae*) have been preserved.

His codification had a practical and a political aim. Its practical impact, though considerable, was limited by the fact that it was wholly in Latin. Hence in the Greek-speaking Byzantine empire few could make proper use of it until the coming of a Greek collection of laws, the *Basilica*, which in the 9th and 10th cents. at last fused the two main sources of law, *Codex* and *Digesta*. In the west Justinian's laws were in force for two centuries in parts of Italy and in North Africa until the expansion of Islam in the 7th cent.

The political aim of the codification was to renew, reform, and extend the Roman empire in its civil aspect. In this Justinian was in the long run successful, but not in the way he foresaw. He thought that the spread of Roman law depended on military conquest. In the west that proved short-lived; and when from the 11th cent. onwards his codification came to be taken as the basis of legal education and administration throughout Europe, it was not by force of arms but through its prestige and inherent rationality that his version of Roman law was adopted.   T. Hon.

Juvenal (Decimus Iunius Iuvenalis), Roman satirist, known primarily for the angry tone of his early *Satires*, although in later poems he developed an ironical and detached superiority as his satiric strategy. The highly rhetorical nature of the *Satires* has long been recognized but only recently has the allied concept of the 'mask' (*persona*) been deployed (primarily by W. Anderson, *Essays on Roman Satire* (1982)) to facilitate assessment of the *Satires* as self-conscious poetic constructs, rather than the reflections of the realities of Roman social life for which they have often been read. This approach is reinforced by rejection of the biographical interpretation, in which Juvenal's 'life' was reconstructed from details in the *Satires*. In fact, virtually nothing is known of his life: he is the addressee of three epigrams of *Martial (themselves highly sophisticated literary constructions) which indicate his skill in oratory. The absence of dedication to a patron in Juvenal's *Satires* may suggest that he was a member of the élite. The few datable references confirm Syme's assessment that the five books were written during the second and third decades of the 2nd cent. AD (or later), at about the same time as *Tacitus was writing his *Annals*. There is no reason to doubt that the *Satires* were written and published in books. Book 1 comprises *Satires* 1–5, book 2 *Satire* 6 alone, book 3 *Satires* 7–9, book 4 *Satires* 10–12, and book 5 *Satires* 13–16 (the last poem is unfinished).

In book 1 Juvenal introduces his indignant speaker who condemns Rome (satire is an urban genre), especially the corruption of the patron–client relationship (*amicitia*, 'friendship') (in *Satires* 1, 3, 4, and 5; see PATRONAGE) and the decadence of the élite (in 1, 2, and 4). *Satire* 1, following predecessors in the genre, provides a justification for satire and a programme of the angry tone and the victims of satirical attack. These include the 'out-groups' (A. Richlin, *The Garden of Priapus* (1983)) who transgress sexual and social boundaries, such as the passive homosexuals of *Satire* 2 (see HOMOSEXUALITY) and the social upstarts, criminals, and foreigners attacked by Umbricius in *Satire* 3 (Umbricius figures himself as the last true Roman, driven from an un-Roman Rome). The Roman élite are portrayed as paradigms of moral corruption: the selfish rich are attacked in *Satires* 1 and 3 and the emperor *Domitian is portrayed as sexual hypocrite and autocrat in 2 and 4. Those dependent on these powerful men are not absolved from blame: the courtiers humiliated by Domitian by being asked to advise on what to do with an enormous fish in *Satire* 4, like the client humiliated by his wealthy patron at a dinner party in 5, are condemned for craven compliance.

The focus upon Roman men in book 1 is complemented by the focus upon Roman women in book 2, which consists of the massive *Satire* 6, comparable in length to a book of epic. The speaker fiercely (but unsuccessfully) attempts to dissuade his addressee from marriage by cataloguing the (alleged) faults of Roman wives. Here Juvenal develops his angry speaker in the ultimate rant which seems to exhaust the possibilities of angry satire; thereafter he adopts a new approach of irony and cynicism. Initially (in book 3) Juvenal's new, calmer *persona* takes up the same topics as treated in book 1, although his detachment invites a less stark perspective: clients and patrons (*Satires* 7 and 9) and the corruption and worthlessness of the élite (8). He then marks his change of direction explicitly at the start of book 4, where the speaker states his preference for detached laughter over tears as a reaction to the follies of the world; in the remainder of *Satire* 10 he accordingly demolishes first the objects of human prayer, then the act of prayer itself. His programmatic declaration is borne out by the 'Horatian' tone and topics (see HORACE) of *Satire* 11 (where an invitation to dinner conveys a condemnation of decadence and a recommendation of self-sufficiency) and 12 (where true friendship is contrasted with the false friendship of legacy-hunters). The speaker of book 5 becomes still more detached and cynical as he turns his attention to the themes of crime and punishment, money and greed. The opening poem, *Satire* 13, offers a programmatic condemnation of anger in the form of a mock consolation, which indicates clearly the development from book 1 where anger was apparently approved.

Juvenal claims that his satire replaces *epic (*Sat.* 1) and *tragedy (6. 634–61): his chief contribution to the genre is his appropriation of the 'grand style' from other more elevated forms of hexameter verse, notably epic. This contrasts markedly with the sometimes coarse language of Lucilius and the tone of refined 'conversation' adopted by Horace in his satirical writings. Juvenal's satiric 'grand style' mingles different lexical levels, ranging from epic and tragedy (e.g. the epic parody in *Satires* 4 and 12) to mundanities, Greek words, and occasional obscenities. His penchant for oxymora, pithy paradoxes, and trenchant questions makes Juvenal a favourite mine for quotations, e.g. *mens sana in corpore sano* (10. 356) and *quis custodiet ipsos custodes?* (6. 347–8): 'a healthy mind in a healthy body' and 'who guards the guards themselves?'. The *Satires* also appropriate the themes and structures of other forms of discourse: they are rhetorical performances which develop for satiric ends material drawn from epic (*Homer, *Virgil, *Ovid) and pastoral poetry; situations and characters of comedy and mime; philosophical ideas and texts (including *Plato and the Hellenistic philosophical schools); and rhetorical set-pieces (consolation, persuasion, farewell speech).

Juvenal's *Satires* apparently present reassuring entertainment for the Roman male élite audience. However, inconsistencies written into the texts allow alternative views of Juvenal's speakers as riddled with bigotry (chauvinism, misogyny, homophobia) or as cynically superior. In literary history, Juvenal's significance is in bringing to fullest development the indignant speaker: his 'savage indignation' had a lasting influence on Renaissance and later satire (as Johnson's imitations of *Satires* 3 and 10, *London* and *The Vanity of Human Wishes*, indicate) and remains central to modern definitions of 'satire'. See SATIRE.

S. M. B.

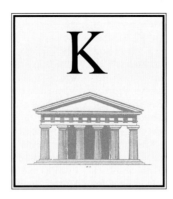

K

kingship (*basileia*) The Mycenaean political system (see MYCENAEAN CIVILIZATION) was monarchic, with the king (*wanax*) at the head of a palace-centred economy; the 10th-cent. BC 'hero's tomb' at *Lefkandi may imply some limited continuity into the Dark Age. Kingship appears to have been rare later: *Homer borrows elements from Mycenae and the near east, but seems essentially to be describing an aristocratic world, in which the word *basileus* is often used in the plural of an office-holding nobility. The earliest true monarchies were the 7th–6th-cent. *tyrannies, which were regarded as aberrations; the Spartan dual 'kingship' (see SPARTA) is a form of hereditary but non-monarchic military leadership. The Classical period knew kingship only from myth and as a *barbarian form of rule, found in tribal areas and in the near east. *Sophists established a theoretical table of constitutions, with kingship and tyranny as the good and bad forms of monarchy, opposed to the rule of the few and the rule of the many (see OLIGARCHY; DEMOCRACY, ATHENIAN; POLITICAL THEORY). In the 4th cent. BC, developments in *Thessaly (Jason of Pherae), *Syracuse (*Dionysius I and II), Caria (Mausolus), and *Cyprus (Nicocles and Evagoras), and especially the rise of Macedon under *Philip II, demonstrated the practical importance of monarchy; and *Plato, *Xenophon, and *Isocrates elaborated theories justifying kingship.

After *Alexander the Great, monarchy became a dominant form of government in the Greek world. The Hellenistic monarchies (see GREECE, PREHISTORY AND HISTORY; HELLENISM) controlled vast territories by conquest ('land won by the spear'), and often made use of existing local administrative practices, presenting themselves as successors to earlier kings; they encouraged and adapted indigenous forms of king-worship (see RULER-CULT). In practice monarchies were hereditary, and claims were made to divine descent. In Greek cities the forms of king-worship were based on the idea of the king as saviour and benefactor (see EUERGETISM), or new founder of the city: the king and sometimes his family were living gods to be worshipped with temples, cult statues, and festivals. In the free cities such honours were often diplomatic, and reflected

the needs of alliances. Roman proconsuls also found themselves honoured; and the emperors accepted and systematized emperor-worship in the Greek provinces of the empire.

A philosophical theory of monarchy developed in the early Hellenistic period: philosophers were often welcomed as advisers at court, and representatives from all major philosophical schools except the *Cynic are known to have written treatises *On Kingship*. These seem to have rested on a common theoretical basis: kingship was 'rule without accountability'; it was justified by the perfect virtue of the king, which should be exemplified in a series of actions towards his subjects. The main virtue was love of his subjects (*philanthrōpia*); others were beneficence (*euergesia*), justice, self-control, wisdom, foresight, courage. Though the king need not be a philosopher, he should listen to their advice. The king's actions would ensure the love of his subjects. The doctrine of the king as 'living law' was not part of the theory, which was singularly weak in legal justification. Apart from some derivative pseudo-Pythagorean fragments of uncertain date (see PYTHAGORAS), no treatise *On Kingship* survives, but their influence can be detected in contemporary literature (most clearly in the pseudonymous Letter of Aristeas to Philocrates on the Greek translation of the Torah), and in the language used in government documents.

It is doubtful whether this theory affected Roman attitudes to the emperor until the mid-1st cent. AD. But thereafter a series of writers describe the duties of the emperor in language derived from Hellenistic kingship theory; the most important of these are Philo Judaeus, the younger *Seneca, *De clementia*, and *Dio of Prusa, *Or.* 1–4. In the high empire a distinction became established between rhetorical speeches addressed 'to a king' and in direct praise of him, and philosophical treatises of advice 'on kingship', presenting an ideal picture even when addressed to a particular king. Fourth-cent. writers (Themistius, *Julian, Libanius, Claudian, Synesius) make much of this distinction. Kingship theory also influenced Christian theology (see CHRISTIANITY), and was used by *Eusebius in the portrayal of *Constantine I, the first Christian emperor. It was therefore an important influence on Byzantine political thought.   O. Mu.

kinship is not treated separately, at full length, in this Companion. 'The promise of a unified and general theory of kinship has not been realized; indeed the very definition of the field is in dispute, some scholars arguing that the project of a comparative science of kinship rests on the illusion that in all societies "kinship" systems are ordered on similar principles': so the anthropologist Adam Kuper begins his entry 'Kinship' in A. and J. Kuper (eds.), *Social Science Encyclopedia*, 2nd edn. (1996), 441–3; the reader is referred to Kuper's article for an up-to-date discussion of the theoretical position. However he concludes that 'the resemblances between domestic institutions in societies all over the world are so remarkable that it is hard to understand why anthropologists should have lost sight of commonalities'. Certainly some modern criticisms ('the cultural critique') of traditional kinship study seem inappropriate to the study of the ancient Greeks and Romans. For instance it has been said that genealogy, an institution which assumes that blood relationships structure social systems, is simply the imposition of western categories on other peoples (see ORIENTALISM). But Greek interest in *genealogy is securely attested (in other words, perhaps, the ancient Greeks were to that extent 'westerners'). And there is no doubt that Greeks of the Classical and Hellenistic periods were themselves very interested in the idea of kinship (*syngeneia*) between peoples or cities, and that they based political claims and requests on such real, exaggerated, or imagined kinship-ties. (For a collection of the relevant inscriptions and a good discussion of Greek words for 'kin' and 'kinship' terminology see O. Curty, *Les Parentés légendaires entre cités grecques* (1995); see also J. Strubbe, *Anc. Soc.* 1984–6, 253–304, and Hornblower, *Comm. on Thuc.* 2 (1996), Introduction, section 4 on 'Thucydides and *Syngeneia*'). The Romans also defined themselves in terms of such kinship connections; see AENEAS. All this might seem to encourage rather than discourage generalization about kinship in the ancient world.

Nevertheless, many of the theoretical problems about such generalization remain. The problems are scarcely less if we confine ourselves *either* to the Greeks (among whom it is only the Classical Athenians who are really well attested, through orators and inscriptions, and thus susceptible to detailed analysis) *or* to the Romans. (On Athens, S. C. Humphreys, *Anthropology and the Greeks* (1978), 193 ff., and the introductory material in R. J. Littman, *Kinship and Politics in Athens 600–400 BC* (1990), may be found helpful.) We therefore prefer to direct readers to those particular entries in this Companion which cover, or have a bearing on, ancient kinship-institutions or ideas about kinship, namely: ADOPTION; FAMILY, ROMAN; GENEALOGY; HOUSEHOLD, GREEK AND ROMAN; INCEST; JUDGES, FOREIGN; MARRIAGE LAW; MATRIARCHY; PROSOPOGRAPHY; TRIBUS; WOMEN.   S. H.

labour, as a factor in the production of wealth, has no equivalent in Greek or Latin. Association of the terms *ponos* and *labor* with drudgery reflects the negative attitudes of ancient élites, for whom 'labour' was the antithesis of *scholē* and *otium* (time available for leisure, politics, education, and culture). Consequently, the labour of theoretically free wage-earners and craftsmen tended to be assimilated to slavery (Arist. *Pol.* 1337ᵇ19 ff.; Cic. *Off.* 1. 159 f.). Wages were seen as purchasing the person as opposed to labour-power; the supposedly degrading nature of craftwork (*banausia*) led to the downgrading of the individual worker (see ART, ANCIENT ATTITUDES TO; ARTISANS AND CRAFTSMEN). Surviving sources reveal nothing resembling modern conceptions of unions or trade-guilds, strikes, or common programmes of action; nor, aside from occasional epitaphs, is there any awareness of the 'dignity of labour'. Striking is the absence of any sustained competition or resentment between types of labour. Throughout the Greek and Roman worlds are found instead shifting, complementary relationships between different forms of exploitation. Already in *Hesiod's *Works and Days* (less clearly in the *Odyssey*) there exist crude equivalents of 'free', 'wage', and 'slave' labourer, combined on the peasant farm. In quantitative terms, the dominant form of labour on the land throughout the ancient world may broadly be described as 'compulsory labour', whereby the politically weak performed obligatory labour dues for the powerful. From the Greek world, the Spartan helots (state slaves) are the best known of these unfree agricultural workforces 'between freedom and slavery' (Pollux). There was a similar pattern in the Roman empire, with Romans in the provinces retaining pre-existing systems of compulsory labour. In cities, the labour of independent artisans and their families would be supplemented by slaves (a permanent workforce) or wage labourers (for casual labour). Large public projects would require extensive hired labour (Plut. *Per.* 12. 5; Suet. *Vesp.* 8. 5). Exceptional were Classical Athens and Roman Italy and Sicily during the late republic, where chattel-*slavery was widespread in the countryside (though supplemented by wage labour at harvest). In both cases, the citizen status of peasants made problematic their direct exploitation by landowning élites. Italian peasants, however, always remained vulnerable. As the number of chattel-slaves gradually (though never completely) diminished, the later centuries of the empire saw a lowering of peasant status and their progressive re-exploitation: tenant farmers were tied to the land as *coloni*. The relationship of the colonate and allied forms of compulsory labour to the eventual emergence of feudalism remains obscure. See CLASS STRUGGLE; INDUSTRY. P. C. M.

Latin language

1. Introduction Latin belongs to the Italic group of Indo-European (IE) languages, which includes Faliscan, Umbrian, and Oscan. It was originally spoken in Latium from 800 BC or earlier and with the spread of Roman power became the common language first of Italy, then of the western Mediterranean and Balkan regions of the Roman empire. The language of the illiterate majority of Latin-speakers, Vulgar Latin (VL), evolved through its regional dialects into the Romance languages. It is known from casual remarks by ancient grammarians, comparative Romance reconstruction, and deviations from classical norms in manuscript and epigraphic texts.

Refined versions of the language were developed early on for specific socio-cultural purposes—legal and ritual texts, public oratory, senatorial and pontifical records, and Saturnian verse. The earliest of these survive in corrupt and fragmentary forms, e.g. the *Twelve Tables and the *Carmen arvale* ('Hymn of the Arval Brethren'). Later examples are the senate's decree (*ILLRP* 519) on the cult of Bacchus (186 BC; see BACCHANALIA) and the Scipio Epitaphs (*c.*250–150 BC; *ILLRP* 309–17). The combination of these native written genres and the influence of Greek models from *c.*240 BC onwards led eventually to the written form of the Roman dialect, *sermo urbanus* 'urban(e) speech', that we know as Classical Latin (CL). In contrast to the dialects of Greek the non-Roman dialects played no part in Latin literary culture or, from the classical period onwards, in local administration.

CL is defined by the characteristics common to literary authors in the period *c*.90 BC–*c*. AD 120. It is a highly artificial construct which must be regarded linguistically as a deviation from the mainstream of the language, namely VL. Nevertheless for centuries a spectrum of usage linked the highest literary compositions through the informal idiom of the letters and conversation of their authors and the plain registers of legal, administrative, and technical writings to the Latin of the masses. The spectrum was ruptured long before the 9th century. The Strasburg Oaths (AD 842), which are in an early form of French, are reported in a contemporary chronicle composed by Nithard in medieval Latin. The regional variants of VL, difficult to infer from the written texts of any period, had now become the Romance languages. The literary tradition, modelled on CL but infiltrated by vulgar elements, was now medieval Latin. Most oral renderings of medieval Latin would have been almost as incomprehensible to *Cicero as the Romance languages.

A spectrum of Latinity did survive however in the various registers of ecclesiastical Latin, which has no linguistic unity apart from its common Christian lexicon— *ecclēsia* 'church', *baptizāre* 'baptize', *presbyter* 'priest', *resurrexiō* 'resurrection', *saluātor* 'saviour', *iūstificāre* 'justify', etc. At one end is the vulgarized idiom of the Scriptures, then the plain technical Latin of the Church bureaucracy and doctrinal pronouncements, finally the language of the early hymns and above all the collects and prayers of the Liturgy.

Sections 2–5 indicate some of the more distinctive characteristics of Latin.

2. Phonology Vowel length was functional in CL, both in the lexicon, e.g. *pŏpulus* 'people', *pōpulus* 'poplar', *lĕuis* 'light', *lēuis* 'smooth', *incĭdere* 'to fall on', *incīdere* 'to incise', and in the grammar, e.g. *rosă* (nom. sing.) 'rose', *rosā* (abl. sing.), *manŭs* 'hand' (nom. sing.), *manūs* (nom. pl.). The rounded front vowel [y], written as *y*, was used to render Greek upsilon, e.g. *tyrannus* 'tyrant'. The relative frequency and distribution of short vowels were affected by raising ('vowel weakening') in non-initial syllables between *c*.450 and *c*.250 BC, e.g. †*obfaciom*>*officium* 'duty', †*abagetes*> *abigitis* 'you drive off', †*exfactos*>*effectus* 'done'. Syncope, the end-point of raising, occurs at all periods, e.g. †*retetolet*>*rettulit* 'brought back', †*opifacīna*>*officīna* 'workshop', *ualidē*>*ualdē* 'very much', later *dominus*>*domnus* 'master'.

Most of the inherited diphthongs survived into early Latin but were reduced to long vowels by 150 BC, e.g. *indoucere* 'to bring in', *oinos* 'one', *deicere* 'to say'>*indūcere*, *ūnus*, *dīcere*. Only two remain frequent, *ae* and *au*. The former (<*ai*) is replaced by *e* in some dialects before 150 BC and the new pronunciation was general by AD 400, though the digraph continued to be written inconsistently. Most dialects of VL seem to have retained *au*, but some Italian dialects already had *o*, as in Sabine *plostru* for *plaustrum* 'cart'.

The glides [w] and [j] were never graphically distinct from [u] and [i], of which they are often regarded merely as positional variants. Even their consonantal reflexes, [v] and [dʒ] etc., continued to be written as *u* and *i* until the Renaissance. The first secure evidence for a phonetic shift is *baliat*, *iuuente* for *ualeat* 'farewell', *iubente* 'ordering' in early imperial VL and *Gianuaria* for *Ianuaria* in the 6th cent.

Of the inherited stops *p*, *d*, *k*, etc., *qu*, a velar *k* with lip-rounding inherited from Proto-Indo-European (PIE), survives uniquely in Latin. Its original voiced equivalent *gu* may already have been a cluster [gw]. Scattered evidence for palatalization occurs already in the 2nd and 3rd cents. AD, e.g. *oze*, *terciae*, *Vincentzus* for *hodie* 'today', *tertiae* 'third', *Vincentius*. These changes were accepted by some 5th-cent. grammarians. By this time spellings like *intcitamento*, *dissessit* for *incitāmentō* 'at the instigation', *discessit* 'he left' were appearing in VL.

Aspirated stops, written as *ph*, *th*, *ch* from *c*.150 BC, were introduced for Greek loanwords like *theātrum*, *māchina*.

Of the two nasals *n* had a positional variant [ŋ] before velars, as in *uncus* 'hook', *tangō* 'I touch'. The sequence *Vns* tended to be replaced by *V̄s*, as in *agrōs* (<†*agrons*) 'fields', *cōsul* (<†*consul*), and this became universal in VL, with *mēsa* for *mensa* 'table', *pēsare* for *pensare* 'to weigh'. A weak articulation of *-m*, reflected in metre, is attested in early *uiro*, *omne* (CL *uirum* 'man', *omnem* 'all'), and in its total disappearance in VL.

The unvoiced sibilant *s* was rhotacized intervocalically before *c*.350 BC, e.g. *āsa*, *Numisios*>*āra* 'altar', *Numerius*. Loss of *-s* in sequences like *omnibu(s) prīnceps* is attested in some dialects and in Ennian epic, but was repaired analogically before the classical period, and *-s* survived in most areas of early Romance. The letter *z*, representing [zː] was imported to render Greek zeta; e.g. *Zephyrus* 'West Wind'. The precarious status of [h] is shown by variants like *nīl*, *mī*, *comprendere* for *nihil*, *mihi*, *comprēhendere* and the grammarians' debates about *(h)erus*, *(h)arēna*, etc.

There were severe restrictions on consonant clusters. Many had been reduced in early Latin, e.g. *iouxmenta*, †*trānsdō*>*iūmenta* 'beasts of burden', *trādō* 'I hand over'. Those that survived were often restricted positionally; thus *gn* occurs medially, e.g. *cognōscō*, but no longer initially, e.g. *nōscō*<*gnōscō*, and never finally; *sp*, *st*, *sk* initially and medially, but in final position only *-st*, as in *est*, *post*; *ps* and *ks* occur initially only in Greek loans, but are often found in medial and final position, e.g. *dīxī*, *ops*; *nt* medially and finally, never initially.

Latin like English and Modern Greek had a stress accent. It originally fell on the initial syllable but before 250 BC had shifted, falling on the penultimate syllable, if heavy, otherwise on the antepenultimate, e.g. *legétis* 'you will read', *legéntēs* 'reading', but *légitis* 'you read', *mílitēs* 'soldiers'. The connection between quantity and stress is seen in early 'iambic' shortening, e.g. *bénĕ* (<†*bénē*) 'well', *égŏ* (<†*égō*) 'I', in syncope (see above), and in the tendency in later Latin for vowel length to correlate with stress, e.g. *quándŏ* 'when', *légitis*, *bénĕ*.

3. Lexicon A high proportion of the basic lexical stock has widespread IE cognates; e.g. *auris* 'ear', *canis* 'dog', *dare* 'to give', *edere* 'to eat', *nouus* 'new', *plēnus* 'full', *quīnque* 'five', *trēs* 'three', *uīuere* 'to live'. Some have assured cognates only in Greek, e.g. *cinis* 'ash'; others only in West IE, e.g. *annus* 'year', *flōs* 'flower', *manus* 'hand', in Celtic, e.g. *loquor* 'I speak', or in Germanic, e.g. *aqua* 'water'. Finally some have no known cognates, e.g. *arbor* 'tree', *mulier* 'woman', *niger* 'black', *caedere* 'to cut'.

The native resources were extended by composition. Complexes, formed by affixation to lexical roots, are frequent. Thus *pater* 'father', *patrius* 'ancestral'; *legere* 'to choose', *leg-iō* 'legion', *lec-tor* 'reader', *lec-tiō* 'a reading'; *fingere* 'to fashion', *fig-mentum* 'image', *fig-ūra* 'shape'; *probus* 'honest', *prob-itās* 'honesty'; *fortis* 'brave', *forti-tūdō* 'bravery'. Some of these formants are distinctively Latin. Denominative verbs were assigned to the first conjugation in all periods, e.g. *dōnāre* 'to give' from *dōnum* 'gift', *pācāre* 'to pacify' from *pāx* 'peace'. Compounds, made up of more than one lexical root, were not as frequent as in Greek but were productive in every period, e.g. *agri-cola* 'field-dweller'>'farmer', *arti-fex* 'maker of craftwork'. Compound-complex forms like *bene-fic-ium* 'benefit', *ad-uen-tus* 'arrival' carry the process even further.

Latin had many loanwords. From Oscan or Sabine came *bōs* 'cow', *multa* 'fine', *nāsus* 'nose'; from *Etruscan *ātrium* 'hall', *fenestra* 'window', *satelles* 'attendant', perhaps even *populus* 'the people'. Greek was a very prolific source, e.g. *āēr* 'air', *balineum* 'bath', *bracchium* 'arm', *cista* 'chest', *gubernāre* 'to direct', *massa* 'lump', *nauta* 'sailor', *poena* 'punishment'. In the learned vocabulary, beside loans such as *grammaticus* 'philologist', *historia* 'history', *mūsica* 'music', *philosophus* 'philosopher', many calques were modelled on Greek, e.g. *essentia* 'essence', *quālitās* 'quality', as were loan translations like *cāsus* 'grammatical case', *ratiō* 'logical argument'.

VL even replaced basic lexemes by Greek loans, e.g. *colpus* (<*kólaphos*) for *ictus* 'blow', *gamba* (<*kampḗ*) for *crūs* 'leg', *parabolāre* (<*parabolḗ*) for *loquī* 'to speak'. Lexical mortality is illustrated by the replacement of *canō* 'I sing', †*speciō* 'I look at', *pleō* 'I fill', †*fendō* 'I ward off' by *cantō*, *spectō* (and *conspiciō*), *impleō*, *dēfendō*. Again VL has many examples: *bellus* (and *formōsus*) for *pulcher* 'beautiful', *bucca* for *ōs* 'mouth', *caballus* for *equus* 'horse', *iectāre* for *iacere* 'to throw', *portāre* for *ferre* 'to carry', etc.

4. Morphology Nouns were organized into six paradigms, e.g. (1) *mensa* 'table', (2) *seruus* 'slave', (3a) *urbs* 'city', (3b) *turris* 'tower', (4) *manus* 'hand', (5) *diēs* 'day'. All were inherited types except (5), which was formed in Italic. The i- stems (3b), which in PIE had been closely parallel to u- stems (4), gradually merged in Latin with the consonant stems (3a). Paradigms (4) and (5) had few members. In VL these were either transferred to (2) and (1), as *manus*, -*ūs* to *manus*, -*ī*, and *diēs* to *dia*, or were replaced by other lexemes, as *rēs* 'thing' by *causa* 'cause'.

The three inherited genders are systematically identifiable only in adjectives. Thus *nauta ualidus* (masc.) 'a sturdy sailor', *humus ūda* (fem.) 'moist ground', *animal formōsum* (neut.) 'a well-formed animal'. Of the three PIE numbers the dual was lost already in Italic, traces surviving only in forms like *duo* and perhaps *duae*.

Seven of the eight PIE cases survived, ablative and instrumental having already merged in Italic. Nominative and vocative remained distinct only in the singular of (2), *Marcus* (nom.) *Marce* (voc.). The locative has no distinct morphology at all; thus *Rōmae* (1) 'at Rome' is identical with genitive and dative, and the locative plural is identical with the dative-ablative in all paradigms. Of the eleven possible case forms (nom. voc. acc. gen. dat. loc. abl. sing.; nom.-voc. acc. gen. dat.-loc.-abl. pl.) paradigm (2) has the most, with eight, paradigm (5) has the least, with six. In VL the cases eventually collapsed to two, a nominative and an oblique.

The gen. sing. -*ī* in (2) *serui* 'of the slave' has a unique correspondent in Old Irish *maqi* 'of the son', while the nom.-voc. pl. of (1) *mensae* 'tables' and (2) *seruī* 'slaves', in which the Italic forms in -*ās* and -*ōs* have been replaced by the pronominal endings, are uniquely paralleled in Greek. The pronouns, as in other IE languages, share only a few of their case-forms with nouns. The anaphoric and deictic pronouns *is* and *ille* supply third-person pronouns beside *ego* 'I' and *tū* 'thou'.

Adjectives all belong to paradigms (1), (2), or (3). In the comparison of adjectives the formants -*ior*-, -*is*-, and -*mo*- are inherited, but the composite formant in e.g. *alt-is-simus* 'highest' seems unique to Latin.

Verbs were organized into five paradigms; e.g. (1) *stāre* 'to stand', (2) *monēre* 'to warn', (3a) *dīcō*, *dīcere* 'to say', (3b) *capiō*, *capere* 'to take', (4) *audīre* 'to hear'. Inherited athematic verbs such as Gk. *histēmi* were reshaped and assigned to conjugations (1) and (2). Thematic verbs like Gk. *légō* are reflected in (3).

All the PIE grammatical categories—person, number, tense, mood, and voice—were retained. Number was determined solely by concord with the subject.

The tense system, as in Greek, distinguishes imperfective and perfective aspect, e.g. *scrībēbam* 'I was writing', *scrīpsī* 'I wrote', also used as a perfect 'I have written'; cf. Gk. *égrapsa* 'I wrote', but *gégrapha* 'I have written'. PIE aorist and perfect formants both appear in the Latin perfect, e.g. *dīxī* 'I (have) said' and *tutudī* 'I (have) struck'. Notable innovations are the -*b*- forms in the future (also in Faliscan) and imperfect (also in Oscan), e.g. *stābō* 'I shall stand', *stābam* 'I was standing', which were periphrastic in origin (<†*stāsi bhwō* 'I am to be in the act of standing'); also the -*w*- perfects, which are used mostly in paradigms (1), (2), and (4); and the creation of new relative-time tenses, past-in-the-future *audīuerō* 'I shall have heard', past-in-the-past *audīueram* 'I had heard'. Important for Romance are the reintroduction of the perfect/past definite distinction by the use of *scrīptum habeō* as a perfect 'I have written', which was already emerging in CL, and the use of *scrībere habeō* in rivalry with *scrībam* 'I shall write', not attested before the late 2nd cent. AD.

The optative and subjunctive moods had already merged in Italic and the Latin subjunctive has traces of both formations: optative in *sim* 'I would be', *dīxerim* 'I would say'; subjunctive in *dīcās* 'you would say', and perhaps *stēs* 'you would stand'. The creation of imperfect and pluperfect subjunctives, *dīcerem, dīxissem*, is an innovation. The medio-passive formant *-r*, also found in Old Irish and Hittite, was already established in Italic. The perfect passive tenses were analytic: *laudāta est* 'she has been praised' beside *laudātur* 'she is being praised'. The middle sense is seen in e.g. *uertor* 'I turn myself' and *indūtus* 'having put on'. It also accounts for 'deponents' like *sequor* 'I follow', *ūtor* 'I use'.

The infinitives reflect PIE verbal nouns. They had however become absorbed into the verb system both in syntax, e.g. *pācem petere* 'to seek peace' beside *pācis petitiō*, and by their marking for tense and voice, e.g. *dīcere* 'to say', pass. *dīcī*, perf. *dīxisse*, etc. The supines in *-tum* and *-tū* are cognate with Sanskrit declined infinitives. The gerund, as in *audiendō* 'by hearing' etc., seems ultimately to be derived from the gerundive *audiendus* 'which is to be heard', a verbal adjective unknown outside Italic. The imperfective participle in *-nt-*, as in *monens* 'warning', and the perfect passive in *-tus*, as in *monitus* 'warned', are both inherited; the future in *-tūrus*, as in *monitūrus*, is peculiar to Latin.

5. Syntax Among distinctively Latin case uses is the extension of the allatival dative of inanimate nouns, e.g. *ūsuī est* 'it is useful', *quindecimuirī sacrīs faciundīs* 'the fifteen commissioners for religious practices'; also the comitative use of the ablative to assign a quality adnominally, e.g. *dux aequō animō* 'a leader with a calm mind'; and to indicate attendant circumstances adverbially, e.g. *dīs fauentibus* 'with the blessing of the gods', *crīnibus dēmissīs* 'with their hair let down', whence the 'absolute' construction, which in Latin acquired, as the Greek genitive absolute also did, fully clausal functions.

As in other IE languages, prepositions had been developed to give precision to 'local' case functions. Thus in the accusative the allatival *ad urbem* 'to the city' and perlatival *per tōtam noctem* 'all through the night' are distinguished from *urbem condidit* 'he founded the city', *proelium pugnābant* 'they were fighting a battle'. In the ablative the instrumental *gladiō pugnābat* 'he fought with a sword' was similarly distinguished from the locatival *in urbe* 'in the city' and the ablatival *ex urbe* 'from the city' and *ab eō condita est* 'it was founded by him'. Abstract extensions, as in the last example, are widespread; cf. *propter* 'because of' (<'close to') and *de* 'concerning' (<'down from') etc. In contrast to Greek most Latin prepositions were confined to one case, thus reducing the semantic importance of the case. Hence VL *cum discentēs suōs* 'with his pupils', with accusative for ablative. In VL these prepositional phrases encroached on simple case uses; as in *dē sagittā percutere* 'to hit with an arrow', for the simple ablative, *uenditiō dē campō* 'sale of the field' for gen. *campī*, and *ad illam dīxit* 'he said to her' for dat. *illī*. All this contributed substantially to the massive case syncretism in late VL (see §4 above).

Latin shares exclusively with Greek the development of the accusative + infinitive construction to render indirect speech. There were not enough infinitives or subjunctives to represent the distinctions required in principal and subordinate clauses respectively, and the whole inefficient construction gave way to clauses with *quod, quia* (perhaps modelled on Gk. *hōs, hóti* 'that'), to a larger extent in the later written language and totally in VL. The subjunctive as the mood of unreality was used in both members of unreal conditional sentences, e.g. *sī hoc dīcās, errēs* 'If you were to say this, you would be wrong'. But it tended in time also to become the mood of subordination generally (hence the name), as in *cum hoc dīxisset, exiit* 'when he had said this, he left', *sciō quid crēdās* 'I know what you think', *adeō clāmābat ut exīrent* 'he shouted so much that they left'.

Latin shares, again exclusively, with Greek the development of complex sentence structure, most notably the periodic form, which was a major legacy to later European languages. Attention to rhythm, especially at clause-ends, and pragmatic considerations of emphasis, anaphora, etc. led to departures from the normal word order, subject–object–verb (SOV), which was inherited from PIE. In VL, where SVO seems to have become established at an early date, the subsequent collapse of the case system precluded variations of the classical kind. R. G. C.

law and procedure, Athenian

1. Legislation Greeks used the same word (*nomos*) for both custom and law, and the beginning of law is hard to define. One reasonable view is that an unwritten rule should be regarded as a law if the community or the ruler approves it and imposes or authorizes punishment for infringement of it. In this sense laws forbidding some offences (e.g. murder, theft, bigamy) must have existed since primitive times. An alternative view is that only rules stated in writing are really laws. The transition from oral to written law began in the 7th cent. BC, but was not completed until the end of the 5th cent. in Athens (and later in other cities). See LITERACY; ORALITY.

The first written laws in any Greek city are said to have been drawn up by Zaleucus for the city of Locri Epizephyrii in south Italy. The first written laws in Athens are attributed to Draco in the year when Aristaechmus was archon (probably 621/0). His laws, except that on homicide, were superseded in 594/3 by those of *Solon. These laws were inscribed on wooden blocks (*axones*) for everyone to read. Later these inscriptions were transferred to stone and many additions and alterations were made, but the Athenians continued to refer to their code as the laws of Solon.

After democracy was established, new laws were made by majority vote in the *ekklēsia* (assembly). For most of the 5th cent. there was no sharp distinction between a law (*nomos*) laying down a permanent rule and a decree (*psēphisma*) for a particular occasion. Legislation was not systematic, and some confusions and contradictions arose.

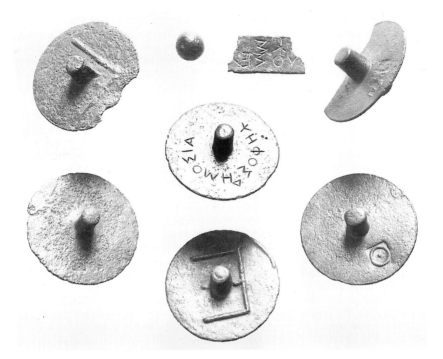

law and procedure, Athenian Archaeological evidence for legal procedure from the *agora at *Athens (5th–4th cent. BC): bronze wheels used as jurors' votes; a fragmentary inscribed plaque serving as a juror's identity card; and a bronze ball from a machine used to allocate jurors randomly to different courts.

From 410 onwards efforts were made to rectify this situation. Existing laws were revised to remove obscurities or inconsistencies, and were all inscribed on stone; henceforth no uninscribed law was to be enforced, and no decree could override a law. New decrees were still made by the *ekklēsia*, but the making of new laws was handed over to groups of citizens known as *nomothetai*.

2. Judicature Until the early 6th cent. BC all verdicts were given by the nine magistrates called *archontes* or archons (see further below) or the Areopagus (the most ancient council at Athens, see ATHENS (TOPOGRAPHY), section on *Environs of the Acropolis*) or the *ephetai* (a jury of 51 members). Solon instituted a system of trial by the *ēliaia*, probably for appeals against the verdicts of the archons or for imposition of penalties above certain limits. The next stages of development are obscure, but presumably appeals became so usual that the archons practically ceased to give verdicts and the *ēliaia* (if it was a single body) did not have time to hear all the cases referred to it. A system of juries was therefore set up, in which each jury consisted of a number of citizens who tried a case on behalf of all the citizens.

For the period after the middle of the 5th cent. we have fuller information. Volunteers for jury service (who had to be citizens over 30 years old) were called for at the beginning of each year, and a list of 6,000 jurors for the year was drawn up. To encourage volunteers, each juror received a small fee for each day on which he sat to try a case. This payment was introduced by *Pericles, who probably fixed it at two obols; it was raised to three obols, probably on the proposal of Cleon, not later than 425. Since the payment was less than an able-bodied man would earn by an ordinary day's work, one of its effects was that many of the volunteers were men who were too old for work. This state of affairs is satirized in *Aristophanes' *Wasps*.

The number of jurors who formed a jury varied according to the type of case, but was normally several hundred. In one trial it is said to have been 6,000. In the 4th cent. odd numbers (e.g. 501) were used, to avoid a tie in the voting, but there is no evidence for odd numbers in the 5th cent. It is not known what method was used in the 5th cent. for allocating jurors to courts (*dikastēria*, sing. *dikastērion*). By the early 4th cent. a system of lot was used for this purpose, and later in the century a more complicated system of lot (described in detail in *Ath. pol.* 63–6) was introduced. The aim was to prevent *bribery by making it impossible to know beforehand which jurors would try which case.

Each trial was arranged and presided over by a magistrate or group of magistrates. Different magistrates had responsibility for different types of case. The (eponymous) archon had charge of cases concerning family and inheritance rights. The *basileus* had charge of homicide cases and most cases connected with religion. The *polemarchos* had charge of cases concerning non-Athenians. The *thesmothetai* had charge of a wide variety of cases; in general any type of public case which did not clearly fall within the province of another magistrate came to them. The 'Eleven' had charge of cases of theft and similar offences.

The *stratēgoi* (generals) had charge of cases concerning military and naval service, and there were several lesser boards of magistrates with responsibility for particular types of case, such as the *apodektai* and the *nautodikai*. In the 4th cent. most types of private case were handled by four judges selected by lot for each of the ten tribes or *phylai* (subdivisions of the citizen body), sometimes known collectively as the Forty.

In the 5th cent. and the first half of the 4th each magistrate sat regularly in the same court. The *ēliaia* was the court of the *thesmothetai*. Other courts, perhaps not all in use at the same time, were the Odeum, the Painted Stoa (*Stoa Poikilē*), the New Court (*to Kainon*), the Inserted Court (*to Parabyston*), the Court at Lykos (*to epi Lykōi*), the Kallion, and the Triangular, Greater, and Middle Courts (*to Trigōnon, to Meizon, to Meson*). In the later 4th cent. magistrates no longer sat regularly in the same courts, but were allocated to courts by lot each day. Distinct from all these courts were the Areopagus and the other special homicide courts, manned by the *ephetai* (a jury of 51), in which a different procedure was followed. A few cases were tried by the *boulē* (Council of 500, see DEMOCRACY, ATHENIAN) or the *ekklēsia*.

3. Actions The law on any particular subject generally specified the action to be raised against a transgressor; for some offences the prosecutor had a choice of actions. The principal distinction was between public actions (*dikai dēmosiai*) and private actions (*dikai idiai* or simply *dikai*). The following were the main differences. (*a*) A private action concerned a wrong or injury done to an individual. A public action concerned an offence which was regarded as affecting the community as a whole. (*b*) A private action could be raised only by the person who claimed that he had suffered wrong or injury. A public action might be raised by a magistrate or official acting on behalf of the state. But the scope of public prosecution was widened by Solon to allow prosecution by 'anyone who wishes' (*ho boulomenos*); this meant any free adult male, except that some actions could not be brought by a non-citizen and none could be brought by a disfranchised citizen. (*c*) In a private action damages or compensation might be awarded to the prosecutor. In a public action any fine or penalty was paid to the state. However, to encourage public-spirited citizens to prosecute offenders on behalf of the state, financial rewards were given to successful prosecutors in certain public actions, notably *phasis* and *apographē*. This had the unintended effect of encouraging the rise of *sycophants (habitual prosecutors). (*d*) To deter sycophants penalties were imposed, in most public actions, on a prosecutor who dropped a case after starting it or who failed to obtain at least one-fifth of the jury's votes; he had to pay a fine of 1,000 drachmas and forfeited the right to bring a similar action in future. These penalties did not apply in private actions.

The various public actions were named after their method of initiation. (*a*) *Graphē* was the most ordinary public action, so named presumably because it had originally been the only one in which the charge had to be put in writing, though by the 4th cent. written charges had become the rule in other actions too. (*b*) *Apagōgē*. The prosecutor began proceedings by arresting the accused and handing him over to the appropriate magistrates, usually the Eleven. This procedure was used especially against thieves caught in the act and against persons caught exercising rights to which they were not entitled. The speeches of *Antiphon *On the Murder of Herodes* and *Lysias *Against Agoratus* concern cases of *apagōgē*. (*c*) *Endeixis*. The prosecutor made a denunciation to the magistrates, and might go on to arrest the accused. This procedure too was used against persons accused of exercising rights to which they were not entitled. The case of *Andocides *On the Mysteries* is the best known example. (*d*) *Ephēgēsis*. The prosecutor led the magistrates to the accused, and they arrested him—a procedure very similar to *apagōgē* and *endeixis*, and used for the same kind of offence. (*e*) *Phasis*. The prosecutor pointed out goods or property involved in an offence, such as goods smuggled into Athens from abroad without payment of customs duties. If he won the case, he was rewarded with half of the fine exacted or property confiscated. This action is satirized in *Aristophanes' *Acharnians*. In the 4th cent. it was extended to some other kinds of offence which we cannot define exactly. (*f*) *Apographē*. The prosecutor listed property which he alleged was due to the state and was being withheld. If he won the case, he was rewarded with three-quarters of the property recovered. Several surviving speeches were written for this type of case, e.g. Lysias *On the Property of Aristophanes* and [*Demosthenes] *Against Nicostratus*. (*g*) *Eisangelia* of the most serious type (a prosecution for treason) was initiated by a denunciation to the *boulē* or the *ekklēsia*, which might either decide to try the case itself or refer it to a jury. (*h*) *Probolē*. The prosecutor made a denunciation to the *ekklēsia*. The *ekklēsia* voted on it, but this hearing did not constitute a trial; if the prosecutor proceeded with the case, it was tried subsequently by a jury. This procedure was used against men accused of sycophancy (see above) or of deceiving the Athenian people, and also for offences concerning festivals. The case of Demosthenes *Against Meidias* is the best-known example. (*i*) In addition, a case arising from an accusation made at a *dokimasia* (examination of candidates for office) or a *euthyna* (examination of accounts) was similar to a public action in some respects.

A special type of private action was *diadikasia*. This was used when a right (e.g. to claim an inheritance) or an obligation (e.g. to perform a *trierarchy) was disputed between two or more persons. Its distinctive feature was that there was no prosecutor or defendant: all the claimants were on equal terms. Another special category of private action was *dikē emmēnos* ('monthly case'), which by the second half of the 4th cent. could be used for most financial cases, including disputes with foreign merchants. It was in some way a faster procedure, probably because it was available every month, but there is doubt about the details.

Homicide cases were treated differently from others. If a person was killed, his relatives were required to prosecute the killer. The prosecution followed a special procedure, including a proclamation to the killer to keep away from sacred and public places, three pre-trials at monthly intervals, and special oaths. The trial, at which the prosecutor and the defendant each made two speeches, was held not in an ordinary court, but at one of several special open-air courts, with the Areopagus or the *ephetai* as the jury.

4. Procedure When anyone wished to raise either a private or a public action, he gave his charge to the appropriate magistrate. It was the responsibility of the prosecutor to deliver the summons to the defendant. The magistrate held an inquiry (*anakrisis*), at which he heard statements and evidence from both parties. Some minor cases could be decided by the magistrate forthwith, but generally the purpose of the inquiry was simply to satisfy him that the case should be taken to court. At this stage a defendant might object by the procedure of *paragraphē* that the wrong form of action had been raised, and then this question had to be decided before the action could proceed further. A private action coming before the tribe judges (the Forty) was referred by them to a public arbitrator, and did not go on to trial by jury unless one or other of the litigants refused to accept the arbitrator's verdict.

At the trial the magistrate presided, but he did not give directions or advice to the jury, and did not perform the functions of a modern judge. The prosecutor spoke first and the defendant afterwards. If either litigant was a woman or child, the speech was made by the nearest adult male relative; but otherwise each litigant had to speak for himself, unless clearly incapable, though he might deliver a speech written for him by a speech-writer (*logographos*), and he might call on friends to speak too in his support. In the course of his speech he could request to have laws or other documents read out to the court. He could also call witnesses. Until some date in the first half of the 4th cent., witnesses gave their evidence orally, and might be questioned by the speaker who called them (but not cross-examined by his opponent). Later in the 4th cent. witnesses gave evidence beforehand in writing, and at the trial merely signified assent when their statements were read out. Disfranchised citizens, women, children, and slaves could not speak as witnesses, although they could be present in court without speaking; a written record of a slave's statement could be produced as evidence if the statement had been made under *torture. A certain length of time, varying according to the type of case, was allowed for each litigant to make his speech, the time being measured by a water-clock.

When the speeches were over, the jury heard no impartial summing-up and had no opportunity for discussion, but voted at once. In the 5th cent. each juror voted by placing a pebble or shell in an urn; there was one urn for conviction and one for acquittal. In the 4th cent. each juror was given two bronze votes, one with a hole through the middle signifying conviction and one unpierced signifying acquittal, and he placed one in a 'valid' (bronze) urn and the other in an 'invalid' (wooden) urn; this method helped to ensure that the voting was secret and that each juror cast only one valid vote. When all had voted, the votes were counted, and the majority decided the verdict. A tie was treated as acquittal. There was no appeal from the jury's verdict. However, a losing litigant who proved that a witness for his opponent had given false evidence could claim compensation from the witness, or in some instances got a case reopened; and there were a few exceptional occasions when the *ekklēsia* decreed that verdicts should be set aside.

For some offences the penalty was laid down by law, but in other cases the penalty or the amount of damages had to be decided by the jury. In such cases, when the verdict had been given against the defendant, the prosecutor proposed a penalty and the defendant proposed another (naturally more lenient). Each spoke in support of his proposal, and the jury voted again to decide between them. Payment of money was the most usual kind of penalty, but other penalties regularly imposed were partial or total disfranchisement, confiscation of property, confinement in the stocks, exile, or death. See PUNISHMENT (GREEK AND ROMAN PRACTICE). Long terms of imprisonment were not normally imposed. Cf. PRISON.

The chief fault of the Athenian courts was that a jury could too easily be swayed by a skilful speaker. Most jurors were men of no special intelligence; yet, without impartial advice or guidance, they had to distinguish true from false statements and valid from invalid arguments, and they had to interpret the law as well as decide the facts. It says much for the Athenians' alertness and critical sense that the system worked as well as it did. The advantages were that the large juries were hard to bribe (see BRIBERY) or browbeat, and that the courts and the people were as nearly as possible identical, so that an accused man felt that he was being judged by the Athenian people, not merely by some government official or according to an obscure written rule. Thus the institution of popular juries was one of the Athenians' greatest democratic achievements. See also DEMOCRACY, ATHENIAN. D. M. M.

law and procedure, Roman *(see facing page)*

law in Greece Modern work on this subject is conditioned by two important considerations. In the first place, it is Rome and not Greece which dominates European legal history: indeed, because the Greek world produced no jurists, its law is perhaps best studied not as a source of juridical principles but rather as a way of understanding how particular ancient societies perceived and regulated themselves. The second constraint is the distribution of our sources, which are rich but geographically and temporally very patchy.

Classical Athenian law (see LAW AND PROCEDURE, ATHENIAN) is well documented from the Attic orators (*c.*420–320

[*continued on p. 409*]

Roman law and procedure

Roman law and procedure The subject is here dealt with in three sections: civil law; civil procedure; and criminal law and procedure.

1. Civil law (*ius civile*) in its broadest sense was the law of the city of Rome as opposed to that of some other city. In a narrower sense it refers to the secular law of Rome, private and public, to the exclusion of sacred law (*ius sacrum*). This section deals, so far as the sources of law are concerned, with civil law in the first sense, but as regards substantive law is confined to the second.

From the standpoint of sources the beginning and end of Roman civil law are conveniently marked by the *Twelve Tables and *Justinian's codification. Dating from about 450 BC the law of the Twelve Tables was treated by the Romans as the starting-point of their legal history. Though much of it became obsolete it was never technically superseded until Justinian's legislation of AD 528–34. These two documents, neither of which is systematic enough to be called a code in the modern sense, were of very different bulk, the first consisting of a few score laconic sentences, the second running to well over a million words.

Four periods of legal history are commonly distinguished in the interval between the Twelve Tables and Justinian's codification: (*a*) the early republic, a period of relatively primitive law ending in the 3rd cent. BC; (*b*) the late republic, a formative period in which an independent legal profession took shape, beginning about 200 BC and ending with the victory of *Augustus in 31 BC; (*c*) the classical period, spanning the first three cents. AD and roughly corresponding with the Principate. Its core was an age of relative stability between 68 and 235, which is often subdivided into three: the early classical period of the Flavian dynasty (68 to 96), the high classical age of the adoptive emperors (96 to 180), and the late classical flowering from Commodus to the fall of the Severan dynasty (180 to 235). See ROME (HISTORY). At this time important treatises (see LEGAL LITERATURE) were being written by lawyers who, particularly in the middle period, were free to give expression to their sense of justice without the distraction of political pressures. There followed 60 years of disorder, up to 300, which have been termed epiclassical. In these, private law changed very little but legal writing almost dried up. The period ends with a determined effort by *Diocletian (284–305) to revive classical law in its essential features. Finally follows (*d*) the post-classical period of the later empire, in which *Constantine and his successors introduced important reforms in public and procedural law and in the religious life of the empire but made only limited changes in private law. In the east this period ends with Justinian's 6th-cent. codification, which introduced some important reforms and simplifications, but often reverted to the law of the classical period. In the west the post-classical period ends with the disintegration of the empire in the 5th cent. AD. It has been seen by some as one of legal decline and vulgarization; but it is doubtful whether this assessment is accurate. Some of the terms mentioned embody a mixture of political, legal, and literary value judgements. They need to be used with caution.

A striking mark of the law of the early Roman republic was its formalism. Both in legal transactions and in litigation solemn oral forms were necessary and sufficient. The will of the parties was denied effect unless clothed in these forms. In this respect Roman law resembled primitive systems elsewhere; but it differed from them in the simplicity and economy of the forms used (see ADOPTION, ROMAN). A small number of these served a wide variety of purposes; *mancipatio* (a solemn transaction with copper and scales) and *stipulatio* (a formal contract concluded orally) are good examples. As in other early systems Roman private law was confined to citizens. The *ius Quiritium* (right of citizens) was all important and the community excluded foreigners from the use of the formulae it had devised. The Roman *family preserved its traditional, exclusive organization in which its male head occupied a central place as the person in whom legal power was concentrated. The state hardly interfered in relations between him and those subject to him, free or unfree, over whom indeed he had the power of life and death.

In the last two to three cents. BC, however, the expansion of Rome's commerce and empire over the Mediterranean world (see IMPERIALISM, ROMAN) made it impossible to maintain the exclusiveness of the old civil law. New, informal institutions appeared, which depended on the intention of the parties rather than the observance of external forms. An important example is the class of agreements binding by consent alone (consensual contract), which provided a way of enforcing the principal commercial transactions, such as sale, lease, and partnership. These new institutions were open to foreigners and citizens alike. The form of *stipulatio*, which could be used to make any lawful agreement legally binding, was also widened so that it was now open to foreigners. Special boards of assessors (*recuperatores*) had early been set up for disputes with non-citizens, and about 242 BC a special magistrate for matters involving foreigners (*praetor peregrinus*; see PROVINCIA) was created with jurisdiction over these cases. In the same period the old rigid procedure for the trial of suits between citizens, called *legis actiones* (actions in law) gave way to the less formal and more flexible 'formulary procedure' (see §2. 4 below). These developments were made possible by a first flowering of legal thought and writing, stimulated by contact with Greek culture but with an insistence on verbal clarity and precision which is markedly Roman.

Legislation played only a minor part in these changes. Apart from the Twelve Tables, legislation did little to develop private law during the republic. Such statutes as were enacted usually touched only the detail of existing institutions. The *lex Aquilia*, which provided a broad range of remedies for damage to property, is a notable exception. Decrees of the *senate (*senatus consulta*) also played little part in private and criminal law, and their legal force was uncertain.

The chief factor in releasing the old civil law from its early rigidity was the development of magisterial law (*ius honorarium*). In the sense explained above this formed part of civil law but in a narrower sense was contrasted with it. The key magistrate in its development was the urban praetor in Rome (see CONSUL). He, like other magistrates, published an annual edict setting out how he proposed to exercise his jurisdiction. In the last century of the republic this became an instrument by which, with the help of lawyers whom he consulted, significant innovations were introduced. A concurrent aspect of the development was the gradual introduction of the formulary procedure, by which the issue to be litigated no longer had to be expressed in one of the small number of ritual modes admitted by the old system of *legis actiones*. Instead it was embodied in a formula drawn up before the magistrate and adapted to the alleged facts of the case, though the actual trial was normally conducted by someone else. Thus the magistrate, who controlled the granting of formulae, the most important of which were incorporated in his edict, in effect acquired the power to reform and develop the law. Formally, it is true, he had no such power; his function was to administer the law and not to change it. But with the introduction of the new procedure he was able to grant new remedies by way of both right of action and defence, and thereby, as the lawyer Aemilius Papinianus (early 3rd cent. AD) was to put it two centuries later, to 'support, supplement, and correct the civil law' (*Dig.* 1. 1. 7. 1). He supported it by giving more effective remedies to enforce existing rights. He supplemented the civil law by recognizing claims which the civil law did not recognize, for example the claims of those legitimate blood relations who were technically not members of the family to the possession of a deceased's estate. He corrected the law by barring claims which it recognized, for example because it would be dishonest in the circumstances to allow their enforcement. In some areas this power to supplement and correct produced a dualism between the old civil and newer magisterial law. There was succession by magisterial law alongside succession by civil law, and magisterial rights of property, regarded by some as amounting to ownership, existed alongside ownership by civil law. Indeed writers in the Principate treat civil law and magisterial law in separate works or successive parts of the same work. Their integration in Justinian's codification is the outcome of the efforts of the law schools and lawyers of the later empire.

Augustus made a serious attempt to adhere to republican forms of legislation (*lex, plebiscitum*) but

law and procedure, Roman Marble portrait of the emperor Theodosius II (*c.* AD 440), an important figure in the later history of Roman law. Under his authority some 2,500 imperial laws were collected and published in AD 438. The Theodosian Code, as it is known, formed the basis for *Justinian's codification of Roman law, which survives today.

they were little used by his successors and disappeared altogether during the course of the 1st cent. AD. As an instrument of legislation *senatus consulta* took their place. Emperors influenced, and even dictated, the content of such of these decrees as were of general importance, and the emperor's speech (*oratio*) proposing the decree came often to be cited in place of the decree itself. Thus the codification of the praetor's edict was effected by a decree of the senate drafted by the lawyer Julianus on *Hadrian's behalf.

The emperor's powers were at first conceived as modelled on those of republican magistrates. Thus the emperor might issue edicts, give instructions to officials, towns, or provincial assemblies, grant charters or citizenship, decide cases as a judge, and reply to petitions from private individuals. By the time of Hadrian these various pronouncements came to be grouped together as constitutions of the emperor (*constitutiones principis*). In the mid-2nd cent. AD the law teacher Gaius treats them as having formally, and not merely in practice, the force of law. Some constitutions, like edicts, could openly innovate, something which with the codification of the praetor's edict in AD 131 other magistrates could no longer do. Thus *Caracalla in 212 employed an edict to grant citizenship to the free inhabitants of the empire (see CITIZENSHIP, ROMAN). But the emperor along with lawyers of authority continued in the Principate to make law indirectly, if interstitially, through rulings made in particular cases. Decisions made by the emperor acting as a judge (*decreta*) and replies or rescripts on his behalf to petitions on points of law (*subscriptiones, rescripta*), though in principle merely interpreting existing law, possessed a force which went beyond the case in point and served to fill gaps in the law and resolve ambiguities. Their force was analogous to but greater than that of the opinions (*responsa*) of lawyers of authority (see LAWYERS). By the end of the late classical period this imperial case law, mainly embodied in rescripts, supplanted the case law embodied in practitioners' opinions as an instrument for developing the law without legislating. After the lawyer Herennius Modestinus in the early 3rd cent. AD, and Aquila who may have been his pupil, collections of *responsa* cease, though lawyers naturally continued to give opinions as before. The change was not as dramatic as it may sound, since in practice lawyers, often those who are known to us from their writings, such as Modestinus himself, Arcadius Charisius (fl. 290), and Hermogenianus (fl. 300), went on drafting the rescripts which issued in the emperor's name. But after Diocletian, though replies on points of law continued to issue from the imperial offices (*scrinia*), they too were no longer collected and published.

The opportunity for lawyers to make an independent contribution to the development of the law therefore disappeared by the end of the 3rd cent. It was the lawyers of the classical period who composed the works which, via Justinian's codification, have proved to be the chief legacy of Roman law to medieval and modern civilization (see LEGAL LITERATURE). Indeed that is the main reason for calling the period 'classical'.

A factor which tended to break the pattern of the earlier law was the development of institutions, for example *fideicommissum* (a provision similar to a trust), which were imperial innovations and so cut across the old lines between civil and magisterial law. To enforce these new institutions 'extraordinary' procedures and jurisdictions were created outside the formulary system. These procedures of extraordinary inquiry (*cognitio extra ordinem* or *cognitio extraordinaria*: see §2. 13, 14 below) gradually spread to jurisdiction over ordinary civil law cases and by the early 4th cent. entirely supplanted the formulary procedure.

Problems had arisen from the conquest of provinces (see PROVINCIA) to which the Romans conceded from the first the right of organizing their legal life according to their own laws. Only those provincials on whom Roman citizenship was conferred, individually or by groups or regions, had to observe Roman private law in their legal relations. Conflicts between Roman and local law were submitted to the emperor, who not infrequently decided in favour of local law. Caracalla's general grant of Roman citizenship in AD 212 in theory abolished these conflicts, but local law continued to a varying extent to be accommodated in the guise of long-standing custom. This was treated as part of Roman law provided that, unlike *incest or polygamy, it did not outrage Roman susceptibilities.

In the reign of Constantine I independent legal writing came to an end (see LEGAL LITERATURE) and the imperial government, now firmly bureaucratized, assumed a monopoly of legal development. Some scholars, influenced by the mystique of decline and fall, have treated the ensuing centuries as a period of legal degeneration, in which classical law was replaced by 'vulgar law'. The detailed evidence hardly supports this view. The law schools of Rome and Berytus (mod. Beirut) flourished in the post-classical period, teaching classical law. Many other towns had their law teachers, and the number of lawyers needed to fill posts such as those of assessor to provincial governors increased. A factor which creates an impression of decline is that the constitutions issuing from the imperial legislature (the consistory) in the later empire were drafted by the emperor's quaestor, an official who had become his principal spokesman. Quaestors were rhetorically skilled but until about AD 400 were seldom lawyers, though they had access to professional advice in the imperial offices (*scrinia*). The language of legislation was therefore untechnical; indeed there was often a conscious avoidance of technicalities. But though this created some danger of misunderstanding, lawyers were at hand to explain what was meant. Hence classical private law continued in force over a wide area, though with some modifications. In particular, contrary to what has sometimes been asserted, the basic distinctions between ownership and possession, contract and conveyance remained intact. Only when invaders overran the west and captured Rome, disrupting the administration of justice along with the imperial administration as a whole, can one properly speak of vulgarization. The Roman law of the successor states such as those of the Visigoths and Burgundians (*lex Romana Visigothorum, lex Romana Burgundionum*) does indeed often present a simplistic version of Roman law.

In the east the invasions were repelled. By the 6th cent. the law school of Berytus had built up a tradition of teaching and analysis of the classical texts over some 300 years; and in 425 Theodosius II imposed imperial control on law teaching in Constantinople. This enabled Justinian to draw for his codification on teachers from both centres along with officials and practising lawyers who had been taught in them. It was therefore inevitable that the tendency of the codification would be to move back towards classical private law, in so far as it had been modified in the post-classical period. The same was not of course true of public or religious law. But even in private law Justinian was a reformer to the extent that with his quaestor Tribonianus' help he eliminated obsolete institutions and over-subtle distinctions and settled points of dispute among the classical lawyers, developing the received tradition in an incremental way. In general Justinian favoured equitable solutions, though sometimes at the cost of certainty. He not infrequently changed his mind. The influence of Christian thinking, hardly noticeable in the codification apart from legislation on religious matters, is more strongly marked in the *Novellae* (new legislation) enacted from 535 onwards. T. Hon.

2. Civil procedure 1. The Roman civil trial was governed in the course of history by three systems of procedure: that of the *legis actiones*, the formulary system, and the *cognitio extra ordinem* or *cognitio extraordinaria*. The periods during which these systems were in use overlapped to some extent, but, broadly speaking, the *legis actiones* prevailed until, probably in the second half of the 2nd cent. BC, they were largely replaced by the formulary system; the *cognitio extraordinaria* gradually encroached on the formulary system during the Principate and finally superseded it under the Dominate (i.e. after AD 284).

2. The first two systems shared a central feature: the division into two stages. The first took place before a magistrate, *in iure*, and its purpose was to define and formulate the issue (i.e. the limits of the dispute between the parties). This stage culminated in joinder of issue (*litis contestatio*), an acceptance by the parties, under the magistrate's supervision, of the issue thus formulated and the nomination, in the usual case, of the *iudex* authorized by the magistrate. It was the *iudex* who presided in the second stage (*apud iudicem*) when the case was heard and argued. He was a private person empowered by the magistrate's order to give judgement, but he was more than a mere private arbitrator, because that judgement was recognized by the state and gave rise to execution proceedings, though in the last resort

it was the successful plaintiff who had to put these into effect. Only in the stage *in iure* were certain formalities observed; the stage *apud iudicem* was entirely informal. The differences between the *legis actio* system and the formulary system lay in the proceedings *in iure*.

3. The procedure by *legis actio* (which existed in the time of the Twelve Tables: Gai. *Inst.* 4. 17a) required the plaintiff and the defendant ritually to assert their rights in one or other of five sets of exactly prescribed formal words (Gai. *Inst.* 4. 11 ff.). Three of these sets of words served to initiate a claim and the other two to obtain execution. Of the former the most general, applicable to claims of ownership and to claims originating in obligations, was the *legis actio sacramento*. This involved in historical times a formal wager between the parties as to the validity of their claims, each party depositing as his stake a fixed sum of money (*sacramentum*). The other forms for initiating a claim were (a) the *legis actio per iudicis arbitrive postulationem*, available only for cases for which it had been specifically authorized by statute; the cases of which we know were claims based on a solemn promise (*stipulatio*) and disputes about property owned by more than one person, but there were apparently others; (b) the *legis actio per condictionem*, introduced by a *lex Silia* and a *lex Calpurnia*, probably in the 3rd cent. BC, for claims for specific sums of money or specific things asserted to be owing by the defendant to the plaintiff. The two forms of *legis actio* for obtaining execution were *per manus iniectionem* and *per pignoris capionem*. By the former the creditor proceeded against the person of the condemned debtor and by the latter against his property.

4. The *legis actio* system had the disadvantage that it was inflexible. In particular it seems that the praetor could neither create new forms of action nor extend the existing *legis actiones* to claims not recognized by the law. These defects were removed by the formulary system. The characteristics of this system were that for each cause of action there was an appropriate form of action, expressed in a set of words or *formula*; and that the praetor had the power to create new *formulae* to meet new needs. The *formula* constituted the pleadings. Thus, if there had been a contract of sale (*emptio venditio*) and the seller refused to deliver what he had sold, the buyer had an action on the purchase (*actio empti*), and conversely if the buyer refused to pay the price, the seller had an action on the sale (*actio venditi*); and each action had an appropriate *formula* in which the issue was defined. But while the *formula* varied from action to action, its structure was based on some permanent essential parts: the *intentio* (concise formulation of the plaintiff's claim) and the *condemnatio*, by which the judge was directed to condemn the defendant if he found after hearing the evidence and the arguments that the plaintiff's case was good, otherwise to acquit him. To suit the complexities of each case the *formula* might be extended by additional clauses, e.g. by a *demonstratio*, which served to determine more precisely the matter at issue where the *intentio* was indefinite (*incerta*), i.e. where the claim was not for a specific sum or thing; or by an *exceptio*, a clause on behalf of the defendant excluding his condemnation if he should prove a fact recognized by the praetor as making such condemnation unjust (e.g. that the plaintiff had been guilty of bad faith: *exceptio doli*; or that the plaintiff had agreed not to sue the defendant: *exceptio pacti*); and the plaintiff might reply to the *exceptio* by a *replicatio* expressing a countervailing plea (e.g. that the defendant had subsequently agreed to waive the agreement not to sue: *replicatio pacti*); and so on. The whole *formula* was framed as a succession of conditional clauses governing an order by the magistrate to the judge to condemn or acquit the defendant. Model *formulae* for all recognized actions, defences, etc. were published with the edict. The principle that each cause of action had its appropriate *formula*, coupled with the power of the praetor to create new *formulae* (or new parts of *formulae*), either generally in the edict or on the facts of a particular case, lay at the root of the law deriving from praetors and other magistrates (*ius honorarium*).

5. All actions, except those intended only to settle a preliminary question (*actiones praeiudiciales*), necessarily led to a *condemnatio* for a money sum. There could therefore be no order for specific performance or for the restitution of a thing, though it was open to the defendant to make such

restitution before judgement. In some actions the *condemnatio* was made conditional on the defendant's not having made restitution, the plaintiff being allowed to make his own assessment of the value. In the ordinary case it was for the *iudex* to make the assessment of the amount which the defendant must pay (*litis aestimatio*), whether it was the value of a thing or damages.

6. The origins of the formulary system are obscure. The 2nd-cent. AD law teacher Gaius (*Inst.* 4. 30) says only that the *legis actiones* were replaced by the *formula* by a *lex Aebutia* (probably in the latter part of the 2nd cent. BC) and by two *leges Iuliae* (17/16 BC), but the part played by each of these pieces of legislation is conjectural. It is likely that the *formula* originated well before the *lex Aebutia* in proceedings between *peregrini* (aliens, to whom the *legis actiones* were not open) under the jurisdiction of the *praetor peregrinus* (first created 242 BC), or in the provinces. In either case the proceedings would depend entirely on the *imperium* of the magistrate authorizing them and would therefore be free of the restrictions imposed on suits between citizens by *legis actio*. It is also likely that the *formula* was admitted before the *lex Aebutia* in suits between citizens arising out of the newer, flexible institutions open to citizens and peregrines alike. If this is so, the *lex Aebutia* would for the first time have allowed the formulary procedure as an alternative to the *legis actio* in cases involving the old *ius civile*, and the *leges Iuliae* would have abolished the *legis actiones* altogether, except for proceedings before the centumviral court.

7. The actions of the formulary system were derived from that part of the functions of the praetor known as *iurisdictio*. There were, however, other remedies which derived from his *imperium*. They are in form orders issued for the purpose of the administration of justice, but since the praetor generally avoided using direct means of enforcing obedience, disputes concerning these orders might lead to an action which would be tried in the ordinary way. From the point of view of the development of the general law the most important of these orders were the interdicts (*interdicta*). Their object was to give immediate protection to threatened or violated interests of the plaintiff. If the defendant ignored the interdict, or disputed the plaintiff's right to it, a procedural wager would, in the usual case, enable the matter to be litigated by an ordinary action. A variety of private interests were protected in this way, but the most important were possession and the praetorian rights of inheritance created by a grant of possession of a deceased estate (*bonorum possessio*). Interdicts also protected rights of a public character, such as public rights of way.

8. In addition to interdicts, praetorian orders included *missiones in possessionem* and *in integrum restitutiones*. A *missio in possessionem* was an authorization to enter into possession either of a particular thing or of the whole of a person's property, with the purpose of putting pressure on that person, e.g. on the owner of a building to give security against the threat of damage caused by the building to a neighbour (*damnum infectum*), or on a losing defendant to an action to comply with the judgement. An *in integrum restitutio* was an order reversing the consequence of a general rule of law which the praetor considered in the particular case to be inequitable. So a minor (i.e. a person under 25 years of age) could seek *in integrum restitutio* if his inexperience had led him to enter into a disadvantageous transaction, even though he could not show that the other party actually took advantage of his youth.

9. The bringing of an action began with an extra-judicial summons, *in ius vocatio*, by which the plaintiff personally summoned the defendant to follow him before the magistrate. The Twelve Tables contained detailed provisions governing this summons. The only way of avoiding an immediate appearance before the magistrate (which could be secured by force in case of resistance) was for the summoned party to give a guarantor (*vindex*).

10. The proceedings *in iure* might begin with preliminary questions, such as whether the magistrate had jurisdiction in the matter or whether the parties had the capacity to appear in court. A negative result of this inquiry would result in a rejection of the case (*denegatio actionis*) and an end to the

proceedings. Normally, however, the stage *in iure* was devoted to defining the issue. There might be discussions about the composition of the *formula*, especially when the case was not provided for in the edict and the plaintiff tried to obtain the grant of a new *formula* (or a new part of a *formula*, such as an *exceptio*) adapted to the particularities of the case. The proceedings ended with *litis contestatio*. This required the co-operation of the parties, but neither of them could prevent the achievement of this act by repeated refusal. The plaintiff would run the risk of *denegatio actionis* and the defendant of *missio in possessionem*. After *litis contestatio* there could not be another trial of the same issue; and it was with reference to the moment of *litis contestatio* that the judge had to decide controverted matters.

11. The trial took place usually before a single *iudex*, but in some cases before several *recuperatores* or before the *centumviri* or the *decemviri stlitibus iudicandis* ('board of ten for judging lawsuits'). The *iudex* was bound of course to consider the issues as they were presented in the *formula* and in so doing to apply the law, but otherwise he was uncontrolled and could take what advice he chose. *Gellius (*NA* 14. 2) records that, when faced, on his first appointment as a *iudex*, with a difficult decision on a matter of fact, he sought the opinion of Favorinus of Arles, a philosopher. At the end of the hearing the *iudex* was bound to announce his verdict to the parties in accordance with the *condemnatio*, unless he was willing (as Aulus Gellius was on that first occasion) to swear an oath that the matter was not clear to him (*rem sibi non liquere*). In that event the case would be remitted to another *iudex* for a retrial.

12. If the unsuccessful defendant did not carry out the terms of the judgement, the plaintiff could not proceed immediately to execution. He must first bring an action on the judgement (*actio iudicati*). In this action the defendant could not dispute the merits of the judgement, but he might plead that it was invalid, e.g. for want of jurisdiction or defect of form, or that he had already satisfied it. In such a case there would be *litis contestatio* and a trial in the usual way. There were, however, two deterrents to frivolous defences: the defendant had to give security; and, if he lost, he would be condemned in double the amount of the original judgement. If the defendant neither satisfied the judgement nor defended the *actio iudicati*, the magistrate would authorize the plaintiff to proceed either to personal or to real execution. In the latter case the magistrate made a decree putting the creditor in possession of all the debtor's property and there followed what was in effect a bankruptcy.

13. The formulary system was the ordinary procedure of the classical period, but from the time of Augustus there developed beside it various other forms of procedure in particular contexts, which are commonly referred to collectively as *cognitio extraordinaria* or *cognitio extra ordinem* (investigation outside the ordinary procedure of the formulary system). The emperor (rarely) or a magistrate or (most commonly) a delegated official conducted the entire trial; there was no division into two stages and no private *iudex*. The process was still, however, a judicial one and the development of a system of appeals served to secure uniformity. The trial had the character more of an investigation than of a hearing of a dispute between adversaries. In this respect it was the forerunner of the procedure which is found on the continent of Europe today.

14. In the republic there was no possibility of appeal, except to the very limited extent that a judgement could be called into question by defending the *actio iudicati*. In the early Principate, however, some appeal to the emperor seems to have been allowed, and in cases dealt with by *cognitio extraordinaria* or *cognitio extra ordinem*, where the trial would normally be before a delegated judge, it would be natural to allow an appeal to the person who had made the delegation. Certainly it soon became a regular institution, with the higher court not only quashing the original decision, but substituting its own. The appeal was made orally or in writing (*libelli appellatorii*) to the trial judge, who sent the entire dossier to the higher official, with a written report (*litterae dimissoriae* or *apostoli*). There were penalties for frivolous appeals. Justinian made an extensive reform of the system of appeal and his *Novella* 82 settled the rule that all judgements were appealable, except those of the praetorian prefect (commander of the imperial bodyguard).   B. N.

3. Criminal law and procedure 1. Criminal law was not originally distinguished from civil law at Rome, as it is in modern legal systems, both by procedure and by the fact that in successful actions judgement is given in favour of the public authority rather than those who have been wronged. Moreover, when this distinction regarding procedure and judgement did come to be made, we find a different categorization of criminal and civil wrongs from those which are normally found in modern systems. Theft for example was originally treated as a private wrong (delict) pursuable by civil action; only much later did it become usual to bring a criminal prosecution. *Adultery was not originally a matter for a civil suit (in Roman society no ground was needed for a divorce), but later became a crime. It is possible to see a progression from private revenge towards a system where public authority and those acting for the public undertake the pursuit of crimes, but this progression was never complete. We can distinguish phases in this development. In the oldest phase of criminal law we find, side by side with private revenge, the practice of settlements between offended and offender, at first voluntary and sporadic, later obligatory. By the end of this phase the beginnings of a new system can be observed: intervention of the community in punishing some crimes, especially those directed against its own structure or existence. Next, the community takes in its hands the repression of offences, not only those which menace the public order or interest directly, but also those affecting private property or interest. The Twelve Tables represent a combination of the first two phases, while in the advanced republic the intervention of public authority, hitherto exceptional, becomes more and more common. Under the Principate it gains dominance, and under the late empire and Justinian it becomes exclusive, having absorbed nearly the whole field of private criminal law. A survival of the idea of vengeance is found in the *noxae deditio*, the surrender of the wrongdoer (slave or son under *patria potestas*) to the person wronged, though by the late empire this practice was limited, when the surrender of sons was abolished.

2. The Romans did not create an organic body of statutes relating to criminal law. The Twelve Tables are primarily concerned with civil actions and even in the fragmentary provisions of tables 8 and 9 we find a mosaic of varied penal provisions rather than a code. They were restricted to such criminal matters as interested a primitive peasant community, and therefore were inadequate when the republic became more sophisticated and powerful. The copious legislation of the republic did not solve the problem as these *leges* dealt only with single crimes or groups of crimes. In the late republic it is noticeable that some offences were treated by several *leges* voted within a short period of time, e.g. the *crimen repetundarum* (extortion by Roman provincial officials) or *ambitus* (see BRIBERY). As *Tacitus later noted (*Ann.* 3. 27), when public affairs were at their worst, there were most laws. The emphasis was on crimes by senators and magistrates, people acting in the public sphere, but elaborate laws were also created against homicide and violence by any person. Some attempt was made under *Sulla to revise comprehensively criminal procedures but the result was no more a systematic treatment or a coherent code than the later legislation of *Caesar, Augustus, and subsequent emperors, however creative this was in particular details. Extensive interpretation of earlier statutes to cover new facts (wherein the senate co-operated as long as it remained active), or modification of penalties in the direction of greater or lesser severity, constitutes all the legislative activity of the empire in substantive criminal law. The procedure *cognitio extra ordinem* or *cognitio extraordinaria*, it is true, caused the introduction of new ideas into the general doctrines of penal law; and imperial constitutions applied some novel conceptions; but all these, being sporadic and exceptional, did not give an impulse to systematic elaboration.

3. The jurists of the 2nd cent. AD—the best period of classical jurisprudence—contributed to the development of criminal law far less than to that of civil law. A compilation analogous to the *edictum perpetuum* in civil law would certainly have roused their interest in criminal matters; and it is noticeable how fertile was their contribution to doctrines of private delicts, with which the praetorian edict dealt (cf. the excellent elaboration of *iniuria*, *Dig.* 47. 10: see below), in comparison with their modest part in

public criminal law. The effect of the interpretative work of all these more or less authoritative elements (imperial rescripts and edicts, *senatus consulta*, practice of *cognitio extraordinaria* or *cognitio extra ordinem* (see §2. 13, 14 above), jurisprudence) was that offences quite different from those which were described and made punishable in republican statutes were subjected to the statutory penalties. The exact terms of the original criminal statute might on occasion become obscure. Thus (*a*) Sulla's *lex Cornelia testamentaria* (*nummaria*, called also *de falsis*), which originally dealt with falsification of wills and of coins, was extended not only to the forgery of documents and the assumption of false names, titles, or official rank, but even to corruption in litigation, as when a juror, accuser, witness, or advocate was bribed, in which case both giver and receiver were punishable. Even a juror who neglected the constitutions of the emperors was punished according to this statute. (*b*) The *lex Iulia de ambitu* was applied to cases of pressure exercised on a juror by the accuser or the accused, though the original field of the statute was electoral *corruption. See BRIBERY, ROMAN. Interestingly, there appears in some jurists of the 2nd cent. AD a desire to return to the exact provisions of the original statute, even at the cost of discarding some later case law.

4. Under the late empire criminal legislation is directed more to penalties than to the doctrinal treatment of offences. The punishableness of some delicts varied under the influence of political or religious points of view; the creation of new categories of crimes in this long period is restricted to abduction and offences against the Christian religion after its recognition by the state. The profession of *Christianity had at one time been prosecuted as *crimen maiestatis* (treason). Justinian's legislative compilations show the first endeavour to collect the scattered provisions of public and private criminal law into a systematic whole (see JUSTINIAN'S CODIFICATION). The *Digest*, books 47–9, and *Codex*, book 9, give a well-arranged design of criminal law, procedure, and penalties. The compilers, of course, found some help in works of the latest classical jurists, who in just appreciation of the difficulties created by this fluctuating and uncertain state of criminal legislation dealt with these matters in monographs: *De iudiciis publicis* (Marcianus, Macer, Paulus), *De poenis* (Paulus, Claudius (or Venuleius) Saturninus, Modestinus), *De cognitionibus* (Callistratus). But all these and similar works, though doubtless meritorious and useful, aimed rather at collecting material than at creative criticism or presentation of new ideas. Even the terminology distinguishing different categories of offences does not show that stability and precision which is so excellent a feature of Roman legal language. The terms most used are *crimen, delictum, maleficium*; but it can hardly be affirmed that these expressions had a particular exclusive sense, though generally *crimen* indicates more serious offences directed against the state or public order, whilst *delictum* is rather used for delicts against private property or personal integrity and of no great harmfulness. The meaning of *maleficium* as a general term is even less technical, especially as it was used for designating sorcery and magic arts. All endeavours to bring order into classical texts by allotting to these terms an exclusive technical sense and removing all inconvenient texts as interpolated break down because of the indiscriminate use of these terms.

5. For the distinction between public and private offences we likewise lack any precise definition or statement of distinguishing marks; and yet it was of fundamental importance for developed Roman criminal law. This distinction rested upon a practical, rather than a doctrinal, differentiation of offended interests, and found its visible consequences in the fields of procedure and penalties, which differed greatly in the two spheres. The Roman jurists dealt more with the distinction between *iudicia publica* and private *actiones poenales* than with that between the interests violated as public or private, and the post-classical and Justinianic classification into *delicta privata, crimina extraordinaria*, and *iudicia publica* (*Rubric to Digest* 47. 1, 47. 11, 48. 1) was also made from a procedural point of view.

6. The private delicts form a group apart: the wrongdoer is exposed to an action under the ordinary civil procedure by the person wronged, the effect of which is that he must pay a pecuniary penalty to the plaintiff (to be distinguished from another *actio* by which the restitution of the *res* or compensation is claimed—*rei persecutio*). The state as such did not show any interest in the prosecution of these

offences, except where the offender was a magistrate or other official (*repetundae*), but the proceedings had a punitive character. By contrast with other civil proceedings (i.e. for *rei persecutio*) they did not lie against the heir if the wrongdoer died before he had been sued, and each of several wrongdoers was liable for the whole penalty. The principal forms were theft (*furtum*); robbery (*rapina*, theft combined with violence); damage to property (*damnum iniuria datum*); assault, and in general all affronts to the plaintiff's dignity and personality (*iniuria*). The praetor also made other wrongs actionable, such as threats (*metus*), deceit (*dolus*), malicious corruption of other people's slaves, and the like. Praetorian law also introduced a category of actions for misdemeanours which affected public interest, e.g. damage to the *album* (public list) of magistrates, violation of sepulchres, and pouring liquids or throwing things out into the streets. In such cases anyone, *quivis ex populo* (hence the names *actiones populares*), could be plaintiff and claim the penalty. Proceedings for private delicts were in later times greatly restricted in favour of the criminal *cognitio extra ordinem* or *cognitio extraordinaria*.

7. The special domain of criminal law is, however, the second group of crimes prosecuted by public organs in *iudicia publica*. The oldest law knew the intervention of the state, as avenger of offences against its security or against public order, only in exceptional cases such as treason (*perduellio*), desertion to the enemy, or special forms of murder (parricide, *parricidium*). For the evolution of this group the series of criminal *leges* of the last two centuries of the republic (especially the *Corneliae* and *Iuliae*, i.e. those of Sulla and Caesar) were of the greatest importance. They instituted special criminal courts for particular crimes, extending in large measure the competence of the state to the prosecution and punishment of criminal acts. A survey of the various kinds of crimes allotted to the *quaestiones perpetuae* (standing courts) shows that they comprehended not only offences against the state, its security, and organization, or public order in the widest sense of the word, but also the more serious offences against life, personal integrity, private interests (falsification of wills and documents, serious injuries), and morality (adultery).

8. However, even with the help of the senate, imperial constitutions, and the jurists, this legislation covered only part of the offences needing repression. Furthermore, the *quaestiones* operated only at Rome and tried Roman citizens only (not women or slaves or aliens (*peregrini*)). Under Augustus we find in *Cyrene trials of *peregrini* by panels of jurors, but we cannot assume that this practice was widespread in the provinces and normally criminal jurisdiction would have been a matter for the provincial governor or his legate. A solution was found for these and other problems with the development of the procedure called *cognitio extra ordinem* or *extraordinaria*, as not being subordinated to the *ordo iudiciorum*. The trials in these *iudicia publica extra ordinem* were always conducted by public officials. Jurisdiction was exercised—apart from political offences and senatorial matters reserved for the senate—chiefly by the emperor and the prefects and in particular provinces by *praesides* and procurators as the emperor's delegates (see PROCURATOR). The sphere of *cognitio extra ordinem* became, thanks to imperial policy, more and more extensive and superseded the *quaestiones*, which are not mentioned after *Severus Alexander. On the strength of new legislative provisions new forms of offences arose (called later *crimina extraordinaria*), e.g. fraud (*stellionatus*), participation in illicit corporations, displacing of boundary stones, special types of theft (*fures balnearii, nocturni*). Whilst in *quaestiones* only the penalty laid down by the statute could be pronounced, the imperial judges had discretion in grading the penalty according to their appreciation of all the facts of the case. Moreover, penalties might vary according to the status (free / slave, man / woman) or rank of the convicted person: in particular, by the early 2nd cent. AD poorer citizens and others of low rank (*humiliores*) came to be punished more severely than those of higher rank (*honestiores*). The increase in the discretion of magistrates during the 3rd and 4th cents. AD made the accused more vulnerable to arbitrary severity.

9. From the earliest times the intention of the wrongdoer was taken into consideration; even the legendary law of King Numa on parricide required that the murderer had acted knowingly with malice (*sciens dolo*); the analogous expression in republican laws was *sciens dolo malo*. More adequate

differentiation between different states of mind was developed in the practice of the *cognitio extra ordinem* or *extraordinaria*, influenced also by imperial constitutions. In appreciating the atrocity of the act and depravity of its author the judge considered the intensity and persistence of the delinquent's will (*dolus*), the question of whether the act had been committed with premeditation or on sudden impulse, whether it had been provoked by a moral offence (e.g. murder of an adulterous wife when caught in the act) or was due to drunkenness ('*per vinum*'). A late classical jurist, Claudius Saturninus, known only by a treatise on penalties, distinguished seven points to be taken into consideration in determining the punishment: reason, person, place, time, quality, quantity, and effect (*Dig.* 48. 19. 16). Judicial liberty, however, gave occasion for arbitrariness: the 3rd cent., with the decline of imperial authority, brought anarchy into criminal jurisdiction. Under the late empire fixed penalties—now more severe than formerly—were restored, the discretion of the judge in the infliction of punishment having been abolished.

10. The magistrates invested with *imperium*, acting personally or by delegates, were in general the organs of criminal justice. From early times their power of punishment was restricted by *provocatio ad populum* (appeal to the people), which on one view required a judgement by an assembly, on another view encouraged but did not compel a reference to an assembly, and on a third only applied when there had been no formal trial, that is, when the magistrate applied coercive measures against disobedient or recalcitrant citizens, e.g. *prison, castigation, and fines (*multae*). Foreigners, slaves (see SLAVERY), and *women were also subjected to this kind of coercion, but had no redress. There were two fundamentally different forms of procedure under the republic, trial before the assembly (the so-called *iudicium populi*) and *quaestio* (tribunal of inquiry). Both were originally based on the inquisitorial principle: before an assembly the magistrate for the most part acted both as prosecutor and president of the assembly simultaneously; in the early *quaestiones* he, aided by a *consilium* of advisers, decided whether an accusation laid before him required investigation, controlled the investigation and production of evidence, and ultimately delivered a verdict and sentence. However, the latter procedure was modified when *quaestiones perpetuae* were set up by statute in the 2nd and 1st cents. BC. In these the investigation of crimes and production of evidence was a matter for the plaintiff or prosecutor; the selection of a jury was regulated by the relevant statute and both plaintiff and defendant had rights of rejection. At the trial itself, although the presiding magistrate might ask questions, procedure was adversarial, the verdict was determined by the jury, and the sentence was either fixed by the statute or a limited discretion was allowed to the jury, especially with financial penalties (*litis aestimatio*). This accusatory system was, however, abolished in trials *extra ordinem* or *extraordinaria*, where, once information had been laid about a crime, the magistrate had once more full initiative in prosecution and conducted the trial from beginning to end. The statutes establishing the *quaestiones* had specifically ruled out any appeal to another authority against verdict or sentence. An unsuccessful proposal was made by Mark *Antony to introduce appeal to the assembly from certain *quaestiones*, but the situation only changed decisively with the advent of the Principate. Augustus' tribunician power (see TRIBUNE) was associated with the right to hear appeals and a prerogative of mercy (according to Cass. Dio, this grant was made in 30 BC). Moreover, the *lex Iulia de vi publica* incorporated sanctions against the disregard of appeals by those subject to coercion or criminal sentences throughout the empire.

11. The Roman penal system was peculiar in its distinction between public and private penalties, reflecting the division into public and private offences. The private penalty seems originally a substitute for private vengeance and retaliation (*talio* = infliction on the delinquent of the same injury as that done by him), but pecuniary composition between the parties (*pacisci*) was already an option at the time of the Twelve Tables and later became compulsory. A private penalty consisted in payment of a sum of money to the person wronged, and is to be distinguished from *multa*, a fine inflicted by a magistrate and paid to the state. Public penalties originated, as in other primitive systems, in the idea of public revenge, or religious expiation for crimes against the community, or religious conceptions

('sacer esto'), and, for serious offences, entailed the elimination of the guilty person from the community. The death penalty (*poena capitis*) was inflicted in different ways. The Twelve Tables refer to burning, for arson, and suspension (perhaps a form of crucifixion) for using magic on crops. We later hear of decapitation, precipitation from the precipitous Tarpeian Rock on Rome's Capitol, and drowning in a sack (for parricide). It should not be thought that the more grotesque penalties were all primitive. In republican times the execution (and even the sentence) could be avoided by voluntary exile of the wrongdoer. Banishment was later applied as an independent penalty in various forms: *aqua et igni interdictio, relegatio, deportatio*. Under the empire we find condemnation to heavy work in mines (*metalla*) or public works (*opus publicum*) or to the gladiatorial training-schools (*in ludos*; see GLADIATORS). These penalties were normally combined with loss of citizenship, while *damnatio in metalla* ('condemnation to the mines', considered as the penalty closest to death) normally also involved loss of liberty and flagellation; an accessory penalty was the total or partial confiscation of property. Execution might take the form of exposure to wild beasts in the arena. It is noticeable that the Romans applied imprisonment only as a coercive or preventive measure, not as a penalty (see PRISON); the Roman conception of penalty laid more stress upon its vindictive and deterrent nature than on correction of the delinquent (see PUNISHMENT (GREEK AND ROMAN PRACTICE)). The advent of Christianity led to some changes in the modalities of punishments but did not mitigate their severity.

A. B.; B. N.; A. W. L.

BC): over 100 lawcourt speeches survive, though we rarely hear the result or even the opponent's case, and our manuscripts do not usually preserve the texts of witnesses' statements or legal statutes. Further information, particularly about judicial procedure, can be gleaned from Athenian comedy (especially *Aristophanes' Wasps*) and from the Aristotelian *Athenaion politeia* (esp. §§63–9); anecdotes in the philosophers or historians occasionally presuppose points of law; and the Athenian habit of recording public decisions on stone has left large numbers of texts, though few of these are strictly legislative.

The other significant body of evidence comprises private documents written on papyrus. Papyrus was widely used throughout classical antiquity, but for climatic reasons virtually none survives except in Egypt, where Greek was the dominant language of administration under Ptolemaic and Roman rule (*c.*320 BC–*c.* AD 630). The range of these texts is vast (wills, letters, agreements, etc.), and though often fragmentary, they give us an unparalleled picture of law operating at ground level.

Otherwise we have only scattered data. Even for such an important *polis* as *Sparta we rely on chance remarks in *Aristotle and *Plutarch about inheritance, or incidental details in historians about the trials of particular kings. The loss of *Theophrastus' *Laws* is keenly felt: surviving fragments suggest that this was a comparative study after the manner of Aristotle's *Politics*, which might have filled many gaps in our knowledge. The study of non-Athenian inscriptions may eventually offer a comparative understanding of judicial procedure throughout the Greek world; but it is an indication of our present ignorance that the Cretan city of Gortyn has the best-known legal system outside Athens and Egypt because of the chance survival of one extensive inscription, the so-called Gortyn code.

Origins The origins of law in Greece are important but hard to distinguish. There are traces of dispute settlement in the earliest surviving literary works (*c.*725–700 BC), most notably *Homer's depiction of a homicide trial on the Shield of *Achilles (*Iliad* 18. 497–508), while *Hesiod's *Works and Days* involves an inheritance dispute between the poet and his (possibly fictitious) brother. It has been argued that the Shield represents a process of voluntary arbitration which by Hesiod's time has become compulsory, but this seems unlikely, given that Hesiod's aristocrats-cum-judges appear politically weaker than their Homeric counterparts. Better perhaps is the suggestion that Homer's judges are not arbitrators: rather, what they hear is the killer taking the initiative in claiming the protection of their community against the threat of summary vengeance from his victim's relatives. But such individual literary portrayals cannot be permitted to sustain theories of legal evolution.

The earliest signs of legislation in the Greek world belong around 600 BC. This is the period in which later Greeks located the activity of semi-mythical legislators in widely spread Greek communities (Zaleucus at Locri Epizephyrii in southern Italy, Charondas at Catana in Sicily, Draco and *Solon at Athens). It also provides the context for the earliest surviving public inscriptions: fragmentary laws (mostly regulating judicial procedure and the holding of public office) from Dreros in *Crete shortly before 600 (ML 2) and from Chios, Eretria on Euboea, and near Naupactus (Gulf of Corinth) over the following century. The joint phenomenon of legislators and inscribed laws invites explanation, but traditional hypotheses appear unsatisfactory: places like Locri and Catana seem remote from near eastern influence, but few of the affected communities were colonies; the needs of traders (see TRADE) do not seem to have concerned the early legislators, while the idea that publication of law is a move towards open government rests on anachronistic assumptions about the nature and spread of writing. See LITERACY; ORALITY. A recent suggestion, indeed, sees writing as a new technology seeking a function, but this may ignore an apparent time-lag between its introduction in private contexts and the subsequent decision to use it for inscribing laws.

Unity Whether it is legitimate to speak of Greek law as a single entity is a long-disputed question. Scholars working on the papyri generally look for unity where those studying the orators perceive diversity; and German and Italian scholars tend to emphasize broad juristic principles held throughout the Greek world, at the cost (in the view of their Anglo-American counterparts) of ignoring real and major differences of detail.

There are underlying problems of *ethnicity, *nationalism, and evolution. What does it mean to be Greek? How far is Greekness a racial, cultural, or linguistic identity, and how strong is its political significance? Herodotus' Athenians (8. 144), admittedly, can appeal to the shared customs which distinguish Greeks from barbarians (non-Greeks). Classical *poleis*, however, were independent communities, each with its own political system and the jealously guarded right to make its own laws. Even in the Hellenistic period the Greek world was never a nation-state, and it is anachronistic to assume that the *poleis* were aiming towards a goal of political unity.

The dispute is significant because of its consequences. Evolutionary theories misleadingly imply that Gortyn represents a stage through which every Greek community passed on its road from Homeric dispute settlement to the law of the orators; they also encourage gap-filling, such that regulations attested only at Athens are predicated of the papyri and vice versa. Greek law, if it existed, was not a national legal system, but a family of systems like Islamic law today. See JUDGES, FOREIGN.   S. C. T.

lawyers, Roman or jurists (*iuris prudentes, iuris consulti, iuris periti, iuris studiosi*) were a specialized professional group in Roman society distinct from those humble clerks and notaries who copied documents and recorded proceedings. That society was unusual in that in the later republic and empire there emerged for the first time in history a class of secular legal experts who, whether they made a living from their profession or not, were regarded as the repositories of a special type of learning useful to the state and private citizens. Until the 3rd cent. BC knowledge of the law and its procedure was a monopoly of the patrician priesthood, the college of *pontifices* (see PRIESTS), whose advice was sought on the law of the state cult but also on secular forms. From then on some who were not members of the priestly college began to give advice on law; but until the end of the republic the same people were often expert in sacred, public, and private law. Their functions resembled those of modern lawyers. They gave opinions to people who consulted them (*respondere*), helped them to draft documents or take other measures to avoid legal pitfalls (*cavere*), and advised on litigation and its proper forms (*agere*). They were consulted by magistrates such as the urban praetor on the formulation of his edict and by lay judges (*iudices*) on the law they should apply in the cases before them. They taught mainly by allowing others to listen to them as they practised, but sometimes actively undertook to instruct pupils. Some lawyers wrote books (see LEGAL LITERATURE), but this was not essential. In principle their services were free, but they were not forbidden to accept gifts from those who consulted or were taught by them, though unlike other professionals such as surveyors and doctors there was even in the empire no procedure by which they could sue for a fee (*honorarium*).

In the republic and early empire the number of lawyers was small. Membership of this élite group of intellectuals depended on being taught by another member and enjoying a sufficient regard from the group as a whole for one's independence of judgement and depth of learning. It continued, even in the empire, to depend on professional opinion and not on official recognition or employment, valuable as the latter might be for the success of the lawyer's career. Legal expertise often ran in families. The existence of such a small, intimate body of specialists explains why in their writings lawyers so often cite one another's opinions. They aim to convince other lawyers. Advocacy was not in the republic and early empire a normal part of a lawyer's career, rhetoric being a separate discipline, but was not ruled out. In the republic and early empire lawyers often came from senatorial families but legal expertise could also be the avenue by which 'new men' (the first of their family to enter the senate) rose in the world. Lawyers often held public office, but Gaius Aquillius Gallus (a patron of *Martial) and Marcus Antistius Labeo (d. between AD 10 and 22) set the precedent of preferring practice or scholarship to public life.

As a prestigious non-political group the legal profession presented *Augustus with a problem since it comprised, for example, not only his supporter Gaius Trebatius Testa but the latter's republican pupil Labeo. He declined to bring the profession directly under his own control (*Res gestae* 6) but devised a system by which certain lawyers were granted the privilege of giving opinions publicly on his authority (*ius respondendi ex auctoritate principis*). *Tiberius gave the first such grant to a non-senator, Masurius Sabinus. The practical working of this scheme is obscure, since in general neither grants nor refusals of the privilege are recorded. In the middle of the 1st cent. AD another division occurred in the profession, the leading lawyers grouping themselves into two schools. The Cassian school was founded by Gaius Cassius Longinus with the help of his teacher Sabinus; a century later its members came to be called Sabinians. Though the matter is controversial, the Proculian school (named from Sempronius Proculus, mid-1st cent. AD) seems to have differed from its rivals in outlook and method, and these differences, though not the organization into schools, went back to Gaius Ateius Capito (consul AD 5) and Antistius Labeo. The Proculians were less tied to tradition and more insistent on logical rigour than their rivals, the Cassians readier to tolerate anomalies and tackle new problems piecemeal. Sextus Pomponius (2nd cent. AD) records the succession of the heads of the two schools well into the 2nd cent. AD, each school at that stage having two or more heads. Around 160 the law teacher Gaius still speaks of 'Sabinus and Cassius and our other teachers'.

Early in the 2nd cent. *Hadrian made some important changes. He ruled that the opinions of privileged lawyers, when in agreement, bound judges, and is said to have discouraged applications for the privilege by senators who were not professionally expert. More important, he reorganized the imperial administration in a way which offered a well-paid career structure to Romans of equestrian status (see EQUITES), who henceforth were to replace *freedmen as heads of the imperial offices. Of these the office of petitions (*libelli*) was held by a lawyer at the latest from *Antoninus Pius onwards. Marcus *Aurelius made the holder of this office, the secretary *a libellis* (later *magister libellorum*), registrar of the emperor's court. Equestrian lawyers could now aspire even to the highest imperial post, that of praetorian prefect, as in the case of Taruttienus Paternus in the reign of Marcus Aurelius, Papinianus, probably Paulus, and Ulpian and Hermogenianus. These opportunities attracted men of talent to the imperial service, and, under an emperor committed to government according to law, created an influential group of lawyers holding public office. This in turn increased the demand for formal law teaching; there now emerge prominent teachers and writers such as Gaius and Sextus Pomponius who did not practice. In the east law teaching in Berytus (mod. Beirut) goes back to the late 2nd or early 3rd cent. and the city remained an important centre of legal study from then onwards.

Around 200 *Septimius Severus, keenly interested in the administration of justice, created more posts for lawyers, and the new Roman citizens enfranchised by Caracalla in 212 (see CITIZENSHIP, ROMAN) swelled the demand for legal advice, especially in the provinces. In the later empire the number of lawyers in official posts again increased, as the number of emperors, praetorian prefects, their deputies (vicars), and provincial officials who needed legal advice multiplied. But though *Diocletian (284–305) attracted able lawyers to his service, *Constantine I kept them at a distance, and for two generations none is known to have risen to high public office. Then in the late 4th and early 5th cents. they again began to do so. The career structure now ran from law school through practice as an advocate or a post as assessor to an official, and service in one or more of the offices of state (*scrinia*) to the quaestorship. In some cases, such as that of Antiochus Chuzon (quaestor to Theodosius II), it ended with a praetorian prefecture, as with his predecessors two hundred years earlier.

In the west the legal profession along with the administration as a whole was disrupted by the 5th-cent. invasions of the Goths and others. In the east it was subjected to extensive state control. In 425 Theodosius II reorganized higher education including law teaching in Constantinople. He divided public from private teaching, allocating public space to only two law professors, who were forbidden to take private pupils. From 460 a candidate wishing to practise before the court of the praetorian prefect of the east needed to produce a certificate from his law teachers. The number of lawyers at the various bars was now fixed, and preference in filling vacancies was given to the sons of existing advocates. Justinian had thus a considerable pool of talent to draw on for his codification (see JUSTINIAN'S CODIFICATION).

That codification was the work of a self-conscious legal élite, inheriting a tradition which, despite the growth of state control, went back in an unbroken line to the republic. Its impact on Roman public life naturally varied from time to time according to the sympathies of different emperors and the felt need to give high priority to civil administration and hence to insist on the legal values of clarity, precision, impartiality, and conformity to rule.   T. Hon.

Lefkandi (see ◀Map 1, Cc▶), a coastal site (ancient name unknown) on the island of Euboea (off central Greece's east coast) between Chalcis and Eretria. Inhabited from the early bronze age until its desertion *c*.700 BC, perhaps following the Lelantine War (see GREECE, HISTORY, *archaic age*), it flourished in the late Helladic IIIC period. During the Dark Ages Lefkandi was an important centre in a region uniting Euboea, *Thessaly, east central Greece, and the Aegean island of Scyros. Cemeteries spanning the 11th to 9th cents. have revealed significant wealth and, from *c*.950 BC, abundant evidence for contact with *Cyprus and the Levant. A unique, massive apsidal building (almost 50 × 14 m. (164 × 46 ft.); *c*.1000 BC), with external and internal colonnades supporting a steep raking roof, represents a new form of monumental architecture following the end of the bronze age and prefigures Greek *temple design (see p. 412). Inside the central hall were buried a man and woman, and four horses: woman and horses had apparently been killed in a chieftain's funeral ceremony. After a short life the building was demolished and covered with a mound. Whether it served as a chieftain's house, destroyed following his burial inside, or as a cult-place erected over a heroic warrior's tomb, is debated.   R. W. V. C.

legal literature refers to those works of Roman *lawyers which in their treatment of legal matters went beyond mere collections of laws and formulae. Legal literature was the most specifically Roman branch of Latin literature, and until the Byzantine age nearly all works on law were in Latin, which remained the language of legislation in the east until AD 535. But they can only be understood in the light of those Greek genres which were imitated in Rome. They were for the most part written in plain but technically accurate language. They consisted of one or more books (*libri*), generally of 10,000–15,000 words

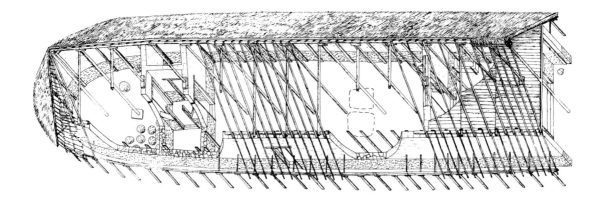

Lefkandi Axonometric reconstruction of the cult building at Lefkandi, c.1000 BC. Its wooden colonnade, apsidal end, and great length (c.50 m. or 164 ft.) anticipate the earliest Greek *temples.

each, divided into titles each with a rubric and often numbered. We depend for their early history mainly on the account given by Sextus Pomponius (2nd cent. AD). About 300 BC Appius Claudius Caecus is said to have written a book *De usurpationibus* ('On Interruption of Title'). A century later Sextus Aelius Paetus besides publishing laws and formulae wrote on the interpretation of the *Twelve Tables. Later in the 2nd cent. BC a number of writers are mentioned, some influenced by Greek philosophy and dialectics. One influential work was Marcus Iunius Brutus' three books (*libri*) in dialogue form *De iure civili* ('On Civil Law'). In the next century Quintus Mucius Scaevola's eighteen books on the same topic became the first standard work on law. Though casuistic, it was incisive enough to remain the subject of commentary 200 years later. At the end of the republic Alfenus Varus' 40 books of *Digesta* ('Ordered Abstracts') remained, despite the title, a bulky collection of opinions (*responsa*) given mainly by himself and his teacher Servius Sulpicius Rufus in particular cases. A few monographs were written, and some short commentaries on the praetor's edict. But with Marcus Antistius Labeo in the early empire an important new genre appears, that of the large-scale commentary.

Little republican writing has survived. The literature of the empire, of which thanks to Justinian's codification (see JUSTINIAN'S CODIFICATION) we have a great deal, included, apart from these genres, critical editions of and commentaries on earlier works and teaching manuals. Discussion of cases still predominates, since lawyers spent most of their time giving opinions and advice on concrete problems to private clients, magistrates, officials, or the emperor himself. Advanced teaching took the similar form of discussing difficult cases, real or imaginary (*quaestiones, disputationes*), and lawyers carried on correspondence with pupils and friends (*epistulae*). Collections of *responsa, quaestiones*, and *epistulae* were published, at first by the lawyer's

pupils, later by himself. Quintus Cervidius Scaevola and Aemilius Papinianus published little else, and even the *Digesta* of Julianus are mainly casuistic.

Large-scale commentaries began as stated with Labeo, who wrote massive treatises on the urban and peregrine praetors' edicts. This genre returned to prominence in the 2nd cent. AD when the climate of opinion set by *Antoninus Pius and Marcus *Aurelius favoured precision in the administration of justice. Sextus Pomponius' edictal commentary of that period ran to about 150 books, a record never surpassed. He and others also wrote large treatises on the *Ius civile* ('Civil Law') of Mucius Scaevola and Sabinus. Shortly before and after 200 Paulus and Ulpian became the last to practise the extended commentary, at about half Pomponius' length. These works, intended for officials and private practitioners, reproduced as much of the basic text as was necessary to understand the commentary.

Monographs were popular and remained so up to Arcadius Charisius at the end of the 3rd cent. AD. They included works on particular branches of the law, like adultery, and offices, like that of consul. Aspiring lawyers seem often to have written one at the start of their career, to put down a professional marker. Another young man's genre was the edition of an earlier work with *notae* (critical comments). Thus Paulus showed his paces by annotating Labeo's *Pithana* ('Persuasive Propositions'). But some monographs were ambitious and innovative. Both Ulpian and especially Paulus composed many, the first setting guidelines for public officers such as provincial governors, the second exploring and refining many branches of law and procedure.

Teaching manuals were slow in developing. An early example is Neratius Priscus' *Regulae* ('Guidelines'). They were in demand in the provinces, but when Roman citizenship was extended in AD 212 leading lawyers in Rome took them up and extended their scale. The textbook (*Institutiones*) of Marcianus, written around 220, ran to sixteen books (*libri*). Other types of work intended mainly for students were *regulae* ('guidelines'), *differentiae* ('distinctions'), and *pandectae* ('encyclopaedia'), the last two titles innovations of Herennius Modestinus.

Three monographs of Arcadius Charisius are to be dated to around 290. But the market for large-scale original works was now saturated. We find instead summaries and epitomes in up to six or seven books. Examples are the *Iuris epitomae* ('Summaries of the Law') of Hermogenianus in six books, *Sententiae receptae* ('Received Views'), attributed to Paulus, in five, and works of *Regulae* ('Guidelines') of similar length attributed to Gaius and Ulpian. There were also of course the semi-official collections of imperial constitutions by Gregorius and Hermogenianus and an unofficial collection of about 320 of uncertain authorship known as *Fragmenta Vaticana*. It consisted of imperial constitutions (legislative enactments) and excerpts from the private writings of lawyers and ran to the equivalent of about twenty books. There was an enlarged edition towards the end of the 4th cent. These were mere compilations, with no element of originality. The last legal treatise was perhaps the *Opiniones* ('Opinions') in six books, falsely attributed to Ulpian, which seems to belong to the reign of *Constantine. Two generations later a more slanted compilation appeared which is perhaps to be seen as a Christian reply to pagan propaganda. The late 4th- or early 5th-cent. *Lex Dei quam Deus precepit ad Moysen* ('Law which God Gave to Moses') is generally known as the *Collatio* ('Comparison') *legum Romanarum et Mosaicarum* since it sets out parallels between the law of Moses and Roman law in order to demonstrate the priority of the Mosaic law. This was a familiar Christian theme at the time.

Constantine I was hostile to what he saw as the undue complexity of classical law and was concerned that the law should be simple, unchallenged, and subject to his control. He ruled that the spurious and recent, but elementary, *Pauli Sententiae* was a genuine work of authority and invalidated Paulus' and Ulpian's sometimes critical notes on Papinianus. The canon of writings of authority was now closed, and the political and ideological climate under Constantine and his sons was hostile to any further private legal publication. T. Hon.

Lepidus (Marcus Aemilius Lepidus), the triumvir, younger son of Marcus Aemilius Lepidus. As praetor 49 BC, he supported *Caesar, then governed Hither Spain (48–7), intervening in the dissensions in Further Spain and returning to triumph. He was consul (46) and Caesar's *magister equitum* (see DICTATOR) (46–44). On Caesar's death he gave armed support to Mark *Antony, who in return contrived his appointment as pontifex maximus (chief of the *pontifices*: see PRIESTS) in Caesar's place. He then left to govern the provinces assigned him by Caesar, Gallia Narbonensis and Hither Spain. When, after the war of Mutina, Antony retreated into Gaul, Lepidus assured Cicero of his loyalty

to the republic but on 29 May 43 joined forces with Antony and was declared a public enemy by the senate. At Bononia in Etruria in October he planned the Triumvirate with Antony and Octavian (the later *Augustus), accepting Further Spain with his existing provinces as his share of the empire; and demanding (or conceding) the proscription of his brother Lucius Aemilius Paullus. After triumphing again *ex Hispania* ('from Spain') he held a second consulship (42) and took charge of Rome and Italy during the campaign of Philippi. After their victory his colleagues deprived him of his provinces, on the rumour of a collusion between him and Sextus Pompeius (son of *Pompey), but nothing serious was proved; and after helping Octavian ineffectively in the war against Lucius Antonius (Pietas), he was allowed by Octavian to govern Africa, where he had sixteen legions and won an imperatorial salutation. Kept out of the discussions at Tarentum over the renewal of the Triumvirate (37) and ignored in the arrangements, he asserted himself when summoned by Octavian to aid in the war against Sextus Pompeius. He tried to take over Sicily, but Octavian won over his army, ousted him from the Triumvirate and banished him to Circeii, though he later contemptuously allowed him to enter Rome. He kept his title of pontifex maximus until his death in 13 or 12, when Augustus took it over. Superior to his two partners in social rank and inherited connections, he lacked their ability to organize support and their total dedication to the pursuit of power.   G. W. R.; T. J. C.; E. B.

Lesbos (now Lesvos or Mytilini) (see ◀Map 1, Db▶), the third largest Aegean island (1,630 sq. km.: 629 sq. mi.) after *Crete and Euboea, 10 km. (6 mi.) from NW *Asia Minor. It is divided into three lobes on the south side by the long, narrow-mouthed gulfs of Kalloni and Gera. The volcanic western and northern mountains rise to 968 m. (3,176 ft.); the SE hills are greener and more fertile. Alluvium (partly marshy) occurs around the gulfs and in the east, where Thermi (an important bronze-age site) has hot springs.

Lesbos was usually divided between five competing *poleis*: Mytilene (the most powerful), Methymna, Pyrrha, Antissa, and Eresus. A sixth, Arisbe (near Kalloni), was absorbed by Methymna in the Archaic period. Some of the towns had land in Asia Minor. Settlement is relatively dispersed: there are important rural sanctuaries at Klopedi (temple of *Apollo), Mesa, and elsewhere, and the frequent rural towers and enclosures may be further evidence of inter-*polis* rivalry.

Proximity to Anatolia and the Hellespont (Dardanelles) partly explains the distinctive early culture. The earliest Greek settlers (10th cent. BC?) may have brought to the island its Aeolian dialect. Mytilene and Pyrrha have protogeometric remains. Lesbian culture retained unusual features, such as the characteristic grey *bucchero* pottery which may imply a continuity of pre-Aeolian Greek population or culture. *Cybele was worshipped in several towns.

The importance of seafaring is indicated by the harbour moles at several of the towns. Lesbian transport amphorae are found throughout the Greek world; amphora kilns have been located on the island. As élite wealth increased, a distinctive aristocratic culture grew up. Lesbos was the home of the poets *Sappho, *Alcaeus, Terpander, and Arion, the historian Hellanicus, and the philosopher Theophrastus. Lesbians founded colonies in the Hellespont and challenged Athens for control of Sigeum c.600 BC. The island came under *Persian domination during the Persian Wars. The cities joined the Athenian alliance (see DELIAN LEAGUE), but their rivalries persisted: Methymna did not back Mytilene's revolt in 428, and was alone in not having an Athenian cleruchy (citizen colony) imposed afterwards. Lesbos revolted again in 412.

After the Peloponnesian War (431–404 BC) the island increasingly has a single history. It oscillated between Athenian, Spartan, and Persian rule until *Alexander the Great's expedition. In the Hellenistic period it came under Ptolemaic domination (see PTOLEMY I and II); after the Macedonian wars the towns formed a league. Mytilene and Methymna were the seats of bishops from the 5th cent. See GREECE (HISTORY). D. G. J. S.

libraries By the end of the 5th cent. BC, *books were in general circulation, even if some regarded them as a fad of intellectuals like *Euripides (Ar. *Ran.* 943, cf. fr. 506 KA); Athens had booksellers (Eup. fr. 327, Aristomenes (2) fr. 9, KA), and exports reached the Black Sea (Xen. *An.* 7. 5. 14). Individuals collected the best-known poets and philosophers (Xen. *Mem.* 4. 2. 1); an imagined collection of the later 4th cent. BC includes *Orpheus, *Hesiod, *tragedies, Choerilus (?of Samos), *Homer, the comedian Epicharmus, and all kinds of prose, including Simus' *Cookery* (Alexis fr. 140 KA). Of famous collectors (Ath. 1. 3a), *Aristotle took first place (Strabo 13. 1. 54); but his library, like that of the other philosophic schools, remained private property (for its chequered history, see Strabo, ibid.; Plut. *Sull.* 26. 1–2).

Institutional libraries begin with the Hellenistic monarchies; the 'public' library of *Pisistratus (Gell. *NA* 7. 17) is no doubt myth. The model was apparently Aristotle's school, the Peripatus (Strabo, as above), rather than the temple and palace libraries of the near east. The first Ptolemies (see PTOLEMY I and II) collected ambitiously and systematically; the Alexandrian Library (see ALEXANDRIA) became legend, and *Callimachus's *Pinakes* made its content accessible. There were rivals at *Macedonian Pella, *Antioch (where the poet Euphorion of Chalcis was librarian), and especially *Pergamum. Holdings were substantial: if the figures can be trusted, Pergamum held at least 200,000 rolls (Plut. *Ant.* 58. 9), the main library at Alexandria nearly 500,000 (Tzetzes, *Prolegomena de comoedia* IIa. 2. 10–11 Koster)—the equivalent, perhaps, of 100,000 modern books. Smaller towns had their own libraries, some at least attached to the *gymnasium: so in the 2nd cent. at *Rhodes, Cos, and Tauromenium, mod. Taormina (*SEG* 26. 1123).

The Romans inherited some libraries direct (Lucius Aemilius Paullus in 167 brought home the Macedonian

libraries The inscribed rules from the so-called 'Library of Pantaenus' (c. AD 110), a privately funded establishment in the *agora of *Athens: 'No book is to be taken out because we have sworn an oath. [The library] is to be open from the first hour until the sixth.' An oath is still required of users of certain modern libraries (e.g. the Bodleian in Oxford).

royal library, *Sulla obtained Aristotle's books after the sack of *Athens), together with the traditions of private collection and public endowment. *Cicero accumulated several libraries (and visited those of *Varro, Faustus Sulla (Sulla's son), and Marcus Licinius Lucullus (d. 42 BC)); the satirist Persius left 700 rolls of the Stoic philosopher Chrysippus. The private library became fashionable: the fictional Trimalchio boasted both Greek and Latin libraries (*Petronius Arbiter *Sat.* 48); *Seneca and *Lucian satirize those whose books serve only for show (Sen. *Dial.* 9. 9. 4–7; Lucian, *Ind.*). Successful Greeks and Romans continued to found libraries in their native cities: Xenophon (*Claudius' doctor) on Cos, ⁺Dio of Prusa at Prusa, ⁺Pliny the Younger at Comum (mod. Como). Excavation has uncovered (among others) the libraries of Flavius Pantaenus at Athens, Julius Aquila at *Ephesus ('library of Celsus'), and Marcus Iulius Quintianus Flavius Rogatianus at Timgad (*Africa). On the monarchic scale, *Caesar planned a public library in Rome, under Varro's direction; Asinius Pollio (d. AD 4) actually founded one in the Atrium Libertatis. There followed (among the grandest) *Augustus' library on the Palatine hill, *Vespasian's near the templum Pacis, *Trajan's in his forum, *Severus Alexander's in the Pantheon; libraries were included in the baths of Trajan, *Caracalla, and *Diocletian (see BATHS). The Constantinian description of Rome counts 28 libraries; in the 2nd cent. AD at least a *procurator bibliothecarum* had overseen the whole system (see PROCURATOR). The new capital Constantinople was provided at short order with a library, which eventually reached 120,000 books. Origen's library at Palestinian Caesarea provided the Christian exemplar.

Hellenistic libraries apparently consisted of simple storage-rooms attached to a stoa (colonnade) or the like; such is the only ancient library to survive *in situ*, that of the Villa of the Papyri at *Herculaneum. The great Roman libraries provide reading-rooms, one for Greek and one for Latin (a challenge to parity), with books in niches round the walls. *Vitruvius (*De arch.* 6. 4. 1) advises that libraries should face east, to provide for good light and against damp; green marble floors might reduce eye-strain, gilded ceilings increase it (Isid. *Etym.* 6. 11. 2). Books would generally be stored in cupboards (*armaria*), which might be numbered for reference (SHA *Tac.* 8. 1). A statue of a divine (or imperial) patron occupied a central niche; busts of authors ('those whose immortal spirits there speak', *Pliny the Elder *HN* 35. 2. 9) adorned the building. Catalogues (*indices*) listed authors under broad subject-headings; attendants fetched the books (borrowing was for a privileged few). The library of Pantaenus at Athens had its rules inscribed on stone: see caption to accompanying illustration. The staff would comprise a librarian; attendants (*prosmenontes* in the library of Celsus at Ephesus), often slaves (as in the Palatine); copyists and restorers (*glutinatores*, Cic. *Att.* 4. 4a. 1; *antiquarii*, *Cod. Theod.* 14. 9. 2; cf. Suet. *Dom.* 20). New acquisitions might be provided by gift (each ephebe (see GYMNASIUM) at the Ptolemaion of Athens gave 100 rolls on leaving), or by purchase; Pliny's library at Comum had an endowment of 100,000 sesterces (*ILS* 2927), the library of Celsus 23,000 denarii (*Inschriften von Ephesos*, 7. 2. 5113).

Libraries came to rank among the grandest civic monuments. In the Bibliotheca Ulpia (forum of Trajan, Rome), each reading-room covered 460 sq. m. (5,000 sq. ft.). The library of Celsus (see above), founded in honour of Julius Celsus Polemaeanus (consul 92) by his son Aquila (consul 110), has a floor area of 180 sq. m. (2,000 sq. ft.), and Celsus' tomb in the basement; the elaborate façade (re-erected) still impresses. Costs were substantial: 1,000,000 sesterces at Comum, 400,000 sesterces at Timgad. Such libraries celebrated the ruling culture, and its representatives. They also preserved its texts. Ancient books were always vulnerable: material fragile, editions small, circulation desultory. The library offered a safe haven: so 1st-cent. AD Heraclitus of Rhodiapolis, 'the Homer of medical poetry', made sure to donate his works to the libraries of Alexandria, *Rhodes, and Athens (*TAM* 2. 3. 910). Acceptance into a great library marked a work as authentic (Dictys Cretensis, p. 3. 11 Eisenhut), or politically acceptable (Hor. *Epist.* 1. 3. 17; Ov. *Tr.* 3. 1. 59 ff.); emperors promoted favourite authors (Suet. *Tib.* 70. 2, *Calig.* 34. 2). But favour could do nothing against fire (the Palatine Library burnt down under *Nero or *Titus, again in AD 191, finally in 363); mould and 'the worst enemy of the Muses' (*Anth. Pal.* 9. 251), worm, put paid to many immortalities. See also ARCHITECTURE.

P. J. P.

Libya (see ◀Map 4, Cd▶), Greek name for the country of the Libyans, the indigenous peoples of North *Africa. In *Homer it was a pastoral land of great fecundity near Egypt (*Od.* 4. 85 f.); later, most commonly the Greek colonial area of Cyrenaica (see CYRENE; COLONIZATION, GREEK), but sometimes other parts, or the whole, of the North African coastal zone, even the whole continent of Africa. Roman informal usage followed Greek; formally it described the Egyptian administrative district west of *Alexandria as the nome of Libya and two Diocletianic provinces (see PROVINCIA; DIOCLETIAN) as Libya Inferior (or *Sicca*), approximately from Alexandria to Darnis (Derna), and Libya Superior (or *Pentapolis*), approximately from Darnis to Arae Philaenorum (mod. Ras el Aali in the Syrtica). On its peoples in the classical period information is currently accruing from anthropological and archaeological surveys. Ancient sources tend to stress their nomadism (see NOMADS), but some always had sizeable settlements; under Greek, Carthaginian (see CARTHAGE), and Roman influence many in the coastal zones seem to have become sedentary farmers. Intermarriage and socio-economic connections with colonists produced racial and cultural mixes here; normally, perhaps, the initiative for raids on the settled areas came from tribes further off.

In Cyrenaica Libya was personified, introduced into the story of the nymph Cyrene and *Apollo (Pind. *Pyth.* 9. 55. 8), and given a family (variable in detail) which connected her both with Egypt and with Greece, perhaps also with *Babylonia. *Pausanias described a (lost) relief at *Delphi (probably of the 5th cent. BC) which showed her crowning Battus, the founder of Cyrene, who stood in a chariot driven by Cyrene (10. 15. 6). Securely identified representations rarely survive. The clearest is on a Roman-period relief on which she crowns Cyrene who is strangling a lion; she is characterized by corkscrew ringlets, short over the temples and shoulder-length at the sides, a cape, fastened between the breasts and so stiff as to suggest leather, an animal beside her (probably a gazelle), and vine-branches above, with bunches of grapes. Hairstyle and cape seem taken from the real styles of Libyan women, the gazelle evokes the fecundity of pre-desert animals, the vine the fertility of cultivated land. The conceptualization is Greek and embodies the tradition that Libyans helped the founders of Cyrene. Whether it had an origin in Libyan belief is debatable. There is no certain evidence for a native cult of Libya and what there is for a Greek cult is of comparatively late date; the most widespread native cults known are those of Ammon, oracular god of Siwa in Egypt's Western Desert, and of Underworld deities.

J. M. R.

limes originated as a surveyor's term for the path that simultaneously marked the boundaries of plots of land and gave access between them. It came to be used in a military sense, first of the roads that penetrated into enemy territory (Tac. *Ann.* 1. 50; Frontin. *Str.* 1. 3. 10), and thence, as further conquest ceased, of the land boundaries that divided Roman territory from non-Roman (SHA *Hadr.* 12). At this stage a whole paraphernalia of border control grew up—frontier roads with intermittent watch-towers and forts and fortlets to house the provincial garrisons which moved up to the frontier line. The term *limes* comes to embrace the totality of the border area and its control system (but note the strictures of B. Isaac, *JRS* 1988, 125–47 on this point). In Europe, where the frontiers faced onto habitable lands, and where they did not coincide with a river or other clear natural obstacle, the frontier line came to be marked off (usually no earlier than *Hadrian) by an artificial running barrier. In Britain this took the form of a stone wall (*wall of Hadrian) or one of turf (wall of Antoninus); in Upper Germany and in Raetia timber palisades were originally built under Hadrian and *Antoninus Pius; these were strengthened in Upper Germany by a rampart and ditch (*Pfahlgraben*), and replaced in Raetia by a narrow (1.3 m. / 4¼ ft.) stone wall (*Teufelsmauer*) at an uncertain date in the later 2nd or early 3rd cent. In Europe beyond Raetia (an Alpine province), the frontier ran along the river Danube except where Dacia (the plateau of Transylvania) projected northwards. Here earthwork barriers were used in discontinuous sectors to the north-west and south-east where there were gaps in the encircling mountain ranges. The Upper German and Raetian frontiers were abandoned under Gallienus (253–68) and the whole of Dacia under Aurelian (270–5), leading to an intensification of military control on the rivers Rhine and Danube. In the eastern and southern parts of the empire the *limites* took a different form. They lay at the limits of cultivable land capable of supporting a sedentary population and were concerned with the supervision of trade routes and the control of cross-frontier migration by nomadic peoples (see NOMADS) whose traditional transhumance routes took them into provincial territory. In the east, military bases were positioned along the major north–south communication line along the edge of the desert (the via nova Traiana), and concentrated on guarding watering-places and points where natural route-ways crossed the frontier line. The threat of raiding Bedouin bands increased in the later Roman period, leading to a considerable build-up of military installations on the desert fringe. The problems were similar in *Africa, where the use of intermittent linear barriers such as the Fossatum Africae was designed to channel and control rather than to halt nomadic movements. In Tripolitania troops were based at intervals along the Limes Tripolitanus, a route that led right into the major city, Lepcis Magna, running around the Gebel escarpment which ran through the richest agricultural zone of the province. Three major caravan routes which converged with this road were likewise guarded by the military, with legionaries being outposted in the Severan period to oasis forts at the desert edge. The intermediate area was peppered with fortified settlements, largely of a civilian rather than a military character. The frontiers as a whole were greatly strengthened

in the Diocletianic period (284–305; see DIOCLETIAN) in response to increasing external pressure.   V. A. M.

literacy The number of people who could read and write in the ancient world is hard to determine. Without statistical evidence, we must rely mostly on chance information and inference: for example, the institution of *ostracism implies that most Athenian citizens could be expected to write a name. Our evidence (written) indicates the literate, not the illiterate, and especially the highly educated élite. The ancient habit of reading aloud meant that written texts could often be shared the more easily by others; the presence of inscriptions does not itself imply that they were read by everyone, since their symbolic value added another dimension to their written contents. There are also many different levels of literacy, which complicate the picture, from the basic ability to figure out a short message, to functional literacy or 'craft literacy', to the skill required for reading a literary papyrus (reading and writing skills may also have been separate). However, certain broad generalizations are possible. The 'mass literacy' of modern industrial countries was never achieved in the ancient world (cf. W. V. Harris, *Ancient Literacy* (1989), who believes a maximum of 20–30 per cent literacy was achieved, and that in Hellenistic cities). Women, slaves, and the lower social levels would usually be less literate. Archaic Greece and particularly Archaic Rome have left fewer instances of writing (graffiti, inscriptions), implying sparse literacy, and Archaic Greek cities sometimes attempt to ensure an official's power over the written word was not abused. However, there were pockets and periods where a higher rate of basic literacy among the adult citizen-body is probable: for instance, under the Athenian *democracy, when there was a relatively high level of reading-matter and incentives to read (even the sausage seller can read a little, Ar. *Eq.* 188–90); Hellenistic cities which made provision for elementary *education, especially *Rhodes; the Roman empire which probably had widespread craft literacy in the cities (cf. POMPEII) with increasingly elaborate use of writing; Roman Egypt, where the society was permeated by the need for written documentation (the administrative category of 'illiterates' (*agrammatoi*) denoted illiteracy in *Greek*). Literacy levels may to some extent be related to the functions of, or needs for, writing: *Sparta used written records very little until the Roman period, hence Classical Spartans were thought illiterate. The contexts in which writing was or could be used are essential in assessing the role or importance of literacy: both Greeks and Romans gave writing a magical, and non-functional role, as well as its more familiar use for preserving literature, public and private records, and inscriptions. It was often supplemented by oral communication and performance (see ARCHIVES; ORALITY; RECORDS AND RECORD-KEEPING). Literacy by itself was not a key to social advancement, and social success was impossible without the accoutrements of high culture. Much reading and writing was done by slaves, especially in Rome, ensuring that it was by itself of low status. However, it was not confined at any point in the Graeco-Roman world to scribes: writing is used from very early on in Greece for widely different purposes, informal graffiti and poetry, then inscriptions, suggesting it was not limited to a narrow social group, or to the public sphere. This spread may be partly linked to the comparative ease with which the alphabet can be learned, but the open nature of Archaic Greek society, and the early use of writing for memorials, should also be taken into account. R. T.

literary criticism in antiquity 1. The arts of formal speech played a great part in ancient life, so that it was natural that vocabularies and conceptual frameworks should be developed for the purposes of evaluation, speculation about the nature and role of poetry, and practical advice for successful composition, especially in oratory. In the resulting body of doctrine, this last element—which is the contribution of rhetoric—is dominant, and it is this which seems the most striking difference between Graeco-Roman 'criticism' and most modern analogues.

2. The first evidences we have of reflection on these subjects are in the early poets. *Homer and *Hesiod speak of their art as a gift of the *Muses, who inspire the poet, know all things, and can tell false tales as well as true (*Il.* 2. 484–92; *Od.* 8. 479 ff.; Hes. *Theog.* 1–104). *Pindar too called himself the 'prophet'—i.e. 'spokesman'—of the Muses (fr. 137 Snell–Maehler), and was proud to think of his 'wisdom' as the product of natural endowment, not of teachable technique, which was for lesser mortals (*Ol.* 2. 83). The poets did not however escape criticism; they were the transmitters of a mythological tradition which had many offensive features—tales of the gods' immorality and the viciousness of heroic figures—and the early philosophers found these an easy target. Allegory—for example the interpretation of the Battle of the Gods in Homer, *Iliad* 21, as a battle of the elements—began as a mode of defence against such attacks, and eventually (especially with the Stoics (see STOICISM) in Hellenistic times and the Neoplatonists later) became the most significant and influential critical approach in all antiquity. The idea of inspiration (of which Democritus of Abdera, it seems, made some rational justification) and the demand for a moral and social commitment are not the only achievements of 'pre-Platonic' poetics. More sophisticated reflection is suggested by the paradox of the sophist Gorgias, that tragedy 'offers a deception such that the deceiver is more just than the non-deceiver, and the deceived wiser than the undeceived' (Plut. *Mor.* 348c); and delicate connoisseurship is displayed by the comparison of 'high' and 'low' styles, as represented by *Aeschylus and *Euripides, in the great debate in *Aristophanes' *Frogs*.

3. *Plato pulled the threads together but in a very radical and paradoxical way, in which there may be a good deal of irony. Inspiration, as claimed by the poets, was for him no road to knowledge, indeed a thing of no great worth; and in so far as poets failed to promote the right moral and social values, they were to be banished from the ideal state altogether. In rationalizing this attitude Plato developed for the first time a concept of 'imitation' (*mimēsis*) which, in various guises, was to be a central theme of later theory. He held strongly that the spectacle of degrading emotion nourished the same emotion in the hearer. Parallel to his attack on the poets was his criticism of contemporary *rhetoric; here too he saw fraud, pretence, and contempt for truth. As a critic of style, he was superb, as is shown, not by any refined vocabulary, but by his marvellous parodies (*Symposium*, *Phaedrus*, *Menexenus*), rivalled only by Aristophanes himself.

4. *Aristotle's *Poetics*, the fountain-head of most later criticism, is in part an answer to Plato; this is the context of the improved and very important analysis of *mimēsis* and of the much-debated doctrine that tragedy effects a *katharsis* of pity and fear. This very crabbed and difficult book has many different themes: a general theory of poetry as a 'mimetic' art, and a speculative account of its origins; a detailed analysis of tragedy, stressing the primary importance of plot (*mythos*) over character and ideas; an account of poetic diction, including a good deal of what we should call grammatical theory; and finally some discussion of *epic and its inferiority (as Aristotle held) to *tragedy as a poetic *genre. A treatment of comedy is lost, but can to some extent be reconstructed from later writings. The *Poetics* is a truly seminal work, not so much for later antiquity (when it was hardly known, though the dialogue *On Poets*, now lost, was much read) as for the Renaissance and for modern criticism.

5. Whereas Aristotle held poetry and rhetoric to be fundamentally distinct—the one was an 'imitative' art, the other a practical skill of persuasion—his successors tended more and more to blur the difference. Theophrastus, Aristotle's pupil, is credited with the observation (fr. 84 Wimmer = 78 Fortenbaugh) that, while philosophers are concerned solely with facts and the validity of deductions, poets and orators alike are concerned with their relation with their audience, and this is why they have to use dignified words, put them together harmoniously, and in general produce pleasure (*hēdonē*) and astonishment (*ekplēxis*) in order to cajole or bully their hearers into conviction. For criticism, the consequence of this kind of approach is that form may be judged apart from content. It is thus no surprise that the main achievement of post-Aristotelian criticism is in the analysis of style, rather than in literary theory. The basic distinction between 'high' and 'low' writing, the 'high' being associated with strong emotion and the 'low' with everyday life and character, goes back to Aristophanes; in terms of effect on the audience, it corresponds to the distinction between *hēdonē* and *ekplēxis*, of which Theophrastus speaks. It was of course refined and modified in various ways. Demetrius (author of 'On Style') for example describes four 'types' of style (*charactēres*), two of which (the 'grand' (*megaloprepēs*) and the 'forceful' (*deinos*)) belong to the higher range, and two (the 'elegant' (*glaphyros*) and the 'plain' (*ischnos*)) to the

lower. Particularly influential, however, was a system of three styles, accommodating not only the two extremes but the smooth, flowing style of *Isocrates. This tripartite division was even supposed to be exemplified by Homer's heroes: *Odysseus, whose words come out 'like winter snows', Menelaus, who spoke little but to the point, and Nestor, whose speech was sweet as honey (Quint. *Inst.* 12. 10. 64). All kinds of writing could be pigeon-holed in this way: e.g. the representative historians were *Xenophon, *Thucydides, and *Herodotus. A *locus classicus* for the system is *Cicero, *Orator* 75–90. In the Greek critics and rhetors of the empire (*Dionysius of Halicarnassus, 'Longinus', Hermogenes) there are many refinements of these ideas. 'Longinus' is unique in concentrating not so much on the stylistic means of achieving *ekplēxis*, but on the kinds of subject-matter, thought, and general moral attitude which alone, in his view, could make success in 'the sublime' possible.

6. Though this rhetorical and stylistic doctrine is the main achievement of critics after Aristotle, there were other developments as well. (*a*) The Stoics (see STOICISM) viewed poetry primarily as an educational instrument, and so in a sense continued Plato's moralizing approach. *Plutarch's essay on *How the Young should Study Poetry* (*Mor.* 14d–37b) is a later example of this tradition: though a Platonist, he tries to overcome Plato's objections to poetry, not (as the Stoics did) by allegory, but by scholarly attention to context and historical circumstances. (*b*) The Epicurean Philodemus (see EPICURUS) is an important witness to Hellenistic theory: in his *On poems*, parts of which are preserved in tantalizingly difficult papyrus texts, he discussed and refuted theories of the Stoic Ariston, the scholar Crates of Mallus, the Peripatetic Neoptolemus, and Aristotle himself. He seems also to have had a positive view of his own, namely that form and content are inseparable, and cannot be judged separately. If this is a right interpretation, Philodemus makes a sharp contrast with the prevailing 'rhetorical tradition'. (*c*) The *Alexandrian scholars who collected and edited Classical poets and orators, and discussed the authenticity of the pieces they found, were also 'critics'. They needed historical, aesthetic, and grammatical insights. Much of Dionysius of Halicarnassus' work on orators is in their tradition; but we know it also from its remains scattered about the many extant commentaries and scholia, all the way down to the Byzantine scholar Eustathius, which contain critical judgements and insights of interest.

7. The Roman contribution is not a mere appendage to Greek criticism, though the two literary worlds are closely connected, and writers like Dionysius and 'Longinus' actually addressed their works to Roman patrons. In the classical period of Latin literature (as in the days of the Attic Old Comedy) criticism appears in topical writing in quite unacademic contexts; in Lucilius and *Horace, and later in Persius and *Petronius Arbiter, it is an ingredient of *satire. Horace not only defended his own literary position and expounded literary history in his *Satires* (1. 4, 1. 10, 2. 1)

and *Epistles* (1. 19, 2. 1, 2. 2), but wrote a humorous didactic poem (*Ars poetica*) in which he combined traditional precepts on the drama and views on the poet's place in society with witty and urbane reflections on his own literary experience. The *Ars* set a fashion followed in the Renaissance and after by Vida, Boileau, and Pope.

8. Cicero's achievement as a judge of oratory is unequalled—naturally, for he was himself a great orator. Political oratory died with him, and the age of the declaimers which followed produced critics of a different cast. Seneca the Elder makes many shrewd points in commenting on his favourite declaimers. The dominant theme in the early empire seems to have been a consciousness of decline. In itself this was nothing new, since Greek critics of music and art as well as of oratory had long been drawing contrasts between admired works of the past and the degenerate efforts of the present. The younger *Seneca (esp. in *Epistle* 114) and *Tacitus (*Dialogus*) reflect interestingly on the causes of 'decline'—moral and political, as well as intellectual. With Quintilian, the writer on rhetoric, there is some renewed optimism and a return to Cicero's ideals. The famous chapter (*Inst.* 10. 1) in which he catalogues the authors to be read by the budding orator summarizes traditional teaching on 'imitation' (his account of the Greek authors is based on Dionysius) but shows a capacity for independent judgement.

9. Greek literature, from the time of Dionysius onwards, was increasingly 'classicizing' and archaistic; the critics almost entirely neglected Hellenistic writers and their own contemporaries. In the Latin world, 'archaism', in the form of a preference for the early poets and pre-Ciceronian orators and historians, was in general a development of the 2nd cent. AD. But the Greek model of concentration on the 'classics' was increasingly followed; and the most significant contribution of the later imperial period to literary criticism is to be found in works like Servius' commentaries on Virgil and Donatus' on *Terence.

10. Late antiquity also saw a development in the philosophical criticism of literature. Stoic allegory and Aristotelian theory gave way to Neoplatonist interpretations, which involved allegory of a new, and more metaphysical, kind, and a serious attempt to 'reconcile Homer to Plato' by new means. Proclus' commentary on the *Republic* of Plato is the main text of this movement. Its importance for the medieval understanding of literature—and especially of biblical texts—can hardly be exaggerated.   D. A. R.

literary theory and classical studies One of the most striking features of 20th-cent. intellectual life has been the attention paid to literary theory, especially from the time of the 1960s. This intellectual ferment has produced a confusing variety of approaches, and especially of terminology, which has in turn given birth to a new minor isagogic genre, that of the 'Introduction to Literary Theory', the modern equivalent of the *Technai rhetorikai* or *Placita philosophorum* of the ancient world. The analogy with the Hellenistic philosophical schools is perhaps particularly close, in that alongside 'school' theorizing there is a mass of more or less eclectic work by practitioners who, like *Horace, would claim to be 'bound to swear by no master's words'. Just as no one would regard Aetius' account of Platonism (1st cent. AD) as an even half-adequate account of what reading *Plato is like, so summary accounts of literary theory are often embarrassed before their own inadequacy. Many of the most significant 20th-cent. theories of language and literature stress a slippery indeterminacy in discourse that is at odds with the pretence to scientific objectivity which is often (wrongly) taken to be the presupposition of a Companion like this one: and any attempt to give a history of literary theory instantly encounters the suspicion of plot which is another of the prevalent characteristics of the 'post-modern' age. The field is also one of particularly rapid change and, as another central dogma puts it, there is no point outside history from which it can be surveyed: what seems important in 1996 may seem a quaint byway by the following millennium. The purpose of this article is to offer not so much a path through the minefield as a way in. It is written by two who believe that 20th-cent. theorizing has a great deal to offer classical studies, and that in any case the time when the discipline could even consider trying to pull up the drawbridge and see out the Dark Ages in comfortable isolation has long gone.

In the United States and some European countries (but not in the United Kingdom, where the word is reserved for historical linguistics) 'philology' is the term which is often taken to sum up the traditional methods of classical scholarship. Both defenders of this tradition and critical theorists opposed to it tend to underestimate the degree to which this approach was theorized, the one group in a desire to make it appear as simply natural, the other out of anger at its lack of self-consciousness. In its most developed form it is clearly a product of 19th-cent. German attempts to grant to literary and historical studies the objectivity which was then seen as central to the increasingly powerful physical sciences, and it received its classic formulations from U. von Wilamowitz-Moellendorff in the course of his quarrel with Nietzsche. The purpose of textual study is to recover the intentions of the authors of the texts, and to this end all conceivable data from the ancient world may be relevant. The fragmentary traces that have come down to us are clues which can enable us to reconstruct the thought processes of the ancients: but the conventions of ancient literature need to be established through painstaking examination of parallels before interpretation can take place. These researches are most typically set forth in editions or especially commentaries, great monuments of learning like Pease's commentaries on *Cicero, Headlam's on the Hellenistic poet Herodas, or on a higher level Fraenkel's on *Aeschylus and those of Nisbet–Hubbard on *Horace.

There is much in traditional philology of which the discipline can be proud, especially the broad definition of text and the interdisciplinary nature of research implied by the detective metaphor, with the massive learning that that in turn entailed. But there are a number of assumptions made by the method which have come under scrutiny from various different theoretical positions in the 20th cent.: the assumed scientific objectivity of the critic, the focus on the surface psychology of the author, the belief that all the 'clues' will point to a single coherent picture, the aspiration to that overall master interpretation, and especially the belief that the hermeneutic tools used to interpret texts are timeless, based on the common-sense rules used in everyday life. These assumptions are not necessarily to be rejected simply because they are assumptions (though we believe they are all unhelpful), but, paradoxically, if the traditional method is to be sustained, they require a considerably more sophisticated theoretical underpinning than has to date been provided.

The theoretical movements which have brought these assumptions into question may be broadly categorized as *foundational* or *methodological*: the former tackle the basic assumptions of critical practice, that is, they are essentially metacritical, while the latter provide new things to do with texts rather than new reasons to do them. These two categories are naturally not sharply distinct, since assumptions about the point of criticism will affect practice and practice has implications for the foundations of theory, but it is a paradox that the theories which most radically challenge basic assumptions may have less of an effect on practice. It has been argued, for instance, that a 'post-structuralist' view of the self as constructed in language can perversely legitimate an apparently old-fashioned interest in the 'personality' of a figure like Horace (C. Martindale and D. Hopkins, *Horace Made New* (1993), 16–18). In contrast, the narratology of Genette and Bal (see below), with a wealth of new terminology and methods, is often seen as the least 'threatening' approach by traditional scholars, except perhaps in relation to historiography. Nevertheless, the various critical theories cannot be represented simply as a smorgasbord of techniques: more is at stake than methodology (cf. K. Ormand, *Bryn Mawr Classical Review*, 1994).

One popular plot for 20th-cent. literary theory sees the focus of interest moving from the author to the text and then to the reader. In contrast to the traditional focus on the personality of the creator of the text, various movements beginning with the Russian Formalists (to whom we owe such basic concepts as the distinction between 'story'—what happened—and 'narrative'—the way it is told) saw literature as a more or less autonomous system whose workings could be analysed in a manner similar to the formal analysis of language whose foundations were being laid by the linguist F. de Saussure with his *Course in General Linguistics* of 1916, perhaps the single most influential book in 20th-cent. literary theory. Saussure's distinction between a *diachronic* approach to language which looked at how it changed over time and a *synchronic* approach which viewed it as a single coherent system, and his insistence that meaning lay in the relationship between the elements of the system rather than in any external reference, led to a focus on the text rather than on the processes of its creation. This new focus of interest could, however, take radically different forms. In Anglo-American 'New Criticism', whose origins lay in I. A. Richards's experiments with the reading practices of English students reported in his *Practical Criticism* of 1929, the central critical act became the 'reading' of an individual text (usually a lyric poem or novel), exposing the way in which its devices, especially irony and ambiguity, contributed to the unity of its effect. In the continental tradition, on the other hand, interest was concentrated on the *langue* or general system rather than the *parole* or individual utterance within it, to use another distinction made by Saussure. This eventually led to the movement known as structuralism, whose founding father was the 'Prague school' linguist Roman Jakobson but whose most famous representatives were the anthropologist Claude Lévi-Strauss and the writer Roland Barthes (the movement of people and ideas from eastern Europe to Paris—and later the USA—is another common plot in the history of theory: another distinguished example is the Rumanian poetician Tzvetan Todorov, whose *Encyclopedic Dictionary of the Sciences of Language* (with Oswald Ducrot), originally published in 1972, provides an extremely useful overview of many central concepts). The movement was popularized in England and America by Jonathan Culler's outstandingly approachable *Structuralist Poetics* of 1975.

Structuralist analysis took many forms, but one essential element was this focus not on the individual text but on the underlying system of which it was a part. The analysis of literary and linguistic systems was only one subspecies of a general science of signs or *semiotics* (a concept going back ultimately to the American philosopher C. S. Peirce, who was directly influenced by the philosophizing poet Philodemus' *On Signs*): a famous early example was Roland Barthes's *System of Fashion* (1985). Myth was particularly a subject of research, as Lévi-Strauss, following in the footsteps of the *Morphology of the Folktale* of the Russian Vladimir Propp (1968; 1st pub. in Russian, 1928), sought, in the bewildering stories told by South American native peoples, the underlying patterns that gave meaning to their lives and enabled them to 'mediate' between the oppositions of nature and culture, men and gods. This phase of structuralism had a particularly profound effect on Greek studies through the 'Paris school' of Jean-Pierre Vernant and Pierre Vidal-Naquet, whose work was based on the earlier pioneering studies of Louis Gernet. Fifth-cent. BC Athenian tragedy and comedy in particular, publicly performed within the context of a religious festival that was also a celebration of social cohesion, proved a fertile ground for analyses which sought common functional patterns in myth, ritual, and literature. It was significant that it was American scholars (particularly Charles Segal and Froma Zeitlin) who did most to welcome the new approaches and put them to use, but their power and suggestiveness were such that they were fairly readily assimilated into the reading practices of Hellenists, as earlier Latin critics had taken to the New Criticism.

One particular offshoot of structuralism, although it took a little longer to establish itself in classical studies, has also been widely employed, that is, the formal study of *narrative known as *narratology*. The term seems to have been coined by Todorov and many of the methods have their origin in the work of Roland Barthes, but the father of the approach was the French poetician Gérard Genette, in a discussion of Proust published in a collection with the punning title *Figures III* in 1972 and later translated into English as *Narrative Discourse* (1980). Genette provided a simple but richly suggestive framework for analysing the relationship between story and narrative which proved of great practical utility for the analysis of a wide range of texts, not simply those most clearly 'narrative' in form. His work was carried forward especially by the Dutch theoretician Mieke Bal (*Narratology: Introduction to the Theory of Narrative* (1985; orig. pub. 1977)), and it was the work on point of view (focalization) in *Homer by one of Bal's pupils, Irene de Jong (*Narrators and Focalizers* (1987)) which encouraged use of the methods by classical scholars, though they had already been employed with great success by, for instance, the Italian critic Massimo Fusillo in his book on *Apollonius Rhodius, *Il tempo delle Argonautiche* (1985). Perhaps the most celebrated narratological study of a classical text, however, is John J. Winkler's book on the author of the Latin novel *The Golden Ass* (Apuleius), *Auctor et Actor* (1985), though that largely eschews the more technical terminology of the approach.

Another aspect of the structuralist emphasis on the system of literature rather than individual texts has been a mass of work on what older critics called 'allusion', the recognition in texts of traces of other texts. The detection of these traces has always played an important part in classical philology, partly as 'parallels' and partly in terms of the notions of imitation and literary rivalry that are prominent in ancient literary critical texts. The focus, however, was on allusion as a conscious or unconscious (the question of whether a particular allusion was 'intended' was hotly debated) metaliterary act in which an author chose to pay homage to or otherwise notice a predecessor. Structuralism replaced this with the insight that because all texts participate in literary systems, all texts (and not only literary ones) are always already of necessity shot through with the presence of other texts. A text which did not participate in any system in this way would be literally unreadable, since we would have no possible codes with which to decipher it. Authors cannot decide whether or not to be allusive: whatever they intend, their texts will be read against the 'matrix of possibilities' created by other texts. This phenomenon by which texts are inescapably and multiply allusive was termed by the French critic Julia Kristeva 'intertextuality' and, although in more general usage the term has lost some of its original emphasis and become domesticated as simply a synonym for 'allusion', it gave a powerful impetus to studies of literary relationships which moved beyond comparing and contrasting related passages to an insight into how the presence of earlier texts, if recognized by a critic, can radically affect interpretation. This approach has been of particular fertility in Latin studies, with an important role played by the Italian Latinist Gian Biagio Conte (*The Rhetoric of Imitation* (1986; orig. pub. 1984–5)) and younger Italian figures such as Alessandro Barchiesi (*La traccia del modello* (1984)), whose works have found an enthusiastic echo in English and American Latin studies. It has been central to the revaluation of Silver Latin, and the Flavian epicists in particular, viewed not as servile imitators of Virgil but as machines for producing striking intertextual complexities.

After structuralism came post-structuralism, though some figures, notably Roland Barthes, straddle the divide. The year before the famous *événements* of 1968 saw the publication of two major works by the philosopher Jacques Derrida which radically altered the direction of French critical theory. In *On Grammatology* and *Writing and Difference* he expounded a theory whose roots were also in Saussure but which moved in a very different direction. Like the structuralists, Derrida insisted that there was nothing outside text, that is, everything that constitutes the world for us comes to us as text, already in language. But language is not a stable, self-consistent *langue* that we can hold still under the microscope, but a restless chain of signifiers whose meaning, depends on further signifiers, whose meaning . . . In the most celebrated (self-reflexive) pun in 20th-cent. theory, meaning is *différance*, difference / deferral, never wholly present. Drawing on Plato's *Phaedrus* (particularly in the essay 'Plato's Pharmacy', which is the most concise introduction to his views), Derrida reversed the terms of the hierarchy that made the unmediated 'presence' of everyday speech the original form of which the disembodied and indeterminate voice of writing was an unwelcome perversion. Writing preceded speech, in the sense that all language, however apparently tied down by context and pragmatics, was nevertheless subject to the free-ranging deferral of full meaning that Plato had seen as so threatening. If all writings needed the help of the father, in one important sense the father was never there.

Derrida was not putting forward a literary theory, but a theory of language in general which was also, because of the role played by language in the theory, a general philosophy. Naturally, given the nature of his views, he has always deprecated attempts to turn what he says into a system or a method, but one aspect of what came to be known as 'deconstruction' did have an important effect on the practice of criticism. The structuralists, following the practice of linguistics, where the method had had its origins in phonology, had analysed complex systems into sets of oppositions, like the famous opposition of nature and culture in Lévi-Strauss's analyses. Typically in these oppositions one side was valued over the other: in terms of Derrida's Platonic metaphor, one had paternal authority over the other. Deconstruction was the process by which it was shown that in these oppositions elements apparently possessed by one side could be shown to occur also on the other, and that the relative value of the terms could be

'flipped' (and reflipped, and flipped again). This dismantling of apparently stable hierarchies was not simply a trick, nor was it suggested that there was some way of thinking which avoided the use of oppositions: the point was to stress that any stopping-place in the process of deferral of meaning would be an arbitrary one. But the deconstructive method became an extremely powerful tool for literary critics wishing to challenge dominant views of the '*closure' (a term popularized within a New Critical framework in another work of the late 1960s, Barbara Herrnstein Smith's *Poetic Closure* of 1968) of the texts they were studying. Derrida's views were again enthusiastically received in the United States, particularly by the 'Yale critics' such as J. Hillis Miller and the controversial Belgian Paul de Man, and they were welcome also to a number of classical literary critics precisely because they offered the opportunity to challenge stifling orthodoxies about the harmony and perfection of the classical moment. A conspicuous example was Simon Goldhill's *Language, Sexuality, Narrative: The Oresteia* (1984), which showed how slippery was the teleology even of what many regarded as the most perfectly closed piece of 5th-cent. drama.

Deconstruction was an important element in, and also perhaps a product of, the wider cultural phenomenon known as post-modernism, defined succinctly by the French philosopher Jean-François Lyotard as 'incredulity towards metanarratives' (*The Postmodern Condition* (1984; orig. pub. 1979), p. xxiv): that is, a belief that there was no fixed plot to human history, no single story that could be told about any human phenomenon, and no 'foundations' outside human discourse that could ground any theory or practice, even those of the supposedly 'hard' sciences. The most important representative of this line in the English-speaking world was the philosopher Richard Rorty. As we mentioned to begin with, however, one paradoxical effect of this radicalism has been to remove the urgency from the question of how to read literary texts. The answer is: however one wants to (in terms of Rorty's pragmatism, 'use' replaces 'meaning' as the central goal of literary study). A central tenet of post-modernism is that there is no single right way to do anything. One aspect of this is that significance is firmly located in the reader, rather than the author or the text, and the reader's own set of beliefs becomes the determining factor in the criticism that he or she produces, rather than any objective features of the text or its historical context: 'meaning is realised at the point of reception.' This leads to a historicism that is the mirror image of the historicism of traditional philology: the emphasis is on the historically determined nature not of the original literary production, but of the modern critic's reading.

In a sense there is no further step beyond post-modernism for criticism to take, no more radical position to adopt than the total denial of foundations. In another sense, however, the question of what an individual reader may wish to do with a text becomes more urgent. There are other 20th-cent. critical traditions that have existed alongside the Saussurean line throughout, and some of these have come into prominence more in the aftermath of post-structuralism. One is the political criticism of literature which has its roots above all in Marxist theory. This has a long history, from the comments on literature of Marx and Engels themselves, through Georg Lukács to the 'Frankfurt school', and beyond to the influential work of Pierre Macherey (*A Theory of Literary Production* (1978; orig. pub. 1966)) and to Marxists writing in English such as Fredric Jameson and Terry Eagleton. The greatest influence on both recent criticism and in particular the criticism of classical literature has come however not so much from what one might term the main line of Marxist criticism as from the work of critics with a more figured relationship to Marxist theory. The most important of these is the philosopher and 'archaeologist' of human culture Michel Foucault, who enjoyed particularly close relations with classical scholars through association with the ancient historians Paul Veyne and Peter Brown: one of his last major works was a *History of Sexuality* (1990; orig. pub. 1978) which dealt in detail with the ancient world. Like many recent thinkers, Foucault is antifoundationalist and radically historicist: even concepts like 'truth' or 'knowledge' change over time, and there is no possibility of standing outside history. His central contribution was to see that in the light of this, *power* becomes crucial, a power, however, exercised not so much directly from above but more diffusely distributed through every aspect of society. Power in this sense is an inescapable feature of social life, and not simply bad: but it is all-encompassing, and any attempt to try to stand outside it is doomed to failure. This insight has been influential in literary studies both directly and through the movement known as 'New Historicism' begun by the American scholar Stephen Greenblatt (e.g. *Renaissance Self-Fashioning* (1980)). Whereas deconstruction tended to figure itself as 'oppositionalist' in the way that it extricated texts from the imprisonment of fixed meanings, the New Historicism saw meaning as necessarily constrained by power. However apparently rebellious a text, it still in the end recapitulates the dominant ideology of the society that produced it: if you shoot the president, you are only confirming that he is setting the agenda for your actions. Methodologically, because power is everywhere in society, New Historicist criticism finds its traces not only in the major official texts of a society but in more marginal texts, and in English studies it has been responsible for a considerable broadening of the range of material which comes under the critic's eye. This has been less important for classical studies, which have always been characterized by the breadth only recently becoming common in 'cultural studies' in other fields, but its influence can be seen in the growing interest in phenomena like drinking, eating, and sex from both a historical and a literary point of view. Again, it is Latin studies where the impact has been greater, particularly in the criticism of Augustan and imperial literature, where the question of the political stance of texts like the *Aeneid* or the *Ars amatoria* is an old one (cf. e.g. T. Habinek and A. Schiesaro (eds.), *The Roman Cultural Revolution* (1995)).

Another Marxist whose views have had especial impact on classical studies is the Russian critic Mikhail Bakhtin, whose work (including some essays published under the names of other scholars but possibly by him, notably V. Voloshinov, *Marxism and the Philosophy of Language* (1973; orig. pub. 1929)) goes back to the 1920s but has had a major impact only more recently (he died in 1975, and his two major studies of Dostoevsky, for instance, were published in 1929 and 1963). Bakhtin's work, which had its origins in Russian Formalism, was wide-ranging, but two related ideas have had the greatest impact. One is the concept of *dialogism*, the manner in which some texts (e.g. *Brothers Karamazov*) are seen as containing many different points of view which are not made subservient to one overall interpretation but coexist as irreducibly multiple: the other is the notion of *carnival*, and the *carnivalesque* text (like that of Rabelais) in which high and low, serious and comic are mixed and all the familiar hierarchies of literature break down. The pre-eminent example of this is the modern novel, which knows no generic boundaries of content or form and can thereby deal with any and every aspect of everyday life. These concepts have been employed in classical literature in relation to genres which are most obviously like Bakhtin's models, such as 5th-cent. Athenian comedy (see COMEDY (GREEK), OLD) and the Latin *novel, but they have also stimulated a more widespread interest in what the philologist Wilhelm Kroll had famously called 'crossing of genres' ('Kreuzung der Gattungen': *Studien zum Verständnis der römischen Literatur* (1924), 202–24), and have been used in relation to the different but still extreme generic complexity of works like *Virgil's *Aeneid* and especially Ovid's *Metamorphoses*.

Although Marxist literary theory represents in some ways a separate tradition from the Saussurean line, it has undergone a similar move from a focus on the production of literary texts by individual artists to an analysis of the interpretative practices of readers, conceived however not as their surface reactions but on a deeper level as their underlying ideological configuration, what the sociologist Pierre Bourdieu called their *habitus* (e.g. *The Field of Cultural Production* (1993; orig. pub. 1968–87)). Another tradition that has undergone the shift away from the author to the text and the reader is the psychoanalytic tradition. Like Marx, Freud himself commented at considerable length on literature and criticism from a variety of points of view, but later psychoanalytic criticism tended to focus solely on the psychology of the author's mental processes, a particularly unrewarding activity in relation to classical antiquity, where our knowledge of the authors is so exiguous. More recent psychoanalytic criticism has turned its attention, again, to the reading process. A particularly sophisticated version of this has been offered by the Italian psychoanalytic critic Francesco Orlando (e.g. *Towards a Freudian Theory of Literature* (1978; orig. pub. 1973)), whose

Lettura freudiana della Phèdre (1971, Eng. trans. in *Towards a Freudian Theory of Literature*) influenced Charles Segal's reading of Seneca's *Phaedra* (*Language and Desire in Seneca's Phaedra* (1986); see SENECA). But the psychoanalyst who has had the most influence on modern theory is the notoriously difficult Jacques Lacan (also an important influence on Segal). For Lacan, there can be no attempt to get beyond language in the psychoanalytic act, and the slippery chains of signifiers seen in Derridan theory *are* the unconscious: he makes extensive use of linguistic concepts such as metaphor and metonymy, but gives them a new, psychological, interpretation. If *power* was the key word for Foucault, for Lacan it is *desire*, but desire working through and in language. The account Lacan gives of this working is complex and his terminology difficult, but one of the important side-effects of his work has been to stimulate interest in a psychological reinterpretation of such typical aspects of the reading process as the desire for and fear of the end and the pleasures of anticipation and recall. This aspect of what has been termed 'reader-response' criticism has been practised with particular suggestiveness by the American critic Peter Brook (*Reading for the Plot: Design and Intention in Narrative* (1984); *Psychoanalysis and Storytelling* (1994)) and has inspired a number of treatments of classical narrative that attempt to go beyond the formalisms of narratology.

Finally, one last tradition of literary theory which will arguably have the greatest impact of all on critical practice but which emphasizes again how difficult it is to confine discussion of theory solely to the contested domain of the 'literary' is feminism, which unites many of the concerns of the other traditions within a new framework. Critical theory both ancient and modern has tended to talk of the author or the reader of a text as a gender-neutral abstraction, in practice often modelled on male responses. But just as the strong historicist line in 20th-cent. criticism has stressed that even the most apparently objective concepts are historically conditioned, so feminist criticism has called into question the universal validity of concepts like reason, coherence, order, and closure: not simply to set against these their opposites as essentially 'feminine' values, but rather to propose the deconstruction of the oppositions. 'Reason' is not a gender-neutral concept, but nor is it simply male and 'emotion' female, though that opposition unconsciously structures unreflective language and thought. The most notable proponent of a new type of 'écriture feminine' is the French critic Hélène Cixous (e.g. *Coming to Writing and Other Essays* (1991); *The Hélène Cixous Reader* (1994)). Early feminist criticism in classics set out either to draw the attention of critics to female writers or subjects previously marginalized, or to expose the more obvious ways in which a literature written by and for men, far from being a model of objective perfection, represented the values of that male world, particularly in relation to sexuality and violence (e.g. A. Richlin, *The Garden of Priapus*, 2nd edn. (1992; orig. pub. 1983)). But more recent criticism has both attempted a deeper analysis of how gendered writing and reading pervade the texts and their interpretation, and has detected more cracks and fissures in the operation of male power within them (cf. E. Oliensis, *Arethusa* 1991, 107–36). See WOMEN.

This has not been a comprehensive survey either of literary theory in the second half of the 20th cent. or of the classical work inspired by the theories and theorists that we have discussed: nothing, for instance, on the German traditions of hermeneutics and reception theory and scholars like Malcolm Heath and Charles Martindale influenced by them, or on a figure like René Girard (e.g. *Violence and the Sacred* (1977)) whose work has influenced both Greek and Latin studies (e.g. P. Hardie, *The Epic Successors of Vergil* (1993)). Those classical scholars who have been most influenced by modern theory, like Martindale or John Henderson in Britain and Froma Zeitlin and Charles Segal in the United States, cannot and should not be pigeon-holed by those theories, not least because like everyone else's their views have changed over time. But we would like the version of the story we have offered to be seen as stressing both the foundational and the methodological importance of modern literary theory for classics, that is, both as an important and salutary invitation to examine the presuppositions and preconceptions of our individual practices, and as a wealth of techniques and approaches which will enable classical scholars to play their full part in the cultural dialogue that is a central justification for the study of antiquity. See also RECEPTION.   D. P. F., P. G. F.

Livia (Livia Drusilla), b. 58 BC, in 43 or 42 married Tiberius Claudius Nero, whom she accompanied on his flight after the Perusine War. She bore him *Tiberius, the future emperor, and Drusus (the later Drusus Iulius Caesar). In 39, in order to marry Octavian (*Augustus), she was divorced though pregnant with her second son. Although she had no further children, she retained Augustus' respect and confidence throughout his life. As consort of the *princeps*, she became an effective model of old-fashioned propriety, her beauty, dignity, intelligence, and tact fitting her for her high position. She played a role in the Augustan system which was unusually formal and conspicuous for a woman, and on Augustus' death became a principal figure in his cult and (by his will) a member of his family, as Julia Augusta. She was believed to have interceded successfully on behalf of conspirators, but some took her influence on Augustus to be malign, and saw her as a ruthless intriguer (her grandson Gaius Caesar called her 'Ulixes stolatus', 'Odysseus in a matron's gown'), while the tradition grew up that she had manipulated the affairs of Augustus' household on behalf of her sons, especially Tiberius, to the extent of involvement in the deaths of Marcus Claudius Marcellus, Gaius Caesar, Lucius Caesar, Agrippa Postumus, and *Germanicus, and even of Augustus himself. But after AD 14 her continuing influence caused discord between her and Tiberius, who was even supposed to have retired from Rome in 26 chiefly to avoid her. She died in 29, but Tiberius' hostility ensured that her will was not executed until Gaius' reign, and that she was not deified until that of *Claudius. N. P.

Livy (see facing page)

Londinium (mod. London) (see ◀Map 5, Bb▶). The Roman settlement had no iron age predecessor and was not established until c. AD 50, earlier routes crossing the Thames up river at Westminster. The settlement stood on Cornhill and Ludgate Hill north of the river, with a suburb across the bridge in Southwark. The original settlement was laid out around the northern bridgehead, beside modern London Bridge; it grew to c.25 ha. (62 acres) by the time of its destruction in the Boudiccan revolt of 60/1, when *Tacitus states that it was an important trading centre (Ann. 14. 33). There is no evidence for any early military presence and the settlement's early status is uncertain. It was most likely a community of traders from other provinces.

Following AD 61 there was a major public building programme including the construction of two successive fora (Flavian and early 2nd cent.), the latter of enormous size, covering c.3.6 ha. (9 acres). There is strong evidence for vibrant economic activity. Substantial timber quays, stretching up to 300 m. (330 yds.) along the river, were constructed from the Flavian period. Epigraphic evidence shows the procurator was based here after 61 (RIB 12 and 2443. 2), whilst a substantial Flavian building overlooking the river is interpreted as the provincial governor's palace, implying that London had become the provincial capital. The governor's guard and a staff seconded from other units were based here, probably in the Cripplegate fort, built c.90. Adjacent to this was an early 2nd-cent. amphitheatre. The settlement suffered an economic decline during the later 2nd cent., and although there is good evidence for later Roman occupation there was no resurgence of the productive economy. The later Roman city was instead dominated by town houses.

In the late 2nd cent. London was surrounded by a landward wall enclosing 133.5 ha. (330 acres), making it the largest town in Britain. The wall was extended along the riverside in the middle of the 3rd cent., whilst external towers were added in the mid-4th. Excavations show the city to have been more cosmopolitan than the others of the province. A mid-3rd-cent. Mithraeum has been excavated and high-quality sculpture has also been found, including material from a monumental arch reused in the riverside wall.

There is no direct evidence for London's status; it is conjectured to have been successively a *municipium* and *colonia*. It became the capital of Upper *Britain in the early 3rd cent. and Maxima Caesariensis under *Diocletian (284–305). The visit of Constantius I in 306 may have occasioned the grant of its later name, Augusta. M. J. M.

Lucan (Marcus Annaeus Lucanus) (AD 39–65), was born at Corduba (mod. Córdoba), 3 November AD 39. His father, Marcus Annaeus Mela, was a Roman knight and brother of the younger *Seneca. Mela came to Rome when his son was about eight months old. There Lucan received the typical élite education, ending with the school of rhetoric, where he was a great success (see EDUCATION, ROMAN); he probably also studied Stoic philosophy under Lucius Annaeus Cornutus, a connection of Seneca. He continued his studies at Athens, but was recalled by *Nero, who admitted him to his inner circle and honoured him with the offices of quaestor and augur. In AD 60, at the first celebration of the games called Neronia, he won a prize for a poem in praise of Nero. In AD 62 or 63 he published three books of his epic on the Civil War. Growing hostility between him and Nero, for which various reasons are given, finally led the emperor to ban him from public recitation of his poetry and from speaking in the law-courts. Early in AD 65 Lucan joined the conspiracy of Gaius Calpurnius Piso, and on its discovery was forced to open his veins in April 65; as he died he recited some of his own lines on the similar death of a soldier.

Works Lucan was a prolific writer. Of the many titles fragments exist of the *Catacthonia* ('Journey to the Underworld'), *Iliaca*, *Orpheus*, and epigrams. The surviving epic *De bello civili* (the alternative title *Pharsalia* is probably based on a misunderstanding of 9. 985) contains ten books covering events in the years 49–48 BC beginning with *Caesar's crossing of the Rubicon; the poem breaks off, almost certainly unfinished, with Caesar in *Alexandria. The historical sources include *Livy's (lost) books on the period and Caesar's own *On the Civil War*, but Lucan freely manipulates historical truth where it suits his purpose, e.g. in introducing Cicero in *Pompey's camp on the eve of the battle of Pharsalus in book 7. The epic has no single hero; the three main characters are Caesar, an amoral embodiment of Achillean (see ACHILLES) and elemental energy; Pompey, figure of the moribund republic and shadow of his own former greatness; and *Cato the Younger, an impossibly virtuous specimen of the Stoic saint (see STOICISM).

The Civil War is narrated as a tale of unspeakable horror and criminality leading to the destruction of the Roman republic and the loss of liberty; this message sits uneasily with the fulsome panegyric of Nero in the proem, unless that is to be read satirically or as the product of an early stage of composition before Lucan fell out with the emperor. From the moment when Caesar is confronted at the Rubicon by a vision of the distraught goddess Roma, in a scene that reworks Aeneas' vision of the ghost of Hector on the night of the sack of Troy, Lucan engages in continuous and detailed allusion to *Virgil's Aeneid, the epic of the birth and growth of Rome, in order to construct the De bello civili as an 'anti-Aeneid', a lament for the death of the Roman body politic as Roman military might is turned against itself. Lucan's rhetorical virtuosity is exploited to the full to involve the audience (defined in the proem as Roman citizens, i.e. those most nearly concerned by the subject of civil war) in his grim tale. In an extension of tendencies present already in Virgil, an extreme of pathos is

[continued on p. 427]

Livy

Livy (Titus Livius), the Roman historian, lived 59 BC–AD 17 (although Syme has argued for 64 BC–AD 12). He was born and died at Patavium (mod. Padua), the most prosperous city of northern Italy, famed for its stern morality. The Augustan historian Gaius Asinius Pollio criticized Livy's *Patavinitas* (Paduanism), but the import of this remark is unclear. An epitaph from Padua recording a Titus Livius with two sons and a wife Cassia Prima may be his (*ILS* 2919). In a letter he urged his son to imitate *Demosthenes and *Cicero, and this or another son wrote a geographical work. A daughter married Lucius Magius, a rhetorician. We do not know when Livy came to Rome or how much time he spent there; but he was on good personal terms with *Augustus (see below) and encouraged the young *Claudius, future emperor, to write history. Apart from, perhaps before beginning, his major work he also wrote philosophical dialogues.

Livy entitled his work *Ab urbe condita libri* ('Books from the Foundation of the City'): it covered Roman history from the origins of Rome to 9 BC in 142 books. Of these only 1–10 and 21–45 survive (and 41 and 43–5 have lacunae caused by the loss of leaves in the 5th-cent. manuscript which alone preserves 41–5). We also have two fragments of manuscripts of late antiquity: one, some 80 lines of print, has been known since the 18th cent.; the other, much damaged and containing parts of a few sentences of book 11, was discovered in 1986. We also have passages cited or referred to by later writers, and two kinds of summary of the history. First, there is the so-called Oxyrhynchus Epitome, covering books 37–40 and 48–55, and preserved in a papyrus written in the first half of the 3rd cent. Second, there are the *Periochae* (summaries) of all books except 136 and 137. The *Periochae* were perhaps composed in the 4th cent. and are preserved in a normal manuscript tradition (the summary of the first book survives in two different versions). It is uncertain whether the authors were working directly from the text of Livy or from an earlier summary (or summaries). Conflicts between the summaries and the text of Livy himself can be attributed to errors by the epitomator or to the use of sources other than Livy. Comparison of the summaries with the extant books indicates that we cannot always assume that the summaries of the lost books provide a reliable indication of their contents. The summaries of the final books are very brief, reporting only some foreign wars and events concerning Augustus' family. Livy was also the major source for, among others, Florus, Eutropius, and Obsequens (the so-called 'Livian tradition'). The whole work seems to have survived into the 6th cent.

From late antiquity, Livy's history was referred to by 'decades'. This is because ten books were the most that could be fitted into a parchment codex (thus the story of the transmission of the surviving parts varies from decade to decade). But it is disputed whether Livy himself conceived his work as consisting of significant units of five (pentads), ten, or even fifteen books. Book 5 ends with the recovery of Rome after the Gallic sack and book 6 begins with a 'second preface'. The First Punic War began in book 16, while the Second War occupies the whole of the third decade, with the war against Philip V of *Macedonia—the start of Rome's domination of the Hellenistic world—beginning in book 31; the war against *Antiochus III begins in book 36, and books 41–5 contain the whole of the reign of the last Macedonian king, Perseus. But there is no obvious break before books 11 and 26, and it is difficult to discern any pattern in the lost books. Livy was probably attracted by the possibility of beginning and/or concluding a pentad or decade with a significant historical event, but was not prepared to achieve that end by damaging the economy of his work—making books excessively long or short, skimping or padding his material.

Internal indications show that books 1–5 were completed between 27 and 25 BC. It may be, however, that some of the passages which date from that time were additions to an early draft. A note in the best manuscripts of the *Periochae* states that book 121 was said to have been published after the death of

Augustus; if that is true (and it may come from Livy's preface) it is likely that this applies to the following books.

Apart from a few references to topography and monuments, indicating autopsy, Livy relied on literary sources; he did not regard it as his duty to consult documents. In books 31–145 it is clear that for events in the east Livy followed *Polybius closely, adapting his narrative for his Roman audience and making additions—sometimes tacitly—and noting variants from the 1st-cent. writers Quintus Claudius Quadrigarius and Valerius Antias. The common view is that his procedure elsewhere was similar; he followed one main source—Antias, Gaius Licinius Macer, and (for books 6–10) Quadrigarius in the first decade, Lucius Coelius Antipater, Antias, or Quadrigarius in books 31–45—for longer or shorter sections, supplementing it from other sources. It is also thought that, apart from Antipater in the third decade, he did not use 2nd-cent. Roman writers directly: references to Quintus Fabius Pictor and Lucius Calpurnius Piso Frugi were derived from the 1st-cent. writers. Neither conclusion is certain: no Roman writer was so obviously superior on western events as was Polybius on eastern ones, and it could be that Livy sometimes produces an amalgam of the various works he had read (which in many cases had virtually the same story). A passage of the fourth decade (32. 6. 8) is hard to reconcile with the view that Livy read only Polybius, Antias, and Quadrigarius for events in Greece. There is a strong case for holding that he used *Cato the Elder directly for the latter's campaign in Spain in 195, and he could well have read other 2nd-cent. writers. Nor can it be excluded that he consulted Polybius directly throughout the third decade (most scholars agree that he did so for parts of books 24–30). If Livy did read 2nd-cent. historians, he did not necessarily conclude that discrepancies between them and later sources were to be resolved in favour of the former, though he was aware that Antias, and to a lesser extent Quadrigarius, were fond of inflating enemy casualty figures.

Livy has been criticized for his failure to inspect the linen corselet which, according to Augustus, proved that Aulus Cornelius Cossus (late 5th cent. BC) was not a military tribune when he dedicated the spolia opima after killing the king of Veii in single combat (4. 20). But Livy was writing tongue in cheek; it would have been out of the question to refute Augustus, who had political reasons for wanting Cossus not to have been a military tribune. Livy is also criticized for not inspecting the libri lintei ('linen books' cited as containing lists of magistrates) when his sources gave differing reports of their evidence (4. 23); it is quite possible that the books were no longer accessible. Nor are Livy's errors—anachronisms, geographical mistakes, misunderstandings of Polybius, and chronological confusions (sometimes caused by fitting Polybius' Olympiad years into a system based on Roman consular years)—all that numerous or striking in relation to the size of his work or in comparison with other writers.

It has often been said that it was Livy who fulfilled Cicero's desire that history should be written by an orator. Cicero wanted a style that 'flowed with a certain even gentleness', and Quintilian was to write of Livy's lactea ubertas ('milky richness'). Livy, reacting against the contorted Thucydideanism of *Sallust (see THUCYDIDES), first introduced fully developed periodic structure into Latin historiography. He had the ability to use language to embellish his material (comparison of Livy with Polybius in individual passages often shows the extent of Livy's originality) to convey an atmosphere and portray emotions. He gives special attention to major episodes, which are particularly numerous in the first decade—e.g. the rape of Lucretia, the attempted rape of Verginia, the stories of *Coriolanus, Spurius Maelius, and Marcus Manlius Capitolinus. The mixture of direct and indirect speech is one of the features of his technique. Elsewhere the speed of action in a battle—his battle scenes are often stereotyped—can be conveyed by short vivid sentences, while the dry style normally adopted for lists of prodigies, elections, and assignments of provinces and armies is perhaps a deliberate imitation of early writers, criticized by Cicero for just this, or of the annales maximi (the chronicle kept by the pontifex maximus).

Part of Livy's style is achieved by the use of poetical or archaic words avoided by Cicero and *Caesar. In this respect he is following in a tradition of historiography to which Sallust also belonged.

These usages are most common in books 1–10, least so in 31–45. This phenomenon, however, is not to be explained on the hypothesis that Livy began under the influence of Sallust, but later moved back to a more Ciceronian vocabulary. Rather, Livy makes particular use of vocabulary of this sort in those episodes which specially attracted him, and these became progressively less common as his work proceeded—the diplomatic and military details of the early 2nd cent. did not compare in excitement with the great (and largely fictional) stories of the first decade. But some such episodes do occur in the later books, and it is precisely there that we find the greatest concentration of non-Ciceronian usages, as for example in the story of the *Bacchanalia in book 39 or the account of the death of Cicero preserved by Seneca the Younger.

Livy was a patriotic writer, though in narrative he never refers to Roman troops as *nostri* or *exercitus noster* ('our men', 'our army'), and often, writing from their opponents' point of view, talks of the Romans as *hostes* ('enemy'). His aim was to chronicle the rise of Rome to mastery first of Italy, then of the rest of the Mediterranean world, and to highlight the virtues which produced this result and enabled Rome to defeat *Hannibal. Livy intended his work to be morally improving (pref. 10), but though there are many passages where he writes with this aim in mind, a moral purpose is not all-pervasive. He believed that a serious moral decline had taken place by his own time, and appears to have lacked confidence that Augustus could reverse it.

Livy doubtless shared Augustus' ideals, but he was by no means a spokesman for the regime. Tacitus (*Ann.* 4. 34) makes the historian Aulus Cremutius Cordus, defending himself on a *maiestas* (treason) charge, claim that Livy felt free to praise *Brutus and Cassius; Cordus also claims that Livy was so lavish in his praise of *Pompey that Augustus called him a Pompeian, and adds that this did not harm their friendship. There are signs that Livy regarded the rule of Augustus as necessary, but only as a short-term measure.   J. Br.

achieved through the use of lengthy speeches, apostrophe of characters in the narrative, and indignant epigrammatic utterances (*sententiae*); in contravention of the objectivity associated with Homeric epic, Lucan as narrator repeatedly intrudes his own reactions, as in the shocked meditation on the death of Pompey in book 8. Related to the goal of *pathos* are the features of hyperbole and paradox. Hyperbole is expressive both of the vast forces involved in the conflict, presented as a 'world war', and of the greatness of the crimes perpetrated. Lucan's use of paradox is rooted in the conceptual and thematic anti-structures of civil war, in which legality is conferred on crime, and the greatest exemplars of Roman military virtue, such as the centurion Scaeva in book 6, are at the same time the greatest criminals; but in this topsy-turvy world paradox also extends to the physical, as in the sea-battle at the end of book 3 which turns into a 'land-battle' because the ships are so tightly packed. Realism is not a goal; Lucan's notorious abolition of the traditional epic divine machinery is not determined by the desire for a historiographical plausibility; rather, Lucan replaces the intelligibility of the anthropomorphic gods of Homer and Virgil with a darker sense of the supernatural, in a world governed by a negative version of Stoic Providence or Fate. Dreams, portents, and prophecies abound, as in the list of omens at Rome at the end of book 1, or in Appius Claudius Pulcher's consultation of the long-silent Delphic oracle in book 5; the Gothick atmosphere reaches a climax with the consultation in book 6 by Sextus Pompeius of the

witch Erichtho and her necromantic resurrection of a corpse. Death fascinates Lucan, in both its destructive and its heroic aspects; a recurrent image is *suicide, viewed both as the symbol of Rome's self-destruction and as the Stoic's praiseworthy exit from an intolerable life (the paradoxes are explored in the Vulteius episode in book 4). The Roman spectacle of ritualized killing in the amphitheatre is reflected in the frequent gladiatorial imagery (see GLADIATORS) of the epic. In all of these features Lucan shows a close affinity with the writings, above all the tragedies, of his uncle the younger Seneca.

Lucan displays his learning in mythological episodes, such as the story of Hercules and Antaeus in book 4, in the geography and ethnography of the catalogues of books 1 and 3 and the description of Thessaly in book 6, and in the 'scientific' passages on the snakes of Libya in book 9 and on the sources of the Nile in book 10; but these 'digressions' usually have a further thematic and symbolic purpose. It is true that Lucan's style lacks the richness and colour of Virgil's, but his limited and repetitive range of vocabulary, often prosaic in tone, is deliberately geared to the bleak, remorseless, and unromantic nature of the subject-matter; a similar response may be made to the criticism of the monotony of Lucan's metre. Stylistic and metrical narrowness as a purposeful inversion of Virgilian norms finds an analogy in the device of 'negative enumeration', the listing of things that do not happen, but which might in normal circumstances be expected to happen, as in the description of the funereal remarriage of Cato and Marcia in book 2.

Lucan's epic was avidly read and imitated for centuries after his death; his admirers include *Statius (whose mythological epic on civil war, the *Thebaid*, is permeated with echoes of Lucan), Dante, Goethe, and Shelley. After a period of critical condemnation and neglect, the sombre baroque brilliance of the work is once more coming to be appreciated.   W. B. A.; P. R. H.

Lucian, of Samosata in SE *Asia Minor (b. *c.* AD 120), accomplished belletrist and wit in the context of the *Second Sophistic. The details of his life are extremely sketchy, and his own presentations of his biography are literary and therefore suspect. His native language was not Greek but probably Aramaic; but he practised in the courts, then as an itinerant lecturer on literary-philosophical themes as far afield as Gaul. He presents a '*conversion' to philosophy around the age of 40, and his natural milieu is Athens. He was known to the doctor Galen of Pergamum for a successful literary fraud. We find him late in life in a minor administrative post in Roman *Egypt; he survived the emperor Marcus *Aurelius.

Works Lucian's work is difficult both to categorize and to assign to any sort of literary 'development'. Throughout he is a master of sensibly flexible Atticism. His *œuvre* runs to some 80 pieces, most of which are genuine. While some can be classified under traditional rhetorical headings such as *meletai* ('exercises') and *prolaliai* ('preambles'), the most characteristic products of his repertoire are literary dialogues which fuse Old Comic (see COMEDY (GREEK), OLD) and popular and/or 'literary' philosophy to produce an apparently novel blend of comic prose dialogue. But he is also an accomplished miniaturist, essayist, and raconteur: the *Enalioi dialogoi* ('Dialogues of the Sea-Gods') are particularly successful in exploiting the art of prose paraphrase of verse classics from *Homer to *Theocritus; the *Pōs dei historian syngraphein* ('How to Write History') gives a wittily commonsensical rather than commonplace treatment of a topical subject; while the *Philopseudeis* ('Lovers of Lies') successfully combines satire of superstition with racy novella. When he chooses he can be a lively and revealing commentator on his cultural and religious environment as when he attacks successful sophists, or figures such as Peregrinus or the oraclemonger Alexander of Abunoteichus whom he sees as charlatans. In the *Alēthē diēgēmata* ('True Histories') he produced a masterpiece of Munchausenesque parody. His literary personality is engaging but elusive: he is cultivated but cynical, perhaps with a chip on his shoulder, but difficult to excel in his chosen field of versatile prose entertainment. His weakest moments to contemporary taste are perhaps as a repetitive and superficial moralist, his most successful when he plays with the full range of Classical Greek literature in a characteristically amusing way.   W. M. E.; R. B.; G. A.

Lucretius (Titus Lucretius Carus), Epicurean poet (see EPICURUS), author of the *De rerum natura* (*DRN*), 'On the Nature of Things' (*c.*94–55 or 51 BC?). We know less about the life of Lucretius than about almost any other Latin poet. His full name is given only in the manuscripts of his work (pun on *Carus*, 1. 730?), and nothing is known of his place of birth or social status, though both have been the subject of much speculation. Jerome's version of the *Chronicle* of *Eusebius puts his birth in 94 BC, and says that he was 44 when he died, but the Donatus *Life of Virgil* puts his death in 55, on the same day that Virgil assumed the *toga virilis (6, though there are textual problems), and a note in a 10th-cent. manuscript (H. Usener *Kl. Schr.* (1913), 156, 196–9) says that he was born 27 years before Virgil, i.e. 97 BC. The only secure date is a reference in a letter of *Cicero to his brother (*QFr.* 2. 10(9). 3) written in February 54, where he praises Lucretius' *poemata* as possessing both flashes of genius (*ingenium*) and great artistry (*ars*), that is, as combining the qualities of an inspired and a craftsmanlike poet. This is certainly a reference to *DRN* (an *Empedoclea* by one Sallustius is mentioned more critically in the same context), and although *poemata* could refer to just selections, the easiest hypothesis is that Lucretius' poem was published by this time. The poem has often been thought to be unfinished (there are problems especially in the prologue to book 4): if so, Lucretius may well have been dead by the time of the letter. But textual corruption rather than incompleteness may be responsible for the problems in the text.

Jerome (whose source was *Suetonius) also reports the story (made famous by Tennyson and others) of Lucretius writing *DRN* in brief intervals of sanity after having been driven mad by a love-potion given him by his wife, and eventually committing suicide. If this story is true, it is surprising that it was not used by *Ovid in his defence of the *Ars Amatoria* in *Tristia* 2 or by the Fathers of the Church attacking paganism and Epicureanism: it may be the result of a biographical reading of parts of books 3 and 4, or of confusion with Lucullus (cf. Plut. *Luc.* 43. 2). Nor is there any reason to believe Jerome's statement that Cicero edited *DRN* after its author's death. More biographical details are provided by the so-called 'Borgia Life' found in a British Museum printed book, but this is a Renaissance compilation (L. Canfora, *Vita di Lucrezio* (1993), 35–6).

The addressee of *DRN* (1. 25–43, 136–48; cf. 1. 411, 1052, 2. 143, 182, 5. 8, 93, 164, 867, 1282) is a Memmius, who must be Gaius Memmius, a prominent politician associated also with *Catullus (28. 9). Memmius was praetor in 58, and a candidate for the consulship of 53: but after a complicated electoral pact that went wrong, he was found guilty of corruption in 52 and went into exile in Athens (E. S. Gruen in *Hommages à Marcel Renard* (1969), 2. 311–21; G. V. Sumner, *Harv. Stud.* 1982, 133–9). In the summer of 51, Cicero wrote to him on behalf of the Epicurean group in Athens, asking him not to demolish what was left of Epicurus' house (*Fam.* 13. 1. 3–4), and suggesting that Memmius was not on good terms with the Epicureans. It is not impossible that he had been annoyed by the dedication of *DRN*: despite its warm praise of him in the prologue, the poem is orthodox in its Epicurean condemnation of political life (3. 59–84, 995–1002, 5. 117–35). But in any case, *DRN* does not imply that Memmius was a convinced Epicurean (cf. 1. 102–3). There can be no clear distinction between Memmius as the didactic addressee and a more generalized second-person, but Memmius' public persona was relevant: *DRN* is not unpolitical (D. Minyard, *Lucretius and the Late Republic* (1985); D. P. Fowler, in M. Griffin and J. Barnes (eds.), *Philosophia Togata* (1989), 120–50).

The poem is in six books of hexameter verse (*c*.7,400 lines, about three-quarters the size of the *Aeneid*) and whether or not it failed to receive the final corrections of its author is substantially complete: it opens with an elaborate prologue, and the prologue to book 6 states explicitly that this is the final book (6. 92–5). The ending is abrupt, and textually corrupt: it is likely that 1247–51 are the actual concluding lines, and should be transposed after 1286, but if this is done, the ending contains a number of closural features, most notably a recall of the end of the funeral of Hector at the end of the *Iliad* (cf. P. G. Fowler, in F. Dunn, D. P. Fowler, and D. Roberts, *Classical Closure* (1997)). The ending on the *plague at Athens and the many deaths it caused is in stark contrast to the opening description of the first day of spring and the appeal for help to *Venus, but the polarity can be made to have point. The recurrent pattern of the cycle of coming-to-be and passing-away makes a final appearance, while the fixed temporal and spatial location in Athens, which represents the peak of civilization according to the opening of book 6, indicates the inevitable failure of the city-state to provide for the ultimate happiness of human beings.

As well as the great initial prologue to book 1, each of the other books also has a prologue, and the concluding section of each book in some way stands apart from the rest of the book (see especially the attack on love in book 4, and the final plague). Each book is a unity in terms both of structure and subject-matter. Book 1 deals with the basic metaphysical and physical premises of Epicureanism, beginning with the proposition that nothing comes to be out of nothing, and concluding with a description of the collapse of our world which is presented as a counterfactual consequence of the belief that all elements tend towards the centre of the earth but which anticipates the Epicurean accounts of the death of our world at the end of book 2 and in book 5. Book 2 deals with the motion and shape of the atoms, and how these are relevant to the relationship between primary and secondary qualities: it concludes with the important Epicurean doctrine of the infinite number of worlds in the universe, and the connected proposition that our world has both a birth and a death (recalling the end of book 1). Book 3 gives an account of the nature of the human soul, and argues both that it is mortal and that, because of this, death is not to be feared. Book 4 discusses a variety of psychological phenomena, especially perception, and argues against scepticism: as

remarked above, it concludes with an attack on love, seen as a mental delusion. Book 5 argues for the mortality of our world, and then gives a rationalist and anti-providentialist account of its creation and early history, concluding with the section on the development of human civilization which is perhaps the most famous part of the poem. Book 6 then proceeds to account for those phenomena of our world which are most likely to lead to false belief in the gods—thunder and lightning, *earthquakes, volcanoes, etc.—and ends with the aetiology of *disease and the plague at Athens.

This clearly defined book-structure is more typical of prose philosophical treatises than of hexameter poetry, and it is replicated at levels both above and below that of the individual book. The books form three pairs, in which books 1 and 2 deal with atomic phenomena up to the level of the compound (see ATOMISM), books 3 and 4 deal with human beings, and books 5 and 6 deal with the world: there is thus a clear sense of expanding horizons, as we move from the atomic to the macroscopic level. The twin targets of the work as a whole are fear of the gods and of death (1. 62–135; cf. Epicurus, *RS* 1–2, *Ep. Men.* 133): the first and last pairs deal more with the former fear, by explaining phenomena that would otherwise be felt to require divine intervention in the world, while the central books, and especially book 3, tackle the fear of death head on. But the two motives are intermingled throughout the work. The six books may also be organized into two halves, with books 1–3 dealing with basic premises, books 4–6 with what follows from those basic premises: the problematic prologue to book 4 (repeated almost verbatim from 1. 921–50), with its stress on Lucretius' role as a poet and philosopher and its Callimachean imagery (see CALLIMACHUS), thus functions as a 'proem in the middle' for the second half (cf. G. B. Conte *YClS* 1992, 147–59). The existence of more than one possible structural analysis in this way is typical of *DRN* as a whole (contrast 3. 31–40 with 5. 55–63).

Below the level of the book, the subject-matter is carefully delineated and individual propositions within sections signposted with markers like *Principio*, 'First', *Deinde*, 'Next', and *Postremo*, 'Finally': the verse, in contrast to both the epic verse-paragraph and the neoteric focus on the single line, tends to group itself into blocks of two or more verses, with careful arrangement of words within the block. This division of the text corresponds to the Epicurean stress on the intelligibility of phenomena: everything has a *ratio* or systematic explanation, the world can be analysed and understood. If we are to believe Cicero, however, this is in marked contrast to the formlessness of earlier Epicurean writing in Latin (Amafinius and Rabirius: cf. Cic. *Acad. post.* 5 with Reid's comm., and esp. *Fin.* 1. 22, 29, 2. 30, 3. 40).

Every major proposition in *DRN* can be paralleled in other Epicurean sources, and it is likely that the majority at least of the arguments for these propositions also existed in the Epicurean tradition. We do not know, however, to what extent the poem had a single main source, and if so, what that source was. The title (cf. 1. 25) recalls that of Epicurus' major treatise, the *Peri physeōs* or 'On Nature', but the structure of that work as we know it from papyrus fragments is not very similar to that of *DRN*, and that presumably also goes for any (lost) epitome. There is a much closer correspondence, however, with the extant *Letter to Herodotus* of Epicurus, passages of which are closely translated (e.g. 1. 159–60 = *Ep. Hdt.* 38), although *DRN* is longer and the order of topics is sometimes changed (e.g. in *Ep. Hdt.* 42–3 Epicurus treats atomic shape before atomic motion (see ATOMISM), while *DRN* reverses the order, 2. 62–729). One plausible hypothesis is that the *Letter to Herodotus* provided the basic core of the poem, but this was expanded from a variety of other sources (cf. also D. Clay, *Lucretius and Epicurus* (1983)). Other prose philosophical and scientific sources are also drawn on (e.g. Plato's *Timaeus*, P. De Lacy in *Syzetesis: Studi Gigante* (1983), 291–307, and the Hippocratic corpus (see MEDICINE §4), C. Segal, *CPhil.* 1970, 180–2) though we can never be certain that some of this had not already been assimilated into the atomist tradition (cf. F. Solmsen, *AJPhil.* 1953, 34–51). The final part of book 3 in particular (cf. also the prologues to 2 and 3 and the end of 4) contains material from the so-called 'diatribe' tradition of practical philosophical rhetoric (cf. B. P. Wallach, *Lucretius and the Diatribe against the Fear of Death: De Rerum Natura III 830–1094* (1970); T. Stork, *Nil igitur est ad nos* (1970); G. B. Conte, *Genres and Readers* (1994)).

But *DRN* also draws on a wide range of literary texts in both Greek (e.g. *Sappho fr. 31 LP in *DRN* 3. 152–8, *Aeschylus fr. 44 Nauck in *DRN* 1. 250–61, *Euripides fr. 839 Nauck in *DRN* 2. 991–1003, Callimachus fr. 260. 41 Pf. in *DRN* 6. 753, Antipater of Sidon, *Anth. Pal.* 7. 713 in *DRN* 4. 181–2, and especially *Thucydides' account of the plague at Athens in 2. 47–53 at the end of *DRN* 6) and Latin (e.g. *Ennius, cf. 1. 117–26, O. Gigon, in *Lucrèce*, Entretiens Hardt 24 (1978), 167–96, Pacuvius, e.g. *Chryses* fr. 86–92 Ribbeck with 5. 318–23). The main model is the lost philosophical didactic poem of Empedocles, the *Peri physeōs* or 'On Nature' (cf. W. Kranz, *Philol.* 1943, 68–107; M. Gale, *Myth and Poetry in Lucretius* (1994), 59–75): Empedocles' doctrine is criticized (1. 705–829), but he is praised as a poet especially for his stance as a 'master of truth' offering an important secret to his audience, in contrast to the stress on form in Hellenistic didactic poetry (Aratus, Nicander, etc.). Lucretius too writes to save humanity (cf. 6. 24–34 on Epicurus): although the work concentrates on *physics and natural philosophy, this ethical purpose is clear throughout (cf. e.g. 2. 1–61, 3. 59–93, 5. 43–54). Epicurus was opposed to poetry as a serious medium of enlightenment, and the Epicurean stress on clarity and simplicity of language and 'sober reasoning' in thought creates problems for an Epicurean didactic poem: by returning to the archaic models of Empedocles and Parmenides, Lucretius was able to place himself in a tradition which made the alliance of philosophy and poetry more natural (though

Empedocles' status as a poet had itself been called into question by *Aristotle, *Poet.* 1447[b] 17 ff.). Many of the resources of poetry, particularly the recall to the phenomenal world implicit in the use of metaphor and simile, can easily be made consonant with the needs of Epicureanism: poet and philosopher alike must make the reader *see* (cf. 2. 112–41, A. Schiesaro, *Simulacrum et Imago* (1990)). The effect is a recontextualization of both the traditional devices of poetry and the basic elements of Epicurean epistemology, particularly the 'first image' (*Ep. Hdt.* 38) or prolepsis associated with each word, the basis for live metaphor (cf. D. Sedley, *Cron. Erc.* 1973, 5–83). The complexity and precision of Lucretius' imagery, always a central part of his claim to poetic excellence (D. West, *The Imagery and Poetry of Lucretius* (1969)), is thus also an aspect of his role as philosopher and scientist.

Nevertheless, the old conception of a conflict between Lucretius the poet and Lucretius the philosopher was not perhaps wholly wrong. The *De rerum natura* became an immensely important text in the Renaissance and modern periods because of its rationalism: when Abraham Cowley celebrated Bacon's victory over 'Authority' and superstition in his ode *To the Royal Society*, it was to Lucretius' image of Epicurus triumphing over *religio* to which he naturally turned (1. 62–79). Similarly, through Pufendorf, Hobbes, and Rousseau (cf. C. Kahn, in G. B. Kerferd (ed.), *The Sophists and their Legacy* (1981), 92–108), the account of the development of civilization in book 5 of *DRN*, and in particular the notion of the 'social contract', enabled historians and philosophers to free themselves from theist models of the foundations of human society. But that very stress on scientific rationalism as providing a single sure and certain (cf. *DRN* 6. 24–34, 4. 507–21) answer to the troubles of life has come under suspicion in the post-modern age. Lucretius the poet offers perhaps more ways of looking at the world than can be accommodated with comfort within the plain and simple truth of Epicureanism. Of necessity, his rationalism has its own sustaining myths, from the clear light of reason which pierces and disperses the clouds of ignorance (2. 55–61, 3. 14–17) to the secure citadel of the wise (2. 7–13), from the nurturing female powers of *Venus, Mother Earth, and Nature (cf. 2. 589–660) to the hellish shadows of 'normal' life (3. 59–86). Nevertheless, those myths in themselves continue to offer a powerful vision of a world by no means providentially ordered for humanity, but in which all humans can find happiness.   P. G. F., D. P. F.

Lycophron The name of Lycophron is associated with two writers of the Hellenistic age, the identity of whom is the subject of much debate. They are here distinguished as (*a*) Lycophron and (*b*) ps.-Lycophron.

(*a*) Lycophron, a native of Chalcis, of the early 3rd cent. BC, active in *Alexandria, a member of the tragic Pleiad (canonical grouping of the city's eight or more tragic poets), author of a number of tragedies and satyr-plays, and also a grammarian and glossographer of the comic poets, of whom a few glosses survive. The titles of some of the plays are conventional, of others topical (including one on his friend Menedemus of Eretria and one called the *Cassandreis*, the theme of which is unknown). Only a few fragments survive.

(*b*) Ps.-Lycophron, author of the 'monodrama' *Alexandra*, written in the immediate aftermath of the victory of *Flamininus at Cynoscephalae over Philip V of Macedon in 197/6 BC. The author, whose true name and place of origin are probably concealed beneath the impenetrably enigmatic biographical tradition concerning Lycophron, probably used the name, and some of the literary substance, of Lycophron (*a*), not in emulation, but as an ironic reminiscence of the earlier writer, who had combined the practice of tragedy and the elucidation of comedy. Only on this assumption of a deliberate pseudepigraphon can the full irony of his work be appreciated. His poem, cast in the form of a prophetic recitation by Cassandra in iambic trimeters, called in the title of the poem Alexandra, has acquired notoriety on account of its obscure and laboured style and vocabulary, in which individual episodes and persons are alike concealed in memorable metaphorical terms, which defy indisputable rationalization. The poem is nevertheless a powerful, indeed brilliant performance, in which tragic intensity, grim irony, and recondite learning combine to create a memorable *tour de force*.

The framework of the poem (ll. 1–30 and 1461–74) is provided by a report to Priam by a guard set to watch over Cassandra. The rest is Cassandra's prophecy, which falls into the following main divisions: ll. 31–364, the fall of *Troy and consequent disasters; 365–1089, the sufferings of the Greeks who do not succeed in returning home; 1090–1225, the sufferings of the Greeks who do return home; 1226–80, the wanderings of *Aeneas and the Trojans; 1283–1450, the struggles between Europe and Asia, culminating in the victory of Rome; 1451–60, Cassandra's lamentation on the uselessness of her prophecy.

Three major questions relate to (1) the sources, (2) the purpose, and (3) the occasion of the poem.

1. Sources: (*a*) stylistic, thematic, and linguistic sources. The use of the iambic trimeter is natural to its tragic theme, and the tragic type of 'monodrama' recitatif (whether iambic or lyric) was current in the Hellenistic age; these features therefore call for no comment here, though they could be illustrated in many ways. (*b*) For the role of Cassandra as prophetess of post-Homeric catastrophes the author could call on numerous Archaic and Classical sources, and it is inevitable that precise debts, probably incurred by direct loan and not through an intermediary compendium of post-Homeric legends, should be largely unassignable. We may also be certain that, the prophecy apart, many other sources also contributed to the substance of the poem, both in general, and in specific passages. For instance, *Herodotus' opening passage on the conflict of east and west probably provided the poet with that theme, essential to his version of Cassandra's prophecy, and *Timaeus may have been the channel

through which many of the abstruse Western legends, based on *Nostoi* ('Returns' from Troy), which form so significant a part of the poem, reached him. The possibilities extend far beyond the range of our limited knowledge. (*c*) The poet's language, monstrously obscure and metaphorical, was no doubt his own: a deliberate and successful attempt to wrap the prophetic, Sibylline theme in language that readers might deem appropriate to the occasion, in which echoes of Homeric, lyric, and especially tragic language are evident. The ancients reckoned the poet as 'dark' (*skoteinos, ater*), and he would no doubt have agreed.

2. Intent. The poet's purpose in choosing the theme is not explicitly stated, but the emphasis on Italian legends, especially those connected with *Odysseus and other Greek heroes (irrespective of whether such legends came to him, for example, from a direct reading of an early poet or poets, from a careful study of Timaeus, in some ways a kindred spirit, from an intermediate handbook, or even perhaps by local traditions regarding the heroic past), and the prominence given to the decisive role played by *Macedonia in subduing *Persia, and of Rome in subduing Macedonia, seem to indicate that the ultimate purpose of the prophecy is to commemorate the recent and apparently decisive change in the world order which he associates with the victory of Roman arms.

3. Date. The date of composition has to be determined in the light of this presumed purpose. It has caused much debate and there is no reason, unless more evidence is forthcoming, why the controversy should cease. The problem is well known. Lycophron, as identified under (*a*), lived in the early 3rd cent. BC, yet the poet clearly refers to a widely recognized Roman supremacy. The two propositions are hardly reconcilable, and the Byzantine commentator Tzetzes suggested that the relevant lines had been written by another Lycophron. Since the debate opened in modern times it has been continually discussed whether the lines referring to Rome are acceptable in the context of a date *c*.275 BC, whether the whole passage relating to Rome should be regarded as an interpolation added after Rome's conquest of Greece had become a reality, or whether the whole poem should be dated to a period when that had happened. The suggestion made here as to authorship is based on the hard-won belief that the reference in the Rome passage to a 'unique Wrestler' refers to (Titus Quinctius) Flamininus, and was made in the immediate aftermath of his victory at Cynoscephalae in 197/6 BC, when his praises were being sung, statues being erected to him, and religious festivals in his honour, Titeia, being inaugurated all over Greece. The impact made by the politic and *philhellene Titus, representative of a new ruling power linked by ties of mythological kinship to the Greek and Trojan past, provides the appropriate background for this speedily produced pro-Roman eulogy from the mouth of the Trojan Cassandra. Independent evidence derived from the use made of 3rd-cent. authors, seems to confirm this date.   P. M. F.

Lycurgus, traditional founder of Classical *Sparta's *eunomia* ('good order'). Ancient accounts of his work evolved according to political circumstance. The earliest, in *Herodotus (1. 65–6), reflects official Spartan views: guardian of the early Agiad-dynasty king, Leobotes, he was responsible for all Sparta's laws, and military and political institutions which he brought from *Crete. Most later writers attached him to the Eurypontid-dynasty king Charillus, perhaps reflecting that royal house's subsequent prominence. A 5th-cent. BC, non-Spartan version that his measures came from *Apollo at *Delphi was later incorporated by making Apollo sanction laws he brought from Crete. The view that the ephorate (a Spartan magistracy) was post-Lycurgan, probably originated by King Pausanias in exile post-395, was invoked by Cleomenes III when abolishing the office in 227 BC. Later accounts became increasingly wide-ranging and detailed as Lycurgus' achievements were expanded to embrace 4th-cent. and Hellenistic philosophical and political programmes. *Plutarch's 'biography' reflects the culmination of this trend.

Although scholars generally accept that Sparta's *eunomia* was the product of coherent design, few now view it as the work of a single legislator. Many elements emerged through a long-term process of adaptation to Sparta's distinctive political and economic situation. Whether purely legendary or a historical person subsequently invoked as a charter for the regime, Lycurgus' absence from the poet Tyrtaeus' 7th-cent. account of the 'Great Rhetra' (see SPARTA § 2) undermines later belief in his significant founding role.   S. J. Ho.

lyric poetry

Greek The term 'lyric' (*lyrikos*) is derived from *lyra*, 'lyre'. As a designation of a category of poetry it is not found before the Hellenistic period (earlier writers term such a poem *melos*, 'song', and the poet *melopoios*, 'composer of song'; hence we find 'melic' used as a synonym for 'lyric'). Its use in the ancient world was more precise than the terms 'lyric' and 'lyrical' as now used with reference either to modern or to ancient poetry. Though the term was extended to poetry sung to other stringed instruments or to the flute, it is always used of sung poetry as distinct from stichic, distichic (elegy included), or epodic poems which were recited or spoken.

The 'lyric' age begins in the 7th cent. BC, though the finished metres of the earliest exponents indicate that they are the heirs to a long tradition of popular song. So does the evidence of *Homer, whose narrative mentions sung paeans (*Il.* 1. 472–3, 22. 391–2; cf. *Hymn. Hom. Ap.* 517–18), dirges (*Il.* 24. 720 ff.; *Od.* 24. 58 ff.), wedding songs (*Il.* 18. 491 ff.), the Linus-song (*Il.* 18. 567 ff.), and more generally choral song and dance (*Il.* 18. 590 ff.). However, the fact that no composer's name survives from this period suggests a context of anonymous folk-song. In the 7th cent. a change occurs, as named poets of distinction emerge. The reasons for this change are not clear.

Modern scholars divide lyric into choral and monodic (solo). There is no evidence of any such division in ancient scholarship, and its validity has been disputed, but it does correspond to broad differences in form and content. Choral poetry was performed by a choir which sang and danced. The element of spectacle was enhanced further by the impressive dress of the chorus (Alcm. 1. 64 ff.; Dem. 21. 16). The collective voice was ideally suited to represent the voice of the community, and consequently choral song in general has a pronounced 'public' quality to it. In origin choral performance was sacral, and even in the Classical period 'dance' may be synonymous with 'worship' (Soph. *OT* 896). Accordingly, most of the attested types of choral song are religious or ritual in character: paean, usually addressed to *Apollo but also attested for other gods, *dithyramb, addressed to *Dionysus, processional song (*prosodion*), maiden-song (*partheneion*), dirge (*thrēnos*), wedding song (*hymenaios*). However, the sacral use was not exclusive, for already in Homer we find choral song and dance as festive entertainment. During the late Archaic period there is a further secularization of choral music, as choral songs are composed in praise of rulers and aristocrats, as in the erotic and laudatory songs of Ibycus and the *encomia* (originally 'party/revel song', then 'song of praise') and *epinicia* (victory odes) of *Simonides, *Pindar, and *Bacchylides. Choral lyric is especially associated with 'Dorian' states (*Alcman, *Stesichorus, Arion, Ibycus, Pindar), though not exclusively (since Simonides and Bacchylides were from Ceos (mod. Kea)). The dialect is an artificial amalgam of West Greek, Aeolic, and Homeric, though within this framework there are differences between authors. Choral compositions are either strophic (composed of stanzas which correspond metrically, strophe and antistrophe, which later writers associate with the movements of the chorus, 'turn' and 'counterturn') or triadic (each triad being composed of matching strophe and antistrophe, with a third stanza, epode, with a different metrical pattern). The metres are usually elaborate, and the metrical schema of each poem is with rare exceptions unique. The songs are almost invariably tied to a particular occasion. But celebration of the human or divine addressee is usually accompanied by succinct generalizations (*gnōmai*) which place the present celebration or its occasion in the broader context of human experience, and regularly a myth is narrated, usually occupying the centre of the ode; though not invariable, this persistent pattern is already established for Alcman in 7th-cent. Sparta. The most striking exception is Stesichorus, whose choral lyric narratives are epic in scale and in their absence of explicit attachment to a specific occasion. The choral lyric tradition reached its peak in the late Archaic and early Classical period in the work of Simonides, Bacchylides, and Pindar, the first 'freelance' professional Panhellenic poets. The same period saw the beginning of the decline of choral lyric as a major literary genre. *Aristophanes (*Nub.* 1355 ff.) and Eupolis (frs. 148, 398 KA) testify to a change in musical tastes at this period. In the age of the *sophists the old practice of learning to sing lyric compositions fell into decline, and so did interest in and knowledge of the choral poets. At the same time, the nature of choral lyric changed, with choral and monody mixed, the abandonment of strophic responsion in the interests of emotional realism, and an increasing dominance of music over words. Choral poems continued to be composed, and major poets emerged who challenged comparison with the old masters (*Xenophon places Melanippides the dithyrambist in the same category as *Homer and *Sophocles, *Mem.* I. 4. 3). But the number of choral genres still being composed was much reduced.

Monodic lyric is particularly associated with eastern Greece. *Sappho and *Alcaeus were natives of *Lesbos and *Anacreon of Teos. The metrical structures of monody are more simple, and unlike choral lyric are repeated from song to song. The dialect tends to be based on the vernacular of the poet. The subject-matter usually derives from the life and circumstances of the poet. The range of solo lyric is very wide. Love, politics, war, wine, abuse of enemies all figure, though to different degrees and with different emphases and approaches from poet to poet. To the modern reader, this personal poetry often seems remarkably impersonal, since there is a marked tendency to generalize personal experience through the medium of myth. As with choral lyric, there is a visible decline in the 5th cent. The latest monodists to be named by Aristophanes are Timocreon and Anacreon, both active in the late 6th and early 5th cent. There must have been many contemporary and subsequent monodists, but none achieved Panhellenic importance.

The age of scholarly research on the lyric poets begins with the generation after Aristotle. Dicaearchus wrote a book about Alcaeus. Clearchus of Soli's book *On Love Poetry* included Sappho and Anacreon. Chamaeleon wrote on Stesichorus, Anacreon, Simonides, and Lasus; his studies embraced Alcman and probably Ibycus. The major lyric poets were edited by the scholars of the *Library at *Alexandria. It is to Alexandrian scholarship that we owe the list of Nine Lyric Poets, Alcman, Alcaeus, Anacreon, Bacchylides, Ibycus, Pindar, Sappho, Simonides, Stesichorus (first attested *c.*100 BC, *Anth. Pal.* 9. 184), identical with those who are studied (*hoi prattomenoi* schol. on Dion. Thrax, p. 21. 18 ff.), i.e. subjected to scholarly exegesis; Corinna of Tanagra in Boeotia is sometimes appended as a tenth, though we do not find a reference to the Ten Lyric Poets as an established grouping before the Byzantine scholar Tzetzes. The list of nine covers the period 650–450 BC. It includes all those who were studied by the Peripatetics (the school of Aristotle), with the exception of Lasus and the inclusion of Bacchylides. It is probably a selection, rather than a collection of all surviving lyric, though the surprising exclusion of Lasus suggests that not all Archaic lyric reached Alexandria.   C. C.

Latin The modern definition of lyric (verse neither epic nor dramatic but characterized by brevity, use of stanzas, and the enthusiastic expression of personal experience and emotion) would have meant little in Roman antiquity.

Greek lyric could be defined by the social settings of its performance, the accompaniment of the lyre, and the use of certain metrical patterns. Already, however, the classification of the corpus of lyric poetry posed special problems for the scholars of *Alexandria, and in the Roman context the only one of these criteria which may be usefully employed is that of metre. The Roman poets knew the Alexandrian canon of Nine Greek Lyricists, and *Horace, who considers himself to be the first Latin lyric poet, memorably asks to be added to the list (*Carm.* I. I. 35). The generic status of *Catullus, who combines lyric and iambic metres in his polymetrics (poems 1–60), is disputed by *Martial, Quintilian, and *Suetonius. For modern scholars the number of lyric poems to be ascribed to him varies between two and sixty-three. Catullan polymetry (and the use of varied metres in a collection can be considered one of the defining features of ancient lyric) may be compared with polymetric experiments involving lyric metres by Laevius in his *Erotopaegnia,* *Varro in his *Menippean Satires,* and Horace in his *Epodes.* It is Horace who first combines Hellenistic technical refinement with the spirit of the lyric of *Alcaeus and *Pindar, and his *Odes* represent the crowning achievement of Latin lyric poetry. Before them the *cantica* of *Plautus provide genuine examples of lyric verse, as do the unfortunately fragmentary choral odes of early Roman tragedy (see TRAGEDY, LATIN). After Horace, *Seneca's tragedies include choral lyric and Statius' *Silvae* contain two lyric poems (4. 5 and 7). *Persius (6. 1 f.) and Quintilian (10. 1. 96) mention the lyric verse of Caesius Bassus, while *Pliny the Younger (*Ep.* 9. 22. 2) praises Passennus Paulus as the equal of Horace and provides evidence (e.g. *Ep.* 3. 1. 7, 7. 4. 9) for a considerable amount of amateur lyric versification. The fragments of a number of 2nd-cent. AD poets, conveniently but misleadingly characterized as the *poetae novelli,* also preserve lyric verse of a metrically innovative but alas now very fragmentary nature. Perhaps the greatest, and certainly the most influential, successors of Horace in the tradition of Latin lyric are the Christian poets Ambrose in his *Hymns* and Prudentius in his *Cathemerinon* and *Peristephanon.* See further under individual authors.   D. P. N.

Lysander (d. 395 BC), Spartan general. His family, though of Heraclid origin (see HERACLES), was poor and when young he was reputedly of *mothax* status, requiring sponsorship through the *agōgē* (state training). He subsequently became the *erastēs* ('lover') of Agesilaus, younger son of King Archidamus II. Appointed admiral in 408 or 407, he gained the friendship and support of the Persian prince Cyrus the Younger, commenced the creation of a personal following, and won a victory at Notion which led to the dismissal of *Alcibiades. Resuming command in 405, he transferred his fleet to the Hellespont (Dardanelles) and destroyed the Athenian fleet at Aegospotami. His personal success was celebrated through several monuments and dedications; at *Samos he was worshipped as a god, perhaps the first living Greek ever to receive divine worship.

See RULER-CULT, *Greek*. Cf. also *Suppl. Hell.* nos. 51, 325, 565.

Lysander established 'decarchies' (ten-man juntas) of his oligarchical partisans in many cities. Obtaining Athens' surrender through blockade (spring 404), he secured the installation there of the Thirty Tyrants, but his policy was overturned by King Pausanias' restoration of democracy in 403. At some (disputed) date before 396 the ephors withdrew support from the faltering decarchies. His continuing influence, however, led Sparta to support Cyrus' attempt at the Persian throne (401) and to make his protégé Agesilaus king. Hoping to restore the decarchies, he obtained for Agesilaus the command against Persia in 396. Resentful of Lysander's personal following, Agesilaus frustrated his plans, but gave him an important Hellespontine command where he persuaded the Persian Spithridates to defect. Back in Sparta in 395, he was instrumental in starting war with Thebes. Invading Boeotia from Phocis, he was surprised and killed at Haliartus before the planned rendezvous with King Pausanias' forces.

An abortive scheme to increase his power by making the kingships elective was 'discovered' after his death by Agesilaus. The sources differ as to whether it was planned in 403 or 395; it may be an invention to discredit his posthumous reputation and supporters. Accurate interpretation of Lysander's career generally is impeded by the hostility of most sources to the imperial system he created.

S. J. Ho.

Lysias, Attic orator. The ancient biographical tradition, that he was born in 459/8 and died *c.*380 BC ([Plut.] *Vit. Lys.* 835c, 836a; Dion. Hal. *Lys.* 1, 12), is clear but problematic. The latter date is plausible; the former less so, and many scholars suggest that a man some fifteen years younger would have been more likely to engage in his range of activities after 403 (the speeches, and cf. also [Dem.] 59. 21–2). He appears as a character in *Plato's Phaedrus*; in the *Republic*, his father Cephalus is an elderly *Syracusan, resident as a *metic in Athens, and friend of assorted Athenian aristocrats: the search for dramatic dates, however, is probably vain.

Lysias and his brother Polemarchus left Athens after Cephalus' death to join the Panhellenic colony of Thurii in southern Italy, where he is said to have studied *rhetoric. They were expelled as Athenian sympathizers after the Sicilian expedition, and returned to Athens as metics in 412/11. In 403 the Thirty Tyrants arrested both brothers, alleging disaffection but really (according to Lys. 12. 6) in order to confiscate their substantial property. Polemarchus was executed; Lysias escaped, and gave financial and physical support to the democratic counter-revolutionaries. He was rewarded by Thrasybulus' decree granting citizenship to all those who assisted in the restoration, but this grant was promptly annulled as unconstitutional.

Works Modern editions contain 34 numbered speeches, although the titles of about 130 others are known, and for several we possess sufficient fragments (either as citations or on papyrus) to determine the nature of the case. Lysias' activity as a speech-writer after 403 was largely confined to that of forensic logographer, like his fellow *metics *Isaeus and Dinarchus, composing speeches for litigants to deliver in court; but his versatility was very great. Like *Demosthenes and *Hyperides, he wrote for both public and private cases. The two categories, however, are not formally distinguished in the corpus, where few private speeches remain: most striking is 1, in which a cuckolded husband pleads justifiable homicide after killing his wife's lover, and the attack in 32 on an allegedly dishonest guardian. Private cases are better represented among the fragments, including for instance the *Hippotherses*, which deals with Lysias' attempts to recover his confiscated property from those who had purchased it under the Thirty Tyrants. Underlying the public speeches are a variety of legal procedures, most notably the *dokimasia* or scrutiny of prospective officials, many of them compromised by their record under the *oligarchies of the Four Hundred or the Thirty Tyrants (16, 25, 26, 31, and the fragmentary *Eryximachus*); other cases concern official malpractice (most notably 12, in which Lysias personally charged Eratosthenes, ex-member of the Thirty, with having killed Polemarchus). The shadow of the Thirty, indeed, hangs over much of Lysias' work, but attempts to discern a consistent political standpoint throughout the corpus have largely foundered.

Lysias' reputation attracted speeches. We are told ([Plut.] *Vit. Lys.* 836a) that no fewer than 425 were circulating in antiquity, but that only 233 of these were agreed to be genuine. Critics since *Dionysius of Halicarnassus (Dion. Hal. *Lys.* 11–12) have attempted to determine authorship on chronological, stylistic, or, more recently, stylometric grounds, but the search has proved largely inconclusive. K. J. Dover (*Lysias and the Corpus Lysiacum* (1968)) has indeed argued that authorship itself may not be a simple concept, and that Lysias and his clients may have collaborated to varying degrees, but this view remains contentious. More important for most purposes (including for instance the use of the speeches as historical sources) is the authenticity not of authorship but of the texts themselves: with the exception of 11, perhaps of 15, and possibly of 6, all the forensic works seem to be genuine speeches, written to be delivered on the occasion they purport to be (though we should allow for the probability of unquantifiable revision).

Characteristics Lysias was noted in antiquity as a master of the language of everyday life: this 'purity' of style led to his being regarded by later rhetoricians as the pre-eminent representative of 'Atticism', as opposed to the florid 'Asiatic' school. Dionysius (*Lys.* 18) criticized him for lacking emotional power in his arguments, but this may be to miss the significance of his admitted mastery in narrative: by the time Lysias has finished telling a story, the audience has been beguiled by his apparent artlessness into accepting as true the most tendentious assertions. Dionysius noted his mastery of *ēthopoiia* (§ 8), by which he evidently meant the ability to portray character attractively, though there are signs in several speeches (notably 1 and 16) of an attempt also to capture the individuality of the speaker in the language given to him.   S. C. T.

Lysimachus (*c*.355–281 BC), Macedonian from Pella (late sources wrongly allege *Thessalian origins), was prominent in the entourage of *Alexander the Great, achieving the rank of Bodyguard by 328. At Babylon (323) he received Thrace as his province, establishing himself with some difficulty against the Thracian dynast, Seuthes (322). He consolidated his power in the eastern coastal districts, suppressing a revolt among the Black Sea cities (313) and founding Lysimacheia in the Chersonese as a bulwark against the Odrysian monarchy (309). Though he assumed royal titulature (306/5), he made no mark in the wars of the Successors (Diadochi) until in 302 he invaded Asia Minor and fought the delaying campaign against *Antigonus the One-eyed which enabled *Seleucus to bring up his army

for the decisive battle of Ipsus (301). His reward was the lands of Asia Minor north of the Taurus range, the source of immense wealth, which he husbanded with legendary tight-fistedness and a degree of fiscal rapacity. These new reserves (*Pergamum alone held 9,000 talents) supported his impressive coinage and allowed him to consolidate in Europe, where he extended his boundaries north until he was captured by the Getic king, Dromichaetes, and forced to surrender his Transdanubian acquisitions (292). In 287 he joined *Pyrrhus in expelling Demetrius (son of Antigonus) from Macedon and two years later occupied the entire kingdom. His writ now ran from the Epirote borders to the Taurus, but dynastic intrigue proved his nemesis, when he killed his heir, Agathocles, at the instigation of his second wife, Arsinoë II, and alienated his nobility (283). Seleucus was invited to intervene and again invaded Asia Minor. The decisive battle at Corupedium (*c.* January 281) cost Lysimachus his life. Asia passed to the Seleucids while *Macedonia dissolved into anarchy.

                                                    A. B. B.

Maccabees The name Maccabee, probably meaning 'the hammer', was the appellation of Judas son of Mattathias, leader of the Judaean Revolt of 168/7 BC against Antiochus IV Epiphanes. See JEWS; SELEUCIDS. The name was given also to Judas' fellow rebels, his father and his four brothers. They were the leaders of the traditionalists, reacting against a process of Hellenization in Jerusalem masterminded by a section of the Jewish aristocracy (see HELLENISM AND HELL-ENIZATION). The high priesthood was usurped by Jason, a member of the Oniad clan, from his brother Menelaus. But the ultimate provocation to the Maccabees was the king's installation of a garrison in the city and a pagan cult in the Temple, and his consequent attempt to suppress Judaism on a wide front. After Mattathias' public killing of an apostate Jew in the act of sacrifice, the Maccabees took to the hills to conduct a guerrilla war, eventually winning concessions from the regent Lysias on behalf of the young Antiochus V. Judas rededicated the Temple on 25 Kislev (December) 164 BC, a date already marked within a few years of the events as the festival of Hanukkah. But he continued to resist the Hellenizers in Jerusalem and successive Seleucid armies. A memorable victory against Nicanor, the Seleucid general, in 161 was followed by the defeat and death of Judas in 160, in battle against Bacchides, after which his brother Jonathan continued the struggle.

The term Maccabees is also applied to the two Greek books in which the revolt and its sequel are narrated and to two associated books. Finally, the name is sometimes given to the seven children and their mother, whose legendary martyrdom in the persecution of Epiphanes, described in 2 Maccabees 7 and embellished in 4 Maccabees, was remembered in rabbinic literature and gave rise to a cult at *Antioch and to a long-lasting Christian tradition (as well as to the word 'macabre').   T. R.

Macedonia (see ◀Map 1, Ba▶) By its geographical position Macedonia forms the connecting link between the Balkans and the Greek peninsula. Four important routes converge on the Macedonian plain: from the Danube via the Morava and Axius valleys, from the Adriatic via Lake Ochrid, from Thrace via Mygdonia, and from the Greek peninsula via Tempe. In climate Macedonia is intermediate between Europe and the Mediterranean. The original Macedonia was Pieria and Mt. Olympus, and from there the Macedonians acquired the coastal plain of the Thermaic Gulf, which has been formed by the rivers Haliacmon, Lydias, and Axius. These rivers, draining the wide plateaux of Upper Macedonia, cut the mountain-ring of the Macedonian plain at Beroea, Edessa, and the defile of Demir Kapu. Of the cantons of Upper Macedonia Elimiotis occupied the middle and Orestis the upper Haliacmon valley, Lyncus and Pelagonia the upper valleys of the Erigon (a tributary of the Axius), Paeonia the upper valley of the Axius, and Eordaea the basin of Lake Arnissa west of Edessa. The Macedonian plain comprised Pieria south of the lower Haliacmon, Bottiaea between the Haliacmon and the Axius, Almopia in the upper Lydias valley, Mygdonia in the Lake Bolbe basin leading towards the Strymon valley, Crestonia and Anthemus north and south respectively of Mygdonia. Upper Macedonia is girt by high mountain-ranges traversed mainly by three important routes mentioned above; when united, it had strong natural defences. The Macedonian plain is vulnerable from the sea and from Mygdonia, but the defiles leading into Upper Macedonia are easily defensible. The natural products were horses, cattle, sheep, crops, *wine, fruit, iron, gold, silver, and *timber, the last two being exported in antiquity.

Prehistoric Macedonia, occupied continuously from early neolithic times, possessed a uniform culture in the bronze age, little influenced by *Mycenaean civilization, and was invaded c.1150 BC by a northern people, of whom a western offshoot may have provoked the semi-legendary Dorian invasion of the *Peloponnese. *Hesiod first mentioned 'Makedon', the eponym of the people and the country, as a son of *Zeus, a grandson of Deucalion, and so a first cousin of Aeolus, Dorus, and Xuthus; in other words he considered the 'Macedones' to be an outlying branch of the Greek-speaking tribes, with a distinctive dialect of their own, 'Macedonian' (see MACEDONIAN LANGUAGE). He gave

Macedonia A richly decorated bronze krater (bowl for mixing wine and water) from a cemetery at Derveni, Macedonia, 4th cent. BC. Heavy drinking was a well-known feature of life at the court of the Macedonian kings, and costly vessels for the service of *wine are a feature of élite-burials in the region. See ALCOHOLISM.

their habitat as 'Pieria and Olympus'. In northern Pieria an early iron age cemetery of 300 tumuli, partly excavated, has revealed the rulers there as probably Phrygians and then Illyrii until *c.*650 BC, when it went out of use. At that time a new dynasty, the Temenidae, ruling the Macedonians, founded their early capital at *Aegae (mod. Vergina), situated above the cemetery, and thereafter gained control of the coastal plain as far as the Axius. The Persian occupation of Macedonia 512–479 BC was beneficial. *Xerxes gave to Alexander I the rule over western Upper Macedonia, which was peopled by Epirotic tribes with their own dialect of Greek; and after Xerxes' flight Alexander gained territory west of the Strymon. His claim to be a Temenid, descended from Heracles and related to the royal house of Argos in the Peloponnese, was recognized at *Olympia; he issued a fine royal coinage and profited from the export of ship-timber.

The potentiality of the Macedonian kingdom was realized by *Philip II. By defeating the northern barbarians and incorporating the Greek-speaking Upper Macedonians he created a superb army (see ARMIES, GREEK), which was supported economically by other peoples who were brought by conquest into the enlarged kingdom: Illyrii, Paeonians, and Thracians—with their own non-Greek languages—and Chalcidians and Bottiaeans, both predominantly Greek-speaking. 'He created a united kingdom from many tribes and nations' (Just. *Epit.* 8. 6. 2) by a policy of tolerance and assimilation. His son *Alexander the Great, inheriting the strongest state in eastern Europe, carried his conquests to the borders of Afghanistan and Pakistan. Later the conquered territories split up into kingdoms ruled mainly by Macedonian royal families, which fought against one another and contended for the original Macedonian kingdom (see ANTIGONUS THE ONE-EYED; ANTIGONUS GONATAS; PTOLEMY I and II; SELEUCUS I). In 167 BC Rome defeated Macedonia and split it into four republics; and in 146 BC it was constituted a Roman province. Thereafter its history merged with that of the Roman empire.

From Philip II onwards the Macedonian court was a leading centre of Greek culture, and the policies of Alexander and his Successors (Diadochi) spread the Greek-based 'Hellenistic' culture in the east, which continued to flourish for centuries after the collapse of Macedonian power. See COLONIZATION, HELLENISTIC; HELLENISM AND HELLENIZATION.　　　　　　　　　　　　　　　N. G. L. H.

Macedonian language The problem of the nature and origin of the Macedonian language is still disputed by modern scholars, but does not seem to have been raised among the ancients. We have a rare adverb *makedonisti* (important passages in *Plutarch, *Alex.* 51 and *Eum.* 14), but the meaning of this form is ambiguous. The adverb cannot tell us whether Plutarch had in mind a language different from Greek (cf. *phoinikisti*, 'in Phoenician'), or a dialect (cf. *megaristi*, 'in Megarian'), or a way of speaking (cf. *attikisti*). We have some 'Macedonian' glosses, particularly in *Hesychius' lexicon, but they are mostly disputed and

some were corrupted in the transmission. Thus ἀβροῦτες, 'eyebrows' probably must be read as ἀβροῦϝες (with τ which renders a digamma). If so, it is a Greek dialect form; yet others (e.g. A. Meillet) see the dental as authentic and think that the word belongs to an Indo-European language different from Greek.

After more than a century we recognize among linguists two schools of thought. Those who reject the Greek affiliation of Macedonian prefer to treat it as an Indo-European language of the Balkans, located geographically and linguistically between Illyrian in the west and Thracian in the east. Some, like G. Bonfante (*Rend. Linc.* 1987, 83–5), look towards Illyrian; others, like I. I. Russu (*Macedonica = Ephemeris Dacoromana* 1938, 105–232), towards 'Thraco-Phrygian' (at the cost, sometimes, of unwarranted segmentations such as that of Ἀλέξανδρος (Alexandros) into †ἀλε- and †ξανδ-). Those who favour a purely Greek nature of Macedonian as a northern Greek dialect are numerous and include early scholars like A. Fick, 'Zum makedonischen Dialecte', *Zeitschrift für vergleichende Sprachforschung* 1874, 193–235 and O. Hoffmann, *Die Makedonen* (1906; repr. 1974). The Greek scholars, like G. Hatzidakis (1897, etc.) and above all J. Kalléris, *Les Anciens Macédoniens* I (1954), 2/1 (1976) [no more published; repr. 1988], have turned this assumption into a real dogma, with at times nationalistic overtones. This should not prevent us, however, from inclining towards this view.

For a long while Macedonian onomastics, which we know relatively well thanks to history, literary authors, and epigraphy, has played a considerable role in the discussion. In our view the Greek character of most names is obvious and it is difficult to think of a Hellenization (see HELLENISM) due to wholesale borrowing. Πτολεμαῖος, (Ptolemaios) is attested as early as *Homer, Ἀλέξανδρος (Alexandros) occurs next to the Mycenaean feminine *a-re-ka-sa-da-ra* (Alexandra), Λάαγος (Laagos), then Λᾶγος (Lagos), matches the Cyprian *Lawagos*, etc. The small minority of names which do not look Greek, like Ἀρριδαῖος (Arrhidaios) or Σαβαττάρας (Sabattaras), may be due to substratum or adstratum influence (as elsewhere in Greece). Macedonian may then be seen as a Greek dialect, characterized by its marginal position and by local pronunciations (like Βερενίκα (Berenika) for Φερενίκα (Pherenika), etc.). Yet in contrast with earlier views which made of it an Aeolic dialect (O. Hoffmann, *Die Makedonen* (1906; repr. 1974) compared Thessalian) we must by now think of a link with North-West Greek (Locrian, Aetolian, Phocidian, Epirote). This view is supported by the recent discovery at Macedonian Pella of a curse tablet (4th cent. BC) which may well be the first 'Macedonian' text attested (provisional publication by E. Voutyras; cf. the *Bulletin Épigraphique* in *Rev. Ét. Grec.* 1994, no. 413); the text includes an adverb ὅποκα (hopoka) which is not Thessalian. We must wait for new discoveries, but we may tentatively conclude that Macedonian is a dialect related to North-West Greek. See GREEK LANGUAGE.　　　　　　　　　O. Ma.

Maecenas, Gaius Maecenas is his *nomen* (hereditary family-name): 'Cilnius' (Tac. *Ann.* 6. 11) may be his mother's name, perhaps descended from an ancient *Etruscan family, the Cilnii of Arretium (Livy 10. 3. 2). The poets call Maecenas scion of Etruscan kings (Hor. *Carm.* 1. 1. 1). Among Octavian's earliest supporters—he fought at Philippi (42 BC)—he was his intimate and trusted friend and agent. (See AUGUSTUS.) His great position rested entirely on this: he never held a magistracy or entered the senate, remaining an *eques* (see EQUITES). He arranged Octavian's marriage with Scribonia, and represented him at the negotiations of the pact of Brundisium (40 BC) and that of Tarentum (37 BC), when he took along his poets (Hor. *Sat.* 1. 5). He went as envoy to Mark *Antony in 38, and in 36–33 and 31–29 he was in control of Rome and Italy in Octavian's absence, an unprecedented position: 'no title, only armed power' (Syme, *AA* 272). In 30, claiming to uncover a conspiracy, he executed the son of the triumvir *Lepidus. His enormous wealth must derive partly from the confiscations: by chance we hear that he acquired part of the possessions of the proscribed Marcus Favonius (schol. Juv. 5. 3; see PROSCRIPTIONS). He bequeathed the emperor everything, including his magnificent house and grounds on Rome's Esquiline hill, the famous *turris Maecenatiana*. Many inscriptions survive of his slaves and *freedmen. Maecenas was famous, or notorious, for his luxury: wines, gourmet dishes (baby donkey, Plin. *HN* 8. 170), gems, fabrics, and love affairs (that with the actor Bathyllus became scandalous: Tac. *Ann.* 1. 54). Astute and vigorous at need, he cultivated an image of softness (Sen. *Ep.* 114). His name became proverbial as the greatest patron of poets (Martial 8. 55. 5). Absent from the *Eclogues*, he is the dedicatee of *Virgil's *Georgics*; unnamed in *Propertius, he is a rewarding and apparently exigent patron in 2. 1. Virgil introduced *Horace (Hor. *Sat.* 1. 6. 54), who dedicated to Maecenas *Satires* 1, *Epodes*, *Odes* 1–3, and *Epistles* 1. Maecenas gave Horace his Sabine estate. Horace gives the fullest picture of Maecenas and his circle, which included Lucius Varius Rufus, Plotius Tucca, Domitius Marsus, and his freedman Melissus. Maecenas wrote poems which recall the metres and to some extent the manner of *Catullus: extant fragments of two are addressed to Horace, intimate in tone. He wrote in prose: *Prometheus* (? a Menippean *satire); *Symposium*, Virgil and Horace being speakers; *De cultu suo*. His style was criticized for affectation: 'the preciosity and neuroticism of the author come through strongly in the fragments' (Courtney, *FLP* 276–81). They contain no trace of politics, but Maecenas must have been influential in inducing Virgil, Horace, and even Propertius to express support for the regime and the values it fostered. His influence is controversial in detail. He was an important intermediary between *princeps* and poets, who lost contact after his death. His wife Terentia, eventually divorced, was Aulus Terentius Varro Murena's sister; apparently Maecenas, departing from his usual discretion, warned her of the detection of her brother's conspiracy (23 BC). Thereafter his relations with Augustus, never openly impaired, seem to have been less close. He died in 8 BC. Two undistinguished *Elegies* on his death survive.   J. Gr.

maenads, women inspired to ritual frenzy by *Dionysus. Maenadic rituals took place in the rough mountains of Greece in the heart of winter every second year. Having ceremonially left the city, maenads (probably upper-class women) would walk into the mountains shouting the cry 'to the mountains'. Here they removed their shoes, left their hair down, and pulled up their fawn-skins. After a sacrifice of *cakes, they started their nightly dances accompanied by *tympanon* and *aulos* (in sound more similar to the oboe than the flute). Stimulated by the high-pitched music, the flicker effects of the torches, the whirling nature of the dances, the shouting of *euhoi*, the headshaking, jumping, and running, the maenads eventually fell to the ground—the euphoric climax of their *ecstasy.

Maenadic ritual strongly stimulated the mythical imagination: the *Bacchae* of *Euripides shows us women who tear animals apart, handle snakes, eat raw meat, and are invulnerable to iron and fire. Most likely, in Euripides' time maenads did not handle snakes or eat raw meat; however, their ecstasy may well have made them insensible to pain. Myth often exaggerates ritual, but the absence of contemporary non-literary sources makes it difficult to separate these two categories in the *Bacchae*, where they are so tightly interwoven.

Maenadism was integrated into the city and should not be seen as a rebellion. It enabled women to leave their houses, to mingle with their 'sisters', and to have a good time. This social aspect, though, could only be expressed through the worship of Dionysus. To separate the social and religious aspect is modern not Greek.

Most likely, maenadism already occurs in *Homer (*Il.* 22. 461 f.). In Athenian art it became popular on pots towards the end of the 6th cent. and again in the 4th cent. BC, with a selective interest expressed in the intervening period by painters of larger pots (see p. 440). Among the tragedians *Aeschylus pictured maenads in various of his lost plays, e.g. the *Bassarai*, as did Euripides, especially in the *Bacchae*. Given these changing periods of interest in maenadism in literature and art, we should be wary of privileging the *Bacchae* by ascribing to it a special influence on later maenadic ritual or by tying it too closely to contemporary new cults. The demise of maenadism started in the Hellenistic period and was complete by the 2nd cent. AD.   J. N. B.

magic

1. The concept Antiquity does not provide clear-cut definitions of what was understood by magic and there is a variety of terms referring to its different aspects. The Greek terms that lie at the roots of the modern term 'magic', *magos*, *mageia*, were ambivalent. Originally they referred to the strange but powerful rites of the Persian magi and their overtones were not necessarily negative (Pl. *Alc.* 1. 122: 'the magian lore of Zoroaster'). Soon, however,

maenads An Athenian vase-painter (c.480 BC) shows maenads inspired to ritual *ecstasy by *Dionysus. Although wine vessels are present, maenadic 'madness' was the result of possession, not alcohol.

magos was associated with the doubtful practices of the Greek *goēs* ('sorcerer') and hence attracted the negative connotations of quack, fraud, and mercenary (e.g. Soph. *OT* 386 f.). Through *Aristotle, his pupil Theophrastus, and Hellenistic authors this negative sense also affected the Latin terms *magus*, *magia*, *magicus*. However, in late antiquity, especially in the *Greek Magical Papyri*, the term *magos* regained an authoritative meaning, somewhat like wizard, and was also embraced by philosophers and theurgists. Since in these late texts prayer, magical formulae, and magical ritual freely intermingle, they challenge modern distinctions between magic and religion (and science). However, definitions being indispensable, we here employ a broad description of the 'family resemblance' of magic: a manipulative strategy to influence the course of nature by supernatural ('occult') means. 'Supernatural means' involves an overlap with religion, 'manipulative (coercive or performative) strategy', as combined with the pursuit of concrete goals, refers rather to a difference from religion.

2. Sources Greek and Roman literature provides abundant examples of magical practice in both narrative and discur-sive texts. Myth affords many instances. Besides gods con-nected with magic (*Hermes and Hecate), we hear of Telchines, skilful but malignant smiths well versed in magic. The Idaean Dactyls were masters of medical charms and music. Thracian *Orpheus was a famous magician, and so were Musaeus, Melampus, and others. But, as elsewhere, the female gender predominates. The most notorious witch was *Medea. *Thessaly boasted an old tradition of witchcraft, the Thessalian witches being notorious for their specialism of 'drawing down the moon'.

The earliest literary examples come from *Homer. The witch Circe (*Od.* 10. 274 ff.) uses potions, salves, and a magic wand to perform magical tricks and teaches *Odysseus how to summon the ghosts from the nether world. Folk magic glimmers through in a scene where an incantation stops the flow of blood from a wound (*Od.* 19. 457). *Hesiod (*Theog.* 411–52) offers an aretalogy (see MIRACLES) of the goddess Hecate. Tragedy contributes magical scenes (e.g. the calling up of the ghost of *Darius I: Aesch. *Pers.* 619–842) as well as whole plays (Eur. *Med.*), while comedy ridicules magicians (e.g. Ar. *Plut.* 649–747; Menander's (lost) *Deisidaimon* and *Theophoroumenos*). *Theocritus'

Pharmakeutria ('Drug- or Poisonmonger', hence 'Sorceress') became a model for many later witch scenes (e.g. Verg. *Ecl.* 8, and Hor. *Epod.* 5, describing the gruesome preparation of a love potion). Similarly, magical motifs in Greek epic tradition (e.g. Ap. Rhod. *Argon. passim*) were continued by Roman epic (e.g. Luc. *Pharsalia* 6. 413–830). Exceptionally informative is Apuleius' *Metamorphoses* (see NOVEL, LATIN) which contains many a picturesque magical scene.

Another illuminating work by Apuleius belongs to the sphere of critical reflection. His *Apologia* (*De magia*) is a defence against the charge of magic and provides a full discussion of various aspects of ancient magic. Other discussions can be found in the satirical works of e.g. Theophrastus (for instance the 16th Character (*Deisidaimon*)), and *Lucian, *passim*. Although early philosophers like Heraclitus, *Pythagoras, Empedocles, and Democritus were often associated with magical experiments, Greek philosophy generally rejected magic. *Plato wants the abuse of magic (*pharmakeia*) to be punished, and Sceptics, Epicureans (see EPICURUS), and *Cynics never tired of contesting magic. The shift towards a more positive appreciation in late antiquity, in, for example, Hermetic writings, Iamblichus, and Proclus (cf. §1 above), was effected by a new cosmology, also apparent in new demonologies, in prophecies, and *astrology.

3. Objectives As to the intended effects, a rough distinction can be made between harmful 'black' magic and innocent or beneficial 'white' magic, although the boundaries cannot be sharply drawn. For the category of black magic curse-tablets are the most conspicuous evidence (see CURSES). Numerous other forms of black magic were widely applied and feared: incantations; the use of drugs and poison (significantly *pharmakon* may refer to magic, poison, and medicine); the practice of 'sympathetic magic' (*similia similibus*), for instance the use of 'voodoo dolls' melted in fire or pierced with needles (Pl. *Leg.* 933b; Theoc. 2; Verg. *Ecl.* 8; Ov. *Her.* 6. 91); and 'contagious magic', the destruction of the victim's hair, nails, part of his cloak, or other possessions as 'part for all', with the aim of harming the victim himself (Theoc. 2. 53 ff.; Verg. *Aen.* 4. 494 ff.).

Some of these practices can function in 'white' magic as well. Its main objectives are protection against any kind of mishap, the attraction of material or non-material benefits, and the healing of illness. The first two are above all pursued by the use of amulets or phylacteries, the last by the application of all sorts of materia medica, often activated by charms and ritual (see § 4 below); also by means of purifications, exorcism, or divine healing.

Mixtures occur: love magic is generally pursued for the benefit of the lover, not for that of the beloved, who is sometimes bewitched in a very aggressive manner and by gruesome means. Other types of magic (e.g. prophecy) are more or less neutral, although uncanny aspects may render them suspect (e.g. nekyomancy or the consultation of spirits of the dead).

4. Techniques Magic is essentially based on secret knowledge of sources of power. The most important are (*a*) utterances, (*b*) material objects, and (*c*) performance.

(*a*) Utterances may consist of inarticulate sounds, cries, various types of noise (e.g. the use of bells), hissing, or whistling. More common are powerful words and formulae. One important category consists of strange, uncanny words not belonging to the Greek or Latin idiom: the 'Ephesian letters' (so called from their alleged origin in *Ephesus), also referred to by terms such as *onomata asēma* ('meaningless names'), or *voces magicae* ('magical names/ words'), whose (alleged) foreign origin and lack of normal communicable meaning were believed to enhance their magical power. Another category of effective words consists of Greek or Latin expressions in which the illness or the cure is compared with a model taken from myth or legend (esp. Homer, Virgil, the Bible) or nature. Stylistic and prosodic devices, such as metre, anaphora, repetition, and rhyme, add emphasis and efficacy to the formulae, as do other magical devices such as writing normal words from right to left or with foreign letters. A copious stock of magical formulae is provided by the so-called *Greek Magical Papyri*, a corpus of papyrus texts from Egypt that contain extended formulae with magical words and names of great gods and demons, including lists of vowels understood as names of archangels, who are invoked or even forced to assist the practitioner.

(*b*) There is practically no limit to the selection of magical ingredients: any object or material may have a magical force—iron, (precious) stones, pieces of wood, parts of animals, nails, hair, the blood of criminals. Most important are herbs and plants, where magic and folk medicine often coalesce in the wisdom of the root-cutter and herbalist. Drawings of foreign gods and demons may be added and, especially in black magic, 'voodoo dolls', sometimes transfixed with needles, could have a role.

(*c*) In the application of these objects and as independent magical acts, various performative actions play a part. The magical objects must be manipulated in a special way, various gestures are prescribed, etc.

These three technical aspects are often combined, exemplarily so in the famous cure of a fracture in *Cato the Elder, *Agr.* 160: a knife is brandished and two pieces of reed are brought together over the fracture while a charm is sung: *motas vaeta daries dardares astataries dissunapiter* (untranslatable).

5. Social setting The social and legal standing of magic is basically ambivalent. (Secret) wisdom and expertise in the application of supernatural means was indispensable and widely resorted to, hence highly valued. Many official 'religious' rites, especially in Rome, contained 'magical' elements, which were accepted because and as long as they were publicly executed on behalf of the state. In the private sphere, however, magic's very secretiveness and association with asocial or even antisocial goals fostered suspicion and condemnation. Already in the 5th cent. BC, the author of *The Sacred Disease* (2. 12 f., 4. 36 ff.) made a clear distinction between religious and magical strategies and censured the latter. Plato (see §2 above) wanted the abuse of magic to be penalized in his ideal state; the Romans, as early as 450 BC, actually did so in the *Twelve Tables. Under the first emperors many laws were issued to repress the growth of magical practices, and the 4th cent. AD saw a renaissance of anti-magical legislation. In this period, however, magic was practically identified with *prava religio* ('bad religion') and *superstitio* ('superstition'), which, together, served as conveniently comprehensive (and vague) classificatory terms to discredit social, political, and/or religious opponents. H. S. V.

magistracy, Greek Magistracies (*archai*) in Greek states were the successors of the *kingships which rarely survived into the Classical period. By a process which cannot now be followed in detail, and which the sources tend to reconstruct in too systematic a fashion, the powers of a hereditary king came to be divided between a plurality of magistrates, normally appointed for one year and often not eligible for reappointment. In addition to general offices of state, more specialized offices were sometimes created, for example to control a treasury or to supervise public works or the market (the office of *agoranomos*). A small state could manage with a small number of magistrates, but in a large one there might be many, and many duties might be given to boards rather than single individuals: Athens in the 5th cent. BC developed a particularly extensive range of offices—700 internal and 700 external, according to the text of *Ath. pol.* 24. 3, though the second 700 is probably corrupt.

Magistrates tended to be more powerful, and to be appointed from a more restricted circle, in *oligarchies than in democracies. Appointment by lot rather than by *election, to civilian posts which were not thought to require special ability, was particularly associated with democracy, but both that and a ban on reappointment to the same office can be found in oligarchies too. Athens and some other democratic states provided small salaries for magistrates (see DEMOCRACY, ATHENIAN, §2). One office might be regarded as the principal office in a state, but in general there was no hierarchy of offices and no *cursus honorum* as in Rome (see CAREERS). The citizens might control their magistrates through such procedures as *dokimasia* (vetting their qualifications before they entered office) and *euthynai* (examining their conduct after they left office), as well as by making them liable to prosecution for misconduct.

The magistrates of the Hellenistic kings were of a very different kind. They were professionals, paid by their king in money, natural produce, or gifts of land. The higher positions were occupied by Macedonians and Greeks, the lower mostly by natives, who did not rise to higher positions before the 2nd cent. The members of the central administration worked in the chief city, but there were numerous higher and lower officials in every part of the

kingdom. The most important provincial officials were usually called *stratēgoi* ('generals'). The administration was strictly centralized in Egypt, but decentralized in the *Seleucid empire. Especially in *Egypt, there was a firm hierarchy, bureaucratically organized. Lower officials were often personally dependent on the higher, as the higher were on the king. V. E.; P. J. R.

magistracy, Roman Magistrates at Rome may be divided in various ways according to various criteria. The most general recognizes a distinction between (*a*) the *ordinarii* (regularly elected), namely *consuls, praetors, censors, curule aediles (these four offices were distinguished by privileges as 'curule', so called because they were entitled to use the official curule chair or *sella curulis*), quaestors, the vigintisexvirate (vigintivirate under the empire), and (not formally magistrates of the whole *populus Romanus* but only of the *plebs) the *tribuni plebis* (see TRIBUNE) and aediles of the *plebs*, and (*b*) the *extraordinarii* (*extra ordinem creati*, occasionally appointed or elected), namely the *interrex*, *praefectus urbi* or city prefect (altered by *Augustus), *dictator, *magister equitum*, and a number of unique commissions (*decemviri legibus scribundis*, *tribuni militum consulari potestate*, *tresviri rei publicae constituendae*, etc.). More important is the distinction between those who possessed *imperium (consuls, praetors, dictators, *magistri equitum*, the *decemviri legibus scribundis*, military tribunes with consular power, and the *tresviri r. p. c.*) and those who did not (the rest). The competences and histories of the individual magistracies varied greatly. Most of them did, however, share certain features. They were elected (apart from the *interrex*, dictator, *magister equitum*, and *praefectus urbi*). They were temporary: all the regular magistracies were annual, apart from the censorship. They were organized in colleges (generally of two, three, or ten members), and thereby subject to the *intercessio* (veto) of their colleagues; the dictatorship is the most significant exception, for which reason tenure of it was restricted to six months, until *Sulla and, especially, *Caesar, whose dictatorship for life effectively re-created the *imperium* of the kings. They were unpaid: magistracy was regarded as an honour (*honos* can be a synonym for *magistratus*). The powers of magistrates with *imperium* were restricted over time, by the creation of the tribunate of the *plebs* and by the development of *provocatio* (appeal to the Roman people against the action of a magistrate). But Roman magistrates, unlike Athenian, were never formally accountable to the people who elected them. Around the middle of the 2nd cent. BC it came to be felt that they ought to be, to the point that *Polybius could say, erroneously, that the consuls had, upon laying down their office, to account for their actions to the people (*euthunas hupechein*, 6. 15. 10). Magistrates and promagistrates could be called to account, but this required special prosecutions which could be (and were) initiated by tribunes. Attempts formally to regulate the conduct, to enforce public scrutiny, and to facilitate public accountability of magistrates and promagistrates were made (chiefly by Gaius *Gracchus and Lucius Appuleius Saturninus), but this initiative foundered as the holders of high office dominant in (and, collectively, as) the senate defended their power and privilege, and as political principle gave way to internecine politics in the late republic. P. S. D.

manuscripts See BOOKS, GREEK AND ROMAN; SCHOLARSHIP, HISTORY OF CLASSICAL.

maps Many cultures, including those of Egypt and Mesopotamia, use visual representations of aspects of space that cannot be directly perceived. The Ionian Greeks (perhaps taking the idea from other traditions) produced the first maps in the classical tradition (*Eratosthenes, *Strabo 1. 1. 11 (7), attributed the first map to Anaximander); the famous one shown to King Cleomenes I of Sparta by Aristagoras of Miletus (Hdt. 5. 49) is an example of such maps: these fit into the context of new world-views that are also found in Hecataeus and *Herodotus. World maps are mentioned at Athens in the late 5th cent. BC, but do not seem to have been widespread.

These early maps were attempts to depict the wider order of the world rather than to survey smaller areas in detail; such local maps, if known, were not related conceptually to the geographers' task. Only the calculation of linear distances on some land routes (such as the Royal Road (see ROADS)) and on *periploi* (lit. 'voyages around': descriptions of coastal itineraries) offered a bridge between the two: but there is no evidence that such linear conceptions of space were represented graphically before the Roman period. The place of maps in the geographical knowledge of *Alexander the Great and his commanders is therefore controversial.

The governmental purposes of the Ptolemies (see PTOLEMY I and II), under whom the ancient agrimensorial techniques of the Nile valley's agriculture were developed, gave a new status to mapping in Alexandrian geography (see ALEXANDRIA). Influence from one of the Hellenistic kingdoms may perhaps be postulated for the development in Rome from the 3rd cent. BC of visual representations, in a context of land-divisions on a large scale, long-distance road-building, and widespread city-foundation; and the greatest development of mapping in antiquity was indeed associated with Roman imperial policy. Cadastral plans, especially of land-allotments, were developed to a high degree of sophistication and accuracy: the best-known examples are fragments of the Flavian marble cadasters of the territory of Arausio (Orange) in the Rhône valley, displayed on the walls of a room near the local forum (see page 183). The most complex known example of ancient surveying is related in technique and perhaps in purpose, but much larger in scale (about 1:300) and more detailed: the *Forma Urbis Romae, a plan of Rome on marble slabs which decorated a hall in the templum Pacis complex at Rome and dates from the Severan period (the numerous fragments are a source of great value for the nature of the

maps Section of the Peutinger Table, a copy made c.1200 of a late-Roman world-map, showing parts of southern Italy with Sicily, North Africa, Macedonia, and southern Greece. In elongated form, the map shows the whole inhabited world from Britain to India. It had a practical value, marking roads, posting stations and inter-city distances.

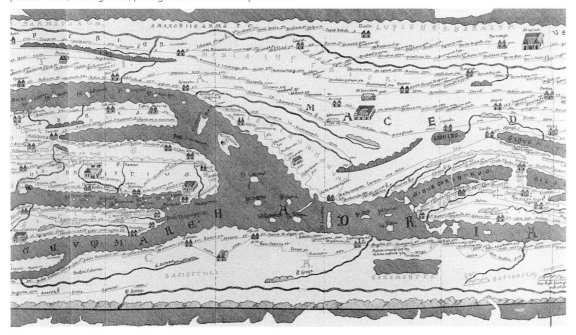

ancient city). A recently discovered fragment of perhaps Flavian date (the 'Via Anicia Fragment') proves that there was an earlier version of neater draftsmanship and greater detail, with records of title to property as well as the names of public buildings.

The scale of Roman land-division (see CENTURIATION) and its connection with world-spanning road-building projects suggested that the wide world of geographic/cosmological description like Eratosthenes' might be represented in this sort of detail, and it is likely that the ambitious plan of world surveying attributed to Caesar was an attempt, and perhaps the first, to realize this grandiose vision and use it as a sign of knowledge and power. *Agrippa's world map, succeeding to *Caesar's vision, in the Porticus Vipsania in Rome was a potent symbol of the control of space by the Augustan regime. It is certain that this calibrated distances as well as representing the whole *oikoumenē* ('inhabited world'), but there is dispute over the shape and layout: was it an Eratosthenic world map, a pictorial version of the world-order of the sort that is represented in Roman and late antique art, the progenitor of the *mappae mundi* of the Middle Ages; or an early version of the road-map of the world known as the Peutinger Table? The practical, as opposed to the symbolic, use of detailed maps in Roman military and governmental planning remains controversial.   N. P.

Marius, Gaius, born *c*.157 BC near Arpinum, of a family probably of recent equestrian standing (see EQUITES), but with good Roman connections, including *Scipio Aemilianus. He served with distinction under Scipio at Numantia and, with his commendation, won a military tribunate by election, perhaps serving under Manius Aquillius in Asia. Quaestor *c*.123, he was helped to a tribunate by the Metelli (119), but fiercely attacked the consul Lucius Caecilius Metellus Delmaticus when he opposed Marius' law ensuring secrecy of individual votes in the *comitia* (assembly). Because of this breach of *fides* (trust) he failed to gain an aedileship, but became (urban) praetor 115, barely securing acquittal on a charge of *ambitus* (see BRIBERY, ROMAN). Sent to Further Spain as proconsul, he showed aptitude at guerrilla warfare and added to his fortune. On his return he married a patrician Julia, a distinguished match. In 109 Quintus Caecilius Metellus Numidicus, sent to fight a guerrilla war against Jugurtha, chose Marius as his senior legate. But when Marius requested leave to seek a consulship, Metellus haughtily rebuffed him. Marius now intrigued against Metellus among his equestrian and Italian friends in Africa and Rome and won election for 107 by playing on suspicions of the aristocracy. He superseded Metellus in Numidia by special legislation. He ended the manpower shortage by the radical step of abolishing the property qualification for service and enrolled a volunteer army. After fighting for two years without decisive success, he captured Jugurtha through the diplomatic skill of his quaestor *Sulla, was elected consul for the second time for 104 by special dispensation, to deal with a threatened German invasion, and triumphed on 1 January.

He found an army reorganized and trained by Publius Rutilius Rufus, his fellow legate under Metellus and his enemy, as consul 105; and, re-elected consul year after year, with friendly colleagues, he improved the army's equipment and organization (see ARMIES, ROMAN) and defeated the Teutones and Ambrones at Aquae Sextiae (mod. Aix-en-Provence) and, with Quintus Lutatius Catulus, the Cimbri at Vercellae (near Rovigo in northern Italy), in 102 and 101 respectively, consenting to celebrate a joint triumph with Catulus. His immense prestige attracted nobles like Catulus into his following and confirmed the loyalty of *equites* and *plebs*. He was elected to a sixth consulship (100), defeating Metellus' quixotic candidacy.

The tribune Lucius Appuleius Saturninus had provided land for his African veterans in 103, and in 100 undertook to do so for the veterans of the German war. Marius gladly accepted his co-operation and was pleased when Metellus' intransigence in opposition led to his exile. But when Saturninus, with the help of Gaius Servilius Glaucia, threatened to establish independent power, Marius turned against them, rejected Glaucia's consular candidacy, and, when they tried to force through a law overruling him, 'saved the republic' by forcibly suppressing them. But his stubborn opposition to Metellus' return, delaying it while his friend Marcus Antonius was consul, alienated his optimate supporters. When the vote for Metellus' recall passed, he left for the east, 'to fulfil a vow', abandoning hope for a censorship. His firm words to *Mithradates VI earned him election to an augurate in absence and, with his *dignitas* restored, he returned. But he had frittered away his overwhelming stature. Some of his friends and clients were now attacked (the younger Manius Aquillius, Gaius Norbanus; the prosecution of Titus Matrinius (Cic. *Balb.* 48 f.)), and although he successfully defended them, his noble friends deserted him. In 92, reaffirming his links with the *equites*, he assisted in the prosecution of Rutilius Rufus, and in 91 he seems to have opposed Marcus Livius Drusus with his equestrian friends, mobilizing his Italian followers against Drusus. When the senate openly expressed support for Sulla by allowing the Numidian ruler Bocchus to dedicate a group showing Jugurtha's surrender on the Capitol, Marius was prevented from violent opposition only by the outbreak of the Social War of 91–89 BC (see ROME (HISTORY), §1.5). In the war he was successful on the northern front, but when not offered supreme command, chose to retire.

With war against Mithradates imminent, Marius hoped to have the command and opposed the attempt of his relative by marriage Gaius Iulius Caesar Strabo Vopiscus to win the consulship for 88. He found an ally in Drusus' friend Publius Sulpicius Rufus, tribune 88, in return for supporting his policies. When the *optimates* (lit. 'the best men') chose Sulla for the consulship and command (he married Caecilia Metella, widow of the *princeps senatus* (designated senior senator) Marcus Aemilius Scaurus), Sulpicius had the *plebs* transfer the command to Marius.

Sulla responded by seizing Rome with his army. Marius, unprepared for this, had to flee (the flight was later embroidered with dramatic detail), finding safety at Cercina, a colony of his veterans off Africa. After the expulsion of Lucius Cornelius Cinna from Rome, Marius returned and joined him with an army collected among his veterans. He sacked Ostia and organized Cinna's capture of Rome. Both were proclaimed consuls for 86 and Marius was to supersede Sulla in the east. He now took terrible vengeance on his enemies, especially on faithless former friends; but his health gave out and he died before taking up his command.

A typical *novus homo* (first of his family to reach the senate and/or consulship), like *Cato the Elder before him and Cicero after him, Marius wanted to beat the nobles at their own game and win acceptance as a leader of their *res publica*. Unlike some aristocrats, from Gaius *Gracchus to *Caesar, he had no plans for reform. Although favouring rewards for soldiers without distinction between citizens and Italians, he opposed Drusus' attempt to enfranchise the Italians and left it to Saturninus to look after his veterans' interests. His reform of enlistment, due to momentary considerations, accidentally created the client army: it was Sulla who taught him the consequences. However, his early career first demonstrated the power inhering in an alliance of a successful commander with a demagogue and a noble following; and his opponents, in their attitude to him and to Sulla, revealed the lack of cohesion and of political principle besetting the *nobilitas* (the senatorial élite descended from consuls).   E. B.

markets and fairs

Greece The arrival of the market as an institution in the 8th cent. BC (see TRADE, GREEK), gradually replacing archaic mechanisms for exchange, along with the concomitant beginnings of urbanization, prompted the *polis* to develop marketing arrangements. The installation of permanent retail-markets in urban centres, signalled in the shift in the meaning of *agora* from 'assembly (place of)' to 'market', is best followed at *Athens, where built shops are attested by c.500 and the first public edifice for commercial purposes by 391 BC (Ar. *Eccl.* 686), although temporary 'booths' (*skēnai*) and 'tables' (*trapezai*) still typified the bazaar-area in the 4th cent.; generally, peristylar (colonnaded) markets (*makella*) are a 3rd-cent. development. Elsewhere, as in the 'new town' at Olynthus (northern Greece), private houses could act as retail outlets. The *polis* controlled the urban market through magistrates called *agoranomoi* and drew revenues from taxing retailers; but it had no larger interest in intervention beyond seeking to assure (for essentially political reasons) an adequate *food supply.

Although urban markets chiefly served an urban populace, additional periodic market-days, attested monthly at Classical Athens (Ar. *Eq.* 43–4; *Vesp.* 169–71), point to their use by peasant farmers; in the 3rd cent. BC one Attic village (Sunium, perhaps exceptional) had its own built market (J Travlos, *Bildlexikon zur Topographie des antiken Attika* (1988), 426–9). Although *Demosthenes (23. 39) speaks of the 'border market' (*agora ephoria*) as a thing of the past, periodic rural markets and fairs are attested in remote parts of Roman *Greece (e.g. Paus. 10. 32. 14–16). Periodic markets as a part of religious festivals (*panēgyreis*), well known from the Hellenistic period, are probably older (as at *Olympia, allegedly existing by c.500 BC: Cic. *Tusc.* 5. 3. 9); while all served pilgrims, some were genuine regional fairs too, encouraged by the lifting of import and export duties, as

markets and fairs Marble relief from *Ostia (mid-2nd cent. AD) showing a woman selling live produce over a 'counter' of chicken- and rabbit-cages. Much selling in classical cities was conducted in this casual fashion, rather than in built shops. The relief suggests the important role of working *women in the retail trade.

on *Delos (Strabo 10. 5. 4). Negotiation of temporary markets outside city walls for exchanges with campaigning armies was a feature of Greek military logistics.

Rome The Forum was originally (*i.a.*) a market-site, the word surviving in this sense in the specialized markets of Rome (e.g. forum Boarium), although by the 1st cent. BC *macellum* was the usual term for an alimentary market. A daily retail market existed in Rome by 210 BC (Livy 26. 27. 1–4) and later was joined by others; wholesaling took place at the riverine Emporium, built in 193 BC (Livy 35. 10. 12). The state supervised Rome's markets through aediles. State-authorized periodic markets and fairs (*nundinae*, *mercatus*) have recently been shown to be commoner than usually thought in the Roman world. In cities they included both weekly ('peasant') markets, as for instance in some 25 towns in central Italy of the 1st cent. AD (attested by inscribed market-calendars), and also regional fairs, as with those following annual games at Rome itself (*Inscr. Ital.* 13. 2. 10) in the same period. In rural areas a distinctly Roman development is the estate market instituted by a landowner, of the type which brought a Roman senator into conflict with an Italian town in 105 (Plin. *Ep.* 5. 4 and 13) and found too in Roman *Africa and *Asia. Supraregional fairs (as at Amm. Marc. 14. 3. 3) seem to have been rare, probably because the long-distance seaborne transport of the Mediterranean was ill-adapted for punctuality.

A. J. S. S.

marriage law

Greek Marriage in Greece was a process of transfer, by which the *kyrios* ('lord' or 'controller') of a woman (normally her father; if he had died, her nearest adult male relative) gave her away to another man for the procreation of children. Originally this was merely a private arrangement between the two men; but, because the procreation of children affected inheritance of property and membership of the community, cities made laws regulating marriage in order to define legitimacy for those purposes.

In Athens a marriage was legal only if it began with *engyē*, a formal statement by the *kyrios* granting the woman to a husband. (A woman with no father or brother living could be awarded to a husband by the archon, the civilian head of state.) The woman's own consent was not legally required. She could not be married to a direct ascendant or descendant, nor to her brother or half-brother by the same mother, but marriage to a half-brother by the same father or to an uncle or cousin was permitted. From 451/0 BC marriage between an Athenian and a foreigner was forbidden (see CITIZENSHIP, GREEK). Bigamy was not allowed; a man could have a concubine as well as a wife, but the concubine's children were not legitimate. A man could divorce his wife by sending her back to her father, who could then give her in marriage to a second husband.

Marriage was often accompanied by gifts of property or money: in Homeric times usually by gifts from the husband to the father, in Classical Athens by a dowry given by the father to support the wife and her future children. But these were customary, not legal requirements.

See also INCEST. D. M. M.

Roman Traditional expressions enshrine the view that a man took a wife for the procreation of children. According to the celebrated definition of the lawyer Herennius Modestinus adopted in the *Digest*, Roman marriage was 'a joining together of a man and a woman, and a partnership (for life) in all areas of life, a sharing in divine and human law' (*Dig.* 23. 2. 1), an ideal rather than a legal definition. No formalities were legally necessary for the inception of a marriage: the usual ceremonies had social and sometimes religious significance. All that was legally necessary was for a man and woman to live together with the intention of forming a lasting union (*affectio maritalis*, the reciprocal attitude of regarding each other as husband or wife). The initial consent was also given by both partners; if one or both was in paternal power (*patria potestas*) that of the respective fathers was needed. The social consequences of marriage (*honor matrimonii*) followed. Wedding ceremonies, especially the transfer of the bride to the husband's house (for the upper classes a procession) normally attested this intention. Moreover, the intention was necessary not merely at the beginning of a marriage, but throughout: hence if the intention ceased, the marriage was in principle at an end (see below). Roman marriage was essentially monogamous, for a man could have only one wife at a time for the purpose of breeding legitimate children, and intended to be lasting (provided that *affectio maritalis* persisted). But although the virtue and good fortune of a woman who in her lifetime had only one husband was valued (*univira*), remarriage was acceptable and necessary.

Marriage in the ancient world was a matter of personal law, and therefore a full Roman marriage (*iustae nuptiae*, *iustum matrimonium*) could exist only if both parties were Roman citizens or had *conubium* (right to contract marriage), either by grant to a group (e.g. Latins) or individually. Only such a marriage could place the children in the father's power and create rights of succession. Further, parties might have this general *conubium* but still lack *conubium* with each other. Impediments varied: (1) Age. Although consent, not consummation, made a marriage, the partners had to be physically capable. The minimum age became fixed at 12 for women and (apparently) 14, puberty, or both for men. (2) Relationship, by blood, adoption, or marriage, within certain degrees. (3) Disparate rank. A probably innovative prohibition of the *Twelve Tables on intermarriage between *patrician and plebeian (see PLEBS) was abolished in 445 BC; the Augustan marriage laws of 18 BC and AD 9 prohibited marriage between senators and their immediate descendants and freed slaves. (4) Considerations of morals or public policy. *Augustus similarly prohibited marriage between free-born citizens and members of disreputable professions, or with a convicted adulteress. Serving soldiers (below a certain rank) were forbidden to marry (a ban perhaps introduced by Augustus, maintained until *Septimius Severus); later, to avoid undue influence, provincial officials were forbidden to marry women of the province during their term, and guardians to marry their wards. Marriage was usually preceded by a formal betrothal (*sponsalia*), in early law by solemn exchange of verbal promises (*sponsio*). Later, it became informal (though marked by celebration) and could be broken without legal penalty. But betrothal created relationships and moral obligations similar to those of marriage. In the 4th cent. AD, in imitation of eastern custom, earnest money (*arrha sponsalicia*) guaranteed the promise to marry.

Except when accompanied by *manus* (when all the wife's property became the husband's and she was under his control), marriage made no difference to the status or property rights of the wife. She remained either in the paternal power of her father or independent (*sui iuris*), with ownership of her property. Ideally, the separation of property of husband and wife was maintained. Dowry (*dos*), on the other hand, was property transferred to the husband for the duration of the marriage, for the maintenance of the wife. *Dos* was not legally necessary, but it was a moral duty to endow a woman so that she might make an eligible marriage. In early law, whoever gave the dowry could stipulate for its return at the end of the marriage; later, there developed a suit for return of dowry after divorce (*actio rei uxoriae*). The husband could retain fractions of the dowry to cover expenses and compensate him for misconduct or (if there were children) unjustified initiation of divorce by the wife. Later, the husband's ownership diminished; by Justinian's time it amounted to usufruct.

Marriage was ended by the withdrawal of *affectio maritalis* by one or both partners. There was no public authority which had to give permission; even receipt of formal notice was not legally necessary, although in practice a husband or wife would usually inform the partner orally or in writing or by messenger and one would leave the marital home and recover personal property, and arrangements would be made about return of dowry. Augustus introduced documented notification, probably only when the husband needed evidence that he had divorced an adulteress. The husband normally kept any children. If the wife was in *manus*, formalities were necessary to free her. Divorce was by the husband or his *paterfamilias* (male head of family) in early times, but by the last century BC could also be decided by the wife (or her *paterfamilias*: the father's powers were gradually curbed). The upper class of the late republic and early Principate exploited the possibility with relative freedom (despite inconvenient economic consequences, possible emotional suffering, e.g. because young children would stay under the father's control, and some public disapproval unless the motives were acceptable, e.g. for *adultery). The Christian emperors penalized unilateral divorce, except on specific grounds; Justinian briefly succeeded in prohibiting consensual divorce (see JUSTINIAN'S CODIFICATION).

A. B.; B. N.; S. M. T.

Mars, next to *Jupiter the chief Italian god. Months were named after him at Rome (*Martius*, mod. Eng. March), Alba Longa, Falerii, Aricia, Tusculum, Lavinium, and among the Italic Hernici, Aequiculi, Paelignians, and Sabines (Ov. *Fast.* 3. 89–95, presumably from Verrius Flaccus). At Rome his festivals came in March and October, with the exception of the first Equirria (27 February). They were the *feriae Marti* on 1 March (old New Year's Day), second Equirria (14 March), *agonium Martiale* (17 March), Quinquatrus (19 March; afterwards extended to five days and supposed to be a festival of *Minerva), and Tubilustrium (23 March). All these may be reasonably explained, so far as their ritual is known, as preparations for the campaigning season, with performance of rites to benefit the horses (Equirria), trumpets (Tubilustrium), and other necessaries for the conduct of war. On 1, 9, and 23 March also, the Salii, an ancient priesthood belonging to Jupiter, Mars, and Quirinus (Servius on *Aen.* 8. 663), danced a sort of war-dance in armour of the fashion of the bronze age and sang their traditional hymn, addressed apparently to all the gods, not to these three only. This is intelligible as further preparation for war. In October the Equus October came on the Ides (15th). A horse-race took place in the Campus Martius; the off horse of the winning team was sacrificed and his head contended for by the inhabitants of the via Sacra and the Suburra. On the 19th was the Armilustrium, presumably the purification of the soldiers' arms before putting them away for the winter. In this month again the Salii performed their dances ('arma ancilia movent', the *ancilia* being archaic shields shaped like the figure 8). Before commencing a war the general shook the sacred spears of Mars in the Regia, saying 'Mars vigila'; it is most probable that these were the original embodiments of the god. His priest is the *flamen Martialis* (see PRIESTS) and his sacred animals the wolf and woodpecker. It is therefore not remarkable that he is usually considered a war-god and was equated with *Ares. Scholars have hesitated over the function of Mars (H. S. Versnel, *Inconsistencies in Greek and Roman Religion* 2 (1992), 290 ff.). Often interpreted as a god of vegetation, Mars is now considered a war- and warrior-god, who exercised his wild function in various contexts, e.g. by his presence on the border of a city, a territory, a field, or a group of citizens. This border-line was materialized, before an action or a period of time, by a lustration, i.e. a circumambulation of three victims—a boar, a ram, a bull—which were then sacrificed.

His mythology is almost entirely borrowed from Ares, the only exception being the comic tale of how he was deceived into marrying Anna Perenna (Ov. *Fast.* 3. 675 ff.). Under *Augustus he obtained an important new title, Ultor, 'Avenger', in recognition of the victory over *Caesar's assassins (Richardson, *Topog. Dict. Ancient Rome*, 244 f. for his other places of worship in Rome).

H. J. R.; J. Sch.

Martial (Marcus Valerius Martialis), Latin poet, was born at Bilbilis in Spain on 1 March in a year between AD 38 and

41 (in 10. 24, written between 95 and 98, he celebrates his fifty-seventh birthday). He died in Spain, probably at Bilbilis, between 101 and 104 (book 12 is later than 101, but Plin. *Ep.* 3. 21 on Martial's death is not later than 104). Brought up in Spain, he came to Rome around AD 64 (10. 103 and 104, datable to AD 98, report that he had lived in Rome for 34 years). In Rome he was supported by the younger *Seneca, then the most celebrated Spaniard in the city, and probably by other important patrons (4. 40, 12. 36): Gaius Calpurnius Piso, Memmius Regulus (consul in 63), and Vibius Crispus (consul in 61). Already in 65, however, the suppression of the Pisonian conspiracy brought ruin to the families of Seneca and Piso. Martial continued to be on friendly terms with the widow of *Lucan, Seneca's nephew and another victim, and with Quintus Ovidius, formerly connected with the circle of Seneca (7. 44, 45): it is possible that Martial's property at Nomentum and the neighbouring estate of Quintus Ovidius were both gifts from Seneca, who had considerable holdings in the area. These links do not, however, mean that Martial was connected with the intellectual opposition to *Domitian, whose favour he assiduously courted. The references to martyrs to republican freedom (*Pompey, *Cicero, *Cato the Younger, *Brutus, Porcia, Thrasea Paetus) that occur from time to time in Martial are common in literature and by this date innocuous, or indeed had been taken over by Flavian propaganda against Nero. We do not know if Martial attempted a legal career: he expresses strong dislike of the idea, even when endorsed by another important Spaniard, the rhetorician Quintilian (2. 90), but it was normally considered the most suitable career for an intellectual on the make. In the fifteen years and more that he spent in Rome before his first publications, he was probably already gaining renown and reward through occasional verse and panegyrics of the rich and powerful. He must already have been well known to have been able in 80 to celebrate with a book of epigrams an important public event, the opening games for the new Flavian amphitheatre (see COLOSSEUM). It was probably on this occasion that *Titus gave him the *ius trium liberorum* (privileges rewarding parents of three children and granted fictitiously as a favour), an honour later confirmed by Domitian. After another two collections with particular purposes (*Xenia* and *Apophoreta*), in 86 he began publishing the series of twelve books of varied epigrams which are his principal claim to fame. They show already in existence a network of patronage and friendship involving a large cross-section of Roman upper-class society. He was also in contact with many of the most significant writers of the period: *Quintilian, *Pliny the Younger, *Silius Italicus, Frontinus, *Juvenal. There is no mention of *Statius, nor does Statius ever mention Martial, and this silence is usually taken to be a sign of personal enmity between two poets competing for the attentions of the same patrons. Martial's success, already apparently noteworthy before his poems were published in book form (2. 6), grew progressively, and he became extremely popular, being read even in the provinces by a wide public. His relationship with Domitian and the powerful *freedmen of the court also grew, as his popular success gave him a central role in the literary scene and made it more and more natural that his epigrams should be used to celebrate official events connected with imperial propaganda. Martial complains that this success did not bring him financial reward: without any copyright in his works, he was dependent on patrons whose lack of generosity towards their clients and refusal to respect the role and dignity of an intellectual and a poet he constantly laments. He represents himself, doubtless with considerable exaggeration, as just another *cliens* (client) forced to roam the streets of Rome in search of tiny recompense for the humiliating attentions that had to be paid to his patrons. For a long time he rented a house like other persons of moderate means, but he had his property at Nomentum, and from 94 at least he also had a house in Rome: he had a number of slaves, and an honorary tribunate (3. 95. 9) conferred on him the social prestige of equestrian rank. After the death of Domitian he showed no hesitation in repudiating his earlier adulation and turning to Nerva (in book 11; an anthology of books 10 and 11 was also dedicated to Nerva, but this has not survived, though its opening epigrams were placed in book 12) and later Trajan (in a second edition of book 10 from which Domitian's name was expunged, the only version to survive, and in book 12). Both his personal position and his poetry were, however, too closely involved with the court of Domitian, and in the new regime Martial must have felt less at home. Tired of city life and, as ever, nostalgic for the idealized 'natural' life in Spain that he had always set against the falsity and conventionality of Rome, he decided to return there in 98. One of his patrons, Pliny the Younger, helped him with the expenses of the journey, and even in Spain he needed to depend on the generosity of friends, especially a widow, Marcella, who gave him a house and farm which finally enabled him to realize his dream of a free and natural existence. The contradictory and unnatural life of the capital was, however, the source of his poetry, and in book 12, composed in Spain, he expresses with a new bitterness his sense of delusion and emptiness at the loss of the cultural and social stimuli that had made him a poet in the first place.

Works *Epigrammaton liber* (modern title, *Liber de spectaculis*), published AD 80. This described the games for the opening of the 'Colosseum': we possess an incomplete selection of about 30 poems from the original volume.

Xenia and *Apophoreta* (now books 13 and 14), published in December of two different years (or less likely a single year) between 83 and 85. They claim to be collections of poetic tickets, each of a single couplet in elegiacs (except for two of the 127 *Xenia* and nine of the 223 *Apophoreta*), and designed to accompany gifts at the Saturnalia festival. They present themselves as collections from which readers can select examples for their own use, and thus form part of the production of works designed to be of practical help to readers during the Saturnalian festivities (cf. Ov. *Tr.* 2. 471 ff.), but they merit literary appreciation for the ingenious brevity with which they characterize everyday objects (in the case of the *Xenia* usually food-stuffs, in the more varied and lively *Apophoreta* every type of gift).

Epigrammaton libri XII (around 1,175 poems in all), published probably as follows. Book 1 at the beginning of 96; 2 in 96–7; 3 in autumn 87, during a long stay at Imola; 4 in December 88; 5 in December 89; 6 in 90–1; 7 in December 92; 8 in January 94; 9 in autumn 94; 10 (lost first edition) in 95; 11 in December 96; 10 (second edition), April–October 98; 12, end of 101/2. Books 1, 2, 8, 9, 12 have prose prefaces.

Martial's production does sometimes include epigrams of the usual Greek type: epitaphs for friends and patrons, dedications celebrating both private and public events, and epideictic poems on contemporary or historical events, unusual happenings, or recoveries from illness. In these cases the traditional conventions are easily recognized, though the treatment may be original. In general, however, Martial's epigrams are very different from those of his Greek predecessors. His main model was *Catullus, not as a love-poet but as a writer who had brought full literary dignity to the minor poetry of autobiography and comic realism. He takes from Catullus many formal elements, above all his metres: as well as the elegiac couplets characteristic of Greek epigram and also predominant in Martial, he includes poems in hendecasyllables and scazons, both common metres in Catullus. Other metres are rare. Catullus had created a genre of minor poetry which joined the influence of the Greek epigram, iambic, and lyric traditions to the Roman tradition (itself influenced by Greek iambic poetry) of satirical verse full of personal and political polemic. Of the other models to whom Martial refers, we know little (Domitius Marsus) or scarcely anything (Albinovanus Pedo, Cornelius Lentulus Gaetulicus), but they presumably continued the Catullan tradition. Certainly this type of minor poetry on sentimental/autobiographical, satirical, polemical, or complimentary themes was widely practised at Rome both by dilettante amateurs and by 'professional' poets as occasional verse for their patrons. Martial also had important models in late Hellenistic Greek epigram (see EPIGRAM, GREEK), which had already developed the tendency towards a clever final 'point' which marks much of his work: the Neronian poet Lucillius and his imitator Nicarchus had cultivated a new type of epigram mocking physical defects and typical characters from social and professional life. Their epigrams are perhaps a little cold and cerebral, but they conclude with striking final effects of surprise.

At first Martial's poems circulated privately, especially through oral delivery (2. 6), or were published in connection with particular events (*Liber de spectaculis*) or for particular 'practical' purposes (*Xenia, Apophoreta*). When he decided to publish them in collections of varied nature divorced from their (real or supposed) occasions, they

ceased to be 'practical' verse and became 'literature', although the new form of presentation in its turn fulfilled roles as entertainment, polemic, or celebration on a higher and more lasting level. Martial's growing success with his readers encouraged the conviction that this type of minor poetry (which he always termed 'epigram', in contrast to the more varied terminology of other writers of the period) corresponded to a real need which the grander and more official genres could not satisfy. It was not a question of formal elegance or emotional intensity—the characteristics that had led *Callimachus and Catullus to affirm the greater dignity of the shorter forms—but of a need for realism, of a closer link between the pages of the text and everyday life (8. 3). The short epigram, able to treat incisively any and every aspect of life, could satisfy this need in a way that the more distant and conventional genres, which continued to produce variations on the same old mythological themes (4. 49, 9. 50, 10. 4), could not. The most typical form of the epigram in Martial, and the reason for his success, is the humorous realistic epigram on contemporary characters and behaviour which moves from witty entertainment to offer a lively and merciless picture of Roman society, revealing its multiple absurdities and contradictions through the mirror of the gestures and behaviour of the various social classes. Martial's attitude, unlike most social description in antiquity, is not moralizing, but he takes pleasure simply in recording with all his verbal art the complexities and contradictions of the spectacle of life. Both as a Spaniard born in a province which still retained a sense of the natural life of the country, and as an intellectual in a world where poets were valued less than he thought their due, Martial observes Rome from the outside. His ambitious view that his chosen poetic form, considered the lowest of all genres (12. 94. 9), might have greater validity than the great works promoted by official culture, and the merciless picture he offers of Roman society together give Martial's work a strongly anti-establishment tone, which, though frequently criticized by opponents, was well received by the general public, and eventually even by the higher classes and the court, albeit with a certain nervousness. A considerable part of his work in fact represents him as well integrated into the life of the upper classes, who were happy to see themselves described and celebrated in his verse even if at the same time it exposed many sordid aspects of the society of which these same classes were the highest representatives. The epigrams which Martial as a 'professional' poet offered to his patrons as a noble and cultured ornament of their lives give to us a particularly concrete and direct representation of Roman high society, with its houses, parks, possessions, and rituals. The many epigrams devoted to Titus and especially to Domitian are a fundamental document for the history of the imperial cult under the Flavians (see RULER-CULT). The first-person of the comic or satirical poems is mostly simply a device to give vividness to the many social observations so that they appear to have been born from one man's experience, but there is also a more autobiographical 'I', not always easy to separate from the more general figure, the personality of a restless and unsatisfied poet who is proud of his merits but disappointed in society and convinced that he could have achieved much more in different circumstances. We are offered the picture of a simple and candid individual, qualities appropriate to a poet who constantly denounces the falsity and paradoxes of a counterfeit life, a man of delicate affections and a strong sense of friendship, both often depicted in Horatian terms (see HORACE). Love (as opposed to sex) plays little part in the poems, but there are some epigrams of a subtle and sophisticated eroticism, mainly directed towards boys.

Martial's production is extremely varied, and offers both realism and fantasy, subtlety and extravagance. It is rarely that one has a sense of a poem having been written solely for piquant entertainment. His poetic language is influenced not only by Catullus but also by Horace, and above all by *Ovid; it has a cool mastery of expression which knows how to preserve the appearance of nature even when artifice is at its most obvious. His celebratory and adulatory poetry is clearly related to the precious mannerism of Flavian epideictic as we find it in some of Statius' *Silvae*, albeit with a greater lightness of touch. His realistic epigrams, while maintaining a high literary quality, open themselves to a lower and cruder language, including obscenity: in this area Martial is one of the boldest Latin poets, and, in general, many everyday objects and acts, and the words that describe them, enter Latin poetry for the first time with Martial. His most celebrated virtue is the technique with which he realizes his comic effects, either placing at the end of his epigrams a novel or surprising conclusion which throws an unexpected light on the situation being described, or else concentrating the entire sense of the poem at the end, in a pointed, antithetical, or paradoxical formulation of extraordinary density and richness of expression. See CLOSURE. This technique derives in part from later Greek epigram (see above), and also shows the same taste for point seen in contemporary rhetoric; Martial's brilliantly inventive use of it made him a model for the modern epigram, and indeed more widely for modern short poetry. The comic mechanisms that he employs, however, are not simply intellectual games, but also the means by which, on each occasion, the reality he is representing can be made the bearer of an intimate contradiction and incongruity, of a violent asymmetry with respect to reason and nature. They are thereby an original and efficacious means to give meaning to the myriad fragments of reality which had attracted his interest and which his large corpus offers in abundance. Within this vast canvas, the generic affinity with real life that epigram derives from its occasional nature is everywhere employed to the full, but realism is in productive tension with fantasy, play, and the grotesque, as the patterns of behaviour of everyday life are turned about in the brilliant paradoxes of Martial's wit.

M. Ci.

Marxism and classical antiquity Having written his doctoral dissertation on the atomic theories of Democritus and *Epicurus (1841, published 1928), Karl Marx retained a lifelong interest in classical antiquity, spicing his writings with a wealth of allusions to ancient texts.

The central concern of Marx's intellectual and practical activity was class conflict, but he never provided a definitive account of what he understood by class, and he applied the term to the ancient world in different ways. In the *Communist Manifesto* (with Engels, 1848), Marx spoke of the conflict between 'freeman and slave', but in the *Eighteenth Brumaire of Louis Bonaparte* (1852) he stressed the struggle between wealthy and poor citizens in antiquity, with slaves forming 'the purely passive pedestal for these combatants'. Later, in the first volume of *Capital* (1867), Marx stated that the class struggle in antiquity 'took the form chiefly of a contest between debtors and creditors'; but in the posthumously published third volume (1894) slave and feudal relations of production were amalgamated to form a contrast with capitalism. See CLASS STRUGGLE.

Marx gave primacy in historical explanation to material economic factors, and in his summation of his theory (preface to *Critique of Political Economy* (1859)) he outlined a schema whereby increasing productive capacities led necessarily to strains in the prevailing social relations and the emergence of a new mode of production or social formation. But in the *Grundrisse* notebooks of 1857–8 and elsewhere, he characterized pre-capitalist societies as essentially static in comparison to the revolutionary nature of capitalist production.

In the exploratory *Grundrisse* drafts (published partially in 1939, in full in 1953), Marx identified the classical city as one of four different social formations by which class society emerged from primitive communalism. Whether a relatively stable slave society may be described as the locus of class struggle has been much debated among Marxists. Since Marx defined exploitation as the extraction by one class of a portion of the value (called *Mehrwert* or 'surplus value') created by the labour of another class, class relations are assumed to be antagonistic. But the antagonism between slaves and slave-owners rarely took the form of overt collective conflict. See SLAVERY.

The authority of Stalin's unscholarly *Dialectical and Historical Materialism* (1938), relying largely on Engels's *Origins of Family, Private Property, and the State* (1884) and other writings, imposed a rigid progressivist schema on orthodox Marxist historiography. According to this 'theory of stages', each historical epoch is defined by the prevailing form of labour relation and yields inexorably to the next 'higher' stage as a result of class struggles. Thus, slave society is supposed universally to give way to feudalism, itself in turn replaced by capitalism and then communism. Since the pluralist 1960s, various models of ancient society have found supporters among Marxist historians.

In Marxist historiography, classical Greece and Rome are commonly understood to have been slave societies, characterized by a mode of production in which slave labour yields the greatest quantity of surplus value. Slavery need not, on this conception, be the predominant form of labour in respect of numbers of labourers or total quantity of production. While peasant farmers may have been responsible for the larger part of the value produced, slavery will have been the chief form in which the value produced by direct labour was expropriated by the class of large landowners, and thus the basis for the leisure and power of the dominant social class.

Considerable disagreement remains over just when and how slavery took hold in earnest as the primary mode of production in classical antiquity, and when and how it was superseded by feudal labour relations. In regard to the Athenian *democracy, for example, some Marxists have stressed the role of slavery in large-scale agriculture, but others have contended that slave labour was marginal to agricultural production and concentrated rather in household services and, importantly, the *mines. On either conception, overt class struggle consisted basically in a conflict between large landowners, who were in a position to exploit slave and other forms of dependent *labour, and smallholders who ran the risk of being degraded into the ranks of dependent labour.

Slavery did not disappear in late antiquity, but it yielded in importance to the colonate (coloni were Roman tenant farmers) and other forms of free or semi-free dependent labour. The reasons for this change are again controversial among Marxists, of whom some have attributed the decline of slavery to the higher cost of slaves (and hence the lower profitability of slavery) under the pax Romana, whereas others have pointed to the availability of alternative sources of dependent labour as a consequence of the earlier expropriation of the small Roman peasantry (itself a function, in part, of the widespread exploitation of slave labour due to Roman imperial expansion).

Marxist theories of culture have generally emphasized that ideas and institutions depend on a society's underlying relations of production (Marx and Engels, The German Ideology (1845–6); Marx's 1859 preface). Marx's own nuanced observations concerning culture were, however, obscured by the mechanical, Stalinist division between base and superstructure, whereby economic relations and interests were held to determine all aspects of culture from morality and the arts to education and law. Neo-Marxist theories, originating especially in Italy and France, have stressed instead the relative autonomy of cultural forms and transcended the purely instrumental view of ideology as a weapon wielded by the ruling class to preserve its hegemony. Marxists have also become increasingly sensitive to analyses of forms of oppression other than the narrowly economic, above all the oppression of *women and other 'outsiders'.

While Marxist historians have been particularly concerned to recover the culture of slaves and other oppressed groups in antiquity directly from the meagre evidence, Marxist critics have also attempted to uncover evidence of class conflict in canonical works of literature, understood to have been shaped by tensions and evasions having their roots in the contradictions of exploitative social relations. Studies of ideology and class relations in the great works of classical antiquity are still rare, but they have contributed substantially to a new interest in the material conditions of the production of classical art. See also LITERARY THEORY AND CLASSICAL STUDIES.   P. A. C., D. K.

Masada (see ◀Map 4, Ed▶) is a small isolated plateau 457 m. (1,500 ft.) high, on the western shore of the Dead Sea, and accessible from there only by the tortuous 'snake path'. King Herod the Great of Judaea, having secured his family in its Hasmonean fortress during the Parthian invasion of 40 BC, later made it the most spectacular of his own fortress residences, with two ornate palaces, one built onto the northern rock terraces. Archaeology supplements *Josephus' detailed description of the architecture, revealing also a garrison-block, baths, storage rooms for quantities of food and weapons, cisterns, a surrounding casemate wall, and (probably) a synagogue. After the murder of their leader, Menahem, in Jerusalem early in the Jewish Revolt, sicarii (Jewish rebels) occupied Masada; and it was the last fortress to hold out after the fall of Jerusalem, succumbing in AD 73 or 74 to a six-month siege by Flavius Silva. See JEWS. The eight Roman *camps and circumvallation are visible, as well as the earth ramp which supported a platform for artillery (see next page). Josephus' graphic account of the mass suicide of the 960 defenders, with their leader, Eleazar ben Yair, after the breaching of the wall, supposedly based on the testimony of two women survivors, has aroused some scepticism. But the remains of the revolutionaries' years of occupation of the site are at any rate extensive. These include domestic and personal objects, as well as Greek papyri and biblical texts of the Qumran type (see DEAD SEA SCROLLS).   E. M. S.; T. R.

mathematics Our knowledge of the origins and early development of mathematics among the Greeks is negligible. In Mesopotamia an advanced mathematics had existed since at least the time of Hammurabi (c.1700 BC). Characteristic of this were problems in arithmetic and algebra, but many facts of elementary geometry were known, e.g. 'Pythagoras' theorem' and the mensuration formulae for a variety of plane and solid figures. It is probable that much of this knowledge reached the Greek world at some time, but the nature of our sources makes it difficult to say what came when, particularly as independent discovery can rarely be excluded. Greek doxographic tradition ascribed the invention of geometry to the Egyptians, whence it was made known to the Greeks in the 6th cent. BC by Thales in Ionia (W. Turkey) or *Pythagoras in Magna Graecia (S. Italy). However, there was little to learn from Egypt beyond elementary mensuration formulae, and since neither Thales nor Pythagoras left writings there could be no foundation for the tradition. The most that can be said is that it is probable that 5th-cent. 'Pythagoreans' such as

Masada Air view of Masada from the north-west. Silva's camp is clearly visible (lower right), as is the Roman ramp in the middle of the west slope.

Philolaus discussed the properties of numbers in the semi-mystical way imitated by Speusippus in the 4th cent. ('Iamblichus', *Theologoumena tes arithmetikes* 82. 10 ff. de Falco).

The first concrete evidence we have concerns the mathematical activity of Hippocrates of Chios at Athens in the late 5th cent. While investigating the problem of squaring the circle (already considered a typical mathematical problem, cf. Ar. *Av.* 1005), he produced some ingenious theorems on the quadrature of lunes. The *content* of these is reasonably certain, but our knowledge of the *form* is derived via two intermediaries, Eudemus and Simplicius (*In Phys.* 60. 22 ff. Diels), and it may have been very different from the Euclidean cast in which we have it. However, these theorems exhibit the concept of proof, the greatest single contribution and the most characteristic feature of

Greek mathematics. There must have been a geometrical tradition before Hippocrates; but how old, and of what kind, we cannot say. It is possible that the arguments of Zeno of Elea in the mid-5th cent., showing that infinite division involved self-contradiction, were in part directed against contemporary mathematical procedures. It is certain that the logical difficulties he raised influenced the later course of Greek mathematics in its care to avoid infinitesimals. That this was a difficulty in the early stages is shown by Democritus asking whether the two contiguous faces of a cone cut by a plane parallel to the base are equal or unequal (DK 68 B 155). Another difficulty was the existence of irrationals, specifically the incommensurability of the diagonal of a square with its side. Both arise only when one deals with continuous magnitudes (geometry), not with discrete (arithmetic in the Greek sense). Perhaps this explains the statement of Archytas in the early 4th cent. that arithmetic can provide proofs where geometry fails (DK 47 B 4). But these logical difficulties did not inhibit the practice of geometry, as is shown by Archytas' own ingenious solution to the problem of finding two mean proportionals (which Hippocrates had already shown to be equivalent to the problem of 'doubling the cube'), and by the work of his contemporary Theaetetus, who made significant discoveries about irrationals and the five regular solids.

The difficulties were solved, or at least circumvented, by Eudoxus, *c*.360. He formulated a general theory of proportion including both commensurable and incommensurable magnitudes, and also invented the method of approach to the limit which became the standard Greek way of dealing with problems involving infinitesimals. Euclid's formulation of this is found in book 10, prop. 1: 'If from the greater of (any) two unequal magnitudes more than its half is subtracted, and from the remainder more than its half, and so on, there will (eventually) be left a magnitude less than the smaller of the original two.' Archimedes (*Quadrature of the Parabola*, pref.) quotes another formulation: 'The amount by which the greater of two unequal areas exceeds the smaller can, by being added continuously to itself, be made to exceed any given finite area.' He says that 'the earlier geometers' used this to prove among other things that pyramid and cone are one-third of prism and cylinder respectively with equal base and height. Since he tells us elsewhere (*Method* pref.) that Eudoxus was the first to prove these theorems (although Democritus had stated them), the second formulation is probably that of Eudoxus. We may guess that Eudoxus, with his interest in logical rigour, was also chiefly responsible for the thorough axiomatization of geometry as we find it in Euclid. The great interest and progress in strict deductive logic during the 4th cent. is best seen in the logical works of *Aristotle, who also provides valuable evidence for the form of contemporary geometry.

From Proclus' summary of the early history of mathematics extracted from Eudemus we know many names of mathematicians active in the 4th cent., but few details of what they did. However, Eutocius (*In Arch. circ. dim.* 78–80 Heiberg) preserves an account of a solution by Menaechmus (mid-4th cent.) to the problem of finding two mean proportionals which is the first attested use of conic sections. Aristaeus wrote a textbook on these not much later, which shows that this branch of higher geometry was rapidly developed.

With the *Elements* of Euclid we come to the first extant mathematical treatise. This, though an introductory textbook, reflects the sophistication of contemporary geometry in both form and content, but the axiomatic method of exposition necessarily obscures the historical development. A particular problem is raised by the propositions concerning the 'application of areas'—6. 28 gives a general solution of which a particular case can be derived from 2. 5 (see Heath's translation, 383): 'To a given straight line (*b*)

to apply a rectangle which shall be equal to a given area (*A*), and fall short of the rectangle formed by the straight line and one of its own sides by a square figure.' In algebraic terms this is $xy = A$, $x + y = b$ (in other words the quadratic equation $bx \div x^2 = A$ is to be solved). This is exactly what one would arrive at if one were to transform the 'normal forms' of *Babylonian numerical problems involving a quadratic equation into geometrical terms, and it is likely, although not demonstrable, that this 'algebraic geometry' is just such a transformation. If so, some knowledge of advanced Babylonian mathematics had reached Greece by the 4th cent. (the same is true of Babylonian astronomy). As well as plane and solid geometry, the *Elements* comprises number theory, which (like other contemporary branches of mathematics) had not attained the same level of systematization as pure geometry. However, some remarkable results were reached, such as the proof that there is no limit to the number of primes.

In the case of conics this deficiency was supplied by Apollonius of Perge (fl. 200 BC), who transformed the approach to the field by extending the 'application of areas' to include it in a *tour de force* of generalization. A generation before him Archimedes created new branches of mathematics by applying the axiomatic approach to statics and hydrostatics, but systematization was not his main interest. Most of his surviving work is in higher geometry, where he proves by traditional methods many theorems which are now proved by integral calculus. But his *Method* shows that he arrived at many of these results by using infinitesimals. This is only one of the ways in which his thought was so far ahead of its time that it had no effect in antiquity: thus the profound concept of a numerical system implicit in the *Sand-reckoner* has no echo in surviving literature. However, many of his results, such as the formula for the volume of a sphere and his approximation to π, became mathematical commonplaces.

The 3rd cent. was the great period of pure geometry, represented not only in the work of Apollonius and Archimedes, but also in that of a number of other mathematicians whose achievements can be judged from references by Pappus and others, although their works are lost. After this, most creative mathematics was done in other fields. Several of these were connected with *astronomy. For instance, the necessity of determining time accurately led to the development of the theory of sundials. Although the sundial itself goes back to the 5th cent. or earlier in Greece, mathematical determination of the hour-lines does not predate the 3rd cent., and the particular application to them of the type of descriptive geometry known by the ancients as *analēmma* does not seem to be older than Diodorus of Alexandria, 1st cent. BC. The most elegant example of this is found in Ptolemy's *Analemma*; earlier, cruder methods appear in the works of Heron and *Vitruvius. The related technique of stereographic projection was probably used by Hipparchus about 140 BC for mapping circles of the heavenly sphere on to a plane in order to solve certain astronomical problems (exemplified in the plane astrolabe). The same problems led to the development of spherical trigonometry, probably by Menelaus about AD 100. Plane trigonometry, with the first computed trigonometrical function (a chord table), had already been created by Hipparchus himself, also for astronomical purposes.

It is in later Greek mathematics too that we find the non-axiomatic, numerical, and algebraic techniques which are typical of Babylonian mathematics. But it is accidental that the first extant examples occur as late as the work of Heron, *c.* AD 60, for we cannot doubt that they are directly descended from Mesopotamian sources in a continuous tradition, which did not hesitate to borrow from the works of the classical mathematicians, although apparently ignored by them. It is also found in mathematical papyri, and was evidently 'popular' mathematics (in Heron it is mostly practical). A different branch of the same tradition is found in Diophantus' *Arithmetica*. This is the Greek work which comes nearest to the modern conception of algebra, although it is not a textbook on the solution of equations, but rather groups of problems, mostly of indeterminate equations. Though the roots of this lie in Mesopotamia, much of the content is probably original, and the form of exposition owes much to the Greek tradition.

In late antiquity, although there were still mathematicians, such as Pappus, Theon, and Eutocius, competent enough to edit, excerpt, and comment on the classical works, mathematics had become sterile, so that the value of these authors lies in what they preserve from earlier periods. It was only after transmission to the Islamic world (translations into Arabic began in the 9th cent.) that the ancient mathematical tradition was revived and enlarged. This happened again, even more fruitfully, in 16th-cent. Europe, after the recovery of the Greek texts, many of them interpreted in the superb Latin translations of Commandino. Rivault's edition of Archimedes with the commentary of Eutocius (1615) and Bachet's edition of Diophantus (1621) were essential to the work of the great 17th-cent. mathematicians, such as Descartes and Fermat.

G. J. T.

matriarchy has since J. J. Bachofen (*Das Mutterrecht* (1861)) been used to denote a quite hypothetical and now long discredited phase in the history of mankind when property was transmitted and descent traced through females, not males. (There has from the outset been a persistent tendency to confuse the specific phenomenon of matrilineal descent on the one hand—a system widely attested among contemporary peoples worldwide—with female supremacy in a more general and altogether less clearly defined sense on the other.) The system of descent is stated by Herodotus (1. 173) to have been operative as a going concern among the non-Greek people of Lycia (SW *Asia Minor) in his own time, but this assertion is flatly contradicted by the conventional family structure reflected in their funeral inscriptions, including well over 150 in the Lycian language itself, many of which go back to the 4th cent. BC.

The statement of *Aristotle (fr. 547 Rose; cited by Polyb. 12. 5–6) that the people of Locri Epizephyrii in southern Italy derived all their ancestral honours from women, not from men, has long been viewed as indicating a similar descent system, but in fact refers to the first generation only. It reflects the ancient tradition that the city was founded by runaway slaves who (unlike the accompanying womenfolk) necessarily and by definition lacked full civic status, from which alone honours of any kind could be derived. Crucial to the correct interpretation of Aristotle's statement (even as summarized: the verb is lacking) is the distinction between the first and second preposition, which on a casual reading it is only too easy, but mistaken, to assimilate: 'among them all ancestral distinction (is derived) from the women, not from the men ...' (πάντα τὰ διὰ προγόνων ἔνδοξα παρ' αὑτοῖς ἀπὸ τῶν γυναικῶν, οὐκ ἀπὸ τῶν ἀνδρῶν ...).

The Greek term 'gynaecocracy' ('women in control'), used much more widely, denotes not a specific set of institutions, or descent system, but a disturbing threat to, and reversal of, the state of masculine supremacy on all fronts, the normality (and desirability) of which is effectively taken for granted by ancient sources, which are throughout antiquity hardly notable for even an incipient feminism. Mythical all-female societies such as the *Amazons or the women of Aegean Lemnos appear to reflect projected male anxiety on this score rather than any sort of recollection (itself a highly questionable notion) of prehistoric data. Equally, ancient speculations as to what preceded the institution of marriage (the invention of the Athenian king Cecrops: Varro in August. *De civ. D.* 18. 9, cf. Just. *Epit.* 2. 6. 7 and the *Suda* entry for Prometheus) are simply imaginative reconstructions for which no real historical foundation was necessary. They were, however, enthusiastically taken up and even generalized in the second half of the 19th cent., which saw a plethora of universal evolutionary schemas along 'matriarchal' lines and speculative reconstruction on a breathtaking scale. (A conspicuous feature of these theories is the constant resort to such dubious (because uncontrollable) hypothetical props as the doctrine of 'survivals'.) These were, or should have been, definitively scotched by anthropological fieldwork at the beginning of the present century (e.g. B. Malinowski, *The Family among the Australian Aborigines* (1913)); regrettably, the theories themselves, though not impossible to disprove, have continued to exercise such an attraction in some quarters as to guarantee them a kind of extended though strictly unhistorical halflife.

S. G. P.

Mausoleum at Halicarnassus, the One of the *Seven Wonders of the ancient world, it was the tomb of the satrap Mausolus of Caria (reigned 377–353 BC). Begun shortly after 367, when Mausolus refounded Halicarnassus (mod. Bodrum, W. Turkey), it was finished after his wife Artemisia died in 351, and is perhaps best interpreted as his hero-shrine as city-founder. Its architect was Pythius of Priene; *Vitruvius (*De arch.* 7 pref. 12) records that he and Mausolus' court sculptor

Mausoleum Reconstruction of the Mausoleum, one of the *Seven Wonders of the ancient world. Although thoroughly Greek in execution, in spirit this lavish tomb owed more to the burials of other non-Greek rulers in W. Asia Minor, notably the Nereid Monument at *Xanthus.

Satyrus wrote a book on the building, and he and *Pliny the Elder (*HN* 36. 31) note that four other sculptors joined them: Scopas, Bryaxis, Leochares, and either Praxiteles or Timotheus. Pliny also outlines the building's form, reports that Scopas and his colleagues each took one side of it, and adds that Pythius made the chariot-group that crowned it. It stood until the 15th cent., when the Knights of Rhodes quarried it for their castle.

Excavation has supplemented and corrected the ancient accounts. The building consisted of a high podium measuring 30 × 36 m. (100 × 120 ft.), a colonnade of 36 Ionic columns, and a pyramid of 24 steps. With the crowning chariot-group, it reached a total height of 42.7 m. (140 ft.). The tomb-chamber was encased in the podium, and sacrificial remains suggest the existence of a hero-cult. The podium's steps carried quantities of freestanding sculpture (hunts, battles, audience scenes, sacrifices, and portraits), and was crowned by an *Amazon frieze; portraits stood between the columns; coffer-reliefs embellished the peristyle's ceiling; lions ringed the cornice; and the base for the chariot carried a *Centaur frieze. The chariot frieze may have ringed the interior of the tomb-chamber. See SCULPTURE, GREEK.   A. F. S.

meals Among the Greeks the times and names of meals varied at different periods. In early times breakfast (*ariston*) was taken shortly after sunrise, followed by a main meal (*deipnon*) at midday and supper (*dorpon*) in the evening. In Classical Athens two meals—a light lunch (*ariston*) and dinner (*deipnon*) in the evening—appear to have been usual. From the 4th cent. BC onwards an earlier breakfast (*akratisma*) was again added, or substituted for lunch.

Among the Romans dinner (*cena*) was eaten in the middle of the day in early times, with a light supper (*vesperna*) in the evening. Eventually an evening *cena*, often commencing in the late afternoon, became usual. Lunch (*prandium*), consisting of fish or eggs and vegetables together with wine, was eaten towards midday and replaced supper. In the morning there was a very light breakfast (*ientaculum*), which might consist of only bread and salt. Cheese and fruit were sometimes added.

The *cena*, the biggest meal of the day, was eaten after the day's work was finished. It consisted of three parts. The hors d'œuvre (*gustatio*), of eggs, shellfish, dormice, and *olives, with honeyed wine (*mulsum*), was followed by the *cena* proper, comprising up to seven courses (*fercula*), with one chief item (*caput cenae*). This might be a whole roasted pig, accompanied by smaller, but substantial courses (e.g. lampreys, turbot, roast veal). The meal ended with dessert (*mensae secundae*), consisting of snails, nuts, shellfish, and fruit. Apicius, *On the Art of Cookery* (Eng. trans. J. Edwards, 1984) describes the meals of the rich, to whom most of our information relates. The appearance of ostriches, peacocks, cranes, etc. on the tables of the rich was largely due to the search for novelty. The pseudo-*Virgilian poem *Moretum* (Eng. trans. E. J. Kenney, 1984) describes a peasant's lunch.

See COOKERY; FOOD AND DRINK.   J. R. S.

Medea, in mythology, granddaughter of *Helios, and daughter of Aeëtes, king of Colchian Aia, and his wife Eidyia; ancient writers frequently associate her name (perhaps rightly) with *mēdesthai*, 'to devise', and she became the archetypal example of the scheming, *barbarian woman. Already in our earliest testimony, *Hesiod's *Theogony*, she is associated with the completion of Jason's challenges in Aia in his quest for the golden fleece, and leaves Aia with him to live in Iolcus (vv. 992–1002), but her mastery of drugs and potions, a skill she shares with her aunt Circe, is not mentioned. This passage appears in a catalogue of goddesses who slept with mortal men, and Medea was clearly always conceived as a divine being (cf. Pind. *Pyth.* 4. 11; West on Hes. *Theog.* 992). In one Archaic legend she married *Achilles in the Elysian Fields (the paradise inhabited by the distinguished dead) after the hero's death (Ap. Rhod. *Argon.* 4. 814–15 with schol.). In the best-known account, that of *Pindar, *Pythian* 4 and *Apollonius of Rhodes, *Argonautica*, Jason succeeds in gaining the golden fleece because Medea is made to fall in love with him and supplies him with a potion to protect him in the tasks Aeëtes sets him; she then charms the dragon which guarded the fleece so that Jason could steal it. In a story first attested for Pherecydes (*FGrH* 3 F 32) and *Sophocles (fr. 343 Radt), Medea protected the Argonauts from the pursuit of the Colchians by killing her baby brother, Apsyrtus, and scattering his limbs either in the palace itself or at the later Tomis ('the cutting') on the Black Sea coast. Apollonius, however, makes Apsyrtus a young man, and Medea plots his murder by Jason on an Adriatic island (4. 395–481). On their return to Iolcus, Medea rejuvenated Jason's aged father, Aeson (first in the cyclic *Nostoi*, fr. 6 Davies, *EGF*), and in some versions also Jason himself (Page, *PMG* 548; Pherec. *FGrH* 3 F 113); as the instrument of Hera's revenge, she then punished Pelias by persuading his daughters to cut him up and boil him so that he too could be rejuvenated (cf. Braswell on Pind. *Pyth.* 4. 250 (c)). After this, Jason and Medea fled to Corinth, the setting of *Euripides' famous *Medea* which, more than any other text, influenced later traditions about and iconographic representations of Medea. If Euripides did not actually invent Medea's deliberate killing of Jason's new bride and her own children to punish Jason for abandoning her, he certainly gave it fixed form; in earlier tradition Medea had sought to make her children immortal, and in the historical period they were the object of cult in Corinth (cf. Eur. *Med.* 1378–83). Her association with that city, attested in a complex variety of stories, goes back at least to the early Archaic period; in his epic *Corinthiaca*, Eumelus (*c*.700) made Aeëtes king first of Corinth and then of Colchis, and the Corinthians subsequently summoned Jason and Medea from Iolcus (frs. 2–3 Davies, *EGF*).

Medea fled from Corinth to Athens in a chariot of the Sun (*Helios) drawn, according to a tradition at least as old as the 4th cent. BC, by dragons; there she took shelter with King Aegeus (cf. Eur. *Med.* 663–758). When Aegeus' son, *Theseus, came to Athens from Troezen, Medea recog-

Medea A vase-painter from Lucania (S. Italy) shows Medea in her dragon-drawn chariot, surrounded by rays (a reference to her grandfather *Helios). She wears a Phrygian helmet—eastern dress stressing her non-Greek, *barbarian, character.

nized him and sought to remove a threat to her position by attempting to poison him or having him sent to fight the bull of Marathon, or both; fragments of *Callimachus's *Hecale* refer to these stories.   R. L. Hu.

Medea in art Medea first appears on an *Etruscan olpe (jug) of *c*.630 BC showing the cauldron of rejuvenation, with which she tricks the Peliads (i.e. daughters of Pelias), on Attic vases from a century later, and on a Roman copy of a Classical relief, probably from the Altar of the Twelve Gods in the Athenian Agora (see ATHENS (TOPOGRAPHY)). The slaughter of the children appears mainly on south Italian vases, also a painting by Timomachus, mid-1st cent. BC (Plin. *HN* 35. 136). From the later 5th cent., Medea usually wears eastern garb and carries potions. She appears in the capture of the animated bronze man Talos. Her snake-chariot is shown. She appears with Theseus. In Roman art, she appears particularly on sarcophagi, contemplating the murder of her children.   K. W. A.

medicine (*see facing page*)

Mediterranean The Mediterranean Sea, very deep and, over substantial areas, out of sight of land, little affected by tides, and less rich in marine life than many of the world's enclosed seas (but see FISHING), provided the coherence which united the classical world. It was regarded as a unity (and distinct from the encircling Ocean) from the Archaic period; both Greeks and Romans named it as being distinctively theirs (the name Mediterranean is not found before Isidorus of Seville).

This sea represents (and has done, in the shape of its predecessor the Tethys, for some 200 million years) the complex and shifting abutment of the tectonic plates, fragmented at their edges, which make up the adjoining continents. This structural instability produces the characteristic tangled chains of high mountains interspersed with deep down-faulted basins, valleys, and plains, and an intricate coastal topography with numerous indentations, and very many islands of every size (as well as volcanoes and frequent *earthquakes).

With its inner branch the Black (Euxine) Sea, the Mediterranean is a major climatic feature (see CLIMATE): the distinctive pattern of summer drought and very variable winter rainfall promotes some uniformity in agricultural production. The sea is very prone to bad weather and notoriously changeable, but its numerous beaches and anchorages make it readily adaptable to the needs of communication and exchange. Contacts by sea have therefore shaped the orientation of most of the cultures of its seaboards at all periods, whether they have identified it with home like Xenophon's Greeks with their famous cry of '*thalatta, thalatta!*' ('the sea, the sea!': *An.* 4. 8); built their power on what was known in systematic historiography as a thalassocracy (sea power); or rejected it like some Romans and some of the Islamic states as an inimical and alien element.   N. P.

mercenaries

Greek and Hellenistic For there to be mercenaries, three conditions are necessary—*warfare, people willing to pay, and others to serve. Warfare existed almost throughout Greek history, and there were probably also always those whom love of adventure, trouble at home, or poverty made willing to serve. *Alcaeus' brother, Antimenidas, and *Xenophon himself are, perhaps, examples of the first; the latter's comrades, the Spartans Clearchus and Dracontius, of the second. But in the heyday of the city-state, when military service was the duty of all citizens, mercenaries usually only found employment with tyrants or with near eastern potentates. The pharaoh Psammetichus I of Egypt, for example, used Carians and Ionian Greeks from western *Asia Minor to seize power around 660 BC, and Pabis of Colophon and Elesibius of Teos were among those who carved their names on the statue of Rameses II at Abu Simbel, while serving Psammetichus II.

There was probably always also a market for specialist troops like Cretan archers and Rhodian slingers, particularly when warfare became more complex. Cleon, for example, took Thracian peltasts (light-armed infantrymen) to Pylos in 425 BC (Thuc. 4. 28. 4), and Cretan archers and Rhodian slingers joined the Sicilian Expedition in 415 (Thuc. 6. 43. 2). By the end of the Peloponnesian War in 404 BC there were enough Greeks eager for mercenary service for the Persian prince, Cyrus, to raise more than 10,000 for his attempt on his brother's throne, including Athenians, Spartans, Arcadians, Achaeans, Boeotians, and Thessalians, as well as the usual Cretan and Rhodian specialists.

Poverty had probably always been the main factor in driving Greeks to become mercenaries—it is significant how many were Arcadians—and the increasing number in the 4th cent. BC was probably partly due to the worsening economic situation (cf. Isoc. 4. 167 ff.). Greek mercenaries were now in great demand in Persia, and it is said that the Persian king promoted the Common Peace of 375 in order to be able to hire Greeks for the reconquest of Egypt. But Greek states also increasingly employed mercenaries. The Thessalian ruler Jason of Pherae is said to have had up to 6,000 (Xen. *Hell.* 6. 1. 5), and the 4th cent. saw many other 'tyrants' who relied on mercenaries to keep them in power, the most conspicuous being *Dionysius I of Syracuse. In the 'Sacred War' of 356–346 (see GREECE (HISTORY)), the Phocians showed how even a small state could rival larger ones provided it had the financial resources—in this case the treasures of *Delphi—to hire troops.

*Philip II and *Alexander the Great of Macedonia certainly employed mercenaries, particularly as specialists and for detached duties such as garrisons, and Alexander's Successors (Diadochi) increasingly employed mercenaries in their phalanxes (massed infantry formations) as the supply of real Macedonians declined. However, as the Hellenistic world settled down after the battle of Ipsus (301), the great powers developed supplies of phalanx-troops from their own national resources—often the

[*continued on p. 466*]

medicine

1. Introductory survey I. Western literature begins with a *disease; in the first book of *Homer's *Iliad* the god *Apollo (associated with the medical arts directly or through his Asclepiad progeny; see ASCLEPIUS) sends a plague on the Greeks camped before Troy to avenge Chryses' treatment at the hands of *Agamemnon. No attempt is made to treat the plague; the activity of doctors in the Homeric epics is generally limited to the treatment of wounds and injuries sustained in combat. Many later authorities (e.g. Cornelius Celsus, early 1st cent. AD) argued that this was a sign of the high moral standards which then prevailed. If disease had its own moral force in literature—note, for example, *Hesiod's account of diseases escaping from Pandora's jar (*Op.* 69–105), the role of illness and deformity in the *Oedipus legends, in *Sophocles' *Philoctetes*, in Attic comedy, and down to the Roman Stoic (see STOICISM) disapproval of over-reliance on medical help—the status and social function of those who treated diseases was similarly a matter for moral ambivalence. Mad doctors in Greek Middle and New *Comedy speak with strange, Doric accents—see Crates, fr. 41 Kock; Epicrates, fr. 11 Kock; Menander, *Aspis* 439 f. (Sicily was the home of an influential group of medical theorists who claimed an ultimate connection with Empedocles of Acragas, and Doric was also spoken on the eastern Aegean island of Cos and Cnidus on *Asia Minor's SW tip.) The first Greek doctor traditionally to arrive in Rome, Archagathus, was nicknamed '*carnifex*' or 'butcher'. On the other hand, Homer had allowed that 'a doctor is worth many other men' (*Il.* 11. 514), and even in post-heroic times the number of inscriptions commemorating doctors suggests to some scholars a possible problem of undersupply. Medicine was never a profession in any strict modern sense; the vast amount of medical literature which survives from the pens of educated, philosophically literate men does not necessarily present a balanced view of the range and diversity of medical traditions, which seem to have competed on more or less equal terms. The pluralism of ancient medicine is very striking. An increasing amount of archaeological evidence which has come to light this century especially from Roman sites—medical instruments, votive objects from temples, prescription stamps, wall-paintings, and so on—goes some way towards providing a fuller picture, but the gulf between the archaeological and literary study of ancient medicine remains wide.

2. Most of the literary evidence for early medical practice and theory is preserved either in the Hippocratic writings (see below) or by Galen of Pergamum (2nd cent. AD), but there is much besides in early literary texts, especially the Homeric epics. From earliest times, therapies might involve incantation (for example, to staunch the flood of blood from a wound sustained fighting a wild boar, at *Od.* 19. 452–8), or the use of analgesic drugs (e.g. by Patroclus at *Il.* 11. 837–48), or the magical herb *moly* to defend *Odysseus against Circe's witchcraft (*Od.* 10. 203–347), down to the use of amulets and charms by the so-called 'purifiers' (*kathartai*) and 'mages' (*magoi*: see MAGIC). Medical treatment and advice was also supplied by drug-sellers (*pharmakopōlai*), 'root-cutters' (*rizotomoi*), midwives (*maiai*), gymnastic trainers, and surgeons. In the absence of formal qualifications, anyone could offer medical services, and the early literary evidence for medical practice shows doctors working hard to distinguish their own ideas and treatments from those of their competitors. Some Hippocratic treatises, like *On the Sacred Disease*, indicate by their hostility the importance of medical services offered by these root-cutters, drug-sellers, and purveyors of amulets, incantations, and charms. If the traditional picture of rational Hippocratic medicine dominating ancient medical practice still attracts many modern scholars, the reality seems to have been a good deal more complicated. See MAGIC.

3. Various authorities, both ancient and modern (starting with *Herodotus), have sought links with Egypt to explain the origins of certain medical practices, especially surgery, in the Greek world. Others have found links with the near east, and with Babylonian medicine in particular, although these have proved very difficult to prove. Some argue that the Hellenistic doctors working in *Alexandria

continued to be influenced by Egyptian traditional medicine in the 4th and 3rd cents. BC. In the 5th cent. BC, when Herodotus told (3. 129–37) the story of *Darius I's Greek physician, Democedes of Croton, the really surprising feature of his career—apart from its conspicuous success—was Democedes' technical superiority over the Egyptian doctors.

4. Medical practitioners often took their skills from town to town, visiting communities in the same way, ironically enough, as the diseases they sought to treat. (The word 'epidemic' (from *epidēmeō*) means 'visitation'.) Little is known of the careers of such doctors. *Thucydides' account of the great *plague at Athens (2. 47) provides one of our few non-medical accounts of reaction to a great public crisis; he has little to say, however, about the doctors who treated the plague beyond the important observation that they were often the first to succumb. Herodotus is aware of the practice followed by various Greek states of hiring public physicians—he notes that Democedes held such a position at Aegina—but very little is known of the exact role of these doctors. The question of just how public these public physicians were is a difficult one; there is little evidence, for instance, to indicate that they were hired to provide free care for the citizenry, and some scholars simply see some kind of semi-official recognition of medical status lying behind these positions.

5. Nor is it clear how common were contracts and agreements like those contained in the Hippocratic Oath. The Oath is probably aimed at a specific, and perhaps rather small, group of doctors—in it, the doctor swears by Apollo, by Health (Hygieia), and Panacea amongst other things to revere his teacher and his teacher's family, and never to administer poison, use the knife, abuse his patients, or breach their confidences. The Oath could be as much a symptom of general medical anarchy, as of a coherent acceptance of general standards. Anyone could choose to practise; some were ex-slaves but many were free-born. In Rome, where traditional Italian medicine competed with foreign imports to an unknown extent, many doctors were Greek. Sometimes training might take the form of an apprenticeship to another doctor, attendance at medical lectures, or even at public anatomical demonstrations.

6. In the 1st cent. AD, Aulus Cornelius Celsus reiterated the traditional division of medical therapy into dietetics, pharmacology, and surgery. The use of exercise and the regulation of one's way of life was traditionally associated with the training of athletes and gymnasts. Some dietetic lore is preserved outside medical writings in cookery books like that of the Roman Apicius and the Greek epicure Athenaeus of Naucratis. Surgery too, was employed from earliest times although dangers in its use meant that the more invasive procedures were generally used as a last resort. The drug lore contained in book 9 of Theophrastus' *Historia plantarum* (written probably in the 4th cent. BC) gives a good idea of the persistence of certain beliefs about the magical powers of drugs and herbs, but Theophrastus also preserves a good deal of information new and old about the very real powers of medicinal plants. This is equally the case with the much later *Materia medica* of Dioscorides (fl. *c.* AD 60). See BOTANY.

2. Temple medicine Shrines and temples to the god *Asclepius formed one important focus for religious medicine. Most of the detailed evidence we have for temple medicine comes from later writers and inscriptions; and it is not altogether clear when Asclepius, rather than his father Apollo, began to become the object of veneration. That the practice of temple medicine was widespread in the 5th and 4th cents. BC, however, seems clear from the extended parody in *Aristophanes' *Plutus* (653–744). The most important temple was at Epidaurus (eastern *Peloponnese). Many inscriptions from here detail the practical help and advice that the faithful received from the god as they slept in the temple precincts (it was called *egkoimēsis*, Lat. *incubatio*, 'incubation': see Diod. Sic. 1. 53). All manner of problems were solved here, not all of them strictly medical—monuments erected by grateful patients record cures for lameness, baldness, infestations with worms, blindness, aphasia, and snakebite. One case involves the god repairing a broken wine-cup brought to the temple by a worried slave. It is widely believed that the development of the cult of Asclepius at Epidaurus received a new impetus after the great plague at Athens.

Relations between temple medicine and the medicine of the Hippocratic corpus are difficult to determine. One later tradition has it that disciples of Hippocrates established a rival temple to Asclepius on Cos but there is considerable disagreement over the antiquity of the cult here; there was another at Tricca in *Thessaly, and throughout antiquity the medical, magical, and religious seem to have coexisted in this context. In Greek and Roman temple sites, many stone and terracotta votive objects survive—models of affected parts of the body which the god was able to cure. Important later accounts of experiences of temple medicine are preserved in the *Sacred Orations* of Aelius Aristides (2nd cent. AD), and the importance of *dreams is shown by the *Onirocritica* of Artemidorus of Daldis (2nd cent. AD). In many cases, it seems, diagnoses of physicians could be rejected in favour of those acquired through dreams.

3. Early medical theory Little is known about the activities of early—pre-Hippocratic—theorists who offered physiological and pathological accounts of the human body. Certain Presocratic philosophers had well-attested interests in medical theory; most important perhaps was Empedocles of Acragas, a version of whose four-element theory was applied to the basic fluid constituents in the body. It is mirrored in a dominant strain of Hippocratic humoral pathology, as well as in the physiological theories of *Plato (in the *Timaeus*) and, in all probability, those of Philistion of Locri. Speculative theories about the origins of man, human reproduction, the internal structure of the body, and the nature of various biological processes are a feature of the cosmologies of Anaxagoras and Diogenes of Apollonia amongst others. An early statement of the idea that health can be ascribed to some kind of balanced state of affairs in the body (the political undertone is significant) is attributed to Alcmaeon of Croton, who is also credited (controversially) with some of the the first anatomical work based on dissection. Nearly all ancient doctors ascribed disease to an imbalance of some kind or other, and Plato's pathological theory in the *Timaeus* (e.g. at 82a) similarly ascribes certain conditions to 'surfeit' or 'lack'.

4. Hippocratic medicine 1. The large and heterogeneous corpus of writings which bears the name of Hippocrates forms the core of our literary evidence for early Greek medicine. It was always agreed, even in antiquity, that the writings were not all by one person, even though some favoured Hippocratic authorship of, or inspiration behind, certain treatises. Galen, for instance, argued that the treatise *On the Nature of Man*, which is partly the work of Polybus, largely represented the views of Hippocrates himself and that other works similar in character could be attributed to Hippocrates' own medical school on Cos. Galen, in fact, may well have encouraged the idea that there are two distinct intellectual strains in the corpus, one 'Hippocratic', 'Coan', philosophically refined, the other more primitive, less theoretically sophisticated, and originating from a rival medical school at Cnidus. This model of medical thought has come under attack in recent years, partly due to more detailed work on the ways in which Galen reacted to his predecessors, and partly through closer analysis of these supposedly 'Cnidian' works. Moreover, although certain places seem to have been a focus for medical activity— various places in Magna Graecia (the Greek settlements of southern Italy) and around *Cyrene especially, as well as Cos and Cnidus—it is not at all clear that they were sites of schools in any formal sense. Intellectually and culturally, the Hippocratic corpus shows signs of influence from all areas of Greek life, not just medical life.

2. The contents of the Hippocratic corpus had apparently stabilized by the time of the Roman emperor *Hadrian, when Artemidorus Capito put together a canon of Hippocratic works. Galen still felt the need to write a treatise (now lost) entitled *The Genuine Hippocratic Treatises*. It seems that the corpus in its present form dates from this time. In common with several other ancient (and modern) authorities, the Hippocratic lexicographer Erotian divided the writings into five categories. These form a useful framework for a brief survey.

(*a*) 'Semiotic' works
(*b*) Aetiological and physiological works
(*c*) Therapeutic works: Surgery; Regimen; Pharmacology
(*d*) 'Mixed' works (treatises which are summaries of others, or compilations)
(*e*) Works on the art of medicine (dealing with medical method, knowledge, deontology)

(*a*) **Semiotic works**

'Expertise at making prognoses seems to me one of the best things for a doctor' (*Prognostic* 1). The ability to interpret the signs presented by the patient and the patient's circumstances is regarded as a skill of the first importance throughout the corpus. The patient, understandably enough, was interested solely in the outcome of the disease, or the preservation of his health. Hippocratic diagnosis had to be based on careful study of a wide range of different phenomena, from the general—age, climate, sex, way of life—to the very specific. The author of *Prognostic* (ch. 2) offers the following advice about observing an acute, potentially fatal, case, which came later to be known as the *Hippocratic facies*: 'In acute diseases, the doctor needs to pursue his investigation thus: first, examine the face of the patient to see if it resembles the face of healthy people, and in particular if it is as it is normally. Such a resemblance is a very good sign; the opposite a very grave one. The opposite signs might appear as a sharp nose, hollow eyes, sunken temples, cold ears drawn in with their lobes turned outwards, and skin hard around the face, tight, and desiccated. The colour of the whole face is pale or dark. If the face is like this at the beginning of the disease, and if one cannot yet build up a complete picture on the basis of the other signs, the doctor needs to ask if the man is having trouble sleeping, if his bowels are disturbed, or if he is hungry. If he answers "yes" to any of these, then the danger can be considered less serious. The crisis occurs after a day and a night, if it is through these causes that the face appears thus. But if the patient does not answer "yes", and if recovery does not take place within the above-mentioned period, one should realize that it is a sign of death.' Apart from *Prognostic*, *Prorrhetic* is an important work in this class, and there is much relevant material, especially on charting the likely course of incurable diseases, in the case histories of the *Epidemics*. Health faddists are catered for in works like *Regimen in Health*, which stand at the head of a long tradition of similar handbooks outlining precepts for healthy living.

(*b*) **Physiology**

Hippocratic doctors, by and large, were committed to the idea that the phenomena of health and disease are explicable in the same way as other natural phenomena. Many treatises, notably *On the Nature of Man*, *Regimen*, *On Fleshes*, *On the Sacred Disease*, and *On Breaths* offer answers to the basic questions that most divided ancient doctors—how is the body constructed? how is it generated? what makes it prey to disease? what is disease? and so on. Whilst concepts of balance and morbid imbalance underly many pathological theories, the nature of the balance and the elements implicated in it could be explained in many ways. For the author of *On the Nature of Man*, the balance was one of fluids or 'juices' in the body ('humours'). In this treatise, the humours are blood, yellow bile, black bile, and phlegm, and they are linked to the four elements earth, air, fire, and water, the four qualities associated with the elements, and the four seasons. Predominance of yellow bile and phlegm is particularly associated with disease. This is not the only humoral pathological system in the Hippocratic corpus— but its adoption and adaptation by Galen much later ensured its subsequent association with 'true' Hippocratic doctrine. *On the Nature of Man* opens with a blistering attack on those who explain disease by reference to one causal agent. The treatise *On Breaths*, for example, attributes all disease to 'breaths'. This debate about the extent to which the search for causes can be narrowed down continued throughout antiquity. Theoretical disagreements apart, the names and symptoms of the major diseases were broadly accepted by Hippocratic doctors. Diseases tended to be named after the affected part, or the seat of the most significant symptoms; so pneumonia (*pneumōn*, 'lung'), pleurisy (*pleura*, 'sides'), hepatitis (*hēpar*, 'liver'), arthritis (*arthron*, 'joint'), and so on; this was even the case for those doctors (like the later Methodists (see §5. 3 below)), who either took a whole-body view of all disease, or denied altogether that diseases exist as specific entities. Difficulties could arise over fundamental terminological disagreements: phrenitis, for example, was named after the *phrēn*, which stood at various times for the diaphragm, the cerebral membranes, and even the lungs.

(c) Therapeutic works

Hippocratic therapy took many forms: treatises like *On Ancient Medicine* and *Airs, Waters, Places* stress the historical and practical debt of medicine to dietetics, which focused attention on the whole of the patient's way of life, diet, and environment. The applications of dietetics were not confined to the sick; 'precepts of health' showed the way to the prevention of disease. Yet the drug-based treatment of disease is also an important strand in Hippocratic therapy. Pharmaceutical therapies and tests (for example, for pregnancy or fertility) are especially characteristic of the gynaecological treatises (see *Diseases of Women* 1–2, *On the Nature of Woman*). Much ingenuity was expended in devising drugs to promote and test for conception—*On Barren Women* provides many examples. Explanations of why these treatments work tell us much about ancient speculative views on the internal structure of the female body (see GYNAECOLOGY). Surgery and invasive physical manipulation were also widely used, although the status of surgery was problematic because of the dangers involved. Several treatises deal with methods of reducing dislocations (*Joints, Instruments of Reduction, Fractures*), bandaging (*In the Surgery*), excision of haemorrhoids (*Haemorrhoids*), treatment of cranial trauma (*Wounds in the Head*), surgical removal of the dead foetus (*Excision of the Foetus*), and so on.

(d) 'Mixed' works

Erotian's category of 'mixed' works includes practical compendia of material dealt with under the other headings. The seven books of *Epidemics* fell into this category, as did the highly influential and pithy summaries of Hippocratic practice contained in the *Aphorisms*.

(e) The art of medicine

Authors of many of the theoretical works in the corpus take care to describe their own epistemological as well as practical methods. They often distinguish their enterprises from those of philosophers on one side, and alternative healers on the other. The author of the treatise *On Ancient Medicine* insists that medicine cannot be approached in the same way as those subjects which 'stand in need of an empty postulate', an attack which seems to be directed at cosmologists and meteorologists, but may also be directed at doctors tempted to import fledgling deductive methods from geometry and mathematics into medicine. The constant concern with establishing the status of medicine as a *technē*, an art, gives us some idea how tenuous this status could be. The difficulty of the task faced by the author of *On Ancient Medicine* can be seen in the use of postulates that he himself seems to make later in the treatise, when he privileges the physiological position of certain qualities such as bitter and sweet in the body. In addition to these studies, a number of works deal with the problem of how the doctor should behave with his patients and in his dealings with society generally (e.g. *In the Surgery*).

5. From the Hippocratics to Galen 1. The dominating figure of Galen eclipsed many of his predecessors, and very little Hellenistic medical writing survives intact. None the less, recent work on Hellenistic and Graeco-Roman medicine has brought to light a great deal of new material and goes some way towards rediscovering the 500-odd years of lost medical research. After the conquests of *Alexander the Great, medicine like so much else spread east to the great new centres of learning and research in the Aegean, Egypt, and Asia Minor whilst remaining in its traditional homes in the west. Medical theorists and doctors like Diocles of Carystus, Plistonicus, Phylotimus, Praxagoras of Cos, Mnesitheus, and Dieuches of Athens were still important enough in the 2nd cent. AD to be cited by Galen. Diocles' anatomy and Praxagoras' study of the diagnostic value of the pulse and the nature of its origins in the blood-vascular system were of great importance. Aristotle's pioneering work on scientific method, psychology, and zoology proved central to much post-Hippocratic medical research, even if figures like Galen insisted that Aristotle was heavily dependent on Hippocrates for his medical and on Plato for the philosophical details. (The physiology of Plato's *Timaeus* proved a rich source of theory throughout the rest of antiquity.) Aristotle's famous exhortations to anatomical research found particular resonances in Ptolemaic Alexandria, where Herophilus and Erasistratus made extraordinary progress in *anatomy and physiology. It seems likely that they even employed highly controversial techniques such as human *vivisection, using condemned criminals as subjects. Herophilus found the Greek language insufficient to the task of describing his discoveries, and he is credited with a series of anatomical coinages, several of which remain in use today. He undertook pioneering work on the anatomy of the eyes, on neural anatomy, and the male and female reproductive systems, and his work on the diagnostic use of the pulse, following on from Praxagoras, is highly elaborate.

2. If most of the doctors mentioned immediately above subscribed to various types of humoral system (though there is some doubt about Herophilus), Erasistratus developed or adopted a strikingly different theory which shows an awareness of post-Aristotelian physical theory. Erasistratus argued that the body is composed of a 'threefold web' of elemental nerve, vein, and artery 'perceptible to the intellect'. The activities of macroscopic nerves, veins, and arteries also figure prominently in his pathological system, which accounted for disease in terms of the morbid seepage of blood into the arteries through anastomoses (a term especially associated with his theory) in their walls. Veins, for him, distributed blood through the body, and arteries the vital *pneuma* (inspired air) which had its origins in inspired air. Erasistratus' anatomical work, in harness with his physical theory, supported him in his conviction that the arteries did not naturally carry blood—a view quite conceivably supported by inspection of corpses. The blood we see in the arteries on dissection rushes in to prevent the formation of an unnatural vacuum, as *pneuma* leaves through the point at which the incision is made. This view was fiercely attacked by Galen in his treatise *On Whether Blood is Naturally Contained in the Arteries*.

3. The literary evidence for later Hellenistic medicine also documents the rise of sectarian groups (*haireseis*) of doctors who espoused different methodological approaches to medicine. If in practice the pool of treatments on which they drew remained more or less constant, the debate over how medicine should be studied, which can be discerned in much Hippocratic writing, became far more vigorous. Much of what is known about their activities is known through Galen; he insisted that he was himself a slave to no sect, often affecting what appears a rather disingenuous respect for 'common sense'. The so-called 'Empiricists', who espoused a medicine in which theory and speculation about diseases had no place, determined treatments on the basis of earlier experience of similar conditions, research into other doctors' experience, and, in special cases, a kind of analogical inference which justified thinking that what works for a complaint afflicting one part of the body may well work on a similar affection in another part. The complex details of their medical method are preserved mainly by Galen in a series of treatises on Empiricism, *On Medical Experience*, *Outline of Empiricism*, and *On Sects for Beginners*. These doctors, including figures like Serapion and Heraclides of Tarentum, saw themselves as quite apart from so-called rationalist or dogmatic physicians who were committed to the value of theory in various ways. This latter group was never strictly a sect—adherents of medical theories hardly make up a coherent group—and frequently the term 'dogmatic' is used in a critical sense.

One sect which went so far as to name itself after its method became particularly successful in Rome. 'Methodism' was grounded on the idea that the whole of the diseased body (and not just the affected part) presents one of two morbid, phenomenally evident states or 'communities', one called 'stricture', the other 'flux'. (Some Methodists allowed a third state, a mixture of the other two.) Theoretical reflection on the origins of these states was unnecessary for many Methodists, and the appropriate treatment followed directly on the correct identification of the general state of the whole body. The most famous Methodist physician was Soranus of Ephesus (early 2nd cent. AD); his work on gynaecology survives in the original Greek, and there is a paraphrastic version of his treatises *On Acute and Chronic Diseases* by Caelius Aurelianus, a 6th-cent. Methodist.

4. However much the medical sects may appear to us as a series of monolithic entities, it should be stressed that sectarian orthodoxy was rare, and a great deal of theoretical and practical variation can be found in all the groupings, including the less well known like the Pneumatists and other more eclectic groups. (It might reasonably be thought that Soranus' Methodism, for instance, would explicitly discourage the anatomical investigation of the human body on the ground that this is an unnecessary luxury in view of the fact that indications for treatment simply follow on from correct visual recognition of the prevailing morbid state. Yet Soranus' highly detailed gynaecological research shows that his methodological faith did not stifle his curiosity.) It should equally be stressed that not all doctors were sectarian; evidence from inscriptions points to the existence of large numbers of independent medical practitioners who were very likely to have been largely innocent of the theoretical debates going on in other quarters. Mention should also be made at this point of the important anatomical work of Rufus of Ephesus.

6. Galen of Pergamum (probably AD 129–99) dominates later Greek medicine, and indeed the whole subsequent western medical tradition. He is our most important source for post-Hippocratic medicine, and the modern appreciation of Hippocratic medicine owes much to his own version of Hippocratic doctrine. A daunting amount of his work survives—nearly three million words in Greek alone—and much remains to be edited and translated to modern standards. He wrote several guides to his own works, one of which, *On the Order of his own Books*, provides a convenient starting-point for this briefest of surveys. Here, surprisingly perhaps, he stresses before anything else the importance of what he calls 'demonstrative knowledge' (*epistēmē apodeiktikē*) in all medical work. He advises those embarking on medical studies to examine the methodological weakness of the medical sectarians who lack, he claims, the logical equipment necessary to tell truth from fiction. (Galen's bluff and bluster and his claim to possess the means to real knowledge need to be treated with caution, but his logical skill is indeed considerable.) He then recommends an introductory study of anatomy and basic physiology. Of his own works which survive, he recommends that anatomy should begin with *On Pulses for Beginners*, and *On Bones for Beginners*, culminating in the great teleological analysis of the human body, *On the Usefulness of the Parts*. Important evidence for the nature of Galen's debt to the Hippocratics, Plato, Aristotle, and the Stoics is presented in *On the Doctrines of Hippocrates and Plato*, in which Galen investigates in very general terms the 'physical and psychical faculties of the body'. *On the Natural Faculties* presents Galen's reaction to the physiology of his Hellenistic medical predecessors.

Galen's physiological theory is based on a four-humour system which closely resembles the theory of the Hippocratic treatise *On the Nature of Man*, although many details of Galen's version draw on Stoic mixture theory—see *On the Elements according to Hippocrates* and *On Mixtures*. The application of the theory to the behaviour of drugs is dealt with in a series of extensive pharmacological treatises which draw together drug lore and theory from a variety of earlier sources. Galen is able to draw on all kinds of pharmacological writers, from the Greek Empiricist Heraclides of Tarentum to Dioscorides, Asclepiades the Pharmacist, and the Roman Scribonius Largus.

7. After Galen important medical compendiums were compiled by Oribasius, Aetius of Amida, Paul of Aegina, Marcellus of Bordeaux, and Alexander of Tralles, to name only a few. Modern scholarship is only now beginning to re-examine these figures in any detail.

See also: ANATOMY AND PHYSIOLOGY; DISEASE; GYNAECOLOGY; VIVISECTION.   J. T. V.

descendants of Greek mercenary settlers—and most mercenaries of the 3rd and 2nd cents. BC appear to have been, once again, light-armed and specialist troops.   J. F. La.

Roman Contact with foreign powers such as *Carthage and Macedon exposed Rome's weakness in cavalry and light-armed troops. This deficiency she remedied principally by obtaining contingents outside Italy. Some came from independent allies like Masinissa of Numidia, others were raised by forced levies or paid as mercenaries. Gauls served in the First Punic War, 600 Cretan archers fought at Lake Trasimene (217 BC), Numidian cavalry turned the scales at Zama (202). During the next two centuries the number and variety of contingents increased. Spain was a favourite recruiting-ground for cavalry and light infantry, while *Caesar obtained his cavalry from Numidia, Gaul, and Germany, and his archers and slingers from Numidia, Crete, and the Balearic Islands.

Under the Principate such troops became formalized within the *auxilia* (auxiliary units), but supplementary irregular troops were always employed on campaign (Germans, Cantabrians, Dacians, Palmyrenes, Sarmatians, Arabs, Armenians, Moors, etc.).   J. C. N. C.

Mercury (Mercurius), patron god of circulation, known as well in Campania (at Capua and in the *Falernus ager*) and Etruria (the *Etruscan deity Turms). According to ancient tradition, in 495 BC Mercury received an official temple on the SW slope of the Aventine, its anniversary falling on 15 May (Festus 135. 4 Lindsay). He was foreign in origin in the view of some scholars, but others see him as an Italic and Roman deity. On any view his cult was old, and it had close links with shopkeepers and transporters of goods, notably grain; also, at the *lectisternium* (ritual banquet of the gods) of 399 BC he was associated with *Neptune, and, at that of 217 BC, with Ceres. But his function was not simply the protection of businessmen or 'the divine power inherent in *merx* [merchandise]'. If all the evidence for his cult, notably Ovid, *Fast.* 5. 681–90, and *ILS* 3200, is taken together, he emerges, like the Greek *Hermes, as the patron god of circulation, the movement of goods, people, and words and their roles. Mediator between gods and mortals, between the dead and the living, and always in motion, Mercury is also a deceiver, since he moves on the boundaries and in the intervening space; he is patron of the shopkeeper as much as the trader, the traveller as well as the brigand (see BRIGANDAGE). Hence it is not astonishing that *Horace, with a certain malice, assigns to *Augustus the traits of this ambiguous mediator (*Carm.* 1. 2. 41 ff.).   J. Sch.

Messal(l)ina (Valeria Messal(l)ina), great-granddaughter of *Augustus' sister Octavia on her father's and mother's sides, was born before AD 20. In AD 39 or 40 she married her second cousin *Claudius, then *c.*50 years old, and bore him two children, Claudia Octavia and Britannicus. Claudius alone was blind to her sexual profligacy (which *Juvenal travestied in Satires 6 and 10), even to her eventual partici-

pation in the formalities of a marriage service with the consul-designate Gaius Silius in AD 48. The *freedman Narcissus turned against her and, while Claudius was in a state of stunned incredulity, ensured that an executioner was sent. Encouraged by her mother Domitia Lepida, she committed suicide.   J. P. B.; M. T. G.

metics As the Greek *polis* evolved it sought to differentiate, amongst its inhabitants, between insiders and outsiders. Insiders *par excellence* were its own members, the citizens; palpable outsiders were its slaves, indigenous or imported (see SLAVERY); but this simple dichotomy would have sufficed only for communities like *Sparta which discouraged immigration. Elsewhere it was necessary to recognize free persons who lived, temporarily or permanently, in the *polis* without becoming its citizens. Several *-oikos* ('abode') words are attested of such persons, with *metoikos* ('changing one's abode', i.e. foreign settler, 'metic') most common. The precise nature and complexity of metic-status doubtless varied from place to place; evidence approaches adequacy only for Athens, atypical in its allure and, consequently, the numbers of those who succumbed thereto (half the size of the (reduced) citizen body of *c.*313 BC (Ath. 272c); perhaps proportionately larger in the 5th cent. BC (R. Duncan-Jones, *Chiron* 1980, 101 ff.)). With *Solon having created only indirect incentives to immigration, Athenian metic-status probably owes its formal origins to *Cleisthenes, after whom the presence of metics was recognized in law and could develop in its details at both city and local level. The dividing line between visitors and residents seems to have been drawn on a common-sense basis in the 5th cent. BC but became more mechanical in the 4th (thus P. Gauthier *Symbola* (1972), ch. 3 and D. Whitehead, *The Ideology of the Athenian Metic* (1977); *contra*, E. Lévy, in L. Raoul (ed.), *L'Étranger dans le monde grec* (1987), 47 ff.). Definition as a metic brought some privileges but many burdens, largely fiscal (including the *metoikion*, 'poll-tax') and military; various exemptions came with higher-status niches such as *isotelēs*. Socio-economically, Athens' metics were highly diverse, and contemporary attitudes to their presence deeply ambivalent.   D. W.

mineralogy The modern term for the systematic study of the character and diversity of chemical elements and compounds which occur naturally within the earth. How far the Greeks could be said to have engaged in this kind of study is highly questionable, yet there is evidence that the diversity of mineral substances was recognized, and names given to a few minerals. There is no doubt that the ancients had experience of the use of ores, precious and semi-precious stones, and building materials. Archaeological evidence for ancient mining and metallurgy, however, suggests degrees of technical sophistication and understanding which are not equally evident in the surviving literary sources.

Epistemologically based hierarchies of nature like those of *Plato and, to a lesser extent, *Aristotle seem effectively to have discouraged the systematic investigation of anything but the most unusual, valuable, or beautiful of mineral substances. Yet speculation about the origins of earth-materials in general is a feature of certain Presocratic cosmologies (notably those of Anaximenes, Heraclitus, Anaxagoras, and Empedocles). There is little sign of any generally accepted distinction between rocks and minerals, but Plato (*Ti.* 59b–60c) distinguishes between the modes of formation of rocks (*petrai*) and metals. He argues that metals (of which the most perfect is gold) are formed when a fusible type of water melts and then congeals in the earth. Varying degrees of admixture with earth explain the variety of the products of the process. Stones are formed when earth is compressed by the air above it. At the end of book 3 of the *Meteorology*, Aristotle divides substances found in the earth into metals (*metalleuta*), characterized by their fusibility and ductility and which result from the action of his 'vaporous exhalation', and 'things dug up' (*orukta*), including what he calls the 'infusible stones'—ochre, sulphur, etc.—which result from the burning action of the so-called dry and fiery exhalation on the earth.

Aristotle's successor Theophrastus preserves the distinction between substances which originate in water and in earth. His short treatise *On Stones*, companion to a lost treatise on metals to which he refers in passing, covers stones and earth-materials with a particular interest in the rare and unusual. He discusses the properties of mineral substances and stones—particularly those endowed with special qualities—without attempting any systematic classification. By modern standards, the number of 'stones' he mentions is remarkably small.

Much of Theophrastus' research was used later by *Pliny the Elder, in books 33–7 of the *Natural History*. Book 33 deals with precious metals, their origins, modes of extraction, and uses. Book 34 covers less valuable metals and alloys, like copper, lead, iron, and bronze, and Book 35 begins the coverage of earths, focusing first on their utility as artists' pigments. Book 36 treats stone, especially architecturally useful varieties like marble, limestone, granite, before moving on to more unusual, in some cases marvellous, substances like the lodestone, and the 'eagle stone'. The introduction of Hellenistic material on the magical and extraordinary properties of certain stones, especially gems, is a striking feature of book 37, which also contains (37. 42) the first surviving account of the true origin of amber. This tradition is preserved and developed in the later, often mystical, Lapidaries. Pedanius Dioscorides (1st cent. AD) treats minerals with medicinal importance in the fifth book of his *Materia medica*, as does Galen of Pergamum (2nd cent. AD) in his great pharmacological treatises.   J. T. V.

Minerva, an Italian goddess of handicrafts, widely worshipped and regularly identified with *Athena. Altheim (*RE* 'Minerva') believes her actually to be Athena, borrowed early through Etruria (see ETRUSCANS); but most scholars think her indigenous, and connect her name with the root of *meminisse* ('to remember') etc. At all events there is no trace of her cult in Rome before the introduction of the Capitoline Triad, where she appears with *Jupiter and *Juno in an Etruscan grouping. Apart from this she was worshipped in a (possibly) very ancient shrine on the Caelian hill, which was called Minerva Capta by *Ovid, from the taking of Falerii in 241 BC (Ov. *Fast.* 3. 835 ff.). But it seems that this name was derived from a statue captured in Falerii and offered to the Caelian Minerva. A much more important cult lay *extra pomerium* ('outside the *pomerium*', or religious boundary) on the Aventine hill; it was supposedly vowed in 263 or 262 BC. The Aventine Minerva was of Greek origin and was the headquarters of a guild of writers and actors during the Second Punic War (Festus 446. 26 ff. Lindsay), and seems to have been generally the centre of organizations of skilled craftsmen. Minerva's worship spread at the expense of *Mars himself, the Quinquatrus coming to be considered her festival, apparently because it was the *natalis* ('anniversary') of her temple (Ov. *Fast.* 3. 812); it was also extended to five days, from a misunderstanding of the meaning ('fifth day after' a given date; see Frazer on Ov. *Fast.* 3. 812). 13 June was called the *Quinquatrus minusculae* ('Lesser Quinquatrus') and was the special feast-day of the professional flute-players (*tibicines*; cf. Ov. *Fast.* 6. 651 ff., and G. Dumézil, *Mythe et épopée* 3 (1973)).   H. J. R.; J. Sch.

mines and mining

Greek Greeks obtained gold and silver and 'utility' metals, copper, tin (for bronze), iron, and lead by mining and by trade; *colonization extended their scope for both. Literary evidence for mining is mainly historical not technical; later references to Egyptian and Roman methods are only partly applicable. Epigraphical, archaeological, and scientific evidence has extended knowledge of industrial organization and techniques, and proved the early exploitation of certain ore-fields. Climate, geography, and geology dictated methods: panning for gold (as in Asia Minor and Black Sea regions) and hushing of (applying jets of water to) placer (alluvial) deposits were rarely practicable in Greece and its islands, while low rainfall reduced mine-drainage problems and accounted for the elaborate catchment channels, cisterns, and ore-washeries designed to recycle water in the Laurium area SE of Athens. There the Athenian lead-silver mines were extremely extensive (copper and iron ores were also exploited). The rural settlement of Thoricus has revealed sherd evidence for mining in the early bronze age (third millennium BC), late Mycenaean (see MYCENAEAN CIVILIZATION), and late Roman times, with marks of prehistoric hammer-stones and later metal chisels and picks. Sporadic mining continued in Laurium till the boom period of the 5th and 4th cents. BC, with small-scale working and re-exploitation of minehead and furnace spoil-heaps thereafter. Opencast pits, oblique and vertical shafts (with cuttings for ladders, stagings, and windlasses), and underground galleries (some only 1 m. (39 in.) high) and chambers mark hillsides and valleys, along with extensive surface-works (cisterns, washeries), some in seemingly haphazard juxtaposition, others segregated in compounds. Cycladic Siphnos, prosperous and famed for its gold- and silver-mines in Archaic times, has also produced evidence for silver-lead mining in the early bronze age, with opencast pits, trenches, shafts, ovoid galleries, and chambers, repacked ritually on abandonment. In northern Greece also, in Macedonia and Thrace (Mt. Pangaeus) and on Thasos, gold and silver were mined. Control of the mainland mines yielded *Philip II of Macedon an income of 1,000 talents annually. See SLAVERY.

J. E. J.

Roman Imperial expansion gave Rome control over a wide variety of mineral resources. The Iberian peninsula (see SPAIN), *Gaul (Transalpine), *Britain, the Danubian provinces (Dalmatia, Noricum, and Dacia), and *Asia Minor came to be the major mining regions of the Roman empire, and gold, silver, copper, lead, and tin the main metals extracted. Iron was found in many parts of the empire and despite the presence of large-scale iron-mining districts in Noricum and the Kentish Weald was usually exploited in smaller local units of production. It is difficult to trace precisely the history of Roman mining, since mining areas and individual mines came into and went out of production, and because archaeological research has been more thorough in some areas than others; but the main lines can be drawn. Italy contained few precious metals, and so Rome initially had to rely on imports from mines controlled by Hellenistic kings in the east and the Carthaginians in the west. After the defeat of *Hannibal in 201 BC, Romans and Italians were soon exploiting the silver-mines in SE Spain around New Carthage. After the conquest of the Macedonian kingdom in 167 BC, Rome regulated the operation of the Macedonian gold-mines to suit its needs. The apogee of production at the major mines of Iberia, Gaul, Britain, and the Danubian provinces took place in the first two centuries AD. After the disruption of the 3rd cent., some mines were operating again in the 4th cent., but, as far as we can tell, on a reduced scale and under a different organizational regime.

The Romans rarely opened up new areas of mining, but often expanded the scale of production and the variety of metals mined in regions already known for their mineral potential. Techniques of prospection relied heavily on observation of visible veins of mineralization in rock deposits and changes in soil colour. Of the precious metals only gold (and to a lesser degree copper) existed in a natural state. Silver, copper, lead, and tin occurred in compound metal deposits (ores) and required metallurgical processing to convert them into usable metals. Three main types of mining were practised: the exploitation of alluvial deposits; opencast mining of rock-deposits found near the surface; and underground mining of deeper-lying rock-deposits. The Romans exploited alluvial deposits (placers) of gold and tin by panning or, if they were larger in scale,

by flushing the alluvium with large quantities of water released at high speed in sluices to separate the metal-bearing sands from the dross. In NW Spain especially deep alluvial deposits were undermined before being flushed with water to separate out the gold-nuggets (Plin. *HN* 33. 70–8). In underground mines vertical shafts were sunk often in pairs occasionally to an impressive depth: 340 m. (1,115 ft.) at one mine near New Carthage. Horizontal galleries, often strengthened with wooden props, connected the shafts, increased ventilation, and allowed ore once mined to be removed from the ore-face. Terracotta oil-lamps were placed in niches to provide lighting. Drainage was a problem in deeper mines. Manual bailing was practised (Plin. *HN* 33. 97), but if possible, drainage adits were cut through sterile rock. In some mines chain-pumps, Archimedean screw-pumps, or a series of water-lifting wheels were used. Mining tools, including picks, hammers, and gads, were mainly of iron, while ore was collected in buckets made of esparto grass before being hauled, in some cases by pulleys, to the surface.

Many mines (especially gold- and silver-mines) over time became the property of the Roman state, but cities and private individuals continued to own and operate mines. In state-owned mines the state either organized production directly, as probably occurred in the gold-mining region of NW Spain, or it leased out contracts to work the mines to individuals, small associations or the larger *societates publicanorum* (see PUBLICANI). Mineworkers were often slaves, but prisoners of war, convicts, and free-born wage labourers also formed part of the workforce. Tombstones from mining settlements show that people often migrated long distances to work at mines. Soldiers were stationed at the larger mines, not just to supervise the labour force, but also to provide technological expertise. Any mining site needed a large number of ancillary workers to keep the labour force fed, clothed, and equipped, and to assist in processing ore into usable metals. J. C. E.

Minoan civilization (*see facing page*)

miracles Stories of the power of the gods were common throughout antiquity, many of them rooted in personal devotion, as appears, for instance, from votive inscriptions expressing gratitude for a miraculous recovery. A large group is linked with particular cults and cult places allegedly founded following miraculous deeds by the deity involved, who thus showed his/her divine power. Early instances can be found in the *Homeric Hymns*, for example those to *Dionysus, *Demeter, and *Apollo. From the 4th cent. BC onwards there is a rapid increase in miracle-stories, and the connection with epiphany (divine appearances) receives ever more emphasis. Under the title *Epiphaneiai* collections of miracles abounded, the term *epiphaneia* signifying both the appearance and the miraculous deeds of the god. Among the epigraphic evidence the miracles performed by *Asclepius in Epidaurus (4th cent. BC) are particularly significant. Slightly earlier, literature reveals a new

[*continued on p. 472*]

Minoan civilization

Minoan civilization, the bronze-age civilization of *Crete (*c.*3500–1100 BC). The term 'Minoan' (after the legendary Cretan King Minos) was coined by Sir Arthur Evans to distinguish the prehistoric culture of Crete revealed in his excavations beginning in 1900 at the site of *Cnossus (*Knōssos*) from the *Mycenaean civilization revealed by Schliemann on the Greek mainland. Evans, using the pottery styles found at Cnossus, divided the civilization into three phases, early, middle, and late Minoan (EM, MM, LM), a scheme subsequently refined to produce complex subdivisions (e.g. EM IIA, LM IIIA1), although a simpler tripartite division into pre-Palatial, Palatial (subdivided into proto- and neo-Palatial), and post-Palatial better reflects cultural developments. The absolute chronology of prehistoric Crete, established through connections with the 'historical' chronology of Egypt, has been refined using radiocarbon dating techniques together with tree-ring calibration. Chief among the refinements are the dates for the earliest permanent settlers on the island (*c.*7000 BC), for the beginning of the bronze age (EM I) (*c.*3500 BC), and for the beginning of the late bronze age (LM I) (*c.*1700 BC, based on a likely date for the destruction of the Akrotiri site on Thera of 1628 BC). The beginning of the iron age is conventionally placed at the end of the sub-Minoan phase (*c.*1000 BC), although functional iron objects are known from LM IIIC onwards.

Pre-Palatial (neolithic to MM IA: *c.*7000–2000 BC). Although humans may have visited Crete earlier, it was first colonized before *c.*7000 BC, possibly from SW Anatolia. The only attested site of that date is Cnossus, some 5 km. (3 mi.) from the sea on the west side of the Kairatos valley—in its earliest phase perhaps only 0.25 ha. (0.6 acre) in size with a population of about 70 (cf. *Antiquity* 1991, 233 ff.). The first colonists there brought with them a fully developed farming lifestyle and the ancestor of one of the island's later languages. For the next 2,500 years very few sites are known until numbers increase dramatically in the late and final neolithic periods (*c.*4500–3500 BC), by which time Cnossus has reached a size of 5 ha. (12.4 acres), its population perhaps as high as 1,500. The rise in site numbers seems too large to be explained solely by indigenous population increase, suggesting some new settlers in a period when many of the smaller Aegean islands were being colonized for the first time. The appearance of new ceramic traditions in the earliest bronze age ('Agios Onouphrios' and 'Pyrgos' wares) and material culture links with the Cyclades have been cited as further evidence for immigration.

Although the EM I phase conventionally marks the beginning of the bronze age, this term is misleading: copper metallurgy was already known in the final neolithic at Cnossus, but true bronze metallurgy does not become widespread until EM II (*c.*2,500 BC). Our understanding of society in EM I–MM IA Crete (*c.*3500–2000 BC) depends to a large extent on burials (particularly those in circular tombs in the Mesara region) and on a handful of small excavated sites, such as Debla, Myrtos Phournou Koriphi (0.09 ha.: 0.25 acres), and Vasiliki (which lends its name to a characteristic ceramic of the EM II period). The evidence of these sites (with populations perhaps in the order of 30–50 individuals) suggests a relatively egalitarian society, in contrast to the larger settlements that certainly existed in this phase (Cnossus, Phaestus, Malia, Mochlus) with populations perhaps ranging from 450 (Phaestus) to 1,500 (Cnossus) (cf. T. Whitelaw, *Minoan Society*, ed. O. Kryszkowska and L. Nixon (1983), 337 ff.). Their sizes, together with poorly understood monumental structures at Cnossus and élite burials at Mochlus, imply the emergence of a social hierarchy already by EM II. In the latest pre-Palatial phase (MM IA in central Crete, EM III in the east), élite burials become more widespread (Archanes, Malia, Gournia, Mochlus), as do indicators of connections with the eastern Mediterranean, suggesting the importance of social stratification and external contacts as factors associated with the emergence of the palaces (cf. *PCPS* 1984, 18 ff.).

Minoan civilization The west court of the Minoan palace at Phaistos, southern *Crete. Monumental, and usually paved, courts were a feature of Minoan palaces and suggest their function as (among other things) ceremonial centres.

Palatial (MM IB to LM IB: *c*.2000–1470 BC). The first structures referred to as 'palaces' are built at the central Cretan sites of Cnossus, Malia, and Phaestus in the MM IB phase. Architecturally they are distinguished by monumentality (floor areas range from 1.3 ha. (3.2 acres) at Cnossus to 0.75 ha. (1.85 acres) at Malia), by their arrangement around a paved central court, with a paved western court, and by sophisticated masonry techniques such as ashlar orthostate blocks. The uniformity of plans of the first palaces is somewhat illusory and Malia in particular seems to have had a more dispersed layout, while it is possible that architecturally distinct palaces did not appear all over the island in MM IB, notably in east Crete, where an extensive network of roads, way-stations, and watch-towers established in MM II, linked the sites of Palaikastro and Kato Zakros with the SE section of the island.

Innovations in economic and social organization of the late pre-Palatial period are more clearly articulated in the architectural environment of the early palaces. The palaces mobilized agricultural surplus within their territories, necessitating the construction of large-scale storage facilities for food to support the élite and their workforce, to provide relief in times of stress, and, probably, to support ritual feasting. To record such storage two scripts were used—so-called Cretan Hieroglyphic (chiefly at Cnossus and Malia) and Linear A (at Phaestus)—while clay sealings were used at Phaestus as a direct means of controlling storage rooms and containers. Élite craft production was centred on the palaces and it seems likely that the palaces also monopolized the acquisition of raw materials, such as copper (from Attica and other sources), tin, and ivory (through Syria). Finds of the polychrome 'Kamares' ware characteristic of the proto-Palatial period are widespread if not numerous at various sites in the eastern Mediterranean and Egypt, suggesting exchange links with the major circum-Mediterranean powers. Overseas contacts with the Greek mainland and the Aegean islands (especially the Cyclades) are intense during the proto-Palatial period and become more so in the neo-Palatial period.

Iconographic and artefactual evidence suggest that the palaces also functioned as centres for ritual, while cult sites, including cave (e.g. the Idaean, Dictaean, and Arkalochori caves), spring (e.g. Kato

Symi), and peak-top sanctuaries—particularly characteristic of Minoan culture (e.g. Iouchtas, Petsophas: *Cambridge Archaeological Journal* 1992, 59 ff.)—were widely distributed in the rural landscape. The alignments of Cnossus on Mount Iouchtas and Phaestus on the Kamares cave suggest a close connection between the palace centres and these rural cult places, which may have functioned to unify territories around a prominent visual marker.

The palaces became focal points for settlement, as the growth of the settlement at Cnossus by the neo-Palatial period to an estimated 75 ha. (185 acres), its population to perhaps 12,000, demonstrates. (By comparison, late Helladic Mycenae was 30 ha. (74 acres) in area, including the walled citadel.) The territories controlled from Cnossus, Phaestus, and Malia may each have been over 1,000 sq. km. (386 sq. mi.) in extent.

The transition from the old or first palaces (the proto-Palatial) to the new or second palaces (the neo-Palatial period) is defined by reconstruction of the palaces, after destructions—perhaps by earthquake—at all three major sites in MM II and IIIA. It is the new palaces that are best understood and which show the greatest architectural similarities. They retain many of the functions of their predecessors: storage, ritual, élite craft production (including the dark-on-light 'Plant'- and 'Marine'-style fine-ware ceramics), also the acquisition of raw materials through contacts with the Greek mainland and the Aegean islands and with the eastern Mediterranean and Egypt. Striking among these links are examples of frescoes in Minoan style at Tel Kabri in Israel and Tell el-Daba'a (ancient Avaris) in the Egyptian Delta.

However, there are changes in the neo-Palatial period. The palaces are extensively decorated with frescos containing figured scenes drawn from the natural world and from ritual, public display and possibly narrative; the best-preserved examples are not from Crete, but the Minoanized settlement of Akrotiri on Thera. It seems that the extent of storage space and access to the central structures was more restricted in this phase, suggesting a devolution of agricultural storage and some administrative control to subordinate settlements, including a new class that appears in the neo-Palatial period, conventionally called 'villas': small, rural settlements with storage and processing facilities for agricultural produce (e.g. Vathypetro) and links to the palaces in architectural details and the use of Linear A script and clay sealings (e.g. Myrtos Pyrgos, Tylissos, Sklavokampos). These 'villas' may have been subordinate to towns, each perhaps controlling specific sectors of the palatial territories and in some cases producing Linear A finds (Archanes, Agia Triada, Gournia, Palaikastro). Ports are also important, notably at Kommos on the western coast of the Mesara plain, 6 km. (3.7 mi.) from Phaestus and Agia Triada, and the small (only 0.31 ha. (0.8 acre) in area) palace constructed at Kato Zakros on the east coast of the island, perhaps over a proto-Palatial predecessor, which may have functioned to control exchange.

The Linear A script is now in almost exclusive use for administrative recording and is also found on items of jewellery (gold and silver pins) and stone offerings-tables found at rural sanctuaries (Iouchtas, Kato Symi), implying close links between the palaces and rural cult sites. The architectural uniformity of the new palaces, together with the widespread use of Linear A and the discovery of near-identical seal impressions at a number of sites has suggested to some a unification of the island under a single authority, probably the palace at Cnossus (e.g. *Kadmos* 1967, 15 ff.), but this need not necessarily have been the case (J. F. Cherry, *Peer Polity Interaction* (1986), 35 ff.).

Post-Palatial (LM II to SM: *c.*1470–1000 BC). The end of the neo-Palatial period is marked by a series of burnt destructions in the pottery phase known as LM IB; sites affected include the palaces of Kato Zakros, Malia, and Phaestus and many smaller sites as far west as Chania. The following period is conventionally referred to as the post-Palatial, although some scholars prefer to extend the term neo-Palatial to include the final destruction of the palace at Cnossus, which continued in use. The date of the final destruction at Cnossus hinges on the material Evans published as belonging to the final palace and has been controversial since the 1960s, when rival dates were proposed of *c.*1375 and *c.*1200 BC. The discovery at the western site of Chania (Linear B *ku-do-ni-ja*) in a LM IIIB context of Linear B tablets, one of them at least probably written by a Cnossian scribe (*Kadmos* 1992, 61 ff.; *BCH* 1993, 19 ff.), not only supports a late date for the Cnossus destruction, but also confirms the existence of close administrative ties between the two sites.

The Linear B documents record the final year of the economic administration centred on Cnossus in an early form of the Greek language, a fact that implies—along with archaeological evidence for features of mainland material culture—that Mycenaean Greeks had taken over control there and had perhaps been responsible for the destructions at the end of the LM IB phase. From the documents it is possible to demonstrate that Cnossus managed the economy of much of central and western Crete, a territory of perhaps 3,000–4,000 sq. km. (1,200–1,500 sq. mi.), incorporating the territories of former palatial centres, which continued to be occupied but were now subordinate to Cnossus.

As in other parts of the Aegean, many sites on Crete are abandoned or destroyed in the latter half of the LM IIIB pottery phase (*c*.1250–1200 BC). The final destruction of Cnossus may be part of this pattern. A number of settlements are founded in inaccessible or easily defensible locations in the LM IIIC—SM periods, notably at Karphi (altitude 1,100 m.: 3,600 ft.), at Vrokastro, and Kavousi, and at Kastri near Palaikastro. Some Minoan settlements continue in use or are reoccupied after the bronze age (Cnossus, Phaestus, Kydonia), while some attract later cult (Kommos, Palaikastro). Relatively few cult sites (notably the Idaean and Dictaean caves) are reused in the iron age, but the spring sanctuary at Kato Symi, dedicated to *Hermes and *Aphrodite in the historical period, is in continuous use.

J. Be.

impetus in the *Bacchae* of *Euripides. Miracles (healing, punitive, and other) are now explicitly pictured as divine instruments to exact worship, obedience, and submission. In the same period the term *aretē*—literally the 'virtue' of a god—develops the meaning 'miracle', which entails the rise of so-called *aretalogiai*, aretalogies: quasi-liturgical enumerations of the qualities, achievements, and power (all could be referred to by the term *dynamis*) of a specific god. All these features abound during and after the Hellenistic period in the cults of great foreign gods, for instance Sarapis and Isis (see EGYPTIAN DEITIES), and no less in Christian texts. The fierce competition between, and radical demand of devout submission to, these new gods fostered a propagandistic tendency to publicize the gods' miraculous deeds. 'Miracle proved deity' (A. D. Nock, *Conversion* (1933)) and as such it was often welcomed with the exclamation *heis ho theos* ('one/unique is the god'), thus contributing to the shaping of 'henotheistic' religiosity.

H. S. V.

Mithradates VI Eupator Dionysus (120–63 BC), elder son of Mithradates V Euergetes (152/1–120 BC), was the greatest, most famous king of Pontus in NE *Asia Minor, and Rome's most dangerous enemy in the 1st cent. BC. After murdering his mother and brother, his first major enterprise was the conquest of the Crimea and northern Black Sea. Ultimate control of most of the circuit of the Black Sea gave him almost inexhaustible supplies of men and materials for his military campaigns. In Cappadocia he continued to try to exert indirect control through agents: his creature Gordius, a Cappadocian noble; his sister

Laodice; her son Ariarathes VII; and eventually his own son, whom he installed as king Ariarathes IX. For the more aggressive annexation of Paphlagonia he took as ally his most powerful neighbour, Nicomedes III of Bithynia, but subsequently fell out with him. A famous meeting with *Marius in 99/8, and the armed intervention of *Sulla in Cappadocia a little later, made it clear that war with Rome was inevitable, and he prepared carefully. While Italy was preoccupied by the Social War of 91–89 BC (see ROME (HISTORY), §1. 5), he annexed Bithynia and Cappadocia. Skilful diplomacy, masterful propaganda and Roman overreaction enabled him to cast Rome in the role of aggressor and cause of the First Mithradatic War which followed (89–85). His armies swept all before them in Asia, where he ordered a massacre of resident Romans and Italians (the 'Asian Vespers'). He failed to capture Rhodes, but was welcomed in *Athens and won over most of Greece. The Roman response came in 87, when Sulla arrived in Greece with five legions. He defeated the Pontic armies, besieged and captured Athens, and took the war to Asia. Mithradates surrendered at the Peace of Dardanus, and was allowed to retire to Pontus. The Second Mithradatic War (*c*.83–81) was no more than a series of skirmishes with Sulla's lieutenant Lucius Licinius Murena, but when Nicomedes IV of Bithynia died in 76 or 75 and bequeathed his kingdom to Rome, Mithradates again prepared for war. Having allied himself with Quintus *Sertorius, the Roman rebel in Spain, he invaded Bithynia in the spring of 73 (possibly 74), thus precipitating the Third Mithradatic War. The advance faltered immediately with a disastrous failure to capture Cyzicus, and the Roman forces, ably commanded by

Lucius Licinius Lucullus, pushed Mithridates out of Pontus into Armenia, where he took refuge with King Tigranes II, his son-in-law. He failed to win Parthian support, but was able to return to Pontus in 68. The great *Pompey, newly appointed to the Mithradatic command, easily defeated him, and forced him to retreat to his Crimean kingdom. He was said to be planning an ambitious invasion of Italy by land, when his son Pharnaces led a revolt against him. Inured to poison by years of practice, he had to ask an obliging Gallic bodyguard to run him through with a sword. Mithradates presented himself both as a civilized philhellene—he consciously copied the portraiture and actions of *Alexander the Great—and as an oriental monarch, and although in many ways he achieved a remarkably successful fusion of east and west, he failed either to understand or to match the power of Rome.

B. C. McG.

Mithras, an ancient Indo-Iranian god adopted in the Roman empire as the principal deity of a mystery cult which flourished in the 2nd and 3rd cents. AD. Iranian Mithra was a god of compact (the literal meaning of his name), cattle-herding, and the dawn light, aspects of which survive (or were re-created) in his western manifestation, since Roman Mithras was a sun-god ('deus sol invictus Mithras', 'invincible sun god Mithras'), a 'bull-killer', and 'cattle-thief', and the saviour of the sworn brothers of his cult.

The cult is known primarily from its archaeological remains. Over 400 find-spots are recorded, many of them excavated meeting-places. These and the c.1,000 dedicatory inscriptions give a good idea of cult life and membership. Some 1,150 pieces of sculpture (and a few frescos) carry an extraordinarily rich sacred art, although the iconography remains frustratingly elusive in default of the explicatory sacred texts. Literary references to Mithras and Mithraism are as scarce as the material remains are abundant.

Mithraism was an organization of cells. Small autonomous groups of initiates, exclusively male, met for fellowship and worship in chambers of modest size and distinctive design which they called 'caves' ('Mithraea', like 'Mithraism' and 'Mithraist', are neologisms). A cave is an 'image of the universe', and according to Porphyry (De antr. nymph. 6) the archetypal Mithraeum was designed and furnished as a kind of microcosmic model. Mithraea were sometimes sited in real caves or set against rock-faces (e.g. at Jajce in Bosnia) or were made to imitate caves by vaulting or decoration or by sequestering them in dim interior or underground rooms (see the Barberini, San Clemente, and Santa Prisca Mithraea in Rome, those at Capua and Marino, and the many Mithraea of *Ostia, among which the 'Seven Spheres' Mithraeum with its mosaic composition of zodiac and planets arguably exemplifies Porphyry's cosmic model). The Mithraeum is the antithesis of the classic temple, totally lacking in exterior decoration and space for solemn public ritual. The Mithraeum's most distinctive (and unvarying) feature is

the pair of platforms flanking a central aisle. It was on these that the initiates reclined for a communal meal. Visual representations (see esp. the Santa Prisca frescos and the relief from Konjic in Bosnia) show that this meal was the human counterpart of a divine banquet shared by Mithras and the sun-god (the latter appearing on the monuments as a separate being) on the hide of the bull killed by the former in his greatest exploit.

As is now known from the Santa Prisca frescos and the pavement of the Felicissimus Mithraeum in Ostia, initiates were ranked in a hierarchy of seven grades, each under the protection of one of the planets: Raven (Mercury), 'Nymphus' (Venus), Soldier (Mars), Lion (Jupiter), Persian (Moon), 'Heliodromus' (Sun), Father (Saturn). It is generally accepted that this was a lay hierarchy, not a professional priesthood. Mithraists, as their monuments attest, remained in and of the secular world. It is unlikely that the full hierarchy was represented in each Mithraeum, although probable that most were presided over by one or more Fathers. The disparate connotations of the various ranks, the two idiosyncratic coinages ('Heliodromus' and 'Nymphus'—the latter would mean, if anything, 'male bride') and the unique planetary order all bespeak an unusually inventive and evocative construct.

Actual Mithraea or traces of the cult have been found in virtually every quarter of the Roman empire, though with two notable areas of concentration. The first was Rome itself and its port of Ostia. In Ostia, some 15 Mithraea have been discovered in the excavated area that comprises about half of the town's total. Extrapolation to Rome, where some 35 locations are known, would yield a total of perhaps as many as 700 Mithraea. The number is impressive (if speculative), but individual Mithraea were small, and even if all were in service contemporaneously they would accommodate no more than 2 per cent of the population—scarcely the great rival to *Christianity that inflated views of the cult have sometimes made it. The other area of concentration was the empire's European frontier from Britain to the mouth of the Danube. As inscriptions confirm, Mithraism's typical recruits were soldiers and minor functionaries, e.g. employees of the Danubian customs service headquartered at Poetovio (mod. Ptuj in Slovenia). Many were *freedmen or slaves. Mithraism did not generally attract the upper classes (except as occasional patrons) until its final days as the rather artificial creature of the pagan aristocracy of 4th-cent. Rome. It was always better represented in the Latin west than the Greek east.

By the middle of the 2nd cent. AD the cult was well established. The routes of its diffusion and its earlier development are much debated, problems complicated by the question of transmission from Iran. Did the cult develop from and perpetuate a stream of Zoroastrianism, or was it essentially a western creation with 'Persian' trimmings? There is no agreement, because there is so little evidence. Almost the only firm datum is *Plutarch's remark that the Cilician pirates suppressed by *Pompey (Pomp. 24) had

Mithras This marble relief from a Mithraic temple at Heddenheim (Germany) depicts the principal icon in the myth of Mithras, his killing of a bull. Although not fully understood, the scene may have been seen by worshippers as an *astrological allegory.

secret initiatory rites (*teletai*) of Mithras which had endured to his own day. These may have been a prototype of the developed *mysteries.

The cult's theology and its sacred myth must be recovered, if at all, from the monuments. Principal among these is the icon of Mithras killing a bull, which was invariably set as a focal point at one end of the Mithraeum. Mithras is shown astride the bull, plunging a dagger into its flank. The victim's tail is metamorphosed into an ear of wheat. Mithras is accompanied by dog, snake, scorpion, and raven; also by two minor deities, dressed like him in 'Persian' attire and each carrying a torch (one raised, the other inverted), whose names, Cautes and Cautopates, are known from dedications. Above the scene, which is enacted in front of a cave, are images of Sol and Luna. This strange assemblage challenges interpretation. Clearly, the killing is an act of sacrifice, but to what end? It has been seen variously as an action which creates or ends the world (support for both can be adduced from Zoroastrian sources) or which in some sense 'saves' the world or at least the initiates within it. The line from Santa Prisca 'et nos servasti [...] sanguine fuso' ('and who saved us with the shed blood') probably refers to the bull-killing Mithras *qua* saviour, though one must beware of reading into this 'salvation' inappropriate Christian connotations.

The bull-killing has also been interpreted as an astrological allegory, the initial warrant for this being the remarkable correspondence, certainly not an unintended coincidence, between elements in the composition and a group of constellations. But there is no consensus on the extent to which learned astrological doctrines should be imputed to the cult, let alone on their theological or soteriological function. This contributor holds that *astrology was central and that its function was to provide the specifics of a doctrine of the soul's celestial journey (descent to earth and ascent to heaven), initiation into which, Porphyry says (*De antr. nymph.* 6), was the ritual enacted in Mithraea.

The bull-killing is but one episode, albeit the most important, in a cycle of Mithraic myth represented (frustratingly, in no set order) on the monuments. Other episodes are Mithras' birth from a rock, the hunt and capture of the bull, and the feast celebrated with Sol. The banquet scene is sometimes shown on the reverse of bull-killing reliefs, as salvific effect from salvific cause. There are fine examples in the Louvre (from Fiano Romano), Wiesbaden (from Heddernheim), and—still, one hopes—Sarajevo (from Konjic).   R. L. B.

monopolies, in the sense of exclusive control of the supply of a product or service, were known in antiquity, but restricted in scope. In no case was the declared aim an increase in productivity through efficient planning or economies of scale. Instead, monopolistic control aimed above all at increasing revenues and was the prerogative of the state: 'cornering the market' by individuals was an almost mythical occurrence (Arist. *Pol.* 1259ᵃ5 ff.). State control and leasing of silver deposits in Attica (the Laurium mines) marks a long-term revenue-raising monopoly. Other Greek states invented and sold monopolies in time of fiscal emergency ([Arist.] *Oec.* 2). In Ptolemaic *Egypt, monopoly control of goods and services, usually by sale and lease of rights, was a way of life (from oil and textiles to beer and goose-breeding). In the Roman empire, sale of monopolies by cities was a regular revenue-raising device. See ECONOMY, GREEK, HELLENISTIC, and ROMAN.   P. C. M.

mosaic Floors paved with natural pebbles arranged in simple geometric designs were used in the near east in the 8th cent. BC. In the Greek world, unpatterned pebble floors were known in the Minoan and Mycenaean periods (see MINOAN and MYCENAEAN CIVILIZATION); decorated pebble mosaics are first attested at the end of the 5th cent., at Corinth and Olynthus. The earliest examples had simple two-dimensional designs, both geometric and figured, usually light on a dark ground. Their use, mainly in private houses, spread throughout Greece during the 4th cent.; by its end a wider range of colours and shades was used, and attempts were made to achieve more three-dimensional

effects. Outstanding examples of this phase come from the palatial houses at Pella in Macedonia, dated to the late 4th cent.; some artificial materials such as strips of lead or terracotta for outlines were used here to reinforce the natural pebbles. See HOUSES, GREEK.

The technique of tessellated mosaic (*opus tessellatum*), in which pieces of stone or marble were cut to approximately cubic shape and fitted closely together in a bed of mortar, was invented in the course of the 3rd cent. BC; the exact date is controversial. There were probably experiments in various places; mosaics at Morgantina in Sicily are often cited as early examples. Tesserae were cut irregularly at first, then with greater precision; by the 2nd cent. the technique sometimes known as *opus vermiculatum* had appeared, in which tiny pieces, sometimes less than 1 mm. square, in a wide range of colours, were fitted so closely together as to imitate the effects of painting. Mosaics in this last technique often took the form of *emblemata*: panels produced in the artists' studios, and then inserted into the floor at the centre of a coarser surround of tessellated mosaic. Outstanding examples have been found near *Alexandria (at mod. Thmuis), and in *Pergamum; *Pliny the Elder (*HN* 36. 184) records the mosaicist Sosus of Pergamum, famous for his representation of an 'unswept floor' (*asarōtos oikos*) littered with the debris of a meal, and for a scene of Drinking Doves, reflected in several Roman copies. The largest number of mosaics of the Hellenistic period is found in *Delos, dating from the late 2nd and beginning of the 1st cent. BC; they range from pavements of unshaped chips to very fine *emblemata*.

In Italy mosaics of Hellenistic style are found in Rome, *Pompeii, and elsewhere from the late 2nd cent. BC onwards; outstanding examples are the Alexander mosaic (see ALEXANDER THE GREAT) from the House of the Faun in Pompeii and the Nile mosaic from Praeneste (mod. Palestrina). Tessellated mosaics with geometric patterns, coloured or black-and-white, became increasingly common in the 1st cent. BC. Alongside them appeared more utilitarian types of floor, especially those of *signinum*, coloured (usually red) mortar-and-aggregate, their surface often decorated with tesserae or other pieces of stone strewn at random or arranged in simple patterns. The antecedents for these may have come from Carthage, where pavements of related type are dated at least as early as the 3rd cent., perhaps to the 4th. Another technique developed in Italy in the late republic is that of *opus sectile* ('cut work'), where larger pieces of stone or marble were cut to the shape of specific parts of a design; this was later used on walls as well as floors, for both ornamental and figured designs.

Under the empire mosaics became mass-produced; they were widespread in private houses and better-quality apartments, and in large public buildings such as *baths. Geometric designs were much more common than figured work, and fine *emblemata*, always objects of luxury, became rare. In Italy throughout the first three centuries AD, the great majority of mosaics were black-and-white, with all-over geometric or floral designs, or with figures in black

mosaic A hunt mosaic from Apamea, restored in AD 539. It illustrates the rich tradition of pictorial mosaic in the eastern empire and particularly (as here) the province of *Syria.

silhouette. The figures might be set in panels, or as abstract all-over designs covering the greater part of the floor; examples are found above all in *Ostia.

Much of the western empire adopted the use of mosaic under Italian influence during the 1st and 2nd cents. AD; a taste for polychromy generally prevailed over the black-and-white style. Each province tended to develop its own regional character, with a repertory of favourite designs and methods of composition. Among the most distinctive are those of North Africa; elaborate polychrome geometric and floral designs were favoured, and figure scenes often formed all-over compositions covering large areas of floor with minimal indication of depth or recession. Subject-matter here was often directly related to the interests and activities of the patrons, with scenes from the amphitheatre, the hunting-field, or the country estate. Closely related are the pavements of the great 4th-cent. villa at Piazza Armerina in Sicily, very probably laid by a workshop from Carthage. In Spain the most striking mosaics come from villas of the late empire: they have much in common with the African floors, but include a higher proportion of mythological or literary subjects. In Britain a number of individual workshops have been distinguished, especially from the 4th cent.

The development in the eastern empire is less well known, but a fine series has been excavated at *Antioch, dating from c. AD 100 to the 6th cent. The Hellenistic tradition of the pictorial figure scene persisted much longer here, and black-and-white mosaics were rare. Very fine pictorial mosaics of the 4th cent. AD have been found at several sites in *Syria (e.g. Shahba-Philippopolis, Apamea). At the end of the 4th cent. these gave way to all-over two-dimensional designs, both geometric and figured, best exemplified by the 5th-cent. 'hunting-carpets' of Antioch. Some eastern (Sasanid) influence is perceptible in these late mosaics, but the dominant influence seems to come from fashions developed slightly earlier in the west.

The use of mosaic on walls and vaults (opus musivum) was a Roman invention. In the late republic grottoes and fountains were decorated with shells, pumice-stone, and pieces of glass, from which the use of regular glass tesserae developed. Numerous small fountains in Pompeii were decorated in this way, and more extensive mosaic decoration on walls is found there and in Rome in the 1st cent. AD; patterns and designs were more closely related to wall-painting than to floor mosaic. The technique was used on a large scale for vaults and walls in buildings such as baths and tombs in the 2nd and 3rd cents. The use of mosaic in Christian churches from the 4th cent. onwards is an extension of this development.   K. M. D. D.

Muses, goddesses upon whom poets—and later other artists, philosophers, and intellectuals generally—depended for the ability to create their works. They were goddesses, not lesser immortals, not only because of their pedigree(s) and their home on Mt. Olympus. They are called goddesses from the earliest sources on, and their attitude to mankind is identical to that of gods: they do not hesitate to destroy a mortal who dares to usurp their place (so Thamyris, whom they maimed and deprived of his skill: Hom. Il. 2. 594–600), and they are divinely contemptuous of humankind (it does not matter to them whether the poetry they inspire is true or false: Hes. Theog. 26–8). Muses appear both singly and in groups of varying sizes (West, on Theog. 60). Homer, for example, addresses a single goddess or Muse but knows there are more (the Thamyris story). The canonical nine and their names probably originated with *Hesiod (West on Theogony 76). They were: Calliope (epic poetry), Clio (history), Euterpe (flute-playing), Terpsichore (lyric poetry and dancing, esp. choral), Erato (lyric poetry), Melpomene (tragedy), Thalia (comedy), Polyhymnia (hymns and pantomime), Urania (astronomy). But their names, functions, and number fluctuated.

The earliest sources locate the Muses at Pieria, just north of Olympus, and on Olympus itself; they are associated with so-called 'Thracian' bards, *Orpheus, Thamyris, and Musaeus. That region appears to have been their first home. A southern group, the Muses of Helicon in Boeotia, is identified by Hesiod with the Muses of Olympia and Pieria, perhaps because of an underlying connection between the two regions (compare Mt. Leibethrion and its nymphs in the Helicon massif with Leibethra in Pieria in *Macedonia), but possibly because the young poet himself saw fit to make the association as a means to enhance his own reputation (on the introduction to the Theogony, see W. G. Thalmann, Conventions of Form and Thought in Early Greek Epic Poetry (1984), 134–52).

Hesiod's influence led eventually—but possibly not before the 4th cent. BC—to the establishment of a formal cult and sanctuary below Mt. Helicon in the Vale of the Muses. This may have been the first 'Mouseion' (i.e. Museum: it housed, in the open air, statues of both legendary and historical notables, and possibly contained an archive of poetic works), and it is not surprising that a Ptolemy (probably Ptolemy IV Philopator, whose queen Arsinoë III was worshipped as the Tenth Muse) was among the benefactors when part of the musical agōn (see GAMES), the Mouseia, was reorganized towards the end of the 3rd cent. BC (for the Heliconian cult, see A. Schachter, Cults of Boeotia 2 (1986), 147–79).

Philosophers, traditionally beginning with *Pythagoras, adopted the Muses as their special goddesses, in some cases organizing their schools as thiasoi (groups of worshippers) under their patronage (P. Boyancé, Le Culte des Muses chez les philosophes grecs (1937), esp. 229–351). From Hellenistic times they were a popular subject, individually or as a group, in sculpture (especially sarcophagi) and *mosaics.

There is no satisfactory etymology (see Frisk and Chantraine).   A. Sch.

music in Greek and Roman life 'Let me not live without music', sings a chorus of greybeards in *Euripides (HF 676). Expressions such as 'without music', 'chorusless',

music in Greek and Roman life Athenian wine-jar (amphora) of the early 5th cent. BC depicting a young man singing to the tune of a box-lyre or *kithara*—the major instrument of professional and public performance in Greece.

'lyreless' evoked the dreary bitterness of war, the Erinyes' curse, or death, 'without wedding song, lyreless, chorusless, death at the end' (Soph. *OC* 1221–3). Poetic pictures of unblemished happiness are correspondingly resonant with music; and in every sort of revel and celebration, Greeks of all social classes sang, danced (see DANCING), and played instruments, besides listening to professional performances. Music was credited with divine origins and mysterious powers, and was the pivot of relations between mortals and gods. It was central to public religious observance, and to such semi-religious occasions as weddings, funerals, and harvests. At the great Panhellenic festivals (see GREECE (PREHISTORY AND HISTORY)) and their many local counterparts, choruses and vocal and instrumental soloists competed no less than athletes for prizes and glory (cf. Pind. *Pyth.* 12): these showcase occasions provided a matrix for the development of sophisticated forms of art-music, and fostered rapid stylistic elaborations and technical advances (see GAMES).

The best Greek soloists and composers were usually in some sense professionals, and professionals are already familiar in *Homer, though apart from Thamyris (*Il.* 2. 594–600) they are neither competitors nor independent agents, but retainers in a noble house. In historical times poet-composers such as Terpander, Thaletas, and *Alcman may have been 'retained' by the public purse in Sparta, and there were eminent musicians in the retinues of 6th-cent. tyrants. Others, *Sappho for example, and many in 5th-cent. Athens, made their living as teachers. But not all public performers were professionals. Choruses of singers and dancers remained citizen-amateurs until Hellenistic times, whether in Homer's Phaeacia (Scheria), in Alcman's Sparta, in Archaic *Delos, or in the dithyrambic and dramatic contests of Classical Athens (see DITHYRAMB; COMEDY (GREEK), OLD; TRAGEDY (GREEK)), and often later, even on occasion in Augustan Rome. Well-bred Greek citizens normally had a competence on an instrument (usually the lyre, sometimes the pipes) as well as in singing and choral dance. When *Achilles, the toughest of the Greek warriors, is found playing the lyre and singing in his tent (*Il.* 9. 186–9), no one is surprised. Humbler folk sang at their work, piped to their flocks, or kept time to music at their oars. Guests at the *symposium listened to girl-pipers and other hired entertainers, but also sang and played instruments. Women made music in their domestic quarters. Music, all in all, was essential to the pattern and texture of Greek life at all social levels, providing a widely available means for the expression of communal identity and values, and a focus for controversy, judgement, and partisanship in which all citizens could enthusiastically engage.

It has generally been held, perhaps rightly, that music was much less important in Roman life than in Archaic or Classical Greece. It was nevertheless indispensable at Rome to all religious rituals and civic celebrations, prominent in public theatrical performance and private merry-making, a fully institutionalized ingredient of military activities, and a common element in the education of well-

bred citizens (see EDUCATION, GREEK, § 3). Professional performers won great acclaim. There are perhaps three main reasons for its apparently less significant status. First, we are ill-informed about relations between music and poetry in early Roman times. Unlike their Greek counterparts, most surviving Latin poets belong to a period in which sophisticated poetry had emancipated itself from occasions of musical performance and was primarily designed to be spoken or read. Secondly, Roman writers on music are typically educated men with a deep respect for Hellenic culture, inclined to compare the deliberate theatricality and the cosmopolitan variousness of contemporary performance unfavourably with the supposedly pure, simple, and ethically edifying music of the Greek past (but Greeks themselves regularly made similar complaints from the 5th cent. onwards). Finally, Greek lore about music's effects on character and its distinctive role in moral education had been elaborately articulated by philosophers and theorists, and such theorizing continued through imperial times: but in whichever language they wrote, Roman intellectuals invariably related these ideas to the older Greek music, seldom reflecting on matters within their own experience. Romans seem to have thought of the musical elements in education either as a source of peripheral gentlemanly adornments, or as part of a thoroughly ungentlemanly professional training. Even where one would most expect it, in the ethical writings of the Roman Stoics (see STOICISM), there are few traces of the doctrine that musical education moulds the moral core of a citizen's dispositions and sensibilities. To most reflective Roman minds, music in their own milieu was no more than trivial entertainment, and the polemics of the Epicurean Philodemus (see EPICURUS) against Greek Stoics' and Platonists' conceptions of music's ethical significance found a ready audience (see PLATO). Technical analyses of musical structures continued similarly to focus wholly on Greek models: we have only the most impressionistic accounts of the music the Romans heard.   A. D. B.

Mycenaean civilization (*see following page*)

mysteries For much of the 20th cent. the term 'mystery religions' has been current, denoting a special form of personal religion linking the fate of a god of Frazer's 'dying-rising' type with the individual believer. The two scholars whose authority made soteriology the central issue were Fr. Cumont (1904) and R. Reitzenstein (1910). The concealed agendum was the question of the uniqueness, and by implication, validity, of Christianity; at the same time, it was the model of that religion which provided the agreed terms of discussion. In this perspective, the earliest and most influential Greek mystery cult, of *Demeter and Kore (see PERSEPHONE) at *Eleusis, appeared a crude forerunner of more developed mystery religions from the near east, which in the Hellenistic period filled a spiritual vacuum left by the etiolation of Archaic and Classical civic cult. 'Mystery' was taken to be the essence of oriental religiosity.

[*continued on p. 483*]

Mycenaean civilization

Mycenaean civilization takes its name from the spectacular finds made by Heinrich Schliemann at Mycenae, and was first systematically defined by Christos Tsountas. He applied the term Mycenaean to all Aegean late bronze-age material, but it is now confined to the culture which developed on the mainland in the late bronze age. The stylistic divisions of the Mycenaean pottery style (LH (late Helladic) I, IIA, etc.) provide a well-defined relative chronology, but historically the Mycenaean age is better divided into a formative period, covering LH I and IIA (c.1575/50–1450 BC), a Palace period, covering LH IIB, IIIA1, IIIA2, IIIB1, and IIIB2 (c.1450–1200 BC), and a post-Palatial period, covering LH IIIC (frequently subdivided into early, middle, and late) and sub-Mycenaean (c.1200–1050/1000 BC).

The most striking feature of the formative period is the emergence of wealthy ruling groups in the southern mainland, who were surely native to the territories that they controlled; theories that they represent alien invaders have not identified the new and consistently occurring cultural assemblage that should appear, or explained the variability of the earliest Mycenaean developments in different regions and the strong links with the preceding middle Helladic culture. Their emergence and acquisition of considerable wealth, displayed mostly in lavish burials (see below), remains hard to explain, but the expanding influence of *Minoan civilization in the Aegean and the increasing involvement of the Aegean with the east Mediterranean trading systems may have been major stimuli. Minoan influence is most marked in the crafts (see below) that they patronized, and was hardly felt at the level of the ordinary settlements.

During the formative period features that were at first localized, like the Messenian tholos-tombs (SW *Peloponnese), were combined into something more like a homogeneous culture; by its end not only the Mycenaean pottery style but the characteristic burial practices had spread through the *Peloponnese and central Greece. The new principalities were organized rather simply—there is no trace of the administrative use of the seal or writing—and the popularity of weapons as high-status grave-goods suggests that society was more turbulent than that of Crete and the south Aegean islands. The discovery of early Mycenaean pottery in the north Aegean and central Mediterranean suggests that the mainlanders could have played a significant role in the expansion of trade connections, but their contacts with the near east will still have been largely indirect while Minoan civilization dominated the Aegean.

Theories of Mycenaean responsibility for the collapse of Minoan civilization c.1450 BC remain questionable, but the following period certainly saw a great expansion of Mycenaean culture and the establishment of a state in *Crete, centred on Cnossus, whose ruling class had strong Mycenaean connections in its burial customs and use of Greek, written in the Linear B script, as the administrative language. The administrative skills of Crete were probably transmitted to the mainland at this time, when the first well-preserved antecedents of the later Mycenaean palaces were built; but tombs continued to be richly provided with grave-goods at both mainland and Cretan sites. The final destruction of Cnossus during the 14th cent. BC removed the last major competitor to the mainland centres, and Mycenaean civilization now reached its zenith, dominating the south Aegean and extending along the Asia Minor coast from Miletus to Cnidus.

The organizing centres of this civilization were the great palaces best preserved at Mycenae, Tiryns, Pylos, and Thebes. While considerably smaller than the Minoan palaces and differently laid out, they evidently functioned similarly, as centres of administration, ceremonial, storage, and craftwork. They presided over societies that were small in scale: most settlements ranged in size from a few households to some hundreds, and even the greatest, with populations probably in the thousands, do not have a very townlike appearance. But there were more settlements on the mainland than ever before;

Mycenaean civilization View of the central hall ('megaron') of the Mycenaean palace at Pylos (SW *Peloponnese). The circular hearth surrounded by four columns, a feature also known from Mycenae and Tiryns, suggests the role of hospitality and feasting in sustaining the primacy of the palace centres.

exploitation of the land was being expanded, probably to provide commodities for trade as well as to support an increasing population. The most recent study (P. Halstead, *PCPS* 1992, 57 ff.) distinguishes between the highly specialized economies of the palaces, which concentrated on large-scale cultivation of a few crops and the production of perfumed olive oil, fine textiles, and other craftwork, and the mixed economies of the ordinary settlements, which were not controlled from the palaces but interacted with them, providing some agricultural products in taxes and others, like pulses, on an irregular basis. To judge from the Pylos texts, which provide most of the documentary information, the palace directly maintained a workforce of many hundreds, and controlled most of the distribution and working of bronze. Resources were now expended mainly on building and engineering projects rather than tombs, though the finest tholoi belong to the period.

The Linear B texts do not make the palaces' administrative system wholly clear, but at the top in Pylos was the *wanax*, a monarch-like figure; below him were various administrators, who may well have been drawn from a class of major landowners. Texts concerning land-holdings indicate that people of very varied status could hold land, generally by some form of lease, including priests, craftsmen, herdsmen, and, at *Pa-ki-ja-ne*, an important religious site relatively near Pylos itself, many 'slaves of the god', both male and female. Land could be leased from different owners and in various ways, but its tenure may always have entailed payment to the palace in taxes or service.

Mycenaean pottery of this period is found in considerable quantities in much of the Mediterranean, reaching rarely as far as northern Italy and eastern Spain. It was clearly popular, for it was widely imitated, but the most significant element may have been containers for perfumed *olive oil and other substances. Its conspicuousness should not lead to overestimation of the Mycenaean position either in

Mediterranean trade, whose most important organizing centres were probably in *Syria and *Cyprus, or politically: there remain difficulties in identifying the state Ahhiyawa, mentioned in Hittite sources, with Mycenaean Greece, and likely references to Mycenaeans are hard to identify in other near eastern sources. The masses of exported Mycenaean pottery may rather symbolize the strenuous effort necessary to maintain the inward flow of raw materials and luxuries necessary to the Mycenaean style of life.

Indications of trouble during the later 13th cent. BC may reflect strains within Mycenaean society rather than any external threat. Some major sites had already suffered severe damage (Thebes) and begun to decline, or been abandoned (Gla), before the main series of destructions around 1200 BC; these have been attributed to earthquakes in the Argolid, but this explanation can hardly apply all over the mainland (e.g. the Menelaion, Pylos, Teikhos Dymaion, Crisa). Subsequently some regions recovered and prospered at a simpler level, centring on large nucleated settlements (Tiryns, *Lefkandi, Perati) that were still essentially Mycenaean in culture and retained contacts with the Aegean and near east. But exchange systems had been badly dislocated, and there seems to have been growing instability; ultimately the surviving centres were abandoned or dwindled to villages. Culture reverted to an essentially pre-Mycenaean level, parochial and impoverished, with limited external contacts, and surviving Mycenaean features disappeared (e.g. figurines, chamber-tomb cemeteries).

Burial customs Most characteristically, an open passage (*dromos*) would be cut to a chamber hollowed in soft rock (chamber-tomb) or built of stone; best known of the latter are the tholos-tombs, which have a circular ground-plan, domed vault, and covering mound, and were probably always high-status tombs. A series of burials, averaging 6–8 but often more or fewer, were inhumed in these chambers, often with complex two-stage rites. Although showing similarities to earlier Aegean forms, these tomb types seem specifically Mycenaean developments. They were used by a variable but increasingly large proportion of the population; the rest may have used cists and pits, but these nowhere occur in large numbers.

Architecture Ordinary houses mostly consisted of a few rooms grouped on various plans, built largely of mud-brick on stone foundations, with timber fittings and some kind of thatched roof. The palaces and some smaller buildings were built in the Minoan style, with fine stone façades, wooden columns, plastered walls around a timber frame, and fresco decoration in major areas. Although clay roof-tiles have been identified at several major sites, they seem a late development hardly used in the palaces, which were probably flat-roofed like the Minoan. Where fully preserved, palace plans centre on the 'megaron' suite of rooms, essentially a hall containing an elaborate hearth and 'throne' emplacement, approached through an ante-room and porch, which surely had a ceremonial purpose. Other rooms open off flanking corridors, and there are traces of an upper storey and further associated structures, including storage buildings and workshops. Also notable architecturally are the 'Cyclopean' fortifications, of two faces of massive blocks containing a rubble fill, generally 5–8 m. (16–26 ft.) thick and averaging 8 m. (26 ft.) high; the same style was used for terraces, dikes, dams, bridges, etc., mainly in the Argolid and Boeotia.

Crafts Many luxury crafts were established on the mainland in the formative period, as demonstrated by the rich grave-goods from many tombs. Their first practitioners may have been largely immigrants: Minoan influence is marked from the beginning in the weapons, precious vessels, seals, and decorated pottery, although native elements can be identified, and this steadily increases in jewellery. As a result, no separate Mycenaean artistic tradition developed; individuality is shown mainly in preferences for particular motifs, themes, or materials (e.g. metal rather than stone for vessels). The crafts of the Palace period maintained high standards technically, but generally repeated the established themes of earlier art; some, like the production of seals, progressively declined. More use was made of *ivory than before, especially for inlays on luxury furniture, but also for occasional works in the round. Decorative stone reliefs are occasionally found in palaces and the finest tholoi, but the Lion Gate relief at Mycenae remains unique. Worth mentioning as particularly characteristic are the clay figurines, especially standing female figures and bovids, which evidently served several ritual purposes. In the post-Palatial period, elaborate classes of pictorial pottery are conspicuous for a while, but all but the most basic crafts eventually disappeared.   O. T. P. K. D.

This entire scenario, and with it the coherence of the notion 'mystery', has now been seriously eroded. U. von Wilamowitz and C. Schneider showed in the 1930s that mysteries in the Greek (Eleusinian) sense were unknown in the homelands of the oriental cults, and were only attached to them on their entry into the Graeco-Roman world. M. P. Nilsson later made a similar point about Dionysiac mysteries (see DIONYSUS); and it is now agreed that all the 'oriental' divinities were thoroughly Hellenized in the process of being assimilated. The validity of Frazer's typology of the 'dying-rising god' (Osiris, Attis, Adonis) was undermined in the 1950s by H. Frankfort and others. The nature of the soteriology of mystery cults has been critically reviewed by the 'School of Rome' since the 1960s, especially by U. Bianchi and his pupils (e.g. U. Bianchi, *The Greek Mysteries* (1976); U. Bianchi and M. J. Vermaseren (eds.), *La soteriologia dei culti orientali nell'impero romano* (1982)), and redefined as 'the mass of benefits and guarantees which the worshipper expected from the celebration of the cult' (Sfameni Gasparro, *Soteriology and Mystic Aspects in the Cult of Cybele and Attis*, 2nd edn. (1985)). In the light of this revisionism, the uniqueness of the claims of Pauline *Christianity (see PAUL, ST) against the background of Judaic Messianism has been re-emphasized, and the issue of the Christianization of the Roman empire opened to fresh debate. The category 'mysteries' is looking decidedly limp. For it is clear that they cannot be considered independent movements, let alone religions, but as merely an ingrained modality of (Greek, later Graeco-Roman) polytheism—they have been compared with a pilgrimage to Santiago di Compostela in the Christian context. And they are only a specialized, often highly local, form of the cult of ill-assorted divinities. Their prominence in modern scholarship is quite disproportionate to their ancient profile.

The most useful recent typology of Graeco-Roman mysteries as forms of personal religious choice is that of Bianchi and others. Three modes are distinguished: 'mystery' proper, an entire initiatory structure of some duration and complexity, of which the type (and in many cases the actual model, e.g. Celeia near Phlius (Paus. 2. 14. 1–4) or the mysteries of Alexander of Abonuteichos (Lucian, *Alex.* 38 f.)) is Eleusis; 'mystic' cult, involving not initiation but rather a relation of intense communion, typically ecstatic or enthusiastic, with the divinity (e.g. Bacchic frenzy (see DIONYSUS), or the *kybēboi* of *Cybele); and 'mys-

teriosophic' cult, offering an anthropology, an eschatology, and a practical means of individual reunion with divinity— the primitive or original form is Orphism (see ORPHEUS, and below), consistently represented as a 'mystery' (e.g. Paus. 9. 30. 4 f., 10. 7. 2), the most typical, Hermeticism and Gnosis, though these are late Egyptian and Judaeo-Christian forms of religiosity. Bianchi himself has sought to provide an element of thematic unity by adapting Frazer's 'dying-rising god' typology: these cults are all focused upon a 'god subject to some vicissitude'. This tack has rightly been criticized, but the scheme has heuristic value without it.

Of their very nature, ideal types simplify to offer insight. The real world is always much more confused. The word *teletē*, which often denotes initiatory rituals of the Eleusinian type, could also be applied to any kind of unusual rite in some way analogous. One of the costs of conceptual clarity is the exclusion from consideration of numerous minor cults of Greece and Asia Minor, such as the *teletē* of *Hera at Nauplion, where she bathed annually to 'become a virgin' (Paus. 2. 38. 3). 'Mystery' shifts uneasily between indigenous term and analytical concept. Further complications are the intermingling of the three types in practice and the clear evidence of changes over time: early Orphic lore cannot be neatly distinguished from Bacchic 'mystic' experience; Orphic texts are intimately connected with the formation of Eleusinian myth; the cult of Cybele and Attis is marked by 'mystic' *ecstasy but also, in the Hellenistic period and after, by mysteries of uncertain content analogous to those of Eleusis, and, from the 2nd cent. AD, by a fusion of sacrifice, substitute-castration, and personal baptism—the *taurobolium* ('bull-sacrifice'); the cult of *Mithras may have taken on a 'mysteriosophic' tone.

The variety of mystery cults makes them exceptionally difficult to summarize both briefly and accurately. The aim of the 'mystic' form is best contrasted with that of the collective, integrative, political value of sacrificial civic religion: the individual seeks through possession/'madness' to transcend the constraints of the everyday and become a member of a privileged but temporary community of bliss (Eur. *Bacch.* 64–169; Strabo 10. 3. 7). Religious imagery and style offer a complex counterpoint to those of civic cult. A brusquer world-rejection inspired the 'mysteriosophic' form, based upon a myth accounting for the separation between god and man, flesh and spirit (Kern, *Orph. frag.*

[continued on p. 486]

mythology

mythology is the field of scholarship dealing with myth but also a particular body of myths. Myth goes back to the Greek word *mythos*, which originally meant 'word, speech, message' but in the 5th cent. BC started to acquire the meaning 'entertaining, if not necessarily trustworthy, tale'. The Romans used the word *fabula*, which was also used in modern discussions until *c*.1760, when the Göttingen classicist C. G. Heyne (1729–1812) coined the word *mythus* in order to stress the inner veracity of myth. No universally accepted definition of myth exists, but Walter Burkert's statement that 'myth is a traditional tale with secondary, partial reference to something of collective importance' gives a good idea of the main characteristics of myth.

Let us start with the problem of tradition. *Homer already mentions the Argonauts, the Theban Cycle (see HOMER, 9), and the deeds of *Heracles. The presence in Mycenaean Linear B texts of the formulae 'Mother of the Gods' and 'Drimius, son of *Zeus' suggests a divine genealogy, and the myths of *Achilles, Helen, and the cattle-raiding Heracles all seem to go back to Indo-European times (and Heracles maybe further back than that). The connection with central institutions or pressing problems of society—initiation, marriage, food—makes their continuity persuasive: Achilles' myth can hardly be separated from rites of initiation, whereas wedding poetry probably stands in the background of Helen's mythology. See INITIATION.

Other myths were certainly also of considerable age, such as the birth of Athenian Erechtheus from the seed of *Hephaestus or the birth of the famous horse Arion from the union of *Poseidon with the goddess Erinys. It is typical of Greek myth that Homer and other Archaic poets tended to suppress such strange and scandalous details, which survived only in locally fixed traditions. The trend of Greek mythology was firmly anthropomorphic and away from the fantastic.

Another ancient complex was constituted by initiatory myths. Strikingly, all early Panhellenic expeditions—the Trojan War (see TROY), Jason and the Argonauts (see MEDEA), and the Calydonian Hunt—contain many male initiatory elements, just as the myths of Iphigenia, Io, Europa, and the daughters of Proetus reflect the final transition into womanhood. Although many other Indo-European peoples had initiatory myths, their prominence is one of the distinctive features of Greek mythology.

A more recent complex of myths came from the east. The Indo-Europeans had at the most only rudimentary theogonical and cosmogonical myths. It is not surprising, therefore, that in this area Greece became very much indebted to the rich mythologies of Anatolia and Mesopotamia. Cronus' castration of his father Uranus ultimately derives from the Hurrians, having passed through Hittite and Phoenician intermediaries; the division of the world between Zeus, Poseidon, and *Hades through the casting of lots, as described in the *Iliad* (15. 187–93), derives from the Akkadian epic *Atrahasis*; and when *Hera, in a speech to deceive Zeus, says that she will go to Oceanus, 'origin of the gods', and Tethys, the 'mother' (*Il.* 14. 201), she mentions a couple derived from the parental pair Apsu and Tiamat in the Babylonian creation epic *Enuma Elish*. New clay tablets will surely present further surprises in this direction.

The fertile contacts with the east probably took place in the early iron age. Somewhat later, the foundations of colonies (see COLONIZATION, GREEK) in the Mediterranean and the Black Sea (*c*.750–600 BC) led to the last great wave of mythological inventions. In particular, the myths about the return of the heroes after the Trojan War, but also the expedition of the Argonauts, enabled many colonies to connect their new foundations to the Panhellenic past as created through these great myths. It is surprising how quickly traditional story-patterns here transformed historical events.

It is clear that poets were always prepared to assimilate or borrow new material. Another way of 'staying in business' was to vary the traditional myths by introducing new details—e.g. new names and motivations—or by restructuring the myth in a different direction. Whereas Archaic myth concentrated more, for example, on dynasties and heroic feats, in a later, more regulated society, myth tended to concentrate on relations within the family and, especially in Athenian tragedy (see TRAGEDY, GREEK), on the relation between individual and *polis or the value of democratic institutions (see DEMOCRACY, ATHENIAN).

Rome, on the other hand, was situated at the margin of the 'civilized' world and was late to assimilate Greek myth (see further below). When the Roman élite started to write down its history at the end of the 3rd cent. BC, it had one fixed mythological complex at its disposal: the foundation of Rome by *Romulus and Remus. A few names, such as *Janus and Picus, hint at the sometime existence of other myths, but nothing suggests an originally rich mythology, and the absence of a Götterapparat has even led some scholars to the suggestion that the Romans lacked a mythology altogether. Moreover, the 'brain drain' of neighbouring élites into Rome did not favour the survival of Italic myths: the founding of Praeneste by Caeculus is the only full myth from Latium that we still have. The foundation myths show that the temporal horizon was not the creation of gods or men but the birth of the native city; the foundation of the city was also the most important mythological theme in public declamations in imperial times.

Unlike Rome, which lacked a native expression for poets and poetry, Greece knew many poets who were the main producers of mythology; the tradition of formal narrative prose, which existed as well, is only discoverable in bare outlines. Poets performed at courts or local festivals in various genres, which successively became popular: epic in the 8th cent., choral lyric in the 6th, and, finally, tragedy, the last public performance of myth, in the 5th. Yet myths were also related in other contexts. Temple friezes, sculptures, and vases (see IMAGERY; PAINTING; SCULPTURE) made myth as a subject visible virtually everywhere. Women told myths during weaving-sessions (Eur. Ion 196 f.); old men will have related them in the leschai (club-like meeting-places), and mothers and nurses told them to children (Eur. fr. 484 Nauck; Pl. Leg. 887d). 'Indoctrination' by mothers and nurses will have been a significant, if usually neglected, factor in the continuing popularity of myth all through antiquity.

The uses of myth varied over time, but the entertainment value was always important. Indeed, Homer himself points to the delight of songs (Od. 17. 385). Choral lyric, with its combination of music, dance, and song, must have been quite a spectacle, and for the thousands of spectators Athenian *tragedy was a welcome break in the winter months. Other uses included the foundation of the social and political order. Myth explained how in Athens males had arrived at their dominant position through the chaos caused by women; how cities originated, such as Thebes through a struggle against a dragon, or how tribal groupings arose, such as the Ionians from Ion and the Aeolians from Aeolus. It explained why, for example, the Spartans ruled their extended territory, or why Athens could claim Aegina.

Myth also helped the Greeks to define the world around them and their own place in relation to the gods. By situating murderous women on mountains, by letting girls in their prime play on flowery meadows, or by ascribing the ancestry of the leading family to a river-god, these features of the landscape were assigned negative or positive values. Moreover, by relating the unhappy endings of love affairs between gods and humans, for example Semele being burnt to ashes through the appearance of Zeus in full glory, myth stressed the unbridgeable gap between mortals and immortals.

Finally, the aetiological function of myth was substantial. Many myths explained the birth or function of rituals; even the tragedian *Euripides often recounted the origins of vital Attic cults. Other myths highlighted or 'explained' unusual features of ritual: the myth of the Lemnian women concentrated on the separation of the sexes but totally left out the new fire, which was actually very prominent in the corresponding ritual. (See W. Burkert, Homo Necans (1983), 190 ff.) The exaggeration by myth of the ritual separation of the sexes into the mythical murder shows up an important difference between myth and *ritual: myth can depict as real what in ritual has to remain symbolic. Over time, myth could free itself from one specific ritual and be connected with other ones, or the ritual could disappear while the myth continued to be narrated: in the 2nd cent. AD the traveller *Pausanias recorded many myths of which the rituals had already long disappeared.

Myth was originally the product of an oral society (see ORALITY), but the arrival of writing brought important changes. Poets had now to share their leading intellectual roles with philosophers and historians—authors who wrote in prose and did not have to subject their opinions to the scrutiny of a public. The new intellectuals soon started to systematize and criticize mythological traditions. On the other hand, the force of tradition weighed heavily and that explains why the two most popular strategies in dealing with mythology were rationalization, which in our sources starts with Hecataeus of Miletus (c.550–480 BC), and allegorization, which probably started with the late 6th-cent. rhapsodist Theagenes of Rhegium; the adoption of this approach by the Stoics (see STOICISM) caused its survival until late antiquity. In this way, intellectuals could have their mythological cake and eat it.

These developments strongly diminished the public influence of poets as prime producers of mythology. In Hellenistic times, the myths recorded and adapted by *Callimachus and his contemporaries were directed at a small circle of connoisseurs, not the general public. However, it was these poets who exercised an enormous influence in Rome, where in the last two centuries of the republic and during the early Principate a proliferation of mythical themes can be noted—to the extent that in *Ovid one ritual can receive several aetiological myths. However, it is hard to say what degree of authority, if any, these myths had in Rome.

In the Hellenistic and early imperial period scholars started to collect myths in order to elucidate allusions in the Classical authors; most important in this respect was the collection of mythological scholia (ancient commentators) on Homer which circulated as a separate book at least from the 1st to the 5th cent. AD. Other collections concentrated on one theme, such as *Eratosthenes' book of star-myths or the famous Library ascribed to Apollodorus of Athens, which organized the mythological material by families. It is especially these collections which have ensured modern knowledge of the less familiar myths of Greece.

The modern study of Greek mythology started in France in the 18th cent., but the centre of interest soon shifted to Germany, where there was more philological expertise. It was the insights of Heyne in particular—myth as history, myth as explanation of natural phenomena, myth as the product of a specific people—which dominated the field in the 19th cent. However, the excesses of the naturalist interpretation were an important factor in the shift of scholarly interest away from mythology towards ritual at the end of the 19th cent. Since the middle 1960s interest in Greek myth has revived, notably through the work of Walter Burkert (1931–   ). The focal points of the new approaches are the relationship between myth and ritual and the explanatory and normative functions of myth. Roman myth has also profited from this revival, but the scarcity of material and the élite's view of myths as *fabulae*, 'fictional stories', make it difficult to see what exactly the place of myth was in Roman society. The differences between Greek and Roman mythology still await further analysis.   J. N. B.

232), evident in the gold plaques from Pelinna in *Thessaly (late 4th cent. BC). The 'mystery' type is much more integrated into dominant social values. The modal form, the Eleusinian mysteries, was a full and regular part of Athenian civic cult from the late 6th cent. BC, institutionalizing many aspects of religious aspiration otherwise excluded from public ceremonial: collective purification, the dramatic representation of mythical narrative, the opportunity for awe, fear, wonder, scurrility, and humour (the *gephyrismoi* (ritual abuse) at the bridge over the Cephissus), explicit exegesis by the *mystagōgoi*, the privilege bestowed by an open secret 'that may not be divulged', and

public reaffirmation of a theodicy of moral desert linked to good fortune. In this perspective, the offer of a blessed existence in the Elysian Fields after death (e.g. *Hymn. Hom. Cer.* 480–9, comm. N. J. Richardson (1974)) received no special emphasis, being a projection of complacency into the world beyond, not a compensation for the sorrows of this one. The point probably holds good for all mystery cults, indigenous or 'oriental' (cf. Diod. Sic. 5. 49. 5 f.), until the 3rd cent. AD.   R. L. G.

mythology (see page 484)

Naevius, Gnaeus, stage poet of Campanian birth (west central Italy) and obscure social attachments, possibly a client of the Claudii Marcelli. He saw military service in the last years of the First Punic War (see ROME (HISTORY), §1.4). His theatrical career began as early as 235 and was over by 204. Many stories were told of the insulting remarks he made about men of the nobility from the stage or in other contexts. Plautus, *Mil.* 210–12 was interpreted to refer to a spell by him in prison. He died in the Punic city of Utica.

Titles of 32 plays on themes of the Attic 'New' Comedy (see COMEDY (GREEK), NEW) are transmitted (*Acontizomenos, Agitatoria, Agrypnuntes, †assitogiola†, Carbonaria, Chlamydaria, Colax, †cemetria†, Corollaria, Dementes, Demetrius, Dolus, Figulus, Glaucoma, Gymnasticus, Hariolus, Lampadio, Leo, Nagido, Neruolaria, †pellicus†, Personata, Proiectus, Quadrigemini, Stalagmus, Stigmatias, Tarentilla, Technicus, Testicularia, †tribacelus†, Triphallus, Tunicularia*). According to *Terence (*An.* 9–21), Naevius was one of those who set a precedent for treating an Attic model with some liberty. He put both dialogues and monologues into musically accompanied metres of the type used by his contemporary *Plautus. On occasion he made his Greek personages allude to features of Italian life. There is thus no need to deduce from an allusion to the tastes of the men of Praeneste and Lanuvium (Macrob. *Sat.* 3. 18. 6) that the *Hariolus* was a play of the kind composed by Titinius and Lucius Afranius, i.e. a *fabula togata* (a drama, usually a comedy, set in Rome or Italy). The *Satyra* cited by Verrius Flaccus (Festus, p. 306. 29, Lindsay) is a mystery.

Six titles (*Danae, Equos Troianus, Hector proficiscens, Hesiona, Iphigenia, Lycurgus*) suggest tragedies of the Attic type. An account of Danae's disgrace (Non. p. 456. 25, Lindsay) seems to have been set in bacchiac verse rather than in spoken senarii. Naevius also composed original tragedies, one on the story of *Romulus the first Roman king, another (the *Clastidium*) on the defeat of a Gallic army in 222 by Marcus Claudius Marcellus. The latter may have been performed at funeral games for Marcellus in 208 or at the dedication in 205 of the temple of Virtus (military courage) vowed by the consul before the battle of Clastidium (fought in 222 BC by Rome against the Celts).

Only one of the plays survived into the 1st-cent. BC stage repertoire. A narrative poem in Saturnian verses concerning the 264–241 war with *Carthage, the *Carmen belli Poenici*, lasted longer. The grammarian Gaius Octavius Lampadio divided it into seven units towards the end of the 2nd cent. Naevius could hardly have been unaware of the pro-Carthaginian account of the war by Philinus of Acragas. Whether he knew of Fabius Pictor's has been the subject of much speculation. A digression filling a large part of the first of Lampadio's units, all the second, and a large part of the third related the early history of Rome and Carthage and provided a divine, perhaps even a cosmic, setting for the 3rd-cent. clash of arms. Naevius claimed inspiration by the Camenae (the Roman *Muses) and used a metrical and verbal style hard now to distinguish from that of Livius Andronicus' translation of *Homer's *Odyssey*.

Despite strong criticism by *Ennius (Cic. *Brut.* 72) Naevius' poem continued to find readers in the 1st cent. BC. Two grammarians, a Cornelius and a Vergilius, composed commentaries on it (Varro, *Ling.* 7. 39). *Horace used its survival to make fun of the claims of Ennius' *Annals* (*Epist.* 2. 1. 53–4). The collectors of 'thefts' in *Virgil's *Aeneid* detected a number from Naevius. The matter was still of interest in the 5th cent. AD (cf. Macrob. *Sat.* 6. 2), but there is no evidence that the older poem itself could be found in any library of this time.   H. D. J.

narrative, narration In the last 30 years, interest in narrative has developed at an incredible pace. Two branches of this 'narratology' may be distinguished. The one is orientated towards the 'story' as signified ('what happened': cf. especially the work of Greimas and Bremond, looking back to Propp's famous *Morphology of the Folktale*); the other is orientated rather towards the narrative as signifier ('the way it is told': Stanzel, Genette, in the line of the Russian formalists, Henry James, and E. M. Forster). Both approaches have been widely applied in classical studies, but the first has perhaps been more successful in the anthropological study of myth (see MYTHOLOGY), the second in literary studies, in that it focuses on the rhetorical construction of the work rather than its underlying functional structure. The sophisticated armoury of methods that is modern narratology is one of the products of structuralism and semiotics, and like those more general movements it has in recent times been subject to qualifications and criticisms from post-structuralists and from reception theorists and students of literary pragmatics with their greater focus on the audience or readership of a work.

An interest in the theory of narrative is already apparent in *Aristotle, whose *Poetics* may be considered the first treatise of narratology. Obviously there are differences between the prescriptive and evaluative character of ancient aesthetics and the descriptive and interpretative character of the semiotic approach: but it is significant that Aristotle assigns a central place to *mythos* or 'plot', which is the criterion (rather than metre) that he uses to distinguish poetry from other forms of discourse. *Mythos*, analysed in terms both of content and of its representation, is required to have an organic unity which calls to mind the concept of *closure as defined in Anglo-American criticism. The Aristotelian theory of narrative includes drama, and many modern theorists such as P. Ricoeur (*Time and Narrative* (1984)) include drama (and historiography) within the boundaries of narrative theory. More recently however, the idiosyncratic nature of the dramatic text, which is realized fully only in performance, has been stressed. One may certainly study narrative elements in non-narrative genres (e.g. *Pindar or the messenger speeches of tragedy; see TRAGEDY, GREEK), but it is important to remember that these genres have different contexts of *reception and different purposes. For this reason, a narrower conception of *fictional* narrative, above all *epic and the *novel, may be preferable. The question of the applicability of narratological approaches to *historiography has been particularly controversial, especially in relation to the work of the American historian Hayden White (see now S. Hornblower in Hornblower (ed.), *Greek Historiography* (1994), ch. 5).

The basic forms of western narrative occur already in Homer. P. Genette (*Narrative Discourse* (1980)) distinguishes four categories: the *order* in which events are narrated, their *duration* at the level of narrative in comparison to that of the underlying story, the mode or *mood* in which the information is conveyed ('focalization', point of view), and the *voice* which delivers it. A fifth category, that of the *frequency* with which an event is related, plays a less central role. Homeric narrative knows various possible ways of manipulating the linearity of story-time, such as the 'analeptic' flashbacks of Nestor in the *Iliad* and the beginning *in medias res* of the *Odyssey*. At the level of duration, 'scenes' with dialogue predominate over more rapid 'summaries': the opposition is a version of the Platonic one (see PLATO) between *mimēsis* 'representation' and *diēgēsis* 'narration', or Henry James's distinction between 'showing' and 'telling'. At the level of mood and voice, we are presented with a narrator who is (on the surface at least) impersonal, objective, and with a point of view superior to that of his characters. In comparison with this model, *Apollonius Rhodius and *Virgil, under the influence of Hellenistic epyllion (narrative poem of up to c.600 hexameters), show a desire for a denser and more 'subjective' mode more orientated towards the present moment of narration: hence the greater use of 'proleptic' anticipation of later events, of summary narration, and of focalization from the point of view of the characters (e.g. *Medea, *Dido).

The equivalence between poetry and fiction established by Aristotle had a long history in antiquity, and prose fiction developed late. The love novel or romance at first used a linear narrative technique (Chariton, Xenophon of Ephesus) but later turned to more complex forms in the phase influenced by the *Second Sophistic (Achilles Tatius, Longus, Heliodorus). In these, we find frequent use of a restricted point of view and 'metadiegesis' (the device of 'stories within stories' used e.g. also by *Ovid). This last technique is particularly prevalent in Heliodorus: the ultimate model is the *Odyssey*. In contrast, the Latin novel, associated more closely with that cultural tradition which the theorist Bakhtin called 'Menippean', tended towards more free and open forms, as in Greek did the *Life of Aesop*. See also LITERARY THEORY AND CLASSICAL STUDIES.　　　M. F.

nationalism

Greece, Archaic and Classical

D. M. Lewis has observed that 'to say that the Athenians built the Parthenon to worship themselves would be an exaggeration, but not a great one' (*CAH* 5² (1992), 139). Such self-worship would make 5th-cent. BC Athenians into 'nationalists' by one modern criterion (cf. E. Gellner, drawing on E. Durkheim: 'in a nationalistic age, societies worship themselves brazenly and openly': *Nations and Nationalism* (1983), 56)). But in the strong sense familiar from the history of the 19th-cent. rise of certain European nation-states, nationalism was hardly a feature of, or problem experienced by, the Classical Greek world. City-state particularism (see POLIS), and the consciousness of the religious and linguistic differences between Dorians and Ionians, are not the same as nationalism. Such feelings are best considered under the heading of *ethnicity. The idea that Greece was a 'nation', in a way that transcended local differences, does occur in our sources, but only at special moments like the Persian Wars (see e.g. Hdt. 8. 144). In the following period the Persian Wars affected Greek thinking (see GREECE (PREHISTORY AND HISTORY)); but the effect was negative rather than positive: in the 5th cent. BC *barbarians' were viewed more disparagingly as a result of the Persian Wars, just as the opposition between Dorians and Ionians became sharper as tensions between Athens and Sparta increased in the same period. But no correspondingly increased sense of Greek national identity is traceable. However, it has been well said (M. I. Finley, *The Use and Abuse of History*, 2nd edn. (1986), 121 f.) that it is pointless to castigate the Greeks for their 'failure to achieve unity' when there is so little evidence that this was an aim they had or even understood. Nationalism, like ethnicity, is a matter of attitude. The rhetorical nature of much of our literary evidence makes the truth about real attitudes hard to reach: before the invading Athenians arrive in *Sicily in 415 BC, the Syracusan Hermocrates in *Thucydides is made to say, in effect, 'let us unite! Sicily for the Sicilians' (4. 61. 2; 6. 34. 4); but once the Athenians have arrived he plays the Dorian card, to create bad feeling against the invading Ionians (6. 77. 1). S. H.

Hellenistic and Roman

The Graeco-Macedonian kingdoms were essentially dynastic states under personal rule. This was true even of the 4th-cent. BC ethnic state of Macedonia, sometimes seen today as a 'national' monarchy: but it is notable that *Alexander the Great's invasion of Asia not only promoted no vital Macedonian interest but led to the undoing of the traditional Macedonian state.

Early Rome did not evolve into a nation because initial expansion was based, not on incorporation, but treaty-relationships; even when she extended her citizenship to all Italy, a Roman citizen belonged to a city, not a country.

Subject-resistance to the Hellenistic and Roman empires is sometimes scanned for 'national feeling'. But there was rarely a tradition of political unity even among ethnic groups sharing a common culture (e.g. the Gauls), so that nationalism in the modern sense could not exist. Important exceptions are the indigenous Egyptians under the Ptolemies, and the *Jews of Judaea, who rebelled under both the *Seleucids and Rome; both groups could look back to a tradition of political independence. Otherwise, revolts against imperial Rome, when not occurring shortly after incorporation and constituting a continuation of the initial armed struggle, were chiefly occasioned by Roman misgovernment (e.g. the revolt of Boudicca in *Britain), the political ambitions of individuals (such as Gaius Avidius Cassius under Marcus *Aurelius), or other factors. Generally, Rome's political integration of subject élites (much more successful, and indeed purposeful, than in the Ptolemaic and Seleucid empires) kept local nationalisms underdeveloped. The assertion of local cultures in (e.g.) the African and Greek-speaking provinces has been thought to be fuelled by anti-Roman sentiment, but this interpretation is controversial (2nd-cent. AD nostalgia among Greek-speakers for the Classical past, for instance, was actually encouraged by Rome); it is no easier here than in the regional schisms of early Christianity to detect provincial quests for political independence. A. J. S. S.

navies The oldest navy in the ancient world was probably that of the Egyptian pharaohs. Very little is known about Egyptian naval development, however, until the dynasty known as the Saites (672–525 BC), one of whom, Necho II (610–595), reorganized the navy to protect Egyptian interests against the Babylonians. The introduction of *triremes, probably under Amasis (570–526), further strengthened Egypt's navy prior to the Persian conquest.

The Persian navy was created under Cambyses (530–522). It utilized triremes and was crewed by the king's maritime subjects, arranged in territorial or ethnic squadrons (e.g. Egyptians, *Phoenicians, Ionians). During much of the 5th cent. BC this navy fought in the eastern Mediterranean against the Greek city-states, led by Athens, whose ships were crewed by her citizens and subject allies. From the battle of Salamis (480) to the battle of Aegospotami (405) the Athenians were the dominant naval power in the region. They developed considerable expertise in trireme warfare, which was put to good use in the Peloponnesian War (431–404 BC). During the 4th cent. the Athenian navy remained a powerful force, although lack of money and manpower prevented a return to its former position of dominance. Defeat by the Macedonians at the battle of Amorgos in 322 BC effectively marked the end of the Athenian navy.

The Hellenistic period saw the development of larger warships as the Hellenistic monarchs apparently tried to outbuild each other in an attempt to achieve supremacy and assert prestige. The Ptolemaic kings (see EGYPT, PTOLEMAIC) used their navies extensively in the effort to secure their overseas possessions, but no single state gained lasting naval dominance until the Romans were forced to create a series of large fleets from the resources of Italy, initially in order to defeat the Carthaginians, and then to fight a series of wars in the Greek East.

Roman naval forces in the 2nd and 1st cents. BC were mainly drawn from allies in Italy and the Greek east. The value of a strong navy had been demonstrated to Octavian in his struggle with Sextus Pompeius. He established permanent naval forces soon after the battle of *Actium. These consisted of a fleet to guard the NW coast of Italy and the Gallic coast, based at Forum Iulii (mod. Fréjus), two praetorian fleets to secure the Italian coasts, based at Ravenna and Misenum, a small fleet based at *Alexandria, and, probably, another at Seleuceia in Pieria. Later emperors added units in the Black (Euxine) Sea, *Africa, *Britain, and on the Rhine and Danube rivers. The Forum Iulii fleet disappeared before the end of the 1st cent. AD, but most of the others seem to have continued to exist well into the 3rd cent. Considerable reorganization took place under *Constantine I who divided the fleets into smaller squadrons and created extra commands.

The duties of the Roman navy included transporting Roman troops, supporting land campaigns, protecting coastal settlements, suppressing *piracy, and dealing with hostile incursions by barbarians into Roman waters. The fleets of the Roman imperial navy contained mainly triremes and smaller vessels, with only a few quinqueremes or larger ships in the two praetorian fleets. After the defeat of Licinius in AD 324 triremes ceased to be the main ships of the imperial fleets, and the navy of the Byzantine empire consisted largely of two-banked galleys, called *dromones*.

Naval craft were expensive to build and maintain. Most warships could not be used for *trade and their crews were normally free men who required payment as well as provisioning. The creation of a navy was, therefore, a momentous step for any ancient state. *Samos acquired its navy during the prosperous period of Polycrates' tyranny, possibly with Egyptian backing. The Athenian navy of the 5th cent. BC was founded on the proceeds of a rich silver strike in the Laurium mines in 483, and maintained through tribute payments and the wealth of private citizens (see TRIERARCHY). During the Peloponnesian War the Spartans were only able to sustain their naval presence in the Aegean with the support of the Persian king, who provided money for the wages of the crews. The achievement of the Rhodians (see RHODES), who maintained a substantial navy from the 4th to the 1st cent. BC, was exceptional and surpassed only by the Roman empire.   P. de S.

navigation can be defined as the art of taking a ship successfully from one chosen point to another. From a very early stage the relatively calm, tideless waters of the Mediterranean encouraged travel by sea. Seagoing ships were not normally used in the winter months, because storms and poor visibility made navigation hazardous, but *Hesiod's suggestion that sailing be limited to July and August is overcautious (Hes. *Op.* 663–5), the period between the vernal and autumnal equinoxes being the best season, with some leeway at either end. Ancient vessels were either paddled, rowed, or sailed. Their speed depended upon size, type of propulsion, and the weather. Sailing speeds of between four and six knots seem to have been the norm with favourable winds. Light or unfavourable winds might reduce speed to less than one knot, making it preferable to lie up and wait for a change in the weather.

Ancient seafarers guided their vessels without the benefit of instruments or charts. Wherever possible they followed the coastline or sailed between fixed points on land. On clear nights the stars could be used to plot a course, as could the moon. Experienced ancient mariners would have had a good, practical understanding of the phases of the moon and the movement of the stars, which they would have passed on by oral transmission. They would also have needed detailed knowledge of local conditions such as prevailing winds and currents, the presence of reefs, rocks, and shallows, and how to follow a course according to local landmarks.

Basic navigational equipment included oars and sails, steering oars, anchors, usually made of stone or wood, or both, and a variety of lines and cables. Leaded lines for checking the depth of the water were common, often featuring a hollow weight that could be used to sample the nature of the seabed. Flags and pennants were used to identify warships, or sometimes deliberately to misidentify them (Polyaenus, *Strat.* 8. 53. 3), and lanterns were employed at night or in fog to enable flotillas to follow a flagship (App. *BCiv.* 2. 89). Although the theoretical skills and the basic knowledge needed to produce quite detailed *maps were available from the early Hellenistic period onwards, there is no evidence that charts intended for use at sea were ever produced. A few descriptions of sea routes

and coastlines (*periploi*) have survived from antiquity, but it is unlikely that they circulated among the mariners themselves.

Navigable rivers were also heavily used, especially the Nile, the Rhine, and the Rhône. In late republican and imperial times the Tiber would have been crowded with vessels carrying people and goods up to Rome from *Ostia. River-craft were mostly rowed, paddled, or sailed, but towing, either by teams of men or animals, or by use of a line fixed on shore and a capstan was also common.
      P. de S.

Nemrut Dag (Mt. Nemrut) (see ◀Map 2, Db▶), the highest mountain in Commagene, its peak—commanding spectacular views over SE Turkey—the site of a monumental *hierothesion* (mausoleum-cum-cult-centre) built *c.*40 BC by the Commagenian king Antiochus I; of interest for its grandiose divinizing (see RULER-CULT, *Greek*) of this Roman client king and for its mix of Greek and Persian imagery and religious ideas. The complex comprised a vast tumulus (probably the royal burial-mound) flanked by two terraces for sculpture, each repeating the same row of colossal enthroned divinities (8–9 m. (26–9 ft.) high), among them Antiochus himself, and the same two series of inscribed relief-slabs portraying respectively his Persian and Macedonian ancestors. In two long (Greek) inscriptions (duplicates), Antiochus expounded his lifelong piety and prescribed details of the cult (*OGI* 383; partial Eng. trans.: S. Burstein, *The Hellenistic Age from the Battle of Ipsos to the Death of Kleopatra VII* (1985), no. 48).   A. J. S. S.

Neptune, Italic god of *water. He extended his protection to watercourses and to expanses of water threatened by evaporation in the heat of summer as well as to human activities linked with water; hence, under the influence of *Poseidon, he could become patron of journeys on water. During *sacrifice (Roman), the cooked *exta* ('entrails') were thrown into water (Livy 29. 27. 5); it is in virtue of this capacity that the absurd identification of Consus with 'Neptunus Equester', i.e. Poseidon Hippios, takes place, Livy 1. 9. 6. The etymology of his name is quite uncertain; in Etruscan it is Neθun(u)s. His festival is of the oldest series (Neptunalia, 23 July); we know concerning its ritual only that arbours, *umbrae*, of boughs were commonly erected (Festus 519, 1 Lindsay), but it may be conjectured that its object was to obtain sufficient water at this hot and dry time of year. Neptune is attested at Rome before the first *lectisternium* or banquet for the gods (399 BC); his association there with *Mercury seems to refer to the circulation of merchandise (Livy 5. 13. 6). His cult-partner is Salacia (Gell. 13. 23. 2); she may be the goddess of 'leaping', i.e. springing water (*salire*), but was identified with Amphitrite as he was with Poseidon.   H. J. R.; J. Sch.

Nero (Nero Claudius Caesar), Roman emperor AD 54–68, was born 15 December 37 of Gnaeus Domitius Ahenobarbus (consul AD 32) and *Agrippina.

To strengthen his doubtful claim to the throne, stories had been spread of his miraculous childhood (Suet. *Ner.* 6; Tac. *Ann.* II. II) and stress laid on his descent from the divine *Augustus. In 49 his mother, as *Claudius' new wife, was able to have the younger *Seneca recalled from exile in order to teach her son rhetoric and to secure his betrothal to Claudius' daughter Octavia; in 50 Lucius Domitius Ahenobarbus was adopted by Claudius, thus becoming Tiberius Claudius Nero Caesar or, as he is sometimes called, Nero Claudius Caesar Drusus Germanicus. In the next year he assumed the *toga virilis* (dress indicating manhood) at the early age of 13 and was clearly marked out for the accession by being given the same privileges as Augustus' grandsons Gaius and Lucius had received. When Claudius died on 13 October 54, Nero was escorted into the praetorian camp by the prefect Sextus Afranius Burrus. The senate then conferred the necessary powers on Nero and declared his adoptive father a god and Agrippina his priestess.

The ancient tradition is unanimous in regarding Nero's initial years of rule as excellent, a period hailed as a golden age by contemporary poets. Two 4th-cent. writers ascribe to the later emperor *Trajan the view that Nero surpassed all other *principes* for a *quinquennium*, apparently referring to the first five years. Of our three major ancient authorities, *Suetonius and *Cassius Dio suggest that the young emperor at first left government to his mother and Dio adds that Seneca and Burrus soon took over control, leaving the emperor to his pleasures. *Tacitus, however, regards the influence of Agrippina (visible on coins of December 54 showing her head facing Nero's on the obverse) as more apparent than real and the role of his advisers as one of guiding his activities, as in Seneca's *De clementia*, and managing court intrigue and public relations. Nero's first speech to the senate, written by Seneca, is described by Suetonius (*Ner.* 10) as a promise to rule according to Augustan precedent; Tacitus (*Ann.* 13. 4) adds a renunciation of the abuses of the Claudian regime—excessive influence of palace minions and monopolization of jurisdiction by the *princeps*, in particular, the trying of (political) cases behind closed doors—and a pledge to share the responsibilities of government with the senate. The historian vouches for the fulfilment of these promises, clearly interpreting the last, not in the sense of a surrender of power by the *princeps* but of an attitude of respect towards that body. Symbolic of the new attitude was the legend '*ex s c*' ('in accordance with a senatorial decree') appearing regularly on the gold and silver coinage for the first ten years, though whether it is an authorization mark or relates to the types and legends is uncertain.

Nero at first heeded his advisers because they protected him from his domineering mother and indulged him within limits. She had always used the menace of rivals to threaten him, and the presence of a considerable number of dynastic claimants was inevitable under the Augustan Principate, which, not being an avowed monarchy, could have no law of succession to regulate the actual practice of hereditary succession. When Agrippina decided to show sympathy for Claudius' natural son Britannicus in 55, she sealed his doom, though the poisoning was not overt and could be dissembled, as by Seneca, who wrote praising Nero's clemency in the next year. In 59 Agrippina's resistance to his affair with Poppaea Sabina led Nero to enlist the prefect of the fleet of Misenum to drown her in a collapsible boat. When that failed, she was stabbed at her villa. This spectacular crime marked the end of the good part of Nero's reign, according to a contemporary view (Tac. *Ann.* 15. 67), echoed in the later tradition of the 'Quinquennium Neronis'. But for Tacitus, the political deterioration did not set in until 62 when a treason charge of the unrepublican sort, based on irreverence towards the emperor, was admitted for the first time in the reign, and Burrus died, thereby ending Seneca's influence as well. One of the new prefects, Ofonius Tigellinus, was seen by Tacitus as Nero's evil genius, rather like *Sejanus to *Tiberius. Nero now divorced his barren wife Octavia and married Poppaea who was pregnant: the child was a girl, Claudia Augusta, who was born in January of 41 and died four months later.

The death of his mother already made him feel freer to indulge his artistic passions. His enthusiasm for art, chariot-racing, and Greek *athletics seems to have been genuine; he wanted to lead Rome from gladiatorial shows (see GLADIATORS) to nobler entertainments. At the Iuvenalia, private games held in 59 to celebrate the first shaving of his beard, he sang and performed on the cithara (lyre) but also encouraged members of the upper classes to take lessons in singing and dancing. A year later he introduced for the first time at Rome public games in the Greek fashion (see GAMES) to be celebrated every five years. In 61 he opened a *gymnasium and distributed free oil to competitors. His interest in re-educating Rome was genuine: it was not until the second celebration of these games in 65 that the *princeps* himself performed, though he had already made his début in the Greek city of Naples a year earlier. His voice, described as 'slight and husky', may have been passable; his poetry was probably his own, for *Suetonius had seen his notebooks with their erasures (*Ner.* 52).

The emperor's popularity with the propertied classes had been further undermined by a fire which devastated the city and strained the economy. It broke out in the early hours of 19 June 64 in shops around the Circus Maximus, and spread north through the valley between the Palatine and the Esquiline. It lasted for nine days in all and reduced three of the fourteen regions (*regiones*) of the city to rubble, leaving only four regions untouched. The emperor provided emergency shelter and helped with reconstruction, but he soon revealed that he would take the opportunity, not only to introduce a new code of safety for buildings, but to use land previously in private occupation for a grand palace and spacious parks (the Golden House or Domus Aurea) in the centre of Rome. The precious metal coinage shows the financial strain, to which the expense of the disastrous revolt of Boudicca (Boadicea) in

*Britain in 60 and the protracted wars with Parthia over Armenia contributed: both the gold and silver were reduced in weight and the silver content of the denarius lowered by more than 10 per cent. With rumours circulating that Nero had instigated the fire and recited his own poems over the burning city, Nero made the Christians scapegoats, burning them alive to make the punishment fit the alleged crime (see CHRISTIANITY).

Nero never lost his popularity with the ordinary people of Rome, who loved his generosity and his games. The threat came from the upper classes and especially from senators governing provinces where the propertied élite had become discontent as a result of confiscations after the Rome fire: they are attested in Gaul, Spain, Africa, Britain, Judaea, and Egypt. But meanwhile his paranoiac prosecutions in Rome led to a conspiracy in 65 to assassinate him and make Gaius Calpurnius Piso emperor. The scheme was betrayed. Piso and his accomplices, senators including *Lucan, knights, officers of the praetorian guard, and one of the prefects, Faenius Rufus, were executed. Nero now suspected all, and more deaths followed, including Seneca, Petronius, and the Stoics Thrasea Paetus and Barea Soranus (see STOICISM). In the year after Poppaea's death, Nero married *Messallina, and, also in 66, Tiridates, a member of the ruling Parthian dynasty, came to Rome to receive the diadem of Armenia from Nero's hand. This represented an adjustment of Roman foreign policy in the east, where independent client kings had always been imposed on this buffer state with Parthia. In September of 66, despite another conspiracy at Beneventum, Nero himself left for Greece, to perform in all the Greek games. The highpoint of his tour was his liberation of Greece from Roman administration and taxation, announced at a special celebration of the Isthmian Games at Corinth on 28 November 67. The text of Nero's speech in Greek is preserved on an inscription (ILS 8794; Syll.³ 814; Sherk, Hadrian 71 for translation).

While in Greece *Vespasian was selected from the emperor's entourage to deal with a revolt in Judaea (see JEWS). But Nero deposed and executed three senatorial commanders, Gnaeus Domitius Corbulo who had served him well in the east, and the Scribonii brothers who governed the two Germanies. Disaffection was rumbling in the west. At last Nero, in response to the warnings of his freedman Helius, returned to Italy. Soon after, in March of 68, Gaius Iulius Vindex, governor of Gallia Lugdunensis (see GAUL, TRANSALPINE), rose in arms. Although he was defeated two months later by the governor of Upper Germany, Nero's failure to respond decisively had encouraged others to defect. In Spain Galba declared himself 'Legate of the Senate and Roman People', and in Africa Lucius Clodius Macer revolted. The praetorians were told that Nero had already fled abroad and were bribed by Gaius Nymphidius Sabinus, one of their prefects, to declare for Galba. The senate followed suit, decreeing Nero a public enemy. Nero took refuge in the villa of his freedman Phaon and there he committed suicide, reputedly lamenting, 'What an artist dies with me!' (Suet. *Ner.* 48–9).

Nero's *philhellenism earned him the devotion of many in the Greek-speaking provinces, and within the next twenty years, three false Neros appeared there, all playing the lyre and all attracting followers. But the Christians naturally hated him for their persecution of 64 and the Jews for the mistreatment that led to the revolt which ultimately lost them the Temple in Jerusalem.

M. P. C.; G. E. F. C.; M. T. G.

Nerva, Marcus Cocceius, Roman emperor AD 96–8, grandson of *Tiberius' friend Marcus Cocceius Nerva, was born possibly in AD 35. His family, which came from the old Latin colony of Narnia and acquired distinction during the Civil Wars, had a remote connection with the Julio-Claudian dynasty. Nerva it seems did not serve as a provincial governor or hold any senior administrative post, but was influential as a confidant of *Nero, who admired his poetry and presented him with triumphal ornaments and other honours after the suppression of the conspiracy of Gaius Calpurnius Piso in 65. Despite this he was high in the Flavians' favour, being ordinary *consul with *Vespasian in 71 and again in 90 with *Domitian.

Nerva was seemingly not party to the plot to murder Domitian and was approached by the conspirators only after several others had rebuffed them. But he had qualities of good birth, a pleasant disposition, and long experience in imperial politics, and immediately set out to be a contrast to Domitian, who had been detested by the upper classes and whose memory was damned by the senate (*damnatio memoriae*). The slogans on Nerva's coinage ('Public Freedom', 'Salvation', 'Equity', 'Justice') reflect his wish to create a new atmosphere. He released those on trial for treason, banned future treason charges, restored exiles, returned property confiscated by Domitian, displayed moderation in the public honours he accepted, and took advice from leading men. He built granaries in Rome, dedicated the forum Transitorium begun by Domitian, distributed a largess to the people and the soldiers, removed the burden of the imperial post (*vehiculatio*, see POSTAL SERVICE) from communities in Italy, and initiated moves to buy up land for distribution to the poorest citizens; he may also have begun the 'alimentary' scheme, which aimed to provide funds for the maintenance of poor children in rural Italy, although major responsibility for its execution probably lay with Trajan. According to Tacitus, Nerva combined two incompatible elements—liberty and imperial rule (*Agr.* 3).

However, Nerva was elderly and infirm and had no children. Naturally there was speculation about the succession, and further problems appeared. The desire for vengeance against supposed agents of Domitian came close to anarchy. The appointment of a senatorial committee in 97 to effect economies suggests that there were some financial difficulties, which arguably were the result of extravagance in Nerva's regime. The most serious signs of disquiet occurred among the soldiers, with whom Domitian had been popular. One army was close to mutiny on the news of his death, and subsequently there were rumours about the intentions of a governor of one of the eastern provinces in command of a substantial army (Philostr. *VS* 488; Plin. *Ep.* 9. 13). Coins celebrating 'Concord of the armies' probably express hope rather than confidence. There was also a plot against the emperor in Rome. Most ominously, rebellion broke out among the praetorians who had been stirred up by their prefect Casperius Aelianus into demanding the execution of the murderers of Domitian. Nerva had to accede, and was forced to give public thanks for the executions, thereby losing much of his authority and prestige. In October 97, amid gathering political crisis, he adopted *Trajan, whom he had previously appointed governor of Upper Germany, as his son, co-emperor, and successor. His own title *Germanicus*, granted for a minor victory over the Germans in Bohemia, was conferred on Trajan. It is impossible to discover the exact circumstances of Trajan's adoption. Pliny suggests that the empire was tottering above the head of an emperor who now regretted his elevation to imperial power (*Pan.* 6. 3, 7. 3), but this may have been exaggerated in order to please Trajan. However if Nerva's regime faced increasing discontent, his advisers would doubtless take into consideration Trajan's distinguished background and career, popularity with the troops, and proximity to Rome. Nerva's death on 28 January 98 marks an important point in the development of the empire, since he was the last strictly Italian emperor. J. B. C.

Nicias (*c*.470–413 BC), Athenian politician and general. During the period after the death of *Pericles he became the principal rival of Cleon in the struggle for political leadership. He was a moderate and opposed the aggressive *imperialism of the extreme democrats, his aim being the conclusion of peace with Sparta as soon as it could be attained on terms favourable to Athens. Elected frequently to serve as *stratēgos* (general), he led several expeditions in which, thanks to his cautious competence, he suffered no serious defeat and won no important victory. He was largely responsible for the armistice concluded in 423, and the Peace of 421 appropriately bears his name.

He now favoured a policy of retrenchment and objected to the ambitious schemes of *Alcibiades, who advocated Athenian intervention in the Peloponnese and later an expedition to Sicily. Despite his disapproval Nicias was appointed with Alcibiades and Lamachus to conduct this enterprise. Alcibiades was soon recalled, and little was accomplished in 415, but in 414 Syracuse was besieged and almost reduced to capitulation. The death of Lamachus, the arrival of the Spartan Gylippus, and the inactivity of Nicias, now seriously ill, transformed the situation, and in spite of the efforts of Demosthenes, who brought reinforcements in 413, the Athenians were themselves blockaded. Nicias, who refused to withdraw by sea until too late, led the vanguard in a desperate attempt to escape by land.

His troops were overwhelmed at the river Assinarus, and he was subsequently executed. The narrative of *Thucydides, though giving due credit to Nicias for his selfless devotion, shows very clearly that the Athenian disaster was largely due to the inadequacy of his military leadership.

He was very wealthy (Xen. *Vect.* 4. 14 says he had 1,000 slaves working in the silver *mines; see SLAVERY) and spent lavishly; see esp. Plut. *Nic.* 3, mentioning the splendid festival procession he led to *Delos, where Athens had recently re-established the festival of the Delia (Thuc. 3. 104). Thucydides may have this in mind when he speaks of Nicias' *aretē* (civic virtue, a notion which could include open-handed outlay on liturgies, i.e. financial services to the city). See Thuc. 7. 86. 5. H. D. W.; S. H.

Nicopolis (see ◀Map 1, Ab▶) in Epirus, situated on the isthmus of the Preveza peninsula opposite *Actium at the entrance to the Ambracian Gulf. It was founded by Octavian (see AUGUSTUS) on the site of his army encampment (specially revered, as at *Alexander the Great's Cilician city of Nicopolis, founded after the battle of Issus in 333 BC, which provided the model for the city in Epirus). Nicopolis was not only a 'victory city' (the Greek name means this), honouring Octavian's defeat of Antony (Mark *Antony) and *Cleopatra in this region, but was also a *synoecism of older cities (Strabo 10. 2. 2; Paus. 5. 23. 3). It was settled soon after 31 BC, and dedicated, perhaps, in 29. A free city minting its own coinage, Nicopolis served as a regional administrative, economic, and religious centre, especially following the creation of a separate province of Epirus. Augustus chose the city as the new site for the Actian Games (*Actia*), an ancient festival once held on Cape Actium, but now celebrated every four years under Spartan stewardship and ranked equal to the major Panhellenic *games; he also enrolled it in the Delphic amphictiony (see DELPHI). Surviving structures include impressive city walls, a theatre, stadium, bath structure, odeum, Actian victory monument, aqueduct, and four early Christian basilicas. It was home to Epictetus. See illustration on following page. N. P., W. M. M.

Nike, the goddess of Victory, is first mentioned by *Hesiod (*Theog.* 383–4) as daughter of the Titan Pallas and Styx, and sister of Zelos, Kratos, and Bia ('Rivalry', 'Strength', and 'Force'). With these she was honoured by *Zeus because she fought with the gods against the Titans. *Bacchylides (11. 1) depicts her standing next to Zeus on Olympus and judging the award for 'areta' (virtue) to gods and men. The victorious athlete sinks into the arms of Nike (Pind. *Nem.* 5. 42). Here Nike is already victory of an athletic, not only a military, contest.

Nike has no mythology of her own, and in cult may be assimilated with other gods, such as Zeus at *Olympia (Paus. 5. 14. 8) or *Athena at Athens, where from *c*.566 BC, she had an altar on the Acropolis, and subsequently a Classical temple. *Pausanias (1. 22. 4) calls this Nike wing-

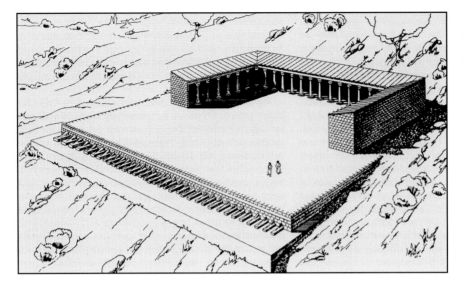

Nicopolis Reconstructed drawing of the naval trophy set up by Octavian (the future *Augustus) on the site of his army encampment at the battle of *Actium. The trophy overlooked the site of Nicopolis, founded by Octavian in imitation of earlier 'victory-cities' built by *Pompey (in Pontus, *Asia Minor) and *Alexander the Great (near Issus).

less, adding (3. 15. 7) that the Athenians and Spartans had a wingless Nike so that she would always stay with them. In art, her winged appearance is readily confused with orientalizing figures, and subsequently with Iris, especially when she holds a *kērykeion* (caduceus). She appears from

Nike A 4th-cent BC gemstone depicts Nike (Victory), winged and scantily draped, alighting to build a *trophy of captured arms on a tree-trunk marking a battle site.

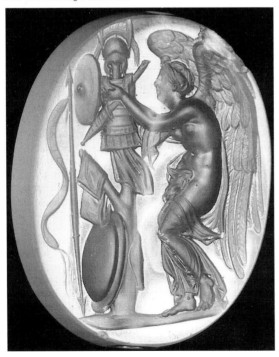

the early 6th cent., on vases, freestanding or as acroteria, always in the 'Knielauf' pose. She may have two or four wings. The Nike of Archermus (supposedly the first to give Nike wings) c.550 BC and that of Callimachus c.480 are representative.

In the Classical period, her iconography is fully developed, attributes including garland, jug, phiale, and *thymiatērion* (censer). She is particularly popular on vases after the Greek victory over Persia at the battle of Marathon (490 BC), often alone, or pouring a libation over an altar, for both gods and men; also in athletic and military contexts, sometimes holding weapons, or decorating a *trophy. She strides, runs, or flies. Sculptural representations attempt to evoke flight, such as the Nike of Paros (c.470) where she hovers or alights; so too the Nike of Paeonius at Olympia of c.420. She was shown alighting on the hand of the Athena Parthenos and the Zeus at Olympia (where she was also an acroterion). The sculpted parapet of her temple on the Acropolis (c.410) shows her as messenger of Victory, setting a trophy, administrating libations, leading bulls to sacrifice, and, characteristically, binding her sandal. She appears as charioteer on Classical vases, especially south Italian.

In the Hellenistic period, Nike is used for political ends by *Alexander the Great and his Successors (the 'Diadochi') on coins and *gems. The striding type is represented by the Nike of Samothrace (c.306–250), and continues in attachments to Canosan vases and terracotta statuettes to the 1st cent. BC.   K. W. A.

nomads Greek (followed by Roman) writers lumped together as nomads (*nomades*, formed on *nomos*, 'pasture') all pastoral groups for whom wandering was a way of life, without distinguishing (as does the modern concept of nomadism) between semi-nomads—including those practising transhumance—and fully nomadic societies of no fixed abode, such as the ancients met on the desert fringes of Libya and Arabia and in Scythia. *Homer's portrayal of the pastoral Cyclopes as uncivilized and savage (*Od.* 9) inaugurates a persistent hostility in Greek literature to nomads, whose lifestyle as 'cultivators of living fields' (Arist. *Pol.* 1256ᵃ34–5), in particular their different diet (in particular their drinking of milk) and their desert habitat, set them apart from the sedentary communities of Greek farmers and encouraged a stereotyping taken to extremes in *Herodotus' account of the nomadic Scythian 'man eaters' (4. 106). Thus to turn nomads into settled agriculturalists ranked among the self-evident achievements of the Macedonian kings *Philip II and *Alexander the Great (Arr. *Anab.* 7. 9. 2, 8. 40. 8). Modern ethnographic work denies this rigid conceptual separation of cultivators from nomads in real life, stressing rather their economic symbiosis, for which there is some ancient evidence from Roman *Africa, where the old view, that the Roman state tried to blockade out the Libyan nomads by means of a *limes* (artificial barrier), is now questioned. See BARBARIAN; PASTORALISM.   A. J. S. S.

Notitia Dignitatum The 'List of Offices' is a late Roman illustrated manuscript which survived in a Carolingian copy. This is lost, but at least four copies were made, which are now in Oxford, Cambridge, Paris, and Munich. The Notitia is divided into two parts, each entitled 'a list of all offices, civil and military' in the eastern and western halves of the empire respectively, as divided in AD 395. Each part was kept by a senior member of the court secretariat, the *primicerius notariorum*, and contains an index followed by more than 40 chapters, one for each of the high officers of state, from the praetorian prefects, masters of the soldiers, and other court dignitaries to the lesser generals (*comites* and *duces*) and the provincial governors, in order of precedence or geographical sequence. For the provincial governors, however, only one specimen of each grade (*consularis*, *corrector*, *praeses*) is given. Each chapter gives the title and rank of the dignitary, a brief description of his functions, including a list of his subordinate officers, if any, and the members of his staff (*officium*); for generals, a list of units under his command, with their stations in the case of *duces*. Each chapter is accompanied by an illustration of *insignia*, a schematic picture of the dignitary's responsibilities; for *magistri militum* ('masters of the soldiers') these are the shields of their regiments, for *duces* ('generals') their forts. The Notitia outlines the late Roman order of battle and administrative structure in great detail, but its date and purpose are obscure. It may have listed dignitaries who received letters of appointment (for a fee), our copy being derived from the western working copy, since some eastern chapters are in abbreviated form and contain nothing that is demonstrably later than 395, whereas the western chapters have been altered thereafter. Both parts contain internal inconsistencies due to piecemeal revision, and material which reached its present form in earlier reigns. Revision later than 395 is most apparent in the western military chapters, which must reflect the supremacy (395–408) and strategy of the *magister militum* Stilicho.   R. S. O. T.

novel, Greek Extended prose narrative fiction is a latecomer to Greek literature. It is first recognizable in a lively account of the Assyrian king Ninus' courtship of a 14-year-old Semiramis, preserved on a papyrus dated by a document on its verso to earlier than AD 100–1 and by its script to between 50 BC and AD 50. Its composition need not be earlier, though some conjecture *c*.100 BC. Of the authors of the five novels to survive complete, Chariton (known, like *Metiochus and Parthenope*, from papyri and oriental descendants) probably belongs to the later 1st cent. AD, though a date as late as *Hadrian is possible; Xenophon of Ephesus to the first half of the 2nd cent., and Achilles Tatius to the second; Longus is perhaps late 2nd or early 3rd cent. AD, while both early 3rd and late 4th cent. AD are claimed for Heliodorus. Only Iamblichus' *Babylonian History*, known from fragments and Photius' epitome, is firmly dated by its author's claimed career, to *c*. AD 165–80.

These narratives (two in eight books, the others in four, five, and ten) vary a shared pattern. Boy and girl fall in love: Xenophon's heroine is also 14, his hero 16, Longus' 13 and 15. Either before marriage (Achilles Tatius, Heliodorus, ? *Ninus*) or soon after (Chariton, Xenophon of Ephesus) they are separated and survive storms, shipwreck, imprisonment, attempted seduction or rape, torture, and even what readers and characters believe to be death, before reunion at the book's end. Their ordeals usually traverse Egypt or other near eastern lands; but Heliodorus' couple have Ethiopian Meroe as their goal, that of Xenophon of Ephesus reach south Italy, and Longus compresses his pastoral couple's adventures into a corner of *Lesbos, substituting sexual naïvety for external forces as obstacles to their union. The heroine typically preserves her virginity/fidelity to her husband, although Chariton's accepts a cultivated Greek as her second husband (to protect the hero's child she is carrying). Achilles' hero, however, succumbs to a married Ephesian, and Longus' receives sexual instruction, crucial to the plot's advancement, from a married city woman.

Love stories are found in earlier Greek literature, both verse (especially of the Hellenistic period) and prose (above all the more famous *Xenophon's *Cyropaedia*); *historiography is evoked by the setting of the *Ninus*, of Chariton's *Chaereas and Callirhoe* (5th/4th-cent. BC *Syracuse), and of a scene from *Metiochus and Parthenope*; the centrality of a young couple's love, their city origins, and some speeches recall New Comedy (see COMEDY, GREEK); analogous story-patterns can be found in Mesopotamian or Egyptian literature. But the novel evolves from none of these. Rather it is a late Hellenistic or early imperial creation, whose literary effects include evocation of all these Greek predecessors and of *Homer's *Odyssey* and Attic tragedy too (see TRAGEDY, GREEK). Elaborate 'documentation' of the story's 'origin' and apparently exact geographical detail entice readers to accept the 'events' as having once happened, albeit in the distant (*Ninus*) and particularly Classical past: only Xenophon of Ephesus' world seems to be that of the empire, though Achilles' might be taken as such, and the élites from which the novels' characters are drawn (even the foundlings Daphnis and Chloe) resemble those of Greek cities of the Roman empire. But all authors exclude Rome and Romans. *Piracy is commoner than in the *pax Romana* ('Roman peace'), coincidences are far-fetched, but the impossible is avoided and only such miraculous events admitted (e.g. prophetic *dreams) as contemporary belief credited.

Characters are less convincing. Anglophone critics often adduce shallow characterization as a reason for denying that these works are 'novels': in continental Europe they are *Roman* (Ger.), *roman* (Fr.), *romanzo* (It.), *romance* (Portug.) rather than *novela* (Sp.). The main characters, albeit morally admirable, are indeed rarely interesting, though the often stronger heroines engage readers more effectively, and some minor characters (e.g. Heliodorus' Calasiris and even Cnemon) are more fascinating because less predictable. Descriptions of actions and thoughts (usually conveyed by dialogue or monologue) are deployed rather to delineate emotion and raise suspense or excitement. The speeches attest rhetorical training, as do *ekphraseis* of scenes or works of art, especially in Achilles Tatius, Longus, and Heliodorus, authors whose mannered and Atticizing style has caused their novels to be classed as 'sophistic' (see SECOND SOPHISTIC). Yet Chariton too, though not Atticizing, both claims to be a rhetor's secretary and deploys rhetorical speeches, while all four avoid hiatus and allude extensively to Classical literature. These features mark literary aspirations as high and the intended readership as educated. Philostratus and *Julian betray knowledge of the genre, but the silence of other writers has puzzled scholars, and been used (along with the lack of an ancient generic name) to argue that it was despised and of low status. Few, however, dispute the dexterity with which all but Xenophon of Ephesus unfold their plot and manipulate their readers. Achilles, Longus, and Heliodorus can be seen as variously parodying the genre's basic tropes, and the complexity, irony, and suspense created by Heliodorus' opening *in mediis rebus*, and gradual unfolding of the couple's story through Calasiris' long and sometimes misleading narrative, mark him as a master of plot-construction, with Calasiris and Fate or Fortune sometimes taking his part.

Such 'ideal' romances were not the only novels. Antonius Diogenes retained romantic love but gave more emphasis to travel in a chinese-box plot occupying 24 books. In the lost *Metamorphoses* ascribed by Photius (cod. 129) to Lucius of Patrae and in its surviving epitome, the Lucianic *Onos* ('Ass'), the first-person narrator who is turned into an ass strings together in a travel-framework incidents involving witchcraft and obscene or titillating sexual escapades in the tradition of *Milesian Tales* (short erotic tales attributed to an Aristides, and conventionally

set in Miletus; see NOVEL, LATIN). Similar coarse and melodramatic treatment of sex is found in the papyrus of Lollianus' *Phoenician Tales* and in a prosimetric scrap in which one Iolaus may intend disguise as a eunuch priest to achieve a boy's seduction (*POxy*. 42. 3010, early 2nd cent. AD). Remoter still, and with only a minor role for love or sex, are Dictys Cretensis' rewriting of the Trojan War and the 'Alexander Romance' (a fictional work, falsely ascribed to *Alexander the Great's historian Callisthenes, hence sometimes called 'pseudo-Callisthenes').

Of the five 'ideal' romances all but Longus were still read in the 6th cent.; in the 9th Photius summarized Antonius, Lucius' *Metamorphoses*, Heliodorus, Iamblichus, and Achilles, commending their Attic style but condemning erotic content. Only the last two, and Xenophon of Ephesus, get entries in the Byzantine dictionary known as *Suidas* or *Suda*, but in the 11th cent. Psellus wrote a comparison of Achilles and Heliodorus, while both they and Longus inspire writers of four 12th-cent. Byzantine novels, three verse and one prose.

In the Renaissance Heliodorus, the first to be printed (1534) and translated (into French, 1547), was most influential; but later the others, especially Longus, were much read too, vernacular translations preceding *editiones principes*.

E. L. B.

novel, Latin The Latin novel is mainly represented for us by two extant texts, the *Satyrica* of *Petronius Arbiter (1st cent. AD) and the *Metamorphoses* or *Golden Ass* of Apuleius (2nd cent. AD); no previous long fictions are known in Latin. An important influence on both was the lubricious *Milesian Tales* of Lucius Cornelius Sisenna in the 1st cent. BC (Ov. *Tr*. 2. 443–4), short stories translated from the Greek *Milēsiaka* of Aristides (2nd cent. BC; cf. Plut. *Crass*. 32, [Lucian], *Amores* 1). The adaptations by *Varro of the prosimetric Greek satires of Menippus of Gadara also contributed something to the prosimetric form and satirical content of Petronius, and were followed by the younger *Seneca in his *Apocolocyntosis*; there is also recent evidence in the Iolaus-papyrus (*POxy*. 42. 3010) that there existed at least one work of low-life prosimetric fiction in Greek.

Petronius' *Satyrica* survives only in parts, but was clearly lengthy, in at least sixteen books. Its plot concerns the comic adventures of a homosexual couple as narrated by one of them, Encolpius; as its title implies, it has connections with Roman *satire, in terms both of its prosimetric form (see above) and of its content, for example the comic meal (the *Cena Trimalchionis*). Two of its inserted tales clearly reflect the tradition of *Milesian Tales* (above)—the Widow of Ephesus (111–12) and the Pergamene Boy (85–7); it also contains literary and social criticism and some complex narrative technique. Apuleius' *Metamorphoses* in eleven books, concerning the metamorphosis of a young man into an ass and his comic adventures before retransformation by the goddess Isis, contains like the *Satyrica* a number of inserted tales, the most famous being that of Cupid and Psyche in two books (4. 28–6. 24). Some of these are clearly *Milesian Tales*, which Apuleius explicitly claims to use (I. I. I, 4. 32. 6); the inserted tales make up a large proportion of the plot but also lend it unity and coherence by their close thematic relation to the main narrative. The *Metamorphoses* has marked Isiac and Platonic elements; in the final book, the conversion of Lucius to Isiac cult and the resulting reassessment of his adventures (II. 15. I–5), coupled with the apparent revelation that the narrator is no longer Lucius but Apuleius himself (II. 27. 9), provide a problematic conclusion in both ideological and narratological terms (see NARRATIVE).

Both Petronius and Apuleius use the existing genre of the Greek ideal novel, but both alter its flavour in a characteristically Roman way, parodying its stress on virtuous young love, adding low-life realism, bawdy humour, and elements from other established literary genres, and using narrators, narrative levels, and inserted tales in a complex way. All these features appear to some extent in Greek novelistic texts, but are fundamentally characteristic of the two main Latin novels. There are two further Latin novels extant from late antiquity, translations from the Greek, belonging essentially to the Greek rather than Latin tradition—the *Story of Apollonius, King of Tyre* (5th–6th cent. AD) and the Alexander Romance of Iulius Valerius (4th cent. AD; for the Romance see NOVEL, GREEK). Christian texts in Latin make use of the ancient novel for fictionalized hagiography: the pseudo-Clementine *Recognitiones* (4th cent. AD), translated from an earlier Greek original, shows many novelistic elements in its melodramatic story of the young Clement, Peter's successor as bishop of Rome, as does Jerome's similar *Life of St Paul the First Hermit* (text in Migne, *PL* 23. 17–30) from the same period. There are also fictionalized histories in Latin with some novelistic colouring from late antiquity, particularly the Troy-narratives of Dictys Cretensis (4th cent. AD) and Dares of Phrygia (5th/6th cent. AD). S. J. Ha.

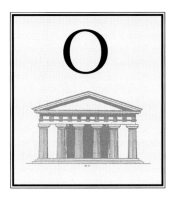

Odysseus (Latin Ulixes from one of several Greek variants; hence English Ulysses), king of Ithaca; son of Laertes and Anticlea; husband of Penelope; hero of *Homer's *Odyssey*.

In Homer's *Iliad*, despite his out-of-the-way kingdom, Odysseus is already one of the most prominent of the Greek heroes. He displays martial prowess (e.g. at II. 310–488, where he delays the rout of the Greeks), courage and resourcefulness (e.g. in the *Doloneia* of book 10, a late addition), and above all wisdom and diplomacy (e.g. at 2. 169–335, where he prevents the Greek army from disbanding, and in the embassy to *Achilles, especially 9. 223–306). He shows little of the skill in deceit which is characteristic of him in the *Odyssey*, but such epithets as 'much-enduring' and 'cunning', which occur in both epics, must refer to his exploits after the Trojan War (see TROY), and show that these were always his principal claim to fame.

In the *Odyssey* he is in some ways the typical 'trickster' of folktales, who uses guile and deception to defeat stronger opponents. His maternal grandfather is the knavish Autolycus (19. 392–466). Besides spear and sword he uses the bow, which was often considered a less manly weapon, and he even procures arrow-poison (1. 261–2). He not only resorts to trickery by necessity but sometimes revels in it, as when he boasts of his triumph over the Cyclops (9. 473–525); and his lying tales on Ithaca are elaborated with relish, as *Athena observes (13. 291–5). But Homer was concerned to make him a worthy hero, not just for a folktale, but for an epic. Books 1–4, where his son Telemachus takes centre-stage, are largely devoted to building up our sense of his greatness: he is the ideal king, whose return is necessary to establish order on Ithaca, and a friend deeply honoured by Nestor and Menelaus. When we first see him in book 5—longing for home after his long detention by Calypso, then no sooner released than shipwrecked—the emphasis is on his noble patience and endurance. At his lowest point, naked and destitute on the shore of Scheria in book 6, he is still resourceful, and can be seen by the princess Nausicaa as an ideal husband (6. 239–45). Even in the fantastic and magical episodes which he relates as bard-like storyteller to the Phaeacians in books 9–12 (the Lotus-Eaters, the Cyclops, the Bag of the Winds, the Laestrygonians, the witch Circe, the visit to the Underworld, the Sirens, Scylla and Charybdis, the Cattle of the Sun), there is pathos as well as adventure. When he finally reaches Ithaca he spends much of the rest of the poem (books 17–21) in the most humiliating condition, disguised as a beggar in his own house; but in his final revenge over Penelope's suitors, although he takes the crafty and necessary precaution of removing their weapons (19. 1–52), the main emphasis is on his strength in stringing the great bow and the skill with which he wields it (books 21–2).

A later epic, the *Telegoneia* of Eugammon of Cyrene, continued the story with further travels and martial adventures for Odysseus, who was finally killed unwittingly by Telegonus, his son by Circe. Other early poetry seems to have presented him less favourably. In the *Cypria* he feigned madness to evade his obligation to join the Trojan expedition, but the trick was exposed by Palamedes. In revenge he and Diomedes later brought about Palamedes' death. In the *Little Iliad* Odysseus and Diomedes stole the Palladium, a Trojan talisman; and by some accounts Odysseus tried to kill Diomedes on the way back. The dispute with *Aias over the arms of Achilles, first mentioned at *Odyssey* 11. 543–51, was related in the *Aethiopis* and *Little Iliad*, and *Pindar (*Nemean* 8. 23–34) claims that Odysseus won the arms by dishonest trickery. The killing of the infant Astyanax was attributed to Neoptolemus by the *Little Iliad* but to Odysseus by the *Capture of Troy*.

The tragedians tended to be similarly unfavourable. *Sophocles, while presenting a noble and magnanimous Odysseus in *Ajax*, makes him an unprincipled cynic in *Philoctetes*. *Euripides depicts the Homeric Odysseus straightforwardly in *Cyclops*, but evidently made him a villain in his lost *Palamedes* (as does the *sophist *Gorgias in his *Defence of Palamedes*), and his character in other plays (on stage in *Hecuba*, reported elsewhere) is in keeping with this. His detractors now often call him the son, not of Laertes, but of the criminal Sisyphus, who had allegedly seduced Anticlea before her marriage.

*Virgil's references to Ulixes in *Aeneid* 2 follow the Euripidean conception (ignoring a tradition which made him a founder of Rome and father of Latinus), as does the younger *Seneca in *Troades*. The dispute over the arms of Achilles, treated as a rhetorical debate by Antisthenes, is again so treated by *Ovid, *Met.* 13.

At a few sites Odysseus was honoured as a cult hero, evidently because of his prestige in epic. His name has been found on a dedication on Ithaca.

In art he is always a popular figure. The more spectacular adventures are illustrated especially often in the Archaic period (the blinding of Polyphemus and the escape under the ram are found as early as the seventh century). Later these are joined by quieter subjects, such as the embassy to Achilles and the dispute over the arms. From the 5th cent. Odysseus is often depicted in a conical hat, the *pilos*.   A. L. B.

Oedipus, son of Laius, the king of Thebes who killed his father and married his mother. The name appears to mean 'with swollen foot', but the reason for this is obscure, as the explanation given by ancient authors—that his feet were swollen because his ankles were pierced when he was exposed as a baby—looks like rationalizing invention.

*Homer's *Iliad* mentions him only (23. 679) in the context of the funeral games held after his death, implying that he died at Thebes and probably in battle. Homer's *Odyssey*, however (11. 271–80), tells how he unwittingly killed his father and married his mother Epicaste (the later Jocasta), but the gods soon made this known (this version allows no time for the couple to have children) and Epicaste hanged herself. Oedipus continued to reign at Thebes, suffering all the woes that a mother's Erinyes ('Furies', chthonian powers of retribution) can inflict.

Of the epic *Oidipodia* we know little except that it mentioned the *Sphinx (also in *Hesiod, *Theog.* 326), who killed Haemon son of Creon and must have been killed (perhaps in fight) by Oedipus, and that Oedipus had children, not by his mother, but by a second wife, Euryganeia. The children must have included Eteocles and Polynices, and probably also Antigone and Ismene.

Another epic, the *Thebais*, told how Oedipus, now probably blind, twice cursed his sons, first when Polynices disobeyed him by serving him wine in a gold cup on a silver table (fr. 2, cf. *TrGF* 2 fr. adesp. 458), and again when his sons served him the wrong joint of meat (fr. 3). He prayed that they would quarrel over their patrimony and die at each other's hands, and the epic went on to describe the Theban War that ensued.

It is uncertain when Oedipus was first said to have had children by his mother (see INCEST), and when the motif of his exile arose. In a fragment of *Stesichorus (*PMGF* 222b) the mother of Eteocles and Polynices attempts to mediate between them, presumably after the death of Oedipus, but she could be either Iocasta (Epicaste) or Euryganeia. Pindar, *Pyth.* 4. 263–9, may allude to Oedipus in exile.

In 467 *Aeschylus produced a tetralogy consisting of *Laius, Oedipus*, the surviving *Seven against Thebes*, and the satyr-play *Sphinx*. Though much is debatable, the outlines of the Oedipus story can be gathered from fragments and from allusions in the *Septem* (esp. 742–91). Laius learned from the *Delphic oracle that to save the city he must die childless. Overcome by lust, however, he begot Oedipus, and sought to have the baby exposed. Oedipus somehow survived to kill his father at a fork in the road near Potniae. He came to Thebes and rid the city of the man-eating Sphinx, probably by answering its riddle. He married Iocasta, became an honoured king, and begot Eteocles and Polynices. The patricide and incest came to light (we do not know how, but the prophet Tiresias may have played a role), and Oedipus in his anguish blinded himself and cursed the sons born of the incest: they were to divide their patrimony with the sword. In the *Septem* Oedipus is dead, having probably died at Thebes.

*Sophocles' *Antigone* (49–54) mentions how Oedipus blinded himself and died and Iocasta hanged herself. But Sophocles' *Oedipus Tyrannus* (*King Oedipus*) became the definitive account. Here Laius received an *oracle from *Apollo that his son would kill him, so he ordered a shepherd to expose the infant Oedipus on Mt. Cithaeron. The shepherd, however, took pity on the baby, and Oedipus survived to be brought up as the son of Polybus, king of Corinth, and his wife Merope. An oracle warned him that he would kill his father and marry his mother, so he fled from Corinth. At a junction of three roads near Daulis he killed Laius in a quarrel, not knowing who he was. Coming to Thebes he answered the riddle of the Sphinx, married Iocasta, and became king. When the play opens, the city is being ravaged by a *plague, caused, so the oracle reveals, by the polluting presence of the killer of Laius (see POLLUTION). Oedipus, an intelligent and benevolent king, pronounces a *curse on the unknown killer and begins an investigation, which ends in the discovery of the whole truth. Iocasta hangs herself and Oedipus blinds himself with pins from her dress. The ending is problematic, as Oedipus does not go into the immediate exile foreshadowed earlier but remains, for the moment, in the palace.

*Euripides too wrote an *Oedipus*, in which the king was blinded by the servants of Laius, not by his own hand. In Euripides' *Phoenissae* he is self-blinded and is still living in the palace at the time of his sons' death.

At the end of his life Sophocles returned to Oedipus with his *Oedipus at Colonus*. Here the blind man, led by Antigone, comes to the grove of the Eumenides (Erinyes) at Colonus near Athens, where he knows that he must die. Protected by *Theseus, he resists the attempts of Polynices and Iocasta's brother Creon, who banished him from Thebes, to bring him back there for their selfish purposes. He curses his sons for their neglect, and finally, called by the gods, he dies mysteriously at a spot known only to Theseus, where his angry corpse will protect Athens against Theban attack. Tombs and hero-cults of Oedipus are reported from Colonos and from Athens itself (among other places), but the antiquity of these, and their relation to Sophocles' play (where he has *no* tomb), are uncertain.

Roman authors of an *Oedipus* tragedy included *Caesar. The *Oedipus* of *Seneca is based on Sophocles' *Oedipus Tyrannus*. The role of Oedipus in *Statius' *Thebaid* is derived from Euripides' *Phoenissae*.

In art the confrontation with the Sphinx is often portrayed, other episodes more rarely. See *LIMC* 7. 1 (1994), 1–15.   A. L. B.

oligarchy ('the rule of the few'), with monarchy (see KINGSHIP) and democracy one of the three basic categories of constitution commonly used by the Greeks from the 5th cent. BC onwards. Whereas a democratic regime gave basic political rights to all adult males in the free non-immigrant population, and had slight or non-existent limitations on eligibility for office, an oligarchic regime excluded some of the free population even from basic political rights, and might exclude even more of them from office-holding and reduce the amount of business which came the way of the full citizen body. In practice those who were admitted to political activity by democracies but not by oligarchies were the poor, and *Aristotle, after listing the three categories of constitution and distinguishing correct and deviant versions of each, went on to say that really oligarchy is the rule of the rich and democracy is the rule of the poor (*Pol.* 3. 1279^{a}22–1280^{a}6).

Before the 5th cent. the constitutions of most states were in fact oligarchic, though the term did not yet exist. In the 5th cent. Athens developed a self-conscious democracy (see DEMOCRACY, ATHENIAN) and posed as a champion of democracy elsewhere in Greece, while those who disliked that labelled themselves oligarchic, and Sparta, though not itself a typical oligarchy, posed as the champion of oligarchies. At the end of the 5th cent. there were oligarchic revolutions in Athens, resulting in the regimes of the Four Hundred (see ATHENS (HISTORY)) and of the (moderate but still not fully democratic) Five Thousand in 411–410, and of the Thirty Tyrants in 404–403. In the Hellenistic period the distinction between oligarchy and democracy was still sometimes taken seriously, but it mattered less than in the Classical period as even states which were democratic in form tended in practice to be run by the rich; and government by the rich was preferred by the Romans.   V. E.; P. J. R.

olive The olive is probably native to the Mediterranean region. It is long-lived and highly drought-resistant, though sensitive to frost, and thrives best at relatively low altitudes. Olives generally only crop every other year, and usually trees are regionally synchronized. Despite the attempts of farmers from antiquity to the present to break this habit, it has never successfully been circumvented.

Olives are easily propagated by cuttings, ovules (trunk growths, Gk. *premna*), or by grafting, a well-known technique in the classical world. Domesticated scions were frequently grafted onto wild stocks. Trees grown from cuttings planted in nursery beds seem to have been more characteristic of Roman than Greek regimes. Greek farmers apparently preferred planting ovules, which have a greater success-rate under conditions of water-stress than cuttings. Olives do not grow true to type from seed. Many varieties were known and cultivated for both oil and table use in classical antiquity.

Rarely grown under a monocultural system, olives were usually part of mixed farming regimes, including arable and other tree crops since cropping and yields can be erratic. Sometimes olive cultivation was combined with *pastoralism, as in *Cato the Elder's (*Agr.* 10) model olive grove which included a shepherd, 100 sheep, and a swineherd. Sheep ate grass and weed growth under trees, while pigs utilized the presscake.

Olives are harvested in autumn and winter. Greeks and Romans felt that the best-quality oil came from 'white' ('green') olives, picked early, a belief not in accord with modern practice. Ripe, 'black' olives contain more oil than green ones—the scarcity of oil in the latter may partially explain why it was more highly valued. Today the crucial factor is felt to be acidity, which increases in oil which is old, or which has been made from olives (black or green) stored for some time between picking and pressing.

Olives can be processed for either table-olives or oil: they are not edible raw. The most basic table-olives are packed in salt, but the Roman agronomists provide other recipes. Olive oil was used for food, medicine, lighting, perfume, and bathing, as well as *athletics.

Producing oil entails crushing, pressing, and separating. Many different devices were known in antiquity for crushing and pressing olives. The simplest crusher is a flat bed with a stone roller. However the Romans (and probably the Greeks) believed that crushing the olive stones (almost inevitable with most machines) lowered oil quality. For luxury-quality oil they tried to keep crushed stones to a minimum, although this reduced the yield. Machines were invented to achieve this end, although it is questionable how effectively they worked. The most common olive crusher found in archaeological contexts is the rotary mill generally known as the *trapetum*, invented around the 4th cent. BC (it is debated whether the earliest examples from Chios and Olynthus used one millstone or two). Machines remained common throughout the Roman world until late antiquity. The most usual presses were beam presses. Earlier examples were weighted with large stones, but later many used capstans. Screw presses came into use during Roman times, though the date of their invention is uncertain, perhaps around the 2nd cent. BC. Crushed olives were placed in bags or frails on the pressbed (many stone examples survive), and the press was fastened. The first pressing produced best-quality 'green' oil, sometimes kept separate and sold at high prices. Hot water was poured on the frails before further, lower quality, pressings.

The mixed oil, water, and olive juice (*amurca*) was left to settle in vats until the oil floated. Then oil was skimmed off the top or the waste let out via a tap from the bottom. Oil was stored in large jars (*dolia*, *pithoi*) or sold in *amphorae*. Though most ordinary oil was probably consumed locally, high-quality oil was a luxury product traded over long distances, like vintage wine. Certain regions, e.g. Attica (Athens' countryside), *Samos, Venafrum in Italy, Baetica in Spain, and Cyrenaica (see CYRENE; LIBYA), became famous for oil. In the case of Attica, the olive was an important symbol of Athena and Athens and oil from the sacred trees (*moiriai*) was given as prizes at the Panathenaic Games. However, it was probably never the most important Attic crop and oil may not have been the primary export. See AGRICULTURE.   L. F.

Olympia (see ◀Map 1, Ac▶), Panhellenic sanctuary of *Zeus located in hill country beside the river Alpheus in Elis (western *Peloponnese).

1. Before 500 BC There is evidence of extensive prehistoric settlement in the vicinity including a large EH tumulus in the Altis which remained visible into the early iron age, MH houses, and Mycenaean tombs (see MYCENAEAN CIVILIZATION) in the vicinity of the archaeological museum.

Votives (tripods and figurines) in an ash layer in the Altis indicate cult activity at least from the late 10th cent. (perhaps with an early ash altar). The first Olympiad was traditionally dated 776 BC (see TIME-RECKONING). According to *Pindar, *Heracles founded the Olympian games; an alternative tradition attributed the foundation to Pelops after his victory over Oenomaus. A sequence of wells on the eastern side of the sanctuary beginning in the late 8th cent. served visitors.

The first temple (ascribed to *Hera) was built *c*.590. A row of eleven treasuries (primarily of west Greek i.e. Italian and Sicilian states) lay under Cronus Hill. The first phase of the *stadium (*c*. mid-6th cent.) consisted of a simple track west of the later stadium, extending into the Altis. The first bouleuterion (building for the *boulē* or council) was built in *c*.520. From at least the 6th cent., sanctuary and festival were managed by Elis.   C. A. M.

2. Classical The Greeks of the west (see (1) above) always had close connections with Olympia, cf. ML 10 of *c*.525 (treaty between Sybaris and the Serdaioi); 29, bronze helmet commemorating Hiero I's victory over the

Olympia Model of the sanctuary of Olympia as it looked by the later 2nd cent. AD, with the row of treasuries lined up top right. Typically of a major sanctuary, a dense accretion of sculptured offerings is visible around the principal temple. At Olympia, a high proportion commemorated athletes victorious in the Olympian *games.

*Etruscans at Cumae in 474 (cf. *BCH* 1960, 721 and *SEG* 33 no. 328); ML 57 (victory dedication of Tarentum over Thurii); and *IVO* 266 (statues dedicated by Praxiteles of *Syracuse and Camarina). But Olympia, the paramount athletic sanctuary (P. *Ol.* 1), was properly Panhellenic. Thus the Persian Wars (see GREECE (HISTORY)) were commemorated at Olympia, though less spectacularly than at *Delphi; for instance (A. Mallwitz, *Olympia und seine Bauten* (1972), 32 ff.) the Athenians dedicated at Olympia a helmet 'taken from the Medes'; another splendid helmet-dedication by Miltiades might be from the Greek victory over Persia at Marathon (490 BC) but is probably earlier. The battle of Plataea (479 BC) prompted a colossal bronze Zeus (Paus. 5. 23), inscribed with a roll of honour of the participating states, including Ionian Athens in second place after Sparta. But the Dorian character of Olympia is marked, even if we deny political symbolism to the labours of *Heracles depicted on the temple metopes of the mid-cent. Zeus temple, the second to be built within the Altis. Thus the Olympian games of 428 were turned by Sparta into an overtly anti-Athenian meeting, Thuc. 3. 8 ff. But Athens was never, even in the Peloponnesian War (431–404), formally denied access to Olympia, any more than to Delphi; and to balance ML 22 (Spartan victory dedication over Messenians, 490s?) we have, from the 420s, ML 74, the lovely *Nike of Paeonius—a dedication by Athens' friends the Messenians of Naupactus (cf. Thuc. 1. 103). We do hear of a classical exclusion from the Olympic games, but of Sparta not Athens: Thuc. 5. 49–50, a rare Thucydidean glimpse of the continuing political importance of *athletics.

S. H.

3. Hellenistic and Roman Hellenistic kings affirmed by their dedications Olympia's Panhellenic standing. New buildings included a palaestra (training-ground), *gymnasium, and (*c.*100 BC) the earliest Roman-style *baths found in Greece. Roman domination, signalled by the dedications of Lucius Mummius (146 BC), at first saw Olympia decline in prestige: by 30 BC the games had dwindled into an essentially local festival. Imperial patronage prompted a marked revival: *Agrippa repaired the temple and both *Tiberius and *Germanicus won chariot-races, to be outdone by *Nero, who performed in person at irregularly convened games (67) including (uniquely) musical contests (full refs.: N. Kennell, *AJPhil.* 1988, 241). In the 2nd cent., with the popularity of the games never greater, Olympia once more attracted orators (see SECOND SOPHISTIC), as well as cultural *tourism (Phidias' statue of Zeus was among the *Seven Wonders of the ancient world); facilities saw a final expansion, including a nymphaeum (fountain-house), attracting conservative attack (Lucian, *Peregr.* 19). From fear of the Heruli, the sanctuary was fortified (*c.*268) at the cost of many classical monuments. Cult survived well into the 4th cent. A Christian basilica was built *c.*400–450; the temple was only toppled by earthquake in the 6th cent.

A. J. S. S.

oracles Among the many forms of divination known to the Greeks, the responses given by a god or hero when consulted at a fixed oracular site were the most prestigious (see e.g. Soph. *OT* 498–501). Such oracles were numerous. *Herodotus lists five in mainland Greece and one in Asia Minor which the Lydian king Croesus supposedly consulted in the 6th cent. BC (1. 46), and at least another five (including one 'oracle of the dead') appear in his pages; *Pausanias mentions four lesser local oracles, and at least five more can be added from epigraphical evidence (cf. C. Michel, *Recueil d'inscriptions grecques* (1900–27), 840–56; *Syll.*[3] 1157–66).

Healing oracles, those of *Asclepius above all, are a specialized group, though even these never confined themselves exclusively to medical questions. The business of a general purpose oracle is best revealed by the lead question-tablets found at *Zeus' oracle at Dodona in Epirus. The majority of enquiries are from individuals; of the minority addressed by states, most ask whether a particular alteration to cult practice is acceptable, or more generally by what sacrifices divine favour is to be maintained; one or two concern political issues. Individuals enquire, for instance, whether their wife will conceive (or conceive a son), whether a proposed marriage or journey or change of career is wise, whether a child is legitimate; they also ask about health problems, and more generally about ways of winning and keeping divine favour. The kind of answer envisaged is either 'yes' or 'no' or 'by sacrificing to X'.

According to *Plutarch (*De Pyth. or.* 408c), similar everyday questions about 'whether to marry or to sail or to lend', or, from cities, about 'crops and herds and health' ('and cults', he might have added) formed the staple of Delphi's business in his day (see DELPHIC ORACLE). Before about 400 BC, states had certainly also consulted Delphi about political issues, but even then a decision, to go to war for instance or dispatch a colony (see COLONIZATION, GREEK), had normally been made by the state before approaching the oracle. What was sought was a divine sanction. And since no mortals were endowed with religious authority in the Greek system, all oracles at all dates had an especially important role in sanctioning adjustments to cult practice.

Techniques by which responses were given were very various. The most prestigious was 'inspired' prophecy, the sayings of a priest or more commonly a priestess who spoke, probably in a state of trance, in the person of the god. This was the method of several oracles of *Apollo in Asia Minor and almost certainly of that of Delphi too, though a process of drawing bean-lots seems also to have played some part there. The prophetic dream was characteristic of healing oracles such as those of Asclepius and Amphiaraus, though not confined to them: the consultant slept a night or nights in the temple (incubation), during which the god in theory appeared in a dream and issued instructions (or even, in pious legend, performed a cure direct). The oracle of Zeus at *Olympia worked by 'empyromancy', signs drawn from the flames on Zeus' altar. To consult the hero Trophonius at Boeotian Lebadea, the client made a simulated descent to the Underworld: how the revelation then occurred is not recorded. Nor do we know anything certain about the practice at Zeus' oracle at Dodona.

Apart from the Egyptian–Libyan oracle of Ammon at the oasis of Siwa in the Sahara, which many Greeks consulted as an oracle of Zeus from the 5th cent. BC onwards, the great oracular shrines were Greek. In Italy, the oracle of the Sibyl at Cumae is well known from *Virgil, Aeneid 6. 9–101, who describes an ecstatic form of prophecy (see ECSTASY). Also prominent was the lot-oracle of Fortuna Primigenia at Praeneste (mod. Palestrina). On extraordinary occasions the Roman government or ruler consulted the Sibylline books, which were kept by the *duoviri* (later *quindecimviri*) *sacris faciundis* i.e. colleges of two (eventually fifteen) *priests whose job it was to look after ritual texts.

R. C. T. P.

Late antiquity The first two centuries AD witnessed a great flourishing of oracular shrines throughout the Greek-speaking portion of the Roman empire. These oracles took many different forms. *Delphi, Didyma, and Claros (both western Asia Minor) delivered responses from a god through a prophet, whose words were interpreted for consultants by priests at the shrine. At Mallus in Cilicia and the sanctuary of Amphiaraus at Oropus (for example), the consultant slept (after a period of some preparation) in the shrine, hoping to have a dream of the god (also interpreted by priests). Other oracles, such as that of Bel at Apamea in *Syria appear to have worked by indicating passages in Classical literature (see also *POxy.* 3831). Lot-oracles of various sorts are known from southern Asia Minor and Egypt. The oracle of Glycon offered a wide variety of methods of consultation.

Many responses are concerned with cult activity and personal crises; others, however, appear to have been more philosophic and provided important material for some pagan opponents of Christianity—they were taken as proof that the gods existed and as a proper guide to religious belief. Two oracles, of Didyma and Zeus Philios, the last opening at *Antioch under Maximin Daia (305–13), also played significant roles in the great persecutions of the early 4th cent. Christians argued in turn that these responses were the work of demons, and those oracular shrines that survived the problems of the 3rd cent. appear to have been closed very soon after *Constantine I's defeat of Valerius Licinius in 324.

D. S. P.

orality Coined as the opposite of *literacy, to denote the phenomenon of extensive reliance on oral communication rather than the written word, it is a useful concept for the ancient world, where writing was often used less than modern readers would assume. Various forms of orality are not incompatible with some use of writing, and it can be helpfully subdivided into (1) oral composition, (2) oral communication, (3) oral transmission.

Oral composition, entirely without the help of writing, is best known in relation to the Homeric poems (see HOMER) and the long tradition of oral poetry through the Greek Dark Ages. The influential work of Parry and Lord sought to show how an oral poet could compose in performance. Spontaneous oral composition can also be found, however, in later symposiastic poetry, and oratory. The importance of oral communication can be seen e.g. in the political activity of democratic Athens (see DEMOCRACY, ATHENIAN); in the use of contracts or wills relying on witnesses, not writing, in Athens and Rome; in the habit of hearing literature. Oral transmission is the transmission without writing of any information, literature, traditions about the past, etc. This usually involves some distortion, especially over generations of oral tradition, unless there is a deliberate effort to maintain the accuracy of the tradition (e.g. through poetry). Until the development of 5th-cent. Greek *historiography, most Greeks knew about their past from oral tradition; and it was crucial in preserving traditions about early Rome. Its character and reliability depends heavily on who is transmitting the traditions and why (e.g. notions of honour, patriotism). Thus Archaic Greece was almost entirely an oral society: even poetry that was written down (e.g. *Sappho) was primarily meant to be heard and performed.

As written documents and the centrality of written literature increase in the 5th and 4th cents., elements of orality still remain fundamental, notably the performance of poetry and prose (e.g. *Herodotus), and oratory and extempore performance; the value of the written word was not uniformly accepted (cf. *Plato's criticisms in *Phaedrus*). The Romans were more book- and library-oriented, but even at the level of high culture one finds literary readings, the accomplishments of oratory, memory, and improvisation (see Quint. *Inst. Or.* 10. 7. 30–2; 11; the skill and advantages of shorthand were despised, Sen. *Ep. Mor.* 90. 25). The balance between oral communication and writing varied immensely over the period and in different areas. Some see a fundamental mentality engendered by orality (e.g. lack of individualism and/or analytical skills), but both Greece and Rome have their own particular manifestations of oral culture, and the theory may be exaggerated.

R. T.

Orientalism *Orientalism* is the title of a study by the distinguished Palestinian literary critic, Edward Said; published in 1978, its impact has been enormous. The central thesis is that the concepts 'Europe' and 'Orient', as polar opposites, have been created by Europeans, particularly in the context of European imperialism, to provide a positive, strong image of Europe, with which eastern civilizations (especially the Muslim world) can be negatively contrasted. The 'Orient' is thus presented as lacking all desirable, active characteristics: it is effeminate, decadent, corrupt, voluptuous, despotic, and incapable of independent creative development. This pervasive perception of 'the east' underlies most studies of Middle Eastern history and culture and has profoundly shaped scholarly analysis. Although most of Said's study is devoted to the 18th to 20th cents. he argues that Oriental stereotypes derive much of their imagery from early Greek literary works (e.g. *Herodotus; *Aeschylus' *Persae*). This has led several classicists and ancient historians to refocus their work and explore consciously the assumptions made in some traditional areas of study. As a result, standard approaches to several subjects are now being scrutinized and radically reassessed. Most prominent among these are: the development of Greek art, in particular the 'orientalizing' phase, Greek tragedy, and Achaemenid and Hellenistic history. An interesting, though in several respects maverick, study of Greek civilization, which adopts part of Said's political agenda, is M. Bernal's *Black Athena* (London 1987–); he takes an extreme position to argue that Greece was colonized by black Africans and *Phoenicians and owed its culture to them.

See also HELLENISM, HELLENIZATION.   A. T. L. K.

Orpheus, the quintessential mythical singer, son of *Apollo and a Muse (see MUSES), whose song has more than human power. In Archaic Greece, Orpheus appears among the Argonauts whom he saves from the Sirens by overcoming their song with his own; other attestations exalt the power of his song (Ibycus, *Simonides). In the 5th cent. Orpheus enlarges his field of competence: his powerful song encompasses epic poetry, healing songs, oracles, and initiatory rites.

His main myth is his tragic love for Eurydice, narrated by *Virgil (*Georg.* 4. 453–525) and *Ovid (*Met.* 10. 1–11. 84) but known already in some form in the 5th cent. BC. In Virgil's version Eurydice, newly wed to Orpheus, died of a snakebite, and the singer descended to Hades to bring her back. His song enchanted *Hades; Eurydice was allowed to return provided Orpheus did not look back when leading her up; he failed, losing Eurydice for ever. He retired into wild nature where his lamenting song moved animals, trees, and rocks; finally a band of Thracian women or Bacchic *maenads (see DIONYSUS) killed him. The first representation of Eurydice, Orpheus, and *Hermes is the relief from the Athenian Altar of the Twelve Gods: earlier is the allusion in Eur. *Alc.* 357–62 (438 BC). Orpheus' death at the hands of maenads is presented in *Aeschylus' drama *Bassarae* as the result of Dionysus' wrath (470/460 BC). Vases depicting Thracian women murdering him are somewhat earlier, without giving a reason for the killing; later, it is the aloofness of the widowed (and turned homosexual) singer which provokes the women. But even after his death, Orpheus' voice was not silenced: his head was carried by the sea to the island of *Lesbos where for a while it gave prophecies.

Generally, Orpheus is called a Thracian. A grave and a cult belong not to Thrace but to Pieria in *Macedonia, north-east of Mt. Olympus, a region which formerly had been inhabited by Thracians and with which the Muses had some relations. It may have been a recent invention, or point to the original home of Orpheus who has no certain place in the web of Greek mythological *genealogy.

An important consequence of his miraculous song was his authorship of the so-called Orphic poetry: as early as the late 6th cent. the powerful singer who went down into Hades was thought especially competent to sing about eschatology and theogony. Pythagoreans (see PYTHAGORAS) and adherents of Bacchic mystery cults adopted him as their figurehead, and the Neoplatonist philosophers especially discerned deep theosophical knowledge in these poems and promoted Orpheus to the role of prime theological thinker. Thus 'Orphic literature' refers to the whole body of pseudepigraphical literature ascribed to Orpheus

Orpheus An Orphic prayer inscribed on a gold leaf supposedly found folded in a cinerary urn from *Thessaly (late 4th cent. BC): 'Parched with thirst am I, and dying. Nay, drink of Me, the ever-flowing spring where on the right is a fair cypress. "Who art thou? where art thou?"—"I am the son of Earth and of star-filled Heaven, but from Heaven alone is my house"' (trans. J. Breslin).

Similar texts from burials in N. Greece, S. Italy, and Crete suggest the widespread circulation of Orphic beliefs about death and the Underworld from the 5th cent. BC on.

(see M. L. West, *The Orphic Poems* (1983)), while 'Orphism' refers to the set of beliefs and religious practices thought to derive from Orphic literature (see R. Parker in A. Powell (ed.), *The Greek World* (1995), 483–510).

In art the myth of Orpheus is treated from *c*.550 BC to late antiquity (main themes: as Argonaut; murder; in Hades; with the animals). F. G.

Ostia (see ◀Map 3, Bb▶), city at the mouth of the Tiber, *colonia* at least by the late 4th cent. BC, heavily involved with Rome's naval history, commerce, and communications, and one of the best-known Roman cities archaeologically. Abandoned in the 5th cent. AD, Ostia was covered with drifting sand from coastal dunes, and the area was sparsely populated until this century because of malaria. With the coast southwards, and the remains of Portus, this therefore makes an archaeological site of the highest importance.

Tradition ascribed the foundation to King Ancus Marcius, and claimed that the trade in salt from the adjacent lagoons (which was certainly significant in historical times) dated back to that epoch (cf. the *via Salaria*). The Latin civilization is well represented in the immediate hinterland by the important discoveries at Castel di Decima on the via Laurentina and Ficana, overlooking the confluence of the Tiber and the Fossa Galeria, an important route leading inland towards Veii, and dominating the coastal plain just inland from Ostia. No remains have been found at Ostia earlier than those of the small (*c*.2 ha.) fortified set-

Ostia The brick-faced House of Diana at Ostia (*c*. AD 150), originally with at least four floors, is a good example of the multi-storeyed apartment blocks (*insulae*) found in the Roman empire's larger cities. In Italy, the use of fired brick (mid-1st cent. AD on) in place of timber-framed mudbrick made this type of structure much safer.

tlement, typical of the *coloniae maritimae* of the time, constructed at the Tiber mouth, from which it took its name at the end of the 4th cent. (the so-called 'Castrum').

The Tiber was the route to the arsenal of Rome, the Navalia, and needed strategic protection throughout the Punic wars (see ROME (HISTORY), §1.4), and on into the age of the depredations of *piracy, which destroyed a Roman fleet at Ostia in 67 BC. Since the 6th cent. BC it had also provided access for travellers and traders to the wharves of Rome (greatly improved and embellished during the 2nd cent.). The imperial power won by Rome at that time gave its sea access new importance, and, as the grain-supply (see FOOD SUPPLY, *Roman*) of the city came under increased governmental supervision from the time of Gaius *Gracchus, a resource of huge political sensitivity began to pass through the difficult and insecure waters of Ostia regularly. A circuit of walls (probably of the end of the 2nd cent. BC) enclosed 69 ha.; *Marius captured Ostia by treachery in 87 and sacked it. In the Civil War the loyalty to Octavian's cause of members of the local élite, Cartilius Poplicola and Lucilius Gamala, benefited the city under the victorious regime. But Strabo describes Ostia in the Augustan period as 'a city without a harbour' (5. 3. 5 (232)), and says that the huge merchant-ships of southern Spain 'make for Puteoli and Ostia, the shipyard of Rome' (3. 2. 6 (145)); the city was still only a way-station on the route up the river, and the ports of Campania (which long received much of the grain trade and retained their prosperity until the third century) were unrivalled until the construction of the basins of *Claudius and *Trajan at Portus.

The good communications of the coastal area attracted the villas of the Roman élite even before the discomfiture of the pirates in the 60s, and there were spacious houses of the Pompeian type within Ostia's new walls as well as large estates in the territory. These increased in number greatly at the end of the republic, and Ostia became the centre of a resort coast which stretched south to Antium, the *litus Laurentinum* where *Pliny the Younger had a maritime *villa. It was to service this community that Ostia became the 'very comfortable and convenient city' (*amoenissima civitas*) of the proem to Minucius Felix's dialogue *Octavius*.

These comforts are very apparent. Most of the houses are good-quality *insulae* (tenement blocks) which, when they were first studied, gave an exaggeratedly optimistic idea of what Roman urban conditions were like (some of the apartments have as many as seven rooms), the streets were often colonnaded or arcaded, and there are areas of very spacious houses, like the area outside the seaward gate (where the synagogue was excavated in 1962). An aqueduct supplied at least 17 bath-houses (some very grand, like the forum baths). Ostia was well-equipped with taverns and similar places of resort, and provides important information about them. A lavish theatre was originally probably a benefaction from *Agrippa, perhaps because of the town's contributions to the war against Sextus Pompeius. The buildings of the forum (first given monumental form under Augustus and his successors; the large

Capitoline temple is Hadrianic) occupied most of the area of the former *colonia*, and are on a magnificent scale.

The principal testimony to Ostia's economic life are the great *horrea* or storehouses, including many used by the *annona* (public grain supply; in the 3rd cent. increasingly transformed into other uses). There are a number of head-quarters of *collegia*, associations among other things connected with commerce, the river, the harbour, or ware-housing; the elaborately decorated premises were intended to provide a place of visible, semi-public social interaction for the bosses rather than the rank and file. The 'Square of the Corporations' is the most remarkable building of this kind, taking the form of a piazza surrounded by colon-nades and *tabernae* (booths) for the representatives of ports involved in the grain-trade, and for others connected with the harbour: its precise function remains unclear. Our understanding of the relationship of the city to the river is hampered by changes in the Tiber's course and erosion of the site: there are some indications that important depen-dencies of the city extended to the north on both banks of the river. But the main extent of the town was a long development beside the via Ostiensis, stretching towards Rome, and dense occupation to the west around two roads which forked beyond the seaward gate and gave access to different parts of the littoral.

Most of what is visible at Ostia is a development of the Flavian, Antonine, and Severan periods. The uniformity of the kiln-fired brick construction and the regularity of the plan suggest wholesale redevelopment, and large-scale investment in urban property. Much of what we know of Ostia refers to the 2nd and 3rd cents. when the city appears to have been home to a social milieu who had made their money in harbour-activities; their descendants and succes-sors saw a further move away from economic activity in the direction of *amoenitas* (amenity) and in late antiquity the *domus*, small and elegant, with elaborate water-decora-tions, returned to the city-centre (e.g. the famous House of Cupid and Psyche).

Ostia is relatively small (there is no sign that the built-up area was ever larger than about 50 ha., and much of this was not primarily dwelling-places). It was overwhelmingly a service-town, for the countryside around, for the spread-out activities of the Tiber-bank, and the harbours of Portus, and for the numerous passers-by on their way to and from Rome (wide horizons are apparent in the diver-sity of its religious cults). Such service functions supported an economically relatively privileged population and a considerable number of their slaves who are archaeologi-cally largely invisible. Otherwise labour is likely to have been available on a seasonal basis from Rome and other parts of the densely populated region around it. Ostia was thus rather a focal point in a port-region rather than a harbour-town in the strict sense, and its importance is much more as an example of the social and economic, architectural and urban conditions prevailing in Rome itself than as either a typical example of a Mediterranean port or a normal Italian regional centre.

The serious study of the site was made possible by the

ostracism This *ostrakon* (potsherd) is incised with the remark 'Cimon son of Miltiades, take Elpinice and go!'. The Athenian leader Cimon was ostracized in 461 BC. The allegation of *incest with his sister Elpinice, known from other ancient evidence, suggests how charges of immoral behaviour, then as now, were used as a means of attack in politics.

eradication of malaria, and very large areas were uncovered during 1938–42, so that about three-quarters of the inner part of the city is visible today. Work has concentrated more recently on the detailed publication of the building-history of sections of the excavated site, on stratigraphic excavation of small areas (the Baths of the Swimmer (Terme del Nuotatore) are a particularly celebrated case), and on the exploration of the urban periphery and territory. See HOUSES, ITALIAN.   N. P.

ostracism in Athens in the 5th cent. BC was a method of banishing a citizen for ten years. Each year in the sixth prytany (one-tenth subdivision of the official year) the question whether an ostracism should be held that year was put to the *ekklēsia* (assembly). If the people voted in favour of holding an ostracism, it was held on a day in the eighth prytany in the *Agora under the supervision of the *archontes* (see LAW AND PROCEDURE, ATHENIAN) and the *boulē* (council). Each citizen who wished to vote wrote on a fragment of pottery (*ostrakon*) the name of the citizen whom he wished to be banished. The voters were marshalled by *phylai* (the ten 'tribes' in the sense of subdivisions of the citizen-body) in an enclosure erected for the occasion, to ensure that no one put in more than one *ostrakon*. When all had voted, the *ostraka* were counted and, provided that there was a total of at least 6,000, the man whose name appeared on the largest number was ostracized. (An alternative view, attributed to Philochorus, *FGrH* 328 F30, is that the ostracism was valid only if at least 6,000 votes were cast against one man.) He had to leave the country within ten days and remain in exile for ten years, but he did not forfeit his citizenship or property, and at the end of the ten years he could return to live in Athens without any disgrace or disability.

The date of the institution of ostracism has been a matter of dispute. According to the standard account (Arist. *Ath. Pol.* 22) the law about it was introduced by *Cleisthenes in 508/7, but the first ostracism was not held until 487. Some modern scholars accept this account and offer various conjectural explanations of the twenty years' interval. Others maintain that the law cannot have been passed until shortly before the first ostracism in 487, and that Cleisthenes therefore was not its author; a statement attributed to the 4th-cent. historian Androtion (*FGrH* 324 F6) has been adduced in support of this view, but its interpretation and value are doubtful. A third view, based on later sources, is that Cleisthenes introduced a different method of ostracism by the *boulē* and was himself ostracized by this method, which was subsequently replaced by the method first used in 487.

The man ostracized in 487 was Hipparchus son of Charmus, a relative of the ex-tyrant Hippias, son of *Pisistratus. He was followed in 486 by Megacles, one of a famous family, the Alcmaeonids, and in 485 by some other adherent of Hippias' family, probably Callias son of Cratius. No doubt these three had all become unpopular because it was thought that they favoured the Persian invaders and the restoration of the tyranny. Xanthippus was ostracized in 484 and Aristides in 482, but both of these returned from exile in 480 when an amnesty was declared in an attempt to muster the full strength of Athens to resist the invasion of Xerxes. Other prominent men known to have been ostracized are *Themistocles about 470, Cimon in 461, and Thucydides (not the historian) son of Melesias in 443. Hyperbolus was the last victim of the system; his ostracism is usually dated in 417, though some scholars have placed it in 416 or 415. Ostracism then fell out of use, although the law authorizing it remained in force in the 4th cent. The *graphē paranomōn* (law against unconstitutional proposals) was found to be a more convenient method of attacking politicians.

It is often hard to tell why a particular man was ostracized. Sometimes, as in the cases of Cimon and Thucydides son of Melesias, the Athenians seem to have ostracized a man to express their rejection of a policy for which he stood and their support for an opposing leader; thus an ostracism might serve a purpose similar to that of a modern general election. But no doubt individual citizens were often actuated by personal malice or other non-political motives, as is illustrated by the story of the yokel who wished to vote against Aristides because he was tired of hearing him called 'the Just' (Plut. *Arist.* 7. 7).

Over 10,000 *ostraka*, dumped in the Agora or Cerameicus (potters' quarter) after use, have now been found. The names include not only men whom we know to have been actually ostracized but also a considerable number of others. Some are men quite unknown to us, and it may well be that they were not prominent politicians but merely had an odd vote cast against them by some malicious personal acquaintance. Particularly interesting is a find of 190 *ostraka* in a well on the north slope of the Acropolis (see ATHENS, TOPOGRAPHY), all inscribed with the name of Themistocles by only a few different hands. Presumably they were prepared for distribution by his opponents. This suggests that he was the victim of an organized campaign, and it illustrates the importance of ostracism as a political weapon in 5th-cent. Athens. See also LITERACY.   D. M. M.

Ovid (*see following page*)

Ovid

Ovid (Publius Ovidius Naso, 43 BC–AD 17), poet, was born at Sulmo in the Abruzzi on 20 March. Our chief source for his life is one of his own poems, *Tr.* 4. 10. As the son of an old equestrian family, Ovid was sent to Rome for his education. His rhetorical studies under Arellius Fuscus and Porcius Latro, in which he evidently acquitted himself with distinction, are described by the elder Seneca (*Controv.* 2. 2. 8–12; cf. 9. 5. 17). His education was rounded off by the usual Grand Tour through Greek lands (*Tr.* 1. 2. 77–8, *Pont.* 2. 10. 21 ff.). After holding some minor judicial posts, he apparently abandoned public life for poetry—thus enacting one of the commonplaces of Roman elegiac autobiography. With early backing from Marcus Valerius Messalla Corvinus (*Pont.* 1. 7. 27–8) Ovid quickly gained prominence as a writer, and by AD 8 he was the leading poet of Rome. In that year he was suddenly banished by *Augustus to Tomis on the Black (Euxine) Sea. Ovid refers to two causes of offence in his exile poetry: *carmen*, a poem, the *Ars Amatoria*; and *error*, an indiscretion. He has much to say concerning the first of these counts, especially in *Tr.* 2; concerning the second he repeatedly refuses to elaborate—though, since the *Ars* had already been out for some years in AD 8, the *error* must have been the more immediate cause. Amid the continuing speculation (cf. J. C. Thibault, *The Mystery of Ovid's Exile* (1964); Syme, *History in Ovid* (1978), 215–22), all that can be reconstructed from Ovid's own hints is a vague picture of involuntary complicity (cf. *Tr.* 2. 103–8) in some scandal affecting the imperial house. Tomis, a superficially Hellenized town with a wretched climate on the extreme edge of the empire, was a singularly cruel place in which to abandon Rome's most urbane poet. Public and private pleading failed to appease Augustus or (later) *Tiberius: Ovid languished in Tomis until his death, probably (so Jerome) in AD 17. Several of the elegies from exile are addressed to his third wife (connected somehow with the *gens Fabia* (the Fabian line): *Pont.* 1. 2. 136), who remained behind him in Rome; Ovid also mentions a daughter and two grandchildren.

Works (all extant poems written in elegiac couplets except the *Metamorphoses*).
Amores, 'Loves'. Three books of elegies (15, 20, and 15 poems) presenting the ostensibly autobiographical misadventures of a poet in love. What we have in this three-book collection is a second edition, published not before 16 BC and perhaps somewhat later (1. 14. 45–9); work on the original five books mentioned in Ovid's playful editorial preface may have begun c.25 BC. (For the vexed chronology of all Ovid's amatory works see J. C. McKeown, *Am.* (1987), 1. 74–89.) The *Amores* continue the distinctive approach to elegy taken by Ovid's older contemporaries *Propertius and *Tibullus and by the shadowy Cornelius Gallus before them (cf. *Tr.* 4. 10. 53–4); the frequent use of mythological illustration recalls especially Propertius. Corinna, the named mistress of Ovid's collection, owes much to Propertius' Cynthia and Tibullus' Delia; her name itself (along with the pet bird mourned in *Am.* 2. 6) acknowledges a debt to an important forerunner of the Augustan elegiac woman, *Catullus' Lesbia ('Lesbia' looks to *Sappho; 'Corinna' names another Greek female poet). Erotic elegy before Ovid had featured a disjunction in the first-person voice between a very knowing poet and a very unknowing lover. Ovid closes this gap, and achieves a closer fit between literary and erotic conventions, by featuring a protagonist who loves as knowingly as he writes. Ovid's lover is familiar with the rules of the genre, understands the necessity for them, and manipulates them to his advantage. The result is not so much a parody of previous erotic elegy as a newly rigorous and zestful exploration of its possibilities.

Heroides, 'Heroines' (so called by Priscian, *Gramm. Lat.* 2. 544 Keil; but cf. *Ars Am.* 3. 345 *Epistula*. The correct form may have been *Epistulae Heroidum*, 'Heroines' Epistles'). Of the 'single *Heroides*' 1–14 are letters from mythological female figures to absent husbands or lovers; *Her.* 15, whose Ovidian authorship is in doubt, is from the historical but heavily mythologized *Sappho. In their argumentative ingenuity these poems show us the Ovid who was a star declaimer in the schools; in that they speak of female subjectivity under pressure they also testify to an admiration for Euripidean tragedy (see EURIPIDES), and give us a glimpse of what we have lost in Ovid's own *Medea*. The heroines tend to be well known rather than obscure: some of the interest of the letters lies in locating the point at which they are to be 'inserted' into prior canonical works, usually epic or tragic, and in considering the operations of revision and recall. The epistolary format is sometimes archly appropriate ('what harm will a letter do?', Phaedra asks Hippolytus), sometimes blithely inappropriate (where on her deserted shore, one wonders, will Ariadne find a postman?); above all, perhaps, it effects a characteristically Alexandrian modernization by Ovid of the dramatic monologue by presenting the heroine as a writer, her impassioned speech as a written text, and the process of poetic composition as itself part of the action. Ovid claims the *Heroides* to be a new kind of literary work (*Ars Am.* 3. 346); they owe something to an experiment in Propertius (4. 3). The idea for the 'double *Heroides*' (16–21) may have come from the replies which Ovid's friend Sabinus is said to have composed for the 'single *Heroides*' (*Am.* 2. 18, a poem which probably places the 'single *Heroides*' between the two editions of the *Amores*). Formerly doubted, 16–21 are now generally accepted as Ovid's own, stylistic discrepancies with 1–14 being explained by a later compositional date (perhaps contemporary with the *Fasti*). Arguably it is in these paired letters that the potential of the epistolary format is most fully realized.

Medicamina Faciei Femineae, 'Cosmetics for the Female Face'. A didactic poem which predates the third book of the *Ars* (*Ars Am.* 3. 205–6). Only the first 100 lines survive, the latter 50 of which, a catalogue of recipes, show Ovid matching the Hellenistic Greek poet Nicander (in the *Theriaca* and *Alexipharmaca*) in virtuoso ability to make poetry out of abstruse drug-lore.

Ars Amatoria, 'Art of Love' (for the title cf. Sen. *Controv.* 3. 7. 2). A didactic poem in three books on the arts of courtship and erotic intrigue; the mechanics of sexual technique receive but limited attention (2. 703–32, 3. 769–808), perhaps reversing the proportions of works such as the manual of Philaenis (*POxy.* 2891). Books 1–2, datable in their present form to about 1 BC (1. 171 ff.), advise men about women; book 3, presented as a sequel (3. 811 may or may not imply a substantial gap in real time), advises women about men—arguably with one eye still firmly upon the interests of the latter. The situations addressed owe much to previous elegy; at times the preceptor seems to explore the rules of love poetry as much as of love (*ars amatoria* functioning as *ars poetica*). Mythological illustration is more fully developed than in the *Amores*, anticipating the full-scale narratives of *Metamorphoses* and *Fasti*. The actors themselves are firmly located in contemporary Rome: the vivid specificity of the social milieux is sometimes more reminiscent of satire than of earlier elegy. As didactic, the *Ars* takes many traits from Virgil's *Georgics* and Lucretius. It has an irreverent and parodic feel, however, deriving not from the theme alone (other didactic poems, as Ovid was to point out (*Tr.* 2. 471 ff.), could be frivolous too) but from the combination of theme and metre. Conventionally, didactic was a subset of epic written in hexameters; Ovid's choice of elegiac couplets, as it signals a continuity with his own *Amores*, signals a felt discontinuity with mainstream didactic. As successor to the *Amores*, the *Ars* achieves much of its novelty through a reversal of the implied roles of poet and reader: in the *Amores* the reader oversees the poet's love affair; in the *Ars* the poet oversees the reader's love affair. It may be (for we cannot but read with hindsight derived from later events) that this newly direct implication of the Roman reader in the erotic text made the *Ars* the poem most likely to be picked on when the climate turned unfavourable to Ovid's work. The poet's attempts to forestall moral criticism in this area (1. 31–4; cf. *Tr.* 2. 245–52) seem disingenuous.

Remedia Amoris, 'Remedies for Love'. A kind of recantation of the *Ars Amatoria*; the poet now instructs his readers how to extricate themselves from a love affair. The *Remedia* (date between 1 BC and AD 2 indicated by 155–8) appropriately concludes Ovid's early career in erotic elegiac experimentation.

Metamorphoses, 'Transformations'. An unorthodox *epic in fifteen books, Ovid's only surviving work in hexameters, composed in the years immediately preceding his exile in AD 8. The poem is a collection of tales from Classical and near eastern myth and legend, each of which describes or somehow alludes to a supernatural change of shape. Metamorphic myths enjoyed an especial vogue in Hellenistic times and had previously been collected in poems (all now lost) by Nicander, by the obscure Boios or Boio (whose *Ornithogonia*, 'Generation of Birds', was apparently adapted by Macer, *Tr.* 4. 10. 43), and by Parthenius. In Ovid's hands metamorphosis involves more than just a taste for the bizarre. Throughout the poem (and with programmatic emphasis in the opening cosmogony) the theme calls attention to the boundaries between divine and human, animal and inanimate, raising fundamental questions about definition and hierarchy in the universe. Structurally the *Metamorphoses* is a paradox. The preface promises an unbroken narrative, epic in its scope, from the creation to the poet's own day; but throughout much of the poem chronological linearity takes second place to patterns of thematic association and contrast, book divisions promote asymmetry over symmetry, and the ingenious transitions (criticized by the classicizing Quintilian: *Inst.* 4. 1. 77) do as much to emphasize the autonomy of individual episodes as to weld them into a continuum. In some ways the poem's closest analogue (structurally; but also for its interest in the mythic explanation of origins) is *Callimachus' Aetia*, whose avowed aesthetic, influential on all Augustan poetry, the *Metamorphoses* seems both to reject and to embrace (1. 4; E. J. Kenney, *PCPS* 1976, 46 ff.). There is a real flirtation with the Augustan model of epic teleology established in the *Aeneid*; but it can be argued that the metamorphic world of Ovid's poem is structurally and ideologically incompatible with such a vision. Wherever his sources are wholly or partly extant, Ovid's dialogues with the literary past repay the closest attention. He engages with an unprecedented range of Greek and Roman writing; every genre, not just epic, leaves its mark in the poem's idiom. But in the final analysis the *Metamorphoses* renders its sources superfluous: with its many internal narrators and internal audiences, with its repeated stress on the processes of report and retelling whereby stories enter the common currency, the primary intertextual reading which the poem insists on is one internal to itself. As narrative it brilliantly captures the infinite variety and patterning of the mythological tradition on which it draws (and which, for many later communities of readers, it effectively supersedes). Ovid's poetic imagination, intensely verbal and intensely visual, finds here its finest expression. The *Metamorphoses* tells utterly memorable stories about the aspirations and sufferings which define and threaten the human condition; from the poem's characteristic aestheticization of those sufferings come both its surface brightness and its profound power to disturb.

Fasti, 'Calendar'. A poetical calendar of the Roman year with one book devoted to each month. At the time of Ovid's exile it was incomplete, and only the first six books (January–June) survive. These show evidence of partial revision at Tomis (e.g. 1. 3, 4. 81–4); the silence which is books 7–12 abides as a reminder of a life interrupted. The poem's astronomy (1. 2) is influenced by Aratus' *Phaenomena*, its aetiological treatment of history and religion (1. 1) by Callimachus. These debts show Ovid at his most overtly Alexandrian; but, like Propertius in his fourth book (4. 2, 4, 9, 10), he is applying Callimachean aetiology to distinctively Roman material. The *Fasti* belongs equally in the tradition of *Varro's lost Antiquitates*; and the figure without whom the poem is ultimately inconceivable is the emperor Augustus, whose recuperation and appropriation of Roman religious discourse constitutes the basis of Ovid's own poetic appropriation (1. 13–14). The restrictiveness of the day-to-day format as a determinant of both subject-matter and structure is repeatedly stressed by the poet (4. 417, 5. 147–8). However, comparison with other calendrical sources (cf. A. Degrassi, *Inscr. Ital.* 13, *Fasti et Elogia* (1963), esp. the *Fasti Praenestini* compiled by Verrius Flaccus) reveals the extent to which Ovid has been free to select and order his emphases; and the very fragmentation of the narrative material (e.g. the life of Romulus is split and chronologically shuffled between five or six different dates) offers an interesting contrast with the contemporaneous (and more fluid) *Metamorphoses*. The poet is a prominent character in his own poem: he appears in expository passages as an eager antiquarian weighing aetiological and etymological variants with himself or with interlocutors who range from the *Muses (as in books 1–2 of Callimachus' *Aetia*) to random bystanders. Long mined for its detailed information about the perceived roots of Roman religion and ritual, the *Fasti* has begun to attract new attention both as a complex work of art and as an exploration of religious thinking at a time of ideological realignment.

Tristia, 'Sorrows'. A series of books dispatched from exile between AD 9 and 12, containing (so *Tr.* 1, 3, 4, 5) poems addressed by Ovid to his wife and to various unnamed persons in Rome. The 'sorrows' of the title are the past, present, and anticipated sufferings associated with the relegation to the Black Sea: the *Tristia*, like the later *Epistulae ex Ponto*, function as open letters in which the poet campaigns from afar for a reconsideration of his sentence. *Tr.* 2, addressed to Augustus, differs in format from the other four books. A single poem of over 500 lines, it uses an ostensibly submissive appeal for imperial clemency as the point of departure for a sustained defence of the poet's career and artistic integrity. The mood of the *Tristia* is deeply introspective, with all the rich opportunities for geography and ethnography subsumed within the narrative of an inner journey: the ships on which Ovid voyages into exile merge with his metaphorical 'ship of fortune' (1. 5. 17–18); the icy torpor and infertility of the Pontic landscape become indices of the poet's own (allegedly) frozen creativity. The books read at times as *post mortem* autobiography, with exile figured as death and the elegiac metre reclaiming its supposed origins in funereal lament. On one level the insistently self-depreciatory poetics (e.g. 1. 1. 3 ff.) offer an artful fiction of incompetence, extending a *topos* of mock modesty familiar from earlier literary programmes in the sub-epic genres. But only on one level. The pervasive imagery of sickness and barrenness, decay and death, though belied by the continued technical perfection of Ovid's writing, captures an erosion of the spirit which feels real enough, in and between the lines, in the later books from Tomis.

Epistulae ex Ponto, 'Epistles from Pontus'. Four books of poems from exile, differing from the *Tristia* only in that the addressees are named (1. 1. 17–18), and characterized with greater individuality. The letters in books 1–3 were gathered into a single collection ('without order': so claims 3. 9. 51–4) in AD 13; book 4 probably appeared posthumously (4. 9 written in AD 16).

Ibis. An elaborate curse-poem in elegiacs (perhaps AD 10 or 11) directed at an enemy whose identity is hidden under the name of a bird of unclean habits; both title and treatment derive from a lost work of Callimachus (55–62). As at the beginning of the *Tristia*, Ovid dramatizes a forced break with his former self: a previously benign poet now seeks to wound; his elegy has become a prelude to Archilochean iambic (see ARCHILOCHUS). In fact, the *Ibis* displays much continuity with Ovid's earlier work. The poem's ferociously dense catalogue of sufferings achieves a mythological comprehensiveness (despite its small compass) comparable to that of the *Metamorphoses* or *Fasti*; even its 'unOvidian' obscurity (57–60) comes across as a thoroughly Ovidian experiment (cf. G. Williams, *PCPS* 1992, 174 ff.).

Lost and spurious works. Our principal loss is Ovid's tragedy *Medea* (*Tr.* 2. 553). Two verses survive, one cited by Quintilian (*Inst.* 8. 5. 6), the other by the elder Seneca (*Suas.* 3. 7). The poet of the *Fasti* was among those who translated Aratus' *Phaenomena* into Latin hexameters; two brief fragments remain. It is most unlikely that either the *Halieutica* or the *Nux* is by Ovid (cf. J. A. Richmond in *ANRW* 2. 31. 4, 2744 ff., with bibliography).

Ovid is not only one of the finest writers of antiquity; he is also one of the finest readers. Not since Callimachus, perhaps, had a poet shown such understanding in depth and in detail of the literary traditions of which he was the inheritor; never was such understanding carried so lightly. In a national literature dominated by anxious gestures towards the past, Ovid's relationship with his predecessors is exuberantly unanxious. Moreover, the same revisionary energy which he brings to alien texts is applied no less to his own. Ovid constantly reworks himself, at the level of the poem (the *Ars* reframes the *Amores*, the *Remedia* the *Ars*), of the episode (cross-referential Persephones in *Metamorphoses* and *Fasti*), and even of the individual line and phrase (cf. A. Lueneburg, *De Ovidio sui imitatore* (1888)). This paradigm of self-imitation, together with the deceptively easy smoothness and symmetry which he bequeaths to the dactylic metres, make his manner (once achieved) endlessly imitable to later generations as a kind of Ovidian *koinē*. What remains inimitable, however, is the sheer wealth of the poet's invention. Ovid devoted most of his career to a single genre, elegy, so that by the time of the *Remedia* he was already able to claim (*Rem. Am.* 395–6) that 'elegy owes as much to me as epic does to

Virgil'. (The *Metamorphoses* still lay ahead, an epic which—although it is much else besides—can justly be said to be the epic of an elegist.) But within elegy he achieved an unparalleled variety of output by exploiting and extending the range of the genre as no poet had before—not by ignoring its traditional norms, but by carrying to new extremes the Alexandrian and Augustan tendency to explore a *genre's potentiality by testing its boundaries.

No Roman poet can equal Ovid's impact upon western art and culture; only the critics, stuffy as Quintilian (*Inst.* 10. 1. 88, 98), have sometimes stood aloof. Especially remarkable in its appropriations has been the *Metamorphoses*—from the Christianizing ingenuities codified in the 14th-cent. *Ovide moralisé* to the bold painterly narratives of Titian's *poesie* in the Renaissance. In the Anglophone world the terms of Ovid's *reception in the modern era have largely been defined by Dryden and Pope; behind these influential Ovids can still be sensed the Naso of Shakespeare's Holofernes, 'smelling out the odoriferous flowers of fancy', and the figure of 'Venus clerk, Ovyde' in Chaucer's *Hous of Fame*. Though not immune to the challenges which the 20th cent. has posed to the continuity of the classical tradition, Ovid's poetry, now entering upon its third millennium, still reaches artists as well as scholars: a 1979 preface to the *Metamorphoses* by Italo Calvino is at once an academic essay and an assimilation of Ovid's narrative aesthetic to Calvino's own 'post-modern' fiction ('Ovid and Universal Contiguity' translated in *The Literature Machine* (1987), 146 ff.). See ELEGIAC POETRY (LATIN).   S. E. H.

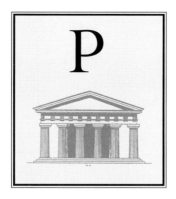

Paestum (mod. Pesto) (see ◀Map 3, Bc▶), a colony of Sybaris, founded as Posidonia *c.*600 BC 60 km. south-east of Naples. It grew rapidly, exploiting its agricultural resources and control of communications, and there was a period of intense urban expansion in the 6th cent., during which a series of temples was constructed (see next page). In 410, it fell to the Lucanians and gradually became Oscanized. In 273 a Latin colony was founded there (see COLONIZATION, ROMAN); it continued to flourish under Roman control. It retained the right to issue coins until the 1st cent. AD. A second colony was founded in AD 71, and inscriptions reveal a thriving civic body until late antiquity, when malaria (see DISEASE) and marshy conditions became a problem. Both the Greek and Roman cities were orthogonally planned, and there are extensive remains of all phases of the city's history, and of extramural sanctuaries at Santa Venere and Foce del Sele.   K. L.

painting, Greek (*see page 516*)

painting, Roman (*see page 518*)

Palmyra (Tadmor) (see ◀Map 4, Ec▶) gained wealth, power, and splendour particularly in Roman times. From it, a central Syrian desert oasis with hills, wadi, and spring (*Efqa*), routes ran in all directions. Efqa yielded stone tools, some *c.*7,500 BC, others neolithic, *c.*7000 BC. A community, Tadmor (of uncertain etymology), enters the records *c.*2000 BC. Puzur-Ishtar the 'Tadmorean' made a contract at Kanesh (Kultepe), Asia Minor (19th cent. BC); Syrian archives mention Tadmoreans, Suteans (nomads) pillaging, and the Amurru king's demand for taxes. The Assyrians (1115–1077) defeated, near Tadmor, Aramaeans (Semites whose language, Aramaic, spread throughout western Asia) and (645–644) Arabs (Semites), who penetrated western Asia and comprised half Roman Tadmor's population. Hellenistic Old Testament *Chronicles* (and Josephus) reported that Solomon 'rebuilt Tadmor'; *c.*150 BC. *Parthia reached the Euphrates, and a Tadmor family built a hypogeum in Hellenized, hybrid 'Parthian' style.

Tadmor rose rapidly after Seleucid extinction (64/3 BC), becoming semi-independent, and exploiting caravans between Roman (coastal) Syria and Parthia. Crafts-people developed Tadmor's 'Parthian' art style. From 44 BC there are Aramaic inscriptions, often with Seleucid-era dating, documented (profile-figured) art and architectural commissions. In 41 Mark *Antony raided Palmyra unsuccessfully; shrines were refurbished and from now on, striking stone tomb towers lined routes. Roman control, from *Tiberius (*Germanicus' eastern mission, AD 17–19), brought soldiery, use of Greek and occasionally Latin alongside Aramaic, the name 'Palmyra', taxation (Tariff Law, 137), administration (tribes, senate, 'city', 'people'), urbanization, and religious syncretism. *Hadrian visited Palmyra *c.*129. Caravans, often organized and policed by Palmyrenes, brought luxuries. The Palmyrenes created a handsome, largely limestone city, combining Semitic, Greek, Roman, and Parthian features (see p. 515). Walls, gates, the great Temple of Bel (32), Romanized temples (Baalshamin, 130/1), a piazza, market (agora), houses, streets (including the Grand Colonnade, with bracket statuary), the Tetrapylon, arch, tower tombs, hypogea, and 'house'-tombs arose. The local, stylized, frontal-figured 'Parthian' art comprised statues depicting deities and notables, reliefs of deities, lion and ceremonial, funerary busts (for closing burial slots) and sarcophagi showing the deceased, wall-paintings, including funerary Roman allegories (Achilles, Ganymede), plaster heads and friezes, and (from *c.*200) coins. Imports included Chinese silks, imperial and Athena marble statues, and mosaicists (Cassiopeia). The Palmyrene king Septimius Odaenathus' (murdered 267–8) and queen Zenobia's brief, Roman-style empire was ended by Aurelian (272–3). *Diocletian (284–305) built a camp, walls and baths; Justinian (527–65) refurbished the walls and churches. Arabs took Tadmor (634); a late medieval fortress arose. Palmyra's 18th-cent. rediscovery influenced European neo-classicism.   M. A. R. C.

Pan, a god whose original home was Arcadia. His name, attested on Mount Lykaion in the form *Paoni* is certainly

Paestum Aerial view of Paestum showing the polygonal line of the city-wall and grid-like street plan. The three well-preserved Doric temples (6th–5th-cent. BC) are clearly visible (centre) and show the wealth of Greek Posidonia.

derived from the root †pa(s), and means 'guardian of flocks' (cf. Latin *pascere*). His appearance is mixed, half man and half goat, not surprising in a region where divine theriomorphism is well attested. His usual attributes of syrinx and *lagobolon* (a device for catching hares) mark him out as a shepherd. Pan became a kind of national god of Arcadia, being shown in the fourth century on the reverse of coins of Zeus Lycaeus type of the Arcadian League. Starting at the beginning of the 5th cent. BC, Pan spreads into Boeotia and Attica, continuing in the 4th cent. to reach the rest of the Greek world.

The principal myths concern his birth, and there are no fewer than fourteen different versions of his parentage. Most often his father is *Hermes, another Arcadian god, but the name of his mother varies, though most often she is a nymph, in harmony with the god's rustic nature. In some versions Pan's mother is Penelope. Otherwise, there are few stories about Pan before Hellenistic times: he loves the nymphs Echo, Pitys, and Syrinx, of whom the last two escape him, and Selene, the moon.

Pan's activities and functions are basically concerned with the pastoral world (see PASTORALISM, GREEK). He is a shepherd god and protector of shepherds, who sacrifice in his honour kids (*Anth. Pal.* 6. 154), goats, or sheep, and who dedicate to him statuettes showing herdsmen, with or without offerings. He is also a hunting god, concerned with small animals such as hares, partridges, and small birds, while it is *Artemis who presides over larger game. This function is illustrated by an Arcadian ritual, whereby after an unsuccessful hunt, young men would beat Pan's statue with squills (Theoc. 7. 106–8, with scholia). In this way they would stimulate Pan's powers of fertility and direct it towards the animal domain. Pan is also linked to the world of those soldiers patrolling the rocky, lonely places where he lives. During the Persian Wars (see GREECE (HISTORY)), he intervened among the Athenian ranks at Marathon (490 BC). *Herodotus (6. 105. 2–3) has the story of his appearance to the runner Phidippides, who was near Mount Parthenion in Arcadia on his way to Laconia to get help from the Spartans; he offered to help the Athenians, in return for which the cult of Pan was established in Athens. From the Hellenistic period onwards, Pan is the god responsible for sowing panic (*paneion*) in the enemy, a sudden, unforeseeable fear. Soldiers therefore pay cult to

Palmyra Air view of Palmyra (mod. Tadmor), showing the great temple of Bel (AD 32), the surrounding sacred space framed by a colonnaded court, and (upper right) the colonnaded street and arched gateway, typical features of Roman *urbanism.

him. In the case of the individual, too, Pan can exercise a type of savage and violent possession (*panolepsia*). In Attica (cf. Menander, *Dyskolos* 571–2), Arcadia, and at the Corycian cave at *Delphi, Pan is credited with oracular and prophetic powers. See ORACLES.

The Greeks liked to worship Pan, together with Hermes and the nymphs, in sacred caves, recalling the figure of the Arcadian goatherd. But in his homeland of Arcadia, though he is fond of mountains, well away from human habitation, Pan does not live in caves, and he is not absent from cities. Little is known of his public cult. In Athens, it involved the sacrifice of a castrated goat and a torch-race. Individual offerings are typified by votives such as vases, golden grasshoppers, oil-lamps (in the cave at Vari in Attica), and reliefs, which show the God in his cave in front of his worshippers, playing the syrinx and accompanied by Hermes, three nymphs, and sometimes the river Achelous. In the *Dyskolos* of Menander, the mother of Sostratos organizes a religious celebration in honour of Pan at Phyle, in Attica, after the god appears to her in a dream. The sacrifice of a sheep is followed by a meal, and the happy and rowdy celebration continues all night at the cave, with drinking and dancing in the presence of the god.

The ancients quite early associated Pan with the word *pān*, 'all' (*Homeric Hymn to Pan* 47). From this, word-play leads to the association which made Pan in the Roman period into a universal god, the All. It is in this context that we should see the well-known story in *Plutarch (*Mor.* 419c), which has sometimes been linked with the rise of Christianity, of a mysterious voice announcing the death of 'great Pan'. Despite these developments, as *Pausanias) bears witness, in cult the god remained the god of shepherds.   M. J.

Parthia, Parthian empire (see ◀Map 2, Fc▶) The people whom Greeks and Romans called Parthians were originally Parni, members of the semi-nomad Dahae confederacy north of Hyrcania. Their Greek name is derived from the Achaemenian *Persian and then *Seleucid satrapy called Parthia (*Parthava*), which they occupied, traditionally in 247 BC, the year with which the Parthian ('Arsacid') era begins; later they ruled from the Euphrates

[*continued on p. 519*]

Greek and Roman painting

Greek painting (see also POTTERY, GREEK). When the Mycenaean palaces fell, *c*.1200 BC (see MYCENAEAN CIVILIZATION), the art of painting was lost. It is next practised in the early Archaic period. Sources for Archaic to Hellenistic are: literary references; artefacts echoing painting (primarily vases); surviving examples, mostly recent discoveries.

Writers of the Roman period are most informative (J. J. Pollitt, *The Art of Greece* (rev. 1990), 124–80). *Pliny the Elder (*HN* 35) gives a history of painting, detailing many works and careers, dividing artists into regional schools, notably (as in sculpture) a 4th-cent. Sicyonian school. Pliny acknowledges debts to Xenocrates of Sicyon, hence the conspicuousness of the Corinthia (i.e. the territory of Corinth in the sources (although much has been found there). *Pausanias' autopsy and interest in art *per se* distinguish him from other writers. Philosophers like *Plato and *Aristotle made moral and aesthetic judgements on art (see ART, ANCIENT ATTITUDES TO); the *ekphrasis* employed by rhetoricians like Philostratus, Lucian, and Aelius Aristides involved describing art for effect, not accuracy.

Classical painters enjoyed high social standing (hence perhaps their prominence in the sources): most notably, Polygnotus' association with Cimon, and Apelles' with *Alexander the Great. Slaves (see SLAVERY) were excluded from painting (*HN* 35. 77); Pliny lists female painters (*HN* 35. 147). Painting was introduced into the school curriculum by Pamphilus (below).

Pliny denies Egyptian influence on early painting, placing its beginnings at Corinth or Sicyon. The invention of linear painting is attributed to Philocles of Egypt or Cleanthes of Corinth, dating early Archaic. The temples at Corinth and neighbouring Isthmia sanctuary, *c*.690–650, have painted walls: the former has blocks of colour, the latter figures *c*.30 cm. (12 in.) high and border patterns on stucco, using several colours. Contemporary is the rare use of a brown wash for flesh on vases from several regions, notably Corinth (Chigi (MacMillan) Painter). However, these are explicable ceramically, as are the clay 'metopes' from Thermum in Aetolia (west central Greece), *c*.630, and Corinthian red-ground vases, *c*.575–550. Also from the Corinthia, the wooden Pitsa plaques, *c*.540–500 (largest, *c*.15×30 cm. (6×12 in.)) use a white ground and a range of colours, including (like Isthmia) blue.

Tomb paintings preserved in Etruria appear to have been undertaken for Greek patrons (see ETRUSCANS); at *Paestum in southern Italy, the Tomb of the Diver, *c*.480, bears close resemblance in pose and (in the *symposium) subject-matter to contemporary Athenian vases. In Lycia (southern Asia Minor), tomb paintings discovered at Elmalı in 1969–70 (M. Mellink, *CR Acad. Inscr.* 1979, 476–96), *c*.525 and *c*.475, include a funeral feast and a hunt, mixing Greek, Persian, and local elements. A painting on a stone plaque from *Persepolis *c*.500 (*JHS* 1980, 204–6) further attests to a mix of Greek and local elements.

Cimon of Cleonae (between Argos and Corinth) is credited with inventing *katagrapha* (three-quarter views) and a new disposition of figures, matching renderings on late 6th-cent. Pioneer vases, a date supported by *Simonides against Pliny's early Archaic. Substantial advances occur *c*.475–450, the age of Polygnotus and Micon. Their work, often on historical and heroic themes in prominent public buildings, was characterized by variable groundlines, grouping, and disposition of figures, reflected in some contemporary vases. Panaenus (brother of Phidias) is said to have painted portraits (among the earliest) in the Marathon painting of the Stoa Poecile (Painted Stoa). The use of perspective was greatly developed by Agatharchus, and *Sophocles is said to have introduced *skene*-painting (Arist. *Poet.* 1449ᵃ) (A. L. Brown, *PCPS* 1984).

Apollodorus of Athens (fl. 407–404 BC) opened 'the door of the art of painting' (Pliny, *HN* 35. 61), developing *skiagraphia*, balancing light and shade. Through the 'door', says Pliny, walked Zeuxis. He is often contrasted with Parrhasius of Ephesus (fl. 397 BC), who worked mainly in Athens. Zeuxis was the painter of shade and mass, Parrhasius of contour lines (Plin. *HN* 35. 65–72), reflected e.g. in the lekythoi

painting, Roman Wall-painting from the House of the Vettii at *Pompeii, AD 63–79. An example of the 'Fourth Style', showing central picture panels, fantastic architecture, and imitation marble veneer.

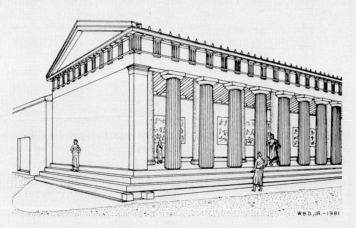

W.B.D.,JR.-1981

painting, Greek Reconstructed drawing of the 5th-cent. BC Stoa Poecile ('Painted Colonnade') in the *Agora of *Athens. A series of wooden panel paintings inside commemorated Athenian military achievements, including the victory at Marathon (490 BC). The Greek *polis* was a patron of public painting, often, as here, exploiting local themes to express civic pride and identity.

of Group R. Euphranor (fl. 364 BC) contrasted himself with Parrhasius, saying that the latter's Theseus was fed on roses, his own on meat (Plin. *HN* 35. 129). A debate on painting styles is reflected in *Xenophon (*Mem.* 3. 10. 1–5) where Parrhasius talks with *Socrates. The most highly regarded of all painters was Apelles (fl. 332 BC), pupil of Ephorus of Ephesus and Pamphilus of Sicyon, and court painter to Alexander. His contemporary, Protogenes of Rhodes, could not quite match Apelles in drawing straight lines freehand.

Classical paintings were (at least mainly) painted on whitened wooden panels (probably hung on a frame by pegs, as in the Stoa of Attalus at *Delphi). The removal of the Stoa Poecile paintings by c. AD 400 supports this. Pliny and *Cicero give (differing) lists of four-colour painters, implying that the Classical range was limited to red, yellow, black, and white. Pliny divides colours into 'austeri' (earth) and 'floridi' (artificial). The absence of blue (used at Archaic Isthmia and Pitsa) may be explained if black acts as a darkening agent. The absence of green is incompatible with Vergina (see AEGAE) and Aineia (below), although the Alexander mosaic (if it accurately reflects a late Classical painting) argues for the four-colour scheme.

Most paintings were done with brushes, but encaustic, applying pigments mixed with heated wax, is regularly used from the 4th cent. (a statue is being painted in encaustic on an Apulian vase of c.370–360, G. Richter, *Handbook of Greek Art*, 288 fig. 403), although Polygnotus used it (Plin. *HN* 35. 122). Pausias of Sicyon first became well-known for encaustic, learning it from Pamphilus, teacher of Apelles. Pausias is said (anachronistically) to have begun the practice of painting on panelled ceilings, and to have painted small panels, but is best known for introducing many kinds of flowers, and for his *stephanoplokos*, or girl making garlands (Plin. *HN* 35. 123–5). 'Pausian' florals occur regularly on contemporary south Italian vases, and on mosaics and paintings from *Macedonia (below), Illyria, and elsewhere. Pausias painted *Eros and Drunkenness at Epidaurus (Paus. 2. 27. 3). Encaustic was used by Nicias (fl. 332) on paintings, and perhaps on the statue he painted for Praxiteles; he was famed for painting women (Plin. *HN* 35. 131), and animals, or living figures in general (Paus. 1. 29. 15).

Recent finds include tomb paintings from Macedonia, notably Vergina (M. Andronikos, *Vergina* (1984)), from 1976. See AEGAE. The smaller tomb (c.340?) contains a *Hades and *Persephone which eschews outline, painted impressionistically, with subtle shades of colour, hatching giving shading and depth. The 'tomb of *Philip II' (if so, soon after c.336) features a hunt where human figures dominate, as in later Hellenistic and early Roman wall-painting. The treatment of landscape is paralleled in the Alexander mosaic from *Pompeii. Hades and Persephone are also painted on the back of a throne found at Vergina in 1987 (*Arch. Rep.* 1988–9, cover, 78–9).

The tombs at Aineia (found 1979–82), c.350–325, use at least six colours, and include 'Pausian' florals (I. Vokotopoulou, Οἱ ταφικοί τυμβοί της Αινείας (1990)). The late-4th-cent. paintings at Lefkadia feature 'Pausian' florals, and imitation relief sculpture, including suggested shadow. The figures are reminiscent of the Roman paintings at Boscoreale. The contemporary tomb at Kazanlak in Bulgarian Thrace (L. Zhivkova, *The Tomb at Kazanlak* (1974)) depicts battle, chariot race, and feast (and 'Pausian' florals). Outline is emphasized, with shading and little subtlety of colour, a different approach from the Macedonian, indicating that several trends were current, as must have been true of all periods of Greek painting. These tomb paintings were apparently executed on wet plaster, with a binding medium. See IMAGERY; PAINTING (Roman); POTTERY (Greek).   K. W. A.

Roman painting In late republican times Roman collectors avidly acquired Greek 'old master' pictures (see ART, ANCIENT ATTITUDES TO), and contemporary painters provided new works for the market; Greek artists such as Metrodorus of Athens in the 2nd cent. BC and Iaia of Cyzicus in the 1st cent. BC were brought to, or migrated to, Rome to meet the demand. Pictures commemorating military campaigns were carried in triumphs (see TRIUMPH). But the advent of the empire saw a gradual shift of interest from portable panels to wall-paintings, a trend lamented by *Pliny the Elder (*HN* 35. 118).

Wall-painting on plaster is attested in tombs at Rome from an early date (a well-known fragment from the Esquiline shows historical episodes from the Samnite wars; and became increasingly normal in private houses. At *Pompeii and *Herculaneum virtually every residence eventually contained extensive paintings, ranging from simple schemes in minor rooms to rich, polychrome schemes in important rooms. The evidence from the Vesuvius region, together with contemporary material from Rome (including remains in *Augustus' properties on the Palatine and Nero's *Domus Aurea* (Golden House), enable us to follow changing fashions up to the late 1st cent. AD. The so-called First Style, the Italian version of a fashion current throughout the Hellenistic world, modelled plaster in relief to imitate drafted masonry and marble veneer. Pictures were admitted in narrow friezes at eye-level, and the veins of imitation marble were occasionally shaped into figures and other motifs. The Second Style began early in the 1st cent. BC and reproduced architectural forms by illusionistic means upon a flat surface; the illusion became increasingly elaborate, with receding planes, baroque forms and rich colouring, but the architecture remained essentially solid and constructible. The painted architecture of the Third Style (c.15 BC–AD 50) was delicate and unreal, and all illusion of depth was removed from the wall, which was now divided into broad areas of colour (red and black especially favoured, but blue and green also becoming more popular) supplemented by fine miniaturist detail; interest was now focused on a central picture, often very large and showing academic groups set against a landscape backcloth. The Fourth Style (extending to the end of the Flavian period) retained both the central pictures, now smaller and squarer, and the unreal architecture, but reintroduced effects of depth, if only as a foil to large 'tapestry' fields framed by stencil-like borders; yellow appeared as a dominant colour alongside red and black.

The evidence from the 2nd, 3rd, and 4th cents. AD is more fragmentary and difficult to date, but includes important decorations from the provinces. Architectural schemes remained popular but often without the organic structure and internal logic of the Pompeian period; sometimes, as in the Inn of the Peacock at *Ostia, they were reduced almost to abstract patterns. Surviving ceiling-decorations show inventive schemes in which emphasis was laid upon the centre and diagonals, reflecting the influence of structural forms such as cross-vaults. In the 3rd cent. AD there was a fashion for a cheap kind of decoration in which walls and ceilings were divided into compartments by a tracery of red and green stripes or lines on a white ground, a style much favoured in the early Christian catacombs. The early 4th cent. saw something of a classical revival. A richly coloured ceiling from the Constantinian palace at Augusta Treverorum (Trier), painstakingly reconstructed from thousands of fragments, was divided into rectangular compartments containing busts of poets or philosophers and nimbed females alternating with pairs of winged Cupids, all on blue backgrounds.

Portable panel-pictures certainly continued to be produced throughout the Roman period, but most are lost; an exception is a wooden roundel found in Egypt which depicts *Septimius Severus with his empress and sons. Also from Egypt comes a series of mummy portraits, usually executed on wooden panels which were inserted in the mummy-case; the painting was done either directly on the wood or on a thin coat of gypsum-plaster. The first known paintings in manuscripts belong to late antiquity; they include the well-known series of illustrations in two 5th-cent. *codices* of Virgil now in the Vatican Library. See IMAGERY; PORTRAITURE (ROMAN); SCULPTURE (ROMAN).   R. J. L.

to the Indus, with Ctesiphon as their main residence. The territorial gains under Mithradates I and II not only changed their former eastern Iranian empire into an ethnically, politically, socially, and culturally diverse one needing new forms of administration and organization, but also deeply influenced the relationship between the Parthian aristocracy and the rulers. It was the conflict between kings and nobles which shaped later history and often allowed foreign powers like Rome to intervene in Parthian affairs. Although we hear of large estates of Parthian aristocrats in the conquered parts of the empire we do not know very much about the way in which their rights of possession and use were transferred to, and retained by them. It is therefore dangerous to call the Parthian state a 'feudal' one. Ambitious members of the great Parthian families (Suren, Karin, Gev, and others), governors, petty and 'vassal' kings temporarily gained total or limited independence (like the rulers of Mesene and Seistan). We do not know very much about Parthian rule in Persis, apart from the fact that in their time south-western Iranian historical and mythical tradition was replaced by eastern Iranian stories and legends, and that Parthian rule was finally brought to an end by local dynasts from Istakhr.

The structure of Parthian society and the titulature of their élite are best known from the administrative documents from Nisa, the Sasanian inscriptions of the 3rd cent. AD and the classical reports of Parthian warfare. They distinguish between a higher and a lower nobility and their dependants (cf. the *ordo probulorum*, *liberi*, and *servi* in Justin), the last group not being slaves but people with the belt of 'vassalage' (Iran. *bandag*). Apart from these groups we find a kind of middle stratum of artists, traders, doctors, bards, and other specialists and the non-Iranian native population of the conquered territories. Scholarship for a long time classified the Parthians as culturally dependent, without great political aspirations and inferior to Rome in almost all respects. New findings (texts from Mesopotamia, archaeological remains) provide a more differentiated view which, e.g., allows us to see the 'Philhellenism' of the kings (on their coins and in cultural affairs; cf. HELLENISM) and the Iranian traits of their rule as ways of ensuring the co-operation of two important groups of subjects. In warfare they were famous for their mailed cavalry (*cataphractarii/clibanarii*) and their horse archers, and they bred the Nisaean horses which were known even in China. The Parthians spoke Parthian, a western Middle Iranian language; they seem to have adopted the Zoroastrian cult of fire and its calendar, but tolerated every other religion.

A stronger emphasis on the Iranian heritage is characteristic of the second half of their empire (cf. the legends on the coins and the role of Vologeses I (?) in the Zoroastrian tradition), but it is very dangerous to see this as a consequence of the revolt of Seleuceia, the reasons for which are not known to us. The Parthians played an important role as middlemen in the trade between China, India, and Syria. Their art—a revived Iranian art, which absorbed both Mesopotamian and Greek elements—spread far and is historically interesting.   J. Wi.

pastoral poetry, Greek For as long as peasants have tended their flocks and herds on grazing lands away from the village, song and music (especially that of the pipe, which is easily cut, fashioned, and carried) have served as an anodyne against rustic tedium and brutality; the Taviani brothers' film *Padre Padrone* (1977) provides a powerful illustration from modern Sardinia. This is especially true of the goatherd, who ranges furthest into the wild territory of *Pan in search of shrubs on which only his chalcenteric and omnivorous charges will browse; and in these lonely wastes it is natural that two herdsmen whose paths cross should not only perform in each other's company but that their songs should be competitive. This real-world situation provided the foundation upon which a literary genre was established by the Sicilian poet *Theocritus in the 3rd

cent. BC and developed by his followers in Hellenistic Greece (Moschus, Bion, and a school of epigrammatists), Rome (*Virgil, Calpurnius Siculus), and the post-Renaissance world.

Bucolic poetry was not created *ex nihilo*. Two piping herdsmen are among the figures depicted on the Shield of Achilles (*Homer, *Il.* 18. 525 f.), and Eumaeus in Homer's *Odyssey* shows early literary interest in peasant characterization; even the Cyclops Polyphemus, communing with his ram, arouses a moment of sympathy which will later stimulate his re-creation as a youthful lover in Philoxenus (frr. 2–4P) and Theocritus (6, 11). The Sicilian lyric poet *Stesichorus is credited by Aelian (*VH* 10. 18) with having been the first to sing of the local bucolic hero Daphnis, back in the 6th cent. (fr. 102P). But the conditions needed for pastoral themes to gain critical mass as a viable genre were not met until literary life became concentrated in the great Hellenistic cities, alienated from the villages in which so many Greek cultural traditions (tales, folksong, dance, ritual competition) had developed. One thread in the cultural amalgam of the 3rd cent. is an understandable nostalgia for the simpler world once dominated by Daphnis, Pan, Priapus, and the Nymphs; a world now largely vanished but whose continued existence could at least be fantasized in the mountains of Magna Graecia (south Italy and Sicily) and Arcadia.

As already mentioned, the basic form elaborated by Theocritus seems to have been essentially agonistic. Theocritus 5 provides the clearest example. Two peasants meet; one proposes a contest; stakes are wagered, and a judge is sought; jockeying for the most favourable ground takes place; and after some preliminary boasting and badinage, each attempting to unsettle the other, the competition begins. This takes the form of an alternating ('amoebean') sequence of couplets or quatrains in which the first singer, as proposer of each subject, has an inbuilt advantage, while the respondent must follow suit and if possible cap each theme. This goes some way to offset the fact that the initiator of the challenge—in this case, Lacon—has chosen the time and place (contrast 6. 5). In poem 5, victory is suddenly and confidently claimed by Comatas at v. 136, and immediately confirmed by the judge. Why? The explanation of G. Serrao (*Problemi di poesia alessandrina* 1 (1971)) is attractive: not only must the respondent follow suit but (to continue the card-game analogy) each singer must remember every trick that has been played; the first one to contradict a previous statement is the loser. There is thus a natural limiting factor to the bucolic agon, for the longer it goes on the harder it gets.

The genius of Theocritus' creativity was to realize the possibilities offered by this half-crude, half-sophisticated model to the modern style of self-conscious urban literature. His chosen form is artificial from the start; the Doric dialect may impart a rustic flavour (see *Greek language), but the metre is the classical Homeric hexameter. Each poem works its own elegant variation on the fundamental pattern. The brief exchanges of the original contest are substituted with single songs (6, 7); rivalry is replaced by a friendly and voluntary exchange of gifts (6); the scenes of peasant life acquire a distancing layer of sophistication by being framed as notional letters (6. 2, *Arate*) or poetic autobiography (7); the dialogue may become an end in itself without ever reaching the stage of competition (4), or may be dropped in favour of a lover's monologue (3). Full circle is reached in poem 1, where the obscene teasing is inverted to become exquisite politeness and in which, though the diptych structure is retained, the first 'performance' is not a competition effort at all but an ekphrastic description (deliberately recalling the Iliadic *Shield of Achilles*, only recast on a miniature scale) of the decorative carving on a wooden cup (see EKPHRASIS) which is freely offered as reward for a song by the other character. The coarse duels of the grubby, garlic-chewing rustics have been alchemically transmuted into allusive mandarin elegance, without ever quite pulling free of their roots in the vigorous Sicilian soil. The literary conventions which lead on to *Virgil, Milton, and Marie-Antoinette are all in place.　　A. H. G.

pastoral poetry, Latin Latin pastoral poetry is, in strict terms, represented by *Virgil's ten eclogues, Calpurnius Siculus' seven, the two Einsiedeln eclogues, and Nemesianus' four. But pastoral (or 'bucolic') is often defined by theorists as a 'mode' rather than a *genre, and, in this sense, one may speak of pastoral colouring or attitudes in *Tibullus, *Lucretius, the *Culex*, *Dirae*, and *Lydia* of the *Appendix Vergiliana*, *Aeneid* 8, and numerous other texts besides. It is unlikely that Virgil's contemporary Cornelius Gallus wrote pastoral elegies, although the tenth *Eclogue* has frequently been interpreted to that effect.

Among Latin pastoralists Virgil stands supreme. He significantly extended the boundaries of the genre which he had inherited from *Theocritus, whose inspiration he explicitly acknowledges, and upon whom he draws extensively in all the *Eclogues*, with the exception of 4 and 6, in which the poet strives to lift pastoral to a higher plane (cf. 4. 1 *Sicelides Musae, paulo maiora canamus*, 'Sicilian Muses, let us sing a somewhat grander strain'). Virgil's innovativeness is proclaimed at the outset of the *Eclogue*-book. Whereas Theocritus had kept pastoral and court poems rigidly distinct, contemporary politics and pastoral are strikingly blended in the first *Eclogue*, which describes, in the persons of Meliboeus and Tityrus, the effects upon the Italian countryside of the triumviral dispossessions of the late 40s BC (see ROME (HISTORY) §1.5). In consequence of this, the pastoral world may be said to exist no longer in a hermetic space, but to suffer encroachments from without, which have the effect of disrupting the shepherds' traditional *otium* ('ease, tranquil existence').

Also to Virgil's credit is the creation of the Arcadian setting—Snell's famous 'spiritual landscape'—which was to prove so influential in European pastoral. But it is important to note that references to Arcadia in the *Eclogues* are actually rather few, and are moreover combined with features of Italian topography (cf. *Eclogue* 7). The precise import of Arcadia is much disputed. It seems best to regard it as a remote, solitary setting for lovers' plaints and for song (at which the Arcadians were especially skilled). Both topics are central to pastoral. It is probably to the former of these that *Horace's famous verdict on the *Eclogues*, *molle atque facetum* ('gentle' and elegant') (*Sat.* 1. 10. 44) refers, though both adjectives have a stylistic connotation as well.

The *Eclogues* are self-reflexive, experimental, and challenging, but none of the authors who follow Virgil can rival him in complexity and suggestiveness. With Calpurnius, and to a lesser extent the Einsiedeln eclogues, one has a sense that pastoral is being pushed to its furthest limits. Indeed, Calpurnius' fifth *Eclogue* is concerned with purely georgic matters, while his seventh provides no more than a pastoral framework for extensive praise of *Nero's Roman amphitheatre. Similarly, both Neronian pastoralists show a readiness to talk explicitly of political matters which are properly extraneous to the pastoral world (though they naturally impinge upon it).

Certain aspects of Virgilian pastoral are taken up and developed by Calpurnius—not necessarily in a felicitous way. Whereas Virgil (in *Ecl.* 1 and 9) had hinted at an opposition between city and country, in Calpurnius' final poem, this opposition is made explicit, and resolved in favour of the former, so that the pastoral ethic is in a sense betrayed by its own representative Corydon. Virgil's youthful 'god' (Octavian) had exercised his (questionable) influence on the land at long range; Calpurnius pictures the city-dwelling Nero as a veritable *deus praesens*, 'god made manifest' in the countryside, at the mere sound of whose name the fields are instinct with joy and fertility (4. 97 ff.). So too the praise which Virgil had proffered to several patrons becomes concentrated, in Neronian pastoral, in the figure of the emperor. The richly textured, prophetic millenarianism of Virgil's fourth *Eclogue* is transmuted into the prosy assertion that the golden age—a favourite theme both of pastoral and imperial *propaganda—has returned under the presidency of Nero. Virgil's experimentation with the possibilities of the genre and his musings on which direction his future work should take are commuted by Calpurnius (*Ecl.* 4) into pastoral encomium, culminating in a baldly-phrased request for imperial patronage. One can only commend Nero for shutting his ears.

The *Eclogues* of Nemesianus, written it seems in the early 280s AD, are far more conventional than those of Calpurnius, whom Nemesianus nevertheless assiduously echoes, and, it is arguable, outshines. Verbally and thematically, the influence of Virgil is paramount. The fourth *Eclogue* restores to pastoral the Theocritean refrain, which Calpurnius had dropped. Also noteworthy is *Eclogue* 2, in which two young shepherds rape the girl of whom both are enamoured while, like Proserpina, she is picking flowers. The motif of sexual violence is new to pastoral poetry, although the idea of erotic conquest—in this case by force—recalls [Theocritus] 27 and, to some extent, anticipates the medieval *pastourelle*.　　L. C. W.

pastoralism, Greek Although animals were ubiquitous throughout the Greek countryside, animal husbandry has until recently received little systematic attention; hence current interpretations are frequently embryonic. Zoo-archaeological studies of animal bone assemblages from the historical period are particularly needed.

Evidence of domesticated animals goes back to the 7th millennium BC. In the early neolithic modest flocks of ovicaprines (sheep and goats), kept primarily for meat, were integrated into small-scale gardening, grazing on fallow and stubble and supplying manure. More specialized stock-keeping arose in the late neolithic and bronze age, with increased exploitation of 'secondary products', especially ox traction and ovicaprine textile fibres, culminating in the large-scale wool production of the Minoan and Mycenaean palaces (see MINOAN and MYCENAEAN CIVILIZATION). Older views of the Dark Age as one of nomadic pastoralism (often associated with the 'Dorian invasions', for which see MACEDONIA) are now under challenge. 'Homeric society' rested upon arable production, with large herds as a store for surplus wealth. The period of independent *poleis* (discussed further below) witnessed smaller herd sizes; Hellenistic and Roman Greece a subsequent increase. Within the Roman, especially later Roman, empire demand for pastoral products made ovicaprine stock-raising (often conducted from isolated, tenant-run farmsteads) important on larger Greek estates.

The animals reared in different regions were partly influenced by environmental conditions, with more larger livestock in the moister north and west. Older studies assumed that environmental conditions also dictated a pattern of long-distance seasonal transhumance, as practised frequently in modern times. Transhumance, however, is now regarded as the product of specific economic and political circumstances (especially weak lowland agriculture and unified political authority) which did not apply under the independent *poleis* (see POLIS). Despite occasional cross-border agreements, seasonal movements were generally limited to upland areas within *polis* boundaries. Many citizens possessed a few 'house' animals; but larger herds (typically not more than 50–100 strong) were owned by wealthy landowners employing individual hired or slave herders, rather than—as recently—by independent, low-status mobile pastoralist groups. Recent research has emphasized the income-generating capacity of such modest-sized ovicaprine flocks reared for their marketable high-quality wool and cheese. The extent of animal husbandry's integration with arable farming is controversial. One opinion stresses the role of agro-pastoral farms whose animals fed at least partly on fodder crops, fallow, and agricultural waste-products, providing manure in return; another asserts greater reliance upon pastures distant from arable cultivation.

Animal husbandry also performed important religious and social functions. The requirements of official sacrificial calendars mirrored the seasonal availability of surplus animals from local flocks and conditioned the age at which animals were sold. War-horses, chariot-horses, and hunting dogs were powerful status symbols, playing important roles in élite lifestyles. (See also BRIGANDAGE; PAN.)

S. J. Ho.

pastoralism, Roman Pastoralism, whether good, bad or indifferent, provided the most lucrative returns, according to *Cato the Elder (Cicero, *Off.* 2. 89; Columella, *Rust.* 6 *praef.* 4–5; Plin. *HN* 8. 29–30). Thus scholars have traditionally focused on such profitable forms of stockbreeding (sometimes described as 'ranching') as *Varro's long-distance, large-scale transhumance of sheep between Apulia and the Abruzzi (*Rust.* 2. 2. 9)—entrepreneurial pastoralism largely divorced from, or even in competition with, settled *agriculture which exploited Rome's post-Hannibalic control of Italy (see ROME (HISTORY) §1.4). More recently, evidence from archaeology (patterns of rural settlement, *villa excavation, and analysis of animal bones and plant remains) and ethnography (the study of still-extant traditional forms of pastoralism), together with a close reading of the Roman *agricultural writers, has begun to round out the picture by emphasizing the more widespread, if less prominent, closer integration of pastoralism with agriculture. Subsistence peasants, who owned a few sheep for clothing, milk, cheese, and manure (Columella, *Rust.* 7. 2. 1) and an ass for transport and the plough (*id.* 7. 1. 1), sowed their limited cultivable land with crops for their own consumption but found pasture for their animals most of the year round in local scrub and woodland (cf. Varro, *Rust.* 2. 5. 11; Columella, *Rust.* 1. 2. 5). A *c*.60 ha. (240 *iugera*) estate with 6 plough-oxen, 4 asses, 100 sheep, and an unspecified number of pigs (Cato, *Agr.* 10) could produce additional fodder resources of its own: surplus grain, forage crops rotated with cereals, dry and/or irrigated meadows (which might also be profitably leased, Cato, *Agr.* 9; 149; Varro, *Rust.* 1. 21), grass grown on fallow land, grazing of the cereal crop while still in the leaf, foliage, and grape pressings. Besides sheep, which were always in the majority—with parts of Apulia and the Po plain gaining reputations for particular breeds (Columella, *Rust.* 7. 2. 3)—Roman pastoralism included cattle, horses, mules, asses, goats, pigs, dogs, and slave herdsmen (Varro, *Rust.* 2. 10. 6; 2 *passim*) and, from the late republic onwards, the specialized breeding, known as *pastio villatica*, of peacocks, dormice, boars, snails, fish, etc. (Varro, *Rust.* 2, esp. 10. 6). See BRIGANDAGE. M. S. Sp.

patricians formed a privileged class of Roman citizens. The word is probably connected with *patres* ('Fathers'), a formal collective term for patrician senators (see SENATE). In the republican period patrician status could be obtained only by birth; and it may be surmised that in early times both parents had to be patricians, if the law of the *Twelve Tables which stated that patricians could not legally marry plebeians (see PLEBS) was a codification of long-established practice rather than an innovation by the Decemviri; this law was repealed by Gaius Canuleius in 445 BC. It is also possible, but not certain, that patrician marriages had to be by *confarreatio* (a special ceremony which took its name from a sacrificial loaf).

The origin of the patriciate is disputed. Tradition made it the creation of *Romulus, but also suggested that it was augmented by the admission of aristocratic clans (*gentes*) from outside Rome, such as the 'Trojan families' (including the Iulii) who were brought to Rome after the sack of Alba Longa, and the Claudii, a Sabine clan that migrated to Rome at the beginning of the republic. The mysterious distinction among the patricians between the 'greater and lesser clans' (*gentes maiores, gentes minores*) was explained as a consequence of the elevation of new men to the patriciate by the kings. These stories suggest not only that the patriciate originated under the monarchy, but also that patrician status was characteristic of whole clans (though the modern view that only patricians had clans is untenable). Even so, many clans developed plebeian branches, for instance the plebeian Claudii Marcelli.

In contrast with the tradition, some modern scholars believe that the patricians emerged only under the republic. Their strongest argument is that the kings themselves do not appear to have been patricians. But the nature of patrician privilege suggests a different interpretation. One of the most notable patrician prerogatives was their control of affairs during an interregnum (when, it was said, the 'auspices returned to the Fathers'—*auspicia ad patres redierunt*). Only a patrician could hold the office of *interrex* ('between-king'), evidently a relic of the regal period. It may be correct to say that it was the patricians who chose the king, but that the king could not himself be a patrician. This would explain both the origin of patrician power and the fact that most of the kings were in some sense outsiders (many of them, indeed, foreigners).

There is some evidence that patricians served in the cavalry, and that six centuries were reserved for them; but it is doubtful if this was the definitive criterion of patrician status. The theory that the republican patricians were the descendants of the royal cavalry is probably mistaken.

We know that the patricians monopolized all the important priesthoods, and it is most probable that they were essentially a group defined by religious prerogatives. The nature of their political power is, by contrast, much less certain. Membership of the senate was not confined to patricians, since the senators were formally known as 'Fathers and Conscripts' (*patres et conscripti*) of whom only the former were patricians (the *patrum auctoritas*, the 'assent given by the fathers' to decisions of the popular assemblies, was confined to them). The most controversial question is whether it was necessary to be a patrician in order to hold a magistracy. Our sources assume that it was, but the Fasti suggest that in the earliest decades of the republic not all consuls were patricians. The patrician monopoly of political office developed gradually in the course of the 5th cent., and was successfully challenged in the 4th by the increasingly powerful *plebs*.

Although by 300 BC the patricians had lost their monop-

oly of office and of the major priestly colleges, they continued to exercise power out of all proportion to their numbers. Until 172 BC one of the two annual consuls was always a patrician, and they continued to hold half the places in the major priestly colleges as of right. Other priesthoods, such as the *flamines maiores* ('priests of the senior Roman gods'), the *rex sacrorum* ('the king for sacred rites'), and the Salii ('college serving Mars'), remained exclusively patrician.

As an aristocracy of birth, the patriciate was unable to reproduce itself, and patrician numbers gradually declined. Of around 50 patrician clans that are known in the 5th cent., only 14 still survived at the end of the republic. *Caesar and Octavian, the future *Augustus, were given the right to create new patricians (the former by a *Lex Cassia*, 45 or 44 BC; the latter by a *Lex Saenia*, 30). Later emperors used their censorial powers to confer patrician status on favoured individuals, who then passed it on to their descendants. The hereditary patriciate seems finally to have disappeared in the third century AD, but *Constantine revived the title *patricius* as a personal honour, in recognition of faithful service to the empire.

A. M.; T. J. Co.

patronage, non-literary Greek and Roman society were both heavily stratified, and many forms of dependence tied people to their superiors in *wealth, power and *status. The study of these relations is a central part of ancient social history. (Classical Athens was perhaps untypical.)

Sources such as the letters of *Cicero and *Pliny the Younger combine with the legal evidence and epigraphy to give a more complete picture of patronage in the Roman world. In addition, the special relationship between patron and client, *patronus* and *cliens*, among Roman citizens was recognized as being distinctive (e.g. Dion. Hal. *Ant. Rom.* 2. 9), and has received a great deal of scholarly attention.

By the Augustan period it could be believed that *Romulus had assigned all the plebeians at Rome to individual aristocratic patrons. In practice, the title of *cliens* was odious (Cicero, *Off.* 2. 69) and the patterns of formal patronage of this type are hard to discern. Much is made of the institution in early imperial literature, but that may be largely a literary reflection in traditional guise on current problems of status. Certainly the role of *clientes* in late republican politics has been much exaggerated. This is partly because of the tendency to confuse it with other Roman social institutions such as *amicitia* (friendship), or *hospitium* (hospitality) and to adduce practices such as the morning *salutatio*, a deferential and potentially humiliating paying of respects, but a practice which entailed only a more general dependence.

Two further forms of patronage, for which the word *patronus* was indeed used, have also complicated the picture. The first is the relationship of the master to a slave or former slave, which had precise definition in Roman law, and which entailed *operae* or duties for *freedmen.

This was of course a common form of dependence everywhere in the ancient world, and in Roman cities there must have been many blurred and difficult borderline cases in mixed freedman and free households as to who owed what kind of duty to which former owners or their relatives. The second is the relationship of Roman leaders to whole communities either in Italy or the provinces, and their protection of influential foreigners, for whom they might even obtain the Roman *citizenship. This relationship essentially derived from the circumstances of Rome's growth as an imperial power, and in many ways drew on the behaviour of Hellenistic kings and their families. Augustus and his successors combined enormous households and very numerous dependents with an unsurpassed range of opportunities for bestowing favours of this second sort on communities and individuals all over the inhabited world. But that did not mean that they ruled through a vast extension of the institution of *clientela*.

Cicero's patronage is our most systematic guide to the late republican practice. He acquired relations with communities in southern Italy on his way to his province of Sicily as quaestor; in the troubles of 63, retainers from Atella, Volaterrae, and particularly Reate gave him their physical support; he had a close tie with the important city of Cales; around his villa at *Pompeii most of the towns were in his *clientela*; his governorship in Cilicia gave him a special relationship with the whole of *Cyprus; and (in an area where his friend *Atticus had important financial interests) he had the city of Buthrotum in Epirus as clients, and so on. All these places could count on Cicero for *commendatio*: a way into the personal politics of Rome, and in particular legal guidance and support. *Civitates* were a natural object of this kind of patronage, but other collectivities, such as *collegia*, acquired patrons in this way too.

The example of Cicero provides us with an insight into the importance of the general phenomenon of patronage. Chains of this sort of relationship offered a way of dealing with the scale of ancient society: with the mechanics of representing, and making decisions concerning the rival interests of, either very numerous individuals in a large community, or thousands of communities in a world-empire. It thus offered a sort of brokerage, and promoted both active communication and reciprocal exchanges of information and esteem, and served to retain a real political role for patrons under a system in which their constitutional political position had been greatly weakened by the advent of the imperial system. *Commendatio*, moreover, could only work if there were in place agreed principles of comparison and standards of assessment, the maintenance of which fostered cultural cohesion. Finally, the system reflected and maintained change in hierarchic order, and worked against sclerotic immobility, since the effectiveness of chains of influence varied, and the fortunes of the client with them. All of these effects ultimately worked in favour of the social stability which is such an interesting feature of the Roman world.

N. P.

Paul, St St Paul was a convert (see CONVERSION) from Pharisaic to Messianic Judaism as a result of a mystical experience (Gal. 1: 12 and 16) when he believed himself called to be the divine agent by whom the biblical promises about the eschatological ingathering of the pagans would be fulfilled. That transference of allegiance led him to renounce his previous religious affiliations (Phil. 3: 6 f.), even though the form of his religion remains in continuity with apocalyptic Judaism. We know him as the result of letters which he wrote over a period of about ten years to maintain communities of Jews and gentiles in Rome and several other urban centres in a pattern of religion which enjoined faithfulness to Jesus Christ as the determining factor in the understanding of the Mosaic Law. This subordination of the Law inevitably led to conflict with Jewish and Christian opponents who suspected him of antinomianism and apostasy. His doctrine of justification by faith was hammered out as a way of explaining his position in relation to the Jewish Law. He commended Christianity as a religion which was both the fulfilment of the Jewish tradition and also the negation of central precepts like food laws and circumcision, though he was emphatic in his rejection of idolatry. In his letters we have clear evidence of the emergence of identifiable Christian communities separate from Judaism with a loose adherence to the Jewish tradition as interpreted by Paul. At the end of his life he organized a financial offering for the poor in Jerusalem from the gentile churches he had founded. According to *Acts his journey to Jerusalem with this collection preceded his journey to Rome where later Christian tradition suggests that he died in the Neronian persecution. The letters in the New Testament which are widely assumed to be authentic are Romans, 1 and 2 Corinthians, Galatians, Philippians, 1 Thessalonians, and Philemon, and possibly Colossians and 2 Thessalonians. Ephesians, and 1 and 2 Timothy and Titus are probably pseudonymous. This last group of documents indicates the direction of the Pauline tradition after the apostle's death when accredited teachers began to be ordained to ensure the preservation of the apostolic traditions and institutions in the face of emerging gnosticism and antinomianism. See also CHRISTIANITY.

C. C. R.

Pausanias, from Magnesia ad Sipylum (?) in Lydia, western Asia Minor (fl. *c.* AD 150), periegetic writer (see TOURISM), wrote an extant *Description of Greece* (*Periēgēsis tēs Hellados*) claiming to describe 'all things Greek' (*panta ta Hellēnika*); in fact limited essentially to the Roman province of Achaia with the omission of Aetolia and the islands. Contents: 1. Attica, Megara; 2. Argolis etc.; 3. Laconia; 4. Messenia; 5–6. Elis, Olympia; 7. Achaea; 8. Arcadia; 9. Boeotia; 10. Phocis, Delphi.

His chief concern in his selective account was with the monuments (especially sculpture and painting) of the Archaic and Classical periods, along with their historical contexts, and the sacred (cults, rituals, beliefs), of which he had a profound sense. His work is organized as a tour of the *poleis* and extra-urban sanctuaries of Achaia, with some interest in topography, but little in the intervening countryside. His concern for objects after 150 BC is slight, although contemporary monuments attracted his attention, especially the benefactions of *Hadrian. He wrote from autopsy, and his accuracy (in spite of demonstrable muddles) has been confirmed by excavation. Although his approach was personal, his admiration for old Greece (Athens, Sparta, Delphi, and Olympia figure prominently) and its great patriots (see 8. 52) belongs to the archaizing enthusiasm for the Greek motherland fanned by the *Second Sophistic and the Panhellenion (the Hadrianic Athens-centred organization of Greek cities), which attracted many overseas (especially Asian) Greeks to Antonine Achaia; presumably Pausanias wrote partly with these in mind.   A. J. S. S.

Peloponnese (see ◀Map 1▶) the large peninsula of southern mainland Greece, joined to Attica and Boeotia by the Isthmus of Corinth, a mountainous area of complex topography. All the north is highland, from the lower chains of the Argolic peninsula westwards successively through Cyllene (*Ziria*), Chelmos, Panachaicum, and to the south Erymanthus and Maenale towards the centre of the Peloponnese: all with extensive areas above 1,500 m. Three chains run southwards from this mass, the lowest to the west beginning with Lykaion and running through Ithome to form the Messenian peninsula; Taygetus in the centre, with the highest summit of the Peloponnese (2,409 m.), forming the peninsula now called the Mani, running to Cape Taenarum (Matapan); and Parnon to the east, running to Cape Malea. The (mainly limestone) mountains are agriculturally unproductive, being densely wooded, and used for forest-grazing and other *pastoralism.

Within this armature are located a number of sizeable alluvial lowlands (especially the plain of Argos; the Eurotas valley; the Pamisus valley and plain of Messenia; the Alpheus valley and plain of Elis; and the central basin of Megalopolis), and many other small basins, including a series of characteristic *polje* in the limestone mountains. Along the north and west coasts are well-watered and well-drained terraces, the uplifted remnants of earlier coastal plains. Except where drainage was very poor, the agriculture of all these lowlands supported nucleated settlements at some period. The deep gulfs between the mountain chains provided some good harbours; the capes were all dangerous, Malea notoriously so. Smaller landfalls were numerous, and are not far apart even on the most mountainous coasts (like eastern Laconia).

The landscape helped the regions retain some identity throughout antiquity. Elis to the north-west with the panhellenic sanctuary of *Olympia was the region of the Alpheus plain and adjacent coasts. The steep northern valleys, their outfalls, and the coastal strip made up Achaea. The central mountains and basins, including the plain of Megalopolis, constituted Arcadia; the south-western peninsula and Pamisus plain Messenia; the

Eurotas valley and south-eastern peninsula Laconia. The Isthmus and its adjacencies were controlled by Corinth; Argos was the principal focus of its plain (and some neighbouring districts: but the Saronic Gulf and the ambiguous allegiances of the island of Aegina confused the political geography of this area).

The siting of major centres has varied, though a perennial factor has been the combination of control of fertile bottomland and routes within and away from the Peloponnese. Thus the sea/land crossroads of the Isthmus gave Corinth rather stable geographical circumstances, but similar natural advantages in the Roman period, when routes to north-western Greece and beyond were of ever greater importance, were enjoyed by Patrae (which became a *colonia*), at the western mouth of the Corinthian gulf and close to the easy crossing from Rhium to Antirrhium. The plain of Argos supported important communities in the bronze age, throughout antiquity, and again in the medieval and early modern periods. To the south Lacedaemon/*Sparta was a central place for the Laconian plain throughout antiquity; its inhabitants fled to the coastal refuge of Monemvasia in the troubles thereafter, but in late Byzantine times Mistra used the resource base of the central Eurotas plain once again. Bronze-age settlements in Messenia were of considerable importance, and after the end of Spartan control, Messene as a city had some prosperity; the Hellenistic and Roman periods saw a growing role for the southern coastal cities of Gythium and Methone which were useful stations on long-haul east–west routes (an importance which Methone in particular retained until the 19th cent.). The inland districts supported a considerable population, particularly the cities of eastern Arcadia, Tegea, Mantinea, and Orchomenus, the three ingredients of Byzantine and early modern Tripolis; internal routes played a part here.

'Peloponnesos' is first attested in the mainly lost epic poem the *Cypria* and in the *Homeric Hymn to Apollo*, and the inhabitants seem to have thought of themselves as really resembling islanders (in Mediterranean comparison slightly smaller than Sicily, twice the size of Cyprus). The fragmentation of the topography encouraged various forms of federalism (see FEDERAL STATES) and *sympoliteia* (joint citizenship); the hegemony of Sparta promoted a regional solidarity, though it was never complete. In later times geographers saw the Peloponnese on a smaller scale, likening it to a plane-tree leaf (the medieval name Morea derives from a similar analogy to the mulberry) or to the acropolis of Greece (Strabo 8. 334).   N. P.

Peloponnesian War See GREECE (PREHISTORY AND HISTORY).

Pergamum (see ◀Map 2, Bb▶) in Mysia (NW Asia Minor) *c*.24 km. (15 miles) from the Aegean, a natural fortress of great strategic importance commanding the rich plain of the river Caïcus; important historically as the capital of the Attalid kings and, later, as one of the three leading cities of

Pergamum In this scene from the main frieze of Pergamum's 'Great Altar' an armed *Athena grapples with a fallen *Giant. In art depictions of the mythical battle between gods and Giants served as an allegory for real-life threats to Greek civilization. Here the sub-text was probably the victory of Eumenes II (ruled 197–158 BC) over the '*barbarian' Galatians, a Celtic population settled in central *Asia Minor in the 3rd–2nd cent. BC.

provincial *Asia, and archaeologically as the best excavated Hellenistic royal capital outside *Macedonia. First attested in Greek sources in 401 BC, Pergamum enters history's mainstream as a treasury of *Lysimachus, who entrusted it (c.302) to Philetaerus, founder of Attalid fortunes. An indigenous community (in spite of the Attalid claim to foundation by the Heraclid Telephus), Pergamum had adopted Greek civic organization (see POLIS) by c.300 (OGI 265) at the latest, and this was upheld by the Attalids, who maintained control in practice through their assumption (from Eumenes I) of the right to appoint the chief magistrates (stratēgoi). As a royal capital as well as a polis, the city was the chief showcase of Attalid patronage. From Attalus I on the kings promoted *Athena, the city's presiding deity, as dynastic protectress, especially of military success; she acquired the title Nikephoros, 'victory-bearer', and her

sanctuary in the upper city was adorned with the famous statues of defeated Galatians. *Strabo (13. 4. 2) credits above all Eumenes II, his power and wealth vastly augmented by the Peace of Apamea, with the enlargement and beautification of the city. To his reign dates the 'Great Altar', masterpiece of the Pergamene 'school' of Greek *sculpture, as well as the royal *libraries and the terraced, fan-shaped plan of the upper city, its focus the royal palace—a remarkable statement of royal absolutism (see URBANISM); an inscription (SEG 13. 521; Eng. trans. in Austin no. 216) preserves a royal law on municipal administration showing the efforts made to keep the city clean and in good repair. This royal programme aimed at transforming Pergamum into a Greek cultural capital, for which the model was *Athens, recipient of generous Attalid patronage in the 2nd cent. BC. Declared free in his will by Attalus

III, Pergamum lost its Roman status of allied city for its support of *Mithradates VI (88–85 BC); ensuing hardship at the hands of Roman troops and businessmen was mitigated by the diplomacy of Diodorus Pasparos, a leading citizen, deified by the grateful city (C. Jones, *Chiron*, 1974, 183 ff. for the redating). Although politically and economically subordinate to *Ephesus, Pergamum under the Principate was head of a *conventus* (assize) and a centre of the (Roman) *ruler-cult. Its prosperity and prestige can be gauged from such new monuments as the temple of *Trajan and *Zeus Philios and, in the lower city, the Asclepieum (see ASCLEPIUS), transformed under *Hadrian, and from its tally of six senatorial families by AD 200 (H. Halfmann, *Die Senatoren aus dem östlichen Teil des Imperium Romanum* (1979), 68). Attacked by the Goths in the mid-3rd cent., the city contracted. Despite unimpressive physical remains from late antiquity, it remained an important intellectual centre, where the future emperor *Julian studied philosophy.   A. J. S. S., C. R.

Pericles (*c*.495–429 BC), Athenian politician, was the son of Xanthippus and Agariste (a member of the noble Alcmaeonid family), niece of *Cleisthenes and granddaughter of Agariste of Sicyon and Megacles. He was *chorēgos* (paying for the production) for *Aeschylus' *Persae* in 472, but first came to prominence as one of the elected prosecutors of Cimon in 463/2. In 462/1 he joined with Ephialtes in the attack on the Areopagus (see DEMOCRACY, ATHENIAN 3).

According to *Plutarch he became popular leader and one of the most influential men in Athens after Ephialtes' death and the *ostracism of Cimon. Little is recorded of him for some years, but it is reasonable to assume that he was in favour of the more ambitious foreign policy pursued by Athens in the 450s and of the further reforms of that decade. He is credited with a campaign in the Gulf of Corinth *c*.454 and with the sending out of cleruchies (colonies retaining citizenship rights in the mother-city) to places in the *Delian League, and with the introduction of pay for jurors and the law limiting citizenship to those with an Athenian mother as well as an Athenian father. His proposal for a congress of all the Greeks, which came to nothing because of opposition from *Sparta (Plut. *Per.* 17: its authenticity has been challenged) perhaps belongs to the early 440s and was an attempt to convert the Delian League into a league of all the Greeks under Athens' leadership now that the Delian League's war against Persia had ended. In 446 he commanded the expedition to put down the revolt of Euboea; he returned to Athens when the Peloponnesians invaded, and was alleged to have bought off the Spartan king Pleistoanax; and he then went back to deal with Euboea.

Pericles was greatly involved in Athens' public building programme of the 440s and 430s. This was the issue on which opposition to him was focused by Thucydides (not the historian), son of Melesias, a relative of Cimon, but Thucydides was ostracized (see OSTRACISM) *c*.443 and the

building continued. According to Plutarch, Pericles was elected general (*stratēgos*) every year after that and was Athens' unchallenged leader; but it seems likely that attacks on Pericles and his friends, probably from the democratic end of the political spectrum, are to be dated to the early 430s. His mistress Aspasia and the *sophist Anaxagoras were perhaps prosecuted, the sculptor Phidias was prosecuted and left Athens, and Pericles himself was charged with embezzlement but presumably acquitted.

In the 430s he led an expedition to the Black (Euxine) Sea. The policies pursued by Athens in the late 430s, which led to the outbreak of the Peloponnesian War (431–404 BC), are presumably his: *Aristophanes represents him as being particularly obstinate over the decree imposing sanctions on Megara, and the historian *Thucydides gives him a speech claiming that a policy of appeasement will not work. According to Thucydides his strategy for the Peloponnesian War was to stay inside the walls when the Peloponnesians invaded, and to rely on Athens' sea power and superior financial resources to outlast the Peloponnesians; but there are indications in the scale of Athens' expenditure and naval activity in the opening years of the war that Thucydides' picture may be distorted. In 430, when the hardship of the war was beginning to be felt, the Athenians deposed him from the generalship and attempted unsuccessfully to negotiate with Sparta; he was afterwards re-elected, but he was one of the many Athenians to suffer from the *plague, and he died in 429.

Pericles was an aristocrat who became a democratic leader. He won the admiration of Cimon's relative, the historian Thucydides, as a man who was incorruptible and far-sighted, and who led the people rather than currying favour with them (2. 65). Plutarch reconciled this with the less favourable picture given by *Plato by supposing that Pericles was a demagogue in the earlier part of his career and a great statesman in the later. He was an impressive orator. His manner was aloof, and he is said to have been uninterested in his family's concerns. His marriage (possibly to his cousin and *Alcibiades' mother, Deinomache) was unhappy, but he formed a liaison with the Milesian Aspasia, and when his two sons by his Athenian wife had died from the plague his son by Aspasia, Pericles, was made an Athenian citizen.   A. W. G.; P. J. R.

Persephone/Kore, goddess, *Demeter's daughter by *Zeus, *Hades' wife and queen of the underworld. Her most important myth is that of her abduction by Hades, her father's brother, who carried her off when she was picking flowers in a meadow and took her to the underworld, Demeter's unsuccessful search for her daughter (which took her to *Eleusis) and consequent withdrawal from her normal functions caused the complete failure of crops, and men would have starved if Zeus had not intervened. When Demeter did not respond to the persuasion of the divine messengers he sent to mediate, Zeus sent Hermes to persuade Hades to release Persephone, which he did; but Hades tricked Persephone and made her eat some pomegranate seeds, with the consequence that she could not leave Hades for ever, but had to spend part of the year with her husband in the underworld and part of the year with her mother in the upper world. The story is told in the *Homeric Hymn to Demeter*, a text which has a complex relationship with what may well have been the most important cult involving Persephone and Demeter, that of the Eleusinian *mysteries, the celebration of which included a ritual search for Kore with torches.

In the images Kore/Persephone is represented as a young woman, often with the addition of attributes, among which torches, stalks of grain, and sceptres are common, while some, like the cock at Locri Epizephyrii in south Italy, are found especially in the iconography of particular cults.

The name Kore stresses her persona as Demeter's daughter, Persephone that as Hades' wife. (Her name also occurs in other forms, for example, Phersephone, or, in Attic (see GREEK LANGUAGE), Pherrephatta). The myth of her rape was perceived as, among many other things, a polarized articulation of some perceptions pertaining to marriage from the viewpoint of the girl. Her cult in some places, notably Locri Epizephyrii, stresses this aspect. Her wedding had an important place in Locrian cult and myth and she was worshipped also as the protector of marriage and the women's sphere, including the protection of children. Demeter does not seem to have had a prominent place in the Locrian cult. Persephone's wedding and the flower-picking that preceded the abduction were also celebrated in other places, as, for example, in Sicily, where her flower-picking and marriage were celebrated, and in the Locrian colony of Hipponium. The Sicilians also celebrated *Korēs katagōgē*, the bringing down of Kore.

Of course she also had an awesome and dread aspect as the queen of the underworld. Everyone will eventually come under her authority. But she was not implacable, and she and Hades listened to reasonable requests, such as that to return to the upper world to request the performance of proper burial or other rites—a trait abused and exploited by the dishonest Sisyphus who refused to return to Hades.

She was often worshipped in association with Demeter; a most important festival in honour of the two goddesses was the Thesmophoria, which was celebrated by women all over the Greek world (Demeter also bore the cult-title Thesmophoros, 'law-giving'). At Cyzicus Persephone was worshipped with the epithet Soteira (Saviour) and her festival was called Pherephattia or Koreia or Soteria. (Cf. also Paus. 8. 31. 1 for Arcadia). Not surprisingly, Persephone had an important place in the texts inscribed on the gold leaves that were buried with people who had been initiated into Orphism (see ORPHEUS). In one strand of belief Persephone was the mother of Dionysus-Zagreus.   C. S.-I.

Persepolis (see ◀Map 2, Fd▶), in Persis (SW Iran), a residence of the Achaemenid *Persian kings. *Alexander the Great in 331 BC took and looted Persepolis and set fire to the palaces (Diod. 17. 71–2); this served to bake a number of clay sealings. The royal quarters, built on a hill-terrace, contained a treasury and symmetrically planned palaces with immense square columnar halls.

Excavations on the site have revealed that *Darius I levelled the rock-terrace and began the great *Apadana* (audience hall), the main palace-buildings, and the 'harem'. These were completed by *Xerxes; Artaxerxes I finished the Hall of a Hundred Pillars and built his own palace. Around the whole complex was a fortification wall, and a great gate and stairway led up to the terrace. The bas-reliefs of these palaces are among the finest extant examples of Achaemenid art. These include the Audience reliefs originally flanked by lions attacking bulls, and 23 delegations of tribute bearers. The tombs of the Achaemenid kings are near by. In the palace and walls two collections of thousands of administrative texts written in Elamite have been found.   M. S. D.; M. V.

Persia (see ◀Map 2▶) In the narrow sense (Persis, Pārsa), Persia defines the country lying in the folds of the southern Zagros mountains. From the start of the first millennium BC, an Iranian population lived in close contact with the Elamite inhabitants here. This led to the emergence of the Persian *ethnos* and the kingdom of Anshan, which appears fully on the historical scene beginning with the conquests of *Cyrus the Great. Even with the extension and consolidation of the Achaemenid empire under *Darius I, Persia proper retained a prominent place in the way in which the Great Kings visualized their territorial power. At the same time, members of the Persian aristocracy received the highest governorships and offices in the central and provincial government. In this respect, the empire created by Cyrus and his successors may be described as Persian.

The history of this large empire has been neglected for a long time: between the fall of Babylon (539) and *Alexander the Great's arrival, the Near East has resembled a gigantic historiographical 'no-man's land'. This neglect cannot be blamed on a lack of documents, and finds of material continue to be made. Besides the archaeological and iconographical evidence, the historian has at his disposal royal inscriptions, thousands of Elamite and Babylonian tablets and Aramaic documents, not to mention Greek accounts and other regional bodies of material. But Achaemenid history has been viewed for a long time through the distorting lenses of Greek authors, not least because the Persians themselves left virtually no narrative accounts of their own history. The find of central government documents (especially the Elamite tablets from *Persepolis, combined with a different vision of Near Eastern history, has given a new and powerful impetus to intensive study of a fascinating period of ancient history.

On the historical scale, the Achaemenid period represents a turning point in Middle Eastern history: for the first time, countries from the Indus to the Balkans, from Central Asia to Elephantine in Upper Egypt were embraced by one, unifying, political structure. This political unification did not result in the disappearance of local ethno-cultural identities. In 334, despite the marked process of acculturation, *Asia Minor, *Egypt, *Babylonia, and *Bactria were still countries clearly distinguishable in terms of language, culture, and religion. This was also true of Persia proper. In spite of partial and/or temporary setbacks (notably the secession of Egypt between 399 and 343), the overall assessment must be that the empire held together for more than two centuries. Alexander himself frequently did little more than take over to his own advantage the Achaemenid ideological heritage and administrative techniques. *Mutatis mutandis*, the splintered geopolitical pattern of the Near East *c*.280 recalls the one which had prevailed before Cyrus the Great's conquests.   P. B.

Persian Wars See GREECE (PREHISTORY AND HISTORY), *Archaic Age*.

Petronius Arbiter, author of the extant *Satyrica*, possibly identical with Petronius, the politician and *arbiter elegantiae* at the court of Nero, forced to suicide in AD 66. Given that scholars now agree that the *Satyrica* belongs stylistically and in terms of factual detail to the Neronian period, and that *Tacitus' account of the courtier Petronius describes a hedonistic, witty, and amoral character which would well suit the author of the *Satyrica* (*Ann.* 16. 17–20), many find it economic to identify the two, but the matter is beyond conclusive proof; the occurrence of the name Titus Petronius Arbiter in the MSS of the *Satyrica* gives no aid, since this may simply be the supplement of a later copyist who had read Tacitus.

Of the *Satyrica* itself we seem to have fragments of books 14, 15, and 16, with book 15 practically complete, containing the *Cena Trimalchionis* (26. 6–78.8). The commonly used but misleading title *Satyricon* (sc. *libri*) conceals not Σατυρικόν (neuter singular) but Σατυρικῶν (neuter genitive plural) and alludes both to influence from Roman *satire and (ironically) to Encolpius' far from satyric sexual capacity (see below for both). The whole work was evidently lengthy; one conjectural reconstruction has suggested twenty books and a length of 400,000 words. It is prosimetric in form, an inheritance from the similar satires of *Varro, though there is now extant a Greek low-life prosimetric fictional text in the Iolaus-papyrus, *POxy.* 42 (1974). The outline of the plot is naturally difficult to reconstruct; the main characters are the homosexual pair Encolpius (the narrator) and the younger Giton, who undergo various adventures in a southern Italian setting. They encounter a number of characters, some of whom, such as the unscrupulous adventurer Ascyltus and the lecherous poet Eumolpus, try to divide the lovers; Giton is not particularly faithful, and this, like the sexual orientation of the lovers and many other elements in the novel, constitutes an evident parody of the chaste fidelity of the boy–girl pairings of the ideal Greek *novel. Encolpius seems to be afflicted with impotence as the result of the wrath of the phallic god Priapus, and there are several episodes describing his sexual failures; the wrath of Priapus is evidently a parody of the wrath of *Poseidon in the *Odyssey* of *Homer, and other parallels between Encolpius and *Odysseus are present, particularly when he encounters a woman named Circe (126 ff).

Many themes familiar from Roman satire appear, such as legacy-hunting (the episode set in Croton (Crotone), 116–41) and the comic meal (the *Cena Trimalchionis*); in the latter Encolpius, Giton, and Ascyltus attend a dinner given by the rich *freedman Trimalchio, probably in Puteoli, in the narrative of which both Trimalchio's vulgar and ignorant display of wealth and the snobbishness of the narrator emerge very forcibly, and which contains in a parody of *Plato's *Symposium* a collection of tales told by Trimalchio's freedman friends which gives some evidence for vulgar Latin, though Petronius has naturally not reproduced colloquial speech exactly. Several other inserted tales are told in the novel, especially those of the Pergamene Boy (85–7) and the Widow of Ephesus (111–12), suitably lubricious stories for their narrator Eumolpus, but also clearly drawing on the Hellenistic tradition of Milesian tales (see NOVEL, LATIN). The inserted poems in various metres sometimes appear to comment on the novel's action; the two longest, presented as the work of the bad poet Eumolpus, seem to relate to other Neronian writers, the 65-line *Troiae Halosis* (89) written in the iambic trimeters of Senecan tragedy, and the *Bellum Civile* in 295 hexameters (119–24), closely recalling *Lucan's homonymous epic on the same subject (and restoring the divine machinery which Lucan had excluded). Literary and cultural criticism is certainly a concern of the novel; there are prominent attacks on contemporary oratory, painting, and poetry (1–5, 88–9, 118).

Petronius' novel seems not to have been widely known in antiquity, though a more extensive text than ours was available; it was rediscovered between the 15th and 17th cents., with great impact. The fragmentary text which has come down to us is likely to have some degree of interpolation, though scholars disagree as to how much. A number of poems in various metres transmitted separately from the *Satyrica* are also attributed to Petronius. See NOVEL, LATIN.   S. J. Ha.

philhellenism (in Roman republican history) refers to the nexus of two developments in the late 3rd and 2nd cent. BC. One of these is cultural, characterized by the actively favourable reception of Greek language, literature, and philosophy within the Roman ruling class. The other, political, is signalled by the adoption of policy and behaviour actively represented as beneficial to, and respectful of, Greece and Greeks. The phenomenon is associated especially with *Flamininus, Lucius Aemilius Paullus (consul 182), and *Scipio Aemilianus and his Scipionic Circle. Instances of approbation of aspects of Greek culture go back a very long way. Advice was taken from *Apollo at *Delphi and thanks rendered to him (398, 394) long before Delphi was 'freed' from Aetolian control (see FEDERAL

STATES) in 189. On instruction from Apollo during the Samnite wars (see ROME (HISTORY) §1.3) statues of *Alcibiades and *Pythagoras were erected in the *Comitium* or chief place of political assembly (Plin. *HN* 34. 26), long before Gaius Laelius welcomed Athenian philosophers (155). The serpent of *Asclepius was brought to Rome from Epidaurus (292) long before the black stone of the Magna Mater (see CYBELE) was imported from Pessinus in *Asia Minor (204). Greek plays (in translation) were first performed in Rome in 240. In the sphere of diplomacy, Lucius Postumius Megellus, when envoy to Tarentum in 282, spoke Greek long before Flamininus dealt with Greeks in their own language, and as early as 228 Rome's victorious treaty with the Illyrian queen Teuta was presented to Greeks as in their interest (Polybius 2. 12). The name 'Atticus' ('Athenian') was first borne by the censor of 247 (and consul 244, 241) Aulus Manlius Torquatus Atticus.

Early instances of 'philhellenic' behaviour, collective and individual, abound, as do indications of 'hellenization' (though it is difficult to say how far this ever happened and what exactly it means to say that it did: see HELLENISM). But these instances are disparate, and the disparate sources for them are not such as to suggest ideological coherence or consistency. From the end of the 3rd cent. the pace quickens and the picture changes. This is partly a matter of evidence—the availability of a comparatively continuous contemporary account (*Polybius) and the tendency of writers of the 1st cent. (esp. Posidonius and *Cicero) to find philhellenism in their favoured Romans of the second, but not only that. Quintus Fabius Pictor wrote his annals in Greek early in the 2nd cent. (see HISTORIOGRAPHY, ROMAN), and by the 160s Greek purveyors of hellenism were flocking to Rome (Polyb. 31. 24. 7); things Greek were much sought and genuinely admired, if occasionally to excess. Aulus Postumius Albinus had his self-imposed literary hellenism castigated by *Cato the Elder; Polybius (39. 1) concurred and more. (Cato's hostility to particular representatives and manifestations of Roman philhellenism should not be taken to indicate general hostility to hellenism.) Titus Albucius was lampooned by Lucilius (see SATIRE) for preferring to be called Greek rather than Roman (Cic. *Fin.* 1. 9).

Alongside all this, the Romans in 200 announced to the Greeks that they would go to war against Philip V of Macedon to prevent him from attacking any Greeks and protected Athens from Macedonian attack. From 198 Flamininus adopted the language of Greek diplomacy and used the rhetoric of Greek freedom to great advantage, most strikingly at the Isthmian games of 196. This was the efflorescence of political philhellenism. It was effective. Philip was defeated, and Greek cities honoured Flamininus; Lampsacus with an embassy (196) and Smyrna (also on the west coast of Asia Minor) with a *templum urbis Romae* (temple of the city of Rome) (195) sought Roman favour and protection against *Antiochus III. But the philhellenic posture was less in evidence during the war with Antiochus and thereafter, as a policy of partisan intervention took hold. In Greece Lucius Aemilius Paullus celebrated his victory (167) over Perseus, the last Macedonian king, in explicitly hellenistic fashion, but he also oversaw the deportation or slaughter of Rome's opponents in the Greek cities and mass enslavement in Epirus. At the same time, the Romans were often referred to in Greek inscriptions of the period as 'common benefactors' (*koinoi euergetai*; see EUERGETISM), and the goddess Roma was worshipped: Greeks participated in the construct that was Rome's political philhellenism and so continued to make it as real as Rome's dominion.   P. S. D.

Philip II (382–336 BC), king of Macedon and architect of Macedonian greatness. In his youth he witnessed the near dissolution of the kingdom through civil war and foreign intervention, and spent some time (probably 369–367) as hostage in *Epaminondas' Thebes. The nadir came when his brother, Perdiccas III, died in battle against Illyrian invaders (360/59), who occupied the north-western borderlands. On his accession (perhaps initially as regent for his nephew, Amyntas) his priority was to save Macedon from dismemberment by hostile powers, poised for the kill; and from the outset he displayed a genius for compromise and intrigue. The Athenians, who backed a pretender (Argaeus), were defeated in a skirmish near *Aegae but wooed by the return of their prisoners (and by hints that he would recognize their claims to Amphipolis). Other belligerents (Paeonians and Thracians) were bought off, and Philip used the time he acquired to train a new citizen army in mass infantry tactics, introducing the 12-cubit pike (*sarisa*) as its basic weaponry (see ARMS AND ARMOUR). His efforts bore fruit in 358, when he decisively defeated the Illyrians near Lake Lychnitis and used his victory to integrate the previously independent principalities of upper Macedonia into his kingdom. Their nobility joined the companions of his court and the commons were recruited into the army. Philip's increased power was immediately deployed against Athens. While the city was enmeshed in the Social War (357–355) he annexed Amphipolis and Pydna in 357, captured Potidaea in 356, ceding it to the Olynthian federation (see Chalcidice; Olynthus) in return for alliance, and acquired Methone (354)—at the cost of his right eye and permanent disfigurement. From the conquests came land which he distributed in part to a new aristocracy, recruited from all parts of the Greek world (e.g. Nearchus of Crete, Laomedon of Mytilene and Androsthenes of Thasos, all settled at Amphipolis). Most important was Crenides, the Thracian settlement by Mt. Pangaeus, which Philip occupied and reinforced in 356, naming it Philippi after himself. The exploitation of the neighbouring gold *mines allegedly engrossed 1,000 talents *per annum*, which enabled him to maintain a large mercenary army and win the services of politicians in southern Greece.

*Thessaly rapidly became an annex of Macedon. An early marriage alliance with the Aleuadae family of Larissa brought an invitation to intervene in the murderous internecine war between the Thessalian League and the tyrants of Pherae. Initial defeats in 353 were redeemed in 352 by the great victory of the Crocus Field and the expulsion of Lycophron and Peitholaus from Pherae. In return Philip was appointed archon of Thessaly with its revenues and superb cavalry at his disposal. In 349 he attacked another traditional enemy, Olynthus, and by September 348 had captured the city through internal treachery. The population was enslaved and Olynthus' land absorbed, but despite the shock of this exemplary treatment there was no response to the Athenian appeal for an international alliance against him, and in despondency the Athenians entered peace negotiations early in 346. Peace and alliance were concluded in April 346 at the same time that Philip accepted an appeal to lead an Amphictionic campaign against the Phocians (allies of Athens). With masterly prevarication he delayed ratifying the peace until he was in the vicinity of Thermopylae, preventing the Athenians reinforcing their allies, and forced the Phocians to terms (July 346). The settlement which resulted left him master of Thermopylae with voting rights in the Amphictiony.

The years after 346 saw further expansion. Campaigns against the Illyrians (notably in 345) brought the Dardanians and Taulantians to subject status, and between 342 and 340 Philip crowned a long series of campaigns against the Thracians with a prolonged war in the Hebrus valley. The old Odrysian kingdom became a dependency under a Macedonian *stratēgos* (military governor); military colonies (notably Philippopolis/Plovdiv) were implanted, and the Thracians supplied his largest pool of auxiliary troops. Meanwhile Philip's influence had expanded in southern Greece. He championed Megalopolis and Messenia against Sparta, supported a coup at Elis (343) and sent mercenaries to Euboea (343/2: date disputed). By 342 Athenian interpretations of his motives had more conviction. In 341 the Euboean regimes at Eretria and Oreos (Histiaea) were overthrown by an Athenian-led invasion and Athenian overtures were sympathetically received in the Peloponnese. The situation became graver in 340, when Philip laid siege to Perinthus and *Byzantium, and open war erupted in the late summer, when he commandeered the Athenian grain fleet. He left the sieges incomplete to launch a successful attack on the Scythian king Ateas, and returned to Macedon in mid-339.

The final act came when he assumed command of an Amphictionic expedition against the Locrians of Amphissa and used the campaign as a fulcrum to attack Thebes and Athens, now united in alliance against him. Its denouement was the battle of Chaeronea (August 338), fought with a fraction of the forces at his disposal, which destroyed Thebes as a military power and made him undisputed master of the Greek world. Garrisons at Corinth, Thebes, Ambracia, and (probably) Chalcis policed the settlement he imposed, and a conference at Corinth (summer 337) approved a common peace which guaranteed the stability of all governments party to it, prohibited constitutional change and entrenched Philip as executive head (*hegemon*) of the council (*synedrion*) which directed its

enforcement. It was intended to perpetuate Macedonian domination and did so effectively. The meeting also witnessed Philip's proclamation of his war of revenge against Persia, a project doubtless long in gestation but only now publicized, and in 336 an expeditionary force crossed the Hellespont (Dardanelles) to begin operations in Asia Minor.

Philip's last year was overshadowed by domestic conflict. His love match with Cleopatra provoked a rift in the royal house which saw his wife Olympias in angry retirement and the heir-apparent, Alexander (see ALEXANDER THE GREAT), in temporary exile in Illyria. There was a formal reconciliation; but tensions persisted, and Philip fell by an assassin's hand in autumn 336. The sources give personal motives, but there are also hints of a multiplicity of conspirators and the background to the murder is beyond speculation. He was interred at *Aegae (many believe, in the splendid barrel-vaulted Tomb II in the Great Tumulus of Vergina), leaving his kingdom a military and economic giant but internally almost as distracted as it had been at his accession.   A. B. B.

philosophers and politics *Plato (*Rep.* 473d) regarded good government as unattainable 'unless either philosophers become kings in our cities or those whom we now call kings and rulers take to the pursuit of philosophy'. He already recognized, however, that philosophers would either be reluctant to leave the contemplation of truth for the task of governing any but an ideal city, or would be ridiculed and rejected if they tried (*Rep.* 516d–517a; 519e–521b).

Philosopher-leaders were rare in the ancient world: *Cicero (*Leg.* 3. 14) named only Demetrius of Phalerum, the Peripatetic (Aristotelian) philosopher who ruled Athens from 317 to 307 BC, ignoring less respectable examples, like the Peripatetic Athenion and the Epicurean Aristion (see EPICURUS) who ruled Athens for brief periods in his youth. The Romans themselves sent philosophers to rule Cilician Tarsus in SE Asia Minor (Strabo 14. 675), but it was in the 2nd cent. AD that admirers of Marcus *Aurelius, the emperor, could claim that Plato's ideal was finally fulfilled (SHA *Marc.* 27. 6–7, cf. *Med.* 9. 29). Philosophers more commonly served their cities by educating and advising rulers or serving as ambassadors. In the 3rd cent. BC Hermippus wrote a treatise entitled 'On Those who Have Converted from Philosophy to Tyrannies and Positions of Power', in which he described such cases as the Stoic Persaeus who served *Antigonus Gonatas (unsuccessfully) as a general. Another Stoic, Sphaerus, advised King Cleomenes III of *Sparta (Plut. *Cleom.* 11). In 155 BC when the Athenians wanted the senate to reduce a fine imposed on the city, they sent as envoys the Stoic Diogenes, the Peripatetic Critolaus and the Academic Carneades. They succeeded in their missions, but also gave such attractive lectures that *Cato the Elder objected that they were seducing Roman youth away from traditional values (Plut. *Cato* 22).

The charge of corrupting the youth, already employed against *Socrates, was used at Rome as a reason for expelling philosophers from the city as early as 161 BC. As a preparation for public life, philosophy was suspect on several counts: (1) Philosophers, as Plato surmised, might reject practical politics. The Epicureans in fact advocated such abstention except in exceptional circumstances, though many of them in fact participated (e.g. Ath. 5. 215b; Cic. *Fin.* 2. 76; *Tusc.* 5. 108; Joseph. *BJ* 19. 32; Epict. 3. 7, cf. Plin. *Ep.* 8. 24). Stoics (see STOICISM) took the opposite line, so that their failure to participate was, or could be construed as, criticism of the existing regime. (2) Philosophers might insist on unrealistic moral standards in public life (e.g. Cic. *Mur.* 60 f.; Sen. *Clem.* 2. 5. 2). The Romans were particularly prone to this view (Tac. *Agr.* 4. 4), so that whereas philosophers, except Epicureans, were regularly honoured at Athens and elsewhere in the Greek world for their contribution to educating the young (e.g. Diog. Laert. 7. 10–12), at Rome they were at first excluded from the privileges offered to doctors and teachers of rhetoric and literature for their services to the community.

It is often said that philosophers made a theoretical contribution to politics only in the age of the independent Greek city-state or *polis*, and that before, and after, Academic and Peripatetic political theory was applied to Rome in the age of the republic, philosophers living under the Hellenistic and Roman monarchical systems limited their concerns to the individual. That is an oversimplification of the fact that the Hellenistic schools were not interested in discussing ideal constitutions, but rather in prescribing moral conduct for rulers of any kind and in teaching their subjects how to preserve their integrity and exercise free speech. See KINGSHIP.   M. T. G.

philosophy See ACADEMY; ARISTOTLE; CYNICS; EPICURUS; PLATO; PYTHAGORAS AND PYTHAGOREANISM; SOCRATES; SOPHISTS; STOICISM

Phoenicians (Gk. *Phoinikes*, Lat. *Poeni*), a people (rather than a nation) occupying the coast of the Levant; they are thus described only in the classical sources and etymologically their name is Greek; their own name for themselves is unknown, although the Bible classes them as Canaanites (for the Greek tradition on Chna see Hecataeus in Steph. Byz.; also Philo of Byblos). The royal Assyrian inscriptions (9th–7th cent. BC) refer to the cities of Tyre, Sidon, Byblos, etc., as (in the form of ethnics) do the Phoenician inscriptions; but they are silent about 'Phoenicia' and 'Phoenicians', which were classical constructs.

A common view derives *Phoinikes* from the Greek *phoinios*, *phoinos*, meaning 'red'. The Phoenicians were so designated (runs this view) from their copper skin, and / or their expertise in the purple industry; other theories relate their name to the copper trade, the palm-tree and dates, textiles (based on a tablet of ambiguous sense from Minoan Cnossus; see MINOAN CIVILIZATION), or to an Egyptian word for 'woodcutters'.

The land of the Phoenicians (Phoenicia) extended along the eastern Mediterranean coast from modern Syria to southern Lebanon and Galilee. Its limits are debated: either from Tarsus to Gaza, or, more conventionally, from Tell Sukas (Syria) south of Ugarit to Akko (Galilee). For the classical Greeks, Phoenicia was no more or less than the Phoenician homeland, without the precise boundaries later assigned by Rome. The Phoenicians were divided into several city-kingdoms, the most famous being Sidon (for 'Sidonian' as a synonym for 'Phoenician' see Hom. *Od.* 4. 84), Tyre, and Byblos, although Aradus, Amrith, Berytus, and Sarepta were important too.

The Phoenicians were said by *Herodotus (1. 1; 2. 44; 7. 89) to have migrated from the Persian Gulf 2,300 years before his time. Whatever the basis of this tradition, it takes the existence of the Phoenicians back to the 3rd millennium, when their presence in Lebanon is well-attested archaeologically. The port of Byblos was known in Early Dynastic Egypt. The history of the Phoenicians is intimately related to the sea, as shown e.g. by their island-harbours at Tyre and Aradus and their harbour-settlements in the western Mediterranean; also by their expertise in ship-building (using *timber from the Lebanon forests) and seafaring. This relationship inspired two dominant trends in their history: their role in international trade—notably metals (both ore and processed), textiles, purple, foodstuffs, exotic materials, and craft-goods (see the trade of Tyre in Ezekiel 27)—and what is misleadingly called Phoenician 'colonization': i.e. the spread of Phoenician settlements (trading posts and farming communities) from Spain via Africa to Egypt; of these *Carthage was the most famous. This movement began early in the 11th cent., reaching its climax in the 9th–8th cents., when Phoenician culture (arts, religion, and inscriptions) left traces almost all over the Mediterranean.

The Phoenicians were also a vital element of the Near East: the maritime strength of the region caused Assyrian and Babylonian kings to conquer it several times, and the Phoenicians formed the backbone of the Persian navy in Achaemenid times. They maintained close links with Palestine, Egypt (along with the Red Sea), Assyria, and Arabia, and their arts were strongly influenced by the east.

From the beginning of their expansion, the Phoenicians came into contact with the Greeks, but it was only after the Persian Wars that the Hellenization of Phoenicia commenced; see HELLENISM, HELLENIZATION. After their conquest (Tyre included) by *Alexander the Great, the Phoenician cities were gradually integrated into the Hellenistic *koinē* or shared culture, first under the Ptolemies (see PTOLEMY I and II), then the *Seleucids and finally Rome; but their political identity (based on their cities) and cultural character (notably their language) were partly preserved, and the Phoenicians maintained their own specific place in the Graeco-Roman world.   J.-F. S.

physics today involves the investigation of the nature and behaviour of matter and energy, and it is often thus distinguished from chemistry and biology. The same term, derived from the Greek word for 'nature', *'physis'*, is used to describe a number of ancient inquiries, including *peri physeos historia* (the inquiry into nature), *'ta physika'* (natural things) and *physikē* [sc. *epistēmē*], where no such distinction is implied. These ancient expressions are to some extent context-relative and they covered a range of interests far wider than that encompassed by modern physics. 'Theory of Nature' might be a reasonable general characterization of ancient physics. Notably, for some ancient authorities 'physics' explicitly excluded mathematics and even mathematical attempts at modelling nature. For early doctors physical inquiry was equivalent to what we might now call physiology; the cognate terms in English, 'physic' and 'physician', tend to relate, on the other hand, to the practice of what is now called pathology.

1. Before Aristotle, physical investigation ranged from the cosmological through to the observation and explanation of discrete natural phenomena. Early studies of the material origins of the world, the position of the earth in space, along with speculation about what we now call magnetism, and the nature of sound and light, could all be thought of as parts of physical inquiry. In the first book of the *Metaphysics*, *Aristotle reports in summary fashion that many of the earliest philosophers based their speculations about nature on the idea that the physical world is reducible to one or more basic starting points or principles. Thales is supposed to have given water a special status, Anaximenes air, and so on. The atomists Leucippus and Democritus (see ATOMISM) invented a theory of matter which, they hoped, would satisfy *both* strict logical demands for certain, immutable, knowledge about reality (laid down by people like Parmenides of Elea) *and* account for the changing and unpredictable phenomena of the visible world. They posited an ontologically real world of first principles—atoms and void—and a secondary world of appearances, the result of the movement of the atoms in the void. (Aristotle praised Democritus for arguing 'physically' and not just 'logically', but criticized nearly all his predecessors for leaving important questions unanswered, notably about the origins of physical motion.)

2. *Plato's physical system is similarly based on a distinction between what is real and intelligible (the Forms) and the particulars we can see in the world around us, which share in different ways (though never completely) in the perfection of the idealized Forms. Doubts about the extent to which the mathematical perfection of ultimate reality can ever be fully present in physical objects lie behind the reservations expressed by Plato about the reliability of the physical theory in the *Timaeus* (5. 27–30). Matter, for Plato, is inherently chaotic, and the creator of Plato's universe had to struggle hard with the recalcitrant material substrate of physical being as he sought to model it in the image of the Forms.

Yet the desire to describe mathematically the behaviour of natural—physical—objects and phenomena did not always clash, even for Plato, and relations between mathematics and the physical world were studied throughout antiquity. Early evidence comes from the Pythagorean investigations into harmonics, but the idea that a mathematically describable order has left its imprint on at least some levels of creation was encouraged by Plato. In *Republic* 9, Plato prescribed a curriculum of physical subjects including astronomy, stereometry, and harmonics for the education of the Guardians of his ideal state, because their study shows that the perfect order of the Forms is reflected to some extent at least in the world around us.

3. Aristotle is the author of the earliest surviving detailed work bearing the title *Physics*. For him, *Physikē* is distinguished (e.g. at *Metaphysics* E 1, 1026[a]) from the abstract study of number and shape in *mathematika* (see MATHEMATICS) and from the science of divinity in *theologikē*. Physics involved going back to the first principles which underlie the phenomenal world of natural objects, and investigating their origins, number, behaviour, and interactions. The 'inquiry into nature' in Aristotle's view is the study of those things which do not exist independently of matter. It can thus be thought to include both the theoretical material contained in the *Physics* itself, the biological and zoological material in, for example, the *History of Animals*, what we might call the geophysical material in the *Meteorology*, along with the inherently more mathematical material of astronomy in *On the Heavens*.

In Aristotle's *Physics*, the first principles governing the behaviour of matter are investigated in great detail. The nature of physical existence, of weight, qualitative variety, different types of motion and their origins, the nature of purpose-directed activity and its sources are all examined. It is here that the four types of causal question necessary for a full account of something's existence are formulated—the formal, final, material, and efficient. Aristotelian ideas about motion—notably his statements implying that the velocity of falling objects is inversely proportional to the resistance they meet and directly proportional to their weight (see *Physics* 4. 8), which made velocity in a void undefinable—were famously criticized and developed by much later commentators, including Simplicius and Philoponus. Aristotle's successors as head of the Lyceum, Theophrastus of Eresus and Strato of Lampsacus, continued to stress the importance of the types of physical inquiry initiated by their master.

4. It is widely believed that Aristotle's criticisms of early atomic physics (especially in *On Generation and Corruption*) led *Epicurus and his followers to modify Democritean atomism in a number of respects. The exact extent of Epicurean innovation is hard to gauge, partly because of our lack of evidence for Democritus' own theory, and partly because Epicurus himself acknowledges few positive debts to any predecessors. Driven by the need to find arguments to dissolve away fear, and especially fear of death, Epicurean physics centres on proving the existence of ungenerated and permanent forms of matter—atoms—whose unpredictable and unpremeditated motion in the

void can explain all natural phenomena. The Epicureans developed new arguments to prove the possibility of indivisible atoms, explain their motion and combination, and found new language to describe void. The phenomena of sensation and action at a distance (magnetic attraction, for instance) are all explained in terms of influxes or effluxes of atoms moving across the void. Purpose-directed activity in the domain of natural phenomena, and the active intervention of divine power in human life for good or ill, are denied. The study of the physical world is of value only insofar as it aids in the search for peace of mind.

5. With ethics and logic, physics was one of the cornerstones of Stoic philosophy. Although there is doctrinal variation within *Stoicism on the level of detail, Diogenes Laertius (7. 132) reports that the Stoics divided physics into the study of the world, of the elements, and the inquiry into causes. Stoic physics is an essential part of the broad Stoic inquiry into our place in the universe, and into the divine and guiding active principle which permeates everything, designing and steering it. Unlike the Epicureans, but following Plato and Aristotle, the Stoics denied the possibility of void within the cosmos, and many of the more sophisticated explanations of action at a distance in a continuum can be laid at their door.

6. Mathematical—geometrical—models of the behaviour of physical bodies developed rapidly in mechanics, and also in what Aristotle calls the more 'physical' branches of *mathematics or the more 'mathematical' branches of physics, such as optics, acoustics and *astronomy. (Mathematical geography, statics and hydrostatics might be added to Aristotle's list.) Quite apart from the mathematical sophistication of these ancient inquiries, the level of methodological controversy, particularly between empiricist and rationalist positions, is striking. In the Aristotelian corpus there is a treatise on mechanics, almost certainly not by Aristotle himself, which deals with the theory and practical uses of balances, pulleys, and levers. Archimedes' theoretical work on the behaviour of basic mechanical elements is characteristic of the subsequent application of strict geometry to the practical explanation of physical contrivances. Archimedes' *On the Equilibrium of Planes* deals amongst other things with the problem of how to determine the centre of gravity in different types of figures. Other important ancient mechanical theoreticians include Heron of Alexandria (*Mechanics*) and Pappus of Alexandria (esp. the *Collectio*, bk. 8).

7. A group of ancient writers dealt with applied as well as theoretical mechanics. Figures like Ctesibius are little more than names to us, but Heron of Alexandria and Philo of Byzantium wrote elaborate works on the subject, Philo dealing with the theory and practice of machines of war, Hero with mechanical automata.

8. The physics of sight, light, and colour occupied both physiologists and mathematicians. Natural philosophers and physiologists offered theories to explain the mechanisms of visual perception (e.g. Plato, *Timaeus*, Aristotle, *On the Soul* 2, and Theophrastus, *On the Senses*, which includes a review of earlier theories of sight). Theoretical debate focused on the nature of light—was it a type of wave, or a tension in the continuum (a Stoic view), or the transport of something through the atomists' void? Geometrical optics was based on the assumption that light—or the visual ray—travels from the eye in straight lines. Systematic research into the behaviour of these lines begins (for us) with Euclid's *Optics*, which also survives in a late version by Theon of Alexandria, but important treatises on optics were also composed by Ptolemy, by Heron of Alexandria and an optician of the 4th cent. AD, Damianus (of Larissa?). Geminus, quoted by Proclus (*Commentary on Euclid's Elements* 1), divides optics into (*a*) the study of problems related to the perception of objects at a distance (including perspective), (*b*) catoptrics, or the study of reflection and refraction, and (*c*) scenography, which dealt originally with the problem of representing in drawing and painting objects of different sizes and at different distances from the observer. In addition, dioptrics (the subject of a work by Heron of Alexandria) was concerned with the construction of optical instruments used to investigate all these phenomena.

9. 'Pythagoras had no faith in the human ear', reports Boethius (*On Music* 1. 10). He sought instead fixed, mathematical ways of measuring consonances; the Pythagoreans were credited even in antiquity with the discovery of the connection between the length of a vibrating body and its pitch. Further work on the subject was done by the Pythagorean Philolaus of Croton, and on the properties of vibrating bodies generally by Archytas, Euclid, Ptolemy, and Nicomachus. Aristotle deals with the physiology of sound, speech and hearing in *On the Soul*, and there is a spurious tract in the Aristotelian corpus entitled *On Things Heard*. Ancient harmonics was profoundly influenced by more general epistemological debates over how far the senses—the ear in this case—should be trusted over reason. There was also a long-running dispute over the fundamental nature of sound itself which mirrors in certain respects disagreements about the nature of light—is sound continuous, or discrete, to be analysed geometrically or arithmetically? The greatest ancient authority on harmonics is the Aristotelian physicist and musicologist Aristoxenus, whose *Elements of Harmonics* provided the basis for most subsequent treatments of both mathematical and practical harmonics. See MUSIC. J. T. V.

physiology See ANATOMY AND PHYSIOLOGY.

pilgrimage (Christian) Despite the New Testament's disavowal of the localized cults of Judaism and the surrounding pagan world—the need was for holy lives rather than holy places—early Christians still clung to their sacred sites. Jesus' followers preserved some memory of the location of his tomb in Jerusalem and (at least by the mid-2nd cent.) of his birthplace in Bethlehem; while further afield the burial places of martyrs on the outskirts of their cities attracted local gatherings. In maintaining these recollections of their sacred past, the first Christian pilgrims tried to assert some communal identity in a world indifferent or hostile to their faith.

As the first emperor to favour Christianity, *Constantine I actively promoted holy places through imperial church-building in the Holy Land, as well as at the shrines of Peter and *Paul and other Roman martyrs; and his mother Helena Augusta personified the official interest in sacred sites by visiting Palestine as part of a tour of the eastern provinces (c. AD 327). Pilgrimages to the Holy Land were no longer just a local preserve, but might bring travellers from the opposite end of the empire. The earliest such journey on record is that of an unknown pilgrim from Bordeaux, who reached Jerusalem in 333: the surviving document is both a 'secular' itinerary of the route and the account of a pilgrimage round the biblical sites of the Holy Land. The religious significance attached not to the journey itself, but to its objective of locating and—with the aid of the 'eyes of faith' and a very literal reading of the text—entering into the scriptural past of both Old and New Testaments.

In 381–4 the western pilgrim Egeria journeyed round the Holy Land and Egypt. Besides visiting martyr-shrines *en route*, she endeavoured to search out 'on the ground' the places of the Bible, attempting e.g. to retrace the movements of the children of Israel out of Egypt. Holy men were as much an object of pilgrimage for her as holy places: the monks who now populated the region formed part of Egeria's scriptural landscape, perceived as successors of the Holy Land's biblical occupants. These 4th-cent. Christian travellers engaged in a species of devotional *tourism which had eyes only for the biblical past re-created in the contemporary Holy Land. The many other associations of pilgrimage—ascetic, therapeutic, penitential—would emerge only later.   E. D. H.

Pindar, lyric poet, native of Cynoscephalae in Boeotia. He was born probably in 518 BC (*Suda*, fr. 193, if the latter refers to Pindar). The tradition (one of several competing accounts) that he lived to the age of eighty is at least roughly correct, since his last datable composition (*Pyth.* 8) belongs in or shortly after 446. On the basis of *Pyth.* 5. 72 it is widely believed that he belonged to the aristocratic family of the Aegeidae. He achieved panhellenic recognition early; at the age of 20 he was commissioned by the ruling family of *Thessaly to celebrate the athletic victory of a favourite youth, Hippocleas (*Pyth.* 10). His commissions covered most of the Greek world, from *Macedonia and Abdera in Thrace in the north (fr. 120–1, *Pae.* 2) to *Cyrene in Africa in the south (*Pyth.* 4, 5, 9), from *Italy and *Sicily in the west (*Ol.* 1–5, 10, 11, *Pyth.* 1, 2, 3, 6, *Nem.* 9, *Isthm.* 2) to the seaboard of *Asia Minor in the east (*Ol.* 7, *Nem.* 11, fr. 123). He probably travelled a great deal, but we have little information on his movements. He is already a classic for *Herodotus (1) (3. 38), and was regarded by many in antiquity as the greatest of the nine poets of the lyric canon (Quint. 10. 1. 61, Dion. Hal. *On imitation* 2).

The *Alexandrian editors divided Pindar's works into 17 books: hymns, paeans, *dithyrambs (2 books), *prosodia* (processional songs, 2 books), *partheneia* (maiden-songs, 3 books), *hyporchemata* (dance songs, 2 books), encomia, *threnoi* (dirges) and *epinicia* (victory songs, 4 books). Of these, the only books to survive intact are the choral victory songs composed for the formal celebration of victories in the four panhellenic athletic festivals (see GAMES). His patrons were the great aristocratic houses of the day, and the ruling families of Cyrene, *Syracuse, and Acragas. The scale of this section of the corpus indicates the value which Pindar, in common with other Greeks, placed on *athletics as a testing ground for the highest human qualities. The victory ode was normally performed either at the athletic festival shortly after the victory or after the victor's return to his native city. Since time for composition and choir training was limited, the former type tends to be brief. Odes composed for performance after the victor's return are usually, though not invariably, lengthier and more elaborate. The longer odes usually have three sections, with the opening and closing sections devoted to the victor and his success and the central section usually containing a mythic narrative. The opening is always striking, often elaborate, consisting either of an abrupt announcement of victory or a focusing process which sets the victory against a general background, usually through a hymnal invocation or a preparatory list of objects, experiences, or achievements (*priamel*). In the sections devoted to the victor conventional elements recur. The god of the games is honoured. Place of victory and event are announced, with details frequently surrendered slowly in order to maintain a forward tension (description of victory is rare, however). Earlier victories by the patron or other members of his family are listed; such lists are carefully crafted to avoid monotony. The city is praised, and in the case of boy victors the father and usually the trainer. Self-praise by the poet is also common. More sombre notes, surprising to the modern reader, are struck. The poet often reminds the victor of his mortality or offers prayers to avert misfortune; these elements reflect the archaic fear of divine envy and awareness of the psychological dangers of success, they function both to warn and to emphasize the extent of the achievement. *Gnomai* (succinct generalizations) are frequent. Recurrent themes are the impossibility of achievement without toil, the need for divine aid for success, the duty to praise victory, the vulnerability of achievement without praise in song, the importance of inborn excellence and the inadequacy of mere learning. The effect of this moralizing is to give the ode a pronounced didactic as well as celebratory quality.

Pindar usually chooses myths dealing with the heroes of the victor's city. As with most Greek *lyric poetry, the myth is not narrated in full. Usually a single incident is selected for narration, with other details dealt with briskly. Even the lengthy quasi-epic myth of *Pyth.* 4 proceeds by a series of scenes, not an even narrative. Audience familiarity with the myth is assumed. Unlike his contemporary

*Bacchylides, Pindar regularly adopts an explicit moral stance with reference to the events narrated. The role of myth in the odes varies. Sometimes the myth has only a broad relevance to the victor, in that the deeds of the city's heroes highlight the tradition which has produced the victor's qualities. On occasion myth presents a negative contrast to the victor (such as the Tantalus myth in *Ol.* 1, the Orestes myth of *Pyth.* 11). Often it appears to reflect an aspect of the victory or the victor's situation as developed in the direct praise.

The fragmentary nature of the rest of the corpus makes it difficult to generalize about other genres. The same moralizing quality is present. The structure where ascertainable corresponds to the tripartite structure of the victory odes. The myth is in most cases uncontroversial, since it arises from the location and occasion of the performance.

His poems are written in regular stanzas, either strophic or triadic. With the exception of *Isthm.* 3 and 4, no two poems are identical metrically. Most are composed in the dactylo-epitrite or aeolic metres. His manner of writing is both dense and elaborate. Words are used sparingly. Compound adjectives abound. The style is rich in metaphor, and rapid shifts of metaphor are common. Transition between themes is rapid, and is often effected by formalized claims to be constrained by time or rules of composition or to have lost the way. As his earliest and last datable compositions (*Pyth.* 10 and 8) show, he adhered throughout his life to a conservative set of standards. His thought impresses not for its originality but the consistency and conviction with which he presents the world view of the aristocrat of the late Archaic period. His religion is the traditional Olympian religion (see RELIGION, GREEK), combined in *Ol.* 2 and the dirges with elements of mystery cult and Orphico-Pythagorean belief (see ORPHEUS; PYTHAGORAS, PYTHAGOREANISM). C. C.

piracy can be defined as armed robbery involving the use of ships. The greater mobility which the sea provides is a major factor in differentiating between piracy and *brigandage, although the Greek and Latin vocabulary for the two was largely the same. It is often very difficult to distinguish piracy from warfare in the ancient sources, especially when the labelling of certain activities as piracy seems to be a way of illegitimizing the perpetrators, similar in some ways to the modern practice of describing political violence as terrorism.

The earliest references to pirates are in the Homeric poems (see HOMER), particularly the *Odyssey*, where piracy is an activity which brings no shame upon its practitioners, although it may be disapproved of for the misery it brings to the victims (e.g. Hom. *Od.* 3. 71–4; 14. 222–34). None of the Homeric heroes is ever called a pirate, but they carry out seaborne raids which are very similar to the actions of those referred to as pirates (e.g. *Od.* 9. 39–52).

Piracy begins to be differentiated from war in the Classical period of Greek history, when the political aims of the Greek city-states began to take precedence over the economic goals of raiding and plundering. Nevertheless, pirates are mentioned frequently by *Thucydides and *Xenophon in their accounts of the wars of the 5th and 4th cents. BC, and the works of the Attic orators show that accusations of piracy were made by both sides in the rivalries between Athens and *Macedonia in the second half of the 4th cent. BC.

In the Hellenistic period the main difference between piracy and warfare was the scale of activity. Many pirates operated on the fringes of wars in this period, taking advantage of the political confusion, but they do not seem to have played a major part in the conflicts of the Hellenistic monarchs. Although attacks on ships at sea are mentioned occasionally in the ancient sources, the main threat from piracy seems to have been to coastal settlements. Numerous inscriptions from this period record sudden attacks by unidentified pirates on the islands and coastal cities of the Aegean, in search of both plunder and prisoners to be ransomed or sold. The abduction of a well-born young man or woman by pirates who sell their captive as a slave (see SLAVERY) became a common theme in Greek and Latin literature.

The custom of plundering enemies, or even third parties, in reprisal for injuries or insults suffered could be used by some groups to justify acts which others might have called piracy. A great deal of the piracy found in sources from the 5th to the 2nd cents. BC involves reprisals. The rules governing reprisals were rather vague, allowing considerable latitude for interpretation. *Polybius criticized the Aetolians in particular for their abuse of this custom (Polyb. 4. 3–6; see FEDERAL STATES). Cities and communities attempted to deter attacks by concluding treaties which guaranteed them immunity from reprisals, but it is unclear how effective this system was in practice.

Thucydides credited the legendary King Minos of Crete with clearing the seas of pirates (Thuc. 1. 4), but, until the 1st cent. BC, no ancient state possessed the resources to suppress piracy on anything more than a local scale, although even small successes might win fulsome praise and help to legitimize political power. A significant problem was the fact that successful suppression of piracy meant depriving pirates of bases on land, which entailed the conquest and control of territory. Without co-operation between states, or the imposition of a policy by a single imperial power, piracy could easily flourish in many parts of the Mediterranean. The Athenians took some action to limit piracy in their own interests in the 5th and 4th cents. BC, as did the Rhodians (see RHODES) in the Hellenistic period. Both were strongly applauded by later writers. The rise of Roman power in the Mediterranean was accompanied by a gradual realization that the Romans should take a stand against those perceived as pirates, but little action had been taken by the 2nd cent. BC, when pirates based in Cilicia (southern Asia Minor) began to cause serious problems in the eastern Mediterranean.

The attitude of the Romans towards piracy in the Mediterranean seems to have changed towards the end of the 2nd cent. BC. The campaign of Marcus Antonius in Cilicia in 102 was specifically directed against pirates, and a law of 100 BC concerning praetorian provinces enjoins all Rome's allies and friends to assist in the suppression of piracy. Further campaigns by Roman magistrates in the 70s and 60s BC, most famously that of *Pompey in 67, reduced the areas from which pirates were able to operate, but piracy remained a problem at the start of Augustus' reign. It was only after the Roman emperors had secured control of the entire coastline of the Mediterranean that they were able to reduce piracy to a minimum, through the use of their powerful army and navy.

Piracy was thus largely confined to the margins of the Roman empire with some strong incursions by *barbarian tribes in the second half of the 3rd cent. AD. When the empire began to break up in the 5th cent. AD, however, piracy again became a serious problem, especially when the Vandals seized *Carthage and used it as a base for their own plundering raids. The Muslim conquests of the 7th cent. were followed by a widespread resurgence of piracy in the Mediterranean.   P. De S.

Pisistratus (*Peisistratos*), tyrant of Athens (see TYRANNY), claimed descent from the Neleids of Homeric Pylos and Pisistratus, archon (civilian head of state) at Athens 669/8 BC. He first came to prominence through his success in the war against Megara (*c*.565). In a period of aristocratic faction between Lycurgus and the *Pedieis* (party 'of the Plain') and Megacles and *Paralioi* (coast party), he created a third faction, the *Hyperakrioi* or *Diakrioi* (referring to 'hill country', probably NE Attica: the factions probably reflect regional bases of support, Hdt. 1. 59). He first seized power with the bodyguard granted him by the Athenians (*c*.560). Ousted by the other two factions, he returned again with Megacles' allegiance and, if we can extract anything from the ruse in *Herodotus (1. 60), a claim to the protection of *Athena. However the Alcmaeonid-family alliance disintegrated and he went into a 10-year exile, settling Rhaecelus in *Macedonia, mustering support from Eretria, other cities (e.g. Thebes) and from the mines of Mt. Pangaeus in Thrace (*Ath. Pol.* 15; Hdt. 1. 64). Armed with money and Argive *mercenaries, he landed near Marathon, *c*.546, defeated opposition at the battle of Pallene, and established the tyranny for 36 years. He died in 527.

Sources agree that Pisistratus' rule, financed by a 5 per cent tax and perhaps family resources from the Strymon area in northern Greece, was benevolent and law-abiding: (esp. Thuc. 6. 54; a 'golden age', *Ath. Pol.* 16. 7). Despite the mention of exiles (Hdt. 1. 64), he seems to have achieved a *modus vivendi* with other aristocratic families (who are later found holding archonships). Strained relations with the Philaids may have been eased by Miltiades' colonization of the Chersonesus (Hdt. 6. 34–41), whose strategic importance suggests it had Pisistratus' blessing. Athenian interests were strengthened by Pisistratus' control of Cycladic Naxos (Hdt. 1. 64), and recapture of Sigeum, foreshadowing Athens' later maritime expansion. He lent money to

poor farmers and instituted travelling judges (*Ath. Pol.* 16).

From the 560s, Athens begins to acquire a monumental appearance and become a panhellenic artistic centre. The archaeological record indicates rapidly increasing prosperity, as Attic black figure becomes (from the 560s) the dominant exported pottery (see POTTERY, GREEK). How much can be linked to Pisistratus' personal efforts, rather than to the indirect effects of internal peace and external expansion, is uncertain and controversial, and purely archaeological evidence is inconclusive. The Panathenaea festival, reorganized in 566/5, and City Dionysia prospered, but Pisistratus cannot securely be credited with establishing the former, nor erecting the (so-called 'old') temple of Athena on the Acropolis built about the same time. The beginning of Athenian *coinage, attested archaeologically by 550, might imply the ruler's support. It is likely, however, that, like other archaic aristocrats, he used religious cult to consolidate his position (Davies *APF* pp. 454–5; D. Lewis, *Hist.* 1963, 22 ff.) or enhance *polis* cohesion; and that he was a great builder, like his sons. He purified the Ionian Greek religious centre of *Delos and instituted a festival there (Thuc. 3. 104). Other cults to Apollo were probably fostered by him in Athens, that of Pythian *Apollo and (perhaps) Apollo Patroos (first temple built, in the Agora, *c*.550); and perhaps other cults (see H. Shapiro, *Art and Culture under the Tyrants in Athens* (1989)). It has been suggested, purely on pottery evidence, that he claimed special association with *Heracles (J. Boardman, *Rev. Arch.* 1972, 57 ff.) as well as Athena's protection. Of secular buildings, as well as the Enneakrounos fountain-house (Paus. 1. 14. 1), he can probably be associated with other building in the Agora in the third quarter of the 6th cent., including the Stoa Basileios and the mysterious 'Building F': in short with the further clearing of the Agora and its development as civic centre. (see ATHENS (TOPOGRAPHY); IMAGERY; PROPAGANDA).   R. T.

plague (GK. *loimos*, Lat. *pestis*), a term confusingly employed by ancient historians to designate epidemics of infectious *diseases. Epidemics in antiquity were not necessarily caused by the disease now called plague (*Yersinia pestis*), although Rufus of Ephesus (1st cent. AD) cites some evidence for true plague in Hellenistic Egypt and Syria. The major epidemic diseases are density-dependent. The 'plague of Athens' (see below) was an isolated event in Greek history, but there is more evidence for great epidemics during the Roman empire. This increase in frequency was a consequence of *population growth in antiquity. Most of the epidemics described by Roman historians, e.g. *Livy who relied on the annalistic tradition, are described so briefly that there is no hope of identifying the diseases in question. Epidemics are neglected in the major theoretical works of ancient medicine (the Hippocratic corpus (see MEDICINE §4) and in the writings of Galen (2nd cent. AD) because doctors had no knowledge of the existence of micro-organisms and had difficulty applying the types of explanation they favoured (in terms of the diet and lifestyle of individuals; also, later, the theory of the four humours) to mass outbreaks of disease.

*Thucydides (2. 47–58, 3. 87) described the so-called 'plague of Athens' (430–426 BC), the most famous epidemic in antiquity. Unfortunately there is no agreement regarding the identification of the disease. Around 30 different diseases have been suggested as the cause. Most of these are highly implausible, either because they do not correspond to Thucydides' description, or because they cannot be transmitted in such a way as to cause large epidemics. Epidemic typhus and smallpox are the strongest candidates, but true plague has also attracted a considerable number of advocates, along with the hypothesis that the disease organism is now extinct. Thucydides recognized the role of contagion in transmitting the infection.

The second famous plague in antiquity was the 'Antonine plague', which attacked the Roman empire in the 2nd cent. AD. Galen, the main source, does not provide a comprehensive description, but gives details which permit a more definite resolution of the problem than in the case of the 'plague of Athens': this evidence indicates smallpox. Subsequently there were other great epidemics, e.g. the 'plague of Cyprian' in the 3rd cent. AD. However, the descriptions are so inadequate that it is impossible to identify them. Typhus and smallpox were probably the most important causes of epidemics in antiquity.   J. R. S.

Plato (see facing page)

Plautus (Titus Maccius Plautus), comic playwright, author of *fabulae palliatae* ('dramas in a Greek cloak') between c.205 and 184 BC; plays by Plautus are the earliest Latin works to have survived complete. The precise form of his name is uncertain, and in any case each element of it may have been a nickname (see A. S. Gratwick, *CQ* 1973, 78 ff.). He is said to have come from Sarsina in Umbria, inland from Ariminum (Jerome, Festus; an inference from the joke at *Mostellaria* 769 f.?), made money in some kind of theatrical employment, lost it in a business venture, and been reduced to working in a mill (Gell. *NA* 3. 3. 14 f., probably all fictitious). Gell. *NA* 3. 3 records that 130 plays were attributed to him but that the authenticity of most was disputed; *Varro had drawn up a list of 21 plays which were generally agreed to be by Plautus, and there can be little doubt that these are the 21 transmitted in our manuscripts and listed at the end below (though Varro himself believed some others to be genuine as well). Nearly 200 further lines survive in later quotations (many of one line or less), attributed to over 30 named plays.

The *didascaliae* (production notices) give dates of 200 BC for *Stichus* (at the Plebeian Games) and 191 for *Pseudolus* (Megalesian Games, on the dedication of the temple of *Cybele). There is general agreement that *Cistellaria* and *Miles Gloriosus* are relatively early plays, *Bacchides*, *Casina*, *Persa*, *Trinummus*, and *Truculentus* late, but the dating of most plays is quite uncertain; the criteria usually invoked are (alleged) contemporary references and relative fre-

quency of *cantica* (see below), but neither yields indisputable results.

The plays are nearly all either known or assumed to be adaptations of (Greek) New Comedy, with plots portraying love affairs, confusion of identity and misunderstandings; the strongest candidates for (Greek) Middle Comedy are *Amphitruo* (Plautus' only mythological comedy) and *Persa* (because of the reference to a Persian expedition into Arabia at line 506). See COMEDY (GREEK), MIDDLE and NEW. For eight plays the prologue names the author or title, or both, of the Greek original: Diphilus is named as the author for *Casina* and *Rudens*, Philemon for *Mercator* and *Trinummus*, the otherwise unknown Demophilus for *Asinaria*; titles alone are given for *Miles Gloriosus* and *Poenulus*; the prologue of *Vidularia* is very fragmentary but seems to have given at least the title of the original. In addition, *Bacchides*, *Cistellaria*, and *Stichus* are known to be based on plays by Menander, and *Aulularia* is widely believed to be. We cannot always be sure what titles Plautus himself gave his plays, but in about half these cases he seems to have changed it from the Greek original, and the titles of nearly all his plays have at least been Latinized. Scholars influenced by *Terence's invocation of Plautine precedent at *Andria* prologue 18 used to think they could show that Plautus had in some cases incorporated material from another Greek play into his adaptation; it is now commoner to believe in free invention of some material by Plautus. Attempts have even been made to show that he sometimes took no specific Greek original as his model, so far without success. But he adapted his models with considerable freedom and wrote plays that are in several respects quite different from anything we know of New Comedy. There is a large increase in the musical element. The roles of stock characters such as the parasite or sponger appear to have been considerably expanded. Consistency of characterization and plot development are cheerfully sacrificed for the sake of an immediate effect. The humour resides less in the irony of the situation than in jokes and puns. There are 'metatheatrical' references to the audience and to the progress of the play (e.g. *Pseudolus* 388, 562 ff., 720–1), or explicit reminders (as at *Stichus* 446–8) that the play is set in Greece. Above all, there is a constant display of verbal fireworks, with alliteration, wordplays, unexpected personifications (e.g. *Rudens* 626, 'Twist the neck of wrongdoing'), and riddling expressions (e.g. *Mercator* 361, 'My father's a fly: you can't keep anything secret from him, he's always buzzing around'). Both the style of humour and the presentation of stock characters may well have been influenced by the *Atellana* (a type of low-life comedy), but the verbal brilliance is Plautus' own.

The Greek originals have not survived, but a tattered papyrus published by Handley in 1968 contains the lines on which *Bacchides* 494–561 are based (from Menander's *Dis Exapaton*, 'The Double Deceiver'), for the first time enabling us to study Plautus' techniques of adaptation at first hand, and confirming the freedom of his approach. Plautus has preserved the basic plot and sequence of

[continued on p. 544]

Plato

Plato of Athens, *c*.429–347 BC, descended from wealthy and influential Athenian families on both sides. His own family, like many, was divided by the disastrous political consequences of the Peloponnesian War (431–404 BC). His stepfather Pyrilampes was a democrat and friend of *Pericles, but two of his uncles, Critias and Charmides, became members of the Thirty Tyrants (see DEMOCRACY, ATHENIAN). At some point Plato renounced ambition for a public career, devoting his life to philosophy. The major philosophical influence on his life was Socrates, but in three important respects Plato turned away from the example of *Socrates. He rejected marriage and the family duty of producing citizen sons; he founded a philosophical school, the *Academy; and he produced large quantities of written philosophical works (as well as the shadowy 'unwritten doctrines' produced at some point in the Academy, for which we have only secondary evidence).

Plato's works are all in the form of dialogues in which he does not himself appear. The philosophical point of this is to detach him from the arguments which are presented. Plato is unique among philosophers in this constant refusal to present ideas as his own, forcing the reader to make up his or her own mind about adopting them—a strategy which works best in the shorter dialogues where arguments are presented in a more lively way. For Plato this detachment and use of dialogue is not a point of style, but an issue of epistemology: despite various changes of position on the issue of knowledge, he remains convinced throughout that anything taken on trust, second-hand, either from others or from books, can never amount to a worthwhile cognitive state; knowledge must be achieved by effort from the person concerned. Plato tries to stimulate thought rather than to hand over doctrines.

This detachment also makes Plato himself elusive, in two ways. First, we know very little about him personally. Later biographies are patently constructed to 'explain' aspects of the dialogues. The seventh of a series of 'letters by Plato' has been accepted as genuine by some scholars, and has been used to create a historical background to the dialogues. But such 'letters' are a recognized fictional genre; it is very unwise to use such material to create a basis for the arguments in the dialogues, which are deliberately presented in a detached way. To try to explain the dialogues by appeal to a 'life and letters', though tempting since antiquity, is to miss the point of Plato's procedure, which is to force us to respond to the ideas in the dialogues themselves, not to judge them by our view of the author.

Second, the dialogues themselves are extremely varied and interpretatively often quite open. Since antiquity there has been a debate as to whether Plato's philosophical legacy should be taken to be one of a set of doctrines, or of continuing debate and argument. The middle, sceptical Academy read Plato for the arguments, and Plato's heritage was taken to be a continuation of the practice of argument against contemporary targets. The dialogue most favourable to this kind of interpretation is the *Theaetetus*, in which Socrates presents himself as a barren midwife, drawing ideas out of others but putting forward none himself. However, even in antiquity we find the competing dogmatic reading of Plato, in which the dialogues are read as presenting pieces of doctrine which the reader is encouraged to put together to produce 'Platonism', a distinctive system of beliefs. The dogmatic reading has to cope with the diverse nature of the dialogues and the unsystematic treatment of many topics, with apparent conflicts between dialogues and with the changing and finally disappearing role of Socrates as the chief figure. These problems are often solved by appeal to some development of Plato's thought, although there have been 'unitarians' about Plato's ideas since Arius Didymus (1st cent. BC) declared, 'Plato has many voices, not, as some think, many doctrines' (Stobaeus, *Eclogae* 2. 55. 5–6).

Since the 19th cent. much energy has been expended on the chronology of the dialogues, but, in spite of computer-based work, no stylistic tests establish a precise order. In any case a chronology of the dialogues is only interesting if it tracks some independently established development of Plato's thought, and attempts to establish this easily fall into circularity where they do not rest on the dubious 'life and letters'. Stylistically, however, the dialogues fall into three comparatively uncontroversial groups: (1) the 'Socratic' dialogues, in which Socrates is the main figure, questioning others about their own positions but arguing for none himself, though characteristic views of his own emerge. This group includes *Ion*, *Laches*, *Lysis*, *Apology*, *Euthyphro*, *Charmides*, *Menexenus*, *Hippias Major*, *Hippias Minor*, *Protagoras*, *Crito*, *Cleitophon*, *Alcibiades*, *Lovers*, *Hipparchus* (the last two are often doubted as Plato's work, and since the 19th cent. this has been true of the *Alcibiades*, never doubted in antiquity). Two dialogues generally regarded as transitional between the Socratic and middle dialogues are *Gorgias* and *Meno*. Two dialogues which use the Socratic format but have much in common with the later works are *Euthydemus* and *Theaetetus*. (2) the 'middle' dialogues, in which Socrates remains the chief figure, but, no longer undermining others' views, sets out, at length, many positive ideas: this group includes *Phaedo*, *Republic*, *Symposium*, and *Phaedrus*. (3) the 'later' dialogues, in which Socrates retreats as the main interlocutor, and Plato deals at length, sometimes critically, with his own ideas and those of other philosophers, in a newly detailed and increasingly technical and 'professional' way: this group includes *Cratylus*, *Parmenides*, *Sophist*, *Statesman*, *Philebus*, and *Laws*. *Timaeus* and *Critias* are most often put in this group, but there are arguments for placing them with the middle dialogues.

There is no uncontroversial way of presenting Plato's thought. Many aspects of his work invite the reader to open-ended pursuit of the philosophical issues; others present her with more developed positions, substantial enough to be characterized as 'Platonic' even for those who reject the more rigid forms of the dogmatic reading. While no brief survey of Plato's varied and fertile thought can be adequate, some major themes recur and can be traced through several works.

Ethical and Political Thought Plato is throughout insistent on the objectivity of values, and on the importance of morality in the individual's life. The 'protreptic' passage in the *Euthydemus* anticipates the Stoics in its claim that what are called 'goods' (health, wealth, and so on) are not really so; the only good thing is the virtuous person's knowledge of how to make use of these things in a way consonant with morality. The assumption is explicitly brought out that everyone pursues happiness, though we have, prior to philosophical reflection, little idea of what it is, and most confuse it with worldly success; the choice of virtue is embodied in the worldly failure of Socrates. Many of the Socratic dialogues show Socrates trying to get people to rethink their priorities, and to live more morally; he is sure that there is such a thing as virtue, though he never claims to have it. He further identifies virtue with the wisdom or understanding that is at its basis, the unified grasp of principles which enables the virtuous to act rightly in a variety of situations, and to explain and justify their decisions and actions.

In the *Protagoras*, we find the claim that this wisdom will be instrumental in achieving pleasure; this view is examined respectfully, and although we find attacks on the idea that pleasure could be our end in the *Phaedo* and *Gorgias*, Plato reverts to some very hedonistic-seeming thoughts in the *Philebus* and *Laws*. Arius Didymus compares Plato with Democritus as a kind of hedonist, and clearly he is tempted at times by the idea that some form of pleasure is inescapably our aim, although after the *Protagoras* he never thinks that our reason might be merely instrumental to achieving it. Apart from cryptic and difficult hints in the *Philebus*, he never achieves a substantive characterization of the virtuous person's understanding.

In some of the early and middle dialogues Plato conflates the wisdom of the virtuous individual with that of the virtuous *ruler*; the skill of running one's own life is run together with that of achieving the happiness of others. The culmination of this is the *Republic*, where individual and state are similar in structure, and the virtuous individual is produced only in the virtuous state. Later Plato divides these concerns again, so that the *Philebus* is concerned with individual, and the *Laws* with social morality.

Plato's treatment of social and political matters is marked by a shift of emphasis between two strands in his thought. One is his conviction that the best solution to political problems is the exercise of expert judgement: in an individual life what is needed is overall grasp based on correct understanding of priorities, and similarly in a state what is needed is expert overall understanding of the common good. This conviction is triumphant in the *Republic*, where the rulers, the Guardians, have power to run the lives of all citizens in the state in a very broadly defined way: laws serve the purpose of applying the Guardians' expert knowledge, but do not stand in its way. Expert knowledge gives its possessor the right to enforce on others what the expert sees to be in their true interests, just as the patient must defer to the doctor and the crew to the ship's captain.

Plato is also, however, aware of the importance of law in ensuring stability and other advantages. In the *Crito* the Laws of Athens claim obedience from Socrates (though on a variety of unharmonized grounds). In the *Statesman* Plato admits that, although laws are in the real world a clog on expertise, they embody the past results of expertise and are therefore to be respected, indeed obeyed absolutely in the absence of an expert. In the *Laws*, where Plato has given up the hope that an actual expert could exist and rule uncorrupted by power, he insists that problems of political division and strife are to be met by complete obedience to laws, which are regarded as the product of rational reflection and expertise, rather than the haphazard product of party strife.

Plato's best-known contribution to political thought is his idea, developed in the *Republic*, that individual (more strictly the individual's *soul) and state are analogous in structure. Justice in the state is the condition in which its three functionally defined parts—the rulers, the rulers' auxiliaries, and the rest of the citizens (the producers)—work in harmony, guided by the expert understanding of the rulers, who, unlike the others, grasp what is in the common interest. Analogously, justice in the individual is the condition where the three parts of the individual's soul work in harmony. What this condition will be will differ for members of the three classes. All the citizens have souls whose parts are: reason, which discerns the interest of the whole or at least can be guided by grasp of someone else's reason which does; 'spirit', the emotional side of the person; and desire, the collection of desires aimed at their own satisfaction regardless of the interests of the whole. For all, justice consists in the rule of reason, and the subordination of spirit and the desires; but what this demands is different for the rulers, who understand and can articulate the requirements of reason, and for the producers, who do not. It is notable that Plato identifies this condition of soul, which he calls psychic harmony, with justice, quite contrary to Greek intuitions about political justice. In the *Republic*, the citizen's justice consists in identifying his or her overall interest, to the extent that that is possible, with the common interest, and this idea is taken to notorious lengths in the central books, where the rulers are to live a life in which individuality is given the least possible scope. Opinions have always differed as to whether the *Republic* is a contribution to political theory, or a rejection of the very basis of political theory, one which refuses to solve political conflicts, but unrealistically eliminates their sources. The *Republic* has always been most inspiring as a 'pattern laid up in heaven' for individuals to use in the pursuit of individual justice.

Knowledge and its Objects In the early dialogues, Socrates is constantly in search for knowledge; this is provoked, not by sceptical worries about knowledge of matters of fact, but by the desire to acquire, on a larger and deeper scale, the kind of expert knowledge displayed by craftspeople. Socrates does not doubt that such globally expert knowledge, which he calls wisdom, exists, nor that it would be most useful in the understanding and running of one's life, but he never claims to have it, and in the Socratic dialogues differences show up between it and everyday kinds of expert knowledge. *Sophists, particularly Hippias, are ridiculed as people who uncontroversially have everyday skills, but are shown up as totally lacking in the kind of global understanding which Socrates is seeking.

Socrates' conception of wisdom is an ambitious one; the person with this expert knowledge has a unified overall grasp of the principles which define his field and (as is stressed in the *Gorgias*) he can give a *logos* or account of what it is that he knows, enabling him to explain and justify the judgements that he makes. In several dialogues this demand for giving a *logos* becomes more stringent, and prior conditions are set on an adequate answer. The person who putatively has knowledge of X is required to give an answer as to what X is which is in some way explanatory of the way particular things and kinds of thing are X. The answer is said to provide a 'form' which is itself in some way X, indeed X in a way which (unlike the Xness of other things) precludes ever being the opposite of X in any way. A number of complex issues arise over these 'forms', hotly disputed by scholars and with respect to which the text gives suggestive but incomplete solutions.

In the Socratic dialogues there is a noteworthy mismatch between the goal of wisdom and the method that Socrates employs; for the latter is the procedure of *elenchus*, the testing of the opponent's views by Socrates' tenacious arguments. But the *elenchus* is a method that shows only inconsistency between beliefs; it has no resources for proving truth. Its result is negative; we have demonstrations as to what friendship, courage, piety, and the like are not, but none as to what they are. In the *Meno* a different approach emerges; the theory of 'recollection' stresses that a person can get knowledge by thinking in a way not dependent on experience, and therefore entirely through his own intellectual resources. Although the *Meno* is careful not to restrict knowledge entirely to such *a priori* knowledge, Plato goes on to develop an account of knowledge in which the model of skill is replaced by that of non-empirical, particularly mathematical reasoning. In the *Phaedo* and *Republic* Plato stresses both the non-empirical nature of the objects of knowledge, the forms, and the structured and hierarchical nature of knowledge. Understanding now requires grasp of an entire connected system of thought, and insight into the difference between the basic and the derived elements, and the ways in which the latter are dependent on the former. As the conditions for having knowledge become higher, knowledge becomes an ever more ideal state; in the *Republic* it is only to be achieved by an intellectually gifted élite, who have spent many years in unremittingly abstract intellectual activities, and have lived a life strenuously devoted to the common good. In the *Republic* Plato's account of knowledge, theoretically demanding yet practically applicable, is his most extensive and ambitious.

In later dialogues this synthesis, though never repudiated, lapses. In the *Statesman* we find that theoretical and practical knowledge are now carefully separated; in the *Laws* a continued stress on the importance of mathematics does little work, and contrasts with the work's extensive and explicit reliance on experience. The *Theaetetus* examines knowledge with a fresh and lively concern, attacking various forms of relativism and subjectivism, but without reference to the *Republic* account.

Plato continues to talk about forms, but in elusive and often puzzling ways. The one sustained passage which appears to discuss forms as they appear in the *Phaedo* and *Republic* is wholly negative— the first part of the *Parmenides*, where various powerful arguments are brought against this conception of forms, and no answers are supplied. Whatever Plato's own opinion of these arguments (some of them resembling arguments in early *Aristotle), forms in later dialogues revert to a role more like their earlier one. They are the objective natures of things, the objects of knowledge, and are to be grasped only by the exercise of thought and enquiry, not by reliance on experience. *Statesman* 262b–263d discusses the way that language can be misleading: there is no form of foreigner, since 'foreigner' simply means 'not Greek', and things are not put into a unified kind by not being Greek. There is no single method, other than the continued use of enquiry, to determine which of our words do in fact pick out kinds that are natural, rather than merely contrived. However, Plato, though never renouncing forms as a demand of objectivity in intellectual enquiry, ceases to attach to them the mystical and exalted attitudes of the middle dialogues.

Soul and the Cosmos Throughout the dialogues Plato expresses many versions of the idea that a person's soul is an entity distinct from the living embodied person, attached to it by a relation which is inevitable but unfortunate. In the *Phaedo* several arguments for the soul's immortality show that Plato is dealing indiscriminately with a number of different positions as to what the soul is: the principle of life, the intellect, the personality. The latter two are the ideas most developed. Soul as the intellect is the basis of Plato's tendency to treat knowledge as what transcends our embodied state; in the *Meno* learning a geometrical proof is identified with the person's soul recollecting what it knew before birth.

Soul as the personality is the basis of Plato's use of myths of transmigration of souls and afterlife rewards and punishments. In the middle dialogues these two ideas are united: the *Phaedrus* gives a vivid picture of souls caught on a wheel of ongoing rebirth, a cycle from which only philosophical understanding promises release.

Plato's use of the idea that souls are immortal and are endlessly reborn into different bodies is a metaphorical expression of a deep body–soul dualism which also takes other forms. He tends to draw sharp oppositions between active thinking and passive reliance on sense-experience, and to think of the senses as giving us merely unreflected and unreliable reports; the middle dialogues contain highly coloured disparagements of the world as revealed to us through the senses. However, there is also a strain in Plato which sets against this a more unified view of the person. In the *Symposium* he develops the idea that erotic love can be sublimated and refined in a way that draws the person to aspire to philosophical truth; in the *Phaedrus* he holds that this need not lead to repudiation of the starting-point. In the *Republic* the soul has three parts, two of which are closely connected with the body; but in the final book only the thinking part achieves immortality.

The *Timaeus*, an account of the natural world cast in the form of a description of how it was made by a creator god, treats the world itself as a living thing, with body and soul, and a fanciful cosmic account is developed. Other later dialogues, particularly the *Philebus*, also introduce the idea that our souls are fragments of a cosmic soul in the world as a whole. Many aspects of the *Timaeus'* cosmology depend on the assumption that the world itself is a living thing.

Later Problems and Methods The later dialogues do not display the same literary concerns as the Socratic and middle ones, nor do they contain the same themes. Rather, Plato moves to engaging with the ideas of other philosophers, and his own earlier ones, in a way strikingly unlike his earlier way of doing philosophy by the use of dialogue. In the later works the dialogue form is often strained by the need for exposition, and they are sometimes heavy and pedagogical. However, dialogue is often used brilliantly for long stretches of argument, as in the *Parmenides* and *Sophist*.

The *Sophist* presents, in a passage of challenging argument, Plato's solution to Parmenides' challenge about the coherence of talking about not-being. The *Timaeus* takes up the challenge of cosmology, replying to earlier thinkers with different cosmological assumptions. More fanciful treatment of cosmology is found in the *Statesman*. The *Cratylus* discusses questions of language and etymology in a semi-playful but systematic way. The unfinished *Critias* and the *Statesman* take up questions of political theory, discussing them by means previously rejected, like fiction and accounts which take folk memory and myth seriously. The *Philebus*, discussing the place of pleasure in the good life, does so in a context of Pythagorean metaphysics. The *Laws* sketches an ideal state with considerable help from the lessons of history and of actual politics. These works show a larger variety of interests than hitherto, and an increased flexibility of methodology. Plato in these works shows both a greater respect for the views of others and an enlarged willingness to learn from experience, tradition, and history. *Laws* 3 is a precursor of Aristotle's detailed research into political history. It is not surprising that we find many ideas which remind us of his pupil Aristotle, and the latter's methods and concerns, from the 'receptacle' of the *Timaeus*, suggestive of matter, to the treatment of the 'mean' in the *Statesman*.

Plato is original, radical, and daring, but also elusive. His ideas are locally clear and uncompromising, and globally fragmented, perennially challenging the reader to join in the dialogue and take up the challenge, following the argument where it leads.
J. A.

scenes, but he has cut two scenes altogether and has contrived to avoid a pause in the action where there was an act-break in the original. The tormented monologue of a young man in love has had some jokes added to it. Passages spoken without musical accompaniment in the original Greek are turned into accompanied passages in longer lines. The play is still set in Athens, and the characters have Greek-sounding names; but Plautus has changed most of them, in particular that of the scheming slave who dominates the action, called Syrus (The Syrian) in Menander's play; Plautus calls him Chrysalus (Goldfinger) and adds some colour elsewhere in the play by punning on this name. Chrysalus even boasts of his superiority to slaves called Syrus (649)!

The plots show considerable variety, ranging from the character study of *Aulularia* (the source of Molière's *L'Avare*) to the transvestite romp of *Casina*, from the comedy of mistaken identity in *Amphitruo* and *Menaechmi* (both used by Shakespeare in *The Comedy of Errors*) to the more movingly ironic recognition comedy of *Captivi* (unusual in having no love interest). *Trinummus* is full of high-minded moralizing; *Truculentus* shows the triumph of an utterly amoral and manipulative prostitute. In several plays it is the authority-figure, the male head of the household, who comes off worst: *Casina* and *Mercator* show father and son competing for the love of the same girl, while at the end of *Asinaria* the father is caught by his wife as he tries to share his son's beloved; other plays (above all *Bacchides*, *Epidicus*, *Mostellaria*, and *Pseudolus*) glorify the roguish slave, generally for outwitting the father. These plays have been seen as providing a holiday release from the tensions of daily life, and their Greek setting must have helped: a world in which young men compete with mercenary soldiers for a long-term relationship with a prostitute was probably quite alien to Plautus' first audiences, a fantasy world in which such aberrations as the domination of citizens by slaves could safely be contemplated as part of the entertainment.

Plautus is at his most exuberant in the *cantica*, operatic arias and duets written in a variety of metres, with considerable technical virtuosity, and displaying many features of high-flown style. They often do little or nothing to advance the action, and we know of nothing like them in Greek New Comedy. *Cantica* come in many contexts, e.g. in the mouths of young men in love (as at *Cistellaria* 203–28, *Mostellaria* 84–156, *Trinummus* 223–75), or of 'running slaves', who rush on to the stage in great excitement to deliver an important piece of news but take the time to deliver a lengthy monologue about its importance (as at *Mercator* 111–30, *Stichus* 274–307, *Trinummus* 1008–58). Chrysalus has two strikingly boastful *cantica* at *Bacchides* 640–66 and 925–77. Some of his boasting is embroidered with triumph-imagery and other peculiarly Roman references; it is part of the fantasy of Plautus' Greek world that it can include Italian elements. Thus at *Pseudolus* 143 and 172 the pimp Ballio in addressing the members of his establishment speaks as a Roman magistrate issuing an official edict, and at *Menaechmi* 571 ff. the complaints about the duties of a patron are concerned entirely with social problems at Rome in Plautus' day. But such explicit comment on Roman matters is rare.

Plautus' plays continued to be performed with success at Rome at least until the time of Horace, and they were read by later generations. The earliest surviving manuscript is the 6th-cent. 'Ambrosian palimpsest'. Plautus was well known in Renaissance Italy, particularly after the rediscovery of twelve plays in a manuscript found in Germany in 1429, and his plays were performed and imitated all over Europe until the seventeenth century, and more sporadically thereafter. Terence was more widely read in schools, but both contributed to the development of the European comic tradition (see COMEDY, LATIN).   P. G. M. B.

plebs, the name given to the mass of Roman citizens, as distinct from the privileged patricians, perhaps related to the Greek term for the masses, *plēthos*. A modern hypothesis that the *plebs* was racially distinct from the *patricians is not supported by ancient evidence; and the view of some ancient writers (Cic. *Rep.* 2. 16; Dion. Hal. 2. 9; Plut. *Rom.* 13) that the plebeians were all clients of the patricians in origin may simply be an overstatement of the truism that clients were plebeians. Although we can confidently believe in the differentiation of an aristocracy of wealthier and more powerful families in the regal period, a clear-cut distinction of birth does not seem to have become important before the foundation of the republic, except perhaps in the field of religion, where the view that the plebeians did not originally have *gentes*, lineages (Livy 10. 8. 9), may be of some value. Our sources maintain that in the early republic the plebeians were excluded from religious colleges, magistracies, and the senate; a law of the *Twelve Tables confirmed an existing ban on their intermarriage with patricians, only to be repealed within a few years by the *lex Cannuleia*. However, they were enrolled in *curiae* (voting units) and *tribus* (tribes), they served at all times in the army and could hold the office of military tribune. The 'Conflict of the Orders', by which the *plebs* (or, more precisely, its wealthier members) achieved political equality with the patricians, is an essential part of the story of the development of Rome. The *plebs* owed its victory to the fact that it organized itself into an association, which held its own assemblies (*concilia plebis*), appointed its own officers, the *tribuni plebis* (see TRIBUNE) and *aediles* (usually selected from the wealthier members of the order) and deposited its own records in the temples of Ceres and *Diana on the Aventine hill. Its major tactic in crises was *secessio*, secession *en masse* from Rome (note that the term *seditio* also means a going apart). During the first secession it secured inviolability for the persons of its officers by a collective undertaking to protect them. In fact the tribunes and aediles became in due course magistrates of the *populus Romanus*. The final secession in 287 BC led to the *lex Hortensia*, which made *plebiscita* (resolutions of the plebeian assembly) binding on the whole community. This is normally regarded as the end of the Conflict of the Orders, since the plebeians were no longer significantly disadvantaged *qua* plebeians. However, there continued to be clashes between the interests of the aristocrats and the wealthy and those of the humbler citizens over issues such as public land, which had first emerged in the early republic. Under the later republic the name 'plebeian' acquired in ordinary parlance its modern sense of a member of the lower social orders. Hence from at least *Augustus' reign onwards those who did not belong to the senatorial or equestrian orders or to the order of the local senate (*decuriones*) in colonies or *municipia* (municipalities) were often called the *plebs*.   A. M., A. W. L.

Pliny the Elder (AD 23/4–79), Gaius Plinius Secundus, prominent Roman equestrian, from Novum Comumin Gallia Cisalpina (see GAUL (CISALPINE)), commander of the fleet at Misenum, and uncle of *Pliny the Younger, best known as the author of the 37-book *Naturalis Historia*, an encyclopaedia of all contemporary knowledge—animal, vegetable, and mineral—but with much that is human included too: *natura, hoc est vita, narratur* ('Nature, which is to say Life, is my subject', *pref.* 13).

Characteristic of his age and background in his range of interests and diverse career, Pliny obtained an equestrian command through the *patronage of Quintus Pomponius Secundus (consul 41), and served in Germany, alongside the future emperor *Titus. Active in legal practice in the reign of *Nero, he was then promoted by the favour of the Flavians (and probably the patronage of Licinius Mucianus, whose works he also often quotes) through a series of high procuratorships (including that of Hispania Tarraconensis), in which he won a reputation for integrity (see PROCURATOR). He became a member of the council of *Vespasian and Titus, and was given the command of the Misenum fleet. When Mt. Vesuvius erupted on 24 August 79, duty and curiosity combined, fatally; he led a detachment to the disaster-area, landed at Stabiae, and died from inhaling fumes. For his career and death two letters of his nephew (Pliny, *Ep.* 3. 5 and 6. 16) are the primary source (also Suet. *Illustr.* fr. 80 Reifferscheid).

Throughout this career Pliny was phenomenally productive of literary work. His cavalry command produced a monograph on the use of the throwing-spear by cavalrymen, piety towards his patron demanded a biography in two books. The *Bella Germaniae* in 20 books recounted Roman campaigns against the Germans, and was used by *Tacitus in the *Annales* and *Germania*. *Studiosi* in 3 long books (two rolls each) was a collection of *sententiae* from *controversiae* for use by orators, and *Dubius sermo*, reconciling the claims of analogy and anomaly in Latin diction, reflect his period of legal employment—and the dangers of composing anything less anodyne in the latter years of Nero. The years of his procuratorships produced a 31-book history continuing Aufidius Bassus (see HISTORIOGRAPHY, ROMAN) and covering the later Julio-Claudian period; and, dedicated to Titus, the *Naturalis Historia*.

Pliny was clearly impressed by scale, number, comprehensiveness, and detail. It is characteristic that he claims that there are 20,000 important facts derived from 2,000 books in his work (*pref.* 17), but this is a severe underestimate. The value of what he preserves of the information available to him (the more so since he usually attributes his material to its source) far outweighs the fact that when he can be checked against the original (as with Theophrastus, for instance), he not infrequently garbles his information through haste or insufficient thought. To give only four examples: our study of ancient *agriculture, *medicine, the techniques of metallurgy, and the canon of great artists in antiquity, would all be impoverished if the work had perished (see ART, ANCIENT ATTITUDES TO). So dependent are we on him for many technical fields, that it becomes essential to remember that, mania for inclusiveness notwithstanding, his was a selection of what was available to him (and is indeed—creditably—slanted where possible towards his own experience). The argument from literary silence about many matters of economic and social importance is thus often essentially an argument from the silence of Pliny, and therefore methodologically very limited. It still has to be said that he can scarcely be blamed for not applying the standards of empirical enquiry to ancient medical lore, or for sharing widespread misconceptions about the world. Indeed, one of the interesting aspects of the work is the eloquent witness that he provides for precisely these pre-scientific ways of thinking.

Pliny was no philosopher. It may indeed be thought refreshing to have a view of the ancient world from an author who did not have some claim to the philosophical viewpoint; certainly the sections where Pliny's thought is least accessible are often those where subject matter such as the Cosmos or the Divine take him away from the relatively concrete. Even here, though, there is an engaging personality at work, and there are enough asides and reflections on the world to give an impression of the author which, though it resembles, to an extent, the persona adopted by other Latin technical writers such as *Vitruvius or Julius Frontinus (and is deeply conscious of what literary work it is proper to expect from an important equestrian, but not a senator) is still highly individual: as is the style and the imagery, which was often misunderstood in later antiquity, and can still baffle today. The standard ethical diatribe against luxury and aristocratic excess of the man from the municipality is given vivid historical and geographical colour, and if the Roman past is idealized it is partly through the evocation of an image of the *populus Romanus* which is among the least hostile treatments of the many in any ancient author. The themes of the sufficient excellence of the natural endowment of Italy, and the terrible moral threat posed by the differential value of the exotic, form a laconic and memorable conclusion to book 37 (described in book 1, end as *Comparatio naturae per terras; comparatio rerum per pretia*, 'nature compared in different lands; products compared as to value').

Vita vigilia est (*pref.* 18): Life is being awake. The *Naturalis*

Historia is a monument to keeping alert, and to the useful employment of time. Pliny's energy and diligence astonished his nephew, were intended to impress his contemporaries, and still amaze today; they were, moreover, not just a contingent habit of mind, but intended as an ethical statement. For all his defects of accuracy, selection, and arrangement, Pliny achieved a real summation of universal knowledge, deeply imbued with the mood of the time, and the greatness of his work was speedily recognized. It was a model for later writers such as Julius Solinus and Isidore of Seville, and attained a position of enormous cultural and intellectual influence in the medieval west.   N. P.

Pliny the Younger (*c.* AD 61–*c.*112), Gaius Plinius Caecilius Secundus, is known from his writings and from inscriptions (e.g. *ILS* 2927). Son of a landowner of Comum, he was brought up by his uncle, *Pliny the Elder, of equestrian rank (see EQUITES), who adopted him, perhaps in his will; see ADOPTION, *Roman Adoptio*. He studied rhetoric at the feet of Quintilian and Nicetes at Rome. After the usual year's service on the staff of a Syrian legion (*c.*81), he entered the senate in the later 80s through the patronage of such distinguished family friends as Verginius Rufus and Julius Frontinus. He practised with distinction in the civil courts all his life, specializing in cases relating to inheritance, and conducted several prosecutions in the senate of provincial governors charged with extortion. He rose up the senatorial ladder, becoming praetor in 93 (or less probably 95) and consul in 100, and he also held a series of imperial administrative appointments, as *praefectus aerari militaris* (prefect in charge of soldiers' pension fund: *c.*94–6), *praefectus aerari Saturni* (prefect in charge of the state treasury: *c.*98–100), and *curator alvei Tiberis*, i.e. in charge of the banks of the river Tiber (*c.*104–6). He was thrice a member of the judicial council of *Trajan (*c.*104–7), who sent him as imperial legate to govern Bithynia-Pontus in NW *Asia Minor (*c.*111), where he apparently died in office (*c.*112). His career, very similar to that of his friend *Tacitus, is the best-documented example from the Principate of municipal origins and continuing ties, of the role of patronage, of the nature of senatorial employment under emperors tyrannical and liberal, and of the landed wealth that underpinned the system.

Pliny published nine books of literary letters between 99 (or 104) and 109 at irregular intervals, singly or in groups of three. Some letters comment elegantly on social, domestic, judicial, and political events, others offer friends advice, others again are references for jobs or requests for support for his own candidates in senatorial elections, while the tone is varied by the inclusion of short courtesy notes and set-piece topographical descriptions. Each letter is carefully composed (*Ep.* 1. 1), with great attention to formal style; Pliny uses the devices of contemporary rhetoric, with intricate arrangement and balance of words and clauses in sentences and paragraphs. Letters are limited either to a single subject treated at appropriate length, or to a single theme illustrated by three examples (cf. *Epp.* 2.

20; 3. 16; 6. 31; 7. 27). Great care was also taken with the sequence of letters within each book. Pliny and his friends regularly exchanged such letters (*Ep.* 9. 28), which Pliny distinguished from boring business letters (*Ep.* 1. 10), from mere trivialites (*Ep.* 3. 20), and from the philosophical abstractions of *Seneca's letters (*Ep.* 9. 2). The letters do have their origins in day-to-day events, but Pliny aimed to create a new type of literature. He set out to write not an annalistic history, but a picture of his times with a strong moral element. He censures the cruelty of slave masters, the dodges of legacy hunters, and the meanness of the wealthy, but the targets of his criticisms are normally anonymous. He dwells for preference on positive aspects of the present, the benign role of Trajan, the merits of friends and acquaintances, the importance of education, and the literary life of Rome. Other letters describe the public life of senatorial debates, elections and trials, without concealing the weaknesses of senators, and recount, in a manner anticipating Tacitus, heroic episodes of the political opposition to *Domitian, with which Pliny liked to claim some connection.

Pliny was also active in other fields of literature. He wrote verses enthusiastically, publishing two volumes in the manner of his protégé *Martial, of which he quotes a few indifferent specimens. His surviving speech, the *Panegyricus*, the only extant Latin speech between *Cicero and the late imperial panegyrics, is an expanded version of the original he delivered in the senate in thanks for his election to the consulship. Rhetorically a success (its popularity in the late-Roman rhetorical schools is responsible for its survival), it contrasts Trajan with the tyrannical Domitian. It is a major statement of the Roman political ideal of the good emperor condescending to play the role of an ordinary senator.

The tenth book of letters contains all of Pliny's correspondence with Trajan: the first fourteen letters date between 98 and *c.*110, the remainder to Pliny's governorship of Bithynia-Pontus. The letters are much simpler in style than those in books 1–9 and were not worked up for publication, which probably occurred after Pliny's death. The provincial letters are the only such dossier surviving entire, and are a major source for understanding Roman provincial government. Each letter concerns a particular problem, such as the status of foundlings or the condition of civic finances, on which Pliny sought a ruling from Trajan. In *Ep.* 10. 96 Pliny gives the earliest external account of Christian worship, and the fullest statement of the reasons for the execution of Christians; see CHRISTIANITY.   A. N. S.-W.; S. R. F. P.

Plutarch (Lucius (?) Mestrius Plutarchus) of Boeotian Chaeronea; b. before AD 50, d. after AD 120; philosopher and biographer. The family had long been established in Chaeronea, and most of Plutarch's life was spent in that historic town, to which he was devoted. He knew Athens well, and visited both Egypt and Italy, lecturing and teaching at Rome. His father, Autobulus, his grandfather,

Lamprias, and other members of his family figure often in his dialogues; his wide circle of influential friends include the consulars Lucius Mestrius Florus (whose gentile name he bore), Quintus Sosius Senecio (to whom the *Parallel Lives* and other works are dedicated), and Gaius Minicius Fundanus, as well as magnates like the exiled Syrian prince Philopappus. For the last thirty years of his life, Plutarch was a priest at *Delphi. A devout believer in the ancient pieties and a profound student of its antiquities, he played a notable part in the revival of the shrine in the time of Trajan and Hadrian; and the people of Delphi joined with Chaeronea in dedicating a portrait bust of him 'in obedience to the decision of the Amphictions', the members of the sanctuary's venerable governing body (*Syll.*³ 843 A). Late authorities (*Suda*, Eusebius) report that he received *ornamenta consularia* (the honorary rank of *consul) from Trajan, and was imperial *procurator in Achaia (the province of Greece) under Hadrian; whatever lies behind this, he was a man of some influence in governing circles, as he was in his writing an active exponent of the concept of a partnership between Greece, the educator, and Rome, the great power, and of the compatibility of the two loyalties.

The 'Catalogue of Lamprias', a list of his works probably dating from the 4th cent., contains 227 items. Extant are 78 miscellaneous works (some not listed in the Catalogue) and 50 Lives. We have lost the Lives of the Caesars (except *Galba* and *Otho*) and some others (notably *Epaminondas*, *Pindar*, *Daiphantus*), and probably two-thirds of the miscellaneous works. Nevertheless, what remains is a formidable mass; Plutarch was a very prolific writer, especially (it seems) in the last twenty years of his life. The relative chronology of his works however is very difficult to establish (C. P. Jones, *JRS* 1966, 61–74). For a complete list of titles, see e.g. any volume of the Loeb *Moralia*, or D. A. Russell, *Select Essays and Dialogues* (World's Classics, 1993), pp. xxiii–xxix. In what follows, we can only mention a few. (The numbers attached to the titles refer to the order of treatises in all editions.)

1. The group of *rhetorical* works—epideictic performances—includes 'The Glory of Athens' (22), 'The Fortune of Rome' (20), 'Against Borrowing Money' (54). Plutarch's richly allusive and metaphorical style does not seem very well adapted to rhetorical performance, and these—with the exception of 'Against Borrowing' which is a powerful, satirical piece—are not very successful; it is often thought, though without clear evidence, that Plutarch's epideictic rhetoric was something that he gave up in later life.

2. The numerous treatises on themes of popular moral philosophy are derivative in content, but homogeneous and characteristic in style. Among the best are 'Friends and Flatterers' (4), 'Progress in Virtue' (5), 'Superstition' (14), 'The Control of Anger' (29), 'Talkativeness' (35), 'Curiosity' (36), and 'Bashfulness' (38). In 'Rules for Politicians' (52), Plutarch draws both on his historical reading and on his own experience, to give advice to a young man entering politics. The warm and sympathetic personality never far beneath the surface appears particularly in 'Consolation to my Wife' (45) and 'Advice on Marriage' (12). Plutarch's teaching is less individualistic than that of many ancient moralists: family affections and friendly loyalties play a large part in it.

3. Many of Plutarch's works are *dialogues*, written not so much in the Platonic tradition as in that of *Aristotle (and indeed *Cicero), with long speeches, a good deal of characterization, and the frequent appearance of the author himself as a participant. The nine books of 'Table Talk' (46) are full of erudite urbanity and curious speculation. 'Socrates' Daimonion' (43) combines exciting narrative (liberation of Boeotian Thebes from Spartan occupation in 379/8) with philosophical conversation about prophecy (a favourite theme) and an elaborate Platonic myth (see PLATO) of the fate of the soul after death (Plutarch attempted such myths elsewhere also, especially in 'God's Slowness to Punish' (41)). 'Eroticus' (47) also combines narrative with argument, this time in a near contemporary setting: the 'kidnapping' of a young man by a widow who wishes to marry him forms the background to a discussion of *heterosexual and *homosexual love in general. Delphi is the scene of four dialogues, all concerned with prophecy, *daimones*, and divine providence; and it is in these (together with *Isis and Osiris* (23)) that the greater part of Plutarch's philosophical and religious speculation is to be sought.

4. He was a Platonist, and a teacher of philosophy; and the more technical side of this activity is to be seen in his interpretation of the *Timaeus* (68) and a series of polemical treatises against the Stoics (70–2) and Epicureans (73–5).

5. We possess also important antiquarian works— 'Roman Questions' and 'Greek Questions' (18), mainly concerned with religious antiquities—and some on literary themes ('On Reading the Poets' (2) is the most significant).

Plutarch's fame led to the inclusion in the corpus of a number of *spuria*, some of which have been very important: 'The Education of Children' (1) was influential in the Renaissance; 'Doctrines of the Philosophers' (58) is a version of a doxographic compilation to which we owe a lot of our knowledge of Greek philosophy, while 'Lives of the Ten Orators' (55) and 'Music' (76) are also important sources of information.

The 'Parallel Lives' remain his greatest achievement. We have 23 pairs, 19 of them with 'comparisons' attached. Plutarch's aims are set out e.g. in *Alexander* 1: his object was not to write continuous political history, but to exemplify individual virtue (or vice) in the careers of great men. Hence he gives attention especially to his heroes' education, to significant anecdotes, and to what he sees as the development or revelation of character. Much depends of course on the sources available to him (*Alcibiades* is full of attested personal detail, *Publicola* is thin and padded out, *Antony* full of glorious narrative, especially about *Cleopatra VII, *Phocion* and *Cato Maior* full of sententious anecdotes), but the general pattern is maintained wherever possible: family, education, début in public life, climaxes, changes of fortune or attitude, latter years and death. The *Lives*, despite the pitfalls for the historian which have sometimes led to despair about their value as source-material, have been the main source of understanding of the ancient world for many readers from the Renaissance to the present day.

Indeed, Plutarch has almost always been popular. He was a 'classic' by the 4th cent., and a popular educational text in Byzantine times. The preservation of so much of his work is due mainly to Byzantine scholars (especially Maximus Planudes). His wider influence dates from Renaissance translations, especially Amyot's French version (*Lives* 1559, *Moralia* 1572) and Sir T. North's English *Lives* (1579; largely based on Amyot) and Philemon Holland's *Moralia* (1603). Montaigne, Shakespeare, Dryden, Rousseau, and Emerson are among Plutarch's principal debtors. In the 19th cent., however, his influence, at least among scholars, diminished: he was seen as a derivative source both in history and in philosophy, and his lack of historical perspective and his rather simple moral attitudes earned him much disrespect. Recent scholarship has done much to reverse this negative view; as understanding of his learning and the aims and methods of his writing has deepened, so he has come again to be seen, not as a marginal figure, but as a thinker whose view of the classical world deserves respect and study. See also BIOGRAPHY, GREEK.

D. A. R.

police In any discussion of police it is necessary to distinguish between the function of policing, that is, maintaining public order and enforcing the law, and the existence of a specialized agency of repression, i.e. a police force, to carry out these tasks on behalf of the state. Police forces as such, though taken for granted as a necessity, or at least a necessary evil, in modern societies, did not exist in the ancient world. They are a creation of the 18th and 19th cents., and reflect the growth of state power in the increasingly complex and bureaucratic societies of the modern industrialized world, and the extent to which mechanisms of social control have been centralized and monopolized by the state.

On the other hand, ancient city-states recognized the need for publicly appointed officials to carry out functions of social regulation. For example, in Classical Athens annual boards of magistrates (*astynomoi* (streets), *agoranomoi* (markets), *sitophylakes* (corn supply), etc.) were charged with keeping the streets clean, supervising market transactions, and controlling grain prices (*Ath. Pol.* 50–1, with Rhodes's commentary). Officials of this kind are attested in Greek cities throughout the Hellenistic and Roman periods, and the same functions were performed in Rome and cities of the Latin west by the aediles and their equivalents.

There were also magistrates appointed to deal with certain aspects of criminal activity. At Athens a board of citizen officials called the Eleven, appointed by lot, had the task of guarding prisoners in the city *prison, carrying out executions and occasionally arresting criminals. In Rome these functions were carried out by minor magistrates called *tresviri capitales*, who may also have exercised summary jurisdiction over slaves and humble citizens. But these magistrates, who were assisted by only a small number of public slaves, had neither the authority nor the resources to act as a police force. At Athens after the Persian Wars (see GREECE, HISTORY) a special force of 300 Scythian slaves, armed with bows, was used to keep order in the assembly and the law courts, but the Scythian archers acted as policemen only in the most rudimentary sense; they were of low status, enjoyed little public respect and had no authority to investigate, arrest or prosecute. At Rome the lictors who attended the senior magistrates were only symbols of the state's authority to discipline and punish; they had no effective power to coerce. The authority of magistrates depended absolutely on the acceptance by the citizens of their political institutions and the men who operated them.

A remarkable feature of ancient societies is how little the authorities were involved in the suppression, investigation, and prosecution of criminal activity. These matters were left to the private initiative of citizens who relied on networks of kin, friends, and dependants in a system of self-help. Small-scale disturbances were resolved locally by neighbours and passers-by, who were expected to take sides and usually did so. The state became involved only when violence had a political dimension or when it became a threat to the community as a whole. In such circumstances the authorities mobilized ordinary citizens who took up arms on behalf of state. This happened in Athens in the crisis of 415 BC (Andocides 1. 45), and in Rome in 186 BC at the time of the Bacchanalian affair (Livy 39. 16. 13; see BACCHANALIA). In the political crises of 121 and 100 BC the senators and knights armed themselves and their dependants in order to crush Gaius *Gracchus and Lucius Appuleius Saturninus. The need to call upon the armed support of the citizens in a crisis was widely recognized, and is for example laid down in Roman colonial charters (e.g. *lex Coloniae Genetivae* 103).

After the breakdown of public order in the late republic the Roman emperors instituted more permanent forces to police the city of Rome. These were the urban cohorts, commanded by the prefect of the city, and the *vigiles*, a corps of 7,000 freed slaves under an equestrian prefect, whose principal task was to act as a fire brigade, but could be used to enforce order if necessary. The praetorian guard was also on hand to suppress major public disturbances. Urban cohorts similar to those at Rome existed at certain large cities, including Lugdunum (Lyon) and *Carthage, and several cities apparently had fire brigades; but these were treated with suspicion by the central government which saw them as potentially subversive. *Trajan advised *Pliny the Younger to provide fire-fighting equipment for the citizens of Nicomedia to use when needed, rather than to set up a permanent fire brigade (Plin. *Ep.* 10. 34, a most revealing document). But these paramilitary forces of the Roman empire, although closer to a police force than anything else in antiquity, were not involved in day-to-day law enforcement, which remained the responsibility of private citizens acting on their own behalf.   T. J. Co.

polis (pl. *poleis*), the Greek city-state. The *polis* is the characteristic form of Greek urban life; its main features are small size, political autonomy, social homogeneity, sense of community and respect for law. It can be contrasted with the earlier Mycenaean palace economy (see MYCENAEAN CIVILIZATION), and with the continuing existence of tribal (*ethnos*) types of organization in many areas of northern Greece. (See ETHNICITY. For a different sense of 'tribe' see below.) The *polis* arose in the late Dark Ages. It is present in *Homer; the archaeological signs of city development (public space, temples, walls, public works, town planning) appear in an increasing number of sites in the 8th–7th cents. (Old Smyrna, Eretria); the peaceful abandonment of smaller sites and the general decline of archaeological evidence from the countryside in the 7th cent. suggest early *synoecism or concentration of population in specific *polis* sites. The foundation of organized settlements in new areas (see COLONIZATION, GREEK) is not distinct, but part of the same process.

Each *polis* controlled a territory (*chōra*) delimited geographically by mountains or sea, or by proximity to another *polis*; border wars were common, as were intercity agreements and attempts to establish religious rights over disputed areas; *Athens and *Sparta were exceptional in possessing large territories. Autonomy was jealously guarded, but the necessities of collaboration made for a proliferation of foreign alliances, leagues, and hegemonies; and a constant struggle for domination or independence developed (see IMPERIALISM, *Greek and Hellenistic*). There was also constant interchange and competition between

cities, so that despite their separate identities a common culture was always maintained.

Economically the *polis* served an agrarian economy as a centre for local exchange, processing and manufacture; many cities were located on the sea, and had also important overseas trading interests (see ECONOMY, GREEK and HELLENISTIC). Socially the citizens comprised an ethnically homogeneous or limited group, organized according to 'tribes' (*phylai*) and smaller *kinship groups, such as phratries, demes (rural villages) and families (see HOUSEHOLD); new cities would replicate these, and they were often reorganized more or less artificially to serve new civic functions. Each city had a specific patron deity and a religious calendar with other lesser cults and festivals; the older priesthoods belonged to specific aristocratic families, later ones were often appointed by the people (see PRIESTS). Animal sacrifice (see SACRIFICE, GREEK) was accompanied by equal distribution of the meat at civic festivals, which from the 6th cent. became the focus for city-organized competitions in sport, dancing, and theatre (see GAMES). New cities required religious authorization, traditionally from the oracle of Apollo at Delphi (see COLONIZATION, GREEK; DELPHIC ORACLE); sacred fire was brought from the mother city, and established at the *prytaneion* (*hôtel de ville*), which in all cities acted as the common hearth, where magistrates and others took meals provided at public expense; the founder of a new city was given heroic honours after death, with a tomb within the walls and public rites.

Economy, kinship groups, and religion were subordinate to the main focus of the *polis*, which was broadly political; and its development may be seen largely in terms of the adaptation of these forces to a political end. Originating as an aristocratic system, the *polis* became a 'guild of warriors', in which the military power of the community (hoplites or heavy infantrymen, and later at

polis Ruins of an Athenian farmhouse near modern Vari (late 5th cent. BC). Most *poleis* were agricultural communities, and at Athens the majority of citizens lived in the Attic countryside until forced to take shelter behind the city-walls in the Peloponnesian War (431–404 BC).

Athens the 'naval mob') controlled the political and institutional life. Women were therefore never admitted to
political rights and were effectively excluded from public
life. In origin all cities seem to have possessed similar institutions: magistrates (see MAGISTRACY, GREEK) elected annually, a council of elders, and a warrior assembly; the
common later contrast between *oligarchy and democracy simply relates to relatively minor differences in the
distribution of powers and eligibility for office. The first
stage in the development of the *polis* (7th–6th cents.) was
usually the establishment of a written or customary
lawcode (often attributed to a named *nomothetēs* or law-
maker (*Lycurgus, *Solon)), which limited the arbitrary
powers of the aristocratic magistrates and regulated social
conflict; the ideal was often referred to as *eunomia* (see
SPARTA §2). The second stage (late 6th cent.) was the evolution of the concept of the citizen with defined privileges
and duties; this often involved the establishment of equality in political rights (*isonomia*, or democracy), but also the
establishment of clear membership rules excluding non-
citizens, and creating subordinate statuses (see CLEIS-
THENES; METICS). The *polis* was indeed always defined in
terms of its members, rather than geographically: the city
of Athens is always called 'the Athenians', and citizenship
generally implied equality and participation in all political,
judicial, and governmental activities. In the 5th and 4th
cents. a fully political society developed, centred on the
making of complex decisions in the citizen assembly (see
POLITICS).

This elaboration of a political culture affected all aspects
of the *polis*. Religious and social institutions were not
autonomous, but were continually being adapted to
conform to the needs of *polis* organization. Sparta is a striking example: an initially normal Greek city substituted universal military commensality (the *syssitia*) in place of
family structures, and adapted all religious *rituals to the
needs of a hoplite *polis*. Other cities underwent less
extreme forms of adaptation, but the constant subordination of family and religious structures and large parts of
the legal system (such as inheritance) to the needs of the
polis is striking, and creates an impression of rationality in
the development of social forms. Equally the dominance
of the political led to an early recognition of the difference
between the various spheres of social activity (Max
Weber's 'formal rationality'), and of the possibility of conflict between them, which is especially exemplified in the
public art of tragedy (see TRAGEDY, GREEK).

In the late 4th cent. the gradual loss of political autonomy eroded the power of the armed citizens, and
increased that of wealthy notables. The Hellenistic *polis*
was marked by a conflict between rich and poor citizens
(see CLASS STRUGGLE), mediated by the willingness of the
rich to spend their *wealth on the duties of office and to
engage in *euergetism, or subsidizing the expenses of
office and of public festivals and culture, and providing
buildings and other public works; this is expressed in the
ideal of *homonoia* (concord). The extension of the *polis* as a

civic form across the areas conquered by *Alexander the
Great under his successors created a colonial-style system,
in which a Greek urbanized élite lived off the labour of a
non-Greek countryside (see COLONIZATION, HELLENISTIC).
The criterion of citizenship became education at the
*gymnasium in Greek letters and sport, and the concept of
the *polis* became as much cultural as political.

The *polis* of the Roman age inherited a tradition of independence and competition within an imperial system, of
civic pride expressed in public building programmes, and
of cultural superiority over Romans and native peasantry;
this was exemplified in the Greek renaissance of the
'*Second Sophistic'. The Greek cities of the eastern empire
were thus able to develop and continue a rich economic,
cultural and social life into the early Byzantine period.

The origins of the rationalization and idealization of the
polis lie deep in the reforming tendencies of the Archaic
age. Greek political philosophy emerged in the fifth
century with various attempts to imagine utopian cities
whose institutions were directed towards specific ends;
*Plato's *Republic* and *Laws* stand in this tradition.
*Aristotle's *Politics* begins from the claim that 'man is by
nature an animal of the *polis*', and seeks to draw conclusions from the whole experience of the *polis*, but fails to
create an ideal philosophical state. Later thinkers (the
*Cynics, Zeno, *Epicurus) rebelled against the conception
of man as subordinate to the *polis*, either by claiming his
freedom from it, or by redefining the institution as a *cos-
mopolis*, in which all wise men were free. It is this mystical
universalization of the *polis* which enabled first the Roman
imperial panegyrists and then the Christian writer
*Augustine to conceive of the *polis* as a transcendental city
embracing all the members of a community, whether
empire or church.

See also CITIZENSHIP, GREEK; ETHNICITY; FEDERAL STATES;
FREEDOM IN THE ANCIENT WORLD; GREECE (PREHISTORY AND
HISTORY); LAW IN GREECE; POLITICAL THEORY; POLITICS;
URBANISM.   O. Mu.

political theory (*see facing page*)

politics

In Greece 1. Politics as power struggle. This is the dominant interpretation of politics in the modern world since
Macchiavelli; it requires organized groups, either operating
out of group self-interest or with differing conceptions of
the common interest. In the archaic age of Greece there is
some evidence for the existence of aristocratic groups supported by retainers, notably in the poetry of *Alcaeus and
at Athens before *Cleisthenes; in the Classical period organized aristocratic *hetairiai* (clubs) occasionally emerged as
politically important, but usually as a consequence of lack
of success in normal political life. Organized political
parties never existed, and political programmes were confined to groups trying to change the constitution.

2. Politics as ritualized decision-making. Specific political institutions and methods for decision-making are first

[*continued on p. 552*]

political theory

political theory Greek and Roman authors reflected constantly about justice, good government, the nature of law. Epic, tragedy, comedy, history, and oratory are rich in political thought, frequently intensely interacting with the thought of the philosophers. To single out the philosophers, as must be done here, is potentially distorting.

Greek and Roman political theory is distinctive in its focus on the *soul. All the major thinkers hold that one cannot reflect well about political institutions without reflecting, first, about human flourishing, and about the psychological structures that facilitate or impede it. Their thought about virtue, education, and the passions is integral to their political theory, since they hold, for the most part, that a just city (*polis) can only be achieved by the formation of balanced and virtuous individuals—although they also hold that institutions shape the passions of individuals and their possibilities for flourishing.

The 5th cent. BC in Athens saw a flowering of political theory and a turning of philosophy from cosmology to human concerns. The *sophists and those influenced by them exchanged arguments about the status of ethical and political norms—whether these norms exist by nature (*physis*) or by convention or law (*nomos*), and whether they are absolute, or relative to the species and/or the individual. Protagoras' famous saying that 'The human being is the measure of all things' was probably not intended as the claim that each individual is the subjective judge of value for himself; the human species is the standard. But even such anthropocentrism constituted a challenge to the primacy of religious sources of value. Other thinkers championed more thoroughgoing forms of relativism. While Protagoras strongly defended conventions of justice as essential to well-being, others offered an immoralist teaching, urging individuals to pursue their own pleasure or power in so far as they could escape the tyranny of constraining law and custom.

*Socrates portrayed his relation to the Athenian democracy (see DEMOCRACY, ATHENIAN) as that of a gadfly on the back of a 'noble but sluggish horse': democracy was on the whole admirable but in need of critical self-examination. Although charged with oligarchic sympathies, he remained on good terms with *Lysias and other prominent democrats after the restoration; it is likely that he preferred democracy to other regimes, while advocating a larger role for expert judgement. In *Plato's *Crito*, he justifies his refusal to escape his penalty by insisting on the obligation of obedience to law imposed by a citizen's acceptance of the benefit and education of those same laws.

Plato's search for a just city, in the *Republic*, begins with the attempt to defend the life of the just person against Thrasymachus' immoralist challenge, showing that this life is more *eudaimōn* (lucky) than the unjust life. In order to understand justice in the individual, the interlocutors imagine an ideal city, in whose class relations justice may be seen. The relation between city and *soul turns out to be more complex than analogy, however, since the institutions of the ideal city prove necessary for the production of full justice in individuals; and the rule of just individuals is necessary for the maintenance of ideal institutions. The just individual is characterized by psychic harmony in which each part of the soul does its proper work, reason ruling and appetite and spirit being ruled; so too, in the just city, the reasoners are to rule and people dominated by appetite are to be ruled. On this basis Plato's Socrates develops his institutional proposals, which include: an education for the ruling class in which all traditional poetry is banished as bad for the soul; the abolition of the nuclear family and a communal scheme of marriage and child-rearing; the equal consideration of women for all functions, including that of ruler; a selective cultivation of the best souls to produce a ruling class of philosophers with knowledge of the good. Plato seems unconcerned about the limits he imposes on free choice, since he views most citizens as psychically immature and in need of permanent supervision.

Plato's later political works, *Statesman* and *Laws*, re-examine these psychic and institutional questions. *Statesman* develops the idea of practical wisdom as a flexible ability to grapple with the changing circumstances of human life, thus anticipating a prominent theme in the thought of *Aristotle. In *Laws* the emphasis on the guiding political role of wisdom is maintained, but, apparently, with a new emphasis on the importance of consent by and rational persuasion of the ruled, who now seem to be judged capable of some sort of fully-fledged virtue. The dialogue reflects at length about the justification and nature of punishment.

Aristotle's political thought includes an account of the nature of human flourishing or *eudaimonia*, since, as he argues, the good things that politics distributes (property, possessions, offices, honours) are good not in themselves but as means to flourishing; an account of flourishing thus gives a 'limit' to the legislator, whose task will be to make an arrangement such that, barring catastrophic accidents, 'anyone whatsoever may do well and live a flourishing life'. Aristotle justifies the *polis* as essential to the complete realization of human ends, and details its development from the household and the village. While critical of 'artificial slavery', he defends a 'natural slavery' whose subjects are beings who 'altogether lack the deliberative faculty'. A more co-operative type of subordination is justified for women, apparently on the grounds that they deliberate ineffectually. Because he holds that virtue requires leisure, he denies citizenship to farmers, craftsmen, and resident aliens. These exclusions aside, Aristotle's preferred regime is that of free and equal citizens, ruling and being ruled by turns. His ideal city subsidizes the participation of poor citizens in common meals and other institutions out of the revenue from publicly held land; on the other hand, Platonic communism of property is thoroughly repudiated, as is Plato's attack on the family. Education is central, and Aristotle seems almost as insensitive as Plato to the issue of state control. In the central books of the *Pol.*, Aristotle describes various types of actual regime and their alternations.

For *Epicurus, justice is a necessary condition for *eudaimonia*, not an end in itself. Political involvement is to be avoided as a source of disturbance. The moderation of bad desires, such as the fear of death and aggressive wishes, will ameliorate many social ills. *Lucretius either preserves or innovates a fuller account of politics, which includes the idea that justice arose out of an implicit contract for the sake of protecting the weak.

The Stoics (see STOICISM) also focus on the therapy of the soul, holding that anger, fear, and the other 'passions' should be extirpated by removing excessive attachments to external goods such as money and reputation. This will change politics by removing various bad forms of contention and self-assertion. Zeno and Chrysippus propose an ideal city in which virtuous citizens will live in concord, inspired by bonds of love. Women are given full equality; the institution of marriage is replaced by free consensual sexual relations. To all Stoics, local and national affiliations are less morally salient than our membership in the worldwide community of reason; this theme of the *kosmou politēs* ('world citizen') is developed vividly in Roman Stoicism, especially in Marcus *Aurelius. Roman Stoics debated the question of the best regime: some preferred monarchy and conceived of the emperor as (ideally) a Stoic sage; others, such as Thrasea Paetus under *Nero, understanding the Stoic ideal of self-command to entail republican government, invoked Stoicism in their anti-imperial politics.

Other major contributors to Hellenistic political theory include *Cicero, with his account of the mixed regime, and *Plutarch, with his wide-ranging reflections on virtue and rulership. See FREEDOM IN THE ANCIENT WORLD; KINGSHIP; OLIGARCHY; POLIS; POLITICS.   M. C. N.

found in the archaic age, and were highly developed by the Classical period; the best-known examples are *Sparta and *Athens (see LYCURGUS; DEMOCRACY, ATHENIAN). They involved a specific location for taking decisions, religious rituals for demarcating space and time, and a fixed procedure. In principle all citizens with full rights could participate in the assembly. The aim was to achieve consensus

through structured discussion; arguments usually took the form of opposed speeches, and speakers were expected to maintain certain conventions of dignified behaviour: scandal was caused when these were infringed by the Athenian demagogues in the late 5th cent. At Athens political leaders were initially of aristocratic birth, but after the death of *Pericles they were simply those who spoke most often (*prostatai tou dēmou, dēmagōgoi, rhētores* ('champions/leaders of the people, public speakers')); they were regarded as responsible for decisions, and prided themselves on consistency of advice. There were four main issues on which they were expected to possess knowledge: city revenues, war and peace, defence, corn supply (Aristotle *Rhet.* I. 4; Xen. *Mem.* 3. 6). Seventeen assembly speeches survive from the period 403–322 BC, by *Lysias, *Andocides and (especially) *Demosthenes; they are brief and well organized; their arguments are based on rational calculation of advantage and consequence, rather than appeals to sentiment, religion, or historical rights. The controls on assembly procedure in the 5th cent. were customary; but in the 4th cent. the formal distinction between laws and decrees, and the limitation of the assembly to the making of decrees, led to the constitutional check of the *graphē paranomōn* (indictment for unconstitutional behaviour), whereby decrees could be challenged in the courts as being contrary to the laws. A decision once taken was accepted as the will of the community expressed in such phrases as 'the Athenians decided', and was binding on all: there was no mechanism for continued dissent.

This absence of a means for structuring permanent political oppositions such as class conflict (see CLASS STRUGGLE) was a basic weakness of Greek political life: *stasis*, armed revolution, had as its aim the overthrow of the existing consensus, in order to return to a different political unity through the extermination of the opposition; it was common in many cities, and focused on the conflict between democracy and oligarchy, or the question of equal or unequal distribution of political privileges in relation to social class; it caused much instability of political life. *Stasis* was regarded as a disease of the body politic, capable of destroying the community (Thuc. 3. 82–3). Philosophers were unable to offer any solution to the problem.

At Rome Roman society had a strong gentilicial framework, and throughout the republic politics was largely based on the *clientela* or kinship group; the late republic saw also the growth of military clientship among the dynasts. Much of Roman political life was concerned with the struggle for election to those offices which gave access to legal power, military command, and the possibility of conquest (see IMPERIUM; MAGISTRACY, ROMAN; PROVINCIA); it therefore involved a measure of participation by the people. Individuals might espouse conservative or radical attitudes and be designated by the political labels, *optimates* (lit. 'the best men', the conservative governing class) and *populares* (popular politicians); but there was much inconsistency, and these claims seldom involved clear differences in policy. Decision-making was divided between the aristocratic *senate and a number of different assemblies, and was therefore complex and open to challenge. Roman political life seems closer to modern practices than does Greek, for it distanced the people from the process of decision-making and possessed a complex constitutional law

based on precedent; but it still lacked the concept of institutionalized party politics. The political leadership was always aristocratic, and much concerned with its own dignity, privileges, and 'equality'. The emperors continued to respect the claims of the senate to play a major role in the political system at least in principle during the 1st cent. AD, but the power of the people was not preserved under the Principate; *libertas* (see FREEDOM) became an aristocratic ideal.

See DEMOCRACY, ATHENIAN; FREEDOM IN THE ANCIENT WORLD; OLIGARCHY; POLIS; TYRANNY. O. Mu.

pollution, the Greek concept of Societies create order by stigmatizing certain disorderly conditions and events and persons as 'polluting', that is, by treating them metaphorically as unclean and dangerous. Very roughly, the pollutions generally recognized by the Greeks were birth, death, to a limited degree sexual activity, homicide except in war, and sacrilege; certain diseases, madness above all, were also sometimes viewed in this way, while mythology abounds in instances of extreme pollutions such as *incest, parricide, and cannibalism.

Different pollutions worked in different ways (local rules also varied). We get some indication of the attendant casuistry from, above all, a long code from *Cyrene (*SEG* 9. 72) and the rules of purity attached to certain Coan priesthoods (F. Sokolowski, *Lois sacrées des cités grecques* (1969), nos. 154, 156). To give some illustrations: contact with a dead person of one's own family pollutes for longer than with an unrelated person; a person entering a house of birth becomes polluted, but does not transmit the pollution further; sexual contact only requires purification if it occurs by day...

Pollution has a complicated relation to the sacred. In one sense they are polar opposites: the main practical consequence of (for instance) the pollutions of birth and death was that the persons affected were excluded from temples for a period of days, and *priests and priestesses had to observe special rules of purity. But offenders against the gods became 'consecrated' to them in the sense of being made over to them for punishment; and such negative consecration (which could also be imposed by a human curse) was comparable to a pollution. This is why *agos* and *enagēs*, words that appear to be related to a root †*hag* conveying the idea of sacredness, to some extent overlap in usage with *miasma* and *miaros*, the standard terms for pollution and polluting. In consequence, the boundaries are blurred between the concepts of 'pollution' and of 'divine anger'.

Since some pollutions are natural and inescapable, rules of purity are obviously not simply rules of morality in disguise. But the very dangerous pollutions were those caused by avoidable (if sometimes unintentional) actions such as bloodshed and sacrilege. In theory, one man's crime could through such pollution bring disaster to a whole state. There is a common mythological schema (best seen at the start of *Sophocles, *OT*), whereby pollution causes plague, crop-failure, infertility of women and of animals. Such pollution is fertility reversed, which is why such powers as the Eumenides (Furies) are double-sided, agents of pollution and also givers of fertility (see above all Aeschylus, *Eum.*). Orators often attempted to brand political opponents as polluting demons, the source of the city's misfortunes; and a question actually put to the *oracle of *Zeus at Dodona shows that this conception of the polluting individual was not a mere anachronism in the historical period: 'is it because of a mortal's pollution that we are suffering the storm?' (*SEG* 19. 427).

But pollution is also often envisaged as working more selectively. According to *Antiphon's *Tetralogies*, for instance, murder pollution threatens the victim's kin until they seek vengeance or prosecute, the jurors until they convict. Thus the threat of pollution encourages action to put right the disorder.

Fear of pollution is often said by modern scholars to be absent from the world of Homer; the emergence of such anxieties becomes therefore a defining mark of the succeeding centuries. But it is wrong to interpret pollution beliefs, an ordering device, as primarily a product of fear; and the natural context for, for instance, a doctrine of blood pollution of the type discussed above is a society such as Homer's where legal sanctions are weak. As we have seen, pollution belief is a complex phenomenon, a vehicle for many different concerns: it has no unified origin or history.   R. C. T. P.

Polybius (*c*.200–*c*.118 BC), Greek historian of Rome's rise to Mediterranean dominion and of the world in which that happened. His father, Lycortas of Megalopolis, was a leading figure of the Achaean Confederacy (see GREECE (HISTORY)) in the 180s and, along with Philopoemen, one of the architects of the doomed Achaean attempt to treat with Rome on a basis of equality during those years. Polybius bore Philopoemen's ashes to burial in 182, was appointed in 180 as envoy to Alexandria, and in 170/69 served as Hipparch of the Confederation. After Rome's victory over Perseus, last king of Macedon, at Pydna (168), he was denounced as insufficiently friendly to the Romans by the Achaean politician Callicrates and became one of the thousand prominent Achaeans deported to Rome and subsequently detained without trial in various towns of Italy. Polybius became friend and mentor to *Scipio Aemilianus, was allowed to remain in Rome during his captivity, and formed part of the 'Scipionic Circle'. He probably accompanied Scipio to Spain (151) and to Africa (where he met Masinissa), returning to Italy over the Alps in *Hannibal's footsteps. After the release of the surviving detainees in 150 Polybius witnessed the destruction of *Carthage (146) in Scipio's company and undertook an exploratory voyage in the Atlantic. He helped to usher in the Roman settlement of Greece after the sack of Corinth (146), visited *Alexandria and Sardis (western Asia Minor), and may have been at Numantia (Spain) in 133. He is reported to have died at the age of 82 after falling from a horse.

His minor works—an early encomiastic biography of Philopoemen, a work on tactics, a history of the Numantine war, and a treatise on the habitability of the equatorial region—are all lost. Of his *Histories* a substantial amount survives; he is the only Hellenistic historian of whom a significant amount does remain. Only books 1–5 of the original forty survive intact. After that we are dependent upon excerpts and occasional quotations by other writers. The 'Excerpta Antiqua' are a continuous abridgement of books 1–18 and provide the majority of what remains of books 6–18. For the remainder the main source is the slightly later collection of excerpts, by a number of hands under various headings and from many Greek historians along with Polybius, made for the emperor Constantine VII Porphyrogenitus (AD 912–50). From five books there are no excerpts at all (17, 19, 26, 37, 40); they were presumably lost already. A few quotations from 19, 26, and 37 are found in other authors. Book 34 (devoted to geographical matters) was much referred to, especially by *Strabo; it survives only in quotations. Books 17 and 40 have perished without trace. For the arrangement of what does survive of books 7–39, a matter beset with difficulty, see Walbank, *HCP* 3. 1–62.

Polybius' original purpose was to tell the story of (that is, to describe and explain) Rome's rise to world dominion, to answer the question 'how and by a state with what sort of constitution almost the whole of the known world was conquered and fell under the single rule of the Romans in a space of not quite 53 years' (1. 1. 5; from the beginning of the 140th Olympiad in 220 to the end of the Macedonian monarchy in 167: books 3–30). He was profoundly impressed by this process, both by the simple fact of the end of the monarchy that had dominated the affairs of Greece for almost two centuries and by the way in which the course of events seemed almost calculated to produce the final result. A metaphor of supernatural guidance is often invoked in the form of *tychē* (fortune), which, though sometimes very close to seeming an active, even a vengeful, agent, is never invoked as an explanation of anything. He later extended his purpose to show how the Romans exercised their dominion, how the world under them reacted to it, and how both were affected (books 30–39; book 40 contained a recapitulation and chronological survey). For his task Polybius developed both a structure and a kind of history. Given his theme and his belief that the process at issue was fundamentally unitary, the structure must allow at once for universality and focus. This was made possible by combining chronological and geographical organization in an original way. Vertically, the arrangement is by Olympiads, each Olympiad containing four numbered years; these years were not rigidly fixed but were adapted to the flow of events. Horizontally, the framework is geographical. Within each year there is a fixed progression from west to east: first, events in Italy (with Sicily, Spain, and Africa), then Greece and Macedonia, then Asia, then Egypt. Books 1 and 2 are something apart. They focused primarily on Rome from the first Punic war to 220, providing a background for those little acquainted with the Romans and an explanation of how the Romans could with reason come to develop the aim for universal dominion (*hē tōn holōn epibolē*, I. 3. 6, etc.) that informed their actions after the Hannibalic war.

For the kind of history he wrote Polybius invented the term *pragmatikē historia*, 'pragmatic history'. This kind of inquiry involves study of documents and written memoirs, geographical study (especially autopsy), first-hand knowledge of some events, and the most careful examination of eye-witnesses about the rest. The focus is upon political actions (*hai praxeis hai politikai*, 12. 25e), but the scope of 'political' was for Polybius very wide indeed, as may be inferred from the breadth of his account of the Roman *politeia* in book 6: this embraced military, economic, religious, social, and political institutions and practice. (It also included the formulation of the theory of a tripartite constitution, incorporating elements of monarchy, aristocracy, and democracy, that influenced political thinking for the next two thousand years.) Apprehension of all these was needed in order to describe things properly and, above all, to explain them. For Polybius the historian's primary task was explanation. 'The mere statement of a fact may interest us, but it is when the reason is added that the study of history becomes fruitful: it is the mental transference of similar circumstances to our own that gives us the means of forming presentiments about what is going to happen …' (12. 25b). This resembles *Thucydides (I. 22), as does Polybius' insistence upon true and accurate narration of historical action (both deed and speech), but Polybius goes beyond his predecessor in his insistence upon the element of explanation and beyond everybody in his explicit formulation (3. 6–7) about beginnings (*archai*) and reasons (*aitiai*). (*Prophasis* is reserved for 'pretext'.) Beginnings are actions; actions are preceded by decisions to act; decisions to act are processes involving various elements: a proper explanation, for Polybius, must delineate these processes and identify these various elements. In dealing with the wars that led to Rome's dominion Polybius adheres rigorously to his principles: he aims to explain in a properly multifaceted way rather than to assign responsibility.

Having brought the writing of history to a methodological acme (and having access to Rome and Romans in a way that his Greek predecessors and contemporaries did not), Polybius was regularly critical of past and contemporary historians, often polemically and sometimes excessively, whether for their method or their bias (book 12 is the most concentrated statement about method and what survives of it contains much hostile criticism of *Timaeus). From bias he was himself manifestly not free, whether positive (as for Philopoemen, Scipio Aemilianus, or the Achaean Confederacy as a whole) or negative (as for *Flamininus, the Aetolian Confederacy, many of Rome's opponents and supporters alike, and the lower classes generally). But he was, though of course not neutral, honest, and he was, above all,

concerned about the effect of undisputed dominion upon the society that wielded it and upon those who inhabited the world in which it was wielded. P. S. D.

Pompeii (see ◀Map 3, Bc▶) Archaeologically the best-known Roman city, this port and regional centre in the Sarnus (mod. Sarno) plain of south Campania in Italy, destroyed by the eruption of AD 79, is central to the study of Roman art and domestic life, but surprisingly hard to fit into general accounts of local politics, or economic and social history.

The oldest architecture (fragments from the Doric Temple and the Temple of *Apollo) belongs in the Greek milieu around the Campanian *apoikiai* (colonies: see COLO-NIZATION, GREEK) of the 6th cent. BC: scattered finds suggest links with the *Etruscan cultures of the Archaic and Classical periods, and the wider Mediterranean world. Pompeii appears as a dependent port-settlement of Nuceria in 310 BC (Livy 9. 38. 2–3), and at no earlier point—either in the Greek, Etruscan, or early Samnite (Oscan-speaking) milieux of 6th, 5th, and 4th cents.—does there seem to have been a substantial urban nucleus or an autonomous political community. Even now there has been little stratigraphic excavation, but the early Pompeii appears at present as a village on the lava hill above the sheltered mouth of the river Sarno, with a couple of prominent sanctuaries and a likely role as an anchorage for coasting vessels and a local market.

There have been suggestions of a 6th-cent. enceinte on the line of the later substantial fortifications (enclosing some 63 ha. on the summit of the lava spur, and perhaps, if so early, a refuge-enclosure). Debate continues, but the walls are most probably to be linked with the introduction of new methods and aspirations in such architecture now widely attested among the indigenous populations of south Italy at the end of the 4th cent., and linked with a widespread urbanizing process. The layout of the greater part of the street-plan is probably also of 4th/3rd-cent. date (perhaps in two phases with rather different orientations), though the 9 ha. nucleus of somewhat irregular lanes and small blocks around the forum may reflect earlier circum-stances.

The impetus for the impressive transformation involved in the creation of streets and walls escapes us: otherwise, the basics of Pompeii as we know it are 2nd cent. Campanians were prominent participants in late Hellenistic economic prosperity, and the Oscan culture of this period is of particular interest for its participation—alongside, and blending with, the similar contemporary experience of Rome—in the currents of fashion and display that were found in the eastern Mediterranean. The formation, out of earlier local prototypes, of the distinc-tive 'Pompeian house', belongs in this setting. Benefactors who could afford dwellings like the palatial House of the Faun equipped the city with the larger theatre, the earlier palaestra, and the temple of Isis, the first *baths, the *gymnasium around the Doric temple, the first systemati-

zation of the forum, and the paving of the main streets. This phase undoubtedly saw activity in the harbour district, of which little is still known.

On this flourishing community, *Sulla imposed a *colonia* of Roman veterans, led by his nephew, as a penalty for siding with the enemy in the Social War of 91–89 BC (during which he had himself laid siege to Pompeii). See COLONIZATION, ROMAN. Latin subsequently replaced Oscan (completing a process that had been at work for some time) in the town's inscriptions, and the *meddix tuticus* (an Oscan magistracy) was replaced by aediles. The new community continued the tradition of architectural benefaction with important monuments: the amphitheatre, the covered theatre, the temple of Jupiter which formed the main feature of the forum. Further important houses date from this period (like that of the Silver Wedding), as do the first monumental tombs of the inner suburbs and the first villas of the territory (*Cicero was one proprietor).

Yet another phase of public building marked the city's response to the initiatives and ideologies of the new Augustan regime. Important monumental complexes like the Macellum or the Porticus of Eumachia (which echoes themes in contemporary architecture in the capital) were added to the forum; the Great Palaestra was built alongside the amphitheatre, and the larger theatre remodelled.

The sudden destruction crystallized a problematic moment: the damage of the earthquake of 62 was still being patchily repaired and the opulence and modishness of some private and public projects of the last phase (the temple of the town's patron Venus and the 'central' baths were both ambitious in scale) contrast with chaos and squalor. The centre of gravity of Campania was shifting towards Puteoli (Pozzuoli), and servicing the luxury villas had perhaps become the town's principal activity. But the painted inscriptions of the walls attest vigorous political life, and the removal of decorative and documentary material from the easily identified public zones in the immediate aftermath of the eruption may have skewed the evidence towards the private sphere. Most important, earlier phases might have looked like this too, if they had been interrupted: the constant disruptions of rebuilding and social discontinuity, and the enormous complexity of the social history of a community like this, are among Pompeii's most important lessons.

Neither the composition by place of origin nor the total size of the population is easily established, though the inscriptions attest frequent links by family-name (implying blood-ties or manumission-relationships) with other cities of the area. Local contacts also included rivalry over spectacles (vividly illuminated by the slogans and notices painted on the walls), like that with Nuceria which caused a major riot in AD 59, untypically attracting attention from Rome (Tac. *Ann.* 14, 17), and the economic relations which stemmed from the city's important function as a port (for Nola, Nuceria, and Acerrae, Strabo 5. 4. 8). The city was the centre of a vigorous and varied cash-crop agriculture (an export *wine of middling reputation was of some

importance); excavation has revealed the intensiveness of cultivation on small garden-lots even within the walls. See GARDENS. The territory had been *centuriated at an uncertain date. The processing of agricultural produce is visible in many small commercial premises, but the extent and economic standing of activities such as textile-manufacture remain controversial. Any assessment of Roman Pompeii must take into account the wealth of Campania, its dense network of overseas contacts (which are reflected in many aspects of the life of the city, especially its religion), and the investment in the area that derived from its popularity as a resort.

The site (only haphazardly reoccupied in antiquity) was first rediscovered in 1748, rapidly acquiring a sensational fame. Systematic recording began in 1861; the new excavations of the 1950s set a new standard; contemporary work today concentrates more on recording, conservation, and analysis, since the discoveries of the first excavators have often decayed irreparably. Some four-fifths of the walled area have been disinterred.   N. P.

Pompey (Gnaeus Pompeius Magnus), b. 106 BC (the official *cognomen* or surname 'Magnus', meaning 'the Great', in imitation of *Alexander the Great, was assumed after 81 BC). He served with his father Gnaeus Pompeius Strabo at Asculum (89) and brought a private army of three legions from his father's veterans and clients in Picenum to win victories for *Sulla in 83. He was then sent *pro praetore* (as a magistrate substituting for a praetor) to Sicily, where he defeated and killed Gnaeus Papirius Carbo, and from there to Africa, where he destroyed Gnaeus Domitius Ahenobarbus and King Iarbas. Though Pompey was still an *eques* (see EQUITES), Sulla grudgingly allowed him to triumph (12 March 81); and in 80, after the death of his wife Aemilia, Sulla's stepdaughter, he married Mucia Tertia, a close connection of the Metellan family. He supported Marcus Aemilius Lepidus for the consulship of 78, for which Sulla cut him out of his will, but assisted Quintus Lutatius Catulus to overcome Lepidus next year. Later in 77 he was sent *pro consule* (i.e. as a magistrate substituting for a *consul) to reinforce Quintus Caecilius Metellus Pius against *Sertorius in Spain. Thence he returned in 71 and attempted to steal from *Crassus the credit for finishing off the Slave War. He was rewarded with a second *triumph and as his first magistracy, despite his youth, the consulship of 70, with Crassus as his colleague. They restored the legislative powers which Sulla had removed from the tribunes; and Lucius Aurelius Cotta reversed another of Sulla's arrangements by ending the senate's monopoly of representation on the courts: judges were now to be drawn equally from senators, *equites*, and *tribuni aerarii* (a group similar to the *equites*).

Pompey took no consular province. But in 67 the Gabinian law empowered him to deal with *piracy. The command, for three years, covered the whole Mediterranean, and gave him unprecedented powers; but Pompey's campaign required only three months. In 66 a

---

Pompeii (previous page) The forum at Pompeii, with Vesuvius in the background. This multi-functional open space, the focal point of most Roman towns in the west, was surrounded by a variety of public buildings, including temples, speakers' platforms, and senate-house, as well as taverns.

law of the tribune Gaius Manilius gave him the Asiatic provinces of Cilicia, Bithynia, and Pontus, earlier held by Lucius Licinius Lucullus, and the conduct of the war against *Mithradates VI. Pompey's eastern campaigns were his greatest achievement. Mithradates was defeated immediately, and though attempts to pursue him over the Caucasus failed, he committed suicide in the Crimea in 63. Pompey founded colonies, annexed *Syria, settled Judaea, and laid the foundation of subsequent Roman organization of the East (though he reached no agreement with Parthia).

In 62 he returned, disbanded his army, and triumphed, no longer a *popularis* (popular politician) as hitherto (for the new role, Cic. *Att.* 2. 1. 6). He made two requests: land for his veterans, and ratification of his eastern arrangements. But he had divorced Mucia for adultery, allegedly with *Caesar; and the Metelli, aided by Lucullus and *Cato the Younger, frustrated him until in 60 Caesar succeeded in reconciling him with Crassus. In 59 the three men formed a coalition and Pompey married Caesar's daughter Julia. His demands were satisfied by Caesar as consul; but his popularity waned, and in 58/7 P. *Clodius Pulcher flouted and attacked him. In 57, after securing *Cicero's return from exile, he received control of the corn-supply for five years with proconsular *imperium* and fifteen legates. But no army was attached, nor could he secure the commission to restore Ptolemy XII Auletes (father of *Cleopatra VII) in Egypt. In April 56 the coalition with Caesar and Crassus was renewed at Luca (mod. Lucca). Pompey became consul with Crassus for 55, and received both Spanish provinces for five years; he governed them through legates, staying in the suburbs of Rome. After Julia's death in 54 he declined a further marriage alliance with Caesar, and the death of Crassus in 53 increased the tension between Caesar and Pompey. In 52 after Clodius' murder Pompey was appointed sole consul, with backing even from Cato. Pompey's immediate actions—the trial of Titus Annius Milo and his legislation on violence, on *bribery, and on the tenure of *magistracies—were not necessarily intended specifically to injure Caesar, but the prolongation of his *imperium* for five years from this date destroyed the balance of power, and he took as his colleague Quintus Caecilius Metellus Pius Scipio, whose daughter Cornelia he married about the time that he became consul. At first he resisted attempts to recall Caesar, but his desire to pose as the arbiter of Caesar's fate was challenged in 50 by Gaius Scribonius Curio, who insisted that both or neither should lay down their commands. Unable to accept the implications of parity, Pompey conditionally accepted from the consul Gaius Claudius Marcellus the command of the republic's forces in Italy. In 49 he transported his army from Brundisium to Greece and spent the year mobilizing in *Macedonia. He met Caesar on the latter's arrival in 48 with a force powerful in every arm, and inflicted a serious reverse when Caesar attempted to blockade him in Dyrrachium. But later (9 August), perhaps under pressure from his senatorial friends, he joined in a pitched battle at Pharsalus, and was heavily defeated. He fled to Egypt, but was stabbed to death as he landed (28 September 48).

The violence and unconstitutional character of Pompey's early career invite comparison with *Augustus whose constitutional position his powers often prefigured: in 67 he had 15 (or even 24) legates; from 55 he governed Spain through legates, and while doing so was made consul in 52. But still more significant was his wealth and his unofficial power: by 62 in Spain, Gaul, Africa and the east, and parts of Italy, there were colonists and clients bound to him by the relationship of *fides* (loyalty) and surrounding him with a magnificence unsurpassed by a Roman senator hitherto; the climax was reached with the dedication of his theatre in Rome's Campus Martius in 55. His military talents are hard to evaluate. Other commanders—Metellus, Crassus, Lucullus—often paved the way to his successes, and at Pharsalus he clearly panicked. Logistics seem to have been his strong point, as in the campaign against the pirates. But in politics he showed a mastery which it was easy for clever men to underrate (e.g., for all its brilliance, the epigram of Marcus Caelius Rufus in Cic. *Fam.* 8. 1. 3: 'he is apt to say one thing and think another, but is not clever enough to keep his real aims from showing'). 'Moderate in everything but in seeking domination' (Sallust, *Histories* 2. 14), by superb skill and timing he rose from his lawless beginnings to a constitutional preeminence in which he could discard the use of naked force. His aim was predominance, but not at the expense of at least the appearance of popularity. He did not wish to overthrow the republican constitution, but was content if its rules were bent almost but not quite to breaking-point to accommodate his extraordinary eminence. His private life was virtually blameless, and two women, Julia and Cornelia, married to him for dynastic ends, became deeply attached to him, and his love for Julia was noted by contemporaries. Cicero, though he never understood Pompey's subtleties, remained a devoted admirer; and despite the disappointments of the war years Pompey's death brought from him a muted but moving tribute: 'I knew him to be a man of good character, clean life, and serious principle' (*Att.* 11. 6. 5). G. E. F. C.; R. J. S.

population, Greek The demography of Greece is a very difficult subject to investigate because of the shortage of statistical data. The Greeks did not have the modern concept of 'population' as a breeding group. Ancient authors did not write any books about demography and give hardly any figures for population sizes. Owing to the stress on war in historiography most estimates relate to the size of military forces or to the manpower available for military purposes, i.e. adult males only. Extrapolations must be attempted from such information to total population sizes because women, children, and slaves were usually not enumerated at all. The Greeks had a very poor grasp of numbers and were prone to exaggeration, for example in relation to the size of Persian armies.

*Thucydides was a notable exception to this rule. Even in Classical Athens it seems unlikely that there was a central register of hoplites (citizen-infantrymen), in addition to the deme registers. Greek states did not have taxes payable by all inhabitants that would have required the maintenance of records for financial purposes. Censuses of citizens were rare in the ancient Greek world.

Estimates of ancient population sizes inevitably involve a lot of guesswork. It is often necessary to use estimates of carrying capacity based on land areas, soil fertility, etc. The assumptions underlying such estimates are usually controversial. Intensive archaeological field surveys are yielding information about changes in settlement patterns in ancient Greece, which are probably connected to population fluctuations. The general pattern is of a thinly populated landscape in the 11th–10th cents. BC, followed by substantial population growth in most areas from the 9th cent. BC, suggesting that *colonization from the eighth century BC onwards was at least partly a product of population growth. A peak was reached in the fifth to the third centuries BC. The period of colonization after *Alexander the Great (see COLONIZATION, HELLENISTIC) was at least partly a consequence of population increase. There was a substantial decline in the last two centuries BC, which continued into the early Roman empire. There were many local variations on this broad pattern in all periods. However it is very striking that the inference drawn from the field surveys, namely that Greece was more densely populated in the classical period than at any time before or since until the late 19th cent. AD, correlates with the fact that even the lowest estimates of the size of the population of Classical Greece made by modern scholars, on the basis of the fragmentary literary sources, are substantially higher than figures derived from census data for parts of late medieval and early modern Greece. The total population in the 4th cent. BC may have been about two million people.

Demography is not just a matter of population size. It is also concerned with the age-structure of populations, which is determined principally by fertility rates and also by mortality rates. Fertility and mortality rates are determined by many factors, especially average age of marriage for fertility, and disease patterns for mortality. There is as little information for vital rates in ancient Greece as for population size.

Excavations of cemeteries suggest a high level of infant and early child mortality in Classical Greece (c.30 per cent at Olynthus in northern Greece). Physical anthropologists attempt to determine the age of death of ancient skeletons. However their methods suffer from various sources of uncertainty, especially in relation to the age of death of adults. Individuals who survived infancy and early childhood (i.e. survived weaning) may have had a reasonable chance of reaching old age. Moreover conclusions drawn from cemeteries about populations, rather than individuals, are often controversial because it is not certain whether the individuals buried there were a representative sample of the whole population. Scholars are suspicious of ages given in literary sources because there were no birth or death certificates. The Greeks in the Classical period seldom recorded ages or causes of death on tombstones.

There is even less evidence for fertility rates than for mortality rates. However, fertility levels were almost certainly much higher than in modern advanced countries. In the context of high infant mortality (see CHILDBIRTH) parents needed several children to ensure that some reached adulthood, to provide an heir to the estate, support for the parents in old age, and additional farm labour. These considerations are also important motives for high fertility in developing countries today. Each adult woman would have had to give birth four or five times to reproduce the population. There is very little evidence for average age of marriage, particularly for women, which is the most important factor influencing fertility levels. There were no marriage certificates. A few passages in literary sources suggest a pattern of late marriage for men (around the age of 30) and early marriage for women (mid- to late-teens). Early marriage for women made very high fertility rates possible. Consequently family limitation measures such as infanticide or *abortion may have been practised in some social classes, regions, or periods. Marriage patterns are themselves influenced by the nature of the economic system, social structure, and even conceivably by political organization.

Apart from calculations based on land areas, and scattered references to army strengths, the main body of information comes from *Athens, especially for the 4th cent. BC. Such promising contemporary epigraphic sources as lists of *ephēboi* (two age-classes of young men undergoing paramilitary training), *bouleutai* (councillors) and *diaitētai* (an age-class of elderly men serving as arbitrators) are usually fragmentary. It is unclear whether these groups were recruited from the entire adult male citizen body or only from the hoplite and upper classes. At Athens every boy at 18 was registered in his father's deme. The total of deme registers formed the list of those entitled to attend the assembly, and the basis of lists of *zeugitai* (the third *Solonian property class) liable to hoplite service and *thētes* (the fourth and lowest property class) liable to service in the Athenian navy. Unfortunately the registers of the demes (constitutional sub-units) were not inscribed on stone. Other methods for calculating population size are hardly any more promising: cereal production (the one extant figure may well refer to a year of drought); cereal imports (one estimate made in a year of drought, which may in any case total the imports for several years). Boys and girls were enrolled in their phratries (kinship groups); but there were no other records of citizen women. *Metics were required to pay a tax and were registered in their deme of residence. The biggest source of uncertainty is the number of slaves (see SLAVERY).

For Classical Athens only one census is recorded, namely that carried out by the Macedonian governor Demetrius of Phaleron in the late 4th cent. BC. According to information preserved by Athenaeus (6. 272c) this census enumerated 21,000 citizens, 10,000 metics, and 400,000 slaves. The number of citizens seems plausible, but it is uncertain whether it includes all citizens or merely those liable and fit for hoplite service. The number of metics is the only preserved figure for this status-group, whose numbers probably varied in accordance with the prosperity of Athens. The number of slaves is incredible, as are similar figures for slaves in Corinth and Aegina. Attempts have been made to emend the text, but it is more likely that these figures for slaves were simply invented. Nevertheless there were probably considerably more slaves in the 5th cent. BC, at the time of the Athenian empire (see DELIAN LEAGUE), than there had been earlier. *Herodotus (5. 97. 2) suggests that there were about 30,000 Athenian citizens in the early 5th cent. BC. This stock figure for the number of citizens was frequently repeated: the citizen body probably did not significantly exceed it during the 4th cent. BC. Multiplication by four to account for women and children indicates a total (citizen) population of around 120,000 then. There is no evidence that the sex-ratio diverged significantly from parity. Evidence for the size of Athenian military forces during the 5th-cent. empire suggests that by c.450 BC there were at least 50,000, or possibly even 60,000, citizens, revealing a substantial increase since the early 5th cent. BC. This level was maintained until the beginning of the Peloponnesian War. According to Thucydides (2. 14) most Athenians still lived in the countryside then, rather than in Athens. During the war the citizen population gradually declined, first because of the great '*plague', and second because of heavy casualties in battle, especially during the Syracusan expedition (415–413).

*Sparta suffered from a serious problem of manpower shortage, which *Aristotle (Politics 1270ª29–34) identified as the reason for her downfall. Herodotus (7. 234. 2; 9. 10. 1) states that Sparta had 8,000 potential soldiers in 480 BC, and 5,000 actually took part in the battle of Plataea in 479 BC. By Aristotle's time Sparta probably had fewer than 1,000 citizens. There is much debate about the causes of this decline. Such diverse factors as the structure of Spartan society, casualties in war, inheritance patterns, and the *earthquake of c.464 BC have been invoked to explain it. In any case, it is clear that the Spartan citizen body was only a small fraction of the total population of the region of Laconia and, before 371 BC, Messenia. Field-survey data suggest that these parts of the *Peloponnese were as densely populated in the 4th cent. BC as the rest of Greece.

There is even less evidence for other parts of Greece. Judging by evidence for military strengths, Argos and Boeotia had citizen bodies not dissimilar in size to that of Athens in the 4th cent. BC, but probably had fewer resident aliens and slaves. Corinth's population was at most half the size of the Athenian population. The mountainous country of Arcadia produced many emigrants. However, migration occurred on a substantial scale from most regions of Greece from the Dark Age until well into the Hellenistic period, resulting in the foundation of many colonies abroad. The Greek colonies in *Sicily and Italy were particularly prosperous. The population of *Syracuse may have exceeded in size all the states of mainland Greece, including Athens. Several other colonies in these areas, such as Acragas and Tarentum, probably also surpassed virtually all states in mainland Greece in respect of population size, although there is little detailed information available.

J. R. S.

population, Roman There are two different kinds of questions which historians might wish to ask about the population of the Roman world: how large was it or any of its constituent parts? and what were the patterns and tendencies of such things as birth rates and death rates? Four kinds of information are available to offer imperfect answers to the first question: census figures, mostly but not exclusively, for the Roman republic and early empire, where they served for the levy and, originally, taxation; figures relating to the feeding of (part of) the population of the city of Rome; occasional references to the population of particular cities or areas, usually without any possibility of knowing on what they were based; and figures for the carrying capacity of different areas of the Roman world in the earliest periods for which reasonably reliable figures exist. The first to collect such material systematically was K. J. Beloch (Die Bevölkerung der griechisch-römischen Welt (1886)) and it is with him that serious study of the population of the Roman world begins. Almost no information is available for the second question; and one has to try to find the best fit of such scraps as there are with the model life tables compiled in the modern period for a variety of populations at different stages of economic development.

As far as the Roman census figures are concerned, they purport to give the adult male population from the early republic to the early empire. Leaving aside the problem of the reliability of the early figures, some scholars have argued that they give for the republic only the adult male population above the property qualification for military service, excluding proletarii (poor citizens exempt from serving). If the figures really were only of those eligible, however, it would be hard to see why the Romans ever had problems of recruitment to the legions. On the other hand, it has also been argued that the rise in the total under Augustus is so large that it can only be explained on the assumption that the figures now included women and children, probably over the age of one:

70/69 BC	910,000
28 BC	4,063,000

This view is principally associated with the name of P. A. Brunt (Italian Manpower (2nd edn. 1987)). It is by no means universally accepted; and the alternative view argues that the difference is to be explained by the enfranchisement of the Transpadanes (see GAUL, CISALPINE) in 49 BC and by the greater efficiency of registration. In any case, the figure of 4,063,000 will have included large numbers of Romans living overseas and comparisons with guesses as to the total (male) population of Italy in any earlier period are hazardous. Similarly, we cannot know how far rises in numbers after *Augustus are due to manumissions of slaves (see SLAVERY) and enfranchisements of provincials (see CITIZENSHIP, ROMAN).

There will always have been some under-registration in the census, probably substantial after *tributum* ceased to be collected after 167 BC. The rise in numbers between 131 and 125 BC is probably to be related to the *Lex agraria* of Tiberius *Gracchus; but it is not clear whether it is due to recipients of plots of land bothering to register for the first time or to men registering in order to prove their eligibility. The relatively low rise in 86 BC, after the enfranchisement of peninsular Italy in 90 is probably to be explained by the difficulty of conditions in the aftermath of the Social War of 91–89 BC.

All arguments about trends are made difficult by uncertainty over the scale of losses due to war casualties and the removal of Roman citizens to Latin colonies (see COLONIZATION, ROMAN), and of additions to citizen numbers through the manumission of slaves and the incorporation of new citizens from other communities.

The conventional view of Rome is that in the imperial period it had a total population of about 1 million; but it seems not to have been widely noticed that a fragment of *Livy, quoted in a scholium (ancient commentary) on *Lucan 1. 319, implies that this figure had already been reached when *Pompey was *curator annonae* (see FOOD SUPPLY) in 57 BC.

Figures exist for a number of other cities, plausibly attesting that *Alexandria, *Carthage, *Antioch, *Pergamum, *Ephesus, Apamea in *Syria, and Lyons (Lugdunum) had free populations in the range 300,000 to 100,000, probably including the free inhabitants of their *chora* or territory. The numbers of slaves to be added to these figures are obviously uncertain, though the 2nd-cent. physician Galen implies that there were as many slaves in Pergamum as free male inhabitants. (Attempts to estimate size of cities from carrying capacity of *aqueducts are hopelessly flawed: many cities never had aqueducts at all and relied on cisterns; aqueducts therefore form an unknowable part of the total water supply.)

For the total population of the Roman empire, Beloch estimated about 54 million at the death of Augustus; it is a plausible guess and compatible with the figure of 7.5 million reported for Egypt, excluding Alexandria. The total may have risen slightly thereafter, declining with the series of *plagues which begin in the 160s AD and culminate in that under Justinian (6th cent. AD).

When we turn to patterns and tendencies in the population as a whole, the best guess is that the population of the Roman world was relatively stable, both in size and in structure, with a high birth-rate and a high death-rate, particularly in infancy. Some confirmation for the use of model life tables as parallels comes from the small number of declarations of death which survive from Egypt, and a few other documents. It should by now be clear that ages of death recorded on tombstones are wholly worthless as

demographic evidence; the surviving evidence is hopelessly skewed by underlying differences in who was commemorated and who was not.

The existence of the *ius (trium) liberorum* (privileges for parents of three children) obviously indicates that three surviving children was regarded as an attainable goal. There is very limited evidence for the sex-ratio at birth or for the scale of infanticide, let alone specifically female infanticide.   M. H. C.

pornography has been defined as material which presents people—particularly women—as mute, available, and subordinate sexual objects, often shown in a context of violence. In its most extreme form, pornography theory argues that all representation produced by men in patriarchal societies is, by very definition, pornographic. In antiquity the rare term *pornographos* is used in a far more limited sense, to mean a writer about, or a painter of, whores (see PROSTITUTION, SECULAR). It first appears in Athenaeus 13. 567b3–8. The lost Hellenistic erotic handbooks, probably written by men despite being assigned to female authors (e.g. Philaenis) suggest that part of their purpose was to teach women to be whores, presenting themselves as objects for male pleasure. It has been argued that at least some forms of representation from the ancient world should be seen as pornographic in a modern sense. In particular, types of production sometimes read in this way include vase paintings, wall paintings, and oil lamps.

Attic red-figure ware includes scenes of abuse and degradation of women, including some sado-masochism, in which women are typically threatened with a sandal. M. F. Kilmer (*Greek Erotica* (1993)) argues that scenes on pottery are deliberately left open-ended, so that the viewer can decide whether to see a figure as male or female, and can use his or her own preferences in deciding what form of sexual activity will happen next. It is possible to read homosexual images on Athenian vases as more 'romantic' in tone than the heterosexual images.

Erotic wall paintings from cities such as *Pompeii were once used to define buildings as brothels, but it is now clear that erotic wall paintings as exemplars were found on the walls of private houses as well. Roman literary references to such images refer to small painted pictures (Ov. *Tr.* 2; Suet. *Tib.* 43) on the bedroom walls of the Julio-Claudian emperors. Mirror covers and oil lamps also show heterosexual couples in a range of poses.

A further category of ancient material used in a rather different way is *Suetonius' *Lives of the Twelve Caesars*. The erotic scenes here were illustrated in the 18th cent. and these images were then passed off as recently discovered ancient cameos. Some scenes were subsequently used to illustrate privately printed sex manuals—an example of using the Classical past as pornography. See HETEROSEXUALITY; HOMOSEXUALITY; PAINTING; SEXUALITY.   H. K.

portraiture, Greek Although archaic gravestones and other sculpture already represented specific individuals,

Greek portraiture proper begins after the Persian invasions of 480. The Tyrannicides were generic representations of men long dead, but the *Themistocles from Ostia (a copy) modifies a pre-existing *Heracles type to make him into a heroic figure (cf. Plut. *Them.* 22. 2). Such 'role' portraiture, whereby standard types were personalized to a greater or lesser degree, was normative during the classical period and into the Hellenistic. Examples (all copies) include *Pericles (*c.*425), *Herodotus, *Thucydides, and *Socrates 'A' (*c.*380), *Xenophon (*c.*350), *Plato (*c.*345), 'Acropolis' *Alexander the Great (*c.*338), *Sophocles (*c.*336), *Aristotle and Socrates 'B' (*c.*320), *Demosthenes (280), *Epicurus (*c.*270), Metrodorus and Hermarchus (*c.*260), and Carneades (*c.*150). Most if not all are Attic. Coiffure, attributes, posture, and gesture helped to locate the subject as belonging to a particular citizen and/or character type within the *polis*.

Though the Athenian sculptor Demetrius of Alopece apparently excelled at specific likenesses, they chiefly appear outside Athens or in other media: good surviving examples are the Porticello 'philosopher' (*c.*400) and an engraved *gem by Dexamenus (*c.*430). Portraits of barbarians, outside the *polis* and its social and characterological norms, also tend to be quite specific: compare the 'Mausolus' from the *Mausoleum and the coins of the early 4th-cent. Lycian and other dynasts.

Alexander's conquests both revolutionized the genre of ruler-portraiture and stimulated a massive demand for portraits at all levels. His preferred sculptor Lysippus idealized his features and blended them with a version of the nude Doryphoros ('spear-bearer') of Polyclitus in order to show him as a latter-day *Achilles, while the court-painter Apelles represented him as a *Zeus on earth, complete with thunderbolt (Plut. *Mor.* 335a f. 360d; *Alex.* 4). They and others also first portrayed the ruler in narrative situations (hunts, battles, processions), and with gods and personifications. Alexander's successors eagerly followed suit, choosing the diadem or head-ribbon (which he had assumed in 330) as their royal symbol. Whether equestrian, armoured, cloaked, or nude; striding, standing, or seated; spear-bearing or with trident, sceptre, or cornucopia; or wearing solar crown, winged *petasos*, panther-scalp, elephant-scalp, or horns, their statues, pictures, coins, and gems represented them as charismatic and often semi-divine rulers in their own right. While most are idealized, this seldom obscures their individuality, for easy recognition is one of their prime aims; indeed, some Bactrian (see BACTRIA) and Asian rulers opted for a no-nonsense realism as an alternative, attention-getting, device.

After Alexander, portraiture became the central Hellenistic art form. While the old categories continue, and bourgeois portraits are mostly conventional, others are markedly original. Most striking are the sharp-featured Menander (*c.*290), the aged Chrysippus (*c.*200), the bronze 'Worried Man' from *Delos (*c.*100), and some inspired 'baroque' portraits: the Antisthenes (*c.*200), the 'pseudo-Seneca' (*c.*150; perhaps *Hesiod), and the Homer IV (*c.*150).

Portraits of Romans conformed both to traditional Greek attitudes about barbarians and the sitters' own tastes: examples range from the aquiline, impetuous *Flamininus (after 197; cf. Plut. *Flam.* 1. 1) to the hard-boiled Italian merchants who settled on Delos between 166 and 88. Athletes represent the opposite pole: surviving examples suggest hardly any individualization in the majority of cases. See PORTRAITURE, ROMAN.   A. F. S.

portraiture, Roman Roman portraiture is especially noted for its verism, the meticulous recording of facial characteristics including such unflattering features as wrinkles, warts, and moles. The origins of the veristic style remain obscure, but republican customs suggest that portraits were used by the Romans to exemplify noble behaviour. *Polybius (6. 53) records the practice at the funeral processions of great men of dressing young men of the family in the clothes and death masks of those distinguished ancestors whom they most resembled; he and *Pliny the Elder describe the ancestral portraits kept in genealogical order in noble houses together with a written record of the achievements of the dead. The right to keep and display such portraits (*imagines*) was restricted to the nobility and to the families of serving magistrates.

Most surviving republican Roman portraits date to the 1st cent. BC, when the ancestral portrait was used in the competitive environment of the intense struggle for political leadership in the late republic. Some aspiring political and military leaders adopted the fashions of Hellenistic court portraiture (see PHILHELLENISM), but *Caesar favoured the veristic style, discrediting its republican origins by becoming the first Roman to have his own portrait on coins minted during his lifetime, and permitting his images to be carried on litters and set up on sacred platforms. *Augustus developed an idealized image drawn from the repertoire of Classical Greece, but recognizably Roman in its often modest presentation. From the beginning of Empire, men and women copied court portraiture from images of the emperor and his family on coins and statues intended for wide use and public view at Rome and in the provinces. The veristic style continued to be used by some nobles, but was also adopted by *freedmen who wished to celebrate the right of their families to Roman citizenship following legislation passed under Augustus; in the conventionalized portraits of freedmen and their families it is difficult to trace the documentation of individual features that was so marked a feature of republican portraiture of the aristocracy. Verism is also marked in the portraiture of emperors of modest origin such as *Vespasian and some of the 3rd-cent. emperors.

The Julio-Claudian emperors and their successors were mostly clean-shaven, though *Nero and *Domitian were occasionally portrayed bearded. It is likely that his beard, comparable to that of *Pericles, expressed *Hadrian's commitment to Greek culture. During his reign women adopted the simple bun worn high on the crown, a revival of Hellenistic Greek fashion and a striking contrast to the elaborate tiered coiffures fashionable from the time of Nero to that of Trajan. Hadrian's adoption of the beard and the contemporary innovation of engraving the pupil and iris of the eye influenced subsequent imperial and private portraiture. Among beards there were idiosyncratic variations: Marcus *Aurelius wore the long beard of the philosopher, and *Septimius Severus the forked beard marking his interest in the cult of the Graeco-Egyptian god Sarapis. The soldier-emperors and tetrarchs of the later 3rd cent. were ill-shaven rather than bearded, with close-cropped hair; Gallienus (253–268), in contrast, presented an image of Hadrianic refinement. The clean-shaven portrait was revived by *Constantine I and his successors. Commemorative and funerary portraits were introduced to many regions under the empire, and proved an influential form of individual commemoration. Portraits, whether of imperial or private subjects, were made in a wide variety of media including silver, bronze, stone, terracotta, glass, mosaic, ivory, bone, and painted wood. Of the last the most striking examples are the mummy portraits made in the Fayûm (Egypt), the only naturalistically coloured portraits to survive from antiquity (see PAINTING, ROMAN). Many of these seem to represent individuals as they appeared in life; some present a type still current in north-east Africa. These and the limestone funerary reliefs of *Palmyra (Syria) offer the best surviving evidence for the wearing of *dress and jewellery.

Roman portrait busts may be dated not only by their relationship to the fashions of the imperial court, but by changes in the shape and size of the bust, which by Flavian times had enlarged from head and neck to incorporate the shoulders, and in the early third century grew to a half-length figure, after which it shrank again. See ART, FUNERARY, ROMAN.   F. N. P.; J. M. C. T.; S. E. C. W.

Poseidon 'All men call Poseidon god of the sea, of *earthquakes, and of horses', wrote *Pausanias (7. 21. 7) in the 2nd cent. AD, describing the three principal aspects of one of the most widely, and anciently, worshipped of the Greek gods. Pausanias' term for god of the sea, *pelagaios*, is descriptive, not cultic, but his epithets for the earthquake god, Asphalcios, 'He who keeps things steady', and god of horses, Hippios, were common cult titles. In the form Posedaon (= *Poseidaōn*, as in epic poetry) he is attested on *Mycenaean tablets from the palace archives at Cnossus on Crete and at Pylos in Messenia, where there are more references to him than to any other divinity; he has a sanctuary (Posidaion) and Posidawes (cult personnel?), while a female figure, Posideia, owes her name to him. His local importance at Pylos is reflected in *Homer's *Odyssey* (3. 4–8, Nestor and nine groups of 500 Pylians sacrifice nine black bulls to the god on the seashore) and in later traditions of the Neleids in Athens and Ionia, who claimed descent from Pylian kings (see PISISTRATUS). According to Homer, in a division of realms, *Zeus received the sky, Poseidon the sea, and *Hades the underworld, while all three shared Mt. Olympus and earth. He is a powerful figure, resistant to pressure from his brother Zeus while acknowledging the latter's seniority (15. 184–99); this is in contrast to the story of Zeus being the last child of Cronus and Rhea (Hes. *Theog.* 454–506, and often later). In Homer he is largely the god of the sea, aside from the implications of earthquake in the epithets *enosichthon*, *ennosigaios* ('earth-skaker'). He causes storms and calms the waters; his wife is Amphitrite, a sea-creature. Poseidon supports the Greeks in the Trojan War (see TROY), but is hostile to *Odysseus, the supreme seafarer. Eventually Odysseus will establish the god's cult far from the sea where an oar is mistaken for a winnowing fan (*Od.* 11. 119–34).

Poseidon begets various monstrous figures such as Odysseus' enemies the Cyclopes. He is not associated, in myth or cult, with civic institutions. The violence of natural phenomena, sea and earthquake, are central to the Greek conception of him. In art he is always a grave, mature male, indistinguishable from Zeus when not accompanied by attributes.

Numerous sanctuaries of the god on coastal sites, such as the 5th-cent. BC marble temple on the promontory of Sunium in Attica, where quadrennial boat races were held in his honour, and the oracular shrine at Taenarum in Laconia which boasted a passage to the underworld, show that his ties to the sea were also prominent in cult, as do the dedications of sailors and fishermen. Many coastal settlements were named after him.

But there were also important cult places inland where clefts in rocks, pools, streams and springs (cf. Aesch. *Sept.* 308–11) were signs of his activity. Heliconius, his title as common god of the Ionian Greeks at the Panionium near Mycale (western Asia Minor), and similar epithets on the Greek mainland (cf. also Mt. Helicon in Boeotia with its spring Hippocrene), may refer to the blackness of deep waters. A concern with fertility is seen in the worship of Poseidon Phytalmios ('of plants') which was said to be almost universal among the Greeks (Plut. *Mor.* 675 f). This aspect of the god may have stemmed from his association with fresh waters and lightning, for which the trident was an instrument. There is, however, in general an emphasis on masculinity and potency in his myths and cults (so stallions, bulls, and uncastrated sheep are sacrificial victims, cf. *Syll.*[3] 1024 from Myconos).

Mating with grim figures (a single Erinys ('Fury') in Boeotia, Schol. *Il.* 23. 347, with *Demeter Erinys at Arcadian Telphusa, she in the form of a mare, he as a stallion, Paus. 8. 25. 4–5), he begets the marvellous horse Arion and, at Telphusa also a daughter with a secret name. Again in Arcadia, at Phigaleia (Paus. 8. 42. 1–2), Black Demeter is represented with a horse's head and her child by Poseidon is Despoina ('Mistress') which is also the public name of the daughter of Demeter and Poseidon Hippios at Arcadian Lycosura (Paus. 8. 37. 9–10). With the Gorgon Medusa he begets Chrysaor and the winged horse Pegasus whose name was connected with the springs (*pēgai*) of Ocean (Hes. *Theog.* 278–83). He had herds of horses in Arcadian Pheneus (Paus. 8. 14. 5–6), and horses were some-

Poseidon View of the Erechtheum *temple on the Acropolis (late 5th cent. BC). It housed a group of Athenian cults, including that of Poseidon Erechtheus. The god's tokens, a salt-water well and the mark of his trident, were displayed inside.

times sacrificed to him (Paus. 8. 7. 2). In his sanctuary at Onchestus in Boeotia a horse with chariot but no driver was allowed to run loose and if the chariot crashed it was dedicated to the god (*Hymn Hom. Ap.* 229–38). This close association with the horse has led to the theory that he was introduced to Greece along with the horse by the speakers of an ancestral form of Greek early in the second millennium BC. Whatever the reasons for the original connection, the aristocratic and non-utilitarian associations of the horse were appropriate for a god often named as the ancestor of aristocratic families.

He was worshipped widely in inland Arcadia and Boeotia ('All Boeotia is sacred to Poseidon', Aristarchus of Samothrace, in *Etym. Magn.* 547. 17) and he had important cults around the Saronic Gulf. In the Archaic period, on the island of Calauria (mod. Poros) off Troezen, his sanctuary was the centre of an amphictiony (cultic league of neighbours) of originally five small *poleis* on the Argolic and Saronic gulfs, together with Athens and Boeotian Orchomenus (Strabo 8. 6. 14; Poseidon's son *Theseus moves in myth, as his cult may have moved historically, from Troezen to Athens). The organization seems to have lapsed in the Classical period but revived briefly in the Hellenistic. The Athenian orator and statesman *Demosthenes killed himself in the sanctuary while fleeing from the Macedonians in 322 BC. Corinth, not a member of the amphictiony, developed the open-air shrine of the god on the Isthmus, dating from the Dark Age, into a major regional and then panhellenic sanctuary with one of the earliest ashlar-built temples (mid-7th cent. BC) and, in the early 6th cent., a biennial festival with *games. It was the seat of the Hellenic League first formed at the time of *Xerxes' invasions and revived more than once by the Macedonian kings. The sanctuary was destroyed by the Romans in 146 BC. and rebuilt by them more than a century later. On the southern tip of Euboea was the sanctuary of Poseidon Geraistius.

In Athens Poseidon was shown contending with *Athena for the patronage of the city in the west pediment of the Parthenon. He bore the epithet Erechtheus while Erechtheus himself (originally a local form of the god?) was regarded as a heroized early king of the city. The same Attic *genos* ('clan') provided the priest of Poseidon Erechtheus and the priestess of Athena Polias (the goddess of the Acropolis). Even so, no major Athenian festival was celebrated in his honour. The annual Posideia, held in the winter month of Posideon, is more likely to have been concerned with his agricultural than his maritime role. His priest, along with the priestess of Athena, also marched to Sciron, west of Athens, the site of a sacred ploughing (Plut. *Mor.* 144b).

The etymology of the name is not certain. The first two syllables seem to contain the Greek word for 'Lord', 'Husband', cf. Sanskrit (*pátī*). *da*, in the second part of his name, may be an alternative form of Ga=Ge, Earth (cf. gaia), for which the Pindaric epithet (see PINDAR) Ennosidas and the first syllable of Damater (Demeter) may provide

support. He would then be 'Husband of Earth' (cf. the epic epithet *gaieochos*, 'holder of the earth'). M. H. J.

postal service The Greek *poleis* communicated by professional messengers (*hemerodromoi*, like Phidippides, on land; there were also messenger-ships), but developed no other general infrastructure for communications. The Assyrian state, however, with its developed and centralized requisitioning system, used relays of mounted couriers. These were the model for the efficient Persian arrangements (e.g. the Royal Road: see ROADS) which were maintained at the expense of local communities. From the first, the carrying of messages, the movement of goods due to the state, and the journeys of the ruler and his representatives were closely linked, and this is the system bequeathed by the Achaemenid *Persian kingdom to the Successors of *Alexander the Great in *Syria and in Egypt, where the Ptolemies (see PTOLEMY I and II) developed it to a high level of complexity and dependability (here the duty to maintain the post was liturgical, i.e. a compulsory service, like military service, though it could be commuted into a tax).

Rome in the republic knew only the essentially private, though quite large scale, networks of messengers (*tabellarii*) maintained by important men, governors, or *publicani* (entitled to requisition in certain circumstances). No doubt most movements of information and materials continued to be organized in this essentially private way: *Augustus' bold introduction (Suet. *Aug.* 49. 3) of a public postal system for the whole empire was modelled rather on the Hellenistic kingdoms, and designed specifically for governmental purposes. The original system (Augustus' experiment made use of long-distance, rather than relay-, messengers called *iuvenes*) and its 1st-cent. development are still relatively little known (our best information derives from legal regulations for the system in the 4th cent.), but its developed form (the so-called *cursus publicus*) was clearly one of the largest-scale administrative initiatives of antiquity. It could only work through a system of local requisitioning of animals, vehicles, and provisions, and the system for arranging this (*vehiculatio*, in Greek *angareia*) rapidly became one of the most burdensome and unpopular forms of state imposition. *Nerva freed Italy from it: a series of measures preserved on inscriptions from different provinces (most recently Galatia in *Asia Minor under Tiberius: S. Mitchell, *JRS* 1976, 106–31) attests the scale of the problem, the level of unrest, the state's concern, and the inefficacy of attempts to reform. The principal check, the limiting of use of the service to those with warrants (*diplomata*) was very prone to abuse, and even *Pliny the Younger defends his use of the system for his wife in a letter to *Trajan (*Ep.* 10, 120). Valid *diplomata* were very valuable documents. The appointment of supervisory officials (*a vehiculis*, later *praefectus vehiculorum*) does not seem to have helped, though the appointment of imperial contractors (*mancipes*, SHA, *Hadrian* 7. 5) relieved local magistrates of burdensome involvement in the running of the system, and various attempts to shift parts of the cost of the system, at least in some places, to the state, are attested.

The system was centred on the posting stations (*mansiones*, originally the larger and most important stations, and *mutationes*) and, naturally on the road network (some visual signalling was used, but with relatively simple content only, cf. Polyb. 10. 45. 6); many of the imperial *maps and itineraries were also probably adjuncts of the *cursus*. Any specialized personnel was military, first *tabellarii*, messengers like those used in the republic, then *speculatores* (scouts), eventually the more secret-agent-like *frumentarii* (lit. 'victuallers', 2nd cent.) and *agentes in rebus* ('agents', 284–305). The existence of this administrative infrastructure invited its use for other state purposes: it rapidly became linked with the wholesale movement of state goods, especially the food-supplies exacted by the development of the *annona* into a tax in kind (see FOOD SUPPLY), for which *Septimius Severus created the *cursus clabularis*, with provision of ox-carts, as opposed to the *cursus velox*; and with troop movements in general.

The government communication network (a better description than 'postal service') was thus potentially very effective (50 miles per day was a not uncommon speed for messages, but the news of the revolt of the Rhine army in 69 travelled to the emperor Galba at the rate of *c*.150 miles per day), and its existence is certainly one of the distinguishing features of the Roman empire. What is more problematic is the question of the density of written communications and their role in day-to-day government: the relationship between potential and actuality remains in need of clarification. N. P.

pottery, Greek

1. General Pottery is a primary source of evidence throughout the Greek period. Pervasive and almost indestructible, its generally predictable development means that it provides a framework to which other arts can be related. The presence of clay in every region fostered local styles, whence trade patterns can be detected. Factors determining origin are clay, shape, and decoration, the latter varying from none (most cookpots, coarsewares, storage amphoras) to the elaborate mythological scenes exemplified by Archaic and Classical Athenian vases (see IMAGERY). Recent advances in clay analysis have further refined provenance studies. Regular inscriptions give names of potters and painters and clues to workshop organization, as do excavations like those in the Athenian Agora, the area of Plato's *Academy, the Potters' Quarter at Corinth, or Figaretto on Corcyra (Corfu). Sir John Beazley (1885–1970) adopted Renaissance attribution methods to reconstruct the careers of many Archaic and Classical Athenian vase-painters, and to gauge master–pupil relations and workshop patterns. The method has been criticized as unduly subjective, but has been extensively applied to Etruscan, S. Italian, Laconian, and Corinthian pottery (D. A. Amyx, *Corinthian Vase-Painting of the Archaic Period* (1988)). Recent trends have moved from attributions towards the social sig-

pottery, Greek Athenian silver-gilt vessel in the form of a winged horse (*c*.450 BC) from the Scythian site of Aul Ulljap, N. of the Caucasus. From time to time, Greek production of fine pottery sought to imitate costly metal vessels, although the strength of this influence is controversial.

nificance of pottery, with renewed interest in factors influencing shapes, imagery, and composition, especially wall-painting (see PAINTING, GREEK). Thus metalwork has been seen as a complete model for Classical vase shapes and decoration, although surviving examples do not permit this conclusion and literary sources are late. The *Corpus Vasorum Antiquorum* (*CVA*) continues publishing vase collections worldwide. Recent advances in computing have facilitated access to extensive archives of Athenian (Oxford) and Corinthian (Amsterdam) vases; computers are now being used for profile and even figure-drawing.

2. Prehistoric During the neolithic period, hand-made burnished wares were characteristic over a wide area (e.g. Cnossus, Saliagos, *Thessaly). The surface is sometimes blackened or reddened and may have relief, incised or impressed decoration (sometimes with white or red paste fill); ripple (MN) and pattern (LN) burnish are especially popular on Crete. On the mainland, painted (abstract linear) designs occur from an early stage; notable are the MN Sesklo (dark-on-light) and LN Dimini (light on dark and bichrome) wares.

In the early bronze age, dark-on-light painted wares with simple geometric designs dominate. On Crete, Ag. Onouphrios and Pyrgos wares (the latter with pattern burnish) were followed by the mottled Vasiliki ware. In the

Cyclades, the Pelos phase (incised ornament) was followed by Syros (stamped and incised) with its characteristic sauceboats and frying pans. Mainland styles were dominated by burnished wares (initially similar to Cycladic). During the middle bronze age (when the fast wheel came into use), matt-painted wares were popular on the Cyclades and the mainland, and dark-on-light was fashionable on Crete. Influences of metalwork are widespread (eg. in mainland grey Minyan ware). During the late bronze age, dark-on-light returned, initially with a naturalistic, Minoan-influenced style (mainly floral and marine subjects), followed by more standard linear decoration uniform over a wide area. Hand-made burnished ware appeared during late LHIIIB, and there was a brief vogue during middle LHIIIC for the elaborate Close, Granary, and Pictorial styles. Thereafter Submycenaean wares were more austerely Geometric (P. A. Mountjoy, *Mycenaean Pottery* (1993)). See MINOAN and MYCENAEAN CIVILIZATION

3. Historic After the austere geometry of Submycenaean, the Protogeometric and Geometric periods (1050–700 BC) saw the addition of new shapes and motifs (notably the meander). From restricted beginnings, decoration came to cover the whole vase in horizontal bands. This period is characterized by local schools, notably Argive and Attic; here the 8th cent. saw the development of figure scenes, including funerary subjects (prothesis and ekphora), chariot processions and battles. From the 8th cent. onwards, it is possible to identify 'hands' such as the Dipylon Master (J. N. Coldstream, *Greek Geometric Pottery* (1968)).

From the late 8th cent. the Geometric style developed into 'Orientalizing', with the addition of motifs including florals and animals (real and fantastic) which replaced Geometric patterns. Although silhouette continued, the black-figure technique (invented in Corinth *c.*720) was most innovative; here lines are incised into a silhouette, with the addition of red and white. The human figure was drawn with increasing naturalism, and mythological representations become complex. The chief 7th-cent. styles are Proto-Corinthian and Proto-Attic; contemporary is the peak of the island and East Greek schools (A. Lemos, *Archaic Pottery of Chios* (1991)). A mid-7th-cent. series of vases of various schools may reflect contemporary free-painting, using such elements as a brown paint for flesh and mass battle scenes (e.g. works of the Corinthian Chigi (MacMillan) Painter).

By 600, black-figure was fully established in Attica (J. D. Beazley, *The Development of Attic Black Figure* (1951/1986); J. Boardman, *Athenian Black-Figure Vases* (1974)), and by soon after 550 Corinth, Athens' main rival, had effectively ceased producing figured wares, continuing with the patterned 'conventionalizing' style. Athenian potters produced a wider range of vases, introducing such shapes as the volute- and kalyx-krater, and a range of cups, such as the Siana, lip, band, and types A and B, which are among the finest of Attic potting. Notable among painters are

Sophilus, the first whose name we know (*c.*580–570), Nearchus (*c.*570–555) and his son Tleson, and the rivals Execias and the Amasis Painter (*c.*560–525). The regular practice of inscribing vases is of inestimable value: the words *epoiesen* and *egrapsen* probably name the potter and painter, although it is possible that the former indicates the workshop owner, often the head of an extended family.

Around 525, the red-figure technique was invented at Athens, possibly by Psiax or the Andocides Painter (perhaps the same man as the black-figure Lysippides Painter) (M. Robertson, *The Art of Vase-Painting in Classical Athens* (1992); J. Boardman, *Athenian Red-Figured Vases: the Archaic Period* (1978), *Athenian Red-Figured Vases: the Classical Period* (1989)). Other innovations of this period include Six's technique, coral or intentional red, and white ground. In red-figure the decoration is left in the clay colour, and the background painted black; inner details are painted with lines of varying thickness. The use of the brush rather than the engraver allowed greater fluidity of drawing. Accessory colours are used sparingly in the 6th cent., white becoming common towards its end. The first generation trained in red-figure (*c.*520–500) Beazley called the Pioneers (e.g. Euphronius, Phintias, Euthymides); they are characterized by adventurous anatomical depictions. Late Archaic vase-painting saw further advances by, for example, the Berlin and Cleophrades Painters (who preferred large vases), and the cup specialists Duris and the Brygus Painter. Black-figure continued in quantity until the end of the Archaic period and, for Panathenaic prize amphorae, until the 2nd cent. BC.

In the early Classical period, some vases of the Niobid Painter and others reflect the free painting recorded in literary sources as current in Athens and elsewhere in the works of such artists as Polygnotus and Micon (*c.*475–450). The later 5th cent. saw the ornate miniaturism of the Meidias Painter (L. Burn, *The Meidias Painter* (1987)) and others, often featuring boudoir scenes. There is a parallel, broader tradition exemplified by the Dinos Painter. White ground, at first mainly on cups, is used in the later 5th cent. for funerary lekythoi, often painted with delicate colours (D. C. Kurtz, *Athenian White Lekythoi* (1975); L. Wehgartner, *Attische Weissgrundige Keramik* (1983)).

4th-cent. vases are characterized by greater use of accessory colours and gilding; red-figure ceased by *c.*320 but although much late work is poor, artists such as the Marsyas and Eleusinian Painters (*c.*350–330) gave unprecedented depth to their figures. In the late 4th cent., fineware production was restricted to cheap clay substitutes for the costly metal vessels which suited Hellenistic taste. Painted decoration was limited to floral scrolls and patterns: both light-on-dark and dark-on-light styles are found, but painted wares are secondary to the new metallic styles in which relief ornament predominates. Moulded reliefs may be added to wheel-made vases or vases may be thrown in a mould (e.g. the particularly widespread Megarian bowls). During the 3rd cent., the black ground colour inherited from Athens was modified in E. Greece into red or bronze, and thence developed terra sigillata, the standardized fine pottery of Roman times.

In Italy, painted wares imitating the contemporary Greek styles appeared from the 8th cent. BC, and by 525 native pottery was largely displaced by Greek (mainly Attic) imports and local copies. Independent schools of pottery in Apulia borrowed painted techniques from Greece, but remained local in style. Red figure production began in S. Italy about 440, perhaps introduced by immigrant Athenian potters. There are five main schools: Apulian, Lucanian, Paestan, Campanian, and Sicilian (A. D. Trendall, *Red Figure Vases of South Italy and Sicily* (1989)). A considerable output of vases, often large and elaborately decorated, continued into the early 3rd cent. Their inspiration was initially Athenian, but they increasingly diverged; their iconography owes much to the theatre, especially the 'phlyax' vases (A. D. Trendall and T. B. L. Webster, *Illustrations of Greek Drama* (1971); O. P. Taplin, *Comic Angels* (1993)). In Gnathian (mid-4th to early 3rd cent.), the pot is painted black and decoration added.

In Hellenistic times, Apulia and Campania were the chief areas of production. Light-on-dark painted ware and vases with applied reliefs were most popular. *Alexandria was the principal source of inspiration, and Italy was long uninfluenced by E. Greek experiments in red glazes and moulded wares; after 30 BC, however, it took the lead with the appearance of Arretine ware.   K. W. A., C. A. M.

pottery, Roman Roman pottery was used for a wider range of purposes than in most periods of prehistory or the Middle Ages, providing a comprehensive range of vessels for table and kitchen functions, and for use in storage and transportation. At the top of the quality scale were vessels with a smooth glossy surface designed for the table, notably the bright red *terra sigillata*, or Samian ware, mass-produced in Italy (Arretine ware) and elsewhere from the 1st cent. BC. Elaborately decorated cups and beakers with coloured surface coatings were used alongside this dinner service, while ornate pottery oil lamps provided light. The majority of Roman pots were plain earthenware vessels designed for everyday household cooking and storage functions. The only really specialized forms were amphorae, containers used for transporting wine and oil, globular *dolia*, employed on farms for storage and fermentation, and *mortaria*, large bowls suitable for grinding and mixing. Many Roman buildings were constructed (wholly or partly) from bricks and roofed with ceramic tiles, while specialized clay elements aided the construction of bath-buildings and vaulted ceilings.

The study of pottery is an essential part of the investigation of sites by excavation, and an important part of Roman 'industrial archaeology'. It reveals details of technology and methods of manufacture, and the analysis of patterns of production and distribution illuminates aspects of society and the economy. Pottery production ranged from a part-time activity that supplemented farming to full-time employment for specialized craft workers. Most

vessels were formed on a potter's wheel and fired in carefully constructed kilns, although some widely distributed kitchen wares were handmade and fired in bonfires. Some industries made ranges of forms, others concentrated on particular categories. Most Roman pottery seems to have been traded, rather than manufactured, for the exclusive consumption of individual households or estates. Distribution patterns of wares varied enormously; Italian *terra sigillata* could be found throughout the empire, whereas unspecialized kitchen wares might only supply a single town and its surrounding region.

Rome conquered areas of Italy that already possessed well-established ceramic traditions—Celtic in the north, Etruscan in central Italy and Greek in the south. In areas north of the Alps, the term 'Roman' may indicate new forms and wares introduced by trade or conquest, in contrast to 'native' pottery of local origin, but the term is best used in its broadest sense, simply to mean pottery of Roman date. The kitchen and storage vessels made in most conquered areas were not markedly different from those of Italy, and they were normally adopted by the invaders once permanent garrison forts had been established. Studies of kiln sites show that some specialized vessel forms, such as flagons, were rapidly added to the repertoire of local potters. However, name-stamps on *terra sigillata*, lamps, and *mortaria* all confirm that some manufacturers either migrated to new provinces or set up branch workshops, presumably to avoid high transport costs involved in supplying distant markets. We are particularly well informed about the diffusion of *terra sigillata* production from Italy to the provinces, for styles of decoration and name-stamps, combined with typological studies of the evolution of plain vessels, allow us to identify production centres that may then be corroborated by scientific analysis of clays.

Roman military units included skilled artisans who frequently established facilities for the manufacture of bricks and rooftiles, commonly stamped the name of their unit or legion. If local pottery supplies were inadequate (e.g. in northern parts of the Rhineland or in northern Britain and Wales) they also turned their hands to potting. Since many soldiers had been recruited in Italy or heavily Romanized provinces, the majority of vessel forms made by military potters are closely comparable to those found in Italy itself, with the addition of some forms that reveal Celtic or other regional influence. Military production tended to be short-lived, for when frontier areas were stabilized, supplies could be brought safely from non-military sources in the hinterland. Alternatively, civilian potters might set up production in a military region in order to take advantage of new markets created by forts and the civilian settlements (*canabae*) which grew up around them.

From the end of the 1st cent. AD, sites around the Mediterranean were increasingly supplied with Red Slip Ware from North *Africa and Asia Minor rather than *terra sigillata* made in Europe. Although sharing common origins, these wares diverged after the 1st cent. AD. In general, recognizably 'Roman' forms and wares still dominated ceramics used around the Mediterranean as late as the 7th cent. AD. K. T. G.

prayer Prayer was the most common form of expression in ancient religion. It could be formal or informal and was often accompanied by other acts of worship, e.g. *sacrifice or vow (the Greek word *euchē* meant both prayer and vow). The earliest instance of an independent formal prayer, namely the prayer of the priest Chryses to *Apollo in *Il.* 1. 37 ff., presents a complete set of the fixed constitutive elements of ancient prayer. These are: (1) *invocation*. The god is addressed with his (cult) name(s), patronymic, habitual residence, functions, and qualities. This part serves both to identify and to glorify the god. (2) The *argument* (in older literature called *pars epica*), consisting of considerations that might persuade a god to help, e.g. a reminder of the praying person's acts of piety, or a reference to the god's earlier benefactions or his natural inclination to help people. This part often expanded into a eulogy with narrative aspects, especially in hymns. (3) The *prayer* proper, the petition. For the great majority of both private and public prayers contain a wish. There is a large variation in 'egoistic' motifs ('Gebetsegoismus'). Drought, epidemics, or hail, for instance, can be prayed away (*apopompē*), but also passed on to enemies or neighbours (*epipompē*). This comes very close to the *curse, which, too, may contain elements of prayer: the term *ara* denoted both prayer and curse. Although feelings of gratitude were not lacking, the prayer of gratitude was extremely rare. It did exist but instead of terms for gratitude (*charis, gratia*) expressions of honour (*timē, epainos, laus*) were generally employed, glorification being the most common expression of gratitude, as in human communication. Private

prayer often lacked these formal aspects, but in public cultic prayer too very simple invocations occurred, as e.g. in the famous Eleusinian prayer (see ELEUSIS): *hue kue* ('rain, conceive' Hippol. *Haer.* 5. 7. 34. 87 Wendland). There were also linguistically meaningless sounds which accompanied certain dances and processions and which could be interpreted as invocations of the god, such as *ololuge, thriambe, euhoi, paian*. They could even develop into the name of a god: the cry *iakche* became the divine name Iacchus.

Although Greek influence is noticeable, especially with respect to the formal aspects, Roman, and generally Italic, prayers (*preces*) distinguished themselves by their elaborate accuracy. Prayers for individual use were often equally formulaic (cf. Cato, *Agr.* 132. 2), but both officially and privately less elaborate prayers occurred as well, e.g. *Mars vigila* ('Mars, wake up', Serv. at *Aen.* 8. 3).

Ancient prayer used to be spoken aloud. Silent or whispered prayer was reserved for offensive, indecent, erotic, or magical uses, but was later adopted as the normal rule in Christian practice. Kneeling down, though not unknown, was unusual, the gesture of entreaty being outstretched arms, with the hands directed to the god invoked (or his cult-statue). H. S. V.

priests (Greek and Roman) Cities in the Graeco-Roman world always had men and women, often of high rank, specially chosen for the service of the gods and goddesses. They might be serving for life or for a fixed term; they might be holding a hereditary position, or be publicly elected or selected by some other method, or the office might (at least in the Greek world) be put up for sale. The offices always carried honour, but often too, especially in later periods, the expectation of high expenditure by the

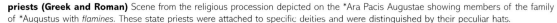

priests (Greek and Roman) Scene from the religious procession depicted on the *Ara Pacis Augustae showing members of the family of *Augustus with *flamines*. These state priests were attached to specific deities and were distinguished by their peculiar hats.

holders. (See EUERGETISM.) The duties varied a great deal, from quite humble service to high authority and power.

Greek and Latin have several terms referring to these positions—*hiereis* and *sacerdotes* are only the most common; in English, 'priest' is used as a generic term for all of them, but implies a potentially misleading unity of conception and an analogy with the roles of priesthood in later religions. Pagan priests did not form a separate group or caste and seldom devoted their whole lives to religious activity; characteristically, they performed their religious duties on special occasions or when required and otherwise continued with the same range of social or political activities as other members of their social groups. Above all, there was no religious community, separate from the civic community, with its own personnel or power-structure. Nor did priests monopolize religious action or communication with the gods and goddesses: fathers of families, leaders of social groups, officials of the city, all had the power of religious action, with priests as advisers or helpers. So far as the city itself was concerned, it might well be the city authorities who took the religious decisions and the magistrates (elected officials), not the priests, who took religious actions on the city's behalf.

To this extent, there was not much difference between the pagan practice of Greece and of Rome; but differences appear on a more detailed examination. Greek cities have female as well as male priests, female for goddesses, male for gods. They do not form priestly groups or colleges, but are attached to particular cults and even to particular temples, sanctuaries, or festivals; there is an alternative pattern where priesthood is carried in families. Priests seldom act as advisers to individuals, who consult ritual experts (*exēgētai*) or diviners. They seem not to have been consulted on religious issues by the state, except the priests of an oracle speaking on behalf of a god or when special purifications or remedies were needed and a religious expert might be brought in.

In Rome on the other hand priests are (with the exception of the Vestal Virgins: see VESTA) males, formed into colleges or brotherhoods. They are not attached to particular deities or temples, but rather to special festivals (as the Luperci to the Lupercalia) or areas of religion (the *augures* to the taking of auspices). The *flamines* are a spectacular exception, perhaps preserving a more archaic and far closer relationship between priest and deity; they therefore provide the model for the priesthood of the emperors after death (the Divi; see RULER-CULT). The most senior colleges were above all expert advisers, consulted by the senate when religious problems were to be dealt with. The *pontifices* are also available to private individuals, in need of advice on the religious law. Their leading member, the *pontifex maximus*, came to be seen as the most prominent and influential of the priests, and, once united by *Augustus with the imperial power, the position—held by all subsequent emperors down to Gratian (367–83)—came to resemble that of a 'High Priest'.

In both Greece and Rome, the powers associated with

priesthood were narrowly defined. They superintended particular cultic activities, but the financing of these activities was often carefully controlled by state officials and the priests controlled no great temple incomes or resources, as equivalent officers did in other parts of the ancient world. The city would often vote funds for religious expenditure and might regard the treasures stored in temples as state reserves to be used in case of emergency (see, famously, Thuc. 2. 13. 3–4) and repaid later. There might also at all periods be city officials taking overall responsibility for state religious expenditure.

In the imperial period, both in the east and west, priesthood became closer than ever to the expression of public power. The flaminate in its new guise of an imperial priesthood became widespread in the provinces and cities, held by the leading members of the local élites as a mark of their authority and an opportunity for public generosity. Meanwhile, the emperor's image in priestly garb became one of the empire-wide expressions of his rule.

Apart from these official civic priesthoods, there was a great range of religious expertise available for private consultation—diviners of all sorts, magicians, and astrologers; these had no official recognition and often attracted criticism. The mystery-cults also had their priests, who might attain to great authority within a less controlled cultic environment than that of the civic priests; religious groups devoted to a particular cult might appoint priests of their own; the Bacchist movement of 186 BC (see BACCHANALIA) had priests and priestesses, differentiated from lay magistrates in the senate's decree; but the clearest example of this development is the figure of the Isis priest in Apuleius' Latin *novel (The Golden Ass* 11), who acts as mentor and spiritual adviser to the hero after his rescue from the spell that turned him into the ass. It seems clear that there were new currents within pagan religious life that corresponded to, if they were not imitating, the new religious types evolving at the same time amongst Jews and Christians. Nothing, however, in pagan religious life corresponded to the Christian hierarchic structure of deacons, priests, and bishops. See ORACLES.   J. A. N.

prison Long-term imprisonment was not a usual *punishment in Greek cities, although Classical Athens had a prison (Thuc. 5.18.7: *to dēosion*, lit. 'the public thing') used for prisoners-of-war and, famously, *Socrates (for tentative identification with a mid-5th cent. structure near the Agora: J. Camp, *The Athenian Agora* (1986), 113–16). Roman criminal law, like that of Athens, did not in general use public imprisonment of free persons as a form of punishment, although under the republic some criminals suffered private imprisonment at the hands of those they had wronged and, occasionally, a special kind of criminal might be detained either inside or outside Rome. The public prison (*carcer, publica vincula*) served normally only for a short incarceration, whether used as a coercive measure by magistrates against disobedience to their orders or for convicted criminals awaiting execution (though such detention lasted several years for Quintus Pleminius, *c*.200 BC). During inquiry in a criminal trial the accused person could be detained so as to be at the disposal of the authorities, but this was not necessarily in a public prison. Larger households had arrangements for imprisoning slaves, especially in workhouses (*ergastula*) in the countryside. These were also used for convicted debtors and (under the republic) thieves, as well as other free men improperly seized.

A. B.; A. W. L.

procurator signified an agent or, in legal proceedings, representative, and under the Principate came to be the distinctive term for the employees of the emperor in civil administration. They might be freedmen from the imperial *familia* (slave household), but the majority, especially of the holders of the more important posts, were normally *equites*. The principal types of procuratorial post were:

1. Praesidial procurators governed minor provinces such as Corsica, Judaea, Noricum, Thrace, and the Mauretanias (see AFRICA, ROMAN). These governors had originally been called *praefecti*; thus Pontius Pilate was officially entitled *Praefectus Iudaeae*, AE 1963, 104. However this term came to be reserved for the equestrian governors of *Egypt and, from 198, Mesopotamia where legionary troops were stationed. Praesidial procurators commanded the auxiliary units in their provinces, exercised full civil and criminal jurisdiction, and supervised all fiscal matters. If at any time legionary forces were permanently stationed in such a province, the role of governor was transferred to a senatorial *legatus pro praetore* (e.g. Judaea from the time of the revolt of AD 66; see JEWS).

2. Procurators of imperial provinces, governed by legates, supervised the collection of direct taxes, indirect taxes (when special officials were not appointed, see below (4)), and of the revenues accruing from imperial properties. They were also responsible for the commissariat and pay of the troops. They had small detachments of troops at their disposal and official entitlement to requisitioned transport.

3. Procurators of the public provinces, governed by annual proconsuls, were originally only in charge of the properties of the emperor. They came, by a process whose details remain obscure, to acquire responsibilities analogous to those of the procurators of the imperial provinces and, thus, to exercise joint supervision, with the proconsuls, of public taxation.

Both of these types of procurators (2 and 3) also acquired legitimate jurisdiction in fiscal litigation. Occasionally they are found exercising powers, in the realms of civil and criminal jurisdiction or of non-fiscal administration (e.g. supervision of construction of roads), which were routinely the preserve of senatorial governors. These occasional extensions of their role are probably best understood as matters of administrative expediency. Also both types of procurator might act in place of the senatorial governor of the province. The first known occasion was in Asia about 88 (after the execution of the incumbent

proconsul), and this function became increasingly common from the first half of the 3rd cent.

4. Procurators of imperial estates were responsible for their general supervision. They issued regulations about the mutual obligations of *coloni* (tenant farmers) and *conductores* (lessees) and possessed wide policing powers.

5. Procurators responsible for the supervision of specific indirect taxes appear in the 1st cent. and more widely in the 2nd. Their responsibility normally encompassed a set of geographically contiguous provinces.

6. Throughout the first two centuries there was a steady accretion of procuratorial posts connected with the organization of matters such as the aqueducts, the *annona* (see FOOD SUPPLY), the mint, and imperial *ludi* or *familiae gladiatoriae* (see GLADIATORS).

Entry to procuratorial posts followed normally on military service, either (for men who were already *equites*), the 'tres militiae' (*praefectus cohortis, tribunus legionis, praefectus alae*), or from the rank of *primipilus bis* (chief centurion of a legion for a second time) for men who had risen from the ranks. The 1st cent. saw the formation of the 'praetorian cursus' or career-path by which a *primipilus* went as tribune of a cohort successively in the three urban units (*vigiles* or fire brigade, urban, and praetorian cohorts), went to another legion as *primipilus bis*, and then moved to important procuratorships. Under *Hadrian we meet for the first time the junior equestrian post of *advocatus fisci* which served as a non-military point of entry to the equestrian cursus. A minority of the most successful procurators could hope to gain promotion to the major prefectures, Egypt, the *annona*, and the praetorian cohorts and from the late 1st cent. to the secretarial posts with the emperor, previously the preserve of imperial freedmen. Procurators were the direct appointees of the emperor and received a codicil of appointment (see AE 1962, 183 for a fine example).

By the reign of *Septimius Severus 163 procuratorial posts are attested; many of those only attested in the 2nd cent. may have existed earlier (our surviving evidence is seriously deficient). A regular hierarchy of promotion evolved (see CAREERS) which by the mid-2nd cent. ran (after military service or the post of *advocatus fisci*) from minor procuratorial posts, to provincial procuratorships, praesidial procuratorships, 'secretarial posts', and major prefectures. In this evolution procuratorial posts came to be graded by level of pay—*sexagenarii* (those receiving 60,000 sesterces per annum), *centenarii* (100,000), *ducenarii* (200,000), and, rarely, *trecenarii* (300,000). The number and the duties of the freedmen procurators are ill known; but most, probably, acted as assistants to equestrian procurators.

In the second half of the 3rd cent. equestrians steadily replaced senators as provincial governors, a process completed by *Diocletian (284–305) (except for the surviving proconsulates of Africa and Asia); the word *praeses*, increasingly common for both types of governor in the 3rd cent., was now universal for equestrian governors.

propaganda Wall of the *temple of Roma and Augustus at Ancyra (Ankara), inscribed with a copy of the *Res gestae* of *Augustus, a first-person record of his achievements and expenditures. The emphases apparent in this piece of imperial self-advertisement (the justification of his superior personal authority, his benefactions, his military glory, etc.) offer a striking mix of agitation and integration propaganda.

Procuratores survived as the officials in charge of imperial mints, mines, factories, and landed properties. See FINANCE, ROMAN; PROVINCE/PROVINCIA. G. P. B.

propaganda is not easy to define. It means active manipulation of opinion and some distortion of the truth; it also perhaps aims at exclusive indoctrination of one set of opinions, contrast ideology (a value-system which may admit the possibility of other value-systems) or mentality (values unconsciously subscribed to rather than actively promoted). Propaganda has been divided (J. Ellul, *Propaganda* (1973)) into agitation propaganda and integration propaganda; the first seeks to change attitudes, the second to reinforce them. This division is helpful (see below) for the understanding of the ancient world.

Lacking modern techniques for the dissemination of information, the ancient world was spared some modern manifestations of propaganda; nor were conditions suitable for the emergence of professional governmental 'propaganda machines' of a modern sort (decision-making was amateur and theoretically in the hands of the citizens). There were however ways of making general proclamations. Thus Rome exploited *Delphi to make pronouncements adverse to King Perseus, *Macedonia's last king (*Syll.*³ 643); this builds on a long Greek tradition of making proclamations at panhellenic *sanctuaries like Delphi and *Olympia. There were other less direct ways of moulding opinion; it has been suggested (Boardman) that vase-paint-

ing and architecture directly reflect *Pisistratus' foreign, domestic, and religious policies, and if so this would be integration propaganda; but the interpretation of the evidence is controversial (see IMAGERY). Pisistratan 'control' of vase-painters was hardly close enough to justify talk of propaganda.

The Spartan educational system or *agōgē* can also be seen as a kind of integration propaganda; equally, Sparta's policy of 'freeing the Greeks' was originally agitation propaganda, a way of undermining Athens' *Delian League. (The 'freedom of the Greeks' motif was later taken up by Hellenistic rulers and eventually by Romans down to *Nero. See FREEDOM IN THE ANCIENT WORLD. The 'agitation' element became less prominent over time.) Classical Athens for its part used religion, myth (esp. Ionian themes), and manipulation of the past, exploiting different types of literary and artistic discourse, to promote its empire (see ATHENS (HISTORY); BARBARIAN; DELIAN LEAGUE). In particular, imperial Athens exploited and exaggerated the idea of *kinship (*syngeneia*) between states, and treated its subject allies as if they were all its Ionian colonists owing quasi-familial obligations: cf. *mētropolis* (mother-city). But 'Athens' and 'Sparta' are abstractions and it is a question how far Athenian or Spartan individuals set out consciously to manipulate opinion. In any case Thuc. 6. 82. 3–4 is strikingly out of line (Euphemus at Camarina justifies Athenians' coercion of their Ionian 'kin' by reference to Ionian participation in *Xerxes' invasion).

Autocrats are more promising propagandists. Hellenistic rulers promoted their regimes through sculpture and spectacle, but not all self-advertisement of this sort is strictly propaganda. We get closer with the Rome of *Augustus, who had the power, the wealth, and the motive to promote a specific set of values and beliefs, using art, architecture, coinage, sculpture, and literature, including and especially Augustus' own *Res gestae. At the outset there was an 'agitation' element to his propaganda, which was aimed at Mark *Antony, but Augustan propaganda turned into the integrative type as opposition became less of a threat. But even the most loyal Augustan poets were not crude propagandists. Subsequent imperial propaganda tends to be of the integrative type, and takes sophisticated forms (thus the Persian-Wars tradition, strictly a story of *Greek* achievement, is taken over by Rome as a way of reconciling Greeks to Roman power). With the aggressive paganism of *Julian we perhaps encounter agitation propaganda again.   S. H.

Propertius, Sextus, Roman poet, born between 54 and 47 BC, at Asisium (mod. Asisi), where his family were local notables (4. 1. 121 ff.). His father died early, and the family property was diminished by Octavian's confiscations of 41–40 BC (4. 1. 127 ff.; see AUGUSTUS; PROSCRIPTION)—not so diminished however that Propertius needed to earn a living. In the two last poems of book 1 the poet notably identifies with the side vanquished by Octavian at Perusia (mod. Perugia) in 41 BC. It is the first sign of a political independence that continues throughout his life, despite involvement in *Maecenas' circle. As the Augustan regime toughened, Propertius' modes of irreverence become more oblique, but irreverence towards the government is maintained none the less: see e.g. 2. 7, 2. 15. 41 ff., 3. 11, 4. 9.

Propertius' first book was probably published before Oct. 28 BC; the latest events mentioned in books 2, 3, and 4 belong to the years 26, 23, and 16 respectively. Propertius was certainly dead by 2 BC (Ov. *Rem. Am.* 764).

It is as a love poet that Propertius is best known. He celebrated his devotion to a mistress whom he called Cynthia (a name with Apolline and Callimachean associations; see APOLLO; CALLIMACHUS). Apuleius says her real name was Hostia (*Apol.* 10). Many of the incidents suggested in the poems seem conventional, but there is no reason to doubt Cynthia's basic reality. Her social status is uncertain.

Characteristic of Propertian love poetry is the claim to be the slave of his mistress (1. 1 etc.), and the claim that love is his life's occupation; it replaces the normal career move of a young equestrian (service in the cohort of a provincial governor, *militia*). Propertius distils this last point by referring to love as his *militia* (esp. 1. 6. 29 f.). Typical too of his love poetry is his use of mythology: he cites figures and events from myth as 'romantic standards', as examples of how things in a romantic world might be.

Book 1, consisting almost entirely of love poems, is addressed to a variety of friends, most prominently a Tullus (1. 1, 1. 6, 1. 14, 1. 22; 9. 3. 22) who seems to have been nephew to Lucius Volcacius Tullus, consul in 33 BC with Octavian. Book 2 (which some think an amalgamation (by a later hand) of two books), still largely devoted to love poems, evidences his entry to the circle of Maecenas (2. 1), but there is no suggestion that he was ever economically dependent on the great patron in the way that *Virgil and *Horace were. Book 3 also contains a prominent poem to Maecenas (3. 9), but book 4 omits all mention of his name. Maecenas fades from Propertius' poetry as he fades from Horace's: this is probably due to the great patron's loss of favour with Augustus in the wake of the conspiracy of 23 BC.

Book 3 shows a greater diversity of subject-matter than the first two books, and it is here that Propertius first makes an ostentatious claim to be a Roman Callimachus (3. 1 and 3. 3). Some scholars think the claim is not very justified: Horace had claimed to be the Roman *Alcaeus (*Ode* 3. 30); with some humour Propertius responds by making his claim to be the first Roman to adopt the mantle of another Greek poet. Among the many non-Cynthia poems in book 3 one might note 3. 18 on the death of Augustus' nephew Marcus Claudius Marcellus. It is hard to imagine Propertius writing this a few years earlier. The toughening of the Augustan regime and the fading influence of the mediating Maecenas was having its effect. But Propertius can still be irreverent (see above). The concluding poems of the book recall book 1 in various ways, and mark the end both of the affair with Cynthia and of his career as a love-poet (or so it seems).

Book 4 is more successful than book 3, and in it Propertius has a more valid claim to be called a Roman Callimachus. It consists partly of poems descended from Callimachus' *Aetia*; but these are Roman *Aetia* (1, 2, 4, 6, 9, and 10), one (6) indeed explaining the *aition* of the Temple of Apollo as a thank-offering for the victory at *Actium. 4. 6 is an example of Propertius' later subtle irreverence. It is largely devoted to an account of the battle of Actium, but tells it all in the manner of Callimachus, a style wholly unsuited to the subject-matter. The total result is amusing to those with literary taste. To these aetiological poems are added poems on various subjects. The two in which he returns to the theme of Cynthia (7 and 8) are among Propertius' most original, and the speech from beyond the grave by Cornelia (11) is moving, though marred by textual corruption.

Some Romans, though not the rhetorician Quintilian, thought Propertius the most 'refined and elegant' of the Roman elegists (Quint. 10. 1. 93; cf. also Plin. *Ep.* 9. 22). Such epithets apply to many of his poems, but others seem to the modern reader obscure and jagged. Part of this is the reader's fault. The poet's wit is a demanding one. Other and real obscurities are due to a very corrupt manuscript tradition. The fact remains that Propertius is difficult in a way that *Tibullus is not, and—perhaps owing to his Callimachean aspirations—often seems to cultivate complexity and convolution.

His vivid recreation of his affair with Cynthia, his literary range, and his political independence make Propertius one of the most captivating of the Latin poets.

R. O. A. M. L.

proscription, the publication of a notice, especially (1) a notice of a sale; (2) a list of Roman citizens who were declared outlaws and whose goods were confiscated. This procedure was used by *Sulla in 82–81 BC, and by Mark *Antony, *Lepidus, and Octavian (the future *Augustus) in 43–42 as a means of getting rid of personal and political opponents and obtaining funds in virtue, or anticipation, of special powers of inappellable jurisdiction conferred on them as *dictator and *triumviri* respectively. The proscribed were hunted down and executed in Rome and throughout Italy by squads of soldiers, and the co-operation of the victims' families and slaves and of the general public was sought by means of rewards and punishments.

Despite some wild exaggeration in ancient sources and modern calculations, Sulla's proscription, in part an act of revenge for massacres in 87 and 82 by *Marius, targeted no more than perhaps 520 persons. The lists were closed on 1 June 81. The sons and grandsons of the proscribed were debarred from public life until restored by *Caesar in 49. The impression left was profound, and similar conduct was feared from Caesar or *Pompey, whichever should win the Civil War: as it was, Caesar's clemency was made an excuse for the proscriptions of the triumvirs (see above). Their lists included about 300 senators and *equites*; but many escaped, and some of these, including a fair proportion of senators, were afterwards restored.

T. J. C.; R. J. S.

prosopography is a modern term for the study of individuals, and is derived from the Greek *prosōpon*, one meaning of which is 'person'. There is no agreed or official definition of prosopography, which goes under different names in different disciplines (to the social scientist, prosopography in one of its manifestations is 'multiple career-line analysis': see L. Stone, 'Prosopography', *Daedalus*, 1971, 46 ff.). Prosopography, as used in ancient history, is a historical method which uses onomastic evidence to establish (i) regional origins of individuals and (ii) family connections, esp. via marriage-ties but also via *adoption (which leaves traces on nomenclature), between individual and individual and between group and group. (In Greece the *genos* and in Rome the *gens*, both translatable as 'lineage', constituted the basic large *kinship units; but 'group' theories of Roman politics, see below, presuppose units made up of more than one *gens*. Thus Scullard (below) posited a 'Fulvian-Claudian group' in late 3rd cent. Rome, drawn from members of two *gentes*, the Fulvii and Claudii.) Conclusions about the origins and family connections of individuals then classically lead to inferences about their likely political sympathies and allegiances.

The prosopographic method is specially associated with Roman history, and in particular with the work of R. Syme (1903–89), who once wrote of 'the science (or rather the art) of prosopography' (*RP* 2. 711). Syme however had his German predecessors at one level (E. Groag, F. Münzer, and the editors of the first edn. of *Prosopographia Imperii Romani*, 1897–). Prosopography of the Syme–Scullard sort has always had its critics; for an early reply to such critics see H. H. Scullard's preface to the 2nd edn. of his *Roman Politics 220–150 BC* (1973, but reprinted from *BICS* 1955. Scullard's book, first published in 1951 and much indebted to Münzer's *Römische Adelsparteien und Adelsfamilien* (1920), had argued for the existence and importance of family 'groups' at Rome in the late 3rd and early 2nd cents. BC. For a more cautious approach to this issue, but still retaining the central idea, see J. Briscoe, *Hist.* 1969, 67 ff., dealing with the mid 2nd cent. BC). But fundamental scepticism persisted, see for instance P. A. Brunt, *Gnomon* 1965, 189 ff. and K. Hopkins, *Death and Renewal* (1983), ch. 2. One obvious line of criticism is that the prosopographic approach is too narrow, thus it is alleged to neglect ideas in favour of 'matrimonial bulletins' (A. N. Sherwin-White, *JRS* 1969, 287, apparently approved by Brunt, *Proc. Brit. Acad.* 1994, 463, cf. *JRS* 1968, 231; see also Stone 63) or in favour of strictly economic evidence about ownership and transmission of property (Stone 59). These are however hardly objections to the prosopographic method itself, but rather to its mechanical and unimaginative implementation. Again, W. V. Harris, *War and Imperialism in Republican Rome 327–70 BC* (1979), 32 explicitly rejects the prosopographic approach of Scullard, by putting the emphasis on the fighting and military success which were the justification for election to political office which in turn made possible further military success, and so on. Another objection (Brunt 1965, see above) is that for the age of *Cicero, where political evidence of a direct sort is for once relatively plentiful, members of the same family go different ways, ties seem generally loose and loyalties changeable. As for individuals, 'we seldom have access to their minds'. Again, this is an argument for sophisticated and flexible use, not for abandonment, of the technique. More generally and recently, some of the assumptions about Roman political life made by Syme (and before him by M. Gelzer, *The Roman Nobility* (1969, Ger. orig. 1912)) are now disputed. Extensive use of prosopographic technique tended to go with a belief in the pervasiveness of *clientela* relationships and political friendships: the powerful individual or group (it was held) was capable of mobilizing vast *clientelae*. But see Brunt, *Fall of the Roman Republic* (1988), chs. 7, 8 for scepticism about the importance of domestic *clientela*. Finally (Stone; Hopkins) traditional prosopography can be criticized for undue attention to the doings of élites and exceptional individuals (Hopkins 41 speaks of the 'Everest fallacy', i.e. the 'tendency to illustrate a category by an example which is exceptional'); but the paucity of evidence for low-status groups and individuals is not a problem peculiar to prosopography but one which faces most attempts to investigate the ancient world. Notwithstanding the above-noted objections, it is arguable that Roman republican history in its human and political complexity cannot be understood without proper and expertly guided attention to prosopographical detail. As for imperial Rome, prosopography, allied with epigraphy, has transformed understanding of the Roman governing class under the Principate, not only by documenting the gradual absorption of subject-élites into the *senate and order of *equites, but also by providing the basis for estimates of the biological maintenance-rates of senatorial families (cf. the statistical approach of Hopkins himself in the book cited above), and discussion of the relative claims of merit versus patronage in advancing individual *careers. At a lower social level, present knowledge of the diffusion and activities of the *negotiatores* (Italian businessmen) owes much to prosopography.

Prosopography has made less impact on Greek history, though the example of *Prosopographia Imperii Romani* was followed by J. Kirchner, *Prosopographia Attica* for Athens (1901), P. Poralla, *Prosopographie der Lakedaimonier* (1913) for Sparta, and by Berve, *Alexanderreich* (1926), a massive study of the extended entourage of *Alexander the Great; see also now Heckel, *The Marshals of Alexander's Empire* (1992). But it was not till E. Badian's acute study of Harpalus, *JHS* 1961, that approaches more familiar from Roman history were applied to Alexander's court. In 1958 C. Habicht made remarkable use of prosopography in aspect (i) above—i.e. the study of the ethnic and regional origins of individuals, rather than aspect (ii), their marriage connections—for the illumination of *Seleucid policy towards indigenous personnel: see HELLENISM, HELLENIZATION. In Athenian history, J. K. Davies, the author of *Athenian Propertied Families* (1971), a family-based study of the Athenian 'liturgical class' i.e. those liable to perform liturgies—compulsory services to the state), has shown that there is a basic mutual incompatibility between 'Athenian history and the method of Münzer': *Rivista Storica Italiana* 1968, 209 ff. (in Italian). But simple prosopographic methods can, naturally, be used for Classical Athens, see for instance Dover, *HCT* 4. 276 ff. on the 'politics and prosopography' of the affairs of the Herms and Mysteries (see ANDOCIDES), with good general cautionary remarks at 288 on the dangers of believing 'that kinsmen and acquaintances consistently support each other's policies'. Another example is the association of the Athenian politician Cleon with the tribute re-assessment of 425 BC (ML 69), the proposer of which was called Thudippus (a rare name). Now the 4th.-cent. orator *Isaeus reveals (9.17) a second Cleon, who is a son of a Thudippus, and it is a plausible inference that Thudippus married the daughter of the famous Cleon. Again, prosopography has shown that there is surprisingly little overlap between politics at deme (local) level and at city level (D. Whitehead, *The Demes of Attica* (1986), 325, cf. 237). Large differences nevertheless remain between Athenian and Roman politics, despite recent shifts (see above) in the study of Roman republican history and despite attempts actually to categorize Rome of the middle and late republic as a democracy with some affinities to the Classical Athenian model. But politics is not the only kind of

history, and, as we have seen, there is more than one way of doing prosopography. Syme, for instance, was as much interested in names as indicators of origin and of social as well as geographical mobility, as in the evidence they provided for family connections. He drew in particular on W. Schulze, *Zur Geschichte lateinischer Eigennamen* (1904). When P. M. Fraser and E. Matthews, *Lexicon of Greek Personal Names* (*LGPN*; so far 2 vols., 1987 and 1994), is complete, the possibilities for the Greek social historian, interested in origins and migration, will be enormous.

S. H., A. J. S. S.

prostitution, sacred is a strictly modern, not ancient, term and misleading in that it transfers to the institution, or rather a variety of institutions, an adjective which in ancient sources denotes only the status of the personnel involved (sometimes also their earnings, which likewise became sacred on dedication). In the cult of *Aphrodite at Corinth, Strabo (8. 6. 20, C378; cf. 12. 3. 36, C559), admittedly writing long after the city's destruction in 146 BC, gives a total of over 1,000 *hetairai* (lit. 'companions', a category of female prostitute) dedicated by both men and women. Much earlier *Pindar (fr. 122; Chamaeleon fr. 31 Wehrli), in a *scolion* (drinking song) which explicitly anticipates a degree of moral opprobrium and seeks to forestall this with a coy invocation to 'necessity' (*anagkē*), celebrates the dedication of up to 100 by the contemporary Xenophon of Corinth (the figure given is strictly a total of limbs rather than of persons). The modern view that their professional activities were ritually significant is not borne out by the down-to-earth, matter-of-fact ancient term 'earning from the body' (*ergazesthai apo tou sōmatos*), elsewhere and no less casually also used of wet-nursing (see CHILDBIRTH). Dedication is also emphasized in the cult of Aphrodite at Eryx in *Sicily (Strabo 6. 2. 6, C272; once again a thing of the past by his time), some women being sent from outside the island; *Diodorus (4. 83. 6) emphasizes relaxation and entertainment rather than religious solemnity. In the cult of Ma at Comana Pontica (Asia Minor), *Strabo (559) says most but not all such women were sacred. In all these cases, the adjective denotes no more than manumission by fictive dedication of a kind already attested in the cult of Poseidon at Laconian Taenarum (southern *Peloponnese in the 5th cent. BC.

A quite distinct institution, reported only from the margins of the Greek world, is the practice of pre-marital sex with strangers, sometimes sustained over a period of time, sometimes strictly delimited, but invariably presented as followed by a lifetime of strict conjugal fidelity, the *locus classicus* being *Herodotus' often hilarious description of Babylon (1. 199, not confirmed but not contradicted by *Babylonian sources; some distinctive features repeated in *LXX Epist. Jerem.* 42–43, c.300 BC). This is a one-off rite, compulsory for all, in the service of the goddess Mylitta, to whom earnings are dedicated, the act itself (by contrast with Corinthian practices) involving a strictly religious obligation (*aposiōsamenē* 199.4, cf. Justin (Trogus) *epit.* 18. 5. 4 (*Cyprus), Val. Max. 2. 6. 15 (Numidian Sicca Veneria, Roman *Africa)). By contrast, Herodotus' picture of Lydian girls earning their dowries by prostitution (and giving themselves away in marriage, 1. 93) could be a strictly secular (economic) phenomenon; not only did the Lydians invent coined money, they were the world's first 'hucksters', *kapēloi* (ibid. 94).

Distinct again but poorly attested (that is to say indirectly and in the rather suspect context of tyrannical misdeeds) is the vow supposedly taken by the citizens of Locri Epizephyrii (S. Italy) to prostitute all their unmarried girls (*virgines*, Justin (Trogus) *epit.* 21. 3. 2) in the event of victory over Rhegium in 477/6 BC, a one-off and clearly desperate measure which must if authentic be explained in quite different terms, perhaps connected with the highly unusual circumstances of the city's foundation. But oriental origins (or influence), so often invoked to exorcise the Hellenist's embarrassment at the Corinthian data (see ORIENTALISM), the real problem remaining the fact of their reception (and naturalization), however comforting on the Greek mainland, are certainly not applicable to Locri.

The *hiaran mistōma*, or 'contract-price of the [pl.] sacred (—)', mentioned in a number of inscriptions from the 4th-cent. archive of the temple of *Zeus at Locri (A. de Franciscis, *Stato e società a Locri Epizefiri* (1972), nos. 22, 30, 31) must certainly denote sacred lands, not sacred women: for the ellipse cf. the *misthōsis tēs neas* ('rental of the new (land)') in F. Sokolowski, *Lois sacrées* (1969), no. 33, ll. 11–18 (Athens, 335/4–330/29 BC).   S. G. P.

prostitution, secular The prostitution of women (broadly defined here as the exchange of a female's sexual service, with or without her consent, for some other resource) may have arisen in Greece out of contact with earlier Near Eastern manifestations of so-called sacred prostitution (see preceding entry); this may have been 'temple prostitution', 'prostitution' in order to gain a dowry, or both. The exchange of sexual service for the economic benefits conferred by marriage is remarked upon by *Hesiod (*Works and Days* 373–5). In both Greece and Rome, prostitution was considered to be as necessary an institution as the institutions of marriage, concubinage, or *slavery. Social attitudes and legislation generally stigmatized the prostitute, who—whether female or male—generally was of low status. In the Greek world there is a constant emphasis on the economic perils of the transaction for men (Archilochus 302 W) and its concomitant provision of sexual release (Philemon, *Adelphoi* fr. 3K–A). The very terms *porneion* (brothel) and *pornē* (whore) are related to *pernēmi* (to sell); cf. Latin *meretrix*, *merx*, *mereo*. The major written sources—fictional literature, historiography, the orators, and law codes—frequently set into collision medical, moralizing, regulatory, tolerant, and oppressive ideologies, and must be analysed with great care. Much work remains to be done on this important aspect of social history. See HOMOSEXUALITY (for male prostitutes); PROSTITUTION, SACRED.   M. M. H.

provincia/province 1. The etymology of the word *provincia* is obscure: it was mistakenly derived from *pro+vincere* by Roman antiquarians. Its basic meaning is the sphere in which a magistrate (perhaps originally a magistrate with *imperium*) is to function. See MAGISTRACY, ROMAN. By the 3rd cent. BC, the two consuls normally had their *provinciae* assigned by the *senate or by mutual agreement (*comparatio*); later allotment was normal. A law of Gaius *Gracchus (123) provided that the senate was to decide, before the consular elections, in a vote protected against tribunician *intercessio* (veto: see TRIBUNE OF THE PLEBS), which *provinciae* were to be consular: this was to prevent personal or political influences on that decision. At the beginning of the year the senate would decide which *provinciae* were to be praetorian (and, before 123, consular): for these, the magistrates would then draw lots. Any others would be filled by designated promagistrates. By the late 3rd cent., a magistrate or promagistrate was expected to confine his activities to his *provincia*, except in emergencies or by special permission. By 171 this had become a formal rule, enforced by the senate (see Livy 43. 1): perhaps in the process of administrative reform that produced the law of Lucius Villius (tribune 180). It was at various times reaffirmed in legislation on provincial administration.

Originally the two consuls normally divided all duties between them. Since they had to campaign nearly every year, a praetor (see CONSUL) with *imperium* was appointed (traditionally in 367) and given the *provincia urbana* (affairs in the city, especially legal business and the presidency of the senate and legislative assemblies when necessary). Until *c.*100, when consuls began most often to stay in Rome, this remained his task, but he came to specialize in civil law and in the end to confine himself to this. A second praetor was created at the end of the First Punic War (264–241 BC), probably to supervise the newly-won territory of Punic *Sicily and perhaps later Sardinia. In 227 two new praetors were created for these overseas *provinciae* and the second praetor, though freely used in fighting in the Second Punic War (218–202 BC), was normally assigned to judicial duties in the city, in due course those affecting aliens (hence the popular title *praetor peregrinus*). Two more praetors were created in 198/7, to command in the two newly won territories in *Spain, hitherto in the charge of private citizens with special *imperium*. Henceforth the word *provincia*, although it never lost its original meaning, was mainly used for overseas territories under permanent Roman administration, i.e. it came mainly to mean 'province'; but the two city *provinciae* were the highest in prestige. By the second century (and probably from the start) provincial commanders were attended by quaestors. The praetor of Sicily, where the territory of *Syracuse, annexed in the Second Punic War (see ROME (HISTORY) §1.4), remained under its traditional administration, separate from that of the originally Punic province, was given two quaestors. Characteristically for Roman conservatism, he retained the two quaestors to the end of the republic, even after the administration of Sicily was unified, in the settlement of Publius Rupilius (consul 132) after a slave war, on the more profitable model of the old kingdom of Syracuse.

After 197 the senate was unwilling to create more praetors and, as a necessary consequence, on the whole to annex more territory. Macedonia was 'freed' after the battle of Pydna (168); Numidia was not annexed after Jugurtha's defeat (see MARIUS); Transalpine *Gaul, which provided the land connection with Spain, was not organized as a province until after the wars with the Cimbri and their allies had shown the danger this presented; *Cyrene, bequeathed by its king (96), was not properly organized until the 60s; and the bequest of Egypt by Ptolemy X (87) was refused by *Sulla. But some annexation became necessary, or was regarded as such: Macedonia and Africa (the territory of *Carthage; see AFRICA, ROMAN) in 146, Asia after the war with Aristonicus (129), Transalpine Gaul after 100. Unwillingness to create more praetors meant that the traditional city-state system of (in principle) annual magistracies was abandoned and promagistrates became an integral part of imperial administration. New quaestors were probably created, since quaestors, at that time not even guaranteed membership of the senate, did not endanger the political system. In 123–2, Gaius Gracchus, reforming the *repetundae* (provincial extortion) court, put a praetor in charge of it. Over the next generation, other *quaestiones* (standing courts) were established on this model, so that by *c*.90 most, perhaps all, praetors were occupied in Rome during their year of office. Since consuls were not involved in routine provincial government, provinces were almost entirely left to promagistrates. As early as 114, the *praetor urbanus* Marius was sent as proconsul to Spain after his year of office—a major innovation as far as our records go. By the 90s praetors serving in the city might expect to be sent overseas the following year. Major foreign wars, the Social War (91–89 BC; see ROME (HISTORY) §1.5) and civil wars added to the strain on the system, and tenures of promagistrates increased until they could reach six years. This, combined with the growth of the client army (see MARIUS), posed a serious danger to the republic, as Sulla soon showed.

Sulla, after his victory, aimed at stabilizing the state under senate control. He added at least two *quaestiones,* but also added two praetorships (and raised the number of quaestors to 20). Consuls (it seems) were encouraged to go to prestigious provinces (like Cisalpina) at the end of their year. It was apparently Sulla's idea that ten magistrates with *imperium,* normally governing provinces after their year of office, would suffice to keep provincial tenures down to a year or at most two. But after 70 various factors—especially the rise of populares (popular politicians) with their programmes and ambitions and increasing, hence increasingly expensive, competition for the consulship—led to accelerated annexation. *Crete was annexed by Quintus Caecilius Metellus (Creticus) to end Cretan *piracy—and to prevent its annexation by *Pompey. *Cyprus was annexed to pay for Publius *Clodius Pulcher's corn distributions; Pompey annexed Syria and added Pontus to Bithynia, as well as first organizing several territories (e.g. Judaea) as dependencies of provinces. He claimed to have added 85 million denarii to Rome's previous revenue of 50 million (Plut. *Pomp.* 45. 4). *Caesar, for reasons of personal ambition, extended Transalpine Gaul to the Rhine and the English Channel. Yet men not seeking glory or fortunes were often unwilling to serve in provinces, and Sulla had omitted to make acceptance of a promagistracy compulsory, as a magistrate's *provincia* always had been. Thus exploitation of provincials for private gain became a necessary incentive, tending to select those eager for it as provincial governors, while major wars and increasingly competitive ambitions for glory led to the granting of large *provinciae* with long tenure to men like Lucius Licinius Lucullus, Pompey, Caesar, and Crassus. To stop the dangers inherent in this, Pompey, on the senate's advice, fixed an interval (perhaps of five years) between magistracy and pro-magistracy and made acceptance of provinces compulsory (52): thus men like *Cicero and Marcus Calpurnius Bibulus belatedly had to accept provincial service. But the plan was nullified when civil wars supervened. It was later essentially restored by *Augustus.

2. A province was not an area under uniform administration. In Sicily, cities that joined the Romans had been declared 'free' when the territory was taken over from Carthage, and 'free' cities, granted various degrees of independence, remained characteristic of eastern and some western provinces. Inevitably their rights tended to be whittled down: by the early 1st cent., the free city of Utica was the seat of the governor of Africa. Many governors were less than scrupulous in respecting the rights of free cities. Tribes could also be granted various degrees of self-government, and from the late 2nd cent. colonies of citizens were founded overseas (see COLONIZATION, ROMAN). A province was therefore a mosaic of territories with different statuses, from complete subjection to nominal independence, and provincial maps were kept in Rome to show this. Most provinces were annexed after wars, and in such cases the victorious commander would organize the peace settlement (including, if appropriate, annexation) with a commission of *legati* (legates) according to a *senatus consultum* (senatorial resolution). (Pompey, characteristically, refused to accept a commission, thereby causing serious anxiety regarding his political intentions.) This settlement, later confirmed by senate or people, was called the *lex provinciae.* (See Cic. 2 *Verr.* 2. 32, 40.) It settled boundaries (though provinces facing *barbarian tribes seem to have had no fixed external frontier), local constitutions, taxation, and the administration of justice, in ways and degrees that differed considerably from one province to another. The *lex* might later be amended in detail, but remained the basis for the organization of the particular province. In the few cases where annexation did not follow upon victory, we do not know what was done, but basic rules were certainly set up (e.g. for Cyprus when it was added to Cilicia (SE Asia Minor).

Within the general framework, each governor issued his edict, normally based on his predecessor's and relevant parts of those of urban magistrates. But this was never compulsory. Quintus Mucius Scaevola in the 90s in Asia and Cicero, modelling himself on him in 51 in Cilicia, introduced major judicial innovations. Scaevola's reforms were made mandatory for Asia by the senate, but any extension to other provinces was haphazard. The edict was not binding on the governor, at least until 67 and perhaps after. Within the limits set by the general framework, he held absolute *imperium* over non-citizens. In fact, he was a commander and not, in the modern sense, a governor or administrator. On his departure from Rome, no matter how peaceful his province, he and his lictors (official attendants) changed to military garb and his friends would escort him with prayers for his safety and success; and his return was accompanied by corresponding ceremonial. He could delegate his power to his quaestor and legates, and within limits to others. He was accompanied to his province by a large *cohors* (a military term) of military and civilian attendants and friends of his and of his officers, many of them young men thus gaining their first experience of public service and rule. Among them and provincial Romans, he would choose his *consilium* (panel of advisers), to advise on, and vouch for, his judicial and other activities. Having *imperium,* he could not be challenged during his tenure, no matter how he behaved, and he could protect the actions of his officers and *cohors,* and also those of businessmen and *publicani,* by armed force and sheer terror, for immense mutual profit. The chances of having him convicted in the *repetundae* court were slim, since he was rich and well connected: nearly all cases in the late republic ended in acquittal. Even conviction might not profit the provincials. The sum voted by the senate for the province offered further opportunities for profit: it was not expected that he would return the surplus, which was normally shared by him with his officers and *cohors.* As we have seen, these opportunities became an integral part of the system and were thus not subject to reform.

3. All indirect taxes were farmed by *publicani.* Direct taxes were originally collected by the quaestor, at greatly varying rates, though farmed at the local level. Gaius Gracchus arranged for the *decuma* (tithe on the grain harvest) of Asia, the wealthiest province, to be sold to *publicani* under five-year contracts. This system was apparently extended by Pompey to the provinces he organized. Asia remained a centre of exploitation and consequent resentment, due more to warfare and the actions of governors than to the *publicani,* though the latter offered easier targets for complaint. Lucius Lucullus tried to save it by restructuring its huge debts, and after further civil war and oppression Caesar greatly reduced its tax and restored its collection to the quaestor. There was no change in other provinces before Augustus.

4. In 27 BC, Augustus was given a large consular *provincia,* originally (it seems) Gaul, Spain, and Syria, which he governed (after 23 as proconsul) through *legati pro praetore*

and which contained nearly all the legions. Its finances were administered by *procurators. The command was regularly renewed and the area changed over time. By the end of the reign the emperor's provinces were an accepted institution. The public (in fact, senatorial) provinces were governed by proconsuls, most (and within a generation all) of them without legions, but still with *imperium* and assisted by quaestors and legates. But the emperor had *imperium maius* (see IMPERIUM), which we find Augustus exercising as early as the Cyrene edicts. He also, of course, had to approve of all proconsular appointments, especially the most prestigious ones to Asia (see ASIA, ROMAN PROVINCE) and Africa. Egypt, though 'subject to the Roman people' (*RG* 27), was forbidden to senators and governed for the emperor by an equestrian prefect with legionary forces. Various minor provinces (e.g. Judaea and Noricum) were governed by prefects (later by procurators) without legions. Direct taxes were directly collected in all provinces; indirect taxes continued to be collected by *publicani,* now subject to strict regulation, but by the 3rd cent. AD were taken over by the central government.

The system established by Augustus was essentially maintained until well into the 3rd cent., although there were many changes in detail, some of them significant. *Britain was annexed by *Claudius and later extended, Dacia and Arabia by *Trajan. (Other conquests proved ephemeral.) As expansion ceased, especially after Trajan, frontiers were gradually marked out and defended by garrisons (see LIMES). Various client kings were succeeded by governors and the subdivision of large provinces, begun by Augustus, was continued, especially since a constant supply of senior men was soon available. Supervision of municipal government, made necessary by AD 100 because of financial incompetence, was gradually extended and stifled civic tradition. The whole system was finally reorganized, after the strains of civil wars and invasions, by *Diocletian (284–305).

In some provinces a *concilium* (assembly) of local notables had developed under the republic: it could serve as a vehicle for distributing the governor's messages and would propose honours for him; it might even occasionally complain about him to the senate. These *concilia,* extended to all provinces, became the organizations in charge of the imperial cult (see RULER-CULT, ROMAN), which grew out of the cult of the goddess Roma under the republic. The councils were headed by native high priests, who in due course could expect to gain citizenship; many of their descendants became *equites* or even senators. As more provincial notables gained the Roman *citizenship, the equestrian service and the senate were gradually opened up to provincials, although over a long time-span and at very varying rates for different provinces. Among the lower classes, Romanization was spread by army service, while the grant of *ius Latii* ('Latin right', a status conferring some of the rights of citizenship) was extended among provincial communities; though the Latin language never spread to the east (see BILINGUALISM). By the time of *Caracalla's edict granting citizenship to most inhabitants of the empire, a unitary Roman state was *de facto* already in existence. See FINANCE, ROMAN. E. B.

Ptolemy I (Ptolemaeus) Soter ('Saviour') (367/6–282 BC), king of Egypt and founder of the Ptolemaic dynasty. The son of Lagus and Arsinoë, he served *Alexander the Great of Macedon as an experienced general and childhood friend. At Susa in 324 he married Artacama (also called Apame), daughter of the Persian noble Artabazus, whom he later divorced. He later married the Macedonian Eurydice (6 children) and subsequently Berenice I, mother of the dynastic line. On Alexander's death (323) he hijacked the conqueror's corpse and, taking it to Memphis in Egypt, established himself as satrap in place of Alexander's appointee Cleomenes. In the following year he took Cyrene and in 321 repulsed the invasion of Perdiccas. In the complex struggles of Alexander's successors (Diadochi) he was not at first particularly successful. In 295 however he recovered Cyprus, lost in 306 to Demetrius Poliorcetes ('the Besieger'), and from 291 he increasingly controlled the Aegean League of Islanders. Ptolemy took the title of King (*basileus*) in 305; this served as the first year of his reign. Responsible for initiating a Greek-speaking administration in Egypt, he consulted Egyptians (the priest Manetho and others), exploiting their local expertise. The cult of Sarapis, in origin the Egyptian Osiris-Apis (see EGYPTIAN DEITIES), was probably developed under Soter as a unifying force. There are few papyri from his reign, but hieroglyphic inscriptions from the Delta (especially the 'Satrap Stele') present him as a traditional pharaoh. In Upper Egypt he founded Ptolemais Hermiou (modern El-Mansha) as a second Greek administrative centre. Moving the capital from Memphis (S. of mod. Cairo) to *Alexandria, he brought Egypt into the mainstream of the Hellenistic world. D. J. T.

Ptolemy I as historian Ptolemy I wrote a history of the reign of *Alexander the Great. Much about it is obscure, notably its title, dimensions and even its date of composition. Apart from a single citation in *Strabo our knowledge of it is wholly due to *Arrian who selected it, along with Aristobulus, as his principal source. The work was evidently comprehensive, covering the period from at least 335 BC to the death of Alexander, and it provided a wealth of 'factual' detail, including most of our information about the terminology and organization of the Macedonian army. The popular theory that Ptolemy based his work upon a court journal rests ultimately on his use of the Ephemerides (royal day-books) for Alexander's last illness. Rather the narrative, as it is reconstructed from Arrian, suggests that Ptolemy had propagandist aims (not surprisingly, given his skill at publicity). He emphasized his personal contribution to the campaign and tended to suppress or denigrate the achievements of his rivals, both important in an age when service under Alexander was a considerable political asset. There is also a tendency to eulogize Alexander (whose body he kept interred in state) and gloss over darker episodes like the 'conspiracy' of the Macedonian general Philotas. The king accordingly appears as a paradigm of generalship, his conquests achieved at minimum cost and maximum profit, and Ptolemy continuously figures in the action. His account is contemporary and valuable; but it is not holy writ and needs to be controlled by other evidence. A. B. B.

Ptolemy II Philadelphus ('Sister-loving') (308–246 BC), son of Ptolemy I and Berenice I, born on Cos, first married *Lysimachus' daughter Arsinoë I, mother to Ptolemy III, Lysimachus, and Berenice, and then his sister Arsinoë II, who brought him her Aegean possessions. He became joint ruler with his father in 285, succeeding to the throne in 282. Externally, he expanded the Ptolemaic overseas empire in *Asia Minor and *Syria, fighting two Syrian Wars, against the *Seleucid king Antiochus I (274–271) and, with less success, against Antiochus II in 260–253; in 252 his daughter Berenice II was married to Antiochus II. The Chremonidean War (267–261) against Macedon in Greece and the western Aegean involved some Ptolemaic losses. *Cyrene was re-established under Ptolemaic rule (250); Red Sea trading-posts were founded. Internally, an increasing number of Greek and demotic papyri illuminate a developing bureaucracy and control of the population through a tax-system based on a census and land-survey. Land, especially in the Fayūm region, was reclaimed and settled with military cleruchs (colonists) and in gift-estates. It was a period of experiment and expansion. Royal patronage benefited *Alexandria; the Pharos lighthouse (see SEVEN WONDERS OF THE ANCIENT WORLD), Museum, Library (see LIBRARIES), and other buildings graced the city, which developed as a centre of artistic and cultural life. Honouring his parents with a festival, the Ptolemaieia (279/8), Philadelphos further instituted a Greek royal cult for himself and Arsinoë II (see RULER-CULT, I. *Greek*). D. J. T.

publicani Since the Roman republic had only a rudimentary 'civil service' and primitive budgeting methods, the collection of public revenue, except for the *tributum*, was sold as a public contract to the highest bidder, who reimbursed himself with what profit he could, at the tax rate set by the state. In addition, as in other states, there were contracts for public works, supplies, and services (*ultro tributa*). The purchasers of these contracts provided the logistic background to the Roman victories in the Punic Wars (see ROME (HISTORY) §1.4) and in the eastern wars of the 2nd cent. BC, and managed the building of the Roman *roads. Roman expansion also expanded their activities; thus the traditional contracts for the exploitation of *mines were extended to the vastly profitable Spanish mines (see e.g. Strabo 3. 2. 10. 147–8c, from Polybius), and the profits of victory also financed a boom in public construction. Tax collection expanded correspondingly, as more harbours and toll stations came under Roman control and much conquered land became *ager publicus* (public land). In Italy there seems to have been a basic shift in sources of revenue between 179 and 167, with indirect taxes (especially *portoria*, customs dues) collected by *publicani* taking the place of *tributum*. The increase in their opportunities led to some conflicts with the senate and the censors (magistrates), in which the latter always prevailed. (See e.g. *Cato the Elder.)

In *Sicily the main tax was collected according to the law of King Hiero II of *Syracuse, which protected the population against serious abuse. In Spain, a *stipendium* (cash tax), originally to pay for the Roman troops, was collected by the quaestors. We do not know how the taxes were collected in the provinces acquired in 146 and originally in Asia, but in 123 Gaius *Gracchus changed history by providing that the tithe of Asia was to be sold in Rome by the censors every five years. The sums involved were spectacular: the companies (*societates publicanorum*) had to become much larger and more complex in organization. Henceforth taxes far surpassed *ultro tributa* as sources of profit, especially when *Pompey extended the Asian system to the provinces he organized. The wealthiest of the *publicani* gained a dominant role in the *repetundae* (provincial extortion) court and other *quaestiones* (standing courts) and in the *ordo* of *equites. They became the most powerful pressure group in Rome, and they dominated finance in the provinces and allied states.

The companies, by special legislation, possessed privileges unknown in normal Roman company law. They consisted of *socii* (partners), who put up the capital and were governed by one or more *magistri*, one of them probably the *manceps* (successful bidder) who bought the contract at auction. Provincial offices were run by a *pro magistro* (who might be an *eques*) and might have large staffs, including *familiae* of hundreds of slaves and freedmen. By the late republic they acted as bankers to the state (avoiding the shipment of large sums in coin) and their messengers would transport mail for officials and important private persons.

Complaints about their abuses were frequent. Proconsuls found it more profitable to co-operate with them in exploitation than to protect the provincials. The fate of Publius Rutilius Rufus (exiled 92) and Lucius Lucullus (command in Asia removed by stages 68–7) shows the risks of opposing them; but these cases were exceptional and partly due to personal character. Cicero showed that tactful and honest governors could gain their co-operation in relieving provincials of unbearable burdens in return for secure profits. Extortion by senatorial commanders and their staffs seems to have far surpassed any due to the *publicani*. In the late republic there was a market for unregistered shares (*partes*) in the companies in Rome, enabling senators (e.g. *Caesar and *Crassus), who were not allowed to be *socii*, to share in the profits of the companies and no doubt to be influential in running them. The largest companies now tended to form a cartel: thus the main company for Bithynia (NW Asia Minor) consisted of all the other companies.

The Civil Wars brought the companies huge losses, as their provincial *fisci* (treasuries) were appropriated by opposing commanders. They never recovered their wealth and power. Caesar somewhat restricted their activities by depriving them of the Asian *decuma* (tithe on the grain harvest). Under the empire, tribute came to be collected by quaestors and *procurators, though *publicani* might be used at the local level. Other revenues continued to be in their hands and we have plentiful evidence for their elaborate organization. Complaints against them continued, but they had little political influence. *Nero strictly regulated their activities, and from the 2nd cent. AD their place was increasingly taken by individual *conductores* (tax farmers). See FINANCE, ROMAN.   E. B.

Punic wars See ROME (HISTORY) §1.4.

punishment, Greek and Roman practice According to *Cicero (*Ad Brut.* 23. 3), it was a dictum of *Solon's that a community was held together by rewards and penalties, and the ascription seems plausible, in so far as Archaic Greek law-codes (see LAW IN GREECE) already show the city asserting its authority in laying down penalties both for universally recognized crimes and for failure to perform the duties imposed by its statutes. Cicero himself argued that the instinct to take vengeance (*vindicatio*) is nature's gift to man to ensure his own and his family's survival (*Inv.* 2. 65). both in Greece and Rome criminal law emerged as an attempt to circumscribe and replace private revenge. Accordingly, just as prosecution in many cases fell to injured persons or their relatives, so the treatment of the convicted man was often closely related to his victims, for example in early homicide law and in matters of physical injury and theft. There are also the religious aspects of punishment, which extend beyond offences against the gods themselves—for example at Athens and Rome in relation to blood-guilt (see POLLUTION) and at Rome in relation to certain political offences.

In fixing penalties legislators were guided to some extent both by the severity of the offence and the intention of the wrongdoer. Another consideration was the *status of the convicted person. Punishment of slaves, for example, was harsher and more humiliating than that of free men (see SLAVERY). Two other factors should be borne in mind: first, limited financial resources made any great expenditure on punishment impossible in practice in the majority of communities, even if it was thinkable; secondly, the high value attached to official membership of a community through citizenship made the removal (or diminution) of this status, i.e. exile or loss of political rights, an effective form of punishment.

The supreme penalty, execution, had a two-way relationship to exile. One might escape execution by voluntary exile, whereupon the self-imposed penalty was aggravated by a ban on return (on pain of death) and confiscation of property. Alternatively one might be condemned to exile with loss of property with the threat of a full capital penalty for illegal return. A form of inflicting dishonour less severe than exile was the removal of some citizen-privileges (*atimia* at Athens, *infamia* at Rome), e.g. loss of the right to speak or vote in an assembly or of membership of the senate at Rome or in a Roman municipality.

Long-term imprisonment by the community is not usually found in Greek cities or under the Roman republic (see PRISON), but a similar effect might be achieved by selling delinquents into chattel-slavery or turning them into virtual slaves to the person they had offended (the fate of condemned thieves under the Roman republic). Under the Principate we find condemnation to the *mines, public works, or gladiatorial schools (see GLADIATORS, COMBATANTS AT GAMES) not only in Italy but the provinces.

Flogging was normally thought appropriate only for the punishment of slaves under Athenian democracy, not for that of free men. Whips were associated with tyrants; thus the Thirty (Spartan-sponsored oligarchy at Athens, 404 BC) had 300 whip-carriers. However, whips were used on free men elsewhere in the Greek world, notably at the *games. At Rome, apart from being an element in the traditional form of execution (symbolized in the *fasces*, bundles of rods, carried before magistrates with capital powers, where the rods surrounded the axe), flogging was apparently inflicted on citizens at Rome as reprisal for disobedience to magistrates until the *lex Porcia*, probably passed by *Cato the Elder in 198 or 195 BC; even after this it remained a feature of military discipline and was employed on non-Romans anywhere.

Financial penalties were both employed to recompense injured parties, as in the Roman *lex de repetundis*, and as fines paid to the community, in some instances being deliberately made so large as to entail the financial ruin of the convicted person—an early example is the ruinous fine imposed on the Athenian general Miltiades in 489 BC (Hdt. 6. 136).

Punishments which seem to us barbarous and grotesque should not be assumed to be primitive. The Roman penalty for parricide—drowning in a sack with a dog, cock, ape, and viper (Cic. *Rosc. Am.* 70; *Dig.* 48. 9. 9)—must have been devised after a distinction was drawn between the killing of parents and grandparents and that of other relatives. A particularly recherché punishment under the Principate was the use of criminals as entertainment, when they were condemned to fight as gladiators or beast-fighters in the arena, often being forced to act mythological characters in dramas of blood which culminated in real death (S. Bartsch, *Actors in the Audience* (1994), 50 ff.).

Revenge, recompense, and the assertion of civic authority are the main themes in the Greek and Roman practice of punishment. The latter involved rewarding the good and punishing the bad, hence encouraging citizens to virtue and deterring them from vice. To this extent only was punishment related to moral reform.   A. W. L.

pygmies, dwarves who live in *Africa, *India, Scythia, or Thrace. They are usually discussed in Greek mythology in connection with their fight against the cranes (geranomachy). *Homer (*Il.* 3. 3–6) says that the cranes flee before the winter to the (southern) stream of Oceanus and bring death to the Pygmies. Hecataeus, who located the pygmies in southern Egypt, Ctesias, and the writers on India (e.g. Megasthenes) considerably elaborated the story. Pygmies disguise themselves as rams, or ride on rams and goats. They battle with the cranes to protect their fields (perhaps a reflection of the farmer's life), and conduct operations to destroy the cranes' eggs and young. Other mythographers invented explanations for the struggle, tracing the enmity to a beautiful pygmy girl transformed into a crane (Boeus in Ath. 9. 393e–f). Philostratus (*Eik.* 2.22) tells of an unsuccessful pygmy attack on *Heracles after he killed Antaeus.

The geranomachy is often shown in Greek art, first on the François vase *c.*570, where the pygmies are shown as midgets battling with clubs, hooked sticks, and slings, and riding goats. On later Archaic and Classical vases they become podgy and grotesquely proportioned. Some 4th-cent. vases show them with pelts and poses like giants; like them, they were earth-born (hence their defence of Antaeus). Pygmies appear on Hellenistic rhyta and, in isolated groups, on *gems. In Hellenistic and Roman art, they occur on Campanian wall-paintings as fully armed warriors with no deformity, and in Nilotic paintings and mosaics deformed, often in humorous confrontations with crocodiles or hippopotami.   K. W. A.

Pyrrhus of Epirus in NW Greece (319–272 BC), son of Aeacides and Phthia, most famous of the Molossian kings, chief architect of a large, powerful, and Hellenized Epirote state (see HELLENISM), and builder of the great theatre at the Zeus-sanctuary at Dodona. After reigning as a minor from 307/6 to 303/2, he was driven out and followed for a time the fortunes of Demetrius Poliorcetes ('the Besieger'). With the support of *Ptolemy I, whose step-daughter Antigone he married, and of Agathocles, tyrant of *Syracuse, he became joint king with Neoptolemus, whom he soon removed. Early in his reign he annexed and retained southern Illyria, probably as far as Epidamnus. He tried to emancipate Epirus from Macedonia. By intervening in a dynastic quarrel in Macedonia Pyrrhus obtained the frontier provinces of Parauaea and Tymphaea, together with Ambracia, Amphilochia, and Acarnania. On the death of Antigone he acquired Corcyra (Corfu) and Leucas (Lefkas) as the dowry of his new wife, Lanassa daughter of Agathocles, and made alliances with the Dardanian chief Bardylis and the Paeonian king Audoleon, whose daughters he also married. Conflict with Demetrius (from 291), now king of Macedon, saw substantial gains in Thessaly and Macedonia, but these were largely lost later to *Lysimachus (284).

Appealed to by the Tarentines (as his uncle Alexander of Epirus and the Spartans King Archidamus III and Cleonymus before him), Pyrrhus went to assist them in their Hellenic struggle against Rome. With a force of

25,000 infantry, 3,000 horse, and 20 elephants he defeated the Romans at Heraclea (mod. Policoro) (280), though not without loss, and won the support of the Samnites, Lucanians, Bruttians, and Greek cities of the south. He marched towards Rome, but prolonged negotiations failed to secure peace. In 279 he defeated the Romans again, at Ausculum, but again with heavy losses. Late in the same year he received an appeal from Syracuse and in 278 sailed to Sicily, where he fought the Carthaginians, then allies of Rome, and Mamertines. In 276 he abandoned the campaign (perhaps by then a lost cause) and returned to Italy, whither he was urgently summoned by his allies in the south. After more losses (including eight elephants and his camp) in battle with the Romans at Malventum (renamed thereafter Beneventum) in 275, he returned to Epirus with less than a third of his original force. A garrison was left behind at Tarentum, signifying perhaps future intent, but the Italian manpower at Rome's disposal had triumphed decisively. Pyrrhus himself embarked upon a new attempt at Macedonia. Initial success and a brief time as king there in 274 gave way to unpopularity after he plundered the royal tombs at *Aegae, and in 273 he marched into the *Peloponnese. Following a failed attack on Sparta he went to Argos, where in 272 he died, struck on the head by a tile thrown from the roof of a house; in the same year Tarentum fell to the Romans. P. S. D.

Pythagoras, Pythagoreanism

1. Pythagoras Pythagoras, son of Mnesarchus, one of the most mysterious and influential figures in Greek intellectual history, was born in *Samos in the mid-6th cent. BC and migrated to Croton (S. Italy) in *c*.530 BC. There he founded the sect or society that bore his name, and that seems to have played an important role in the political life of Magna Graecia (the Greek settlements of S. Italy) for several generations. Pythagoras himself is said to have died as a refugee in Metapontum. Pythagorean political influence is attested well into the 4th cent., with Archytas of Tarentum.

The name of Pythagoras is connected with two parallel traditions, one religious and one scientific. Pythagoras is said to have introduced the doctrine of transmigration of *souls into Greece, and his religious influence is reflected in the cult organization of the Pythagorean society, with periods of initiation, secret doctrines and passwords (*akousmata* and *symbola*), special dietary restrictions (see ANIMALS, ATTITUDES TO), and burial rites. Pythagoras seems to have become a legendary figure in his own lifetime and was identified by some with the Hyperborean *Apollo. His supernatural status was confirmed by a golden thigh, the gift of bilocation, and the capacity to recall his previous incarnations. Classical authors imagine him studying in Egypt; in the later tradition he gains universal wisdom by travels in the east. Pythagoras becomes the pattern of the 'divine man': at once a sage, a seer, a teacher, and a benefactor of the human race.

The scientific tradition ascribes to Pythagoras a number of important discoveries, including the famous geometric theorem that still bears his name. Even more significant for Pythagorean thought is the discovery of the musical consonances: the ratios 2:1, 3:2, and 4:3 representing the length of strings corresponding to the octave and the basic harmonies (the fifth and the fourth). These ratios are displayed in the *tetractys*, an equilateral triangle composed of 10 dots; the Pythagoreans swear an oath by Pythagoras as author of the *tetractys*. The same ratios are presumably reflected in the music of the spheres, which Pythagoras alone was said to hear.

In the absence of written records before Philolaus in the late 5th cent., it is impossible to tell how much of the Pythagorean tradition in *mathematics, music, and *astronomy can be traced back to the founder and his early followers. Since the fundamental work of Walter Burkert, it has been generally recognized that the conception of Pythagorean philosophy preserved in later antiquity was the creation of *Plato and his school, and that the only reliable pre-Platonic account of Pythagorean thought is the system of Philolaus. *Aristotle reports that for the Pythagoreans all things are numbers or imitate numbers. In Philolaus we read that it is by number and proportion that the world becomes organized and knowable. The basic principles are the Unlimited (*apeira*) and the Limiting (*perainonta*). The generation of the numbers, beginning with One in the centre, seems to coincide with the structuring of the cosmos. There must be enough cosmic bodies to correspond to the perfect number 10; the earth is a kind of heavenly body, revolving around an invisible central fire. This fact permitted Copernicus to name 'Philolaus the Pythagorean' as one of his predecessors.

Plato was deeply influenced by the Pythagorean tradition in his judgement myths, in his conception of the soul as transcending the body, and in the mathematical interpretation of nature. The *Phaedo* and the *Timaeus*, respectively, became the classical formulations for the religious and cosmological aspects of the Pythagorean world view. In the *Philebus* (16c) begins the transformation of Pythagoras into the archetype of philosophy. This view is developed by Speusippus, who replaces Plato's Forms by Pythagorean numbers. Hence Aristotle's successor Theophrastus can assign to Pythagoras the late Platonic 'unwritten doctrines' of the One and the Infinite Dyad, and these two principles appear in all later versions of Pythagorean philosophy.

In the 1st cent. BC, the Roman scholar and mystic Publius Nigidius Figulus revived the Pythagorean tradition in Rome, while in *Alexandria the Platonist Eudorus attributed to the Pythagoreans a supreme One, above the two older principles of One and Dyad. This monistic Platonism was developed by the Neopythagoreans: Moderatus of Gades in the 1st cent. AD, Nicomachus of Gerasa and Numenius of Apamea in the 2nd cent. Their innovations were absorbed into the great Neoplatonic synthesis of Plotinus, and thereafter no distinction can be drawn between Pythagoreans and Neoplatonists.

Porphyry and Iamblichus both composed lives of Pythagoras in which he is represented as the source of Platonic philosophy.

There is an important pseudonymous literature of texts ascribed to Pythagoras, Archytas, and other members of the school. This begins in the 3rd cent. BC and continues down to Byzantine times. A number of these texts have survived, thanks to the prestige of their supposed authors.

C. H. K.

2. Pythagoreanism (Religious Aspects) Pythagoreanism is the name given to the philosophical and religious movement(s) allegedly derived from the teachings of Pythagoras. Reliable tradition on the early form of Pythagoreanism, coming chiefly from *Aristotle and his school, presents Pythagoras and his followers as a religious and political association in S. Italy (chiefly Croton) where they gained considerable political influence, until their power was broken in a catastrophe in about 450 BC. From then on, Pythagoreanism survived in two distinct forms, a scientific, philosophical form (the so-called *mathēmatikoi*) which in the 4th cent. manifested itself in the thinking of Philolaus and Archytas of Tarentum and the Pythagoreans whom Plato knew and followed, and a religious, sectarian form (*akousmatikoi*), those following certain oral teachings (*akousmata* or *symbola*), which manifested itself in the migrant Pythagoristai of Middle Comedy. After the analysis of W. Burkert (*Lore and Science in Ancient Pythagoreanism* (1972, Ger. orig. 1962)), it is universally recognized that scientific Pythagoreanism is a reform of its earlier, religious way ascribed to Hippasus of Metapontum around 450 BC.

Despite the fact that many pseudepigraphical Pythagorean writings are dated to Hellenistic times, the continuity of any form of Pythagoreanism after the Classical age is disputed. Neopythagoreanism existed at any rate in the late Hellenistic (the Roman Nigidius Figulus, founder of Neoplatonism according to Cic. *Tim.* 1) and early imperial epochs (*Apollonius of Tyana); through the alleged derivation of the legendary King Numa's teaching from that of Pythagoras, it gained popularity in Rome (see Ov. *Met.* 15. 60–496). It continued into the related Neoplatonist movement (see Neoplatonism); prominent

Neoplatonists such as Porpyhry and his pupil Iamblichus wrote on Pythagoreanism (*De vita Pythagorica*). The hexametrical collection of life rules, under the title Golden Words (*Chrysē Epē*) ascribed to Pythagoras himself, appears at the same date.

While among the philosophical disciplines of the mathematici, arithmetic, theory of number and music are prominent and influential, the doctrines of the acusmatici laid down rules for a distinctive life style, the 'Pythagorean life'. The originally oral *akousmata* (collected by later authors; a list in Iambl. *V. Pyth.* 82–6) contained unrelated and often strange answers to the questions 'What exists?', 'What is the best thing?', 'What should one do?' Prominent among the rules of life is a complicated (and in our sources not consistent) vegetarianism, based on the doctrine of metempsychosis and already ascribed to Pythagoras himself during his lifetime (Xenophanes, DK 21 B 7); total vegetarianism excludes participation in sacrifice and marginalizes those who profess it, at the same time all the more efficiently binding them together in their own sectarian group. Metempsychosis and, more generally, an interest in the afterlife connects Pythagoreanism with Orphism; Plato associates vegetarianism with the Orphic life-style (*bios Orphikos* Plat. *Laws* 6. 783 C), and authors from about 400 BC onwards name Pythagoreans as authors of certain Orphic texts.

See ANIMALS, ATTITUDES TO; ORPHEUS.   F. G.

Pytheas (*c.*310–306 BC), Greek navigator of Massalia (Marseille), author of a lost work 'About the Ocean', object of ancient distrust. From *Strabo, *Diodorus, and *Pliny the Elder mostly we learn that, sailing from Gades (Cadiz) past Cape Ortegal, the Loire, north-west France, and Uxisame (Ushant), he visited Belerium (Cornwall) and the tin-depot at Ictis (St Michael's Mount), circumnavigated *Britain, described its inhabitants and climate, reported an island Thule (Norway or Iceland), sailed perhaps to the Vistula, and reported an estuary (Frisian Bight?) and an island (Heligoland?) abounding in amber. Pytheas calculated closely the latitude of Massalia and laid bases for cartographic parallels through north France and Britain.

E. H. W.; A. J. S. S.

Quintilian (c. AD 35–sometime in the 90s). See LITERARY CRITICISM IN ANTIQUITY, §8; RHETORIC, LATIN.

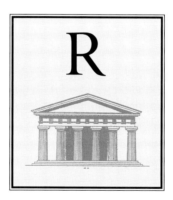

race Greeks and Romans were avid observers in art and text of departures among foreigners (*allophyloi*, *alienigeni*) from their own somatic norms. But it is difficult to discern any lasting ascription of general inferiority to any ethnic group in antiquity solely on the basis of body-type. The explanation is partly conceptual: although *Aristotle realized that pigmentation was biologically transmitted (*Gen. An.* 1. 18, 722ª), popular *anthropology understood cultural variation among humankind in terms, not of nature (i.e. heredity), but nurture, and specifically environment (thus the Hippocratic *Air, Waters, Places* 12. 17–24; see MEDICINE, §4), which shaped 'customs, appearance, and colour' (Polyb. 4. 21), the sunny south generating blackness, the north 'glacial whiteness' (Plin. *HN* 2. 80. 189); thus, as *Strabo implies, it was only their poor soil which debarred the Arians of E. Iran from the pleasures of civilization (25. 32). Although profoundly ethnocentric and, along the way, idealizing one somatic norm (Graeco-Roman) over others, this outlook none the less inhibited the emergence of 'white' as a privileged somatic category (with 'black' as its antithesis), as did the fact that both Greeks and Romans defined themselves in opposition to a *cultural* construct, the *barbarian, which embraced mainly peoples of similarly pale skin-tone. A variety of ancient sensory responses can be detected to the physiognomies of Mediterranean blacks (usually from Nilotic or NW Africa and, whatever their hue, classed generally as *Aethiopes*), ranging from the negative (e.g. the description of a negroid woman in the (?Virgilian) *Moretum*, ed. E. J. Kenney, 1984, ll. 31–5) to the admiring (the dignified negroid head-vases of Attic Greek *pottery, or the Mauretanian with skin 'like Corinthian bronze' of a Roman epitaph, *SEG* 40. 397); more problematic is the extent to which ancient colour-symbolism linked blackness stereotypically with the ill-omened—death, demons (in Christian thought), and so on. Less often remarked on are the hints of Roman somatic distaste for northerners, in particular the paleness (*pallor*) of the men and their superior height (Caes. *BGall.* 2. 30. 4; 4. 1. 9). Racism must be distinguished from—even if somatic judgements may form an element in—*cultural* prejudice (ethnocentrism), which by contrast certainly *was* a historical motor in antiquity, shaping (e.g.) a Graeco-Roman *Orientalism to an extent, and in ways, which scholars have yet to map fully. See ETHNICITY; JEWS; NATIONALISM.

A. J. S. S.

rape See HETEROSEXUALITY; HUBRIS; and E. M. Harris, *CQ* 1990; S. Cole, *CP* 1984; S. Deacy and K. Pierce, *Rape in Antiquity* (1997).

reception 'Our literature is characterized by the pitiless divorce which the literary institution maintains between the producer of the text and its user ... between its author and its reader. This reader is thereby plunged into a kind of idleness—he is intransitive' (Roland Barthes). 'Reception', in the specialized sense used within literary theory, is a concept of German origin, associated primarily with the Constance school of critics led by H. R. Jauss and W. Iser, and is often now used to replace words like tradition, heritage, influence, etc., each key-word having its own implied agenda. Studies of reception-history (*Rezeptionsgeschichte*) are studies of the reading, interpretation, (re)fashioning, appropriation, use, and abuse of past texts over the centuries, reception-theory the theory underpinning such studies. Jauss starts from the proposition, previously advanced within German hermeneutics, e.g. in Hans-Georg Gadamer's *Truth and Method* (1960; Eng. trans. 1975), that interpretation always takes place *within history*, and is subject to the contingencies of its historical moment; there is no permanently 'correct' reading of a text, but an ever-changing 'fusion of horizons' between text and interpreter. Thus reception-theory, like other modern theories of reading (including the 'reader-response criticism' associated with the American scholar Stanley Fish, with his dictum (*Is There a Text in This Class?* (1980)) that 'the reader's response is not *to* the meaning, it *is* the meaning'), stresses the importance of the reader, within the triangle writer–text–reader, for the construction of meaning. So *Horace, as a man, as a body of texts, as an authority for different ways of living, has been diversely read in the west over the last 500 years, by scholars, poets, and 'men of letters', and our current images are shaped in response to that reception-history.

Some scholars argue that the proper meaning of a text is the meaning (meanings?) assigned by its original readers. Ancient theorists certainly stress the response of audiences; Aristotle makes the arousal of pity and fear crucial for tragic effect, while the rhetoricians expound the use of tropes and figures to control more effectively the reactions of auditors. Ancient *literary criticism is in that sense primarily *affective*, more concerned with emotional response than with interpretation. A famous anecdote describes the extraordinary impact of *Cicero's *Pro Ligario* on a reluctant *Caesar (Plut. *Cic.* 39). But we know virtually nothing in detail about contemporary responses to ancient texts, so that appeals to them become circular arguments. Much of the evidence is from late antiquity; we should remember that e.g. the 4th-cent. AD grammarian Servius' commentary postdates *Virgil by several centuries (had it been written 200 years later it would doubtless be dismissed as medieval).

Reception-study is necessarily of importance to all classicists, but the nature of that importance can be differently conceived. Reception-study can be seen as a historical study in its own right, casting fresh light on the past and underlining the difference of its reading practices from those of the present (no one today would subscribe to Neoplatonic readings of *Homer or Christian allegorizations of *Ovid). But, by revealing different perspectives on classical texts, it can also change the way we look at the classical world and its productions. The changing responses to antiquity can be seen as strategies for mediating cultural change and (re)negotiating relationships with the past which are significant for the receivers (so, e.g., Virgil was used in the Renaissance to justify princely rule or in the 19th cent. to underwrite British imperialism). Our own readings too are analysable in these terms, readings which have been affected by post-classical interpretations and constructed in turn as a further link in the chain of receptions (e.g. T. S. Eliot's influential view of Virgil was partly based on his interpretation of Dante's Virgil). Reception-theory thus dissolves the distinction between texts in their initial contexts, read 'in their own terms', and the after-life of those texts, in a way which threatens traditional positivistic attempts to reconstitute 'original' meanings as the only true meanings. To a reception-theorist this dictionary is not a compendium of timeless, unmediated, unsituated 'facts' about antiquity but another small chapter in its never-to-be-stilled reception-history. See also LITERARY THEORY AND CLASSICAL STUDIES.

C. A. Ma.

reciprocity (Greece) The idea that giving goods or rendering services imposed upon the recipient a moral obligation to respond pervaded Greek thought from its earliest documented history. Linguistically, the idea is most commonly signalled by the preposition *anti*, either by itself or attached to a noun or verb.

Reciprocity was one of the central issues around which the moral existence of the Homeric heroes revolved; see HOMER. In the poems, it is consistently implied and sometimes plainly stated that a gift or service should be repaid with a counter-gift or a counter-service. This need not be forthcoming immediately, and may not be in the same category as the original gift or service. In the long run, however, allowing for slight temporary imbalances, the gifts and services exchanged must be equal in value and bestow equal benefits upon both parties. In making this assumption the Homeric world differs significantly from that of the Old Testament, in which God rather than the recipient is said to requite both good and bad deeds. Gain, profit, and loss belonged in Homer to the world of traders, or to that of aristocrats engaged in plunder and spoliation. Reciprocity aimed at the forging of binding relationships (see FRIENDSHIP, RITUALIZED; MARRIAGE LAW) between status equals, from which a long series of unspecified mutual acts of assistance could be expected to flow.

The assumption of equivalence did not extend into the realm of hostile encounters. Here there was no taking of an eye for an eye. Instead, what Kenneth Dover has called the 'head for an eye' principle prevailed: upon being provoked, offended, or injured, the hero was expected to give free rein to his passionate desire for revenge. Although the more peaceful alternative of material compensation for an insult or an injury was also available (see e.g. *Il.* 9. 634), over-retaliation was undoubtedly the norm.

A system of thought striving at equivalence of give and take faces a practical difficulty: how to assess the values of exchangeable items with any precision. It is presumably this difficulty that precipitated the invention, at some time after Homer's day, of *coinage.

The *polis* brought about a threefold change in the operation of reciprocity. First, it turned communal interest into a new standard of individual morality, reinterpreting the norms inherited from the past accordingly. When *Themistocles tells King Artaxerxes I of Persia, 'I deserve to be repaid for the help I gave you' (Thuc. 1. 137), *Thucydides makes it clear that the first half of this reciprocal action gave rise to the suspicion that its other half was to be Themistocles' recruitment to the Persian court. This, in turn, posed a threat to the community to which no Athenian could be indifferent. In Homer no moral norms which compete with the unhindered exercise of reciprocity are visible. Secondly, the *polis* promoted the ideal of communal altruism: the performance of actions beneficial to the community but potentially detrimental to the individual performing them (e.g. nursing the sick during a plague or donating money as liturgies (compulsory services to the state)). The pre-*polis* equation dictating equivalence of give and take here breaks down in favour of individual sacrifices for the benefit of the community. (Individual benefit derived from communal benefit is of another order.) Thirdly, the *polis* in general, and Athens in particular, endorsed the ideal of self-restraint as a means of checking hostile encounters. When provoked, offended, or injured, the citizen was expected to refrain from retaliating or taking revenge, relinquishing the right to inflict punishment to the civic authorities.   G. H.

records and record-keeping, attitudes to Greeks and Romans kept records on stone or bronze, lead, wooden tablets (waxed or whitened), papyrus (see BOOKS, GREEK AND ROMAN), ostraca (potsherds), even precious metals. The different materials often bear certain associations and reflect ancient attitudes to records: e.g. bronze documents in Athens have religious associations, as do the bronze tablets of Roman laws. Stone inscriptions promised permanence and importance, publicly visible reminders of the decree (etc.) they record: in *Athens, matters of particular concern to the gods went up on stone (e.g. the Athenian tribute lists). Athenian inscriptions are read and referred to, but they may also serve as memorials of the decision they record, so that their destruction signifies the end of that transaction (e.g. Dem. 16. 27); inscribed laws are often dedicated to a god. The relation of the inscribed records to those in the archives is therefore complex. Some scholars believe that archival texts are the originals, the inscriptions merely copies, and that there were always archival copies. The situation changes in the Hellenistic period, but the terminology, even then, is inconsistent and inscribed texts are treated as authoritative, indicating a less archive-oriented attitude to records. Archive organization, where we have evidence, is often primitive, and not all archive documents are preserved: in classical Athens certain documents are destroyed when the transaction is complete (e.g. records of state debtors), or for political reasons (e.g. *IG* I³ 127, 27 ff., for *Samos), or as a *damnatio memoriae* (erasing the memory of enemies of the state), as in Rome. Certain information was not recorded at all. However written documentation increasingly takes over from memory and oral proof in Athens during the 4th cent., and the archives came to be used more extensively.

Romans generally attach more importance to written record than Classical Greece, and archives are more sophisticated. The public inscriptions, especially those on the Capitol, have powerful symbolic value, however (see Suet. *Vesp.* 8. 5), as well as being fundamental records: as in Greece, their removal would annul the transaction they record (e.g. Plut. *Cic.* 34. 1). The extent of centralization may have been exaggerated, and evidence for reforms in the *aerarium* (treasury) imply negligence, falsification, and loss of documents (Plut. *Cat. Min.* 16–18; Dio 54. 36. 1, 57. 16. 2). *Cicero lamented the lack of a proper guardianship and public record of the laws (*Leg.* 3. 20. 46). The extent to which the *aerarium* was really used for reference is controversial; senatorial writers consulted individuals or private records (including private collections of laws) as well as state archives. Political facts may lie behind these differing attitudes to written record. Apart from the *senatus consulta* (decrees of the *senate), there were no official records of senatorial business until *Caesar proposed the *acta* (official record of proceedings) be published (59 BC, Suet. *Div. Jul.*

20; rescinded, *Aug.* 36). Provincial cities keep their own copies of relevant documents, sometimes not reliably (cf. *Pliny the Younger, *Ep.* 10. 65–6, 72–3, who sends back to *Trajan for accurate versions). Even in the elaborate bureaucracy of the late empire, it has been argued (Mommsen) that the Theodosian Code, a collection of *c*.2,500 imperial laws published under Theodosius II (408–450), was partly compiled not from a central imperial archive but from individuals, law schools, and provincial archives.

See also ARCHIVES. R. T.

religion, Greek (*see page 590*)

religion, Jewish (*see page 592*)

religion, Roman (*see page 594*)

Res gestae (of *Augustus). Augustus left four documents with the Vestal virgins (see VESTA) to be read, after his death, in the senate (Suet. *Aug.* 101). One of these was a record of his achievements (*Index rerum a se gestarum*), in the style of the claims of the *triumphatores* of the Roman past, which was to be erected on bronze pillars at the entrance of his mausoleum in the Campus Martius at Rome. This is known to us from a copy, updated after Augustus' death, which was piously affixed (with a Greek translation) to the *antae* of the front of the *cella* of the temple of Rome and Augustus at Ancyra (mod. Ankara), capital of Galatia and therefore centre of the imperial cult of the province. Small fragments of other copies have been found at Apollonia and Antioch in Pisidia (also in the province of Galatia); it is likely but not established that copies were widely set up in the provinces.

As it stands, the document seems to have been composed immediately before Augustus' death, but it is certain that it was in existence in some form in AD 13 and likely that it existed considerably before that. It is remarkable for the claims that it makes for the legality and constitutional propriety of Augustus' position, and plays down a number of considerations, relating especially to the period before *Actium, which might be seen less favourably.

The emphases are extremely interesting: first, the bestowal of honours on Augustus by the community is stressed, consensus being a striking theme; second, the expenditures made, as a great benefactor, by Augustus, are outlined (this is announced in the opening words, which entitle the document a Record of the Achievements and Expenses of the Divine Augustus); third, the military achievements of the age, with the emphasis on *imperium* and the personal glory of Augustus, a historic and unthreatening boast in terms of Roman politics; and a final summary of the position with a justification of the superior *auctoritas* which all of this entailed, and particular notice, accordingly, of the title *pater patriae* ('Father of the Fatherland'). This is a record in the tradition of self-advertisement used by great men under the republic, and not a royal manifesto; it omits anything which might suggest an unconstitutional overall guidance of Roman decision-making, and is not a complete record of either his legislation or his administrative innovations. The document illustrates very well the speciously libertarian traditionalism which *Tacitus so deftly punctures in the opening chapters of the *Annals*; but it is also a very important source for a great deal of detail not attested elsewhere.

N. P.

Rhamnus (see ◀Map 1, Cc▶), an Athenian deme (rural district) of moderate size on the north-east coast of Attica, overlooking the narrow waters to the island of Euboea. It was the site of an important fort, constructed in the 5th cent. BC and enlarged in the 4th, on an acropolis by the coast and including a *gymnasium and *theatre within its walls. A road lined with a series of monumental tombs runs inland from this acropolis to the sanctuary of the goddess Nemesis with its two 5th-cent. temples. The late 5th-cent. temple of Nemesis is relatively well preserved, and it has been possible to reconstruct its entablature and a large part of the famous cult statue, attributed to the sculptor Agoracritus, with its base. Neolithic and late bronze-age finds have also been made at the sanctuary site. The epigraphic record from 5th–3rd-cent. Rhamnus gives uniquely rich coverage of the interactions between garrison troops and local population. C. W. J. E.; R. G. O.

rhetoric, Greek The art of public speaking (*rhētorikē* (sc. *technē*)) was vitally important in ancient city-states, and it was generally supposed to be teachable, at least to some extent. This article surveys the development of this teaching in the Greek-speaking world, and offers a summary of the system in which it was generally organized. The concepts and terminology of rhetoric are almost entirely Greek: the Romans provided a wider field of activity for the teachers, and certain new emphases in response to practical needs.

Effective speaking of course existed long before any theory or teaching. Later rhetors wisely referred pupils to the speeches in *Homer (see Quintilian 10. 1. 46 ff.), and his descriptions of the oratory of the heroes (see LITERARY CRITICISM IN ANTIQUITY, §2) were taken as evidence that 'rhetoric' was known in his day. In fact, the teaching of these skills probably began (as *Aristotle thought) under the pressure of social and political needs in the 5th-cent. democracies of Syracuse and Athens (see GORGIAS). Even if the first mode of teaching was primarily by example (as in the demonstration pieces of Gorgias, Thrasymachus, and *Antiphon), this presupposes some theory of the parts of a speech (prologue, narrative, argument, counter-argument, epilogue) and some discussion of probable arguments and the value of different kinds of evidence. The early teachers cannot be responsible for the brilliant achievements of Attic orators from *Lysias to *Hyperides; these are due to individual genius and political stimulus. Behind the great orators, however, stood the mass of

Rhamnus Reconstructed drawing of the late 5th-cent. BC cult-statue by Agoracritus (a follower of Phidias; see SCULPTURE, GREEK) in the *temple of Nemesis at Rhamnus. Like some other Athenian demes (country villages), Rhamnus resembled a mini-*polis* in its array of public buildings.

average Athenians, dependent for their success in life, and often for their personal safety, on the exertions of speech-writers (*logographoi*; Lysias and *Demosthenes both wrote speeches for others) or on the teaching they could pick up themselves. The large jury-courts made forensic oratory almost as much a matter of mass appeal as deliberative speeches in the assembly, but there were naturally substantial differences between these two genres which the teachers recognized. Ceremonial speeches (like the public funeral speeches) again made different demands—less argument, more emotion, more ornamentation. The *Rhetorica ad Alexandrum* gives an idea of the type of teaching available in the late 4th cent.: systematic, but arid, and with no attention to basic principles. But questions about the status and value of rhetoric were already being asked; and both *Isocrates and the philosophers made important contributions. Isocrates wrote speeches for litigants, and is credited (probably wrongly) with having written a textbook. His importance is as an educator, whose 'philosophy' (*philosophia*) was distinct from the *sophists' logic and rhetoric and also from the dialectic and mathematics of *Plato. He wished to give his pupils the right moral and political attitudes, and his method was to make them write about such things and criticize and discuss his own work (5. 17 ff., 12. 200 ff.). This was to make a claim for instruction in writing and speaking, under the name of 'philosophy', as a complete education in itself. For Plato, Isocrates' approach was hardly more valid than that of the sophists and rhetoricians of the previous age. He attacks them all (*Gorgias, Phaedrus*) as deceivers and perverters of the truth.

A 'philosophical' rhetoric, he says (*Phaedrus* 271c ff.), would be based on an adequate psychology; this at least would have some value. Plato's hint was taken up by his pupil, Aristotle, who gave instruction in rhetoric as well as in philosophy, and wrote the most influential of all treatises on the subject. This work, the *Rhetoric*, the product of many years and some changes of mind, deals in its three books with three main topics: (*a*) the theory of rhetorical, as distinct from philosophical, argument—*enthymeme* and example; (*b*) the state of mind of the audience and the ways of appealing to their prejudices and emotions; (*c*) style, its basic virtues (clarity, appropriateness), and the use of metaphor. Much of what Aristotle left inchoate (delivery (*hypokrisis*), the virtues and types of style) was developed by his pupil Theophrastus (see LITERARY CRITICISM IN ANTIQUITY, §5).

When forensic and political oratory became less important, under the Hellenistic monarchies and later, rhetoric still continued; outliving its original function, it became the principal educational instrument in the spread of Greek culture. Isocrates' attitudes triumphed. We know little about the technical rhetoric of Hellenistic times. Hermagoras, with his doctrine of types of issue (*staseis*), is probably the most important figure. The philosophical schools, especially the Stoics (see STOICISM), were also concerned with the subject. It is the *Rhetoric* of Philodemus (d. *c*.45–40 BC) that gives us our best Greek evidence for the discussion of wider questions, e.g. whether rhetoric is an art, and whether forensic and epideictic oratory can be regarded as species of the same activity. The stimulus of

[*continued on p. 596*]

religion

Greek religion Despite the diversity of the Greek world, which is fully reflected in its approach to things divine, the cult practices and pantheons current among different communities have enough in common to be seen as essentially one system, and were generally understood as such by the Greeks. This is not to say that the Greeks were familiar with the concept of 'a religion', a set of beliefs and practices espoused by its adherents as a matter of conscious choice, more or less to the exclusion of others; such a framework was not applied to Greek religion before late antiquity, and then under pressure from Christianity. Boundaries between Greek and non-Greek religion were far less sharp than is generally the case in comparable modern situations, but they were perceived to exist. The tone is set by *Herodotus (8. 144. 2), who characterizes 'Greekness' (*to Hellēnikon*) as having common temples and rituals (as well as common descent, language, and customs). Thus, despite his willingness to identify individual Persian or *Egyptian deities with Greek ones (a practice followed by most Greek ethnographers), and indeed despite his attribution of most of the system of divine nomenclature to the Egyptians (2. 50–2), he still sees a body of religious thought and practice which is distinctively Greek. Many modern scholars go further and see a certain overall coherence in this body which enables us to speak of a 'system' despite the lack of formal dogma or canonical ritual.

Origins The system, then, as known to Herodotus, had clearly developed over a long period. The origins of some ritual acts may even predate the human species itself. More definitely, we can clearly trace some Greek deities to Indo-European origins: *Zeus, like *Jupiter, has evolved from an original Sky Father, while the relation between the Dioscuri (Castor and Polydeuces, the 'Heavenly Twins') and the Aśvins, the twin horsemen of the Vedas, is too close for coincidence. Another source of input will have been the indigenous religious forms of Greece, originating before the arrival of Greek-speakers. Sorting such elements from 'Greek' ones in the amalgam we call Minoan-Mycenaean religion is an impossible task; it is easier to trace Minoan-Mycenaean elements in the religion of later periods. See MINOAN and MYCENAEAN CIVILIZATION. Most obviously, many of the names of the major Greek gods are found already in Mycenaean Linear B documents, but recent discoveries also indicate that some elements of classical cult practice have their roots in this period. It remains true, however, that the total complex of cult presents a very different aspect.

At various periods the religion of Greece came under substantial influence from the near east. Much in the traditions of creation and theogony represented for us in *Hesiod has very striking parallels in several west Asian sources, probably reflecting contact in the Minoan-Mycenaean period. Cult practice, however, does not seem to have been open to influence from the east much before the Geometric period, when we begin to find the construction of large temples containing cult images, a form which is likely to owe more to near eastern/West Semitic culture than to the bronze age in Greece. Elements of the Classical form of sacrificial ritual can also be derived from the east. A final 'source' for later Greek religion is formed by the poems of *Homer and Hesiod, who though they did not, as Herodotus claims, give the gods their cult titles and forms (2. 53. 2), certainly fixed in Greek consciousness a highly anthropomorphic and more or less stable picture of divine society, a pattern extremely influential throughout antiquity despite its frequent incompatibility with ritual practices and local beliefs.

General characteristics Turning to the analysis of Greek religion as it appears in the post-Geometric period, we find in common with most pre-modern societies a strong link between religion and society, to the extent that the sacred/secular dichotomy as we know it has little meaning for the Greek world. Greek religion is community-based, and to the extent that the *polis* forms the most conspicuous of communities, it is therefore *polis*-based. The importance of this connection began to wane somewhat in the Hellenistic period and later, but to the end of antiquity it remains true to say that Greek religion is primarily a public religion rather than a religion of the individual. Reciprocally, religious observances contributed to the structuring of society, as kinship groups (real or fictitious), local habitations, or less obviously related groups of friends constructed their corporate identity around shared deities and cults. One major difference in the socio-religious organization of Greece from that of many other cultures concerns priestly office, not in the Greek world a special status indicating integration in a special group or caste, but rather parallel to a magistracy, even where, as often, a particular priesthood is hereditary. See PRIESTS.

Cult Specific religious practices are described more fully under separate headings (see also RITUAL); the following is a very brief résumé. Probably the central ritual act in Greek cult, certainly the most conspicuous, is animal *sacrifice, featured in the overwhelming majority of religious gatherings. Its overlapping layers of significance have been much debated, but it is clear that sacrifice relates both to human–divine relations (the celebration of and offering to a deity) and to a bonding of the human community (the shared sacrificial meal). The act might take place at most times, but on certain dates it was celebrated regularly at a particular sanctuary, usually in combination with a special and distinctive ritual complex; the word 'festival' is loosely but conveniently applied to such rites, whether Panhellenic like the *games at *Olympia or intimate and secret like the Arrephoria (in honour of Athena Polias) in Athens. Festivals, at least those of the more public type, articulated the calendar year and provided an opportunity for communal recreation. A more specialized type of gathering was provided by rites known as *mysteries, participation in which was usually felt to confer special benefits, often a better fate after death. Secrecy was a prominent characteristic of these rites, and the experience was often a profoundly emotional one. There were of course more basic methods of communicating with the divine. Most obviously, *prayer was an indispensable part of any public ritual, but was also used on other occasions, often by individuals. Votive offerings were a very common individual religious act throughout the Greek world (see ART, ANCIENT ATTITUDES TO). On a day-to-day basis, individuals would greet deities whose shrines they were passing, and might also show piety by garlanding an image or making a personal, unscheduled sacrifice—often bloodless, consisting of *cakes or other vegetarian foods, or a pinch of incense. Sometimes they might experience a divine epiphany in the form of a dream (see DREAMS) or a waking vision. Both individuals and *poleis* might make use of various types of prophecies; methods were very various, but generally the process was understood as another form of divine–human communication.

Gods and other cult figures The pantheon certainly showed some local variations, but presented a recognizable picture throughout the Greek world. Zeus, *Demeter, *Hermes, for instance, were names to which any Greek could respond. Again, the fundamental qualities or 'personality' of a deity remained to some extent consistent across different areas of Greece, but exceptions spring readily to mind; *Persephone (Kore), typically an Underworld goddess, is at Locri Epizephyrii (in S. Italy) more concerned with human fertility and the life of women, while the normally strong connection of *Artemis with her brother *Apollo is virtually absent in her Arcadian manifestations. Looking at this another way, we might speak of a multiplicity of deities in different locations, who share their name with others of partially similar character. This analysis, although incomplete, accounts better for the existence of certain local deities who are not, or not completely, identified with the great Panhellenic gods. Thus for instance at Aegina and elsewhere we find Damia and Auxesia, clearly goddesses very roughly of the Demeter-Kore type, but too different to be readily identified with them. Cretan Britomartis appears both as herself and as a form of Artemis. More generally, we might ask in what sense, and to what extent, *Hera of *Samos is identical with Hera of Argos, or indeed within the same city whether Apollo Pythius is 'the same' god as Apollo Agyieus. From one point of view it could be said that every sanctuary housed a 'different' god. On the other hand, the desire to schematize was clearly a strong centripetal force, as was the anthropomorphizing concept of the gods exemplified and promoted by the Homeric poems and their milieu. The boundaries of divine individuality could be drawn in quite different ways depending on context and circumstance.

An anthropomorphic view of the gods also encouraged a concept of a divine society, probably influenced by west Asian models and very prominent in Homer. Prayer formulae locate deities in their sanctuaries or favourite place on earth, but much mythology creates a picture of a group of gods living more or less together in (albeit rather eccentric) family relationships. Since their home was traditionally Mt. Olympus (N. Greece), the gods most prone to this presentation were the 'Olympians', by and large those who were most widely known and worshipped. Sometimes these deities were schematized into the 'Twelve Gods', a group whose composition varied slightly and might include such figures as *Hades/Pluto (widely known, but not situated on Olympus) and Hestia, the hearth (Olympian, but scarcely personified), whose presence is due to their Homeric or Hesiodic status as siblings of Zeus. (The twelve on the frieze of the Parthenon at Athens are *Aphrodite, Apollo, *Ares, Artemis, *Athena, Demeter, Dionysus, *Hephaestus, Hera, Hermes, *Poseidon, Zeus.) However, any local pantheon would also exhibit deities who were not so universally known or who, though the object of widespread cult, were scarcely perceived as personal mythological figures. As examples of the former we could adduce Eleusinian Da(e)ira or Arcadian Despoina ('Mistress'); of the latter, such well-known divinities as Gaia/Ge (who seems scarcely affected by her presentation in Hesiod) and Kourotrophos. There were also 'new', 'foreign' Gods such as Adonis or Sabazius who were difficult to place in the pre-existing framework of divine personalities; and there were deities like the Cabiri who had a Panhellenic reputation although their cult remained confined to a very few locations. More localized still were the 'minor' figures of cult such as female nymphs and heroes, for here there was much less tendency to assimilate figures with others more universally known. True, local heroes were sometimes identified with characters in Panhellenic mythology, but such identifications often remained speculative and were by no means the invariable rule. Nymphs and heroes were generally thought of as residing in one specific place, and though in that place their powers were often considerable, they were usually perceived as ranking lower than gods. They were, however, a characteristic and indispensable part of the circle of superhuman beings.

Later developments The above sketch is based mainly on evidence from before the 3rd cent. BC. Much of the picture is applicable also to Greece in the Hellenistic and Roman periods; religious thought and practice were constantly evolving rather than undergoing sudden transformation. But during the period of *Alexander the Great and his successors, the Greek world acquired a vastly greater geographical extent, and at the same time the significance of the *polis* was gradually changing. These changes inevitably had an influence on religious development. Overall, it seems that many distinctive local practices were giving way to wider trends. It is easy to exaggerate the extent to which this occurred; *Pausanias, writing in the 2nd cent. AD, still found a vast diversity of cult in old Greece. On the other hand, it is undeniable that the worship of certain 'new' deities was steadily gaining in popularity over the Greek world as a whole. One of the most spectacular examples is the cult of Tyche (Chance, Fortune), while also conspicuous in the later period were Egyptian and Anatolian deities such as Isis, Sarapis, and Men, whose cults showed a large admixture of Greek elements. The payment of divine honours to rulers (see RULER-CULT), originating with Alexander, soon became standard, modifying pre-existing religious forms in a new direction. E. Ke.

Jewish religion Judaism in Graeco-Roman antiquity is better known than any other ancient religion apart from Christianity, primarily because of the survival to modern times of traditions about ancient Judaism through rabbinic and Christian literature. However, this same factor creates its own problems of bias in the selection and interpretation of evidence.

The main sources of knowledge about Judaism are the Old and New Testaments and other religious texts preserved in Greek within the Christian Church: the apocrypha and pseudepigrapha, and the writings of Philo of Alexandria and *Josephus. The works composed in Hebrew and Aramaic produced by the rabbis after AD 70 stress rather different aspects. A fresh light has been shone on Judaism by the chance discovery of Jewish papyri in Elephantine and especially by the *Dead Sea Scrolls, which revealed the incompleteness of the later Jewish and Christian traditions even about the 1st cent. AD, the period for which most evidence survives. Pagan Greek and Latin writers emphasized the aspects of Judaism most surprising to outsiders but many of their comments were ignorant and prejudiced.

Many of the basic elements of Jewish worship were shared with other religions of classical antiquity. The prime form of worship was by sacrifices and other offerings in the Jerusalem Temple. In this respect the Jewish cult differed from most in the Greek and Roman world only in the exceptional scrupulousness of its observance; in the assumption of most Jews that sacrifices were only valid if performed in Jerusalem, even though this meant that the sacrificial cult was for many only known from a distance; in the role of the priestly caste, who inherited the prerogative to serve in the sanctuary under the authority of an autocratic high priest who at certain periods also operated as political leader of the nation; and in their strong sense of the special sanctity of the land of Israel and the city of Jerusalem and its shrine.

Of the special elements of Judaism noted in antiquity, most striking to pagans was the exclusive monotheism of Jews: most Jews worshipped only their own deity and either asserted that other gods did not exist or chose to ignore them. Equally strange was the lack of any cult image and the insistence of most Jews by the Hellenistic period that Jewish sacrificial worship was only permitted in the Jerusalem Temple, despite the existence of Jewish temples at Elephantine in Egypt in the 5th cent. BC and at Leontopolis in the Nile delta from the mid-2nd cent. BC to AD 72, and the Samaritan temple on Mt. Gerizim, which was destroyed only in the 120s BC.

Jews were in general believed by outsiders to be specially devoted to their religion, a trait interpreted sometimes negatively as superstition, sometimes positively as philosophy. The foundation of this devotion lay in the Torah, the law governing all aspects of Jewish life which Jews considered had been handed down to them through Moses on Mt. Sinai as part of the covenant between God and Israel. The Torah is enshrined in the Hebrew Bible, and pre-eminently in the Pentateuch (the first five books). Jews treated the scrolls on which the Torah was recorded with exceptional reverence; if written in the correct fashion, such scrolls were holy objects in themselves. The covenant, marked by circumcision for males, involved the observance of moral and ethical laws as well as taboos about food and sacred time (especially, the sabbath).

The main elements of Judaism as here presented were already in place by the 3rd and 2nd cents. BC, when the final books of the Hebrew Bible were composed, but the Jewish religion was to undergo much change over the following centuries. One new development was the gradual emergence of the notion of a canon of scripture treated as more authoritative than other writings.

Agreement about the authority of particular books did not lead to uniformity, or even the notion of orthodoxy. The Hebrew Bible left many opportunities for diversity of interpretation. The extent of variety, at least up to AD 70, is clear from the Dead Sea Scrolls. Disagreements may have been fuelled in part by diverse reactions to the surrounding Hellenistic culture. The continuation of variety after *c.* AD 100, after which Christians ceased to preserve Jewish texts and Judaism is known almost only through the rabbinic tradition, is uncertain.

From the 2nd cent. BC self-aware philosophies began to proclaim themselves within Judaism: Pharisees, Sadducees, and Essenes, and perhaps others. These groups differed on correct practice in the Jerusalem cult as well as on quite fundamental issues of theology, such as the role of fate and the existence of an after-life. However, apart perhaps from the Dead Sea sectarians, who saw themselves as the True Israel, all these Jews believed that they belonged within a united religion: Josephus, who described the three main Jewish philosophies in detail (*BJ* 2. 119–66; *AJ* 18. 11–22), elsewhere boasted that Jews are remarkable for their unanimity on religious issues (*Ap.* 2. 181). The earliest followers of Jesus are best considered in the context of such variety within Judaism.

In the Hellenistic and early Roman periods some aspects of the biblical tradition were particularly emphasized by Jews. Ritual purity as a metaphor for holiness was stressed by Jews of all persuasions: *mikvaoth* (ritual baths) have been excavated in many Jewish sites in the land of Israel, both Pharisees and Essenes elaborated complex elucidations of the biblical purity rules, and restrictions on the use of gentile foodstuffs became more widespread.

Some Jews indulged in speculation about the end of days, which was variously envisaged as a victory of Israel over the nations under God's suzerainty or the total cessation of mundane life. In some texts a leading role was accorded to a messianic figure, but ideas about the personality and function of a messiah or messiahs varied greatly, and the extent to which messianic expectations dominated Judaism in any period is debated. Much of the extant eschatological literature is composed in the form of apocalyptic, in which a vision is said to have been vouchsafed to a holy seer. All the apocalyptic texts from the post-biblical period are either anonymous or pseudepigraphic, reflecting a general belief that the reliability of prophetic inspiration had declined since biblical times.

Religious ideas of all kinds within Judaism were generated or confirmed by study and midrash (a type of exegesis) of the biblical books. According to Josephus in his defence and summary of Judaism in *Ap*. 2. 181–220, Jews were uniquely concerned to learn their own law. The primary locus of teaching was the *synagogue, where the Pentateuch was read and explained at least once a week, on sabbaths. Special buildings for such teaching, and probably for public prayer, are first attested in Egypt in the 3rd cent. BC. In the late Roman period some synagogue buildings were designed with monumental architecture similar to pagan temples and were treated as sacred places.

The increased ascription of sanctity to synagogues was in part a reaction to the destruction of the Jerusalem Temple by Roman forces under *Titus in AD 70 (see JEWS). The destruction, at the end of the great Jewish revolt of AD 66–70, was eventually to have important consequences for the development of Judaism, although new theologies were slow to emerge: Josephus in the 90s AD still assumed that God is best worshipped by sacrifices in Jerusalem, and about a third of the Mishnah (collection of legal opinions), redacted *c*. AD 200, is concerned with the Temple cult.

In the diaspora the Temple had in any case always dominated more as an idea than as an element in religious practice, since only occasional pilgrimage was ever possible. The synagogues at Dura Europus (Mesopotamia) and Sardis (W. Asia Minor) may reveal Judaisms based on synagogue liturgy. An honorific inscription probably of the 3rd cent. AD from *Aphrodisias reveals that, in that Jewish community at least, gentile God-fearers may have participated in Jewish religious institutions.

The Judaism of the rabbis differed from other forms of Judaism mainly in its emphasis on learning as a form of worship. Rabbinic academies, first in Yavneh (Jamnia) on the coast of Judaea immediately after AD 70, but from the mid-2nd cent. mainly in Galilee and (from the 3rd cent.) in *Babylonia, specialized in the elucidation of Jewish law, producing a huge literature by the end of antiquity. Their most important products were the Mishnah, composed in Hebrew *c.* AD 200, and the two Talmuds, redacted (mainly in Aramaic) in Palestine in *c.* AD 400 and in Babylonia in *c.* AD 500; but they also produced a large corpus of midrashic texts commenting on the Bible, and they or others in late antiquity composed the Hekhalot texts, which attest to a continued mystical tradition. See CHRISTIANITY.

M. D. G.

Roman religion The history of Roman religion might be said to begin with *Varro's *Human and Divine Antiquities* (47 BC), of which the second half, 16 books on Divine Antiquities, codified for the first time Roman religious institutions: priests, temples, festivals, rites, and gods. This work, which may have had the unsettling effect of enabling people to see how imperfectly the existing system corresponded to the 'ideal', was extremely influential on traditionalists, and provided ammunition for Christians such as *Augustine in the *City of God*. Nineteenth-cent. scholarship on Roman religion, in attempting a diachronic history down to the age of Varro, assumed an ideal phase, in which religion was perfectly attuned to the agricultural year, from which republican religion was a sorry decline:

religion, Roman An engraved Etruscan mirror showing the mythical diviner Calchas observing the liver of a sacrificial victim (*c*.400 BC). When the need arose the Roman state would summon Etruscan diviners (haruspices, members of the Etruscan aristocracy) to explain prodigies and portents. Generally, the religious expertise of the *Etruscans made a lasting impression on the Romans.

politics increasingly obtruded on religion, and scepticism was rife. This decline model, which underlies the two standard handbooks of Wissowa and Latte, has become increasingly unpopular. In its place scholars now prefer to stress the dynamic changes of republican religion, including its position in public life, and also the continuing significance of public religion in the imperial age.

Defining 'Roman religion' is harder than it might seem. The emphasis of scholars has generally been on the public festivals and institutions, on the ground that they provided the framework within which private rituals were constructed; only those committed to a Protestant view of personal piety will argue that public rituals lack real religious feeling or significance. The geographical focus of the phrase changes radically over time, from the regal period when Rome was an individual city-state through to Rome's acquisition of an empire stretching from Scotland to Syria. Two related themes run through that expansion: the role of specifically Roman cults outside Rome, and the religious impact of empire on Rome itself.

Our knowledge of the early phase of Roman religion is patchy, and subject, like all early Roman history, to later myth-making. For the regal period archaeology casts some light, for example on the extent of Greek influence in the area; the principal festivals of the regal calendar are all attested, in all probability, in the calendar of the late republic. For the republic, archaeological evidence, for example of temples, remains important, and the literary tradition becomes increasingly reliable, especially from the mid-4th or 3rd down to the 1st cent. BC. It becomes possible to produce a diachronic history of the changes to the public cults of the city of Rome, such as the introduction of the cult of Magna Mater (204 BC; see CYBELE; PHILHELLENISM), the suppression of the *Bacchanalia (186 BC), the creation in Italy and the provinces of *coloniae* (Roman citizen-colonies) whose religious institutions were modelled on those of Rome, and the increasing divine aura assumed by dynasts of the late republic.

The Augustan 'restoration' of religion (see AUGUSTUS) was in reality more a restructuring, with the figure of the emperor incorporated at many points. Some 'ancient' cults were given a fresh impetus, while Augustus also built major new temples in the city (*Apollo; *Mars Ultor), which expressed his relationship to the divine. This Augustan system remained fundamental to the public religious life of Rome to the end of antiquity. The religious life of the city also became increasingly cosmopolitan under the empire, with a flourishing of associations focused on gods both Roman and foreign, some within individual households, others drawing their membership from a wider circle. In the high empire the civic cults of Rome operated alongside associations devoted to Isis, *Mithras, Jahveh, or Christ. Outside Rome, civic cults of the Greek east continued to offer a sense of identity to Greeks under Roman rule, but hardly fall under the rubric 'Roman religion'; civic cults in the Latin west, however, took on a strongly Roman cast. Pre-Roman gods were reinterpreted and local pantheons modelled on the Roman. In the 3rd and 4th cents., there was an increasing conceptual opposition between Roman religion and Christianity, but elements of the Roman system proved to be very enduring: in Rome the Lupercalia festival was still celebrated in the late 5th cent. AD.

See also: RELIGION, GREEK; RULER-CULT; also individual deities.   S. R. F. P.

Rome, where significant political activity was in the hands of an aristocracy eager to learn, led to a revival of rhetoric in the 1st cent. BC (see RHETORIC, LATIN). The work of people like Apollodorus of Pergamum, Apollonius Molon, and Theodorus of Gadara, is only to be understood against a Roman background. With the revival of a more independent Greek literature in imperial times, Greek rhetoric (especially epideictic) took on a new lease of life; success in the schools might lead to a brilliant career as a sophist; see SECOND SOPHISTIC. The bulk of the extant works on rhetoric comes from this period, or later. The last great system-atizer was Hermogenes of Tarsus (2nd cent. AD); his work and the voluminous later commentaries on it (especially those of Syrianus) afford the best extant synthesis in Greek, though R. Volkmann (*Die Rhetorik der Griechen und Römer* (2nd. edn. 1885)) was surely right to find in the more humane Roman Quintilian (see next entry) the only 'Ariadne's clue' to the labyrinth of confusing terminology and theory.

Volkmann (and e.g. J. Martin (*Antike Rhetorik* (1974))) are able to set out a description of ancient rhetorical teaching which would be roughly valid for the whole Hellenistic and Roman period, because the conservatism of the educational system ensured that, whatever refinements individual teachers or schools introduced, the main lines of instruction remained the same. The basic divisions of a speech (prologue, etc.) and the basic classification of oratory (forensic, deliberative, epideictic) go back, as we have seen, to the 4th cent. BC. They continue to fulfil a useful function in all later writers; but the method of organizing the whole subject which prevailed later derives ultimately from Aristotle's *Rhetoric*, and comprises five divisions:

1. 'Invention' (*heuresis*) is the most important, and corresponds essentially to Aristotle's 'proofs' (*pisteis*). It teaches how to 'find' (*heuriskein*) things to say to meet the question at issue. The central doctrine is that of 'issue' (*stasis*, Lat. *status*), developed by Hermagoras and refined by many later writers. Hermagoras distinguished four 'issues': 'conjecture' (*stochasmos*), e.g. 'Did X kill Y?'; 'definition' (*horos*), e.g. 'Was it murder?'; 'quality' (*poiotēs*), e.g. 'Was it honourable or expedient?'; 'transference' (*metalēpsis*), e.g. 'It was all Y's fault.' Such analyses, obviously useful to advocates and debaters and for interpreting the orators, inevitably led into great scholastic complexities, as in Hermogenes or Sopater.

2. 'Disposition' (*oikonomia*) comprises prescriptions for the division of subject-matter within the 'parts' of a speech, and some common-sense advice about arrangement—e.g. 'put your weakest points in the middle'.

3. Diction (*lexis*, *phrasis*) was the area where rhetoric comes closest to literary criticism as it was practised in ancient times. Not only types of style, but figures, tropes, word-order, rhythm, and euphony were discussed. Figures (*schēmata*), at least in the developed systems, were generally regarded as deviant or unnatural (*para physin*) forms of expression or thought; tropes (*tropoi*) were similarly deviant (abnormal, non-literal) uses of words, such as occur in metaphor, metonymy, hyperbole, etc.

4. Delivery (*hypokrisis*) was clearly a vital skill, and ancient taste approved of much artifice in pronunciation and gesture, so long as the orator's dignity was preserved.

5. 'Memory' (*mnēmē*) was also a subject of instruction and various forms of 'arts of memory' were taught, involving memorization of visual features (e.g. columns in a colonnade) and the trick of associating these with the points to be made. It was bad form to read from a text, and speeches in court could be very long.

Naturally, the order in which these skills were taught did not follow this pattern. One cannot teach 'invention' and 'diction' quite separately. There was however a recognized course of exercises, and if we look for the influence of rhetorical teaching on literary practice, it is here that it is principally to be found.   D. A. R.

rhetoric, Latin Oratory at Rome was born early. Rhetoric —reduced to a method—came later, an import from Greece

that aroused suspicion. *Cato the Elder, himself a distinguished speaker, pronounced *rem tene, verba sequentur*, 'get a grip on the content: the words will follow'; and rhetoricians professing to supply the words risked expulsion (as in 161 BC). But Greek teachers trained the Gracchi; the satirist Lucilius teased Titus Albucius for the intricacy of his Graecizing mosaics in words; and *Cicero marks out Marcus Aemilius Lepidus Porcina (consul 137) as the first master of a smoothness and periodic structure that rivalled the Greeks. In the last quarter of the 2nd cent. prose rhythms based on contemporary Hellenistic practice appear unmistakably in the orators' fragments. In 92 BC Latin rhetoricians came under the castigation of the censors; Cicero for one wanted to be taught by them, but was kept by his elders to the normal path of instruction in Greek exercises, doubtless declamation. The respectable orator Marcus Antonius (consul 99) wrote a *libellus* that showed knowledge of Hermagoras' *status*-lore. Soon came both the *Rhetorica ad Herennium* and Cicero's *De inventione*: the former a complete manual, the latter, closely related to it, only partial, but both evidence of the sophisticated declamation-based rhetoric taught by Greeks in Rome in the 80s.

Cicero never came nearer than this to writing a rhetorical handbook, though his *Partitiones oratoriae* and *Topica* handled aspects of the subject. In his major rhetorical work, the *De oratore* (55), dialogue form militates against technical exposition; moreover, Cicero was concerned to inculcate his idea of the philosophic orator, with the widest possible education, able to speak 'ornately and copiously' (1. 21) on any topic, and this naturally went with criticism of those who thought that one could become an orator by reading a textbook. Nevertheless, the *De oratore* contained much traditional material; as did the later *Orator* (46 BC), in which Cicero contrasted the 'perfect orator', well educated and commanding every kind of style, modelled on Demosthenes and, implicitly, on Cicero himself, with the so-called Atticists, contemporaries who had a narrower and more austere ideal of oratory. Cicero thus was here defending his own oratorical practice, especially in the matter of wordplay and rhythm; and this practice, no less than the precepts educed from his rhetorical works, was carefully studied by later rhetoricians.

The *Philippics* of Cicero, however, were the last examples of great oratory used to influence political action at Rome. Oratory of course went on under the Principate, but its practical effect was mainly in the lawcourts. Declamation continued to dominate the schools, fascinating even grown men; and it increasingly imparted a crisper style not only to public oratory but also to literature in general. As in the period after the death of *Demosthenes, rhetorical theory, which had always concentrated on forensic oratory, was if anything encouraged by the new political climate. The dispute of Apollodorus of Pergamum and Theodorus of Gadara about the rigidity with which rhetorical rules were to be observed was typical of the new mood; and Gaius Valgius Rufus brought Apollodorus' precepts to Latin readers. The first half of the 1st cent. AD was marked by the contribution of Cornelius Celsus (early 1st cent. AD), whose encyclopaedia went into some detail on rhetoric, and by Rutilius Lupus' translation (of which part survives) of a Greek work on figures. A little later *Pliny the Elder wrote a (lost) work giving detailed instructions on the education of an orator.

The massive *Institutio* of Quintilian (d. 90s AD) takes account of this earlier work, if only to reject it; but, more important, it looks back over it to Cicero, and amidst all its detail retains Cicero's enthusiasm for a wide training and his dislike of trivial technicality. There was much in the *Institutio* that reflected contemporary conditions, especially its concern with declamation; but it maintained, in defiance of history, the ideal of the 'good man skilled in speaking' (*vir bonus dicendi peritus*: Cato the Elder's phrase), whose eloquence should guide the senate and people of Rome (12. 1. 26). For a more realistic assessment of oratory under the early empire we have to look to *Tacitus' more or less contemporary *Dialogus*. Despite all this, the *Institutio* retained interest, particularly in the Renaissance, as a handbook on style and a repository of rhetorical wisdom.

Halm's collection of *Rhetores Latini Minores* may illustrate the ossification and puerility of Latin rhetoric after the 1st cent., in the pat question-and-answer of Fortunatianus and the derivative compendium of Julius Victor. Oratory of this period is represented by the *Panegyrici Latini* that have come down to us; and the letters of Cornelius Fronto in the 2nd cent. reflect the new importance of eulogy. From the schoolroom we have the extravagances of the *Major Declamations*. Rhetoricians continued to flourish, and even found themselves celebrated in the poetry of the 4th-cent. Ausonius; their pupils were in demand as barristers and imperial officials. Many of the Church fathers started out teaching the subject; and rhetoric was turned to Christian uses in the *De Doctrina Christiana* of *Augustine and Cassiodorus' *Institutiones*.

For a summary of ancient rhetorical doctrine, which was usually Greek in origin but found some of its best surviving expositors in Latin, see RHETORIC, GREEK. See also TOPOS.   M. W.

Rhodes (see ◀Map 1, Ed▶), largest island of the mod. Dodecanese (c.1400 sq. km.), lying close to the mainland of Caria.

The earlier prehistory of Rhodes is unclear, but by the 16th cent. (LM I) the Minoans (see MINOAN CIVILIZATION) had established a settlement at Trianda on the NW coast, presumably to facilitate trade between *Crete and the eastern Mediterranean. The Minoans were followed in the 14th cent. (LH IIIA1) by Mycenaeans, apparently from the *Peloponnese, whose numerous chamber-tomb cemeteries suggest a more thorough colonization of the island. Although no Mycenaean settlements have as yet been excavated, the grave offerings, from the cemetery at Ialysus in particular, indicate considerable prosperity.

Dark-Age Rhodes was settled by Dorian Greeks who formed three city-states, Lindus, Ialysus, and Camirus. Their development in the Archaic period was typical for the time and place: they sent out colonies (Gela in Sicily and Phaselis in Lycia (SW Asia Minor) were Lindian foundations), they were ruled by local tyrants, they submitted to Persia in 490. In the 5th cent., they were members of the Athenian Confederacy (see DELIAN LEAGUE), and all appear in the Athenian tribute-lists. The cities revolted from Athens in 412/11, perhaps under the influence of Dorieus, an Ialysian aristocrat of the Diagoridai clan who had been exiled by Athens at the beginning of the Peloponnesian War and turned to Sparta. In 408/7 the three cities renounced their independent political status, synoecized (see SYNOECISM), and founded a *federal state, Rhodes. The reason for this decision was probably commercial rather than military. Existing alongside the new federal capital (also called Rhodes) built on the northern tip of the island in Ialysian territory, the cities retained autonomy in local civic and religious matters and continued to be inhabited, although in the course of time much of the population would naturally have moved to the capital.

Rhodes remained loyal to Sparta until 395, when the pro-Athenian faction drove out the Diagoridai. Severe internal *stasis* (civil war) between rival factions continued, but the next decades saw the establishment of the democratic constitution and probably also the organization of the population into demes divided among the three old cities. Rhodes became a member of the Second Athenian Confederacy (see ATHENS (HISTORY)) in 378/7, but was detached from it by the intervention of the Carian satrap Mausolus, eager to extend his influence into the Aegean. The Social War against Athens broke out in 357 and Rhodes was granted independence, only to suffer Carian domination until the arrival of *Alexander the Great in 332. Relations with Alexander are obscure, but an unpopular Macedonian garrison was installed on Rhodes.

Rhodes flourished in the age of the Successors of Alexander. The foundation of new cities in the East meant the transfer of trade to the eastern Mediterranean, and Rhodes with its five harbours was ideally placed for this commercial traffic. The famous year-long siege of Rhodes by Demetrius Poliorcetes ('the Besieger') in 305/4 (Diod. Sic. 20. 81–8; 91–100) arose when Demetrius tried to win the Rhodian fleet and dockyards for himself, thereby threatening a favourable Rhodian alliance with the Ptolemies of *Egypt. The Rhodians resisted heroically. Demetrius was forced to withdraw after wasting a year, and from the sale of his siege equipment the Rhodians financed the Colossus, a 33 m.-tall statue of their patron god Helios (see SEVEN WONDERS OF THE ANCIENT WORLD). Rhodes' survival on this occasion increased its prestige and self-confidence, so that throughout the 3rd cent. it successfully avoided subservience to any of the larger powers, although close political and commercial ties with Egypt were maintained. By the second half of the century the distinguished Rhodian fleet replaced the Ptolemaic navy as the enemy of piracy on the high seas and as protector of the island communities.

Rhodes owned substantial territory on the opposite mainland or *peraia* (some probably acquired by the old cities before the synoecism). The communities which were integral parts of the Rhodian state became demes (constitutional sub-units) assigned to one of the three old cities and their citizens ranked equally with those of the island. This so-called 'Incorporated Peraea' is distinct from outlying territory which was controlled by Rhodes, the 'Subject Peraea', the population of which were not citizens of the Rhodian state and were governed by Rhodian officials. In time Rhodes gained control of the islands of Syme, Carpathos, Casos, Nisyros, Telos, Chalce, and Megiste (Castellorizo), and these were also incorporated as demes of the old cities in the Rhodian state.

Rhodes (with *Pergamum) played a role in the first major intervention of Rome in eastern affairs. It co-operated with Rome (not previously an ally) in the wars against Philip V of Macedon and *Antiochus III, and was rewarded after Apamea (see SELEUCIDS) with territory in Caria and Lycia (SW Asia Minor). Ancient sources vividly attest the *stasis* (civil strife) between the pro- and anti-Roman factions in the Rhodian assembly in the complex political manœuvrings of these years. Rome punished the equivocal attitude of Rhodes in the Third Macedonian War by depriving it of this extra territory and more besides, and by proclaiming *Delos a free port (167), thereby ending Rhodian commercial supremacy as the centre of the Mediterranean transit trade. Rhodes sought safety within an unequal alliance with Rome (164), which effectively ended its political independence and role as a major Mediterranean power. It successfully withstood a siege by *Mithradates VI in 88, but was captured and pillaged by Gaius Cassius Longinus in 43. Nevertheless, under Roman rule Rhodes retained her democratic constitution and social cohesiveness, and traditional civic life continued in the capital as well as in the three old cities. Rhodes remained prosperous and was known as a centre of cultural activity. The Rhodian school of Stoic philosophy (see STOICISM) boasted Panaetius and Posidonius among its distinguished members, and *Cicero studied there. There was a flourishing school of local sculpture, and the epic poet *Apollonius of Rhodes was a native. *Strabo (14. 2. 5 [652]) lavishly praises the city and Rhodian civic institutions, *Dio of Prusa (Dio Chrys. *Or.* 31) the pre-eminent wealth of the city, and [ps.] Aristides (25 [43]) its outstanding beauty before the severe *earthquake damage of *c.* AD 142.

Much of the ancient city, built on a rectangular grid, lies under the medieval walled town of the Knights of St John and the modern town, but identifiable remains include stretches of the city wall, several temples, harbour installations, the acropolis, a stadium, odeum, and extensive necropolis areas which have produced rich finds.

C. B. M., E. E. R.

'Riace warriors', two masterpieces of Greek bronze-casting, from (it seems) an ancient shipwreck; found off the toe of Italy in 1972. Standing nudes, 1.97–8 m. high, they originally held weapons; on technical grounds they are thought to come from the same workshop (see following page). A dating round the mid-5th cent. BC is gaining ground; later dates have advocates. Attempts to see in them famous lost works are, by their nature, highly speculative. See SCULPTURE, GREEK.

A. J. S. S.

ritual Both definition and interpretation of ritual are highly debated among social scientists. On a minimal definition (at least in the context of Greek and Roman cultures), ritual could be seen as symbolic activity in a religious context. A ritual (or ceremony) is composed of several single acts, the rites. Ritual is an activity whose imminent practical aim has become secondary, replaced by the aim of communication; this does not preclude ritual from having other, less immediate practical goals. Form and meaning of ritual are determined by tradition; they are malleable according to the needs of any present situation, as long as the performers understand them as being traditional. As to interpretation, in an era where often loosely associated Frazerian meanings dominated the field, the seminal work of A. van Gennep (*Les Rites de passage* (1909)) made it clear that rituals with seemingly widely different goals have common structures; this developed the insight, deepened by structuralism, that in ritual, structures are prior to meaning. French sociology (E. Durkheim) and British social anthropology (E. E. Evans-Pritchard) saw society as the main frame of reference for the interpretation of ritual meaning; V. Turner analysed the anti-structural aspects of Van Gennepian ritual. Insights from social anthropology have been applied to classical studies by J. E. Harrison, *Themis* (1911, 1927), and W. Burkert, *Structure and History in Greek Mythology and Ritual* (1979).

The study of ritual in Greek and Roman religion, as in most religions of the past, is hampered by lack of sufficient data. Social anthropology developed its interpretative models with societies where the rituals are documented in all their details, both the ordinary and the uncommon ceremonies and rites. Ancient sources, local historians and antiquarians, as well as sacred laws, recorded only the exceptional and aberrant rituals, not the familiar and ordinary ones which were part of daily life; and because they recorded only the salient features, entire scenarios are very rare. Further, instruction in the correct performance of ritual was part of an oral tradition, from generation to generation or from priest to priest, esp. in the Greek sacerdotal families like the Eumolpidae in *Eleusis or the Iamidae in *Olympia, or in the *collegia* (religious associations) in Rome. See PRIESTS. Elaborate ritual texts such as those known from near eastern, notably Hittite sources, are therefore absent in Greece and Rome. The exception, the Greek magical papyri, confirms the rule; magical rituals

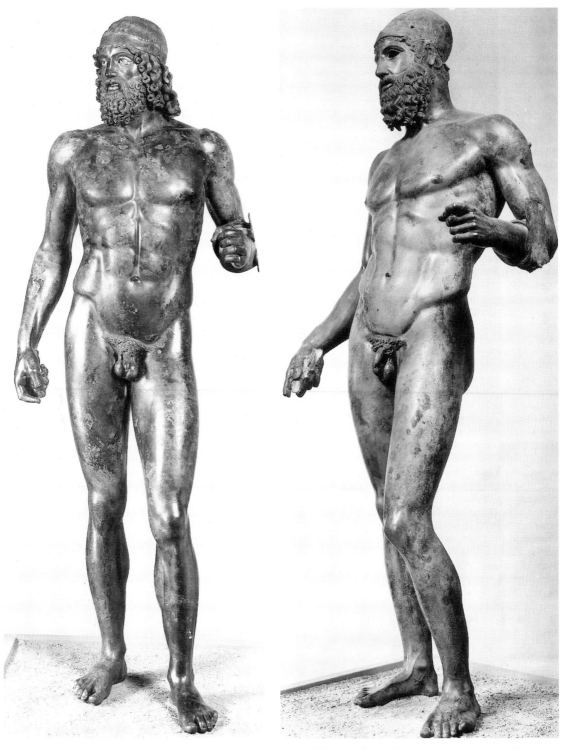

'Riace warriors' Warriors 'B' (left, thought to represent a younger man) and 'A'. The nipples and lips are coated in copper, teeth are silver. Ancient bronzes like this were kept bright to resemble gold. The dull patina of museum-bronzes is the result of time and neglect.

were transmitted in books from one practitioner to another one because these individual practices lacked any organizational form. But the magical papyri, combining different religious traditions, are of only limited value for a study of Greek and Roman ritual; see MAGIC.

Neither Greek nor Roman cultures analysed ritual as a specific category of religious activity. In Greek, the closest equivalent is *teletē*, but this term tended to be used in a much narrower sense for specific rituals of an exceptional nature, like those of the mystery cults (see C. Zijderveld, *TELETĒ: Bijdrage tot de kennis der religieuze terminologie in het Grieks* (1934)); other terms, as the frequent *hiera*, 'sacred things', or (*theōn*) *therapeia*, 'service (of the gods)' (Plat. *Rep.* 427b), are much wider; a term often used in Attic texts, *ta nomizomena*, 'what is customary', underscores the importance of tradition (J. Rudhardt, *Notions fondamentales de la pensée religieuse et actes constitutifs du culte dans la Grèce classique* (1958)). In Rome, the closest equivalents are *caerimonia* and *ritus*; both, however, rather mean subjectively the 'manner of a religious (or profane) observance'.

In modern discussions of ancient ritual, the dichotomy Olympian (see RELIGION, GREEK) versus chthonian (gods of the earth) often plays an important role: rituals destined for Olympian gods would be categorically distinguished from those of chthonian gods or heroes. This dichotomy is the product of late antique scholarship, not of observation of religious usage; it might have some explicatory value in late antiquity, much less for the Archaic and Classical epochs.

The central rite of Greek and Roman religion is animal *sacrifice. Whatever the theories about its origin, Greek and Roman analysis understood it as a gift to the gods; the myth of its institution by the trickster Prometheus (Hes. *Th.* 535–616) explained less its function as communication between man and god than the deficiency of something which should have been a nourishing gift from man to god. Beyond this indigenous interpretation, ordinary animal sacrifice with its ensuing meal repeated and reinforced the structure of society and was used to express societal values; changes of ritual reflected changes in values. Specific significations went together with specific forms of the ritual: the change from ordinary sheep or goat sacrifice to extraordinary sacrifice of bovines expressed a heightening of expense, festivity, and social status (religious reformers exposed the fundamental lack of moral values in such a differentiation, Philostr. *VA* 1. 11); more specific animals were used for specific deities, chiefly as a function of their relationship to the central *polis* values (dog sacrifice to Enyalius (see ARES)). Holocaust sacrifice, which destroyed the entire animal, was offered in marginal contexts, but not only with extraordinary animals.

Besides animal sacrifice, there existed different kinds of bloodless sacrifice. A common gift was the cake (see CAKES), in specific forms which again were determined by the character of the divinity and its position in society (C. A. Lobeck, *Aglaophamus* (1829), 1050–1985, gives a still useful *pemmatologia sacra*). Other sacrifices comprised

fruits or grains, often mixed and even cooked as a specific ritual dish (*kykeōn* in *Eleusis, 'hot-pot' of the Pyanopsia or Thargelia festivals, *puls* in Rome), as a function of the specific value of the festival. Libation (pouring a liquid offering) was used combined with animal sacrifice, but also as a ritual of its own. Again, the use of different liquids was determined by the function of the ritual; the main opposition was between mixed wine, the ordinary libation liquid as it was the ordinary drink, and unmixed *wine, milk, *water, oil (see OLIVE), or honey. Already Peripatetic (Aristotelian) cultural theory explained many of the substances as survivals from an earlier period without wine libations and animal sacrifice.

Another important group are purificatory rituals. Their aim is to remove *pollution, either on a regular basis, as in the ritual of the *pharmakos* (scapegoat) of the Greek Thargelia or in the festivals of the Roman month Februarius which derived its name from *februa*, a twig bundle used in purificatory rites, or in specific cases, to heal misfortune caused by pollution, as in the rites to cure epilepsy (see ps.-Hippocrates, *De morbo sacro*; cf. MEDICINE, §4), or in the many rites instituted by oracles to avert a *plague. Cathartic rituals precede any new beginning; therefore, they belong to New Year cycles (Februarius precedes the new beginning of the Kalends of March) or initiatory rites. The forms of apotropaic rituals vary from ritual washing to holocaust sacrifices, and many forms used are not specific to cathartic rituals. A common idea, though, is to identify the pollution with an object and then to destroy it, by either burning it entirely (holocaust sacrifice of pigs) or expelling it (*pharmakos*; cure of epilepsy, where the *katharmata*, the unclean substances, are carried beyond the borders of the *polis*).

A further group of rituals which has attracted scholarly interest is *initiation rituals, or rather rituals which can be seen as transformation from rituals which, in a hypothetical earlier phase of Greek or Roman society, fulfilled the function tribal initiation fulfils in ethnological societies; in them, the Van Gennepian tripartite structure is particularly visible. In historical Greece, the possible transformations were many. One group of rituals retains the function of introducing the young generation into the community; beside the rituals in the archaic Spartan and Cretan societies, the institution of the *ephēbeia* (see GYMNASIUM) belongs to this group. Other rituals concentrate upon a few elected members, like the Arrephori in the cult of the Athenian Athena, or the Roman Salii where some rites preserve traces of their respective practical functions, namely to initiate women into weaving as the main female technology, or to initiate young men into armed dancing as training for hoplite (heavy infantryman) combat. A specific group of rituals whose roots, at least partly, lie in initiation, are the *mystery cults of Eleusis, Samothrace, and the Theban and Lemnian Cabiri; here, earlier initiation into a family group or a secret society has been transformed into a Panhellenic ritual by emphasizing and elaborating the anti-structural aspect.

The social function of ritual was used by Hellenistic kings and Roman emperors alike to legitimate and base their rule on a religious foundation; in ruler-cult, traditional forms like sacrifice were taken up to express these new concerns; modern negative judgements of such cults misunderstand the fundamental social and political meaning of much of ancient religion, where refusal of such rites by Christians was rightly understood as refusal to recognize the political supremacy of the ruler. See RULER-CULT; CHRISTIANITY.   F. G.

roads Ancient road-theory divides into two categories: the art of enhancing communications through built or dug works; and the planning and maintaining of large-scale communications networks based on such works.

Ramps, cuttings, stone pavements, zig-zags, and pull-offs are found on local roads from Archaic Greek times, and were clearly designed to facilitate wheeled traction: there are *Mycenaean precursors, and parallels in many parts of the Mediterranean, such as Etruria. Improved routes for specialized purposes such as the haulage-route to Athens from the marble quarries of Mt. Pentelicon, or the *diolkos across the isthmus of Corinth, are found, and fine paved processional ways like the Athenian Sacred Way or the approaches to great *sanctuaries like *Delphi. The technological repertoire was greatly increased by the deployment of arched construction on a large scale, which made bridges and viaducts feasible; and where labour was cheap, and petrology favourable, major cuttings and tunnels could be contemplated. Such things like the deployment of the older road technologies on any very large scale required large-scale organization, intercommunity co-operation, voluntary or enforced, and very large resources, all of which escaped the Greek world of the Archaic and Classical periods.

The Royal Road of the Achaemenid *Persian empire did not, in all likelihood, comprise a continuous line of built structure; but what the scope of Persian power made distinctively possible along this 1,600-mile stretch was the vision of a line joining distinct regions. This second category of ancient road-theory is first and foremost a way of looking at the layout of the world and expressing the power of the state or the individual in relation to it. The manifold technologies of improving the route are deployed in the service of that aim.

In this the road-building of the Roman republic was strikingly original. Between 312 (the date of the first stretch of the via Appia) and 147 BC (when the via Postumia joined Adriatic to Tyrrhenian and spanned Cisalpine Gaul) Roman planners had perfected a way of turning the military journey-routes of commanders with *imperium (itinera) into a theoretically sophisticated network which formally linked Roman communities with Rome, and (linked as the road-building and city-foundation alike were with land-division: see CENTURIATION) spectacularly expressed Rome's power over the landscape. The system already involved using the available technological skills to make showily

roads Milestones, usually cylindrical and about 1.8 m. (6 ft.) high, were a feature of Roman (not Greek) road-building. Typically, this example from N. Wales in *Britain is inscribed with the name of the emperor (*Hadrian) and the distance (eight Roman miles) from the nearest important centre (Caerhun).

straight connections across natural obstacles, and that was a precedent taken up with enthusiasm in the road plans of Gaius *Gracchus. Around the same time the first large-scale application of milestones (though they are attested on Thasos in the 5th cent.), docketing and measuring the domains of Rome, and the first really ambitious roads of the provincial empire are found, notably the via Egnatia linking the Adriatic with the Aegean and eventually the Bosporus, and the via Domitia running from the Alps across the Rhône and Pyrenees into *Spain.

The origins of the idea remain obscure: locally the layout of Roman roads resembles *Etruscan practice, for instance in preferring to follow the summits of long ridges, but in the crucial scale of the geographical vision, which is already there in the via Appia, even the Royal Road does not really provide a precedent. The ancient routes of west central Italy like the via Salaria and via Latina, which may have an economic origin, are a possible precedent, but their date is uncertain.

The early emperors made road-building their own. *Augustus rebuilt the via Flaminia as the highway to his *provincia* in the settlement of 27; *Claudius commemorated his triumphal journey back to Rome from *Britain by piously completing the road which his father Drusus had begun on his own military expeditions across the Alps. The imitation of their practice by governors, and of both by municipal benefactors, spread a dense capillary net of roads across the whole empire. While the routes of Augustus and Claudius were single highways (*Agrippa's great highway from Lugdunum (Lyons) to the Channel should also be mentioned), there is a growing sense of the application of a blueprint (developed long before in Italy), of boxing in territories with crisscross roads on a huge scale. These are the *limites* which were eventually to give their name to the frontier works of the empire (see LIMES). Strategic road-building on a scale large enough to cross provincial boundaries reaches its peak under the Flavians, Trajan, and Hadrian, with the systematic reshaping of the networks of Anatolia and the whole eastern frontier, eventually down to Aqaba. Something similar happens in the Balkans at the same period.   N. P.

Romanization

I. In the west. This term describes the processes by which indigenous peoples incorporated into the empire acquired cultural attributes which made them appear as Romans. Since the Romans had no single unitary culture but rather absorbed traits from others, including the conquered, the process was not a one-way passing of ideas and styles from Roman to indigene but rather an exchange which led to the metropolitan mix of styles which characterized the Roman world. Styles of art and architecture, town-planning and villa-living, as well as the adoption of Latin and the worship of the Roman pantheon, are all amongst its expressions. The result of Romanization was not homogeneity, since indigenous characteristics blended to create hybrids like Romano-Celtic religion or Gallo-Roman sculpture.

Its manifestations were not uniform, and there is debate over the relative importance of directed policy and local initiative. Rome promoted aspects of her culture to integrate the provinces and facilitate government with least effort. Provincial centres like Tarraco in *Spain and Lugdunum (Lyons) in Transalpine *Gaul were created to promote loyalty to the state through the worship of Roman gods, and their priesthoods became a focus for the ambitions of provincials. *Tacitus (*Agr.* 21) states that Gnaeus Iulius Agricola in *Britain promoted public building and education for these purposes. Roman culture was also spread less deliberately by Roman actions. Mass movements of soldiers brought goods and ideas to newly con-

quered areas, whilst the construction of new *roads in their wake speeded communication and facilitated further cultural exchange. *Trade both within and beyond the frontiers brought Roman culture to new peoples. Equally, conquered people themselves sought to acquire Roman goods and values to curry favour with their conquerors and confer or maintain status within their own societies. In Gaul local aristocrats were obtaining Roman *citizenship in the Julio-Claudian period, establishing for themselves a new status in relation to Rome and their own peoples. Emulation of Roman customs and styles accompanied their rise. Thus in Claudian Britain, the client-king Cogidubnus almost certainly constructed the highly sophisticated Roman villa at Fishbourne, and presided over a client kingdom where a temple of Neptune and Minerva was built. This copying of things Roman by indigenes was probably the most important motive for these cultural changes.   M. J. M.

II. In the east. No ancient writer provides any general description or explanation of the impact of Roman culture and institutions on the eastern provinces of the empire. The term Romanization is best applied to specific developments which can be traced to the patterns of Roman rule.

Military The language used by the legions and most auxiliary regiments, both officially and privately, was Latin. Building inscriptions, gravestones, dedications, and casual graffiti provide evidence for a Latin-speaking culture in and around fortresses and also in towns which were accustomed to heavy military traffic on the roads to the eastern frontiers.

Administrative practices The staff of a provincial governor or of a provincial procurator was too small to have any significant effect on the culture of the communities where they resided or which they visited. Many officials, in any case, were Greek-speaking by birth or by inclination. Latin, however, seems to have been widely used for the administration of imperial estates; Latin gravestones are the rule for the freedmen and imperial slaves who ran them.

Citizenship and law Roman *citizenship spread rapidly in the Greek east, and became almost universal with the Antonine constitution of AD 212. Roman citizens were notionally entitled to be tried or to conduct cases within the framework of Roman law. This will have swiftly led the Greek cities and other communities of the east to bring their own legal practices into conformity with Roman law.

Urbanization and architecture The most characteristic form of Roman town, the colony, was introduced on a large scale to the Greek east. *Caesar and *Augustus settled veterans in colonies in Macedonia, Asia Minor, and Syria. The practice of introducing new settlers became rare under their successors, but existing communities were often raised to the status of colonies, particularly from the Severan period through the 3rd cent. More important than the practice of founding colonies (see COLONIZATION,

ROMAN) was the fact that Roman provincial administration could only function in regions where an infrastructure of self-governing cities existed. Since much of the area between the Aegean and the Euphrates, especially the interior of Asia Minor, was only thinly urbanized in the Hellenistic age, Roman rule led to the creation of hundreds of new cities. Although these had the constitution and institutions of Greek *poleis* (see POLIS) they owed their existence directly to Roman control (see URBANISM). Civic culture, in both colonies and cities, also underwent radical changes. Since civic independence was now a thing of the past, much more emphasis was laid on the externals of city life, above all splendid public buildings, which were the hallmark of a Roman city, especially in the 1st and 2nd cents. AD. Certain building types reflected specific Roman influence: temples and other structures associated with the imperial cult often dominated both old and newly founded cities; not only *amphitheatres (which were relatively infrequent in the Greek east) but theatres were built to accommodate gladiatorial shows and other forms of public entertainment; above all, the *baths, *aqueducts, and spectacular fountain houses, which were present everywhere and served almost as a defining characteristic of city life, were specifically Roman supplements to the existing character of a city.

Language Although no attempt was made to introduce or impose Latin as the spoken language of the population of the eastern provinces, it was the language of the army, of administration, and of the lawyers. During the 3rd and 4th cents. the attractions of a local career in a city were far outweighed by the prospect and possibilities of imperial service, as a soldier, an officer, or as a member of the imperial administrative cadre. Knowledge of Latin was effectively a precondition for anyone who wished to enter this world. The law school at Berytus (Beirut), whose students needed to master the language as well as the niceties of Roman law, provided a focal point where members of the Hellenized upper classes of the later empire acquired these two essential elements of the new, Romanized culture.

Religion and cult Specifically Roman cults, such as that of *Jupiter Optimus Maximus or of the Capitoline Triad (Jupiter, Juno, and Minerva), made little impact on the Greek east outside military camps. The Roman *ruler-cult, however, whose origins lay in a collaboration between the Roman authorities, especially provincial governors, and the upper classes of the eastern provinces, and which evolved a new form of politico-religious expression within the framework of imperial rule, had an enormous impact. Imperial temples and other buildings often dominated the cities; priesthoods and other offices concerned with the cult became the peak of a local political career; games and festivals in honour of the emperors dominated civic calendars. Much of the 'Romanness' of a city of the eastern provinces during the imperial period could therefore be traced directly to the institution of emperor-worship.

S. M.

Rome (history) (*see facing page*)

Rome (topography) (see ◀Map 3, Bb▶) The Tiber valley at Rome is a deep trough, from 1 to 3 km. wide, cut into the soft tufa floor of the river's lower basin. The edges of the trough are formed by steep weathered cliffs, seamed and even isolated by tributary streams. In this way the famous hills of Rome were formed: the Caelian, Oppian (not counted as one of Rome's Seven Hills), Esquiline, Viminal, and Quirinal were flat-topped spurs, while the Capitol, Palatine and Aventine were cut off from the main hinterland. On the valley floor itself the river meanders in an S-shaped curve, the northern twist containing the Campus Martius and skirting the Vatican plain, the southern curve skirting the Capitol, forum Boarium, and Aventine, and enclosing Transtiberim, a smaller plain at the foot of the Janiculan ridge. Just below the middle of the S-curve the river runs shallow and divides at Tiber island. The ford here was the only feasible crossing-point between Rome and the sea, or for many miles upstream; so hills and spurs provided the natural strongholds suitable for defended settlement, and traffic across the heavily populated Latian plain concentrated at the Tiber ford, which was to be the key to Rome's predominance.

Archaeology has revealed the presence of bronze-age settlement on the Capitol, and iron-age settlements here and on many of the other hills, notably the Palatine, Esquiline, and Quirinal. Cemeteries crowded the edges of the marshy valley of the forum Romanum; burials cease by the late 7th cent. BC, attesting the *synoecism of these different communities brought about as the area was drained by means of the *cloaca maxima* and the forum was created as a market-place. The fortification of Servius on the Viminal, and cliffs elsewhere, made this unified Rome a great promontory-fortress comparable with Veii or Ardea; during the regal period, it grew to become one of the most substantial cities in the Mediterranean. Projects associated with the kings include the Regia in the forum, the temple of Jupiter Capitolinus, the temple of Diana on the Aventine, and the pons Sublicius which replaced the Tiber ford.

The forum was the centre of civic life in republican Rome; political, religious, and commercial activities took place in a square which was also surrounded by housing and shops. As the city grew, however, ceremonial activities came to play an increasingly important role there; the Palatine became a centre of aristocratic housing, and the shops moved to the periphery of the forum, as well as the Velabrum and forum Boarium areas, close to the Tiber port. Popular housing was concentrated in overcrowded and squalid areas such as the Subura. As Rome's power in Italy and overseas grew, the Campus Martius (where the centuriate assembly met) was increasingly characterized by competitive building, as rival aristocrats sought to impress gods and voters with temples. Similarly, the construction of basilicas around the forum in the 2nd cent. BC provides an indication of aristocratic rivalry, while at the

[*continued on p. 623*]

history of Rome

Rome (history) (see ◀Map 3, Bb▶)

1. From the Origins to 31 BC
1. The origins of Rome
Surviving literary accounts of the beginnings of Rome are based entirely on legend. The stories provide evidence of what the Romans at various times thought about their own origins and how they liked to see themselves. The developed version of the story contained two main legends, those of *Aeneas and *Romulus, which were artificially combined at an unknown date (but certainly before 300 BC). Although both legends are very ancient, they are, as far as we can tell, quite unhistorical, although certain incidental details (e.g. the idea that Romulus founded his settlement on Rome's Palatine hill) are consistent with the archaeological facts.

The archaeological evidence now available shows that one or more villages were established on the hills of Rome (including the Palatine) from the end of the bronze age (c.1000 BC). These communities were similar to other hilltop settlements that have been identified throughout Latium Vetus, whose cemeteries provide evidence of a distinct form of material culture known as the *cultura laziale*. In the earliest phases (10th and 9th cents. BC) the settlements were small, isolated villages consisting of a few thatched huts. During the 8th and 7th cents. they grew in size and sophistication, with the development of external trade (including contacts with the Greek world), specialized craft production, and the emergence of a wealthy aristocracy. At Rome the Palatine settlement expanded by 700 to include the forum valley and possibly the Quirinal hill, and the main cemetery moved from the forum to the Esquiline hill. Towards the end of the 7th cent. the forum was laid out as a public meeting place (see FORUM ROMANUM), and monumental buildings made their first appearance. At this point Rome was transformed into an organized city-state.

As befits a frontier town on an important river crossing, Rome seems to have had a mixed population, including Sabines, Greeks and, it seems, large numbers of *Etruscans. Two of the kings were traditionally of Etruscan origin, but this does not mean that Rome was conquered by the Etruscans or that it became in any other sense an 'Etruscan city'. This is a false deduction from the fact that it shared the same (Hellenizing) material culture as the cities of southern Etruria (see HELLENISM, HELLENIZATION). Although heavily influenced by contacts with the outside world (including Greece and the near east, as well as Etruria and Campania, Rome remained fundamentally a Latin city. This is borne out by an ever-increasing body of Latin inscriptions, which also prove incidentally that Roman culture had been literate from probably before 600 BC.

What passes for the history of Rome at this early period is recorded in literary sources of the 1st cent. BC and later, which are unlikely to contain much reliable information about events hundreds of years earlier. According to the sources the city was originally ruled by kings, which is likely enough, but no confidence can be placed in the complex dynastic history or the dating of the canonical seven: Romulus, Numa Pompilius, Tullus Hostilius, Ancus Marcius, Tarquinius Priscus, Servius *Tullius, and *Tarquinius Superbus. With the exception of the eponymous Romulus these names may be those of genuine kings, but the notion that their reigns occupied the whole of the period from the 8th cent. BC to the end of the 6th is unacceptable. The conventional foundation date, fixed at 753 BC by *Varro, is the result of artificial manipulation, and does not accord with any archaeological starting-point; the earliest settlement is much earlier than 753, and the formation of an urbanized city-state considerably later. It is necessary to suppose either that the regal period was much shorter than the conventional 250 years, or that there were more kings than the conventional seven. As it happens there are good reasons for doing both, since alternative traditions record the names of kings not in the canonical list (e.g. Titus Tatius and Mastarna).

The detailed narratives of their reigns must be regarded largely as fictitious elaboration; but it is nevertheless possible that some elements are based, however dimly, on genuine memory. For instance, accounts of the Roman conquest of the Alban hills region (traditionally attributed to Tullus Hostilius) and the lower Tiber valley (Ancus Marcius) describe an extension of Roman territory that must have occurred before the end of the 6th cent. Similarly the organization of the calendar and the major priesthoods, traditionally the work of Numa, can be dated with some confidence to the 6th cent. or even earlier. The belief that the Roman monarchy was elective rather than hereditary is unlikely to be an invention, and many institutions associated with the election process, such as the *interrex*, the *lex curiata de imperio* (see IMPERIUM), and the ceremony of inauguration, were probably genuine relics of the time of the kings. The earliest institutions of the state, the three pre-Servian tribes and the thirty *curiae* (groupings for voting), of which only residual traces survived in the later republic, almost certainly go back to the early monarchic period (tradition ascribes them to Romulus). The centuriate reform attributed to Servius Tullius, as it is described in the surviving narratives, belongs to the middle republic, but a simpler system dividing the citizens according to their capacity to arm themselves may well be a genuine reform of the 6th cent.; it is also likely that the innovation of locally based tribes is of pre-republican origin.

The last two kings are presented as tyrants—illegal usurpers who adopted a flamboyant and populist style of rule similar to that of the contemporary Greek tyrants (see TYRANNY). Like the latter, they pursued an ambitious foreign policy, patronized the arts, and embarked on extensive and grandiose building projects. In view of the extent to which 6th-cent. Rome was subject to Greek influence, this need not surprise us; moreover the archaeological evidence confirms that Rome was indeed a powerful, sophisticated, and cosmopolitan city at this time—in the well-known phrase that has recently become something of a cliché: *la grande Roma dei Tarquini* ('the great Rome of the Tarquins'). Finally, Tarquinius Superbus is said to have created a miniature 'empire' in Latium, a state of affairs that is also presupposed in the first Carthaginian treaty (Polyb. 3. 22); this coincidence between the annalistic tradition and an apparently contemporary document tends to confirm the authenticity of both.

2. The early republic and the 'Conflict of the Orders'
The portrayal of the later kings as tyrannical populists is consistent with the story that the last of them, Tarquinius Superbus, was expelled in an aristocratic coup, and replaced by a republic under two annually elected *consuls. These basic elements of the traditional story are more credible than an alternative modern theory that the monarchy was not overthrown in a sudden coup, but slowly faded away, the king being gradually reduced to a purely ceremonial figure (the *rex sacrorum*, 'king for sacred rites'), and replaced as ruler by a supreme magistrate (see MAGISTRACY, ROMAN), variously defined as *dictator, magister populi*, or *praetor maximus*. The dual consulship, on this view, was a later development.

The principal objection to this ingenious theory is that it conflicts with the evidence of the *Fasti*, the list of consuls preserved in a number of sources (with only minor variations) and widely regarded as authentic. The *Fasti* list the two consuls of each year going back to around 500 BC (the version of the *Fasti Capitolini*, based on the researches of *Varro, places the beginning of the list, and therefore the beginning of the republic, in 509 BC; this Varronian system of dating, though incorrect in places, is conventionally followed by modern historians). A late 6th-cent. date for the beginning of the republic is likely to be correct in general terms, and seems to be confirmed by independent Greek sources.

In this connection it is worth noting that the sources for the republic are in general more soundly based than for the preceding monarchic period. The accounts we can read all date from the late republic and early empire (the most important ones from the second half of the 1st cent. BC). These sources are in their turn based on earlier accounts, now lost, the earliest of which were written at the end of the 3rd cent. BC. Where the earliest Roman historians obtained their material is largely a matter for conjecture, but their sources undoubtedly included the following: accounts of Greek historians, oral memory, the traditions of the great noble families (at least partly preserved in written form), and public documents such as laws, treaties, and senatorial decrees. It is also evident that they had access to archival documents in chronicle form, above all the *annales maximi*, a chronicle kept by the *pontifex maximus* (see PRIESTS) which included the magistrates of each year together with other information about public events. Naturally the 5th-cent. notices were meagre and uncertain, and the later literary narratives introduced much secondary elaboration and perhaps even invention; but there is no reason to doubt that a basic structure of documentary material lies behind the accounts of our sources for the history of the republic.

During the early republic power rested in the hands of an aristocratic clique known as the patriciate (see PATRICIANS). Patricians were members of certain privileged clans (*gentes*; see GENS) which had probably obtained special status under the kings. This would seem to follow from the fact that only patricians could hold the office of *interrex*, an obvious relic of the monarchy. The patricians had an exclusive hold on all the chief religious offices, and it was they who gave their assent (the *auctoritas patrum*) to decisions of the *comitia* (assembly) before they became binding. Most consuls were patricians, but it appears from the *Fasti* that they did not have a monopoly of political office until the middle of the 5th cent.

The early republic appears to have been a period when Rome experienced military difficulties and economic recession. Not surprisingly it was the poorer citizens who suffered most, especially without the protection of the kings who had relied on their support. Debt, land-hunger, and food shortages are recorded as the main grievances. Some of these poorer citizens are said to have taken matters into their own hands in 494 BC, when they withdrew from the city and formed their own alternative state. The **plebs*, as they were called, formed an assembly (the *concilium plebis*), elected their own officers (*tribuni plebis*—see TRIBUNE OF THE PLEBS—and aediles), and set up their own cult (of Ceres, Liber, and Libera). For the next two centuries this remarkable plebeian organization fought to improve the lot of its members, by passing resolutions (*plebiscita*), by backing the authority of the tribunes, whose sacrosanctity enabled them to frustrate the actions of magistrates through personal intervention, and if necessary by secession.

The principal demands of the *plebs* were for debt relief and a more equitable distribution of economic resources, especially land. Tradition maintained that the codification of the **Twelve Tables* in 450 BC was also a product of plebeian agitation. The plebeian organization was gradually recognized, and obtained a limited right to pass plebiscites binding on the whole people (in 449, extended in 339). Its membership seems to have increased, and to have come to include growing numbers of wealthy and politically ambitious citizens. In the 4th cent. (if not earlier) these richer plebeians began to use the organization as a means to break down the exclusive privileges of the patricians. It was only at this secondary stage that the struggle became a direct conflict between patricians and plebeians.

In 367 BC the Licinio-Sextian laws made plebeians eligible for the consulship, and in 342 the rule was established that one of the two consuls must be a plebeian. A similar rule was extended to the censorship in 339, the same year as the *auctoritas patrum* was reduced to a formality; and in 300 the major priestly colleges were divided between the two orders. By these and similar measures the plebeians were gradually reintegrated into the state, a process that was completed in *c*.287 BC when plebiscites were made binding on the people and became equivalent to laws.

The plebeians also succeeded in obtaining relief from debt (by a series of measures in the 4th cent.), and particularly from the institution of debt-bondage (*nexum*), which was abolished by statute in 326. They also gained increased access to *ager publicus* (public land) by limiting the amounts an individual could hold (a *lex Licinia Sextia* of 367 set the maximum at 500 *iugera c*.330 acres; 133 ha.)). But the most important factor in the emancipation of the *plebs* was the redistribution of newly conquered territory in allotments to poorer citizens. It was the programme of colonization and settlement during the late 4th cent. that did most to relieve the burdens of the poor and to end the plebeian struggle as a radical movement.

The main political result was the rise of the nobility, consisting of both patricians and plebeians, who formed a new ruling class based on tenure of office and descent from former office-holders. By the mid-4th cent. a hierarchy of magistracies had been established, resulting from the gradual creation of additional offices alongside the consulship: the quaestors (before 447), the censors (443), the praetor and curule aediles (367). Successful nobles expected to hold a succession of these offices, and a rudimentary *career path (cursus honorum) was established. With the end of the plebeian struggle and the integration of its institutions, the posts of plebeian tribune and aedile became equivalent to magistracies, and were frequently held by young plebeian nobles who used them as stepping-stones to the consulship. After the lex Ovinia in the later 4th cent. the *senate became an independent body of permanent life-members, most of them ex-magistrates, and took an increasingly important role in the routine administration of the state and the formation of policy. This was in part an inevitable consequence of the increasing complexity of government as Rome expanded at the expense of its neighbours.

3. The Roman conquest of Italy

After the fall of the monarchy Rome was faced with a revolt of the Latins which led to the battle of Lake Regillus and the treaty of Spurius Cassius Vecellinus (493 BC). The result was a military alliance which enabled Rome and the Latins to resist the incursions of threatening neighbours, the Sabines, Aequi, and Volsci. By the second half of the 5th cent. the regular raids by these peoples gradually ceased, and the Romans (with allied support) were able to take the offensive. During the last years of the 5th cent. they were engaged in the conquest and colonization of southern Latium. They also gained the upper hand against the Etruscan city of Veii, a long-standing rival, which they captured and destroyed in 396. Rome's advance continued in the 4th cent., despite the sack of the city by a Celtic war-band in 390 (Varronian; the true date is probably 386), which proved only a temporary setback. Rome's recovery was rapid, and in the following decades the setting of Roman military activity shifted to Samnium and Campania in the south, and to the territory of Tarquinii and Caere in the north. Relations with the Latins also deteriorated, as the Romans' imperialist intentions became clear. The great Latin war which broke out in 341 BC was crucial, and the Roman victory and subsequent settlement (338 BC) marked a decisive stage in the process of Roman expansion.

The Romans followed up their victory by further conquests and a programme of colonization which led to the foundation of Cales (334) and Fregellae (328); the second of these colonies provoked the great conflict known to moderns as the Second Samnite War (326–304), in which the Romans, after a major setback at the Caudine Forks (321 BC), strengthened their hold on Campania, made alliances in northern Apulia, Etruria, and Umbria, and advanced into central Italy, where they overcame the Hernici and Aequi, and made alliances with the Marsi, Paeligni, Marrucini, Frentani, and Vestini. These military alliances greatly extended the warlike capacity of Rome, which by 300 was the dominant power in Italy. A few years later the Samnite leader Gellius Egnatius succeeded in forming an anti-Roman alliance of Samnites, Gauls, Etruscans, and Umbrians, but their joint forces were destroyed at Sentinum in 296, a battle that decided the fate of Italy. In the following decades, which are poorly documented in the surviving literature, Rome completed the conquest of peninsular Italy by forcing all its peoples to become allies, either by defeating them in war or compelling them to surrender in advance. The last to succumb were the Greek cities of the south, particularly Tarentum, which in 280 BC summoned *Pyrrhus to Italy to lead the war against Rome. The defeat of Pyrrhus in 275 was a turning-point, not only because it was virtually the final act in the Roman conquest of Italy (Tarentum held out for a few years, but was captured in 272), but because it brought Rome to the attention of a wider world; the defeat of a powerful king with a fully trained professional army by a hitherto unknown Italian republic created a sensation in the Hellenistic east. A new world power had emerged.

The final stages of the conquest had been completed extremely quickly; barely fifty years elapsed between the outbreak of the Second Samnite War and the fall of Tarentum. And yet the Romans' hold

Rome (history), §3.2 The city wall of Rome, constructed by the emperor Aurelian in AD 271–5 in anticipation of a sudden barbarian inroad, and repaired and elaborated by later emperors. The refortification of the capital, part of a more general fortification of the cities of the empire, reflects the military stress of the 3rd cent. AD.

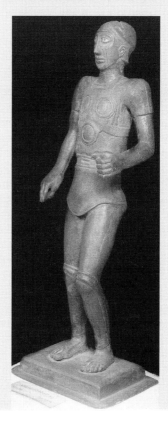

Rome (history), §1.3 Bronze statuette of a Samnite warrior, 6th–5th cent. BC. Organized as a confederation and led to war by a generalissimo, the Samnites were the Romans' doughtiest foes among the peoples of *Italy.

over the Italian allies proved remarkably thorough and lasting. Their success was partly due to the policy of founding colonies throughout the peninsula (19 were established between 334 and 263), on strategic sites linked by a network of well-constructed military roads. A second factor that secured the loyalty of the allies was Rome's support for local aristocracies, who saw the oligarchic republic as their natural ally, and relied on Roman backing to keep them in power at home. Finally, the cohesiveness of the system of alliances was a result of continuous and successful warfare, in which the allies took part and from which they gained a share of the profits. The system was a remarkably effective military machine. War was its *raison d'être*, and its inevitable product. This fact bears directly on the much debated question of Roman imperialism. Roman *imperialism was the result of continuous war, and continuous war was the result of the Roman system of alliances in Italy.

4. Roman imperialism and its consequences

It was inevitable that, after completing the conquest of peninsular Italy, the Romans would embark on military adventures beyond its borders. Less than a decade after the fall of Tarentum they became involved in a major overseas war, when they challenged the Carthaginians for the control of Sicily. In spite of immense losses Rome finally emerged as the victor in this First Punic War (264–241 BC), and *Sicily became the first province. A second was added shortly afterwards, when Sardinia was seized from an enfeebled Carthage (238). Twenty years later the Second Punic War began when the Romans declared war over the Saguntum affair and *Hannibal invaded Italy (218). In spite of spectacular victories in the field Hannibal failed to win over Rome's Italian allies, most of whom remained loyal, and was gradually worn down; he withdrew from Italy in 204 and was finally defeated at Zama in 202.

As a result the Romans obtained further provinces from the former Carthaginian possessions in Spain, and were drawn into imperialistic ventures in the eastern Mediterranean. They also resumed the conquest of northern Italy, which had begun in 224 but had been interrupted by Hannibal's invasion (see GAUL, CISALPINE). In the period to c.175 BC Roman armies overran the Po Valley, Liguria, and the Istrian peninsula. At the same time they were engaged in fierce fighting in Spain, which continued intermittently until 133 and led to the conquest of Lusitania and Celtiberia, although the north-west corner of the Iberian peninsula remained unconquered until the time of Augustus. Finally, campaigns in southern Gaul from 125 to 121 BC resulted in the conquest of Gallia Narbonensis (Provence).

During the same period Rome became increasingly involved in the affairs of the eastern Mediterranean. The first Roman venture east of the Adriatic was in Illyria during the 220s. A Second Illyrian War occurred in 219, and was viewed with alarm by the Macedonian king, Philip V. In 215 Philip made an alliance with Hannibal, which provoked the Romans into the so-called First Macedonian War (214–205), a half-hearted affair to which they were unable or unwilling to commit large military forces. After Zama, however, they felt free to give more attention to the east, and embarked on the Second Macedonian War in 200. Roman troops invaded the Balkans and defeated Philip at Cynoscephalae (197), but these forces were withdrawn in 194 after *Flamininus had confined Philip to Macedonia and pronounced 'the freedom of the Greeks'. Roman efforts to control events in the Greek world by diplomacy and threats were eventually unsuccessful, however, and further military interventions occurred in 191–188, when the Romans invaded Asia Minor and defeated *Antiochus III, and in the Third Macedonian War (171–167), when the kingdom of Macedon was destroyed by the Roman victory at Pydna. Finally, in the 140s, Roman armies crushed revolts in *Macedonia and Greece, which were made into provinces ruled directly from Rome. The Romans emphasized their dominance by ruthlessness, the most brutal example of which was the destruction of Corinth in 146 BC. In the same year Carthage was destroyed after a Third Punic War (149–146), and its territory became the Roman province of Africa (see AFRICA, ROMAN). Further annexations occurred in Asia (133; see ASIA, ROMAN PROVINCE), Cilicia (SE Asia Minor) (101), and *Cyrene (96).

The successful pattern of overseas conquests had dramatic effects on all aspects of life in Rome and Italy. In the first place it consolidated the power of the patrician-plebeian élite, which dominated the senate and virtually monopolized the senior offices of state. The *plebs* were happy to acquiesce in this as long as they benefited from the proceeds of military conquest, as were the Italian allies. Secondly the growth of empire vastly increased the wealth of the upper classes, which began to adopt luxurious and increasingly sophisticated habits. The influence of Greek culture became pervasive, and wealthy Romans began to affect the leisured style of the great centres of the Hellenistic world; see HELLENISM. Architecture and the visual arts flourished, as the Romans imitated all the trappings of Greek civilization. One of the results was the development of Roman literature on the Greek model, including drama, epic poetry, and, not least, historiography.

But overseas conquests also had unforeseen and sometimes damaging effects on the economy and society of Italy. The conspicuous consumption of the élite was fuelled by investment in Italian land. This led to the growth of large landed estates in Italy, worked by war captives who were imported as slaves. The slave-worked estates introduced new methods of farming, designed to provide absentee landlords with an income from the sale of cash crops (a regime described in the handbook *On Agriculture* by *Cato the Elder). Large-scale grazing was also a profitable form of investment, particularly in southern Italy, where much land had been made available by the devastations and confiscations associated with the Hannibalic War. Some of the land in question was technically *ager publicus* (public land), but the Roman government turned a blind eye to its expropriation by the rich, and did not enforce the legal limits on the size of holdings.

There has been much discussion about the nature of these large estates, the extent of their spread in various regions of Italy, their impact on existing agrarian structures, and their effect on the growth of urban markets. The result of modern research, involving new theoretical models and the use of archaeological evidence, has been to produce a complex picture of varying types of land-use, tenure, and labour exploitation. Nevertheless, it is probable that our sources (particularly Appian, *Civil Wars* I) are right to stress that one of the effects of the changes was large-scale peasant displacement. This had alarming implications for the government, because small peasant proprietors formed the backbone of the Roman army; the situation was aggravated by the fact that prolonged military service in distant theatres made it increasingly difficult for such men to maintain their farms. Roman and Italian peasant-soldiers were thus the victims of their own success, and were driven off the land to a life of penury and unemployment. Since the law laid down a property qualification for army service, the displaced and impoverished peasants were no longer available for recruitment. The result was a manpower crisis, as well as discontent and growing social tension, which came increasingly to threaten the long-standing political consensus. See AGRICULTURE, ROMAN.

5. The Roman revolution

The widening gulf between rich and poor eventually gave rise to social conflict and political breakdown. In 133 BC a tribune, Tiberius *Gracchus, introduced a land reform which proposed to enforce the ancient and long-neglected limit of 500 *iugera* on holdings of *ager publicus*, and to redistribute the reclaimed surplus in allotments to the poor (see AGRARIAN LAWS AND POLICY). Not surprisingly there was furious opposition, and Gracchus was eventually murdered in an outbreak of political violence instigated by the *optimates* (conservative senators). Ten years later his brother, Gaius *Gracchus suffered the same fate, when he attempted to bring in a series of reforms, which ranged far more widely than his brother's single law. Gaius' legislation embraced provincial administration and taxation, the urban grain supply, judicial reform, and the extension of Roman citizenship to the Italian allies. His aim was to ensure that all citizens, not just the ruling class, should benefit from the proceeds of empire, and that those who governed it should be made accountable for their actions. But his efforts were in vain; most of the measures that he succeeded in passing into law were repealed after his murder (121 BC).

In the following generation Rome faced military difficulties in every part of the empire. These included a war in Africa, a slave revolt in Sicily (103–101 BC; an earlier revolt there had been crushed in

132), and an invasion of Italy by migrating German tribes, the Cimbri and Teutones. In attempting to respond to these crises the ruling oligarchy showed itself corrupt and incompetent, and they were only resolved by allowing an able and ambitious parvenu, *Marius, to hold an unprecedented succession of consulships, and to recruit a professional army from the proletariat.

These measures solved the military problems, but had fatal long-term consequences, because they provided the poor with a means to redress their grievances, and ambitious nobles with the chance to gain personal power by means of armed force. Matters were brought to a head in the aftermath of the Social War (91–89 BC), the revolt of the Italian allies who had taken up arms in order to obtain the Roman citizenship, and by an invasion of the eastern provinces by *Mithradates VI of Pontus, who was welcomed as a liberator by many provincials. These events created political chaos at Rome. *Sulla, the consul of 88, was appointed by the senate to lead an expedition against Mithradates; but the plebeian assembly, at the bidding of the tribune Gaius Sulpicius, overturned this arrangement and gave the command instead to Marius. Sulla responded by marching on the city and imposing his will by force. Marius was driven out and Sulpicius murdered. But when Sulla and his army left for the east, Marius and his followers marched on the city in their turn, massacred their opponents and seized power (87 BC). When Sulla returned after defeating Mithradates at the end of 83, the stage was set for a full-scale civil war between his army and those of Marius' successors (Marius himself had died in 86).

After a series of extremely bloody encounters, Sulla emerged victorious and set himself up as dictator in 81. He purged his opponents by means of the notorious *proscriptions and attempted to reform the constitution, in particular by strengthening the position of the senate and abolishing most of the powers of the tribunes. These efforts were ineffectual, however, since they addressed the symptoms, not the cause, of the problem, and the same lethal trends continued. A fresh series of military crises in the 70s (see SERTORIUS, QUINTUS) brought the popular generals *Pompey and *Crassus to power. As consuls in 70 they repealed most of Sulla's laws and restored the powers of the tribunes.

These events, combined with scandals such as the trial of Verres, ex-governor of Sicily (see CICERO), left the senate with little power and even less authority, at a time when military difficulties and economic crises continued to afflict the empire. In 67 Pompey was given (by a tribunician plebiscite) an overriding command against the pirates, and in 66 was appointed, again by plebiscite and in place of Lucius Licinius Lucullus, the senate's commander, to take charge of a war in the east against Mithradates. This he quickly brought to an end, and settled by a complete reorganization of the east, annexing territory, founding cities, and disposing kingdoms. In Italy meanwhile social unrest and discontent erupted in the conspiracy of *Catiline (63), which was ruthlessly put down by the consul *Cicero, who himself portrayed the outcome as a triumph for moderation.

In 62 Pompey returned, a conquering hero, to a magnificent triumph and what he no doubt hoped would be a life of ease and dignity as Rome's leading statesman. If so he was disappointed, since the *optimates* (the conservative ruling class), led by Lucullus and *Cato the Younger, frustrated his efforts to gain the land allotments he had promised as a reward for his veterans. The effect was to drive Pompey into an informal pact with Crassus and *Caesar, sometimes called (in modern books, not in the ancient sources) the First Triumvirate. This alliance proved irresistible. Pompey had overwhelming popular support, Crassus had unlimited money, and Caesar, who was even more unscrupulous than his partners, turned out to have the brains. As consul in 59 Caesar enacted all the measures his partners wanted, and rewarded himself with a special command in Gaul, which he proceeded to conquer in a brilliant (if brutal) campaign (58–51 BC).

In Rome during the 50s the senate was powerless in the face of the dynasts, but the latter had less control over the tribunes, as the activities of Publius *Clodius Pulcher demonstrated. Towards the end of the decade order threatened to break down completely, and in 52 Pompey was appointed sole consul when riots prevented elections. By this time relations between Pompey and Caesar were becoming strained (Crassus had been killed in battle in 53). Fear of Caesar drove Pompey and the *optimates* closer together, as they attempted to frustrate Caesar's aim of passing directly from his Gallic command to a second consulship. Caesar refused to lay down his arms, and in 49 he invaded Italy at the head of an army and once again plunged the empire into civil war. Pompey, who presented himself as defender of the republic, had some initial successes, but was eventually beaten at Pharsalus (48), and was murdered after fleeing to Egypt. Caesar then overcame the republicans in Africa and Spain, before returning to Italy where he became consul and dictator for life.

Caesar embarked on a series of grandiose and visionary schemes, but his monarchical tendencies went against republican tradition and offended the nobles. On 15 March, 44 BC, he was stabbed to death by a group of senators led by *Brutus and Cassius. The conspirators were unable to restore the republic, however, because Caesar's chief aides, Mark *Antony and *Lepidus, had the support of his armies; in 43 they joined together with Caesar's heir, the 19-year-old Caesar Octavian (see AUGUSTUS), to form a Triumvirate (a formally constituted board of three for the organization of the state), whereupon they divided the empire between them, and purged their opponents (including Cicero) by reviving Sulla's device of proscriptions. Lepidus was soon squeezed out, and the empire was uneasily divided between Octavian and Antony until 31 BC, when the issue was finally decided in Octavian's favour at the battle of *Actium. Mark Antony and his mistress *Cleopatra VII committed suicide, leaving Octavian in complete control of the Roman empire.   T. J. Co.

2. From Augustus to the Antonines (31 BC–AD 192)
1. Augustus and the foundation of imperial rule
After victory over the forces of Mark *Antony and *Cleopatra VII at *Actium (31 BC) and the subsequent annexation of Egypt in the summer of 30 BC, Octavian (see AUGUSTUS) and his generals were masters of the Mediterranean world. To create a system of permanent rule they needed both to gain the acceptance of their power by the majority of the senatorial and equestrian élite, even if a majority of die-hard republicans could not be won over, and to maintain the loyalty of the soldiery. The armed forces in turn were to revert to their traditional role of war against foreign enemies. The great and successful wars of conquest initiated by Augustus and *Agrippa became one of the key sources of legitimacy and prestige of the new regime (see below, §3).

Octavian and his key political allies (such as Agrippa and Titus Statilius Taurus) proceeded cautiously and by trial and error in their search for an enduring political settlement. Already in 32 BC 700 senators (out of a total of about 1,000) had sworn a personal oath of loyalty to Octavian. In 28 BC Octavian and Agrippa assumed censorial powers, completed the first full census of the citizen body since 69, and revised the rolls of the *senate. One hundred and ninety 'unworthy' members were removed. Grants of special powers by senate and people, most notably in 28 and 23 BC, ensued, which formalized and legitimated Augustus' pre-eminent position. Augustus, 'revered', was a title conferred on Octavian in 27 BC. Augustus' most important right was that of directly appointing all senior army officers and the governors of key (especially military) provinces. At all times he ensured that any new powers were formally voted to him and made a great show of rejecting anything which hinted at monarchy or dictatorship. Among his fellow aristocrats he portrayed himself as 'first among equals'. The lessons of *Caesar's fate had been well learnt. In the years up to his death in 13 BC Agrippa acted as almost co-regent of the empire. He was also the recipient of grants of special powers in 23 and 18 BC. Together they took active measures to reconstruct the state's financial infrastructure. Both men spent long periods touring the provinces especially in the decade after the political settlement of 23 BC. In the long term their most important administrative innovation was the introduction of provincial censuses which were designed to map out the resources of the provinces and provide a more rational framework for the assessment and levying of direct taxation, 'the sinews of the state'. See FINANCE, ROMAN.

The senate, from whose ranks generals and most provincial governors were drawn, remained the most important political element in the state, even though its corporate powers were restricted through the *de facto* transfer of the formulation of fiscal and military policy to Augustus and his advisers. The new regime also saw the entrenchment of the equestrian order (see EQUITES, *Imperial period*) as the empire's second estate. At Rome important new positions of public authority (the prefect of the corn supply, the prefects of the praetorian guard) were created and allotted to equestrians. In the provinces equestrian administrators (*procuratores*; see PROCURATOR) oversaw fiscal affairs. In the armed forces young equestrians came to form the junior officer corps as commanders of auxiliary units and as military tribunes in the legions. Augustus and his advisers thus exercised rule over the empire through the collaboration of the political élite. In turn the public careers of individual senators and equestrians were dependent on the favour of the emperor. Loyalty brought reward and success, disloyalty (real or imagined) disgrace, even execution.

The land question in general and the material demands of the veteran troops in particular had fatally undermined oligarchic rule in the late republic (see AGRARIAN LAWS AND POLICY). Augustus and his advisers took determined and decisive steps to resolve this problem. Mass demobilization immediately followed the end of the civil wars. Land in Italy and the provinces was purchased, via the vast private resources of Octavian Augustus, and distributed to these veterans. In the medium term the practice of routine distribution of land or cash to veterans was established. The creation of a special military treasury in AD 6, funded by a new tax on inheritances, marked the culmination of this development. The process of overseas civil and military colonization, first adumbrated by Caesar and taken to its logical conclusion by Augustus, brought about the transfer to the provinces of about 250,000 adult male Italians, roughly one-fifth of the total free adult male population of Italy. In a parallel process vast resources were also expended to underpin the material interests of the free population of Rome. The regular distribution of free rations of grain, acquired by provincial taxation, became a normal feature of imperial Rome. Augustus also used his own personal fortune to make periodic distributions of cash to the inhabitants of Rome. On his own account hundreds of millions of sesterces were spent in this way between 30 BC and his death, a sum greater than the total annual revenues of the Roman state in the early 50s BC.

2. High politics, the succession, and the emperors

The resolution of the land question via overseas *colonization and the underpinning of the material livelihood of the massive population of Rome removed from the political agenda two issues which had dominated the history of the late republic. Under the emperors high politics came to centre on two interconnected issues, namely the relationship of individual emperors to the political élite, and the imperial succession. Extreme tension between sections of the political élite and the emperor, expressed most dramatically in treason-trials and executions, became the hallmark of high politics under Augustus' immediate successors, *Tiberius (AD 14–37), *Gaius or Caligula (37–41), *Claudius (41–54), and *Nero (54–68), the Julio-Claudian dynasty. This tension derived structurally from the claim that the emperor was only first among his aristocratic equals, from lingering republicanism, and from the absence of any established law of succession. Consequently leading aristocrats, especially if connected by blood or marriage to the imperial family, could be regarded as threatening an individual emperor's rule. The contingent factor of the personalities and backgrounds of the Julio-Claudian emperors sharpened this structural tension. So the suspicious Tiberius had become Augustus' chosen successor only by default after the death of Augustus' two grandsons; the autocratic Caligula is said to have made senators kiss his feet; Claudius was completely without experience of public life at his accession; Nero came to power at the age of 16. Each turned to court-favourites to buttress his position. But the open use, especially, of imperial slaves and freedmen as confidants merely served to strengthen the antagonism of the political élite.

The first imperial dynasty succumbed to insurrection and civil war in 68. Nero had both profoundly alienated the political élite by converting the imperial role into a vehicle for indulging his private interests (e.g. singing and chariot-racing) and fatally neglected to cultivate the armed forces and their commanders. When Gaius Iulius Vindex, governor of Gallia Lugdunensis, revolted, support for Nero melted away. His suicide in June 68 opened the way to civil war as leading senators vied for the purple. After the brief reigns of Galba (68–9), Otho (69), and Vitellius (69), order and stability were restored by *Vespasian (69–79).

The new Flavian dynasty initiated by Vespasian was short-lived. His elder son *Titus ruled for two years (79–81) and was succeeded by Vespasian's younger son *Domitian (81–96). Under Domitian, who liked to style himself 'Lord and God', tension quickly resurfaced. A serious *putsch* was attempted by the governor of Upper Germany in 89, and in September 96 Domitian was murdered in a palace coup. The senate nominated as his successor a leading, if elderly, senator *Nerva (96–8).

The ensuing 90 years represented a high-water mark of stability. The succession problem was resolved by the chance that a series of emperors had no surviving sons. So Nerva adopted *Trajan (98–118). Trajan adopted *Hadrian (117–38), and Hadrian adopted *Antoninus Pius (138–61). All had been leading senators before their accession. The transfer of key political offices at Rome (such as those in charge of imperial correspondence and finances) from freedmen to senior equestrians further served to ameliorate relations between emperors and the élite. In 161 Marcus *Aurelius, adopted son of Pius, succeeded and immediately associated his adoptive brother Lucius Verus (161–9) as co-emperor. Two tests of political stability now ensued. First, incursions by the Parthians in 162 and by northern tribes from 166 precipitated a period of intense and systematic military campaigning more serious than any seen since the reign of Augustus (see below, § 3). Secondly, the problem of the succession resurfaced. Marcus had a surviving son, *Commodus. Commodus was made co-emperor in 177 and succeeded in March 180. His reign reawakened political tensions reminiscent of the 1st cent. He quickly abandoned his father's senior advisers and placed his trust in confidants of servile status. Like Nero he used the imperial role to indulge his private whims, most notably fighting as a *gladiator. The result was predictable. On New Year's Eve 192 he was assassinated in a palace *coup*. Official propaganda justified his murder by claiming that he intended on New Year's Day 193 to murder the incoming consuls and leading senators.

Whatever the vicissitudes of high politics the rulers of Rome in the two centuries from the accession of Augustus achieved two great objectives. Militarily they further extended the empire and protected it from external assault. Politically they maintained uninterrupted administrative control over its vast territory. Fission and secession, the normal fate of great pre-industrial empires, were conspicuous by their absence.

3. The army and military policy

The Roman imperial armed forces were a formidable institution. The state routinely mobilized an average *c*.350,000 men. The army was the largest element in the state's budget. It was the guarantor of the empire's security, the means for its further expansion. In the last analysis the security of any emperor depended on the loyalty of the troops and their commanders.

Augustus for the first time in Roman history had created a fully professional army with fixed terms and conditions of service. The troops swore a personal oath of loyalty to the reigning emperor. Above all, the loyalty of the troops was grounded in a system of material rewards (pay and donatives) which privileged them in comparison to the mass of the free inhabitants of the empire. Although no emperors could count in principle on the absolute loyalty of all their military commanders (recruited as in the republic from the senatorial and equestrian orders), a variety of devices limited the potential for revolt. All senior commanders were personally appointed by the emperor. Tenure of key positions, such as legionary commander or governor of a military province, was normally restricted to three years, while no military governor normally had above three legions under his command. That only two civil wars (68–9 and 193–7) occurred up to the end of the 2nd cent. is testimony to the success of these devices.

After twenty years of civil war Augustus set his new model army to the most traditional of Roman purposes, conquest and expansion. By the end of his reign the classic geographic contours of the empire had been set. Augustus had inherited a fundamentally Mediterranean empire; the main objectives of the campaigns fought under his auspices were conquest and expansion in continental Europe. Campaigns under Augustus and then Agrippa ensured the final subjugation, after 200 years, of Spain in 19 BC. All efforts were then directed to the north. By 14 BC all the Alpine regions were under Roman control; in the same year a series of campaigns began which led to the conquest of the Balkan peninsula up to the Danube. Roman control was also extended beyond the Rhine up to the Elbe. In AD 6 large-scale preparations were made for further expansion via the invasion of Bohemia by two army groups. These preparations were interrupted by a serious revolt in Pannonia which took three years of hard fighting, under the command of Tiberius, to suppress. Celebration of this victory in AD 9 was cut short by the news of the loss of three complete legions in the area between the Rhine and the Elbe. Attempts at continued expansion were then abandoned and the line of the Rhine–Danube *de facto* became the empire's northern frontier.

Augustus, despite the great conquests of his reign, left to his successors the advice to keep the empire within its current territorial limits. For nearly a century they adhered, in general, to this advice. Consolidation, rather than conquest, came to epitomize Roman policy. Some new accretion of territory occurred through the assimilation as provinces of previously client territory (Cappadocia in AD 17, the Mauretanias in 42, Thrace in 46, all of Judaea by 44, Commagene in 72, and Nabataea in 106). On the northern frontier an important development was the occupation under the Flavians of the Rhine–Danube re-entrant. The only clear exception to this process of consolidation was Claudius' invasion of *Britain in 43. Britain was never to be fully conquered. In the longer term its garrison of three legions represented an anomalous diversion of resources to a strategically unimportant area.

The reign of Trajan marked a temporary return to determined expansionism. In the north two major expeditions were mounted on the Danube in 101–2 and 105–6 which saw the annexation of Dacia and its attendant gold-mines. In the east Trajan was the first emperor to try to destroy the military capacity of the Parthian kingdom and to annex territory east of the Euphrates. The expedition of 113–17 was at first successful, but a serious revolt in Mesopotamia in 116–17 and the death of Trajan in 117 led his successor Hadrian to abandon the attempt. No major campaigns against external enemies occurred again until the reign of Marcus Aurelius when invasion from the east and then from the north posed a classic two-pronged strategic threat. In 161 the Parthian king declared war and invaded. The counter-expedition of Lucius Verus of 162–6 was militarily successful although no attempt was made to repeat Trajan's plan of annexing Mesopotamia. In 166–7 northern tribes breached the weakened defences on the Danube, and triggered the so-called northern wars of Marcus Aurelius. By the time of Marcus' death at Vienna in 180 plans had probably been made to annex further territory north of the Danube. Commodus, however, opted for peace, and by his death the territorial extent of the empire was very much, with the exception of Britain and Dacia, as Augustus had left it in AD 14.

Given the limited number of major expansionary campaigns the prime function of the Roman armed forces became the routine defence of the empire. For the first time the territorial empire acquired clearly demarcated frontiers, especially to the north (Rhine–Danube) and the east (Euphrates). The majority of legions and auxiliary units came to be stationed on or near the frontiers in permanent fortified positions. Artificial barriers, such as Hadrian's wall (see WALL OF HADRIAN), were sometimes constructed when the frontiers were not naturally delimited. An elaborate network of roads was built up to facilitate communications and the movement of troops and supplies. The frontiers, natural or artificial, functioned as symbolic demarcation of direct Roman rule and as barriers to minor incursions rather than as major obstacles to serious attacks (see LIMES). Across time there was also a significant shift in the strategic disposition of Rome's forces. Under Tiberius there were eight legions stationed on the Rhine, six in the Balkans/Danube theatre, and only four in Syria. By the accession of Hadrian only four remained on the Rhine, twelve were now stationed in the Danube area, and six in the east. This shift of forces to the Danube–Euphrates axis represented a significant step in the process culminating in the removal of the capital of the empire from Rome to Byzantium.

4. Running an empire

The mature empire of the 2nd cent. embraced a territory of about 5 million sq. km. with a population conventionally estimated at about 55 million. Despite rudimentary technology and limited means of communication the territorial integrity of the empire was not seriously threatened in our period. The two great Jewish revolts of 66–74 and 132–5 (see JEWS) represented the only exceptions to this generalization. The principal aims of imperial rule were to maintain internal order and to extract resources, via taxation, to underpin state expenditure, especially the funding of the massive standing army. Given these limited aims, no large-scale bureaucratic apparatus was elaborated, and routine administration was predicated on the co-operation of the local élites of the provinces.

At the apex of the exercise of public authority stood the emperor. The emperor was the key source of binding rules affecting individuals, corporate groups, and the subject population as a whole; he adjudicated serious disputes and granted ideal and material privileges to both individuals and corporate groups (especially cities). His court was the supreme tribunal of the empire both at first instance and at appeal. Decision-making by the emperor was normally mediated through the mechanism of an advisory body, the *consilium principis*, whose members were drawn from the senatorial and equestrian élite. Although the senate also maintained some parallel authoritative powers they were comparatively limited in scope.

The empire was divided administratively into a series of territorial circumscriptions, of unequal size and population, called provinces (44 at the time of Trajan). In each province a governor of senatorial status exercised overall responsibility, although Egypt and some minor provinces had equestrian governors. For fiscal purposes governors were normally aided by equestrian officials called procurators. The number of élite Roman officials allotted to the provinces was very small, about 160 in the mid-2nd cent., and each had only a small administrative apparatus to help him. Consequently routine administrative activity was devolved on local cities and their magistrates and councils who formed the prime intermediary mechanism linking the state to the mass of its subjects. Each province operated administratively as an agglomeration of civic units, each unit having responsibility for the territorial hinterland and population attached to it.

In the fiscal sphere the Roman officials exercised a supervisory and adjudicatory authority. They organized the periodic censuses, made global tax-assessments for each city, and adjudicated disputes which arose in the processes of assessment and collection of taxes. In turn each city had the responsibility of collecting its own tax-assessment. The individual paid to the city, the city paid to the state. Provincial governors had supreme authority for the maintenance of order and monopolized the legitimate use of violence. Only they had the right, through both formal proceedings and summary jurisdiction, to impose capital penalties. Their tribunal operated as the prime mechanism for the resolution both of private disputes, especially those concerning Roman citizens and individuals of high social status, and of disputes between rival civic communities over their ideal and material rights. The local civic authorities underpinned the governor's role in four distinct ways. They were responsible for hunting down serious criminals (e.g. brigands, Christians, rustlers) and holding them for trial by the governor. Within their own territories they exercised a lower-level jurisdiction to resolve minor private disputes and to punish minor crimes. Administratively they supervised the internal affairs (e.g. raising and reallocating local revenues, supervising public buildings, regulating local markets) of their own cities. Finally each province had a provincial council whose members were recruited from individual cities' élites. The provincial councils had a double function. They were responsible for the organization of the religious ceremonies and festivals associated with the imperial cult, and members of the council acted as high-priests of the cult, a role of great prestige; diplomatically the councils could send embassies to the emperor to make representations about matters of common interest to a province or to lay accusations of misgovernment by Roman officials. This crucial intermediary role of the local élites of the provinces was recognized by privileges they came to acquire in the social order.

5. The social order

The imperial social order was deeply stratified and characterized by a marked congruence of wealth and status and by very limited opportunities for upward social mobility. At the apex of the social pyramid stood three aristocratic orders, namely (in descending rank) the senatorial order, the equestrian order, and the local élites of civic councillors and magistrates. Each had differential property-qualifications for membership; each possessed distinct status symbols in terms of dress and legal privilege. Below stood the vast mass of the humble free and the slaves, the latter in strict law the chattels of their owners. Although the total number of slaves is not known, the probable proportion in Egypt of 10 per cent (inferred from census-data) is a reasonable estimate for the whole empire.

The most important social development of our period was the process by which the local élites across the empire came to acquire a common and coherent privileged status. At first the local élites were rewarded by individual grants of Roman citizenship. In the course of the 2nd cent. a series of imperial rulings granted all local councillors and magistrates a bundle of legal privileges (e.g. less severe and degrading punishments for serious crimes) which set them apart from the mass of the provincial population. In turn new recruits into the equestrian and senatorial orders normally came from the ranks of local élites. Only two institutionalized avenues of upward social mobility, namely the army and the emancipation of slaves, existed. The economic and social status of the soldiery was enhanced by the material rewards of service and by the privileges granted to veterans. Furthermore a small minority of ranking legionaries could achieve the post of centurion and, even more spectacularly, the post of chief centurion which automatically conferred equestrian status. Private owners had the right to emancipate their slaves, and a small minority of *freedmen (ex-slaves) are found entering the ranks of the local élites.

Within this stable social order dissent and desperation among the poor and immiserated expressed themselves primarily in *brigandage and piracy. No serious political ideologies of opposition existed or were developed, while the state for reasons of internal security tightly regulated freedom of association. The most important ideological developments occurred in the religious sphere notably through the dissemination of Mithraism and Christianity. But even by the late 2nd cent. the nascent world religion had had only a limited impact. It remained primarily an urban phenomenon, and even then most widely spread in the empire's Mediterranean heartlands. Christian ideology and practices had scarcely touched the north and north-west of the empire or rural areas in general.

By the late 2nd cent. 'the immeasurable majesty of the Roman peace' (as the elder Pliny had termed it) still appeared settled and unchallenged. The political and institutional characteristics of Roman rule, even the territorial extent of the empire itself, were little different from the situation at the end of Augustus' reign. It was to be the combination of the intense civil wars that ensued on the murder of Commodus, and the advent of new and aggressive enemies to the north and east of the empire, which were to put the imperial state to its first great test in the 3rd cent., to transform its political and institutional structures, and to open the way for the triumph of the new world religion.   G. P. B.

3. From Septimius Severus to Constantine (AD 193–337)
1. Political and dynastic history

The period from the Severans to Constantine the Great begins and ends with strong government, separated by a period of political instability and military stress through which shine the heroic achievements of great (but short-lived) individual emperors. *Septimius Severus (193–211) rose to power in civil wars reminiscent of those of 68–70. Proclaimed in Pannonia, he at once marched to Italy to suppress Marcus Didius Severus Iulianus, after which he quickly defeated his rivals Pescennius Niger in the east and Decimus Clodius Septimius Albinus in the west. After a determined and in some ways ruthless reign which did not endear him to senatorial opinion, he was succeeded at York by his son *Caracalla, who was killed in 217 during an eastern campaign by the supporters of his praetorian prefect Marcus Opellius Macrinus, the first candidate of equestrian rank to achieve the imperial dignity.

Macrinus was quickly displaced by an eastern relative of Severus' wife, the eccentric religious innovator *Elagabalus, and he in 222 by *Severus Alexander, whose persistent ineffectiveness eventually alienated the army. His assassination in 235 and replacement by a tough military officer from Thrace, Gaius Iulius Verus Maximinus, was an uncomfortable reminder that what the Roman empire needed was not dilettante sportsmen, exuberant child priests, or likeable youths, but disciplined officers who knew armies. The period from Maximinus to the rise of *Diocletian in 284 is traditionally known as the 'period of anarchy' of the Roman empire, and this is true if one takes as a criterion the traditional historian's task of reconstructing a narrative of events in the correct order—a task made infinitely more difficult by the deficiencies in the ancient narrative sources. In this half-century there were at least eighteen 'legitimate' emperors, and far more if one counts the numerous usurpers of the period. Nearly all met violent deaths after short reigns. What does emerge from the period, in the response of Diocletian (284–305), is a conception of the imperial office as divisible, authority in different regions being devolved to separate emperors who, instead of fighting each other for sole power, would concede each others' dignity and collaborate. This conception is at the heart of the so-called Tetrarchy, in which Diocletian first (in 285) shared his power as Augustus with a single colleague, Maximian, and (in 293) added to the Augusti two Caesars who would both share the burden of warfare and government and ensure an orderly succession. The first of these aims was achieved by Diocletian, but the second was not, as the planned succession was disrupted by the ambitions of rival contenders. From the complicated series of civil wars, executions, and suicides following the joint retirements of Diocletian and Maximian in 305 emerged the figures of (the newly converted) Constantine in the west, and Licinius in the east. It was they who in 312 jointly issued the so-called 'edict of Milan' restoring peace to the Church after the persecutions of Diocletian and Galerius, and restoring to Christians their confiscated property, but Constantine's defeat of Licinius at Chrysopolis in 324 put him and his sons in sole control of the Roman empire.

2. Military policy and government
Despite political difficulties and frequent military reverses the territorial integrity of the Roman empire was maintained with surprising success. Septimius Severus had converted his early civil war against Pescennius Niger into a war of conquest in which he annexed Mesopotamia; this provided a solution to the problem of Armenia, a perennial cause of conflict between Rome and Persia. The rise of the Sasanian dynasty in Persia under Ardashir I (c.223–c.240) and especially Sapor I (c.240–c.270) posed new problems for the Roman empire in the east. The campaign against Persia of *Gordian III ended in defeat and the emperor's death, some thought by treachery of his praetorian prefect Philip, who succeeded him (244). In the mid-250s Sapor's invasion of the empire resulted in his penetration of Roman territories (*Antioch was occupied for a time), and in 260 in the capture of the emperor Valerian, but no territory was permanently lost, and the campaign of Galerius in the last decade of the century resulted in a settlement weighted heavily in favour of Rome. On the lower Danube the empire was confronted, also in the 250s, by invasions of Goths, who penetrated parts of Thrace and Asia Minor (this was when the ancestors of the Gothic missionary Ulfila were taken prisoner); the death of the emperor Decius took place in battle against this new enemy. In the 260s and 270s much was achieved in the name of Rome by the usurping regimes of Postumus and his successors in Gaul (260–74), and in the east by the Palmyrene 'empire' of Odaenathus and Zenobia (see PALMYRA). Both rebellions were suppressed by Aurelian (270–5), another of the great Illyrian emperors of the third century; but Aurelian was obliged to abandon Dacia to Gothic occupation. The only other territorial cession made in the period was the abandonment, also by Aurelian, of the *Agri Decumates*, the re-entrant angle between Rhine and Danube annexed in the Flavian period.

The principle of the devolution of imperial power, referred to in § 1 above, is clearly inherent in these events. The rise of the Gallic and Palmyrene empires under Gallienus (sole ruler 260–8) secured frontiers which he could not have defended himself while also maintaining control in Italy and

Illyricum. The situation that obtained under Gallienus, when the Balkans and Italy (with the addition of Africa), and separate administrations among the Gauls and in the east, were financed and governed independently of each other, clearly anticipates the regional prefectures of the 4th cent. Also anticipated in the 3rd cent. is a progressive increase in the number, and reduction in the size, of provinces. After Diocletian there were more than 100 of these, compared with fewer than 50 in the time of Trajan. They were governed to an increasing extent by equestrian rather than senatorial governors. By a supposed decree of Gallienus, indeed, senators were formally excluded from military commands in order to keep them away from armies. Whether the edict is historical or not, it represents a process of change that can be traced in the developing career patterns of senators and equestrians. The army itself underwent considerable changes, the distinction between legionaries and auxiliaries disappearing as the emperors made increasing use of barbarian federates for their field armies. It was also much enlarged, a process that continued into the 4th cent. It is, however, far from clear that one can talk of a 'militarization' of the Roman empire, and still less so that one can assign the beginning of such a process to Septimius Severus. The legal and financial benefits offered to the army by that emperor are not out of line with their times. The right to contract legal marriages, for example, recognizes the long custom of soldiers to acquire 'common-law' wives and raise children with them in stable unions.

3. The economy
The economic history of the 3rd cent., like its political history, is one of distress and recovery, the extent of both being debated by historians. The conventional picture is of a monetary decline leading to the brink of collapse, and of a transition to a largely natural economy in which the emperors secured their needs and paid their salaries by requisitions in kind rather than from the products of monetary taxation. The rampant inflation of the later part of the period can in part be attributed to the emperors' own debasement of their coin in order to meet the ever-increasing prices caused by its diminishing value as currency. But *Diocletian and *Constantine I were able to restore a stable gold currency based on the *solidus* minted first at 60, then at 72 to the pound. This coin, one of the most successful ever produced, was the foundation of the late Roman and Byzantine monetary economy (see COINAGE, ROMAN). The picture is also one of urban decline, but with many variations and exceptions. Britain, largely exempt from the wars of the period, does not seem to have suffered from it, and over the longer term the prosperity of frontier regions benefited from the shift from the centre to the periphery of those resources necessary for defence. As the emperors spent more of their time in the frontier regions, their presence acted as a stimulant to the economies of these regions. And the cities which were promoted by the emperors—such as Trier, Serdica, Naissus, Thessalonica, Nicomedia, and of course Constantinople—both became great and contributed to the economic development of their hinterlands. The Antonine constitution of 212, in which Caracalla extended Roman *citizenship to all free inhabitants of the Roman empire, is presented by the historian Cassius Dio as inspired by fiscal motives; but another effect was to remove this once great privilege from the status of gift or grant to communities and individuals, and to make the city of Rome marginal to their social and legal position. Fulfilling a long development, the *civitas Romana* was now without any ambiguity citizenship of the Roman empire and not of its capital.

4. Culture
The Severan period saw the continued efflorescence of the literary culture known as the '*Second Sophistic' (the inventor of the phrase, the biographer of the sophists Philostratus, published his work under Alexander Severus). Literary accomplishment was still important in the relations of cities with their rulers through embassies, and literary men were still rewarded and promoted to imperial office. Most notable is the juristic culture of the Severan age, with great *lawyers like Ulpian and Papinian (both of whom were killed in the dynastic upheavals of the later Severan period), but this is one of the great continuums of Roman culture. Preserving and systematizing the case law of the later 1st and 2nd

cents. as propounded in imperial judgements, the Classical jurists were themselves preserved for posterity by the codifications of Justinian (see JUSTINIAN'S CODIFICATION). The middle and later years of the 3rd cent. produced the philosopher Plotinus and his pupil and biographer Porphyry; and the historian Dexippus of Athens attests the continuing prestige of a great intellectual capital despite the physical impact of the Herulian invasion. Of immediate relevance to the future, the Christian Church expanded considerably. At the opening of the 3rd cent. Tertullian of Carthage preached opposition to the world and secular culture, at the end of it *Eusebius of Caesarea documents the expansion of the Church and its acceptance, in the conversion of Constantine, by the empire and the world-order. See CHRISTIANITY. In the mid-3rd cent. Cyprian, later executed in the persecution of Valerian, attests 87 bishops in North Africa, and in Rome seven deacons looked after the interests of 1,500 widows and orphans.

4. The Late Empire

1. Political and dynastic history

The three sons of Constantine who emerged from a co-ordinated killing of the more distant claimants at their father's death in 337 competed among themselves for pre-eminence; Constantine II, who succeeded in Gaul (with Britain and Spain), was eliminated in 340 by his brother Constans II, who had inherited Illyricum. He was in turn defeated by the usurper Magnentius (350), and he by the surviving brother Constantius II (353). Constantius, preoccupied in the west, appointed Gallus Caesar to deputize in the East, and after Gallus' execution (354) tried to rule as sole emperor. Again, however, he was confronted by usurpation while he himself was committed to war with Persia, and reluctantly accepted his cousin *Julian as Caesar in Gaul. Julian's military successes and his army's growing discontent at his treatment by his senior partner led to his proclamation against Constantius, but he was spared a war which he would probably not have won by Constantius' death (361). Julian's famous attempt to restore the pagan cults of the Roman empire was cut short by his death in Persia (363), and the short reign of Jovian was succeeded in 364 by the firm military government of the brothers Valentinian and Valens. Valens' death at Adrianople (378) brought to the throne Theodosius I, a former general whose successes both in foreign and in civil war have tended to be overshadowed by his pro-Nicene religious policies and by his religious confrontations with St Ambrose. The accession of Valentinian and Valens had been followed by a division of the resources of eastern and western empires, and this was repeated after Theodosius' death in 395. Theodosius' sons Arcadius (in the east) and Honorius (in the west), and their respective successors Theodosius II and Valentinian III, were, however, weak emperors, coming to power in their minority, surrounded by powerful courtiers and—especially in the west—by competing warlords and barbarian leaders who cared little for imperial authority. The ascendancy over emperors of such figures as Stilicho, Bonifatius, Flavius Aetius, and Ricimer well presages the replacement of the imperial office by the kings of Italy, Odoacer and Theoderic. In the east, the death of Theodosius II was followed by a disruptive period of competition, but the competitors were on the whole vigorous, effective war leaders, and under Anastasius (491–518), Justin I (518–27), and his formidable nephew and successor Justinian (527–65) the Byzantine empire was able to hold its own and even, under Justinian, to attempt to make good its losses by reconquest.

2. Military policy

The 4th-cent. west was threatened on the Rhine front by the Germanic federation known as the Alamanni and on the Danube by the Quadi and their allies and, in particular, by the Goths. The Alamanni succeeded in the 350s in occupying large areas of eastern Gaul, but the ground was recovered by the early campaigns of Julian (356–60) and maintained by the strenuous work of Valentinian, both in campaigning and in a building programme well attested by archaeology. In the east, traditional Roman policy, of containing Persian aggression and responding by measured counter-attacks (with tremendous sieges), was followed by Constantine (who died while setting out on a Persian campaign) and Constantius II, but broken by the invasion of Persia conducted by Julian with disastrous results; Jovian was forced after Julian's death to cede to the Persians much of what had been gained by the success of Galerius. Under Theodosius I Armenia was partitioned between Rome and Persia, and thereafter relations between the two powers took on a more familiar pattern until the time of Justinian. The real crisis of the Roman empire was generated on the Danube, as the Goths, under pressure from the Huns, negotiated or forced their way across the river, a process leading to the momentous defeat at Adrianople. Despite the treaty concluded in 382 by Theodosius I, the Romans were never able fully to recover, and the ensuing fragility of their command of the Balkans is the most important strategic consideration in the division of the empire into eastern and western parts. In the 5th cent., the west was overrun by mainly Germanic invaders—Goths and then Franks in Gaul, Goths and Suebi in the Spanish peninsula, Vandals in North Africa—permitting greater or lesser degrees of Roman continuity. The Gallic upper classes and Church preserved much of what was important to them—including the Latin language—and the reign of Theoderic the Ostrogoth in north Italy marks something of a cultural high point. Despite pressure from the Avars and other northern peoples, the eastern empire retained its territorial integrity until the expansion of Islam in the early 7th cent. Justinian's programme of recovery of the western provinces was in the short term successful, but it is debatable whether the recovery of Gothic Italy benefited or impoverished its inhabitants, and Justinian's prolonged campaigns there were shortly followed by the invasions of the Lombards from the north.

3. Government

The military and administrative achievements of later Roman government were based on structural reforms and changes that make it look very unlike the government of the early empire. It was a strongly bureaucratized state, with large and systematically organized departments of administration staffed (often, no doubt, over-staffed) by career officials who spent their lives in a service characterized by demarcations of duties and by hierarchies of seniority within and between departments. It has been calculated that more than 30,000 men were employed in the civil branches of the service, but this figure must be set beside the vast size of the empire and the greatly increased level of governmental intervention required for its administration; since the military stresses of the 2nd and 3rd cents., the 'consensual' mode of government of the early empire had been replaced by one much more authoritarian, and given the needs of empire it is hard to see that it could have been otherwise. The old aristocracies of Italy and the west, willing participants in the government of the early empire, largely stood aloof except in so far as was required to defend their essential interests; in the east they were more effectively drawn into government as its agents and allies. The foundation of Constantinople had much to do with this different pattern in the east. The whole institution of government was glorified, from the emperor to his lowliest official, by an elaborate system of ceremonial which has its culmination in Byzantine handbooks, and is beautifully expressed in visual imagery (the Ravenna mosaics).

There was a price to pay—the late Roman penal code was one of an unprecedented brutality, quite unmoderated by Christianity—but the success in practice of the system of government is evident. The later Roman empire enjoyed a stable currency in precious metals and limited inflation, regular taxation, good transport, and an adequate flow of supplies. Until the last decades of the 4th cent. in the west and for much longer in the east, its borders were maintained intact, trade between its regions and with the outside world flourished, and despite predictable *corruption its administrative and legal systems were stable and effective. Cities maintained their prosperity and even, in the east, increased it, and the countryside was productive and free of major disruption and banditry. Education was maintained, and the period was marked by an efflorescence of literary and artistic culture, both Christian and pagan; it produced the Gallic panegyrists, the history of *Ammianus Marcellinus and the poetry of Ausonius and Claudian, the speeches of Libanius and Themistius, the letters of Symmachus, Christian exegesis exceeding by an order of magnitude everything that had been produced before, and mountains of documentary material. Sidonius Apollinaris and the Greek Church historians in the 5th cent. are followed in the 6th by Cassiodorus and the histories of Procopius, not to mention those monuments to Roman juristic culture, the Theodosian Code and the codification of Justinian (see JUSTINIAN'S CODIFICATION).

4. The impact of Christianity

It is hard to exaggerate the importance of the conversion to Christianity of Constantine, and after him the Roman empire. Constantine's hopes that loyal bishops would deliver to him obedient tax-paying cities were disappointed by the levels of mutual disagreement (of which his historian Eusebius might have warned him) within the Christian Church. The emperors of the whole period were haunted by this problem, which they tended to exacerbate by taking sides themselves. Paganism also proved unexpectedly recalcitrant, especially in its associations with classical culture and established patterns of life such as public games (see GAMES). But Christianity gave common ground in a literate culture to rulers and ruled, and provided for imperial ideologists such as Eusebius a rhetoric of power, and a model of imperial as deriving from divine authority. It gave to bishops an enhanced secular role, exemplified in their appointment as arbitrators in civil jurisdiction, an activity well documented in the letters of bishops such as Basil of Caesarea and *Augustine of Hippo. The consequences, in an influx of Christian 'converts' using their religion to advance their personal and family interests (some Roman senatorial families were among the worst offenders), were clearly seen by some Christian writers— such as Jerome, who proposed to write a history of the Church in which he would show how it had become materially richer and more powerful but poorer in virtue. At the beginning of the 4th cent. Eusebius could offer a Christian triumphalism, in which the conversion of Constantine and the participation in government of pious Christian magistrates were seen as providential and the fulfilment of Old Testament prophecy; at the beginning of the 5th, Augustine, having used the imperial power to force Donatist schismatics into the Catholic Church, developed in the *City of God* a theory of a mixed earthly society of the virtuous and the wicked, whom only God could separate. As a reading of Ammianus Marcellinus or the Theodosian Code will show, the conversion of Constantine to Christianity did not bring about Heaven on earth, and many a Christian sermon—such as Ambrose on usury—will cause one to doubt whether it brought earth much closer to Heaven. It could indeed be a double-edged weapon, but as an instrument of power it appealed to emperors and churchmen alike.   J. F. Ma.

same time their architectural style demonstrates the Hellenization of the public spaces of the city. Meanwhile, *aqueducts were built to provide the city with an adequate water-supply, together with bridges, quays, and newly paved roads. The rise of the dynasts in the 1st cent. BC was likewise reflected in the buildings of the city; *Sulla reconstructed the Curia (senate-house) to reflect the increasing authority he granted to the senate; *Pompey built Rome's first permanent stone theatre, together with an impressive portico, on the Campus Martius, while of *Caesar's grandiose schemes, including a plan to divert the Tiber, only the forum Caesaris, Basilica Iulia, and the Saepta remain, finished by *Augustus.

Most of the surviving monuments of ancient Rome are, however, largely the work of the emperors, whose rebuildings or additions transformed or eclipsed the older monuments. Augustus built a new forum Augustum, decorated with statues of Roman heroes and members of the gens

Iulia; his palace on the Palatine was associated with the new temple of *Apollo, while many new monuments in the Campus, including the Mausoleum, were erected by him or *Agrippa, or by his *viri triumphales*. The combination of Saepta, Pantheon, and Agrippa's baths rivalled Pompey's theatre and portico for scale and grandeur. The eastern end of the forum Romanum was remodelled, with the temple of the Divine Iulius a new focal point, but ancient cult buildings were respected and in many cases restored; and the city was divided into fourteen new *regiones*. Tiberius' contributions to the urban landscape were limited, the Castra Praetoria on the outskirts of the Viminal reflecting the growing importance of the praetorians (imperial guard). *Gaius and *Nero, however, both sought to expand the imperial palace beyond Augustus' relatively modest habitation; Gaius linked it to the forum by means of the temple of Castor and Pollux. When Nero's first palace, the Domus Transitoria, was destroyed in the fire of AD 64, he built another, the lavish Domus Aurea (Golden House), on a site which extended from the Palatine to the Esquiline. The effect of these building schemes was to drive the residential quarters off the Palatine to the villas and parks of the Quirinal, Pincian, and Aventine, and to make both emperors highly unpopular with the Roman élite; the Flavians spent much energy in returning the site of the Domus Aurea to the people of Rome, by replacing it with the *Colosseum and baths of Titus, and removing many of its treasures to the new temple of Peace. Later, the baths of Trajan were built on the site. Domitian rebuilt the Palatine palace, further extending it to overlook the Circus Maximus; two new fora were built by *Nerva and Trajan. The centrepiece of the latter was *Trajan's Column, probably of Hadrianic date; the complex also included the 'Markets of Trajan', which deliberately separated the commercial functions of the forum from the ceremonial. Hadrian sought to establish parallels between his rule and that of Augustus (and thereby legitimate his authority) by erecting a new Mausoleum, and rebuilding the Pantheon and baths of Agrippa in the Campus; his creation of a new temple to Venus and Rome (a deity worshipped in the provinces, but not previously in the city) demonstrated that Rome had now become the capital of an empire, not Italy alone.

Then followed a pause in building activities: the Antonines could afford to live upon the prestige of their predecessors, adding only triumphal monuments and temples of the deified emperors. Later building schemes, apart from repairs, take the form of isolated monumental buildings, chiefly utilitarian in scope; typical among these are the great *thermae* (see BATHS). These tended to be on the outskirts of the city, near residential areas, *Caracalla picking the low ground outside porta Capena, *Diocletian and *Constantine I choosing the Quirinal. Great fires offered the only chance of rebuilding in the older regions: thus, the *thermae Alexandrinae* were an enlargement of Nero's baths in the Campus, while the fire of Carinus in 283 created space for the *basilica* of Maxentius, the noblest experiment in vaulting in the ancient world. The city had now reached the climax of its development; soon it was to give way to Constantinople as imperial capital.

I. A. R.; F. C.; J. R. P.

Romulus and **Remus,** mythical founders of Rome. Their legend, though probably as old as the late 4th cent. BC in one form or another (the Ogulnii dedicated a statue of the she-wolf with the twins in 206 BC, Livy 10. 23. 12; see further C. Duliere, *Lupa Romana* (1979); F. Coarelli, *Il Foro Romano: Periodo repubblicano e augusteo* (1985), 89 ff.), cannot be very old nor contain any popular element, unless it be the almost universal one of the exposed children who rise to a great position. The name of Romulus means simply 'Roman', cf. the two forms *Sicanus* and *Siculus*; Remus (who in the Latin tradition replaces the Rhomos of most Greek authors), if not a back-formation from local place-names such as Remurinus ager, Remona (Festus 344. 25 and 345. 10 Lindsay), is possibly formed from *Roma* by false analogy with such doublets as *Kerkura*, *Corcyra*, where the o is short. The origin of the legend of Romulus and Remus has often been debated since the 19th cent. (see C. J. Classen, *Historia* 1963, 447 ff.). The discussion focuses above all on three problems: the antiquity of the myth, its meaning, and the death of Romulus. The majority opinion today is that the legend of the twins already existed by the beginning of the 3rd cent. BC (T. Cornell, *PCPS* 1975, 1 ff.), but some scholars, e.g. J. Bremmer, have no hesitation in dating its origin to the first quarter of the 6th cent., while the comparativists liken it to the Vedic Nāsataya-Ásvin (Dumézil, *ARR* 253 ff.; R. Schilling, *Rites, cultes, dieux de Rome* (1971), 103 ff.) or the creation (B. Lincoln, *HR* 1975–6, 121 ff., and *Priests, Warriors and Cattle* (1981)). Interpretations vary. While all scholars recognize that the myth narrates the foundation of Roman institutions, one version even making Romulus a Greek *ktistēs* (city-founder), historians stress variously the schemata known from anthropology (e.g. the bands of youths), the Indo-European concept of twins (Dumézil, Lincoln), or the political realities of the republican period. As to the different versions of the death of Romulus (sudden disappearance or murder followed by

Rome (topography) Reconstructed drawing of the northern Campus Martius in Rome showing the area's transformation by the public works of *Augustus. The obelisk (centre) formed the gnomon (pointer) of a great sundial, with the *Ara Pacis (right) at the end of one of its meridians. Augustus' grandiose mausoleum is on the left.

dismemberment), the light has yet to penetrate. The assimilation of Romulus to the god Quirinus could go back, like the tradition about his apotheosis, to the 3rd cent. BC. Romulus did not receive cult.

In its normal form (Livy 1. 3. 10 ff.; Dion. Hal. *Ant. Rom.* 1. 76. 1 ff.; Plut. *Rom.* 3 ff.; more in Bremmer in *Roman Myth and Mythography* (1987), 25 ff., which article is an excellent summary of the whole matter, with relevant literature) the story runs thus. Numitor, king of Alba Longa, had a younger brother Amulius who deposed him. To prevent the rise of avengers he made Numitor's daughter, R(h)ea Silvia, a Vestal virgin (see VESTA). But she was violated by *Mars himself, and bore twins. Amulius, who had imprisoned her, ordered the infants to be thrown into the Tiber. The river was in flood, and the receptacle in which they had been placed drifted ashore near the Ficus Ruminalis. There a she-wolf (Plut. *Rom.* 4 adds a woodpecker, both being sacred to Mars) tended and suckled them, until they were found by Faustulus the royal herdsman. He and his wife Acca Larentia brought them up as their own; they increased mightily in strength and boldness, and became leaders of the young men in daring exploits. In one of these Remus was captured and brought before Numitor; Romulus came to the rescue, the relationship was made known, they rose together against Amulius, killed him, and made Numitor king again. The twins then founded a city of their own on the site of Rome, beginning with a settlement on the Palatine; Romulus walled it, and he or his lieutenant Celer killed Remus for leaping over the walls. He offered asylum on the Capitol to all fugitives, and got wives for them by stealing women from the Sabines, whom he invited to a festival. After a successful reign of some forty years he mysteriously vanished in a storm at Goat's Marsh and became the god Quirinus.   H. J. R.; J. Sch.

ruler-cult

I. Greek The essential characteristic of Greek ruler-worship is the rendering, as to a god or hero, of honours to individuals deemed superior to other people because of their achievements, position, or power. The roots of this lie in Greece, though parallels are to be found in other near eastern societies.

In the aristocratic society of the Archaic age, as in the Classical *polis* of the 5th cent. BC, no person could reach a position of such generally acknowledged pre-eminence as to cause the granting of divine honours to be thought appropriate: posthumous heroization, rather than deification, was the honour for city-founders. The first case of divine honours occurred in the confused period at the end of the Peloponnesian War (431–404 BC), when *Lysander, the most powerful man in the Aegean, received divine cult on *Samos. There are some other, 4th-cent., examples.

Ruler-cult in a developed form first appears during the reign of *Alexander the Great, and is directly inspired by his conquests, personality, and in particular his absolute and undisputed power. Alexander's attempt to force the Greeks and Macedonians in his entourage to adopt the Persian custom of prostration before the king (*proskynēsis*), which for the Persians did not imply worship, was an isolated and unsuccessful experiment without consequence. Much more important is his encounter with the priest of Ammon at Siwa (Egypt's Western Desert) in 331 BC. The priest seemingly addressed Alexander as the son of Amon-Ra, the traditional salutation due to any Pharaoh of Egypt, but the prestige which the oracle of Ammon then enjoyed throughout the Greek world had a decisive effect, not only on the Greeks, but also and in particular on the romantic imagination of the young king himself. It is probably the progressive development of these emotions which caused Alexander in 324, when he ordered the restoration of political exiles, to apply pressure on the Greek cities to offer him divine cult; some cities certainly responded, though contemporary evidence remains thin. Alexander also secured heroic honours for his dead intimate Hephaestion, as official recognition of his outstanding achievements.

The cults of Alexander's successors (Diadochoi) are found in various different contexts. The principal context was that of the Greek cities dependent on particular kings, both ancient cities and those founded by the king himself. The cities acknowledged benefactions received from a king by the establishment of a cult, with temple or altar, priest, sacrifices, and games, modelled on that granted to the Olympian gods (*isotheoi timai*). Rulers were also honoured by having their statues placed in an already existing temple. The king was thought to share the temple with the god (as *sunnaos theos*, 'temple-sharing god'), and thus to partake in the honours rendered to the deity and, on occasion, in the deity's qualities.

The other main context was that of the court itself. The Greek monarchies of the east in time created their own official cults. The dynastic cult of the Ptolemies at *Alexandria (a cult founded by 285/4) in its developed form by the end of the 3rd cent. BC consisted of priests of Alexander, of each pair of deceased rulers, and of the reigning king and queen. In 280 Antiochus I deified his dead father *Seleucus I and dedicated to him a temple and precinct at Seleuceia in Pieria in *Syria; *Antiochus III extended a court cult throughout his newly reconquered Seleucid empire, with high priests of the living king and his divine ancestors in each province of the empire. In the later dynastic cult of the Attalids (see PERGAMUM) the kings were deified only after death.

Cults are also found outside strictly Greek contexts. In the kingdom of Commagene (SE Asia Minor) a complex cult, organized by the Commagenian king Antiochus I (1st cent. BC: see NEMRUT DAG) round different cult centres, was a blend of Greek and Persian traditions. In Egyptian temples cult of the Ptolemies continued on the model of Pharaonic practice. Incorporation of Greek practice might, however, be controversial: the erection of a statue of the Seleucid Antiochus IV in the Temple at Jerusalem stimulated the writing of the Book of Daniel, with its attack on Nebuchadnezzar's demand for worship, and was one factor that provoked the Maccabean Revolt (see MACCABEES).

Even within Greek contexts, at the outset there were debates about the propriety of divine honours for human beings, though the cults gradually became an accepted practice. That it became accepted does not prove it was essentially a political and not a religious phenomenon: to press the distinction is to deny significance to the creation of a symbolic system calqued on the cult of the gods. Those responsible for the cults, whether at court or in cities, were attempting to articulate an understanding of the power of the king.　　　　　　C. F. E.; S. R. F. P.

II. Roman The offering of divine honours to humans was not indigenous to Italy. The Romans had long sacrificed to the ghosts of the dead (*Manes*) and conceived of a semi-independent spirit (*genius*) attached to living people. But the myth of a deified founder, *Romulus, was invented only in or after the 4th cent. BC, under Greek influence, and developed in the new political circumstances of the late republic. From the time of Marcus Claudius Marcellus' conquest of *Syracuse in 212 BC, Roman officials received divine honours in Greek cities; a notable instance is the 'liberator' of Greece, *Flamininus (*c*.191 BC), whose cult survived into the imperial period. At Rome such honours are met only from the late 2nd cent. BC, and then exceptionally, e.g. those offered privately to *Marius (101 BC) and popularly to the demagogue Marius Gratidianus (86 BC). Under Stoic influence (see STOICISM) the idea that worthy individuals might become divine after death appeared in *Cicero's *Somnium Scipionis* (*c*.51 BC) and in the shrine he planned for his daughter Tullia (d. 45 BC). Though the evidence is controversial, *Caesar as dictator in 45–44 BC probably received divine honours, based on Roman models (cults of *Alexander the Great and Hellenistic kings took different forms). After his assassination the triumvirs, supported by popular agitation, secured from the senate his formal deification in 42 BC as Divus Iulius.

Worship of emperors and members of their families has two aspects, the worship of the living, including identification with the gods, and the apotheosis of the dead. It took different forms in different contexts: Rome; provincial assemblies; towns; and in private. At Rome *Augustus and later 'good' emperors avoided official deification in their lifetimes; *Gaius Caligula and *Commodus were exceptional in seeking to emphasize their own divinity. Augustus was *divi filius* (son of the deified one), and enjoyed a mediating role with the divine, as implied by his name, and as a result of becoming *pontifex maximus* (see PRIESTS) in 12 BC. He also in 7 BC reorganized the cults of the 265 wards (*vici*) of the city: henceforth the officials of the wards, mainly *freedmen, worshipped the Augustan Lares and the *genius* of Augustus. The worship appropriate for a household was now performed throughout the city. Poets played with the association of Augustus with the gods, and assumed that he would be deified posthumously. In AD 14 Augustus' funeral managed both to evoke, on a grand scale, traditional aristocratic funerals and to permit his formal deification by the senate; it was the precedent for all subsequent emperors up to *Constantine I. After *Livia in AD 41, imperial relatives, male and female, could also be deified posthumously. After Constantine's avowal of *Christianity, it became increasingly difficult for traditional practices to continue: Christ alone had combined human and divine, and the prevalent doctrine, formulated by *Eusebius, was that the emperor ruled by divine favour.

In the Greek east provincial assemblies (*koina*) were permitted to establish cults of Roma and Augustus: the precedent was set in Asia (see ASIA, ROMAN PROVINCE) at *Pergamum and in Bithynia at Nicomedia in 29 BC. In 'civilized' western provinces provincial assemblies (*concilia*) followed the Roman model, on the precedent of Hispania Tarraconensis which was granted permission to establish a temple and a priest (*flamen*) to Divus Augustus at Tarraco in AD 15. Assemblies in more recently conquered western provinces had cults of the living Augustus and Roma (Three Gauls at Lugdunum (Lyons), 12 BC; Germany near Cologne (Colonia Agrippinensis), 8–7 BC?); these centred on altars, not temples, and had *sacerdotes* not *flamines* (the title indicating that they were not Roman priesthoods).

Below the provincial level different forms of cult are found, depending in part on local traditions. In the (non-Greek) Egyptian temples Augustus and other emperors were accorded the position of high priest, like the Ptolemies and the Pharaohs before them. In Greek contexts, in Egypt and the rest of the Greek east, emperors were generally accommodated within the context of the ordinary cult of the Olympian gods (see RELIGION, GREEK). In cities throughout the east living emperors were granted temples and cult statues, priests and processions, sacrifices and games. At first the cult focused specifically on Augustus, and then often became a general cult of the emperors. Though some cults of Hellenistic kings did survive through to Roman times, the imperial cult was more varied and more dynamic than Hellenistic cults had been. Towns in Italy and the west also established cults of the living Augustus (not his *genius*) and his successors; some, especially *coloniae*, chose to follow the Roman model.

Private households in Rome and elsewhere included associations of worshippers of Augustus (Tac. *Ann.* 1. 73), who will mainly have been the slaves and freedmen of the house. *Ovid in exile makes great play of his piety in praying at dawn each day before his household shrine with images of Augustus, Livia, *Tiberius, *Germanicus, and Drusus (*Pont.* 4. 9). In Italy and the west there were also the Augustales, a high-ranking status for Roman freedmen, whose officials are sometimes associated with the imperial cult.

The significance of the imperial cult has been much debated. Was it a form of *Graeca adulatio* (Tac. *Ann.* 6. 18: divine honours to a human as Greek adulation), a system that was really political and not religious? On the other side it has been argued that to impose a distinction between religion and politics is anachronistic and Christianizing, and that it is illegitimate to undercut the implicit meanings of the rituals by claims about insincerity and flattery. The way forward is to investigate the different ritual systems that honoured the emperor in their different social and cultural contexts. As the cult was in general not imposed from above, it is essential to examine the contexts from which it sprang and which gave it meaning. There is a profound difference between a Greek city with its stable Olympian pantheon within which the emperor was accommodated and a town in Gaul whose pre-Roman pantheon was restructured on Roman models before the emperor found a place in it. Focus on actual divinization of the emperor is also too narrow. There was a whole range of religious honours, only some of which placed the emperor unambiguously among the gods. In some sense there was no such thing as 'the imperial cult'. See CHRISTIANITY.

M. H.; S. R. F. P.

sacrifice, Greek Sacrifice was the most important form of action in Greek religion (see RELIGION, GREEK), but we should note at once that there is no single Greek equivalent to the English word 'sacrifice'. The practices we bring together under this heading were described by a series of overlapping terms conveying ideas such as 'killing', 'destroying', 'burning', 'cutting', 'consecrating', 'performing sacred acts', 'giving', 'presenting', but not at all the idea present in 'it was a great sacrifice for him'. As occasions for sacrifice Theophrastus distinguished 'honour, gratitude, and need' (in Porphyry, *Abst.* 2. 24), but his categories do not correspond to fixed types, and in fact the rite could be performed on almost any occasion.

Vegetable products, savoury *cakes above all, were occasionally 'sacrificed' (the same vocabulary is used as for animal sacrifice) in lieu of animals or, much more commonly, in addition to them. But animal sacrifice was the standard type. The main species used were sheep, goats, pigs, and cattle. In a few cults fish and fowl were offered, wild animals still more rarely; dogs and horses appear in a few sacrifices of special type that were not followed by a feast. Human sacrifice occurred only in myth and scandalous story. The choice between the main species was largely a matter of cost and scale, a piglet costing about 3 drachmae, a sheep or goat 12, a pig 20 or more, a cow up to 80. Within the species symbolic factors were sometimes also relevant: the virgins *Athena and *Artemis might require unbroken cattle, fertile Earth a pregnant sow.

The most important step-by-step accounts of a standard sacrifice are a series of Homeric scenes, of which the fullest is *Od.* 3. 430–63. Attic practice differs or may have differed from Homeric in several significant details, but the basic articulations of the rite are the same in all sources. Vase-paintings and votive reliefs provide extremely important supplementary evidence, though by their nature they very rarely depict the full succession of actions as a sequence. Three main stages can be distinguished:

1. Preparatory. An animal was led to the altar, usually in procession. The participants assembled in a circle, rinsed their hands in lustral water, and took a handful of barley grain from a basket. Water was sprinkled on the victim to force it to 'nod' agreement to its own sacrifice. The main sacrificer (not necessarily a priest) then cut hair from the victim, put it on the altar fire, and uttered a *prayer which defined the return that was desired (e.g. 'health and safety') for the offering. The other participants threw forwards their barley grains.

2. The kill. The victim's throat was cut with a knife; larger victims had been stunned with a blow from an axe first. Women participants raised the cry known as *ololygē*. In Attic practice it was important to 'bloody the altar'; small animals were held over it to be killed, the blood from larger ones was caught in a bowl and poured out over it.

3. Treatment of the meat, which itself had three stages. First the god's portion, typically the thigh bones wrapped in fat with (in Homer) small portions of meat cut 'from all the limbs' set on top, was burnt on the altar fire. *Wine was poured on as it burnt. (Further portions for the gods were sometimes put on a table or even on the knees or in the hands of their statues; in practice, these became priests' perquisites.) Then the entrails were roasted on skewers and shared among all the participants. Finally the rest of the meat was boiled and distributed (normally in equal portions); in contrast to the entrails, this boiled meat was occasionally taken away for consumption at home, though a communal feast on the spot was the norm. Omens were often taken both from the burning of the god's portion and from the condition of the entrails.

A distinction is drawn in Herodotus (2. 44) between sacrifice to the gods, *thuein*, and to heroes, *enagizein*. It used to be common to draw a contrast between the normal Olympian sacrifice outlined and a 'chthonian' ('earthly') type which supposedly diverged from the other systematically: the victim would be dark, not light; it would be killed with its head pressed down into a low pit or hearth, not drawn back over a high altar; the accompanying libations would be 'wineless'; and, above all, the animal's flesh would not be eaten. But it is now clear that these divergences from the standard type more often occurred individually than as a group, and also that they might be

sacrifice, Greek A sacrificial scene from an Athenian pottery bowl (c.400 BC). The moment shown is preparatory. While a participant calms the victim, the priest is about to sprinkle water on the sheep to force a 'nod' of assent.

present in 'Olympian' sacrifice, absent (largely or wholly) from sacrifice to chthonian gods or heroes.

There were also certain 'quasi-sacrifices' which contained several of the actions listed above and could be described by some, though not all, of the group of words that denote sacrifice. The killing of animals to ratify an oath, for instance, followed many of the stages mentioned under 1 and 2 above; stage 3, however, was omitted entirely, the carcass being carried away or thrown in the sea (cf. Hom. *Il.* 3. 245–313, 19. 250–68). And similar quasi-sacrificial ritual killings occurred in certain purifications and before battle.

Explicit early reflection on sacrifice is sparse. (But see too ANIMALS, ATTITUDES TO.) The division whereby men received most of the meat was explained by a trick played on *Zeus by the man-loving god Prometheus at the time of the first sacrifice (Hes. *Theog.* 535–61). The rite of Bouphonia (part of the Attic festival Dipolieia) raised the issue of the institution's moral legitimacy: an ox sacrifice was followed by a 'trial' at which guilt for the killing was eventually fixed on the sacrificial axe or knife. *Plato's Euthyphro no doubt echoes popular usage in describing sacrifice as a form of 'gift' to the gods (*Euthyphro* 14c).

Recent interpretations are largely divided between those which see sacrifice (perhaps with reference to its hypothetical origins among prehistoric hunters) as a dramatization of killing, violence, and the associated guilt, and those for which by contrast it is a way of legitimizing meat-eating by treating the taking of life that necessarily precedes it as a ritual, i.e. a licensed act: the former approach stresses that rituals such as the Bouphonia raise the issue of sacrificial guilt, the latter that they resolve it. Sacrifice is normally killing followed by eating, but where does the emphasis lie? In the vast majority of cases, clearly, on the eating; but all the uneaten sacrifices and quasi-sacrifices have to be set aside if the institution is to be understood by reference to the communal feast alone.   R. C. T. P.

sacrifice, Roman Roman sacrificial practices were not functionally different from Greek, although there are no sources for them earlier than the 2nd cent. BC, and the *modalités* of Roman sacrifice were complex, since several rites existed (Roman, Greek, and Etruscan). In any case, as in the Greek world, sacrifice was a central act of religion. The expression *rem divinam facere*, 'to make a thing sacred', often abridged to *facere* ('to sacrifice'), and the etymology of the words designating sacrificial activity, *sacrificare*, *sacrificium* (*sacrum facere*, 'to perform a religious ceremony'), show the importance of these acts and signal that sacrifice was an act of transfer of ownership. On its own or part of larger celebrations, the typical sacrifice embraced four phases: the *praefatio*, the *immolatio*, the slaughtering, and the banquet.

1. After the purification of the participants and of the

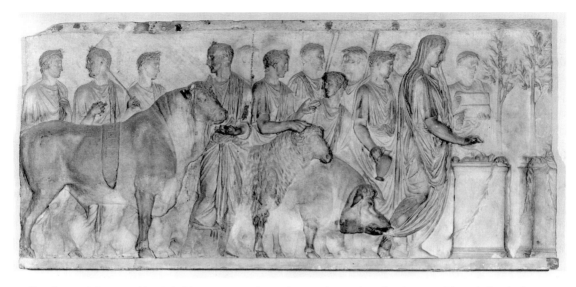

sacrifice, Roman A Roman marble relief of the 1st cent. AD depicts the special type of sacrifice (*suovetaurilia*) concluding the Roman ritual of purification and averting evil known as *lustratio*. In the republic this ceremony—denoting a new beginning—concluded the taking of the census of Roman citizens and marked the arrival of a new army-commander.

victims (always domestic animals) chosen in accordance with the divinity's function and the context, a procession led them to the altar of the divinity. There the presiding figure celebrated the *praefatio* ('preface') on a portable hearth (*focus, foculus*) set up beside the sacrificial altar (*ara*). This rite consisted of offering incense and *wine, and, according to the ancient commentators, was the equivalent of a solemn salutation affirming the superiority of the gods. At the same time this rite opened a ritual space and announced what was to follow.

2. The second stage of the sacrifice was the *immolatio*. The presiding figure poured wine on the victim's brow, sprinkled its back with salted flour (*mola salsa*, whence *immolare*), doubtless prepared by the *Vestals, and finally passed a sacrificial knife over the victim's spine. According to ancient commentators and the *prayer spoken during this rite, immolation transferred the victim from human possession into the divine.

3. Once this transfer was effected, the sacrificers (*popae, victimarii*; cf. Gr. *mageiroi*) felled the victim, butchered it, and opened the corpse, now on its back. The presiding figure then performed the *extispicina*, the inspection of the *exta* (vital organs: the peritoneum, liver, gall bladder, lungs, and, from the beginning of the 3rd cent. BC (Plin. *HN* 11. 186), the heart), to decide if they were in the good shape which would signal the deity's acceptance (*litatio*) of the sacrifice. If the victim was unacceptable, the sacrifice had to begin again.

4. The banquet comprised two phases. Once acceptance was obtained, the sacrificers beheaded the victim, set aside the *exta*, and prepared them for offering: the *exta* of bovines were boiled in cooking pots (*ollae extares*), those of ovines and the pig-family were grilled on spits. This cooking done, the *exta* were offered to the divinity (*porricere; pollucere* for Hercules), i.e. burnt, basted with *mola salsa* and wine, sometimes along with pieces of meat designated on the victim in advance (*magmentum*). This was done on the altar if celestial divinities were in question; offerings to aquatic deities were thrown into the water, those for epichthonic or chthonic divinities were placed on the ground or in ditches. Offerings for the *di manes* (spirits of the dead) were made on a pyre itself resting on the ground (*ILS* 139, 16 ff.; *CIL* 11. 5047). When the offering to the deity had been consumed, the rest of the victim was seized (*profanare*) by the presiding figure, no doubt by imposition of the hand, and thus rendered fit for human consumption. In principle all sacrifices, except those addressed to divinities of the underworld, were followed by a sacrificial banquet (*cena, visceratio*). But the procedures at these banquets are ill-understood, because of both the complexity of communal banquets in Rome's strongly hierarchical society, and the enormous numbers having the right to take part (e.g. the citizens). Sometimes the banquet was celebrated (doubtless on behalf of all) by just the immediate participants and their helpers, along with those possessing privileges in a particular sanctuary (e.g. the flute-players at the temple of Jupiter); sometimes the banquet united the chief sections of society (e.g. the Roman élite for the *epulum Jovis*); sometimes the meat was sold in butchers' shops (i.e. it was accessible to all); sometimes, finally, it was eaten at great communal banquets, ultimately financed by benefactors. At the *ara maxima* of Hercules, sacrificial meat had to be eaten or burnt before nightfall, a requirement giving rise to a very generous

form of sacrificial banquet even if the cult's foundation-myth barred one of the families in charge of the cult, the Pinarii, from taking part.

In public sacrifices conducted in accordance with Greek ritual (*Graeco ritu*), the details of which are very poorly known, the conduct of the presiding figure was different. While in the Roman rite he wore the *toga praetexta, draped in such a way as to allow a flap of cloth to cover the head, in the Greek ritual he sometimes removed the praetexta before proceeding with the *immolatio*, and for the rest of the proceedings; he certainly sacrificed with head uncovered, sometimes wearing a laurel-wreath. The commentators on the Secular Games show that sacrifice according to the Greek rite was no different functionally from the Roman rite. Only the *immolatio* differed, since the presiding figure burnt hairs cut from the animal's brow and offered crowns, and in addition the *exta* were called *splanchna* (G. Pighi, *De ludis saecularibus* (1965), 154 f.); but it is not known whether the rules for the division of the victims differed from the 'Roman' ones. At any rate, Roman sacrifices according to the 'Greek ritual' were much more complicated than has been thought, although the state of the sources prevents a full understanding of them. Of sacrifices according to Etruscan ritual we know even less, save that the inspection of the *exta* (*haruspicatio*) permitted divination. Even if they had no special name, the sacrificial rituals of certain cults of the imperial age differed from traditional sacrifices, at least to judge from the evidence of imagery. If we are to believe the sources, the *taurobolium* (or *criobolium*) in some way reproduced the myth of Attis (the youthful consort of *Cybele), by creating a central role for blood and for the setting aside of the testicles of the sacrificial victim. Of Mithraic sacrifice, represented on numerous altars of *Mithras, too little is known for comparison with traditional Roman sacrifice. All that can be said is that Mithraic imagery emphasizes violence where representations of traditional sacrifice underline calm.

Communal sacrifices were celebrated by those who exercised power in the community in question: the paterfamilias (male head of the family), magistrates and *priests, and the presidents (*magistri*) of clubs. In spite of a few exceptions, women could not sacrifice on behalf of the whole community. Many sacrifices were part of much larger celebrations, and in certain cases the sacrifices themselves were celebrated in more spectacular fashion (e.g. at the lectisternium, ritual feeding of the gods). Occasions for sacrifice were innumerable, from regular acts of homage shaped by sacred calendars and the ritual obligations of the city and its constituent associations to thanks-offerings or contractual sacrifices (*vota*, vows). Faults and involuntary oversights committed in the celebration of the cult, or the involuntary deterioration of the patrimony of the gods, were expiated by *piacula*, sacrifices the purpose of which was to present excuses for past or imminent action (e.g. maintenance works in a sanctuary).

By way of a global view of what traditional Roman sac-

rifice articulated and realized, it can be understood as establishing—with the help of a solemn sharing of food—a hierarchy between three partners: gods, humans, and animals. To the gods was assured absolute priority in the course of a symbolic feast, during which they shared with humans an animal victim or a vegetable-offering. The different Roman myths which commented on sacrificial practices—those concerning the *instauratio* (repetition of a religious ceremony) of the cult of the Ara Maxima, the two groups of Luperci, and the Vinalia, as well as those revealing the origin of sacrifice (Ov. *Met.* 15. 60 ff.; *Fast.* 1. 335 ff.)—all insist on the fact that, by the privilege of priority, essential in Roman society, and the quality of the offerings (the *exta*, seat of the animal's vitality, the incense and the pure wine, all reserved for the immortals), sacrifice fixed the superiority and immortality of the gods, along with the mortal condition and the pious submission of their human partners, at the expense of the animal victims. At the same time the sacrificial rite was capable of expressing, by the right to take part in the banquet and by the privilege of priority, the hierarchy among mortals. J. Sch.

Sadducees, a religious group within Judaism attested in Judaea from the 2nd cent. BC to the 1st cent. AD. The Sadducees are described by *Josephus and are mentioned in the New Testament and in rabbinic texts, usually as opponents of the Pharisees in matters concerning law or theology. According to the generally unfavourable picture given by Josephus, their distinctive tenets consisted in a refusal to accept the unwritten religious traditions championed by the Pharisees, an unwillingness to ascribe human fortunes to the operations of fate, and unwillingness to accept the notion of life after death. Josephus also accused them of harshness in judgement and claimed that they had little influence over the people.

Josephus stated that most Sadducees came from the rich and powerful part of Judaean society. This assertion, together with the evidence of Acts 5: 17 and the probable derivation of the name 'Sadducees' from Zadok, the ancestor of the high priests in earlier times, has led many scholars to identify the Sadducees with the ruling priests in Jerusalem. Some overlap between these groups is certain, but some influential priests (including high priests) were not Sadducees, and there is no reason to doubt that some Sadducees were not priests.

Some of the legal views ascribed to Sadducees in early rabbinic texts have been paralleled in sectarian writings found among the *Dead Sea Scrolls, but the view that the Qumran sectarians should be classified as a type of Sadducee is debated. See RELIGION, JEWISH. M. D. G.

Sallust (Gaius Sallustius Crispus), Roman historian, probably 86–35 BC. A Sabine from Amiternum, he probably derived from the municipal aristocracy. The earliest certain information of his career concerns his tribunate in 52 (see TRIBUNES OF THE PLEBS), when he acted against *Cicero and Titus Annius Milo (Asc. *Mil.* 37, 45, 49, 51 C). He was expelled from the senate in 50; the anonymous *Invectio in Sallustium* 16 alleges immorality, but the real grounds were probably his actions in 52. He now joined *Caesar, commanding a legion in 49. As praetor in 46 he took part in the African campaign, and was appointed the first governor of Africa Nova. On his return to Rome he was charged with malpractice, allegedly escaping only on Caesar's intervention (Cass. Dio 43. 9. 2, *Inv. in Sall.* 19). With no immediate prospect of advancement, Sallust withdrew from public life—the proems of both *Cat.* and *Iug.* defend that decision—and turned to historiography.

In his first two works he avoided the usual annalistic presentation, preferring the monograph form introduced to Rome by Coelius Antipater. The first, the *Bellum Catilinae* (*c*.42/1 BC), treats the conspiracy of *Catiline, 'especially memorable for the unprecedented quality of the crime and the danger' (*Cat.* 4. 4). This is set against, and illustrates, the political and moral decline of Rome, begun after the fall of *Carthage, quickening after *Sulla's dictatorship, and spreading from the dissolute nobility to infect all Roman politics (*Cat.* 6–14, 36–9). There are no doubts about the guilt of the 'conspirators', and Sallust so far accepts the assessment of Cicero, who must have been one of his principal sources (supplemented by oral testimony, *Cat.* 48. 9). But Cicero himself is less prominent than might be expected; the heroes are Caesar and *Cato the Younger, the two examples of *virtus* ('excellence') which stand out from the moral gloom of their day (53–4), and their speeches in the final debate are presented at a length which risks unbalancing the whole (51–2). Sallust's even-handedness between the two men would have struck contemporaries familiar with the fiercely polarized propaganda since Cato's death.

The second monograph, the more ambitious and assured *Bellum Iugurthinum* (*c*.41–40 BC), again emphasizes moral decline. The Jugurthan War is chosen 'both because it was great, bloody, and of shifting fortunes, and because it represented the first challenge to the arrogance of the nobility' (*Iug.* 5. 1): a strange judgement, but one which reflects the work's interest in the interrelation of domestic strife and external warfare. The military narrative is patchy and selective. Politics are presented simply but vigorously, with decline again spreading from the venal nobility. This decline is presented more dynamically than in *Cat.*, as several individuals fail to live up to promising beginnings: the Numidian king Jugurtha himself, *Marius, *Sulla, and even Quintus Caecilius Metellus Numidicus, who comes closest to being a hero. Speeches and especially digressions divide the work into distinct panels, and implied comparisons—Gaius Memmius and Marius, Metellus and Marius, Marius and Sulla—further plot the changes in political and military style. For sources Sallust perhaps used a general history and the autobiographies of Marcus Aemilius Scaurus, Publius Rutilius Rufus, and Sulla; some geographical notions, but not much more, may derive from Posidonius. Little seems owed to the 'Punic books' mentioned at 17. 7.

Sallust's last work, the *Histories*, was annalistic (year by year in arrangement). It covered events from 78, perhaps continuing Sisenna, though it included a retrospect of earlier events. The last datable fragment, from book 5, concerns the year 67, hardly his chosen terminus. Speeches and letters survive entire, though the other fragments are scrappy. He again emphasized the decline of the state after Sulla, and was not generous to Pompey.

The 'Invective against Cicero' ascribed to Sallust in the manuscripts and cited as genuine by the rhetorician Quintilian (4. 1. 68, 9. 3. 89) is not appropriate to Sallust in 54 (its ostensible date); its author was probably an Augustan rhetorician. The authenticity question is more difficult with the two 'Letters to the elderly Caesar', purportedly of 46 (or 48) and *c*.50 BC, but they too are most likely later works, probably declamations of the early empire.

As a historian Sallust has weaknesses. His leading theme is decline, but this is presented schematically and unsubtly; his characters have vigour, but seldom convince. The interpretation of Roman politics is often crude; but if the *nobiles* (élite of senators descended from consuls) come in for most criticism, this is because they set the pattern; their more popular opponents were no better. Still, the choice of the monograph form was enterprising, and he avoids the danger of drifting into biography; the use of particular episodes to illuminate a general theme is deft; he shows an increasing grasp of structure; the rhetoric, especially in speeches and letters, has concentration and verve; and the man has style. The influence of *Thucydides is pervasive, though he cannot match his model's intellectual depth. Many stylistic features are also owed to the Roman tradition, particularly *Cato the Younger. The characteristics are noted by ancient writers (*testimonia* in Kurfess edn., pp. xxvi ff.): archaisms, 'truncated epigrams, words coming before expected, obscure brevity' (Sen. *Ep.* 114. 17), recherché vocabulary, rapidity. He won many admirers in later antiquity and was the greatest single influence on *Tacitus.

C. B. R. P.

Samos (see ◀Map 1, Dc▶), an important *polis* on the large Aegean island of the same name (476 sq. km.), only 1.8 km. from Asia Minor. Though western Samos is dominated by Mt. Kerkis (1, 433 m.; ancient Cerceteus) and the centre by Mt. Karvounis (1, 153 m.)—whose ancient name (Ampelus) implies viticulture—Samos has arable slopes and coastal plains, and was considered fertile. Wheat was grown in the *peraia* (mainland territory) in Asia Minor, possibly by a serf population. Exports included olive oil and Samian Earth (a clay used in fulling); Samian transport amphorae (enclosed jars) are a distinct type.

The city was in the south-eastern lowlands, at modern Pythagorio (or Tigani); 8 km. to the west along a sacred road, at the site of a bronze-age cult, lay the Heraion or sanctuary of Hera, the city's patron goddess. Both sites have Mycenaean remains. Samos was reputedly peopled by Carians (from SW Asia Minor) before Ionian Greeks arrived, perhaps in the 10th cent.; classical Samians spoke a local version of Ionic Greek. The first Hera temple (early 8th cent.) was one of the earliest stone temples in Greece, receiving lavish dedications as an emerging élite developed overseas contacts. Samians colonized Cilicia (SE Asia Minor), the Propontis (mod. sea of Marmara), and the Black (Euxine) Sea, helped found *Cyrene, and built a temple at Naucratis (see COLONIZATION, GREEK).

Detailed history is lacking before the tyranny of Polycrates (c.550–522). His warships dominated nearby islands and towns, and his court was frequented by artists and poets (including Ibycus and *Anacreon). Refugees from the tyranny included the philosopher *Pythagoras, who settled in Italy; others founded Dicaearchia (mod. Pozzuoli). Polycrates probably commissioned the three constructions mentioned by *Herodotus (3. 60), all of them still extant: a long harbour mole, the resplendent fortification walls, and a tunnel over 1 km. long, driven through the acropolis by Eupalinus of Megara to bring piped water into the city (see AQUEDUCTS). A new Hera temple begun earlier by the artist Rhoecus had proved unstable: its replacement, by Theodorus, probably dates to Polycrates' reign (like the colossal *kouros*, or nude male statue, recently found there). Though never finished, it was the largest Greek temple known to Herodotus.

The Persians killed Polycrates and installed tyrants friendly to themselves. Many Samian captains deserted the Ionians at Lade. Prominent in the *Delian League, Samos contributed ships until its revolt in 440, which took *Pericles eight months to suppress. Cleruchs (citizen colonists) were installed, and the ruling élite remained pro-Athenian in the Peloponnesian War (431–404 BC). For a time Samians shared Athens' radical democracy: in 405 they even received Athenian citizenship. After the war *Lysander installed a decarchy and received divine honours. After the fall of his regime Samos was generally pro-Athenian until the satrap Mausolus of Caria renewed Persian domination. In 365 the Athenians again cleruchized the island, allegedly expelling the entire population. Liberated by *Alexander the Great's exiles decree, Samos was disputed between the Successors (Diadochoi); the historian Duris became tyrant of his own city. From 281 it was a Ptolemaic base; after being attacked by Philip V of Macedon it came under Rhodian hegemony (see RHODES), confirmed by Rome in 188.

In the period after Alexander, power once more lay with a landed élite. They redesigned the town and built fine houses; the Heraion saw its first major additions since Polycrates. Samos suffered occasional wheat shortages, but continued to exploit the *peraia* as well as Corsiae (the nearby Phoúrnoi islets), Icaros, and Amorgos. Exports to *Alexandria, documented on papyri, were perhaps aimed at Greeks: Samian émigrés there were numerous and included intellectuals such as Aristarchus, Asclepiades, and Conon the mathematician.

In 129 Samos became part of the Roman province of Asia (see ASIA, ROMAN PROVINCE); élite contacts with Rome

were cultivated. The Heraion suffered at Verres' hands; his prosecutor *Cicero was later honoured in Samos. Octavian turned down a request for tribute remission, but as *Augustus he declared Samos free. Though *Vespasian reduced the island's privileges, its prosperity increased in Roman times, to judge by the new public buildings (including a bath complex, gymnasium, and basilicas) and the expansion of rural settlement into the west.   D. G. J. S.

sanctuaries Sanctuaries in the Greek world were areas set aside for religious purposes and separate from the normal secular world. The boundary (*peribolos*) might be an actual wall, but more often would be indicated by boundary markers. Traditional Greek and Roman worship was not restricted to initiates (except for the *mysteries at *Eleusis and elsewhere) who had to be accommodated in closeable buildings suitable for private ritual: the open space of the sanctuary was where the worshippers congregated to observe and participate in the ritual which was enacted on their behalf; for this, the main requisite was sufficient space.

The festivals which were the occasion for such worship were normally annual, though sanctuaries would be accessible for individual acts of worship and the performance of vows. Within the sanctuary space were the buildings and other structures dedicated to the use of the god, especially the altar at which the burnt *sacrifice, essential to the religious functioning of the sanctuary, was made. Other buildings responded to various religious needs, and are not always found. There is normally a *temple to house the image which was the god, which watched and so received the sacrifice. The temple was itself both an offering to the god, and a store room for votive offerings. The open area of the sanctuary round the altar was the place where, at the god's festival, worshippers would witness the sacrifices. The meat from these was then divided amongst them, and normally consumed within the sanctuary: some sanctuaries had laws which stipulated that the meat had to be consumed within their boundaries. Most worshippers seem to have feasted al fresco, but certain sanctuaries contained special dining rooms (*hestiatoria*) for at least a privileged section of the worshippers. Other religious functions accommodated include contests of song and dance, as well as athletic ones (see GAMES). Specialized structures (see THEATRE; STADIUM) eventually developed for these.

The size and arrangement of a sanctuary depended on the importance and nature of the cult. In large sanctuaries it is often possible to distinguish between an innermost sacred area round the altar as place of sacrifice and the temple as the abode of the god, and an outer area given over to human activity, the feasting and contests. As a result theatres and stadia are often on the periphery. In healing sanctuaries, such as the Asclepieion at Epidaurus, or the sanctuary of Amphiaraus at Oropus, buildings where those seeking the god's cure might spend the night in the sanctuary were normally adjacent to the temple itself. In some sanctuaries the distinction between the two

sanctuaries This small shrine (2nd cent. BC?) of *Artemis at Messene in the SW *Peloponnese, crowded with bases for statues, was one of several cult-places within a sanctuary-complex dedicated to *Asclepius. The statues, as their inscribed bases show, commemorated service by priestesses and other female servitors of the goddess.

areas is clearly marked: at Olympia a wall was eventually built round the innermost sanctuary, leaving outside gymnasia, stadium, and the course for the chariot races. Here and at Epidaurus a vaulted passage leads from the inner area into the stadium. In other sanctuaries the distinction is not so clear cut. At the sanctuary of *Poseidon at Isthmia the original running track has been found very close to the temple; later it was removed to a nearby valley which perhaps afforded a better locality for the spectators.

Though undoubtedly there were shrines and religious places in the Greek settlements of the *Mycenaean civilization, the sanctuaries of the Classical period develop at the earliest in the 8th cent. BC, as far as can be judged from the archaeological evidence. Reasons for the choice of a sanctuary site are quite unclear. Some are based on places of late bronze-age occupation, though it is not known whether this in any way denotes continuity of cult or rather a sense of awe inspired by the visible remains of an earlier age. Natural features such as springs may be the attraction; *water is an important element in the performance of cult. A spring in the sanctuary, or its vicinity, was often embellished with a fountain house. Water may have to be provided artifically, as at Perachora, or by the construction of wells. It was needed for ritual purification, but also, when feasting buildings were provided, for more normal cleaning purposes. Sometimes the reason for the location of a sanctuary may be nothing more than an awareness of some unusual character of a place. Shrines in bronze-age Crete (see MINOAN CIVILIZATION), in the palaces and elsewhere, were often aligned with 'peak sanctuaries' on a prominent visible mountain top; the idea that similar alignments may explain Classical sanctuaries has been promoted, but is unconvincing. Some sanctuaries are developed for particular communities, and each *polis would possess one of major significance to it, dedicated to its pro-

tecting deity. Others belong to less important gods, or serve only limited sections of the community, classes in society, or villages outside the urban centre of the state. Within the *polis*-context, the location of major extra-urban sanctuaries could serve to demarcate a community's territory in the face of competing claims by neighbours. Other sanctuaries develop to serve more than one community, up to the 'international' sanctuary such as *Delphi or *Olympia which attract support and worshippers from all over Greece.

The earliest stages of the sanctuaries, where known, are often small and simple. Increasing popularity, larger numbers of worshippers, and the acquisition of greater wealth lead to discernible expansion. Control over the sanctuary, and responsibility for its development, rests extensively with the community at large (see POLIS), through its political bodies, supervising finance, approving and supporting building programmes, and passing all necessary legislation for the conduct of its affairs. Immediate direction is often vested in groups of officials (who have a religious function but are not *priests): in democratic Athens, and elsewhere, the accounts were scrutinized and published as inscriptions. Smaller sanctuaries were of lower, or minimal, public concern. Many major sanctuaries were not limited to single cults. The Acropolis of Athens within the surrounding walls and the gateway, the Propylaea, was a sacred area, the pivot of which was the altar to Athena. *Pausanias lists a whole succession of cult-places within the sacred area, including, for example, a precinct of Brauronian Artemis (see ARTEMIS; BRAURON; ATHENS, TOPOGRAPHY). Asclepius at Epidaurus shared his sanctuary with his father, Apollo (probably the original owner), as well as Hera.

The sanctuary would contain 'sacred property'. This might include the utensils and other paraphernalia of sacrifice and feasting, recorded on inscriptions. These both belonged to the god and were used by the god, or his worshippers. They include, at times, valuable plate, in gold or silver, which in itself constitutes a special offering, but is still essentially a possession to be used. Other offerings are often described as votives, strictly gifts made in response to the successful outcome of a vow, but even with these there may be a related purpose. A statue may well constitute an offering, but is also a commemoration, of service by priests or priestesses (especially those whose office was temporary), of successful achievement whether by the community in war or the individual in athletic contest. In 'international' sanctuaries, individual cities might dedicate '*thesauroi*'; the term means treasury, but this is a misleading translation, since they are not mere storehouses but offerings in their own right, often dedicated to the god to commemorate a victory in war. Some sanctuaries are oracular (see ORACLES) and thus needed to provide for the appropriate consultation process; these might require modification of the temple plan (as at Delphi) with perhaps, in addition, special office-type buildings, as at Didyma.

The sanctuaries of the Roman period represent an essential continuation of these concepts. An important right, confirmed by the Roman authorities in a limited number of cases, is that of asylum, though strictly all sanctuaries, being sacred places, offered potential refuge. In the early 5th cent. BC the regent Pausanias, condemned by his fellow Spartiates, sought refuge in Sparta's sanctuary of Athena Chalcioecus, where he could not be put to death, or even allowed to die when he was starved out. In form, Roman sanctuaries are often more regularly planned, a characteristic inherited from Hellenistic architectural concepts, typified by the sanctuary of Artemis at Magnesia ad Maeandrum (W. Asia Minor) in its redeveloped, 2nd-cent. BC form. Such sanctuaries are normally a strict rectangle in plan, surrounded by porticoes round the boundaries, and with formal gateway buildings which can be closed. The temple, with its altar directly in front, is placed within the resulting courtyard, and often situated to the back of it. The Severan marble plan (see FORMA URBIS) of the city of Rome shows several such sanctuaries for which other archaeological evidence is inadequate; but this form also characterizes the so-called imperial fora, such as those of Caesar, Augustus, and Trajan, which are essentially courtyard sanctuaries. See ROME (TOPOGRAPHY). This concept, of the chief temple in its precinct, which continues over a road and frequently a barrier to form the forum (civic centre), is typical of towns in the western Roman provinces.

In Roman *Syria these precincts assume a complex form: large rectangles with formal entrances on all four sides, the principal 'Golden Gate' to the east, and the whole structure embellished with towers. The formalism of such sanctuaries may owe something to local cult needs, and the political significance of the priests who control them, but the underlying concepts are general to the entire classical world. See BOOTY; MARKETS AND FAIRS; PAINTING; PRIESTS; SCULPTURE; TEMPLE.   R. A. T.

sanitation

Greek Developed arrangements in Greek towns for sanitation are a relatively late phenomenon, coming in with the planned cities in the 4th cent. BC. Scenes of the *symposium on Greek vases depict the use of the chamber-pot, whose contents would be thrown out of the house, probably into open channels along the road surfaces. No recognizable system of drainage exists in Athens, other than the canalized stream which flows through the area of houses west of the Areopagus. The houses of Olynthus (N. Greece) provide evidence for bathrooms and tubs, with terracotta drainpipes leading the waste away from the house and along the streets. What appears to be a fixed latrine was found in house A vii 9; it had an extended spout passing through the wall of the house, to empty directly onto the street. A similar example has been found in the Xenon at Nemea. The streets of Pella (Macedonia) have substantial covered sewers into which all waste from the adjacent houses drained. Such arrangements also existed at Priene (W. Asia Minor), in conjunction with a piped water-supply, though only four actual latrines were found in the houses. The fullest evidence comes from the houses at *Delos; by the later Hellenistic period houses generally have a recognizable built-in latrine, linked to covered drains running along the streets. The latrines empty into narrow channels, and are flushed by water used to wash down the floors. *Antioch had a sewage system, emptying into the river Orontes (Polyb. 5. 58), while excavations at *Alexandria have produced evidence for drainage systems in the streets.

R. A. T.

Roman Despite Roman proficiency in hydraulic engineering, sanitation through the provision of a clean water-supply and the hygienic removal of human and other waste was a low priority. The role of impure *water and ordure in causing *disease was little understood, and sewage was abhorred rather because it was noisome and might 'taint' other substances.

Private water-supplies were usually obtained from wells, and also from cisterns in dry climates. Only the wealthy could afford to tap the public *aqueducts. Domestic sanitation was provided by the cesspit (which might be near the well). Multi-storey buildings (*insulae*) could be linked by gravity-fed pipes to a main cesspit. Night-soil was taken out to be spread on the fields. Chamber-pots, empty amphorae (transport jars), and the public gutters were also commonly used.

City aqueducts afforded a supply of drinkable water to street fountains. Covered sewers and drains were usually multi-purpose, combining sanitation with land- and rainfall-drainage, as in the Cloaca Maxima (Great Drain) of Rome. Excess aqueduct water was used to flush these sewers. Open sewers and gutters ran down the centre or sides of streets. Bath-houses commonly contained latrines, using their water-supply. The latrines consisted of benches with holes over drains. Water for users' cleanliness was supplied in basins or channels. At Rome large urinal pots stood at street corners, the contents being used by the fullers (see TEXTILE PRODUCTION). When these were taxed by *Vespasian the pots were nicknamed after him.

The army understood the value of hygiene in maintaining military effectiveness. Some temporary camps had cesspits, permanent forts had a clean water-supply and latrines which flushed outside the defences.   A. S. E. C.

Sappho, lyric poet. Born on *Lesbos in the second half of the 7th cent. BC, she was hailed in antiquity as 'the tenth Muse' (*Anth. Pal.* 9. 506), and her poetry was collected into nine books (arranged according to metre) in the canonical Alexandrian edition. Only one complete poem and some substantial fragments survive, culled from quotations in other writers or from papyrus finds.

Most of her poems were for solo performance, and many refer to love between women or girls. Other subjects include hymns to deities and apparently personal concerns such as her brother's safety (fr. 5). Wedding songs, and snatches from a lament for Adonis (fr. 140) are clearly for several singers. Fr. 44, describing the marriage of *Hector and Andromache, is unusual in its narrative length and proximity to *epic.

Little about her life is certain: biographies (*POxy.* 1800, *Suda*, 'Sappho') are late and sometimes contradictory. She may have had some involvement in the aristocratic power struggles of Lesbos (fr. 71), leading to a period of exile in Sicily (*Marm. Par.* 36). She was probably married, though only a brother and (probably) a daughter, Cleis, figure in the poems. The story of her suicide for love of Phaon is almost certainly fictional.

Her sexual inclinations have occasioned much speculation from antiquity to the present. From Attic comedy onwards she was credited with an implausible selection of male lovers. She is described as a lover of women only in post-Classical times, and in later European tradition was often regarded as heterosexual. See HOMOSEXUALITY.

Her own poetry remains the major source for the controversial question of how she related to the companions (fr. 160) who formed her audience. An important parallel is *Alcman's *partheneia* (maiden-songs) written for girls' choruses, in which the singers praise each other in erotic terms. Sappho's term for her companions is *parthenos* (girl). This, and the frequent references to partings and absence in her poems, suggest that most of her circle shared their lives for only a limited period before marriage. Homoeroticism was probably institutionalized at this stage of life, as it was elsewhere for young men. The group's preoccupations—love, beauty, poetry—are indicated by the divinities most often invoked in Sappho: *Aphrodite, the Graces, and the *Muses.

But despite the likely educational and religious function of her group, Sappho herself emerges from the poems as far from the chaste headmistress figure constructed by 19th- and early 20th-cent. German philology. In fr. 1, the poet names herself in a prayer enlisting Aphrodite's help in winning the love of an unresponsive girl. In fr. 16 the singer links her own love for the absent Anactoria with that of Helen for Paris, and fr. 31 famously charts the singer's despair as she watches a beloved girl sitting next to a man. Sappho's love poetry differs from that of male writers in the almost complete absence of a sharp distinction between lover and beloved.

Poems such as these reveal an accomplished poet who can achieve effects of great subtlety beneath an apparently simple surface; other, less complex poems (frs. 102, 114) seem influenced by folk-song. Like her contemporary *Alcaeus she writes in a literary Aeolic dialect (see GREEK LANGUAGE §4). Her work was admired in antiquity for its euphony (Dion. Hal. *Comp.* 23) and she was credited with musical invention; the Sapphic stanza was used by later poets such as *Horace. Notable imitations include *Catullus 51, 61, and 62, while *Ovid's imaginary epistle from Sappho to Phaon (*Her.* 15) was the progenitor of many subsequent fictions about her.   M. Wil.

satire (*satura*) was first classified as a literary form in Rome. 'Satire, at any rate, is all our own,' boasted Quintilian (10. 1. 93) of the genre that depicted Rome in the least flattering light. Originally simply a hotch-potch (in verse, or in prose and verse mixed), satire soon acquired its specific character as a humorous or malicious exposé of hypocrisy and pretension; however, it continued to be a hold-all for mismatched subjects, written in an uneven style and overlapping with other genres. The author himself figured prominently in a variety of shifting roles: civic watchdog, sneering cynic, mocking or indignant observer, and social outcast.

Name *Satura* is the feminine of *satur*, 'full', and was transferred to literary miscellanies from *lanx satura*, a dish crammed with first fruits, or from *satura*, a mixed stuffing or sausage. *Juvenal, for example, claims (1. 86) to be filling his writing tablets with a *farrago* (mixed mash) of urban vice. Mixture and variety remained constant features of satire: many satirical techniques—parody, exaggeration, deflation, caricature—depend on incongruous juxtapositions, and satirists were self-conscious about the uneven qualities of their writing. Shared elements of irreverence and burlesque gave rise to an alternative, though false, derivation, from *satyri*, 'satyrs': hence *Horace's pose as Priapus (*Sat.* 1. 8) and the punning title of *Petronius Arbiter's satirical novel *Satyrica*, 'Adventures of Satyrs'. *Livy's assertion (7. 2) that variety shows called *saturae* were an early form of Roman drama looks like a spurious attempt to link Roman satire with Greek satyr-plays. In the 2nd cent. BC, while the first satires were being written, the name *lex per saturam* was given to any suspiciously mixed political bill, which increased the reputation of satire as a dubious concoction. Both Horace (*Sat.* 2. 1. 1–2) and Juvenal (6. 635) speak of transgressing a 'law' of satire, partly as a pun on these bills, partly as a joke, as satire was a law unto itself, and partly in earnest, as satire was genuinely constrained by external laws. Finally, a bogus link was drawn with the similar-sounding festival of the Saturnalia, the Romans' temporary season for free abuse, which satire often adopted as a dramatic context (Hor. *Sat.* 2. 3, 2. 7; Petr. *Sat.* 44, 58, 69).

Influences Greece

The idea of the satirist as a vindictive member of society originated with the iambics of *Archilochus and Hipponax. Athenian Old Comedy, especially that of *Aristophanes, was often cited as a model for outspoken abuse of other citizens (e.g. Hor. *Sat.* I. 4. I–5; see COMEDY (GREEK), OLD). However, both iambics and comedy also inspired defensive apologies with which Roman satirists deflected charges of spite on to their critics.

The Hellenistic diatribe, a lecture which popularized moral philosophy with jokes, parody, fables, and split dialogue, was also a strong influence (Horace acknowledges a specific debt to the itinerant philosopher Bion of Borysthenes, *Ep.* 2. 2. 60). Its conscious mixture of serious and humorous elements (also known as *spoudogeloion*) lies behind Horace's laughing candour (*ridentem dicere verum* 'to tell the truth smiling' *Sat.* I. I. 24) as well as the bitterer invective of Persius (AD 34–62) and Juvenal. The *Cynic philosopher Menippus of Gadara was associated with so-called Menippean satire, a mixture of prose and verse which inspired experiments by *Varro, Petronius, and *Seneca; he also presides over several of the satirical dialogues of *Lucian.

Rome

Satire, for the Romans, enshrined a national characteristic, blunt free speech, and was later a reminder of the republican past. They were proud of traditional social outlets for satirical feeling—the Saturnalia, *Fescennini* (songs of ribald abuse at weddings), lampoons, pillorying of army commanders after a triumph. Yet in practice literary satire only pays lip-service to these. It was dangerous to write undiluted satire in all periods of Roman history, right from the *Twelve Tables' ban on malicious imprecations (*mala carmina*); and libel usually carried severe penalties. That is why satire is more of a discussion of the limits imposed on aggression, and why satirists tend to equivocate rather than take risks. Roman satire's bark was always worse than its bite.

Development *Ennius wrote the first *saturae*, up to six books in various metres, of which only 31 lines survive. A sideline from his monumental *Annales*, they were miscellanies of Hellenistic culture which, though not noticeably acerbic, contained many ingredients of later satire in embryo: animal fables, moral censure, ethical dialogue, and the self-conscious presence of the author himself.

Lucilius (d. 102/1 BC), according to ancient tradition, was the true father of satire: he specialized in outspoken criticism of contemporaries, and fixed the hexameter as the conventional satirical metre. His prolific writings (30 books, of which about 1300 lines survive) reveal a strong autobiographical element and an earthy, conversational style which is less spontaneous than it seems. Already the satirical personality is split between moral censor (e.g. in the mock 'trials' of Lentulus Lupus and Mucius Scaevola and the exposure of urban dinner-parties) and rollicking adventurer. Horace thought Lucilius prolix, but admired him for stripping the skin off a corrupt society. He was unanimously held up as a symbol of republican liberty, especially during the civil wars, but in reality he owed his freedom of expression to his patrons, *Scipio Aemilianus and Laelius.

Varro added a new dimension to the principle of variety with his 150 books of Menippean satires, in verse and prose mixed, also now in fragments. Their titles—e.g. 'False Aeneas', 'Split Varro', 'Socratic Hercules'—give a clue to their hybrid contents—'a dash of philosophy, with a pinch of dialogue and humour thrown in' (Cic. *Acad.* 1. 8).

At the end of the republic, satire became yet more constrained. Horace's *Satires* (or *Sermones*, 'Conversations') are a sensitive gauge of the political changes through which he lived. Book 1, ten satires written during the transition from civil war to new civic order, is a tight blend of ingredients based on principles of moderation, finesse, and inoffensiveness, in direct contrast with Lucilius. Although Horace rejects the venom of traditional satire ('black squid-ink' and 'Italian vinegar', *Sat.* I. 4. 100, I. 7. 32), and claims to be satisfied with his humble status, the odd trace of nostalgia for republican free speech remains below the surface. In Book 2, eight satires written in the more restricted environment of the Augustan regime, Horace symbolically hands over Saturnalian opportunities for free speech to pundits on various controversial themes: gastronomy, legacy-hunting, Stoic philosophy (see STOICISM). The book ends on an unsatisfying note with an unfinished feast.

In imperial Rome, satirists risked reprisals from their capricious rulers. The tyranny of *Nero, surprisingly, was a fruitful period. However, Persius switches his focus from political to philosophical freedom, and confines his secrets to a hole in the ground or a darkened study. His six poems are puzzlingly disjointed Stoic diatribes, where satirical language reaches a new pitch of concentration. Two Menippean satires date from the same time. The courtier Petronius' picaresque novel, *Satyrica*, is a loosely Epicurean mock-epic (see EPICURUS), where the narrator appears to be pursued by a wrathful Priapus; but it is hard to find any strong moral basis when Encolpius himself is a victim of the decay he observes in society. The longest extended fragment, the 'Cena Trimalchionis', dissects a tasteless Saturnalian dinner hosted by an ex-slave. *Seneca's *Apocolocyntosis* ('Pumpkinification') is an inverted apotheosis-myth, depicting the emperor *Claudius as a carnival king, prematurely senile, with filthy habits and a penchant for dicing. It is significant that it was probably written for the first Saturnalia of Nero's reign, not during the lifetime of its subject. Two lines survive from the Flavian satirist Turnus, exposing one of Nero's own crimes, the murder of Claudius' son Britannicus, after the event.

With Juvenal, imperial satire seems to have been stretched to its full potential. His sixteen satires, spanning the reigns of *Domitian, *Nerva, *Trajan, and *Hadrian, take in not only a bloated metropolis but also the ends of the earth. The satirist now adopts a posture of savage indignation: only hyperbole is adequate for describing the depravity of modern Rome, where vice has reached mythic proportions. Despite his sense of outrage, Juvenal's moral standpoint is strangely unstable: his language swells into tragic bombast, then plunges just as dramatically into bathos. These extremes of indignation are best seen in Satire 3, on the tottering city of Rome, the monstrous Satire 6, on women, and Satire 10, on ambition, with its striking images, such as that of the statue of *Sejanus melted down into chamber-pots. However, Juvenal's claim to be returning to Lucilius is another rhetorical posture: most of his victims are either stereotypical ones—women, homosexuals, foreigners—or ghosts from the reign of Domitian.

*Lucian gave a satirical flavour to Greek dialogue, which he claims to have corrupted under the influence of iambics, Old Comedy, and the Cynicism of Menippus ('a dog who laughs when he bites'). Although he specialized in fantastical, timeless perspectives on terrestrial folly (seen from above and below in *Icaromenippus* and *Menippus*), his own viewpoint as a subject-Greek inspired some pointed satires on Roman culture (e.g. *Nigrinus, De Mercede Conductis*).

The history of Roman satire reached an apt conclusion two centuries later with the last classical Menippean satire, *Julian's *Caesars*, a character-assessment of his dead predecessors written (in Greek) by the emperor himself.

E. J. G.

satyrs and silens Satyrs at play on an Athenian pottery wine-cooler (early 5th cent. BC). The scene conveys the (simultaneous) desire for both wine and sex which the Greeks attributed to these 'wild men' of *Dionysus.

satyrs and **silens** are imaginary male inhabitants of the wild, comparable to the 'wild men' of the European folk tradition, with some animal features, unrestrained in their desire for sex and wine, and generally represented naked. The first mention in literature of 'silens' is as making love to *nymphs in caves (*Hymn. Hom. Ven.* 262–3); of 'satyrs' it is as 'worthless and mischievous' (Hes. fr. 123). On the Attic François vase (*c.*570 BC) the horse–human hybrids accompanying *Hephaestus (with *Dionysus) back to Mt. Olympus are labelled as silens. It seems that in the course of the 6th cent. BC the (Attic-Ionic) silens were amalgamated with the (Peloponnesian) satyrs (so that the names were used interchangeably) to form, along with nymphs or maenads, the sacred band (*thiasos*) of Dionysus. It is a *thiasos* of young satyrs that, in the 5th cent., forms the chorus of satyric drama, with Silenus (in keeping with the ancient belief in individual silens) as father of the satyrs. In vase-painting satyrs are at first present in a limited number of myths (the Return of Hephaestus, the Gigantomachy (see GIANTS), etc.), but in the 5th cent. this number grows considerably, at least partly under the influence of satyric drama.

People dressed up as satyrs, e.g. at the Athenian Anthesteria festival, where their frolics are depicted on the 'Choes' vases. Also at the Anthesteria was the procession in which Dionysus arrived in a ship-cart accompanied by satyrs, who are prominent also in great processions at *Alexandria (Ath. 196a–203b) and Rome (Dion. Hal. 7. 72). In contrast to this public presence, satyrs also conducted mystic *initiation (e.g. Pl. *Leg.* 815c, and the paintings at the Villa of the Mysteries at *Pompeii; see MYSTERIES). To be initiated might be to join a satyric *thiasos*, a community of this world and the next. Hence the occurrence of satyrs in funerary art throughout most of antiquity.

Analogous to this contrast is the ambiguity of the satyrs as grotesque hedonists and yet the immortal companions of a god, cruder than men and yet somehow wiser, combining mischief with wisdom, lewdness with skill in music, animality with divinity. In satyric drama they are the first to sample the creation of culture out of nature in the invention of *wine, of the lyre, of the pipe, and so on. Silenus is the educator of Dionysus. King Midas of Phrygia extracted from a silen, whom he had trapped in his garden, the wisdom that for men it is best never to have been born, second best to die as soon as possible (Hdt. 8. 138; Arist. fr. 44). And Virgil's shepherds extract from

Silenus a song of great beauty and wisdom (*Ecl.* 6). This ambiguity is exploited in *Alcibiades' famous comparison of *Socrates to the musical satyr Marsyas (Pl. *Symp.* 215).

At first somewhat equine, the satyrs become progressively more human in appearance (though from the Hellenistic period more caprine than equine, perhaps through association with *Pan), and may decorate a pastoral landscape or embody, for the visual artist, the charm of a not quite human body, as in the sculpted sleeping satyr known as the 'Barberini Faun'. Popular belief in the presence of satyrs in the wild no doubt persisted throughout antiquity (e.g. Plut. *Sull.* 27), as did the practice of imitating them in urban festivals, which was banned in Constantinople in AD 692. R. A. S. S.

scholarship, ancient

Greek In one sense of the term scholarship began when literature became a central element of education and the prescribed texts had to be explained and interpreted to pupils in a class. An early reflex of this activity is the reported invention by Theagenes of Rhegium (late 6th cent. BC) of the allegorical method of interpretation, which could be used to deny the literal meaning of supposedly objectionable passages of *Homer. But scholarship, like literary criticism, was slow to develop in the Classical period. In the Peripatos *Aristotle and his disciples were not primarily concerned with literature or history, but their discussions of Homer and concern with the chronology of Athenian dramatic festivals was a step forward. Recognizably scholarly work, including the composition of books or pamphlets about literary texts, began early in the 3rd cent. BC in *Alexandria under the patronage of the Ptolemies (see PTOLEMY I and II); to what extent the ideals of the Peripatos were influential, possibly through the influence of Demetrius of Phalerum (late 4th cent. BC), is a disputed question. The Museum, where scholars enjoyed good working conditions, became a centre where literary topics were discussed regularly; according to one report a record was kept of the discussions. Its library (see LIBRARIES) acquired a virtually complete collection of books written in Greek, to which *Callimachus wrote an enormous bibliographical guide, and it looks as if copies of the classics, such as Homer, which reflected the results of work done in the Museum, came to be regarded as standard. Between *c.*285 and 145 BC a series of Alexandrian scholars, who variously combined one or more of the professions of poet, tutor to the children of the royal family, and librarian of the Museum, brought scholarship to a high level. They edited texts by comparing different exemplars, commented on them by writing either notes on difficult passages or extended running commentaries, and composed innumerable treatises on individual problems, some of them historical and antiquarian rather than literary. Questions of authenticity also had to be addressed. The leading figures in this process were Zenodotus, Callimachus, *Eratosthenes, Aristophanes of Byzantium, and Aristarchus. Not all their decisions about puzzles in Homer win the

approval of a modern reader, and they seem to have been too prone to reject lines as being unworthy of Homer or inconsistent with the context; but luckily they did not remove such lines from the texts in circulation. Good copies of leading authors were often equipped with a kind of *apparatus criticus* in the margin; this consisted of signs indicating e.g. the dubious status of a line of verse, or some point of general interest in the text, on which the reader could expect to find guidance in a note in a separate book containing a commentary. During part of the Hellenistic period there was also a rival school in *Pergamum, but very little is known in detail about it, and it does not seem to have achieved the prestige of the Museum.

Much ancient scholarship can be seen as the response to the difficulties created by the handwritten book (see BOOKS). Different copies of the same text diverged. Although this was most notable in the case of Homer, it was true of all texts in some degree, and even by Hellenistic times a number of passages in other classical authors had become obscure or unintelligible. Scribal error was recognized as a factor to be reckoned with; the term *graphikon hamartēma* (lit. 'mistake in writing') is found e.g. in Harpocration (2nd cent. AD), and the Homer scholia discuss variant readings, while from time to time we find that scholars ventured upon emendation in passages they believed to be meaningless. The best critics, however, did not content themselves with the removal of obvious corruptions. They devised principles of interpretation, a famous case being the maxim traditionally but perhaps wrongly attributed to Aristarchus, that one should interpret an author by reference to his own usage elsewhere (*Homēron ex Homērou saphēnizein* (lit. 'clarify Homer through Homer')). Another good rule was that a unique word should not be deleted from a poetic text just because it was unique. They also attempted aesthetic appreciation: the scholia on Homer contain many remarks of this kind which a modern reader will agree with and respect. These notes employ such concepts as poetic licence, the scale, structure, unity, and variety in the composition of the epic, the characterization and the stylistic level. Since none of the works of the greatest scholars survive, and there is very little left even of what their lesser contemporaries and successors wrote, it is hard to write a convincing account of the development of scholarship; to concentrate on the relatively few known facts about the leading figures risks neglect of all the achievements that cannot be safely attributed to an individual. Our main source of information is the material known as scholia, i.e. notes written in the margins of ancient and medieval copies of our texts.

From late Hellenistic and Roman times there is less to report about literary scholarship. As specimens of what scholars wrote we have the *Technē grammatikē* of Dionysius 'the Thracian' (though many authorities now believe it to be a product of late antiquity), the short essay on allegory in Homer by Heraclitus, and a substantial papyrus fragment of a work by Didymus on *Demosthenes, which does not cast a flattering light on his standards of scholarship. In the Roman empire literary life altered under the influence of the new fashion of Atticism and much effort was spent on compiling manuals that would ensure accurate imitation of the classics, such as the extant lexicographical guides of Pollux, Phrynichus, and Moeris. The grammatical writings of Herodian and Apollonius Dyscolus, especially the latter's long book on syntax, were also a serious contribution to their subject. The Christians soon learned to adopt the techniques that had served the pagans well, and we find in Origen much that is reminiscent of Alexandrian philology, both in the handling of details—he needed to establish the text of the Septuagint—and in the use of the allegorical method. The later rival school of *Antioch was if anything even closer in its adherence to Alexandrian methods.

Early in the 3rd cent. AD we find the first important representative of another group of scholars whose work is extant in substantial quantities, the commentators on *Plato and Aristotle. From Alexander of Aphrodisias, who began lecturing on Aristotle *c.* AD 198, to the middle of the 6th cent. the philosophical schools in *Athens and Alexandria (the latter had no connection with the Museum, by now defunct) were highly productive. There are two other developments dating from late antiquity which deserve mention. One is the invention, perhaps to be credited to Procopius of Gaza (*c.*500), of the *catena*, which is made up of short excerpts from two or more existing commentaries on a given book of the Bible, with the name of each author normally prefixed to each excerpt. This type of compilation is akin to, though it was not necessarily the model for, the scholia. The formation of the extant corpora of scholia probably took place in late antiquity, and the process may have been continued in the early centuries of Byzantium. Original works of Hellenistic and later scholarship were the raw material for this process, and once a compilation had been made from them they were discarded. Unfortunately the scholia do not often name the authorities responsible for the views or information presented, nor do they give what look like verbatim quotations. This is the main reason why, given the loss of the original texts, it is still so difficult to reconstruct the history of scholarship from material that does in large part ultimately derive from such texts.   N. G. W.

Latin The origins of scholarship at Rome are lost to view, along with much of Rome's earliest scholarly writing. *Suetonius' attempt (*Gramm.* 2) to trace Rome's first experience of Hellenistic scholarship to the visit of Crates of Mallos around 167 BC is more colourful than reliable; it no doubt captures, however, the *kind* of contact that was influential in the course of the 2nd cent., when a 'great flock' of learned men came to Rome from Greece (Polyb. 31. 24. 6 f.). By the end of the 2nd cent. and the start of the 1st not only was there substantial learning displayed in the *Didascalica* of Accius and the *satires of Lucilius, but Lucius Aelius had developed what would be the three main

foci of Roman scholarship: 'antiquities', treating the institutions and beliefs of Rome and her neighbours; literary studies, including questions of authenticity and literary history (but little that we would recognize as 'literary criticism'); and the more or less systematic study of language, especially (in this early period) etymology and semantics. Aelius, Rome's first true scholar, in turn influenced *Varro, Rome's greatest scholar, whose antiquarian research (*Antiquitates rerum humanarum et divinarum*), study of Latinity (*De lingua Latina*), and investigations of literary history (*De poetis*) provided a model and a resource for all other scholars (e.g. Cornelius Nepos, Verrius Flaccus) and some authors of imaginative literature (e.g. *Ovid).

Varro and Aelius, who were not professional teachers, established a tradition of 'amateur' scholarship that continued throughout later antiquity and included (to note only authors of works still extant) *Pliny the Elder, who extended the methods of antiquarian scholarship to the investigation of the natural world (*Historia Naturalis*); Aulus *Gellius, whose *Attic Nights* gathered edifying or beguiling excerpts from his varied reading; Censorinus, who wrote on the reckoning of human life and time (*De die natali*) in the 3rd cent.; Nonius Marcellus (4th cent. AD?), whose encyclopaedic dictionary (*De compendiosa doctrina*) embraces both linguistic oddments and *Realien*; and two 5th-cent. authors, Macrobius (*Saturnalia*) and Martianus Capella (*De nuptiis Philologiae et Mercurii*), whose learned compilations are cast (respectively) as an elaborate dialogue and an allegory. Though arising from different motives in different milieux, all such works are alike in suggesting which elements of their culture the authors thought it worthwhile to explain and preserve for their posterity.

The transmission of culture was also central to the second main stream of Latin scholarship, which arose from the schools of *grammaticē* and rhetoric that began to proliferate in the 1st cent. BC. Here commentaries on literary texts and handbooks surveying grammatical and rhetorical doctrine were the chief staple. Precepts on Latin rhetoric were being compiled as early as the 80s BC, when the anonymous *Rhetorica ad Herennium* was written; the main surviving example of the genre is Quintilian's great survey of the education suitable for an orator (*c.* AD 95). Quintilian's older contemporary Remmius Palaemon wins the credit for writing the first *ars grammatica* of which we are specifically informed, though examples of the type almost certainly existed by the mid-1st cent. BC. Commentaries on literary texts, especially those read in schools, are also attested for the 1st cent. BC, though it is not until Pomponius Porphyrio's commentary on Horace (3rd cent. AD) that we have an example surviving in something resembling its original form. In later antiquity the teachers Aelius Donatus (mid-4th cent. AD), Servius (late 4th–early 5th cent.), and Priscian (late 5th–early 6th cent.) are the emblematic figures: the first as author of commentaries on *Terence and *Virgil and of two highly influential grammars (the *Ars minor* and the *Ars maior*), the second as author of extant commentaries on Virgil and Donatus' *artes*, the third as author of the greatest compilation of Latin linguistic knowledge to survive from antiquity.

See also LITERARY CRITICISM IN ANTIQUITY.   R. A. K.

scholarship, history of classical *(see following page)*

Scipio Aemilianus, Publius Cornelius Scipio Aemilianus Africanus (Numantinus), born 185/4 BC as second son of Lucius Aemilius Paullus (consul 182), adopted as a child by Publius Cornelius Scipio, son of *Scipio Africanus, as his elder brother was by a Quintus Fabius Maximus. In 168 he fought under Paullus at Pydna (see ROME (HISTORY) §1.4). Back in Rome, he met *Polybius, who became his friend and his mentor in preparing him for a public career. (See esp. Polyb. 31. 23 ff.) In 151, though asked by the Macedonians, as Paullus' son, to settle their problems that soon led to the war with the royal pretender Andriscus, he instead volunteered for arduous service as a military tribune under Lucius Licinius Lucullus (consul 151) in Spain, thus persuading others to volunteer. In the fighting he won a major decoration, the *corona muralis* (for the first man to scale an enemy wall in battle). When sent to request *elephants from the Numidian king Masinissa, he renewed Africanus' patronal relations with him and vainly tried to mediate peace between him and *Carthage after a battle he had witnessed. In 149 and 148 he served as a military tribune under Manius Manilius in Africa and again distinguished himself both in the fighting, where he won a rare distinction, the *corona graminea*, a grass crown for a soldier who raised a siege (Plin. *HN* 22. 6 ff., 13), and in diplomacy, persuading a Carthaginian commander to defect. After Masinissa's death he divided the kingdom among his three legitimate sons according to the king's request. Coming to Rome to stand for a lower magistracy (the aedileship) for 147, he was elected *consul, contrary to the rules for the *cursus honorum* (Roman career path), by a well-organized popular demand that forced the senate to suspend the rules. He was assigned *Africa by special legislation and, after restoring discipline and closing off the enemy's harbour, he overcame long and desperate resistance and early in 146 captured Carthage after days of street-fighting. After letting his soldiers collect the booty, he destroyed the city and sold the inhabitants into slavery. Anyone who should resettle the site was solemnly cursed. With the help of the usual senate commission he organized the province of Africa and after giving magnificent games returned to celebrate a splendid triumph, earning the name 'Africanus' to which his adoptive descent entitled him. He distributed some captured works of art among cities in Sicily and Italy (Cic. *Verr. passim*; *Syll.*³ 677; *ILLRP* 326).

Probably in 144–3 he headed an embassy to the kings and cities of the east, perhaps even as far as the territory contested between Parthians and *Seleucids (Lucil. 464 Marx), with the Greek philosopher Panaetius as his personal companion. After his return he presumably guided senate policy in those areas, especially towards *Pergamum, the Seleucids, and the *Jews. (We have no evidence on its for-

mulation and little on its execution.) In 142 he was censor with Lucius Mummius (consul 146), who mitigated some of his severity. They restored the Aemilian Bridge over the Tiber and adorned the Capitol (temple of Jupiter).

In 136 he secured the rejection of the peace in Spain negotiated for Gaius Hostilius Mancinus (consul 137) by his cousin and brother-in-law Tiberius *Gracchus. This deeply offended Gracchus, even though Scipio saved him from personal disgrace. In 135, again by special dispensation and without campaigning for the office, he was elected consul 134 and sent to Numantia in Spain, with an army consisting chiefly of his own clients because of the shortage of military manpower. He starved Numantia into surrender in just over a year, destroyed it, and sold the survivors into slavery, returning in 132 to celebrate a second triumph and acquire the (unofficial) name 'Numantinus'. By approving of Gracchus' murder he incurred great unpopularity. It was increased when, in 129, defending the interests of Italian clients holding public land, he was responsible for a senate decree that paralysed the agrarian commission by transferring its judiciary powers to the consuls, usually hostile or absent. When, soon after, he was found dead, various prominent persons, including his wife (Gracchus' sister) and Cornelia (Gracchus' mother), were suspected of responsibility, though the funeral laudation written by his friend Gaius Laelius (consul 140) specified natural death. (See E. Badian, *JRS* 1956, 220.)

His personal morality and civil and military courage made him an unlikely friend of *Cato the Elder. But he was a patron of poets and philosophers, with a genuine interest in literature (he was himself an able orator) and in Greek philosophy, as transmitted by Polybius, which he combined with a traditional aristocratic Roman outlook. He believed in the 'balanced constitution', with the people entitled to choose their leaders (Polyb. 6. 14. 4 and 8: hence his willingness to accept extraordinary appointments) and to take charge of criminal trials (Polyb. 6. 14. 5 ff.: hence his support for the ballot law of Lucius Cassius Longinus Ravilla (as tribune 135)). But he could foresee the ultimate fall of Rome (cf. Polyb. 6. 9. 12 ff.), which could be delayed by stopping signs of decay, especially the decline in aristocratic morality (see *ORF*⁴ 21, esp. nos. 13, 17, 30, and cf. Polyb. 6. 8. 4 f.) and the danger of the democratic element, under the tribunes (cf. Polyb. 6. 16. 5 ff.), leading the state into anarchy and tyranny (cf. Polyb. 6. 9. 2 ff.—and an aristocratic Roman fear of a leader's excessive popularity producing *regnum*, 'monarchy'). Utterly ruthless towards Rome's enemies, he believed in loyal patronage (both for Rome and for himself) over client-friends, whether monarchs like Attalus II of Pergamum and Masinissa or Italian allies. Cicero, in *De republica*, depicts him as the ideal Roman statesman (cf. also *De senectute* and *De amicitia*) and sets him in a group of aristocrats and their cultured clients (esp. *Amic.* 69) that modern scholars turned into the 'Scipionic Circle'.   E. B.

history of classical scholarship (from the Renaissance) Classical texts formed the core of the arts curriculum in medieval schools and universities and were central to two of the three higher faculties, law and medicine, as well. But modern classical scholarship—the systematic effort to collect and study the written and material remains of the ancient world as a whole—came into being in 14th-cent. northern Italy. Here teachers of rhetoric began to teach from *Cicero rather than the 'modern'—i.e. medieval—texts they had previously used. Formal imitation of the classics became systematic. Scholars began to see classical Latin texts as distinctively better than later ones: they copied, read, and studied a wide range of literary and historical texts that had generally not been read in the Middle Ages. Access to new material created new questions: problems of attribution and dating that had not interested medieval scholars cropped up and new techniques were devised to solve them. Before 1320 Giovanni de Matociis of Verona had established in a formal essay that the Pliny who wrote the *Natural History* could not have written the *Letters* as well (SEE PLINY THE ELDER and YOUNGER). He also wrote a history of the Roman emperors in which he drew on the evidence of coins as well as that of the ancient historians.

The poet and philosopher Petrarch (Francesco Petrarca, 1304–74) knitted these technical threads together into the programme for a new scholarship. Convinced that 'all history was but the praise of Rome' and that he himself lived in an inferior, 'dark' age, he dedicated his life to the study and imitation of the ancients—by which, as a list of his favourite books that he drew up reveals, he meant Romans like *Livy and *Virgil and Saint *Augustine. Thanks to his connections with the papal curia, which spent much of the 14th cent. in Avignon, and with influential Italian clerics and statesmen, he gained access to the treasures of both Italian and northern libraries. Petrarch assembled a remarkable library of his own: his copy of Livy, for example, brought together from diverse sources three decades (groups of 10 books; see LIVY), the bulk of the text that survives today, and though he never learned Greek, he had manuscripts of *Plato and *Homer. He studied and annotated his books with care and intelligence, hunted for other texts that they mentioned, and explored the ruins of Rome as well as its literary canon. His own works—which included an epic, bucolics, philosophical dialogues, historical compilations, and lively letters modelled on those of Cicero—represented a dramatic effort to revive the main genres of Latin literature. He insisted that the literature, history, and moral philosophy of the classical world could form a more solid and satisfactory basis for education and a better model for modern writers than the technical philosophy of Aristotle and his medieval commentators, which dominated the universities of northern Europe and were also becoming fashionable in Italian universities. He thus provided both a model for classical studies and a new justification for them: both proved vastly influential.

For the next century, Italian humanists followed the lines Petrarch had laid down. They hunted little-known classical texts all over Europe, copying what they discovered and stealing what they had no chance to copy; gradually they assembled what remains the basic canon of Latin texts. They established schools, both in republican Florence and Venice and at the courts of Ferrara, Mantua, and Milan, where young men could master the grammar and literature of classical Latin and learn the lessons of ancient history and moral philosophy. The correction of textual errors became a fashion and gave rise to sharp debates. Before the middle of the 15th cent. Lorenzo Valla wrote the first modern manual of classical Latin usage; unmasked a medieval legal text, the *Donation of Constantine*, as written in a non-classical Latin and therefore forged; and brilliantly corrected the text (and the content) of Livy. Meanwhile specialist antiquaries like Cyriacus of Ancona explored ancient sites and filled notebooks with drawings of ruins and texts of inscriptions. The study of Greek revived as well, first of all in Florence, where Emanuel Chrysoloras taught for three years from 1397. He also produced a practical

Greek grammar. Unsystematic but energetic efforts at translation brought Plato and *Lucian, Homer and *Aristophanes into Latin, and a modest command of Greek became part of the normal scholar's arsenal.

From the middle of the 15th cent. new public libraries like that of the Vatican gave the new canon of classical texts permanent homes. The support of patrons like Cosimo de' Medici and Pope Nicholas V made possible the translation of the major works of Greek prose: Plato and Plotinus were translated for the Medici by Marsilio Ficino, *Thucydides and *Herodotus for Nicholas V by Valla. The invention of printing ensured the survival, first of the major Latin works and, from the 1480s, of the Greek classics as well. Meanwhile commentators tried, at increasing length, to remedy the corruptions, explain the difficulties, and emphasize the beauties of the classical texts. Much of the scholarly work of this period was done too rapidly. Angelo Poliziano, who devised before his early death in 1494 the basic principles of textual criticism, insisting that before trying to correct a given text one must examine all the manuscripts and eliminate from consideration those copied from other extant ones, argued this thesis so forcefully precisely because he held that the editions of his time were based on randomly chosen manuscripts, silently emended and wilfully explained. With few exceptions, he was right.

None the less, by the end of the 15th cent. many central techniques of classical scholarship had been formulated and applied. Poliziano's *Miscellanea* of 1489, Ermolao Barbaro's *Castigationes Plinianae* of 1492–3, and many less ambitious works deployed a vast range of Greek and Latin sources to correct and explicate texts and solve problems in every field of ancient culture. Poliziano showed how to compare Latin writers systematically with their Greek sources. More generally, he and others insisted that only the philologist could correct and explicate classical texts—even the technical classics of law, medicine, and philosophy, which had long been the province of professional practitioners of those disciplines. A new critical and historical method had come into being. At the same time, however, classical scholarship revived old myths and created new ones. Ficino, Pico, and others developed from their reading of Neoplatonic texts like the *Hermetic Corpus* what became the popular theory that the Greek philosophers had derived their central ideas from the Egyptians and Chaldeans. And the papal theologian Annius of Viterbo, who published what he described as the fragments of the lost histories of Berosus, Manetho, and others in 1498, embedded in a huge commentary, foisted actual forgeries on a Europe-wide public. Spanish and English readers delighted in his meticulously argued demonstration that their nations were directly descended from exiled Trojans.

The later 15th and 16th cents. saw all of these new methods and interests spread to northern Europe. Some northern scholars—like Beatus Rhenanus—continued the technical efforts of Poliziano and others, working with librarians and printers to produce clean editions of texts based on the best sources. Others continued the more contentious effort to show that humanistic methods could be applied to all ancient texts. Guillaume Budé wrote the first full humanistic commentary on the *Digest*, founding what became a French speciality. Biblical scholarship developed even more rapidly. Valla had already argued that the text of the New Testament needed the same sort of critical treatment as the classics. The great Dutch scholar Erasmus, who printed Valla's New Testament commentary, produced and printed a full new Latin translation of the New Testament, with a Greek text to support it. He also argued that the historical and philological methods of the humanists could yield the best understanding of the biblical text. The Reformation and Counter-Reformation, though Erasmus and others initially saw them as a threat to the humanities, ultimately reinforced their enterprise. Catholics and Protestants alike accepted the need to study the Bible in its original languages, while Protestant academies and Jesuit colleges both adopted and systematized the humanist curriculum.

In the second half of the 16th cent. scholarship in several technical disciplines reached maturity. Textual criticism, of Greek as well as Latin, found many original practitioners, like Jean Dorat, and a few theorists, like Francesco Robortello, who wrote the first manual of the art. Denys Lambin and others drew up spectacularly detailed commentaries on the central Latin texts and their Greek literary background. Students of Roman history and Greek poetry and philosophy compiled the first collections of fragments of authors whose works had been wholly or partially lost. Antiquarians and Roman lawyers like Antonio Agustìn, Carlo Sigonio, and Jacques Cujas traced the development of the Roman constitution and legal system over the centuries, from the *Twelve Tables to the *Corpus Iuris Civilis*, which received critical editions and elaborate commentary (see JUSTINIAN'S CODIFICATION). Antiquaries also collected, organized, and published the first corpora of inscriptions and wrote systematic treatises on virtually every aspect of ancient social and cultural life. Justus Lipsius, for example, reconstructed the military and organizational practices of the Roman army. Systematic descriptions made the main ancient ruins and artworks of Rome and other cities widely known: especially important were the Roman consular *Fasti* and *Triumphs*, discovered and reassembled in the 1540s, which inspired Sigonio and others to rework the chronology of Roman history. Joseph Scaliger and other chronologers extended this enterprise, establishing what remains the chronological framework of ancient history, Greek and near eastern as well as Roman. They also reconstructed the central ancient calendars and their development.

By the end of the 16th cent. most of the classical texts now known had been printed, an enormous technical literature had been produced, and central problems of ancient political and literary history—like that of the origins of Rome—had begun to be studied in a critical, open-minded way that owed little to ancient precedent. The Dutch universities—above all Leiden, where Lipsius taught and Scaliger enjoyed the first full-time research post created in the modern world—became centres of classical research, with remarkable libraries and publishing facilities. At the same time, however, the historical texts forged by Annius of Viterbo still outsold Herodotus. Jean Bodin, who wrote the first manual on how to read and assess the sources of ancient and modern history, took central theses from them. The myth of a glamorous Egyptian *prisca philosophia* found adherents across Europe. Though a few scholars, like Isaac Casaubon, saw that the *Hermetic Corpus* was neither Egyptian nor ancient, most continued to treat it as the source from which Plato drew his central theses.

The 17th and 18th cents. saw the gains of the Renaissance consolidated, especially in the Netherlands. Huge collections of historical and antiquarian treatises enabled readers to follow the growth of debate over Athenian festivals or the Roman constitution, and variorum editions collected the results of textual criticism and explanatory comments, text by text. Some new texts, like the *Cena Trimalchionis* (see PETRONIUS ARBITER), were discovered: textual critics like Gronovius and Heinsius continued to explore manuscript traditions and propose brilliant conjectural emendations; and a vast range of late Greek texts, like those of many Church Fathers and Byzantine historians, saw print for the first time. The good money of the genuine ancient historians gradually drove Annius' bad money off the market. Much attention was also paid to relics that did not come from classical Greece or Rome—like the Egyptian obelisks, sometimes adorned with hieroglyphic inscriptions, found in Rome, in which many scholars thought they could see the relics of the *prisca philosophia*, or the Roman catacombs, in which ecclesiastical historians found the visual remains of an ancient world very different from that presented in the literary canon. Enormous effort went into assembling and interpreting the sources of the history of ancient philosophy, but debate still raged over the extent of the Greek thinkers' debt to the ancient near east.

Despite this intense continued activity, the significance of classical learning was challenged more profoundly than ever before. Bacon, Galileo, and Descartes insisted, in different ways, that knowledge of nature had more to offer than knowledge of texts, and that a modern philosophy and curriculum could not rest on the study of books written in what had actually been a more primitive time. The rise of modern languages and literatures challenged the pre-eminence of the classics. A reading public grew up which felt less at ease with Greek and Latin than with French, English, or Italian. And the undeniable fact that many issues in ancient literature, history, and philosophy had remained the objects of endless debate for centuries called the intellectual validity of classical studies into question. The scholarly response to this challenge took varied forms. Some antiquaries and archaeologists claimed—

not without exaggeration—that their first-hand study of material remains rested on the same methods of exact measurement as the experiments of the scientists. The late 17th and 18th cents. certainly witnessed an intensive effort to explore and record Greek and Roman ruins, as well as the vastly important excavation of *Herculaneum and *Pompeii. Textual criticism benefited from the systematic efforts of Mabillon, Montfaucon, and Maffei to date manuscripts systematically, on the basis of their materials and script.

But the most profound changes took place in what had traditionally been seen as the central areas of classical studies. Historians like Giambattista Vico and Jacobus Perizonius and philologists like Jean Leclerc and Richard Bentley worked in radically different contexts and from radically different assumptions. All of them agreed, however, that the study of the ancient world must become as modern as the New Philosophy. The scholar must read the classics in a critical spirit; must eliminate or alter any passage in a text, however familiar, if the evidence of the manuscripts and of 'reason' did not support its presence; must abandon the traditional narrative of Roman history or the traditional view that Homer had written elaborate works of high literature, if the sources, rationally considered, did not justify them. It became clear that every text—even those of the Old and New Testaments—had changed over time, thanks to human action and intervention: also that the ancients themselves had not fully understood the development of their languages, literatures, and societies. The modern Dutch or English scholar knew his ancient texts too well to believe that they encompassed all knowledge—or even all the tools needed to analyse them. Homer himself, long seen as the first and greatest of classics, was re-imagined as a primitive poet, more like a modern Bedouin than a modern Englishman.

This approach, with its stress on the otherness of the Greek and Roman past, might seem to undermine the value of classical studies. In later 18th-cent. Germany, however, it became the core of the intellectual programme that restored classical scholarship to a central position in higher education. The art historian Winckelmann, the Göttingen professor Heyne, and his brilliant, rebellious pupil Friedrich August Wolf admitted that the ancient world was very different from their own. Only by dropping all familiar assumptions and undertaking a comprehensive study of every aspect of antiquity, from literature to history to archaeology and religion, they held, could a scholar hope to interpret a given text or solve a given problem. But they also insisted that this exercise had a unique intellectual value. By working his way into every nook and cranny of ancient life, by coming to understand the Greek spirit as a whole, the scholar—and the student—would develop his own sensibility and intellect in a uniquely rich and rewarding way, for which the study of the natural world offered no parallel. The value of this new approach was dramatized by a series of brilliant, iconoclastic publications, including Winckelmann's *History of Art in Antiquity*, Wolf's *Prolegomena to Homer*, and Barthold Georg Niebuhr's *History of Rome*. It won the support of the reformer of Prussian education, Wilhelm von Humboldt, and found institutional homes in the Prussian universities and Gymnasien. And it led to the creation of new methods and new literatures in every field: to the production of vast new series of publications, from corpora of Roman and Greek inscriptions and the Teubner texts to classical journals in which specialized results could be presented and debated; to the rise of a newly rigorous textual criticism; to the effort, never wholly successful, to create histories of Greece and Rome that integrated the traditional historian's effort to provide a narrative account of central events with what had been the antiquarian tradition of systematic analysis of laws, institutions, and rituals.

The German classicists were not, in fact, as original as they claimed. Their approach to textual criticism was modelled on that of 18th-cent. biblical scholars, and their efforts to write a new history of the ancient world came after the pioneering models established by two English amateurs, Edward Gibbon and George Grote. England, France, and Italy continued to foster partly or wholly independent scholarly methods and enterprises. In the course of the 19th and 20th centuries, however, the comprehensive programme known as *Altertumswissenschaft* gradually put its stamp on classical studies throughout the western world. Even the sharpest critics of particular German scholars—like A. E. Housman—generally learned their trade by mastering what they saw as the core of the German tradition. Even Hitler's expulsion of the Jews, which did incalculable harm to German scholarship, paradoxically conveyed its methods and results to universities and scholarly communities in France, England, the United States, and elsewhere.

The new scholarship proved as fertile a ground for debates and polemics as the old. Schools developed, whose members proved incapable of seeing outsiders' points of view, and both substantive and methodological questions proved capable of serving as the occasions of philological warfare. The increasing specialization and technicality of the new scholarship also provoked criticism—most notably and influentially from Friedrich Nietzsche, himself a product of it. Meanwhile the competition of modern forms of secondary education chipped away, slowly but inevitably, at the central position of classical studies in the university. None the less, classical scholarship finished the 20th cent. in a condition that would have been recognizable two hundred years before: as an interdisciplinary, rigorous, and creative enterprise.

A. T. G.

Scipio Africanus (the elder), Publius Cornelius Scipio Africanus, son of Publius Cornelius Scipio (consul 218 BC), husband of the daughter of Lucius Aemilius Paullus (consul 219), father of Publius Cornelius Scipio (the father of *Scipio Aemilianus) and of one other son, and of two daughters, one married to Tiberius Sempronius Gracchus, father of the *Gracchi. He was born in 236 BC and is said to have saved his father's life at the battle of the Ticinus in 218 and, as military tribune, to have rallied the survivors of the battle of Cannae (see HANNIBAL) at Canusium. He was curule aedile 213, and in 210 was appointed by the people to the command in Spain, the first person to have received consular *imperium* without having previously been *consul or praetor. In Spain he resumed the aggressive policy of his father and uncle; in 209 he captured Carthago Nova (mod. Cartagena), the main Carthaginian supply base in Spain, by sending a wading party across the lagoon, which, he had discovered, normally ebbed in the evening. In 208, employing tactics which marked a major break with traditional Roman practice, he defeated the Carthaginian general Hasdrubal Barca at Baecula (Bailen), north of the Baetis (Guadalquivir). When Hasdrubal escaped towards the Pyrenees and the route to Italy, he decided not to pursue him. In 206 he defeated Mago and Hasdrubal the son of Gisgo at Ilipa, just north of Seville. Thereafter only mopping-up operations remained in Spain; a mutiny in his army was quelled, and the ringleaders executed. Scipio crossed to Africa to solicit the support of Syphax, and met Masinissa (another Numidian ruler) in western Spain.

Elected *consul for 205, Scipio wanted to carry the war to Africa. Opposition in the senate was led by *Fabius Maximus and Quintus Fulvius Flaccus (consul 237), but he was assigned Sicily with permission to invade Africa if he saw fit. Denied the right to levy new troops, he crossed to Sicily accompanied only by volunteers, returning to southern Italy to recapture Locri (Epizephyrii); the subsequent behaviour of the commander Quintus Pleminius briefly threatened Scipio's own position. In 204 he landed in Africa, began the siege of Utica, and wintered on a nearby headland. Hasdrubal and Syphax encamped a few miles to the south; in the course of feigned peace negotiations Scipio discovered the details of their camps, which were made of wood or reeds, and in the spring of 203 a night attack led to their destruction by fire and the death of large numbers of Carthaginian troops. Later Scipio defeated Hasdrubal and Syphax at the battle of the Great Plains, c.120 km. (75 mi.) west of Carthage. He now occupied Tunis, but was forced to use his transport ships to block a Carthaginian attack on his fleet at Utica, losing 60 transports. During an armistice, peace terms were agreed, and accepted at Rome, but in the spring of 202 an attack by Carthage on Roman ships, and subsequently on envoys sent by Scipio to protest, led to the resumption of hostilities. Hannibal had now returned to Carthage, and after further abortive peace negotiations Scipio defeated him at the battle of Zama (202); peace was concluded on Rome's terms. Scipio received the *cognomen* (surname) Africanus and returned to Rome to celebrate a triumph.

Scipio now had great prestige at Rome. The so-called 'Scipionic legend' (in its later form Scipio is the son of Jupiter) had already come into existence. The capture of Carthago Nova, when Scipio is said to have told his troops that *Neptune had appeared to him in a dream and promised him help, led to the belief that he was divinely inspired. The Iberians had saluted him as a king, but there is no evidence that he ever envisaged playing other than a traditional role in Roman politics. His success, however, meant that he had many enemies among the nobility, some alarmed by the stories circulating about him, others merely jealous of his success. He was elected censor in 199 but his tenure of the office was unremarkable: he became *princeps senatus* (senior senator), a position confirmed by the following two pairs of censors. Consul for the second time in 194, he wanted to succeed Flamininus in Greece, believing that a continued military presence was necessary as security against *Antiochus III, but the senate voted that the army should be withdrawn. Scipio campaigned in northern Italy during his consulship, but achieved little. As an ambassador to Africa in 193 he failed, perhaps deliberately, to settle a dispute between Carthage and Masinissa;

the story that he also went to Asia in that year and met Hannibal should be rejected. In 190 he volunteered to go to Asia as a legate under his brother Lucius Cornelius Scipio Asiagenes. He rejected a bribe, which Antiochus offered him in order to secure a favourable peace; shortly before the battle of Magnesia (188) Antiochus returned his captive son Lucius. He took no part in the battle itself because of illness, but was chosen to present the Roman peace terms after Antiochus' defeat. At Rome there now began a series of conflicts between the Scipio brothers (and their allies) and their opponents, among whom *Cato the Elder was prominent, culminating in the much-debated 'trials of the Scipios'. The accusations involved the embezzlement of public funds and, perhaps, the taking of bribes from Antiochus. It is probable that Publius was attacked in the senate in 187, and Lucius put on trial (in what way and with what result is uncertain), and that Publius was accused in 184, but avoided trial by retiring into voluntary exile at Liternum (in Campania), where he died the following year.

J. Br.

sculpture, Greek (see following page)

sculpture, Roman (see page 651)

Second Sophistic is the term regularly applied in modern scholarship to the period c. AD 60–230 when declamation became the most prestigious literary activity in the Greek world. Philostratus of Athens (early 3rd cent.) coined the term in his Lives of the Sophists, claiming a link between the Classical *sophists and the movement whose first member he identified as Nicetes of Smyrna in the reign of *Nero (Lives 1. 19). The term sophist (sophistēs; verb sophisteuein) seems restricted to rhetors (public speakers, see RHETORIC, GREEK) who entered upon a career of public displays, though usage even in the Digest is erratic, and Philostratus' Dionysius of Miletus (Lives 1. 22) is simply rhētōr on his sarcophagus at Ephesus (Inschriften von Ephesos 426).

On the evidence of Philostratus, whose 40 lives of imperial sophists include several Severan contemporaries, and of other literary and epigraphic texts, it is clear that for these 170 years declamation was not simply an exercise for teachers of rhetoric and their pupils but a major art form in its own right. It flourished especially in Athens and the great cities of western Asia Minor, above all *Pergamum, Smyrna, and *Ephesus. Rhetors (rhētores), whether resident teachers of rhetoric or touring eminences, would draw aficionados in large numbers to private or imperial mansions, lecture halls in libraries, bouleuteria, odeia, and even theatres. After a less formal discourse (dialexis, lalia) which acted as a prelude (prolalia), their formal speech (meletē) was more usually deliberative (Latin suasoria; see RHETORIC, LATIN), recreating a historical situation, invariably from before 323 BC (e.g. Artabanus urges *Xerxes not to invade Greece, Lives 2. 5, cf. Hdt. 7. 10), than forensic (controversia—e.g. should a man who both started and then halted civil war be rewarded or punished? Lives 1. 26), often

involving tyrants, pirates, or rape. Rhetors also had opportunities to deliver diverse epideictic speeches: e.g. Polemon of Smyrna's speech commemorating the dedication of the Athenian Olympieum in AD 131/2, or Aelius Aristides' praise of Rome (26 Keil) and lament (monōidia) for Smyrna devastated by an earthquake (18 Keil). Aristides also claimed to innovate in composing prose hymns to gods. Although many of *Dio of Prusa's over 70 surviving speeches are sophistic, of Philostratus' sophists only Aristides has a substantial surviving corpus (over 40 speeches, the longest running to 230 modern pages) which demonstrates the range covered by sophistic speeches: otherwise we have only a pair of Polemon's declamations ('Who was the best fighter at Marathon?'), a few by *Lucian, and perhaps one each from Herodes Atticus (below) and Adrianus of Tyre.

Many sophists, especially of those written up by Philostratus, were influential in their cities and even provinces, intervening to check civic disorder or inter-city rivalry (e.g. Aristides 23K), or dispatched as envoys to congratulate emperors on their accession or to win or secure privileges for their cities (and often themselves). We know of some omitted by Philostratus who, like his sophists, held city offices or were honoured with statues.

But for the majority teaching must have taken more time and energy than declamation, and it was to encourage education that *Vespasian gave rhetors, like grammatici and doctors, immunities from city offices, judicial service, and priesthoods whether city or provincial, immunities confirmed by his successors and extended to philosophers by *Nerva or *Trajan. *Antoninus Pius limited holders to between three and five according to the city's size (and excluded philosophers), though those deemed of special excellence (agan epistēmones) were supernumerary and, unlike the others, immune even when teaching outside their city. Emperors also established salaried chairs of rhetoric: Vespasian of both Greek and Latin at Rome, Pius allegedly throughout the empire (SHA Ant. Pius 11. 3). To the civic chair of Greek rhetoric then founded at Athens with a salary of a talent (Lives 2. 20, 600), Marcus *Aurelius added c. AD 170 an imperial chair salaried at 10,000 drachmae. From no later than *Hadrian the equestrian post (see EQUITES, Imperial period) ab epistulis graecis or secretary for Greek correspondence was, appropriately, often held by a distinguished rhetor, and this led to a procuratorial career (see PROCURATOR) and further rewards. Some posts, however, and the elevation of sophists to the senate, like their authority within city or province, may be as much attributable to their birth into their cities' governing élites as to their skill in manipulating enthusiastic audiences.

Competition for such distinctions encouraged professional quarrels in a breed already competitive. Such rivalry added spice to performances and tempted fans to trap their hero's rival, as when Herodes' pupils spoiled a supposedly extempore performance of Philagrus by reading out the speech, which had already been published (Lives 2. 8, 579).

Many rhetors' intellectual activities extended beyond

[continued on p. 653]

Greek and Roman sculpture

Greek sculpture *Origins (c.1000–c.600 BC)* Of Dark-Age sculpture, only small bronzes and terracottas survive; unpretentious at first, by the 8th cent. they tend to favour the rigorously analytical forms of contemporary vase-painting. Some wooden cult images certainly existed, though most were perhaps aniconic or semi-iconic. Yet *Homer describes an *Athena at *Troy that was probably lifesize and fully human in form (*Il.* 6. 297 ff.); and a half-lifesize *Apollo, a Leto, and an *Artemis, bronze-plated over a wooden core, survive from Cretan Drerus (see CRETE) as confirmation (*c.*750). This *sphyrelaton* technique is near-eastern in origin. On close inspection the works reveal a careful attention to proportions, a command of volume and mass, and a strong sense of articulation (based on the natural jointing of the core). Converting the flux of appearance into a regular, harmonious, yet visually credible form, this unknown artist is a true pioneer.

The Cretan *poleis* (see POLIS) were socially and politically precocious, and their eastern trade, in which Corinth soon joined, set off a new cycle of experimentation *c.*700. In sculpture, the most popular of these orientalizing styles is usually called 'Daedalic' after the mythical founder of Greek sculpture, Daedalus. Diffused through terracotta plaques and popular in a wide variety of media and scales, Daedalic is characterized by a strict frontality and an equally strict adherence to stylized, angular forms; coiffures are elaborately layered in the Syrian manner. When employed on temples (Gortyn, Prinias), it often follows near-eastern precedent in both placement and iconography.

Meanwhile, Cycladic sculptors were looking to Egypt, receptive to foreigners from 664. After *c.*650 the walking, kilted Egyptian males were adapted to form the *kouros* type, nude and free-standing— supposedly a 'discovery' of Daedalus (Diod. Sic. 1. 97. 5, etc.). Marble was the preferred medium, and adherence to the shape of the quarried block tended to make the finished work look like a four-sided relief. The type soon spread to east Greece and the mainland. In the earliest *kouroi*, as in their draped female counterparts, the *korai*, the Daedalic style predominated, but by *c.*600 its rigid stylization was breaking down as sculptors sought new ways of communicating male and female beauty, to delight the gods or to commemorate the dead.

Archaic sculpture (c.600–c.480 BC) Archaic sculpture seeks exemplary patterns for reality, somewhat akin to the formulae of Homeric and Archaic poetry. The aim was still to make sense of the phenomenal world, to generalize from experience, but in a more flexible and direct way. Each local school developed its own preferences in ideal male beauty. Naxians liked a sinuous contour and clear-cut, elegantly stylized anatomy; Samians massively rounded forms and powerfully articulated joints; Boeotians a craggy masculinity; and so on. Only in Athens did a thoroughgoing naturalism evolve, as a by-product of a desire to understand the tectonics of the perfect human body in their entirety. By *c.*500 Athenian *kouroi* were fully developed human beings, their anatomy closely observed, clearly articulated, and skilfully integrated with the underlying physical and geometric structure of the body.

Korai offered fewer opportunities for detailed physical observation, but just as many for displays of beauty appropriate to their subjects' station in life and value to a male-dominated world. Their sculptors concentrated upon refining the facial features, creating a truly feminine proportional canon, and indicating the curves of the body beneath the drapery. The mainland tunic or *peplos* offered little here, but from *c.*560 the possibilities of the more complex Ionian chiton and himation began to fascinate the eastern Greeks. Soon, refugees fleeing from the Persians helped the fashion to catch on elsewhere, particularly in Attica. Yet by *c.*500, serious interest in the behaviour of cloth had given way to a passion for novelty: sculptors now pursued a decorative brilliance enhanced by a lavish application of colour.

Both types could be adapted for cult statues, and the sources recount much work in this genre, often associated with the new stone *temples that now served as focal points of *polis* religion. Gold and ivory (*chryselephantine*) statues also begin to appear; several have been found at Delphi. From *c*.600, temple exteriors were often embellished with architectural sculpture, first in limestone, then in marble; treasuries for votives were soon enhanced in the same way. Mythological narratives first supplemented, then supplanted primitive power-symbols like gorgons and lions (Corfu (Corcyra), 'Hekatompedon', and Hydra pediments at Athens). Sculptors soon adapted their subjects to their frames, whether triangular (see above), rectangular (Ionic friezes at *Ephesus, *Samos, and *Delphi), or square (metopes of the Sicyonian treasury at Delphi and temples at *Paestum and Selinus); to carve pediments in higher relief and even in the round ('Old temple' pediments at Athens; Apollo temple at Delphi); and to dramatize the story by judicious timing, lively postures and gestures, and compelling rendering of detail.

By *c*.500 the drive to narrate convincingly had permeated virtually all sculptural genres, from gravestones to statue-bases. Hollow-cast bronze also began to replace marble, at least in free-standing sculpture. Its greater tensile strength now removed any technical restraint in the handling of narrative action poses. Only the *kouroi* and *korai* remained aloof—and look increasingly old-fashioned in consequence. A revolution was brewing, and could not be long delayed.

Classical sculpture (c.480–c.330 BC) 'The dynamic of the subject-matter'—the living body, unencumbered by arcane symbolism or religious inhibitions—had always played an important part in modifying the formulaic style, and surely contributed signally to its abandonment, but other factors also helped. Three stand out: a strong commitment to credible narration, prompting sculptors to think of the body as an integrated organism, not a mechanism assembled from discrete parts; a feeling that naturalism was a mixed blessing, requiring corrective measures to preserve the statue's monumentality; and a new quest for interiority, for exploring man's inner self. Around 480 even the automaton-like *kouros* gave way to more subtly mobile, narrative-oriented figures, monumental in physique and grave of countenance, pausing as if to think, like the 'Critius' boy, or resolute in action, like the Tyrannicides.

This more flexible, holistic, and contextual view of man was abetted by a simultaneous repudiation of late Archaic 'excess' in decorative patterning in favour of a rigorously applied doctrine of formal restraint. The new style strongly recalls the *sōphrosynē* or 'wise moderation' urged by the poets. This was an ethic much in vogue after the replacement of aristocracies at Athens and elsewhere by limited democracies, and particularly after the spectacular defeat of the hybristic and excessive Persians in 490 and 480. This early Classical phase is often (appropriately) called 'Severe'.

Sōphrosynē is best exemplified in the sculptures of the temple of *Zeus at *Olympia, carved between 470 and 457 (Paus. 5. 10). Their themes bespeak *hubris* overcome by divinely inspired wisdom, and the participants act out their characters like participants in a tragedy. The expansive rendering brings power to the narrative, while a self-imposed economy of means allows bold distinctions in characterization, unhampered by distracting clutter. The same is true of bronzes like the Zeus from Artemisium (Euboea) and *Riace Warrior A, whose carefully calculated postures are eloquent, respectively, of divine might and heroic potency; and of works known only in copy like the Discobolos (Discus Thrower) of Myron, whose swinging curves capture the essence of athletic endeavour.

Throughout, the aim is to find forms or modes that express the general or typical, yet are open to some variation for individuality's sake: witness the differences between the two Riace warriors. Further progress was the work of two geniuses, Polyclitus of Argos and Phidias of Athens (active *c*.470–420). In his bronze *Doryphoros* or 'Spearbearer', Polyclitus created a new standard or canon (also written up as a treatise) for the youthful nude male. Powerfully muscled, proportioned with meticulous exactitude, composed around carefully calibrated cross-relationships among the limbs, and finished with painstaking precision, it was a paradigm of measured humanity. The Mean personified, it was restrained yet limber, self-controlled yet ever-ready for action. Polyclitus produced many variations on this theme and future generations were to follow it 'like a law' (Plin. *HN* 34. 55).

Polyclitus was remembered as supreme in the rendering of mortals, Phidias as the unsurpassed interpreter of the divine, master of chryselephantine, and propagandist for Periclean Athens (Quint. 12. 10. 9; cf. PERICLES). In his Athena Parthenos and Zeus at Olympia he sought to convey the majesty of the gods by subtle manipulation of the rendering, and by surrounding them with mythological sagas to demonstrate their power. On the Parthenon (447–432) he extended this technique to the exterior sculpture. Athena's power and reach are proclaimed by a closely co-ordinated programme of narratives, and her chosen people, the Athenians, are exalted by a rendering unsurpassed in Greek sculpture for its fluency, grace, harmony of body and clothing, and perfection of formal design. In this way the typical became the citizen ideal.

Phidias' followers, active during the Peloponnesian War (431–404), both pressed his style to its limits and turned it to other ends, e.g. Agoracritus at *Rhamnus. The *Nike of another follower, Paeonius, and the parapet of the Nike Temple on the Athenian Acropolis manipulate drapery to create a surface brilliance that seduces the spectator into believing that what he sees is truth: victory scintillates before his eyes. Hitherto a more-or-less objective analysis of reality, here sculpture becomes a vehicle for the subjective and rhetorical, initiating yet another phase of restless experiment. The pendulum was to swing back somewhat with the 4th-cent. masters, but henceforth, as the ancient critics realized (Quint. 12. 10. 9), it is the phenomena that tend to coerce the sculptor, not vice versa. The war was not wholly to blame: the *sophists had done their work well, particularly in Athens.

Whereas in the Peloponnese the war only benefited the conservative pupils of Polyclitus, in postwar Athens, demand for sculpture was virtually restricted to gravestones, revived around 430 (see ART, FUNERARY, GREEK). Not until c.370 could the Athenians celebrate recovery by commissioning a bronze Eirene and Plutus (Peace and Wealth) from Cephisodotus, a work that exudes Phidian majesty and harmony. Also seeking new ways to the divine, Cephisodotus' son Praxiteles created his revolutionary Aphrodite of Cnidus, proclaiming the power of the love goddess through total nudity and a beguiling radiance of feature and surface. Meanwhile, his contemporary Scopas sought to perfect an acceptable formula for conveying the passions of gods and men.

Scopas was a leading sculptor in the team engaged by Mausolus of Caria for his gigantic tomb, the *Mausoleum. Its unparalleled magnificence announced the advent of the Hellenistic world; a pointer, too, was the hiring away of the best artistic talent by a '*barbarian' patron. The real revolutionary, though, was Lysippus of Sicyon (active c.370–310), who radically transformed Greek sculpture's central genre, the male nude. His Apoxyomenos or 'Body-scraper' not only rocks back and forth before our eyes and extends an arm into our space, but was planned according to a new canon which sought slimness, elegance, and the appearance of greater height (Plin. HN. 34. 65). This and his minute attention to details made him popular as a portraitist, particularly with *Alexander the Great (reigned 336–323), from whose features he created a new ideal that was firmly rooted in reality. Greek portraiture, which had hitherto veered between slight modifications to standard types and a sometimes trenchant realism, was transformed at a stroke (see PORTRAITURE, GREEK).

Hellenistic sculpture (c.330–c.30 BC) The phenomenal expansion of the Greek world under Alexander created a bonanza of opportunity for sculptors. Lysippus' pupils and others were hired to create commemorative, votive, and cult statues for the new kingdoms. Portraitists were particularly in demand to render and where necessary improve the features of Successor kings (Diadochoi), generals, and dignitaries.

Yet the political chaos after Alexander's death, together with the transformations being undergone by the independent *polis in old Greece, sculpture's homeland, undermined the art's social and religious foundations. Furthermore, Lysippus' commitment to the subjective had severely compromised whatever shared artistic values still existed; together with a feeling that little now remained to be discovered, this often tended to promote either eclectic blends of Scopaic, Praxitelean, and Lysippic (in portraiture) or a cautious neo-classicism.

Lysippus' school dominated the Peloponnese and was popular with the Successors, while more conservative patrons could choose the Athenians. As Athens declined, her sculptors increasingly sought permanent employment abroad: *Alexandria, *Rhodes, and the Asian cities were the main beneficiaries. In Alexandria, Attic-style gravestones were popular for a while, and the comfortably-off soon became avid consumers of grotesques; meanwhile, Ptolemaic royal portraits (PTOLEMY I and II) exude an aura of suprahuman calm. In *Pergamum, a liking for the vigorous realism of the local sculptor Epigonus, in monuments celebrating the defeats of the Celts and *Seleucids (237 and after), did not preclude the hiring of the Athenian Phyromachus to create cult-images, portraits, and battle-groups in a turbulent 'baroque' style derived from late 4th-cent. art. Style was now a matter of choice, and form could follow function—or not, as the patron wished.

The devastating wars of the years around 200 mark a watershed in Hellenistic sculpture. Following Pergamene precedent, the victorious Romans looted hundreds of statues and began to entice Greek sculptors west to work directly for them; realistic portraiture and Athenian neo-classical cult-images were most in demand. As the Roman market grew, Greek workshops also began to respond with decorative copies and reworkings of Classical masterpieces for direct shipment to Italy (see PHILHELLENISM).

Meanwhile the main beneficiaries of Rome's intervention, Pergamum and Achaea, celebrated in style. Eumenes II of Pergamum built the Great Altar, probably after Macedon's final defeat in 168, embellishing it with a 'baroque' Gigantomachy (see GIANTS) and a quasi-pictorial inner frieze narrating the life of the city's mythical founder, Telephus. He also installed a copy of the Athena Parthenos in the Pergamene library to advertise his claim to rule the 'Athens of the east'. Neo-classical sculpture was also favoured in the Achaean cities, where Damophon of Messene sought to update the style of Phidias. Athens preferred an even more rigid classicism, while on *Delos from 166 to *Mithradates VI's sack of 88 the Italian business community erected hard-boiled portraits of each other and bought dainty statuettes for their homes.

Attalus III of Pergamum willed his domains to Rome in 133, bringing its sculptural tradition to a close, but the most crushing blow was dealt by the Mithradatic Wars (88–66), which left Greece and Asia devastated and impoverished. Though some striking work was still produced, largely in portraiture, sculptors now moved to Italy in large numbers, creating the last of the great Hellenistic schools, but now on foreign soil and pledged to foreign masters. When the Carrara quarries (NW Italy) opened c.50 and *Augustus officially endorsed imperial classicism after *Cleopatra VII's defeat in 31, the west at last reigned supreme.

See IMAGERY.   A. F. S.

Roman sculpture Roman sculpture was produced in a variety of materials (bronze, marble, other stones, precious metals, terracotta) but it is marble that is seen as typically Roman because so much that survives is in this medium. Sculpture was used for commemorative purposes (for display in public and in private contexts, especially the tomb), for state *propaganda, in religious settings, and for decorative purposes, and various different forms were developed: statues and busts, relief friezes and panels, and architectural embellishments.

Early sculpture in Rome (e.g. the bronze she-wolf of c.500 BC) was heavily influenced by *Etruscan work, and Etruscan sculptors would appear to have worked in Rome in the regal period and the early republic. Rome's contacts with the Greek world, at first with the colonies of southern Italy and later through wars of conquest in Greece and Asia Minor, resulted in a knowledge of and growing taste for Greek sculpture: at first statues arrived as war *booty, but growing demand created a flourishing trade in new work. The taste for sculpture in the Classical Greek style was fostered by the Augustan regime (see AUGUSTUS), and had periodic revivals, most notably in the reign of *Hadrian, but from the late republic onwards there were developments in subject-matter and style that are distinctly Roman, though owing much to Greek precursors. This is seen for example in the development of portraiture in late republican Rome (see PORTRAITURE, ROMAN).

sculpture, Roman Roman marble relief with youth and horse. Although from the 2nd cent. AD, it imitates the Classical style of the Parthenon sculptures at Athens. It was found in the Tibur villa of the philhellene *Hadrian, under whose patronage neoclassicism flourished at Rome.

Perhaps the most original Roman developments occurred in the series of historical reliefs used to decorate major state monuments and to express current ideologies. The taste for the representation of contemporary events first appears in the late republic (e.g. the relief from the so-called 'altar of Domitius Ahenobarbus' in the Louvre, with its scene of a sacrifice at the closure of the census): such a documentary approach continues under the empire, and can be seen at its most developed on the columns of *Trajan and Marcus *Aurelius, where the stories of Rome's wars with the barbarians are represented on a long relief spiralling round the column. These use 'continuous narrative': the episodes run into one another without obvious breaks between scenes, and those on Trajan's Column in particular show great attention to the factual recording of details. However, a more allegorical approach also developed alongside this realism, and some reliefs show a love of drama derived from the art of Hellenistic Greece (e.g. the Great Trajanic Frieze). Realism and allegory appear side by side on one of the most complex and subtle Roman propaganda monuments, the *Ara Pacis Augustae, where 'realistic' procession scenes are placed next to mythological, allegorical, and decorative panels to express the ideals of the Augustan regime. Later state reliefs might combine the two approaches, as in the panels inside the arch of *Titus representing the Judaean *triumph (see JEWS): the carrying of the spoils of Jerusalem is represented in a realistic (if dramatic) way, whereas the emperor in his triumphal chariot is accompanied by deities and allegorical figures. The deep, many-layered relief of these scenes was further developed in the 2nd cent. AD, with experiments in the representation of perspective, overlapping crowds, and the pictorial effects of light and shade. Towards the end of the century (Severan period) repetition and frontality of poses began to be used as a means of clarifying the narrative and isolating and emphasizing the emperor. This tendency is more marked by the time of the tetrarchs and *Constantine I, and is a hallmark of late antique sculpture. The origins of frontality have been variously ascribed to a 'popular' or 'plebeian' style of art in Rome and to the influence of the east, but its adoption certainly accorded with late antique imperial ideology.

Sculptured relief was also produced for private patrons, especially for the tomb: relief panels decorated the exterior walls, and ash chests, grave altars, and sarcophagi were placed inside. A rich repertoire of motifs was used, including mythological (and later, Christian) themes, battles, hunts, genre scenes, and portraits, drawing on Classical and Hellenistic Greek art and contemporary state reliefs as sources of inspiration. Sculpture was also widely used to decorate public buildings, temples, and private homes and *gardens.

In the provinces local styles and schools of sculpture developed. The sculptors of the eastern provinces, especially Greece and Asia Minor, continued and developed the Classical and Hellenistic styles: they travelled widely around the empire, working on major monuments such as the 'Sebasteion' at *Aphrodisias or the forum of *Septimius Severus at Lepcis Magna in Roman *Africa: they also created the large series of eastern sarcophagi exported to Rome and elsewhere. In the northern and western provinces Celtic traditions fused with Roman to produce interesting hybrids, such as the pediment of the temple of Sulis Minerva at Bath (*Britain). On the frontiers the lively but unsophisticated sculpture produced by and for the military (e.g. the Tropaeum Traiani at Adamklissi in Romania) form an instructive contrast to the polished monuments in the Classical style at Rome and in the eastern provinces. See ART, ANCIENT ATTITUDES TO; ART, FUNERARY, ROMAN; IMAGERY; PAINTING, ROMAN.   G. D.

declamation. Some composed poetry, whether shorter pieces, where extempore composition was similarly esteemed, or epic and tragedy. Others, classified apart by Philostratus (Lives 1. 1–8), also lectured or wrote on philosophical issues, whether throughout their career, like the Hellenized eunuch from Arles, Favorinus, or after a 'conversion' from sophistic, as claimed by his teacher Dio of Prusa. Herodes Atticus not only combined teaching and declamation with unusual wealth and power, exercised in an Athenian and a Roman senatorial career (consul 143), but argued knowledgeably with philosophers and grammarians in the circle of Aulus *Gellius. Others wrote history, like Antiochus of Aegeae (Lives 2. 4, 570).

Such literary products need not have been strongly influenced by rhetorical training or the declamatory milieu. Others were: for instance, the exercise of *ekphrasis (set-piece description) found in rhetorical handbooks spawned a whole genre, the descriptions of imaginary paintings, exemplified by the Imagines of the two Philostrati (3rd cent. AD), and influenced Aelian of Praeneste's Varia historia, History of Animals, and (imaginary) Letters. Ekphrasis is also prominent in novelists, two of whom (Longus and Achilles Tatius; see NOVEL, GREEK) are described as sophists by their manuscripts, and in Philostratus' novelistic work on *Apollonius of Tyana. Lucian not only exploits ekphrasis in some prolaliai but developed the dialexis into a humorous art-form: its use for lighter entertainment is already discernible in Dio, but only from Lucian (who claimed to have started as a rhetor) do we have a wide

range of entertaining works of which it is often hard to know whether they were delivered to an audience, circulated as letters or pamphlets, or both. There are other writers, not attested as sophists, whose works' manner and style would surely have been different had they not lived in the Second Sophistic—the periegete *Pausanias, the historian Herodian.

It is clear, however, that the prominence of declamatory rhetoric was not limited to Philostratus' favoured period. It continued as a major cultural phenomenon, little abated by the 3rd-cent. crisis, into the 4th and 5th cents., whose properly sophistic texts are more voluminous than those surviving from AD 60–230. We also already find rhetors active in Greek city politics by the late 1st cent. BC, and the declaimers of Augustan and Tiberian Rome (see AUGUSTUS; TIBERIUS) are documented by the elder Seneca. The change about the time of *Nero may not have been so much one of the rhetors' role as of the theatre in which they played. The Greek world was recovering from Roman expansion and civil wars, Nero's short-lived gift of 'freedom' to old Greece stirred consciousness, and Philostratus' period saw an economic, cultural, and even (in limited terms) political recovery in the Greek world that has fairly been termed a renaissance and is even (loosely) called the Second Sophistic. What was uttered and done by rhetors in this period breathed more confidence and had a wider impact than what went before, and they themselves were prominent among the many elements of Greek culture that found a high place in Roman esteem and society. E. L. B.

Sejanus (Lucius Aelius Seianus), d. AD 31, of Volsinii (mod. Bolsena) in Etruria. Sejanus' father was an *eques* (see EQUITES), Lucius Seius Strabo, his mother the sister of Quintus Iunius Blaesus, suffect consul (see CONSUL) AD 10, and connected with Aelii Tuberones and Cassii Longini. Sejanus, who had attended Augustus' grandson Gaius Caesar in the east, was made Strabo's colleague as prefect of the guard by *Tiberius in AD 14, and soon, on his father's appointment as prefect of Egypt, became sole commander; by 23 he had concentrated the guard in barracks near the porta Viminalis. After the death of Tiberius' son Drusus in 23 his influence was paramount; a succession of prosecutions eliminated opponents (chiefly adherents of the elder Agrippina). Tiberius allegedly refused to allow a marriage with Drusus' widow Livia Iulia (25), but retired from Rome in 26, further increasing Sejanus' influence (he allegedly encouraged the move); honours and oaths were offered to him as to Tiberius. In 29 Agrippina and her eldest son Nero Iulius Caesar were deported; her second, Drusus Iulius Caesar, was imprisoned in 30. That year Sejanus was elected consul for 31 with Tiberius amid engineered demonstrations; proconsular *imperium* followed, and he hoped for tribunician power. In October, however, Tiberius, allegedly warned by his sister-in-law Antonia, sent a letter to the senate which ended by denouncing him (certainly of plotting against *Germanicus' youngest son, *Gaius 'Caligula' (the future emperor)). Sejanus was arrested, the guard having been transferred to Macro, 'tried' in the senate, and executed; the punishment of Livilla and of adherents, real or alleged, followed; even his youngest children were killed. Tiberius acted quickly and in fear of the outcome. Sejanus has been suspected of planning a coup against him; more probably he intended a gradual accession to partnership, involving Livia Iulia's son Tiberius Iulius Caesar Nero 'Gemellus'.   J. P. B.; B. M. L.

Seleucids, rulers of the empire founded by *Seleucus I, governing a vast realm, stretching from Anatolia, via *Syria and *Babylonia to Iran and thence to central Asia. The Seleucids from the start continued (and adapted) Achaemenid *Persian institutions in the army (use of local peoples), in administration (e.g. taxation and satrapal organization), colonizing policies, the use of plural 'royal capitals' (Seleuceia on Tigris, *Antioch, Sardis), the use of local languages (and people) in local bureaucracy; also, from the beginning, Babylon, Babylonia, and the Babylonian kingship were central, in Seleucid planning, to an empire, the pivotal point of which, joining east and west, was the Fertile Crescent.

By the peace of Apamea (188), negotiated between *Antiochus III and Rome, the Seleucids gave up possessions north of the Taurus mountains in Anatolia, retaining Pamphylia, Cilicia in southern Turkey, plus their large empire in the east. It was the complex interaction of dynastic strife, from the later 2nd cent., the advance of the Parthians, under Mithradates I of *Parthia, who had conquered Babylonia by the 120s, and the interference of

Rome, that gradually destroyed the Seleucid empire. Pompey annexed Syria in 64 BC, ending just over two and a half centuries of Seleucid rule.

Rulers: *Seleucus I Nicator, 305–281 BC; Antiochus I Soter, 281–261; Antiochus II Theos, 261–246; Seleucus II Callinicus, 246–225; Seleucus III Soter, 225–223; *Antiochus III the Great, 223–187; Seleucus IV Philopator, 187–175; Antiochus IV Epiphanes, 175–164; Antiochus V Eupator, 164–162; Demetrius I Soter, 162–150; Alexander Balas, 150–145; Demetrius II Nicator, 145–141; Antiochus VI Epiphanes, 145–142; Antiochus VII Sidetes, 138–129; Demetrius II Nicator, 129–125; Cleopatra Thea, 126; Cleopatra Thea and Antiochus VIII Grypus, 125–121; Seleucus V, 125; Antiochus VIII Grypus, 121–96; Antiochus IX Cyzicenus, 115–95; Seleucus VI, Antiochus X, *c.*95; Antiochus XI, *c.*95; Demetrius III, *c.*95–88; Philip I, *c.*95–84/3; Antiochus XII, 87; the final turbulent phase included Philip II and Antiochus XIII Asiaticus, who was deposed in 64 BC by *Pompey.   S. S.-W.

Seleucus I (Nicator: Conqueror) (*c.*358–281 BC), son of Antiochus (unknown), fought with *Alexander the Great in the latter's campaigns from *Asia Minor to *Persia, *Bactria, Sogdiana and, 'India', as a general. Subsequently he was to replay this 'conquest' as he, and his son, Antiochus I, brought the eastern 'Upper Satrapies' of the former Achaemenid *Persian empire gradually under Seleucid control and colonization, wisely negotiating after invasion (*c.*306) of the Indus region a settlement with Sandracottus, founder of the empire of the Mauryas. The detailed interpretation of the terms of this peace is uncertain, but Seleucus ceded the Indus valley, desert Gedrosia, Gandhara, the Swat valley tribes of the Parapamisadae, and east (i.e. desert) Arachosia. See INDIA.

After Alexander's death, Seleucus gained the satrapy of *Babylonia (321), which was to form the core of his later kingdom. There he initially supported *Antigonus the One-eyed, but was ousted by him (316) and fled to Egypt. He regained Babylonia (312) with a small task force in a spectacular exploit and thence took Media, Susiana, and perhaps Persis too; as a Babylonian chronicle shows, fighting against Antigonus continued until a battle (308) left Seleucus in control of Babylonia. Seleucus then embarked on further campaigns to the 'Upper (i.e. eastern) Satrapies', to Bactria-Sogdiana, and the Indus region (above). He founded Seleuceia on Tigris in Babylonia (*c.*305) as a royal capital, returning westwards to join the coalition of 'separatist' generals against Antigonus.

The victory of Ipsus (301) gave Seleucus north Syria and access to the Mediterranean through Syria and Cilicia. He built *Antioch (300) as another of his royal capitals to serve the then limits of his kingdom. Campaigns and colonization by Seleucus, Antiochus, and their officers, continued in the Upper Satrapies (e.g. Media, Bactria-Sogdiana, the Arab-Persian Gulf). See COLONIZATION, HELLENISTIC. Seleucus finally won Asia Minor with the victory of Corupedium over *Lysimachus (281). A new Babylonian chronicle fragment reveals Seleucus' military objectives after Corupedium as 'Macedon, his land,' apparently aiming at the reconstitution of Alexander's unified empire of Macedon and Asia. He launched a campaign, but was assassinated by Ptolemy Ceraunus, who wanted Macedonia for himself.

Seleucus was married to the Bactrian princess Apame, mother of his successor and eldest son, the half-Iranian Antiochus I, a prototype of the dynastic-marriage alliances with non-Greek dynasties that the Seleucids pursued as a continuing policy in their relations with non-Greek peoples in and beyond their realms. Seleucus had prepared Antiochus for the throne since he acted as crown prince (*mār šarri*) in Babylonia before he was appointed co-regent (292/1–281/0), a mechanism that facilitated the Seleucid succession and continued to be utilized. Seleucus' second marriage to Stratonice, daughter of Antigonus' son Demetrius Poliorcetes (290s), seems mainly to have been directed by politics, i.e. a (temporary) pact with Demetrius. It is uncertain if Apame was still alive. However, Stratonice was passed to Antiochus as queen and wife, and Antiochus was dispatched to the eastern satrapies as king with full royal authority (and armies). This is probably to be understood as a recognition of the need to consolidate in the Upper Satrapies and for royal authority to do it, leaving Seleucus free to deal with problems in Syria and Anatolia.

Seleucus was certainly one of the ablest of the Successors ('the greatest king of those who succeeded Alexander': Arr. *Anab.* 7. 22. 5). Apart from his military victories, he took great care to 'respect' and utilize local traditions (e.g. the Babylonian kingship and Babylonian traditions) and to proffer patronage to non-Greek communities and their sanctuaries as well as Greek ones.

G. T. G.; S. S.-W.

senate

Regal and republican Age Composition

In the time of the *Gracchi (*c.*133–121 BC) the senate was a body of around 300 wealthy men of aristocratic birth, most of them ex-magistrates. Although the sources tend to assume that this state of affairs had always existed, in fact it was the product of historical development and change. Since in the early republic there were very few magistrates, and iteration of office was common, it follows that there was a time when either the majority of senators had never held a magistracy, or their number was considerably less than 300. Probably both conclusions are true for the 5th cent. This must cast doubt on the notion that the number 300 is connected with the three tribes and thirty *curiae* (voting groupings); in fact there is no basis for this theory in the ancient sources, and tradition itself implicitly denies it in maintaining that *Romulus, who founded the tribes and *curiae*, chose 100 men to form the first senate.

Very little is actually known about the origins and early history of the senate. Traditionally it was the council of the kings, then of the consuls. There is no reason to think that it was ever an exclusively patrician body. Collectively

the senators were addressed as *patres et conscripti*; since the *patres* were *patricians, it would seem to follow that the *conscripti* were not. The distinction was certainly very ancient, and it may go back to the monarchy. Senators were chosen first by the kings, then by the consuls. Festus (p. 290 Lindsay) tells us that they had a free choice, and that before the *lex Ovinia* it was not considered disgraceful to be omitted from the senate. This can only mean that membership was not fixed, but depended on the whim of the magistrates in office; it clearly implies that before the *lex Ovinia* the senate was little more than an *ad hoc* advisory council. Festus may or may not be right; but his statement is the only evidence we have.

The date of the *lex Ovinia* is unknown, but it was probably after 339 and certainly before 318 BC. It laid down that the censors were to choose the senate according to fixed criteria; only men guilty of serious misconduct could be omitted from the list. As a result membership became effectively lifelong, and expulsion from the senate meant disgrace. The criteria of selection are unfortunately not recorded, but it was probably as a consequence of this reform that ex-magistrates were chosen automatically. By the later 3rd cent. ex-magistrates were permitted to take part in sessions before being formally enrolled at the census. The censors nevertheless retained the right to make up numbers by choosing additional senators, and to exclude persons considered guilty of immoral behaviour or following disreputable professions. *Freedmen and sons of freedmen were usually not admitted. It is also evident that senators had to be qualified for membership of the equestrian order, which meant ownership of landed property worth 400,000 sesterces. *Sulla increased the size of the senate by adding 300 new members and making entry dependent on tenure of the quaestorship; the number of quaestors was raised to twenty to maintain numbers thenceforth. *Caesar rewarded his supporters by admitting them to the senate, which in 45 BC had 900 members; under the triumvirate the figure rose to over a thousand, but was reduced to around 600 by *Augustus.

Senators wore the *latus clavus* (broad purple stripe on the *toga) and special shoes. They had reserved seats at religious ceremonies and games. They were not allowed to leave Italy without the senate's permission. Being excluded from state contracts and ownership of large ships, they were predominantly a landowning class. Although heredity was a strong recommendation for magisterial office, the senate was far from being an exclusively hereditary body; it seems always to have contained numbers of 'new men' (i.e. first-generation senators), particularly among the lower ranks (though for a new man to rise to high office was naturally unusual).

Procedure

The senate was summoned by the presiding magistrates, either holders of *imperium* or, later, tribunes, according to an order of precedence. Sessions were held between dawn and sunset, but were forbidden by a *lex Pupia* (2nd or 1st cent. BC) during the *comitia* (citizen-assembly). Meetings had to take place in Rome or within a mile of the city boundary, in a place both public and consecrated. The first sitting of the year was in the temple of Jupiter Capitolinus.

Sittings were held in private, but with open doors, the *tribunes of the *plebs* sitting in the vestibule in the period before their admission to sessions (4th cent. BC?). A session opened with a statement by the chairman or another magistrate, outlining the matter for discussion. Each senator then gave his opinion (*sententia*) in order of rank—beginning with ex-censors (*censorii*), followed by *consulares, praetorii*, and so on. The senior patrician ex-censor, who gave his opinion first, was known as the *princeps senatus*. After Sulla the magistrate gave precedence to the consuls designate or, in their absence, to a senator of consular rank, and *princeps senatus* became a purely social title open to plebeians. Each senator spoke from his seat. Freedom of speech was unlimited in the republic, but Augustus imposed a time-limit. After the debate a vote was taken; the decree resulting from a positive vote was known as a *senatus consultum* (senatorial decree). Sometimes a vote was taken directly after the opening statement with no intervening debate; and on some issues a quorum was required. A *senatus consultum* could be vetoed by the tribunes. Records of proceedings were kept by the urban quaestors in the *aerarium* (treasury), and in 59 BC Caesar ordered them to be published (Suet. *Caes.* 20).

Functions

The senate's formal role was to advise the magistrates. Its advice covered all matters of domestic and foreign policy, finance, and religion. In the 3rd and 2nd cents. it was customary, but not obligatory, for magistrates (and tribunes) to submit legislative proposals to the senate for discussion, and to obtain a *senatus consultum* before presenting a bill to the *comitia*. The senate could also invalidate laws already passed by pointing out technical flaws in procedure.

Since the senate included ex-magistrates who were effectively (after the *lex Ovinia*) members for life, its decisions inevitably came to bind those of its members who happened to be holding senior magistracies at any given time. And by the start of the 3rd cent. the growth of the Roman state and the increasing complexity of its affairs gave the senate an ever greater control of government business. It was the only permanent body with the necessary knowledge and experience to supervise policy in a wide range of fields. It controlled the state's finances, the levying and disposal of military forces, the allocation of magisterial tasks ('provinces'; see PROVINCIA), relations with foreign powers, and the maintenance of law and order in Rome and Italy. It was the senate that decided whether to extend the period of a magistrate's command (*prorogatio imperii*), and although the people in the *comitia centuriata* had the final say on declarations of war and the ratification of treaties, it is clear that, by the end of the 3rd cent. at least, they merely gave formal assent to decisions taken in advance by the senate. The senate supervised the religious life of the community, and the major priestly colleges consisted largely of senators. The senate received reports of prodigies and decided on the appropriate action; and it was the senate that ordered the performance of special religious ceremonies and decided on the introduction of new cults.

In the late republic the senate claimed the right to wield absolute power in certain circumstances. It could order dispensation from the observance of law, and during the Gracchan period it asserted the right to declare a state of emergency by passing its 'ultimate decree' (*senatus consultum ultimum*), which gave the magistrates unfettered power to act as they saw fit. But these developments occurred at a time when the senate's authority was being challenged by the *populares* (popular politicians), and in the succeeding decades it was completely undermined by armed force. The collapse of the senate's authority marked the end of the republic.   A. M.; T. J. Co.

The Imperial Age Under *Augustus and his successors far-reaching modifications of the social origins and the corporate and individual functions of senators occurred. Despite those changes the senatorial *ordo* remained the most important political and social body in the empire, its first estate.

The *ordo* and its recruitment

By the end of the civil wars the ranks of senators had increased to about 1,000. Augustus initiated a series of revisions of the senate of which the most important occurred in 28 BC and 18 BC. After the latter the size of the senate was fixed at 600, which remained its normal figure through the first two and a half centuries of the Principate. A new property qualification of 1 million sesterces was introduced, which served to differentiate more clearly the senatorial from the equestrian order (see EQUITES). Sons of senators gained the automatic right to assume the *latus clavus* at 17 years of age and to stand, later, for membership of the senate. Sons of senators normally served for one year as a military tribune, then held a post in the vigintivirate before standing for election to the senate (through the quaestorship) at 25. Twenty quaestors were elected each year; from the beginning of *Tiberius' reign the election of junior magistrates (most notably the quaestors and praetors) was transferred to the senate.

The main thrust of Augustus' reforms was to introduce *de iure* a strong hereditary element into the senate. However throughout the Principate some senatorial families were impoverished by over-expenditure, others fell into political disfavour or were eliminated; still other senatorial families had no surviving sons. In addition some sons of senators probably (though this issue is disputed) chose not to try to follow in their fathers' footsteps. Consequently in each generation opportunities arose for new families, through the patronage of the emperors, to enter the senate. Emperors promoted new men into the senate either through the grant of the *latus clavus*, which gave individuals the right to stand for the quaestorship, or through direct adlection. By these means imperial *patronage continuously transformed the social origins of senators.

The influx of new families recruited from the élites of the provinces transformed the geographic composition of the order. Under Augustus the senate remained primarily Italian in origin. Under the Julio-Claudian emperors provincial senators, especially from Baetica and Gallia Narbonensis (see GAUL (TRANSALPINE)), emerged. In the course of the later 1st and 2nd cents. new families emerged from the North African and eastern provinces, though very few senators ever came from the northern and Danubian provinces. By the time of the Severan emperors over 50 per cent of senators were of non-Italian origin. In the long term the social and geographic transformation of the senate allowed the socio-political élite of the conquered to be gradually fused with the élite of the conquerors. See next entry.

Functions and roles

Although financial policy, diplomacy, and military policy became the preserve of the emperors, the senate still exercised certain important corporate functions. It acted as a source of binding rule-making, as *senatus consulta* (senatorial decrees) acquired the full force of law; surviving legislation predominantly concerns the rules of status and of inheritance and the maintenance of public order. As a court it tried its own members, chiefly on charges of extortion. Most importantly it formally conferred powers on new emperors (and members of their families), and the acknowledgement of the senate was, therefore, the condition of legitimacy of any emperor. It also claimed the right to declare them public enemies, condemn their memory (*damnatio memoriae*), and rescind their acts.

Senatorial membership, as in the republic, continued to be a precondition for exercising key individual political and administrative roles. For example the civil and military administration of the majority of the provinces lay in the hands of individual senators in their role as provincial governors (proconsuls and *legati Augusti*). Even in AD 200 29 out of 33 legions were still commanded by senators. The civil and military posts, in Rome and the provinces, allocated to senators were ranked in a clear hierarchy; some were reserved for ex-praetors, others for ex-consuls. The most successful senators politically were those who governed the senior provinces reserved for ex-consuls. Senators also exercised direct influence on the administration, jurisdiction, and military policy of the emperors through their membership of the *consilium principis* (body of imperial advisers). In short, imperial rule was predicated on the active participation of the empire's political élite formed by the senate. Indeed in the 1st and 2nd cents. emperors, when they had no male heir, adopted a senator as their successor (so *Nerva adopted *Trajan who, in turn, adopted *Hadrian). When political legitimacy at Rome broke down and civil war occurred (as in 68–9 and 193–7), it was senior senators who vied for the purple.

The third-century crisis and the later empire

The crisis of the 3rd cent. and major reforms by *Diocletian (284–305) and *Constantine I modified profoundly the political role and social characteristics of the senatorial order. During the crisis many political and military offices were transferred on an *ad hoc* basis to equestrians. This process was first codified by Gallienus and then carried further by Diocletian. By the end of his reign only a few civilian posts, such as proconsul of Africa or Asia and prefect of the city of Rome (*praefectus urbi*), remained open to senators.

Further substantial and complex reforms were introduced through the 4th cent. Under Constantine a general fusion of the senatorial and equestrian orders occurred whereby high-ranking equestrians were enrolled in the senate and senior equestrian officers were converted into senatorial ones. In turn it became normal practice to confer senatorial status on the holders of key military (e.g. *duces, magistri militum*) and fiscal (e.g. *comites* of the *sacrae largitiones* and *res privata*) offices. In consequence the number of senators increased to about 2,000 in the 4th cent. In a parallel development Constantine created a second senate at the newly founded capital of Constantinople whose membership also quickly rose to about 2,000. A new socio-political hierarchy evolved within the senatorial order. By a law of Valentinian I of 372 three grades were codified, namely, in descending status, the *illustres*, the *spectabiles*, and the *clarissimi*.

The senate of the later empire exhibits strong contrasts to its predecessors. Politically, as a corporate body, it ceased to be an effective council of state. Power lay with the emperor, his court, the *consistorium* (imperial council), and the *comitatus* (field army). The residence of emperors at sites such as Ravenna and Milan (Mediolanum) of itself diminished the importance of Rome and its senate. Socially, the enlarged order was far more heterogeneous. Traditional aristocratic families coexisted with *parvenu* military men of humble origin. Although a senator's son was by right a senator (at the level of a *clarissimus*), the higher grades of the order were achieved by the tenure of the appropriate office. Status had become a reward for, rather than a precondition of, high office.   G. P. B.

Seneca (see following page)

Septimius Severus, Lucius, emperor AD 193–211. The Septimii were of Punic African origin, his mother's family (Fulvii) of Italian descent. His equestrian (see EQUITES) grandfather, probably identical with the poet *Statius' friend Septimius Severus, was the leading figure at Lepcis Magna under *Trajan; his father held no office, but two Septimii were already senators when Severus was born (145). One of them secured senatorial rank for him from Marcus *Aurelius; he and his brother Geta had normal careers under Marcus and Commodus. Consul in 190, by now with a second wife, Julia Domna, and two young sons, he became governor of Pannonia Superior in 191 through

[continued on p. 661]

Seneca

Seneca (Lucius Annaeus Seneca, Seneca the Younger) was born at Corduba (mod. Córdoba) in southern Spain between 4 BC and AD 1. He was born into a wealthy equestrian family of Italian stock, being the second son of the elder Seneca and Helvia; his brothers were Lucius Annaeus Novatus, later known as Iunius Gallio after his adoption by the orator of that name, and Lucius Annaeus Mela, the father of the poet Lucan. He was happily married to a woman younger than himself, Pompeia Paulina; the evidence for an earlier marriage is tenuous. He had one son, who died in 41.

He was brought to Rome by his mother's stepsister, the wife of Gaius Galerius, prefect of Egypt from 16 to 31. Little is known about his life before AD 41. In Rome by AD 5, he studied grammar and rhetoric and was attracted at an early age to philosophy. His philosophical training was varied. He attended lectures by Attalus the Stoic and by Sotion and Papirius Fabianus, both followers of Sextius who had founded the only native Roman sect a generation before: Seneca was to describe it as a type of Stoicism. It is not known when he met Demetrius the Cynic, whom he was to write about in his Neronian works. At some time he joined his aunt in Egypt, who nursed him through a period of ill health. About 31 he returned with her, survivors of a shipwreck in which his uncle died. Some time later, through her influence, he was elected quaestor, considerably after the minimum age of 25. By the reign of *Gaius, he had achieved a considerable reputation as an orator, perhaps also as a writer (if some of the lost works can be dated so early), and in 39, according to a story in *Cassius Dio, his brilliance so offended the emperor's megalomania that it nearly cost him his life (political motives have been conjectured). In 41 under *Claudius he was banished to Corsica for alleged adultery with Iulia Livilla, a sister of Gaius, and remained in exile until 49, when he was recalled through the influence of the younger *Agrippina and made praetor. He was appointed tutor to her son *Nero, then 12 years old and ready to embark on the study of rhetoric. In 51 Burrus, who was to become Seneca's congenial ally and colleague during his years of political influence, was made prefect of the praetorian guard (*praefectus praetorio*); and with Nero's accession in 54, Seneca exchanged the role of tutor for that of political adviser and minister.

During the next eight years, Seneca and Burrus managed to guide and cajole Nero sufficiently to ensure a period of good government, in which the influence of his mother was reduced and the worst abuses of the Claudian regime, the irregularities in jurisdiction and the excessive influence and venality of the court, were corrected. Though he ensured that Nero treated the senate with deference, and was himself a senior senator, having held office as suffect consul for the unusual term of six months in 55 or 56, he did not regularly attend senatorial meetings. Nor is Dio's conception of his role as initiating legislation and reform plausible. Rather, as 'emperor's friend' (*amicus principis*), writing the emperor's speeches, exercising patronage, and managing intrigue, Seneca's power was ill-defined but real. His relatives received important posts, as did the *equites* to whom he addressed most of his works. *De clementia* probably gives some idea of the way in which Nero was encouraged to behave himself, but Seneca's reputation was tarnished by Nero's suspected murder of Britannicus in 55 and certain murder of his mother in 59. As Nero fell under the influence of people more willing to flatter him and to encourage his inclination to seek popularity through exhibitionism and security through crime, Seneca's authority declined and his position became intolerable. In 62 the death of Burrus snapped his power, and Seneca asked to retire and offered to relinquish his vast wealth to Nero. The retirement was formally refused and the wealth not accepted until later; in practice he withdrew from public life and spent much time away from Rome. In 64, after Nero's sacrilegious thefts following the Great Fire in July, Seneca virtually retired to his chamber and handed over a great part of his wealth. He devoted these years to philosophy, writing, and the company of a circle of congenial friends. In 65 he was forced to commit suicide for alleged participation in the unsuccessful Pisonian conspiracy (see NERO); his death, explicitly modelled on that of *Socrates, is vividly described by Tacitus (*Ann*. 15. 62–4) who, though sympathetic, clearly found it rather histrionic and preferred the ironic behaviour of Petronius a year later.

Seneca's extant works comprise, first, the ten ethical treatises which are found in the Ambrosian MS (C. 90 inf.) under the name *dialogi*. They are, with the exception of the *De ira* ('on anger'), comparatively short, and their general content is readily inferred from their traditional titles; the dating is in many cases controversial. They comprise (in the manuscript order): *De providentia* ('on providence'), undatable and dedicated to Gaius Lucilius (Iunior), maintaining that no evil can befall the good man; *De constantia sapientis* ('on the constancy of the wise man'), addressed to Annaeus Serenus, written sometime after 47 and probably before 62; *De ira* in three books, dedicated to Seneca's brother Novatus, probably in the early years of Claudius' reign (before 52); *Ad Marciam de consolatione* ('to Marcia, on consolation'), a belated and politically inspired attempt to console the daughter of Aulus Cremutius Cordus for the death of her son, probably his earliest extant work written in 39 or 40; *De vita beata* ('on the good life'), incomplete, addressed to Novatus (now called Gallio) and probably in part an apologia, dating to after the attack on Seneca by Publius Suillius Rufus in 58 (Tac. *Ann*. 13. 42); *De otio* ('on peace and leisure'), of which only eight chapters survive, dating before 62, if addressed to Serenus (whose name has been erased in the MS), like *De tranquillitate animi* ('on tranquillity of mind'), which begins with Serenus describing his moral conflicts; *De brevitate vitae* ('on the brevity of life'), addressed to Paulinus, *praefectus annonae* (in charge of the corn supply) under Claudius and Nero and (now or later) Seneca's father-in-law, dated by some to 49, more plausibly to 55; *Ad Polybium de consolatione*, written about 43 to Claudius' freedman Polybius, in hopes of flattering him into supporting Seneca's recall from exile; *Ad Helviam de consolatione*, addressed to his mother who is consoled on his exile.

Beside the Ambrosian *dialogi*, we have four other prose works. *De clementia* recommends the practice of the virtue to Nero in December 55/6 (after many suspected he had murdered Britannicus): of the original three books, only the first (which has affinities with Hellenistic essays On *kingship*) and the beginning of the second (a technical philosophical analysis of the virtue) survive. The codex Nazarianus (Vat. Pal. 1547), the fundamental source for the text of this treatise, also contains the *De beneficiis*, an elaborate work in seven books, often dry but informative about the Roman social code. It is addressed to Aebutius Liberalis and was written sometime after the death of Claudius, with 56 as a *terminus post quem* for book 2, and before *Ep*. 81. 3 (summer of 64). The *Natural questions*, dedicated to Lucilius and written during the period of Seneca's retirement, deals mainly with natural phenomena, though ethics often impinge on physics, and is of great scientific and some literary interest. The text is corrupt and broken, and the original books, apparently eight in number, have a disturbed sequence. To the same period belongs the longest of the prose works, the *Epistulae morales*, consisting of 124 letters divided into 20 books; more were extant in antiquity. Their advertised recipient is again Lucilius, but the fiction of a genuine correspondence is only sporadically maintained. Though the form was inspired by *Cicero's letters to *Atticus (cited by Seneca), their antecedents are to be found rather in the philosophical letters of *Epicurus and *Horace and in the tradition of popular philosophical discourse (sometimes misleadingly called 'diatribe'). Despite the artificiality of the letter-form, the variety and informality of these essays have made them the most popular of Seneca's prose works at all times.

In a category of its own is the obscurely entitled *Apocolocyntosis*, a Menippean satire written in a medley of prose and verse. It is an original and amusing skit on the deification of Claudius, containing serious political criticism and clever literary parody (even of Seneca himself).

Other prose works have been lost, for the titles or fragments of over a dozen survive. These included letters and speeches, a *Vita patris*, some ethical works, geographical treatises on India and Egypt, and books on physics and natural history.

The bulk of Seneca's prose work is philosophical in content and an important source for the history of *Stoicism. He put his literary skills, human experience, and common sense at the service of his protreptic and paedagogic purpose: though orthodox in doctrine and sometimes learned and technical, his works aim primarily at moral exhortation. The moralizing is given all the force which an accomplished rhetorician can provide and is enlivened by anecdote, hyperbole, and vigorous denunciation. The style is brilliant, exploiting to the full the literary fashions of the day while remaining essentially individual, and has an important place in the history of European prose. Non-periodic and highly rhythmical, antithetical, and abrupt, it relies for its effect on rhetorical device, vivid metaphor, striking vocabulary, paradox and point; the point, a product of the philosophical as much as the rhetorical tradition, is at times refined to excess by the unflagging ingenuity of the writer. Aimed at immediate impact, the structure is often deliberately loose and need not imply an inability to develop a sustained theme. Seneca's contribution to forging a philosophical vocabulary in Latin (see LUCRETIUS) was considerable. The ultimate beneficiaries were the Latin Church Fathers.

His most important poetical works are his tragedies: the corpus contains *Hercules [furens]*, based generally on the *Hercules furens* of *Euripides; *Troades*, combining the sacrificial plot elements from Euripides' *Troades* and *Hecuba*; *Phoenissae*, an unfinished text without choral odes whose two long acts recall both *Sophocles' *OC* and Euripides' *Phoenissae*; *Medea*, close in action and characterization to Euripides' *Medea*; *Phaedra*, the Euripidean myth, but with a Phaedra both more shameless and more repentant than in the *Hippolytus Stephanephorus*; *Oedipus*, close in action to Sophocles' play; *Agamemnon*, unlike *Aeschylus' play in the role played by Aegisthus, the scenes between Cassandra and the Trojan chorus, and the final act; *Thyestes*, with no known model; and *Hercules Oetaeus*, a pagan passion-play whose derivative language and over-extended action suggest rather an imitator than Seneca himself. A tenth drama (the only surviving *praetexta* (historical drama)), *Octavia*, based on the events of AD 62, can hardly be by Seneca, who is a character of the drama. Absent from the oldest MS (Etruscus), it implies knowledge of events that occurred after Seneca's death, and lacks Seneca's richness of verbal invention and dramatic development.

Recent scholarship has argued against judging the tragedies in relation to their famous Greek predecessors, realizing that Seneca did not adapt individual Greek tragedies, but drew inspiration from the whole tragic corpus, especially from *Euripides. More significant is his debt to Roman poetry: he did not admire and probably did not use the now lost republican tragedians; it is more likely that he learned from the metrical and dramatic techniques of Varius Rufus' *Thyestes* or *Ovid's *Medea*. There is unmistakable influence from Ovid's *Heroides* (*Medea*, *Phaedra*) and from episodes of violence and passion in the *Aeneid* and *Metamorphoses*: thus *Troades* makes full use of *Aeneid* 2, and *Thyestes*, while it may reflect Ennius' or Varius' lost versions of the myth, undoubtedly adapts the language and psychology of Ovid's Tereus in *Met.* 6.

The tragedies cannot be dated absolutely, though the parody of the lament from *Hercules furens* in *Apocolocyntosis* implies dating of that early play before 54: Fitch's relative dating based on metrical practice (*AJPhil.* 1981, 289–307) suggests that at least *Thyestes* and *Phoenissae* may be Neronian.

Seneca largely observes a post-classical pattern of five acts, opening with an expository monologue or prologue scene. Acts are divided by choral odes in anapaests, sapphics, or asclepiads: lyric is also used for special scenes, such as the glyconics of the wedding procession and Medea's own polymetric incantations in *Medea*, and the anapaestic monodies of Hippolytus' hymn to Artemis and Andromache's supplication. While the plays show many features of post-classical stagecraft (cf. Tarrant, *Harv. Stud.* 1978, 213–63), and could be staged, discontinuity of action, with unanswered speeches and unexplained exits, suggests rather that they were primarily intended to be recited (wholly or in excerpts) or read. This is also consistent with Seneca's variable practice in indicating when the chorus is a witness to or absent from dialogue scenes and specifying its group identity: *Agamemnon* and *Hercules Oetaeus* have two different choruses.

The plays have been called 'rhetorical': certainly their most conspicuous feature is the passionate rhetoric of the leading characters, displayed both in terse stichomythia and extended harangues. They have been claimed as Stoic, since the dominant theme is the triumph of evil released by uncontrolled passion and the spread of destruction from man to the world of nature around him. Certainly Seneca both praises the beneficial persuasive effect of poetry (*Ep.* 108. 9, citing Cleanthes on the power of verse to concentrate the impact and brilliance of a thought) and exonerates drama from the charge of fostering harmful emotions (*De ira* 2. 2. 5, distinguishing the audience's emotional response as preliminary or conditional). However, although the plays reflect Stoic psychology, ethics, and physical theories, their predominantly negative tone and representation of life makes it unlikely that they were composed as Stoic lessons (*contra* Marti *TAPA* 1945, 216–45.)

The tragedies exercised a powerful influence over the Renaissance theatres of Italy, France, and Elizabethan England, where the 'Tenne Tragedies' adapted from Seneca by various translators coloured the diction and psychology of Marlowe, Shakespeare, and Ben Jonson. Compared with both life and entertainment in the late 20th cent. the violence and extravagance of Senecan as of Elizabethan tragedy no longer seem as shocking, grotesque, or incredible as they did to readers in earlier generations.

Besides the tragedies we have 77 epigrams, a few handed down under Seneca's name, and others attributed to him. Apart from the three epigrams specified as Seneca's in the Codex Salmasianus, their authenticity is highly dubious.

Seneca was a talented orator, statesman, diplomat, financier, and viticulturist, a prolific and versatile writer, a learned yet eloquent philosopher. Yet his style can weary us, as it did the generation of Quintilian and *Tacitus, and as a man, he has continued to be criticized as a hypocrite as he was in antiquity: he preached the unimportance of wealth but did not surrender his until the end; he compromised the principles he preached by flattering those in power and by condoning many of Nero's crimes. Yet, as he says himself, effective exhortation can include preaching higher standards than can be realistically expected, and most moral teachers have urged attention to their words rather than to their example. Moreover, his teaching is more subtle and complex than is sometimes appreciated: he does not require the sacrifice of wealth, only the achievement of spiritual detachment from worldly goods; he advocates giving honest advice to rulers, while avoiding offence and provocation. Moreover, he confesses to having abandoned his youthful asceticism, to giving in on occasion to grief and anger, to being only on the first rung of moral progress. Above all, he conveys, as few moralists have, a sympathy with human weakness and an awareness of how hard it is to be good. For his disciples, then and later, Seneca's power as a healer of souls has more than made up for his shortcomings as a model of virtue.

L. D. R.; M. T. G.; E. F.

the praetorian prefect Quintus Aemilius Laetus, a fellow-African. Twelve days after Pertinax's murder (28 March 193) he was proclaimed emperor at Carnuntum (9 April) as avenger of Pertinax, whose name he assumed. Backed by all sixteen Rhine and Danube legions he marched on Rome, securing the support of Albinus, governor of Britain, by granting him the title *Caesar*. By 1 June, 60 miles north of Rome, Severus was recognized by the senate; Pertinax's successor Didius Severus Julianus was murdered, and Severus entered Rome without opposition on 9 June 193. The praetorians (imperial guard) were dismissed and a new guard, twice as large, was formed from the Danubian legions; three new legions (I–III Parthicae) were raised, one of which (II Parthica) was to be based at Alba, near Rome. This, together with increases in the *vigiles*, urban cohorts, and other units, radically enlarged the capital's garrison. Army pay was raised (for the first time since AD 84) and the men gained new privileges, e.g. the

right to marry. Then Severus moved against Pescennius Niger, proclaimed emperor in Syria in April 193. Advance forces under Fabius Cilo halted Niger at Perinthus; his base at Byzantium was besieged by Marius Maximus with troops from Moesia. By the end of 193 Severan generals defeated Niger at Cyzicus and Nicaea; Egypt had recognized Severus by February 194. The final encounter (spring 194), near Issus, was followed by Niger's death. Syria was divided into two provinces, Coele and Phoenice, *Antioch and other cities that had supported Niger being punished. Severus now launched a campaign against the *Parthian vassals who had backed Niger. Most of Osroëne was annexed, perhaps other parts of N. Mesopotamia too. Severus became *Parthicus Arabicus* and *Parthicus Adiabenicus* in 195. In the same year he proclaimed himself son of the deified Marcus and brother of the deified Commodus, renamed his elder son (*Caracalla) Marcus Aurelius Antoninus and made him Caesar, and gave his wife the title

Septimius Severus, Lucius A scene from the commemorative arch set up by Septimius Severus in his native Lepcis Magna (AD 203), showing the emperor and his two sons conveyed by chariot in a triumphal procession. Military success and its advertisement helped to legitimate imperial rule, especially when (as here) the emperor was a usurper.

'mother of the camp'. This clearly dynastic move led his ally Albinus Caesar to rebel and cross to Gaul with the British army. Severus hurried back west for this final civil war, won at the battle of Lugdunum (Lyon) (19 February 197).

In a purge of Albinus' supporters 29 senators, and numerous others in Gaul, Spain, and Africa, were executed. Severus left for the east in summer 197 for his Second Parthian War, invading in winter and capturing Ctesiphon, on 28 January 198. On this day, the centenary of Trajan's accession, he became *Parthicus Maximus*, raised Caracalla to the rank of Augustus, and made Geta Caesar. The new province of Mesopotamia was garrisoned by two of the new legions (I and III Parthicae), with an equestrian prefect as governor. Two attempts to capture Hatra failed. After a lengthy stay in Syria, the imperial party entered Egypt before the end of 199, remaining for about twelve months: the province was reorganized, notably by the grant of a city council to *Alexandria. At the end of 200 Severus returned to Syria for another year; he was consul for the third time at Antioch, with Caracalla as colleague, on 1 January 202.

Back at Rome in early summer 202 he celebrated *decennalia* with lavish victory games (declining a triumph, although the arch in the Forum had already been voted by the senate), followed by Caracalla's marriage to Fulvia Plautilla, daughter of the seemingly all-powerful praetorian prefect Gaius Fulvius Plautianus. In the autumn the imperial family sailed for Africa: their native Lepcis, *Carthage, and Utica received *ius Italicum* (legal equality with, and privileges of, towns in Italy) while Severus crushed the desert tribes beyond Tripolitania. From 203 to 208 he remained in Italy, holding Secular Games in 204. Early in 205 Plautianus was killed and replaced by Papinian, who, with his fellow-jurists Ulpian and Paulus (see LAWYERS, ROMAN), made the Severan era a golden age of Roman jurisprudence. In 208 minor hostilities in Britain gave an excuse for another war, which Severus supposedly thought would benefit his quarrelling sons. The entire family, with Papinian, elements of the guard, and other troops, crossed to Britain that year and took up residence at Eburacum (York). Severus and Caracalla led two campaigns in northern Scotland, with the professed intention of conquering the whole of Britain; a new advance base was built at Carpow on the Tay, and victory was claimed in 210 with the title *Britannicus* for Severus and his sons, the younger becoming Augustus at last to ensure a joint succession. Long a victim of gout, Severus died at York on 4 February 211, leaving his sons the advice 'not to disagree, give money to the soldiers, and ignore the rest'. See BRITAIN, ROMAN.   A. R. Bi.

Sertorius, Quintus (*c.*126–73 BC), an *eques* (see EQUITES) from Sabine Nursia (Norcia), distinguished himself in the Cimbrian Wars under Quintus Servilius Caepio and *Marius, and under Titus Didius in Spain. Quaestor in 91, then a senior officer in the Social War (91–89 BC: see ROME (HISTORY) §1.5), he was thwarted by *Sulla in his candidacy for a tribunate (89 or 88) and joined Cinna. He shared responsibility for the capture of Rome (87) and subsequent executions, but ended the indiscriminate terror of Marius' slave-bands. He became praetor (probably) in 85; kept in Italy by Sulla's impending return, he criticized, unsuccessfully, the Cinno-Marian leaders for their conduct of the civil war and finally took command of Spain (winter 83/2). Proscribed and driven out (81), he went to Mauretania as a *condottiere*. Invited by the Lusitanians and anti-Sullan Roman exiles, he returned to Spain (80) and soon gained widespread support among the natives, owing to his bravery, justice, and skill in exploiting their religious beliefs. (His white doe was regarded as a sign of divine inspiration.) Through crafty employment of guerrilla methods (and, for naval support, 'Cilician' pirates: see PIRACY) he was successful against many Roman commanders, notably Quintus Caecilius Metellus Pius in Farther Spain, and by 77 he held most of Roman Spain. He tried to Romanize Hispanian leaders and acted throughout as a Roman proconsul, relying heavily on Roman and Italian exiles in the province; creating a 'counter-senate' from among them, he made Spain the focal point of resistance against the post-Sullan regime in Rome. When approached by *Mithradates VI he concluded an alliance, yet refused to surrender Asia to him (76/5). The arrival of Marcus Perperna Veiento with substantial remnants of the army of Marcus Aemilius Lepidus enabled him to take the offensive against *Pompey—now commanding in Hither Spain—whom he defeated at Lauro (77). But costly failures, of his own and his lieutenants, in several pitched battles (76) soon forced him to revert to guerrilla warfare, with waning success after 75. Losing the confidence of his Roman and Hispanian followers alike and embittered by failure, he became increasingly despotic and was assassinated by Perperna.   C. F. K.

Seven Wonders of the ancient world, canon of seven 'sights' (*theamata*) of art and architecture. First attested in the 2nd cent. BC in the *Laterculi Alexandrini* (*PBerol.* 13044ᵛ, col. 8–9) and in Antipater of Sidon (*Anth. Pal.* 9. 58), the canon comprises the pyramids of Egypt, the city walls of Babylon (see BABYLONIA), the hanging gardens of the semi-legendary Assyrian queen Semiramis there, the temple of Artemis at *Ephesus, the statue of Zeus at *Olympia, the *Mausoleum of Halicarnassus, and the colossus of *Rhodes. The concept was developed in individual references to a single wonder and especially in complete lists of seven, sometimes drawn up to celebrate an 'eighth' wonder (like the *Colosseum in Rome in Martial, *Spect.* 1, or Saint Basil's hospital in Gregory of Nazianzus, *Or.* 43. 63 = PG 36. 577).

Later lists keep the number, but not always the identity of the wonders. While a late antique rhetorical treatise purporting to be a guidebook to the seven wonders for the armchair traveller and attributed to the engineer Philon of Byzantium still refers to the seven of the old canon, other wonders like the Pharus of *Alexandria, the labyrinth of King Minos of *Crete, Egyptian Thebes (mod. Luxor), and the temple of Zeus at Cyzicus (NW Asia Minor) first feature in *Pliny the Elder's list (*HN* 36. 75 ff.), the altar of horns at *Delos first in Martial (as above), the Ecbatana palace of *Cyrus the Great first in Ampelius (*Liber memorialis* 8), the Asclepieum of *Pergamum and the Capitol of Rome (see ROME, TOPOGRAPHY) first in *Anth. Pal.* 9. 656.

Christian authors replace pagan sanctuaries with Noah's ark and Solomon's temple (Gregory of Tours, *De cursu stellarum* 1 ff.) or add the Hagia Sophia church in Constantinople (Cosmas of Jerusalem, *PG* 38. 547), eventually listing up to sixteen to accommodate both traditional and new wonders.   K. B.

Severus Alexander (Marcus Aurelius Severus Alexander), Roman emperor AD 222–35. Son of Julia Avita Mamaea by her second husband, the procurator Gessius Marcianus of Arca Caesarea in Syria, b. *c.* AD 209, his names were Gessius Alexianus Bassianus until his adoption in 221 by his cousin *Elagabalus, when he became Marcus Aurelius Alexander Caesar. Made emperor on Elagabalus' murder in March 222, he took the further name Severus and was called 'son of the deified Antoninus' (Caracalla). His mother, under whose influence he remained throughout his reign, set out to recreate a 'senatorial regime', with a council of sixteen. Elderly senators such as Marius Maximus and *Cassius Dio were prominent. The jurist Ulpian became praetorian prefect but, at latest in early 224, was killed by the guard; Dio was obliged to hold his second consulship (229) outside Rome to avoid the same fate and expressed concern at growing military indiscipline at the end of his *History* (bk. 80). Alexander was married in late 225 to Gnaea Seia Herennia Sallustia Orba Barbia Orbiana Augusta, whose father may even have been made Caesar; but she was banished two years later when her father attempted a coup. A major new threat resulted from the collapse of *Parthia and the revival of Persia under the Sasanid dynasty, *c.*224–5. In 231 Alexander launched a Persian expedition. The war, in which he took only a nominal part, ended in 233; although not a great success, it maintained Roman control over the province of Mesopotamia. Meanwhile the Germanic Alamanni were threatening Upper Germany and Raetia. A further expedition was necessary. Alexander wintered in Germany in 234–5, but before the campaign could begin was murdered outside Mainz, with his mother, in an uprising led by the equestrian commander Gaius Iulius Verus Maximinus (February or March 235). His memory was condemned, but he was deified in 238 after Maximinus' death.   A. R. Bi.

Sicily (see ◀Map 3, Bd▶)
1. Prehistory Ancient writers distinguished three indigenous peoples—Sicani in central, Sicels in eastern, and Elymi in western Sicily. *Thucydides (6. 2) attributes an Iberian origin to the Sicans, an Italic to the Sicels, and a Trojan to the Elymi. Archaeologically there is no differentiation of culture between east and west corresponding to the Sicel–Sican distinction, but the Italian origin of immigrants to Sicily in the late bronze age is confirmed by evidence from the Aeolian islands and NE Sicily, showing phases of the Apennine culture known as Ausonian. Surviving Sicel linguistic elements argue in the same direction. In south-east Sicily the pre-Greek culture does not show the same clear Italic affinities.

2. The Greek settlement Despite Thucydides' account, the *Phoenicians did not apparently settle in Sicily before the Greeks, and their colonization was limited to Motya, Panormus, and Soloeis. The Elymi, whose principal centres were Segesta, Eryx, and Entella, became traditional allies of the Carthaginians. From *c.*735 BC (Thucydides' date-indications in 6. 3–5 form the chronological basis) there followed a prolonged period of Greek *colonization. The indigenes were sometimes ejected from the colonized sites or reduced to dependent status; occasionally (as at Leontini) there was peaceful coexistence. Once established, the Greeks and their civilization gradually penetrated and transformed the indigenous area; in many places the process was quite rapid. By the Hellenistic period the island was a Siculo-Greek amalgam. The Greeks exploited the island's economic potential, and Corinthian, East Greek, and (later) Laconian and especially Attic imported pottery (see POTTERY, GREEK) illustrates the considerable trade with Greece. Markets in Africa, south Italy, and (after *c.*500) Rome were also available. Temple-building and rapid urbanization attest the wealth and culture of the Archaic period, and the first Sicilian coinage (see COINAGE, GREEK) belongs to the second half of the 6th cent. The Phoenicians acquiesced in the Greek settlement, but defended their enclave against Pentathlus (*c.*580) and the Spartan Dorieus (*c.*510).

3. Early tyrannies As in Greece, *tyranny emerged, but the aristocracies were tenacious, while the threat, potential or actual, of *Carthage and the Sicels affected internal politics; this in turn produced greater social instability. Early tyrannies in Acragas and elsewhere foreshadowed the despotism of Hippocrates of Gela (d. 491), who was the first of the great tyrants in Sicily. His successor Gelon transferred his capital to *Syracuse. A Carthaginian attempt, at the instigation of some still independent Greek cities, to check Gelon and his ally Theron of Acragas, met with disaster at Himera (480). Under Gelon and Hieron Siceliot-Greek culture reached its classical zenith. It penetrated the Phoenician colonies, and the cities of the interior became increasingly Hellenized. After the deaths of Theron and Hieron the tyrannies soon came to an end. The attempt of the Sicel leader Ducetius to organize a national movement proved abortive.

4. The age of Dionysius In the latter part of the 5th cent. the cities maintained their mutual independence and were democratically governed. But democracy did not strike such deep roots in Sicily as in Greece, and external dangers demanded a more authoritarian organization. The Athenians twice intervened in the island (427–424 and 415–413) on the basis of alliances with Leontini and Segesta, with hopes of ultimately controlling it; the first intervention did not succeed, and the second ('Great') expedition ended in utter failure. Carthage now profited by the exhaustion of Syracuse to attempt the complete conquest of Sicily (409). Selinus and Himera fell in 409, Acragas and Gela in 406/5. In the days of crisis *Dionysius I succeeded in establishing himself as tyrant of Syracuse; the Carthaginians were

repulsed, and Syracuse, which came to control all Sicily outside Carthage's *epikrateia* ('dominion') in the far west, prospered; but the cost was tyranny and the loss of political freedom. (Settlement patterns were altered by all this turmoil; from a remarkable dossier of inscriptions published in 1980, we know that some troops from Campania who settled forcibly at Entella in 404, Diod. Sic. 14. 9. 9, cf. *FGrH* 70 Ephorus F 68, were still there in perhaps the 280s. Their names are partly Oscan but their language is Greek and their constitutional forms look Greek too.) Dionysius' death (367) was followed, after a decade, by civil war; petty tyrants established themselves in the various cities, and the Carthaginians again intervened.

5. The Hellenistic period At this low ebb in their fortunes the Syracusans sent for the Corinthian Timoleon, who defeated the Carthaginians at the river Crimisus (probably in 341) and re-established settled government. His arrangements did not long survive his retirement (*c.*336), and oligarchy prevailed. In 317 Agathocles seized the Syracusan tyranny and subjugated most of the island. When he died (289) fresh anarchy ensued; there were more local tyrants, Carthage again threatened, and the tyrant's ex-mercenaries (Mamertines) carved out a dominion for themselves in Messana. City-state Sicily was in fact in dissolution. *Pyrrhus of Epirus was called in, but despite quick successes produced no lasting effect. Hieron II of Syracuse to some extent halted the decline, but his defeat of the Mamertines brought on a Carthaginian occupation of Messana and was the occasion for Roman interference and the First Punic War (264–41), after which most of the island became a Roman province (see PROVINCIA). Hieron's kingdom remained autonomous and prosperous until his death in 215, when Syracuse went over to Carthage. After the Roman capture of Syracuse (211), all Sicily was unified as a Roman province.

6. The Roman republican period The province was under the control of a governor (praetor) with a quaestor in Syracuse and another in Lilybaeum, but the cities continued to enjoy a large measure of independence with their own self-government. A provincial Sicilian council had no real power. Messana, Tauromenium, and Netum, which had voluntarily accepted Rome's alliance, were distinguished as 'allied' communities (*civitates foederatae*); and five others were 'free' cities (Centuripae, Halaesa, Halicyae, Panormus, and Segesta). Of the remainder some paid a tithe of their grain harvest (*civitates decumanae*) on a system established by Hieron II; the land of others became *ager publicus* (Roman public land), for which they paid rent in addition to the tithe (*civitates censoriae*). Local autonomy was infringed by governors such as Verres (73–1; see CICERO) but generally respected; many cities issued small-denomination coinage until the early empire. Under the republic wheat-growing, vital to Rome's *food supply, was fostered; large *latifundia* (domains) grew up, as a result of big Roman (and Sicilian) purchases of landed estates. These were worked by slaves whose conditions provoked

Sicily Silver coin of Acragas (mod. Agrigento), c.420–415 BC. Coinage and a spectacular series of temples reflect the prosperity of the 6th–5th-cent. BC city, ended—as elsewhere in Greek Sicily—with conquest by Carthage.

the serious rebellions of 135–132 and 104–100 BC. Some of the urban centres were attacked and damaged, but despite these setbacks a majority of the Sicilian towns flourished in the 2nd and 1st cents. BC. The north-east of the island also suffered in 36 when Octavian (see AUGUSTUS) expelled Sextus Pompeius, in whose occupation of Sicily (from 42) he and Antony had acquiesced in 39.

7. The imperial period The island continued to prosper under the empire, governed by a proconsul (later a *corrector*, then a *consularis*), and Latin and Greek culture long coexisted. *Caesar granted the Sicilians Latin rights, and Mark *Antony claimed that Caesar intended to make them full citizens (see CITIZENSHIP, ROMAN), but Octavian was less generous. As Augustus he founded veteran colonies at Catana, Panormus, Syracuse, Tauromenium, Thermae, and Tyndaris (see COLONIZATION, ROMAN), and he gave Latin rights (i.e. some of the privileges of Roman citizenship) to a handful of others. It is possible that a later emperor extended this to all Sicilian communities, but the evidence is fragile. A fixed levy replaced the tithe. *Latifundia*, among them large imperial estates, remained an important feature of the agricultural pattern. Yet village life and smallholdings evidently flourished also, and the population in general was more dispersed in the countryside than hitherto, especially with the decline and abandonment of many of the old hill-towns of the interior. The coastal cities by contrast flourished, at least until the late empire, and the prosperity of the countryside in the 4th cent. is witnessed by luxury villas such as those of Piazza Armerina, Patti Marina, and Tellaro. Grain continued to be the most significant export, although Sicily was now less important to Rome's food supply than Africa and Egypt; other exports included *wine, *timber, wool, and sulphur.

A. M.; A. G. W.; R. J. A. W.

Silius Italicus (Tiberius Catius Asconius Silius Italicus) (*c.* AD 26–102), Roman politician and poet, author of the *Punica*, an *epic of 17 books on the Second Punic War (264–241 BC: see ROME (HISTORY) §1.4), at over 12,000 lines the longest poem in Latin. Before turning to the composition of poetry in retirement Silius had an outstanding public career (the evidence for his life comes from *Martial's epigrams and a distinctly tepid death-notice in *Pliny the Younger, *Ep.* 3. 7). Zealous in prosecution under *Nero, he was the last *consul appointed by the emperor in AD 68, at an early age for a *novus homo* (first-generation senator). In the turmoil of the next year ('the year of the four emperors') he was engaged in tense high-level negotiations between Aulus Vitellius and *Vespasian's brother (Tac. *Hist.* 3. 65); his support for Vitellius did not harm him, for he reached the peak of a senator's career under Vespasian, as proconsul of Asia (*c.*77). One of his sons followed him to the consulate, and there were hopes for the second son, disappointed by death (Mart. 8. 66, 9. 86). He retired to Campania, where he owned many *villas, and spent his last years as an artistic connoisseur, attracting adverse comment for conspicuous consumption. He owned one of *Cicero's villas and the tomb of *Virgil, whose memory he revered (Mart. 11. 48). Many assume that he began his poem in the late 80s on the rather shaky grounds that only then does Martial start referring to his poetic activity (4. 14); the praise of the Flavian dynasty at 3. 593–629 suggests that the poem was either published before Domitian's death (September 96) or, more probably, still not fully revised at the poet's death some years later. Afflicted by an incurable ailment, Silius starved himself to death at the age of 76, perhaps as late as 103. The *Stoicism often attributed to him is based on no external evidence other than a hostile story told by the Stoic philosopher Epictetus about one Italicus, whom there is no need to identify with the poet (Arr. *Epict. Diss.* 3. 8. 7).

With *Livy's third decade (set of 10 books) as the principal historical source, and Virgil's *Aeneid* as the principal poetic model, the *Punica* traverses the entire Second Punic War, casting itself as the fulfilment of the curse with which Queen Dido of Carthage conjures eternal enmity between her people and *Aeneas' (*Aen.* 4. 622–9). A mythological dimension is immediately present, therefore: Hannibal is not just a formidable human antagonist but the hellish tool of Juno's unassuaged hate, and the gods participate throughout. Silius' decision not to follow *Lucan's removal of the gods as characters has attracted the censure of modern critics, but it is symptomatic of his forswearing of Lucan's nihilism in favour of a more traditional view of divine sanction for imperial destiny (debts to Lucan are ubiquitous, however, especially in the Caesarian portrayal of Hannibal). The poem celebrates Roman fortitude by displaying such mighty heroes as Marcus Atilius Regulus, *Fabius Maximus Verrucosus, Marcus Claudius Marcellus, and *Scipio Africanus, and by organizing the mass of 15 years' history to centre on the catastrophic Roman defeat at Cannae in 216 BC (bks. 8–10, with seven books before and after): nostalgia for a simpler and nobler past is shot through with the apprehension that Rome's victory over Carthage held the seeds of contemporary decline.

Discovered only in 1417, the *Punica* had some esteem as a paradigm of courtly virtue until the end of the 16th cent., but for centuries its reputation has been in steep decline, and it is now scarcely read. Recent attempts at rehabilitation have concentrated on Silius' thematic concerns, structural skill, and professional engagement with his tradition. Further systematic and detailed study, especially of his language, is needed before Silius' achievement and stature can be convincingly reassessed.   D. C. F.

Simonides, Greek poet, from Iulis on Ceos (mod. Kéa); son of Leoprepes, grandson or descendant of Hylichus (Callim. frr. 64. 8; 222), uncle of *Bacchylides (Strabo 10. 5. 6). If he worked at the court of Hipparchus, the son of *Pisistratus ([Pl.], *Hipparch.* 228c; Arist., *Ath. Pol.* 18. 1), his career began before 514 BC; his praises of Eualcidas of Eretria (fr. 518) date before 498, his *Battle of Plataea* (frr. 10–17 W²) in or after 479; he finished at the court of Hieron of *Syracuse, and his tomb was shown at Acragas (Callim. fr. 64. 4). Tradition made him live to be 90; most sources set his birth *c*.556 (others *c*.532).

No poem of Simonides survives intact, except the epigrams attributed to him (see EPIGRAM, GREEK); even the *Suda*'s list of works (which should preserve the outlines of the Alexandrian edition) is garbled. But the fragments make it clear that Simonides commanded a wide variety of genres. In choral lyric (see LYRIC POETRY, GREEK), he composed epinicians, of which he and perhaps Ibycus are the first known practitioners; *dithyrambs, with which according to a (Hellenistic) epigram (xxvii Page) he won at least 57 competitions; *thrēnoi* (laments); *paeans; encomia; Partheneia ('maiden songs') and the like (cf. Ar. *Av.* 919). His elegies, which occupied at least one book, included some sympotic pieces (see SYMPOSIUM), and some historical (on the battles of Artemisium, 480 BC, and Plataea, 479 BC). Many epigrams, especially epigrams relating to the Persian Wars (see GREECE (HISTORY)), were collected under Simonides' name; the epitaph for the seer Megistias (vi Page) may be genuine (cf. Hdt. 7. 228. 4). Simonides' clients included cities, individual athletes like Eualcidas and Astylus of Croton (fr. 506), tyrants like Anaxilas of Rhegium (fr. 515), and various *Thessalian dynasts, e.g. the Aleuadae and the Scopadae (Theoc. 16. 42–7). Xenocrates of Acragas (fr. 513) and the Corinthian Oligaethidae (fr. 519A, 21+22) commissioned poems from him, and also from *Pindar (*Isthm.* 2, *Pyth.* 6, *Ol.* 13). Tradition connected him with *Themistocles and the regent Pausanias of *Sparta; poetic enemies included Timocreon (fr. 10 W; Arist. fr. 75).

For the next generation, Simonides belonged to the classic (old-fashioned) poets (Ar. *Nub.* 1355; Eup. fr. 148 KA). He had the reputation of a money-grubber (Xenoph. fr. 21 W; Ar. *Pax* 698 f.), and at some stage Pindar's attack on the 'Muse for hire' was applied to him (*Isthm.* 2. 6, Callim. fr. 222). He acquired also the reputation of a sage, like Bias and Pittacus (Pl. *Resp.* 335e); various apophthegms were ascribed to him, mostly cynical; the saying 'painting is silent poetry and poetry painting that speaks' (Plut. *Mor.* 346f) forms the starting-point of Lessing's *Laokoon*. He was credited further with discovering the third note of the lyre; the long and double letters; and the art of memory (Callim. fr. 64; *Suda*).

What little remains of Simonides shows a professional poet of great scope and range, much in demand over his long life, spanning the tyrants and the new democracy (see DEMOCRACY, ATHENIAN). Ancient critics admired him for simple pathos (Quint. *Inst.* 10. 1. 64), and that appears in noble verses for the dead of the battle of Thermopylae (fr. 531). But the tragic threnody of Danaë (fr. 543), and the devious gnomic textures of *To Scopas* (fr. 542), show other talents; in the elegies, lush eroticism (frr. 21–2 W²) contrasts with the pocket epic *Plataea*, whose form (a hymn to *Achilles introducing a narrative of the campaign) enforces the parallel between the Trojan and Persian Wars, and between *Homer and Simonides.   P. J. P.

sin The modern term has no equivalent in either Greek or Latin. The Christian concept of sin accommodates two basic and coherent senses: offence against moral codes, and action against the laws or the will of God. It presupposes conscious voluntariness, while remorse may be associated with its consequences, interpreted as an expression of estrangement from God. Although some of these characteristics can be found in the Archaic and Classical religions of Greece and Rome, as a whole this complex is not clearly represented. Various aspects are denoted by different terms such as Greek *adikia* (wrongdoing, injustice), *anomia* (lawless conduct), *hamartia*, *hamartēma* (failure, fault, error), or Latin *vitium* (fault, blemish), *scelus* (evil deed, crime), *peccatum* (fault, error), etc. The term *syneidēsis* (Lat. *conscientia*), originally 'awareness, consciousness', developed the sense 'consciousness of right and wrong, conscience' (adopted by early Christianity) only in the Hellenistic and more especially imperial period. The Greek term *hamartia* approximates most closely (but cannot be identified with) our concept 'sin' and was adopted in the Septuagint (the collection of Jewish texts forming the Old Testament) and early Christian scriptures for rendering and developing the biblical concept of sin (cf. Lat. *peccare*, *peccatum*, etc.).

Three of the most remarkable ancient characteristics, as opposed to modern ones, are:

1. In the earlier period voluntary and involuntary offences against moral or divine laws were both equally reprehensible and hence liable to divine vengeance. Evil intention is not necessarily implied in the ancient definition of wrongdoing. The Greek concept of *atē* (delusion, infatuation, through which 'the evil appears good' Soph. *Ant.* 622), which in the early period was often held responsible for human error, was either understood as divinely inspired—thus providing an escape from the problem of human responsibility, though *not* from divine punishment—or as rooted in personal (and condemnable) rashness, being a corollary of *hubris.

2. Closely related is the ancient belief that as far as effects are concerned no clear distinction can be drawn between offences against ethical, legal, and social prescriptions on the one hand and violation of ritual rules on the other.

3. Accordingly, it is often impossible to draw a sharp line between the state of impurity (see POLLUTION) as result of a ritual fault and the state of moral blemish. Murder is a case in point. The earliest phases of (Greek and Roman) civilization did privilege an emphasis on the ritual aspects, and through the ages a gradual development can be perceived towards a more personally felt ethical experience of guilt. That said, even in our earliest source, Homer, there are unmistakable traces of ethical codes warranted by the gods.

Greece In Homer it was especially *Zeus who had the domain of guarding the laws of hospitality in the house and the court and of protecting strangers and suppliants. What happened on the other side of the boundary did not affect him, except in cases of either ritual offence or personal acts of *hubris* defying his honour. *Dikē* (man's duty to his fellows) is not synonymous with *themis* (man's duty according to divine institution). But the two may coincide, e.g. in the sin of *hubris* or disregard of the right of others

(both mortals and gods). However, Hesiod pictures *dikē* as Zeus' central responsibility, even making Dikē the daughter of Zeus. He also presents an interesting mixture of ethical and ritual aspects. In his view, divine vengeance will equally follow both transgression of a certain branch of moral offences, such as ill-treatment of orphans or one's own parents (*Op.* 330 ff.), and purely ritual offences such as omitting to wash one's hands before pouring libation (*Op.* 724). In fact the core of his poem is an appeal to the justice of Zeus: whoever offends human or divine laws will encounter divine anger.

Divine punishment

Early Greece made impressive attempts to bracket together two eternal problems: that of the cause of illness and disaster and that of theodicy, the question of the justice of the gods. In the expression 'By day and night diseases of themselves come upon man, and do him harm silently, for cunning Zeus took out their voice' (Hes. *Op.* 102–4), Zeus can be seen as a designation of blind fate or fortune, making man a plaything of an arbitrary and unfathomable divine power. Otherwise illness is a penalty for evil acts, sent by Zeus in his quality of divine judge. Both options were eagerly exploited, the first being a typical expression of so-called 'archaic pessimism', so characteristic of much *lyric poetry (Greek), the latter providing an explanation that permits control, in cases of sudden unaccountable illness, more especially of epidemics (see DISEASE). These disasters were often seen as caused by the sin of one person (Hes. *Op.* 238 ff., 260 f.), even by a sin unwittingly committed: 'Not willingly am I detained, but I must have sinned (*alitesthai*: the Homeric term for offending a god) against the deathless gods', says *Odysseus (Hom. *Od.* 4. 377 f.). An oracle then might be consulted as to the nature of the unknown sin and the manner of its expiation.

The interpretation of illness as the punishment of sin cannot but raise another question of theodicy: what if patent sinners do *not* fall ill? 'How, O son of Cronus, does your mind manage to award the same portion to evil-doers and just men?' (Hes. *Theog.* 373–8, cf. 1110–11). By way of solution, Archaic literature offers three variations on the theme of temporary postponement: evil-doers will be punished but not always immediately (*Op.* 218 ff., 333; *Theog.* 201 ff.), or the penalty will strike a later generation (*Op.* 284 f.; Solon, fr. 36. 3 West). Combinations occur (Hom. *Il.* 4. 160 ff.; *Theog.* 203 ff.). Although these solutions share the belief that the sinner literally must 'pay' *(apo)tinō* (the common word for being punished), it is obvious that no uniform and consistent doctrine can be vindicated for Archaic and Classical Greece. Various options concerning sin and retaliation coexisted, sometimes in the mind of one person. This is particularly marked in the third variant: the idea of retaliation in the afterlife and the netherworld.

Punishment in the hereafter

As early as in Homer three different conceptions are faintly discernible: (1) the netherworld as a cheerless and gloomy place where all souls assemble, without any connotation of retaliation or reward; (2) the Islands of the Blessed, reserved for the (heroic) happy few, likewise without clear references to any ordeal; and (3) a place where the divine judges Aeacus, Minos, and Rhadamanthys judge the dead. However, with one exception (Hom. *Il.* 3. 278 ff.: general punishment of perjury in the netherworld), the only condemned persons mentioned, Orion, Tityus, Tantalus, and Sisyphus (Hom. *Od.* 11. 576–600, perhaps a later interpolation), are sentenced not for 'normal' moral offences, but as a result of their defying the gods. Their offence is an act of *hubris* against the honour of the Homeric gods.

Remarkably enough the early doctrine of the Eleusinian mysteries (see ELEUSIS), as represented in the *Homeric Hymn to Demeter* (*c.*700 BC), though promising the initiated a blissful stay in the underworld, did not require any proof of good behaviour; from a later period we learn that in this respect there was only one requirement: not to have impure hands tainted with blood. On the other hand, we hear that the Samothracian mysteries required a confession of sins as a preliminary to the initiation: nothing more was apparently needed, the confession being an expiation of the state of sinfulness and impurity.

Most probably it was the Orphic movement (see ORPHEUS) that helped two different solutions to develop: the first was the construction of something that can be called 'hell', with penalties through eternal suffering in mud, etc. Basically different, and no doubt inspired by influences from Pythagoreanism (see PYTHAGORAS), was the idea that evil was a corollary of bodily existence, the body being the prison for the *soul, which is thus punished for sins in previous lives. If these sins are not expiated during one incarnation, the soul transmigrates to another body. Thus, this doctrine of reincarnation provided an elegant solution to the dilemma of divine justice and human suffering. Moreover, it opened an avenue to personal responsibility and an escape from the ritualist group solidarity which involved vicarious suffering for another's fault. Overall, however, the idea of punishment in the afterlife never attained the refinement and popularity that it later enjoyed in Christianity.

Classical developments

The 5th and 4th cents. BC reflected and expanded on earlier Archaic initiatives. We can only indicate superficially the most important tendencies. Fifth-cent. Greek *tragedy problematized all existing ideas on sin, retaliation, and theodicy. *Aeschylus (esp. in his *Oresteia*), fascinated by the idea of hereditary curses, tested ways in which a descendant from a doomed house could escape his fate. *Sophocles explored both the question of guiltless guilt (*OT*) and the tensions between human and divine law (*Ant.*). *Euripides added a theological critique: gods who make unfair demands cannot be gods. Like other thinkers under the influence of the ideas of the *sophists, he demonstrated that gods and ethics are often very difficult to reconcile. In the late 5th cent. this could (but in only a

few scattered instances actually did) lead to atheistic expressions (Diagoras). In this same period the debate about the distinction between the laws of man and those of the gods begins (for instance Xen. *Mem.* 4. 4). It is argued that the unwritten laws are in the hands of the gods and carry their own unavoidable punishment, whereas penalties resulting from violation of human law are avoidable. Others argued that the gods were the invention of a clever politician in order to bind people to laws which could not otherwise be enforced (most emphatically in the satyr-play *Sisyphos* by Euripides or Critias; also in Arist. *Metaph.* 1074^{b}1–8; Isoc. *Bus.* 25).

From the 4th cent. onwards the major philosophical schools inherited from *Plato's *Socrates the basic conviction that 'no one sins willingly', wrongdoing being regarded as an error of judgement. *Stoicism especially puts the emphasis on individual autonomy within a human communion whose cement is the divine principle of Reason (*logos*) which permeates the whole. Here universal laws are identical with divine laws, human life being a divine service. Sin is error, the violation of cosmic laws.

Confession of sins

A wrongdoer was either punished by the law or by the gods (or not at all), but (public) confession of sins was not in vogue in Greek culture. The earliest hints of something of this kind (apart from recognition of *hamartia* in tragedy) can be found in the 4th-cent. *iamata* of Epidaurus: cure-inscriptions detailing the healing miracles of *Asclepius (see MEDICINE §2). In the same period curse tablets (see CURSES) develop a special variant: the prayer to the gods for (judicial) help in cases of theft, black magic, slander, etc., where sometimes the wish is added that the culprit should publicly confess his misdeed. The same idea takes pride of place in the so-called confession inscriptions from Maeonia in Lydia and the bordering area of Phrygia in W. Asia Minor, 2nd and 3rd cents. AD, where we read accounts of private offences resulting in punishment by the god, redressal of the crime or a sacrifice of atonement, and public confession, followed by praise of the power of the god. The influence either of indigenous Anatolian traditions or of oriental cults is probable, as the sin- and guilt-culture of, for instance, the cult of Atargatis, including sackcloth and ashes, seems to be related.

Rome For early Rome a similar state of things can be detected to that of early Greece. Legends abound about the grave consequences resulting from wholly accidental *vitia* in ritual matters. In the Roman *ius divinum* ('divine law'), as in the secular law, a casual slip in a ceremonial action or utterance might entail dire consequences comparable to those assigned to arrogant neglect of the deity. One of the earliest attestations of a movement towards more enlightened views can be found in the *Twelve Tables: they make provision for lenient treatment of a merely accidental homicide (Cicero, *Top.* 64). In Rome no independent reflection on the nature and origin of evil or disaster developed; but from the 2nd cent. BC onwards Stoicism (see above) deeply influenced Roman thought in the field of (social) ethics. See also CHRISTIANITY.

H. S. V.

slavery (*see following page*)

Social Wars See ROME (HISTORY) §1.5.

Socrates (*see page 674*)

Solon, Athenian politician and poet, was of noble descent but, whether or not the tradition that he was of moderate means is correct, came to sympathize with the poor. He was prominent in the war against Athens' neighbour Megara for the possession of Salamis island, urging the Athenians to renewed effort when they despaired of success (*c.*600 BC). In 594/3 he was archon (civilian head of state), and the link between his archonship and his reforms is probably to be accepted, though some have wanted to put the reforms 20 years later. He is said to have spent the 10 years after his reforms in overseas travel, during which his measures were not to be altered: if he continued to travel after that, he may have met Pharaoh Amasis of Egypt and Philocyprus of Cyprus, but if he died *c.*560/59 he is unlikely to have met King Croesus of Lydia (though that tradition is as old as Hdt. 1. 29–33). It may be true that he was in Athens at the time of the troubles in which *Pisistratus first seized power, and tried to warn the Athenians against Pisistratus.

For *Herodotus Solon was a sage, a lawgiver, and a poet; *Thucydides does not mention him. It was at the end of the 5th cent. that the democrats began to think of him as their founding hero: if 4th-cent. writers had access not only to his poems but also to the *axones* (revolving pillars) on which the laws were inscribed, they will have had a firm basis for their accounts of him, even though they were capable of anachronistic misinterpretation, and though the orators tended to ascribe to him all the laws current in the 4th cent.

Solon's *seisachtheia* ('shaking-off of burdens') is represented as a cancellation of all *debts, but should probably be seen as the liberation of the *hektēmoroi* ('sixth-parters'), men in a state of servitude who had to give a sixth of their produce to an overlord: their obligation was abolished and they became the absolute owners of their land; men who had been enslaved for debt (many of them, perhaps, *hektēmoroi* who had defaulted on their obligation) were freed, and for the future enslavement for debt was banned. Grants of *citizenship to immigrant craftsmen, and a ban on the export of agricultural products other than olive oil, encouraging the growth of *olives, will have helped to move Athens from a largely self-contained towards a trading economy (see TRADE). Behind an alleged series of changes in Athens' measures, weights, and *coinage we should perhaps see legislation for the use of standard measures and weights (not necessarily different from those already in

use in Attica); but even the earliest coins are almost certainly later than the time of Solon.

Solon organized the Athenian citizens in four property classes (*pentakosiomedimnoi, hippeis, zeugitai, thētes*), and made these the basis of all political rights, to break the monopoly of the noble families: the major offices were reserved for the two highest classes; the *zeugitai* were eligible for the minor offices; the *thētes* could not hold office but could attend the assembly and *ēliaia* (below). He may have included an element of allotment in the appointment of the archons, to improve the chances of candidates who were rich but not noble. He probably created a new council of 400 to prepare business for the assembly, and provided for regular meetings of the assembly.

He compiled a new code of laws, superseding the more severe laws of Draco except in the area of homicide, and probably extending written laws into areas not touched by Draco. He created a category of public lawsuits, in which any citizen might prosecute, in contrast to the private lawsuits in which only the injured party or his family could prosecute; and he provided for appeals against the verdicts of magistrates to the *ēliaia* (possibly a judicial meeting of the assembly).

Solon shows in his poems that he was trying to achieve a compromise between the demands of the rich and privileged and of the poor and unprivileged, and that he satisfied neither: the *hektēmoroi* were not given the total redistribution of land which some had wanted, but their liberation angered the deprived overlords; the nobles were reluctant to share political power with the non-nobles, and there was trouble over appointments to the archonship in the years that followed; tension continued until the three seizures of power by *Pisistratus, between *c.*561/0 and *c.*546/5. Nevertheless, in the creation of a free peasantry, the weakening of the aristocracy, and the strengthening of the assembly and the judicial system, Solon laid the foundations for the successful and stable society of Classical Athens.

See also DEMOCRACY, ATHENIAN.

A. W. G.; T. J. C.; P. J. R.

sophists, itinerant professors of higher education. From its original senses of 'sage' and 'expert' the word came to be applied in the 5th. cent. BC in the technical sense given above to a number of individuals who travelled widely through the Greek world, giving popular lectures and specialized instruction in a wide range of topics. They were not a school, nor even a single movement, having neither a common set of doctrines nor any shared organization.

Their activities included the popularization of Ionian natural philosophy, *mathematics, and the 'social sciences' of history, *geography, and speculative *anthropology; Hippias was active in all and Protagoras in at least some of these fields. They pioneered the systematic study of techniques of persuasion and argument, which embraced various forms of the study of language, including grammar, literary criticism, and semantics. Protagoras was reputedly

[*continued on p. 673*]

slavery

Greek From *Homer's claim that a man loses half his selfhood when 'the day of slavery' comes upon him (*Il.* 6. 463) to *Aristotle's doctrine of 'natural slavery' (*Pol.* bk. 1), Greek life and thought were inextricably bound up with the ideology and practice of human servitude. Eventually, and incompletely, the notion became established that it was not right for Greeks to enslave their fellow-Greeks, and the correlative idea prevailed that non-Greek 'barbarians' were fitted for servitude by their very nature (not just social or political organization). See BARBARIAN. But that did not prevent the continuing enslavement of Greeks by Greeks, and the language of slavery in the Greek New Testament was by no means a dead metaphor.

'Slavery', however, covered a multitude of sins and life-chances. The ideal type of the slave is the socially dead chattel, ripped forcibly from organic ties of kin and community, transported to an alien environment there to be treated as merely a piece of property or as a factor of production to be used and abused at will, an animate tool or beast of burden with no sense of self other than that allowed by the slave-owner and no legal, let alone civic, personality whatsoever. Societies with large numbers of such slaves, let alone societies based on them, have been very few. The city of Athens and central Roman Italy for periods in antiquity, and in modern times the slave states of the American Old South, the Caribbean, and Brazil, are the only known instances. But even in Athens there were gradations of status and degrees of exploitation regardless of uniformity of legal status.

At the top of the heap were the few hundreds of publicly owned slaves (*dēmosioi*), who served as a token *police force or as other sorts of public functionary such as official coin-tester (*dokimastēs*) in the Agora or clerk to a jury-court. Below them were the privately owned, skilled slaves who 'lived apart' (*chōris oikountes*) in craft workshops established with start-up capital by their owners to whom they remitted a share of their profits, or who were hired out for specific tasks such as harvesting (*sōmata misthophorounta*). Then there were household slaves (*oiketai*), male and female, of whom the males of a smaller household might also work in the fields. Harder was the lot of the agricultural slaves of a rich citizen householder. But worst of all was that of the mine-slaves who were either directly employed by or hired out to work the state-owned silver *mines of Laurium SE of Athens city: for them an early death might be considered a happy release. Reliable statistics of numbers are not available, but a reasonable guess would be that between 450 and 320 BC about 80,000–100,000 slaves of all kinds were active in Attica at any one time (out of a total population of perhaps a quarter of a million).

The Athenian model of chattel slavery became widely diffused in the Greek world, although the size and complexity of the original were never emulated or even approached. The prevalence of inter-Greek warfare ensured that Greek slave-dealers (*andrapodistai, andrapodokapēloi*) had plenty of custom, even if it was rare for a Greek to be removed from his or her native community into permanent servitude elsewhere in the Greek or non-Greek world. On the other hand, the flow of non-Greek slaves into the Greek world continued unabated, giving rise to the popular identification (and Aristotle's flawed justification thereof) of 'barbarians' as 'natural' slaves.

Despite the impression created by imprecision of terminology, or inadequate use of such relatively precise terms as did exist, by no means all those broadly labelled *douloi* ('unfree') in Greece were chattel-slave *douloi*. The two largest classes of these other unfree persons were respectively those enslaved for *debt and the communally enslaved helot-type populations (below). Debt-bondsmen technically forfeited their liberty only temporarily, pending repayment of their debt; in practice, the condition might be permanent and hereditary, and on occasion prompted violent political upheaval, as at Athens in about 600 BC. *Solon's response to that crisis was remarkable in several ways, not least in that he outlawed debt-bondage for citizens altogether. Elsewhere in the Greek world the practice continued and constituted a principal source of exploited labour-power for Greek propertied classes in default of or as a complement to slave *labour.

There were apparently some chattel-slaves in *Sparta, but the overwhelming majority of its servile labour force was constituted by the native helot class. The fact that they were Greek and enjoyed some signal privileges, above all a family life, suggested to one ancient commentator that they ought to be classified as somewhere between outright chattel-slaves and completely free people. But this picture of relative privilege is darkened by the knowledge that at any time their masters might legally kill them with impunity. More important for classificatory purposes is that the helots were enslaved collectively as a community, a feature they shared with several other Greek and native servile populations ranging from Heraclea on the Black Sea to *Syracuse in Sicily by way of *Thessaly and *Crete. There may still be room for argument whether Greek civilization as a whole was 'based' on 'slavery', but the ubiquitousness and centrality of servitude in the Greek imagination as in Greek everyday reality are beyond question.   P. A. C.

Roman Slavery in the strict sense of chattel-slavery, whereby the slave-owner enjoyed complete mastery (*dominium*) over the slave's physical being (*Dig.* 1. 5. 4. 1), the power of life and death included (Gai. *Inst.* 1. 52), was evident throughout the central era of Roman history, and in Roman no less than Greek thought was regarded as both the necessary antithesis of civic freedom and the guarantee of their civic superiority to those who enjoyed it. From this structural point of view Roman society, like Greek, was a genuine slave-society.

Although for no period of antiquity is it possible to determine accurately the size of the slave population, the necessary statistical information being simply unavailable, modern estimates of 2,000,000 slaves in Italy at the close of the republic conform to a slave : free ratio of roughly 1 : 3 in evidence from the major slave-societies of the New World. Slave-ownership was a prerogative of the wealthy, although the scale of ownership was larger in the Roman world than the Greek, and the élite could possess hundreds of slaves. *Pompey's son Gnaeus Pompeius Magnus recruited 800 of his personal slaves and shepherds for the war against *Caesar (Caes. *BCiv.* 3. 4. 4), and the city prefect Lucius Pedanius Secundus maintained under *Nero some 400 slaves in his urban residence alone (Tac. *Ann.* 14. 42. 45). Slave-owning, however, was not confined to the very rich. There is evidence to suggest that artisans in Roman Egypt regularly kept two or three slaves. The Roman naval veteran Gaius Longinus Castor identified just three slaves in his possession in his will in AD 194 (*FIRA* 3, no. 50). Slave-owning was a mark of status to be sought for its own sake, and even slaves and ex-slaves became slave-owners, especially those at Rome who belonged to the *familia Caesaris* and prospered from their favoured status (and see Plin. *HN* 33. 134 for the Augustan freedman Gaius Caecilius Isidorus, said to have owned 4,116 slaves at his death). While the evidence on slave numbers is obviously no more than anecdotal, it suffices to show that there was no social limit on the desire to exercise absolute power over others.

Slaves were procured chiefly as captives in war (see BOOTY), as the victims of organized *piracy and *brigandage, through natural reproduction, and through *trade. The growth of the Roman empire in the 2nd and 1st cents. BC produced vast numbers of prisoners who were transported as slaves to the Italian heartland. Romans, like Greeks, tended to shun enslavement of co-nationals, assimilating slavery to the 'barbarian' character of other peoples; consequently Syrians and Jews were peoples born for enslavement (although, unlike New World slavery, classical slavery was never in itself racially grounded). Piracy is best illustrated from the activities of the Cilician bandits of the late republic, notorious for discharging great quantities of enslaved victims in the port of *Delos, where traders swiftly redistributed them, particularly to the west (Strabo 14. 5. 2). But a recently discovered letter of St *Augustine (*Ep.* 10) indicates how piracy and brigandage were still rampant in late antiquity, and also how demand for slaves had in no way diminished then. Children born to a slave mother (*vernae*) were typically themselves slaves (the status of the father was immaterial); so natural reproduction constantly contributed to the slave supply. To judge from random remarks like those of Columella (*Rust.* 1. 8. 19; cf. Varro, *Rust.* 2. 10. 6; see also AGRICULTURAL WRITERS), slave-owners were sometimes prepared to sanction, if not encourage, reproduction among their slaves when it suited them, and they might allow slaves to enter into informal unions of marriage as a prelude. But the degree of conscious slave-breeding, a highly charged term, is impossible to ascertain in Graeco-Roman society. Slave-traders like Aulus Kapreilius Timotheus (*AE* 1946, 229) operated throughout the Mediterranean, in war and peace, as distributors of captives and home-born slaves alike, at times combining their interests in slaves with trade in other commodities (cf. Petron. *Sat.* 76. 6). At no time are complaints heard of slaves being in short supply, even in late antiquity.

Slaves can be observed in almost every area of human activity, the holding of public office apart, and in a world where capitalist ideas were unknown, there was no concept of competition between slave and free labour; in fact it was conventional in certain contexts (e.g. manufacturing) for slave and free to work side by side. In late republican Italy the extensive development of slave-run *latifundia* (domains) consequent on the growth of the empire (cf. App. *BCiv.* 1. 7) meant that the rural slave presence was very high (although the survival of independent smallholders is now well attested from archaeological survey), and, to judge from Columella's handbook on farming, which gives more attention to slave management than the earlier treatises of *Cato the Elder and *Varro, it was still high, in some regions of Italy at least, under the Principate (see AGRICULTURE, ROMAN). Domestic labour and the dangerous and heavily exploitative work in the *mines were something of a slave preserve; the gold and silver mines in Roman Spain consumed human labour at a prodigious rate.

The slave-owner's prerogative of setting the slave free was frequently exercised in classical antiquity, and at Rome, contrary to Greek practice, the slave could even be admitted to citizenship (see FREEDMEN), although a high frequency should not be equated with a high incidence of manumission, and most slaves were probably not set free; many who were paid their owners a price for their freedom from savings.

Practically all knowledge of classical slavery derives from sources representing the attitudes and ideology of slave-owners. It is impossible therefore to understand fully the nature of life in slavery in Graeco-Roman society. Given the patterns of behaviour observable in New World slave societies, it is likely that ancient slaves were at all times obliged to come to terms with the oppression they constantly endured by adopting strategies of accommodation and resistance in their daily lives. Many slaves must have responded with conscious obedience to the rewards for good behaviour—time off from work, superior rations of food and clothing, freedom—that owners offered them as incentives (Varro, *Rust.* 1. 17. 5–7; Col. *Rust.* 1. 8. 15–20; cf. Xen. *Oec.* 13. 9–12; Arist. [*Oec.*] 1. 5. 3–6), knowing that physical coercion was always predictable if acquiescence were not forthcoming. The element of calculation this required, however, suggests that obedience was not altogether synonymous with passivity, thus offsetting the dominant stereotype. As for resistance, it is most easily recognized in the occasional episodes of open revolt, notably the movement led by Spartacus in Italy in the late 70s BC (see CRASSUS) Their object was not to eradicate slavery but to extricate the disaffected from its rigours. Revolt was a dangerous form of resistance, however, jeopardizing prospects of emancipation and the family relationships slaves constructed. Slaves therefore tended to display resistance more commonly by running away, playing truant, working inefficiently, pilfering, or sabotaging property—annoying and frustrating tactics for owners, but less personally threatening for the perpetrators (e.g. Col. *Rust.* 1. 7. 6–7). Running away was endemic (e.g. *Cicero's slave Dionysius: Cic. *Fam.* 13. 77. 3; cf. the mass flight of 20,000 slaves from Decelea near Athens in 413 BC: Thuc. 7. 27. 5), and slave-owners had to advertise rewards for the return of their runaways, engage professional slave-catchers (*fugitivarii*) to track them down, or do the job themselves.

At no time was there any serious questioning of the structural role of slavery in Graeco-Roman society. At Rome *Stoicism is said to have mitigated attitudes towards slaves and to have inspired humane legislation rendering slavery more tolerable, especially under the Principate. In reality Stoic moralists (cf. Sen. *Ep.* 47) were more concerned with the effects of slaveholding on the moral health of the slave-owners than with the conditions under which slaves lived, while Roman legislation, although showing an increasing interest in the public regulation of slavery, was primarily driven by the aim of perpetuating the slavery system as it was and did little to effect permanent improvement. *Christianity likewise displayed no interest in social change from which slaves might benefit, and the result of the Christian attitude symbolized by the repeated injunction that slaves should obey their masters 'with fear and trembling' (e.g. Eph. 6: 5; *Didache* 4: 11)—a vigorous reaffirmation that slavery was an institution based essentially on violence—was to make slavery even harsher in late antiquity than in earlier eras. See also MARXISM AND CLASSICAL ANTIQUITY.   K. R. B.

the first person to write a treatise on techniques of argument, and was notorious for his claim to 'make the weaker argument the stronger'.

The sophists aroused strong reactions, both positive and negative. On the positive side, the highly successful careers of the most celebrated testify to a considerable demand for their services, especially in providing rhetorical training for aspiring politicians. On the negative, they were regarded, especially by those of conservative views, as subversive of morality and tradition, in view both of their naturalistic outlook on morality and religion, and of their teaching (especially to the young) of techniques of argument.

Various sophists did indeed subject morality to critical scrutiny. Protagoras maintained (apparently inconsistently with his universal subjectivism) a form of moral relativism, in which moral beliefs are true for those communities in which they are maintained. *Plato represents more radical critics of morality in the persons of the sophist Thrasymachus and of Callicles, a pupil of *Gorgias. It is, however, oversimplified to regard the sophists as a group as having shared a generally sceptical or radical outlook on morality. *Xenophon reports Hippias as maintaining the traditional doctrine that there exist certain natural laws common to all societies, while Plato reports Protagoras as holding that the sophist complements, rather than subverts, the traditional educational institutions of the community in their task of imparting the basic social virtues.

As the writings of the sophists are lost, we depend for our information on others, principally Plato, who is a hostile witness. He believed, very probably truly, that the suspicion which certain sophists had attracted had contributed to the unpopularity and ultimately to the condemnation of *Socrates, and therefore depicts the sophists predominantly as charlatans, in contrast to Socrates, the paradigm of the true philosopher. See EDUCATION, GREEK, §3.   C. C. W. T.

Sophocles *(see page 677)*

soul The term in Greek nearest to English 'soul', *psyche* (Latin *anima*), has a long history and a wide variety of senses in both philosophical and non-philosophical contexts. In *Homer, the psyche is what leaves the *body on death (i.e. life, or breath?), but also an insubstantial image

of the dead person, existing in *Hades and emphatically not something alive. But some vague idea of psyche as the essence of the individual, capable of surviving the body (and perhaps entering another) is well established by the 5th cent. (e.g. *IG* I³. 1179. 6; Pindar, *Ol.* 2. 56–80), though without necessarily displacing the older idea and even being combined with it (Pindar, fr. 131 *b* Snell–Maehler). Simultaneously, in medical contexts and elsewhere, psyche begins to be found regularly in contrast with *sōma*, suggesting something like the modern contrast between 'mind' and body.

All of these ideas are found, separately or in combination, in the philosophers. Democritus stresses the interconnectedness of psyche ('mind') and body, while *Socrates regards the psyche primarily as our essence *qua* moral beings. Socrates was probably agnostic about whether it was something capable of surviving death; *Plato, by contrast, offers repeated arguments for the immortality of the psyche, which he combines with the (originally Pythagorean) idea that it transmigrates, after the death of the person, into another body, human or animal. See PYTHAGORAS. Sometimes he represents the psyche as something purely (or ultimately) rational, sometimes as irrevocably including irrational elements. At the same time his myths include many aspects of Homeric eschatology, which may have retained an important place in popular belief. *Aristotle is at the furthest remove from non-philosophical attitudes, adopting a largely biological approach which says that the psyche is the 'form' of the living creature, i.e. the combination of powers or capacities to do the things which are characteristic of its species.

In philosophical contexts, the primary connotations of psyche are probably life, consciousness, and 'self-caused' movement. Psyche, or an aspect of it, is typically made the ultimate cause of all or most movement, whether in the shape of a world soul, as in Platonism (see PLATO), or of god, as in Aristotle and *Stoicism. The chief exception is Epicureanism (see EPICURUS), which makes the movements of atoms themselves primary. It was also the Epicureans, among the philosophers, who most resolutely opposed the idea of an immortal psyche (even Aristotle allowed that the highest aspect of reason might be immortal and divine). Outside philosophy, until the Christian era, the idea, or notions more or less vaguely resembling it, are found

[continued on p. 676]

Socrates

Socrates (469–399 BC), Athenian public figure and central participant in the intellectual debates so common in the city in the middle and late 5th cent. His influence has been enormous, although he himself wrote nothing.

Socrates' philosophy and personality reached a broad ancient audience mainly through the dialogues a number of his associates wrote with him as protagonist. These were numerous and popular enough for *Aristotle to classify them in the *Poetics* as a species of fiction in their own right. But apart from the works of *Plato, only a few fragments survive of the dialogues of Antisthenes, Aeschines of Sphettus, and Phaedon of Elis, and nothing of the dialogues of Aristippus, Cebes of Thebes, and many others. In addition to Plato, most of our own information about Socrates comes from *Aristophanes and *Xenophon, both of whom also knew him personally, and from Aristotle, who did not.

Socrates was the son of Sophroniscus and Phaenarete, of the deme (rural district) of Alopece. Though Plato and Xenophon depict him as a poor man, he must at some time have owned sufficient property to qualify for service as a hoplite (heavy infantryman) in the battles of Potidaea, Amphipolis, and Delium, through which he acquired a reputation for courage. He was married to Xanthippe and was the father of two sons.

As a citizen, Socrates seems to have avoided active participation in politics. He was, however, one of the Presidents (*prytaneis*) of the assembly when the generals at the sea-battle at Arginusae (406 BC) were put to trial for abandoning the bodies of the Athenian dead there. Socrates (who was foreman or *epistatēs* of the *prytaneis* on the crucial day, Xen. *Hell.* 1. 7. 15 and *Mem.* 1. 1. 18, 4. 4. 2; Pl. *Ap.* 32b) alone voted against the illegal motion to try the generals as a single group, and the generals were executed. After the defeat of Athens in the Peloponnesian War (404 BC), he openly ignored an order by the Thirty Tyrants to arrest an innocent citizen (Pl. *Ap.* 32c–d).

Socrates' circle included a number of figures who turned against democracy in Athens, including Critias, Charmides, and *Alcibiades. (See OLIGARCHY; DEMOCRACY, ATHENIAN.) This may well have been the underlying reason why he himself was tried and put to death by drinking hemlock in 399 BC. He was charged with impiety, specifically with introducing new gods and corrupting young men. This charge may have masked the political motives of his accusers, since the amnesty of 403 BC prohibited prosecution for political offences committed before that date.

Socrates' execution prompted Plato and Xenophon to create portraits intended to refute the formal charge under which he was tried and to counter his popular image, which may have been inspired by Aristophanes' *Clouds*. Aristophanes had depicted Socrates engaged in natural philosophy and willing to

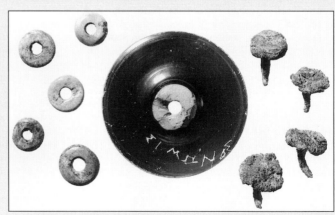

Socrates Shoe nails and the foot of a 5th-cent. cup inscribed 'Simon's'. The findspot, just off the *agora of Athens, is plausibly identified as the shop of Simon the cobbler where Socrates taught. The setting brings out the extreme informality of the Socratic 'classroom'. Specialized buildings for Greek higher education only begin to appear in the 4th cent. BC (see ACADEMY).

teach his students how 'to make the weaker argument stronger'—a commonplace charge against the *sophists. Both Plato and Xenophon were intent on distinguishing Socrates as radically as possible from other members of the sophistic movement, with whom he may actually have had some affinities. But their strategies differ. In both authors, Socrates devotes himself, like the sophists, to dialectical argument and the drawing of distinctions. In both, he refuses, unlike the sophists, to receive payment. In Xenophon, however, he uses argument to support, in contrast to the sophists, a traditional and conventional understanding of the virtues. In Plato, on the other hand, it is a serious question whether he holds any views of his own, and his main difference from the sophists is that, unlike them, he never presents himself as a teacher of any subject.

Plato's and Xenophon's portraits, inconsistent as they are with Aristophanes', are also inconsistent with each other. This is the root of 'the Socratic problem', the question whether we can ever capture the personality and philosophy of the historical Socrates or whether we must limit ourselves to the interpretation of one or another of his literary representations. For various reasons, in the mid-19th cent. Plato replaced Xenophon as the most reliable witness for the historical Socrates, even though it is accepted that our knowledge of the latter can be at best a matter of speculation. And, though recent attempts to rehabilitate Xenophon are not lacking, most contemporary scholars turn to Plato for information on Socrates' ideas and character.

That character is cool, distant, reticent, and ironic, in contrast to Xenophon's more conventional, straightforward, almost avuncular figure. Plato's Socrates refrains from expounding complicated positive views of his own, preferring instead to question those who claim to have such views themselves. In Plato's early or 'Socratic' dialogues his questions mainly concern the nature and teachability of *aretē* ('virtue', 'excellence', or perhaps 'success') and what produces it, both in one's person and in one's activities, and its species—courage, wisdom, piety, self-control, and the like. By means of the procedure of question and answer which came to be known as the *elenchus*, Socrates refutes all those who claim to know what *aretē* is by showing their views to be internally inconsistent.

The Platonic Socrates is utterly serious about *aretē* and the nature of the good and happy life. His commitment to do what is, by his best lights, the right thing to do in all cases is unwavering. This commitment ultimately cost him his life: according to Plato's *Apology*, he antagonized his jury by insisting that his life had been as good as any human being's and that far from having committed any wrongs he had brought the greatest benefits to Athens.

Socrates seems to have been convinced that wisdom and virtue were ultimately the same—that if one knows what the good is, one will always do it. His argument was that the good, or *aretē*, either leads to or is itself part of the happy life. Since everyone wants to be happy above everything else, no one who knows what the good is will not choose to do it. This 'intellectualist' approach to ethics implies that there is no such thing as 'weakness of the will'. It is impossible to know the better and choose the worse: the only reason people choose a worse course of action is that they are ignorant of what is better. This is one of the 'Socratic paradoxes', which contradict everyday experience but have proved surprisingly intransigent to analysis and refutation.

Plato's Socrates consistently denied that he had the knowledge of *aretē* that he considered necessary for the good and happy life. He sometimes referred to this knowledge as 'divine', in opposition to the 'human' knowledge he himself possessed and which consisted in his awareness of his own ignorance. This, he claimed, made him wiser than others, who were both ignorant of *aretē* and ignorant of their very ignorance. In the *Apology*, he claimed that this was the meaning of the *Delphic oracle saying that no one in Athens was wiser that he was.

Socrates often, in both Plato and Xenophon, referred to a 'divine sign', a *daimonion*, which prevented him from taking certain courses of action—he attributes his reluctance to participate in active politics to this sign's intervention. His religious views, even though they sometimes overlapped with those of tradition (he acknowledged the authority of *Apollo, for example, when he received the Delphic oracle), must have been quite novel, since he appears to have thought that the gods could never cause evil or misery to each other or to human beings. He also seems, as we see in Plato's *Euthyphro*, to claim that the gods' approval or disapproval does not render actions right or wrong. On the contrary, rightness and wrongness are established independently, and the gods, knowing what these are, both engage in the former and shun the latter and approve of human beings for acting likewise.

Socrates' moral seriousness is counterbalanced by a worldly personality who enjoys good food and company—goods which he is also willing to forgo without complaint if they are not available or if they conflict with the much more important pursuit of *aretē*. He had an uncanny ability, as we see in both Plato and Xenophon, not to do anything wrong, and his relation to positive philosophical views was fundamentally ambiguous. These features, along with the vividness with which Plato portrays his complex personality, are doubtless responsible for the fact that so many ancient philosophical schools, from the Academic Sceptics and the Cyrenaics to the Stoics (see STOICISM) and the *Cynics, considered him as the person most closely approximating their respective ideal.

With the renewed study of Greek texts in the Renaissance, Socrates became an influence on modern philosophy as well. He provides the first model of a philosopher primarily devoted to the pursuit of ethical issues. His pursuit is systematic, and his emphasis on the necessity of knowing the definitions of the virtues if we are to decide securely what does and what does not fall under them provided an impetus for the development of logic. In addition, he still constitutes the paradigmatic figure in whom philosophy, even in its most abstract manifestations, is never severed from the concerns of life. He lived and—most importantly—he died in accordance with his philosophical principles. Plato's lively portrait makes it believable that such a life is possible. But since his principles are not always clear and we cannot be certain whether he himself knew exactly what they were, Socrates continues to constitute a mystery with which anyone interested in philosophy or in the writings of the Greeks must contend.   A. N.

chiefly in the context of mystery or ecstatic religion (see ECSTASY; MYSTERIES), and in literature reflecting influence from such sources.   C. J. R.

Spain (see ◀Map 5▶)

Prehistory The geographical diversity of the Iberian peninsula enforced cultural heterogeneity. Native peoples drew upon abundant metal resources and rich agricultural areas to achieve a cultural balance between tradition and foreign influence. This was the basis for the emergence of the bronze-age Argaric culture (2nd millennium BC) of the south-east, the Atlantic bronze-age complex (early 1st millennium BC), and the arrival of the Urnfields in the north-east (early 1st millennium BC). Contact with the *Phoenicians and Greeks gave rise to the Tartessus cultural grouping and eventually the urbanized Iberian peoples (5th cent. BC onwards) of the Mediterranean coast. The culture and later urbanization of central (including the Celtiberians), western, northern, and some parts of southern Iberia were conditioned by the movement of Celtic peoples or cultural types from *c*.500 BC onwards.

Phoenicians, Greeks, Carthaginians Traditionally Phoenicians from Tyre founded Gades (Cadiz) *c*.1100 BC, although archaeologists have lowered the date to the 8th cent. BC. Nine further colonies were later established along the coast of southern Spain between Abdera and the river Guadalhorce, and at Ebusus (Ibiza). These traded with Tartessus until the 6th cent. BC, when waning Phoenician power was replaced by that of *Carthage. In the mid-6th cent. BC Greeks from Phocaea founded colonies in Iberia, notably at Emporion, Rhode (Roses), and Maenace (near Málaga), the latter perhaps an attempt to profit from the Phoenician decline. Carthaginian power in Iberia was enhanced with the conquests in the south by Hamilcar Barca and *Hannibal from 237 BC. These culminated in the foundation of Carthago Nova (Cartagena), as Carthage mobilized Iberian manpower and metal resources for the attack on Rome. The Second Punic War (see ROME (HISTORY) §1.4), starting from Hannibal's siege of Rome's ally Saguntum and his approach to the Ebro, continued in the Iberian theatre until Carthage was driven out by *Scipio Africanus in 206 BC.

The Roman provinces Roman territory was formally constituted as two separate provinces, Hispania Citerior (the eastern coastal strip) and Hispania Ulterior (the south-east coast and the Guadalquivir valley) in 197 BC. Both provinces were gradually extended inland in rapacious and reactive campaigns against native peoples and tribes bordering the provinces, culminating in the Lusitanian (155–139 BC) and Celtiberian (155–133 BC) wars. This left the greater part of Iberia in Roman hands. Further conquest was halted and further operations—sorties by triumph-hunting generals, and *Caesar's civil war against the Pompeians (49–45 BC)—were not attempts at expansion. Systematic exploitation of the provinces appears not to have begun before the 170s BC. Tribute eventually comprised a fixed money payment and

[*continued on p. 681*]

Sophocles

Sophocles, Athenian tragic playwright.

Career Sophocles' career in the theatre was a remarkably long one. He first competed against *Aeschylus in 468 BC (*FGrH* 239 *Marm. Par.* A 56; Plut. *Cim.* 8. 7: also his first victory in the competition) more than a decade before Aeschylus' death; he lived to compete for the last time at the Dionysia festival of 406 BC dressing his chorus and actors in mourning, we are told, to mark the death of *Euripides, news of which had just reached Athens (*Life of Eur.* 3. 11 ff., ed. E. Schwartz, *Scholia in Euripidem*, 1 (1887)). He died a few months later (Ar. *Frogs* 82; hyp. 2 (second hypothesis ('preface')) to the *Oedipus at Colonos*); he was born in the 490s BC (probably 496 or 495: *Marm. Par.* A 56).

He wrote more than 120 plays (*Suda*) and won at least 20 victories, 18 at the City Dionysia (*IG* 2². 2325): he was thus markedly the most successful of the three great 5th-cent. playwrights. He was second often and never third (i.e. last). He is said to have given up acting in his own plays early in his career (because he did not have a sufficiently powerful voice) and to have written frequently for a particular actor, Tlepolemus, so as to draw on his strengths as a performer (Schol. Ar. *Clouds* 1267). He also figures in the public life of Athens when already in his fifties: he was one of the Treasurers of Athena in 443–442 BC and a general (*stratēgos*), with *Pericles, probably in 441/0 (*FGrH* 324 Androtion F 38), during the revolt of *Samos. In the political crisis that followed the defeat of the Athenian armada at Syracuse in 413 he is said to have been one of the ten 'advisers' (*symbouloi*) appointed to deal with the state of emergency (Arist. *Rhet.* 1419ª25). There are a number of stories of his friendships with other leading figures of the day, e.g. with the younger tragic playwright, Ion of Chios, who wrote a memoir of his conversations with him (Athen. 13. 603 ff.: cf. the scene in *Plato in which Cephalus, the father of the orator *Lysias, reports having been present at a conversation which included the aged Sophocles (Pl. *Resp.* 1. 329a–c)). He was apparently a priest of the hero Halon (Life) and welcomed the new cult of the healing god *Asclepius and the snake which symbolized him into his own house while a sanctuary was built (Plut. *Num.* 3: probably in 420–419). After his death he was given the honours of a hero cult himself, with the new name Dexion (*Etym. Magn.*). We must be wary of ancient 'biographical' data (many of which are cautionary fictions: M. Lefkowitz, *Lives of the Greek Poets* (1981)) but with Sophocles there seems to be just enough reliable material to construct a public persona.

Plays Paradoxically facts are scarcer when it comes to Sophocles' theatrical output. We have dates for only two of the seven surviving plays (the last two): a victory with *Philoctetes* in 409 (hyp.) and another with *Oedipus at Colonos* in 401 (a posthumous victory, the play being produced by his grandson, also called Sophocles: hyp. 2). We know of victories in 447 (*IG* 2². 2318: plays unknown) and 438 (over Euripides: hyp. Eur. *Alc.*: plays again unknown); and with *Antigone* at a date unknown; also of defeats in 459 (*POxy.* 2256, fr. 3; by Aeschylus with the *Supplices* trilogy; Sophocles' plays of this year are uncertain); in 431 (hyp. Eur. *Med.*; by Euphorion, Aeschylus' son: Euripides was third) and in the year of *Oedipus Tyrannus* (by Philocles, Aeschylus' nephew; date unknown). We have no evidence at all for the dates of *Ajax, Oedipus Tyrannus, Electra*, and *Trachiniae* and only unreliable and unconvincing anecdotal evidence for *Antigone*.

Theatricality Readings of Sophocles in the earlier part of this century tended to be determined by the influence of *Aristophanes' passing remark about him, only months after his death, as 'easy-going' or 'relaxed' (*Frogs* 82) and by the judgement of later ancient critics of style which identified Sophocles' with the 'middle, well-blended' style, neither grand and austere (like Aeschylus and *Thucydides) nor smooth and pedestrian (like *Isocrates and Euripides: Dion. Hal., *Comp.* 21–4; cf. Dio Chrys. *Or.* 52. 15, for a reading of *Philoctetes* which sets Sophocles 'midway between' Aeschylus and Euripides). Sophocles thus emerged as 'middling'—stable, harmonious, and at ease with experience. Such readings ignored the frequently discomforting nature of much Sophoclean theatre (esp. in *Antigone*, *Oedipus Tyrannus*, and *Trachiniae*, for example) and largely denied his insistent theatricality. Sophocles is the master of the enacted metaphor—metaphors of blindness in the two *Oedipus plays and *Antigone*, of bestiality in *Trachiniae*—which is momentarily 'realized' in the text as it is performed. The theatricality of such pervasive dramatic metaphors emerges in moments such as the messenger speech of *Oedipus Tyrannus* and the immediately following scene with the entry of the now blinded but 'seeing' Oedipus (*OT* 1223–1415), and in the first stasimon of the chorus in *Trachiniae* (497–530), where Deianira herself is imagined as an 'abandoned calf' helplessly watching two beast-men fighting in a 'game' (like a wrestling match at *Olympia) for the right to take her. Such moments are moments of stunning theatrical power, and 'middling' is not a word to apply to them. Sophocles can produce equally powerful effects of the eerie and uncanny: e.g. in the opening scene of *Ajax*, where the unseen *Athena manipulates a puppet-like Ajax (see AIAS) and is resisted by the matching subtlety of *Odysseus (1–133: the scene becomes even eerier in retrospect when Tecmessa reports it as if Ajax had been speaking to a vacancy, 301–6).

Much of Sophoclean theatricality resides in his dramatic use of significant objects and significant actions, especially exits and entrances. *Electra*, for example, is a play of thwarted recognition and its centrepiece enacts a sinister game of illusion, of disguises and deceptions. The game involves not only a brilliantly theatrical messenger speech evoking and narrating, in the bravura style of such speeches, distant events which culminate in the violent death of Orestes and which we know have not occurred (680–763), but also the bringing of Orestes' 'ashes', carried in an urn by the unrecognized Orestes himself. The urn is taken by *Electra whose grief for her dead brother and lament for the irreparable loss of her own hoped-for future are directed to it, focused on the 'little weight' which is his tomb and which she now holds in her hands (1126–69). She begs to be allowed to join him in it, 'nothing with nothing', and even when Orestes struggles to disclose himself and to be recognized, she will not let go of it. The urn is 'what is closest' to her (1205–8). The fusing of game-playing, irony, and intensity of tragic emotion is mediated through the simple 'prop'. Other such powerfully meaningful props are the sword in *Ajax* and the bow in *Philoctetes*. Sophocles' dramatic imagination is before all else physical and concrete. It reveals much about him that in *Philoctetes* the isolation and the loss of identity of the hero is figured in physical terms by the deserted, uninhabited island with its cave and sea, its springs, rocks, and wild animals, whereas in the Philoctetes plays of Aeschylus and Euripides Lemnos remains the inhabited island of ordinary experience.

Entrances and exits were always, given the layout of the theatre space, of more importance in Greek tragedy than in later forms of built theatre. Sophocles' use of them is, however, markedly his own. The entrance of the self-blinded Oedipus in *Oedipus Tyrannus*, immediately after one of Sophocles' most powerful messenger speeches, has already been mentioned (*OT* 1287 ff.). The final entrance of Creon, carrying the body of his son, in *Antigone* (1257 ff.) is another *coup-de-théâtre*: it follows almost without pause on the exit of his wife, turning away in silence from the messenger's narrative of her son's death. As Creon enters, he is instantly met by the same messenger emerging from the palace to announce his wife's death and by the 'rolling out' of the theatrical device called the *ekkyklēma* (a wheeled platform), carrying a tableau of his wife's body and the sword with which she has this moment killed herself. Entering and carrying one body, he confronts another.

Sophocles' last two plays offer a unique sense of space and 'place where', in relation to which alone the action has meaning. The deserted island of Lemnos in *Philoctetes* and the grove of the Semnai at Colonos in *Oedipus at Colonos* are heavily loaded with meaning as places to be left or reached. In both plays entrances and exits are thus equally full of significance. In *Oedipus at Colonos* the act of entering unknowingly upon sacred ground and above all that of leaving it are given dramatic weight by the slow measured extension of the blind Oedipus' movements (153–202). Later in the play the entry of

Ismene is similarly extended, this time from the moment the figures on stage first catch sight of her (in the approach to the acting area) until she is within range of speech and touch (310–29). These are adagio movements; in *Philoctetes*, it is the suddenness, for example, of Odysseus' entries at 974 (in mid-line) and 1293 that gives them their theatrical quality. But in *Philoctetes* it is above all the thwarted exit that defines the theatricality of the play. The play's action requires that Philoctetes leave Lemnos for Troy. That exit is four times launched, delayed, and then thwarted (645–750; 877–926; 982–1056; 1362–1410: the final exit, at *Heracles' urging, at 1449–71). Each thwarted exit is different in its implications from each of the others and the last, completed exit is itself ambiguous in its meaning.

Language, form, and structure The language that Sophocles deploys in his plays has, arguably, a greater range than that of either Aeschylus or Euripides, from the baroque sonorities of Ajax's great 'deception speech' (*Ajax* 646–92) or the messenger's opening proclamation of his news in *Oedipus Tyrannus* (1223–31) to the rambling, self-defensive preambles of the guard in *Antigone* (223–47; 388–405). It is a language which is often difficult, even inscrutable (especially in its syntax and particularly in the songs of the chorus); it is never less than formal and it does not yield its sense easily. But it has a flexibility that is very much Sophocles'. It is a mark of Sophoclean writing that it operates within highly formalized structures but uses those structures with masterly tact and subtlety. Sophocles uses the iambic trimeter of tragic dialogue for the most part in its severe form (without, that is, the fluid resolutions that Euripides increasingly used to free the verse) but he treats such formal boundaries as line-end, for example, with a relaxed ease; clauses, even prepositional phrases, may run over into the next line; occasionally a final vowel at the end of one line may be elided (i.e. run into) the opening vowel of the next. The pulse of the verse is kept steady but the rhythmical structure of the whole speech is given a new fluidity by Sophocles' informal treatment of metrical pause. So too with dialogue: like the other tragedians, Sophocles only divides a line between speakers as a sign of greatly heightened emotional tension, but the length of the speeches that are exchanged is left much more fluid than those of Euripides, for example.

The fusion of formal symmetries with a more 'naturalistic' use of speech is well illustrated by the pivotal scene of *Oedipus Tyrannus* which embraces the quarrel between Oedipus and Creon, the entry and intervention of Jocasta, and the following dialogue between Oedipus and Jocasta (512–833). With the entry first of Creon and then of Oedipus the quarrel develops from Oedipus' opening speech of denunciation into a rapid, heated exchange of short speeches which keeps drifting into and out of the formal severities of *stichomythia* (the tightly controlled exchange of single lines); it culminates in Creon's long speech of reasoned self-defence and Oedipus' curt proclamation of death, not exile, as Creon's punishment. This in turn leads at once into a vicious exchange of tense, broken lines, a choral intervention in spoken iambics and Jocasta's entry. The three characters now present (most of our sources attribute to Sophocles the innovation of using three actors: Arist. *Poetics* 1449^{a}15) engage in dialogue with a marked tendency towards symmetry. The formal severity of the scene is suddenly tightened still more when the chorus break in again, this time in song, and confront, first Oedipus, then Jocasta in a mixture of sung and spoken dialogue; the two confrontations, which respond with precise symmetry, are separated by the final, spoken exchanges between Oedipus and Creon, ending in another broken verse and Creon's exit. The chorus in song briefly assure Oedipus of their absolute loyalty, and Jocasta then begins a new scene of spoken, loosely structured dialogue in which it gradually emerges, with a high degree of psychologically persuasive 'naturalness', that it may be Oedipus himself who killed his own predecessor as king, Jocasta's first husband, Laius.

The idea of flexibility in the deployment of a tightly controlled formal structure applies also to resonances and responses between plays. Sophocles turned three times to the cycle of traditional stories associated with Boeotian Thebes, not to produce a continuous 'trilogy' in the manner of Aeschylus but to explore certain recurring themes (the plays are sometimes called the 'Theban plays' or even the 'Theban trilogy'; both titles mislead, the second grossly: if the traditional chronology has any basis in fact the plays were written in the order: *Antigone*, *Oedipus Tyrannus*, *Oedipus at Colonos* and may well have been separated by decades). *Antigone* is often taken to be a broken-backed and structureless play (who is its 'hero'—Antigone, who disappears barely two-thirds of the way through the play, at l. 943 and never reappears, or Creon, who is alienated from us almost from the first by the brutal autocracy of his language? Similar questions have been raised over *Trachiniae*); *Oedipus Tyrannus*, ever since *Aristotle (*Poetics* 1452ª17–32), has been read as the paradigm of a well-structured play. But in important ways Sophocles uses these two differently structured theatrical experiences to explore closely related themes. *Oedipus Tyrannus* has a smoothly pivotal structure in which, with no appearance of discontinuity, we turn from one issue (the salvation of Thebes from plague brought on by *pollution) to another (is Oedipus guilty of both parricide and incest?). *Antigone* seems very different: it is more like a revolving stage on which, from Antigone's exit under sentence of death at 582, one character is replaced by another (Antigone—Haemon—Antigone—Tiresias—Messenger—Eurydice—Creon) until in the closing scene of the play all but Tiresias and the dead Antigone are assembled together in final confrontation with death and, for Creon, tragic recognition. But the two plays are tightly bound together by common themes (pollution through violent death; human blindness to truth; the impenetrability of the divine and the opaqueness of the riddling language of divinity); in both plays humans are left for carrion to devour, and boundaries between the two worlds of gods and men are thereby crossed with deadly results; in both the bonds of kinship have been distorted into horrific travesties of family. *Antigone* ends in inescapable bleakness; *Oedipus Tyrannus*, more positively, with Oedipus re-confronting the world in his blindness.

Tragedy and 'recognition' Aristotle in the *Poetics* makes much use of the idea of 'recognition' (*anagnōrisis*) in his analysis of the tragic effect. The idea is not of much help in reading Aeschylus and of intermittent usefulness in Euripides. But in Sophocles (as arguably in *Homer's *Iliad*) it is an illuminating critical tool. In play after play, one or more characters is brought to a realization that he or she has misperceived the nature of reality and the realization is almost always associated with pain, suffering, and death. The idea of recognition is more often than not also associated with relationships between man and divinity. Between the two worlds of gods and men there is communication, in the imagined world of Sophoclean theatre: it comes in the form of dreams, oracles, and the reading of signs by seers such as Tiresias. Men and women try to guide their decisions by their understanding of such communications. But such understanding is almost always false: the language and the signs used by divinity are everywhere ambiguous, however simple in appearance, and they are systematically and readily misunderstandable, even if they are to hand. In *Ajax*, at a crucial moment, men learn too late of the seer's reading of Athena's intentions and Ajax dies; in *Trachiniae* both Deianira and Heracles only perceive the true meaning of a series of oracles and non-human communications when it is too late and the recognition cannot save them from the consequences of catastrophically mistaken action. In *Antigone*, both Antigone and Creon believe that they are acting as the gods require of them: Antigone dies with that belief shaken and perhaps foundering (919–27) and Creon confronts his misreading of the requirements of divinity only when not just Antigone but his son and wife also are already dead (1257–76). In *Philoctetes* the oracle is never brought sharply into focus but none the less haunts the play; in *Oedipus Tyrannus* the simplicities of the oracle's language become utterly opaque when read through the lens of Oedipus' 'knowledge' of the truth about himself. The recurring pattern of Sophoclean tragedy is that all falls into place and coheres only in retrospect: recognition comes after the event.

Reception Successful in his lifetime, Sophocles continued to be a powerful presence in the Greek tragic theatre in the following century. His plays seem to have been frequently revived, and the leading parts in them were taken by great actors of the period, such as Polus and Theodorus (Dem. *De falsa legatione* 246–7; Epictetus, *Dissertationes* fr. 11, ed. H. Schenkl (1894); Gell. *NA* 6. 5). For Aristotle, the *Oedipus*

Tyrannus is a paradigm of how to maximize the tragic effect, even in reading (*Poetics* 1453ᵇ2). Indeed Sophocles seems to have been read and performed through much of European history. *Oedipus Tyrannus* was the first drama to be performed in Palladio's Teatro Olimpico at Vicenza in the 17th cent. *Antigone* has haunted the European imagination for centuries (George Steiner, *Antigones* (1984)) and in the last century and subsequently Freud's reading of *Oedipus Tyrannus* as the enactment of a universal male fantasy has been widely influential (though not among classical scholars: for a rebuttal of Freudian readings of the play, see J.-P. Vernant, 'Oedipus without the complex', in *Myth and Tragedy in Ancient Greece*, Eng. trans. (1988), 85 ff.). In this century, *Electra* caught the imagination of Hugo von Hofmannsthal and of Richard Strauss, *Trachiniae* that of Ezra Pound. The readings that such continuous interest in Sophocles has led to have been extremely various: they attest the richness, as well as the inscrutability, of his text. See also TRAGEDY, GREEK.   J. P. A. G.

one-twentieth of the grain crop, and prompted the silver and bronze issues minted by native communities in northern Citerior and Ulterior (bronze only) at Rome's behest. Cases of misgovernment led in 171 to the institution of trials *de repetundis* (i.e. for charges of provincial extortion), but the picture of oppression was exaggerated by unreliable sources. *Mines (those of Carthago Nova yielded 2,500 *drachmae* daily) were rented out, for a fixed payment related to production, to Italian businessmen, who settled in moderate numbers in centres like Carthago Nova, Corduba, and Tarraco. There were also substantial bodies of Roman settlers at Italica (206) and Valentia (138), half-Iberian *libertini* (*freedman) at Carteia (171), and *hybridae* (half-Spanish settlers) and natives at Palma and Pollentia (122/1), and possibly in other centres. Elsewhere Rome fostered new native towns (e.g. Gracchuris, founded in 179 by Tiberius Sempronius Gracchus (father of Gaius and Tiberius *Gracchus). In general terms, however, there is little evidence that Rome either systematically urbanized the provinces or attempted to enhance native agriculture before the mid-1st cent. BC.

The conquest of Iberia was completed by *Augustus in the Cantabrian Wars (26–19 BC). This resulted in a largely new province of Lusitania and a great new extension of Citerior (renamed Tarraconensis) to the north and west ocean. These provinces were assigned to the emperor; most of Ulterior (renamed Baetica) was returned to the senate in 27 BC. The new Augustan conquest required three legions in north-west Tarraconensis; by the time of *Vespasian they had been reduced to VII Gemina only. Twenty-two colonies were founded (see COLONIZATION, ROMAN), and a large number of *municipia* (municipalities) created, under Caesar and Augustus, forming the basis for a Roman urban network within juridical *conventus* (assizes) in each province. Following the development of a municipal imperial cult at Tarraco (AD 15), there soon followed the establishment of a conventual (Tarraconensis) and provincial imperial cult (under the Flavians). See RULER-CULT.

The density and sophistication of Hispano-Roman towns varied greatly from region to region. However, a substantial number of the 1st-cent. provincial senators at Rome came from the colonies of the Hispaniae. In literature they pro-

duced the Senecas (see SENECA) and *Lucan; Columella (see AGRICULTURAL WRITERS), Quintilian (see RHETORIC, LATIN), and *Martial were of native stock. The emperors *Trajan, *Hadrian, and Marcus *Aurelius had Spanish ancestry. However, despite *Vespasian's grant of Latin rights (i.e. some of the privileges of Roman citizenship) to all Spanish communities, many retained native cultural traits. The systematic and large-scale exploitation of gold in north-west Tarraconensis, as well as silver (especially near Castulo) and other metals (as at Río Tinto), provided important revenue for Rome and was underwritten by an extensive road network (notably the via Augusta, the Asturica to Emerita Augusta road). Wine (from Tarraconensis) and fish-sauce were widely distributed, while the state monitored the production of Baetican olive oil for Rome and the frontiers.

The mid-3rd-cent. Frankish invasions were of little consequence for the long-term development of the provinces. However, this century saw the diminution of Spanish exports and accelerating municipal decline. *Diocletian (284–305) divided Hispania Tarraconensis into three and added Tingitana: the Balearics were added in 395. The rewalling and continued decline of many towns in the 4th cent. was matched by the flourishing of large residential country villas and the emergence of powerful country-based aristocracies, like the family of emperor Theodosius I. A powerful church by the early 4th cent. is evident from the council of Elvira (Illiberis, mod. Granada), and its position was enhanced by Hosius (Ossius), bishop of Corduba; it also produced Prudentius and Orosius. The barbarian invasions of 409 rapidly led to the loss of Roman control in all provinces, except the Balearics (by 455) and Tarraconensis (by 475). Unified Visigothic control was established by 586, although parts of southern Spain were held by the Byzantines between 552 and 624.   S. J. K.

Sparta (*see page 685*)

sphinx, a hybrid creature, like the chimaera (fire-breathing monster) and the griffin. Illustrations can be traced back to Egypt and Mesopotamia in the mid-3rd millennium BC (impossible to accord priority, although the Egyptian version is known to be a late-comer to local iconography).

sphinx Terracotta incense burner in the shape of a sphinx, c.680 BC.

Basically the Sphinx possessed the body of an animal (usually a lion) and a human head (male or female). Variations include wings (common) and horns.

The Egyptian and Mesopotamian sphinx is depicted in religious and/or heraldic contexts, from the monumental (i.e. the Sphinx at Giza) to the minute. The Egyptian is held to embody the king as the god Horus supplicating the sun god Re. Both are sometimes shown slaying humans, presumably enemies of the king (the foregoing based on H. Demisch, *Die Sphinx* (1977)).

Sphinxes appear in Minoan and Mycenaean art (see MINOAN and MYCENAEAN CIVILIZATION), in Crete and the mainland, the ultimate inspiration probably Egypt. The sphinx later becomes a popular figure in Greek art—monumental and funerary—of the archaic and later periods. This is an extension of her role as guardian spirit.

The only literary references are to the Greek sphinx, whence the name, which came from a monster of Theban legend, (S)phix, that inhabited a mountain at the western edge of Theban territory (central Greece), waylaid passers-by, and wrought havoc on the Cadmeans (the story is referred to by Hesiod, *Theogony* 326, where she is daughter of Echidna and Orthos, and sister of the Nemean lion). Popular Greek etymologizing derived the name from the verb *sphingein* ('bind/hold fast'), perhaps influenced by the story (see West on *Theog.* 326 and P. Chantraine, *Dictionnaire étymologique de la langue grecque* 4 (1977), 1077).

Her hostility to the Thebans may be connected with the traditional war between Minyan Orchomenus and Cadmean Thebes, which was begun and ended near Mt. Phicion, at Onchestus and the Teneric plain respectively. She would have been performing her accustomed role as guardian, this time of Minyan territory (it is to be remarked that as one approaches the mountain from the west—that is, from the direction of Orchomenus—it resembles in outline a crouching beast: this might have caused the connection to be made). Eventually she met her match in *Oedipus, who either answered her riddle, causing her to commit suicide (e.g. Apollod. 3. 5. 8), or actually killed her (Corinna, fr. 672 *PMG*). The attachment of the sphinx to the Oedipus legend is regarded as secondary, and may have been grafted on to it from its original place in the story of the war.   A. Sch.

stadium (Greek *stadion*), running track, about 200 m. long (the term also signifies a comparable unit of linear measurement i.e. a 'stade'). Athletic activity often antedates the surviving stadia (e.g. at Nemea); presumably any area of flat ground was used. One of the earliest definable stadia, that in the sanctuary of *Poseidon at Isthmia, consists simply of a starting gate on the relatively level ground of the sanctuary, with a bank raised artificially to one side for spectators. The architectural development of stadia can be seen by the 4th cent. BC with the running track and seats to one or, preferably, either side. Early examples may have both ends straight or near straight (*Olympia, Epidaurus). Later the end is semicircular. Double races (the diaulos) and other long-distance races, however, started at a straight

starting line at this closed end. This definitive form is still used in structures of the Roman period (see illustration on p. 684). One of the first examples is that at Nemea (*c*.325 BC). A vaulted passage under the seating area gives convenient access to the running tracks; similar passages, Hellenistic in date, are at Epidaurus and Olympia.

Whether the seating rests on natural hill slopes, artificial terraces, or built vaulted substructures (the stadium of the Roman period at Perge, S. Turkey) stadia served as natural catchment areas for rainwater, and required drainage. This often takes the form of a channel at the edge of the running track, perhaps punctuated with water basins at intervals. These probably facilitated cleaning of the channels rather than the provision of water for either spectators or athletes.

See ATHLETICS; SANCTUARIES.   R. A. T.

Statius, Publius Papinius, Roman poet. Born between AD 45 and the early 50s in the distinctively Greek city of Naples, Statius was the son of a man who had a glittering career first as a professional poet on the Greek festival circuit (see GAMES), and then as a teacher in Naples and in Rome, where the family moved when Statius was in his teens (*Silv.* 5. 3). Although Statius did not follow either of these careers, his debt to his father's inheritance is manifest particularly in the *Silvae*, where the often impromptu praise-displays of the Greek festivals blend with the Roman tradition of friendship poetry to produce something new in Latin literature. Popular from a young age as a poet in Rome, he may have composed a pantomime libretto for Paris, *Domitian's favourite (executed AD 83: Juv. 7. 82–7). He was victorious in the poetry competition at Domitian's annual Alban games (prob. March 90), but suffered a mortifying failure in the much more prestigious Capitoline games, almost certainly later in the same year (*Silv.* 3. 5. 31–3). By now he had married Claudia, widow of another poet, who brought him a stepdaughter (he had no children of his own). The poem to Claudia (*Silv.* 3. 5), persuading her to leave Rome and follow him to Naples, speaks of her devoted support, and her nursing of Statius in illness. His epic, the *Thebaid*, was published in 91/2, after many partial recitations and many years of work (one for each of the twelve books he says, with suspicious symmetry, *Theb.* 12. 811–12). There followed the occasional poems of the *Silvae*. Books 1–3 were published together in 93 or 94; Book 4 was published in 95, by which time he had left Rome for Naples; and Book 5 (together with his unfinished second epic, the *Achilleid*) was published after his death, which is conventionally dated before the assassination of Domitian (Sept. 96).

Works Lost Works

The pantomime libretto *Agave* has not survived (if it was ever written); nor have his poems for the Neapolitan, Alban, or Capitoline games, although we may have a fragment of the Alban piece in four hexameter lines from a

stadium Air view of the Piazza Navona, Rome, with the outline of the stadium of *Domitian, who founded the first permanent Greek *games—including athletic contests—at Rome.

Statian poem on Domitian's German wars quoted by Valla on Juvenal 4. 94 (cf. *Silv.* 4. 2. 65–7).

Thebaid

The only surviving Roman *epic which can securely be said to have been published as a completed work by its author, the *Thebaid* recounts the war between the sons of *Oedipus over the kingship of Thebes. Statius may well have begun the poem before he turned 30; it is an acutely self-conscious masterpiece, which has only recently begun to emerge from the neglect that overtook it after its prolonged popularity in the Middle Ages and Renaissance. The poem extravagantly explores human violence and madness. Its cosmic framework draws upon *Ovid's *Metamorphoses* to chart the problematic boundaries of human possibilities, and its political framework draws upon *Virgil and *Lucan (Statius' near-contemporary) to probe the imperial themes of absolutism and civil war. *Seneca's tragedies are the principal source for the atmosphere of doomed familial insanity. The diverse problems of succession and authority which face the brothers, the audience, and the poet reflect upon one another throughout, and this self-awareness renders nugatory the traditional criticism of Statius as derivative. In the divine action above all Statius shows himself to be a bold critic and innovator, undermining his inherited epic apparatus and experimenting with allegorical modes in ways which were to be profoundly influential in the Middle Ages. The verse is superbly accomplished, the style too aestheticized for many. In both respects Statius is rather nearer to Ovid, and further from Virgil, than his contemporaries *Valerius Flaccus and *Silius Italicus.

[*continued on p. 688*]

Sparta

Sparta (see ◀Map 1, Bd▶)

1. Prehistory Sparta ('the sown land'?) lies *c*.56 km. (35 mi.) south of Tegea, and 48 km. (30 mi.) north of Gytheum, at the heart of the fertile alluvial valley of the Eurotas in the district of Laconia (SW *Peloponnese). Very few prehistoric remains are known from the site of historical Sparta, but there was a substantial neolithic community not far south, and a major late bronze age settlement about 3 km. north-east (the 'Menelaion' site at Therapne). The circumstances of the settlement of Sparta town are enveloped in the fog of myth and legend: the 'Return of the Heraclids' (the descendants of *Heracles), as the ancients put it, and the 'Dorian Invasion', in modern parlance (see MACEDONIA). Archaeology as currently understood suggests a cultural break with the bronze age and a humble new beginning somewhere in the darkness of the 10th cent.; the initial relationship between Sparta and nearby Amyclae, which by 700 had been incorporated on equal terms with the other four villages comprising Sparta town, is no less obscure.

2. Archaic and Classical In a long war, usually placed in the later 8th cent., much of neighbouring Messenia was annexed and its population helotized (see SLAVERY). The conquest transformed Sparta into a leading Greek state, culturally as well as militarily, as attested by the wealth of dedications at the sanctuary of *Artemis Orthia and numerous visits by foreign poets. But it also prompted the (poorly understood) dispute surrounding the Partheniai, who departed to found Taras (Tarentum, mod. Taranto) *c*.700; and it saddled Sparta with lasting problems of security, both internal and external. During the 7th cent. Sparta was confronted with a major Messenian revolt (the 'Second Messenian War'), internal discontent from poor citizens, and probably military defeat by Argos at Hysiae in 669. During the 6th cent. the external problem was solved by several successful wars—especially against Argos *c*.545 and, after a serious defeat, against Tegea—followed by a new policy that created a system of unequal alliances which developed into the 'Peloponnesian League'. The League, which underpinned Sparta's dominance until the mid-4th cent., provided external co-operation against the helots in return for support for broadly based oligarchies. An alliance with King Croesus of Lydia (W. Asia Minor) and an expedition against Polycrates of *Samos *c*.525 are signs of Sparta's prominence among Greek states.

Sparta's internal problems were tackled by extending her control over the whole of Messenia and through a thoroughgoing reorganization of Spartan institutions and way of life which embodied a social compromise between rich and poor citizens. The exact chronology of this reorganization is uncertain. Later Spartans attributed it to a single, early lawgiver, *Lycurgus. Most current opinion, while agreeing that the fundamental changes were consciously planned following a common logic, views them as being implemented in a continuing process of adaptation between the 7th and 5th cents. There were three essential elements of the 'remodelled' Spartan society. First, an economic system, according to which *citizenship was extended to a body of several thousand men who, as full-time hoplites supported by produce delivered by helots who worked their private estates, were debarred from agricultural labour, business activity, and a range of expenditures for consumption and display. Secondly, a political system initiated by the 7th-cent. 'Great Rhetra' (Plut. *Lyc.* 6) which combined a limited right of veto for the citizen assembly with the strong executive powers of the five magistrates called ephors, the extra-constitutional influence of the two kings, and the formidable, conservative authority of the *gerousia* (council of elders). Thirdly, a social and ritual system, as part of which every Spartiate (except the two kings and their immediate heirs) underwent an austere public upbringing (the *agōgē*) followed by a common lifestyle of participation in the messes (*syssitia*) and in military training and service in the army.

The result was the creation of the famous *eunomia* ('good order'), admired by both contemporaries and later generations for its long-term stability. Few of its specific institutions were in themselves unique; many were transformations of earlier institutions or were paralleled elsewhere in Greece. What was distinctive was their combination into a coherent structure which attempted to produce a unified citizen body of *homoioi* ('Peers' rather than 'Equals') whose subservience to collective interests and military training would ensure effective policing of the helots. The reorganization had its limits. The cultural impact was gradual: Olympic athletic victories continued until *c*.550 (see OLYMPIA), and Laconian painted pottery and bronze vessel production until a generation later. Several spheres of Spartiate society were only partially affected, especially the strength of family allegiances and more independent role of citizen women. Although the subject is controversial, land tenure probably remained essentially private and its distribution very unequal.

During the reign of Cleomenes I (*c*.520–490) Sparta ousted the tyrants from Athens, but failed to control the subsequent democracy and declined various external appeals for assistance, especially against Persia. Sparta commanded the Greek resistance to *Xerxes' invasion (480/79); but afterwards its leadership of the Greek alliance and campaigns against medizing states in northern Greece foundered amidst the disgrace of the regent Pausanias and King Leotychidas II. The 470s and 460s were decades of crisis marked by conflict with her Arcadian allies and a long helot revolt following losses in the severe earthquake of *c*.465. The remainder of the 5th cent. was dominated by wars with Athens (the so-called 'First' Peloponnesian War *c*.460–446 being conventionally distinguished from that of 431–404). Their controversial origins were, on Sparta's side, connected with her fear that Athenian imperialism would destabilize the Peloponnesian League. Sparta's traditional strategy of invading Attic territory failed; but Athens was ultimately starved into surrender after *Lysander, with Persian financial help, destroyed her fleet at Aegospotami (405). Sparta's subsequent imperialist activities in Asia Minor, central and northern Greece, and even in *Sicily and (possibly) Egypt, led to the Corinthian War (394–387) against a hostile Graeco-Persian coalition. In the King's Peace (387/6) Sparta traded her overseas empire for domination in mainland Greece, which was pursued vigorously against Thebes by King Agesilaus II; but her supremacy was destroyed by defeat at Leuctra (371). Ensuing Theban invasions brought the liberation of Messenia (370/69), the foundation of Megalopolis (368) in south-western Arcadia, and the demise of the Peloponnesian League (366), thereby reducing her to a second-rate power.

The roots of Sparta's international decline lay in internal difficulties. Inequalities in landholding developed during the 5th cent. as the employment of wealth for élite activities such as chariot racing became increasingly significant as a determinant of status. Many poorer Spartiates became unable to provide their contributions to the common messes which were a necessary condition of citizenship. The *homoioi*, 8,000 strong in 480, dwindled to *c*.1,500 by 371. The sources' claim that Sparta was ruined by the influx of imperial wealth may be merely moralizing commonplace; but the development of independent foreign commands and of competing internal factions during the period of empire did mean enlarged opportunities for economic patronage. Unwilling to address the problems of poor Spartiates, the authorities' increasing reliance on non-Spartiate troops left Sparta unable to resist her enemies' dismantling of her power.

3. Hellenistic and Roman Down to the early 2nd cent. BC Sparta intermittently—and unsuccessfully—launched attempts to regain her old hegemony by challenging successively the domination of the Peloponnese by *Macedonia and the Achaean Confederacy; in the same period the Spartan polity and way of life lost much of its distinctiveness (in the mid-3rd cent. the *agōgē* lapsed; and Areus refashioned the royal dyarchy into a Hellenistic-style kingship). Cleomenes III (reigned 235–222) sought a root-and-branch internal reform in a (failed) attempt to revitalize Sparta's military machine; in doing so he claimed to be recreating the laws of Lycurgus, many of which, as recorded by *Plutarch and other later writers, were probably invented at this time. The reign of Nabis (207–192) marks the last glow of

Spartan independence; his assassination, and Sparta's subsequent forced inclusion in the Achaean Confederacy (195 BC), marks its final extinction; in 147 BC, in response to Spartan complaints, Rome allowed the city to leave the confederacy, a development prompting the Achaean War and *Greece's partial provincialization. After 146 Sparta remained on good terms with the Romans, admirers of Classical Sparta, and counted among provincial Greece's 'free' cities. Under Augustus his partisan Gaius Iulius Eurycles founded a Spartan client-dynasty lasting (with breaks) until Nero. Roman Sparta, its 'Lycurgan customs' now an object of cultural *tourism, is a particularly well-documented example of the archaism marking Greek civic life in the age of the *Second Sophistic. There are extensive remains of the Roman city, which survived, spatially much reduced, a sack by Alaric and his Visigoths (AD 396).

KING-LIST. Before c.800 BC the list is very hypothetical. Until 491/0, the Spartans claimed, son had succeeded father; though it is difficult to believe, there is no evidence to refute the claim. Thereafter relationship is indicated in brackets, the reference being to the preceding king. On the problems of the king-lists in their early reaches (Hdt. 7. 204 and 8. 131) see P. Cartledge, *Sparta and Lakonia* (1979), app. 3 and *Agesilaos and the Crisis of Sparta* (1987), 22 f. 102 f., and fig. 7.

Agiads	Eurypontids
Agis, 930–900.	Eurypon, 890–860.
Echestratus, 900–870.	Prytanis, 860–830.
Leobotes, 870–840.	Polydectes, 830–800.
Dorussus, 840–820.	Eunomus, 800–780.
Agesilaus I, 820–790.	Charillus, c.780–750.
Archelaus, c.790–760.	Nicandrus, c.750–720.
Teleclus, c.760–740.	Theopompus, c.720–675.
Alcamenes, c.740–700.	Anaxandridas, c.675–665.
Polydorus, c.700–665.	Archidamus I, c.665–645.
Eurycrates, c.665–640.	Anaxilas, c.645–625.
Anaxandrus, c.640–615.	Leotychidas I, c.625–600.
Eurycratidas, c.615–590.	Hippocratides, c.600–575.
Leon, c.590–560.	Agasicles, c.575–550.
Anaxandridas, c.560–520.	Ariston, c.550–515.
Cleomenes I, c.520–490.	Demaratus, c.515–491.
Leonidas I (brother), 490–480.	Leotychidas II (cousin—great-grandson of Hippocratidas), 491–469.
Pleistarchus (son), 480–459.	Archidamus II (grandson), 469–427.
Pleistoanax (son), 459–409.	Agis II (son), 427–400.
Pausanias (son), 409–395.	Agesilaus II (brother), 400–360.
Agesipolis I (son), 395–380.	Archidamus III (son), 360–338.
Cleombrotus I (brother), 380–371.	Agis III (son), 338–330.
Agesipolis II (son), 371–370.	Eudamidas I (brother), 330–c.305.
Cleomenes II (brother), 370–309.	Archidamus IV (son), c.305–275.
Areus I (grandson), 309–265.	Eudamidas II (son), c.275–244.
Acrotatus (son), 265–262.	Agis IV (son), c.244–241.
Areus II (son), 262–254.	Eudamidas III (son), 241–c.228.
Leonidas II (grandson of Cleomenes II), 254–235.	Archidamus V (uncle), 228–227.
Cleomenes III (son), 235–222.	Eucleidas (Agiad—brother of Cleomenes III), 227–222.
Agesipolis III (grandson of Cleombrotus II), 219–215.	

P. A. C., S. J. Ho., A. J. S. S.

Silvae

Thirty-two poems, of which twenty-six are in hexameters, the standard metre for post-Classical Greek encomiastic poetry. The only popular poem in the collection has been the exceptional poem to Sleep (5. 4). The poems evince a not very intimate acquaintance with a not very large or eminent group, marking noteworthy moments such as marriage, official advancement, or bereavement, and celebrating the taste shown in artistic acquisition or architectural construction. In the service of these quasi-professional relationships Statius marshals the panoply of Greek praise-poetry inherited from his father, boasting self-deprecatingly of the impromptu production of the requisite verses (*Silv.* 1 Pr.). Generally knowing and light in touch, rather than ponderous, the poems nonetheless usually avoid banter and ease. Domitian, an intimidating and distant personality, receives six poems which modern taste has found repellent for sycophancy, though a more charitable reading might focus on the anxiety behind them: 4. 2, thanking the emperor for an invitation to dinner in 94, betrays relief after four long years since the last sign of favour at Alba.

Achilleid

The plan was to tell the whole life of *Achilles, but the poet died before even getting his hero to Troy, and the epic breaks off some 160 lines into the second book. The charming, almost novelistic fragment represents a striking departure from the more elevated and passionate *Thebaid*.

D. C. F.

status, legal and social

Greek Greek social and legal status terminology was rich, complex, and confused. There was a multiplicity of Greek communities, often very different in character, which although typically small in scale were yet complex in organization. The consequent confusion was not clarified by the Greek equivalent of Roman jurisprudents and jurisconsults, since such persons did not exist. In all Greek societies at all periods the fundamental status division was between the free and the unfree. But whereas the former could be divided fairly simply into citizen and non-citizen, men and women, adults and children, the Greeks devised no fewer than a dozen words for various types and degrees of unfree people.

Everywhere in the Greek world the normative type of the high-status person was the citizen (*politēs*), free, adult, and male (see CITIZENSHIP, GREEK). Qualifications for citizenship (*politeia*) varied from community to community, but in all birth—membership of a corporate descent-group—was assumed to be primary. Only in Sparta was this coupled with a test of achievement, successful passage through the compulsory state educational curriculum and consequent election to a common mess. Further distinctions between active and passive, or first-class and second-class, citizenship might be drawn on grounds of age, gender, or wealth. Democratic Athens thus pioneered the idea that to be a full active citizen it was enough for a man to be of legitimate Athenian birth and duly registered with the appropriate authorities to qualify for the exercise of full public and private citizen prerogatives (the most extensive then available anywhere). But even Athens insisted (after 451 BC) on double descent, from a citizen-status mother as well as father. Elsewhere the exercise of citizenship typically remained conditional upon property-ownership in various ways.

No Greek city permitted women the political rights of citizenship, but Athens may have been unusual in the rigour with which physically mature, married citizen women were nevertheless treated virtually as minors at law throughout their lives. Yet, paradoxically, one of the most important public religious functionaries at Athens, the priestess of the city's chief divinity Athena Polias, was by ascribed prerogative a woman from a specified noble lineage. Even in democratic Athens distinctions of birth continued to count for something, as they did more obviously in Sparta, another ideologically egalitarian peer-group society. Indeed, in Sparta there were not only noble families but also two hereditary royal houses.

Between the citizen and the free but non-resident foreigner came the free resident alien or *metic (metoikos)*. This status is attested in some seventy communities but most extensively at Athens, where it can be seen not to have been especially privileged. Metics were required to pay a poll tax and to be represented at law by a citizen patron; metic status, moreover, was that assigned to privately manumitted slaves, most of whom were non-Greek. It was exceedingly rare for an ex-slave such as Pasion, father of Apollodorus (see BANKS), to crash the barrier of full citizen status.

Of the dozen or so current Greek words for the unfree, *doulos* was the most general and the most common. Yet the term could be applied with liberal abandon both to the chattel-slaves of Athens, for example, and to the quite different helot bondsmen of Sparta (see SLAVERY, Greek). The chattel-slave was a socially dead being, categorizable as 'an animate tool'; but even chattel-slaves were granted some legal protection, if only in virtue of their master's rights of property. Besides the helots, there were some other local collective groups of unfree persons each defined by a distinctive name, of which the best attested if ill understood are those of *Crete. The classification of all such groups as 'between free people and *douloi*' perfectly illustrates both the complexity of Greek societies and the inadequacy of Greek social terminology. See FREEDMEN.

P. A. C.

Roman In Roman law, *status* describes the 'legal position' of an individual with respect to both that person's household (*familia*) and the broader civic community of Rome. The concept of *status* is linked to *caput* or *persona*, an individual's legal 'personality'. Personality roughly defines the limits of what an individual is legally able to do: marry, make contracts, commit crimes or delicts, bring lawsuits, and so on. In modern law, such issues are treated as aspects of legal capacity; but the Roman jurists lack this more sophisticated concept.

The most systematic exposition of *status* comes in Roman sources discussing change of status, what *Cicero (*Top.* 18, 29) and the jurists (esp. Gaius, *Inst.* 1. 158–63; *Dig.* 4. 5) call *capitis deminutio*. Three issues are paramount, and they are arranged hierarchically: freedom, citizenship, and membership in a household. The most fundamental division is between free persons and slaves (Gaius, 1. 9; see SLAVERY, *Roman*); then, among free persons, between Roman citizens and others; and finally, especially among Roman citizens, between those who head households (the *sui iuris*) and those subject to the power of a head (the *alieni iuris*).

The complex rules of *capitis deminutio* determine what happens when an individual's legal status changes; the consequences may concern not only the individual but others as well. For example, under the *senatusconsultum Claudianum* (senatorial decree of Claudius) of AD 52, a woman who despite warning cohabits with another's slave can herself become that person's slave, thereby simultaneously losing her freedom, citizenship, and position as a household member; but legal questions may then arise about the enslaved woman's property, her former family relationships, and so on. The jurists decide such questions pragmatically (e.g. Gaius, *Inst.* 1. 91, 160).

Legal status is central to Roman private law and much more significant than in modern law. Other areas of Roman law, such as property, contracts, and testamentary succession, often appear remarkably liberal by modern standards; but all are subject to limitations that status imposes on legal capacity to act. For instance, although in principle Roman jurists permit owners to deal in virtually unrestricted fashion with their property, only sane *sui iuris* persons have completely effective legal ownership of property. When resolution of a lawsuit hinges in part on a question of status (*quaestio status*), especially whether an individual is free or a slave, this issue is always tried first (*Dig.* 40. 12).

Granted the importance of status, the Romans were surprisingly casual in providing means to prove it. Beginning with *Augustus, children of a legitimate marriage were registered soon after birth; from Marcus *Aurelius, illegitimate children were also registered. But these evidently incomplete or inaccurate records did not have conclusive legal force. Marriages, upon the legitimacy of which the civil status of children depended, were not registered at all.

Proving one's freedom or citizenship could be challenging, as is shown by a remarkable set of trial documents preserved from Herculaneum. The jurist Paulus drily observes that 'distinguishing a free person from a slave can be difficult' (*Dig.* 18. 1. 5); just how difficult is demonstrated by many legal sources dealing with a free person 'serving in good faith' (*bona fide serviens*), held as a slave by an 'owner' unaware of the person's true status. Free persons held as slaves could not assert their own freedom and had to find an outsider willing to take up the burden of proof.

As a result, civil status, though a cornerstone of Roman law, was always potentially at risk; at any moment it might be challenged, and it could disappear overnight. None the less, Roman citizens clung tenaciously to the belief that their civil status protected them from harm; as Cicero puts it, the cry 'I am a Roman citizen' brought safety the world over (2 *Verr.* 5. 147, 165; cf. Acts 22: 25–9).

In the modern social sciences, status has a more than purely legal meaning: it refers to social position, particularly as determined by birth, wealth, and external markers such as honour, place of residence, or badges of distinction. The Roman empire's small social élite was highly stratified by status: the 'orders' (*ordines*) of senators (see SENATE), *equites, and municipal councillors. All three orders had minimum wealth requirements, but were also to a large extent hereditary. The rest of the free population was less formally stratified, though quasi-status groups often formed around a common occupation, residence, or civil status; of special note is the order of *freedmen (*ordo libertinorum*), attested from the late republic on.

Such status groups played a significant social, political, and economic role, but were at first not clearly recognized by law; in theory, Roman citizens were equal before the law. However, during the early empire, through a process still not entirely understood, civic equality began to erode, especially in criminal law; criminal procedure and punishment distinguished the 'more upright' (*honestiores*) from the 'more base' (*humiliores*). By the early 2nd cent. AD, this distinction was hardening into law; the *honestiores*, generally defined as the three uppermost social orders, received better legal treatment and milder penalties. In private law, prohibitions on intermarriage and status-based penalties for anti-social behaviour also furthered the bifurcation of society.

The society of the high and late empire was not simply bifurcated, however. Particularly the late imperial bureaucracy saw a profusion of titles and distinctions of rank, all deriving ultimately from the emperor and his court.

B. W. F.

Stesichorus, Greek lyric poet, active *c.*600–550 BC. Greek tradition made him later than *Alcman, and contemporary with *Sappho and *Alcaeus (*Suda*); Simonides (fr. 564) referred back to him and to *Homer. He was connected with Mataurus in Bruttium, S. Italy (Steph. Byz., *Suda*), and with Himera in Sicily (already Pl. *Phdr.* 244a); Arist. *Rh.* 1393[b] tells an anecdote of him and Phalaris. His tomb was shown at Himera (Poll. 9. 100) or Catana (Antipater of Thessalonica, *Anth. Pal.* 7. 75, etc.). Some said that his real name was Teisias (*Suda*).

Stesichorus' works were collected in 26 books (*Suda*); nothing now survives but quotations and some fragmentary papyri. The poems are cited by title, not by book-number. That suggests substantial pieces, and what detail we know confirms it. *Geryoneis* apparently reached at least 1,300 lines; *Oresteia*, and perhaps *Helen*, occupied two books. The titles cover a whole range of major myths: *Helen*, *Wooden Horse*, *Sack of Troy*, *Homecomings*, *Oresteia* belong to the Trojan cycle, *Geryoneis*, *Cycnus*, and *Cerberus*

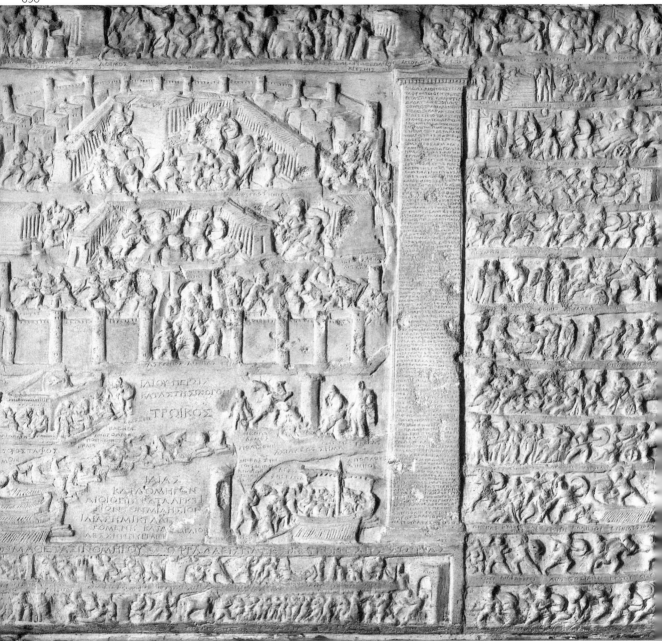

Stesichorus Detail of a 1st-cent. AD Roman monument, the Tabulae Iliacae, with a purported representation of Stesichorus' *Sack of Troy*.

to the adventures of *Heracles, *Eriphyle, Europia,* and the untitled fragment about Eteocles and Polynices to the Theban story; *Boar-hunters* was concerned with Meleager, *Funeral Games for Pelias* with the Argonauts.

These poems represent a kind of lyric *epic. Their metre, 'Doric' dialect, and triadic form seem to attach them to the 'choral lyric' tradition represented by Alcman and *Pindar. But their large scale and narrative sweep recall the traditional epic; their language is often Homeric, their metres dactylic (fr. 222A even has some quasi-hexameters); it has been argued that such long pieces must have been performed, like epic, by a solo poet or reciter, not by a chorus. The prehistory of this form is obscure, and Stesichorus seems to have no successors: perhaps this was a unique attempt to transfuse epic material into a new medium. Not only is his diction 'Homeric' in general; he seems to know at least individual passages of the *Iliad* and *Odyssey* as we have them. Thus fr. 209 reworks the departure of Telemachus from Sparta (*Od.* 15. 164 ff.); Geryones borrows rhetoric from Sarpedon (S11; *Il.* 12. 322 ff.) and dies like Gorgythion (S14; *Il.* 8. 306–8), his mother speaks as Hecuba (S13; *Il.* 22. 83). Ancient critics duly called Stesichorus 'Homeric'; the orator Quintilian (*Inst.* 10. 1. 62) praises his dignity but criticizes his diffuseness. Certainly the few continuous pieces suggest a narrative well spaced with direct speech. In the '*Thebaid*' (fr. 222A) *Oedipus' widow proposes a compromise between her warring sons, the sons agree, Tiresias predicts disaster if the bargain is broken, Polynices leaves, and travels towards Argos: this takes 100 lines, of which the speeches occupy 70. In *Geryoneis* Heracles crosses Ocean in the cup of the Sun, kills the triple Geryones, and drives away his cattle: there is time for a heroic speech by Geryones, and a lament by his mother, before Heracles destroys his heads one by one. Stesichorus came from the fringes of the Greek world: that may explain the idiosyncratic form, and the idiosyncratic versions of myth which the tragedians later borrowed (see frs. 193, 217). His influence has been suspected in the metopes of the temple of Hera at Foce del Sele (see PAESTUM), and in Attic vase-painting of the later 6th cent.; one of the Tabulae Iliacae (a Roman monument of the 1st cent. AD found near Bovillae, for which see N. Horsfall, *JHS* 1979, 26 ff.) claims to represent his *Sack of Troy*. P. J. P.

Stoicism, philosophical movement, founded by Zeno of Citium on *Cyprus, who came to Athens in 313 BC, and, after studying with various philosophers, taught in his own right in the Stoa Poecile (Painted Porch; see PAINTING, GREEK). Zeno developed a distinctive philosophical position divided into three parts, logic, physics, and ethics. We know little of the institutional organization of the school, except that at Zeno's death one of his pupils, Cleanthes, took over the 'headship' of the school. He was not, however, the most famous of Zeno's pupils, and the original position got developed in different directions. Ariston of Chios stressed ethics to the exclusion of physics and logic; Herillus emphasized knowledge at the expense of moral action. Cleanthes stressed a religious view of the world, interpreting Stoic ideas in works like his *Hymn to Zeus*. Stoicism was in danger of dissolving into a number of different positions, but was rescued by Cleanthes' pupil Chrysippus of Soli. He restated and recast Zeno's position in his voluminous writings, defending it with powerful arguments. It was correctly thought later that 'if there had been no Chrysippus there would have been no Stoa'; the work of Zeno's earlier pupils came to be seen as unorthodox, and Chrysippus' works became the standard formulation of Stoicism. Although Chrysippus claimed to adhere to Zeno's ideas, modern scholars have often held that there are divergences between them; but this is hazardous given the fragmentary state of our sources. Chrysippus'

own innovations were mainly in the technical area of logic.

The methodology of Stoicism is holistic: there is no foundational part which supports the others. Different Stoics disagreed radically both over the correct structure of their position and the correct order of teaching it. Thus the theory can be fully understood only as a whole, one of the respects in which it is markedly 'ideal' and makes high demands on the student. However, logic, physics, and ethics are distinguishable at a preliminary stage, and in fact the Stoics developed them with great sophistication. Logic includes logic in the technical sense, in which the Stoics made great advances in what is now called the logic of propositions. It also includes philosophy of language, including grammar and rhetoric, and epistemology. The Stoics are radically empiricist; they give an account of knowledge which traces it from the impact made on the human mind by 'appearances' from the outside world. Some of these appearances, they claim, are such that they could not be wrong; this gave rise to a debate with the Academic Sceptics (who held no doctrine and suspended judgement on everything). Knowledge proper, however, requires understanding of the principles which define the area in question.

Stoic *physics gives an account of the world which is strongly materialist. It is also determinist; the world as a whole is made up of material objects and their interactions, which occur according to exceptionless laws, which are called 'fate'. However, their account is also strongly teleological; everything happens according to providence, which is identified with fate. Further, they are compatibilists; human action is free and morally responsible despite fate. The Stoics defended this problematic set of ideas with sophistication and power. The details of their physical account are more naïve: they take fire to be the basic substrate from which things are produced, though Chrysippus, possibly influenced by contemporary medicine, used the mechanism of differing degrees of tension of *pneuma* or 'breath'.

Stoic ethics is marked by a set of uncompromising theses: virtue is sufficient for happiness; nothing except virtue is good; emotions are always bad. Easily ridiculed in isolation, these theses can be defended when seen as contributing to an overall theory in which what is most important is the difference in kind between the value of virtue and other, 'non-moral' value, virtue being conceived of as the skill of putting other things to correct use. The Stoics give the most demanding account of virtue in ancient ethics, and put the most strain on their account of the happiness which is the virtuous person's aim.

In all areas of philosophy there is appeal to the notions of nature and of reason, which have two roles, in the world as a whole and in us humans. Humans should live in accordance with human nature, which is, for them, to live in accordance with human reason, humans being rational animals. Properly used, human reason will enable us to understand the role of reason in the world, and thus of the world's nature. Nature and reason are in Stoicism objective notions: for us to think rationally is for us to think in ways which converge with other rational thinkers and reach the truth. Those who use their reason form a kind of community of reason, which is sometimes characterized as the only true community, transcending mere earthly bonds.

Early Stoicism remained essentially unmodified in form until Diogenes of Babylon, who, as is increasingly clear from the *Herculaneum papyri, began changes of detail and presentation usually associated with his pupil Panaetius (d. 109), and by Posidonius (d. *c.*51 BC) and Hecaton. The so-called 'Middle Stoa' attempted to make the position more accessible to educated Romans (successfully in the case of Panaetius) and was more hospitable to ideas from other philosophers, particularly *Plato and *Aristotle. Posidonius had much independent interest in science and causality, and Panaetius and Hecaton develop more interest in 'applied ethics' than their predecessors.

In the later period Stoicism survived in its standard form, as we can see from a textbook like Hierocles, and continued to be an object of philosophical discussion; some of the Church Fathers, such as Tertullian, were influenced by it. We also find writers less interested in philosophical argument than in presenting Stoicism as an attitude or way of life. The letters and essays of *Seneca, the essays of Musonius Rufus, the reported lectures of Epictetus, and the meditations of Marcus *Aurelius are examples of this. They tend to edifying and moralizing discussion and give little indication of the philosophical structure of their positions.   J. A.

Strabo of Amaseia (Pontus, N. Turkey), author of a *Geographia* in 17 books, by far the most important source for ancient *geography, a priceless document of the Augustan age, and a compendium of important material derived from lost authors.

His family was prominent in the politics of Pontus since before the time of *Mithradates VI. Born about 64 BC, he studied grammar under Aristodemus of Nysa, and later at Rome under Tyrannio of Amisus, and philosophy under Xenarchus of Seleuceia (his teachers were Peripatetic (Aristotelian); his views align him with the Stoics; see STOICISM). He knew Posidonius, whose work he used, and from whom he may have drawn his idea of a conjoint interest in history (with its ethical implications) and geography (historical notes (*hypomnēmata*) in 47 books, 43 after the conclusion of *Polybius, were his first work). The empires of Romans and Parthians allowed him to do for the Augustan empire what *Eratosthenes had been able to do in the aftermath of *Alexander the Great (1. 2. 1 [14]).

In the debate over how to do geography, however, he is very critical of Eratosthenes (and many other experts), though, compared with them, he is inclined to be amateurish about mathematics and cosmology, in general preferring the practical to the theoretical and the particular to the general, which locates him in the *periēgēsis* tradition pioneered by Hecataeus of Miletus (*c.*500 BC), and leads

him to call his work 'chorography'. He therefore lays little stress on geographical wonders, and in searching for detailed information retails long passages of by then out-of-date description, which can make the interpretation of his evidence very hazardous. He travelled extensively, but does not bother to make very frequent boasts about autopsy (but see 2. 5. 11 [117]); a long stay in *Egypt in the 20s when his patron Aelius Gallus was prefect (i.e. governor), and several visits to Rome, are noteworthy; he has been thought to have returned to Amaseia and remained there until his death (after AD 21). Parts at least of the *Geographia* were composed under Tiberius.

This experience of the patronage of Roman leaders and education among the foremost intellectuals (many Greeks of Asia like himself) made Strabo (almost certainly a Roman citizen, with a Latin *cognomen*) an eloquent witness of the ways in which the Augustan settlement related to, depended on, and forever changed the plurifarious Mediterranean world of the late republic. Accommodation to Rome was part of the training of all his contemporaries, and he inherited the tradition of Panaetius, Polybius, and Posidonius. Beside the historian Nicolaus of Damascus and *Dionysius of Halicarnassus and in the same circles of patronage as the latter (Aelius Gallus, Quintus Aelius Tubero, the circle of *Sejanus and *Tiberius) he made his job the interpretation of Greek and Roman to each other in a way that looks forward to *Plutarch and *Cassius Dio, and at the same time uses the geographical necessities of Roman power to justify and explain the patriarchal hegemony of Augustus. It is no coincidence that this turning-point in Roman imperial power produced the *chef d'œuvre* of ancient geography.

Strabo emphasizes the usefulness of geography for statesmen and generals, those 'who bring together cities and peoples into a single empire and political management' (1. 1. 16 [9]). He speaks from knowledge of the central concerns of Roman government and is a precious witness to them (as on the lack of profit to be had from lands on the fringes of the inhabited world such as *Britain, 2. 5. 8 [115–16]). It is now clear (against the once influential view of Ettore Pais, which relegated him to an Anatolian milieu) that he is speaking from and about the centre of imperial power. The work is an extraordinary achievement—he likens it himself, apologetically (1. 1. 23 [13–14], *kolossourgia*), to a colossal statue whose detailing is less significant than the overall effect—and justifies his more ambitious claim to have fused the disciplines to produce out of a historical and chorographical framework a philosophy of geography. See also GEOGRAPHY.   N. P.

Suetonius (Gaius Suetonius Tranquillus) (b. *c.* AD 70), Latin biographer. Suetonius was the son of the equestrian (see EQUITES, *Imperial period*) Suetonius Laetus, tribune of Legio XIII at Bedriacum in AD 69, and originated perhaps from Pisaurum in Umbria or, more likely, Hippo Regius (mod. Bône) in Numidia (Roman *Africa). From the correspondence of *Pliny the Younger, he appears already to have attracted attention in Rome as an author and scholar by *c.* AD 97, and also to have gained experience in advocacy. Perhaps intending to pursue the equestrian *cursus*, he secured through Pliny's patronage a military tribunate in Britain *c.*102, which in the event he declined to hold; *c.* AD 110, however, he probably travelled with Pliny to Bithynia (NW Turkey) as a member of the provincial governor's retinue, gaining soon after, again through Pliny's intercession, the *ius trium liberorum* (fictional grant of the privileges conferred on parents of three children). In the late years of *Trajan's reign and under *Hadrian, Suetonius held three important posts in the imperial administration, the secretaryships *a studiis*, *a bibliothecis*, and *ab epistulis* (in charge of literary matters, the imperial libraries, and correspondence), as a fragmentary inscription found in 1952 at Hippo Regius records (*AE* 1953. 73). As *ab epistulis* he is likely to have accompanied Hadrian to Gaul, Germany, and Britain in AD 121–2, but then for unknown reasons was dismissed from office when Hadrian simultaneously deposed as praetorian prefect Gaius Septicius Clarus, the dedicant of Suetonius' collection of imperial biographies, the *Caesares*. He presumably continued to write until his death, perhaps *c.* AD 130, but if a public career continued nothing is known of it.

Works 1. *De viris illustribus*, a now incomplete set of biographies of Roman men of letters arranged in categories—grammarians and rhetoricians, poets, orators, historians, philosophers—probably written before the *Caesares* (below). The segment *De grammaticis et rhetoribus* is preserved independently, and a few other lives, variously abbreviated or corrupted, are known from manuscripts of other authors' works: thus *Terence*, *Horace*, *Lucan*, and the Donatus *Virgil* are generally regarded as deriving from the section on poets. Jerome drew on the work in his *Chronicle*, naming from it 32 poets, from *Ennius to *Lucan, fifteen orators, from *Cicero to Gnaeus Domitius Afer, and six historians, from *Sallust to *Pliny the Elder. The full collection, however, may have contained as many as a hundred lives. A particular interest in the age of Cicero and *Augustus and, to a lesser extent, in the Julio-Claudian era has been discerned in the work, while the relationship between authors and the public world in which they lived may have been its principal theme.

2. *De vita Caesarum* (the *Caesares*), a set of twelve imperial biographies from *Caesar to *Domitian, composed in the early 2nd cent. and complete except for the first few chapters of Caesar (lost between the 6th and 9th cents.).

3. Lost works, in Greek as well as Latin, some known from a list in the *Suda* (under 'Trankullos'), others from random citations in later authors. They included other apparently biographical works, on kings and famous courtesans; works on such institutions as Greek games, the Roman year, Roman customs, spectacles, and public offices; and works perhaps of a lexicographical sort, on the names and types of clothes, on physical defects, on weather-signs, on the names of seas and rivers, and on the names of winds. There was too a work on Cicero's *Republic*. Several of these may have comprised the *Pratum* or *Prata* (*Meadows*), a miscellany probably also known as *De variis rebus* (*On Various Subjects*).

Suetonius was a scholar of wide-ranging antiquarian interests. But it is as an imperial biographer that he must be principally judged. Little that is safe can be said of the literary tradition, or traditions, in which he worked, since apart from Cornelius Nepos he is the first Latin biographer whose work has survived. Consequently the *Caesares* have to be evaluated largely in their own historical context, with Suetonius' exposure to the heart of imperial government during his years of administrative service very much in the forefront of consideration.

A striking feature of the biographies is their thematic, rather than strictly chronological, arrangement: after an introductory section on ancestry and a second on the subject's early life and pre-accession career, a sequence of recurring rubrics follows, in which Suetonius details the emperor's accomplishments and his personal characteristics, often providing anecdotes to illustrate general statements. The lives conclude with an account of the subject's death, sometimes accompanied by a description of his physical appearance and personal idiosyncracies. Though the framework of presentation varies from life to life, the principle of organization is consistent throughout.

The repetition from life to life of common topics, especially those such as the building operations or the public entertainments for which a particular emperor was responsible, suggests that the topics themselves had special significance for Suetonius and his contemporaries; and through comparison with other sources such as the *Res gestae* of Augustus and the *Panegyric* of *Pliny the Younger, where an ideal standard of imperial comportment is clearly perceptible, it emerges that Suetonius used the topics to judge his subjects against a set of popular expectations of imperial behaviour that had taken shape by the time the *Caesares* was composed. *Tiberius, for example, is repeatedly criticized for having failed to live up to expectation, whereas even *Nero and Domitian, rulers on whom Suetonius' final judgement is damning, can nevertheless be commended for having successfully met some of their imperial responsibilities. Suetonius' concern with such aspects of private behaviour as the subject's sexual and religious tastes has been taken also to reflect the increasing Hellenization of upper-class Roman society (see HELLENISM).

In modern times, simplicity has been seen as the main characteristic of Suetonius' writing, in the absence of any obvious literary artistry. He is notable for citing earlier writers verbatim and quotes liberally from various documents—the letters of Augustus for instance—in Greek as well as Latin. (Suetonius may have exploited his period of administrative service under Trajan and Hadrian to seek out archival material for his biographies.) The Flavian lives are much shorter than those of the Julio-Claudians, and they in turn are less substantial than those of Caesar and Augustus. This again suggests that Suetonius' main historical preoccupation was the period from which the Principate ultimately appeared as a new form of government.

Suetonius, however, was not in the first instance a historian, and he should not therefore be compared with Sallust, Livy, or Tacitus. His principal concern was to collect and present material pertinent to the biographical goal of realistically illustrating imperial performance and personality, and in this he stands apart from the historians; for while fully capable of detailed analysis and sustained narrative composition if he wished, he had no interest in the moralistic or didactic as they had. As one author later expressed it, while the historians wrote *diserte* ('eloquently'), Suetonius wrote *vere* ('truthfully') (SHA *Prob.* 2. 7). Suetonius was followed as an imperial biographer by Marius Maximus, who wrote a sequence of imperial biographies, no longer extant, from Trajan to *Commodus, and by the author, or authors, of the 4th-cent. *Historia Augusta*. He served also as the model for Einhard's *Life of Charlemagne* in the 9th cent., and lost his position in Europe as the classic biographer only when Plutarch's lives were translated into the vernacular languages. See BIOGRAPHY, ROMAN.   K. R. B.

suicide The Latin word *suicidium*, from which the English derives, is not classical Latin: pronouns were not used as prefixes in compounds, and the word could only have meant 'the killing of a pig'. The first uses of *suicidium* found so far are by Gauthier de Saint-Victor in 1177/8 and, in English, by Sir Thomas Browne in *Religio Medici* published in 1643, who probably invented it afresh. The nearest to a technical term in antiquity was *mors voluntaria* (voluntary death) and the Greek equivalent, verbal phrases being used for the most part. Some ancient terminology reveals that suicide was often subsumed in categories regarded as more fundamental: thus a *biaiothanatos* (Latin *biothanatos*) was any victim of premature, violent death, and an *autocheir* was someone who kills his kin.

The limited and unsystematic nature of our evidence for Greek and Roman suicide does not allow for quantitative studies. Reliant as we are for the most part on literary accounts (some fictional, even mythical, all artistically shaped), we can only draw conclusions about attitudes and values. If a sociological approach is difficult, so is a psychiatric one, for in antiquity suicide was described on the assumption that it was a conscious intentional act: mental imbalance, though occasionally given as a cause of suicide, was not the central case it has become in the modern world. The ancients, including hard-headed Roman jurists who needed to distinguish suicides motivated by fear of condemnation from others that brought exemption from confiscation, felt confident that they could distinguish individual motives. They were not troubled by notions of unconscious motivation. This fact, in combination with the lack of reversible methods, may explain why the suicide attempts reported in the ancient sources are relatively few when compared with the modern ratio of attempted to accomplished suicides.

Some of the chief motives mentioned are shame (typically, for men, because of defeat; for women, loss of chastity); severe pain, incurable illness, or old age; self-sacrifice for country or friend. Suicide was neither wholly approved or wholly condemned: everything depended on the motive, the manner, and the method. When arising from shame and dishonour, suicide was regarded as appropriate; self-sacrifice was admired; impulsive suicide was less esteemed than a calculated, rational act; death by jumping from a height (including drowning) or by hanging was despised and regarded as fit only for women, slaves, or the lower classes, apparently because it was disfiguring; death by weapons was regarded as more respectable, even heroic.

The concern of philosophers with minimizing the fear of death by the application of reason led them to discuss suicide, and to consider, alongside obvious cases, compulsory suicide at one extreme and martyrdom at the other (a combination also covered by Durkheim's definition, 'any death which is the direct or indirect result of a positive or negative act accomplished by the victim himself, which he knows should produce this result', though he wished to exclude the criterion of intention). The *locus classicus* for philosophical discussions of suicide was the death of *Socrates (which exemplifies both extremes), as described by *Plato in the *Phaedo*. Although suicide, except under necessity, is there condemned, Socrates was adopted as a model, not only by *Seneca who was ordered to kill himself, but by *Cato the Younger, who chose to refuse *Caesar's pardon. These were adherents of the Stoa, which advocated the rational exit from life, provided certain conditions were fulfilled (see STOICISM). Plato and *Aristotle had been more negative, though Plato in *The Laws* admitted inevitable misfortune and intolerable shame as justifications and Aristotle allowed self-sacrifice for country or friends, while otherwise rejecting suicide as an injustice to society. The Epicureans (see EPICURUS) reluctantly permitted suicide when the balance of pleasure over pain could not be maintained. A calm demeanour and the giving of reasons to friends and relatives were the hallmark of the philosophically justified suicide: they could be histrionic, not only in literature but in life, for the jurists recognized 'showing off' as a motive for suicide characteristic of philosophers (*Dig.* 28. 3. 6. 7).

At all levels of society, then, there seems to have been no blanket approval or condemnation of suicide, even though it was occasionally compared to murder (Elder Seneca, *Controv.* 8. 4; Quint. 7. 3. 7). It was left to 4th-cent. *Christianity, confronting the incentive to suicide presented by the heavenly rewards of martyrdom, to throw its authority behind the Platonic belief that man must not pre-empt God's decision.   M. T. G.

Sulla (Lucius Cornelius Sulla), surnamed Felix, 'Lucky', born *c*.138 BC of an old, but not recently prominent, *patrician family, after a dissolute youth inherited a fortune from his stepmother, which enabled him to enter the aristocratic career. Chosen by *Marius as his quaestor (107) he distinguished himself in the Numidian War, finally securing the surrender of the Numidian king Jugurtha by his kinsman Bocchus I through diplomacy and thus ending the war. He again served under Marius against the Germans in 104 and 103, then joined the army of Quintus Lutatius Catulus (consul 78), probably dispatched by Marius to advise Catulus, and enabled him to join in the final victory. Omitting the aedileship, he failed to become praetor (see CONSUL) for 98, but succeeded through lavish bribery in becoming urban praetor (i.e. hearing cases of law at Rome) 97. He was assigned Cilicia (SE Asia Minor) *pro consule* (in place of a consul), then instructed to instal Ariobarzanes as king in Cappadocia. He accomplished this largely with local levies and displayed Roman power to the eastern kingdoms, including (for the first time) Parthia. A Chaldaean's prophecy that he would attain greatness and die at the height of good fortune influenced him for the rest of his life. He stayed in Cilicia for several years, perhaps until 92. On his return he was prosecuted, but the prosecution was abandoned. In 91 the senate, promoting him against Marius, granted Bocchus permission to dedicate a group showing the surrender of Jugurtha on the Capitol. Marius' reaction almost led to fighting, but the Social War (see ROME (HISTORY) §1.5) supervened (Plut. *Sull*. 6).

In the war Sulla distinguished himself on the southern front and in 89, promoted especially by the Metelli, gained the consulship of 88 with Quintus Pompeius Rufus, whose son married Sulla's daughter. Sulla himself married Caecilia Metella, widow of Marcus Aemilius Scaurus (consul 115), and was now one of the leading men in the state.

Given the command gainst *Mithradates by the senate, he was deprived of it by the *tribune Publius Sulpicius Rufus, who transferred it to Marius in order to gain Marius' aid for his political plans. Sulla pretended to acquiesce, but finding support among his troops, who hoped for rich booty in Asia, he marched on Rome and took the unprepared city by force. His officers, except for his quaestor (his relative Lucius Licinius Lucullus), deserted him, and his methods shocked even his supporters. He had Sulpicius killed in office and his allies hunted down (Marius escaped to Africa), then passed several laws by armed force. General opposition compelled him to send his army away and allow the election of his enemy Lucius Cornelius Cinna as consul 87, over his own candidate Publius Servilius Vatia; and he failed to gain control of the army of Gnaeus Pompeius Strabo. Leaving Rome and ignoring a summons to stand trial, he embarked for Greece, where Quintus Braetius Sura, a legate of the commander in Macedonia, had already driven the enemy back to the sea. Sulla's hope of safety lay in winning the eastern war: he ordered Sura to return to Macedonia and took charge.

Outlawed, but not molested, under Cinna, he agreed (it seems) to refrain from attacking Lucius Valerius Flaccus (suffect *consul 86) on his march against Mithradates. He himself twice defeated the Mithradatic general Archelaus

and sacked the Piraeus and (in part) *Athens. After Lucullus had saved Mithradates from Gaius Flavius Fimbria, who had taken over Flaccus' army, he made peace with the king at Dardanus (85), granting him his territory, recognition as an ally, and impunity for his adherents in return for surrender of his conquests and support for Sulla with money and supplies. He then dealt with Fimbria, reconciled his own army (disgruntled at the peace with the enemy of Rome) by quartering it on the cities of Asia, which he bled of their wealth, and on hearing of Cinna's death abandoned negotiations with the government and openly rebelled (84). Invading Italy, he was soon joined by most aristocrats—especially Quintus Caecilius Metellus Pius, Marcus Licinius Crassus, and *Pompey—and within a year defeated all the loyalist forces. Finding the Italians hostile, he swore not to diminish their rights of citizenship, but massacred those who continued resistance (especially the Samnites) and imposed severe penalties and confiscations on whole communities. After securing Rome through his victory at the Colline gate, he was appointed dictator under a law of the *interrex* Valerius Flaccus, whom he made his *magister equitum* (master of the horse), and was voted immunity for all his actions, past and future. He continued and legalized his massacres by publishing proscription lists (sometimes fraudulently added to by subordinates).

During 81 he enacted a legislative programme designed to put power firmly in the hands of the senate, whose numbers (traditionally 300, but now much reduced) he raised to 600 by adlecting *equites* supporting him. In addition to minor reforms, he (1) curbed the tribunate by requiring the senate's approval for tribunician bills, limiting the veto (*intercessio*) and debarring ex-tribunes from other magistracies, thus making the office unattractive to ambitious men; (2) restored the *quaestiones* (standing courts), the number of which he raised to at least seven, to the enlarged senate; (3) increased the number of praetors to eight and that of quaestors to twenty, chiefly to ensure that tenure of provinces was not (in general) prolonged beyond one year; (4) laid down a stricter *cursus honorum* (career path for senators), making the quaestorship as well as the praetorship compulsory before the consulship could be reached at a minimum age of 42; (5) made quaestors automatically members of the senate, thus abolishing the censors' right of selection, and did away with the powerful post of *princeps senatus* (acknowledged senior senator); (6) subjected holders of *imperium* outside Italy to stricter control by the senate. His veterans were settled on confiscated land (especially in Campania and Etruria, see ETRUSCANS) as guarantors of his order. Then, believing in the old prophecy that he now had not long to live, he gradually divested himself of power and restored constitutional government, becoming consul (with Metellus Pius) in 80 and returning to private status in 79. He retired to Campania, where he died of a long-standing disease in 79. His funeral was impressively staged to display the power of his veterans, especially in view of the agitation of the consul Marcus Aemilius Lepidus. In fact, his constitutional settlement, weakened by concessions during the 70s, was overthrown in 70 by his old adherents *Pompey and *Crassus; but his administrative reforms survived to the end of the republic and beyond.

Despite his mystical belief in his luck (hence his surname 'Felix' and the *praenomina* (forenames) of his twin children, from *faustus*, 'fortunate'), despite his arrogance and ruthlessness, Sulla never aimed at permanent tyranny: he did not even put his portrait on his coins. He wished his settlement to succeed, and he thought it out carefully, no doubt with the help of his associates (some of the group that had supported Marcus Livius Drusus (tribune 91)), to eliminate the 'two-headedness' (thus *Varro) that Gaius *Gracchus had introduced into the republic and to restore a strengthened senate to unchallenged power. His arrangements were consistent, practical, and neither visionary nor reactionary. Yet he had no appreciation of deep-seated problems: he made no attempt to remove the threat of client armies, such as had supported his own rebellion, by putting the senate in charge of providing for veterans, and he seems actually to have abolished the provision of corn to the poor at a controlled price. His own example not only set a precedent for the use of client armies against the republic, but helped to destroy the morale of those on whom resistance to an imitator would depend. After sparing the only powerful enemy of Rome for his personal advantage, he had prepared the ground for that enemy's resurgence by ruining the cities of Asia; he had weeded out those most loyal to the republic in Rome and Italy and rewarded and promoted those who, for whatever reason, had joined in his rebellion. A sense of duty and public service could not be expected of those now making up the senate who had welcomed the opportunities for power and enrichment provided by a rebel; and a generation later it became clear that Italy, having suffered for its loyalty to the republic, was unwilling to defend Sulla's beneficiaries and their corrupt successors against Caesar when he followed Sulla's example.

That example did instil a horror of civil war that lasted for a generation: his beneficiaries praised his rebellion that had brought them to power, but shuddered at his cruelty after victory. Yet that memory was bound to fade. His career and the effects of his victory ultimately made another civil war almost inevitable, and a politic *clementia* now made a successful rebel unobjectionable to the majority.

The main sources are *Plutarch's *Sulla* and *Appian (*Civil Wars* 1 and *Mithridatica*). Sulla's memoirs, edited by Lucius Licinius Lucullus, pervade the tradition: both Plutarch and Appian's source read and to a considerable extent followed them. The tradition of those who joined Sulla on his return was conveyed in the widely-read history of the historian Lucius Cornelius Sisenna, traceable especially in Appian and historians based on Livy. For a sympathetic portrait of Sulla and recent bibliography, especially of the author's own numerous contributions, see A.

Keaveney, *Sulla, the Last Republican* (1982). For the main problems of detail recently discussed, see Broughton, *MRR* 3. 73 ff. The date of his praetorship and proconsulate: T. C. Brennan, *Chiron* 1992, 103 ff. (with bibliography) supersedes earlier discussion. The date of his formal abdication of the dictatorship and assumption of the consulship still seems best put at the beginning of 80, rather than in the middle, especially since he is never given both titles. (For other recent views see Broughton, *MRR* 3. 73 ff. The older view that he remained dictator until 79 has been abandoned.) On his priesthoods see A. Keaveney, *AJAH* 1982, 150 ff. For the persistence of his reforms, U. Laffi, *Athenaeum* 1967, 177 ff., 255 ff.

E. B.

sycophants (Gk. *sykophantai*), habitual prosecutors. In Athens there were, for most offences, no public prosecutors, but anyone (for some offences, any citizen) who wished was allowed to prosecute in a public action. Some individuals made a habit of bringing prosecutions, either to gain the financial rewards given to successful prosecutors in certain actions (notably *phasis* and *apographē*; see LAW AND PROCEDURE, ATHENIAN), or to gain money by blackmailing a man who was willing to pay to avoid prosecution, or to earn payment from someone who had reasons for wanting a man to be prosecuted, or to make a political or oratorical reputation. Such persons came to be called sycophants (lit. 'fig-revealers'; the origin of the usage is obscure). The word is often used as a term of disparagement or abuse in the Attic orators and in *Aristophanes, who shows sycophants in action in *Acharnians*.

The Athenians wished to check sycophants, who prosecuted without good reason, but not to discourage public-spirited prosecutors. Therefore the rewards for successful prosecution were not abolished, but penalties were introduced in most public actions for a prosecutor who dropped a case after starting it, or whose case was so weak that he failed to obtain one-fifth of the jury's votes. In addition sycophancy was an offence for which a man could be prosecuted. *Graphē*, *probolē*, *eisangelia*, *apagōgē*, and *endeixis* are all said to have been possible methods of accusing sycophants (see LAW AND PROCEDURE, ATHENIAN), but it is not known how the offence was defined; perhaps there was no legal definition.

Nobody has yet come up with a good explanation of how the word got its modern sense of 'flatterers'.

D. M. M.

symposium Commensality in Greece was focused both on the public civic or sacrificial meal and on the activities of smaller exclusive groups. The warrior feast was already central to the Homeric image of society (see HOMER); under the influence of the near east in the period 750–650 BC more complex rituals of pleasure arose. The time of 'drinking together' (*symposion*) was separated from the meal before it (*deipnon*) and became the main focus of attention. The male participants wore garlands, and libations and prayers began and ended the proceedings. The

Greeks adopted the practice of reclining on the left elbow (one or two to a couch); from this evolved a characteristic shape of room, and a standard size for the drinking group of between fourteen and thirty: the *andrōn* or men's room was square, arranged with a door off centre to fit usually seven or fifteen couches; larger sizes (though known) tended to destroy the unity of sympotic space. Many such rooms have been recognized archaeologically, but the best representation is the painted Tomb of the Diver at *Paestum. They were supplied with low tables, cushions, decorated couches, and wall-hangings. By the late 6th cent. a repertoire of vessels had been elaborated, including different cup shapes, jugs, wine coolers, and mixing-vessels: the decoration of these vases offers a set of self-conscious images related to the activities of the drinking group (see POTTERY, GREEK). Water was mixed with the *wine in a central crater to a strength determined by the president (usually three or four to one, or about the strength of modern beer); it was served by slave boys. Equality and order in distribution were maintained: each crater measured a stage in the progress towards drunkenness. At the end of the session a procession (*kōmos*) in the streets would demonstrate the cohesion and power of the group.

The symposium was a male and aristocratic activity, originally based on the warrior group; its earliest poetry was the *elegiac poetry of war, and the Spartan reclining *syssition* (mess) remained the basis of its military organization. Citizen women were excluded. It was a centre for the transmission of traditional values and for the *homosexual bonding of young males; it could provide the organization for political action in the aristocratic *hetaireia* (private club). But it was also a place of pleasure; *kottabos* ('Wine Throw') was a favourite pastime; professional entertainers were hired. *Dionysus was accompanied by *Aphrodite and the *Muses, in the form of female slave companions (*hetairai*) and monodic lyric poetry, which was composed for performance at symposia—at first by gifted amateurs, later by skilled professional poets. In the Archaic age the symposium was the focus for an artistic patronage which reached its heights under the tyrants (see TYRANNY); together with wine, 'drinking in the Greek style' was exported throughout the Mediterranean in a process of acculturation that profoundly affected Etruscans, Romans, and many other peoples.

The artistic and cultural importance of the symposium declined during the Classical age, but it remained important in social life well into the Hellenistic period. Later it fused with Roman customs. The reclining symposium survives today in the ritual of the Seder or Passover Meal.

O. Mu.

synagogue (Gk. *synagōgē*), the name used by Greek-speaking *Jews to describe both their communities in the diaspora and their meeting places for regular public recital and teaching of the Torah (the Law of Moses, as embodied especially in the Pentateuch).

The belief of Jews that they have a duty to hear the law being read at least on occasion can be found already in Nehemiah 8: 1–8, composed probably in the 4th cent. BC, but the first evidence of Jews dedicating buildings to this or a similar institution is found in Ptolemaic *Egypt, where Jewish inscriptions recording the erection of prayer-houses

symposium A clay drinking cup from Athens (early 5th cent. BC) showing an imaginary symposium-scene. Garlanded males entertain themselves with wine, women, and song.

(*proseuchai*) have been found, dated to the 3rd cent. BC and after. *Josephus' use of the term *proseuchē* to describe the building in Tiberias in Galilee where sabbath meetings were held during the revolt against Rome in AD 67 (*Vita* 277) confirms the identity of the *proseuchē* with the *synagogē*. The New Testament and Philo of Alexandria take synagogue meetings for granted as part of Jewish life in the 1st cent. AD both in Galilee and in the east Mediterranean diaspora. A 1st-cent. AD inscription records the erection of a synagogue in Jerusalem by a certain Theodotus (*CIJ* 1404). Rather more tentative should be the identification as synagogues of public buildings dated before AD 70 at Gamla (on the Golan), *Masada and Herodium (in Judaea), and at *Delos.

The term *proseuchē* ('prayer') found in the Egyptian evidence suggests that public prayer may have been part of the function of synagogues, alongside the reading and teaching of the law, at least in the diaspora. However, there is no evidence of a formal public liturgy in synagogues in the land of Israel until the late Roman period. Rabbinic texts of the 2nd cent. AD are silent about any such liturgy, and according to the Gospels (Matt. 6: 5) it was a sign of hypocrisy to pray publicly in the synagogues in order to be admired. Literary references to prayer suggest that it was a private business. It is possible that proximity to the Jerusalem Temple, where formal liturgy accompanied sacrifices, discouraged the use of synagogues for similar purposes in the land of Israel, but the evidence is inconclusive.

By contrast, distance from the Jerusalem Temple may have encouraged treatment of diaspora synagogues as sacred places as far back as the Hellenistic period. Thus the synagogue in *Antioch in Syria was described by Josephus as a temple (*hieron*) (*BJ* 7. 41). Synagogues in Palestine were described on inscriptions as sacred places only in late Roman and Byzantine times, when Jews began to erect numerous synagogues in Judaea, Galilee, and the Golan in monumental style and often with elaborate mosaics. Synagogue architecture was very varied even within Palestine, and in the diaspora the wall frescos of the Dura-Europus synagogue (middle Euphrates), and the huge basilica found at Sardis (W. Asia Minor), have no parallel.

In Babylonia and the land of Israel the teaching function of synagogues was fulfilled by weekly recitation of the Pentateuch in a regular (eventually annual) cycle. Explanation took the form of translation into Aramaic (*targum*) and elucidation and elaboration (*midrash*). In the western diaspora, the law was often read in Greek, either in the Septuagint (the Jewish texts constituting the Old Testament of Greek Christians) or in one of the later versions.

Among diaspora Jews the synagogue often functioned as a community centre as well as a place for worship. The *archisynagōgos* ('ruler of the synagogue') was often the senior magistrate of the community. He and other synagogue officials enforced discipline and adjudicated between members in cases of dispute. See RELIGION, JEWISH.

M. D. G.

synoecism (*synoikismos*), in the Greek world, the combination of several smaller communities to form a single larger community. Sometimes the union was purely political and did not affect the pattern of settlement or the physical existence of the separate communities: this is what the Athenians supposed to have happened when they attributed a synoecism to *Theseus (Thuc. 2. 15), commemorated by a festival in Classical times (the Synoecia). On other occasions it involved the migration of citizens to the new city, as in the case of Megalopolis in Arcadia *c.*370 BC. Sometimes a union might be undone (*dioikismos*) by an enemy which resented the power of the united state: Mantinea, also in Arcadia, was formed out of five villages, perhaps *c.*470, in what appears from the archaeological evidence to have been a purely political union; in 385 *Sparta used the King's Peace of 386 BC (see GREECE, HISTORY) as a pretext for splitting it into separate villages once more; in 370, when Sparta was no longer strong enough to interfere, the single *polis* was recreated.

For the unions of the Hellenistic period, often made at the demand of a king, we tend to encounter the term *sympoliteia* (lit. 'joint *citizenship') rather than synoecism.

V. E.; P. J. R.

Syracuse (Gk. *Syrakousai*, mod. Siracusa) (see ◀Map 3, Bd▶), on the east coast of *Sicily, was founded by the Corinthians (see COLONIZATION, GREEK), led by Archias, *c.*734 BC. The original foundation lay on the island of Ortygia, with an abundant spring and flanked by two fine natural harbours, but almost immediately, as demonstrated by the distribution of 8th-cent. pottery, the settlement spread up to a kilometre inland on the adjacent mainland (Achradina); the two were joined by an artificial causeway. Its early government was aristocratic, the *gamoroi* forming an élite whose lands were worked by underprivileged indigenes (*killyrioi*: see SLAVERY). Prosperity in the Archaic period is attested by colonies at Helorus, Acrae, and Camarina, and at Casmenae (Monte Casale), as well as by architectural remains: temples of Apollo, Olympian Zeus, and Athena, and an Ionic temple of unknown dedication, all belong to the 6th cent. (see TEMPLE). Defeated by the tyrant Hippocrates of Gela (d. 491), the *gamoroi* were expelled in a democratic revolution. Gelon espoused their cause, making himself tyrant (see TYRANNY) of the city, of whose empire he thus became the founder. His brother Hieron confirmed Syracusan primacy and added a cultural splendour: *Aeschylus, *Simonides, and *Pindar all spent time at his court. After the battle of Himera (480) he rebuilt the temple of Athena, the shell of which still stands, remarkably, within the cathedral of Syracuse. The city expanded northwards from Achradina and took in areas known as Tyche and Temenites, the latter also referred to as Neapolis.

Soon after Hieron's death Syracuse regained democratic freedom but lost her empire. The democracy operated through an assembly and council; annual *stratēgoi* ('generals'), whose number varied, formed the chief executive.

For a short time a device resembling *ostracism, called *petalismos*, sought to check abuses of power. In 412, after Athens' defeat, the democracy became more complete by the reforms of Diocles, but *Dionysius I soon established his tyranny, preserving nevertheless the accepted organs of the constitution.

The new democracy after 466 had difficulties with the tyrants' ex-soldiers and new citizens, and faced wars with Acragas and with the indigenous Sicels under Ducetius. But these were overcome, as later were the wars with Athens (427–424 and 415–413), in which the statesmanship of Hermocrates was influential. After 406 *Carthage was the chief enemy. Dionysius I fought four Carthaginian wars, and more than once the Syracusans were in great difficulties. But the early 4th cent. was a period of great prosperity, and it was now that the enormous girdle of fortifications, an astonishing 27 km. (17 mi.) long, were built to include the plateau of Epipolae (to the north of the city) within the defended area. Rigorously but astutely guided by its tyrant, Syracuse now controlled the greater part of Sicily and much of southern Italy. Dionysius II enjoyed ten peaceful years before his kinsman Dion challenged his rule (356); thereafter Syracusan affairs became increasingly anarchic, and the city's power and population declined. Timoleon of Corinth restored the situation, introducing a moderately oligarchic government on the Corinthian model, but after twenty years this was overthrown by Agathocles, who made himself first tyrant (317) and later king (305/4).

At Agathocles' death (289) a further period of instability ensued. A new tyrant Hicetas (288–278) was defeated by Carthage; *Pyrrhus remedied the situation but was unable to revive the empire of Dionysius and Agathocles. After his withdrawal from the scene, conflict with the Mamertines (a band of Campanian mercenaries) in Messana produced a new leader, who as Hieron II (d. 216) led Syracuse into a prosperous Indian summer, when the city became a significant intellectual and artistic centre. The economy prospered, with commercial contacts in both the eastern and western Mediterranean as well as with Carthage; and ambitious building projects included the great theatre (238/215 BC), one of the largest in the Greek world (diameter 138 m. (127 yds.)), a grandiose π-shaped stoa (portico) with sides 100 m. (92 yds.) long above the theatre, and a gigantic altar to Zeus Eleutherius, 200 m. (184 yds.) long. By now, however, Syracusan independence existed by courtesy of the Romans, and when in 215 Hieronymus, Hieron's successor, preferred Carthage to Rome, its end was at hand. After a long siege (213–211), in which the mathematician and inventor Archimedes played a substantial part, Marcus Claudius Marcellus sacked the city.

Under the Roman republic Syracuse became a *civitas decumana* (city liable to pay a tithe) and the centre of provincial government, retaining both its beauty and a certain importance. It suffered at the corrupt governor Verres' hands (see *Cicero), and in 21 BC received an Augustan *colonia* (citizen colony); a new public square near

Hieron's altar, a monumental arch, and the amphitheatre belong to this period. Although the topography of Roman Syracuse is poorly known (a 2nd-cent. AD theatre-temple complex being the only other major surviving public monument), there is little doubt that Syracusan prosperity continued beyond the Frankish raid of AD 278 to its capture by the Arabs in 878. Extensive catacombs attest its populousness in the early Christian period (3rd–7th cents.).

A. G. W.; R. J. A. W.

Syria (see ◀Map 2, Cc▶)

Pre-Roman This region was a satrapy ('Beyond the River', i.e. the *Euphrates) of the Achaemenid Persian empire (see PERSIA) until it was conquered by *Alexander the Great in 332 BC. On his death (323) it was assigned to the Macedonian Laomedon, who was in 319–318 ejected by *Ptolemy I. Thereafter it was disputed between Ptolemy and *Antigonus the One-eyed. After the battle of Ipsus (301), Seleucus gained north Syria (from the Amanus mountains in the north to the river Eleutherus in the south), which he kept, as well as 'on paper' Coele ('Hollow') Syria (the country behind the Lebanese coastal plain) and the Phoenician cities. However, Ptolemy I was already in occupation, and claimed control, of these last two areas; Seleucus I chose to drop his rights to Coele Syria and *Phoenicia, with the southern border dividing off Ptolemaic possessions set at the river Eleutherus. The whole region suffered from repeated wars between the Ptolemies and the *Seleucids in the 3rd cent. until *Antiochus III won (in campaigns, 202–198 BC) the strategically and economically important sectors of Coele Syria and the Phoenician cities, along with Judaea and Transjordania, bringing the southern borders of Seleucid rule in this area for the first time to the Sinai desert. *Pompey annexed Seleucid Syria in 64 BC, and it became a Roman province.

The Seleucids, especially Seleucus I, as part of the physical occupation of this region and a policy of gaining control over major strategic routes, founded many colonies and cities in north Syria, including the tetrapolis of Seleuceia, *Antioch (one of the Seleucid royal capitals), Apamea in the middle Orontes valley, and Laodicea-Mare (mod. Latakiye), which like Seleuceia was developed as a naval base, as well as e.g. Beroea (Aleppo), Cyrrhus, and Zeugma.

This region had been open to Greek trade and to Greek (and other) cultural influences for centuries before Alexander. It is a moot point whether the lack of archaeological evidence from the Hellenistic period is accidental, the result mainly of the fact that the great Roman sites of north Syria obliterated almost completely the remains of the earlier Hellenistic cities; at any rate, the impact of 'Hellenism' on local cultures, under Seleucid rule, is hard to assess, quite apart from the fact that there is no reason to assume any longer that 'Hellenization' was a particular aim of the Seleucid kings (see HELLENISM, HELLENIZATION).

Roman The Roman province comprised besides the cities, a few of which were free, the client kingdoms of Commagene (see NEMRUT DAG) and Arabia, the ethnarchy of the *Jews (Judaea), the tetrarchy of the Ituraeans, and many minor tetrarchies in the north. Mark *Antony gave to *Cleopatra the Ituraean tetrarchy, the coast up to the Eleutherus (except Tyre and Sidon), Damascus and Coele Syria, and parts of the Jewish and Nabataean Arab kingdoms.

Syria (which probably included Cilicia Pedias (roughly the plain around mod. Adana, SE Turkey) from *c.*44 BC to AD 72) was under the Principate an important military command; its imperial governor or legate, a consular, had down to AD 70 normally four legions at his disposal. The client kingdoms were gradually annexed. Commagene was finally incorporated in the province in AD 72, Ituraea partly in 24 BC, partly (Agrippa II's kingdom) *c.* AD 93. Judaea, at first governed by *procurators, became in AD 70 a regular province ruled by a praetorian legate, who commanded a legion withdrawn from Syria; under *Hadrian the province, henceforth usually known as Syria Palaestina, became consular, a second legion being added. The Nabataean kingdom became in AD 105 the province of Arabia, ruled by a praetorian legate with one legion. *Septimius Severus divided Syria into a northern province with two legions (Syria Coele) and a southern with one legion (Syria Phoenice). Urbanization made little progress under the empire. Commagene and Arabia were on annexation partitioned into city-territories, but much of Ituraea was added to the territories of Berytus (mod. Beirut), Sidon, and Damascus, and in the rest the villages became the units of government. In Judaea the centralized bureaucracy established by the Ptolemies and maintained by the Seleucids, *Maccabees, and Herodians survived in some areas throughout the Principate; in others cities were founded by Vespasian, Hadrian, and the Severan emperors. Of the minor principalities some, such as Chalcis ad Belum, Emesa, and Arca, became cities, but most seem to have been incorporated in the territories of existing towns. In late antiquity, Syria was split into four with Antioch, Apamea, Tyre, and Damascus as provincial capitals. Large and well-built villages developed up to the desert edge. Impressive remains survive. Cities, of which Apamea is best known through excavations, flourished up to the mid-6th cent. Then earthquakes, plague, and Persian invasions greatly weakened the province, which easily fell to the Arabs after the battle of the Yarmuk in 636. The leading classes in city and country were Hellenized, and Greek-speaking or bilingual, but Aramaic was widely spoken in the countryside. In the 3rd cent. in eastern Syria and Mesopotamia Aramaic developed into a literary language (Syriac), producing a literature, including translations from the Greek, but also much, mainly religious, original writing. Aramaic became the language in numerous monophysite monasteries.

Olives were produced for export in many parts, also wine. Other agricultural products were nuts, plums of Damascus, the dates of Jericho, and Ascalonite onions. The principal industries were linen-weaving (at Laodicea and in several Phoenician and north Palestinian towns), wool-weaving (at Damascus), purple-dyeing (on the Phoenician and Palestinian coast), and glass-blowing (at Sidon). The transit trade from Babylonia, Arabia Felix, and the far east passed by caravan over the Arabian desert, via such *emporia* (trading places) as *Palmyra, Damascus, Bostra or Petra, to the coastal ports.   A. H. M. J.; H. S.; S. S.-W., W. L.

Tacitus (*see following page*)

Tadmor in Syria. See PALMYRA.

Tarquinius Superbus, Lucius, traditionally the last king of Rome (534–510 BC). According to the oldest sources (Fabius Pictor fr. 11 Peter) he was the son of Tarquinius Priscus, the fifth king of Rome, although on the traditional chronology that is impossible (Dion. Hal. 4. 6–7). It follows either that Superbus was in fact the grandson of Priscus (thus Piso fr. 15 P. = Dion. Hal. 4. 6–7), or, more probably, that the traditional chronology of the regal period is unsound. Tarquin is said to have pursued an aggressive foreign policy; he captured several Latin towns and reorganized the Latin League into a regular military alliance under Roman leadership (Livy 1. 52), a state of affairs that is reflected in the first treaty between Rome and Carthage (Polyb. 3. 22: 509 BC). The text of the treaty he made with the Latin town of Gabii is supposed to have survived until the time of *Augustus. He is also famous for having completed the temple of Capitoline Jupiter (see ROME (TOPOGRAPHY)), and notorious for his tyrannical rule which eventually led to his downfall. Terracottas from the temple site at Sant'Omobono may belong to the reign of Superbus; in any event they confirm that the later Roman kings were flamboyant rulers who modelled themselves on contemporary Greek tyrants (see TYRANNY). This proves that Superbus' reputation as a tyrant is not (or not entirely) the result of secondary elaboration in the annalistic tradition in an artificial attempt to assimilate Rome and Greece.

His accession was supposedly engineered by his sister-in-law Tullia, younger daughter of King Servius *Tullius, who impelled him to murder her husband and sister, marry her, and seize power by killing her father. His son's rape of Lucretia, wife of Lucius Tarquinius Collatinus, who then committed suicide, was the catalyst for the expulsion of the Tarquins from Rome by Lucius Iunius Brutus (alleged ancestor of *Brutus). Tarquin fled to Caere, and persuaded Veii and Tarquinii to attack Rome. After their defeat at Silva Arsia, he appealed to Lars Porsenna, king of Clusium, whose assault on Rome is said to have been aimed at restoring Tarquin to power; but this cannot have been so if Porsenna succeeded in taking the city, and it is hard to reconcile with the story that Tarquin then turned to his son-in-law Octavius Mamilius, *dictator of the Latins, since the Latins had vanquished Porsenna. After the defeat of Mamilius at Lake Regillus, Tarquin took refuge with Aristodemus of Cumae, where he died in 495 BC.

T. J. Co.

technology Modern definitions of technology merely stress the systematic application of knowledge, and underline the difficulty of addressing ancient technology with concepts relevant to antiquity. Lynn White Jr. observed that 'no Greek or Roman ever told us, either in words or in iconography, what he or his society wanted from technology, or why they wanted it', and Moses Finley criticized 'an artificial insistence on isolating technology as an autonomous subject'. The problem of definition is exacerbated by relative judgements made about the success, or failure, of ancient technology. Whatever the practical significance of ancient philosophical concepts of progress may have been, there has been general agreement amongst historians of technology that the modest number of items that can be claimed as Greek or Roman inventions were not exploited, and that this failure was attributable to social factors. A potent assertion maintained by many commentators on supposed advances in medieval technology is that not until Rome was converted to *Christianity could liberation from animism be achieved, and value consequently placed upon *labour and production. However, this kind of 'Darwinian' concept of ancient technology, which assumes that technical progress was a natural path of development towards the Industrial Revolution, seems inappropriate on empirical, as well as theoretical, grounds. If we *must* judge ancient technology, should success be measured by showing that inventions known from documentary sources actually existed, or should we demand that they were widely and productively employed? Whose needs should we consider—the state, the army, a social élite, or the multitude?

[*continued on p. 705*]

Tacitus

Tacitus, Roman historian.

1. Publius (?) Cornelius Tacitus was born *c.* AD 56, probably in Narbonese or Cisalpine Gaul (see GAUL (TRANSALPINE) and GAUL (CISALPINE)). He was in Rome at latest by 75, where an uninterrupted career under *Vespasian, Titus, and *Domitian (*Hist.* 1. 1. 3) brought him to the praetorship in 88, by which time he was also a member of the prestigious priesthood, the college of the *quindecimviri sacris faciundis* (guardians of the Sybilline books: see ORACLES). During 89–93 he was absent from Rome (*Agr.* 45. 5), presumably holding government posts. In 97 he was suffect consul and pronounced the funeral oration upon Lucius Verginius Rufus. We know of no other office held by Tacitus, till seniority brought him the proconsulship of Asia (see ASIA, ROMAN PROVINCE) for 112–13 (*IMylasa* 365, with W. Eck, *ZPE* 45 (1982), 139–53). The date of his death is unknown, but can scarcely have been before 118 (see below).

2. Early in 98 Tacitus published his first work, the *Agricola* (*De vita Iulii Agricolae*), a biography of his father-in-law Gnaeus Iulius Agricola, governor of *Britain for seven years from 77 (or 78). That governorship, culminating in the decisive victory of mons Graupius, forms the work's central core (chs. 18–38). But the work is more than a panegyric of a dead man. The opening chapters, without naming Domitian, declare that recent times were hostile both to the performance and to the chronicling of great deeds. The final chapters develop that theme: a fierce invective against Domitian is followed by a moving *consolatio* for the dead Agricola; and the final words, again linking subject and biographer, affirm that Agricola will live on through Tacitus' biography.

Later in the same year came the *Germania* (*De origine et situ Germanorum*). In its first half (to 27. 1), after arguing briefly that the Germans are indigenous and racially pure, Tacitus describes their public and private life. Comparisons, implicit and explicit, between Germans and contemporary Roman society abound, not always to the advantage of the latter. However, the *Germania* is not to be seen as a mirror of morals (or, as some have argued, a historical excursus): its second half, devoted entirely to describing individual tribes, confirms that it is an ethnographical monograph, in which (naturally enough) a foreign people is viewed through Roman eyes.

The third of Tacitus' *opera minora*, the *Dialogus* (*Dialogus de oratoribus*), was perhaps written *c.*101/2; the belief that its neo-Ciceronian style (see CICERO) indicates an early, pre-Domitianic, date has now been discarded. It is an urbane and good-natured discussion about the causes of the contemporary decline in oratory; following the fiction of Cicero's *De oratore*, Tacitus affects to recall a discussion he heard as a young man in 75. Of its three speakers Marcus Aper champions modern oratory, while Vipstanus Messalla affirms that the decline can be remedied by a return to old-fashioned morals and education. Curiatius Maternus, in whose house the discussion takes place, ascribes the decline to political changes: in the late republic oratory had flourished amid virtual anarchy; now, under a benevolent and all-wise ruler, great oratory was no longer needed. While that may come closest to Tacitus' own view, it is simplistic to equate Maternus with Tacitus. Ambivalences attach to the opinions of all three speakers, and Tacitus characteristically leaves readers to elicit their own answers.

3. By about 105–6 Tacitus was collecting material for a historical work, almost certainly the *Histories* (Plin. *Ep.* 6. 16 and 20); the date of its completion is unknown, but may be *c.*109–10. When complete it comprised twelve or fourteen books, covering the years 69–96; only the first four and a quarter books survive, bringing the narrative to 70.

The subject-matter of bks. 1–3, dealing with the civil wars between Galba, Otho, Aulus Vitellius, and Vespasian (see ROME (HISTORY) §2.2), is predominantly military, and it is for his handling of this material that Mommsen called Tacitus 'most unmilitary of writers'. It is true that the reader is repeatedly puzzled or irritated by the absence of information on chronology, topography, strategy, and logistics.

But Tacitus did not write according to the canons of modern historiography. His aim is to provide a narrative that will hold the reader's attention. By that standard chs. 12–49 of bk. 1 (perhaps matched by the graphic description of the night battle of Cremona and the storming and sacking of the city in 3. 19–34) present a sustained narrative of unsurpassed pace and brilliance. From the moment when a handful of soldiers proclaim Otho emperor (27. 2) till Tacitus delivers his obituary over the murdered Galba (49. 4 'omnium consensu capax imperii, nisi imperasset': 'by universal consent fitted to rule—had he not ruled') the ebb and flow of fortune and emotion are portrayed with masterly skill.

The loss of the later books is particularly frustrating, since they deal with a time when Tacitus was himself close to the centre of political activity. From what survives we can surmise that he was no less hostile to Domitian than he had been in the *Agricola*, and that the senate, despite loud professions of independence, was quick to back down when faced by imperial opposition (4. 44. 1). And though Vespasian alone of emperors is said to have changed for the better (1. 50. 4), it is unlikely that Tacitus thought his reign without blemish.

4. At the beginning of the *Histories* (1. 1. 4) Tacitus had spoken of going on to write of *Nerva and *Trajan. In the event he chose to go back to the Julio-Claudian dynasty from the accession of *Tiberius. The *Annals* (more exactly *Ab excessu divi Augusti*, 'From the decease of the deified Augustus'; the titles *Historiae* and *Annales* date only from the 16th cent.) originally consisted of eighteen (or sixteen) books—six for Tiberius, six for Gaius and Claudius, six (or four) for Nero. Of these there are lost most of 5, all of 7–10, the first half of 11, and everything after the middle of 16. Whether Tacitus completed the *Annals* is not known; nor do we know the date of composition, though two passages (2. 56. 1 and 4. 5. 2) seem datable to 114 and 115 respectively. That would suggest that the last books can scarcely have been written before the early years of *Hadrian's reign, perhaps *c*.120.

The six books of Tiberius' reign are structured as two triads. The dichotomy, marked by the striking opening of bk. 4, emphasizes that the reign took a decisive turn for the worse in AD 23 with the rise to power of the ambitious *Sejanus. But even the excellence of the earlier years is attributed to Tiberius' concealment (*dissimulatio*) of his true character. Whether that explanation, which does not originate with Tacitus, is consistent with Tacitus' claim to write impartially (*Ann.* 1. 1. 3 'sine ira et studio') is open to question; but it is skilfully used to probe the ambiguities of Tiberius' behaviour, as the emperor sought to combine a *de facto* autocracy with a show of constitutional republicanism.

For *Claudius, Tacitus accepted the traditional picture of an emperor dominated by his wives and freedmen and gave great (perhaps excessive) prominence to the sexual scandals of *Messa(l)lina and the dynastic scheming of *Agrippina. But in much of his dealings with the senate Claudius emerges as a pedantically thoughtful personality, e.g. 11. 13 and 24 (in the latter case uniquely we can compare Tacitus' version with the speech that Claudius actually delivered (*ILS* 212)).

*Nero's portrait also is simple: an initial quinquennium of mostly good government ends with the murder of Agrippina in 59, which frees Nero to follow his own desires (14. 13. 2). His extravagance, sexual depravity, and un-Roman innovations are depicted with verve and disapproval. Tacitus also pillories the servility of a senate that congratulates Nero when his mother is murdered (14. 12; cf. 59. 4 and 16. 16), while Thrasea Paetus' attempts to uphold senatorial independence (13. 49; 14. 12, 48–9; 15. 20 and 23) lead only to his condemnation.

If political debate is less sharp in the Neronian books, foreign affairs and Nero's flamboyant behaviour fully extend Tacitus' descriptive powers. Their impact is strengthened by the organization of incidents into larger continuous units, a structural feature first observable in the Claudian books (so Messalina's final excesses in 11. 26–38 and the account of British affairs, covering several years, in 12. 31–40); similarly in the Neronian books: British affairs in 14. 29–39 and the annual accounts of Gnaeus Domitius Corbulo's eastern campaigns, and (at home) Agrippina's murder (14. 1–13), the Great Fire of Rome and its aftermath (15. 38–45), and the Pisonian conspiracy (15. 48–74).

5. Though none of the sources used by Tacitus has survived, many scholars from Mommsen onwards have held that for continuous sections of his narrative Tacitus followed an unnamed single

source; Cluvius Rufus, *Pliny the Elder, Aufidius Bassus, and Fabius Rusticus are among the names that have been suggested. Close and sustained similarities between Tacitus and *Plutarch for the reigns of Galba and Otho make the theory plausible for the period of the civil war, but it is unlikely that Tacitus restricted himself to a single source thereafter, since already at *Hist.* 2. 101 he expresses scepticism of pro-Flavian accounts. For the *Annals*, especially from bk. 6, similarities between Tacitus, *Suetonius, and *Cassius Dio suggest frequent, though not continuous, use of a common source (see also Tacitus' own statement at 13. 20. 2). However, it is probable that Tacitus proceeded differently with different types of material. For senatorial business the *acta senatus* (official record of proceedings) would provide a starting-point, but no more; their bureaucratic language and official version of events would be repugnant to Tacitus. For the private life of the emperor and his family the more lurid and sensational items could be published only after his death, when different versions would multiply (see *Ann.* 14. 2. 1–2 for Agrippina, and *Hist.* 1. 13 and *Ann.* 13. 45 for Poppaea Sabina, Nero's wife). For military matters formal reports in the *acta senatus* could be supplemented from elsewhere (e.g. the elder Pliny's twenty volumes on wars in Germany or Domitius Corbulo's memoirs of his eastern campaigns). But convention also allowed the ancient historian licence to elaborate or invent incidents to make his narrative more colourful and exciting (cf. *Ann.* 4. 46–51 with Caesar, *BGall.* 7. 69 ff. and Sallust, *H.* 2. 87). Yet, whatever the source, the resulting narrative is, by selection, arrangement, and interpretation, wholly Tacitean.

6. Though regret for the lost freedoms of the republic is evident throughout Tacitus, he accepted the necessity of the rule of one man (*Hist.* 1. 1. 1; *Ann.* 4. 33. 2) and praised those few who served the state honourably but without servility (*Ann.* 4. 20. 3; cf. *Agr.* 42. 4). Yet pessimism and hints of a darker underlying reality are ever-present: motives are rarely simple; innuendo often suggests that the less creditable explanation is the more probable; and an awareness of the gulf in political life between what was professed and what was practised informs all his writing and finds fitting expression in a unique prose style.

7. Tacitus' style is marked by a fastidious and continuous avoidance of the trite and hackneyed. Elevation is lent to his language by archaic and poetic words and an admixture of neologisms, while his extensive use of metaphor more closely resembles poetic than prose usage. In much of this he follows *Sallust, at times even echoing whole passages: so at *Ann.* 4. 1. 3 his portrait of Sejanus recalls (but modifies) Sallust's picture of *Catiline at *Cat.* 5. But to Sallust's renowned brevity Tacitus adds a greater compression of thought. The sinewy strength of his language is reinforced by a deliberate rejection of balance (*concinnitas*) in favour of syntactical disruption (*variatio*), a device he uses with special effectiveness to underline alternative motives. The same aim is served by a peculiarly Tacitean type of sentence construction in which the main syntactical statement stands at or near the beginning, and then has appended to it (by various syntactical means, of which the ablative absolute is one of the most common) comments that suggest motives or record men's reactions (for extended examples cf. *Ann.* 3. 3. 1 and 14. 49. 3). This type of sentence allows Tacitus to concentrate, often with sardonic comment, on the underlying psychology of men's actions and is tellingly employed in his portrait of Tiberius.

8. The surviving texts of Tacitus' works reached the age of printing by three tenuous threads. A Carolingian manuscript of the minor works came from Hersfeld in Germany to Rome *c.*1455, but disappeared after numerous 15th-cent. copies had been made; whether the 9th-cent. quire of the *Agricola* that survived till the 1940s was part of that manuscript is uncertain. *Annals* 1–6 depend on a single manuscript, the first Medicean, written in Germany (possibly Fulda) *c.*850, and now in the Laurentian Library in Florence. *Annals* 11–16 and *Histories* 1–5 (numbered consecutively as bks. 11–21) also depend on a single manuscript, the second Medicean, written in a Beneventan script in the 11th cent.; modern attempts to show that any 15th-cent. manuscript is independent of the second Medicean seem unfounded.   R. H. M.

Most elements of Graeco-Roman technology were either inherited from prehistoric times, or adopted from '*barbarian' peoples. Some significant inventions were made, such as hydraulic concrete, the geared 'Vitruvian' water-mill, blown *glass, the screw-press, and a remarkable harvesting machine, the *vallus*. Inventions that were applied included items for use in essential activities such as draining mines, and, above all, in processing the products of the single most important industry—agriculture. The study of their date and application is complicated by the survival of a mere handful of detailed works by technical writers such as Heron of Alexandria (fl. AD 62) or *Vitruvius, and the comparative inattention to technical matters by others, such as *Pliny the Elder. Archaeological evidence plays a growing role in establishing the date and diffusion of applied technology, and it also provides examples of devices that do not appear in the written sources, which (for example) give an incomplete view of the range of pumps. Interpretation is complicated by a tendency amongst classical scholars to approach Roman technology in the light of its Greek background, without adjusting the context from city-state to empire. A persistent stereotype contrasts Greek theory and invention with Roman practical application, and overlooks the fact that much of the engineering associated with 'Greek science' was Roman in date, and developed in *Alexandria.

Technology remained stable (which does not mean stagnant) in most areas of metallurgy (see MINES), stoneworking, ceramics, engineering, *architecture, *agriculture, and transport. Extraction and processing of silver at the Athenian mines at Laurium varied in scale, not technique, from Classical Greek to Byzantine times. Finds from Egypt, Spain, and Wales show that the same techniques were applied across the entire empire in the Roman period. The Roman army evidently acted as an important agent of technology-transfer by spreading *literacy and skills to frontier regions. Thus, intensification rather than innovation characterized Roman technology, assisted by the geographical expansion of Rome and the reliance of its administration on secure and effective transport of men, foodstuffs, and both raw materials and finished goods. It is no accident that Roman engineers are remembered primarily because of the number of *roads, bridges, and harbours that survive; archaeological evidence shows that these facilities were used by a comprehensive range of vehicles and ships whose size and technical complexity were matched to varying requirements. A similar flexibility—and availability—of building materials and construction skills was able to create farms, workshops, and accommodation in rural and urban environments to house producers and consumers alike.

Greece and Rome constructed marble buildings on an unprecedented scale, and minted millions of gold, silver, and bronze coins. Thousands of ordinary farmers and urban craft-workers possessed more iron tools, architectural stonework, and fine tableware than ever before, to an extent that would not be matched again until the post-medieval period. A combination of effective transport and appropriate coin denominations helped to sustain trade in these materials, far beyond the requirements of the state and the army alone. None of this caused, or resulted from, an Industrial Revolution; the significant growth factor was proliferation and intensification as a result of expanding conquest and trade. Evidence for extensive industries and widespread application of technology in the ancient world can be accepted without having to explain why they did not cause economic 'take-off'. See ECONOMY; INDUSTRY; TRADE.　　　　　　　　　　　　　　　K. T. G.

temple The Greek temple was the house of the god, whose image it contained, usually placed so that at the annual festival it could watch through the open door the burning of the sacrifice at the altar which stood outside. It was not a congregational building, the worshippers instead gathering round the altar in the open air, where they would be given the meat of the victims to consume (see SACRIFICE, GREEK). Orientation was generally towards the east, and often towards that point on the skyline where (allowing for the vagaries of ancient Greek calendars) the sun rose on the day of the festival. The temple also served as a repository for the property of the god, especially the more valuable possessions of gold and silver plate.

The core of the temple is the cella, a rectangular room whose side walls are prolonged beyond one end to form a porch, either with columns between them (in antis) or in a row across the front (prostyle). More prestigious temples surround this with an external colonnade (and are described as peripteral). They generally duplicate the porch with a corresponding prolongation of the walls at the rear of the cella, *without*, however, making another doorway into the cella (the opisthodomus, or false porch). Some temples, such as the Parthenon at Athens, have a double cella with a western as well as an eastern room, in which case the porch has a door in it.

The origins of this are uncertain. No provable temples exist (excluding the very different shrine buildings of the late bronze age) before the 8th cent. BC. (See LEFKANDI.)

By the end of the 7th cent. the rectangular form is normal. Cut stone replaces the earlier mudbrick structures, and important temples are peripteral 'hundred footers' (*hekatompeda*); the 6th cent. sees a handful of exceptionally large 85 m. (300-ft.) examples, such as *Artemis at *Ephesus and the Hera-temple on *Samos. From the 6th cent. stone-built temples are normal; marble begins to be utilized where readily available. Doric temples generally stand on a base (*crēpis*) with three steps, though the enlarged dimensions of the building make these excessively high for human use; they have to be doubled at the east-end approach, or replaced there by a ramp; Ionic temples often have more steps. Roofs are generally now of terracotta tiles; gutters occur infrequently in Doric temples, regularly in Ionic. Marble tiles (introduced first in Ionic) are used in the Parthenon. The roof is supported on beams and rafters. Wider buildings require internal supports within the cella; these may also be added as decoration, even when the span is too small to require their support. Some of the very large Ionic temples do not seem to have had internal supports in their cellas, which must therefore have been unroofed or 'hypaethral', though the surrounding colonnades were roofed up to the cella wall.

There are recognizable regional variations, even within the broad distinctions of Doric and Ionic. Approach ramps at the east end are regular in Peloponnesian temples, which often restrict carved decoration in the Doric metopes to those of the inner entablatures over the porch. Sicilian Doric temples may have four rather than three steps, and frequently have narrower cellas, without any internal supports.

Only exceptional buildings, such as the Parthenon, have full pedimental sculpture, let alone carved figures on every metope of the external entablature, while the frieze which replaces the metope frieze over the prostyle porches, and is continued along both sides of the cella, is a unique additional embellishment.

Roman temples derive from Etruscan prototypes, themselves possibly influenced by the simple Greek temples of the 8th and 7th cents. BC. They stand on high *podia*, with stepped approaches only at the front (temples of the Roman period in the Greek part of the empire often continue the tradition of the lower Greek stepped *crēpis*). Roofs are steeper (reflecting perhaps the wetter climate of Etruria); more lavish carved decoration may derive from western Greek taste. The Corinthian order, used for some Hellenistic temples, became the preferred form. Marble is common in the Augustan period, white, with fluted columns; later polished smooth shafts of variegated marbles, granites, etc. are preferred. Regional variations continue to be important. The western provinces generally follow the example of Rome. See ARCHITECTURE; PAINTING; SANCTUARIES; SCULPTURE. R. A. T.

Terence (Publius Terentius Afer), the Roman playwright, author of *fabulae palliatae* ('dramas in a Greek cloak') in the 160s BC. The *Life* by *Suetonius records that he was born at Carthage, came to Rome as a slave in the household of a senator called Terentius Lucanus, was soon freed, but died still young on a visit to Greece in 159. As usual, we have no way to check this information; his Carthaginian birth (see CARTHAGE) may have been an incorrect deduction from his *cognomen* or surname (*Afer*, 'the African'). He was patronized by prominent Romans, and his last play, *Adelphoe*, was commissioned by *Scipio Aemilianus and his brother for performance at the funeral games for their father Lucius Aemilius Paullus in 160. The previous year, his *Eunuchus* had been an outstanding success, marked by a repeat performance and an unprecedentedly large financial reward. His one known failure was *Hecyra*, which twice had to be abandoned in the face of competition from rival attractions (first a tightrope walker and boxers, then a gladiatorial show); Terence's account of these misfortunes in his prologue for the third production is exceptional evidence for conditions of performance at the time.

All his six plays survive. Their dates are given by the *didascaliae* (production notices), which are generally accepted as reliable in spite of some difficulties: *Andria* ('The Girl from Andros', Megalesian Games 166); *Hecyra* ('The Mother-in-Law', Megalesian Games 165, revived in 160 at Aemilius Paullus' funeral games and again later that year); *Heautontimorumenos* ('The Self-Tormentor', Megalesian Games 163); *Eunuchus* ('The Eunuch', Megalesian Games 161); *Phormio* (Roman Games 161); and *Adelphoe* ('The Brothers', Aemilius Paullus' funeral games in 160). *Hecyra* and *Phormio* were based on originals by Apollodorus of Carystus, the other four on plays by Menander; Terence preserved the Greek titles of all but *Phormio* (named after the main character; Apollodorus' title was *Epidikazomenos*, 'The Claimant at Law'). See COMEDY (GREEK), NEW. All the plays were produced by Ambivius Turpio, with music by one Flaccus, slave of Claudius.

In adapting *Andria*, Terence added material from Menander's *Perinthia* ('The Girl from Perinthos'); for his *Eunuchus* he added the characters of the parasite and the soldier from Menander's *Kolax* ('The Toady'); and in *Adelphoe* he added a scene from Diphilus' *Synapothnēskontes* ('Comrades in Death'). We learn this from the prologues to these plays, where he defends himself against charges of 'spoiling' the Greek plays and of 'theft' from earlier Latin plays. But he made more radical changes than these. The commentary by the grammarian Donatus (4th cent AD) provides some further information, e.g. that the first 20 lines of *Andria* are an entirely original creation, and that Terence has converted monologue to dialogue in the central scene of *Eunuchus* (539–614). The extent and implications of these and other changes are much disputed; it is a mark of Terence's skill that we cannot be sure of the boundaries of inserted material even when he tells us that it has been added. It is widely believed that he made significant changes to the endings of several plays (particularly *Eun.* and *Ad.*), but the meagre fragments that survive of his Greek originals force us to rely heavily on intuition about what Menander and Apollodorus are likely to have done.

One clear innovation was Terence's use of a prologue to conduct feuds with his critics; he never used one to tell the spectators about the background to the plot. It has been suggested that he preferred to exploit effects of surprise rather than irony and to involve his audience more directly in the emotions of the characters (most notably in *Hecyra*, where it is laid bare how women are misunderstood, maligned, and mistreated by men). But the scope for ironic effect varies from play to play; in some cases he includes essential background information in the mouths of the characters at an early stage. It seems more likely that he dispensed with expository prologues because he regarded them as an unrealistic device. Consistent with this is his avoidance of direct audience address in his plays, though he does include some 'metatheatrical' remarks at *An.* 474–94 and *Hec.* 865–8.

There is a world of difference between Terence and *Plautus. In general, Terence seems to have preserved the

CIE absquiuir homine cum est opus beneficium accipere gaudeas: uerum enim uero iddemū
iuuat: siquem aequum est bene facere if benefacit: o frater frater quidego tenunc lau
dem satis certo scio: numquam itamagnifice quicqua dicam id uirtus quin super et tua:
itaq. unam hanc rem me habere praeter alias praecipuam arbitror fratrem homini
neminem esse primarium artium magis principem: SYR o ctesipho CIE o frre aeschi
nus ubiest: SYR ellū te exspectat domi: CIE hem SYR quidest: CIE quid sit illius
opera frre nunc uiuo festiuum caput quin omnia sibi post putarit esse p meo commodo.
maledicta famam meam amore & peccatu in se transtulit: nihil supra potest: quis na
fores crepuit: SYR mane mane ipse exit foras:

AESCHINUS   CTESIPHO II   SYRUS SERUUS   SANNIO II
ADULES
CENS

AES ubiest ille sacrilegus: SAN men quaerit nū quid nam effert occidi nihil uideo:
AES ehem opportune te ipsū quaerito quid fit ctesipho intuto est omnis res omitte uero tris
tiam tuā: CIE ego illa facile uero omitto quiquidem te habeam fratre omi aeschine
omi germane uereor corā in os te laudare amplius ne id ad sen tandi magis quā qd
habeam gratum facere & iftimes AES age in epte quasi nunc non norimus nos inter nos
ctesipho sed hoc mihi dolet nos paene sero scisse & paene meū locu redisse ut si omnes
cuperent tibi nihil possent auxiliarier CIE pudebat AES aha stultitia est istaec
non pudor tam ob paruolā rem paene & patria turpe dictum deos quaeso ut iftec phibeant
CIE peccaui AES quid ait tande nobis sannio SYR iam mitis est AES ego ad forum ibo
ut hunc absoluam tu intro adillā ctesipho SAN frre infta SYR eamus nāq hic p
petat incr prium SAN ne tā quidem quā uis & iā maneo otiosus hic SYR reddetur
netime SAN at ut omne reddat SYR omne reddet tace modo ac sequere hac:
SAN sequor CIE heus heus frre SYR hem quidest CIE obsecro hercle te hominem istum

Terence An illustrated manuscript, AD 872–6, of Terence's last play, *Adelphoe*. His style and and moral sentiments gave his plays a favourable *reception throughout the Middle Ages and beyond.

ethos of his originals more faithfully, with well-constructed plots, consistent characterization, and very few overtly Roman intrusions into the Greek setting. Like Plautus, he increased the proportion of lines with musical accompaniment; but he hardly ever used lyric metres, and he was more sparing in his use of set-piece cantica (operatic interludes). His plays repay thoughtful study and give a sympathetic portrayal of human relationships (*Haut.* and *Ad.* both deal with questions of openness and tolerance between fathers and adolescent sons). On the other hand, he added stock characters and boisterous scenes to *Eun.* and *Ad.*, and he appealed to the precedent of Plautus and others when accused of *contaminatio* (i.e. incorporating material from another Greek play into the primary play being adapted); he was not faithful enough to the Greek originals for some of his contemporaries. He deserves his reputation for *humanitas*, a humane sympathy for the predicaments of human beings, but his plays are also lively and entertaining situation comedies.

Terence's greatest contribution to the development of literary Latin was the creation of a naturalistic style far closer to the language of everyday conversation than that of Plautus or the other authors of *palliatae*, with much exclamation, aposiopesis, and ellipsis; many of its features are paralleled in *Cicero's letters and *Catullus' shorter poems. But he did also sometimes use a more ornate and repetitive style, both in the plays themselves and above all in the prologues, which are highly elaborate rhetorical pieces with much antithesis, alliteration, etc. He does not reproduce the fantastic verbal exuberance of Plautus.

Terence was widely read for many centuries after his death, above all for his style and moral sentiments. Over 650 manuscripts of his plays survive, including a number with famous miniature illustrations. In the 10th cent. the nun Hrothswitha of Gandersheim wrote six Christian comedies in imitation of Terence, and he was both imitated and revived in the Renaissance. He held a central place in the European school curriculum until the 19th cent. See COMEDY, LATIN. P. G. M. B.

textile production 1. *Social significance* Spinning and weaving held considerable symbolic and economic importance for women. In the 5th-cent. BC law code from Gortyn on *Crete (3. 17), a woman who was widowed or divorced could keep half of what she had woven in the marriage. Women took pride in men's praise of their skills (e.g. Hom. *Od.* 2. 104–5, 117; 19. 241–2; Pl. *Resp.* 455c) and to 'keep the house and work in wool' was also a typical way of praising a woman after her death (epitaph of Claudia, 2nd cent. BC Rome, *CIL* 6. 15346). Weaving also carries the suggestion of deception; in Athenian tragedy, Deianira and *Medea trap men with fatal robes. The association with women is so strong that to accuse a man of weaving is to suggest that he is effeminate (e.g. Cleisthenes (Ar. *Av.* 831), Egilius (Cic. *De or.* 2. 277)).

In the Roman empire, the strong gender connotations of spinning and weaving weakened; most weaving was done by men, although women were still clothes-makers and menders. H. K.

2. *Production* Once the raw textile fibres had been removed from the parent body and prepared they were ready for spinning. (Wool was dyed before spinning, flax afterwards.) Wool was sometimes converted first into rovings, loose rolls of fibre half-way to yarn. In a Classical Greek context that was achieved by rolling the fibres out on an *epinētron*, a terracotta sheath that fitted over the knee. The principal spinning implement was the spindle (Gk. *atraktos*, Lat. *fusus*), a tapered rod of wood or bone about 20 cm. (8 in.) long with a swelling towards one end on which the whorl (Gk. *sphondylos*, Lat. *turbo*) was jammed. The latter, a circle with central hole cut from a potsherd or shaped from bone, jet, or terracotta, gave the required momentum to the rotation of the spindle: north of the Mediterranean it was mounted at the bottom; to the south and east, at the top of the shaft. The unspun fibre was loaded on a distaff (Gk. *ēlakatē* (probably), Lat. *colus*), a short carrying staff made at its simplest from a (forked) stick and at its most refined from jet or amber segments. Holding the distaff in her left hand the spinner drew out unspun fibres, a few at a time, fastened them to the tip of the spindle and set the latter rotating. The spindle, hanging free and spinning round, imparted twist and hence strength to the yarn. Spinning—seated, standing, or walking—was a chore for all women from materfamilias to slave girl as their tombstones and epitaphs attest, and their level of competence demonstrated by surviving textiles is remarkable. The direction of rotation, clockwise or anticlockwise, was a matter of long-standing convention: yarns spun clockwise, for example, are found everywhere, but in northern and western Europe they were used for warp, while in the eastern Mediterranean they might appear as weft or in a tapestry band. Yarns were sometimes plied for strength, usually in the opposite direction from the spin. A fine gold or silver ribbon could be wound round a textile fibre core to make metal thread for fancy textiles, like the gold and purple coverlet from a Macedonian royal tomb at Vergina (see AEGAE).

Graeco-Roman weaving technology changed radically in the centuries between Homer and Justinian; in the Roman empire particularly there was considerable regional diversity reflecting varied climatic factors and cultural influences. The underlying trend was to develop and enhance the pattern-making capacity of even the simplest looms: the ultimate achievements are the late Roman silks with their breathtakingly complex polychrome decorative schemes. From Archaic Greece to the early Roman empire the basic loom was vertical and warp-weighted, consisting of two upright timbers (perhaps 2m. (6½ ft.) long) (*histopodes*) joined across the top by a horizontal cloth-beam. It did not stand vertically, but was made to lean against a roof strut or wall at a slight angle. The warp-threads were secured to the cloth-beam by a specially pre-woven starting-border or starting-cord. Half of the warp (all the even-numbered or odd-numbered threads) was fastened to loomweights and hung straight down behind the loom. The rest of the warp was tied to a front row of weights and passed over a fixed horizontal shed-rod that linked the uprights at about knee height: these warp-threads remained therefore in the same plane as the tilted uprights. The 'natural shed', the angle between the two sheets of warp in this position, was changed by means of heddles, loops of string that fastened each individual rear warp-thread to a heddle-rod which rested on brackets projecting from the uprights at the front of the loom. When the heddle-rod was lifted forward, it brought the rear warp between, and to a position in advance of, the front warp, creating the second, 'artificial', shed. The process of weaving then consisted of the weaver introducing a ball or spool of weft thread from the side into and through the first shed, changing to the 'artificial' shed and passing the weft back through that. By repeating the process 1/1 tabby weave, the simplest and commonest weave structure, was achieved. Freshly inserted weft was beaten hard against the web of cloth already woven by means of a weaving sword thrust into the shed: the bare warp was kept in order by running a pin-beater (Gk. *kerkis*, Lat. *radius*), a small pointed implement, lightly across it, making it 'sing' (Soph. *Tr.* 890). Loomweights (Gk. *agnuthes*, Lat. *pondera*), usually of terracotta, are found in lenticular, conical, or pyramidal shapes, with a hole for suspension: the form varies with time and place.

By the end of the 2nd cent. AD the warp-weighted loom (at which the weaver stood and pushed the weft upwards) had been largely replaced by the two-beam vertical loom at which the weaver sat and beat the weft downwards with a short-toothed wooden comb. The two-beam loom was ideal for tapestry weaving whereby a 'mosaic' is built by hand from yarns of contrasting colours. As time passed, ever more advanced devices for the mechanical shedding of patterns were introduced. Simple geometric damasks in wool had appeared by AD 100 (later than that in silk), together with compound weaves in which the pattern weft could be selectively drawn to the surface or concealed within its structure. Compound twill, in production by the 5th cent. AD, came to dominate the silk industry of late antiquity. At some point during this development sequence the loom became horizontal. On a smaller scale bands could be woven without a loom-frame using three- or four-hole tablets (like a pack of cards which twisted the warp into parallel cords) or the rigid heddle on which the warp passed alternately through holes in slats or between slats. The warp-interlace technique of *sprang* carried out on a small frame was employed, as finds show, for hairnets. An ever-lengthening list of textile-finds demonstrates the ancient weaver's skill and range. Garments were regularly woven to shape on the loom with integral ornament where relevant: the role of the tailor was minimal. In the west twill weaves in wool were pre-eminent: decoration was in subtle checks or occasionally tapestry-woven bands. The Greek-speaking east was much more diverse, exploit-

ing to the full the properties of both dyed wool and natural linen. At Phrygian Gordium in the 8th cent. BC there were decorative bands in warp pick-up weave and tapestry-woven fabrics. An aristocratic grave of *c.*1000 BC at *Lefkandi on Euboea contained a tunic decorated with looped pile. The beginnings of fancy damask and compound weaving belong to the late Hellenistic or early Roman period. Embroidery was rare. In the west most weaving was on a domestic scale, with occasional production for profit, but in the east there were professional weavers and specialized workshops.

Wool cloth was taken direct from the loom to the fuller (Gk. *gnapheus*, Lat. *fullo*) for cleaning and shrinking. He also acted as laundryman. Fullers' workshops uncovered in *Pompeii and *Ostia show how he operated. Clothing was trodden underfoot in wooden or terracotta tubs in a mixture of water, stale urine, and fuller's earth to disperse the grease and dirt, then rinsed in tanks. The nap on a woollen garment could be raised with a spiked board (*aena*) and trimmed with cropping shears to give a soft finish (*vestis pexa*). Cloth could be bleached over sulphur for enhanced whiteness. Finally, garments were carefully folded and pressed in a screw-press to make the neat creases which fashion demanded. See also DRESS.

J. P. W.

theatres (Greek and Roman), structure The Greek theatre consisted essentially of the orchestra, the flat dancing-place for the choral song and dance out of which grew tragedy and comedy; and the auditorium (the *theatron* proper, Latin *cavea*), normally a convenient slope on which spectators could sit or stand. In early theatres wooden seating was constructed, though it is not clear how this was done. Seats were sometimes cut in the rock; by the time theatres reached a more definitive form, in the 4th cent. BC, seats consisted of stone benches of simple form, rising in tiers. These were curved, reflecting the normal circular shape of the orchestra. A rectangular orchestra survives at the well-preserved theatre at Thoricus, in the territory of Athens, partly faced by seats in a straight line, curving only at the ends. The orchestra consisted of hard earth—paving was not introduced till Roman times. The *skēnē* (tent or hut) was in origin a simple structure for the convenience of the performers, which could also form a background for the plays. In the course of the 5th cent. it became a more solid building, ultimately acquiring a handsome architectural form sometimes with projecting wings. The fully developed auditorium was wherever possible rather more than a semicircle in plan, opening out a little at the outer ends, where the line of seats was drawn on a slightly greater radius. The outer sectors required embankments and solid retaining walls, while the inner was hollowed out of the hillside; there were no elaborate substructures as in Roman theatres. The auditorium did not link up with the *skēnē*, except perhaps by means of light gateways, and the intervening passages on either side were called *parodoi*. Stairways radiated from the orchestra, dividing the seating into 'wedges', and in large theatres there were horizontal passages too (*diazōma*). The front tiers were sometimes provided with more elaborate and comfortable seating for priests and officials (so-called *proedria*).

In the 5th cent., since archaeological evidence is lacking, the level at which the action took place is not certain: probably at orchestra level, with at most a low wooden platform, easily accessible by steps, in front of the *skēnē*, which provided the door openings necessary for the action of all classical drama. Later, the *proskēnion* was introduced, a row of columns in front of the *skēnē* supporting a high platform (seen to good advantage at Oropus, where it has been reconstructed). This came to be used as a raised stage, a feature appropriate to New Comedy (see COMEDY (GREEK), NEW), which would have been out of place in the theatre of *Sophocles or *Aristophanes. *Proskēnia* were usual in Hellenistic theatres, and were added to old theatres at Athens and elsewhere. At Athens itself tradition speaks of an early theatre in the *Agora. The theatre attached to the shrine of *Dionysus Eleuthereus on the south slope of the Acropolis developed from crude beginnings in the latter part of the 6th cent. BC; its peculiar and complicated history is the subject of much dispute. Architecturally it was still simple and undeveloped in the time of the great 5th-cent. dramatists. The theatre at the shrine of Asclepius near Epidaurus shows the perfection of design achieved in the 4th cent. Even then the theatre was by no means standardized and there are many local variations.

Roman theatres conformed to a type which made a complete building, though, in larger examples, the auditorium—a semicircle—was not roofed; instead, awnings (*vela*) could be drawn on ropes over the auditorium as necessary. The stage, certainly roofed and close to the semicircular orchestra, was a wide and fairly deep raised platform, backed by a wall (*scaenae frons*) as high as the top of the *cavea*, treated as an elaborate front towards the stage, with columns, niches, and the requisite doors. Substructures of *cavea* and stage often consisted of vaulted passages, etc., with staircases, and the outer walls enclosing the back of the *cavea*, sometimes squared, were of arched construction in tiers, with order-treatments, though where the auditorium could rest directly on the hillside, this could be used for part of the auditorium. Simple theatres in the western provinces might have auditoria resting on terraces of earth fill supported by walls. The best-preserved Roman theatres are at Aspendus and Perge in Pamphylia (eastern type, with flat *scaenae frons*) and at Arausio (mod. Orange, in France) (western type, with indented *scaenae frons*).

R. A. T.

Themistocles (c.524–459 BC), Athenian politician, was a member of the ancient Lycomid family but by a non-Athenian mother. *Herodotus' informants accused him of corruption and said that in 480 he had 'recently come to the fore', though he was archon in 493/2; but *Thucydides admired him for his far-sightedness and considered him one of the greatest men of his generation.

As archon, Themistocles began the development of the Piraeus as Athens' harbour; it may be that Phrynichus' *Capture of Miletus* and subsequent trial, and Miltiades' return to Athens from the Chersonesus (Gallipoli peninsula) and his subsequent trial, belong to 493/2 and that Themistocles was involved in these episodes. In the *ostracisms of the 480s he regularly attracted votes but was not himself ostracized (altogether, 2,264 ostraca against him are known, including a set of 190 prepared by fourteen hands): the expulsion of Xanthippus in 484 and Aristides in 482 may represent a three-cornered battle in which Themistocles was the winner. Attempts to connect him with a change from direct election to partial sortition in the appointment of the *archontes* (see LAW AND PROCEDURE, ATHENIAN), in 487/6, have no foundation in the sources; but he was behind the decision in 483/2 to spend a surplus from the silver mines on enlarging Athens' navy from 70 to 200 ships—allegedly for use against Aegina, but these ships played a crucial part in the defeat of the Persian navy in 480.

In 480 he was the general who commanded Athens' contingents in the Greek forces against the invading Persians: on land in *Thessaly, and then on sea at Artemisium and at Salamis; he interpreted an oracle to predict victory at Salamis, argued for staying at Salamis rather than retiring beyond the isthmus of Corinth, and tricked the Persians into throwing away their advantage by entering the straits. The Decree of Themistocles inscribed at Troezen in the 3rd cent. probably contains authentic material but has at least undergone substantial editing. In the winter of 480/79 he received unprecedented honours at Sparta, but in 479 we hear nothing of him and Athens' forces were commanded by Aristides and Xanthippus.

After the Persian War there are various stories of his coming into conflict with Sparta (in the best-attested he took delaying action at Sparta while the Athenians rebuilt their city walls), while the *Delian League was built up by the pro-Spartan Cimon. In the main tradition the cunning, democratic Themistocles is opposed to the upright, aristocratic Aristides, but there are indications that Aristides was now a supporter rather than an opponent of Themistocles. About the end of the 470s Themistocles was ostracized (see OSTRACISM), went to live at Argos, and 'visited other places in the Peloponnese' (Thuc. 1. 135. 3), where an anti-Spartan alliance was growing. When Sparta became alarmed, and claimed to have evidence that he was involved with the Spartan regent Pausanias in intrigues with Persia, he fled, first westwards to Corcyra and Epirus but then via *Macedonia and the Aegean Sea to *Asia Minor. The Athenians condemned him to death in his absence; after 465 the new Persian king, Artaxerxes I, made him governor of Magnesia on the Maeander, where coins bearing his name and portrait were issued. He probably died a natural death, though there was a legend that he committed suicide; after his death, his family returned to Athens. Democracy did not become an issue while he was in Athens (see DEMOCRACY, ATHENIAN), but there are links between him and the democratic, anti-Spartan politicians who came to power at the end of the 460s.

A. R. B.; P. J. R.

Theocritus, poet from *Syracuse, early 3rd cent. BC (working at the Alexandrian court in the 270s); creator of the bucolic genre, but a writer who drew inspiration from many earlier literary forms, cleverly blending them into a new amalgam which nevertheless displays constant invention and seeks variety rather than homogeneity. Thirty poems and a few fragments, together with twenty-four epigrams, are ascribed to him, several (e.g. 19, 20, 21, 23) clearly spurious and others (e.g. 25, 26) of doubtful authenticity. A scholar called Artemidorus boasts in an epigram transmitted along with the ancient scholia (which are very full and learned) that he has rounded up 'the Pastoral Muses' so that 'scattered once, all are now a single fold and flock'; his edition no doubt included a good deal of anonymous material in the most distinctive of the various Theocritean styles (rural sketches written in the Doric dialect; see GREEK LANGUAGE §4) alongside the master's work, and authorship is sometimes hard to determine.

A near-contemporary of the great innovator *Callimachus, Theocritus too was a remaker of the Greek poetic tradition, though his own method of propagating the gospel of tightly organized, perfectly finished writing on a miniature scale was to demonstrate by implicit example rather than engage in neurotic combat against real or imaginary enemies. The closest he comes to a manifesto, and a text that is central for understanding his art, is poem 7 in the collection, which bears the title *Thalysia*, 'The Harvest Home'. Cast in elusively autobiographical form, it describes a journey undertaken by a conveniently assumed persona, 'Simichidas', during his younger days on the SE Aegean island of Cos. On the road he meets a Cretan called Lycidas, 'a goatherd—nor could anyone have mistaken him for anything else, since he looked so very like a goatherd'. The two engage in a song contest, preceded by a discussion of the current state of poetry; Philitas and 'Sicelidas of Samos' (a near-anagram for Asclepiades) are mentioned, and Lycidas praises his young companion for his refusal to write Homeric pastiche (see HOMER). The result of the 'competition' is a foregone conclusion, for Simichidas is promised his prize in advance; just as well, since his clumsy party-piece is no match for the smiling Lycidas' sophisticated song. And no wonder: for as F. Williams showed, focusing earlier partial insights into a conclusive picture, Lycidas is *Apollo, the god of poetry himself, and his epiphany in the poem marks it out as an account of the 'poet's consecration' (*Dichterweihe*) of the kind *Hesiod and *Archilochus had received from the Muses (*CQ* 1971, 137–45).

Other poems in the bucolic main sequence (1–7) also contain passages with programmatic implications—in particular the meticulous description of the wonderfully carved cup in poem 1, whose scenes (especially the culmi-

nating picture of the boy concentrating on weaving a tiny cage for a singing cricket, oblivious to all else) seem intended as a visual correlative of Theocritus' poetic agenda. There are also pieces which refer more directly to the problems of the writer in the Hellenistic world. Poem 16 imaginatively reworks themes from *Simonides in appealing for patronage to Hiero II of Syracuse, and 17 is a similar request to *Ptolemy II Philadelphus, less inspired overall but with a splendidly impish portrayal of the afterlife which the king's father is fancied to be enjoying on Olympus with *Alexander the Great and *Heracles as his heavenly drinking-companions (16–33). Life in contemporary *Alexandria, and praise of its enlightened ruler, is again the theme of 14, an exploratory transposition of a scene of New Comedy (see COMEDY (GREEK), NEW) into hexameter form; while 15, one of the two 'urban mimes' in the collection which develop the form invented by Sophron in the 5th cent., gives us a glimpse of the annual Adonis festival in Ptolemy's palace. We watch the celebration, and hear the hymn (T. is fond of encapsulated song) through the eyes and ears of a pair of suburban housewives, Gorgo and Praxinoa, who have spent the first part of the poem (he is no less fond of diptychal composition) stunning the reader by the banality of their conversation.

The other mime (2) is also a diptych, this time cast as a monologue. A young Alexandrian woman, Simaetha, instructs her servant Thestylis in the performance of a *magic ritual designed to charm back a wandering lover— or else destroy him; then, after the slave's departure with the drug, she recalls the occasion of her first sight of the youth, and her seduction. Both the incantations and the first part of the solo scene are punctuated with refrains appropriate to the situation, a hypnotic feature that recurs in the song on the death of Daphnis in 1. The poem is an excellent example of Theocritus' originality in expanding the catchment area of material to be considered 'fit for poetry'; the effect was permanent, and echoes of the double perspective here (the ironic yet fundamentally humane vision of the author laid over the distressed naïveté of the girl; cf. 11) can still be traced in Tiresias' description of the similarly squalid seduction in Eliot's *The Waste Land*. Though (like all of Theocritus' work) the piece is primarily designed for an audience of sophisticated readers, there is an emotional power here that makes it performable.

But Theocritus was also interested in staking a claim on more 'mainstream' territory, as his choice of the hexameter as his regular vehicle suggests (the only exceptions to this rule are three rather contrived experiments in Aeolic lyric, 28–30 cf. GREEK LANGUAGE §4). *Epic remained the ultimate challenge. Two poems (13, on Hylas; and 22, the second part of which narrates the fight between Polydeuces and Amycus) take up Argonautic subjects, and must relate somehow to the contemporary long poem by *Apollonius of Rhodes—perhaps Theocritus is showing his less radical rival how to do it properly. *Pindar (*Nem.* 1) is recast into epic and updated in the treatment of Heracles' cradle-confrontation with the snakes in 24; only as babies or lovers (cf. Menelaus in the Spartan epithalamium, 18) can the traditional heroes retain their tenuous grasp on the Hellenistic imagination. The rhetorical sequence at 16. 47–57 makes all clear: two lines for Homer's *Iliad* (and even here the emphasis is given to the losers, and to the *hand-somest* Greek fighter at Troy, Cycnus, never even mentioned in Homer's poem) are followed by six for the *Odyssey*, with the peasants given pride of place over the eponymous hero.

New, yet in some ways older, characters are brought forward to supplant the epic warrior: Daphnis (1), Hylas (13), and Adonis (15), each of whom swoons in erotic death, and Polyphemus (6, 11), who joins Simaetha and the goatherd in 3 as a failed lover and displaces *Odysseus from centre-stage. Instead of the bloody duels of epic, the new model of competition is the agonistic singing of the goatherds (for which see PASTORAL POETRY, GREEK). Old false ideals and fantasies are pared away, and the new ones that Theocritus puts in their place are justified, paradoxically, by their very self-conscious artificiality. In an age of uncertainty and unbelief, Theocritus offers three beacons by which life may be orientated: love (which must ultimately fail, through rejection or death), personal determination, and art. Each of these is symbolically figured in turn on the cup, the *aipolikon thaēma* ('marvel for goatherds'), at 1. 27–55.

At some point in the ancient tradition Theocritus' poems acquired the generic title *eidyllia*, 'vignettes'; in so far as the transliteration 'idylls' may conjure up a misleading image of rustic languor and passivity it is perhaps best avoided as a label for the poems of this energetic, engaged, and acutely intelligent writer.   A. H. G.

Theopompus of Chios, important Greek historian of the 4th cent. BC, the main exponent of rhetorical historiography alongside *Ephorus (see HISTORIOGRAPHY, GREEK). According to a short *vita* (life) by Photius (*Bibl.* 176 = T 2) he was born in 378/7, and was still young when he and his father Damasistratus were exiled from Chios for *lakōnismos* (sympathizing with Sparta). At the instigation of *Alexander the Great he was allowed to return in 333/2 when he was 45 years old. After Alexander's death he was exiled a second time; 'driven out from everywhere' he eventually reached the court of *Ptolemy I, who wished to have the 'troublemaker' done away with. Theopompus was saved by the intervention of some friends and died probably shortly after 320. According to ancient tradition (cf. T 1, 5 a) he was a pupil of *Isocrates and worked for a long time as an orator (fr. 25). Extant titles of epideictic speeches are (T 48): *To Euagoras, Panathenaicus, Laconicus, Olympicus*; in addition he wrote political pamphlets (T 48): *Letters from Chios, Panegyric on *Philip II, Advice for Alexander*; and also an *Invective against *Plato and his School* (T 7. 48; fr. 259).

Historical works (1) *Epitome of *Herodotus* in two books (T 1, fr. 1–4), the first demonstrable epitome of an earlier work in antiquity; (2) *Hellenica* in twelve books: a continuation of *Thucydides from 411 to 394, namely the sea battle of Cnidus (394 BC), which marked the end of Sparta's short-lived hegemony (T 13 and 14). With this work Th. entered into competition with *Xenophon, *Hellenica* (1–4. 2), but he wrote in far greater detail than Xenophon. Only nineteen partly trivial fragments are extant (frs. 5–23), hence it is impossible to draw any definite conclusions as to contents, arrangement, bias, style, and quality. The *Hellenica* of the Oxyrhynchus Historian, frequently ascribed to Theopompus by modern scholars, is certainly not identical with this work; (3) *Philippica* or rather *Philippikai historiai* ('The History of Philip') in 58 books, Theopompus' main work, published late, after 324 (fr. 330); numerous fragments (frs. 24–396) and *c*.500 lines of verbal quotations are extant. It was not merely a history of Philip of Macedon, but a universal history including 'the deeds of Greeks and barbarians' (fr. 25) centring on Philip II: when Philip V later had only the accounts of Philip II's exploits excerpted, the number of books was reduced to fifteen (T 31).

Characteristics (1) Theopompus had a universal conception of history; he focused not only on political and military events but showed an interest in ethnography, geography, cultural history, history of religion, day-to-day life, memorabilia, *thaumasia* (marvels), even myth (fr. 381). (2) He was fond of extensive digressions of all kinds: especially noteworthy are the digressions on *thaumasia* (bk. 8 and part of 9; frs. 64–84); 'On the Athenian demagogues' (bk. 10; frs. 85–100); and the three books on Sicilian history, covering the tyranny of *Dionysius I and Dionysius II, 406/5–344/3 (cf. frs. 184, 183–205). (3) The rhetorical character of Theopompus' historical writing was very marked. He goes in for meticulous and skilful stylization, including numerous Gorgianic (see GORGIAS) figures of speech (cf. e.g. 34, frs. 225, 263). (4) There is much moralizing in Theopompus. He incessantly denounced the moral depravity of leading politicians. (5) Political tendencies: Theopompus' attitude was that of a conservative aristocrat with Spartan sympathies. Philip II's patriarchal monarchy came closest to a realization of his ideal political and social system. Theopompus venerated him: 'Europe had never before produced such a man as Philip son of Amyntas' (fr. 27).

Sources The accounts of contemporary history are frequently based on autopsy, personal research, and experiences (test. 20a): Theopompus spent some considerable time at Philip's court (T 7) and travelled throughout Greece (fr. 25); for the earlier periods he used historical and literary material such as speeches, comedies, and pamphlets. He was one of the most widely read and influential Greek historians in Graeco-Roman times. *Dionysius of Halicarnassus (*Pomp.* 6 = T 20) praises him for veracity, erudition, meticulous research, versatility, and his personal enthusiasm as well as for the purity, magnificence, and grandeur of his style. He does, however, find fault with

Theopompus' invectives and excessive digressions. Pompeius Trogus, in Augustan times, called his own history *Historiae Philippicae* in imitation of Theopompus.

K. M.

Theseus, a legendary king of Athens, who came to embody many of the qualities Athenians thought important about their city. Apparently originating without special Attic connections, he may perhaps have merged with a local hero of northern Attica, where several of his myths are situated, and his prominence in Athenian tradition seems not to pre-date the 6th cent. BC, deriving at least in part from an epic or epics; the developed tradition of his life indicates a very different figure from older Athenian heroes such as Cecrops or Erechtheus. Detailed accounts of his life are given in Apollod. 3. 16. 1 continued by *Epit.* 1. 24 and *Plutarch's *Life of Theseus*.

Theseus' claim to membership of the Athenian royal line is somewhat shaky, since his father king Aegeus was probably a late addition to the stemma, made precisely to accommodate Theseus. The alternative version, that his real father was *Poseidon, scarcely helps. In either case, his mother was Aethra, daughter of Pittheus of Troezen. With her, Aegeus left instructions that if on reaching manhood their son was able to lift a certain rock under which Aegeus had placed sandals and a sword, he was to take the tokens and travel to Athens. This Theseus did, choosing the dangerous land-route, on which he encountered and defeated many dangerous brigands and monsters, such as Procrustes, Sciron, and the wild sow of Crommyon. On arrival in Athens, Theseus faced more dangers from *Medea, his father's new wife, and from his cousins the Pallantidae, but escaped their respective attempts at poisoning and ambush. He next defeated the

Theseus The deeds of Theseus shown on an Athenian clay cup of the early 5th cent. BC. The popularity of Theseus in Athenian art at this time reflects his transformation into the proto-founder of Athenian *democracy.

troublesome Marathonian bull; it was on this expedition that he was given hospitality by Hecale. But the major exploit of this part of his life was the journey to Crete and killing of the Minotaur. In revenge for the death of his son Androgeus, Minos had laid upon Athens an annual tribute of seven youths and seven maidens to be given to the Minotaur; Theseus now travelled to Crete as one of the youths and killed the beast, escaping from the labyrinth in which it was kept, with the help of a thread given him by Minos' daughter Ariadne. He then fled Crete with Ariadne, but for reasons variously given abandoned her on Naxos. On his return to Athens with his companions, he was unwittingly responsible for his father's death, by forgetting to hoist the white sails indicating his survival; Aegeus, thinking his son was dead, hurled himself off the Acropolis or into the sea.

Theseus thus became king. His greatest achievement as such was the *synoecism of Attica—the conversion of numerous small towns into one political unit centred on Athens. This was accomplished by persuasion, but other exploits, not all respectable, relied on force. Like (sometimes with) *Heracles, he undertook an expedition against the *Amazons, winning Antiope or Hippolyte for himself, but provoking an Amazon invasion of Attica, which was finally defeated. His friendship with the Lapith Pirithous led him to join the fight against the *Centaurs, and later to attempt to carry off *Persephone from the Underworld (rationalizing alternative in Plut. *Thes.* 31). In the usual version, after their failure and imprisonment, Theseus was rescued by Heracles, but Pirithous remained below. Theseus also kidnapped the child Helen and kept her in the care of his mother until she should mature—though Iphigenia was said by *Stesichorus (Page, *PMG* fr. 191) and others to be the child of this union. In either case, he was forced to hand her back to her brothers the Dioscuri (Castor and Pollux / Polydeuces) when they invaded Attica. This gave Theseus' enemies, headed by Menestheus, their chance, and in the ensuing political confusion Theseus sent his sons Acamas and Demophon to Euboea and himself fled to Scyros, where he was treacherously killed by King Lycomedes.

The formation of this tradition has clearly been influenced at several points by the figure of Heracles, notably in the monster-killing episodes at the beginning of his career (which, according to Plutarch, ch. 9, he undertook in emulation of his great contemporary). Evidently the developed Theseus saga was built up from pre-existing snippets to satisfy Athenian desire for a home-grown and clearly non-Dorian hero of Heraclean type, a process which should be dated to roughly the last quarter, even the last decade, of the 6th cent., when there is a dramatic increase in the popularity of Theseus in the visual arts (see below). It is quite possible that the interest of *Pisistratus and / or his sons (Hippias and Hipparchus) may have been a factor contributing to this growth, but it seems very likely that the political significance of the 'new' hero soon became linked with *Cleisthenes, whose

regional reforms could be seen as similar in spirit to the synoecism. Later, it seems we can trace a connection with the family of Miltiades and Cimon, culminating in the latter's transferral of the hero's bones from Scyros to Athens. But by the time of the tragedies of the last 30 or so years of the 5th cent., far from being the property of any one party Theseus is clearly a universally respected figure, the heroic representative of his city's greatness. True, *Euripides' *Hippolytus* presents him as incautious and mistaken (and outside drama, the distinctly negative traditions of the rape of Helen and the attempt on *Persephone survived) but the usual picture of him in tragedy is of a strong, fair-minded, and compassionate man presiding with perfect confidence over a proto-democracy (see DEMOCRACY, ATHENIAN), the antithesis of the tragic tyrant.

Coming to prominence relatively late, Theseus had few major sanctuaries in Attica. This was explained by the view that the living Theseus had handed over all, or almost all, of his lands (*temenē*) to Heracles (Eur. *HF* 1328–33; Philochorus *FGrH* 328 F 18), whose cult is in fact clearly older in Attica. On the other hand, Theseus became deeply embedded in the festival cycle. As well as having his own festival, the Theseia, on 8th Pyanopsion, he was honoured to a lesser extent on the eighth day of every month (the day also sacred to Poseidon). Moreover, his journey to and return from Crete came to be associated with several cult-complexes and *rituals. Among these were the Oschophoria, where ritual transvestism was explained by the story that two of the 'girls' sent to Crete had been young men in disguise, and the juxtaposed cries of joy and grief by the coincidence of Theseus' return with Aegeus' death; and the Pyanopsia, an Apolline festival (see APOLLO) said to derive from Theseus' *sacrifice in payment of a vow. It is possible to see Theseus here and elsewhere as the heroic prototype of the young men whose transition to adulthood seems to be one concern of the rites. Outside Athens, Theseus was said on his return from Crete to have established various sacrifices and the 'crane-dance' on *Delos, a tradition helpful to the Athenians in their claim to Ionian primacy (see PROPAGANDA). E. Ke.

Theseus in art The fight with the Minotaur, the only Theseus story regularly shown in Archaic art, is among the most popular of all scenes, continuing to imperial times in many media. The Minotaur is shown with bull's head (early, with human head), being killed; on the Amyclaean throne (mid-6th cent.), it was merely captured (Paus. 3. 18. 11). Roman paintings often show the aftermath rather than the fight.

From the late 6th cent. a cycle of Theseus' adventures on the road from Troezen appears, perhaps derived from poetry, or the adoption of Theseus as hero of the new democracy, resulting in the creation of a complementary series of 'Labours' to those of the Pisistratid hero, Heracles. Such cycles appear on the metopes of the late Archaic Athenian treasury at Delphi, the Hephaisteion in Athens c.450 (see ATHENS, TOPOGRAPHY), and the frieze of

Gjölbaschi-Trysa (Lycia), c.370. Several vases depict cycles, but the scenes generally appear in groups or individually, mostly c.520–420. Theseus may be naked or wear a short cloak, and his weapons vary; his opponent is bearded and naked. Frequently, rocks and trees suggest Theseus' travels.

The lifting of the rock appears also on imperial Campana reliefs (also Sinis, Sciron, the Marathonian bull) and *gems. On Classical vases, Theseus attacks a woman who may be Medea (rather than Aethra), and Medea may be identified watching Theseus and the Marathonian bull on a series of late Classical vases; her attempt to poison Theseus is shown on Classical vases and Roman copies of Classical reliefs.

Theseus in the Underworld was painted in the Cnidian Lesche or club-house for the people of Cnidus at Delphi (Paus. 10. 29. 9–10); in the Stoa of Zeus with Democracy and the Demos (people) (1. 3. 3); in the Stoa Poecile (Painted Stoa) fighting the Amazons (also on the temple of Apollo at Euboian Eretria, the Zeus at *Olympia, Athena Parthenos, Trysa, and some Classical vases), and rising from the plain of Marathon; and in the Theseion. The visit to the sea in the latter appears on Classical vases. Euphranor and Parrhasius painted Theseus. *Pausanias notes sculptures of Sciron (1. 3. 1), the Minotaur (1. 24. 1), the Marathonian bull (1. 27. 9–10), and Theseus in the Calydonian boarhunt (8. 45. 6).   K. W. A.

Thessaly (see ◀Map 1, Bb▶), region of N. Greece, divided into the four *tetrades* (districts) of Thessaliotis, Hestiaeotis, Pelasgiotis, and Phthiotis, along with the so-called perioecic (neighbouring) regions of Perrhaebia, Magnesia, Achaea Phthiotis, and Dolopia. Comprising two vast plains divided by the modern Revenia hills, Thessaly is enclosed by mountains (notably Olympus, Ossa, Pelion, Othrys, and Pindus) which, far from forming obstacles to communication with neighbours, are pierced by valleys and passes with the generic ancient name of *tempē*, by which, in all periods, travellers, merchants, and armies have reached the Thessalian plains. Thessaly has access to the sea only by the gulf of Pagasae, with its two neighbouring ports, the one in the bay of Volos, in antiquity successively Iolcus, Pagasai, and Demetrias, the other in the bay of Halmyrus (Pyrasus, or Demetrieum, absorbed c.300 BC into the city of Thebes in Achaea Phthiotis); a third port, Phalara near Lamia, was accessible to the Thessalians of the Spercheios valley. Thessaly has a continental climate, far more marked than in the coastal plains further south, with extremely fertile soils; it was rich in grain, horses, and other livestock, although its relative coolness precluded (with exceptions) cultivation of the vine and olive.

Over the last 30 years archaeology has greatly improved our knowledge of ancient Thessaly. Human activity is now attested from the end of the palaeolithic age, and the eastern plain was densely settled in the neolithic, with more than 400 sites so far known (see GREECE, *Stone age*); in late Helladic times Mycenaean culture spread via Iolcus into the two plains and the peripheral mountains.

In the southern half of the eastern plain a population of pastoralists and peasant-farmers calling themselves *Thessaloi* (probably coming from the Balkans) gradually emerged with a distinctive identity based on Greek culture and a 'mixed' language, proto-Aeolian (see GREEK LANGUAGE). From c.1000 BC these Thessalians progressively took over more and more land, eventually coming to dominate (over the passage of almost a thousand years) the two plains and also the surrounding mountains. The Thessalian *ethnos* early on formed itself into an organized state, with cities led by aristocratic families and grouped into a federation under the authority of a chief called *archos* or *archōn* (not *tagos*, as used to be thought).

Their military power first gave the Thessalians access to the Peneus basin and part of the eastern plain, as well as the southern regions of the Othrys range, the Spercheios valley, and the coasts of the Maliac Gulf; then central Greece. Winning control of the amphictyony (see DELPHI) formed by the population of these districts and based first at Anthela, then at Delphi, the Thessalians were for a while a dominant power in central Greece. But from c.600 BC they were forced to fall back on Thessaly proper. In the second half of the 6th cent. BC the Thessalian state was reorganized by Aleuas the Red, who created the four tetrads, each of four cities; the federal chief now received the title of tetrarch. Aleuas adapted the territories of each city for military mobilization by creating land-allotments (*klēroi*) controlled by the *tagoi*, officials charged with organizing the state's military units, and thus created an effective army.

In the 5th cent. BC the Thessalians strengthened their hold on Thessaly as a whole; of the population of the two plains a part was now integrated into the cities (which increased in number), the rest expelled to the mountains. Federal ties weakened following the rise to political and economic dominance over their neighbours of the cities of Larissa, Pherae, and Pharsalus. Urbanization progressed and wealth accumulated; aristocratic families engaged in their rivalries, but also were forced to cede to political pressure from ordinary citizens seeking a say in local government, which became progressively more democratic.

Inter-city rivalries worsened c.400 BC. The Aleuadae of Larissa directly opposed the tyrant Lycophron of Pherae with the help of the kings of Macedon, to whom they thereby gave the means of intervening in Thessaly. Lycophron's successor, Jason, sought to become master of all Thessaly, using the federal army; after initiating an important military reform (whence his title of *tagos*) he attempted to reassert federal power. After his assassination and the coming to power of Alexander in Pherae, internal wrangling brought Thessalian politics to a new low and facilitated the intervention of *Philip II of Macedon, who assumed control of the federation. Philip delegated his authority to his own appointees, four tetradarchs, through whom the submission of the Thessalians was assured. The Thessalian cavalry fought with distinction in Asia under *Alexander the Great, but in the Lamian War the

Thessalians actively sided with the Greeks. In the 3rd cent. BC Thessaly was effectively partitioned, with some areas in Macedonian hands and others controlled by the Aetolian Confederacy; it now became a theatre for the military engagements of other powers, including, from the end of the century, the Romans.

The declaration of Greek freedom by *Flamininus in 196 BC ostensibly liberated the Thessalian cities, but Rome kept control of them. Enlarged after 146 BC and again under *Augustus to include the perioecic regions, the Thessalian federation survived as a Roman administrative tool until the end of the 4th cent. AD.   B. H.

Thucydides (see facing page)

Tiberius (Tiberius Iulius Caesar Augustus), emperor (b. 16 Nov. 42 BC; d. 16 Mar. AD 37). He was the son of Tiberius Claudius Nero and *Livia. His mother Livia was divorced and married Octavian, the future *Augustus, in 38 shortly before the birth of Tiberius' brother Nero Claudius Drusus. After public service in Spain with Augustus (Suet. *Tib.* 8), Tiberius was quaestor in 23 BC, five years earlier than normal. From 20 BC, when he crowned the Roman nominee Tigranes in Armenia, until AD 12, when he returned to Rome after retrieving the situation on the Rhine after the Varian disaster (AD 9; Publius Quinctilius Varus lost three legions), Tiberius' military career was uniformly successful. In 15 and 14 BC he completed with Drusus the conquest of the Alps; from *Agrippa's death in 12 until 9 BC he was reducing Pannonia; from Drusus' death to 7 BC and again from AD 4 to 6 he campaigned in Germany. Between AD 6 and 9 he was engaged in suppressing the revolts of Pannonia and Illyricum.

After Agrippa's death Tiberius divorced Vipsania Agrippina (the 'Elder Agrippina') to marry Augustus' daughter *Julia; their son died in infancy. After his second consulship (7 BC), Tiberius was granted tribunician power and *imperium* in the east for five years for a diplomatic mission, the restoration of Roman authority in Armenia, but the attempt to advance Augustus' grandson and adopted son Gaius Caesar to a premature consulship, made with or without the emperor's approval, helped provoke Tiberius' withdrawal to *Rhodes. He returned to Rome, still out of favour, in AD 2. By spring AD 4 both Augustus' adopted sons were dead and he adopted Tiberius, together with Agrippa Postumus, while Tiberius adopted his nephew *Germanicus. Tiberius received tribunician power (see TRIBUNE OF THE PLEBS) for ten years, renewed in AD 13 for a further ten; concurrently he held proconsular *imperium*, in 13 made equal to that of Augustus.

When Augustus died in AD 14 Tiberius was thus in full power. The nature of the embarrassing 'accession debate' (Tac. *Ann.* 1. 10–13) of 17 September remains unclear: a fresh conferment of power, or a political discussion of the (less autocratic) form to be taken by the new Principate. Certainly, he abolished Augustus' advisory council (*consilium principis*), which in his last months had made authori-

tative decisions; matters came directly to the senate. Abroad, Tiberius' dislike of extravagant honours (Tac. *Ann.* 4. 37 f.) was tempered by precedent and a need to conciliate his subjects which could prevent him making his wishes clear, as to Gytheum in Laconia in AD 15 (EJ 102 (trans. D. Braund, *Augustus to Nero, 31 B.C.–A.D. 68* (1985), 127)).

Tiberius respected Augustus and exploited his memory when taking unpopular steps (Tac. *Ann.* 1. 14. 6–15. 1). In dealing with the Germans he followed the policy of containing the empire that Augustus laid down in his political testament (Tiberius may have helped to draft it). This conflicted with the views of Germanicus, who was recalled in AD 16. Augustus' methods of coping with *Britain and Armenia were also followed: on his mission to the east (AD 17–19) Germanicus established another Roman nominee in Armenia, who survived successfully until 35; further negotiations, backed up by the threat of force, were conducted by Lucius Vitellius. Tiberius did not shrink from annexing dependent monarchies: Germanicus took over Commagene and Cappadocia, which made it possible to halve the Roman sales tax.

Two innovations in provincial administration are credited to Tiberius: prorogations of governors, and governorships in absence. Both were due to a shortage of satisfactory candidates, deplored by Tiberius (Tac. *Ann.* 6. 27). The second was clearly deleterious and the first kept some poor governors in office (e.g. Pontius Pilate in Judaea).

The most notorious feature of Tiberius' principate was the incidence of trials before the senate (introduced by Augustus), some *extra ordinem* (Marcus Scribonius Libo Drusus in 16; *Sejanus in 31), most for diminishing the majesty (*maiestas*) of the Roman people, the emperor, his family, or other notables, by whatever means, however trivial; at first some were discouraged by the emperor (e.g. Tac. *Ann.* 1. 73 f.). That of Gnaeus Calpurnius Piso, also accused in AD 20 of extortion and of poisoning Germanicus, is documented not only in Tac. *Ann.* 3. 8–19, but in the decree embodying the senate's decisions and approved by the emperor (W. Eck and others, *SC de Cn. Pisone patre* (1996)), which affords an unappetizing insight into the atmosphere of the reign.

Tiberius' reign opened with army mutinies, soon suppressed; the revolt in Gaul (AD 21; see GAUL (TRANSALPINE)) was minor. Two factors undermined his principate. Tiberius inherited a poor military and economic situation: the German war was unprofitable; politicians were short of cash and were resorting to prosecutions to obtain it (cf. Tac. *Ann.* 2. 34), there was unrest at Rome due to grain shortages, and provincials were chafing under tax burdens (cf. the revolt of 21). Tiberius' answers (gifts to individuals, treasury disbursements when senators became unable to pay their debts in 33 (Tac. *Ann.* 6, 16 f.), and public economy) were inadequate, and his marked frugality (though personally generous, he built little, and gave donations and games sparingly) increased his unpopularity.

Second, there had been family jealousy since 7 BC, and

[*continued on p. 724*]

Thucydides

Thucydides, author of the (incomplete) History of the War (Peloponnesian War) between Athens and Sparta, 431–404 BC, in eight books.

Life He was born probably between 460 and 455 BC: he was general (*stratēgos*) in 424 (4. 104) and must then have been at least 30 years old; while his claim in 5. 26. 5 that he was of years of discretion from beginning to end of the war perhaps suggests that he was not much more than grown up in 431. He probably died about 400. He shows no knowledge of 4th-cent. events. The revival of Athenian sea power under Conon and Thrasybulus, from 394 on, made the decision of Aegospotami (405: see ATHENS, HISTORY) less decisive than it seemed to Thucydides (compare e.g. 5. 26. 1 with Xen. *Hell.* 5. 1. 35). Of the three writers who undertook to complete his History, only *Xenophon took his view that the story ended in 404 (or 401). *Theopompus took it down to 394, and so probably did Cratippus (Plut. *Mor.* 345d). If, as seems likely, the very respectable author Oxyrhynchus Historian is Cratippus, then both his work and Theopompus' are on a very much larger scale than Xenophon's, a scale like Thucydides' own. This fact, as well as considerations of language and outlook, makes it likely that Xenophon wrote his continuation (*Hell.* books 1–2) earlier than the others, and indeed, before the battle of Coronea in 394. But if this be so, then Thucydides cannot have lived more than a year or so into the 4th cent. Marcellinus, in his Life, ch. 34, says that Thucydides was 'over 50' when he died. If he was born about 455 and died about 400, this will be true. The figure may be from Cratippus, who evidently gave some biographical data: Marcellinus quotes him just before (33) for the view that Thucydides died in Thrace.

Thucydides, then, was part of that ardent youth whose abundance on both sides seemed to him to distinguish the war he wrote of. Something of his ardour may be felt in 2. 31: his pride in the soldier's profession and his devotion to the great commander, *Pericles.

He caught the *plague, some time between 430 and 427, but recovered, and in 424 failed in the task of saving Amphipolis from Brasidas. Not to have been a match for Brasidas does not prove him a bad soldier: from his history one receives the impression of a first-rate regimental officer, ashore or afloat, who saw war as a matter of style; perhaps his defence of the generals before Megara in 4. 73. 4 (cf. 108. 5) says worse of his judgement of problems of high command than his failure against Brasidas. He was exiled for this (424 winter) and returned twenty years later, after the war was over, and died within a few years.

He had property and influence in the mining district of Thrace (4. 105. 1). His father's name was Olorus (4. 104. 4), the name of Cimon's Thracian grandfather; his tomb was in Cimon's family vault. It is almost certain he was related by blood to Cimon, and probably to Thucydides son of Melesias, the statesman (*JHS* 1932, 210); born in the anti-Pericles opposition, he followed Pericles with a convert's zeal.

Parts of the History The incomplete history falls into five parts: A, an introduction (book 1); B, the ten years war (2. 1–5. 24); C, the precarious peace (5. 25–end); D, the Sicilian War (6 and 7); E, fragment of the Decelean War (8). It is convenient to take first B and D, the two complete wars.

B is enclosed between two statements that 'the continuous war has herein been described'. It was therefore provisionally finished (if these are Thucydides' words). It contains one allusion to the fall of Athens (2. 65. 12) and several allusions to events late in the twenty-seven years: these are no doubt additions made to an already existing narrative, since one passage certainly (2. 23. 3) was not written as late as the last decade of the century. The narrative gets rather more summary after Thucydides' exile (424): e.g. after the futile embassy to Artaxerxes I of *Persia (4. 50) nothing is said of the important negotiations with Darius II.

D is the most finished portion. As it stands it is adapted to a history of the whole war (6. 7. 4, 6. 93. 4, 7. 18. 4, cf. 7. 9 etc., also 7. 44. 1, 7. 87. 5), and twice at least refers to events of 404 or later (7. 57. 2, 6. 15. 3–4). But these may be revisions and it has been suggested that Thucydides published it separately; and this opinion, though little held now, is not disproved. B and D are connected by C, sequel to B and introduction to D, and provided accordingly with a second preface. For symptoms of incompleteness, see below. C covers five and a half years, very unequally. Its two outstanding features are the description of the Mantinea campaign, and the Melian Dialogue. The former should perhaps be regarded, with B and D, as a third completed episode. The latter foreshadows the dramatic style of D; but if we read 5. 111 with 8. 27 we shall draw no facile moral (see 8. 27. 5).

E has the same symptoms of incompleteness as C and, moreover, stops abruptly in the middle of a narrative. It is very full, covering barely two years in its 109 chapters.

A consists of (1) 1. 1–23, a long preface, illustrating the importance of Thucydides' subject by comparison with earlier history (the so-called 'archaeology') and stating his historical principles; (2) the causes of the war—that is, for the most part, an account of the political manœuvres of 433–432; he adds important digressions, especially 1. 89–117, a history of the years 479/8–440/39 (the so-called *pentekontaetia*), partly to illustrate his view that the war was an inevitable result of Athens' power, partly to make his history follow without interval on that of *Herodotus (1. 97. 2). The second motive perhaps explains the length of another digression (1. 128–38) on the fate of Pausanias the Spartan regent and of *Themistocles.

Incompleteness E stops in mid-narrative, in winter 411: Thucydides intended to go down to 404 (5. 26. 1). It shares with (roughly) C two peculiarities, absence of speeches and presence of documents, which are thought to show incompleteness; for these see below. The plan to make of BCDE a continuous history of the twenty-seven years is only superficially achieved, even to 411: e.g. there is nothing of Atheno-Persian relations between 424 and 412, vital though these were (2. 65. 12). We shall see below that Thucydides kept his work by him and revised continually; so he left double treatments of the same theme, one of which he meant no doubt to suppress—e.g. the tyrannicides, the killers of *Pisistratus' son Hipparchus (1. 20, 6. 54–59); possibly 1. 23. 1–3 is a short early variant of 1. 1–19; 3. 84 of part of 82–3 (E. Schwartz, *Das Geschichtswerk des Thukydides* (1919), 286f.). It may be even suspected that 8. 82. 2 is a less accurately informed version of 86. 4–5 and the two have been merely harmonized by 85. 4. If this last suspicion were just, it would be good evidence that Thucydides' remains were put into shape by an editor, whose hand may be further suspected in the misplacement of 3. 17, in 1. 56–7 (whose author—as it stands—surely misconceived the course of events), perhaps even in 1. 118. 2 (where the last sentence seems to leap from the 450s to 432); an editorial hand has, indeed, been suspected wholesale. Though no single case is quite decisive, it is unlikely Thucydides left his unfinished work in need of no editing. If we look for an editor, one thinks naturally of Xenophon, who wrote the continuation (it seems) immediately after Thucydides' death; the suggestion was made in antiquity (Diog. Laert. 2. 57). His soldierly (if not his intellectual) qualities might commend him to Thucydides, but if it was indeed he, he worked with extreme piety, and his hand is very little apparent. Xenophon's limits and virtues alike disqualify him for the authorship of 1. 56–7.

Speeches and Documents Ancient craftsmen, and Thucydides notably, aimed at exactness; but in his speeches, Thucydides admits (1. 22. 1) that exactness was beyond his powers of memory. Here, then, as in reconstructing the far past (1. 20–1), he had to trust to his historical imagination, whose use generally he planned to avoid (ὡς ἂν ἐδόκουν ἐμοὶ εἰπεῖν, 'what I think they would have said': this meant applying to the speeches the sort of rationalizing schematism that, e.g., Hecataeus of Miletus applied to *geography); and even here, he promises he will control its use as rigorously as he can by the tenor of the actual words. It is much debated whether he made this profession early or late; and it has been much explained away. But it is unreasonable to doubt that from the start Thucydides took notes himself, or sought for hearers' notes, of the speeches he considered important. But since he used speeches dramatically, to reveal the workings of men's minds and the impact of circumstance, it is clear that verbatim reports would not have served even if he could have managed to get them, and he was bound to compromise (unconsciously) between dramatic and literal truth. It is likely that, as his technique developed, dramatic truth would tend to prevail; it is tempting to put his profession of method early, a young man's intention. Even so, while we cannot suppose that, at a moment when morale was vital, Pericles used the words in 2. 64. 3; while it is unlikely that the Athenian debater at Melos developed exactly the same vein of thought as Phrynichus before Miletus (5. 111–8. 27); while Pericles' first speech (1. 140 ff.) is perhaps composite, and hard to assign to a single occasion; it is yet dangerous to treat the speeches as free fiction: their dramatic truth was combined with the greatest degree of literal truth of which Thucydides was capable. He tried to recreate real occasions.

There are no speeches in E, and (except the Melian Dialogue) none in C: Cratippus (a younger contemporary) says Thucydides had decided to drop their use. Modern critics treat their absence as a symptom of incompleteness; they would have been added had he lived. But it is possible that these parts without speeches are experiments in new techniques. Thucydides may have felt, as many readers do, that the narrative of the ten years is a compromise between the methods of tragedy and of a laboratory notebook, so that between the profoundest issues and the particular detail, the middle ranges (e.g. an intelligible account of strategy) are neglected. In the later narrative the methods are more separated. The Sicilian War was capable of almost purely dramatic treatment; C and E evidently not. And in consequence in E at least a new technique is developed, less like either drama or chronicle, more of an organized narrative, with more of the writer's own judgements of values and interpretations of events. It is questionable if E would be improved by speeches, that is, could be profitably (or at all?) transformed into the style of B or D: was Cratippus perhaps right about Thucydides' intention?

This would not prevent some of the speeches in books 1–4 being composed (or revised) very late. The new experiment would not entail eliminating the dramatic from those books; Thucydides experimented to the end and never solved his problem. It is commonly thought that the Funeral Speech (2. 35 ff.) was written or rewritten after Athens' fall; and 2. 64. 3 surely was. The Corcyra debate (1. 31–44), on the contrary, has good chances of being an actual report, written up soon after delivery. Though some speeches aim at dramatic characterization (Gorgiastic (see GORGIAS), 4. 61. 7: Laconic i.e. Spartan, 1. 86), all are in Thucydides' idiom. But the personalness of this idiom is often overestimated (J. H. Finley, *Thucydides*[2] (1947)).

It is noteworthy that those portions which lack speeches have (instead?) transcriptions of documents: that is, E and (roughly speaking) C.[1] If, then, we take C and E as experiments in a new method, the experiment begins in the latter part of B. These documents are usually thought (like the absence of speeches) a sign of incompleteness, since they offend against a 'law of style' which forbids the verbatim use of foreign matter in serious prose. We need not debate the general validity of this law: with so inventive a writer as Thucydides, his laws of style are to be deduced from his practice, and 5. 24. 2 (cf. 2. 1) suggests that the end of B is provisionally finished. Are they part of the experiment? One may be surprised (though grateful) that Thucydides thought the full text of the Armistice (4. 118–19) worth its room. One of the documents (5. 47) is extant in fragments (*IG* 1[3]. 83) and confirms the substantial accuracy of the copies. One conflicts gravely with the narrative (5. 23, 5. 39. 3): it would seem the narrative was written in ignorance of the exact terms, and has not been revised.

'Early' and 'Late' Thucydides says (1. 1. 1) he began to write his history as soon as war started; and it is at least arguable that much of the existing narrative, in all five parts of the work, was written, substantially as we have it, very soon after the events. But he worked slowly, and, as he says at 1. 22. 3, laboriously; correcting in the light of better information (we only detect this process where it is

---

[1] Not exactly C: C ends with the Melian Dialogue (which in colour belongs to D?) and B has documents instead of speeches in its latter part, i.e. after the occasion of Thucydides' exile.

incomplete; e.g. 5. 39. 3 was due for correction in the light of 5. 23) or of later events (1. 97. 2; 4. 48. 5, where the qualification ὅσα γε may have been put merely *ex abundanti cautela*, from excess of caution, but more likely when the troubles started again in 410). If his point of view, or his method, changed materially during this process, it becomes of importance to know from which point of view this or that portion is written. More than a century ago, Ullrich called attention to this, believing that an important change of approach came with his discovery (announced in the second preface, 5. 26) that the war had not ended in 421.

Two criteria have been used to determine earliness or lateness: (*a*) reference to, or ignorance of, datable events or conditions; (*b*) the stage in Thucydides' own development which a passage reveals.

(*a*) References to late events cannot be written early, but they may be inserted in early contexts: e.g. those who think D early regard 6. 15. 3–4 and 7. 57. 2 as additions. Ignorance of late events is very much harder to establish: those same who think D early may suspect in 6. 41. 3 ignorance of *Dionysius I's tyranny, or even (a very slippery question) in 6. 54. 1 ignorance of Herodotus' history—but cannot prove their suspicions; yet where such ignorance is certain (see below), we may be sure that the narrative (or line of thought) which warrants them was conceived early. The results of this method are modest: e.g. (1) 1. 10. 2 was not written after the catastrophe of 404: therefore the war against which earlier wars are being measured is not the completed twenty-seven years, and the 'end of war' mentioned in 1. 13. 3–4, 1. 18. 1, is presumably 421; (2) 2. 23. 3 was not written after the loss of Oropus in 411: therefore some of the narrative of B was written much as we have it before 411; (3) 2. 65. 12 refers to the fall of Athens: therefore B received additions down to 404 at least.

(*b*) More has been hoped from the second method. Thucydides worked from his twenties to his fifties, his material growing under his eyes: there must surely be some intellectual or spiritual growth, some change of outlook. The best exponent of this method is Schwartz, who gives (*Das Geschichtswerk des T.,* 217–42) an eloquent account of Thucydides' growth. The danger of this method is evident: in the ablest hands it yields quite different results (Meyer, Schwartz), and its first postulate may be doubted, namely, that Thucydides' opinion on the 'true cause' of the war (1. 23. 6) was not formed till after the fall of Athens. No doubt that was his view after 404; no doubt 1. 23. 6 and 1. 88 were written (inserted?) pretty late. But much the same view is expressed by the Corcyran envoy in 1. 33. 3 (cf. 42. 2); and whether the envoy said it or not it was surely Pericles' view. Pericles believed that if Athens used her opportunity in 433 she was bound to provoke in Sparta an enmity that must be faced; all his career, against Cimon and his successors, he had fought for his conviction that Athens and Sparta were natural enemies and Greece not large enough for both. His admirers held that this clear principle (1. 140. 1) was obscured in debate by the irrelevant particulars (1. 140. 4–141. 1). We have not to consider whether Pericles was right: rather, the effect on Thucydides. The devout disciple saw the story unfold in the terms his master had foreseen (2. 65). How far such a 'Pericles-fixation' may have warped Thucydides' judgement, see below.

If this first postulate go, the second will follow it, namely that only after 404 was Pericles given the importance he now has in books 1–2, since after 404 Thucydides started to rewrite his History as a 'defence of Pericles' (Schwartz 239). It hardly needs to be said that many hold to these postulates and the present writer's disbelief is as subjective as their belief. If these are untrue, truer postulates may be found: the attempt to recreate Thucydides' experience should (and will) never be dropped.

Truthfulness Perhaps no good historian is impartial; Thucydides certainly not, though singularly candid. His tastes are clear: he liked Pericles and disliked Cleon. He had for Pericles a regard comparable to Plato's for *Socrates and an equal regard for Pericles' Athens. These things were personal: but in principle, concentrations of energy (like Athens or *Alcibiades) were to his taste. Their impact on a less dynamic world was likely to be disastrous—but whose fault was that? The world's, he says, consistently (1. 99; 1. 23. 6 etc.; 6. 15; 6. 28; cf. 2. 64. 3–5): and though this consistency may surprise us, we need not quarrel with it. Such judgements are rare, since Thucydides conceives his task as like medical research (see below, and cf. 3. 82. 2) where blame is irrelevant; the disconcerting simplicity of 2. 64. 3 (power and energy are absolute goods) is the more striking.

We need not here investigate Thucydides' possible mistakes. The present writer believes that Pericles (having planned an offensive war) lost his striking power, first because Potidaea revolted, next because of the plague. Forced to the defensive, he left that as his testament. Thucydides was reluctant to face the fact of this failure, and accepted the testament, siding with the defeatist officer class against the revived offensive of Cleon (4. 27. 5, 28. 5, 65. 4, 73. 4; cf. 5. 7. 2). This is why Pericles' huge effort against Epidaurus (6. 31. 2; motive, cf. 5. 53) is recorded as a minor futility (2. 56. 4); why Phormio's first campaign in Acarnania (2. 68. 7–9; of 432?) is left timeless; why we hear nothing of the purpose of the Megara decree; why, when that nearly bore fruit at last, Thucydides suggests that the capture of Megara was of no great moment (4. 73. 4; but cf. 72. 1).

Such criticisms hardly detract much from his singular truthfulness. Readers of all opinions will probably agree that he saw more truly, inquired more responsibly, and reported more faithfully than any other ancient historian. That is a symptom of his greatness, but not its core. Another symptom is his style: it is innocent of those clichés of which *Isocrates hoped to make the norm of Attic style; in its 'old-fashioned wilful beauty' (*Dionysius of Halicarnassus) every word tells. Like English prose before Dryden and Addison, it uses a language largely moulded by poets: its precision is a poet's precision, a union of passion and candour. After Thucydides history mostly practised the corrupting art of persuasion (cf. Isoc. 4. 8): his scientific tradition survived in the antiquarians, of whom he is the pioneer (1. 8. 1, 2. 15. 2, 3. 104. 4–6, 6, 55. 1), but the instinctive exactness of early Greek observation was lost. To combine his predecessors' candour of vision with his successors' apparatus of scholarship was a necessity laid on him by his sense of the greatness of his subject: he could no more distort or compromise with what he wished to convey than Shakespeare or Michelangelo could.

Thucydides would no doubt prefer to substitute, for these great names, the practice of any honest doctor. He was not modest, but in his statement of his principles he is singularly unaware of his unique equipment, and claims rather that he has spared no pains. The proper context for this statement (1. 20–2) is, first, his very similar statement about his own account of the plague (2. 48. 3), and then the physician Hippocrates' maxim, 'ars longa vita brevis'. The 'art' which outlasts individual lives is the scientific study of man: the physician studied his clinical, Thucydides his political, behaviour. To know either so well that you can control it (and civilization is largely made up of such controls) is a task for many generations: a piece of that task well done is something gained for ever (1. 22. 4).   H. T. W.-G.

Style In a famous sentence (*Thuc.* 24) *Dionysius of Halicarnassus gives as the four 'tools' in Thucydides' workshop τὸ ποιητικὸν τῶν ὀνομάτων, τὸ πολυειδὲς τῶν σχημάτων, τὸ τραχὺ τῆς ἁρμονίας, τὸ τάχος τῶν σμασιῶν 'poetical vocabulary, great variety of figures, harshness of word-order, swiftness in saying what he has to say'. The first, third, and fourth of these criticisms are undoubtedly true. Thucydides' style has a poetical and archaistic flavour (it is often difficult to distinguish clearly between the two), as a reader sees at once when he turns from Thucydides to *Andocides and *Lysias. His consistent use of αἰεί for ἀεί, ξύν, for σύν and σσ, for ττ is one of the signs of this tendency. 'Roughness' is to be seen in his bold changes of construction and his violent hyperbata, in which he wrests an emphatic word from its natural place in the sentence to give it more prominence (1. 19 κατ' ὀλιγαρχίαν, 1. 93. 4 τῆς θαλάσσης). 'Speed' is perhaps the most striking of all his characteristics. He achieves an extreme concision, hardly to be paralleled in Greek prose except in the gnomic utterances of Democritus. A sentence like δοκεῖ . . . καταστροφή (2. 42. 2) is gone in a flash, and no orator, composing for the ear, could have risked such brevity. At 2. 37. 1 (μέτεστι . . . προτιμᾶται) two antitheses are telescoped into one. τὸ πολυειδὲς τῶν σχημάτων is much more open to question, especially as Dionysius has just before credited Thucydides with the use of the θεατρικὰ σχήματα (parisosis (balance of clauses), paronomasia (play on words), and antithesis) affected by *Gorgias and other writers of the sophistic school (see SOPHISTS). Thucydides' thought is, it is true, markedly antithetical in cast (e.g. 1. 70. 6), and antithesis is sometimes strained (e.g. 2. 43. 3). But, unlike the Gorgianists, he has no affection for merely external antithesis, and he often deliberately avoids formal balance (e.g. 4. 59. 2). He eschews almost entirely certain other common adornments of style. He is too austere to use metaphor at all freely, or asyndeton (more suited to the spoken word). He does employ certain devices of assonance, neither, like Gorgias, as ἡδύσματα nor, like Demosthenes, for emphasis pure and simple, but for the emphasizing of a contrast (3. 82. 8 εὐσεβεία … εὐπρεπεία, 6. 76. 2 κατοικίσαι … ἐξοικίσαι, 76. 4 ἀξυνετωτέρου … κακοξυνετωτέρου). He has a strong leaning, as Dionysius observed (Amm. 2. 5), towards abstract expression (e.g. 3. 82–3), sometimes carried to the length of personification (πόλεμος 1. 122. 1, ἐλπίς 5. 103. 1). He probably coined abstracts (especially in -σις) freely, as *Euripides did, according to the fashion of the late 5th cent., and sometimes used them out of season (7. 70. 6 ἀποστέρησιν, and the odd-looking negatived abstracts, 1. 137. 4 οὐ διάλυσιν, etc.). Like *Antiphon, he experimented freely with the use of neuter adjective, or even participle (1. 142. 8 ἐν τῷ μὴ μελετῶντι), to convey an abstract idea. His periods are usually loosely constructed (e.g. 3. 38. 4–7), of clauses longer in actual words, and far richer in content, than those of other Greek prose-writers (e.g. 2. 43. 2–6).   J. D. D.

[The above entry by Wade-Gery and Denniston, which goes back essentially to the first edition of the big OCD of 1949, and was more or less reproduced in the second edn. of 1970, is an established classic and it seems an impertinence to attempt to replace it. But merely to reprint it would be unhelpful when Thucydides has been so intensively worked on. What follows is therefore a sketch of work on Thucydides in the quarter-century since 1970. We do not attempt a survey of work up to 1970, confining ourselves to a mention of the great historical commentary on Thucydides (HCT), begun by A. W. Gomme (bk. 1, 1945; bks. 2–5.24, 1956) and then completed by A. Andrewes and K. J. Dover (bks. 5. 25–7 (1970); bk. 8 (1981). Note also the important new edition of the text of Thucydides by G. Alberti (so far bks. 1–2, 1972; bks. 3–5, 1992). But the standard edn. of the whole of Thucydides remains the Oxford Classical Text by H. Stuart-Jones, repr. 1942 with critical apparatus revised by J. E. Powell.]

The most noticeable feature of Thucydidean scholarship since 1970 is the move away from preoccupation with the 'composition question' (the identification of layers of the History, with attempts to date them) to study of Thucydides' text as a complete literary whole. There is a parallel here with the move in Homeric scholarship (see HOMER) over the same period away from 'analytical' approaches and towards a 'unitarian' interest in the architecture of the two great poems. Of the 1970 Thucydides bibliography (not reprinted here), it is striking how many items addressed themselves to questions of composition, a topic to which Wade-Gery's OCD article was itself an influential contribution. One discussion which appeared just too late for the 2nd edn. was the relevant section of O. Luschnat's long 1970 survey, RE Suppl. 12, 1147 ff. The related question, whether Thucydides' work was finished, has continued to attract study, notably in Andrewes's contribution to the final (1981) volume of A. W. Gomme, A. Andrewes, and K. J. Dover, HCT, with the reply by H. Erbse, Thukydidesinterpretationen (1989). (See also ch. 5 of Dover, Greece and Rome New Survey no. 7 (1973), an admirable general survey of Thucydides.) And H. H. Rawlings III, The Structure of Thucydides' History (1981) has speculated about the possible content of the unwritten books 9 and 10. But even this was part of a wider attempt to detect patterning within the larger existing structure.

F. M. Cornford, Thucydides Mythistoricus (1907) was an early attempt to treat Thucydides as a literary text to which methods used on tragedy and epic could be applied. More recent works include H.-P. Stahl, Thukydides: Die Stellung des Menschen im geschichtlichen Prozess (1966), a book which allotted as much space to narrative as to speeches, and H. Strasburger's studies of the 1950s (collected now in Strasburger, Studien zur alten Geschichte (1982)), and H. Kitto, Poiesis 1966. V. Hunter in 1973 set the tone for two decades by her title of her book Thucydides the Artful Reporter; Herodotus had for centuries found himself periodically in the pillory for alleged distortion and invention, but Thucydides' authoritative and apparently scientific manner had usually been respected. Now it was suggested that

Thucydides might simply have made things up, particularly his imputations of motive. This approach was also pursued by C. Schneider, *Information und Absicht bei Thukydides* (1974). (Cf. below on the narratological problem of 'restricted access'.) Historical as well as historiographic issues are affected: thus whereas G. E. M. de Ste. Croix, *The Origins of the Peloponnesian War* (1972) had sought to justify Thucydides (and threw in an excellent introductory section on Thucydidean methodology), E. Badian, *From Plataea to Potidaea* (1993), a collection of essays going back to the 1980s, is in complete contrast, an acute demonstration by a historian of the consequences of distrusting Thucydides.

Now the lid was off. One way of going further was to challenge the premiss that ancient historiography had pretensions to being an exact or any sort of science: perhaps (A. J. Woodman, *Rhetoric in Classical Historiography* (1988)) it was merely a branch of rhetoric with a different aim from factual description; perhaps, indeed, the 'facts' are nothing of the sort. (This is not just an 'ancient' problem; but enough documentary evidence exists to control Thucydides and reassure us that there was indeed a Peloponnesian War.)

Another more acceptable approach has been to disregard the signs of incompleteness in Thucydides and insist in post-modern fashion (W. R. Connor, *CJ* 1977) on the autonomy of the text: whatever the authorial intention, we have a long speech-punctuated narrative of Greek prose containing patterns, significant repetitions, ring-composition, etc. See Connor, *Thucydides* (1984), but cf. also S. Hornblower, *Thucydides* (1987) for an attempt to combine literary criteria with recognition of the composition problem and its implications.

The detailed work of Colin Macleod (*Collected Essays* 1983)) deserves a special word; there has been no finer treatment of the rhetoric of the Thucydidean speeches. On rhetorical issues note also W. K. Pritchett's excellent *Dionysius of Halicarnassus on Thucydides* (1975).

More recently still narratology has been tried on Thucydides. Narratology is nothing more frightening than the study of a branch of rhetoric, specifically of the principles underlying narrative texts. First used on modern, then on ancient, novels, it was applied in 1987 to Homer by I. de Jong (see HOMER; LITERARY THEORY AND CLASSICAL STUDIES; NARRATIVE), who demonstrated how narratology can help us see how Homer achieves his famously objective manner. The technique has been most fully applied to Thucydides by Hornblower in S. Hornblower (ed.), *Greek Historiography* (1994), ch. 5), but see already the short essay by Connor in M. Jameson (ed.), *The Greek Historians* (1985), using, however, the term 'narrative discourse' not narratology. Some narratological terms and insights are familiar to Thucydideans under other names; e.g. 'restricted access' means the difficulty encountered by a non-omniscient narrator interested in an agent's motives. The usual response, e.g. in messenger speeches in tragedy (and in Thucydides?) is for the narrator silently to assume an omniscient pose. But the greatest narratological weapon has been focalization, i.e. the point of view or perspective from which an event is described. Choice of Homeric (and Thucydidean?) vocabulary can sometimes be explained by the wish to present events or express emotions from a certain standpoint, which may or may not be that of the author rather than that of the imagined or historical agent. (Dover, *The Greeks and their Legacy* (1988), 74 ff. has ingeniously pointed to one purely linguistic way of determining whether a motive reflects Thucydides' own view or that of an agent's.) Again, all this is not quite new: in the 18th cent. Adam Smith in lectures on rhetoric distinguished between 'direct' and 'indirect' narration. And H. D. Westlake, *Studies in Thucydides and Greek History* (1989), ch. 14 shows that problems of 'personal motives in Thucydides' can be usefully studied in very plain language. There is much work still to be done, but provided it is recognized that there was a relation between what Thucydides says and a real world which existed in the 5th cent. BC, only good can come of the recognition that his text is susceptible to literary 'close reading'. (A valuable survey of the impact of new literary approaches is J. L. Moles, JACT *Bulletin*, autumn 1993.)

The broad trends indicated above do not at all exhaust recent Thucydidean work. There have been full-length commentaries on bks. 1–3 (1991) and 4–5.24 (1996) by S. Hornblower (translates all Greek commented on). See also the commentaries on bk. 2 by J. S. Rusten (1988: markedly linguistic) and

Rhodes (1988: markedly historical; see also his commentary on book 3, 1994); these two illuminate by exact methods traditionally applied, as does the outstanding monograph of K. Maurer, *Interpolation in Thucydides* (1995). On the important topic of the 4th-cent. and Hellenistic reception of Thucydides, Luschnat 1970 (see above) is less good than the older but shorter work of H. Strebel, *Wertung und Wirkung des Thukydideischen Geschichtswerkes* (1935): see Hornblower, *JHS* 1995. Other monographs include: L. Edmunds, *Chance and Intelligence in Thucydides* (1975); M. Ostwald, *ANAΓKH in Thucydides* (1988); Hornblower, *Harv. Stud.* 1992 (on religion esp. Delphi); L. Kallet-Marx, *Money, Expense and Naval Power in Thucydides' History 1–5.26* (1993); J. Ziolkowski, *Thucydides and the Tradition of the Funeral Oration at Athens* (1981); N. Loraux, *The Invention of Athens* (1986). On Thucydides' indebtedness to Herodotus see C. Pelling in M. Flower and M. Toher (eds.), *Georgica* (1991) and Hornblower, *Thucydides Commentary on Thucydides,* vol. 2 (1996), Introduction, section 2 and annexes A and B. This survey may end with the suggestion that two areas needing more work are Thucydides' detailed intertextual relation to Homer and to Herodotus. S. H.

the people and many senators favoured his stepsons. Rivalry after AD 4 led to the downfall of Agrippa Postumus and his adherents. Feared by former opponents, Tiberius could not make politicians trust his *moderatio* and *clementia* (moderation and clemency). They looked forward to the succession of Germanicus (Tiberius was 55 in AD 14). On his death in AD 19 and that of Tiberius' son Drusus Iulius Caesar in 23 the succession question opened up again, with the sons of Germanicus pitted against Sejanus, who seems to have supported Drusus' surviving son Tiberius Iulius Caesar Nero Gemellus. Instead of confronting the problem, Tiberius, encouraged by Sejanus, retired to Campania and then to Capreae (Capri: AD 27), never to enter Rome again. While he was at the mercy of Sejanus and his freedmen, the struggle went on at Rome, until Nero Iulius Caesar and Drusus Iulius Caesar and their mother Vipsania Agrippina were disgraced (AD 29–30) and Tiberius was given evidence that Sejanus was attempting the downfall of Germanicus' youngest son *Gaius (31; Suet. *Tib.* 61), who then became the only likely successor. A purge of Sejanus' followers (and of supporters of Gemellus and rivals of Gaius' chief aide Macro) continued until Tiberius' death on 16 March 37, which was greeted with rejoicing.

Tacitus delivers a favourable verdict on Tiberius' principate down to Sejanus' ascendancy; the five 'ages' ending with a death are another device for moving from promising beginning to disastrous end, like the hypocrisy (*dissimulatio*) also imputed to him.

Tiberius was a forceful orator, a poet (neoteric), a connoisseur, and perhaps a Sceptic (he was careless of religious ritual); he kept his intellect and relish for irony (Philo, *Leg.* 142; Tac. *Ann.* 6. 6). Stories of vice on Capreae (and *Rhodes) may be discounted; real defects, a cultivated sense of superiority, relentlessness and lack of affability, meditated ambiguity of language, remained.

J. P. B.; B. M. L.

Tibullus, Albius, born between 55 and 48 BC. An anonymous and corrupt Life, possibly derived from *Suetonius,

tells us that he was good-looking (confirmed by Hor. *Epist.* 1. 4. 6) and something of a dandy; also that he was of equestrian rank (see EQUITES) and won *dona militaria* (military awards). The Life is preceded by an epigram of Domitius Marsus, which fixes the date of Tibullus' death in 19 BC (cf. also the lament in Ov. *Am.* 3. 9).

Tibullus implies that his patrimony was diminished, presumably by Octavian's confiscations of 41–40 BC (1. 1. 41 f.; see AUGUSTUS; PROSCRIPTION); cf. Propertius. But his claims to poverty, *paupertas*, should not be taken too seriously. He no more than *Propertius seems to have been reduced to economic dependence. *Horace indeed suggests that he was well-off, and possessed a *villa at Pedum (c. 32 km. (20 mi.) E. of Rome) between Tibur and Praeneste (*Epist.* 1. 4; he is also probably the addressee of *Odes* 1. 33). Tibullus refused, or did not attract, the patronage of *Maecenas, and instead addresses himself to Marcus Valerius Messalla Corvinus. He set out to the east in Messalla's entourage, but fell ill at Corcyra and returned to Italy (1. 3); it is uncertain whether he served under him in Gaul (1. 7. 9 and Life).

Tibullus' MSS contain three books, of which the third was divided into two by Italian scholars of the 15th cent.; these are commonly called the *Corpus Tibullianum* and only the first two belong to Tibullus himself. The dates of publication are uncertain: book 1 refers to Messalla's triumph (25 September 27 BC), book 2 to the installation of his son as one of the *quindecimviri sacris faciundis*, a college of fifteen men whose job it was to look after certain ritual texts (this happened perhaps not long before Tibullus' death). It seems likely that Tibullus' first book appeared after Propertius' first, but before the completion of Propertius' second. Propertius 2. 5. 25 ff. seems a retort to Tibullus 1. 10. 61 ff. (on the question of the acceptability of violence in love-affairs).

Tibullus' first book deals with his love for a mistress, Delia (1, 2, 3, 5, 6); surprisingly and provocatively it professes comparable devotion to a boy, Marathus, too (4, 8, 9). Apuleius tells us that Delia existed and that her name was Plania (*Apol.* 10). We need not doubt this, though her attributes (and those of Marathus, for that matter) seem pretty conventional. Book 2 celebrates a different mistress, whom the poet calls Nemesis (3, 4, 6). Nothing certain can be said about the social status of any of these lovers (but for Delia cf. 1. 6. 68, which suggests that she is not a *matrona*).

Tibullus, like Propertius, expresses the belief that love must be his life's occupation (e.g. 1. 1. 45 ff.), and, like Propertius, he claims love to be his *militia* (1. 1. 75 f.), in spite of his actual forays into the world of action; like Propertius too he presents himself as the slave of his lovers (1. 5. 5 f., 1. 9. 21 f.). In his use both of military and servile figures Tibullus is more specific than Propertius. For example his servile declarations express willingness to undergo servile punishments, and some scholars detect an intended, almost Ovidian humour (cf. OVID) in his use of both figures.

Unlike Propertius, Tibullus makes virtually no use of mythology. Propertius' romantic, impossible dream had been that Cynthia would be like heroines of myth. Tibullus' impossible dream is that Delia will join him in his country estate to enjoy a rural idyll (esp. 1. 5. 21 ff.). Tibullus' aspirations to live the country life, expressed in more than one poem, separate him from the urban *Catullus and Propertius.

Apart from the love poems, books 1 and 2 contain poems in honour of Messalla (1. 7, 2. 5), an elegy on the blessings of peace (1. 10), and a charming representation of a rustic festival and the poet's song at it (2. 1). Book 2 is only just over 400 lines long, and may be either defective or posthumous.

The third book is a collection of poems from the circle of Messalla. It begins with six elegies by Lygdamus, and also contains the *Panegyricus Messallae*, five poems on the love of Sulpicia for Cerinthus (known as the Garland of Sulpicia), and six short poems by Sulpicia herself. The poems on Sulpicia are conceivably by Tibullus. The book concludes with an elegy of quality purportedly by Tibullus, and an anonymous epigram.

In Quintilian's view, Tibullus was the most 'refined and elegant' of the Roman elegists (10. 1. 93). The judgement is justified by the smooth finish of his poems; no other Roman poet writes with such refined plainness. Yet his simplicity is sometimes deceptive: the transitions by which he glides from one scene or subject to another often baffle analysis.

The almost total loss of Cornelius Gallus makes it difficult to estimate Tibullus' originality, but it was probably considerable. Certainly his plainness, his eschewal of myth, and his rural emphasis contrast strongly with Catullus and Propertius.   R. O. A. M. L.

Timaeus of Tauromenium (mod. Taormina) in *Sicily, *c*.350–260 BC, the most important western Greek historian; son of Andromachus, the dynast who refounded Tauromenium in 358. Andromachus gave Timoleon (see SICILY §5) a warm welcome in 345 and lent him his support

(T 3). Timaeus was exiled in *c*.315 probably on account of his hostility towards the tyrant Agathocles after he had captured Tauromenium (fr. 124d) and spent at least fifty years of his exile at Athens (fr. 34), where he studied under Philiscus of Miletus, a pupil of *Isocrates (T 1), and wrote his great work of history. It is conceivable that he returned to Sicily in *c*.265 but not certain. Timaeus died, allegedly at the age of 96 (T 5), shortly after 264 (see below).

Works 1. *Olympionikai*: a synchronic list of Olympian victors, Spartan kings and ephors (magistrates), the Athenian *archontes* (see LAW AND PROCEDURE, ATHENIAN), and the priestesses of *Hera in Argos (Polyb. 12. 11. 1 = T 11, frs. 125–8). Thereafter it became standard practice to date historical events by the years of the Olympian Games; see TIME-RECKONING. 2. (*Sikelikai*) *Historiai* = Sicilian History in 38 books from mythical times to the death of Agathocles 289/8 (T 6–8). He also wrote a 'separate account' on the '(Roman) Wars against *Pyrrhus' and the events until the epochal year 264 (T 9), where *Polybius' history starts, 'a fine Timaei' (from where Timaeus left off) (cf. Polyb. 1. 5. 1; 39. 8. 4 = T 6).

The arrangement is known only in outline: the five books of the introduction (*prokataskeuē*) dealt with the *geography and ethnography of the west and accounts of 'colonies, the foundation of cities, and their relations' (T 7). Books 6–15 contained the earlier history of Sicily until *Dionysius I's accession to power in 406/5; books 16–33 treated the tyranny of Dionysius I and II (406/5–344/3) and events down to Agathocles. The last five books (34–8) were devoted to the history of Agathocles (T 8). The work is known through 164 fragments, the extensive use made of it by *Diodorus Siculus (4–21 for the Sicilian passages), and Polybius' criticism in book 12.

Characteristics 1. *Subject-matter*: Timaeus did not restrict his treatment to Sicily but dealt with the whole west including Carthage. Most importantly he was the first Greek historian to give a comprehensive if summary account of Roman history until 264 (T 9b). Hence Aulus *Gellius (*NA* 2. 1. 1 = T 9c) even talks of 'historical works which Timaeus wrote in Greek on the history of the Roman people'. 2. *Conception of history*: Timaeus took an extremely broad view of history, including myth, geography, ethnography, political and military events, culture, religion, marvels, and *paradoxa* (the unexpected or unbelievable). 3. *Sicilian patriotism*: Timaeus frequently distorted events in favour of the Siceliots (fr. 94) and conversely wrote less favourably about the Athenians and Carthaginians (on the Sicilian expedition, cf. K. Meister, *Gymnasium* 1970, 508 ff.); he always emphasized the contribution of the western Greeks to Greek intellectual life (e.g. *Pythagoras, frs. 12 ff., 131 f.; Empedocles, frs. 14, 134; *Gorgias, fr. 137). 4. *Hatred of tyrants*: Timaeus, a conservative aristocrat, distorted not only the historical picture of Agathocles, who had exiled him (fr. 124), but also of other tyrants, e.g. Hiero I and Dionysius I (frs. 29, 105). 5. *Historical classification of his work*: Timaeus' work displays rhetorical, tragic, and 'pragmatic' (frs. 7, 151) features (cf. Polyb. 12. 25; frs. 22, 31) in equal proportion, hence it is an excellent example of the early blend of different kinds of historiography. 6. *Historical criticism*: Timaeus was the first Greek historian critically to appraise almost all of his predecessors, historians and other writers alike. He frequently went too far, which earned him the nickname *Epitimaeus* ('slanderer'); he was first so called by Ister (T 1, 11, 16). He was especially vehement in the attacks on his immediate predecessor Philistus (fr. 38, T 18, fr. 154).

Timaeus in turn was criticized by Polybius (book 12) for factual errors, his harsh criticism, and his historical methods (mere book-learning, want of autopsy, lack of political and military experience).

Timaeus was 'the most important historian between *Ephorus and Polybius' and became 'the standard authority on the history of the Greek West for nearly five centuries' (Pearson). Of Greek authors he was used by e.g. *Callimachus, *Lycophron, *Eratosthenes, Agatharchides, Polybius, Posidonius, *Diodorus, *Strabo, and *Plutarch; of Roman writers by Quintus Fabius Pictor, M. *Cato the Elder, *Cicero, Cornelius Nepos, *Ovid, and *Gellius. The writings of Ister (T 10), Polemon of Ilium (T 26), in reaction to his work as well as Polybius, book 12, bear witness to Timaeus' great impact on historiography.

For names mentioned in this article, see also the entries on HISTORIOGRAPHY, GREEK and HELLENISTIC. K. M.

timber was a valuable economic product in Greece and Rome. Many Mediterranean lands were forested in ancient times, but these timber stands were drastically reduced by human exploitation and by the grazing of animals, especially goats. The Mediterranean climate is capable of sustaining forests so long as they are intact, but once the trees are cut, the combination of marginal rainfall and grazing animals makes forest regeneration difficult, if not impossible. In general, the history of timber supplies is one of gradual depletion, with little effort in antiquity to replant harvested lands. Only in those areas of continental rainfall conditions which lie at some distance from dense human settlement (e.g. the mountains of *Macedonia) have forests survived into modern times. Thus lacking much apparent physical correlation between modern scrubland and ancient forests we are dependent upon references in the ancient authors (e.g. Theophrastus and *Pliny the Elder) for a description of the location and abundance of ancient timberland. Moreover, recent advances in palaeobotany as an archaeological tool have assisted in locating and describing some ancient forests not otherwise known to us. For example, *Cyprus was quite heavily forested from the central Troodos mountains down to its shorelines. Cypriot cedars of Lebanon and tall pines were much in demand for heavy construction and shipbuilding. The clearing of forest land for a variety of common uses (see below) was compounded in Cyprus by the extensive use of wood as fuel for the island's renowned smelting of copper. The result was the virtually complete stripping of the island of its famous forest cover. Much of the timberland in Cyprus today is the result of modern reforestation.

With the growth and spread of the human population throughout the Mediterranean in antiquity, there were commensurate pressures on forest lands. They were cleared for conversion to agriculture, wood was harvested for fuel—either to be burned directly or to be converted into charcoal—and used for furniture, tools, and other domestic needs. Coniferous tall timbers—which were light and strong—were used for the construction of private and public buildings and ships. With the disappearance of nearby forests by late prehistoric times, the timber-starved cities of the Mediterranean turned further afield for their supplies. Beginning in the Classical period, the main sources were Macedonia and Thrace (especially for the pines and oaks necessary for shipbuilding, oars, and pitch), Achaea, parts of *Crete and Cyprus, the south coast of the Black (Euxine) Sea, Cilicia, the mountains of the Levant, southern *Italy, and *Sicily.

As tall timbers became scarcer, the competition among Greek city-states for remaining supplies increased. For example, when the forest products of Achaea were denied to Athens because of depletion and politics, the Athenians turned increasingly to Macedonia, as several surviving inscriptions inform us. The Spartan general Brasidas' prolonged campaigns in Macedonia during the Peloponnesian War (431–404 BC) can be seen in part as a Spartan attempt to prevent Athenian access to the timberlands necessary to maintain the Athenian fleet (see NAVIES). Other inscriptions tell of the importation of heavy construction timbers into Greece during the Hellenistic era. While there is no doubt, however, about the economic, military, and diplomatic importance of timber resources, we are rather poorly informed about the details of forest management, the harvesting of wood, and its transport by land and sea. Inscriptions inform us that the kings of Macedon exercised a royal monopoly over forest resources, and let contracts for the harvest and export of timber. Many Hellenistic dynasts in the eastern Mediterranean exercised similar prerogatives over the timberland under their control.

The timber shortage was never so acute for the Roman republic as for the Greek cities, due to the ample forest resources of lowland Italy, Sicily, and the accessible lower slopes of the Apennine and Alpine ranges. As wealth increased and tastes became more exotic, the Roman timber trade (like the trade in decorative building stone) went further afield to satisfy the demand for more exquisite and rare woods. E. N. B.

time-reckoning Ancient culture knew a range of expedients for dividing the twenty-four hours of the day, for marking the succession of days in the month or year, and for dating important historical events. *Hesiod already used the rising of particular constellations to mark the changing seasons, and ascribed propitious and impropitious qualities to the days of the month that corresponded to the phases of the moon. By the 5th cent. BC, Athenian astronomers—like their Babylonian colleagues—knew that the lunar month is approximately 29¼ and the tropical year approximately 365¼ days long, and could divide the day and night up into twelve 'seasonal' hours that varied with the length of daylight. Astronomers (see ASTRONOMY) from Meton to Hipparchus and Claudius Ptolemy developed increasingly accurate luni-solar cycles and learned to explain and predict solar and lunar eclipses. They also created *parapēgmata*, or public calendars, which traced the risings and settings of stars and predicted weather throughout the year. Civil practices, however, were never guided solely by astronomical expertise. Most people continued to divide the day and night into rough sections rather than precise hours. The Athenian calendar's failure to correspond with the actual movements of the moon was notorious, while the Roman months, before *Caesar reformed the calendar, deviated by a quarter of a year and more from what should have been their place in the seasons. Intercalation was often practised for political rather than calendrical ends. Only in the 1st cent. BC and after, when the spread of *astrology made it urgent to know the year, day, and hour of an individual's birth, did an interest in precise calendar dates become widespread outside scientific circles. The chief motive for interest in the calendar lay, normally, in its days of ritual or ominous import rather than in its technical basis.

Historical events were at first normally dated, by both Greeks and Romans, by the year of a given priest or magistrate into which they fell: rough lengths for a single generation were used to date past dynasties of rulers. *Thucydides protested (5. 20) against the first of these methods, but he himself (esp. in his introductory *Archaeology*) seems to have used the second, generation-count, method; and the temptation, to compute dates by means of assumptions about the length of human life, was persistent. Thus even in the 2nd cent. BC, Apollodorus used an *'acme'* system to date famous but poorly attested individuals like philosophers and historians; that is, he assumed that an individual reached his acme (conventionally put at age 40) at the date of some well-known external event which had occurred in the life of that individual (see F. Jacoby, *Apollodors Chronik* (1902)). From the end of the 4th cent. BC, however, when the *Seleucid era of 312/11 BC came into widespread use, more precise eras and methods gradually came into use. Scholars like *Eratosthenes and *Timaeus tried to co-ordinate historical dates from different societies by measuring their distance from some single, common era, like that of the first Olympian Games in 776 BC or the founding of Rome in 753/2 BC. Other eras sometimes used included that of the Trojan War (normally given as 1183/2 BC) and the astronomers' era of Nabonassar, 26 January 747 BC.   A. T. G.

Titus (Titus Flavius Vespasianus), Roman emperor, AD 79–81. Born on 30 December 39, he was the elder son of *Vespasian and was brought up at court along with Britannicus, *Claudius' son. He had considerable physical and intellectual gifts, especially in music and singing, so that at one stage some viewed him as potentially a second *Nero. He married Arrecina Tertulla, daughter of the praetorian prefect of *Gaius (Caligula); and she bore him a daughter, Julia. After her death he married Marcia Furnilla, whom he later divorced. He spent his early career as a military tribune in Germany and Britain, and it was probably in Lower Germany that he established his friendship with *Pliny the Elder, who subsequently dedicated the *Natural History* to him. Although only of quaestorian rank, he joined his father in 67 in his mission to suppress the Jewish revolt (see JEWS), taking command of legio XV Apollinaris and displaying great personal bravery. He was dispatched to convey Vespasian's congratulations to the newly-acclaimed emperor Galba, but turned back on hearing of the turmoil in Rome, pausing to consult the *oracle of Venus at Paphos on Cyprus, whose allegedly encouraging response he brought to his father. He was closely involved in preparations for the Flavian bid for power which culminated on 1 July 69 when Vespasian was first acclaimed emperor by the troops in Egypt. Titus, however, remained in Judaea to take charge of the military operations and after the Flavian victory was created consul in his absence and given proconsular *imperium*. In 70 he captured Jerusalem and was hailed as *imperator* by his troops. His exploits on campaign were recorded by the Jewish historian *Josephus, who had been befriended by the Flavians.

Hostile observers thought that Titus might use the affection of his troops to seize power for himself, since the soldiers in the east were demanding that he take them all back with him, but there is no sign of any disloyalty to his father. Once back in Rome he celebrated a *triumph with Vespasian and was elevated to share his position, receiving the tribunician power (dated from 1 July 71), holding seven consulships with him, and sharing the office of censor; he also became leader of the young men (*princeps iuventutis*) along with his brother, *Domitian. He was appointed praetorian prefect, a post normally held by equestrians (see EQUITES), and incurred hostility because of his ruthless suppression of the alleged conspiracy of the senators Aulus Caecina Alienus and Eprius Marcellus. He was also disliked for his liaison with Berenice (daughter of the Jewish king Agrippa II), whom he had met in Judaea and who came to Rome in 75, where she probably remained until 79.

Titus succeeded smoothly after Vespasian's death on 23 June 79, and belied the fears of some by the quality of his administration. He ended, however unwillingly, his affair with Berenice, banished informers, and refused to accept treason charges. He declined to put any senator to death or confiscate property, and had a courteous relationship with the senate. Titus once memorably remarked, on observing that he had benefited no one all day, 'Friends, I have lost a day' (Suet. *Tit.* 8). He dedicated the *Colosseum begun by Vespasian, built baths, and provided lavish public spectacles. He reacted energetically to alleviate the natural disasters which occurred during his reign, the eruption of Mt. Vesuvius in 79 and a serious fire and plague in Rome in 80.

There were rumours that Titus' relationship with his brother Domitian was sometimes strained and even that he was poisoned, but his death on 13 September 81 is likely to have been from natural causes. He was remembered with affection as the 'delight and darling of the human race' (Suet. *Tit.* 1), though *Cassius Dio shrewdly commented that had he lived longer his regime might not have been judged so successful. J. B. C.

toga The toga was the principal garment of the free-born Roman male. It was also worn by *Etruscan men and originally also by women. It was usually made of undyed light wool, but for mourning was of dark wool, the *toga pulla*, and, for boys of high birth and the holders of certain offices, it had a purple *praetexta* border along its upper edge. A decorated version worn by victorious commanders in triumphal processions (see TRIUMPH), the *toga picta* or *trabea triumphalis*, was made of purple wool and gold thread.

In shape the toga was a very large semicircle, a single piece of cloth which in the 1st cent. AD measured up to 5.5 × 2.75 m. (19¼ × 10 ft.). It was worn without a fastening and the wearer had to keep his left arm crooked to support its voluminous drapery. It was put on thus: one corner was placed before the feet and the straight edge was taken up and over the left shoulder, across the back and under or over the right arm, across the chest, and over the left shoulder again, the second corner hanging behind the knees; the curved edge became the garment's hem. By the imperial period, two features had developed which helped to accommodate the garment's increased size: an *umbo* or 'navel' at the waist, resulting from the upper part of the under layer being pulled over the second layer, and a *sinus* or 'lap', created by folding down the straight edge where it passed under the right arm. In the 3rd cent. AD the *umbo* was generally folded into a band lying across the wearer's chest, and in the 4th cent. the *sinus* was usually long enough to be thrown over the left forearm.

As a result of Roman conquests the toga spread to some extent into the Roman western provinces, but in the east it never replaced the Greek rectangular mantle, the *himation* or *pallium*. Its increased size and cost caused it to decline among ordinary Romans, but portrait statues record its use by wealthier citizens at least until the end of the 4th cent. AD. A late version, smaller and decorated, is familiar from the ivory diptychs of the consuls. In the long term the toga developed into the sash-like *loros*, a vestment exclusive to the Byzantine emperor. See DRESS. H. G.-T.

topos, a standard form of rhetorical argumentation or a variably expressible literary commonplace.

In classical rhetoric, *inventio* aids the orator to find elements of persuasion: *topoi* or *loci* are both the places where such elements (especially plausible argumentative patterns) lurk, and those patterns themselves (e.g. Arist. *Rh.* 2. 22–3; Quint. *Inst.* 5. 10); if universally applicable (in various senses) they can be called *topoi* or *loci communes*. They are

the habitual tools of ordinary thought but can also be studied and technically applied. No two rhetoricians provide the same catalogue, but some of the more familiar *topoi* include arguments *ad hominem* or *a fortiori*, from homonymy or etymology, from antecedents or effects.

Although in this sense the ancient discussions remain important for contemporary analyses of everyday argumentation, the general decline of rhetoric in modern culture has led *topoi*, like other rhetorical concepts, to seek refuge in literary studies. The recent critical *topos* of applying the term also, and especially, to commonly but variably expressed literary contents (clichéd metaphors and commonplace thoughts) ultimately derives from E. R. Curtius, who sought in his *European Literature and the Latin Middle Ages* (1990; Ger. orig. 1948) to refound the cultural unity of Europe upon the heritage of Latin rhetoric. Correspondingly, many of Curtius's own examples—'brevitas-formula', the composition of a poem as a nautical voyage, 'emphasis on inability to do justice to the topic', 'I bring things never said before', 'praise of forebears and their deeds', etc.—remain closely linked to traditional rhetorical structures. But his extension of the concept from rhetorical forms to literary contents paved the way for the banalizing inclusion of unformalized commonplaces (already Curtius, who sometimes linked *topoi* with unconscious 'archetypes', included 'all must die', 'ape as metaphor', *locus amoenus* ('charming place'), 'perpetual spring', *puer senex* ('boy/old man' i.e. roughly 'old head on young shoulders', 'the world upside-down'. To be sure, communication both ordinary and literary depends upon shared premisses, and novelty, like familiarity, can only be perceived against the background of what is already known. Ancient authors, perhaps because their audience was more restricted and shared with them a more limited cultural background, seem to have been fonder of such commonplaces than modern ones and to have drawn upon a smaller stock (sometimes doubtless supplied by appropriate rhetorical manuals). But they can use them for very different purposes (e.g. to create complicity with the audience, to advertise generic affiliations, to vary surprisingly in detail or context, to provide reassurance by not varying) and may often have believed in their truth.

G. W. M., G. B. C.

torture at Athens and under the Roman republic was normally thought inappropriate for citizens. It might be used on slaves (see SLAVERY) and perhaps on foreigners, for example prisoners of war. Slaves might be tortured in order to extract confessions of their own guilt or evidence against other persons (the unreliability of this second kind of evidence seems to have been recognized in practice at Athens). At Rome the investigation by torture was called *quaestio*; the evidence of the tortured was not *testimonium* (evidence). Evidence under torture by slaves was not accepted against their own masters, except in matters such as treason and sacrilege, as with the Catilinarian conspirators (see CATILINE) (Cic. *Part. Or.* 118). Augustus extended these exceptions to include *adultery in certain situations (*Dig.* 48. 5. 28 pref.) but preserved the letter of the principle by having the slaves sold to a representative of the public (Cass. Dio 55. 5; the change is wrongly ascribed to *Tiberius by Tac. *Ann.* 2. 30, cf. 3. 67). A master might prefer to liberate slaves liable to torture and it is perhaps for this reason that we first hear of the torture of free men of humble status under the Principate (Cass. Dio 57. 19; *Dig.* 48. 18. 1. 13). But we also find occasionally the torture of men of status suspected of conspiracy (Tac. *Ann.* 11. 22; 15. 56)—a practice with a long history: thus *Alexander the Great had Philotas tortured. In general we find emperors during the Principate urging that the use of torture be confined to serious cases and arguing that evidence taken under torture was fragile (*Dig.* 48. 18. 1 *pass.*); the general line taken is that torture should not be resorted to unless there is other evidence of guilt. However, we can draw no secure inference from this about what happened in practice. In the late empire torture of humbler citizens seems to have become accepted and was even extended to civil proceedings, though there was never much use of torture in civil suits (*Cod. Theod.* 2. 27. 1. 2a; *Cod. Just.* 9. 41. 15).

A. W. L.

tourism Well-known Greek tourists include *Solon, said (Hdt. 1. 30) to have visited Egypt and Lydia 'for the sake of seeing' (*theōria*), and *Herodotus himself. Sea-borne *trade and sightseeing were surely companions from an early date, as they still were in the 4th cent. (Isoc. *Trapeziticus* 17. 4). A genre of Greek periegetic ('travel') literature arose by the 3rd cent., from which date fragments survive of a descriptive work, *On the Cities in Greece*, by Heraclides Criticus (ed. F. Pfister (1951); for partial trans. see Austin 83); the only fully preserved work of this type is the Roman *Pausanias. Under Rome ancient sightseeing came into its own. A papyrus (*PTeb.* 1. 33 = Bagnall and Derow 58) of 112 BC gives instructions to prepare for a Roman senator's visit to the Fayūm, including titbits for the crocodiles; the colossi of Memnon and other pharaonic monuments are encrusted with Greek and Latin graffiti. Greece too was a firm favourite (for the itinerary see Livy 45. 27–8). Roman tourists were wealthy, their numbers restrained (cf. the 18th-cent. Grand Tour in Europe); they might combine sightseeing (artworks, monuments, natural phenomena) with overseas study (as with *Cicero), thermal cures, and visits to *sanctuaries. See PILGRIMAGE (CHRISTIAN).

A. J. S. S.

trade, Greek Exchange in some form has probably existed since the emergence of the first properly human social groups. Trade, whether local, regional, or international, is a much later development. It is a certain inference from the extant documentary records in Linear B script that the world of Mycenaean age palace-economy knew all three main forms of commerce (see MYCENAEAN CIVILIZATION), and a reasonable guess that a considerable portion of the long-distance carrying trade was in the hands of spe-

cialized professional traders. But whether that trade was 'administered' or 'free-enterprise' is impossible to say. It is one sign among many of the economic recession experienced by the Greek world generally between about 1200 and 800 BC that in these dark centuries regional and international trade dwindled to vanishing-point; the few known professional traders were typically men of non-Greek, especially *Phoenician, origin.

In book 8 of *Homer's *Odyssey* the sea-battered hero finds his way at last to the comparative calm and safety of Phaeacia, a never-never land set somewhere in the golden west, only to be roundly abused by a Phaeacian aristocrat for looking like a sordidly mercenary merchant skipper rather than a gentleman amateur sportsman. *Hesiod, composing perhaps about the same time (*c*.700 BC) in inland, rural Boeotia, was prepared to concede that a moderately prosperous peasant farmer might load the surplus of the grain-crop produced by himself and his small workforce into his own modest boat and dispose of it down the nearby coast during the dead season of the agricultural year immediately after the grain-harvest. But to be a full-time trader was no more acceptable to Hesiod than to Homer's Phaeacian aristocrat. Each in his way was waging an ideological polemic against the development of professional trading (*emporia*) and traders (*emporoi*).

This prejudice issued from a world ruled and dominated by landed aristocrats. It was perfectly all right for a Greek aristocrat to visit his peers in other communities, then just acquiring the newfangled constitutional form of the *polis, bearing gifts of richly woven garments or finely wrought metalwork, and to come home laden with comparable or even more lavish exchange gifts. It was quite another matter to spend most of the recognized sailing season (late March to late September) plying the Mediterranean with a mixed cargo of, say, perfume flasks from Corinth, hides from Euboea, salt fish from the Black (Euxine) Sea, and wine-amphorae from Chios, making only a humble living and precluded from participating in the military and political activities that defined the status of an élite leader of his *polis*. Such trading was considered an occupation suitable only for the lower orders of Greek society, the dependants (possibly unfree) of a great landlord.

Yet the significance of traders in the early *polis* era of Homer and Hesiod must not be confused with the significance of trade, especially long-distance sea-borne commerce. Without the latter there would have been no opening from the Aegean to both east (for example, the multinational emporion (trading place) at Al Mina on the Orontes) and west (notably Ischia-Pithecusae (Pithekoussai)), beginning in the half-century from 825 to 775, no movement of colonization to southern Italy, Sicily, and the Black Sea (see COLONIZATION, GREEK), no comparative knowledge of other, non-Greek cultures and thus no alphabet—and so, maybe, no Homer and Hesiod. By 600 BC the economic position and social status of traders may have improved, with the development of purpose-built sail-driven, round-hulled merchantmen, the creation of institutions and techniques designed to facilitate multinational commerce, and the establishment of permanent *emporia* in Egypt and Etruria.

Naucratis in the Nile delta was founded in about 630 by Greek traders from western Asia Minor, the adjacent Greek islands, and Aegina, under the auspices of the Egyptian pharaoh Psammetichus (Psamtik). In return for Greek oil, wine, and luxury goods the Greek traders of Naucratis received Egyptian grain, metals, and slaves, from which exchange the Egyptian treasury derived extra value in taxes. Permanent transnational market-centres and ports of trade were thus established under official governmental direction, linking economies of dissimilar type. Soon Naucratis had an Italian counterpart at Gravisca in Etruria, the happy hunting-ground of one Sostratus of Aegina.

This Sostratus, who may be identical with the Sostratus of *Herodotus (4. 152), specialized in the run between Etruria and the Aegean by way of the haulway (*diolkos*) built across the isthmus of Corinth in about 600. He was a free citizen, literate (in addition to his dedication to *Apollo at Gravisca he used personalized merchant-marks on the pots he carried), and an independent entrepreneur who presumably owned his own merchant ship (or ships). Perhaps he knew some Etruscan, as the Phocaean and Samian merchants who traded further westwards to the south of France and Spain knew the local Celtic languages and, as surviving business letters on lead attest, employed locals in their import–export businesses. A similar lead letter of the 6th cent. has survived from the other, eastern end of the world of Archaic Greek commerce, at Berezan (Olbia) in the Black Sea. But this tells an apparently darker and possibly more typical tale of (allegedly) illicit detention and confiscation; and one of the traders involved seems to have been a dependent agent-trader not a free trader working on his own behalf.

By the middle of the 5th cent. the place of Al Mina, Naucratis, and Gravisca had been taken by Athens' newly developed port city of Piraeus. It was the Athenians' famous victory over the Persians at Salamis (480 BC) that enabled the development of Piraeus into a commercial as well as military harbour facility. A century later, *Isocrates hailed its creation: 'for Athens established the Piraeus as a market in the centre of Hellas—a market of such abundance that the articles which it is difficult to obtain, one here, one there, from the rest of the world, all these it is easy to produce from Athens' (*Panegyricus* 42). This testimony is corroborated by archaeology and echoed by writers as diverse as *Thucydides, the pamphlet known as the 'Old Oligarch', and Athenian comic playwrights. As early as 421, we learn from Eupolis' *Marikas*, the characteristic institution of the maritime or bottomry loan had been developed to finance long-distance trade, above all in the staple necessity, grain, on the regular large-scale importation of which Athens had come to depend both economically and (since it was the poor majority of citizens who mainly benefited) politically.

During the currency of her 5th-cent. empire Athens, thanks to her permanently commissioned fleet of *trireme warships, was able to suppress *piracy, one of the major threats to peaceful commerce throughout antiquity, as well as to direct trade towards the Piraeus on economically favourable terms. Loss of empire was among other things bad for Aegean Greek trade generally, and bad for Athens' access to staple grain and the raising of taxes and dues on shipping and goods in particular. Over the course of the 4th cent. a whole series of legal measures was enacted by Athens to compensate for loss of military power (several mentioned in the *Athenaion politeia* attributed to *Aristotle). A combination of the stick (penalties for residents who contracted loans on cargoes of grain bound elsewhere than to Piraeus, or for not offloading a certain minimum percentage of a cargo there, and so on) and the carrot (establishment for the benefit of Athens-based traders of new specialized maritime courts; granting permission to foreign traders to set up on Attic soil sanctuaries for their native gods—Isis and Astarte) was employed to good effect.

One measure practised by trading communities in other periods was significantly conspicuous by its absence: the Athenians never discriminated in favour of their own citizen merchants. This was partly no doubt because they constituted a small minority of the trading and commercial population, but it was also because the barriers between citizen status and the status of the majority (*metics, slaves) involved were high and sturdy—as the exceptional breach in the case of Pasion amply proves. (See CITIZENSHIP, GREEK; SLAVERY.) See also MARKETS AND FAIRS.

P. A. C.

trade, Roman The central issue for historians has long been, and remains, how to characterize properly the scale and importance of trade and commerce in the overall economy of the Roman empire. Some seek to emphasize how different, and essentially backward, the Roman *economy was in comparison to the modern. They point to the Roman élite's apparent snobbish contempt for commerce (Cic. *Off.* 1. 150–1). The primacy of *agriculture cannot be denied, and it is noteworthy that the Roman *agricultural writers, with the large landowner in mind, betray both very little interest in markets and an aversion to risk which did not inspire entrepreneurial experiments. Factories in the modern sense did not exist in the ancient world (see INDUSTRY). Cities did not grow up as centres of manufacturing; far from it, they can be represented merely as centres of consumption (see URBANISM). The cost and difficulty of transport, particularly over land, are claimed to have made it uneconomic to trade over long distances anything other than luxury products. Of course, basic goods, such as *wine, *olive oil, and grain, also *pottery of all kinds, can be demonstrated to have been carried in large quantities over long distances. But, it is argued, something other than the free-market mechanism is at work here. First, there was the considerable circulation of goods

trade, Roman This Latin inscription for a Roman general in the first war against *Mithradates was set up *c*.87 BC by 'the Italians and Greeks who conduct business (*negotiantur*) on Delos'. Roman trade largely depended on the investments and credit of Italian *negotiatores* or 'money-men', who often settled in Mediterranean ports. The community at *Delos, a major entrepôt in the decades around 100 BC, was particularly large and rich.

within the extensive households of the rich, from their estates to their town houses, to their retinues and clients. Further, staples could be exchanged in large quantities as gifts between members of the élite. Examples can be identified at all periods and it has been demonstrated plausibly that such a mechanism was particularly important in the later Roman empire. The circulation of goods within the household of the emperor is the same phenomenon writ large. Secondly, and more importantly, it is claimed that the movement of staples was primarily an act of redistribution, organized by the central government, and on a smaller scale by local communities, to ensure the supply of essentials to the large cities, such as Rome, and to maintain the Roman armies, precisely because the private sector was not up to meeting needs on such a scale (see FOOD SUPPLY).

A different model has been proposed. While it is true that the Roman aristocracy on the whole maintained a distance from direct involvement in trade, even they can, and did, benefit from its profits through intermediaries (see e.g. Plut. *Cat. Mai.* 21). Besides, beyond Rome, it is much less clear that local élites shared the same distaste for trade, with investments, frequently managed by their *freedmen, in potteries, *mines, *textile production, and the like. The landowners needed markets for their products, but were able to affect a lack of interest in trade, because the whole process, often starting with a contract to gather the crop, lay in the hands of *negotiatores* (businessmen). The landowner was provided with a certain return, while the *negotiator* had to organize the trade and to take the risks (for an example of miscalculation of those risks see Plin. *Ep.* 8. 2). The number of shipwrecks in the Mediterranean recorded for the period 100 BC to AD 300 is much larger than for either the preceding period or the Dark Ages; this suggests a level of operation which was not to be reached again until the high Renaissance. The greatest spur to the development of this trade was the creation of a fully monetarized economy throughout the empire. Exchanges in kind, of course, continued to exist; but it is quite clear from Egyptian papyri that the use of money in transactions was the norm. Strabo (7. 5. 5), in the early empire, could go out of his way to note the lack of use of coin among the Dalmatians, as a characteristic of barbarian peoples. The availability of coin could vary from place to place and time to time. This made the existence of bankers (see BANKS) who could provide credit to facilitate deals essential. It is true that the empire did not see the growth of large international banks; but at the local level money-lenders were the key to exchanges both large and small. There are those historians who see in the spread of the use of money the creation of a Roman unified 'world economy'. This is a clear exaggeration. The empire consisted of a range of regional economies at different stages of development, which linked up with each other in ways which changed with time.

At the regional level regular markets (*nundinae*) were vital. They are found throughout the empire and were as important, perhaps more so, to the peasant as to the large landowner. The existence of these markets was strictly regulated. The senate had to be petitioned for permission to hold markets; many such requests came from large landowners who wished to hold markets on their estates. The reason for the control was probably to limit competition with well-established markets in the local towns (Plin. *Ep.* 5. 4, 5. 13). This suggests that at this local level the volume of trade in the countryside was somewhat limited. There are signs that some products circulated largely on a regional basis (the distribution of Roman lamps, which were traded over surprising distances, nevertheless reveals several broad regional patterns of trade) (see MARKETS AND FAIRS).

At the other end of the scale came the huge cities, such as Rome. These constituted enormous markets. Much is made of the state-sponsored system for supplying Rome with corn. However, state grain met no more than a portion of the city's annual grain needs. The rest had to be supplied by the free market. Furthermore, the importation of the state grain depended upon private traders, who in times of crisis had to be offered considerable incentives to involve themselves in the trade (Suet. *Claud.* 18). Monte Testaccio, the dump of Spanish oil amphorae, behind the port on the Tiber in Rome, is testimony to the enormous trade in oil (estimated at some 23 million kg. per year). The annual consumption of wine in the city has been put at between 1 and 1.8 million hectolitres. For much of the empire all this was provided by the free market. Only later did oil and wine become part of the *annona* (see FOOD SUPPLY). The city of Rome was an enormous stimulus to trade.

The expansion of the empire itself could open up major new markets to be exploited. The most researched example is the large market among the Gauls for Italian wine, particularly from the west coast of Italy. However, it is all too easy to exaggerate the effect of these new markets on the agrarian economy of Italy. There were transformations, but they were confined largely to coastal regions within easy reach of ports, and they were limited in time. By the 1st cent. AD these regions were having to compete with expanding trade in wine from Spain and south Gaul.

Because pottery survives on archaeological sites, its importance in trade can be exaggerated. However, it is clear that the industrial scale of production of *terra sigillata* in Gaul presupposes something more than a local market. Pottery on the whole was not often the primary cargo of ships, but it was frequently a part-cargo and could be an important commodity for the return leg of voyages, whose primary concern was the transport of more valuable goods. See POTTERY, ROMAN.

Trade was carried on beyond the limits of the Roman empire. Most notable was the trade in luxuries, spices, ivories (see ELEPHANTS; IVORY), etc. beyond the Red Sea with the East Coast of *Africa and *India. A Greek papyrus in Vienna (*PVindob.* G40822) records one such transaction, involving nard, ivory, and textiles to a value of over 130 talents. When it is realized that some of the large ships on the eastern run could carry up to 150 such cargoes, the potential profitability of the trade is amply demonstrated. However, the handbook from the 1st cent. AD, the *Periplus Maris Erythraei* ('The Voyages round the Red Sea'), shows that although the primary interest was in these very valuable goods, shippers were also on the look-out for more mundane staples to fill their holds.

Large-scale trade continued right through the late empire. In some ways traders became less independent, more tied into work for the imperial government or for the great aristocratic houses. The patterns changed somewhat, with more regional trade and less international. This, however, should not be taken as a sign of a major decline in the system which constituted such an important part of the overall economy of the Roman empire.   J. J. P.

tragedy, Greek (*see facing page*)

tragedy, Latin *Varro and *Atticus put the first performance of a Latin tragedy in the year 240 BC at *Jupiter's September festival. Performances continued at this and other public festivals down to the end of the 1st cent. BC and perhaps into the 1st cent. AD. Celebrations of temple dedications and funerals of men of the aristocracy also provided occasions of performance. In 240 new plays were

still being staged at the Athenian festivals of *Dionysus, but the practice had grown up of reviving each year a number of old ones. Travelling companies of 'artists of Dionysus' performed tragedy as well as comedy at festivals in other Greek cities and perhaps also in private houses. Three 5th-cent. poets, *Aeschylus, *Sophocles, and *Euripides, enjoyed the greatest continuing prestige both in the theatre and in the syllabus of the grammatical schools. There is no sign that the seven tragic poets of the court of *Ptolemy II Philadelphus(285–246) won any widespread fame outside *Alexandria. At Rome adaptations of the better-known Attic works were offered at first under the names of the original authors. The makers of the adaptations sometimes took part in the performance of their own works.

Roman theatres probably never had much space in front of the stage platform for elaborate choral dancing. Little is known about those who performed at the pre-240 festivals (the *histriones*), or the character of their performances. The surviving scripts of Euripides' *Hecuba*, *Iphigenia in Aulis*, and *Medea* and the remnants of *Ennius' adaptations permit, however, a number of deductions about how the early Latin tragedians went about their business. The Greek choral odes did not disappear, but the volume of singing and dancing assigned to the subordinate group of bystanders was sharply reduced. The speeches of the heroic personages on the other hand were given much more musical accompaniment. The metrical structure of the Latin script was usually more varied and complex than that of its Attic model and obeyed in detail conventions long established among local theatrical performers.

Themes from Roman legend and history were taken up as early as the 3rd cent. BC and developed within the dramatic structure which had arisen from the fusion of Attic script and local theatrical tradition. Accius presented Tarquin (see TARQUINIUS SUPERBUS, LUCIUS) talking with his councillors (Cicero, *Div.* 1. 44–5) much as Aeschylus had dramatized the dialogue between Atossa and the chorus in the *Persae* (vv. 159–225).

Despite continuing popularity at the public festivals the 3rd- and 2nd-cent. plays ran into considerable academic condemnation as a result of close comparison with their Attic originals and of acceptance of the generic schemes established in Hellenistic criticism. The apparent licentiousness of early Latin metrical practice aroused particular complaint. The *Thyestes* composed by Lucius Varius Rufus for performance at the festival celebrating Octavian's victory at *Actium (see AUGUSTUS) pleased the young, and *Ovid won praise for a *Medea* written in the new style.

Composing for the public festivals continued in the 1st cent. AD (see Tacitus, *Ann.* 11. 13). Some men preferred, however, to compose poems they called tragedies for recitation to small groups in private. The pieces transmitted under the name of *Seneca are each divided into five units separated by choral odes, and show a metrical practice obedient to the demands made in the Augustan period. Argument rages as to what kind of audience their authors

[*continued on p. 739*]

Greek tragedy

Greek tragedy Tragedy, one of the most influential literary forms that originated in Greece, is particularly associated with Athens in the 5th cent. BC, the period that saw its most distinctive development. All but one of the surviving plays date from the 5th cent. (the exception, *Rhesus*, attributed to *Euripides, is probably 4th cent.), but these represent only a tiny sample of the vast body of material produced from the late 6th cent. onwards; new plays were still being composed as late as the 2nd cent. AD. The popularity of the dramatic festivals at Athens attracted interest in other cities, with the result that performances of tragedy rapidly became common elsewhere, and what began as a medium reflecting the life of a particular community acquired universal appeal in the Greek-speaking world. By the end of the 3rd cent. BC, Roman translations and adaptations began to extend the range of its influence still further.

The material that follows is divided into two sections.

    I Tragedy at Athens in the 5th cent. and earlier
      1. Origins
      2. Early history
      3. Dramatic festivals
      4. Form and performance
      5. Subject-matter and interpretation
    II Tragedy in the Greek-speaking world and beyond
      1. The formation of a repertoire
      2. Actors and festivals
      3. Tragedy in adaptation and translation

I. 1. Origins Much the most valuable information about how Athenian tragedy came into being is preserved in the fourth chapter of *Aristotle's *Poetics*. In particular, he states that (*a*) tragedy came into being from an improvisatory origin, from the leaders (*exarchontes*) of the *dithyramb; (*b*) *Aeschylus increased the number of actors from one to two, reduced the choral part, and made the (spoken) word 'protagonist'; (*c*) *Sophocles introduced the third actor and scene-painting; (*d*) because tragedy developed from the 'satyr-play-like' (*ek satyrikou*), it was slow to become serious, abandoning its small plots and ridiculous diction; (*e*) because of the satyric and more dance-like nature of the poetry, the first metre to be used was the trochaic tetrameter, which was then replaced by the iambic trimeter.

Although it has been maintained that this account is mere hypothesis, there are good reasons for lending it some credence. One is that Aristotle was in a position to know much more than we do about the matter. And indeed in the next chapter he says that the changes that occurred in tragedy are, unlike the case of comedy, known. Moreover, the development of serious drama from boisterous performance (for this there are non-Greek parallels) is unlikely to be Aristotle's hypothesis, partly because it does in fact contradict the theoretical framework he sets out earlier in the same chapter, in which there is an early historical division between serious and trivial poetry. Some have seen an inconsistency in the development of tragedy both from the dithyramb and from the *satyrikon*. But in fact the early processional dithyramb in honour of *Dionysus would naturally be performed by *satyrs, and there is evidence that satyrs did indeed perform the dithyramb. In any case *satyrikon* means 'satyr-play-like', i.e. not necessarily a performance by the satyrs themselves. The word *tragōidia* probably originally meant the song sung by singers at the sacrifice of a goat (in which the goat also may have been a prize), and has no inherent connection with the satyrs, who anyway were at this period more like horses than goats.

tragedy, Greek A ceramic water jar from S. Italy (350–325 BC) with a scene based on a stage performance of a tragedy, showing the mythical Alcestis on her death bed. Figured scenes on Greek *pottery from S. Italy drew heavily——but shed ambiguous light—on the Greek theatre.

There are several advantages to Aristotle's view that he does not mention. An origin of tragedy in the dithyramb, which was a Dionysiac hymn, coheres with the fact that tragedy was performed (along with dithyramb) in the cult of Dionysus. The cult is marked by the participants' change of identity, a change that may be achieved by the use of masks (notably satyr-masks), and this makes it a likely context for the genesis of drama. Further, Aristotle's account coheres well both with the formal structure of extant tragedy (see §2) and with the practice of performing a satyr-play, written by the tragedian, after each tragic trilogy (thereby forming a tetralogy). According to an ancient tradition, satyric drama was instituted so as to preserve the Dionysiac element that had been lost from tragedy (Chamaeleon fr. 38; etc.). Such a development may well have occurred, and is not inconsistent with the Alexandrian view, to be found in *Horace's *Ars Poetica* (220–1), that satyric drama was a later addition to tragedy. But the possibility remains nevertheless that it was invented to complement the Aristotelian theory.

Another ancient tradition locates the origin of tragedy in the northern *Peloponnese. *Herodotus (1. 23) tells us that the first known composition of dithyrambs was in Corinth, by Arion of Methymna (c.600 BC). A late notice (*Suda, Ariōn*) says both that Arion invented the *tragikos tropos* (i.e. probably the style or mode of music which afterwards belonged to tragedy) and that he was the first to name what was sung by the dithyrambic chorus and to bring on satyrs speaking verse (these may or may not be meant to refer to separate kinds of performance). Another late notice attributes to *Solon's elegies the statement that Arion composed the first *drāma tēs tragōidias* (fr. 30a West). Further, Herodotus (5. 67) records that at Sicyon the tyrant Cleisthenes transferred *tragikoi choroi* honouring the sufferings of the hero Adrastus to the cult of Dionysus, and the rest of the sacrifice to another hero, Melanippus. (The implication of this, that a crucial stage in the genesis of tragedy was the coalescence of hero-cult with the cult of Dionysus, is for various reasons an attractive one.) Sicyon was also the birthplace of Epigenes, whom *Suda* (*Thespis*) calls the first tragic poet. Support for an origin in the northern Peloponnese is provided by an apparently Doric feature of tragic language, the use of long α for η, especially in the lyric portions.

I. 2. Early history Little is known about Athenian tragedy before Aeschylus. We have four names (Thespis, Choerilus, Pratinas, and Phrynichus), to whom are attributed a few extant fragments, at least some of which are spurious. Especially suspect are the traditions about the Attic Thespis as the inventor of tragedy. Here the general unreliability of traditions about 'first inventors' is compounded by the suspicion that with Thespis the Athenians attempted to reclaim the invention of tragedy from the Dorians. Even the view often stated in modern handbooks that Thespis first produced tragedy at the City Dionysia in one of the years 535–533 BC has recently been shown to be suspect. It is equally possible that tragedy was instituted at the City Dionysia by the new democratic regime at the very end of the 6th cent. If anything in the tradition about Thespis deserves any credence, it is the remark attributed to Aristotle that he added prologue and speech to what had been a choral performance (Themistius 26. 316d). Although Aeschylus introduced the second actor (see above), his dialogue is (in contrast to Sophocles and Euripides) still mostly between an actor and chorus leader—even in the *Oresteia*, in which he employed the third actor recently introduced by Sophocles. All this, taken together with the fact that in Aeschylus the lyric portions generally form a greater proportion of the drama than they do in Sophocles and Euripides, suggests that the early development of tragedy was the gradual transformation of a choral performance into the structure of choral odes alternating with spoken scenes familiar from extant tragedy. This is supported also by the word for actor, *hypokritēs*, which almost certainly meant 'interpreter' (although it has been claimed that it meant 'answerer'). Perhaps the 'leader' of the dithyrambic performance also interpreted it. Scholars also used to argue (from the fact that there are 50 Danaids in Aeschylus' *Suppliants*, taken together with Pollux 4. 110) that the number of the chorus members in early tragedy was 50, and so considerably larger than the twelve or fifteen of later tragedy. But this view has fallen out of favour, not least because of the discovery of a papyrus (*POxy*. 2256 fr. 3) showing the relatively late dating of Aesch. *Supp*. A respect in which Aeschylus is undoubtedly distinct from Sophocles and Euripides is his tendency to devote the whole trilogy to a single story (e.g. the *Oresteia*).

I. 3. Dramatic festivals The production of tragedy was not confined to Attica, but it was in Attica that tragedy acquired its definitive form, and it is from Attica that we have almost everything that we know about it. From the end of the 6th cent. BC, if not before, tragedies were performed in the Athenian spring festival of Dionysus Eleuthereus, the City Dionysia. This remained the main context for tragic performances, although they occurred also at the Rural Dionysia, and (probably in the 430s) a competition for two tragedians each with two tragedies was introduced into the Lenaea. In all these festivals the tragic performances were one feature of a programme of events which, at the City Dionysia, included processions, sacrifice in the theatre, libations, the parade of war orphans, performances of dithyramb and comedy, and a final assembly to review the conduct of the festival.

At the City Dionysia three tragedians generally competed each with three tragedies and a satyr-play. In charge of the festival was a leading state official, the eponymous archon (see LAW AND PROCEDURE, ATHENIAN), who chose the three tragedians (perhaps after hearing them read their plays, Pl. *Leg*. 817d). He also appointed the three wealthy *chorēgoi* who bore the expenses of training and equipping the choruses. Originally the tragedian acted in his own play, but later we find tragedians employing actors, as well as the appointment of protagonists by the state. This last method may have been instituted when prizes were introduced for actors in 449 BC. In a preliminary ceremony called the *proagōn* it seems that each tragedian appeared with his actors on a platform to announce the themes of his plays. Ten judges were chosen, one from each of the tribes (*phylai*), in a complex process involving an element of chance. The victorious poet was crowned with ivy in the theatre.

R. A. S. S.

I. 4. Form and performance Some features of the tragic performances are best understood if set in the context of Greek festival practice. The notion of performers in sports and the arts competing in honour of the gods was familiar throughout the Greek world (see GAMES). Individuals entered for athletic events like running or boxing or for musical contests as solo instrumentalists, and groups participated in many forms of song and dance or in team activities such as relay races. In the case of the City Dionysia the emphasis was on competition by choruses, whether for dithyramb, tragedy and satyr-play, or comedy; thus despite the novelty of dramatic representation there was a strong element of continuity with established practice, and the competition for the best leading actor (*prōtagōnistēs*), introduced in the mid-5th cent., can be compared with competitions among solo musicians or rhapsodes.

The importance of the choral element is shown by the fact that the main responsibility of each of the financial sponsors (*chorēgoi*) was the recruiting and maintenance, costuming and training of the chorus, while the city paid the leading actors and the poets. Given the competitive nature of the events it was important to have rules governing (e.g.) the choice of playwrights, the allocation of leading actors, and the procedures for judging; the apparent limitation on the number of speaking actors (often called the 'three-actor rule') may have been less a matter of strict regulation than a practical consequence of using masks. In masked drama it is natural to confine the speaking in any one scene to a limited number of parts so that the audience can tell where each voice is coming from, and since the masks (with wigs attached) completely covered the actors' heads one performer could easily play several different roles. All the surviving plays were evidently composed to be performed (with minor, mainly musical, exceptions) by not more than three speakers at a time, and the doubling of roles was certainly standard. Dramatists may well have exploited the effects to be gained from giving two related leading parts to the same actor (e.g. Deianira and *Heracles in Soph. *Trach.* or Pentheus and Agave in Eur. *Bacch.*). Non-speaking roles for attendants, bodyguards, trains of captives, etc. were a different matter—powerful visual effects could be achieved by bringing groups on stage—and occasional extra solo singers (e.g. the child at Eur. *Andr.* 504–36) or supplementary choruses (e.g. the huntsmen at Eur. *Hipp.* 61–71) might also be used.

The metrical patterns of the surviving plays show that the typical 5th-cent. tragedy was formally much more complex than most modern drama. There was a strong musical element which bears some comparison with modern opera, most noticeably the sequences of song (and dance) performed by a chorus on its own which mark a break of some kind in the action and cover any necessary (usually short) lapse of time. Audiences could expect to see about five such performances within a single play, with the chorus in the orchestra as the centre of attention. Then there were the sung exchanges, or exchanges of alternating speech and recitative or song (*amoibaia*), between the chorus and one or more of the actors: these belonged to the same time-frame as the spoken dialogue and were used to intensify emotion or give a scene a ritual dimension, as in a shared lament or song of celebration. Singing by individual actors became more and more important as time went on; Euripides was famous for his monodies (cf. e.g. *Aristophanes, *Frogs* 1329–63), but there were striking examples from earlier tragedy, like the solo by the mad Io at Aesch. (?) *Prometheus Bound* 561–88. The musical accompaniment was provided by a player on a double pipe (*aulos*), who often appears in vase-paintings of dramatic scenes.

Virtuoso performance was not only musical: the speeches and dialogues in iambic trimeters intended for spoken delivery were carefully designed to have an emotive impact, whether in the narrating of shocking off-stage events, the presentation of sharply conflicting points of view in formal debate (*agōn*) scenes, or the cut and thrust of symmetrically alternating lines or pairs of lines (*stichomythia*). All the surviving plays are designed to give the leading actor a series of 'big speeches', in which to show off his talent as an interpreter of character and feeling.

The physical circumstances of Greek theatres—open-air auditoria with a more or less central dancing-space for the chorus—had important consequences for acting style and dramatic design (see THEATRES (GREEK AND ROMAN), STRUCTURE). The sense of the watching community must have been strong in open-air daylight performances in front of large crowds, and the constant presence of a choral group as witnesses to the action contributed to the public character of the events portrayed. This was not drama on an intimate scale, although it could deal with intimate subject-matter: it depended on large effects of gesture and movement that could be 'read' by very diverse audiences, and all the evidence suggests that it was considered to have popular, not élitist, appeal. The comic poets would certainly not have spent so much time parodying tragedy if tragedy had not been a familiar medium that meant something important to their audiences.

I. 5. Subject-matter and interpretation All but one of the plots of the surviving sample of tragedies are drawn from heroic myth, familiar to 5th-cent. audiences from epic poetry. Aeschylus' *Persians* (472 BC) deals with the events of 480 (the Persian Wars, see GREECE (HISTORY)), but these are refracted through a Persian setting, and no Greeks are named. Other examples are known of plays on contemporary subjects; at the other extreme Aristotle (*Poet.* 1451^b) cites Agathon's *Antheus* as an example of a play with entirely fictitious characters and plot. But the normal choice of material was from the heroic past, handled without any sign of antiquarian interest; it must have come naturally to tragedians to use the habits familiar to the lyric poets and to contemporary vase-painters and sculptors. Epic story-telling by rhapsodes must have been a shared experience, and many of the heroes continued to be deeply implicated in Greek life through their worship in cult. It is no accident that Athenian tragedy often deals with heroes who were the object of cult in Attica: *Theseus, *Heracles, *Aias (1), Erechtheus and his family, Iphigenia, *Oedipus.

*Plato called *Homer 'first of the tragic poets' (*Rep.* 607a), and it is true that his poetry, particularly the *Iliad*, offered tragic interpretations of events as well as the raw material for dramatic plots, but the plays that have survived all have a strongly contemporary application to the problems of the Athenian *polis*. Stories of intra-familial conflict like that of Oedipus could be re-cast to lay stress on the tensions between family and city, or the Argonautic tale of Jason and *Medea could be shaped in such a way as to make an Athenian audience look closely at the problematic categories of citizen and foreigner, male and female, civilized and barbarian as defined in their society.

Recent criticism has emphasized the ideological content and didactic function of 5th-cent. tragedy, linking it as a form of public discourse with debates and decision-making in the assembly (*ekklēsia*) and with the speeches aimed at popular juries in the law courts (see DEMOCRACY, ATHENIAN). The importance of *rhetoric is obvious in all these contexts; the tragedies themselves contain much self-conscious reference to rhetorical techniques and to their own strategies of persuasion. Drama in all its forms could function as a powerful medium for the communication of ideas; the tragedians of the 5th cent. seem to have aimed at a balance between displacement (through the choice of a time and place different from the here and now) and the explicit linking of the play with the audience's world, as in the use of aetiology (e.g. the foundation of the Areopagus (see DEMOCRACY, ATHENIAN, §2) in Aesch. *Eum.* or the prophecy of Athenian and Ionian prosperity at the end of Eur. *Ion*) and in appeals through *ritual to their sense of community (e.g. the burial procession at the end of Soph. *Aj.*). There is often a similar tension of opposites in the way in which noble characters who speak in ornate and elevated language are set in plots entailing transgressive desires and actions such as kin-killing, *incest, civil conflict, treachery, or irrational violence. Comparison between early and late plays based on the same stories can help critics to trace changing patterns of attitude and perception reflected in subtle changes of language.

The study of ritual practice and of ritual patterns in drama has helped to redefine the questions that it is appropriate to ask about the gods in Greek tragedy. As in Homeric epic, the gods are everywhere, but the plays are not about theology, and critics are less ready than they used to be to identify the religious beliefs of the individual dramatists. Even a more than usually god-focused play like Eur. *Heracles* asks questions rather than finding answers, combining sceptical challenges to divine morality with aetiological reminders of Attic hero-cult. But it would be wrong to underestimate the religious intensity of plays like Aesch. *Ag.*, Soph. *OC*, or Eur. *Bacch.*; as always, it is through the use of language that the plays achieve their deepest effects. Existential issues like time and mortality, and questions that apply to individuals as well as to communities (such as 'Who am I?' and 'How should I behave?') are strongly represented in tragedy alongside questions relating to contemporary society. This must have been an important factor in the spread of the medium beyond Attica and even outside the Greek-speaking world.

II. 1. The formation of a repertoire Interest in Attic drama outside Athens can be traced to an early stage in its history: Aeschylus was invited to Sicily to compose a drama celebrating the foundation of the city of Aetna in 476/5 and returned to Sicily late in his life. Euripides had links with *Macedonia, particularly reflected in his lost play *Archelaus*; so too did Agathon, and Eur. *Andr.*, with its references to the history of the Molossian royal family, offers a further hint that patrons from elsewhere might take an interest in commissioning plays. But the most extensive range of evidence comes from the end of the 5th cent. onwards and is seen (e.g.) in theatre-building in different parts of the Greek world and in the production in southern Italy and Sicily of large quantities of painted pottery showing tragic scenes. This evidence needs to be combined with what is known from Attica about revivals of plays at the Rural Dionysia (beginning in the 5th cent.: evidence in *DFA*[3] 42–56; D. Whitehead, *The Demes of Attica* (1986), 212–22) and eventually in the city as well. (The first recorded instance at the City Dionysia was in 386 BC, when an old tragedy was put on by the *tragōidoi* (tragic actors; *IG* 2². 2320), but revivals of Aeschylus' plays had exceptionally been allowed in the city since his death; *Life of Aesch.* 12.) The fact that revivals became popular does not have to mean that tragedy was in decline: it is hard to imagine an acting profession developing without a repertoire, and the wider the demand from different communities, whether local audiences in the Attic demes (local districts), or cities outside Attica eager to build a theatrical tradition, the greater must have been the incentive to re-perform successful plays.

There seems to have been no shortage of new writing, however, and the competition for new plays continued for centuries (evidence in *TGF* I). Many names are known of tragic poets from other cities who came to Athens to compete, e.g. Theodectes from Phaselis in Asia Minor, one of the most admired of the 4th-cent. dramatists. From the 5th cent. Aeschylus, Sophocles, and Euripides held pride of place as 'classic' writers and were honoured with statues in Lycurgus' remodelled theatre of Dionysus at Athens. The fact that Lycurgus found it necessary to decree that official copies of the texts of their plays were to be preserved as a protection against interpolation by actors (Plut. *Mor.* 841f) is further evidence of their popularity. But they were not the only ones to survive: others of their contemporaries, e.g. Ion of Chios and Achaeus, had a lasting reputation, and some of the new plays themselves acquired classic status. Aristotle's familiar references to such plays as Astydamas' *Alcmaeon* (*Poet.* 1453[b]) or Theodectes' *Lynceus* (*Poet.* 1452[a], 1455[b]) show how well known they were in his time, and papyrus fragments make clear that some went on being read and re-copied by later generations. The fact that only a very small proportion of the most celebrated tragedies has survived may have more to do with the constraints of the school curriculum in late antiquity and the early Byzantine period than with the intrinsic quality of some of the lost material.

None the less, as tragedy became an 'international' medium changes were certainly taking place, and some of them may have contributed to the eventual decline in its ideological importance. Some developments noted by Aristotle were the increasing influence and prestige of actors at the expense of dramatists (*Rh.* 1403[b]), the habit of some tragedians of writing plays for reading rather than performance (*Rh.* 1413^b), and the growing tendency to use choral songs unconnected with the action of a particular play (*embolima*, *Poet.* 1456^a). This last may not be evidence for a decline in the musical element in tragedy, even if the chorus was indeed tending to be less fully integrated in the action, but it may suggest a trend towards the development of a more adaptable and independent repertoire of song and dance. This should perhaps be associated with the growth of professional troupes, who might on some occasions take the place of specially recruited chorusmen. Aristotle also noted (*Rh.* 1404^b) that Euripides had 'shown the way' to more natural diction in tragedy, which he evidently felt to be a desirable modern feature.

In the Hellenistic period the very thorough scholarly work done by the Alexandrian critics on what they could locate of earlier tragedy was ultimately more important than the output of new plays, although there were many tragedians still active, enough of them winning distinction at Alexandria to constitute a 'Pleiad' (*TGF* I CAT A 5). The most remarkable surviving text from the period is the *Exagōgē* of Ezechiel, a product of the union of Greek and Hebrew traditions.

II. 2. Actors and festivals Growing professionalism must have been an important factor as the influence of tragedy began to spread, and it may have been helped at an early stage by the fact that the crafts of play-writing and producing, and of acting, often ran in families. It was actors who had the best opportunities of becoming well known in the Greek cities; as star performers they could command large fees for performances, and it was they who evidently took the initiative in putting on revivals. The organization of actors from the 3rd cent. onwards into powerful regionally defined guilds (the artists of Dionysus) gave them protection, immunities, and privileges as well as better access to the patronage of rulers and cities (evidence in *DFA*³ 279–321). This is the decisive development for the history of performance in Hellenistic and Roman times, and it linked tragic performers with comic actors, rhapsodes, and musicians of all kinds. Along with the growth in the power and influence of performers went the development of festivals. Dramatic performances were regularly put on not only at festivals of Dionysus, now very common in the Greek-speaking world, but also at many other events: special occasions such as the 'Olympian festival' held by *Philip II of Macedon after he took Olynthus in 348, a pattern followed by many other victorious generals, and regular festivals in honour of other deities, such as the Mouseia at Thespiae, the Naia at Dodona, the Soteria at Delphi, and others in Asia Minor, the Aegean islands, and Egypt. Over time it probably became common to act selected scenes or speeches, 'highlights' from famous plays; inscriptions often do not make clear what the *tragōidoi* performed, but they confirm the impression given by other sources that there was a vigorous theatrical life in the Greek-speaking cities of the Roman empire long after tragedy had ceased to have any importance as a major literary genre.

II. 3. Tragedy in adaptation and translation Greek tragedy first reached Roman audiences through the plays of *Ennius, Accius, and Pacuvius; in the 1st cent. AD *Seneca's tragedies offered a new reading of the same models, and it was through Seneca that the playwrights of the Renaissance made their first contact with the Greeks. The surviving Greek plays have had a profound influence on subsequent literature and culture, and the detailed story of their reception and influence is still waiting to be told. This task grows more complex as performance of the plays becomes more important in the modern media. In the 20th cent. influential experiments in performance in Britain, France, Germany, Greece, Italy, Japan, and North America have begun to change perceptions of the ancient material.   P. E. E.

sought. Tragedy was not among the poetic genres attempted in late antiquity.   H. D. J.

Trajan (Marcus Ulpius Traianus), Roman emperor AD 98–117, was born probably in 53 at Italica in Spain, the son of Marcus Ulpius Traianus, a distinguished consular under the Flavians. His unusually long period of service as a military tribune (though hardly ten years as *Pliny the Younger alleges) included a time in *Syria during the governorship of his father *c.*75. While legionary legate in Spain

Trajan Detail of the frieze spiralling round Trajan's Column, at Rome, dedicated in AD 113. With reliefs depicting Trajan's Dacian Wars, and 28.9 m. (95 ft.) in height, the column is the most spectacular example of Roman (narrative) *sculpture placed at the service of imperial *propaganda. The pedestal was employed as Trajan's mausoleum.

he marched against Lucius Antonius Saturninus, governor of Upper Germany, who revolted against *Domitian in 89. He was consul in 91, and then having been appointed by *Nerva in 97 as governor of Upper Germany, was adopted by that emperor, who faced growing discontent among the praetorians, as his son and co-ruler, and became *consul ordinarius* (see CONSUL) for the second time in 98. After Nerva's death Trajan first inspected the armies in Pannonia and Moesia, and on his arrival in Rome re-established strict discipline by disposing of the praetorian mutineers against Nerva.

As emperor his personal conduct was restrained and unassuming, qualities also exhibited by his wife Plotina, who from about 105 had the title *Augusta*. He was courteous and friendly with individual senators, and treated the senate with respect, avoiding confiscations of property and executions. Pliny's speech (*Panegyric*), delivered in 100, the year of Trajan's third consulship, gives a senatorial appreciation of his excellent qualities. Trajan intervened to help children who had been maltreated by their fathers, and free-born children exposed at birth, and made further exemptions from the inheritance tax. He required that candidates for public office in Rome should have at least one third of their capital invested in Italian land, and he perpetuated the alimentary scheme, probably instituted by Nerva, through which sustenance was provided for poor children in Italian communities. Trajan undertook many utilitarian and celebratory building projects, including baths, a canal to prevent the river Tiber from flooding, a new harbour at *Ostia, the via Traiana which extended the via Appia from Beneventum to Brundisium, a forum and basilica in Rome dedicated in 112 (*forum Traiani*), and a column depicting the Dacian Wars. He was generous to the Roman people, extending the corn doles, paying out enormous largesse partly financed by the booty of the Dacian Wars and the treasure of the Dacian king Decebalus, and providing lavish spectacles; to celebrate the Dacian victory he gave games on one hundred and twenty-three days in which ten thousand gladiators fought.

The correspondence between Trajan and Pliny, who had been specially appointed to resolve administrative and financial problems in the communities in Bithynia, shows the kind of attitude towards provincial administration that the emperor had inspired in his officials, even if the emperor's replies were not directly composed by Trajan himself. They exhibit justice, fairness, and personal probity: 'You know very well that it is my established rule not to obtain respect for my name either from people's fears and anxieties or from charges of treason' (Plin. *Ep.* 10. 82). The letters about the treatment of Christians (10. 96–7; see CHRISTIANITY) illustrate the fair-minded attitude of the emperor and his governor.

Experienced in military command, Trajan took a personal interest in the troops, whom he described as 'my excellent and most loyal fellow-soldiers', in instructions issued to governors about the soldiers' testatory privileges (*Digest* 29. 1). Two new legions were formed, both named

after himself—II Traianic Brave and XXX Ulpian Victorious, and on campaign the emperor took personal charge, marching on foot at the head of his men. Trajan's reign was marked by two great wars of conquest, in Dacia and *Parthia. His invasion in 101 of Decebalus' Dacian kingdom beyond the Danube could be justified on the grounds that the accommodation with the Dacians reached by Domitian was unsatisfactory for long-term Roman interests, and that Decebalus' power was increasing. However his principal motive may have been to win military glory. Trajan crossed the Danube at Lederata and marched north-east to Tibiscum and Tapae; there is insufficient evidence to demonstrate the presence of a second invasion column. The Dacians resisted with great determination and courage and inflicted heavy losses on the Romans in a pitched battle. In 102 Trajan resumed campaigning and by threatening Decebalus' capital at Sarmizegethusa forced the king to accept a peace by which he surrendered some territory and became a vassal of the Romans (Cass. Dio, 68. 9). Leaving garrisons behind, Trajan returned to Rome where he celebrated a triumph, accepted the title *Dacicus*, and issued coins depicting the defeat of Dacia. In 105 the emperor renewed the war, ostensibly because Decebalus was contravening the treaty, and crossed the Danube on a bridge built by Apollodorus at Drobeta (mod. Turnu-Severin). After Sarmizegethusa had fallen to the Romans, Decebalus committed suicide and his treasure was captured. Coins now proclaimed 'the capture of Dacia', and the area was turned into a Roman province with a consular governor and two legions (IV Flavia Felix and XIII Gemina). On the site of a legionary fortress about 30 km. (18 mi.) to the west of the Dacian fortress of Sarmizegethusa a new colony was established, which served as the capital of the province. At Adamklissi a community called *Municipium Tropaeum Traiani* was set up, and a trophy containing a dedication to *Mars the Avenger made by Trajan in 107/8. In Rome, Trajan's column celebrated the emperor's prowess and the glorious achievement of the Roman army; his ashes were to be deposited in its base.

Expansion continued with the annexation of Arabia in 106 by Aulus Cornelius Palma Frontonianus, the governor of Syria. Elsewhere in the east, contacts between Rome and Parthia, the only sophisticated empire on the periphery of Roman territory, had been characterized by diplomatic rapport and avoidance of serious warfare during the previous 150 years. The kingdom of Armenia, between the two empires on the upper Euphrates, though sometimes prey to Parthian influence and intervention, was generally ruled by a Roman nominee. Trajan took exception to the attempts of King Osroes of Parthia to establish control of Armenia, and refusing all diplomatic advances arrived in *Antioch early in 114. Without major opposition he incorporated Armenia into the empire and then launched an attack on Parthia through Mesopotamia while the Parthian king was beset with civil strife. In the campaigns of 115–16, the Romans crossed the Tigris into Adiabene and then advanced down the Euphrates, capturing the Parthian capital, Ctesiphon. Trajan was acclaimed *imperator* (victorious commander), and accepted the title *Parthicus*. At least one new province (Mesopotamia) was created, and possibly another (Assyria); coins celebrated the 'capture of Parthia', and 'Armenia and Mesopotamia brought into the power of the Roman People'. The emperor advanced to the Persian Gulf, but his success proved transitory as serious uprisings occurred in the captured territory to the army's rear, and a major insurrection of the *Jews in the eastern provinces spread to Mesopotamia in 116. Trajan tried to contain the military situation, and Lusius Quietus had some success in northern Mesopotamia while a vassal king, Parthamaspates, was imposed on the Parthians. However, as the situation remained precarious, Trajan decided to retreat. Parthamaspates proved short-lived, despite grandiloquent Roman coins proclaiming a 'king granted to the Parthians', and with his health declining Trajan decided to return to Italy; but in early August he died suddenly at Selinus. *Cassius Dio explained Trajan's aggrandisement in the east as a desire to win glory, and this remains the most likely explanation for a man who had already achieved great military success. The policy was a disastrous failure but criticism was muted because he was generally popular with senators. By 114 the appellation 'Best' (*Optimus*), which had appeared early in the reign, had become one of his official titles, and is recalled in the ritual acclamation of the senate—'May you be even luckier than Augustus and even better than Trajan.'   J. B. C.

translation 'Translation is so far removed from the sterile equation of two dead languages that of all literary forms it is the one charged with the special mission of watching over the maturing process of the original language and the birth pangs of its own' (Walter Benjamin, 'The Task of the Translator', trans. H. Zohn). In just this way the developing literature and culture of Rome can be seen as a series of acts of translation from Greek sources. Translation mediated the relationship between Greece and Rome and, thereafter, Rome and the European vernaculars; Isidorus of Seville (10. 123) etymologizes *interpres*, 'translator', as one standing *inter partes* 'between the two sides'. Members of the Roman élite learned, read, and spoke Greek, competing with each other in the cultural fruits of Hellenization (see HELLENISM): *Cato the Elder ostentatiously addressed a Greek audience in Latin, using a translator, but could easily have spoken in Greek (Plutarch, *Cato Maior* 12. 4). Latin literature may be said to begin with Livius Andronicus' versions of Greek plays and of *Homer's *Odyssey* in native Saturnian verse. The republican dramatists closely adapted Greek comedy and tragedy for the Roman people. In the view of Aulus *Gellius, *Virgil 'translated' *Theocritus, *Hesiod, and Homer (the boundary between translation and imitation is, in practice, impossible to police). Knowledge of the Greek language aided the expansion of Roman power; e.g. *Cicero, himself an experienced translator (he produced, *inter alia*,

a version of Aratus' influential *Phaenomena*), sought a unified Graeco-Roman culture as the basis of an ordered polity, while standardization of Latin grammar on the model of Greek helped to cement a language for empire. Public documents were translated into Greek, often with adjustment to the different conceptual worlds (so Augustus' **Res gestae*, and cf. the famous trilingual inscription set up by Cornelius Gallus in Egypt). A number of prominent Roman authors came from non-Latin-speaking municipalities, while *Ennius famously spoke three languages: Latin, Greek, and Oscan. Translation also encouraged Roman self-consciousness about Latin and its limitations, fuelling a sense of both inferiority and competition; so *Lucretius (1. 139) complains of the poverty of the language, *egestas linguae*.

The Greeks of the Classical and Hellenistic eras, by contrast, seem to have been primarily monoglot (with obvious exceptions like *Polybius or Philodemus)—foreigners were *barbaroi* (see BARBARIAN), i.e. people who did not speak Greek (in this respect at least the Romans emerge as more urbane and civilized). Colonization (see COLONIZATION, GREEK and HELLENISTIC) and contact with the empires of Asia Minor must have created a need for translation, but e.g. *Herodotus appears to have been dependent on native interpreters for his knowledge of matters Persian, Egyptian, etc. Initially most Greeks showed scant interest in reading the great Roman authors (though some claimed that Latin was a dialect form of Greek). It was not until the 3rd cent. AD, apparently, that Greeks in the eastern part of the empire, seeking employment in the Roman administration and needing Latin for competence in law, started to study Latin literary texts on any scale; a writer like Claudian would have studied the same syllabus in Egypt as someone educated in Italy (and there are practical bilingual textbooks from this period known as *hermeneumata*). See BILINGUALISM.

It was the Romans, not the Greeks, who conceptualized the process of translation, establishing the framework and norms of western translation practice until the end of the 18th cent.; words used include *vertere, mutare, transferre, Latine exprimere*. *Pliny the Younger (*Ep.* 7. 9. 1) recommends practice in translating between Latin and Greek for promoting verbal fluency and critical discernment. The canonical case against undue 'literalism' is put by *Horace (*Ars P.* 133–4) and by *Cicero, who describes translating speeches by *Demosthenes and *Aeschines not word for word (*non verbum pro verbo*), but so as to retain style and impact (*De optimo genere oratorum*, 14); St Jerome (letter 57. 5) gave the classic formulation: 'not word for word but sense for sense' (*non verbum e verbo, sed sensum exprimere de sensu*).

Translation must be a matter of concern to all students of antiquity. It is often thought of as the substitution for a foreign word of a word of the same or similar meaning, on the model of a dictionary: *amor* 'means' love. Indeed translatability, the idea that alien cultural and linguistic systems can be made intelligible to us, lies at the root of humanistic inquiry (often in conflict with a counter-claim that certain terms, e.g. *pietas* or *aretē*, are untranslatable). However, the semantic field of a word in one language is never identical with that of a word in another (*amor*, it can be argued, has different connotations and affiliations from *love*); and words are constantly changing their significations according to shifting context and use. So it may be better to think in terms of semantic 'equivalence' rather than identity; translation involves simultaneous sameness *and* difference, and can be seen as the process of appropriating the Other. Indeed, any theory of translation obviously implies, is dependent upon, a theory of language, and is thus a philosophical or even metaphysical matter.

Translation has often been marginalized as a second-order activity, lacking in originality (though translations can become classics in their own right). The first extended study in English is Alexander Tytler's *Essay on the Principles of Translation* (1790). Before that the best discussions are to be found in prefatory remarks by practising translators; in the *Preface to Ovid's Epistles* (1680) Dryden gives his famous threefold model—metaphrase (word for word), paraphrase (retaining the sense), and imitation (modernization and adaptation). Translation studies have enhanced the subject's academic standing, producing an armoury of terms of art (source and target language, formal and dynamic equivalence, etc.), and seeking more objective, 'scientific' accounts, but translation remains obstinately immired in history and usage. For George Steiner (*After Babel* (1970)) it is the best model for interpretation and human communication in general. We can say, with L. G. Kelly (*The True Interpreter* (1979)), that 'Western Europe owes its civilization to its translators'.　　　　C. A. Ma.

transport, wheeled The wheel played a prominent role in traction in the ancient Mediterranean lands (contrast its absence in pre-Columbian societies of the Americas). It is more difficult to gauge its economic and social efficacy.

The role of chariots in the poems of *Homer (an echo of the late 2nd-millennium fashion for this form of warfare, also apparent in Indian epic) established an élite function for light wheeled vehicles: this was reinforced by their use for a variety of ritual movements of cult-personnel or objects. Such vehicles were essentially for use over short distances, whether in war or religion. The war-chariot continued to be of social and military significance in the La Tène cultures (cf. that of the Vix burial, *c.*500 BC, near Mont Lassois, Côte d'Or), which may have had some influence on Italic and Roman practice, in which the *tensa* for religious images, and *carpentum* or *pilentum* for privileged participants (such as *matronae* from 395 BC, Livy 5. 25. 9), were important. The light cart (*zeugos*, a yoke) for relatively rapid movement of people was a luxury but quite widespread where the terrain was suitable. Roman practice adapted from the Celtic chariot the *essedum* and *cisium* for light rapid transit (a 90-km. (56-mi.) journey in 10 hours at night with a relay of *cisia*, Cic. *Rosc. Am.* 19).

2. Carts and wagons (*hamaxa*, *plaustrum*) for the movement of heavy materials, particularly bulk foodstuffs, are attested in the cultures of the Fertile Crescent, and in Danubian Europe, from an early period, and remained in constant use in the Greek and Roman countryside, as well as for transporting goods for state-purposes as at war. The heavy *raeda* (up to 1,000 lbs. burden in late-antique legislation) was an important example: note also the *angaria* or heavy wagons of the *cursus publicus* (see POSTAL SERVICE).

3. Much of the Roman vocabulary for wheeled vehicles was of Celtic origin, but it remains unclear when, to what extent, and for what purpose which Celtic-speaking peoples disseminated the designs and their names. Nor is it clear whether the origin is to be sought more in the nomadic social forms of La Tène Europe (cf. Caesar, *BGall.* 1, 3, on the Helvetii) or in the needs of temperate agricultural production and marketing.

Three factors govern the history of wheeled traction: vehicle design, source of traction energy, and environmental modification. For the first two we are very heavily dependent on the often inadequate representations of ancient stone reliefs: archaeological finds are beginning to correct the pessimistic picture derived from these. The technology of load-bearing wheels and axles, like so many practical deployments of *technology in antiquity, seems to have been discontinuous and unsystematic, but occasionally sophisticated: suspension was less often disregarded than was once thought. Harnessing techniques were primarily orientated towards the ox (large ox-teams were the principal traction for very heavy loads like building materials), but they were less ill-adapted towards horses and mules than was once thought. Road-building (see ROADS) was not primarily designed to aid long-distance wheeled transport, and the extent to which even the Roman road-network at its greatest extent and pitch of maintenance did so is disputed.

Other sources of traction therefore remained important: human porterage (of individuals in sedan-chair, *diphros*/*sella* or litter, *phoreion*/*lectica*; or of goods, particularly over short distances in cities); trains of beasts of burden, horses, donkeys, mules, and increasingly in the east, camels (as a means of carrying humans, horses retained a certain cachet, and wheeled transport was sometimes considered unmasculine or soft). Both of these were relatively efficient, but for certain very heavy loads (such as ships on the Corinthian *diolkos* or haulway) there was no alternative to dragging, which was not. River-transport (see NAVIGATION) and coastal trans-shipment were naturally preferred. Descriptions such as *Strabo's of the Alpine passes under *Augustus suggest that wagons would be used on stretches of road between trans-shipment points and the steepest sections where baggage animals or porters must have taken over (e.g. 4. 6. 10–11).

In moneyed circles vehicles became very elaborate. They were a regular feature of urban existence, as can be deduced from the rutted pavements of urban roads: civic regulations governed the hours of access and regulated the type of user. But the élite came to disregard the former disapproval of the litter (which had also been subject to attempted control by legislation from time to time) and *lecticarii* (of whom eight might be required for an ornate litter) were a normal part of very rich households (cf. Quint. *Inst.* 1. 2. 7). The emperors in particular expressed their standing through the opulence of their travelling-equipment. N. P.

tribune of the plebs The 'tribuni plebis' (or 'plebi') were the officers of the *plebs first created in 500–450 BC (traditionally in 494, the date of the first secession of the *plebs* and their corporate recognition; see ROME (HISTORY) §1.2). The word is evidently connected with *tribus, but it is uncertain whether the tribunes were at first chiefs of the tribes who later became officers of the *plebs* (they are sometimes *phylarchoi* in Greek, but *dēmarchoi* is standard), or whether the title imitated that of the military tribunes (*tribuni militum*) already existing. The original number of the tribunes is variously given as two, four, or five; by 449 it had certainly risen to ten. The tribunes were charged with the defence of the persons and property of the plebeians (*ius auxilii*). Their power derived not from statute (initially, at least) but from the oath sworn by the plebeians to guarantee their *sacrosanctitas*, or inviolability. Elected by the plebeian assembly (*concilium plebis*, more usually called *comitia plebis tributa*) and exercising their power within the precincts of the city, the tribunes could summon the *plebs* to assembly (*ius agendi*) and elicit resolutions (*plebiscita*). They asserted a right of enforcing the decrees of the *plebs* and their own rights (*coercitio*); connected with *coercitio* was a measure of jurisdiction, including, probably, capital. They possessed, moreover, though perhaps not from the very first, a right of veto (*intercessio*) against any act performed by a magistrate (or by another tribune), against elections, laws, *senatus consulta* (decrees of the senate). From this veto only the *dictator (until *c.*300 BC) and, perhaps, the *interrex* were exempt (*interreges* were men with temporary consular powers, appointed to supervise the election of new consuls if both consulships became unexpectedly vacant).

This revolutionary power was gradually recognized by the state. The tribunes became indistinguishable from magistrates of the state, although without *imperium* or insignia. The full acknowledgement of their power came with the recognition of *plebiscita* as laws binding upon the whole *populus* and not just the *plebs* (by the *lex Hortensia* of 287). Tribunes were first admitted to listen to senatorial debates; at least from the 3rd cent. BC they had the right to convoke the senate; in the 2nd cent. the tribunate became sufficient qualification for membership of the senate (probably by a *lex Atinia* of 149). From the 4th and 3rd cents. the tribunate became in part an instrument by which the senate could control magistrates through the veto and the right to summon the senate. But the revolutionary potential and popular origins of the office did not disappear. In the first surviving contemporary discussion of the

tribunes, from about the middle of the 2nd cent., *Polybius (6. 16) states that 'they are bound to do what the people resolve and chiefly to focus upon their wishes'. Succeeding years saw the tribunate active in the pursuit of the people's interest and the principles of popular sovereignty and public accountability, as evidenced by the beginning of the practice of addressing the people in the forum directly (145), the introduction of the secret ballot in assemblies (139 and 137), concern with the corn supply (138), the agrarian legislation of Tiberius *Gracchus (133), and above all by the legislation and speeches, for which contemporary evidence survives, of Gaius *Gracchus (123–122). This movement continued sporadically into the tribunates of Lucius Appuleius Saturninus at the end of the 2nd cent. but did not long survive the domestic chaos of 100 and the convulsion of the Social War of 91–89 BC (see ROME (HISTORY) §1.5) and consequent enfranchisement of peninsular Italy. Active tribunes came increasingly to be associated with the particular interests and grievances of the urban *plebs* (and frequently with those of one or another of the emergent dynasts); the effective popular instrument was now the army. From the 130s on attempts were made to limit the legislative potential of the tribunate as well as the use of the veto. *Sulla excluded tribunes from the magistracies of the Roman People and abolished, or severely curtailed, their power to legislate, their judicial powers, and their veto. In 75 the bar from magistracies was removed, and in 70 the full *tribunicia potestas* was restored to the tribunes. This tribunician power, divorced from the office but retaining its associations, was valued by the architects of the imperial state in the construction of their personal power. *Caesar assumed at least the tribunician *sacrosanctitas*, and *Augustus, probably in three steps (36, 30, 23 BC), gained a permanent *tribunicia potestas*. Reft of its power and all independence, the tribunate itself remained as a step in the senatorial career for plebeians alternatively with the aedileship until the 3rd cent. AD, and there is still evidence for the title in the 5th. P. S. D.

tribus, division of the Roman people. In early times the Roman people were supposedly divided into three tribes (the word *tribus* may be connected with Latin *tres* = three) called Ramnes, Tities, and Luceres. There is no known parallel for this structure elsewhere in Italy. The suggestion that *Virgil (*Aen.* 10. 202, with Servius' comm.) refers to a tribal division at Mantua is doubtful, while in the Iguvine tables (religious inscriptions on bronze from Iguvium in Umbria, modern Gubbio), *trifu* (= *tribus*?) means the whole community. Everything about the three original Roman tribes is obscure. The modern theory that they represent different ethnic groups (e.g. Latins, Sabines, and *Etruscans) is unfounded and improbable. The three tribes were subdivided into *curiae* and were supposedly the basis of the earliest military organization of the state. A vestige of this system survived in the Roman cavalry; the six oldest centuries of cavalry comprised two each of Ramnes, Tities, and Luceres.

In republican times these original tribes had been

replaced by a system of local tribes, to which Roman citizens belonged by virtue of residence. Tradition ascribes the local tribes to Servius *Tullius, who divided the city into four tribes, and the countryside into a number of 'rustic' tribes. By 495 BC there were seventeen rustic tribes. As Rome expanded during the 4th and 3rd cents., further tribes were created to incorporate newly won territory in which Roman citizens were settled or citizenship was conferred on the native inhabitants. By 241 BC the number of tribes had reached 35 (4 urban, 31 rustic). After that it was decided not to create any further tribes, but to include all additional territory in the existing 35. As a result the tribes ceased to be confined to single districts, and came to include separate territories in different parts of Italy.

This process became more marked when Roman citizenship was extended to all of peninsular Italy after the Social War of 91–89 BC (see ROME (HISTORY) §1.5). An attempt to restrict the new citizens to a small number of tribes (in order to diminish their voting power in the *comitia*) was thwarted, and they were distributed among the existing 31 rustic tribes.

The distribution of citizens among the tribes was always a sensitive political issue. In 312 BC the censor Appius Claudius Caecus caused a storm when he registered lower-class citizens (probably including *freedmen) in the rustic tribes. This act, the precise significance of which is not certain, was reversed in 304, and in general during the republic freedmen were confined to the urban tribes, which came to be regarded as socially inferior and politically disadvantaged. The punishment of 'removal from a tribe' (*tribu movere*), which the censors could inflict, in effect meant relegation to an urban tribe.

Every citizen had to belong to a tribe, a rule which continued in imperial times even for provincials who attained the Roman citizenship. It is not known how or why particular tribes were chosen in such cases, and no consistent rule was followed, although certain tribes tended to be favoured in certain provinces. Thus citizens from Gallia Narbonensis (see GAUL (TRANSALPINE)) were enrolled by preference in the tribus Voltinia, and those from the eastern provinces in the Collina and Quirina. From the Ciceronian age it was normal for a Roman citizen to include his tribe (written in abbreviated form) as part of his formal nomenclature.

The tribes were used as constituent voting units in political assemblies, and as the basis of army recruitment, the census, and taxation. During the early republic officials called *tribuni aerarii* had charge of the financial obligations of the tribe. Officers called *curatores tribuum* are also attested, but their role is uncertain (as is their relation to the *tribuni aerarii*).   A. M.; T. J. Co.

tributum was a direct tax paid by individuals to the Roman state. Until 167 BC citizens of Rome were liable to pay a *tributum* which was in principle an extraordinary (in contrast to the regular *vectigalia*) levy on their property and might be repaid. The total size of the levy was decided by the senate and varied from year to year. In some years, e.g. 347–345, no *tributum* was levied. After its suspension in 167 BC this form of *tributum* was only again levied in the exigencies of the civil wars after *Caesar's murder. Under the emperors Rome and Roman Italy were exempt from direct taxation. After 167 BC *tributum* came to denote the direct taxes raised in the provinces, either in the form of a land-tax (*tributum soli*) or poll-tax (*tributum capitis*). These were paid by all inhabitants of the provinces, whether Roman citizens or not, except by citizens of *coloniae* (see COLONIZATION, ROMAN) which normally possessed the *ius Italicum* (a privilege by which provincial land was deemed for some purposes to be in Italy) and were consequently exempt, usually from both taxes (*Dig.* 50. 15. 1 and 8), by citizens of cities which had been granted immunity (*immunitas*) by special dispensation, or by persons specifically exempted by a *lex*, *senatus consultum*, or imperial decree (*SEG* 9. 8. 3).

The *tributum soli*, under the republic, was normally either a fixed sum (*stipendium*) as in Spain and Africa, or a tithe (*decuma*) paid in kind and leased by the censors in Rome to *publicani*, as in Asia (see ASIA, ROMAN PROVINCE) after the *lex Sempronia* (see GRACCHUS, GAIUS) of 123 BC (App. *BCiv.* 5. 4. 17–20). Under the emperors the system of leasing of direct taxes to *publicani* was abandoned. *Augustus instituted periodic provincial censuses which formed the basis of assessment. Each provincial city normally received a bloc assessment. The individual provincial was liable to his city, the city to the Roman government. Local magistrates were responsible for collection in their city and its territory. The tax was levied in cash or kind according to custom and regional circumstances.

The *tributum capitis* seems first to have been imposed, along with *tributum soli*, in Africa in 146 BC (App. *Pun.* 135; see AFRICA, ROMAN); otherwise it is not attested before the period of the civil wars. Under the emperors details of its character and incidence are exiguous, although it was almost certainly universal in the provinces. In *Syria we happen to know (*Dig.* 50. 15. 3) that inhabitants were liable from age 14 for men and 12 for women to 65.

In *Egypt the Romans raised a complex pattern of taxes in cash and kind (especially in grain) on the land and its produce, and also imposed a poll-tax (*laographia*) paid by native Egyptian males from 14 to 60, by the inhabitants of the *metropoleis* at reduced rates, but not by the citizens of the Greek cities.   G. P. B.

trierarchy The word *trierarchos* means '*trireme-commander', but at Athens in the 5th and 4th cents. BC the trierarchy was a liturgy (work for the state at one's own expense), which the richest citizens could be called on to perform for a year. The state provided the ship and its basic equipment, and normally paid for the crew, but the trierarch had not only to command the ship but also to bear the costs of maintenance and repair, which could amount to as much as one talent. After 411 it became common for two men to share responsibility for a ship, and contractors could be found who would relieve the trierarchs of their personal involvement; reforms in 357 and later involved the organization of those liable in so-called *symmoriai* ('partnerships'). The liturgy was abolished by Demetrius of Phalerum (see ATHENS, HISTORY) in 317–307.

The institution is found in some other states (*Rhodes, Arist. *Pol.* 5. 1304^b; Teos and Lebedus (both in Asia Minor), *SIG*³ 344, 66; Priene (Asia Minor again), *SIG*³ 1003, 29), but elsewhere *trierarchos* denotes simply the captain of a warship, and that is perhaps the meaning of the word in *Herodotus (e.g. 6. 14. 2).   C. G. S.; P. J. R.

trireme The trireme (Gk. *triērēs*, Lat. *triremis*) was the standard warship of the classical world for much of the time from the 5th cent. BC to the 4th cent. AD. A long rowing-ship, its principal weapon was a bronze ram, fixed on the prow at the water-line. It was rowed by oarsmen arranged in groups of three, sitting one above the other and each oarsman pulling a single oar of equal length. The topmost level of men were called in Greek *thranitai*, the middle ones *zygioi*, and the lowest ones *thalamioi*. On an Athenian trireme of the Classical period there were 170 oarsmen, ten marines, four archers, and sixteen sailors, including the helmsman, making a total of 200. Trials of a

modern reconstruction of an Athenian trireme have shown that speeds in excess of 9 knots are possible. Triremes could be rowed with only some of the oars manned, but this reduced speed considerably. For long sailing passages sails were used, but masts were usually removed and left on the shore before battle.

The origins of the trireme are uncertain. There is no reliable evidence as to where the ship was first developed, although modern scholars tend to favour either Phoenicia (see PHOENICIANS) or Egypt as its birthplace, and to date its invention to the second half of the 6th cent. BC. The heyday of the trireme was the 5th cent. BC, when the finest practitioners of trireme warfare were the Athenians, who perfected the art of manœuvring at speed to ram and disable enemy ships.

From the mid-4th cent. BC larger warships with oarsmen arranged in groups of four, five, six, or more were developed. These ships relied far less on ramming and high-speed manœuvring, and more on boarding and missile weapons. Thus the trireme became less important in Mediterranean fleets until the creation of the Roman imperial navy, which used triremes extensively until the 4th cent. AD. See NAVIES   P. de S.

trireme The *Olympias*, a modern replica of a trireme, under oars off Poros (Greece) in 1992. Painstakingly researched, and built using (as far as possible) authentic techniques and materials, it has provided valuable insights into seaworthiness and speed.

triumph, the procession of a Roman general who had won a major victory to the temple of *Jupiter on the Capitol. The word came to the Romans from Greek (*thriambos*) via Etruscan and appears in Etruscan form (*triumpe*) in the *Carmen arvale* (hymn of the arval brethren, predating 4th cent. BC). The origin of the triumph cannot be recovered. In Roman tradition, all the kings except for the peaceful Pompilius Numa celebrated triumphs, followed by the founding consul, Publius Valerius Poplicola, but in its developed form it owed much to *Etruscan influence, and Etruscan paintings show similar rituals which we cannot fully interpret. In Classical times, the procession entered Rome through the *porta triumphalis* ('triumphal gate') through which no one else might enter. (It may have been part of the porta Carmentalis.) It made its way to the Capitol by a long route including open spaces where large numbers could see it. It comprised, essentially, the *triumphator* (dressed in the costume said to have been the kings' and close to Jupiter's) on a four-horse chariot, with any sons of suitable age as outriders; eminent captives (normally destined for execution) and freed Roman prisoners of war dressed as the *triumphator*'s freedmen; the major spoils captured; his army; and animals for sacrifice. The whole senate and all the magistrates were supposed to escort it. Increasingly costly and elaborate details were added from *c*.200 BC, including banners, paintings of sieges and battles, musicians, and torch-bearers. The *triumphator* was preceded by his lictors (attendants who carried the *fasces* or rods of office), and a slave rode with him, holding a laurel wreath over his head and reminding him that he was mortal. The soldiers chanted insulting verses, no doubt to avert the gods' displeasure. The right to triumph depended on a special vote of the people allowing him to retain his military *imperium* in the city, and so in fact on the senate's decision to ask for this vote.

In classical times the prerequisites for expecting such a decision were a victory in a declared war over a foreign enemy, with at least 5,000 of them killed and the termination of the war; the *triumphator* must have fought under his own auspices (*auspicia*) in his own *provincia* and as a magistrate (or, later, as a promagistrate). In the late republic acclamation as *imperator* (victorious commander) was the first step, holding out hope of a triumph. Interpretation of entitlement was elastic and subject to intrigue, and the senate might even be bypassed. From the 3rd cent. BC, some generals refused a triumph celebrated one at their own expense in a procession to Jupiter Latiaris on the Alban Mount, probably after the supposed precedent of such ceremonies in the days of the Latin League. If the entitlement was judged defective, the general might be awarded a 'lesser triumph' (Plin. *HN* 15. 19) called *ovatio*. This has been claimed to be an old pre-Etruscan form of triumph, but in Roman tradition it was a lesser substitute, first celebrated in 503 BC (Plin. *HN* 15. 125). All forms of triumph could be equally counted in the record of a man's career, but the Capitoline triumph was the summit of a Roman aristocrat's ambition.

In the late republic interpretation of the rules came to be dominated by power and influence. Thus *Pompey celebrated two triumphs without having been a magistrate, and Caesar allowed two of his *legati* to triumph. Under the empire, triumphs soon became a monopoly of the emperor and (with his permission) his family, while the actual commander would be granted 'triumphal ornaments'. But as early as the 1st cent. AD these were deliberately cheapened and gradually lost their connection with military exploits.

E. B.

trophies (Gk. *tropaia*, Lat. *trophaea*, from Gk. *tropē,* a turning i.e. rout of the enemy). The act of dedicating on the field of battle a suit of enemy armour set upon a stake is a specifically Greek practice. Originally intended as a miraculous image of the *theos tropaios* who had brought about the defeat of the enemy, a trophy marked the spot where the enemy had been routed. Trophies were also dedicated in the sanctuary of the deity to whom victory was ascribed. They appear in art at the end of the 6th cent. BC and were certainly in use during the Persian Wars (see GREECE (HISTORY)).

The trophies of the 4th cent. became permanent monu-

trophies Relief slab from from the Tropaeum Traiani ('Trophy of Trajan') at Adamklissi (in modern Romania), erected by *Trajan in 108/9 to celebrate his conquest of Dacia. The slab depicts hand-to-hand combat between a Roman legionary and two trousered '*barbarians'. Representations of contemporary events were a feature of Roman *sculpture.

ments. The battle of Leuctra (371 BC) was commemorated by a tower surmounted by a trophy of arms, and from this period onwards the name was applied to various kinds of towers and buildings commemorating military and naval victories. Trophies became a common motif of art; sculptured trophies accompanied by statues of captives and victors decorated the buildings of Hellenistic kings and took an important place in Roman triumphal art from the 1st cent. BC. The word trophy is also applied, though not with strict accuracy, to the masses of arms on sculptured monuments which appear first at Pergamum and later on a number of Roman commemorative monuments. The best-known Roman trophy monuments are those of Augustus at La Turbie and of Trajan at Adamklissi.

D. E. S.

Troy (mod. Hisarlık) (see ◀Map 1, Db▶) lies in NW *Asia Minor, about 6¼ km. (4 mi.) from the Aegean coast and rather less from the Hellespont. The site consists of a small citadel mound with c.25 m. of gradually accumulated debris from human habitation, and a lower town at least 1 km. square. It was first identified as Troy by Charles Maclaren in 1820. After initial soundings by Frank Calvert in 1863 and 1865, much of the mound was excavated by H. Schliemann between 1870 and 1890. After his death digging by W. Dörpfeld in 1893 and 1894 and by the University of Cincinnati from 1932 to 1938 greatly supplemented what had previously been learned; and further illumination is expected from new excavations by an international team under M. Korfmann, begun in 1988. The site was occupied from c.3000 BC to c. AD 1200, perhaps with some intervals, and has revealed well over 46 building phases. These are conventionally grouped in nine bands, sometimes misleadingly called 'cities'.

Layers I to III, counting from the bottom, belong to the early bronze age; Layers IV and V probably belong to the middle bronze age; Layer VI, thought by Blegen to have begun in the middle bronze age, is now more probably assigned to the late bronze age to the last portion of which Layers VIIa and VIIb also belong. Layers VIII and IX are of Hellenistic, Roman, and Byzantine date.

Founded on a limestone spur projecting into a marine bay, since silted up, the citadel was fortified from an early stage. In Troy I three successive stone walls supported battlements of mudbrick; an entrance gate was flanked by projecting towers. Within was a system of parallel longhouses with party walls and flat roofs; these were built of mudbrick on stone footings. Pottery was all handmade. Copper, stone, and bone were used for tools and weapons. The bay was exploited for fish and seafood. Culturally Troy I belongs to a north-west Anatolian variant within a Thracian–Anatolian continuum. The culture of Troy I developed without a break but with increasing grandeur into Troy II. Three or more successive fortification walls were erected, each surpassing its predecessor, and each with gates and towers of stone and mudbrick. Inside the citadel a palatial hall or 'megaron' and other buildings were

approached across a colonnaded courtyard. But after a devastating fire the citadel was filled in the final phases of Troy II with densely built village houses, a style of architecture which continued throughout Troy III. From Troy II Schliemann recovered weapons of bronze and precious stone, vessels of gold, silver, bronze, and copper, and, like Blegen, gold jewellery. The potter's wheel appears early in Troy II but makes little impact before the middle and late phases. During Troy II–III there was increasing contact with other parts of Anatolia, the Aegean, and north Syria. The early bronze age at Troy ended c.2000 BC.

Troy IV and V are little known, but the continuing expansion of the citadel and rebuildings of the fortifications suggest a continuing increase of importance and prosperity. Architecture, pottery, and comparative stratigraphy indicate a probable date for IV–V in the Anatolian middle bronze age, ending c.1700 BC.

Troy VI introduced sudden changes: monumental architecture, grey pottery, use of the horse. Blegen saw in these the advent of Indo-European invaders, but the new pottery could have local origins. Three successive citadel walls of increasing strength and magnificence survive. There were at least four gateways, two protected by towers. Inside the citadel the ground rose in concentric terraces: the royal palace no doubt stood at the summit, but no remains are left since much of the top of the hill was sliced away in Hellenistic or Roman times to create a platform for the temple of Athena. Spacious free-standing houses occupied the lower terraces, many equipped with stone bases for interior wooden columns. Outside the citadel walls is evidence for a meaner lower town and, further south, for a cremation cemetery. Fallen masonry and traces of fire show that about 1270 BC Troy VI was violently destroyed.

Survivors maintaining the same culture patched the defensive walls and built modest new houses inside the fortress. This was Troy VIIa which lasted until perhaps c.1190 BC when it too was destroyed as, once again, fallen masonry and traces of fire—and this time remnants of human bones in houses and streets—show.

Once more the citadel was rebuilt and reoccupied in Troy VIIb until perhaps c.1050 BC; but alongside continuation of earlier Troy VI traditions the pottery now introduced fabrics and styles related to widespread Thracian and east European types. There may be evidence for continued occupation of the citadel on a very modest scale until it was resettled by early Greek colonists c.700 BC or earlier. The succeeding Hellenistic and Roman Troy IX gained importance as a sacred site of the classical world, but declined after c. AD 550. There are traces of later occupation until c. AD 1200.

Hisarlık's identification with the Troy of Priam has never been proved, but a ruined castle would have been visible in *Homer's day and its situation agrees with that of Troy in most classical tradition, *Strabo excepted. It is generally assumed that some residue of historical truth persists in the legends concerning the Trojan War, although how much and where is uncertain. Mycenaean Greeks (see

MYCENAEAN CIVILIZATION) could plausibly have destroyed Troy VI, VIIa, or VIIb. Of these Troy VI would fit best as dating to the peak of power at both Mycenae and Troy. An earthquake held by Blegen to have destroyed Troy VI is perhaps to be dated to VIIa instead.   C. W. B.; D. F. E.

Tullius, Servius, the sixth king of Rome (conventionally 578–535 BC), murdered by *Tarquinius Superbus at the instigation of his daughter Tullia. *Claudius identified him with the Etruscan adventurer Mastarna but Roman sources, deriving Servius from *servus* ('slave'), made him the son of a Latin captive Ocrisia and brought up in the household of Tarquinius Priscus. Because of his supposed slave ancestry he was credited with the enfranchisement of freedmen, the creation of the Compitalia, a close association with Fortuna (cf. Degrassi, *ILLRP* 1070 (3rd cent.?)), and perhaps the establishment of the (certainly archaic) federal Latin sanctuary of *Diana on the Aventine (whose dedication date coincided with a slave festival). As the penultimate king he was credited (probably by the time of *Timaeus) with political and military institutions that were deemed fundamental to the republic but believed to antedate it: the centuriate organization, the first territorial tribes (see TRIBUS), and the census. Although their initial phases may well date from the 6th cent., the form in which our sources present these innovations is anachronistic, as is the associated ascription to Servius of the first Roman *coinage, direct taxation (*tributum*), and army pay. The 'Servian wall' of Rome dates from the early 4th cent. (earlier 6th-cent. defences have not been securely identified) but two phases of the Sant'Omobono sanctuary (with which Servius was associated) do belong to the 6th cent. Accius already celebrated Servius as establishing 'liberty' for the citizens, but later writers offer varying interpretations of his reforms: as concentrating political power in the hands of the wealthy (Cic. *Rep.* 2. 37 ff.), as creating a timocratic socio-political hierarchy (Livy 1. 42 ff.), or simply as the work of a skilful pragmatic populist (Dion. Hal. *Ant. Rom.* 4. 1 ff.). Recent speculation has seen him as (in part) attempting to combat the power of the nascent patriciate.

A. D.

Twelve Tables (For the historical background, see ROME (HISTORY) §1.2.) According to Roman tradition, popular pressure led to the appointment for 451 BC of ten men with consular *imperium*, for writing down statutes, *legibus scribundis*, in order to put an end to the patrician and priestly monopoly of the law. They compiled ten tables, were reappointed for 450 BC, and compiled two more, including the ban on intermarriage between patricians and plebeians, which was rapidly abrogated by the *lex Canuleia* of 445 BC. An attempt to remain in office for 449 BC also failed. The fundamental consequence was that customary law was now enacted by statute and given legislative basis; and the Twelve Tables were seen as the starting-point of the development of Roman law.

We have no way of verifying this tradition; and it may

be that the impetus came rather from a desire for self-regulation within the élite. But the legal, antiquarian, oratorical, and historical tradition preserves a remarkably consistent view of the content of the Twelve Tables, even if the language has been modernized. And it is reasonably certain both that they underlay the colonial charters of the late 4th cent. BC onwards and that legislation to revise them began in the early 3rd cent. BC.

Three points remain controversial: there is little evidence for the order of the different provisions and modern editions largely classify them perforce according to the later divisions of the law; it is uncertain how complete is the record preserved by our sources; and it is disputed how far they contained what was later regarded as public law. Our knowledge of the order depends on the fragments of the commentary by the legal teacher Gaius quoted in the *Digest* and on the occasional attribution of particular provisions to particular tables; but it is at least certain that the provision conventionally printed as Tabula I, 1, *is* the first. As far as the second point is concerned, there seem to be few areas of the private law of the late republic where a provision of the Twelve Tables is not at some point invoked and it is unlikely that whole fields covered by the Twelve Tables have disappeared without trace. And if one thinks in less rigid terms about the third problem, a consistent view of our tradition must lead to the conclusion that even if the Twelve Tables mostly concerned themselves with relations between individuals, they also at times concerned themselves with relations between individuals and the community.

The Twelve Tables were presumably not much systematized and perhaps put together largely from material which was readily to hand and which the ten men supposed to be actually or potentially useful, not unlike the later praetor's edict. It would be exaggerated to describe the Twelve Tables as a code. They attracted commentary from the middle republic onwards, but gradually became more and more obsolete as the praetor's edict developed, becoming progressively the province of antiquarians.

M. H. C.

tyranny (*tyrannos*, 'tyrant', was perhaps a Lydian word) is the name given to the form of monarchy set up by usurpers in many Greek states in the 7th and 6th cents. BC. The earliest occurrence of the term is in *Archilochus (*tyrannis*, fr. 19. 3 West). Tyranny was not a special form of constitution, or necessarily a reign of terror; the tyrant might either rule directly or retain the existing political institutions but exercise a preponderant influence over their working, and his rule might be benevolent or malevolent. Tyranny was given a bad sense especially by *Plato and *Aristotle, for whom it was the worst possible form of constitution.

Among the best known of the early tyrants were Pheidon of Argos, Cypselus and Periander of Corinth, Cleisthenes of Sicyon, *Pisistratus and his sons Hippias and Hipparchus in Athens, and Polycrates of Samos.

Archaic tyranny seems to have been a response to the development of the city-states: typically a fringe member of the ruling aristocracy would seize power with the support of discontented members of the community; but after a time the rule of the tyrant in turn became a cause of discontent, and tyranny hardly ever lasted more than two generations. These tyrants ruled in a period of growing confidence and prosperity: by encouraging national cults, by sponsoring public works, and by acting as patrons to writers and artists, they glorified both their cities and themselves. Later tyrants were military dictators, among them Gelo and Hiero of *Syracuse and Thero of Acragas at the beginning of the 5th cent. and *Dionysius I and Dionysius II of Syracuse in the late 5th and 4th cents.

V. E.; P. J. R.

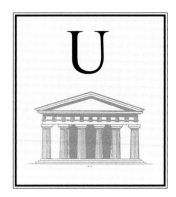

Ulysses See ODYSSEUS.

urbanism

I. Greek and Hellenistic Urban units are to be distinguished not simply by the size of the community, but by its topographical organization, occupational pattern, and cultural sophistication. The formation of towns is not therefore simply a matter of the agglomeration of communities, but of the forging of a community of distinct character. Archaeologists have sometimes been too willing to call early bronze-age settlements towns as a result of overestimating the size of the community involved, but both the archaeological remains and the evidence of the Linear B tablets show that late bronze-age palace centres of the *Minoan and *Mycenaean civilizations were essentially urban units in their size, occupational diversity, and culture. Particularly important seems to be the role of the palaces as centres for the storage and redistribution of agricultural produce: it may not be coincidental that both the bronze-age palaces and the earliest towns develop in areas marginal for agriculture and where accumulation and storage of produce is vital if a stable community of any size is to be maintained and is a source of political power.

No Dark-Age community deserves to be called a town, and the growth of towns in the 8th and 7th cents. seems in many cases to be a result of separate village communities coalescing for political and economic reasons (*synoecism). At Corinth, for example, the creation of a single town, with a specific area devoted to burial of the dead, and the creation of a separate potters' quarter go closely together, and are followed within half a century by temple-building and by *tyranny. Corinthian pottery already follows an independent tradition before the grouping of potting activity into the potters' quarter. The impetus to urbanism in Corinth may in fact have come in part from the sending out of colonizing expeditions, which probably formed communities recognizably urban in their organization of civic space from the outset, to judge from the way in which areas were reserved from the beginning for 'civic' activities at the Megarian colony of Megara Hyblaea (in *Sicily). The members of a new community, formed from scratch, must have given thought in the abstract to the requirements and organization of communal life. This may in turn have led to changes at home as well as in the daughter-community. Unification for defence seems to play little part in the urbanization of this period, and many early towns seem to have been without walls; but it is significant that colonizing and urbanism are at this stage phenomena of agriculturally marginal southern Greece, as also is that characteristic political unit, the *polis*.

Greek political thought did not recognize the existence of urban communities which were not also politically independent: *Aristotle in *Politics* 1 sees the *polis* as the natural evolutionary product of the growth of the village. Urbanism and political independence should therefore be seen as going closely together. One mark of both is the focusing of the community's religious life upon certain particular *sanctuaries, both central sanctuaries and those at the margins of a city's territory which stake out claims to territorial control as well as providing a proving ground for future citizens and citizen wives. The development of functionally specific sanctuaries, including these out-of-town sanctuaries, is part of the occupational diversity characteristic of urban life and can be observed both in southern Greece and in Greek colonies from the later 8th cent. onwards.

The assumption that urban units should also enjoy political independence had consequences for urban development across a single political territory. The main settlement tends to be very much the largest settlement in a political territory, and even when there are other populous centres they tend not to develop the full range of characteristically urban services—theatres, palaestras, diverse sanctuaries, dedicated community meeting-places. This is seen particularly clearly in the case of Athens, where some of the demes (local districts, see DEMOCRACY, ATHENIAN) were very much larger than *poleis* elsewhere in Greece (Acharnae may have had a population of 8,000–10,000), but where none of them seems to have developed the topographical organization, service facilities, or occupational pattern of a town.

urbanism, Greek Reconstructed drawing of the 4th-cent. BC city of Priene on the W. coast of *Asia Minor. German excavations have revealed one of the best surviving examples of a Greek planned city laid out on a 'Hippodamian' grid, a hallmark of Greek urbanism.

It is characteristic of Classical towns that further attention is devoted to the space within which non-religious civic activities take place and that there are buildings specifically designed for such activities. The development of the stoa, from the mid-6th cent. onwards, had an important part to play in this: the stoa originated as a place of shelter in sanctuaries, but came to be used as a flexible meeting-place suitable both for official gatherings, such as lawcourts, and for unofficial civic activities. Flanking the *agora with stoas became a popular way of marking out the civic centre.

During the 5th, 4th, and 3rd cents. urban forms spread to mainland northern Greece, both to the seaboard under the direct influence of southern cities, and inland in Macedonia, Thessaly, and even Epirus, in association with the greater political unification of those territories. Archaeological remains from Pella (in *Macedonia), for example, show it to have been culturally sophisticated in the 4th and 3rd cents. These new towns were all marked by regular land division such as had marked most new developments since the 6th cent. and which had by this time become one of the hallmarks of a Greek city. It is such regular planning, as well as specific Greek building types, that is exported to the near east with *Alexander the Great and embodied in such Hellenistic cities as Dura-Europus on the Euphrates.

The degree to which Greek urban types were bound up with Greek political arrangements emerges clearly in the very different sort of town which the Attalids created at *Pergamum as their capital city. Here it is not the terrain alone that precludes a regular grid plan, but the political requirement that the city focus upon its autocratic rulers. The irregularities of the landscape are exploited to produce a monumental architecture where some elements are clearly subordinated to others, and each element is visually dependent upon those around it, regardless of their functional relations. Familiar architectural forms are here combined in an entirely new way.

See ARCHITECTURE, *Greek*; COLONIZATION; ECONOMY, GREEK and HELLENISTIC; HOUSES; MARKETS AND FAIRS; SANITATION; WATER SUPPLY. R. G. O.

II. Roman The Romans, 'the most city-proud people known', in Procopius' late description (*Goth*. 8. 22. 7), founded their city-policy and urban ideology principally on their own city. Already in the 6th cent. BC extensive in surface-area, imposing in its public buildings and private houses, and complex in its management of space, Rome both resembled the cities of the *Etruscans and Latins (Latini) in many respects, and functioned as a show-case and pioneer of urban form.

In the 4th cent. BC Rome's urban functions were transformed, through the economic and prestige gains of military success, the organization of a huge territory with the expanding tribal system, and new types of relations with neighbouring cities which foreshadowed the incorporative and co-operative citizenship strategies on which a large urban population ultimately depended: the future megalopolis was conceived.

It is only from the perspective of the super-city that the long-lasting tradition of Roman urban policy can be understood. Other ancient cities produced offshoot communities which were essentially new cities. Rome alone deployed its population resources, citizen or Latin, in planned locations, maintaining a superior position in terms of status, and a continuing political and governmental relationship which went far beyond any Greek or Carthaginian *mētropolis–apoikia* tie (i.e. tie between mother- and daughter-city, founding and founded); cf. CARTHAGE).

The successes of the Roman élite from the Latin War to the Pyrrhic transformed Rome, under the physical influence of the developing urban tradition of Greek south Italy and Sicily (to which the Romans attributed their prison and provision-market; we may add the circular *comitium* (assembly place) and porticoed *forum Romanum of the end of the 4th cent.). The new foundations (Cosa, 273, or Alba Fucens, 303, are well-preserved examples of the early stages of the process) adopted from the centre a repertoire of institutional architecture—forum, porticoes, comitium, *temples, streets, sewers (see SANITATION, *Roman*), monuments—which expanded as the city grew in grandeur through the 2nd cent. BC. In mainly military installations, such as the *coloniae maritimae* or maritime colonies (the surviving walls of Pyrgi are an example), we are reminded of the fortifications which many Italic peoples were building in the 4th and 3rd cents. on the model of Hellenic military engineering (see COLONIZATION, ROMAN).

In these cities a citizen egalitarianism (also found in the division of the territory: see CENTURIATION) was derived from Roman constitutional theory and (therefore) linked to military needs. It was particularly apparent in the regularity and uniformity of the plan, which have become the most famous features of Roman cities, and which share a theoretical parentage with the socio-aesthetic ideas of Hippodamus of Miletus; but is also reflected in the legal and political institutions and their architecture (comitium and basilica, for instance), and increasingly by the late republic, the provision of the latest in the people's perks or *commoda*, such as *baths and places for spectacles.

By the age of *Cicero, the local élites of many Italian towns, even places as insignificant as Aletrium, enriched by a century of imperial success, had embellished their communities with the latest in Hellenistic taste, in a way that was still intermittent at Rome. Swollen by centuries of opportunistic influx and impossible to plan (Livy also blamed haphazard redevelopment after the Gallic sack), the metropolis was less beautiful than its old enemy Capua. *Sulla, *Pompey, and *Caesar made strenuous efforts to remedy this, and *Augustus completed the process of making Rome a worthy model for the founding and embellishing of cities everywhere.

The legacy of rectilinear planning and subdivision of space apart, Roman urbanism and its apparent uniformity in the early imperial period are the product of the imitation in local communities of canons of monumentality made fashionable by people further up the chain of patronage. Cities in the provinces came to have an ideological role, as exemplars of the values of Hellenic/Roman culture and a symbol of conversion from barbarism. Fortified settlements were moved from impregnable heights to the plain (like the creation of Virunum below the Magdalensberg in Noricum, or the replacement of Wheathampstead with Verulamium (St Albans) in *Britain), gaining the easy communications and plain-land investment agriculture which were also signs of what the *pax Romana* offered local élites. Roman institutional statuses helped the process, and the bases of the army and the veteran *coloniae* which resembled them in function and planning, provided further examples, as at Augusta Praetoria (Aosta), Arelate (Arles), Merida (Emerita Augusta in *Spain), Timgad (Thamugadi) (but the 'chequerboard' plan should be seen as a legacy of republican thinking rather than as something distinctively military). Meanwhile Rome itself came to resemble the other cities more. Fires and expansion into the periphery made possible the development of large areas of the city on a more regular plan. The great baths and prestige projects like the *Colosseum or Pantheon were imitated in favoured centres; in projects like the *forum Traiani*, however, or the great temples of the reigns from Hadrian to Aurelian, it is the grandiose architecture of the provinces that was being recreated on a grander scale in the centre.

Cities in more civilized places had always been the organs of communication, and the respecting (or not) of privileges, age, beauty, and so on became an important part of Roman government. Thus the destruction of cities (*Carthage, Corinth, Jerusalem) must be considered part of Roman urban policy, throwing into relief the more desirable role of the Roman leader as *pater urbium*. Posing as the first or new founder of a city was a potent image that came to be frequently used. New imitations of the centre were made on an ambitious scale, and certain cities were singled out to enjoy the full benefit of imperial favour (Lepcis in *Africa, Italica in Spain, Augusta Treverorum (Trier)). The whole question of the standing of cities and their claims to favour, based on the past and present attainments of their citizens, became a central feature of life under the empire. The rhetoric in which the cities competed, and which is so apparent in Antonine literature, is a part of Roman urbanism, and relevant to its extension even into remote provinces. The aspirations of communities for a higher place in the formal hierarchy of city status is a real feature of this state of affairs, and the spreading of municipal status, the upgrading of villages to cities, *municipia* to *coloniae* (see COLONIZATION, ROMAN), and the increase in city institutions in places like *Egypt and *Syria where they had been less widespread, owes more to this competition than it does to imperial vision. The city was usually the focus of administration and the base for supervision, a role which it bequeathed, despite diminished populations, to late antiquity, and through the episcopate, to the Christian Middle Ages.

In general, then, we should not credit Rome with planning the efflorescence of cities or their cultural uniformity, let alone with a set of social and economic goals to be achieved through urbanization. The symbolic importance of the city often in fact concealed situations of small structural change in the organization of the productive environment. Many cities probably had quite small permanent populations, and their demise in late antiquity, where this happened, may often have been the collapse of a façade rather than the catastrophe of a structure.   N. P.

III. Late Roman The traditional picture of overall decline is being modified by excavations and surveys which show wide variations in place and time, and by partly semantic disputes: are we confronting the death of civic life, or transformations that show its resilience? Is the city an Aristotelian *polis* (see §I above), an agency of central government, or simply a large settlement?

Imperial supervision of the cities increased greatly from the 3rd cent. The hereditary councils of local gentry that ran them (*decuriones*), and collected and underwrote imperial taxes, were more closely watched by governors of now smaller provinces; their task was complicated by taxes now demanded in kind, though probably little heavier (see FINANCE, ROMAN). New provincial capitals might prosper (often at others' expense), but the immunities of the growing imperial bureaucracies and clergy tempted away many of the curial class; a handful of rich councillors (*principales*) dominated and exploited their remaining colleagues. Civic *gymnasia* (see GYMNASIUM) gave way to rhetorical schools, orientated to imperial careers. Curial wealth and authority in town and country was challenged by soldiers and officials, active or retired, by bishops, monasteries, and hermits; these deployed new sources of wealth, or offered new types of patronage. Many councils, none the less, proved durable; tax-collecting was often profitable; and their numerous complaints in the law-codes reflect their political influence. Their slow decline, moreover, does not imply urban disintegration: new structures of government evolved. Bishops and retired imperial officials (*honorati*) shared increasingly in civic administration, furnishing and electing new officials: the *defensor* ('defender of the municipality', i.e. of peasants against local landowners), the corn-buyer, the Father of the City. Even tax-collecting devolved on to great aristocratic houses in 5th–6th-cent. Egypt, and perhaps elsewhere in the east. Bishops used their own and imperial resources to maintain civic food-supplies, and negotiated for their cities with emperors or invaders, inheriting the rhetor's role. Although new ruling élites, like the old, often provided festivals and buildings, their interests and loyalties also belonged to Church or court. The values of the *polis* were alien to Christianity, although many bishops, like Basil of Cappadocian Caesarea, still imbibed them with their classical education. Christian charities both inherited and challenged the tradition of civic *euergetism, being directed to the poor, rather than fellow-citizens.

Urban building reflects these changes. In the 3rd cent. this declined markedly, except for walls. A glut of existing monuments was one reason; also economic or military problems; but the more stable and prosperous 4th cent. also saw imperial confiscation of civic lands and taxes. Governors and senators tended to feature as benefactors, while local noblemen merely built lavish town-houses. From the late 4th cent., however, cities regained some control over their revenue; in the east, the Father of the City deployed it for new building. Thus, Corinth replanned and rebuilt its forum after Visigothic sack. Moreover, as in 4th-cent. *Africa, or 6th-cent. Arabia, local benefactors may have been partly responsible for buildings for which senators, governors, or emperors took epigraphic credit. Bishops and laity who built churches, hospices, and *martyria* (mainly during the 5th and 6th cents.) thereby increased or replaced urban monuments, but radically altered civic plans and character: declining cities might show islands of settlement around major churches or even shift site to ecclesiastical centres outside the walls. Where possible, though, bishops would occupy and redevelop town centres. Although some cities, like Gaza, long remained obstinately pagan, an important relic, or simply an episcopal establishment, might confer a new communal identity and means of survival.

Public entertainments are another reflection. Imperial taxes increasingly sustained them, while local funds were often diverted by governors, or usurped by private persons. In the 5th cent. the organization of all public spectacles (except Christian festivals) was put under the Blue and Green chariot factions, which also had important roles in imperial ceremonial, communication between governors and subjects, and local defence; typically civic activities were thus integrated with the imperial system. Factions might also absorb the loyalties of traditional civic subgroups (thus, *Jews were often Blues), increasing tensions and violence (see GAMES).

Changes in civic economies and population are hard to estimate. With exceptions, decline was earlier and deeper northward and westward. Many cities developed fields and gardens within their walls; but some eastern cities in the 5th and 6th cents. (e.g. Palestinian Caesarea) were more populated and prosperous than in the early empire. A reduced wall circuit need not imply reduced numbers; some cities, like Corinth and Burdigala, had large extramural settlements. Decline in one urban quarter might mean growth in another, as at *Ephesus. The 6th–7th-cent. transformation of colonnades into souks in some eastern cities indicates lively commerce, though also loss of the classical urban ideal. Some cities (at least in *Egypt) were major producers, especially of textiles, but most were probably consumers, dependent on rents, taxes, immigrants, and through-trade from the countryside. Bishops might extend the city's rural influence, but rural monasteries could challenge their dominance; in the north and west, the rich resided increasingly on their estates; and, in *Syria and elsewhere, villages grew in size and independence. When plague, war, or earthquake decimated a city, it might be hard to replace the population from the peasantry. (Bubonic plague and 6th-cent. urban decline are plausibly linked.) Imperial salaries and largesse might enhance cities that combined an official presence with agricultural and commercial resources; thus, Anastasius restored the harbour of Palestinian Caesarea, a provincial capital. But cities existing largely for official needs might become or remain fortified 'administrative villages', dependent for survival on the state. Justiniana Prima, Illyria (founded 535), praised by Procopius for its large population and traditional buildings, housed only officials and clergy; it was abandoned in the 7th cent. This trend appears in the generally new and fragile cities of Britain, north Gaul, and the north Balkans from the 3rd cent., but was affecting even pre-Roman eastern cities by the early 7th.

While many cities (even western; e.g. Marseille and Córdoba) survived the empire with some prosperity, and many subsequently revived, their character, c.650, would have been unrecognizable to Aristotle, Plutarch, or even Libanius.   S. J. B. B.

Valerius Flaccus (Gaius Valerius Flaccus Setinus Balbus), Roman poet, author of the *Argonautica*, an epic poem on the voyage of Jason and the Argonauts to Colchis in search of the Golden Fleece. There is no external evidence for his biography apart from Quintilian's remark (*c.* AD 95) that 'we have recently suffered a great loss in Valerius Flaccus' (10. 1. 90); since Quintilian can use 'recent' of Caesius Bassus' death in AD 79 (10. 1. 96), the conventional dating of Valerius' death to the early 90s is without foundation. The evidence of the poem itself is controversial. The conventional claim that Valerius was a *quindecimvir sacris faciundis* (member of a college of fifteen men whose job it was to look after certain ritual texts) is based on lines in the proem which by no means dictate such a conclusion (1. 5–7). The one certainty is the reference in a simile to the eruption of Vesuvius, which occurred on 24 August 79 (4. 507–9; cf. 3. 208–9). The date of the composition of the proem, which alludes to *Vespasian, *Titus, and *Domitian, is keenly contested, with advocates for a date under each of the three. The most that can be securely stated is that the *Argonautica* is a Flavian epic (a fact of more than chronological importance).

Indebted to the *Argonautica* of *Apollonius of Rhodes (and perhaps of Publius Terentius Varro Atacinus), but moulded above all by *Virgil, Valerius' poem follows the Argonauts' expedition through many famous adventures to the point where Jason absconds from Colchis with *Medea. The poem breaks off at 8. 467 as Medea is persuading Jason not to hand her back to her brother Absyrtus. The conventional view is that the poet died before finishing his work, although the latest editor believes that the poem was completed in eight books, with the second half of the last book lost in transmission.

The poem owes much to Apollonius' *Argonautica* as a quest with a strong interest in the problems of epic heroism. Valerius, though, departs radically from Apollonius when he concentrates on Argo as the first ship, harbinger of human civilization (1. 1–4), placing his poem in a long and energetic Roman tradition of appropriation of the golden age and iron age myths. A cosmic frame is provided by Jupiter's concern for the expedition, which will reproduce on earth the patterns of order and dominance guaranteed universally by his own recent victory in the Gigantomachy. The cycles set in train by Argo's voyage will carry on down to the contemporary world of the Roman empire (1. 537–60), where the Flavian house likewise rules after the chaos of civil war. Hyperbolically inflating Apollonius' interest in aetiology, Valerius recounts the origin of warfare and imperial institutions, so that the poem is studded with overt references to contemporary Roman practices (in marked contrast with *Statius' *Thebaid*). Valerius exploits Virgil's *Georgics* and *Seneca's *Medea* to stress the ambivalence of iron age achievement, for navigation is a violation of natural boundaries, and hence either magnificent or impious in its audacity. In cunning and ironic counterpoint to these grand themes is the love story which overtakes the narrative in book 5. Valerius rises to the daunting challenge of going where Apollonius, Virgil, and Ovid had gone before, exploiting his great goddesses to present a sombre and frightening image of Medea's passion.

Valerius has unjustly suffered from being viewed as a doggedly earnest imitator of mightier models; his self-awareness and wry humour have gone largely unnoticed, although he has been commended for the poise of his versification and the acuity of his observation.   D. C. F.

Varro (Marcus Terentius Varro, 116–27 BC), was born at Reate, in the Sabine territory north-east of Rome. After studying at Rome with Lucius Aelius, the first true scholar of Latin literature and antiquities, and at Athens with the Academic philosopher Antiochus of Ascalon, Varro began a public career that brought him to the praetorship and, ultimately, to service on the side of *Pompey in the Civil War. Having received *Caesar's clemency after the battle of Pharsalus (48 BC), he was asked to plan and organize the first public library (see LIBRARIES) at Rome. But this project went unrealized, and after Caesar's assassination he was proscribed by Mark *Antony: his library at Casinum was plundered, but he escaped to live the rest of his life in scholarly retirement. He had completed 490 books by the start of his 78th year (Gell. 3. 10. 17): 55 titles are known in all, and his *œuvre* has been estimated to include nearly 75 different works totalling *c.*620 books (Ritschl, *Opuscula* 3. 485 ff.).

Works Varro's combination of methodical analysis, vast range, and original learning made him Rome's greatest scholar. His writings covered nearly every branch of inquiry: history (*De vita populi Romani*, on Roman 'social history'; *De gente populi Romani*, placing Rome's remote past in a Greek context), geography, rhetoric, law (*De iure civili lib. XV*), philosophy, music, medicine, architecture, literary history (*De poetis, De comoediis Plautinis*), religion, agriculture, and language (at least 10 works on this last alone). The achievements of the Augustans and of later authors, in both poetry and prose, are scarcely conceivable without the groundwork that he laid. See also SCHOLARSHIP, ANCIENT, *Latin*.

Only two of his works survive substantially:

1. *De lingua Latina*, in 25 books, of which books 5–10 are partly extant (5 and 6 entirely). Book 1 provided an introduction; 2–7 dealt with etymology, and the connection between words and the entities they represent; 8–13, with inflectional morphology and the conflict (which Varro probably exaggerated) between 'anomalists' and 'analogists' (an argument about language: how far can regularity, 'analogy' be recognized in linguistic rules, and how far must exceptions, 'anomalies', be accepted); 14–25, with syntax and the proper formation of 'propositions' (*proloquia*, a topic derived from Stoic dialectic; see STOICISM). Varro dedicated books 2–4 to his quaestor, the subsequent books to Cicero; the work was published before *Cicero's death, probably in 43.

2. *De re rustica* (3 books: 37 BC), a treatise on farming in dialogue form, intended as an agreeable entertainment for men of Varro's own class. It deals with agriculture in general (book 1), cattle- and sheep-breeding (book 2), and smaller farm-animals (birds, bees, etc.: book 3). The work, which survives entirely and shows some amusing strokes of characterization, reveals very strikingly Varro's fondness for analysing his subjects into their parts, and those parts into their sub-parts: though this analysis is sometimes carried to unhelpful lengths, it also represents a new stage in the logical organization of prose at Rome. See AGRICULTURAL WRITERS; AGRICULTURE, ROMAN.

Among Varro's lost works the following are especially noteworthy:

1. *Saturae Menippeae* (150 books: prob. 81–67 BC), humorous essays on topics of contemporary vice and folly, mingling verse with prose; Varro professed to imitate the 3rd-cent. *Cynic philosopher Menippus of Gadara. Ninety titles and 600 fragments survive.

2. *Antiquitates rerum humanarum et divinarum* (41 books: 47 BC). Of the first 25 books, on human (i.e. Roman) antiquities, little is known: the introductory book was followed by four segments of (probably) six books each, on persons (*de hominibus*: the inhabitants of Italy), places (*de locis*), times (*de temporibus*), and things (*de rebus*). The remaining sixteen books, dedicated to *Caesar as *pontifex maximus* (head of one of the main colleges of *priests), took up the human construction of the divine: another book of general introduction, then five triads, on priesthoods (27–9), holy places (30–2), holy times (33–5), rites (36–8), and kinds of gods (39–41). Among the lost works of republican prose, the *Antiquitates* is perhaps the one we most sorely miss.

3. *Logistorici* (76 books: 44 BC?), a series of dialogues on various subjects, each taking its name from a noted person: e.g. *Marius de fortuna, Tubero de origine humana, Curio de cultu*.

4. *Hebdomades vel de imaginibus* (15 books: 39 BC), a collection of 700 portraits of celebrated Greeks and Romans, in which each portrait was accompanied by an epigram; the number 7 played an important (if now obscure) role in the work's organization (cf. Gell. 3. 10. 1).

5. *Disciplinae* (9 books), a late work surveying the essential terms and principles of the learned 'disciplines' that a free man should command: these *artes liberales* ('liberal arts') included 'grammar', rhetoric, dialectic, arithmetic, geometry, astronomy, music, medicine, and architecture.

R. A. K.

Velleius Paterculus, Roman historical writer, provides details of himself in his work. Among his maternal ancestors were Minatus Magius of Aeclanum and Decius Magius of Capua (2. 16. 2–3); his paternal grandfather was Gaius Velleius, *praefectus fabrum* (chief of engineers) to *Pompey, *Brutus, and Tiberius Claudius Nero, father of the emperor *Tiberius (2. 76. 1); the senator Capito, who helped to prosecute the Caesaricide Cassius in 43 BC, was a paternal uncle (2. 69. 5). Velleius himself was born in (probably) 20 or 19 BC. Having begun his career as military tribune around the turn of the millennium (2. 101. 3), he joined the staff of *Augustus' grandson Gaius Caesar in the east (2. 101–102. 1); later he became *praefectus equitum* (commander of cavalry), as his father had been, and spent AD 4–12 serving under the future emperor Tiberius in Germany (twice), Pannonia, and Dalmatia (2. 104. 3, 111. 3, 114. 2, 115. 5). In AD 6, having completed his service as an equestrian officer (see EQUITES, *Imperial period*), he returned briefly to Rome and was elected quaestor for AD 7 (2. 111. 4); in AD 12 he and his brother Magius Celer Velleianus, who had also served in Dalmatia (2. 115. 1), took part in Tiberius' Illyrian *triumph; and, when Augustus died in AD 14, both brothers were already designated 'candidates of Caesar' (*candidati Caesaris*) for the praetorship of AD 15 (2. 124. 4). Nothing further is certainly known of him, except that he dedicated his work to Marcus Vinicius, the consul of AD 30, the presumed year of its publication. There is no evidence for the suggestion that he was executed in the aftermath of *Sejanus' fall in AD 31; the suffect consuls (see CONSUL) of AD 60 and 61 are thought to be two sons.

Velleius' work begins with Greek mythology and ends in AD 29, a span of time which he encompassed in only two volumes. 'I hardly know any historical work of which the scale is so small, and the subject so extensive', said Macaulay. Like Cornelius Nepos and Florus he is thus a writer of summary history, something to which he draws frequent attention (1. 16. 1, 2. 29. 2, 38. 1, 41. 1, 52. 3, 55. 1, 66. 3, 86. 1, 89. 1, 96. 3, 99. 4, 108. 2, 124. 1). Almost all of book 1 is now lost: not only do we lack the preface and very beginning of the narrative but a vast lacuna has deprived us of his history of Rome between the time of *Romulus (1. 8. 4–6) and the battle of Pydna in 168 BC (1. 9), although a stray fragment on Cimon (1. 8. 6) shows that he continued to refer to Greek history at least as late as the 5th cent. BC. Book 1 is separated from book 2 by two excursuses, which would be notable even in a full-length history (1. 14–15 on Roman colonization, see COLONIZATION, ROMAN; 1. 16–18 on Greek and Latin literature); and book 2 begins, as the narrative part of book 1 had ended (12–13), with the destruction of *Carthage in 146 BC, which Velleius, like *Sallust, saw as a turning-point in Roman history. Although the following years to 59 BC are dispatched in a mere 40 chapters, which notably include three further excursuses of varying length (2. 9 and 36. 2–3 on Roman authors, 2. 38–9 on Roman provincialization), Velleius devotes increasing amounts of space to *Caesar (2. 41–59), Augustus (2. 59–93), and especially Tiberius (2. 94–131), whose career forms the climax of his work. Whether he intended seriously to write his own full-length history, as he often promises (2. 48. 5, 89. 1, 96. 3, 99. 3, 103. 4, 114. 4, 119. 1), is uncertain.

Though Velleius constantly imitates the phraseology of both Sallust and *Cicero, it is the fullness and balance (*concinnitas*) of the latter's style that he aimed generally to reproduce. His sentences, replete with antithesis and point, are often long and involved; and he has a gift for pithy characterization. Yet readers have been dismayed by the successive rhetorical questions (e.g. 2. 122) and exclamations (e.g. 2. 129–30) in his account of Tiberius, which in general, like his treatment of Sejanus (2. 127–8), has been regarded as mere panegyric. On such grounds Sir Ronald Syme and most other 20th-cent. scholars have dismissed with contempt his work as a whole.

Yet in imperial times the traditional patriotism of Roman historians was inevitably focused on the emperor of the day, who in Velleius' case was also his former commander; and his account of Tiberius is valuable in presenting the establishment view of events for which Tacitus, from the safer perspective of the 2nd cent. AD, supplies an opposition view. Even so the prayer, which forms the unconventional conclusion to his work (2. 131), is arguably a recognition of the political crisis of AD 29, while the treatment of Sejanus, which is not a panegyric of the man but a defence of his elevation by Tiberius, betrays some of the very unease which it seems designed to dispel.

Velleius, like *Polybius, travelled widely (cf. 2. 101. 3); he was a senator, like Sallust and *Tacitus, and held magister-ial office; like *Thucydides he witnessed and took part in a significant number of the events he describes (cf. 2. 104. 3, 106. 1, 113. 3, 118. 1). He thus enjoyed many of the advantages conventionally associated with the ideal historian. He regularly provides information on topics about which we would otherwise be ignorant; and he is the only Latin historian of Roman affairs to have survived from the period between *Livy and Tacitus. These seem reasons enough to justify his more favourable assessment in recent years.

Velleius' text depends upon a single codex, designated M, discovered by Beatus Rhenanus at Murbach in 1515 but now lost. From a lost copy of the codex derive both Amerbach's apograph (1516) and Rhenanus' first edition (dated 1520, Basel), the latter containing Burer's collation of the edition with M. The relative merits of apograph and first edition are disputed.   A. J. W.

Venus The debate over the original nature of this goddess, who does not belong to Rome's oldest pantheon but is attested fairly early at Lavinium, has been partly resolved (Schilling, *La Religion romaine de Vénus* (1954)). It is now accepted that the neuter †*venus*, 'charm', cannot be separated from the terms *venia*, *venerari*, *venenum* ('gracefulness', 'to exercise a persuasive charm', 'poison', against Radke, *Götter* 311 ff.). How this neuter was transformed into a feminine, a process attested for the Osco-Umbrian goddess Herentas, is ill-understood in the absence of evidence. Schilling thinks that it took place at the federal sanctuary of Lavinium, a city with old and well-attested links with the Greek world and the legend of *Troy. Whatever the case, from the 3rd cent. BC, Venus was the patron of all persuasive seductions, between gods and mortals, and between men and women (Venus Verticordia). Because of her links with the extraordinary power of *wine, Venus is presented in the rites and myth of the Vinalia as a powerful mediatrix between *Jupiter and the Romans. The first known temple is that of Venus Obsequens ('Propitious'), vowed in 295 BC and built some years later. During the Punic Wars (see ROME (HISTORY) §1.4), the tutelary and diplomatic role of Venus grew continually, in proportion to the process of her assimilation to Greek *Aphrodite. In the 1st cent. BC she even acquired a political value. She was claimed by *Sulla as his protectress (his *agnomen* Epaphroditus means 'favoured by Venus'), as by *Pompey (Venus Victrix) and *Caesar (Venus Genetrix), while *Aphrodisias in Caria benefited progressively from important privileges. Under the empire Venus became one of the major divinities of the official pantheon.   J. Sch.

Vergina in N. Greece. See AEGAE.

Vespasian (Titus Flavius Vespasianus), emperor AD 69–79, was born on 9 November AD 9, at Sabine Reate. His father, Flavius Sabinus was a tax-gatherer; his mother also was of equestrian family, but her brother entered the senate, reaching the praetorship. Vespasian was military tribune in 27, serving in Thrace, quaestor in Crete in the mid-30s, aedile (at the second attempt) in 38, and praetor in 40. Claudius' *freedman, Narcissus, now advanced his undistinguished career, and he became legate of legion II Augusta, commanding it in the invasion of *Britain in 43 and subduing the south-west as far as Exeter (43–7); for this he won triumphal ornaments, and two priesthoods (see PRIESTS (GREEK AND ROMAN)). He was suffect consul (see CONSUL) in November–December 51 and is next heard of as an unpopular proconsul of Africa (*c*.62 (see AFRICA, ROMAN)); any unemployment may be due to the deaths of Narcissus and Lucius Vitellius and the eclipse of other supporters during the ascendancy of *Agrippina. In 66 he accompanied Nero to Greece and allegedly offended him by falling asleep at one of his recitals, but at the end of the year he was entrusted with suppressing the rebellion in Judaea. By mid-68 he had largely subdued Judaea apart from Jerusalem itself but conducted no further large-scale campaigns.

Vespasian now settled his differences with the governor of Syria, Gaius Licinius Mucianus. They successively recognized Galba, Otho, and Aulus Vitellius, but the idea of using the eastern legions to attain power became a plan in the spring of 69. On 1 July the two Egyptian legions under Tiberius Iulius Alexander proclaimed Vespasian; those in Judaea did so on 3 July, and the Syrian legions a little later. Mucianus set out with a task-force against Italy while Vespasian was to hold up the grain ships at *Alexandria and probably *Carthage. However, the Danubian legions declared for Vespasian, and the legionary legate Marcus Antonius Primus invaded Italy. After his crushing victory at Cremona the city was brutally sacked. Primus fell from favour in 70 and took the blame. It was alleged that Primus' invasion was against orders (certainly Mucianus would have opposed his action), but victory could never have been bloodless. Primus pressed on, entering Rome on 21 December, the day after Vitellius' death. The senate immediately conferred all the usual powers on Vespasian, though he dated his tribunician years from 1 July, negating the acts of senate and people and treating his legions as an electoral college.

A fragment of an enabling law has survived (*ILS* 244 = EJ 364, trans. D. Braund, *Augustus to Nero* no. 293) conferring powers, privileges, and exemptions, most with Julio-Claudian precedents. It is disputed whether this was part of the original tralatician grant of powers, surviving only in Vespasian's case, or of a supplementary grant, due to difficulties with the senate, conferring by law the right to perform acts never questioned in a Julio-Claudian but which from Vespasian might be challenged. It sanctioned all he had done up to the passing of the law and empowered him to act in whatever way he deemed advantageous to the Roman people. Vespasian's standing was lower than that of any of his predecessors and the law took the place of the *auctoritas* (prestige, influence) he lacked. Vespasian was careful to publicize a number of divine omens which portended his accession; he frequently took the consulship, however briefly, and accumulated imperatorial salutations.

Vespasian insisted that the succession would devolve on his son (Suet. *Div. Vesp.* 25; sons, Dio Cass. 65. 12). Controversy over the dynastic principle, part of a wider controversy over the role of the senate in government, may have caused his quarrel with doctrinaire senators like Helvidius Priscus, who was exiled and later executed.

Vespasian returned to Italy in the late summer of 70. While at Alexandria he had been concerned with raising money, and his sales of imperial estates and new taxes caused discontent there. He claimed that forty thousand million sesterces (so Suet. *Div. Vesp.* 16. 3) were needed to support the state. He increased, sometimes doubled, provincial taxation and revoked imperial immunities. Such measures were essential after the costs incurred by Nero and the devastation of the civil wars; contemporaries inevitably charged Vespasian with 'avarice'. He was able to restore the Capitol, burnt in December 69, to build his forum and temple of Peace, and to begin the *Colosseum. An attempt by senators in 70 to diminish expenditure by the state treasury (*aerarium*), so promoting senatorial independence, was promptly vetoed.

It may have been in part for financial reasons that in 73–4 he held the censorship with his son *Titus. But both as censor and previously, he recruited many new members, Italian and provincial, to the senate, and conferred rights on communities abroad, notably a grant of Latin rights (*ius Latii*, the right to Roman *citizenship after holding local office) to all native communities in Spain.

Vespasian restored discipline to the armies after the events of 68–9. Before his return Mucianus had reduced the praetorian guard, enlarged by Vitellius, to approximately its old size, and they were entrusted to Titus on his return. The legions were regrouped so that Vitellian troops would not occupy dangerous positions. In the east Vespasian by the end of his reign had substituted three armies (six legions) in Syria, Cappadocia, and Judaea for the single army (until Nero's time only four legions) in Syria. After the Jewish and Rhineland rebellions had been suppressed, Vespasian continued imperial expansion with the annexation of northern England, the pacification of Wales, and an advance into Scotland (see BRITAIN), as well as in SW Germany between Rhine and Danube.

On his death on 23 June 79 he was accorded deification, though Titus did not act at once (he had been Vespasian's colleague since 71 and the ceremony, last held on Claudius' death in 54, may have seemed discredited). Unassuming behaviour had partially conciliated the aristocracy, although some of his friends were informers or otherwise disreputable; Tacitus, *Hist.* 1. 50, claims that he was the first man to improve after becoming emperor, and the reign seems to have been tranquil after conflicts with the senate had been won. The years after 75 were marred (as far as is known) only by Titus' execution of Aulus Caecina Alienus and his forcing Marcellus to suicide.

Vespasian was industrious, and his simple life a model for contemporaries. Matching his rugged features he cultivated a bluff manner, parading humble origins and ridiculing a man who corrected his accent. His initial appointments (Lucius Caesennius Paetus; Quintus Petillius Cerialis Caesius Rufus) show astuteness in building a powerful party of which the core was his own family. To have ended the wars was an achievement, and *Pax* (peace) was a principal motif on his coinage. His proclaimed purposes were the restoration and enhancement of the state, and he made no great break with tradition. In style of government, however, and in the composition of the governing class, the reign paved the way for the 2nd cent.

Nothing is known of Vespasian's education (he was no orator, but could quote *Homer), but his sons were cultivated, and he attended to the needs of Rome and the empire by founding chairs of rhetoric and philosophy and by granting fiscal privileges to teachers and doctors.

Vespasian's wife Flavia Domitilla was alleged to be only of Latin status until her father Liberalis proved her Roman citizenship. Besides his two sons she bore a daughter also named Flavia Domitilla; wife and daughter died before Vespasian's accession. He then lived with an earlier mistress, Caenis, a freedwoman of Antonia.

G. E. F. C.; B. M. L.

Vesta, Vestals Vesta was the Roman goddess of (the hearth-) fire, *custos flammae* (Ov. *Fast.* 6. 258, comm. F. Bömer), one of the twelve *di consentes*. The cult is also known from *Pompeii and Latium: it was believed to have been introduced into Rome by Pompilius Numa—or *Romulus—from Alba Longa (Dion. Hal. *Ant. Rom.* 2. 64. 5 ff.; Serv. on *Aen.* 1. 273). An ancient etymology linked Vesta to Greek Hestia (Cic. *Nat. D.* 2. 67): her cult expressed and guaranteed Rome's permanence. Vesta's main public shrine, never inaugurated *certis verbis* and so never a true *templum* (temple), was a circular building just south-east of Augustus' arch in the *forum Romanum (the original 7th-cent. BC shape is unknown). In the late republic its form was taken to be that of a primitive house, intimating a connection between public and private cults of the hearth. In the historical period, the state cult (Vestalia, 9 June) effectively displaced private cults. There was no statue of Vesta within the shrine (Ov. *Fast.* 295–8): it contained only the fire and, in the *penus* (inner sanctum), the 'sacred things that may not be divulged'—esp. the Palladium (Livy, 26. 27. 14), and the *fascinum*, the erect phallus that averted evil. On being elected *pontifex maximus* (head of one of the major colleges of *priests) in 12 BC, Augustus created another shrine for Vesta on the Palatine.

Though she bore the title *mater*, Vesta was thought of as virgin, by contrast with her sisters *Juno and Ceres. She was 'the same as the earth', which also contains fire, and was sacrificed to on low altars; she protected all altar-fires. Her character gains contour from a contrast with *Vulcan. The sacral status of the six *sacerdotes Vestales*, the Vestal virgins (the sole female priesthood in Rome), was manifested in many ways. Though they were required to maintain strict sexual purity during their minimum of 30 years' service, their dress (*stola*, *vittae*) alluded to matrons' wear,

their hair-style probably to a bride's. They were excised from their own family (freed from their father's *potestas*, ineligible to inherit under the rules of intestacy) without acceding to another. It was a capital offence to pass beneath their litter in the street.

There were several restrictions upon eligibility (Gell. 1. 12. 1–7); most known Vestals are of senatorial family. Though they had many ceremonial roles, their main ritual tasks were the preparation of the grain mixed with salt (*mola salsa*) for public sacrifices (Serv. *Ecl.* 8. 82) and the tending of Vesta's 'undying fire' (*ignis inextinctus*). The extinction of the fire provided the prima facie evidence that a Vestal was impure: impurity spelled danger to Rome. The last known case of living entombment in the Campus Sceleratus (near Colline gate) occurred under *Domitian in AD ?89 (Plin. *Ep.* 4. 11; cf. Plut. *Num.* 10. 4–7). The last known chief vestal (*vestalis maxima*) is Coelia Concordia (AD 380); the cult was finally abandoned in 394. R. L. G.

villa was the Latin word for a rural dwelling associated with an estate, and ranging in character from functional farms to the luxurious country seats of the élite (Varro, *Rust.* 1. 11. 1–12. 4; 3. 2. 1–2. 18). Most of the literary evidence relates to Italy and primarily described farms run for the benefit of urban-based proprietors (Vitr. *De arch.* 6. 6. 1), though the most opulent seaside villas of the Roman aristocracy were sometimes built solely for pleasure. Aristocratic enjoyment of rural retreats and pride in creating architectural splendours there are well attested (Pliny, *Ep.* 2. 17). However, the classic Italian villa, comprising a luxurious dwelling for the use of the owner on visits to the estate (*pars urbana*), the working farm buildings (*pars rustica*), and the storage buildings and barns (*pars fructuaria*), is perfectly illustrated by the excavations at Settefinestre, with its aristocratic *domus* (mansion), baths, slave quarters, wine and olive presses, piggery, substantial granary, and formal gardens (A. Carandini and others, *Settefinestre* (1985); cf. Columella, *Rust.* 1. 4. 6–6. 24). The development of villas in different regions of Italy from the 2nd cent. BC is generally equated with the rise of large slave-run estates, though these regions commonly exhibit divergent patterns of rural settlement and varied types of villa (from simple farmhouses to 'palaces'). Similarly the relative success and longevity of villas differed from one part of Italy to another: certain coastal areas famous for viticulture in the late republic had declined markedly by the 2nd cent. AD, whereas villas in some inland areas survived into late antiquity.

Provincial villa studies suffer from a geographical imbalance, with far more excavated and published sites in north-western Europe than from the Mediterranean countries. In peripheral territories such as *Britain, where it can be exceedingly difficult to decide whether a particular structure would have been considered a villa by the Romans themselves, different criteria have commonly been used to define villas, encompassing aspects of Romanized construction or lifestyle (characterized by mosaics, painted

villas Reconstructed drawing of the Roman villa (later 1st cent. BC) excavated at mod. Settefinestre near Cosa (Tuscany). Fronted by a miniature 'town wall' with turrets, it is a classic Italian villa, combining elegant accommodation with a working farm.

plaster, hypocausts, baths, use of dressed stone and tile, etc.). Mediterranean-style peristyle houses are uncommon in Britain and Belgica (see GAUL (TRANSALPINE)), where winged corridor and aisled buildings tend to predominate, and other regions reveal their own characteristic styles. Important new approaches to villas in Britain look beyond their main Romanized buildings, to explore subsidiary farm buildings, field systems, pre-Roman and sub-Roman phases, and palaeoeconomic evidence for crops and livestock. See AGRICULTURE, ROMAN.

D. J. Ma.

Vindolanda tablets During the 1970s and 1980s several hundred wooden writing-tablets were discovered at the Roman fort of Vindolanda near Hadrian's Wall (see WALL OF HADRIAN); a further 400 turned up in 1993. Of the earlier finds, some were of the well-known stylus type, but the vast majority were made of thin, wooden leaves, written in ink with a pen. Only a handful of tablets of this type was previously known, and the concentration of such numbers at one site is unique. They date between *c.* AD 90 and 120, when the fort was occupied first by Cohors (cohort) I Tungrorum and later by Cohors IX Batavorum.

The Vindolanda material includes the largest group of Latin letters ever discovered. There are also literary fragments, shorthand texts, military reports, applications for leave, and accounts. The letters often bear on the official and private concerns of the officers, their families, and slaves, while the military documents tell us much about the way the Romans organized a newly acquired frontier area. In addition the tablets provide valuable information on palaeography and the *Latin language.

J. D. T.

Virgil (*see page 764*)

Vitruvius (Pol(l)io), a Roman architect and military engineer, in which capacity he served *Caesar. He built a basilica at Fanum Fortunae in Umbria; but his fame rests chiefly on a treatise, *De architectura*, on architecture and engineering, compiled partly from his own experience, partly from work by Hermogenes (to whom he is heavily indebted) and other Greek authors to which his own experiences have been added, sometimes in a disjointed fashion. It is hardly a handbook for architects: rather a book for people who need to understand architecture. Perhaps its main function was place-seeking from Octavian (see AUGUSTUS), to whom it is addressed. His outlook is essentially Hellenistic, and there is a marked absence of reference to important buildings of *Augustus' reign, though he knows of Roman technical developments, such as concrete construction (which he mistrusts). *De architectura*, the only work of its kind which has survived, is divided into ten books. Book 1 treats of town-planning, architecture in general, and of the qualifications proper in an architect; 2 of building-materials; 3 and 4 of temples and of the 'orders'; 5 of other civic buildings; 6 of domestic buildings; 7 of pavements and decorative plaster-work; 8 of water-supplies; 9 of geometry, mensuration, *astronomy, etc.; 10 of machines, civil and military. The information on materials and methods of construction in 2 and 7, and on rules of proportion in 3 and 4, is of great value.

Vitruvius' importance as an architect is very nearly matched by his significance as a historian of many different departments of ancient science and philosophy, ranging from mathematics to astronomy, to meteorology and medicine. Just as the Hippocratic doctors appreciated the

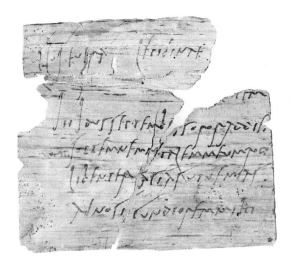

Vindolanda tablets A wooden tablet from Vindolanda containing an invitation to a party from Claudia Severa to Sulpicia Lepidina. Women clearly played their part in efforts to maintain a Roman home-from-home on the northern frontier.

importance of environment to good health, Vitruvius appreciated that in its general and most humane form, architecture included everything which touches on the physical and intellectual life of man and his surroundings.

Often, his encyclopaedic concern with covering a subject thoroughly seems odd to us. In book 2. 1–2 of the *On Architecture* he suggests that the architect who uses bricks needs to be familiar with pre-Socratic theories of matter if he is to understand how his materials can be expected to behave. The doxographies are combed for suitable information. In book 9, the highly abstract geometry of Plato is put to the use of the surveyor—something of which Plato himself might hardly have approved. Similar practical use is made of the mathematics of Archytas, *Eratosthenes, Democritus, and Archimedes, and Vitruvius remains an important source for our knowledge of a great many early Greek scientists. (It was Vitruvius who preserved the famous story of Archimedes' discovery in his bathtub of a way of detecting the adulteration of king Hieron II of *Syracuse's golden crown (9, Pref. 9–12).) And so Vitruvius goes on, often employing the theories of the most anti-banausic Greek thinkers to elucidate his very practical subject. Astronomy is necessary for an understanding of the use of sundials, and surveying instruments; astrology for the insights it offers into the organization of human life; machines and their principles (book 10) because of their utility in the manipulation of materials. As he notes at 10. 1. 4, all machines are created by nature, and the revolutions of the universe ultimately set them in motion. For a man with interests practical and theoretical in equal measure, understanding the nature of nature was central to all.   R. A. T., J. T. V.

vivisection Squeamishness about the dissection (let alone vivisection) of animals is a mark of much ancient medicine and zoology, and there is no firm evidence for vivisection in those Hippocratic works (see MEDICINE §4) which are generally dated to the 5th or 4th cent. BC. (The passage in the Hippocratic treatise *On the Heart* describing the vivisection of a pig (9. 80 Littré) is generally dated to the 3rd cent. BC.) Physicians and zoologists from *Aristotle onwards do, however, seem to have vivisected animals and in some cases even humans. Practitioners themselves rarely show signs of concern with the morality of causing animals suffering in the name of knowledge, although such concern was voiced in other quarters (see ANIMALS, ATTITUDES TO and KNOWLEDGE ABOUT).

Two ancient physicians are notoriously connected with the practice of human vivisection. Aulus Cornelius Celsus reports that the Alexandrian anatomists Herophilus and Erasistratus vivisected criminals provided for them by the king (see ANATOMY AND PHYSIOLOGY §IV). Erasistratus at least seems to have been motivated by the belief that the bodies of the living and the dead differ in important physical respects, and that conclusions drawn from the study of a cadaver will not necessarily hold for a living man. Celsus remarks (*De medicina* 1, Proem 26) that the practice had its supporters, who argued that agony for a few is justified by the widespread benefits that accrue from increased understanding of the body's vital functions, but Celsus himself regards it with distaste. The other major ancient witness, Tertullian (*De anima* 10), manifests his Christian horror at the practice. The truth of these reports has been fiercely disputed in modern times. Some feel that it is difficult to *prove* that human subjects were ever used—and they add

[*continued on p. 772*]

Virgil

Virgil (Publius Vergilius Maro) (70–19 BC), Latin poet. The contemporary spelling of Virgil's name was with an *e*: the first occurrence with an *i* is on an honorific inscription to Claudian in Greek (*CIL* 6. 1710 = *ILS* 1. 2949). Virgil is traditional in English, but the slightly historicizing Vergil is preferred by some modern critics. Virgil and his friends in any case punned on *virgo*, a virgin (*G*. 4. 564, perhaps 1. 430, Donatus' 'Life' of Virgil 11). Varius Rufus is said to have written on Virgil (Quint. 10. 3. 8) and there were other accounts by friends and acquaintances (cf. Gell. *NA* 17. 10. 2): the extant lives go back in part to *Suetonius, *De poetis*. Much (but not all) of the information in them derives from interpretation of the poems (including the spurious ones in the *Appendix Vergiliana*), and few details, however circumstantial, can be regarded as certain.

Nevertheless, Virgil is said to have been born on 15 October 70 BC in Andes, a village near Mantua. Macrobius (*Sat*. 5. 2. 1) says that he was 'born in the Veneto of country parents and brought up amongst the woods and shrubs', and his father is variously described as a potter and a courier who married the boss's daughter (Donat. *Vit. Verg*. 1), but the real status of the family is uncertain. His mother was a Magia: both the *gentes* (families) covered a spectrum of social levels. Virgil is said to have been educated in Cremona and Milan (Mediolanum) before coming to Rome (Donat. *Vit. Verg*. 7) and the family would clearly have had to be sufficiently well-off for such an education to be feasible. At some stage Virgil was associated with the Epicurean (see EPICURUS) community in Naples (Neapolis; see M. Gigante, *Stud. Ital*. 1989, 3–6: his name appears in a papyrus from *Herculaneum with Plotius Tucca, Varius Rufus, and Publius Quinctilius Varus); *Catalepton* 5 and 8, if either genuine or based on a sound biographical tradition, have him fleeing from the normal rhetorical education of a Roman to Epicurean retirement (cf. *G*. 4. 563–4, where he is again (?) enjoying *otium*, leisure, in Naples).

After the defeat of the tyrannicides (the murderers of *Caesar) in 42 BC, Octavian (see AUGUSTUS) attempted to settle members of his army on confiscated land, a controversial move which led to the so-called Perusine War (named after Perusia, mod. Perugia): full-scale war between Mark *Antony and Octavian was only narrowly (and temporarily) avoided by the treaty of Brundisium in 40 BC. Virgil's first collection of poems, the *Eclogues*, probably appeared around 39–38 BC (controversial: see R. J. Tarrant and G. W. Bowersock in *Harv. Stud*. 1978, 197–202) in the midst of the turmoil: the confiscations are a central topic in *Eclogues* 1 and 9. In the first poem, a slave Tityrus says that he has to thank a young man for freedom and security (1. 42): in the context of the times, this can only be Octavian. Other poems mention a Varus (6. 7, 9. 27), presumably the jurist Publius Alfenus Varus, suffect consul (see CONSUL) 39 BC, Gaius Asinius Pollio (4. 12, and probably the addressee of 8—for the controversy, see Tarrant and Bowersock), consul 40 BC, one of Antony's most important supporters and an architect of the Peace of Brundisium, and the important *eques* and poet C. Cornelius Gallus (6. 64–73, 10 *passim*). These three men are said to have been involved in the distribution of land, though the arrangements are uncertain and the Virgilian commentators our only source (cf. *MRR* 2. 377–8). The biographical tradition says that Virgil's father's land was amongst the land confiscated, and some personal experience of loss is suggested by *Ecl*. 9. 27–9 'Mantua, all too near to unhappy Cremona' and *G*. 2. 198 'the land unfortunate Mantua lost', but it is impossible to know how many of the details derive from allegorical reading of the poems.

At some time after the publication of the *Eclogues*, Virgil entered the circle of *Maecenas, and thus of the future Augustus. He is mentioned several times in the first book of *Horace's *Satires*, published at the end of the decade; in 1. 6. 55 he is said to have introduced Horace to Maecenas, and in 1. 5 (40, 48) he is described as joining the 'journey to Brundisium'. The dramatic date of the latter poem is 38 or 37, depending on which of the two possible diplomatic missions it is associated with (cf. I. M. Le M. DuQuesnay, in T. Woodman and D. West, *Poetry and Politics in the Age of Augustus* (1984), 39–43). In the concluding satire of the book (1. 10. 45, cf. 81) Virgil is one of the poets whose achievements Horace contrasts with his own: 'to Virgil the Muses who delight in the countryside have granted tenderness and charm' (*molle atque facetum*, trans. P. M. Brown). The sixteenth of Horace's *Epodes* (*Iambi*), also published at the end of the 30s, parodies *Ecl.* 4 in a context which highlights the violent alternation of hope and despair which characterized the decade.

The publication of Virgil's second major work, the *Georgics*, is usually dated to 29 BC; the battle of *Actium (31 BC) is referred to in *Georgics* 3. 28–9 and according to the Donatus Life, Virgil read the poem to Octavian 'after his return from the victory at Actium' (Donat. *Vit. Verg.* 27): Octavian reached Italy in the summer of 29 BC, and celebrated a great 'triple triumph' in August of that year, though the description of his achievements as depicted on the metaphorical temple at the opening of *Georgic* 3 (26–39) can plausibly be dated before or after this triumph. There was a story that the work had originally ended with praise of Cornelius Gallus, which was removed after his fall and suicide in 26 BC (Servius on *Ecl.* 10. 1; *G.* 4. 1) but this is unlikely to be true (J. Griffin, *Latin Poets and Roman Life* (1985), 180–2).

Like the *Eclogues*, the *Georgics* are a constant presence in the poetry of the 20s BC, but by the time that the final poem of *Propertius' second (?) book of elegies is published some time after Gallus' death (2. 34. 91–2), 'something greater than the *Iliad* is being brought to birth' (2. 34. 66), that is, the *Aeneid*. Macrobius quotes a letter from Virgil to Augustus declining to send any samples as more work is needed; this may be a reply to the letter of Augustus quoted at Donat. *Vit. Verg.* 31 asking for a sketch or fragment, and to be dated to 27–25 BC since Augustus is described as away from Rome in Spain. It is possible, however, that more scepticism as to the genuineness of these letters is in order. Horace, *Odes* 1. 3 addresses a ship carrying a Vergilius to Greece; if this is taken to be Virgil, the bold enterprise of the ship's journey may also be read metapoetically of the vast undertaking of the *Aeneid*. The tradition claims that books 2 (or 3), 4, and 6 were recited to Augustus, the reference to the young Marcus Claudius Marcellus in 6 causing Marcellus' mother Octavia to faint (*Vit. Don.* 32; Servius on *Aen.* 4. 323, 6. 861); this episode, whether true or not, must be set after the death of Marcellus in 23 BC. Virgil himself, however, died in 19 BC, with the poem apparently felt to be unfinished: 'in the 42nd year of his life, intending to finish the *Aeneid*, he decided to go off to Greece and Asia Minor, and to spend three straight years simply in correcting the poem, to leave the rest of his life free for philosophy. But when he had set out on his trip, he met Augustus in Athens returning to Rome from the east, and decided not to go off, and even to return with Augustus. He visited a small town near Megara in very hot sun and caught a fever; this was made worse by his continued journey, to the extent that he was somewhat sicker when he put into Brundisium, where he died on 20 September' (Donat. *Vit. Verg.* 35). He was buried at Naples 'within the second milestone on the road to Puteoli' (Donat. *Vit. Verg.* 36: this does not fit the tomb known to tradition), and is said to have composed his own epitaph on his death-bed:

> Mantua me genuit, Calabri rapuere, tenet nunc
> Parthenope; cecini pascua rura duces.

> Mantua bore me, Calabria snatched me away, now
> Naples holds me; I sang of pastures, fields, and kings.

Varius Rufus and Plotius Tucca were said to have 'emended' the *Aeneid* after Virgil's death, but without making any additions. The tradition also preserves the famous story that Virgil wished to burn the *Aeneid* on his death-bed: like everything else in the tradition, this may or may not be true.

Propertius' prophecy came to pass on the publication of the *Aeneid*: Virgil became the Roman *Homer, the *Aeneid* in particular serving as the great Roman classic against which later epic poets and in a sense all Latin poets had to situate themselves (cf. P. Hardie, *The Epic Successors of Vergil* (1993), cf. e.g. Pliny, *Ep.* 3. 7. 8 on Silius' veneration). Schoolboys studied it, even in Roman Egypt (R. Cavenaile,

Corpus Papyrorum Latinorum (1958), 7–70), and its opening words became a common graffito on the walls of *Pompeii (R. P. Hoogma, *Der Einfluss Vergils auf die Carmina Latina Epigraphica* (1952)). Already in his lifetime Virgil is said to have been famous (Tac. *Dial.* 13. 3) and his friendship with the great brought him considerable wealth: according to Valerius Probus' Life (15–16) he was given ten million sesterces by Augustus (cf. Hor. *Epist.* 2. 1. 245–7 with Helenius Acro's comm.). As with Homer, all human learning came to be seen as condensed in the *Aeneid*, a view which finds full expression in Macrobius' *Saturnalia*: the ancient biographical tradition already shows a tendency to see Virgil as a *theios anēr*, a divine genius, and this became pronounced in the Middle Ages, with the legends of Virgil the Magician (D. Comparetti, *Virgilio nel Medievo²*, ed. G. Pasquali (1937–41; 1st edn. trans. E. F. Benecke 1895); cf. also C. G. Leland, *The Unpublished Legends of Virgil* (1879); J. W. Spargo, *Virgil the Necromancer* (1934); V. Zabughin, *Virgilio nel rinascimento italiano* (1921–3)). The text of the *Aeneid* was consulted as an *oracle in the *sortes Vergilianae* (cf. SHA *Hadr.* 2. 8).

A number of portraits of Virgil are known (*Enc. Virg.* V** 103–4; there is no reason to believe that any are based on a genuine likeness, but the tradition describes him as a valetudinarian who never married and preferred sex with boys (variously identified amongst the characters of the poems). All of this, naturally, tells us more about Roman constructions of gender and culture than about 'the man Virgil'.

The Literary Works The Eclogues

If any of the poems in the *Appendix Vergiliana* are genuine (which is unlikely), they may have been juvenilia, but essentially Virgil enters world literature with his first collection, the *Eclogues*, published probably around 39–38 BC (see above): ten short hexameter poems (the longest is 111 lines long) in the pastoral genre. The original title was *Bucolica*, 'cowherd songs' (*Eclogae*, N. Horsfall, *BICS* 1981, 108); *eclogae* means 'selections (from a larger corpus)' and it is unfortunate that a version of this later title has become usual in English. *Bucolica* as a title signals a clear allusion to pastoral (in Greek *ta bukolika*) and to *Theocritus in particular (cf. the refrain 'begin the bucolic song' in *Idyll* 1; in Moschus 3. 11 the pastoral poet Bion is called a cowherd, *boukolos*), and the collection makes constant reference to Theocritus' *Idylls*: commentators note four separate echoes in the first line. But the intertextuality with earlier Roman poetry is as dense: the opening lines are also significantly Lucretian (cf. G. Castelli, *RSC* 1966, 313–42; 1967, 14–39; see LUCRETIUS) and the 'Song of Silenus' in the sixth poem seems to interact with a broad selection of contemporary poetry, hints of only some of which are we able to pick up (cf. D. O. Ross, *Backgrounds to Augustan Poetry* (1975), 25; P. E. Knox, *Ovid's Metamorphoses and the Tradition of Augustan Poetry* (1986), 11–26).

This combination of the Greek and the Roman, the ancient and the contemporary, and the rustic and the sophisticated is typical of the collection as a whole. Although we do not know exactly in what form the poems of Theocritus and the other bucolic poets circulated in Rome (cf. A. F. S. Gow, *Theocritus* (1952), i. lix–lxii, lxvi–lxxii), it is likely that any edition included both the strictly pastoral poems like the first idyll, urban mimes like 15, and the encomiastic poems 16 and 17. In one sense, Virgil carries this mixture further: just as Theocritus addresses his friend Nicias in the frame of *Idyll* 11, Virgil addresses Varus in 6 (though there Virgil is called 'Tityrus' himself by Apollo) and Pollio (?) in 8, but his contemporaries also make an appearance *within* the bucolic setting (3. 84–91, 6. 64–73, 9. 47, 10 *passim*). *Idyll* 7, the nearest equivalent in Theocritus, is much less explicit. In another sense, however, Virgil is more consistently pastoral: the encomiastic birth poem 4, explicitly *paulo maiora*, 'a little greater (in theme)', is still more consistently pastoral than Theocritus 16 or 17 (cf. *Ecl.* 4. 3, 21–2, 42–5, 55–9).

The ten poems are intricately arranged around the central poem 5; the first and ninth poems deal with the subject of the land confiscations, 2 and 8 contain long laments by star-crossed lovers, 3 and 7 are both 'amoebean' (i.e. with exchanges of song), and 4 and 6 are the most obviously 'elevated' of the collection. Poem 5, another amoebean exchange, describes the apotheosis of Daphnis; 10 concludes the collection with Cornelius Gallus taking on the role of dying lover played by Daphnis in Theocritus, *Idyll* 1. Some supplement this patterning with numerological correspondences, of varying suggestiveness (cf. J. Van Sickle, *The Design of Virgil's Bucolics* (1978)); certainly *Eclogue* 4, which is 63 (9×17) lines long, is structured around the magical number seven, but this has special point in relation to its oracular tone and subject-matter. The collection equally responds, however, to a serial reading. There is a clear movement from the first poem, where Tityrus describes how his land was saved, to the ninth, where Moeris says that he was not so fortunate: 'our poems, Lycidas, have as much power amongst the weapons of *Mars as they say the Chaonian doves have when the eagle comes' (9. 11–13, with a pun on the 'eagle' of the legionary standard). Poem 6 opens with a 'proem in the middle' (cf. G. B. Conte, *YClS* 1992, 147–59) which echoes the opening of *Callimachus' *Aetia* and establishes the pastoral *deductum carmen*, 'fine-spun song', as the equivalent to Callimachus' 'slender muse' (*Ecl.* 6. 5, cf. 6. 8). At the end of the collection, Gallus gives in to love (10. 69), the poet rises from his pastoral ease in the shade (75–6), and the goats are told to go home, now fed to satiety (77).

As this suggests, the *Eclogues* are highly 'artificial' and metaliterary, and the relation of the world of song to the world outside is a central concern. Virgil toys with a variety of partial identifications in the poems: in 5. 86–7 Menalcas claims to have written *Eclogues* 2 and 3 and in 9. 10 Lycidas says that the same character 'saved all with his poems' but *Apollo calls the narrator Tityrus in 6. 4 and it is not hard to see him in the idle singer of an empty day in the first poem (cf. *G.* 565–6); in a broader sense he is also the helpless Corydon of 2 and the magical Silenus (see SATYRS AND SILENS) of 6. Interwoven with and inseparable from the literary texture are the celebrated descriptive passages that so appealed to Romantic enthusiasts like Samuel Palmer, the buzzing bees and cool springs of the pastoral world (cf. e.g. 1. 51–8). The union of the two was an inheritance from Theocritus which Virgil passed on to the west, particularly through Renaissance imitators like Mantuan and especially Sannazaro; although 'Arcadia' is mentioned only rarely in the poems (7. 4, 26, 10. 31, 33, cf. 4. 58–9, 10. 26) and its significance is disputed (B. Snell, *The Discovery of the Mind*, trans. T. G. Rosenmeyer, ch. 13; D. Kennedy, *Hermathena* 1984, 47–59; R. Jenkyns, *JRS* 1989, 26–39), the *Eclogues* came to signify Arcady as a place where poetry and love meet with or avoid the worlds of politics, cities, and empires.

One of the *Eclogues* came to have particular significance for later readers: *Eclogue* 4, with its description of the birth of a child whose lifetime will see a return of the world to the golden age. There were several possible candidates for the identification of the child even for contemporary readers (cf. E. Coleiro, *An Introduction to Vergil's Bucolics with an Edition of the Text* (1979), 222–32: the modern favourite is an anticipated son of Mark *Antony and Octavia, a hope already dashed by the time of the *Eclogues'* publication), but the poem can equally be read as a broader allegory of renewal; Christian readers naturally saw reference to the birth of Jesus (cf. Coleiro, 232–3; Constantine, *Oratio ad sanctum coetum* 19–21, *PL* 8. 454–66). The influence of Jewish messianic writing on the poem is nowhere a required hypothesis, but is not in itself unlikely (cf. R. G. M. Nisbet, *BICS* 1978, 59–78). See PASTORAL POETRY, GREEK and LATIN.

The Georgics

Virgil's call to himself to 'rise' at the end of the *Eclogues* (10. 75 *surgamus*) was answered by a rise in generic level with his next work, the *Georgics*, a didactic poem in four books on farming (book 1: crops, book 2: trees and shrubs, book 3: livestock, book 4: bees). Again there are Hellenistic Greek models: little can be said of the lost *Georgica* of Nicander (fragments in A. F. S. Gow and A. F. Scholfield, *Nicander* (1953), 145–61), but it is clear even from the fragments that we have of Callimachus' *Aetia* that that was an important model (four-book structure, and especially the links between the proem to the third and conclusion to the fourth book of each work: R. F. Thomas, *CQ* 1983, 92–113) and Aratus, *Phaenomena* was both a central Hellenistic text (translated by *Cicero and Publius Terentius Varro Atacinus) and of particular relevance to the discussion of weather in book 1 (cf. also the translation of a passage from *Eratosthenes at *G.* 1. 233–51). But there was also now an important archaic model in

*Hesiod's *Works and Days* (cf. 2. 176 *Ascraeum ... carmen*, 'Hesiodic song'), and the relationship to Lucretius' *De rerum natura* is so central that the *Georgics* may be seen as an *anti-Lucretius* (cf. P. R. Hardie, *Virgil's Aeneid: Cosmos and Imperium* (1986), 157–67, and in general J. Farrell, *Vergil's Georgics and the Traditions of Ancient Epic* (1991)). Lucretius' confident exposition of the power of reason is 'remythologized' into a more sceptical and yet more accepting attitude towards the natural world and its traditional divinities (2. 490–4).

Just as Aratus' *Phaenomena* had been based on a prose treatise of Eudoxus and the *De rerum natura* on Epicurean texts, especially the *Letter to Herodotus*, so the *Georgics* also have important prose models, though none is as central as in those texts. Virgil's sources for the agricultural lore were various (L. A. Jermyn, *G&R* 1949, 50) but the most significant was *Varro's *Res rusticae*, published in 37 BC and influential especially in books 3 and 4 (but note also *Rust.* 1. 1. 4–7 with the opening invocation of the gods in *G.* 1. 8–23, and *Rust.* 1. 69. 2–3 with the end of the first book). The didactic narrator is portrayed as a saviour-sage, taking pity on 'the farmers ... ignorant of the path' (1. 41, with Lucretian overtones: cf. Hardie, 158) but the practical advice avoids technical precision (in contrast to the fragments of Nicander) and the addressee is the extremely unrustic Maecenas (1. 2, 2. 41, 3. 41, 5. 2; cf. also L. P. Wilkinson, *The Georgics of Virgil* (1969), 52–5; S. Spurr, *G&R* 1986, 171–5). As with the *De rerum natura*, the central concern is rather the place in the world of human beings and their possibilities of happiness.

In the established manner of didactic poetry, passages of direct instruction are interspersed with 'digressions', descriptive or reflective passages with a more figured relationship to the main theme, such as *Jupiter's paternal disruption of the golden age (1. 121–59) or the 'praises of Italy' (2. 136–77). In particular, on the Lucretian model, the concluding section of each book stands out: the troubles of Italy in 1 (464–514), the virtues of the country life in 2 (475–540), the Noric plague in 3 (478–566, imitating the end of the *De rerum natura*: for book 3 as a microcosm of that work, cf. M. Gale, *CQ* 1991, 414–26), and especially the 'epyllion' (mini-epic) of Aristaeus and *Orpheus that ends book 4 (315–58). This last section dramatizes (but also in part deconstructs) the opposition between the successful conquest of nature through hard work (Aristaeus) and the pathos of loss and failure (Orpheus) which can be traced throughout the *Georgics* and which has led to a debate over the 'optimism' or 'pessimism' of the work which parallels similar disputes over the *Aeneid* (cf. D. O. Ross, *Virgil's Elements* (1987); C. Perkell, *The Poet's Truth* (1989); T. Habinek, in M. Griffith and D. J. Mastronarde (eds.), *Cabinet of the Muses* (1990), 209–23; and R. F. Thomas, *CPhil.* 1991, 211–18). The contemporary relevance of this is reinforced by a constant comparison between the bee society of book 4 and Rome (cf. J. Griffin, *Latin Poets* (1985), 163–82).

The poem concludes with an epilogue (modelled in part on the conclusion to Callimachus' *Aetia*) in which Virgil contrasts Augustus' 'thundering' on the Euphrates (cf. R. F. Thomas and R. Scodel, *AJPhil.* 1984, 339; J. Clauss, *AJPhil.* 1988, 309–20) with his own easeful retirement in Naples (4. 559–64) and looks back to the *Eclogues*, depicted as the playful work of his youth (565–6). At the opening of *Georgics* 3 he had promised to write a political epic (3. 46–8), a familiar enough turn in the *recusatio* (refusal to handle a topic), but just as Callimachus at the end of the *Aetia* prophesies a move 'down' to the *Iambi* (fr. 112), so at the end of the *Georgics* we are left feeling that for Virgil the next move would be 'up' in the hierarchy of genres (cf. Farrell, *Vergil's Georgics*).

Aeneid

Virgil's final work was the *Aeneid* (in Latin *Aeneis*), an account in twelve books of hexameter verse of the flight of *Aeneas from *Troy and his battles in Italy against Turnus to found a new home, the origin of Rome. As an *epic, the *Aeneid* occupies the summit of ancient generic classification. Epic was the sustained narration of great events ('kings and heroes' according to Callimachus fr. 1) by an inspired, omniscient, but distanced narrator; it was also the genre in which the anxiety of influence was greatest, since any epic was inevitably read against Homer's *Iliad* and *Odyssey*, by common consent the greatest poems of antiquity. Intertextuality with both poems is intense: the standard study takes 60 pages just to list the most obvious parallels (G. N. Knauer, *Die Aeneis und Homer* (1964), 371–431). The basic armature is that of the *Odyssey* (note also the focus on the hero in the title, though that has other implications: cf. *Aristotle, *Poetics* 1451ᵃ 20): the first half of each epic describes the wanderings of the hero, the second his fight for victory in his home (cf. also the 'overlap' in the book-structure in the middle of each: *Od*. 13. 1–91 with *Aen*. 7. 1–36, and contrast *Apollonius Rhodius, 3. 1), and Aeneas is harried by *Juno as *Odysseus is by *Poseidon, but the anger of Juno (cf. 1. 4, 11) also corresponds to the anger of *Achilles (and Apollo) in the *Iliad*, and the end of the poem is more like the battle between Achilles and *Hector in *Iliad* 22 than the killing of the suitors in *Odyssey* 22 (*contra* F. Cairns, *Virgil's Augustan Epic* (1989), 177–214). One may also contrast the first six books as 'Odyssean' with the second half as 'Iliadic' (cf. K. W. Gransden, *Virgil's Second Iliad* (1984): for a different version of this opposition, cf. D. Quint, *Epic and Empire* (1993)). But the correspondences with both epics go much further and much deeper (cf. Knauer, *Aeneis*; *ANRW* 2. 31. 2 (1981), 870–918; A. Barchiesi, *La traccia del modello* (1985); R. R. Schlunk, *The Homeric Scholia and the Aeneid* (1974)). The relationship is signalled in the famous opening words of the poem, *arma virumque cano*, 'arms and the man I sing', where 'arms' points to the *Iliad*, 'man' to the *Odyssey* (and 'I sing' perhaps to 'Cyclic' epic, cf. *Ilias parva* fr. 1).

Two other epics are also of importance: the *Argonautica* of Apollonius Rhodius (cf. D. P. Nelis, *The Aeneid and the Argonautica of Apollonius Rhodius* (1997)) and *Ennius' *Annales* (E. Norden (ed.), *Aen*. 6 (1926), 365–75; M. Wigodsky, *Vergil and Early Latin Poetry* (1972), 40–79). The relationship with Ennius is of great ideological significance (cf. G. B. Conte, *The Rhetoric of Imitation* (1986), 141–84). But the range of material whose traces may be interpreted in the *Aeneid* is vast: other earlier epics like Greek 'cyclic' epic (E. Christian Kopff, *ANRW* 2. 31. 2 (1981), 919–47) and *Naevius' *Punica* (M. Barchiesi, *Nevio Epico* (1962), 50–1 and *passim*), Greek and Roman tragedy (Wigodsky, 80–97; A. König, *Die Aeneis und die griechische Tragödie* (1970); P. Hardie, *PVS* 1991, 29–45), Hellenistic poetry (W. Clausen, *Virgil's Aeneid and the Tradition of Hellenistic Poetry* (1987)), lyric and elegy (F. Cairns, 129–76), and many other *genres (cf. N. Horsfall, *G&R* 1991, 203–11). The *Aeneid* thus both preserves the narrower generic norms of epic and expands the genre towards the variety that critics like M. Bakhtin have reserved for the modern novel, a process taken further by *Ovid (J. B. Solodow, *The World of Ovid's Metamorphoses* (1988), 25). The included genres maintain, however, their separate ideological implications.

Although the particular version of the Aeneas legend presented in the *Aeneid* has become canonical, the versions of the myth in the preceding tradition were many and varied (N. M. Horsfall, in J. N. Bremmer and N. M. Horsfall, *Roman Myth and Mythography*, *BICS* Suppl. 52 (1987), 12–24), and the reconstruction of the matrix of possibilities against which the *Aeneid* situates itself has always been a standard critical procedure (cf. esp. R. Heinze, *Virgil's Epic Technique*, trans. H. and D. Harvey and F. Robertson (1993); N. Horsfall, *Virgilio: l'epopea in alambicco* (1991)). It is clear that many of the details offered by Virgil were by no means the standard ones in his day, that his 'sources' were multiple, and that there was no compunction against free invention. The *Aeneid* is not therefore a 'safe' text to use for the investigation of early Latin history and cult. The story as told by Virgil takes the reader, as in the *Odyssey, in medias res*. Aeneas on his way to Italy is blown off course to North Africa by a storm instigated by Juno (book 1). There he meets Dido, and tells her the story of the fall of Troy (book 2) and his subsequent wanderings (book 3). He and Dido become lovers, and he forgets his mission; Mercury is sent to remind him, and his departure leads to Dido's tragic suicide (book 4). In book 5, the threat of another storm forces Aeneas to put into Sicily, where funeral games are celebrated for his dead father Anchises; after Juno instigates the Trojan women to burn the ships, part of the group are left behind in Sicily and Anchises appears in a dream to urge Aeneas to visit the Sibyl of Cumae (near Naples). The first half of the epic concludes with the consultation of the Sibyl and their visit to the underworld, where Aeneas meets his father and receives a vision of the future of Rome (book 6).

The events of the second half are described by Virgil as a 'greater work' (7. 44, *maius opus*). Landing in Latium, Aeneas sends a successful embassy of peace to the Latin king Latinus; but Juno uses the

Fury Allecto to stir up the young Rutulian king Turnus and Latinus' wife Amata to encourage war. Aeneas' son Iulus kills a pet stag while hunting, and from that small spark a full-blown war develops. Before battle commences we are given a catalogue of Italian forces (book 7). In book 8 Aeneas, advised by the god of the river Tiber in a dream, visits the Arcadian king Evander, who is living on the future site of Rome; Evander's young son Pallas joins the Trojan forces, and Aeneas receives a gift of armour from his mother Venus, including a shield which again depicts future events in the history of Rome, most notably the battle of Actium (book 8). In the succeeding books of fighting, emphasis falls on the terrible cost of the war, as the young lovers Nisus and Euryalus die in a night expedition (book 9), Turnus kills Pallas, and Aeneas kills both the equally tragic youth Lausus and his father the evil Mezentius (book 10), and Turnus' ally the female warrior Camilla is killed by an arrow to her breast (book 11). Finally in book 12 Aeneas and Turnus meet in single combat, despite Juno's attempts to delay the duel; Aeneas is victorious, and hesitates over sparing Turnus until he sees the sword-belt that Turnus had taken from the dead Pallas. In a paroxysm of love and anger, he slaughters Turnus.

Throughout the *Aeneid*, as this summary suggests, there is a strong narrative teleology, reaching beyond the events of the story to the future Rome. 'Fate' is a central concept; it coincides with the will of Jupiter, though the exact relationship is kept vague (C. Bailey, *Religion in Vergil* (1935), 204–40). Juno, pained and angry at past events (1. 25–8), attempts always to retard the progress of the story, as a sort of 'counter-fate' (7. 294, 313–16). She is always doomed to failure; at the end of the epic she is reconciled to the fate of Aeneas (12. 808–28) but we know that this is only temporary (10. 11–15: D. Feeney, in *Oxford Readings in Virgil's Aeneid* (1992), 339–62). Onto the opposition between the king and queen (1. 9) of heaven may be projected many other oppositions in the poem: heaven and hell, order and disorder, reason and emotion, success and failure, future and past, epic and tragedy. The treatment of these oppositions has been the central issue in the criticism of the *Aeneid*. It is clear that although many of them coincide, the contrast is never absolute: if Juno naturally turns to Allecto and the underworld (7. 312), Jupiter god of the bright sky (1. 253) also uses the infernal Dirae as the instruments of his wrath (12. 849–52); if Aeneas like Hercules (see *Heracles) (cf. 8. 299, contrast 2. 314) represents reason and self-control, he also concludes the epic with an act of passion (12. 946–7). It is possible to see these inconsistencies as 'energising contradictions' (C. Martindale, *Redeeming the Text* (1993), 51) which forge a successful viewpoint on the world; or to see them as undermining or subverting the claims to dominance of Roman order, as in the 'two-voices' school of criticism that came to prominence in Harvard in the 1960s (cf. A. Parry, *Arion* 1963, 66–80; W. Clausen, *Harv. Stud.* 1964, 139–47; M. C. J. Putnam, *The Poetry of the Aeneid* (1965); R. O. A. M. Lyne, *Further Voices in Vergil's Aeneid* (1987)); or more generally to see the oppositions (like all oppositions) as inherently unstable and liable to deconstruction. Naturally, simple appeal to the text or its historical setting cannot settle which of these approaches is adopted.

Three particular aspects of the debate may, however, be mentioned. First, the opposition between Jupiter and Juno is a gendered one, and many of the other contrasts drawn relate to ancient (and modern) conceptions of typically male or female characteristics, such as reason and emotion. Women in the *Aeneid* feature predominantly as suffering victims opposed to the progress of history (Juno, Dido, Amata, Camilla, Juturna), and this may be read either as an affront to the values of martial epic or as reinforcing them. At any rate, Virgil's treatment of gender is distinctive and central to the interpretation of the poem, though it is idle to use it to speculate about his own sexuality.

Second, the political aspects of the oppositions are more than implicit. The hero of the epic is *pius Aeneas* (1. 378), a man marked out by attachment to communal values who at the fall of Troy turns away from individual heroism to save his father and in *Carthage rejects personal happiness for the sake of his son's future and the destiny of Rome (4. 267–76). This subordination of the individual to the collective is often seen as a prime component of Roman ideology, and its embodiment in Aeneas a central feature of the epic. At the same time, as in Virgil's earlier work (J. Griffin, *Latin Poets* (1985), 163–82), the pain and loss suffered by individuals are at least equally as prominent in the poem. The question of the relationship between individual and community is raised in a different form by the question of the poem's relationship to the new autocratic rule of Augustus. The purpose of the *Aeneid* was commonly seen in antiquity as to praise Augustus (Servius, *Aen.* pref.), who receives explicit eulogy from Jupiter (1. 286–96, though *Caesar* in 286 is ambiguous), Anchises (6. 791–805), and the primary narrator in the description of Aeneas' divine shield (8. 671–728). Much of the imagery of the *Aeneid* can be related to Augustan symbolic discourse (P. Hardie, *Virgil's Aeneid: Cosmos and Imperium*; P. Zanker, *The Power of Images in the Age of Augustus* (1988)) and there are many typological links between Augustus and Aeneas and other figures such as Hercules (cf. G. Binder, *Aeneas und Augustus* (1971); K. W. Gransden, *PVS* 1973–4, 14–27; J. Griffin, *Latin Poets* (1985), 183–97). On the other hand, many have again seen the poem's tragic elements as incompatible with a celebration of power. It is impossible to separate the question of the *Aeneid*'s political tendency—in its crudest form, whether we make it pro- or anti-Augustan—from the wider ideological issues mentioned above, and again the debate cannot be resolved by an appeal to text or history (cf. D. Kennedy, in A. Powell (ed.), *Roman Poetry and Propaganda in the Age of Augustus* (1992), 26–58). See PROPAGANDA.

Finally, these same issues have also surfaced in relation to the philosophical aspects of the *Aeneid*. Just as the *Georgics* may be read as a reply to the *De rerum natura*, so the *Aeneid* may be seen as again 'remythologizing' Lucretian rationalism (P. Hardie, *Virgil's Aeneid: Cosmos and Imperium*, *passim*); as Aeneas rejects retirement in Carthage or Sicily for his fate in Italy, so the *Aeneid* turns from 'ignoble ease' to harsh commitment (cf. 6. 851 with *De rerum natura* 5. 1130, though there is more than one way of reading the intertextuality). Several passages of the *Aeneid* are explicitly philosophical in their language, most notably Anchises' account of the *soul in 6. 724–51; this contains both Stoic and Platonic elements (see STOICISM; PLATO), and such eclecticism is typical and unsurprising in a period where the two schools pulled closer with figures such as Antiochus of Ascalon and Posidonius. But the debates over the philosophy of the *Aeneid* have concentrated on ethics and the theory of the passions, especially anger. Is the *Aeneid* essentially a Stoic text, which deprecates emotion? Or is it rather Peripatetic (i.e. Aristotelian, see ARISTOTLE), and thereby endorsing a right measure of anger (A. Thornton, *The Living Universe* (1976), esp. 159–63)? Others have looked to Cynicism (see CYNICS) (F. Cairns, *Virgil's Augustan Epic* (1989), 33–8) or the Epicurean theory of anger as presented in Philodemus' *De ira* (cf. G. K. Galinsky *AJPhil.* 1988, 321–48; M. Erler, *GB* (1991)). Any decision on these matters involves a consideration of the poem's imagery, as well as explicit statement by characters and the narrator; and once again the evaluation of these images is not a simple one. A similar ambivalence attends the depiction of the gods: although they may at times function as metaphors for psychological activity on the human plane (G. W. Williams, *Technique and Ideas in the Aeneid* (1983)), they cannot simply be reduced to allegory (D. Feeney, *The Gods in Epic* (1991), 129–87).

The classic status of the *Aeneid* is at once apparent from the parody of its opening line (and 7. 41) as the epitome of epic openings in the first of Ovid's *Amores* (date uncertain, but perhaps before 7 BC: cf. Mckeown on *Am.* I. 1. 1–2). Intertextuality with the *Aeneid* is the central way in which Ovid's *Metamorphoses*, Lucan's *De bello civili* (see LUCAN), and especially the works of the Flavian epicists generate meaning: the *Aeneid* is figured as the official voice of the empire, to be subverted or recuperated (cf. P. Hardie, *The Epic Successors of Virgil*). But just as all Greek literature everywhere of necessity situates itself against Homer, so traces of the *Aeneid* can be seen in every genre of verse and prose, Christian as well as pagan (cf. W. Suerbaum, *ANRW* 2. 31. 1 (1986), 308–37; W. F. Jackson Knight, *Roman Virgil* (1966), 362–98). Inevitably, this role as a machine for generating meaning in others, a stable backdrop for new dramas, may lead to a simplification of the possibilities of the original text, but equally the links between parts of the *Aeneid* established by imitations often offer the possibility of new critical insights into the *Aeneid* itself (cf. P. Hardie, in A. J. Boyle (ed.), *The Imperial Muse: Flavian Epicist to Claudian* (1990), 3–20).

Fortuna

Virgil's works, but especially the *Aeneid*, retained their classic status throughout the Middle Ages and Renaissance as prime examples of pastoral (cf. A. M. Patterson, *Pastoral and Ideology* (1988); S. Chaudhuri, *Renaissance Pastoral and its English Developments* (1989)), didactic (cf. J. Calker, *The English Georgic* (1969)), and most obviously epic, from Dante to Milton (cf. T. M. Green, *The Light in Troy* (1982); D. Quint, *Epic and Empire* (1993)). Many aspects of this *reception in the various vernaculars were studied in the publications connected with the bimillenary celebrations of 1981–2 (lists in A. Wlosok, *Gnomon* 1985, 127–34 and *Enc. Virg.* V** (1991), 114–18: cf. C. Martindale, *Virgil and his Influence* (1984) and *Redeeming the Text* (1993)). Although in English literature the Augustan period is most obviously an *aetas Vergiliana*, he has played a surprisingly important role in the modern period, from Eliot to Hermann Broch (T. Ziolkowski, *Virgil and the Moderns* (1991)); if no major work stands in relation to the *Aeneid* as Joyce's *Ulysses* does to the *Odyssey*, the tactics that novel adopts towards its model are entirely Virgilian. For Eliot as for Milton and Dryden Virgil was *the* classic; if this centrality has given way first before vernacular heroes (Shakespeare, Dante) and then before a more general scepticism towards the canon, Virgil continues to possess the alternative canonic virtue of continual reinterpretation and cultural reuse (cf. W. Suerbaum, *Vergils Aeneis, Beiträge zu ihrer Rezeption in Gegenwart und Geschichte* (1981)).   D. P. F., P. G. F.

---

that there is very little evidence that the practice was subsequently used in antiquity. Moreover, Galen himself based much of his own human anatomy on his dissections and vivisections of the Barbary ape and the Rhesus monkey, creatures which he thought most closely resembled humans. The implication is that, for Galen at least, humans were not possible subjects. The balance of modern opinion, however, seems to be in favour of accepting the veracity of Celsus' and Tertullian's reports.   J. T. V.

Vulcan (Volcanus, Volkanus, Vulcanus), an ancient Roman god of destructive, devouring fire, in both the human environment and in nature: e.g. in volcanoes (see Strabo 5. 246 for his worship at the *Solfatare* of Puteoli, and Plin. *HN* 2. 240 for fire coming out of the ground near Mutina), which explains why his temple should always stand outside a city (Vitr. 1. 7. 1), on the authority of the *Etruscan haruspices (diviners). He was associated with Maia (Gell. *NA* 13. 23. 2 'Maiam Volcani'), the goddess of the irrepressible development of the fire, and was worshipped at Rome from the earliest-known times, having a *flamen* (see PRIESTS) and a festival, the Volcanalia, on 23 August. His shrine, the Volcanal, stood in the Area Volcani in the *forum Romanum at the foot of the Capitol; it may therefore go back to a time when the Forum was still outside the city (see F. Coarelli, *Il Foro Romano*, 1: *Periodo arcaico* (1983), 164 ff.). A newer temple (before 214 BC) stood in the Campus Martius. His name is certainly not Latin, the nearest to it in sound being the Cretan Ϝελχανός (for whom see Cook, *Zeus* 2. 946 ff.), who, however, seems to have no resemblance to him in functions. For Etruscan names suggesting Volcanus see F. Altheim, *Griechische Götter* (1930), 172. It is thus possible, but unproved, that he came in from the eastern Mediterranean, through Etruria. He seems to have been worshipped principally to avert fires, hence his by-name Mulciber ('qui ignem mulcet', 'he who mitigates fire'), his title Quietus, and his association with Stata Mater (Dessau, *ILS* 3295, 3306), apparently the goddess who makes fires stand still. On the Volcanalia, when sacrifice (see SACRIFICE, ROMAN) was also made to Juturna, the Nymphs, Ops Opifera, and Quirinus, he was given a curious and (at least for Rome) unexampled sacrifice, live fish from the Tiber being flung into a fire (see Varro, *Ling.* 6. 20, Festus, 274. 35 ff. Lindsay). This also can be readily explained as an offering of creatures usually safe from him to induce him to spare those things which at so hot a time of year are particularly liable to be burned. He had a considerable cult at *Ostia, where he seems to have been the chief god (R. Meiggs, *Roman Ostia* (1960), 337 ff.). In classical times he is fully identified with *Hephaestus.
                                                                          H. J. R.; J. Sch.

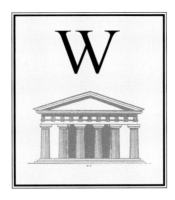

wall of Hadrian (see ◀Map 5, Ba▶) a frontier-wall (see LIMES) of Roman *Britain, running for 80 Roman miles (118 km.; 73 mi.) from Wallsend-on-Tyne to Bowness-on-Solway. Erected under the governor Aulus Platorius Nepos in *c.* AD 122–6, it was first designed to start at Pons Aelius, Newcastle upon Tyne, the eastern 67 km. (42 mi.) being in stone (3 m. (10 ft.) thick and perhaps 4.2 m. (13½ ft.) high) and the western 46 km. (31 mi.) in turf (6 m. (19½ ft.) broad at the base and some 4.2 m. (13½ ft.) high). Six metres (19½ ft.) in front of the wall ran a V-shaped ditch (generally 8.2 m. (26½ ft.) wide and 3 m. (10 ft.) deep). Fortified gateways (milecastles), with towered gates to the north, occurred every Roman mile (1,481 m.; 1,620 yds.) and there were intermediate turrets (observation towers) every third of a mile (494 m.; 540 yds.). Milecastles and turrets continued to the west down the Cumbrian coast to St Bees Head. Similar provisions may have existed on the south bank of the Tyne from Newcastle to the South Shields fort. North of the barrier were three outpost forts at Bewcastle, Netherby, and Birrens. As construction progressed, changes came. The stone wall was reduced to 2.5 m. (7½ ft.) in width, and extended 6 km. (4 mi.) eastwards to Wallsend, and 6 km. westward (replacing the Turf Wall).

As planned, garrison forts remained behind the barrier on the Stanegate, the Trajanic road from Corbridge to Carlisle. At an early stage in construction the decision was taken to build a series of twelve forts astride the wall. These were at Wallsend (1.6 ha.), Benwell (2.2 ha.), Rudchester (1.8 ha.), Halton Chesters (1.7 ha.), Chesters (2.3 ha.), Housesteads (2.0 ha.), Great Chesters (1.35 ha.), Birdoswald (2.15 ha.), Castlesteads (1.5 ha.), Stanwix (3.7 ha.), Burgh-by-Sands (2 ha.) and Bowness-on-Solway (2.8 ha.). On the Cumbrian coast Beckford (1.0 ha.) and Moresby (1.4 ha.) were also added on either side of the existing fort at Maryport. After the decision to move forts onto the line of the frontier the so-called vallum was added to the south of the Wall. The vallum was a flat-bottomed ditch 6 m. (19½ ft.) wide and 3 m. (10 ft.) deep with the upcast disposed in two turf-curbed mounds, one on either side, set back 9 m. (29½ ft.) from the lip of the ditch. This provided a continuous cleared area behind the forts along the full length of the frontier, presumably designed to ensure security. Crossings were limited to causeways at the forts. Lateral communication was first supplied by branches from the Stanegate; only later did the Military Way, between vallum and wall, connect forts and milecastles. Before the end of the reign of *Hadrian further forts were added to the system at Carrawburgh (1.6 ha.), Carvoran (1.4 ha.), and Drumburgh (0.8 ha.), bringing the garrison to *c.*9,090 men (excluding the Cumbrian coast) in auxiliary units.

After the accession of *Antoninus Pius the frontier was advanced to the wall of Antoninus on the Forth–Clyde line. Hadrian's wall was rendered open to traffic by removing the gates from milecastles and slighting the vallum. In the 160s the wall was brought back into full use with the abandonment of the Antonine wall. There was extensive rebuilding and repair, but forts were reoccupied by units of similar size and type to those previously present. Decreasing emphasis was placed on turrets and milecastles, with those on the Cumbrian coast apparently abandoned. The pattern so established endured for almost two hundred years with only gradual modification, piecemeal rebuilding, and a slow decline in the effective size of the garrisons. The lack of evidence for the late Roman field army suggests that the wall remained effective. There is no sound evidence for any violent destruction or wholesale removal of the garrison in the late 4th or early 5th cent.

I. A. R.; S. S. F.; M. J. M.

warfare, attitudes to (Greek and Hellenistic)
*Homer's *Iliad*, a poem about war, does not glorify war: it celebrates martial prowess but also portrays the sufferings caused by war, and *Ares, god of war, is rebuked by Zeus as the most hateful of all the gods, to whom strife, wars, and slaughter are forever dear (*Il.* 5. 890 f.). The same ambivalence pervades Greek attitudes to warfare. War in Greece was a recurring phenomenon, and conflicts multiplied in numbers and scale as larger power blocks emerged. Greek history (see GREECE (HISTORY)) divides according to

major conflicts: the Persian Wars, the Peloponnesian War and its sequels, the rise of *Macedonia, *Alexander the Great's conquest of Asia and the wars of the successor kingdoms. These provide the subject-matter of much of Greek historical writing. There were also innumerable local wars, less prominent in the record. 'War is the father of all things' (Heraclitus, DK 22 B 53). It shaped the institutions, society, and economy of the Greek world. Military function and social and political *status were closely related (Arist. *Pol.* 4. 1297ᵇ10–24; cf. already *Il.* 12. 309–28), hence the predominance in the classical period of the male citizen-warrior, the exclusion of *women from the political sphere, and the constant celebration in literature of military valour. Success in war was ascribed to divine favour and ostentatiously commemorated in *sanctuaries through dedications and offerings from enemy spoils, including captured weapons. In Classical Athens the war dead received burial every year in a public ceremony, and the funeral oration (*epitaphios*) linked the fallen warriors with the collective achievements of the *polis. On the other hand, the destructive aspects of war receive constant emphasis in literature. 'No one is so foolish as to prefer war to peace: in peace children bury their fathers, while in war fathers bury their children' (Hdt. 1. 87. 4). Tragedy and comedy exploited the theme in many ways (Aesch. *Ag.*; Eur. *Tro.* and *Hec.*; Ar. *Ach.*, *Pax*, and *Lys.*). For *Thucydides, war was 'a violent teacher' (3. 82. 2). Later historians often used the sacking of cities and the fate of the defeated for pathos and sensational effect (cf. the critique of *Polybius 2. 56–63). But attempts to limit war were few and ineffective, and it is doubtful whether there was any successful move towards humanizing warfare, even between Greeks. With the Persian Wars and the emergence of the antithesis between Greek and *barbarian, the view gained ground that Greeks should not fight wars against other Greeks or enslave Greek war captives (cf. Pl. *Resp.* 5. 469b–470c). After the failure of Athens in 355 in the Social War (357–355 BC; see ATHENS, HISTORY) voices were raised in condemnation of Athenian imperialism and in favour of peace (Xen. *Vect.*; Isoc. *De Pace* and *Areopagiticus*). But the legitimacy of war itself was not challenged: the same writers preached a profitable war of aggression against the Persian empire as an alternative to wars among Greeks (Xen. *An.* 3. 2. 4–6; Isoc. *Paneg.* and *Philip*; cf. already Hdt. 5. 49). In short, throughout Greek history 'war was a part of the fabric of society, on a par with earthquakes, droughts, destructive storms, and slavery' (W. K. Pritchett). See also BOOTY; IMPERIALISM, *Greek and Hellenistic*; TROPHIES.   M. M. A.

water (Gk. *hudōr*, Lat. *aqua*) in the mostly arid Mediterranean climate by its local availability shaped patterns of settlement and, as erratic rainfall, determined harvest-fluctuations and food-shortages (see FAMINE; FOOD SUPPLY). In *agriculture, although dry-farming was the norm in ancient Greece and Italy, irrigation was by no means unknown (e.g. at Hellenistic Sparta: *SEG* 40. 348.

For the Persian empire see AI KHANOUM). The use of hydraulic technology to increase the water supply was an early concern of the *polis; some of the most spectacular installations (e.g. on *Samos) were the work of the Archaic tyrants (see also TYRANNY); Rome pioneered raised *aqueducts. Communal fountains were a social focus (e.g. Eur. *Med.* 68–9, about Corinth's Pirene); in Roman times they were civic status-symbols liable to lavish architectural embellishment. Apart from drinking and *sanitation, ancient cities needed water for reasons of personal health (directions about baths figure in the Hippocratic *On Regimen and Health* 6. 72 ff. Littré; see MEDICINE §4) as well as hygiene. In Greece domestic baths were increasingly common by the 4th cent. BC (terracotta bath-tubs or special bathrooms were found in one-third of the houses at Olynthus). Public (including hot) *baths were common by the mid-5th cent. BC; baths were among the standard amenities of the Greek *gymnasium; in Roman cities they were a central social and cultural institution and, when based on therapeutic springs, the *raison d'être* of spa-towns. The play of water was an integral part of ancient, especially Roman, gardens and of the Roman idea of the *locus amoenus* (pleasant place). In mythology spring-water had sacred power; in real life springs often prompted cult. Together with fire, water was widely used in cult for purification (see POLLUTION), including bathing, in libations, and in *sacrifice; extra-urban *sanctuaries were as concerned as cities to secure a good supply. Purificatory water was also used in rites of birth, marriage, and death, the dead being considered 'thirsty'. In the so-called 'Orphic' texts on gold plates (see ORPHEUS), the soul is 'parched with thirst' and wants to drink the water of Memory; in the eschatological myths of *Plato and *Virgil (*Aen.* 6. 714, 749), the *souls drink the water of Oblivion. Finally, water was a primal element in cosmogonic thought; this applies equally to philosophy and to the early mythical cosmogonies (on which see Kirk–Raven–Schofield, *Presocratic Philosophers* ch. 1; and for Oceanus as the source of all, 11 ff.). See also NEPTUNE.   J. H. C.; A. J. S. S.

wealth, attitudes to Classical societies developed a range of responses to the universal ambition of individuals to amass property and possessions. One extreme response, characteristic of societies where the wealthy had retained or regained preponderant influence in public affairs, was to impose little or no restriction on accumulation: early Hellenistic Sparta and late republican Rome were examples. Conversely, Greek colonies were often founded on an 'equal and like' basis, and Roman colonial foundations regularly assigned the same land-area to each colonist. However, few colonies remained egalitarian for long (Diod. Sic. 5. 9. 4–5 for an exception, Lipara, one of the Eolian islands). See COLONIZATION, GREEK and ROMAN.

More normally, attitudes oscillated unsystematically within such extremes. Amassing wealth, possessing it, and spending it aroused differing responses, and varied also with the nature and the status of the gainful activity (Cato,

Agr. pref.; Cic. *Off.* 1. 150 ff. and 2. 52 ff.). Greeks saw the rich as potentially hubristic, extravagant, profiteering, and soft, probably dishonest if newly wealthy and lucky rather than worthy if of longer standing, but also as prudent and as potentially generous and magnanimous benefactors (cf. Arist. *Pol.* 1. 8–9). Romans likewise might profess contempt for usury while legally requiring guardians to use their wards' spare capital profitably (*Dig.* 26. 7 *passim*); might be represented as vaunting their wealth, as *Petronius Arbiter's Trimalchio did or as the shippers of Trier (Augusta Treverorum) did on their grave-monuments, or as hoarding it Scrooge-fashion (Hor. *Sat.* 1); or might combine positive and negative attitudes in the same treatise, as *Seneca did repeatedly. Behind some such inconsistencies lay the influence of Greek philosophies. *Cynics preferred poverty and refused possessions, a pattern later followed by some wealthy Christians (see CHRISTIANITY), while some exponents of Stoicism associated joy with the use of wealth. Mainstream *Stoicism counted wealth among the 'useful indifferents', and Aristotelian tradition (see ARISTOTLE) saw at least a comfortable independence as essential to the virtuous life. Other attitudes were less coherent. The idea that poverty had made Rome great, while wealth and luxury would ruin her, was a cliché of late republican ideology, explicit in *Sallust, *Horace, and *Livy, just when the wealthy of Rome and Italy were energetically exploiting every opportunity for investment and accumulation.

Some public policies, expressed in law or custom, attempted to restrain such behaviour. Partible inheritance ensured that an eldest son had no economic advantage, and the revocability of dowries checked some accumulation strategies, though the later freedoms of bequest and adoption largely eroded such restraints. The military need for citizen soldiers long kept the number of free smallholders high, but was overtaken by army professionalization for centuries until the barbarian settlements reinstated the practice. Sumptuary laws, or officials such as the *gynaikonomoi* ('women's wardens'), attempted to restrict extravagant display, especially at funerals or festivals. Most effective of all was the expectation that the wealthy would use at least some of their wealth for public benefit. The idea came closest to enforceable obligation in the institution of liturgies at Athens (see e.g. TRIERARCHY) and elsewhere, but normally emphasized the voluntariness of such benefaction and the goodwill thereby accruing to the benefactor (see EUERGETISM). In Greek contexts the objectives might be contributions to corn-buying or building funds, educational or cult foundations, help in manumission costs, or the ransoming of captives. In Roman contexts expenditure on games, public spectacles, and food handouts tended to predominate, along with expenditure on alimentary-schemes, temple building, the patronage of *collegia* (clubs), and later the endowment of churches and monasteries.   J. K. D.

wheel, wheeled transport See TRANSPORT, WHEELED.

wine (Greek and Roman) The grape vine, which grows naturally in the highlands between the 10° C and 20° C annual isotherms (approximately between 30° and 50° north), had appeared in a cultivated form (*vitis vinifera sativa*) in the Caucasus at least by the neolithic period. Viticulture had become fully established in the Greek world by Mycenaean times, as it had even earlier in its near eastern neighbours. By the earliest historical period wine had already become a fundamental component of classical culture. This is not simply the result of ecological determinism; viticulture represented an important cultural and social choice. Contemporaries were aware that the considerable geographical expansion of vine-growing which happened throughout classical history (in the Black (Euxine) Sea region in the Hellenistic period and, most notably, in southern Spain and France after the Roman conquest) was closely associated with the dissemination of classical culture. So the Phocaean settlers of Massalia (Marseille; see COLONIZATION, GREEK) are represented by Justin (43. 4) as teaching the Gauls not just the pleasures of urban life and constitutional government, but also viticulture.

The evidence, particularly the literary sources, for viticulture in Classical Greece is inadequate; not even Theophrastus offers much detail. On the other hand, the techniques of wine-production figure prominently in the Roman *agricultural writers and *Pliny the Elder (*HN* 14 and 17), whose information is derived not just from personal experience, but also the numerous handbooks produced in the Hellenistic period. Yet, even in Classical Greece it was already acknowledged that the particular character of a wine depended primarily on a combination of the type of vine, the soil, and the climate. Most of the modern methods of training and pruning vines were already known, from the free-standing bush, propped vines, to trellising, and most notably the growing of vines up trees. This last was such a distinctive feature of some of the most prized vineyards of Roman Italy (e.g. Caecuban and Falernian) that Pliny (*HN* 17. 199) could claim that 'classic wines can only be produced from vines grown on trees'. Cited yields varied enormously; but these depended on grape type and the density of planting. The choices here depended on which market the producer was aiming at: young wines for mass consumption or fine wines for the élite.

The descriptive lists of wines which can be found in authors, such as Pliny and Athenaeus, must be used with caution, because many of them are not the judgements of connoisseurs, but are derived from the accounts of medical writers, who assessed wines for their effects as remedies. Athenaeus (1. 27d) has the most useful account of Greek wines with a wide selection of citations from ancient authors. Among the most noted Greek wines were those of Cos, Chios, Thasos, *Lesbos, and *Rhodes. A distinctive feature of several of these wines, particularly Coan, was the practice of cutting the must with quantities of sea water 'to enliven a wine's smoothness' (Plin. *HN* 14. 120) (presumably to increase its acidity). So many of Greece's

wine A wine shop in *Pompeii. The transport jars (amphorae) in which the wine was stored are clearly visible. A modest establishment like this is a reminder that wine was the everyday drink of all classes in Greece and Rome, not just the élite.

most prominent wines and the ones which were exported on a large scale down to the Roman imperial period came from the islands. Viticulture probably played a greater role in their economy than that of mainland areas such as Attica (the territory of *Athens. Two fragmentary inscriptions from 5th-cent. Thasos, an important producer and exporter, contain elaborate regulations about the sale of wine. Sometimes interpreted as trade protection, they are more likely a cumbersome attempt to assure the consumer of the genuineness and quality of their purchase.

In Roman Italy there was a close link between prestige vineyards and the favoured locations of the Roman élite's country estates, most particularly the Alban hills or Albanus mons (Alban, Velletri, Setian wine), further south in Latium (Caecuban), the northern borders of Campania (Massic, Falernian), and round the bay of Naples (Gauranum, Surrentinum). In the reign of *Augustus there was a great interest in the wines of NE Italy. Most of the prized wines were sweet whites. Characteristically they were aged for a considerable number of years, with a resul-

tant darkening of colour as a result of madderization. This process of ageing was often accelerated by exposing the wine to heat by storing it in lofts above hearths. While it was accepted that wine ideally should be unadulterated, the long lists of additives in Pliny and Columella suggest that producers were frequently forced to disguise a deteriorating product.

The widespread finds of Italian amphorae are testimony to the success of Italian wines in the growing markets of the city of Rome itself, in Spain and Gaul, and even in the Greek east. But Italian dominance of this trade lasted for only a fairly short time, from the late 2nd cent. BC to the mid-1st cent. AD. By then the wines of south Spain and southern Gaul were competing successfully in these markets, so much so that Columella (*Rust.* 3. 3) was forced to produce a detailed argument for the continued profitability of viticulture to counter growing scepticism in Italy.

Wine was the everyday drink of all classes in Greece and Rome. It was also a key component of one of the central social institutions of the élite, the dinner and drinking party (see SYMPOSIUM). On such occasions large quantities of wine were drunk, but it was invariably heavily diluted with water. It was considered a mark of uncivilized peoples, untouched by classical culture, that they drank wine neat with supposed disastrous effects on their mental and physical health (Ammianus Marcellinus, 15. 12). See AGRICULTURE; ALCOHOLISM; DIONYSUS.   J. J. P.

women

women Almost all information about women in antiquity comes to us from male sources. Some women could read and write (see LITERACY), at least to the level needed for their role as guardians of the *household stores (e.g. Xen. *Oec.* 7. 5 and 9. 10; see HOUSEWORK) but, although there are many references to literary works by women, very few texts survive. The 'exceptions' to male authorship include women poets (e.g. *Sappho, Corinna, Erinna, Nossis, two women poets called Sulpicia), early philosophers (some Hellenistic pamphlets are attributed to Pythagorean women), personal letters from women, and the 5th-cent. AD travel diary of Egeria (*Itinerarium Egeriae*). Many attributions to women are problematic. Were women's letters written by scribes? Is a text ascribed to a woman simply in order to attack a man (e.g. Aspasia's alleged authorship of *Pericles' speeches)?

The central source problems, and the strategies developed to overcome them, underpin the large amount of work on ancient women produced in the last twenty years. First, every type of evidence has had to be re-examined in order to discover what it can contribute. This has led many scholars to concentrate on very small areas of specialism, leaving the work of synthesis to the reader of the collections of essays in which much recent work has been published. Secondly, the indirect nature of much of the evidence has made necessary a theoretically sophisticated approach, open to methods developed in cognate disciplines.

The source problems used to be solved by dividing material up according to its 'level'; for example, seeing drama as fantasy, legal materials as nearer to the reality of daily life. In considering ancient women under the heading 'women, position of', the 2nd, 1970, edn. of the big *OCD* reflected the dominant questions of the age; first, whether 5th-cent. Athenian women were kept in 'oriental seclusion' or allowed 'freedom', and secondly, whether this meant that they were 'despised' or 'honoured'. Whereas literature and the visual arts were thought to assign women a prominent role, legal and historical material suggested that, in practice, women were seen as perpetual minors. A comparable approach divides the statements of the ideal situation from the incidental, apparently naïve, remarks about women's lives which are thought to reveal the reality.

The problem in both cases is how to weight different types of source material. For example, Creon orders Antigone and Ismene to 'be women' and stay 'inside' (Soph. *Ant.* 578 ff.). Is this evidence that women's domain was normally the home? The 'norm' is only stated because of the perception that it is being breached, so how would we know about a norm which remained unbreached and was therefore unstated? Other sources (drama, philosophy, lawcourt speeches) suggest that Athenian women left the *oikos* to visit relatives, work in the fields, fetch water, and attend weddings and religious festivals. So is this not a norm, but an ideal practised by a very few wealthy households? Or should we argue that what was said did not match what was done?

There is currently an increased awareness that all types of source material were produced by the same society, and that none gives direct access to reality. For example, funerary inscriptions may seem less value-laden than plays, but they operate by their own rules; a woman is praised for her appearance and her personal qualities, a man for what he has done. Fourth-cent. Greek lawcourt speeches are not transparent, but are public discourses designed to win a case by appealing to a shared social ideal of

women This rolled-out drawing of an Athenian vase-painting (about 500 BC) shows a young girl carrying a ritual basket in a sacrificial procession. Participation in public religion marked a significant breach in the ideal 'invisibility' of women in the Classical *polis.

female nature and behaviour. From the late republic onwards, Roman sources praise maternal *breast-feeding, yet discuss the use of a wet-nurse.

Much recent work on women in antiquity looks not at 'the position of women' but at the creation of the concept 'woman'. Woman is deeply ambiguous, a 'beautiful evil' who is both wild and tamed, essential to the continuation of the human race while herself being a member of the separate 'race of women' (Hes. *Theog.* 585–90). Her dual role is reflected in medical and philosophical texts which focus on the reproductive function while seeing women as physically and mentally falling short of the ideal which is the adult male citizen. It is also increasingly recognized that 'women' are not a unified group. For example, rituals may divide women by social status or sexual availability; at the Matuta Mater festival, restricted to women married only once, Roman matrons bring a slave woman into the enclosure and then drive her out with blows and slaps (Plut. *Mor.* 267d, *Cam.* 5).

In certain areas of life the similarities between the position and the experience of Greek and Roman women in all historical periods outweigh the differences, so that a number of generalizations may be made. For all women, their main role was as bearers of legitimate children; even when Spartan women, seen as radically 'different' by the Athenian and Roman men who wrote about them, engaged in physical training it was to strengthen their bodies for *childbirth (e.g. Xen. *Spartan Constitution* 1. 49). Concern with ensuring legitimacy of heirs led both to tight control of women's sexuality—including early marriage, at or before puberty—and fear of the power of that sexuality. Women must be tamed, instructed, and watched.

Ancient women lacked political rights; they could not attend, speak at, or vote in political assemblies, nor could they hold office. However, they could exert influence through men. In the Roman empire it has been argued that their political exclusion meant less after the decline in the roles of senate and assemblies, while the importance of the imperial family gave increased influence to its women. By the 2nd cent. AD the status of imperial women declined in a reaction against the roles of *Livia and *Agrippina. When women are represented in Roman sources as taking a public role, this tends to be accompanied by allusions to female spite, treachery, or lack of self-control. References to women's political action are intended to discredit the men associated with them (e.g. *Clodia, in Cic. *Cael.*).

Because they were thought to be easily deceived and thus unable to make sensible judgements (Gai.

Inst. 144, 190–1), women were supposed to have a guardian; in the absence of a father or husband, a *kyrios* or *tutor* acted for them in economic transactions. In the Roman world the exceptions were the Vestals (see VESTA) and, after Augustus, free-born women who had given birth to three children (*ius liberorum*), and freedwomen with four, who were not under the tutelage of a father or husband. However, the system could be used purely as a matter of form, to give the appearance of male control over property; on the death of their husbands, widows would take over their businesses, while in the eastern provinces women made contracts and used their wealth as benefactors of their communities from the Hellenistic period onwards (see EUERGETISM). By imperial times, male guardianship of Roman women had become a formality.

Although lower-class women in the ancient world often worked outside the home, in agriculture, as market-traders, and as craftswomen (see ARTISANS AND CRAFTSMEN), as well as in more obviously 'female' roles such as midwives and wet-nurses, women were traditionally praised for silence and invisibility. Their appearances in lawcourts were restricted to displays of grief in support of male relatives; in Athens, their evidence was only used when a free woman swore an oath on the heads of her children. In Classical Greece a woman's name was not given in public unless she was dead, or of ill repute, and glory for a woman was defined in *Thucydides' Funeral Speech of Pericles as 'not to be spoken of, whether in praise or blame' (2. 45). In Roman society, naming reflected this invisibility; women took the name of their father, but in time they acquired a *cognomen*, so that sisters were differentiated as (e.g.) Iulia Agrippina and Iulia Drusilla.

In both the Greek and Roman worlds, discrepancies seem to have existed between norms and practice, with 'real' women—if it is possible to separate these out from the multiple images of the sources—apparently acting in ways which were contrary to the stated ideals.

Current work concerns non-élite women, working women, slave-women and the relationship between status and gender. Some attempts are also being made to discover how ancient women saw their world, rather than stopping at how men saw women. The ancient sources suggest that women simply reproduced the values of their culture. *Plutarch's *Sayings of Spartan Women* consist of statements on the traditional role of women as mothers and affirmations of Spartan values ('Come home with your shield or on it'). Roman women were represented as the guardians of Roman culture and traditional morality; for example, Lucretia, the model of chastity, and Marcius Coriolanus' mother Veturia.

Now, however, there is interest in seeing women as agents with their own culture. One example of this work is J. Winkler's analysis (*The Constraints of Desire* (1992)) of the Greek festivals of *Aphrodite and *Demeter (the Adonia, Stenia, Haloa, and Thesmophoria) which included rituals restricted to women and which involved sexual humour (cf. the Roman Consualia). Where Detienne saw these as emphasizing women's approved social role in reproducing the city, Winkler proposes that women's own understanding of them could have been far more subversive. Doubting whether women would celebrate their alleged inferiority, he instead argues that women were laughing at the limitations of male sexuality. In a comparable study, L. Dean-Jones, *Women's Bodies in Classical Greece* (1992), suggests that women saw the opposition between men who fight and may die for the city, and women who give birth and may die for the city, differently from men. For women, their bodies were superior, men's expendable, and even seclusion could thus be seen as a way of expressing their value. Finally, R. Osborne (in I. Morris (ed.), *Classical Greece: Ancient Histories and Modern Archaeologies* (1994), 81–96) investigates how women would have responded to sculpted images of mortal women and goddesses. He argues that, while Classical statues spoke only to the male viewer, late Archaic images of *korai* (see SCULPTURE, GREEK) made female viewers see themselves as tokens of exchange in male systems. This role could give women power, as agents, because the system could not continue without them as tokens linking male households in marriage. See GYNAECOLOGY; HETEROSEXUALITY; HOMOSEXUALITY; MARRIAGE LAW; PROSTITUTION.

H. K.

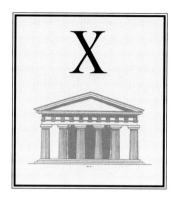

Xanthus (see ◀Map 1, Fd▶) was called the largest city in Lycia (southern *Asia Minor) by *Strabo (14. 3. 6, 666), a claim borne out by its extensive remains; prosperity was based on the fertile plain of the river Xanthus, with access to the sea at Patara. The city was known to Homer, and *Herodotus describes its capitulation to Persia in the famous siege of 545 BC (1. 176); in the 5th cent. it was ruled by a line of Persian client-dynasts (the self-styled 'genos of Karika'). There are impressive and highly distinctive tombs of the 5th and early 4th cents., notably that of the dynast Gergis, with a trilingual (Greek and two types of Lycian) inscription detailing Xanthian involvement in the Peloponnesian War (ML 93; *c.*410 BC; for the war see GREECE (HISTORY)), and the famous Nereid Monument (see ART, FUNERARY, GREEK, *Classical period*), thought to be the heroon of the dynast Arbinas (*c.*390: cp. SEG 39. 1414). In the territory was a major sanctuary of Leto, later the cult-centre of the Lycian League, where the finds include a trilingual inscription (Greek, Lycian, Aramaic) relating to the foundation of a cult of 'King Caunius' during a period of Hecatomnid control (SEG 27. 942, of 337 BC). Falling to *Alexander the Great in 333 BC, the city became a Ptolemaic dependency (see EGYPT, *Ptolemaic*); an interesting 108-line inscription from the Letoon (208 BC) records the diplomatic niceties of a (failed) request for financial assistance from Cytinium in central Greece (SEG 37. 1476). The siege by *Brutus (42 BC) prompted mass self-immolation by the citizens according to App. *BCiv.* 4. 76. But the city prospered under the Roman empire. Limyra (E. Lycia), under its 4th-cent. dynast Pericles (named after the famous *Pericles), was a rival of Xanthus.   S. M., A. J. S. S.

Xenophon *(see facing page)*

Xerxes I (OP Khšāyaršā), son of *Darius and Atossa, king of *Persia 486–465 BC, chosen by his father as successor (XPf ll. 31 ff.; Hdt. 7. 2–3). At the beginning of his reign he crushed a revolt in Egypt (Hdt. 7. 3) and later two rebellions in Babylon (see BABYLONIA). Plans for an expedition against Greece were inherited from Darius: for the course of the 'Persian Wars' see GREECE (HISTORY). No Persian document mentions the expedition.

The more important palaces on the terrace of *Persepolis were built in Xerxes' reign, including the Apadana with its impressive reliefs, illustrating the structure and the extent of the empire: king, court, and subject populations with their ethnographic characteristics. In the Daiva-inscription (XPh ll. 28–41) rebellion is equated with the neglect of Ahuramazda and the worship of *daiva*'s ('bad gods'). Xerxes' destruction of the *daiva*-sanctuary marks no breach with his ancestors' presumed religious tolerance, as is often thought, since DB 5 already contains similar phraseology. Xerxes' reputation as a weakling and a womanizer depends on certain recognizably novelistic passages in Herodotus (7. 2–3, 9. 108–13) and on the reading of royal inscriptions as personal messages by the kings, rather than as formulaic royal statements. Seen from the heartland, his reign forms a period of consolidation, not of incipient decay. Xerxes was murdered in 465.

H. S.-W.

Xenophon

Life Xenophon, son of Gryllus, from the Athenian deme (local district; see DEMOCRACY, ATHENIAN) of Erchia, was born into a wealthy but politically inactive family around 430 BC. He presumably served in the cavalry and certainly (like other affluent young men) associated with *Socrates. This background did not encourage enthusiasm for democracy (see DEMOCRACY, ATHENIAN). He apparently stayed in Athens under the Thirty Tyrants (see ATHENS, HISTORY) and fought the democratic insurgents in the civil war (404–403). The political amnesty of 403/2 theoretically protected him, and material in *Hellenica* and *Memorabilia* shows that (like *Plato) he was critical of the Thirty, but insecurity was surely one reason why he accepted the suggestion of a Boeotian friend, Proxenus, to enrol as a mercenary with Cyrus the Younger (second son of king Darius II of Persia), who made an attempt on the Persian throne after his father's death. Xenophon was thus among the 10,000 Greeks involved in Cyrus' defeat at the battle of Cunaxa (401). When the Persian satrap Tissaphernes liquidated the Greek generals, Xenophon emerged as a replacement and led the survivors through Mesopotamia, Armenia, and northern Anatolia to Byzantium and then into service with the Thracian Seuthes. He alleges a wish to go home at this stage but for various reasons neither did so nor availed himself of Seuthes' offers of land and marriage-alliance. Consequently, when the Spartans under Thibron arrived in Anatolia for a war of 'liberation' (399) and took over the Cyreans (i.e. Cyrus' veterans), he became a Spartan mercenary. Nothing is known of his role in ensuing campaigns except that he self-defensively endorsed criticisms which led to Thibron's dismissal. Subsequent Spartan commanders, Dercylidas and Agesilaus, were more to his taste and he forged close associations with them. In 394 Agesilaus returned home to confront rebellion amongst Sparta's allies and Xenophon fought for the Spartan cause at the battle of Coronea (394 BC) against, among others, his fellow-Athenians. Exiled as a result of this (if not, as some think, earlier, as part of an Athenian attempt to win Persian goodwill) he was settled by the Spartans at Scillus, near *Olympia. (His estate and the sanctuary funded by booty from his Asiatic adventures are described idyllically in *Anab.* 5. 3. 5 ff.). As a Spartan protégé (he was their *proxenos* (diplomatic representative) at Olympia and his children were allegedly educated in Sparta) he became vulnerable during the disturbances which followed the battle of Leuctra (371 BC), was expelled, and spent the rest of his life in Corinth. There was, however, a reconciliation with Athens. Works such as *Cavalry Commander* and *Ways and Means* disclose a sympathetic interest in the city; and in 362 his son Gryllus was killed fighting in the Athenian cavalry at the battle of Mantinea (362 BC). The posthumous eulogies this earned were in part a tribute to his father.

Works Most famous in antiquity as a 'philosopher' or mercenary-leader (ostensibly regarded as a perfect model for the young by *Dio of Prusa, and systematically 'imitated' by *Arrian), Xenophon produced a large output, all known parts of which survive. The chronology is only vaguely established. Most works fall into three categories: long (quasi-)historical narratives, Socratic texts (surely Athenocentric works, not mere by-products of contact with supposed Socratic 'cells' in Elis or Phlius), and technical treatises. There are also monographs (encomium; non-Socratic political dialogue; politico-economic pamphlet; institutional analysis), though their secondary relation to the major categories is obvious. Many are the earliest (or earliest surviving) examples of particular *genres. The clearest common features are (1) intimate relationship with Xenophon's personal experiences and (2) taste for didactic discourse. Xenophon's moral system is conventional, underpinned by belief in the gods and the importance of omen and ritual: divine power (often anonymous and not infrequently singular) is everywhere in Xenophon's writings, though not absolutely stultifyingly—when consulting the oracle at Delphi (see DELPHIC ORACLE) about going to Asia he famously framed the question so as to get the 'right' answer; and at the climactic moment in *Anabasis* where the Greeks reach the sea they are too excited to think of sacrificing to the gods. But it is not these things in their own right so much as issues of leadership (by states as well as individuals) or military skill which engage his didactic muse. That even purely practical pursuits have a moral component because they have social implications is a characteristic Xenophontic perception; and the would-be leader must, whatever else, earn his right to lead by superior wisdom and a capacity to match or outdo his subordinates in all the tasks which he demands of them.

In antiquity his style was judged to be simple, sweet, persuasive, graceful, poetic, and a model of Attic purity (see GREEK LANGUAGE). This is understandable, though there are deviations from standard Attic and some would call the style jejune; both rhetoric (e.g. *Hell*. 7. 5. 1–27) and narrative can sometimes be awkward. The range of stylistic figures employed is modest (simile is quite common, with a penchant for animal comparisons). The overall effect (style *and* content) can seem naïve. A (perhaps *the*) central question, which divides modern readers into two camps, is how far style and content are really *faux-naïf* and informed by humour and irony. One should perhaps reflect that (*a*) Xenophon's emergence as a leader in N. Mesopotamia in late summer 401 must disclose special qualities and (*b*) 4th-cent. Greece was full of men of 'upper-class' origin and of (ex-)mercenaries, and possibly not short of men who were both, but only one of them produced five (modern) volumes of varied, sometimes innovatory, writing. We should give Xenophon the benefit of the doubt, and conclude that there was more, not less, to him than there appears.

Hellenica. A seven-book history of Greek affairs, in two linguistically distinguishable parts, perhaps created at widely differing times, the first possibly as early as the 380s, the second in the mid-350s. (*a*) 1. 1. 1–2. 3. 10 covers the Peloponnesian War (see GREECE (HISTORY)) from 411 to the destruction of Athens' walls, the overthrow of democracy, and the surrender of *Samos (404). The opening narrative links imperfectly with Thuc. 8. 109, but the intention can only be to 'complete' the Thucydidean account (see THUCYDIDES), though this is achieved with little reproduction of Thucydides' historiographical characteristics. (*b*) 2. 3. 11–7. 5. 27 continues the story, covering the Thirty Tyrants (404–403), Sparta's Asiatic campaigns (399–394), the Corinthian War (395–386) and King's Peace (387/6), Spartan imperialism in Greece (386–379), the rise of Thebes (379–371) and the Peloponnesian consequences of Leuctra (371–362). The text ends at Mantinea (362 BC), with Greece in an unabated state of uncertainty and confusion. The account is centred on Sparta and characterized by surprising omissions (e.g. the name of *Epaminondas the architect of Leuctra is not given at all in book 6 where the battle is described; the liberation of Messenia (see SPARTA); Athens' Aegean policies in 378–362), a tendency to expose the shortcomings of all states, including Sparta, and recurrent hostility to imperial aspirations. A curious amalgam of straight history and political pamphlet, it was relatively little read in antiquity, and its modern status has declined in recent years. But it remains an indispensable source, and the tendency to regard the presumed qualities of *Hellenica Oxyrhynchia* as a reason for simply preferring alternative historical traditions should be questioned.

Anabasis. An account (date uncertain)—perhaps initially circulated under the name Themistogenes (cf. *Hell*. 3. 1. 2)—of Cyrus' rebellion and the fate of his Greek mercenaries, dominated in 3–7 by Xenophon's personal role in rescuing the army. The work's motive is not overtly stated. Apologia and self-advertisement are evident (there were other, and different, accounts in circulation); there is implicit endorsement of the panhellenist thesis that Persia was vulnerable to concerted attack and of a more general view about Greek superiority over *barbarians (the army is an emblematic *polis* on the move); and a didactic interest in leadership and military stratagem is obvious (though the account of Cunaxa is strangely flawed). Equally striking is the care taken to construct a varied and genuinely arresting narrative. The work's modern reputation has suffered from traditional use in language learning (cf. *Caesar's Gallic War*).

Cyropaedia. A pseudo-historical account of the life of *Cyrus the Great, often invoked in accounts of the background of the Greek *novel. (There is even a significant, though sketchily narrated, 'love interest' in the story of Panthea and Abradatas.) The institutional framework preserves useful

Achaemenid (see PERSIA) information (though the oriental decor is not as pronounced as it might be; need for compromise with Greek suspicion of the orient makes difficulties here; see ORIENTALISM), but the story-line as it stands flagrantly contradicts other source material (e.g. Cyrus acquires Media by inheritance not conquest, and he dies in bed not battle); suggestions that it may sometimes represent alternative historical tradition (not mere invention) are optimistic. The chief concern (cf. 1. 1. 1) is with techniques of military and political leadership, which are exposed both paradigmatically and through passages of explicit instruction (often involving dialogue). There is also some suggestion that even Cyrus can be corrupted by the acquisition of empire, and a final chapter (post-362) excoriates contemporary Persian vices. Very popular in antiquity (and sometimes thought important enough to have prompted a response from Plato in parts of *Laws*), *Cyropaedia* has been found dull in modern times. But a revival of interest is under way, and it is arguably a litmus-test for true appreciation of Xenophon in general.

Apology. A brief (perhaps very early) work with a purported extract from the court-room defence of Socrates against charges of religious deviance and corruption of the young sandwiched between a preliminary dialogue with Hermogenes and various carefree observations made after the trial was over. The stated purpose is to explain the *megalēgoria* ('big-talking') which previous writers agreed was a feature of Socrates' reaction to prosecution and show why he did not fear death. (Opportunity is also found to note the prosecutor Anytus' son's history of alcohol abuse.)

Symposium. 'In writing of great men it is proper to record not only their serious activities but their diversions' (1. 1), and entertainment at Callias' party is a mixture of cabaret (music, song, and dance, a sexually titillating tableau of *Dionysus and Ariadne) and more-or-less serious conversation about the guests' account of their most prized assets (e.g. beauty, wealth, poverty, making people better, recitation, joke-telling, skill at procuring). There is much explicit or implicit reference to personal relationships (doubtless a feature of real sympotic conversation), so Socrates' eventual discourse on common and celestial love is an unsurprising development, though the Platonic model is probably relevant. See SYMPOSIUM.

Socratic Memoirs. A collection of conversations, probably not planned as a coherent whole. 1. 1–2 explicitly address charges advanced at Socrates' trial, but the whole work presents him as respecting the gods and helping (not corrupting) his fellow-men. Broad thematic patterns are visible—1 dwells on religion and moderate life-style, 2 on friendship and family, and 3 on Socrates' help to 'those ambitious of good things', while 4 is more disparate (education; the existence of god; temperance; justice) and pretentious—but the pleasure of the work is in its individual vignettes and convincing (not necessarily authentic) picture of a down-to-earth Socrates equally happy debating with sophists, courtesans, and victims of the collapse of Athenian imperialism, and concerned with practicalities as well as philosophy. (As with Plato, drawing the line between genuine Socratic conversational subjects and Xenophontic ones is not easy.)

Oeconomicus. A conversation with Critobulus (1–6) establishes the importance of *agriculture. Socrates then reports a conversation with Ischomachus—itself containing a conversation between Ischomachus and his wife (7–10)—covering household organization, the daily pursuits of a rich Athenian, the role of bailiffs, and technical details of cereal and fruit cultivation. Much of it is effectively about leadership—a harder skill than agriculture, as Ischomachus remarks. The work is an important (though, given Socratic—and Xenophontic—unconventionality, slippery) source for social history. Particularly notable is Ischomachus' wife, married young so she will be a *tabula rasa* on which her husband can write what he will, but accorded a significant—if sex-stereotyped—role in the running of the household (see HOUSEWORK; WOMEN).

Cavalry Commander deals with the management and improvement of the Athenian cavalry force (which ought—9. 3—to include foreign mercenaries). After comments on recruitment (1. 2, 9–13), securing good horses (1. 3–4, 14–16), general horsemanship (1. 5–6, 17–21), armament (1. 7, 22–3), discipline (1. 7, 24), the need for good phylarchs (brigade-commanders) and political allies (1. 8, 25–6) and tactical formations (2. 1–9) Xenophon formally turns to the cavalry-commander's duties (3. 1 ff.). There follow sections on festival performances (3), conduct of marches and intelligence-gathering (4), deception (5), inducing respect of subordinates by knowledge and example (6), the defence of Attica (the territory of *Athens) and more general tactical/strategic points (7, 8. 17–25), horsemanship (8. 1–8), questions of numerical advantage (8. 9–16). Treatment of topics is inexhaustive, unsystematic and inclined to repetition (e.g. numerical issues appear in 5. 1 f., 7. 5 f., 8. 9 f.). Characteristically Xenophon begins and ends with the gods, asserts that no art should be practised more than warfare (8. 7)—gymnastics are frivolous—and stresses the importance of leadership qualities.

On Horsemanship. 'Instruction and exercises' for the private and apparently rather ignorant individual (the specific addressees are 'younger friends': 1. 1). It is the earliest surviving such work (one by Simon is an acknowledged predecessor) and covers purchase, housing and grooming (1–6), mounting, riding, galloping and jumping (7–8), correction of vivacity and sluggishness (9), dressage and manipulation of appearance (10–11), and equestrian armour and weaponry (12). Its precepts are well regarded by modern experts.

On Hunting. A technical treatise dealing with nets (2), dogs and their training (3, 4. 11, 7) and the timing and conduct of the hunt (5–6, 8). The hunter is on foot, the normal prey a hare (an animal of notably good organic design: 5. 29), though Xenophon also mentions deer, boar and the wild cats of *Macedonia, Mysia and *Syria (9–11). He disapproves of the hunting of foxes (6. 3). The activity is non-utilitarian (quick capture shows perseverance, but is not real hunting: 6. 8), intensely pleasurable—the sight of a hare running is so charming that to see one tracked, found, pursued, and caught is enough to make a man forget all other passions (5. 33)—and a divine invention which promotes military, intellectual, and moral excellence (1, 12). A contrast is drawn with the corrupt verbal wisdom of '*sophists' (a group not treated elsewhere in Xenophon as a coherent evil), and the hunter beats the politician in point of ethical standing and social value (13). Suspicions about the work's authenticity are unfounded.

Agesilaus. Posthumous encomium of 'a perfectly good man' (1. 1). An uneven chronological account (long stretches in close verbal parallel to passages of *Hellenica*) is followed by a survey (with some anecdotal examples) of principal virtues (piety, justice, continence, courage, wisdom, patriotism, charm, dignity, austerity). Little solid information is offered which is not in *Hellenica*, but a new gloss (sometimes Panhellenic, occasionally critical) is put on already familiar facts. The work (like *Isocrates' *Evagoras*) is normally regarded as an important contribution to the development of biography. See BIOGRAPHY, GREEK.

Hiero. A dialogue version of the 'wise man meets autocrat' scenario (cf. *Herodotus on *Solon and Croesus, see Hdt. 1. 29 ff.) in which, contrary to expectation, Hiero refutes Simonides' claim that it is pleasant to be a *tyrant, while Simonides supplies suggestions for improving the situation, not least by manipulation of public opinion. The original readers will inevitably have thought of 4th-cent. Syracusan tyranny (*Dionysius I and II), but this may not be a specifically intended subtext.

Ways and Means. Politicians claim that poverty compels Athens to treat other cities unjustly. So Xenophon advises alleviation of that poverty through innocent means, particularly (*a*) attracting revenue-creating foreign residents and (*b*) using state-owned slaves in the Laurium silver *mines to increase income and generate a dole (*trophē*) for citizens. The economic plan (a curious mixture of the apparently familiar and completely alien) has been much criticized; but the primary imperative is political—to devise a new imperialism based on peace and consensual hegemony.

Constitution of the Spartans. An account of the Spartan system (attributed to a single lawgiver, Lycurgus) which demonstrates the rationality of its consistent contradiction of normal Greek practices. The tone is laudatory except in a final chapter (misplaced in the manuscripts) which notes the decline from Lycurgan values associated with 4th-cent. imperialism.

(The non-Xenophontic *Constitution of the Athenians*, conceding that democracy, though repellent, was rational in Athenian circumstances, was allowed into the corpus by a later editor as a companion piece. The treatise is often called the 'Old Oligarch'.)   C. J. T.

Zeus, the main divinity of the Greek pantheon (see RELI-GION, GREEK) and the only major Greek god whose Indo-European origin is undisputed. His name is connected with Latin *Iu-p-piter*, Rigveda *Dyaus pitar*, derived from the root †*diéu-*, 'day (as opposed to night)' (Lat. *dies*), '(clear) sky'; as the Rigveda and Latin parallels suggest, his role as father, not in a theogonical or anthropogonical sense, but as having the power of a father in a patriarchal system, is Indo-European too. Thus in *Homer, Zeus is both πατήρ, *patēr*, 'father', and ἄναξ, *anax*, 'king' or 'lord'. His cult is attested in bronze-age Greece; the Linear B texts attest several sanctuaries (Pylos, Chania) and, at Minoan Cnossus, a month name or a festival, if in fact the Mycenaean names of months derive from festivals (KN Fp 5, 1). Another Cnossian text attests the epiclesis Dictaeus, Zeus of Mt. Dicte (KN Fp 1, 2), which remained an important place of cult in the first millennium. A text from Chania gives a common cult of Zeus and *Dionysus, a Pylos text (PY Tn 316, 8–10) one of Zeus, *Hera, and (a figure later unknown) Drimios son of Zeus, which suggests Hera as the consort of Zeus, as in later mythology.

Zeus, the Indo-European god of the bright sky, is transformed in Greece into Zeus the weather god, whose paramount and specific place of worship is a mountain top (Hdt. 1. 131. 1). Among his mountains (list: Cook, *Zeus* 2. 8. 68–987), the most important is Mt. Olympus, a real mountain which was already a mythical place before Homer. Many mountain cults are reflected only in an epiclesis, which does not necessarily imply the existence of a peak sanctuary. Few such sanctuaries are excavated (e.g. on Mt. Hymettus in Attica, the territory of ATHENS); those attested in literature are mostly connected with rain rituals (Zeus Hyetios or Ombrios); the sanctuary on the Arcadian Mt. Lycaeum had an initiatory function as well. As νεφελ-ηγερέτα, *nephelēgereta*, 'the gatherer of clouds' (a common Homeric epithet), he was generally believed to cause rain (comic parody: Aristoph. *Nub.* 373). With the god of clouds comes the god of thunder (ὑψιβρεμέτης, *hupsibremetēs*) and of lightning (τερπικέραυνος, *terpikeraunos*); a spot struck by lightning is inviolable (ἄβατον, *abaton*) and often

sacred to Zeus Καταιβάτης, *Kataibatēs*, 'He who comes down'. As the master of tempest, he is supposed to give signs through thunder and lightning and to strike evildoers, as at the beginning of his reign he struck the Giants and the monstrous Typhon.

But already for the early archaic Greeks (as, presumably, for the Mycenaeans), Zeus had much more fundamental functions. According to the succession myth in Hes. *Theog.* (whose main elements are also known to Homer), Zeus deposed his father Cronus, who had deposed and castrated his father Uranus; after his accession to power, Zeus fought the Giants and the monster Typhon who challenged his reign, and drew up the present world-order by attributing to each divinity his or her respective sphere: to his brothers *Poseidon and *Hades-Pluton, he allotted two thirds of the cosmos, to the one the sea, to the other the nether-world, to his sisters Hera (also his wife) and *Demeter, and to his many divine children their respective domains in the human world; mankind had existed before Zeus' reign. Thus, Zeus became the ruler over both the other gods and the human world; the order of things as it is now is Zeus' work.

Closely related succession myths are attested from Hittite Anatolia and from Mesopotamia. In Hittite mythology, the succession passes through Anu, 'Sky', who is deposed and castrated by Kumarbi, finally to Teshub, the Storm God, who would correspond to Zeus; other myths narrate the attacks of Kumarbi and his followers on Teshub's reign. Myths from Mesopotamia present a similar, though more varied structure; the Babylonian Enūma Elish moves from a primeval pair, Apsu and Tiamat, to the reign of Marduk, the city god of Babylon and in many respects comparable to Ba'al and Zeus; a later version of the Typhon myth (Apollod. *Bibl.* 1. 6. 3) locates part of it on Syrian Mt. Kasion, seat of a peak cult of Ba'al Zaphon (Zeus Kasios). The conception of Zeus as the kingly ruler of the present world is unthinkable without oriental influence. In a similar way, the shift from Indo-European god of the bright sky to the Greek master of sky and storms is inconceivable without the influence of the

Zeus Clay water jar from Italy (c.540 BC) depicting Zeus in battle with the monster Typhon. He is shown with his usual attribute in art, the thunderbolt.

weather gods of Anatolia and Syria-Palestine with whom he was later identified (Zeus Βεελσάμημ, Beelsamēm, Philo in Euseb. *Praep. evang.* 1. 10. 7).

Zeus is a king, not a tyrant. One of his main domains is right and justice: any transgression of his cosmic order is injustice; if necessary, Zeus punishes transgressors. Human kings are under his special protection, but they have to endorse his justice (Hes. *Theog.* 80 ff.). Zeus himself protects those outside ordinary social bonds—strangers, suppliants (Hom. *Od.* 9. 296 ff.) and beggars (*Od.* 6. 207 f.; 14. 57 ff.); cult attests Zeus Ξένιος, Xenios, and Zeus Ἱκέσιος, Hikesios. To preserve his order, he is himself subject to it: he is committed to Fate.

In many instances (e.g. the Trojan War), human affairs follow the plan of Zeus despite apparent setbacks. He might hasten perfection, if asked in prayer to do so (Zeus Τέλειος, Teleios, Aesch. *Ag.* 973), and he might signal his will, either asked for or unasked, in dreams, augural signs, thunder and lightning (Hom. *Il.* 2. 353, 3. 242), but also by provoking ominous human utterances (thunder and utterance, φήμη, phēmē, in Hom. *Od.* 20. 95 ff.). In cult, this function is expressed in rare epicleses (additional names) like Φαντήρ, Phantēr, 'he who signals', Τεράστιος, Terastios 'he of the omens', Φήμιος (Phēios) or Κληδόνιος (Klēdonios), 'who gives oracular sayings'.

In these cases, the prophetic power of Zeus is occasional and accessory. It becomes central in the only Greek *oracle of Zeus, Dodona in Epirus, reputed to be the oldest Greek oracle, known already to Homer (*Il.* 16. 233 ff.; *Od.* 14. 327 f.). It was active until late Hellenistic times; though consulted by cities too, its main clients were private individuals from NW Greece. Zeus is here paired with Dione, mother of *Aphrodite in ordinary Greek myth. Homer mentions the Selloi as prophets, 'barefoot, sleeping on the earth' (*Il.* 16. 234 f.). They disappear without a trace; later authors add that they prophesy in *ecstasy (Aristid. *Or.* 45. 11). Zeus manifested himself in the sounds of the holy oak-tree (*Od.* 14. 27 f., 19. 296 f.) and in doves, whose call from the holy oak-tree or whose flight are used as divine signs (Hdt. 2. 55–8); other sources know also divination by lots (cleromancy), water vessels (hydromancy), and by the sounds of a gong.

Zeus has only a few major *polis festivals; and though he often is called Πολιεύς, Polieus, he has no major temple on an acropolis, unlike the Roman *Jupiter Capitolinus. A few month names attest early festivals: the bronze-age month Diwos (Cnossus) to which corresponds the Macedonian, Aetolian, and Thessalian Δῖος (Dīos), the Attic Maimakterion which pertains to the festival of a shadowy Zeus Μαιμάκτης (Maimaktēs), and the Cretan (V)elchanios which derives from the Cretan (Zeus) Velchanos. Of some importance for the *poleis* in question were the sacrifice of a bull of Zeus Polieus on Cos and the festival of Zeus Sosipolis at Magnesia on the Maeander, both attested in Hellenistic sacred laws. Athenian festivals of Zeus are less self-asserting. The Diisoteria featured a sacrifice and a procession for Zeus Soter and Athena Soteira—it was a festi-

val to honour Zeus 'Saviour of the City'. As to date and place, however, it was more marginal than the Coan festival: it was celebrated outside the city in Piraeus, although with the participation of the city. Closer to the centre were the Dipolieia and Diasia. The Dipolieia featured the strange and guilt-ridden sacrifice of an ox on the altar of Zeus Polieus on the acropolis, the Bouphonia; they belong among the rituals around New Year. *Aristophanes thought it rather old-fashioned (*Nub.* 984): the ritual killing of the ox, the myth which makes all participants guilty, with the ensuing prosecution of the killer with the formal condemnation of axe and knife, enacts a crisis, not a bright festival.

The Diasia, 'the greatest Athenian festival of Zeus' (Thuc. 1. 126. 6), had an even less auspicious character. The festival took place in honour of Zeus Meilichios who appears in reliefs in the shape of a huge snake. His cult took place outside the town, with animal sacrifice or bloodless cakes; the sacrificial animals were burnt whole. This meant no common meal to release the tension of the sacrifice; instead, there were banquets in small family circles and gifts to the children: the *polis* community passes through a phase of disintegration, characteristic of the entire month, Anthesterion, whose festival, the Anthesteria, had an even more marked character of uncanny disintegration.

This apparent paucity of *polis* festivals is not out of tune with the general image of Zeus. The *polis* has to be under the protection of a specific patron deity, *Athena or *Apollo, while Zeus is the overall protector and cannot confine himself to one *polis* only; his protection adds itself to that of the specific *polis* deities. From early on, he is prominent as a panhellenic deity. The founding hero of Dodona, Deucalion, father of Hellen, discloses the oracle's panhellenic aspirations. But Zeus' main Greek festival is the penteteric Olympian Games with the splendid sacrifice to Zeus Olympios and the ensuing panhellenic *agōn* (see GAMES). Their introduction in 776 BC, according to tradition, marked the end of the isolation of the Dark-Age communities; the common festival took place at a spot outside an individual *polis* and under the protection of a superior god. Analysis of the sacrifices points to an origin in *initiation rituals of young warriors which had been widened and generalized in an epoch not too distant from the Homeric poems, with their own universalist conception of Zeus.

In the *polis* at large, Zeus' own province is the *agora, where he presides, as Zeus Ἀγοραῖος (Agoraios), over both the political and the commercial life of the community; thus, he can be counted among the main divinities of a city, like Hestia Prytaneia and Athena Poliouchos or Polias. Among the smaller social units, he is one of the patrons of phratries (kinship groups) and clans (Zeus Φράτριος (Phratrios) or Πατρῷος (Patrōios)/Πάτριος (Patrios), sometimes together with Athena Phratria or Patr(o)ia, Plat. *Euthyd.* 302d). He also protects individual households: as Zeus Ἑρκεῖος (Herkeios), he receives sacrifices on an altar in the courtyard (Hom. *Il.* 11. 772 ff.; *Od.* 22. 334 ff.; every Athenian family had to have one, Arist. *Ath. Pol.* 55), as Zeus Ἐφέστιος (*Ephestios*), on the hearth of a house.

There are functions of Zeus at the level of the family which are easily extended both to individuals and to the *polis*. Since property is indispensable for the constitution of a household, Zeus is also protector of property (Κτήσιος, *Ktēsios*); as such, he receives cults from families (Thasos: Zeus Ktesios Patroios), from cities (Athens: a sacrifice by the *prytaneis*—the presidents of the Council of 500—in 174/3 BC) and from individuals (Stratonicea in Caria: to Zeus Ktesios and Tyche (Fortune)). In many places Zeus Ktesios has the appearance of a snake (Athens, Boeotian Thespiae): property is bound to the ground, at least in the still agrarian mentality of ancient Greece, and its protectors belong to the earth. The same holds true for Zeus Μειλίχιος (*Meilichios*). For the individual, Xenophon attests his efficiency in providing funds (*Anab.* 7. 8. 1 ff.), while in many communities Zeus Meilichios protects families or clans; in Athens, he receives the *polis* festival of the Diasia; here also and elsewhere, he has the form of a snake. And finally, one might add Zeus Φίλιος (*Philios*), protector of friendship between individuals and also between entire communities.

As the most powerful god, Zeus has a very general function which cuts across all groups and gains in importance in the course of time: he is Σωτήρ (*Sōtēr*), the 'Saviour' par excellence. As such, he receives prayers and dedications from individuals, groups, and entire towns. These dedications reflect different possible situations of crisis, from very private ones (where Zeus competes with *Asclepius Soter, see e.g. Zeus Soter Asclepius in *Pergamum, *Altertümer von Pergamum* 8. 3 no. 63) to political troubles (Athens: *SEG* 26 no. 106, 7), natural catastrophes (earthquake: *BCH* 102, 1978, 399) or military attacks (*Delphi, Soteria after the attack by the Gauls).

The Zeus cults of *Crete fit only partially into this picture (see H. Verbruggen, *Le Zeus crétois* (1981)). Myth places both his birth and his grave in Crete: according to *Hesiod, in order to save him from Cronus, Rhea gave birth to Zeus and entrusted the baby to Gaia, who hid it in a cave near Lyctus, on Mt. Aegaeum (Hes. *Theog.* 468 ff.).

Later authors replace Gaia by the Curetes, armed demons, whose noisy dance kept Cronus away, and name other mountains, usually Mt. Ida or Mt. Dicte. This complex of myths reflects cult in caves, which partly go back to Minoan times, and armed dances by young Cretan warriors like those attested in the famous hymn to Zeus from Palaikastro (sanctuary of Zeus Δικταῖος, *Diktaios*), which belong to the context of initiatory rituals of young warriors; in the actual oaths of Cretan *ephēboi* (see GYMNASIUM), Zeus plays an important role. In this function, Zeus (exceptionally) can be young—the Palaikastro hymn calls him κοῦρος (*kouros*), 'youngster'; the statue in the sanctuary of Zeus Dictaeus was beardless, and coins from Cnossus show a beardless (Zeus) Welchanos. There certainly are Minoan (and presumably Mycenaean) elements present in the complex, but it would be wrong to separate Cretan Zeus too radically from the rest of the Greek evidence; both the cults of Mt. Lycaeum and of Olympia contain initiatory features.

Already in Homer (much more than in actual cult), Zeus had reached a very dominant position. During the Classical and Hellenistic age, religious thinkers developed this into a sort of 'Zeus monotheism'. To *Aeschylus, Zeus had begun to move away from the object of simple human knowledge ('Zeus, whoever you are …', *Ag.* 160 ff.) to a nearly universal function ('Zeus is ether, Zeus is earth, Zeus is sky, Zeus is everything and more than that', fr. 105); *Sophocles sees Zeus' hand in all human affairs ('Nothing of this is not Zeus', *Trach.* 1278). The main document of this monotheism, however, is the hymn to Zeus by the Stoic philosopher Cleanthes (*SVF* I 121 no. 537); Zeus, mythical image of the Stoic logos (see STOICISM), becomes the commander of the entire cosmos and its 'universal law', and at the same time the guarantor of goodness and benign protector of man. This marks the high point of a development—other gods, though briefly mentioned, become insignificant besides this Zeus.

Neoplatonist speculation marks something of a regression: in the elaborate chains of divine beings, Zeus is never set at the very top; the Neoplatonists allegorize the succession from Uranus through Cronus to Zeus and consequently assign him to a lower level.   F. G.

Chronology

Greece and the East

BC

*c.*1575–1200 Mycenaean civilization in Greece
*c.*1575–1100 New Kingdom in Egypt
*c.*1450 Mycenaeans take over palace settlements of Minoan Crete

*c.*1270 Troy VI, perhaps the Troy of legend, destroyed
*c.*1100–776 'Dark Age' of Greece
*c.*1050–950 Migration of Ionian Greeks to the eastern Aegean

*c.*825–730 Colonization of the West begins
776 First Olympian Games
*c.*750–700 Homer and Hesiod active
*c.*744–612 Assyrian empire at its height
*c.*740 Greek alphabet created from a Phoenician (Semitic) source
*c.*700 Greeks begin to colonize Black Sea area

*c.*700–600 Society remodelled at Sparta (Lycurgus)
*c.*680–625 The first tyrannies: Pheidon at Argos and Cypselus at Corinth
621/20 Draco's laws at Athens
*c.*610–575 Alcaeus and Sappho active on Lesbos
594/3 Solon's reforms at Athens
587 Capture of Jerusalem by Nebuchadnezzar; beginning of Jewish Diaspora
585 Thales of Miletus predicts eclipse of the sun
*c.*560–510 Tyranny of Pisistratus and his sons at Athens
*c.*557–530 Cyrus founds Persian empire
*c.*546/5 Persians conquer Ionian Greeks
*c.*534 First tragedy performed at City Dionysia in Athens
*c.*530 Pythagoras emigrates to South Italy
508 Reforms of Cleisthenes at Athens
499 Ionian Revolt against Persian rule
*c.*499–458 Aeschylus active (d. 456/5)
498–446 Pindar active

490 First Persian invasion of Greece; Battle of Marathon
*c.*487 State provision of comedies at City Dionysia in Athens begins
480–479 Second Persian invasion of Greece; battles of Thermopylae, Salamis, Plataea, and Mycale

Rome and the West

BC

*c.*1500–1200 Bronze-age 'Apennine' culture in western central Italy

*c.*1300 Earliest Celtic culture emerges on Upper Danube

*c.*1000 Hill-top settlements are established on the hills of Rome, including the Palatine
*c.*900–600 Iron-age 'Villanovan' culture in western central Italy
*c.*800–700 Celtic culture spreads to Spain and Britain

753 Traditional date for founding of Rome

*c.*700 Palatine settlement expands; the Forum is laid out as a public meeting place
700–500 Etruscan civilization in Italy; their alphabet stimulates the spread of writing in Italy

*c.*600 Latin city states begin to emerge in central Italy; organization of Roman calendar and major priesthoods

509 Expulsion of last king and founding of the Republic

494 First secession of the plebeians
493 Treaty between Rome and Latins establishes peace and military alliance

Greece and the East

BC

478/7 Athens founds Delian League against Persia

c. 468–406 Sophocles active (d. 406)

467 Cimon defeats Persians at Eurymedon

c. 465–425 Phidias active

462/1 Ephialtes and Pericles initiate political reform at Athens

c. 461–446 First Peloponnesian War

c. 460–430 Herodotus writes his history

c. 460–410 Polyclitus active

c. 455–408 Euripides active (d. 406)

454 Treasury of the Delian League moved to Athens; growth of Athenian empire

447 Building of the Parthenon begins

431 Second Peloponnesian War begins

c. 431–400 Thucydides writes his history

c. 430 Democritus, Hippocrates, Socrates, and Protagoras active

430–426 Plague at Athens; death of Pericles (429)

c. 427–388 Aristophanes active

415–413 Athenian expedition to Sicily

405 Battle of Aegospotami

405–367 Dionysius I is tyrant of Syracuse

404 Athens surrenders to Sparta; the Thirty Tyrants

c. 404–355 Xenophon active

403 Democracy restored at Athens

399 Trial and execution of Socrates

395–386 Corinthian War

387 Plato (c. 429–347) founds the Academy

386 King's Peace allows Persia to rule in Asia Minor

378 Foundation of Second Athenian Confederacy

377–353 Mausolus rules Caria

c. 375–330 Praxiteles active

371 Sparta defeated by Thebes at Battle of Leuctra

c. 370–315 Lysippus active

c. 360–324 Diogenes the Cynic active

359–336 Philip II is king of Macedon

338 Philip defeats Athens and Thebes at Chaeronea

336 Alexander ('the Great') becomes king of Macedon (d. 323)

335 Aristotle (384–322) founds the Lyceum

334 Alexander crosses into Asia

331 Foundation of Alexandria

326 Alexander crosses the Indus

c. 324–292 Menander active

c. 323–281 Alexander's 'Successors' divide his empire

Rome and the West

BC

c. 450 Codification of the Twelve Tables; Rome on the offensive against neighbouring tribes

c. 400 Earliest genuine archival records in Rome

396 Romans destroy Veii, inaugurating conquest of Etruria

390/386 Sack of Rome by Celts brings only temporary setback to Roman expansion

341–338 Latin War; Latin League is dissolved

326–304 Second Samnite War

Greece and the East

BC

323–31 Egypt ruled by the Ptolemies
322 Death of Demosthenes (b. 384)
321 Seleucus gains satrapy of Babylon; beginning of
 Seleucid empire

***c.*310** Zeno (335–263) founds Stoicism
***c.*307** Epicurus (341–270) founds his school at Athens
301 Antigonus I killed at Battle of Ipsus
***c.*300** Euclid active

***c.*287** Theophrastus dies (b. *c.*371)
281 Battle of Corupedium: Seleucus finally wins Asia
 Minor
281/80 Achaean Confederacy revived
***c.*277/6–239** Antigonus Gonatas is king of Macedon
274–217 Four Syrian Wars fought between Ptolemies and
 Seleucids
***c.*270–245** Apollonius of Rhodes writes Argonautica

***c.*247– AD 224** Arsacids rule Parthia
241–197 Attalus I rules Pergamum
229 Illyrian piracy attracts Roman intervention in the East
227/6 Cleomenes III reforms Spartan state

200 Palestine comes under Seleucid rule

194 Eratosthenes, natural philosopher, dies (b. *c.*285)

***after* 184** Great Altar of Pergamum
171–167 Third Macedonian War
168/7 Judaean Revolt against Antiochus IV Epiphanes, led
 by the Maccabees
166–188 Delos flourishes as free port

146 Macedonia a Roman province; Achaean War;
 destruction of Corinth

Rome and the West

BC

300 All Latium under Roman control
298–290 Third Samnite War
295 Battle of Sentinum, decisive for supremacy in Italy

275 Pyrrhus driven back to Epirus by the Romans
272 Capture of Tarentum, the final act in the Roman
 conquest of Italy

264–241 First Punic War; first gladiatorial games (264)
 in Rome
260 Rome builds large navy

241 Sicily becomes first Roman province

218–201 Second Punic War; Hannibal invades Italy
216 Crushing victory over Romans at Cannae
206 Carthaginians defeated in Spain
***c.*205–184** Career of Plautus
204 Scipio invades Africa
***c.*204–169** Career of Ennius
202 Scipio defeats Hannibal at Zama
200–197 Second Macedonian War between Rome and
 Philip V

192–188 Syrian War between Rome and Antiochus III
191 Rome completes conquest of Cisalpine Gaul

167 Kingdom of Macedon destroyed at Battle of Pydna

166–160 Plays of Terence
155–133 Celtiberian War leaves most of Iberia in
 Roman hands
149–146 Third Punic War; Carthage destroyed

Greece and the East

Rome and the West

Greece and the East

AD

c. 30 Philon ('Philo'), Jewish writer, active; traditional date for crucifixion of Jesus of Nazareth

37/8 Josephus, Jewish Greek historian, born
c. 48 Birth of Plutarch

66 First Jewish revolt begins against Roman rule
66–8 Nero's tour of Greece
70 Destruction of the Temple at Jerusalem

73/4 Fall of Masada ends first Jewish Revolt

106 Arabia a Roman province

135 Revolt of Bar Kokhba in Palestine suppressed
146–*c.* 170 Ptolemy's writings on astronomy and geography
150 Pausanias the travel writer flourishes

c. 200 Mishnah, the first great Rabbinic compilation, is written
224/5 Origen (b. *c* 184/5) dies, Sasanid dynasty seizes power in Persia (224)
267 Athens sacked by Herulian Goths

c. 300 Eusebius of Caesarea, Christian apologist, active; Christianity takes hold in Asia Minor
324 Constantinople founded

393 Olympian games abolished

420 Jerome, biblical translator (b. 347), dies in Palestine

Rome and the West

AD

14–37 Tiberius emperor
17 Death of Livy (b. 59 BC); death of Ovid (b. 43 BC)

37–41 Gaius ('Caligula') emperor
41–54 Claudius emperor
54–68 Nero emperor
64 Fire in Rome
65 Suicides of Seneca (b. 4 BC/AD 1) and Lucan (b. 39)
c. 65 Death of St Paul in Rome
69 Civil war
69–79 Vespasian emperor

79 Pompeii and Herculaneum destroyed by the eruption of Vesuvius; death of Pliny the Elder (b. 23/4)
81–96 Domitian emperor
98–117 Trajan emperor
c. 110–120 Tacitus writes Histories and Annals
c. 112 Death of Pliny the Younger (b. *c.* 61)
113 Trajan's Column dedicated
117–138 Hadrian emperor; Suetonius and Juvenal active; the Pantheon built; Hadrian's Wall built (Britain); Soranus (physician) active
138–161 Antoninus Pius emperor

161–180 Marcus Aurelius emperor; Galen is court physician
180–192 Commodus emperor
193–211 Septimius Severus emperor
198–217 Aurelius Antoninus ('Caracalla') emperor
c. 202 Cassius Dio begins his Roman History
222–235 Aurelius Severus Alexander emperor
235–284 Period of anarchy
284–305 Diocletian emperor
293 Tetrarchy established
306–337 Constantine I emperor
313 Edict of Milan: Christianity tolerated

354 Augustine of Hippo born (d. 430)
395 Division of the empire between East and West
410 Sack of Rome by Alaric the Goth

476 Last Roman emperor in the West deposed
527–565 Justinian eastern emperor; codification of Roman law

Select Bibliography

General encyclopaedias and other works of reference

S. Hornblower and A. Spawforth, *Oxford Classical Dictionary*, 3rd edn. revised (2003).

A. Pauly, G. Wissowa, and W. Kroll, *Realencyclopädie der klassischen Altertumswissenschaft* (1893–).

Archaeology and Art

J. Boardman (ed.), *Oxford History of Classical Art* (1993).

Enciclopedia dell' arte antica, classica et orientale (1958–).

H. A. Ackermann and J.-R. Gisler (eds.), *Lexicon iconographicum mythologiae classicae* (1981–).

A. W. Lawrence, revised by R. A. Tomlinson, *Greek Architecture* (1996).

R. Osborne, *Archaic and Classical Greek Art* (1998).

B. Sparkes, *Greek Art* (1991) (*Greece & Rome New Surveys in the Classics* 22).

R. Stillwell and others, *Princeton Encyclopedia of Classical Sites* (1976).

History

Aufstieg und Niedergang der römischen Welt (1972–).

Cambridge Ancient History, now in a '2nd' (actually completely new) edition (1961–). The most relevant vols. are: Vol. 3, parts 1 and 3 (both 1982), esp. part 3 on the 8th to 6th cents. BC; Vol. 3 part 2 (1991), Near East; Vol. 4 (1988), 525–479 BC; Vol. 5 (1992), The Fifth Century BC; Vol. 6 (1994), The Fourth Century BC; Vol. 7, part 1 (1984), The Hellenistic World; Vol. 7, part 2 (1989), The Rise of Rome to 220 BC; Vol. 8 (1989), Rome and the Mediterranean to 133BC; Vol. 9 (1994), The Last Age of the Roman Republic, 146–43 BC; Vol. 10 (1996), The Augustan Empire 43 BC–AD 69; Vol. 11 (2000), The High Empire AD 70–192; Vol. 13 (1998), The Late Empire AD 337–425; Vol. 14 (2000), Late Antiquity: Empire and Successors AD 425–600.

A. Kazhdan (ed.) *Oxford Dictionary of Byzantium* (1991).

J. Boardman, J. Griffin, and O. Murray (eds.), *Oxford History of the Classical World* (1986). Useful bibliographies.

Good introductions:

A. Cameron, *The Later Roman Empire*, AD 284–430 (1993).

T. J. Cornell, *The Beginnings of Rome* (1995).

M. Crawford, *The Roman Republic*, 2nd edn. (1992).

J. K. Davies, *Democracy and Classical Greece*, 2nd edn. (1993).

M. Goodman, *The Roman World 44 BC–AD 180* (1997).

S. Hornblower, *The Greek World 479–323 BC*, 3rd edn. (2002).

A. Kuhrt, *The Ancient Near East* (1995).

O. Murray, *Early Greece*, 2nd edn. (1993).

R. Osborne, *Greece in the Making* (1996).

G. Shipley, *The Greek World after Alexander* (2000).

F. W. Walbank, *The Hellenistic World,* 2nd edn. (1993).

C. Wells, *The Roman Empire*, 2nd edn. (1992).

Judaism and Christianity

A. di Berardino (ed.), *Encyclopedia of the Early Church* (1992).

F. L. Cross and E. Livingstone (eds.), *Oxford Dictionary of the Christian Church,* 3rd edn. (1997).

F. Schürer, *History of the Jewish People in the Age of Jesus Christ*, rev. and ed. G. Vermes, F. Millar, and M. Goodman (1973–87).

R. J. Z. Werblowsky and G. Wigoder (eds.), *Oxford Dictionary of the Jewish Religion* (1997).

Language and Literature

Cambridge History of Classical Literature, vol. 1, *Greek Literature,* ed. P. E. Easterling and B. M. W. Knox (1985); vol. 2, *Latin Literature,* ed. E. J. Kenney and W. V. Clausen (1982). Useful bibliographies.

P. Easterling (ed.), *Cambridge Companion to Greek Tragedy* (1997).

Greece & Rome New Surveys in the Classics: see esp. nos. 14 (C. Collard, *Euripides* (1981)); 16 (R. Buxton, *Sophocles* (1995)); 18 (S. Ireland, *Aeschylus* (1986)); 24 (R. B. Rutherford, *Homer* (1996)); 27 (C. Kraus and A. J. Woodman, *Latin Historians* (1997); P. Hardie, *Virgil* (1998)

Law

W. W. Buckland, *Textbook of Roman Law*, 3rd edn. by P. G. Stein (1963).

M. Gagarin, *Early Greek Law* (1986).

H. F. Jolowicz and B. Nicholas, *Historical Introduction to the Study of Roman Law*, 3rd edn. (1972).

J. A. C. Thomas, *Textbook of Roman Law* (1976).

S. C. Todd, *The Shape of Athenian Law* (1993).

Philosophy

W. K. C. Guthrie, *History of Greek Philosophy* (1965–81).

G. S. Kirk, J. E. Raven, and M. Schofield, *The Pre-Socratic Philosophers*, 2nd edn. (1983).

Religion

M. Beard, J. North, and S. Price, *Religions of Rome* (1995).

J. Bremmer, *Greek Religion: Greece & Rome New Survey in the Classics* 24 (1994); J. North, *Roman Religion: Greece & Rome New Survey in the Classics* (2000).

S. Price and E. Kearns (eds.) *Oxford Dictionary of Classical Myth and Religion* (2003).

Science and Technology

T. L. Heath, *History of Greek Mathematics* (1921).

O. Neugebauer, *A History of Ancient Mathematical Astronomy* (1975).

P. Potter, *A Short Handbook of Hippocratic Medicine* (1988). General bibliographical guide.

K. D. White, *Greek and Roman Technology* (1984).

Ancient Society

M. M. Austin and P. Vidal-Naquet, *Economic and Social History of Ancient Greece: An Introduction* (1977).

G. Clark, *Women in the Ancient World: Greece & Rome New Survey in the Classics* 21 (1993).

P. Garnsey and R. Saller, *The Roman Empire, Economy, Society and Culture* (1987).

J.-P. Vernant (ed.), *The Greeks* (1995).

A. Giardina (ed.), *The Romans* (1993; Italian original 1989).

MAPS

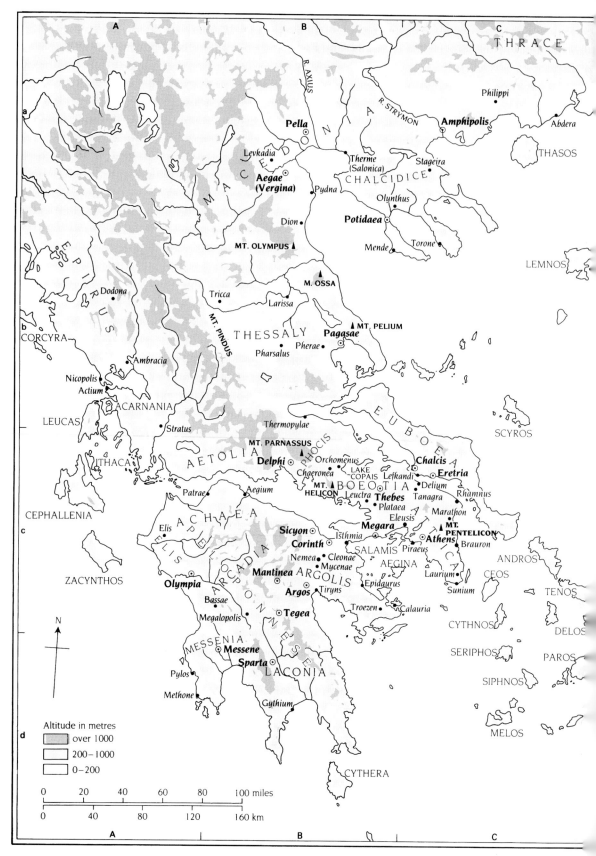

THRACE

Philippi

R. AXIUS

R. STRYMON

Amphipolis *Abdera*

THASOS

Levkadia

Pella

Therme (Salonica) *Stageira*

M A C E D O N I A

CHALCIDICE

Aegae (Vergina) *Pydna*

Olynthus

LEMNOS

Dion **Potidaea**

MT. OLYMPUS

Mende *Torone*

E P I R U S

Dodona

M. OSSA

CORCYRA

Tricca

MT. PELIUM

THESSALY **Pagasae**

MT. PINDUS

Larissa

Ambracia

Pherae

Pharsalus

Nicopolis

Actium

ACARNANIA

EUBOEA

SCYROS

LEUCAS

Stratus

Thermopylae

MT. PARNASSUS

ITHACA

A E T O L I A

Delphi PHOCIS *Orchomenus*

Chaeronea LAKE COPAIS *Lefkandi*

Chalcis

Eretria

Patrae

Aegium

MT. HELICON B O E O T I A *Delium*

Leuctra *Tanagra* *Rhamnus*

CEPHALLENIA

Thebes

Plataea *Marathon*

A C H A E A

Elis

A P

Isthmia **Megara** *Eleusis*

MT. PENTELICON

Sicyon

Athens *Brauron*

ZACYNTHOS

ELIS

A R C A D I A

Corinth

Nemea *Cleonae*

SALAMIS *Piraeus*

ANDROS

Mycenae

AEGINA

CEOS

Mantinea

ARGOLIS *Laurium*

TENOS

Olympia

Bassae

Argos *Tiryns*

Epidaurus

Sunium

P E L O P O N N E S E

Troezen *Calauria*

CYTHNOS

DELOS

Megalopolis

Tegea

SERIPHOS

PAROS

N

MESSENIA **Messene**

Sparta LACONIA

SIPHNOS

Pylos

Methone

Gythium

MELOS

Altitude in metres

over 1000

200–1000

0–200

CYTHERA

0 20 40 60 80 100 miles

0 40 80 120 160 km

MAP I GREECE AND THE AEGEAN WORLD

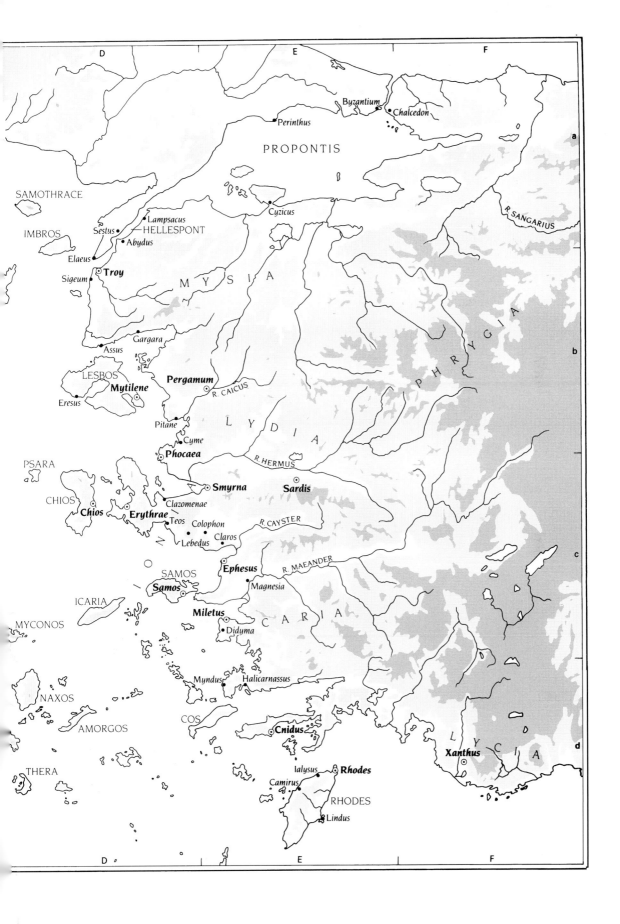

MAP 2 THE HELLENISTIC WORLD

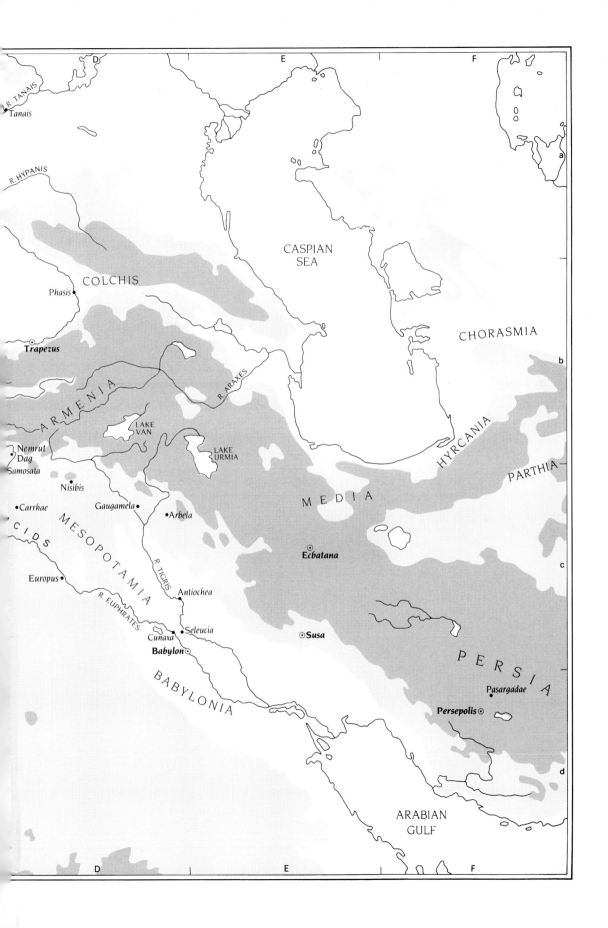

D   E   F

R. TANAIS
Tanais

R. HYPANIS

a

COLCHIS

Phasis •

CASPIAN
SEA

CHORASMIA

b

Trapezus ⊙

A R M E N I A

R. ARAXES

LAKE
VAN

LAKE
URMIA

HYRCANIA

PARTHIA

• Nemrut
Dag
Samosata

Nisibis •

• Carrhae

Gaugamela •

M E D I A

• Arbela

CIDS

M E S O P O T A M I A

R. TIGRIS

⊙
Ecbatana

c

Europus •

R. EUPHRATES

Antiochea •

Cunaxa •

Seleucia •

⊙ **Susa**

P E R S I A

Babylon ⊙

B A B Y L O N I A

Pasargadae •

Persepolis ⊙

d

ARABIAN
GULF

D   E   F

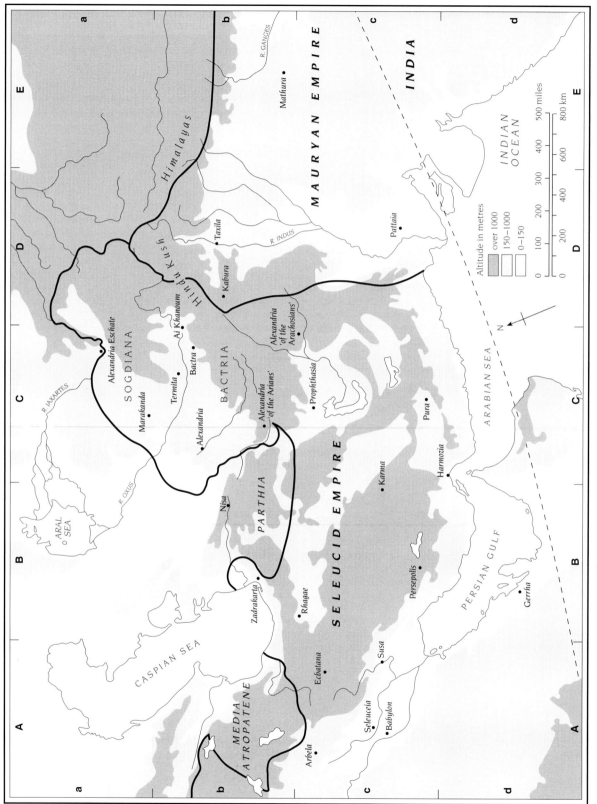

MAP 2a THE HELLENISTIC WORLD (*contd.*)

A
B
C

TRANSPADANA
VENETIA
PANNONIA
R. DANUBE

a
Mediolanum
Sirmio•
Verona•
Patavium
•Tergeste
ISTRIA
a

Cremona
•Mantua
•Bedriacum
•Pola
DALMATIA

Placentia
AEMILIA
R. PADUS

•Parma

•Genua
Ravenna

Carrara•
R. RUBICON
Salonae (Split)

Pisa•
Faesulae
•Ariminum

R. ARNUS
Florentia
UMBRIA
Ancona

Volterra•
Arretium
•Iguvium
PICENUM

b
Populonia•
Cortona•
•Perusia
b

Vetulonia•
Clusium•
•Asculum

Volsinii•
Spoletium
SABINES

Cosa•
•Volci
TIBER

Aleria•
•Falerii
R. LIRIS
Alba
Fucens
Corfinium

CORSICA
Tarquinii
Veii•
LATIUM
SAMNIUM

Rome
•Praeneste
•Luceria
•Sipontum

Ostia
•Arpinum
•Fregellae
APULIA

Velitrae•
CAMPANIA
Cales•
•Beneventum
•Cannae
•Barium

c
Antium•
Minturnae•
•Capua
Nola•
CALABRIA
c

Olbia•
Neapolis•
MT. VESUVIUS
•Brundisium

Cumae
Pompeii
Tarentum

PITHECUSAE
Puteoli•
Metapontum•

SARDINIA
Herculaneum
Paestum•
LUCANIA
Heraclea•

Elea•

Caralis•
Laus•
Thurii•
•Sybaris

•Croton

Terina•
BRUTTIUM

Hipponium•

Medma•

•Lipara
Messana

d
Panormus•
Tyndaris•
Locri•
N
d

Segesta•
Himera•
Tauromenium•
Rhegium

Lilybaeum•
Motya•
MT. ETNA
•Naxos
Altitude in metres

SICILY
Centuripae•
Calana•
Over 1000

•Enna
200–1000

Selinus
Leontini•
Syracuse
0–200

Agrigentum
Gela
0 25 50 75 100 miles

Utica•
•Camarina
0   50   100   150 km

Carthage

A
B
C

MAP 3 ITALY

Map labels (as they appear on the map):

A   B   C

a

RAETIA

Augusta
(Augsburg)

NORICUM

Carnuntum

Aquincum
(Budapest)

DACIA

Pavia

Aquileia

PANNONIA

Drobeta

R. DANUBE

Adamklissi

Arretium

Ancona

ILLYRICUM

Salonae
(Split)

DALMATIA

MOESIA

b

Perusia

ITALY

Rome

Capua

MACEDONIA

THRACE

Doriscus

Thessalonica

Brundisium

Tarentum

EPIRUS

Pergamu

LESBOS

Thebes

CHIOS

Messana

SAMO

SICILY

Catana

Corinth

Athens

Carthage

Agrigentum

Syracuse

ACHAIA

Sparta

c

Hadrumetum

Thapsus

MELITA (MALTA)

CRETE

BYZACIUM

N

Sabratha

Oea

Lepcis Magna

Ptolemais

Apollonia

Berenice
(Benghazi)

Barca

Cyrene

AFRICA

TRIPOLITANIA

CYRENAICA

d

LIBYA

Altitude in metres

over 1000

200–1000

0–200

0   100   200   300 miles

0   100   200   300   400   500 km

A   B   C

MAP 4 THE ROMAN EMPIRE (CENTRAL AND EASTERN PROVINCES)

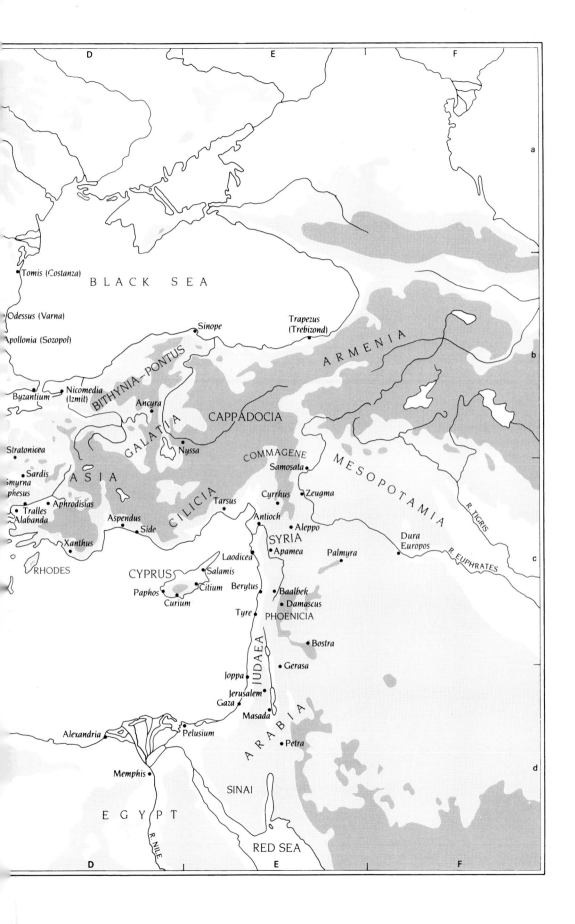

D   E   F

a

• Tomis (Costanza)

B L A C K   S E A

• Odessus (Varna)

• Apollonia (Sozopol)

• Sinope

Trapezus
(Trebizond)

A R M E N I A

b

Byzantium •   • Nicomedia
(Izmit)

BITHYNIA–PONTUS

• Ancyra

G A L A T I A

CAPPADOCIA

• Stratonicea

A S I A

• Sardis

Smyrna
Ephesus

• Tralles
Alabanda

• Aphrodisias

Aspendus

• Side

• Xanthus

C I L I C I A

• Nyssa

COMMAGENE

Samosata •

M E S O P O T A M I A

• Tarsus

Cyrrhus •   • Zeugma

R. TIGRIS

Antioch •

• Aleppo

SYRIA

• Apamea

• Palmyra

Dura
Europos

R. EUPHRATES

c

RHODES

CYPRUS

Laodicea •

• Salamis

Paphos •

• Citium

Curium

Berytus •

Tyre •

• Baalbek

• Damascus

PHOENICIA

• Bostra

J U D A E A

Joppa •

• Gerasa

Jerusalem •

Gaza •

• Masada

A R A B I A

Alexandria •

• Pelusium

• Petra

d

Memphis •

SINAI

E G Y P T

R. NILE

RED SEA

D   E   F

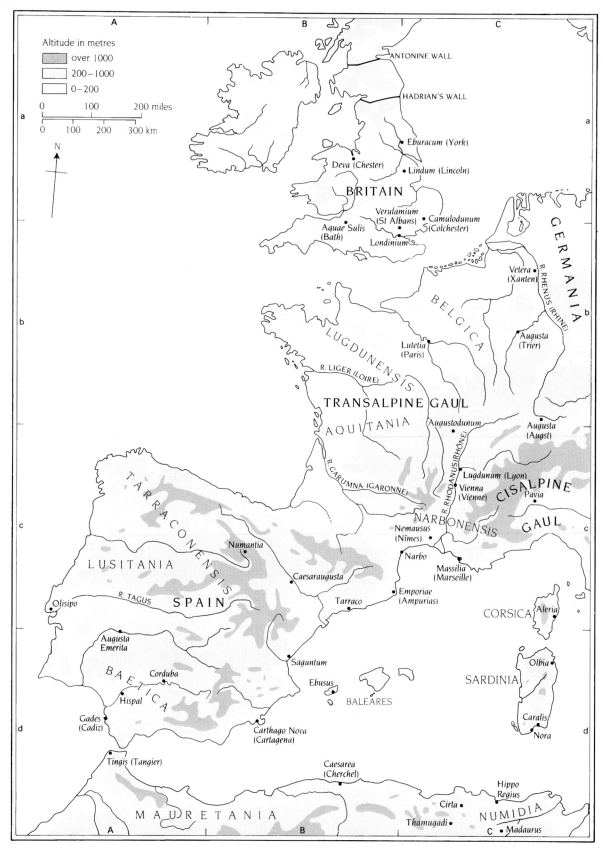

Altitude in metres

over 1000

200 – 1000

0 – 200

0   100   200 miles

0   50   100   200   300 km

N

ANTONINE WALL

HADRIAN'S WALL

Eburacum (York)

Deva (Chester)

Lindum (Lincoln)

BRITAIN

GERMANIA

Verulamium
(St Albans)

Camulodunum
(Colchester)

Aquae Sulis
(Bath)

Londinium

Vetera
(Xanten)

R. RHENUS (RHINE)

BELGICA

LUGDUNENSIS

Lutetia
(Paris)

Augusta
(Trier)

R. LIGER (LOIRE)

TRANSALPINE GAUL

AQUITANIA

Augustodunum

Augusta
(Augst)

R. GARUMNA (GARONNE)

R. RHODANUS (RHÔNE)

Lugdunum (Lyon)

Vienna
(Vienne)

CISALPINE

Pavia

NARBONENSIS

GAUL

Nemausus
(Nîmes)

TARRACONENSIS

Numantia

Narbo

Massilia
(Marseille)

CORSICA

Aleria

LUSITANIA

Caesaraugusta

SPAIN

R. TAGUS

Tarraco

Emporiae
(Ampurias)

Olisipo

SARDINIA

Olbia

Augusta
Emerita

Corduba

Hispal

Saguntum

BAETICA

Ebusus

BALEARES

Caralis

Gades
(Cadiz)

Carthago Nova
(Cartagena)

Nora

Tingis (Tangier)

Caesarea
(Cherchel)

Hippo
Regius

MAURETANIA

Cirta

NUMIDIA

Thamugadi

Madaurus

MAP 5 THE ROMAN EMPIRE (WESTERN PROVINCES)

Illustration Sources